PHILIP'S
WORLD ATLAS

Philip's are grateful to the following for acting as specialist
geography consultants on 'The World in Focus' front section:

Professor D. Brunsden, Kings College, University of London, UK
Dr C. Clarke, Oxford University, UK
Dr I. S. Evans, Durham University, UK
Professor P. Haggett, University of Bristol, UK
Professor K. McLachlan, University of London, UK
Professor M. Monmonier, Syracuse University, New York, USA
Professor M-L. Hsu, University of Minnesota, Minnesota, USA
Professor M. J. Tooley, University of St Andrews, UK
Dr T. Unwin, Royal Holloway, University of London, UK

THE WORLD IN FOCUS
Cartography by Philip's

Picture Acknowledgements
Robin Scagell/Galaxy page 3

Illustrations: Stefan Chabluk

WORLD CITIES
Cartography by Philip's

**Page 10, Dublin: The town plan of Dublin is based on Ordnance Survey
Ireland by permission of the Government Permit Number 8621. © Ordnance
Survey Ireland and Government of Ireland.**

**Page 11, Edinburgh, and page 15, London:
This product includes mapping data licensed from
Ordnance Survey® with the permission of the Controller of Her Majesty's
Stationery Office. © Crown copyright 2008. All rights reserved. Licence
number 100011710.**

Vector data courtesy of Gräfe and Unser Verlag GmbH, München, Germany
(city-centre maps of Bangkok, Beijing, Cape Town, Jerusalem, Mexico City, Moscow,
Singapore, Sydney, Tokyo and Washington D.C.)
**The following city maps utilize base data supplied courtesy of MapQuest.com,
Inc. (© MapQuest)** (Las Vegas, New Orleans, Orlando)

**All satellite images in this section courtesy of NPA Group, Edenbridge, Kent
(www.satmaps.com)**

First published in Great Britain in 2008 by Philip's,
a division of Octopus Publishing Group Limited

This edition published in 2010 by Bounty Books,
a division of Octopus Publishing Group Ltd
Endeavour House
189 Shaftesbury Avenue
London WC2H 8JY

www.octopusbooks.co.uk

An Hachette UK Company
www.hachette.co.uk

ISBN: 978-0-753719-96-1

A CIP catalogue record for this book is available from the British Library

Printed and bound in Hong Kong

PHILIP'S
WORLD ATLAS

Contents

World Statistics

Countries   vi
Physical Dimensions   vii
User Guide   viii

The World in Focus

Planet Earth   2–3
Restless Earth   4–5
Landforms   6–7
Oceans   8–9
Climate   10–11
Water and Vegetation   12–13
Environment   14–15
Population   16–17
The Human Family   18–19
Wealth   20–21
Quality of Life   22–23
Energy   24–25
Production   26–27
Trade   28–29
Travel and Tourism   30–31

World Cities

Amsterdam   2
Athens   2
Atlanta   3
Baghdad   3
Bangkok   3
Barcelona   4
Beijing   4
Berlin   5
Boston   6
Brussels   6
Budapest   7
Buenos Aires   7
Cairo   7
Cape Town   8
Copenhagen   8
Chicago   9
Delhi   10
Dublin   10
Edinburgh   11
Guangzhou   11
Helsinki   11
Hong Kong   12
Istanbul   12
Jakarta   12
Jerusalem   13
Johannesburg   13
Karachi   13
Kolkata   14
Lagos   14
Las Vegas   14
Lima   14
London   15
Lisbon   16
Los Angeles   16
Madrid   17
Manila   17
Melbourne   18
Mexico City   18
Miami   18
Milan   19
Moscow   19
Montréal   20
Mumbai   20
Munich   21
New Orleans   21
New York   22
Orlando   23
Osaka   23
Oslo   23
Paris   24
Prague   25
Rio de Janeiro   25
Rome   26
San Francisco   26
St Petersburg   27
Santiago   27
São Paulo   27
Seoul   27
Shanghai   28
Singapore   28
Stockholm   29
Sydney   29
Tokyo   30
Tehran   31
Toronto   31
Vienna   32
Warsaw   32
Washington   33
Wellington   33
Index to City Maps   34–39
World Cities Satellite Images   40–48

World Maps

Map Symbols   1

The World: Political
1:95 000 000   2–3

Arctic Ocean
1:35 000 000   4

Antarctica
1:35 000 000   5

Europe

Europe: Physical
1:20 000 000   6

Europe: Political
1:20 000 000   7

Scandinavia 1:6 000 000
Iceland 1:6 000 000
Færoe Islands 1:6 000 000
                                   8–9

Ireland 1:2 000 000
                                   10

Scotland 1:2 000 000
                                   11

England and Wales
1:2 000 000
                                   12–13

British Isles 1:5 000 000
                                   14

Netherlands, Belgium and
Luxembourg 1:2 500 000
                                   15

Central Europe 1:5 000 000
                                   16–17

Eastern Europe and Turkey
1:10 000 000
                                   18–19

France 1:5 000 000
                                   20

Spain and Portugal
1:5 000 000
                                   21

Italy and the Balkan States
1:5 000 000
                                   22–23

The Balearics, the Canaries and
Madeira 1:1 000 000 / 1:2 000 000
                                   24

Malta, Crete, Corfu, Rhodes
and Cyprus
1:1 000 000 / 1:1 300 000
                                   25

Asia

Asia: Physical 1:47 000 000   26

Asia: Political 1:47 000 000   27

Russia and Central Asia
1:20 000 000
                                   28–29

Japan 1:5 000 000
                                   30–31

China and the Far East
1:15 000 000
Hong Kong and Macau 1:1 000 000
                                   32–33

Northern China and Korea
1:6 000 000
                                   34–35

Indonesia and the Philippines
1:12 500 000
Java and Madura 1:7 500 000
Bali 1:2 000 000
                                   36–37

Mainland South-east Asia
1:6 000 000
Ko Phuket 1:1 000 000
Ko Samui 1:1 000 000
Pinang 1:1 000 000
Singapore 1:1 000 000
                                   38–39

South Asia 1:10 000 000
                                   40–41

Northern India, Pakistan and Nepal
1:6 000 000
Jammu and Kashmir 1:6 000 000

42–43

The Middle East
1:7 000 000

44–45

The Near East 1:2 500 000

46

Arabia and the Horn of Africa 1:15 000 000

47

Africa

Africa: Physical
1:42 000 000   48

Africa: Political
1:42 000 000   49

Northern Africa
1:15 000 000
Azores 1:15 000 000
Cape Verde Islands 1:10 000 000

50–51

Central and Southern Africa
1:15 000 000
Seychelles 1:2 500 000
Réunion 1:2 500 000
Mauritius 1:2 500 000
Comoros 1:8 000 000

52–53

East Africa 1:8 000 000

54–55

Southern Africa
1:8 000 000
Madagascar 1:8 000 000

56–57

Australia and Oceania

Australia and Oceania: Physical and Political
1:50 000 000   58

New Zealand 1:6 000 000
Samoan Islands 1:6 000 000
Fiji 1:6 000 000
Tonga 1:6 000 000
Tahiti and Moorea 1:1 000 000

59

Western Australia
1:8 000 000

60–61

Eastern Australia
1:8 000 000
Torres Strait 1:8 000 000
Whitsunday Islands 1:2 500 000
Tasmania 1:8 000 000

62–63

Pacific Ocean
1:54 000 000   64–65

North America

North America: Physical
1:35 000 000   66

North America: Political
1:35 000 000   67

Canada 1:15 000 000

68–69

Western Canada 1:7 000 000

70–71

Eastern Canada 1:7 000 000

72–73

United States 1:15 000 000
Hawai'i 1:15 000 000
Alaska 1:15 000 000

74–75

United States – West
1:6 700 000

76–77

Central and Southern California and Western Washington
1:2 500 000

78–79

United States – Midwest and North-east
1:6 700 000

80–81

North-eastern United States
1:2 500 000

82–83

United States – South
1:6 700 000

84–85

Mexico 1:8 000 000

86–87

Central America and the West Indies 1:8 000 000
Jamaica 1:3 000 000
Guadeloupe 1:2 000 000
Martinique 1:2 000 000
Puerto Rico 1:3 000 000
Virgin Islands 1:2 000 000
St Lucia 1:2 000 000
Barbados 1:2 000 000

88–89

South America

South America: Physical
1:35 000 000   90

South America: Political
1:35 000 000   91

South America – North
1:16 000 000
Trinidad and Tobago 1:2 500 000

92–93

Central South America
1:8 000 000

94–95

South America – South
1:16 000 000

96

Index to World Maps

97–176

World Statistics: Countries

This alphabetical list includes the principal countries and territories of the world. If a territory is not completely independent, the country it is associated with is named. The area figures give the total area of land, inland water and ice. The population figures are 2007 estimates where available. The annual income is the Gross Domestic Product per capita in US dollars. The figures are the latest available, usually 2007 estimates.

Country/Territory	Area km² Thousands	Area miles² Thousands	Population Thousands	Capital	Annual Income US $
Afghanistan	652	252	31,890	Kabul	800
Albania	28.7	11.1	3,601	Tirana	5,500
Algeria	2,382	920	33,333	Algiers	8,100
American Samoa (US)	0.20	0.08	58	Pago Pago	5,800
Andorra	0.47	0.18	72	Andorra La Vella	38,800
Angola	1,247	481	12,264	Luanda	6,500
Anguilla (UK)	0.10	0.04	14	The Valley	8,800
Antigua & Barbuda	0.44	0.17	69	St John's	10,900
Argentina	2,780	1,074	40,302	Buenos Aires	13,000
Armenia	29.8	11.5	2,972	Yerevan	5,700
Aruba (Netherlands)	0.19	0.07	100	Oranjestad	21,800
Australia	7,741	2,989	20,434	Canberra	37,500
Austria	83.9	32.4	8,200	Vienna	39,000
Azerbaijan	86.6	33.4	8,120	Baku	9,000
Azores (Portugal)	2.2	0.86	236	Ponta Delgada	15,000
Bahamas	13.9	5.4	306	Nassau	22,700
Bahrain	0.69	0.27	709	Manama	34,700
Bangladesh	144	55.6	150,448	Dhaka	1,400
Barbados	0.43	0.17	281	Bridgetown	19,700
Belarus	208	80.2	9,725	Minsk	10,200
Belgium	30.5	11.8	10,392	Brussels	36,500
Belize	23.0	8.9	294	Belmopan	7,800
Benin	113	43.5	9,078	Porto-Novo	1,500
Bermuda (UK)	0.05	0.02	66	Hamilton	69,900
Bhutan	47.0	18.1	2,328	Thimphu	1,400
Bolivia	1,099	424	9,119	La Paz/Sucre	4,400
Bosnia-Herzegovina	51.2	19.8	4,552	Sarajevo	6,600
Botswana	582	225	1,816	Gaborone	14,700
Brazil	8,514	3,287	190,011	Brasília	9,700
Brunei	5.8	2.2	375	Bandar Seri Begawan	25,600
Bulgaria	111	42.8	7,323	Sofia	11,800
Burkina Faso	274	106	14,326	Ouagadougou	1,200
Burma (=Myanmar)	677	261	47,374	Rangoon/Naypyidaw	1,900
Burundi	27.8	10.7	8,391	Bujumbura	800
Cambodia	181	69.9	13,996	Phnom Penh	1,800
Cameroon	475	184	18,060	Yaoundé	2,300
Canada	9,971	3,850	33,390	Ottawa	38,200
Canary Is. (Spain)	7.2	2.8	1,682	Las Palmas/Santa Cruz	19,900
Cape Verde Is.	4.0	1.6	424	Praia	7,000
Cayman Is. (UK)	0.26	0.10	47	George Town	43,800
Central African Republic	623	241	4,369	Bangui	700
Chad	1,284	496	9,886	Ndjaména	1,600
Chile	757	292	16,285	Santiago	14,400
China	9,597	3,705	1,321,852	Beijing	5,300
Colombia	1,139	440	44,380	Bogotá	7,200
Comoros	2.2	0.86	711	Moroni	600
Congo	342	132	3,801	Brazzaville	3,700
Congo (Dem. Rep. of the)	2,345	905	65,752	Kinshasa	300
Cook Is. (NZ)	0.24	0.09	22	Avarua	9,100
Costa Rica	51.1	19.7	4,134	San José	13,500
Croatia	56.5	21.8	4,493	Zagreb	15,500
Cuba	111	42.8	11,394	Havana	4,500
Cyprus	9.3	3.6	788	Nicosia	24,600
Czech Republic	78.9	30.5	10,229	Prague	24,400
Denmark	43.1	16.6	5,468	Copenhagen	37,400
Djibouti	23.2	9.0	496	Djibouti	1,000
Dominica	0.75	0.29	72	Roseau	3,800
Dominican Republic	48.5	18.7	9,366	Santo Domingo	9,200
East Timor	14.9	5.7	1,085	Dili	800
Ecuador	284	109	13,756	Quito	7,100
Egypt	1,001	387	80,335	Cairo	5,400
El Salvador	21.0	8.1	6,948	San Salvador	5,200
Equatorial Guinea	28.1	10.8	551	Malabo	4,100
Eritrea	118	45.4	4,907	Asmara	1,000
Estonia	45.1	17.4	1,316	Tallinn	21,800
Ethiopia	1,104	426	76,512	Addis Ababa	700
Faroe Is. (Denmark)	1.4	0.54	48	Tórshavn	31,000
Fiji	18.3	7.1	919	Suva	4,100
Finland	338	131	5,238	Helsinki	35,500
France	552	213	60,876	Paris	33,800
French Guiana (France)	90.0	34.7	200	Cayenne	8,300
French Polynesia (France)	4.0	1.5	279	Papeete	17,500
Gabon	268	103	1,455	Libreville	13,800
Gambia, The	11.3	4.4	1,688	Banjul	800
Gaza Strip (OPT)*	0.36	0.14	1,482	–	1,100
Georgia	69.7	26.9	4,646	Tbilisi	4,200
Germany	357	138	82,401	Berlin	34,400
Ghana	239	92.1	22,931	Accra	1,400
Gibraltar (UK)	0.006	0.002	28	Gibraltar Town	38,200
Greece	132	50.9	10,706	Athens	30,500
Greenland (Denmark)	2,176	840	56	Nuuk	20,000
Grenada	0.34	0.13	90	St George's	3,900
Guadeloupe (France)	1.7	0.66	453	Basse-Terre	7,900
Guam (US)	0.55	0.21	173	Agana	15,000
Guatemala	109	42.0	12,728	Guatemala City	5,400
Guinea	246	94.9	9,948	Conakry	1,000
Guinea-Bissau	36.1	13.9	1,473	Bissau	600
Guyana	215	83.0	769	Georgetown	5,300
Haiti	27.8	10.7	8,706	Port-au-Prince	1,900
Honduras	112	43.3	7,484	Tegucigalpa	3,300
Hungary	93.0	35.9	9,956	Budapest	19,500
Iceland	103	39.8	302	Reykjavik	39,400
India	3,287	1,269	1,129,866	New Delhi	2,700
Indonesia	1,905	735	234,694	Jakarta	3,400
Iran	1,648	636	65,398	Tehran	12,300
Iraq	438	169	27,500	Baghdad	3,600
Ireland	70.3	27.1	4,109	Dublin	45,600
Israel	20.6	8.0	6,427	Jerusalem	28,800
Italy	301	116	58,148	Rome	31,000
Ivory Coast (=Côte d'Ivoire)	322	125	18,013	Yamoussoukro	1,800
Jamaica	11.0	4.2	2,780	Kingston	4,800
Japan	378	146	127,433	Tokyo	33,800
Jordan	89.3	34.5	6,053	Amman	4,700
Kazakhstan	2,725	1,052	15,285	Astana	11,100
Kenya	580	224	36,914	Nairobi	1,600
Kiribati	0.73	0.28	108	Tarawa	1,800
Korea, North	121	46.5	23,302	Pyŏngyang	1,900
Korea, South	99.3	38.3	49,045	Seoul	24,600
Kosovo	10.9	4.2	2,127	Pristina	1,800
Kuwait	17.8	6.9	2,506	Kuwait City	55,300
Kyrgyzstan	200	77.2	5,284	Bishkek	2,000
Laos	237	91.4	6,522	Vientiane	1,900
Latvia	64.6	24.9	2,260	Riga	17,700
Lebanon	10.4	4.0	3,926	Beirut	10,400
Lesotho	30.4	11.7	2,125	Maseru	1,500
Liberia	111	43.0	3,196	Monrovia	500
Libya	1,760	679	6,037	Tripoli	13,100
Liechtenstein	0.16	0.06	34	Vaduz	25,000
Lithuania	65.2	25.2	3,575	Vilnius	16,700
Luxembourg	2.6	1.0	480	Luxembourg	80,800
Macedonia (FYROM)	25.7	9.9	2,056	Skopje	8,400
Madagascar	587	227	19,449	Antananarivo	1,000
Madeira (Portugal)	0.78	0.30	241	Funchal	22,700
Malawi	118	45.7	13,603	Lilongwe	800
Malaysia	330	127	24,821	Kuala Lumpur/Putrajaya	14,400
Maldives	0.30	0.12	369	Malé	3,900
Mali	1,240	479	11,995	Bamako	1,200
Malta	0.32	0.12	402	Valletta	23,700
Marshall Is.	0.18	0.07	62	Majuro	2,900
Martinique (France)	1.1	0.43	436	Fort-de-France	14,400
Mauritania	1,026	396	3,270	Nouakchott	1,800
Mauritius	2.0	0.79	1,251	Port Louis	11,900
Mayotte (France)	0.37	0.14	209	Mamoudzou	4,900
Mexico	1,958	756	108,701	Mexico City	12,500
Micronesia, Fed. States of	0.70	0.27	108	Palikir	2,300
Moldova	33.9	13.1	4,320	Chişinău	2,200
Monaco	0.001	0.0004	33	Monaco	30,000
Mongolia	1,567	605	2,952	Ulan Bator	2,900
Montenegro	14.0	5.4	685	Podgorica	3,800
Morocco	447	172	33,757	Rabat	3,800
Mozambique	802	309	20,906	Maputo	900
Namibia	824	318	2,055	Windhoek	5,200
Nauru	0.02	0.008	14	Yaren District	5,000
Nepal	147	56.8	28,902	Katmandu	1,100
Netherlands	41.5	16.0	16,571	Amsterdam/The Hague	38,600
Netherlands Antilles (Neths)	0.80	0.31	224	Willemstad	16,000
New Caledonia (France)	18.6	7.2	222	Nouméa	15,000
New Zealand	271	104	4,116	Wellington	27,300
Nicaragua	130	50.2	5,675	Managua	3,200
Niger	1,267	489	12,895	Niamey	700
Nigeria	924	357	135,031	Abuja	2,200
Northern Mariana Is. (US)	0.46	0.18	85	Saipan	12,500
Norway	324	125	4,628	Oslo	55,600
Oman	310	119	3,205	Muscat	19,100
Pakistan	796	307	164,742	Islamabad	2,600
Palau	0.46	0.18	21	Melekeok	7,600
Panama	75.5	29.2	3,242	Panamá	9,000
Papua New Guinea	463	179	5,796	Port Moresby	2,900
Paraguay	407	157	6,669	Asunción	4,000
Peru	1,285	496	28,675	Lima	7,600
Philippines	300	116	91,077	Manila	3,300
Poland	323	125	38,518	Warsaw	16,200
Portugal	88.8	34.3	10,643	Lisbon	21,800
Puerto Rico (US)	8.9	3.4	3,944	San Juan	19,600
Qatar	11.0	4.2	907	Doha	29,400
Réunion (France)	2.5	0.97	788	St-Denis	6,200
Romania	238	92.0	22,276	Bucharest	11,100
Russia	17,075	6,593	141,378	Moscow	14,600
Rwanda	26.3	10.2	9,908	Kigali	1,000
St Kitts & Nevis	0.26	0.10	39	Basseterre	8,200
St Lucia	0.54	0.21	171	Castries	4,800
St Vincent & Grenadines	0.39	0.15	118	Kingstown	3,600
Samoa	2.8	1.1	214	Apia	2,100
San Marino	0.06	0.02	30	San Marino	34,100
São Tomé & Príncipe	0.96	0.37	200	São Tomé	1,200
Saudi Arabia	2,150	830	27,601	Riyadh	20,700
Senegal	197	76.0	12,522	Dakar	1,700
Serbia	77.5	29.9	8,024	Belgrade	7,700
Seychelles	0.46	0.18	82	Victoria	18,400
Sierra Leone	71.7	27.7	6,145	Freetown	800
Singapore	0.68	0.26	4,553	Singapore City	48,900
Slovak Republic	49.0	18.9	5,448	Bratislava	19,800
Slovenia	20.3	7.8	2,009	Ljubljana	27,300
Solomon Is.	28.9	11.2	567	Honiara	600
Somalia	638	246	9,119	Mogadishu	600
South Africa	1,221	471	43,998	Cape Town/Pretoria	10,600
Spain	498	192	40,448	Madrid	33,700
Sri Lanka	65.6	25.3	20,926	Colombo	4,100
Sudan	2,506	967	39,379	Khartoum	2,500
Suriname	163	63.0	471	Paramaribo	7,800
Swaziland	17.4	6.7	1,133	Mbabane	4,800
Sweden	450	174	9,031	Stockholm	36,900
Switzerland	41.3	15.9	7,555	Bern	39,800
Syria	185	71.5	19,315	Damascus	4,500
Taiwan	36.0	13.9	22,859	Taipei	29,800
Tajikistan	143	55.3	7,077	Dushanbe	1,600
Tanzania	945	365	39,384	Dodoma	1,100
Thailand	513	198	65,068	Bangkok	8,000
Togo	56.8	21.9	5,702	Lomé	900
Tonga	0.65	0.25	117	Nuku'alofa	2,200
Trinidad & Tobago	5.1	2.0	1,057	Port of Spain	21,700
Tunisia	164	63.2	10,276	Tunis	7,500
Turkey	775	299	71,159	Ankara	9,400
Turkmenistan	488	188	5,097	Ashkhabad	9,200
Turks & Caicos Is. (UK)	0.43	0.17	22	Cockburn Town	11,500
Tuvalu	0.03	0.01	12	Fongafale	1,600
Uganda	241	93.1	30,263	Kampala	1,100
Ukraine	604	233	46,300	Kiev	6,900
United Arab Emirates	83.6	32.3	4,444	Abu Dhabi	55,200
United Kingdom	242	93.4	60,776	London	35,300
United States of America	9,629	3,718	301,140	Washington, DC	46,000
Uruguay	175	67.6	3,461	Montevideo	10,700
Uzbekistan	447	173	27,780	Tashkent	2,200
Vanuatu	12.2	4.7	212	Port-Vila	2,900
Venezuela	912	352	26,024	Caracas	12,800
Vietnam	332	128	85,262	Hanoi	2,600
Virgin Is. (UK)	0.15	0.06	24	Road Town	38,500
Virgin Is. (US)	0.35	0.13	108	Charlotte Amalie	14,500
Wallis & Futuna Is. (France)	0.20	0.08	16	Mata-Utu	3,800
West Bank (OPT)*	5.9	2.3	2,536	–	1,100
Western Sahara	266	103	383	El Aaiún	N/A
Yemen	528	204	22,231	Sana'	2,400
Zambia	753	291	11,477	Lusaka	1,400
Zimbabwe	391	151	12,311	Harare	500

*OPT = Occupied Palestinian Territory   N/A = Not available

World Statistics: Physical Dimensions

Each topic list is divided into continents and within a continent the items are listed in order of size. The bottom part of many of the lists is selective in order to give examples from as many different countries as possible. The order of the continents is the same as in the atlas, beginning with Europe and ending with South America. The figures are rounded as appropriate.

World, Continents, Oceans

	km²	miles²	%
The World	509,450,000	196,672,000	–
Land	149,450,000	57,688,000	29.3
Water	360,000,000	138,984,000	70.7
Asia	44,500,000	17,177,000	29.8
Africa	30,302,000	11,697,000	20.3
North America	24,241,000	9,357,000	16.2
South America	17,793,000	6,868,000	11.9
Antarctica	14,100,000	5,443,000	9.4
Europe	9,957,000	3,843,000	6.7
Australia & Oceania	8,557,000	3,303,000	5.7
Pacific Ocean	155,557,000	60,061,000	46.4
Atlantic Ocean	76,762,000	29,638,000	22.9
Indian Ocean	68,556,000	26,470,000	20.4
Southern Ocean	20,327,000	7,848,000	6.1
Arctic Ocean	14,056,000	5,427,000	4.2

Ocean Depths

Atlantic Ocean		m	ft
Puerto Rico (Milwaukee) Deep		8,605	28,232
Cayman Trench		7,680	25,197
Gulf of Mexico		5,203	17,070
Mediterranean Sea		5,121	16,801
Black Sea		2,211	7,254
North Sea		660	2,165

Indian Ocean		m	ft
Java Trench		7,450	24,442
Red Sea		2,635	8,454

Pacific Ocean		m	ft
Mariana Trench		11,022	36,161
Tonga Trench		10,882	35,702
Japan Trench		10,554	34,626
Kuril Trench		10,542	34,587

Arctic Ocean		m	ft
Molloy Deep		5,608	18,399

Southern Ocean		m	ft
South Sandwich Trench		7,235	23,737

Mountains

Europe		m	ft
Elbrus	Russia	5,642	18,510
Dykh-Tau	Russia	5,205	17,076
Shkhara	Russia/Georgia	5,201	17,064
Koshtan-Tau	Russia	5,152	16,903
Kazbek	Russia/Georgia	5,047	16,558
Pushkin	Russia/Georgia	5,033	16,512
Katyn-Tau	Russia/Georgia	4,979	16,335
Shota Rustaveli	Russia/Georgia	4,860	15,945
Mont Blanc	France/Italy	4,808	15,774
Monte Rosa	Italy/Switzerland	4,634	15,203
Dom	Switzerland	4,545	14,911
Liskamm	Switzerland	4,527	14,852
Weisshorn	Switzerland	4,505	14,780
Taschorn	Switzerland	4,490	14,730
Matterhorn/Cervino	Italy/Switzerland	4,478	14,691
Grossglockner	Austria	3,797	12,457
Mulhacén	Spain	3,478	11,411
Zugspitze	Germany	2,962	9,718
Olympus	Greece	2,917	9,570
Galdhøpiggen	Norway	2,469	8,100
Ben Nevis	UK	1,342	4,403

Asia		m	ft
Everest	China/Nepal	8,850	29,035
K2 (Godwin Austen)	China/Kashmir	8,611	28,251
Kanchenjunga	India/Nepal	8,598	28,208
Lhotse	China/Nepal	8,516	27,939
Makalu	China/Nepal	8,481	27,824
Cho Oyu	China/Nepal	8,201	26,906
Dhaulagiri	Nepal	8,167	26,795
Manaslu	Nepal	8,156	26,758
Nanga Parbat	Kashmir	8,126	26,660
Annapurna	Nepal	8,078	26,502
Gasherbrum	China/Kashmir	8,068	26,469
Broad Peak	China/Kashmir	8,051	26,414
Xixabangma	China	8,012	26,286
Kangbachen	Nepal	7,858	25,781
Trivor	Pakistan	7,720	25,328
Pik Imeni Ismail Samani	Tajikistan	7,495	24,590
Demavend	Iran	5,604	18,386
Ararat	Turkey	5,165	16,945
Gunong Kinabalu	Malaysia (Borneo)	4,101	13,455
Fuji-San	Japan	3,776	12,388

Africa		m	ft
Kilimanjaro	Tanzania	5,895	19,340
Mt Kenya	Kenya	5,199	17,057
Ruwenzori (Margherita)	Ug./Congo (D.R.)	5,109	16,762
Meru	Tanzania	4,565	14,977
Ras Dashen	Ethiopia	4,533	14,872
Karisimbi	Rwanda/Congo (D.R.)	4,507	14,787
Mt Elgon	Kenya/Uganda	4,321	14,176
Batu	Ethiopia	4,307	14,130
Toubkal	Morocco	4,165	13,665
Mt Cameroun	Cameroon	4,070	13,353

Oceania		m	ft
Puncak Jaya	Indonesia	5,029	16,499
Puncak Trikora	Indonesia	4,730	15,518
Puncak Mandala	Indonesia	4,702	15,427
Mt Wilhelm	Papua New Guinea	4,508	14,790
Mauna Kea	USA (Hawai'i)	4,205	13,796
Mauna Loa	USA (Hawai'i)	4,169	13,681
Aoraki Mt Cook	New Zealand	3,753	12,313
Mt Kosciuszko	Australia	2,228	7,310

North America		m	ft
Mt McKinley (Denali)	USA (Alaska)	6,194	20,321
Mt Logan	Canada	5,959	19,551
Pico de Orizaba	Mexico	5,610	18,405
Mt St Elias	USA/Canada	5,489	18,008
Popocatépetl	Mexico	5,452	17,887
Mt Foraker	USA (Alaska)	5,304	17,401
Iztaccihuatl	Mexico	5,286	17,343
Mt Lucania	Canada	5,226	17,146
Mt Steele	Canada	5,073	16,644
Mt Bona	USA (Alaska)	5,005	16,420
Mt Whitney	USA	4,418	14,495
Tajumulco	Guatemala	4,220	13,845
Chirripó Grande	Costa Rica	3,837	12,589
Pico Duarte	Dominican Rep.	3,175	10,417

South America		m	ft
Aconcagua	Argentina	6,962	22,841
Bonete	Argentina	6,872	22,546
Ojos del Salado	Argentina/Chile	6,863	22,516
Pissis	Argentina	6,779	22,241
Mercedario	Argentina/Chile	6,770	22,211
Huascarán	Peru	6,768	22,204
Llullaillaco	Argentina/Chile	6,723	22,057
Nevado de Cachi	Argentina	6,720	22,047
Yerupaja	Peru	6,632	21,758
Sajama	Bolivia	6,520	21,391
Chimborazo	Ecuador	6,267	20,561
Pico Cristóbal Colón	Colombia	5,800	19,029
Pico Bolivar	Venezuela	5,007	16,427

Antarctica		m	ft
Vinson Massif		4,897	16,066
Mt Kirkpatrick		4,528	14,855

Rivers

Europe		km	miles
Volga	Caspian Sea	3,700	2,300
Danube	Black Sea	2,850	1,770
Ural	Caspian Sea	2,535	1,575
Dnepr (Dnipro)	Black Sea	2,285	1,420
Kama	Volga	2,030	1,260
Don	Black Sea	1,990	1,240
Petchora	Arctic Ocean	1,790	1,110
Oka	Volga	1,480	920
Dnister (Dniester)	Black Sea	1,400	870
Vyatka	Kama	1,370	850
Rhine	North Sea	1,320	820
N. Dvina	Arctic Ocean	1,290	800
Elbe	North Sea	1,145	710

Asia		km	miles
Yangtze	Pacific Ocean	6,380	3,960
Yenisey–Angara	Arctic Ocean	5,550	3,445
Huang He	Pacific Ocean	5,464	3,395
Ob–Irtysh	Arctic Ocean	5,410	3,360
Mekong	Pacific Ocean	4,500	2,795
Amur	Pacific Ocean	4,442	2,760
Lena	Arctic Ocean	4,402	2,735
Irtysh	Ob	4,250	2,640
Yenisey	Arctic Ocean	4,090	2,540
Ob	Arctic Ocean	3,680	2,285
Indus	Indian Ocean	3,100	1,925
Brahmaputra	Indian Ocean	2,900	1,800
Syrdarya	Aral Sea	2,860	1,775
Salween	Indian Ocean	2,800	1,740
Euphrates	Indian Ocean	2,700	1,675
Amudarya	Aral Sea	2,540	1,575

Africa		km	miles
Nile	Mediterranean	6,695	4,160
Congo	Atlantic Ocean	4,670	2,900
Niger	Atlantic Ocean	4,180	2,595
Zambezi	Indian Ocean	3,540	2,200
Oubangi/Uele	Congo (D.R.)	2,250	1,400
Kasai	Congo (D.R.)	1,950	1,210
Shaballe	Indian Ocean	1,930	1,200
Orange	Atlantic Ocean	1,860	1,155
Cubango	Okavango Delta	1,800	1,120
Limpopo	Indian Ocean	1,770	1,100
Senegal	Atlantic Ocean	1,640	1,020

Australia		km	miles
Murray–Darling	Southern Ocean	3,750	2,330
Darling	Murray	3,070	1,905
Murray	Southern Ocean	2,575	1,600
Murrumbidgee	Murray	1,690	1,050

North America		km	miles
Mississippi–Missouri	Gulf of Mexico	5,971	3,710
Mackenzie	Arctic Ocean	4,240	2,630
Missouri	Mississippi	4,088	2,540
Mississippi	Gulf of Mexico	3,782	2,350
Yukon	Pacific Ocean	3,185	1,980
Rio Grande	Gulf of Mexico	3,030	1,880
Arkansas	Mississippi	2,340	1,450
Colorado	Pacific Ocean	2,330	1,445
Red	Mississippi	2,040	1,270
Columbia	Pacific Ocean	1,950	1,210
Saskatchewan	Lake Winnipeg	1,940	1,205

South America		km	miles
Amazon	Atlantic Ocean	6,450	4,010
Paraná–Plate	Atlantic Ocean	4,500	2,800
Purus	Amazon	3,350	2,080
Madeira	Amazon	3,200	1,990
São Francisco	Atlantic Ocean	2,900	1,800
Paraná	Plate	2,800	1,740
Tocantins	Atlantic Ocean	2,750	1,710
Orinoco	Atlantic Ocean	2,740	1,700
Paraguay	Paraná	2,550	1,580
Pilcomayo	Paraná	2,500	1,550
Araguaia	Tocantins	2,250	1,400

Lakes

Europe		km²	miles²
Lake Ladoga	Russia	17,700	6,800
Lake Onega	Russia	9,700	3,700
Saimaa system	Finland	8,000	3,100
Vänern	Sweden	5,500	2,100

Asia		km²	miles²
Caspian Sea	Asia	371,000	143,000
Lake Baikal	Russia	30,500	11,780
Tonlé Sap	Cambodia	20,000	7,700
Lake Balqash	Kazakhstan	18,500	7,100
Aral Sea	Kazakhstan/Uzbekistan	17,160	6,625

Africa		km²	miles²
Lake Victoria	East Africa	68,000	26,300
Lake Tanganyika	Central Africa	33,000	13,000
Lake Malawi/Nyasa	East Africa	29,600	11,430
Lake Chad	Central Africa	25,000	9,700
Lake Bangweulu	Zambia	9,840	3,800
Lake Turkana	Ethiopia/Kenya	8,500	3,290

Australia		km²	miles²
Lake Eyre	Australia	8,900	3,400
Lake Torrens	Australia	5,800	2,200
Lake Gairdner	Australia	4,800	1,900

North America		km²	miles²
Lake Superior	Canada/USA	82,350	31,800
Lake Huron	Canada/USA	59,600	23,010
Lake Michigan	USA	58,000	22,400
Great Bear Lake	Canada	31,800	12,280
Great Slave Lake	Canada	28,500	11,000
Lake Erie	Canada/USA	25,700	9,900
Lake Winnipeg	Canada	24,400	9,400
Lake Ontario	Canada/USA	19,500	7,500
Lake Nicaragua	Nicaragua	8,200	3,200

South America		km²	miles²
Lake Titicaca	Bolivia/Peru	8,300	3,200
Lake Poopo	Bolivia	2,800	1,100

Islands

Europe		km²	miles²
Great Britain	UK	229,880	88,700
Iceland	Atlantic Ocean	103,000	39,800
Ireland	Ireland/UK	84,400	32,600
Novaya Zemlya (N.)	Russia	48,200	18,600
Sicily	Italy	25,500	9,800
Corsica	France	8,700	3,400

Asia		km²	miles²
Borneo	South-east Asia	744,360	287,400
Sumatra	Indonesia	473,600	182,860
Honshu	Japan	230,500	88,980
Sulawesi (Celebes)	Indonesia	189,000	73,000
Java	Indonesia	126,700	48,900
Luzon	Philippines	104,700	40,400
Hokkaido	Japan	78,400	30,300

Africa		km²	miles²
Madagascar	Indian Ocean	587,040	226,660
Socotra	Indian Ocean	3,600	1,400
Réunion	Indian Ocean	2,500	965

Oceania		km²	miles²
New Guinea	Indonesia/Papua NG	821,030	317,000
New Zealand (S.)	Pacific Ocean	150,500	58,100
New Zealand (N.)	Pacific Ocean	114,700	44,300
Tasmania	Australia	67,800	26,200
Hawai'i	Pacific Ocean	10,450	4,000

North America		km²	miles²
Greenland	Atlantic Ocean	2,175,600	839,800
Baffin Is.	Canada	508,000	196,100
Victoria Is.	Canada	212,200	81,900
Ellesmere Is.	Canada	212,000	81,800
Cuba	Caribbean Sea	110,860	42,800
Hispaniola	Dominican Rep./Haiti	76,200	29,400
Jamaica	Caribbean Sea	11,400	4,400
Puerto Rico	Atlantic Ocean	8,900	3,400

South America		km²	miles²
Tierra del Fuego	Argentina/Chile	47,000	18,100
Falkland Is. (E.)	Atlantic Ocean	6,800	2,600

User Guide

The reference maps which form the main body of this atlas have been prepared in accordance with the highest standards of international cartography to provide an accurate and detailed representation of the Earth. The scales and projections used have been carefully chosen to give balanced coverage of the world, while emphasizing the most densely populated and economically significant regions. A hallmark of Philip's mapping is the use of hill shading and relief colouring to create a graphic impression of landforms: this makes the maps exceptionally easy to read. However, knowledge of the key features employed in the construction and presentation of the maps will enable the reader to derive the fullest benefit from the atlas.

Map sequence

The atlas covers the Earth continent by continent: first Europe; then its land neighbour Asia (mapped north before south, in a clockwise sequence), then Africa, Australia and Oceania, North America and South America. This is the classic arrangement adopted by most cartographers since the 16th century. For each continent, there are maps at a variety of scales. First, physical relief and political maps of the whole continent; then a series of larger-scale maps of the regions within the continent, each followed, where required, by still larger-scale maps of the most important or densely populated areas. The governing principle is that by turning the pages of the atlas, the reader moves steadily from north to south through each continent, with each map overlapping its neighbours.

Map presentation

With very few exceptions (for example, for the Arctic and Antarctica), the maps are drawn with north at the top, regardless of whether they are presented upright or sideways on the page. In the borders will be found the map title; a locator diagram showing the area covered; continuation arrows showing the page numbers for maps of adjacent areas; the scale; the projection used; the degrees of latitude and longitude; and the letters and figures used in the index for locating place names and geographical features. Physical relief maps also have a height reference panel identifying the colours used for each layer of contouring.

Map symbols

Each map contains a vast amount of detail which can only be conveyed clearly and accurately by the use of symbols. Points and circles of varying sizes locate and identify the relative importance of towns and cities; different styles of type are employed for administrative, geographical and regional place names. A variety of pictorial symbols denote features such as glaciers and marshes, as well as man-made structures including roads, railways, airports and canals.

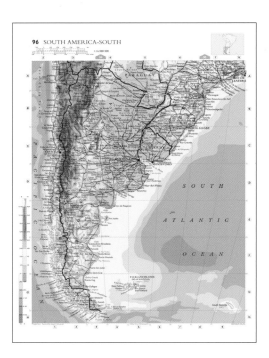

International borders are shown by red lines. Where neighbouring countries are in dispute, for example in the Middle East, the maps show the *de facto* boundary between nations, regardless of the legal or historical situation. The symbols are explained on the first page of the World Maps section of the atlas.

Map scales

The scale of each map is given in the numerical form known as the 'representative fraction'. The first figure is always one, signifying one unit of distance on the map; the second figure, usually in millions, is the number by which the map unit must be multiplied to give the equivalent distance on the Earth's surface. Calculations can easily be made in centimetres and kilometres, by dividing the Earth units figure by 100 000 (i.e. deleting the last five 0s). Thus 1:1 000 000 means 1 cm = 10 km. The calculation for inches and miles is more laborious, but 1 000 000 divided by 63 360 (the number of inches in a mile) shows that the ratio 1:1 000 000 means approximately 1 inch = 16 miles. The table below provides distance equivalents for scales down to 1:50 000 000.

LARGE SCALE		
1:1 000 000	1 cm = 10 km	1 inch = 16 miles
1:2 500 000	1 cm = 25 km	1 inch = 39.5 miles
1:5 000 000	1 cm = 50 km	1 inch = 79 miles
1:6 000 000	1 cm = 60 km	1 inch = 95 miles
1:8 000 000	1 cm = 80 km	1 inch = 126 miles
1:10 000 000	1 cm = 100 km	1 inch = 158 miles
1:15 000 000	1 cm = 150 km	1 inch = 237 miles
1:20 000 000	1 cm = 200 km	1 inch = 316 miles
1:50 000 000	1 cm = 500 km	1 inch = 790 miles
SMALL SCALE		

Measuring distances

Although each map is accompanied by a scale bar, distances cannot always be measured with confidence because of the distortions involved in portraying the curved surface of the Earth on a flat page. As a general rule, the larger the map scale (i.e. the lower the number of Earth units in the representative fraction), the more accurate and reliable will be the distance measured. On small-scale maps such as those of the world and of entire continents, measurement may only be accurate along the 'standard parallels', or central axes, and should not be attempted without considering the map projection.

Latitude and longitude

Accurate positioning of individual points on the Earth's surface is made possible by reference to the geometrical system of latitude and longitude. Latitude *parallels* are drawn west–east around the Earth and numbered by degrees north and south of the Equator, which is designated 0° of latitude. Longitude *meridians* are drawn north–south and numbered by degrees east and west of the *prime meridian*, 0° of longitude, which passes through Greenwich in England. By referring to these co-ordinates and their subdivisions of minutes ($1/60$th of a degree) and seconds ($1/60$th of a minute), any place on Earth can be located to within a few hundred metres. Latitude and longitude are indicated by blue lines on the maps; they are straight or curved according to the projection employed. Reference to these lines is the easiest way of determining the relative positions of places on different maps, and for plotting compass directions.

Name forms

For ease of reference, both English and local name forms appear in the atlas. Oceans, seas and countries are shown in English throughout the atlas; country names may be abbreviated to their commonly accepted form (for example, Germany, not The Federal Republic of Germany). Conventional English forms are also used for place names on the smaller-scale maps of the continents. However, local name forms are used on all large-scale and regional maps, with the English form given in brackets only for important cities – the large-scale map of Russia and Central Asia thus shows Moskva (Moscow). For countries which do not use a Roman script, place names have been transcribed according to the systems adopted by the British and US Geographic Names Authorities. For China, the Pin Yin system has been used, with some more widely known forms appearing in brackets, as with Beijing (Peking). Both English and local names appear in the index, the English form being cross-referenced to the local form.

THE
WORLD
IN FOCUS

PLANET EARTH	2	WATER & VEGETATION	12	QUALITY OF LIFE	22
RESTLESS EARTH	4	ENVIRONMENT	14	ENERGY	24
LANDFORMS	6	POPULATION	16	PRODUCTION	26
OCEANS	8	THE HUMAN FAMILY	18	TRADE	28
CLIMATE	10	WEALTH	20	TRAVEL & TOURISM	30

Planet Earth

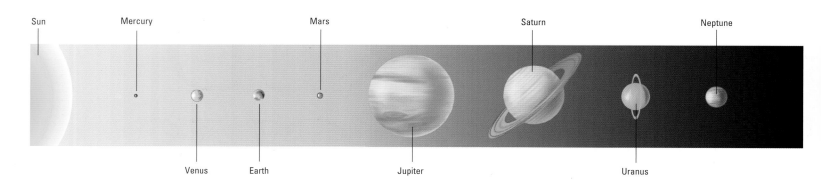

Sun Mercury Mars Saturn Neptune
Venus Earth Jupiter Uranus

The Solar System

A minute part of one of the billions of galaxies (collections of stars) that populate the Universe, the Solar System lies about 26,000 light-years from the centre of our own galaxy, the 'Milky Way'. Thought to be about 5 billion years old, it consists of a central Sun with eight planets and their moons revolving around it, attracted by its gravitational pull. The planets orbit the Sun in the same direction – anti-clockwise when viewed from above the Sun's north pole – and almost in the same plane. Their orbital distances, however, vary enormously.

The Sun's diameter is 109 times that of the Earth, and the temperature at its core – caused by continuous thermonuclear fusions of hydrogen into helium – is estimated to be 15 million degrees Celsius. It is the Solar System's only source of light and heat.

Profile of the Planets

	Mean distance from Sun (million km)	Mass (Earth = 1)	Period of orbit (Earth days/years)	Period of rotation (Earth days)	Equatorial diameter (km)	Number of known satellites*
Mercury	57.9	0.06	87.97 days	58.65	4,879	0
Venus	108.2	0.82	224.7 days	243.02	12,104	0
Earth	149.6	1.00	365.3 days	1.00	12,756	1
Mars	227.9	0.11	687.0 days	1.029	6,792	2
Jupiter	778	317.8	11.86 years	0.411	142,984	63
Saturn	1,427	95.2	29.45 years	0.428	120,536	60
Uranus	2,871	14.5	84.02 years	0.720	51,118	27
Neptune	4,498	17.2	164.8 years	0.673	49,528	13

* Number of known satellites at mid-2008

All planetary orbits are elliptical in form, but only Mercury follows a path that deviates noticeably from a circular one. In 2006, Pluto was demoted from its former status as a planet and is now regarded as a member of the Kuiper Belt of icy bodies at the fringes of the Solar System.

The Seasons

Seasons occur because the Earth's axis is tilted at an angle of approximately 23½°. When the northern hemisphere is tilted to a maximum extent towards the Sun, on 21 June, the Sun is overhead at the Tropic of Cancer (latitude 23½° North). This is midsummer, or the summer solstice, in the northern hemisphere.

On 22 or 23 September, the Sun is overhead at the equator, and day and night are of equal length throughout the world. This is the autumnal equinox in the northern hemisphere. On 21 or 22 December, the Sun is overhead at the Tropic of Capricorn (23½° South), the winter solstice in the northern hemisphere. The overhead Sun then tracks north until, on 21 March, it is overhead at the equator. This is the spring (vernal) equinox in the northern hemisphere.

In the southern hemisphere, the seasons are the reverse of those in the north.

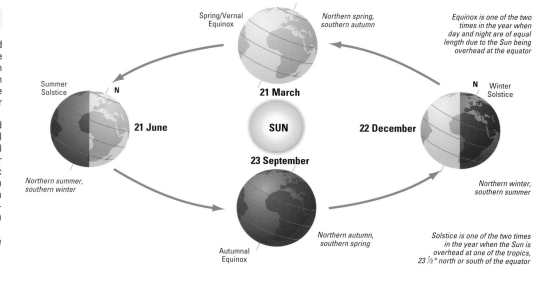

Day and Night

The Sun appears to rise in the east, reach its highest point at noon, and then set in the west, to be followed by night. In reality, it is not the Sun that is moving but the Earth rotating from west to east. The moment when the Sun's upper limb first appears above the horizon is termed sunrise; the moment when the Sun's upper limb disappears below the horizon is sunset.

At the summer solstice in the northern hemisphere (21 June), the Arctic has total daylight and the Antarctic total darkness. The opposite occurs at the winter solstice (21 or 22 December). At the equator, the length of day and night are almost equal all year.

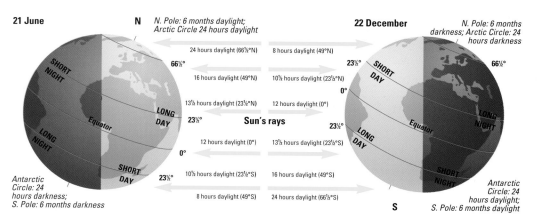

Time

Year: The time taken by the Earth to revolve around the Sun, or 365.24 days.

Leap Year: A calendar year of 366 days, 29 February being the additional day. It offsets the difference between the calendar and the solar year.

Month: The 12 calendar months of the year are approximately equal in length to a lunar month.

Week: An artificial period of 7 days, not based on astronomical time.

Day: The time taken by the Earth to complete one rotation on its axis.

Hour: 24 hours make one day. The day is divided into hours a.m. (ante meridiem or before noon) and p.m. (post meridiem or after noon), although most time-tables now use the 24-hour system, from midnight to midnight.

Sunrise

Sunset

The Moon

The Moon rotates more slowly than the Earth, taking just over 27 days to make one complete rotation on its axis. Since this corresponds to the Moon's orbital period around the Earth, the Moon always presents the same hemisphere towards us, and we never see the far side. The interval between one New Moon and the next is 29½ days – this is called a lunation, or lunar month. The Moon shines only by reflected sunlight, and emits no light of its own. During each lunation the Moon displays a complete cycle of phases, caused by the changing angle of illumination from the Sun.

Phases of the Moon

Mean distance from Earth: 384,401 km; Mean diameter: 3,475 km;
Mass: approximately 1/80 that of Earth; Surface gravity: one-sixth of Earth's;
Daily range of temperature at lunar equator: 280°C; Average orbital speed: 3,681 km/h

| New Moon | Waxing Crescent | First Quarter | Gibbous | Full Moon | Gibbous | Last Quarter | Waning Crescent | New Moon |

Eclipses

When the Moon passes between the Sun and the Earth, the Sun becomes partially eclipsed (1). A partial eclipse becomes a total eclipse if the Moon proceeds to cover the Sun completely (2) and the dark central part of the lunar shadow touches the Earth. The broad geographical zone covered by the Moon's outer shadow (P), has only a very small central area (often less than 100 km wide) that experiences totality. Totality can never last for more than 7½ minutes at maximum, but is usually much briefer than this. Lunar eclipses take place when the Moon moves through the shadow of the Earth, and can be partial or total. Any single location on Earth can experience a maximum of four solar and three lunar eclipses in any single year, while a total solar eclipse occurs an average of once every 360 years for any given location.

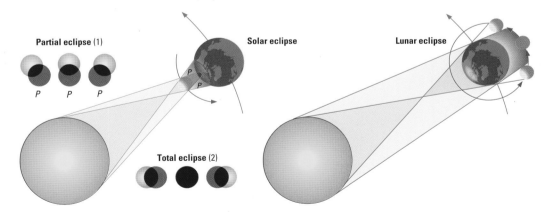

Tides

The daily rise and fall of the ocean's tides are the result of the gravitational pull of the Moon and that of the Sun, though the effect of the latter is not as strong as that of the Moon. This effect is greatest on the hemisphere facing the Moon and causes a tidal 'bulge'.

Spring tides occur when the Sun, Earth and Moon are aligned; high tides are at their highest, and low tides fall to their lowest. When the Moon and Sun are furthest out of line (near the Moon's First and Last Quarters), neap tides occur, producing the smallest range between high and low tides.

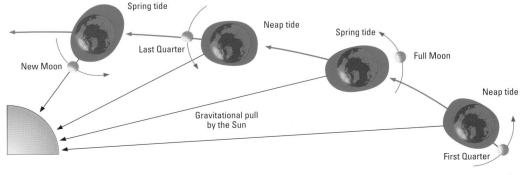

Restless Earth

The Earth's Structure

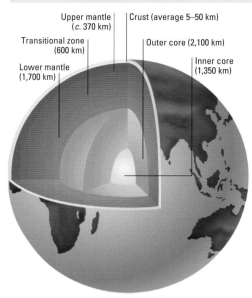

Upper mantle (c. 370 km)

Crust (average 5–50 km)

Transitional zone (600 km)

Outer core (2,100 km)

Lower mantle (1,700 km)

Inner core (1,350 km)

Continental Drift

About 200 million years ago the original Pangaea landmass began to split into two continental groups, which further separated over time to produce the present-day configuration.

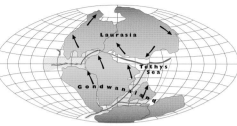

180 million years ago

135 million years ago

Trench

Rift

New ocean floor

Zones of slippage

Present day

Notable Earthquakes Since 1900

Year	Location	Richter Scale	Deaths
1906	San Francisco, USA	8.3	3,000
1906	Valparaiso, Chile	8.6	22,000
1908	Messina, Italy	7.5	83,000
1915	Avezzano, Italy	7.5	30,000
1920	Gansu (Kansu), China	8.6	180,000
1923	Yokohama, Japan	8.3	143,000
1927	Nan Shan, China	8.3	200,000
1932	Gansu (Kansu), China	7.6	70,000
1933	Sanriku, Japan	8.9	2,990
1934	Bihar, India/Nepal	8.4	10,700
1935	Quetta, India (now Pakistan)	7.5	60,000
1939	Chillan, Chile	8.3	28,000
1939	Erzincan, Turkey	7.9	30,000
1960	S. W. Chile	9.5	2,200
1960	Agadir, Morocco	5.8	12,000
1962	Khorasan, Iran	7.1	12,230
1964	Anchorage, USA	9.2	125
1968	N. E. Iran	7.4	12,000
1970	N. Peru	7.8	70,000
1972	Managua, Nicaragua	6.2	5,000
1974	N. Pakistan	6.3	5,200
1976	Guatemala	7.5	22,500
1976	Tangshan, China	8.2	255,000
1978	Tabas, Iran	7.7	25,000
1980	El Asnam, Algeria	7.3	20,000
1980	S. Italy	7.2	4,800
1985	Mexico City, Mexico	8.1	4,200
1988	N.W. Armenia	6.8	55,000
1990	N. Iran	7.7	36,000
1993	Maharashtra, India	6.4	30,000
1994	Los Angeles, USA	6.6	51
1995	Kobe, Japan	7.2	5,000
1995	Sakhalin Is., Russia	7.5	2,000
1997	N. E. Iran	7.1	2,400
1998	Takhar, Afghanistan	6.1	4,200
1998	Rostaq, Afghanistan	7.0	5,000
1999	Izmit, Turkey	7.4	15,000
1999	Taipei, Taiwan	7.6	1,700
2001	Gujarat, India	7.7	14,000
2002	Baghlan, Afghanistan	6.1	1,000
2003	Boumerdes, Algeria	6.8	2,200
2003	Bam, Iran	6.6	30,000
2004	Sumatra, Indonesia	9.0	250,000
2005	N. Pakistan	7.6	74,000
2006	Java, Indonesia	6.4	6,200
2007	S. Peru	8.0	600
2008	Sichuan, China	7.9	70,000

Earthquakes

Earthquake magnitude is usually rated according to either the Richter or the Modified Mercalli scale, both devised by seismologists in the 1930s. The Richter scale measures absolute earthquake power with mathematical precision: each step upwards represents a tenfold increase in shockwave amplitude. Theoretically, there is no upper limit, but most of the largest earthquakes measured have been rated at between 8.8 and 8.9. The 12–point Mercalli scale, based on observed effects, is often more meaningful, ranging from I (earthquakes noticed only by seismographs) to XII (total destruction); intermediate points include V (people awakened at night; unstable objects overturned), VII (collapse of ordinary buildings; chimneys and monuments fall), and IX (conspicuous cracks in ground; serious damage to reservoirs).

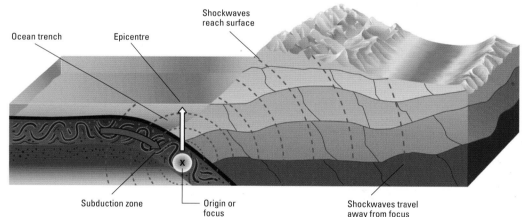

Shockwaves reach surface

Ocean trench

Epicentre

Subduction zone

Origin or focus

Shockwaves travel away from focus

Structure and Earthquakes

Mobile land areas

Submarine zones of mobile land areas

Stable land platforms

Submarine extensions of stable land platforms

Mid-oceanic volcanic ridges

Oceanic platforms

1976 ○ Principal earthquakes and dates (since 1900)

Earthquakes are a series of rapid vibrations originating from the slipping or faulting of parts of the Earth's crust when stresses within build up to breaking point. They usually happen at depths varying from 8 km to 30 km. Severe earthquakes cause extensive damage when they take place in populated areas, destroying structures and severing communications. Most initial loss of life occurs due to secondary causes such as falling masonry, fires and flooding.

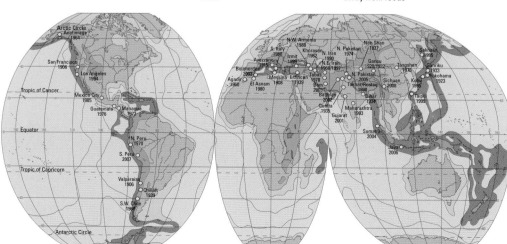

Projection: Interrupted Mollweide

4

Plate Tectonics

—— Plate boundaries   PACIFIC Major plates

→ Direction of plate movements and rate of movement (cm/year)

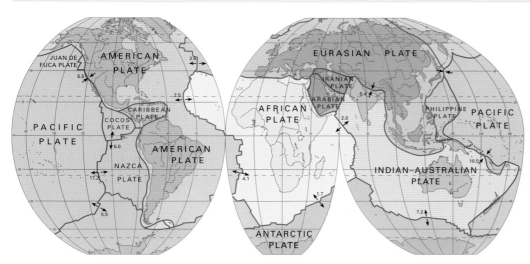

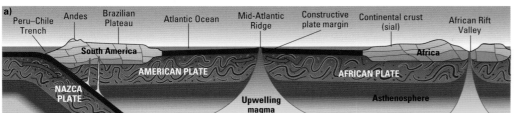

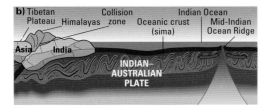

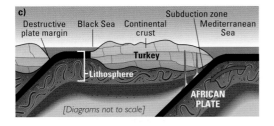

The drifting of the continents is a feature that is unique to Planet Earth. The complementary, almost jigsaw-puzzle fit of the coastlines on each side of the Atlantic Ocean inspired Alfred Wegener's theory of continental drift in 1915. The theory suggested that the ancient super-continent, which Wegener named Pangaea, incorporated all of the Earth's landmasses and gradually split up to form today's continents.

The original debate about continental drift was a prelude to a more radical idea: plate tectonics. The basic theory is that the Earth's crust is made up of a series of rigid plates which float on a soft layer of the mantle and are moved about by continental convection currents within the Earth's interior. These plates diverge and converge along margins marked by seismic activity. Plates diverge from mid-ocean ridges where molten lava pushes upwards and forces the plates apart at rates of up to 40 mm [1.6 in] a year.

The three diagrams, left, give some examples of plate boundaries from around the world. Diagram (a) shows sea-floor spreading at the Mid-Atlantic Ridge as the American and African plates slowly diverge. The same thing is happening in (b) where sea-floor spreading at the Mid-Indian Ocean Ridge is forcing the Indian–Australian plate to collide into the Eurasian plate. In (c) oceanic crust (sima) is being subducted beneath lighter continental crust (sial).

Volcanoes

Volcanoes occur when hot liquefied rock beneath the Earth's crust is pushed up by pressure to the surface as molten lava. Some volcanoes erupt in an explosive way, throwing out rocks and ash, whilst others are effusive and lava flows out of the vent. There are volcanoes which are both, such as Mount Fuji. An accumulation of lava and cinders creates cones of variable size and shape. As a result of many eruptions over centuries, Mount Etna in Sicily has a circumference of more than 120 km [75 miles].

Climatologists believe that volcanic ash, if ejected high into the atmosphere, can influence temperature and weather for several years afterwards. The 1991 eruption of Mount Pinatubo in the Philippines ejected more than 20 million tonnes of dust and ash 32 km [20 miles] into the atmosphere and is believed to have accelerated ozone depletion over a large part of the globe.

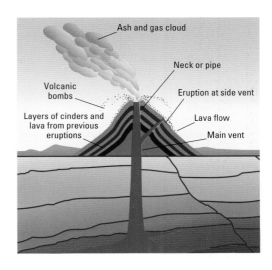

Distribution of Volcanoes

Volcanoes today may be the subject of considerable scientific study but they remain both dramatic and unpredictable: in 1991 Mount Pinatubo, 100 km [62 miles] north of the Philippines capital Manila, suddenly burst into life after lying dormant for more than six centuries. Most of the world's active volcanoes occur in a belt around the Pacific Ocean, on the edge of the Pacific plate, called the 'ring of fire'. Indonesia has the greatest concentration with 90 volcanoes, 12 of which are active. The most famous, Krakatoa, erupted in 1883 with such force that the resulting tidal wave killed 36,000 people and tremors were felt as far away as Australia.

⊙ Submarine volcanoes

▲ Land volcanoes active since 1700

—— Boundaries of tectonic plates

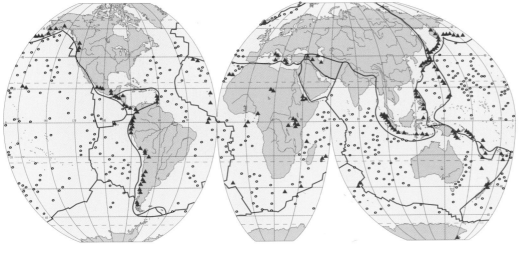

Landforms

The Rock Cycle

James Hutton first proposed the rock cycle in the late 1700s after he observed the slow but steady effects of erosion.

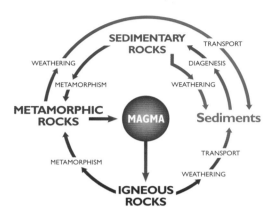

Above and below the surface of the oceans, the features of the Earth's crust are constantly changing. The phenomenal forces generated by convection currents in the molten core of our planet carry the vast segments or 'plates' of the crust across the globe in an endless cycle of creation and destruction. A continent may travel little more than 25 mm [1 in] per year, yet in the vast span of geological time this process throws up giant mountain ranges and creates new land.

Destruction of the landscape, however, begins as soon as it is formed. Wind, water, ice and sea, the main agents of erosion, mount a constant assault that even the most resistant rocks cannot withstand. Mountain peaks may dwindle by as little as a few millimetres each year, but if they are not uplifted by further movements of the crust they will eventually be reduced to rubble and transported away.

Water is the most powerful agent of erosion – it has been estimated that 100 billion tonnes of sediment are washed into the oceans every year. Three

Asian rivers account for 20% of this total; the Huang He, in China, and the Brahmaputra and Ganges in Bangladesh.

Rivers and glaciers, like the sea itself, generate much of their effect through abrasion – pounding the land with the debris they carry with them. But as well as destroying they also create new landforms, many of them spectacular: vast deltas like those of the Mississippi and the Nile, or the deep fjords cut by glaciers in British Columbia, Norway and New Zealand.

Geologists once considered that landscapes evolved from 'young', newly uplifted mountainous areas, through a 'mature' hilly stage, to an 'old age' stage when the land was reduced to an almost flat plain, or peneplain. This theory, called the 'cycle of erosion', fell into disuse when it became evident that so many factors, including the effects of plate tectonics and climatic change, constantly interrupt the cycle, which takes no account of the highly complex interactions that shape the surface of our planet.

Mountain Building

Mountains are formed when pressures on the Earth's crust caused by continental drift become so intense that the surface buckles or cracks. This happens where oceanic crust is subducted by continental crust or, more dramatically, where two tectonic plates collide: the Rockies, Andes, Alps, Urals and Himalayas resulted from such impacts. These are all known as fold mountains because they were formed by the compression of the rocks, forcing the surface to bend and fold like a crumpled rug. The Himalayas are formed from the folded former sediments of the Tethys Sea which was trapped in the collision zone between the Indian and Eurasian plates.

The other main mountain-building process occurs when the crust fractures to create faults, allowing rock to be forced upwards in large blocks; or when the pressure of magma within the crust forces the surface to bulge into a dome, or erupts to form a volcano. Large mountain ranges may reveal a combination of these features; the Alps, for example, have been compressed so violently that the folds are fragmented by numerous faults and intrusions of molten igneous rock.

Over millions of years, even the greatest mountain ranges can be reduced by the agents of erosion (most notably rivers) to a low rugged landscape known as a peneplain.

Types of faults: Faults occur where the crust is being stretched or compressed so violently that the rock strata break in a horizontal or vertical movement. They are classified by the direction in which the blocks of rock have moved. A normal fault results when a vertical movement causes the surface to break apart; compression causes a reverse fault. Horizontal movement causes shearing, known as a strike-slip fault. When the rock breaks in two places, the central block may be pushed up in a horst fault, or sink (creating a rift valley) in a graben fault.

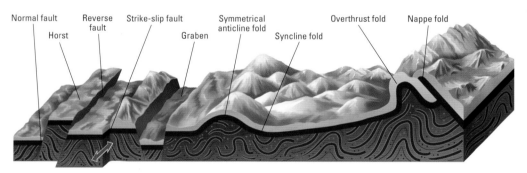

Types of fold: Folds occur when rock strata are squeezed and compressed. They are common, therefore, at destructive plate margins and where plates have collided, forcing the rocks to buckle into mountain ranges. Geographers give different names to the degrees of fold that result from continuing pressure on the rock. A simple fold may be symmetric, with even slopes on either side, but as the pressure builds up, one slope becomes steeper and the fold becomes asymmetric. Later, the ridge or 'anticline' at the top of the fold may slide over the lower ground or 'syncline' to form a recumbent fold. Eventually, the rock strata may break under the pressure to form an overthrust and finally a nappe fold.

Continental Glaciation

Ice sheets were at their greatest extent about 200,000 years ago. The maximum advance of the last Ice Age was about 18,000 years ago, when ice covered virtually all of Canada and reached as far south as the Bristol Channel in Britain.

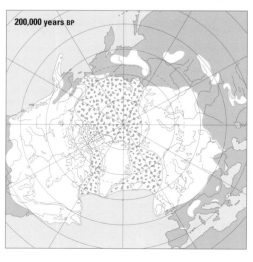

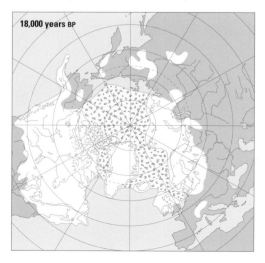

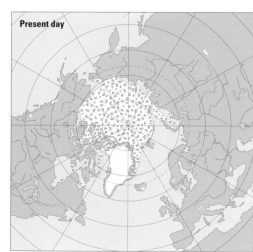

Natural Landforms

A stylized diagram to show a selection of landforms found in the mid-latitudes.

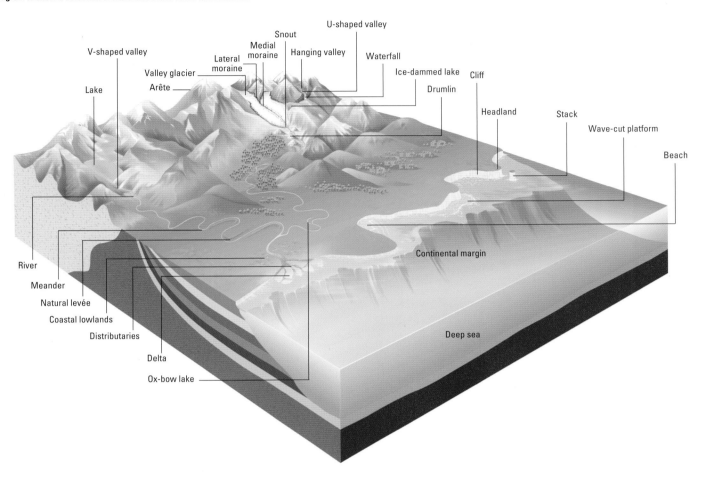

V-shaped valley · Lake · Valley glacier · Arête · Lateral moraine · Medial moraine · Snout · Hanging valley · U-shaped valley · Waterfall · Ice-dammed lake · Drumlin · Cliff · Headland · Stack · Wave-cut platform · Beach · Continental margin · River · Meander · Natural levée · Coastal lowlands · Distributaries · Delta · Ox-bow lake · Deep sea

Desert Landscapes

The popular image that deserts are all huge expanses of sand is wrong. Despite harsh conditions, deserts contain some of the most varied and interesting landscapes in the world. They are also one of the most extensive environments – the hot and cold deserts together cover almost 40% of the Earth's surface.

The three types of hot desert are known by their Arabic names: sand desert, called *erg*, covers only about one-fifth of the world's desert; the rest is divided between *hammada* (areas of bare rock) and *reg* (broad plains covered by loose gravel or pebbles).

In areas of *erg*, such as the Namib Desert, the shape of the dunes reflects the character of local winds. Where winds are constant in direction, crescent-shaped *barchan* dunes form. In areas of bare rock, wind-blown sand is a major agent of erosion. The erosion is mainly confined to within 2 m [6.5 ft] of the surface, producing characteristic mushroom-shaped rocks.

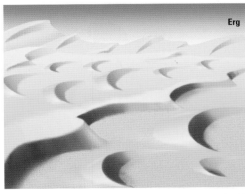

Erg

Hammada

Reg

Surface Processes

Catastrophic changes to natural landforms are periodically caused by such phenomena as avalanches, landslides and volcanic eruptions, but most of the processes that shape the Earth's surface operate extremely slowly in human terms. One estimate, based on a study in the United States, suggested that 1 m [3 ft] of land was removed from the entire surface of the country, on average, every 29,500 years. However, the time-scale varies from 1,300 years to 154,200 years depending on the terrain and climate.

In hot, dry climates, mechanical weathering, a result of rapid temperature changes, causes the outer layers of rock to peel away, while in cold mountainous regions, boulders are prised apart when water freezes in cracks in rocks. Chemical weathering, at its greatest in warm, humid regions, is responsible for hollowing out limestone caves and decomposing granites.

The erosion of soil and rock is greatest on sloping land and the steeper the slope, the greater the tendency for mass wasting – the movement of soil and rock downhill under the influence of gravity. The mechanisms of mass wasting (ranging from very slow to very rapid) vary with the type of material, but the presence of water as a lubricant is usually an important factor.

Running water is the world's leading agent of erosion and transportation. The energy of a river depends on several factors, including its velocity and volume, and its erosive power is at its peak when it is in full flood. Sea waves also exert tremendous erosive power during storms when they hurl pebbles against the shore, undercutting cliffs and hollowing out caves.

Glacier ice forms in mountain hollows and spills out to form valley glaciers, which transport rocks shattered by frost action. As glaciers move, rocks embedded into the ice erode steep-sided, U-shaped valleys. Evidence of glaciation in mountain regions includes cirques, knife-edged ridges, or arêtes, and pyramidal peaks.

Oceans

The Great Oceans

Relative sizes of the world's oceans

- Pacific
- Atlantic
- Indian
- Southern
- Arctic

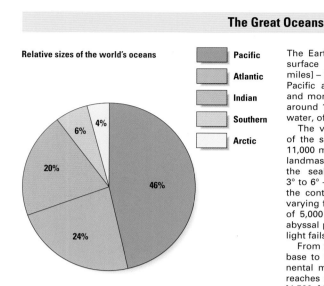

From ancient times to about the 15th century, the legendary 'Seven Seas' comprised the Red Sea, Mediterranean Sea, Persian Gulf, Black Sea, Adriatic Sea, Caspian Sea and Indian Sea.

The Earth is a watery planet: more than 70% of its surface – over 360,000,000 sq km [140,000,000 sq miles] – is covered by the oceans and seas. The mighty Pacific alone accounts for nearly 36% of the total, and more than 46% of the sea area. Gravity holds in around 1,400 million cu. km [320 million cu. miles] of water, of which over 97% is saline.

The vast underwater world starts in the shallows of the seaside and plunges to depths of more than 11,000 m [36,000 ft]. The continental shelf, part of the landmass, drops gently to around 200 m [650 ft]; here the seabed falls away suddenly at an angle of 3° to 6° – the continental slope. The third stage, called the continental rise, is more gradual with gradients varying from 1 in 100 to 1 in 700. At an average depth of 5,000 m [16,500 ft] there begins the aptly-named abyssal plain – massive submarine depths where sunlight fails to penetrate and few creatures can survive.

From these plains rise volcanoes which, taken from base to top, rival and even surpass the tallest continental mountains in height. Mauna Kea, on Hawai'i, reaches a total of 10,203 m [33,400 ft], some 1,355 m [4,500 ft] more than Mount Everest, though scarcely 40% is visible above sea level.

In addition, there are underwater mountain chains up to 1,000 km [600 miles] across, whose peaks sometimes appear above sea level as islands, such as Iceland and Tristan da Cunha.

The Ocean Depths

Average and maximum depths of the world's great oceans, in metres

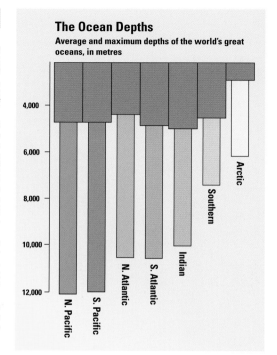

Ocean Currents

January ocean currents

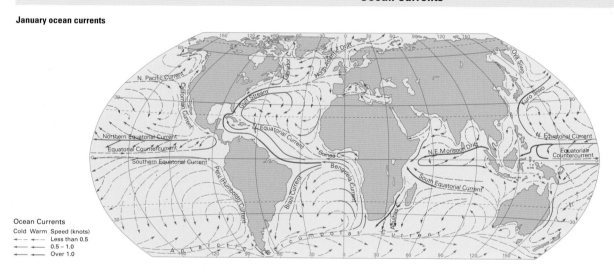

Ocean Currents
Cold Warm Speed (knots)
- Less than 0.5
- 0.5 – 1.0
- Over 1.0

July ocean currents

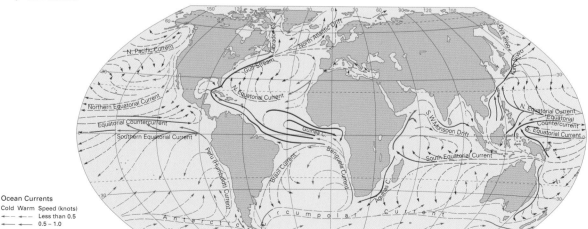

Ocean Currents
Cold Warm Speed (knots)
- Less than 0.5
- 0.5 – 1.0
- Over 1.0

Moving immense quantities of energy as well as billions of tonnes of water every hour, the ocean currents are a vital part of the great heat engine that drives the Earth's climate. They themselves are produced by a twofold mechanism. At the surface, winds push huge masses of water before them; in the deep ocean, below an abrupt temperature gradient that separates the churning surface waters from the still depths, density variations cause slow vertical movements.

The pattern of circulation of the great surface currents is determined by the displacement known as the Coriolis effect. As the Earth turns beneath a moving object – whether it is a tennis ball or a vast mass of water – it appears to be deflected to one side. The deflection is most obvious near the Equator, where the Earth's surface is spinning eastwards at 1,700 km/h [1,050 mph]; currents moving polewards are curved clockwise in the northern hemisphere and anti-clockwise in the southern.

The result is a system of spinning circles known as gyres. The Coriolis effect piles up water on the left of each gyre, creating a narrow, fast-moving stream that is matched by a slower, broader returning current on the right. North and south of the Equator, the fastest currents are located in the west and in the east respectively. In each case, warm water moves from the Equator and cold water returns to it. Cold currents often bring an upwelling of nutrients with them, supporting the world's most economically important fisheries.

Depending on the prevailing winds, some currents on or near the Equator may reverse their direction in the course of the year – a seasonal variation on which Asian monsoon rains depend, and whose occasional failure can bring disaster to millions.

World Fishing Areas

Main commercial fishing areas (numbered FAO regions)

Catch by top marine fishing areas, million tonnes (2005)

1.	Pacific, NW	[61]	21.6	22.7%
2.	Pacific, SE	[87]	15.5	16.3%
3.	Pacific, WC	[71]	11.0	11.6%
4.	Atlantic, NE	[27]	10.0	10.5%
5.	Indian, E	[57]	5.6	5.9%
6.	Indian, W	[51]	4.1	4.3%
7.	Atlantic, EC	[34]	3.4	3.6%
8.	Pacific, NE	[67]	3.1	3.3%
9.	Atlantic, NW	[21]	2.4	2.5%
10.	Atlantic, WC	[31]	2.1	2.2%

Principal fishing areas

Leading fishing nations

China 17.8% Peru 10.1% USA 5.3% Chile 5.2% Indonesia 5.1% Japan 4.6% India 3.8%

World total (2005): 93,800,000 tonnes
(Marine catch 89.8% Inland catch 10.2%)

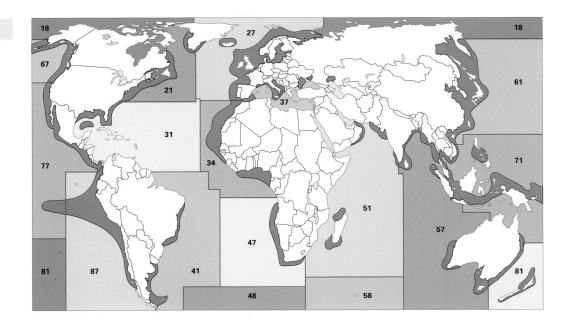

Marine Pollution

Sources of marine oil pollution

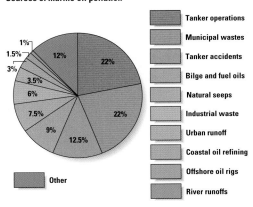

22%, 12%, 1%, 1.5%, 3%, 3.5%, 6%, 7.5%, 9%, 12.5%, 22%

- Tanker operations
- Municipal wastes
- Tanker accidents
- Bilge and fuel oils
- Natural seeps
- Industrial waste
- Urban runoff
- Coastal oil refining
- Offshore oil rigs
- River runoffs
- Other

Oil Spills

Major oil spills from tankers and combined carriers

Year	Vessel	Location	Spill (barrels) *	Cause
1979	Atlantic Empress	West Indies	1,890,000	collision
1983	Castillo De Bellver	South Africa	1,760,000	fire
1978	Amoco Cadiz	France	1,628,000	grounding
1991	Haven	Italy	1,029,000	explosion
1988	Odyssey	Canada	1,000,000	fire
1967	Torrey Canyon	UK	909,000	grounding
1972	Sea Star	Gulf of Oman	902,250	collision
1977	Hawaiian Patriot	Hawaiian Is.	742,500	fire
1979	Independenta	Turkey	696,350	collision
1993	Braer	UK	625,000	grounding
1996	Sea Empress	UK	515,000	grounding
2002	Prestige	Spain	463,250	storm

Other sources of major oil spills

1983	Nowruz oilfield	Persian Gulf	4,250,000[†]	war
1979	Ixtoc 1 oilwell	Gulf of Mexico	4,200,000	blow-out
1991	Kuwait	Persian Gulf	2,500,000[†]	war

* 1 barrel = 0.136 tonnes/159 lit./35 Imperial gal./42 US gal. [†] estimated

River Pollution

Sources of river pollution, USA

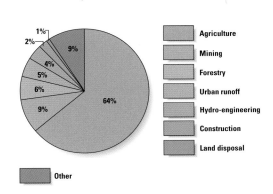

64%, 9%, 1%, 2%, 4%, 5%, 6%, 9%

- Agriculture
- Mining
- Forestry
- Urban runoff
- Hydro-engineering
- Construction
- Land disposal
- Other

Water Pollution

Severely polluted sea areas and lakes

Polluted sea areas and lakes

Areas of frequent oil pollution by shipping

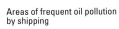
Major oil tanker spills

▲ Major oil rig blow-outs

▼ Offshore dumpsites for industrial and municipal waste

Severely polluted rivers and estuaries

The most notorious tanker spillage of the 1980s occurred when the *Exxon Valdez* ran aground in Prince William Sound, Alaska, in 1989, spilling 267,000 barrels of crude oil close to shore in a sensitive ecological area. This rates as the world's 28th worst spill in terms of volume.

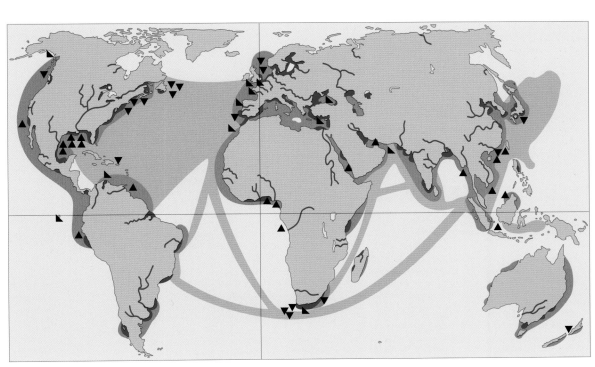

Climate

Climatic Regions

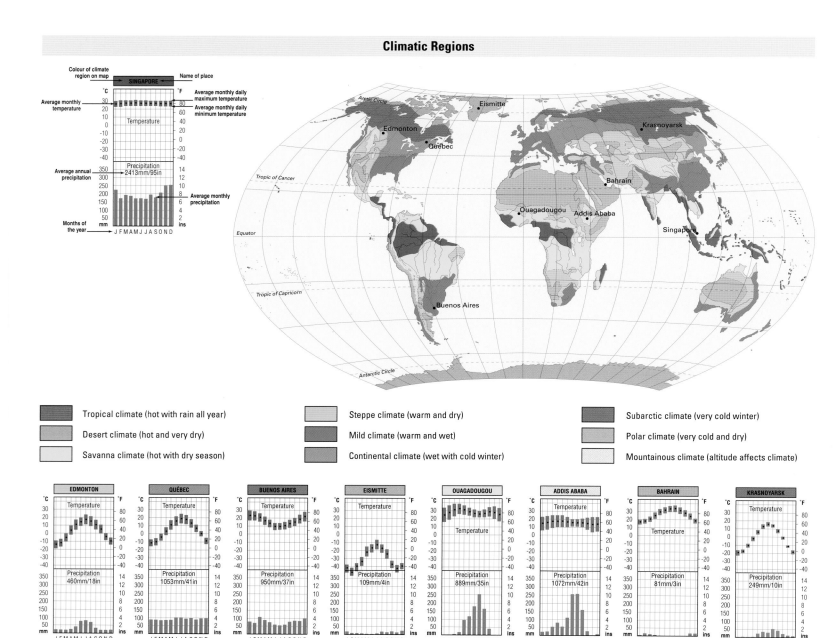

Tropical climate (hot with rain all year)

Desert climate (hot and very dry)

Savanna climate (hot with dry season)

Steppe climate (warm and dry)

Mild climate (warm and wet)

Continental climate (wet with cold winter)

Subarctic climate (very cold winter)

Polar climate (very cold and dry)

Mountainous climate (altitude affects climate)

Climate Records

Temperature
Highest recorded shade temperature: Al Aziziyah, Libya, 57.7°C [135.9°F], 13 September 1922.

Highest mean annual temperature: Dallol, Ethiopia, 34.4°C [94°F], 1960–66.

Longest heatwave: Marble Bar, W. Australia, 162 days over 38°C [100°F], 23 October 1923 to 7 April 1924.

Lowest recorded temperature (outside poles): Verkhoyansk, Siberia, –68°C [–93.6°F], 7 February 1982.

Lowest mean annual temperature: Polus Nedostupnosti, Pole of Cold, Antarctica, –57.8°C [–72°F].

Precipitation
Driest place: Quillagua, Chile, mean annual rainfall 0.5 mm [0.02 in], 1964–2001.

Wettest place (12 months): Cherrapunji, Meghalaya, N. E. India, 26,461 mm [1,042 in], August 1860 to July 1861. Cherrapunji also holds the record for the most rainfall in one month: 2,930 mm [115 in], July 1861.

Wettest place (average): Mt Wai-ale-ale, Hawai'i, USA, mean annual rainfall 11,680 mm [459.8 in].

Wettest place (24 hours): Fac Fac, Réunion, Indian Ocean, 1,825 mm [71.9 in], 15–16 March 1952.

Heaviest hailstones: Gopalganj, Bangladesh, up to 1.02 kg [2.25 lb], 14 April 1986 (killed 92 people).

Heaviest snowfall (continuous): Bessans, Savoie, France, 1,730 mm [68 in] in 19 hours, 5–6 April 1969.

Heaviest snowfall (season/year): Mt Baker, Washington, USA, 28,956 mm [1,140 in], June 1998 to June 1999.

Pressure and winds
Highest barometric pressure: Agata, Siberia (at 262 m [862 ft] altitude), 1,083.8 mb, 31 December 1968.

Lowest barometric pressure: Typhoon Tip, Guam, Pacific Ocean, 870 mb, 12 October 1979.

Highest recorded wind speed: Bridge Creek, Oklahoma, USA, 512 km/h [318 mph], 3 May 1999. Measured by Doppler radar monitoring a tornado.

Windiest place: Port Martin, Antarctica, where winds of more than 64 km/h [40 mph] occur for not less than 100 days a year.

Climate

Climate is weather in the long term: the seasonal pattern of hot and cold, wet and dry, averaged over time (usually 30 years). At the simplest level, it is caused by the uneven heating of the Earth. Surplus heat at the Equator passes towards the poles, levelling out the energy differential. Its passage is marked by a ceaseless churning of the atmosphere and the oceans, further agitated by the Earth's diurnal spin and the motion it imparts to moving air and water. The heat's means of transport – by winds and ocean currents, by the continual evaporation and recondensation of water molecules – is the weather itself. There are four basic types of climate, each of which can be further subdivided: tropical, desert (dry), temperate and polar.

Composition of Dry Air

Nitrogen	78.09%	Sulphur dioxide	trace
Oxygen	20.95%	Nitrogen oxide	trace
Argon	0.93%	Methane	trace
Water vapour	0.2–4.0%	Dust	trace
Carbon dioxide	0.03%	Helium	trace
Ozone	0.00006%	Neon	trace

El Niño

In a normal year, south-easterly trade winds drive surface waters westwards off the coast of South America, drawing cold, nutrient-rich water up from below. In an El Niño year (which occurs every 2–7 years), warm water from the west Pacific suppresses up-welling in the east, depriving the region of nutrients. The water is warmed by as much as 7°C [12°F], disturbing the tropical atmospheric circulation. During an intense El Niño, the south-east trade winds change direction and become equatorial westerlies, resulting in climatic extremes in many regions of the world, such as drought in parts of Australia and India, and heavy rainfall in south-eastern USA. An intense El Niño occurred in 1997–8, with resultant freak weather conditions across the entire Pacific region.

Normal year

El Niño event

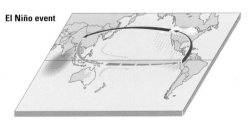

Beaufort Wind Scale

Named after the 19th-century British naval officer who devised it, the Beaufort Scale assesses wind speed according to its effects. It was originally designed as an aid for sailors, but has since been adapted for use on the land.

Scale	Wind speed km/h	mph	Effect
0	0–1	0–1	**Calm** Smoke rises vertically
1	1–5	1–3	**Light air** Wind direction shown only by smoke drift
2	6–11	4–7	**Light breeze** Wind felt on face; leaves rustle; vanes moved by wind
3	12–19	8–12	**Gentle breeze** Leaves and small twigs in constant motion; wind extends small flag
4	20–28	13–18	**Moderate** Raises dust and loose paper; small branches move
5	29–38	19–24	**Fresh** Small trees in leaf sway; wavelets on inland waters
6	39–49	25–31	**Strong** Large branches move; difficult to use umbrellas
7	50–61	32–38	**Near gale** Whole trees in motion; difficult to walk against wind
8	62–74	39–46	**Gale** Twigs break from trees; walking very difficult
9	75–88	47–54	**Strong gale** Slight structural damage
10	89–102	55–63	**Storm** Trees uprooted; serious structural damage
11	103–117	64–72	**Violent storm** Widespread damage
12	118+	73+	**Hurricane**

Conversions
°C = (°F − 32) × 5/9; °F = (°C × 9/5) + 32; 0°C = 32°F
1 in = 25.4 mm; 1 mm = 0.0394 in; 100 mm = 3.94 in

Temperature

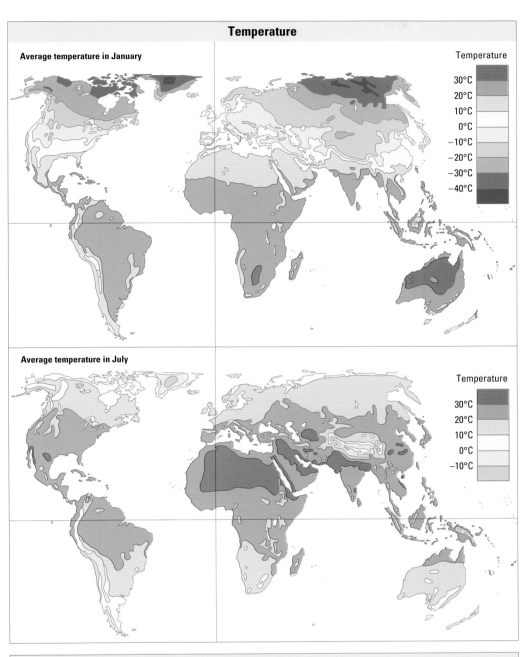

Average temperature in January

Temperature
30°C
20°C
10°C
0°C
−10°C
−20°C
−30°C
−40°C

Average temperature in July

Temperature
30°C
20°C
10°C
0°C
−10°C

Precipitation

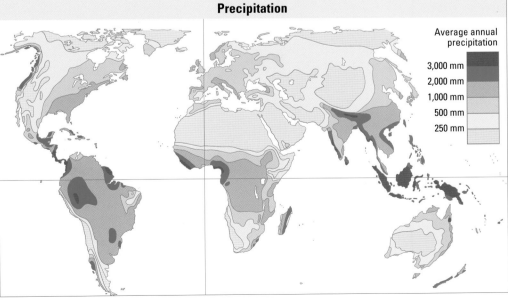

Average annual precipitation
3,000 mm
2,000 mm
1,000 mm
500 mm
250 mm

Water and Vegetation

The Hydrological Cycle

The world's water balance is regulated by the constant recycling of water between the oceans, atmosphere and land. The movement of water between these three reservoirs is known as the hydrological cycle. The oceans play a vital role in the hydrological cycle: 74% of the total precipitation falls over the oceans and 84% of the total evaporation comes from the oceans.

Water Distribution

The distribution of planetary water, by percentage. Oceans and ice caps together account for more than 99% of the total; the breakdown of the remainder is estimated.

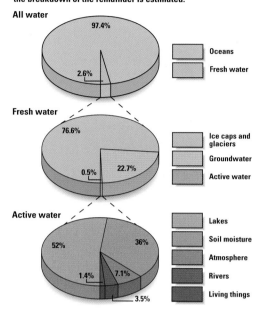

All water
- 97.4%
- 2.6%
  - Oceans
  - Fresh water

Fresh water
- 76.6%
- 0.5%
- 22.7%
  - Ice caps and glaciers
  - Groundwater
  - Active water

Active water
- 52%
- 36%
- 1.4%
- 7.1%
- 3.5%
  - Lakes
  - Soil moisture
  - Atmosphere
  - Rivers
  - Living things

Water Utilization

Domestic Industrial Agriculture

The percentage breakdown of water usage by sector, selected countries (2007)

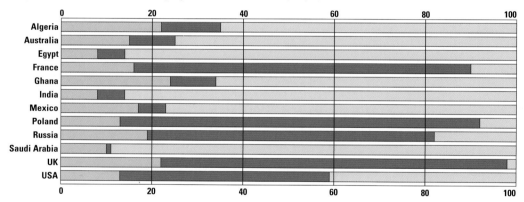

Algeria
Australia
Egypt
France
Ghana
India
Mexico
Poland
Russia
Saudi Arabia
UK
USA

Water Usage

Almost all the world's water is 3,000 million years old, and all of it cycles endlessly through the hydrosphere, though at different rates. Water vapour circulates over days, even hours, deep ocean water circulates over millennia, and ice-cap water remains solid for millions of years.

Fresh water is essential to all terrestrial life. Humans cannot survive more than a few days without it, and even the hardiest desert plants and animals could not exist without some water. Agriculture requires huge quantities of fresh water: without large-scale irrigation most of the world's people would starve. In the USA, agriculture uses 41% and industry 46% of all water withdrawals.

According to the latest figures, the average North American uses 1.3 million litres per year. This is more than six times the average African, who uses just 186,000 litres of water each year. Europeans and Australians use 694,000 litres per year.

Water Supply

Percentage of total population with access to safe drinking water (2005)

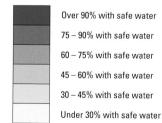

- Over 90% with safe water
- 75 – 90% with safe water
- 60 – 75% with safe water
- 45 – 60% with safe water
- 30 – 45% with safe water
- Under 30% with safe water

- ◊ Under 80 litres per person per day domestic water consumption
- ▲ Over 320 litres per person per day domestic water consumption

NB: 80 litres of water a day is considered necessary for a reasonable quality of life.

Least well-provided countries

Afghanistan	13%	Papua New Guinea	39%
Ethiopia	22%	Cambodia	41%
Western Sahara	26%	Somalia	42%

Natural Vegetation

Regional variation in vegetation

- Tundra and mountain vegetation
- Needleleaf evergreen forest
- Mixed needleleaf evergreen & broadleaf deciduous trees
- Broadleaf deciduous woodland
- Mid-latitude grassland
- Evergreen broadleaf and deciduous trees & shrubs
- Semi-desert scrub
- Desert
- Tropical grassland (savanna)
- Tropical broadleaf rainforest and monsoon forest
- Subtropical broadleaf and needleleaf forest

The map shows the natural 'climax vegetation' of regions, as dictated by climate and topography. In most cases, however, agricultural activity has drastically altered the vegetation pattern. Western Europe, for example, lost most of its broadleaf forest many centuries ago, while irrigation has turned some natural semi-desert into productive land.

Land Use by Continent (2005)

- Forest
- Permanent pasture
- Permanent crops
- Arable
- Other

North America: 26.0%, 16.4%, 0.7%, 12.0%, 45.0%

Europe: 46.0%, 8.3%, 0.8%, 12.9%, 32.0%

Asia: 17.8%, 35.8%, 2.1%, 16.4%, 28.0%

South America: 50.5%, 26.4%, 0.8%, 6.1%, 16.0%

Africa: 21.8%, 31.1%, 0.9%, 6.7%, 39.5%

Oceania: 23.3%, 47.8%, 0.4%, 5.9%, 23.0%

Forestry: Production

	Forest and woodland (million hectares)	Annual production (2006, million cubic metres)	
		Fuelwood	Industrial roundwood*
World	*3,869.5*	*1,948.7*	*1762.6*
Europe	1,039.3	152.6	516.7
S. America	885.6	274.6	157.0
Africa	649.9	588.4	66.4
N. & C. America	549.3	131.4	741.9
Asia	547.8	788.9	231.0
Oceania	197.6	12.8	49.6

Paper and Board

Top producers (2006)**		Top exporters (2006)**	
USA	84,317	Canada	14,260
China	57,983	Germany	13,058
Japan	29,473	Finland	12,906
Germany	22,655	Sweden	10,849
Canada	18,176	USA	9,644

* roundwood is timber as it is felled
** in thousand tonnes

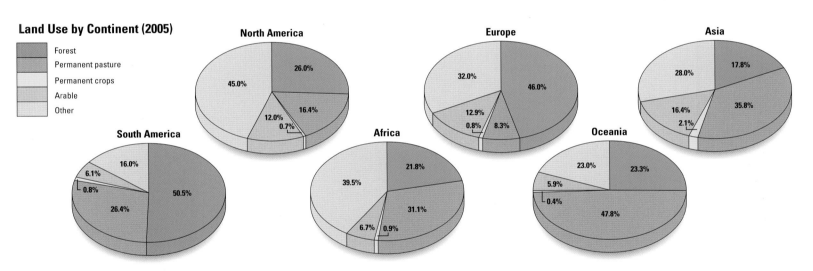

Forestry: Distribution

- Main areas of coniferous production
- Main areas of non-coniferous production
- 🌲 = 5% of world production of coniferous roundwood (2006)
- ♣ = 5% of world production of non-coniferous roundwood (2006)

Environment

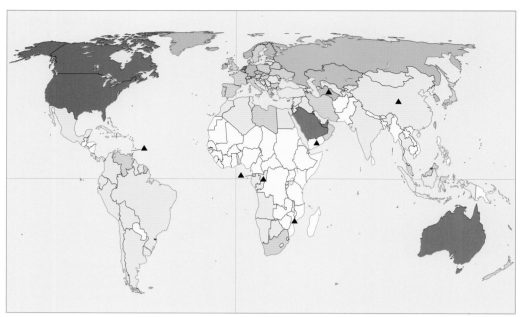

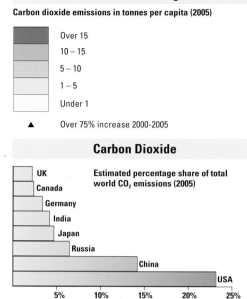

Carbon Dioxide

UK

Canada

Germany

India

Japan

Russia

China

USA

Estimated percentage share of total world CO$_2$ emissions (2005)

5%   10%   15%   20%   25%

Predicted Change in Precipitation

The difference between actual annual average precipitation, 1960-1990, and the predicted annual average precipitation, 2070-2100.
It should be noted that these predicted annual mean changes mask quite significant seasonal detail.

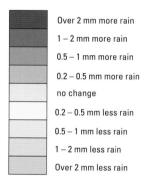

Over 2 mm more rain

1 – 2 mm more rain

0.5 – 1 mm more rain

0.2 – 0.5 mm more rain

no change

0.2 – 0.5 mm less rain

0.5 – 1 mm less rain

1 – 2 mm less rain

Over 2 mm less rain

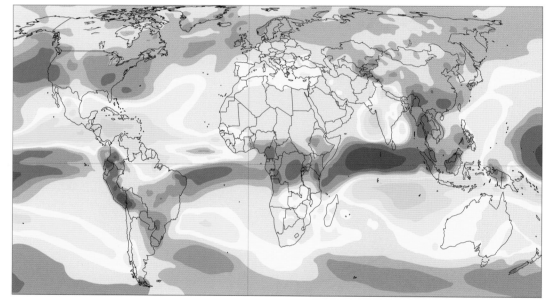

Predicted Change in Temperature

The difference between actual annual average surface air temperature, 1960-1990, and the predicted annual average surface air temperature, 2070-2100.
This map shows the predicted increase, assuming a 'medium growth' of global economy and assuming that no measures to combat the emission of greenhouse gases are taken.

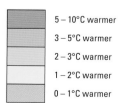

5 – 10°C warmer

3 – 5°C warmer

2 – 3°C warmer

1 – 2°C warmer

0 – 1°C warmer

Source: The Hadley Centre of Climate Prediction and Research, The Met. Office

Projected Change in Global Warming

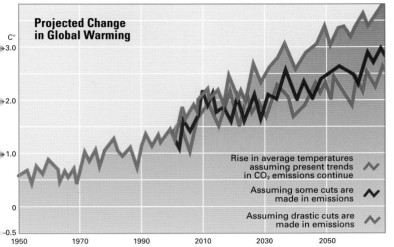

C°
+3.0
+2.0
+1.0
0
-0.5

Rise in average temperatures assuming present trends in CO₂ emissions continue

Assuming some cuts are made in emissions

Assuming drastic cuts are made in emissions

1950   1970   1990   2010   2030   2050

Possible Effect of Sea Level Rise in Florida

Sea levels have risen worldwide by about 2 cm since 1900. If CO₂ emissions continue at the same rate, the sea level is expected to rise by 7.4 m by 2200. The map shows the dramatic effects that such a rise could have on the southern part of Florida in the USA.

Submerged land area if sea level rises 4.5 m

Submerged land area if sea level rises 7.4 m

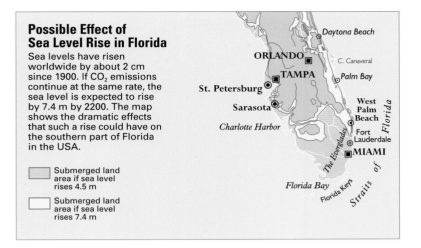

The Greenhouse Effect

Carbon dioxide is increased by burning fossil fuels and cutting forests

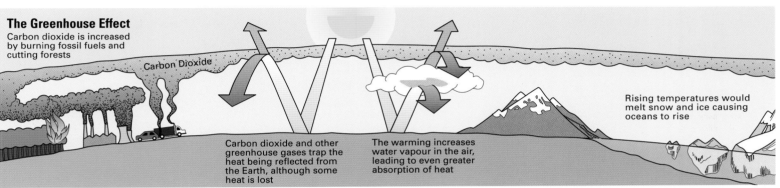

Carbon Dioxide

Carbon dioxide and other greenhouse gases trap the heat being reflected from the Earth, although some heat is lost

The warming increases water vapour in the air, leading to even greater absorption of heat

Rising temperatures would melt snow and ice causing oceans to rise

Desertification

- Existing deserts
- Areas with a high risk of desertification
- Areas with a moderate risk of desertification
- Former areas of rainforest
- Existing rainforest

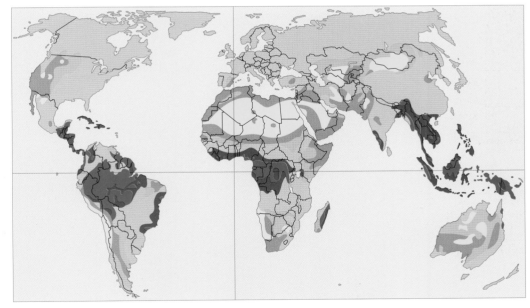

Forest Clearance

Thousands of hectares of forest cleared annually, tropical countries surveyed 1980–85, 1990–95 and 2000–05. Loss as a percentage of remaining stocks is shown in figures on each column. Gain is indicated as a minus figure.

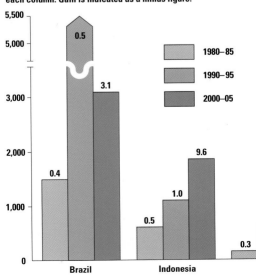

5,500
5,000
3,000
2,000
1,000
0

1980–85
1990–95
2000–05

Brazil: 0.4, 0.5, 3.1
Indonesia: 0.5, 1.0, 9.6
India: 0.3, 0.0, 0.7
Burma: 0.3, 1.4, 4.7
Thailand: 2.4, 2.6, 2.0
Vietnam: 0.7, 1.4, –12.2
Philippines: 1.0, 3.5, 4.2
Costa Rica: 4.0, 3.0, –0.6

Deforestation

The Earth's remaining forests are under attack from three directions: expanding agriculture, logging, and growing consumption of fuelwood, often in combination. Sometimes deforestation is the direct result of government policy, as in the efforts made to resettle the urban poor in some parts of Brazil; just as often, it comes about despite state attempts at conservation. Loggers, licensed or unlicensed, blaze a trail into virgin forest, often destroying twice as many trees as they harvest. Landless farmers follow, burning away most of what remains to plant their crops, completing the destruction. Some countries such as Vietnam and Costa Rica have successfully implemented reafforestation programmes.

Population

Demographic Profiles

Developed nations such as the UK have populations evenly spread across the age groups and, usually, a growing proportion of elderly people. The great majority of the people in developing nations, however, are in the younger age groups, about to enter their most fertile years. In time, these population profiles should resemble the world profile (even Nigeria has made recent progress by reducing its birth rate), but the transition will come about only after a few more generations of rapid population growth.

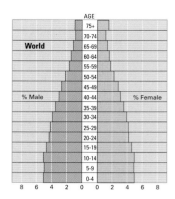

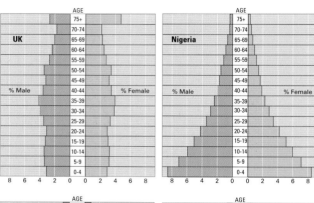

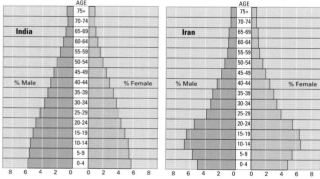

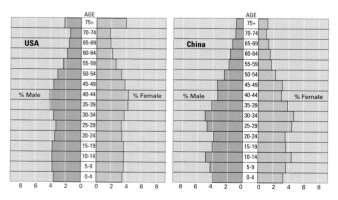

Most Populous Nations, in millions (2007 estimates)

1.	China	1,322	9. Nigeria	135	17. Turkey	71
2.	India	1,130	10. Japan	127	18. Congo (Dem. Rep.)	66
3.	USA	301	11. Mexico	109	19. Iran	65
4.	Indonesia	235	12. Philippines	91	20. Thailand	65
5.	Brazil	190	13. Vietnam	85	21. France	61
6.	Pakistan	165	14. Germany	82	22. UK	61
7.	Bangladesh	150	15. Egypt	80	23. Italy	58
8.	Russia	141	16. Ethiopia	77	24. South Korea	49

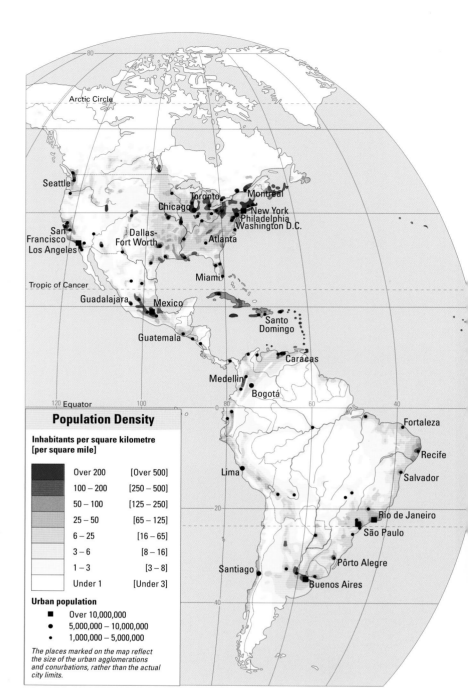

Population Density

Inhabitants per square kilometre [per square mile]

Over 200	[Over 500]
100 – 200	[250 – 500]
50 – 100	[125 – 250]
25 – 50	[65 – 125]
6 – 25	[16 – 65]
3 – 6	[8 – 16]
1 – 3	[3 – 8]
Under 1	[Under 3]

Urban population

- ■ Over 10,000,000
- ● 5,000,000 – 10,000,000
- • 1,000,000 – 5,000,000

The places marked on the map reflect the size of the urban agglomerations and conurbations, rather than the actual city limits.

Continental Comparisons

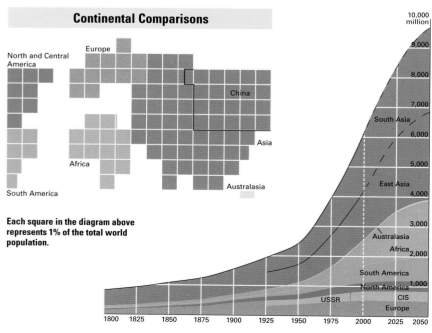

Each square in the diagram above represents 1% of the total world population.

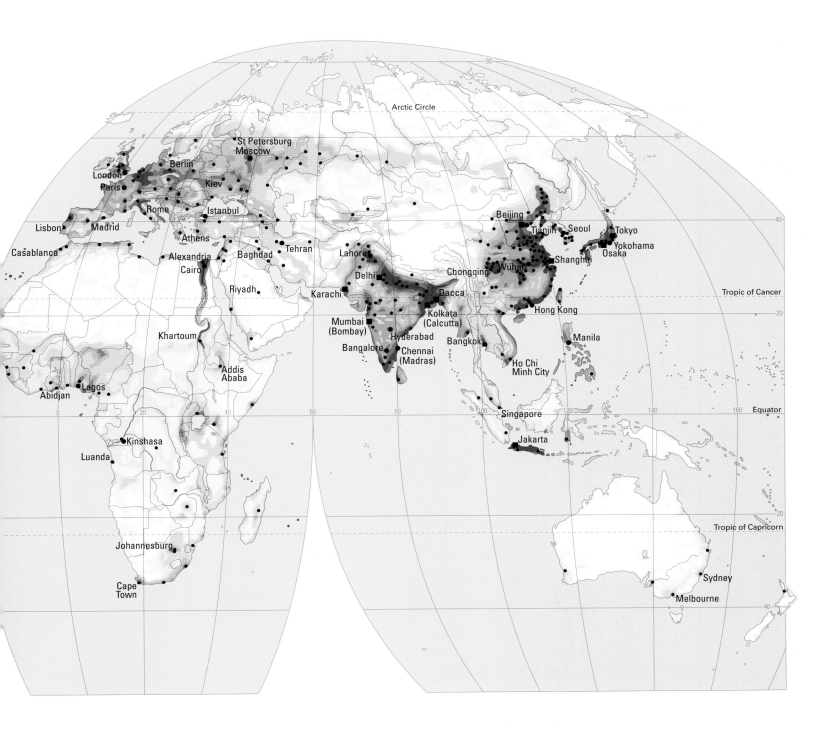

Arctic Circle

St Petersburg
Moscow
Berlin
London
Paris
Kiev
Rome
Istanbul
Lisbon
Madrid
Athens
Casablanca
Alexandria
Baghdad
Tehran
Cairo
Lahore
Delhi
Riyadh
Karachi
Chongqing
Dacca
Khartoum
Mumbai
(Bombay)
Kolkata
(Calcutta)
Hyderabad
Bangkok
Bangalore
Chennai
(Madras)
Addis
Ababa
Lagos
Abidjan
Kinshasa
Luanda

Beijing
Tianjin
Seoul
Tokyo
Yokohama
Osaka
Wuhan
Shanghai
Hong Kong
Manila
Ho Chi
Minh City
Singapore
Jakarta

Tropic of Cancer

Equator

Johannesburg

Cape
Town

Tropic of Capricorn

Sydney
Melbourne

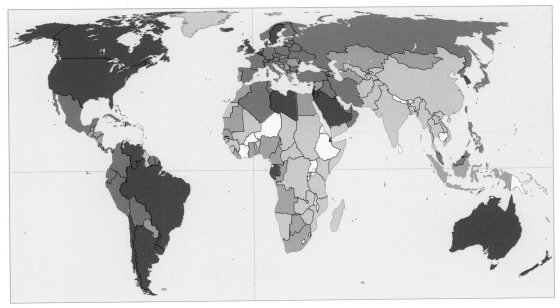

Urban Population

Percentage of total population living in towns and cities (2005)

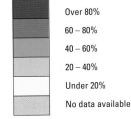

Over 80%

60 – 80%

40 – 60%

20 – 40%

Under 20%

No data available

Most urbanized		Least urbanized	
Singapore	100%	Burundi	10%
Kuwait	97%	Bhutan	11%
Belgium	97%	Trinidad & Tobago	12%
Bahrain	96%	Uganda	13%
Qatar	95%	Papua New Guinea	13%

The Human Family

Predominant Languages

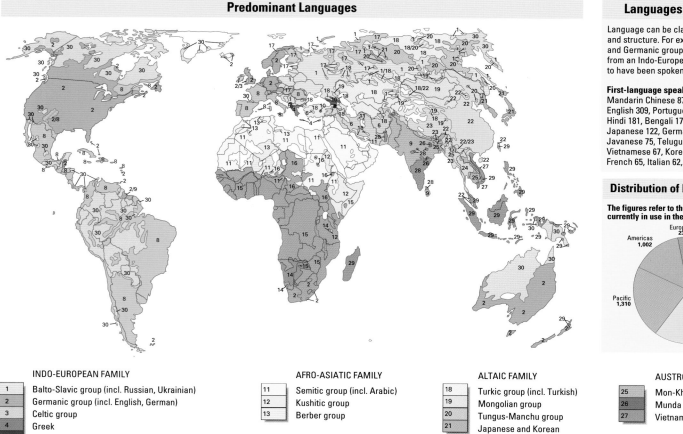

Languages of the World

Language can be classified by ancestry and structure. For example, the Romance and Germanic groups are both derived from an Indo-European language believed to have been spoken 5,000 years ago.

First-language speakers in millions (2005)
Mandarin Chinese 873, Spanish 322, English 309, Portuguese 230, Arabic 206, Hindi 181, Bengali 171, Russian 145, Japanese 122, German 95, Wu Chinese 77, Javanese 75, Telugu 70, Marathi 68, Vietnamese 67, Korean 67, Tamil 65, French 65, Italian 62, Punjabi 60.

Distribution of Living Languages

The figures refer to the number of languages currently in use in the regions shown

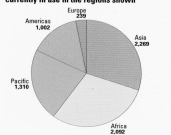

Europe 239
Americas 1,002
Asia 2,269
Pacific 1,310
Africa 2,092

INDO-EUROPEAN FAMILY

1	Balto-Slavic group (incl. Russian, Ukrainian)
2	Germanic group (incl. English, German)
3	Celtic group
4	Greek
5	Albanian
6	Iranian group
7	Armenian
8	Romance group (incl. Spanish, Portuguese, French, Italian)
9	Indo-Aryan group (incl. Hindi, Bengali, Urdu, Punjabi, Marathi)
10	CAUCASIAN FAMILY

AFRO-ASIATIC FAMILY

11	Semitic group (incl. Arabic)
12	Kushitic group
13	Berber group

14	KHOISAN FAMILY
15	NIGER-CONGO FAMILY
16	NILO-SAHARAN FAMILY
17	URALIC FAMILY

ALTAIC FAMILY

18	Turkic group (incl. Turkish)
19	Mongolian group
20	Tungus-Manchu group
21	Japanese and Korean

SINO-TIBETAN FAMILY

| 22 | Sinitic (Chinese) languages (incl. Mandarin, Wu, Yue) |
| 23 | Tibetic-Burmic languages |

| 24 | TAI FAMILY |

AUSTRO-ASIATIC FAMILY

25	Mon-Khmer group
26	Munda group
27	Vietnamese

28	DRAVIDIAN FAMILY (incl. Telugu, Tamil)
29	AUSTRONESIAN FAMILY (incl. Malay-Indonesian, Javanese)
30	OTHER LANGUAGES

Predominant Religions

Religious Adherents

Religious adherents in millions (2006)

Christianity	2,100	Hindu	900
Roman Catholic	1,050	Chinese folk	394
Protestant	396	Buddhism	376
Orthodox	240	Ethnic religions	300
Anglican	73	New religions	103
Others	341	Sikhism	23
Islam	1,070	Spiritism	15
Sunni	940	Judaism	14
Shi'ite	120	Baha'i	7
Others	10	Confucianism	6
Non-religious/		Jainism	4
Agnostic/Atheist	1,100	Shintoism	4

▲	Roman Catholicism
	Orthodox and other Eastern Churches
•	Protestantism
	Sunni Islam
	Shi'ite Islam
	Buddhism
	Hinduism
	Confucianism
✡	Judaism
	Shintoism
	Tribal Religions

United Nations

Created in 1945 to promote peace and co-operation and based in New York, the United Nations is the world's largest international organization, with 192 members and an annual budget of US $2.1 billion (2007). Each member of the General Assembly has one vote, while the five permanent members of the 15-nation Security Council – China, France, Russia, UK and USA – hold a veto. The Secretariat is the UN's principal administrative arm. The 54 members of the Economic and Social Council are responsible for economic, social, cultural, educational, health and related matters. The UN has 16 specialized agencies – based in Canada, France, Switzerland and Italy, as well as the USA – which help members in fields such as education (UNESCO), agriculture (FAO), medicine (WHO) and finance (IFC). By the end of 1994, all the original 11 trust territories of the Trusteeship Council had become independent.

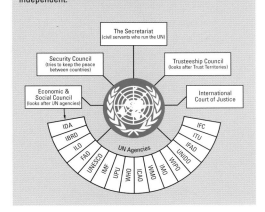

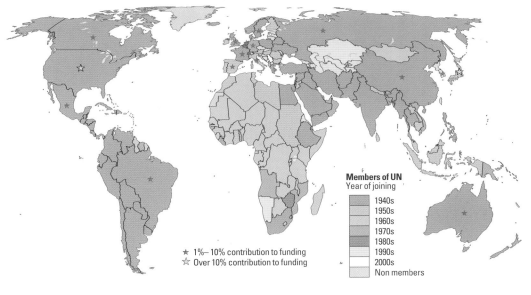

Members of UN
Year of joining
- 1940s
- 1950s
- 1960s
- 1970s
- 1980s
- 1990s
- 2000s
- Non members

★ 1%– 10% contribution to funding
☆ Over 10% contribution to funding

MEMBERSHIP OF THE UN In 1945 there were 51 members; by the end of 2006 membership had increased to 192 following the admission of East Timor, Switzerland and Montenegro. There are 2 independent states which are not members of the UN – Taiwan and the Vatican City. All the successor states of the former USSR had joined by the end of 1992. The official languages of the UN are Chinese, English, French, Russian, Spanish and Arabic.

FUNDING The UN regular budget for 2007 was US$ 2.1 billion. Contributions are assessed by the members' ability to pay, with the maximum 24% of the total (USA's share), the minimum 0.01%. The European Union pays over 37% of the budget.

PEACEKEEPING The UN has been involved in 65 peacekeeping operations worldwide since 1948.

International Organizations

ACP African-Caribbean-Pacific (formed in 1963). Members have economic ties with the EU.
APEC Asia-Pacific Economic Co-operation (formed in 1989). It aims to enhance economic growth and prosperity for the region and to strengthen the Asia-Pacific community. APEC is the only intergovernmental grouping in the world operating on the basis of non-binding commitments, open dialogue, and equal respect for the views of all participants. There are 21 member economies.
ARAB LEAGUE (formed in 1945). The League's aim is to promote economic, social, political and military co-operation. There are 22 member nations.
ASEAN Association of South-east Asian Nations (formed in 1967). Cambodia joined in 1999.
AU The African Union replaced the Organization of African Unity (formed in 1963) in 2002. Its 53 members represent over 94% of Africa's population. Arabic, French, Portuguese and English are recognized as working languages.
COLOMBO PLAN (formed in 1951). Its 25 members aim to promote economic and social development in Asia and the Pacific.
COMMONWEALTH The Commonwealth of Nations evolved from the British Empire. Pakistan was suspended in 1999, and Zimbabwe in 2002. In response to its continued suspension, Zimbabwe left the Commonwealth in December 2003. Pakistan was reinstated in 2004, but Fiji Islands was suspended in December 2006 following a military coup. It now comprises 16 Queen's realms, 31 republics and 6 indigenous monarchies, giving a total of 53 member states.
EU European Union (evolved from the European Community in 1993). Cyprus, the Czech Republic, Estonia, Hungary, Latvia, Lithuania, Malta, Poland, the Slovak Republic and Slovenia joined the EU in May 2004; Bulgaria and Romania joined in January 2007. The other members are Austria, Belgium, Denmark, Finland, France, Germany, Greece, Ireland, Italy, Luxembourg, Netherlands, Portugal, Spain, Sweden and the UK – together these 27 countries aim to integrate economies, co-ordinate social developments and bring about political union.
LAIA Latin American Integration Association (1980). Its aim is to promote freer regional trade.
NATO North Atlantic Treaty Organization (formed in 1949). It continues after 1991 despite the winding up of the Warsaw Pact. Bulgaria, Estonia, Latvia, Lithuania, Romania, the Slovak Republic and Slovenia became members in 2004.

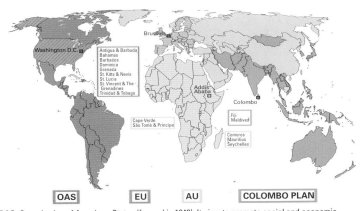

OAS Organization of American States (formed in 1948). It aims to promote social and economic co-operation between developed countries of North America and developing nations of Latin America.
OECD Organization for Economic Co-operation and Development (formed in 1961). It comprises 30 major free-market economies. Poland, Hungary and South Korea joined in 1996, and the Slovak Republic in 2000. 'G8' is its 'inner group' of leading industrial nations, comprising Canada, France, Germany, Italy, Japan, Russia, UK and USA.
OPEC Organization of Petroleum Exporting Countries (formed in 1960). It controls about three-quarters of the world's oil supply. Gabon left the organization in 1996.

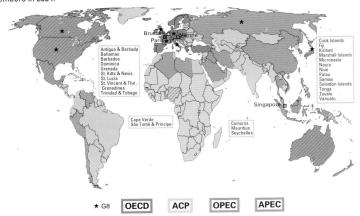

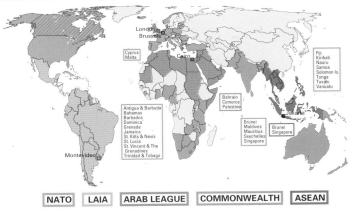

Wealth

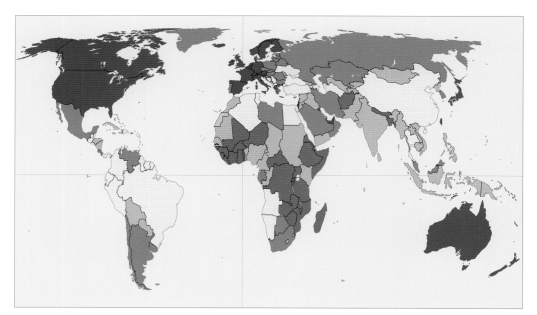

Wealth Creation

The Gross Domestic Product (GDP) of the world's largest economies, US$ million (2007)

1.	USA	13,860,000	23.	Argentina	524,000
2.	China	7,043,000	24.	Thailand	520,000
3.	Japan	4,346,000	25.	South Africa	468,000
4.	India	2,965,000	26.	Pakistan	446,000
5.	Germany	2,833,000	27.	Egypt	432,000
6.	UK	2,147,000	28.	Belgium	379,000
7.	Russia	2,076,000	29.	Malaysia	358,000
8.	France	2,067,000	30.	Venezuela	335,000
9.	Brazil	1,838,000	31.	Sweden	333,000
10.	Italy	1,800,000	32.	Greece	326,000
11.	Spain	1,362,000	33.	Ukraine	321,000
12.	Mexico	1,353,000	34.	Colombia	320,000
13.	Canada	1,274,000	35.	Austria	320,000
14.	South Korea	1,206,000	36.	Switzerland	301,000
15.	Iran	853,000	37.	Philippines	299,000
16.	Indonesia	846,000	38.	Nigeria	295,000
17.	Australia	767,000	39.	Hong Kong	293,000
18.	Taiwan	690,000	40.	Algeria	269,000
19.	Turkey	668,000	41.	Norway	257,000
20.	Netherlands	639,000	42.	Czech Republic	249,000
21.	Poland	624,000	43.	Romania	247,000
22.	Saudi Arabia	572,000	44.	Chile	234,000

The Wealth Gap

The world's richest and poorest countries, by Gross Domestic Product per capita in US $ (2007)

Richest countries			Poorest countries		
1.	Luxembourg	80,800	1.	Congo (Dem. Rep.)	300
2.	Norway	55,600	2.	Liberia	500
3.	Kuwait	55,300	3.	Zimbabwe	500
4.	UAE	55,200	4.	Comoros	600
5.	Singapore	48,900	5.	Guinea-Bissau	600
6.	USA	46,000	6.	Solomon Islands	600
7.	Ireland	45,600	7.	Somalia	600
8.	Hong Kong (China)	42,000	8.	Central African Rep.	700
9.	Switzerland	39,800	9.	Ethiopia	700
10.	Iceland	39,400	10.	Niger	700
11.	Austria	39,000	11.	Afghanistan	800
12.	Andorra	38,800	12.	Burundi	800
13.	Netherlands	38,600	13.	East Timor	800
14.	Canada	38,200	14.	Gambia	800
15.	Australia	37,500	15.	Malawi	800
16.	Denmark	37,400	16.	Sierra Leone	800
17.	Sweden	36,900	17.	Mozambique	900
18.	Belgium	36,500	18.	Togo	900
19.	Finland	35,500	19.	Djibouti	1,000
20.	UK	35,000	20.	Eritrea	1,000
21.	Bahrain	34,700	21.	Guinea	1,000

Continental Shares

Shares of population and of wealth (GNI) by continent

Population
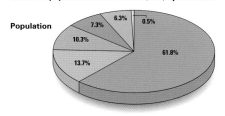

GNI
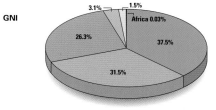

 Europe
 Asia
 South America
 Australia   Africa   North America

Inflation

Highest inflation		Lowest inflation	
Zimbabwe	.....26,470%	Nauru	...........–3.6%
Burma (Myanmar)	. .40%	Vanuatu	.........–1.6%
Venezuela	.........21%	San Marino	......–1.5%
Guinea	...........20%	Dominica	........–0.1%
Tajikistan	..........20%	Japan	..............0%

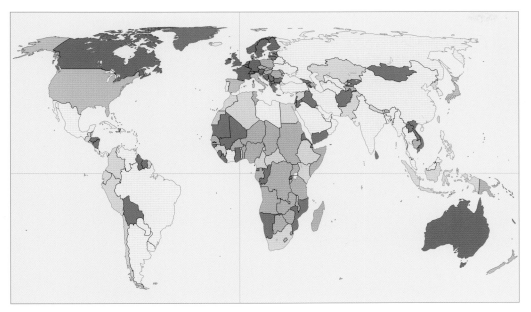

International Aid

Official Development Assistance (ODA) provided and received, per capita (2007)

- Over $100 per person
- $50 – $100 per person
- $20 – $50 per person

Providers

- Under $10 per person
- $10 – $25 per person
- $25 – $50 per person
- Over $50 per person

Receivers

- No data available

Debt and Aid

International debtors and the aid they receive

Although aid grants make a vital contribution to many of the world's poorer countries, they are usually dwarfed by the burden of debt that the developing economies are expected to repay. It is estimated that the total debt burden of developing countries is US$523 billion.

Debt, US $ per capita (2007)

Aid, US $ per capita (2007)

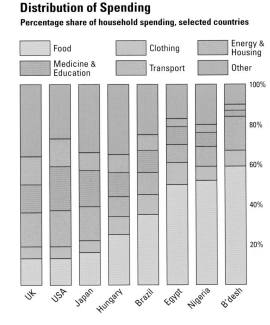

Distribution of Spending

Percentage share of household spending, selected countries

- Food
- Clothing
- Energy & Housing
- Medicine & Education
- Transport
- Other

UK, USA, Japan, Hungary, Brazil, Egypt, Nigeria, B'desh

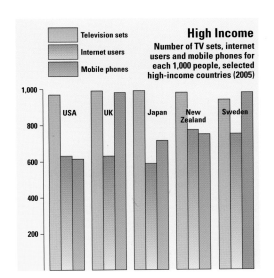

High Income
Number of TV sets, internet users and mobile phones for each 1,000 people, selected high-income countries (2005)

- Television sets
- Internet users
- Mobile phones

USA, UK, Japan, New Zealand, Sweden

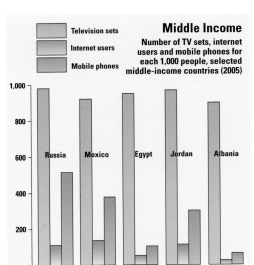

Middle Income
Number of TV sets, internet users and mobile phones for each 1,000 people, selected middle-income countries (2005)

- Television sets
- Internet users
- Mobile phones

Russia, Mexico, Egypt, Jordan, Albania

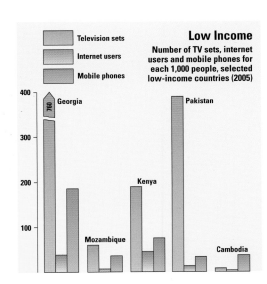

Low Income
Number of TV sets, internet users and mobile phones for each 1,000 people, selected low-income countries (2005)

- Television sets
- Internet users
- Mobile phones

Georgia, Pakistan, Kenya, Mozambique, Cambodia

Quality of Life

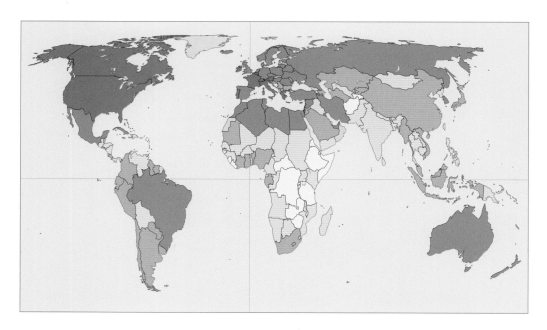

Daily Food Consumption

Average daily food intake in calories per person (2003)

Over 3,500 calories per person

3,000 – 3,500 calories per person

2,500 – 3,000 calories per person

2,000 – 2,500 calories per person

Under 2,000 calories per person

No data available

Hospital Capacity

Hospital beds available for each 1,000 people (2007)

Highest capacity		Lowest capacity	
Japan	14.1	Angola	0.1
Belarus	11.1	Cambodia	0.1
Russia	9.7	Malawi	0.1
Ukraine	8.7	Senegal	0.1
South Korea	8.6	Ethiopia	0.2
Czech Republic	8.4	Nepal	0.2
Germany	8.3	Bangladesh	0.3
Azerbaijan	8.1	Guinea	0.3
Lithuania	8.0	Madagascar	0.3
Hungary	7.9	Mali	0.3
Kazakhstan	7.8	Afghanistan	0.4
Austria	7.6	Chad	0.4
Latvia	7.6	Sierra Leone	0.4
Malta	7.6	Benin	0.5
Iceland	7.5	Nigeria	0.5

Although the ratio of people to hospital beds gives a good approximation of a country's health provision, it is not an absolute indicator. Raw numbers may mask inefficiency and other weaknesses: the high availability of beds in Belarus, for example, has not prevented infant mortality rates over three times as high as in the United Kingdom and the United States.

Life Expectancy

Years of life expectancy at birth, selected countries (2007)

The chart shows combined data for both sexes. On average, women live longer than men worldwide, even in developing countries with high maternal mortality rates. Overall, life expectancy is steadily rising, though the difference between rich and poor nations remains dramatic.

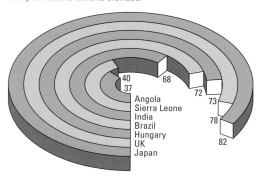

Angola 40
Sierra Leone 37
India 68
Brazil 72
Hungary 73
UK 78
Japan 82

Causes of Death

Causes of death for selected countries by percentage

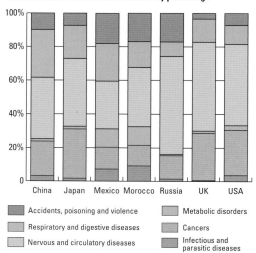

China Japan Mexico Morocco Russia UK USA

- Accidents, poisoning and violence
- Respiratory and digestive diseases
- Nervous and circulatory diseases
- Metabolic disorders
- Cancers
- Infectious and parasitic diseases

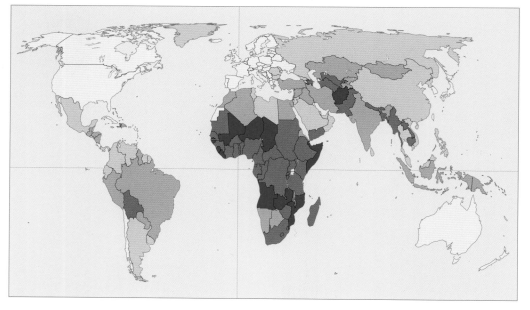

Infant Mortality

Number of babies who died under the age of one, per 1,000 live births (2007)

Over 100 deaths per 1,000 births

50 – 100 deaths per 1,000 births

25 – 50 deaths per 1,000 births

10 – 25 deaths per 1,000 births

Under 10 deaths per 1,000 births

No data available

Highest infant mortality		Lowest infant mortality	
Angola	184 deaths	Singapore	2 deaths
Sierra Leone	158 deaths	Sweden	3 deaths
Afghanistan	157 deaths	Hong Kong (China)	3 deaths
Liberia	150 deaths	Japan	3 deaths
Niger	117 deaths	Iceland	3 deaths

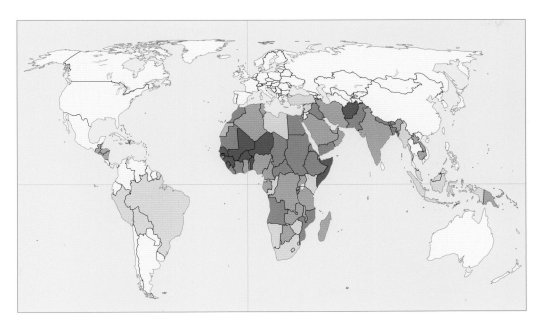

Illiteracy

Percentage of the total adult population unable to read or write (2005)

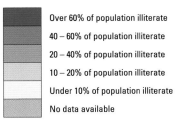

- Over 60% of population illiterate
- 40 – 60% of population illiterate
- 20 – 40% of population illiterate
- 10 – 20% of population illiterate
- Under 10% of population illiterate
- No data available

Countries with the highest and lowest illiteracy rates

Highest		Lowest	
Burkina Faso	87	Australia	0
Niger	83	Denmark	0
Mali	81	Finland	0
Sierra Leone	69	Liechtenstein	0
Guinea	64	Luxembourg	0

Fertility and Education

Fertility rates compared with female education, selected countries (2000–05)

Percentage of females aged 12–17 in secondary education

Fertility rate: average number of children borne per woman

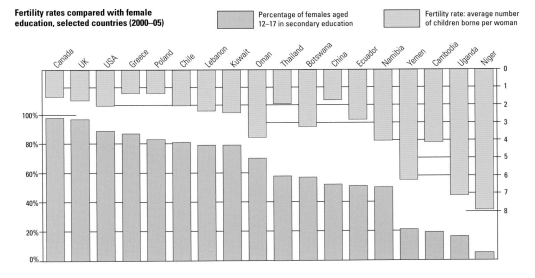

Living Standards

At first sight, most international contrasts in living standards are swamped by differences in wealth. The rich not only have more money, they have more of everything, including years of life. Those with only a little money are obliged to spend most of it on food and clothing, the basic maintenance costs of their existence; air travel and tourism are unlikely to feature on their expenditure lists. However, poverty and wealth are both relative: slum dwellers living on social security payments in an affluent industrial country have far more resources at their disposal than an average African peasant, but feel their own poverty nonetheless. A middle-class Indian lawyer cannot command a fraction of the earnings of a counterpart living in New York, London or Rome; nevertheless, he rightly sees himself as prosperous.

The rich not only live longer, on average, than the poor, they also die from different causes. Infectious and parasitic diseases, all but eliminated in the developed world, remain a scourge in the developing nations. On the other hand, more than two-thirds of the populations of OECD nations eventually succumb to cancer or circulatory disease.

Human Development Index

The Human Development Index (HDI), calculated by the UN Development Programme, gives a value to countries using indicators of life expectancy, education and standards of living (2005). Higher values show more developed countries.

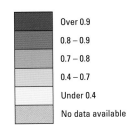

- Over 0.9
- 0.8 – 0.9
- 0.7 – 0.8
- 0.4 – 0.7
- Under 0.4
- No data available

Highest values		Lowest values	
Iceland	0.968	Sierra Leone	0.336
Norway	0.968	Burkina Faso	0.370
Australia	0.962	Guinea-Bissau	0.374
Ireland	0.959	Niger	0.374
Sweden	0.95	Mali	0.380

Energy

Production

Each square represents 1% of world energy production (2006)

North America • Europe • Russia
Middle East • Asia • Japan
Africa
South America • Australasia

Consumption

Each square represents 1% of world energy consumption (2006)

North America • Europe • Russia
Middle East • Asia
Africa
South America • Japan • Australasia

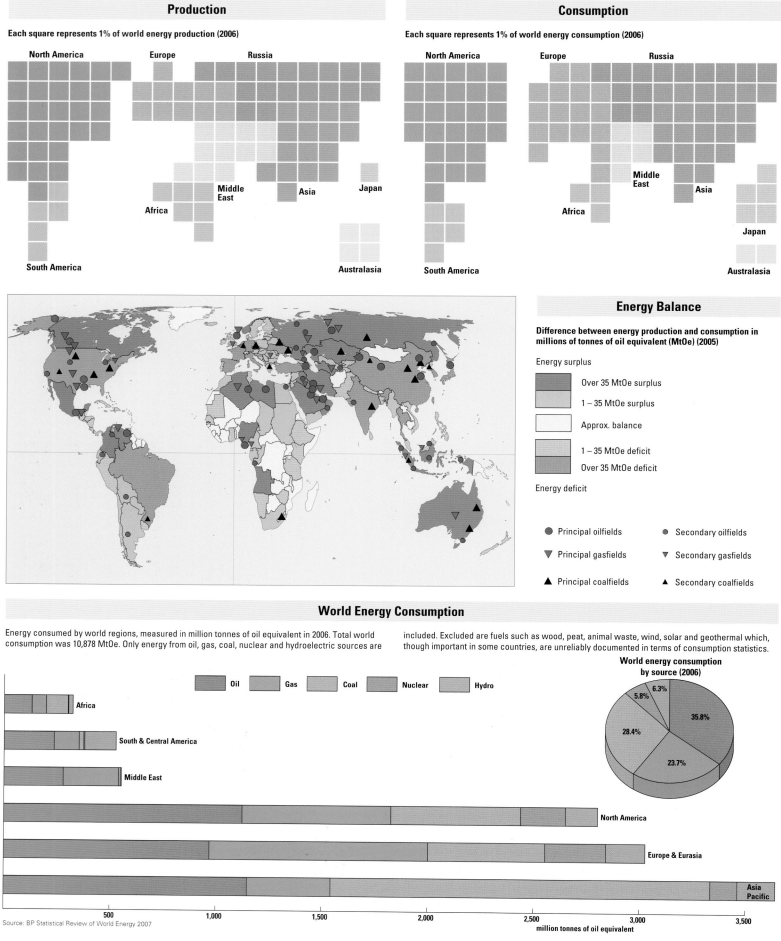

Energy Balance

Difference between energy production and consumption in millions of tonnes of oil equivalent (MtOe) (2005)

Energy surplus

Over 35 MtOe surplus
1 – 35 MtOe surplus
Approx. balance
1 – 35 MtOe deficit
Over 35 MtOe deficit

Energy deficit

● Principal oilfields   ● Secondary oilfields
▽ Principal gasfields   ▽ Secondary gasfields
▲ Principal coalfields   ▲ Secondary coalfields

World Energy Consumption

Energy consumed by world regions, measured in million tonnes of oil equivalent in 2006. Total world consumption was 10,878 MtOe. Only energy from oil, gas, coal, nuclear and hydroelectric sources are included. Excluded are fuels such as wood, peat, animal waste, wind, solar and geothermal which, though important in some countries, are unreliably documented in terms of consumption statistics.

Oil ■ Gas ■ Coal ■ Nuclear ■ Hydro

Africa
South & Central America
Middle East
North America
Europe & Eurasia
Asia Pacific

World energy consumption by source (2006)

6.3%
5.8%
35.8%
28.4%
23.7%

500   1,000   1,500   2,000   2,500   3,000   3,500

million tonnes of oil equivalent

Source: BP Statistical Review of World Energy 2007

Energy

Energy is used to keep us warm or cool, fuel our industries and our transport systems, and even feed us; high-intensity agriculture, with its use of fertilizers, pesticides and machinery, is heavily energy-dependent. Although we live in a high-energy society, there are vast discrepancies between rich and poor; for example, a North American consumes 13 times as much energy as a Chinese person. But even developing nations have more power at their disposal than was imaginable a century ago.

The distribution of energy supplies, most importantly fossil fuels (coal, oil and natural gas), is very uneven. In addition, the diagrams and map opposite show that the largest producers of energy are not necessarily the largest consumers. The movement of energy supplies around the world is therefore an important component of international trade. In 2006, total world movements in oil amounted to 2,590 million tonnes.

As the finite reserves of fossil fuels are depleted, renewable energy sources, such as solar, hydro-thermal, wind, tidal and biomass, will become increasingly important around the world.

Nuclear Power

Major producers by percentage of world total and by percentage of domestic electricity generation (2006)

Country	% of world total production	Country	% of nuclear as proportion of domestic electricity
1. USA	29.6%	1. France	78.7%
2. France	16.1%	2. Lithuania	64.2%
3. Japan	10.9%	3. Slovak Rep.	57.3%
4. Germany	6.0%	4. Belgium	54.7%
5. Russia	5.4%	5. Ukraine	48.4%
6. South Korea	5.3%	6. Switzerland	47.1%
7. Canada	3.4%	7. Bulgaria	43.4%
8. Ukraine	3.2%	8. Sweden	41.5%
9. UK	2.6%	9. Armenia	40.5%
10. Sweden	2.4%	10. South Korea	38.6%

Although the 1980s were a bad time for the nuclear power industry (fears of long-term environmental damage were heavily reinforced by the 1986 disaster at Chernobyl), the industry picked up in the early 1990s. Sixteen countries currently rely on nuclear power to supply over 25% of their electricity requirements. There are over 400 operating nuclear power stations worldwide, with over 100 more planned or under construction.

Hydroelectricity

Major producers by percentage of world total and by percentage of domestic electricity generation (2004)

Country	% of world total production	Country	% of hydroelectric as proportion of domestic electricity
1. Canada	12.2%	1. Bhutan	100%
2. China	11.9%	= Paraguay	100%
3. Brazil	11.6%	= Lesotho	100%
4. USA	9.8%	4. Mozambique	99.8%
5. Russia	6.0%	5. Congo	99.7%
6. Norway	3.9%	= Congo (Dem. Rep.)	99.7%
7. Japan	3.4%	= Uganda	99.7%
8. India	3.0%	8. Nepal	99.6%
9. Sweden	2.3%	9. Zambia	99.5%
10. France	2.2%	10. Norway	98.8%

Countries heavily reliant on hydroelectricity are usually small and non-industrial: a high proportion of hydroelectric power more often reflects a modest energy budget than vast hydroelectric resources. The USA, for instance, produces only 6.7% of its power requirements from hydroelectricity; yet that 6.7% amounts to more than seven times the hydropower generated by most of Africa.

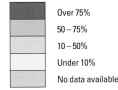

Fuel Exports

Fuels as a percentage of total value of exports (2005)

- Over 75%
- 50 – 75%
- 10 – 50%
- Under 10%
- No data available

In the 1970s, oil exports became a political issue when OPEC sought to increase the influence of developing countries in world affairs by raising oil prices and restricting production. But its power was short-lived, following a fall in demand for oil in the 1980s, due to an increase in energy efficiency and development of alternative resources. However, with the heavy energy demands of the Asian economies early in the 21st century, both oil and gas prices have risen sharply.

Conversion Rates

1 barrel = 0.136 tonnes or 159 litres or 35 Imperial gallons or 42 US gallons

1 tonne = 7.33 barrels or 1,185 litres or 256 Imperial gallons or 261 US gallons

1 tonne oil = 1.5 tonnes hard coal or 3.0 tonnes lignite or 12,000 kWh

1 Imperial gallon = 1.201 US gallons or 4.546 litres or 277.4 cubic inches

Measurements

For historical reasons, oil is traded in 'barrels'. The weight and volume equivalents (shown right) are all based on average-density 'Arabian light' crude oil.

The energy equivalents given for a tonne of oil are also somewhat imprecise: oil and coal of different qualities will have varying energy contents, a fact usually reflected in their price on world markets.

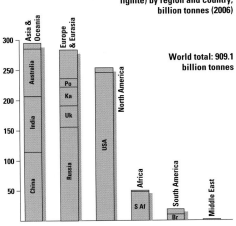

World Coal Reserves

World coal reserves (including lignite) by region and country, billion tonnes (2006)

World total: 909.1 billion tonnes

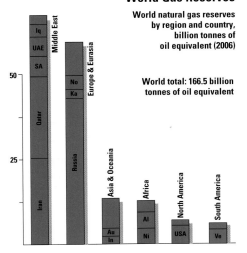

World Gas Reserves

World natural gas reserves by region and country, billion tonnes of oil equivalent (2006)

World total: 166.5 billion tonnes of oil equivalent

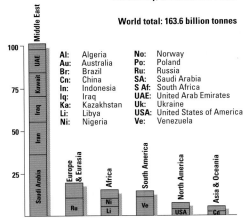

World Oil Reserves

World oil reserves by region and country, billion tonnes (2006)

World total: 163.6 billion tonnes

Al:	Algeria
Au:	Australia
Br:	Brazil
Cn:	China
In:	Indonesia
Iq:	Iraq
Ka:	Kazakhstan
Li:	Libya
Ni:	Nigeria

No:	Norway
Po:	Poland
Ru:	Russia
SA:	Saudi Arabia
S Af:	South Africa
UAE:	United Arab Emirates
Uk:	Ukraine
USA:	United States of America
Ve:	Venezuela

Production

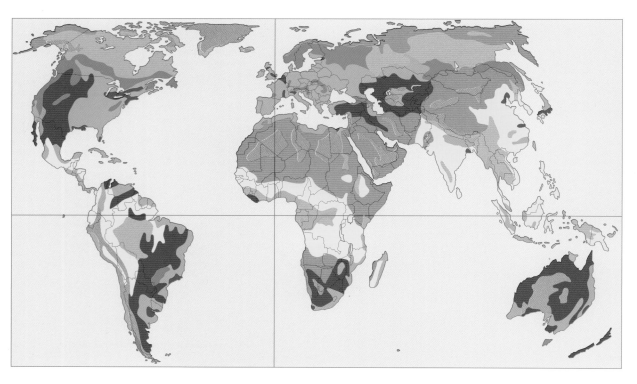

CARTOGRAPHY BY PHILIP'S. COPYRIGHT PHILIP'S

Agriculture

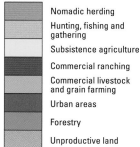

Predominant type of farming or land use

- Nomadic herding
- Hunting, fishing and gathering
- Subsistence agriculture
- Commercial ranching
- Commercial livestock and grain farming
- Urban areas
- Forestry
- Unproductive land

The development of agriculture has transformed human existence more than any other. The whole business of farming is constantly developing: due mainly to the new varieties of rice and wheat, world grain production has more than doubled since 1965. New machinery and modern agricultural techniques enable relatively few farmers to produce enough food for the world's 6 billion or so people.

Staple Crops

Wheat
China 17.2% | India 11.4% | USA 9.5% | Russia 7.4% | France 5.8% | Canada 4.5% | Germany 3.7%

World total (2006): 605,946,000 tonnes

Maize
USA 38.5% | China 20.9% | Brazil 6.1%

World total (2006): 695,228,000 tonnes

Oats
Russia 21.1% | Canada 15.6% | Australia 6.1% | USA 5.9% | China 5.0% | Poland 4.5% | Finland 4.5% | Spain 4.0%

World total (2006): 23,101,000 tonnes

Millet
India 31.8% | Nigeria 24.2% | Niger 10.1% | China 5.7%

World total (2006): 31,781,000 tonnes

Rice
China 29.0% | India 21.5% | Indonesia 8.6% | Bangladesh 6.9% | Vietnam 5.6% | Thailand 4.6% | Burma 4.0%

World total (2006): 634,606,000 tonnes

Potatoes
China 22.3% | Russia 12.2% | India 7.6% | USA 6.3% | Ukraine 6.2%

World total (2006): 315,100,000 tonnes

Soya
USA 38.6% | Brazil 23.6% | Argentina 18.3% | China 7.0%

World total (2006): 221,501,000 tonnes

Cassava
Nigeria 20.2% | Brazil 11.8% | Thailand 10.0% | Indonesia 8.8% | Congo (D.R.) 6.6% | Mozambique 5.1%

World total (2006): 226,337,000 tonnes

Sugars

Sugar cane
Brazil 32.7% | India 20.2% | China 7.2% | Mexico 3.6% | Thailand 3.5% | Pakistan 3.2%

World total (2006): 1,392,365,000 tonnes

Sugar beet
Russia 12.0% | France 11.7% | USA 11.3% | Ukraine 8.7% | Germany 8.1% | Turkey 5.6% | Poland 4.5% | Italy 4.2%

World total (2006): 256,407,000 tonnes

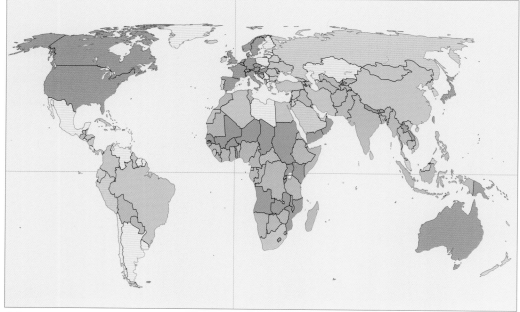

Employment

The number of workers employed in manufacturing for every 100 workers engaged in agriculture (2006)

- Under 10 ┐
- 10 – 50 ├ Mainly agricultural countries
- 50 – 100 ┘
- 100 – 200 ┐
- 200 – 500 ├ Mainly industrial countries
- Over 500 ┘
- No data available

Countries with the highest and lowest number of workers employed in manufacturing per 100 workers engaged in agriculture (2006)

Highest		Lowest	
Bahrain	7,900	Burundi	2.5
San Marino	4,200	Yemen	5.0
Micronesia	3,822	Oman	5.0
USA	3,271	Rwanda	5.6
Liechtenstein	2,350	Malawi	5.6

Mineral Production

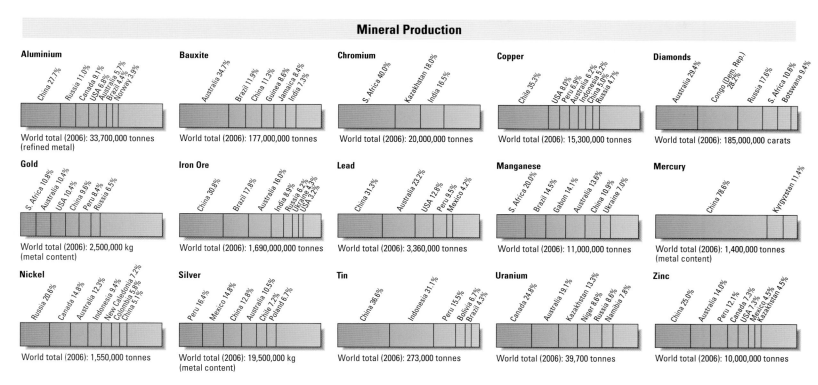

Aluminium
China 27.7% · Russia 11.0% · Canada 9.1% · USA 6.8% · Australia 5.7% · Brazil 4.4% · Norway 3.9%
World total (2006): 33,700,000 tonnes (refined metal)

Bauxite
Australia 34.7% · Brazil 11.9% · China 11.3% · Guinea 8.6% · Jamaica 8.4% · India 7.3%
World total (2006): 177,000,000 tonnes

Chromium
S. Africa 40.0% · Kazakhstan 18.0% · India 16.5%
World total (2006): 20,000,000 tonnes

Copper
Chile 35.3% · USA 8.0% · Peru 6.9% · Australia 6.2% · Indonesia 5.2% · China 5.0% · Russia 4.7%
World total (2006): 15,300,000 tonnes

Diamonds
Australia 29.4% · Congo (Dem. Rep.) 28.2% · Russia 17.6% · S. Africa 10.6% · Botswana 9.4%
World total (2006): 185,000,000 carats

Gold
S. Africa 10.8% · Australia 10.4% · USA 9.6% · China 9.6% · Peru 8.4% · Russia 6.5%
World total (2006): 2,500,000 kg (metal content)

Iron Ore
China 30.8% · Brazil 17.8% · Australia 16.0% · India 8.9% · Russia 6.2% · Ukraine 4.3% · USA 3.2%
World total (2006): 1,690,000,000 tonnes

Lead
China 31.3% · Australia 23.2% · USA 12.8% · Peru 9.5% · Mexico 4.2%
World total (2006): 3,360,000 tonnes

Manganese
S. Africa 20.0% · Brazil 14.5% · Gabon 14.1% · Australia 13.6% · China 10.9% · Ukraine 7.0%
World total (2006): 11,000,000 tonnes

Mercury
China 78.6% · Kyrgyzstan 11.4%
World total (2006): 1,400,000 tonnes (metal content)

Nickel
Russia 20.6% · Canada 14.8% · Australia 12.3% · Indonesia 9.4% · New Caledonia 7.2% · Colombia 5.8% · China 5.1%
World total (2006): 1,550,000 tonnes

Silver
Peru 16.4% · Mexico 14.8% · China 12.8% · Australia 10.5% · Chile 7.2% · Poland 6.7%
World total (2006): 19,500,000 kg (metal content)

Tin
China 36.6% · Indonesia 31.1% · Peru 15.5% · Bolivia 6.7% · Brazil 4.3%
World total (2006): 273,000 tonnes

Uranium
Canada 24.8% · Australia 19.1% · Kazakhstan 13.3% · Niger 8.6% · Russia 8.6% · Namibia 7.8%
World total (2006): 39,700 tonnes

Zinc
China 25.0% · Australia 14.0% · Peru 12.1% · Canada 7.3% · USA 7.3% · Mexico 4.5% · Kazakhstan 4.5%
World total (2006): 10,000,000 tonnes

Mineral Distribution

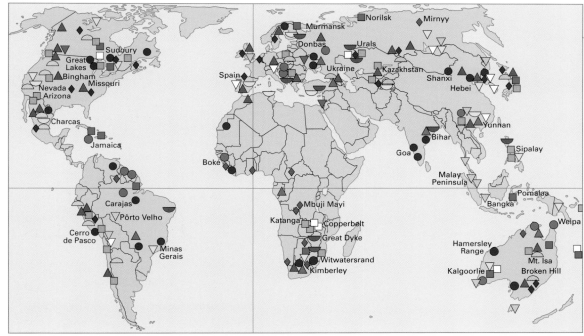

The map shows the richest sources of the most important minerals (major mineral locations are named)

- ● Bauxite
- ⏢ Chromium
- □ Cobalt
- ■ Copper
- ◆ Diamonds
- ▽ Gold
- ● Iron ore
- ▲ Lead
- ▲ Manganese
- ▽ Mercury
- ▲ Molybdenum
- ■ Nickel
- ▼ Potash
- ◠ Silver
- ▽ Tin
- ▽ Tungsten
- ◆ Zinc

The map does not show undersea deposits, most of which are considered inaccessible.

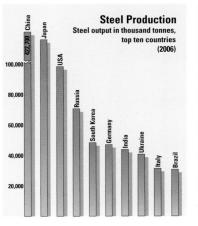

Steel Production
Steel output in thousand tonnes, top ten countries (2006)
China 422,700 · Japan · USA · Russia · South Korea · Germany · India · Ukraine · Italy · Brazil

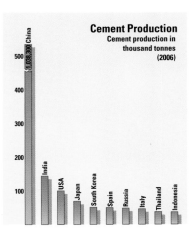

Cement Production
Cement production in thousand tonnes (2006)
China 1,038,300 · India · USA · Japan · South Korea · Spain · Russia · Italy · Thailand · Indonesia

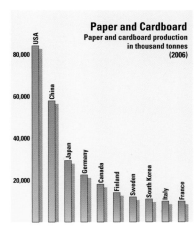

Paper and Cardboard
Paper and cardboard production in thousand tonnes (2006)
USA · China · Japan · Germany · Canada · Finland · Sweden · South Korea · Italy · France

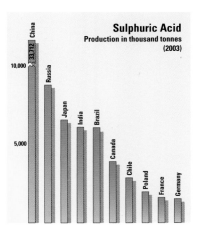

Sulphuric Acid
Production in thousand tonnes (2003)
China 33,712 · Russia · Japan · India · Brazil · Canada · Chile · Poland · France · Germany

Trade

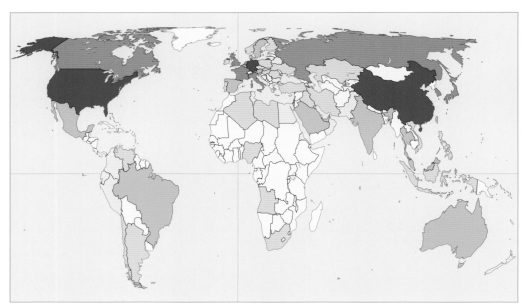

Share of World Trade

Percentage share of total world exports by value (2007)

- Over 5% of world trade
- 2.5 – 5% of world trade
- 1 – 2.5% of world trade
- 0.25 – 1% of world trade
- 0.1 – 0.25% of world trade
- Under 0.1% of world trade

Largest share of world trade		Smallest share of world trade	
Germany	.9.8%	East Timor	.0.0%
China	.8.8%	Eritrea	.0.0%
USA	.8.2%	Burundi	.0.0%
Japan	.4.8%	Rwanda	.0.0%
France	.4.0%	Guinea-Bissau	.0.0%

The Main Trading Nations

The imports and exports of the top ten trading nations as a percentage of world trade (2006). Each country's trade in manufactured goods is shown in dark blue

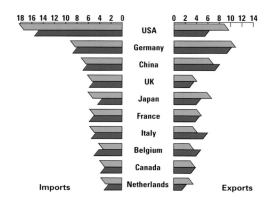

USA
Germany
China
UK
Japan
France
Italy
Belgium
Canada
Netherlands

Imports   Exports

Major exports

Leading manufactured items and their exporters (2007)

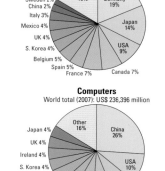

Motor Vehicles
World total (2007): US$ 2,706,511 million

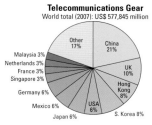

Telecommunications Gear
World total (2007): US$ 577,845 million

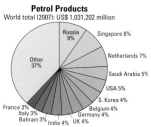

Petrol Products
World total (2007): US$ 1,031,202 million

Computers
World total (2007): US$ 236,396 million

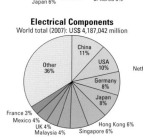

Electrical Components
World total (2007): US$ 4,187,042 million

Pharmaceuticals
World total (2007): US$ 1,042,778 million

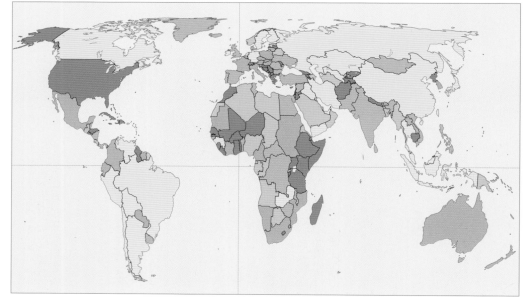

Balance of Trade

Value of exports in proportion to the value of imports (2007)

- More than 40%
- 10 – 40%
- 10% either side
- 10 – 40%
- More than 40%
- No data available

Imports exceed exports by:

Exports exceed imports by:

The total world trade balance should amount to zero, since exports must equal imports on a global scale. In practice, at least $100 billion in exports go unrecorded, leaving the world with an apparent deficit and many countries in a better position than public accounting reveals. However, a favourable trade balance is not necessarily a sign of prosperity: many poorer countries must maintain a high surplus in order to service debts, and do so by restricting imports below the levels needed to sustain successful economies.

Trade in Primary Exports

Primary exports as a percentage of total export value (2005)

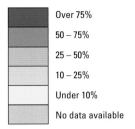

- Over 75%
- 50 – 75%
- 25 – 50%
- 10 – 25%
- Under 10%
- No data available

Primary exports are raw materials or partly processed products that form the basis for manufacturing. They are the necessary requirements of industries and include agricultural products, minerals, fuels and timber, as well as many semi-manufactured goods such as cotton, which has been spun but not woven, wood pulp or flour. Many developed countries have few natural resources and rely on imports for the majority of their primary products. The countries of South-east Asia export hardwoods to the rest of the world, while many South American countries are heavily dependent on coffee exports.

Merchant Fleets

Merchant fleets in thousand gross registered tonnage (2006). Although a large number of vessels are registered in Liberia and Panama, they are not part of the national fleet

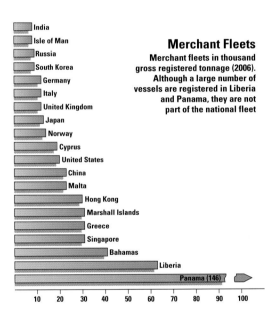

India
Isle of Man
Russia
South Korea
Germany
Italy
United Kingdom
Japan
Norway
Cyprus
United States
China
Malta
Hong Kong
Marshall Islands
Greece
Singapore
Bahamas
Liberia
Panama (146)

Top Ten Ports

Total container traffic, in million TEU (2006) ('TEU' stands for Twenty-foot Equivalent Unit, the equivalent of a standard container)

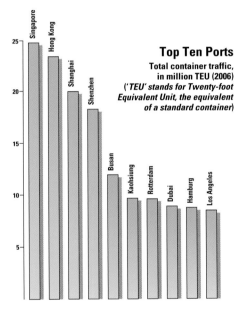

Types of Vessels

World fleet by type of vessel (2006)

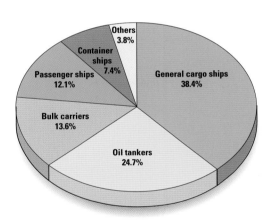

Others 3.8%
Container ships 7.4%
General cargo ships 38.4%
Passenger ships 12.1%
Bulk carriers 13.6%
Oil tankers 24.7%

Exports Per Capita

Value of exports in US $, divided by total population (2006)

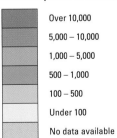

- Over 10,000
- 5,000 – 10,000
- 1,000 – 5,000
- 500 – 1,000
- 100 – 500
- Under 100
- No data available

Highest per capita

Hong Kong	$88,121
Liechtenstein	$72,675
Singapore	$63,132
United Arab Emirates	$52,676
Luxembourg	$41,209

Travel and Tourism

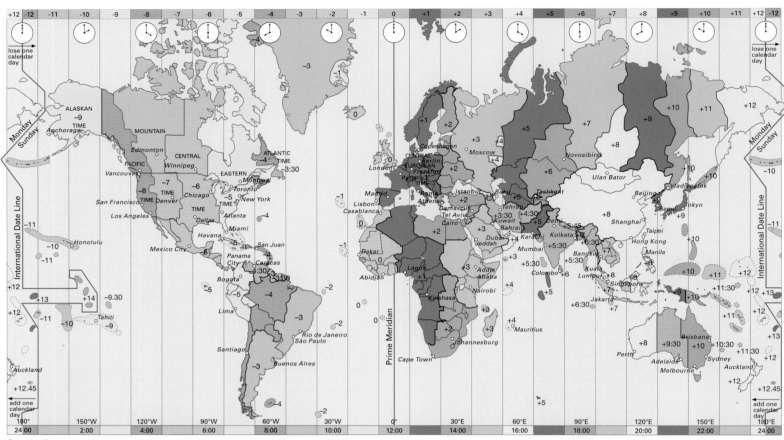

Projection: Mercator

Time Zones

Zones using UT (GMT)	Zones ahead of UT (GMT)
Zones behind UT (GMT)	Half-hour zones
International boundaries	Time-zone boundaries
10 Hours fast or slow of UT or Co-ordinated Universal Time	International Date Line

Certain time zones are affected by the incidence of daylight saving time in countries where it is adopted.

Actual solar time, when it is noon at Greenwich, is shown along the top of the map.

The world is divided into 24 time zones, each centred on meridians at 15° intervals, which is the longitudinal distance the sun travels every hour. The meridian running through Greenwich, London, passes through the middle of the first zone.

Rail and Road: The Leading Nations

Total rail network ('000 km)	Passenger km per head per year	Total road network ('000 km)	Vehicle km per head per year	Number of vehicles per km of roads
1. USA 233.8	Japan 1,891	USA 6,378.3	USA....................12,505	Hong Kong..........287
2. Russia 85.5	Switzerland 1,751	India 3,319.6	Luxembourg 7,989	Qatar....................284
3. Canada 73.2	Belarus..............1,334	China 1,765.2	Kuwait 7,251	UAE.....................232
4. India 63.1	France 1,203	Brazil 1,724.9	France 7,142	Germany 195
5. China.................60.5	Ukraine..............1,100	Canada............1,408.8	Sweden................6,991	Lebanon 191
6. Germany 36.1	Russia 1,080	Japan 1,171.4	Germany..............6,806	Macau..................172
7. Argentina 34.2	Austria 1,008	France 893.1	Denmark..............6,764	Singapore 167
8. France................29.3	Denmark 999	Australia 811.6	Austria.................6,518	South Korea 160
9. Mexico...............26.5	Netherlands 855	Spain 664.9	Netherlands 5,984	Kuwait 156
10. South Africa........22.7	Germany 842	Russia 537.3	UK 5,738	Taiwan 150
11. Brazil.................22.1	Italy 811	Italy....................479.7	Canada................5,493	Israel 111
12. Ukraine 22.1	Belgium 795	UK 371.9	Italy.....................4,852	Malta 110

Air Travel

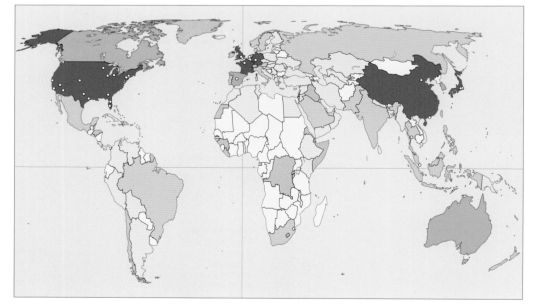

Passenger kilometres flown on scheduled flights (the number of passengers in thousands – international and domestic – multiplied by the distance flown from the airport of origin)

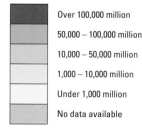

	Over 100,000 million
	50,000 – 100,000 million
	10,000 – 50,000 million
	1,000 – 10,000 million
	Under 1,000 million
	No data available
○	Major airports (handling over 30 million passengers)

World's busiest airports (total passengers)
1. Atlanta (Hartsfield)
2. Chicago (O'Hare)
3. London (Heathrow)
4. Tokyo (Haneda)
5. Los Angeles (International)

World's busiest airports (international passengers)
1. London (Heathrow)
2. Paris (Charles de Gaulle)
3. Amsterdam (Schipol))
4. Frankfurt (International)
5. Hong Kong (International)

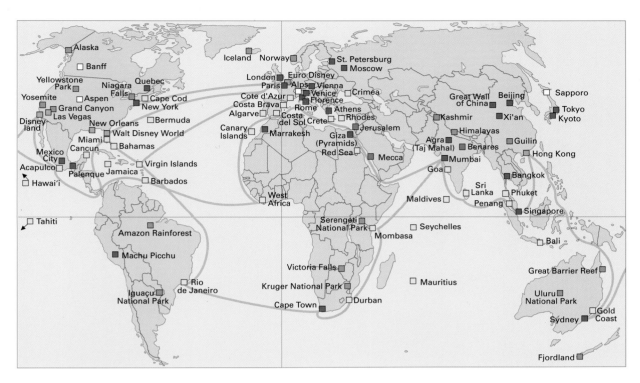

Destinations

- Cultural and historical centres
- Coastal resorts
- Ski resorts
- Centres of entertainment
- Places of pilgrimage
- Places of great natural beauty
- Popular holiday cruise routes

Visitors to the USA

Overseas arrivals to the USA, in thousands (2006)

1.	Canada	15,995
2.	Mexico	13,400
3.	UK	4,176
4.	Japan	3,673
5.	Germany	1,386
6.	France	790
7.	South Korea	758
8.	Australia	603
9.	Italy	533
10.	Brazil	525

Tourist Spending

Countries spending the most on overseas tourism, US$ million (2006)

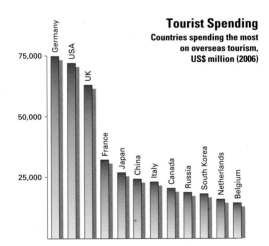

Importance of Tourism

		Arrivals from abroad (2006)	% of world total (2006)
1.	France	76,001,000	9.0%
2.	Spain	55,577,000	6.6%
3.	USA	46,085,000	5.4%
4.	China	41,761,000	4.9%
5.	Italy	36,513,000	4.3%
6.	UK	29,970,000	3.5%
7.	Germany	21,500,000	2.5%
8.	Mexico	20,617,000	2.4%
9.	Turkey	20,273,000	2.4%
10.	Austria	19,952,000	2.4%
11.	Russia	19,940,000	2.4%
12.	Canada	19,152,000	2.3%

The 846 million international arrivals in 2006 represented an additional 43 million over 2005's level – making a new record year for the industry. Growth was common to all regions, but particularly strong in Asia and the Pacific, and in the Middle East.

Tourist Earnings

Countries receiving the most from overseas tourism, US$ million (2006)

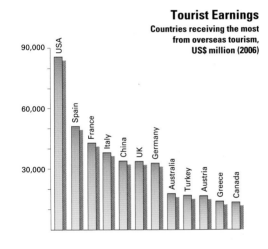

Tourism

Tourism receipts as a percentage of Gross National Income (2005)

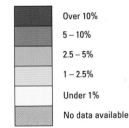

- Over 10%
- 5 – 10%
- 2.5 – 5%
- 1 – 2.5%
- Under 1%
- No data available

Countries most dependent on tourism (highest tourism receipts as a percentage of GNI, 2005)

1.	Palau	63.0%
2.	St Lucia	44.8%
3.	Bahamas	40.2%
4.	Antigua & Barbuda	36.9%
5.	Maldives	36.5%

– MT EVEREST, CHINA/NEPAL –

Part of the Himalaya range, Mt Everest – the highest mountain in the world at 8,850 m (29,035 ft) – lies just north of centre in this image. The two arms of the Rongbuk glacier flow away from the triangular shaded north wall, with the Kangshung glacier due east. The international boundary between China and Nepal bisects the peak, which was first climbed on 28 May 1953.

WORLD CITIES

AMSTERDAM	2	HONG KONG	12	MUMBAI	20	TEHRAN	31
ATHENS	2	ISTANBUL	12	MUNICH	21	TORONTO	31
ATLANTA	3	JAKARTA	12	NEW ORLEANS	21	VIENNA	32
BAGHDAD	3	JERUSALEM	13	NEW YORK	22	WARSAW	32
BANGKOK	3	JOHANNESBURG	13	ORLANDO	23	WASHINGTON	33
BARCELONA	4	KARACHI	13	OSAKA	23	WELLINGTON	33
BEIJING	4	KOLKATA	14	OSLO	23		
BERLIN	5	LAGOS	14	PARIS	24	INDEX	34–39
BOSTON	6	LAS VEGAS	14	PRAGUE	25		
BRUSSELS	6	LIMA	14	RIO DE JANEIRO	25		
BUDAPEST	7	LONDON	15	ROME	26	WORLD CITIES	
BUENOS AIRES	7	LOS ANGELES	16	SAN FRANCISCO	26	SATELLITE IMAGES	
CAIRO	7	LISBON	16	ST PETERSBURG	27	CAPE TOWN	40
CAPE TOWN	8	MADRID	17	SANTIAGO	27	KARACHI	41
COPENHAGEN	8	MANILA	17	SÃO PAULO	27	LONDON	42
CHICAGO	9	MELBOURNE	18	SEOUL	27	MELBOURNE	43
DELHI	10	MEXICO CITY	18	SHANGHAI	28	NEW ORLEANS	44
DUBLIN	10	MIAMI	18	SINGAPORE	28	NEW YORK	45
EDINBURGH	11	MILAN	19	STOCKHOLM	29	SAN FRANCISCO	46
GUANGZHOU	11	MOSCOW	19	SYDNEY	29	SANTIAGO	47
HELSINKI	11	MONTRÉAL	20	TOKYO	30	TOKYO	48

CITY MAPS

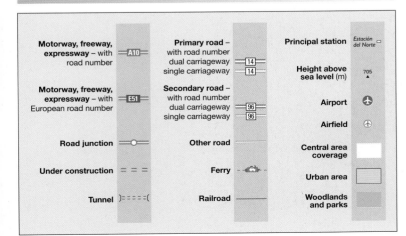

Motorway, freeway, expressway – with road number — A10

Motorway, freeway, expressway – with European road number — E51

Road junction

Under construction

Tunnel

Primary road –
with road number
dual carriageway — 14
single carriageway — 14

Secondary road –
with road number
dual carriageway — 96
single carriageway — 96

Other road

Ferry

Railroad

Principal station — Estación del Norte

Height above sea level (m) — 705

Airport

Airfield

Central area coverage

Urban area

Woodlands and parks

CENTRAL AREA MAPS

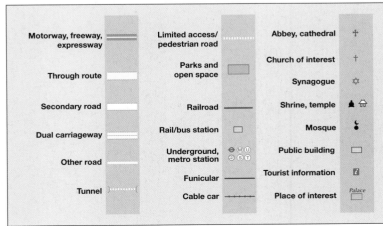

Motorway, freeway, expressway

Through route

Secondary road

Dual carriageway

Other road

Tunnel

Limited access/ pedestrian road

Parks and open space

Railroad

Rail/bus station

Underground, metro station

Funicular

Cable car

Abbey, cathedral

Church of interest

Synagogue

Shrine, temple

Mosque

Public building

Tourist information

Place of interest — Palace

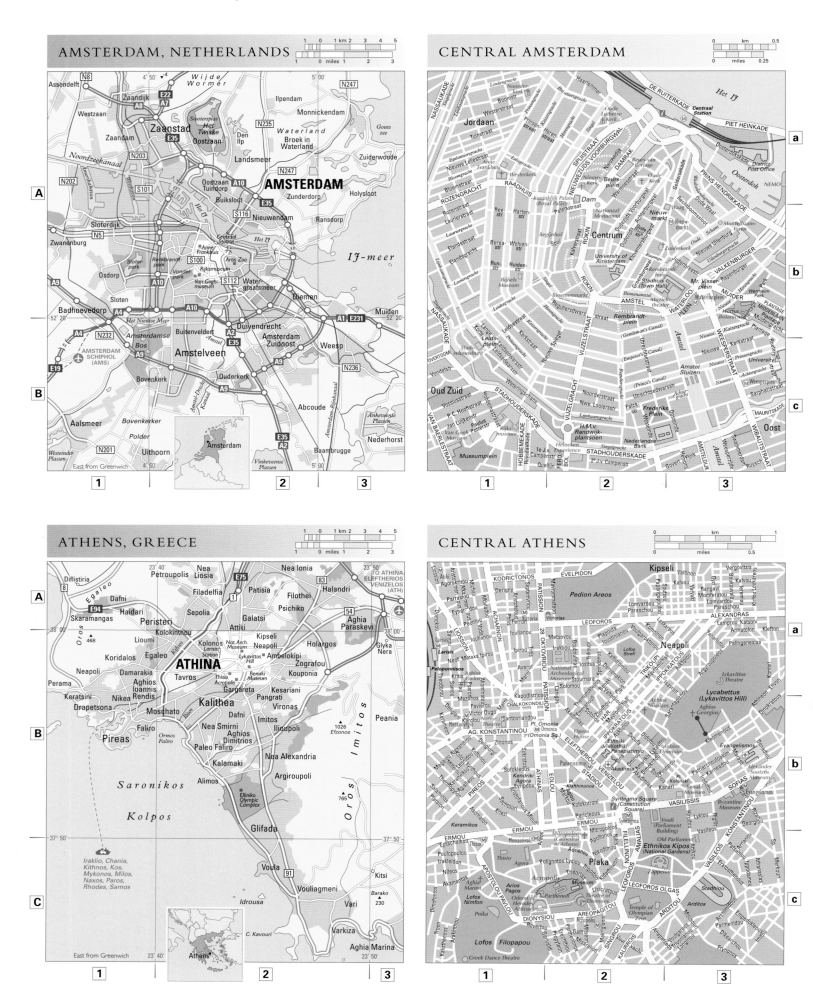

AMSTERDAM, NETHERLANDS

CENTRAL AMSTERDAM

ATHENS, GREECE

CENTRAL ATHENS

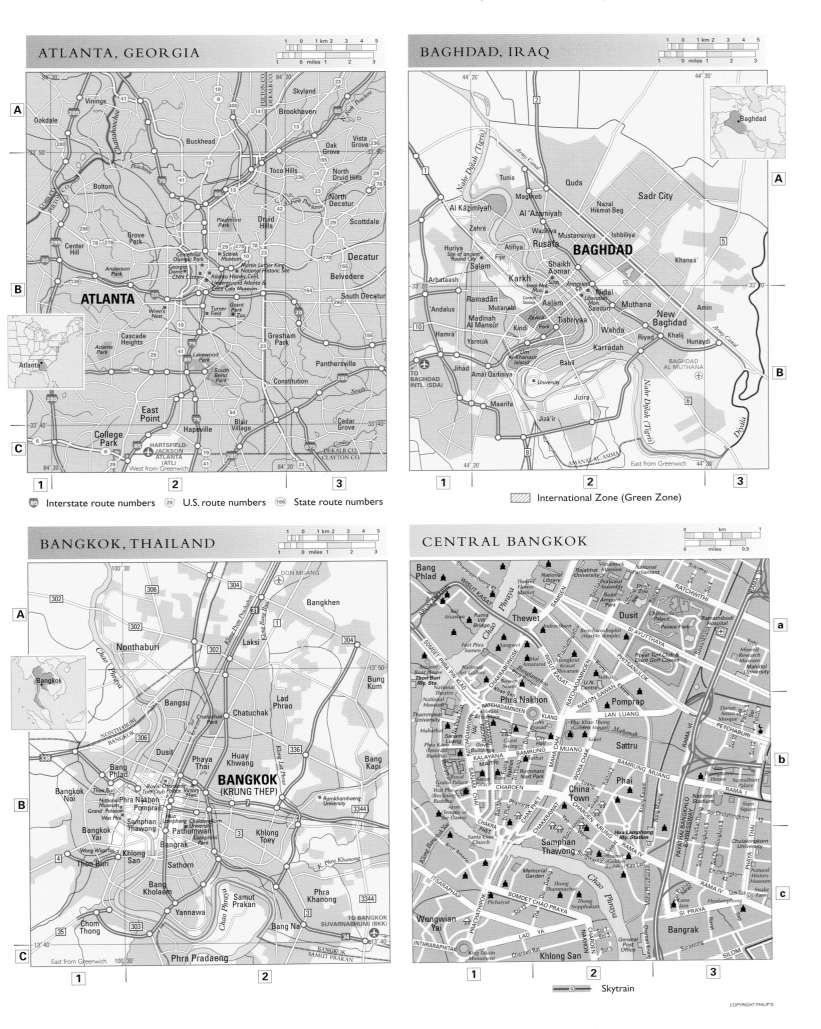

ATLANTA, GEORGIA

85 Interstate route numbers   29 U.S. route numbers   166 State route numbers

BAGHDAD, IRAQ

International Zone (Green Zone)

BANGKOK, THAILAND

CENTRAL BANGKOK

—S— Skytrain

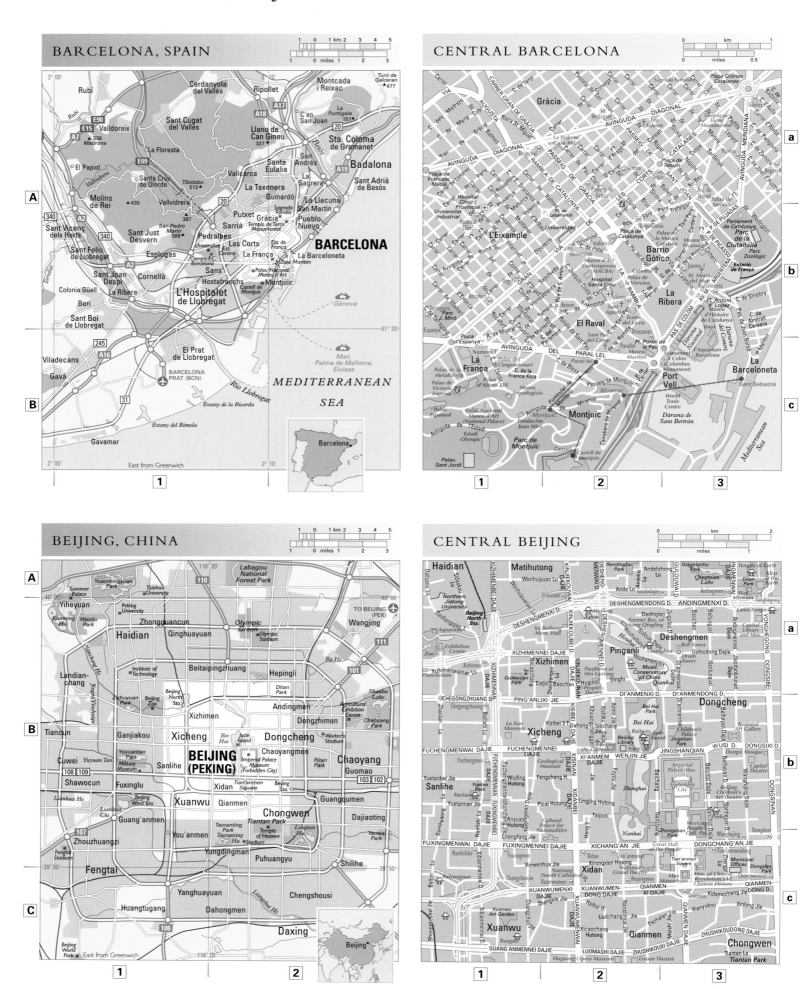

BERLIN, GERMANY

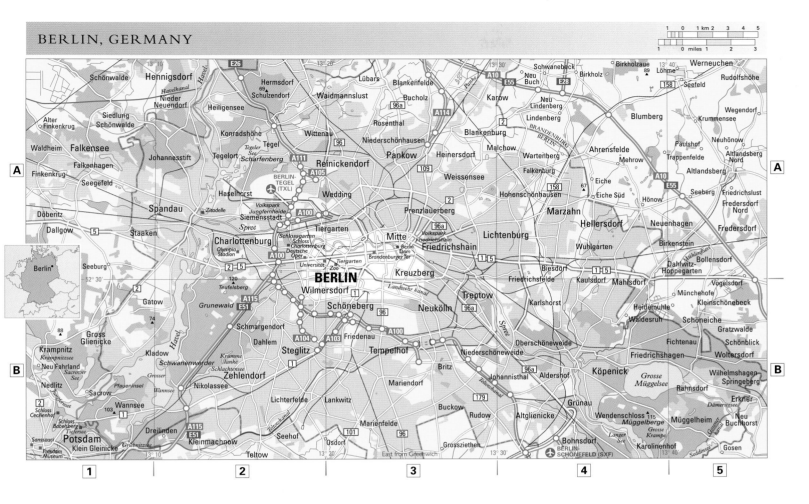

CENTRAL BERLIN

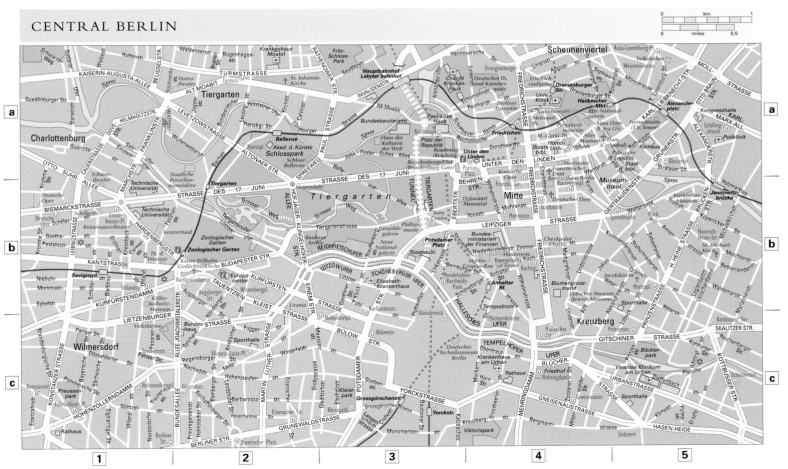

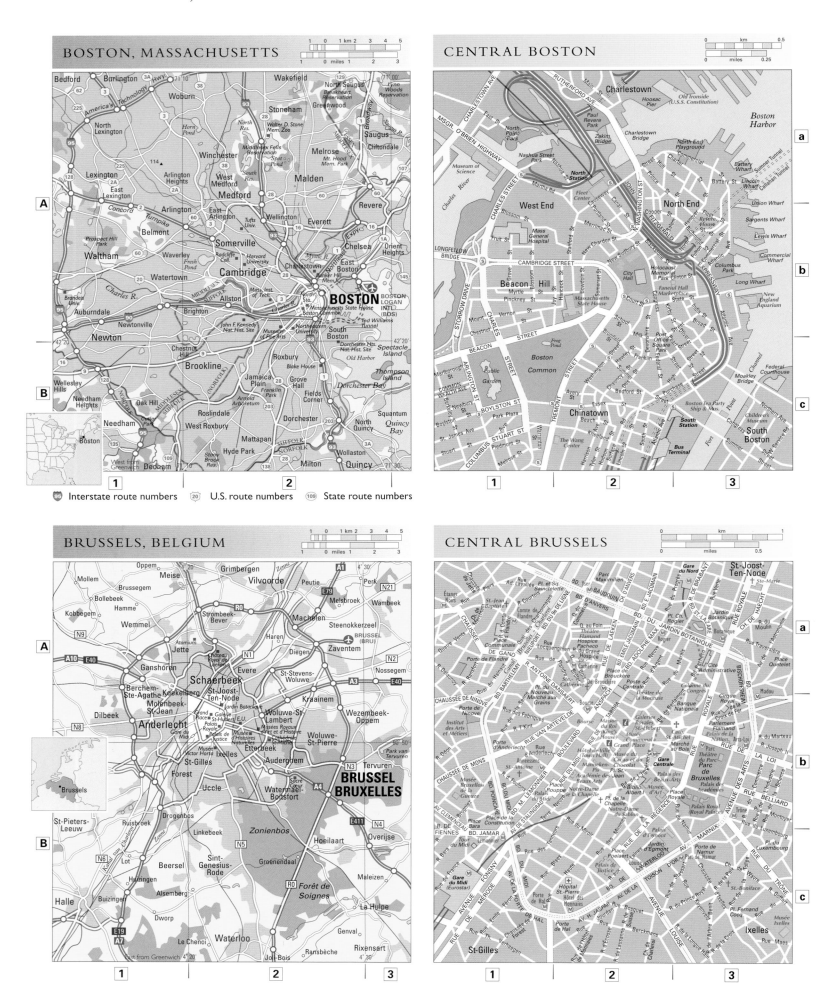

BOSTON, MASSACHUSETTS

1 0 1 km 2 3 4 5
1 0 miles 1 2 3

Bedford · Burlington · 3A HWY · 71'10' · Wakefield · 129 · North Saugus Breakheart Reservation · Lynn Woods Reservation · 71'00'

62 · America's Technology · 3 · Woburn · Stoneham · Greenwood · Broadway · 93

225 · North Lexington · Horn Pond · North Res. · Walter D. Stone Mem. Zoo · Saugus R.

95 · Lexington · 225 · Winchester · Middlesex Fells Reservation · Spot Pond · Mt. Hood Mem. Park · Melrose · 107

128 · East Lexington · 2A · Arlington Heights · 38 · West Medford · Medford · 28 · 60 · Revere · EXPWY · 16 · 1A

A · Concord · 2 · 60 · East Arlington · Tufts Univ. · Wellington · 93 · 16 · Orient Heights

Prospect Hill Park · Belmont · Somerville · Radcliffe Coll. · Harvard University · Mystic R. · Charlestown · East Boston · BOSTON LOGAN INTL (BOS)

Waltham · Charles R. · Watertown · Mass. Inst. of Tech. · Bunker Hill Mem. · North Sta. · **BOSTON** · Massachusetts State House · Boston Common · Ted Williams Tunnel

95 · 90 · Auburndale · Newtonville · Brighton · Allston · Charles R. · John F. Kennedy Nat. Hist. Site · Northeastern University · South Boston · 42'20'

16 · Newton · Chestnut Hill · Museum of Fine Arts · Dorchester Hts. Nat. Hist. Site · Spectacle Island

9 · Wellesley Hills · 128 · Brookline · Blake House · Roxbury · Jamaica Plain · Grove Hall · Fields Corner · Dorchester Bay · Old Harbor · Thompson Island

B · Needham Heights · Oak Hill · NORFOLK · Roslindale · Franklin Park · Arnold Arboretum · 203 · Dorchester · Squantum · Quincy Bay

Needham · 135 · 95 · West Roxbury · Mattapan · SUFFOLK · NORFOLK · 203 · North Quincy · Wollaston

109 · West from Greenwich · Dedham · 10 · Hyde Park · Stony Brook Res. · 138 · 28 · Milton · 3A · Quincy · 71'00'

Boston

1 · **2**

95 Interstate route numbers   20 U.S. route numbers   109 State route numbers

CENTRAL BOSTON

0 km 0.5
0 miles 0.25

Charlestown · Old Ironside (U.S.S. Constitution) · Hoosac Pier · Boston Harbor

MSGR. O'BRIEN HIGHWAY · RUTHERFORD AVE · Paul Revere Park · Zakim Bridge · Charlestown Bridge · North End Playground · **a**

Museum of Science · Nashua Street Park · **North Station** · Fleet Center · North End · Battery Wharf · Union Wharf · Sargents Wharf · Lewis Wharf

Charles River · CHARLES STREET · West End · Mass General Hospital · WASHINGTON ST · Commercial Wharf · **b**

LONGFELLOW BRIDGE · CAMBRIDGE STREET · City Hall · Faneuil Hall Marketplace · Holocaust Memorial Park · Columbus Park · Long Wharf · New England Aquarium

STORROW DRIVE · Beacon Hill · Massachusetts State House · CHARLES STREET · Boston Common · Public Garden · TREMONT STREET · Post Office Square Park · Federal Courthouse · Moakley Bridge

COMMONWEALTH AVE · ARLINGTON ST · BOYLSTON ST · Park Plaza · Chinatown · STUART ST · The Wang Center · Boston Tea Party Ship & Mus. · **South Station** · Children's Museum · South Boston · **c**

COLUMBUS AVE · Bus Terminal

1 · **2** · **3**

BRUSSELS, BELGIUM

1 0 1 km 2 3 4 5
1 0 miles 1 2 3

Oppem · A1 · 4'30' · Perk · N21

Mollem · Meise · Grimbergen · Vilvoorde · Peutie · E79 · Melsbroek · Wambeek

Brussegem · Strombeek-Bever · R0 · Machelen · Steenokkerzeel

Bollebeek · Hamme · Wemmel · Haren · Diegem · **BRUSSEL (BRU)** · N2

Kobbegem · N9 · Atomium · Jette · Zaventem · Nossegem · E40

A · A10 · E40 · Ganshoren · Evere · St-Stevens-Woluwe · A3 · E40

Berchem-Ste-Agathe · Koekelberg · Schaerbeek · St-Joost-Ten-Node · Kraainem · Wezembeek-Oppem

Molenbeek-St-Jean · Grand Place · Jardin Botanique · E.U. · Woluwe-St-Lambert · Woluwe-St-Pierre

Dilbeek · N8 · Anderlecht · Palais Royale · Musée d'Histoires Naturelles · Cathédrale St-Michel · Park van Tervuren

Musée Victor Horta · Ixelles · Etterbeek · Auderghem · 60'50'

St-Gilles · N3 · Tervuren

St-Pieters-Leeuw · Forest · Uccle · Sacré Coeur · Watermael-Boitsfort · A4 · N4 · Overijse

B · Ruisbroek · Drogenbos · Zenne · Linkebeek · **BRUSSEL BRUXELLES** · E411

N6 · Lot · Zonienbos · Hoeilaart

Halle · Buizingen · Huizingen · Beersel · N5 · Sint-Genesius-Rode · Groenendaal · Maleizen

Alsemberg · R0 · Forêt de Soignes · La Hulpe

E19 · A7 · Dworp · Waterloo · Genval · Rixensart

East from Greenwich 4'20' · Le Chenoi · Ransbèche · 4'30' · Joli-Bois

1 · **2** · **3**

CENTRAL BRUSSELS

0 km 1
0 miles 0.5

Gare du Nord · St-Joost-Ten-Node · Ste-Marie

Parc Maximilien · BD BAUDOUIN · CH D'ANVERS · RUE ROYALE · CH DE HAECHT

Étangs Noirs · BD D'ANVERS · Jardin Botanique · Botanique · RUE DU MOULIN · **a**

CHAUSSÉE DE GAND · Place Communale · NIEUPORT · Poste Centrale · Cité Administrative · Madou · Place Quetelet

Porte de Flandre · Rue Antoine Dansaert · Théâtre de la Monnaie · Banque Nationale · Colonne du Congrès · Cirque Royal

CHAUSSÉE DE NINOVE · Bourse · Galeries Royales St-Hubert · Parlement Flamand · Palais de la Nation · RUE DE LA LOI

Institut des Arts et Métiers · Maison du Roi · Grand Place · Hôtel de Ville Town Hall · Théâtre du Parc · Parc de Bruxelles · **b**

Porte d'Anderlecht · Manneken Pis · Gare Centrale · Palais des Académies · AVENUE DES ARTS

CHAUSSÉE DE MONS · Musée Bruxellois de la Gueuze · BD LEMONNIER · Notre-Dame du Sablon · Place Royale · RUE BELLIARD

Palais de Justice · Palais d'Egmont · Porte de Namur · RUE DU TRÔNE

Gare du Midi (Eurostar) · Tour du Midi · Hôpital St-Pierre · AVENUE LOUISE · Ixelles · **c**

Porte de Hal · St-Gilles · Musée Ixelles

1 · **2** · **3**

COPYRIGHT PHILIP'S

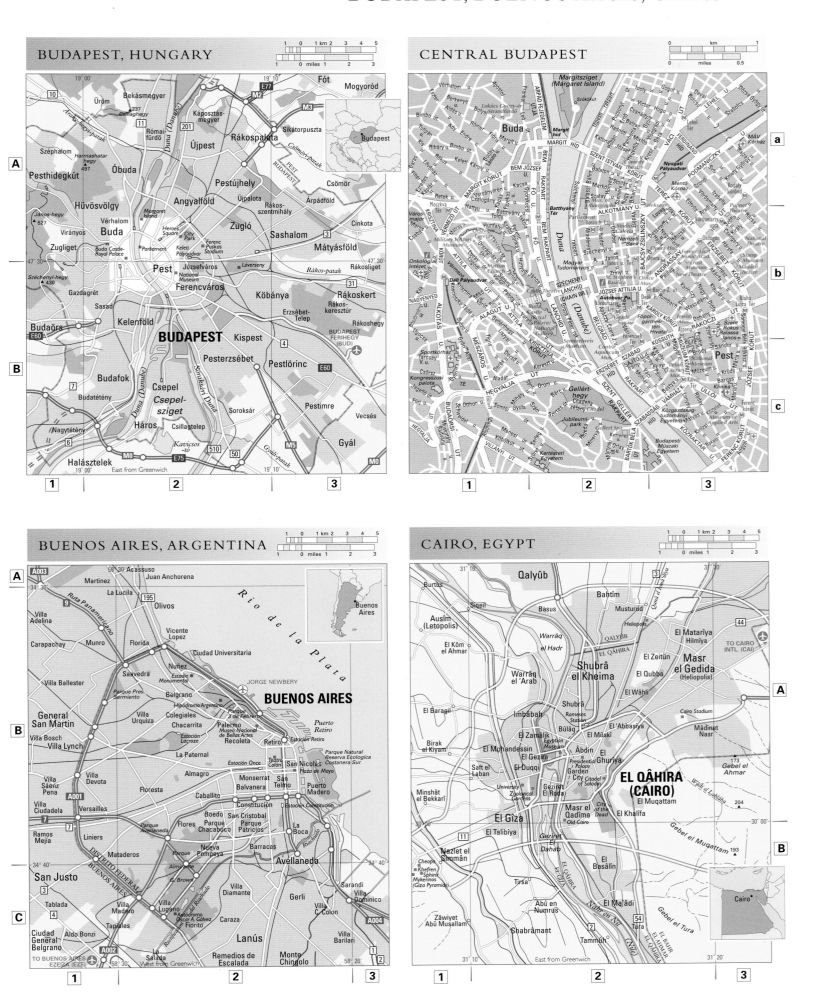

BUDAPEST, HUNGARY

CENTRAL BUDAPEST

BUENOS AIRES, ARGENTINA

CAIRO, EGYPT

COPYRIGHT PHILIP'S

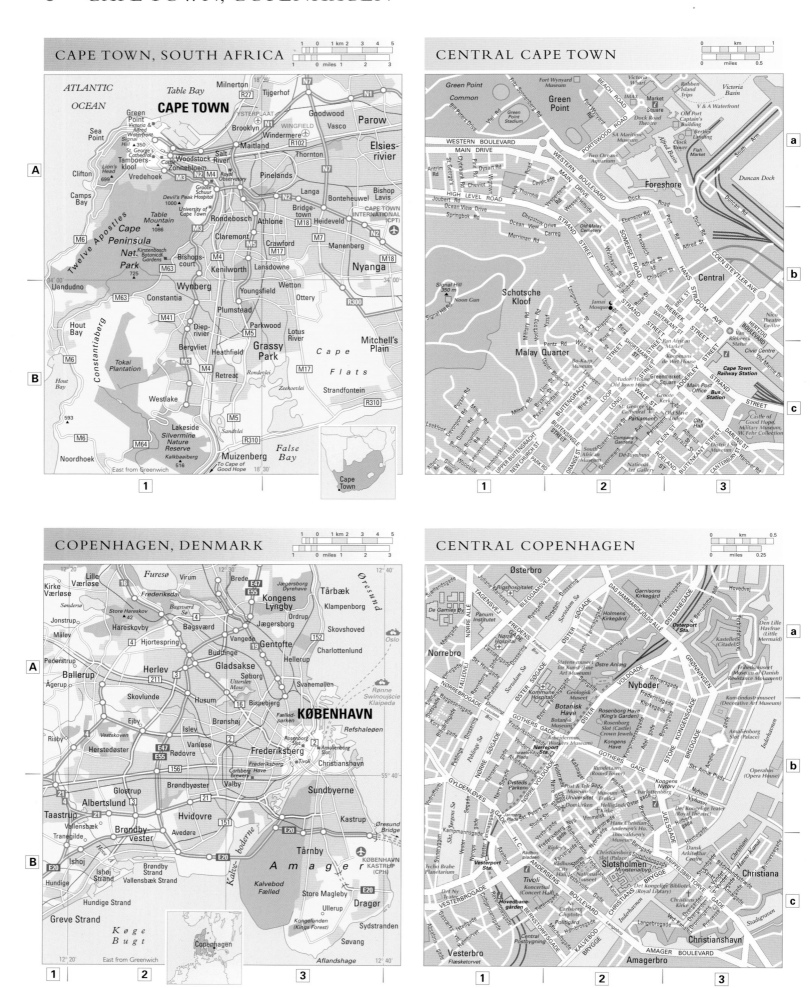

CAPE TOWN, SOUTH AFRICA

CENTRAL CAPE TOWN

COPENHAGEN, DENMARK

CENTRAL COPENHAGEN

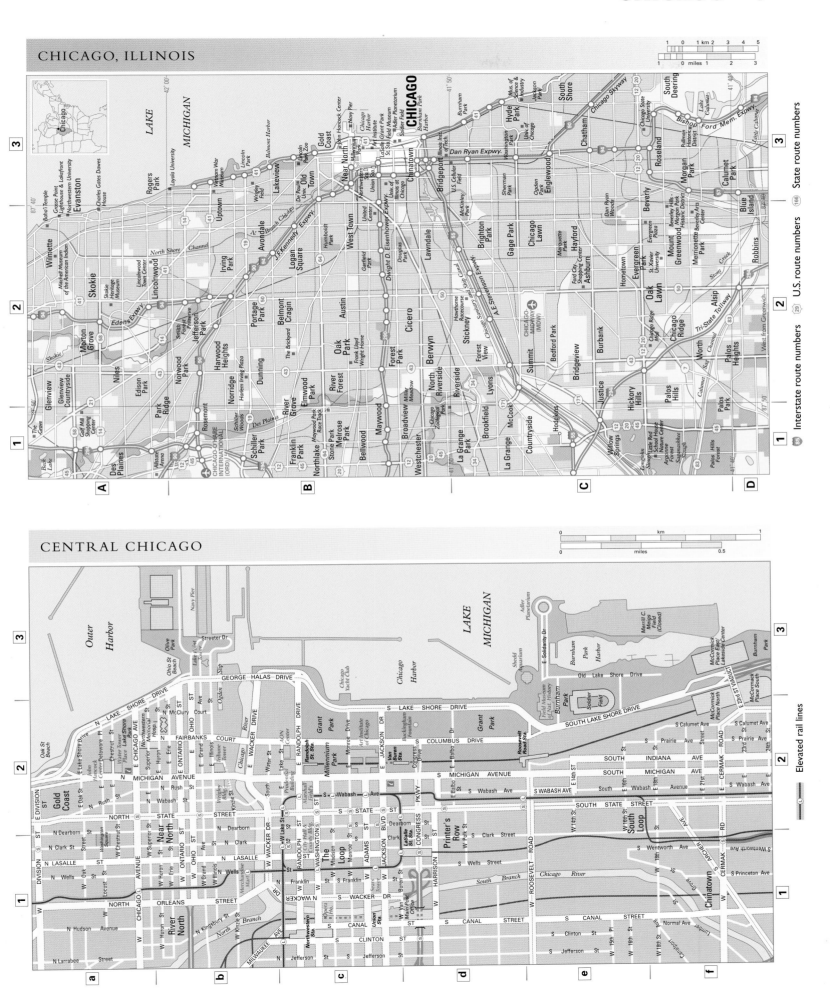

CHICAGO, ILLINOIS

CENTRAL CHICAGO

State route numbers

U.S. route numbers

Interstate route numbers

Elevated rail lines

COPYRIGHT PHILIP'S

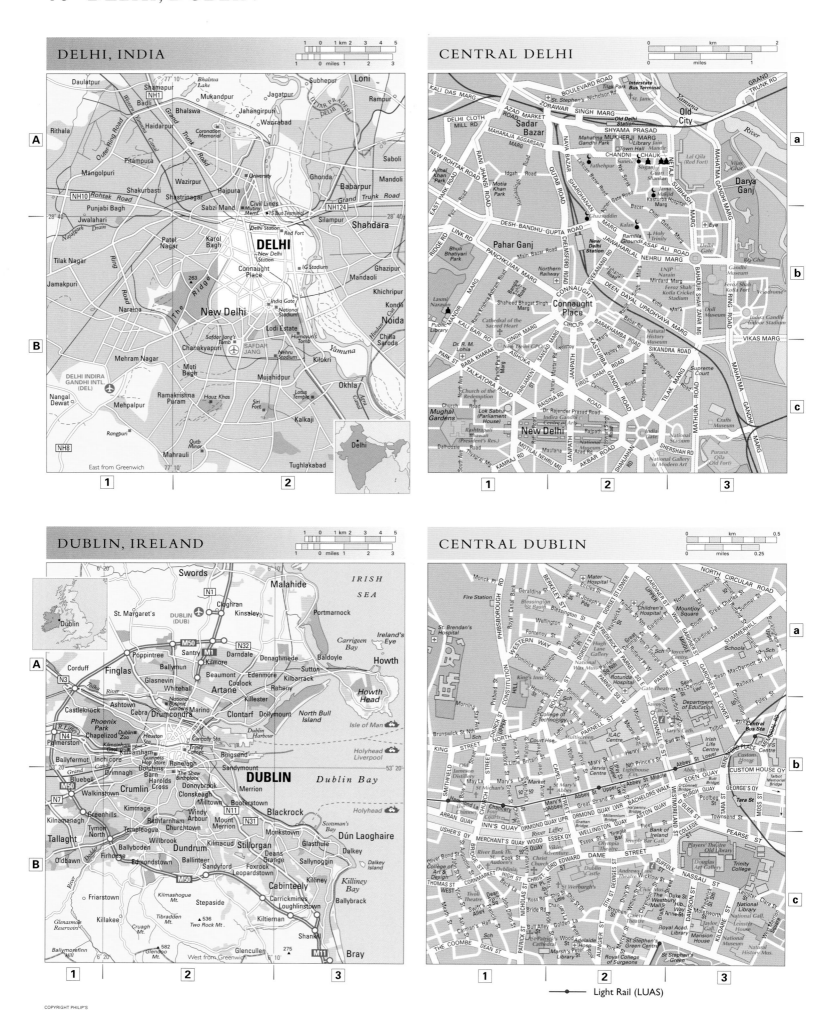

DELHI, INDIA

CENTRAL DELHI

DUBLIN, IRELAND

CENTRAL DUBLIN

Light Rail (LUAS)

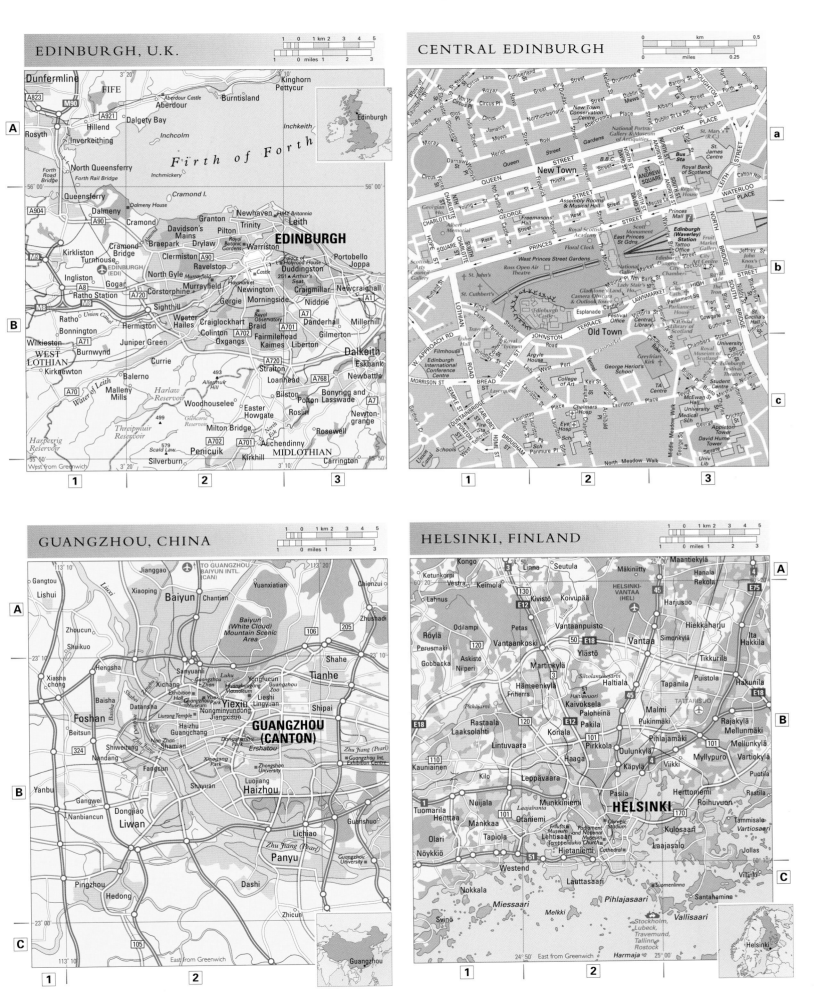

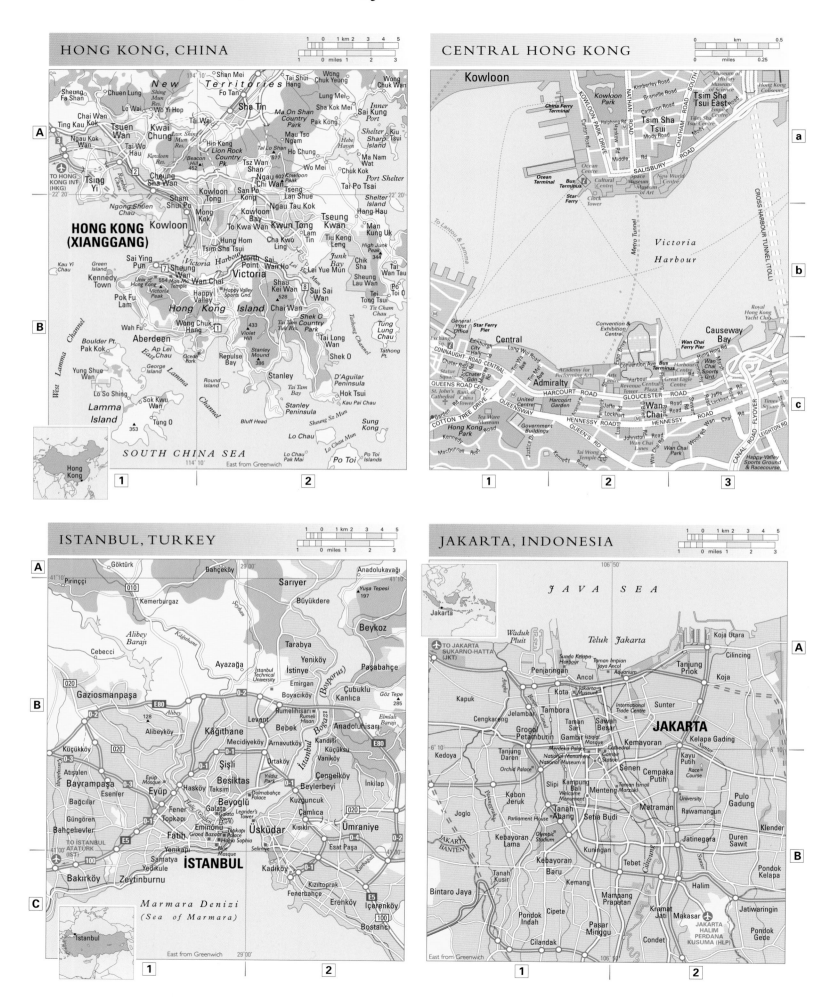

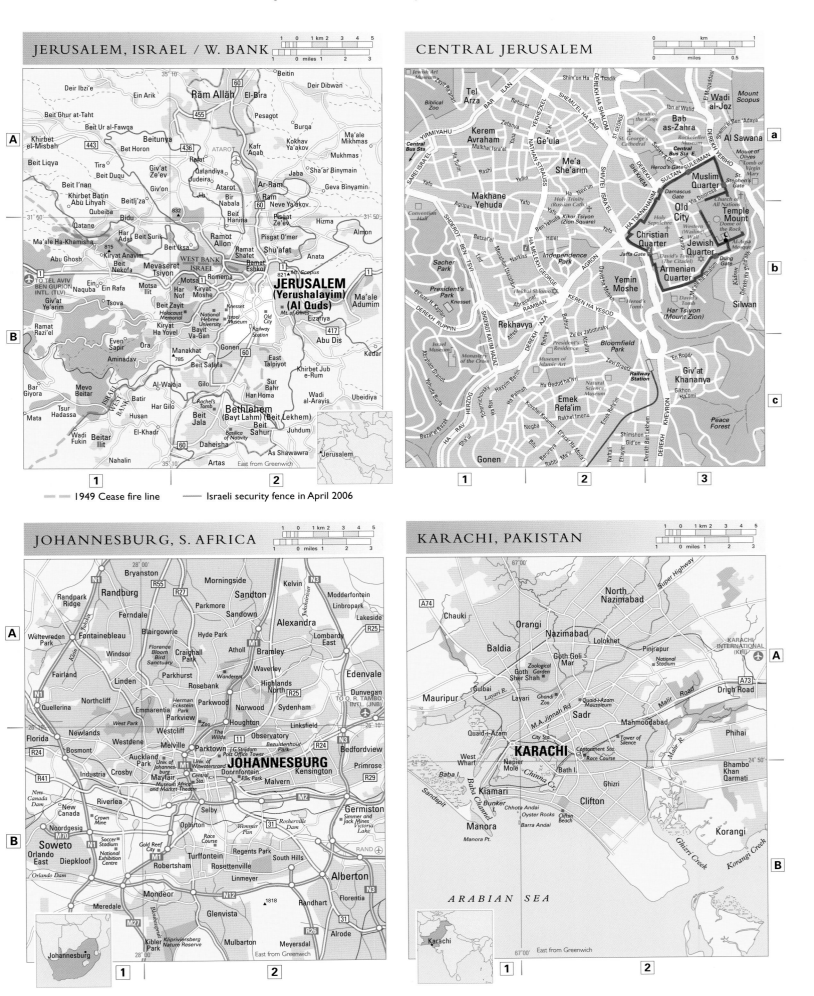

JERUSALEM, ISRAEL / W. BANK

Deir Ibzi'e
Beitin
Ein Arik
Râm Allāh
El-Bira
Deir Dibwan
Beit Ghur at-Taht
Pesagot
Burqa
Beit Ur al-Fawqa
Ma'ale
Mikhmas
Beitunya
Khirbet
el-Misbah
Kokhav
Ya'akov
Kafr
'Aqab
Bet Horon
Khirbet el-Misbah
Beit Liqya
Qalandiya
Mukhmas
Tira
Beit Duqu
Giv'at
Ze'ev
Judeira
Jaba
Sha'ar Binymain
Geva Binyamin
Beit I'nan
Giv'on
Atarot
Ar-Ram
Khirbet Batin
Abū Lihyah
Beitlj'za
Jib
Bir
Nabala
Neve Ya'akov
Qubeiba
Bidu
Beit
Hanina
Hizma
Almon
Qatane
Har Adaf
Beit Surik
Pisgat O'mer
Mt Scopus
Ma'ale Ha-Khamisha
Kiryat Anavim
Beit Iksa
Ramot Allon
Ramat Shafet
Anata
Abu Ghosh
Beit Nekofa
Mevaseret Tsiyon
Ramat Eshkol
Giv'at Ye'arim
Motsa
Romema
JERUSALEM (Yerushalayim) (Al Quds)
Tsova
Motsa Ilit
Har Nof
Kiryat Moshe
Ma'ale Adumim
Even Sapir
Ein Naquba
Ein Rafa
Kiryat Ha Yovel
Bayit Va-Gan
Old City
Eizariya
Ora
Aminadav
Manakhat
Gonen
East Talpiyot
Abu Dis
Ramat Razi'el
Beit Zayit
Beit Safafa
Kedar
Bar Giyora
Mevo Beitar
Al-Walaja
Gilo
Sur Bahr
Khirbet Jub e-Rum
Tsur Hadassa
Har Gilo
Batir
Rachel's Tomb
Har Homa
Ubeidiya
Mata
Husan
Beit Jala
Bethlehem (Bayt Lahm) (Beit Lekhem)
Beit Sahur
Wadi al-Arayis
Wadi Fukin
Beitar Ilit
El-Khadr
Daheisha
Juhdum
Nahalin
Artas
As Shawawra

--- 1949 Cease fire line   —— Israeli security fence in April 2006

CENTRAL JERUSALEM

Jewish Art Museum
Shim'on Ha Tsadik
Mount Scopus
Tel Arza
Biblical Zoo
Bar Ilan
Rehovot
Wadi al-Joz
Kerem Avraham
Ge'ula
Tomb of the Kings
Bab as-Zahra
Al Sawana
Central Bus Sta E
Yirmiyahu
St George Cathedral
Rockefeller Museum
Central Bus Sta. E.
Mount of Olives
Me'a She'arim
Herod's Gate
St Stephen's Gate
Makhane Yehuda
Muslim Quarter
Old City
Temple Mount
Dome of the Rock
Sacher Park
Holy Sepulchre
Christian Quarter
Jewish Quarter
Al-Aqsa Mosque
Independence Park
Jaffa Gate
Armenian Quarter
Dung Gate
Silwan
President's Park
Yemin Moshe
David's Tower (The Citadel)
Rekhavya
Herod's Tomb
Har Tsiyon (Mount Zion)
Israel Museum
Monastery of the Cross
Museum of Islamic Art
President's Residence
Bloomfield Park
Giv'at Khananya
Peace Forest
Emek Refa'im
Natural Science Museum
Railway Station
Gonen

JOHANNESBURG, S. AFRICA

Bryanston
Morningside
Kelvin
Randpark Ridge
Randburg
Sandton
Modderfontein
Linbropark
Parkmore
Sandown
Lakeside
Ferndale
Blairgowrie
Hyde Park
Alexandra
Fontainebleau
Weltevreden Park
Craighall Park
Atholl
Bramley
Lombardy East
Windsor
Florence Bloom Bird Sanctuary
Waverley
Fairland
Linden
Parkhurst
Rosebank
Highlands North
Edenvale
Northcliff
Emmarentia
Parkwood
Norwood
Sydenham
Dunvegan
Quellerina
Herman Eckstein Park
Parkview
Zoo
Houghton
Linksfield
Newlands
West Park
Westcliff
Observatory
Bedfordview
Florida
Bosmont
Westdene
Melville
Parktown
Bezuidenhout Park
Primrose
Industria
Crosby
Univ. of Witwatersrand
JOHANNESBURG
Kensington
New Canada Dam
Mayfair
Doornfontein
Malvern
Germiston
New Canada
Riverlea
Selby
Ellis Park
Noordgesig
Crown Mine
Ophirton
Simmer and Jack Mines Victoria Lake
Soweto
Soccer Stadium
Gold Reef City
Wemmer Pan
Orlando East
Diepkloof
Turffontein
Regents Park
South Hills
Alberton
Mondeor
Robertsham
Rosettenville
Linmeyer
Meredale
Glenvista
Randhart
Florentia
Kibler Park
Klipriviersberg Nature Reserve
Mulbarton
Meyersdal
Alrode

KARACHI, PAKISTAN

North Nazimabad
Super Highway
Chauki
Orangi
Nazimabad
Lolokhet
Karachi International (KHI)
Baldia
Goth Goli Mar
Pinjrapur
Mauripur
Zoological Garden Sher Shah
Gulbai
National Stadium
Ghandi Zoo
Quaid-i-Azam Mausoleum
Drigh Road
Layari
M.A. Jinnah Rd
Malir Road
West Wharf
Sadr
Mahmoodabad
Phihai
Quaid-i-Azam
City Sta.
KARACHI
Cantonment Sta. Race Course
Bhambo Khan Qarmati
Napier Mole
Tower of Silence
Baba I.
China Cr.
Bath I.
Ghizri
West Wharf
Kiamari
Clifton
Sandspit
Bunker
Chhota Andai
Oyster Rocks
Clifton Beach
Korangi
Manora
Barra Andai
Manora Pt.
Ghizri Creek
Korangi Creek

ARABIAN SEA

Karachi

COPYRIGHT PHILIP'S

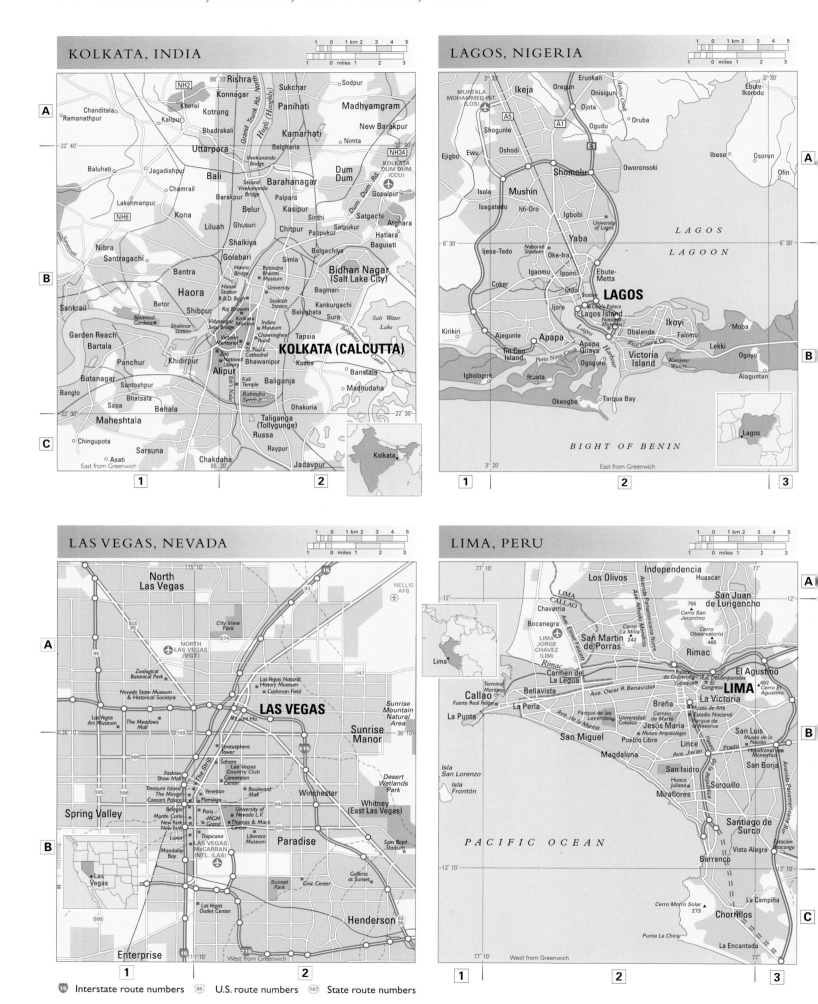

KOLKATA, INDIA

LAGOS, NIGERIA

LAS VEGAS, NEVADA

LIMA, PERU

🛡15 Interstate route numbers   ⬭95 U.S. route numbers   ⬭147 State route numbers

COPYRIGHT PHILIP'S

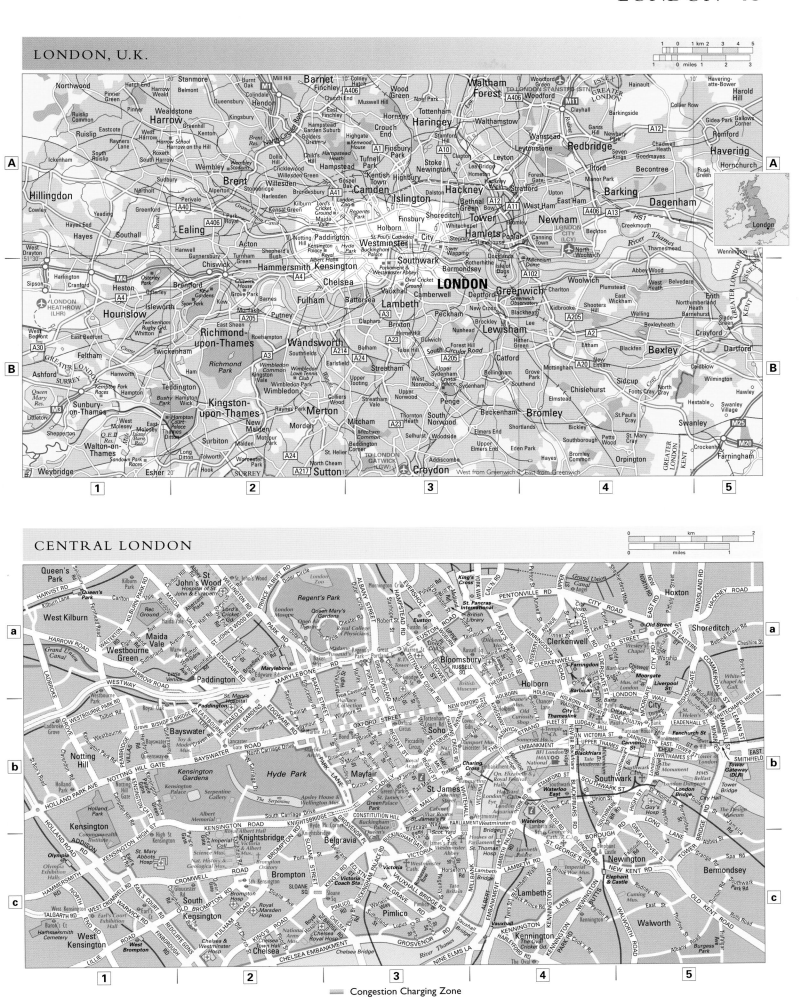

LONDON, U.K.

Congestion Charging Zone

CENTRAL LONDON

COPYRIGHT PHILIP'S

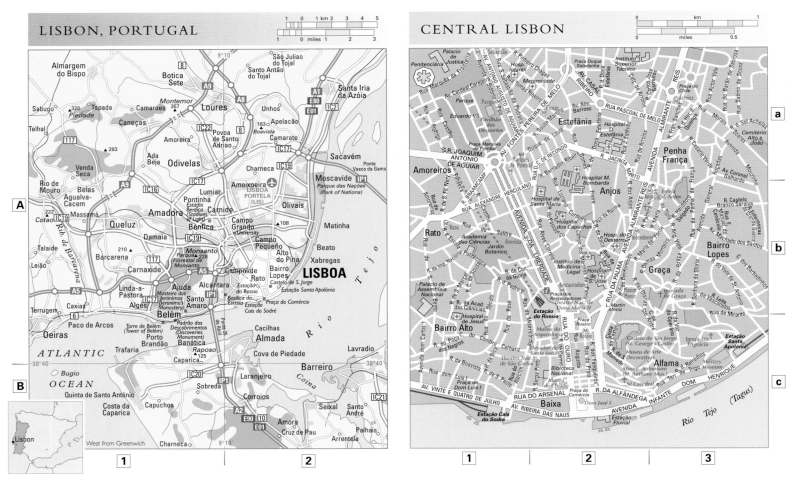

LISBON, PORTUGAL

CENTRAL LISBON

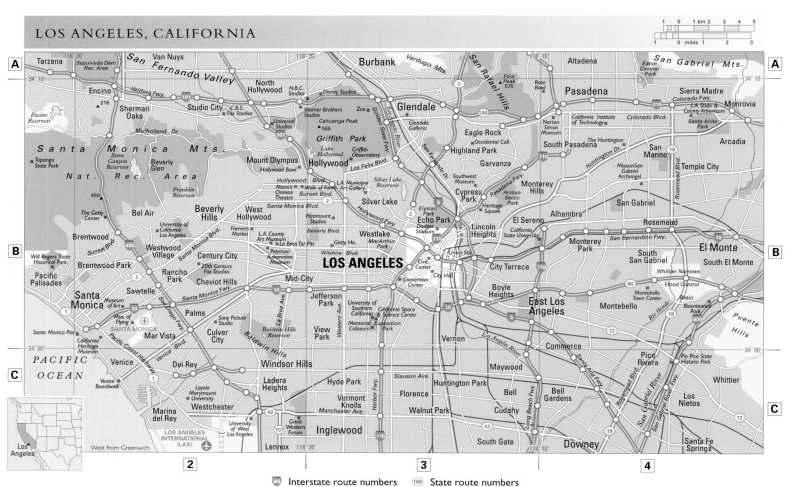

LOS ANGELES, CALIFORNIA

85 Interstate route numbers   166 State route numbers

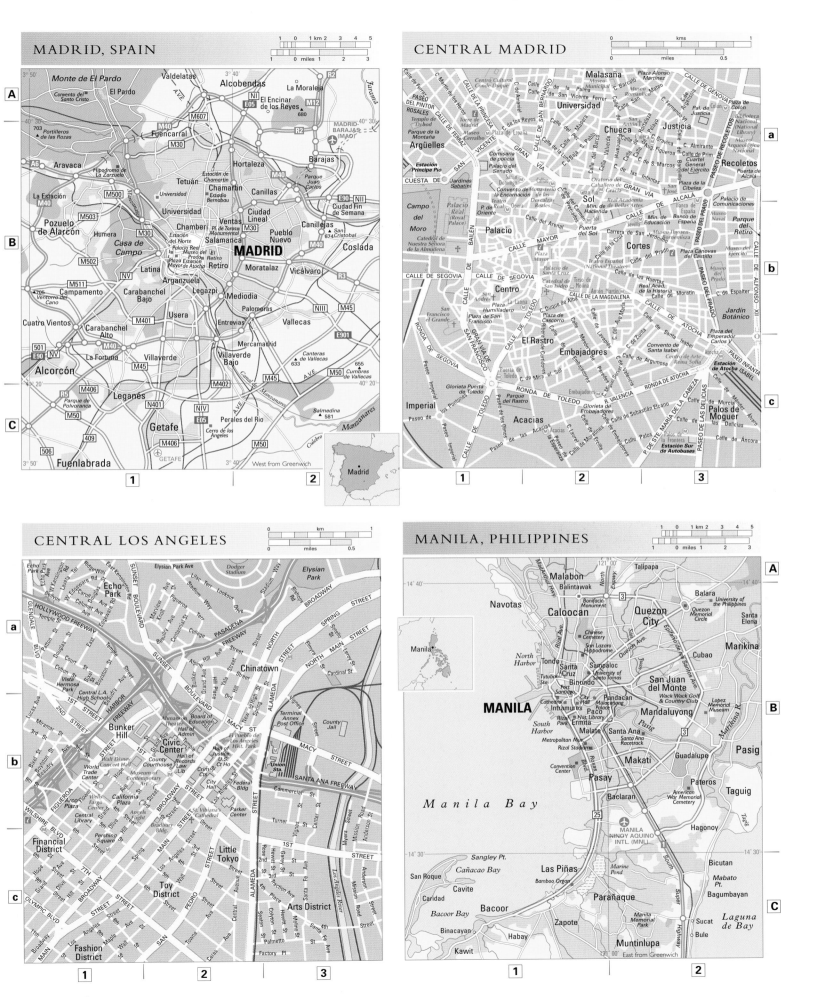

MADRID, SPAIN

1 0 1 km 2 3 4 5
1 0 miles 1 2 3

Monte de El Pardo
3° 50'
3° 40'
Valdelatas
Alcobendas
La Moraleja
Jarama
R2
A
Convento del Santo Cristo
El Pardo
N1
El Encinar de los Reyes
M12
M607
AVE.
E05
680
M40
MADRID 40° 30'
BARAJAS (MAD)
40° 30'
703
Portilleros de las Rozas
Fuencarral
M30
R2
A6
Aravaca
Hortaleza
M40
E90
NII
La Estación
Estación de Chamartín
Canillas
Ciudad Fin de Semana
Tetuán
Chamartín
Parque Juan Carlos
M500
Estadio Bernabéu
Universidad
Ciudad Lineal
E90
N II
Pozuelo de Alarcón
Humera
M30
Chamberí
Ventas
Canillejas
San Cristóbal
674
B
M503
Casa de Campo
Estación del Norte
Pl. de Toros Monumental
M30
Pueblo Nuevo
Coslada
M502
Palacio Real Museo del Prado
Salamanca
M40
Latina
NV
El Retiro
Plaza Estación Mayor de Atocha
MADRID
Moratalaz
Vicálvaro
R3
705
Campamento
Carabanchel Bajo
Legazpi
Mediodía
M401
Usera
Palomeras
N III
M45
Cuatro Vientos
Entrevías
Vallecas
E901
Carabanchel Alto
501
M40
Mercamadrid
Canteras de Vallecas
633
50
Alcorcón
La Fortuna
Villaverde
M45
Villaverde Bajo
655
Cumbres de Vallecas
E90 NV
40° 20'
R5
M406
M45
M50
A.V.E.
40° 20'
C
Parque de Polvoranca
Leganés
M402
Glorieta de Embajadores
Salmedina
581
M50
N401
NIV
Manzanares
Getafe
E05
Perales del Río
GETAFE
Cerro de los Ángeles
506
409
M406
M50
Fuenlabrada
3° 50'
3° 40'
West from Greenwich

1 **2**

Madrid

CENTRAL MADRID

0 kms 1
0 miles 0.5

Malasaña
Plaza Alonso Martínez
CALLE DE GENOVA
Centro Cultural Conde Duque
Universidad
CALLE DE LA PALMA
Justicia
Pza. de Colón
PASEO DEL PINTOR ROSALES
Chueca
Biblioteca Nacional (National Library)
Museo Arqueológico Nacional
Torre de Madrid
Plaza de España
GRAN VIA
Recoletos
Argüelles
Estación Príncipe Pío
CUESTA DE
Jardines Sabatini
Sol
PASEO DE RECOLETOS
Puerta de Alcalá
Campo del Moro
Palacio Real (Royal Palace)
Opera
Min. de Bellas Artes
CALLE
Plaza de la Cibeles
Palacio de Comunicaciones
Palacio
Catedral de Nuestra Sra. de la Almudena
BAILEN
Puerta del Sol
Carrera de San Jerónimo
Banco de España
Museo Naval
Plaza Mayor
Cortes
Museo Thyssen-Bornemisza
Parque del Retiro
CALLE MAYOR
Teatro Español (National Theatre)
Museo del Ejército
CALLE DE SEGOVIA
CALLE DE SEGOVIA
Catedral de San Isidro
CALLE DE LAS HUERTAS
Plaza Cánovas del Castillo
PASEO DEL PRADO
CALLE DE ALFONSO XII
Centro
RONDA DE SEGOVIA
GRAN VIA DE SAN FRANCISCO
CALLE DE LA MAGDALENA
Real Acad. de la Historia
Jardín Botánico
San Francisco el Grande
CALLE DE TOLEDO
Antón Martín
Centro de Arte Reina Sofía
El Rastro
CALLE DE ATOCHA
Estación de Atocha
Embajadores
CALLE DE VALENCIA
RONDA DE ATOCHA
Estación Infanta Isabel
Imperial
Glorieta Puerta de Toledo
Puerta de Toledo
RONDA DE TOLEDO
Glorieta de Embajadores
PASEO INFANTA ISABEL
Acacias
Paseo del Rastro
Palos de Moguer
Estación Sur de Autobuses
PASEO DE LAS DELICIAS

1 **2** **3**

CENTRAL LOS ANGELES

0 km 1
0 miles 0.5

Echo Park
Elysian Park Ave
Dodger Stadium
Elysian Park
Echo Park
SUNSET BOULEVARD
HOLLYWOOD FREEWAY
Chinatown
PASADENA FREEWAY
GLENDALE BLVD
Central L.A. High School
NORTH MAIN STREET
Bunker Hill
Board of Education
Terminal Annex Post Office
County Jail
Civic Center
Hall of Admin
Union Sta.
Walt Disney Concert Hall
County Courthouse
Hall of Records
El Pueblo de Los Angeles Hist. Park
SANTA ANA FREEWAY
MACY ST
World Trade Center
Museum of Contemporary Art
U.S. Ct Ho
Federal Bldg
WILSHIRE BLVD
FIGUEROA
Arco Plaza
Wells Fargo Center
California Plaza
Angels Flight
Bradbury Bldg.
St. Vibiana's Cathedral
Financial District
Central Library
Pershing Square
Little Tokyo
ALAMEDA STREET
BROADWAY
MAIN STREET
Toy District
Arts District
OLYMPIC BLVD
SAN PEDRO ST
Fashion District
Los Angeles River

1 **2** **3**

MANILA, PHILIPPINES

1 0 1 km 2 3 4 5
1 0 miles 1 2 3

121° 00'
Talipapa
Malabon
Balintawak
14° 40'
14° 40'
Balara
A
Navotas
Bonifacio Monument
University of the Philippines
Caloocan
Quezon City
Santa Elena
Chinese Cemetery
Quezon Memorial Circle
Cubao
Marikina
North Harbor
San Lazaro Hippodrome
Sampaloc
Tondo
Santa Cruz
University of Santo Tomas
San Juan del Monte
Manila
Binondo
Wack Wack Golf & Country Club
B
MANILA
Cathedral
Intramuros
Pandacan
Malacañang Palace
City Hall
Santiago
Lopez Memorial Museum
Rizal Park
Nat. Library
Mandaluyong
Pasig
South Harbor
Ermita
Paco
Malate
Santa Ana
Santa Ana Racetrack
Metropolitan Mus.
Rizal Stadium
Guadalupe
Pasig
Convention Center
Makati
Pasay
Pateros
Taguig
Manila Bay
Baclaran
American War Memorial Cemetery
Hagonoy
MANILA NINOY AQUINO INTL. (MNL)
25
14° 30'
14° 30'
Sangley Pt.
Las Piñas
Marine Pond
Bicutan
San Roque
Cañacao Bay
Bamboo Organ
Mabato Pt.
Cavite
Caridad
Parañaque
Bagumbayan
C
Bacoor Bay
Manila Memorial Park
Sucat
Bacoor
Zapote
Laguna de Bay
Binacayan
Habay
Muntinlupa
Bule
Kawit
121° 00'
East from Greenwich

1 **2**

Manila

COPYRIGHT PHILIP'S

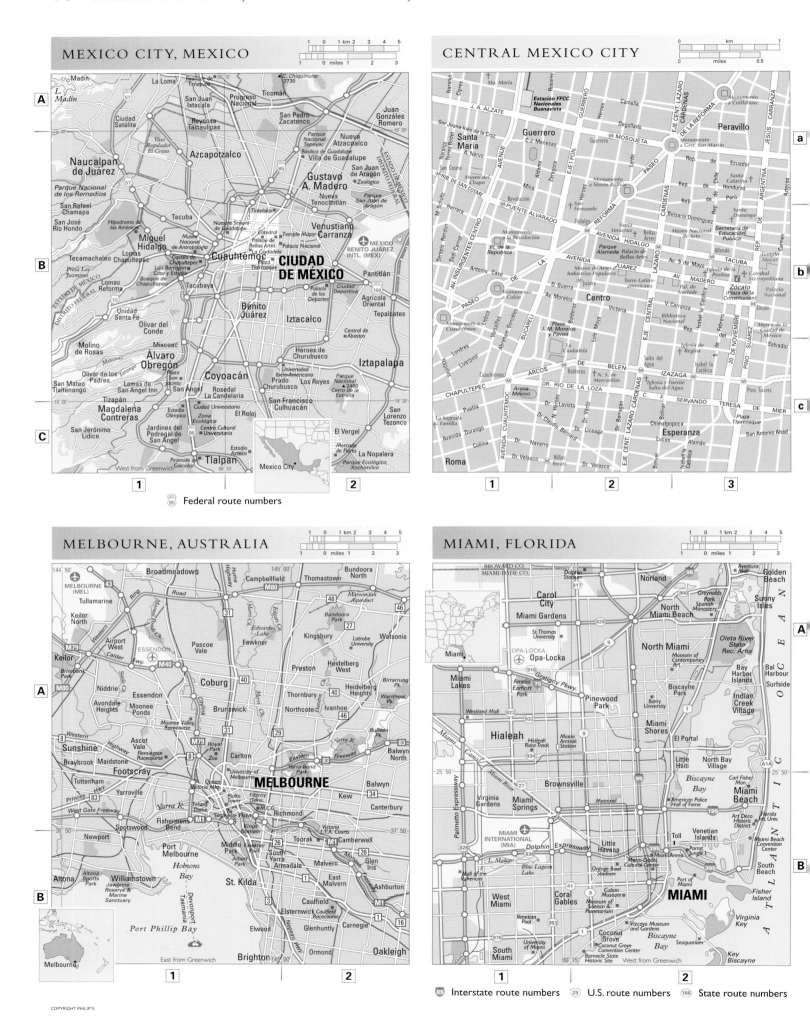

MEXICO CITY, MEXICO

Federal route numbers

CENTRAL MEXICO CITY

MELBOURNE, AUSTRALIA

MIAMI, FLORIDA

Interstate route numbers   U.S. route numbers   State route numbers

COPYRIGHT PHILIP'S

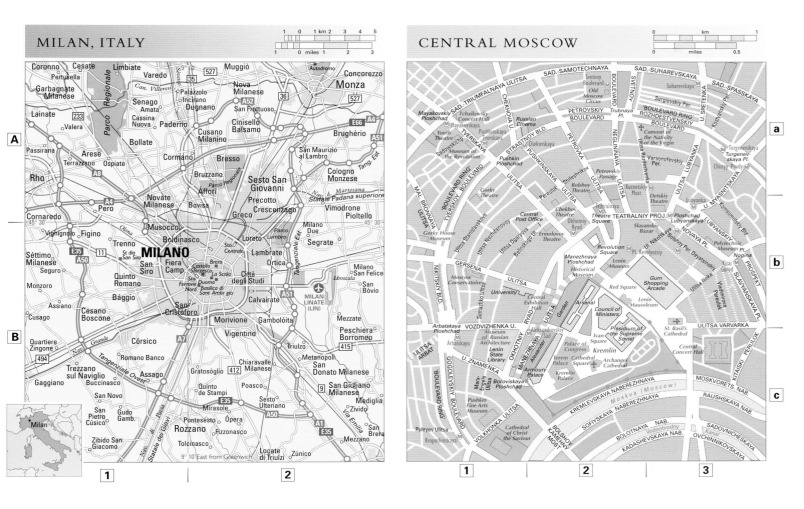

MILAN, ITALY

Coronno Cesate Limbiate Varedo Muggiò Concorezzo Autodromo
Pertusella Garbagnate Milanese Senago Palazzolo Nova Milanese Monza
Lainate Amata Incirano Dugnano San Fruttuoso Brughério
Valera Cassina Nuova Paderno Cinisello Balsamo
Passirana Arese Ospiate Cormano San Maurizio al Lambro
Rho Terrazzano Bollate Bresso Cologno Monzese
Novate Milanese Bruzzano Sesto San Giovanni Vimodrone Pioltello
Cornaredo Pero Affori Precotto Crescenzago
Musocco Bovisa Greco Segrate
Vighignolo Figino Trenno Boldinasco Loreto Milano Due
MILANO Sta Centrale Lambrate
Séttimo Milanese San Siro Fiera Camp. Brera Ortica Milano San Felice
Seguro Quinto Romano Ferrovie Nord Duomo Città degli Studi San Bóvio
Monzoro La Scala Idroscalo MILAN LINATE (LIN)
Bággio San Cristóforo Basilica di Sant'Ambrogio Calvairate
Assiano Cesano Boscone Morivione Gambolóita Mezzate
Cusago Córsico Vigentino Peschiera Borromeo
Quartiere Zingone Romano Banco Chiaravalle Milanese Triulzo
Trezzano sul Naviglio Assago Gratosóglio San Donato Milanese Metanopoli
Gaggiano Buccinasco Quinto de' Stampi Poasco San Giuliano Milanese
San Novo Mirasole Sesto Ulteriano Medíglia
San Pietro Cúsico Gudo Gamb. Ópera Zivido
Rozzano Pontesésto Fizzonasco Mezzano
Zibido San Giacomo Tolcinasco Locate di Triulzi Zúnico

9° 10' East from Greenwich

CENTRAL MOSCOW

SAD.-SAMOTECHNAYA SAD.-SUHAREVSKAYA SAD.-SPASSKAYA
SAD.-TRIUMFALNAYA ULITSA CHEKHOVA U. Svetnoy Boulevard Suharevskaya U. SRETENKA
Mayakovskovo Ploshchad Tchaikovsky Concert Hall Old Moscow Circus Sergievsky Per. Turgenevskaya
Mayakovskaya Pushkinskaya PETROVSKIY BOULEVARD RING Turgenevskaya Pl.
Youth Theatre Russian Cinema Trubnaya Pl. ROZHDESTVENSKIY Chistyy Prudy
Museum of the Revolution STRASTNOY BLVD. Convent of the Nativity of the Virgin
Sadovskovo Pushkin Ploshchad Varsonofyevsky Per. U. MYASNITSKAYA
Gorky Theatre Petrovsky Passage Detskiy Theatre LUBYANKA
Pushkinskaya Bolshoy Theatre Kuznetsky Most NOVAYA PL.
MAL. BRONNAYA Chekhov Theatre Teatralnaya TEATRALNIY PROJ. Polytechnic Museum
ULITSA Central Post Office THEATRE Ploshchad Lyubyanskaya Nogina
Gorky House Museum Ermolovoy Theatre Lenin Museum SLAVYANSKAYA PL.
Revolution Square Gum Shopping Arcade PROSPEKT
GERSENA ULITSA PL. Revolyutsii Red Square ULITSA IIinka
NIKITSKIY BLVD. Central Exhibition Hall Arsenal Lenin Mausoleum Vladimirov Peredalok
Moscow Conservatoire Council of Ministers Kitai Gorod
University Historical Museum Kremlin ULITSA VARVARKA
Arbatskaya Ploshchad VOZDVIZHENKA U. Presidium of the Supreme Soviet St. Basil's Cathedral
Museum of Russian Architecture Ivan Square Central Concert Hall
ULITSA ARBAT Arbatskaya Lenin State Library Palace of Congress MOSKVORETS. NAB.
U. ZNAMENKA Terem Palace Cathedral Square Archangel Cathedral RAUSHSKAYA NAB.
GOGOLEVSKIY BOULEVARD Armoury Palace Kremlin Palace KITAISKI PERULOK
Marx-Engels Ulitsa Borovitskaya Ploshchad KREMLEVSKAYA NABEREZHNAYA SADOVNICHESKAYA
BOULEVARD RING Pushkin Fine Arts Museum Moskva (Moscow) OVCHINNIKOVSKAYA
Ryleyev Ulitsa Cathedral of Christ the Saviour SOFIYSKAYA NABEREZHNAYA
Kropotkinskaya BOLOTNAYA NAB. Vodootvodny
BOLSHOY KAMENNI MOST KADASHEVSKAYA NAB.

MOSCOW, RUSSIA

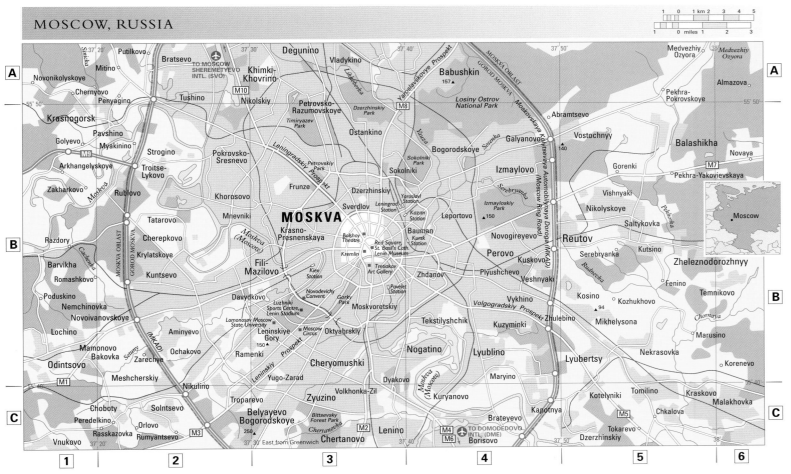

Putilkovo TO MOSCOW SHEREMETYEVO INTL. (SVO) Degunino Vladykino Medvezhiy Ozyora
Novonikolyskoye Mitino Bratsevo Khimki-Khovrino Babushkin GOROD MOSKVA Almazova
Chernyovo Penyagino Tushino Nikolskiy Losiny Ostrov National Park Pekhra-Pokrovskoye
Krasnogorsk Petrovsko-Razumovskoye Dzerzhinskiy Park Abramtsevo Balashikha
Golyevo Pavshino Strogino Timiryazev Park MOSKOVSKAYA OBLAST Novaya
Arkhangelskoye Myakinino Pokrovskoye-Sresnevo Ostankino Galyanovoc Vostochnyy Pekhra-Yakovievskaya
Troitse-Lykovo Petrovsky Park Leningradskiy Prospkt Izmaylovo Gorenki
Zakharkovo Rublovo Khorosovo Frunze Sokolniki Izmaylovskiy Park Vishnyaki
Tatarovo Mnevniki Dzerzhinskiy Ostankino Nikolskoye
MOSKVA OBLAST GOROD MOSKVA Cherepkovo **MOSKVA** Yaroslavl Station Serebryanka Saltykovka
Barvikha Krylatskoye Krasno-Presnenskaya Leningrad Station Bauman Novogireyevo Reutov Zheleznodorozhnyy
Razdory Kuntsevo Bolshoy Theatre Kazan Station Kursk Station Perovo
Romashkovo Fili-Mazilovo Kremlin Red Square, St. Basil's Cath. Kuskovo Veshnyaki Fenino
Poduskino Kiev Station Lenin Museum Zhdanov Plyushchevo Temnikovo
Nemchinovka Davydkovo Novodevichy Convent Tretiakov Art Gallery Vykhino
Novoivanovskoye Lomonosov Moscow State University Gorky Park Volgogradskiy Prospekt Kosino Kozhukhovo Marusino
Lochino Luzhniki Sports Centre, Lenin Stadium Pavelet Station Zhulebino Mikhelysona
Mamonovo Aminyevo Leninskiye Gory Moscow Circus Kuzyminki
Bakovka Ochakovo Oktyabrskiy Nekrasovka Korenevo
Odintsovo Zarechya Ramenki Moskvoretskiy Lyublino Lyubertsy Kraskovo
Meshcherskiy Yugo-Zarad Nogatino Kotelniki Tomilino
Nikulino Troparevo Volkhonka-Zil Maryino Kuryanovo Malakhovka
Choboty Solntsevo Zyuzino Bittsevsky Forest Park Brateyevo Kapotnya Chkalova
Peredelkino Orlovo Belyayevo Bogorodskoye TO DOMODEDOVO INTL. (DME) Tokarevo
Rasskazovo Rumyantsevo Chertanovo Lenin Borisovo Dzerzhinskiy
Vnukovo 37° 30' East from Greenwich

37° 40' Yaroslavskoye Prospekt MOSKVA OBLAST Moskovskaya Avtosuyava Automobilnaya Doroga (Moscow Ring Road) (MKAD) Moskva (Moscow)

COPYRIGHT PHILIP'S

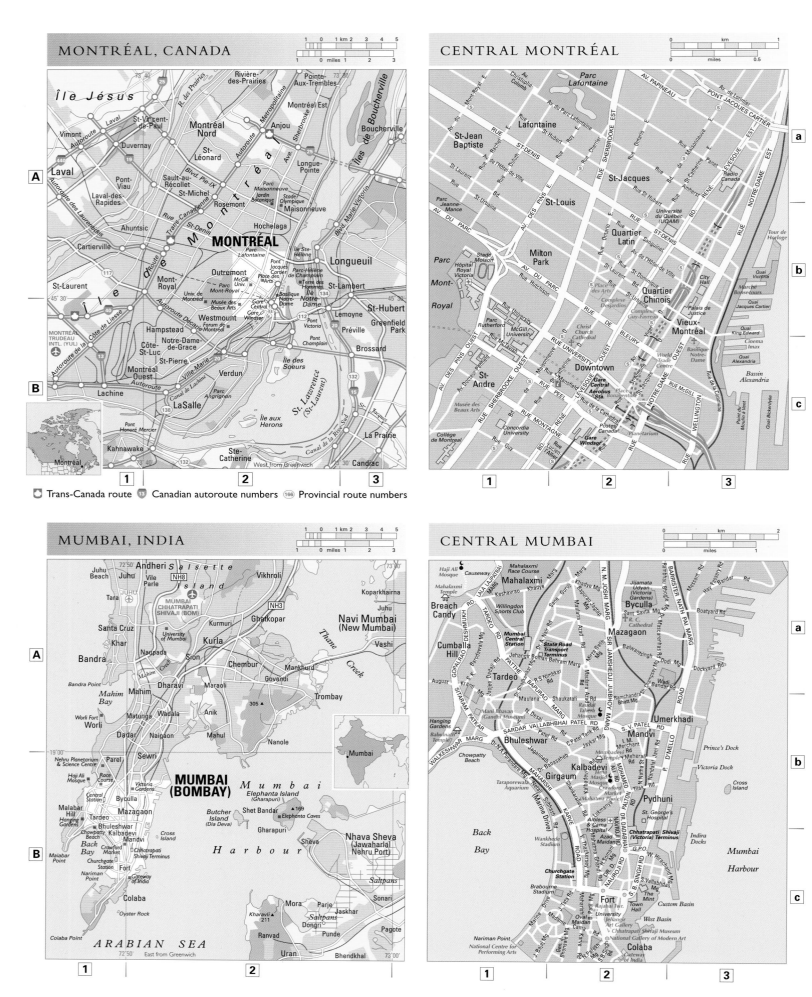

MONTRÉAL, CANADA

CENTRAL MONTRÉAL

Trans-Canada route · Canadian autoroute numbers · Provincial route numbers

MUMBAI, INDIA

CENTRAL MUMBAI

COPYRIGHT PHILIP'S

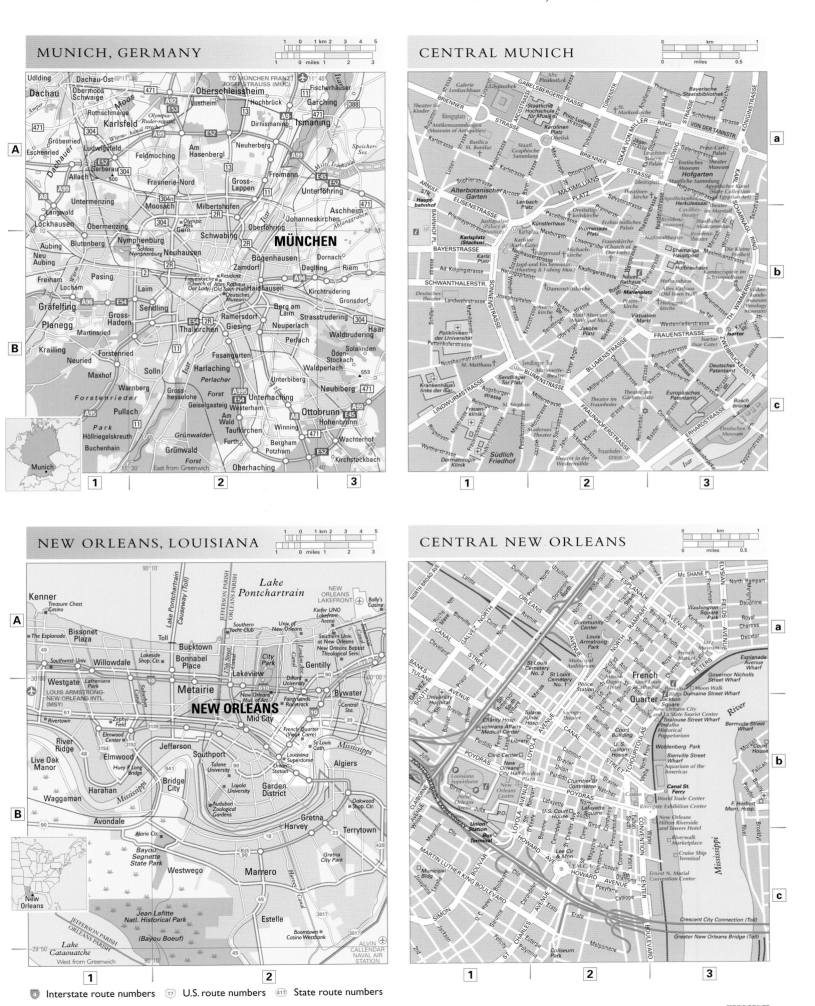

MUNICH, GERMANY

Scale: 1 0 1 km 2 3 4 5 / 1 0 miles 1 2 3

CENTRAL MUNICH

Scale: 0 km 1 / 0 miles 0.5

NEW ORLEANS, LOUISIANA

Scale: 1 0 1 km 2 3 4 5 / 1 0 miles 1 2 3

CENTRAL NEW ORLEANS

Scale: 0 km 1 / 0 miles 0.5

🛡 Interstate route numbers   ⑰ U.S. route numbers   ④₁₇ State route numbers

COPYRIGHT PHILIP'S

NEW YORK, NEW YORK

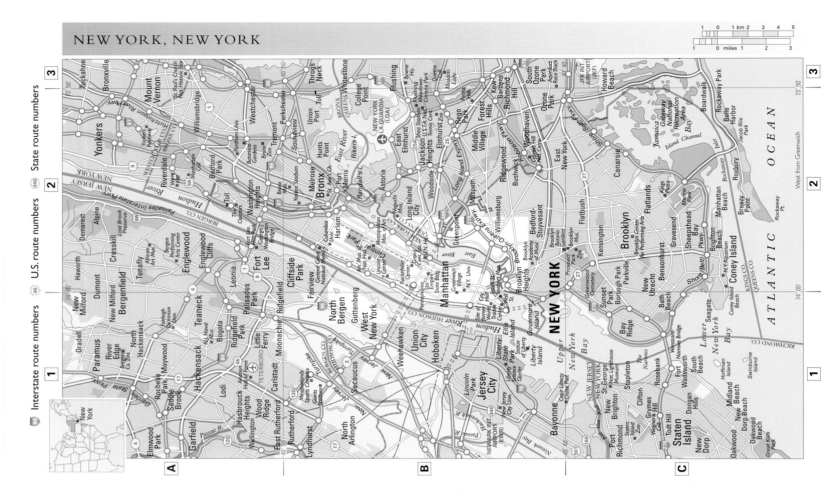

CENTRAL NEW YORK

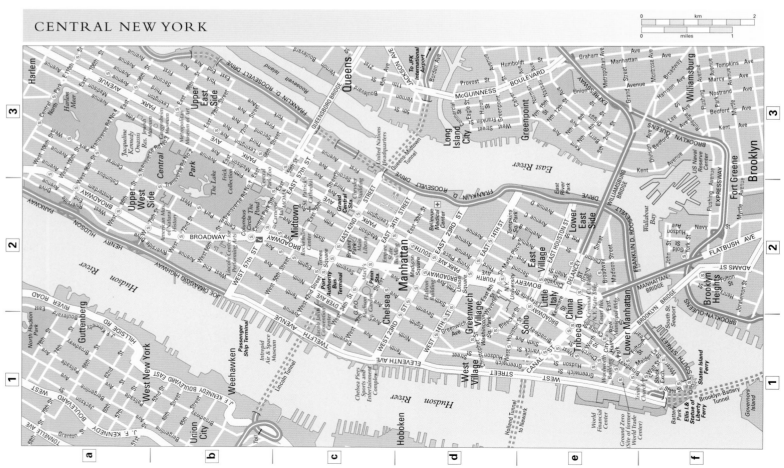

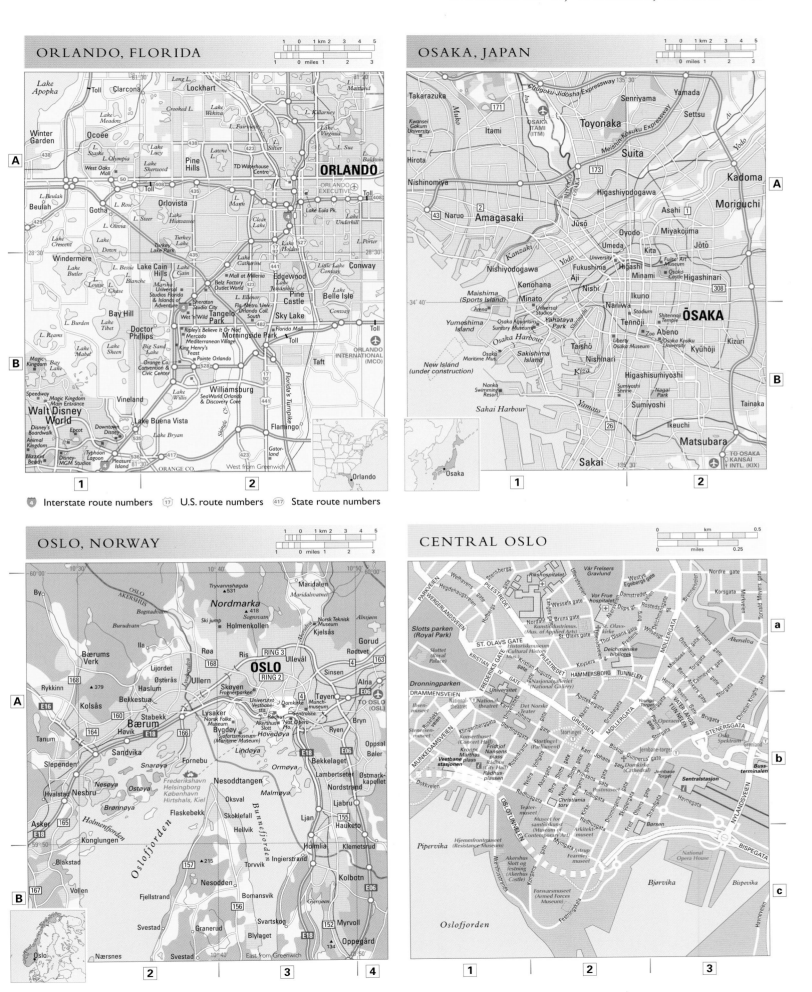

PARIS, FRANCE

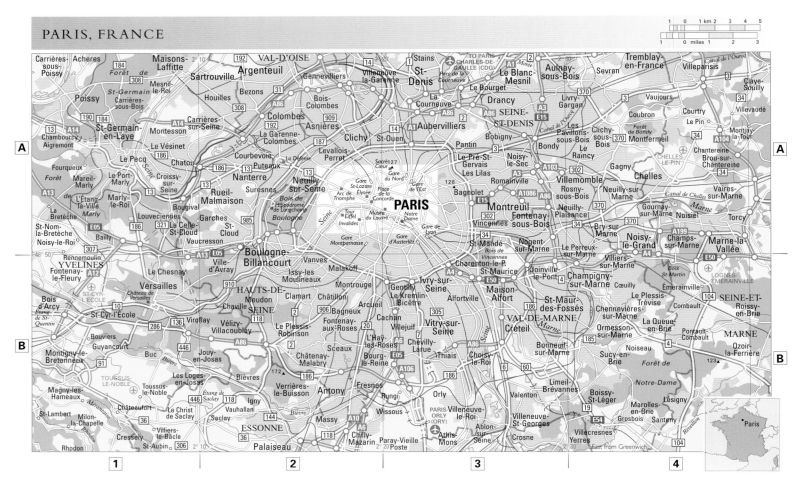

CENTRAL PARIS

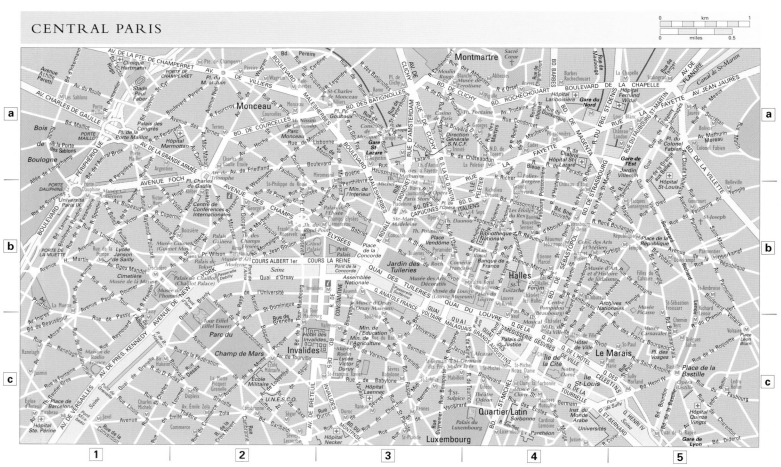

PRAGUE, CZECH REPUBLIC

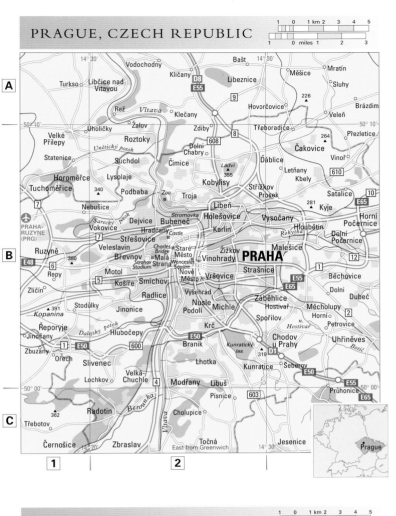

CENTRAL PRAGUE

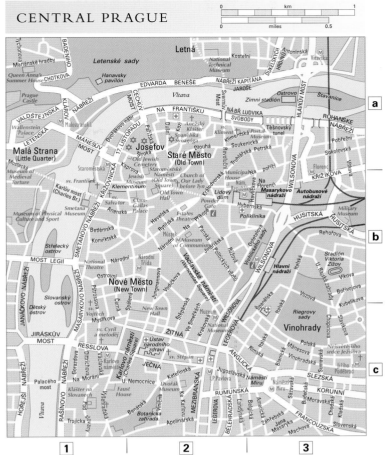

RIO DE JANEIRO, BRAZIL

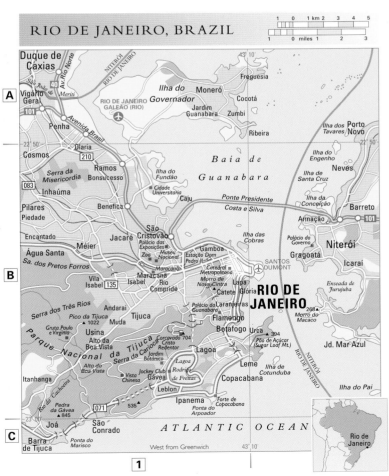

CENTRAL RIO DE JANEIRO

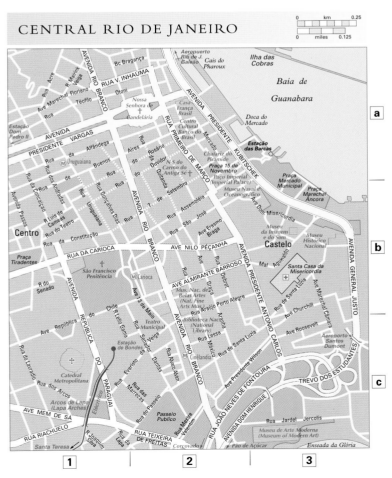

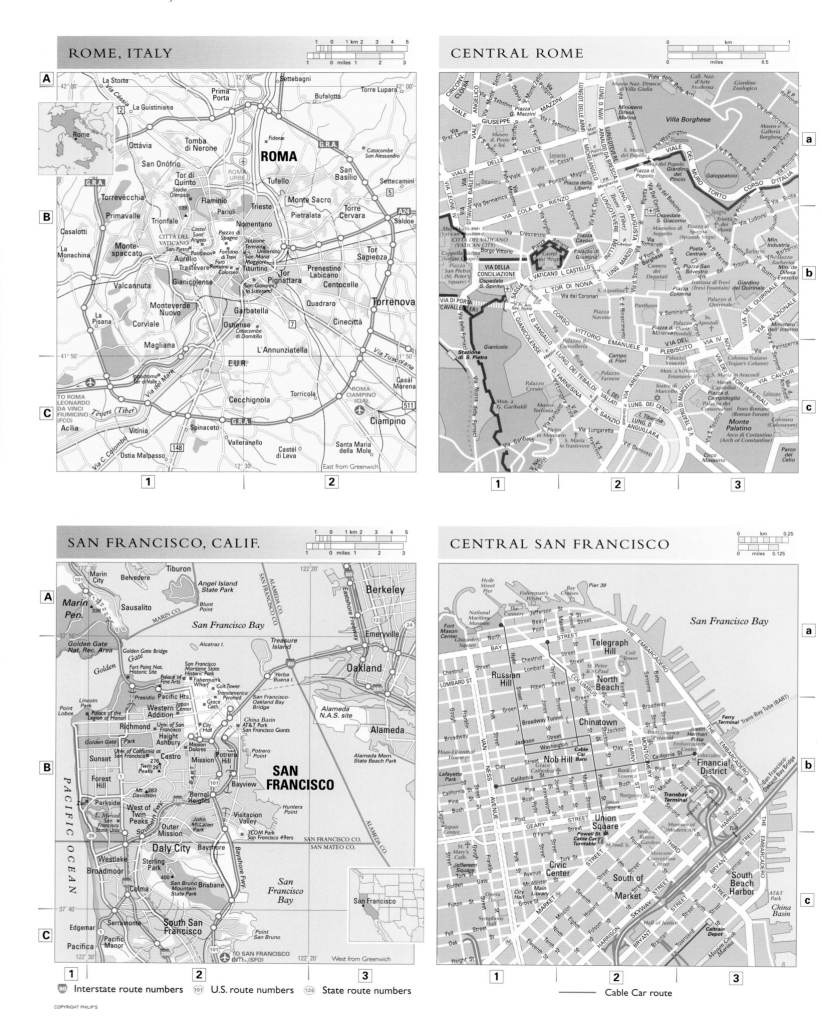

ROME, ITALY

CENTRAL ROME

SAN FRANCISCO, CALIF.

CENTRAL SAN FRANCISCO

Interstate route numbers   U.S. route numbers   State route numbers

Cable Car route

COPYRIGHT PHILIP'S

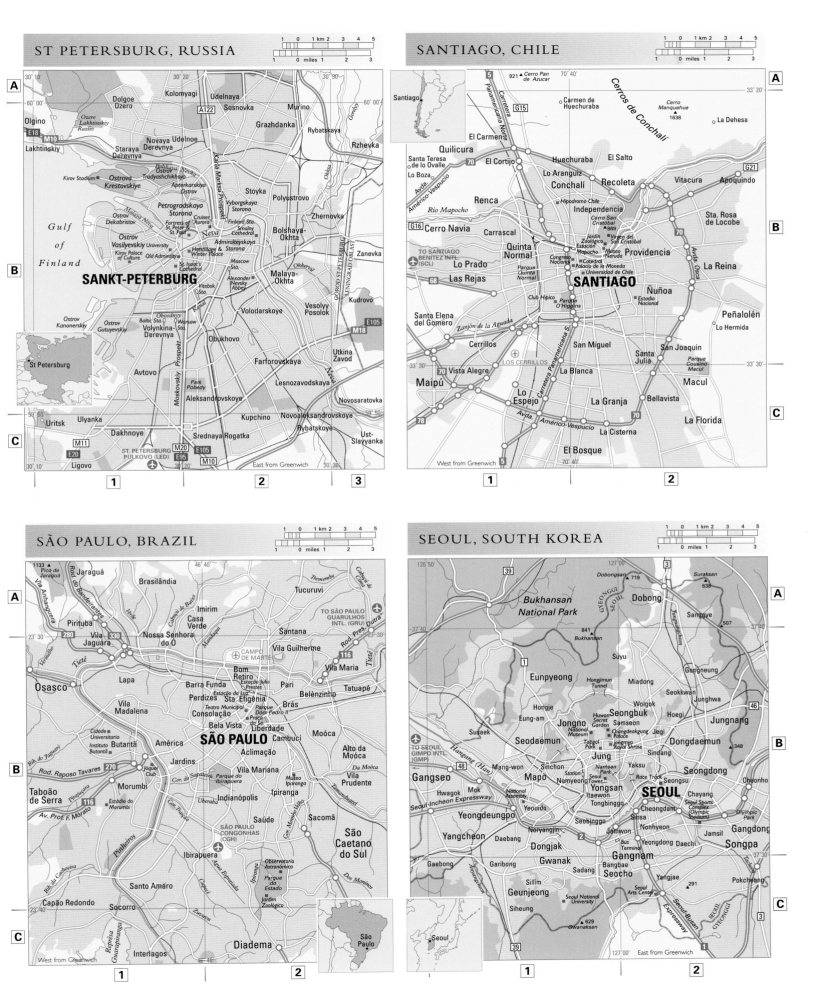

COPYRIGHT PHILIP'S

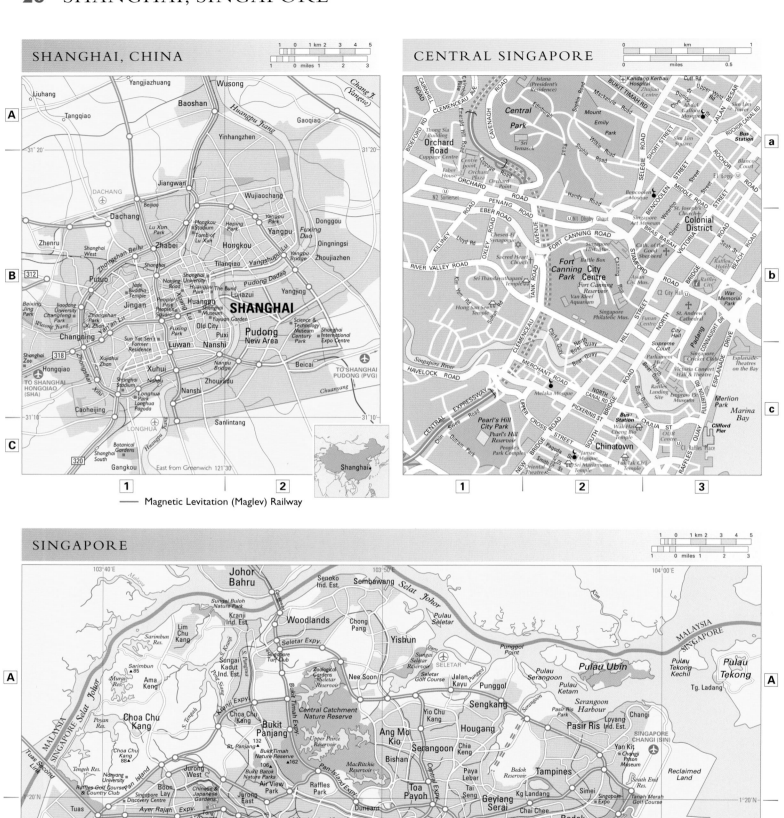

SHANGHAI, CHINA

A

B

C

1   2

— Magnetic Levitation (Maglev) Railway

Liuhang
Yangjiazhuang
Wusong
Tangqiao
Baoshan
Gaoqiao
Yinhangzhen
Huangpu Jiang
Chang J. (Yangtse)

Jiangwan
Wujiaochang
Donggou
Qingningsi

DACHANG
Beijiao
Dachang
Yangpu Park
Fuxing Dao
Zhenru
Hongkou Stadium
Tomb of Lu Xun
Yangpu
Zhoujiazhen

Shanghai West
Zhongshan Beilu
Zhabei
Lu Xun Park
Heping Park
Pudong Dadao
Yangjing

312
Putuo
Shanghai
Nanjing Road
Huangpu Park
The Bund
Luijazui

Jade Buddha Temple
Shanghai University
Jingan
People's Park
People's Square
Huangpu
Shanghai Museum

Beixing Jing Park
Jiaotong University
Chang'eng Park
Zhongshan Park
Xi Zhan'an Lu
Fuxing Park
Old City
Yuyuan Garden
Science & Technology Museum
Shanghai International Expo Centre

318
Changning
Sun Yat Sen's Former Residence
Puxi
Luwan
Nanshi
Pudong New Area
Century Park

Hongqiao
Xujiahui
Zhongshan Xilu
Nanpu Bridge
Beicai

Shanghai Zoo
Xujiahui Zhan
Shanghai Stadium
Naihui
Zhoujiadu
TO SHANGHAI PUDONG (PVG)

TO SHANGHAI HONGQIAO (SHA)
Nanshi
Chuanyang

Longhua
Longhua Park
Longhua Pagoda
Caoheijing
Sanlintang

320
Botanical Gardens
Shanghai South
Gangkou
East from Greenwich 121°30

31°20
31°10

SHANGHAI

Shanghai

CENTRAL SINGAPORE

a

b

c

1   2   3

Kandang Kerbau Hospital
Istana (President's Residence)
Zhujiao Centre
BUKIT TIMAH RD
Cuff Rd
Upper Wold
Sim Lim Tower

CAIRNHILL ROAD
CLEMENCEAU AVE
ROAD
Edinburgh
Sophia Road
Mount Emily Park
SELEGIE ROAD
SHORT STREET
Dunlop Abdul Gafoor Mosque
JALAN BESAR

Central Park

BIDEFORD RD
Emerald Hill
Cavenagh
Mackenzie Road
Emily Road
White Road
Sophia Road
Sim Lim Square
Bus Station

Orchard Road
Thong Sia Building
Sri Temasek
Handy Road
Bencoolen Mosque
Bencoolen
MIDDLE ROAD
Blanco Court

Cuppage Centre
Centre Point
Orchard Plaza
Oppenheim Road
Orchard Point
Faber House
ORCHARD ROAD
Waterloo
Singapore Art Museum
St. Joseph's Church
ROCHOR ROAD
Bugis
Raffles Hotel

N2 Somerset
PENANG ROAD
Handy Road
U N1 Dhoby Ghaut
BRAS BASAH
Colonial District
BEACH ROAD
Seah St

KILLINEY ROAD
EBER ROAD
Chesed-El Synagogue
FORT CANNING ROAD
STAMFORD
Cath. of the Good Shepherd
VICTORIA
Raffles City

Lloyd Rd
OXLEY ROAD
Sacred Heart Church
Battle Box
CANNING
Asian Civ. Mus.
War Memorial Park

RIVER VALLEY ROAD
Sri Thandayuthapani Temple
TANK ROAD
Fort Canning Park
City Centre
Fort Canning Reservoir
Van Kleef Aquarium
HILL STREET
NORTH BRIDGE
St. Andrew's Cathedral
CONNAUGHT DR

Kim Yam Rd
Hong San See Temple
Sultan Rd
Singapore Philatelic Mus.
Funan Centre
C2 City Hall
City Hall
Padang

CLEMENCEAU
Clarke Quay
North Boat Quay
Supreme Court
Parliament
Singapore Cricket Club
Victoria Concert Hall & Theatre
ESPLANADE
Esplanade-Theatres on the Bay

MERCHANT ROAD
North Boat Quay
South Boat Quay
Raffles Landing Site
Empress Place Mus.
Merlion Park

HAVELOCK ROAD
Singapore River
Melaka Mosque
NORTH CANAL RD
BOAT
FULLERTON RD
Marina Bay

CENTRAL EXPRESSWAY
Pearl's Hill City Park
UPPER CROSS ROAD
PICKERING ST
NORTH CANAL RD
SOUTH BRIDGE
CHULIA ST
Raffles Place
QUAY
Clifford Pier

Chin Swee Rd
Pearl's Hill Reservoir
Pagoda
Wak Hai Cheng Bio Temple
Bus Station
OUB Centre

People's Park Complex
NEW BRIDGE ROAD
Jamae Mosque
Chinatown
Fuk Tak Chi Temple

New Oriental Theatre
Smith St
Sri Mariamman Temple
East from Greenwich

103°40'E   103°50'E   104°00'E

SINGAPORE

A

B

1   2   3   4

Johor Bahru
Senoko Ind. Est.
Sembawang
Selat Johor

Sungei Buloh Nature Park
Kranji Ind. Est.
Woodlands
Chong Pang
Kim
MALAYSIA SINGAPORE

Sarimbun Res.
Lim Chu Kang
Seletar Expy.
Yishun
Punggol Point
Pulau Seletar

Sarimbun 85
Murai Res.
Sungai Kadut Ind. Est.
Singapore Turf Club
Zoological Gardens
Seletar Reservoir
SELETAR
Pulau Serangoon
Pulau Ubin
Pulau Tekong Kechil
Pulau Tekong

Ama Keng
Kranji Expy.
Seletar Golf Course
Jalan Kayu
Punggol
Pulau Ketam
Tg. Ladang

Choa Chu Kang
Poyan Res.
Choa Chu Kang
Bukit Panjang
Central Catchment Nature Reserve
Yio Chu Kang
Sengkang
Serangoon Harbour
Pasir Ris Park
Changi

Tengeh Res.
Choa Chu Kang 88
132 Bt. Panjang
Upper Peirce Reservoir
Hougang
Chia Keng
Loyang Ind. Est.
SINGAPORE CHANGI (SIN)

Nanyang University
Pan Island
106, Bukit Timah Nature Reserve
Ang Mo Kio
Bishan
Serangoon
Pasir Ris
Changi Prison Museum

Raffles Golf Course & Country Club
Singapore Discovery Centre
Jurong West
Bukit Batok Nature Parks
Air View Park
162
MacRitchie Reservoir
Pan-Island Expy.
Paya Lebar
Bedok Reservoir
Tampines
South End Res.
Reclaimed Land

Boon Lay
Chinese & Japanese Gardens
Jurong East
Raffles Park
Toa Payoh
Tai Seng
Kg Landang
Simei

Ayer Rajah Expy.
Tang Dynasty Museum
Pandan Res.
Clementi
Maryland
Holland Village
Victoria Park
University of Singapore
Dunearn
Geylang Serai
Chai Chee
Singapore Expo
Tanah Merah Golf Course

Jurong
Jurong Bird Park
Kg Tanjong Penjuru
National University of Singapore
Pasir Panjang
Ayer Rajah Expy.
Botanic Gardens
Queenstown
Telok Blangah
National Museum
Katong
Frankel
Bedok
East Coast Park

Tuas
Jurong Industrial Estate
Pulau Jurong
Seraya
Pasir Panjang Terminal
Buona Vista Park
Mt. 105 Faber
St. Andrew's Cathedral
City Hall
National Stadium
Kallang Park
East Coast Pkwy.

Reclaimed Land
Selat Jurong
Sakra
Pulau Busing
Pulau Bukum
Selat Pandan
Cable Car
Underwater World
Sentosa Gardens
Sentosa
World Trade Centre
Keppel Harbour
P. Brani
Thian Hock Keng Temple
SINGAPORE
Tanjong Golf Course
Straits of Singapore

103°40'E   103°50'E   104°00'E
East from Greenwich

1°20'N

Singapore

COPYRIGHT PHILIP'S

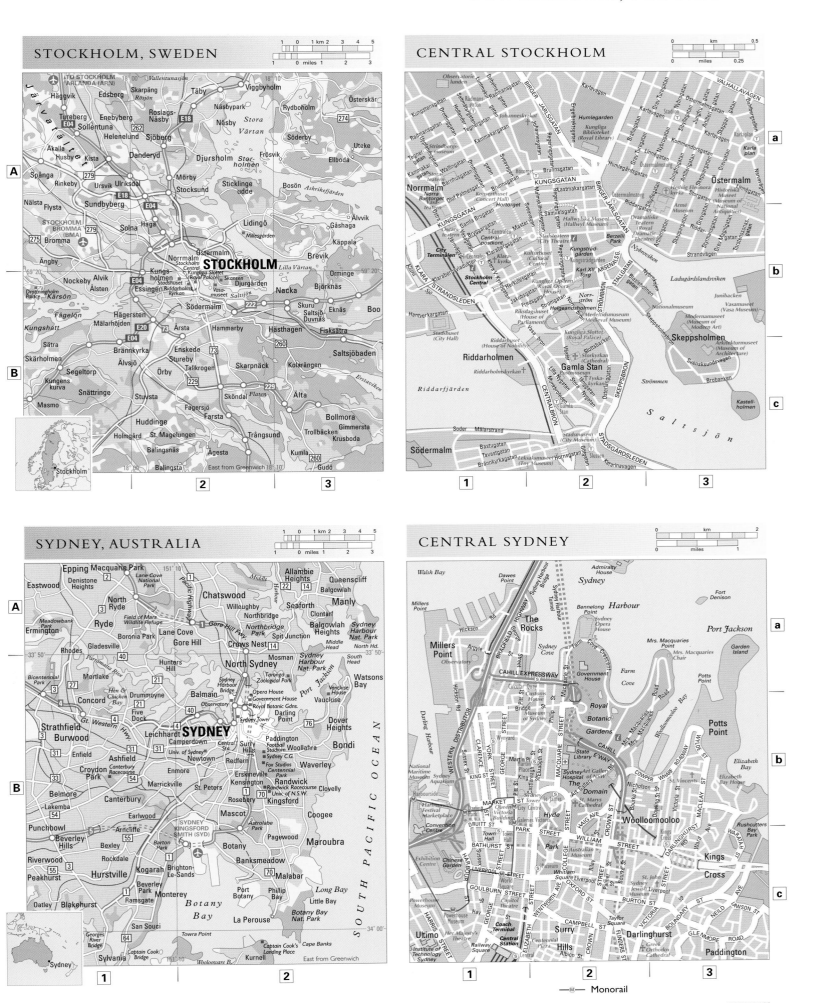

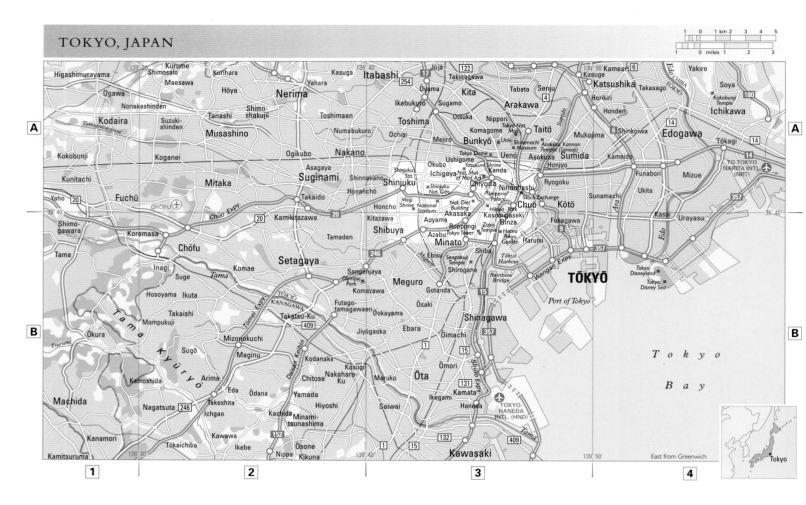

TOKYO, JAPAN

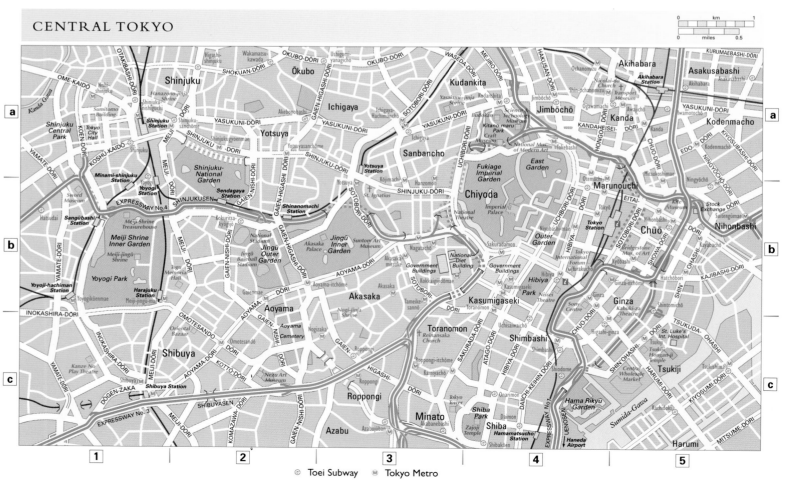

CENTRAL TOKYO

Ⓣ Toei Subway   Ⓜ Tokyo Metro

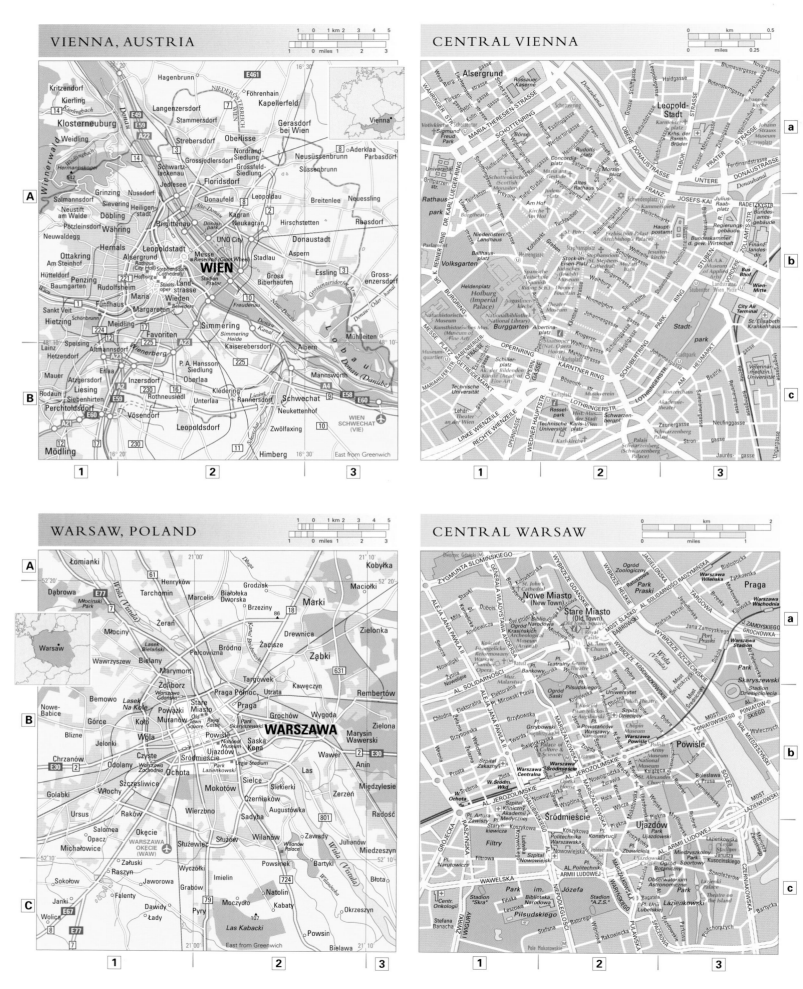

VIENNA, AUSTRIA

CENTRAL VIENNA

WARSAW, POLAND

CENTRAL WARSAW

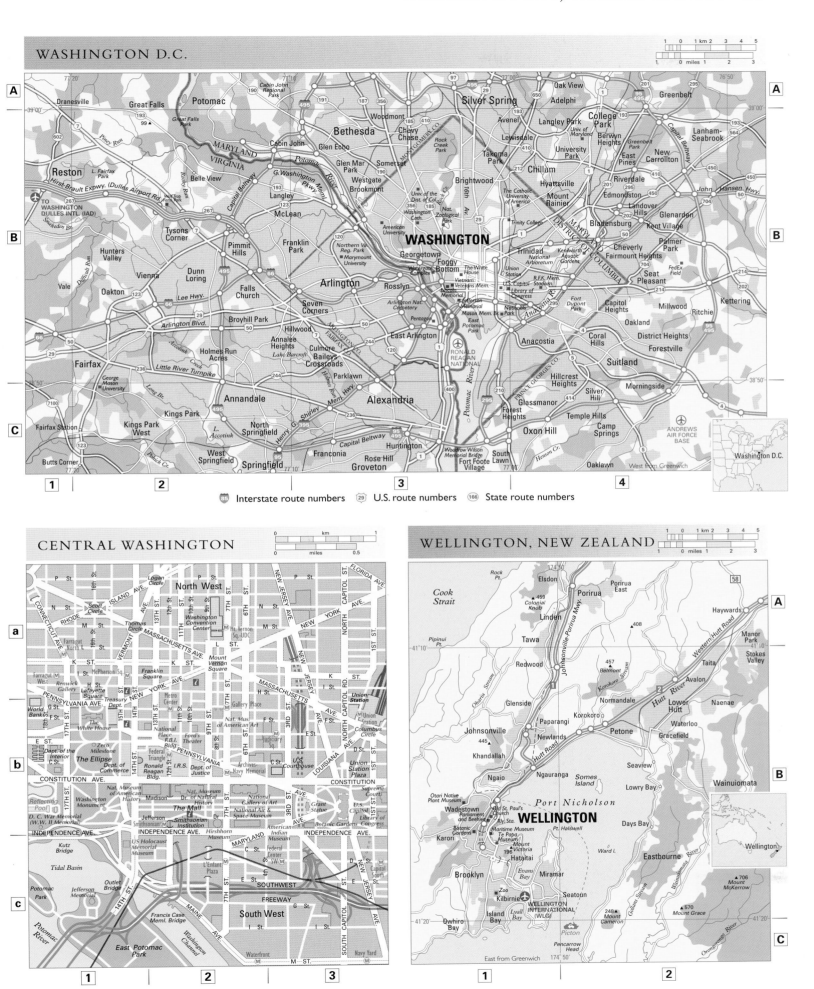

INDEX TO CITY MAPS

The index contains the names of all the principal places and features shown on the City Maps. Each name is followed by an additional entry in italics giving the name of the City Map within which it is located.

The number in bold type which follows each name refers to the number of the City Map page where that feature or place will be found.

The letter and figure which are immediately after the page number give the grid square on the map within which the feature or place is situated.

The letter represents the latitude and the figure the longitude. The full geographic reference is provided in the border of the City Maps.

The location given is the centre of the city, suburb or feature and is not necessarily the name. Rivers, canals and roads are indexed to their name. Rivers carry the symbol → after their name.

An explanation of the alphabetical order rules and a list of the abbreviations used are to be found at the beginning of the World Map Index.

A

Aalām *Baghdad* **3** B2
Aalsmeer *Amsterdam* **2** B1
Abbey Wood *London* **15** B4
Abcoude *Amsterdam* **2** B2
Âbdin *Cairo* **7** A2
Abeno *Osaka* **23** B2
Aberdeen *Hong Kong* **12** B1
Aberdour *Edinburgh* **11** A2
Aberdour Castle *Edinburgh* **11** A2
Abfanggraben → *Munich* **21** A3
Ablon-sur-Seine *Paris* **24** B3
Abramtsevo *Moscow* **19** B3
Abu Dis *Jerusalem* **13** B2
Abû en Numrus *Cairo* **7** B2
Abu Ghosh *Jerusalem* **13** B1
Acassuso *Buenos Aires* **7** A2
Accotink, L. *Washington* **33** C2
Accotink Cr. → *Washington* **33** B2
Achères *Paris* **24** A1
Acília *Rome* **26** C1
Aclimação *São Paulo* **27** B2
Acropolis *Athens* **2** B2
Acton *London* **15** A2
Açúcar, Pão de *Rio de Janeiro* **25** B2
Ada Beja *Lisbon* **16** A1
Adams Park *Atlanta* **3** B2
Addiscombe *London* **15** B3
Adelphi *Washington* **33** A4
Aderklaa *Vienna* **32** A3
Adler Planetarium *Chicago* **9** B3
Admiralteyskaya Storona *St. Petersburg* **27** B2
Áffori *Milan* **19** A2
Aflandshage *Copenhagen* **8** B3
Afsarīyeh *Tehran* **31** B2
Agboyi Cr. → *Lagos* **14** A2
Ågerup *Copenhagen* **8** A1
Ågesta *Stockholm* **29** B2
Aghia Marina *Athens* **2** C3
Aghia Paraskevi *Athens* **2** A2
Aghios Dimitrios *Athens* **2** B2
Aghios Ioannis Rendis *Athens* **2** B1
Agincourt *Toronto* **31** A3
Agra Canal *Delhi* **10** B2
Agricola Oriental *Mexico City* **18** B2
Água Espraiada → *São Paulo* **27** B2
Agualva-Cacem *Lisbon* **16** A1
Ahrensfelde *Berlin* **5** A4
Ahuntsic *Montreal* **20** A1
Ai → *Osaka* **23** A2
Aigremont *Paris* **24** A1
Air View Park *Singapore* **28** A2
Airport West *Melbourne* **18** A1
Ajegunle *Lagos* **14** B2
Aji *Osaka* **23** A1
Ajuda *Lisbon* **16** A1
Akalla *Stockholm* **29** A1
Akasaka *Tokyo* **30** A3
Akbarābād *Tehran* **31** A2
Akershus Slott *Oslo* **23** A3
Al 'Aẓamīyah *Baghdad* **3** A2
Al Quds = Jerusalem *Jerusalem* **13** B2
Al-Walaja *Jerusalem* **13** B1
Alaguntan *Lagos* **14** B2
Alameda *San Francisco* **26** B3
Alameda Memorial State Beach Park *San Francisco* **26** B3
Albern *Vienna* **32** B2
Albert Park *Melbourne* **18** B1
Alberton *Johannesburg* **13** B2
Albertslund *Copenhagen* **8** B2
Alcantara *Lisbon* **16** A1
Alcatraz I. *San Francisco* **26** B2
Alcobendas *Madrid* **17** A2
Alcorcón *Madrid* **17** B1
Aldershof *Berlin* **5** B4
Aldo Bonzi *Buenos Aires* **7** C1
Aleksandrovskoye *St. Petersburg* **27** B2
Alexander Nevsky Abbey *St. Petersburg* **27** B2
Alexandra *Johannesburg* **13** A2
Alexandra *Singapore* **28** B2
Alexandria *Washington* **33** C3
Alfortville *Paris* **24** B3
Algés *Lisbon* **16** A1
Algiers *New Orleans* **21** B2
Alhambra *Los Angeles* **16** B4
Alibey → *Istanbul* **12** B1
Alibey Barajı *Istanbul* **12** B1
Alibeyköy *Istanbul* **12** B1
Alimos *Athens* **2** B2
Alipur *Kolkata* **14** B1
Allach *Munich* **21** A1
Allambie Heights *Sydney* **29** A2
Allermuir Hill *Edinburgh* **11** B2
Allstate Arena *Chicago* **9** A1
Allston *Boston* **6** A2
Almada *Lisbon* **16** A2
Almagro *Buenos Aires* **7** B2
Almargem do Bispo *Lisbon* **16** A1
Almirante G. Brown, Parque *Buenos Aires* **7** C2
Almon *Jerusalem* **13** B2
Almond → *Edinburgh* **11** B2
Alna *Oslo* **23** A4
Alnsjøen *Oslo* **23** A4
Alperton *London* **15** A2
Alpine *New York* **22** A2
Alrode *Johannesburg* **13** B2
Alsemberg *Brussels* **6** B2
Alsergrund *Vienna* **32** A2
Alsip *Chicago* **9** C2
Ålsten *Stockholm* **29** B1
Älta *Stockholm* **29** B3
Altadena *Los Angeles* **16** A4
Alte-Donau → *Vienna* **32** A2
Alter Finkenkrug *Berlin* **5** A1
Altes Rathaus *Munich* **21** B2
Altglienicke *Berlin* **5** B4
Altlandsberg *Berlin* **5** A5
Altlandsberg Nord *Berlin* **5** A5
Altmannsdorf *Vienna* **32** B1
Alto da Boa Vista *Rio de Janeiro* **25** B1
Alto da Moóca *São Paulo* **27** B2
Alto do Pina *Lisbon* **16** A2
Altona *Melbourne* **18** B1
Alvik *Stockholm* **29** B1
Alvin Callendar Naval Air Station *New Orleans* **21** B2
Älvsjo *Stockholm* **29** B2
Älvvik *Stockholm* **29** A3
Am Hasenbergl *Munich* **21** A2
Am Steinhof *Vienna* **32** A1
Am Wald *Munich* **21** B2
Ama Keng *Singapore* **28** A2
Amadora *Lisbon* **16** A1
Amagasaki *Osaka* **23** A1
Amager *Copenhagen* **8** B3
Amāl Qādisiya *Baghdad* **3** B2
Amalienborg Slot *Copenhagen* **8** A3
Amata *Milan* **19** A1
Ambelokipi *Athens* **2** B2
Ameixoeira *Lisbon* **16** A2
América *São Paulo* **27** B1
American Police Hall of Fame *Miami* **18** B2
American Univ. *Washington* **33** B3
Amin *Baghdad* **3** B2
Aminadav *Jerusalem* **13** B1
Amīrābād *Tehran* **31** A2
Amora *Lisbon* **16** B2
Amoreira *Lisbon* **16** A1
Amper → *Munich* **21** A1
Amstel-Drecht-Kanaal *Amsterdam* **2** B2
Amstelveen *Amsterdam* **2** B2
Amsterdam *Amsterdam* **2** A2
Amsterdam ✈ (AMS) *Amsterdam* **2** B1
Amsterdam-Rijnkanaal *Amsterdam* **2** B3
Amsterdam Zuidoost *Amsterdam* **2** B2
Amsterdamse Bos *Amsterdam* **2** B1
Anacosta → *Washington* **33** B4
Anacostia *Washington* **33** B4
Anadoluhisarı *Istanbul* **12** B2
Anadolukavağı *Istanbul* **12** A2
Anata *Jerusalem* **13** B2
Ancol *Jakarta* **12** A1
'Andalus *Baghdad* **3** B1
Andaraí *Rio de Janeiro* **25** B1
Anderlecht *Brussels* **6** A1
Anderson Park *Atlanta* **3** B2
Andingmen *Beijing* **4** B2
Ang Mo Kio *Singapore* **28** A3
Ängby *Stockholm* **29** A1
Angel I. *San Francisco* **26** A2
Angel Island State Park ⌓ *San Francisco* **26** A2
Angke, Kali → *Jakarta* **12** A1
Angyalföld *Budapest* **7** A2
Anik *Mumbai* **20** A2
Anin *Warsaw* **32** B2
Anjou *Montreal* **20** A2
Annalee Heights *Washington* **33** B2
Annandale *Washington* **33** C2
Anne Frankhuis *Amsterdam* **2** A2
Antony *Paris* **24** B2
Aoyama *Tokyo* **30** B3
Ap Lei Chau *Hong Kong* **12** B1
Apapa *Lagos* **14** B2
Apapa Quays *Lagos* **14** B2
Apelacão *Lisbon* **16** A2
Apopka, L. *Orlando* **23** A1
Apoquindo *Santiago* **27** B2
Apterkarskiy Ostrov *St. Petersburg* **27** B2
Ar Kazimiyah *Baghdad* **3** B1
Ar Ram *Jerusalem* **13** A2
Ara → *Tokyo* **30** A4
Arakawa *Tokyo* **30** A3
Arany-hegyi-patak → *Budapest* **7** A2
Aravaca *Madrid* **17** B1
Arbataash *Baghdad* **3** A1
Arc de Triomphe *Paris* **24** A2
Arcadia *Los Angeles* **16** B4
Arcueil *Paris* **24** B2
Arese *Milan* **19** A1
Arganzuela *Madrid* **17** B1
Argenteuil *Paris* **24** A2
Argiroupoli *Athens* **2** B2
Argonne Forest *Chicago* **9** C1
Arima *Tokyo* **30** B2
Arlanda, Stockholm ✈ (ARN) *Stockholm* **29** A1
Arlington *Boston* **6** A1
Arlington *Washington* **33** B3
Arlington Heights *Boston* **6** A1
Arlington Nat. Cemetery *Washington* **33** B3
Armação *Rio de Janeiro* **25** B2
Armadale *Melbourne* **18** B2
Armour Heights *Toronto* **31** A2
Arncliffe *Sydney* **29** B1
Arnold Arboretum *Boston* **6** B2
Árpádföld *Budapest* **7** A3
Arrentela *Lisbon* **16** B2
Arroyo Seco Park *Los Angeles* **16** B3
Årsta *Stockholm* **29** B2
Artane *Dublin* **10** A2
Artas *Jerusalem* **13** B2
Arthur's Seat *Edinburgh* **11** B3
Arts, Place des *Montreal* **20** A2
As Shawawra *Jerusalem* **13** B2
Asagaya *Tokyo* **30** A2
Asahi *Osaka* **23** A2
Asakusa *Tokyo* **30** A3
Asati *Kolkata* **14** C1
Aschheim *Munich* **21** A3
Ascot Vale *Melbourne* **18** A1
Ashbridge's Bay Park *Toronto* **31** B3
Ashburn *Chicago* **9** C2
Ashburton *Melbourne* **18** B2
Ashfield *Sydney* **29** B1
Ashford *London* **15** B1
Ashtown *Dublin* **10** A2
Askisto *Helsinki* **11** B1
Askrikefjärden *Stockholm* **29** A3
Asnières *Paris* **24** A2
Aspern *Vienna* **32** A2
Assago *Milan* **19** B1
Assendelft *Amsterdam* **2** A1
Assiano *Milan* **19** B1
Astoria *New York* **22** B2
Astrolabe Park *Sydney* **29** B2
Atarot *Jerusalem* **13** A2
Atarot ✈ (JRS) *Jerusalem* **13** A2
Atghara *Kolkata* **14** B2
Athens = Athina *Athens* **2** B2
Athina *Athens* **2** B2
Athina ✈ (ATH) *Athens* **2** A3
Athínai = Athina *Athens* **2** B2
Athis-Mons *Paris* **24** B3
Athlone *Cape Town* **8** A2
Atholl *Johannesburg* **13** A2
Atīfiya *Baghdad* **3** A2
Atişalen *Istanbul* **12** B1
Atlanta *Atlanta* **3** B2
Atlanta Hartsfield Int. ✈ (ATL) *Atlanta* **3** C2
Atlanta Zoo *Atlanta* **3** B2
Atomium *Brussels* **6** A2
Attiki *Athens* **2** A2
Atzgersdorf *Vienna* **32** B1
Aubervilliers *Paris* **24** A3
Aubing *Munich* **21** B1
Auburndale *Boston* **6** A1
Auchendinny *Edinburgh* **11** B2
Auckland Park *Johannesburg* **13** B2
Auderghem *Brussels* **6** B2
Augustówka *Warsaw* **32** B2
Aulnay-sous-Bois *Paris* **24** A3
Aurelio *Rome* **26** B1
Ausîm *Cairo* **7** A1
Austerlitz, Gare d' *Paris* **24** A3
Austin *Chicago* **9** B2
Avalon *Wellington* **33** B2
Avedøre *Copenhagen* **8** B2
Avellaneda *Buenos Aires* **7** C2
Avenel *Washington* **33** B4
Avondale *Chicago* **9** B2
Avondale *New Orleans* **21** B1
Avondale Heights *Melbourne* **18** A1
Avtovo *St. Petersburg* **27** B1
Ayazağa *Istanbul* **12** B1
Ayer Chawan, Pulau *Singapore* **28** B2
Ayer Merbau, Pulau *Singapore* **28** B2
Azabu *Tokyo* **30** B3
Azcapotzalco *Mexico City* **18** B1
Azteca, Estadia *Mexico City* **18** C2
Azucar, Cerro Pan de *Santiago* **27** A1

B

Baambrugge *Amsterdam* **2** B2
Baba Channel *Karachi* **13** B1
Baba I. *Karachi* **13** B1
Babarpur *Delhi* **10** A2
Babushkin *Moscow* **19** A3
Back B. *Mumbai* **20** B1
Baclaran *Manila* **17** B2
Bacoor *Manila* **17** C1
Bacoor B. *Manila* **17** C1
Badalona *Barcelona* **4** A2
Badhoevedorp *Amsterdam* **2** A1
Badli *Delhi* **10** A1
Bærum *Oslo* **23** A2
Bağcılar *Istanbul* **12** B1
Bággio *Milan* **19** B1
Bāgh-e-Feyz *Tehran* **31** A1
Baghdād *Baghdad* **3** A2
Baghdād al Muthana ✈ (BGW) *Baghdad* **3** B2
Baghdad Int. ✈ (SDA) *Baghdad* **3** B1
Bagmari *Kolkata* **14** B2
Bagneux *Paris* **24** B2
Bagnolet *Paris* **24** A3
Bagsværd *Copenhagen* **8** A2
Bagsværd Sø *Copenhagen* **8** A2
Baguiati *Kolkata* **14** B2
Bagumbayan *Manila* **17** C2
Baha'i Temple *Chicago* **9** A2
Bahçeköy *Istanbul* **12** A1
Bahçelievler *Istanbul* **12** B1
Bahtîm *Cairo* **7** A2
Baile Átha Cliath = Dublin *Dublin* **10** A2
Baileys Crossroads *Washington* **33** B3
Bailly *Paris* **24** A1
Bairro Lopes *Lisbon* **16** A2
Baisha *Guangzhou* **11** B2
Baiyun *Guangzhou* **11** A2
Baiyun Hill *Guangzhou* **11** B2
Baiyun Mountain Scenic Area *Guangzhou* **11** A2
Bakırköy *Istanbul* **12** C1
Bal Harbor *Miami* **18** A2
Balara *Manila* **17** B2
Baldia *Karachi* **13** A1
Baldoyle *Dublin* **10** A3
Baldwin, L. *Orlando* **23** A3
Baldwin Hills *Los Angeles* **16** B2
Baldwin Hills Res. *Los Angeles* **16** B2
Balgowlah *Sydney* **29** A2
Balgowlah Heights *Sydney* **29** A2
Balham *London* **15** B3
Bali *Kolkata* **14** B1
Baliganja *Kolkata* **14** B2
Balingsnäs *Stockholm* **29** B2
Balingsta *Stockholm* **29** B2
Balintawak *Manila* **17** B1
Ballerup *Copenhagen* **8** A2
Ballinteer *Dublin* **10** B2
Ballyboden *Dublin* **10** B2
Ballybrack *Dublin* **10** B3
Ballyfermot *Dublin* **10** A1
Ballymorefinn Hill *Dublin* **10** B1
Ballymun *Dublin* **10** A2
Balmain *Sydney* **29** B2
Baluhati *Kolkata* **14** B1
Balvanera *Buenos Aires* **7** B2
Balwyn *Melbourne* **18** A2
Balwyn North *Melbourne* **18** A2
Banática *Lisbon* **16** A1
Bandra *Mumbai* **20** A1
Bandra Pt. *Mumbai* **20** A1
Bang Kapi *Bangkok* **3** B2
Bang Na *Bangkok* **3** B2
Bangbae *Seoul* **27** C1
Bangkhen *Bangkok* **3** A2
Bangkok *Bangkok* **3** B2
Bangkok Don Muang Int. ✈ (BKK) *Bangkok* **3** A2
Bangkok Noi *Bangkok* **3** B1
Bangkok Yai *Bangkok* **3** B1
Banglo *Kolkata* **14** B1
Bangrak *Bangkok* **3** B2
Bangsu *Bangkok* **3** B2
Banks, C. *Sydney* **29** C2
Banksmeadow *Sydney* **29** B2
Banstala *Kolkata* **14** B2
Bantra *Kolkata* **14** B1
Baoshan *Shanghai* **28** A1
Bar Giyora *Jerusalem* **13** B1
Barahanagar *Kolkata* **14** B2
Barajas *Madrid* **17** B2
Barajas, Madrid ✈ (MAD) *Madrid* **17** B2
Barakpur *Kolkata* **14** A2
Barcarena *Lisbon* **16** A1
Barcarena, Rib. de → *Lisbon* **16** A1
Barcelona *Barcelona* **4** A2
Barcelona-Prat ✈ (BCN) *Barcelona* **4** B1
Barcroft, L. *Washington* **33** B3
Barking *London* **15** A4
Barkingside *London* **15** A4
Barnes *London* **15** B2
Barnet *London* **15** A2
Barra Andai *Karachi* **13** B2
Barra Funda *São Paulo* **27** B2
Barracas *Buenos Aires* **7** B2
Barrackpur = Barakpur *Kolkata* **14** A2
Barranco *Lima* **14** B2
Barreiro *Lisbon* **16** B2
Barreto *Rio de Janeiro* **25** B2
Bartala *Kolkata* **14** B1
Barton Park *Sydney* **29** B1
Bartyki *Warsaw* **32** C2
Basus *Cairo* **7** A2
Batanagar *Kolkata* **14** B1
Bath Beach *New York* **22** C1
Bath I. *Karachi* **13** B2
Batir *Jerusalem* **13** B1
Batok, Bukit *Singapore* **28** A2
Battersea *London* **15** B3
Bauman *Moscow* **19** B3
Baumgarten *Vienna* **32** A1
Bay, L. *Orlando* **23** A2
Bay Harbor Islands *Miami* **18** A2
Bay Hill *Orlando* **23** B1
Bay Ridge *New York* **22** C1
Bayit Va-Gan *Jerusalem* **13** B2
Bayonne *New York* **22** B1
Bayou Boeuf *New Orleans* **21** B1
Bayou Segnette State Park ⌓ *New Orleans* **21** B2
Bayrampaşa *Istanbul* **12** B1
Bayshore *San Francisco* **26** B2
Bayt Lahm *Jerusalem* **13** B2
Bayview *San Francisco* **26** B2
Bāzār *Tehran* **31** A2
Beacon Hill *Hong Kong* **12** A2
Beato *Lisbon* **16** A2
Beaumont *Dublin* **10** A2
Beaumonte Heights *Toronto* **31** A1
Bebek *Istanbul* **12** B2
Běchovice *Prague* **25** B3
Beck L. *Chicago* **9** A1
Beckenham *London* **15** B3
Beckton *London* **15** A4
Becontree *London* **15** A4
Beddington Corner *London* **15** B3
Bedford *Boston* **6** A1
Bedford Park *Chicago* **9** C2
Bedford Park *New York* **22** A2
Bedford Stuyvesant *New York* **22** B2
Bedford View *Johannesburg* **13** B2
Bedok *Singapore* **28** B3
Bedok, Res. *Singapore* **28** A3
Beersel *Brussels* **6** B1
Behala *Kolkata* **14** B1
Bei Hai *Beijing* **4** B2
Beicai *Shanghai* **28** B2
Beijing *Beijing* **4** B1
Beit Duqu *Jerusalem* **13** A1
Beit Ghur at-Taht *Jerusalem* **13** A1
Beit Ghur el-Fawqa *Jerusalem* **13** A1
Beit Hanina *Jerusalem* **13** B2
Beit Ij'za *Jerusalem* **13** A1
Beit Iksa *Jerusalem* **13** B2
Beit I'nan *Jerusalem* **13** A1
Beit Jala *Jerusalem* **13** B2
Beit Lekhem = Bayt Lahm *Jerusalem* **13** B2
Beit Liqya *Jerusalem* **13** A1
Beit Nekofa *Jerusalem* **13** B1
Beit Sahur *Jerusalem* **13** B2
Beit Sofafa *Jerusalem* **13** B2
Beit Surik *Jerusalem* **13** B1
Beit Ur al-Fawqa *Jerusalem* **13** A1
Beit Zayit *Jerusalem* **13** B1
Beitaipingzhuan *Beijing* **4** B1
Beitar Ilit *Jerusalem* **13** B1
Beitin *Jerusalem* **13** A2
Beitsun *Guangzhou* **11** B2
Beitunya *Jerusalem* **13** A2
Beixing Jing Park *Shanghai* **28** B1
Békásmegyer *Budapest* **7** A2
Bekkelaget *Oslo* **23** A3
Bekkestua *Oslo* **23** A2
Bel Air *Los Angeles* **16** B2
Bela Vista *São Paulo* **27** B2
Bélanger *Montreal* **20** A1
Belas *Lisbon* **16** A1
Beleghata *Kolkata* **14** B2
Belém *Lisbon* **16** A1
Belém, Torre de *Lisbon* **16** A1
Belènzinho *São Paulo* **27** B2
Belgachiya *Kolkata* **14** B2
Belgharia *Kolkata* **14** B2
Belgrano *Buenos Aires* **7** B2
Bell *Los Angeles* **16** C3
Bell Gardens *Los Angeles* **16** C4
Bellavista *Lima* **14** B2
Bellavista *Santiago* **27** C2
Belle Harbor *New York* **22** C2
Belle Isle *Orlando* **23** B2
Belle View *Washington* **33** B2
Bellingham *London* **15** B3
Bellwood *Chicago* **9** B1
Belmont *Boston* **6** A1
Belmont *London* **15** A2
Belmont, Mt. *Wellington* **33** B2
Belmont Cragin *Chicago* **9** B2
Belmont Harbor *Chicago* **9** B3
Belmore *Sydney* **29** B1
Belur *Kolkata* **14** B2
Belvedere *Atlanta* **3** B3
Belvedere *London* **15** B4
Belvedere *San Francisco* **26** A2
Belyayevo Bogorodskoye *Moscow* **19** C2
Bemowo *Warsaw* **32** B1
Benaki Museum *Athens* **2** B2
Bendale *Toronto* **31** A3
Benefica *Rio de Janeiro* **25** B1
Benfica *Lisbon* **16** A1
Benitez Int. ✈ (SCL) *Santiago* **27** B1
Benito Juárez, Int. ✈ (MEX) *Mexico City* **18** B2
Bensonhurst *New York* **22** C2
Berchem-Ste-Agathe *Brussels* **6** A1
Berg am Laim *Munich* **21** B2
Bergenfield *New York* **22** A2
Bergham *Munich* **21** B2
Bergvliet *Cape Town* **8** B1
Beri *Barcelona* **4** A1
Berkeley *San Francisco* **26** A3
Berlin *Berlin* **5** A3
Berlin Dom *Berlin* **5** A3
Berlin Tegel ✈ (TXL) *Berlin* **5** A2
Bermondsey *London* **15** B3
Bernabeu, Estadio *Madrid* **17** B1
Bernal Heights *San Francisco* **26** B2
Berwyn *Chicago* **9** B2
Berwyn Heights *Washington* **33** B4
Besiktas *Istanbul* **12** B2
Besós → *Barcelona* **4** A2
Bessie, L. *Orlando* **23** B1
Bet Horon *Jerusalem* **13** A1
Bethesda *Washington* **33** B3
Bethlehem = Bayt Lahm *Jerusalem* **13** B2
Bethnal Green *London* **15** A3
Betor *Kolkata* **14** B1
Beulah *Orlando* **23** A1
Beulah, L. *Orlando* **23** A1
Beverley Hills *Sydney* **29** B1
Beverley Park *Sydney* **29** B1
Beverly *Chicago* **9** C3
Beverly Arts Center *Chicago* **9** C2
Beverly Glen *Los Angeles* **16** B2
Beverly Hills *Los Angeles* **16** B2
Beverly Hills -Morgan Park Historic District *Chicago* **9** C2
Bexley *Sydney* **29** B1
Bexley □ *London* **15** B4
Bexleyheath *London* **15** B4
Beykoz *Istanbul* **12** B2
Beylerbeyi *Istanbul* **12** B2
Beyoğlu *Istanbul* **12** B1
Bezons *Paris* **24** A2
Bezuidenhout Park *Johannesburg* **13** B2
Bhadrakali *Kolkata* **14** A2
Bhalswa *Delhi* **10** A2
Bhambo Khan Qarmati *Karachi* **13** B2
Bhatsala *Kolkata* **14** B1
Bhawanipur *Kolkata* **14** B2
Bhendkhal *Mumbai* **20** B2
Bhuleshwar *Mumbai* **20** B1
Białołeka Dworska *Warsaw* **32** B2
Bicentennial Park *Los Angeles* **16** B4
Bicentennial Park *Sydney* **29** B1
Bickley *London* **15** B4
Bicutan *Manila* **17** C2
Bidhan Nagar *Kolkata* **14** B2
Bidu *Jerusalem* **13** B1
Bielany *Warsaw* **32** B1
Bielawa *Warsaw* **32** C2
Biesdorf *Berlin* **5** A4
Bièvre → *Paris* **24** B1
Bièvres *Paris* **24** B2
Big Sand Lake *Orlando* **23** B2
Bilston *Edinburgh* **11** B2
Binacayan *Manila* **17** C1
Binondo *Manila* **17** B1
Bintaro Jaya *Jakarta* **12** B1
Bir Nabala *Jerusalem* **13** A2
Birak el Kiyam *Cairo* **7** A1
Birch Cliff *Toronto* **31** A3
Birkenstein *Berlin* **5** A5
Birkholz *Berlin* **5** A4
Birkholzaue *Berlin* **5** A4
Birrarrung Park *Melbourne* **18** A2
Biscayne Park *Miami* **18** A2
Bishop Lavis *Cape Town* **8** A2
Bishopscourt *Cape Town* **8** A1
Bispebjerg *Copenhagen* **8** A3
Bissonet Plaza *New Orleans* **21** A1
Bittsevsky Forest Park *Moscow* **19** C2
Björknas *Stockholm* **29** B3
Black Cr. → *Toronto* **31** A2
Black Creek Pioneer Village *Toronto* **31** A1
Blackfen *London* **15** B4
Blackheath *London* **15** B4
Blackrock *Dublin* **10** B2
Bladensburg *Washington* **33** B4
Blair Village *Atlanta* **3** C2
Blairgowrie *Johannesburg* **13** A2
Blake House *Boston* **6** B2
Blakehurst *Sydney* **29** B1
Blakstad *Oslo* **23** B1
Blanche, L. *Orlando* **23** B1
Blankenburg *Berlin* **5** A3
Blankenfelde *Berlin* **5** A3
Blizne *Warsaw* **32** B1
Blota *Warsaw* **32** C3
Blue Island *Chicago* **9** D2
Blue Mosque = Sultanahme Camil *Istanbul* **12** B1
Bluebell *Dublin* **10** B1
Bluff Hd. *Hong Kong* **12** B2
Bluffers Park *Toronto* **31** A3
Blumberg *Berlin* **5** A4
Blunt Pt. *San Francisco* **26** A2
Blutenberg *Munich* **21** B1
Blylaget *Oslo* **23** B3
Boa Vista, Alto do *Rio de Janeiro* **25** B1
Boardwalk *New York* **22** C3
Boavista *Lisbon* **16** A2
Bobigny *Paris* **24** A3
Bocanegra *Lima* **14** B2
Boedo *Buenos Aires* **7** B2
Bogenhausen *Munich* **21** B2
Bogorodskoye *Moscow* **19** B3
Bogota *New York* **22** A1
Bogstadvatnet *Oslo* **23** A2
Bohnsdorf *Berlin* **5** B4
Bois-Colombes *Paris* **24** A2
Bois-d'Arcy *Paris* **24** B1
Boissy-St-Léger *Paris* **24** B4
Boldinasco *Milan* **19** B1
Bøler *Oslo* **23** A4
Bollate *Milan* **19** A1
Bollebeek *Brussels* **6** A1
Bollensdorf *Berlin* **5** A5
Bollmora *Stockholm* **29** B3
Bolshaya Okhta *St. Petersburg* **27** B2
Bolton *Atlanta* **3** B2
Bom Retiro *São Paulo* **27** B2
Bombay = Mumbai *Mumbai* **20** B2
Bondi *Sydney* **29** B2
Bondy *Paris* **24** A3
Bondy, Forêt de *Paris* **24** A4
Bonifacio Monument *Manila* **17** B1
Bonnabel Place *New Orleans* **21** A2
Bonneuil-sur-Marne *Paris* **24** B4
Bonnington *Edinburgh* **11** B1
Bonnyrigg and Lasswade *Edinburgh* **11** B3
Bonsucesso *Rio de Janeiro* **25** B1
Bonteheuwel *Cape Town* **8** A2
Boo *Stockholm* **29** A3
Booterstown *Dublin* **10** B2
Borisovo *Moscow* **19** C3
Borle *Mumbai* **20** A2
Boronia Park *Sydney* **29** A1
Bosmont *Johannesburg* **13** B1
Bosön *Stockholm* **29** A3
Bosporus = İstanbul Boğazı *Istanbul* **12** B2
Bostancı *Istanbul* **12** C2
Boston *Boston* **6** A2
Boston Common *Boston* **6** A2
Boston Logan Int. ✈ (BOS) *Boston* **6** A2
Botafogo *Rio de Janeiro* **25** B1
Botany *Sydney* **29** B2
Botany B. *Sydney* **29** B2
Botany Bay △ *Sydney* **29** B2
Botič → *Prague* **25** B3
Botica Sete *Lisbon* **16** A1
Boucherville *Montreal* **20** A3
Boucherville, Îs. de *Montreal* **20** A3
Bougival *Paris* **24** A1
Boulder Pt. *Hong Kong* **12** B1
Boulogne, Bois de *Paris* **24** A2
Boulogne-Billancourt *Paris* **24** A2
Bourg-la-Reine *Paris* **24** B2
Bouviers *Paris* **24** B1
Bovenkerk *Amsterdam* **2** B2
Bovenkerker Polder *Amsterdam* **2** B2
Bovisa *Milan* **19** A2
Bow *London* **15** A3
Boyacıköy *Istanbul* **12** B2
Boyd Conservation Area *Toronto* **31** A1
Boyle Heights *Los Angeles* **16** B3
Braepark *Edinburgh* **11** B2
Braid *Edinburgh* **11** B2
Bramley *Johannesburg* **13** A2
Brandeis Univ. *Boston* **6** A1
Brandenburger Tor *Berlin* **5** A3
Brani, Pulau *Singapore* **28** B3
Branik *Prague* **25** B2
Brännkyrka *Stockholm* **29** B2
Brás *São Paulo* **27** B2
Brasilândia *São Paulo* **27** A1
Brateyevo *Moscow* **19** C3
Braybrook *Melbourne* **18** A1
Brázdim *Prague* **25** A3
Breakheart Reservation *Boston* **6** A2
Brede *Copenhagen* **8** A3
Breezy Point *New York* **22** C2
Breitenlee *Vienna* **32** A3
Breña *Lima* **14** B2
Brent □ *London* **15** A2
Brent Res. *London* **15** A2
Brentford *London* **15** B2
Brentwood *Los Angeles* **16** B2
Brentwood Park *Los Angeles* **16** B2
Brera *Milan* **19** B2
Bresso *Milan* **19** A2
Brevik *Stockholm* **29** A3
Břevnov *Prague* **25** B2
Brickyard, The *Chicago* **9** B2
Bridge City *New Orleans* **21** B2
Bridgeport *Chicago* **9** B3
Bridgetown *Cape Town* **8** A2
Bridgeview *Chicago* **9** C2
Brighton *Boston* **6** A2
Brighton *Melbourne* **18** B1
Brighton Beach *New York* **22** C2
Brighton-Le-Sands *Sydney* **29** B1
Brighton Park *Chicago* **9** C2
Brightwood *Washington* **33** B3
Brigittenau *Vienna* **32** A2
Brimbank Park *Melbourne* **18** A1
Brisbane *San Francisco* **26** B2
Britz *Berlin* **5** B3
Brixton *London* **15** B3
Broadmeadows *Melbourne* **18** A1
Broadmoor *San Francisco* **26** B2
Broadview *Chicago* **9** B1
Brockley *London* **15** B3
Bródno *Warsaw* **32** B2
Bródnowski, Kanal *Warsaw* **32** B2
Broek *Amsterdam* **2** A2
Bromley □ *London* **15** B4
Bromley Common *London* **15** B4
Bromma *Stockholm* **29** A1
Bromma ✈ (BMA) *Stockholm* **29** A1
Brøndby Strand *Copenhagen* **8** B2
Brøndbyøster *Copenhagen* **8** B2
Brøndbyvester *Copenhagen* **8** B2
Brondesbury *London* **15** A2
Brønnøya *Oslo* **23** A2
Brønshøj *Copenhagen* **8** A2
Bronxville *New York* **22** A3
Brookfield *Chicago* **9** C1
Brookhaven *Atlanta* **3** A2
Brookline *Boston* **6** B2
Brooklyn *Cape Town* **8** A1
Brooklyn *New York* **22** C2
Brooklyn *Wellington* **33** B1
Brooklyn Heights *New York* **22** B2
Brookmont *Washington* **33** B3
Brossard *Montreal* **20** B3
Brou-sur-Chantereine *Paris* **24** A4
Brown *Toronto* **31** A3
Broyhill Park *Washington* **33** B2
Brughério *Milan* **19** A2
Brunswick *Melbourne* **18** A1
Brussegem *Brussels* **6** A1
Brussel *Brussels* **6** A2
Brussel ✈ (BRU) *Brussels* **6** A2
Brussels = Brussel *Brussels* **6** A2
Bruxelles = Brussel *Brussels* **6** A2
Bruzzano *Milan* **19** A2
Bry-sur-Marne *Paris* **24** A4
Bryan, L. *Orlando* **23** B2
Bryanston *Johannesburg* **13** A1
Bryn *Oslo* **23** A1
Brzeziny *Warsaw* **32** B2
Bubeneč *Prague* **25** B2
Buc *Paris* **24** B1
Buchenhain *Munich* **21** B1
Buchholz *Berlin* **5** A3
Buckhead *Atlanta* **3** A2
Buckingham Palace *London* **15** A3
Buckow *Berlin* **5** B3
Bucktown *New Orleans* **21** A2
Buda *Budapest* **7** A2
Buda Castle = Budaváripalota *Budapest* **7** A2
Budafok *Budapest* **7** B2
Budaörs *Budapest* **7** B1
Budapest *Budapest* **7** B2
Budapest ✈ (BUD) *Budapest* **7** B3
Budatétény *Budapest* **7** B2
Budaváripalota *Budapest* **7** A2
Buddinge *Copenhagen* **8** A3
Buena Vista *San Francisco* **26** B2
Buenos Aires *Buenos Aires* **7** B2
Buenos Aires Ezeiza ✈ (EZE) *Buenos Aires* **7** C1
Bufalotta *Rome* **26** B2
Bugio *Lisbon* **16** B1
Buiksloot *Amsterdam* **2** A2
Buitenveldert *Amsterdam* **2** B2
Buizingen *Brussels* **6** B1
Bukhansan *Seoul* **27** B1
Bukit Panjang Nature Reserve *Singapore* **28** A2
Bukit Timah Nature Reserve *Singapore* **28** A2
Bukum, Pulau *Singapore* **28** B2
Bûlâq *Cairo* **7** A2
Bule *Manila* **17** C2
Bulim *Singapore* **28** A2
Bullen Park *Melbourne* **18** A2
Bund, The *Shanghai* **28** B1
Bundoora North *Melbourne* **18** A2
Bundoora Park *Melbourne* **18** A2
Bunker Hill Memorial *Boston* **6** A2
Bunker I. *Karachi* **13** B1
Bunkyō *Tokyo* **30** A3
Bunnefjorden *Oslo* **23** A3
Buona Vista Park *Singapore* **28** B2
Burbank *Chicago* **9** C2
Burbank *Los Angeles* **16** A3
Burden, L. *Orlando* **23** B1
Burlington *Boston* **6** A1
Burnham Park *Chicago* **9** C3
Burnham Park Harbor *Chicago* **9** B3
Burnhamthorpe *Toronto* **31** B1
Burnt Oak *London* **15** A2
Burntisland *Edinburgh* **11** A2
Burnwynd *Edinburgh* **11** B1
Burqa *Jerusalem* **13** A2
Burtus *Cairo* **7** A1
Burudvatn *Oslo* **23** A2
Burwood *Sydney* **29** B1
Bushwick *New York* **22** B2
Bushy Park *London* **15** B1
Butantã *São Paulo* **27** B1
Butcher I. *Mumbai* **20** B2
Butler, L. *Orlando* **23** B1
Butts Corner *Washington* **33** C2
Büyükdere *Istanbul* **12** B2
Byculla *Mumbai* **20** B2
Bygdøy *Oslo* **23** A3
Bywater *New Orleans* **21** B2

C

C.B.S. Fox Studios *Los Angeles* **16** B2
C.N.N. Center *Atlanta* **3** B2
C.N. Tower *Toronto* **31** B2
Caballito *Buenos Aires* **7** B2
Cabin John *Washington* **33** B2
Cabin John Regional Park ⌓ *Washington* **33** A2
Cabinteely *Dublin* **10** B3
Cabra *Dublin* **10** A2
Cabuçú de Baixo → *São Paulo* **27** A1
Cabuçú de Cima → *São Paulo* **27** A2
Cachan *Paris* **24** B2
Cachoeira, Rib. da → *São Paulo* **27** B1
Cacilhas *Lisbon* **16** A2
Cahuenga Park *Los Angeles* **16** B3
Cain, L. *Orlando* **23** B2
Cairo = El Qâhira *Cairo* **7** A2
Cairo Int. ✈ (CAI) *Cairo* **7** A3
Caju *Rio de Janeiro* **25** B1
Čakovice *Prague* **25** B3
Calcutta = Kolkata *Kolkata* **14** B2
California Inst. of Tech. *Los Angeles* **16** B4
California Los Angeles, Univ. of *Los Angeles* **16** B2
California State Univ. *Los Angeles* **16** B3
Callao *Lima* **14** B2
Caloocan *Manila* **17** B1
Calumet L. *Chicago* **9** C3
Calumet Park *Chicago* **9** C3
Calumet Sag Channel → *Chicago* **9** C2
Calvairate *Milan* **19** B2
Camarate *Lisbon* **16** A2
Camaroes *Lisbon* **16** A1
Camberwell *London* **15** B3
Camberwell *Melbourne* **18** B2
Cambridge *Boston* **6** A2

Cambuci *São Paulo* 27 B2
Camden □ *London* 15 A3
Cameron, Mt. *Wellington* 33 B2
Çamlıca *Istanbul* 12 B2
Camp Springs *Washington* 33 C4
Campamento *Madrid* 17 B1
Campbellfield *Melbourne* 18 A1
Camperdown *Sydney* 29 B2
Campo, Casa de *Madrid* 17 B1
Campo F.C. Barcelona
　Barcelona 4 A1
Campo Grando *Lisbon* 16 A2
Campo Pequeño *Lisbon* 16 A2
Campolide *Lisbon* 16 A2
Camps Bay *Cape Town* 8 A1
C'an San Joan *Barcelona* 4 A2
Cañacao B. *Manila* 17 C1
Canarsie *New York* 22 C2
Candiac *Montreal* 20 B3
Caneças *Lisbon* 16 A1
Canillas *Madrid* 17 B2
Canillejas *Madrid* 17 B2
Canning Town *London* 15 A4
Canteras de Vallecas
　Madrid 17 B2
Canterbury *Melbourne* 18 A2
Canterbury *Sydney* 29 B1
Canton = Guangzhou
　Guangzhou 11 B2
Caohejing *Shanghai* 28 B1
Capão Redondo *São Paulo* 27 B1
Caparica *Lisbon* 16 A2
Caparica, Costa da *Lisbon* 16 B1
Cape Flats *Cape Town* 8 B2
Cape Town *Cape Town* 8 A1
Cape Town Int. ✈ (CPT)
　Cape Town 8 A2
Capitol Heights *Washington* 33 B4
Captain Cook Bridge
　Sydney 29 C2
Captain Cook Landing
　Place Park *Sydney* 29 C2
Capuchos *Lisbon* 16 B1
Carabanchel Alto *Madrid* 17 B1
Carabanchel Bajo *Madrid* 17 B1
Carapachay *Buenos Aires* 7 B2
Caraza *Buenos Aires* 7 C2
Caridad *Manila* 17 C1
Carioca, Sa. da *Rio de Janeiro* 25 B1
Carlstadt *New York* 22 A1
Carlton *Melbourne* 18 A1
Carmen de Huechuraba
　Santiago 27 B1
Carmen de la Legua *Lima* 14 B2
Carnaxide *Lisbon* 16 A1
Carnegie *Melbourne* 18 B2
Carnide *Lisbon* 16 A1
Carol City *Miami* 18 A1
Carrascal *Santiago* 27 B2
Carrickmines *Dublin* 10 B3
Carrières-sous-Bois *Paris* 24 A1
Carrières-sous-Poissy *Paris* 24 A1
Carrières-sur-Seine *Paris* 24 A2
Carrigeen B. *Dublin* 10 A3
Cartierville *Montreal* 20 A1
Casa Loma *Toronto* 31 A2
Casa Verde *São Paulo* 27 B1
Casál Morena *Rome* 26 C2
Casalotti *Rome* 26 B1
Cascade Heights *Atlanta* 3 B2
Castèl di Leva *Rome* 26 C2
Castèl Sant'Angelo *Rome* 26 B1
Castleknock *Dublin* 10 A1
Castleton Corners *New York* 22 C1
Cataouatche, L. *New Orleans* 21 B1
Catete *Rio de Janeiro* 25 B1
Catford *London* 15 B3
Catherine, L. *Orlando* 23 B2
Caulfield *Melbourne* 18 B2
Cavite *Manila* 17 C1
Caxias *Lisbon* 16 A1
Cebecci *Istanbul* 12 B1
Cecchignola *Rome* 26 C2
Cecilienhof, Schloss *Berlin* 5 B1
Cedar Grove *Atlanta* 3 C3
Cedarvale Park *Toronto* 31 A2
Cempaka Putih *Jakarta* 12 B2
Çengelköy *Istanbul* 12 B2
Cengkareng *Jakarta* 12 A1
Centennial Olympic Park
　Atlanta 3 B2
Centennial Park *Sydney* 29 B2
Center Hill *Atlanta* 3 B2
Centocelle *Rome* 26 B2
Central, Gare *Montreal* 20 B2
Central Park *New York* 22 B2
Century City *Los Angeles* 16 B2
Cerdanyola del Vallès
　Barcelona 4 A1
Cerillos *Santiago* 27 B1
Cerro de la Estrella △
　Mexico City 18 B2
Cerro de los Angeles *Madrid* 17 C1
Cerro Navia *Santiago* 27 B1
Cesano Boscone *Milan* 19 B1
Cesate *Milan* 19 A1
Cha Kwo Ling *Hong Kong* 12 B2
Chacarrita *Buenos Aires* 7 B2
Chadwell Heath *London* 15 A4
Chai Chee *Singapore* 28 B3
Chai Wan *Hong Kong* 12 B2
Chai Wan Kok *Hong Kong* 12 A1
Chakdaha *Kolkata* 14 B1
Chamartin *Madrid* 17 B1
Chamberí *Madrid* 17 B1
Chambourcy *Paris* 24 A1
Champigny-sur-Marne
　Paris 24 B4
Champlain, Pont *Montreal* 20 B2
Champs-sur-Marne *Paris* 24 A4
Chamrail *Kolkata* 14 B1
Chanakyapuri *Delhi* 10 B2
Chanditala *Kolkata* 14 A1
Changfeng Park *Shanghai* 28 B1
Changhai = Shanghai
　Shanghai 28 B1
Changi *Singapore* 28 A3
Changi, Singapore ✈
　(SIN) *Singapore* 28 A3
Changning *Shanghai* 28 B1
Changtereine *Paris* 24 A3
Chantian *Guangzhou* 11 A2
Chaoyang *Beijing* 4 B2
Chaoyangmen *Beijing* 4 B2
Chapelzoal *Dublin* 10 A1
Chapultepec, Bosque de
　Mexico City 18 B1
Chapultepec, Castillo de
　Mexico City 18 B2
Charenton-le-Pont *Paris* 24 B3
Charleroi, Kanal de ➝
　Brussels 6 B1
Charles Bridge = Karlův
　most *Prague* 25 B2
Charles Dawes
　House *Chicago* 9 A2
Charlottenburg *Berlin* 5 A2
Charlottenburg, Schloss
　Berlin 5 A2
Charlottenlund *Copenhagen* 8 A3

Charlton *London* 15 B4
Charneca *Lisbon* 16 A2
Charneca *Lisbon* 16 A2
Chase, L. *Orlando* 23 B1
Châteaufort *Paris* 24 B1
Châtenay-Malabry *Paris* 24 B2
Chatham *Chicago* 9 C3
Châtillon *Paris* 24 B2
Chatou *Paris* 24 A1
Chatpur *Kolkata* 14 B2
Chatswood *Sydney* 29 A2
Chatuchak *Bangkok* 3 B2
Chatuchak Park *Bangkok* 3 B2
Chauki *Karachi* 13 A1
Chavarria *Lima* 14 B2
Chaville *Paris* 24 B2
Chayang *Seoul* 27 B2
Chelles *Paris* 24 A4
Chelles, Canal de *Paris* 24 A4
Chells-le-Pin ✈ *Paris* 24 A4
Chelsea *Boston* 6 A2
Chelsea *London* 15 B2
Chembur *Mumbai* 20 A2
Chengshuoi *Beijing* 4 C2
Chennevières-sur-Marne
　Paris 24 B4
Cheongdam *Seoul* 27 B2
Cheonho *Seoul* 27 B2
Cheops *Cairo* 7 B1
Chertanovka ➝ *Moscow* 19 C2
Chertanovo *Moscow* 19 C2
Cheryomushki *Moscow* 19 B2
Chestnut Hill *Boston* 6 B1
Cheung Sha Wan
　Hong Kong 12 A1
Cheverly *Washington* 33 B4
Chevilly-Larue *Paris* 24 B3
Cheviot Hills *Los Angeles* 16 B2
Chevy Chase *Washington* 33 B3
Chhatrapati Shivaji,
　Mumbai ✈ (BOM)
　Mumbai 20 A2
Chia Keng *Singapore* 28 A3
Chiaravalle Milanese *Milan* 19 B2
Chicago *Chicago* 9 B2
Chicago, Univ. of *Chicago* 9 C3
Chicago Harbor *Chicago* 9 B3
Chicago Lawn *Chicago* 9 C2
Chicago-Midway ✈
　(MDW) *Chicago* 9 C2
Chicago O'Hare Int. ✈
　(ORD) *Chicago* 9 B1
Chicago Ridge *Chicago* 9 C2
Chicago River, North
　Branch ➝ *Chicago* 9 B2
Chicago Sanitary and Ship
　Canal *Chicago* 9 C2
Chicago State Univ. *Chicago* 9 C3
Chicago Zoo *Chicago* 9 B1
Chienzui *Guangzhou* 11 B2
Chik Sha *Hong Kong* 12 B2
Child's Hill *London* 15 A2
Chile, Univ. de *Santiago* 27 B2
Chilla Saroda *Delhi* 10 B2
Chillum *Washington* 33 B4
Chilly-Mazarin *Paris* 24 B2
Chingupota *Kolkata* 14 C1
Chinna Cr. ➝ *Karachi* 13 B2
Chiquihuite, Cerro
　Mexico City 18 A2
Chislehurst *London* 15 B4
Chiswick *London* 15 B2
Chiswick House *London* 15 B2
Chitose *Tokyo* 30 B2
Chitralada Palace *Bangkok* 3 B2
Chiyoda *Tokyo* 30 A3
Choa Chu Kang *Singapore* 28 A2
Chodov u Prahy *Prague* 25 B3
Chōfu *Tokyo* 30 B2
Choisy-le-Roi *Paris* 24 B3
Chok Chey *Orlando* 23 B2
Chom Thong *Bangkok* 3 B1
Chong Pang *Singapore* 28 A2
Chongwen *Beijing* 4 B2
Chorrillos *Lima* 14 C2
Chotupice *Prague* 25 C2
Chowpatty Beach *Mumbai* 20 B1
Christianshavn *Copenhagen* 8 A3
Chrzanów *Warsaw* 32 B1
Chuen Lung *Hong Kong* 12 A1
Chuk Kok *Hong Kong* 12 A2
Chulalongkorn Univ.
　Bangkok 3 B2
Chūō *Tokyo* 30 A3
Church End *London* 15 A2
Church of our Lady =
　Frauenkirche *Munich* 21 B2
Churchtown *Dublin* 10 B2
Ciampino *Rome* 26 C2
Ciampino ✈ (CIA) *Rome* 26 C2
Cicero *Chicago* 9 B2
Cilandak *Jakarta* 12 B1
Cilincing *Jakarta* 12 A2
Ciliwung ➝ *Jakarta* 12 B2
Čimice *Prague* 25 B2
Cinecittà *Rome* 26 B2
Cinisello Bálsamo *Milan* 19 A2
Cinkota *Budapest* 7 A3
Cipete *Jakarta* 12 B1
Citta degli Studi *Milan* 19 B2
Città del Vaticano =
　Vatican City ■ *Rome* 26 B1
Cities, The *London* 15 A2
City Hall = Rådhus *Oslo* 23 A3
City Hall = Stadshuset
　Stockholm 29 B2
City of the Dead *Cairo* 7 A2
City Park *New Orleans* 21 A2
City Terrace *Los Angeles* 16 B3
Ciudad de México
　Mexico City 18 B2
Ciudad Deportiva
　Mexico City 18 B2
Ciudad Fin de Semana
　Madrid 17 B2
Ciudad General Belgrano
　Buenos Aires 7 C1
Ciudad Lineál *Madrid* 17 B2
Ciudad Satélite *Mexico City* 18 A1
Ciudad Universitaria
　Buenos Aires 7 B1
Ciudad Universitaria
　Mexico City 18 C1
Claireville Res. *Toronto* 31 A1
Clamart *Paris* 24 B2
Clapham *London* 15 B3
Clapton *London* 15 A3
Claremont *Cape Town* 8 A1
Clayhall *London* 15 A4
Clear, L. *Orlando* 23 A2
Clermiston *Edinburgh* 11 B2
Clichy *Paris* 24 A2
Clichy-sous-Bois *Paris* 24 A4
Cliffside *Toronto* 31 A3
Cliffside Park *New York* 22 B1
Clifton *Cape Town* 8 A1
Clifton *New York* 22 C1
Clifton *Karachi* 13 B2
Clifton Beach *Karachi* 13 B2
Cliftondale *Boston* 6 A2
Cloghran *Dublin* 10 A2
Clonskeagh *Dublin* 10 B2

Clontarf *Dublin* 10 A2
Clontarf *Sydney* 29 A2
Clovelly *Sydney* 29 B2
Cobras, I. das *Rio de Janeiro* 25 B2
Coburg *Melbourne* 18 A1
Cocotá *Rio de Janeiro* 25 A1
Cœuilly *Paris* 24 B4
Coker *Lagos* 14 B2
Colaba *Mumbai* 20 B1
Colaba Pt. *Mumbai* 20 B1
Colegiales *Buenos Aires* 7 B2
Colindale *London* 15 A2
Colinton *Edinburgh* 11 B2
College Park *Atlanta* 3 C2
College Point *New York* 22 B2
Collégien *Paris* 24 A4
Collier Row *London* 15 A4
Colliers Wood *London* 15 B2
Colma *San Francisco* 26 B2
Colney Hatch *London* 15 A3
Cologno Monzese *Milan* 19 A2
Colombes *Paris* 24 A2
Colonia Güell *Barcelona* 4 A1
Colonial Knob *Wellington* 33 A1
Colosseo = Colosseum
　Rome 26 B1
Colosseum = Colosseo
　Rome 26 B1
Combault *Paris* 24 B4
Comércio, Praça do *Lisbon* 16 A2
Commerce *Los Angeles* 16 B4
Conceição, I. da
　Rio de Janeiro 25 B2
Conchali *Santiago* 27 B2
Concord *Sydney* 29 B1
Concord *Toronto* 31 A2
Concorde, Place de la *Paris* 24 A2
Concorezzo *Milan* 19 A2
Condet *Jakarta* 12 B2
Coney Island *New York* 22 C2
Congonhas *São Paulo* ✈
　(CGH) *São Paulo* 27 B2
Conley ➝ *Atlanta* 3 C2
Connaught Place *Delhi* 10 B2
Consolação *São Paulo* 27 B2
Constantia *Cape Town* 8 B1
Constitución *Buenos Aires* 7 B2
Constitution *Atlanta* 3 B2
Convention Center
　Los Angeles 16 B2
Conway *Orlando* 23 B2
Conway, L. *Orlando* 23 B2
Coogee *Sydney* 29 B2
Cooksville *Toronto* 31 B1
Coolock *Dublin* 10 A2
Copacabana *Rio de Janeiro* 25 B1
Copenhagen =
　København *Copenhagen* 8 A2
Copenhagen ✈
　St. Petersburg 27 B1
Coral Gables *Miami* 18 B1
Coral Hills *Washington* 33 B4
Corcovado, Cristo
　Redentor *Rio de Janeiro* 25 B1
Corduff *Dublin* 10 A1
Cormano *Milan* 19 A2
Cornaredo *Milan* 19 A1
Córsico *Milan* 19 B1
Corstorphine *Edinburgh* 11 B2
Corviale *Rome* 26 B1
Coslada *Madrid* 17 B2
Cossigny *Paris* 24 B4
Cotao *Lisbon* 16 A1
Côte-St-Luc *Montreal* 20 B2
Cotunduba, I. de
　Rio de Janeiro 25 B2
Coubron *Paris* 24 A4
Countryside *Chicago* 9 C1
County Art Museum
　Los Angeles 16 B2
Courbevoie *Paris* 24 A2
Courtry *Paris* 24 A4
Cowley *London* 15 A1
Coyoacán *Mexico City* 18 B2
Craighall Park *Johannesburg* 13 A2
Craiglockhart *Edinburgh* 11 B2
Craigmillar *Edinburgh* 11 B3
Cramond *Edinburgh* 11 B2
Cramond, River *Edinburgh* 11 B2
Cramond I. *Edinburgh* 11 B2
Cranford *London* 15 B1
Crawford *Cape Town* 8 A2
Crayford *London* 15 B5
Creekmouth *London* 15 A4
Crescent, L. *Orlando* 23 A1
Crescenzago *Milan* 19 A2
Cresseliy *Paris* 24 B1
Cresskill *New York* 22 A2
Créteil *Paris* 24 B3
Cricklewood *London* 15 A2
Cristo Redentor,
　Corcovado *Rio de Janeiro* 25 B1
Crockenhill *London* 15 B4
Croissy-Beaubourg *Paris* 24 B4
Croissy-sur-Seine *Paris* 24 A1
Crosby *Johannesburg* 13 B1
Crosne *Paris* 24 B3
Cross I. *Mumbai* 20 B2
Crouch End *London* 15 A3
Crown Mine *Johannesburg* 13 B1
Crows Nest *Sydney* 29 B2
Croydon *London* 15 B3
Croydon Park *Sydney* 29 B1
Cruagh Mt. *Dublin* 10 B2
Crumlin *Dublin* 10 B2
Cruz de Pau *Lisbon* 16 B2
Crystal Palace *London* 15 B3
Csepel *Budapest* 7 B2
Csepelsziget *Budapest* 7 B2
Csillaghegy *Budapest* 7 A2
Csillagtelep *Budapest* 7 B2
Csömör *Budapest* 7 A3
Csömöri-patak ➝ *Budapest* 7 A3
Cuatro Vientos *Madrid* 17 B1
Cuauhtémoc *Mexico City* 18 B2
Cuban Museum *Miami* 18 B2
Cubao *Manila* 17 B2
Çubuklu *Istanbul* 12 B2
Cudahy *Los Angeles* 16 C3
Cuicuilco, Pirámide de
　Mexico City 18 C1
Culmore *Washington* 33 B3
Culver City *Los Angeles* 16 B2
Cupecê ➝ *São Paulo* 27 B1
Currie *Edinburgh* 11 B2
Cusago *Milan* 19 B1
Cusano Milanino *Milan* 19 A2
Cutler Park *Boston* 6 B1
Çuvuşabaşi ➝ *Istanbul* 12 B1
Cuwei *Beijing* 4 B2
Cypress Hills *New York* 22 B2
Cypress Park *Los Angeles* 16 B3
Czernikówów *Warsaw* 32 B2
Czyste *Warsaw* 32 B1

D

Da Mooca ➝ *São Paulo* 27 B2
Ďáblice *Prague* 25 B2
Ďabrowa *Warsaw* 32 B1
Dachang *Shanghai* 28 B1

Dachang ✈ *Shanghai* 28 B1
Dachau *Munich* 21 A1
Dachau-Ost *Munich* 21 A1
Dachauer Moos *Munich* 21 A1
Dadar *Mumbai* 20 A1
Daebang *Seoul* 27 B1
Daechi *Seoul* 27 B2
Dafni *Athens* 2 B1
Dagenham *London* 15 A4
Daglfing *Munich* 21 B2
Dahab, Gezîret el *Cairo* 7 B2
Daheisha *Jerusalem* 13 B2
Dahlem *Berlin* 5 B2
Dahlwitz-Hoppegarten
　Berlin 5 A5
Dahongmen *Beijing* 4 C2
Dajiaoting *Beijing* 4 B2
Dakhnoye *St. Petersburg* 27 C1
Dalejsky potok ➝ *Prague* 25 B2
Dalgety Bay *Edinburgh* 11 A1
Dalkeith *Edinburgh* 11 B3
Dalkey *Dublin* 10 B3
Dalkey I. *Dublin* 10 B3
Dallgow *Berlin* 5 A1
Dalmeny *Edinburgh* 11 B1
Dalston *London* 15 A3
Daly City *San Francisco* 26 B2
Damaia *Lisbon* 16 A1
Damarakia *Athens* 2 B1
Dämeritzsee *Berlin* 5 B5
Dan Ryan Woods *Chicago* 9 C2
Danderhall *Edinburgh* 11 B3
Danderyd *Stockholm* 29 A2
Danforth *Toronto* 31 A3
Darakeh *Tehran* 31 A2
Darband *Tehran* 31 A2
Darling Point *Sydney* 29 B2
Darndale *Dublin* 10 A2
Darrûs *Tehran* 31 A2
Dartford *London* 15 B5
Dashi *Guangzhou* 11 B2
Datansha *Guangzhou* 11 B2
Datun *Beijing* 4 B2
Daulatpur *Delhi* 10 A1
Dāvüdiyeh *Tehran* 31 A2
Davydkovo *Moscow* 19 B1
Dawidy *Warsaw* 32 C1
Daxing *Beijing* 4 C2
Days Bay *Wellington* 33 B2
Decatur *Atlanta* 3 B3
Dedham *Boston* 6 B1
Degunino *Moscow* 19 A2
Deir Dibwan *Jerusalem* 13 A2
Deir Ibzi'e *Jerusalem* 13 A1
Dejvice *Prague* 25 B2
Dekabristov, Ostrov
　St. Petersburg 27 B1
Del Rey *Los Angeles* 16 C2
Delhi *Delhi* 10 B2
Delhi Indira Gandhi Int. ✈
　(DEL) *Delhi* 10 B1
Demarest *New York* 22 A2
Den Ilp *Amsterdam* 2 A2
Denistone Heights *Sydney* 29 A1
Dentonia Park *Toronto* 31 A3
DePaul Univ. *Chicago* 9 B3
Deptford *London* 15 B3
Des Plaines *Chicago* 9 A1
Desert Wetlands Park
　Las Vegas 14 B2
Deutsche Oper *Berlin* 5 A2
Deutsches Museum *Munich* 21 B2
Devil's Peak *Cape Town* 8 A1
Dhakuria *Kolkata* 14 B2
Dharavi *Mumbai* 20 A2
Diadema *São Paulo* 27 C2
Diegen *Brussels* 6 A2
Diemen *Amsterdam* 2 A2
Diepkloof *Johannesburg* 13 B1
Dieprivier *Cape Town* 8 B1
Difficult Run ➝
　Washington 33 B2
Dilbeek *Brussels* 6 A1
Dilli = Delhi *Delhi* 10 B2
Dirnismaning *Munich* 21 A2
Disney-M.G.M. Studios
　Orlando 23 B1
Disney Studios *Los Angeles* 16 B3
District Heights *Washington* 33 B4
Djakarta = Jakarta *Jakarta* 12 B1
Djurshólm *Stockholm* 29 A2
Döberitz *Berlin* 5 A1
Döbling *Vienna* 32 A2
Dobong *Seoul* 27 B1
Dobongsan *Seoul* 27 B1
Docklands *London* 15 A3
Doctor Phillips *Orlando* 23 B1
Dodder ➝ *Dublin* 10 B2
Dodger Stadium *Los Angeles* 16 B3
Dogs, Isle of *London* 15 B3
Dogo Ozero *St. Petersburg* 27 A1
Dollis Hill *London* 15 A2
Dollymount *Dublin* 10 A2
Dolni *Prague* 25 B3
Dolni Chabry *Prague* 25 B2
Dolni Počernice *Prague* 25 B3
Dolphins Barn *Dublin* 10 B2
Dom Pedro II, Parque
　São Paulo 27 B2
Don Mills *Toronto* 31 A3
Don Muang Int. ✈ (BKK)
　Bangkok 3 A2
Donaghmede *Dublin* 10 A3
Donau-Oder Kanal *Vienna* 32 A3
Donaufeld *Vienna* 32 A2
Donaupark *Vienna* 32 A2
Donaustadt *Vienna* 32 A2
Dongan Hills *New York* 22 C1
Dongcheng *Beijing* 4 B2
Dongdaemung *Seoul* 27 B2
Donggou *Shanghai* 28 B2
Dongjiak *Seoul* 27 B1
Dongjiao *Guangzhou* 11 B2
Dongri *Mumbai* 20 B2
Dongshanhu Park
　Guangzhou 11 B2
Dongzhimen *Beijing* 4 B2
Donnybrook *Dublin* 10 B2
Doornfontein *Johannesburg* 13 B2
Dorchester *Boston* 6 B2
Dorchester B. *Boston* 6 B2
Dorchester Heights Nat.
　Historical Site △ *Boston* 6 B2
Dornach *Munich* 21 B3
Dorval Int., Montréal ✈
　(YUL) *Montreal* 20 B2
Dos Moninos ➝ *São Paulo* 27 C2
Douglas Park *Chicago* 9 B2
Dover Heights *Sydney* 29 B2
Dowlatābād *Tehran* 31 B2
Down, L. *Orlando* 23 A1
Downey *Los Angeles* 16 C4
Downsview *Toronto* 31 A2
Dragør *Copenhagen* 8 B3
Drancy *Paris* 24 A3
Dranesville *Washington* 33 A1
Drapetsona *Athens* 2 B1

Drewnica *Warsaw* 32 B2
Drigh Road *Karachi* 13 A2
Drimnagh *Dublin* 10 B2
Drogenbos *Brussels* 6 B1
Druid Hills *Atlanta* 3 B2
Drumcondra *Dublin* 10 A2
Drummoyne *Sydney* 29 B1
Drylaw *Edinburgh* 11 B2
Dubeč *Prague* 25 B3
Dublin *Dublin* 10 A2
Dublin ✈ (DUB) *Dublin* 10 A1
Dublin B. *Dublin* 10 A2
Dublin Harbour *Dublin* 10 A2
Duddingston *Edinburgh* 11 B3
Dugnano *Milan* 19 A1
Duivendrecht *Amsterdam* 2 B2
Dūlāb *Tehran* 31 A2
Dulles Int. ✈ (IAD)
　Washington 33 B1
Dulwich *London* 15 B3
Dum Dum *Kolkata* 14 B2
Dum Dum Int. ✈ (CCU)
　Kolkata 14 B2
Dumont *New York* 22 A2
Dún Laoghaire *Dublin* 10 B3
Dundrum *Dublin* 10 B2
Dunearn *Singapore* 28 B2
Dúnleary = Dún
　Laoghaire *Dublin* 10 B3
Dunn Loring *Washington* 33 B2
Dunning *Chicago* 9 B2
Dunvegan *Johannesburg* 13 A2
Duomo *Milan* 19 B2
Duque de Caxias
　Rio de Janeiro 25 A1
Duren Sawit *Jakarta* 12 A2
Dusit *Bangkok* 3 B2
Dworp *Brussels* 6 B1
Dyakovo *Moscow* 19 B2
Dyker Beach Park
　New York 22 C1
Dzerzhinskiy *Moscow* 19 B2
Dzerzhinskiy Park *Moscow* 19 B2

E

E.U.R. = Esposizione
　Universale di Roma
　Rome 26 C1
Eagle Rock *Los Angeles* 16 B3
Ealing □ *London* 15 A2
Earlsfield *London* 15 B2
Earlwood *Sydney* 29 B1
Engenho, I. do *Rio de Janeiro* 25 B2
Englewood *Chicago* 9 C3
Englewood *New York* 22 A2
Englewood Park *Chicago* 9 B2
Englewood Cliffs *New York* 22 A2
Enmore *Sydney* 29 B1
Enterprise *Las Vegas* 14 B1
Entrevias *Madrid* 17 B1
Epcot *Orlando* 23 B1
Epping *Sydney* 29 A1
Erenköy *Istanbul* 12 C2
Erith *London* 15 B5
Erlaa *Vienna* 32 B1
Ermington *Sydney* 29 A1
Ermita *Madrid* 17 B1
Ershanou *Guangzhou* 11 B2
Erskineville *Sydney* 29 B2
Erunkan *Lagos* 14 B2
Erzsébet-Telep *Budapest* 7 B3
Eschenried *Munich* 21 A1
Esenler *Istanbul* 12 B1
Esher *London* 15 B1
Eskbank *Edinburgh* 11 B3
Esplugas *Barcelona* 4 A1
Esposizione Universale di
　Roma *Rome* 26 C1
Essendon *Melbourne* 18 A1
Essendon ✈ (MEB)
　Melbourne 18 A1
Essingen *Stockholm* 29 B1
Essling *Vienna* 32 A3
Est, Gare de l' *Paris* 24 A3
Estado, Parque do *São Paulo* 27 B2
Estelle *New Orleans* 21 B1
Estrela, Basilica da *Lisbon* 16 A2
Etobicoke *Toronto* 31 B1
Etobicoke Cr. ➝ *Toronto* 31 B1
Etterbeek *Brussels* 6 B2
Eung-am *Seoul* 27 B1
Eunpyeong *Seoul* 27 B1
Evanston *Chicago* 9 A2
Even Sapir *Jerusalem* 13 B1
Evere *Brussels* 6 A2
Everett *Boston* 6 A2
Evergreen Park *Chicago* 9 C2
Evin *Tehran* 31 A2
Ewu *Lagos* 14 A1
Exhibition Place *Toronto* 31 B2
Eyüp *Istanbul* 12 B1
Ezeiza ✈ (EZE) *Buenos Aires* 7 C1

F

Fabour, Mt. *Singapore* 28 B2
Faelledparken *Copenhagen* 8 A3
Fågelön *Stockholm* 29 B1
Fagersjö *Stockholm* 29 C2
Fairfax *New York* 22 A4
Fairfax Station *Washington* 33 C2
Fairland *Johannesburg* 13 A1
Fairmilehead *Edinburgh* 11 B2
Fairmount Heights
　Washington 33 B4
Fairport *Toronto* 31 A4
Fairview *New York* 22 B1
Fairview, L. *Orlando* 23 A2
Falenty *Warsaw* 32 C1
Faliro, Órmos *Athens* 2 B2
Falkenburg *Berlin* 5 A4
Falkenhagen *Berlin* 5 A1
Falkensee *Berlin* 5 A1
Falls Church *Washington* 33 B3
Falomo *Lagos* 14 B2
False Bay *Cape Town* 8 B2
Fangcun *Guangzhou* 11 B2
Farāḥābād *Tehran* 31 A2
Farmingham *London* 15 B5
Farsta *Stockholm* 29 C2
Fasanerie-Nord *Munich* 21 A2
Fasangarten *Munich* 21 B2
Fatih *Istanbul* 12 B1
Favoriten *Vienna* 32 B2
Fawkner *Melbourne* 18 A1
Fawkner Park *Melbourne* 18 B1
FedEx Stadium *Washington* 33 B4
Feijó *Lisbon* 16 A2
Feldkirchen *Munich* 21 B3
Feltham *London* 15 B1
Fener *Istanbul* 12 B1
Fenerbahçe *Istanbul* 12 C2
Fengtai *Beijing* 4 C1
Fengtai Stadium *Beijing* 4 B1
Ferencváros *Budapest* 7 B2

Ferihegy, Budapest ✈
　(BUD) *Budapest* 7 B3
Ferndale *Johannesburg* 13 A2
Fichtenau *Berlin* 5 B5
Field Museum of Natural
　History *Chicago* 9 C3
Fields Corner *Boston* 6 B2
Fiera Camp *Milan* 19 B1
Figino *Milan* 19 B1
Fijir *Baghdad* 3 A2
Filadélfia *Athens* 2 A2
Fili-Mazilovo *Moscow* 19 B1
Filothei *Athens* 2 A2
Finchley *London* 15 A2
Fine Arts, Museum of *Boston* 6 A2
Finglas *Dublin* 10 A2
Finsbury *London* 15 A3
Finsbury Park *London* 15 A3
Fiorito *Buenos Aires* 7 C2
Fischerhäuser *Munich* 21 A3
Fisher Island *Miami* 18 B2
Fishermans Bend *Melbourne* 18 A1
Fisherville *Toronto* 31 A2
Fisksätra *Stockholm* 29 B3
Fitzroy Gardens *Melbourne* 18 A1
Five Cowrie Cr. ➝ *Lagos* 14 B2
Five Dock *Sydney* 29 B1
Fjellstrand *Oslo* 23 B2
Flamengo *Rio de Janeiro* 25 B1
Flamingo *Orlando* 23 B2
Flaminio *Rome* 26 B1
Flaskebekk *Oslo* 23 A2
Flatbush *New York* 22 C2
Flaten *Stockholm* 29 B2
Flatlands *New York* 22 C2
Flemington Racecourse
　Melbourne 18 A1
Flint Pk. *Los Angeles* 16 B3
Florence *Los Angeles* 16 C3
Florence Bloom Bird
　Sanctuary ○
　Johannesburg 13 A2
Florentia *Johannesburg* 13 B2
Flores *Buenos Aires* 7 B2
Flores, Mercado de
　Mexico City 18 C2
Floresta *Buenos Aires* 7 B1
Florida *Buenos Aires* 7 B2
Florida *Johannesburg* 13 B1
Floridsdorf *Vienna* 32 A2
Flushing *New York* 22 B3
Flushing Meadows
　Corona Park *New York* 22 B3
Flysta *Stockholm* 29 A1
Fo Tan *Hong Kong* 12 A1
Foggy Bottom *Washington* 33 B3
Föhrenhain *Vienna* 32 A3
Fontainebleau *Johannesburg* 13 A1
Fontenay-aux-Roses *Paris* 24 B2
Fontenay-le-Fleury *Paris* 24 A1
Fontenay-sous-Bois *Paris* 24 A3
Foots Cray *London* 15 B4
Footscray *Melbourne* 18 A1
Forbidden City = Imperial
　Palace Museum *Beijing* 4 B2
Forest Brussels 6 B1
Forest Gate *London* 15 A4
Forest Heights *Washington* 33 C3
Forest Hill *London* 15 B3
Forest Hill *Toronto* 31 A2
Forest Hills *New York* 22 B2
Forest Park *Chicago* 9 B2
Forest View *Chicago* 9 C2
Forestville *Washington* 33 B4
Fornebu *Oslo* 23 A2
Foro Romano *Rome* 26 B1
Forstenried *Munich* 21 B1
Forstenrieder Park *Munich* 21 B1
Fort Mumbai *Mumbai* 20 B2
Fort Dupont Park
　Washington 33 B4
Fort Foote Village
　Washington 33 C3
Fort Lee *New York* 22 B1
Fort Road Bridge *Edinburgh* 11 A3
Forth Road Bridge
　Edinburgh 11 A1
Foshan *Guangzhou* 11 B2
Fôt *Budapest* 7 A3
Fourqueux *Paris* 24 A1
Fox Studios *Sydney* 29 B2
Foxrock *Dublin* 10 B2
Franconia *Washington* 33 C3
Frank Lloyd Wright Home
　Chicago 9 B2
Frankel *Singapore* 28 B3
Franklin Park *Boston* 6 B2
Franklin Park *Chicago* 9 B1
Franklin Park *Washington* 33 B3
Franklin Res. *Los Angeles* 16 B2
Franz Josef Strauss ✈
　(MUC) *Munich* 21 A3
Frauenkirche *Munich* 21 B2
Fredriksberg *Copenhagen* 8 A3
Frederiksdal *Copenhagen* 8 A3
Fredersdorf *Berlin* 5 A5
Freguesia *Rio de Janeiro* 25 A1
Freidrichshain, Volkspark
　Berlin 5 A3
Freiham *Munich* 21 B1
Freimann *Munich* 21 A2
Fresh Ponds *New York* 22 B2
Fresh Pond Reservation ○
　Boston 6 A1
Fresnes *Paris* 24 B2
Freudenau *Vienna* 32 A2
Friarstown *Dublin* 10 B1
Friedenau *Berlin* 5 B3
Friedrichsfelde *Berlin* 5 A4
Friedrichshagen *Berlin* 5 B4
Friedrichshain *Berlin* 5 A3
Friedrichslust *Berlin* 5 A5
Friherrs *Helsinki* 11 B1
Friluffs Museum *Helsinki* 11 B2
Frontón, I. *Lima* 14 C1
Frunze *Moscow* 19 B2
Fuchū *Tokyo* 30 A1
Fuencarral *Madrid* 17 B1
Fuenlabrada *Madrid* 17 C1
Fukagawa *Tokyo* 30 A4
Fukushima *Osaka* 23 A1
Fulham *London* 15 B2
Funabori *Tokyo* 30 A4
Fundão, I. do *Rio de Janeiro* 25 B1
Fünfhaus *Vienna* 32 A2
Fureso *Copenhagen* 8 A2
Fürth *Munich* 21 B2
Futago-tamagawaen *Tokyo* 30 B2
Fuxing Dao *Shanghai* 28 B2
Fuxing Park *Shanghai* 28 B1
Fuxinglu *Beijing* 4 B1

G

G. Ross Lord Park *Toronto* 31 A2
Gaebong *Seoul* 27 C1
Gage Park *Chicago* 9 C2
Gagny *Paris* 24 A4

Galata *Istanbul* 12 B1
Galata Tower *Istanbul* 12 B1
Galatsi *Athens* 2 A2
Galeão, Int. de ✈ (GIG)
　Rio de Janeiro 25 B1
Galyanovo *Moscow* 19 B3
Gambir *Jakarta* 12 A1
Gamboa *Rio de Janeiro* 25 B1
Gambolóita *Milan* 19 B2
Gamlebyen *Oslo* 23 A3
Gangdong *Seoul* 27 B2
Gangnam *Seoul* 27 B2
Gangseo *Seoul* 27 B1
Gangtou *Guangzhou* 11 A1
Gangwei *Guangzhou* 11 B2
Ganjiakou *Beijing* 4 B1
Ganshoren *Brussels* 6 A1
Gants Hill *London* 15 A4
Gaoqiao *Shanghai* 28 B2
Garbagnate Milanese *Milan* 19 A1
Garbatella *Rome* 26 B2
Garches *Paris* 24 A2
Garching *Munich* 21 A3
Garden City *Cairo* 7 A2
Garden Reach *Kolkata* 14 B1
Garder *Oslo* 23 A2
Garfield *New York* 22 A1
Garfield Park *Chicago* 9 B2
Gargareta *Athens* 2 B2
Garibong *Seoul* 27 C1
Garvanza *Los Angeles* 16 B3
Gâshaga *Stockholm* 29 A3
Gateway △ *New York* 22 C2
Gateway of India *Mumbai* 20 B2
Gatow *Berlin* 5 B1
Gavà *Barcelona* 4 B1
Gavamar *Barcelona* 4 B1
Gávea *Rio de Janeiro* 25 B1
Gávea, Pedra da
　Rio de Janeiro 25 B1
Gazdagrét *Budapest* 7 B1
Gaziosmanpaşa *Istanbul* 12 B1
Gebel el Ahmar *Cairo* 7 A2
Gebel el Muqattam *Cairo* 7 A2
Gebel el Tura *Cairo* 7 B2
Gebelgasteig *Munich* 21 B2
Geiselgasteig *Munich* 21 B2
General San Martín
　Buenos Aires 7 B2
Gennevilliers *Paris* 24 A2
Gentilly *New Orleans* 21 A2
Gentilly *Paris* 24 B2
Gentofte *Copenhagen* 8 A3
Genval *Brussels* 6 B2
George I. *Hong Kong* 12 B1
Georges River Bridge
　Sydney 29 C1
Georgetown *Washington* 33 B3
Georgia Dome *Atlanta* 3 B2
Gerasdorf bei Wien *Vienna* 32 A2
Gerberau *Munich* 21 A1
Gerli *Buenos Aires* 7 C2
Germiston *Johannesburg* 13 B2
Gern *Munich* 21 B2
Getafe *Madrid* 17 C1
Getty Center, The
　Los Angeles 16 B2
Geunjeong *Seoul* 27 C1
Geva Binyamin *Jerusalem* 13 A2
Geylang Serai *Singapore* 28 B3
Gharapuri *Mumbai* 20 B2
Gharb = Shahrak-e Qods
　Tehran 31 A2
Ghatkopar *Mumbai* 20 A2
Ghazipur *Delhi* 10 B2
Ghizri *Karachi* 13 B2
Ghizri Cr. ➝ *Karachi* 13 B2
Ghonda *Delhi* 10 A2
Ghusuri *Kolkata* 14 B2
Gianicolense *Rome* 26 B1
Giant Wheel = Riesenrad
　Vienna 32 A2
Gibraltar Pt. *Toronto* 31 B2
Gidea Park *London* 15 A5
Giesing *Munich* 21 B2
Gilmerton *Edinburgh* 11 B3
Gilo *Jerusalem* 13 B2
Gimmersta *Stockholm* 29 B3
Ginza *Tokyo* 30 A3
Giv'at Ram *Jerusalem* 13 B2
Giv'at Ye'arim *Jerusalem* 13 B1
Giv'at Ze'ev *Jerusalem* 13 A2
Giv'on *Jerusalem* 13 A2
Giza = El Gîza *Cairo* 7 A2
Giza Pyramids *Cairo* 7 B1
Gjersjøen *Oslo* 23 B3
Gladesville *Sydney* 29 B1
Gladsaxe *Copenhagen* 8 A2
Glasnevin *Dublin* 10 A2
Glassmanor *Washington* 33 C4
Glasthule *Dublin* 10 B3
Glen Iris *Melbourne* 18 B2
Glen Mar Park *Washington* 33 B3
Glen Rouge Park *Toronto* 31 A4
Glenanden *Washington* 33 B4
Glenasmole Reservoirs
　Dublin 10 B1
Glencorse Res. *Edinburgh* 11 B2
Glenculien *Dublin* 10 B2
Glendale *Los Angeles* 16 B3
Glendoo Mt. *Dublin* 10 B2
Glenhuntly *Melbourne* 18 B2
Glenside *Wellington* 33 B1
Glenview *Chicago* 9 A1
Glenview Countryside
　Chicago 9 A2
Glenvista *Johannesburg* 13 B2
Glifada *Athens* 2 B2
Glostrup *Copenhagen* 8 B2
Gogar *Edinburgh* 11 B2
Göktürk *Istanbul* 12 B1
Golabári *Kolkata* 14 B2
Golabki *Warsaw* 32 B1
Gold Coast *Chicago* 9 B3
Golden Gate *San Francisco* 26 B2
Golden Gate = *San Francisco* 26 B2
Golden Gate Bridge
　San Francisco 26 B2
Golden Gate Park
　San Francisco 26 B2
Golden Horn = Haliç
　Istanbul 12 B1
Golders Green *London* 15 A2
Golestan Palace *Tehran* 31 A2
Gollans Stream ➝
　Wellington 33 B2
Gongneung *Seoul* 27 B2
Goodmayes *London* 15 A4
Goodwood *Cape Town* 8 A2
Gopalpur *Kolkata* 14 B2
Görce *Warsaw* 32 B1
Gore Hill *Sydney* 29 A2
Gorelyy ➝ *St. Petersburg* 27 B2
Gorgie *Edinburgh* 11 B2
Gorky Park *Moscow* 19 B2
Gosen *Berlin* 5 B5
Gosener kanal *Berlin* 5 B5
Gospel Oak *London* 15 B2
Gotanda *Tokyo* 30 B3
Goth Goli Mar *Karachi* 13 A2
Goth Sher Shah *Karachi* 13 A1

Gotha *Orlando* 23 A1
Gournay-sur-Marne *Paris* 24 A4
Governador, I. do
  Rio de Janeiro 25 A1
Governors I. *New York* 22 B1
Grabów *Warsaw* 32 C1
Grace, Mt. *Wellington* 33 B2
Gracefield *Wellington* 33 B2
Gràcia *Barcelona* 4 A2
Gräfelfing *Munich* 21 B1
Gragoatá *Rio de Janeiro* 25 B2
Grand Bazaar = Kapali
  Carsi Istanbul 12 B1
Grand Central Station
  New York 22 B2
Grand Palace *Bangkok* 3 B1
Grande Place *Brussels* 6 A2
Grankulla = Kauniainen
  Helsinki 11 B1
Grant Park *Chicago* 9 B3
Granton *Edinburgh* 11 B2
Grassy Park *Cape Town* 8 B2
Gratosóglio *Milan* 19 B2
Gratzwalde *Berlin* 5 B5
Gravesend *New York* 22 C2
Grazhdanka *St. Petersburg* 27 B2
Great Falls *Washington* 33 B2
Great Falls Park *Washington* 33 B2
Great Western Forum
  Los Angeles 16 C2
Greco *Milan* 19 A2
Green I. *Hong Kong* 12 B1
Green Point *Cape Town* 8 A1
Greenbelt *Washington* 33 A4
Greenbelt Park *Washington* 33 B4
Greenfield Park *Montreal* 20 B3
Greenford *London* 15 A1
Greenhill *London* 15 A2
Greenhills *Dublin* 10 B1
Greenwich □ *London* 15 B3
Greenwich Observatory
  London 15 B3
Greenwich Village
  New York 22 B2
Greenwood *Boston* 6 A2
Grefsen *Oslo* 23 A3
Gresham Park *Atlanta* 3 B2
Gretna *New Orleans* 21 B2
Gretna City Park
  New Orleans 21 B2
Greve Strand *Copenhagen* 8 B1
Griebnitzsee *Berlin* 5 B1
Griffith Park *Los Angeles* 16 B3
Grimbergen *Brussels* 6 A2
Grinzing *Vienna* 32 A2
Gröbenried *Munich* 21 A1
Grochów *Warsaw* 32 B2
Grodzisk *Warsaw* 32 B2
Groenendaal *Brussels* 6 B2
Grogol Petamburin *Jakarta* 12 A1
Gronsdorf *Munich* 21 B3
Gorud *Oslo* 23 A4
Gross-Glienicke *Berlin* 5 B1
Gross-Hadern *Munich* 21 B1
Gross-Lappen *Munich* 21 A2
Grosse Krampe *Berlin* 5 B5
Grosse Müggelsee *Berlin* 5 B4
Grosse Point Lighthouse
  Chicago 9 A2
Grossenzersdorf *Vienna* 32 A3
Grossenzersdorfer Arm →
  Vienna 32 A3
Grosser Biberhaufen *Vienna* 32 A2
Grosser Wannsee *Berlin* 5 B2
Grossfeld-Siedlung *Vienna* 32 A2
Grosshesselohe *Munich* 21 B2
Grossjedlersdorf *Vienna* 32 A2
Grossziethen *Berlin* 5 B3
Ground Zero *New York* 22 B1
Grove, The *Chicago* 9 A1
Grove Hall *Boston* 6 B2
Grove Park *Atlanta* 3 B2
Grove Park *London* 15 B4
Grove Park *London* 15 B2
Groveton *Washington* 33 C3
Grünau *Berlin* 5 B4
Grunewald *Berlin* 5 B2
Grünwald *Munich* 21 B2
Grünwalder Forst *Munich* 21 B2
Grymes Hill *New York* 22 C1
Guadalupe *Manila* 17 B2
Guadalupe, Basílica de
  Mexico City 18 B2
Guanabara, B. de
  Rio de Janeiro 25 B2
Guanabara, Jardim
  Rio de Janeiro 25 B2
Guanabara, Palácio da
  Rio de Janeiro 25 B1
Guang'anmen *Beijing* 4 B2
Guangqumen *Beijing* 4 B2
Guangzhou *Guangzhou* 11 B2
Guanshuo *Guangzhou* 11 B3
Gudö *Stockholm* 29 B3
Güell, Parque de *Barcelona* 4 A2
Guinardó *Barcelona* 4 A2
Gulbai *Karachi* 13 A1
Güngören *Istanbul* 12 B1
Gunnersbury *London* 15 B2
Guomao *Beijing* 4 B2
Gustavo A. Madero
  Mexico City 18 B2
Guttenberg *New York* 22 B1
Gutuyevskiy, Ostrov
  St. Petersburg 27 B1
Guyancourt *Paris* 24 B1
Gwanak *Seoul* 27 C1
Gwanaksan *Seoul* 27 C1
Gyál *Budapest* 7 B3
Gyáli-patak → *Budapest* 7 B2

H

Haaga *Helsinki* 11 B2
Haar *Munich* 21 B3
Habay *Manila* 17 C1
Hackbridge *London* 15 B3
Hackensack *New York* 22 A1
Hackensack → *New York* 22 B1
Hackney □ *London* 15 A3
Hackney Wick *London* 15 A3
Hadr, Warrâq el *Cairo* 7 A2
Haga *Stockholm* 29 A2
Hagenbrunn *Vienna* 32 A2
Hägersten *Stockholm* 29 B1
Häggvik *Stockholm* 29 A1
Hagonoy *Manila* 17 B2
Hague Park *Toronto* 31 A3
Haidari *Athens* 2 A1
Haidarpur *Delhi* 10 A1
Haidhausen *Munich* 21 B2
Haidian *Beijing* 4 B1
Haight-Ashbury
  San Francisco 26 B2
Hainault *London* 15 A4
Haizhou *Guangzhou* 11 B2
Haizhu Guangcheng
  Guangzhou 11 B2
Hakunila *Helsinki* 11 B3
Halandri *Athens* 2 A2

Halásztelek *Budapest* 7 B1
Haliç *Istanbul* 12 B1
Halim Perdana Kusuma
  Int. ✈ (HLP) *Jakarta* 12 B2
Halle *Brussels* 6 B1
Haltiala *Helsinki* 11 B2
Haltiavuori *Helsinki* 11 B2
Ham *London* 15 B2
Hämeenkylä *Helsinki* 11 B1
Hamme *Brussels* 6 A1
Hammarby *Stockholm* 29 B2
Hammersmith *London* 15 B2
Hampstead *London* 15 A2
Hampstead *Montreal* 20 B2
Hampstead Garden
  Suburb *London* 15 A2
Hampton *London* 15 B1
Hampton Court Palace
  London 15 B1
Hampton Wick *London* 15 B2
Hamrā' *Baghdad* 3 B1
Hanala *Helsinki* 11 A3
Haneda *Tokyo* 30 B3
Haneda, Tôkyô ✈ (HND)
  Tokyo 30 B3
Hang Hau *Hong Kong* 12 B2
Hanging Gardens *Mumbai* 20 B1
Hanlon *Toronto* 31 B1
Hanwell *London* 15 A1
Hanworth *London* 15 B1
Haora *Kolkata* 14 B1
Hapeville *Atlanta* 3 C2
Happy Valley *Hong Kong* 12 B2
Har Adar *Jerusalem* 13 B1
Har Gilo *Jerusalem* 13 B2
Har Homa *Jerusalem* 13 B2
Har Nof *Jerusalem* 13 B2
Harahan *New Orleans* 21 B1
Haren *Brussels* 6 A2
Hareskovby *Copenhagen* 8 A2
Haringey □ *London* 15 A3
Harjusuo *Helsinki* 11 B3
Harlaching *Munich* 21 B2
Harlaw Res. *Edinburgh* 11 B2
Harlem *New York* 22 B2
Harlesden *London* 15 A2
Harlington *London* 15 B1
Harmaja *Helsinki* 11 C2
Harmashatar hegy *Budapest* 7 A2
Harolds Cross *Dublin* 10 B2
Háros *Budapest* 7 B2
Harperrig Res. *Edinburgh* 11 B1
Harrow □ *London* 15 A1
Harrow on the Hill *London* 15 A1
Harrow School *London* 15 A1
Harrow Weald *London* 15 A1
Hartsfield-Atlanta Int. ✈
  (ATL) *Atlanta* 3 C2
Harumi *Tokyo* 30 B3
Harvard Univ. *Boston* 6 A1
Harvey *New Orleans* 21 B1
Harwood Heights *Chicago* 9 B2
Ijasanábád *Tehran* 31 A1
Hasbrouck Heights
  New York 22 A1
Haselhorst *Berlin* 5 B1
Haskôy *Istanbul* 12 B1
Hasle *Oslo* 23 A3
Haslum *Oslo* 23 A2
Hästhagen *Stockholm* 29 B2
Hataitai *Wellington* 33 B2
Hatch End *London* 15 A1
Hatiara *Kolkata* 14 B2
Hauketo *Oslo* 23 A3
Hauz Khas *Delhi* 10 B2
Havel → *Berlin* 5 B2
Havelkanal *Berlin* 5 A1
Havering □ *London* 15 A5
Havering-atte-Bower
  London 15 A5
Haworth *New York* 22 A2
Hawthorne Racecourse
  Chicago 9 C2
Hayes *London* 15 B4
Hayes *London* 15 A1
Hayes End *London* 15 A1
Hayford *Chicago* 9 C2
Haywards *Wellington* 33 A2
Heathfield *London* 15 B1
Heathrow, London ✈
  (LHR) *London* 15 B1
Hebe Haven *Hong Kong* 12 A2
Hedong *Guangzhou* 11 B2
Heidelberg Heights
  Melbourne 18 A2
Heidelberg West *Melbourne* 18 A2
Heidemühle *Berlin* 5 B5
Heideveld *Cape Town* 8 A2
Heiligensee *Berlin* 5 A2
Heiligenstadt *Vienna* 32 A2
Heinersdorf *Berlin* 5 A3
Hélène de Champlain,
  Parc △ *Montreal* 20 A2
Helenenhof *Stockholm* 29 A1
Heliopolis = Masr el
  Gedida *Cairo* 7 A2
Hellersdorf *Berlin* 5 A4
Hellerup *Copenhagen* 8 A3
Helsingfors = Helsinki
  Helsinki 11 B2
Helsinki *Helsinki* 11 B2
Helsinki-Vantaa ✈ (HEL)
  Helsinki 11 B2
Hen and Chicken B. *Sydney* 29 B1
Henderson *Las Vegas* 14 B2
Hendon *London* 15 A2
Hengsha *Guangzhou* 11 B2
Hennigsdorf *Berlin* 5 A2
Henryków *Warsaw* 32 B1
Henson Cr. → *Washington* 33 C4
Henttaa *Helsinki* 11 B1
Heping Park *Shanghai* 28 B2
Hepingli *Beijing* 4 B2
Herlev *Copenhagen* 8 A2
Herman Eckstein Park
  Johannesburg 13 A2
Hermannskogel *Vienna* 32 A1
Hermiston *Edinburgh* 11 B2
Hermitage and Winter
  Palace *St. Petersburg* 27 B2
Hermsdorf *Berlin* 5 A3
Hernals *Vienna* 32 A2
Herne Hill *London* 15 B3
Héroes de Churubusco
  Mexico City 18 B2
Herons, Î. aux *Montreal* 20 B2
Herstedøster *Copenhagen* 8 A2
Herttoniemi *Helsinki* 11 B3
Iļešárak *Tehran* 31 A2
Heston *London* 15 B1
Hetzendorf *Vienna* 32 B1
Hextable *London* 15 B5
Hialeah *Miami* 18 A1
Hiawassa, L. *Orlando* 23 A1
Hickory Hills *Chicago* 9 C1
Hiekkaharju *Helsinki* 11 B3
Hietaniemi *Helsinki* 11 B2
Hietzing *Vienna* 32 A1
Higashi *Osaka* 23 A2
Hidøvre *Oslo* 23 A3
Higashimurayama *Tokyo* 30 A3

Higashinari *Osaka* 23 A2
Higashisumiyoshi *Osaka* 23 B2
Higashiyodogawa *Osaka* 23 A1
High Park *Toronto* 31 B2
Highbury *London* 15 A3
Highgate *London* 15 A3
Highland Cr. → *Toronto* 31 A3
Highland Creek *Toronto* 31 A3
Highland Park *Los Angeles* 16 B3
Highlands North
  Johannesburg 13 A2
Hillcrest Heights
  Washington 33 C4
Hilled *Edinburgh* 11 A1
Hillingdon □ *London* 15 A1
Hillwood *Washington* 33 B3
Hilmîya *Cairo* 7 A2
Hin Keng *Hong Kong* 12 A2
Hirota *Osaka* 23 A1
Hirschstetten *Vienna* 32 A2
History Center *Atlanta* 3 B2
Hither Green *London* 15 B3
Hiyoshi *Tokyo* 30 B2
Hizma *Jerusalem* 13 B2
Hjortekær *Copenhagen* 8 A3
Hjortespring *Copenhagen* 8 A2
Hlubočepy *Prague* 25 B2
Ho Chung *Hong Kong* 12 A2
Hoboken *New York* 22 B1
Hobsons B. *Melbourne* 18 B1
Hochbrück *Munich* 21 A2
Hochelaga *Montreal* 20 A2
Hodgkins *Chicago* 9 C1
Hoegi *Seoul* 27 B2
Hoeilaart *Brussels* 6 B2
Hoffman I. *New York* 22 C1
Hohenbrunn *Munich* 21 B3
Hohenschönhausen *Berlin* 5 A4
Holargos *Athens* 2 A2
Holborn *London* 15 A3
Holden, L. *Orlando* 23 B2
Holešovice *Prague* 25 B2
Holland Village *Singapore* 28 B2
Höllriegelskreuth *Munich* 21 B1
Hollywood *Los Angeles* 16 B3
Hollywood Bowl *Los Angeles* 16 B2
Holmenkollen *Oslo* 23 A3
Holmes Run Acres
  Washington 33 B3
Holmgård *Stockholm* 29 B3
Holmlia *Oslo* 23 B3
Holocaust Memorial
  Jerusalem 13 B1
Holyrood House, Palace of
  Edinburgh 11 B3
Holysloot *Amsterdam* 2 A3
Homerton *London* 15 A3
Hometown *Chicago* 9 C2
Hônanchô *Tokyo* 30 A3
Honcho *Tokyo* 30 A3
Honden *Tokyo* 30 A4
Hondo, Rio → *Los Angeles* 16 B4
Hong Kong *Hong Kong* 12 B1
Hong Kong, Univ. of
  Hong Kong 12 B1
Hong Kong I. *Hong Kong* 12 B2
Hongje *Seoul* 27 B1
Hongjiao *Shanghai* 28 B1
Hongkou *Shanghai* 28 B1
Hongqiao *Shanghai* 28 B1
Honjyo *Tokyo* 30 A3
Honoré Mercier, Pont
  Montreal 20 B1
Hônow *Berlin* 5 A4
Hook *London* 15 B2
Horikiri *Tokyo* 30 A4
Horn Pond *Boston* 6 A1
Hornchurch *London* 15 A5
Horni *Prague* 25 B3
Horni Počernice *Prague* 25 B3
Hornsey *London* 15 A3
Horoměřice *Prague* 25 B1
Hortaleza *Madrid* 17 B2
Hosoyama *Tokyo* 30 B2
Hostafranchs *Barcelona* 4 A1
Hostivař *Prague* 25 B3
Houbětin *Prague* 25 B3
Houghton *Johannesburg* 13 B2
Houilles *Paris* 24 A2
Hounslow □ *London* 15 B1
Hout Bay *Cape Town* 8 B1
Hovedøya *Oslo* 23 A3
Hovik *Oslo* 23 A2
Honorčovice *Prague* 25 A3
Howard Beach *New York* 22 C2
Howrah = Haora *Kolkata* 14 B1
Howth *Dublin* 10 A3
Howth Hd. *Dublin* 10 A3
Höya *Tokyo* 30 A3
Hradčany *Prague* 25 B2
Huahuagang
  Mausoleum *Guangzhou* 11 B2
Huangpu *Shanghai* 28 B2
Huangpu Jiang → *Shanghai* 28 B1
Huangpu Park *Shanghai* 28 B1
Huascar *Lima* 14 A2
Huay Khwang *Bangkok* 3 B2
Huddinge *Stockholm* 29 B2
Huechuraba *Santiago* 27 B1
Huertas de San Beltran
  Barcelona 4 A1
Huizingen *Brussels* 6 B1
Humayun's Tomb *Delhi* 10 B2
Humber B. *Toronto* 31 A1
Humber B. *Toronto* 31 B2
Humber Bay Park *Toronto* 31 B2
Humber College *Toronto* 31 A1
Humber Summit *Toronto* 31 A1
Humber Valley Village
  Toronto 31 A1
Humberlea *Toronto* 31 A1
Humberwood Park *Toronto* 31 A1
Humboldt Park *Chicago* 9 B2
Humera *Madrid* 17 B1
Hunaydî *Baghdad* 3 B2
Hundige *Copenhagen* 8 B2
Hundige Strand *Copenhagen* 8 B2
Hung Hom *Hong Kong* 12 B2
Hunters Hill *Sydney* 29 B1
Hunters Valley *Washington* 33 B2
Huntington *Washington* 33 C3
Huntington Park
  Los Angeles 16 C3
Hurîya *Baghdad* 3 A1
Hurstville *Sydney* 29 B1
Husan *Jerusalem* 13 B1
Husby *Stockholm* 29 A2
Husum *Copenhagen* 8 A2
Hutt → *Wellington* 33 B2
Hütteldorf *Vienna* 32 A1
Hüvösvölgy *Budapest* 7 A2
Huwon Secret Garden *Seoul* 27 B1
Hvalstad *Oslo* 23 A1
Hvidøre *Copenhagen* 8 A3
Hwagok *Seoul* 27 B1

Hyattsville *Washington* 33 B4
Hyde Park *Boston* 6 B2
Hyde Park *Chicago* 9 C3
Hyde Park *Johannesburg* 13 A2
Hyde Park *London* 15 A2
Hyde Park *Los Angeles* 16 C3
Hyde Park *Sydney* 29 B2

I

Ibese *Lagos* 14 A2
Ibirapuera *São Paulo* 27 B1
Ibirapuera, Parque do
  São Paulo 27 B2
Icarai *Rio de Janeiro* 25 B2
Içerenköy *Istanbul* 12 C2
Ichgao *Tokyo* 30 B2
Ichigaya *Tokyo* 30 A3
Ichikawa *Tokyo* 30 A4
Ickenham *London* 15 A1
Iddo *Lagos* 14 B2
Idi-Oro *Lagos* 14 A2
Iganmu *Lagos* 14 B2
Igbobi *Lagos* 14 A2
Igbologun *Lagos* 14 B1
Igny *Paris* 24 B2
Ikebe *Tokyo* 30 B2
Ikebukuro *Tokyo* 30 A3
Ikegami *Tokyo* 30 B3
Ikeja *Lagos* 14 A2
Ikeuchi *Osaka* 23 B2
Ikoyi *Lagos* 14 B2
Ikuata *Lagos* 14 B2
Ikuno *Osaka* 23 A2
Ikuta *Tokyo* 30 B2
Ila *Oslo* 23 A2
Ilford *London* 15 A4
Ilioupoli *Athens* 2 B2
Imbâbah *Cairo* 7 A2
Imielin *Warsaw* 32 B2
Imirim *São Paulo* 27 A2
Imitos *Athens* 2 B2
Imitos, Oros *Athens* 2 B2
Imperial Palace Museum
  Beijing 4 B2
Inagi *Tokyo* 30 B2
Inchcolm *Edinburgh* 11 A2
Inchicore *Dublin* 10 A1
Inchkeith *Edinburgh* 11 A3
Inchmickery *Edinburgh* 11 A2
Incirano *Milan* 19 A1
Independencia *Lima* 14 A2
Independencia *Santiago* 27 B2
India Gate *Delhi* 10 B2
Indian Creek Village *Miami* 18 A2
Indianópolis *São Paulo* 27 B2
Indira Gandhi Int. ✈
  (DEL) *Delhi* 10 B1
Industria *Johannesburg* 13 B1
Industrial Canal
  New Orleans 21 A2
Inggerstrand *Oslo* 23 B3
Inglewood *Los Angeles* 16 C3
Ingliston *Edinburgh* 11 B1
Inhaúma *Rio de Janeiro* 25 B1
Inner Port Shelter
  Hong Kong 12 A2
Interlagos *São Paulo* 27 C1
Intramuros *Manila* 17 B1
Invalides *Paris* 24 A2
Inverkeithing *Edinburgh* 11 A1
Inzersdorf *Vienna* 32 B2
Ipanema *Rio de Janeiro* 25 B1
Ipiranga *São Paulo* 27 B2
Ipiranga → *São Paulo* 27 B2
Iponri *Lagos* 14 B2
Ireland's Eye *Dublin* 10 A3
Irving Park *Chicago* 9 B2
Isabel *Rio de Janeiro* 25 B1
Isagateko *Lagos* 14 A1
Isar → *Munich* 21 A2
Ishbilîya *Baghdad* 3 A2
Ishoi Strand *Copenhagen* 8 B2
Island Bay *Wellington* 33 B1
Island Park *Toronto* 31 B2
Islev *Copenhagen* 8 A2
Isleworth *London* 15 B2
Islington *Toronto* 31 B1
Islington □ *London* 15 A3
Ismaning *Munich* 21 A3
Ismayloskiy Park *Moscow* 19 B3
Isolo *Lagos* 14 A1
Issy-les-Moulineaux *Paris* 24 A2
İstanbul *Istanbul* 12 B1
İstanbul Boğaz *Istanbul* 12 B2
İstinye *Istanbul* 12 A2
İtä Hakkila *Helsinki* 11 B3
Itaewon *Seoul* 27 B1
Itami *Osaka* 23 A1
Itanhanga *Rio de Janeiro* 25 B1
Ivanhoe *Melbourne* 18 A2
Ivry-sur-Seine *Paris* 24 B3
Ixelles *Brussels* 6 A2
Izmaylovo *Moscow* 19 B3
Iztacalco *Mexico City* 18 B2
Iztapalapa *Mexico City* 18 B2

J

Jaba *Jerusalem* 13 A2
Jacaré *Rio de Janeiro* 25 B1
Jackson Heights *New York* 22 B2
Jackson Park *Chicago* 9 C3
Jacques-Cartier *Montreal* 20 A3
Jacques-Cartier, Pont
  Montreal 20 A2
Jadavpur *Kolkata* 14 B2
Jade Buddha Temple
  Shanghai 28 B1
Jægersborg *Copenhagen* 8 A3
Jægersborg Dyrehave
  Copenhagen 8 A3
Jagadishpur *Kolkata* 14 A1
Jagatpur *Delhi* 10 A2
Jaguaré, Rib. do →
  São Paulo 27 B1
Jahangirpur *Delhi* 10 A2
Jakarta *Jakarta* 12 A1
Jakarta, Teluk *Jakarta* 12 A1
Jakarta Hakim Perdana
  Kusuma Int. ✈ (HLP)
  Jakarta 12 B2
Jalan Kayu *Singapore* 28 A3
Jamaica *New York* 22 B2
Jamaica Plain *Boston* 6 B2
Jamakpuri *Delhi* 10 B1
Jamshîdîyeh *Tehran* 31 A2
Jamsil *Seoul* 27 B2
Jamwon *Seoul* 27 B2

Janki *Warsaw* 32 C1
Jaraguá *São Paulo* 27 A1
Jaraguá, Pico de *São Paulo* 27 A1
Jardim Paulista *São Paulo* 27 B1
Järvastättet *Stockholm* 29 A1
Jaskhar *Mumbai* 20 B2
Jatinegara *Jakarta* 12 B2
Javádíyeh *Tehran* 31 B2
Jaworowa *Warsaw* 32 C1
Jean Lafitte Nat. Historical
  Park △ *New Orleans* 21 B1
Jedlesee *Vienna* 32 A2
Jefferson *New Orleans* 21 B1
Jefferson Memorial
  Washington 33 B3
Jefferson Park *Chicago* 9 B2
Jefferson Park *Los Angeles* 16 B3
Jegi *Seoul* 27 B2
Jelambar *Jakarta* 12 A1
Jelonki *Warsaw* 32 B1
Jerónimos, Mosteiro dos
  Lisbon 16 A1
Jersey City *New York* 22 B1
Jerusalem *Jerusalem* 13 B2
Jessamine, L. *Orlando* 23 B2
Jésus, Î. *Montreal* 20 A2
Jesús Maria *Lima* 14 B2
Jette *Brussels* 6 A1
Jey *Tehran* 31 B2
Jiangqao *Guangzhou* 11 B1
Jiangwan *Shanghai* 28 B1
Jib *Jerusalem* 13 A2
Jingan *Shanghai* 28 B1
Jinočany *Prague* 25 B1
Jinonice *Prague* 25 B2
Jiulong = Kowloon
  Hong Kong 12 B1
Jiyūgaoka *Tokyo* 30 B3
Jîzah = Baghdad *Baghdad* 3 B2
Jízíra *Baghdad* 3 B2
Joglo *Jakarta* 12 B1
Johannesburg *Johannesburg* 13 B2
Johannesburg, Univ. of
  Johannesburg 13 B2
Johanneskirchen *Munich* 21 A2
Johannesstift *Berlin* 5 A2
Johannisthal *Berlin* 5 B4
John F. Kennedy Int. ✈
  New York 22 C3
John McLaren Park
  San Francisco 26 B2
Johnsonville *Wellington* 33 B1
Joinville-le-Pont *Paris* 24 B3
Joli-Bois *Brussels* 6 B2
Jollas *Helsinki* 11 B3
Jongmyo Royal Shrine
  Seoul 27 B1
Jongno *Seoul* 27 B1
Jonstrup *Copenhagen* 8 A2
Joppa *Edinburgh* 11 B3
Jorge Chavez, Int. ✈ (LIM)
  Lima 14 B2
Jorge Newbery ✈ (AEP)
  Buenos Aires 7 B2
Jósefa Piłsudskiego Park
  Warsaw 32 B1
Jôtô *Osaka* 23 A2
Jouy-en-Josas *Paris* 24 B2
Juan Anchorena
  Buenos Aires 7 B2
Juan Gonzales Romero
  Mexico City 18 A2
Juárez Int. ✈ (MEX)
  Mexico City 18 B2
Judeira *Jerusalem* 13 A2
Juhdum *Jerusalem* 13 B2
Jūjū *Tokyo* 30 A3
Jukskeirivier →
  Johannesburg 13 A2
Julianów *Warsaw* 32 B2
Jung *Seoul* 27 B1
Jungfernheide, Volkspark
  Berlin 5 A2
Jungfernsee *Berlin* 5 B1
Junghwa *Seoul* 27 B2
Jungnang *Seoul* 27 B2
Jungnangcheon → *Seoul* 27 B1
Junk B. *Hong Kong* 12 B2
Jurong *Singapore* 28 B2
Jurong, Selat *Singapore* 28 B2
Jurong Industrial Estate
  Singapore 28 B2
Jurujuba, Enseada de
  Rio de Janeiro 25 B2
Jûsô *Osaka* 23 A1
Justice *Chicago* 9 C2
Jwalahari *Delhi* 10 B1

K

Kaapstad = Cape Town
  Cape Town 8 A1
Kabaty *Warsaw* 32 C2
Kadıköy *Istanbul* 12 C2
Kadoma *Osaka* 23 A2
Kafr 'Aqab *Jerusalem* 13 A2
Kâğıthane *Istanbul* 12 B1
Kâğıthane → *Istanbul* 12 B1
Kagran *Vienna* 32 A2
Kahnawake *Montreal* 20 B1
Kaimes *Edinburgh* 11 B2
Kaiserebersdorf *Vienna* 32 B2
Kaivoksela *Helsinki* 11 B2
Kalamaki *Athens* 2 B2
Kalbadevi *Mumbai* 20 B1
Kalipur *Kolkata* 14 A1
Kalithea *Athens* 2 B1
Kalkaji *Delhi* 10 B2
Kalookan = Caloocan
  Manila 17 B1
Kalveboderne *Copenhagen* 8 B3
Kalvebod Fælled *Copenhagen* 8 B3
Kamarhati *Kolkata* 14 A2
Kamata *Tokyo* 30 B3
Kameido *Tokyo* 30 A4
Kameari *Tokyo* 30 A4
Kami-Itabashi *Tokyo* 30 A3
Kamikitazawa *Tokyo* 30 B3
Kamoshida *Tokyo* 30 B2
Kampong Landang
  Singapore 28 A3
Kampong Tanjong
  Penjuru *Singapore* 28 B2
Kampung Bali *Jakarta* 12 B1
Kanamori *Tokyo* 30 B1
Kanda *Tokyo* 30 A3
Kandilli *Istanbul* 12 B2
Kankurgachi *Kolkata* 14 A2
Kanonerskiy, Ostrov
  St. Petersburg 27 B1
Kansai Int. ✈ (KIX) *Osaka* 23 B1
Kanzaki → *Osaka* 23 A1
Kapali Carsi *Istanbul* 12 B1
Kapelleveld *Brussels* 6 A2
Kápolnásmegyer *Budapest* 7 A2

Kapotnya *Moscow* 19 C3
Käppala *Stockholm* 29 A3
Kapuk *Jakarta* 12 A1
Käpylä *Helsinki* 11 B2
Karachi *Karachi* 13 A2
Karachi Int. ✈ (KHI)
  Karachi 13 B2
Karkh *Baghdad* 3 A2
Karlın *Prague* 25 B2
Karlsfeld *Munich* 21 A1
Karlshorst *Berlin* 5 B4
Karlův most *Prague* 25 B2
Karol Bagh *Delhi* 10 B2
Karolinenhof *Berlin* 5 B4
Karori *Wellington* 33 B1
Karori *Wellington* 33 B1
Karow *Berlin* 5 A3
Karrâdah *Baghdad* 3 B2
Kârsôn *Stockholm* 29 B1
Kasai *Tokyo* 30 A4
Kasimpur *Kolkata* 14 A1
Kastrup *Copenhagen* 8 B3
Kastrup, København ✈
  (CPH) *Copenhagen* 8 B3
Kasuga *Tokyo* 30 A3
Kasuge *Tokyo* 30 A3
Kasumigaseki *Tokyo* 30 B3
Katong *Singapore* 28 B3
Katsushika *Tokyo* 30 A4
Kau Pai Chau *Hong Kong* 12 B2
Kau Yi Chau *Hong Kong* 12 B1
Kaulsdorf *Berlin* 5 B4
Kauniainen *Helsinki* 11 B1
Kawasaki *Tokyo* 30 B3
Kawawa *Tokyo* 30 B2
Kawęczyn *Warsaw* 32 B2
Kayu Putih *Jakarta* 12 B2
Kbely *Prague* 25 B3
Kebayoran Baru *Jakarta* 12 B1
Kebayoran Lama *Jakarta* 12 B1
Kebon Jeruk *Jakarta* 12 B1
Kedar *Jerusalem* 13 B2
Kedoya *Jakarta* 12 B1
Keilor *Melbourne* 18 A1
Keilor North *Melbourne* 18 A1
Keimola *Helsinki* 11 A1
Kelapa Gading *Jakarta* 12 A2
Kelenföld *Budapest* 7 B2
Kelvin *Johannesburg* 13 A2
Kemang *Jakarta* 12 B1
Kemayoran *Jakarta* 12 A2
Kemang → *São Paulo* 27 B2
Kemerburgaz *Istanbul* 12 B1
Kempton Park Races
  London 15 B1
Kenilworth *Cape Town* 8 A1
Kennedy Town *Hong Kong* 12 B1
Kenner *New Orleans* 21 A1
Kensal Green *London* 15 A2
Kensington *Johannesburg* 13 B2
Kensington *London* 15 B2
Kensington *New York* 22 C2
Kensington *Sydney* 29 B2
Kensington Palace *London* 15 A2
Kent Village *Washington* 33 B4
Kentish Town *London* 15 A3
Kenton *London* 15 A2
Kenwood House *London* 15 A3
Kepa *Warsaw* 32 B2
Keppel Harbour *Singapore* 28 B2
Kesariani *Athens* 2 B2
Kettering *Washington* 33 B5
Kew *Melbourne* 18 A2
Kew *London* 15 B2
Kew Gardens *London* 15 B2
Kew Gardens *Toronto* 31 B3
Key Biscayne *Miami* 18 B2
Khalîj *Baghdad* 3 B2
Khandallah *Wellington* 33 B1
Khansâ' *Baghdad* 3 A2
Kharavli *Mumbai* 20 B2
Khefren *Cairo* 7 B1
Khichripur *Delhi* 10 B2
Khidirpur *Kolkata* 14 B1
Khimki-Khovrino *Moscow* 19 A2
Khirbet Batin Abu Lihyah
  Jerusalem 13 A1
Khirbet el-Misbah *Jerusalem* 13 A1
Khirbet Jub e-Rum
  Jerusalem 13 B2
Khlong San *Bangkok* 3 B2
Khlong Toey *Bangkok* 3 B2
Khorel *Kolkata* 14 A1
Khorosovo *Moscow* 19 B2
Kiamari *Karachi* 13 B1
Kierling *Vienna* 32 A1
Kierlingbach → *Vienna* 32 A1
Kikuna *Tokyo* 30 B2
Kilbarrack *Dublin* 10 A3
Kilbirnie *Wellington* 33 B1
Kilburn *London* 15 A2
Kilkakee *Dublin* 10 B1
Kilester *Dublin* 10 A2
Killiney *Dublin* 10 B3
Killiney B. *Dublin* 10 B3
Kilmacud *Dublin* 10 B2
Kilmainham *Dublin* 10 A2
Kilmainham Gaol *Dublin* 10 A2
Kilmashogue Mt. *Dublin* 10 B2
Kilmore *Dublin* 10 A2
Kilnamanagh *Dublin* 10 B1
Kilo *Helsinki* 11 B1
Kilokri *Delhi* 10 B2
Kiltiernan *Dublin* 10 B2
Kimmage *Dublin* 10 B2
Kindi *Baghdad* 3 B1
Kinghorn *Edinburgh* 11 A2
Kings Domain *Melbourne* 18 B2
Kings Forest =
  Kongelunden *Copenhagen* 8 B3
Kings Park *Washington* 33 C2
Kings Park West
  Washington 33 C2
Kingsbury *London* 15 A2
Kingsbury *Melbourne* 18 A2
Kingsford *Sydney* 29 B2
Kingsford Smith,
  Sydney ✈ (SYD) *Sydney* 29 B2
Kingston-upon-Thames □
  London 15 B2
Kingston Vale *London* 15 B2
Kingsway *Toronto* 31 A1
Kinsaley *Dublin* 10 A3
Kipling Heights *Toronto* 31 A1
Kipseli *Athens* 2 B2
Kirchnorbach *Munich* 21 B3
Kirchtruderding *Munich* 21 B3
Kirikiri *Lagos* 14 B1
Kirke Værløse *Copenhagen* 8 A1
Kirkhill *Edinburgh* 11 B2
Kirkliston *Edinburgh* 11 B1
Kirknewton *Edinburgh* 11 B1
Kirov Palace of Culture
  St. Petersburg 27 B1
Kiryat Anavim *Jerusalem* 13 B1
Kiryat Ha Yovel *Jerusalem* 13 B1
Kısıklı *Istanbul* 12 B2
Kispest *Budapest* 7 B2
Kita *Osaka* 23 A1
Kita *Tokyo* 30 A3
Kitazawa *Tokyo* 30 B3

Kiu Tsiu *Hong Kong* 12 A2
Kivistö *Helsinki* 11 B1
Kızıltoprak *Istanbul* 12 C2
Kizuri *Osaka* 23 B2
Klampenborg *Copenhagen* 8 A3
Klečany *Prague* 25 A2
Kledering *Vienna* 32 B2
Klein Jukskei →
  Johannesburg 13 A1
Kleinmachnow *Berlin* 5 B2
Kleinschönebeck *Berlin* 5 B5
Klemetsrud *Oslo* 23 A4
Kličany *Prague* 25 A2
Kličany *Prague* 25 A2
Klipriversberg Nature
  Reserve *Johannesburg* 13 B2
Klosterneuburg *Vienna* 32 A1
Kôbánya *Budapest* 7 B2
Kobbegem *Brussels* 6 A1
Kôbánya → *Budapest* 7 B2
Kôbánya *Copenhagen* 8 A3
København ✈ (CPH)
  Copenhagen 8 B3
Kobylisy *Prague* 25 B2
Kobyłka *Warsaw* 32 A3
Kodaira *Tokyo* 30 A2
Kodanaka *Tokyo* 30 B3
Koekelberg *Brussels* 6 A1
Koganei *Tokyo* 30 A2
Kogarah *Sydney* 29 B1
Koivupää *Helsinki* 11 B2
Koja *Jakarta* 12 A2
Koja Utara *Jakarta* 12 A2
Kokhav Ya'akov *Jerusalem* 13 A2
Kokobunji *Tokyo* 30 A2
Kokobunji-Temple *Tokyo* 30 A4
Kolarängen *Stockholm* 29 B3
Kolbotn *Oslo* 23 B3
Kolkata *Kolkata* 14 B2
Kolkata Dum Dum ✈
  (CCU) *Kolkata* 14 A2
Kolkata Maidan *Kolkata* 14 B1
Kolo *Warsaw* 32 B1
Kolokinthou *Athens* 2 B2
Kolomyagi *St. Petersburg* 27 A1
Kolonos *Athens* 2 B2
Kolsâs *Oslo* 23 A2
Komae *Tokyo* 30 B3
Komagome *Tokyo* 30 A3
Komazawa *Tokyo* 30 B3
Kona *Kolkata* 14 B1
Konala *Helsinki* 11 B2
Kondli *Delhi* 10 B2
Kongelunden *Copenhagen* 8 B3
Kongens Lyngby *Copenhagen* 8 A3
Kongo *Helsinki* 11 A1
Konnagar *Kolkata* 14 A2
Konohana *Osaka* 23 A1
Konradshöhe *Berlin* 5 A2
Kopanina *Prague* 25 B1
Koparkhairna *Mumbai* 20 A2
Köpenick *Berlin* 5 B4
Korangi *Karachi* 13 B2
Koremasa *Tokyo* 30 B1
Koridalos *Athens* 2 B1
Korokoro *Wellington* 33 B2
Korokoro Stream →
  Wellington 33 B2
Kosino *Moscow* 19 B4
Kosugi *Tokyo* 30 B3
Kota *Jakarta* 12 A2
Kôtô *Tokyo* 30 A3
Kotrung *Kolkata* 14 A2
Kouponia *Athens* 2 B2
Kowloon *Hong Kong* 12 B1
Kowloon Peak *Hong Kong* 12 A2
Kowloon Res. *Hong Kong* 12 A1
Kowloon Tong *Hong Kong* 12 B2
Kraainem *Brussels* 6 A2
Krailling *Munich* 21 B1
Krampnitz *Berlin* 5 A1
Krampnitzsee *Berlin* 5 B1
Kranji, Sungei → *Singapore* 28 A2
Kranji Industrial Estate
  Singapore 28 A2
Krasno-Presnenskaya
  Moscow 19 B2
Krč *Prague* 25 B2
Kremlin *Moscow* 19 B2
Krestovskiye, Ostrov
  St. Petersburg 27 B1
Kreuzberg *Berlin* 5 A3
Kritzendorf *Vienna* 32 A1
Krumme Lanke *Berlin* 5 B2
Krummensee *Berlin* 5 A5
Krung Thep = Bangkok
  Bangkok 3 B2
Krusboda *Stockholm* 29 B3
Kuangchou = Guangzhou
  Guangzhou 11 B2
Küçükçöy *Istanbul* 12 B1
Küçüksu *Istanbul* 12 B2
Kudrovo *St. Petersburg* 27 B2
Kulosaari *Helsinki* 11 B3
Kumla *Stockholm* 29 B2
Kungens kurva *Stockholm* 29 B1
Kungliga Slottet *Stockholm* 29 B2
Kungshatt *Stockholm* 29 B1
Kungsholmen *Stockholm* 29 A2
Kunitachi *Tokyo* 30 A1
Kunming Hu *Beijing* 4 B1
Kunratice *Prague* 25 B2
Kupchino *St. Petersburg* 27 B2
Kuramo Waters *Lagos* 14 B2
Kurbağalı → *Istanbul* 12 C2
Kurihara *Tokyo* 30 B1
Kurla *Mumbai* 20 A2
Kurmuri *Mumbai* 20 A2
Kuryanovo *Moscow* 19 C3
Kuskovo *Moscow* 19 B3
Kustia *Kolkata* 14 B2
Kuzguncuk *Istanbul* 12 B2
Kuzminki *Moscow* 19 B3
Kwai Chung *Hong Kong* 12 A1
Kwanghow =
  Guangzhou *Guangzhou* 11 B2
Kwun Tong *Hong Kong* 12 B2
Kyje *Prague* 25 B3
Kyûhôji *Osaka* 23 B2

L

La Barceloneta *Barcelona* 4 A2
La Blanca *Santiago* 27 C2
La Boca *Buenos Aires* 7 B2
La Bretèche *Paris* 24 A1
La Celle-St-Cloud *Paris* 24 A1
La Courneuve *Paris* 24 A3
La Dehesa *Santiago* 27 B2
La Encantada *Lima* 14 C2
La Estación *Madrid* 17 B1
La Floresta *Barcelona* 4 A1
La Florida *Santiago* 27 C2
La Fortuna *Madrid* 17 B1
La França *Barcelona* 4 A1

La Garenne-Colombes *Paris* 24 A2
La Giustiniana *Rome* 26 B1
La Grange *Chicago* 9 C1
La Grange Park *Chicago* 9 C1
La Granja *Santiago* 27 C2
La Guardia ✈ (LGA) *New York* 22 B2
La Hulpe *Brussels* 6 B2
La Llacuna *Barcelona* 4 A1
La Loma *Mexico City* 18 A1
La Lucila *Buenos Aires* 7 B2
La Maladrerie *Paris* 24 A1
La Milla, Cerro *Lima* 14 A2
La Monachina *Rome* 26 B1
La Moraleja *Madrid* 17 A2
La Nopalera *Mexico City* 18 C2
La Paternal *Buenos Aires* 7 B2
La Perla *Lima* 14 B2
La Perouse *Sydney* 29 B2
La Pisana *Rome* 26 B1
La Prairie *Montreal* 20 B3
La Punta *Lima* 14 B1
La Puntigala *Barcelona* 4 A1
La Queue-en-Brie *Paris* 24 B4
La Reina *Santiago* 27 B2
La Ribera *Barcelona* 4 A2
La Sagrera *Barcelona* 4 A2
La Salada *Buenos Aires* 7 C2
La Scala *Milan* 19 B1
La Storta *Rome* 26 B1
La Taxonera *Barcelona* 4 A2
La Victoria *Lima* 14 B2
Laajalahti *Helsinki* 11 B1
Laajasalo *Helsinki* 11 B3
Laaksolahti *Helsinki* 11 B1
Labagou National Forest
  Park *Beijing* 4 B1
Lablâba, W. el → *Cairo* 7 A2
Lachine *Montreal* 20 B1
Lachine, Canal de *Montreal* 20 B2
Lad Phrao *Bangkok* 3 B2
Ladera Heights *Los Angeles* 16 C2
Lâdvi *Prague* 25 B2
Lady *Warsaw* 32 C1
Lafontaine, Parc *Montreal* 20 A2
Lagoa *Rio de Janeiro* 25 B1
Lagos *Lagos* 14 B2
Lagos-Ikeja ✈ (LOS) *Lagos* 14 A1
Lagos Island *Lagos* 14 B2
Lagos Lagoon *Lagos* 14 B2
Laguna de B. *Manila* 17 C2
Laim *Munich* 21 B2
Lainate *Milan* 19 A1
Lainz *Vienna* 32 B1
Lake Buena Vista *Orlando* 23 B1
Lake Cain Hills *Orlando* 23 B2
Lake Fairfax Park
  Washington 33 B2
Lakemba *Sydney* 29 B1
Lakeside *Cape Town* 8 B1
Lakeside *Johannesburg* 13 A2
Lakeview *Chicago* 9 B3
Lakeview *New Orleans* 21 A2
Lakewood Park *Atlanta* 3 B2
Lakhtinskiy *St. Petersburg* 27 B1
Lakhtinskiy Razliv, Oz.
  St. Petersburg 27 B1
Lakshmanpur *Kolkata* 14 B1
Laksi *Bangkok* 3 A2
Lal Qila *Delhi* 10 B2
Lam Tin *Hong Kong* 12 B2
Lambert *Oslo* 23 A3
Lambeth □ *London* 15 B3
Lambrate *Milan* 19 B2
Lambro, Parco *Milan* 19 B2
Lambton Mills *Toronto* 31 B1
Lamma I. *Hong Kong* 12 B1
Landiunchang *Beijing* 4 B1
Landover Hills *Washington* 33 B4
Landsmeer *Amsterdam* 2 A2
Landstrasse *Vienna* 32 A2
Landwehr kanal *Berlin* 5 B3
Lane Cove *Sydney* 29 A1
Lane Cove Nat. Park △
  Sydney 29 A1
Langa *Cape Town* 8 A2
Langenzersdorf *Vienna* 32 A2
Langer See *Berlin* 5 B4
Langley *Washington* 33 B2
Langley Park *Washington* 33 B4
Langwald *Munich* 21 A1
Lanham *Washington* 33 B4
L'Annunziatella *Rome* 26 C2
Lansdowne *Cape Town* 8 A2
Lansing *Toronto* 31 A2
Lanus *Buenos Aires* 7 C2
Lapa *Rio de Janeiro* 25 B1
Laranjeiras *Rio de Janeiro* 25 B1
Las *Warsaw* 32 B2
Las Corts *Barcelona* 4 A1
Las Pinas *Manila* 17 C1
Las Rejas *Santiago* 27 B1
Las Vegas *Las Vegas* 14 B2
Las Vegas McCarran
  Int. ✈ (LAS) *Las Vegas* 14 B2
LaSalle *Montreal* 20 B2
LaSalle Street Station
  Chicago 9 B3
Lasek Bielański *Warsaw* 32 B1
Lasek Na Kole *Warsaw* 32 B1
Latina *Madrid* 17 B1
Lauttasaari *Helsinki* 11 C2
Laval-des-Rapides *Montreal* 20 A2
Lavízán *Tehran* 31 A2
Lavradio *Lisbon* 16 A2
Lawndale *Chicago* 9 B2
Lawne L. *Orlando* 23 A2
Lawrence Heights *Toronto* 31 A2
Layari *Karachi* 13 A1
Layari → *Karachi* 13 A2
Łazienkowski Park *Warsaw* 32 B2
Le Blanc-Mesnil *Paris* 24 A3
Le Bourget *Paris* 24 A3
Le Chenoi *Brussels* 6 B2
Le Christ de Saclay *Paris* 24 B1
Le Mesnil-le-Roi *Paris* 24 A1
Le Pecq *Paris* 24 A1
Le Perreux *Paris* 24 A4
Le Pin *Paris* 24 A4
Le Plessis-Robinson *Paris* 24 B2
Le Plessis-Trévise *Paris* 24 A4
Le Port-Marly *Paris* 24 A1
Le Pré-St-Gervais *Paris* 24 A3
Le Raincy *Paris* 24 A4
Le Vésinet *Paris* 24 A1
Lea Bridge *London* 15 A3
Leaside *Toronto* 31 A2
Leblon *Rio de Janeiro* 25 B1
Lee *London* 15 B4
Leganés *Madrid* 17 C1
Legazpi *Madrid* 17 B1
Lehtisaari *Helsinki* 11 B2
Lei Yue Mun *Hong Kong* 12 B2
Leião *Lisbon* 16 A1
Leichhardt *Sydney* 29 B1
Leith *Edinburgh* 11 B3

Lekki *Lagos* **14** B2
Leme *Rio de Janeiro* **25** B1
Lemoyne *Montreal* **20** B3
Lenin *Moscow* **19** B2
Lenino *Moscow* **19** C2
Leninskiye Gory *Moscow* **19** B2
Lennox *Los Angeles* **16** C2
Leonia *New York* **22** A2
Leopardstown *Dublin* **10** B2
Leopoldau *Vienna* **32** B1
Leopoldsdorf *Vienna* **32** B2
Leopoldstadt *Vienna* **32** A2
Leporovo *Moscow* **19** B3
Leppävaara *Helsinki* **11** B1
Les Lilas *Paris* **24** A3
Les Loges-en-Josas *Paris* **24** B1
Les Pavillons-sous-Bois
  Paris **24** A4
Lésigny *Paris* **24** B4
Lesnozavodskaya
  St. Petersburg **27** B2
Lester B. Pearson Int.,
  Toronto ✈ (YYZ) *Toronto* **31** A1
L'Étang-la-Ville *Paris* **24** A1
Letňany *Prague* **25** B3
Letopolis = Ausim *Cairo* **7** A1
Levallois-Perret *Paris* **24** A2
Levent *Istanbul* **12** B2
Lewisdale *Washington* **33** B4
Lewisham □ *London* **15** B3
Lexington *Boston* **6** A1
Leyton *London* **15** A3
Leytonstone *London* **15** A4
L'Haÿ-les-Roses *Paris* **24** B3
L'Hospitalet de Llobregat
  Barcelona **4** A1
Lhotka *Prague* **25** B2
Liangshui He ⇌ *Beijing* **4** C2
Lianhua Chi *Beijing* **4** B2
Lianhua He ⇌ *Beijing* **4** B1
Libčice nad Vltavou *Prague* **25** A2
Liberň *Prague* **25** B2
Liberdade *São Paulo* **27** B2
Liberton *Edinburgh* **11** B3
Liberty I. *New York* **22** B1
Liberty Osaka Museum
  Osaka **23** B1
Liberty State Park △
  New York **22** B1
Libeznice *Prague* **25** A2
Libuš *Prague* **25** B2
Lichiao *Guangzhou* **11** B2
Lichtenberg *Berlin* **5** A4
Lichtenfelde *Berlin* **5** B2
Lidingö *Stockholm* **29** A2
Lieshi Lingyuan *Guangzhou* **11** B2
Liesing *Vienna* **32** B1
Liesing ⇌ *Vienna* **32** B2
Ligovo *St. Petersburg* **27** C1
Lijordet *Oslo* **23** A2
Likhoborka ⇌ *Moscow* **19** A2
Lilla Värtan *Stockholm* **29** A3
Lille Værløse *Copenhagen* **8** A2
Liluah *Kolkata* **14** B1
Lim Chu Kang *Singapore* **28** A2
Lima *Lima* **14** B2
Lima Jorge Chavez, Int. ✈
  (LIM) *Lima* **14** B2
Limbiate *Milan* **19** A1
Limehouse *London* **15** A3
Limeil-Brévannes *Paris* **24** B3
Linate, Milano ✈ (LIN)
  Milan **19** B2
Linbropark *Johannesburg* **13** A2
Lincoln Center for
  Performing Arts
  New York **22** B2
Lincoln Heights *Los Angeles* **16** B3
Lincoln Memorial
  Washington **33** B3
Lincoln Park *Chicago* **9** B3
Lincoln Park *New York* **22** B1
Lincoln Park *San Francisco* **26** B1
Lincoln Park Zoo *Chicago* **9** B3
Lincolnwood *Chicago* **9** B2
Linda-a-Pastora *Lisbon* **16** A1
Linden *Johannesburg* **13** A2
Linden *Wellington* **33** A1
Lindenberg *Berlin* **5** A4
Lindoya *Oslo* **23** A3
Liniers *Buenos Aires* **7** B1
Linkebeek *Brussels* **6** B2
Linksfield *Johannesburg* **13** A2
Linmeyer *Johannesburg* **13** B2
Linna *Helsinki* **11** A2
Lintuvaara *Helsinki* **11** B1
Lion Rock Country
  Park ⌂ *Hong Kong* **12** A2
Lion's Head *Cape Town* **8** A1
Lioumi *Athens* **2** A2
Lisboa *Lisbon* **16** A1
Lisboa ✈ (LIS) *Lisbon* **16** A2
Lisbon = Lisboa *Lisbon* **16** A1
Lishui *Guangzhou* **11** A1
Little B. *Sydney* **29** B2
Little Calumet ⇌ *Chicago* **9** D3
Little Ferry *New York* **22** A1
Little Lake Conway *Orlando* **23** B2
Little Red School House
  Nature Center *Chicago* **9** C1
Little Rouge ⇌ *Toronto* **31** A4
Liuhang *Shanghai* **28** B1
Liurong Temple *Guangzhou* **11** B2
Live Oak Manor
  New Orleans **21** B1
Livry-Gargan *Paris* **24** A4
Liwan *Guangzhou* **11** B2
Ljan *Oslo* **23** A3
Llano de Can Gineu
  Barcelona **4** A2
Lo Aranguiz *Santiago* **27** B2
Lo Boza *Santiago* **27** B1
Lo Chau *Hong Kong* **12** B2
Lo Chau Pak Mai
  Hong Kong **12** B2
Lo Espejo *Santiago* **27** C1
Lo Hermida *Santiago* **27** B2
Lo Prado *Santiago* **27** B1
Lo So Shing *Hong Kong* **12** B1
Lo Wai *Hong Kong* **12** A1
Loanhead *Edinburgh* **11** B3
Lobau *Vienna* **32** A2
Lobos, Pt. *San Francisco* **26** B1
Locham *Munich* **21** B1
Lochkov *Prague* **25** B2
Lockhausen *Munich* **21** A1
Lodi *New York* **22** A1
Lodi Estate *Delhi* **10** B2
Logan Int. ✈, Boston ✈
  (BOS) *Boston* **6** A2
Logan Square *Chicago* **9** B2
Lognes-Émerainville ✈
  (XLG) *Paris* **24** B4
Löhme *Berlin* **5** A5
Lolokhet *Karachi* **13** B1
Lomas Chapultepec
  Mexico City **18** B1
Lomas de San Angel Inn
  Mexico City **18** B1
Lombardy East *Johannesburg* **13** A2
Lomianki *Warsaw* **32** A1

Lomus Reforma *Mexico City* **18** B1
London *London* **15** B3
London Avenue Canal
  New Orleans **21** B2
London City ✈ (LCY)
  London **15** A4
London Heathrow ✈
  (LHR) *London* **15** B1
London Zoo *London* **15** A3
Long B. *Sydney* **29** B2
Long Branch *Toronto* **31** B1
Long Brook ⇌ *Washington* **33** C2
Long Ditton *London* **15** B2
Long Island *New York* **22** B2
Longchamp, Hippodrome
  de *Paris* **24** A2
Longhua Pagoda *Shanghai* **28** B1
Longhua Park *Shanghai* **28** B1
Longtan Hu ⇌ *Beijing* **4** B2
Longue-Pointe *Montreal* **20** A2
Longueuil *Montreal* **20** A3
Loni *Delhi* **10** A2
Loop, The *Chicago* **9** B3
Los Angeles *Los Angeles* **16** B3
Los Angeles Int. ✈ (LAX)
  Los Angeles **16** C2
Los Cerrillos ✈ (ULC)
  Santiago **27** B2
Los Nietos *Los Angeles* **16** C4
Los Olivos *Lima* **14** A2
Los Remedios △ *Mexico City* **18** B1
Los Reyes *Mexico City* **18** B2
Lossy Ostrov △ *Moscow* **19** A3
Lot *Brussels* **6** B1
Lotus River *Cape Town* **8** B2
Lotus Temple *Delhi* **10** B2
Loughlinstown *Dublin* **10** B3
Louis Armstrong New
  Orleans Int. ✈ (MSY)
  New Orleans **21** A1
Louise, L. *Orlando* **23** A1
Louisiana Superdome
  New Orleans **21** B2
Loures *Lisbon* **16** A1
Louveciennes *Paris* **24** A1
Louvre, Musée du *Paris* **24** A3
Lower B. *New York* **22** C1
Lower Hutt *Wellington* **33** B2
Lower New York B. =
  Lower B. *New York* **22** C1
Lower Shing Mun Res.
  Hong Kong **12** A1
Lowry Bay *Wellington* **33** B2
Loyola Univ. *Chicago* **9** B3
Lu Xun, Tomb of *Shanghai* **28** B1
Lu Xun Park *Shanghai* **28** B1
Lübars *Berlin* **5** A3
Lucy, L. *Orlando* **23** A1
Ludwigsfeld *Munich* **21** A1
Luha *Guangzhou* **11** B2
Lumiar *Lisbon* **16** A1
Lundtofte *Copenhagen* **8** A3
Lung Mei *Hong Kong* **12** A2
Luojiang *Guangzhou* **11** B2
Lustheim *Munich* **21** A2
Luwan *Shanghai* **28** B1
Luzhniki Sports Centre
  Moscow **19** B2
Lyndhurst *New York* **22** B1
Lynn Woods Res. *Boston* **6** A2
Lyon, Gare de *Paris* **24** A3
Lyons *Chicago* **9** C2
Lysaker *Oslo* **23** A2
Lysakerselva ⇌ *Oslo* **23** A2
Lysolaje *Prague* **25** B2
Lyublino *Moscow* **19** B3

M

Ma Nam Wat *Hong Kong* **12** A2
Ma On Shan Country
  Park ⌂ *Hong Kong* **12** A2
Ma'ale Adumim *Jerusalem* **13** B2
Ma'ale Ha Khamisha
  Jerusalem **13** B1
Ma'ale Mikhmas *Jerusalem* **13** A2
Maantiekylä *Helsinki* **11** A3
Maarifa *Baghdad* **3** A2
Mabato Pt. *Manila* **17** C2
Mabel, L. *Orlando* **23** A1
Macaco, Morro do
  Rio de Janeiro **25** B2
McCarran Int., Las
  Vegas ✈ (LAS) *Las Vegas* **14** B2
McCook *Chicago* **9** C2
McGill Univ. *Montreal* **20** A2
Machelen *Brussels* **6** A2
Machida *Tokyo* **30** B1
Maciolki *Warsaw* **32** A2
McKerrow, Mt. *Wellington* **33** B2
McKinley Park *Chicago* **9** C2
McLean *Washington* **33** B2
Macopocho ⇌ *Santiago* **27** B1
MacRitchie Res. *Singapore* **28** A2
Macul *Santiago* **27** C2
Madhudaha *Kolkata* **14** B2
Madhyamgram *Kolkata* **14** A2
Madin *Mexico City* **18** A1
Madin, L. *Mexico City* **18** A1
Madinah Al Mansūr
  Baghdad **3** B2
Mâdînet Nasr *Cairo* **7** A2
Madrid *Madrid* **17** B1
Madrid Barajas ✈ (MAD)
  Madrid **17** B2
Madrona *Barcelona* **4** A1
Maesawa *Tokyo* **30** A2
Magdalena *Lima* **14** B2
Magdalena Contreras
  Mexico City **18** C1
Maghreb *Baghdad* **3** B1
Maginu *Tokyo* **30** B2
Magliana *Rome* **26** B1
Magny-les-Hameaux *Paris* **24** B1
Maheshtala *Kolkata* **14** C1
Mahim *Mumbai* **20** A1
Mahim B. *Mumbai* **20** A1
Mahlsdorf *Berlin* **5** B4
Mahmoodabad *Karachi* **13** A2
Mahrauli *Delhi* **10** B2
Mahul *Mumbai* **20** A2
Maida Vale *London* **15** A2
Maidstone *Melbourne* **18** A1
Maipú *Santiago* **27** C1
Maisonneuve, Parc
  Montreal **20** A2
Maisons-Alfort *Paris* **24** B3
Maisons-Laffitte *Paris* **24** A1
Maissonneuve *Montreal* **20** A1
Maitland *Cape Town* **8** A1
Makasar *Jakarta* **12** B2
Makati *Manila* **17** B2
Mäkiniitty *Helsinki* **11** B2
Malá Strana *Prague* **25** B2
Malabar *Sydney* **29** B2
Malabar Hill *Mumbai* **20** B1

Malabar Pt. *Mumbai* **20** B1
Malabon *Manila* **17** B1
Malacañang Palace *Manila* **17** B1
Malahide *Dublin* **10** A3
Malakoff *Paris* **24** B2
Mälarhöjaen *Stockholm* **29** B1
Malate *Manila* **17** B1
Malaya Neva *St. Petersburg* **27** B1
Malaya Okhta
  St. Petersburg **27** B2
Malchow *Berlin* **5** A4
Malden *Boston* **6** A2
Malden *London* **15** B2
Maleizen *Brussels* **6** B3
Malešice *Prague* **25** B3
Malir ⇌ *Karachi* **13** B2
Malleny Mills *Edinburgh* **11** B2
Malmi *Helsinki* **11** B2
Malmøya *Oslo* **23** A3
Måløv *Copenhagen* **8** A2
Malton *Toronto* **31** A1
Malvern *Johannesburg* **13** B2
Malvern *Melbourne* **18** B2
Malvern *Toronto* **31** A3
Mampang Prapatan *Jakarta* **12** B1
Mampukuji *Tokyo* **30** B2
Man Budrukh *Mumbai* **20** A2
Man Khurd *Mumbai* **20** A2
Manakhat *Jerusalem* **13** B2
Mandaluyong *Manila* **17** B2
Mandaoli *Delhi* **10** B2
Mandaqui ⇌ *São Paulo* **27** A2
Mandoli *Delhi* **10** A2
Mandvi *Mumbai* **20** B1
Manenberg *Cape Town* **8** A2
Mang Kung Uk *Hong Kong* **12** B2
Mang-won *Seoul* **27** B1
Mangolpuri *Delhi* **10** A1
Manguinhos ✈
  Rio de Janeiro **25** B1
Manhattan *New York* **22** B2
Manhattan Beach
  New York **22** C2
Manila *Manila* **17** B1
Manila Ninoy Aquino
  Int. ✈ (MNL) *Manila* **17** B1
Mankkaa *Helsinki* **11** B1
Manly *Sydney* **29** A2
Mann, L. *Orlando* **23** A1
Mann's Chinese Theatre
  Los Angeles **16** B2
Mannswörth *Vienna* **32** B2
Manor Park *London* **15** A4
Manor Park *Wellington* **33** A4
Manora *Karachi* **13** B1
Manora Pt. *Karachi* **13** B1
Manqueue, Cerro *Santiago* **27** B2
Manzanares, Canal de
  Madrid **17** C2
Mapo *Seoul* **27** B1
Mar Vista *Los Angeles* **16** B2
Maracanã *Rio de Janeiro* **25** B1
Maraoli *Mumbai* **20** A2
Marcelin *Warsaw* **32** B1
Mareil-Marly *Paris* **24** A1
Margareten *Vienna* **32** A2
Maria *Vienna* **32** A2
Maridalen *Oslo* **23** A3
Maridalsvatnet *Oslo* **23** A3
Mariendorf *Berlin* **5** B3
Marienfelde *Berlin* **5** B3
Marikina *Manila* **17** B2
Marikina ⇌ *Manila* **17** B2
Marin City *San Francisco* **26** A1
Marin Pen. *San Francisco* **26** A1
Marina del Rey *Los Angeles* **16** C2
Marino *Dublin* **10** A2
Marisco, Ponta do
  Rio de Janeiro **25** C1
Markham *Toronto* **31** A2
Marki *Warsaw* **32** A2
Markland Wood *Toronto* **31** B1
Marly, Forêt de *Paris* **24** A1
Marly-le-Roi *Paris* **24** A1
Marne-la-Vallée *Paris* **24** A4
Marolles-en-Brie *Paris* **24** B4
Maroubra *Sydney* **29** B2
Marquette Park *Chicago* **9** C2
Marrero *New Orleans* **21** B1
Marrickville *Sydney* **29** B1
Marsfield *Sydney* **29** A1
Marsha, L. *Orlando* **23** A1
Marte, Campo de *São Paulo* **27** B2
Martesana, Naviglio della
  Milan **19** A2
Martin Luther King Nat.
  Historic Site ⌂ *Atlanta* **3** B2
Martinez *Buenos Aires* **7** A1
Martinkylä *Helsinki* **11** B2
Martinsried *Munich* **21** B1
Maruko *Tokyo* **30** B3
Maryino *Moscow* **19** B3
Maryland *Singapore* **28** B2
Marymont *Warsaw* **32** B2
Marysin Wawerski *Warsaw* **32** B2
Marzahn *Berlin* **5** A4
Mascot *Sydney* **29** B1
Masmo *Stockholm* **29** B1
Maspeth *New York* **22** B2
Masr el Gedida *Cairo* **7** A2
Masr el Qadîma *Cairo* **7** A2
Massachusetts Inst. of
  Tech. *Boston* **6** A2
Massamá *Lisbon* **16** A1
Massey ⇌ *Toronto* **31** A3
Massy *Paris* **24** B2
Mata *Jerusalem* **13** B1
Matinha *Lisbon* **16** A2
Matramam *Jakarta* **12** B2
Matsubara *Osaka* **23** B2
Mattapan *Boston* **6** B2
Mátyásföld *Budapest* **7** A3
Mau Tso Ngam *Hong Kong* **12** A2
Mauer *Vienna* **32** B1
Mauripur *Karachi* **13** B1
Maxhof *Munich* **21** B1
Mayfair *Johannesburg* **13** B2
Maywood *Chicago* **9** B1
Maywood *Los Angeles* **16** C3
Maywood *New York* **22** A1
Maywood Park Race
  Track *Chicago* **9** B1
Mazagaon *Mumbai* **20** B2
Meadowbank Park *Sydney* **29** A1
Mêchoupy ⇌ *Paris* **24** A1
Mêčíce *Prague* **25** A2
Mecidiyeköy *Istanbul* **12** B2
Medford *Boston* **6** A2
Mediodia *Madrid* **17** B2
Meguro *Tokyo* **30** B3
Meguro ⇌ *Tokyo* **30** B3
Mehpalpur *Delhi* **10** B1
Mehrābād ✈ (THR) *Tehran* **31** A1
Mehram Nagar *Delhi* **10** B1
Mehrow *Berlin* **5** A4
Meidling *Vienna* **32** A2
Mëier *Rio de Janeiro* **25** B1
Meiji Shrine *Tokyo* **30** A3
Meise *Brussels* **6** A1
Mejiro *Tokyo* **30** A3
Melbourne *Melbourne* **18** A1

Melbourne ✈ (MEL)
  Melbourne **18** A1
Melki *Helsinki* **11** C2
Mellunkylä *Helsinki* **11** B3
Mellunmäki *Helsinki* **11** B3
Melrose *Boston* **6** A2
Melrose *New York* **22** B2
Melrose Park *Chicago* **9** B1
Melsbroek *Brussels* **6** A2
Melville *Johannesburg* **13** B2
Menteng *Jakarta* **12** B1
Mérantaise ⇌ *Paris* **24** B2
Mercamadrid *Madrid* **17** B2
Merced, L. *San Francisco* **26** B2
Meredale *Johannesburg* **13** B2
Merlimau, Pulau *Singapore* **28** B2
Merri Cr. ⇌ *Melbourne* **18** A1
Merrion *Dublin* **10** B2
Merrionette Park *Chicago* **9** C2
Merton □ *London* **15** B2
Mesgarābād *Tehran* **31** B3
Messe *Vienna* **32** A2
Metairie *New Orleans* **21** A2
Metanópoli *Milan* **19** B2
Metro-Dade Cultural
  Centre *Miami* **18** B2
Metro Toronto Zoo *Toronto* **31** A3
Metropolitan Museum of
  Art *New York* **22** B2
Meudon *Paris* **24** B2
Mevaseret Tsiyon *Jerusalem* **13** B1
Mevo Beitar *Jerusalem* **13** B1
México *Mexico City* **18** B2
México, Ciudad de
  Mexico City **18** B1
Mexico City Int. ✈ (MEX)
  Mexico City **18** B2
Meyerdal *Johannesburg* **13** B2
Mezzate *Milan* **19** B2
Miadong *Seoul* **27** B2
Michałowice *Warsaw* **32** B1
Michle *Prague* **25** B2
Mid-City *Los Angeles* **16** B2
Mid City *New Orleans* **21** B2
Middle Harbour *Sydney* **29** A2
Middle Hd. *Sydney* **29** A2
Middle Park *Melbourne* **18** B1
Middle Village *New York* **22** B2
Middlesex Fells
  Reservation *Boston* **6** A2
Midland Beach *New York* **22** C1
Midwood *New York* **22** C2
Miedzeszyn *Warsaw* **32** B2
Międzylesie *Warsaw* **32** B2
Miessuari *Helsinki* **11** C1
Miguel Hidalgo *Mexico City* **18** B1
Milan = Milano *Milan* **19** B1
Milanese, Parco
  Regionale △ *Milan* **19** A1
Milano *Milan* **19** B1
Milano Due *Milan* **19** B2
Milano Linate ✈ (LIN)
  Milan **19** B2
Milano San Felice *Milan* **19** B2
Milbertshofen *Munich* **21** A2
Mill Hill *London* **15** A2
Millennium Dome *London* **15** A4
Miller Meadow *Chicago* **9** B2
Millerhill *Edinburgh* **11** B3
Milltown *Dublin* **10** B2
Millwood *Washington* **33** B3
Milnerton *Cape Town* **8** A1
Milon-la-Chapelle *Paris* **24** B1
Milton *Boston* **6** B2
Milton Bridge *Edinburgh* **11** B2
Mimico *Toronto* **31** B1
Mimico Creek ⇌ *Toronto* **31** B1
Minami *Osaka* **23** A2
Minamitsunashima *Tokyo* **30** B2
Minato *Osaka* **23** B1
Minato *Tokyo* **30** B3
Minshât el Bekkarî *Cairo* **7** A1
Miraflores *Lima* **14** B2
Miramar *Wellington* **33** B2
Misericordia, Sa. da
  Rio de Janeiro **25** B1
Mission *San Francisco* **26** B2
Mississauga *Toronto* **31** B1
Mitaka *Tokyo* **30** A2
Mitcham *London* **15** B2
Mitcham Common *London* **15** B3
Mitchell Museum of the
  American Indian *Chicago* **9** A2
Mitchell's Plain *Cape Town* **8** B2
Mitte *Berlin* **5** A3
Mittel Isarkanal ⇌ *Munich* **21** A3
Mixcoac *Mexico City* **18** B1
Miyakojima *Osaka* **23** A2
Mizonokuchi *Tokyo* **30** B2
Mizue *Tokyo* **30** A4
Mlocinski Park *Warsaw* **32** A1
Mlociny *Warsaw* **32** A1
Mnevniki *Moscow* **19** B2
Moba *Lagos* **14** B2
Moczydlo *Warsaw* **32** B1
Modderfontein *Johannesburg* **13** A2
Modřany *Prague* **25** B2
Mogyoród *Budapest* **7** A3
Moinho Velho, Cor. ⇌
  São Paulo **27** B2
Mok *Seoul* **27** B1
Mokotów *Warsaw* **32** B1
Molenbeek-St-Jean *Brussels* **6** A1
Molino de Rosas
  Mexico City **18** B1
Mollem *Brussels* **6** A1
Mollins de Rey *Barcelona* **4** A1
Mondeor *Johannesburg* **13** B2
Moneda, Palacio de la
  Santiago **27** B2
Monerò *Rio de Janeiro* **25** A1
Mong Kok *Hong Kong* **12** B2
Monkstown *Dublin* **10** B3
Monnickendam *Amsterdam* **2** A3
Monrovia *Los Angeles* **16** B4
Monsanto *Lisbon* **16** A1
Monsanto, Parque
  Florestal de *Lisbon* **16** A1
Mont-Royal *Montreal* **20** A2
Mont-Royal, Parc *Montreal* **20** A2
Montana de Montjuich
  Barcelona **4** A1
Montcada i Reixac *Barcelona* **4** A2
Monte Chingolo *Buenos Aires* **7** C2
Montebello *Los Angeles* **16** B4
Montemor *Lisbon* **16** A1
Monterey Hills *Los Angeles* **16** B3
Monterey Park *Los Angeles* **16** B4
Montespaccato *Rome* **26** B1
Montesson *Paris* **24** A1
Monteverde Nuovo *Rome* **26** B1
Montfermeil *Paris* **24** A4
Montigny-le-Bretonneux
  Paris **24** B1
Montjay-la-Tour *Paris* **24** A4

Montjuïc *Barcelona* **4** A2
Montparnasse, Gare *Paris* **24** A2
Montréal *Montreal* **20** A1
Naviglio di Pavia *Milan* **19** B1
Naviglio Grande *Milan* **19** B1
Montréal, Î. de *Montreal* **20** A2
Montréal, Univ. de *Montreal* **20** B2
Montréal-Nord *Montreal* **20** A2
Montréal-Trudeau Int. ✈
  (YUL) *Montreal* **20** A1
Montreal Trudeau, Int. ✈
  Montreal **20** A1
Montserrat *Buenos Aires* **7** B2
Monza *Milan* **19** A2
Monzoro *Milan* **19** B1
Mooca *São Paulo* **27** B2
Moonachie *New York* **22** B1
Moonee Ponds *Melbourne* **18** A1
Moonee Valley
  Racecourse *Melbourne* **18** A1
Moosach *Munich* **21** A2
Mora *Mumbai* **20** B2
Moratalaz *Madrid* **17** B1
Mörby *Stockholm* **29** A2
Morden *London* **15** B2
Morée ⇌ *Paris* **24** A3
Morgan Park *Chicago* **9** C3
Moriguchi *Osaka* **23** A2
Morivione *Milan* **19** B2
Morningside *Edinburgh* **11** B2
Morningside *Johannesburg* **13** A2
Morningside *Orlando* **23** B2
Morningside Park *Orlando* **23** B2
Morro Solar, Cerro *Lima* **14** C2
Mortlake *London* **15** B2
Mortlake *Sydney* **29** B1
Morton Grove *Chicago* **9** A2
Morumbi *São Paulo* **27** B1
Moscavide *Lisbon* **16** A2
Moschato *Athens* **2** B2
Moscow = Moskva *Moscow* **19** B3
Moskva *Moscow* **19** B2
Moskvoretskiy *Moscow* **19** B2
Mosman *Sydney* **29** B2
Moti Bagh *Delhi* **10** B2
Motol *Prague* **25** B2
Motsa *Jerusalem* **13** B2
Motsa Ilit *Jerusalem* **13** B1
Motspur Park *London* **15** B2
Mottingham *London* **15** B4
Mount Dennis *Toronto* **31** A2
Mount Greenwood *Chicago* **9** C2
Mount Hood Memorial
  Park △ *Boston* **6** A2
Mount Merrion *Dublin* **10** B2
Mount Olympus *Los Angeles* **16** B2
Mount Rainier *Washington* **33** B4
Mount Vernon *New York* **22** A2
Mount Hood Memorial
Müggelberge *Berlin* **5** B4
Müggelheim *Berlin* **5** B5
Muggiò *Milan* **19** A2
Mühleiten *Vienna* **32** A3
Mühlenfliess ⇌ *Berlin* **5** A5
Muiden *Amsterdam* **2** A3
Muizenberg *Cape Town* **8** B1
Mujahidpur *Delhi* **10** B2
Mukandpur *Delhi* **10** A2
Mukhmas *Jerusalem* **13** A2
Muko ⇌ *Osaka* **23** A1
Mukojima *Tokyo* **30** A3
Mulbarton *Johannesburg* **13** B2
Mullach Ide = Malahide
  Dublin **10** A3
Mumbai *Mumbai* **20** B2
Mumbai Chhatrapati
  Shivaji Int. ✈ (BOM)
  Mumbai **20** A2
Mumbai Harbour *Mumbai* **20** B2
Munch-museum *Oslo* **23** A3
Münchehofe *Berlin* **5** B5
München *Munich* **21** B2
München Franz Josef
  Strauss Int. ✈ (MUC)
  Munich **21** A3
Munich = München
  Munich **21** B2
Munkkiniemi *Helsinki* **11** B2
Munro *Buenos Aires* **7** B1
Muntinlupa *Manila* **17** C2
Murai Res. *Singapore* **28** A2
Murino *St. Petersburg* **27** B2
Murrayfield *Edinburgh* **11** B2
Murtala Mohammed
  International ✈ (LOS)
  Lagos **14** A2
Musashino *Tokyo* **30** A2
Museu Nacional
  Rio de Janeiro **25** B1
Mushin *Lagos* **14** A2
Musocco *Milan* **19** A1
Mustansiriya *Baghdad* **3** A2
Musturud *Cairo* **7** A2
Muswell Hill *London* **15** A3
Mutanabi *Baghdad* **3** B2
Muthana *Baghdad* **3** A2
Mykerinos *Cairo* **7** B1
Myllypuro *Helsinki* **11** B3
Mystic ⇌ *Boston* **6** A2

N

Nacka *Stockholm* **29** B3
Naenae *Wellington* **33** B2
Nersnes *Oslo* **23** B2
Nagatsuta *Tokyo* **30** B2
Nagytétény *Budapest* **7** B1
Nahalin *Jerusalem* **13** B1
Najafgarh Drain ⇌ *Delhi* **10** B1
Nakahara *Tokyo* **30** B2
Nakano *Tokyo* **30** A2
Naksan Park *Seoul* **27** B1
Namyeong *Seoul* **27** B1
Nanbiancun *Guangzhou* **11** B1
Nanchang He ⇌ *Beijing* **4** B2
Nandang *Guangzhou* **11** B1
Nangal Dewat *Delhi* **10** B1
Naniwa *Osaka* **23** B1
Nanole *Mumbai* **20** A2
Nanpu Bridge *Shanghai* **28** B1
Nanshi *Shanghai* **28** B1
Nanterre *Paris* **24** A2
Napier Mole *Karachi* **13** B1
Naraina *Delhi* **10** B1
Narayan Point *Mumbai* **20** B1
Nariman Pt. *Mumbai* **20** B1
Närmak *Tehran* **31** A2
Naroco *Osaka* **23** A1
Näsby *Stockholm* **29** A2
Näsbypark *Stockholm* **29** A2
Nationaal Arboretum
  Washington **33** B4
National Zoological Park
  Washington **33** B3
Nativity, Basilica of
  Jerusalem **13** B2
Natolin *Warsaw* **32** C2
Naucalpan de Juárez
  Mexico City **18** B1

Naupada *Mumbai* **20** A2
Navi Mumbai *Mumbai* **20** A2
Navotas *Manila* **17** B1
Navy Pier *Chicago* **9** B3
Nazal Hikmat Beg *Baghdad* **3** A2
Nazimabad *Karachi* **13** A1
Nazlet el Simmân *Cairo* **7** B1
Nea Alexandria *Athens* **2** A2
Nea Ionia *Athens* **2** A2
Nea Liosia *Athens* **2** A2
Nea Smirni *Athens* **2** B2
Neapoli *Athens* **2** B2
Near North *Chicago* **9** B3
Nebušice *Prague* **25** B1
Nederhorst *Amsterdam* **2** B3
Nedlitz *Berlin* **5** B1
Nee Soon *Singapore* **28** A2
Needham *Boston* **6** B1
Needham Heights *Boston* **6** B1
Nellis Air Force Base ✈
  (LSV) *Las Vegas* **14** A2
Nellis Air Force Base ✈
Nerima *Tokyo* **30** A3
Nesodden *Oslo* **23** B3
Nesoddtangen *Oslo* **23** A3
Nesoya *Oslo* **23** A2
Neu Aubing *Munich* **21** B1
Neu Buch *Berlin* **5** A4
Neu Buchhorst *Berlin* **5** B5
Neu Fahrland *Berlin* **5** B1
Neu Lindenberg *Berlin* **5** A4
Neubiberg *Munich* **21** B3
Neuenhagen *Berlin* **5** A4
Neuessen *Munich* **21** A2
Neuherberg *Munich* **21** A2
Neuhönow *Berlin* **5** A5
Neuilly-Plaisance *Paris* **24** A4
Neuilly-sur-Marne *Paris* **24** A4
Neuilly-sur-Seine *Paris* **24** A2
Neukagran *Vienna* **32** A2
Neukettenhof *Vienna* **32** B2
Neukölln *Berlin* **5** B3
Neuperlach *Munich* **21** B2
Neuried *Munich* **21** B1
Neustift am Walde *Vienna* **32** A1
Neusüssenbrunn *Vienna* **32** A2
Neuwaldegg *Vienna* **32** A1
Neve Ya'akov *Jerusalem* **13** A2
Neve Sha'anan *Tel Aviv* **31** ?
Neves *Rio de Janeiro* **25** B2
New Baghdad *Baghdad* **3** B2
New Barakpur *Kolkata* **14** A2
New Brighton *New York* **22** C1
New Canada *Johannesburg* **13** B1
New Canada Dam
  Johannesburg **13** B1
New Carrollton *Washington* **33** B4
New Cross *London* **15** B3
New Delhi *Delhi* **10** B2
New Dorp *New York* **22** C1
New Dorp Beach *New York* **22** C1
New Malden *London* **15** B2
New Milford *New York* **22** A1
New Mumbai = Navi
  Mumbai *Mumbai* **20** A2
New Orleans *New Orleans* **21** B2
New Orleans Int. ✈ (MSY)
  New Orleans **21** A1
New Territories *Hong Kong* **12** A1
New Toronto *Toronto* **31** B1
New Utrecht *New York* **22** C2
New York *New York* **22** B2
New York La Guardia ✈
  (LGA) *New York* **22** B2
Newark B. *New York* **22** B1
Newbattle *Edinburgh* **11** B3
Newbury Park *London* **15** A4
Newcraighall *Edinburgh* **11** B3
Newhaven *Edinburgh* **11** B2
Newington *Edinburgh* **11** B2
Newlands *Johannesburg* **13** B1
Newlands *Wellington* **33** B1
Newport *Melbourne* **18** B1
Newton *Boston* **6** B1
Newtonbrook *Toronto* **31** A2
Newtongrange *Edinburgh* **11** B3
Newtonville *Boston* **6** A1
Newtown *Sydney* **29** B2
Ngaio *Wellington* **33** B1
Ngau Chi Wan *Hong Kong* **12** A2
Ngau Tau Kok *Hong Kong* **12** B2
Ngauranga *Wellington* **33** B1
Ngong Shuen Chau
  Hong Kong **12** B1
Ngua Kok Wan *Hong Kong* **12** A1
Nhava Sheva *Mumbai* **20** B2
Niävarän *Tehran* **31** A2
Nibra *Kolkata* **14** B1
Nidal *Baghdad* **3** B2
Niddrie *Edinburgh* **11** B3
Niddrie *Melbourne* **18** A1
Nieder Neuendorf *Berlin* **5** A2
Niederschönhausen *Berlin* **5** A3
Niemeyer *Rio de Janeiro* **25** B1
Nieuwendam *Amsterdam* **2** A2
Nihonbashi *Tokyo* **30** A3
Niipperi *Helsinki* **11** B1
Nikea *Athens* **2** B1
Nikolassee *Berlin* **5** B2
Nikolskiy *Moscow* **19** B1
Niles *Chicago* **9** A2
Nimta *Kolkata* **14** A2
Ninoy Aquino Int. ✈
  (MNL) *Manila* **17** B2
Nippa *Tokyo* **30** B2
Nippori *Tokyo* **30** A3
Nishi *Osaka* **23** B1
Nishinari *Osaka* **23** B1
Nishinomiya *Osaka* **23** A1
Nishiyodogawa *Osaka* **23** A1
Niterói *Rio de Janeiro* **25** B2
Nockeby *Stockholm* **29** B1
Noel Park *London* **15** A3
Nogatino *Moscow* **19** B3
Nogent-sur-Marne *Paris* **24** A3
Noida *Delhi* **10** B2
Nois-le-Grand *Paris* **24** A4
Noisiel *Paris* **24** A4
Noisy-le-Roi *Paris* **24** A1
Noisy-les-Sec *Paris* **24** A3
Nokkala *Helsinki* **11** C1
Nonakashinden *Tokyo* **30** A2
Nongminyundong
  Jiangxisuo *Guangzhou* **11** B2
Nonhyeon *Seoul* **27** B2
Nonthaburi *Bangkok* **3** B1
Noordzeekanaal ⇌ *Amsterdam* **2** A1
Nord, Gare du *Paris* **24** A3
Nordmarka *Oslo* **23** A3
Nordrand-Siedlung *Vienna* **32** A2
Nordstrand *Oslo* **23** A3
Norridge *Chicago* **9** B2
Norrmalm *Stockholm* **29** A2
North Arlington *New York* **22** B1

Ohariu Stream ⇌
  Wellington **33** B1
O'Higgins, Parque *Santiago* **27** B2
Oimachi *Tokyo* **30** B3
Ojota *Lagos* **14** A2
Oke-Ira *Lagos* **14** A1
Okęcie *Warsaw* **32** B1
Okęcie, Warszawa ✈
  (WAW) *Warsaw* **32** B1
Okeogbe *Lagos* **14** B2
Okhla *Delhi* **10** B2
Okko ⇌ *St. Petersburg* **27** B2
Okkervil ⇌ *St. Petersburg* **27** B2
Okrzeszyn *Warsaw* **32** C2
Oksval *Oslo* **23** A2
Oktyabrskiy *Moscow* **19** B2
Ōkubo *Tokyo* **30** A3
Ōkura *Tokyo* **30** B2
Olari *Helsinki* **11** B1
Olaria *Rio de Janeiro* **25** B1
Old Admiralty *St. Petersburg* **27** B1
Old City *Jerusalem* **13** B2
Old City *Shanghai* **28** B1
Old Fort York *Toronto* **31** B2
Old Harbor *Boston* **6** A2
Old Town = Stare Miasto
  Warsaw **32** B2
Old Town *Chicago* **9** B3
Old Town Hall = Altes
  Rathaus *Munich* **21** B2
Oldbawn *Dublin* **10** B1
Olgino *St. Petersburg* **27** A1
Olímpico, Estadio
  Mexico City **18** C1
Olivais *Lisbon* **16** A2
Olivar de los Padres
  Mexico City **18** B1
Olivar del Conde
  Mexico City **18** B1
Olives, Mt. of *Jerusalem* **13** B2
Olivia, L. *Orlando* **23** A1
Olivos *Buenos Aires* **7** B1
Olona ⇌ *Milan* **19** A1
Olympia, L. *Orlando* **23** A1
Olympic Green *Beijing* **4** B2
Olympic Stadium =
  Turner Field *Atlanta* **3** B2
Olympic Stadium *Beijing* **4** B2
Olympic Stadium *Helsinki* **11** B2
Olympique, Stade *Montreal* **20** A2
Ōmori *Tokyo* **30** B3
Onisigun *Lagos* **14** A2
Ontario Science Centre
  Toronto **31** A2
Ōokayama *Tokyo* **30** B3
Oostzaan *Amsterdam* **2** A2
Opa-Locka *Miami* **18** A1
Opa-Locka ✈ (OPF) *Miami* **18** A1
Opacz *Warsaw* **32** B1
Ophirton *Johannesburg* **13** B2
Opgård *Oslo* **23** B3
Oppem *Brussels* **6** A1
Oppsal *Oslo* **23** A3
Ora *Jerusalem* **13** B1
Oradell *New York* **22** A1
Oradell Res. *New York* **22** A1
Orange Bowl Stadium
  Miami **18** B2
Orangi *Karachi* **13** A1
Ordrup *Copenhagen* **8** A3
Orech *Prague* **25** B1
Oregun *Lagos* **14** A2
Orient Heights *Boston* **6** A3
Orlando *Orlando* **23** A2
Orlando Dam *Johannesburg* **13** B1
Orlando East *Johannesburg* **13** B1
Orlando Executive ✈
  (ORL) *Orlando* **23** A2
Orlando Int. ✈ (MCO)
  Orlando **23** B3
Orlovista *Orlando* **23** A2
Orly *Paris* **24** B3
Orly, Paris ✈ (ORY) *Paris* **24** B3
Ormesson-sur-Marne *Paris* **24** B4
Ormond *Melbourne* **18** B2
Ormøya *Oslo* **23** A3
Orpington *London* **15** B4
Ortaköy *Istanbul* **12** B2
Ortica *Milan* **19** B2
Oruba *Lagos* **14** A2
Ōsaka *Osaka* **23** A2
Ōsaka Castle *Osaka* **23** A2
Ōsaka Harbour *Osaka* **23** B1
Ōsaka Itami Int. ✈ (ITM)
  Osaka **23** A1
Ōsaka Kansai Int. ✈ (KIX)
  Osaka **23** B2
Ōsaki *Tokyo* **30** B3
Osasco *São Paulo* **27** B1
Osdorf *Berlin* **5** B1
Osdorp *Amsterdam* **2** A1
Oshodi *Lagos* **14** A2
Oslo *Oslo* **23** A3
Oslo ✈ (OSL) *Oslo* **23** A1
Osorun *Lagos* **14** A2
Ospiate *Milan* **19** A1
Ostankino *Moscow* **19** B2
Osterley *London* **15** B1
Osterley Park *London* **15** B1
Östermalm *Stockholm* **29** A2
Österskär *Stockholm* **29** A3
Óstia Malpasso *Rome* **26** B1
Ostiense *Rome* **26** B1
Ostmarkkapellet *Oslo* **23** A4
Ostoya *Oslo* **23** A1
Østre Aker *Oslo* **23** A3
Ōta *Tokyo* **30** B3
Otaniemi *Helsinki* **11** B1
Otari Open Air Museum
  Wellington **33** B1
Otira *Oslo* **23** A3
Ōtsuka *Tokyo* **30** A3
Ōtávia *Rome* **26** B1
Ottery *Cape Town* **8** B2
Ottobrunn *Munich* **21** B3
Ouderkerk *Amsterdam* **2** B2
Oulunkylä *Helsinki* **11** B2
Ourcq, Canal de l' *Paris* **24** A3
Outer Mission *San Francisco* **26** B2
Outremont *Montreal* **20** A2
Overijse *Brussels* **6** B3
Owhiro Bay *Wellington* **33** C1
Oworonsoki *Lagos* **14** A2
Oxgangs *Edinburgh* **11** B2
Oxon Hill *Washington* **33** C4
Oyodo *Osaka* **23** A1
Oyster Rock *Mumbai* **20** B1
Oyster Rocks *Karachi* **13** B2
Ozoir-la-Ferrière *Paris* **24** B4
Ozone Park *New York* **22** B2

P

Pacific Heights
  San Francisco **26** B2
Pacific Manor *San Francisco* **26** C2
Pacific Palisades *Los Angeles* **16** B1
Pacifica *San Francisco* **26** C2
Paco *Manila* **17** B1

Paco de Arcos *Lisbon* 16 A1
Paddington *London* 15 A2
Paddington *Sydney* 29 B2
Paderno *Milan* 19 A1
Pagewood *Sydney* 29 B2
Pagote *Mumbai* 20 B2
Pai, I. do *Rio de Janeiro* 25 B2
Pak Kok *Hong Kong* 12 B1
Pak Kong *Hong Kong* 12 A2
Pakila *Helsinki* 11 B2
Palacio Real *Madrid* 17 B1
Palaiseau *Paris* 24 B2
Palazzolo *Milan* 19 A1
Paleo Faliro *Athens* 2 B2
Palermo *Buenos Aires* 7 B2
Palhais *Lisbon* 16 B2
Palisades Park *New York* 22 A1
Palmer Park *Washington* 33 B4
Palmerston *Dublin* 10 A1
Palms *Los Angeles* 16 B2
Paloheinä *Helsinki* 11 B2
Palomeras *Madrid* 17 B2
Palos Heights *Chicago* 9 D2
Palos Hills *Chicago* 9 C2
Palos Hills Forest *Chicago* 9 C1
Palos Park *Chicago* 9 C1
Palpara *Kolkata* 14 B2
Panchur *Kolkata* 14 B1
Pandacan *Manila* 17 B2
Pandan, Selat *Singapore* 28 B2
Pandan Res. *Singapore* 28 B2
Pangrati *Athens* 2 B2
Pangsua, Sungei → *Singapore* 28 A2
Panihati *Kolkata* 14 A2
Panjang, Bukit *Singapore* 28 A2
Panke → *Berlin* 5 A3
Pankow *Berlin* 5 A3
Pantheon *Rome* 26 B1
Panthersville *Atlanta* 3 B3
Pantin *Paris* 24 A3
Pantitlán *Mexico City* 18 B2
Panyu *Guangzhou* 11 B2
Paparangi *Wellington* 33 B1
Papiol *Barcelona* 4 A1
Paradise *Las Vegas* 14 B2
Paramount Studios *Los Angeles* 16 B3
Paramus *New York* 22 A1
Paranaque *Manila* 17 B1
Paray-Vieille-Poste *Paris* 24 B3
Pardisān Nature Park *Tehran* 31 A2
Parel *Mumbai* 20 B1
Pari *São Paulo* 27 B2
Parioli *Rome* 26 B1
Paris *Paris* 24 A3
Paris Orly ✈ (ORY) *Paris* 24 B3
Parje *Mumbai* 20 B2
Pārk-e Āzādegān *Tehran* 31 B2
Pārk-e Mellat *Tehran* 31 A2
Park Ridge *Chicago* 9 A1
Park Royal *London* 15 A2
Parkchester *New York* 22 B2
Parkdale *Toronto* 31 B2
Parkhurst *Johannesburg* 13 A2
Parklawn *Washington* 33 B3
Parkmore *Johannesburg* 13 A2
Parkside *San Francisco* 26 B2
Parktown *Johannesburg* 13 B2
Parkview *Johannesburg* 13 A2
Parkville *New York* 22 C2
Parkwood *Cape Town* 8 B1
Parkwood *Johannesburg* 13 A2
Parow *Cape Town* 8 A2
Parque Chacabuco *Buenos Aires* 7 B2
Parque Patricios *Buenos Aires* 7 B2
Parramatta → *Sydney* 29 A1
Paşabahçe *Istanbul* 12 B2
Pasadena *Los Angeles* 16 B4
Pasar Minggu *Jakarta* 12 B1
Pasay *Manila* 17 B1
Pascoe Vale *Melbourne* 18 A1
Pasig *Manila* 17 B2
Pasig → *Manila* 17 B2
Pasila *Helsinki* 11 B2
Pasing *Munich* 21 B1
Pasir Panjang *Singapore* 28 B2
Pasir Ris *Singapore* 28 A3
Passaic *New York* 22 A1
Passaic → *New York* 22 B1
Passirana *Milan* 19 A1
Patel Nagar *Delhi* 10 B1
Pateros *Manila* 17 B2
Pathumwan *Bangkok* 3 B2
Patipukur *Kolkata* 14 B2
Patisia *Athens* 2 A2
Paulo E. Virginia, Gruta *Rio de Janeiro* 25 B1
Paulshof *Berlin* 5 A5
Paya Lebar *Singapore* 28 A3
Peakhurst *Sydney* 29 B1
Peania *Athens* 2 B3
Pearson Int. Toronto ✈ (YYZ) *Toronto* 31 A1
Peckham *London* 15 B3
Pederstrup *Copenhagen* 8 A2
Pedralbes *Barcelona* 4 A1
Pedregal de San Angel, Jardines del *Mexico City* 18 C1
Peip'ing = Beijing *Beijing* 4 B1
Peking = Beijing *Beijing* 4 B1
Pelcowizna *Warsaw* 32 B2
Peñalolén *Santiago* 27 B2
Pencarrow Hd. *Wellington* 33 C2
Peng Siang → *Singapore* 28 A2
Penge *London* 15 B3
Penha *Rio de Janeiro* 25 A1
Penicuik *Edinburgh* 11 B2
Penjaringan *Jakarta* 12 A1
Pentagon *Washington* 33 B3
Penzing *Vienna* 32 A1
People's Park *Shanghai* 28 B1
People's Square *Shanghai* 28 B1
Perales del Rio *Madrid* 17 C2
Perchtoldsdorf *Vienna* 32 B1
Perdizes *São Paulo* 27 B2
Peristeri *Athens* 2 A2
Perivale *London* 15 A2
Perk *Brussels* 6 A2
Perlach *Munich* 21 B2
Perlacher Forst *Munich* 21 B2
Pero *Milan* 19 A1
Peropok, Bukit *Singapore* 28 B2
Perovo *Moscow* 19 B3
Pertusella *Milan* 19 A1
Pesagot *Jerusalem* 13 A2
Pesanggrahag, Kali → *Jakarta* 12 B1
Peschiera Borromeo *Milan* 19 B2
Pesek, Pulau *Singapore* 28 B2
Pest *Budapest* 7 B2
Pesterzsébet *Budapest* 7 B2
Pesthidegkút *Budapest* 7 A1
Pestimre *Budapest* 7 B3
Pestlőrinc *Budapest* 7 B3
Pestújhely *Budapest* 7 A2
Petas *Helsinki* 11 B2
Petone *Wellington* 33 B2
Petrogradskaya Storona *St. Petersburg* 27 B2
Petroupoli *Athens* 2 A2
Petrovice *Prague* 25 B3
Petrovskiy Park *Moscow* 19 B2
Petrovsko-Razumovskoye *Moscow* 19 B2
Pettycur *Edinburgh* 11 A2
Peutie *Brussels* 6 A2
Pfaueninsel *Berlin* 5 B1
Phaya Thai *Bangkok* 3 B2
Phihai *Karachi* 13 A2
Phillip B. *Sydney* 29 B2
Phoenix Park *Dublin* 10 A2
Phra Khanong *Bangkok* 3 B2
Phra Nakhon *Bangkok* 3 B2
Phra Pradaeng *Bangkok* 3 C2
Phranakhon *Bangkok* 3 B1
Pico Rivera *Los Angeles* 16 C4
Piedade *Lisbon* 16 A1
Piedade *Rio de Janeiro* 25 B1
Piedade, Cova da *Lisbon* 16 A2
Piedmont Park *Atlanta* 3 B2
Pierre Elliott Trudeau ✈ (YUL) *Montreal* 20 B1
Pietralata *Rome* 26 B2
Pihlajamäki *Helsinki* 11 B2
Pihlajasaari *Helsinki* 11 C2
Pilares *Rio de Janeiro* 25 B1
Pilton *Edinburgh* 11 B2
Pimmit Hills *Washington* 33 B2
Pine Castle *Orlando* 23 B2
Pine Grove *Toronto* 31 A1
Pine Hills *Orlando* 23 A2
Pinewood Park *Miami* 18 A2
Piney Run → *Washington* 33 B2
Pingzhou *Guangzhou* 11 B2
Pinheiros → *São Paulo* 27 B1
Pinjrapur *Karachi* 13 A2
Pinner *London* 15 A1
Pinner Green *London* 15 A1
Pioltello *Milan* 19 A2
Pipinui Pt. *Wellington* 33 A1
Piræus = Pireas *Athens* 2 B1
Piraiévs = Pireas *Athens* 2 B1
Pirajuçara → *São Paulo* 27 B1
Pireas *Athens* 2 B1
Pirinçci *Istanbul* 12 B1
Pirituba *São Paulo* 27 A1
Pirkkola *Helsinki* 11 B2
Pisgat O'mer *Jerusalem* 13 B2
Pisgat Ze'ev *Jerusalem* 13 B2
Pisnice *Prague* 25 C2
Pitampura *Delhi* 10 A1
Pitkäjärvi *Helsinki* 11 B1
Planegg *Munich* 21 B1
Plaza Mayor *Madrid* 17 B1
Pleasure Island *Orlando* 23 B1
Plumstead *Cape Town* 8 B1
Plumstead *London* 15 B4
Plyushchevo *Moscow* 19 B3
Po Toi *Hong Kong* 12 B2
Po Toi O *Hong Kong* 12 B2
Poasco *Milan* 19 B2
Podbaba *Prague* 25 B2
Podoli *Prague* 25 B2
Pohick Creek → *Washington* 33 C2
Pointe-Aux-Trembles *Montreal* 20 A2
Poissy *Paris* 24 A1
Pok Fu Lam *Hong Kong* 12 B1
Pokcheong *Seoul* 27 C2
Polton *Edinburgh* 11 B3
Polvoranca, Parque de *Madrid* 17 C1
Polyustrovo *St. Petersburg* 27 B2
Pomprap *Bangkok* 3 B2
Pondok Gede *Jakarta* 12 A2
Pondok Indah *Jakarta* 12 B1
Pont-Viau *Montreal* 20 A1
Pontault-Combault *Paris* 24 B4
Pontinha *Lisbon* 16 A1
Poplar *London* 15 A3
Poppintree *Dublin* 10 A2
Porirua *Wellington* 33 A2
Porirua East *Wellington* 33 A2
Port Botany *Sydney* 29 B2
Port Mearnóg = Portmarnock *Dublin* 10 A3
Port Melbourne *Melbourne* 18 B1
Port Nicholson *Wellington* 33 B2
Port Richmond *New York* 22 C1
Port Shelter *Hong Kong* 12 A2
Port Union *Toronto* 31 A4
Portage Park *Chicago* 9 B2
Portela, Lisboa ✈ (LIS) *Lisbon* 16 A2
Porter, L. *Orlando* 23 B2
Portmarnock *Dublin* 10 A3
Porto Brandão *Lisbon* 16 A1
Pôrto Novo *Rio de Janeiro* 25 A2
Porto Novo Cr. → *Lagos* 14 B2
Portobello *Edinburgh* 11 B3
Portrero *San Francisco* 26 B3
Potomac *Washington* 33 A2
Potrero Pt. *San Francisco* 26 B2
Potsdam *Berlin* 5 B1
Potzham *Munich* 21 B2
Pötzleinsdorf *Vienna* 32 A1
Póvoa de Santo Adriao *Lisbon* 16 A2
Powązki *Warsaw* 32 B1
Powisle *Warsaw* 32 B2
Powsin *Warsaw* 32 C2
Powsinek *Warsaw* 32 C2
Poyan Res. *Singapore* 28 A2
Pozuelo de Alarcón *Madrid* 17 B1
Prado, Museo del *Madrid* 17 B1
Prado Churubusco *Mexico City* 18 B2
Praga *Warsaw* 32 B2
Prague = Praha *Prague* 25 B2
Praha *Prague* 25 B2
Praha ✈ (PRG) *Prague* 25 B1
Praires, R. des → *Montreal* 20 A2
Prater *Vienna* 32 A2
Precotto *Milan* 19 A2
Prenestino Labicano *Rome* 26 B2
Prenzlauerberg *Berlin* 5 A3
Preston *Melbourne* 18 A1
Pretos Forros, Sa. dos *Rio de Janeiro* 25 B1
Préville *Montreal* 20 B3
Přezletice *Prague* 25 B3
Prima Porta *Rome* 26 B1
Primavalle *Rome* 26 B1
Primrose *Johannesburg* 13 B2
Progreso Nacional *Mexico City* 18 A2
Prosek *Prague* 25 B3
Prospect Hill Park *Boston* 6 A1
Providencia *Santiago* 27 B2
Průhonice *Prague* 25 C3
Psichiko *Athens* 2 A2
Pudong New Area *Shanghai* 28 B2
Pueblo Libre *Lima* 14 B2
Pueblo Nuevo *Barcelona* 4 A2
Pueblo Nuevo *Madrid* 17 B2
Puerto Madero *Buenos Aires* 7 B2
Puhuangyu *Beijing* 4 B2
Puistola *Helsinki* 11 B3
Pukinmäki *Helsinki* 11 B2
Pulkovo Int. ✈ (LED) *St. Petersburg* 27 C1
Pullach *Munich* 21 B1
Pullman Historic District *Chicago* 9 C3
Pulo Gadung *Jakarta* 12 B2
Pūnak *Tehran* 31 A2
Punchbowl *Sydney* 29 B1
Punde *Mumbai* 20 B2
Punggol *Singapore* 28 A3
Punggol, Sungei → *Singapore* 28 A3
Punggol Pt. *Singapore* 28 A3
Punjabi Bagh *Delhi* 10 A1
Puotila *Helsinki* 11 B3
Puteaux *Paris* 24 A2
Putney *London* 15 B2
Putuo *Shanghai* 28 B1
Putxet *Barcelona* 4 A1
Puxi *Shanghai* 28 B1
Pyramids *Cairo* 7 B1
Pyry *Warsaw* 32 C1

Q

Qalandiya *Jerusalem* 13 A2
Qal'eh Morghī *Tehran* 31 B2
Qanâ el Ismâ'ilîya *Cairo* 7 A2
Qāsemābād *Tehran* 31 A3
Qasr-e Fīrūzeh *Tehran* 31 B3
Qatane *Jerusalem* 13 B1
Qianmen *Beijing* 4 B2
Qinghuayuan *Beijing* 4 A1
Qingningsi *Shanghai* 28 B2
Qolhak *Tehran* 31 A2
Quadraro *Rome* 26 B2
Quaid-i-Azam *Karachi* 13 A1
Quartiere Zingone *Milan* 19 B1
Qubeiba *Jerusalem* 13 A1
Quds *Baghdad* 3 A2
Queen Mary Res. *London* 15 B1
Queen Victoria Market *Melbourne* 18 A1
Queensbury *London* 15 A2
Queenscliffe *Sydney* 29 A2
Queensferry *Edinburgh* 11 B1
Queenstown *Singapore* 28 B2
Quellerina *Johannesburg* 13 A1
Queluz *Lisbon* 16 A1
Quezon City *Manila* 17 B2
Quilicura *Santiago* 27 B1
Quincy *Boston* 6 B2
Quincy B. *Boston* 6 B3
Quinta Normal *Santiago* 27 B1
Quinto de Stampi *Milan* 19 B2
Quinto Romano *Milan* 19 B1
Quirinale *Rome* 26 B1

R

R.F.K. Memorial Stadium *Washington* 33 B4
Raasdorf *Vienna* 32 A3
Radcliffe College *Boston* 6 A2
Rådhus *Oslo* 23 A3
Radlice *Prague* 25 B2
Radość *Warsaw* 32 B3
Radotín *Prague* 25 C2
Rafat *Jerusalem* 13 A2
Raffles Park *Singapore* 28 B2
Raheny *Dublin* 10 A3
Rahnsdorf *Berlin* 5 B5
Rajakylä *Helsinki* 11 B3
Rajpura *Delhi* 10 A2
Rákos-patak → *Budapest* 7 B3
Rákoshegy *Budapest* 7 B3
Rákoskeresztúr *Budapest* 7 B3
Rákoskert *Budapest* 7 B3
Rákosliget *Budapest* 7 B3
Rákospalota *Budapest* 7 A2
Rákosszentmihály *Budapest* 7 A2
Raków *Warsaw* 32 B1
Ram *Jerusalem* 13 A2
Rām Allāh *Jerusalem* 13 A2
Ramadān *Baghdad* 3 B2
Ramakrishna Puram *Delhi* 10 B1
Rāmallāh = Rām Allāh *Jerusalem* 13 A2
Ramanathpur *Kolkata* 14 A1
Ramat Allon *Jerusalem* 13 B2
Ramat Eshkol *Jerusalem* 13 B2
Ramat Razi'el *Jerusalem* 13 B1
Ramat Shafet *Jerusalem* 13 B2
Rambler Channel *Hong Kong* 12 A1
Ramenki *Moscow* 19 B1
Ramersdorf *Munich* 21 B2
Rameses Station *Cairo* 7 A2
Ramos *Rio de Janeiro* 25 B1
Ramos Mejía *Buenos Aires* 7 B1
Ramot *Jerusalem* 13 B2
Rampur *Delhi* 10 A2
Ramsgate *Sydney* 29 B1
Rancho Park *Los Angeles* 16 B2
Rand ✈ (QRA) *Johannesburg* 13 B2
Randalls I. *New York* 22 B2
Randburg *Johannesburg* 13 A1
Randhart *Johannesburg* 13 B2
Randpark Ridge *Johannesburg* 13 A1
Randwick *Sydney* 29 B2
Ranelagh *Dublin* 10 A2
Rangpuri *Delhi* 10 B1
Rannersdorf *Vienna* 32 B2
Ransbèche *Brussels* 6 B2
Ransdorp *Amsterdam* 2 A2
Ranvad *Mumbai* 20 B2
Raposo *Lisbon* 16 A1
Rastaala *Helsinki* 11 B1
Rastila *Helsinki* 11 B3
Raszyn *Warsaw* 32 C1
Rathfarnham *Dublin* 10 B2
Ratho *Edinburgh* 11 B1
Ratho Station *Edinburgh* 11 B1
Rato *Lisbon* 16 A2
Ravelston *Edinburgh* 11 B2
Rawamangun *Jakarta* 12 B2
Rayners Lane *London* 15 A1
Raynes Park *London* 15 B2
Raypur *Kolkata* 14 C2
Real Felipe, Fuerte *Lima* 14 B2
Reams, L. *Orlando* 23 B1
Reclining Buddha = Wat Pho *Bangkok* 3 B1
Recoleta *Buenos Aires* 7 B2
Recoleta *Santiago* 27 B2
Red Fort = Lal Qila *Delhi* 10 B2
Red Square *Moscow* 19 B2
Redbridge □ *London* 15 A4
Redfern *Sydney* 29 B2
Redwood *Wellington* 33 B1
Refshaleøen *Copenhagen* 8 A3
Regents Park *Johannesburg* 13 B2
Regent's Park *London* 15 A3
Rego Park *New York* 22 B2
Reinickendorf *Berlin* 5 A3
Rekola *Helsinki* 11 B3
Rembertów *Warsaw* 32 B2
Rembrandtpark *Amsterdam* 2 A2
Remedios de Escalada *Buenos Aires* 7 C2
Rèmola, Estany del *Barcelona* 4 B1
Renca *Santiago* 27 B1
Rennemoulin *Paris* 24 A1
Řeporyje *Prague* 25 B1
Repulse Bay *Hong Kong* 12 B2
Repy *Prague* 25 B1
Residenz *Munich* 21 B2
Reston *Washington* 33 B2
Retiro *Buenos Aires* 7 B2
Retiro *Madrid* 17 B1
Retiro, Puerto *Buenos Aires* 7 B2
Retreat *Cape Town* 8 B1
Reutov *Moscow* 19 B4
Réveillon → *Paris* 24 B4
Revere *Boston* 6 A2
Rexdale *Toronto* 31 A1
Reynosa Tamaulipas *Mexico City* 18 A1
Rho *Milan* 19 A1
Rhodes *Sydney* 29 A1
Rhodon *Paris* 24 B1
Rhodon → *Paris* 24 B1
Rialto Towers *Melbourne* 18 A1
Ribeira *Rio de Janeiro* 25 A1
Ricarda, Estany de la *Barcelona* 4 B1
Richmond *Melbourne* 18 A2
Richmond *San Francisco* 26 B2
Richmond Hill *New York* 22 B2
Richmond Park *London* 15 B2
Richmond-upon-Thames □ *London* 15 B2
Ridge, The *Delhi* 10 B2
Ridgefield *New York* 22 B1
Ridgefield Park *New York* 22 A1
Ridgewood *New York* 22 B2
Riem *Munich* 21 B3
Riesenrad *Vienna* 32 A2
Rijksmuseum *Amsterdam* 2 A2
Rikers I. *New York* 22 B2
Rímac *Lima* 14 B2
Ringsend *Dublin* 10 A2
Rinkeby *Stockholm* 29 A1
Rio Comprido *Rio de Janeiro* 25 B1
Rio de Janeiro *Rio de Janeiro* 25 B1
Rio de Janeiro Galeão ✈ (GIG) *Rio de Janeiro* 25 A1
Rio de Mouro *Lisbon* 16 A1
Ripollet *Barcelona* 4 A1
Ris *Oslo* 23 A3
Risby *Copenhagen* 8 A1
Rishra *Kolkata* 14 A2
Ritchie *Washington* 33 B4
Rithala *Delhi* 10 A1
Rive Sud, Canal de la *Montreal* 20 B2
River Edge *New York* 22 A1
River Forest *Chicago* 9 B2
River Grove *Chicago* 9 B1
River Ridge *New Orleans* 21 B1
Riverdale *New York* 22 A2
Riverdale *Washington* 33 B4
Riverdale Park *Toronto* 31 A2
Riverlea *Johannesburg* 13 B1
Riverside *Chicago* 9 C2
Riverwood *Sydney* 29 B1
Rivière-des-Prairies *Montreal* 20 A2
Rixensart *Brussels* 6 B3
Riyad *Baghdad* 3 B2
Rizal Park *Manila* 17 B1
Rizal Stadium *Manila* 17 B1
Røa *Oslo* 23 A2
Robbins *Chicago* 9 D2
Robertsham *Johannesburg* 13 B2
Rochelle Park *New York* 22 A1
Rock Cr. → *Washington* 33 B3
Rock Creek Park *Washington* 33 B3
Rock Pt. *Wellington* 33 A1
Rockaway Beach *New York* 22 C3
Rockaway Pt. *New York* 22 C2
Rockdale *Sydney* 29 B1
Rockefeller Center *New York* 22 B2
Rocky Run → *Washington* 33 B2
Roda, Gezîret el *Cairo* 7 A2
Roda I. = Roda, Gezîret el *Cairo* 7 A2
Rodaon *Vienna* 32 B1
Rødovre *Copenhagen* 8 A2
Rodrigo de Freitas, L. *Rio de Janeiro* 25 B1
Roehampton *London* 15 B2
Rogers Park *Chicago* 9 A3
Roihuvuori *Helsinki* 11 B3
Roissy-en-Brie *Paris* 24 B4
Rokytka → *Prague* 25 B3
Roma *Rome* 26 B1
Roma Urbe ✈ *Rome* 26 B2
Római-Fürdő *Budapest* 7 A2
Romainville *Paris* 24 A3
Roman Forum = Foro Romano *Rome* 26 B1
Romano Banco *Milan* 19 B1
Rome = Roma *Rome* 26 B1
Romema *Jerusalem* 13 B2
Romford *London* 15 A5
Ronald Reagan Nat. Washington ✈ (DCA) *Washington* 33 B3
Rondebosch *Cape Town* 8 A1
Roppongi *Tokyo* 30 B3
Rose, L. *Orlando* 23 A1
Rose Bowl *Los Angeles* 16 B4
Rose Hill *Washington* 33 C3
Rosebank *Johannesburg* 13 A2
Rosebank *New York* 22 C1
Rosebery *Sydney* 29 B2
Rosedal La Candelaria *Mexico City* 18 B2
Roseland *Chicago* 9 C3
Rosemead *Los Angeles* 16 B4
Rosemont *Chicago* 9 B1
Rosemont *Montreal* 20 A2
Rosenborg Slot *Copenhagen* 8 A3
Rosenthal *Berlin* 5 A3
Rosettenville *Johannesburg* 13 B2
Rosewell *Edinburgh* 11 B3
Rosherville Dam *Johannesburg* 13 B2
Rösjön *Stockholm* 29 A2
Roslags-Näsby *Stockholm* 29 A2
Roslin *Edinburgh* 11 B3
Roslindale *Boston* 6 B2
Rosny-sous-Bois *Paris* 24 A4
Rosslyn *Washington* 33 B3
Rosyth *Edinburgh* 11 A1
Rotherhithe *London* 15 B3
Rothneusiedl *Vienna* 32 B2
Rothschmaige *Munich* 21 A1
Rouge Hill *Toronto* 31 A4
Round I. *Hong Kong* 12 B2
Roxbury *Boston* 6 B2
Roxeth *London* 15 A1
Royal Botanic Gardens *Edinburgh* 11 B2
Royal Observatory *Edinburgh* 11 B2
Royal Palace = Kungliga Slottet *Stockholm* 29 B2
Royal Palace = Palacio Real *Madrid* 17 B1
Royal Park *Melbourne* 18 A1
Röylä *Helsinki* 11 B1
Rozas, Portilleros de las *Madrid* 17 B1
Roztoky *Prague* 25 B2
Rozzano *Milan* 19 B1
Rubí → *Barcelona* 4 A1
Rudolfsheim *Vienna* 32 A2
Rudolfshöhe *Berlin* 5 A5
Rudow *Berlin* 5 B3
Rueil-Malmaison *Paris* 24 A2
Ruisbroek *Brussels* 6 B1
Ruislip *London* 15 A1
Rumelihisarı *Istanbul* 12 B2
Rungis *Paris* 24 B3
Rusāfa *Baghdad* 3 A2
Rush Green *London* 15 A5
Russa *Kolkata* 14 C2
Rutherford *New York* 22 B1
Ruzyně *Prague* 25 B1
Ruzyne, Praha ✈ (PRG) *Prague* 25 B1
Rybatskaya *St. Petersburg* 27 B2
Rydboholm *Stockholm* 29 A3
Ryde *Sydney* 29 A1
Ryogoku *Tokyo* 30 A3
Rzhevka *St. Petersburg* 27 B3

S

Sa'ādatābād *Tehran* 31 A2
Saadūn *Baghdad* 3 B2
Saavedra *Buenos Aires* 7 B2
Saboli *Delhi* 10 A2
Sabugo *Lisbon* 16 A1
Sabzi Mand *Delhi* 10 A2
Sacavém *Lisbon* 16 A2
Saclay *Paris* 24 B2
Saclay, Étang de *Paris* 24 B1
Sacomã *São Paulo* 27 B2
Sacré Cœur *Paris* 24 A3
Sacrow *Berlin* 5 B1
Sacrower See *Berlin* 5 B1
Sadang *Seoul* 27 C1
Saddle → *New York* 22 A1
Saddle Brook *New York* 22 A1
Sadr *Karachi* 13 A2
Sadr City *Baghdad* 3 A2
Sadyba *Warsaw* 32 B2
Safdar Jang's Tomb *Delhi* 10 B2
Saft el Laban *Cairo* 7 A2
Saganashkee Slough *Chicago* 9 C1
Sagene *Oslo* 23 A3
Sagrada Familia, Templo de *Barcelona* 4 A2
Sahar, Mumbai ✈ (BOM) *Mumbai* 20 A2
Sai Kung *Hong Kong* 12 A2
Sai Wan Ho *Hong Kong* 12 B2
Sai Ying Pun *Hong Kong* 12 B1
St-Aubin *Paris* 24 B1
St-Cloud *Paris* 24 A2
St-Cyr-l'École *Paris* 24 B1
St-Cyr-l'École ✈ *Paris* 24 B1
St-Denis *Paris* 24 A3
St-Germain, Forêt de *Paris* 24 A1
St-Germain-en-Laye *Paris* 24 A1
St-Gilles *Brussels* 6 B2
St. Helier *London* 15 B2
St-Hubert *Montreal* 20 B3
St. Hubert, Galeries Royales *Brussels* 6 A2
St. Isaac's Cathedral *St. Petersburg* 27 B1
St-Jacques → *Montreal* 20 B3
St-Joost-Ten-Node *Brussels* 6 A2
St. Kilda *Melbourne* 18 B1
St-Lambert *Montreal* 20 A3
St-Lambert *Paris* 24 B1
St-Laurent *Montreal* 20 A1
St-Léonard *Montreal* 20 A2
St. Magelungen *Stockholm* 29 B2
St-Mandé *Paris* 24 A3
St. Margaret's *Dublin* 10 A2
St-Martin, Bois *Paris* 24 B4
St. Mary Cray *London* 15 B4
St-Maur-des-Fossés *Paris* 24 B3
St-Maurice *Paris* 24 B3
St-Michel *Montreal* 20 A2
St. Nikolaus-Kirken *Prague* 25 B2
St-Ouen *Paris* 24 A3
St. Paul's Cray *London* 15 B4
St. Peters *Sydney* 29 B2
St. Peter's Square = San Pietro, Piazza *Rome* 26 B1
St. Petersburg = Sankt-Peterburg *St. Petersburg* 27 B1
St. Petersburg Pulkovo Int. ✈ (LED) *St. Petersburg* 27 C1
St-Pierre *Montreal* 20 B2
St-Pieters Leew *Brussels* 6 B1
St-Quentin, Étang de *Paris* 24 B1
St. Stephens Cathedral = Stephansdom *Vienna* 32 A2
St-Stevens-Woluwe *Brussels* 6 A2
St-Vincent-de-Paul *Montreal* 20 A2
St. Xavier Univ. *Chicago* 9 C2
Ste-Catherine *Montreal* 20 B2
Ste-Hélène, Î. *Montreal* 20 A2
Saiwai *Tokyo* 30 B3
Sakai *Osaka* 23 B1
Sakai Harbour *Osaka* 23 B1
Sakra, Pulau *Singapore* 28 B2
Salam *Baghdad* 3 A2
Salamanca *Madrid* 17 B1
Sallynoggin *Dublin* 10 B3
Salmannsdorf *Vienna* 32 A1
Salmedina *Madrid* 17 C2
Salomea *Warsaw* 32 B1
Salsette I. *Mumbai* 20 A2
Salt Lake City = Bidhan Nagar *Kolkata* 14 B2
Salt River *Cape Town* 8 A1
Salt Water L. *Kolkata* 14 B2
Saltsjö-Duvnäs *Stockholm* 29 B3
Samatya *Istanbul* 12 C1
Sampaloc *Manila* 17 B1
Samphan Thawong *Bangkok* 3 B2
Samseon *Seoul* 27 B2
Samuel Smith Park *Toronto* 31 B1
Samut Prakan *Bangkok* 3 B2
San Andrés *Barcelona* 4 A2
San Angel *Mexico City* 18 B1
San Basilio *Rome* 26 B2
San Borja *Lima* 14 B3
San Bóvio *Milan* 19 B2
San Bruno, Pt. *San Francisco* 26 C2
San Bruno Mountain State Park ⌂ *San Francisco* 26 B2
San Cristóbal *Buenos Aires* 7 B2
San Cristóbal *Madrid* 17 B2
San Cristóbal, Cerro *Santiago* 27 B2
San Cristóbal, Virgen del *Santiago* 27 B2
San Cristoforo *Milan* 19 B1
San Donato Milanese *Milan* 19 B2
San Francisco *San Francisco* 26 B2
San Francisco B. *San Francisco* 26 B3
San Francisco Culhuacán *Mexico City* 18 C2
San Fruttuoso *Milan* 19 A2
San Gabriel *Los Angeles* 16 B4
San Gabriel → *Los Angeles* 16 C4
San Giuliano Milanese *Milan* 19 B2
San Isidro *Lima* 14 B2
San Jerónimo Lídice *Mexico City* 18 C1
San Joaquín *Santiago* 27 B2
San José Río Hondo *Mexico City* 18 B1
San Juan → *Manila* 17 B2
San Juan de Aragón *Mexico City* 18 B2
San Juan de Aragón, Parque *Mexico City* 18 B2
San Juan de Lurigancho *Lima* 14 A2
San Juan del Monte *Manila* 17 B2
San Juan Ixtacala *Mexico City* 18 A1
San Just Desvern *Barcelona* 4 A1
San Justo *Buenos Aires* 7 C1
San Lorenzo Tezonco *Mexico City* 18 C2
San Luis *Lima* 14 B2
San Marino *Los Angeles* 16 B4
San Martin *Barcelona* 4 A2
San Martín de Porras *Lima* 14 B2
San Mateo Tlaltenango *Mexico City* 18 B1
San Miguel *Lima* 14 B2
San Miguel *Santiago* 27 B2
San Nicolás *Buenos Aires* 7 B2
San Onófrio *Rome* 26 B1
San Pedro Mártir *Barcelona* 4 A1
San Pedro Zacatenco *Mexico City* 18 A2
San Pietro, Piazza *Rome* 26 B1
San Po Kong *Hong Kong* 12 A2
San Rafael Chamapa *Mexico City* 18 B1
San Rafael Hills *Los Angeles* 16 A3
San Roque *Manila* 17 B2
San Siro *Milan* 19 B1
San Souci *Sydney* 29 B1
San Telmo *Buenos Aires* 7 B2
San Vicenç dels Horts *Barcelona* 4 A1
Sandown *Johannesburg* 13 A2
Sandown Park Races *London* 15 B1
Sandton *Johannesburg* 13 A2
Sandvika *Oslo* 23 A2
Sandyford *Dublin* 10 B2
Sandymount *Dublin* 10 B2
Sangenjaya *Tokyo* 30 B2
Sanggye *Seoul* 27 B2
Sangley Pt. *Manila* 17 C1
Sankrail *Kolkata* 14 B1
Sankt-Peterburg *St. Petersburg* 27 B1
Sankt Veit *Vienna* 32 A1
Sanlihe *Beijing* 4 B1
Sanlintang *Shanghai* 28 C1
Sans *Barcelona* 4 A1
Sanssouci *Berlin* 5 B1
Sant Ambrogio, Basilica di *Milan* 19 B2
Sant Boi de Llobregat *Barcelona* 4 A1
Sant Cugat *Barcelona* 4 A1
Sant Feliu de Llobregat *Barcelona* 4 A1
Sant Joan Despi *Barcelona* 4 A1
Santa Ana *Manila* 17 B2
Santa Anita Park *Los Angeles* 16 B4
Santa Coloma de Gramenet *Barcelona* 4 A2
Santa Cruz *Manila* 17 B1
Santa Cruz *Mumbai* 20 A1
Santa Cruz, I. de *Rio de Janeiro* 25 B2
Santa Cruz de Olorde *Barcelona* 4 A1
Santa Efigênia *São Paulo* 27 B2
Santa Elena *Manila* 17 B2
Santa Elena del Gomero *Santiago* 27 B1
Santa Eulàlia *Barcelona* 4 A2
Santa Fe Springs *Los Angeles* 16 C4
Santa Iria da Azóia *Lisbon* 16 A2
Santa Julia *Santiago* 27 C2
Santa Monica *Los Angeles* 16 B2
Santa Monica Mts. *Los Angeles* 16 B2
Santa Rosa de Locobe *Santiago* 27 B2
Santa Teresa de la Ovalle *Santiago* 27 B1
Santahamina *Helsinki* 11 C3
Santana *São Paulo* 27 A2
Santeny *Paris* 24 B4
Santiago *Santiago* 27 B2
Santiago Benitez ✈ (SCL) *Santiago* 27 B1
Santiago de Surco *Lima* 14 B2
Santo Amaro *Lisbon* 16 A1
Santo Amaro *São Paulo* 27 B1
Santo André *Lisbon* 16 B2
Santo Antão do Tojal *Lisbon* 16 A2
Santo Antônio, Cabo de *Lisbon* 16 B1
Santo Tomas, Univ. of *Manila* 17 B1
Santos Dumont ✈ (SDU) *Rio de Janeiro* 25 B2
Santoshpur *Kolkata* 14 B1
Santragachi *Kolkata* 14 B1
Santry *Dublin* 10 A2
Sanyuanli *Guangzhou* 11 B2
São Caetano do Sul *São Paulo* 27 B2
São Conrado *Rio de Janeiro* 25 B1
São Cristóvão *Rio de Janeiro* 25 B1
São Jorge, Castelo de *Lisbon* 16 A2
São Julião do Tojal *Lisbon* 16 A2
São Paulo *São Paulo* 27 B2
São Paulo Congonhas ✈ (CGH) *São Paulo* 27 B2
Sapa *Kolkata* 14 B1
Sapateiro, Cor. do → *São Paulo* 27 B1
Sarandi *Buenos Aires* 7 C2
Saraswati → *Kolkata* 14 A1
Sarecky potok → *Prague* 25 B2
Sarimbun *Singapore* 28 A2
Sarimbun Res. *Singapore* 28 A2
Sarıyer *Istanbul* 12 A2
Sarrià *Barcelona* 4 A1
Sarsuna *Kolkata* 14 C1
Sartrouville *Paris* 24 A2
Sasad *Budapest* 7 B2
Sashalom *Budapest* 7 A3
Saska *Warsaw* 32 B2
Satalice *Prague* 25 B3
Satgachi *Kolkata* 14 B2
Satpukur *Kolkata* 14 B2
Sätra *Stockholm* 29 B1
Saúde *São Paulo* 27 B2
Saugus *Boston* 6 A2
Saugus → *Boston* 6 A2
Sault-au-Récollet *Montreal* 20 A2
Sausalito *San Francisco* 26 A2
Sawah Besar *Jakarta* 12 A1
Sawtelle *Los Angeles* 16 B2
Scald Law *Edinburgh* 11 B2
Scarborough *Toronto* 31 A3
Scarborough Bluffs *Toronto* 31 A3
Sceaux *Paris* 24 B2
Schaerbeek *Brussels* 6 A2
Scharfenberg *Berlin* 5 A2
Schiller Park *Chicago* 9 B1
Schiller Woods *Chicago* 9 B1
Schiphol, Amsterdam ✈ (AMS) *Amsterdam* 2 B1
Schlachtensee *Berlin* 5 B2
Schlossgarten *Berlin* 5 A2
Schmargendorf *Berlin* 5 B2
Schönblick *Berlin* 5 B5
Schönbrunn *Vienna* 32 A1
Schöneberg *Berlin* 5 B3
Schönefeld *Berlin* 5 B4
Schöneiche *Berlin* 5 B5
Schönwalde *Berlin* 5 A1
Schulzendorf *Berlin* 5 A2
Schwabing *Munich* 21 B2
Schwanebeck *Berlin* 5 A4
Schwanenwerder *Berlin* 5 B2
Schwarzlackenau *Vienna* 32 A2
Schwechat *Vienna* 32 B2
Schwechat, Wien ✈ (VIE) *Vienna* 32 B3
Science and Industry, Museum of *Chicago* 9 C3
Scitrek Museum *Atlanta* 3 B2
Scopus, Mt. *Jerusalem* 13 B2
Scottdale *Atlanta* 3 B3
Scutari = Üsküdar *Istanbul* 12 B2
Sea Point *Cape Town* 8 A1
Seabrook *Washington* 33 B5
Seacliff *San Francisco* 26 B2
Seaforth *Sydney* 29 A2
Seagate *New York* 22 C1
Seat Pleasant *Washington* 33 B4
Seaview *Wellington* 33 B2
SeaWorld *Orlando* 23 B2
Šeberov *Prague* 25 B3
Secaucus *New York* 22 B1
Seddinsee *Berlin* 5 B5
Seeberg *Berlin* 5 A5
Seeburg *Berlin* 5 A1
Seefeld *Berlin* 5 A5
Seegefeld *Berlin* 5 A1
Seehof *Berlin* 5 B2
Segeltorp *Stockholm* 29 B1
Segrate *Milan* 19 B2
Seguro *Milan* 19 B1
Seixal *Lisbon* 16 B2
Selby *Johannesburg* 13 B2
Seletar, Pulau *Singapore* 28 A3
Seletar Hills *Singapore* 28 A3
Seletar Res. *Singapore* 28 A2
Selhurst *London* 15 B3
Sembawang *Singapore* 28 A2
Senago *Milan* 19 A1
Sendling *Munich* 21 B2
Senju *Tokyo* 30 A3
Senriyama *Osaka* 23 A2
Sentosa *Singapore* 28 B2
Seobinggo *Seoul* 27 B1
Seocho *Seoul* 27 C1
Seodaemun *Seoul* 27 B1
Seokkwan *Seoul* 27 B2
Seongbuk *Seoul* 27 B2
Seongdong *Seoul* 27 B2
Seongsu *Seoul* 27 B2
Seoul *Seoul* 27 B2
Seoul Nat. Univ. *Seoul* 27 C1
Seoul Tower *Seoul* 27 B1
Sepolia *Athens* 2 A2
Sepulveda Dam Rec. Area ⌂ *Los Angeles* 16 A2
Serangoon *Singapore* 28 A3
Serangoon, Pulau *Singapore* 28 A3
Serangoon, Sungei → *Singapore* 28 A3
Serangoon Harbour *Singapore* 28 A3
Seraya, Pulau *Singapore* 28 B2
Serebryanka → *Moscow* 19 B3
Serramonte *San Francisco* 26 C2
Sesto San Giovanni *Milan* 19 A2
Sesto Ulteriano *Milan* 19 B2
Setagaya *Tokyo* 30 B2
Seter *Oslo* 23 A3
Setia Budi *Jakarta* 12 B1
Settebagni *Rome* 26 A2
Settecamini *Rome* 26 B2
Séttimo Milanese *Milan* 19 B1
Settsu *Osaka* 23 A2
Seutula *Helsinki* 11 A2
Seven Corners *Washington* 33 B3
Seven Kings *London* 15 A4
Seventeenth Street Canal *New Orleans* 21 A2
Sévesco → *Milan* 19 A1
Sevran *Paris* 24 A4
Sewri *Mumbai* 20 B2
Sforzesco, Castello *Milan* 19 B2
Sha Kok Mei *Hong Kong* 12 A2
Sha Tin *Hong Kong* 12 A2
Sha'ar Binyamin *Jerusalem* 13 A2
Shabrâmant *Cairo* 7 B2
Shah Mosque *Tehran* 31 A2
Shahdara *Delhi* 10 A2
Shahe *Guangzhou* 11 B2
Shahr-e Rey *Tehran* 31 B2
Shahrak-e Golshahr *Tehran* 31 B1
Shahrak-e Qods *Tehran* 31 A2
Shaikh Aomar *Baghdad* 3 A2
Shakurbasti *Delhi* 10 A1
Shalkiya *Kolkata* 14 B2
Sham Shui Po *Hong Kong* 12 B1
Shamapur *Delhi* 10 A1
Shamian *Guangzhou* 11 B2
Shan Mei *Hong Kong* 12 A2
Shanghai *Shanghai* 28 B2
Shanghai Hongqiao ✈ (SHA) *Shanghai* 28 B1
Shanghai Pudong ✈ (PVG) *Shanghai* 28 B2
Shankill *Dublin* 10 B3
Sharp I. *Hong Kong* 12 A2
Shastrinagar *Delhi* 10 A2
Shau Kei Wan *Hong Kong* 12 B2
Shawocun *Beijing* 4 B1
Shayuan *Guangzhou* 11 B2
Sheen, L. *Orlando* 23 B1
Sheepshead Bay *New York* 22 C2
Shek O *Hong Kong* 12 B2
Shelter I. *Hong Kong* 12 B2
Shepherds Bush *London* 15 A2
Shepperton *London* 15 B1
Sheremetyevo ✈ (SVO) *Moscow* 19 A2
Sherman Oaks *Los Angeles* 16 B2
Sherman Park *Chicago* 9 C2
Sherwood, L. *Orlando* 23 A2
Shet Bandar *Mumbai* 20 B2
Sheung Fa Shan *Hong Kong* 12 A1
Sheung Lau Wan *Hong Kong* 12 B2
Sheung Wan *Hong Kong* 12 B1
Sheva *Mumbai* 20 B2
Sheva Nhava *Mumbai* 20 B2
Shiba *Tokyo* 30 B3
Shibpur *Kolkata* 14 B1
Shibuya *Tokyo* 30 B3
Shilihe *Beijing* 4 B2
Shimogawara *Tokyo* 30 B1
Shimosalo *Tokyo* 30 A2
Shimoshakujii *Tokyo* 30 A2
Shinagawa *Tokyo* 30 B3
Shing Mun Res. *Hong Kong* 12 A1
Shinjuku *Tokyo* 30 A3
Shinjuku Nat. Garden *Tokyo* 30 A3
Shinkoiwa *Tokyo* 30 A4
Shinnakano *Tokyo* 30 A3
Shipai *Guangzhou* 11 B3
Shirinashi → *Osaka* 23 B1
Shirogane *Tokyo* 30 B3
Shitennoji Temple *Osaka* 23 B2
Shiweitang *Guangzhou* 11 B2
Shogunle *Lagos* 14 A2
Shomolu *Lagos* 14 A2
Shooters Hill *London* 15 B4
Shoreditch *London* 15 A3
Shortlands *London* 15 B4
Shu'afat *Jerusalem* 13 B2
Shubrâ *Cairo* 7 A2
Shubrâ el Kheima *Cairo* 7 A2
Shuikou *Guangzhou* 11 A2
Sidcup *London* 15 B4
Siebenhirten *Vienna* 32 B1
Siedlung *Berlin* 5 A1
Siekierki *Warsaw* 32 B2
Sielce *Warsaw* 32 B2
Siemensstadt *Berlin* 5 A2
Sierra Madre *Los Angeles* 16 B4
Sievering *Vienna* 32 A2
Sighthill *Edinburgh* 11 B2
Signal Hill *Cape Town* 8 A1
Siheung *Seoul* 27 C1
Sikátorpuszta *Budapest* 7 A3
Silampur *Delhi* 10 B2
Sillim *Seoul* 27 C1
Silver, L. *Orlando* 23 A2
Silver Hill *Washington* 33 C4
Silver Lake *Los Angeles* 16 B3
Silver Spring *Washington* 33 A3
Silvermine Nature Reserve *Cape Town* 8 B1
Silvolantekojärvi *Helsinki* 11 B2
Simei *Singapore* 28 A3
Simla *Kolkata* 14 B2
Simmering *Vienna* 32 A2
Simmering Heide *Vienna* 32 A2
Simonkylä *Helsinki* 11 B3
Sinchon *Seoul* 27 B1
Sindang *Seoul* 27 B2
Singapore ■ *Singapore* 28 B3
Singapore, Univ. of *Singapore* 28 B2
Singapore Changi ✈ (SIN) *Singapore* 28 A3
Sinki, Selat *Singapore* 28 B2
Sinsa *Seoul* 27 B2
Sint-Genesius-Rode *Brussels* 6 B2
Sion *Mumbai* 20 A2
Sipson *London* 15 B1
Siqeil *Cairo* 7 A1
Şişli *Istanbul* 12 B1
Skansen *Stockholm* 29 B2
Skärholmen *Stockholm* 29 B1
Skarpäng *Stockholm* 29 A2
Skarpnäck *Stockholm* 29 B2
Skaryszewski, Park *Warsaw* 32 B2
Skokie *Chicago* 9 A2
Skokie → *Chicago* 9 A2
Skokie Heritage Museum *Chicago* 9 A2
Skoklefall *Oslo* 23 A3
Skøndal *Stockholm* 29 B2
Skovlunde *Copenhagen* 8 A2
Skovshoved *Copenhagen* 8 A3
Skuru *Stockholm* 29 B3
Sky Lake *Orlando* 23 B2
Skyland *Atlanta* 3 A3
Slade Green *London* 15 B5
Slependen *Oslo* 23 A2
Slipi *Jakarta* 12 B1
Slivenec *Prague* 25 B2
Sloten *Amsterdam* 2 A1
Sloterdijk *Amsterdam* 2 A1
Sloterpark *Amsterdam* 2 A1
Sluhy *Prague* 25 A3
Służew *Warsaw* 32 B2
Służewiec *Warsaw* 32 B2
Smíchov *Prague* 25 B2
Smith Forest Preserve *Chicago* 9 B2
Smolny *St. Petersburg* 27 B2
Smolny Cathedral *St. Petersburg* 27 B2
Snake Creek Canal *Miami* 18 A2
Snakeden Branch → *Washington* 33 B1
Snarøya *Oslo* 23 A2
Snättringe *Stockholm* 29 B1
Søborg *Copenhagen* 8 A2
Sobreda *Lisbon* 16 B1
Söderby *Stockholm* 29 A3
Södermalm *Stockholm* 29 B2
Sodpur *Kolkata* 14 A2
Soeurs, Î. des *Montreal* 20 B2
Sognsvatn *Oslo* 23 A3
Soignes, Forêt de *Brussels* 6 B2
Sok Kwu Wan *Hong Kong* 12 B1
Sokolniki *Moscow* 19 B3
Sokolniki Park *Moscow* 19 B3
Sokołów *Warsaw* 32 C1
Solalinden *Munich* 21 B3
Sollentuna *Stockholm* 29 A1
Solln *Munich* 21 B2
Solna *Stockholm* 29 A1
Somerset *Washington* 33 B3
Somerville *Boston* 6 A2
Somes I. *Wellington* 33 B2
Sonari *Mumbai* 20 B2
Sønderso *Copenhagen* 8 A2
Songpa *Seoul* 27 B2
Sony Picture Studio *Los Angeles* 16 B2
Sord = Swords *Dublin* 10 A2
Soroksár *Budapest* 7 B2
Soroksari Duna → *Budapest* 7 B2
Sosenka → *Moscow* 19 B3
Sosnovka *St. Petersburg* 27 B2
Sŏul = Seoul *Seoul* 27 B2

Soundview New York 22 B2
South Beach New York 22 C1
South Bend Park Atlanta 3 B2
South Boston Boston 6 A2
South Decatur Atlanta 3 B3
South Deering Chicago 9 C3
South El Monte Los Angeles 16 B4
South Gate Los Angeles 16 C3
South Harbor Manila 17 B1
South Harrow London 15 A1
South Hd. Sydney 29 B2
South Hills Johannesburg 13 B2
South Lawn Washington 33 C3
South Miami Miami 18 B1
South Norwood London 15 B3
South of Market San Francisco 26 B2
South Ozone Park New York 22 B3
South Pasadena Los Angeles 16 B4
South Res. Boston 6 A2
South Ruislip London 15 A1
South San Francisco San Francisco 26 C2
South San Gabriel Los Angeles 16 B4
South Shore Chicago 9 C3
Southall London 15 A1
Southborough London 15 B4
Southend London 15 B3
Southern California, Univ. of Los Angeles 16 B3
Southfields London 15 B2
Southport New Orleans 21 B2
Southwark □ London 15 B3
Southwest Museum Los Angeles 16 B3
Søvang Copenhagen 8 B3
Soweto Johannesburg 13 B1
Sowhānak Tehran 31 A3
Soya Tokyo 30 A4
Spandau Berlin 5 A1
Spånga Stockholm 29 A1
Spanish Monastery Miami 18 A2
Spectacle I. Boston 6 A3
Speicher-See Munich 21 A3
Speising Vienna 32 B1
Sphinx Cairo 7 B1
Spinaceto Rome 26 C1
Spit Junction Sydney 29 A2
Spořilov Prague 25 B3
Spot Pond Boston 6 A2
Spotswood Melbourne 18 B1
Spring Valley Las Vegas 14 B1
Springeberg Berlin 5 B5
Springfield Washington 33 C2
Squantum Boston 6 B2
Srednaya Rogatka St. Petersburg 27 C2
Śródmieście Warsaw 32 B2
Staaken Berlin 5 A1
Stabekk Oslo 23 A2
Stadlau Vienna 32 A2
Stadshuset Stockholm 29 B2
Stains Paris 24 A3
Stamford Hill London 15 A3
Stammersdorf Vienna 32 A2
Stanley Hong Kong 12 B2
Stanley Pen. Hong Kong 12 B2
Stanmore London 15 A2
Stapleton New York 22 C1
Staraya Derevnya St. Petersburg 27 B1
Staré Město Prague 25 B2
Stare Miasto Warsaw 32 B2
Starke, L. Orlando 23 A1
Staten Island Zoo New York 22 C1
Staten Islands Ferry Terminal New York 22 C1
Statenice Prague 25 B1
Stedelijk Museum Amsterdam 2 A2
Steele Creek Melbourne 18 A1
Steenokkerzeel Brussels 6 A2
Steer, L. Orlando 23 A2
Steglitz Berlin 5 B2
Stepaside Dublin 10 B2
Stephansdom Vienna 32 A2
Stepney London 15 A3
Sterling Park San Francisco 26 B2
Sticklinge udde Stockholm 29 A2
Stickney Chicago 9 C2
Stillorgan Dublin 10 B2
Stockholm Stockholm 29 B2
Stockholm Arlanda ✕ (ARN) Stockholm 29 A1
Stocksund Stockholm 29 A2
Stodůlky Prague 25 B1
Stoke Newington London 15 A3
Stokes Valley Wellington 33 B2
Stone Canyon Res. Los Angeles 16 B2
Stone Park Chicago 9 B1
Stonebridge London 15 A2
Stoneham Boston 6 A2
Stony Brook Res. Boston 6 B2
Stony Creek → Chicago 9 C2
Stora Värtan Stockholm 29 A2
Store Hareskov Copenhagen 8 A2
Store Magleby Copenhagen 8 B3
Storholmen Stockholm 29 A2
Stoyka St. Petersburg 27 B2
Straiton Edinburgh 11 B3
Strandfontein Cape Town 8 B2
Strašnice Prague 25 B2
Strasstrudering Munich 21 B3
Stratford London 15 A4
Strathfield Sydney 29 B1
Streatham London 15 B3
Streatham Vale London 15 B3
Strebersdorf Vienna 32 A2
Střešovice Prague 25 B2
Strip, The Las Vegas 14 B2
Střížkov Prague 25 B2
Strombeek-Bever Brussels 6 A2
Stromovka Prague 25 B2
Studio City Los Angeles 16 B2
Stureby Stockholm 29 B2
Stuvsta Stockholm 29 B2
Subhepur Delhi 10 A2
Suburban Canal New Orleans 21 B1
Sucat Manila 17 C2
Suchdol Prague 25 B2
Sucy-en-Brie Paris 24 B4
Sue, L. Orlando 23 A2
Sugamo Tokyo 30 A3
Sugar Loaf Mt. = Açúcar, Pão de Rio de Janeiro 25 B2
Suge Tokyo 30 B2
Suginami Tokyo 30 A2
Sugō Tokyo 30 B2
Sui Sai Wan Hong Kong 12 B1
Suita Osaka 23 A2
Suitland Washington 33 B4
Sukchar Kolkata 14 A2
Sultanahme Camil Istanbul 12 B1
Sumida Tokyo 30 A3
Sumida → Tokyo 30 A3
Sumiyoshi Osaka 23 B2
Sumiyoshi Shrine Osaka 23 B1
Summerville Toronto 31 B1
Summit Chicago 9 C2
Sunamachi Tokyo 30 A4
Sunbury-on-Thames London 15 B1
Sundbyberg Stockholm 29 A1
Sundbyerne Copenhagen 8 B3
Sung Kong Hong Kong 12 B2
Sungei Kadut Industrial Estate Singapore 28 A2
Sungei Selatar Res. Singapore 28 A3
Sunrise Manor Las Vegas 14 A2
Sunrise Mountain Natural Area Las Vegas 14 A2
Sunset Park Las Vegas 14 B2
Sunset Park New York 22 C2
Sunter Jakarta 12 A2
Sunter, Kali → Jakarta 12 B2
Suomenlinna Helsinki 11 C2
Sur Bahr Jerusalem 13 B2
Sura Kolkata 14 B2
Suraksan Seoul 27 A2
Surbiton London 15 B2
Suresnes Paris 24 A2
Surfside Miami 18 A2
Surquillo Lima 14 B2
Surrey Hills Sydney 29 B2
Susaek Seoul 27 B1
Süssenbrunn Vienna 32 A2
Sutton Dublin 10 A3
Sutton London 15 B2
Suyu Seoul 27 B2
Suzukishinden Tokyo 30 A2
Svanemøllen Copenhagen 8 A3
Sveaborg = Suomenlinna Helsinki 11 C2
Sverdlov Moscow 19 B2
Svestad Oslo 23 B2
Svinö Helsinki 11 C1
Swanley London 15 B4
Swansea Toronto 31 B2
Swinburne I. New York 22 C1
Swords Dublin 10 A2
Sydenham Johannesburg 13 A2
Sydney Sydney 29 B2
Sydney, Univ. of Sydney 29 B2
Sydney Harbour △ Sydney 29 B2
Sydney Harbour Bridge Sydney 29 B2
Sydney Kingsford Smith ✕ (SYD) Sydney 29 B2
Sydstranden Copenhagen 8 B3
Sylvania Sydney 29 C1
Syon Park London 15 B2
Szczęśliwice Warsaw 32 B1
Széchnenyi-hegy Budapest 7 B1
Széphalom Budapest 7 A1

T

Taastrup Copenhagen 8 B1
Tabata Tokyo 30 A3
Tablada Buenos Aires 7 C1
Table B. Cape Town 8 A1
Table Mountain △ Cape Town 8 A1
Taboão da Serra São Paulo 27 B1
Täby Stockholm 29 A2
Tacuba Mexico City 18 B1
Tacubaya Mexico City 18 B1
Tafelbaai = Table B. Cape Town 8 A1
Taft Orlando 23 B2
Tagig → Manila 17 B2
Taguig Manila 17 B2
Tai Lo Shan Hong Kong 12 A2
Tai Po Tsai Hong Kong 12 A2
Tai Seng Singapore 28 A3
Tai Shui Hang Hong Kong 12 A2
Tai Tam B. Hong Kong 12 B2
Tai Tam Tuk Res. Hong Kong 12 B2
Tai Wai Hong Kong 12 A2
Tai Wan Tau Hong Kong 12 B2
Tai Wo Hau Hong Kong 12 A1
Tainaka Osaka 23 B2
Taishō Osaka 23 B1
Taita Wellington 33 B2
Tajrish Tehran 31 A2
Takaido Tokyo 30 A2
Takaishi Tokyo 30 B2
Takarazuka Osaka 23 A1
Takasago Tokyo 30 A4
Takatsu Tokyo 30 B2
Takeshita Tokyo 30 B2
Takinegawa Tokyo 30 A3
Takoma Park Washington 33 B3
Taksim Istanbul 12 B1
Talaide Lisbon 16 A1
Taliganga Kolkata 14 B2
Talipapa Manila 17 A2
Tallaght Dublin 10 B1
Tallkrogen Stockholm 29 B2
Tama Tokyo 30 B1
Tama → Tokyo 30 B2
Tama Kyūryō Tokyo 30 B2
Tamaden Tokyo 30 B2
Tamagawa-josui → Tokyo 30 A1
Taman Sari Jakarta 12 A1
Tamanduateí → São Paulo 27 B2
Tamboerskloof Cape Town 8 A1
Tambora Jakarta 12 A1
Tammisalo Helsinki 11 B3
Tammūh Cairo 7 B2
Tampines Singapore 28 A3
Tanah Abang Jakarta 12 B1
Tanah Kusir Jakarta 12 B1
Tangelo Park Orlando 23 B2
Tanjung Duren Jakarta 12 B1
Tanjung Priok Jakarta 12 A2
Tanum Oslo 23 A1
Tapada Lisbon 16 A1
Tapanila Helsinki 11 B3
Tapiales Buenos Aires 7 C1
Tapiola Helsinki 11 B1
Tapsia Kolkata 14 B2
Tara Mumbai 20 A1
Tarabya Istanbul 12 B2
Tårbæk Copenhagen 8 A3
Tarchomin Warsaw 32 B1
Tardeo Mumbai 20 B1
Targówek Warsaw 32 B2
Tårnby Copenhagen 8 B3
Tarqua Bay Lagos 14 B2
Tathong Channel Hong Kong 12 B2
Tathong Pt. Hong Kong 12 B2
Tatuapé São Paulo 27 B2
Taufkirchen Munich 21 B2
Tavares, I. dos Rio de Janeiro 25 A2
Tavros Athens 2 B2
Tawa Wellington 33 A1
Te Papa Museum Wellington 33 B1
Teaneck New York 22 A1
Tebet Jakarta 12 B2
Tecamachalco Mexico City 18 B1
Ted Williams Tunnel Boston 6 A2
Teddington London 15 B1
Tegel Berlin 5 A2
Tegel, Berlin ✕ (TXL) Berlin 5 A2
Tegeler See Berlin 5 A2
Tegelort Berlin 5 A2
Teheran = Tehrān Tehran 31 A2
Tehrān Tehran 31 A2
Tehrān Mehrābād ✕ (THR) Tehran 31 A1
Tehrān Pārs Tehran 31 A3
Tei Tong Tsui Hong Kong 12 B2
Tejo, Rio → Lisbon 16 A2
Tekstilyshchik Moscow 19 B3
Telhal Lisbon 16 A1
Telok Blangah Singapore 28 B2
Teltow Berlin 5 B2
Teltow kanal Berlin 5 B3
Tempelhof Berlin 5 B3
Temple City Los Angeles 16 B4
Temple Hills Washington 33 C4
Temple of Heaven Beijing 4 B2
Templeogue Dublin 10 B2
Temppeliaukio Church Helsinki 11 B2
Tenafly New York 22 A2
Tenayuca, Pirámide de Mexico City 18 A1
Tengah → Singapore 28 A2
Tennoji Osaka 23 B2
Tepalcates Mexico City 18 B2
Tepeyac △ Mexico City 18 B2
Terrazzano Milan 19 A1
Terre des Hommes Montreal 20 A2
Terrugem Lisbon 16 A1
Terrytown New Orleans 21 B2
Tervuren Brussels 6 B3
Tervuren, Park van Brussels 6 B3
Tetuán Madrid 17 B1
Teufelsberg Berlin 5 B2
Thalkirchen Munich 21 B2
Thames Ditton London 15 B1
Thamesmead London 15 A4
Thana Cr. → Mumbai 20 A2
Thiais Paris 24 B3
Thisio Athens 2 B2
Thistletown Toronto 31 A1
Thomastown Melbourne 18 A2
Thompson I. Boston 6 B3
Thon Buri Bangkok 3 B1
Thornbury Melbourne 18 A2
Thorncliffe Toronto 31 A2
Thornhill Toronto 31 A2
Thornton Cape Town 8 A2
Thornton Heath London 15 B3
Threipmuir Res. Edinburgh 11 B2
Throgs Neck New York 22 B3
Tiancun Beijing 4 B1
Tianhe Guangzhou 11 B3
Tibet, L. Orlando 23 B1
Tibidabo Barcelona 4 A1
Tibradden Mt. Dublin 10 B2
Tiburon San Francisco 26 A2
Tiburtino Rome 26 B2
Ticomán Mexico City 18 A2
Tiefersee Berlin 5 B1
Tiergarten Berlin 5 A3
Tijgerhof Cape Town 8 A2
Tijuca Rio de Janeiro 25 B1
Tijuca, Pico da Rio de Janeiro 25 B1
Tijuca △ Rio de Janeiro 25 B1
Tikkurila Helsinki 11 B3
Tilak Nagar Delhi 10 B1
Tilanqiao Shanghai 28 B1
Timah, Bukit Singapore 28 A2
Timiryazev Park Moscow 19 B2
Tin Can I. Lagos 14 B2
Ting Kau Hong Kong 12 A1
Tira Jerusalem 13 A1
Tirsa Cairo 7 B2
Tishrīyaa Baghdad 3 B2
Tiu Keng Leng Hong Kong 12 B2
Tizapán Mexico City 18 C1
Tlalnepantla → Mexico City 18 A1
Tlalpan Mexico City 18 C2
To Kwai Wan Hong Kong 12 B2
Toa Payoh Singapore 28 A3
Točná Prague 25 C2
Toco Hills Atlanta 3 B2
Todt Hill New York 22 C1
Togaki Tokyo 30 A4
Tokai Plantation Cape Town 8 B1
Tōkaichiba Tokyo 30 B2
Tōkyō Tokyo 30 B3
Tōkyō B. = Tōkyō-Wan Tokyo 30 B4
Tōkyō Disneyland Tokyo 30 B4
Tōkyō Haneda ✕ (HND) Tokyo 30 B3
Tōkyō Harbour Tokyo 30 B3
Tōkyō-Wan Tokyo 30 B4
Tolka → Dublin 10 A1
Tollygunge = Taliganga Kolkata 14 B2
Tolworth London 15 B2
Tomba di Nerone Rome 26 B1
Tommy Thompson Park Toronto 31 B3
Tondo Manila 17 B1
Tongbinggo Seoul 27 B1
Tongqiao Shanghai 28 B1
Toorak Melbourne 18 B2
Topanga State Park ⌂ Los Angeles 16 B1
Topkapı Istanbul 12 B1
Topkapı Palaca Istanbul 12 B1
Tor di Quinto Rome 26 B1
Tor Pignattara Rome 26 B2
Tor Sapienza Rome 26 B2
Torcy Paris 24 A4
Toronto Toronto 31 B2
Toronto, Univ. of Toronto 31 B2
Toronto City Centre ✕ (YTZ) Toronto 31 B2
Toronto Harbour Toronto 31 B2
Toronto I. Toronto 31 B2
Toronto Lester B. Pearson Int. ✕ (YYZ) Toronto 31 A1
Torre Lupara Rome 26 B2
Torre Nova Rome 26 B2
Torrellas → Barcelona 4 A1
Torrevécchia Rome 26 B1
Toshima Tokyo 30 A3
Toshimaen Tokyo 30 A2
Tottenham London 15 A3
Tottenham Melbourne 18 A1
Toussus-le-Noble Paris 24 B1
Toussus-le-Noble ✕ (TNF) Paris 24 B1
Towchāl Cable Car Tehran 31 A2
Tower Hamlets □ London 15 A3
Tower of London London 15 A3
Towra Pt. Sydney 29 C2
Tøyen Oslo 23 A3
Toyonaka Osaka 23 A1
Trafaria Lisbon 16 A1
Traição, Cor. → São Paulo 27 B2
Tranegilde Copenhagen 8 B2
Trångsund Stockholm 29 B2
Trappenfelde Berlin 5 A4
Trastévere Rome 26 B1
Treasure I. San Francisco 26 B2
Třeboradice Prague 25 B3
Třebotov Prague 25 B1
Tremblay-en-France Paris 24 A4
Tremembe → São Paulo 27 A2
Tremont New York 22 A2
Trenno Milan 19 B1
Treptow Berlin 5 B3
Três Rios, Sa. dos Rio de Janeiro 25 B1
Trevi, Fontana di Rome 26 B1
Trezzano sul Naviglio Milan 19 B1
Trieste Rome 26 B2
Trinidad Washington 33 B4
Trinity Edinburgh 11 B2
Trinity College Dublin 10 A2
Trionfale Rome 26 B1
Triulzo Milan 19 B2
Troja Prague 25 B2
Trollbäcken Stockholm 29 B3
Trombay Mumbai 20 A2
Troparevo Moscow 19 C1
Trudeau, Montréal ✕ (YUL) Montreal 20 B1
Trudyashchikhsya, Ostrov St. Petersburg 27 B1
Tryvasshøgda Oslo 23 A3
Tseng Lan Shue Hong Kong 12 A2
Tseung Kwan Hong Kong 12 B2
Tsim Sha Tsui Hong Kong 12 B2
Tsing Yi Hong Kong 12 A1
Tsova Jerusalem 13 B1
Tsuen Wan Hong Kong 12 A1
Tsur Hadassa Jerusalem 13 B1
Tsurumi → Tokyo 30 B3
Tsz Wan Shan Hong Kong 12 A2
Tuas Singapore 28 B1
Tuchoměřice Prague 25 B1
Tuckahoe New York 22 A3
Tucuruvi São Paulo 27 A2
Tufello Rome 26 B2
Tufnell Park London 15 A3
Tufts Univ. Boston 6 A2
Tughlakabad Delhi 10 B2
Tullamarine Melbourne 18 A1
Tulse Hill London 15 B3
Tung Lung Chau Hong Kong 12 B2
Tung O Hong Kong 12 B1
Tunis Baghdad 3 A2
Tuomarila Helsinki 11 B1
Tureberg Stockholm 29 A1
Turffontein Johannesburg 13 B2
Turkey L. Orlando 23 A2
Turkey Lake Park Orlando 23 A2
Turner Field Atlanta 3 B2
Turnham Green London 15 B2
Turnhouse Edinburgh 11 B1
Tuscolana, Via Rome 26 B2
Twelve Apostles Cape Town 8 A1
Twentieth Century Fox Studios Los Angeles 16 B2
Twickenham London 15 B1
Twickenham Rugby Ground London 15 B1
Twin Peaks San Francisco 26 B2
Two Rock Mt. Dublin 10 B2
Tymon North Dublin 10 B1
Tysons Corner Washington 33 B2

U

U.S. Capitol Washington 33 B3
U.S. Cellular Field Chicago 9 C3
Ubeidiya Jerusalem 13 B2
Uberaba → São Paulo 27 B2
Ubin, Pulau Singapore 28 A3
Uccle Brussels 6 B2
Udelnaya St. Petersburg 27 A2
Udelnoe St. Petersburg 27 B1
Udling Munich 21 A1
Ueno Tokyo 30 A3
Úholičky Prague 25 B1
Uhříněves Prague 25 B3
Uithoorn Amsterdam 2 B1
Ujazdów Warsaw 32 B2
Újpalota Budapest 7 A2
Újpest Budapest 7 A2
Ukita Tokyo 30 A4
Ullerup Copenhagen 8 B3
Ullevål Oslo 23 A3
Ulriksdal Stockholm 29 A1
Ulyanka St. Petersburg 27 B1
Um Al-Khanazir Island Baghdad 3 B2
Umeda Osaka 23 A1
Ümraniye Istanbul 12 B2
Underground Atlanta Atlanta 3 B2
Underhill, L. Orlando 23 A3
Unětický potok → Prague 25 B2
Unhos Lisbon 16 A2
Unidad Santa Fe Mexico City 18 B1
Union City New York 22 B1
Union Port New York 22 B2
Union Station Toronto 31 B2
United Center Chicago 9 B2
United Nations Headquarters New York 22 B2
Universal Studios Los Angeles 16 B2
Universal Studios Orlando 23 B2
Universidad Madrid 17 B1
University Park Washington 33 B4
Unterbiberg Munich 21 B2
Unterföhring Munich 21 A3
Unterhaching Munich 21 B2
Unterlaa Vienna 32 B2
Untermenzing Munich 21 A1
Upper B. New York 22 C1
Upper Elmers End London 15 B3
Upper New York B. = Upper B. New York 22 C1
Upper Norwood London 15 B3
Upper Peirce Res. Singapore 28 A2
Upper Sydenham London 15 B3
Upper Tooting London 15 B3
Upton London 15 A4
Uptown Chicago 9 B2
Uran Mumbai 20 B2
Urayasu Tokyo 30 B4
Urbe ✕ Rome 26 B2
Urca Rio de Janeiro 25 B2
Uritsk St. Petersburg 27 C1
Üröm Budapest 7 A2
Ursus Warsaw 32 B1
Ursvik Stockholm 29 A1
Usera Madrid 17 B1
Ushigome Tokyo 30 A3
Usina Rio de Janeiro 25 B1
Üsküdar Istanbul 12 B2
Ust-Slavyanka St. Petersburg 27 C3
Uteke Stockholm 29 A3
Utrata Warsaw 32 B2
Uttarpara Kolkata 14 B1
Utterslev Mose Copenhagen 8 A2

V

Vaclavské náměstí Prague 25 B2
Vadaul Mumbai 20 A2
Vaires-sur-Marne Paris 24 A4
Valby Copenhagen 8 B2
Valcannuta Rome 26 B1
Valdelatas Madrid 17 A1
Vale Washington 33 B1
Valenton Paris 24 B3
Valera Milan 19 A1
Vallcarca Barcelona 4 A1
Valldoreix Barcelona 4 A1
Vallecas Madrid 17 B2
Vallecas, Cumbres de Madrid 17 B2
Vallensbæk Copenhagen 8 B2
Vallensbæk Strand Copenhagen 8 B2
Vallentunasjön Stockholm 29 A2
Valleranello Rome 26 C1
Vallisaari Helsinki 11 C3
Vallvidrera Barcelona 4 A1
Valvidrera → Barcelona 4 A1
Van Gogh Museum Amsterdam 2 A2
Vanak Tehran 31 A2
Vanda = Vantaa Helsinki 11 B2
Vangede Copenhagen 8 A3
Vaniköy Istanbul 12 B2
Vanløse Copenhagen 8 A2
Vantaa Helsinki 11 B2
Vantaankoski Helsinki 11 B2
Vantaanpuisto Helsinki 11 B2
Vanves Paris 24 B2
Varedo Milan 19 A1
Varkiza Athens 2 C2
Vartiokylä Helsinki 11 B3
Vartiosaari Helsinki 11 B3
Vasamuseet Stockholm 29 B2
Vasco Cape Town 8 A2
Vasfanārd Tehran 31 B2
Vashi Mumbai 20 A2
Vasilyevskiy, Ostrov St. Petersburg 27 B1
Vatican City ■ Rome 26 B1
Vaucluse Sydney 29 B2
Vaucluse House Sydney 29 B2
Vaucresson Paris 24 A1
Vaughan Toronto 31 A1
Vauhallan Paris 24 B2
Vaujours Paris 24 A4
Vauxhall London 15 B3
Vecsés Budapest 7 B3
Veleň Prague 25 A3
Veleslavin Prague 25 B2
Vélizy-Villacoublay Paris 24 B2
Velka-Chuchle Prague 25 B2
Velké Přílepy Prague 25 B1
Venda Seca Lisbon 16 A1
Venetian Islands Miami 18 B2
Venice Los Angeles 16 C2
Ventas Madrid 17 B1
Ventorro del Cano Madrid 17 B1
Venustiano Carranza Mexico City 18 B2
Verde → São Paulo 27 A1
Verdi Athens 2 A2
Verdugo Mts. Los Angeles 16 A2
Verdun Montreal 20 B2
Vérhalom Budapest 7 A2
Vermelho → São Paulo 27 B1
Vermont Knolls Los Angeles 16 C3
Vernon Los Angeles 16 B3
Verrières-le-Buisson Paris 24 B2
Versailles Buenos Aires 7 B1
Versailles Paris 24 B1
Veshnyaki Moscow 19 B3
Vesolyy Posolok St. Petersburg 27 B2
Vestra Helsinki 11 B1
Vestskoven Copenhagen 8 A2
Vicálvaro Madrid 17 B2
Vicente López Buenos Aires 7 B2
Victoria Hong Kong 12 B2
Victoria, Mt. Wellington 33 B1
Victoria, Pont Montreal 20 B2
Victoria and Alfred Waterfront Cape Town 8 A1
Victoria Gardens Mumbai 20 B2
Victoria Harbour Hong Kong 12 B1
Victoria Island Lagos 14 B2
Victoria, L. Johannesburg 13 B2
Victoria Lawn Tennis Courts Melbourne 18 B2
Victoria Park Singapore 28 B2
Victoria Peak Hong Kong 12 B1
Vienna = Wien Vienna 32 A2
Vienna Washington 33 B2
Vietnam Veterans Memorial Washington 33 B3
Vietnam War Museum Chicago 9 B3
Vieux Carré = French Quarter New Orleans 21 B2
View Park Los Angeles 16 B3
Vigário Geral Rio de Janeiro 25 A1
Vigentino Milan 19 B2
Viggbyholm Stockholm 29 A2
Vighignolo Milan 19 B1
Viikki Helsinki 11 B3
Vikhroli Mumbai 20 A2
Vila Guilherme São Paulo 27 B2
Vila Isabel Rio de Janeiro 25 B1
Vila Jaguára São Paulo 27 B1
Vila Madalena São Paulo 27 B1
Vila Maria São Paulo 27 B2
Vila Mariana São Paulo 27 B2
Vila Prudente São Paulo 27 B2
Viladecans Barcelona 4 B1
Vile Parle Mumbai 20 A2
Villa Adelina Buenos Aires 7 B1
Villa Ballester Buenos Aires 7 B1
Villa Barilari Buenos Aires 7 C2
Villa Bosch Buenos Aires 7 B1
Villa C. Colon Buenos Aires 7 C2
Villa Ciudadela Buenos Aires 7 B1
Villa de Guadalupe Mexico City 18 B2
Villa Devoto Buenos Aires 7 B1
Villa Diamante Buenos Aires 7 C2
Villa Dominico Buenos Aires 7 C3
Villa Lugano Buenos Aires 7 C2
Villa Lynch Buenos Aires 7 B1
Villa Madero Buenos Aires 7 C1
Villa Sáenz Pena Buenos Aires 7 B1
Villa Urquiza Buenos Aires 7 B2
Villaverde Madrid 17 B1
Villaverde Bajo Madrid 17 B1
Ville-d'Avray Paris 24 B2
Villecresnes Paris 24 B4
Villejuif Paris 24 B3
Villemomble Paris 24 A4
Villeneuve-la-Garenne Paris 24 A2
Villeneuve-le-Roi Paris 24 B3
Villeneuve-St-Georges Paris 24 B3
Villeparisis Paris 24 A4
Villevaudé Paris 24 A4
Villiers-le-Bâcle Paris 24 B1
Villiers-sur-Marne Paris 24 B4
Villinki Helsinki 11 C3
Villoresi, Canale Milan 19 A1
Vilvoorde Brussels 6 A2
Vimodrone Milan 19 A2
Vimont Montreal 20 A1
Vincennes Paris 24 A3
Vincennes, Bois de Paris 24 B3
Vineland Orlando 23 B1
Vinings Atlanta 3 A2
Vinohrady Prague 25 B2
Vinoř Prague 25 B3
Violet Hill Hong Kong 12 B2
Virányos Budapest 7 A1
Virginia, L. Orlando 23 A2
Virginia Gardens Miami 18 B1
Virginia Key Miami 18 B2
Viroflay Paris 24 B2
Vironas Athens 2 B2
Virum Copenhagen 8 A2
Visitacion Valley San Francisco 26 B2
Vista Alegre Lima 14 B3
Vista Alegre Santiago 27 C1
Vista Grove Atlanta 3 A3
Vitacura Santiago 27 B2
Vitínia Rome 26 C1
Vitry-sur-Seine Paris 24 B3
Vizcaya Museum and Gardens Miami 18 B2
Vladykino Moscow 19 A2
Vokovice Prague 25 B2
Volgelsdorf Berlin 5 B5
Volkhonka-Zil Moscow 19 C2
Vollen Oslo 23 B1
Volodarskoye St. Petersburg 27 B2
Volynkina-Derevnya St. Petersburg 27 B1
Vondelpark Amsterdam 2 A2
Vösendorf Vienna 32 B2
Voula Athens 2 C2
Vouliagmeni Athens 2 C2
Vredehoek Cape Town 8 A1
Vršovice Prague 25 B2
Vyborgskaya Storona St. Petersburg 27 B2
Vykhino Moscow 19 B3
Vyšehrad Prague 25 B2

W

Wachterhof Munich 21 B3
Wadala Mumbai 20 A2
Wadestown Wellington 33 B1
Wadi al-Arayis Jerusalem 13 B2
Wadi Fukin Jerusalem 13 B1
Waduk Pluit Jakarta 12 A1
Waggaman New Orleans 21 B1
Wah Fu Hong Kong 12 B1
Wahda Baghdad 3 B2
Währing Vienna 32 A2
Waidmannslust Berlin 5 A3
Wainuiomata Wellington 33 B2
Wainuiomata → Wellington 33 B2
Wakefield Boston 6 A2
Waldesruh Berlin 5 B4
Waldperlach Munich 21 B3
Waldtrudering Munich 21 B3
Walkinstown Dublin 10 B1
Wall Street New York 22 B1
Walt Disney World Orlando 23 B1
Walter D. Stone Memorial Zoo Boston 6 A2
Waltham Boston 6 A1
Waltham Forest □ London 15 A3
Walthamstow London 15 A3
Walton-on-Thames London 15 B1
Wambeek Brussels 6 A3
Wan Chai Hong Kong 12 B2
Wandle → London 15 B2
Wandsworth □ London 15 B2
Wangjing Beijing 4 B2
Wannsee Berlin 5 B1
Wansdorf Berlin 5 A1
Wanstead London 15 A4
Wapping London 15 A3
Ward I. Wellington 33 B2
Wards I. New York 22 B2
Warnberg Munich 21 B2
Warner Brothers Studios Los Angeles 16 B2
Warrâq el 'Arab Cairo 7 A2
Warringal Park Melbourne 18 A2
Warriston Edinburgh 11 B2
Warsaw = Warszawa Warsaw 32 B2
Warszawa Warsaw 32 B2
Warszawa ✕ (WAW) Warsaw 32 B1
Wartenberg Berlin 5 A4
Washington Washington 33 B3
Washington Dulles Int. ✕ (IAD) Washington 33 B1
Washington Heights New York 22 A2
Washington Park Chicago 9 C3
Washington Ronald Reagan Nat. ✕ (DCA) Washington 33 B3
Wat Pho Bangkok 3 B1
Water of Leith → Edinburgh 11 B1
Watergraafsmeer Amsterdam 2 A2
Waterland Amsterdam 2 A2
Waterloo Brussels 6 B2
Waterloo Wellington 33 B2
Watermael-Boitsfort Brussels 6 B2
Watertown Boston 6 A1
Watsonia Melbourne 18 A2
Waverley Boston 6 A1
Waverley Johannesburg 13 A2
Waverley Sydney 29 B2
Wawer Warsaw 32 B2
Wawrzyszew Warsaw 32 B1
Wazirabad Delhi 10 A2
Wazīrīya Baghdad 3 A2
Wazirpur Delhi 10 A2
Wealdstone London 15 A1
Wedding Berlin 5 A3
Weehawken New York 22 B1
Weesp Amsterdam 2 B3
Weidling Vienna 32 A1
Weidlingbach Vienna 32 A1
Weissensee Berlin 5 A3
Wellesley Hills Boston 6 B1
Welling London 15 B4
Wellington Boston 6 A2
Wellington Wellington 33 B1
Wellington Int. ✕ (WLE) Wellington 33 B1
Weltevreden Park Johannesburg 13 A1
Wembley London 15 A2
Wemmel Brussels 6 A1
Wemmer Pan Johannesburg 13 B2
Wenceslas Square = Vaclavské náměstí Prague 25 B2
Wendenschloss Berlin 5 B4
Wennington London 15 A5
Werneuchen Berlin 5 A5
West Don → Toronto 31 A2
West Drayton London 15 A1
West Ham London 15 A4
West Harrow London 15 A1
West Heath London 15 B4
West Hill Toronto 31 A3
West Hollywood Los Angeles 16 B2
West Lamma Channel Hong Kong 12 B1
West Los Angeles, Univ. of Los Angeles 16 C2
West Medford Boston 6 A2
West Miami Miami 18 B1
West Molesey London 15 B1
West New York New York 22 B1
West of Twin Peaks San Francisco 26 B2
West Park Johannesburg 13 A1
West Rouge Toronto 31 A4
West Roxbury Boston 6 B2
West Springfield Washington 33 C2
West Town Chicago 9 B2
West Wharf Karachi 13 B1
Westchester Chicago 9 B1
Westchester Los Angeles 16 C2
Westchester New York 22 A2
Westcliff Johannesburg 13 B2
Westdene Johannesburg 13 B1
Westend Helsinki 11 C1
Wester Hailes Edinburgh 11 B2
Westerham Munich 21 B2
Western Addition San Francisco 26 B2
Westgate New Orleans 21 A1
Westgate Washington 33 B3
Westlake Cape Town 8 B1
Westlake Los Angeles 16 B3
Westlake San Francisco 26 B2
Westminster London 15 A3
Westmount Montreal 20 B2
Weston Toronto 31 A1
Westwego New Orleans 21 B2
Westwood Village Los Angeles 16 B2
Westzaan Amsterdam 2 A1
Wetton Cape Town 8 B2
Wexford Toronto 31 A3
Weybridge London 15 B1
Wezembeek-Oppem Brussels 6 A2
White Cloud Hill = Baiyun Hill Guangzhou 11 B2
White House, The Washington 33 B3
Whitechapel London 15 A3
Whitehall Dublin 10 A2
Whitney Las Vegas 14 B2
Whittier Los Angeles 16 C4
Whitton London 15 B1
Wieden Vienna 32 A2
Wien Vienna 32 A2
Wien-Schwechat ✕ (VIE) Vienna 32 B3
Wienerberg Vienna 32 B2
Wierzbno Warsaw 32 B2
Wijde Wormer Amsterdam 2 A2
Wilanów Warsaw 32 B2
Wilanówka → Warsaw 32 C2
Wilds, The Johannesburg 13 B2
Wilhelmshagen Berlin 5 B5
Wilket Creek Park Toronto 31 A2
Wilkieston Edinburgh 11 B1
Will Rogers State Historical Park ⌂ Los Angeles 16 B1
Willbrook Dublin 10 B2
Willesden London 15 A2
Willesden Green London 15 A2
Williamsbridge New York 22 A2
Williamsburg New York 22 B2
Williamsburg Orlando 23 B2
Williamstown Melbourne 18 B1
Willis, L. Orlando 23 B2
Willoughby Sydney 29 A2
Willow Springs Chicago 9 C1
Willowdale New Orleans 21 A1
Willowdale Toronto 31 A2
Wilmersdorf Berlin 5 B2
Wilmette Chicago 9 A2
Wilmington London 15 B5
Wimbledon London 15 B2
Wimbledon Common London 15 B2
Wimbledon Park London 15 B2
Wimbledon Tennis Ground London 15 B2
Winchester Boston 6 A2
Winchester Las Vegas 14 B2
Windermere Cape Town 8 A2
Windermere Orlando 23 B1
Windsor Johannesburg 13 A1
Windsor, Gare Montreal 20 B2
Windsor Hills Los Angeles 16 C2
Windy Arbour Dublin 10 B2
Winning Munich 21 B2
Wissous Paris 24 B2
Wittenau Berlin 5 A2
Witwatersrand, Univ. of Johannesburg 13 B2
Włochy Warsaw 32 B1
Wo Mei Hong Kong 12 A2
Wo Yi Hop Hong Kong 12 A1
Woburn Boston 6 A2
Woburn Toronto 31 A3
Wola Warsaw 32 B1
Wolf Trap Farm Park Washington 33 B2
Wolgok Seoul 27 B2
Wolica Warsaw 32 C2
Wolica Warsaw 32 B2
Wollaston Boston 6 B2
Woltersdorf Berlin 5 B5
Woluwe-St-Lambert Brussels 6 A2
Woluwe-St-Pierre Brussels 6 A2
Wong Chuk Hang Hong Kong 12 B2
Wong Chuk Wan Hong Kong 12 A2
Wong Chuk Yeung Hong Kong 12 A2
Wood Green London 15 A3
Wood Ridge New York 22 A1
Woodbine Race Track Toronto 31 A1
Woodbridge Toronto 31 A1
Woodford London 15 A4
Woodford Bridge London 15 A4
Woodford Green London 15 A4
Woodhaven New York 22 B2
Woodhouselee Edinburgh 11 B2
Woodlands Singapore 28 A2
Woodmont Washington 33 B3
Woodside London 15 A2
Woodside New York 22 B2
Woodstock Cape Town 8 A1
Woollahra Sydney 29 B2
Wooloowere B. Sydney 29 C1
Woolwich London 15 B4
Worker's Stadium Beijing 4 B2
World Trade Center, Site of former = Ground Zero New York 22 B1
Worli Mumbai 20 A1
Worth Chicago 9 C2
Wren's Nest Atlanta 3 B2
Wrigley Field Chicago 9 B3
Wuhlgarten Berlin 5 A4
Wujiaochang Shanghai 28 B2
Würm → Munich 21 B1
Würm-kanal Munich 21 A1
Wusong Shanghai 28 A1
Wyczółki Warsaw 32 C1
Wygoda Warsaw 32 B2
Wynberg Cape Town 8 B1

X

Xabregas Lisbon 16 A2
Xianggang = Hong Kong Hong Kong 12 B1
Xiaogang Park Guangzhou 11 B2
Xiaoping Guangzhou 11 A2
Xiasha chong Guangzhou 11 B1
Xichang Guangzhou 11 B2
Xicheng Beijing 4 B1
Xidan Beijing 4 B2
Xizhimen Beijing 4 B1
Xochimilco, Parque Ecológico Mexico City 18 C2
Xuanwu Beijing 4 B1
Xuhui Shanghai 28 B1

Y

Yaba Lagos 14 A2
Yaftābād Tehran 31 B1
Yahara Tokyo 30 A2
Yaho Tokyo 30 A1
Yakire Tokyo 30 A4
Yaksu Seoul 27 B2
Yamada Osaka 23 A2
Yamada Tokyo 30 B2
Yamato → Osaka 23 B1
Yan Kit Singapore 28 A3
Yanbu Guangzhou 11 B1
Yangcheon Seoul 27 B1
Yanghuayuan Beijing 4 C1
Yangjae Seoul 27 C2
Yangjiazhuang Shanghai 28 A1
Yangjing Shanghai 28 B2
Yangpu Shanghai 28 B2
Yangpu Park Shanghai 28 B2
Yannawa Bangkok 3 B2
Yarmūk Baghdad 3 B1
Yarra Bend Park Melbourne 18 A2
Yarraville Melbourne 18 A1
Yauza → Moscow 19 B4
Yeading London 15 A1
Yedikule Istanbul 12 C1
Yenikapı Istanbul 12 B1
Yeniköy Istanbul 12 B2
Yeongdeungpo Seoul 27 B1
Yeongdong Seoul 27 B2
Yeouido Seoul 27 B1
Yerba Buena I. San Francisco 26 B2
Yerres Paris 24 B4
Yerushalayim = Jerusalem Jerusalem 13 B2
Yiexiu Guangzhou 11 B2
Yiheyuan Beijing 4 B1
Yıldız Park Istanbul 12 B2
Yinhangzhen Shanghai 28 A2
Yishun Singapore 28 A3
Ylästö Helsinki 11 B2
Yodo → Osaka 23 A2
Yongdingmen Beijing 4 B2
Yongfucun Guangzhou 11 B2
Yongsan Seoul 27 B1
Yonkers New York 22 A2
York Toronto 31 A2
York Mills Toronto 31 A2
York Univ. Toronto 31 A2
You'anmen Beijing 4 B1
Youngsfield Cape Town 8 B1
Yuanmingyuan Park Beijing 4 A1
Yuanxiatian Guangzhou 11 A2
Yuexiu Park Guangzhou 11 B2
Yugo-Zarad Moscow 19 B2
Yuhalixqui, Volcan Mexico City 18 C2
Yung Shue Wan Hong Kong 12 B1
Yūsofābād Tehran 31 A2

Z

Zaandam Amsterdam 2 A1
Zaandijk Amsterdam 2 A1
Zaanstad Amsterdam 2 A1
Záběhlice Prague 25 B2
Zabki Warsaw 32 B2
Żacisze Warsaw 32 B2
Zahrā Baghdad 3 A1
Žalov Prague 25 A2
Załuski Warsaw 32 C1
Zamdorf Munich 21 B2
Zanevka St. Petersburg 27 B3
Zapote Manila 17 C1
Zaventem Brussels 6 A2
Zawady Warsaw 32 B2
Zāwiyet Abū Musallam Cairo 7 B1
Zawrā' Park Baghdad 3 B2
Zbraslav Prague 25 C2
Zbuzany Prague 25 B1
Zdiby Prague 25 B2
Zeekoevlei Cape Town 8 B2
Zehlendorf Berlin 5 B2
Zenne → Brussels 6 A2
Zephyr Field New Orleans 21 B1
Żerań Warsaw 32 B2
Żerzeń Warsaw 32 B2
Zeytinburnu Istanbul 12 C1
Zhabei Shanghai 28 B1
Zhdanov Moscow 19 B3
Zhenru Shanghai 28 B1
Zhernovka St. Petersburg 27 B2
Zhicun Guangzhou 11 B2
Zhongguancun Beijing 4 B1
Zhongshan Park Shanghai 28 B1
Zhoucun Guangzhou 11 B1
Zhoujiadu Shanghai 28 B1
Zhoujiazhen Shanghai 28 B2
Zhouzhuangjia Beijing 4 B1
Zhulebino Moscow 19 B4
Zhushadi Guangzhou 11 A3
Zielona Warsaw 32 B3
Zielonka Warsaw 32 B2
Zizhuyuan Park Beijing 4 B1
Žižkov Prague 25 B2
Zličín Prague 25 B1
Zografou Athens 2 B2
Żoliborz Warsaw 32 B2
Zonnebloem Cape Town 8 A1
Zugliget Budapest 7 B1
Zugló Budapest 7 A2
Zuiderwoude Amsterdam 2 A3
Zumbi Rio de Janeiro 25 A1
Zunderdorp Amsterdam 2 A2
Zuvuvu → São Paulo 27 C1
Zwanenburg Amsterdam 2 A1
Zwölfaxing Vienna 32 B2

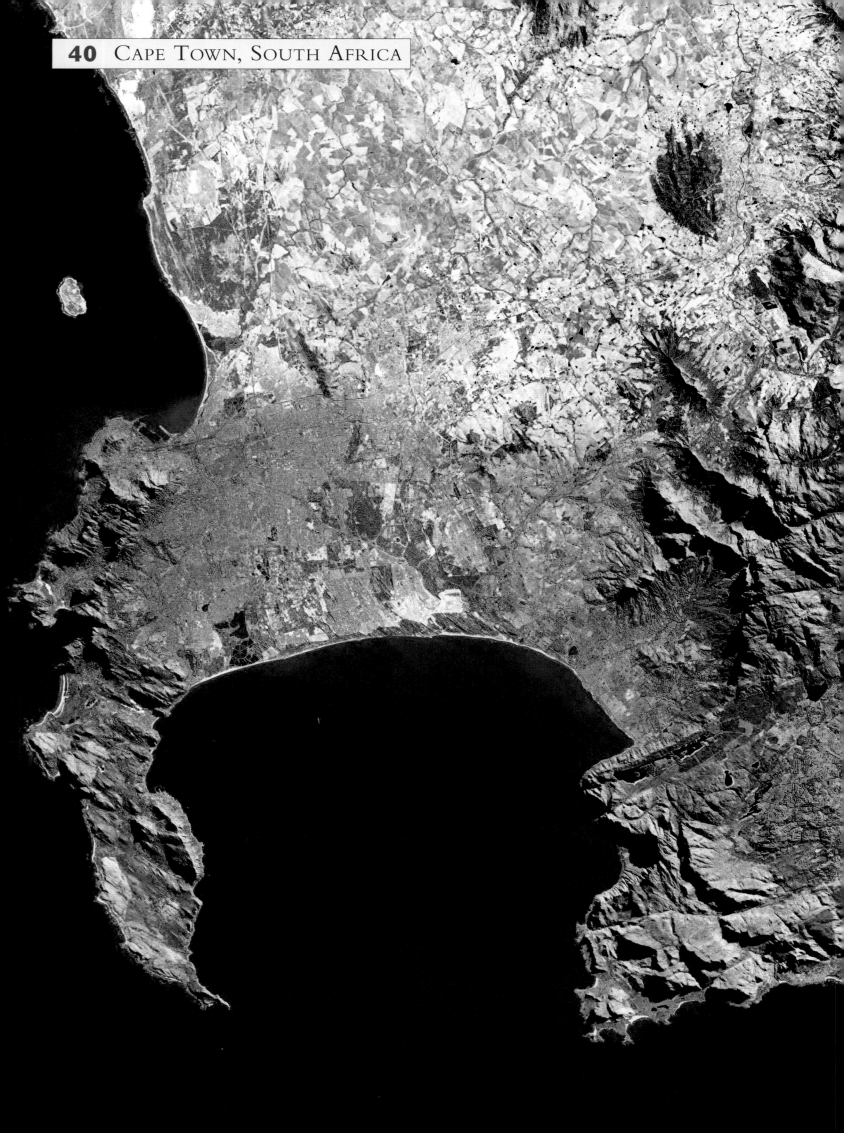

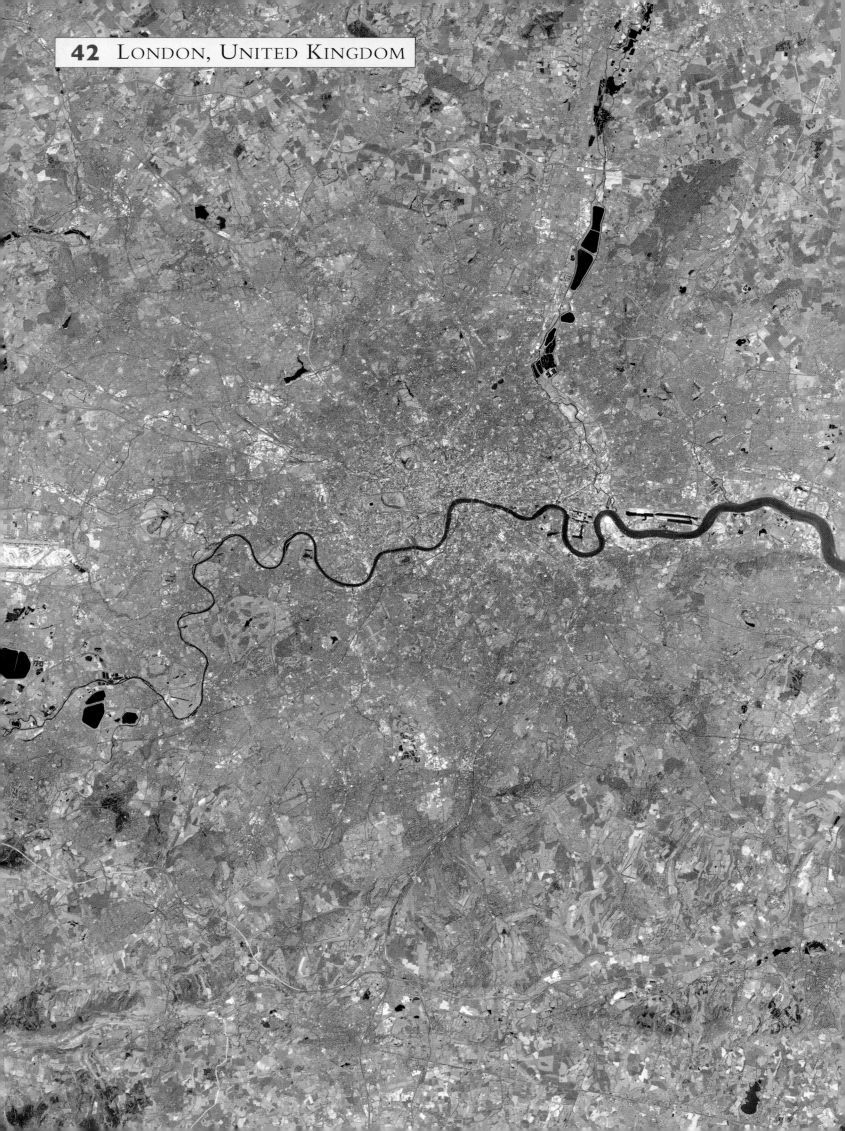

WORLD
MAPS

SETTLEMENTS

■ **PARIS**   ◉ **Rotterdam**   ◉ **Livorno**   ◉ **Brugge**   ◉ Exeter   ◦ *Torremolinos*   ○ *Oberammergau*   ○ *Thira*

Settlement symbols and type styles vary according to the scale of each map and indicate the importance of towns on the map rather than specific population figures

● *Vaduz*   Capital cities have red infills

∴   Ruins or archaeological sites

⬠   Urban agglomerations

᷅   Wells in desert

ADMINISTRATION

——— International boundaries

········· Internal boundaries

PERU   Country names

- - - - International boundaries (undefined or disputed)

⬟ National parks

KENT   Administrative area names

International boundaries show the *de facto* situation where there are rival claims to territory

COMMUNICATIONS

═══ Motorways, freeways and expressways

——— Principal roads

——— Other roads

+--+ Road tunnels

——— Principal railways

- - - Railways under construction

——— Other railways

+--+ Railway tunnels

LHR ✈ Principal airports

⊕ Other airports

·········· Principal canals

⚒ Passes

PHYSICAL FEATURES

⌐⌐ Perennial streams

- - - Intermittent streams

⬭ Perennial lakes

⋯ Sand deserts

◌ Intermittent lakes

⚶ Swamps and marshes

⧈ Permanent ice and glaciers

▲ 8850   Elevations in metres

▼ 8500   Sea depths in metres

1134   Height of lake surface above sea level in metres

ELEVATION AND DEPTH TINTS

Height of land above sea level

in metres	6000	4000	3000	2000	1500	1000	400	200	0				
in feet	18 000	12 000	9000	6000	4500	3000	1200	600					

Land below sea level

Depth of sea

6000	12 000	15 000	18 000	24 000	in feet
0	2000	4000	5000	6000	8000	in metres

Some of the maps have different contours to highlight and clarify the principal relief features

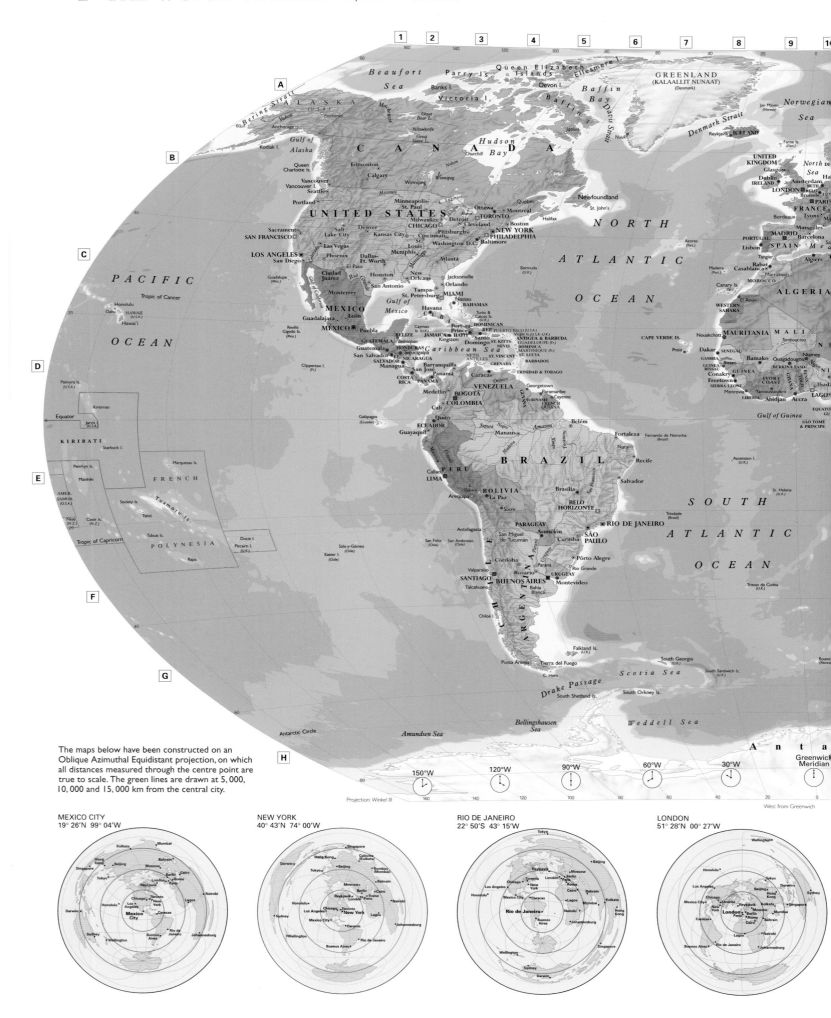

The maps below have been constructed on an Oblique Azimuthal Equidistant projection, on which all distances measured through the centre point are true to scale. The green lines are drawn at 5, 000, 10, 000 and 15, 000 km from the central city.

Projection: Winkel III

West from Greenwich

MEXICO CITY
19° 26'N 99° 04'W

NEW YORK
40° 43'N 74° 00'W

RIO DE JANEIRO
22° 50'S 43° 15'W

LONDON
51° 28'N 00° 27'W

Equatorial Scale 1:95 000 000

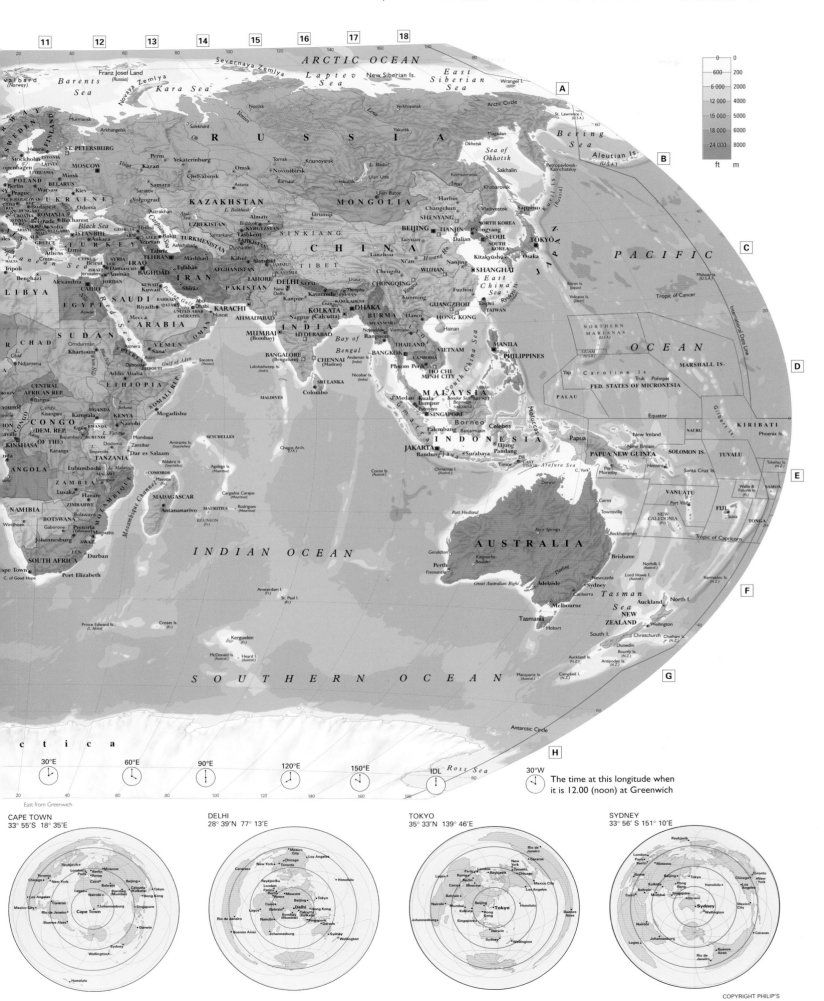

ft	m			
0	0			
600	200			
6 000	2000			
12 000	4000			
15 000	5000			
18 000	6000			
24 000	8000			

The time at this longitude when it is 12.00 (noon) at Greenwich

East from Greenwich

CAPE TOWN
33° 55'S 18° 35'E

DELHI
28° 39'N 77° 13'E

TOKYO
35° 33'N 139° 46'E

SYDNEY
33° 56'S 151° 10'E

COPYRIGHT PHILIP'S

1:35 000 000

Projection : Zenithal Equidistant

COPYRIGHT PHILIP'S

Legend:
- Maximum extent of sea ice
- Minimum extent of sea ice (September 2007)
- Ice caps and permanent ice shelf

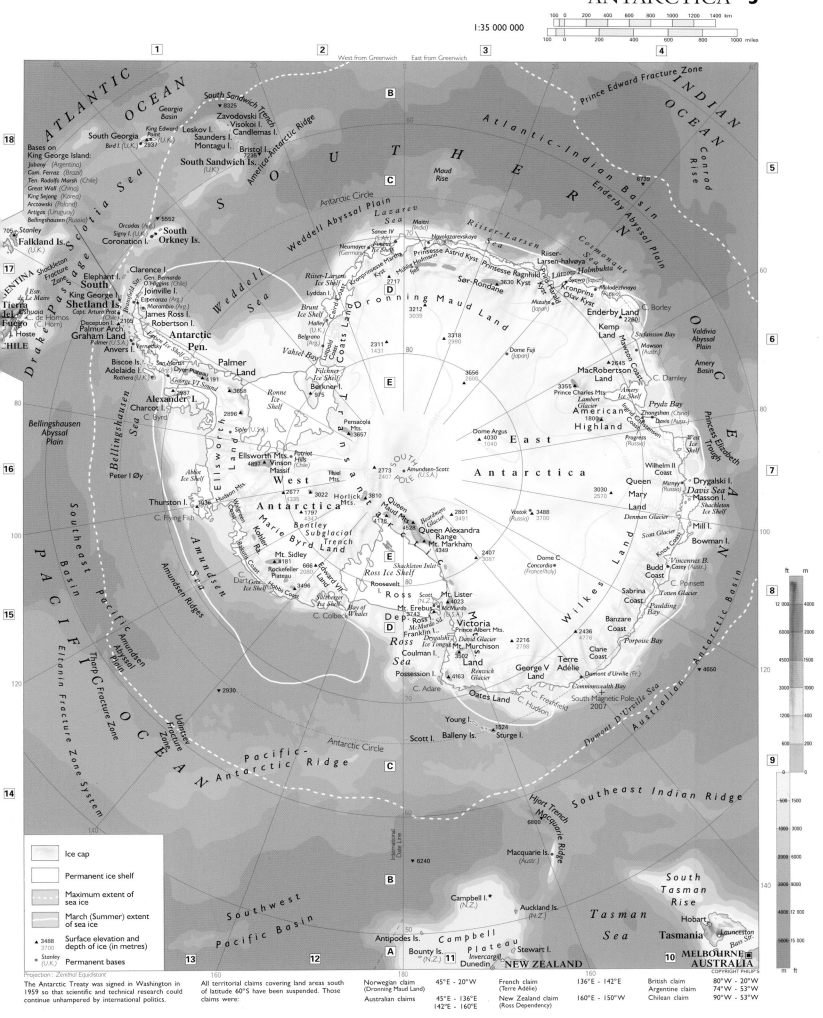

ANTARCTICA 5

1:35 000 000

Legend
- Ice cap
- Permanent ice shelf
- Maximum extent of sea ice
- March (Summer) extent of sea ice
- ▲ 3488 / 3700 Surface elevation and depth of ice (in metres)
- ● Stanley (U.K.) Permanent bases

Projection: Zenithal Equidistant

The Antarctic Treaty was signed in Washington in 1959 so that scientific and technical research could continue unhampered by international politics.

All territorial claims covering land areas south of latitude 60°S have been suspended. Those claims were:

Norwegian claim (Dronning Maud Land)	45°E – 20°W
Australian claims	45°E – 136°E / 142°E – 160°E
French claim (Terre Adélie)	136°E – 142°E
New Zealand claim (Ross Dependency)	160°E – 150°W
British claim	80°W – 20°W
Argentine claim	74°W – 53°W
Chilean claim	90°W – 53°W

100 0 100 200 300 400 500 600 700 800 km

1:20 000 000

100 0 100 200 300 400 500 miles

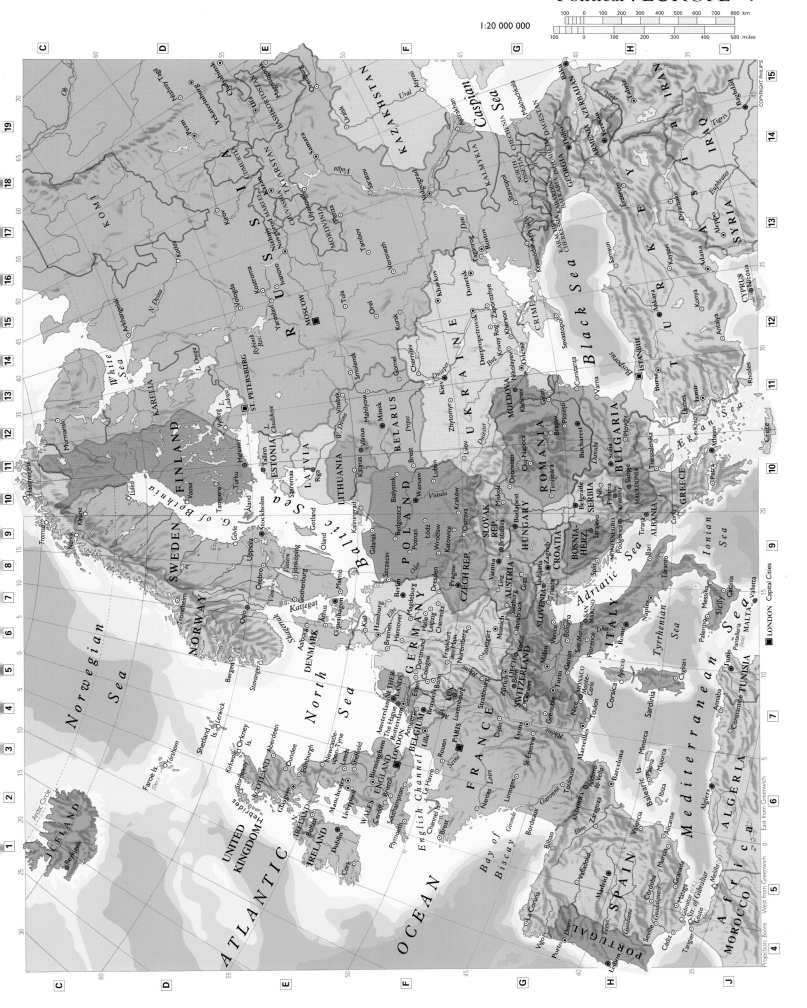

1:20 000 000

100 0 100 200 300 400 500 600 700 800 km
100 0 100 200 300 400 500 miles

COPYRIGHT PHILIP'S

■ LONDON Capital Cities

Projection: Bonne   West from Greenwich   East from Greenwich

ICELAND on same scale

FÆROE ISLANDS on same scale

ATLANTIC OCEAN

BARENTS SEA

NORWEGIAN SEA

RUSSIA

KARELIA

FINLAND

LAPLAND

Gulf of Bothnia

1:6 000

50   0   25   50   75   100   125   150   175 km

50   0   25   50   75   100   125 miles

1:2 000 000

10 0 10 20 30 40 50 60 70 80 km
10 0 10 20 30 40 50 miles

SCOTLAND
Kintyre
Brodick
Arran
Campbeltown
Mull of Oa
Mull of Kintyre
Ailsa Craig
Firth of Clyde

ATLANTIC OCEAN

NORTH CHANNEL

Malin Hd.
Inishtrahull
Malin Pen.
Trawbreaga B.
Lough Swilly
Fanad Hd.
Carndonagh
Moville
Buncrana
Inishowen Pen.
Giants Causeway
Rathlin I.
Fair Hd.
Ballycastle
Ballymoney
Cushendall
Garron Pt.
Portstewart
Portrush
Coleraine
Limavady
GLENARIFF
554
Larne
Carncastle

Tory I.
Horn Hd.
Bloody Foreland
Sheep Haven
Mulroy B.
Dunfanaghy
Glengad Hd.
L. Foyle
Roe
L. Ryan
Cairnryan
Stranraer
Portpatrick
269

Inishfree B.
Gweedore
Errigal 752
The Rosses
Aran I.
Dunglow
Crohy Hd.
Gweebarra B.
Dawros Hd.
Rossan Pt.
Killybegs
Slieve League 601
St. John's Pt.
DONEGAL
Glenties
Ardara
Glencolumbkille
Letterkenny
Rathmelton
GLENVEAGH
683
Lifford
Strabane
Sion Mills
Newtownstewart
Castlederg
Londonderry
LONDONDERRY
Sawel Mt. 683
Sperrin Mts.
Magherafelt
Randalstown
Ballyclare
Moneymore
Cookstown
NORTHERN IRELAND
Antrim
Lough Neagh
Belfast
Bangor
Newtownards
Lisburn
Comber
Donaghadee
Ards Pen.

Ulster
TYRONE
Omagh
Dungannon
Coalisland
Craigavon
Portadown
Lurgan
Armagh
Middletown
Keady
Newry
DOWN
Banbridge
Ballynahinch
Dundrum
Downpatrick
Ardglass
Ballyquintin Pt.
Strangford Lough
Portaferry

Downpatrick Hd.
Killala B.
Lenadoon Pt.
Belderg
Belmullet
Bellanaleck
Sligo Bay
Drumcliff
Manorhamilton
Enniskillen
FERMANAGH
Upper L. Erne
Lower L. Erne
L. Melvin
MONAGHAN
Clones
Castleblaney
Cootehill
Slieve Gullion 577
Crossmaglen
Dundalk
Carlingford L.
Mourne Mts.
Slieve Donard 852
Warrenpoint
Kilkeel
Newcastle
Greenore
Dundrum B.

Erris Hd.
Mullet Pen.
Inishkea North
Inishkea South
Blacksod Bay
Achill Hd.
Achill I. 672
Corraun Pen.
Clare I.
Clew Bay
Inishturk
Inishbofin
Inishshark
Killary Harbour
Croagh Patrick 765
Mweelrea 819

MAYO
Nephin Beg Range
Nephin 806
Crossmolina
Ballina
Killala
Foxford
Swinford
Castlebar
Newport
Westport
Louisburgh
Claremorris
Ballinrobe
L. Carra
L. Mask
Knock
Ballyhaunis
Castlerea
ROSCOMMON
Strokestown
Boyle
Carrick-on-Shannon
L. Gara
Ballaghaderreen
Charlestown
Ballymote
SLIGO
Sligo
Colooney
Lackagh Hills
544
L. Arrow
L. Key
LEITRIM
Leitrim
L. Allen
L. Oughter
Belturbet
CAVAN
Cavan
Annalee
L. Sheelin
Carrickmacross
Kingscourt
Oldcastle
Ceanannus Mor (Kells)
Blackwater
Clogher Hd.
Drogheda
Dunleer
Ardee
LOUTH
Louth
Dundalk Bay

Connacht
CONNEMARA
Clifden
Roundstone
Slyne Hd.
Bertraghboy B.
Kilkieran B.
Oughterard
Lough Corrib
Tuam
Mount Bellew Bridge
Glennamaddy
Roscommon
LONGFORD
Longford
Granard
Castlepollard
Mullingar
WESTMEATH
Athlone
Moate
Ferbane
Clara
Kilbeggan
Edenderry
Royal Canal
MEATH
An Uaimh (Navan)
Trim
Athboy
Dunshaughlin
Balbriggan
Skerries
Rush
Lambay I.
Swords
Malahide
Howth Hd.
DUBLIN
Dun Laoghaire
Bray
Greystones
123

GALWAY
Galway
Galway Bay
Black Hd.
Burren
Spiddle
Aran Is.
Inishmore
Inishmaan
Inisheer
Lisdoonvarna
BURREN
Cliffs of Moher
Hags Hd.
Ennistimon
Crusheen
Feakle
Slieve Aughty
Gort
Kinvarra
Loughrea
Athenry
Aughrim
Ballinasloe
Shannonbridge
Portumna
368
Lough Derg
Birr
Roscrea
OFFALY
Tullamore
Portarlington
Mountmellick
Port Laoise
Daingean
Rathangan
Kildare
KILDARE
Monasterevin
Droichead Nua
Naas
Clondalkin
DUBLIN
Kippure
Clane
Maynooth
Leinster
Grand Canal
Bog of Allen
Slieve Bloom 529
Arderin

Loop Hd.
Kilkee
Mutton I.
Mal Bay
Milltown Malbay
Liscannor Bay
CLARE
Ennis
Tulla
Sixmilebridge
Silvermine Mts. 694
Keeper Hill
Nenagh
Killaloe
Templemore
Thurles
Durrow
LAOIS
Abbeyleix
Carlow
CARLOW
Muine Bheag
Tullow
Shillelagh
Mt. Leinster 796
WICKLOW
Wicklow Mts.
Lugnaquilla 926
Wicklow
Wicklow Hd.
Rathdrum
Avoca
Arklow
Mizen Hd.
Gorey
Ballycanew
Cahore Pt.

Kerry Hd.
Ballybunion
Tarbert
Foynes
Glin
Mouth of the Shannon
Shannon Airport
Limerick
LIMERICK
Rathkeale
Newcastle West
Abbeyfeale
Listowel
Feale
Golden Vale
Tipperary
TIPPERARY
Cashel
Slievenamon 722
Clonmel
Carrick-on-Suir
KILKENNY
Kilkenny
Callan
Thomastown
Mullinavat
Graiguenamanagh
WEXFORD
New Ross
Enniscorthy
Wexford
Wexford Harbour
Rosslare
Rosslare Harbour
Greenore Pt.
Carnsore Pt.

Munster
Tralee
Tralee B.
Brandon B.
Brandon Mt. 953
Smerwick Harbour
Dunmore Hd.
Dingle
Dingle Bay
Slieve Mish 853
Castlemaine
Killorglin
Killarney
Macgillycuddy's Reeks
Carrauntoohil 1041
KERRY
Valencia I.
Cahirciveen
Puffin I.
Great Skellig
Ballinskelligs B.
Sneem
Kenmare
Kenmare River
Caha Mts. 686
Glengarriff
Castletown Bearhaven
Bear I.
Whiddy I.
Dursey I.
Crow Hd.
Bantry Bay
Dunmanus B.
Skull
Mizen Hd.
Long I.
Sherkin I.
Clear I.
C. Clear
Fastnet Rock

Newmarket
Kanturk
Mallow
Millstreet
Boggeragh Mts. 646
Macroom
Blarney
Nagles Mts. 429
Fermoy
Mitchelstown
Galty Mts. 920
Kilfinnane
Buttevant
Doneraile
Rath Luirc (Charleville)
519
Knockmealdown Mts. 795
Comeragh Mts. 792
Dungarvan
Dungarvan Harbour
Waterford Harbour
Tramore
Tramore B.
Dunmore East
Hook Hd.
Passage East
Kilmore Quay
Saltee Is.

CORK
Cork
Lee
Passage West
Cobh
Crosshaven
Cork Harbour
Midleton
Youghal
Youghal B.
Blackwater
Lismore
WATERFORD
Waterford
Bandon
Kinsale
Old Head of Kinsale
Timoleague
Clonakilty
Clonakilty B.
Galley Hd.
Skibbereen
Ballydehob
Baltimore

CELTIC SEA

IRISH SEA

St. George's Channel

WALES
St. David's Hd.
St. David's
St. Bride's Bay
115
13

Projection: Lambert's Conformal Conic
West from Greenwich
COPYRIGHT PHILIP'S

ft m
1500 500
600 200
300 100
0 0
50 150
100 300
200 600
500 1500
1000 3000
2000 6000
m ft

1:2 000 000

10 0 10 20 30 40 50 60 70 80 km
10 0 10 20 30 40 50 miles

Key to English unitary authorities on map

25 HARTLEPOOL
26 DARLINGTON
27 STOCKTON-ON-TEES
28 MIDDLESBROUGH
29 REDCAR AND CLEVELAND
30 BLACKPOOL
31 BLACKBURN WITH DARWEN
32 HALTON
33 WARRINGTON
34 KINGSTON UPON HULL
35 NORTH EAST LINCOLNSHIRE
36 STOKE-ON-TRENT
37 TELFORD AND WREKIN
38 DERBY CITY
39 CITY OF NOTTINGHAM
40 LEICESTER CITY
41 RUTLAND
42 PETERBOROUGH
43 MILTON KEYNES
44 LUTON
45 NORTH SOMERSET
46 CITY OF BRISTOL
47 BATH AND NORTH EAST SOMERSET
48 SWINDON
49 READING
50 WOKINGHAM
51 WINDSOR AND MAIDENHEAD
52 SLOUGH
53 BRACKNELL FOREST
54 THURROCK
55 SOUTHEND-ON-SEA
56 MEDWAY
57 TORBAY
58 POOLE
59 BOURNEMOUTH
60 SOUTHAMPTON
61 PORTSMOUTH
62 PLYMOUTH
63 BRIGHTON AND HOVE

Key to Welsh unitary authorities on map

15 SWANSEA
16 NEATH PORT TALBOT
17 BRIDGEND
18 RHONDDA CYNON TAFF
19 MERTHYR TYDFIL
20 CAERPHILLY
21 BLAENAU GWENT
22 TORFAEN
23 CARDIFF
24 NEWPORT

NORTH SEA

IRISH SEA

NORTHERN IRELAND

North Channel

SCOTLAND

NORTHUMBERLAND

CUMBRIA

LAKE DISTRICT

Newcastle-upon-Tyne
Sunderland
Hartlepool
Middlesbrough
Darlington
Carlisle
Edinburgh
Glasgow
Belfast
Liverpool
MANCHESTER
Leeds
Bradford
Sheffield
York
Kingston upon Hull
Lincoln
Nottingham
Derby
Chester
Preston
Blackpool

ISLE OF MAN

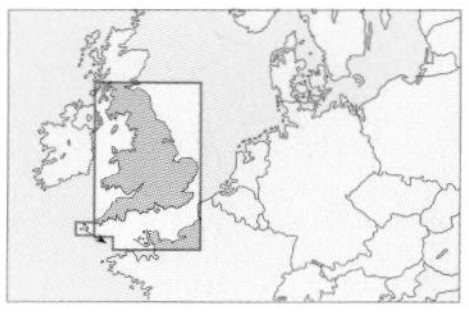

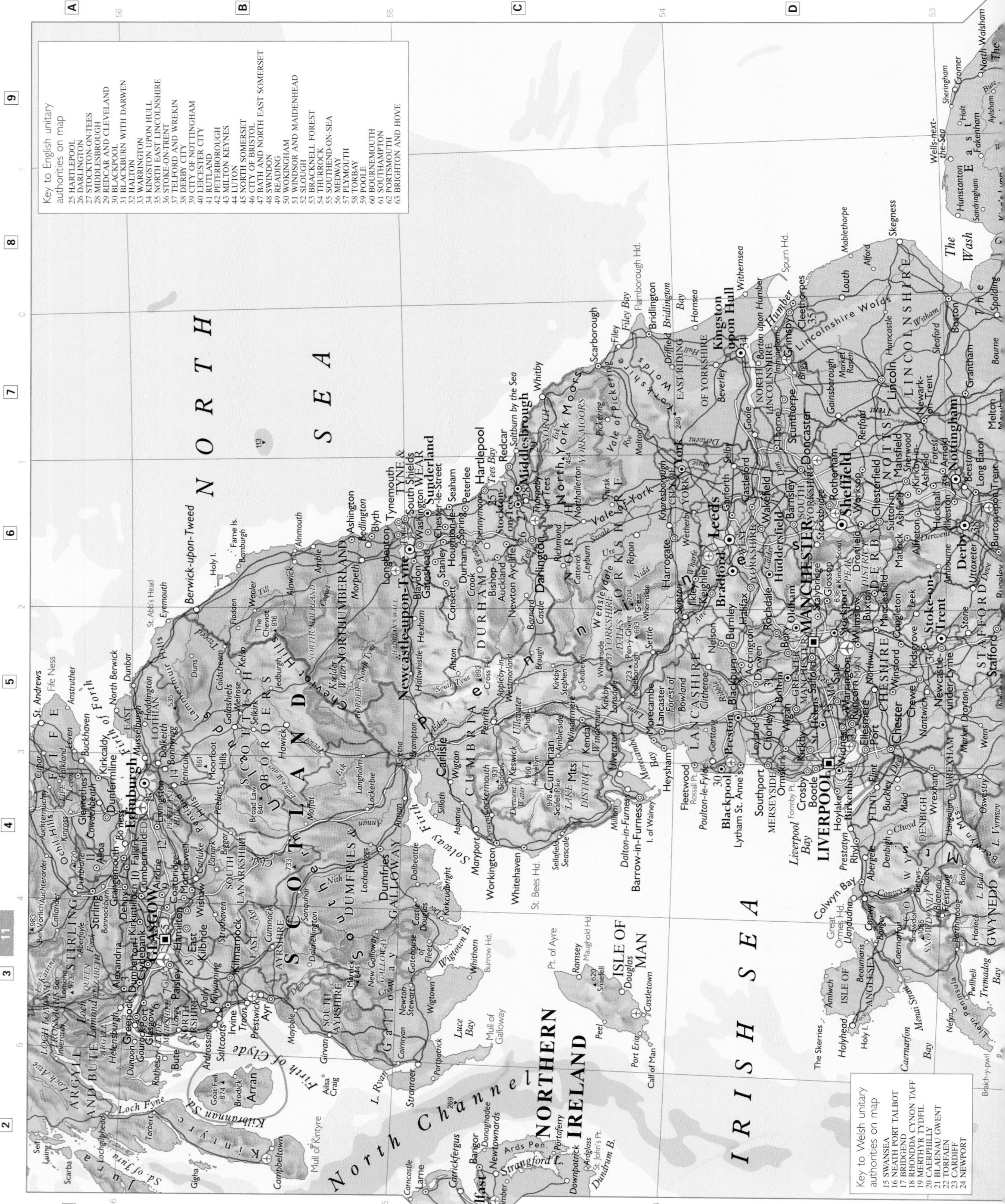

ISLES OF SCILLY
on same scale

Projection: Lambert's Conformal Conic

COPYRIGHT PHILIP'S

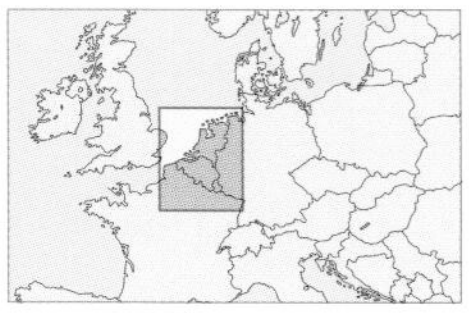

1:2 500 000

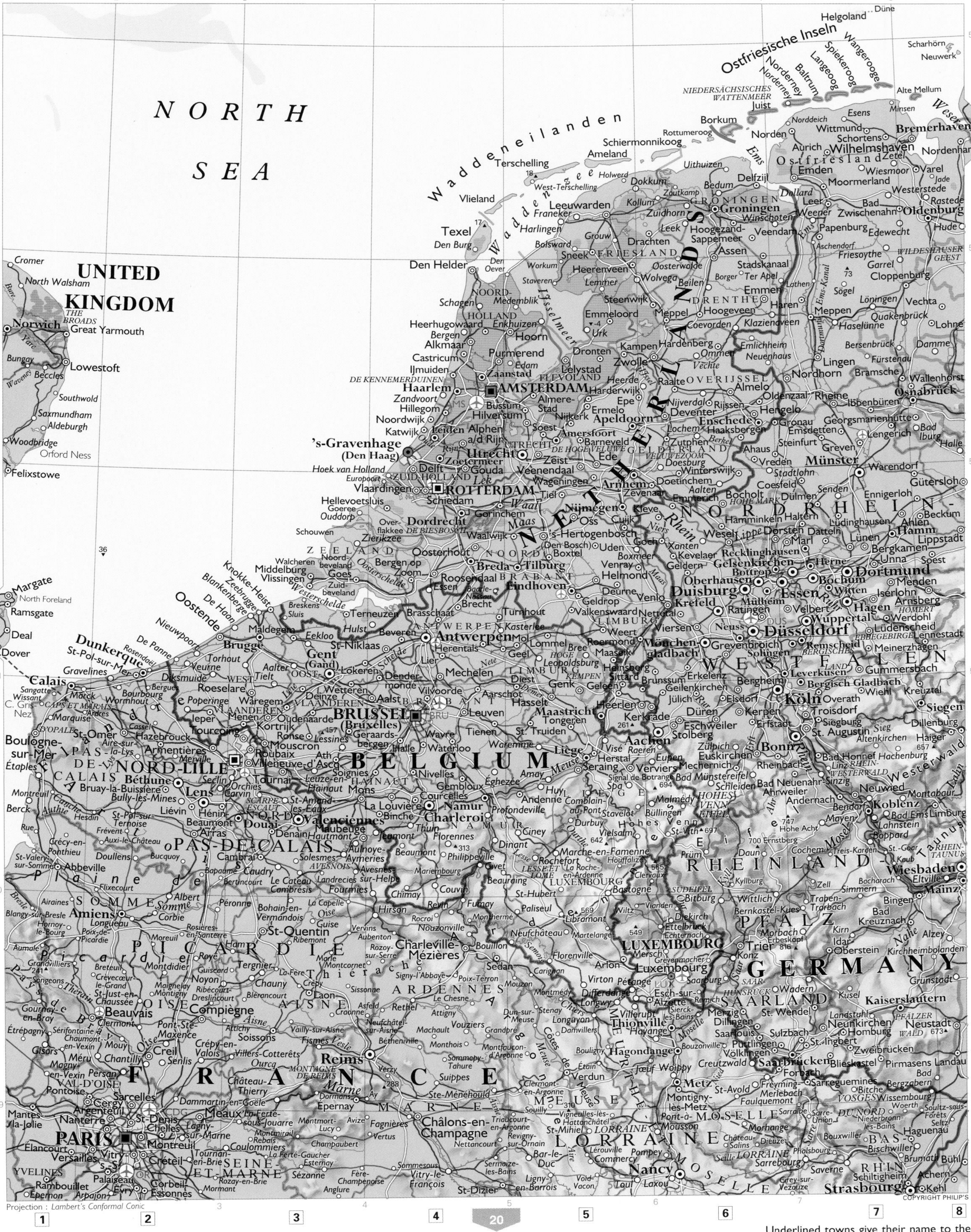

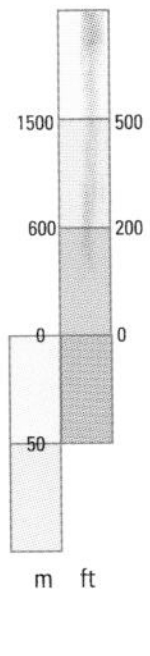

Underlined towns give their name to the administrative area in which they stand.

Projection : Lambert's Conformal Conic

COPYRIGHT PHILIP'S

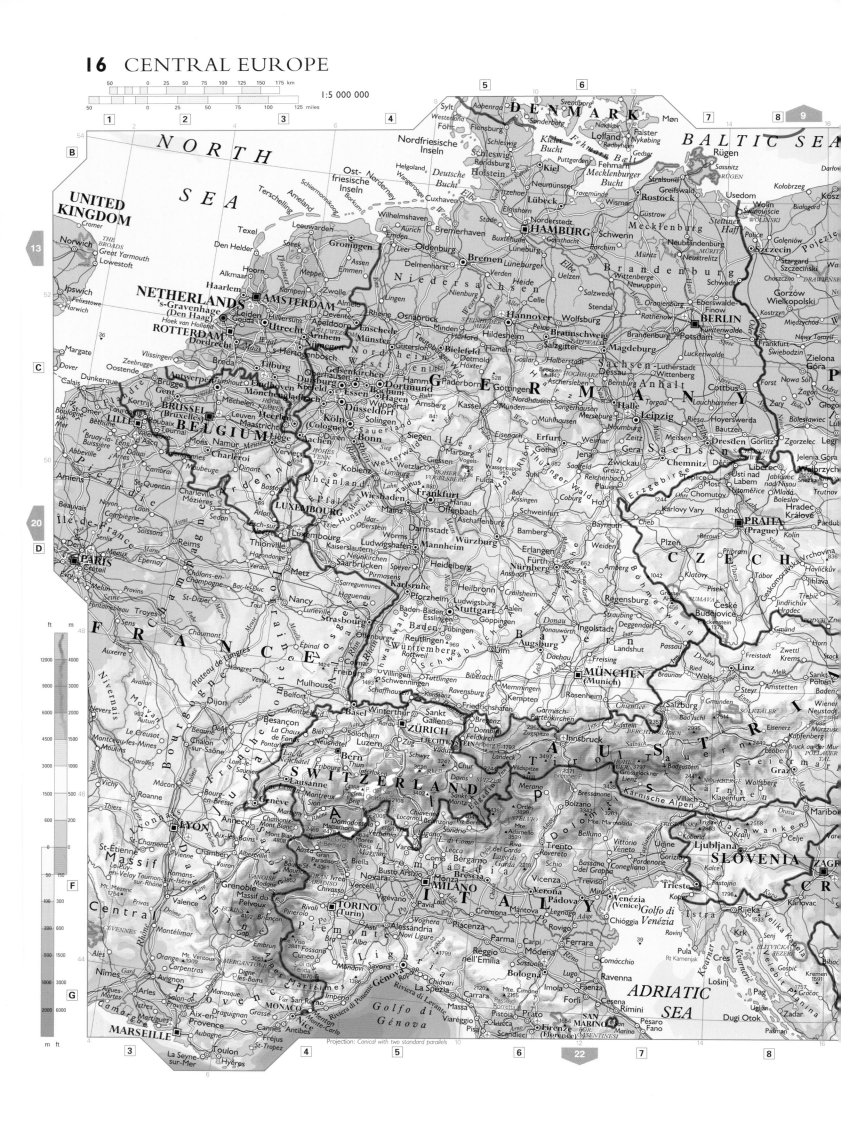

50 0 25 50 75 100 125 150 175 km
50 0 25 50 75 100 125 miles

1:5 000 000

Projection: Conical with two standard parallels

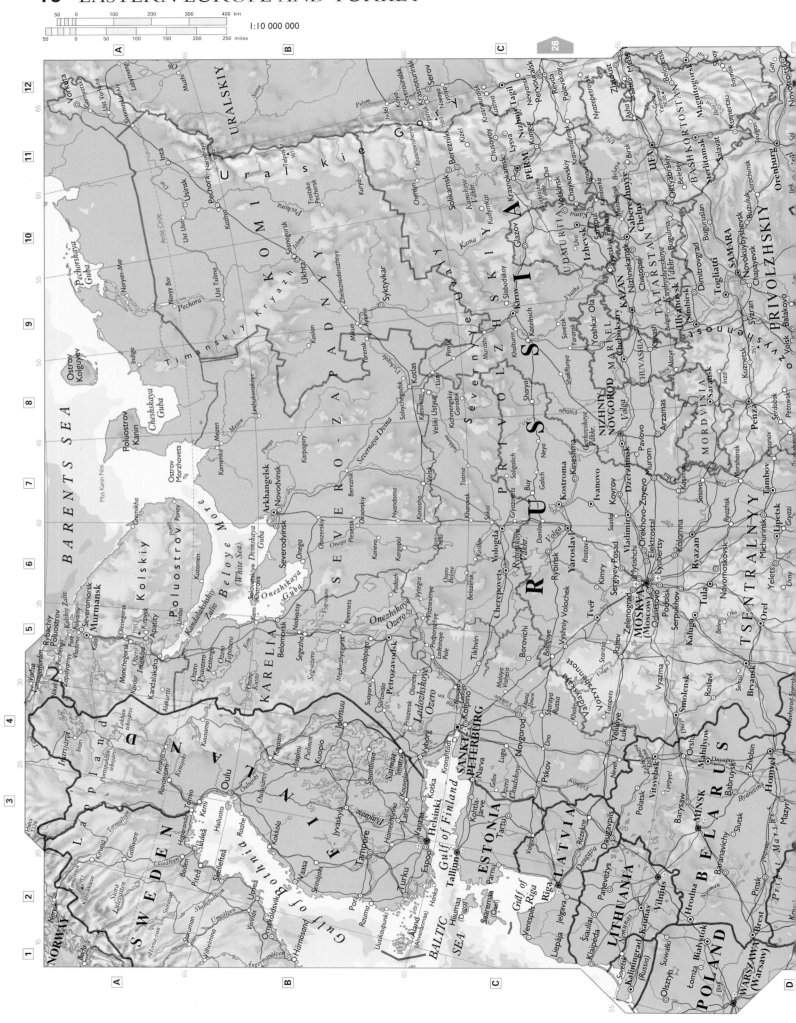

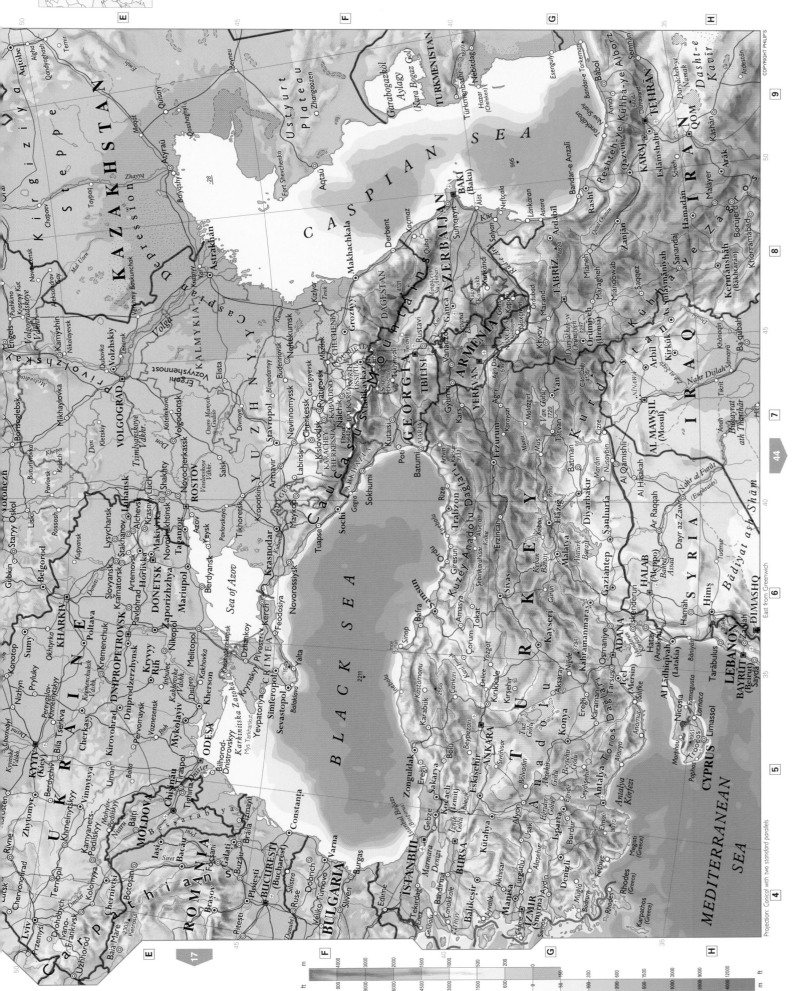

1:5 000 000

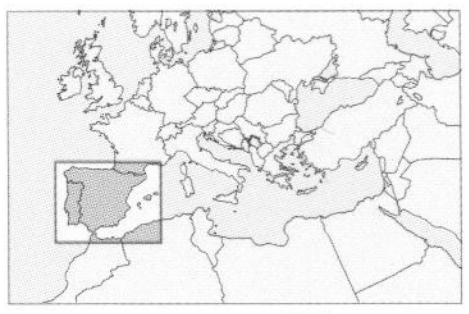

1:5 000 000

Projection: Conical with two standard parallels

COPYRIGHT PHILIP'S

East from Greenwich

West from Greenwich

F R A N C E

S P A I N

P O R T U G A L

M O R O C C O

A L G E R I A

Pyrenees

ANDORRA

Castilla y León

Castilla - La Mancha

Valencia

Murcia

ATLANTIC OCEAN

MEDITERRANEAN SEA

BALEARIC SEA

Bay of Biscay

Golfe du Lion

Mallorca

Menorca

Evissa (Ibiza)

Formentera

Costa Brava

Costa Dorada

Costa Blanca

Costa del Sol

Str. of Gibraltar

MADRID

LISBOA

BARCELONA

Valencia

Sevilla

Málaga

Zaragoza

Bilbao

ALGER (Algiers)

Oran

Gibraltar (U.K.)

Ceuta (Sp.)

Melilla (Sp.)

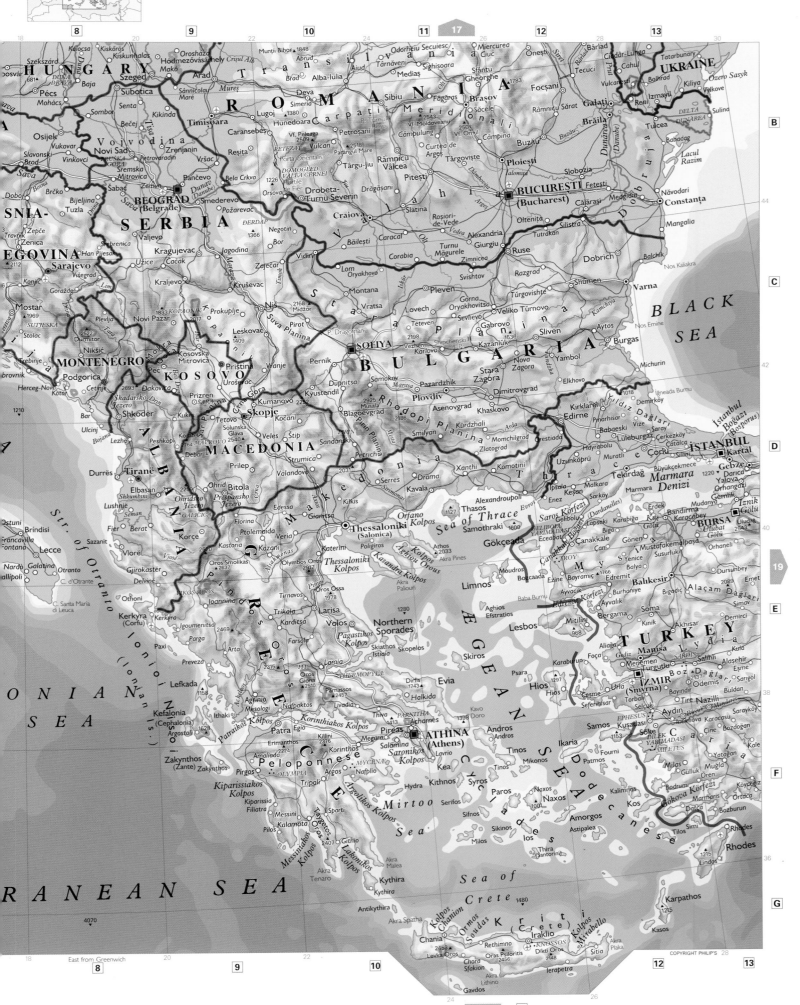

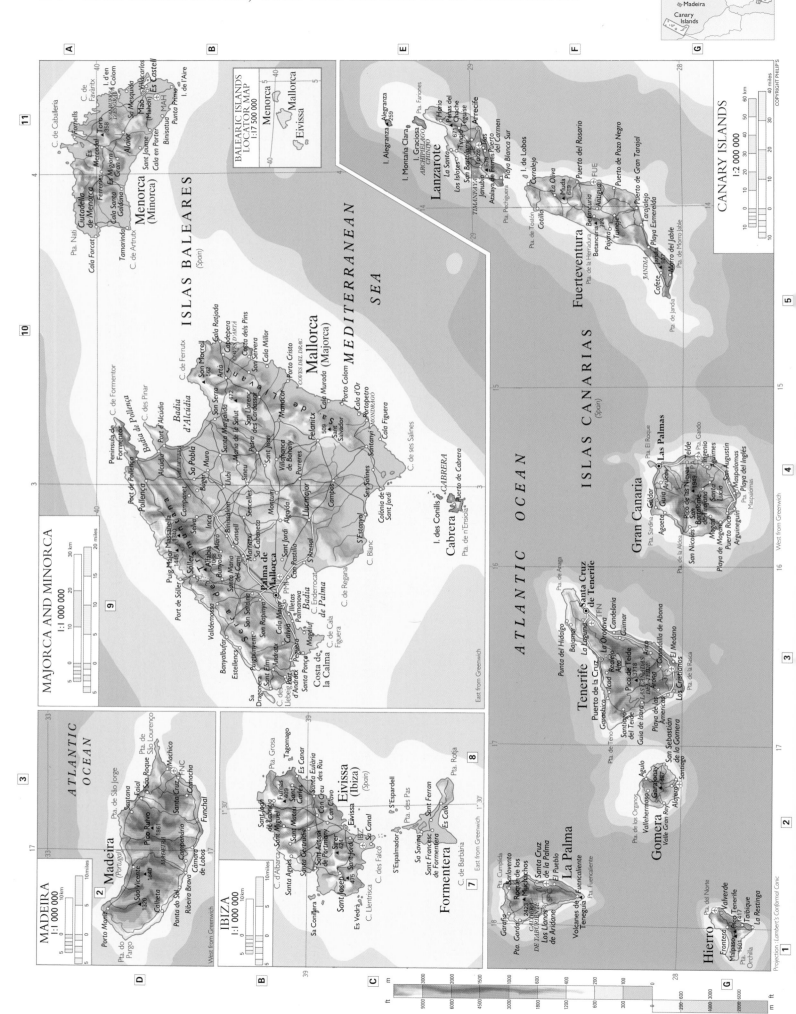

Madeira

Canary
Islands

Balearic
Islands

A B E F G

MEDITERRANEAN SEA

ISLAS BALEARES
(Spain)

Menorca
(Minorca)

BALEARIC ISLANDS
LOCATOR MAP
1:17 500 000

Menorca

Mallorca

Eivissa

Mallorca (Majorca)

Palma de Mallorca

Cabrera

ATLANTIC OCEAN

MAJORCA AND MINORCA
1:1 000 000

MADEIRA
1:1 000 000

Madeira
(Portugal)

ATLANTIC
OCEAN

IBIZA
1:1 000 000

Eivissa
(Ibiza) (Spain)

Formentera

Lanzarote

Fuerteventura

ISLAS CANARIAS
(Spain)

Gran Canaria

Las Palmas

CANARY ISLANDS
1:2 000 000

Tenerife

Santa Cruz
de Tenerife

Gomera

La Palma

Hierro

COPYRIGHT PHILIP'S

Projection: Lambert's Conformal Conic

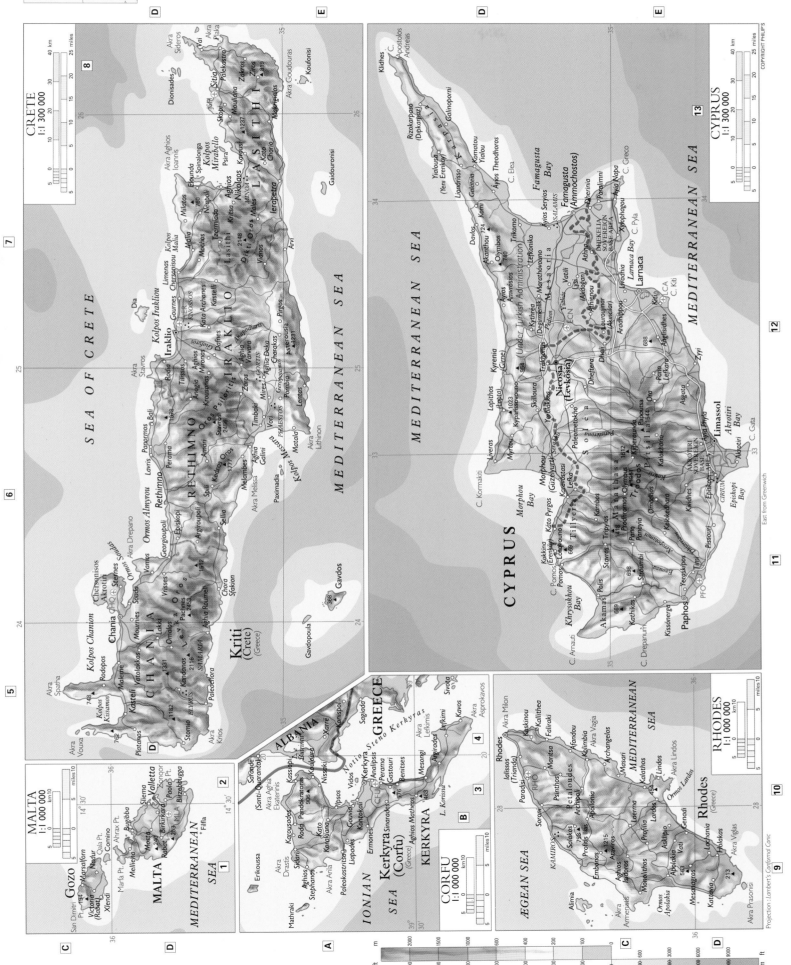

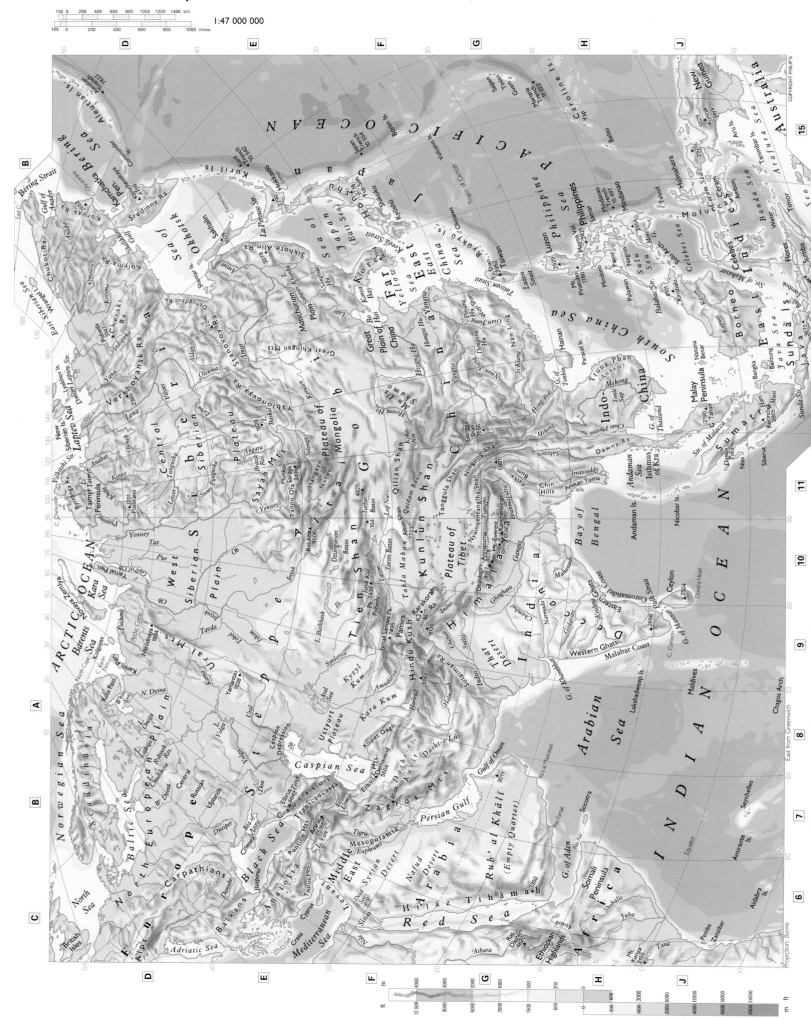

1:47 000 000

1:47 000 000

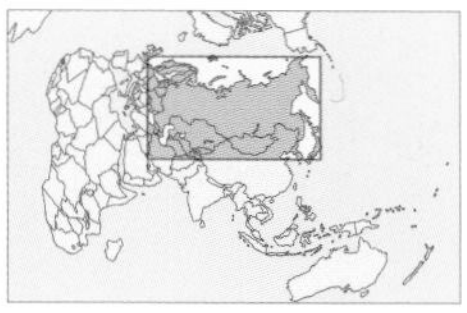

OCEAN

Severnaya Zemlya

Laptev Sea

East Siberian Sea

Bering Sea

Bering Strait

Chukchi Sea

Novosibirskiye Ostrova

Poluostrov Taymyr

Gory Byrranga

Sea of Okhotsk

Poluostrov Kamchatka

Sakhalin

Kurilskiye Ostrova

R U S S I A

Verkhoyanskiy Khrebet

Khrebet Cherskogo

Kolymskoye Nagorye

Koryakskoye Nagorye

Sredinnyy Khrebet

Stanovoy Khrebet

Khrebet Dzhugdzur

Sikhote Alin

Yablonovyy Khrebet

Norilsk

Krasnoyarsk

Irkutsk

Bratsk

Ulan Ude

Chita

Yakutsk

Vilyuysk

Olekminsk

Tiksi

Khatanga

Tura

Mirnyy

Lensk

Neryungri

Tynda

Skovorodino

Blagoveshchensk

Khabarovsk

Komsomolsk-na-Amur

Yuzhno-Sakhalinsk

Magadan

Okhotsk

Petropavlovsk-Kamchatskiy

Anadyr

Pevek

M O N G O L I A

Ulaanbaatar

Hangayn Nuruu

Hentiyn Nuruu

Gobi

(Aerhtai Shan)

C H I N A

(Manchuria)

Da Hinggan Ling

BEIJING

HOHHOT

BAOTOU

ZHANGJIAKOU

TANGSHAN

SHENYANG

ANSHAN

FUSHUN

CHANGCHUN

JILIN

HARBIN

QIQIHAR

DAQING

JIAMUSI

JIXI

MUDANJIANG

Vladivostok

NORTH KOREA

PYONGYANG

SOUTH KOREA

SEOUL

INCHEON

DAEJEON

DAEGU

BUSAN

GWANGJU

J A P A N

Honshū

Hokkaidō

SAPPORO

Hakodate

TOKYO

KYOTO

OSAKA

KOBE

Sea of Japan (East Sea)

COPYRIGHT PHILIP'S

1:5 000 000

SEA OF OKHOTSK

Sakhalin

La Perouse Strait

HOKKAIDŌ

SAPPORO

HONSHŪ

TŌHOKU

SENDAI

Sendai-Wan

RUSSIA

PRIMORSKIY KRAY

SIKHOTE-ALIN

Lake Khanka

Vladivostok

Zaliv Petra Velikogo

CHINA

HEILONGJIANG

Dongbei

Manchuria

JILIN

NORTH KOREA

SEA OF JAPAN

(EAST SEA)

Yamato Rise

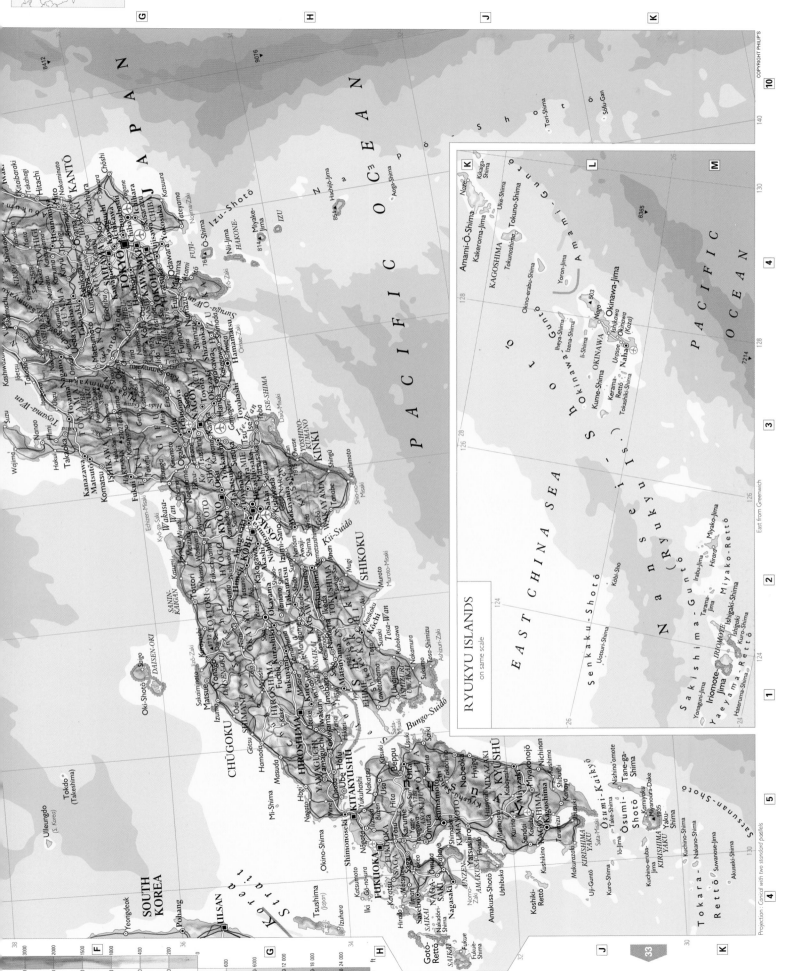

RYUKYU ISLANDS
on same scale

PACIFIC OCEAN

EAST CHINA SEA

SOUTH KOREA

Projection: Conical with two standard parallels

East from Greenwich

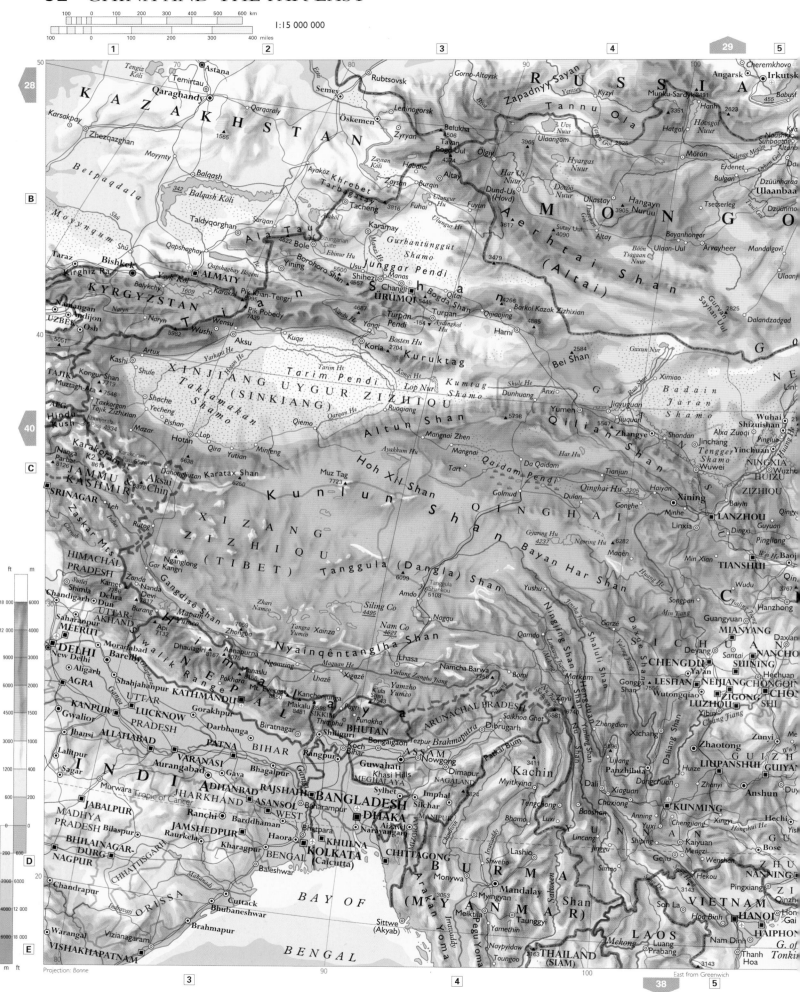

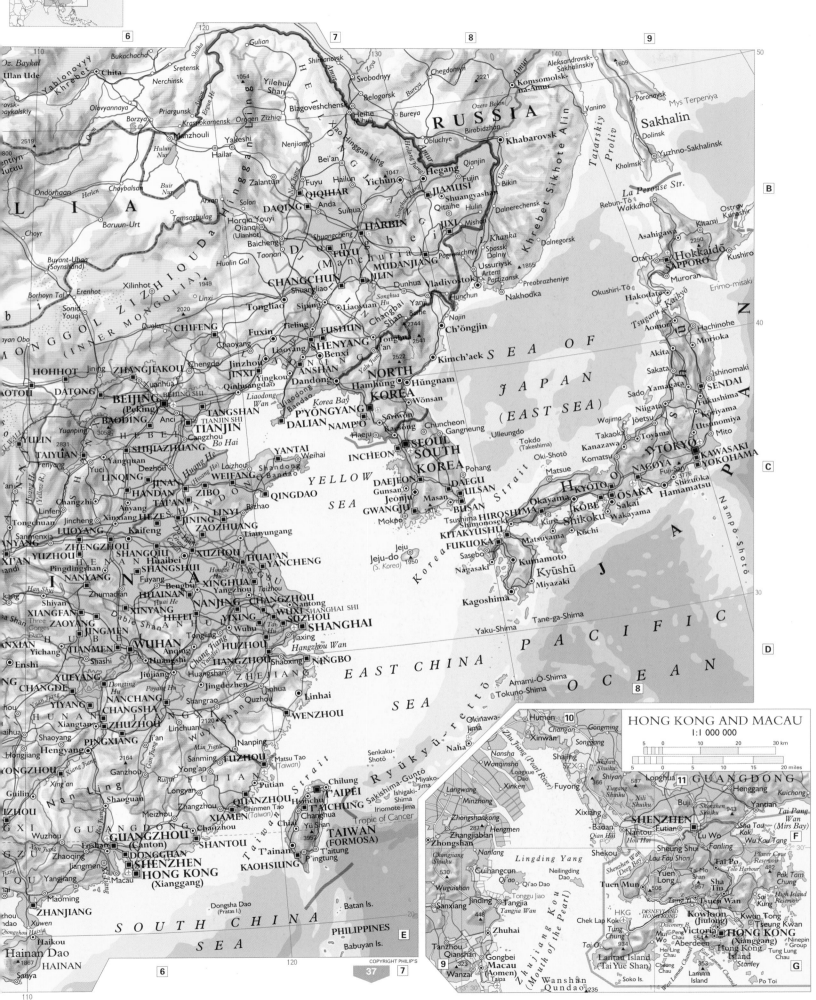

HONG KONG AND MACAU

1:1 000 000

5 0   10   20   30 km

5   0   5   10   15   20 miles

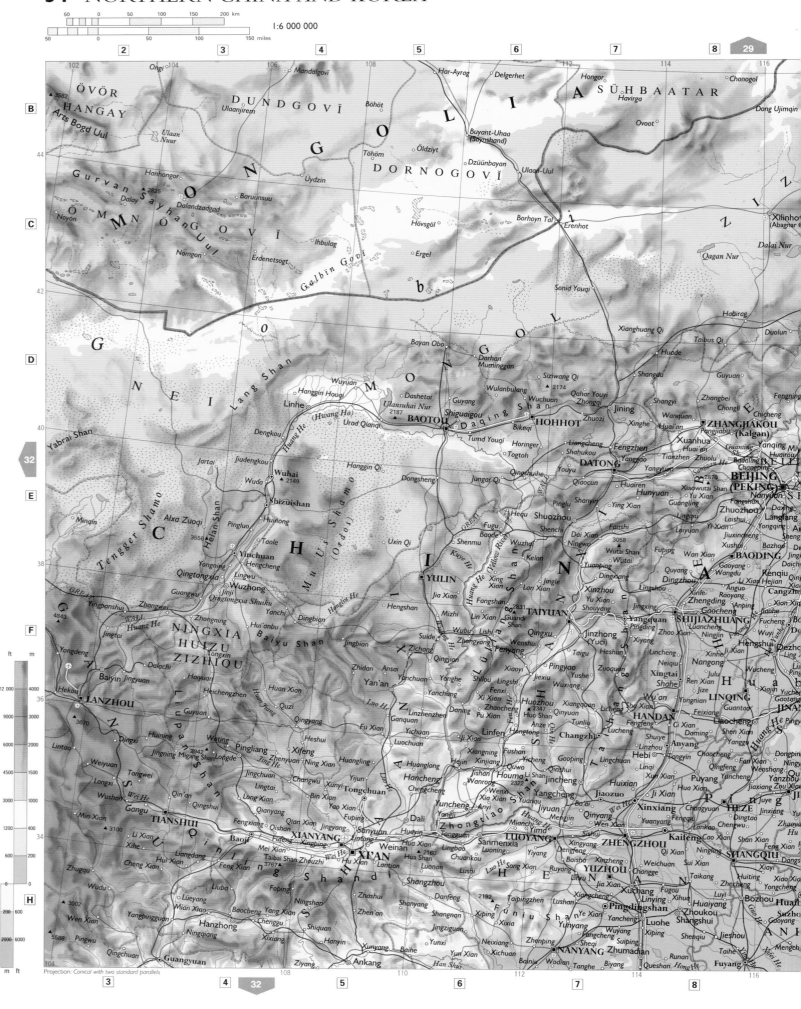

1:6 000 000

Projection: Conical with two standard parallels

HIUQ

Horqin Youyi Qianqi
(Ulanhot)

Zhenlai　Nen　HARBIN　Bin Xian
Maoxing　Zhaoyuan　Shuangcheng　Acheng　Yanshou　Shangzhi
Huolin Gol　Baicheng　Da'an　Songhua Jiang　Changchunling　HEILONGJIANG　Turiy Rog　JIXI　69
Hulin He　Taonan　Fuyu　Beitaolaizhou　Sanchahe　Wuchang　Yimianpo　Hengdaohezi　Maqiaohe　Linkou
Jarud Qi　Tuquan　Anguang　Oagan Nur Qian　Yushu　Shanhetun　Hailin　Pogranichnyy　RUSSIA
Qian an　Shenjingzi　Dehui　Shulan　Zhangguangcailing　MUDANJIANG　Muling　Ussuriysk
Tongyu　Beizhengzhen　Fulongquan　Nung'an　1690　Hailin　Suiyang　Suifenhe　Golenki
Xinkai He　Changling　Horqin Zuoyi Zhongqi　Jiutai　Gangyu　Ning'an　Dongjingcheng　Dongning　44
1949　Huaidezhen　CHANGCHUN　JILIN　Jiaohe　Emu　Jingpo Hu　Chunyang　Daxinggou　Luozigou
Bairin Zuoqi　Kailu　Tongliao　Shuangliao　Lishu　Gongzhuling　Yitong　Panshi　Huadian　Wangqing　Shixian　Vladivostok　C
Linxi　Xilao He　Jargalang　Siping　Liaoyuan　Dongfeng　Huinan　Baishan　Fusong　Antu　Tumen　Kanji　Hunchun　Slavyanka
Xar Moron He　Bamiancheng　Xifeng　Jingyu　Quanyang　Songjianghe　Helong　Longjing　Namyang　Kraskino
Bairin Youqi　Laoha He　Kangping　Zhangwu　Kaiyuan　Meihekou　Shanchengzhen　Shiren　Linjiang　Chunggang-ŭp　2744　Paektu-san　Hoeryŏng　Posyet
Ongniud Qi　Wutonghaolji　Hure Qi　Tiefa　Qingyuan　Huinan　Hunjiang　1677　Changbai　Muson　Aoji　Sŏsura
2020　Xiawa　Faku　Tieling　Jiangyuan　Kasan-dong　Hyesan　Hapsu　Puryŏng　Unggi　Pugodong
CHIFENG (Ulanhad)　Heishui　Fuxin　Xinlitun　Xinmin　Piao ertun　Xinbin　Tonghua　Ji'an　Yalu　Changjin　Kapsan　P'ungsan　Kilchu　Najin　42
Weichang　Beipiao　Qinghemen　Liu He　Liao He　Kaiyuan　Wiwon　Manp'o　Hŭch'ang　Kanggye　Puksubaek-san　Iwŏn　Kimch'aek (Sŏngjin)
Longhua　Chaoyang　Beizhen　SHENYANG　FUSHUN　Qinghecheng　Huanren　1846　Ch'osan　Koin　2522　Pujŏn-ho　Iwŏn　Tanch'ŏn　Musudan
1885　Ningcheng　Liaozhong　Sujiatun　Benxi　Tianshifu　Ji'an　Changjin-ho　Kwangdaeri　Iwŏn　Pukch'ŏng
1029　Chengde　Lingyuan　Jinzhou　Liaoyang　Anping　Gongchangling　Supung Shuiku　Pyŏktong　Kangye　Changjin　Changhŭngni　Sinhŭng　Sinch'ang　30
Luanhe　Pingquan　Jianchang　Panjin　ANSHAN　Lianshanguan　Kuandian　Sakchu　Taegwan　Kujang　Changjin-ni　Hongwon
Liugou　Huludao　Niuzhuang　Haicheng　Xiuyan　Cao He　Uiju　Pukchin　Huich'on　Oro　Hamhŭng　40
Shuiku　Shangbancheng　JINXI　Tianzhuangtai　Dashiqiao　Fengcheng　Dandong　Sinŭiju　Yongamp'o　Kusŏng　Koin　Sinanju　Oro　Hŭngnam　SEA OF
Zunhua　Kuancheng　Xingcheng　Yingkou　Gaizhou　Xiuyan　Langtou　Chŏngju　Pakch'ŏn　Tŏkch'ŏn　NORTH　Hongwon　JAPAN
Xianglong　Fengrun　Lulong　Qinhuangdao　Liaodong　Gushan　Donggou　Sŏnch'ŏn　Chŏngju　Sunch'on　KOREA　Tongjosŏn Man
Yatian　Funing　Leting　Changli　Wan　Xiongyuecheng　Bryun Shan　Wanfu　1131　Zhuanghe　Yalu Tuan　Sinmi-do　Sukch'ŏn　Yŏnghŭng　E
Baodi　Jingtanggang　Wafangdian　Baod　Changshan　Pikou　Qundao　Sŏnch'ŏn　Sanch'ŏn　Kowŏn　Munch'ŏn
TIANJIN　Tangshan　Pulandian (Xinjin)　Jinzhou (Jin Xian)　Zhuanghe　Cho-do　P'YŎNGYANG　Chunghwa　Kangdong　Tongyang　Anbyŏn　Wŏnsan
Dagu　Lüshun　DALIAN (Lüda)　Korea Bay　NAMP'O　Pyŏngsong　Kangdong　Koksan　Sepo-ri　Hoeyang　Kosŏng
Tanggu　Miaodao Qundao　Cho-do　Sariwŏn　Sinmak　Pyŏnggang　1638　Changdo-ri　Gangseong　38
Oikou　Bo Hai　Sunan　Chaeryŏng　Sinch'ŏn　Kŭmch'on　Cheorwon　Hwacheon　Chuncheon　Jumunjin
Huanghua　Huang He　Changyŏn　Haeju　Yonan　Kaesŏng　Panmunjŏm　Munsan　Ujeongbu　1708　Yang-yang
Xincun　Longkou　Penglai　Baengnyeongdo (S. Korea)　Ongjin　Kŭmch'on　GOYANG　SEOUL　Hongcheon　Gangneung
Yanshan　Laizhou Wan　Huang Xian　Daxindian　YANTAI　Weihai　Chengshan Jiao　INCHEON　SEONGNAM　Hoengseong　Donghae　Samcheok
Qingyun　Zhanhua　Dongying Wan　Fushan　Muping　Wendeng　Ansan　Anyang　Jcheon　Yeoju　Wonju　Jecheon　Yeongwol-up　Uljin　F
Wudi　Binzhou　Dajiawa　Guangrao　Qixia　923　Rongcheng　Suwon　Icheon　Chungju　Yeongju　Ulleungdo (S. Korea)
Huimin　Kenli　Dongying　Laizhou　Xenia　Laiyang　Rushan　Shidao　Pyeongtaek　Cheonan　Yecheon　Yeongdeok
Shanghe　Zhoucun　ZIBO　Huantai　Shouguang　Changle　Shandong Bandao　Nanhuang　Haiyang　Seosan　Hongseong　SOUTH　Andong　Heunghae
Jiyang　Mashang　Hongshan　Linzi　Fangzi　Pingdu　Laixi　Cheonan　Gongju　Cheongju　Yecheon　Pohang　36
Boshan　Yidu　Hanting　WEIFANG　Gaomi　Lancun　Jimo　Chengyang　Anmyeondo　Baryeong　DAEJEON　Gimcheon　Gumi　Uiseong
Jinan　Laiwu　Zhucheng　Jiaozhou　Jiaozhou Wan　QINGDAO　Gongju　Yeongdong　Sangju　Gyeongju
1108　Mengyin　Yishui　Wulian　Huangdao　Anmyeondo　Nonsan　Yeongdong　Seonsan　Gyeongju
Tai'an　XINTAI　Linqu　Tangtou　Gunsan　Iksan　Jeonju　Waegwan　DAEGU　Cheongdo　Miryang　ULSAN
Ning　Pingyi　Ju Xian　Liangcheng　Gimje　Gochang　Jeonju　Geochang　Goryeong　Yeongcheon　Dongnae　G
Feng　Fei Xian　Ganyu　Rizhao　Shijiusuo　YELLOW SEA　Damyang 1915　Jinju　Masan　Gimhae　Busan
LINYI　Tancheng　Andongwei　Haizhou Wan　GWANGJU　Namwon　Chang-won　Sacheon　Tong-yeong　BUSAN
ZAOZHUANG　Hanzhuang　Pizhou　Lianyungang　(Huang Hai)　Naju　Hadong　Sacheon　Korea Strait　Tsushima (Japan)
Jiawang　Haizhou　Guanyun　Chenjiagang　Suncheon　Boseong　Beolgyo　Yeosu　Izuhara
XINYI　Shuyang　Xiangshui　Heuksando (S. Korea)　Mokpo　Jangheung　Haenam　Jindo　34
XUZHOU　Guannan　Binhai　Jindo　Korea Strait　Iki　Karatsu
SUQIAN　Lianshui　Funing　Sheyang　JIANGSU　Jeju　Jeju-do (S. Korea)　JAPAN　31
Suining　Do Yanhe　Hallim　Hallasan　Namju　Nakadori-Shima　Karatsu　Imari
Lingbi　Huaiyin　HUAI'AN　Chuzhou　Baoying　Daejeong　Seogwipo　Seogwipo　Sasebo　Omuro　Isahaya
Guzhen　Hongze Hu　Liuzhuang　YANCHENG　Fukue-Shima　Nagasaki　Kuchinotsu　H
Sixian　Wuhe　Gaoyou Hu　Gaoyou　Dongtai　Nakadori-Shima　Omura
Bengbu　Fengyang　XINGHUA　Dongtai　COPYRIGHT PHILIP'S

1:12 500 000

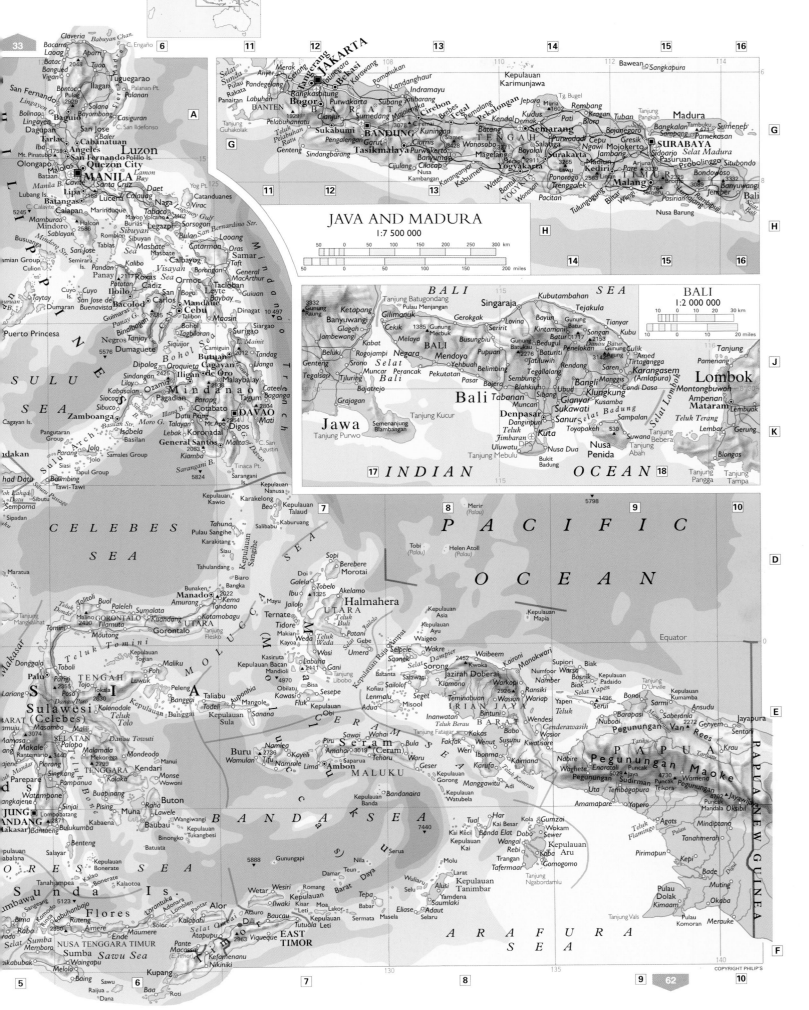

JAVA AND MADURA
1:7 500 000

BALI
1:2 000 000

1:6 000 000

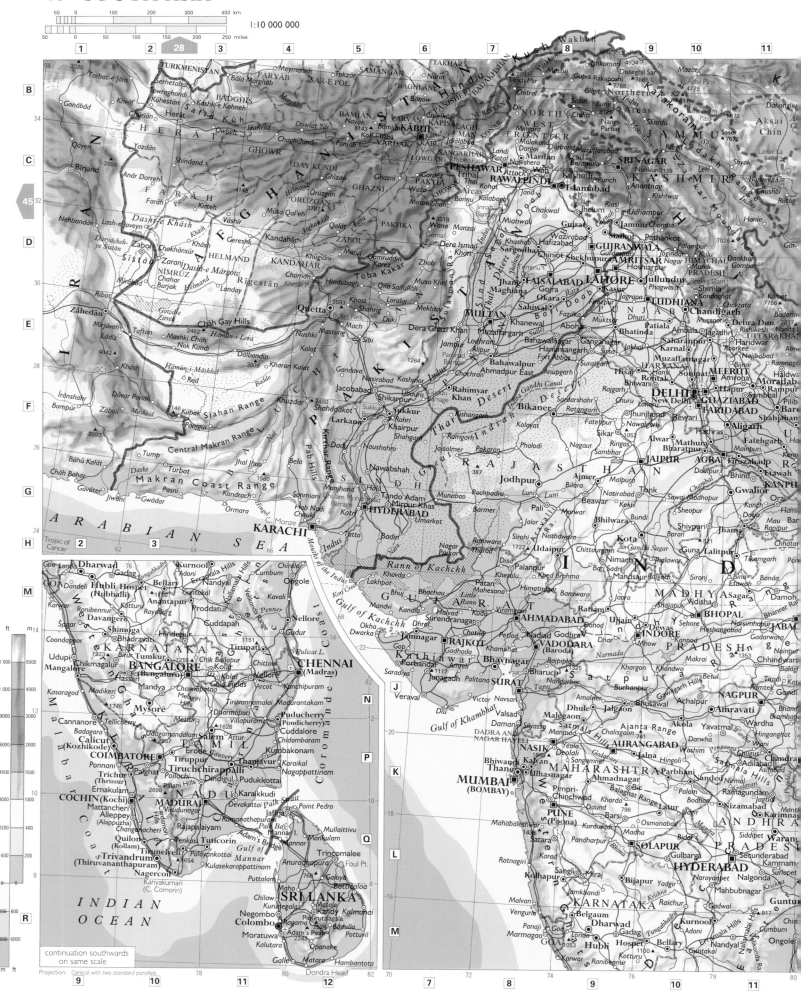

continuation southwards
on same scale

Projection: Conical with two standard parallels

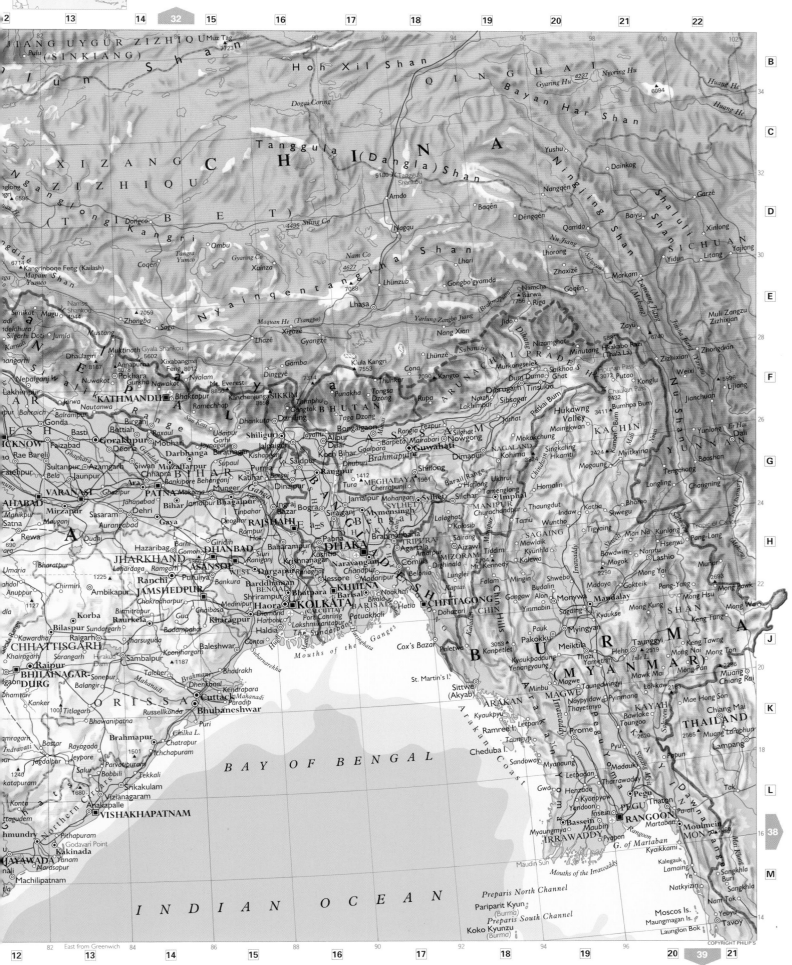

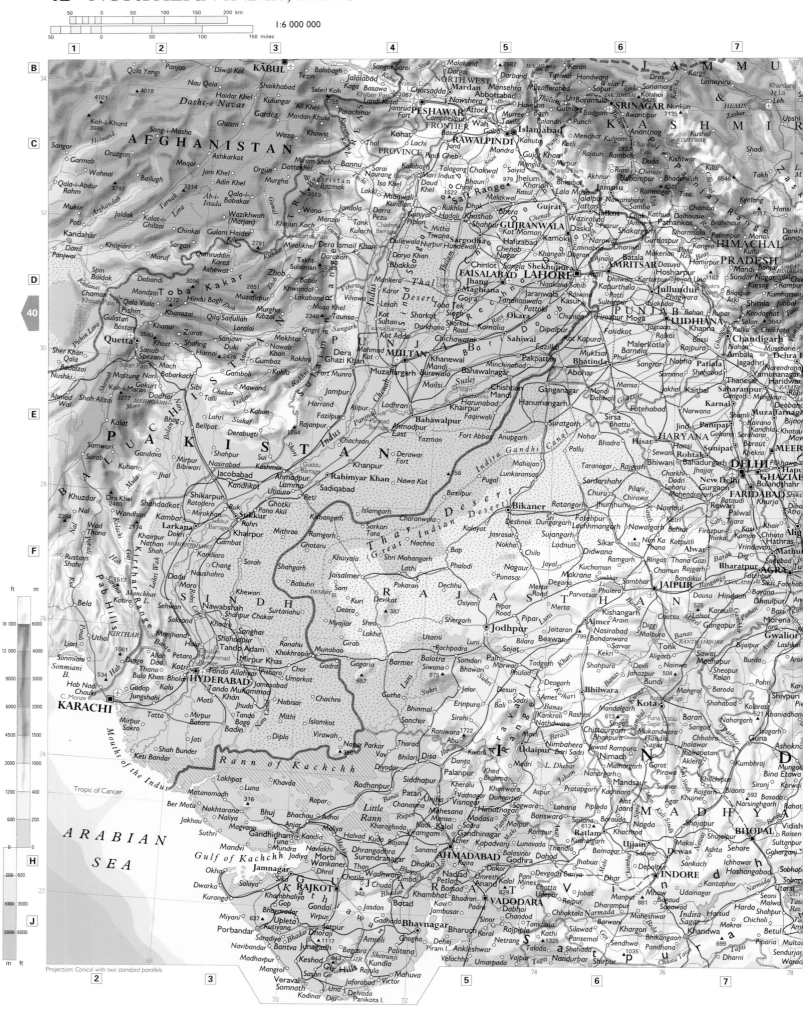

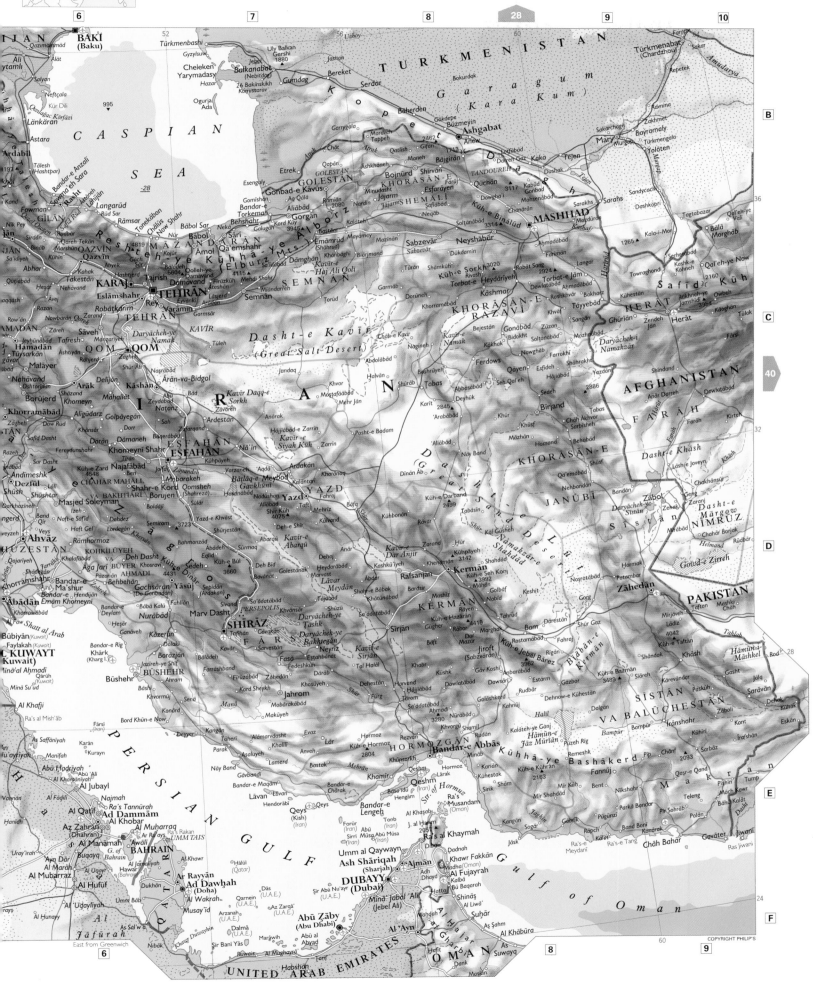

1:2 500 000

10 0 10 20 30 40 50 60 70 80 100 km
10 0 10 20 30 40 50 60 miles

44

CYPRUS

Paphos · Episkopi · Kivides · Zyyi
Episkopi Bay · Limassol · Akrotiri Bay · C. Gata

M E D I T E R R A N E A N

S E A

2775
2089

LEBANON

Al Hamidiyah · Al Mina · Tarabulus (Tripoli) · Zghartā · Qurnat as Sawdā 3088 · Bsharri
Al Batrūn · Qartābā · Jubayl · Ibrāhim · Bikfayyā 2628 · J. Sannin
BAYRŪT (Beirut) · Jūniyah
Ash Shuwayfāt · Alayh · Zahlah
Ad Dāmūr · **JABAL LUBNĀN** · Hawsh Mūssā · 1942 al Bāriq
Saydā (Sidon) · Jazzin · ash Shaykh (Mt. Hermon) 2814
An Nabaṭiyah at Tahta · **AL JANŪB** · Marj 'Uyūn · Al Khiyām
Ṣūr (Tyre) · Qiryat Shemona · Golan Hts · Mas'ada
Nahariyya · Me'ona · Ḥagalil (Galilee) 1208 · Zefat · 1197
'Akko (Acre) · Mifraẓ Hefa · Qiryat · Karmi'el · Yam Kinneret (Sea of Galilee)
Hefa (Haifa) · Qiryat Ata · Teverya (Tiberias) · -210
Dāliyat el Karmel · **EL KARMEL** · Nazerat (Nazareth)
HEFA · TEL MEGIDDO · Afula · Tayiba
Umm el Fahm · **Shōmrōn**
CAESAREA · Pardes · Jenin · Bet She'an
Hadera · Hanna-Karkur · Ṭulkarm · Tūbās · SAMARIA
ISRAEL · Netanya · Nābulus
HAMERKAZ · Ra'anana · N. az Zarqā
Herzliyya · Kefar Sava
Benē Beraq · Petah Tiqva · SHILO
TEL AVIV-YAFO · Ramat Gan · As Salt
Bat Yam · Lod · **WEST BANK** · Wadi as Sir
Holon · Ram · Karama
Rishon le Ziyyon · Ramla · Ram Allāh · 289
Yavne · Rehovot · El Arīḥa (Jericho)
Ashdod · Qiryat Mal'akhi · Bet Shemesh · **Jerusalem** (Yerushalayim) (Al Quds)
Ashqelon · Qiryat Gat · Bayt Laḥm (Bethlehem) · Ma'daba
LAKHISH · **MA'DABA**
Gaza · N. Shiqma · Al Khalil (Hebron)
GAZA STRIP · Sederot · Az Zāhiriyah
Khān Yūnis · ESHKOL · Arad · En Gedi -418
Rafaḥ · Be'er Sheva (Beersheba) · MASADA
El Daheir · Bor Mashash · Sedom -333
El 'Arīsh · Dimona · W. al Ḥasā
HADAROM · 1305 · **AL KARAK**
Ramāni · Bir el 'Abd · El Qusayma · At Ṭafilah
SHAMÂL SÎNÎ · Abu 'Aweigila · Qezi'ot · Sedé Boqér · **AT TAFILAH** · Dana
El Qantara · Birein · Muweilih · Mizpe Ramon
Wāḥid · Bir el Mālḥi · El Qadi
Ismâ'iliya · ISMA'ILIYA · Khamsa · 892 · G. Yi 'Allaq 1094 · **Hanegev** (Negev Desert)
El Buheirat el Murrat el Kubra (Great Bitter L.) · Bir Ḥasana · Bir Beiḍa · PETRA · Wādi Mūsā · Ma'ān
E G Y P T · **S Î N Â** (Sinai) · Bir el Thamâda · El 'Agrūd · Mamarr Mitla · N. Paran
Gineifa · Bir Gebeil Hisn · Nakhl · El Thamad · **M A 'Ā N**
El Suweis (Suez) · Bûr Taufiq · Ain Sudr · Gebel el Tih · El Kuntilla · Yotvata
Adabiya · 'Uyūn Mûsa · 948 G. el Kabrit · 'En Avrona · Rumm 1754 · **WADI RUM**
E S S Î N Â · **JANÛB SÎNÎ** · Elat · Al 'Aqaba · Ra's an Naqb 1435
Ghubbet el Bûs · El Wabeira · 1592 · Baṭn al Ghūl
1272 · Ras Matarma · Bir Ṭāba · Haql · **S A U D I**
EL SUWEIS · Bîr Wuseit · 1165 · Al Mudawwarah · **A R A B I A** · At Ṭubayq

SYRIA
Al Ḥirmil · An Nabk · Al Qaryatayn
Al Labwah 2464 · Al Burayj
Ba'labakk · Yabrūd · Bi'r Ghadir
ASH SHAMĀLS · **AL BIQĀ** · Khān Abū Shāmat
Az Zabadāni · Dumayr · Jayrūd
DIMASHQ (Damascus) · Dārayyā · Jaramānah
Qatanā · Al Kiswah · Al Ḥājānah · Burāq · Ṣafā
DAR'Ā · As Sanamayn · **AS SUWĀYDĀ**
Figr · Shaykh Miskin · Shahbā 1800
IRBID · Saḥam al Jawlān · Dar'ā · Salkhad
Al Mafraq · Umm al Qiṭṭayn · Jarash
AL MAFRAQ · Az Zarqā
'Ammān · **AMMĀN** · Azraq ash Shishan · **AZ ZARQĀ**
Madaba · Ma'daba · J. ash Shawmari 1072
Dhibān · W. al Ḥaydān · W. al Mawjib · Al Hadithah
Al Mazar · Al Qaṭrānah · W. al Ghadir
J O R D A N · W. Bā'ir · Bā'ir
Mahattat 'Unayzah · Nijil 1736 · Rujm Tal'at al Jamā'ah · Al Jafr · Qa'el Jafr
HIMS

ft m
9000 3000
6000 2000
4500 1500
3000 1000
1200 400
600 200
0 0
100 300
290 600
500 1500
1000 3000
2000 6000
m ft

Projection: Polyconic
East from Greenwich
COPYRIGHT PHILIP'S

▭ ▭ ▭ 1974 Cease Fire Lines

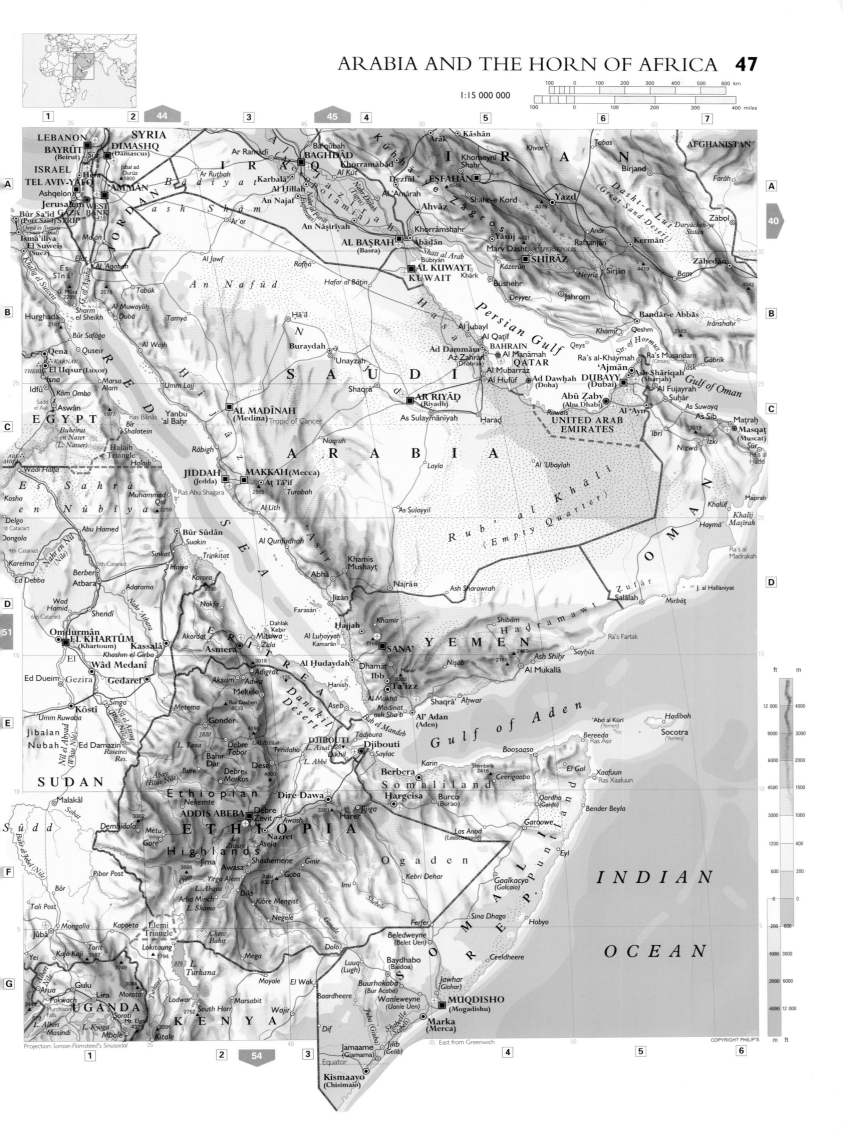

1:15 000 000

1:42 000 000

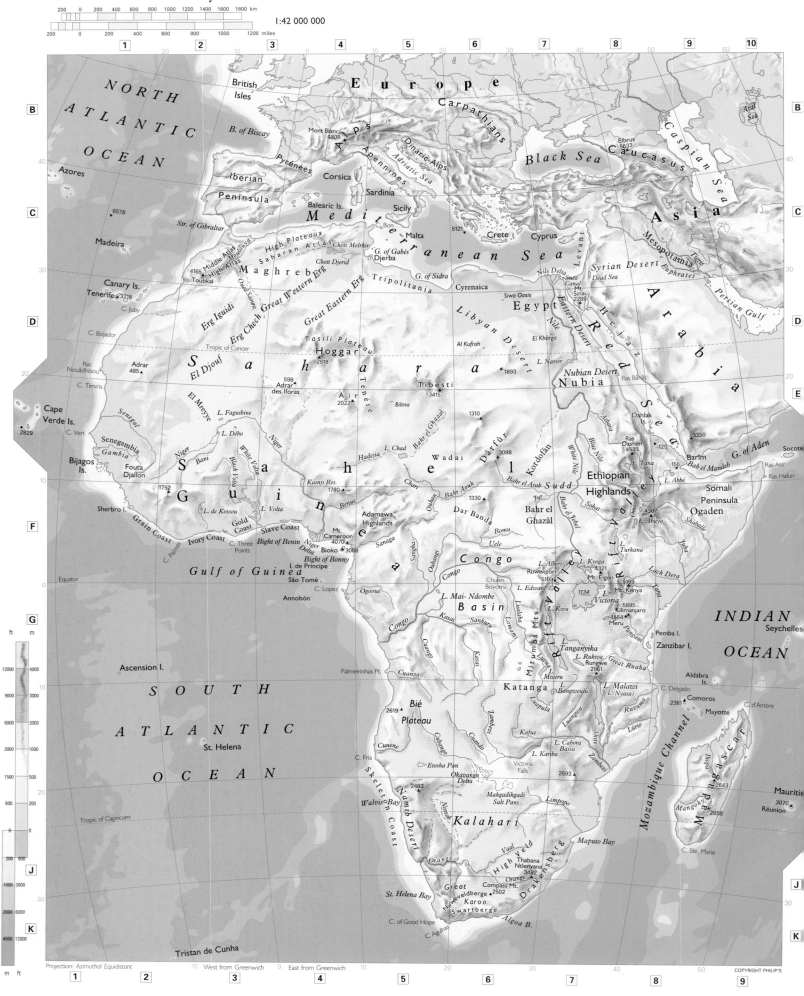

Projection: Azimuthal Equidistant

West from Greenwich   East from Greenwich

COPYRIGHT PHILIP'S

1:42 000 000

200 0 200 400 600 800 1000 1200 1400 1600 1800 km
200 0 200 400 600 800 1000 1200 miles

NORTH ATLANTIC OCEAN

UNITED KINGDOM
LONDON
NETH.
BELG.
GERMANY POLAND
Warsaw
Kiev
RUSSIA
Volgograd
KAZAKHSTAN
Prague
Paris
CZECH REP.
Vienna
SLOVAK REP.
AUSTRIA HUNGARY
UKRAINE
Odessa
Aral Sea
FRANCE
SWITZ.
CROATIA
BOS.-HERZ.
SERBIA
MONT. KOS.
ROMANIA
MAC.
BULGARIA
GEORGIA
ARM. AZER.
Baku
TURKMEN.
B. of Biscay
Marseilles
ITALY
Adriatic Sea
Black Sea
Ankara
Mosul
Tehrán
Madrid
Corsica
Rome
GREECE
Athens
TURKEY
Aleppo
Esfahán
PORTUGAL
SPAIN
Sardinia
Sicily
Crete
CYPRUS
SYRIA
Tigris
Baghdád
IRAN
Lisbon
Gibraltar (U.K.)
Algiers
Annaba
Constantine
Tunis
MALTA
Mediterranean Sea
LEB.
Damascus
Euphrates
Basra
Oran
Ceuta (Sp.)
Melilla (Sp.)
Sfax
Tripoli
Mişrátah
Benghazi
Alexandria
Port Said
Tel Aviv-Jaffa
Jerusalem
ISRAEL
JORDAN
IRAQ
KUWAIT
Madeira (Port.)
Funchal
Rabat
Casablanca
Fès
Marrakesh
TUNISIA
CAIRO
Suez
El Faiyûm
Syrian Desert
SAUDI
BAHRAIN
Persian Gulf
QATAR
MOROCCO
Santa Cruz de Tenerife
Canary Is. (Sp.)
Las Palmas
El Aaiún
In Salah
ALGERIA
Sabhá
LIBYA
EGYPT
Asyût
Al Jawf
Aswân
Medina
Riyadh
ARABIA
Dakhla
WESTERN SAHARA
Fdérik
Tropic of Cancer
Sahara
Wadi Halfa
Jedda
Mecca
Ras Nouâdhibou
Port Sudan
Red Sea
MAURITANIA
Nouakchott
NIGER
Agadès
CHAD
Abéché
SUDAN
El Fásher
El Obeid
Omdurmân
Khartoum
Atbara
Wád Medani
Asmera
ERITREA
Massawa
Sana'
YEMEN
Socotra (Yemen)
CAPE VERDE IS.
St-Louis
Senegal
Tombouctou
MALI
Niamey
Niger
Kano
Kaduna
Maiduguri
Ndjamena
L. Chad
Chari
Blue Nile
White Nile
L. Tana
DJIBOUTI
Djibouti
Berbera
SOMALILAND
G. of Aden
Ras Asir
Praia
C. Vert
Dakar
SENEGAL
GAMBIA
Banjul
GUINEA-BISSAU
Bissau
BURKINA FASO
Ouagadougou
Bobo-Dioulasso
Bamako
BENIN
NIGERIA
Abuja
Enugu
Benue
Malakâl
Wâw
Bahr el Jebel
Addis Ababa
ETHIOPIA
Harer
L. Turkana
SOMALI REP.
Conakry
Freetown
SIERRA LEONE
GUINEA
IVORY COAST
GHANA
Kumasi
Bouaké
TOGO
Ibadan
LAGOS
Lomé
CAMEROON
CENTRAL AFRICAN REP.
Bangui
Shabelle
Mogadishu
Monrovia
LIBERIA
Yamoussoukro
Abidjan
Sekondi-Takoradi
Accra
Porto Novo
Benin City
Douala
Rey Malabo
Yaoundé
Congo
Ubangi
Kisangani
L. Albert
UGANDA
Kampala
L. Edward
KENYA
Juba
Nairobi
Kismayu
Bight of Benin
Port Harcourt
EQUATORIAL GUINEA
SÃO TOMÉ & PRÍNCIPE
Libreville
GABON
CONGO
(DEM. REP. OF THE)
Mbandaka
RWANDA
Kigali
BURUNDI
Bujumbura
L. Victoria
Kisumu
Mombasa
Gulf of Guinea
C. Lopez
Equator
Annobón (Eq. Guinea)
Brazzaville
Pointe-Noire
CABINDA (Angola)
Congo
KINSHASA
Matadi
Kasai
Kananga
Mbuji-Mayi
TANZANIA
Dodoma
Zanzibar
Dar es Salaam
L. Kivu
L. Tanganyika
INDIAN OCEAN
Victoria
SEYCHELLES
Luanda
Cuango
Kolwezi
L. Mweru
Likasi
Lubumbashi
Aldabra Is. (Seychelles)
C. Delgado
COMOROS
Moroni
Mamoudzou
Mayotte (Fr.)
Antsiranana
Ascension I. (U.K.)
SOUTH ATLANTIC OCEAN
Lobito
ANGOLA
Huambo
Ndola
ZAMBIA
Lusaka
Lilongwe
MALAWI
L. Malawi
Blantyre
MOZAMBIQUE
Moçambique
Mahajanga
St. Helena (U.K.)
Namibe
Cunene
Zambezi
Livingstone
Harare
ZIMBABWE
Beira
Mozambique Channel
Toamasina
Antananarivo
MADAGASCAR
MAURITIUS
NAMIBIA
BOTSWANA
Bulawayo
Limpopo
Fianarantsoa
St-Denis
Réunion (Fr.)
Port Louis
C. Fria
Windhoek
Gaborone
Pretoria (Tshwane)
Maputo
Johannesburg
Vaal
Mbabane SWAZ.
Orange
Kimberley
Maseru
LESOTHO
Durban (eThekwini)
SOUTH AFRICA
Cape Town
C. of Good Hope
C. Agulhas
East London
Port Elizabeth

Tropic of Capricorn
Tristan da Cunha (U.K.)

Projection: Azimuthal Equidistant
West from Greenwich
East from Greenwich
COPYRIGHT PHILIP'S

● Dakar Capital Cities

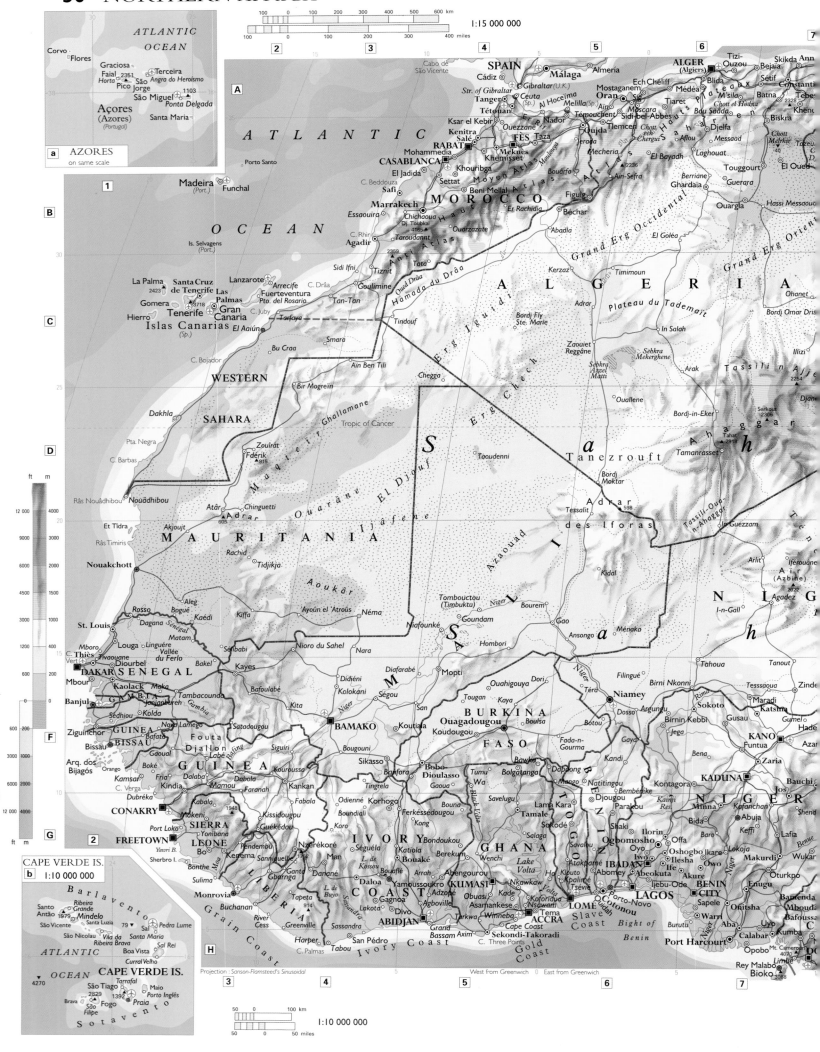

1:15 000 000

ATLANTIC OCEAN

Corvo • Flores
Graciosa
Faial ▲2351 Terceira
Horta • São ⊕ Angra do Heroísmo
Pico Jorge
São Miguel ▲1103
Ponta Delgada
Santa Maria

Açores
(Azores)
(Portugal)

a **AZORES**
on same scale

b **CAPE VERDE IS.** 1:10 000 000

Barlavento

Santo
Antão Ribeira
Grande Mindelo
1979 Santa Luzia
São Vicente São Nicolau Santa Maria
Ribeira Brava Sal Rei
79 Sal
Pedra Lume

ATLANTIC

OCEAN **CAPE VERDE IS.**
4270 Tarrafal
São Tiago Maio
2829 Praia Porto Inglês
Brava 1392
São Fogo
Filipe Sotavento

Projection : Sanson-Flamsteed's Sinusoidal

1:10 000 000

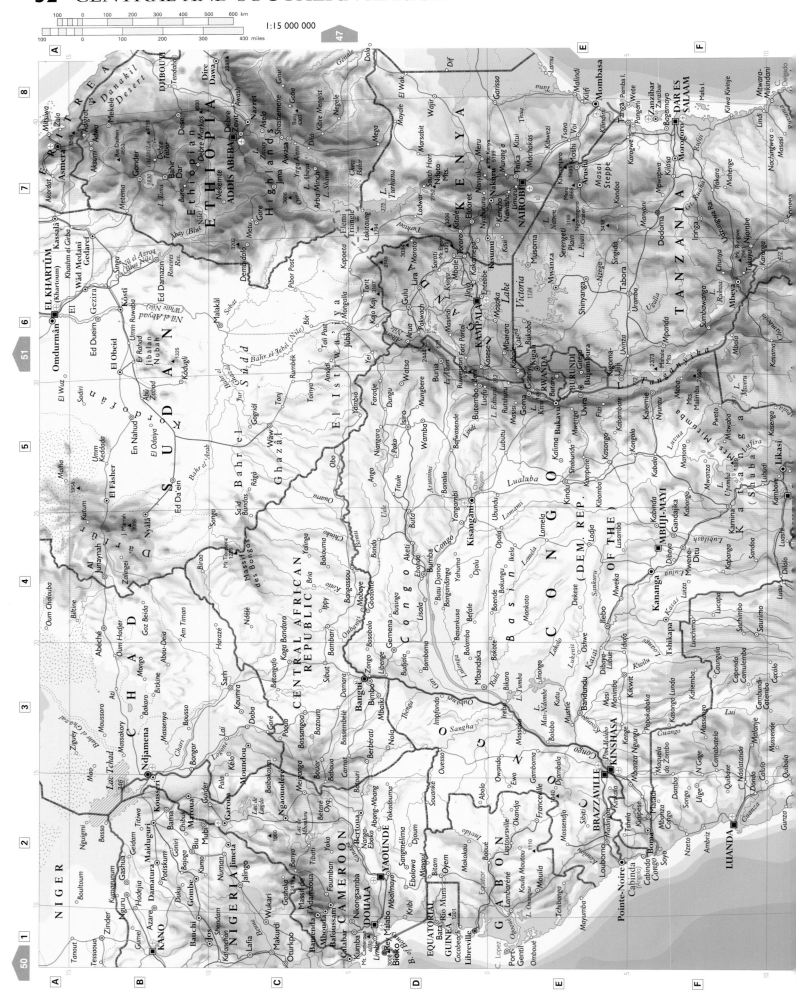

1:15 000 000

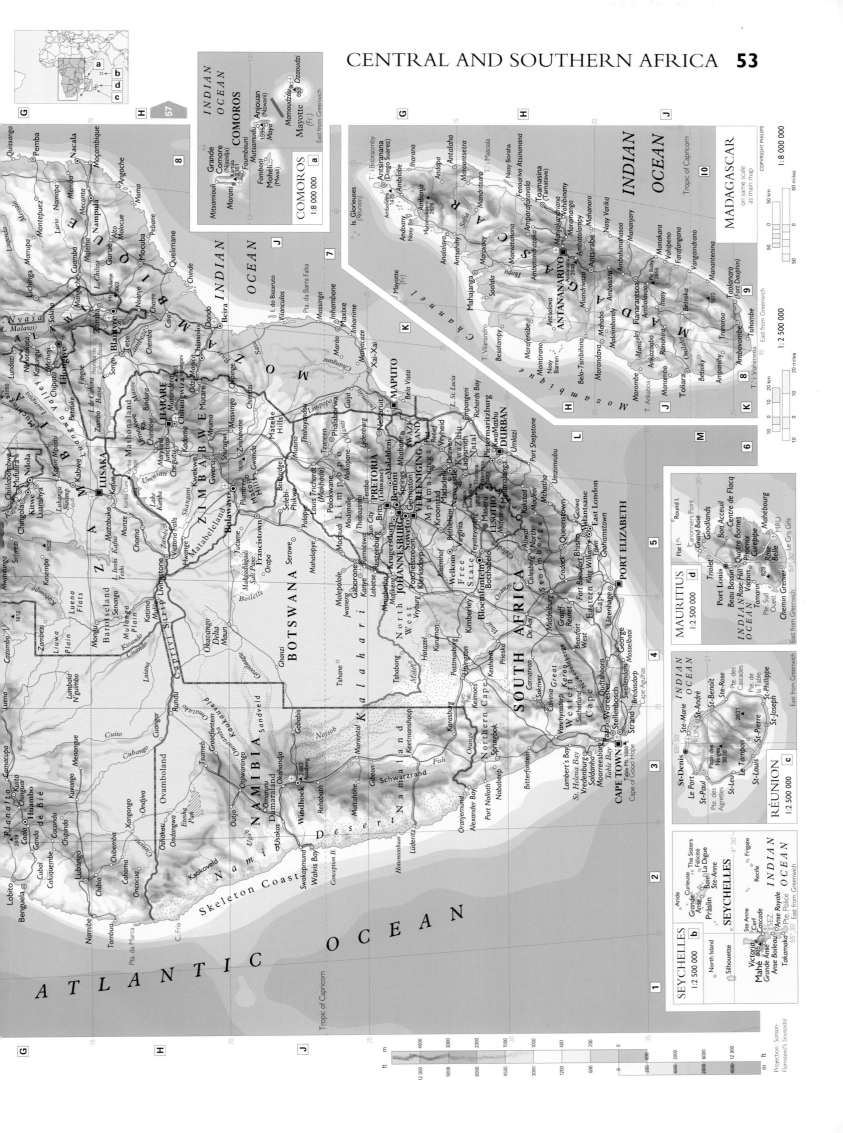

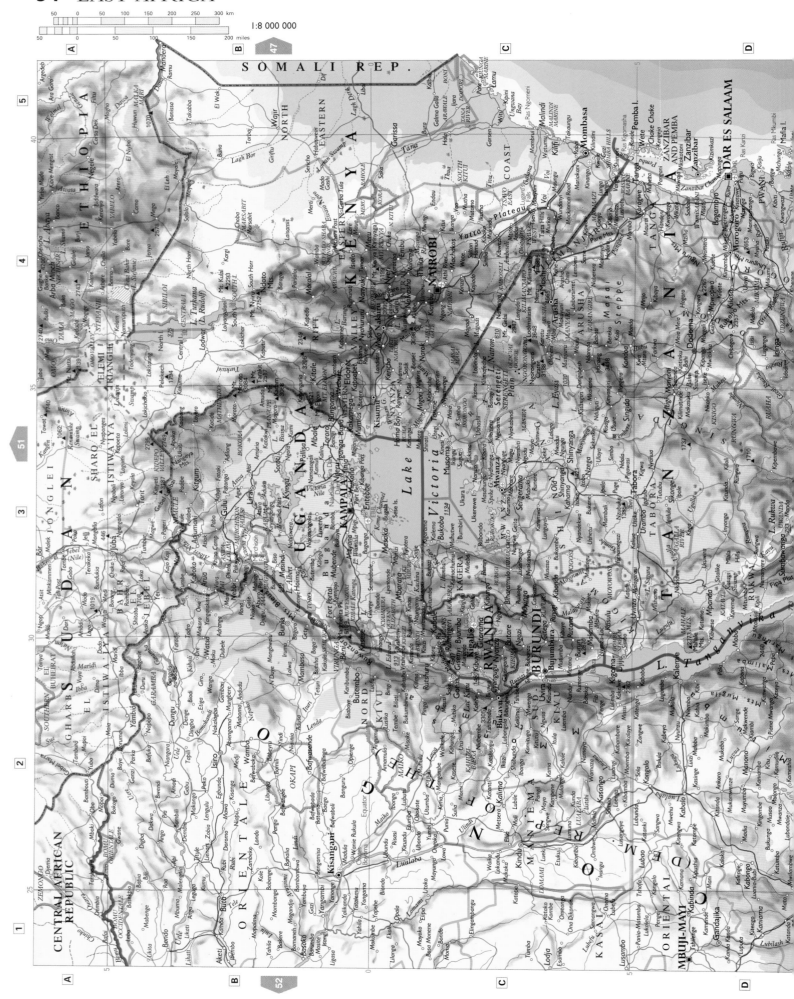

1:8 000 000

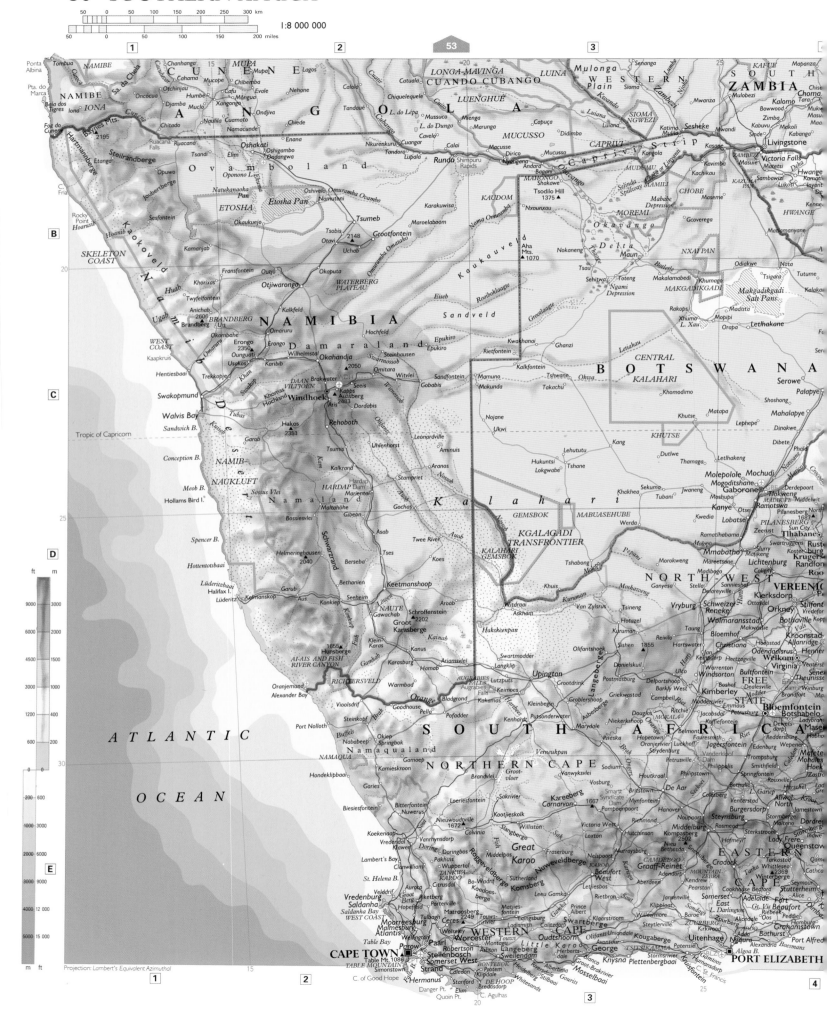

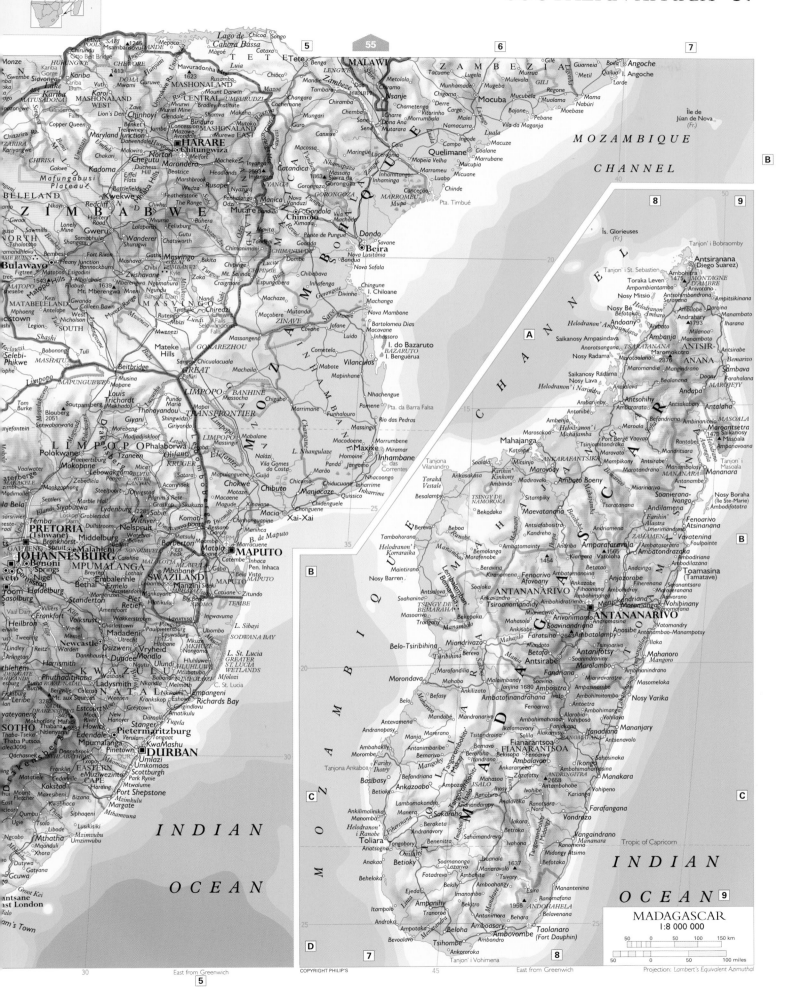

MOZAMBIQUE CHANNEL

I N D I A N   O C E A N

MOZAMBIQUE

I N D I A N   O C E A N

MADAGASCAR
1:8 000 000

COPYRIGHT PHILIP'S

East from Greenwich

Projection: *Lambert's Equivalent Azimuthal*

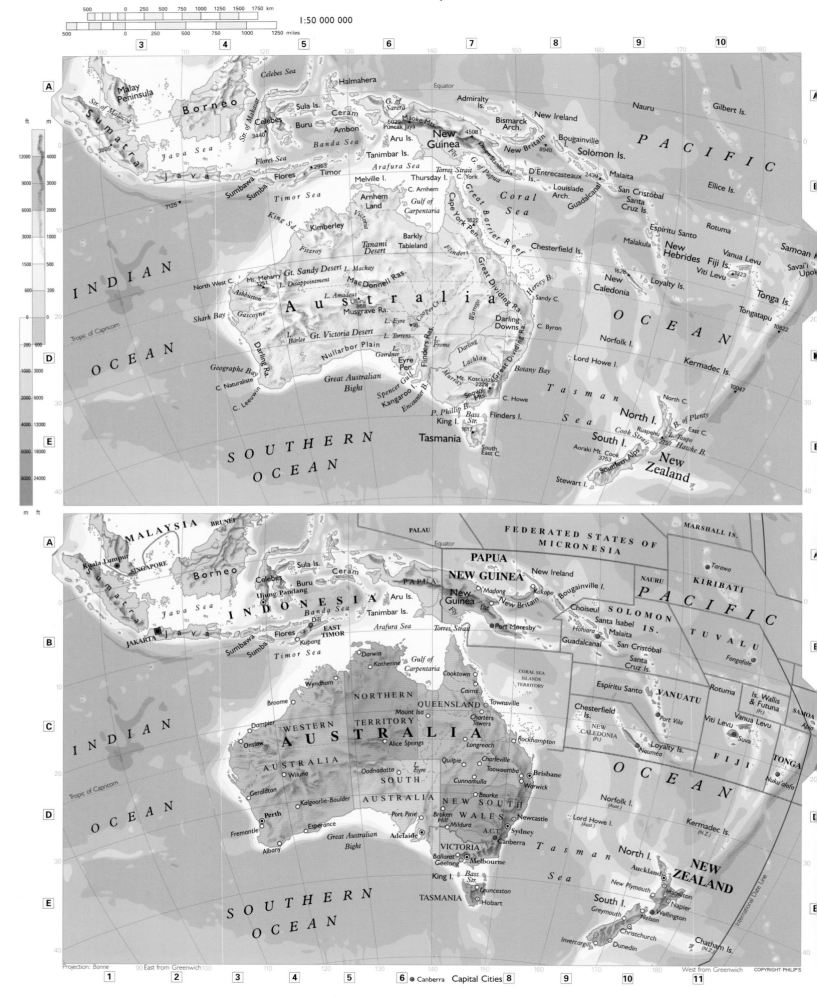

500   0 250 500 750 1000 1250 1500 1750 km

1:50 000 000

500   0   250   500   750   1000   1250 miles

Physical Map (top)

INDIAN OCEAN

SOUTHERN OCEAN

PACIFIC OCEAN

Tropic of Capricorn

Equator

Malay Peninsula
Str. of Malacca
Sumatra
Borneo
Celebes Sea
Str. of Macassar
Sula Is.
Halmahera
Celebes
Buru
Ceram
Ambon
Aru Is.
G. of Sarera
Maoke Mts.
Puncak Jaya
New Guinea
Admiralty Is.
New Ireland
Bismarck Arch.
New Britain
Bougainville I.
Solomon Is.
D'Entrecasteaux
Malaita
San Cristóbal
Santa Cruz Is.
Nauru
Gilbert Is.
Ellice Is.
Java
Java Sea
Flores Sea
Banda Sea
Sumbawa
Sumba
Flores
Timor
Tanimbar Is.
Arafura Sea
Thursday I.
C. York
Torres Strait
G. of Papua
Owen Stanley Ra.
Coral Sea
Louisiade Arch.
Guadalcanal
Espíritu Santo
Rotuma
Samoan
Savai'i
Upo
Timor Sea
Melville I.
C. Arnhem
Arnhem Land
Gulf of Carpentaria
Cape York Pen.
Great Barrier Reef
Chesterfield Is.
New Hebrides
Malakula
Fiji Is.
Vanua Levu
Viti Levu
Tonga Is.
King Sd.
Kimberley
Fitzroy
Tanami Desert
Barkly Tableland
Flinders
New Caledonia
Loyalty Is.
Norfolk I.
Tongatapu
North West C.
Mt. Meharry
Ashburton
Gt. Sandy Desert
L. Disappointment
L. Mackay
MacDonnell Ras.
Great Dividing Ra.
Hervey B.
Sandy C.
Australia
Uluru
L. Amadeus
Musgrave Ra.
Cooper Cr.
Warrego
Darling Downs
C. Byron
Kermadec Is.
Shark Bay
Gascoyne
L. Barlee
Gt. Victoria Desert
L. Eyre
L. Torrens
Darling
Lachlan
Lord Howe I.
Botany Bay
Geographe Bay
C. Naturaliste
Darling Ra.
Nullarbor Plain
L. Gairdner
Eyre Pen.
Flinders Ras.
L. Frome
Murray
Mt. Kosciuszko
Snowy Mts.
Great Dividing Ra.
Tasman Sea
North C.
C. Leeuwin
Great Australian Bight
Spencer Gulf
Kangaroo I.
Encounter B.
C. Howe
P. Phillip B.
Bass Str.
Flinders I.
King I.
Tasmania
South East C.
North I.
South I.
Cook Strait
Ruapehu
Hawke B.
B. of Plenty
East C.
Aoraki Mt. Cook
Southern Alps
Stewart I.
New Zealand

Political Map (bottom)

INDIAN OCEAN

SOUTHERN OCEAN

PACIFIC OCEAN

Tropic of Capricorn

Equator

MALAYSIA
BRUNEI
Kuala Lumpur
SINGAPORE
Sumatra
Borneo
PALAU
FEDERATED STATES OF MICRONESIA
MARSHALL IS.
Celebes
Ujung Pandang
Buru
Ceram
PAPUA
Sula Is.
Aru Is.
PAPUA NEW GUINEA
New Ireland
Madang
Kokopo
New Britain
Bougainville I.
Tarawa
NAURU
KIRIBATI
INDONESIA
New Guinea
Lae
Fly
SOLOMON IS.
Choiseul
Santa Isabel
JAKARTA
Java
Dili
EAST TIMOR
Tanimbar Is.
Port Moresby
Malaita
Guadalcanal
San Cristóbal
PACIFIC
TUVALU
Sumbawa
Sumba
Flores
Kupang
Arafura Sea
Torres Strait
Santa Cruz Is.
Fongafale
Timor Sea
Darwin
Katherine
Gulf of Carpentaria
Cooktown
Cairns
CORAL SEA ISLANDS TERRITORY
Espíritu Santo
Rotuma
SAMOA
Wyndham
NORTHERN
Townsville
VANUATU
Is. Wallis & Futuna (Fr.)
Broome
WESTERN
TERRITORY
QUEENSLAND
Mount Isa
Charters Towers
Chesterfield Is.
Port Vila
Viti Levu
Vanua Levu
Dampier
AUSTRALIA
Alice Springs
Longreach
Rockhampton
NEW CALEDONIA (Fr.)
Loyalty Is.
Nouméa
Suva
FIJI
Onslow
AUSTRALIA
SOUTH
Oodnadatta
L. Eyre
Quilpie
Charleville
Toowoomba
Brisbane
INDIAN
Wiluna
Cunnamulla
Warwick
OCEAN
Geraldton
AUSTRALIA
Bourke
Norfolk I. (Aust.)
TONGA
Nuku'alofa
Kalgoorlie-Boulder
Port Pirie
NEW SOUTH
Broken Hill
Mildura
WALES
Newcastle
Lord Howe I. (Aust.)
Perth
Fremantle
Esperance
Adelaide
A.C.T.
Sydney
Canberra
Kermadec Is. (N.Z.)
Albany
Great Australian Bight
VICTORIA
Ballarat
Melbourne
Geelong
Tasman Sea
North I.
NEW ZEALAND
Auckland
King I.
Bass Str.
New Plymouth
Hamilton
Napier
TASMANIA
Launceston
Hobart
South I.
Greymouth
Wellington
Nelson
Invercargill
Dunedin
Christchurch
Chatham Is. (N.Z.)

1:6 000 000

50 0 50 100 150 200 km
50 0 50 100 150 miles

FIJI [a]
on same scale

PACIFIC OCEAN

Great Sea Reef · Kia · Udu Pt. · Ringgold Is.
Yaqaga · Labasa · Rabi
Vanua Levu · Savusavu Bay · Buca · Qamea · Taveuni
Yasawa Group · Yadua · Bua · Naitaba · Vanua Balavu
Nacula · Nabouwalu · Namuka Passage · Vatu · Mago · Northern Lau Group
Naviti · Vomo · Tavua · Lawaki · Vanuavatu · Lakeba
Waya · Nadi · Tomanini 1323 · Levuka · Wakaya · Cicia · Lakeba Passage
Mamanuca Group · Malolo · Viti Levu · Yunidawa · Ovalau · Batiki · Nairai · Nayau
Sigatoka · Korolevu · Navua · Keiyasi · Nausori · Tuvuca
Vatulele · Beqa · Suva · **FIJI** · Gau · Vanua Vatu · Lakeba · Oneata · Moce
Yanuca · Kadavu Passage · Moala · Namuka-i-Lau · Yagasa Cluster
Kadavu · Ono · Totoya · Matuku · Fulaga · Ogea · Ogea Driki

KORO SEA
18 S
178 E 180 East from Greenwich West from Greenwich

SAMOA
Savai'i · Asau · Safune · Pu'apu'a · Falefa
Taga · Mulifanua · Apia · Falefatai · Amaile
OLE PUPU PU'E · 'Upolu · Strand

AMERICAN SAMOA (U.S.A.)
Tutuila · Pago Pago · Leone · Ofu · Olosega · Ta'u
Vaitogi · Luma · Manu'a Is.

PACIFIC OCEAN
14 S
West from Greenwich

SAMOAN ISLANDS [b]
on same scale

TONGA [c]
on same scale

PACIFIC OCEAN
Fonualei · Toku
Vava'u · Vava'u Group · Neiafu
Late · Home Reef
Disney Reef
Tofua · Kao · Ha'ano · Foa · Ha'apai · Lifuka · Uiha
Ofolanga · Ha'apai Group
Fonuafo'ou · Kotu Group · Mango · Oto Tolu Group
Hunga Ha'apai · Nomuka · Nomuka Group · Tonumea
TONGA
Nuku'alofa · **Tongatapu** · Eua
Tongatapu Group
West from Greenwich
18 S
20 S

TASMAN SEA

PACIFIC OCEAN

North Island

C. Reinga · C. Maria van Diemen · North C.
Houhora Heads · Rangaunu B. · Doubtless B.
Ahipara B. · Kaitaia · Mangonui · Whangaroa Harb.
Tauroa Pt. · Rawene · Okaihau · C. Brett · B. of Islands
Hokianga Harbour · Kaikohe · Hikurangi
Waipoua Forest · Waipu · Whangarei · Whangarei Harb.
Dargaville · Bream Hd. · Bream B.
Little Barrier I.
Kaipara Harbour · Warkworth · C. Rodney · Great Barrier I.
Helensville · C. Colville · Cuvier I.
Hauraki Gulf · Coromandel · Whitianga
Takapuna · **AUCKLAND** · Thames · Whangamata
Manukau · Papakura · Waihi · Mayor I.
Waiuku · Pukekohe · Mercer · Whangamata · Mount Maunganui
Waikato · Huntly · Te Aroha · Tauranga Harb. · Whakaari (White I.)
Hamilton · Morrinsville · **Tauranga** · Whakatane · C. Runaway
Raglan · Cambridge · Te Puke · Opotiki · Hikurangi 1753
Kawhia Harbour · Te Awamutu · **Rotorua** · Kawerau · Raukumara Ra. · East C.
Kowhai · Otorohanga · Putaruru · Waipiro
Waitomo Caves · Te Kuiti · Kinleith · Taneatua · UREWERA · Tolaga Bay
Mokau · Taupo · Murupara · Ormond
North Taranaki Bight · Ongarue · Wairakei · Waikaremoana · **Gisborne**
Waitara · Taumarunui · L. Taupo · Poverty Bay
New Plymouth · Inglewood · Turangi · Ruatahuna · Nuhaka · Waikohu
Mt. Taranaki or Mt. Egmont 2518 · WHANGANUI · Rangitikei Mts. · Wairoa
Opunake · Stratford · EGMONT · Raetihi · TONGARIRO · Bay View
Kaponga · Eltham · Ohakune · Waiouru · **Napier**
Hawera · South Taranaki Bight · Taihape · Ruahine Ra. · **Hastings** · C. Kidnappers
Patea · Waverley · Mangaweka · Waipukurau · Hawke Bay
Wanganui · Marton · Hunterville · Waipawa
Bulls · Halcombe · Feilding · Dannevirke
Palmerston North · Woodville · Pahiatua
Foxton · Shannon · Levin · C. Turnagain
Paraparaumu · Otaki · Eketahuna · Masterton
Kapiti I. · **Upper Hutt** · Featherston · Cartertown · Greytown
Petone · **Lower Hutt** · **Wellington** · Martinborough
Cook Strait

40
38
36
34
174 176 178

South Island

C. Farewell · D'Urville I.
Collingwood · Golden B. · ABEL TASMAN · Tasman B.
Takaka · KAHURANGI · Tasman Mts. · Motueka
Karamea · Karamea Bight · **Nelson** · Havelock · Picton
Granity · Tadmor · Richmond · Wakefield · **Blenheim** · Seddon
Seddonville · Wakefield · NELSON LAKES · Ward
Westport · Lyell · Murchison · Inangahua · Wairau · 2885 Tapuae-o-Uenuku
Denniston · Reefton · L. Rotoroa · Kaikoura
PAPAROA · Punakaiki · Mt. Travers 2337 · Spenser Mts. · Hanmer Springs
Blackball · Lewis Pass · Clarence
Runanga · Greymouth · Stillwater · Culverden · Waiau
Kumara · L. Brunner · Jacksons · Waikari · Waipara
Hokitika · ARTHUR'S PASS · Hurunui · Amberley · Pegasus Bay
Ross · Arthur's · Hawarden · Oxford · Kaiapoi · New Brighton
Abut Hd. · Springfield · Rangiora · **Christchurch**
Westland Bight · WESTLAND · Whitecliffs · Riccarton · Lyttelton
Aoraki · Mt. Cook 3753 · Methven · Lincoln · Banks Pen.
Mt. Cook · MT. COOK · Staveley · Little River · Akaroa
Jackson B. · Fairlie · Ashburton · Rakaia
MOUNT ASPIRING · Mt. Aspiring 3033 · Pukaki · Temuka · Canterbury Bight
Milford Sd. · Mt. Earnslaw 2819 · Tekapo · **Timaru**
Sutherland Falls · L. Wanaka · Ohau · Waimate
Milford Sound · Wanaka · Kurow · St. Andrews
George Sound · Arrowtown · Cromwell · Otago · Palmerston
Secretary I. · Anau · Kingston · Clyde · Maheno · Dunback
Doubtful Sd. · Eyre Mts. · Alexandra · Oamaru · Otago Harbour
Breaksea Sd. · FIORDLAND · L. Te Anau · Garvie Mts. · Roxburgh · Waikouaiti
Resolution I. · Manapouri · Umbrella Mts. · Ranfurly · C. Saunders
Dusky Sd. · L. Manapouri · Ettrick · Lawrence · **Dunedin**
SOUTHLAND · Mossburn · Waikaia · Balclutha
Chalky Inlet · Lumsden · Ohai · Nightcaps · Kaitangata
Preservation Inlet · Clifden · Tuatapere · Mataura · Owaka
Te Waewae B. · Hedgehope · Gore · Clinton · Nugget Pt.
Solander I. · Winton · Wyndham · Tokanui · Tahakopa
Riverton · **Invercargill** · South Invercargill · Ruapuke I.
Bluff · Foveaux Str.
Halfmoon Bay · Stewart I. (Rakiura) · RAKIURA · Port Pegasus · South West C.

44
46
42
166 168 170 172

E
F
G

Projection: Conical with two standard parallels
East from Greenwich

TAHITI & MOOREA [d]
1:1 000 000

Pte. Aroa · B. de Matavai · Pte. Vénus · Mahina
Papetoai · **Papeete** · Arue · Papenoo
Mt. Tohiea 1207 · Pirae · Tiarei
Moorea (France) · Afareaitu · Faaa · Mt. Aorai 2060 · Mt. Orohena 2241 · Hitiaa
Haapiti · Pte. Nuupere · Punaauia · **Tahiti** (France) · Faaone
PACIFIC OCEAN · Paea · Mt. Teatara 1798 · Lac Vaihiria · Faaone
Maraa · Papara · Taravao · Isthme de Taravao
Atimaono · Mataiea · Afaahiti · Pte. Tatatua
Mt. Rooniu 1332 · Vairao
Teahupoo · Presqu'île de Taiarapu

17°30'S
17°45'S
149°30'W · 149°15'W
West from Greenwich
COPYRIGHT PHILIP'S

1:1 000 000
10 0 10 km
10 0 10 miles

ft m
9000 3000
6000 2000
3000 1000
1200 400
600 200
0 0
200 600
2000 6000
4000 12 000
6000 18 000
m ft

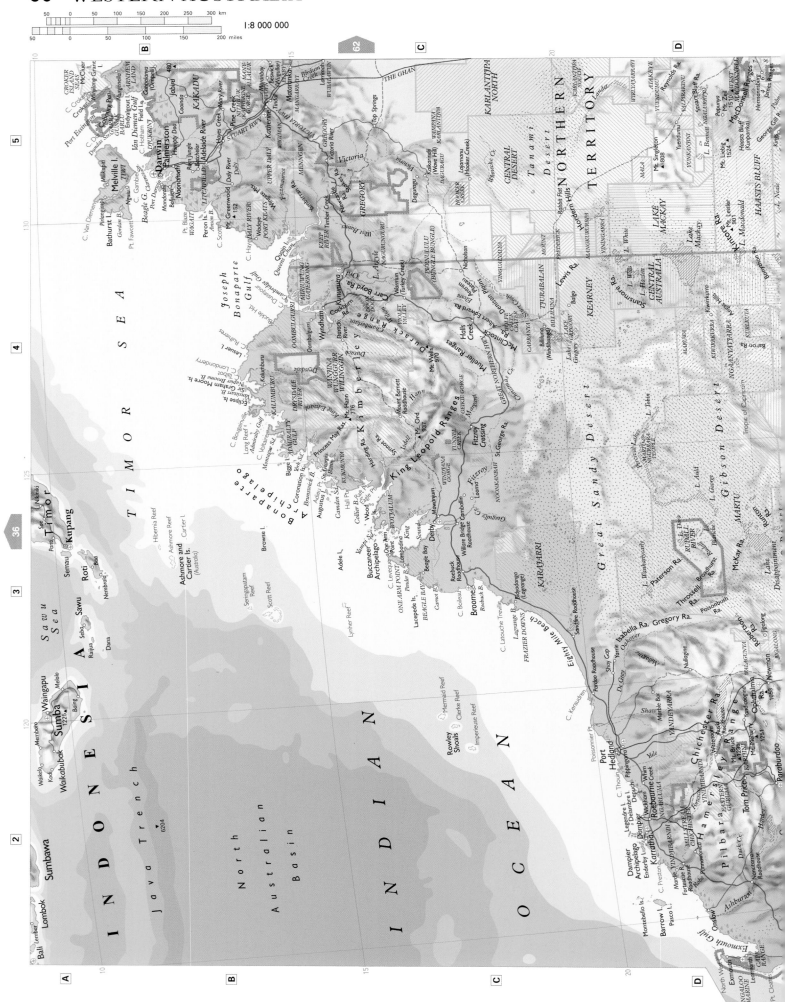

1:8 000 000

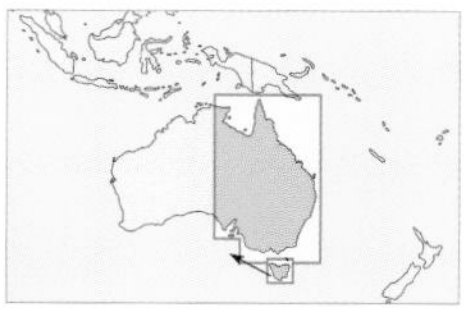

TASMAN SEA

QUEENSLAND

NEW SOUTH WALES

SOUTH AUSTRALIA

VICTORIA

TASMANIA

BRISBANE
SYDNEY
Canberra
AUSTRALIAN CAPITAL TERRITORY
Newcastle
Wollongong
MELBOURNE
ADELAIDE
Hobart

Great Dividing Range
Darling Range
Grey Range
Barrier Range
Flinders Ranges
Gawler Ranges
Sturt Stony Desert
Strzelecki Desert
Tirari Desert
Pedirka Desert
Simpson Desert

Lake Eyre (North)
Lake Eyre (South)
Lake Torrens
Lake Gairdner
Lake Frome
Lake Blanche
Lake Gregory

Gulf of St Vincent
Spencer Gulf
Eyre Peninsula
Yorke Peninsula
Kangaroo I.

Bass Strait
King Island
Flinders Island
Cape Barren I.
Furneaux Group
Kent Group

Gold Coast
Sunshine Coast
Coffs Harbour
Port Macquarie

Coober Pedy
Woomera
Port Augusta
Port Pirie
Whyalla
Port Lincoln
Broken Hill
Dubbo
Orange
Bathurst
Wagga Wagga
Albury
Bendigo
Ballarat
Geelong
Warrnambool
Mount Gambier

East from Greenwich

on same scale

Aboriginal lands

Projection: Bonne

Equatorial Scale 1:54 000 000

RUSSIA

Yekaterinburg · Tomsk
Moskva · Novosibirsk
Volga · Irkutsk · Chita · Blagoveshchensk · *Amur* · Sea of Okhotsk · Okhotsk · Poluostrov Kamchatka
Astana (Aqmola) · Semey · Oz. Baykal · Khabarovsk · Sakhalin · Kurilskiye Ostrova *(Russia)* · Petropavlovsk-Kamchatskiy · Komandorskiye Ostrova *(Russia)* · Near Is. *(U.S.A.)* · Andreanof · Aleutian Basin · Ber Sea
KAZAKHSTAN · *Balqash Köl* · Ulaanbaatar · La Pérouse Str. · Kuril-Kamchatka Trench · Aleutians · Aleutian Trench
Aral Sea · **MONGOLIA** · Harbin · Sapporo · Hakodate · 10,542 · Emperor Trough · Chinook Tr
Almaty · Ürümqi · Altai · Changchun · Vladivostok · Sea of Japan · Northwest
Toshkent · **KYRGYZSTAN** · Shenyang · Sea of Japan · Emperor Seamount Chain · How
TAJIKISTAN · Beijing · NORTH KOREA · Sendai · Shatsky Rise · Pacific
Kabul · Srinagar · **CHINA** · Tianjin · SOUTH KOREA · Seoul · Nagoya · Tōkyō · Yokohama · **Midway Is.** *(U.S.A.)*
AFGHANISTAN · Lanzhou · Taiyuan · Dalian · Fuji-San 3776 · Kyōto · Osaka · **JAPAN** · Basin
PAKISTAN · Kunlun Shan · Xi'an · Qingdao · Shikoku · Yokohama · Minami-Tori-Shima *(Japan)*
Lahore · *Himalaya* · Nanjing · Yellow Sea · Kyūshū · 10,554 · Japan Trench · Lisianski I. *(U.S.A.)*
Delhi · Chongqing · Wuhan · **Shanghai** · East China Sea · Iwo-Jima *(Japan)* · Ogasawara Gunto *(Japan)*
Kanpur · Everest 8850 · Changsha · Hangzhou · Okinawa · Kazan-Rettō *(Japan)* · Wake I. *(U.S.A.)*
NEPAL · Lhasa · **XIZANG** · Chang J. · Fuzhou · Ryūkyū-rettō *(Japan)* · NORTHERN MARIANAS *(U.S.A.)*
BANGLADESH · Kunming · **Taipei** · West Mariana Basin · East Mariana Basin · MARSHALL IS.
Kolkata (Calcutta) · Dhaka · **TAIWAN** · Tinian · Saipan · Enewetak Atoll · P
Hyderabad · **BURMA** · Guangzhou · Macau · Hong Kong · *Philippine Sea* · GUAM *(U.S.A.)* · Bikini Atoll
INDIA · Mandalay · Hanoi · Hainan · Luzon · Philippine Basin · Challenger 11,022 Deep · Kwajalein · Ralik Chain · Majuro · A
Bay of Bengal · Rangoon · **LAOS** · Paracel Is. · **Manila** · Mariana Trench · Yap · **Micronesia** · Jaluit I. · Centr
Chennai (Madras) · **THAILAND** · Bangkok · Mindoro · **PHILIPPINES** · Caroline Is. · Chuuk · Pohnpei · Pacific
Andaman Is. *(India)* · **CAMBODIA** · Phnom Penh · Palawan · Samar 10,497 · Melekeok · FED. STATES OF MICRONESIA · Palikir · Butaritari
Nicobar Is. *(India)* · South China Sea · Sulu Sea · Mindanao · Davao · Mindanao Trench · PALAU · East Caroline Basin · Tarawa · Gilbert Is. · Howland I.
SRI LANKA · Thanh Pho Ho Chi Minh · G. of Thailand · West Caroline Basin · Eauripik Rise · Solomon Rise · Melanesian Basin · Banaba · Baker I.
Colombo · **MALAYSIA** · *Celebes Sea* · 4101 · **Melanesia** · Abariringa · Phoenix Is. · Enderbur
Kuala Lumpur · PEN. MALAYSIA · SARAWAK · SABAH · BRUNEI · Halmahera · **PAPUA NEW GUINEA** · Admiralty Is. · NAURU · KI
Singapore · Borneo · Sulawesi · Seram · Puncak Jaya 5029 · Bismarck Arch. · New Ireland · New Britain · SOLOMON IS. · Fongafale · TUVALU · Tokelau *(N.Z.)*
INDONESIA · Palembang · Ujung Pandang · Buru · **PAPUA** · **New Guinea** · Kokopo · Bougainville · Honiara · Guadalcanal · Is. Wallis & Futuna *(Fr.)* · SAMOA
Sumatera · Jakarta · Java Sea · Flores Sea · Banda Sea · 7440 · Lae · 8940 · Santa Cruz I. 9165 · Rotuma · Apia
Selat Sunda · Surabaya · Bali · Flores · Dili · EAST TIMOR · Torres Strait · Port Moresby · VANUATU · Vanua Levu · SAMO
Jawa · Sumbawa · Sumba · Timor · Arafura Sea · C. York · Louisiade Arch. · Espíritu Santo · Port Vila · Viti Levu · FIJI · Suva
INDIAN · Christmas I. *(Austral.)* · North Australian Basin · C. Arnhem · Darwin · Gulf of Carpentaria · Coral Sea Basin · Is. Chesterfield · West Fiji Basin · Nuku'alofa · TON
Cocos Is. *(Austral.)* · Broome · Exmouth Plateau · Cairns · *Coral Sea* · 7570 · Is. Loyauté · Tonga Trench 10,822
OCEAN · Wharton Basin · North West C. · Mount Isa · Townsville · NEW CALEDONIA *(Fr.)* · Nouméa · South Fiji Basin
Broken Ridge · Geraldton · Perth Basin · **AUSTRALIA** · Alice Springs · Rockhampton · Lord Howe Rise · Middleton Reef · Kermadec Is. *(N.Z.)* · Kermadec Trench 10,047
Perth · Naturaliste Plateau · L. Eyre · Brisbane · Lord Howe I. *(Austral.)* · Norfolk I. *(Austral.)* · South Fiji Basin
Nouvelle Amsterdam *(Fr.)* · I. St. Paul *(Fr.)* · Albany · Great Australian Bight · Adelaide · Darling · Sydney · Canberra · Mt Kosciuszko 2228 · *Tasman Sea* · **NEW ZEALAND** · Auckland
Is. Crozet *(Fr.)* · Mid-Indian Ridge · South Australian Basin · Melbourne · Bass Str. · Murray · East Tasman Plateau · Aoraki Mt. Cook 3753 · Christchurch · Chatham Is. *(N.Z.)*
SOUTHERN · Kerguelen *(Fr.)* · Tasmania · Hobart · Tasman Basin · South Tasman Rise · South Tasman Basin · Wellington · Dunedin · Bounty Trough
Heard I. *(Austral.)* · **OCEAN** · Invercargill · Antipodes Is. *(N.Z.)* · Bounty Is. *(N.Z.)*
Auckland Is. *(N.Z.)* · Campbell Is. *(N.Z.)* · Campbell Plateau · Macquarie I. *(N.Z.)*

Ninetyeast Ridge · *Sunda Island* · *Java Trench*

ft m scale:
12 000 / 4000
9000 / 3000
6000 / 2000
3000 / 1000
1500 / 500
600 / 200
0 / 0
200 / 600
1000 / 3000
2000 / 6000
4000 / 12000
6000 / 18000
8000 / 24000
m ft

Projection: Mollweide's Homolographic · East from Greenwich

Arctic Circle

11 **12** **13** **14** **15** **16** **17** **18** **19** **20**

ALASKA
(U.S.A.)
Anchorage

Bristol Bay

Gulf of Alaska

Juneau

Prince of Wales I.
(U.S.A.) Prince Rupert
Queen Charlotte Is.
(Canada)

CANADA

Edmonton   L. Winnipeg
Calgary
Vancouver   Regina   Winnipeg
Vancouver I.   Victoria
Seattle
Portland   Boise

NORTH

Newfoundland

St. Lawrence
Québec   St. John's
Montréal
Ottawa
Toronto   Boston
Detroit   Buffalo
Minneapolis
Chicago   New York
Pittsburgh   Philadelphia
Denver   Cincinnati   Baltimore
Kansas City   Washington D.C.
Salt Lake   St. Louis
City
Sacramento
San Francisco   **UNITED STATES**
Oklahoma City   Memphis   Atlanta   C. Hatteras
Los Angeles   Phoenix   Dallas
San Diego   Houston
Ciudad
Juárez   San Antonio   New
Orleans   Tampa
Guadalupe
(Mex.)   Gulf of Mexico   Miami   BAHAMAS
Monterrey
La Habana
Guadalajara   Mérida
Mexico
Puebla   JAMAICA
Acapulco   GUATEMALA   BELIZE   Kingston
HONDURAS
Guatemala
San Salvador   NICARAGUA
EL SALVADOR   Managua   Barranquilla   Maracaíbo
San José   Panamá   Caracas
COSTA   Colón   VENEZUELA
RICA   PANAMA
Medellín   Bogotá
Cali
COLOMBIA
Quito
ECUADOR
Guayaquil
Iquitos

ATLANTIC

Bermuda
(U.K.)

Sargasso Sea

OCEAN

West Indies

CUBA
HAITI   DOMINICAN REP.
PUERTO   Leeward
RICO   Is.
(U.S.A.)   BARBADOS
Caribbean Sea   Windward Is.

BRAZIL

Trujillo
PERU
Lima
Cuzco
Arequipa
La Paz
BOLIVIA
Iquique
Chile
Antofagasta   PARAGUAY
San Felix   San Miguel   Asunción
(Chile)   de Tucumán
San Ambrosio
(Chile)   Córdoba   Porto
Alegre
Valparaíso   Rosario
Santiago   Buenos   URUGUAY
Aires   Montevideo
Concepción   **ARGENTINA**   Río de la Plata

Tropic of Cancer

Honolulu
Kauai
Oahu   Maui
HAWAIIAN IS.
Hilo   (U.S.A.)
Hawaii

Palmyra Is.
(U.S.A.)
Teraina
Tabuaeran
Kiritimati

Jarvis I.
(U.S.A.)

Equator

Penrhyn
(Tongareva)
Manihiki
Pukapuka
Manihiki   Malden I.
Plateau   Starbuck I.
Suwarrow Is.   Vostok I.
Caroline I.
(Millennium I.)
Flint I.

Nuku Hiva   Îs. Marquises
Hiva Oa

Îs. de la Société
Bora Bora   Rangiroa
Huahine
Raiatea   Tahiti   Îs. Tuamotu
Papeete

FRENCH POLYNESIA   Îs. Gambier
Mururoa
Cook Is.   Atiu
(N.Z.)   Aitutaki
Rarotonga   Îs. Tubuai
Mangaia

Oeno I.
Henderson I.
Pitcairn I.   Ducie I.
(U.K.)
Rapa

Tropic of Capricorn

SOUTH

ATLANTIC

Falkland Is.
(U.K.)

South Georgia
(U.K.)

OCEAN

Punta Arenas   South
Est. de Magallanes   Georgia
Tierra del Fuego
C. de Hornos   Drake Passage

11 **12** **13** **14** **15** **16** **17** **18** **19** **20**

West from Greenwich   COPYRIGHT PHILIP'S

B
C
D
E
F
G
H
J
K
L
M
N

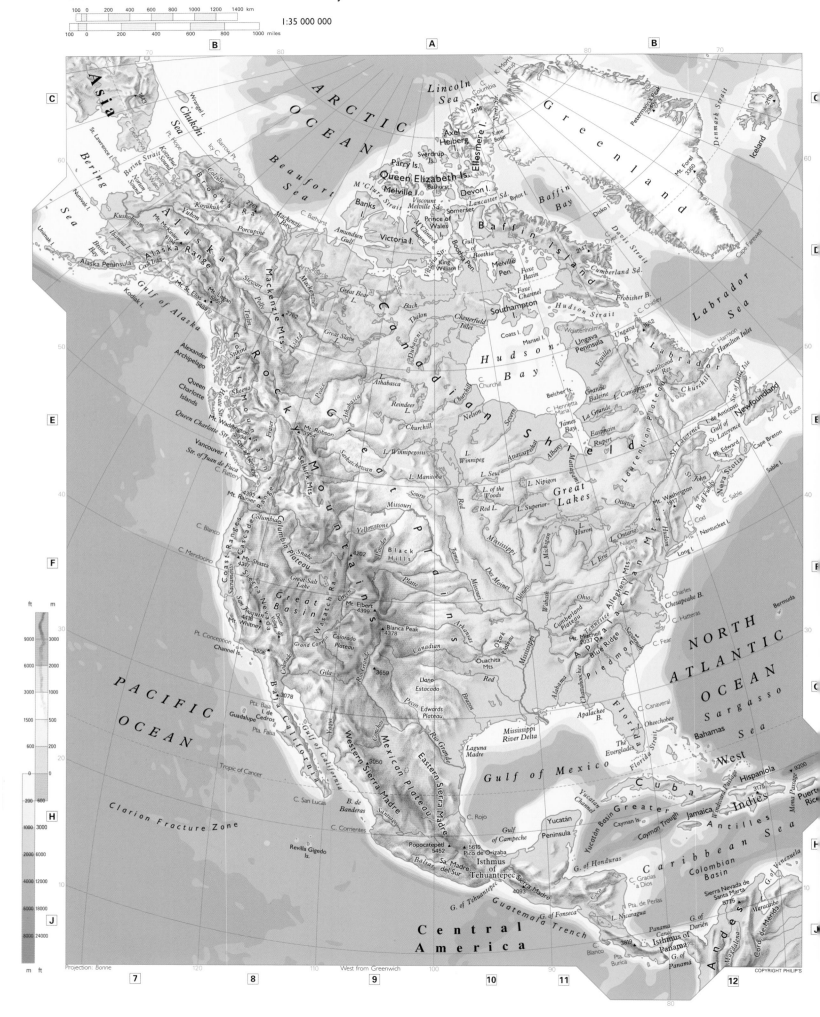

1:35 000 000

Projection: Bonne

West from Greenwich

COPYRIGHT PHILIP'S

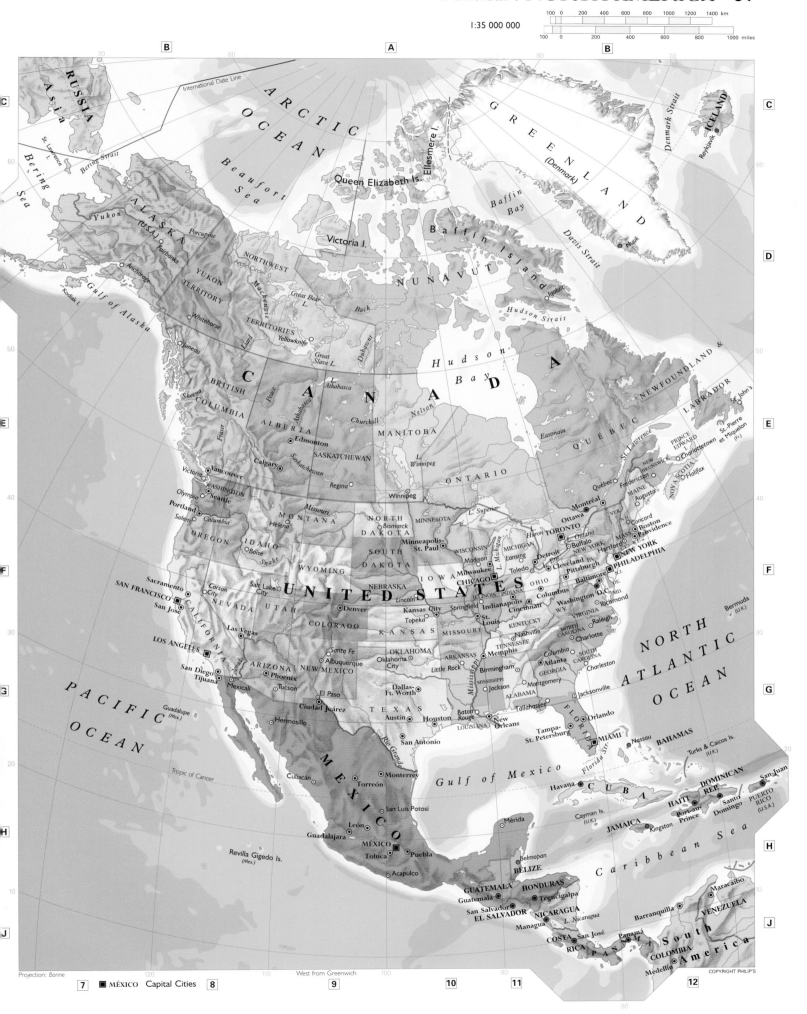

1:35 000 000

100 0 200 400 600 800 1000 1200 1400 km
100 0 200 400 600 800 1000 miles

B **A** **B**

C ASIA RUSSIA ARCTIC OCEAN GREENLAND (Denmark) ICELAND **C**

St. Lawrence
Bering Strait
Bering Sea
Beaufort Sea
Queen Elizabeth Is.
Ellesmere I.
Baffin Bay
Denmark Strait
Reykjavik
Nuuk

D Yukon ALASKA (USA) Porcupine Victoria I. Baffin Island Davis Strait **D**
Anchorage
Kodiak I.
Gulf of Alaska
Fairbanks
YUKON TERRITORY
NORTHWEST
Arctic Circle
Mackenzie
NUNAVUT
Iqaluit
Hudson Strait

E Whitehorse TERRITORIES Great Bear L. Back NEWFOUNDLAND & **E**
Juneau
Liard
Yellowknife
Great Slave L.
Dubawnt
Hudson Bay
LABRADOR
St. John's
Skeena
BRITISH COLUMBIA
Peace
Athabasca
L. Athabasca
CANADA
Churchill
Nelson
Eastmain
QUÉBEC
St. Lawrence
PRINCE EDWARD
Charlottetown
St-Pierre et Miquelon (Fr.)
Fraser
ALBERTA
Edmonton
SASKATCHEWAN
MANITOBA
L. Winnipeg
NEW BRUNSWICK
NOVA SCOTIA
Halifax
Victoria
Vancouver
Calgary
Saskatchewan
Regina
ONTARIO
Winnipeg
Québec
Fredericton
MAINE
Augusta

F Olympia WASHINGTON Seattle Missouri MONTANA NORTH DAKOTA MINNESOTA L. Superior Ottawa Montréal VER. N.H. Concord Boston **F**
Portland
Salem
OREGON
Columbia
Helena
Bismarck
WISCONSIN
Madison
L. Michigan
L. Huron
TORONTO
L. Ontario
Buffalo
NEW YORK
MASS.
Providence
Hartford
CONN.
R.I.
Sacramento
Carson City
IDAHO
Boise
Snake
SOUTH DAKOTA
WYOMING
IOWA
Milwaukee
Minneapolis-St. Paul
MICHIGAN
Lansing
Detroit
Erie
Cleveland
Pittsburgh
PA.
NEW YORK
PHILADELPHIA
N.J.
San Francisco
San Jose
NEVADA
Salt Lake City
UTAH
NEBRASKA
Lincoln
CHICAGO
ILLINOIS
Toledo
OHIO
Columbus
W.VA.
Baltimore
Washington D.C.
DE.
MD.

G Las Vegas Denver COLORADO KANSAS Topeka Kansas City St. Louis MISSOURI Springfield INDIANA Indianapolis Cincinnati KENTUCKY VIRGINIA Richmond NORTH ATLANTIC OCEAN **G**
LOS ANGELES
CALIFORNIA
San Diego
Tijuana
ARIZONA
Phoenix
Tucson
Santa Fe
Albuquerque
NEW MEXICO
OKLAHOMA
Oklahoma City
ARKANSAS
Little Rock
Memphis
TENNESSEE
Nashville
NORTH CAROLINA
Raleigh
Charlotte
Bermuda (U.K.)
Mexicali
El Paso
Ciudad Juárez
TEXAS
Dallas-Ft. Worth
MISSISSIPPI
Birmingham
ALABAMA
GEORGIA
Atlanta
Columbia
SOUTH CAROLINA
Charleston
Guadalupe (Mex.)
Hermosillo
Rio Grande
Austin
Houston
San Antonio
Baton Rouge
LOUISIANA
Jackson
Montgomery
Jacksonville
New Orleans
Tallahassee

H PACIFIC OCEAN MÉXICO Tropic of Cancer Culiacán Monterrey Gulf of Mexico Havana CUBA BAHAMAS Nassau Turks & Caicos Is. (U.K.) DOMINICAN REP. San Juan **H**
Torreón
San Luis Potosí
Mérida
Florida Str.
Tampa-St. Petersburg
Orlando
FLORIDA
MIAMI
Cayman Is. (U.K.)
HAITI
Port-au-Prince
Santo Domingo
PUERTO RICO (U.S.A.)
León
Guadalajara
Revilla Gigedo Is. (Mex.)
MÉXICO
Toluca
Puebla
Acapulco
BELIZE
Belmopan
JAMAICA
Kingston
Caribbean Sea

J GUATEMALA HONDURAS Maracaibo VENEZUELA **J**
Guatemala
San Salvador
EL SALVADOR
Tegucigalpa
NICARAGUA
Managua
L. Nicaragua
COSTA RICA
San José
PANAMA
Panamá
COLOMBIA
Medellín
Barranquilla
South America

Projection: Bonne
West from Greenwich
COPYRIGHT PHILIP'S

7 ■ MÉXICO Capital Cities **8** **9** **10** **11** **12**

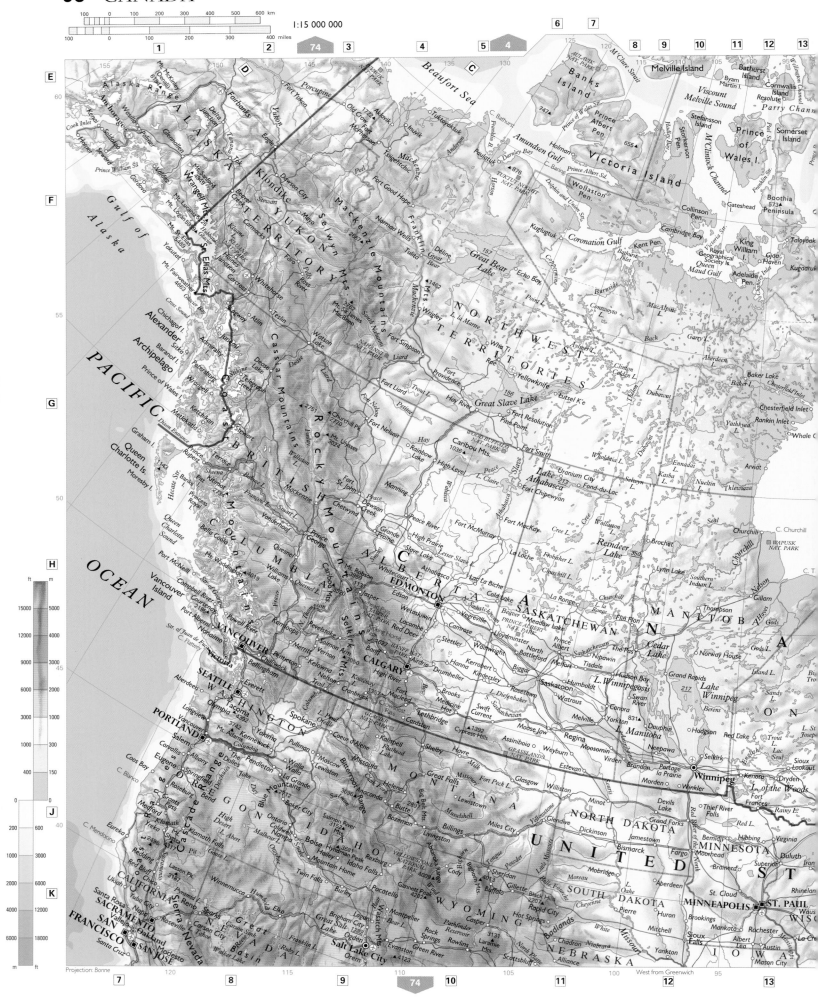

1:15 000 000

Projection: Bonne

West from Greenwich

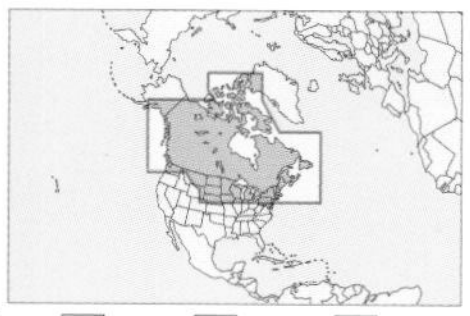

NORTHERN CANADA
continuation northwards on same scale as main map
ARCTIC OCEAN
North Magnetic Pole 2007
GREENLAND (KALAALLIT NUNAAT) (Denmark)
Kronprins Frederik Land
Nyeboe Land
Lincoln Sea
Alert
QUTTINIRPAAQ NAT. PARK
Barbeau Pk.
Lake Hazen
Ellesmere Island
Axel Heiberg Island
Eureka
Sverdrup Islands
Meighen I.
Borden Island
Brock I.
Mackenzie King I.
Ellef Ringnes Island
Amund Ringnes I.
King Christian I.
Lougheed I.
Queen Elizabeth Islands
Prince Patrick Island
Eglinton I.
Emerald I.
N.W.T.
Parry Islands
Melville Island
M'Clure Strait
NUNAVUT
Cornwall
Graham I.
Norwegian Bay
Grinnell Pen.
Bathurst Island
Byam Martin I.
Cornwallis Island
Resolute
Viscount Melville Sound
Lowther I.
Parry Channel
Stefansson Island
Prince of Wales I.
Peel Sd.
Somerset Island
Prince Regent Inlet
Brodeur Pen.
Arctic Bay
Nanisivik
Borden Pen.
Bylot I.
Eclipse Sd.
Pond Inlet
Devon Island
Jones Sound
Grise Fiord
Coburg I.
Lancaster Sound
Baffin Bay
Wellington Channel
Nares Strait
Kane Basin
Knud Rasmussen Land
Sermersuaq (Humboldt Gletscher)
Petermann Gletscher
Hans I.
Qeqertarsuaq
Qaanaaq (Thule)
Uummannaq (Dundas)
Lauge Koch Kyst
Kap York
Melville Bugt
Greely Fiord
Agassiz Icecap
Prince of Wales Icefield
C. Columbia
C. Thomas Hubbard
C. Isachsen
Nunavik
Baffin Island
SIRMILIK NAT. PARK
Clyde River
C. Adair
C. Raper
Davis Strait
Home B.
Fury and Hecla Str.
Igloolik
Rowley I.
Hall Beach
Spicer Is.
Prince Charles I.
Air Force I.
Melville Peninsula
Foxe Basin
Repulse Bay
Qikiqtarjuaq
AUYUITTUQ NAT. PARK
Cumberland Peninsula
Pangnirtung
Cumberland Sd.
Hoare B.
C. Dyer
C. Mercy
Koukdjuak
Nettilling L.
Amadjuak L.
Foxe Pen.
Vansittart I.
C. Dorchester
Foxe Channel
Roes Welcome Sd.
Southampton I.
Coral Harbour
Bell Pen.
Mill I.
Kinngait
Salisbury I.
Iqaluit
Hall Peninsula
Meta Incognita Peninsula
Frobisher Bay
Kimmirut
Resolution I.
Nottingham I.
Charles I.
Hudson Strait
Digges Is.
Salluit
Ivujivik
Coats I.
Mansel I.
Kangiqsujuaq
Cratère du Nouveau-Québec
Péninsule d'Ungava
Quaqtaq
Akpatok I.
Kangirsuk
Ungava Bay
C. Chidley
Torngat Mts.
Mt. d'Iberville
Mt. Caubvick
Kangiqsualujjuaq
Hebron
Labrador Sea
Sea
ATLANTIC OCEAN
Smith I.
Puvirnituq
L. Payne
Arnaud
Ottawa Is.
Hudson Bay
Inukjuak
Kuujjuaq
Koksoak
Feuilles
George
Nain
Hopedale
C. Harrison
L. Minto
Caniapiscau
Rigolet
Cartwright
NEWFOUNDLAND & LABRADOR
Port Hope Simpson
Sleeper Is.
King George Is.
Bakers Dozen Is.
Sanikiluaq
Belcher Is.
L. à l'Eau Claire
Smallwood Res.
Labrador
North West River
Happy Valley-Goose Bay
Kawawachikamach
Schefferville
Churchill Falls
Petitsikapau L.
Esker
L. Bienville
Grande Baleine
Kuujjuarapik
Labrador City
Wabush
Fermont
L. Caniapiscau
Belle Isle
C. Bauld
St. Anthony
Grey Is.
Str. of Belle Isle
Long Range Mts.
Baie Verte
Notre Dame B.
Lewisporte
Gander
Bonavista
Grand Falls-Windsor
Newfoundland
Deer Lake
Corner Brook
Stephenville
Carbonear
St. John's
Trinity B.
Placentia B.
Placentia
Avalon Pen.
C. Race
Marystown
Channel-Port aux Basques
ST-PIERRE et MIQUELON (Fr.)
C. Ray
Cabot Strait
Gulf of St. Lawrence
C. North
Cape Breton I.
Glace Bay
Sydney
Port Hawkesbury
Antigonish
New Glasgow
Sable I. (Nova Scotia)
C. Henrietta Maria
Pte. Louis XIV
Peawanuck
Winisk
James Bay
Chisasibi
La Grande
Kanaaupscow
Twin Is.
Akimiski I.
Wemindji
Attawapiskat
Eastmain
Charlton I.
Fort Albany
Moosonee
Waskaganish
Rupert
L. Mistassini
Nottaway
Harricana
Chibougamau
L. Albanel
QUEBEC
Plateau Laurentien
Mts. Otish
Rés. Manicouagan
Mts. Groulx
Gagnon
Moisie
Sept-Îles
Port-Cartier
Havre-St-Pierre
Natashquan
Romaine
St-Augustin
Î. d'Anticosti
Dét. de Jacques-Cartier
Dét. d'Honguedo
Baie-Comeau
Manicouagan
Péribonka
Dolbeau-Mistassini
Alma
Chicoutimi
Saguenay
Jonquière
Roberval
L. St-Jean
Gaspé
Pén. de la Gaspésie
Matane
Rimouski
St. Lawrence (St-Laurent)
Chaleur B.
Campbellton
Bathurst
Rivière-du-Loup
Edmundston
Îs. de la Madeleine
PRINCE EDWARD I.
Summerside
Charlottetown
Northumberland Str.
NEW BRUNSWICK
Miramichi
Moncton
Amherst
Truro
NOVA SCOTIA
Grand Falls
Woodstock
Fredericton
Saint John
B. of Fundy
Digby
Kentville
Dartmouth
Halifax
Bridgewater
Liverpool
Yarmouth
C. Sable
Nakina
Kenogami
Hearst
Greenstone
Kapuskasing
Cochrane
L. Abitibi
Amos
Val-d'Or
Rés. Gouin
Rés. Cabonga
Timmins
Kirkland Lake
Rouyn-Noranda
Marathon
Wawa
Chapleau
New Liskeard
Thunder Bay
Lake Superior
L. Matagami
Matagami
Missinaibi
Mattagami
La Tuque
Québec
Lévis
Shawinigan
Trois-Rivières
Thetford Mines
St-Georges
Drummondville
Joliette
St-Hyacinthe
Sherbrooke
Granby
MONTRÉAL
Mont-Laurier
Hull
OTTAWA
Outaouais
MAINE
Augusta
Bangor
Lewiston
Portland
Sault Ste. Marie
Elliot Lake
Sudbury
North Bay
Nipissing
Pembroke
Manitoulin I.
Parry Sound
Georgian Bay
Huntsville
Orillia
Lake Huron
Owen Sound
Barrie
Peterborough
Brockville
Cornwall
Kingston
Belleville
Oshawa
TORONTO
L. Ontario
Kitchener
Hamilton
London
Niagara Falls
Buffalo
Rochester
Syracuse
Adirondack Mts.
Albany
NEW YORK
Burlington
Montpelier
VERMONT
NEW HAMPSHIRE
Concord
Manchester
Lowell
BOSTON
C. Cod
MASS.
PROVIDENCE
R.I.
Springfield
Hartford
New Haven
CONN.
Houghton
Marquette
Manistique
Escanaba
Petoskey
Traverse City
Cadillac
Green Bay
Sheboygan
MICHIGAN
L. Michigan
Grand Rapids
Saginaw
Flint
MILWAUKEE
Madison
Lansing
Sarnia
DETROIT
Windsor
Toledo
L. Erie
Erie
Jamestown
PENNSYLVANIA
CLEVELAND
Elmira
Binghamton
UNITED STATES
ONTARIO
COPYRIGHT PHILIP'S

1:7 000 000

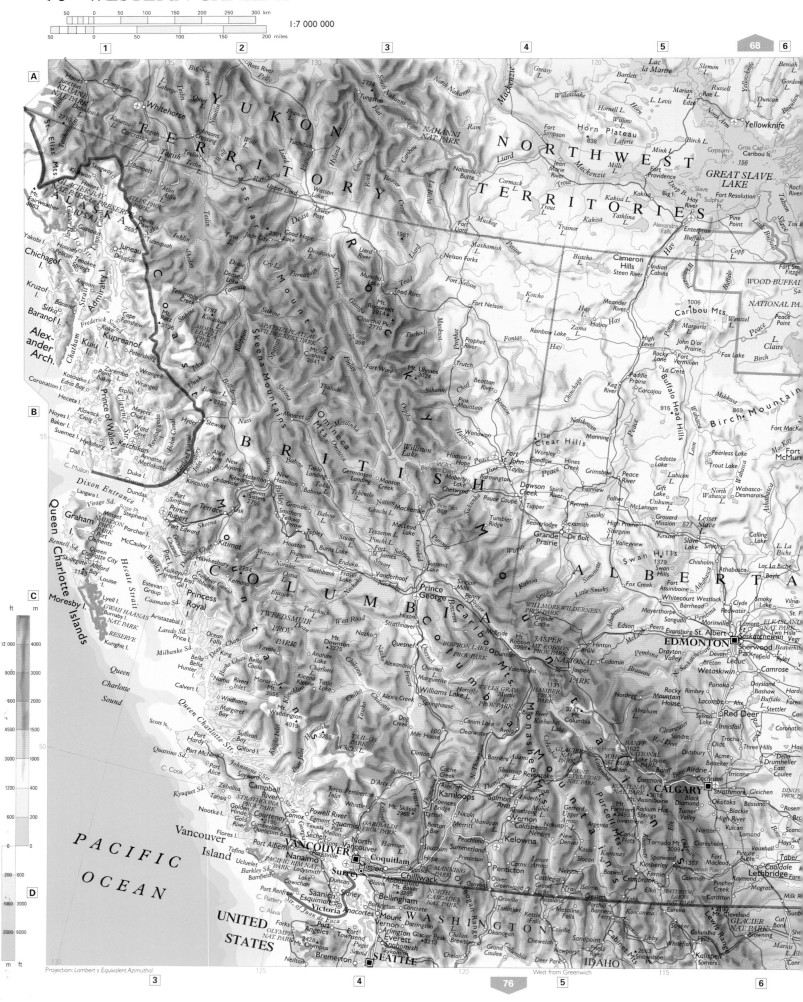

Projection: Lambert's Equivalent Azimuthal

West from Greenwich

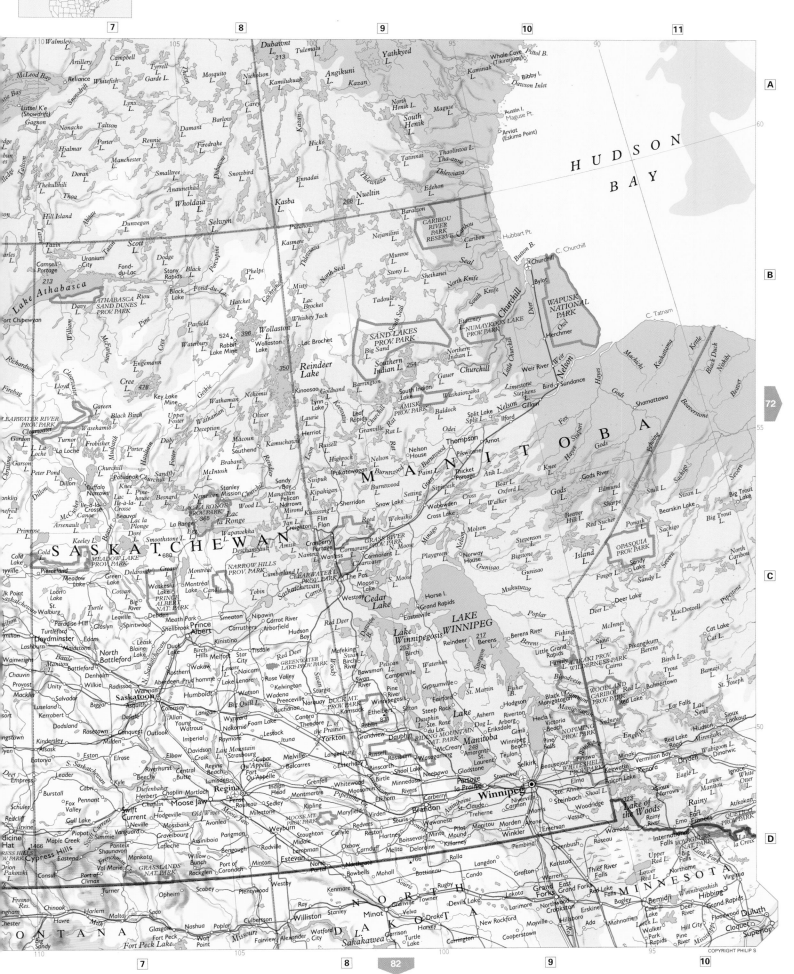

50 0 50 100 150 200 250 300 km
1:7 000 000
50 0 50 100 150 200 miles

Projection: Lambert's Equivalent Azimuthal

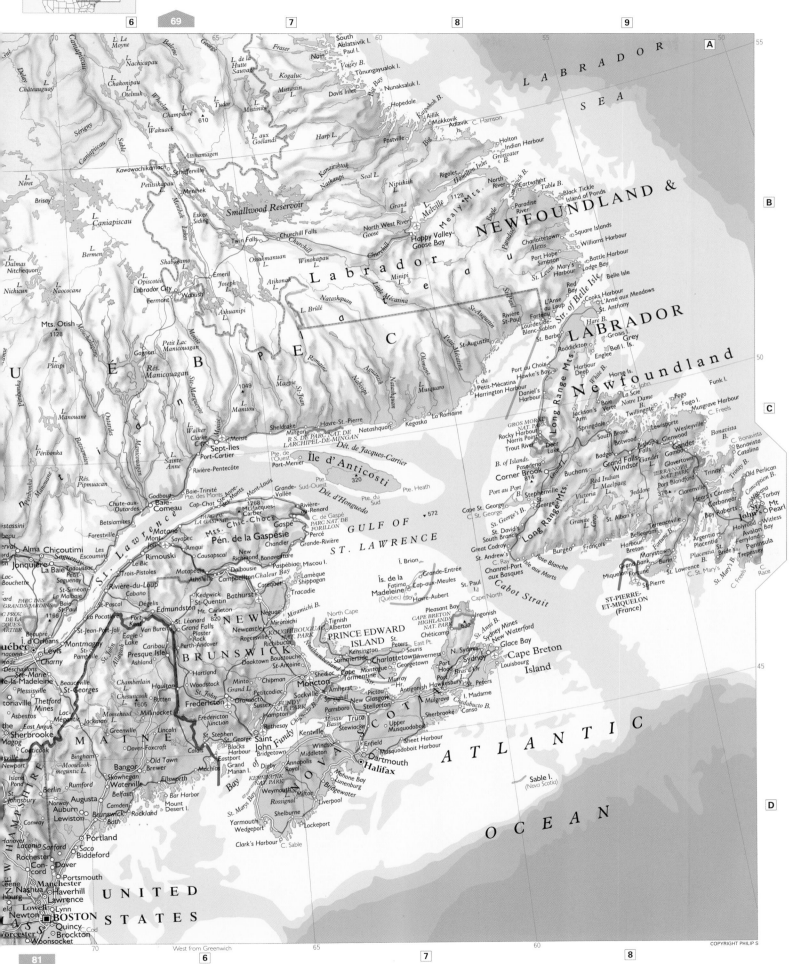

100 0 100 200 300 400 500 km

1:15 000 000

100 0 50 100 150 200 250 300 350 miles

11 12 13 14 16 68 17

PACIFIC OCEAN

3363 miles
5412 km

Anchorage Washington D.C.

2010 miles
3224 km

2438 miles
3923 km

2785 miles
4482 km

San Francisco

2395 miles
3854 km

Honolulu

Tropic of Cancer

ALASKA
on same scale

RUSSIA

Koryakskoye
Nagorye

BERING SEA

Aleutian Islands

Andreanof Islands

Fox Islands

Projection: Albers' Equal Area with two standard parallels

West from Greenwich

ARCTIC OCEAN

CHUKCHI SEA

Bering Strait

ALASKA

Seward Peninsula

Brooks Range

North Slope

Yukon Flats

Kuskokwim Mountains

Alaska Range

Mt. McKinley

Anchorage

Gulf of Alaska

Alaska Peninsula

Kodiak

3 4 5 6 7 8 9 10 11 12

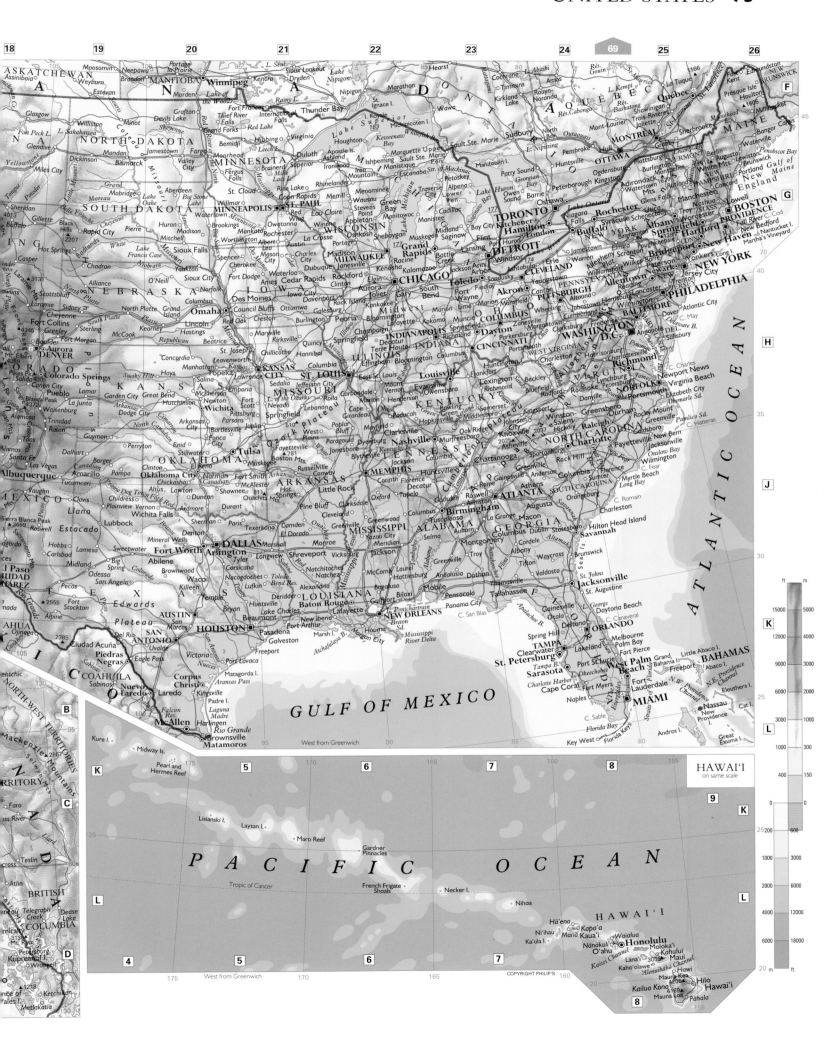

1:6 700 000

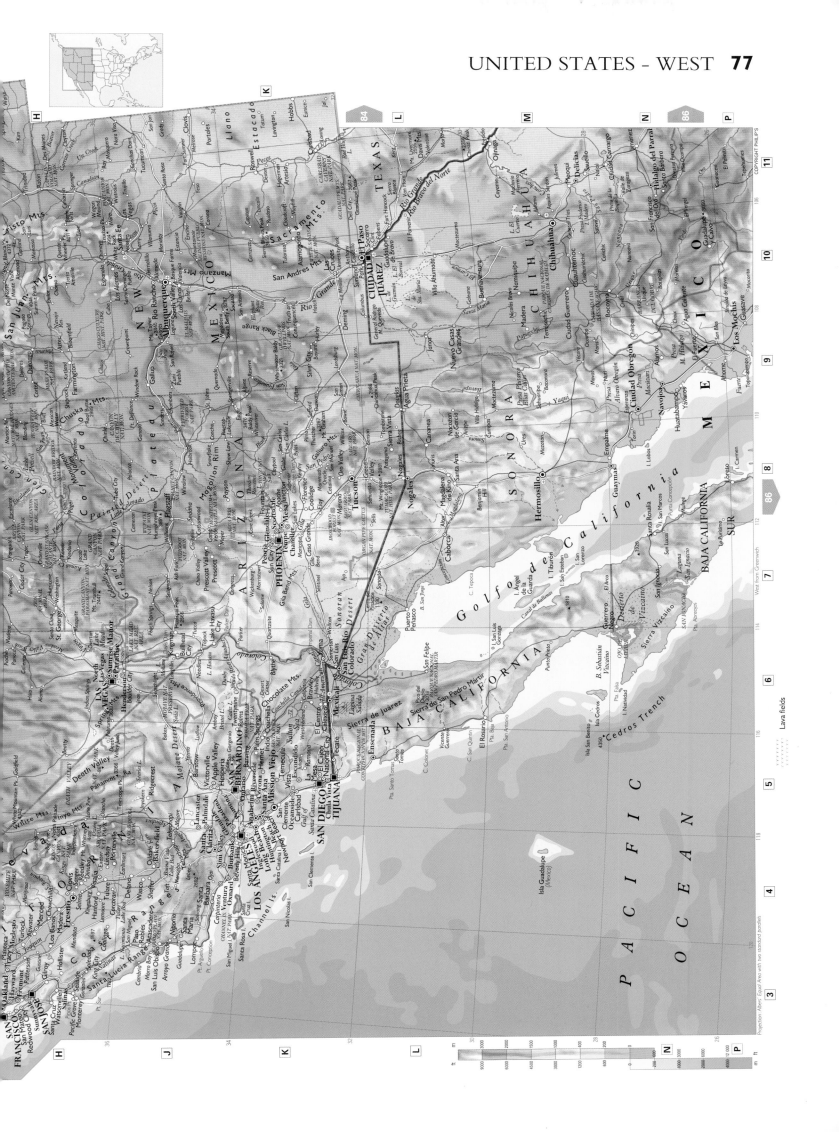

1:2 500 000

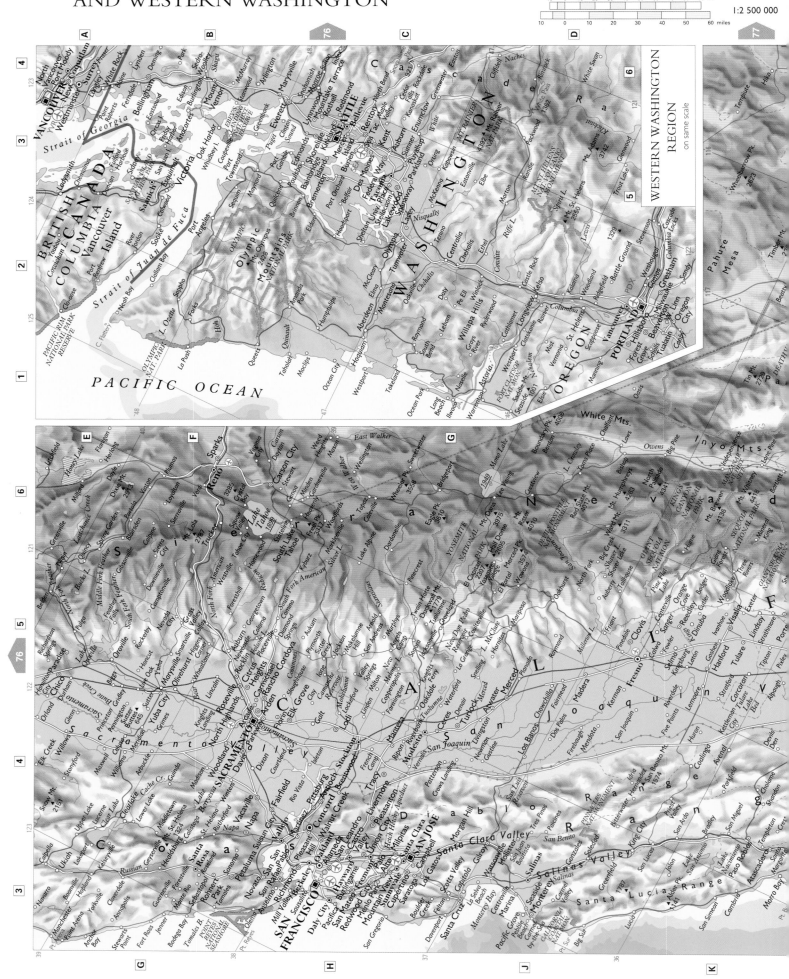

WESTERN WASHINGTON REGION
on same scale

PACIFIC OCEAN

Lava fields

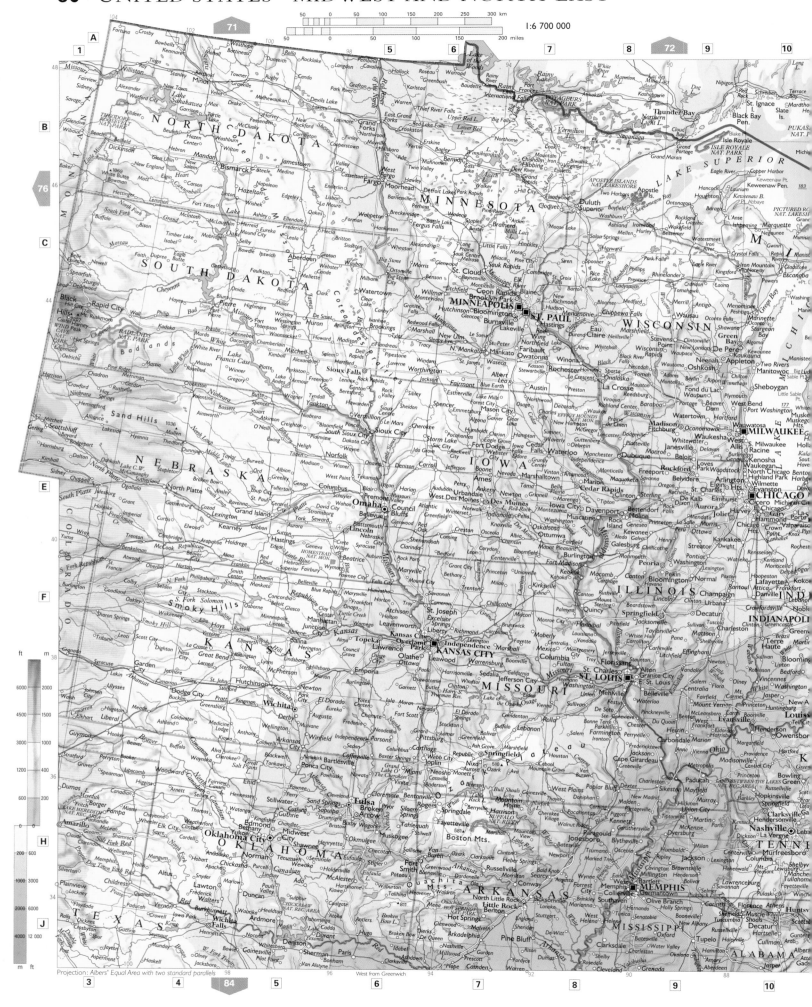

1:6 700 000

Projection: Albers' Equal Area with two standard parallels

West from Greenwich

1:2 500 000

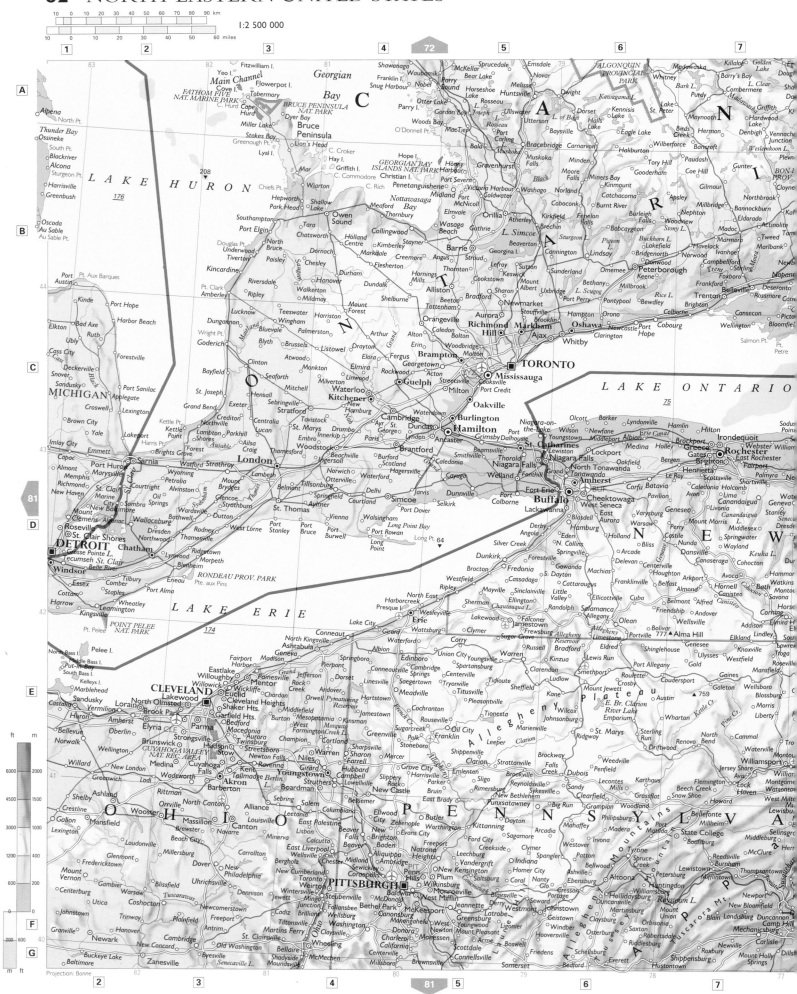

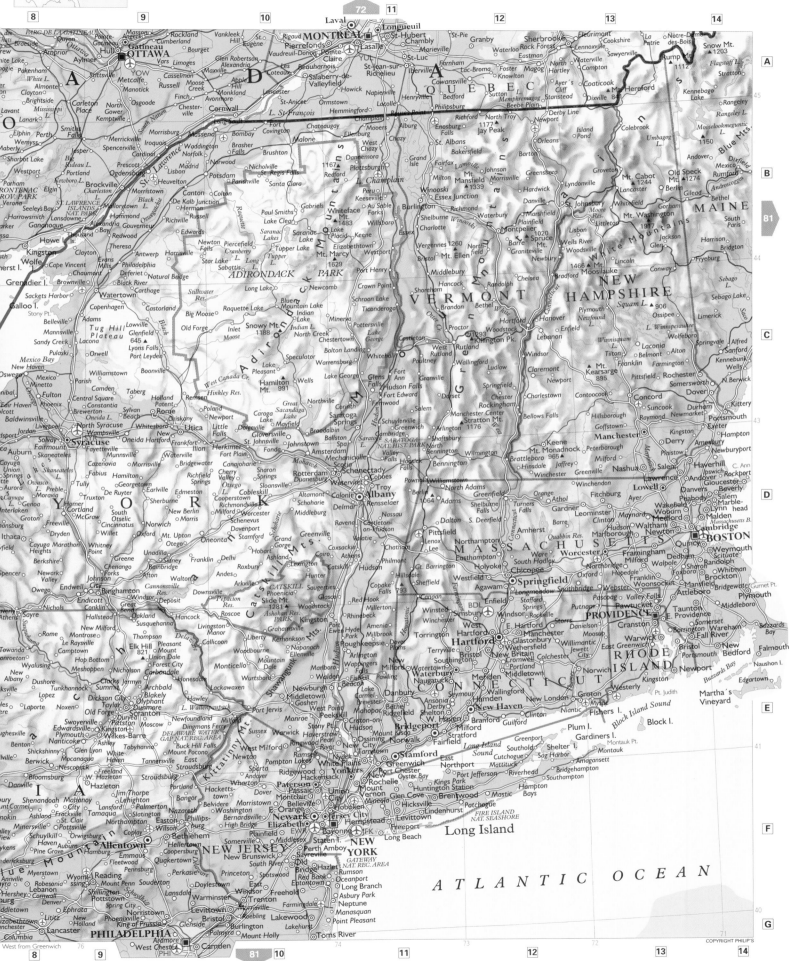

1:6 700 000

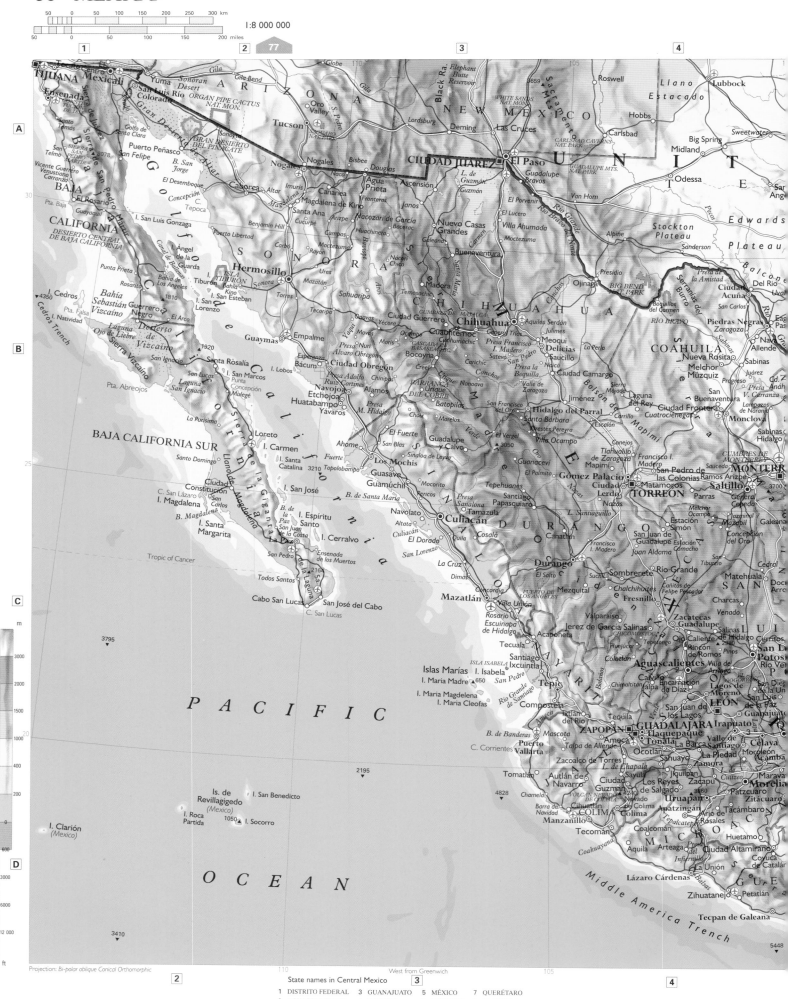

1:8 000 000

Projection: Bi-polar oblique Conical Orthomorphic

West from Greenwich

State names in Central Mexico
1 DISTRITO FEDERAL   3 GUANAJUATO   5 MÉXICO   7 QUERÉTARO
2 AGUASCALIENTES   4 HIDALGO   6 MORELOS   8 TLAXCALA

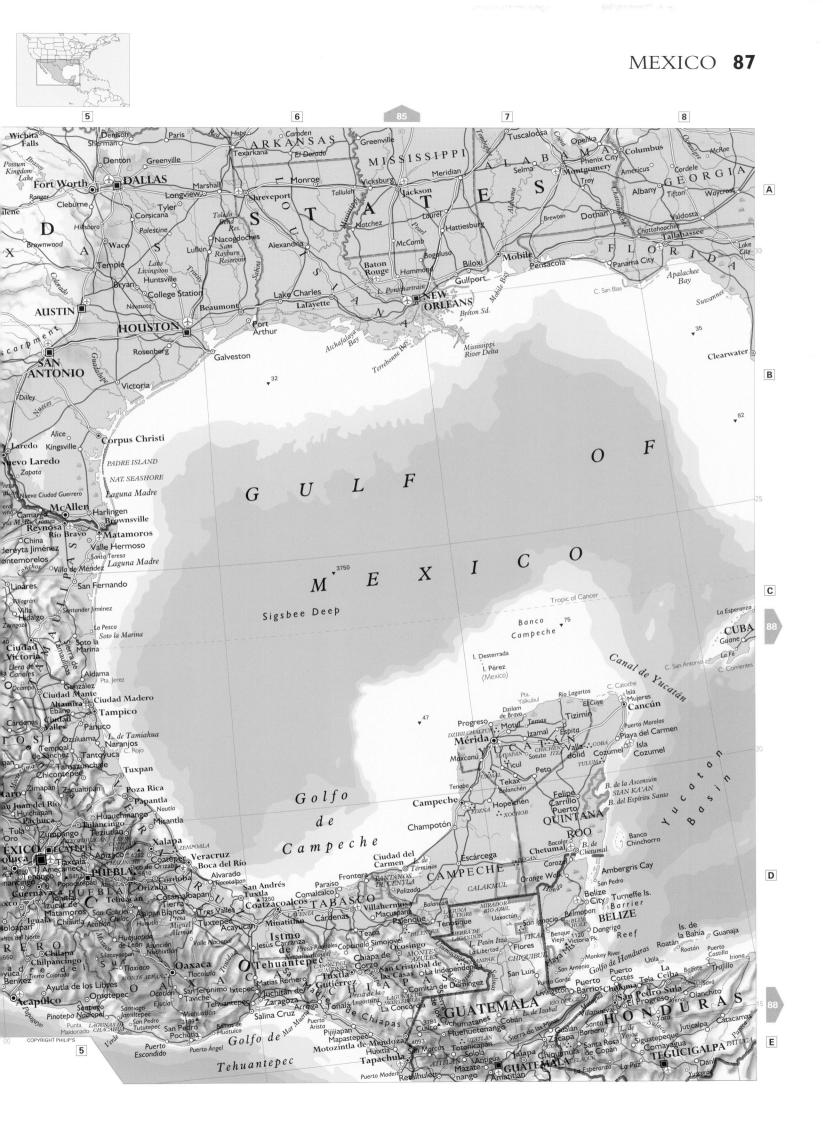

1:8 000

50 0 50 100 150 200 250 300 km
50 0 50 100 150 200 miles

JAMAICA
1:3 000 000
10 0 10 20 30 40 50 km
10 0 10 20 30 miles

CARIBBEAN SEA

Montego Bay · Falmouth · Runaway Bay · St. Ann's Bay · Port Maria · Port Antonio
Lucea · Negril · Wakefield · Ocho Rios · Annotto Bay · John Crow
South Negril Pt. · Cambridge · The Cockpit Country · Mount Denham 985 · Moneague · Linstead · Blue Mountains 2256 Blue Mountain Peak · Morant Point
Savanna-la-Mar · Maggotty · Don Figuero Mts. · Dry Harbour Mountains · Spanish Town · Portmore · Morant Bay · Port Morant
Black River · Mandeville · Santa Cruz Mts. · May Pen · KINGSTON · Morant Bay
Great Pedro Bluff · Alligator Pond · Portland Bight · Portland Point

FLORIDA L. Okeechobee · West Palm Beach · West End · Little Abaco I.
Cape Coral · Fort Myers · Boca Raton · Free port · Grand Bahama · Hope Town · Abaco I.
U.S.A. · Naples · The Everglades · Fort Lauderdale · Northwest Providence Channel
C. Romano · Hialeah · **MIAMI** · Bimini Is. · Berry Is. · Eleuthera I. · Nassau · New Providence · Andros Town
EVERGLADES NAT. PARK · C. Sable · Florida Bay · Nicolls Town · Andros Island
Dry Tortugas (U.S.A.) · Key West · Florida Keys · Straits of Florida · Great Bahama Bank · Exuma

GULF OF MEXICO

LA HABANA (Havana) · Guanabacoa · Santa Cruz del Norte · Canal Nicholás · Cay Sal Bank
Bahía Honda · Guanajay · Matanzas · Cárdenas · Arch. de Sabana
La Esperanza · Güines · Havellanos · Sagua la Grande
Pinar del Río · San Antonio de los Baños · Batabanó · Colón · Jagüey Grande · Caibarién · Arch. de Camagüey
Guane · San Luis · La Fé · Nueva Gerona · Cienfuegos · Santa Clara · Placetas · Cayo Romano
I. de la Juventud · Arch. de los Canarreos · B. de Cochinos · Trinidad · Sancti Spíritus · Ciego de Ávila · Nuevitas
Pen. de Zapata · Corrientes · Júcaro · Florida · Camagüey
CUBA · Tunas de Zaza · Golfo de Ana María · Las Tunas · Gibara
Golfo de Guacanayabo · Santa Cruz del Sur · Bayamo · Holg
Sierra Maestra · Manzanillo · Pico Turqui 1972 · Santi
C. Cruz · de C

Yucatan Basin

Progreso · Dzilam de Bravo · Río Lagartos · C. Catoche · Isla Mujeres
Punta Yalkukul · Motul · Temax · Tizimín · El Cuyo · Cancún
Mérida · Maxcanú · Izamal · Espita · Puerto Morelos · Playa del Carmen
YUCATÁN · Sotuta · CHICHÉN ITZÁ · Valladolid · Cozumel · Isla Cozumel
Calkiní · Tenabo · Ticul · Tekax · Peto · **QUINTANA ROO**
Campeche · Champotón · Hopelchén · Felipe Carrillo Puerto · B. de la Ascensión · SIAN KA'AN · B. del Espíritu Santo
Ciudad del Carmen · Balancán · CALAKMUL · Bacalar · Chetumal · B. de Chetumal · Banco Chinchorro
PANTANOS DE CENTLA · Palizada · **MEXICO** · **CAMPECHE** · Corozal · Orange Walk · Ambergris Cay
Tenosique · MIRADOR-RÍO AZUL · San Pedro · Turneffe Is.
Ocosingo · LAGUNA DEL TIGRE · Uaxactún · **Belize City** · Barrier Reef
Comitán de Domínguez · San Ignacio · Belmopan · Middlesex · Dangriga
MONTES AZULES · L. Petén Itzá · TIKAL · **BELIZE** · Benque Viejo 1120 · Victoria Peak 1120
Flores · La Libertad · CARACOL · CHIQUIBUL · Monkey River
Sebol · Maya Mts. · San Antonio · Is. de la Bahía · Guanaja
GUATEMALA 3784 · Cuilco · Sayaxché · Punta Gorda · Puerto Barrios · Livingston · Utila · Roatán · Puerto Castilla · Iriona · C. Camarón
Huehuetenango · Cobán · Puerto Cortés · Tela · La Ceiba · Trujillo · Brus Laguna
Totonicapán · Salamá · San Pedro Sula · Choloma · Olanchito · Sává · Sico · El Carbón · Laguna de Caratasca
Quetzaltenango · Sololá · Chiquimula · El Progreso · Santa Bárbara · Arenal · Mosquitia · C. Falso
Antigua · **GUATEMALA** · Jalapa · Sierra de las Minas · **HONDURAS** · Yoro · Sierra de Agalta · C. Gracias a Dios
San Marcos · Amatitlán · Chiquimula · Zacapa · L. de Yojoa · Juticalpa · Catacamas · Coco (Segovia) · Puerto Cabo Gracias á Dios
Mazatenango · Escuintla · Santa Rosa de Copán · La Esperanza · Comayagua · Leimus
San José · **TEGUCIGALPA** · Pespire · Danlí · Puerto Cabezas
Ahuachapán · Santa Ana · Sonsonate · Cojutepeque · Yuscarán · Ocotal · Cayos Miskitos (Nicaragua)
Nueva San Salvador · Apopa · Nacaome · Choluteca · Somoto · Siuna · Pta. Gorda
SAN SALVADOR · Zacatecoluca · San Miguel · La Unión · Estelí · Jinotega · Tungla · Prinzapolca
EL SALVADOR · Usulután · G. de Fonseca · El Sauce · Matagalpa · Muy Muy · La Barra
Chinandega · Corinto · León · Boaco · Santo Domingo · Bluefields · El Bluff
NICARAGUA · Tipitapa · Masaya · Juigalpa · Rama · Pta. de Perlas
MANAGUA · Diriamba · Granada · Siquia · I. de San Andrés (Colombia)
Jinotepe · Lago de Nicaragua · Cord. de Yolaina · Is. del Maíz (Nicaragua)
Rivas · I. de Ometepe 1610 · San Carlos · Cayos de Albuquerque (Colombia)
San Juan del Sur · B. de Salinas · La Cruz · Los Chiles · San Juan del Norte
GUANACASTE · SANTA ROSA · G. de Papagayo · **COSTA RICA** · TORTUGUERO
Liberia · PALO VERDE · Cord. de Guanacaste · Guápiles · Siquirres · Limón
Santa Cruz · Nicoya · Cord. Central · San José · Cartago · Bribri
Carmona · Puntarenas · Esparza · Alajuela · LA AMISTAD · Bocas del Toro
Pen. de Nicoya · C. Blanco · Quepos · Chirripó 3819 · Almirante · **PANAMÁ**
PACIFIC OCEAN · Puerto Quepos · Buenos Aires · Volcán Barú 3475 · David · Chepo · Portobelo
B. de Coronado · Ciudad Cortés · San Vito · Boquete · Santiago · Penonomé
CORCOVADO · Pen. de Osa · Golfito · La Concepción · Aguadulce · Chitré
G. Dulce · Puerto Armuelles · Remedios · Sona · Pocrí · El Real de Sta. Maria
Pta. Burica · G. de Chiriquí · Las Tablas · **DARIÉN**
ISLA COIBA · I. de Coiba · CERRO HOYA · Punta Mariato · Golfo de Panamá

Cayman Islands (U.K.) · George Town · Grand Cayman · Little Cayman · Cayman Brac
Cayman Trench 7680
Misteriosa Bank · Is. Santanilla (Swan Islands) (Honduras)
Pedro Bank · Pedro Cays (Jamaica)
Rosalind Bank · Serranilla Bank · Bajo Nuevo (Colombia)
Banco Gorda · Bajo Nuevo (Colombia)
CARIB
Montego Bay · Falmouth · St. Ann's Bay · Port Maria
Lucea · Negril · **JAMAICA** · Cambridge
South Negril Pt. · Savanna-la-Mar · Black River · Mandeville · May Pen · Spanish Town · **Kingston**
I. de Providencia (Colombia) · Cayos Roncador (Colombia)

Isthmus of Panama
I. de San Bernardo · **CARTA**
Nombre de Dios · Archipiélago de San Blas · Golfo del Darién
Colón · Portobelo · Serranía de San Blas · G. Morros
PANAMÁ · Canal de Panamá · L. Gatún · Chiman · San Miguel · La Palma · Yaviza · G. de Urabá
Manzanillo · Pta. Garachiné

GUADELOUPE
Pte. de la Grande Vigie
Port-Louis · Grande-Terre · La Désirade
Pointe Allègre · Petit-Canal · Le Moule
Ste-Rose · Pointe-à-Pitre · Ste-Anne · Pointe des Châteaux
Pointe-Noire · Le Gosier · Îles de la Petite Terre
Basse-Terre · **GUADELOUPE** (Fr.)
Bouillante · Capesterre-Belle-Eau · Marie-Galante
Soufrière 1467 · St-Louis · Capesterre
Basse-Terre · Trois-Rivières · Grand-Bourg · Pte. des Basses
Îles des Saintes

MARTINIQUE
Cap St-Martin · Basse-Pointe
Le Prêcheur · Montagne Pelée 1463 · Ste-Marie · Presqu'île de la Caravelle
St-Pierre · La Trinité
Schoelcher · Le Robert
Fort-de-France · Le Lamentin · Le François · Le St-Esprit
MARTINIQUE (Fr.) · Rivière-Salée · Le Marin · Ste-Luce
Pte. d'Enfer

GUADELOUPE AND MARTINIQUE
1:2 000 000
10 0 10 20 30 40 50 60 km
10 0 10 20 30 40 miles

Projection: Bi-polar oblique Conical Orthomorphic

ATLANTIC OCEAN

PUERTO RICO d
1:3 000 000

PUERTO RICO
(U.S.A.)

Pta. Aguijereada
Isabela
Aguadilla
Barceloneta
San Sebastian
Arecibo
Manati
Vega Baja
SAN JUAN
SJU
Mayagüez
Utuado
Bayamón
Carolina
Río Grande
Adjuntas
Cordillera Central
Sierra de Luquillo
Fajardo
Dewey
Pta. Culebra
San German
Mts. de
Uroyan
1338 Cerro de Punta
Cayey
Humacoa
Naguabo
Puerca
Vieques
Yauco
Coamo
Esperanza
Pta. Aguila
Guanica
Ponce
Yabucoa
I. Caja de Muertos
Guayama

VIRGIN ISLANDS e
1:2 000 000

Rufling Pt.
The Settlement
Anegada
East Pt.
Virgin Islands
(U.K.)
Great Camanoe
Jost Van Dyke I.
Guana I.
521
Virgin Gorda
Virgin Is.
(U.S.A.)
Hans Lollik I.
Beef I.
Spanish Town
Tortola
Road Town
Peter I.
Charlotte Amalie
St. Cruz Bay
St. John I.
VIRGIN IS.
Thomas I.

ST. LUCIA f
1:1 000 000

Cap Point
Gros Islet
Pte. Hardy
Esperance Bay
Castries
Marquis
Anse la Raye
Girard
Canaries
Millet
Dennery
Soufrière
Mt. Gimie
950
Trou Gras Pt.
Soufrière Bay
750
Petit Piton
Micoud
Gros Piton Pt.
796
Gros Piton
Vierge Pt.
Choiseul
ST. LUCIA
Laborie
Vieux Fort
C. Moule à Chique

BARBADOS
North Point
Crab Hill
Spring Hall
Fustic
Boscobelle
Portland
245
Belleplaine
Speightstown
Bathsheba
Westmoreland
Alleynes Bay
340
BARBADOS
Mt. Hillaby
Martin's Bay
Holetown
Hillcrest
Massiah Street
Jackson
Bridgefield
Ragged Pt.
Black Rock
Ellerton
Six Cross Roads
Edey
The Crane
Bridgetown
Ivy
St. Martins
Carlisle Bay
Oistins
Worthing
Oistins Bay
BGI
Chancery Lane
South Point

BARBADOS g
1:1 000 000

ATLANTIC OCEAN

MAS

Arthur's Town
New Bight
Cat I.
San Salvador I.
Conception I.
Rum Cay
Long I.
Clarence Town
Samana Cay
Albert Town
Snug Corner
Plana Cays
Mayaguana I.
Acklins I.
Mira por vos Cay
Cay Verde
Hogsty Reef
Little Inagua I.
Turks & Caicos Is.
(U.K.)
Caicos Is.
Cockburn Town
Turks Is.
Lake Rose
Great Inagua I.
Matthew Town
INAGUA
Mouchoir Bank
Guantánamo
Baracoa
Maisi
Pta. de Maisi
Î. de la Tortue
Navidad Bank
Silver Bank
Cap-Haïtien
Monte Cristi
LA ISABELA
Santiago de los Caballeros
San Francisco de Macorís
Port-de-Paix
Jean Rabel
Fort Liberté
Puerto Plata
La Vega
Milwaukee Deep 9200
Puerto Rico Trench
Gonaïves
Hinche
Central
Nagua
Samana
Sabana de la Mar
San Juan
HAITI
DOMINICAN REP.
San Pedro de Macorís
Hato Mayor
Higüey
Bayamón
SAN JUAN
Carolina
PORT-AU-PRINCE
SANTO DOMINGO
La Romana
C. Engaño
Arecibo
Fajardo
Anegada
Virgin Is.
Sombrero (U.K.)
Jérémie
L. Enriquillo
San Cristóbal
B. de Yuma
Mayagüez
Ponce
Caguas
Virgin Is.
Anguilla (U.K.)
Les Cayes
Aquin
Barahona
Isla Saona
PUERTO RICO
Guayama
Charlotte Amalie
St.-Martin (Fr.)
Pointe-à-Gravois
Pedernales
I. Beata
C. Beata
Isla Mona (U.S.A.)
(U.S.A.)
Christiansted
St. Eustatius
St.-Barthélemy (Fr.)
Hispaniola
Frederiksted
St. Croix (U.S.A.)
Saba (Neth.)
Barbuda
Antilles
Montserrat (U.K.)
Basseterre
ANTIGUA & BARBUDA
Redonda
914
Guadeloupe Passage
St. John's
Antigua
Ste.-Rose
Le Moule
Beata Ridge
La Désirade
GUADELOUPE (Fr.)
1467
Pointe-à-Pitre
Venezuelan
Basse-Terre
Marie-Galante (Fr.)
I. des Saintes (Fr.)
Grand-Bourg
CARIBBEAN SEA
Dominica Passage
Portsmouth
DOMINICA
1447
Morne
I. de Aves (Venezuela)
Diablotin
MORNE TROIS PITONS
Basin
Roseau
Martinique Passage
Mt. Pelée
Ste.-Marie
1397
Le François
Fort-de-France
Rivière-Pilote
MARTINIQUE (Fr.)
St. Lucia Channel
Castries
ST. LUCIA
Soufrière
St. Vincent Passage
St. Vincent
Speightstown 340
Soufrière 1234
ABC Lesser Islands
Aruba (Neth.)
Kingstown
BARBADOS
Bequia
Bridgetown
Oranjestad
Curaçao
Canouan
Willemstad
Bonaire
ST. VINCENT & THE GRENADINES
NETH. ANTILLES
Carriacou
The Grenadines
Is. Las Aves
I. de Aves (Ven.)
840
GRENADA
St. George's
COLOMBIA
Pta. Gallinas
Pen. de la Guajira
Is. Los Roques (Ven.)
I. Orchila (Ven.)
I. Blanquilla (Ven.)
Is. Los Hermanos (Ven.)
Tobago
C. San Román
Pta. Espada
Is. Los Testigos (Ven.)
Scarborough
Paraguaná
Punto Fijo
NUEVA ESPARTA
Galera Pt.
Santa Marta
Riohacha
Uribia
Punta Cardón
I. La Tortuga (Ven.)
I. de Margarita
Port of Spain
TAYRONA
Coro
La Vela
Cerro El Copey
Porlamar
Arima
Rio Claro
Ciénaga
San Rafael
Tucacas
La Asunción
TRINIDAD & TOBAGO
Soledad
MACURIA
Puerto Cabello
Maracay
La Guaira
Cumaná
Güiria
San Fernando
Sabanalarga
MARACAIBO
FALCON
CARACAS
Carúpano
G. de Paria
Fundación
Altagracia
Mene de Mauroa
Puerto La Cruz
Barcelona
Maturín
Calamar
Ciudad Ojeda
LARA
Los Teques
Río Chico
Caripito
MONAGAS
MAGDALENA
Santa Rita
Cabimas
SUCRE
DELTA
Zambrano
BARQUISIMETO
VALENCIA
San Juan de los Morros
Anaco
Tucupita
ZULIA
Lago de Maracaibo
Villa de Cura
El Tigre
AMACURO
Mene Grande
TRUJILLO
Acarigua
Valle de la Pascua
Los Barrancos
Valera
PORTUGUESA
El Baúl
Calabozo
Santa María de Ipire
ANZOÁTEGUI
MÉRIDA
Guanare
GUÁRICO
Soledad
Ciudad Guayana
Ciudad Bolívar
El Banco
Barinas
San Carlos
Libertad
Sierra Imataca
Ocaña
BARINAS
Ciudad Bolivia
San Fernando de Apure
El Pao
Upata
NORTE DE SANTANDER
TÁCHIRA
Achaguas
Apure
Guasipati
El Callao
Cúcuta
VENEZUELA
Caicara
Embalse de Guri
Tumeremo

COPYRIGHT PHILIP'S

West from Greenwich

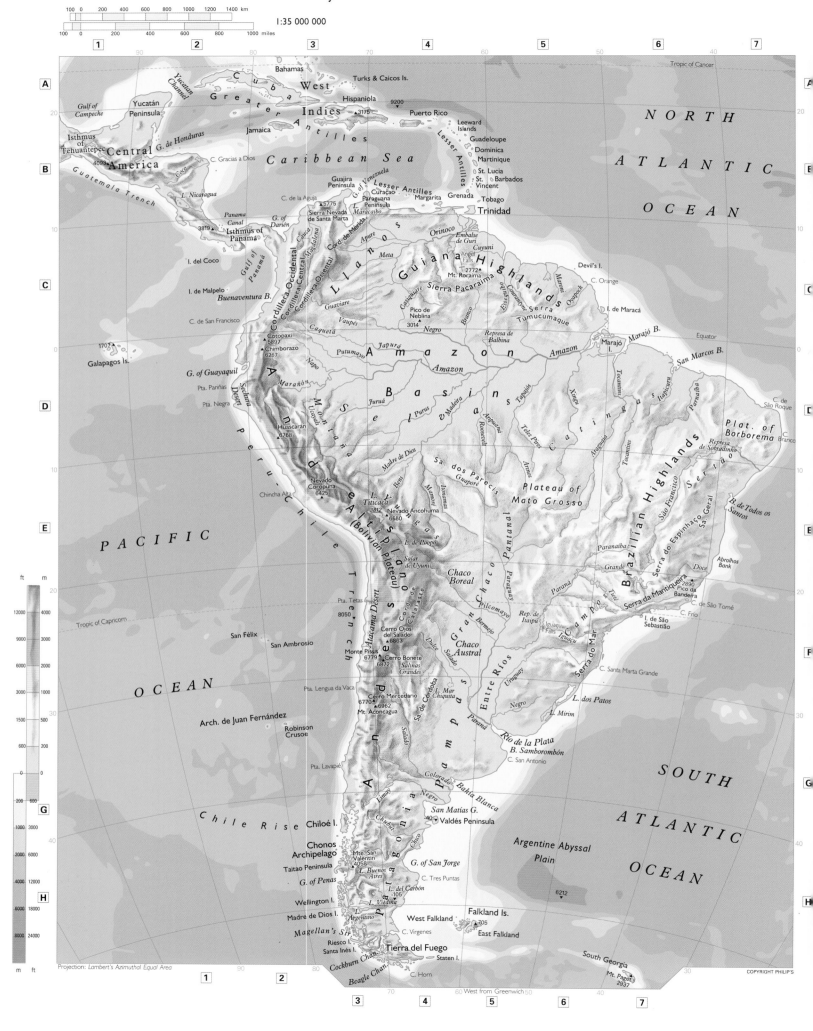

1:35 000 000

Projection: Lambert's Azimuthal Equal Area

COPYRIGHT PHILIP'S

1:35 000 000

100 0   200 400 600 800 1000 1200 1400 km

100 0   200   400   600   800   1000 miles

Tropic of Cancer

A

Havana
CUBA   BAHAMAS   Turks & Caicos Is.
(U.K.)

Cayman Is.
(U.K.)
HAITI   DOMINICAN   San Juan   Virgin Is. (U.S.A. - U.K.)
JAMAICA   Port-au-   REP.   Anguilla (U.K.)
Kingston   Prince   Santo   PUERTO   St. Martin (Fr. - Neth.)
Domingo   RICO   ANTIGUA &
(U.S.A.)   ST. KITTS   BARBUDA
MEXICO   & NEVIS   GUADELOUPE
Basse-Terre   (Fr.)
DOMINICA   MARTINIQUE
GUATEMALA   BELIZE   Fort-de-France   (Fr.)
Caribbean Sea   Castries   ST. LUCIA
HONDURAS   Tegucigalpa   ST. VINCENT   BARBADOS
Guatemala   Kingstown   Bridgetown
San Salvador   NICARAGUA   Aruba   GRENADA   St. George's
EL SALVADOR   Oranjestad   NETH.   Port of
Managua   (Neth.)   ANTILLES   TRINIDAD &
COSTA   Barranquilla   Willemstad   Spain   TOBAGO
San José   G. of   Maracaibo   Caracas
RICA   Panamá   Darién   Cartagena   Valencia
PANAMA   Barquisimeto
I. del Coco   Cúcuta   San Cristóbal   Orinoco   Ciudad Guayana
(Costa Rica)   Medellín   Bucaramanga   VENEZUELA   Georgetown
Gulf of Panamá   Cali   BOGOTÁ   GUYANA   Paramaribo
RORAIMA   SURINAME   Cayenne
I. de Malpelo   COLOMBIA   FRENCH   C. Orange
(Colombia)   Branco   GUIANA
Quito   AMAPÁ
Galapagos Is.   ECUADOR   Equator
(Ecuador)   Guayaquil   Napo   Putumayo   Japurá   Marajó   Belém
G. of Guayaquil   Iquitos   Amazon   I.
Marañón   AMAZONAS   Amazon   Manaus   Santarém   São Luís
Chiclayo   Juruá   Madeira   PARÁ   Fortaleza
Trujillo   Purus   Tapajós   Xingu   MARANHÃO   Teresina   CEARÁ
Chimbote   ACRE   Pôrto Velho   RIO G.
PERU   Madre de Dios   RONDÔNIA   Parnaíba   PIAUÍ   DO NORTE   Natal
Callao   LIMA   Mamoré   B R A Z I L   TOCANTINS   PARAÍBA
Cuzco   Campina Grande
L.   BOLIVIA   MATO GROSSO   PERNAMBUCO   Recife
Titicaca   Arequipa   La Paz   GOIÁS   ALAGOAS   Maceió
Cochabamba   Cuiabá   DIS. FED.   Brasília   SERGIPE
Santa Cruz   Goiânia   BAHÍA   Aracaju
Sucre   São Francisco   Salvador
Iquique   MATO GROSSO   MINAS GERAIS
DO SUL   Belo   ESPÍRITO
Horizonte   SANTO
Tropic of Capricorn   Antofagasta   PARAGUAY   Paraná   Ribeirão   Juiz   Vitória
Prêto   de Fora   R. DE J.   Campos
SÃO PAULO
Salta   Pilcomayo   Asunción   SÃO   Campinas   RIO DE
San Félix   PARANÁ   PAULO   Niterói   JANEIRO
(Chile)   San Miguel   Curitiba   Santos
San Ambrosio   de Tucumán   Salado   SANTA CATARINA
(Chile)   Resistencia   Corrientes   Uruguay
RIO GRANDE
Córdoba   Santa Fé   DO SUL   Pôrto Alegre
Arch. de Juan Fernández   San Juan   Paraná   Pelotas
Robinson   Rosario   URUGUAY
Crusoe   Viña del Mar   Mendoza   Montevideo
Valparaíso   SANTIAGO   BUENOS AIRES
Talca   La Plata   Río de la Plata
Concepción   Bahía   Mar del Plata
Blanca
Valdivia   Colorado
Negro   Viedma
Puerto Montt

NORTH

ATLANTIC

OCEAN

PACIFIC

OCEAN

SOUTH

ATLANTIC

OCEAN

Comodoro Rivadavia
Gulf of San Jorge

Gulf of Penas

Chubut

ARGENTINA

CHILE

West Falkland   FALKLAND IS.
(U.K.)
Stanley
East Falkland
Magellan's Str.   South Georgia
Punta Arenas   (U.K.)
Tierra del Fuego
C. Horn

A **B** **C** **D** **E** **F** **G** **H**

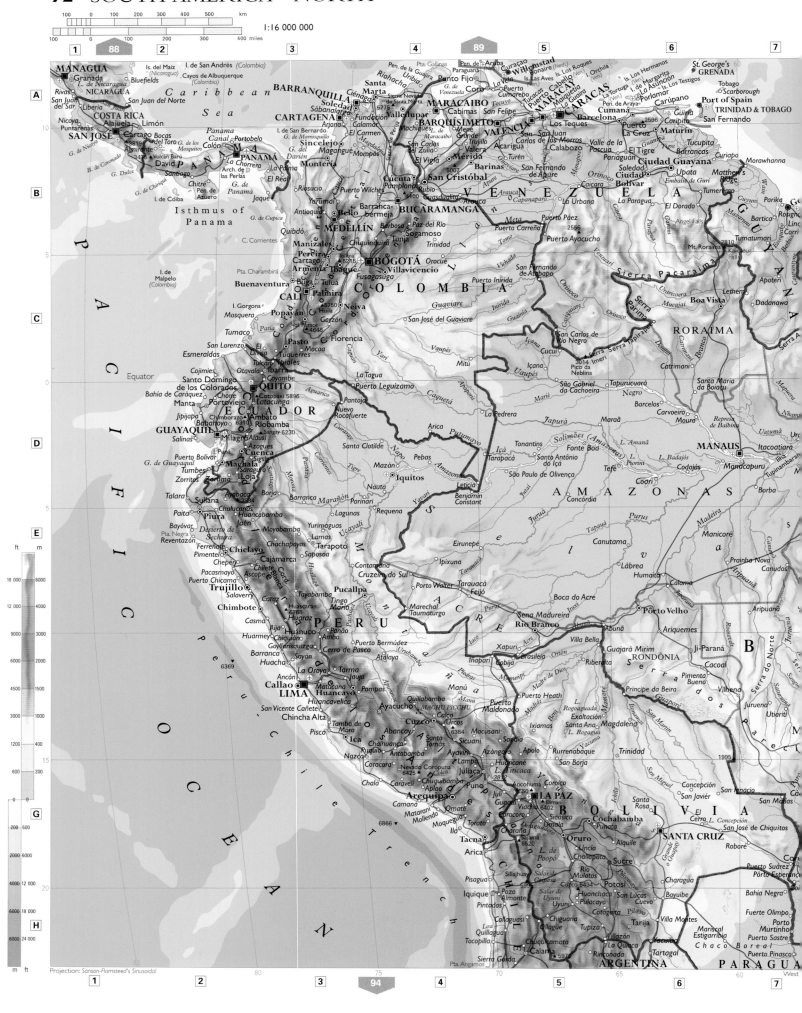

1:16 000 000

Projection: Sanson-Flamsteed's Sinusoidal

ATLANTIC

OCEAN

TRINIDAD AND TOBAGO
1:2 500 000

Tobago
Charlotteville
Plymouth   Castara   Main Ridge   565   Little Tobago
Buccoo Reef   Scarborough   Roxborough
Crown Pt.   Rockly Bay

J

VENEZUELA
Pen. de
Paria
Corozal
Pt.
Macuro
Güiria

ATLANTIC

OCEAN

Trinidad

Dragon's Mouths
Monos I.
Maraval
La Vache Pt.
Chupara Pt.
Blanchisseuse
Marecas Bay
Sans Souci
Matelot
Toco
Galera Pt.
Northern Range
Redhead
936   940 ▲ Mt. Aripo
Tunapuna   Salybia
**Port of
Spain**   San Juan   Valencia
Arima
Caroni   Sangre Grande
Chaguanas   Guaico   Upper Manzanilla
Couva   Talparo   Narival Swamp
Cocos Bay
Point Lisas   Gasparillo   Rio Claro   Guatuaro Pt.
Otaheite Bay
San Fernando   Pierreville
Brighton   La Brea   Princes Town   Mayaro Bay
Guap Bay   Pitch Lake   Penal   Basse Terre   Guayaguayare
Point Fortin   Siparia   Galeota Pt.
Cedros Bay   Palo Seco   La Lune   304 ▲   Moruga   Trinity Hills
Bonasse
Icacos Pt.   Erin Pt.   Moruga

Serpent's Mouth

K

L

VENEZUELA
Pta. Bombedor
West from Greenwich

ATLANTIC

OCEAN

Paramaribo
Nickerie   Nieuw Amsterdam
Totness   Albina   Moengo   St-Laurent du Maroni
koegroni   W. J. Van   Iracoubo   Sinnamary
Blommestein   Kourou
Meer   Kaw   Cayenne
SURINAME   Mana
1230   FRENCH
atop   St-Georges   GUIANA
C. Orange   Oiapoque
Approuague
Camopi

AMAPÁ   Amapá
I. de Maracá
Merirumã   Serra do
Navio
Macapá   I. Caviana
Mazagão   I. Mexiana
Afuá   Chaves
I. Grande   I. de   Soure
de Gurupá   Marajó   Curuçá   Salinópolis
Óbidos   Breves   Vigia   Bragança
Monte   Almeirim   Gurupá   **BELÉM**
Alegre   Porto de Moz   Castanhal   Turiaçu
Alenquer   Santarém   Cametá   Abaetetuba
Juruti   Belterra   Baião   Alcântara   **São Luís**
Aveiro   Altamira   Curralinho   Pinheiro   Rosário
Brasília Legal   Tucuruí   Viana
Itaituba   P A R Á   Santa Inês   Bacabal

EQUATOR

D

Barreirinhas
Tutóia
Parnaíba   Luís Correia
Cururupu   Granja   Itapipoca
B. de São Marcos   Brejo   Caucaia
Itapecuru-Mirim   Piracuruca   Sobral   **FORTALEZA**
Coroatá   Codó   Piripiri   Maranguape   Cascavel
Pedreiras   Caxias   Ipu   Quixadá   Aracati
MARANHÃO   Campo   Crateús   Baturité   Russas
Imperatriz   Maior   C E A R Á
Teresina   Areia Branca
Barra do   Senador Pompeu   Mossoró   Macau
Corda   Caraúbas   Ceará-Mirim
Amarante   Valença   RIO GRANDE   **NATAL**
Colinas   do Piauí   Iguatu   DO NORTE
Floriano   Oeiras   Cedro   Currais   Canguaretama
Nova Iorque   Picos   Souza   Novos   Mamanguape
Uruçuí   P I A U Í   Cajazeiras   Alagoa   Cabedelo
Paulistana   Crato   PARAÍBA   **João Pessoa**
Juàzeiro do Norte   **Campina**   Olinda
Ouricuri   **Grande**   **RECIFE**
PERNAMBUCO   Caruaru   Jaboatão

E

5

São João
do Piauí
Caracol   Sa. Dois Irmãos
Casa Nova   Petrolina   Garanhuns   Vitória de Santo Antão
Remanso   Juàzeiro   Salgueiro   Palmares   Rio Largo
Senhor-do-   Paulo Afonso   **MACEIÓ**
Bonfim   Propriá   ALAGOAS
Jacobina   Penedo   6059
Xique-Xique   Queimadas   Copela   **Aracaju**
Mundo   São Cristóvão
Novo   Serrinha   Estância
B A H I A   Feira de   SERGIPE
Barreiras   Santana   Alagoinhas
Ibotirama   Itaberaba   Cachoeira   Santo Amaro
Bom Jesus   Castro   **SALVADOR**
da Lapa   Alves   Nazaré
Santa Maria   Valença
da Vitória   Jequié
São Domingos   Caetité   B. de Todos os Santos
Posse   Carinhanha   Brumado   Ubaitaba
Condeúba   Vitória da   Itabuna
Januária   Monte Azul   Conquista   Ilhéus
Formosa   São Francisco   Canavieiras
BRASÍLIA   Januária   Pedra Azul   Belmonte
Luziânia   Salinas   Porto Seguro
Jequitinhonha
Araçuaí   Itamaraju
Teófilo Otoni   Prado   Caravelas
Nanuque   Banco dos
Diamantina   Governador   Mucuri   Abrolhos
Valadares   Conceição da Barra
Ipatinga   Nova   São Mateus
BELO HORIZONTE   Colatina   Linhares
Sabará   Caratinga   Cariacica   **VITÓRIA**
VITÓRIA   Vila Velha
Cachoeiro de Itapemirim

F

G

10

15

TOCANTINS
Palmas
Porto Nacional
Gurupi
Peixe
Paranã
Campos Belos

Trindade
(Braz.)

H

20

São Pedro &
São Paulo
(Braz.)

0

Rocas
Fernando de Noronha
(Braz.)

COPYRIGHT PHILIP'S

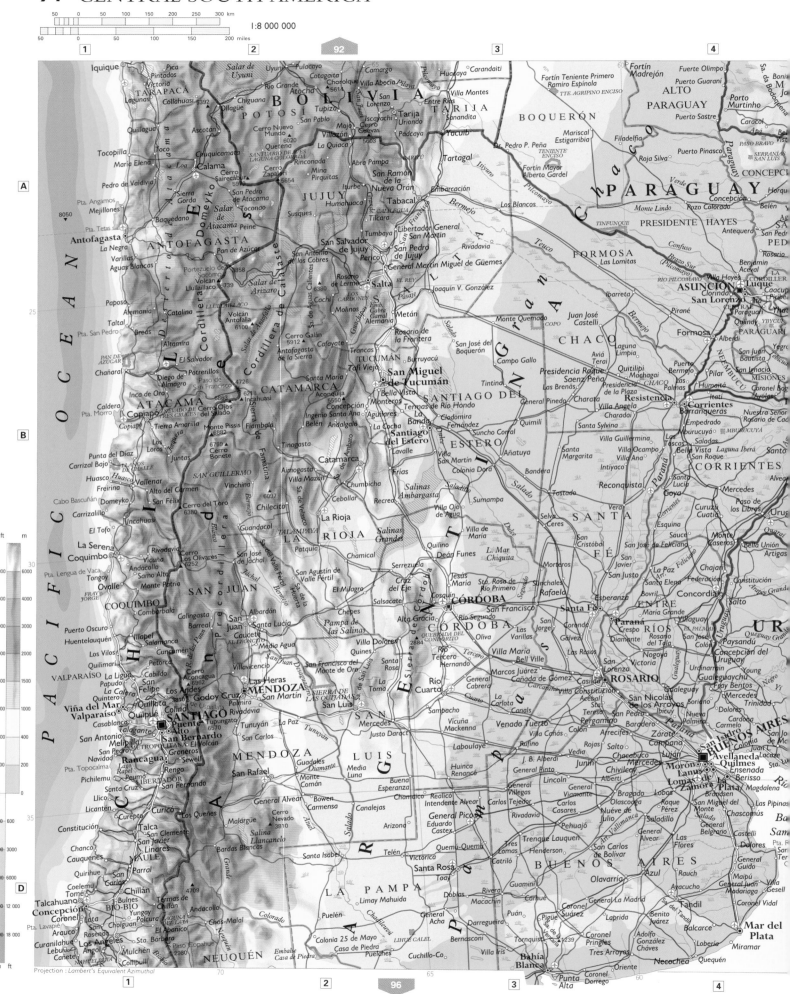

1:8 000 000

Projection : Lambert's Equivalent Azimuthal

A

B

C

D

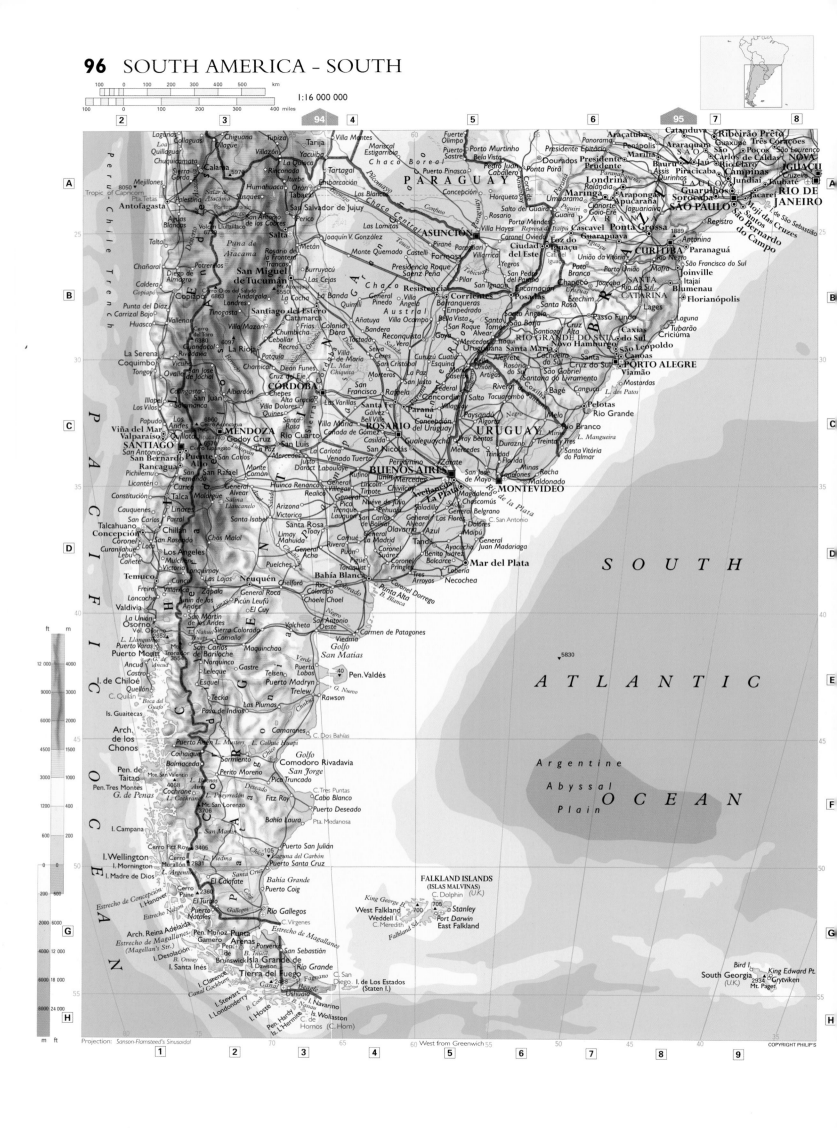

INDEX TO WORLD MAPS

The index contains the names of all the principal places and features shown on the World Maps. Each name is followed by an additional entry in italics giving the country or region within which it is located. The alphabetical order of names composed of two or more words is governed primarily by the first word, then by the second, and then by the country or region name that follows. This is an example of the rule:

Mīr Kūh *Iran*	26°22N 58°55E	**45** E8	
Mīr Shahdād *Iran*	26°15N 58°29E	**45** E8	
Mira *Italy*	45°26N 12°8E	**22** B5	
Mira por vos Cay *Bahamas*	22°9N 74°30W	**89** B5	

Physical features composed of a proper name (Erie) and a description (Lake) are positioned alphabetically by the proper name. The description is positioned after the proper name and is usually abbreviated:

Erie, L. *N. Amer.* 42°15N 81°0W **82** D4

Where a description forms part of a settlement or administrative name, however, it is always written in full and put in its true alphabetical position:

Mount Morris *U.S.A.* 42°44N 77°52W **82** D7

Names beginning with M' and Mc are indexed as if they were spelled Mac. Names beginning St. are alphabetized under Saint, but Sankt, Sint, Sant', Santa and San are all spelt in full and are alphabetized accordingly. If the same place name occurs two or more times in the index and all are in the same country, each is followed by the name of the administrative subdivision in which it is located.

The geographical co-ordinates which follow each name in the index give the latitude and longitude of each place. The first co-ordinate indicates latitude – the distance north or south of the Equator. The second co-ordinate indicates longitude – the distance east or west of the Greenwich Meridian. Both latitude and longitude are measured in degrees and minutes (there are 60 minutes in a degree).

The latitude is followed by N(orth) or S(outh) and the longitude by E(ast) or W(est).

The number in bold type which follows the geographical co-ordinates refers to the number of the map page where that feature or place will be found. This is usually the largest scale at which the place or feature appears.

The letter and figure that are immediately after the page number give the grid square on the map page, within which the feature is situated. The letter represents the latitude and the figure the longitude. A lower-case letter immediately after the page number refers to an inset map on that page.

In some cases the feature itself may fall within the specified square, while the name is outside. This is usually the case only with features that are larger than a grid square.

Rivers are indexed to their mouths or confluences, and carry the symbol ➜ after their names. The following symbols are also used in the index: ■ country, ☑ overseas territory or dependency, □ first-order administrative area, △ national park, ⌂ other park (provincial park, nature reserve or game reserve), ✗ (LHR) principal airport (and location identifier), ⌖ Australian aboriginal land.

Abbreviations used in the index

A.C.T. – Australian Capital Territory
A.R. – Autonomous Region
Afghan. – Afghanistan
Afr. – Africa
Ala. – Alabama
Alta. – Alberta
Amer. – America(n)
Ant. – Antilles
Arch. – Archipelago
Ariz. – Arizona
Ark. – Arkansas
Atl. Oc. – Atlantic Ocean
B. – Baie, Bahía, Bay, Bucht, Bugt
B.C. – British Columbia
Bangla. – Bangladesh
Barr. – Barrage
Bos.-H. – Bosnia-Herzegovina
C. – Cabo, Cap, Cape, Coast
C.A.R. – Central African Republic
C. Prov. – Cape Province
Calif. – California
Cat. – Catarata
Cent. – Central
Chan. – Channel
Colo. – Colorado
Conn. – Connecticut
Cord. – Cordillera
Cr. – Creek
Czech. – Czech Republic
D.C. – District of Columbia
Del. – Delaware
Dem. – Democratic
Dep. – Dependency
Des. – Desert
Dét. – Détroit
Dist. – District
Dj. – Djebel
Dom. Rep. – Dominican Republic

E. – East
El Salv. – El Salvador
Eq. Guin. – Equatorial Guinea
Est. – Estrecho
Falk. Is. – Falkland Is.
Fd. – Fjord
Fla. – Florida
Fr. – French
G. – Golfe, Golfo, Gulf, Guba, Gebel
Ga. – Georgia
Gt. – Great, Greater
Guinea-Biss. – Guinea-Bissau
H.K. – Hong Kong
H.P. – Himachal Pradesh
Hants. – Hampshire
Harb. – Harbor, Harbour
Hd. – Head
Hts. – Heights
I.(s). – Île, Ilha, Insel, Isla, Island, Isle
Ill. – Illinois
Ind. – Indiana
Ind. Oc. – Indian Ocean
Ivory C. – Ivory Coast
J. – Jabal, Jebel
Jaz. – Jazīrah
Junc. – Junction
K. – Kap, Kapp
Kans. – Kansas
Kep. – Kepulauan
Ky. – Kentucky
L. – Lac, Lacul, Lago, Lagoa, Lake, Limni, Loch, Lough
La. – Louisiana
Ld. – Land
Liech. – Liechtenstein
Lux. – Luxembourg
Mad. P. – Madhya Pradesh
Madag. – Madagascar
Man. – Manitoba
Mass. – Massachusetts

Md. – Maryland
Me. – Maine
Medit. S. – Mediterranean Sea
Mich. – Michigan
Minn. – Minnesota
Miss. – Mississippi
Mo. – Missouri
Mont. – Montana
Mozam. – Mozambique
Mt.(s) – Mont, Montaña, Mountain
Mte. – Monte
Mti. – Monti
N. – Nord, Norte, North, Northern, Nouveau, Nahal, Nahr
N.B. – New Brunswick
N.C. – North Carolina
N. Cal. – New Caledonia
N. Dak. – North Dakota
N.H. – New Hampshire
N.I. – North Island
N.J. – New Jersey
N. Mex. – New Mexico
N.S. – Nova Scotia
N.S.W. – New South Wales
N.W.T. – North West Territory
N.Y. – New York
N.Z. – New Zealand
Nac. – Nacional
Nat. – National
Nebr. – Nebraska
Neths. – Netherlands
Nev. – Nevada
Nfld & L. – Newfoundland and Labrador
Nic. – Nicaragua
O. – Oued, Ouadi
Occ. – Occidentale
Okla. – Oklahoma
Ont. – Ontario
Or. – Orientale

Oreg. – Oregon
Os. – Ostrov
Oz. – Ozero
P. – Pass, Passo, Pasul, Pulau
P.E.I. – Prince Edward Island
Pa. – Pennsylvania
Pac. Oc. – Pacific Ocean
Papua N.G. – Papua New Guinea
Pass. – Passage
Peg. – Pegunungan
Pen. – Peninsula, Péninsule
Phil. – Philippines
Pk. – Peak
Plat. – Plateau
Prov. – Province, Provincial
Pt. – Point
Pta. – Ponta, Punta
Pte. – Pointe
Qué. – Québec
Queens. – Queensland
R. – Rio, River
R.I. – Rhode Island
Ra. – Range
Raj. – Rajasthan
Recr. – Recreational, Récréatif
Reg. – Region
Rep. – Republic
Res. – Reserve, Reservoir
Rhld-Pfz. – Rheinland-Pfalz
S. – South, Southern, Sur
Si. Arabia – Saudi Arabia
S.C. – South Carolina
S. Dak. – South Dakota
S.I. – South Island
S. Leone – Sierra Leone
Sa. – Serra, Sierra
Sask. – Saskatchewan
Scot. – Scotland
Sd. – Sound
Sev. – Severnaya
Sib. – Siberia

Sprs. – Springs
St. – Saint
Sta. – Santa
Ste. – Sainte
Sto. – Santo
Str. – Strait, Stretto
Switz. – Switzerland
Tas. – Tasmania
Tenn. – Tennessee
Terr. – Territory, Territoire
Tex. – Texas
Tg. – Tanjung
Trin. & Tob. – Trinidad & Tobago
U.A.E. – United Arab Emirates
U.K. – United Kingdom
U.S.A. – United States of America
Ut. P. – Uttar Pradesh
Va. – Virginia
Vdkhr. – Vodokhranilishche
Vdskh. – Vodoskhovyshche
Vf. – Vîrful
Vic. – Victoria
Vol. – Volcano
Vt. – Vermont
W. – Wadi, West
W. Va. – West Virginia
Wall. & F. Is. – Wallis and Futuna Is.
Wash. – Washington
Wis. – Wisconsin
Wlkp. – Wielkopolski
Wyo. – Wyoming
Yorks. – Yorkshire

A

A Coruña Spain 43°20N 8°25W 21 A1
A Estrada Spain 42°43N 8°27W 21 A1
A Fonsagrada Spain 43°8N 7°4W 21 A2
Aabenraa Denmark 55°3N 9°25E 9 J13
Aachen Germany 50°45N 6°6E 16 C4
Aalborg Denmark 57°2N 9°54E 9 H13
Aalen Germany 48°51N 10°6E 16 D6
Aalst Belgium 50°56N 4°2E 15 D4
Aalten Neths. 51°56N 6°35E 15 C6
Aalter Belgium 51°5N 3°28E 15 C3
Äänekoski Finland 62°36N 25°44E 8 E21
Aarau Switz. 47°23N 8°4E 20 C8
Aare → Switz. 47°33N 8°14E 20 C8
Aarhus = Århus Denmark 56°8N 10°11E 9 H14
Aarschot Belgium 50°59N 4°49E 15 D4
Aba Dem. Rep. of the Congo 3°58N 30°17E 54 B3
Aba Nigeria 5°10N 7°19E 50 G7
Abaco I. Bahamas 26°25N 77°10W 88 A4
Ābādān Iran 30°22N 48°20E 45 D6
Ābādeh Iran 31°8N 52°40E 45 D7
Abadla Algeria 31°2N 2°45W 50 B5
Abaetetuba Brazil 1°40S 48°50W 93 D9
Abagnar Qi = Xilinhot China 43°52N 116°2E 34 C9
Abah, Tanjung Indonesia 8°46S 115°38E 37 K18
Abai Paraguay 25°58S 55°54W 95 B4
Abakan Russia 53°40N 91°10E 29 D10
Abancay Peru 13°35S 72°55W 92 F4
Abariringa Kiribati 2°50S 171°40W 64 H10
Abarqū Iran 31°10N 53°20E 45 D7
Abashiri Japan 44°0N 144°15E 30 B12
Abashiri-Wan Japan 44°0N 144°30E 30 C12
Ābay = Nîl el Azraq → Sudan 15°38N 32°31E 51 E12
Abay Kazakhstan 49°38N 72°53E 28 E8
Abaya, L. Ethiopia 6°30N 37°50E 47 F2
Abaza Russia 52°39N 90°6E 28 D9
'Abbāsābād Iran 33°34N 58°23E 45 C8
Abbay = Nîl el Azraq → Sudan 15°38N 32°31E 51 E12
Abbaye, Pt. U.S.A. 46°58N 88°8W 80 B9
Abbé, L. Ethiopia 11°8N 41°47E 47 E3
Abbeville France 50°6N 1°49E 20 A4
Abbeville Ala., U.S.A. 31°34N 85°15W 85 F12
Abbeville La., U.S.A. 29°58N 92°8W 84 G8
Abbeville S.C., U.S.A. 34°11N 82°23W 85 D13
Abbeyfeale Ireland 52°23N 9°18W 10 D2
Abbot Ice Shelf Antarctica 73°0S 92°0W 5 D16
Abbotsford Canada 49°5N 122°20W 70 D4
Abbottabad Pakistan 34°10N 73°15E 42 B5
ABC Islands = Netherlands Antilles ☑ W. Indies 12°15N 69°0W 92 A5
Abd al Kūrī Yemen 12°5N 52°20E 47 E5
Ābdar Iran 30°16N 55°19E 45 D7
'Abdolābād Iran 34°12N 56°30E 45 C8
Abdulpur Bangla. 24°15N 88°59E 43 G13
Abéché Chad 13°50N 20°35E 51 F10
Abel Tasman △ N.Z. 40°59S 173°3E 59 D4
Abengourou Ivory C. 6°42N 3°27W 50 G5
Åbenrå = Aabenraa Denmark 55°3N 9°25E 9 J13
Abeokuta Nigeria 7°3N 3°19E 50 G6
Aberaeron U.K. 52°15N 4°15W 13 E3
Aberayron = Aberaeron U.K. 52°15N 4°15W 13 E3
Aberchirder U.K. 57°34N 2°37W 11 D6
Abercorn Australia 25°12S 151°5E 63 D5
Aberdare U.K. 51°43N 3°27W 13 F4
Aberdare △ Kenya 0°22S 36°44E 54 C4
Aberdare Ra. Kenya 0°15S 36°50E 54 C4
Aberdeen Australia 32°9S 150°56E 63 E5
Aberdeen Canada 52°20N 106°8W 71 C7
Aberdeen China 22°14N 114°8E 33 G11
Aberdeen S. Africa 32°28S 24°2E 56 E3
Aberdeen U.K. 57°9N 2°5W 11 D6
Aberdeen Idaho, U.S.A. 42°57N 112°50W 76 E7
Aberdeen Md., U.S.A. 39°31N 76°10W 81 F15
Aberdeen Miss., U.S.A. 33°49N 88°33W 85 E10
Aberdeen S. Dak., U.S.A. 45°28N 98°29W 80 C4
Aberdeen Wash., U.S.A. 46°59N 123°50W 78 D3
Aberdeen, City of ☑ U.K. 57°10N 2°10W 11 D6
Aberdeen L. Canada 64°30N 99°0W 68 E12
Aberdeenshire ☑ U.K. 57°17N 2°36W 11 D6
Aberdovey = Aberdyfi U.K. 52°33N 4°3W 13 E3
Aberdyfi U.K. 52°33N 4°3W 13 E3
Aberfeldy U.K. 56°37N 3°51W 11 E5
Aberfoyle U.K. 56°11N 4°23W 11 E4
Abergavenny U.K. 51°49N 3°1W 13 F4
Abergele U.K. 53°17N 3°35W 12 D4
Abernathy U.S.A. 33°50N 101°51W 84 E4
Abert, L. U.S.A. 42°38N 120°14W 76 E3
Aberystwyth U.K. 52°25N 4°5W 13 E3
Abhā Si. Arabia 18°0N 42°34E 47 D3
Abhar Iran 36°9N 49°13E 45 B6
Abhayapuri India 26°24N 90°38E 43 F14
Abidjan Ivory C. 5°26N 3°58W 50 G5
Abilene Kans., U.S.A. 38°55N 97°13W 80 F5
Abilene Tex., U.S.A. 32°28N 99°43W 84 E5
Abingdon U.K. 51°40N 1°17W 13 F6
Abingdon U.S.A. 36°43N 81°59W 81 G13
Abington Reef Australia 18°0S 149°35E 62 B4
Abitau → Canada 59°53N 109°3W 71 B7
Abitibi → Canada 51°3N 80°55W 72 B3
Abitibi, L. Canada 48°40N 79°40W 72 C4
Abkhaz Republic = Abkhazia ☑ Georgia 43°12N 41°5E 19 F7
Abkhazia ☑ Georgia 43°12N 41°5E 19 F7
Abminga Australia 26°8S 134°51E 63 D1
Åbo = Turku Finland 60°30N 22°19E 9 F20
Abohar India 30°10N 74°10E 42 D6
Abomey Benin 7°10N 2°5E 50 G6
Abong-Mbang Cameroon 4°0N 13°8E 52 D2
Abou-Deïa Chad 11°20N 19°20E 51 F9

Aboyne U.K. 57°4N 2°47W 11 D6
Abra Pampa Argentina 22°43S 65°42W 94 A2
Abraham L. Canada 52°15N 116°35W 70 C5
Abreojos, Pta. Mexico 26°50N 113°40W 86 B2
Abrolhos, Banco dos Brazil 18°0S 38°0W 93 F11
Abrud Romania 46°19N 23°5E 17 E12
Absaroka Range U.S.A. 44°45N 109°50W 76 D9
Abu India 24°41N 72°50E 42 G5
Abū al Abyad U.A.E. 24°11N 53°50E 45 E7
Abū al Khaṣīb Iraq 30°25N 48°0E 45 D6
Abu 'Alī Si. Arabia 27°20N 49°27E 45 E6
Abū 'Alī → Lebanon 34°25N 35°50E 46 A4
Abu Dhabi = Abū Ẓāby U.A.E. 24°28N 54°22E 45 E7
Abu Du'ān Syria 36°25N 38°15E 44 B3
Abu el Gaïn, W. → Egypt 29°35N 33°30E 46 F2
Abū Ga'da, W. → Egypt 29°15N 32°53E 46 F1
Abu Hamed Sudan 19°32N 33°13E 51 E12
Abū Kamāl Syria 34°30N 41°0E 44 C4
Abū Madd, Ra's Si. Arabia 24°50N 37°7E 44 E3
Abū Mūsā Iran 25°52N 55°3E 45 E7
Abū Qaşr Si. Arabia 30°21N 38°34E 44 D3
Abū Shagara, Ras Sudan 21°4N 37°19E 51 D13
Abu Simbel Egypt 22°18N 31°40E 51 D12
Abū Şukhayr Iraq 31°54N 44°30E 44 D5
Abū Zabad Sudan 12°25N 29°10E 51 F11
Abū Ẓāby U.A.E. 24°28N 54°22E 45 E7
Abū Zeydābād Iran 33°54N 51°45E 45 C6
Abuja Nigeria 9°5N 7°32E 50 G7
Abukuma-Gawa → Japan 38°6N 140°52E 30 E10
Abukuma-Sammyaku Japan 37°30N 140°45E 30 F10
Abuná Brazil 9°40S 65°20W 92 E5
Abuná → Brazil 9°41S 65°20W 92 E5
Aburo Dem. Rep. of the Congo 2°4N 30°53E 54 B3
Abut Hd. N.Z. 43°7S 170°15E 59 E3
Ābyek Iran 36°4N 50°33E 45 B6
Acadia △ U.S.A. 44°20N 68°13W 81 C19
Açailândia Brazil 4°57S 47°0W 93 D9
Acajutla El Salv. 13°36N 89°50W 88 D2
Acámbaro Mexico 20°2N 100°44W 86 D4
Acaponeta Mexico 22°30N 105°22W 86 C3
Acapulco Mexico 16°51N 99°55W 87 D5
Acaraí, Serra Brazil 1°50N 57°50W 92 C7
Acarigua Venezuela 9°33N 69°12W 92 B5
Acatlán Mexico 18°12N 98°3W 87 D5
Acayucán Mexico 17°57N 94°55W 87 D6
Accomac U.S.A. 37°43N 75°40W 81 G16
Accra Ghana 5°35N 0°6W 50 G5
Accrington U.K. 53°45N 2°22W 12 D5
Acebal Argentina 33°20S 60°50W 94 C3
Aceh ☑ Indonesia 4°15N 97°30E 36 D1
Achalpur India 21°22N 77°32E 40 J10
Acharnes Greece 38°5N 23°44E 23 E10
Acheloos → Greece 38°19N 21°7E 23 E9
Acheng China 45°30N 126°58E 35 B14
Acher India 23°10N 72°32E 42 H5
Achill Hd. Ireland 53°58N 10°15W 10 C1
Achill I. Ireland 53°58N 10°1W 10 C1
Achinsk Russia 56°20N 90°20E 29 D10
Acireale Italy 37°37N 15°10E 22 F6
Ackerman U.S.A. 33°19N 89°11W 85 E10
Acklins I. Bahamas 22°30N 74°0W 89 B5
Acme Canada 51°33N 113°30W 70 C6
Acme U.S.A. 40°8N 79°26W 82 F5
Aconcagua, Cerro Argentina 32°39S 70°0W 94 C2
Aconquija, Mt. Argentina 27°0S 66°0W 94 B2
Açores, Is. dos Atl. Oc. 38°0N 27°0W 50 a
Acornhoek S. Africa 24°37S 31°2E 57 C5
Acraman, L. Australia 32°2S 135°23E 63 E2
Acre = 'Akko Israel 32°55N 35°4E 46 C4
Acre ☑ Brazil 9°1S 71°0W 92 E4
Acre → Brazil 8°45S 67°22W 92 E5
Actinolite Canada 44°32N 77°19W 82 B7
Acton Canada 43°38N 80°3W 82 C4
Ad Dammām Si. Arabia 26°20N 50°5E 45 E6
Ad Dāmūr Lebanon 33°43N 35°27E 46 B4
Ad Dawādimī Si. Arabia 24°35N 44°15E 44 E5
Ad Dawḥah Qatar 25°15N 51°35E 45 E6
Ad Dawr Iraq 34°27N 43°47E 44 C4
Ad Dir'īyah Si. Arabia 24°44N 46°35E 44 E5
Ad Dīwānīyah Iraq 32°0N 45°0E 44 D5
Ad Dujayl Iraq 33°51N 44°14E 44 C5
Ad Duwayd Si. Arabia 30°15N 42°17E 44 D4
Ada Minn., U.S.A. 47°18N 96°31W 80 B5
Ada Okla., U.S.A. 34°46N 96°41W 84 D6
Adabiya Egypt 29°53N 32°28E 46 F1
Adair, C. Canada 71°30N 71°34W 69 C17
Adaja → Spain 41°32N 4°52W 21 B3
Adak U.S.A. 51°45N 176°45W 74 E4
Adak I. U.S.A. 51°45N 176°45W 74 E4
Adamaoua, Massif de l' Cameroon 7°20N 12°20E 51 G8
Adamawa Highlands = Adamaoua, Massif de l' Cameroon 7°20N 12°20E 51 G8
Adamello, Mte. Italy 46°9N 10°30E 20 C7
Adaminaby Australia 36°0S 148°45E 63 F4
Adams Mass., U.S.A. 42°38N 73°7W 83 D11
Adams N.Y., U.S.A. 43°49N 76°1W 83 C8
Adams Wis., U.S.A. 43°57N 89°49W 80 D9
Adams, L. Canada 51°10N 119°40W 70 C5
Adam's Bridge Sri Lanka 9°15N 79°40E 40 Q11
Adams, Mt. U.S.A. 46°12N 121°30W 78 D5
Adam's Peak Sri Lanka 6°48N 80°30E 40 R12
Adana Turkey 37°0N 35°16E 44 B2
Adapazarı = Sakarya Turkey 40°48N 30°25E 19 F5
Adarama Sudan 17°10N 34°52E 51 E12
Adare, C. Antarctica 71°0S 171°0E 5 D11
Adaut Indonesia 8°8S 131°7E 37 F8
Adavale Australia 25°52S 144°32E 63 D3

Adda → Italy 45°8N 9°53E 20 D8
Addis Ababa = Addis Abeba Ethiopia 9°2N 38°42E 47 F2
Addis Abeba Ethiopia 9°2N 38°42E 47 F2
Addison U.S.A. 42°1N 77°14W 82 D7
Addo S. Africa 33°32S 25°45E 56 E4
Addo △ S. Africa 33°30S 25°50E 56 E4
Ādeh Iran 37°42N 45°11E 44 B5
Adel U.S.A. 31°8N 83°25W 85 F13
Adelaide Australia 34°52S 138°30E 63 E2
Adelaide S. Africa 32°42S 26°20E 56 E4
Adelaide I. Antarctica 67°15S 68°30W 5 C17
Adelaide Pen. Canada 68°15N 97°30W 68 D12
Adelaide River Australia 13°15S 131°7E 60 B5
Adelaide Village Bahamas 25°0N 77°31W 88 A4
Adelanto U.S.A. 34°35N 117°22W 79 L9
Adele I. Australia 15°32S 123°9E 60 C3
Adélie, Terre Antarctica 68°0S 140°0E 5 C10
Adelie Land = Adélie, Terre Antarctica 68°0S 140°0E 5 C10
Aden = Al 'Adan Yemen 12°45N 45°0E 47 E4
Aden, G. of Ind. Oc. 12°30N 47°30E 47 E4
Adendorp S. Africa 32°15S 24°30E 56 E3
Adh Dhayd U.A.E. 25°17N 55°53E 45 E7
Adhoi India 23°26N 70°32E 42 H4
Adi Indonesia 4°15S 133°30E 37 E8
Adieu, C. Australia 32°0S 132°10E 61 F5
Adieu Pt. Australia 15°14S 124°35E 60 C3
Adige → Italy 45°9N 12°20E 22 B5
Adigrat Ethiopia 14°20N 39°26E 47 E2
Adilabad India 19°33N 78°20E 40 K11
Adirondack △ U.S.A. 44°0N 74°20W 83 C10
Adirondack Mts. U.S.A. 44°0N 74°0W 83 C10
Adis Abeba = Addis Abeba Ethiopia 9°2N 38°42E 47 F2
Adjumani Uganda 3°20N 31°50E 54 B3
Adjuntas Puerto Rico 18°10N 66°43W 89 d
Adlavik Is. Canada 55°0N 58°40W 73 B8
Admiralty G. Australia 14°20S 125°55E 60 B4
Admiralty Gulf ☼ Australia 14°16S 125°50E 60 B4
Admiralty I. U.S.A. 57°30N 134°30W 70 B2
Admiralty Inlet Canada 72°30N 86°0W 69 C14
Admiralty Is. Papua N. G. 2°0S 147°0E 58 B7
Adolfo González Chaves Argentina 38°2S 60°5W 94 D3
Adolfo Ruiz Cortines, Presa Mexico 27°15N 109°6W 86 B3
Adonara Indonesia 8°15S 123°5E 37 F6
Adoni India 15°33N 77°18E 40 M10
Adour → France 43°32N 1°32W 20 E3
Adra India 23°30N 86°42E 43 H12
Adra Spain 36°43N 3°3W 21 D4
Adrano Italy 37°40N 14°50E 22 F6
Adrar Algeria 27°51N 0°11E 50 C6
Adrar Mauritania 20°30N 7°30W 50 D3
Adrar des Iforas Africa 19°40N 1°40E 50 E6
Adrian Mich., U.S.A. 41°54N 84°2W 81 E11
Adrian Tex., U.S.A. 35°16N 102°40W 84 D3
Adriatic Sea Medit. S. 43°0N 16°0E 22 C6
Adua Indonesia 1°45S 129°50E 37 E7
Adwa Ethiopia 14°15N 38°52E 47 E2
Adygea ☑ Russia 45°0N 40°0E 19 F7
Adzhar Republic = Ajaria ☑ Georgia 41°30N 42°0E 19 F7
Adzopé Ivory C. 6°7N 3°49W 50 G5
Ægean Sea Medit. S. 38°30N 25°0E 23 E11
Aerhtai Shan Mongolia 46°40N 92°45E 32 B4
Afaahiti Tahiti 17°45S 149°17W 59 d
'Afak Iraq 32°4N 45°15E 44 C5
Afandou Greece 36°18N 28°12E 25 C10
Afareaitu Moorea 17°33S 149°47W 59 d
Afghanistan ■ Asia 33°0N 65°0E 40 C4
Aflou Algeria 34°7N 2°3E 50 B6
Afognak I. U.S.A. 58°15N 152°30W 74 D9
Africa 10°0N 20°0E 48 E6
'Afrīn Syria 36°32N 36°50E 44 B3
Afton N.Y., U.S.A. 42°14N 75°32W 83 D9
Afton Wyo., U.S.A. 42°44N 110°56W 76 E8
Afuá Brazil 0°15S 50°20W 93 D8
'Afula Israel 32°37N 35°17E 46 C4
Afyon Turkey 38°45N 30°33E 19 G5
Afyonkarahisar = Afyon Turkey 38°45N 30°33E 19 G5
Agadès = Agadez Niger 16°58N 7°59E 50 E7
Agadez Niger 16°58N 7°59E 50 E7
Agadir Morocco 30°28N 9°55W 50 B4
Agaete Canary Is. 28°6N 15°43W 24 F4
Agalega Is. Mauritius 11°0S 57°0E 3 E12
Agar India 23°40N 76°2E 42 H7
Agartala India 23°50N 91°23E 41 H17
Agassiz Canada 49°14N 121°46W 70 D4
Agassiz Icecap Canada 80°15N 76°0W 69 A16
Agats Indonesia 5°33S 138°0E 37 F9
Agattu I. U.S.A. 52°25N 173°35E 74 E2
Agawam U.S.A. 42°5N 72°37W 83 D12
Agboville Ivory C. 5°55N 4°15W 50 G5
Ağdam Azerbaijan 40°0N 46°58E 44 B5
Agde France 43°19N 3°28E 20 E5
Agen France 44°12N 0°38E 20 D4
Āgh Kand Iran 37°15N 48°4E 45 B6
Aghia Deka Greece 35°3N 24°58E 25 D6
Aghia Ekaterinis, Akra Greece 39°50N 19°50E 25 B3
Aghia Galini Greece 35°6N 24°41E 25 D6
Aghia Varvara Greece 35°8N 25°1E 25 D7
Aghios Ioannis, Akra Greece 35°20N 25°40E 25 D7
Aghios Isidoros Greece 36°9N 27°51E 25 C9
Aghios Matheos Greece 39°30N 19°47E 25 B3
Aghios Stephanos Greece 39°46N 19°39E 25 A3
Aghiou Orous, Kolpos Greece 40°6N 24°0E 23 D11
Aginskoye Russia 51°6N 114°32E 29 D12
Agnew Australia 28°1S 120°31E 61 E3
Agori India 24°33N 82°57E 43 G10

Agra India 27°17N 77°58E 42 F7
Ağri Turkey 39°44N 43°3E 19 G7
Agri → Italy 40°13N 16°44E 22 D7
Ağri Daği Turkey 39°50N 44°15E 44 B5
Ağri Karakose = Ağri Turkey 39°44N 43°3E 19 G7
Agrigento Italy 37°19N 13°34E 22 F5
Agrinio Greece 38°37N 21°27E 23 E9
Agua Caliente Mexico 29°32N 116°59W 79 N10
Agua Caliente Springs U.S.A. 32°56N 116°19W 79 N10
Água Clara Brazil 20°25S 52°45W 93 H8
Agua Fria △ U.S.A. 34°14N 112°0W 77 J8
Agua Hechicera Mexico 32°28N 116°15W 79 N10
Agua Prieta Mexico 31°18N 109°34W 86 A3
Aguadilla Puerto Rico 18°26N 67°10W 89 d
Aguadulce Panama 8°15N 80°32W 88 E3
Aguanga U.S.A. 33°27N 116°51W 79 M10
Aguanish Canada 50°14N 62°2W 73 B7
Aguanish → Canada 50°13N 62°5W 73 B7
Aguapey → Argentina 29°7S 56°36W 94 B4
Aguaray Guazú → Paraguay 24°47S 57°19W 94 A4
Aguarico → Ecuador 0°59S 75°11W 92 D3
Aguaro-Guariquito △ Venezuela 8°20N 66°35W 89 E6
Aguas Blancas Chile 24°15S 69°55W 94 A2
Aguas Calientes, Sierra de Argentina 25°26S 66°40W 94 B2
Aguascalientes Mexico 21°53N 102°18W 86 C4
Aguascalientes ☑ Mexico 22°0N 102°20W 86 C4
Aguila, Punta Puerto Rico 17°57N 67°13W 89 d
Aguilares Argentina 27°26S 65°35W 94 B2
Águilas Spain 37°23N 1°35W 21 D5
Agüimes Canary Is. 27°58N 15°27W 24 G4
Aguja, C. de la Colombia 11°18N 74°12W 90 B3
Agujereada, Pta. Puerto Rico 18°30N 67°8W 89 d
Agulhas, C. S. Africa 34°52S 20°0E 56 E3
Agulo Canary Is. 28°11N 17°12W 24 F2
Agung, Gunung Indonesia 8°20S 115°28E 37 J18
Agur Uganda 2°28N 32°55E 54 B3
Agusan → Phil. 9°0N 125°30E 37 C7
Aha Mts. Botswana 19°45S 21°0E 56 B3
Ahaggar Algeria 23°0N 6°30E 50 D7
Ahar Iran 38°35N 47°0E 44 B5
Ahiara B. N.Z. 35°5S 173°5E 59 A4
Ahipara B. N.Z. 35°5S 173°5E 59 A4
Ahiri India 19°30N 80°0E 40 K12
Ahmad Wal Pakistan 29°18N 65°58E 42 E1
Ahmadabad India 23°0N 72°40E 42 H5
Ahmadābād Khorāsān, Iran 35°3N 60°50E 45 C9
Aḥmadābād Khorāsān, Iran 35°49N 59°42E 45 C8
Aḥmadī Iran 27°56N 56°42E 45 E8
Ahmadnagar India 19°7N 74°46E 40 K9
Ahmadpur East Pakistan 29°12N 71°10E 42 E4
Ahmadpur Lamma Pakistan 28°19N 70°3E 42 E4
Ahmedabad = Ahmadabad India 23°0N 72°40E 42 H5
Ahmednagar = Ahmadnagar India 19°7N 74°46E 40 K9
Ahome Mexico 25°55N 109°11W 86 B3
Ahoskie U.S.A. 36°17N 76°59W 85 C16
Ahram Iran 28°52N 51°16E 45 D6
Ahrax Pt. Malta 36°0N 14°22E 25 D1
Ahuachapán El Salv. 13°54N 89°52W 88 D2
Ahvāz Iran 31°20N 48°40E 45 D6
Ahvenanmaa = Åland Finland 60°15N 20°0E 9 F19
Aḥwar Yemen 13°30N 46°40E 47 E4
Ai → India 26°26N 90°44E 43 F14
Ai-Ais Namibia 27°54S 17°59E 56 D2
Ai-Ais and Fish River Canyon △ Namibia 24°45S 17°15E 56 C2
Aichi ☑ Japan 35°0N 137°15E 31 G8
Aigrettes, Pte. des Réunion 21°3S 55°13E 53 c
Aiguá Uruguay 34°13S 54°46W 95 C5
Aigues-Mortes France 43°35N 4°12E 20 E6
Aihui = Heihe China 50°10N 127°30E 33 A7
Aija Peru 9°50S 77°45W 92 E3
Aikawa Japan 38°2N 138°15E 30 E9
Aiken U.S.A. 33°34N 81°43W 85 E14
Aileron Australia 22°39S 133°20E 62 C1
Aillik Canada 55°11N 59°18W 73 A8
Ailsa Craig Canada 43°8N 81°33W 82 C3
Ailsa Craig U.K. 55°15N 5°6W 11 F3
Aim Russia 59°0N 133°55E 29 D14
Aimere Indonesia 8°45S 121°3E 37 F6
Aimogasta Argentina 28°33S 66°50W 94 B2
Aïn Ben Tili Mauritania 25°59N 9°27W 50 C4
Aïn-Sefra Algeria 32°47N 0°37W 50 B5
Ain Sudr Egypt 29°50N 33°6E 46 F2
Aïn Témouchent Algeria 35°16N 1°8W 50 A5
Ainaži Latvia 57°50N 24°24E 9 H21
Ainsworth U.S.A. 42°33N 99°52W 80 D4
Aiquile Bolivia 18°10S 65°10W 92 G5
Aïr Niger 18°30N 8°0E 50 E7
Air Force I. Canada 67°58N 74°5W 69 D17
Air Hitam Malaysia 1°55N 103°11E 39 M4
Airdrie Canada 51°18N 114°2W 70 C6
Airdrie U.K. 55°52N 3°57W 11 F5
Aire → U.K. 53°43N 0°55W 12 D7
Aire, I. de l' Spain 39°48N 4°16E 24 B11
Aire → France 49°26N 5°0E 20 B6
Ait India 25°54N 79°14E 43 G8
Aitkin U.S.A. 46°32N 93°42W 80 B7
Aitutaki Cook Is. 18°13S 159°45W 65 J12
Aiud Romania 46°19N 23°44E 17 E12
Aix-en-Provence France 43°32N 5°27E 20 E6
Aix-la-Chapelle = Aachen Germany 50°45N 6°6E 16 C4
Aix-les-Bains France 45°41N 5°53E 20 D6
Aizawl India 23°40N 92°44E 41 H18

Aizkraukle Latvia 56°36N 25°11E 9 H21
Aizpute Latvia 56°43N 21°40E 9 H19
Aizuwakamatsu Japan 37°30N 139°56E 30 F9
Ajaccio France 41°55N 8°40E 20 F8
Ajai △ Uganda 2°52N 31°16E 54 B3
Ajaigarh India 24°52N 80°16E 43 G9
Ajalpan Mexico 18°22N 97°15W 87 D5
Ajanta Ra. India 20°28N 75°50E 40 J9
Ajari Rep. = Ajaria ☑ Georgia 41°30N 42°0E 19 F7
Ajaria ☑ Georgia 41°30N 42°0E 19 F7
Ajax Canada 43°50N 79°1W 82 C5
Ajdābiyā Libya 30°54N 20°4E 51 B10
Ajka Hungary 47°4N 17°31E 17 E9
'Ajlūn Jordan 32°18N 35°47E 46 C4
'Ajlūn ☑ Jordan 32°18N 35°47E 46 C4
'Ajman U.A.E. 25°25N 55°30E 45 E7
Ajmer India 26°28N 74°37E 42 F5
Ajnala India 31°50N 74°48E 42 D6
Ajo U.S.A. 32°22N 112°52W 77 K7
Ajo, C. de Spain 43°31N 3°35W 21 A4
Akabira Japan 43°33N 142°5E 30 C11
Akamas △ Cyprus 35°3N 32°18E 25 D11
Akan △ Japan 43°20N 144°20E 30 C12
Akanthou Cyprus 35°22N 33°45E 25 D12
Akaroa N.Z. 43°49S 172°59E 59 E4
Akashi Japan 34°45N 134°58E 31 G7
Akbarpur Bihar, India 24°39N 83°58E 43 G10
Akbarpur Ut. P., India 26°25N 82°32E 43 F10
Akçakale Turkey 36°41N 38°56E 44 B3
Akdoğan = Lysi Cyprus 35°6N 33°41E 25 D12
Akelamo Indonesia 1°35N 129°40E 37 D7
Aketi Dem. Rep. of the Congo 2°38N 23°47E 52 D4
Akhisar Turkey 38°56N 27°48E 23 E12
Akhnur India 32°52N 74°45E 43 C6
Akhtyrka = Okhtyrka Ukraine 50°25N 35°0E 19 D5
Aki Japan 33°30N 133°54E 31 H6
Akimiski I. Canada 52°50N 81°30W 72 B3
Akincilar = Louroujina Cyprus 35°0N 33°28E 25 E12
Akita Japan 39°45N 140°7E 30 E10
Akita ☑ Japan 39°40N 140°30E 30 E10
Akjoujt Mauritania 19°45N 14°15W 50 E3
Akkeshi Japan 43°2N 144°51E 30 C12
'Akko Israel 32°55N 35°4E 46 C4
Aklavik Canada 68°12N 135°0W 68 D4
Aklera India 24°26N 76°32E 42 G7
Akola India 20°42N 77°2E 40 J10
Akordat Eritrea 15°30N 37°40E 47 D2
Akpatok I. Canada 60°25N 68°8W 69 E18
Åkrahamn Norway 59°15N 5°10E 9 G11
Akranes Iceland 64°19N 22°5W 8 D2
Akron Colo., U.S.A. 40°10N 103°13W 76 F12
Akron Ohio, U.S.A. 41°5N 81°31W 82 E3
Akrotiri Cyprus 34°36N 32°57E 25 E11
Akrotiri Bay Cyprus 34°35S 33°10E 25 E12
Aksai Chin China 35°15N 79°55E 43 B8
Aksaray Turkey 38°25N 34°2E 44 B2
Aksay = Aqsay Kazakhstan 51°11N 53°0E 19 D9
Akşehir Turkey 38°18N 31°30E 44 B1
Akşehir Gölü Turkey 38°30N 31°25E 19 G5
Aksu China 41°5N 80°10E 32 B3
Aksum Ethiopia 14°5N 38°40E 47 E2
Aktsyabrski Belarus 52°38N 28°53E 17 B15
Aktyubinsk = Aqtöbe Kazakhstan 50°17N 57°10E 19 D10
Akure Nigeria 7°15N 5°5E 50 G7
Akureyri Iceland 65°40N 18°6W 8 D4
Akuseki-Shima Japan 29°27N 129°37E 31 K4
Akyab = Sittwe Burma 20°18N 92°45E 41 J18
Al 'Adan Yemen 12°45N 45°0E 47 E4
Al Aḥsā = Hasa Si. Arabia 25°50N 49°0E 45 E6
Al Ajfar Si. Arabia 27°26N 43°0E 44 E4
Al Amādīyah Iraq 37°5N 43°30E 44 B4
Al 'Amārah Iraq 31°55N 47°15E 44 D5
Al Anbār ☑ Iraq 33°25N 42°0E 44 C4
Al 'Aqabah Jordan 29°31N 35°0E 46 F4
Al 'Aqabah ☑ Jordan 29°30N 35°0E 46 F4
Al Arak Syria 34°38N 38°35E 44 C3
Al 'Aramah Si. Arabia 25°30N 46°0E 44 E5
Al 'Arṭāwīyah Si. Arabia 26°31N 45°20E 44 E5
Al 'Aşimah = 'Amman ☑ Jordan 31°40N 36°30E 46 D5
Al 'Assāfiyah Si. Arabia 28°17N 38°59E 44 D3
Al 'Awdah Si. Arabia 25°32N 45°41E 44 E5
Al 'Ayn Si. Arabia 25°4N 38°6E 44 E3
Al 'Ayn U.A.E. 24°15N 55°45E 45 E7
Al 'Azīzīyah Iraq 32°54N 45°4E 44 C5
Al Bāb Syria 36°23N 37°29E 44 B3
Al Bad' Si. Arabia 28°28N 35°1E 44 D2
Al Bādī Iraq 35°56N 41°32E 44 C4
Al Baḥrah Kuwait 29°40N 47°52E 44 D5
Al Baḥral Mayyit = Dead Sea Asia 31°30N 35°30E 46 D4
Al Balqā' ☑ Jordan 32°5N 35°45E 46 C4
Al Bārūk, J. Lebanon 33°39N 35°40E 46 B4
Al Başrah Iraq 30°30N 47°50E 44 D5
Al Baṭhā Iraq 31°6N 45°53E 44 D5
Al Batrūn Lebanon 34°15N 35°40E 46 A4
Al Bayḍā Libya 32°50N 21°44E 51 B10
Al Bi'r Si. Arabia 28°51N 36°16E 44 D3
Al Bukayrīyah Si. Arabia 26°9N 43°40E 44 E4
Al Burayj Syria 34°15N 36°46E 46 A5
Al Faḍilī Si. Arabia 26°58N 49°10E 45 E6
Al Fallūjah Iraq 33°20N 43°55E 44 C4
Al Fāw Iraq 30°0N 48°30E 45 D6
Al Fujayrah U.A.E. 25°7N 56°18E 45 E8
Al Ghadaf, W. → Jordan 31°26N 36°43E 46 D5
Al Ghammās Iraq 31°45N 44°37E 44 D5
Al Ghazālah Si. Arabia 26°48N 41°19E 44 E4
Al Ḥadīthah Iraq 34°0N 41°13E 44 C4
Al Ḥadīthah Si. Arabia 31°28N 37°8E 46 D3
Al Ḥadr Iraq 35°35N 42°44E 44 C4

Al Ḥājānah *Syria* 33°20N 36°33E **46** B5
Al Ḥajar al Gharbī *Oman* 24°10N 56°15E **45** E8
Al Ḥamad *Si. Arabia* 31°30N 39°30E **44** D3
Al Ḥamdānīyah *Syria* 35°25N 36°50E **46** A3
Al Ḥamīdīyah *Syria* 34°42N 35°57E **46** A4
Al Ḥammār *Iraq* 30°57N 46°51E **44** D5
Al Ḥamrā' *Si. Arabia* 24°2N 38°55E **44** E3
Al Ḥamzah *Iraq* 31°43N 44°58E **44** D5
Al Ḥanākīyah *Si. Arabia* 24°51N 40°31E **44** E4
Al Ḥarūj al Aswad *Libya* 27°0N 17°10E **51** C9
Al Ḥasakah *Syria* 36°35N 40°45E **44** B4
Al Ḥayy *Iraq* 32°5N 46°5E **44** C5
Al Ḥijarah *Asia* 30°0N 44°0E **44** D4
Al Ḥillah *Iraq* 32°30N 44°25E **44** C5
Al Ḥillah *Si. Arabia* 23°35N 46°50E **47** B4
Al Ḥindīyah *Iraq* 32°30N 44°10E **44** C5
Al Ḥirmil *Lebanon* 34°26N 36°24E **46** A5
Al Hoceïma *Morocco* 35°8N 3°58W **50** A5
Al Ḥudaydah *Yemen* 14°50N 43°0E **47** E3
Al Ḥudūd ash Shamālīyah □
  Si. Arabia 29°10N 42°30E **44** D4
Al Ḥufūf *Si. Arabia* 25°25N 49°45E **45** E6
Al Ḥumaydah *Si. Arabia* 29°14N 34°56E **44** D2
Al Ḥunayy *Si. Arabia* 25°58N 48°45E **45** E6
Al Īsāwīyah *Si. Arabia* 30°43N 37°59E **44** D3
Al Jafr *Jordan* 30°18N 36°14E **46** E5
Al Jaghbūb *Libya* 29°42N 24°38E **51** C10
Al Jahrah *Kuwait* 29°25N 47°40E **44** D5
Al Jalāmīd *Si. Arabia* 31°20N 40°6E **44** D3
Al Jamalīyah *Qatar* 25°37N 51°5E **45** E6
Al Janūb □ *Lebanon* 33°20N 35°20E **46** B4
Al Jawf *Libya* 24°10N 23°24E **51** D10
Al Jawf *Si. Arabia* 29°55N 39°40E **44** D3
Al Jazair = Algeria ■
  Africa 28°30N 2°0E **50** C6
Al Jazirah *Iraq* 33°30N 44°0E **44** C5
Al Jithāmīyah *Si. Arabia* 27°41N 41°43E **44** E4
Al Jubayl *Si. Arabia* 27°0N 49°50E **45** E6
Al Jubaylah *Si. Arabia* 24°55N 46°25E **44** E5
Al Jubb *Si. Arabia* 27°11N 42°17E **44** E4
Al Junaynah *Sudan* 13°27N 22°45E **51** F10
Al Kabā'ish *Iraq* 30°58N 47°0E **44** D5
Al Karak *Jordan* 31°11N 35°42E **46** D4
Al Karak □ *Jordan* 31°0N 36°0E **46** E5
Al Kāẓimīyah *Iraq* 33°22N 44°18E **44** C5
Al Khāburah *Oman* 23°57N 57°5E **45** F8
Al Khafji *Si. Arabia* 28°24N 48°29E **45** E6
Al Khalīl *West Bank* 31°32N 35°6E **46** D4
Al Khāliṣ *Iraq* 33°49N 44°32E **44** C5
Al Kharsānīyah
  Si. Arabia 27°13N 49°18E **45** E6
Al Khaṣab *Oman* 26°14N 56°15E **45** E8
Al Khawr *Qatar* 25°41N 51°30E **45** E6
Al Khiḍr *Iraq* 31°12N 45°33E **44** D5
Al Khiyām *Lebanon* 33°20N 35°36E **46** B4
Al Khobar *Si. Arabia* 26°17N 50°12E **45** E6
Al Khums *Libya* 32°40N 14°17E **51** B8
Al Kiswah *Syria* 33°23N 36°14E **46** B5
Al Kūfah *Iraq* 32°2N 44°24E **44** C5
Al Kufrah *Libya* 24°17N 23°15E **51** D10
Al Kuhayfīyah *Si. Arabia* 27°12N 43°3E **44** E4
Al Kūt *Iraq* 32°30N 46°0E **44** C5
Al Kuwayt *Kuwait* 29°30N 48°0E **44** D5
Al Labwah *Lebanon* 34°11N 36°20E **46** A5
Al Lādhiqīyah *Syria* 35°30N 35°45E **44** C2
Al Līth *Si. Arabia* 20°9N 40°15E **47** C3
Al Liwā' *Oman* 24°31N 56°36E **45** E8
Al Luḥayyah *Yemen* 15°45N 42°40E **47** D3
Al Madīnah *Iraq* 30°57N 47°16E **44** D5
Al Madīnah *Si. Arabia* 24°35N 39°52E **44** E3
Al Mafraq *Jordan* 32°17N 36°14E **46** C5
Al Mafraq □ *Jordan* 32°0N 37°0E **46** C5
Al Maghreb = Morocco ■
  N. Afr. 32°0N 5°50W **50** B4
Al Maḥmūdīyah *Iraq* 33°3N 44°21E **44** C5
Al Majma'ah *Si. Arabia* 25°57N 45°22E **44** E5
Al Makhruq, W. ↠
  Jordan 31°28N 37°0E **46** D6
Al Makhūl *Si. Arabia* 26°37N 42°39E **44** E4
Al Manāmah *Bahrain* 26°10N 50°30E **45** E6
Al Maqwa' *Kuwait* 29°10N 47°59E **44** D5
Al Marāḥ *Si. Arabia* 25°35N 49°35E **44** E6
Al Marj *Libya* 32°25N 20°30E **51** B10
Al Maṭlā *Kuwait* 29°24N 47°40E **44** D5
Al Mawṣil *Iraq* 36°15N 43°5E **44** B4
Al Mayādin *Syria* 35°1N 40°27E **44** C4
Al Mazār *Jordan* 31°4N 35°41E **46** D4
Al Midhnab *Si. Arabia* 25°50N 44°18E **44** E5
Al Minā' *Lebanon* 34°24N 35°49E **46** A4
Al Miqdādīyah *Iraq* 34°0N 45°0E **44** C5
Al Mubarraz *Si. Arabia* 25°30N 49°40E **45** E6
Al Mudawwarah *Jordan* 29°19N 36°0E **46** F5
Al Mughayrā' *U.A.E.* 24°5N 53°32E **45** E7
Al Muḥarraq *Bahrain* 26°15N 50°40E **45** E6
Al Mukallā *Yemen* 14°33N 49°2E **47** E4
Al Mukhā *Yemen* 13°18N 43°15E **47** E3
Al Musayjīd *Si. Arabia* 24°5N 39°5E **44** E3
Al Musayyib *Iraq* 32°49N 44°20E **44** C5
Al Muthanná □ *Iraq* 29°40N 45°15E **44** D5
Al Muwayliḥ *Si. Arabia* 27°40N 35°30E **44** E2
Al Qā'im *Iraq* 34°21N 41°7E **44** C4
Al Qalībah *Si. Arabia* 28°24N 37°42E **44** D3
Al Qāmishlī *Syria* 37°2N 41°14E **44** B4
Al Qaryatayn *Syria* 34°12N 37°13E **46** A6
Al Qaṣīm □ *Si. Arabia* 26°0N 43°0E **44** E4
Al Qaṭ'ā *Syria* 34°40N 40°48E **44** C4
Al Qaṭīf *Si. Arabia* 26°35N 50°0E **45** E6
Al Qaṭrūn *Libya* 31°12N 36°6E **46** C5
Al Qayṣūmah *Si. Arabia* 28°20N 46°7E **44** D5
Al Quds = Jerusalem
  Israel/West Bank 31°47N 35°10E **46** D4
Al Qunayṭirah *Syria* 32°55N 35°45E **46** B4
Al Qunfudhah *Si. Arabia* 19°3N 41°4E **47** D3
Al Qurnah *Iraq* 31°1N 47°25E **44** D5
Al Quṣayr *Iraq* 30°45N 45°50E **44** D5

Al Quṣayr *Syria* 34°31N 36°34E **46** A5
Al Qutayfah *Syria* 33°44N 36°36E **46** B5
Al 'Ubaylah *Si. Arabia* 21°59N 50°57E **47** C5
Al 'Uḍaylīyah *Si. Arabia* 25°8N 49°18E **45** E6
Al 'Ulā *Si. Arabia* 26°35N 38°0E **44** E3
Al 'Uqayr *Si. Arabia* 25°40N 50°15E **45** E6
Al 'Uwaynid *Si. Arabia* 24°50N 46°0E **44** E5
Al 'Uwayqīlah *Si. Arabia* 30°30N 42°10E **44** D4
Al 'Uyūn *Ḥijāz, Si. Arabia* 24°33N 39°35E **44** E3
Al 'Uyūn *Najd, Si. Arabia* 26°30N 43°50E **44** E4
Al 'Uzayr *Iraq* 31°19N 47°25E **44** D5
Al Wajh *Si. Arabia* 26°10N 36°30E **44** E3
Al Wakrah *Qatar* 25°10N 51°40E **45** E6
Al Waqbah *Si. Arabia* 28°48N 45°33E **44** D5
Al Wari'āh *Si. Arabia* 27°51N 47°25E **44** E5
Al Yaman = Yemen ■
  Asia 15°0N 44°0E **47** E3
Ala Dağ *Turkey* 37°44N 35°9E **44** B2
Ala Tau *Asia* 45°30N 80°40E **28** E9
Ala Tau Shankou = Dzungarian
  Gate *Asia* 45°10N 82°0E **32** B3
Alabama □ *U.S.A.* 33°0N 87°0W **85** J11
Alabama ↠ *U.S.A.* 31°8N 87°57W **85** F11
Alabaster *U.S.A.* 33°15N 86°49W **85** J2
Alaçam Dağları *Turkey* 39°18N 28°49E **23** E13
Alachua *U.S.A.* 29°47N 82°30W **85** G13
Alagoa Grande *Brazil* 7°3S 35°35W **93** E11
Alagoas □ *Brazil* 9°0S 36°0W **93** E11
Alagoinhas *Brazil* 12°7S 38°20W **93** F11
Alaior *Spain* 39°57N 4°8E **24** B11
Alajero *Canary Is.* 28°3N 17°13W **24** F2
Alajuela *Costa Rica* 10°2N 84°8W **88** D3
Alakamisy *Madag.* 21°19S 47°14E **57** C8
Alaknanda ↠ *India* 30°8N 78°36E **43** D8
Alakurtti *Russia* 66°58N 30°25E **8** C24
Alamarvdasht *Iran* 27°37N 52°59E **45** E7
Alameda *Calif., U.S.A.* 37°46N 122°15W **78** H4
Alameda *N. Mex.,*
  U.S.A. 35°11N 106°37W **77** J10
Alamo *U.S.A.* 37°22N 115°10W **79** H11
Alamogordo *U.S.A.* 32°54N 105°57W **77** K11
Alamos *Mexico* 27°1N 108°56W **86** B3
Alamosa *U.S.A.* 37°28N 105°52W **77** H11
Åland *Finland* 60°15N 20°0E **9** F19
Ålands hav *Europe* 60°0N 19°30E **9** G18
Alania = North Ossetia □
  Russia 43°30N 44°30E **19** F7
Alanya *Turkey* 36°38N 32°0E **44** B1
Alaotra, Farihin' *Madag.* 17°30S 48°30E **57** B8
Alapayevsk *Russia* 57°52N 61°42E **28** D7
Alappuzha = Alleppey
  India 9°30N 76°28E **40** Q10
Alaró *Spain* 39°42N 2°47E **24** B9
Alarobia-Vohiposa
  Madag. 20°59S 47°9E **57** C8
Alaşehir *Turkey* 38°23N 28°30E **23** E13
Alaska □ *U.S.A.* 64°0N 154°0W **74** C9
Alaska, G. of *Pac. Oc.* 58°0N 145°0W **68** F3
Alaska Peninsula *U.S.A.* 56°0N 159°0W **74** D8
Alaska Range *U.S.A.* 62°50N 151°0W **68** E1
Ălāt *Azerbaijan* 39°58N 49°25E **45** B6
Alatau Shan = Ala Tau
  Asia 45°30N 80°40E **28** E9
Alatyr *Russia* 54°55N 46°35E **18** D8
Alausi *Ecuador* 2°0S 78°50W **92** D3
Alava, C. *U.S.A.* 48°10N 124°44W **76** B1
Alavo = Alavus *Finland* 62°35N 23°36E **8** E20
Alavus *Finland* 62°35N 23°36E **8** E20
Alawa ◊ *Australia* 15°42S 134°39E **62** B1
Alawoona *Australia* 34°45S 140°30E **63** E3
Alayawarra ◊ *Australia* 22°0S 134°30E **62** C1
'Alayh *Lebanon* 33°46N 35°33E **46** B4
Alba *Italy* 44°42N 8°2E **20** D8
Alba-Iulia *Romania* 46°8N 23°39E **17** E12
Albacete *Spain* 39°0N 1°50W **21** C5
Albacutya, L. *Australia* 35°45S 141°58E **63** F3
Albanel, L. *Canada* 50°55N 73°12W **72** B5
Albania ■ *Europe* 41°0N 20°0E **23** D9
Albany *Australia* 35°1S 117°58E **61** G2
Albany *Ga., U.S.A.* 31°35N 84°10W **85** F12
Albany *N.Y., U.S.A.* 42°39N 73°45W **83** D11
Albany *Oreg., U.S.A.* 44°38N 123°6W **76** D2
Albany *Tex., U.S.A.* 32°44N 99°18W **84** E5
Albany ↠ *Canada* 52°17N 81°31W **72** B3
Albarca, C. d' *Spain* 39°4N 1°22E **24** B7
Albardón *Argentina* 31°20S 68°30W **94** C2
Albatross B. *Australia* 12°45S 141°30E **62** A3
Albemarle *U.S.A.* 35°21N 80°12W **85** D14
Albemarle Sd. *U.S.A.* 36°5N 76°0W **85** C16
Alberche ↠ *Spain* 39°58N 4°46W **21** C3
Alberdi *Paraguay* 26°14S 58°20W **94** B4
Alberga ↠ *Australia* 27°6S 135°33E **63** D2
Albert, L. *Africa* 1°30N 31°0E **54** B3
Albert, L. *Australia* 35°30S 139°10E **63** F2
Albert Edward Ra.
  Australia 18°17S 127°57E **60** C4
Albert Lea *U.S.A.* 43°39N 93°22W **80** D7
Albert Nile ↠ *Uganda* 3°36N 32°2E **54** B3
Albert Town *Bahamas* 22°37N 74°33W **89** B5
Alberta □ *Canada* 54°40N 115°0W **70** C6
Alberti *Argentina* 35°1S 60°16W **94** D3
Albertinia *S. Africa* 34°11S 21°34E **56** E3
Alberton *Canada* 46°50N 64°0W **73** C7
Albertville *France* 45°40N 6°22E **20** D7
Albertville *U.S.A.* 34°16N 86°13W **85** D11
Albi *France* 43°56N 2°9E **20** E5
Albia *U.S.A.* 41°2N 92°48W **80** E7
Albina *Suriname* 5°37N 54°15W **93** B8
Albina, Ponta *Angola* 15°52S 11°44E **56** B1
Albion *Mich., U.S.A.* 42°15N 84°45W **81** D11
Albion *Nebr., U.S.A.* 41°42N 98°0W **80** E4
Albion *Pa., U.S.A.* 41°53N 80°22W **82** E4
Alborán *Medit. S.* 35°57N 3°0W **21** E4
Ålborg = Aalborg *Denmark* 57°2N 9°54E **9** H13
Alborz, Reshteh-ye Kūhhā-ye
  Iran 36°0N 52°0E **45** C7
Albufeira *Portugal* 37°5N 8°15W **21** D1
Albuquerque *U.S.A.* 35°5N 106°39W **77** J10

Albuquerque, Cayos de
  Caribbean 12°10N 81°50W **88** D3
Alburg *U.S.A.* 44°59N 73°18W **83** B11
Albury *Australia* 36°3S 146°56E **63** F4
Alcalá de Henares *Spain* 40°28N 3°22W **21** B4
Alcalá la Real *Spain* 37°27N 3°57W **21** D4
Álcamo *Italy* 37°59N 12°55E **22** F5
Alcañiz *Spain* 41°2N 0°8W **21** B5
Alcântara *Brazil* 2°0S 44°30W **93** D10
Alcántara, Embalse de
  Spain 39°44N 6°50W **21** C2
Alcantarilla *Spain* 37°59N 1°12W **21** D5
Alcaraz, Sierra de *Spain* 38°40N 2°20W **21** C4
Alcaudete *Spain* 37°35N 4°5W **21** D3
Alcázar de San Juan
  Spain 39°24N 3°12W **21** C4
Alchevsk *Ukraine* 48°30N 38°45E **19** E6
Alcira = Alzira *Spain* 39°9N 0°30W **21** C5
Alcova *U.S.A.* 42°34N 106°43W **76** E10
Alcoy *Spain* 38°43N 0°30W **21** C5
Alcúdia *Spain* 39°51N 3°7E **24** B10
Alcúdia, B. d' *Spain* 39°47N 3°15E **24** B10
Aldama *Mexico* 23°0N 98°4W **87** C5
Aldan *Russia* 58°40N 125°30E **29** D13
Aldan ↠ *Russia* 63°28N 129°35E **29** C13
Aldea, Pta. de la
  Canary Is. 28°0N 15°50W **24** G4
Aldeburgh *U.K.* 52°10N 1°37E **13** E9
Alder Pk. *U.S.A.* 35°53N 121°22W **78** K5
Alderney *U.K.* 49°42N 2°11W **13** H5
Aldershot *U.K.* 51°15N 0°44W **13** F7
Aledo *U.S.A.* 41°12N 90°45W **80** E8
Aleg *Mauritania* 17°3N 13°55W **50** E3
Alegranza *Canary Is.* 29°23N 13°32W **24** E6
Alegranza, I. *Canary Is.* 29°23N 13°32W **24** E6
Alegre *Brazil* 20°50S 41°30W **95** A7
Alegrete *Brazil* 29°40S 56°0W **95** B4
Aleksandriya = Oleksandriya
  Ukraine 50°37N 26°19E **17** C14
Allah Dad *Pakistan* 25°38N 67°34E **42** G2
Aleksandrov Gay *Russia* 50°9N 48°34E **19** D8
Aleksandrovsk-Sakhalinskiy
  Russia 50°50N 142°20E **29** D15
Aleksandry, Zemlya
  Russia 80°25N 48°0E **28** A5
Além Paraíba *Brazil* 21°52S 42°41W **95** A7
Alemania *Argentina* 25°40S 65°30W **94** B2
Alemania *Chile* 25°10S 69°55W **94** B2
Alençon *France* 48°27N 0°4E **20** B4
Alenquer *Brazil* 1°56S 54°46W **93** D8
'Alenuihāhā Channel
  U.S.A. 20°30N 156°0W **75** L8
Aleppo = Ḥalab *Syria* 36°10N 37°15E **44** B3
Aléria *France* 42°5N 9°26E **20** E9
Alert *Canada* 83°2N 60°0W **69** A20
Alès *France* 44°9N 4°5E **20** D6
Alessándria *Italy* 44°54N 8°37E **20** D8
Ålesund *Norway* 62°28N 6°12E **8** E12
Aleutian Basin *Pac. Oc.* 57°0N 177°0E **64** B9
Aleutian Is. *Pac. Oc.* 52°0N 175°0W **74** E5
Aleutian Range *U.S.A.* 60°0N 154°0W **74** D9
Aleutian Trench *Pac. Oc.* 48°0N 180°0E **4** D17
Alexander *U.S.A.* 47°51N 103°39W **80** B2
Alexander, Mt.
  Australia 28°58S 120°16E **61** E3
Alexander Arch. *U.S.A.* 56°0N 136°0W **68** F4
Alexander Bay *S. Africa* 28°40S 16°30E **56** D2
Alexander City *U.S.A.* 32°56N 85°58W **85** E12
Alexander I. *Antarctica* 69°0S 70°0W **5** C17
Alexandra *Australia* 37°8S 145°40E **63** F4
Alexandra *N.Z.* 45°14S 169°25E **59** F2
Alexandra Falls *Canada* 60°29N 116°18W **70** A5
Alexandria = El Iskandarîya
  Egypt 31°13N 29°58E **51** B11
Alexandria *B.C.,*
  Canada 52°35N 122°27W **70** C4
Alexandria *Ont.,*
  Canada 45°19N 74°38W **83** A10
Alexandria *Romania* 43°57N 25°24E **17** G13
Alexandria *S. Africa* 33°38S 26°28E **56** E4
Alexandria *U.K.* 55°59N 4°35W **11** F4
Alexandria *La., U.S.A.* 31°18N 92°27W **84** F8
Alexandria *Minn.,*
  U.S.A. 45°53N 95°22W **80** C6
Alexandria *S. Dak.,*
  U.S.A. 43°39N 97°47W **80** D5
Alexandria *Va., U.S.A.* 38°49N 77°5W **81** F15
Alexandria Bay *U.S.A.* 44°20N 75°55W **83** B9
Alexandrina, L.
  Australia 35°25S 139°10E **63** F2
Alexandroupoli *Greece* 40°50N 25°54E **23** D11
Alexis ↠ *Canada* 52°33N 56°8W **73** B8
Alexis Creek *Canada* 52°10N 123°20W **70** C4
Aleysk *Russia* 52°40N 83°0E **28** D9
Alfabia *Spain* 39°44N 2°44E **24** B9
Alfenas *Brazil* 21°20S 46°10W **95** A6
Alford *Aberds., U.K.* 57°14N 2°41W **11** D6
Alford *Lincs., U.K.* 53°15N 0°10E **12** D8
Alfred *Maine, U.S.A.* 43°29N 70°43W **83** C14
Alfred *N.Y., U.S.A.* 42°16N 77°48W **82** D7
Alfreton *U.K.* 53°6N 1°24W **12** D6
Algaida *Spain* 39°33N 2°53E **24** B9
Algarve *Portugal* 36°58N 8°20W **21** D1
Algeciras *Spain* 36°9N 5°28W **21** D3
Algemesí *Spain* 39°11N 0°27W **21** C5
Alger *Algeria* 36°42N 3°8E **50** A6
Algeria ■ *Africa* 28°30N 2°0E **50** C6
Alghero *Italy* 40°33N 8°19E **22** D3
Algiers = Alger *Algeria* 36°42N 3°8E **50** A6
Algoa B. *S. Africa* 33°50S 25°45E **56** E4
Algoma *U.S.A.* 44°36N 87°26W **80** C10
Algona *U.S.A.* 43°4N 94°14W **80** D6
Algonac *U.S.A.* 42°37N 82°32W **82** D2
Algonquin △ *Canada* 45°50N 78°30W **72** C4
Alhama de Murcia
  Spain 37°51N 1°25W **21** D5
Alhambra *U.S.A.* 34°5N 118°7W **79** L8
Alhucemas = Al Hoceïma
  Morocco 35°8N 3°58W **50** A5

'Alī al Gharbī *Iraq* 32°30N 46°45E **44** C5
'Alī ash Sharqī *Iraq* 32°7N 46°44E **44** C5
Äli Bayramlı *Azerbaijan* 39°59N 48°52E **45** B6
Alī Khēl *Afghan.* 33°57N 69°43E **42** C3
Alī Shāh *Iran* 38°9N 45°50E **44** B5
'Alīābād *Golestān, Iran* 36°40N 54°33E **45** B7
'Alīābād *Khorāsān, Iran* 32°30N 57°30E **45** C8
'Alīābād *Kordestān, Iran* 35°4N 46°58E **44** C5
'Alīābād *Yazd, Iran* 31°41N 53°49E **45** D7
Aliağa *Turkey* 38°47N 26°59E **23** E12
Aliákmonas ↠ *Greece* 40°30N 22°36E **23** D10
Alicante *Spain* 38°23N 0°30W **21** C5
Alice *S. Africa* 32°48S 26°55E **56** E4
Alice *U.S.A.* 27°45N 98°5W **84** H5
Alice ↠ *Queens.,*
  Australia 24°2S 144°50E **62** C3
Alice ↠ *Queens.,*
  Australia 15°35S 142°20E **62** B3
Alice Arm *Canada* 55°29N 129°31W **70** B3
Alice Springs *Australia* 23°40S 133°50E **62** C1
Alicedale *S. Africa* 33°15S 26°4E **56** E4
Aliceville *U.S.A.* 33°8N 88°9W **85** E10
Aliganj *India* 27°30N 79°10E **43** F8
Aligarh *Raj., India* 25°55N 76°15E **42** G7
Aligarh *Ut. P., India* 27°55N 78°10E **42** F8
Alīgūdarz *Iran* 33°25N 49°45E **45** C6
Alimia *Greece* 36°16N 27°43E **25** C9
Alingsås *Sweden* 57°56N 12°31E **9** H15
Alipur *Pakistan* 29°25N 70°55E **42** E4
Alipur Duar *India* 26°30N 89°35E **41** F16
Aliquippa *U.S.A.* 40°37N 80°15W **82** F4
Aliwal North *S. Africa* 30°45S 26°45E **56** E4
Aliwal South = Alytus *Lithuania* 54°24N 24°3E **9** J21
Alix *Canada* 52°24N 113°11W **70** C6
Aljustrel *Portugal* 37°55N 8°10W **21** D1
Alkmaar *Neths.* 52°37N 4°45E **15** B4
All American Canal
  U.S.A. 32°45N 115°15W **77** K6
Allagash ↠ *U.S.A.* 47°5N 69°3W **81** B19
Allah Dad *Pakistan* 25°38N 67°34E **42** G2
Allahabad *India* 25°25N 81°58E **43** G9
Allan *Canada* 51°53N 106°4W **71** C7
Allanridge *S. Africa* 27°45S 26°40E **56** D4
Allegany *U.S.A.* 42°6N 78°30E **82** D6
Alleghany ↠ *U.S.A.* 40°27N 80°1W **82** F5
Allegheny Mts. *U.S.A.* 38°15N 80°10W **81** F13
Allegheny Plateau
  U.S.A. 41°30N 78°30W **81** E14
Allegheny Res. *U.S.A.* 41°50N 79°0W **82** E6
Allègre, Pte. *Guadeloupe* 16°22N 61°46W **88** b
Allen, Bog of *Ireland* 53°15N 7°0W **10** C5
Allen, L. *Ireland* 54°8N 8°4W **10** B3
Allendale *U.S.A.* 33°1N 81°18W **85** E14
Allende *Mexico* 28°20N 100°51W **86** B4
Allentown *U.S.A.* 40°37N 75°29W **83** F9
Alleppey *India* 9°30N 76°28E **40** Q10
Aller ↠ *Germany* 52°56N 9°12E **16** B5
Alleynes B. *Barbados* 13°13S 59°39W **89** g
Alliance *Nebr., U.S.A.* 42°6N 102°52W **80** D2
Alliance *Ohio, U.S.A.* 40°55N 81°6W **82** F3
Allier ↠ *France* 46°57N 3°4E **20** C5
Alliford Bay *Canada* 53°12N 131°58W **70** C2
Alligator Pond *Jamaica* 17°52N 77°34W **88** a
Alliston *Canada* 44°9N 79°52W **82** B5
Alloa *U.K.* 56°7N 3°47W **11** E5
Allora *Australia* 28°2S 152°0E **63** D5
Alluitsup Paa *Greenland* 60°30N 45°35W **4** C5
Alma *Canada* 48°35N 71°40W **73** C5
Alma *Ga., U.S.A.* 31°33N 82°28W **85** F13
Alma *Kans., U.S.A.* 39°1N 96°17W **80** F5
Alma *Mich., U.S.A.* 43°23N 84°39W **81** D11
Alma *Nebr., U.S.A.* 40°6N 99°22W **80** E4
Alma *Wis., U.S.A.* 44°20N 91°55W **80** C8
Alma Ata = Almaty
  Kazakhstan 43°15N 76°57E **28** E8
Alma Hill *U.S.A.* 42°2N 78°0W **82** D7
Almada *Portugal* 38°41N 9°8W **21** C1
Almaden *Australia* 17°22S 144°40E **62** B3
Almadén *Spain* 38°49N 4°52E **21** C3
Almalyk = Olmaliq
  Uzbekistan 40°50N 69°35E **28** E7
Almanor, L. *U.S.A.* 40°14N 121°9W **76** F3
Almansa *Spain* 38°51N 1°5W **21** C5
Almanzor, Pico *Spain* 40°15N 5°18W **21** B3
Almanzora ↠ *Spain* 37°14N 1°46W **21** D5
Almaty *Kazakhstan* 43°15N 76°57E **28** E8
Almazán *Spain* 41°30N 2°30W **21** B4
Almeirim *Brazil* 1°30S 52°34W **93** D8
Almelo *Neths.* 52°22N 6°42E **15** B6
Almendralejo *Spain* 38°41N 6°26W **21** C2
Almere-Stad *Neths.* 52°20N 5°15E **15** B5
Almería *Spain* 36°52N 2°27W **21** D4
Almirante *Panama* 9°10N 82°30W **88** E3
Almond ↠ *U.S.A.* 42°19N 77°44W **82** D7
Almont *U.S.A.* 42°55N 83°3W **82** D1
Almonte *Canada* 45°14N 76°12W **83** A8
Almora *India* 29°38N 79°40E **43** E8
Almyrou, Ormos *Greece* 35°23N 24°20E **25** D6
Alness *U.K.* 57°41N 4°16W **11** D4
Alnmouth *U.K.* 55°24N 1°37W **12** B6
Alnwick *U.K.* 55°24N 1°42W **12** B6
Aloi *Uganda* 2°16N 33°10E **54** B3
Alon *Burma* 22°12N 95°5E **41** H19
Alor *Indonesia* 8°15S 124°30E **37** F6
Alor Setar *Malaysia* 6°7N 100°22E **39** c
Alot *India* 23°56N 75°40E **42** H6
Aloysius, Mt. *Australia* 26°0S 128°38E **61** E4
Alpaugh *U.S.A.* 35°53N 119°29W **78** K7
Alpena *U.S.A.* 45°4N 83°27W **81** C12
Alpha *Australia* 23°39S 146°37E **62** C4
Alpha Ridge *Arctic* 84°0N 118°0W **4** A2
Alphen aan den Rijn
  Neths. 52°7N 4°40E **15** B4
Alpine *Ariz., U.S.A.* 33°51N 109°9W **77** K9
Alpine *Calif., U.S.A.* 32°50N 116°46W **79** N10
Alpine *Tex., U.S.A.* 30°22N 103°40W **84** F3
Alps *Europe* 46°30N 9°30E **20** C8
Alpurrurulam *Australia* 20°59S 137°50E **62** C2
Alsace □ *France* 48°15N 7°25E **20** B7

Alsask *Canada* 51°21N 109°59W **71** C7
Alsásua *Spain* 42°54N 2°10W **21** A4
Alsek ↠ *U.S.A.* 59°10N 138°12W **70** B1
Alsta *Norway* 65°58N 12°40E **8** D15
Alston *U.K.* 54°49N 2°25W **12** C5
Alta *Norway* 69°57N 23°10E **8** B20
Alta Gracia *Argentina* 31°40S 64°30W **94** C3
Alta Sierra *U.S.A.* 35°42N 118°33W **79** K8
Altaelva ↠ *Norway* 69°54N 23°17E **8** B20
Altafjorden *Norway* 70°5N 23°5E **8** A20
Altai = Aerhtai Shan
  Mongolia 46°40N 92°45E **32** B4
Altai = Gorno-Altay □
  Russia 51°0N 86°0E **28** D9
Altamaha ↠ *U.S.A.* 31°20N 81°20W **85** F14
Altamira *Brazil* 3°12S 52°10W **93** D8
Altamira *Chile* 25°47S 69°51W **94** B2
Altamira *Mexico* 22°24N 97°55W **87** C5
Altamont *U.S.A.* 42°42N 74°3W **83** D10
Altamura *Italy* 40°49N 16°33E **22** D7
Altanbulag *Mongolia* 50°16N 106°30E **32** A5
Altar *Mexico* 30°43N 111°44W **86** A2
Altar, Gran Desierto de
  Mexico 31°50N 114°10W **86** D2
Altata *Mexico* 24°40N 107°55W **86** C3
Altavista *U.S.A.* 37°6N 79°17W **81** G14
Altay *China* 47°48N 88°10E **32** B3
Altea *Spain* 38°38N 0°2W **21** C5
Altiplano *Bolivia* 17°0S 68°0W **92** G5
Alto Araguaia *Brazil* 17°15S 53°20W **93** G8
Alto Cuchumatanes =
  Cuchumatanes, Sierra de los
  Guatemala 15°35N 91°25W **88** C1
Alto del Carmen *Chile* 28°46S 70°30W **94** B1
Alto Ligonha *Mozam.* 15°30S 38°11E **55** F4
Alto Molocue *Mozam.* 15°50S 37°35E **55** F4
Alto Paraguay □
  Paraguay 21°0S 58°30W **94** A4
Alto Paraná □ *Paraguay* 25°30S 54°50W **95** B5
Alton *Canada* 43°54N 80°5W **82** C4
Alton *U.K.* 51°9N 0°59W **13** F7
Alton *Ill., U.S.A.* 38°53N 90°11W **80** F8
Alton *N.H., U.S.A.* 43°27N 71°13W **83** C13
Altona *Canada* 49°6N 97°33W **71** D9
Altoona *U.S.A.* 40°31N 78°24W **82** F6
Altun Kupri *Iraq* 35°45N 44°9E **44** C5
Altun Shan *China* 38°30N 88°0E **32** C3
Alturas *U.S.A.* 41°29N 120°32W **76** F3
Altus *U.S.A.* 34°38N 99°20W **84** D5
Alucra *Turkey* 40°22N 38°47E **19** F6
Alūksne *Latvia* 57°24N 27°3E **9** H22
Alunite *U.S.A.* 35°59N 114°55W **79** K12
Alusi *Indonesia* 7°35S 131°40E **37** F8
Alva *U.S.A.* 36°48N 98°40W **84** C5
Alvarado *Mexico* 18°46N 95°46W **87** D5
Alvarado *U.S.A.* 32°24N 97°13W **84** E6
Alvaro Obregón, Presa
  Mexico 27°52N 109°52W **86** B3
Alvear *Argentina* 29°5S 56°30W **94** B4
Alvesta *Sweden* 56°54N 14°35E **9** H16
Alvin *U.S.A.* 29°26N 95°15W **84** G7
Alvinston *Canada* 42°49N 81°52W **82** D3
Älvkarleby *Sweden* 60°34N 17°26E **9** F17
Alvord Desert *U.S.A.* 42°30N 118°25W **76** E4
Älvsbyn *Sweden* 65°40N 21°0E **8** D19
Alwar *India* 27°38N 76°34E **42** F7
Alxa Zuoqi *China* 38°50N 105°40E **34** E3
Alyangula *Australia* 13°55S 136°30E **62** A2
Alyata = Ălät *Azerbaijan* 39°58N 49°25E **45** B6
Alyth *U.K.* 56°38N 3°13W **11** E5
Alytus *Lithuania* 54°24N 24°3E **9** J21
Alzada *U.S.A.* 45°2N 104°25W **76** D11
Alzamay *Russia* 55°33N 98°39E **29** D10
Alzira *Spain* 39°9N 0°30W **21** C5
Am Timan *Chad* 11°0N 20°10E **51** F10
Amadeus, L. *Australia* 24°54S 131°0E **61** D5
Amadi
  Dem. Rep. of the Congo 3°40N 26°40E **54** B2
Amâdi *Sudan* 5°29N 30°25E **51** G12
Amadjuak L. *Canada* 65°0N 71°8W **69** E17
Amagansett *U.S.A.* 40°59N 72°9W **83** F12
Amagasaki *Japan* 34°42N 135°23E **31** G7
Amahai *Indonesia* 3°20S 128°55E **37** E7
Amaile *Samoa* 13°59S 171°22W **59** b
Amakusa-Shotō *Japan* 32°15N 130°10E **31** H5
Åmål *Sweden* 59°3N 12°42E **9** G15
Amaliada *Greece* 37°47N 21°22E **23** F9
Amalner *India* 21°5N 75°5E **40** J9
Amamapare *Indonesia* 4°53S 136°38E **37** E9
Amambaí *Brazil* 23°5S 55°13W **95** A4
Amambaí ↠ *Brazil* 23°22S 53°56W **95** A5
Amambay □ *Paraguay* 23°0S 56°0W **95** A4
Amambay, Cordillera de
  S. Amer. 23°0S 55°45W **95** A4
Amami-Guntō *Japan* 27°16N 129°21E **31** L4
Amami-Ō-Shima *Japan* 28°16N 129°21E **31** K4
Aman, Pulau *Malaysia* 5°16N 100°24E **39** c
Amaná, L. *Brazil* 2°35S 64°40W **92** D6
Amanat ↠ *India* 24°7N 84°4E **43** G11
Amanda Park *U.S.A.* 47°28N 123°55W **78** C3
Amankeldi *Kazakhstan* 50°10N 65°10E **28** D7
Amapá *Brazil* 2°5N 50°50W **93** C8
Amapá □ *Brazil* 1°40N 52°0W **93** C8
Amarante *Brazil* 6°14S 42°50W **93** E10
Amaranth *Canada* 50°36N 98°43W **71** C9
Amargosa ↠ *U.S.A.* 36°14N 116°51W **79** J10
Amargosa Desert
  U.S.A. 36°40N 116°30W **79** J10
Amargosa Range
  U.S.A. 36°20N 116°45W **79** J10
Amari *Greece* 35°13N 24°40E **25** D6
Amarillo *U.S.A.* 35°13N 101°50W **84** D4
Amarkantak *India* 22°40N 81°45E **43** H9
Amaro, Mte. *Italy* 42°5N 14°5E **22** C6
Amarpur *India* 25°5N 87°0E **43** G12
Amarwara *India* 22°18N 79°10E **43** H8
Amasya *Turkey* 40°40N 35°50E **19** F6
Amata *Australia* 26°9S 131°9E **61** E5
Amatikulu *S. Africa* 29°3S 31°33E **57** D5

Amatitlán *Guatemala* 14°29N 90°38W **88** D1
Amay *Belgium* 50°33N 5°19E **15** D5
Amazon = Amazonas ➤
  S. Amer. 0°5S 50°0W **93** D8
Amazonas □ *Brazil* 5°0S 65°0W **92** E6
Amazonas ➤ *S. Amer.* 0°5S 50°0W **93** D8
Ambah *India* 26°43N 78°13E **42** F8
Ambahakily *Madag.* 21°36S 43°41E **57** C7
Ambahita *Madag.* 24°1S 45°16E **57** C8
Ambala *India* 30°23N 76°56E **42** D7
Ambanja *Madag.* 13°40S 48°27E **57** A8
Ambararata *Madag.* 15°3S 48°33E **57** B8
Ambarchik *Russia* 69°40N 162°20E **29** C17
Ambarijeby *Madag.* 14°56S 47°41E **57** A8
Ambaro, Helodranon'
  Madag. 13°23S 48°38E **57** A8
Ambato *Ecuador* 1°5S 78°42W **92** D3
Ambato *Madag.* 13°24S 48°29E **57** A8
Ambato, Sierra de
  Argentina 28°25S 66°10W **94** B2
Ambato Boeny *Madag.* 16°28S 46°43E **57** B8
Ambatofinandrahana
  Madag. 20°33S 46°48E **57** C8
Ambatolampy *Madag.* 19°20S 47°35E **57** B8
Ambatomainty *Madag.* 17°41S 45°40E **57** B8
Ambatomanoina *Madag.* 18°18S 47°37E **57** B8
Ambatondrazaka
  Madag. 17°55S 48°28E **57** B8
Ambatosoratra *Madag.* 17°37S 48°31E **57** B8
Ambenja *Madag.* 15°17S 46°58E **57** B8
Amberg *Germany* 49°26N 11°52E **16** D6
Ambergris Cay *Belize* 18°0N 87°55W **87** D7
Amberley *Canada* 44°2N 81°42W **82** B3
Amberley *N.Z.* 43°9S 172°44E **59** E4
Ambikapur *India* 23°15N 83°15E **43** H10
Ambilobé *Madag.* 13°10S 49°3E **57** A8
Ambinanindrano *Madag.* 20°5S 48°23E **57** C8
Ambinanitelo *Madag.* 15°21S 49°35E **57** B8
Ambinda *Madag.* 16°25S 45°52E **57** B8
Amble *U.K.* 55°20N 1°36W **12** B6
Ambleside *U.K.* 54°26N 2°58W **12** C5
Ambo *Peru* 10°5S 76°10W **92** F3
Amboahangy *Madag.* 24°15S 46°22E **57** C8
Ambodifototra *Madag.* 16°59S 49°52E **57** B8
Ambodilazana *Madag.* 18°6S 49°10E **57** B8
Ambodiriana *Madag.* 17°55S 49°18E **57** B8
Ambohidratrimo *Madag.* 18°50S 47°26E **57** B8
Ambohidray *Madag.* 18°36S 48°18E **57** B8
Ambohimahamasina
  Madag. 21°56S 47°11E **57** C8
Ambohimahasoa *Madag.* 21°7S 47°13E **57** C8
Ambohimanga *Madag.* 20°52S 47°36E **57** C8
Ambohimitombo *Madag.* 20°43S 47°26E **57** C8
Ambohitra *Madag.* 12°30S 49°10E **57** A8
Amboise *France* 47°24N 1°2E **20** C4
Ambon *Indonesia* 3°43S 128°12E **37** E7
Ambondro *Madag.* 25°13S 45°44E **57** D8
Amboseli, L. *Kenya* 2°40S 37°10E **54** C4
Amboseli △ *Kenya* 2°37S 37°13E **54** C4
Ambositra *Madag.* 20°31S 47°25E **57** C8
Ambovombe *Madag.* 25°11S 46°5E **57** D8
Amboy *U.S.A.* 34°33N 115°45W **79** L11
Amboyna Cay
  S. China Sea 7°50N 112°50E **36** C4
Ambridge *U.S.A.* 40°36N 80°14W **82** F4
Ambriz *Angola* 7°48S 13°8E **52** F2
Amchitka I. *U.S.A.* 51°32N 179°0E **74** E3
Amderma *Russia* 69°45N 61°30E **28** C7
Amdhi *India* 23°51N 81°27E **43** H9
Ameca *Mexico* 20°33N 104°2W **86** C4
Ameca ➤ *Mexico* 20°41N 105°18W **86** C3
Amecameca de Juárez
  Mexico 19°8N 98°46W **87** D5
Ameland *Neths.* 53°27N 5°45E **15** A5
Amenia *U.S.A.* 41°51N 73°33W **83** E11
America-Antarctica Ridge
  S. Ocean 59°0S 16°0W **5** B2
American Falls *U.S.A.* 42°47N 112°51W **76** E7
American Falls Res.
  U.S.A. 42°47N 112°52W **76** E7
American Fork *U.S.A.* 40°23N 111°48W **76** F8
American Highland
  Antarctica 73°0S 75°0E **5** D6
American Samoa ☑
  Pac. Oc. 14°20S 170°0W **59** b
American Samoa △
  Amer. Samoa 14°15S 170°28W **59** b
Americana *Brazil* 22°45S 47°20W **95** A6
Americus *U.S.A.* 32°4N 84°14W **85** E12
Amersfoort *Neths.* 52°9N 5°23E **15** B5
Amersfoort *S. Africa* 26°59S 29°53E **57** D4
Amery Basin *S. Ocean* 68°15S 74°30E **5** C6
Amery Ice Shelf *Antarctica* 69°30S 72°0E **5** C6
Ames *U.S.A.* 42°2N 93°37W **80** D7
Amesbury *U.S.A.* 42°51N 70°56W **83** D14
Amet *India* 25°18N 73°56E **42** G5
Amga *Russia* 60°50N 132°0E **29** C14
Amga ➤ *Russia* 62°38N 134°32E **29** C14
Amgu *Russia* 45°45N 137°15E **30** B8
Amgun ➤ *Russia* 52°56N 139°38E **29** D14
Amherst *Canada* 45°48N 64°8W **73** C7
Amherst *Mass., U.S.A.* 42°23N 72°31W **83** D12
Amherst *N.Y., U.S.A.* 42°59N 78°48W **82** D6
Amherst *Ohio, U.S.A.* 41°24N 82°14W **82** E2
Amherst I. *Canada* 44°8N 76°43W **83** B8
Amherstburg *Canada* 42°6N 83°6W **72** D3
Amiata, Mte. *Italy* 42°53N 11°37E **22** C4
Amidon *U.S.A.* 46°29N 103°19W **80** B2
Amiens *France* 49°54N 2°16E **20** B5
Aminuis *Namibia* 23°43S 19°21E **56** C2
Amīrābād *Iran* 33°20N 46°16E **44** C5
Amirante Is. *Seychelles* 6°0S 53°0E **26** J7
Amisk *Canada* 56°43N 98°0W **71** B9
Amisk L. *Canada* 54°35N 102°15W **71** C8
Amistad, Presa de la
  Mexico 29°26N 101°3W **86** B4
Amistad △ *U.S.A.* 29°32N 101°12W **84** G4
Amite *U.S.A.* 30°44N 90°30W **85** F9

Amla *India* 21°56N 78°7E **42** J8
Amlapura = Karangasem
  Indonesia 8°27S 115°37E **37** J18
Amlia I. *U.S.A.* 52°4N 173°30W **74** E5
Amlwch *U.K.* 53°24N 4°20W **12** D3
'Ammān *Jordan* 31°57N 35°52E **46** D4
'Ammān □ *Jordan* 31°40N 36°30E **46** D5
'Ammān ✈ (AMM)
  Jordan 31°45N 36°2E **46** D5
Ammanford *U.K.* 51°48N 3°59W **13** F4
Ammassalik = Tasiilaq
  Greenland 65°40N 37°20W **4** C6
Ammochostos = Famagusta
  Cyprus 35°8N 33°55E **25** D12
Ammon *U.S.A.* 43°28N 111°58W **76** E8
Amnat Charoen
  Thailand 15°51N 104°38E **38** E5
Amnura *Bangla.* 24°37N 88°25E **43** G13
Āmol *Iran* 36°23N 52°20E **45** B7
Amorgós *Greece* 36°50N 25°57E **23** F11
Amory *U.S.A.* 33°59N 88°29W **85** E10
Amos *Canada* 48°35N 78°5W **72** C4
Åmot *Norway* 59°57N 9°54E **9** G13
Amoy = Xiamen *China* 24°25N 118°4E **33** D6
Ampanavoana *Madag.* 15°41S 50°22E **57** B9
Ampang *Malaysia* 3°8N 101°45E **39** L3
Ampangalana, Lakandranon'
  Madag. 22°48S 47°50E **57** C8
Ampanihy *Madag.* 24°40S 44°45E **57** C7
Amparafaravola *Madag.* 17°35S 48°13E **57** B8
Ampasinambo *Madag.* 20°31S 48°0E **57** C8
Ampasindava, Helodranon'
  Madag. 13°40S 48°15E **57** A8
Ampasindava, Saikanosy
  Madag. 13°42S 47°55E **57** A8
Ampenan *Indonesia* 8°34S 116°4E **37** K18
Amper ➤ *Germany* 48°29N 11°55E **16** D6
Amphoe Kathu *Thailand* 7°55N 98°21E **39** a
Amphoe Thalang *Thailand* 8°1N 98°20E **39** a
Ampitsikinana *Madag.* 12°57S 49°49E **57** A8
Ampombiantambo
  Madag. 12°42S 48°57E **57** A8
Ampotaka *Madag.* 25°3S 44°41E **57** D7
Ampoza *Madag.* 22°20S 44°44E **57** C7
Amqui *Canada* 48°28N 67°27W **73** C6
Amravati *India* 20°55N 77°45E **40** J10
Amreli *India* 21°35N 71°17E **42** J4
Amritsar *India* 31°35N 74°57E **42** D6
Amroha *India* 28°53N 78°30E **43** E8
Amsterdam *Neths.* 52°23N 4°54E **15** B4
Amsterdam *U.S.A.* 42°56N 74°11W **83** D10
Amsterdam ✈ (AMS)
  Neths. 52°18N 4°45E **15** B4
Amsterdam, I. = Nouvelle
  Amsterdam, Î. *Ind. Oc.* 38°30S 77°30E **3** F13
Amstetten *Austria* 48°7N 14°51E **16** D8
Amudarya ➤ *Uzbekistan* 43°58N 59°34E **28** E6
Amund Ringnes I.
  Canada 78°20N 96°25W **69** B12
Amundsen Abyssal Plain
  S. Ocean 65°0S 125°0W **5** C14
Amundsen Basin *Arctic* 87°30N 80°0E **4** A
Amundsen Gulf *Canada* 71°0N 124°0W **68** C7
Amundsen Ridges
  S. Ocean 69°15S 123°0W **5** C14
Amundsen-Scott *Antarctica* 90°0S 166°0E **5** E
Amundsen Sea *Antarctica* 72°0S 115°0W **5** D15
Amuntai *Indonesia* 2°28S 115°25E **36** E5
Amur ➤ *Russia* 52°56N 141°10E **29** D15
Amurang *Indonesia* 1°5N 124°40E **37** D6
Amursk *Russia* 50°14N 136°54E **29** D14
Amyderya = Amudarya ➤
  Uzbekistan 43°58N 59°34E **28** E6
An Bien *Vietnam* 9°45N 105°0E **39** H5
An Cabhán = Cavan
  Ireland 54°0N 7°22W **10** B4
An Cóbh = Cóbh *Ireland* 51°51N 8°17W **10** E3
An Daingean = Dingle
  Ireland 52°9N 10°17W **10** D1
An Hoa *Vietnam* 15°40N 108°5E **38** E7
An Longfort = Longford
  Ireland 53°43N 7°49W **10** C4
An Muileann gCearr = Mullingar
  Ireland 53°31N 7°21W **10** C4
An Nabatīyah at Tahta
  Lebanon 33°23N 35°27E **46** B4
An Nabk *Si. Arabia* 31°20N 37°20E **44** D3
An Nabk *Syria* 34°2N 36°44E **46** A5
An Nafūd *Si. Arabia* 28°15N 41°0E **44** D4
An Najaf *Iraq* 32°3N 44°15E **44** C5
An Nás = Naas *Ireland* 53°12N 6°40W **10** C5
An Nāşirīyah *Iraq* 31°0N 46°15E **44** D5
An Nhon *Vietnam* 13°55N 109°7E **38** F7
An Nu'ayrīyah *Si. Arabia* 27°30N 48°30E **45** E6
An Nu'mānīyah *Iraq* 32°32N 45°25E **44** C5
An Ros = Rush *Ireland* 53°31N 6°6W **10** C5
An tAonach = Nenagh
  Ireland 52°52N 8°11W **10** D3
An Thoi, Dao *Vietnam* 9°58N 104°0E **39** H5
An tInbhear Mór = Arklow
  Ireland 52°48N 6°10W **10** D5
An Uaimh = Navan *Ireland* 53°39N 6°41W **10** C5
'Anabtā *West Bank* 32°19N 35°7E **46** C4
Anaconda *U.S.A.* 46°8N 112°57W **76** C7
Anacortes *U.S.A.* 48°30N 122°37W **78** B4
Anadarko *U.S.A.* 35°4N 98°15W **84** D5
Anadolu *Turkey* 39°0N 30°0E **19** G5
Anadyr *Russia* 64°35N 177°20E **29** C18
Anadyr ➤ *Russia* 64°55N 176°5E **29** C18
Anadyrskiy Zaliv *Russia* 64°0N 180°0E **29** C19
Anaga, Pta. de *Canary Is.* 28°34N 16°9W **24** F3
'Ānah *Iraq* 34°25N 42°0E **44** C4
Anaheim *U.S.A.* 33°50N 117°55W **79** M9
Anahim Lake *Canada* 52°28N 125°18W **70** C3
Anakapalle *India* 17°42N 83°6E **41** L13
Anakie *Australia* 23°32S 147°45E **62** C4
Analalava *Madag.* 14°35S 48°0E **57** A8
Analavoka *Madag.* 22°23S 46°30E **57** C8

Analipsis *Greece* 39°36N 19°55E **25** A3
Anambar ➤ *Pakistan* 30°15N 68°50E **42** D3
Anambas, Kepulauan
  Indonesia 3°20N 106°30E **36** D3
Anambas Is. = Anambas,
  Kepulauan *Indonesia* 3°20N 106°30E **36** D3
Anamosa *U.S.A.* 42°7N 91°17W **80** D8
Anamur *Turkey* 36°8N 32°58E **44** B2
Anan *Japan* 33°54N 134°40E **31** H7
Anand *India* 22°32N 72°59E **42** H5
Anangu Pitjantjatjara ◎
  Australia 27°0S 132°0E **61** E5
Anantapur *India* 14°39N 77°42E **40** M10
Anantnag *India* 33°45N 75°10E **43** C6
Ananyiv *Ukraine* 47°44N 29°58E **17** E15
Anapa *Russia* 44°53N 37°28E **19** F6
Anápolis *Brazil* 16°15S 48°50W **93** G9
Anapu ➤ *Brazil* 1°53S 50°53W **93** D8
Anār *Iran* 30°55N 55°13E **45** D7
Anārak *Iran* 33°25N 53°40E **45** C7
Anas ➤ *India* 23°26N 74°0E **42** H5
Anatolia = Anadolu
  Turkey 39°0N 30°0E **19** G5
Anatsogno *Madag.* 23°33S 43°46E **57** C7
Añatuya *Argentina* 28°20S 62°50W **94** B3
Anatye ◎ *Australia* 22°29S 137°3E **62** C2
Anaunethad L. *Canada* 60°55N 104°25W **71** A8
Anbyŏn *N. Korea* 39°1N 127°35E **35** E14
Ancaster *Canada* 43°13N 79°59W **82** C5
Anchor Bay *U.S.A.* 38°48N 123°34W **78** G3
Anchorage *U.S.A.* 61°13N 149°54W **68** E2
Anci *China* 39°20N 116°40E **34** E9
Ancohuma, Nevado
  Bolivia 16°0S 68°50W **92** G5
Ancón *Peru* 11°50S 77°10W **92** F3
Ancona *Italy* 43°38N 13°30E **22** C5
Ancud *Chile* 42°0S 73°50W **96** E2
Ancud, G. de *Chile* 42°0S 73°0W **96** E2
Anda *China* 46°24N 125°19E **33** B7
Andacollo *Argentina* 37°10S 70°42W **94** D1
Andacollo *Chile* 30°14S 71°6W **94** C1
Andaingo *Madag.* 18°12S 48°17E **57** B8
Andalgalá *Argentina* 27°40S 66°30W **94** B2
Åndalsnes *Norway* 62°35N 7°43E **8** E12
Andalucía □ *Spain* 37°35N 5°0W **21** D3
Andalusia = Andalucía □
  Spain 37°35N 5°0W **21** D3
Andalusia *U.S.A.* 31°18N 86°29W **85** F11
Andaman Is. *Ind. Oc.* 12°30N 92°45E **27** G11
Andaman Sea *Ind. Oc.* 13°0N 96°0E **36** B1
Andamooka *Australia* 30°27S 137°9E **63** E2
Andapa *Madag.* 14°39S 49°39E **57** A8
Andara *Namibia* 18°2S 21°9E **56** B3
Andenes *Norway* 69°19N 16°18E **8** B17
Andenne *Belgium* 50°28N 5°5E **15** D5
Anderson *Alaska,*
  U.S.A. 64°25N 149°15W **74** C10
Anderson *Calif., U.S.A.* 40°27N 122°18W **76** F2
Anderson *Ind., U.S.A.* 40°10N 85°41W **81** E11
Anderson *Mo., U.S.A.* 36°39N 94°27W **80** G6
Anderson *S.C., U.S.A.* 34°31N 82°39W **85** D13
Anderson ➤ *Canada* 69°42N 129°0W **68** D6
Andes *U.S.A.* 42°12N 74°47W **83** D10
Andes, Cord. de los
  S. Amer. 20°0S 68°0W **92** H5
Andfjorden *Norway* 69°10N 16°20E **8** B17
Andhra Pradesh □ *India* 18°0N 79°0E **40** L11
Andijon *Uzbekistan* 41°10N 72°15E **28** E8
Andikíthira = Antikythira
  Greece 35°52N 23°15E **23** G10
Andilamena *Madag.* 17°1S 48°35E **57** B8
Andīmeshk *Iran* 32°27N 48°21E **45** C6
Andizhan = Andijon
  Uzbekistan 41°10N 72°15E **28** E8
Andoany *Madag.* 13°25S 48°16E **57** A8
Andohahela △ *Madag.* 24°4S 46°44E **57** C8
Andong *S. Korea* 36°40N 128°43E **35** F15
Andongwei *China* 35°6N 119°20E **35** G10
Andorra ■ *Europe* 42°30N 1°30E **20** E4
Andorra La Vella *Andorra* 42°31N 1°32E **20** E4
Andover *U.K.* 51°12N 1°29W **13** F6
Andover *Maine, U.S.A.* 44°38N 70°45W **83** B14
Andover *Mass., U.S.A.* 42°40N 71°8W **83** D13
Andover *N.J., U.S.A.* 40°59N 74°45W **83** F10
Andover *N.Y., U.S.A.* 42°10N 77°48W **82** D7
Andover *Ohio, U.S.A.* 41°36N 80°34W **82** E4
Andøya *Norway* 69°10N 15°50E **8** B16
Andradina *Brazil* 20°54S 51°23W **93** H8
Andrahary *Madag.* 13°37S 49°17E **57** A8
Andramasina *Madag.* 19°11S 47°35E **57** B8
Andranopasy *Madag.* 21°17S 43°44E **57** C7
Andranovory *Madag.* 23°8S 44°10E **57** C7
Andratx *Spain* 39°39N 2°25E **24** B9
Andreanof Is. *U.S.A.* 51°30N 176°0W **74** E4
Andrews *S.C., U.S.A.* 33°27N 79°34W **85** E15
Andrews *Tex., U.S.A.* 32°19N 102°33W **84** E3
Ándria *Italy* 41°13N 16°17E **22** D7
Andriamena *Madag.* 17°26S 47°30E **57** B8
Andriba *Madag.* 17°30S 46°58E **57** B8
Andringitra △ *Madag.* 22°13S 46°56E **57** C8
Androka *Madag.* 24°58S 44°2E **57** C7
Andros *Greece* 37°50N 24°57E **23** F11
Andros I. *Bahamas* 24°30N 78°0W **88** B4
Andros Town *Bahamas* 24°43N 77°47W **88** B4
Androscoggin ➤
  U.S.A. 43°58N 69°52W **83** C14
Andselv *Norway* 69°4N 18°34E **8** B18
Andújar *Spain* 38°3N 4°5W **21** C3
Andulo *Angola* 11°25S 16°45E **52** G3
Anegada *Br. Virgin Is.* 18°45N 64°20W **89** e
Anegada Passage
  W. Indies 18°15N 63°45W **89** D7
Aneto, Pico de *Spain* 42°37N 0°40E **21** A6
Ang Mo Kio *Singapore* 1°23N 103°50E **39** d
Ang Thong *Thailand* 14°35N 100°31E **38** E3
Ang Thong, Ko *Thailand* 9°37N 99°41E **39** b
Ang Thong △ *Thailand* 9°40N 99°43E **39** H2
Angamos, Punta *Chile* 23°1S 70°32W **94** A1

Angara ➤ *Russia* 58°5N 94°20E **29** D10
Angarsk *Russia* 52°30N 104°0E **29** D11
Angas Hills *Australia* 23°0S 127°50E **60** D4
Angaston *Australia* 34°30S 139°8E **63** E2
Ånge *Sweden* 62°31N 15°35E **8** E16
Ángel, Salto = Angel Falls
  Venezuela 5°57N 62°30W **92** B6
Ángel de la Guarda, I.
  Mexico 29°20N 113°25W **86** B2
Angel Falls *Venezuela* 5°57N 62°30W **92** B6
Angeles *Phil.* 15°9N 120°33E **37** A6
Ängelholm *Sweden* 56°15N 12°58E **9** H15
Angels Camp *U.S.A.* 38°4N 120°32W **78** G6
Ångermanälven ➤
  Sweden 64°0N 17°20E **8** E17
Ångermanland *Sweden* 63°36N 17°45E **8** E17
Angers *Canada* 45°31N 75°29W **83** A9
Angers *France* 47°30N 0°35W **20** C3
Ängesån ➤ *Sweden* 66°16N 22°47E **8** C20
Angikuni L. *Canada* 62°12N 99°59W **71** A9
Angkor *Cambodia* 13°22N 103°50E **38** F4
Angledool *Australia* 29°5S 147°55E **63** D4
Anglesey *U.K.* 53°17N 4°20W **12** D3
Anglesey, Isle of □ *U.K.* 53°16N 4°18W **12** D3
Angleton *U.S.A.* 29°10N 95°26W **84** G7
Anglisidhes *Cyprus* 34°51N 33°27E **25** E12
Angmagssalik = Tasiilaq
  Greenland 65°40N 37°20W **4** C6
Ango *Dem. Rep. of the Congo* 4°10N 26°5E **54** B2
Angoche *Mozam.* 16°8S 39°55E **55** F4
Angoche, I. *Mozam.* 16°20S 39°50E **55** F4
Angol *Chile* 37°56S 72°45W **94** D1
Angola *Ind., U.S.A.* 41°38N 85°0W **81** E11
Angola *N.Y., U.S.A.* 42°38N 79°2W **82** D5
Angola ■ *Africa* 12°0S 18°0E **53** G3
Angoulême *France* 45°39N 0°10E **20** D4
Angoumois *France* 45°50N 0°25E **20** D3
Angra do Heroísmo
  Azores 38°39N 27°13W **50** a
Angra dos Reis *Brazil* 23°0S 44°10W **95** A7
Angtassom *Cambodia* 11°1N 104°41E **39** G5
Angu
  Dem. Rep. of the Congo 3°23N 24°30E **54** B1
Anguang *China* 45°15N 123°45E **35** B12
Anguilla ☑ *W. Indies* 18°14N 63°5W **89** C7
Anguo *China* 38°28N 115°15E **34** E8
Angurugu *Australia* 14°0S 136°25E **62** A2
Angus *Canada* 44°19N 79°53W **82** B5
Angus □ *U.K.* 56°46N 2°56W **11** E6
Angwa ➤ *Zimbabwe* 16°0S 30°23E **57** B5
Anhanduí ➤ *Brazil* 21°46S 52°9W **95** A5
Anholt *Denmark* 56°42N 11°33E **9** H14
Anhui □ *China* 32°0N 117°0E **33** C6
Anhwei = Anhui □ *China* 32°0N 117°0E **33** C6
Anichab *Namibia* 21°0S 14°46E **56** C1
Animas ➤ *U.S.A.* 36°43N 108°13W **77** H9
Anivorano *Madag.* 18°44S 48°58E **57** B8
Anjalankoski *Finland* 60°45N 26°51E **8** F22
Anjar *India* 23°6N 70°10E **42** H4
Anjou *France* 47°20N 0°15W **20** C3
Anjouan *Comoros Is.* 12°15S 44°20E **53** a
Anjozorobe *Madag.* 18°22S 47°52E **57** B8
Anju *N. Korea* 39°36N 125°40E **35** E13
Ankaboa, Tanjona
  Madag. 21°58S 43°20E **57** C7
Ankang *China* 32°40N 109°1E **34** H5
Ankara *Turkey* 39°57N 32°54E **19** G5
Ankarafantsika △ *Madag.* 16°8S 47°5E **57** B8
Ankaramena *Madag.* 21°57S 46°39E **57** C8
Ankaratra *Madag.* 19°25S 47°12E **53** H9
Ankasakasa *Madag.* 16°21S 44°52E **57** B7
Ankavandra *Madag.* 18°46S 45°18E **57** B8
Ankazoabo *Madag.* 22°18S 44°31E **57** C7
Ankazobe *Madag.* 18°20S 47°10E **57** B8
Ankeny *U.S.A.* 41°44N 93°36W **80** E7
Ankilimalinika *Madag.* 22°58S 43°45E **57** C7
Ankilizato *Madag.* 20°25S 45°1E **57** C8
Ankisabe *Madag.* 19°17S 46°29E **57** B8
Ankoro
  Dem. Rep. of the Congo 6°45S 26°55E **54** D2
Ankororoka *Madag.* 25°30S 45°11E **57** D8
Anlong Veng *Cambodia* 14°14N 104°5E **38** E5
Anmyeondo *S. Korea* 36°25N 126°25E **35** F14
Ann, C. *U.S.A.* 42°38N 70°35W **83** D14
Ann Arbor *U.S.A.* 42°17N 83°45W **81** D12
Anna *U.S.A.* 37°28N 89°15W **80** G9
Annaba *Algeria* 36°50N 7°46E **50** A7
Annalee ➤ *Ireland* 54°2N 7°24W **10** B4
Annam *Vietnam* 16°0N 108°0E **38** E7
Annamitique, Chaîne
  Asia 17°0N 106°0E **38** D6
Annan *U.K.* 54°59N 3°16W **11** G5
Annan ➤ *U.K.* 54°58N 3°16W **11** G5
Annapolis *U.S.A.* 38°59N 76°30W **81** F15
Annapolis Royal *Canada* 44°44N 65°32W **73** D6
Annapurna *Nepal* 28°34N 83°50E **43** E10
Annean, L. *Australia* 26°54S 118°14E **61** E2
Annecy *France* 45°55N 6°8E **20** D7
Annette I. *U.S.A.* 55°9N 131°28W **70** B2
Anning *China* 24°55N 102°26E **32** D5
Anniston *U.S.A.* 33°39N 85°50W **85** E12
Annobón *Atl. Oc.* 1°25S 5°36E **49** G4
Annotto B. *Jamaica* 18°17N 76°45W **88** a
Annville *U.S.A.* 40°20N 76°31W **83** F8
Anogia *Greece* 35°16N 24°52E **25** D6
Anorotsangana *Madag.* 13°56S 47°55E **57** A8
Anosibe *Madag.* 19°26S 48°13E **57** B8
Anping *Hebei, China* 38°15N 115°30E **34** E8
Anping *Liaoning, China* 41°5N 123°30E **35** D12
Anqing *China* 30°30N 117°3E **33** C6
Anqiu *China* 36°25N 119°10E **35** F10
Ansai *China* 36°50N 109°20E **34** F5
Ansan *S. Korea* 37°21N 126°52E **35** F14
Ansbach *Germany* 49°28N 10°34E **16** D6
Anse Boileau *Seychelles* 4°43S 55°29E **53** b
Anse Royale *Seychelles* 4°44S 55°31E **53** b
Anshan *China* 41°5N 122°58E **35** D12
Anshun *China* 26°18N 105°57E **32** D5
Ansley *U.S.A.* 41°18N 99°23W **80** E4

Anson *U.S.A.* 32°45N 99°54W **84** E5
Anson B. *Australia* 13°20S 130°6E **60** B5
Ansongo *Mali* 15°25N 0°35E **50** E6
Ansonia *U.S.A.* 41°21N 73°5W **83** E11
Anstruther *U.K.* 56°14N 2°41W **11** E6
Ansudu *Indonesia* 2°11S 139°22E **37** E9
Antabamba *Peru* 14°40S 73°0W **92** F4
Antakya = Hatay *Turkey* 36°14N 36°10E **44** B3
Antalaha *Madag.* 14°57S 50°20E **57** A9
Antalya *Turkey* 36°52N 30°45E **19** G5
Antalya Körfezi *Turkey* 36°15N 31°30E **19** G5
Antambohobe *Madag.* 22°20S 46°47E **57** C8
Antanambao-Manampotsy
  Madag. 19°29S 48°34E **57** B8
Antanambe *Madag.* 16°26S 49°52E **57** B8
Antananarivo *Madag.* 18°55S 47°31E **57** B8
Antananarivo □ *Madag.* 19°0S 47°0E **57** B8
Antanifotsy *Madag.* 19°39S 47°19E **57** B8
Antanimbaribe *Madag.* 21°30S 44°48E **57** C7
Antanimora *Madag.* 24°49S 45°40E **57** C8
Antarctic Pen. *Antarctica* 67°0S 60°0W **5** C18
Antarctica 90°0S 0°0 **5** E
Antelope *Zimbabwe* 21°2S 28°31E **55** G2
Antequera *Paraguay* 24°8S 57°7W **94** A4
Antequera *Spain* 37°5N 4°33W **21** D3
Antero, Mt. *U.S.A.* 38°41N 106°15W **76** G10
Anthemana *Madag.* 21°2S 44°8E **57** C7
Anthony *Kans., U.S.A.* 37°9N 98°2W **80** G4
Anthony *N. Mex.,*
  U.S.A. 32°0N 106°36W **77** K10
Anti Atlas *Morocco* 30°0N 8°30W **50** C4
Anti-Lebanon = Sharqi, Al Jabal
  ash *Lebanon* 33°40N 36°10E **46** B5
Antibes *France* 43°34N 7°6E **20** E7
Anticosti, Î. d' *Canada* 49°30N 63°0W **73** C7
Antigo *U.S.A.* 45°9N 89°9W **80** C9
Antigonish *Canada* 45°38N 61°58W **73** C7
Antigua *Canary Is.* 28°24N 14°1W **24** F5
Antigua *Guatemala* 14°34N 90°41W **88** D1
Antigua *W. Indies* 17°0N 61°50W **89** C7
Antigua & Barbuda ■
  W. Indies 17°20N 61°48W **89** C7
Antikythira *Greece* 35°52N 23°15E **23** G10
Antilla *Cuba* 20°40N 75°50W **88** B4
Antilles = West Indies
  Cent. Amer. 15°0N 65°0W **89** D7
Antioch *U.S.A.* 38°1N 121°48W **78** G5
Antioquia *Colombia* 6°40N 75°55W **92** B3
Antipodes Is. *Pac. Oc.* 49°45S 178°40E **64** M9
Antlers *U.S.A.* 34°14N 95°37W **84** D7
Antoetra *Madag.* 20°46S 47°20E **57** C8
Antofagasta *Chile* 23°50S 70°30W **94** A1
Antofagasta □ *Chile* 24°0S 69°0W **94** A2
Antofagasta de la Sierra
  Argentina 26°5S 67°20W **94** B2
Antofalla *Argentina* 25°30S 68°5W **94** B2
Antofalla, Salar de
  Argentina 25°40S 67°45W **94** B2
Anton *U.S.A.* 33°49N 102°10W **84** E3
Antongila, Helodrano
  Madag. 15°30S 49°50E **57** B8
Antonibé *Madag.* 15°7S 47°24E **57** B8
Antonibé, Presqu'île d'
  Madag. 14°55S 47°20E **57** A8
Antonina *Brazil* 25°26S 48°42W **95** B6
Antrim *U.K.* 54°43N 6°14W **10** B5
Antrim *U.S.A.* 40°7N 81°21W **82** F3
Antrim □ *U.K.* 54°56N 6°25W **10** B5
Antrim, Mts. of *U.K.* 55°3N 6°14W **10** A5
Antrim Plateau *Australia* 18°8S 128°20E **60** C4
Antsakabary *Madag.* 15°3S 48°56E **57** B8
Antsalova *Madag.* 18°40S 44°37E **57** B7
Antsenavolo *Madag.* 21°24S 48°3E **57** C8
Antsiafabositra *Madag.* 17°18S 46°57E **57** B8
Antsirabe *Antananarivo,*
  Madag. 19°55S 47°2E **57** B8
Antsirabe *Antsiranana,*
  Madag. 12°16S 49°17E **57** A8
Antsirabe *Mahajanga,*
  Madag. 15°57S 48°58E **57** B8
Antsiranana *Madag.* 12°25S 49°20E **57** A8
Antsiranana □ *Madag.* 12°16S 49°17E **57** A8
Antsohihy *Madag.* 14°50S 47°59E **57** A8
Antsohimbondrona Serranana
  Madag. 13°7S 48°48E **57** A8
Antu *China* 42°30N 128°20E **35** C15
Antwerp = Antwerpen
  Belgium 51°13N 4°25E **15** C4
Antwerp *U.S.A.* 44°12N 75°37W **83** B9
Antwerpen *Belgium* 51°13N 4°25E **15** C4
Antwerpen □ *Belgium* 51°15N 4°40E **15** C4
Anupgarh *India* 29°10N 73°10E **42** E5
Anuppur *India* 23°6N 81°41E **43** H9
Anuradhapura *Sri Lanka* 8°22N 80°28E **40** Q12
Anurrete ◎ *Australia* 20°50S 135°38E **62** C2
Anveh *Iran* 27°23N 54°11E **45** E7
Anvers = Antwerpen
  Belgium 51°13N 4°25E **15** C4
Anvers I. *Antarctica* 64°30S 63°40W **5** C17
Anxi *China* 40°30N 95°43E **32** B4
Anxious B. *Australia* 33°24S 134°45E **63** E1
Anyang *China* 36°5N 114°21E **34** F8
Anyang *S. Korea* 37°23N 126°55E **35** F14
Anyer *Indonesia* 6°4S 105°53E **37** G11
Anyi *China* 35°2N 111°2E **34** G6
Anza *U.S.A.* 33°35N 116°39W **79** M10
Anze *China* 36°10N 112°12E **34** F7
Anzhero-Sudzhensk
  Russia 56°10N 86°0E **28** D9
Ánzio *Italy* 41°27N 12°37E **22** D5
Ao Makham *Thailand* 7°50N 98°24E **39** a
Ao Phangnga △ *Thailand* 8°10N 98°32E **39** a
Aoga-Shima *Japan* 32°28N 139°46E **31** H9
Aoji *N. Korea* 42°31N 130°23E **35** C16
Aomen = Macau
  China 22°12N 113°33E **33** G10
Aomori *Japan* 40°45N 140°45E **30** D10
Aomori □ *Japan* 40°45N 140°40E **30** D10
Aonla *India* 28°16N 79°11E **43** E8

Aorai, Mt. _Tahiti_ 17°34S 149°30W **59 d**
Aoraki Mount Cook _N.Z._ 43°36S 170°9E **59 E3**
Aoral, Phnum _Cambodia_ 12°0N 104°15E **39 G5**
Aosta _Italy_ 45°45N 7°20E **20 D7**
Aotearoa = New Zealand ■ _Oceania_ 40°0S 176°0E **59 D6**
Aoukâr _Mauritania_ 17°40N 10°0W **50 E4**
Aozou Strip _Chad_ 22°0N 19°0E **51 D9**
Apá → _S. Amer._ 22°6S 58°2W **94 A4**
Apache _U.S.A._ 34°54N 98°22W **84 D5**
Apache Junction _U.S.A._ 33°25N 111°33W **77 K8**
Apalachee B. _U.S.A._ 30°0N 84°0W **85 G13**
Apalachicola _U.S.A._ 29°43N 84°59W **85 G12**
Apalachicola → _U.S.A._ 29°43N 84°58W **85 G12**
Apaporis → _Colombia_ 1°23S 69°25W **92 D5**
Aparados da Serra △ _Brazil_ 29°10S 50°8W **95 B5**
Aparri _Phil._ 18°22N 121°38E **37 A6**
Apatity _Russia_ 67°34N 33°22E **8 C25**
Apatula = Finke _Australia_ 25°34S 134°35E **62 D1**
Apatzingán _Mexico_ 19°5N 102°21W **86 D4**
Apeldoorn _Neths._ 52°13N 5°57E **15 B5**
Apennines = Appennini _Italy_ 44°30N 10°0E **22 B4**
Api _Nepal_ 30°0N 80°57E **32 C3**
Apia _Samoa_ 13°50S 171°50W **59 b**
Apiacás, Serra dos _Brazil_ 9°50S 57°0W **92 E7**
Apies → _S. Africa_ 25°15S 28°8E **57 D4**
Apizaco _Mexico_ 19°25N 98°8W **87 D5**
Aplao _Peru_ 16°0S 72°40W **92 G4**
Apo, Mt. _Phil._ 6°53N 125°14E **37 C7**
Apolakia _Greece_ 36°5N 27°48E **25 C9**
Apolakia, Ormos _Greece_ 36°5N 27°45E **25 C9**
Apollonia = Sūsah _Libya_ 32°52N 21°59E **51 B10**
Apollonia _Greece_ 36°15N 27°58E **25 C9**
Apolo _Bolivia_ 14°30S 68°30W **92 F5**
Apopa _El Salv._ 13°48N 89°10W **88 D2**
Aporé → _Brazil_ 19°27S 50°57W **93 G8**
Apostle Is. _U.S.A._ 47°0N 90°40W **80 B8**
Apostle Islands △ _U.S.A._ 46°55N 91°0W **80 B8**
Apóstoles _Argentina_ 28°0S 56°0W **95 B4**
Apostolos Andreas, C. _Cyprus_ 35°42N 34°35E **25 D13**
Apoteri _Guyana_ 4°2N 58°32W **92 C7**
Appalachian Mts. _U.S.A._ 38°0N 80°0W **81 G14**
Appennini _Italy_ 44°30N 10°0E **22 B4**
Apple Hill _Canada_ 45°13N 74°46W **83 A10**
Apple Valley _U.S.A._ 34°32N 117°14W **79 L9**
Appleby-in-Westmorland _U.K._ 54°35N 2°29W **12 C5**
Appledore _U.K._ 51°3N 4°13W **13 F3**
Appleton _U.S.A._ 44°16N 88°25W **80 C9**
Approuague → _Fr. Guiana_ 4°30N 51°57W **93 C8**
Aprília _Italy_ 41°36N 12°39E **22 D5**
Apsley _Canada_ 44°45N 78°6W **82 B6**
Apucarana _Brazil_ 23°55S 51°33W **95 A5**
Apure → _Venezuela_ 7°37N 66°25W **92 B5**
Apurímac → _Peru_ 12°17S 73°56W **92 F4**
Āq Qālā _Iran_ 37°10N 54°30E **45 B7**
Aqaba = Al 'Aqabah _Jordan_ 29°31N 35°0E **46 F4**
Aqaba, G. of _Red Sea_ 29°0N 34°40E **44 D2**
'Aqabah, Khalīj al = Aqaba, G. of _Red Sea_ 29°0N 34°40E **44 D2**
'Aqdā _Iran_ 32°26N 53°37E **45 C7**
'Aqrah _Iraq_ 36°46N 43°45E **44 B4**
Aqsay _Kazakhstan_ 51°11N 53°0E **19 D9**
Aqtaū _Kazakhstan_ 43°39N 51°12E **19 F9**
Aqtöbe _Kazakhstan_ 50°17N 57°10E **19 D10**
Aqtoghay _Kazakhstan_ 46°57N 79°40E **28 E8**
Aquidauana _Brazil_ 20°30S 55°50W **93 H7**
Aquila _Mexico_ 18°36N 103°30W **86 D4**
Aquiles Serdán _Mexico_ 28°36N 105°53W **86 B3**
Aquin _Haiti_ 18°16N 73°24W **89 C5**
Aquitain, Bassin _France_ 44°0N 0°30W **20 D3**
Ar Rafid _Syria_ 32°57N 35°52E **46 C4**
Ar Raḩḩālīyah _Iraq_ 32°44N 43°23E **44 C4**
Ar Ramādī _Iraq_ 33°25N 43°20E **44 C4**
Ar Ramthā _Jordan_ 32°34N 36°0E **46 C5**
Ar Raqqah _Syria_ 35°59N 39°8E **44 C3**
Ar Rashidiya = Er Rachidia _Morocco_ 31°58N 4°20W **50 B5**
Ar Rass _Si. Arabia_ 25°50N 43°40E **44 E4**
Ar Rayyan _Qatar_ 25°17N 51°25E **45 E6**
Ar Rifā'ī _Iraq_ 31°50N 46°10E **44 D5**
Ar Riyāḍ _Si. Arabia_ 24°41N 46°42E **44 E5**
Ar Ru'ays _Qatar_ 26°8N 51°12E **45 E6**
Ar Rukhaymīyah _Iraq_ 29°22N 45°38E **44 D5**
Ar Rumaythah _Iraq_ 31°31N 45°12E **44 D5**
Ar Rusāfah _Syria_ 35°45N 38°49E **44 C3**
Ar Ruṭbah _Iraq_ 33°0N 40°15E **44 C4**
Ara _India_ 25°35N 84°32E **43 G11**
Arab _U.S.A._ 34°19N 86°30W **85 D11**
'Arab, Bahr el → _Sudan_ 9°0N 29°30E **51 G11**
Arab, Shatt al → _Asia_ 29°57N 48°34E **45 D6**
'Arabābād _Iran_ 33°2N 57°41E **45 C8**
Arabia _Asia_ 25°0N 45°0E **26 F6**
Arabian Desert = Es Sahrâ' Esh Sharqîya _Egypt_ 27°30N 32°30E **51 C12**
Arabian Gulf = Persian Gulf _Asia_ 27°0N 50°0E **45 E6**
Arabian Sea _Ind. Oc._ 16°0N 65°0E **26 G8**
Aracaju _Brazil_ 10°55S 37°4W **93 F11**
Aracati _Brazil_ 4°30S 37°44W **93 D11**
Araçatuba _Brazil_ 21°10S 50°30W **95 A5**
Aracena _Brazil_ 16°52S 42°4W **93 G10**
Araçuaí _Brazil_ 16°52S 42°4W **93 G10**
'Arad _Israel_ 31°15N 35°12E **46 D4**
Arad _Romania_ 46°10N 21°20E **17 E11**
Arādān _Iran_ 35°21N 52°30E **45 C7**
Arādhippou _Cyprus_ 34°57N 33°36E **25 E12**
Arafura Sea _E. Indies_ 9°0S 135°0E **58 B6**
Aragón □ _Spain_ 41°25N 0°40W **21 B5**

Aragón → _Spain_ 42°13N 1°44W **21 A5**
Araguacema _Brazil_ 8°50S 49°20W **93 E9**
Araguaia → _Brazil_ 5°21S 48°41W **93 E9**
Araguaína _Brazil_ 7°12S 48°12W **93 E9**
Araguari _Brazil_ 18°38S 48°11W **93 G9**
Araguari → _Brazil_ 1°15N 49°55W **93 C9**
Arain _India_ 26°27N 75°2E **42 F6**
Arak _Algeria_ 25°20N 3°45E **50 C6**
Arāk _Iran_ 34°0N 49°40E **45 C6**
Arakan Coast _Burma_ 19°0N 94°0E **41 K19**
Arakan Yoma _Burma_ 20°0N 94°40E **41 K19**
Araks = Aras, Rūd-e → _Asia_ 40°5N 48°29E **44 B5**
Aral _Kazakhstan_ 46°41N 61°45E **28 E7**
Aral Sea _Asia_ 44°30N 60°0E **28 E7**
Aral Tengizi = Aral Sea _Asia_ 44°30N 60°0E **28 E7**
Aralsk = Aral _Kazakhstan_ 46°41N 61°45E **28 E7**
Aralskoye More = Aral Sea _Asia_ 44°30N 60°0E **28 E7**
Aramac _Australia_ 22°58S 145°14E **62 C4**
Aran I. _Ireland_ 55°0N 8°30W **10 A3**
Aran Is. _Ireland_ 53°6N 9°38W **10 C2**
Aranda de Duero _Spain_ 41°39N 3°42W **21 B4**
Arandān _Iran_ 35°23N 46°55E **44 C5**
Aranjuez _Spain_ 40°1N 3°40W **21 B4**
Aranos _Namibia_ 24°9S 19°7E **56 C2**
Aransas Pass _U.S.A._ 27°55N 97°9W **84 H6**
Aranyaprathet _Thailand_ 13°41N 102°30E **38 F4**
Arapahoe _U.S.A._ 40°18N 99°54W **80 E4**
Arapey Grande → _Uruguay_ 30°55S 57°49W **94 C4**
Arapgir _Turkey_ 39°5N 38°30E **44 B3**
Arapiraca _Brazil_ 9°45S 36°39W **93 E11**
Arapongas _Brazil_ 23°29S 51°28W **95 A5**
Ar'ar _Si. Arabia_ 30°59N 41°2E **44 D4**
Araranguá _Brazil_ 29°0S 49°30W **95 B6**
Araraquara _Brazil_ 21°50S 48°0W **93 H9**
Araras, Serra das _Brazil_ 25°0S 53°10W **95 B5**
Ararat _Australia_ 37°16S 142°58E **63 F3**
Ararat, Mt. = Ağrı Dağı _Turkey_ 39°50N 44°15E **44 B5**
Araria _India_ 26°9N 87°33E **43 F12**
Araripe, Chapada do _Brazil_ 7°20S 40°0W **93 E11**
Araruama, L. de _Brazil_ 22°53S 42°12W **95 A7**
Aras = Aras, Rūd-e → _Asia_ 40°5N 48°29E **44 B5**
Aras, Rūd-e → _Asia_ 40°5N 48°29E **44 B5**
Arauca _Colombia_ 7°0N 70°40W **92 B4**
Arauca → _Venezuela_ 7°24N 66°35W **92 B5**
Arauco _Chile_ 37°16S 73°25W **94 D1**
Aravalli Range _India_ 25°0N 73°30E **42 G5**
Arawale → _Kenya_ 1°24S 40°9E **54 C5**
Araxá _Brazil_ 19°35S 46°55W **93 G9**
Araxes = Aras, Rūd-e → _Asia_ 40°5N 48°29E **44 B5**
Araya, Pen. de _Venezuela_ 10°40N 64°0W **92 A6**
Araz = Aras, Rūd-e → _Asia_ 40°5N 48°29E **44 B5**
Arba Minch _Ethiopia_ 6°0N 37°30E **47 F2**
Arbat _Iraq_ 35°25N 45°35E **44 C5**
Árbatax _Italy_ 39°56N 9°42E **22 E3**
Arbīl _Iraq_ 36°15N 44°5E **44 B5**
Arborfield _Canada_ 53°6N 103°39W **71 C8**
Arborg _Canada_ 50°54N 97°13W **71 C9**
Arbroath _U.K._ 56°34N 2°35W **11 E6**
Arbuckle _U.S.A._ 39°1N 122°3W **78 F4**
Arcachon _France_ 44°40N 1°10W **20 D3**
Arcade _U.S.A._ 42°32N 78°25W **82 D6**
Arcadia _Fla., U.S.A._ 27°13N 81°52W **85 H14**
Arcadia _La., U.S.A._ 32°33N 92°55W **84 E8**
Arcadia _Pa., U.S.A._ 40°47N 78°51W **82 F6**
Arcata _U.S.A._ 40°52N 124°5W **76 F1**
Archangel = Arkhangelsk _Russia_ 64°38N 40°36E **18 B7**
Archangelos _Greece_ 36°13N 28°7E **25 C10**
Archbald _U.S.A._ 41°30N 75°32W **83 E9**
Archer → _Australia_ 13°28S 141°41E **62 A3**
Archer B. _Australia_ 13°20S 141°30E **62 A3**
Archer Bend = Mungkan Kandju △ _Australia_ 13°35S 142°52E **62 A3**
Archers Post _Kenya_ 0°35N 37°35E **54 B4**
Arches △ _U.S.A._ 38°45N 109°25W **76 G9**
Archipel-de-Mingan △ _Canada_ 50°13N 63°10W **73 B7**
Archipiélago Chinijo △ _Canary Is._ 29°20N 13°30W **24 E6**
Archipiélago Los Roques △ _Venezuela_ 11°50N 66°44W **89 D6**
Arckaringa Cr. → _Australia_ 28°10S 135°22E **63 D2**
Arco _U.S.A._ 43°38N 113°18W **76 E7**
Arcos de la Frontera _Spain_ 36°45N 5°49W **21 D3**
Arcot _India_ 12°53N 79°20E **40 N11**
Arctic Bay _Canada_ 73°1N 85°7W **69 C14**
Arctic Mid-Ocean Ridge _Arctic_ 87°0N 90°0E **4 A**
Arctic Ocean _Arctic_ 78°0N 160°0W **4 B18**
Arctic Red River = Tsiigehtchic _Canada_ 67°15N 134°0W **68 D5**
Arctowski _Antarctica_ 62°30S 58°0W **5 C18**
Arda → _Bulgaria_ 41°40N 26°30E **23 D12**
Ardabīl _Iran_ 38°15N 48°18E **45 B6**
Ardakān = Sepīdān _Iran_ 30°20N 52°5E **45 D7**
Ardakān _Iran_ 32°19N 53°59E **45 C7**
Ardara _Ireland_ 54°46N 8°25W **10 B3**
Ardee _Ireland_ 53°52N 6°33W **10 C5**
Arden _Canada_ 44°43N 76°56W **82 B8**
Arden _Calif., U.S.A._ 38°36N 121°33W **78 G5**
Arden _Nev., U.S.A._ 36°1N 115°14W **79 J11**
Ardennes _Belgium_ 49°50N 5°5E **15 E5**
Ardennes = Ardenne _Belgium_ 49°50N 5°5E **15 E5**
Arderin _Ireland_ 53°2N 7°39W **10 C4**
Ardestān _Iran_ 33°20N 52°25E **45 C7**
Ardfert _Ireland_ 52°20N 9°47W **10 D2**

Ardglass _U.K._ 54°17N 5°36W **10 B6**
Ardivachar Pt. _U.K._ 57°23N 7°26W **11 D1**
Ardlethan _Australia_ 34°22S 146°53E **63 E4**
Ardmore _Okla., U.S.A._ 34°10N 97°8W **84 D6**
Ardmore _Pa., U.S.A._ 40°2N 75°17W **83 F9**
Ardnamurchan, Pt. of _U.K._ 56°43N 6°14W **11 E2**
Ardnave Pt. _U.K._ 55°53N 6°20W **11 F2**
Ardrossan _Australia_ 34°26S 137°53E **63 E2**
Ardrossan _U.K._ 55°39N 4°49W **11 F4**
Ards Pen. _U.K._ 54°33N 5°34W **10 B6**
Arecibo _Puerto Rico_ 18°29N 66°43W **89 d**
Areia Branca _Brazil_ 5°0S 37°0W **93 E11**
Arena, Pt. _U.S.A._ 38°57N 123°44W **78 G3**
Arenal _Honduras_ 15°21N 86°50W **88 C2**
Arendal _Norway_ 58°28N 8°46E **9 G13**
Arequipa _Peru_ 16°20S 71°30W **92 G4**
Arévalo _Spain_ 41°3N 4°43W **21 B3**
Arezzo _Italy_ 43°25N 11°53E **22 C4**
Arga _Turkey_ 38°21N 37°59E **44 B3**
Arganda del Rey _Spain_ 40°19N 3°26W **21 B4**
Argarapa ⊙ _Australia_ 22°20S 134°58E **62 C1**
Argenta _Canada_ 50°11N 116°56W **70 C5**
Argentan _France_ 48°45N 0°1W **20 B3**
Argentário, Mte. _Italy_ 42°24N 11°9E **22 C4**
Argentia _Canada_ 47°18N 53°58W **73 C9**
Argentina ■ _S. Amer._ 35°0S 66°0W **96 D3**
Argentine Basin _Atl. Oc._ 45°0S 45°0W **96 H5**
Argentino, L. _Argentina_ 50°10S 73°0W **96 G2**
Argeş → _Romania_ 44°5N 26°38E **17 F14**
Arghandab → _Afghan._ 31°30N 64°15E **42 D1**
Argirades _Greece_ 39°27N 19°58E **25 B3**
Argiroupoli _Greece_ 35°17N 24°20E **25 D6**
Argolikos Kolpos _Greece_ 37°20N 22°52E **23 F10**
Argos _Greece_ 37°40N 22°43E **23 F10**
Argostoli _Greece_ 38°11N 20°29E **23 E9**
Arguello, Pt. _U.S.A._ 34°35N 120°39W **79 L6**
Arguineguín _Canary Is._ 27°46N 15°41W **24 G4**
Argun → _Russia_ 53°20N 121°28E **29 D13**
Argungu _Nigeria_ 12°40N 4°31E **50 F6**
Argus Pk. _U.S.A._ 35°52N 117°26W **79 K9**
Argyle, L. _Australia_ 16°20S 128°40E **60 C4**
Argyll & Bute □ _U.K._ 56°13N 5°28W **11 E3**
Århus _Denmark_ 56°8N 10°11E **9 H14**
Ariadnoye _Russia_ 45°8N 134°25E **30 B7**
Ariamsvlei _Namibia_ 28°9S 19°51E **56 D2**
Ariana _Tunisia_ 36°52N 10°12E **51 A8**
Arica _Chile_ 18°32S 70°20W **92 G4**
Arica _Colombia_ 2°0S 71°50W **92 D4**
Arico _Spain_ 28°9N 16°29W **24 F3**
Arid, C. _Australia_ 34°1S 123°10E **61 F3**
Arida _Japan_ 34°5N 135°8E **31 G7**
Aride _Seychelles_ 4°13S 55°40E **53 b**
Ariège → _France_ 43°30N 1°25E **20 E4**
Arila, Akra _Greece_ 39°43N 19°39E **25 A3**
Arima _Trin. & Tob._ 10°38N 61°17W **93 K15**
Arinos → _Brazil_ 10°25S 58°20W **92 F7**
Ario de Rosales _Mexico_ 19°12N 101°43W **86 D4**
Aripo, Mt. _Trin. & Tob._ 10°45N 61°15W **93 K15**
Aripuanã _Brazil_ 9°25S 60°30W **92 E6**
Aripuanã → _Brazil_ 5°7S 60°25W **92 E6**
Ariquemes _Brazil_ 9°55S 63°6W **92 E6**
Arisaig _U.K._ 56°55N 5°51W **11 E3**
Aristazabal I. _Canada_ 52°40N 129°10W **70 C3**
Arivonimamo _Madag._ 19°1S 47°11E **57 B8**
Arizaro, Salar de _Argentina_ 24°40S 67°50W **94 A2**
Arizona _Argentina_ 35°45S 65°25W **94 D2**
Arizona □ _U.S.A._ 34°0N 112°0W **77 J8**
Arizpe _Mexico_ 30°20N 110°10W **86 A2**
'Arjah _Si. Arabia_ 24°43N 44°17E **44 E5**
Arjeplog _Sweden_ 66°3N 17°54E **8 C17**
Arjepluovve = Arjeplog _Sweden_ 66°3N 17°54E **8 C17**
Arjona _Colombia_ 10°14N 75°22W **92 A3**
Arjuna _Indonesia_ 7°49S 112°34E **37 G15**
Arka _Russia_ 60°15N 142°0E **29 C15**
Arkadelphia _U.S.A._ 34°7N 93°4W **84 D8**
Arkalyk = Arqalyk _Kazakhstan_ 50°13N 66°50E **28 D7**
Arkansas □ _U.S.A._ 35°0N 92°30W **84 D8**
Arkansas → _U.S.A._ 33°47N 91°4W **84 E9**
Arkansas City _U.S.A._ 37°4N 97°2W **80 G5**
Arkaroola _Australia_ 30°20S 139°22E **63 E2**
Arkhangelsk _Russia_ 64°38N 40°36E **18 B7**
Arki _India_ 31°9N 76°58E **42 D7**
Arklow _Ireland_ 52°48N 6°10W **10 D5**
Arkport _U.S.A._ 42°24N 77°42W **82 D7**
Arkticheskiy, Mys _Russia_ 81°10N 95°0E **29 A10**
Arkville _U.S.A._ 42°9N 74°37W **83 D10**
Arlanzón → _Spain_ 42°3N 4°17W **21 A3**
Arlbergpass _Austria_ 47°9N 10°12E **16 E6**
Arlbergtunnel _Austria_ 47°9N 10°12E **16 E6**
Arles _France_ 43°41N 4°40E **20 E6**
Arlington _S. Africa_ 28°1S 27°53E **57 D4**
Arlington _N.Y., U.S.A._ 41°42N 73°54W **83 E11**
Arlington _Oreg., U.S.A._ 45°43N 120°12W **76 D3**
Arlington _S. Dak., U.S.A._ 44°22N 97°8W **80 C5**
Arlington _Tex., U.S.A._ 32°44N 97°6W **84 E6**
Arlington _Va., U.S.A._ 38°53N 77°7W **81 F15**
Arlington _Vt., U.S.A._ 43°5N 73°9W **83 C11**
Arlington _Wash., U.S.A._ 48°12N 122°8W **78 B4**
Arlington Heights _U.S.A._ 42°5N 87°59W **80 D10**

Armenistis, Akra _Greece_ 36°8N 27°42E **25 C9**
Armidale _Australia_ 30°30S 151°40E **63 E5**
Armour _U.S.A._ 43°19N 98°21W **80 D4**
Armstrong _B.C., Canada_ 50°25N 119°10W **70 C5**
Armstrong _Ont., Canada_ 50°18N 89°4W **72 B2**
Arnarfjörður _Iceland_ 65°48N 23°40W **8 D2**
Arnaud → _Canada_ 59°59N 69°46W **69 F18**
Arnauti, C. _Cyprus_ 35°6N 32°17E **25 D11**
Arnett _U.S.A._ 36°8N 99°46W **84 C5**
Arnhem _Neths._ 51°58N 5°55E **15 C5**
Arnhem, C. _Australia_ 12°20S 137°30E **62 A2**
Arnhem B. _Australia_ 12°20S 136°10E **62 A2**
Arnhem Land _Australia_ 13°10S 134°30E **62 A1**
Arnhem Land ⊙ _Australia_ 12°50S 134°50E **62 A1**
Arno → _Italy_ 43°41N 10°17E **22 C4**
Arno Bay _Australia_ 33°54S 136°34E **63 E2**
Arnold _U.K._ 53°1N 1°7W **12 D6**
Arnold _U.S.A._ 38°15N 120°21W **78 G6**
Arnot _Canada_ 55°56N 96°41W **71 B9**
Arnøya _Norway_ 70°9N 20°40E **8 A19**
Arnprior _Canada_ 45°26N 76°21W **83 A8**
Arnsberg _Germany_ 51°24N 8°5E **16 C5**
Aroa, Pte. _Moorea_ 17°28S 149°46W **59 d**
Aroab _Namibia_ 26°41S 19°39E **56 D2**
Aron _India_ 25°57N 77°56E **42 G6**
Arona _Canary Is._ 28°6N 16°40W **24 F3**
Aros → _Mexico_ 29°9N 107°57W **86 B3**
Arqalyk _Kazakhstan_ 50°13N 66°50E **28 D7**
Arrah = Ara _India_ 25°35N 84°32E **43 G11**
Arrah _Ivory C._ 6°40N 3°58W **50 G5**
Arran _U.K._ 55°34N 5°12W **11 F3**
Arras _France_ 50°17N 2°46E **20 A5**
Arrecife _Canary Is._ 28°57N 13°37W **24 F6**
Arrecifes _Argentina_ 34°6S 60°9W **94 C3**
Arrée, Mts. d' _France_ 48°26N 3°55W **20 B2**
Arriaga _Mexico_ 16°14N 93°54W **87 D6**
Arrilalah _Australia_ 23°43S 143°54E **62 C3**
Arrino _Australia_ 29°30S 115°40E **61 E2**
Arrow, L. _Ireland_ 54°3N 8°19W **10 B3**
Arrowtown _N.Z._ 44°57S 168°50E **59 F2**
Arroyo Grande _U.S.A._ 35°7N 120°35W **79 K6**
Ars _Iran_ 37°9N 47°46E **44 B5**
Arsenault L. _Canada_ 55°6N 108°32W **71 B7**
Arsenev _Russia_ 44°10N 133°15E **30 B6**
Arta _Greece_ 39°8N 21°2E **23 E9**
Artà _Spain_ 39°41N 3°21E **24 B10**
Artà, Coves d' _Spain_ 39°40N 3°24E **24 B10**
Arteaga _Mexico_ 18°28N 102°25W **86 D4**
Artem _Russia_ 43°22N 132°13E **30 C6**
Artemovsk _Russia_ 54°45N 93°35E **29 D10**
Artemovsk _Ukraine_ 48°35N 38°0E **19 E6**
Artesia = Mosomane _Botswana_ 24°2S 26°19E **56 C4**
Artesia _U.S.A._ 32°51N 104°24W **77 K11**
Arthur _Canada_ 43°50N 80°32W **82 C4**
Arthur → _Australia_ 41°2S 144°40E **63 G3**
Arthur Cr. → _Australia_ 22°30S 136°25E **62 C2**
Arthur Pt. _Australia_ 22°7S 150°3E **62 C5**
Arthur River _Australia_ 33°20S 117°2E **61 F2**
Arthur's Pass _N.Z._ 42°54S 171°35E **59 E3**
Arthur's Pass △ _N.Z._ 42°53S 171°42E **59 E3**
Arthur's Town _Bahamas_ 24°38N 75°42W **89 B4**
Artigas _Antarctica_ 62°30S 58°0W **5 C18**
Artigas _Uruguay_ 30°20S 56°30W **94 C4**
Artillery L. _Canada_ 63°9N 107°52W **71 A7**
Artois _France_ 50°20N 2°30E **20 A5**
Artrutx, C. de _Spain_ 39°55N 3°49E **24 B10**
Artsyz _Ukraine_ 46°4N 29°26E **17 E15**
Artux _China_ 39°40N 76°10E **32 C2**
Artvin _Turkey_ 41°14N 41°44E **19 F7**
Aru, Kepulauan _Indonesia_ 6°0S 134°30E **37 F8**
Aru Is. = Aru, Kepulauan _Indonesia_ 6°0S 134°30E **37 F8**
Arua _Uganda_ 3°1N 30°58E **54 B3**
Aruanã _Brazil_ 14°54S 51°10W **93 F8**
Aruba ☑ _W. Indies_ 12°30N 70°0W **89 D6**
Arucas _Canary Is._ 28°7N 15°32W **24 F4**
Arué _Tahiti_ 17°31S 149°30W **59 d**
Arun → _Nepal_ 26°55N 87°10E **43 F12**
Arun → _U.K._ 50°49N 0°33W **13 G7**
Arunachal Pradesh □ _India_ 28°0N 95°0E **41 F19**
Arusha _Tanzania_ 3°20S 36°40E **54 C4**
Arusha □ _Tanzania_ 4°0S 36°30E **54 C4**
Arusha △ _Tanzania_ 3°16S 36°47E **54 C4**
Arusha Chini _Tanzania_ 3°32S 37°20E **54 C4**
Aruwimi → _Dem. Rep. of the Congo_ 1°13N 23°36E **54 B1**
Arvada _Colo., U.S.A._ 39°48N 105°5W **76 G11**
Arvada _Wyo., U.S.A._ 44°39N 106°8W **76 D10**
Arvayheer _Mongolia_ 46°15N 102°48E **32 B5**
Arvi _Greece_ 34°59N 25°28E **25 E7**
Arviat _Canada_ 61°6N 93°59W **71 A10**
Arvidsjaur _Sweden_ 65°35N 19°10E **8 D18**
Arvika _Sweden_ 59°40N 12°36E **9 G15**
Arvin _U.S.A._ 35°12N 118°50W **79 K8**
Arwal _India_ 25°15N 84°41E **43 G11**
Arxan _China_ 47°11N 119°57E **33 B6**
Arzamas _Russia_ 55°27N 43°55E **18 C7**
Arzanah _U.A.E._ 24°47N 52°34E **45 E7**
Aş Şafā _Syria_ 33°10N 37°0E **46 B6**
Aş Saffānīyah _Si. Arabia_ 27°55N 48°50E **45 E6**
As Safīrah _Syria_ 36°5N 37°21E **44 B3**
Aş Şahm _Oman_ 24°10N 56°53E **45 E8**
As Sājir _Si. Arabia_ 25°11N 44°36E **44 E5**
As Salamīyah _Syria_ 35°1N 37°2E **44 C3**
As Salmān _Iraq_ 30°30N 44°32E **44 D5**
As Salṭ _Jordan_ 32°2N 35°43E **46 C4**
As Sal'w'a _Qatar_ 24°23N 50°50E **45 E6**
As Samāwah _Iraq_ 31°15N 45°15E **44 D5**
As Sanamayn _Syria_ 33°3N 36°10E **46 B5**
As Sohar = Şuḩār _Oman_ 24°20N 56°40E **45 E8**
As Sukhnah _Syria_ 34°52N 38°52E **44 C3**
As Sulaymānīyah _Iraq_ 35°35N 45°29E **44 C5**
As Sulaymī _Si. Arabia_ 26°17N 41°21E **44 E4**

As Sulayyil _Si. Arabia_ 20°27N 45°34E **47 C4**
As Summān _Si. Arabia_ 25°0N 47°0E **44 E5**
As Suwaydā' _Syria_ 32°40N 36°30E **46 C5**
As Suwaydā' □ _Syria_ 32°45N 36°45E **46 C5**
As Suwayq _Oman_ 23°51N 57°26E **45 F8**
Aş Şuwayrah _Iraq_ 32°55N 45°0E **44 C5**
Asab _Namibia_ 25°30S 18°0E **56 D2**
Asad, Buḩayrat al _Syria_ 36°0N 38°15E **44 C3**
Asahi-Gawa → _Japan_ 34°36N 133°58E **31 G6**
Asahigawa = Asahikawa _Japan_ 43°46N 142°22E **30 C11**
Asaluyeh _Iran_ 27°29N 52°37E **45 E7**
Asamankese _Ghana_ 5°50N 0°40W **50 G5**
Asan → _India_ 26°37N 78°24E **43 F8**
Asansol _India_ 23°40N 87°1E **43 H12**
Asau _Samoa_ 13°27S 172°33W **59 b**
Asbesberge _S. Africa_ 29°0S 23°0E **56 D3**
Asbestos _Canada_ 45°47N 71°58W **83 A13**
Asbury Park _U.S.A._ 40°13N 74°1W **83 F10**
Ascension _Mexico_ 31°6N 107°59W **86 A3**
Ascensión, B. de la _Mexico_ 19°40N 87°30W **87 D7**
Ascension I. _Atl. Oc._ 7°57S 14°23W **49 G2**
Aschaffenburg _Germany_ 49°58N 9°6E **16 D5**
Aschersleben _Germany_ 51°45N 11°29E **16 C6**
Áscoli Piceno _Italy_ 42°51N 13°34E **22 C5**
Ascope _Peru_ 7°46S 79°8W **92 E3**
Ascotán _Chile_ 21°45S 68°17W **94 A2**
Aseb _Eritrea_ 13°0N 42°40E **47 E3**
Asela _Ethiopia_ 8°0N 39°0E **47 F2**
Asenovgrad _Bulgaria_ 42°1N 24°51E **23 C11**
Aşgabat = Ashgabat _Turkmenistan_ 38°0N 57°50E **45 B8**
Asgata _Cyprus_ 34°46N 33°15E **25 E12**
Ash Fork _U.S.A._ 35°13N 112°29W **77 J7**
Ash Grove _U.S.A._ 37°19N 93°35W **80 G7**
Ash Shabakah _Iraq_ 30°49N 43°39E **44 D4**
Ash Shamāl □ _Lebanon_ 34°25N 36°0E **46 A5**
Ash Shāmīyah _Iraq_ 31°55N 44°35E **44 D5**
Ash Shāriqah _U.A.E._ 25°23N 55°26E **45 E7**
Ash Sharqāt _Iraq_ 35°27N 43°16E **44 C4**
Ash Sharmah _Si. Arabia_ 28°1N 35°16E **44 D2**
Ash Shaṭrah _Iraq_ 31°30N 46°10E **44 D5**
Ash Shawbak _Jordan_ 30°32N 35°34E **44 D2**
Ash Shiḩr _Yemen_ 14°45N 49°36E **47 E4**
Ash Shināfiyah _Iraq_ 31°35N 44°39E **44 D5**
Ash Shu'bah _Si. Arabia_ 28°54N 44°44E **44 D5**
Ash Shumlūl _Si. Arabia_ 26°31N 47°20E **44 E5**
Ash Shūr'a _Iraq_ 35°58N 43°13E **44 C4**
Ash Shurayf _Si. Arabia_ 25°43N 39°14E **44 E3**
Ash Shuwayfāt _Lebanon_ 33°45N 35°30E **46 B4**
Asha _Russia_ 55°0N 57°16E **18 D10**
Ashau _Vietnam_ 16°6N 107°22E **38 D6**
Ashbourne _U.K._ 53°2N 1°43W **12 D6**
Ashburn _U.S.A._ 31°43N 83°39W **85 F13**
Ashburton _N.Z._ 43°53S 171°48E **59 E3**
Ashburton → _Australia_ 21°40S 114°56E **60 D1**
Ashcroft _Canada_ 50°40N 121°20W **70 C4**
Ashdod _Israel_ 31°49N 34°35E **46 D3**
Ashdown _U.S.A._ 33°40N 94°8W **84 E7**
Asheboro _U.S.A._ 35°43N 79°49W **85 D15**
Ashern _Canada_ 51°11N 98°21W **71 C9**
Asherton _U.S.A._ 28°27N 99°46W **84 G5**
Asheville _U.S.A._ 35°36N 82°33W **85 D13**
Ashewat _Pakistan_ 31°22N 68°32E **42 D3**
Asheweig → _Canada_ 54°17N 87°12W **72 B2**
Ashford _Australia_ 29°15S 151°3E **63 D5**
Ashford _U.K._ 51°8N 0°53E **13 F8**
Ashgabat _Turkmenistan_ 38°0N 57°50E **45 B8**
Ashibetsu _Japan_ 43°31N 142°11E **30 C11**
Ashikaga _Japan_ 36°28N 139°29E **31 F9**
Ashington _U.K._ 55°11N 1°33W **12 B6**
Ashizuri-Uwakai △ _Japan_ 32°56N 132°32E **31 H6**
Ashizuri-Zaki _Japan_ 32°44N 133°0E **31 H6**
Ashkarkot _Afghan._ 33°3N 67°58E **42 C2**
Ashkhabad = Ashgabat _Turkmenistan_ 38°0N 57°50E **45 B8**
Āshkhāneh _Iran_ 37°26N 56°55E **45 B8**
Ashland _Kans., U.S.A._ 37°11N 99°46W **80 G4**
Ashland _Ky., U.S.A._ 38°28N 82°38W **81 F12**
Ashland _Maine, U.S.A._ 46°38N 68°24W **81 B19**
Ashland _Mont., U.S.A._ 45°36N 106°16W **76 D10**
Ashland _Ohio, U.S.A._ 40°52N 82°19W **82 F2**
Ashland _Oreg., U.S.A._ 42°12N 122°43W **76 E2**
Ashland _Pa., U.S.A._ 40°45N 76°22W **83 F8**
Ashland _Va., U.S.A._ 37°46N 77°29W **81 G15**
Ashland _Wis., U.S.A._ 46°35N 90°53W **80 B8**
Ashley _N. Dak., U.S.A._ 46°2N 99°22W **80 B4**
Ashley _Pa., U.S.A._ 41°12N 75°55W **83 E9**
Ashmore and Cartier Is. _Ind. Oc._ 12°15S 123°0E **60 B3**
Ashmore Reef _Australia_ 12°14S 123°5E **60 B3**
Ashmyany _Belarus_ 54°30N 25°58E **17 A13**
Ashokan Res. _U.S.A._ 41°56N 74°13W **83 E10**
Ashoknagar _India_ 24°34N 77°43E **42 G7**
Ashqelon _Israel_ 31°42N 34°35E **46 D3**
Ashta _India_ 23°1N 76°43E **42 H7**
Ashtabula _U.S.A._ 41°52N 80°47W **82 E4**
Ashton _S. Africa_ 33°50S 20°5E **56 E3**
Ashton _U.S.A._ 44°4N 111°27W **76 D8**
Ashuanipi, L. _Canada_ 52°45N 66°15W **73 B6**
Ashuapmushuan → _Canada_ 48°37N 72°20W **72 C5**
Ashville _U.S.A._ 40°34N 78°33W **82 F6**
Asia 45°0N 75°0E **26 E9**
Asia, Kepulauan _Indonesia_ 1°0N 131°13E **37 D8**
Asifabad _India_ 19°20N 79°24E **40 K11**
Asinara _Italy_ 41°4N 8°16E **22 D3**
Asinara, G. dell' _Italy_ 41°0N 8°30E **22 D3**
Asino _Russia_ 57°0N 86°0E **28 D9**
Asipovichy _Belarus_ 53°19N 28°33E **17 B15**
'Asīr □ _Si. Arabia_ 18°40N 42°30E **47 D3**
Asir, Ras _Somali Rep._ 11°55N 51°10E **47 E5**
Askham _S. Africa_ 26°59S 20°47E **56 D3**
Askim _Norway_ 59°35N 11°10E **9 G14**
Askja _Iceland_ 65°3N 16°48W **8 D5**
Asklipio _Greece_ 36°4N 27°56E **25 C9**

Askøyna *Norway* 60°29N 5°10E **8 F11**
Asmara = Asmera
  Eritrea 15°19N 38°55E **47 D2**
Asmera *Eritrea* 15°19N 38°55E **47 D2**
Åsnen *Sweden* 56°37N 14°45E **9 H16**
Aso Kuju △ *Japan* 32°53N 131°6E **31 H5**
Aspatria *U.K.* 54°47N 3°19W **12 C4**
Aspen *U.S.A.* 39°11N 106°49W **76 G10**
Aspermont *U.S.A.* 33°8N 100°14W **84 E4**
Aspiring, Mt. *N.Z.* 44°23S 168°46E **59 F2**
Aspur *India* 23°58N 74°7E **42 H6**
Asquith *Canada* 52°8N 107°13W **71 C7**
Assab = Aseb *Eritrea* 13°0N 42°40E **47 E3**
Assal, L. *Djibouti* 11°40N 42°26E **47 E3**
Assam □ *India* 26°0N 93°0E **41 G18**
Assateague Island △
  U.S.A. 38°15N 75°10W **81 F16**
Asse *Belgium* 50°24N 4°10E **15 D4**
Assen *Neths.* 53°0N 6°35E **15 A6**
Assiniboia *Canada* 49°40N 105°59W **71 D7**
Assiniboine ➤ *Canada* 49°53N 97°8W **71 D9**
Assiniboine, Mt.
  Canada 50°52N 115°39W **70 C5**
Assis *Brazil* 22°40S 50°20W **95 A5**
Assisi *Italy* 43°4N 12°37E **22 C5**
Assynt, L. *U.K.* 58°10N 5°3W **11 C3**
Astana *Kazakhstan* 51°10N 71°30E **32 A2**
Ăstăneh *Iran* 37°17N 49°59E **45 B6**
Astara *Azerbaijan* 38°30N 48°50E **45 B6**
Astarabad = Gorgān
  Iran 36°55N 54°30E **45 B7**
Asterousia *Greece* 34°59N 25°3E **25 E7**
Asti *Italy* 44°54N 8°12E **20 D8**
Astipalea *Greece* 36°32N 26°22E **23 F12**
Astorga *Spain* 42°29N 6°8W **21 A2**
Astoria *U.S.A.* 46°11N 123°50W **78 D3**
Astrakhan *Russia* 46°25N 48°5E **19 E8**
Astrebla Downs
  Australia 24°12S 140°34E **62 C3**
Asturias □ *Spain* 43°15N 6°0W **21 A3**
Asunción *Paraguay* 25°10S 57°30W **94 B4**
Asunción Nochixtlán
  Mexico 17°28N 97°14W **87 D5**
Aswa ➤ *Uganda* 3°43N 31°55E **54 B3**
Aswa-Lolim △ *Uganda* 2°43N 31°55E **54 B3**
Aswân *Egypt* 24°4N 32°57E **51 D12**
Aswan High Dam = Sadd el Aali
  Egypt 23°54N 32°54E **51 D12**
Asyût *Egypt* 27°11N 31°4E **51 C12**
At Tafilah *Jordan* 30°45N 35°30E **46 E4**
At Tafilah □ *Jordan* 30°45N 35°30E **46 E4**
At Tā'if *Si. Arabia* 21°5N 40°27E **47 C3**
At Ta'mim □ *Iraq* 35°30N 44°50E **44 C5**
At Ţirāq *Si. Arabia* 27°19N 44°33E **44 E5**
At Tubayq *Si. Arabia* 29°30N 37°0E **44 D3**
At Ţunayb *Jordan* 31°48N 35°57E **46 D4**
Atacama □ *Chile* 27°30S 70°0W **94 B2**
Atacama, Desierto de
  Chile 24°0S 69°20W **94 A2**
Atacama, Salar de *Chile* 23°30S 68°20W **94 A2**
Atakeye ◎ *Australia* 22°30S 133°45E **60 D5**
Atakpamé *Togo* 7°31N 1°13E **50 G6**
Atalaya *Peru* 10°45S 73°50W **92 F4**
Atalaya de Femes
  Canary Is. 28°56N 13°47W **24 F6**
Atami *Japan* 35°5N 139°4E **31 G9**
Atamyrat *Turkmenistan* 37°50N 65°12E **28 F7**
Atapupu *Indonesia* 9°0S 124°51E **37 F6**
Atâr *Mauritania* 20°30N 13°5W **50 D3**
Atari *Pakistan* 30°56N 74°2E **42 D6**
Atascadero *U.S.A.* 35°29N 120°40W **78 K6**
Atasu *Kazakhstan* 48°30N 71°0E **28 E8**
Atatürk Baraji *Turkey* 37°28N 38°30E **19 G6**
Atauro *E. Timor* 8°10S 125°30E **37 F7**
Atbara *Sudan* 17°42N 33°59E **51 E12**
'Atbara, Nahr ➤ *Sudan* 17°40N 33°56E **51 E12**
Atbasar *Kazakhstan* 51°48N 68°20E **28 D7**
Atchafalaya B. *U.S.A.* 29°25N 91°25W **84 G9**
Atchison *U.S.A.* 39°34N 95°7W **80 F6**
Ăteshān *Iran* 35°35N 52°37E **45 C7**
Ath *Belgium* 50°38N 3°47E **15 D3**
Athabasca *Canada* 54°45N 113°20W **70 C6**
Athabasca ➤ *Canada* 58°40N 110°50W **71 B6**
Athabasca, L. *Canada* 59°15N 109°15W **71 B7**
Athabasca Sand Dunes △
  Canada 59°4N 108°43W **71 B7**
Athboy *Ireland* 53°37N 6°56W **10 C5**
Athenry *Ireland* 53°18N 8°44W **10 C3**
Athens = Athina *Greece* 37°58N 23°43E **23 F10**
Athens *Ala., U.S.A.* 34°48N 86°58W **85 D11**
Athens *Ga., U.S.A.* 33°57N 83°23W **85 E13**
Athens *N.Y., U.S.A.* 42°16N 73°49W **83 D11**
Athens *Ohio, U.S.A.* 39°20N 82°6W **81 F12**
Athens *Pa., U.S.A.* 41°57N 76°31W **83 E8**
Athens *Tenn., U.S.A.* 35°27N 84°36W **85 D12**
Athens *Tex., U.S.A.* 32°12N 95°51W **84 E7**
Atherley *Canada* 44°37N 79°20W **82 B5**
Atherton *Australia* 17°17S 145°30E **62 B4**
Athi River *Kenya* 1°28S 36°58E **54 C4**
Athienou *Cyprus* 35°3N 33°32E **25 D12**
Athina *Greece* 37°58N 23°43E **23 F10**
Athinai = Athina
  Greece 37°58N 23°43E **23 F10**
Athlone *Ireland* 53°25N 7°56W **10 C4**
Athol *U.S.A.* 42°36N 72°14W **83 D12**
Atholl, Forest of *U.K.* 56°51N 3°50W **11 E5**
Atholville *Canada* 47°59N 66°43W **73 C6**
Athos *Greece* 40°9N 24°22E **23 D11**
Athy *Ireland* 53°0N 7°0W **10 C5**
Ati *Chad* 13°13N 18°20E **51 F9**
Atiak *Uganda* 3°12N 32°2E **54 B3**
Atikaki △ *Canada* 51°30N 95°31W **71 C9**
Atikameg ➤ *Canada* 52°30N 82°46W **72 B3**
Atikokan *Canada* 48°45N 91°37W **72 C1**
Atikonak L. *Canada* 52°40N 64°32W **73 B7**

Atimaono *Tahiti* 17°46S 149°28W **59 d**
Atitlán △ *Cent. Amer.* 14°38N 91°10W **87 E6**
Atiu *Cook Is.* 20°0S 158°10W **65 J12**
Atka *Russia* 60°50N 151°48E **29 C16**
Atka I. *U.S.A.* 52°7N 174°30W **74 E5**
Atlanta *U.S.A.* 33°45N 84°23W **85 E12**
Atlanta *Tex., U.S.A.* 33°7N 94°10W **84 E7**
Atlantic *U.S.A.* 41°24N 95°1W **80 E6**
Atlantic City *U.S.A.* 39°21N 74°27W **81 F16**
Atlantic-Indian Basin
  Antarctica 60°0S 30°0E **5 B4**
Atlantic Ocean 0°0 20°0W **2 D8**
Atlas Mts. = Haut Atlas
  Morocco 32°30N 5°0W **50 B4**
Atlin *Canada* 59°31N 133°41W **70 B2**
Atlin, L. *Canada* 59°26N 133°45W **70 B2**
Atlin △ *Canada* 59°10N 134°30W **70 B2**
Atmore *U.S.A.* 31°2N 87°29W **85 F11**
Atoka *U.S.A.* 34°23N 96°8W **84 D6**
Atolia *U.S.A.* 35°19N 117°37W **79 K9**
Atrai ➤ *Bangla.* 24°7N 89°22E **43 G13**
Atrak = Atrek ➤
  Turkmenistan 37°35N 53°58E **45 B8**
Atrauli *India* 28°2N 78°20E **42 E8**
Atrek ➤ *Turkmenistan* 37°35N 53°58E **45 B8**
Atsuta *Japan* 43°24N 141°26E **30 C10**
Attalla *U.S.A.* 34°1N 86°6W **85 D11**
Attapu *Laos* 14°48N 106°50E **38 E6**
Attawapiskat *Canada* 52°56N 82°24W **72 B3**
Attawapiskat ➤
  Canada 52°57N 82°18W **72 B3**
Attawapiskat L. *Canada* 52°18N 87°54W **72 B2**
Attica *Ind., U.S.A.* 40°18N 87°15W **80 E10**
Attica *Ohio, U.S.A.* 41°4N 82°53W **82 E2**
Attikamagen L. *Canada* 55°0N 66°30W **73 B6**
Attleboro *U.S.A.* 41°57N 71°17W **83 E13**
Attock *Pakistan* 33°52N 72°20E **42 C5**
Attopeu = Attapu *Laos* 14°48N 106°50E **38 E6**
Attur *I. U.S.A.* 52°55N 172°55E **74 E2**
Attur *India* 11°35N 78°30E **40 P11**
Atuel ➤ *Argentina* 36°17S 66°50W **94 D2**
Atura *Uganda* 2°7N 32°20E **54 B3**
Åtvidaberg *Sweden* 58°12N 16°0E **9 G17**
Atwater *U.S.A.* 37°21N 120°37W **78 H6**
Atwood *Canada* 43°40N 81°1W **82 C3**
Atwood *U.S.A.* 39°48N 101°3W **80 F3**
Atyraū *Kazakhstan* 47°5N 52°0E **19 E9**
Au Sable ➤ *U.S.A.* 44°25N 83°20W **82 B1**
Au Sable *U.S.A.* 44°25N 83°20W **81 C12**
Au Sable Forks *U.S.A.* 44°27N 73°41W **83 B11**
Au Sable Pt. *U.S.A.* 44°20N 83°20W **82 B1**
Auas *Honduras* 15°29N 84°20W **88 C3**
Auasberg *Namibia* 22°37S 17°13E **56 C2**
Aubagne *France* 43°17N 5°37E **20 E6**
Aube □ *France* 48°34N 3°43E **20 B5**
Auberry *U.S.A.* 37°7N 119°29W **78 H7**
Auburn *Ala., U.S.A.* 32°36N 85°29W **85 E12**
Auburn *Calif., U.S.A.* 38°54N 121°4W **78 G5**
Auburn *Ind., U.S.A.* 41°22N 85°4W **81 E11**
Auburn *Maine, U.S.A.* 44°6N 70°14W **81 C18**
Auburn *N.Y., U.S.A.* 42°56N 76°34W **83 D8**
Auburn *Nebr., U.S.A.* 40°23N 95°51W **80 E6**
Auburn *Pa., U.S.A.* 40°36N 76°6W **83 F8**
Auburn *Wash., U.S.A.* 47°18N 122°14W **78 C4**
Auburn Ra. *Australia* 25°15S 150°30E **63 D5**
Auburndale *U.S.A.* 28°4N 81°48W **85 G14**
Aubusson *France* 45°57N 2°11E **20 D5**
Auch *France* 43°39N 0°36E **20 E4**
Auchterarder *U.K.* 56°18N 3°41W **11 E5**
Auchtermuchty *U.K.* 56°18N 3°13W **11 E5**
Auckland *N.Z.* 36°52S 174°46E **59 B5**
Auckland Is. *Pac. Oc.* 50°40S 166°5E **64 N8**
Aude □ *France* 43°13N 3°14E **20 E5**
Auden *Canada* 50°14N 87°53W **72 B2**
Audubon *U.S.A.* 41°43N 94°56W **80 E6**
Augathella *Australia* 25°48S 146°35E **63 D4**
Aughnacloy *U.K.* 54°25N 6°59W **10 B5**
Aughrim *Ireland* 52°51N 6°20W **10 D5**
Augrabies Falls *S. Africa* 28°35S 20°20E **56 D3**
Augrabies Falls △
  S. Africa 28°40S 20°22E **56 D3**
Augsburg *Germany* 48°25N 10°52E **16 D6**
Augusta *Australia* 34°19S 115°9E **61 F2**
Augusta *Italy* 37°13N 15°13E **22 F6**
Augusta *Ark., U.S.A.* 35°17N 91°22W **84 D9**
Augusta *Ga., U.S.A.* 33°28N 81°58W **85 E14**
Augusta *Kans., U.S.A.* 37°41N 96°59W **80 G5**
Augusta *Maine, U.S.A.* 44°19N 69°47W **81 C19**
Augusta *Mont., U.S.A.* 47°30N 112°24W **76 C7**
Augustów *Poland* 53°51N 23°0E **17 B12**
Augustus, Mt. *Australia* 24°20S 116°50E **61 D2**
Augustus I. *Australia* 15°20S 124°30E **60 C3**
Aujuittuq = Grise Fiord
  Canada 76°25N 82°57W **69 B15**
Aukštaitija △ *Lithuania* 55°15N 26°0E **9 J22**
Aukum *U.S.A.* 38°34N 120°43W **78 G6**
Aulavik △ *Canada* 73°42N 119°55W **68 C8**
Auld, L. *Australia* 22°25S 123°50E **60 D3**
Ault *U.S.A.* 40°35N 104°44W **76 F11**
Aunis *France* 46°5N 0°50W **20 C3**
Aunu'u *Amer. Samoa* 14°20S 170°31W **59 b**
Auponhia *Indonesia* 1°58S 125°27E **37 E7**
Aur, Pulau *Malaysia* 2°35N 104°10E **39 L5**
Auraiya *India* 26°28N 79°33E **43 F8**
Aurangabad *Bihar, India* 24°45N 84°18E **43 G11**
Aurangabad *Maharashtra, India* 19°50N 75°23E **40 K9**
Aurich *Germany* 53°28N 7°28E **16 B4**
Aurillac *France* 44°55N 2°26E **20 D5**
Aurora *Canada* 44°0N 79°28W **82 C5**
Aurora *S. Africa* 32°40S 18°29E **56 E2**
Aurora *Colo., U.S.A.* 39°43N 104°49W **76 G11**
Aurora *Ill., U.S.A.* 41°45N 88°19W **80 E9**
Aurora *Mo., U.S.A.* 36°58N 93°43W **80 G7**
Aurora *N.Y., U.S.A.* 42°45N 76°42W **83 D8**
Aurora *Nebr., U.S.A.* 40°52N 98°0W **80 E5**

Aurora *Ohio, U.S.A.* 41°21N 81°20W **82 E3**
Aurukun *Australia* 13°20S 141°45E **62 A3**
Aurukun ◎ *Australia* 13°36S 141°48E **62 A3**
Aus *Namibia* 26°35S 16°12E **56 D2**
Ausable ➤ *Canada* 43°19N 81°46W **82 C3**
Auschwitz = Oświęcim
  Poland 50°2N 19°11E **17 C10**
Auski Roadhouse
  Australia 22°22S 118°41E **60 D2**
Austin *Minn., U.S.A.* 43°40N 92°58W **80 D7**
Austin *Nev., U.S.A.* 39°30N 117°4W **76 G5**
Austin *Pa., U.S.A.* 41°38N 78°6W **82 E6**
Austin *Tex., U.S.A.* 30°17N 97°45W **84 F6**
Austin, L. *Australia* 27°40S 118°0E **61 E2**
Austin I. *Canada* 61°10N 94°0W **71 A10**
Austra *Norway* 65°8N 11°55E **8 D14**
Austral Is. = Tubuaï, Îs.
  French Polynesia 25°0S 150°0W **65 K13**
Austral Seamount Chain
  Pac. Oc. 24°0S 150°0W **65 K13**
Australia ■ *Oceania* 23°0S 135°0E **58 D6**
Australian-Antarctic Basin
  S. Ocean 60°0S 120°0E **5 C9**
Australian Capital Territory □
  Australia 35°30S 149°0E **63 F4**
Australind *Australia* 33°17S 115°42E **61 F2**
Austria ■ *Europe* 47°0N 14°0E **16 E8**
Austvågøya *Norway* 68°20N 14°40E **8 B16**
Autlán de Navarro
  Mexico 19°46N 104°22W **86 D4**
Autun *France* 46°58N 4°17E **20 C6**
Auvergne □ *France* 45°20N 3°15E **20 D5**
Auvergne, Mts. d' *France* 45°20N 2°55E **20 D5**
Auxerre *France* 47°48N 3°32E **20 C5**
Auyuittuq △ *Canada* 67°30N 66°0W **69 D18**
Av-Dovurak *Russia* 51°17N 91°35E **29 D10**
Ava *U.S.A.* 36°57N 92°40W **80 G7**
Avallon *France* 47°30N 3°53E **20 C5**
Avalon *U.S.A.* 33°21N 118°20W **79 M8**
Avalon Pen. *Canada* 47°30N 53°20W **73 C9**
Avanos *Turkey* 38°43N 34°51E **44 B5**
Avaré *Brazil* 23°4S 48°58W **95 A6**
Avawatz Mts. *U.S.A.* 35°40N 116°30W **79 K10**
Aveiro *Brazil* 3°10S 55°5W **93 D7**
Aveiro *Portugal* 40°37N 8°38W **21 B1**
Avej *Iran* 35°40N 49°15E **45 C6**
Avellaneda *Argentina* 34°40S 58°22W **94 C4**
Avellino *Italy* 40°54N 14°47E **22 D6**
Avenal *U.S.A.* 36°0N 120°8W **78 K6**
Aversa *Italy* 40°58N 14°12E **22 D6**
Avery *U.S.A.* 47°15N 115°49W **76 C6**
Aves, I. de *W. Indies* 15°45N 63°55W **89 C7**
Aves, Is. las *Venezuela* 12°0N 67°30W **89 D6**
Avesta *Sweden* 60°9N 16°10E **9 F17**
Aveyron ➤ *France* 44°5N 1°16E **20 D4**
Avezzano *Italy* 42°2N 13°25E **22 C5**
Aviá Terai *Argentina* 26°45S 60°50W **94 B3**
Aviemore *U.K.* 57°12N 3°50W **11 D5**
Avignon *France* 43°57N 4°50E **20 E6**
Ávila *Spain* 40°39N 4°43W **21 B3**
Avila Beach *U.S.A.* 35°11N 120°44W **79 K6**
Avilés *Spain* 43°35N 5°57W **21 A3**
Avis *U.S.A.* 41°11N 77°19W **82 E7**
Avoca ➤ *Australia* 35°40S 143°43E **63 F3**
Avoca ➤ *Ireland* 52°48N 6°10W **10 D5**
Avola *Canada* 51°45N 119°19W **70 C5**
Avola *Italy* 36°56N 15°7E **22 F6**
Avon ➤ *Australia* 31°40S 116°7E **61 F2**
Avon *U.S.A.* 42°55N 77°45W **82 D7**
Avon ➤ *Bristol, U.K.* 51°29N 2°41W **13 F5**
Avon ➤ *Dorset, U.K.* 50°44N 1°46W **13 G6**
Avon ➤ *Warks., U.K.* 52°0N 2°8W **13 E5**
Avon Park *U.S.A.* 27°36N 81°31W **85 H14**
Avondale *Zimbabwe* 17°43S 30°58E **55 F3**
Avonlea *Canada* 50°0N 105°0W **71 D8**
Avonmore *Canada* 45°10N 74°58W **83 A10**
Avonmouth *U.K.* 51°30N 2°42W **13 F5**
Avranches *France* 48°40N 1°20W **20 B3**
Awa-Shima *Japan* 38°27N 139°14E **30 E9**
A'waj ➤ *Syria* 33°23N 36°20E **46 B5**
Awaji-Shima *Japan* 34°30N 134°50E **31 G7**
'Awālī *Bahrain* 26°0N 50°30E **45 E6**
Awantipur *India* 33°55N 75°3E **43 C6**
Awasa *Ethiopia* 7°2N 38°28E **47 F2**
Awash *Ethiopia* 9°1N 40°10E **47 F3**
Awatere ➤ *N.Z.* 41°37S 174°10E **59 D5**
Awbārī *Libya* 26°46N 12°57E **51 C8**
Awbārī, Idehan *Libya* 27°10N 11°30E **51 C8**
Awe, L. *U.K.* 56°17N 5°16W **11 E3**
Awjilah *Libya* 29°8N 21°7E **51 C10**
Axe ➤ *U.K.* 50°42N 3°4W **13 G4**
Axel Heiberg I. *Canada* 80°0N 90°0W **69 F14**
Axim *Ghana* 4°51N 2°15W **50 H5**
Axios ➤ *Greece* 40°57N 22°35E **23 D10**
Axminster *U.K.* 50°46N 3°0W **13 G4**
Ayabaca *Peru* 4°40S 79°53W **92 D3**
Ayabe *Japan* 35°20N 135°20E **31 G7**
Ayacucho *Argentina* 37°5S 58°20W **94 D4**
Ayacucho *Peru* 13°0S 74°0W **92 F4**
Ayaguz = Ayaköz
  Kazakhstan 48°10N 80°10E **32 B3**
Ayaköz *Kazakhstan* 48°10N 80°10E **32 B3**
Ayamonte *Spain* 37°12N 7°24W **21 D2**
Ayan *Russia* 56°30N 138°16E **29 D14**
Ayaviri *Peru* 14°50S 70°35W **92 F4**
Aydın *Turkey* 37°51N 27°51E **23 F12**
Aydingkol Hu *China* 42°40N 89°15E **32 B3**
Ayer *U.S.A.* 42°34N 71°35W **83 D13**
Ayer Hitam *Malaysia* 5°24N 100°16E **39 c**
Ayer's Cliff *Canada* 45°10N 72°3W **83 A12**
Ayers Rock = Uluru
  Australia 25°23S 131°5E **61 E5**
Ayeyarwady = Irrawaddy ➤
  Burma 15°50N 95°6E **41 M19**
Áyia Napa *Cyprus* 34°59N 34°0E **25 E13**
Áyia Phyla *Cyprus* 34°45N 33°1E **25 E12**
Áyios Amvrósios
  Cyprus 35°20N 33°35E **25 D12**

Áyios Seryios *Cyprus* 35°12N 33°53E **25 D12**
Áyios Theodhoros
  Cyprus 35°22N 34°1E **25 D13**
Aykhal *Russia* 66°0N 111°30E **29 C12**
Aykino *Russia* 62°15N 49°56E **18 B8**
Aylesbury *U.K.* 51°49N 0°49W **13 F7**
Aylmer *Canada* 42°46N 80°59W **82 D4**
Aylmer, L. *Canada* 64°5N 108°30W **68 E10**
'Ayn, Wādī al *Oman* 22°15N 55°28E **45 F7**
Ayn Dār *Si. Arabia* 25°55N 49°10E **45 E7**
Ayn Zālah *Iraq* 36°45N 42°35E **44 B4**
Ayolas *Paraguay* 27°10S 56°59W **94 B4**
Ayon, Ostrov *Russia* 69°50N 169°0E **29 C17**
'Ayoûn el 'Atroûs
  Mauritania 16°38N 9°37W **50 E4**
Ayr *Australia* 19°35S 147°25E **62 B4**
Ayr *Canada* 43°17N 80°27W **82 C4**
Ayr *U.K.* 55°28N 4°38W **11 F4**
Ayr ➤ *U.K.* 55°28N 4°38W **11 F4**
Ayre, Pt. of *I. of Man* 54°25N 4°21W **12 C3**
Ayton *Australia* 15°56S 145°22E **62 B4**
Aytos *Bulgaria* 42°42N 27°16E **23 C12**
Ayu, Kepulauan
  Indonesia 0°35N 131°5E **37 D8**
Ayutla *Guatemala* 14°40N 92°10W **88 D1**
Ayutla de los Libres
  Mexico 16°54N 99°13W **87 D5**
Ayvacık *Turkey* 39°36N 26°24E **23 E12**
Ayvalık *Turkey* 39°20N 26°46E **23 E12**
Az Zabadānī *Syria* 33°43N 36°5E **46 B5**
Az Zāhiriyah *West Bank* 31°25N 34°58E **46 D3**
Az Zahrān *Si. Arabia* 26°10N 50°7E **45 E6**
Az Zarqā *Jordan* 32°5N 36°4E **46 C5**
Az Zarqā □ *Jordan* 32°5N 36°4E **46 C5**
Az Zarqā' *U.A.E.* 24°53N 53°4E **45 E7**
Az Zāwiyah *Libya* 32°52N 12°56E **51 B8**
Az Zībār *Iraq* 36°52N 44°4E **44 B5**
Az Zilfī *Si. Arabia* 26°12N 44°52E **44 E5**
Az Zubayr *Iraq* 30°26N 47°40E **44 D5**
Azad Kashmir □
  Pakistan 33°50N 73°50E **43 C5**
Azamgarh *India* 26°5N 83°13E **43 F10**
Azangaro *Peru* 14°55S 70°13W **92 F4**
Azaouad *Mali* 19°0N 3°0W **50 E5**
Āzar Shahr *Iran* 37°45N 45°59E **44 B5**
Azarān *Iran* 37°25N 47°16E **44 B5**
Ãzarbāyjān = Azerbaijan ■
  Asia 40°20N 48°0E **19 F8**
Ãzarbāyjān-e Gharbī □
  Iran 37°0N 44°30E **44 B5**
Ãzarbāyjān-e Sharqī □
  Iran 37°20N 47°0E **44 B5**
Azare *Nigeria* 11°55N 10°10E **50 F8**
A'zāz *Syria* 36°36N 37°4E **44 B3**
Azbine = Aïr *Niger* 18°30N 8°0E **50 E7**
Azerbaijan ■ *Asia* 40°20N 48°0E **19 F8**
Azimganj *India* 24°14N 88°16E **43 G13**
Azogues *Ecuador* 2°35S 78°0W **92 D3**
Azores = Açores, Is. dos
  Atl. Oc. 38°0N 27°0W **50 a**
Azov *Russia* 47°3N 39°25E **19 E6**
Azov, Sea of *Europe* 46°0N 36°30E **19 E6**
Azovskoye More = Azov, Sea of
  Europe 46°0N 36°30E **19 E6**
Azraq ash Shīshān
  Jordan 31°50N 36°49E **46 D5**
Aztec *U.S.A.* 36°49N 107°59W **77 H10**
Azúa de Compostela
  Dom. Rep. 18°25N 70°44W **89 C5**
Azuaga *Spain* 38°16N 5°39W **21 C3**
Azuero, Pen. de *Panama* 7°30N 80°30W **88 E3**
Azul *Argentina* 36°42S 59°43W **94 D4**
Azusa *U.S.A.* 34°8N 117°52W **79 L9**
Azzel Matti, Sebkra
  Algeria 26°10N 0°43E **50 C6**

B

Ba Be △ *Vietnam* 22°25N 105°37E **38 A5**
Ba Don *Vietnam* 17°45N 106°26E **38 D6**
Ba Ngoi = Cam Lam
  Vietnam 11°54N 109°10E **39 G7**
Ba Tri *Vietnam* 10°2N 106°36E **39 G6**
Ba Vi ➤ *Vietnam* 21°1N 105°22E **38 B5**
Ba Xian = Bazhou *China* 39°8N 116°22E **34 E9**
Baa *Indonesia* 10°50S 123°0E **60 B3**
Baardheere *Somali Rep.* 2°20N 42°27E **47 G3**
Baarle-Nassau *Belgium* 51°27N 4°56E **15 C4**
Bab el Mandeb *Red Sea* 12°35N 43°25E **47 E3**
Bābā, Koh-i- *Afghan.* 34°30N 67°0E **40 B5**
Baba Burnu *Turkey* 39°29N 26°2E **23 E12**
Bābā Kalū *Iran* 30°7N 50°49E **45 D6**
Babadag *Romania* 44°54N 28°44E **17 F15**
Babaeski *Turkey* 41°26N 27°6E **23 D12**
Babahoyo *Ecuador* 1°40S 79°30W **92 D3**
Babai = Sarju ➤ *India* 27°21N 81°23E **43 F9**
Babar *Indonesia* 8°0S 129°30E **37 F7**
Babar *Pakistan* 31°7N 69°32E **42 D3**
Babarkach *Pakistan* 29°45N 68°0E **42 E3**
Babb *U.S.A.* 48°51N 113°27W **76 B7**
Baberu *India* 25°33N 80°43E **43 G9**
Babi Besar, Pulau
  Malaysia 2°25N 103°59E **39 L4**
Bābil □ *Iraq* 32°30N 44°30E **44 C5**
Babinda *Australia* 17°20S 145°56E **62 B4**
Babine *Canada* 55°22N 126°37W **70 B3**
Babine ➤ *Canada* 55°45N 127°44W **70 B3**
Babine L. *Canada* 54°48N 126°0W **70 C3**
Babo *Indonesia* 2°30S 133°30E **37 E8**
Bābol *Iran* 36°40N 52°50E **45 B7**
Bābol Sar *Iran* 36°45N 52°45E **45 B7**
Baboua *C.A.R.* 5°49N 14°58E **52 C2**
Babruysk *Belarus* 53°10N 29°15E **17 B15**
Babuhri *India* 26°49N 69°43E **42 F3**
Babusar Pass *Pakistan* 35°12N 73°59E **43 B5**
Babuyan Chan. *Phil.* 18°40N 121°30E **37 A6**
Babylon *Iraq* 32°34N 44°22E **44 C5**

Bac Can *Vietnam* 22°8N 105°49E **38 A5**
Bac Giang *Vietnam* 21°16N 106°11E **38 B6**
Bac Lieu *Vietnam* 9°17N 105°43E **39 H5**
Bac Ninh *Vietnam* 21°13N 106°4E **38 B6**
Bac Phan *Vietnam* 22°0N 105°0E **38 B5**
Bac Quang *Vietnam* 22°30N 104°48E **38 A5**
Bacabal *Brazil* 4°15S 44°45W **93 D10**
Bacalar *Mexico* 18°43N 88°27W **87 D7**
Bacan, Kepulauan
  Indonesia 0°35S 127°30E **37 E7**
Bacarra *Phil.* 18°15N 120°37E **37 A6**
Bacău *Romania* 46°35N 26°55E **17 E14**
Bacerac *Mexico* 30°18N 108°50W **86 A3**
Bach Long Vi, Dao
  Vietnam 20°10N 107°40E **38 B6**
Bach Ma △ *Vietnam* 16°11N 107°49E **38 D6**
Bachhwara *India* 25°35N 85°54E **43 G11**
Back ➤ *Canada* 65°10N 104°0W **68 D11**
Bacolod *Phil.* 10°40N 122°57E **37 B6**
Bacuk *Malaysia* 6°4N 102°25E **39 J4**
Bácum *Mexico* 27°33N 110°5W **86 B2**
Bād *Iran* 33°41N 52°1E **45 C7**
Bad ➤ *U.S.A.* 44°21N 100°22W **80 C3**
Bad Axe *U.S.A.* 43°48N 83°0W **82 C2**
Bad Ischl *Austria* 47°44N 13°38E **16 E7**
Bad Kissingen *Germany* 50°11N 10°4E **16 C6**
Bada Barabil *India* 22°7N 85°24E **43 H11**
Badagara *India* 11°35N 75°40E **40 P9**
Badain Jaran Shamo
  China 40°23N 102°0E **32 B5**
Badajós, L. *Brazil* 3°15S 62°50W **92 D6**
Badajoz *Spain* 38°50N 6°59W **21 C2**
Badakhshān □ *Afghan.* 36°30N 71°0E **40 A7**
Badaling *China* 40°21N 116°0E **33 B6**
Badalona *Spain* 41°26N 2°15E **21 B7**
Badalzai *Afghan.* 29°50N 65°35E **42 E1**
Badampahar *India* 22°10N 86°10E **41 H15**
Badanah *Si. Arabia* 30°58N 41°30E **44 D4**
Badarinath *India* 30°45N 79°30E **43 D8**
Badas, Kepulauan
  Indonesia 0°45N 107°5E **36 D3**
Baddo ➤ *Pakistan* 28°0N 64°20E **40 F4**
Bade *Indonesia* 7°10S 139°35E **37 F9**
Baden *Austria* 48°1N 16°13E **16 D9**
Baden *U.S.A.* 40°38N 80°14W **82 F4**
Baden-Baden *Germany* 48°44N 8°13E **16 D5**
Baden-Württemberg □
  Germany 48°20N 8°40E **16 D5**
Badgam *India* 34°1N 74°45E **43 B6**
Badgastein *Austria* 47°7N 13°9E **16 E7**
Badger *Canada* 49°0N 56°4W **73 C8**
Badger *U.S.A.* 36°38N 119°1W **78 J7**
Bādghīs □ *Afghan.* 35°0N 63°0E **40 B3**
Badgingarra △
  Australia 30°23S 115°22E **61 F2**
Badin *Pakistan* 24°38N 68°54E **42 G3**
Badlands *U.S.A.* 43°55N 102°30W **80 D2**
Badlands △ *U.S.A.* 43°38N 102°56W **80 D2**
Badrah *Iraq* 33°6N 45°58E **44 C5**
Badrinath *India* 30°44N 79°29E **43 D8**
Badu *Australia* 10°7S 142°11E **62 a**
Badulla *Sri Lanka* 7°1N 81°7E **40 R12**
Badung, Selat *Indonesia* 8°40S 115°22E **37 K18**
Baena *Spain* 37°37N 4°20W **21 D3**
Baengnyeongdo
  S. Korea 37°57N 124°40E **35 F13**
Baeza *Spain* 37°57N 3°25W **21 D4**
Bafatá *Guinea-Biss.* 12°8N 14°40W **50 F3**
Baffin B. *N. Amer.* 72°0N 64°0W **69 C19**
Baffin I. *Canada* 68°0N 75°0W **69 D17**
Bafing ➤ *Mali* 13°49N 10°50W **50 F3**
Bafliyūn *Syria* 36°37N 36°59E **44 B3**
Bafoulabé *Mali* 13°50N 10°55W **50 F3**
Bafoussam *Cameroon* 5°28N 10°25E **52 C2**
Bāfq *Iran* 31°40N 55°25E **45 D7**
Bafra *Turkey* 41°34N 35°54E **19 F6**
Bāft *Iran* 29°15N 56°38E **45 D8**
Bafwasende
  Dem. Rep. of the Congo 1°3N 27°5E **54 B2**
Bagaha *India* 27°6N 84°5E **43 F11**
Bagamoyo *Tanzania* 6°28S 38°55E **54 D4**
Bagan Datoh *Malaysia* 3°59N 100°47E **39 L3**
Bagan Serai *Malaysia* 5°1N 100°32E **39 K3**
Baganga *Phil.* 7°34N 126°33E **37 C7**
Bagani *Namibia* 18°7S 21°41E **56 B3**
Bagansiapiapi *Indonesia* 2°12N 100°50E **36 D2**
Bagasra *India* 21°30N 71°0E **42 J4**
Bagaud *India* 22°19N 75°53E **42 H6**
Bagdad *U.S.A.* 34°35N 115°53W **79 L11**
Bagdarin *Russia* 54°26N 113°36E **29 D12**
Bagé *Brazil* 31°20S 54°15W **95 C5**
Bagenalstown = Muine Bheag
  Ireland 52°42N 6°58W **10 D5**
Baggs *U.S.A.* 41°2N 107°39W **76 F10**
Bagh *Pakistan* 33°59N 73°45E **43 C5**
Baghain ➤ *India* 25°32N 81°1E **43 G9**
Baghdād *Iraq* 33°20N 44°23E **44 C5**
Bagheria *Italy* 38°5N 13°30E **22 E5**
Baghlān *Afghan.* 32°12N 68°46E **40 A6**
Baghlān □ *Afghan.* 36°0N 68°30E **40 B6**
Bagley *U.S.A.* 47°32N 95°24W **80 B6**
Bago = Pegu *Burma* 17°20N 96°29E **41 L20**
Bagodar *India* 24°5N 85°52E **43 G11**
Baguio *Phil.* 16°26N 120°34E **37 A6**
Bah *India* 26°53N 78°36E **43 F8**
Bahadurganj *India* 26°16N 87°49E **43 F12**
Bahadurgarh *India* 28°40N 76°57E **42 E7**
Bahama, Canal Viejo de
  W. Indies 22°10N 77°30W **88 B4**
Bahamas ■ *N. Amer.* 24°0N 75°0W **89 B5**
Bahār *Iran* 34°54N 48°26E **45 C6**
Baharampur *India* 24°2N 88°27E **43 G13**
Baharu Pandan = Pandan
  Malaysia 1°32N 103°46E **39 d**
Bahawalnagar *Pakistan* 30°0N 73°15E **42 E5**
Bahawalpur *Pakistan* 29°24N 71°40E **42 E4**
Bāherden *Turkmenistan* 38°25N 57°26E **45 B8**
Baheri *India* 28°45N 79°34E **43 E8**

Bahgul ➤ *India* 27°45N 79°36E **43** F8
Bahi *Tanzania* 5°58S 35°21E **54** D4
Bahi Swamp *Tanzania* 6°10S 35°0E **54** D4
Bahía = Salvador *Brazil* 13°0S 38°30W **93** F11
Bahía □ *Brazil* 12°0S 42°0W **93** F10
Bahía, Is. de la *Honduras* 16°45N 86°15W **88** C2
Bahía Blanca *Argentina* 38°35S 62°13W **94** D3
Bahía de Caráquez
    Ecuador 0°40S 80°27W **92** D2
Bahía Kino *Mexico* 28°47N 111°58W **86** B2
Bahía Laura *Argentina* 48°10S 66°30W **96** F3
Bahía Negra *Paraguay* 20°5S 58°5W **92** H7
Bahir Dar *Ethiopia* 11°37N 37°10E **47** E2
Bahmanzād *Iran* 31°15N 54°7E **45** D6
Bahraich *India* 27°38N 81°37E **43** F9
Bahrain ■ *Asia* 26°0N 50°35E **45** E6
Bahror *India* 27°51N 76°20E **42** F7
Bāhū Kalāt *Iran* 25°43N 61°25E **45** E9
Bai Bung, Mui = Ca Mau, Mui
    Vietnam 8°38N 104°44E **39** H5
Bai Duc *Vietnam* 18°3N 105°49E **38** C5
Bai Thuong *Vietnam* 19°54N 105°23E **38** C5
Baia Mare *Romania* 47°40N 23°35E **17** E12
Baião *Brazil* 2°40S 49°40W **93** D9
Baïbokoum *Chad* 7°46N 15°43E **51** G9
Baidoa = Baydhabo
    Somali Rep. 3°8N 43°30E **47** G3
Baie-Comeau *Canada* 49°12N 68°10W **73** C6
Baie-St-Paul *Canada* 47°28N 70°32W **73** C5
Baie Ste-Anne *Seychelles* 4°18S 55°45E **53** b
Baie-Trinité *Canada* 49°25N 67°20W **73** C6
Baie Verte *Canada* 49°55N 56°12W **73** C8
Baihar *India* 22°6N 80°33E **43** H9
Baihe *China* 32°50N 110°5E **34** H6
Ba'iji *Iraq* 35°0N 43°30E **44** C4
Baijnath *India* 29°55N 79°37E **43** E8
Baikal, L. = Baykal, Oz.
    Russia 53°0N 108°0E **29** D11
Baikonur = Bayqongyr
    Kazakhstan 45°40N 63°20E **28** E7
Baikunthpur *India* 23°15N 82°33E **43** H10
Baile Átha Cliath = Dublin
    Ireland 53°21N 6°15W **10** C5
Baile Átha Fhirdhia = Ardee
    Ireland 53°52N 6°33W **10** C5
Baile Átha I = Athy *Ireland* 53°0N 7°0W **10** C5
Baile Átha Luain = Athlone
    Ireland 53°25N 7°56W **10** C4
Baile Átha Troim = Trim
    Ireland 53°33N 6°48W **10** C5
Baile Brigín = Balbriggan
    Ireland 53°37N 6°11W **10** C5
Băilești *Romania* 44°1N 23°20E **17** F12
Bainbridge *Ga., U.S.A.* 30°55N 84°35W **85** F12
Bainbridge *N.Y., U.S.A.* 42°18N 75°29W **83** D9
Bainbridge Island
    U.S.A. 47°38N 122°32W **78** C4
Baing *Indonesia* 10°14S 120°34E **37** F6
Bā'ir *Jordan* 30°45N 36°55E **46** E5
Baird Mts. *U.S.A.* 67°0N 160°0W **74** B8
Bairiki = Tarawa *Kiribati* 1°30N 173°0E **64** G9
Bairin Youqi *China* 43°30N 118°35E **35** C10
Bairin Zuoqi *China* 43°58N 119°15E **35** C10
Bairnsdale *Australia* 37°48S 147°36E **63** F4
Baisha *China* 34°20N 112°32E **34** G7
Baitadi *Nepal* 29°35N 80°25E **43** E9
Baiyin *China* 36°45N 104°14E **34** F3
Baiyu Shan *China* 37°15N 107°30E **34** F4
Baj Baj *India* 22°30N 88°5E **43** H13
Baja *Hungary* 46°12N 18°59E **17** E10
Baja California *Mexico* 31°10N 115°12W **86** A1
Baja California □ *Mexico* 30°0N 115°0W **86** B2
Baja California Sur □
    Mexico 25°50N 111°50W **86** B2
Bajag *India* 22°40N 81°21E **43** H9
Bajamar *Canary Is.* 28°33N 16°20W **24** F3
Bajana *India* 23°7N 71°49E **42** H4
Bajatrejo *Indonesia* 8°29S 114°19E **37** J17
Bajera *India* 8°13S 115°2E **37** J18
Bājgīrān *Iran* 37°36N 58°24E **45** B8
Bajimba, Mt. *Australia* 29°17S 152°6E **63** D5
Bajo Boquete *Panama* 8°46N 82°27W **88** E3
Bajo Nuevo *Caribbean* 15°40N 78°50W **88** C4
Bajoga *Nigeria* 10°57N 11°20E **51** F8
Bajool *Australia* 23°40S 150°35E **62** C5
Bakel *Senegal* 14°56N 12°20W **50** F3
Baker *Calif., U.S.A.* 35°16N 116°4W **79** K10
Baker *Mont., U.S.A.* 46°22N 104°17W **76** C11
Baker, L. *Canada* 64°0N 96°0W **68** E12
Baker, Mt. *U.S.A.* 48°50N 121°49W **76** B3
Baker I. *Pac. Oc.* 0°10N 176°35W **64** G10
Baker I. *U.S.A.* 55°20N 133°40W **70** B2
Baker L. *Australia* 26°54S 126°5E **61** E4
Baker Lake *Canada* 64°20N 96°3W **68** E12
Bakers Creek *Australia* 21°13S 149°7E **62** C4
Bakers Dozen Is. *Canada* 56°45N 78°45W **72** A4
Bakersfield *Calif., U.S.A.* 35°23N 119°1W **79** K8
Bakersfield *Vt., U.S.A.* 44°45N 72°48W **83** B12
Bakharden = Bäherden
    Turkmenistan 38°25N 57°26E **45** B8
Bākhtarān = Kermānshāh
    Iran 34°23N 47°0E **44** C5
Bākhtarān = Kermānshāh □
    Iran 34°0N 46°30E **44** C5
Baki *Azerbaijan* 40°29N 49°56E **45** A6
Bakkafjörður *Iceland* 66°2N 14°48W **8** C6
Bakouma *C.A.R.* 5°40N 22°56E **52** C4
Bakswaho *India* 24°15N 79°18E **43** G8
Baku = Bakı *Azerbaijan* 40°29N 49°56E **45** A6
Bakutis Coast *Antarctica* 74°0S 120°0W **5** D15
Baky = Bakı *Azerbaijan* 40°29N 49°56E **45** A6
Bala *Canada* 45°1N 79°37W **82** A5
Bala *U.K.* 52°54N 3°36W **12** E4
Bala, L. *U.K.* 52°53N 3°37W **12** E4
Balabac I. *Phil.* 8°0N 117°0E **36** C5

Balabac Str. *E. Indies* 7°53N 117°5E **36** C5
Balabagh *Afghan.* 34°25N 70°12E **42** B4
Ba'labakk *Lebanon* 34°0N 36°10E **46** B5
Balabalangan, Kepulauan
    Indonesia 2°20S 117°30E **36** E5
Balad *Iraq* 34°0N 44°9E **44** C5
Balad Rūz *Iraq* 33°42N 45°5E **44** C5
Bālādeh *Fārs, Iran* 29°17N 51°56E **45** D6
Bālādeh *Māzandaran, Iran* 36°12N 51°48E **45** B6
Balaghat *India* 21°49N 80°12E **40** J12
Balaghat Ra. *India* 18°50N 76°30E **40** K10
Balaguer *Spain* 41°50N 0°50E **21** B6
Balaklava *Ukraine* 44°30N 33°30E **19** F5
Balakovo *Russia* 52°4N 47°55E **18** D8
Balamau *India* 27°10N 80°21E **43** F9
Balancán *Mexico* 17°48N 91°32W **87** D6
Balasbino *Russia* 51°30N 43°10E **19** D7
Balasinor *India* 22°57N 73°23E **42** H5
Balasore = Baleshwar
    India 21°35N 87°3E **41** J15
Balaton *Hungary* 46°50N 17°40E **17** E9
Balbina, Represa de *Brazil* 2°0S 59°30W **92** D7
Balboa *Panama* 8°57N 79°34W **88** E4
Balbriggan *Ireland* 53°37N 6°11W **10** C5
Balcarce *Argentina* 38°0S 58°10W **94** D4
Balcarres *Canada* 50°50N 103°35W **71** C8
Balchik *Bulgaria* 43°28N 28°11E **23** C13
Balclutha *N.Z.* 46°15S 169°45E **59** G2
Balcones Escarpment
    U.S.A. 29°30N 99°15W **84** G5
Bald I. *Australia* 34°57S 118°27E **61** F2
Bald Knob *U.S.A.* 35°19N 91°34W **84** D9
Baldock L. *Canada* 56°33N 97°57W **71** B9
Baldwin *Mich., U.S.A.* 43°54N 85°51W **81** D11
Baldwin *Pa., U.S.A.* 40°21N 79°58W **82** F5
Baldwinsville *U.S.A.* 43°10N 76°20W **83** C8
Baldy Peak *U.S.A.* 33°54N 109°34W **77** K9
Baleares, Is. *Spain* 39°30N 3°0E **24** B10
Baleares = Baleares, Is.
    Spain 39°30N 3°0E **24** B10
Baleine ➤ *Canada* 58°15N 67°40W **73** A6
Baleine, Petite R. de la ➤
    Canada 56°0N 76°45W **72** A4
Baler *Phil.* 15°46N 121°34E **37** A6
Baleshare *U.K.* 57°31N 7°22W **11** D1
Baleshwar *India* 21°35N 87°3E **41** J15
Baley *Russia* 51°36N 116°37E **29** D12
Balfate *Honduras* 15°48N 86°25W **88** C2
Balgo *Australia* 20°9S 127°58E **60** D4
Bali *Greece* 35°25N 24°47E **25** D6
Bali *India* 25°11N 73°17E **42** G5
Bali *Indonesia* 8°20S 115°0E **37** J18
Bali □ *Indonesia* 8°20S 115°0E **37** J18
Bali, Selat *Indonesia* 8°18S 114°25E **37** J17
Bali Sea *Indonesia* 8°0S 115°0E **37** J17
Baliapal *India* 21°40N 87°17E **43** J12
Balige *Indonesia* 2°14N 99°7E **39** L2
Balık Pulau *Malaysia* 5°21N 100°14E **39** c
Balıkesir *Turkey* 39°39N 27°53E **23** E12
Balikpapan *Indonesia* 1°10S 116°55E **36** E5
Balimbing *Phil.* 5°5N 119°58E **37** C5
Baling *Malaysia* 5°41N 100°55E **39** K3
Balkan Mts. = Stara Planina
    Bulgaria 43°15N 23°0E **23** C10
Balkanabat *Turkmenistan* 39°30N 54°22E **45** B7
Balkhash = Balqash
    Kazakhstan 46°50N 74°50E **28** E8
Balkhash, Ozero = Balqash Köli
    Kazakhstan 46°0N 74°50E **28** E8
Ballachulish *U.K.* 56°41N 5°8W **11** E3
Balladonia *Australia* 32°27S 123°51E **61** F3
Ballaghaderreen *Ireland* 53°55N 8°34W **10** C3
Ballarat *Australia* 37°33S 143°50E **63** F3
Ballard, L. *Australia* 29°20S 120°40E **61** E3
Ballater *U.K.* 57°3N 3°3W **11** D5
Ballenas, Canal de
    Mexico 29°10N 113°29W **86** B2
Balleny Is. *Antarctica* 66°30S 163°0E **5** C11
Ballia *India* 25°46N 84°12E **43** G11
Ballina *Australia* 28°50S 153°31E **63** D5
Ballina *Ireland* 54°7N 9°9W **10** B2
Ballinasloe *Ireland* 53°20N 8°13W **10** C3
Ballinger *U.S.A.* 31°45N 99°57W **84** F5
Ballinrobe *Ireland* 53°38N 9°13W **10** C2
Ballinskelligs B. *Ireland* 51°48N 10°13W **10** E1
Ballston Spa *U.S.A.* 43°0N 73°51W **83** D11
Ballyboghil *Ireland* 53°32N 6°16W **10** C5
Ballybunion *Ireland* 52°31N 9°40W **10** D2
Ballycanew *Ireland* 52°37N 6°19W **10** D5
Ballycastle *U.K.* 55°12N 6°15W **10** A5
Ballyclare *U.K.* 54°46N 6°0W **10** B5
Ballydehob *Ireland* 51°34N 9°28W **10** E2
Ballygawley *U.K.* 54°27N 7°2W **10** B4
Ballyhaunis *Ireland* 53°46N 8°46W **10** C3
Ballyheige *Ireland* 52°23N 9°49W **10** D2
Ballymena *U.K.* 54°52N 6°17W **10** B5
Ballymoney *U.K.* 55°5N 6°31W **10** A5
Ballymote *Ireland* 54°5N 8°31W **10** B3
Ballynahinch *U.K.* 54°24N 5°54W **10** B6
Ballyquintin Pt. *U.K.* 54°20N 5°30W **10** B6
Ballyshannon *Ireland* 54°30N 8°11W **10** B3
Balmaceda *Chile* 46°0S 71°50W **96** F2
Balmertown *Canada* 51°4N 93°41W **71** C10
Balmoral *Australia* 37°15S 141°48E **63** F3
Balmoral *U.K.* 57°2N 3°13W **11** D5
Balochistan = Baluchistan □
    Pakistan 27°30N 65°0E **40** F4
Balochistan = Baluchistan □
    Pakistan 27°30N 65°0E **40** F4
Balonne ➤ *Australia* 28°47S 147°56E **63** D4
Balotra *India* 25°50N 72°14E **42** G5
Balqash *Kazakhstan* 46°50N 74°50E **28** E8
Balqash Köli *Kazakhstan* 46°0N 74°50E **28** E8
Balrampur *India* 27°30N 82°20E **43** F10
Balranald *Australia* 34°38S 143°33E **63** E3
Balsas ➤ *Brazil* 7°15S 44°35W **93** E9
Balsas *Brazil* 7°15S 44°35W **93** E9
Balsas ➤ *Mexico* 17°55N 102°10W **86** D4
Balsas del Norte *Mexico* 18°0N 99°46W **87** D5
Balta *Ukraine* 48°2N 29°45E **17** D15
Balti *Moldova* 47°48N 27°58E **17** E14
Baltic Sea *Europe* 57°0N 19°0E **9** H18

Baltimore *Ireland* 51°29N 9°22W **10** E2
Baltimore *Md., U.S.A.* 39°17N 76°36W **81** F15
Baltimore *Ohio, U.S.A.* 39°51N 82°36W **82** G2
Baltinglass *Ireland* 52°56N 6°43W **10** D5
Baltit *Pakistan* 36°15N 74°40E **43** A6
Baltiysk *Russia* 54°41N 19°58E **9** J18
Baluchistan □ *Pakistan* 27°30N 65°0E **40** F4
Balurghat *India* 25°15N 88°44E **43** G13
Balvi *Latvia* 57°8N 27°15E **9** H22
Balya *Turkey* 39°44N 27°35E **23** E12
Balykchy *Kyrgyzstan* 42°26N 76°12E **32** B2
Balyqshi *Kazakhstan* 47°4N 51°52E **19** E9
Bam *Iran* 29°7N 58°14E **45** D8
Bama *Nigeria* 11°33N 13°41E **51** F8
Bamaga *Australia* 10°50S 142°25E **62** A3
Bamaji L. *Canada* 51°9N 91°25W **72** B1
Bamako *Mali* 12°34N 7°55W **50** F4
Bambari *C.A.R.* 5°40N 20°35E **52** C4
Bamberg *Germany* 49°54N 10°54E **16** D6
Bamberg *U.S.A.* 33°18N 81°2W **85** E14
Bambili
    Dem. Rep. of the Congo 3°40N 26°0E **54** B2
Bamburgh *U.K.* 55°37N 1°43W **12** B6
Bamenda *Cameroon* 5°57N 10°11E **52** C2
Bamfield *Canada* 48°45N 125°10W **70** D3
Bāmīān □ *Afghan.* 35°0N 67°0E **40** B5
Bamiancheng *China* 43°15N 124°2E **35** C13
Bampūr ➤ *Iran* 27°15N 60°21E **45** E9
Bampūr *Iran* 27°24N 59°0E **45** E8
Ban Ao Tu Khun *Thailand* 8°9N 98°20E **39** a
Ban Ban *Laos* 19°31N 103°30E **38** C4
Ban Bang Hin *Thailand* 9°32N 98°35E **39** H2
Ban Bang Khu *Thailand* 7°57N 98°23E **39** a
Ban Bang Rong *Thailand* 8°3N 98°25E **39** a
Ban Bo Phut *Thailand* 9°33N 100°2E **39** b
Ban Chaweng *Thailand* 9°32N 100°3E **39** b
Ban Chiang Klang
    Thailand 19°25N 100°55E **38** C3
Ban Choho *Thailand* 15°2N 102°9E **38** E4
Ban Dan Lan Hoi *Thailand* 17°0N 99°35E **38** D2
Ban Don = Surat Thani
    Thailand 9°6N 99°20E **39** H2
Ban Don *Vietnam* 12°53N 107°48E **38** F6
Ban Don, Ao ➤ *Thailand* 9°20N 99°25E **39** H2
Ban Dong *Thailand* 19°30N 100°59E **38** C3
Ban Hong *Thailand* 18°18N 98°50E **38** C2
Ban Hua Thanon *Thailand* 9°26N 100°1E **39** b
Ban Kantang *Thailand* 7°25N 99°31E **39** J2
Ban Karon *Thailand* 7°51N 98°18E **39** a
Ban Kata *Thailand* 7°50N 98°18E **39** a
Ban Keun *Laos* 18°22N 102°35E **38** C4
Ban Khai *Thailand* 12°46N 101°18E **38** F3
Ban Kheun *Laos* 20°13N 101°7E **38** B3
Ban Khlong Khian
    Thailand 8°10N 98°26E **39** a
Ban Khlong Kua *Thailand* 6°57N 100°8E **39** J3
Ban Khuan *Thailand* 8°20N 98°25E **39** a
Ban Khuan Mao *Thailand* 7°50N 99°37E **39** J2
Ban Ko Yai Chim
    Thailand 11°17N 99°26E **39** G2
Ban Laem *Thailand* 13°13N 99°59E **38** F2
Ban Lamai *Thailand* 9°28N 100°3E **39** b
Ban Lao Ngam *Laos* 15°28N 106°10E **38** E6
Ban Le Kathe *Thailand* 15°49N 98°53E **38** E2
Ban Lo Po Noi *Thailand* 8°1N 98°34E **39** a
Ban Mae Chedi *Thailand* 19°11N 99°31E **38** C2
Ban Mae Nam *Thailand* 9°34N 100°0E **39** b
Ban Mae Sariang
    Thailand 18°10N 97°56E **38** C1
Ban Mê Thuột = Buon Ma Thuot
    Vietnam 12°40N 108°3E **38** F7
Ban Mi *Thailand* 15°3N 100°32E **38** E3
Ban Muong Mo *Laos* 19°4N 103°58E **38** C4
Ban Na Bo *Thailand* 9°19N 99°41E **39** b
Ban Na Mo *Laos* 17°7N 105°40E **38** D5
Ban Na San *Thailand* 8°53N 99°52E **39** H2
Ban Na Tong *Laos* 20°56N 101°47E **38** B3
Ban Nam Bac *Laos* 20°38N 102°20E **38** B4
Ban Nam Ma *Laos* 22°2N 101°37E **38** A3
Ban Ngang *Laos* 15°59N 106°11E **38** E6
Ban Nong Bok *Laos* 17°5N 104°48E **38** D5
Ban Nong Boua *Laos* 15°40N 106°33E **38** E6
Ban Nong Pling
    Thailand 15°40N 100°10E **38** E3
Ban Pak Chan *Thailand* 10°32N 98°51E **39** G2
Ban Patong *Thailand* 7°54N 98°18E **39** a
Ban Phai *Thailand* 16°4N 102°44E **38** D4
Ban Phak Chit *Thailand* 8°0N 98°24E **39** a
Ban Pong *Thailand* 13°50N 99°55E **38** F2
Ban Ron Phibun *Thailand* 8°9N 99°51E **39** H2
Ban Sakhu *Thailand* 8°4N 98°18E **39** a
Ban Sanam Chai
    Thailand 7°33N 100°25E **39** J3
Ban Sangkha *Thailand* 14°37N 103°52E **38** E4
Ban Tak *Thailand* 17°2N 99°4E **38** D2
Ban Tako *Thailand* 14°5N 102°40E **38** E4
Ban Tha Dua *Thailand* 17°59N 98°39E **38** D2
Ban Tha Nun *Thailand* 8°12N 98°18E **39** a
Ban Tha Rua *Thailand* 7°59N 98°22E **39** a
Ban Tha Yu *Thailand* 8°17N 98°22E **39** a
Ban Thahine *Laos* 14°12N 105°33E **38** E5
Ban Thong Krut *Thailand* 9°25N 99°57E **39** b
Ban Xien Kok *Laos* 20°54N 100°39E **38** B3
Ban Yen Nhan *Vietnam* 20°57N 106°2E **38** B6
Banaba *Kiribati* 0°45S 169°50E **64** H8
Banalia
    Dem. Rep. of the Congo 1°32N 25°5E **54** B2
Banam *Cambodia* 11°20N 105°17E **39** G5
Bananal, I. do *Brazil* 11°30S 50°30W **93** F8
Banaras = Varanasi
    India 25°22N 83°0E **43** G10
Banas ➤ *Gujarat, India* 23°45N 71°25E **42** H4
Banas ➤ *Mad. P., India* 24°15N 81°30E **43** G9
Bânâs, Ras *Egypt* 23°57N 35°59E **51** D13
Banbridge *U.K.* 54°22N 6°16W **10** B5
Banbury *U.K.* 52°4N 1°20W **13** E6
Banchory *U.K.* 57°3N 2°29W **11** D6

Bancroft *Canada* 45°3N 77°51W **82** A7
Band Bonī *Iran* 25°30N 59°33E **45** E8
Band Qīr *Iran* 31°39N 48°53E **45** D6
Banda *Mad. P., India* 24°3N 78°57E **43** G8
Banda Ut. P., India* 25°30N 80°26E **43** G9
Banda, Kepulauan
    Indonesia 4°37S 129°50E **37** E7
Banda Aceh *Indonesia* 5°35N 95°20E **36** C1
Banda Banda, Mt.
    Australia 31°10S 152°28E **63** E5
Banda Elat *Indonesia* 5°40S 133°5E **37** F8
Banda Is. = Banda, Kepulauan
    Indonesia 4°37S 129°50E **37** E7
Banda Sea *Indonesia* 6°0S 130°0E **37** F7
Bandai-Asahi △ *Japan* 37°38N 140°5E **30** F10
Bandai-San *Japan* 37°36N 140°4E **30** F10
Bandān *Iran* 31°23N 60°44E **45** D9
Bandanaira *Indonesia* 4°32S 129°54E **37** E7
Bandanwara *India* 26°9N 74°38E **42** F6
Bandar = Machilipatnam
    India 16°12N 81°8E **41** L12
Bandar-e Abbās *Iran* 27°15N 56°15E **45** E8
Bandar-e Anzalī *Iran* 37°30N 49°30E **45** B6
Bandar-e Bushehr = Būshehr
    Iran 28°55N 50°55E **45** D6
Bandar-e Chārak *Iran* 26°45N 54°20E **45** E7
Bandar-e Deylam *Iran* 30°5N 50°10E **45** D6
Bandar-e Emām Khomeynī
    Iran 30°30N 49°5E **45** D6
Bandar-e Lengeh *Iran* 26°35N 54°58E **45** E7
Bandar-e Maqām *Iran* 26°56N 53°29E **45** E7
Bandar-e Ma'shur *Iran* 30°35N 49°10E **45** D6
Bandar-e Rīg *Iran* 29°29N 50°38E **45** D6
Bandar-e Torkeman *Iran* 37°0N 54°10E **45** B7
Bandar Lampung
    Indonesia 5°20S 105°10E **36** F3
Bandar Maharani = Muar
    Malaysia 2°3N 102°34E **39** L4
Bandar Penggaram = Batu Pahat
    Malaysia 1°50N 102°56E **39** M4
Bandar Seri Begawan
    Brunei 4°52N 115°0E **36** D5
Bandar Sri Aman = Sri Aman
    Malaysia 1°15N 111°32E **36** D4
Bandawe *Malawi* 11°58S 34°5E **55** E3
Bandeira, Pico da *Brazil* 20°26S 41°47W **95** A7
Bandera *Argentina* 28°55S 62°20W **94** B3
Banderas, B. de *Mexico* 20°40N 105°25W **86** C3
Bandhavgarh *India* 23°40N 81°2E **43** H9
Bandi ➤ *India* 26°12N 75°47E **42** F6
Bandikui *India* 27°3N 76°34E **42** F7
Bandırma *Turkey* 40°20N 28°0E **23** D13
Bandjarmasin = Banjarmasin
    Indonesia 3°20S 114°35E **36** E4
Bandon *Ireland* 51°44N 8°44W **10** E3
Bandon ➤ *Ireland* 51°43N 8°37W **10** E3
Bandula *Mozam.* 19°0S 33°7E **55** F3
Bandundu
    Dem. Rep. of the Congo 3°15S 17°22E **52** E3
Bandung *Indonesia* 6°54S 107°36E **37** G12
Bāneh *Iran* 35°59N 45°53E **44** C5
Banes *Cuba* 21°0N 75°42W **89** B4
Banff *Canada* 51°10N 115°34W **70** C5
Banff *U.K.* 57°40N 2°33W **11** D6
Banff △ *Canada* 51°30N 116°15W **70** C5
Bang Fai ➤ *Laos* 16°57N 104°45E **38** D5
Bang Hieng ➤ *Laos* 16°10N 105°10E **38** D5
Bang Krathum *Thailand* 16°34N 100°18E **38** D3
Bang Lamung *Thailand* 13°3N 100°56E **38** F3
Bang Mun Nak *Thailand* 16°2N 100°23E **38** D3
Bang Pa In *Thailand* 14°14N 100°35E **38** E3
Bang Rakam *Thailand* 16°45N 100°7E **38** D3
Bang Saphan *Thailand* 11°14N 99°28E **39** G2
Bang Thao *Thailand* 7°59N 98°18E **39** a
Banganduni I. *India* 21°34N 88°52E **43** J13
Bangala Dam *Zimbabwe* 21°7S 31°25E **55** G3
Bangalore *India* 12°59N 77°40E **40** N10
Banganga ➤ *India* 27°6N 77°25E **42** F6
Bangaon *India* 23°0N 88°47E **43** H13
Bangassou *C.A.R.* 4°55N 23°7E **52** D4
Banggai *Indonesia* 1°34S 123°30E **37** E6
Banggai, Kepulauan
    Indonesia 1°40S 123°30E **37** E6
Banggai Arch. = Banggai,
    Kepulauan *Indonesia* 1°40S 123°30E **37** E6
Banggi, Pulau *Malaysia* 7°17N 117°12E **36** C5
Banghāzī *Libya* 32°11N 20°3E **51** B10
Bangka *Sulawesi, Indonesia* 1°50N 125°5E **37** D7
Bangka *Sumatera,
    Indonesia* 2°0S 105°50E **36** E3
Bangka, Selat *Indonesia* 2°30S 105°30E **36** E3
Bangka-Belitung □
    Indonesia 2°30S 107°0E **36** E3
Bangkalan *Indonesia* 7°2S 112°46E **37** G15
Bangkinang *Indonesia* 0°18N 101°5E **36** D2
Bangko *Indonesia* 2°5S 102°9E **36** E2
Bangkok *Thailand* 13°45N 100°35E **38** F3
Bangla = West Bengal □
    India 23°0N 88°0E **43** H13
Bangladesh ■ *Asia* 24°0N 90°0E **41** H17
Bangli *Indonesia* 8°27S 115°21E **37** J18
Bangong Co *China* 33°45N 78°43E **43** B8
Bangor *Down, U.K.* 54°40N 5°40W **10** B6
Bangor *Gwynedd, U.K.* 53°14N 4°8W **12** D3
Bangor *Maine, U.S.A.* 44°48N 68°46W **81** C19
Bangor *Pa., U.S.A.* 40°52N 75°13W **83** F9
Bangued *Phil.* 17°40N 120°37E **37** A6
Bangui *C.A.R.* 4°23N 18°35E **52** D3
Banguru
    Dem. Rep. of the Congo 0°30N 27°10E **54** B2
Bangweulu, L. *Zambia* 11°0S 30°0E **55** E3
Bangweulu Swamp
    Zambia 11°20S 30°15E **55** E3
Banhine △ *Mozam.* 22°49S 32°55E **57** C5
Baní *Dom. Rep.* 18°16N 70°22E **89** C5
Banī Sa'd *Iraq* 33°34N 44°32E **44** C5
Banihal Pass *India* 33°30N 75°12E **43** C6
Banissa *Kenya* 3°55N 40°19E **54** B4
Bāniyās *Syria* 35°10N 36°0E **44** C3

Banja Luka *Bos.-H.* 44°49N 17°11E **22** B7
Banjar *India* 31°38N 77°21E **42** D7
Banjar ➤ *India* 22°36N 80°22E **43** H9
Banjarmasin *Indonesia* 3°20S 114°35E **36** E4
Banjul *Gambia* 13°28N 16°40W **50** F2
Banka *India* 24°53N 86°55E **43** G12
Banket *Zimbabwe* 17°27S 30°19E **55** F3
Bankipore *India* 25°35N 85°10E **41** G14
Banks I. = Moa *Australia* 10°11S 142°16E **62** a
Banks I. B.C., Canada* 53°20N 130°0W **70** C3
Banks I. N.W.T., Canada* 73°15N 121°30W **68** C7
Banks Pen. *N.Z.* 43°45S 173°15E **59** E4
Banks Str. *Australia* 40°40S 148°10E **63** G4
Bankura *India* 23°11N 87°18E **43** H12
Banmankhi *India* 25°53N 87°11E **43** G12
Bann ➤ *L'derry., U.K.* 55°8N 6°41W **10** A5
Bann ➤ *Armagh, U.K.* 54°30N 6°31W **10** B5
Bannang Sata *Thailand* 6°16N 101°16E **39** J3
Banning *U.S.A.* 33°56N 116°53W **79** M10
Bannockburn *Canada* 44°39N 77°33W **82** B7
Bannockburn *U.K.* 56°5N 3°55W **11** E5
Bannockburn *Zimbabwe* 20°17S 29°48E **55** G2
Bannu *Pakistan* 33°0N 70°18E **40** C7
Bano *India* 22°40N 84°55E **43** H11
Bansgaon *India* 26°33N 83°21E **43** F10
Banská Bystrica
    Slovak Rep. 48°46N 19°14E **17** D10
Banswara *India* 23°32N 74°24E **42** H6
Bantaeng *Indonesia* 5°32S 119°56E **37** F5
Banten □ *Indonesia* 6°30S 106°0E **37** G11
Bantry *Ireland* 51°41N 9°27W **10** E2
Bantry B. *Ireland* 51°37N 9°44W **10** E2
Bantul *Indonesia* 7°55S 110°19E **37** G14
Bantva *India* 21°29N 70°12E **42** J4
Banyak, Kepulauan
    Indonesia 2°10N 97°10E **36** D1
Banyalbufar *Spain* 39°42N 2°31E **24** B9
Banyo *Cameroon* 6°52N 11°45E **52** C2
Banyumas *Indonesia* 7°32S 109°18E **37** G13
Banyuwangi *Indonesia* 8°13S 114°21E **37** J17
Banzare Coast *Antarctica* 68°0S 125°0E **5** C9
Bao Ha *Vietnam* 22°11N 104°21E **38** A5
Bao Lac *Vietnam* 22°57N 105°40E **38** A5
Bao Loc *Vietnam* 11°32N 107°48E **39** G6
Bao'an = Shenzhen
    China 22°32N 114°5E **33** F10
Baocheng *China* 33°12N 106°56E **34** H4
Baode *China* 39°1N 111°5E **34** E6
Baodi *China* 39°38N 117°20E **35** E9
Baoding *China* 38°50N 115°28E **34** E8
Baoji *China* 34°20N 107°5E **34** G4
Baoshan *China* 25°10N 99°5E **32** D4
Baotou *China* 40°32N 110°2E **34** D6
Baoying *China* 33°17N 119°20E **35** H10
Baoyou = Ledong *China* 18°50N 109°20E **38** C7
Bap *India* 27°23N 72°18E **42** F5
Bapatla *India* 15°55N 80°30E **41** M12
Bāqerābād *Iran* 33°2N 51°58E **45** C6
Ba'qūbah *Iraq* 33°45N 44°50E **44** C5
Baquedano *Chile* 23°20S 69°52W **94** A2
Bar *Montenegro* 42°8N 19°6E **23** C8
Bar *Ukraine* 49°4N 27°40E **17** D14
Bar Bigha *India* 25°21N 85°47E **43** G11
Bar Harbor *U.S.A.* 44°23N 68°13W **81** C19
Bar-le-Duc *France* 48°47N 5°10E **20** B6
Bara *India* 25°16N 81°43E **43** G9
Bara Banki *India* 26°55N 81°12E **43** F9
Barabai *Indonesia* 2°32S 115°34E **36** E5
Baraboo *U.S.A.* 43°28N 89°45W **80** D9
Baracoa *Cuba* 20°20N 74°30W **89** B5
Baradā ➤ *Syria* 33°33N 36°34E **46** B5
Baradero *Argentina* 33°52S 59°29W **94** C4
Baraga *U.S.A.* 46°47N 88°30W **80** B9
Baragoi *Kenya* 1°47N 36°47E **54** B4
Barah ➤ *India* 27°42N 77°5E **42** F6
Barahona *Dom. Rep.* 18°13N 71°7W **89** C5
Barail Range *India* 25°15N 93°20E **41** G18
Barakaldo *Spain* 43°18N 2°59W **21** A4
Barakar ➤ *India* 24°7N 86°14E **43** G12
Barakot *India* 21°33N 84°59E **43** J11
Barakpur *India* 22°47N 88°21E **43** H13
Baralaba *Australia* 24°13S 149°50E **62** C4
Baralzon L. *Canada* 60°0N 98°3W **71** B9
Baramati *India* 18°11N 74°33E **40** L8
Baramula *India* 34°15N 74°20E **43** B6
Baran *India* 25°9N 76°40E **42** G7
Baran ➤ *Pakistan* 25°13N 68°17E **42** G3
Baranavichy *Belarus* 53°10N 26°0E **17** B14
Baranof *U.S.A.* 57°5N 134°50W **70** B2
Baranof I. *U.S.A.* 57°0N 135°0W **68** F4
Barapasi *Indonesia* 2°15S 137°5E **37** E9
Barasat *India* 22°46N 88°31E **43** H13
Barat Daya, Kepulauan
    Indonesia 7°30S 128°0E **37** F7
Barataria B. *U.S.A.* 29°20N 89°55W **85** G10
Barauda *India* 23°33N 75°15E **42** H6
Baraut *India* 29°13N 77°7E **42** E7
Barbacena *Brazil* 21°15S 43°56W **95** A7
Barbados ■ *W. Indies* 13°10N 59°30W **89** g
Barbària, C. de *Spain* 38°39N 1°24E **24** C7
Barbas, C. *W. Sahara* 22°20N 16°42W **50** D2
Barbastro *Spain* 42°2N 0°5E **21** A6
Barbeau Pk. *Canada* 81°54N 75°1W **69** A16
Barberton *S. Africa* 25°42S 31°2E **57** D5
Barberton *U.S.A.* 41°1N 81°39W **82** E3
Barbosa *Colombia* 5°57N 73°37W **92** B4
Barbuda *W. Indies* 17°30N 61°40W **89** C7
Barcaldine *Australia* 23°43S 145°6E **62** C4
Barcellona Pozzo di Gotto
    Italy 38°9N 15°13E **22** E6
Barcelona *Spain* 41°22N 2°10E **21** B7
Barcelona *Venezuela* 10°10N 64°40W **92** A6
Barceloneta *Puerto Rico* 18°27N 66°32W **89** d
Barcelos *Brazil* 1°0S 63°0W **92** D6
Barcoo ➤ *Australia* 25°30S 142°50E **62** D3
Bardaï *Chad* 21°25N 17°0E **51** D9
Bardas Blancas
    Argentina 35°49S 69°45W **94** D2
Bardawîl, Sabkhet el
    Egypt 31°10N 33°15E **46** D2

Barddhaman *India* 23°14N 87°39E **43** H12
Bardejov *Slovak Rep.* 49°18N 21°15E **17** D11
Bardera = Baardheere
 Somali Rep. 2°20N 42°27E **47** G3
Bardīyah *Libya* 31°45N 25°5E **51** B10
Bardsey I. *U.K.* 52°45N 4°47W **12** E3
Bardstown *U.S.A.* 37°49N 85°28W **81** G11
Bareilly *India* 28°22N 79°27E **43** E8
Barela *India* 23°6N 80°3E **43** H9
Barents Sea *Arctic* 73°0N 39°0E **4** B9
Barfleur, Pte. de *France* 49°42N 1°16W **20** B3
Bargara *Australia* 24°50S 152°25E **63** C5
Bargi Dam *India* 22°59N 80°0E **43** H9
Barguzin *Russia* 53°37N 109°37E **29** D11
Barh *India* 25°29N 85°46E **43** G11
Barhaj *India* 26°18N 83°44E **43** F10
Barharwa *India* 24°52N 87°47E **43** G12
Barhi *India* 24°15N 85°25E **43** G11
Bari *India* 26°39N 77°39E **42** F7
Bari *Italy* 41°8N 16°51E **22** D7
Bari Doab *Pakistan* 30°20N 73°0E **42** D5
Bari Sadri *India* 24°28N 74°30E **42** G6
Barīdī, Ra's *Si. Arabia* 24°17N 37°31E **44** E3
Barīm *Yemen* 12°39N 43°25E **48** E8
Barinas *Venezuela* 8°36N 70°15W **92** B4
Baring, C. *Canada* 70°0N 117°30W **68** D8
Baringo, L. *Kenya* 0°47N 36°16E **54** B4
Barisal *Bangla.* 22°45N 90°20E **41** H17
Barisal □ *Bangla.* 22°45N 90°20E **41** H17
Barisan, Pegunungan
 Indonesia 3°30S 102°15E **36** E2
Barito → *Indonesia* 4°0S 114°50E **36** E4
Baritú △ *Argentina* 23°43S 64°40W **94** A3
Barjūj, Wadi → *Libya* 25°26N 12°12E **51** C8
Bark L. *Canada* 45°27N 77°51W **82** A7
Barkakana *India* 23°37N 85°29E **43** H11
Barker *U.S.A.* 43°20N 78°33W **82** C6
Barkley, L. *U.S.A.* 37°1N 88°14W **85** C10
Barkley Sound *Canada* 48°50N 125°10W **70** D3
Barkly East *S. Africa* 30°58S 27°33E **56** E4
Barkly Homestead
 Australia 19°52S 135°50E **62** B2
Barkly Tableland
 Australia 17°50S 136°40E **62** B2
Barkly West *S. Africa* 28°5S 24°31E **56** D3
Barkol Kazak Zizhixian
 China 43°37N 93°2E **32** B4
Bârlad *Romania* 46°15N 27°38E **17** E14
Bârlad → *Romania* 45°38N 27°32E **17** F14
Barlee, L. *Australia* 29°15S 119°30E **61** E2
Barlee, Mt. *Australia* 24°38S 128°13E **61** D4
Barletta *Italy* 41°19N 16°17E **22** D7
Barlovento *Canary Is.* 28°48N 17°48W **24** F2
Barlovento *C. Verde Is.* 17°0N 25°0W **50** b
Barlow L. *Canada* 62°0N 103°0W **71** A8
Barmedman *Australia* 34°9S 147°21E **63** E4
Barmer *India* 25°45N 71°20E **42** G4
Barmera *Australia* 34°15S 140°28E **63** E3
Barmouth *U.K.* 52°44N 4°4W **12** E3
Barna → *India* 25°21N 83°3E **43** G10
Barnagar *India* 23°7N 75°19E **42** H6
Barnala *India* 30°23N 75°33E **42** D6
Barnard Castle *U.K.* 54°33N 1°55W **12** C6
Barnaul *Russia* 53°20N 83°40E **28** D9
Barnesville *Ga., U.S.A.* 33°3N 84°9W **85** E12
Barnesville *Minn.,*
 U.S.A. 46°43N 96°28W **80** B5
Barnet □ *U.K.* 51°38N 0°9W **13** F7
Barneveld *Neths.* 52°7N 5°36E **15** B5
Barnhart *U.S.A.* 31°8N 101°10W **84** F4
Barnsley *U.K.* 53°34N 1°27W **12** D6
Barnstable *U.S.A.* 41°42N 70°18W **81** E18
Barnstaple *U.K.* 51°5N 4°4W **13** F3
Barnstaple Bay = Bideford Bay
 U.K. 51°5N 4°20W **13** F3
Barnwell *U.S.A.* 33°15N 81°23W **85** E14
Baro *Nigeria* 8°35N 6°18E **50** G7
Baroda = Vadodara
 India 22°20N 73°10E **42** H5
Baroda *India* 25°29N 76°35E **42** G7
Baroe *S. Africa* 33°13S 24°33E **56** E3
Baron Ra. *Australia* 23°30S 127°45E **60** D4
Barpeta *India* 26°20N 91°10E **41** F17
Barqa *Libya* 27°0N 23°0E **51** C10
Barques, Pt. Aux *U.S.A.* 44°4N 82°58W **82** B2
Barquísimeto *Venezuela* 10°4N 69°19W **92** A5
Barr Smith Range
 Australia 27°4S 120°20E **61** E3
Barra *Brazil* 11°5S 43°10W **93** F10
Barra *U.K.* 57°0N 7°29W **11** E1
Barra, Sd. of *U.K.* 57°4N 7°25W **11** D1
Barra de Navidad
 Mexico 19°12N 104°41W **86** D4
Barra do Corda *Brazil* 5°30S 45°10W **93** E9
Barra do Garças *Brazil* 15°54S 52°16W **93** G8
Barra do Piraí *Brazil* 22°30S 43°50W **95** A7
Barra Falsa, Pta. da
 Mozam. 22°58S 35°37E **57** C6
Barra Hd. *U.K.* 56°47N 7°40W **11** E1
Barra Mansa *Brazil* 22°35S 44°12W **95** A7
Barraba *Australia* 30°21S 150°35E **63** E5
Barrackpur = Barakpur
 India 22°47N 88°21E **43** H13
Barraigh = Barra *U.K.* 57°0N 7°29W **11** E1
Barranca *Lima, Peru* 10°45S 77°50W **92** F3
Barranca *Loreto, Peru* 4°50S 76°50W **92** D3
Barranca del Cobre △
 Mexico 27°18N 107°40W **86** B3
Barrancabermeja
 Colombia 7°0N 73°50W **92** B4
Barrancas *Venezuela* 8°55N 62°5W **92** B6
Barrancos *Portugal* 38°10N 6°58W **21** C2
Barranqueras *Argentina* 27°30S 59°0W **94** B4
Barranquilla *Colombia* 11°0N 74°50W **92** A4
Barraute *Canada* 48°26N 77°38W **72** C4
Barre *Mass., U.S.A.* 42°25N 72°6W **83** D12
Barre *Vt., U.S.A.* 44°12N 72°30W **83** B12
Barreal *Argentina* 31°33S 69°28W **94** C2

Barreiras *Brazil* 12°8S 45°0W **93** F10
Barreirinhas *Brazil* 2°30S 42°50W **93** D10
Barreiro *Portugal* 38°39N 9°5W **21** C1
Barren, Nosy *Madag.* 18°25S 43°40E **57** B7
Barretos *Brazil* 20°30S 48°35W **93** H9
Barrhead *Canada* 54°10N 114°24W **70** C6
Barrie *Canada* 44°24N 79°40W **82** B5
Barrier Ra. *Australia* 31°0S 141°30E **63** E3
Barrier Reef *Belize* 17°9N 88°3W **87** D7
Barrière *Canada* 51°12N 120°7W **70** C4
Barrington *U.S.A.* 41°44N 71°18W **83** E13
Barrington L. *Canada* 56°55N 100°15W **71** B8
Barrington Tops
 Australia 32°6S 151°28E **63** E5
Barringun *Australia* 29°1S 145°41E **63** D4
Barron *U.S.A.* 45°24N 91°51W **80** C8
Barrow → *Ireland* 52°25N 6°58W **10** D5
Barrow, Pt. *U.S.A.* 71°23N 156°29W **74** A4
Barrow Creek *Australia* 21°30S 133°55E **62** C1
Barrow I. *Australia* 20°45S 115°20E **60** D2
Barrow-in-Furness *U.K.* 54°7N 3°14W **12** C4
Barrow Pt. *Australia* 14°20S 144°40E **62** A3
Barrow Ra. *Australia* 26°0S 127°40E **61** E4
Barrow Str. *Canada* 74°20N 95°0W **4** B3
Barry *U.K.* 51°24N 3°16W **13** F4
Barry's Bay *Canada* 45°29N 77°41W **82** A7
Barsat *Pakistan* 36°10N 72°45E **43** A5
Barsi *India* 18°10N 75°50E **40** K9
Barstow *U.S.A.* 34°54N 117°1W **79** L9
Barthélemy, Col *Vietnam* 19°26N 104°6E **38** C5
Bartica *Guyana* 6°25N 58°40W **92** B7
Bartle Frere *Australia* 17°27S 145°50E **62** B4
Bartlesville *U.S.A.* 36°45N 95°59W **84** C7
Bartlett *Calif., U.S.A.* 36°29N 118°2W **78** J8
Bartlett *Tenn., U.S.A.* 35°12N 89°52W **85** D10
Bartlett, L. *Canada* 63°5N 118°20W **70** A5
Barton → *Australia*
Barton *U.S.A.* 44°45N 72°11W **83** B12
Barton upon Humber
 U.K. 53°41N 0°25W **12** D7
Bartow *U.S.A.* 27°54N 81°50W **85** H14
Barú, Volcan *Panama* 8°55N 82°35W **88** E3
Barumba
 Dem. Rep. of the Congo 1°3N 23°37E **54** B1
Baruun Urt *Mongolia* 46°46N 113°15E **29** E12
Baruunsuu *Mongolia* 43°43N 105°35E **34** C3
Barwani *India* 22°2N 74°57E **42** H6
Barzān *Iraq* 36°55N 44°3E **46** B5
Bāsa'idū *Iran* 26°35N 55°20E **45** E7
Basal *Pakistan* 33°33N 72°13E **42** C5
Basankusa
 Dem. Rep. of the Congo 1°5N 19°50E **52** D3
Basarabeasca *Moldova* 46°21N 28°58E **17** E15
Basarabia = Bessarabiya
 Moldova 47°0N 28°10E **17** E15
Basawa *Afghan.* 34°15N 70°50E **42** B4
Bascuñán, C. *Chile* 28°52S 71°35W **94** B1
Basel *Switz.* 47°35N 7°35E **20** C7
Bashäkerd, Kühhä-ye
 Iran 26°42N 58°35E **45** E8
Bashaw *Canada* 52°35N 112°58W **70** C6
Bāshī *Iran* 28°41N 51°4E **45** D6
Bashkir Republic =
 Bashkortostan □
 Russia 54°0N 57°0E **18** D10
Bashkortostan □ *Russia* 54°0N 57°0E **18** D10
Basibasy *Madag.* 22°10S 43°40E **57** C7
Basilan *Phil.* 6°35N 122°0E **37** C6
Basilan Str. *Phil.* 6°50N 122°0E **37** C6
Basildon *U.K.* 51°34N 0°28E **13** F8
Basim = Washim *India* 20°3N 77°0E **40** J10
Basin *U.S.A.* 44°23N 108°2W **76** D9
Basingstoke *U.K.* 51°15N 1°5W **13** F6
Baskatong, Rés. *Canada* 46°46N 75°50W **72** C4
Basle = Basel *Switz.* 47°35N 7°35E **20** C7
Basoda *India* 23°52N 77°54E **42** H7
Basoko
 Dem. Rep. of the Congo 1°16N 23°40E **54** B1
Basque Provinces = País Vasco □
 Spain 42°50N 2°45W **21** A4
Basra = Al Başrah *Iraq* 30°30N 47°50E **44** D5
Bass Str. *Australia* 39°15S 146°30E **63** F4
Bassano *Canada* 50°48N 112°20W **70** C6
Bassano del Grappa *Italy* 45°46N 11°44E **22** B4
Bassas da India *Ind. Oc.* 22°0S 39°0E **55** G4
Basse-Pointe *Martinique* 14°52N 61°8W **88** c
Basse-Terre *Guadeloupe* 16°0N 61°44W **88** b
Basse Terre *Trin. & Tob.* 10°7N 61°19W **93** K15
Bassein *Burma* 16°45N 94°30E **41** L19
Basses, Pte. des
 Guadeloupe 15°52N 61°17W **88** b
Basseterre
 St. Kitts & Nevis 17°17N 62°43W **89** C7
Bassett *U.S.A.* 42°35N 99°32W **80** D4
Bassi *India* 30°44N 76°21E **42** D7
Bastak *Iran* 27°15N 54°25E **45** E7
Baştām *Iran* 36°29N 55°4E **45** B7
Bastar *India* 19°15N 81°40E **41** K12
Basti *India* 26°52N 82°55E **43** F10
Bastia *France* 42°40N 9°30E **20** E8
Bastogne *Belgium* 50°1N 5°43E **15** D5
Bastrop *La., U.S.A.* 32°47N 91°55W **84** E9
Bastrop *Tex., U.S.A.* 30°7N 97°19W **84** F6
Basuo = Dongfang
 China 18°50N 108°33E **38** C7
Bat Yam *Israel* 32°2N 34°44E **46** C3
Bata *Eq. Guin.* 1°57N 9°50E **52** D1
Bataan □ *Phil.* 14°40N 120°25E **37** B6
Batabanó *Cuba* 22°41N 82°18W **88** B3
Batabanó, G. de *Cuba* 22°30N 82°30W **88** B3
Batac *Phil.* 18°3N 120°34E **37** A6
Batagai *Russia* 67°38N 134°38E **29** C14
Batala *India* 31°48N 75°12E **42** D6
Batama
 Dem. Rep. of the Congo 0°58N 26°33E **54** B2
Batamay *Russia* 63°30N 129°15E **29** C13

Batang *Indonesia* 6°55S 109°45E **37** G13
Batangafo *C.A.R.* 7°25N 18°20E **52** C3
Batangas *Phil.* 13°35N 121°10E **37** B6
Batanta *Indonesia* 0°55S 130°40E **37** E8
Batatais *Brazil* 20°54S 47°37W **95** A6
Batavia *U.S.A.* 43°0N 78°11W **82** D6
Batchelor *Australia* 13°4S 131°1E **60** B5
Batdambang *Cambodia* 13°7N 103°12E **38** F4
Batemans B. *Australia* 35°40S 150°12E **63** F5
Batemans Bay *Australia* 35°44S 150°11E **63** F5
Batesburg-Leesville
 U.S.A. 33°54N 81°33W **85** E14
Batesville *Ark., U.S.A.* 35°46N 91°39W **84** D9
Batesville *Miss., U.S.A.* 34°19N 89°57W **85** D10
Batesville *Tex., U.S.A.* 28°58N 99°37W **84** G5
Bath *Canada* 44°11N 76°47W **83** B8
Bath *U.K.* 51°23N 2°22W **13** F5
Bath *Maine, U.S.A.* 43°55N 69°49W **81** D19
Bath *N.Y., U.S.A.* 42°20N 77°19W **82** D7
Bath & North East Somerset □
 U.K. 51°21N 2°27W **13** F5
Batheay *Cambodia* 11°59N 104°57E **39** G5
Bathsheba *Barbados* 13°13N 59°32W **89** g
Bathurst *Australia* 33°25S 149°31E **63** E4
Bathurst *Canada* 47°37N 65°43W **73** C6
Bathurst *S. Africa* 33°30S 26°50E **56** E4
Bathurst, C. *Canada* 70°34N 128°0W **68** C6
Bathurst B. *Australia* 14°16S 144°25E **62** A3
Bathurst Harb.
 Australia 43°15S 146°10E **63** G4
Bathurst I. *Australia* 11°30S 130°10E **60** B5
Bathurst I. *Canada* 76°0N 100°30W **69** B11
Bathurst Inlet *Canada* 66°50N 108°1W **68** D10
Batiki *Fiji* 17°48S 179°10E **59** a
Batlow *Australia* 35°31S 148°9E **63** F4
Batman *Turkey* 37°55N 41°5E **44** B4
Baṭn al Ghūl *Jordan* 29°36N 35°56E **46** F4
Batna *Algeria* 35°34N 6°15E **50** A7
Batoka *Zambia* 16°45S 27°15E **55** F2
Baton Rouge *U.S.A.* 30°27N 91°11W **84** F9
Batong, Ko *Thailand* 6°32N 99°12E **39** J2
Batopilas *Mexico* 27°1N 107°44W **86** B3
Batouri *Cameroon* 4°30N 14°25E **52** D2
Båtsfjord *Norway* 70°38N 29°39E **8** A23
Battambang = Batdambang
 Cambodia 13°7N 103°12E **38** F4
Batticaloa *Sri Lanka* 7°43N 81°45E **40** R12
Battipáglia *Italy* 40°37N 14°58E **22** D6
Battle *U.K.* 50°55N 0°30E **13** G8
Battle → *Canada* 52°43N 108°15W **71** C7
Battle Creek *U.S.A.* 42°19N 85°11W **81** D11
Battle Ground *U.S.A.* 45°47N 122°32W **78** E4
Battle Harbour *Canada* 52°16N 55°35W **73** B8
Battle Lake *U.S.A.* 46°17N 95°43W **80** B6
Battle Mountain
 U.S.A. 40°38N 116°56W **76** F5
Battlefields *Zimbabwe* 18°37S 29°47E **55** F2
Battleford *Canada* 52°45N 108°15W **71** C7
Batu *Ethiopia* 6°55N 39°45E **47** F2
Batu *Malaysia* 3°15N 101°40E **39** L3
Batu, Kepulauan
 Indonesia 0°30S 98°25E **36** E1
Batu Ferringhi *Malaysia* 5°28N 100°15E **39** c
Batu Gajah *Malaysia* 4°28N 101°3E **39** K3
Batu Is. = Batu, Kepulauan
 Indonesia 0°30S 98°25E **36** E1
Batu Pahat *Malaysia* 1°50N 102°56E **39** M4
Batuata *Indonesia* 6°12S 122°42E **37** F6
Batugondang, Tanjung
 Indonesia 8°6S 114°29E **37** J17
Batukau, Gunung
 Indonesia 8°20S 115°5E **37** J18
Batumi *Georgia* 41°39N 41°44E **19** F7
Batur, Danau *Indonesia* 8°15S 115°24E **37** J18
Batur, Gunung
 Indonesia 8°14S 115°23E **37** J18
Baturaja *Indonesia* 4°11S 104°15E **36** E2
Baturité *Brazil* 4°28S 38°45W **93** D11
Baturi *Indonesia* 8°19S 115°11E **37** J18
Bau *Malaysia* 1°25N 110°9E **36** D4
Baubau *Indonesia* 5°25S 122°38E **37** F6
Baucau *E. Timor* 8°27S 126°27E **37** F7
Baudette *U.S.A.* 48°43N 94°36W **80** A6
Bauer, C. *Australia* 32°44S 134°4E **63** E1
Bauhinia *Australia* 24°35S 149°18E **62** C4
Baukau = Baucau
 E. Timor 8°27S 126°27E **37** F7
Bauld, C. *Canada* 51°38N 55°26W **69** G20
Baurú *Brazil* 22°10S 49°0W **95** A6
Bausi *India* 24°48N 87°1E **43** G12
Bauska *Latvia* 56°24N 24°15E **9** H21
Bautzen *Germany* 51°10N 14°26E **16** C8
Bavānāt *Iran* 30°28N 53°27E **45** D7
Bavaria = Bayern □
 Germany 48°50N 12°0E **16** D6
Bavispe → *Mexico* 29°15N 109°11W **86** B3
Bawdwin *Burma* 23°5N 97°20E **41** H20
Bawean *Indonesia* 5°46S 112°35E **36** F4
Bawku *Ghana* 11°3N 0°19W **50** F5
Bawlake *Burma* 19°11N 97°21E **41** K20
Baxley *U.S.A.* 31°47N 82°21W **85** F13
Baxter *U.S.A.* 46°21N 94°17W **80** B6
Baxter Springs *U.S.A.* 37°2N 94°44W **80** G6
Baxter State △ *U.S.A.* 46°5N 68°57W **81** B19
Bay City *Mich., U.S.A.* 43°36N 83°54W **81** D12
Bay City *Tex., U.S.A.* 28°59N 95°58W **84** G7
Bay Minette *U.S.A.* 30°53N 87°46W **85** F11
Bay Roberts *Canada* 47°36N 53°16W **73** C9
Bay St. Louis *U.S.A.* 30°19N 89°20W **85** F10
Bay Springs *U.S.A.* 31°59N 89°17W **85** F10
Bay View *N.Z.* 39°25S 176°50E **59** C6
Baya
 Dem. Rep. of the Congo 11°53S 27°25E **55** E2
Bayamo *Cuba* 20°20N 76°40W **88** B4
Bayamón *Puerto Rico* 18°24N 66°9W **89** d
Bayan Har Shan *China* 34°0N 98°0E **32** C4

Bayan Hot = Alxa Zuoqi
 China 38°50N 105°40E **34** E3
Bayan Lepas *Malaysia* 5°17N 100°16E **39** c
Bayan-Ovoo *China* 42°55N 106°5E **34** C4
Bayan-Ovoo = Erdenetsogt
 Mongolia 42°55N 106°5E **34** C4
Bayana *India* 26°55N 77°18E **42** F7
Bayanaūyl *Kazakhstan* 50°45N 75°45E **28** D8
Bayandalay *Mongolia* 43°30N 103°29E **34** C2
Bayanhongor *Mongolia* 46°8N 102°43E **32** B5
Bayard *N. Mex., U.S.A.* 32°46N 108°8W **77** K9
Bayard *Nebr., U.S.A.* 41°45N 103°20W **80** E2
Baybay *Phil.* 10°40N 124°55E **37** B6
Baydaratskaya Guba
 Russia 69°0N 67°30E **28** C7
Baydhabo *Somali Rep.* 3°8N 43°30E **47** G3
Bayern □ *Germany* 48°50N 12°0E **16** D6
Bayeux *France* 49°17N 0°42W **20** B3
Bayfield *Canada* 43°34N 81°42W **82** C3
Bayfield *U.S.A.* 46°49N 90°49W **80** B8
Bayındır *Turkey* 38°13N 27°39E **23** E12
Baykal, Oz. *Russia* 53°0N 108°0E **29** D11
Baykan *Turkey* 38°7N 41°44E **44** B4
Baymak *Russia* 52°36N 58°19E **18** D10
Baynes Mts. *Namibia* 17°15S 13°0E **56** B1
Bayombong *Phil.* 16°30N 121°10E **37** A6
Bayonne *France* 43°30N 1°28W **20** E3
Bayonne *U.S.A.* 40°40N 74°6W **83** F10
Bayovar *Peru* 5°50S 81°0W **92** E2
Bayqongyr *Kazakhstan* 45°40N 63°20E **28** E7
Bayram-Ali = Baýramaly
 Turkmenistan 37°37N 62°10E **45** B9
Baýramaly *Turkmenistan* 37°37N 62°10E **45** B9
Bayramiç *Turkey* 39°48N 26°36E **23** E12
Bayreuth *Germany* 49°56N 11°35E **16** D6
Bayrūt *Lebanon* 33°53N 35°31E **46** B4
Bays, L. of *Canada* 45°15N 79°4W **82** A5
Baysville *Canada* 45°9N 79°7W **82** A5
Bayt Lahm *West Bank* 31°43N 35°12E **46** D4
Baytown *U.S.A.* 29°43N 94°59W **84** G7
Bayun *Indonesia* 8°11S 115°16E **37** J18
Baza *Spain* 37°30N 2°47W **21** D4
Bazaruto, I. do *Mozam.* 21°40S 35°28E **57** C6
Bazaruto △ *Mozam.* 21°42S 35°26E **57** C6
Bazhou *China* 39°8N 116°22E **34** E9
Bazmān, Küh-e *Iran* 28°4N 60°1E **45** D9
Beach *U.S.A.* 46°58N 104°0W **80** B2
Beach City *U.S.A.* 40°39N 81°35W **82** F3
Beachport *Australia* 37°29S 140°0E **63** F3
Beachville *Canada* 43°5N 80°49W **82** C4
Beachy Hd. *U.K.* 50°44N 0°15E **13** G8
Beacon *Australia* 30°26S 117°52E **61** F2
Beacon *U.S.A.* 41°30N 73°58W **83** E11
Beaconsfield *Australia* 41°11S 146°48E **63** G4
Beagle, Canal *S. Amer.* 55°0S 68°30W **96** H3
Beagle Bay *Australia* 16°58S 122°40E **60** C3
Beagle Bay ۞ *Australia* 16°53S 122°40E **60** C3
Beagle G. *Australia* 12°15S 130°25E **60** B5
Béal an Átha = Ballina
 Ireland 54°7N 9°9W **10** B2
Béal Átha na Sluaighe =
 Ballinasloe *Ireland* 53°20N 8°13W **10** C3
Bealanana *Madag.* 14°33S 48°44E **57** A8
Beals Cr. → *U.S.A.* 32°10N 100°51W **84** E4
Beamsville *Canada* 43°12N 79°28W **82** C5
Bear → *Calif., U.S.A.* 38°56N 121°36W **78** G5
Bear → *Utah, U.S.A.* 41°30N 112°8W **74** G17
Bear I. *Ireland* 51°38N 9°50W **10** E2
Bear L. *Canada* 55°8N 96°0W **71** B9
Bear Lake *U.S.A.* 41°59N 111°21W **76** F8
Beardmore *Canada* 49°36N 87°57W **72** C2
Beardmore Glacier
 Antarctica 84°30S 170°0E **5** E11
Beardstown *U.S.A.* 40°1N 90°26W **80** E8
Bearma → *India* 24°20N 79°51E **43** G8
Béarn *France* 43°20N 0°30W **20** E3
Bearpaw Mts. *U.S.A.* 48°12N 109°30W **76** B9
Bearskin Lake *Canada* 53°58N 91°2W **72** B1
Beas → *India* 31°10N 74°59E **42** D6
Beata, C. *Dom. Rep.* 17°40N 71°30W **89** C5
Beata, I. *Dom. Rep.* 17°34N 71°31W **89** C5
Beatrice *U.S.A.* 40°16N 96°45W **80** E6
Beatrice *Zimbabwe* 18°15S 30°55E **55** F3
Beatrice, C. *Australia* 14°20S 136°55E **62** A2
Beatton → *Canada* 56°15N 120°45W **70** B4
Beatton River *Canada* 57°26N 121°20W **70** B4
Beatty *U.S.A.* 36°54N 116°46W **78** J10
Beau Bassin *Mauritius* 20°13S 57°27E **53** d
Beauce, Plaine de la
 France 48°10N 1°45E **20** B4
Beauceville *Canada* 46°13N 70°46W **73** C5
Beaudesert *Australia* 27°59S 153°0E **63** D5
Beaufort *Malaysia* 5°30N 115°40E **36** C5
Beaufort *N.C., U.S.A.* 34°43N 76°40W **85** D16
Beaufort *S.C., U.S.A.* 32°26N 80°40W **85** E14
Beaufort Sea *Arctic* 72°0N 140°0W **66** B5
Beaufort West *S. Africa* 32°18S 22°36E **56** E3
Beauharnois *Canada* 45°20N 73°52W **83** A11
Beaulieu → *Canada* 62°3N 113°11W **70** A6
Beauly *U.K.* 57°30N 4°28W **11** D4
Beauly → *U.K.* 57°29N 4°27W **11** D4
Beaumaris *U.K.* 53°16N 4°6W **12** D3
Beaumont *Belgium* 50°15N 4°14E **15** D4
Beaumont *U.S.A.* 30°5N 94°6W **84** F7
Beaune *France* 47°2N 4°50E **20** C6
Beaupré *Canada* 47°3N 70°54W **73** C5
Beauraing *Belgium* 50°7N 4°57E **15** D4
Beausejour *Canada* 50°5N 96°35W **71** C9
Beauvais *France* 49°25N 2°8E **20** B5
Beauval *Canada* 55°9N 107°37W **71** B7
Beaver *Okla., U.S.A.* 36°49N 100°31W **84** C4
Beaver *Pa., U.S.A.* 40°42N 80°19W **82** F4
Beaver *Utah, U.S.A.* 38°17N 112°38W **76** G7
Beaver → *B.C., Canada* 59°52N 124°20W **70** B4
Beaver → *Ont., Canada* 55°55N 87°48W **72** A2
Beaver → *Sask., Canada* 55°26N 107°45W **71** B7
Beaver City *U.S.A.* 40°8N 99°50W **80** E4

Beaver Creek *Canada* 63°0N 141°0W **68** E3
Beaver Dam *U.S.A.* 43°28N 88°50W **80** D9
Beaver Falls *U.S.A.* 40°46N 80°20W **82** F4
Beaver Hill L. *Canada* 54°5N 94°50W **71** C10
Beaver I. *U.S.A.* 45°40N 85°33W **81** C11
Beavercreek *U.S.A.* 39°43N 84°11W **81** F11
Beaverhill L. *Canada* 53°27N 112°32W **70** C6
Beaverlodge *Canada* 55°11N 119°29W **70** B5
Beaverstone → *Canada* 54°59N 89°25W **72** B2
Beaverton *Canada* 44°26N 79°9W **82** B5
Beaverton *U.S.A.* 45°29N 122°48W **78** E4
Beawar *India* 26°3N 74°18E **42** F6
Bebedouro *Brazil* 21°0S 48°25W **95** A6
Bebera, Tanjung
 Indonesia 8°44S 115°51E **37** K18
Becán *Mexico* 18°34N 89°31W **87** D7
Bécancour *Canada* 46°20N 72°26W **81** B12
Beccles *U.K.* 52°27N 1°35E **13** E9
Bečej *Serbia* 45°36N 20°3E **23** B9
Béchar *Algeria* 31°38N 2°18W **50** B5
Becharof L. *U.S.A.* 57°56N 156°23W **74** D8
Beckley *U.S.A.* 37°47N 81°11W **81** G13
Beddouza, C. *Morocco* 32°33N 9°9W **50** B4
Bedford *Canada* 45°7N 72°59W **83** A12
Bedford *S. Africa* 32°40S 26°10E **56** E4
Bedford *U.K.* 52°8N 0°28W **13** E7
Bedford *Ind., U.S.A.* 38°52N 86°29W **80** F10
Bedford *Iowa, U.S.A.* 40°40N 94°44W **80** E6
Bedford *Ohio, U.S.A.* 41°23N 81°32W **82** E3
Bedford *Pa., U.S.A.* 40°1N 78°30W **82** F6
Bedford *Va., U.S.A.* 37°20N 79°31W **81** G14
Bedford, C. *Australia* 15°14S 145°21E **62** B4
Bedfordshire □ *U.K.* 52°4N 0°28W **13** E7
Bedok *Singapore* 1°19N 103°56E **39** d
Bedourie *Australia* 24°30S 139°30E **62** C2
Bedum *Neths.* 53°18N 6°36E **15** A6
Beebe Plain *Canada* 45°1N 72°9W **83** A12
Beech Creek *U.S.A.* 41°5N 77°36W **82** E7
Beechy *Canada* 50°53N 107°24W **71** C7
Beed = Bir *India* 19°4N 75°46E **40** K9
Beef I. *Br. Virgin Is.* 18°26N 64°30W **89** e
Beenleigh *Australia* 27°43S 153°10E **63** D5
Beer Menuha *Israel* 30°19N 35°8E **44** D2
Be'er Sheva *Israel* 31°15N 34°48E **46** D3
Beersheba = Be'er Sheva
 Israel 31°15N 34°48E **46** D3
Beestekraal *S. Africa* 25°23S 27°38E **57** D4
Beeston *U.K.* 52°56N 1°14W **12** E6
Beeton *Canada* 44°5N 79°47W **82** B5
Beeville *U.S.A.* 28°24N 97°45W **84** G6
Befale
 Dem. Rep. of the Congo 0°25N 20°45E **52** D4
Befandriana *Mahajanga,*
 Madag. 15°16S 48°32E **57** B8
Befandriana *Toliara,*
 Madag. 21°55S 44°0E **57** C7
Befasy *Madag.* 20°33S 44°23E **57** C7
Befotaka *Antsiranana,*
 Madag. 13°15S 48°16E **57** A8
Befotaka *Fianarantsoa,*
 Madag. 23°49S 47°0E **57** C8
Bega *Australia* 36°41S 149°51E **63** F4
Begusarai *India* 25°24N 86°9E **43** G12
Behābād *Iran* 32°24N 59°47E **45** C8
Behala *India* 22°30N 88°18E **43** H13
Behara *Madag.* 24°55S 46°20E **57** C8
Behbehān *Iran* 30°30N 50°15E **45** D6
Behm Canal *U.S.A.* 55°10N 131°0W **70** B2
Behshahr *Iran* 36°45N 53°35E **45** B7
Bei Jiang → *China* 23°2N 112°58E **33** D6
Bei Shan *China* 41°30N 96°0E **32** B4
Bei'an *China* 48°10N 126°20E **33** B7
Beihai *China* 21°28N 109°6E **33** D5
Beijing *China* 39°53N 116°21E **34** E9
Beijing □ *China* 39°55N 116°20E **34** E9
Beilen *Neths.* 52°52N 6°27E **15** B6
Beilpajah *Australia* 32°54S 143°52E **63** E3
Beinn na Faoghla = Benbecula
 U.K. 57°26N 7°21W **11** D1
Beipiao *China* 41°52N 120°32E **35** D11
Beira *Mozam.* 19°50S 34°52E **55** F3
Beirut = Bayrūt *Lebanon* 33°53N 35°31E **46** B4
Beiseker *Canada* 51°23N 113°32W **70** C6
Beit Lekhem = Bayt Lahm
 West Bank 31°43N 35°12E **46** D4
Beitaolaizhao *China* 44°58N 125°58E **35** B13
Beitbridge *Zimbabwe* 22°12S 30°0E **55** G3
Beizhen = Binzhou
 China 37°20N 118°2E **35** F10
Beizhen *China* 41°38N 121°54E **35** D11
Beizhengzhen *China* 44°31N 123°30E **35** B12
Beja *Portugal* 38°2N 7°53W **21** C2
Béja *Tunisia* 36°43N 9°12E **51** A7
Bejaïa *Algeria* 36°42N 5°2E **50** A7
Béjar *Spain* 40°23N 5°46W **21** B3
Bejestān *Iran* 34°30N 58°5E **45** C8
Bekaa Valley = Al Biqā
 Lebanon 34°10N 36°10E **46** A5
Békéscsaba *Hungary* 46°40N 21°5E **17** E11
Bekily *Madag.* 24°13S 45°19E **57** C8
Bekisopa *Madag.* 21°40S 45°54E **57** C8
Bekitro *Madag.* 24°33S 45°18E **57** C8
Bekodoka *Madag.* 16°58S 45°7E **57** B8
Bekopaka *Madag.* 2°20N 103°7E **39** L4
Bekuli *Indonesia* 8°22S 114°13E **37** J17
Bela *India* 25°50N 82°0E **43** G10
Bela *Pakistan* 26°12N 66°20E **42** F2
Bela Bela *S. Africa* 24°51S 28°19E **57** C4
Bela Crkva *Serbia* 44°55N 21°27E **23** B9
Bela Vista *Brazil* 22°12S 56°20W **94** A4
Bela Vista *Mozam.* 26°10S 32°44E **57** D5
Belan → *India* 24°2N 81°45E **43** G9
Belarus ■ *Europe* 53°30N 27°0E **17** B14
Belau = Palau ■ *Palau* 7°30N 134°30E **58** A6
Belavenona *Madag.* 24°50S 47°4E **57** C8
Belawan *Indonesia* 3°33N 98°32E **36** D1
Belaya → *Russia* 54°40N 56°0E **18** C9

Belaya Tserkov = Bila Tserkva
  Ukraine   49°45N 30°10E 17 D16
Belaya Zemlya, Ostrova
  Russia   81°36N 62°18E 28 A7
Belcher Is. Canada   56°15N 78°45W 72 C4
Belden U.S.A.   40°2N 121°17W 78 E5
Belebey Russia   54°7N 54°7E 18 D9
Beledweyne Somali Rep.   4°30N 45°5E 47 G4
Belém Brazil   1°20S 48°30W 93 D9
Belén Argentina   27°40S 67°5W 94 B2
Belén Paraguay   23°30S 57°6W 94 A4
Belen U.S.A.   34°40N 106°46W 77 J10
Belet Uen = Beledweyne
  Somali Rep.   4°30N 45°5E 47 G4
Belev Russia   53°50N 36°5E 18 D6
Belfair U.S.A.   47°27N 122°50W 78 C4
Belfast S. Africa   25°42S 30°2E 57 D5
Belfast U.K.   54°37N 5°56W 10 B6
Belfast Maine, U.S.A.   44°26N 69°1W 81 C19
Belfast N.Y., U.S.A.   42°21N 78°7W 82 D6
Belfield U.S.A.   46°53N 103°12W 80 B2
Belfort France   47°38N 6°50E 20 C7
Belfry U.S.A.   45°9N 109°1W 76 D9
Belgaum India   15°55N 74°35E 40 M9
Belgavi = Belgaum India 15°55N 74°35E 40 M9
Belgium ■ Europe   50°30N 5°0E 15 D4
Belgorod Russia   50°35N 36°35E 19 D6
Belgorod-Dnestrovskiy =
  Bilhorod-Dnistrovskyy
  Ukraine   46°11N 30°23E 19 E5
Belgrade = Beograd
  Serbia   44°50N 20°37E 23 B9
Belgrade U.S.A.   45°47N 111°11W 76 D8
Belgrano Antarctica   77°52S 34°37W 5 D1
Belhaven U.S.A.   35°33N 76°37W 85 D16
Beli Drim → Europe   42°6N 20°25E 23 C9
Belimbing Indonesia   8°24S 115°2E 37 J18
Belinyu Indonesia   1°35S 105°50E 36 E3
Beliton Is. = Belitung
  Indonesia   3°10S 107°50E 36 E3
Belitung Indonesia   3°10S 107°50E 36 E3
Belize ■ Cent. Amer.   17°0N 88°30W 87 D7
Belize City Belize   17°25N 88°10W 87 D7
Belkovskiy, Ostrov
  Russia   75°32N 135°44E 29 B14
Bell → Canada   49°48N 77°38W 72 C4
Bell I. Canada   50°46N 55°35W 73 B8
Bell-Irving → Canada   56°12N 129°5W 70 B3
Bell Peninsula Canada   63°50N 82°0W 69 E15
Bell Ville Argentina   32°40S 62°40W 94 C3
Bella Bella Canada   52°10N 128°10W 70 C3
Bella Coola Canada   52°25N 126°40W 70 C3
Bella Unión Uruguay   30°15S 57°40W 94 C4
Bella Vista Corrientes,
  Argentina   28°33S 59°0W 94 B4
Bella Vista Tucuman,
  Argentina   27°10S 65°25W 94 B2
Bellaire U.S.A.   40°1N 80°45W 82 F4
Bellary India   15°10N 76°56E 40 M10
Bellata Australia   29°53S 149°46E 63 D4
Belle Fourche U.S.A.   44°40N 103°51W 80 C2
Belle Fourche →
  U.S.A.   44°26N 102°18W 75 G19
Belle Glade U.S.A.   26°41N 80°40W 85 H14
Belle-Île France   47°20N 3°10W 20 C2
Belle Isle Canada   51°57N 55°25W 73 B8
Belle Isle, Str. of Canada 51°30N 56°30W 73 B8
Belle Plaine U.S.A.   41°54N 92°17W 80 E7
Belle River Canada   42°18N 82°43W 82 D2
Bellefontaine U.S.A.   40°22N 83°46W 81 E12
Bellefonte U.S.A.   40°55N 77°47W 82 F7
Belleoram Canada   47°31N 55°25W 73 C8
Belleplaine Barbados   13°15N 59°34W 89 g
Belleville Canada   44°10N 77°23W 82 B7
Belleville Ill., U.S.A. 38°31N 89°59W 80 F7
Belleville Kans., U.S.A. 39°50N 97°38W 80 F5
Belleville N.J., U.S.A. 40°47N 74°9W 83 F10
Belleville N.Y., U.S.A. 43°46N 76°10W 83 C8
Bellevue Idaho, U.S.A.   43°28N 114°16W 76 E6
Bellevue Nebr., U.S.A.   41°9N 95°54W 80 E6
Bellevue Ohio, U.S.A.   41°17N 82°51W 82 E2
Bellevue Wash., U.S.A.   47°37N 122°12W 78 C4
Bellin = Kangirsuk
  Canada   60°0N 70°0W 69 F18
Bellingen Australia   30°25S 152°50E 63 E5
Bellingham U.S.A.   48°46N 122°29W 78 B4
Bellingshausen Abyssal Plain
  S. Ocean   64°0S 90°0W 5 C16
Bellingshausen Sea
  Antarctica   66°0S 80°0W 5 C17
Bellinzona Switz.   46°11N 9°1E 20 C8
Bello Colombia   6°20N 75°33W 92 B3
Bellows Falls U.S.A.   43°8N 72°27W 83 C12
Bellpat Pakistan   29°0N 68°5E 42 E3
Belluno Italy   46°9N 12°13E 22 A5
Bellwood U.S.A.   40°36N 78°20W 82 F6
Belmont Canada   42°53N 81°5W 82 D3
Belmont S. Africa   29°28S 24°22E 56 D3
Belmont U.S.A.   42°14N 78°2W 82 D6
Belmonte Brazil   16°0S 39°0W 93 G11
Belmopan Belize   17°18N 88°30W 87 D7
Belmullet Ireland   54°14N 9°58W 10 B2
Belo Horizonte Brazil   19°55S 43°56W 93 G10
Belo-sur-Mer Madag.   20°42S 44°0E 57 C7
Belo-Tsiribihina Madag. 19°40S 44°30E 57 B7
Belogorsk Russia   51°0N 128°20E 29 D13
Beloha Madag.   25°10S 45°3E 57 D8
Beloit Kans., U.S.A.   39°28N 98°6W 80 F4
Beloit Wis., U.S.A.   42°31N 89°2W 80 D9
Belokorovichi Ukraine   51°7N 28°2E 17 C15
Belomorsk Russia   64°35N 34°54E 18 B5
Belonia India   23°15N 91°30E 41 H17
Beloretsk Russia   53°58N 58°24E 18 D10
Belorussia = Belarus ■
  Europe   53°30N 27°0E 17 B14
Belovo Russia   54°30N 86°0E 28 D9
Beloyarskiy Russia   63°42N 66°40E 28 C7
Beloye, Ozero Russia   60°10N 37°35E 18 B6

Beloye More Russia   66°30N 38°0E 8 C25
Belozersk Russia   60°1N 37°45E 18 B6
Belpre U.S.A.   39°17N 81°34W 81 F13
Belrain India   28°23N 80°55E 43 E9
Belt U.S.A.   47°23N 110°55W 76 C8
Beltana Australia   30°48S 138°25E 63 E2
Belterra Brazil   2°45S 55°0W 93 D8
Belton U.S.A.   31°3N 97°28W 84 F6
Belton L. U.S.A.   31°6N 97°28W 84 F6
Beltsy = Bălți Moldova   47°48N 27°58E 17 E14
Belturbet Ireland   54°6N 7°26W 10 B4
Belukha Russia   49°50N 86°50E 28 E9
Beluran Malaysia   5°48N 117°35E 36 C5
Belushya Guba Russia   71°32N 52°19E 28 B6
Belvidere Ill., U.S.A.   42°15N 88°50W 80 D9
Belvidere N.J., U.S.A.   40°50N 75°5W 83 F9
Belyando → Australia   21°38S 146°50E 62 C4
Belyando Crossing
  Australia   21°32S 146°51E 62 C4
Belyuen Australia   12°34S 130°42E 60 B5
Bely, Ostrov Russia   73°30N 71°0E 28 B8
Belyy Yar Russia   58°26N 84°39E 28 D9
Belzoni U.S.A.   33°11N 90°29W 85 E9
Bemaraha, Lembalemban′ i
  Madag.   18°40S 44°45E 57 B7
Bemarivo Madag.   21°45S 44°45E 57 C7
Bemarivo → Antsiranana,
  Madag.   14°9S 50°9E 57 A9
Bemarivo → Mahajanga,
  Madag.   15°27S 47°40E 57 B8
Bemavo Madag.   21°33S 45°25E 57 C8
Bembéréke Benin   10°11N 2°43E 50 F6
Bembesi Zimbabwe   20°0S 28°58E 55 G2
Bembesi → Zimbabwe   18°57S 27°47E 55 F2
Bemetara India   21°42N 81°32E 43 J9
Bemidji U.S.A.   47°28N 94°53W 80 B6
Bemolanga Madag.   17°44S 45°6E 57 B8
Ben Iran   32°32N 50°45E 45 C6
Ben Cruachan U.K.   56°26N 5°8W 11 E3
Ben Dearg U.K.   57°47N 4°56W 11 D4
Ben En △ Vietnam   19°37N 105°30E 38 C5
Ben Gardane Tunisia   33°11N 11°11E 51 B8
Ben Hope U.K.   58°25N 4°36W 11 C4
Ben Lawers U.K.   56°32N 4°14W 11 E4
Ben Lomond N.S.W.,
  Australia   30°1S 151°43E 63 E5
Ben Lomond Tas.,
  Australia   41°38S 147°42E 63 G4
Ben Lomond U.K.   56°11N 4°38W 11 E4
Ben Lomond △
  Australia   41°33S 147°39E 63 G4
Ben Luc Vietnam   10°39N 106°29E 39 G6
Ben Macdhui U.K.   57°4N 3°40W 11 D5
Ben Mhor U.K.   57°15N 7°18W 11 D1
Ben More Argyll & Bute,
  U.K.   56°26N 6°1W 11 E2
Ben More Stirling, U.K. 56°23N 4°32W 11 E4
Ben More Assynt U.K.   58°8N 4°52W 11 C4
Ben Nevis U.K.   56°48N 5°1W 11 E3
Ben Quang Vietnam   17°3N 106°55E 38 D6
Ben Tre Vietnam   10°14N 106°23E 39 G6
Ben Vorlich U.K.   56°21N 4°14W 11 E4
Ben Wyvis U.K.   57°40N 4°35W 11 D4
Bena Nigeria   11°20N 5°50E 50 F7
Benalla Australia   36°30S 146°0E 63 F4
Benares = Varanasi
  India   25°22N 83°0E 43 G10
Benavente Spain   42°2N 5°43W 21 A3
Benavides U.S.A.   27°36N 98°25W 84 H5
Benbecula U.K.   57°26N 7°21W 11 D1
Benbonyathe Hill
  Australia   30°25S 139°11E 63 E2
Bend U.S.A.   44°4N 121°19W 76 D3
Bender Beyla Somali Rep. 9°30N 50°48E 47 F5
Bendery = Tighina
  Moldova   46°50N 29°30E 17 E15
Bendigo Australia   36°40S 144°15E 63 F3
Benē Beraq Israel   32°6N 34°51E 46 C3
Benenitra Madag.   23°27S 45°5E 57 C8
Benevento Italy   41°8N 14°45E 22 D6
Benga Mozam.   16°11S 33°40E 55 F3
Bengal, Bay of Ind. Oc. 15°0N 90°0E 41 M17
Bengaluru = Bangalore
  India   12°59N 77°40E 40 N10
Bengbu China   32°58N 117°20E 35 H9
Benghazi = Banghāzī
  Libya   32°11N 20°3E 51 B10
Bengkalis Indonesia   1°30N 102°10E 39 M4
Bengkulu Indonesia   3°50S 102°12E 36 E2
Bengkulu □ Indonesia   3°48S 102°16E 36 E2
Bengough Canada   49°25N 105°10W 71 D7
Benguela Angola   12°37S 13°25E 53 G2
Benguérua, I. Mozam.   21°58S 35°28E 57 C6
Beni Dem. Rep. of the Congo 0°30N 29°27E 54 B2
Beni → Bolivia   10°23S 65°24W 92 F5
Beni Mellal Morocco   32°21N 6°21W 50 B4
Beni Suef Egypt   29°5N 31°6E 51 C12
Beniah L. Canada   63°23N 112°17W 70 A6
Benidorm Spain   38°33N 0°9W 21 C5
Benin ■ Africa   10°0N 2°0E 50 G6
Benin, Bight of W. Afr. 5°0N 3°0E 50 H6
Benin City Nigeria   6°20N 5°31E 50 G7
Benito Juárez Argentina 37°40S 59°43W 94 D4
Benitses Greece   39°32N 19°55E 25 A3
Benjamin Aceval
  Paraguay   24°58S 57°34W 94 A4
Benjamin Constant
  Brazil   4°40S 70°15W 92 D4
Benjamín Hill Mexico   30°9N 111°7W 86 A2
Benkelman U.S.A.   40°3N 101°32W 80 E3
Benlidi Australia   24°35S 144°50E 62 C3
Bennett Canada   59°51N 135°0W 70 B2
Bennett, L. Australia   22°50S 131°2E 60 D5
Bennetta, Ostrov
  Russia   76°21N 148°56E 29 B15
Bennettsville U.S.A.   34°37N 79°41W 85 D15
Bennington N.H., U.S.A. 43°0N 71°55W 83 D13
Bennington Vt., U.S.A.   42°53N 73°12W 83 D11
Benom Malaysia   3°50N 102°6E 39 L4
Benoni S. Africa   26°11S 28°18E 57 D4

Benque Viejo Belize   17°5N 89°8W 87 D7
Benson Ariz., U.S.A.   31°58N 110°18W 77 L8
Benson Minn., U.S.A.   45°19N 95°36W 80 C6
Bent Iran   26°20N 59°31E 45 E8
Benteng Indonesia   6°10S 120°30E 37 F6
Bentinck I. Australia   17°3S 139°35E 62 B2
Bentley Subglacial Trench
  Antarctica   80°0S 115°0W 5 E15
Bento Gonçalves Brazil   29°10S 51°31W 95 B5
Benton Ark., U.S.A.   34°34N 92°35W 84 D8
Benton Calif., U.S.A.   37°48N 118°32W 78 H8
Benton Ill., U.S.A.   38°0N 88°55W 80 F9
Benton Pa., U.S.A.   41°12N 76°23W 83 E8
Benton Harbor U.S.A.   42°6N 86°27W 80 D10
Bentong Malaysia   3°31N 101°55E 39 L3
Bentonville U.S.A.   36°22N 94°13W 84 C7
Benue → Nigeria   7°48N 6°46E 50 G7
Benxi China   41°20N 123°48E 35 D12
Beo Indonesia   4°25N 126°50E 37 D7
Beograd Serbia   44°50N 20°37E 23 B9
Beolgyo S. Korea   34°51N 127°21E 35 G14
Beppu Japan   33°15N 131°30E 31 H5
Beqa Fiji   18°23S 178°8E 59 a
Beqaa Valley = Al Biqā
  Lebanon   34°10N 36°10E 46 A5
Ber Mota India   23°27N 68°34E 42 H3
Bera, Tasik Malaysia   3°5N 102°38E 39 L4
Berach → India   25°15N 75°2E 42 G6
Beraketa Madag.   23°7S 44°25E 57 C7
Berastagi Indonesia   3°11N 98°31E 39 L2
Berat Albania   40°43N 19°59E 23 D8
Berau = Tanjungredeb
  Indonesia   2°9N 117°29E 36 D5
Berau, Teluk Indonesia   2°30S 132°30E 37 E8
Beravina Madag.   18°10S 45°14E 57 B8
Berber Sudan   18°0N 34°0E 51 E12
Berbera Somali Rep.   10°30N 45°2E 47 E4
Berbérati C.A.R.   4°15N 15°40E 52 D3
Berbice → Guyana   6°20N 57°32W 92 B7
Berdichev = Berdychiv
  Ukraine   49°57N 28°30E 17 D15
Berdsk Russia   54°47N 83°2E 28 D9
Berdyansk Ukraine   46°45N 36°50E 19 E6
Berdychiv Ukraine   49°57N 28°30E 17 D15
Berea U.S.A.   37°34N 84°17W 81 G11
Berebere Indonesia   2°25N 128°45E 37 D7
Bereeda Somali Rep.   11°45N 51°0E 47 E5
Berehove Ukraine   48°15N 22°35E 17 D12
Bereket Turkmenistan   39°16N 55°32E 45 B7
Berekum Ghana   7°29N 2°34W 50 G5
Berens → Canada   52°25N 97°2W 71 C9
Berens I. Canada   52°18N 97°18W 71 C9
Berens River Canada   52°25N 97°0W 71 C9
Beresford U.S.A.   43°5N 96°47W 80 D5
Berestechko Ukraine   50°22N 25°5E 17 C13
Berevo Mahajanga,
  Madag.   17°14S 44°17E 57 B7
Berevo Toliara, Madag.   19°44S 44°58E 57 B7
Berezhany Ukraine   49°26N 24°58E 17 D13
Berezina = Byarezina →
  Belarus   52°33N 30°14E 17 B16
Bereznik Russia   62°51N 42°40E 18 B7
Berezniki Russia   59°24N 56°46E 18 C10
Berezovo Russia   64°0N 65°0E 28 C7
Berga Spain   42°6N 1°48E 21 A6
Bérgamo Turkey   39°8N 27°11E 23 E12
Bérgamo Italy   45°41N 9°43E 20 D8
Bergen Neths.   52°40N 4°43E 15 B4
Bergen Norway   60°20N 5°20E 8 F11
Bergen U.S.A.   43°5N 77°57W 82 C7
Bergen op Zoom Neths.   51°28N 4°18E 15 C4
Bergerac France   44°51N 0°30E 20 D4
Bergholz U.S.A.   40°31N 80°53W 82 F4
Bergisch Gladbach
  Germany   50°59N 7°8E 15 D7
Bergville S. Africa   28°52S 29°18E 57 D4
Berhala, Selat Indonesia 1°0S 104°15E 36 E2
Berhampore = Baharampur
  India   24°2N 88°27E 43 G13
Berhampur = Brahmapur
  India   19°15N 84°54E 41 K14
Bering Glacier U.S.A.   60°20N 143°30W 74 C11
Bering Sea Pac. Oc.   58°0N 171°0W 74 C1
Bering Strait Pac. Oc.   65°30N 169°0W 74 B6
Beringovskiy Russia   63°3N 179°19E 29 C18
Berisso Argentina   34°56S 57°50W 94 C4
Berja Spain   36°50N 2°56W 21 D4
Berkeley U.S.A.   37°51N 122°16W 78 H4
Berkner I. Antarctica   79°30S 50°0W 5 D18
Berkshire U.S.A.   42°19N 76°11W 83 D8
Berkshire Downs U.K.   51°33N 1°29W 13 F6
Berlin Germany   52°31N 13°23E 16 B7
Berlin Md., U.S.A.   38°20N 75°13W 81 F16
Berlin N.H., U.S.A.   44°28N 71°11W 83 B13
Berlin N.Y., U.S.A.   42°42N 73°23W 83 D11
Berlin Wis., U.S.A.   43°58N 88°57W 80 D9
Berlin L. U.S.A.   41°3N 81°0W 82 E4
Bermejo → Formosa,
  Argentina   26°51S 58°23W 94 B4
Bermejo → San Juan,
  Argentina   32°30S 67°30W 94 C2
Bermejo, Paso = Uspallata, P. de
  Argentina   32°37S 69°22W 94 C2
Bermen, L. Canada   53°35N 68°55W 73 B6
Bermuda ☑ Atl. Oc.   32°18N 64°45W 67 F13
Bern Switz.   46°57N 7°28E 20 C7
Bernalillo U.S.A.   35°18N 106°33W 77 J10
Bernardo de Irigoyen
  Argentina   26°15S 53°40W 95 B5
Bernardsville U.S.A.   40°43N 74°34W 83 F10
Bernasconi Argentina   37°55S 63°44W 94 D3
Bernburg Germany   51°47N 11°44E 16 C6
Berne = Bern Switz.   46°57N 7°28E 20 C7
Bernerray U.K.   57°43N 7°11W 11 D1
Bernier I. Australia   24°50S 113°12E 61 D1
Bernina, Piz Switz.   46°20N 9°54E 20 C8
Beroroha Madag.   21°40S 45°10E 57 C8
Beroun Czech Rep.   49°57N 14°5E 16 D8
Berri Australia   34°14S 140°35E 63 E3

Berriane Algeria   32°50N 3°46E 50 B6
Berry Australia   34°46S 150°43E 63 E5
Berry France   46°50N 2°0E 20 C5
Berry Is. Bahamas   25°40N 77°50W 88 A4
Berryessa, L. U.S.A.   38°31N 122°6W 78 G4
Berryville U.S.A.   36°22N 93°34W 84 C8
Berseba Namibia   26°0S 17°46E 56 D2
Bershad Ukraine   48°22N 29°31E 17 D15
Berthold U.S.A.   48°19N 101°44W 80 A3
Berthoud U.S.A.   40°19N 105°5W 76 F11
Bertoua Cameroon   4°30N 13°45E 52 D2
Bertraghboy B. Ireland   53°22N 9°54W 10 C2
Berwick U.S.A.   41°3N 76°14W 83 E8
Berwick-upon-Tweed
  U.K.   55°46N 2°0W 12 B6
Berwyn Mts. U.K.   52°54N 3°26W 12 E4
Besal Pakistan   35°4N 73°56E 43 B5
Besalampy Madag.   16°43S 44°29E 57 B7
Besançon France   47°15N 6°2E 20 C7
Besar Indonesia   2°40S 116°0E 36 E5
Besnard L. Canada   55°25N 106°0W 71 B7
Besni Turkey   37°41N 37°52E 44 B3
Besor, N. → Egypt   31°28N 34°22E 46 D3
Bessarabiya Moldova   47°0N 28°10E 17 E15
Bessarabka = Basarabeasca
  Moldova   46°21N 28°58E 17 E15
Bessemer Ala., U.S.A.   33°24N 86°58W 85 E11
Bessemer Mich., U.S.A.   46°29N 90°3W 80 B8
Bessemer Pa., U.S.A.   40°59N 80°30W 82 F4
Beswick Australia   14°34S 132°53E 60 B5
Beswick ◊ Australia   14°3S 132°51E 60 B5
Bet She'an Israel   32°30N 35°30E 46 C4
Bet Shemesh Israel   31°44N 35°0E 46 D4
Betafo Madag.   19°50S 46°51E 57 B8
Betancuria Canary Is.   28°25N 14°3W 24 F5
Betanzos Spain   43°15N 8°12W 21 A1
Bétaré Oya Cameroon   5°40N 14°5E 52 C2
Betatao Madag.   18°11S 47°52E 57 B8
Bethal S. Africa   26°27S 29°28E 57 D4
Bethanien Namibia   26°31S 17°8E 56 D2
Bethany Canada   44°11N 78°34W 82 B6
Bethany Mo., U.S.A.   40°16N 94°2W 80 E6
Bethany Okla., U.S.A.   35°31N 97°38W 84 D6
Bethel Alaska, U.S.A.   60°48N 161°45W 74 C7
Bethel Conn., U.S.A.   41°22N 73°25W 83 E11
Bethel Maine, U.S.A.   44°25N 70°47W 83 B14
Bethel Vt., U.S.A.   43°50N 72°38W 83 C12
Bethel Park U.S.A.   40°19N 80°2W 82 F4
Bethlehem = Bayt Lahm
  West Bank   31°43N 35°12E 46 D4
Bethlehem S. Africa   28°14S 28°18E 57 D4
Bethlehem U.S.A.   40°37N 75°23W 83 F9
Bethulie S. Africa   30°30S 25°59E 56 E4
Béthune France   50°30N 2°38E 20 A5
Betioky Madag.   23°48S 44°20E 57 C7
Betong Malaysia   1°24N 111°31E 36 D4
Betong Thailand   5°45N 101°5E 39 K3
Betoota Australia   23°0S 122°0E 62 D3
Betpaqdala Kazakhstan   45°45N 70°30E 32 B2
Betroka Madag.   23°16S 46°0E 57 C8
Betsiamites Canada   48°56N 68°40W 73 C6
Betsiamites → Canada   48°56N 68°38W 73 C6
Betsiboka → Madag.   16°3S 46°36E 57 B8
Bettendorf U.S.A.   41°32N 90°30W 80 E8
Bettiah India   26°48N 84°33E 43 F11
Betul India   21°58N 77°59E 40 J10
Betws-y-Coed U.K.   53°5N 3°48W 12 D4
Beulah Mich., U.S.A.   44°38N 86°6W 80 C10
Beulah N. Dak., U.S.A.   47°16N 101°47W 80 B3
Beveren Belgium   51°12N 4°16E 15 C4
Beverley Australia   32°9S 116°56E 61 F2
Beverley U.K.   53°51N 0°26W 12 D7
Beverly U.S.A.   42°33N 70°53W 83 D14
Beverly Hills Calif.,
  U.S.A.   34°5N 118°24W 79 L8
Beverly Hills Fla.,
  U.S.A.   28°55N 82°28W 85 G13
Bevoalavo Madag.   25°13S 45°26E 57 D7
Bewas → India   23°59N 79°21E 43 H8
Bewdley Canada   44°5N 78°19W 82 B6
Bexhill U.K.   50°51N 0°29E 13 G8
Beyānlū Iran   36°0N 47°51E 44 C5
Beyneu Kazakhstan   45°18N 55°9E 19 E10
Beypazarı Turkey   40°10N 31°56E 19 F5
Beyşehir Gölü Turkey   37°41N 31°33E 44 B1
Bezwada = Vijayawada
  India   16°31N 80°39E 41 L12
Bhabua India   25°3N 83°37E 43 G10
Bhachau India   23°20N 70°16E 42 H4
Bhadar → Gujarat, India 22°17N 72°20E 42 H5
Bhadar → Gujarat, India 21°27N 69°47E 42 J3
Bhadarwah India   32°58N 75°46E 43 C6
Bhadgaon = Bhaktapur
  Nepal   27°38N 85°24E 43 F11
Bhadohi India   25°25N 82°34E 43 G10
Bhadra India   29°8N 75°14E 42 E6
Bhadrakh India   21°10N 86°30E 41 J15
Bhadran India   22°19N 72°6E 42 H5
Bhadravati India   13°49N 75°40E 40 N9
Bhag Pakistan   29°2N 67°49E 42 E2
Bhagalpur India   25°10N 87°0E 43 G12
Bhagirathi → Uttarakhand,
  India   30°8N 78°35E 43 D8
Bhagirathi → W. Bengal,
  India   23°25N 88°23E 43 H13
Bhakkar Pakistan   31°40N 71°5E 42 D4
Bhakra Dam India   31°30N 76°45E 42 D7
Bhaktapur Nepal   27°38N 85°24E 43 F11
Bhamo Burma   24°15N 97°15E 41 G20
Bhandara India   21°5N 79°42E 40 J11
Bhanpura India   24°31N 75°44E 42 G6
Bhanrer Ra. India   23°40N 79°45E 43 H8
Bhaptiahi India   26°19N 86°44E 43 F12
Bharat = India ■ Asia   20°0N 78°0E 40 K11
Bharatpur Chhattisgarh,
  India   23°44N 81°46E 43 H9
Bharatpur Raj., India   27°15N 77°30E 42 F7
Bharatpur Nepal   27°34N 84°10E 43 F11

Bharno India   23°14N 84°53E 43 H11
Bharuch India   21°47N 73°0E 40 J8
Bhatinda India   30°15N 74°57E 42 D6
Bhatpara India   22°50N 88°25E 43 H13
Bhattu India   29°36N 75°19E 42 E6
Bhaun Pakistan   32°55N 72°40E 42 C5
Bhaunagar = Bhavnagar
  India   21°45N 72°10E 40 J8
Bhavnagar India   21°45N 72°10E 40 J8
Bhawari India   25°42N 73°4E 42 G5
Bhayavadar India   21°51N 70°15E 42 J4
Bhera Pakistan   32°29N 72°57E 42 C5
Bhikangaon India   21°52N 75°57E 42 J6
Bhilai = Bhilainagar-Durg
  India   21°13N 81°26E 41 J12
Bhilainagar-Durg India   21°13N 81°26E 41 J12
Bhilsa = Vidisha India   23°28N 77°53E 42 H7
Bhilwara India   25°25N 74°38E 42 G6
Bhima → India   16°25N 77°17E 40 L10
Bhimbar Pakistan   32°59N 74°3E 43 C6
Bhind India   26°30N 78°46E 43 F8
Bhinga India   27°43N 81°56E 43 F9
Bhinmal India   25°0N 72°15E 42 G5
Bhisho S. Africa   32°50S 27°23E 57 E4
Bhiwandi India   19°20N 73°0E 40 K8
Bhiwani India   28°50N 76°9E 42 E7
Bhogava → India   22°26N 72°20E 42 H5
Bhola Bangla.   22°45N 90°35E 41 H17
Bholari Pakistan   25°19N 68°13E 42 G3
Bhopal India   23°20N 77°30E 42 H7
Bhubaneshwar India   20°15N 85°50E 41 J14
Bhuj India   23°15N 69°49E 42 H3
Bhumiphol Res. Thailand 17°20N 98°40E 38 D2
Bhusawal India   21°3N 75°46E 40 J9
Bhutan ■ Asia   27°25N 90°30E 41 F17
Biafra, B. of = Bonny, Bight of
  Africa   3°30N 9°20E 52 D1
Biak Indonesia   1°10S 136°6E 37 E9
Biała Podlaska Poland   52°4N 23°6E 17 B12
Białogard Poland   54°2N 15°58E 16 A8
Białystok Poland   53°10N 23°10E 17 B12
Biaora India   23°56N 76°56E 42 H7
Biärjmand Iran   36°6N 55°53E 45 B7
Biaro Indonesia   2°5N 125°26E 37 D7
Biarritz France   43°29N 1°33W 20 E3
Bias Indonesia   8°24S 115°36E 37 J18
Bibai Japan   43°19N 141°52E 30 C10
Bibby I. Canada   61°55N 93°0W 71 A10
Biberach Germany   48°5N 9°47E 16 D5
Bibungwa
  Dem. Rep. of the Congo 2°40S 28°15E 54 C2
Bicester U.K.   51°54N 1°9W 13 F6
Bicheno Australia   41°52S 148°18E 63 G4
Bichia India   22°27N 80°42E 43 H9
Bickerton I. Australia   13°45S 136°10E 62 A2
Bid = Bir India   19°4N 75°46E 40 K9
Bida Nigeria   9°3N 5°58E 50 G7
Bidar India   17°55N 77°35E 40 L10
Biddeford U.S.A.   43°30N 70°28W 81 D18
Bideford U.K.   51°1N 4°13W 13 F3
Bideford Bay U.K.   51°5N 4°20W 13 F3
Bidhuna India   26°49N 79°31E 43 F8
Bidokht Iran   34°20N 58°46E 45 C8
Bidor Malaysia   4°6N 101°15E 39 K3
Bidyadanga Australia   18°45S 121°43E 60 C3
Bié, Planalto de Angola 12°0S 16°0E 53 G3
Bieber U.S.A.   41°7N 121°8W 76 F3
Biel Switz.   47°8N 7°14E 20 C7
Bielefeld Germany   52°1N 8°33E 16 B5
Biella Italy   45°34N 8°3E 20 D8
Bielsk Podlaski Poland   52°47N 23°12E 17 B12
Bielsko-Biała Poland   49°50N 19°2E 17 D10
Bien Hoa Vietnam   10°57N 106°49E 39 G6
Bienne = Biel Switz.   47°8N 7°14E 20 C7
Bienville, L. Canada   55°5N 72°40W 72 A5
Biesiesfontein S. Africa 30°57S 17°58E 56 E2
Big → Canada   54°50N 58°55W 73 B8
Big B. Canada   55°43N 60°35W 73 A7
Big Bear City U.S.A.   34°16N 116°51W 79 L10
Big Bear Lake U.S.A.   34°15N 116°56W 79 L10
Big Belt Mts. U.S.A.   46°30N 111°25W 76 C8
Big Bend Swaziland   26°50S 31°58E 57 D5
Big Bend △ U.S.A.   29°20N 103°5W 84 G3
Big Black → U.S.A.   32°3N 91°4W 85 E9
Big Blue → U.S.A.   39°35N 96°34W 80 F5
Big Creek U.S.A.   37°11N 119°14W 78 H7
Big Cypress △ U.S.A.   26°0N 81°0W 85 H14
Big Desert Australia   35°45S 141°10E 63 F3
Big Falls U.S.A.   48°12N 93°48W 80 A7
Big Fork → U.S.A.   48°31N 93°43W 80 A7
Big Horn Mts. = Bighorn Mts.
  U.S.A.   44°25N 107°0W 76 D10
Big I. Canada   61°7N 116°45W 70 A5
Big Lake U.S.A.   31°12N 101°28W 84 F4
Big Moose U.S.A.   43°49N 74°58W 83 C10
Big Muddy Cr. → U.S.A.   48°8N 104°36W 76 B11
Big Pine U.S.A.   37°10N 118°17W 78 H8
Big Piney U.S.A.   42°32N 110°7W 76 E8
Big Quill L. Canada   51°55N 104°30W 71 C8
Big Rapids U.S.A.   43°42N 85°29W 81 D11
Big Rideau L. Canada   44°40N 76°15W 83 B8
Big River Canada   53°50N 107°0W 71 C7
Big Run U.S.A.   40°57N 78°55W 82 F6
Big Sable Pt. U.S.A.   44°3N 86°1W 80 C10
Big Salmon → Canada   61°52N 134°55W 70 A2
Big Sand L. Canada   57°45N 99°45W 71 B9
Big Sandy U.S.A.   48°11N 110°7W 76 B8
Big Sandy → U.S.A.   38°25N 82°36W 81 F12
Big Sandy Cr. = Sandy Cr. →
  U.S.A.   41°51N 109°47W 76 F9
Big Sandy Cr. →
  U.S.A.   38°7N 102°29W 76 G12
Big Sioux → U.S.A.   42°29N 96°27W 80 D5
Big South Fork △
  U.S.A.   36°27N 84°47W 85 C12
Big Spring U.S.A.   32°15N 101°28W 84 E4
Big Stone City U.S.A.   45°18N 96°28W 80 C5
Big Stone Gap U.S.A.   36°52N 82°47W 81 G12

Big Stone L. *U.S.A.* 45°18N 96°27W **80 C5**
Big Sur *U.S.A.* 36°15N 121°48W **78 J5**
Big Timber *U.S.A.* 45°50N 109°57W **76 D9**
Big Trout L. *Canada* 53°40N 90°0W **72 B2**
Big Trout Lake *Canada* 53°45N 90°0W **72 B2**
Biğa *Turkey* 40°13N 27°14E **23 D12**
Bigadiç *Turkey* 39°22N 28°7E **23 E13**
Biggar *Canada* 52°4N 108°0W **71 C7**
Biggar *U.K.* 55°38N 3°32W **11 F5**
Bigge I. *Australia* 14°35S 125°10E **60 B4**
Biggenden *Australia* 25°31S 152°4E **63 D5**
Biggleswade *U.K.* 52°5N 0°14W **13 E7**
Biggs *U.S.A.* 39°25N 121°43W **78 F5**
Bighorn *U.S.A.* 46°10N 107°27W **76 C10**
Bighorn → *U.S.A.* 46°10N 107°28W **76 C10**
Bighorn Canyon △
  U.S.A. 45°10N 108°0W **76 D10**
Bighorn L. *U.S.A.* 44°55N 108°15W **76 D9**
Bighorn Mts. *U.S.A.* 44°25N 107°0W **76 D10**
Bigstone L. *Canada* 53°42N 95°44W **71 C9**
Bigwa *Tanzania* 7°10S 39°10E **54 D4**
Bihać *Bos.-H.* 44°49N 15°57E **16 F8**
Bihar *India* 25°5N 85°40E **43 G11**
Bihar □ *India* 25°0N 86°0E **43 G12**
Biharamulo *Tanzania* 2°25S 31°25E **54 C3**
Biharamulo △ *Tanzania* 2°24S 31°26E **54 C3**
Bihariganj *India* 25°44N 86°59E **43 G12**
Bihor, Munţii *Romania* 46°29N 22°47E **17 E12**
Bijagós, Arquipélago dos
  Guinea-Biss. 11°15N 16°10W **50 F2**
Bijaipur *India* 26°2N 77°20E **42 F7**
Bijapur *Chhattisgarh,*
  India 18°50N 80°50E **41 K12**
Bijapur *Karnataka, India* 16°50N 75°55E **40 L9**
Bījār *Iran* 35°52N 47°35E **44 C5**
Bijawar *India* 24°38N 79°30E **43 G8**
Bijeljina *Bos.-H.* 44°46N 19°14E **23 B8**
Bijnor *India* 29°27N 78°11E **42 E8**
Bikaner *India* 28°2N 73°18E **42 E5**
Bikapur *India* 26°30N 82°7E **43 F10**
Bikeqi *China* 40°43N 111°20E **34 D6**
Bikfayyā *Lebanon* 33°55N 35°41E **46 B4**
Bikin *Russia* 46°50N 134°20E **30 A7**
Bikin → *Russia* 46°51N 134°2E **30 A7**
Bikini Atoll *Marshall Is.* 12°0N 167°30E **64 F8**
Bikita *Zimbabwe* 20°6S 31°41E **57 C5**
Bīkkū Bīttī *Libya* 22°0N 19°12E **51 D9**
Bila Tserkva *Ukraine* 49°45N 30°10E **17 D16**
Bilara *India* 26°14N 73°53E **42 F5**
Bilaspur *Chhattisgarh,*
  India 22°2N 82°15E **43 H10**
Bilaspur *Punjab, India* 31°19N 76°50E **42 D7**
Bilauk Taungdan *Thailand* 13°0N 99°0E **38 F2**
Bilbao *Spain* 43°16N 2°56W **21 A4**
Bilbo = Bilbao *Spain* 43°16N 2°56W **21 A4**
Bildudalur *Iceland* 65°41N 23°36W **8 D2**
Bílé Karpaty *Europe* 49°5N 18°0E **17 D9**
Bilecik *Turkey* 40°5N 30°5E **19 F5**
Bilgram *India* 27°11N 80°2E **43 F9**
Bilhaur *India* 26°51N 80°5E **43 F9**
Bilhorod-Dnistrovskyy
  Ukraine 46°11N 30°23E **19 E5**
Bilibino *Russia* 68°3N 166°20E **29 C17**
Bilibiza *Mozam.* 12°30S 40°20E **55 E5**
Billiluna *Australia* 19°37S 127°41E **60 C4**
Billings *U.S.A.* 45°47N 108°30W **76 D9**
Billiton Is. = Belitung
  Indonesia 3°10S 107°50E **36 E3**
Bilma *Niger* 18°50N 13°30E **51 E8**
Biloela *Australia* 24°24S 150°31E **62 C5**
Biloxi *U.S.A.* 30°24N 88°53W **85 F10**
Bilpa Morea Claypan
  Australia 25°0S 140°0E **62 D3**
Biltine *Chad* 14°40N 20°50E **51 F10**
Bima *Indonesia* 8°22S 118°49E **37 F5**
Bimbo *C.A.R.* 4°15N 18°33E **52 D3**
Bimini Is. *Bahamas* 25°42N 79°25W **88 A4**
Bin Xian *Heilongjiang,*
  China 45°42N 127°32E **35 B14**
Bin Xian *Shaanxi, China* 35°2N 108°4E **34 G5**
Bina-Etawah *India* 24°13N 78°14E **42 G8**
Binalbagan *Phil.* 10°12N 122°50E **37 B6**
Binalong *Australia* 34°40S 148°39E **63 E4**
Bīnālūd, Kūh-e *Iran* 36°30N 58°30E **45 B8**
Binatang = Bintangau
  Malaysia 2°10N 111°40E **36 D4**
Binche *Belgium* 50°26N 4°10E **15 D4**
Bindki *India* 26°2N 80°36E **43 F9**
Bindura *Zimbabwe* 17°18S 31°18E **55 F3**
Bingara *Australia* 29°52S 150°36E **63 D5**
Bingham *U.S.A.* 45°3N 69°53W **81 C19**
Binghamton *U.S.A.* 42°6N 75°55W **83 D9**
Bingöl *Turkey* 38°53N 40°29E **44 B4**
Binh Dinh = An Nhon
  Vietnam 13°55N 109°7E **38 F7**
Binh Khe *Vietnam* 13°57N 108°51E **38 F7**
Binh Son *Vietnam* 15°20N 108°40E **38 E7**
Binhai *China* 34°2N 119°49E **35 G10**
Binisatua *Spain* 39°50N 4°11E **24 B11**
Binissalem *Spain* 39°41N 2°50E **24 B9**
Binjai *Indonesia* 3°20N 98°30E **36 D1**
Binnaway *Australia* 31°28S 149°24E **63 E4**
Binongko *Indonesia* 5°57S 124°2E **37 F6**
Binscarth *Canada* 50°37N 101°17W **71 C8**
Bintan *Indonesia* 1°0N 104°0E **36 D2**
Bintangau *Malaysia* 2°10N 111°40E **36 D4**
Bintuni *Indonesia* 2°7S 133°32E **37 E8**
Binzert = Bizerte *Tunisia* 37°15N 9°50E **51 A7**
Binzhou *China* 37°20N 118°2E **35 F10**
Bío Bío □ *Chile* 37°35S 72°0W **94 D1**
Bíobío → *Chile* 36°49S 73°10W **94 D1**
Bioko *Eq. Guin.* 3°30N 8°40E **52 D1**
Bir *India* 19°4N 75°46E **40 K9**
Bîr Abu Muḥammad
  Egypt 29°44N 34°14E **46 F3**
Bi'r ad Dabbāghāt *Jordan* 30°26N 35°32E **46 E4**
Bi'r al Butayyihāt *Jordan* 29°47N 35°20E **46 F4**
Bi'r al Mārī *Jordan* 30°4N 35°33E **46 E4**

Bi'r al Qaṭṭār *Jordan* 29°47N 35°32E **46 F4**
Bîr Atrun *Sudan* 18°15N 26°40E **51 E11**
Bîr Beida *Egypt* 30°25N 34°29E **46 E3**
Bîr el 'Abd *Egypt* 31°2N 33°0E **46 D2**
Bîr el Biarât *Egypt* 29°30N 34°43E **46 F3**
Bîr el Duweidar *Egypt* 30°56N 32°32E **46 E1**
Bîr el Garârât *Egypt* 31°3N 33°34E **46 D2**
Bîr el Heisi *Egypt* 29°22N 34°36E **46 F3**
Bîr el Jafir *Egypt* 30°50N 32°41E **46 E1**
Bîr el Mâlḥi *Egypt* 30°38N 33°19E **46 E2**
Bîr el Thamâda *Egypt* 30°12N 33°27E **46 E2**
Bîr Gebeil Ḥişn *Egypt* 30°2N 33°18E **46 E2**
Bi'r Ghadīr *Syria* 34°6N 37°3E **46 A6**
Bîr Ḥasana *Egypt* 30°29N 33°46E **46 E2**
Bîr Kaseiba *Egypt* 31°0N 33°17E **46 E2**
Bîr Lahfân *Egypt* 31°0N 33°51E **46 E2**
Bîr Madkûr *Egypt* 30°44N 32°33E **46 E1**
Bîr Mogreïn *Mauritania* 25°10N 11°25W **50 C3**
Bîr Qaṭia *Egypt* 30°58N 32°45E **46 E1**
Bîr Shalatein *Egypt* 23°5N 35°25E **51 D13**
Birāk *Libya* 27°31N 14°20E **51 C8**
Biratnagar *Nepal* 26°27N 87°17E **43 F12**
Birawa
  Dem. Rep. of the Congo 2°20S 28°48E **54 C2**
Birch → *Canada* 58°28N 112°17W **70 B6**
Birch Hills *Canada* 52°59N 105°25W **71 C7**
Birch I. *Canada* 52°26N 99°54W **71 C9**
Birch L. *N.W.T., Canada* 62°4N 116°33W **70 A5**
Birch L. *Ont., Canada* 51°23N 92°18W **72 B1**
Birch Mts. *Canada* 57°30N 113°10W **70 B6**
Birch River *Canada* 52°24N 101°6W **71 C8**
Birchip *Australia* 35°56S 142°55E **63 F3**
Bird *Canada* 56°30N 94°13W **71 B10**
Bird I. = Aves, I. de
  W. Indies 15°45N 63°55W **89 C7**
Bird I. *S. Georgia* 54°0S 38°3W **96 G9**
Birds Creek *Canada* 45°6N 77°52W **82 A7**
Birdsville *Australia* 25°51S 139°20E **62 D2**
Birdum Cr. → *Australia* 15°14S 133°0E **60 C5**
Birecik *Turkey* 37°2N 38°0E **44 B3**
Birein *Israel* 30°50N 34°28E **46 E3**
Bireuen *Indonesia* 5°14N 96°39E **36 C1**
Birigüi *Brazil* 21°18S 50°16W **95 A5**
Bīrjand *Iran* 32°53N 59°13E **45 C8**
Birkenhead *U.K.* 53°23N 3°2W **12 D4**
Bîrlad = Bârlad
  Romania 46°15N 27°38E **17 E14**
Birmingham *U.K.* 52°29N 1°52W **13 E6**
Birmingham *U.S.A.* 33°31N 86°48W **85 E11**
Birmingham Int. ✈ (BHX)
  U.K. 52°26N 1°45W **13 E6**
Birmitrapur *India* 22°24N 84°46E **41 H14**
Birni Nkonni *Niger* 13°55N 5°15E **50 F7**
Birnin Kebbi *Nigeria* 12°32N 4°12E **50 F6**
Birobidzhan *Russia* 48°50N 132°50E **29 E14**
Birr *Ireland* 53°6N 7°54W **10 C4**
Birrie → *Australia* 29°43S 146°37E **63 D4**
Birsilpur *India* 28°11N 72°15E **42 E5**
Birsk *Russia* 55°25N 55°30E **18 C10**
Birtle *Canada* 50°30N 101°5W **71 C8**
Birur *India* 13°30N 75°55E **40 N9**
Biržai *Lithuania* 56°11N 24°45E **9 H21**
Birzebbugga *Malta* 35°50N 14°32E **25 D2**
Bisa *Indonesia* 1°15S 127°28E **37 E7**
Bisalpur *India* 28°14N 79°48E **43 E8**
Bisbee *U.S.A.* 31°27N 109°55W **77 L9**
Biscarrosse *France* 44°22N 1°20W **20 D3**
Biscay, B. of *Atl. Oc.* 45°0N 2°0W **20 D1**
Biscayne B. *U.S.A.* 25°40N 80°12W **85 J14**
Biscoe Is. *Antarctica* 66°0S 67°0W **5 C17**
Biscostasing *Canada* 47°18N 82°9W **72 C3**
Bishkek *Kyrgyzstan* 42°54N 74°46E **28 E8**
Bishnupur *India* 23°8N 87°20E **43 H12**
Bisho = Bhisho *S. Africa* 32°50S 27°23E **57 E4**
Bishop *Calif., U.S.A.* 37°22N 118°24W **78 H8**
Bishop *Tex., U.S.A.* 27°35N 97°48W **84 H6**
Bishop Auckland *U.K.* 54°39N 1°40W **12 C6**
Bishop's Falls *Canada* 49°2N 55°30W **73 C8**
Bishop's Stortford *U.K.* 51°52N 0°10E **13 F8**
Bisina, L. *Uganda* 1°38N 33°56E **54 B3**
Biskra *Algeria* 34°50N 5°44E **50 B7**
Bismarck *U.S.A.* 46°48N 100°47W **80 B3**
Bismarck Arch.
  Papua N. G. 2°30S 150°0E **58 B7**
Biso *Uganda* 1°44N 31°26E **54 B3**
Bison *U.S.A.* 45°31N 102°28W **80 C2**
Bisotūn *Iran* 34°23N 47°26E **44 C5**
Bissagos = Bijagós, Arquipélago
  dos *Guinea-Biss.* 11°15N 16°10W **50 F2**
Bissau *Guinea-Biss.* 11°45N 15°45W **50 F2**
Bistcho L. *Canada* 59°45N 118°50W **70 B5**
Bistriţa *Romania* 47°9N 24°35E **17 E13**
Bistriţa → *Romania* 46°30N 26°57E **17 E14**
Biswan *India* 27°29N 81°2E **43 F9**
Bitam *Gabon* 2°5N 11°25E **52 D2**
Bitkine *Chad* 11°59N 18°13E **51 F9**
Bitlis *Turkey* 38°20N 42°3E **44 B4**
Bitola *Macedonia* 41°1N 21°20E **23 D9**
Bitolj = Bitola *Macedonia* 41°1N 21°20E **23 D9**
Bitter Creek *U.S.A.* 41°33N 108°33W **76 F9**
Bitterfontein *S. Africa* 31°1S 18°32E **56 E2**
Bitterroot → *U.S.A.* 46°52N 114°7W **76 C6**
Bitterroot Range *U.S.A.* 46°0N 114°20W **76 C6**
Bitterwater *U.S.A.* 36°23N 121°0W **78 J6**
Biu *Nigeria* 10°40N 12°3E **51 F8**
Biwa-Ko *Japan* 35°15N 136°10E **31 G8**
Biwabik *U.S.A.* 47°32N 92°21W **80 B7**
Bixby *U.S.A.* 35°57N 95°53W **84 D7**
Biyang *China* 32°38N 113°21E **34 H7**
Biysk *Russia* 52°40N 85°0E **28 D9**
Bizana *S. Africa* 30°50S 29°52E **57 E4**
Bizen *Japan* 34°43N 134°8E **31 G7**
Bizerte *Tunisia* 37°15N 9°50E **51 A7**
Blanco *S. Africa* 33°55S 22°23E **56 E3**
Blanco → *Argentina* 30°20S 68°42W **94 C2**
Blanco → *Costa Rica* 9°34N 85°8E **88 E2**
Blanco, C. *Spain* 42°51N 124°34W **94 T1**
Blanda → *Iceland* 65°37N 20°9W **8 D3**
Blandford Forum *U.K.* 50°51N 2°9W **13 G5**

Bjørnøya *Arctic* 74°30N 19°0E **4 B8**
Black = Da → *Vietnam* 21°15N 105°20E **38 B5**
Black → *Canada* 44°42N 79°19W **82 B5**
Black → *Ariz., U.S.A.* 33°44N 110°13W **77 K8**
Black → *Ark., U.S.A.* 35°38N 91°50W **84 D9**
Black → *La., U.S.A.* 31°16N 91°50W **84 F9**
Black → *Mich., U.S.A.* 43°59N 76°4W **83 C8**
Black → *N.Y., U.S.A.* 43°59N 76°4W **83 C8**
Black → *Wis., U.S.A.* 43°57N 91°22W **80 D8**
Black Bay Pen. *Canada* 48°38N 88°21W **72 C2**
Black Birch L. *Canada* 56°53N 107°45W **71 B7**
Black Canyon of the Gunnison △
  U.S.A. 38°30N 107°35W **76 G10**
Black Diamond *Canada* 50°45N 114°14W **70 C6**
Black Duck → *Canada* 56°51N 89°2W **72 A2**
Black Forest = Schwarzwald
  Germany 48°30N 8°20E **16 D5**
Black Forest *U.S.A.* 39°0N 104°43W **76 G11**
Black Hd. *Ireland* 53°9N 9°16W **10 C2**
Black Hills *U.S.A.* 44°0N 103°45W **80 D2**
Black I. *Canada* 51°12N 96°30W **71 C9**
Black L. *Canada* 59°12N 105°15W **71 B7**
Black L. *Mich., U.S.A.* 45°28N 84°16W **81 C11**
Black L. *N.Y., U.S.A.* 44°31N 75°36W **83 B9**
Black Lake *Canada* 59°11N 105°20W **71 B7**
Black Mesa *U.S.A.* 36°58N 102°58W **84 C3**
Black Mt. = Mynydd Du
  U.K. 51°52N 3°50W **13 F4**
Black Mts. *U.K.* 51°55N 3°7W **13 F4**
Black Range *U.S.A.* 33°15N 107°50W **77 K10**
Black River *Jamaica* 18°0N 77°50W **88 a**
Black River *U.S.A.* 44°0N 75°47W **83 C9**
Black River Falls *U.S.A.* 44°18N 90°51W **80 C8**
Black Rock *Barbados* 13°7N 59°37W **89 g**
Black Rock Desert
  U.S.A. 41°10N 118°50W **76 F4**
Black Sea *Eurasia* 43°30N 35°0E **19 F6**
Black Tickle *Canada* 53°28N 55°45W **73 B8**
Black Volta → *Africa* 8°41N 1°33W **50 G5**
Black Warrior →
  U.S.A. 32°32N 87°51W **85 E11**
Blackall *Australia* 24°25S 145°45E **62 C4**
Blackball *N.Z.* 42°22S 171°26E **59 E3**
Blackbraes △ *Australia* 19°10S 144°10E **62 B3**
Blackbull *Australia* 17°55S 141°45E **62 B3**
Blackburn *U.K.* 53°45N 2°29W **12 D5**
Blackburn, Mt. *U.S.A.* 61°44N 143°26W **74 C11**
Blackburn with Darwen □
  U.K. 53°45N 2°29W **12 D5**
Blackdown Tableland △
  Australia 23°52S 149°8E **62 C4**
Blackfoot *U.S.A.* 43°11N 112°21W **76 E7**
Blackfoot → *U.S.A.* 46°52N 113°53W **76 C7**
Blackfoot Res. *U.S.A.* 42°55N 111°39W **76 E8**
Blackpool *U.K.* 53°49N 3°3W **12 D4**
Blackpool □ *U.K.* 53°49N 3°3W **12 D4**
Blackriver *U.S.A.* 44°46N 83°17W **82 B1**
Blacks Harbour *Canada* 45°3N 66°49W **73 C6**
Blacksburg *U.S.A.* 37°14N 80°25W **81 G13**
Blacksod B. *Ireland* 54°6N 10°0W **10 B1**
Blackstairs Mt. *Ireland* 52°33N 6°48W **10 D5**
Blackstone *U.S.A.* 37°5N 78°0W **81 G14**
Blackstone Ra. *Australia* 26°0S 128°30E **61 E4**
Blackwater = West Road →
  Canada 53°18N 122°53W **70 C4**
Blackwater *Australia* 23°35S 148°53E **62 C4**
Blackwater → *Meath,*
  Ireland 53°39N 6°41W **10 C4**
Blackwater → *Waterford,*
  Ireland 52°4N 7°52W **10 D4**
Blackwater → *U.K.* 54°31N 6°35W **10 B5**
Blackwell *U.S.A.* 36°48N 97°17W **84 C6**
Blackwells Corner
  U.S.A. 35°37N 119°47W **79 K7**
Bladensburg △
  Australia 22°30S 142°59E **62 C3**
Blaenau Ffestiniog *U.K.* 53°0N 3°56W **12 E4**
Blaenau Gwent □ *U.K.* 51°48N 3°12W **13 F4**
Blagdarnoye = Blagodarnyy
  Russia 45°7N 43°37E **19 E7**
Blagodarnyy *Russia* 45°7N 43°37E **19 E7**
Blagoevgrad *Bulgaria* 42°2N 23°5E **23 C10**
Blagoveshchensk
  Russia 50°20N 127°30E **29 D13**
Blahkiuh *Indonesia* 8°31S 115°12E **37 J18**
Blain *U.S.A.* 40°20N 77°31W **82 F7**
Blaine *Minn., U.S.A.* 45°10N 93°13W **80 C7**
Blaine *Wash., U.S.A.* 48°59N 122°45W **78 B4**
Blaine Lake *Canada* 52°51N 106°52W **71 C7**
Blair *U.S.A.* 41°33N 96°8W **80 E5**
Blair Athol *Australia* 22°42S 147°31E **62 C4**
Blair Atholl *U.K.* 56°46N 3°50W **11 E5**
Blairgowrie *U.K.* 56°35N 3°21W **11 E5**
Blairsden *U.S.A.* 39°47N 120°37W **78 F6**
Blairsville *U.S.A.* 40°26N 79°16W **82 F5**
Blakang Mati, Pulau
  Singapore 1°15N 103°50E **39 d**
Blake Pt. *U.S.A.* 48°11N 88°25W **80 A9**
Blakely *Ga., U.S.A.* 31°23N 84°56W **85 F12**
Blakely *Pa., U.S.A.* 41°28N 75°37W **83 E9**
Blanc, C. *Spain* 39°21N 2°51E **24 B9**
Blanc, Mont *Europe* 45°48N 6°50E **20 D7**
Blanca, B. *Argentina* 39°10S 61°30W **96 D4**
Blanca, Cord. *Peru* 9°10S 77°35W **92 E3**
Blanca Peak *U.S.A.* 37°35N 105°29W **77 H11**
Blanche, C. *Australia* 33°1S 134°9E **63 E1**
Blanche, L. *S. Austral.,*
  Australia 29°15S 139°40E **63 D2**
Blanche, L. *W. Austral.,*
  Australia 22°25S 123°17E **60 D3**
Blanchisseuse
  Trin. & Tob. 10°48N 61°18W **93 K15**

Blanding *U.S.A.* 37°37N 109°29W **77 H9**
Blanes *Spain* 41°40N 2°48E **21 B7**
Blankenberge *Belgium* 51°20N 3°9E **15 C3**
Blanquilla *Venezuela* 11°51N 64°37W **89 D7**
Blanquillo *Uruguay* 32°53S 55°37W **95 C4**
Blantyre *Malawi* 15°45S 35°0E **55 F4**
Blarney *Ireland* 51°56N 8°33W **10 E3**
Blasdell *U.S.A.* 42°48N 78°50W **82 D6**
Blåvands Huk *Denmark* 55°33N 8°4E **9 J13**
Blaydon *U.K.* 54°58N 1°42W **12 C6**
Blaze, Pt. *Australia* 12°56S 130°11E **60 B5**
Blekinge *Sweden* 56°25N 15°20E **9 H16**
Blenheim *Canada* 42°20N 82°0W **82 D3**
Blenheim *N.Z.* 41°38S 173°57E **59 D4**
Bletchley *U.K.* 51°59N 0°44W **13 F7**
Bleus, Monts
  Dem. Rep. of the Congo 1°30N 30°30E **54 B3**
Blida *Algeria* 36°30N 2°49E **50 A6**
Bligh Sound *N.Z.* 44°47S 167°32E **59 F1**
Bligh Water *Fiji* 17°0S 178°0E **59 a**
Blind River *Canada* 46°10N 82°58W **72 C3**
Bliss *Idaho, U.S.A.* 42°56N 114°57W **76 E6**
Bliss *N.Y., U.S.A.* 42°34N 78°15W **82 D6**
Blissfield *U.S.A.* 40°24N 81°58W **82 F3**
Blitar *Indonesia* 8°5S 112°11E **37 H15**
Block I. *U.S.A.* 41°11N 71°35W **83 E13**
Block Island Sd. *U.S.A.* 41°15N 71°40W **83 E13**
Bloemfontein *S. Africa* 29°6S 26°7E **56 D4**
Bloemhof *S. Africa* 27°38S 25°32E **56 D4**
Blois *France* 47°35N 1°20E **20 C4**
Blönduós *Iceland* 65°40N 20°12W **8 D3**
Blongas *Indonesia* 8°53S 116°2E **37 K19**
Bloodvein → *Canada* 51°47N 96°43W **71 C9**
Bloody Foreland *Ireland* 55°10N 8°17W **10 A3**
Bloomer *U.S.A.* 45°6N 91°29W **80 C8**
Bloomfield *Canada* 43°59N 77°14W **82 C7**
Bloomfield *Iowa, U.S.A.* 40°45N 92°25W **80 E7**
Bloomfield *N. Mex.,*
  U.S.A. 36°43N 107°59W **77 H10**
Bloomfield *Nebr., U.S.A.* 42°36N 97°39W **80 D5**
Bloomington *Ill., U.S.A.* 40°28N 89°0W **80 E9**
Bloomington *Ind.,*
  U.S.A. 39°10N 86°32W **80 F10**
Bloomington *Minn.,*
  U.S.A. 44°50N 93°17W **80 C7**
Bloomsburg *U.S.A.* 41°0N 76°27W **83 F8**
Bloomsbury *Australia* 20°48S 148°38E **62 b**
Blora *Indonesia* 6°57S 111°25E **37 G14**
Blossburg *U.S.A.* 41°41N 77°4W **82 E7**
Blouberg *S. Africa* 23°8S 28°59E **57 C4**
Blountstown *U.S.A.* 30°27N 85°3W **85 F12**
Blue Earth *U.S.A.* 43°38N 94°6W **80 D6**
Blue Hole △ *Belize* 17°24N 88°30W **88 C2**
Blue Lagoon △ *Zambia* 15°28S 27°26E **55 F2**
Blue Mesa Res. *U.S.A.* 38°28N 107°20W **76 G10**
Blue Mountain Lake
  U.S.A. 43°51N 74°27W **83 C10**
Blue Mountain Pk.
  Jamaica 18°3N 76°36W **88 a**
Blue Mt. *U.S.A.* 40°30N 76°30W **83 F8**
Blue Mts. *Jamaica* 18°3N 76°36W **88 a**
Blue Mts. *Maine, U.S.A.* 44°50N 70°35W **83 B14**
Blue Mts. *Oreg., U.S.A.* 45°0N 118°20W **76 D4**
Blue Mud B. *Australia* 13°30S 136°0E **62 A2**
Blue Mud Bay ◎
  Australia 13°25S 136°2E **62 A2**
Blue Nile = Nîl el Azraq →
  Sudan 15°38N 32°31E **51 E12**
Blue Rapids *U.S.A.* 39°41N 96°39W **80 F5**
Blue Ridge *U.S.A.* 36°40N 80°50W **81 G13**
Blue River *Canada* 52°6N 119°18W **70 C5**
Bluefield *U.S.A.* 37°15N 81°17W **81 G13**
Bluefields *Nic.* 12°20N 83°50W **88 D3**
Bluevale *Canada* 43°51N 81°15W **82 C3**
Bluff *Australia* 23°35S 149°4E **62 C4**
Bluff *N.Z.* 46°37S 168°20E **59 G2**
Bluff *U.S.A.* 37°17N 109°33W **77 H9**
Bluff Knoll *Australia* 34°24S 118°15E **61 F2**
Bluff Pt. *Australia* 27°50S 114°5E **61 E1**
Bluffton *U.S.A.* 40°44N 85°11W **81 E11**
Blumenau *Brazil* 27°0S 49°0W **95 B6**
Blunt *U.S.A.* 44°31N 99°59W **80 C4**
Bly *U.S.A.* 42°24N 121°3W **76 E3**
Blyde River Canyon △
  S. Africa 24°37S 31°2E **57 C5**
Blyth *Canada* 43°44N 81°26W **82 C3**
Blyth *U.K.* 55°8N 1°31W **12 B6**
Blythe *U.S.A.* 33°37N 114°36W **79 M12**
Blytheville *U.S.A.* 35°56N 89°55W **85 D10**
Bo *S. Leone* 7°55N 11°50W **50 G3**
Bo Duc *Vietnam* 11°58N 106°50E **39 G6**
Bo Hai *China* 39°0N 119°0E **35 E10**
Bo Xian = Bozhou
  China 33°55N 115°41E **34 H8**
Boa Vista *Brazil* 2°48N 60°30W **92 C6**
Boa Vista *C. Verde Is.* 16°0N 22°49W **50 b**
Boaco *Nic.* 12°29N 85°35W **88 D2**
Bo'ai *China* 35°10N 113°3E **34 G7**
Boalsburg *U.S.A.* 40°47N 77°49W **82 F7**
Boane *Mozam.* 26°6S 32°19E **57 D5**
Boardman *U.S.A.* 41°2N 80°40W **82 E4**
Bobadah *Australia* 32°19S 146°41E **63 E4**
Bobbili *India* 18°35N 83°30E **41 K13**
Bobcaygeon *Canada* 44°33N 78°33W **82 B6**
Bobo-Dioulasso
  Burkina Faso 11°8N 4°13W **50 F5**
Bobonong *Botswana* 21°58S 28°20E **55 G2**
Bóbr → *Poland* 52°4N 15°4E **16 B8**
Bobraomby, Tanjon' i
  Madag. 12°40S 49°10E **57 A8**
Bobruysk = Babruysk
  Belarus 53°10N 29°15E **17 B15**
Boby, Pic *Madag.* 22°12S 46°55E **53 J9**
Boca del Río *Mexico* 19°5N 96°4W **87 D5**
Boca do Acre *Brazil* 8°50S 67°27W **92 E5**
Boca Raton *U.S.A.* 26°21N 80°5W **85 H14**
Bocas del Dragón = Dragon's
  Mouths *Venezuela* 11°0N 61°50W **93 K15**

Bocas del Toro *Panama* 9°15N 82°20W **88 E3**
Bochnia *Poland* 49°58N 20°27E **17 D11**
Bochum *Germany* 51°28N 7°13E **16 C4**
Bocoyna *Mexico* 27°52N 107°35W **86 B3**
Boda *Central Africa* 7°55S 147°40E **61 F2**
Bodaybo *Russia* 57°50N 114°0E **29 D12**
Boddam *U.K.* 59°56N 1°17W **11 B7**
Boddington *Australia* 32°50S 116°30E **61 F2**
Bodega Bay *U.S.A.* 38°20N 123°3W **78 G3**
Boden *Sweden* 65°50N 21°42E **8 D19**
Bodensee *Europe* 47°35N 9°25E **20 C8**
Bodhan *India* 18°40N 77°44E **40 K10**
Bodmin *U.K.* 50°28N 4°43W **13 G3**
Bodmin Moor *U.K.* 50°33N 4°36W **13 G3**
Bodø *Norway* 67°17N 14°24E **8 C16**
Bodrog → *Hungary* 48°11N 21°22E **17 D11**
Bodrum *Turkey* 37°3N 27°30E **23 F12**
Boende
  Dem. Rep. of the Congo 0°24S 21°12E **52 E4**
Boerne *U.S.A.* 29°47N 98°44W **84 G5**
Boesmans → *S. Africa* 33°42S 26°39E **56 E4**
Bogalusa *U.S.A.* 30°47N 89°52W **85 F10**
Bogan → *Australia* 30°20S 146°55E **63 D4**
Bogan Gate *Australia* 33°7S 147°49E **63 E4**
Bogantungan *Australia* 23°41S 147°17E **62 C4**
Bogata *U.S.A.* 33°28N 95°13W **84 E7**
Bogda Shan *China* 43°35N 89°40E **32 B3**
Boggabilla *Australia* 28°36S 150°24E **63 D5**
Boggabri *Australia* 30°45S 150°5E **63 E5**
Boggeragh Mts. *Ireland* 52°2N 8°55W **10 D3**
Boglan = Solhan *Turkey* 38°57N 41°3E **44 B4**
Bognor Regis *U.K.* 50°47N 0°40W **13 G7**
Bogo *Phil.* 11°3N 124°0E **37 B6**
Bogong, Mt. *Australia* 36°47S 147°17E **63 F4**
Bogor *Indonesia* 6°36S 106°48E **37 G12**
Bogotá *Colombia* 4°34N 74°0W **92 C4**
Bogotol *Russia* 56°15N 89°50E **28 D9**
Bogra *Bangla.* 24°51N 89°22E **41 G16**
Boguchany *Russia* 58°40N 97°30E **29 D10**
Bogué *Mauritania* 16°45N 14°10W **50 E3**
Bohemian Forest = Böhmerwald
  Germany 49°8N 13°14E **16 D7**
Böhmerwald *Germany* 49°8N 13°14E **16 D7**
Bohol □ *Phil.* 9°50N 124°10E **37 C6**
Bohol Sea *Phil.* 9°0N 124°0E **37 C6**
Bohorok *Indonesia* 3°30N 98°12E **39 L2**
Bohuslän *Sweden* 58°25N 12°0E **9 G14**
Boi, Pta. do *Brazil* 23°55S 45°15W **95 A6**
Boiaçu *Brazil* 0°27S 61°46W **92 D6**
Boigu *Australia* 9°16S 142°13E **62 a**
Boileau, C. *Australia* 17°40S 122°7E **60 C3**
Boise *U.S.A.* 43°37N 116°13W **76 E5**
Boise City *U.S.A.* 36°44N 102°31W **84 C3**
Boissevain *Canada* 49°15N 100°5W **71 D8**
Bojador, C. *W. Sahara* 26°0N 14°30W **50 C3**
Bojana → *Albania* 41°52N 19°22E **23 D8**
Bojnūrd *Iran* 37°30N 57°20E **45 B8**
Bojonegoro *Indonesia* 7°11S 111°54E **37 G14**
Bokaro *India* 23°46N 85°55E **43 H11**
Boké *Guinea* 10°56N 14°17W **50 F3**
Bokhara → *Australia* 29°55S 146°42E **63 D4**
Boknafjorden *Norway* 59°14N 5°40E **9 G11**
Bokor △ *Cambodia* 10°50N 104°1E **39 G5**
Bokora → *Uganda* 2°12N 31°32E **54 B3**
Bokoro *Chad* 12°25N 17°14E **51 F9**
Bokpyin *Burma* 11°18N 98°42E **39 G2**
Bokungu
  Dem. Rep. of the Congo 0°35S 22°50E **52 E4**
Bolan → *Pakistan* 28°38N 67°42E **42 E2**
Bolan Pass *Pakistan* 29°50N 67°20E **42 E5**
Bolaños → *Mexico* 21°12N 104°5W **86 C4**
Bolbec *France* 49°30N 0°30E **20 B4**
Boldājī *Iran* 31°56N 51°3E **45 D6**
Bole *China* 45°11N 81°37E **32 B3**
Bolekhiv *Ukraine* 49°0N 23°57E **17 D12**
Bolesławiec *Poland* 51°17N 15°37E **16 C8**
Bolgatanga *Ghana* 10°44N 0°53W **50 F5**
Bolgrad = Bolhrad
  Ukraine 45°40N 28°32E **17 F15**
Bolhrad *Ukraine* 45°40N 28°32E **17 F15**
Bolivar *Mo., U.S.A.* 37°37N 93°25W **80 G7**
Bolivar *N.Y., U.S.A.* 42°4N 78°10W **82 D6**
Bolivar *Tenn., U.S.A.* 35°12N 89°0W **85 D10**
Bolivia ■ *S. Amer.* 17°6S 64°0W **92 G6**
Bolivian Plateau = Altiplano
  Bolivia 17°0S 68°0W **92 G5**
Bollnäs *Sweden* 61°21N 16°24E **8 F17**
Bollon *Australia* 28°2S 147°29E **63 D4**
Bolmen *Sweden* 56°55N 13°40E **9 H15**
Bolobo
  Dem. Rep. of the Congo 2°6S 16°20E **52 E3**
Bologna *Italy* 44°29N 11°20E **22 B4**
Bologoye *Russia* 57°55N 34°5E **18 C5**
Bolomba
  Dem. Rep. of the Congo 0°35N 19°0E **52 D3**
Bolonchén *Mexico* 20°1N 89°45W **87 D7**
Boloven, Cao Nguyen
  Laos 15°10N 106°30E **38 E6**
Bolpur *India* 23°40N 87°45E **43 H12**
Bolsena, L. di *Italy* 42°36N 11°56E **22 C4**
Bolshevik, Ostrov
  Russia 78°30N 102°0E **29 B11**
Bolshoy Anyuy →
  Russia 68°30N 160°49E **29 C17**
Bolshoy Begichev, Ostrov
  Russia 74°20N 112°30E **29 B12**
Bolshoy Kamen *Russia* 43°7N 132°19E **30 C6**
Bolshoy Kavkas = Caucasus
  Mountains *Eurasia* 42°50N 44°0E **19 F7**
Bolshoy Lyakhovskiy, Ostrov
  Russia 73°35N 142°0E **29 B15**
Bolshoy Tyuters, Ostrov
  Russia 59°51N 27°13E **9 G22**
Bolsward *Neths.* 53°3N 5°32E **15 A5**
Bolt Head *U.K.* 50°12N 3°48W **13 G4**
Bolton *Canada* 43°54N 79°45W **82 C5**
Bolton *U.K.* 53°35N 2°26W **12 D5**
Bolton Landing *U.S.A.* 43°32N 73°35W **83 C11**
Bolu *Turkey* 40°45N 31°35E **19 F5**
Bolungavík *Iceland* 66°9N 23°15W **8 C2**

Bolvadin *Turkey* 38°45N 31°4E **44** B1
Bolzano *Italy* 46°31N 11°22E **22** A4
Bom Jesus da Lapa
  Brazil 13°15S 43°25W **93** F10
Boma *Dem. Rep. of the Congo* 5°50S 13°4E **52** F2
Bombala *Australia* 36°56S 149°15E **63** F4
Bombay = Mumbai
  India 18°56N 72°50E **40** K8
Bombay *U.S.A.* 44°56N 74°34W **83** B10
Bombedor, Pta.
  Venezuela 9°53N 61°37W **93** L15
Bomboma
  Dem. Rep. of the Congo 2°25N 18°55E **52** D3
Bombombwa
  Dem. Rep. of the Congo 1°40N 25°40E **54** B2
Bomili
  Dem. Rep. of the Congo 1°45N 27°5E **54** B2
Bømlo *Norway* 59°37N 5°13E **9** G11
Bomokandi →
  Dem. Rep. of the Congo 3°39N 26°8E **54** B2
Bomu → *C.A.R.* 4°40N 22°30E **52** D4
Bon, C. = Ra's aţ Tib
  Tunisia 37°1N 11°2E **22** F4
Bon Acceuil *Mauritius* 20°10S 57°39E **53** d
Bon Echo △ *Canada* 44°55N 77°16W **82** B7
Bon Sar Pa *Vietnam* 12°24N 107°35E **38** F6
Bonāb *Iran* 36°35N 48°41E **45** B6
Bonaigarh *India* 21°50N 84°57E **43** J11
Bonaire *Neth. Ant.* 12°10N 68°15W **89** D6
Bonampak *Mexico* 16°44N 91°5W **87** D6
Bonang *Australia* 37°11S 148°41E **63** F4
Bonanza *Nic.* 13°54N 84°35W **88** D3
Bonaparte Arch.
  Australia 14°0S 124°30E **60** B3
Bonar Bridge *U.K.* 57°54N 4°20W **11** D4
Bonasse *Trin. & Tob.* 10°5N 61°54W **93** K15
Bonaventure *Canada* 48°5N 65°32W **73** C6
Bonavista *Canada* 48°40N 53°5W **73** C9
Bonavista, C. *Canada* 48°42N 53°5W **73** C9
Bonavista B. *Canada* 48°45N 53°25W **73** C9
Bondo
  Dem. Rep. of the Congo 3°55N 23°53E **54** B1
Bondoukou *Ivory C.* 8°2N 2°47W **50** G5
Bondowoso *Indonesia* 7°55S 113°49E **37** G15
Bone, Teluk *Indonesia* 4°10S 120°50E **37** E6
Bonerate *Indonesia* 7°25S 121°5E **37** F6
Bonerate, Kepulauan
  Indonesia 6°30S 121°10E **37** F6
Bo'ness *U.K.* 56°1N 3°37W **11** E5
Bonete, Cerro *Argentina* 27°55S 68°40W **94** B2
Bong Son = Hoai Nhon
  Vietnam 14°28N 109°1E **38** E7
Bongaigaon *India* 26°28N 90°34E **32** D4
Bongandanga
  Dem. Rep. of the Congo 1°24N 21°3E **52** D4
Bongor *Chad* 10°35N 15°20E **51** F9
Bongos, Massif des *C.A.R.* 8°40N 22°25E **52** C4
Bonham *U.S.A.* 33°35N 96°11W **84** E6
Boni *Kenya* 1°35S 41°18E **54** C5
Bonifacio *France* 41°24N 9°10E **20** F8
Bonifacio, Bouches de
  Medit. S. 41°12N 9°15E **22** D3
Bonin Is. = Ogasawara Gunto
  Pac. Oc. 27°0N 142°0E **27** F16
Bonn *Germany* 50°46N 7°6E **16** C4
Bonne Terre *U.S.A.* 37°55N 90°33W **80** G8
Bonners Ferry *U.S.A.* 48°42N 116°19W **76** B5
Bonney, L. *Australia* 37°50S 140°20E **63** F3
Bonnie Rock *Australia* 30°29S 118°22E **61** F2
Bonny, Bight of *Africa* 3°30N 9°20E **52** D1
Bonnyrigg *U.K.* 55°53N 3°6W **11** F5
Bonnyville *Canada* 54°20N 110°45W **71** C6
Bonoi *Indonesia* 1°45S 137°41E **37** E9
Bonsall *U.S.A.* 33°16N 117°14W **79** M9
Bontang *Indonesia* 0°10N 117°30E **36** D5
Bontebok △ *S. Africa* 34°5S 20°28E **56** E3
Bonthe *S. Leone* 7°30N 12°33W **50** G3
Bontoc *Phil.* 17°7N 120°58E **37** A6
Bonython Ra. *Australia* 23°40S 128°45E **60** D4
Boodjamulla △ *Australia* 18°15S 138°6E **62** B2
Bookabie *Australia* 31°50S 132°41E **61** F5
Booker *U.S.A.* 36°27N 100°32W **84** C4
Booligal *Australia* 33°58S 144°53E **63** E3
Böön Tsagaan Nuur
  Mongolia 45°35N 99°9E **32** B4
Boonah *Australia* 27°58S 152°41E **63** D5
Boone *Iowa, U.S.A.* 42°4N 93°53W **80** D7
Boone *N.C., U.S.A.* 36°13N 81°41W **85** C14
Booneville *Ark., U.S.A.* 35°8N 93°55W **84** D8
Booneville *Miss., U.S.A.* 34°39N 88°34W **85** D10
Boonville *Calif., U.S.A.* 39°1N 123°22W **78** F3
Boonville *Ind., U.S.A.* 38°3N 87°16W **80** F10
Boonville *Mo., U.S.A.* 38°58N 92°44W **80** F7
Boonville *N.Y., U.S.A.* 43°29N 75°20W **83** C9
Boorabbin △ *Australia* 31°30S 120°10E **61** F3
Boorindal *Australia* 30°22S 146°11E **63** E4
Boorowa *Australia* 34°28S 148°44E **63** E4
Boosaaso *Somali Rep.* 11°12N 49°18E **47** E4
Boothia, Gulf of *Canada* 71°0N 90°0W **68** C14
Boothia Pen. *Canada* 71°0N 94°0W **68** C13
Bootle *U.K.* 53°28N 3°1W **12** D4
Booué *Gabon* 0°5S 11°55E **52** E2
Boquilla, Presa de la
  Mexico 27°31N 105°30W **86** B3
Boquillas del Carmen
  Mexico 29°11N 102°58W **86** B4
Bor *Serbia* 44°5N 22°7E **23** B10
Bôr *Sudan* 6°10N 31°40E **51** G12
Bor Mashash *Israel* 31°7N 34°50E **46** D3
Bora Bora
  French Polynesia 16°30S 151°45W **65** J12
Borah Peak *U.S.A.* 44°8N 113°47W **76** D7
Borås *Sweden* 57°43N 12°56E **9** H15
Borāzjān *Iran* 29°22N 51°10E **45** D6
Borba *Brazil* 4°12S 59°34W **92** D7
Borborema, Planalto da
  Brazil 7°0S 37°0W **90** D7
Bord Khûn-e Now *Iran* 28°3N 51°28E **45** D6
Borda, C. *Australia* 35°45S 136°34E **63** F2

Bordeaux *France* 44°50N 0°36W **20** D3
Borden *Australia* 34°3S 118°12E **61** F2
Borden-Carleton *Canada* 46°18N 63°47W **73** C7
Borden I. *Canada* 78°30N 111°30W **69** B9
Borden Pen. *Canada* 73°0N 83°0W **69** C15
Border Ranges △
  Australia 28°24S 152°56E **63** D5
Borders = Scottish Borders □
  U.K. 55°35N 2°50W **11** F6
Bordertown *Australia* 36°19S 140°45E **63** F3
Borðeyri *Iceland* 65°12N 21°6W **8** D3
Bordj Fly Ste. Marie
  Algeria 27°19N 2°32W **50** C5
Bordj-in-Eker *Algeria* 24°9N 5°3E **50** D7
Bordj Mokhtar *Algeria* 21°20N 0°56E **50** D6
Bordj Omar Driss *Algeria* 28°10N 6°40E **50** C7
Borehamwood *U.K.* 51°40N 0°15W **13** F7
Borgarfjörður *Iceland* 65°33N 13°47W **8** D7
Borgarnes *Iceland* 64°32N 21°55W **8** D3
Borgefjellet *Norway* 65°20N 13°45E **8** D15
Borger *Neths.* 52°54N 6°44E **15** B6
Borger *U.S.A.* 35°39N 101°24W **84** D4
Borgholm *Sweden* 56°52N 16°39E **9** H17
Borhoyn Tal *Mongolia* 43°50N 111°58E **34** C6
Borikhane *Laos* 18°33N 103°43E **38** C4
Borisoglebsk *Russia* 51°27N 42°5E **19** D7
Borisov = Barysaw
  Belarus 54°17N 28°28E **17** A15
Borja *Peru* 4°20S 77°40W **92** D3
Borkou *Chad* 18°15N 18°50E **51** E9
Borkum *Germany* 53°34N 6°40E **16** B4
Borlänge *Sweden* 60°29N 15°26E **9** F16
Borley, C. *Antarctica* 66°15S 52°30E **5** C5
Borneo *E. Indies* 1°0N 115°0E **36** D5
Bornholm *Denmark* 55°10N 15°0E **9** J16
Borogontsy *Russia* 62°42N 131°8E **29** C14
Borohoro Shan *China* 44°6N 83°10E **32** B3
Boron *U.S.A.* 35°0N 117°39W **79** L9
Borongan *Phil.* 11°37N 125°26E **37** B7
Borovichi *Russia* 58°25N 33°55E **18** C5
Borrego Springs
  U.S.A. 33°15N 116°23W **79** M10
Borrisokane *Ireland* 53°0N 8°7W **10** D3
Borroloola *Australia* 16°4S 136°17E **62** B2
Borşa *Romania* 47°41N 24°50E **17** E13
Borsad *India* 22°25N 72°54E **42** H5
Borth *U.K.* 52°29N 4°2W **13** E3
Borūjerd *Iran* 33°55N 48°50E **45** C6
Boryeong *S. Korea* 36°21N 126°36E **35** F14
Boryslav *Ukraine* 49°18N 23°28E **17** D12
Borzya *Russia* 50°24N 116°31E **29** D12
Bosa *Italy* 40°18N 8°30E **22** D3
Bosanska Gradiška
  Bos.-H. 45°10N 17°15E **22** B7
Boscastle *U.K.* 50°41N 4°42W **13** G3
Boscobelle *Barbados* 13°17N 59°35W **89** g
Bose *China* 23°53N 106°35E **32** D5
Boseong *S. Korea* 34°46N 127°5E **35** G14
Boshan *China* 36°28N 117°49E **35** F9
Boshof *S. Africa* 28°31S 25°13E **56** D4
Boshrūyeh *Iran* 33°50N 57°30E **45** C8
Bosna → *Bos.-H.* 45°4N 18°29E **23** B8
Bosna i Hercegovina = Bosnia-
  Herzegovina ■ *Europe* 44°0N 18°0E **22** B7
Bosnia-Herzegovina ■
  Europe 44°0N 18°0E **22** B7
Bosnik *Indonesia* 1°5S 136°10E **37** E9
Bosobolo
  Dem. Rep. of the Congo 4°15N 19°50E **52** D3
Bosporus = İstanbul Boğazı
  Turkey 41°5N 29°3E **23** D13
Bosque Farms *U.S.A.* 35°51N 106°42W **77** J10
Bossangoa *C.A.R.* 6°35N 17°30E **52** C3
Bossier City *U.S.A.* 32°31N 93°44W **84** E8
Bosso *Niger* 13°43N 13°19E **51** F8
Bostan *Pakistan* 30°26N 67°2E **42** D2
Bostānābād *Iran* 37°50N 46°50E **44** B5
Bosten Hu *China* 41°55N 87°40E **32** B3
Boston *U.K.* 52°59N 0°2W **12** E7
Boston Bar *Canada* 49°52N 121°30W **70** D4
Boston Mts. *U.S.A.* 35°42N 93°15W **84** D8
Boswell *Canada* 49°28N 116°45W **70** D5
Boswell *U.S.A.* 40°10N 79°2W **82** F5
Botad *India* 22°15N 71°40E **42** H4
Botany B. *Australia* 33°58S 151°11E **58** E8
Botene *Laos* 17°35N 101°12E **38** D3
Bothaville *S. Africa* 27°23S 26°34E **56** D4
Bothnia, G. of *Europe* 62°0N 20°0E **8** F19
Bothwell *Australia* 42°20S 147°1E **63** G4
Bothwell *Canada* 42°38N 81°52W **82** D3
Botletle → *Botswana* 20°10S 23°15E **56** C3
Botoşani *Romania* 47°42N 26°41E **17** E14
Botou *Burkina Faso* 12°42N 1°59E **50** F6
Botshabelo *S. Africa* 29°14S 26°44E **56** D4
Botswana ■ *Africa* 22°0S 24°0E **56** C3
Bottineau *U.S.A.* 48°50N 100°27W **80** A3
Bottrop *Germany* 51°31N 6°58E **15** C6
Botucatu *Brazil* 22°55S 48°30W **95** A6
Botum Sakor △
  Cambodia 11°5N 103°15E **39** G4
Botwood *Canada* 49°6N 55°23W **73** C8
Bou Saâda *Algeria* 35°11N 4°9E **50** A6
Bouaflé *Ivory C.* 7°1N 5°47W **50** G4
Bouaké *Ivory C.* 7°40N 5°2W **50** G4
Bouar *C.A.R.* 6°0N 15°40E **52** C3
Bouârfa *Morocco* 32°32N 1°58W **50** B5
Boucaut B. *Australia* 12°0S 134°25E **62** A1
Bouctouche *Canada* 46°30N 64°45W **73** C7
Bougainville, C. *Australia* 13°57S 126°4E **60** B4
Bougainville I. *Papua N. G.* 6°0S 155°0E **58** B8
Bougainville Reef
  Australia 15°30S 147°5E **62** B4
Bougie = Bejaïa *Algeria* 36°42N 5°2E **50** A7
Bougouni *Mali* 11°30N 7°20W **50** F4
Bouillon *Belgium* 49°44N 5°3E **15** E5
Boulder *Colo., U.S.A.* 40°1N 105°17W **76** F11
Boulder *Mont., U.S.A.* 46°14N 112°7W **76** C7
Boulder City *U.S.A.* 35°58N 114°49W **79** K12

Boulder Creek *U.S.A.* 37°7N 122°7W **78** H4
Boulder Dam = Hoover Dam
  U.S.A. 36°1N 114°44W **79** K12
Boulia *Australia* 22°52S 139°51E **62** C2
Boulogne-sur-Mer *France* 50°42N 1°36E **20** A4
Boulsa *Burkina Faso* 12°39N 0°34W **50** F5
Boultoum *Niger* 14°45N 10°25E **51** F8
Bouma △ *Fiji* 16°50S 179°52E **59** a
Boun Neua *Laos* 21°38N 101°54E **38** B3
Boun Tai *Laos* 21°23N 101°58E **38** B3
Boundary Peak *U.S.A.* 37°51N 118°21W **78** H8
Boundiali *Ivory C.* 9°30N 6°20W **50** G4
Bountiful *U.S.A.* 40°53N 111°52W **76** F8
Bounty Is. *Pac. Oc.* 48°0S 178°30E **64** M9
Bounty Trough *Pac. Oc.* 46°0S 178°0E **64** M9
Bourbonnais *France* 46°28N 3°0E **20** C5
Bourbonnais *U.S.A.* 41°1N 87°52W **80** E10
Bourdel L. *Canada* 56°43N 74°10W **72** A5
Bourem *Mali* 17°0N 0°24W **50** E5
Bourg-en-Bresse *France* 46°13N 5°12E **20** C6
Bourg-St-Maurice *France* 45°35N 6°46E **20** D7
Bourgas = Burgas
  Bulgaria 42°33N 27°29E **23** C12
Bourges *France* 47°9N 2°25E **20** C5
Bourget *Canada* 45°26N 75°9W **83** A9
Bourgogne □ *France* 47°0N 4°50E **20** C6
Bourke *Australia* 30°8S 145°55E **63** E4
Bourne *U.K.* 52°47N 0°22W **12** E7
Bournemouth *U.K.* 50°43N 1°52W **13** G6
Bournemouth □ *U.K.* 50°43N 1°52W **13** G6
Bouse *U.S.A.* 33°56N 114°0W **79** M13
Bousso *Chad* 10°34N 16°52E **51** F9
Bouvet I. = Bouvetøya
  Antarctica 54°26S 3°24E **2** G10
Bouvetøya *Antarctica* 54°26S 3°24E **2** G10
Bovill *U.S.A.* 46°51N 116°24W **76** C5
Bovril *Argentina* 31°21S 59°26W **94** C4
Bow → *Canada* 49°57N 111°41W **70** C6
Bow Island *Canada* 49°50N 111°23W **70** B8
Bowbells *U.S.A.* 48°48N 102°15W **80** A2
Bowdle *U.S.A.* 45°27N 99°39W **80** C4
Bowelling *Australia* 33°25S 116°30E **61** F2
Bowen *Argentina* 35°0S 67°31W **94** D2
Bowen *Australia* 20°0S 148°16E **62** J6
Bowen Mts. *Australia* 37°0S 147°50E **63** F4
Bowers Basin *Pac. Oc.* 54°0N 176°0E **4** D16
Bowers Ridge *Pac. Oc.* 54°0N 180°0E **4** D17
Bowie *Ariz., U.S.A.* 32°19N 109°29W **77** K9
Bowie *Tex., U.S.A.* 33°34N 97°51W **84** E6
Bowkān *Iran* 36°31N 46°12E **44** B5
Bowland, Forest of *U.K.* 54°0N 2°30W **12** D5
Bowling Green *Ky.,*
  U.S.A. 36°59N 86°27W **80** G10
Bowling Green *Ohio,*
  U.S.A. 41°23N 83°39W **81** E12
Bowling Green, C.
  Australia 19°19S 147°25E **62** B4
Bowling Green Bay △
  Australia 19°26S 146°57E **62** B4
Bowman *U.S.A.* 46°11N 103°24W **80** B2
Bowman I. *Antarctica* 65°0S 104°0E **5** C8
Bowmanville = Clarington
  Canada 43°55N 78°41W **82** C6
Bowmore *U.K.* 55°45N 6°17W **11** F2
Bowral *Australia* 34°26S 150°27E **63** E5
Bowraville *Australia* 30°37S 152°52E **63** E5
Bowron → *Canada* 54°3N 121°50W **70** C4
Bowron Lake △ *Canada* 53°10N 121°5W **70** C4
Bowser L. *Canada* 56°30N 129°30W **70** B3
Bowsman *Canada* 52°14N 101°12W **71** C8
Bowwood *Zambia* 17°5S 26°20E **55** F2
Box Cr. → *Australia* 34°10S 143°50E **63** E3
Boxmeer *Neths.* 51°38N 5°56E **15** C5
Boxtel *Neths.* 51°36N 5°20E **15** C5
Boyce *U.S.A.* 31°23N 92°40W **84** F8
Boyd L. *Canada* 52°46N 76°42W **72** B4
Boyle *Canada* 54°35N 112°49W **70** C6
Boyle *Ireland* 53°59N 8°18W **10** C3
Boyne → *Ireland* 53°43N 6°15W **10** C5
Boyne City *U.S.A.* 45°13N 85°1W **81** C11
Boynton Beach *U.S.A.* 26°32N 80°4W **85** H14
Boyolali *Indonesia* 7°32S 110°35E **37** G14
Boyoma, Chutes
  Dem. Rep. of the Congo 0°35N 25°23E **54** B2
Boysen Res. *U.S.A.* 43°25N 108°11W **76** E9
Boyuibe *Bolivia* 20°25S 63°17W **92** G6
Boyup Brook *Australia* 33°50S 116°23E **61** F2
Boz Dağları *Turkey* 38°20N 28°0E **23** E13
Bozburun *Turkey* 36°43N 28°4E **23** F13
Bozcaada *Turkey* 39°49N 26°3E **23** E12
Bozdoğan *Turkey* 37°40N 28°17E **23** F13
Bozeman *U.S.A.* 45°41N 111°2W **76** D8
Bozen = Bolzano *Italy* 46°31N 11°22E **22** A4
Bozhou *China* 33°55N 115°41E **34** H8
Bozoum *C.A.R.* 6°25N 16°35E **52** C3
Bozyazı *Turkey* 36°6N 33°0E **44** B2
Bra *Italy* 44°42N 7°51E **20** D7
Brabant □ *Belgium* 50°46N 4°30E **15** D4
Brabant L. *Canada* 55°58N 103°43W **71** B8
Brač *Croatia* 43°20N 16°40E **22** C7
Bracadale, L. *U.K.* 57°20N 6°30W **11** D2
Bracciano, L. di *Italy* 42°7N 12°14E **22** C5
Bracebridge *Canada* 45°2N 79°19W **82** A5
Bräcke *Sweden* 62°45N 15°26E **8** E16
Brackettville *U.S.A.* 29°19N 100°25W **84** G4
Bracknell *U.K.* 51°25N 0°43W **13** F7
Bracknell Forest □ *U.K.* 51°25N 0°44W **13** F7
Brad *Romania* 46°10N 22°50E **17** E12
Bradenton *U.S.A.* 27°30N 82°34W **85** H13
Bradford *Canada* 44°7N 79°34W **82** B5
Bradford *U.K.* 53°47N 1°45W **12** D6
Bradford *Pa., U.S.A.* 41°58N 78°38W **82** E6
Bradford *Vt., U.S.A.* 43°59N 72°9W **83** C12
Bradley *Ark., U.S.A.* 33°6N 93°39W **84** E8
Bradley *Calif., U.S.A.* 35°52N 120°48W **78** K6
Bradley Institute
  Zimbabwe 17°7S 31°25E **55** F3
Brady *U.S.A.* 31°9N 99°20W **84** F5
Braeside *Canada* 86°7N 26°24W **83** A8

Braga *Portugal* 41°35N 8°25W **21** B1
Bragado *Argentina* 35°2S 60°27W **94** D3
Bragança *Brazil* 1°0S 47°2W **93** D9
Bragança *Portugal* 41°48N 6°50W **21** B2
Bragança Paulista
  Brazil 22°55S 46°32W **95** A6
Brahestad = Raahe
  Finland 64°40N 24°28E **8** D21
Brahmanbaria *Bangla.* 23°58N 91°15E **41** H17
Brahmani → *India* 20°39N 86°46E **41** J15
Brahmapur *India* 19°15N 84°54E **41** K14
Brahmaputra → *Asia* 23°40N 90°35E **43** H13
Braich-y-pwll *U.K.* 52°47N 4°46W **12** E3
Braidwood *Australia* 35°27S 149°49E **63** F4
Brăila *Romania* 45°19N 27°59E **17** F14
Brainerd *U.S.A.* 46°22N 94°12W **80** B6
Braintree *U.K.* 51°53N 0°34E **13** F8
Braintree *U.S.A.* 42°13N 71°0W **83** D14
Brak → *S. Africa* 29°35S 22°55E **56** D3
Brakwater *Namibia* 22°28S 17°3E **56** C2
Brampton *Canada* 43°45N 79°45W **82** C5
Brampton *U.K.* 54°57N 2°44W **12** C5
Brampton I. *Australia* 20°49S 149°16E **62** b
Branco → *Brazil* 1°20S 61°50W **92** D6
Brandberg → *Namibia* 21°10S 14°33E **56** C1
Brandberg △ *Namibia* 21°10S 14°30E **56** C1
Brandenburg = Neubrandenburg
  Germany 53°33N 13°15E **16** B7
Brandenburg *Germany* 52°25N 12°33E **16** B7
Brandenburg □ *Germany* 52°50N 13°0E **16** B6
Brandfort *S. Africa* 28°40S 26°30E **56** D4
Brandon *Canada* 49°50N 99°57W **71** D9
Brandon *U.S.A.* 43°48N 73°6W **83** C11
Brandon B. *Ireland* 52°17N 10°8W **10** D1
Brandon Mt. *Ireland* 52°15N 10°15W **10** D1
Brandsen *Argentina* 35°10S 58°15W **94** D4
Brandvlei *S. Africa* 30°25S 20°30E **56** E3
Branford *U.S.A.* 41°17N 72°49W **83** E12
Braniewo *Poland* 54°25N 19°50E **17** A10
Bransfield Str. *Antarctica* 63°0S 59°0W **5** C18
Branson *U.S.A.* 36°39N 93°13W **80** G7
Brantford *Canada* 43°10N 80°15W **82** C4
Bras d'Or L. *Canada* 45°50N 60°50W **73** C7
Brasher Falls *U.S.A.* 44°49N 74°47W **83** B10
Brasil = Brazil ■ *S. Amer.* 12°0S 50°0W **93** F9
Brasil, Planalto *Brazil* 18°0S 46°30W **90** E6
Brasília *Brazil* 15°47S 47°55W **93** G9
Brasília Legal *Brazil* 3°49S 55°36W **93** D7
Braslaw *Belarus* 55°38N 27°0E **9** J22
Braşov *Romania* 45°38N 25°35E **17** F13
Brasschaat *Belgium* 51°19N 4°27E **15** C4
Brassey, Banjaran
  Malaysia 5°0N 117°15E **36** D5
Brassey Ra. *Australia* 25°8S 122°15E **61** E3
Brasstown Bald *U.S.A.* 34°53N 83°49W **85** D13
Brastad *Sweden* 58°23N 11°30E **9** G14
Bratislava *Slovak Rep.* 48°10N 17°7E **17** D9
Bratsk *Russia* 56°10N 101°30E **29** D11
Brattleboro *U.S.A.* 42°51N 72°34W **83** D12
Braunau *Austria* 48°15N 13°3E **16** D7
Braunschweig *Germany* 52°15N 10°31E **16** B6
Braunton *U.K.* 51°7N 4°10W **13** F3
Brava *C. Verde Is.* 14°52N 24°40W **50** b
Bravo del Norte, Rio → = Grande,
  Rio → *N. Amer.* 25°58N 97°9W **84** J6
Brawley *U.S.A.* 32°59N 115°31W **79** N11
Bray *Ireland* 53°13N 6°7W **10** C5
Bray, Mt. *Australia* 14°0S 134°30E **62** A1
Bray, Pays de *France* 49°46N 1°26E **20** B4
Brazeau → *Canada* 52°55N 115°14W **70** C5
Brazil *U.S.A.* 39°32N 87°8W **80** F10
Brazil ■ *S. Amer.* 12°0S 50°0W **93** F9
Brazilian Highlands = Brasil,
  Planalto *Brazil* 18°0S 46°30W **90** E6
Brazo Sur → *S. Amer.* 25°21S 57°42W **94** B4
Brazos → *U.S.A.* 28°53N 95°23W **84** G7
Brazzaville *Congo* 4°9S 15°12E **52** E3
Brčko *Bos.-H.* 44°54N 18°46E **23** B8
Bré = Bray *Ireland* 53°13N 6°7W **10** C5
Breaden, L. *Australia* 25°51S 125°28E **61** E4
Breaksea Sd. *N.Z.* 45°35S 166°35E **59** F1
Bream B. *N.Z.* 35°56S 174°28E **59** A5
Bream Hd. *N.Z.* 35°51S 174°36E **59** A5
Breas *Chile* 25°29S 70°24W **94** B1
Brebes *Indonesia* 6°52S 109°3E **37** G13
Brechin *Canada* 44°32N 79°10W **82** B5
Brechin *U.K.* 56°44N 2°39W **11** E6
Brecht *Belgium* 51°21N 4°38E **15** C4
Breckenridge *Colo.,*
  U.S.A. 39°29N 106°3W **76** G10
Breckenridge *Minn.,*
  U.S.A. 46°16N 96°35W **80** B5
Breckenridge *Tex.,*
  U.S.A. 32°45N 98°54W **84** E5
Breckland *U.K.* 52°30N 0°40E **13** E8
Brecon *U.K.* 51°57N 3°23W **13** F4
Brecon Beacons *U.K.* 51°53N 3°26W **13** F4
Brecon Beacons △ *U.K.* 51°50N 3°30W **13** F4
Breda *Neths.* 51°35N 4°45E **15** C4
Bredasdorp *S. Africa* 34°33S 20°2E **56** E3
Bree *Belgium* 51°8N 5°35E **15** C5
Bregenz *Austria* 47°30N 9°45E **16** E5
Breiðafjörður *Iceland* 65°15N 23°15W **8** D2
Brejo *Brazil* 3°41S 42°47W **93** D10
Bremen *Germany* 53°4N 8°47E **16** B5
Bremer Bay *Australia* 34°21S 119°20E **61** F2
Bremer I. *Australia* 12°5S 136°45E **62** A2
Bremerhaven *Germany* 53°33N 8°36E **16** B5
Bremerton *U.S.A.* 47°34N 122°37W **78** C4
Brenham *U.S.A.* 30°10N 96°24W **84** F6
Brennerpass *Austria* 47°2N 11°30E **16** E6
Brent *U.S.A.* 32°56N 87°10E **85** E11
Brentwood *U.K.* 51°37N 0°19E **13** F8
Brentwood *Calif.,*
  U.S.A. 37°56N 121°42W **78** H5
Brentwood *N.Y., U.S.A.* 40°47N 73°15W **83** F11
Bréscia *Italy* 45°33N 10°15E **20** D9
Breskens *Neths.* 51°23N 3°33E **15** C3

Breslau = Wrocław *Poland* 51°5N 17°5E **17** C9
Bressanone *Italy* 46°43N 11°39E **22** A4
Bressay *U.K.* 60°9N 1°6W **11** A7
Brest *Belarus* 52°10N 23°40E **17** B12
Brest *France* 48°24N 4°31W **20** B1
Brest-Litovsk = Brest
  Belarus 52°10N 23°40E **17** B12
Bretagne □ *France* 48°10N 3°0W **20** B2
Breton *Canada* 53°7N 114°28W **70** C6
Breton Sd. *U.S.A.* 29°35N 89°15W **85** G10
Brett, C. *N.Z.* 35°10S 174°20E **59** A5
Brevard *U.S.A.* 35°14N 82°44W **85** D13
Breves *Brazil* 1°40S 50°29W **93** D8
Brewarrina *Australia* 44°48S 68°46W **81** C19
Brewer *U.S.A.* 44°48N 68°46W **81** C19
Brewer, Mt. *U.S.A.* 36°44N 118°28W **78** J8
Brewster *N.Y., U.S.A.* 41°23N 73°36W **83** E11
Brewster *Ohio, U.S.A.* 40°43N 81°36W **82** F3
Brewster *Wash., U.S.A.* 48°6N 119°47W **76** B4
Brewster, Kap = Kangikajik
  Greenland 70°7N 22°0W **4** B6
Brewton *U.S.A.* 31°7N 87°4W **85** F11
Breyten *S. Africa* 26°16S 30°0E **57** D5
Bria *C.A.R.* 6°30N 21°58E **52** C4
Briançon *France* 44°54N 6°39E **20** D7
Bribie I. *Australia* 27°0S 153°10E **63** D5
Bribri *Costa Rica* 9°38N 82°50W **88** E3
Bridgefield *Barbados* 13°9N 59°36W **89** g
Bridgehampton *U.S.A.* 40°56N 72°19W **83** F12
Bridgend *U.K.* 51°30N 3°34W **13** F4
Bridgend □ *U.K.* 51°36N 3°36W **13** F4
Bridgenorth *Canada* 44°23N 78°23W **82** B6
Bridgeport *Calif., U.S.A.* 38°15N 119°14W **78** G7
Bridgeport *Conn.,*
  U.S.A. 41°11N 73°12W **83** E11
Bridgeport *N.Y., U.S.A.* 43°9N 75°58W **83** C9
Bridgeport *Nebr., U.S.A.* 41°40N 103°6W **80** E2
Bridgeport *Tex., U.S.A.* 33°13N 97°45W **84** E6
Bridger *U.S.A.* 45°18N 108°55W **76** D9
Bridgeton *U.S.A.* 39°26N 75°14W **81** F16
Bridgetown *Australia* 33°58S 116°7E **61** F2
Bridgetown *Barbados* 13°6N 59°37W **89** g
Bridgetown *Canada* 44°55N 65°18W **73** D6
Bridgewater *Australia* 42°44S 147°14E **63** G4
Bridgewater *Canada* 44°25N 64°31W **73** D7
Bridgewater *Mass.,*
  U.S.A. 41°59N 70°58W **83** E14
Bridgewater *N.Y.,*
  U.S.A. 42°53N 75°15W **83** D9
Bridgewater, C.
  Australia 38°23S 141°23E **63** F3
Bridgnorth *U.K.* 52°32N 2°25W **13** E5
Bridgton *U.S.A.* 44°3N 70°42W **83** B14
Bridgwater *U.K.* 51°8N 2°59W **13** F5
Bridgwater B. *U.K.* 51°15N 3°15W **13** F4
Bridlington *U.K.* 54°5N 0°12W **12** C7
Bridlington B. *U.K.* 54°4N 0°10W **12** C7
Bridport *Australia* 40°59S 147°23E **63** G4
Bridport *U.K.* 50°44N 2°45W **13** G5
Brig *Switz.* 46°18N 7°59E **20** C7
Brigg *U.K.* 53°34N 0°28W **12** D7
Brigham City *U.S.A.* 41°31N 112°1W **76** F7
Bright *Australia* 36°42S 146°56E **63** F4
Brighton *Australia* 35°5S 138°30E **63** F2
Brighton *Canada* 44°2N 77°44W **82** B7
Brighton *Trin. & Tob.* 10°13N 61°39W **93** K15
Brighton *U.K.* 50°49N 0°7W **13** G7
Brighton *U.S.A.* 43°8N 77°34W **82** C7
Brightside *Canada* 45°7N 76°29W **83** A8
Brilliant *U.S.A.* 40°15N 80°39W **82** F4
Brindisi *Italy* 40°39N 17°55E **22** D7
Brinkley *U.S.A.* 34°53N 91°12W **84** D9
Brinnon *U.S.A.* 47°41N 122°54W **78** C4
Brion, Î. *Canada* 47°46N 61°26W **73** C7
Brisay *Canada* 54°26N 70°31W **73** B5
Brisbane *Australia* 27°25S 153°2E **63** D5
Brisbane → *Australia* 27°24S 153°9E **63** D5
Bristol *U.K.* 51°26N 2°35W **13** F5
Bristol *Conn., U.S.A.* 41°40N 72°57W **83** E12
Bristol *Pa., U.S.A.* 40°6N 74°51W **83** F10
Bristol *R.I., U.S.A.* 41°40N 71°16W **83** E13
Bristol *Tenn., U.S.A.* 36°36N 82°11W **85** C13
Bristol *Vt., U.S.A.* 44°8N 73°4W **83** B11
Bristol, City of □ *U.K.* 51°27N 2°36W **13** F5
Bristol B. *U.S.A.* 58°0N 160°0W **74** D7
Bristol Channel *U.K.* 51°18N 4°30W **13** F3
Bristol I. *Antarctica* 58°45S 28°0W **5** B1
Bristol L. *U.S.A.* 34°28N 115°41W **77** J6
Bristow *U.S.A.* 35°50N 96°23W **84** D6
Britain = Great Britain
  Europe 54°0N 2°15W **6** E5
British Columbia □
  Canada 55°0N 125°15W **70** C3
British Indian Ocean Terr. =
  Chagos Arch. ☒ *Ind. Oc.* 6°0S 72°0E **26** J9
British Isles *Europe* 54°0N 4°0W **14** D5
British Mts. *N. Amer.* 68°50N 140°0W **74** B12
British Virgin Is. ☒
  W. Indies 18°30N 64°30W **89** e
Brits *S. Africa* 25°37S 27°48E **57** D4
Britstown *S. Africa* 30°37S 23°30E **56** E3
Britt *Canada* 45°46N 80°34W **72** C3
Brittany = Bretagne □
  France 48°10N 3°0W **20** B2
Britton *U.S.A.* 45°48N 97°45W **80** C5
Brive-la-Gaillarde *France* 45°10N 1°32E **20** D4
Brixen = Bressanone
  Italy 46°43N 11°39E **22** A4
Brixham *U.K.* 50°23N 3°31W **13** G4
Brno *Czech Rep.* 49°10N 16°35E **17** D9
Broach = Bharuch *India* 21°47N 73°0E **40** J8
Broad → *U.S.A.* 34°1N 81°4W **85** D14
Broad Arrow *Australia* 30°23S 121°15E **61** F3
Broad B. *U.K.* 58°14N 6°18W **11** C2
Broad Haven *Ireland* 54°20N 9°55W **10** B2
Broad Law *U.K.* 55°30N 3°21W **11** F5
Broad Pk. = Faichan Kangri
  India 35°48N 76°34E **43** B7
Broad Sd. *Australia* 22°0S 149°45E **62** C4

Broadalbin *U.S.A.* 43°4N 74°12W **83** C10
Broadback → *Canada* 51°21N 78°52W **72** B4
Broadhurst Ra.
 Australia 22°30S 122°30E **60** D3
Broads, The *U.K.* 52°45N 1°30E **12** E9
Broadus *U.S.A.* 45°27N 105°25W **76** D11
Brochet *Canada* 57°53N 101°40W **71** B8
Brochet, L. *Canada* 58°36N 101°35W **71** B8
Brock I. *Canada* 77°52N 114°19W **69** B9
Brocken *Germany* 51°47N 10°37E **16** C6
Brockport *U.S.A.* 43°13N 77°56W **82** C7
Brockton *U.S.A.* 42°5N 71°1W **83** D13
Brockville *Canada* 44°35N 75°41W **83** B9
Brockway *Mont.,*
 U.S.A. 47°18N 105°45W **76** C11
Brockway *Pa., U.S.A.* 41°15N 78°47W **82** E6
Brocton *U.S.A.* 42°23N 79°26W **82** D5
Brodeur Pen. *Canada* 72°30N 88°10W **69** C14
Brodick *U.K.* 55°35N 5°9W **11** F3
Brodnica *Poland* 53°15N 19°25E **17** B10
Brody *Ukraine* 50°5N 25°10E **17** C13
Brogan *U.S.A.* 44°15N 117°31W **76** D5
Broken Arrow *U.S.A.* 36°3N 95°48W **84** C7
Broken Bow *Nebr.,*
 U.S.A. 41°24N 99°38W **80** E4
Broken Bow *Okla., U.S.A.* 34°2N 94°44W **84** D7
Broken Bow Lake *U.S.A.* 34°9N 94°40W **84** D7
Broken Hill *Australia* 31°58S 141°29E **63** E3
Broken Ridge *Ind. Oc.* 30°0S 94°0E **64** L1
Broken River Ra.
 Australia 21°0S 148°22E **62** b
Bromley □ *U.K.* 51°24N 0°2E **13** F8
Bromo *Indonesia* 7°55S 112°55E **37** G15
Bromsgrove *U.K.* 52°21N 2°2W **13** E5
Brønderslev *Denmark* 57°16N 9°57E **9** H13
Bronkhorstspruit
 S. Africa 25°46S 28°45E **57** D4
Brønnøysund *Norway* 65°28N 12°14E **8** D15
Brook Park *U.S.A.* 41°23N 81°48W **82** E4
Brookhaven *U.S.A.* 31°35N 90°26W **85** F9
Brookings *Oreg., U.S.A.* 42°3N 124°17W **76** E1
Brookings *S. Dak.,*
 U.S.A. 44°19N 96°48W **80** C5
Brooklin *Canada* 43°55N 78°55W **82** C6
Brooklyn Park *U.S.A.* 45°6N 93°23W **80** C7
Brooks *Canada* 50°35N 111°55W **70** C6
Brooks Range *U.S.A.* 68°0N 152°0W **74** B9
Brooksville *U.S.A.* 28°33N 82°23W **85** G13
Brookton *Australia* 32°22S 117°0E **61** F2
Brookville *U.S.A.* 41°10N 79°5W **82** E5
Broom, L. *U.K.* 57°55N 5°15W **11** D3
Broome *Australia* 18°0S 122°15E **60** C3
Brora *U.K.* 58°0N 3°52W **11** C5
Brora → *U.K.* 58°0N 3°51W **11** C5
Brosna → *Ireland* 53°14N 7°58W **10** C4
Brothers *U.S.A.* 43°49N 120°36W **76** E3
Brough *U.K.* 54°32N 2°18W **12** C5
Brough Hd. *U.K.* 59°8N 3°20W **11** B5
Broughton Island = Qikiqtarjuaq
 Canada 67°33N 63°0W **69** D19
Brown, L. *Australia* 31°5S 118°15E **61** F2
Brown, Pt. *Australia* 32°32S 133°50E **63** E1
Brown City *U.S.A.* 43°13N 82°59W **82** C2
Brown Willy *U.K.* 50°35N 4°37W **13** G3
Brownfield *U.S.A.* 33°11N 102°17W **84** E3
Browning *U.S.A.* 48°34N 113°1W **76** B7
Brownsville *Oreg.,*
 U.S.A. 44°24N 122°59W **76** D2
Brownsville *Pa., U.S.A.* 40°1N 79°53W **82** F5
Brownsville *Tenn.,*
 U.S.A. 35°36N 89°16W **85** D10
Brownsville *Tex., U.S.A.* 25°54N 97°30W **84** J6
Brownville *U.S.A.* 44°0N 75°59W **83** C9
Brownwood *U.S.A.* 31°43N 98°59W **84** F5
Browse I. *Australia* 14°7S 123°33E **60** B3
Bruas *Malaysia* 4°30N 100°47E **39** K3
Bruay-la-Buissière *France* 50°29N 2°33E **20** A5
Bruce, Mt. *Australia* 22°37S 118°8E **60** D2
Bruce Pen. *Canada* 45°0N 81°30W **82** B3
Bruce Peninsula △
 Canada 45°14N 81°36W **82** A3
Bruce Rock *Australia* 31°52S 118°8E **61** F2
Bruck an der Leitha
 Austria 48°1N 16°47E **17** D9
Bruck an der Mur
 Austria 47°24N 15°16E **16** E8
Brue → *U.K.* 51°13N 2°59W **13** F5
Bruges = Brugge *Belgium* 51°13N 3°13E **15** C3
Brugge *Belgium* 51°13N 3°13E **15** C3
Bruin *U.S.A.* 41°3N 79°43W **82** E5
Brûk, W. el → *Egypt* 30°15N 33°50E **46** E2
Brûlé *Canada* 53°15N 117°58W **70** C5
Brûlé, L. *Canada* 53°35N 64°4W **73** B7
Brumado *Brazil* 14°14S 41°40W **93** F10
Brumunddal *Norway* 60°53N 10°56E **8** F14
Bruneau *U.S.A.* 42°53N 115°48W **76** E6
Bruneau → *U.S.A.* 42°56N 115°57W **76** E6
Brunei = Bandar Seri Begawan
 Brunei 4°52N 115°0E **36** D5
Brunei ■ *Asia* 4°50N 115°0E **36** D5
Brunner, L. *N.Z.* 42°37S 171°27E **59** E3
Brunssum *Neths.* 50°57N 5°59E **15** D5
Brunswick = Braunschweig
 Germany 52°15N 10°31E **16** B6
Brunswick *Ga., U.S.A.* 31°10N 81°30W **85** F14
Brunswick *Maine,*
 U.S.A. 43°55N 69°58W **81** D19
Brunswick *Md., U.S.A.* 39°19N 77°38W **81** F15
Brunswick *Mo., U.S.A.* 39°26N 93°8W **80** F7
Brunswick *Ohio, U.S.A.* 41°14N 81°51W **82** E3
Brunswick, Pen. de
 Chile 53°30S 71°30W **96** G2
Brunswick B. *Australia* 15°15S 124°50E **60** C3
Brunswick Junction
 Australia 33°15S 115°50E **61** F2
Brunt Ice Shelf *Antarctica* 75°30S 25°0W **5** D2
Brus Laguna *Honduras* 15°47N 84°35W **88** C3
Brush *U.S.A.* 40°15N 103°37W **76** F12
Brushton *U.S.A.* 44°50N 74°31W **83** B10

Brusque *Brazil* 27°5S 49°0W **95** B6
Brussel *Belgium* 50°51N 4°21E **15** D4
Brussel ✈ (BRU) *Belgium* 50°54N 4°29E **15** D5
Brussels = Brussel
 Belgium 50°51N 4°21E **15** D4
Brussels *Canada* 43°44N 81°15W **82** C3
Bruthen *Australia* 37°42S 147°50E **63** F4
Bruxelles = Brussel
 Belgium 50°51N 4°21E **15** D4
Bryan *Ohio, U.S.A.* 41°28N 84°33W **81** E11
Bryan *Tex., U.S.A.* 30°40N 96°22W **84** F6
Bryan, Mt. *Australia* 33°30S 139°5E **63** E2
Bryansk *Russia* 53°13N 34°25E **18** D4
Bryce Canyon △
 U.S.A. 37°30N 112°10W **77** H7
Bryne *Norway* 58°44N 5°38E **9** G11
Bryson City *U.S.A.* 35°26N 83°27W **85** D13
Bsharri *Lebanon* 34°15N 36°0E **46** A5
Bū Baqarah *U.A.E.* 25°35N 56°25E **45** E8
Bu Craa *W. Sahara* 26°45N 12°50W **52** C3
Bū Ḥasā *U.A.E.* 23°30N 53°20E **45** F7
Bua *Fiji* 16°48S 178°37E **59** a
Bua → *Malaysia* 12°45S 34°16E **55** E3
Bua Yai *Thailand* 15°33N 102°26E **38** E4
Buan *S. Korea* 35°44N 126°44E **35** G14
Buapinang *Indonesia* 4°40S 121°30E **37** E6
Bubanza *Burundi* 3°6S 29°23E **54** C2
Bubi → *Zimbabwe* 22°20S 31°7E **55** G3
Būbiyān *Kuwait* 29°45N 48°15E **45** D6
Buca *Fiji* 16°38S 179°52E **59** a
Bucaramanga *Colombia* 7°0N 73°0W **92** B4
Bucasia *Australia* 21°2S 149°10E **62** b
Buccaneer Arch.
 Australia 16°7S 123°20E **60** C3
Buccoo Reef
 Trin. & Tob. 11°10N 60°51W **93** J16
Buchach *Ukraine* 49°5N 25°25E **17** D13
Buchan *U.K.* 57°32N 2°21W **11** D6
Buchan Ness *U.K.* 57°29N 1°46W **11** D7
Buchanan *Canada* 51°40N 102°45W **71** C8
Buchanan *Liberia* 5°57N 10°2W **50** G3
Buchanan, L. *Queens.,*
 Australia 21°35S 145°52E **62** C4
Buchanan, L. *W. Austral.,*
 Australia 25°33S 123°2E **61** E3
Buchanan, L. *U.S.A.* 30°45N 98°25W **84** F5
Buchanan Cr. →
 Australia 19°13S 136°33E **62** B2
Buchans *Canada* 48°50N 56°52W **73** C8
Bucharest = București
 Romania 44°27N 26°10E **17** F14
Bucheon *S. Korea* 37°28N 126°45E **35** F14
Buchon, Pt. *U.S.A.* 35°15N 120°54W **78** K6
Buck Hill Falls *U.S.A.* 41°11N 75°16W **83** E9
Buckeye Lake *U.S.A.* 39°55N 82°29W **82** G2
Buckhannon *U.S.A.* 39°0N 80°8W **81** F13
Buckhaven *U.K.* 56°11N 3°3W **11** E5
Buckhorn L. *Canada* 44°29N 78°23W **82** B6
Buckie *U.K.* 57°41N 2°58W **11** D6
Buckingham *Canada* 45°37N 75°24W **72** C4
Buckingham *U.K.* 51°59N 0°57W **13** F7
Buckingham B.
 Australia 12°10S 135°40E **62** A2
Buckinghamshire □
 U.K. 51°53N 0°55W **13** F7
Buckle Hd. *Australia* 14°26S 127°52E **60** B4
Buckleboo *Australia* 32°54S 136°12E **63** E2
Buckley *U.K.* 53°10N 3°5W **12** D4
Buckley → *Australia* 20°10S 138°49E **62** C2
Bucklin *U.S.A.* 37°33N 99°38W **80** G4
Bucks L. *U.S.A.* 39°54N 121°12W **78** F5
București *Romania* 44°27N 26°10E **17** F14
Bucyrus *U.S.A.* 40°48N 82°59W **81** E12
Budalin *Burma* 22°20N 95°10E **41** H19
Budaun *India* 28°5N 79°10E **43** E8
Budapest *Hungary* 47°29N 19°3E **17** E10
Budaun *India* 28°5N 79°10E **43** E8
Budd Coast *Antarctica* 68°0S 112°0E **5** C8
Bude *U.K.* 50°49N 4°34W **13** G3
Budennovsk *Russia* 44°50N 44°10E **19** F7
Budge Budge = Baj Baj
 India 22°30N 88°5E **43** H13
Budgewoi *Australia* 33°13S 151°34E **63** E5
Budjala
 Dem. Rep. of the Congo 2°50N 19°40E **52** D3
Buellton *U.S.A.* 34°37N 120°12W **79** L6
Buena Esperanza
 Argentina 34°45S 65°15W **94** C2
Buena Park *U.S.A.* 33°52N 117°59W **79** M9
Buena Vista *Colo.,*
 U.S.A. 38°51N 106°8W **76** G10
Buena Vista *Va., U.S.A.* 37°44N 79°21W **81** G14
Buena Vista Lake Bed
 U.S.A. 35°12N 119°18W **79** K7
Buenaventura *Colombia* 3°53N 77°4W **92** C3
Buenaventura *Mexico* 29°51N 107°29W **86** B3
Buenos Aires *Argentina* 34°36S 58°22W **94** C4
Buenos Aires *Costa Rica* 9°10N 83°20W **88** E3
Buenos Aires □ *Argentina* 36°30S 60°0W **94** D4
Buenos Aires, L.
 Argentina 46°35S 72°30W **96** F2
Buffalo *Mo., U.S.A.* 37°39N 93°6W **80** G7
Buffalo *N.Y., U.S.A.* 42°53N 78°53W **82** D6
Buffalo *Okla., U.S.A.* 36°50N 99°38W **84** C5
Buffalo *S. Dak., U.S.A.* 45°35N 103°33W **80** C2
Buffalo *Wyo., U.S.A.* 44°21N 106°42W **76** D10
Buffalo → *U.S.A.* 60°5N 115°5W **70** A5
Buffalo → *S. Africa* 28°43S 30°37E **57** D5
Buffalo → *U.S.A.* 36°14N 92°36W **84** C8
Buffalo Head Hills
 Canada 57°25N 115°55W **70** B5
Buffalo L. *Alta., Canada* 52°27N 112°54W **70** C6
Buffalo L. *N.W.T.,*
 Canada 60°12N 115°25W **70** A5
Buffalo Narrows
 Canada 55°51N 108°29W **71** B7
Buffalo Springs △ *Kenya* 0°32N 37°35E **54** B4
Buffels → *S. Africa* 29°36S 17°3E **56** D2
Buford *U.S.A.* 34°10N 84°0W **85** D12
Bug → *Poland* 52°31N 21°5E **17** B11
Bug = Buh → *Ukraine* 46°59N 31°58E **19** E5

Bug → *Poland* 52°31N 21°5E **17** B11
Buga *Colombia* 4°0N 76°15W **92** C3
Bugala I. *Uganda* 0°40S 32°20E **54** C3
Buganda *Uganda* 0°0 31°30E **54** C3
Buganga *Uganda* 0°3S 32°0E **54** C3
Bugel, Tanjung *Indonesia* 6°26S 111°3E **37** G14
Būger *Spain* 39°45N 2°59E **24** B9
Bugibba *Malta* 35°57N 14°25E **25** D1
Bugsuk I. *Phil.* 8°12N 117°18E **36** C5
Bugulma *Russia* 54°33N 52°48E **18** D9
Bugungu *Uganda* 2°17N 31°50E **54** B3
Buguruslan *Russia* 53°39N 52°26E **18** D9
Buh → *Ukraine* 46°59N 31°58E **19** E5
Buhera *Zimbabwe* 19°18S 31°29E **57** B5
Buhl *U.S.A.* 42°36N 114°46W **76** E6
Buir Nur *Mongolia* 47°50N 117°42E **33** B6
Buji *China* 22°37N 114°5E **33** F11
Bujumbura *Burundi* 3°16S 29°18E **54** C2
Bukachacha *Russia* 52°55N 116°50E **29** D12
Bukama
 Dem. Rep. of the Congo 9°10S 25°50E **55** D2
Bukavu
 Dem. Rep. of the Congo 2°20S 28°52E **54** C2
Bukene *Tanzania* 4°15S 32°48E **54** C3
Bukhara = Buxoro
 Uzbekistan 39°48N 64°25E **28** F7
Bukhoro = Buxoro
 Uzbekistan 39°48N 64°25E **28** F7
Bukima *Tanzania* 1°50S 33°25E **54** C3
Bukit Badung *Indonesia* 8°49S 115°10E **37** K18
Bukit Kerajaan *Malaysia* 5°25N 100°15E **39** c
Bukit Mertajam *Malaysia* 5°22N 100°28E **39** c
Bukit Ni *Malaysia* 1°22N 104°12E **39** d
Bukit Panjang *Singapore* 1°23N 103°46E **39** d
Bukit Tengah *Malaysia* 5°22N 100°25E **39** c
Bukoba *Tanzania* 1°20S 31°49E **54** C3
Bukum, Pulau *Singapore* 1°14N 103°46E **39** d
Bukuya *Uganda* 0°40N 31°52E **54** B3
Būl, Kuh-e *Iran* 30°48N 52°45E **45** D7
Bula *Indonesia* 3°6S 130°30E **37** E8
Bulahdelah *Australia* 32°23S 152°13E **63** E5
Bulandshahr *India* 28°28N 77°51E **42** E7
Bulawayo *Zimbabwe* 20°7S 28°32E **55** G2
Buldan *Turkey* 38°2N 28°50E **23** E13
Buldi I. *U.S.A.* 52°21N 175°56E **74** E3
Bulgan *Mongolia* 48°45N 103°34E **32** B5
Bulgar *Russia* 54°57N 49°4E **18** D8
Bulgaria ■ *Europe* 42°35N 25°30E **23** C11
Buli, Teluk *Indonesia* 0°48N 128°25E **37** D7
Buliluyan, C. *Phil.* 8°20N 117°15E **36** C5
Bulim *Singapore* 1°22N 103°43E **39** d
Bulkley → *Canada* 55°15N 127°40W **70** B3
Bull Shoals L. *U.S.A.* 36°22N 92°35W **84** C8
Bulleringa △ *Australia* 17°39S 143°56E **62** B3
Bullhead City *U.S.A.* 35°8N 114°32W **79** K12
Büllingen *Belgium* 50°25N 6°16E **15** D6
Bullock Creek *Australia* 17°43S 144°31E **62** B3
Bulloo → *Australia* 28°43S 142°30E **63** D3
Bulloo L. *Australia* 28°43S 142°25E **63** D3
Bulls *N.Z.* 40°10S 175°24E **59** D5
Bulman *Australia* 13°39S 134°20E **62** A1
Bulnes *Chile* 36°42S 72°19W **94** D1
Bulsar = Valsad *India* 20°40N 72°58E **40** J8
Bultfontein *S. Africa* 28°18S 26°10E **56** D4
Bulukumba *Indonesia* 5°33S 120°11E **37** F6
Bulun *Russia* 70°37N 127°30E **29** B13
Bumba
 Dem. Rep. of the Congo 2°13N 22°30E **52** D4
Bumbah, Khalīj *Libya* 32°20N 23°15E **51** B10
Bumbiri I. *Tanzania* 1°40S 31°55E **54** C3
Bumhpa Bum *Burma* 26°51N 97°14E **41** F20
Bumi → *Zimbabwe* 17°0S 28°20E **55** F2
Buna *Kenya* 2°58N 39°30E **54** B4
Bunaken *Indonesia* 1°37N 124°46E **37** D6
Bunazi *Tanzania* 1°3S 31°23E **54** C3
Bunbury *Australia* 33°20S 115°35E **61** F2
Bunclody *Ireland* 52°39N 6°40W **10** D5
Buncrana *Ireland* 55°8N 7°27W **10** A4
Bundaberg *Australia* 24°54S 152°22E **63** C5
Bundey → *Australia* 21°46S 135°37E **62** C2
Bundi *India* 25°30N 75°35E **42** G6
Bundjalung △ *Australia* 29°16S 153°21E **63** D5
Bundoran *Ireland* 54°28N 8°16W **10** B3
Bung Kan *Thailand* 18°23N 103°37E **38** C4
Bungay *U.K.* 52°27N 1°28E **13** E9
Bungil Cr. → *Australia* 27°5S 149°5E **63** D4
Bungle Bungle = Purnululu △
 Australia 17°20S 128°20E **60** C4
Bungo-Suidō *Japan* 33°0N 132°15E **31** H6
Bungoma *Kenya* 0°34N 34°34E **54** B3
Bungotakada *Japan* 33°35N 131°25E **31** H5
Bungu *Tanzania* 7°35S 39°0E **54** D4
Bunia
 Dem. Rep. of the Congo 1°35N 30°20E **54** B3
Bunji *Pakistan* 35°45N 74°40E **43** B6
Bunkie *U.S.A.* 30°57N 92°11W **84** F8
Bunnell *U.S.A.* 29°28N 81°16W **85** G14
Buntok *Indonesia* 1°40S 114°58E **36** E4
Bunya Mts. △ *Australia* 26°51S 151°34E **63** D5
Bunyola *Spain* 39°41N 2°42E **24** B9
Bunyu *Indonesia* 3°35N 117°50E **36** D5
Buol *Indonesia* 1°15N 121°32E **37** D6
Buon Brieng *Vietnam* 13°9N 108°12E **38** F7
Buon Ma Thuot *Vietnam* 12°40N 108°3E **38** F7
Buong Long *Cambodia* 13°44N 106°59E **38** F6
Buorkhaya, Mys
 Russia 71°50N 132°40E **29** B14
Buqayq *Si. Arabia* 26°0N 49°45E **45** E6
Bur Acaba = Buurhakaba
 Somali Rep. 3°12N 44°20E **47** G3
Bûr Safâga *Egypt* 26°43N 33°57E **44** E2
Bûr Sa'îd *Egypt* 31°16N 32°18E **51** B12
Bûr Sûdân *Sudan* 19°32N 37°9E **51** E13
Bura *Kenya* 1°4S 39°58E **54** C5
Burakin *Australia* 30°31S 117°10E **61** F2
Burao = Burco *Somali Rep.* 9°32N 45°32E **47** F4

Burāq *Syria* 33°11N 36°29E **46** B5
Buraydah *Si. Arabia* 26°20N 43°59E **44** E4
Burbank *U.S.A.* 34°12N 118°18W **79** L8
Burco *Somali Rep.* 9°32N 45°32E **47** F4
Burda *India* 25°50N 77°35E **42** G6
Burdekin → *Australia* 19°38S 147°25E **62** B4
Burdur *Turkey* 37°45N 30°17E **19** G5
Burdwan = Barddhaman
 India 23°14N 87°39E **43** H12
Bure *Ethiopia* 10°40N 37°4E **47** E2
Bure → *U.K.* 52°38N 1°43E **12** E9
Bureya → *Russia* 49°27N 129°30E **29** E13
Burford *Canada* 43°7N 80°27W **82** C4
Burgas *Bulgaria* 42°33N 27°29E **23** C12
Burgeo *Canada* 47°37N 57°38W **73** C8
Burgersdorp *S. Africa* 31°0S 26°20E **56** E4
Burgess, Mt. *Australia* 30°50S 121°5E **61** F3
Burghead *U.K.* 57°43N 3°30W **11** D5
Burgos *Spain* 42°21N 3°41W **21** A4
Burgsvik *Sweden* 57°3N 18°19E **9** H18
Burhaniye *Turkey* 39°30N 26°58E **23** E12
Burhanpur *India* 21°18N 76°14E **40** J10
Burhi Gandak → *India* 25°20N 86°37E **43** G12
Burhner → *India* 22°43N 80°31E **43** H9
Burias I. *Phil.* 12°55N 123°5E **37** B6
Burica, Pta. *Costa Rica* 8°3N 82°51W **88** E3
Burien *U.S.A.* 47°28N 122°20W **78** C4
Burigi, L. *Tanzania* 2°2S 31°22E **54** C3
Burigi △ *Tanzania* 2°20S 31°6E **54** C3
Burin *Canada* 47°1N 55°14W **73** C8
Buriram *Thailand* 15°0N 103°0E **38** E4
Burkburnett *U.S.A.* 34°6N 98°34W **84** D5
Burke → *Australia* 23°12S 139°33E **62** C2
Burke Chan. *Canada* 52°10N 127°30W **70** C3
Burketown *Australia* 17°45S 139°33E **62** B2
Burkina Faso ■ *Africa* 12°0N 1°0W **50** F5
Burk's Falls *Canada* 45°37N 79°24W **72** C4
Burleigh Falls *Canada* 44°33N 78°12W **82** B6
Burley *U.S.A.* 42°32N 113°48W **76** E7
Burlingame *U.S.A.* 37°35N 122°21W **78** H4
Burlington *Canada* 43°18N 79°45W **82** C5
Burlington *Colo.,*
 U.S.A. 39°18N 102°16W **76** G12
Burlington *Iowa, U.S.A.* 40°49N 91°14W **80** E8
Burlington *Kans., U.S.A.* 38°12N 95°45W **80** F6
Burlington *N.C., U.S.A.* 36°6N 79°26W **85** C15
Burlington *N.J., U.S.A.* 40°4N 74°51W **83** F10
Burlington *Vt., U.S.A.* 44°29N 73°12W **83** B11
Burlington *Wash.,*
 U.S.A. 48°28N 122°20W **78** B4
Burlington *Wis., U.S.A.* 42°41N 88°17W **80** D9
Burma ■ *Asia* 21°0N 96°30E **41** J20
Burnaby I. *Canada* 52°25N 131°19W **70** C2
Burnet *U.S.A.* 30°45N 98°14W **84** F5
Burney *U.S.A.* 40°53N 121°40W **76** F3
Burnham *U.S.A.* 40°38N 77°34W **82** F7
Burnham-on-Sea *U.K.* 51°14N 3°0W **13** F5
Burnie *Australia* 41°4S 145°56E **63** G4
Burnley *U.K.* 53°47N 2°14W **12** D5
Burns *U.S.A.* 43°35N 119°3W **76** E4
Burns Junction *U.S.A.* 42°47N 117°51W **76** E5
Burns Lake *Canada* 54°14N 125°45W **70** C3
Burnside → *Canada* 66°51N 108°4W **68** D10
Burnside, L. *Australia* 25°22S 123°0E **61** E3
Burnsville *U.S.A.* 44°47N 93°17W **80** C7
Burnt River *Canada* 44°41N 78°42W **82** B6
Burntwood → *Canada* 56°8N 96°34W **71** B9
Burntwood L. *Canada* 55°22N 100°26W **71** B8
Burqān *Kuwait* 29°0N 47°57E **44** D5
Burqin *China* 47°43N 87°0E **32** B3
Burra *Australia* 33°40S 138°55E **63** E2
Burray *U.K.* 58°51N 2°54W **11** C6
Burren *Ireland* 53°9N 9°5W **10** C2
Burren △ *Ireland* 53°1N 8°58W **10** C3
Burren Junction
 Australia 30°7S 148°58E **63** E4
Burrinjuck, L. *Australia* 35°0S 148°36E **63** F4
Burro, Serranías del
 Mexico 28°56N 102°5W **86** B4
Burrow Hd. *U.K.* 54°41N 4°24W **11** G4
Burrum Coast △
 Australia 25°13S 152°36E **63** D5
Burruyacú *Argentina* 26°30S 64°40W **94** B3
Burry Port *U.K.* 51°41N 4°15W **13** F3
Bursa *Turkey* 40°15N 29°5E **23** D13
Burstall *Canada* 50°39N 109°54W **71** C7
Burton *Ohio, U.S.A.* 41°28N 81°8W **82** E3
Burton *S.C., U.S.A.* 32°26N 80°43W **85** E14
Burton, L. *Canada* 54°45N 78°20W **72** B4
Burton upon Trent *U.K.* 52°48N 1°38W **12** E6
Buru *Indonesia* 3°30S 126°30E **37** E7
Burûn, Râs *Egypt* 31°14N 33°7E **46** D2
Burundi ■ *Africa* 3°15S 30°0E **54** C3
Bururi *Burundi* 3°57S 29°37E **54** C2
Burutu *Nigeria* 5°20N 5°29E **50** G7
Burwell *U.S.A.* 41°47N 99°8W **80** E4
Burwick *U.K.* 58°45N 2°58W **11** C5
Bury *U.K.* 53°35N 2°17W **12** D5
Bury St. Edmunds *U.K.* 52°15N 0°43E **13** E8
Buryatia □ *Russia* 53°0N 110°0E **29** D12
Busan *S. Korea* 35°5N 129°0E **35** G15
Busango Swamp *Zambia* 14°15S 25°45E **55** E2
Busawal *Nigeria* 11°12N 49°18E **47** E4
Büsheh *Iran* 28°55N 50°55E **45** D6
Büshehr *Iran* 28°55N 50°55E **45** D6
Bushenyi *Uganda* 0°35S 30°10E **54** C3
Bushire = Büshehr *Iran* 28°55N 50°55E **45** D6
Businga
 Dem. Rep. of the Congo 3°16N 20°59E **52** D4
Buşra ash Shām *Syria* 32°30N 36°25E **46** C5
Busselton *Australia* 33°42S 115°15E **61** F2
Bussum *Neths.* 52°16N 5°10E **15** B5
Busto Arsízio *Italy* 45°37N 8°51E **20** D8
Busu Djanoa
 Dem. Rep. of the Congo 1°43N 21°23E **52** D4

Busuanga I. *Phil.* 12°10N 120°0E **37** B6
Busungbiu *Indonesia* 8°16S 114°58E **37** J17
Buta *Dem. Rep. of the Congo* 2°50N 24°53E **54** B1
Butare *Rwanda* 2°31S 29°52E **54** C2
Butaritari *Kiribati* 3°30N 174°0E **64** G9
Bute *U.K.* 55°48N 5°2W **11** F3
Bute Inlet *Canada* 50°40N 124°53W **70** C4
Butemba *Uganda* 1°9N 31°37E **54** B3
Butembo
 Dem. Rep. of the Congo 0°9N 29°18E **54** B2
Butere *Kenya* 0°13N 34°30E **54** B3
Butha Qi *China* 48°0N 122°32E **33** B7
Butiaba *Uganda* 1°50N 31°20E **54** B3
Butler *Mo., U.S.A.* 38°16N 94°20W **80** F6
Butler *Pa., U.S.A.* 40°52N 79°54W **82** F5
Buton *Indonesia* 5°0S 122°45E **37** F6
Butte *Mont., U.S.A.* 46°0N 112°32W **76** C7
Butte *Nebr., U.S.A.* 42°58N 98°51W **80** D4
Butte Creek → *U.S.A.* 39°12N 121°56W **78** F5
Butterworth = Gcuwa
 S. Africa 32°20S 28°11E **57** E4
Butterworth *Malaysia* 5°24N 100°23E **39** c
Buttevant *Ireland* 52°14N 8°40W **10** D3
Buttfield, Mt. *Australia* 24°45S 128°9E **61** D4
Button B. *Canada* 58°45N 94°23W **71** B10
Buttonwillow *U.S.A.* 35°24N 119°28W **79** K7
Butty Hd. *Australia* 33°54S 121°39E **61** F3
Butuan *Phil.* 8°57N 125°33E **37** C7
Butung = Buton *Indonesia* 5°0S 122°45E **37** F6
Buturlinovka *Russia* 50°50N 40°35E **19** D7
Buurhakaba *Somali Rep.* 3°12N 44°20E **47** G3
Buxa Duar *India* 27°45N 89°35E **43** F13
Buxar *India* 25°34N 83°58E **43** G10
Buxoro *Uzbekistan* 39°48N 64°25E **28** F7
Buxtehude *Germany* 53°28N 9°39E **16** B5
Buxton *U.K.* 53°16N 1°54W **12** D6
Buy *Russia* 58°28N 41°28E **18** C7
Buyant-Uhaa *Mongolia* 44°55N 110°11E **33** B6
Buyo, L. de *Ivory C.* 6°16N 7°10W **50** G4
Büyük Menderes →
 Turkey 37°28N 27°11E **23** F12
Büyükçekmece *Turkey* 41°2N 28°35E **23** D13
Buzău *Romania* 45°10N 26°50E **17** F14
Buzău → *Romania* 45°26N 27°44E **17** F14
Buzen *Japan* 33°35N 131°5E **31** H5
Buzi → *Mozam.* 19°50S 34°43E **55** F3
Bûzmeyin *Turkmenistan* 38°3N 58°12E **45** B8
Buzuluk *Russia* 52°48N 52°12E **18** D9
Buzzards Bay *U.S.A.* 41°45N 70°37W **83** E14
Bwana Mkubwe
 Dem. Rep. of the Congo 13°8S 28°38E **55** E2
Bwindi □ *Uganda* 1°2S 29°42E **54** C2
Byam Martin I.
 Canada 75°15N 104°15W **69** B11
Byarezina → *Belarus* 52°33N 30°14E **17** B16
Bydgoszcz *Poland* 53°10N 18°0E **17** B9
Byelorussia = Belarus ■
 Europe 53°30N 27°0E **17** B14
Byers *U.S.A.* 39°43N 104°14W **76** G11
Byesville *U.S.A.* 39°58N 81°32W **82** G3
Byfield □ *Australia* 22°52S 150°45E **62** C5
Bykhaw *Belarus* 53°31N 30°14E **17** B16
Bykhov = Bykhaw
 Belarus 53°31N 30°14E **17** B16
Bylas *U.S.A.* 33°8N 110°7W **77** K8
Bylot *Canada* 58°25N 94°8W **71** B10
Bylot I. *Canada* 73°13N 78°34W **69** C16
Byrd, C. *Antarctica* 69°38S 76°7W **5** C17
Byrock *Australia* 30°40S 146°27E **63** E4
Byron, C. *Australia* 28°43S 153°38E **63** D5
Byron Bay *Australia* 28°43S 153°37E **63** D5
Byrranga, Gory *Russia* 75°0N 100°0E **29** B11
Byrranga Mts. = Byrranga, Gory
 Russia 75°0N 100°0E **29** B11
Byske *Sweden* 64°57N 21°11E **8** D19
Byskeälven → *Sweden* 64°57N 21°13E **8** D19
Bytom *Poland* 50°25N 18°54E **17** C10
Bytów *Poland* 54°10N 17°30E **17** A9
Byumba *Rwanda* 1°35S 30°4E **54** C3

C

C.W. McConaughy, L.
 U.S.A. 41°14N 101°40W **80** E3
Ca → *Vietnam* 18°45N 105°45E **38** C5
Ca Mau *Vietnam* 9°7N 105°8E **39** H5
Ca Mau, Mui *Vietnam* 8°38N 104°44E **39** H5
Ca Na *Vietnam* 11°20N 108°54E **39** G7
Caacupé *Paraguay* 25°23S 57°5W **94** B4
Caaguazú □ *Paraguay* 26°5S 55°31W **95** B4
Caála *Angola* 12°46S 15°30E **53** G3
Caamaño Sd. *Canada* 52°55N 129°25W **70** C3
Caazapá *Paraguay* 26°8S 56°19W **94** B4
Caazapá □ *Paraguay* 26°10S 56°0W **95** B4
Caballeria, C. de *Spain* 40°5N 4°5E **24** A11
Cabanatuan *Phil.* 15°30N 120°58E **37** A6
Cabano *Canada* 47°40N 68°56W **73** C6
Cabazon *U.S.A.* 33°55N 116°47W **79** M10
Cabedelo *Brazil* 7°0S 34°50W **93** E12
Cabildo *Chile* 32°30S 71°5W **94** C1
Cabimas *Venezuela* 10°23N 71°25W **92** A4
Cabinda *Angola* 5°33S 12°11E **52** F2
Cabinda □ *Angola* 5°0S 12°30E **52** F2
Cabinet Mts. *U.S.A.* 48°10N 115°49W **76** B6
Cabo Blanco *Argentina* 47°15S 65°47W **96** F3
Cabo Frio *Brazil* 22°51S 42°3W **95** A7
Cabo Pantoja *Peru* 1°0S 75°10W **92** D3
Cabo San Lucas *Mexico* 22°53N 109°54W **86** C3
Cabo Verde = Cape Verde Is. ■
 Atl. Oc. 16°0N 24°0W **50** b
Cabonga, Réservoir
 Canada 47°20N 76°40W **72** C4
Cabool *U.S.A.* 37°7N 92°6W **80** G8
Caboolture *Australia* 27°5S 152°58E **63** D5
Cabora Bassa Dam = Cahora
 Bassa, Lago de *Mozam.* 15°20S 32°50E **55** F3
Caborca *Mexico* 30°37N 112°6W **86** A2
Cabot, Mt. *U.S.A.* 44°30N 71°25W **83** B13

Cabot Hd. *Canada* 45°14N 81°17W **82 A3**
Cabot Str. *Canada* 47°15N 59°40W **73 C8**
Cabra *Spain* 37°30N 4°28W **21 D3**
Cabrera *Spain* 39°8N 2°57E **24 B9**
Cabri *Canada* 50°35N 108°25W **71 C7**
Cabriel → *Spain* 39°14N 1°3W **21 C5**
Caçador *Brazil* 26°47S 51°0W **95 B5**
Caçapava do Sul *Brazil* 30°30S 53°30W **95 C5**
Cáceres *Brazil* 16°5S 57°40W **92 G7**
Cáceres *Spain* 39°26N 6°23W **21 C2**
Cache Bay *Canada* 46°22N 80°0W **72 C4**
Cache Cr. → *U.S.A.* 38°42N 121°42W **78 G5**
Cache Creek *Canada* 50°48N 121°19W **70 C4**
Cachi *Argentina* 25°5S 66°10W **94 B2**
Cachimbo, Serra do
 Brazil 9°30S 55°30W **93 E7**
Cachinal de la Sierra
 Chile 24°58S 69°32W **94 A2**
Cachoeira *Brazil* 12°30S 39°0W **93 F11**
Cachoeira do Sul *Brazil* 30°3S 52°53W **95 C5**
Cachoeiro de Itapemirim
 Brazil 20°51S 41°7W **95 A7**
Cacoal *Brazil* 11°32S 61°18W **92 E6**
Cacólo *Angola* 10°9S 19°21E **52 G3**
Caconda *Angola* 13°48S 15°8E **53 G3**
Caddo *U.S.A.* 34°7N 96°16W **84 D6**
Cader Idris *U.K.* 52°42N 3°53W **13 E4**
Cadereyta de Jiménez
 Mexico 25°36N 100°0W **86 B5**
Cadibarrawirracanna, L.
 Australia 28°52S 135°27E **63 D2**
Cadillac *U.S.A.* 44°15N 85°24W **81 C11**
Cadiz *Phil.* 10°57N 123°15E **37 B6**
Cádiz *Spain* 36°30N 6°20W **21 D2**
Cadiz *Calif., U.S.A.* 34°30N 115°28W **79 L11**
Cadiz *Ohio, U.S.A.* 40°22N 81°0W **82 F4**
Cádiz, G. de *Spain* 36°40N 7°0W **21 D2**
Cadiz L. *U.S.A.* 34°18N 115°24W **77 J6**
Cadney Park *Australia* 27°55S 134°3E **63 D1**
Cadomin *Canada* 53°2N 117°20W **70 C5**
Cadotte Lake *Canada* 56°26N 116°23W **70 B5**
Cadoux *Australia* 30°46S 117°7E **61 F2**
Caen *France* 49°10N 0°22W **20 B3**
Caernarfon *U.K.* 53°8N 4°16W **12 D3**
Caernarfon B. *U.K.* 53°4N 4°40W **12 D3**
Caernarvon = Caernarfon
 U.K. 53°8N 4°16W **12 D3**
Caerphilly *U.K.* 51°35N 3°13W **13 F4**
Caerphilly □ *U.K.* 51°37N 3°12W **13 F4**
Caesarea *Israel* 32°30N 34°53E **46 C3**
Caetité *Brazil* 13°50S 42°32W **93 F10**
Cafayate *Argentina* 26°2S 66°0W **94 B2**
Cafu *Angola* 16°30S 15°8E **56 B2**
Cagayan de Oro *Phil.* 8°30N 124°40E **37 C6**
Cagayan Is. *Phil.* 9°40N 121°16E **37 C5**
Cágliari *Italy* 39°13N 9°7E **22 E3**
Cágliari, G. di *Italy* 39°8N 9°11E **22 E3**
Caguán → *Colombia* 0°8S 74°18W **92 D4**
Caguas *Puerto Rico* 18°14N 66°2W **89 d**
Caha Mts. *Ireland* 51°45N 9°40W **10 E2**
Cahama *Angola* 16°17S 14°19E **56 B1**
Caher *Ireland* 52°22N 7°56W **10 D4**
Cahersiveen *Ireland* 51°56N 10°14W **10 E1**
Cahora Bassa, Lago de
 Mozam. 15°20S 32°50E **55 F3**
Cahore Pt. *Ireland* 52°33N 6°12W **10 D5**
Cahors *France* 44°27N 1°27E **20 D4**
Cahul *Moldova* 45°50N 28°15E **17 F15**
Cai Bau, Dao *Vietnam* 21°10N 107°27E **38 B6**
Cai Nuoc *Vietnam* 8°56N 105°1E **39 H5**
Caia *Mozam.* 17°51S 35°24E **55 F4**
Caianda *Angola* 11°2S 23°31E **55 E1**
Caibarién *Cuba* 22°30N 79°30W **88 B4**
Caicara *Venezuela* 7°38N 66°10W **92 B5**
Caicó *Brazil* 6°20S 37°0W **93 E11**
Caicos Is. *Turks & Caicos* 21°40N 71°40W **89 B5**
Caicos Passage *W. Indies* 22°45N 72°45W **89 B5**
Caiguna *Australia* 32°16S 125°29E **61 F4**
Caird Coast *Antarctica* 75°0S 25°0W **5 D1**
Cairn Gorm *U.K.* 57°7N 3°39W **11 D5**
Cairngorm Mts. *U.K.* 57°6N 3°42W **11 D5**
Cairngorms △ *U.K.* 57°10N 3°50W **11 D5**
Cairnryan *U.K.* 54°59N 5°1W **11 G3**
Cairns *Australia* 16°57S 145°45E **62 B4**
Cairns L. *Canada* 51°42N 94°30W **71 C10**
Cairo = El Qâhira *Egypt* 30°2N 31°13E **51 B12**
Cairo *Ga., U.S.A.* 30°52N 84°13W **85 F12**
Cairo *Ill., U.S.A.* 37°0N 89°11W **80 G9**
Cairo *N.Y., U.S.A.* 42°18N 74°0W **83 D10**
Caiseal = Cashel *Ireland* 52°30N 7°53W **10 D4**
Caisleán an Bharraigh = Castlebar
 Ireland 53°52N 9°18W **10 C2**
Caithness *U.K.* 58°25N 3°35W **11 C5**
Caithness, Ord of *U.K.* 58°8N 3°36W **11 C5**
Caja de Muertos, I.
 Puerto Rico 17°54N 66°32W **89 d**
Cajamarca *Peru* 7°5S 78°28W **92 E3**
Cajazeiras *Brazil* 6°52S 38°30W **93 E11**
Cala d'Or *Spain* 39°23N 3°14E **24 B10**
Cala en Porter *Spain* 39°52N 4°8E **24 B11**
Cala Figuera *Spain* 39°20N 3°10E **24 B10**
Cala Figuera, C. de *Spain* 39°27N 2°31E **24 B9**
Cala Forcat *Spain* 40°0N 3°47E **24 B10**
Cala Major *Spain* 39°33N 2°37E **24 B9**
Cala Mezquida = Sa Mesquida
 Spain 39°55N 4°16E **24 B11**
Cala Millor *Spain* 39°35N 3°22E **24 B10**
Cala Murada *Spain* 39°27N 3°17E **24 B10**
Cala Ratjada *Spain* 39°43N 3°27E **24 B10**
Cala Santa Galdana
 Spain 39°56N 3°58E **24 B10**
Calabar *Nigeria* 4°57N 8°20E **50 H7**
Calabogie *Canada* 45°18N 76°43W **83 A8**
Calabozo *Venezuela* 9°0N 67°28W **92 B5**
Calábria □ *Italy* 39°0N 16°30E **22 E7**
Calahorra *Spain* 42°18N 1°59W **21 A5**
Calais *France* 50°57N 1°56E **20 A4**
Calais *U.S.A.* 45°11N 67°17W **81 C20**

Calakmul → *Mexico* 18°14N 89°48W **87 D7**
Calalaste, Cord. de
 Argentina 25°0S 67°0W **94 B2**
Calama *Brazil* 8°0S 62°50W **92 E6**
Calama *Chile* 22°30S 68°55W **94 A2**
Calamar *Colombia* 10°15N 74°55W **92 A4**
Calamian Group *Phil.* 11°50N 119°55E **37 B5**
Calamocha *Spain* 40°50N 1°17W **21 B5**
Calang *Indonesia* 4°37N 95°37E **36 D1**
Calapan *Phil.* 13°25N 121°7E **37 B6**
Călăraşi *Romania* 44°12N 27°20E **17 F14**
Calatayud *Spain* 41°20N 1°40W **21 B5**
Calauag *Phil.* 13°55N 122°15E **37 B6**
Calavite, C. *Phil.* 13°26N 120°20E **37 B6**
Calbayog *Phil.* 12°4N 124°38E **37 B6**
Calca *Peru* 13°22S 72°0W **92 F4**
Calcasieu L. *U.S.A.* 29°55N 93°18W **84 G8**
Calcium *U.S.A.* 44°1N 75°50W **83 B9**
Calcutta = Kolkata
 India 22°34N 88°21E **43 H13**
Calcutta *U.S.A.* 40°40N 80°34W **82 F4**
Caldas da Rainha *Portugal* 39°24N 9°8W **21 C1**
Calder → *U.K.* 53°44N 1°22W **12 D6**
Caldera *Chile* 27°5S 70°55W **94 B1**
Caldera de Taburiente △
 Canary Is. 28°43N 17°52W **24 F2**
Caldwell *Idaho, U.S.A.* 43°40N 116°41W **76 E5**
Caldwell *Kans., U.S.A.* 37°2N 97°37W **80 G5**
Caldwell *Tex., U.S.A.* 30°32N 96°42W **84 F6**
Caledon *Canada* 43°51N 79°51W **82 C5**
Caledon *S. Africa* 34°14S 19°26E **56 E2**
Caledon → *S. Africa* 30°31S 26°5E **56 E4**
Caledon B. *Australia* 12°45S 137°0E **62 A2**
Caledonia *Canada* 43°7N 79°58W **82 C5**
Caledonia *U.S.A.* 42°58N 77°51W **82 D7**
Calella *Angola* 16°0S 15°44E **56 B2**
Calen *Australia* 20°56S 148°48E **62 b**
Caletones *Chile* 34°6S 70°27W **94 C1**
Calexico *U.S.A.* 32°40N 115°30W **79 N11**
Calf of Man *I. of Man* 54°3N 4°48W **12 C3**
Calgary *Canada* 51°0N 114°10W **70 C6**
Calheta *Madeira* 32°44N 17°11W **24 D2**
Calhoun *U.S.A.* 34°30N 84°57W **85 D12**
Cali *Colombia* 3°25N 76°35W **92 C3**
Calicut *India* 11°15N 75°43E **40 P9**
Caliente *U.S.A.* 37°37N 114°31W **77 H6**
California *Mo., U.S.A.* 38°38N 92°34W **80 F7**
California *Pa., U.S.A.* 40°4N 79°54W **82 F5**
California □ *U.S.A.* 37°30N 119°30W **78 H7**
California, Baja, T.N. = Baja
 California □ *Mexico* 30°0N 115°0W **86 B2**
California, Baja, T.S. = Baja
 California Sur □
 Mexico 25°50N 111°50W **86 B2**
California, G. de *Mexico* 27°0N 111°0W **86 B2**
California City *U.S.A.* 35°10N 117°55W **79 K9**
California Hot Springs
 U.S.A. 35°51N 118°41W **79 K8**
Calilegua △ *Argentina* 25°36S 64°50W **94 B3**
Calingasta *Argentina* 31°15S 69°30W **94 C2**
Calipatria *U.S.A.* 33°8N 115°31W **79 M11**
Calistoga *U.S.A.* 38°35N 122°35W **78 G4**
Calitzdorp *S. Africa* 33°33S 21°42E **56 E3**
Callabonna, L. *Australia* 29°40S 140°5E **63 D3**
Callan *Ireland* 52°32N 7°24W **10 D4**
Callander *U.K.* 56°15N 4°13W **11 E4**
Callao *Peru* 12°3S 77°8W **92 F3**
Callicoon *U.S.A.* 41°46N 75°3W **83 E9**
Calling Lake *Canada* 55°15N 113°12W **70 B6**
Calliope *Australia* 24°0S 151°16E **62 C5**
Calma, Costa de la *Spain* 39°28N 2°26E **24 B9**
Calne *U.K.* 51°26N 2°0W **13 F6**
Calola *Angola* 16°25S 17°48E **56 B2**
Caloundra *Australia* 26°45S 153°10E **63 D5**
Calpella *U.S.A.* 39°14N 123°12W **78 F3**
Calpine *U.S.A.* 39°40N 120°27W **78 F6**
Calstock *Canada* 49°47N 84°9W **72 C3**
Caltagirone *Italy* 37°14N 14°31E **22 F6**
Caltanissetta *Italy* 37°29N 14°4E **22 F6**
Calulo *Angola* 10°1S 14°56E **52 G2**
Calulu *Angola* 10°1S 14°56E **52 G2**
Calvert → *Australia* 16°17S 137°44E **62 B2**
Calvert I. *Canada* 51°30N 128°0W **70 C3**
Calvert Ra. *Australia* 24°0S 122°30E **60 D3**
Calvi *France* 42°34N 8°45E **20 E8**
Calvià *Spain* 39°34N 2°31E **24 B9**
Calvillo *Mexico* 21°51N 102°43W **86 C4**
Calvinia *S. Africa* 31°28S 19°45E **56 E2**
Calwa *U.S.A.* 36°42N 119°46W **78 J7**
Cam → *U.K.* 52°21N 0°16E **13 E8**
Cam Lam *Vietnam* 11°54N 109°10E **39 G7**
Cam Pha *Vietnam* 21°7N 107°18E **38 B6**
Cam Ranh *Vietnam* 11°54N 109°12E **39 G7**
Cam Xuyen *Vietnam* 18°15N 106°0E **38 C6**
Camabatela *Angola* 8°20S 15°26E **52 F3**
Camacha *Madeira* 32°41N 16°49W **24 D3**
Camacupa *Angola* 11°58S 17°22E **53 G3**
Camagüey *Cuba* 21°20N 77°55W **88 B4**
Camaná *Peru* 16°30S 72°50W **92 G4**
Camanche Res. *U.S.A.* 38°14N 121°1W **78 G6**
Camaquã *Brazil* 30°51S 51°49W **95 C5**
Camaquã → *Brazil* 31°17S 51°47W **95 C5**
Câmara de Lobos
 Madeira 32°39N 16°59W **24 D3**
Camargo *Mexico* 26°19N 98°50W **87 B5**
Camarón, C. *Honduras* 16°0N 85°5W **88 C2**
Camarones *Argentina* 44°50S 65°40W **96 E3**
Camas *U.S.A.* 45°35N 122°24W **78 E4**
Camas Valley *U.S.A.* 43°2N 123°40W **76 E2**
Camballin *Australia* 17°59S 124°12E **60 C3**
Cambará *Brazil* 23°2S 50°5W **95 A5**
Cambay = Khambhat
 India 22°23N 72°33E **42 H5**
Cambay, G. of = Khambhat, G. of
 India 20°45N 72°30E **40 J8**
Cambodia ■ *Asia* 12°15N 105°0E **38 F5**
Camborne *U.K.* 50°12N 5°19W **13 G2**
Cambrai *France* 50°11N 3°14E **20 A5**

Cambria *U.S.A.* 35°34N 121°5W **78 K5**
Cambrian Mts. *U.K.* 52°3N 3°57W **13 E4**
Cambridge *Canada* 43°23N 80°15W **82 C4**
Cambridge *Jamaica* 18°18N 77°54W **88 a**
Cambridge *N.Z.* 37°54S 175°29E **59 B5**
Cambridge *U.K.* 52°12N 0°8E **13 E8**
Cambridge *Mass., U.S.A.* 42°23N 71°7W **83 D13**
Cambridge *Minn., U.S.A.* 45°34N 93°13W **80 C7**
Cambridge *N.Y., U.S.A.* 43°2N 73°22W **83 C11**
Cambridge *Nebr.,
 U.S.A.* 40°17N 100°10W **80 E3**
Cambridge *Ohio, U.S.A.* 40°2N 81°35W **82 F3**
Cambridge Bay *Canada* 69°10N 105°0W **68 D11**
Cambridge G. *Australia* 14°55S 128°15E **60 B4**
Cambridge Springs
 U.S.A. 41°48N 80°4W **82 E4**
Cambridgeshire □ *U.K.* 52°25N 0°7W **13 E7**
Cambuci *Brazil* 21°35S 41°55W **95 A7**
Cambundi-Catembo
 Angola 10°10S 17°35E **52 G3**
Camden *Australia* 34°1S 150°43E **63 B5**
Camden *Ala., U.S.A.* 31°59N 87°17W **85 F11**
Camden *Ark., U.S.A.* 33°35N 92°50W **84 E8**
Camden *Maine, U.S.A.* 44°13N 69°4W **81 C19**
Camden *N.J., U.S.A.* 39°55N 75°7W **83 G9**
Camden *N.Y., U.S.A.* 43°20N 75°45W **83 C9**
Camden *S.C., U.S.A.* 34°16N 80°36W **85 D14**
Camden Sd. *Australia* 15°27S 124°25E **60 C3**
Camdenton *U.S.A.* 38°1N 92°45W **80 F7**
Camelford *U.K.* 50°37N 4°42W **13 G3**
Cameron *Ariz., U.S.A.* 35°53N 111°25W **77 J8**
Cameron *La., U.S.A.* 29°48N 93°20W **84 G8**
Cameron *Mo., U.S.A.* 39°44N 94°14W **80 F6**
Cameron *Tex., U.S.A.* 30°51N 96°59W **84 F6**
Cameron Highlands
 Malaysia 4°27N 101°22E **39 K3**
Cameron Hills *Canada* 59°48N 118°0W **70 B5**
Cameroon ■ *Africa* 6°0N 12°30E **51 G7**
Cameroun, Mt. *Cameroon* 4°13N 9°10E **52 D1**
Cametá *Brazil* 2°12S 49°30W **93 D9**
Camiguin I. *Phil.* 18°56N 121°55E **37 C6**
Camilla *U.S.A.* 31°14N 84°12W **85 F12**
Caminha *Portugal* 41°50N 8°50W **21 B1**
Camino *U.S.A.* 38°44N 120°41W **78 G6**
Cammal *U.S.A.* 41°24N 77°28W **82 E7**
Camocim *Brazil* 2°55S 40°50W **93 D10**
Camooweal *Australia* 19°56S 138°7E **62 B2**
Camooweal Caves △
 Australia 20°1S 138°11E **62 C2**
Camopi *Fr. Guiana* 3°12N 52°17W **93 C8**
Camp Hill *U.S.A.* 40°14N 76°55W **82 F8**
Camp Nelson *U.S.A.* 36°8N 118°39W **79 J8**
Camp Pendleton
 U.S.A. 33°13N 117°24W **79 M9**
Camp Verde *U.S.A.* 34°34N 111°51W **77 J8**
Camp Wood *U.S.A.* 29°40N 100°1W **84 G4**
Campana *Argentina* 34°10S 58°55W **94 C4**
Campana, I. *Chile* 48°20S 75°20W **96 F1**
Campanário *Madeira* 32°39N 17°2W **24 D2**
Campánia □ *Italy* 41°0N 14°30E **22 D6**
Campbell *S. Africa* 28°48S 23°44E **56 D3**
Campbell *Calif., U.S.A.* 37°17N 121°57W **78 H5**
Campbell *Ohio, U.S.A.* 41°5N 80°37W **82 E4**
Campbell I. *Pac. Oc.* 52°30S 169°0E **64 N8**
Campbell L. *Canada* 63°14N 106°55W **71 A7**
Campbell Plateau *S. Ocean* 50°0S 170°0E **5 A11**
Campbell River *Canada* 50°5N 125°20W **70 C3**
Campbellford *Canada* 44°18N 77°48W **82 B7**
Campbellpur *Pakistan* 33°46N 72°26E **42 C5**
Campbellsville *U.S.A.* 37°21N 85°20W **81 G11**
Campbellton *Canada* 47°57N 66°43W **73 C6**
Campbelltown *Australia* 34°4S 150°49E **63 B5**
Campbeltown *U.K.* 55°26N 5°36W **11 F3**
Campeche *Mexico* 19°51N 90°32W **87 D6**
Campeche □ *Mexico* 19°0N 90°30W **87 D6**
Campeche, Golfo de
 Mexico 19°30N 93°0W **87 D6**
Camperdown *Australia* 38°14S 143°9E **63 F3**
Camperville *Canada* 51°59N 100°9W **71 C8**
Câmpina *Romania* 45°10N 25°45E **17 F13**
Campina Grande *Brazil* 7°20S 35°47W **93 E11**
Campinas *Brazil* 22°50S 47°0W **95 A6**
Campo Grande *Brazil* 20°25S 54°40W **93 H8**
Campo Maior *Brazil* 4°50S 42°12W **93 D10**
Campo Mourão *Brazil* 24°3S 52°22W **95 A5**
Campobasso *Italy* 41°34N 14°39E **22 D6**
Campos *Brazil* 21°50S 41°20W **95 A7**
Campos *Spain* 39°26N 3°1E **24 B10**
Campos Belos *Brazil* 13°10S 47°3W **93 F9**
Campos Novos *Brazil* 27°21S 51°50W **95 B5**
Camptonville *U.S.A.* 39°27N 121°3W **78 F5**
Camrose *Canada* 53°0N 112°50W **70 C6**
Camsell Portage
 Canada 59°37N 109°15W **71 B7**
Can *Turkey* 40°2N 27°3E **23 D12**
Can Clavo *Spain* 38°57N 1°27E **24 C7**
Can Creu *Spain* 38°58N 1°28E **24 C7**
Can Gio *Vietnam* 10°25N 106°58E **39 G6**
Can Pastilla *Spain* 39°32N 2°42E **24 B9**
Can Tho *Vietnam* 10°2N 105°46E **39 G5**
Canaan *U.S.A.* 42°2N 73°20W **83 D11**
Canada ■ *N. Amer.* 60°0N 100°0W **68 C10**
Canada Abyssal Plain
 Arctic 80°0N 140°0W **4 B18**
Canada Basin *Arctic* 80°0N 145°0W **4 B18**
Cañada de Gómez
 Argentina 32°40S 61°30W **94 C3**
Canadian *U.S.A.* 35°55N 100°23W **84 D4**
Canadian → *U.S.A.* 35°28N 95°3W **84 D7**
Canadian Shield *Canada* 53°0N 75°0W **66 D12**
Canajoharie *U.S.A.* 42°54N 74°35W **83 D10**
Çanakkale *Turkey* 40°8N 26°24E **23 D12**
Çanakkale Boğazı
 Turkey 40°17N 26°32E **23 D12**
Canal Flats *Canada* 50°10N 115°48W **70 C5**
Canalejas *Argentina* 35°15S 66°34W **94 D2**

Canals *Argentina* 33°35S 62°53W **94 C3**
Canandaigua *U.S.A.* 42°54N 77°17W **82 D7**
Canandaigua L. *U.S.A.* 42°47N 77°19W **82 D7**
Cananea *Mexico* 31°0N 110°18W **86 A2**
Canarias, Is. *Atl. Oc.* 28°30N 16°0W **24 F4**
Canaries *St. Lucia* 13°55N 61°4W **89 f**
Canarreos, Arch. de los
 Cuba 21°35N 81°40W **88 B3**
Canary Is. = Canarias, Is.
 Atl. Oc. 28°30N 16°0W **24 F4**
Canaseraga *U.S.A.* 42°27N 77°45W **82 D7**
Canatlán *Mexico* 24°31N 104°47W **86 C4**
Canaveral, C. *U.S.A.* 28°27N 80°32W **85 G14**
Canaveral △ *U.S.A.* 28°28N 80°34W **85 G14**
Canavieiras *Brazil* 15°39S 39°0W **93 G11**
Canberra *Australia* 35°15S 149°8E **63 F4**
Canby *Calif., U.S.A.* 41°27N 120°52W **76 F3**
Canby *Minn., U.S.A.* 44°43N 96°16W **80 C5**
Canby *Oreg., U.S.A.* 45°16N 122°42W **78 E4**
Cancún *Mexico* 21°8N 86°44W **87 C7**
Candelaria *Argentina* 27°29S 55°44W **95 B4**
Candelaria *Canary Is.* 28°22N 16°22W **24 F3**
Candelo *Australia* 36°47S 149°43E **63 F4**
Candi Dasa *Indonesia* 8°30S 115°34E **37 J18**
Candia = Iraklio *Greece* 35°20N 25°12E **25 D7**
Candle L. *Canada* 53°50N 105°18W **71 C7**
Candlemas I. *Antarctica* 57°3S 26°40W **5 B1**
Cando *U.S.A.* 48°32N 99°12W **80 A4**
Canea = Chania *Greece* 35°30N 24°4E **25 D6**
Canelones *Uruguay* 34°32S 56°17W **95 C4**
Cañete *Chile* 37°50S 73°30W **94 D1**
Cangas del Narcea *Spain* 43°10N 6°32W **21 A2**
Canguaretama *Brazil* 6°20S 35°5W **93 E11**
Canguçu *Brazil* 31°22S 52°43W **95 C5**
Canguçu, Serra do
 Brazil 31°20S 52°40W **95 C5**
Cangzhou *China* 38°19N 116°52E **34 E9**
Caniapiscau → *Canada* 56°40N 69°30W **73 A6**
Caniapiscau, L. *Canada* 54°10N 69°55W **73 B6**
Canicattì *Italy* 37°21N 13°51E **22 F5**
Canim Lake *Canada* 51°47N 120°54W **70 C4**
Canindeyu □ *Paraguay* 24°10S 55°0W **95 A5**
Canisteo *U.S.A.* 42°16N 77°36W **82 D7**
Canisteo → *U.S.A.* 42°7N 77°8W **82 D7**
Cañitas de Felipe Pescador
 Mexico 23°36N 102°43W **86 C4**
Çankırı *Turkey* 40°40N 33°37E **19 F5**
Cankuzo *Burundi* 3°10S 30°31E **54 C3**
Canmore *Canada* 51°7N 115°18W **70 C5**
Cann River *Australia* 37°35S 149°7E **63 F4**
Canna *U.K.* 57°3N 6°33W **11 D2**
Cannanore *India* 11°53N 75°27E **40 P9**
Cannes *France* 43°32N 7°1E **20 E7**
Canning Town = Port Canning
 India 22°23N 88°40E **43 H13**
Cannington *Canada* 44°20N 79°2W **82 B5**
Cannock *U.K.* 52°41N 2°1W **13 E5**
Cannonball → *U.S.A.* 46°26N 100°35W **80 B3**
Cannonvale *Australia* 20°17S 148°43E **62 b**
Canoas *Brazil* 29°56S 51°11W **95 B5**
Canoe L. *Canada* 55°10N 108°15W **71 B7**
Cañon City *U.S.A.* 38°27N 105°14W **76 G11**
Cañón de Río Blanco △
 Mexico 18°43N 97°15W **87 D5**
Cañón del Sumidero △
 Mexico 16°50N 93°0W **87 D6**
Canonniers Pt. *Mauritius* 20°2S 57°32E **53 d**
Canora *Canada* 51°40N 102°30W **71 C8**
Canowindra *Australia* 33°35S 148°38E **63 E4**
Canso *Canada* 45°20N 61°0W **73 C7**
Cantabria □ *Spain* 43°10N 4°0W **21 A4**
Cantabrian Mts. = Cantábrica,
 Cordillera *Spain* 43°0N 5°10W **21 A3**
Cantábrica, Cordillera
 Spain 43°0N 5°10W **21 A3**
Cantal, Plomb du *France* 45°3N 2°45E **20 D5**
Canterbury *Australia* 25°23S 141°53E **62 D3**
Canterbury *U.K.* 51°16N 1°6E **13 F9**
Canterbury Bight *N.Z.* 44°16S 171°55E **59 F3**
Canterbury Plains *N.Z.* 43°55S 171°22E **59 E3**
Cantil *U.S.A.* 35°18N 117°58W **79 K9**
Canton = Guangzhou
 China 23°6N 113°13E **33 D6**
Canton *Ga., U.S.A.* 34°14N 84°29W **85 D12**
Canton *Ill., U.S.A.* 40°33N 90°2W **80 E8**
Canton *Miss., U.S.A.* 32°37N 90°2W **85 E9**
Canton *Mo., U.S.A.* 40°8N 91°32W **80 E8**
Canton *N.Y., U.S.A.* 44°36N 75°10W **83 B9**
Canton *Ohio, U.S.A.* 40°48N 81°23W **82 F3**
Canton *Pa., U.S.A.* 41°39N 76°51W **82 E8**
Canton *S. Dak., U.S.A.* 43°18N 96°35W **80 D5**
Canton L. *U.S.A.* 36°6N 98°35W **84 C5**
Canudos *Brazil* 7°13S 58°5W **92 E7**
Canumã → *Brazil* 3°55S 59°10W **92 D7**
Canutama *Brazil* 6°30S 64°20W **92 E6**
Canutillo *U.S.A.* 31°55N 106°36W **84 F1**
Canvey *U.K.* 51°31N 0°37E **13 F8**
Canyon *U.S.A.* 34°59N 101°55W **84 D4**
Canyon De Chelly △
 U.S.A. 36°10N 109°20W **77 H9**
Canyonlands △ *U.S.A.* 38°15N 110°0W **77 G9**
Canyons of the Ancients △
 U.S.A. 37°30N 108°55W **77 H9**
Canyonville *U.S.A.* 42°56N 123°17W **76 E2**
Cao Bang *Vietnam* 22°40N 106°15E **38 A6**
Cao He → *China* 40°10N 124°32E **35 D13**
Cao Lanh *Vietnam* 10°27N 105°38E **39 G5**
Cao Xian *China* 34°50N 115°35E **34 G8**
Cap-aux-Meules *Canada* 47°23N 61°52W **73 C7**
Cap-Chat *Canada* 49°6N 66°40W **73 C6**
Cap-de-la-Madeleine
 Canada 46°22N 72°31W **72 C5**
Cap-Haïtien *Haiti* 19°40N 72°20W **89 C5**
Cap Pt. *St. Lucia* 14°7N 60°57W **89 f**
Capac *U.S.A.* 43°1N 82°56W **82 D2**
Capanaparo → *Venezuela* 7°1N 67°7W **92 B5**

Cape → *Australia* 20°59S 146°51E **62 C4**
Cape Arid △ *Australia* 33°58S 123°13E **61 F3**
Cape Barren I. *Australia* 40°25S 148°15E **63 G4**
Cape Breton Highlands
 Canada 46°50N 60°40W **73 C7**
Cape Breton I. *Canada* 46°0N 60°30W **73 C7**
Cape Charles *U.S.A.* 37°16N 76°1W **81 G15**
Cape Coast *Ghana* 5°5N 1°15W **50 G5**
Cape Cod △ *U.S.A.* 41°56N 70°6W **81 E18**
Cape Coral *U.S.A.* 26°33N 81°57W **85 H14**
Cape Crawford *Australia* 16°41S 135°43E **62 B2**
Cape Dorset = Kinngait
 Canada 64°14N 76°32W **69 E16**
Cape Fear → *U.S.A.* 33°53N 78°1W **85 D15**
Cape Girardeau *U.S.A.* 37°19N 89°32W **80 G9**
Cape Hatteras △
 U.S.A. 35°30N 75°28W **85 D17**
Cape Hillsborough △
 Australia 20°54S 149°2E **62 b**
Cape Le Grand △
 Australia 33°54S 122°26E **61 F3**
Cape Lookout △
 U.S.A. 35°45N 76°25W **85 D16**
Cape May *U.S.A.* 38°56N 74°56W **81 F16**
Cape May Point *U.S.A.* 38°56N 74°58W **81 F16**
Cape Melville △
 Australia 14°26S 144°28E **62 A3**
Cape Range △ *Australia* 22°3S 114°0E **60 D1**
Cape St. George *Canada* 48°28N 59°14W **73 C8**
Cape Tormentine *Canada* 46°8N 63°47W **73 C7**
Cape Town *S. Africa* 33°55S 18°22E **56 E2**
Cape Upstart △
 Australia 19°45S 147°48E **62 B4**
Cape Verde Is. ■ *Atl. Oc.* 16°0N 24°0W **50 b**
Cape Vincent *U.S.A.* 44°8N 76°20W **83 B8**
Cape York Peninsula
 Australia 12°0S 142°30E **62 A3**
Capela *Brazil* 10°30S 37°0W **93 F11**
Capella *Australia* 23°2S 148°1E **62 C4**
Capesterre-Belle-Eau
 Guadeloupe 16°4N 61°36W **88 b**
Capesterre-de-Marie-Galante
 Guadeloupe 15°53N 61°14W **88 b**
Capim → *Brazil* 1°40S 47°47W **93 D9**
Capitan *U.S.A.* 33°35N 105°35W **77 K11**
Capitán Arturo Prat
 Antarctica 63°0S 61°0W **5 C17**
Capitol Reef △ *U.S.A.* 38°15N 111°10W **77 G8**
Capitola *U.S.A.* 36°59N 121°57W **78 J5**
Capoche → *Mozam.* 15°35S 33°0E **55 F3**
Capraia *Italy* 43°2N 9°50E **20 E8**
Capreol *Canada* 46°43N 80°56W **72 C3**
Capri *Italy* 40°33N 14°14E **22 D6**
Capricorn Coast
 Australia 23°16S 150°49E **62 C5**
Capricorn Group
 Australia 23°30S 151°55E **62 C5**
Capricorn Ra. *Australia* 23°20S 116°50E **60 D2**
Caprivi Game △ *Namibia* 17°55S 22°37E **56 B3**
Caprivi Strip *Namibia* 18°0S 23°0E **56 B3**
Captains Flat *Australia* 35°35S 149°27E **63 F4**
Capulin Volcano △
 U.S.A. 36°47N 103°58W **84 C3**
Caquetá → *Colombia* 1°15S 69°15W **92 D5**
Caracal *Romania* 44°8N 24°22E **17 F13**
Caracas *Venezuela* 10°30N 66°55W **92 A5**
Caracol *Belize* 16°45N 89°6W **88 C2**
Caracol *Mato Grosso do Sul,
 Brazil* 22°18S 57°1W **94 A4**
Caracol *Piauí, Brazil* 9°15S 43°22W **93 E10**
Carajas *Brazil* 6°5S 50°23W **93 E8**
Carajás, Serra dos *Brazil* 6°0S 51°30W **93 E8**
Carangola *Brazil* 20°44S 42°5W **95 A7**
Caransebeş *Romania* 45°28N 22°18E **17 F12**
Caraquet *Canada* 47°48N 64°57W **73 C6**
Caratasca, L. de
 Honduras 15°20N 83°40W **88 C3**
Caratinga *Brazil* 19°50S 42°10W **93 G10**
Caraúbas *Brazil* 5°43S 37°33W **93 E11**
Caravaca de la Cruz *Spain* 38°8N 1°52W **21 C5**
Caravelas *Brazil* 17°45S 39°15W **93 G11**
Caraveli *Peru* 15°45S 73°25W **92 G4**
Caravelle, Presqu'île de la
 Martinique 14°46N 60°48W **88 c**
Caraz *Peru* 9°3S 77°47W **92 E3**
Carazinho *Brazil* 28°16S 52°46W **95 B5**
Carballo *Spain* 43°13N 8°41W **21 A1**
Carberry *Canada* 49°50N 99°25W **71 D9**
Carbó *Mexico* 29°42N 110°58W **86 B2**
Carbón, L. del *Argentina* 49°35S 68°21W **90 F3**
Carbonara, C. *Italy* 39°6N 9°31E **22 E3**
Carbondale *Colo.,
 U.S.A.* 39°24N 107°13W **76 G10**
Carbondale *Ill., U.S.A.* 37°44N 89°13W **80 G9**
Carbondale *Pa., U.S.A.* 41°35N 75°30W **83 E9**
Carbonear *Canada* 47°42N 53°13W **73 C9**
Carbónia *Italy* 39°10N 8°30E **22 E3**
Carcajou *Canada* 57°47N 117°6W **70 B5**
Carcarana → *Argentina* 32°27S 60°48W **94 C3**
Carcasse, C. *Haiti* 18°30N 74°28W **89 C5**
Carcassonne *France* 43°13N 2°20E **20 E5**
Carcross *Canada* 60°13N 134°45W **70 A2**
Cardamom Hills *India* 9°30N 77°15E **40 Q10**
Cardamon Mts. = Kravanh,
 Chuor Phnum
 Cambodia 12°0N 103°32E **39 G4**
Cárdenas *Cuba* 23°0N 81°30W **88 B3**
Cárdenas *San Luis Potosí,
 Mexico* 22°0N 99°38W **87 C5**
Cárdenas *Tabasco,
 Mexico* 17°59N 93°22W **87 D6**
Cardiff *U.K.* 51°29N 3°10W **13 F4**
Cardiff □ *U.K.* 51°31N 3°12W **13 F4**
Cardiff-by-the-Sea
 U.S.A. 33°1N 117°17W **79 M9**
Cardigan *U.K.* 52°5N 4°40W **13 E3**
Cardigan B. *U.K.* 52°30N 4°30W **13 E3**
Cardinal *Canada* 44°47N 75°23W **83 B9**
Cardona *Uruguay* 33°53S 57°18W **94 C4**

Cardoso, Ilha do *Brazil* 25°8S 47°58W **95** B5
Cardston *Canada* 49°15N 113°20W **70** D6
Cardwell *Australia* 18°14S 146°2E **62** B4
Careen L. *Canada* 57°0N 108°11W **71** B7
Carei *Romania* 47°40N 22°29E **17** E12
Careme = Ciremay
  Indonesia 6°55S 108°27E **37** G13
Carey *U.S.A.* 43°19N 113°57W **76** E7
Carey, L. *Australia* 29°0S 122°15E **61** E3
Carhué *Argentina* 37°10S 62°50W **94** D3
Caria *Turkey* 37°20N 28°10E **23** F13
Cariacica *Brazil* 20°16S 40°25W **93** H10
Caribbean Sea *W. Indies* 15°0N 75°0W **89** D5
Cariboo Mts. *Canada* 53°0N 121°0W **70** C4
Caribou *U.S.A.* 46°52N 68°1W **81** B19
Caribou → *Man.,*
  Canada 59°20N 94°44W **71** B10
Caribou → *N.W.T.,*
  Canada 61°27N 125°45W **70** A3
Caribou I. *Canada* 47°22N 85°49W **72** C2
Caribou Is. *Canada* 61°55N 113°15W **70** A6
Caribou L. *Man., Canada* 59°21N 96°10W **71** B9
Caribou L. *Ont., Canada* 50°25N 89°5W **72** B2
Caribou Mts. *Canada* 59°12N 115°40W **70** B5
Caribou River △ *Canada* 59°35N 96°35W **71** B9
Carichíc *Mexico* 27°56N 107°3W **86** B3
Carinda *Australia* 30°28S 147°41E **63** E4
Carinhanha *Brazil* 14°15S 44°46W **93** F10
Carinhanha → *Brazil* 14°20S 43°47W **93** F10
Carinthia = Kärnten □
  Austria 46°52N 13°30E **16** E8
Caripito *Venezuela* 10°8N 63°6W **92** A6
Carleton, Mt. *Canada* 47°23N 66°53W **73** C6
Carleton Place *Canada* 45°8N 76°9W **83** A8
Carletonville *S. Africa* 26°23S 27°22E **56** D4
Carlin *U.S.A.* 40°43N 116°7W **76** F5
Carlingford L. *U.K.* 54°3N 6°9W **10** B5
Carlinville *U.S.A.* 39°17N 89°53W **80** F9
Carlisle *U.K.* 54°54N 2°56W **12** C5
Carlisle *U.S.A.* 40°12N 77°12W **82** F7
Carlisle B. *Barbados* 13°5N 59°37W **89** g
Carlisle I. *Australia* 20°49S 149°18E **62** b
Carlos Casares *Argentina* 35°32S 61°20W **94** D3
Carlos Tejedor *Argentina* 35°25S 62°25W **94** D3
Carlow *Ireland* 52°50N 6°56W **10** D5
Carlow □ *Ireland* 52°43N 6°50W **10** D5
Carlsbad *Calif., U.S.A.* 33°10N 117°21W **79** M9
Carlsbad *N. Mex.,*
  U.S.A. 32°25N 104°14W **77** K11
Carlsbad Caverns △
  U.S.A. 32°10N 104°35W **77** K11
Carluke *U.K.* 55°45N 3°50W **11** F5
Carlyle *Canada* 49°40N 102°20W **71** D8
Carmacks *Canada* 62°5N 136°16W **68** C4
Carman *Canada* 49°30N 98°0W **71** D9
Carmarthen *U.K.* 51°52N 4°19W **13** F3
Carmarthen B. *U.K.* 51°40N 4°30W **13** F3
Carmarthenshire □ *U.K.* 51°55N 4°13W **13** F3
Carmaux *France* 44°3N 2°10E **20** D5
Carmel *U.S.A.* 41°26N 73°41W **83** E11
Carmel-by-the-Sea
  U.S.A. 36°33N 121°55W **78** J5
Carmel Valley *U.S.A.* 36°29N 121°43W **78** J5
Carmelo *Uruguay* 34°0S 58°20W **94** C4
Carmen *Paraguay* 27°13S 56°12W **95** B4
Carmen → *Mexico* 30°42N 106°29W **86** A3
Carmen, I. *Mexico* 25°57N 111°12W **86** B2
Carmen de Patagones
  Argentina 40°50S 63°0W **96** E4
Carmensa *Argentina* 35°15S 67°40W **94** D2
Carmi *Canada* 49°36N 119°8W **70** D5
Carmi *U.S.A.* 38°5N 88°10W **80** F9
Carmichael *U.S.A.* 38°38N 121°19W **78** G5
Carmila *Australia* 21°55S 149°24E **62** C4
Carmona *Costa Rica* 10°0N 85°15W **88** E2
Carmona *Spain* 37°28N 5°42W **21** D3
Carn Ban *U.K.* 57°7N 4°15W **11** D4
Carn Eige *U.K.* 57°17N 5°8W **11** D3
Carnamah *Australia* 29°41S 115°53E **61** E2
Carnarvon *Australia* 24°51S 113°42E **61** D1
Carnarvon *Canada* 45°3N 78°41W **82** A6
Carnarvon *S. Africa* 30°56S 22°8E **56** E3
Carnarvon △ *Australia* 24°54S 148°2E **62** C4
Carnarvon Ra. *Queens.,*
  Australia 25°15S 148°30E **62** D4
Carnarvon Ra. *W. Austral.,*
  Australia 25°20S 120°45E **61** E3
Carnation *U.S.A.* 47°39N 121°55W **78** C5
Carncastle *U.K.* 54°54N 5°53W **10** B6
Carndonagh *Ireland* 55°16N 7°15W **10** A4
Carnduff *Canada* 49°10N 101°50W **71** D8
Carnegie *U.S.A.* 40°24N 80°5W **82** F4
Carnegie, L. *Australia* 26°5S 122°30E **61** E3
Carnegie Ridge *Pac. Oc.* 1°0S 87°0W **65** H19
Carnic Alps = Karnische Alpen
  Europe 46°36N 13°0E **16** E7
Carniche Alpi = Karnische Alpen
  Europe 46°36N 13°0E **16** E7
Carnot *C.A.R.* 4°59N 15°56E **52** D3
Carnot, C. *Australia* 34°57S 135°38E **63** E2
Carnot B. *Australia* 17°20S 122°15E **60** C3
Carnoustie *U.K.* 56°30N 2°42W **11** E6
Carnsore Pt. *Ireland* 52°10N 6°22W **10** D5
Caro *U.S.A.* 43°29N 83°24W **81** D12
Caroga Lake *U.S.A.* 43°8N 74°28W **83** D10
Carol City *U.S.A.* 25°56N 80°14W **85** J14
Carolina *Brazil* 7°10S 47°30W **93** E9
Carolina *Puerto Rico* 18°23N 65°58W **89** d
Carolina *S. Africa* 26°5S 30°6E **57** D5
Caroline I. *Kiribati* 9°58S 150°13W **65** H12
Caroline Is. *Micronesia* 8°0N 150°0E **64** G6
Caroní → *Venezuela* 10°34N 61°23W **93** K15
Caroní → *Venezuela* 8°21N 62°43W **92** B6
Caronie = Nébrodi, Monti
  Italy 37°54N 14°35E **22** F6
Caroona *Australia* 31°24S 150°26E **63** E5
Carpathians *Europe* 49°30N 21°0E **17** D11
Carpaţii Meridionali
  Romania 45°30N 25°0E **17** F13

Carpentaria, G. of
  Australia 14°0S 139°0E **62** A2
Carpentras *France* 44°3N 5°2E **20** D6
Carpi *Italy* 44°47N 10°53E **22** B4
Carpinteria *U.S.A.* 34°24N 119°31W **79** L7
Carr Boyd Ra. *Australia* 16°15S 128°35E **60** C4
Carra, L. *Ireland* 53°41N 9°14W **10** C2
Carrabelle *U.S.A.* 29°51N 84°40W **85** G12
Carraig Mhachdire Rois =
  Carrickmacross
  Ireland 53°59N 6°43W **10** C5
Carraig na Siúire = Carrick-on-
  Suir *Ireland* 52°21N 7°24W **10** D4
Carranya ○ *Australia* 19°13S 127°46E **60** C4
Carranza, Presa V.
  Mexico 27°20N 100°50W **86** B4
Carrara *Italy* 44°5N 10°6E **20** D9
Carrauntoohill *Ireland* 52°0N 9°45W **10** D2
Carrick-on-Shannon
  Ireland 53°57N 8°5W **10** C3
Carrick-on-Suir *Ireland* 52°21N 7°24W **10** D4
Carrickfergus *U.K.* 54°43N 5°49W **10** B6
Carrickmacross *Ireland* 53°59N 6°43W **10** C5
Carrieton *Australia* 32°25S 138°31E **63** E2
Carrillo *Mexico* 26°54N 103°55W **86** B4
Carrington *U.S.A.* 47°27N 99°8W **80** B4
Carrizal Bajo *Chile* 28°5S 71°20W **94** B1
Carrizalillo *Chile* 29°5S 71°30W **94** B1
Carrizo Cr. → *U.S.A.* 36°55N 103°55W **77** H12
Carrizo Plain △ *U.S.A.* 35°11N 119°47W **78** K7
Carrizo Springs *U.S.A.* 28°31N 99°52W **84** G5
Carrizozo *U.S.A.* 33°38N 105°53W **77** K11
Carroll *U.S.A.* 42°4N 94°52W **80** D6
Carrollton *Ga., U.S.A.* 33°35N 85°5W **85** E12
Carrollton *Ill., U.S.A.* 39°18N 90°24W **80** F8
Carrollton *Ky., U.S.A.* 38°41N 85°11W **81** F11
Carrollton *Mo., U.S.A.* 39°22N 93°30W **80** F7
Carrollton *Ohio, U.S.A.* 40°34N 81°5W **82** F3
Carron → *U.K.* 57°53N 4°22W **11** D4
Carron, L. *U.K.* 57°22N 5°35W **11** D3
Carrot → *Canada* 53°50N 101°17W **71** C8
Carrot River *Canada* 53°17N 103°35W **71** C8
Carruthers *Canada* 52°52N 109°16W **71** C7
Carson *Calif., U.S.A.* 33°49N 118°16W **79** M8
Carson *N. Dak., U.S.A.* 46°25N 101°34W **80** B3
Carson → *U.S.A.* 39°45N 118°40W **78** F8
Carson City *U.S.A.* 39°10N 119°46W **78** F7
Carson Sink *U.S.A.* 39°50N 118°25W **76** G4
Cartagena *Colombia* 10°25N 75°33W **92** A3
Cartagena *Spain* 37°38N 0°59W **21** D5
Cartago *Colombia* 4°45N 75°55W **92** C3
Cartago *Costa Rica* 9°50N 83°55W **88** E3
Cartersville *U.S.A.* 34°10N 84°48W **85** D12
Carterton *N.Z.* 41°2S 175°31E **59** D5
Carthage *Tunisia* 36°52N 10°20E **22** F4
Carthage *Ill., U.S.A.* 40°25N 91°8W **80** E8
Carthage *Mo., U.S.A.* 37°11N 94°19W **80** G6
Carthage *N.Y., U.S.A.* 43°59N 75°37W **81** D16
Carthage *Tex., U.S.A.* 32°9N 94°20W **84** E7
Cartier I. *Australia* 12°31S 123°29E **60** B3
Cartwright *Canada* 53°41N 56°58W **73** B8
Caruaru *Brazil* 8°15S 35°55W **93** E11
Carúpano *Venezuela* 10°39N 63°15W **92** A6
Caruthersville *U.S.A.* 36°11N 89°39W **80** G9
Carvoeiro *Brazil* 1°30S 61°59W **92** D6
Carvoeiro, C. *Portugal* 39°21N 9°24W **21** C1
Cary *U.S.A.* 35°47N 78°46W **85** D15
Casa de Piedra *Argentina* 38°55S 67°28W **94** D2
Casa de Piedra, Embalse
  Argentina 38°55S 67°32W **94** D2
Casa Grande *U.S.A.* 32°53N 111°45W **77** K8
Casa Nova *Brazil* 9°25S 41°5W **93** E10
Casablanca *Chile* 33°20S 71°25W **94** C1
Casablanca *Morocco* 33°36N 7°36W **52** B4
Cascada de Basaseachic △
  Mexico 28°9N 108°15W **86** B3
Cascade *Seychelles* 4°39S 55°29E **53** b
Cascade *Idaho, U.S.A.* 44°31N 116°2W **76** D5
Cascade *Mont., U.S.A.* 47°16N 111°42W **76** C8
Cascade Locks *U.S.A.* 45°40N 121°54W **78** E5
Cascade Ra. *U.S.A.* 47°0N 121°30W **78** D5
Cascade Res. *U.S.A.* 44°32N 116°3W **76** D5
Cascades, Pte. des *Réunion* 21°9S 55°51E **53** c
Cascais *Portugal* 38°41N 9°25W **21** C1
Cascavel *Brazil* 24°57S 53°28W **95** A5
Cáscina *Italy* 43°41N 10°33E **22** C4
Casco B. *U.S.A.* 43°45N 70°0W **81** D19
Caserta *Italy* 41°4N 14°20E **22** D6
Casey *Antarctica* 66°0S 76°0E **5** C8
Caseyr, Raas = Asir, Ras
  Somali Rep. 11°55N 51°10E **47** E5
Cashel *Ireland* 52°30N 7°53W **10** D4
Casiguran *Phil.* 16°22N 122°7E **37** A6
Casilda *Argentina* 33°10S 61°10W **94** C3
Casino *Australia* 28°52S 153°3E **63** D5
Casiquiare → *Venezuela* 2°1N 67°7W **92** C5
Casma *Peru* 9°30S 78°20W **92** E3
Casmalia *U.S.A.* 34°50N 120°32W **79** L6
Caspe *Spain* 41°14N 0°1W **21** B5
Casper *U.S.A.* 42°51N 106°19W **76** E10
Caspian Depression
  Eurasia 47°0N 48°0E **19** E8
Caspian Sea *Eurasia* 43°0N 50°0E **19** F9
Cass City *U.S.A.* 43°36N 83°10W **82** C1
Cass Lake *U.S.A.* 47°23N 94°37W **80** B6
Cassadaga *U.S.A.* 42°20N 79°19W **82** D5
Casselman *Canada* 45°19N 75°5W **83** A9
Casselton *U.S.A.* 46°54N 97°13W **80** B5
Cassiar Mts. *Canada* 59°30N 130°30W **70** B2
Cassino *Italy* 41°30N 13°49E **22** D5
Cassville *U.S.A.* 36°41N 93°52W **80** G7
Castaic *U.S.A.* 34°30N 118°38W **79** L8
Castalia *U.S.A.* 41°24N 82°49W **82** E2
Castanhal *Brazil* 1°18S 47°55W **93** D9
Castara *Trin. & Tob.* 11°17N 60°42W **93** J16
Castellammare di Stábia
  Italy 40°42N 14°29E **22** D6
Castelli *Argentina* 36°7S 57°47W **94** D4
Castelló de la Plana *Spain* 39°58N 0°3W **21** C5

Castelo *Brazil* 20°33S 41°14W **95** A7
Castelo Branco *Portugal* 39°50N 7°31W **21** C2
Castelsarrasin *France* 44°2N 1°7E **20** E4
Castelvetrano *Italy* 37°41N 12°47E **22** F5
Castile *U.S.A.* 42°38N 78°3W **82** D6
Castilla-La Mancha □
  Spain 39°30N 3°30W **21** C4
Castilla y Leon □ *Spain* 42°0N 5°0W **21** B3
Castillos *Uruguay* 34°12S 53°52W **95** C5
Castle Dale *U.S.A.* 39°13N 111°1W **76** G8
Castle Douglas *U.K.* 54°56N 3°56W **11** G5
Castle Rock *Colo.,*
  U.S.A. 39°22N 104°51W **76** G11
Castle Rock *Wash.,*
  U.S.A. 46°17N 122°54W **78** D4
Castlebar *Ireland* 53°52N 9°18W **10** C2
Castlebay *U.K.* 56°57N 7°31W **11** E1
Castleblaney *Ireland* 54°7N 6°44W **10** B5
Castlederg *U.K.* 54°42N 7°35W **10** B4
Castleford *U.K.* 53°43N 1°21W **12** D6
Castlegar *Canada* 49°20N 117°40W **70** D5
Castlemaine *Australia* 37°2S 144°12E **63** F3
Castlemaine *Ireland* 52°10N 9°42W **10** D2
Castlepollard *Ireland* 53°41N 7°19W **10** C4
Castlerea *Ireland* 53°46N 8°29W **10** C3
Castlereagh □
  Australia 30°12S 147°32E **63** E4
Castlereagh B. *Australia* 12°10S 135°10E **62** A2
Castleton *U.S.A.* 43°37N 73°11W **83** C11
Castleton-on-Hudson
  U.S.A. 42°31N 73°45W **83** D11
Castletown *I. of Man* 54°5N 4°38W **12** C3
Castletown Bearhaven
  Ireland 51°39N 9°55W **10** E2
Castor *Canada* 52°15N 111°50W **70** C6
Castor → *Canada* 53°24N 78°58W **72** B4
Castorland *U.S.A.* 43°53N 75°31W **83** C9
Castres *France* 43°37N 2°13E **20** E5
Castricum *Neths.* 52°33N 4°40E **15** B4
Castries *St. Lucia* 14°2N 60°58W **89** f
Castro *Brazil* 24°45S 50°0W **95** A6
Castro *Chile* 42°30S 73°50W **96** E2
Castro Alves *Brazil* 12°46S 39°33W **93** F11
Castro Valley *U.S.A.* 37°41N 122°5W **78** H4
Castroville *U.S.A.* 36°46N 121°45W **78** J5
Castuera *Spain* 38°43N 5°37W **21** C3
Cat Ba, Dao *Vietnam* 20°50N 107°0E **38** B6
Cat Ba △ *Vietnam* 20°47N 107°3E **38** B6
Cat I. *Bahamas* 24°30N 75°30W **89** B4
Cat L. *Canada* 51°40N 91°50W **72** B1
Cat Lake *Canada* 51°40N 91°50W **72** B1
Cat Tien △ *Vietnam* 11°25N 107°17E **39** G6
Catacamas *Honduras* 14°54N 85°56W **88** D2
Cataguases *Brazil* 21°23S 42°39W **95** A7
Catalão *Brazil* 18°10S 47°57W **93** G9
Çatalca *Turkey* 41°8N 28°27E **23** D13
Catalina *Canada* 48°31N 53°4W **73** C9
Catalina *Chile* 25°13S 69°43W **94** B2
Catalina *U.S.A.* 32°30N 110°50W **77** K8
Catalonia = Cataluña □
  Spain 41°40N 1°15E **21** B6
Cataluña □ *Spain* 41°40N 1°15E **21** B6
Catamarca *Argentina* 28°30S 65°50W **94** B2
Catamarca □ *Argentina* 27°0S 65°50W **94** B2
Catanduanes □ *Phil.* 13°50N 124°20E **37** B6
Catanduva *Brazil* 21°5S 48°58W **95** A6
Catánia *Italy* 37°30N 15°6E **22** F6
Catanzaro *Italy* 38°54N 16°35E **22** E7
Cataratman *Phil.* 12°28N 124°35E **37** B6
Catatumbo-Bari △
  Colombia 9°3N 73°12W **89** E5
Catchacoma *Canada* 44°44N 78°19W **82** B6
Cateel *Phil.* 7°47N 126°24E **37** C7
Catembe *Mozam.* 26°0S 32°33E **57** D5
Caterham *U.K.* 51°15N 0°4W **13** F7
Cathair na Mart = Westport
  Ireland 53°48N 9°31W **10** C2
Cathair Saidhbhín = Cahersiveen
  Ireland 51°56N 10°14W **10** E1
Cathcart *S. Africa* 32°18S 27°10E **56** E4
Cathedral City *U.S.A.* 33°47N 116°28W **79** M10
Cathlamet *U.S.A.* 46°12N 123°23W **78** D3
Catlettsburg *U.S.A.* 38°25N 82°36W **81** F12
Catoche, C. *Mexico* 21°35N 87°5W **87** C7
Catriló *Argentina* 36°26S 63°24W **94** D3
Catrimani *Brazil* 0°27N 61°41W **92** C6
Catrimani → *Brazil* 0°28N 61°44W **92** C6
Catskill *U.S.A.* 42°14N 73°52W **83** D11
Catskill Mts. *U.S.A.* 42°10N 74°25W **83** D10
Catt, Mt. *Australia* 13°49S 134°23E **62** A1
Cattaraugus *U.S.A.* 42°20N 78°52W **82** D6
Catterick *U.K.* 54°23N 1°37W **12** C6
Catuala *Angola* 16°25S 19°2E **56** B2
Catuane *Mozam.* 26°48S 32°18E **57** D5
Catur *Mozam.* 13°45S 35°30E **55** E4
Caubvick, Mt. = Iberville, Mt. d'
  Canada 58°50N 63°50W **69** F19
Cauca → *Colombia* 8°54N 74°28W **92** B4
Caucaia *Brazil* 3°40S 38°35W **93** D11
Caucasus Mountains
  Eurasia 42°50N 44°0E **19** F7
Caucete *Argentina* 31°38S 68°20W **94** C2
Cauese Mts. *Mozam.* 15°14S 30°33E **55** F3
Caungula *Angola* 8°26S 18°38E **52** F3
Cauquenes *Chile* 36°0S 72°22W **94** D1
Caura → *Venezuela* 7°38N 64°53W **92** B6
Cauresi → *Mozam.* 17°8S 33°0E **55** F3
Causapscal *Canada* 48°19N 67°12W **73** C6
Cauvery → *India* 11°9N 78°52E **40** P11
Caux, Pays de *France* 49°38N 0°35E **20** B4
Cavalier *U.S.A.* 48°48N 97°37W **80** A6
Cavan *Ireland* 54°0N 7°22W **10** B4
Cavan □ *Ireland* 54°1N 7°16W **10** C4
Cave Creek *U.S.A.* 33°50N 111°57W **77** K8
Cavenagh Ra. *Australia* 26°12S 127°55E **61** E4
Cavendish *Australia* 37°31S 142°2E **63** F3
Caviana, I. *Brazil* 0°10N 50°10W **93** C8

Cavite *Phil.* 14°29N 120°54E **37** B6
Cawndilla L. *Australia* 32°30S 142°15E **63** E3
Cawnpore = Kanpur
  India 26°28N 80°20E **43** F9
Caxias *Brazil* 4°55S 43°20W **93** D10
Caxias do Sul *Brazil* 29°10S 51°10W **95** B5
Cay Sal Bank *Bahamas* 23°45N 80°0W **88** B4
Cayambe *Ecuador* 0°3N 78°8W **92** C3
Cayenne *Fr. Guiana* 5°5N 52°18W **93** B8
Cayey *Puerto Rico* 18°7N 66°10W **89** d
Cayman Brac
  Cayman Is. 19°43N 79°49W **88** C4
Cayman Is. ☑ *W. Indies* 19°40N 80°30W **88** C3
Cayman Trough
  Caribbean 19°0N 81°0W **66** H11
Cayuga *Canada* 42°59N 79°50W **82** D5
Cayuga *U.S.A.* 42°54N 76°44W **83** D8
Cayuga Heights *U.S.A.* 42°27N 76°29W **83** D8
Cayuga L. *U.S.A.* 42°41N 76°41W **83** D8
Cazenovia *U.S.A.* 42°56N 75°51W **83** D9
Cazombo *Angola* 11°54S 22°56E **53** G4
Ceanannus Mor *Ireland* 53°44N 6°53E **10** C5
Ceará = Fortaleza *Brazil* 3°45S 38°35W **93** D11
Ceará □ *Brazil* 5°0S 40°0W **93** E11
Ceará-Mirim *Brazil* 5°38S 35°25W **93** E11
Ceatharlach = Carlow
  Ireland 52°50N 6°56W **10** D5
Cébaco, I. de *Panama* 7°33N 81°9W **88** E3
Cebollar *Argentina* 29°10S 66°35W **94** B2
Cebu *Phil.* 10°18N 123°54E **37** B6
Cecil Plains *Australia* 27°30S 151°11E **63** D5
Cedar → *U.S.A.* 41°17N 91°21W **80** E8
Cedar City *U.S.A.* 37°41N 113°4W **77** H7
Cedar Creek Res. *U.S.A.* 32°11N 96°4W **84** E6
Cedar Falls *Iowa, U.S.A.* 42°32N 92°27W **80** D7
Cedar Falls *Wash.,*
  U.S.A. 47°25N 121°45W **78** C5
Cedar Key *U.S.A.* 29°8N 83°2W **85** G13
Cedar L. *Canada* 53°10N 100°0W **71** C9
Cedar Rapids *U.S.A.* 41°59N 91°40W **80** E8
Cedartown *U.S.A.* 34°1N 85°15W **85** D12
Cedarvale *Canada* 55°1N 128°22W **70** B3
Cedarville *S. Africa* 30°23S 29°3E **57** E4
Cedral *Mexico* 23°50N 100°45W **86** C4
Cedro *Brazil* 6°34S 39°3W **93** E11
Cedros, I. *Mexico* 28°12N 115°15W **86** B1
Cedros B. *Trin. & Tob.* 10°15N 62°30W **93** K15
Ceduna *Australia* 32°7S 133°46E **63** E1
Ceel Gaal *Somali Rep.* 10°58N 50°20E **47** E5
Ceel Waaq *Kenya* 2°49N 40°56E **54** B5
Ceelbuur *Somali Rep.* 3°50N 47°8E **47** G4
Ceerigaabo *Somali Rep.* 10°35N 47°20E **47** E4
Cefalù *Italy* 38°2N 14°1E **22** E6
Ceglèd *Hungary* 47°11N 19°47E **17** E10
Cekik *Indonesia* 8°12S 114°27E **37** J17
Celaque △ *Honduras* 14°30N 88°43W **88** D2
Celaya *Mexico* 20°31N 100°37W **86** C4
Celebes = Sulawesi
  Indonesia 2°0S 120°0E **37** E6
Celebes Sea *Indonesia* 3°0N 123°0E **37** D6
Celina *U.S.A.* 40°33N 84°35W **81** E11
Celje *Slovenia* 46°16N 15°18E **16** E8
Celle *Germany* 52°37N 10°4E **16** B6
Celtic Sea *Atl. Oc.* 50°9N 9°34W **14** F2
Cenderwasih, Teluk
  Indonesia 3°0S 135°20E **37** E9
Center *N. Dak., U.S.A.* 47°7N 101°18W **80** B3
Center *Tex., U.S.A.* 31°48N 94°11W **84** F7
Centerburg *U.S.A.* 40°18N 82°42W **82** F2
Centerville *Calif., U.S.A.* 36°44N 119°30W **78** J7
Centerville *Iowa, U.S.A.* 40°44N 92°52W **80** E7
Centerville *Pa., U.S.A.* 40°3N 79°59W **82** F5
Centerville *Tenn.,*
  U.S.A. 35°47N 87°28W **85** D11
Centerville *Tex., U.S.A.* 31°16N 95°59W **84** F7
Central = Tsentralnyy □
  Russia 52°0N 40°0E **28** D4
Central □ *Kenya* 0°30S 37°30E **54** C4
Central □ *Malawi* 13°30S 33°30E **55** E3
Central □ *Zambia* 14°25S 28°50E **55** E2
Central, Cordillera
  Colombia 5°0N 75°0W **92** C4
Central, Cordillera
  Costa Rica 10°10N 84°5W **88** D3
Central, Cordillera
  Dom. Rep. 19°15N 71°0W **89** C5
Central, Cordillera
  Puerto Rico 18°8N 66°35W **89** d
Central African Rep. ■
  Africa 7°0N 20°0E **51** G9
Central America *America* 12°0N 85°0W **66** H11
Central Australia ◇
  Australia 22°30S 128°30E **60** D4
Central Butte *Canada* 50°48N 106°31W **71** C7
Central City *Colo.,*
  U.S.A. 39°48N 105°31W **76** G11
Central City *Ky., U.S.A.* 37°18N 87°7W **80** G10
Central City *Nebr., U.S.A.* 41°7N 98°0W **80** E4
Central Desert ◇
  Australia 19°56S 130°46E **60** C5
Central I. *Kenya* 3°30N 36°0E **54** B4
Central Island △ *Kenya* 2°33N 36°1E **54** B4
Central Kalahari
  Botswana 22°36S 23°58E **56** C3
Central Makran Range
  Pakistan 26°30N 64°15E **40** F4
Central Pacific Basin
  Pac. Oc. 8°0N 175°0W **64** G10
Central Patricia *Canada* 51°30N 90°9W **72** B1
Central Point *U.S.A.* 42°23N 122°52W **76** E2
Central Russian Uplands
  Europe 54°0N 36°0E **6** E13
Central Siberian Plateau
  Russia 65°0N 105°0E **26** B12
Central Square *U.S.A.* 43°17N 76°9W **83** C8
Centralia *Canada* 43°17N 81°28W **82** C3
Centralia *Ill., U.S.A.* 38°32N 89°8W **80** F9
Centralia *Mo., U.S.A.* 39°13N 92°8W **80** F7

Centralia *Wash., U.S.A.* 46°43N 122°58W **78** D4
Centre de Flacq *Mauritius* 20°12S 57°43E **53** d
Centreville *N.Y., U.S.A.* 42°28N 78°14W **82** D6
Centreville *Pa., U.S.A.* 41°44N 79°45W **82** E5
Cephalonia = Kefalonia
  Greece 38°15N 20°30E **23** E9
Cepu *Indonesia* 7°9S 111°35E **37** G14
Ceram = Seram *Indonesia* 3°10S 129°0E **37** E7
Ceram Sea = Seram Sea
  Indonesia 2°30S 128°30E **37** E7
Ceredigion □ *U.K.* 52°16N 4°15E **13** E3
Ceres *Argentina* 29°55S 61°55W **94** B3
Ceres *S. Africa* 33°21S 19°18E **56** E2
Ceres *U.S.A.* 37°35N 120°57W **78** H6
Cerf *Seychelles* 4°38S 55°40E **53** b
Cerignola *Italy* 41°17N 15°53E **22** D6
Cerigo = Kythira *Greece* 36°8N 23°0E **23** F10
Çerkezköy *Turkey* 41°17N 28°0E **23** D12
Cerralvo, I. *Mexico* 24°15N 109°55W **86** C3
Cerritos *Mexico* 22°26N 100°16W **86** C4
Cerro Chato *Uruguay* 33°6S 55°8W **95** C4
Cerro Cofre de Perote △
  Mexico 19°29N 97°8W **87** D5
Cerro Corá △ *Paraguay* 22°35S 56°2W **95** A4
Cerro de Pasco *Peru* 10°45S 76°10W **92** F3
Cerro el Copey △
  Venezuela 10°59N 63°53W **89** D7
Cerro Hoya △ *Panama* 7°17N 80°45W **88** E3
Cerro Saroche △
  Venezuela 10°8N 69°38W **89** D6
Cervantes *Australia* 30°31S 115°3E **61** F2
Cervera *Spain* 41°40N 1°16E **21** B6
Cesena *Italy* 44°8N 12°15E **22** B5
Cēsis *Latvia* 57°18N 25°15E **9** H21
Česká Rep. = Czech Rep. ■
  Europe 50°0N 15°0E **16** D8
České Budějovice
  Czech Rep. 48°55N 14°25E **16** D8
Českomoravská Vrchovina
  Czech Rep. 49°30N 15°40E **16** D8
Çeşme *Turkey* 38°20N 26°23E **23** E12
Cessnock *Australia* 32°50S 151°21E **63** E5
Cetinje *Montenegro* 42°23N 18°59E **23** C8
Cetraro *Italy* 39°31N 15°55E **22** E6
Ceuta *N. Afr.* 35°52N 5°18W **21** E3
Cévennes *France* 44°10N 3°50E **20** D5
Ceyhan *Turkey* 37°4N 35°47E **44** B2
Ceylanpinar *Turkey* 36°50N 40°2E **44** B4
Ceylon = Sri Lanka ■
  Asia 7°30N 80°50E **40** R12
Cha-am *Thailand* 12°48N 99°58E **38** F2
Chacabuco *Argentina* 34°40S 60°27W **94** C3
Chachapoyas *Peru* 6°15S 77°50W **92** E3
Chachoengsao *Thailand* 13°42N 101°5E **38** F3
Chachran *Pakistan* 28°55N 70°30E **42** E4
Chachro *Pakistan* 25°5N 70°15E **42** G4
Chaco □ *Argentina* 26°30S 61°0W **94** B3
Chaco □ *Paraguay* 26°0S 60°0W **94** B3
Chaco → *U.S.A.* 36°46N 108°39W **77** H9
Chaco △ *Argentina* 27°0S 59°30W **94** B4
Chaco Austral *S. Amer.* 27°0S 61°30W **96** B4
Chaco Boreal *S. Amer.* 22°0S 60°0W **92** H6
Chaco Central *S. Amer.* 24°0S 61°0W **96** A4
Chaco Culture △
  U.S.A. 36°3N 107°58W **77** H10
Chacon, C. *U.S.A.* 54°42N 132°0W **70** C2
Chad ■ *Africa* 15°0N 17°15E **51** F8
Chad, L. = Tchad, L.
  Chad 13°30N 14°30E **51** F8
Chadileuvú → *Argentina* 37°46S 66°0W **94** D2
Chadiza *Zambia* 14°45S 32°27E **55** E3
Chadron *U.S.A.* 42°50N 103°0W **80** D2
Chadyr-Lunga = Ciadâr-Lunga
  Moldova 46°3N 28°51E **17** E15
Chae Hom *Thailand* 18°43N 99°35E **38** C2
Chae Son △ *Thailand* 18°42N 99°20E **38** C2
Chaem → *Thailand* 18°11N 98°38E **38** C2
Chaeryŏng *N. Korea* 38°24N 125°36E **35** E13
Chagai Hills = Chāh Gay Hills
  Afghan. 29°30N 64°0E **40** E3
Chagda *Russia* 58°45N 130°38E **29** D14
Chaghcharān *Afghan.* 34°31N 65°15E **40** B4
Chagos Arch. ☑ *Ind. Oc.* 6°0S 72°0E **26** J9
Chagres → *Panama* 9°33N 79°37E **88** E4
Chaguanas *Trin. & Tob.* 10°30N 61°26W **93** K15
Chāh Ākhvor *Iran* 32°41N 59°40E **45** C8
Chāh Bahar *Iran* 25°20N 60°40E **45** E9
Chāh-e Kavīr *Iran* 34°29N 56°52E **45** C8
Chāh Gay Hills *Afghan.* 29°30N 64°0E **40** E3
Chahār Borjak *Afghan.* 30°17N 62°3E **40** D3
Chahār Mahāll va Bakhtīarī □
  Iran 32°0N 49°0E **45** C6
Chai Badan *Thailand* 15°12N 101°8E **38** E3
Chai Wan *China* 22°16N 114°14E **33** G11
Chaibasa *India* 22°42S 85°49E **43** H11
Chainat *Thailand* 15°11N 100°8E **38** E3
Chaiya *Thailand* 9°23N 99°14E **39** H2
Chaiyaphum *Thailand* 15°48N 102°2E **38** E4
Chaj Doab *Pakistan* 32°15N 73°0E **42** C5
Chajari *Argentina* 30°42S 58°0W **94** C4
Chak Amru *Pakistan* 32°22N 75°11E **42** C6
Chakar → *Pakistan* 29°29N 68°2E **42** E3
Chakari *Zimbabwe* 18°5S 29°51E **57** B4
Chake Chake *Tanzania* 5°15S 39°45E **54** D4
Chakhānsūr *Afghan.* 31°10N 62°0E **40** D3
Chakonipau, L. *Canada* 56°18N 68°30W **73** A6
Chakradharpur *India* 22°45N 85°40E **43** H11
Chakrata *India* 30°42N 77°51E **42** D7
Chakwal *Pakistan* 32°56N 72°53E **42** C5
Chala *Peru* 15°48S 74°20W **92** G4
Chalchihuites *Mexico* 23°29N 103°53W **86** C4
Chalcis = Halkida
  Greece 38°27N 23°42E **23** E10
Chalfant *U.S.A.* 37°32N 118°21W **78** H8
Chalhuanca *Peru* 14°15S 73°15W **92** F4
Chalisgaon *India* 20°30N 75°10E **40** J9
Chalk River *Canada* 46°1N 77°27W **72** C4
Chalky Inlet *N.Z.* 46°3S 166°31E **59** G1

Challapata *Bolivia* 18°53S 66°50W **92 G5**
Challenger Deep *Pac. Oc.* 11°30N 142°0E **64 F6**
Challenger Fracture Zone
  Pac. Oc. 35°0S 105°0W **65 L17**
Challis *U.S.A.* 44°30N 114°14W **76 D6**
Chalmette *U.S.A.* 29°56N 89°57W **85 G10**
Chalong *Thailand* 7°50N 98°22E **39 a**
Châlons-en-Champagne
  France 48°58N 4°20E **20 B6**
Chálten, Cerro = Fitz Roy, Cerro
  Argentina 49°17S 73°5W **96 F2**
Chālūs *Iran* 36°38N 51°26E **45 B6**
Cham, Cu Lao *Vietnam* 15°57N 108°30E **38 E7**
Chama → *U.S.A.* 36°54N 106°35W **77 H10**
Chamaicó *Argentina* 35°3S 64°58W **94 D3**
Chaman *Pakistan* 30°58N 66°25E **40 D5**
Chamba *India* 32°35N 76°10E **42 C7**
Chamba *Tanzania* 11°37S 37°0E **55 E4**
Chambal → *India* 26°29N 79°15E **43 F8**
Chamberlain → *U.S.A.* 43°49N 99°20W **80 D4**
Chamberlain →
  Australia 15°30S 127°54E **60 C4**
Chamberlain L. *U.S.A.* 46°14N 69°19W **81 B19**
Chambers *U.S.A.* 35°11N 109°26W **77 J9**
Chambersburg *U.S.A.* 39°56N 77°40W **81 F15**
Chambéry *France* 45°34N 5°55E **20 D6**
Chambeshi → *Zambia* 11°53S 29°48E **52 G6**
Chambly *Canada* 45°27N 73°17W **83 A11**
Chambord *Canada* 48°25N 72°6W **73 C5**
Chamchamal *Iraq* 35°32N 44°50E **44 C5**
Chamela *Mexico* 19°32N 105°5W **86 D3**
Chamical *Argentina* 30°22S 66°27W **94 C2**
Chamkar Luong
  Cambodia 11°0N 103°45E **39 G4**
Chamoli *India* 30°24N 79°21E **43 D8**
Chamonix-Mont Blanc
  France 45°55N 6°51E **20 D7**
Chamouchouane =
  Ashuapmushuan →
  Canada 48°37N 72°20W **72 C5**
Champa *India* 22°2N 82°43E **43 H10**
Champagne *Canada* 60°49N 136°30W **70 A1**
Champagne *France* 48°40N 4°20E **20 B6**
Champaign *U.S.A.* 40°7N 88°15W **80 E9**
Champassak *Laos* 14°53N 105°52E **38 E5**
Champawat *India* 29°20N 80°6E **43 E9**
Champdoré, L. *Canada* 55°55N 65°49W **73 A6**
Champion *U.S.A.* 41°19N 80°51W **82 E4**
Champlain *U.S.A.* 44°59N 73°27W **83 B11**
Champlain, L. *U.S.A.* 44°40N 73°20W **83 B11**
Champotón *Mexico* 19°21N 90°43W **87 D6**
Champua *India* 22°5N 85°40E **43 H11**
Chana *Thailand* 6°55N 100°44E **39 J3**
Chañaral *Chile* 26°23S 70°40W **94 B1**
Chanārān *Iran* 36°39N 59°6E **45 B8**
Chanasma *India* 23°44N 72°5E **42 H5**
Chancery Lane *Barbados* 13°3N 59°30W **89 g**
Chanco *Chile* 35°44S 72°32W **94 D1**
Chand *India* 21°57N 79°7E **43 J8**
Chandan *India* 24°38N 86°40E **43 G12**
Chandan Chauki *India* 28°33N 80°47E **43 E9**
Chandannagar *India* 22°52N 88°24E **43 H13**
Chandausi *India* 28°27N 78°49E **43 E8**
Chandeleur Is. *U.S.A.* 29°55N 88°57W **85 G10**
Chandeleur Sd. *U.S.A.* 29°55N 89°0W **85 G10**
Chandigarh *India* 30°43N 76°47E **42 D7**
Chandil *India* 22°58N 86°3E **43 H12**
Chandler *Australia* 27°0S 133°19E **63 D1**
Chandler *Canada* 48°18N 64°46W **73 C7**
Chandler *Ariz., U.S.A.* 33°18N 111°50W **77 K8**
Chandler *Okla., U.S.A.* 35°42N 96°53W **84 D6**
Chandod *India* 21°59N 73°28E **42 J5**
Chandpur *Bangla.* 23°8N 90°45E **41 H17**
Chandrapur *India* 19°57N 79°25E **40 K11**
Chānf *Iran* 26°38N 60°29E **45 E9**
Chang *Pakistan* 26°59N 68°30E **42 F3**
Chang, Ko *Thailand* 12°0N 102°23E **39 G4**
Ch'ang Chiang = Chang Jiang →
  China 31°48N 121°10E **33 C7**
Chang Jiang → *China* 31°48N 121°10E **33 C7**
Changa *India* 33°53N 77°35E **43 C7**
Changanacheri *India* 9°25N 76°31E **40 Q10**
Changanacheri = Changanacheri
  India 9°25N 76°31E **40 Q10**
Changane → *Mozam.* 24°30S 33°30E **57 C5**
Changbai *China* 41°25N 128°5E **35 D15**
Changbai Shan *China* 42°20N 129°0E **35 C15**
Changchiak'ou = Zhangjiakou
  China 40°48N 114°55E **34 D8**
Ch'angchou = Changzhou
  China 31°47N 119°58E **33 C6**
Changchun *China* 43°57N 125°17E **35 C13**
Changchunling *China* 45°18N 125°53E **35 B13**
Changde *China* 29°4N 111°35E **33 D6**
Changdo-ri *N. Korea* 38°30N 127°40E **35 E14**
Changhai = Shanghai
  China 31°15N 121°26E **33 C7**
Changhua *Taiwan* 24°2N 120°30E **33 D7**
Changhūngni
  N. Korea 40°24N 128°19E **35 D15**
Changi *Singapore* 1°23N 103°59E **39 d**
Changi, Singapore ✈ (SIN)
  Singapore 1°23N 103°59E **39 M4**
Changji *China* 44°1N 87°19E **32 B3**
Changjiang *China* 19°20N 108°55E **38 C7**
Changjiang Shuiku
  China 22°29N 113°27E **33 G10**
Changjin *N. Korea* 40°23N 127°15E **35 D14**
Changjin-ho *N. Korea* 40°30N 127°15E **35 D14**
Changli *China* 39°40N 119°13E **35 E10**
Changling *China* 44°20N 123°58E **35 B12**
Changlun *Malaysia* 6°25N 100°26E **39 J3**
Changping *China* 40°14N 116°12E **34 D9**
Changsha *China* 28°12N 113°0E **33 D6**
Changshan Qundao
  China 39°11N 122°32E **35 E12**

Changuinola *Panama* 9°26N 82°31W **88 E3**
Changwu *China* 35°10N 107°45E **34 G4**
Changyi *China* 36°40N 119°30E **35 F10**
Changyŏn *N. Korea* 38°15N 125°6E **35 E13**
Changyuan *China* 35°15N 114°42E **34 G8**
Changzhi *China* 36°10N 113°6E **34 F7**
Changzhou *China* 31°47N 119°58E **33 C6**
Chanhanga *Angola* 16°0S 14°8E **56 B1**
Chania *Greece* 35°30N 24°4E **25 D6**
Chania □ *Greece* 35°30N 24°0E **25 D6**
Chanion, Kolpos *Greece* 35°33N 23°55E **25 D5**
Channapatna *India* 12°40N 77°15E **40 N10**
Channel Is. *U.K.* 49°19N 2°24W **13 H5**
Channel Is. *U.S.A.* 33°40N 119°15W **79 M7**
Channel Islands △
  U.S.A. 34°0N 119°24W **79 L7**
Channel-Port aux Basques
  Canada 47°30N 59°9W **73 C8**
Channel Tunnel *Europe* 51°0N 1°30E **13 F9**
Channing *U.S.A.* 35°41N 102°20W **84 D3**
Chantada *Spain* 42°36N 7°46W **21 A2**
Chanthaburi *Thailand* 12°38N 102°12E **38 F4**
Chantrey Inlet *Canada* 67°48N 96°20W **68 D12**
Chanute *U.S.A.* 37°41N 95°27W **80 G6**
Chao Phraya →
  Thailand 13°40N 100°31E **38 F3**
Chao Phraya Lowlands
  Thailand 15°30N 100°0E **38 E3**
Chaocheng *China* 36°4N 115°37E **34 F8**
Chaoyang *China* 41°35N 120°22E **35 D11**
Chaozhou *China* 23°42N 116°32E **33 D6**
Chapaev *Kazakhstan* 50°25N 51°10E **19 D9**
Chapais *Canada* 49°47N 74°51W **72 C5**
Chapala *Mozam.* 15°50S 37°35E **55 F4**
Chapala, L. de *Mexico* 20°15N 103°0W **86 C4**
Chapayevsk *Russia* 53°0N 49°40E **18 D8**
Chapecó *Brazil* 27°14S 52°41W **95 B5**
Chapel Hill *U.S.A.* 35°55N 79°4W **85 D15**
Chapleau *Canada* 47°50N 83°24W **72 C3**
Chaplin *Canada* 50°28N 106°40W **71 C7**
Chaplin L. *Canada* 50°22N 106°36W **71 C7**
Chappell *U.S.A.* 41°6N 102°28W **80 E2**
Chapra = Chhapra
  India 25°48N 84°44E **43 G11**
Chara *Russia* 56°54N 118°20E **29 D12**
Charadai *Argentina* 27°35S 59°55W **94 B4**
Charagua *Bolivia* 19°45S 63°10W **92 G6**
Charakas *Greece* 35°1N 25°7E **25 D7**
Charambirá, Punta
  Colombia 4°16N 77°32W **92 C3**
Charaña *Bolivia* 17°30S 69°25W **92 G5**
Charanwala *India* 27°51N 72°10E **42 F5**
Charata *Argentina* 27°13S 61°14W **94 B3**
Charcas *Mexico* 23°8N 101°7W **86 C4**
Charcot I. *Antarctica* 70°0S 75°0W **5 C17**
Chard *U.K.* 50°52N 2°58W **13 G5**
Chardon *U.S.A.* 41°35N 81°12W **82 E3**
Chardzhou = Türkmenabat
  Turkmenistan 39°6N 63°34E **45 B9**
Charente → *France* 45°57N 1°5W **20 D3**
Chari → *Chad* 12°58N 14°31E **51 F8**
Chārīkār *Afghan.* 35°0N 69°10E **40 B6**
Chariton → *U.S.A.* 41°1N 93°19W **80 E7**
Chariton → *U.S.A.* 39°19N 92°58W **80 F7**
Chärjew = Türkmenabat
  Turkmenistan 39°6N 63°34E **45 B9**
Charkhari *India* 25°24N 79°45E **43 G8**
Charkhi Dadri *India* 28°37N 76°17E **42 E7**
Charleroi *Belgium* 50°24N 4°27E **15 D4**
Charleroi *U.S.A.* 40°9N 79°57W **82 F5**
Charles, C. *U.S.A.* 37°7N 75°58W **81 G16**
Charles, Peak *Australia* 32°52S 121°11E **61 F3**
Charles City *U.S.A.* 43°4N 92°41W **80 D7**
Charles I. *Canada* 62°39N 74°15W **69 E17**
Charles L. *Canada* 59°50N 110°33W **71 B6**
Charles Town *U.S.A.* 39°17N 77°52W **81 F15**
Charlesbourg *Canada* 46°51N 71°16W **81 B18**
Charleston *Ill., U.S.A.* 39°30N 88°10W **80 F9**
Charleston *Miss., U.S.A.* 34°1N 90°4W **85 D9**
Charleston *Mo., U.S.A.* 36°55N 89°21W **80 G9**
Charleston *S.C., U.S.A.* 32°46N 79°56W **85 E15**
Charleston *W. Va.,
  U.S.A.* 38°21N 81°38W **81 F13**
Charleston L. *Canada* 44°32N 76°0W **83 B9**
Charleston Peak
  U.S.A. 36°16N 115°42W **79 J11**
Charlestown *Ireland* 53°58N 8°48W **10 C3**
Charlestown *S. Africa* 27°26S 29°53E **57 D4**
Charlestown *Ind.,
  U.S.A.* 38°27N 85°40W **81 F11**
Charlestown *N.H.,
  U.S.A.* 43°14N 72°25W **83 C12**
Charlestown of Aberlour
  U.K. 57°28N 3°14W **11 D5**
Charleville = Rath Luirc
  Ireland 52°21N 8°40W **10 D3**
Charleville *Australia* 26°24S 146°15E **63 D4**
Charleville-Mézières
  France 49°44N 4°40E **20 B6**
Charlevoix *U.S.A.* 45°19N 85°16W **81 C11**
Charlotte *Mich., U.S.A.* 42°34N 84°50W **81 D11**
Charlotte *N.C., U.S.A.* 35°13N 80°50W **85 D14**
Charlotte *Vt., U.S.A.* 44°19N 73°16W **83 B11**
Charlotte Amalie
  U.S. Virgin Is. 18°21N 64°56W **89 e**
Charlotte Harbor *U.S.A.* 26°57N 82°4W **85 H13**
Charlotte L. *Canada* 52°12N 125°19W **70 C3**
Charlottesville *U.S.A.* 38°2N 78°30W **81 F14**
Charlottetown *Nfld. & L.,
  Canada* 52°46N 56°7W **73 B8**
Charlottetown *P.E.I.,
  Canada* 46°14N 63°8W **73 C7**
Charlotteville
  Trin. & Tob. 11°20N 60°33W **93 J16**
Charlton *Australia* 36°16S 143°24E **63 F3**
Charlton I. *Canada* 52°0N 79°20W **72 B4**
Charny *Canada* 46°43N 71°15W **73 C5**
Charolles *France* 46°27N 4°16E **20 C6**
Charre *Mozam.* 17°13S 35°10E **55 F4**

Charsadda *Pakistan* 34°7N 71°45E **42 B4**
Charters Towers
  Australia 20°5S 146°13E **62 C4**
Chartres *France* 48°29N 1°30E **20 B4**
Chascomús *Argentina* 35°30S 58°0W **94 D4**
Chase *Canada* 50°50N 119°41W **70 C5**
Chasefu *Zambia* 11°55S 33°8E **55 E3**
Chashma Barrage
  Pakistan 32°27N 71°20E **42 C4**
Chāt *Iran* 37°59N 55°16E **45 B7**
Châteaubriant *France* 47°43N 1°23W **20 C3**
Chateaugay *U.S.A.* 44°56N 74°5W **83 B10**
Chepo *Panama* 9°10N 79°6W **88 E4**
Chepstow *U.K.* 51°38N 2°41W **13 F5**
Chequamegon B. *U.S.A.* 46°39N 90°51W **80 B8**
Cher → *France* 47°21N 0°29E **20 C4**
Cheraw *U.S.A.* 34°42N 79°53W **85 D15**
Cherbourg *France* 49°39N 1°40W **20 B3**
Cherdyn *Russia* 60°24N 56°29E **18 B10**
Cheremkhovo *Russia* 53°8N 103°1E **29 D11**
Cherepovets *Russia* 59°5N 37°55E **18 C6**
Chergui, Chott ech
  Algeria 34°21N 0°25E **50 B6**
Cherikov = Cherykaw
  Belarus 53°32N 31°20E **17 B16**
Cherkasy *Ukraine* 49°27N 32°4E **19 E5**
Cherkessk *Russia* 44°15N 42°5E **19 F7**
Cherlak *Russia* 54°15N 74°55E **28 D8**
Chernaya *Russia* 70°30N 89°10E **29 B9**
Chernigov = Chernihiv
  Ukraine 51°28N 31°20E **18 D5**
Chernigovka *Russia* 44°19N 132°34E **30 B6**
Chernihiv *Ukraine* 51°28N 31°20E **18 D5**
Chernivtsi *Ukraine* 48°15N 25°52E **17 D13**
Chernobyl = Chornobyl
  Ukraine 51°20N 30°15E **17 C16**
Chernogorsk *Russia* 53°49N 91°18E **29 D10**
Chernovtsy = Chernivtsi
  Ukraine 48°15N 25°52E **17 D13**
Chernyakhovsk *Russia* 54°36N 21°48E **9 J19**
Chernysheyskiy *Russia* 63°0N 112°30E **29 C12**
Cherokee *Iowa, U.S.A.* 42°45N 95°33W **80 D6**
Cherokee *Okla., U.S.A.* 36°45N 98°21W **84 C5**
Cherokee Village *U.S.A.* 36°17N 91°31W **84 C9**
Cherokees, Grand Lake O' The
  U.S.A. 36°28N 94°55W **84 C7**
Cherrapunji *India* 25°17N 91°47E **41 G17**
Cherry Valley *U.S.A.* 42°48N 74°45W **83 D10**
Cherskiy *Russia* 68°45N 161°18E **29 C17**
Cherskogo Khrebet
  Russia 65°0N 143°0E **29 C15**
Chersonisos *Greece* 35°18N 25°22E **25 D7**
Chersonisos Akrotiri
  Greece 35°30N 24°10E **25 D6**
Cherven *Belarus* 53°45N 28°28E **17 B15**
Chervonohrad *Ukraine* 50°25N 24°10E **17 C13**
Cherwell → *U.K.* 51°44N 1°14W **13 F6**
Cherykaw *Belarus* 53°32N 31°20E **17 B16**
Chesapeake *U.S.A.* 36°49N 76°16W **81 G15**
Chesapeake B. *U.S.A.* 38°0N 76°10W **81 F14**
Cheshire □ *U.K.* 53°14N 2°30W **12 D5**
Cheshskaya Guba *Russia* 67°20N 47°0E **18 A8**
Cheshunt *U.K.* 51°43N 0°1W **13 F7**
Chesil Beach *U.K.* 50°37N 2°33W **13 G5**
Chesley *Canada* 44°17N 81°5W **82 B3**
Chester *U.K.* 53°12N 2°53W **12 D5**
Chester *Calif., U.S.A.* 40°19N 121°14W **76 F3**
Chester *Ill., U.S.A.* 37°55N 89°49W **80 G9**
Chester *Mont., U.S.A.* 48°31N 110°58W **76 B8**
Chester *Pa., U.S.A.* 39°51N 75°22W **81 F16**
Chester *S.C., U.S.A.* 34°43N 81°12W **85 D14**
Chester *Vt., U.S.A.* 43°16N 72°36W **83 C12**
Chester W. *U.S.A.* 33°31N 126°32E **35 H14**
Chester-le-Street *U.K.* 54°51N 1°34W **12 C6**
Chesterfield *U.K.* 53°15N 1°25W **12 D6**
Chesterfield, Îs. *N. Cal.* 19°52S 158°15E **58 C8**
Chesterfield Inlet
  Canada 63°30N 90°45W **68 E13**
Chesterton Ra.
  Australia 25°30S 147°27E **63 D4**
Chesterton Range △
  Australia 26°16S 147°22E **63 D4**
Chestertown *U.S.A.* 43°40N 73°48W **83 C11**
Chesterville *Canada* 45°6N 75°14W **83 A9**
Chesuncook L. *U.S.A.* 46°0N 69°21W **81 C19**
Chéticamp *Canada* 46°37N 60°59W **73 C7**
Chetumal *Mexico* 18°30N 88°20W **87 D7**
Chetumal, B. de
  Cent. Amer. 18°40N 88°10W **87 D7**
Chetwynd *Canada* 55°45N 121°36W **70 B4**
Cheviot, The *U.K.* 55°29N 2°9W **12 B5**
Cheviot Hills *U.K.* 55°20N 2°30W **12 B5**
Cheviot Ra. *Australia* 25°20S 143°45E **62 D3**
Chew Bahir *Ethiopia* 4°40N 36°50E **47 G2**
Chewelah *U.S.A.* 48°17N 117°43W **76 B5**
Cheyenne *Okla., U.S.A.* 35°37N 99°40W **84 D5**
Cheyenne *Wyo., U.S.A.* 41°8N 104°49W **76 F11**
Cheyenne → *U.S.A.* 44°41N 101°18W **80 C4**
Cheyenne Wells
  U.S.A. 38°49N 102°21W **76 G12**
Cheyne B. *Australia* 34°35S 118°50E **61 F2**
Chhabra *India* 24°40N 76°54E **42 G7**
Chhaktala *India* 22°6N 74°11E **42 H6**
Chhapra *India* 25°48N 84°44E **43 G11**
Chhata *India* 27°42N 77°30E **42 F7**
Chhatarpur *Jharkhand,
  India* 24°23N 84°11E **43 G11**
Chhatarpur *Mad. P.,
  India* 24°55N 79°35E **43 G8**
Chhattisgarh □ *India* 22°0N 82°0E **43 J10**
Chhep *Cambodia* 13°45N 105°24E **38 F5**
Chhindwara *Mad. P.,
  India* 23°3N 79°29E **43 H8**
Chhindwara *Mad. P.,
  India* 22°2N 78°59E **43 H8**
Chhlong *Cambodia* 12°15N 105°58E **39 F5**
Chhota Tawa → *India* 22°14N 76°36E **42 H7**
Chhoti Kali Sindh →
  India 24°2N 75°31E **42 G6**

Chenjiagang *China* 34°23N 119°47E **35 G10**
Chennai *India* 13°8N 80°19E **40 N12**
Cheò, Eilean a' = Skye
  U.K. 57°15N 6°10W **11 D2**
Cheom Ksan *Cambodia* 14°13N 104°56E **38 E5**
Cheonan *S. Korea* 36°48N 127°9E **35 F14**
Cheongdo *S. Korea* 35°38N 128°42E **35 G15**
Cheongju *S. Korea* 36°39N 127°27E **35 F14**
Cheorwon *S. Korea* 38°15N 127°10E **35 E14**
Chepén *Peru* 7°15S 79°23W **92 E3**
Chepes *Argentina* 31°20S 66°35W **94 C2**
Chepo *Panama* 9°10N 79°6W **88 E4**
Chequamegon B. *U.S.A.* 46°39N 90°51W **80 B8**
Cherbourg *France* 49°39N 1°40W **20 B3**
Cherdyn *Russia* 60°24N 56°29E **18 B10**
Cheremkhovo *Russia* 53°8N 103°1E **29 D11**
Cherepovets *Russia* 59°5N 37°55E **18 C6**
Chergui, Chott ech
  Algeria 34°21N 0°25E **50 B6**
Cherikov = Cherykaw
  Belarus 53°32N 31°20E **17 B16**
Cherkasy *Ukraine* 49°27N 32°4E **19 E5**
Cherkessk *Russia* 44°15N 42°5E **19 F7**
Cherlak *Russia* 54°15N 74°55E **28 D8**
Chernaya *Russia* 70°30N 89°10E **29 B9**
Chernigov = Chernihiv
  Ukraine 51°28N 31°20E **18 D5**
Chernigovka *Russia* 44°19N 132°34E **30 B6**
Chernihiv *Ukraine* 51°28N 31°20E **18 D5**
Chernivtsi *Ukraine* 48°15N 25°52E **17 D13**
Chernobyl = Chornobyl
  Ukraine 51°20N 30°15E **17 C16**
Chernogorsk *Russia* 53°49N 91°18E **29 D10**
Chernovtsy = Chernivtsi
  Ukraine 48°15N 25°52E **17 D13**
Chernyakhovsk *Russia* 54°36N 21°48E **9 J19**
Chernysheyskiy *Russia* 63°0N 112°30E **29 C12**
Cherokee *Iowa, U.S.A.* 42°45N 95°33W **80 D6**
Cherokee *Okla., U.S.A.* 36°45N 98°21W **84 C5**
Cherokee Village *U.S.A.* 36°17N 91°31W **84 C9**
Cherokees, Grand Lake O' The
  U.S.A. 36°28N 94°55W **84 C7**
Cherrapunji *India* 25°17N 91°47E **41 G17**
Cherry Valley *U.S.A.* 42°48N 74°45W **83 D10**
Cherskiy *Russia* 68°45N 161°18E **29 C17**
Cherskogo Khrebet
  Russia 65°0N 143°0E **29 C15**
Chersonisos *Greece* 35°18N 25°22E **25 D7**
Chersonisos Akrotiri
  Greece 35°30N 24°10E **25 D6**
Cherven *Belarus* 53°45N 28°28E **17 B15**
Chervonohrad *Ukraine* 50°25N 24°10E **17 C13**
Cherwell → *U.K.* 51°44N 1°14W **13 F6**
Cherykaw *Belarus* 53°32N 31°20E **17 B16**
Chesapeake *U.S.A.* 36°49N 76°16W **81 G15**
Chesapeake B. *U.S.A.* 38°0N 76°10W **81 F14**
Cheshire □ *U.K.* 53°14N 2°30W **12 D5**
Cheshskaya Guba *Russia* 67°20N 47°0E **18 A8**
Cheshunt *U.K.* 51°43N 0°1W **13 F7**
Chesil Beach *U.K.* 50°37N 2°33W **13 G5**
Chesley *Canada* 44°17N 81°5W **82 B3**
Chester *U.K.* 53°12N 2°53W **12 D5**
Chester *Calif., U.S.A.* 40°19N 121°14W **76 F3**
Chester *Ill., U.S.A.* 37°55N 89°49W **80 G9**
Chester *Mont., U.S.A.* 48°31N 110°58W **76 B8**
Chester *Pa., U.S.A.* 39°51N 75°22W **81 F16**
Chester *S.C., U.S.A.* 34°43N 81°12W **85 D14**
Chester *Vt., U.S.A.* 43°16N 72°36W **83 C12**
Chester W. *U.S.A.* 33°31N 126°32E **35 H14**
Chester-le-Street *U.K.* 54°51N 1°34W **12 C6**
Chesterfield *U.K.* 53°15N 1°25W **12 D6**
Chesterfield, Îs. *N. Cal.* 19°52S 158°15E **58 C8**
Chesterfield Inlet
  Canada 63°30N 90°45W **68 E13**
Chesterton Ra.
  Australia 25°30S 147°27E **63 D4**
Chesterton Range △
  Australia 26°16S 147°22E **63 D4**
Chestertown *U.S.A.* 43°40N 73°48W **83 C11**
Chesterville *Canada* 45°6N 75°14W **83 A9**
Chesuncook L. *U.S.A.* 46°0N 69°21W **81 C19**
Chéticamp *Canada* 46°37N 60°59W **73 C7**
Chetumal *Mexico* 18°30N 88°20W **87 D7**
Chetumal, B. de
  Cent. Amer. 18°40N 88°10W **87 D7**
Chetwynd *Canada* 55°45N 121°36W **70 B4**
Cheviot, The *U.K.* 55°29N 2°9W **12 B5**
Cheviot Hills *U.K.* 55°20N 2°30W **12 B5**
Cheviot Ra. *Australia* 25°20S 143°45E **62 D3**
Chew Bahir *Ethiopia* 4°40N 36°50E **47 G2**
Chewelah *U.S.A.* 48°17N 117°43W **76 B5**
Cheyenne *Okla., U.S.A.* 35°37N 99°40W **84 D5**
Cheyenne *Wyo., U.S.A.* 41°8N 104°49W **76 F11**
Cheyenne → *U.S.A.* 44°41N 101°18W **80 C4**
Cheyenne Wells
  U.S.A. 38°49N 102°21W **76 G12**
Cheyne B. *Australia* 34°35S 118°50E **61 F2**
Chhabra *India* 24°40N 76°54E **42 G7**
Chhaktala *India* 22°6N 74°11E **42 H6**
Chhapra *India* 25°48N 84°44E **43 G11**
Chhata *India* 27°42N 77°30E **42 F7**
Chhatarpur *Jharkhand,
  India* 24°23N 84°11E **43 G11**
Chhatarpur *Mad. P.,
  India* 24°55N 79°35E **43 G8**
Chhattisgarh □ *India* 22°0N 82°0E **43 J10**
Chhep *Cambodia* 13°45N 105°24E **38 F5**
Chhindwara *Mad. P.,
  India* 23°3N 79°29E **43 H8**
Chhindwara *Mad. P.,
  India* 22°2N 78°59E **43 H8**
Chhlong *Cambodia* 12°15N 105°58E **39 F5**
Chhota Tawa → *India* 22°14N 76°36E **42 H7**
Chhoti Kali Sindh →
  India 24°2N 75°31E **42 G6**

Chhuikhadan *India* 21°32N 80°59E **43 J9**
Chhuk *Cambodia* 10°46N 104°28E **39 G5**
Chi → *Thailand* 15°11N 104°43E **38 E5**
Chiai *Taiwan* 23°29N 120°25E **33 D7**
Chiamboni *Somali Rep.* 1°39S 41°35E **52 E8**
Chiang Dao *Thailand* 19°22N 98°58E **38 C2**
Chiang Kham *Thailand* 19°32N 100°18E **38 C3**
Chiang Khan *Thailand* 17°52N 101°36E **38 D3**
Chiang Khong *Thailand* 20°17N 100°24E **38 B3**
Chiang Mai *Thailand* 18°47N 98°59E **38 C2**
Chiang Rai *Thailand* 19°52N 99°50E **38 C2**
Chiang Saen *Thailand* 20°16N 100°5E **38 B3**
Chiapa → *Mexico* 16°42N 93°0W **87 D6**
Chiapa de Corzo *Mexico* 16°42N 93°0W **87 D6**
Chiapas □ *Mexico* 16°30N 92°30W **87 D6**
Chiapas, Sa. Madre de
  Mexico 15°40N 93°0W **87 D6**
Chiautla de Tapia
  Mexico 18°18N 98°36W **87 D5**
Chiávari *Italy* 44°19N 9°19E **20 D8**
Chiavenna *Italy* 46°19N 9°24E **20 C8**
Chiba *Japan* 35°30N 140°7E **31 G10**
Chiba □ *Japan* 35°30N 140°20E **31 G10**
Chibabava *Mozam.* 20°17S 33°35E **57 C5**
Chibemba *Cunene, Angola* 15°48S 14°8E **53 H2**
Chibemba *Huila, Angola* 16°20S 15°20E **56 B2**
Chibi *Zimbabwe* 20°18S 30°25E **57 C5**
Chibia *Angola* 15°10S 13°42E **53 H2**
Chibougamau *Canada* 49°56N 74°24W **72 C5**
Chibougamau, L.
  Canada 49°50N 74°20W **72 C5**
Chibuk *Nigeria* 10°52N 12°50E **51 F8**
Chibuto *Mozam.* 24°40S 33°33E **57 C5**
Chicacole = Srikakulam
  India 18°14N 83°58E **41 K13**
Chicago *U.S.A.* 41°52N 87°38W **80 E10**
Chicago Heights *U.S.A.* 41°30N 87°38W **80 E10**
Chichagof I. *U.S.A.* 57°30N 135°30W **68 F4**
Chichaoua *Morocco* 31°32N 8°44W **50 B4**
Chichawatni *Pakistan* 30°32N 72°42E **42 D5**
Chichén-Itzá *Mexico* 20°37N 88°35W **87 C7**
Chicheng *China* 40°55N 115°55E **34 D8**
Chichester *U.K.* 50°50N 0°47W **13 G7**
Chichester Ra. *Australia* 22°12S 119°15E **60 D2**
Chichibu *Japan* 35°59N 139°10E **31 F9**
Chichibu-Tama △
  Japan 35°52N 138°42E **31 G9**
Ch'ich'ihaerh = Qiqihar
  China 47°26N 124°0E **33 B7**
Chicholi *India* 22°1N 77°40E **42 H8**
Chickasaw △ *U.S.A.* 34°26N 97°0W **84 D6**
Chickasha *U.S.A.* 35°3N 97°58W **84 D6**
Chiclana de la Frontera
  Spain 36°26N 6°9W **21 D2**
Chiclayo *Peru* 6°42S 79°50W **92 E3**
Chico *U.S.A.* 39°44N 121°50W **78 F5**
Chico → *Chubut, Argentina* 44°0S 67°0W **96 E3**
Chico → *Santa Cruz,
  Argentina* 50°0S 68°30W **96 F3**
Chicoa *Mozam.* 15°36S 32°20E **55 F3**
Chicomo *Mozam.* 24°31S 34°6E **57 C5**
Chicomostoc *Mexico* 22°28N 102°46W **86 C4**
Chicontepec *Mexico* 20°58N 98°10W **87 C5**
Chicopee *U.S.A.* 42°9N 72°37W **83 D12**
Chicoutimi *Canada* 48°28N 71°5W **73 C5**
Chicualacuala *Mozam.* 22°6S 31°42E **57 C5**
Chidambaram *India* 11°20N 79°45E **40 P11**
Chidenguele *Mozam.* 24°55S 34°11E **57 C5**
Chidley, C. *Canada* 60°23N 64°26W **69 E19**
Chiducuane *Mozam.* 24°35S 34°25E **57 C5**
Chiede *Angola* 17°15S 16°22E **56 B2**
Chiefs Pt. *Canada* 44°41N 81°18W **82 B3**
Chiem Hoa *Vietnam* 22°12N 105°17E **38 A5**
Chiemsee *Germany* 47°53N 12°28E **16 E7**
Chiengi *Zambia* 8°45S 29°10E **55 D2**
Chiengmai = Chiang Mai
  Thailand 18°47N 98°59E **38 C2**
Chiese → *Italy* 45°8N 10°25E **20 D9**
Chieti *Italy* 42°21N 14°10E **22 C6**
Chifeng *China* 42°18N 118°58E **35 C10**
Chignecto B. *Canada* 45°30N 64°40W **73 C7**
Chiguana *Bolivia* 21°0S 67°58W **94 A2**
Chigwell *U.K.* 51°37N 0°6E **13 F8**
Chihli, G. of = Bo Hai
  China 39°0N 119°0E **35 E10**
Chihuahua *Mexico* 28°38N 106°5W **86 B3**
Chihuahua □ *Mexico* 28°30N 106°0W **86 B3**
Chiili = Shieli *Kazakhstan* 44°20N 66°15E **28 E7**
Chik Bollapur *India* 13°25N 77°45E **40 N10**
Chikmagalur *India* 13°15N 75°45E **40 N9**
Chikwawa *Malawi* 16°2S 34°50E **55 F3**
Chilanga *Zambia* 15°33S 28°16E **55 F2**
Chilapa *Mexico* 17°36N 99°10W **87 D5**
Chilas *Pakistan* 35°25N 74°5E **43 B6**
Chilaw *Sri Lanka* 7°30N 79°50E **40 R11**
Chilcotin → *Canada* 51°44N 122°23W **70 C4**
Childers *Australia* 25°15S 152°17E **63 D5**
Childress *U.S.A.* 34°25N 100°13W **84 D4**
Chile ■ *S. Amer.* 35°0S 72°0W **96 D2**
Chile Rise *Pac. Oc.* 38°0S 92°0W **65 L18**
Chilecito *Argentina* 29°10S 67°30W **94 B2**
Chilete *Peru* 7°10S 78°50W **92 E3**
Chililabombwe *Zambia* 12°18S 27°43E **55 E2**
Chilim *Pakistan* 35°5N 75°5E **43 B6**
Chilin = Jilin *China* 43°44N 126°30E **35 C14**
Chilka L. *India* 19°40N 85°25E **41 K14**
Chilko → *Canada* 52°0N 123°40W **70 C4**
Chilko L. *Canada* 51°20N 124°10W **70 C4**
Chillagoe *Australia* 17°7S 144°33E **62 B3**
Chillán *Chile* 36°40S 72°10W **94 D1**
Chillicothe *Ill., U.S.A.* 40°55N 89°29W **80 E9**
Chillicothe *Mo., U.S.A.* 39°48N 93°33W **80 F7**
Chillicothe *Ohio, U.S.A.* 39°20N 82°59W **81 F12**
Chilliwack *Canada* 49°10N 121°54W **70 D4**
Chilo *India* 27°25N 73°32E **42 F5**
Chiloane, I. *Mozam.* 20°40S 34°55E **57 C5**
Chiloé, I. de *Chile* 42°30S 73°50W **96 E2**
Chilpancingo *Mexico* 17°33N 99°30W **87 D5**

Chiltern Hills *U.K.* 51°40N 0°53W **13** F7
Chilton *U.S.A.* 44°2N 88°10W **80** C9
Chilubi *Zambia* 11°5S 29°58E **55** E2
Chilubula *Zambia* 10°14S 30°51E **55** E3
Chilumba *Malawi* 10°28S 34°12E **55** E3
Chilung *Taiwan* 25°3N 121°45E **33** D7
Chilwa, L. *Malawi* 15°15S 35°40E **55** F4
Chimaltitán *Mexico* 21°35N 103°50W **86** C4
Chimán *Panama* 8°45N 78°40W **88** E4
Chimanimani *Zimbabwe* 19°48S 32°52E **57** B5
Chimay *Belgium* 50°3N 4°20E **15** D4
Chimayo *U.S.A.* 36°0N 105°56W **77** J11
Chimba *Zambia* 9°54S 31°28E **55** D3
Chimbay *Uzbekistan* 42°57N 59°47E **28** E6
Chimborazo *Ecuador* 1°29S 78°55W **92** D3
Chimbote *Peru* 9°0S 78°35W **92** E3
Chimkent = Shymkent
Kazakhstan 42°18N 69°36E **28** E7
Chimoio *Mozam.* 19°4S 33°30E **55** F3
Chimpembe *Zambia* 9°31S 29°33E **55** D2
Chin □ *Burma* 22°0N 93°0E **41** J18
Chin Hills *Burma* 22°30N 93°30E **41** H18
Chin Ling Shan = Qinling Shandi
China 33°50N 108°10E **34** H5
China *Mexico* 25°42N 99°14W **87** B5
China ■ *Asia* 30°0N 100°0E **33** C6
China, Great Plain of
Asia 35°0N 115°0E **26** E13
China Lake *U.S.A.* 35°44N 117°37W **79** K9
Chinan = Jinan *China* 36°38N 117°1E **34** F9
Chinandega *Nic.* 12°35N 87°12W **88** D2
Chinati Peak *U.S.A.* 29°57N 104°29W **84** G2
Chincha Alta *Peru* 13°25S 76°7W **92** F3
Chinchaga → *Canada* 58°53N 118°20W **70** B5
Chinchilla *Australia* 26°45S 150°38E **63** D5
Chinchorro, Banco
Mexico 18°35N 87°22W **87** D7
Chinchou = Jinzhou
China 41°5N 121°3E **35** D11
Chincoteague *U.S.A.* 37°56N 75°23W **81** G16
Chinde *Mozam.* 18°35S 36°30E **55** F4
Chindwin → *Burma* 21°26N 95°15E **41** J19
Chineni *India* 33°2N 75°15E **43** C6
Chinga *Mozam.* 15°13S 38°35E **55** F4
Chingola *Zambia* 12°31S 27°53E **55** E2
Chingole *Malawi* 13°4S 34°17E **55** E3
Ch'ingtao = Qingdao
China 36°5N 120°20E **35** F11
Chinguetti *Mauritania* 20°25N 12°24W **50** D3
Chingune *Mozam.* 20°33S 34°58E **57** C5
Chinhanguanine
Mozam. 25°21S 32°30E **57** D5
Chinhoyi *Zimbabwe* 17°20S 30°8E **55** F3
Chini *India* 31°32N 78°15E **42** D8
Chiniot *Pakistan* 31°45N 73°0E **42** D5
Chínipas *Mexico* 27°23N 108°32W **86** B3
Chinji *Pakistan* 32°42N 72°22E **42** C5
Chinju = Jinju *S. Korea* 35°12N 128°2E **35** G15
Chinko → *C.A.R.* 4°50N 23°53E **52** D4
Chinle *U.S.A.* 36°9N 109°33W **77** H9
Chinnampo = Namp'o
N. Korea 38°52N 125°10E **35** E13
Chino *Japan* 35°59N 138°9E **31** G9
Chino *U.S.A.* 34°1N 117°41W **79** L9
Chino Valley *U.S.A.* 34°45N 112°27W **77** J7
Chinon *France* 47°10N 0°15E **20** C4
Chinook *U.S.A.* 48°35N 109°14W **76** B9
Chinook Trough
Pac. Oc. 44°0N 175°0W **64** C10
Chinsali *Zambia* 10°30S 32°2E **55** E3
Chinsura = Chunchura
India 22°53N 88°27E **43** H13
Chióggia *Italy* 45°13N 12°17E **22** B5
Chíos = Hios *Greece* 38°27N 26°9E **23** E12
Chipata *Zambia* 13°38S 32°28E **55** E3
Chipindo *Angola* 13°49S 15°48E **53** G3
Chipinge *Zimbabwe* 20°13S 32°28E **55** G3
Chipinge △ *Zimbabwe* 20°14S 33°0E **55** G3
Chipley *U.S.A.* 30°47N 85°32W **85** F12
Chipman *Canada* 46°6N 65°53W **73** C6
Chipoka *Malawi* 13°57S 34°28E **55** E3
Chippenham *U.K.* 51°27N 2°6W **13** F5
Chippewa → *U.S.A.* 44°25N 92°5W **80** C7
Chippewa Falls *U.S.A.* 44°56N 91°24W **80** C8
Chipping Norton *U.K.* 51°56N 1°32W **13** F6
Chiputneticook Lakes
N. Amer. 45°35N 67°35W **81** C20
Chiquián *Peru* 10°10S 77°0W **92** F3
Chiquibul △ *Belize* 16°49N 88°52W **88** C2
Chiquimula *Guatemala* 14°51N 89°37W **88** D2
Chiquinquira *Colombia* 5°37N 73°50W **92** B4
Chirala *India* 15°50N 80°26E **40** M12
Chiramba *Mozam.* 16°55S 34°39E **55** F3
Chirawa *India* 28°14N 75°42E **42** E6
Chirchiq *Uzbekistan* 41°29N 69°35E **28** E7
Chiredzi *Zimbabwe* 21°0S 31°38E **57** C5
Chiricahua △ *U.S.A.* 32°0N 109°20W **77** K9
Chiricahua Peak
U.S.A. 31°51N 109°18W **77** L9
Chirikof I. *U.S.A.* 55°50N 155°40W **74** D8
Chiriquí, G. de *Panama* 8°0N 82°10W **88** E3
Chiriquí, L. de *Panama* 9°10N 82°0W **88** E3
Chirisa △ *Zimbabwe* 17°53S 28°15E **55** F2
Chirivira Falls *Zimbabwe* 21°10S 32°12E **55** G3
Chirmiri *India* 23°15N 82°20E **43** H10
Chirripó Grande, Cerro
Costa Rica 9°29N 83°29W **88** E3
Chirundu *Zimbabwe* 16°3S 28°50E **57** B4
Chisamba *Zambia* 14°55S 28°20E **55** E2
Chisapani *Nepal* 28°37N 81°16E **43** E9
Chisasibi *Canada* 53°50N 79°0W **72** B4
Chisholm *U.S.A.* 47°29N 92°53W **80** B7
Chishtian Mandi
Pakistan 29°50N 72°55E **42** E5
Chisimaio = Kismaayo
Somali Rep. 0°22S 42°32E **47** H3
Chisimba Falls *Zambia* 10°12S 30°56E **55** E3
Chişinău *Moldova* 47°2N 28°50E **17** E15

Chisos Mts. *U.S.A.* 29°5N 103°15W **84** G3
Chistopol *Russia* 55°25N 50°38E **18** C9
Chita *Russia* 52°0N 113°35E **29** D12
Chitipa *Malawi* 9°41S 33°19E **55** D3
Chitose *Japan* 42°49N 141°39E **30** C10
Chitral *Pakistan* 35°50N 71°56E **40** B7
Chitré *Panama* 7°59N 80°27W **88** E3
Chittagong *Bangla.* 22°19N 91°48E **41** H17
Chittagong □ *Bangla.* 24°5N 91°0E **41** G17
Chittaurgarh *India* 24°52N 74°38E **42** G6
Chittoor *India* 13°15N 79°5E **40** N11
Chitungwiza *Zimbabwe* 18°0S 31°6E **55** F3
Chiusi *Italy* 43°1N 11°57E **22** C4
Chivasso *Italy* 45°11N 7°53E **20** D7
Chivhu *Zimbabwe* 19°2S 30°52E **55** F3
Chivilcoy *Argentina* 34°55S 60°0W **94** C4
Chiwanda *Tanzania* 11°23S 34°55E **55** E3
Chizarira *Zimbabwe* 17°36S 27°45E **55** F2
Chizarira △ *Zimbabwe* 17°44S 27°52E **55** F2
Chizela *Zambia* 13°8S 25°0E **55** E2
Chkalov = Orenburg
Russia 51°45N 55°6E **18** D10
Chloride *U.S.A.* 35°25N 114°12W **79** K12
Cho Bo *Vietnam* 20°46N 105°10E **38** B5
Cho-do *N. Korea* 38°30N 124°40E **35** E13
Cho Phuoc Hai *Vietnam* 10°26N 107°18E **39** G6
Choa Chu Kang *Singapore* 1°22N 103°41E **39** d
Choba *Kenya* 2°30N 38°5E **54** B4
Chochoele Choel *Argentina* 39°11S 65°40W **96** D3
Choiseul *St. Lucia* 13°47N 61°3W **89** f
Choiseul *Solomon Is.* 7°0S 156°40E **58** B8
Choix *Mexico* 26°43N 108°17W **86** B3
Chojnice *Poland* 53°42N 17°32E **17** B9
Chok Chai *Thailand* 14°44N 102°10E **38** E4
Chōkai-San *Japan* 39°6N 140°3E **30** E10
Choke Canyon Res.
U.S.A. 28°30N 98°20W **84** G5
Chokurdakh *Russia* 70°38N 147°55E **29** B15
Cholame *U.S.A.* 35°44N 120°18W **78** K6
Cholet *France* 47°4N 0°52W **20** C3
Cholguan *Chile* 37°10S 72°3W **94** D1
Choloma *Honduras* 15°37N 87°57W **88** C2
Choluteca *Honduras* 13°20N 87°14W **88** D2
Choluteca → *Honduras* 13°0N 87°20W **88** D2
Chom Bung *Thailand* 13°37N 99°36E **38** F2
Chom Thong *Thailand* 18°25N 98°41E **38** C2
Choma *Zambia* 16°48S 26°59E **55** F2
Chomolungma = Everest, Mt.
Nepal 28°5N 86°58E **43** E12
Chomun *India* 27°15N 75°40E **42** F6
Chomutov *Czech Rep.* 50°28N 13°23E **16** C7
Chon Buri *Thailand* 13°21N 101°1E **38** F3
Chon Thanh *Vietnam* 11°24N 106°36E **39** G6
Chone *Ecuador* 0°40S 80°0W **92** D3
Chong Kai *Cambodia* 13°57N 103°35E **38** F4
Chong Mek *Thailand* 15°10N 105°27E **38** E5
Chong Phangan *Thailand* 9°39N 100°0E **39** b
Chong Samui *Thailand* 9°21N 99°50E **39** b
Ch'ŏngjin *N. Korea* 41°47N 129°50E **35** D15
Chongju *N. Korea* 39°40N 125°5E **35** E13
Chongli *China* 40°58N 115°15E **34** D8
Chongqing *China* 29°35N 106°25E **32** D5
Chongqing Shi □ *China* 30°0N 108°0E **32** C5
Chonguene *Mozam.* 25°3S 33°49E **57** C5
Chongwe *Zambia* 15°21S 28°42E **55** F2
Chonos, Arch. de los *Chile* 45°0S 75°0W **96** F2
Chop *Ukraine* 48°26N 22°12E **17** D12
Chopim → *Brazil* 25°35S 53°5W **95** B5
Chor *Pakistan* 25°31N 69°46E **42** G3
Chora Sfakion *Greece* 35°15N 24°9E **25** D6
Chorbat La *India* 34°42N 76°37E **43** B7
Chorley *U.K.* 53°39N 2°38W **12** D5
Chornobyl *Ukraine* 51°20N 30°15E **17** C16
Chorolque, Cerro *Bolivia* 20°59S 66°5W **94** A2
Chorregon *Australia* 22°40S 143°32E **62** C3
Chorro el Indio △
Venezuela 7°43N 72°9W **89** E5
Chortkiv *Ukraine* 49°2N 25°46E **17** D13
Chorzów *Poland* 50°18N 18°57E **17** C10
Chos-Malal *Argentina* 37°20S 70°15W **94** D1
Ch'osan *N. Korea* 40°50N 125°47E **35** D13
Choszczno *Poland* 53°7N 15°25E **16** B8
Choteau *U.S.A.* 47°49N 112°11W **76** C7
Chotila *India* 22°23N 71°15E **42** H4
Chotta Udepur *India* 22°19N 74°1E **42** H6
Chowchilla *U.S.A.* 37°7N 120°16W **78** H6
Choybalsan *Mongolia* 48°4N 114°30E **33** B6
Choyr *Mongolia* 46°24N 108°30E **29** E11
Christchurch *N.Z.* 43°33S 172°47E **59** E4
Christchurch *U.K.* 50°44N 1°47W **13** G6
Christian I. *Canada* 44°50N 80°12W **82** B4
Christian Sd. *U.S.A.* 55°56N 134°40W **75** D13
Christiana *S. Africa* 27°52S 25°8E **56** D4
Christiansted
U.S. Virgin Is. 17°45N 64°42W **89** C7
Christie B. *Canada* 62°32N 111°10W **71** A6
Christina → *Canada* 56°40N 111°3W **71** B6
Christmas Cr. →
Australia 18°29S 125°23E **60** C4
Christmas I. = Kiritimati
Kiribati 1°58N 157°27W **65** G12
Christmas I. *Ind. Oc.* 10°30S 105°40E **64** J2
Christopher, L.
Australia 24°49S 127°42E **61** D4
Chtimba *Malawi* 10°35S 34°13E **55** E3
Chü = Shū *Kazakhstan* 43°36N 73°42E **28** E8
Chu → *Vietnam* 19°53N 105°45E **38** C5
Chu Lai *Vietnam* 15°28N 108°45E **38** E7
Chuadanga *Bangla.* 23°38N 88°51E **43** H13
Chuak, Ko *Thailand* 9°28N 99°41E **39** b
Ch'uanchou = Quanzhou
China 24°55N 118°34E **33** D6
Chuankou *China* 34°20N 110°59E **34** G6
Chubbuck *U.S.A.* 42°55N 112°28W **76** E7

Chūbu □ *Japan* 36°45N 137°30E **31** F8
Chubu-Sangaku △
Japan 36°30N 137°40E **31** F8
Chubut → *Argentina* 43°20S 65°5W **96** E3
Chuchi L. *Canada* 55°12N 124°30W **70** B4
Chuda *Japan* 22°29N 71°41E **42** H4
Chudskoye, Ozero
Russia 58°13N 27°30E **9** G22
Chugach Mts. *U.S.A.* 60°45N 147°0W **74** C10
Chūgoku □ *Japan* 35°0N 133°0E **31** G6
Chūgoku-Sanchi *Japan* 35°0N 133°0E **31** G6
Chugwater *U.S.A.* 41°46N 104°50W **76** F11
Chuka *Kenya* 0°20S 37°39E **54** C4
Chukchi Plateau *Arctic* 78°0N 165°0W **4** B17
Chukchi Sea *Russia* 68°0N 175°0W **29** C19
Chukotskiy Mys *Russia* 64°14N 173°8W **74** C5
Chukotskiy Poluostrov
Russia 66°0N 174°0W **74** B5
Chukotskoye Nagorye
Russia 68°0N 175°0E **29** C18
Chula Vista *U.S.A.* 32°38N 117°5W **79** N9
Chulucanas *Peru* 5°8S 80°10W **92** E2
Chulym → *Russia* 57°43N 83°51E **28** D9
Chum Phae *Thailand* 16°40N 102°6E **38** D4
Chum Saeng *Thailand* 15°55N 100°15E **38** E3
Chumar *India* 32°40N 78°35E **43** C8
Chumbicha *Argentina* 29°0S 66°10W **94** B2
Chumikan *Russia* 54°40N 135°10E **29** D14
Chumphon *Thailand* 10°35N 99°14E **39** G2
Chumuare *Mozam.* 14°31S 31°50E **55** E3
Chuna → *Russia* 57°47N 94°37E **29** D10
Chuncheon *S. Korea* 37°58N 127°44E **35** F14
Chunchura *India* 22°53N 88°27E **43** H13
Chunga *Zambia* 15°0S 26°2E **55** F2
Chunggang-ŭp
N. Korea 41°48N 126°48E **35** D14
Chunghwa *N. Korea* 38°52N 125°47E **35** E13
Chungju *S. Korea* 36°58N 127°58E **35** F14
Chungking = Chongqing
China 29°35N 106°25E **32** D5
Chungt'iaoshan = Zhongtiao
Shan *China* 35°0N 111°10E **34** G6
Chunian *Pakistan* 30°57N 74°0E **42** D6
Chunya *Tanzania* 8°30S 33°27E **55** D3
Chunyang *China* 43°38N 129°23E **35** C15
Chupara Pt.
Trin. & Tob. 10°49N 61°22W **93** K15
Chuquibamba *Peru* 15°47S 72°44W **92** G4
Chuquicamata *Chile* 22°15S 69°0W **94** A2
Chur *Switz.* 46°52N 9°32E **20** C8
Churachandpur *India* 24°20N 93°40E **41** G18
Church Stretton *U.K.* 52°32N 2°48W **13** E5
Churchill *Canada* 58°47N 94°11W **71** B10
Churchill → *Man.*,
Canada 58°47N 94°12W **71** B10
Churchill → *Nfld. & L.*,
Canada 53°19N 60°10W **73** B7
Churchill, C. *Canada* 58°46N 93°12W **71** B10
Churchill Falls *Canada* 53°36N 64°19W **73** B7
Churchill L. *Canada* 55°55N 108°20W **71** B7
Churchill Pk. *Canada* 58°10N 125°10W **70** B3
Churki *India* 23°50N 83°12E **43** H10
Churu *India* 28°20N 74°50E **42** E6
Churún Merú = Angel Falls
Venezuela 5°57N 62°30W **92** B6
Chushal *India* 33°40N 78°40E **43** C8
Chuska Mts. *U.S.A.* 36°15N 108°50W **77** H9
Chusovoy *Russia* 58°22N 57°50E **18** C10
Chute-aux-Outardes
Canada 49°7N 68°24W **73** C6
Chuuk = Truk
Micronesia 7°25N 151°46E **64** G7
Chuvash Republic = Chuvashia □
Russia 55°30N 47°0E **18** C8
Chuvashia □ *Russia* 55°30N 47°0E **18** C8
Chuwārtah *Iraq* 35°43N 45°34E **44** C5
Chuy *Uruguay* 33°41S 53°27W **95** C5
Ci Xian *China* 36°20N 114°25E **34** F8
Ciadâr-Lunga *Moldova* 46°3N 28°51E **17** E15
Ciamis *Indonesia* 7°20S 108°21E **37** G13
Cianjur *Indonesia* 6°49S 107°8E **37** G12
Cianorte *Brazil* 23°37S 52°37W **95** A5
Cibola *U.S.A.* 33°17N 114°42W **79** M12
Cicero *U.S.A.* 41°51N 87°44W **80** E2
Cicia *Fiji* 17°45S 179°18W **59** a
Ciéagas del Cataumbo △
Venezuela 9°25N 71°54W **89** E5
Ciechanów *Poland* 52°52N 20°38E **17** B11
Ciego de Ávila *Cuba* 21°50N 78°50W **88** B4
Ciénaga *Colombia* 11°1N 74°15W **92** A4
Cienfuegos *Cuba* 22°10N 80°30W **88** B3
Cieszyn *Poland* 49°45N 18°35E **17** D10
Cieza *Spain* 38°17N 1°23W **21** C5
Cihuatlán *Mexico* 19°14N 104°35W **86** D4
Cijara, Embalse de *Spain* 39°18N 4°52W **21** C3
Cijulang *Indonesia* 7°42S 108°27E **37** G13
Cilacap *Indonesia* 7°43S 109°0E **37** G13
Cill Airne = Killarney
Ireland 52°4N 9°30W **10** D2
Cill Chainnigh = Kilkenny
Ireland 52°39N 7°15W **10** D4
Cill Dara = Kildare *Ireland* 53°9N 6°55W **10** C5
Cill Mhantáin = Wicklow
Ireland 52°59N 6°3W **10** D5
Cilo Dağı *Turkey* 37°28N 43°55E **19** G7
Cima *U.S.A.* 35°14N 115°30W **79** K11
Cimarron *Kans., U.S.A.* 37°48N 100°21W **80** G3
Cimarron *N. Mex.,
U.S.A.* 36°31N 104°55W **77** H11
Cimarron → *U.S.A.* 36°10N 96°16W **84** C6
Cimişlia *Moldova* 46°34N 28°44E **17** E15
Cimone, Mte. *Italy* 44°12N 10°42E **22** B4
Cinca → *Spain* 41°26N 0°21E **21** B6
Cincar *Bos.-H.* 43°55N 17°5E **22** C7
Cincinnati *U.S.A.* 39°9N 84°27W **81** F11
Cincinnatus *U.S.A.* 42°33N 75°54W **83** D9
Çine *Turkey* 37°37N 28°2E **23** F13
Ciney *Belgium* 50°18N 5°5E **15** D5
Cinto, Mte. *France* 42°24N 8°54E **20** E8

Circle *Alaska, U.S.A.* 65°50N 144°4W **74** B11
Circle *Mont., U.S.A.* 47°25N 105°35W **76** C11
Circleville *U.S.A.* 39°36N 82°57W **81** F12
Cirebon *Indonesia* 6°45S 108°32E **37** G13
Ciremay *Indonesia* 6°55S 108°27E **37** G13
Cirencester *U.K.* 51°43N 1°57W **13** F6
Cirium *Cyprus* 34°40N 32°53E **25** E11
Cisco *U.S.A.* 32°23N 98°59W **84** E5
Citlaltépetl = Orizaba, Pico de
Mexico 18°58N 97°15W **87** D5
Citrus Heights *U.S.A.* 38°42N 121°17W **78** G5
Citrusdal *S. Africa* 32°35S 19°0E **56** E2
Città del Vaticano = Vatican
City ■ *Europe* 41°54N 12°27E **22** D5
Città di Castello *Italy* 43°27N 12°14E **22** C5
Ciudad Acuña *Mexico* 29°18N 100°55W **86** B4
Ciudad Altamirano
Mexico 18°20N 100°40W **86** D4
Ciudad Anáhuac
Mexico 27°14N 100°7W **86** B4
Ciudad Bolívar *Venezuela* 8°5N 63°36W **92** B6
Ciudad Camargo
Mexico 27°40N 105°10W **86** B3
Ciudad Cortés *Costa Rica* 8°55N 84°0W **88** E3
Ciudad de México *Mexico* 19°24N 99°9W **87** D5
Ciudad de Valles *Mexico* 22°0N 99°0W **87** C5
Ciudad del Carmen
Mexico 18°38N 91°50W **87** D6
Ciudad del Este *Paraguay* 25°30S 54°50W **95** B5
Ciudad Delicias = Delicias
Mexico 28°13N 105°28W **86** B3
Ciudad Frontera
Mexico 26°56N 101°27W **86** B4
Ciudad Guayana
Venezuela 8°0N 62°30W **92** B6
Ciudad Guerrero
Mexico 28°33N 107°30W **86** B3
Ciudad Guzmán
Mexico 19°41N 103°29W **86** D4
Ciudad Juárez *Mexico* 31°44N 106°29W **86** A3
Ciudad Lerdo *Mexico* 25°32N 103°32W **86** B4
Ciudad Madero *Mexico* 22°19N 97°50W **87** C5
Ciudad Mante *Mexico* 22°44N 98°59W **87** C5
Ciudad Obregón
Mexico 27°29N 109°56W **86** B3
Ciudad Real *Spain* 38°59N 3°55W **21** C4
Ciudad Rodrigo *Spain* 40°35N 6°32W **21** B2
Ciudad Victoria *Mexico* 23°44N 99°8W **87** C5
Ciudadela *Spain* 40°0N 3°50E **24** B10
Civitanova Marche *Italy* 43°18N 13°44E **22** C5
Civitavécchia *Italy* 42°6N 11°48E **22** C4
Cizre *Turkey* 37°19N 42°10E **44** B4
Clackmannanshire □
U.K. 56°10N 3°43W **11** E5
Clacton-on-Sea *U.K.* 51°47N 1°11E **13** F9
Claire, L. *Canada* 58°35N 112°5W **70** B6
Clairton *U.S.A.* 40°18N 79°53W **82** F5
Clallam Bay *U.S.A.* 48°15N 124°16W **78** B2
Clanton *U.S.A.* 32°51N 86°38W **85** E11
Clanwilliam *S. Africa* 32°11S 18°52E **56** E2
Clara *Ireland* 53°21N 7°37W **10** C4
Claraville *U.S.A.* 35°24N 118°20W **79** K8
Clare *Australia* 33°50S 138°37E **63** E2
Clare *U.S.A.* 43°49N 84°46W **81** D11
Clare □ *Ireland* 52°45N 9°0W **10** D3
Clare → *Ireland* 53°20N 9°2W **10** C2
Clare I. *Ireland* 53°49N 10°0W **10** C1
Claremont *Calif., U.S.A.* 34°6N 117°43W **79** L9
Claremont *N.H., U.S.A.* 43°23N 72°20W **83** C12
Claremont Pt. *Australia* 14°1S 143°41E **62** A3
Claremore *U.S.A.* 36°19N 95°36W **84** C7
Claremorris *Ireland* 53°45N 9°0W **10** C3
Clarence → *Australia* 29°25S 153°22E **63** D5
Clarence → *N.Z.* 42°10S 173°56E **59** E4
Clarence, I. *Chile* 54°0S 72°0W **96** G2
Clarence I. *Antarctica* 61°10S 54°0W **5** C18
Clarence Str. *U.S.A.* 12°0S 131°0E **60** B5
Clarence Town *Bahamas* 23°6N 74°59W **89** B5
Clarendon *Pa., U.S.A.* 41°47N 79°6W **82** E5
Clarendon *Tex., U.S.A.* 34°56N 100°53W **84** D4
Clarenville *Canada* 48°10N 54°1W **73** C9
Claresholm *Canada* 50°2N 113°33W **70** C6
Clarie Coast *Antarctica* 68°0S 135°0E **5** C9
Clarinda *U.S.A.* 40°44N 95°2W **80** E6
Clarington *Canada* 43°55N 78°41W **82** C6
Clarion *Iowa, U.S.A.* 42°44N 93°44W **80** D7
Clarion *Pa., U.S.A.* 41°13N 79°23W **82** E5
Clarion → *U.S.A.* 41°7N 79°41W **82** E5
Clarion Fracture Zone
Pac. Oc. 20°0N 120°0W **66** H7
Clark *U.S.A.* 44°53N 97°44W **80** C5
Clark, Pt. *Canada* 44°4N 81°45W **82** B3
Clark Fork *U.S.A.* 48°9N 116°11W **76** B5
Clark Fork → *U.S.A.* 48°9N 116°15W **76** B5
Clarkdale *U.S.A.* 34°46N 112°3W **77** J7
Clarke City *Canada* 50°12N 66°38W **73** B6
Clarke I. *Australia* 40°32S 148°10E **63** G4
Clarke → *Australia* 19°45S 148°30E **62** B3
Clarks Fork Yellowstone →
U.S.A. 45°39N 108°43W **76** D9
Clark's Harbour *Canada* 43°25N 65°38W **73** D6
Clarks Hill L. = J. Strom
Thurmond L. *U.S.A.* 33°40N 82°12W **85** E13
Clarks Summit *U.S.A.* 41°30N 75°42W **83** E9
Clarksburg *U.S.A.* 39°17N 80°30W **81** F13
Clarksdale *U.S.A.* 34°12N 90°35W **85** D9
Clarkston *U.S.A.* 46°25N 117°3W **76** C5
Clarksville *Ark., U.S.A.* 35°28N 93°28W **84** D8
Clarksville *Tenn.,
U.S.A.* 36°32N 87°21W **85** C11
Clarksville *Tex., U.S.A.* 33°37N 95°3W **84** E7
Clatskanie *U.S.A.* 46°6N 123°12W **78** D3
Claude *U.S.A.* 35°7N 101°22W **84** D4
Claveria *Phil.* 18°37N 121°4E **37** A6
Clay *U.S.A.* 38°17N 121°10W **78** G5
Clay Center *U.S.A.* 39°23N 97°8W **80** F5
Claypool *U.S.A.* 33°25N 110°51W **77** K8
Claysburg *U.S.A.* 40°17N 78°27W **82** F6
Claysville *U.S.A.* 40°7N 80°25W **82** F4

Clayton *Canada* 45°11N 76°19W **83** A8
Clayton *N. Mex.,
U.S.A.* 36°27N 103°11W **77** H12
Clayton *N.Y., U.S.A.* 44°14N 76°5W **83** B8
Clear, C. *Ireland* 51°25N 9°32W **10** E2
Clear, L. *Canada* 45°26N 77°12W **82** A7
Clear Hills *Canada* 56°40N 119°30W **70** B5
Clear I. *Ireland* 51°26N 9°30W **10** E2
Clear L. *U.S.A.* 39°2N 122°47W **78** F4
Clear Lake *Iowa, U.S.A.* 43°8N 93°23W **80** D7
Clear Lake *S. Dak.,
U.S.A.* 44°45N 96°41W **80** C5
Clear Lake Res. *U.S.A.* 41°56N 121°5W **76** F3
Clearfield *Pa., U.S.A.* 41°2N 78°27W **82** E6
Clearfield *Utah, U.S.A.* 41°7N 112°2W **76** F7
Clearlake *U.S.A.* 38°57N 122°38W **78** G4
Clearwater *Canada* 51°38N 120°2W **70** C4
Clearwater *U.S.A.* 27°59N 82°48W **85** H13
Clearwater → *Alta.,*
Canada 52°22N 114°57W **70** C6
Clearwater → *Alta.,*
Canada 56°44N 111°23W **71** B6
Clearwater L. *Canada* 53°34N 99°49W **71** C9
Clearwater Lake △
Canada 54°0N 101°0W **71** C8
Clearwater Mts. *U.S.A.* 46°5N 115°20W **76** C6
Clearwater River △
Canada 56°55N 109°10W **71** B7
Cleburne *U.S.A.* 32°21N 97°23W **84** E6
Clee Hills *U.K.* 52°26N 2°35W **13** E5
Cleethorpes *U.K.* 53°33N 0°3W **12** D7
Cleeve Cloud *U.K.* 51°56N 2°0W **13** F6
Clemson *U.S.A.* 34°41N 82°50W **85** D13
Clerke Reef *Australia* 17°22S 119°20E **60** C2
Clermont *Australia* 22°49S 147°39E **62** C4
Clermont *U.S.A.* 28°33N 81°46W **85** G14
Clermont-Ferrand *France* 45°46N 3°4E **20** D5
Clervaux *Lux.* 50°4N 6°2E **15** D6
Clevedon *U.K.* 51°26N 2°52W **13** F5
Cleveland *Miss., U.S.A.* 33°45N 90°43W **85** E9
Cleveland *Ohio, U.S.A.* 41°29N 81°41W **82** E3
Cleveland *Okla., U.S.A.* 36°19N 96°28W **84** C6
Cleveland *Tenn., U.S.A.* 35°10N 84°53W **85** D12
Cleveland *Tex., U.S.A.* 30°21N 95°5W **84** F7
Cleveland, C. *Australia* 19°11S 147°1E **62** B4
Cleveland, Mt. *U.S.A.* 48°56N 113°51W **76** B7
Cleveland Heights
U.S.A. 41°31N 81°33W **82** E3
Clevelândia *Brazil* 26°24S 52°23W **95** B5
Clew B. *Ireland* 53°50N 9°49W **10** C2
Clewiston *U.S.A.* 26°45N 80°56W **85** H14
Clifden *Ireland* 53°29N 10°1W **10** C1
Clifden *N.Z.* 46°1S 167°42E **59** G1
Cliffdell *U.S.A.* 46°56N 121°5W **78** D5
Cliffy Hd. *Australia* 35°1S 116°29E **61** G2
Clifton *Australia* 27°59S 151°53E **63** D5
Clifton *Ariz., U.S.A.* 33°3N 109°18W **77** K9
Clifton *Colo., U.S.A.* 39°7N 108°25W **76** G9
Clifton *Tex., U.S.A.* 31°47N 97°35W **84** F6
Clifton Beach *Australia* 16°46S 145°39E **62** B4
Clinch → *U.S.A.* 35°53N 84°29W **85** D12
Clingmans Dome
U.S.A. 35°34N 83°30W **85** D13
Clint *U.S.A.* 31°35N 106°14W **84** F1
Clinton *B.C., Canada* 51°6N 121°35W **70** C4
Clinton *Ont., Canada* 43°37N 81°32W **82** C3
Clinton *N.Z.* 46°12S 169°23E **59** G2
Clinton *Ark., U.S.A.* 35°36N 92°28W **84** D8
Clinton *Conn., U.S.A.* 41°17N 72°32W **83** E12
Clinton *Ill., U.S.A.* 40°9N 88°57W **80** E9
Clinton *Ind., U.S.A.* 39°40N 87°24W **80** F10
Clinton *Iowa, U.S.A.* 41°51N 90°12W **80** E8
Clinton *Mass., U.S.A.* 42°25N 71°41W **83** D13
Clinton *Miss., U.S.A.* 32°20N 90°20W **85** E9
Clinton *Mo., U.S.A.* 38°22N 93°46W **80** F7
Clinton *N.C., U.S.A.* 35°0N 78°22W **85** D15
Clinton *Okla., U.S.A.* 35°31N 98°58W **84** D5
Clinton *S.C., U.S.A.* 34°29N 81°53W **85** D14
Clinton *Tenn., U.S.A.* 36°6N 84°8W **85** C12
Clinton *Wash., U.S.A.* 47°59N 122°21W **78** C4
Clinton, C. *Australia* 22°30S 150°45E **62** C5
Clinton Colden L.
Canada 63°58N 107°27W **68** E10
Clintonville *U.S.A.* 44°37N 88°46W **80** C9
Clipperton, I. *Pac. Oc.* 10°18N 109°13W **65** F17
Clipperton Fracture Zone
Pac. Oc. 19°0N 122°0W **65** G16
Clisham *U.K.* 57°58N 6°49W **11** D2
Clitheroe *U.K.* 53°53N 2°22W **12** D5
Clo-oose *Canada* 48°39N 124°49W **78** B2
Cloates, Pt. *Australia* 22°43S 113°40E **60** D1
Clocolan *S. Africa* 28°55S 27°34E **57** D4
Clodomira *Argentina* 27°35S 64°14W **94** B3
Clogher Hd. *Ireland* 53°48N 6°14W **10** C5
Clonakilty *Ireland* 51°37N 8°53W **10** E3
Clonakilty B. *Ireland* 51°35N 8°51W **10** E3
Cloncurry *Australia* 20°40S 140°28E **62** C3
Cloncurry *Ireland* 53°19N 6°25W **10** C5
Cloncurry → *Australia* 18°37S 140°40E **62** B3
Clondalkin *Ireland* 53°19N 6°25W **10** C5
Clones *Ireland* 54°11N 7°15W **10** B4
Clonmel *Ireland* 52°21N 7°42W **10** D4
Cloquet *U.S.A.* 46°43N 92°28W **80** B7
Clorinda *Argentina* 25°16S 57°45W **94** B4
Cloud Bay *Canada* 48°5N 89°26W **72** C2
Cloud Peak *U.S.A.* 44°23N 107°11W **76** D10
Cloudcroft *U.S.A.* 32°58N 105°45W **77** K11
Cloverdale *U.S.A.* 38°48N 123°1W **78** G4
Clovis *Calif., U.S.A.* 36°49N 119°42W **78** J7
Clovis *N. Mex., U.S.A.* 34°24N 103°12W **77** J12
Cloyne *Canada* 44°49N 77°11W **82** B7
Cluain Meala = Clonmel
Ireland 52°21N 7°42W **10** D4
Cluj-Napoca *Romania* 46°47N 23°38E **17** E12
Clunes *Australia* 37°20S 143°45E **63** F3
Clutha → *N.Z.* 46°20S 169°49E **59** G2
Clwyd → *U.K.* 53°19N 3°31W **12** D4
Clyde *Canada* 54°9N 113°39W **70** C6
Clyde *N.Z.* 45°12S 169°20E **59** F2

Clyde *U.S.A.* 43°5N 76°52W 82 C8
Clyde → *U.K.* 55°55N 4°30W 11 F4
Clyde, Firth of *U.K.* 55°22N 5°1W 11 F3
Clyde Muirshiel △ *U.K.* 55°50N 4°40W 11 F4
Clyde River *Canada* 70°30N 68°30W 69 C18
Clydebank *U.K.* 55°54N 4°23W 11 F4
Clymer *N.Y., U.S.A.* 42°1N 79°37W 82 D5
Clymer *Pa., U.S.A.* 40°40N 79°1W 82 D5
Coachella *U.S.A.* 33°41N 116°10W 79 M10
Coachella Canal
 U.S.A. 32°43N 114°57W 79 N12
Coahoma *U.S.A.* 32°18N 101°18W 84 E4
Coahuayana →
 Mexico 18°41N 103°45W 86 D4
Coahuila □ *Mexico* 27°20N 102°0W 86 B4
Coal → *Canada* 59°39N 126°57W 70 B3
Coalane *Mozam.* 17°48S 37°2E 55 F4
Coalcomán *Mexico* 18°47N 103°9W 86 D4
Coaldale *Canada* 49°45N 112°35W 70 D6
Coalgate *U.S.A.* 34°32N 96°13W 84 D6
Coalinga *U.S.A.* 36°9N 120°21W 78 J6
Coalisland *U.K.* 54°33N 6°42W 10 B5
Coalville *U.K.* 52°44N 1°23W 12 E6
Coalville *U.S.A.* 40°55N 111°24W 76 F8
Coamo *Puerto Rico* 18°5N 66°22W 89 d
Coari *Brazil* 4°8S 63°7W 92 D6
Coast □ *Kenya* 2°40S 39°45E 54 C4
Coast Mts. *Canada* 55°0N 129°20W 70 C3
Coast Ranges *U.S.A.* 39°0N 123°0W 78 G4
Coatbridge *U.K.* 55°52N 4°6W 11 F4
Coatepec *Mexico* 19°27N 96°58W 87 D5
Coatepeque *Guatemala* 14°46N 91°55W 88 D1
Coatesville *U.S.A.* 39°59N 75°50W 81 F16
Coats I. *Canada* 62°30N 83°0W 69 E15
Coats Land *Antarctica* 77°0S 25°0W 5 D1
Coatzacoalcos *Mexico* 18°7N 94°25W 87 D6
Cobá *Mexico* 20°31N 87°45W 87 C7
Cobalt *Canada* 47°25N 79°42W 72 C4
Cobán *Guatemala* 15°30N 90°21W 88 C1
Cobar *Australia* 31°27S 145°48E 63 E4
Cóbh *Ireland* 51°51N 8°17W 10 E3
Cobija *Bolivia* 11°0S 68°50W 92 F5
Cobleskill *U.S.A.* 42°41N 74°29W 83 D10
Coboconk *Canada* 44°39N 78°48W 82 B6
Cobourg *Canada* 43°58N 78°10W 82 C6
Cobourg Pen. *Australia* 11°20S 132°15E 60 B5
Cobram *Australia* 35°54S 145°40E 63 F4
Cóbué *Mozam.* 12°0S 34°58E 55 E3
Coburg *Germany* 50°15N 10°58E 16 C6
Coburg I. *Canada* 75°57N 79°26W 69 B16
Cocanada = Kakinada
 India 16°57N 82°11E 41 L13
Cochabamba *Bolivia* 17°26S 66°10W 92 G5
Cochemane *Mozam.* 17°0S 32°54E 55 F3
Cochin *India* 9°58N 76°20E 40 Q10
Cochin China = Nam-Phan
 Vietnam 10°30N 106°0E 39 G6
Cochran *U.S.A.* 32°23N 83°21W 85 E13
Cochrane *Alta., Canada* 51°11N 114°30W 70 C6
Cochrane *Ont., Canada* 49°0N 81°0W 72 C3
Cochrane → *Canada* 59°0N 103°40W 71 B8
Cochrane, L. *Chile* 47°10S 72°0W 96 F2
Cochranton *U.S.A.* 41°31N 80°3W 82 E4
Cockburn *Australia* 32°5S 141°0E 63 E3
Cockburn, Canal *Chile* 54°30S 72°0W 96 G2
Cockburn I. *Canada* 45°55N 83°22W 72 C3
Cockburn Ra. *Australia* 15°46S 128°0E 60 C4
Cockermouth *U.K.* 54°40N 3°22W 12 C4
Cocklebiddy *Australia* 32°0S 126°3E 61 F4
Cockpit Country, The
 Jamaica 18°15N 77°45W 88 a
Coco → *Cent. Amer.* 15°0N 83°8W 88 D3
Coco, I. del *Pac. Oc.* 5°25N 87°55W 65 G19
Cocoa *U.S.A.* 28°21N 80°44W 85 G14
Cocobeach *Gabon* 0°59N 9°34E 52 D1
Cocos B. *Trin. & Tob.* 10°25N 61°2W 93 K15
Cocos Is. *Ind. Oc.* 12°10S 96°55E 64 J11
Cocos Ridge *Pac. Oc.* 4°0N 88°0W 65 G19
Cod, C. *U.S.A.* 42°5N 70°10W 81 D18
Codajás *Brazil* 3°55S 62°0W 92 D6
Codó *Brazil* 4°30S 43°55W 93 D10
Cody *U.S.A.* 44°32N 109°3W 76 D9
Coe Hill *Canada* 44°52N 77°50W 82 B7
Coelemu *Chile* 36°30S 72°48W 94 D1
Coen *Australia* 13°52S 143°12E 62 A3
Coeur d'Alene *U.S.A.* 47°41N 116°46W 76 C5
Coeur d'Alene L.
 U.S.A. 47°32N 116°49W 76 C5
Coevorden *Neths.* 52°40N 6°44E 15 B6
Cofete *Canary Is.* 28°6N 14°23W 24 F5
Coffeyville *U.S.A.* 37°2N 95°37W 84 D7
Coffin B. *Australia* 34°38S 135°28E 63 E2
Coffin Bay *Australia* 34°37S 135°29E 63 E2
Coffin Bay △ *Australia* 34°34S 135°19E 63 E2
Coffin Bay Peninsula
 Australia 34°32S 135°15E 63 E2
Coffs Harbour *Australia* 30°16S 153°5E 63 E5
Cognac *France* 45°41N 0°20W 20 D3
Cohocton *U.S.A.* 42°30N 77°30W 82 D7
Cohocton → *U.S.A.* 42°9N 77°6W 82 D7
Cohoes *U.S.A.* 42°46N 73°42W 83 D11
Cohuna *Australia* 35°45S 144°15E 63 F3
Coiba, I. de *Panama* 7°30N 81°40W 88 E3
Coig → *Argentina* 51°0S 69°10W 96 G3
Coigeach, Rubha *U.K.* 58°6N 5°26W 11 C3
Coihaique *Chile* 45°30S 71°45W 96 F2
Coimbatore *India* 11°2N 76°59E 40 P10
Coimbra *Brazil* 19°55S 57°48W 92 G7
Coimbra *Portugal* 40°15N 8°27W 21 B1
Coín *Spain* 36°40N 4°48W 21 D3
Coipasa, Salar de *Bolivia* 19°26S 68°9W 92 G5
Cojimies *Ecuador* 0°20N 80°0W 92 C3
Cojutepeque *El Salv.* 13°41N 88°54W 88 D2
Cokeville *U.S.A.* 42°5N 110°57W 76 E8
Colac *Australia* 38°21S 143°35E 63 F3
Colatina *Brazil* 19°32S 40°37W 93 G10
Colbeck, C. *Antarctica* 77°6S 157°48W 5 D13

Colborne *Canada* 44°0N 77°53W 82 C7
Colby *U.S.A.* 39°24N 101°3W 80 F3
Colca → *Peru* 15°5S 72°43W 92 G4
Colchester *U.K.* 51°54N 0°55E 13 F8
Colchester *U.S.A.* 41°35N 72°20W 83 E12
Cold L. *Canada* 54°33N 110°5W 71 C7
Cold Lake *Canada* 54°27N 110°10W 71 C6
Coldstream *Canada* 50°13N 119°11W 70 C5
Coldstream *U.K.* 55°39N 2°15W 11 F6
Coldwater *Canada* 44°42N 79°40W 82 B5
Coldwater *Kans., U.S.A.* 37°16N 99°20W 80 G4
Coldwater *Mich., U.S.A.* 41°57N 85°0W 81 E11
Colebrook *U.S.A.* 44°54N 71°30W 83 B13
Coleman *Canada* 49°40N 114°30W 70 D6
Coleman *U.S.A.* 31°50N 99°26W 84 F5
Coleman → *Australia* 15°6S 141°38E 62 B3
Colenso *S. Africa* 28°44S 29°50E 57 D4
Coleraine *Australia* 37°36S 141°40E 63 F3
Coleraine *U.K.* 55°8N 6°41W 10 A5
Coleridge, L. *N.Z.* 43°17S 171°30E 59 E3
Coleville *U.S.A.* 38°34N 119°30W 78 G7
Colfax *Calif., U.S.A.* 39°6N 120°57W 78 F6
Colfax *La., U.S.A.* 31°31N 92°42W 84 F8
Colfax *Wash., U.S.A.* 46°53N 117°22W 76 C5
Colhué Huapi, L.
 Argentina 45°30S 69°0W 96 F3
Coligny *S. Africa* 26°17S 26°15E 57 D4
Colima *Mexico* 19°14N 103°43W 86 D4
Colima □ *Mexico* 19°10N 104°0W 86 D4
Colima, Nevado de
 Mexico 19°33N 103°38W 86 D4
Colina *Chile* 33°13S 70°45W 94 C1
Colinas *Brazil* 6°0S 44°10W 93 E10
Coll *U.K.* 56°39N 6°34W 11 E2
Collahuasi *Chile* 21°5S 68°45W 94 A2
Collarenebri *Australia* 29°33S 148°34E 63 D4
Colleen Bawn *Zimbabwe* 21°0S 29°12E 55 G2
College *U.S.A.* 64°52N 147°49W 74 C10
College Park *U.S.A.* 33°39N 84°27W 85 E12
College Station *U.S.A.* 30°37N 96°21W 84 F6
Collie *Australia* 33°22S 116°8E 61 F2
Collier B. *Australia* 16°10S 124°15E 60 C3
Collier Ra. *Australia* 24°45S 119°10E 61 D2
Collier Range △
 Australia 24°39S 119°7E 61 D2
Collierville *U.S.A.* 35°3N 89°40W 85 D10
Collina, Passo di *Italy* 44°2N 10°56E 22 B4
Collingwood *Canada* 44°29N 80°13W 82 B4
Collingwood *N.Z.* 40°41S 172°40E 59 D4
Collins *Canada* 50°17N 89°27W 72 B2
Collins Bay *Canada* 44°14N 76°36W 83 B8
Collinson Pen. *Canada* 69°58N 101°24W 68 D11
Collinsville *Australia* 20°30S 147°56E 62 C4
Collipulli *Chile* 37°55S 72°30W 94 D1
Collooney *Ireland* 54°11N 8°29W 10 B3
Colmar *France* 48°5N 7°20E 20 B7
Colo → *Australia* 33°25S 150°52E 63 E5
Cologne = Köln *Germany* 50°56N 6°57E 16 C4
Colom, I. d'en *Spain* 39°58N 4°16E 24 B11
Coloma *U.S.A.* 38°48N 120°53W 78 G6
Colomb-Béchar = Béchar
 Algeria 31°38N 2°18W 50 B5
Colombia ■ *S. Amer.* 3°45N 73°0W 92 C4
Colombian Basin
 S. Amer. 14°0N 76°0W 66 H12
Colombo *Sri Lanka* 6°56N 79°58E 40 R11
Colón *B. Aires, Argentina* 33°53S 61°7W 94 C3
Colón *Entre Ríos,*
 Argentina 32°12S 58°10W 94 C4
Colón *Cuba* 22°42N 80°54W 88 B3
Colón *Panama* 9°20N 79°54W 88 E4
Colón, Arch. de *Ecuador* 0°0 91°0W 90 D1
Colònia de Sant Jordi
 Spain 39°19N 2°59E 24 B9
Colonia del Sacramento
 Uruguay 34°25S 57°50W 94 C4
Colonia Dora *Argentina* 28°34S 62°59W 94 B3
Colonial Beach *U.S.A.* 38°15N 76°58W 81 F15
Colonie *U.S.A.* 42°43N 73°50W 83 D11
Colonsay *Canada* 51°59N 105°52W 71 C7
Colonsay *U.K.* 56°5N 6°12W 11 E2
Colorado □ *U.S.A.* 39°30N 105°30W 76 G11
Colorado → *Argentina* 39°50S 62°8W 96 D4
Colorado → *N. Amer.* 31°45N 114°40W 77 L6
Colorado → *U.S.A.* 28°36N 95°59W 84 G7
Colorado City *U.S.A.* 32°24N 100°52W 84 E4
Colorado Plateau *U.S.A.* 37°0N 111°0W 77 H8
Colorado River Aqueduct
 U.S.A. 33°50N 117°23W 79 L12
Colorado Springs
 U.S.A. 38°50N 104°49W 76 G11
Colotlán *Mexico* 22°6N 103°16W 86 C4
Colstrip *U.S.A.* 45°53N 106°38W 76 D10
Colton *U.S.A.* 44°33N 74°56W 83 B10
Columbia *Ky., U.S.A.* 37°6N 85°18W 81 G11
Columbia *La., U.S.A.* 32°6N 92°5W 84 E8
Columbia *Miss., U.S.A.* 31°15N 89°50W 85 F10
Columbia *Mo., U.S.A.* 38°57N 92°20W 80 F7
Columbia *Pa., U.S.A.* 40°2N 76°30W 83 F8
Columbia *S.C., U.S.A.* 34°0N 81°2W 85 D14
Columbia *Tenn., U.S.A.* 35°37N 87°2W 85 D11
Columbia → *N. Amer.* 46°15N 124°5W 78 D2
Columbia, C. *Canada* 83°6N 69°57W 69 A18
Columbia, District of □
 U.S.A. 38°55N 77°0W 81 F15
Columbia, Mt. *Canada* 52°8N 117°20W 70 C5
Columbia Basin *U.S.A.* 46°45N 119°5W 76 C4
Columbia Falls *U.S.A.* 48°23N 114°11W 76 B6
Columbia Mts. *U.S.A.* 52°0N 119°0W 70 C5
Columbia Plateau
 U.S.A. 44°0N 117°30W 76 F5
Columbiana *U.S.A.* 40°53N 80°42W 82 F4
Columbretes, Is. *Spain* 39°50N 0°50E 21 C6
Columbus *Ga., U.S.A.* 32°28N 84°59W 85 E12
Columbus *Ind., U.S.A.* 39°13N 85°55W 81 F11
Columbus *Kans., U.S.A.* 37°10N 94°50W 80 G6
Columbus *Miss., U.S.A.* 33°30N 88°25W 85 E10
Columbus *Mont.,*
 U.S.A. 45°38N 109°15W 76 D9

Columbus *N. Mex.,*
 U.S.A. 31°50N 107°38W 77 L10
Columbus *Nebr., U.S.A.* 41°26N 97°22W 80 E5
Columbus *Ohio, U.S.A.* 39°58N 83°0W 81 F12
Columbus *Tex., U.S.A.* 29°42N 96°33W 84 G6
Colusa *U.S.A.* 39°13N 122°1W 78 F4
Colville *U.S.A.* 48°33N 117°54W 76 B5
Colville → *U.S.A.* 70°25N 150°30W 74 A9
Colville, C. *N.Z.* 36°29S 175°21E 59 B5
Colwood *Canada* 48°26N 123°29W 78 B3
Colwyn Bay *U.K.* 53°18N 3°44W 12 D4
Comácchio *Italy* 44°42N 12°11E 22 B5
Comalcalco *Mexico* 18°16N 93°13W 87 D6
Comallo *Argentina* 41°0S 70°5W 96 E2
Comanche *U.S.A.* 31°54N 98°36W 84 F5
Comandante Ferraz
 Antarctica 62°5S 58°0W 5 C18
Comayagua *Honduras* 14°25N 87°37W 88 D2
Combahee → *U.S.A.* 32°31N 80°31W 85 E14
Combarbalá *Chile* 31°11S 71°2W 94 C1
Combe Martin *U.K.* 51°12N 4°3W 13 F3
Comber *Canada* 42°14N 82°33W 82 D2
Comber *U.K.* 54°33N 5°45W 10 B6
Combermere *Canada* 45°22N 77°37W 82 A7
Comblain-au-Pont
 Belgium 50°29N 5°35E 15 D5
Comeragh Mts. *Ireland* 52°18N 7°34W 10 D4
Comet *Australia* 23°36S 148°38E 62 C4
Comilla *Bangla.* 23°28N 91°10E 41 H17
Comino *Malta* 36°1N 14°20E 25 C1
Comino, C. *Italy* 40°32N 9°49E 22 D3
Comitán de Domínguez
 Mexico 16°15N 92°8W 87 D6
Commerce *Ga., U.S.A.* 34°12N 83°28W 85 D13
Commerce *Tex., U.S.A.* 33°15N 95°54W 84 E7
Committee B. *Canada* 68°30N 86°30W 69 D14
Commodore, C. *Canada* 44°47N 80°54W 82 B4
Commonwealth B.
 Antarctica 67°0S 144°0E 5 C10
Commoron Cr. →
 Australia 28°22S 150°8E 63 D5
Communism Pk. = imeni Ismail
 Samani, Pik *Tajikistan* 39°0N 72°2E 28 F8
Como *Italy* 45°47N 9°5E 20 D8
Como, Lago di *Italy* 46°0N 9°11E 20 D8
Comodoro Rivadavia
 Argentina 45°50S 67°40W 96 F3
Comorin, C. = Kannyakumari
 India 8°3N 77°40E 40 Q10
Comoros ■ *Ind. Oc.* 12°10S 44°15E 53 a
Comox *Canada* 49°42N 124°55W 70 D4
Compiègne *France* 49°24N 2°50E 20 B5
Compostela *Mexico* 21°14N 104°55W 86 C4
Comprida, I. *Brazil* 24°50S 47°42W 95 A6
Compton *Canada* 45°14N 71°49W 83 A13
Compton *U.S.A.* 33°53N 118°13W 79 M8
Comrat *Moldova* 46°18N 28°40E 17 E15
Con Cuong *Vietnam* 19°2N 104°54E 38 C5
Con Dao *Vietnam* 8°42N 106°3E 39 H6
Con Son *Vietnam* 8°41N 106°37E 39 H6
Conakry *Guinea* 9°29N 13°49W 50 G3
Conara *Australia* 41°50S 147°26E 63 G4
Concarneau *France* 47°52N 3°56W 20 C2
Conceição *Mozam.* 18°47S 36°7E 55 F4
Conceição da Barra
 Brazil 18°35S 39°45W 93 G11
Conceição do Araguaia
 Brazil 8°0S 49°2W 93 E9
Concepción *Argentina* 27°20S 65°35W 94 B2
Concepción *Bolivia* 16°15S 62°8W 92 G6
Concepción *Chile* 36°50S 73°0W 94 D1
Concepción *Mexico* 18°15N 90°5W 87 D6
Concepción *Paraguay* 23°22S 57°26W 94 A4
Concepción □ *Chile* 37°0S 72°30W 94 D1
Concepción → *Mexico* 30°32N 113°2W 86 A2
Concepción, Est. de
 Chile 50°30S 74°55W 96 G2
Concepción, L. *Bolivia* 17°20S 61°20W 92 G6
Concepción, Pta.
 Mexico 26°53N 111°50W 86 B2
Concepción del Oro
 Mexico 24°38N 101°25W 86 C4
Concepción del Uruguay
 Argentina 32°35S 58°20W 94 C4
Conception, Pt. *U.S.A.* 34°27N 120°28W 79 L6
Conception B. *Canada* 47°45N 53°0W 73 C9
Conception B. *Namibia* 23°55S 14°22E 56 C1
Conception I. *Bahamas* 23°52N 75°9W 89 B4
Concession *Zimbabwe* 17°27S 30°56E 55 F3
Conchas Dam *U.S.A.* 35°22N 104°11W 77 J11
Concho *U.S.A.* 34°28N 109°36W 77 J9
Concho → *U.S.A.* 31°34N 99°43W 84 F5
Conchos → *Chihuahua,*
 Mexico 29°35N 104°25W 86 B4
Conchos → *Chihuahua,*
 Mexico 27°29N 105°45W 86 B3
Conchos → *Tamaulipas,*
 Mexico 24°55N 97°38W 87 B5
Concord *Calif., U.S.A.* 37°59N 122°2W 78 H4
Concord *N.C., U.S.A.* 35°25N 80°35W 85 D14
Concord *N.H., U.S.A.* 43°12N 71°32W 83 C13
Concordia *Antarctica* 75°6S 123°23E 5 D17
Concórdia *Amazonas,*
 Brazil 4°36S 66°36W 92 D5
Concórdia *Sta. Catarina,*
 Brazil 27°14S 52°1W 95 B5
Concordia *Mexico* 23°17N 106°4W 86 C3
Concordia *U.S.A.* 39°34N 97°40W 80 F5
Concrete *U.S.A.* 48°32N 121°45W 76 B3
Condamine *Australia* 26°56S 150°9E 63 D5
Conde *U.S.A.* 45°9N 98°6W 80 C4
Condeúba *Brazil* 14°52S 42°0W 93 F10
Condobolin *Australia* 33°4S 147°6E 63 E4
Condon *U.S.A.* 45°14N 120°11W 76 D3
Conegliano *Italy* 45°53N 12°18E 22 B5
Conejera, I. = Conills, I. des
 Spain 39°11N 2°58E 24 B9
Conejos *Mexico* 26°14N 103°53W 86 B4

Conemaugh → *U.S.A.* 40°28N 79°19W 82 F5
Confuso → *Paraguay* 25°9S 57°34W 94 B4
Congleton *U.K.* 53°10N 2°13W 12 D5
Congo (Brazzaville) = Congo ■
 Africa 1°0S 16°0E 52 E3
Congo (Kinshasa) = Congo, Dem.
 Rep. of the ■ *Africa* 3°0S 23°0E 52 E4
Congo ■ *Africa* 1°0S 16°0E 52 E3
Congo → *Africa* 6°4S 12°24E 52 F2
Congo, Dem. Rep. of the ■
 Africa 3°0S 23°0E 52 E4
Congo Basin *Africa* 0°10S 24°30E 52 E4
Congonhas *Brazil* 20°30S 43°52W 95 A7
Congress *U.S.A.* 34°9N 112°51W 77 J7
Conills, I. des *Spain* 39°11N 2°58E 24 B9
Coniston *Canada* 46°29N 80°51W 72 C3
Conjeeveram = Kanchipuram
 India 12°52N 79°45E 40 N11
Conklin *Canada* 55°38N 111°5W 71 B6
Conklin *U.S.A.* 42°2N 75°49W 83 D9
Conn, L. *Ireland* 54°3N 9°15W 10 B2
Connacht □ *Ireland* 53°43N 9°12W 10 C2
Conneaut *U.S.A.* 41°57N 80°34W 82 E4
Conneautville *U.S.A.* 41°45N 80°22W 82 E4
Connecticut □ *U.S.A.* 41°30N 72°45W 83 E12
Connecticut → *U.S.A.* 41°16N 72°20W 83 E12
Connell *U.S.A.* 46°40N 118°52W 76 C4
Connellsville *U.S.A.* 40°1N 79°35W 82 F5
Connemara *Ireland* 53°29N 9°45W 10 C2
Connemara △ *Ireland* 53°32N 9°52W 10 C2
Connersville *U.S.A.* 39°39N 85°8W 81 F11
Connors Ra. *Australia* 21°40S 149°10E 62 C4
Conoweame 5°48N 55°55W *Suriname* 93 B7
Conquest *Canada* 51°32N 107°14W 71 C7
Conrad *U.S.A.* 48°10N 111°57W 76 B8
Conrad Rise *S. Ocean* 53°0S 41°0E 5 B5
Conran, C. *Australia* 37°49S 148°44E 63 F4
Conroe *U.S.A.* 30°19N 95°27W 84 F7
Consecon *Canada* 44°0N 77°31W 82 C7
Conselheiro Lafaiete
 Brazil 20°40S 43°48W 95 A7
Consell *Spain* 39°40N 2°49E 24 B9
Consett *U.K.* 54°51N 1°50W 12 C6
Consort *Canada* 52°1N 110°46W 71 C6
Constance = Konstanz
 Germany 47°40N 9°10E 16 E5
Constance, L. = Bodensee
 Europe 47°35N 9°25E 20 C8
Constanţa *Romania* 44°14N 28°38E 17 F15
Constantine *Algeria* 36°25N 6°42E 50 A7
Constitución *Chile* 35°20S 72°30W 94 D1
Constitución *Uruguay* 31°0S 57°50W 94 C4
Constitución de 1857 △
 Mexico 32°4N 115°55W 86 A1
Consul *Canada* 49°20N 109°30W 71 D7
Contact *U.S.A.* 41°46N 114°45W 76 F6
Contai *India* 21°54N 87°46E 43 J12
Contamana *Peru* 7°19S 74°55W 92 E4
Contas → *Brazil* 14°17S 39°1W 93 F11
Contoocook *U.S.A.* 43°13N 71°45W 83 C13
Contra Costa *Mozam.* 25°9S 33°30E 57 D5
Contwoyto L. *Canada* 65°42N 110°50W 68 D9
Conway = Conwy *U.K.* 53°17N 3°50W 12 D4
Conway *Australia* 20°24S 148°41E 62 b
Conway *Canada* 44°6N 76°54W 82 B8
Conway *Ark., U.S.A.* 35°5N 92°26W 84 D8
Conway *N.H., U.S.A.* 43°59N 71°7W 83 C13
Conway *S.C., U.S.A.* 33°51N 79°3W 85 E15
Conway, C. *Australia* 20°34S 148°46E 62 b
Conwy *U.K.* 53°17N 3°50W 12 D4
Conwy □ *U.K.* 53°10N 3°44W 12 D4
Conwy → *U.K.* 53°17N 3°50W 12 D4
Coober Pedy *Australia* 29°1S 134°43E 63 D1
Cooch Behar = Koch Bihar
 India 26°22N 89°29E 41 F16
Cooinda *Australia* 13°15S 130°5E 60 B5
Cook *Australia* 30°37S 130°25E 61 F5
Cook *U.S.A.* 47°51N 92°41W 80 B7
Cook, B. *Chile* 55°10S 70°0W 96 H3
Cook, C. *Canada* 50°8N 127°55W 70 C3
Cook, Mt. = Aoraki Mount Cook
 N.Z. 43°36S 170°9E 59 E3
Cook Inlet *U.S.A.* 60°0N 152°0W 68 F1
Cook Is. *Pac. Oc.* 17°0S 160°0W 65 J12
Cook Strait *N.Z.* 41°15S 174°29E 59 D5
Cookeville *U.S.A.* 36°10N 85°30W 85 C12
Cookhouse *S. Africa* 32°44S 25°47E 56 E4
Cooks Harbour *Canada* 51°36N 55°52W 73 B8
Cookshire *Canada* 45°25N 71°38W 83 A13
Cookstown *Canada* 54°11N 79°42W 82 B5
Cookstown *U.K.* 54°39N 6°45W 10 B5
Cooksville *Canada* 43°35N 79°38W 82 C5
Cooktown *Australia* 15°30S 145°16E 62 B4
Coolabah *Australia* 31°1S 146°43E 63 E4
Cooladdi *Australia* 26°37S 145°23E 63 D4
Coolah *Australia* 31°48S 149°41E 63 E4
Coolamon *Australia* 34°46S 147°8E 63 E4
Coolgardie *Australia* 30°55S 121°8E 61 F3
Coolidge *U.S.A.* 32°59N 111°31W 77 K8
Coolidge Dam *U.S.A.* 33°10N 110°32W 77 K8
Cooma *Australia* 36°12S 149°8E 63 F4
Coon Rapids *U.S.A.* 45°9N 93°19W 80 C7
Coonabarabran
 Australia 31°14S 149°18E 63 E4
Coonamble *Australia* 30°56S 148°27E 63 E4
Coonana *Australia* 31°0S 123°0E 61 F3
Coonana ۞ *Australia* 30°51S 122°53E 61 F3
Coondapoor *India* 13°42N 74°40E 40 N9
Cooninie, L. *Australia* 26°4S 139°59E 63 D2
Coonoor *India* 11°21N 76°45E 40 P10
Cooper *U.S.A.* 33°23N 95°42W 84 E7
Cooper Cr. → *Australia* 28°29S 137°46E 63 D2
Cooper Ridge *Pac. Oc.* 10°0N 150°30W 65 G12
Coopersburg *U.S.A.* 40°30N 75°23W 83 F9
Cooperstown *N. Dak.,*
 U.S.A. 47°27N 98°8W 80 B4
Cooperstown *N.Y.,*
 U.S.A. 42°42N 74°56W 83 D10

Coorabie *Australia* 31°54S 132°18E 61 F5
Coorong, The *Australia* 35°50S 139°20E 63 F2
Coorow *Australia* 29°53S 116°2E 61 E2
Cooroy *Australia* 26°22S 152°54E 63 D5
Coos Bay *U.S.A.* 43°22N 124°13W 76 E1
Coosa → *U.S.A.* 32°30N 86°16W 85 E11
Cootamundra *Australia* 34°36S 148°1E 63 E4
Cootehill *Ireland* 54°4N 7°5W 10 B4
Copahue Paso *Argentina* 37°49S 71°8W 94 D1
Copainalá *Mexico* 17°4N 93°18W 87 D6
Copake *U.S.A.* 42°7N 73°31W 83 D11
Copán *Honduras* 14°50N 89°9W 88 D2
Cope *U.S.A.* 39°40N 102°51W 76 G12
Copenhagen = København
 Denmark 55°40N 12°26E 9 J15
Copenhagen *U.S.A.* 43°54N 75°41W 83 C9
Copiapó *Chile* 27°19S 70°56W 94 B1
Copiapó → *Chile* 27°19S 70°56W 94 B1
Coplay *U.S.A.* 40°44N 75°29W 83 F9
Copo △ *Argentina* 25°53S 61°41W 94 B3
Copp L. *Canada* 60°14N 114°40W 70 A6
Copper Canyon = Barranca del
 Cobre △ *Mexico* 27°18N 107°40W 86 B3
Copper Center *U.S.A.* 61°58N 145°18W 74 C10
Copper Harbor *U.S.A.* 47°28N 87°53W 80 B10
Copper Queen *Zimbabwe* 17°29S 29°18E 55 F2
Copperas Cove *U.S.A.* 31°8N 97°54W 84 F6
Copperbelt □ *Zambia* 13°15S 27°30E 55 E2
Coppermine = Kugluktuk
 Canada 67°50N 115°5W 68 D8
Coppermine → *Canada* 67°49N 116°4W 68 D8
Copperopolis *U.S.A.* 37°58N 120°38W 78 H6
Coquet → *U.K.* 55°20N 1°32W 12 B6
Coquille *U.S.A.* 43°11N 124°11W 76 E1
Coquimbo *Chile* 30°0S 71°20W 94 C1
Coquimbo □ *Chile* 31°0S 71°0W 94 C1
Coquitlam *Canada* 49°17N 122°45W 70 D4
Corabia *Romania* 43°48N 24°30E 17 G13
Coracora *Peru* 15°5S 73°45W 92 G4
Coraki *Australia* 29°39S 153°17E 63 D5
Coral *U.S.A.* 40°29N 79°10W 82 F5
Coral Bay *Australia* 23°8S 113°46E 60 D1
Coral Gables *U.S.A.* 25°43N 80°16W 85 J14
Coral Harbour *Canada* 64°8N 83°10W 69 E15
Coral Sea *Pac. Oc.* 15°0S 150°0E 58 C8
Coral Sea Basin *Pac. Oc.* 14°0S 152°0E 64 J7
Coral Sea Islands Terr. □
 Australia 20°0S 155°0E 58 C8
Coral Springs *U.S.A.* 26°16N 80°16W 85 H14
Coraopolis *U.S.A.* 40°31N 80°10W 82 F4
Corato *Italy* 41°9N 16°25E 22 D7
Corbett △ *India* 29°20N 79°0E 43 E8
Corbin *U.S.A.* 36°57N 84°6W 81 G11
Corby *U.K.* 52°30N 0°41W 13 E7
Corby Glen *U.K.* 52°49N 0°30W 12 E7
Corcaigh = Cork *Ireland* 51°54N 8°29W 10 E3
Corcoran *U.S.A.* 36°6N 119°33W 78 J7
Corcovado △ *Costa Rica* 8°33N 83°35W 88 E3
Corcubión *Spain* 42°56N 9°12W 21 A1
Cordele *U.S.A.* 31°58N 83°47W 85 F13
Cordell *U.S.A.* 35°17N 98°59W 84 D5
Córdoba *Argentina* 31°20S 64°10W 94 C3
Córdoba *Mexico* 18°53N 96°56W 87 D5
Córdoba *Spain* 37°50N 4°50W 21 D3
Córdoba □ *Argentina* 31°22S 64°15W 94 C3
Córdoba, Sierra de
 Argentina 31°10S 64°25W 94 C3
Cordova *U.S.A.* 60°33N 145°45W 68 E2
Corella → *Australia* 19°34S 140°47E 62 B3
Corfield *Australia* 21°40S 143°21E 62 C3
Corfu = Kerkyra *Greece* 39°38N 19°50E 25 A3
Corfu *U.S.A.* 42°57N 78°24W 82 D6
Corfu, Str. of = Kerkyras, Notio
 Steno *Greece* 39°34N 20°0E 25 A4
Coria *Spain* 39°58N 6°33E 21 C2
Corigliano Cálabro *Italy* 39°36N 16°31E 22 E7
Coringa Is. *Australia* 16°58S 149°58E 62 B4
Corinth = Korinthos
 Greece 37°56N 22°55E 23 F10
Corinth *Miss., U.S.A.* 34°56N 88°31W 85 D10
Corinth *N.Y., U.S.A.* 43°15N 73°49W 83 C11
Corinth, G. of = Korinthiakos
 Kolpos *Greece* 38°16N 22°30E 23 E10
Corinto *Brazil* 18°20S 44°30W 93 G10
Corinto *Nic.* 12°30N 87°10W 88 D2
Cork *Ireland* 51°54N 8°29W 10 E3
Cork □ *Ireland* 51°57N 8°40W 10 E3
Cork Harbour *Ireland* 51°47N 8°16W 10 E3
Çorlu *Turkey* 41°11N 27°49E 23 D12
Cormack L. *Canada* 60°56N 121°37W 70 A4
Cormorant *Canada* 54°14N 100°35W 71 C8
Cormorant L. *Canada* 54°15N 100°50W 71 C8
Corn Is. = Maíz, Is. del
 Nic. 12°15N 83°4W 88 D3
Cornélio Procópio *Brazil* 23°7S 50°40W 95 A5
Corner Brook *Canada* 48°57N 57°58W 73 C8
Corneşti *Moldova* 47°21N 28°1E 17 E15
Corning *Ark., U.S.A.* 36°25N 90°35W 85 C9
Corning *Calif., U.S.A.* 39°56N 122°11W 76 G2
Corning *Iowa, U.S.A.* 40°59N 94°44W 80 E6
Corning *N.Y., U.S.A.* 42°9N 77°3W 82 D7
Cornwall *Canada* 45°2N 74°44W 83 A10
Cornwall *U.S.A.* 40°17N 76°25W 83 F8
Cornwall □ *U.K.* 50°26N 4°40W 13 G3
Cornwall I. *Canada* 77°37N 94°38W 69 B13
Cornwallis I. *Canada* 75°8N 95°0W 69 B13
Corny Pt. *Australia* 34°55S 137°0E 63 E2
Coro *Venezuela* 11°25N 69°41W 92 A5
Coroatá *Brazil* 4°8S 44°0W 93 D10
Corocoro *Bolivia* 17°15S 68°28W 92 G5
Coroico *Bolivia* 16°0S 67°50W 92 G5
Coromandel *N.Z.* 36°45S 175°31E 59 B5
Coromandel Coast *India* 12°30N 81°0E 40 N12
Corona *Calif., U.S.A.* 33°53N 117°34W 79 M9
Corona *N. Mex., U.S.A.* 34°15N 105°36W 77 J11
Coronado *U.S.A.* 32°41N 117°10W 79 N9
Coronado, B. de *Costa Rica* 9°0N 83°40W 88 E3
Coronados, Is. Los
 Mexico 32°26N 117°19W 79 N9
Coronation *Canada* 52°5N 111°27W 70 C6

Coronation Gulf
  Canada 68°25N 110°0W **68** D10
Coronation I. Antarctica 60°45S 46°0W **5** C18
Coronation Is. Australia 14°57S 124°55E **60** B3
Coronda Argentina 31°58S 60°56W **94** C3
Coronel Chile 37°0S 73°10W **94** D1
Coronel Bogado
  Paraguay 27°11S 56°18W **94** B4
Coronel Dorrego
  Argentina 38°40S 61°10W **94** D3
Coronel Oviedo
  Paraguay 25°24S 56°30W **94** B4
Coronel Pringles
  Argentina 38°0S 61°30W **94** D3
Coronel Suárez
  Argentina 37°30S 61°52W **94** D3
Coronel Vidal Argentina 37°28S 57°45W **94** D4
Coropuna, Nevado Peru 15°30S 72°41W **92** G4
Corowa Australia 35°58S 146°21E **63** F4
Corozal □ Belize 18°23N 88°23W **87** D7
Corozal Pt. Trin. & Tob. 10°45N 61°37W **93** K15
Corpus Argentina 27°10S 55°30W **95** B4
Corpus Christi U.S.A. 27°47N 97°24W **84** H6
Corpus Christi, L. U.S.A. 28°2N 97°52W **84** G6
Corralejo Canary Is. 28°43N 13°53W **24** F6
Corraun Pen. Ireland 53°54N 9°54W **10** C2
Correntes, C. das Mozam. 24°6S 35°34E **57** C6
Corrib, L. Ireland 53°27N 9°16W **10** C2
Corrientes Argentina 27°30S 58°45W **94** B4
Corrientes □ Argentina 28°0S 57°0W **94** B4
Corrientes → Argentina 30°42S 59°38W **94** C4
Corrientes → Peru 3°43S 74°35W **92** D4
Corrientes, C. Colombia 5°30N 77°34W **92** B3
Corrientes, C. Cuba 21°43N 84°30W **88** B3
Corrientes, C. Mexico 20°25N 105°42W **86** C3
Corrigan U.S.A. 31°0N 94°52W **84** F7
Corrigin Australia 32°20S 117°53E **61** F2
Corriverton Guyana 5°55N 57°20W **92** B7
Corry U.S.A. 41°55N 79°39W **82** E5
Corse □ France 42°0N 9°0E **20** F8
Corse, C. France 43°1N 9°25E **20** E8
Corsica = Corse □ France 42°0N 9°0E **20** F8
Corsicana U.S.A. 32°6N 96°28W **84** E6
Corte France 42°19N 9°11E **20** E8
Cortés, Mar de = California, G. de
  Mexico 27°0N 111°0W **86** B2
Cortez U.S.A. 37°21N 108°35W **77** H9
Cortland N.Y., U.S.A. 42°36N 76°11W **83** D8
Cortland Ohio, U.S.A. 41°20N 80°44W **82** E4
Çorum Turkey 40°30N 34°57E **19** F5
Corumbá Brazil 19°0S 57°30W **92** G7
Corunna = A Coruña
  Spain 43°20N 8°25W **21** A1
Corvallis U.S.A. 44°34N 123°16W **76** D2
Corvette, L. de la Canada 53°25N 74°3W **72** B5
Corvo Azores 39°43N 31°8W **50** a
Corydon U.S.A. 40°46N 93°19W **80** E7
Cosalá Mexico 24°23N 106°41W **86** C3
Cosamaloapan de Carpio
  Mexico 18°22N 95°48W **87** D5
Cosenza Italy 39°18N 16°15E **22** E7
Coshocton U.S.A. 40°16N 81°51W **82** F3
Cosmo Newberry
  Australia 28°0S 122°54E **61** E3
Cosmo Newberry ○
  Australia 27°59S 122°53E **61** E3
Cosmonaut Sea S. Ocean 66°30S 40°0E **5** C5
Coso Junction U.S.A. 36°3N 117°57W **79** J9
Coso Pk. U.S.A. 36°13N 117°44W **79** J9
Cosquín Argentina 31°15S 64°30W **94** C3
Costa Blanca Spain 38°25N 0°10W **21** C5
Costa Brava Spain 41°30N 3°0E **21** B7
Costa Daurada Spain 41°12N 1°15E **21** B6
Costa del Sol Spain 36°30N 4°30W **21** D3
Costa dels Pins Spain 39°38N 3°26E **24** B10
Costa Mesa U.S.A. 33°38N 117°55W **79** M9
Costa Rica ■ Cent. Amer. 10°0N 84°0W **88** E3
Costa Smeralda Italy 41°5N 9°35E **22** D3
Cosumnes → U.S.A. 38°16N 121°26W **78** G5
Cotabato Phil. 7°14N 124°15E **37** C6
Cotagaita Bolivia 20°45S 65°40W **94** A2
Côte d'Azur France 43°25N 7°10E **20** E7
Coteau des Prairies
  U.S.A. 45°20N 97°50W **80** C5
Coteau du Missouri
  U.S.A. 47°0N 100°0W **80** B4
Cotentin France 49°15N 1°30W **20** B3
Cotillo Canary Is. 28°41N 14°1W **24** F5
Cotonou Benin 6°20N 2°25E **50** G6
Cotopaxi Ecuador 0°40S 78°30W **92** D3
Cotswold Hills U.K. 51°42N 2°10W **13** F5
Cottage Grove U.S.A. 43°48N 123°3W **76** E2
Cottam Canada 42°8N 82°45W **82** D2
Cottbus Germany 51°45N 14°20E **16** C8
Cottonwood U.S.A. 34°45N 112°1W **77** J7
Cotulla U.S.A. 28°26N 99°14W **84** G5
Coudersport U.S.A. 41°46N 78°1W **82** E6
Couedic, C. du Australia 36°5S 136°40E **63** F2
Coulee City U.S.A. 47°37N 119°17W **76** C4
Coulee Dam Nat. Recr. Area =
Lake Roosevelt ○
  U.S.A. 48°5N 118°14W **76** B4
Coulman I. Antarctica 73°35S 170°0E **5** D11
Coulonge → Canada 45°52N 76°46W **72** C4
Coulterville U.S.A. 37°43N 120°12W **78** H6
Council Alaska, U.S.A. 64°53N 163°41W **74** C7
Council Idaho, U.S.A. 44°44N 116°26W **76** D5
Council Bluffs U.S.A. 41°16N 95°52W **80** E6
Council Grove U.S.A. 38°40N 96°29W **80** F5
Coupeville U.S.A. 48°13N 122°41W **78** B4
Courantyne → S. Amer. 5°55N 57°5W **92** B7
Courcelles Belgium 50°28N 4°22E **15** D4
Courtenay Canada 49°45N 125°0W **70** D4
Courtland Canada 42°51N 80°38W **82** D4
Courtland U.S.A. 38°20N 121°34W **78** G5
Courtrai = Kortrijk
  Belgium 50°50N 3°17E **15** D3

Courtright Canada 42°49N 82°28W **82** D2
Coushatta U.S.A. 32°1N 93°21W **84** E8
Coutts Crossing
  Australia 29°49S 152°55E **63** D5
Couva Trin. & Tob. 10°25N 61°27W **93** K15
Couvin Belgium 50°3N 4°29E **15** D4
Cove I. Canada 45°17N 81°44W **82** A3
Coventry U.K. 52°25N 1°28W **13** E6
Covilhã Portugal 40°17N 7°31W **21** B2
Covington Ga., U.S.A. 33°36N 83°51W **85** E13
Covington Ky., U.S.A. 39°5N 84°30W **81** F11
Covington Tenn., U.S.A. 35°34N 89°39W **85** D10
Covington Va., U.S.A. 37°47N 79°59W **81** G14
Cowal, L. Australia 33°40S 147°25E **63** E4
Cowan, L. Australia 31°45S 121°45E **61** F3
Cowan L. Canada 54°0N 107°15W **71** C7
Cowangie Australia 35°12S 141°26E **63** F3
Cowansville Canada 45°14N 72°46W **83** A12
Coward Springs
  Australia 29°24S 136°49E **63** D2
Cowcowing Lakes
  Australia 30°55S 117°20E **61** F2
Cowdenbeath U.K. 56°7N 3°21W **11** E5
Cowell Australia 33°39S 136°56E **63** E2
Cowes U.K. 50°45N 1°18W **13** G6
Cowichan L. Canada 48°53N 124°17W **78** B2
Cowlitz → U.S.A. 46°6N 122°55W **78** D4
Cowra Australia 33°49S 148°42E **63** E4
Coxilha Grande Brazil 28°18S 51°30W **95** B5
Coxim Brazil 18°30S 54°55W **93** G8
Cox's Bazar Bangla. 21°26N 91°59E **41** J17
Coyote Wells U.S.A. 32°44N 115°58W **79** N11
Coyuca de Benitez
  Mexico 17°2N 100°4W **87** D4
Coyuca de Catalán
  Mexico 18°20N 100°39W **86** D4
Cozad U.S.A. 40°52N 99°59W **80** E4
Cozumel Mexico 20°31N 86°55W **87** C7
Cozumel, Isla Mexico 20°30N 86°40W **87** C7
Crab Hill Barbados 13°19N 59°38W **89** g
Cracow = Kraków
  Poland 50°4N 19°57E **17** C10
Cracow Australia 25°17S 150°17E **63** D5
Cradle Mt.-Lake St. Clair △
  Australia 41°49S 147°56E **63** G4
Cradock Australia 32°6S 138°31E **63** E2
Cradock S. Africa 32°8S 25°36E **56** E4
Craig U.S.A. 40°31N 107°33W **76** F10
Craigavon U.K. 54°27N 6°23W **10** B5
Craigmore Zimbabwe 20°28S 32°50E **55** G3
Craik Canada 51°3N 105°49W **71** C7
Crailsheim Germany 49°8N 10°5E **16** D6
Craiova Romania 44°21N 23°48E **17** F12
Cramsie Australia 23°20S 144°15E **62** C3
Cranberry L. U.S.A. 44°11N 74°50W **83** B10
Cranberry Portage
  Canada 54°35N 101°23W **71** C8
Cranbrook Australia 34°18S 117°33E **61** F2
Cranbrook Canada 49°30N 115°46W **70** D5
Crandon U.S.A. 45°34N 88°54W **80** C9
Crane Oreg., U.S.A. 43°25N 118°35W **76** E4
Crane Tex., U.S.A. 31°24N 102°21W **84** F3
Crane, The Barbados 13°6N 59°27W **89** g
Cranston U.S.A. 41°47N 71°26W **83** E13
Crater L. U.S.A. 42°56N 122°6W **76** E2
Crater Lake △ U.S.A. 42°55N 122°10W **76** E2
Craters of the Moon ○
  U.S.A. 43°25N 113°30W **76** E7
Crateús Brazil 5°10S 40°39W **93** E10
Crato Brazil 7°10S 39°25W **93** E11
Craven, L. Canada 54°20N 76°56W **72** B4
Crawford U.S.A. 42°41N 103°25W **80** D2
Crawfordsville U.S.A. 40°2N 86°54W **80** E10
Crawley U.K. 51°7N 0°11W **13** F7
Crazy Mts. U.S.A. 46°12N 110°20W **76** C8
Crean L. Canada 54°5N 106°9W **71** C7
Crediton Canada 43°17N 81°33W **82** C3
Crediton U.K. 50°47N 3°40W **13** G4
Cree → Canada 58°57N 105°47W **71** B7
Cree → U.K. 54°55N 4°25W **11** G4
Cree L. Canada 57°30N 106°30W **71** B7
Creede U.S.A. 37°51N 106°56W **77** H10
Creekside U.S.A. 40°40N 79°11W **82** F5
Creel Mexico 27°45N 107°38W **86** B3
Creemore Canada 44°19N 80°6W **82** B4
Creighton Canada 54°45N 101°54W **71** C8
Creighton U.S.A. 42°28N 97°54W **80** D5
Crema Italy 45°22N 9°41E **20** D8
Cremona Italy 45°7N 10°2E **20** D9
Cres Croatia 44°58N 14°25E **16** F8
Crescent City U.S.A. 41°45N 124°12W **76** F1
Crespo Argentina 32°2S 60°19W **94** C3
Cresson U.S.A. 40°28N 78°36W **82** F6
Crestline Calif., U.S.A. 34°14N 117°18W **79** L9
Crestline Ohio, U.S.A. 40°47N 82°44W **82** F2
Creston Canada 49°10N 116°31W **70** D5
Creston Calif., U.S.A. 35°32N 120°33W **78** K6
Creston Iowa, U.S.A. 41°4N 94°22W **80** E7
Crestview Calif., U.S.A. 37°46N 118°58W **78** H8
Crestview Fla., U.S.A. 30°46N 86°34W **85** F11
Crete = Kriti Greece 35°15N 25°0E **25** D7
Crete U.S.A. 40°38N 96°58W **80** E5
Créteil France 48°47N 2°27E **20** B5
Creus, C. de Spain 42°20N 3°19E **21** A7
Creuse → France 47°0N 0°34E **20** C4
Crewe U.K. 53°6N 2°26W **12** D5
Crewkerne U.K. 50°53N 2°48W **13** G5
Crianlarich U.K. 56°24N 4°37W **11** E4
Criciúma Brazil 28°40S 49°23W **95** B6
Crieff U.K. 56°22N 3°50W **11** E5
Crimea □ Ukraine 45°30N 33°10E **19** E5
Crimean Pen. = Krymskyy
Pivostriv Ukraine 45°0N 34°0E **19** F5
Crișul Alb → Romania 46°42N 21°17E **17** E11
Crișul Negru →
  Romania 46°42N 21°16E **17** E11
Crna → Macedonia 41°33N 21°59E **23** D9
Crna Gora = Montenegro ■
  Europe 42°40N 19°20E **23** C8

Crna Gora Macedonia 42°10N 21°30E **23** C9
Crna Reka = Crna →
  Macedonia 41°33N 21°59E **23** D9
Croagh Patrick Ireland 53°46N 9°40W **10** C2
Croatia ■ Europe 45°20N 16°0E **16** F9
Crocker, Banjaran
  Malaysia 5°40N 116°30E **36** C5
Crockett U.S.A. 31°19N 95°27W **84** F7
Crocodile = Umgwenya →
  Mozam. 25°14S 32°18E **57** D5
Crocodile Is. Australia 12°3S 134°58E **62** A1
Crohy Hd. Ireland 54°55N 8°26W **10** B3
Croix, L. la Canada 48°20N 92°15W **72** C1
Croker, C. Canada 10°58S 132°35E **60** B5
Croker, C. Canada 44°58N 80°59W **82** B4
Croker I. Australia 11°12S 132°32E **60** B5
Croker Islands Seas ○
  Australia 11°20S 132°30E **60** B5
Cromarty U.K. 57°40N 4°2W **11** D4
Cromer U.K. 52°56N 1°17E **12** E9
Cromwell N.Z. 45°3S 169°14E **59** F2
Cromwell U.S.A. 41°36N 72°39W **83** E12
Crook U.K. 54°43N 1°45W **12** C6
Crooked → Canada 54°50N 122°54W **70** C4
Crooked → U.S.A. 44°32N 121°16W **76** D3
Crooked I. Bahamas 22°50N 74°10W **89** B5
Crooked Island Passage
  Bahamas 22°55N 74°35W **89** B5
Crookston Minn., U.S.A. 47°47N 96°37W **80** B5
Crookston Nebr., U.S.A. 42°56N 100°45W **80** D3
Crookwell Australia 34°28S 149°24E **63** E4
Crosby U.K. 53°30N 3°3W **12** D4
Crosby N. Dak., U.S.A. 48°55N 103°18W **80** A2
Crosby Pa., U.S.A. 41°45N 78°23W **82** E6
Crosbyton U.S.A. 33°40N 101°14W **84** E4
Cross City U.S.A. 29°38N 83°7W **85** G13
Cross Fell U.K. 54°43N 2°28W **12** C5
Cross L. Canada 54°45N 97°30W **71** C9
Cross Lake Canada 54°37N 97°47W **71** C9
Cross Sound U.S.A. 58°0N 135°0W **68** F4
Crossett U.S.A. 33°8N 91°58W **84** E9
Crosshaven Ireland 51°47N 8°17W **10** E3
Crossmaglen U.K. 54°5N 6°36W **10** B5
Crossmolina Ireland 54°6N 9°20W **10** B2
Crossville U.S.A. 35°57N 85°2W **85** D12
Croswell U.S.A. 43°16N 82°37W **82** C2
Croton-on-Hudson
  U.S.A. 41°12N 73°55W **83** E11
Crotone Italy 39°5N 17°8E **22** E7
Crow → Canada 59°41N 124°20W **70** B4
Crow Agency U.S.A. 45°36N 107°28W **76** D10
Crow Hd. Ireland 51°35N 10°9W **10** E1
Crowell U.S.A. 33°59N 99°43W **84** E5
Crowley U.S.A. 30°13N 92°22W **84** F8
Crowley, L. U.S.A. 37°35N 118°42W **78** H8
Crown Point Ind.,
  U.S.A. 41°25N 87°22W **80** E10
Crown Point N.Y.,
  U.S.A. 43°57N 73°26W **83** C11
Crown Pt. Trin. & Tob. 11°18N 60°51W **93** J16
Crownpoint U.S.A. 35°41N 108°9W **77** J9
Crows Landing U.S.A. 37°23N 121°6W **78** H5
Crows Nest Australia 27°16S 152°4E **63** D5
Crowsnest Pass Canada 49°40N 114°40W **70** D6
Croydon Australia 18°13S 142°14E **62** B3
Croydon □ U.K. 51°22N 0°5W **13** F7
Crozet, Is. Ind. Oc. 46°27S 52°0E **3** G12
Crusheen Ireland 52°57N 8°53W **10** D3
Cruz, C. Cuba 19°50N 77°50W **88** C4
Cruz Alta Brazil 28°45S 53°40W **95** B5
Cruz Bay U.S. Virgin Is. 18°20N 64°48W **89** e
Cruz del Eje Argentina 30°45S 64°50W **94** C3
Cruzeiro Brazil 22°33S 45°0W **95** A7
Cruzeiro do Oeste Brazil 23°46S 53°4W **95** A5
Cruzeiro do Sul Brazil 7°35S 72°35W **92** E4
Cry L. Canada 58°45N 129°0W **70** B3
Crystal Bay U.S.A. 39°15N 120°0W **78** F7
Crystal Brook Australia 33°21S 138°12E **63** E2
Crystal City U.S.A. 28°41N 99°50W **84** G5
Crystal Falls U.S.A. 46°5N 88°20W **80** B9
Crystal River U.S.A. 28°54N 82°35W **85** G13
Crystal Springs U.S.A. 31°59N 90°21W **85** F9
Csongrád Hungary 46°43N 20°12E **17** E11
Cu Lao Hon Vietnam 10°54N 108°18E **39** G7
Cua Rao Vietnam 19°16N 104°27E **38** C5
Cuácua → Mozam. 17°54S 37°0E **55** F4
Cuamato Angola 17°2S 15°7E **56** B2
Cuamba Mozam. 14°45S 36°22E **55** E4
Cuando → Angola 17°30S 23°15E **53** H4
Cuando Cubango □
  Angola 16°25S 20°0E **56** B3
Cuangar Angola 17°36S 18°39E **56** B2
Cuango = Kwango →
  Dem. Rep. of the Congo 3°14S 17°22E **52** E3
Cuanza → Angola 9°21S 13°9E **52** F2
Cuarto → Argentina 33°25S 63°2W **94** C3
Cuatrociénegas Mexico 26°59N 102°5W **86** B4
Cuauhtémoc Mexico 28°25N 106°52W **86** B3
Cuba N. Mex., U.S.A. 36°1N 107°4W **77** H10
Cuba N.Y., U.S.A. 42°13N 78°17W **82** D6
Cuba ■ W. Indies 22°0N 79°0W **88** B4
Cubango → Africa 18°50S 22°25E **56** B3
Cuc Phuong △ Vietnam 20°17N 105°38E **38** B5
Cuchumatanes, Sierra de los
  Guatemala 15°35N 91°25W **88** C1
Cuckfield U.K. 51°1N 0°8W **13** F7
Cucuí Brazil 1°12N 66°50W **92** C5
Cucurpé Mexico 30°20N 110°43W **86** A2
Cúcuta Colombia 7°54N 72°31W **92** B4
Cuddalore India 11°46N 79°45E **40** P11
Cuddapah India 14°30N 78°47E **40** M11
Cuddapan, L. Australia 25°45S 141°26E **62** D3
Cue Australia 27°25S 117°54E **61** E2
Cuenca Ecuador 2°50S 79°9W **92** D3
Cuenca Spain 40°5N 2°10W **21** B4
Cuenca, Serranía de
  Spain 39°55N 1°50W **21** C5
Cuernavaca Mexico 18°55N 99°15W **87** D5
Cuero U.S.A. 29°6N 97°17W **84** G6

Cueva de la Quebrada del Toro △
  Venezuela 10°46N 69°3W **89** D6
Cuevas del Almanzora
  Spain 37°18N 1°58W **21** D5
Cuevo Bolivia 20°15S 63°30W **92** H6
Cuiabá Brazil 15°30S 56°0W **93** G7
Cuiabá → Brazil 17°5S 56°36W **93** G7
Cuihangcun China 22°27N 113°32E **33** G10
Cuijk Neths. 51°44N 5°50E **15** C5
Cuilco Guatemala 15°24N 91°58W **88** C1
Cuillin Hills U.K. 57°13N 6°15W **11** D2
Cuillin Sd. U.K. 57°4N 6°20W **11** D2
Cuilo = Kwilu →
  Dem. Rep. of the Congo 3°22S 17°22E **52** E3
Cuito → Angola 18°1S 20°48E **56** B3
Cuitzeo, L. de Mexico 19°55N 101°5W **86** D4
Cukai Malaysia 4°13N 103°25E **39** K4
Culbertson U.S.A. 48°9N 104°31W **76** B11
Culcairn Australia 35°41S 147°3E **63** F4
Culebra Puerto Rico 18°19N 65°18W **89** d
Culgoa → Australia 29°56S 146°20E **63** D4
Culgoa Flood Plain △
  Australia 28°58S 147°5E **63** D4
Culiacán Mexico 24°50N 107°23W **86** C3
Culiacán → Mexico 24°30N 107°42W **86** C3
Culik Indonesia 8°21S 115°37E **37** J18
Culion Phil. 11°54N 119°58E **37** B6
Cullarin Ra. Australia 34°30S 149°30E **63** E4
Cullen U.K. 57°42N 2°49W **11** D6
Cullen Pt. Australia 11°57S 141°54E **62** A3
Cullera Spain 39°9N 0°17W **21** C5
Cullman U.S.A. 34°11N 86°51W **85** D11
Cullompton U.K. 50°51N 3°24W **13** G4
Culpeper U.S.A. 38°30N 78°0W **81** F14
Culuene → Brazil 12°56S 52°51W **93** F8
Culver, Pt. Australia 32°54S 124°43E **61** F3
Culverden N.Z. 42°47S 172°49E **59** E4
Cumaná Venezuela 10°30N 64°5W **92** A6
Cumberland B.C.,
  Canada 49°40N 125°0W **70** D4
Cumberland Ont.,
  Canada 45°29N 75°24W **83** A9
Cumberland U.S.A. 39°39N 78°46W **81** F14
Cumberland → U.S.A. 37°9N 88°25W **80** G9
Cumberland Gap △
  U.S.A. 36°36N 83°40W **81** G12
Cumberland I. U.S.A. 30°50N 81°25W **85** F14
Cumberland Is. Australia 20°35S 149°10E **62** b
Cumberland Island △
  U.S.A. 30°12N 81°24W **85** F14
Cumberland L. Canada 54°3N 102°18W **71** C8
Cumberland Pen. Canada 67°0N 64°0W **69** D19
Cumberland Plateau
  U.S.A. 36°0N 85°0W **85** D12
Cumberland Sd. Canada 65°30N 66°0W **69** D18
Cumbernauld U.K. 55°57N 3°58W **11** F5
Cumborah Australia 29°40S 147°45E **63** D4
Cumbres de Majalca △
  Mexico 28°48N 106°30W **86** B3
Cumbres de Monterrey △
  Mexico 25°26N 100°25W **86** B4
Cumbria □ U.K. 54°42N 2°52W **12** C5
Cumbrian Mts. U.K. 54°30N 3°0W **12** C5
Cumbum India 15°40N 79°10E **40** M11
Cuminá → Brazil 1°30S 56°0W **93** D7
Cummings Mt. U.S.A. 35°2N 118°34W **79** K8
Cummins Australia 34°16S 135°43E **63** E2
Cumnock Australia 32°59S 148°46E **63** E4
Cumnock U.K. 55°28N 4°17W **11** F4
Cumpas Mexico 30°2N 109°48W **86** B3
Cumplida, Pta.
  Canary Is. 28°50N 17°48W **24** F2
Cunco Chile 38°55S 72°2W **96** D2
Cuncumén Chile 31°53S 70°38W **94** C1
Cunderdin Australia 31°37S 117°12E **61** F2
Cunene → Angola 17°20S 11°50E **56** B1
Cúneo Italy 44°23N 7°32E **20** D7
Çüngüş Turkey 38°13N 39°17E **44** B3
Cunnamulla Australia 28°2S 145°38E **63** D4
Cupar Canada 50°57N 104°10W **71** C8
Cupar U.K. 56°19N 3°1W **11** E5
Cupertino U.S.A. 37°19N 122°2W **78** H4
Cupica, G. de Colombia 6°25N 77°30W **92** B3
Curaçao Neth. Ant. 12°10N 69°0W **89** D6
Curanilahue Chile 37°29S 73°28W **94** D1
Curaray → Peru 2°20S 74°5W **92** D4
Curepto Chile 35°8S 72°1W **94** D1
Curiapo Venezuela 8°33N 61°5W **92** B6
Curicó Chile 34°55S 71°20W **94** C1
Curieuse Seychelles 4°15S 55°44E **53** b
Curitiba Brazil 25°20S 49°10W **95** B6
Curitibanos Brazil 27°18S 50°36W **95** B5
Currabubula Australia 31°16S 150°44E **63** E5
Currais Novos Brazil 6°13S 36°30W **93** E11
Curral Velho C. Verde Is. 16°8N 22°48W **50** b
Curralinho Brazil 1°45S 49°46W **93** D9
Currane, L. Ireland 51°49N 10°4W **10** E1
Currant → U.S.A. 38°51N 115°28W **78** G11
Currarong Australia 35°1N 150°4W **63** E5
Currawinya △ Australia 28°55S 144°27E **63** D3
Current → U.S.A. 36°15N 90°55W **84** C9
Currie Australia 39°56S 143°53E **63** F3
Currie U.S.A. 40°16N 114°45W **76** F6
Curtea de Argeş
  Romania 45°12N 24°42E **17** F13
Curtin Springs Australia 25°20S 131°45E **61** E5
Curtis U.S.A. 40°38N 100°31W **80** E3
Curtis Group Australia 39°30S 146°37E **63** F4
Curtis I. Australia 23°35S 151°10E **62** C5
Curuápanema → Brazil 2°25S 55°2W **93** D7
Curuçá Brazil 0°43S 47°50W **93** D9
Curuguaty Paraguay 24°31S 55°42W **95** A4

Cururupu Brazil 1°50S 44°50W **93** D10
Curuzú Cuatiá Argentina 29°50S 58°5W **94** B4
Curvelo Brazil 18°45S 44°27W **93** G10
Cusco = Cuzco Peru 13°32S 72°0W **92** F4
Cushendall U.K. 55°5N 6°4W **10** A5
Cushing U.S.A. 35°59N 96°46W **84** D6
Cushing, Mt. Canada 57°35N 126°57W **70** B3
Cusihuiriáchic Mexico 28°14N 106°50W **86** B3
Custer U.S.A. 43°46N 103°36W **80** D2
Cut Bank U.S.A. 48°38N 112°20W **76** B7
Cutchogue U.S.A. 41°1N 72°30W **83** E12
Cuthbert U.S.A. 31°46N 84°48W **85** F12
Cutler U.S.A. 36°31N 119°17W **78** J7
Cuttaburra → Australia 29°43S 144°22E **63** D3
Cuttack India 20°25N 85°57E **41** J14
Cuvier, C. Australia 23°14S 113°22E **61** D1
Cuvier I. N.Z. 36°27S 175°50E **59** B5
Cuxhaven Germany 53°51N 8°41E **16** B5
Cuyahoga Falls U.S.A. 41°8N 81°29W **82** E3
Cuyahoga Valley △
  U.S.A. 41°24N 81°33W **82** E3
Cuyo Phil. 10°51N 121°2E **37** B6
Cuyuni → Guyana 6°23N 58°41W **92** B7
Cuzco Bolivia 20°0S 66°50W **92** H5
Cuzco Peru 13°32S 72°0W **92** F4
Cwmbran U.K. 51°39N 3°2W **13** F4
Cyangugu Rwanda 2°29S 28°54E **54** C2
Cyclades Greece 37°0N 24°30E **23** F11
Cygnet Australia 43°8S 147°1E **63** G4
Cynthiana U.S.A. 38°23N 84°18W **81** F11
Cypress Hills Canada 49°40N 109°30W **71** D7
Cypress Hills △ Canada 49°40N 109°30W **71** D7
Cyprus ■ Asia 35°0N 33°0E **25** E12
Cyrenaica = Barqa Libya 27°0N 23°0E **51** C10
Cyrene Libya 32°53N 21°52E **51** B10
Czar Canada 52°27N 110°50W **71** C6
Czech Rep. ■ Europe 50°0N 15°0E **16** D8
Częstochowa Poland 50°49N 19°7E **17** C10

D

Da → Vietnam 21°15N 105°20E **38** B5
Da Hinggan Ling China 48°0N 121°0E **33** B7
Da Lat Vietnam 11°56N 108°25E **39** G7
Da Nang Vietnam 16°4N 108°13E **38** D7
Da Qaidam China 37°50N 95°15E **32** C4
Da Yunhe → Hopei,
  China 39°10N 117°10E **35** E9
Da Yunhe → Jiangsu,
  China 34°25N 120°5E **35** H11
Da'an China 45°30N 124°7E **35** B13
Daan Viljoen △ Namibia 22°2S 16°45E **56** C2
Daba Shan China 32°0N 109°0E **33** C5
Dabbagh, Jabal Si. Arabia 27°52N 35°45E **44** E2
Dabhoi India 22°10N 73°20E **42** H5
Dabo = Pasirkuning
  Indonesia 0°30S 104°33E **36** E2
Dabola Guinea 10°50N 11°5W **50** F3
Dabung Malaysia 5°23N 102°1E **39** K4
Dacca = Dhaka Bangla. 23°43N 90°26E **43** H14
Dacca = Dhaka □
  Bangla. 24°25N 90°25E **43** G14
Dachau Germany 48°15N 11°26E **16** D6
Dachigam △ India 34°10N 75°0E **42** B6
Dacre Canada 45°22N 76°57W **82** A8
Dadanawa Guyana 2°50N 59°30W **92** C7
Dade City U.S.A. 28°22N 82°11W **85** G13
Dadhar Pakistan 29°28N 67°39E **42** E2
Dadnah U.A.E. 25°32N 56°22E **45** E8
Dadra & Nagar Haveli □
  India 20°5N 73°0E **40** J8
Dadri = Charkhi Dadri
  India 28°37N 76°17E **42** E7
Dadu Pakistan 26°45N 67°45E **42** F2
Daegu S. Korea 35°50N 128°37E **35** G15
Daejeon S. Korea 36°20N 127°28E **35** F14
Daejeong S. Korea 33°8N 126°17E **35** H14
Daet Phil. 14°2N 122°55E **37** B6
Dafnes Greece 35°13N 25°3E **25** D7
Dagana Senegal 16°30N 15°35W **50** E2
Dagestan □ Russia 42°30N 47°0E **19** F8
Daghestan Republic =
Dagestan □ Russia 42°30N 47°0E **19** F8
Dağlıq Qarabağ =
Nagorno-Karabakh □
  Azerbaijan 39°55N 46°45E **44** B5
Dagö = Hiiumaa Estonia 58°50N 22°45E **9** G20
Dagu China 38°59N 117°40E **35** E9
Dagupan Phil. 16°3N 120°20E **37** A6
Daguragu Australia 17°33S 130°30E **60** C5
Daguragu ○ Australia 17°24S 130°48E **60** C5
Dahab Egypt 28°31N 34°31E **44** D2
Dahlak Kebir Eritrea 15°50N 40°10E **47** D3
Dahlonega U.S.A. 34°32N 83°59W **85** D13
Dahod India 22°50N 74°15E **42** H6
Dahongliutan China 35°45N 79°20E **43** B8
Dahra Libya 29°30N 17°50E **51** C9
Dahûk Iraq 36°50N 43°1E **44** B3
Dai Hao Vietnam 18°1N 106°25E **38** C6
Dai-Sen Japan 35°22N 133°32E **31** G6
Dai Xian China 39°4N 112°58E **34** E7
Daichengi China 38°42N 116°38E **34** E9
Daikondi = Day Kundī □
  Afghan. 34°0N 66°0E **40** C5
Daingean Ireland 53°18N 7°17W **10** C4
Daintree Australia 16°20S 145°20E **62** B4
Daintree △ Australia 16°8S 145°2E **62** B4
Daiō-Misaki Japan 34°15N 136°45E **31** G8
Daisen-Oki △ Japan 35°18N 133°20E **31** G6
Daisetsu-Zan Japan 43°30N 142°57E **30** C11
Daisetsu-Zan △ Japan 43°30N 142°55E **30** C11
Dajarra Australia 21°42S 139°30E **62** C2
Dajiawa China 37°9N 119°0E **35** F10
Dak Dam Cambodia 12°20N 107°21E **38** F6
Dak Nhe Vietnam 15°28N 107°48E **38** E6
Dak Pek Vietnam 15°4N 107°44E **38** E6
Dak Song Vietnam 12°19N 107°35E **39** F6

Dak Sui Vietnam 14°55N 107°43E 38 E6
Dakar Senegal 14°34N 17°29W 50 F2
Dakhla W. Sahara 23°50N 15°53W 50 D2
Dakhla, El Wâhât el
  Egypt 25°30N 28°50E 51 C11
Dakor India 22°45N 73°11E 42 H5
Dakota City U.S.A. 42°25N 96°25W 80 D5
Dalachi China 36°48N 105°0E 34 F3
Dalai Nur China 43°20N 116°45E 34 C9
Dālakī Iran 29°26N 51°17E 45 D6
Dalälven → Sweden 60°12N 16°43E 9 F17
Dalaman → Turkey 36°41N 28°43E 23 F13
Dalandzadgad Mongolia 43°27N 104°30E 34 C3
Dalap-Uliga-Darrit = Majuro
  Marshall Is. 7°9N 171°12E 64 G9
Dalarna Sweden 61°0N 14°0E 8 F16
Dālbandīn Pakistan 29°0N 64°23E 40 E4
Dalbeattie U.K. 54°56N 3°50W 11 G5
Dalbeg Australia 20°16S 147°18E 62 C4
Dalby Australia 27°10S 151°17E 63 D5
Dale City U.S.A. 38°38N 77°19W 81 F15
Dale Hollow L. U.S.A. 36°32N 85°27W 85 C12
Dalgān Iran 27°31N 59°19E 45 E8
Dalhart U.S.A. 36°4N 102°31W 84 C3
Dalhousie Canada 48°5N 66°26W 73 C6
Dalhousie India 32°38N 75°58E 42 C6
Dali Shaanxi, China 34°48N 109°58E 34 G5
Dali Yunnan, China 25°40N 100°10E 41 G22
Dalian China 38°50N 121°40E 35 E11
Daliang Shan China 28°0N 102°45E 32 D5
Daling He → China 40°55N 121°40E 35 D11
Dāliyat el Karmel Israel 32°43N 35°2E 46 C4
Dalkeith U.K. 55°54N 3°4W 11 F5
Dallas Oreg., U.S.A. 44°55N 123°19W 76 D2
Dallas Tex., U.S.A. 32°47N 96°48W 84 E6
Dalles, The U.S.A. 45°36N 121°10W 76 D3
Dalmā U.A.E. 24°30N 52°20E 45 E7
Dalmacija Croatia 43°20N 17°0E 22 C7
Dalmas, L. Canada 53°30N 71°50W 73 B5
Dalmatia = Dalmacija
  Croatia 43°20N 17°0E 22 C7
Dalmau India 26°4N 81°2E 43 F9
Dalmellington U.K. 55°19N 4°23W 11 F4
Dalnegorsk Russia 44°32N 135°33E 30 B8
Dalnerechensk Russia 45°50N 133°40E 30 B6
Dalnevostochnyy □
  Russia 67°0N 140°0E 29 C14
Daloa Ivory C. 7°0N 6°30W 50 G4
Dalry U.K. 55°42N 4°43W 11 F4
Dalrymple, L. Australia 20°40S 147°0E 62 C4
Dalrymple, Mt. Australia 21°1S 148°39E 62 b
Dalsland Sweden 58°50N 12°15E 9 G15
Daltenganj India 24°0N 84°4E 43 H11
Dalton Ga., U.S.A. 34°46N 84°58W 85 D12
Dalton Mass., U.S.A. 42°28N 73°11W 83 D11
Dalton Nebr., U.S.A. 41°25N 102°58W 80 E2
Dalton-in-Furness U.K. 54°10N 3°11W 12 C4
Dalvík Iceland 65°58N 18°32W 8 D4
Dálvvadis = Jokkmokk
  Sweden 66°35N 19°50E 8 C18
Dalwallinu Australia 30°17S 116°40E 61 F2
Daly → Australia 13°35S 130°19E 60 B5
Daly City U.S.A. 37°42N 122°27W 78 H4
Daly L. Canada 56°32N 105°39W 71 B7
Daly River Australia 13°46S 130°42E 60 B5
Daly River-Port Keats ◌
  Australia 14°13S 129°36E 60 B4
Daly Waters Australia 16°15S 133°24E 62 B1
Dam Doi Vietnam 8°50N 105°12E 39 H5
Dam Ha Vietnam 21°21N 107°36E 38 B6
Daman India 20°25N 72°57E 40 J8
Dāmaneh Iran 33°1N 50°29E 45 C6
Damanhûr Egypt 31°0N 30°30E 51 B12
Damanzhuang China 38°5N 116°35E 34 E9
Damar Indonesia 7°7S 128°40E 37 F7
Damara C.A.R. 4°58N 18°42E 52 D3
Damaraland Namibia 20°0S 15°0E 56 C2
Damascus = Dimashq
  Syria 33°30N 36°18E 46 B5
Damaturu Nigeria 11°45N 11°55E 52 B2
Damāvand Iran 35°47N 52°0E 45 C7
Damāvand, Qolleh-ye
  Iran 35°56N 52°10E 45 C7
Damba Angola 6°44S 15°20E 52 F3
Dâmbovița → Romania 44°12N 26°26E 17 F14
Dame Marie Haiti 18°36N 74°26W 89 C5
Dāmghān Iran 36°10N 54°17E 45 B7
Damiel Spain 39°4N 3°37W 21 C4
Damietta = Dumyât
  Egypt 31°24N 31°48E 51 B12
Daming China 36°15N 115°6E 34 F8
Damīr Qābū Syria 36°58N 41°51E 44 B4
Dammam = Ad Dammām
  Si. Arabia 26°20N 50°5E 45 E6
Damodar → India 23°17N 87°35E 43 H12
Damoh India 23°50N 79°28E 43 H8
Dampier Australia 20°41S 116°42E 60 D2
Dampier, Selat Indonesia 0°40S 131°0E 37 E8
Dampier Arch.
  Australia 20°38S 116°32E 60 D2
Damrei, Chuor Phnum
  Cambodia 11°30N 103°0E 39 G4
Damyang S. Korea 35°19N 126°59E 35 G14
Dana Indonesia 11°0S 122°52E 37 F6
Dana Jordan 30°41N 35°37E 46 E4
Dana, L. Canada 50°53N 77°20W 72 B4
Dana, Mt. U.S.A. 37°54N 119°12W 78 H7
Danakil Desert Ethiopia 12°45N 41°0E 47 E3
Danané Ivory C. 7°16N 8°9W 50 G4
Danau Poso Indonesia 1°52S 120°35E 37 E6
Danbury U.S.A. 41°24N 73°28W 83 E11
Danby L. U.S.A. 34°13N 115°5W 77 J6
Dand Afghan. 31°28N 65°32E 42 D1
Dande → Zimbabwe 15°56S 30°15E 55 F3
Dandeldhura Nepal 29°20N 80°35E 43 E9
Dandeli India 15°5N 74°30E 40 M9
Dandenong Australia 38°0S 145°15E 63 F4

Dandong China 40°10N 124°20E 35 D13
Danfeng China 33°45N 110°25E 34 H6
Danger Is. = Pukapuka
  Cook Is. 10°53S 165°49W 65 J11
Danger Pt. S. Africa 34°40S 19°17E 56 E2
Danginpuri Indonesia 8°40S 115°13E 37 K18
Dangla Shan = Tanggula Shan
  China 32°40N 92°10E 32 C4
Dangrek, Mts. = Dangrek, Phnom
  Thailand 14°20N 104°0E 38 E5
Dangrek, Phnom
  Thailand 14°20N 104°0E 38 E5
Dangriga Belize 17°0N 88°13W 87 D7
Dangshan China 34°27N 116°22E 34 G9
Daniel U.S.A. 42°52N 110°4W 76 E8
Daniel's Harbour
  Canada 50°13N 57°35W 73 B8
Danielskuil S. Africa 28°11S 23°33E 56 D3
Danielson U.S.A. 41°48N 71°53W 83 E13
Danilov Russia 58°16N 40°13E 18 C7
Daning China 36°28N 110°45E 34 F6
Dank Oman 23°33N 56°16E 45 F8
Dankhar Gompa India 32°10N 78°10E 42 C8
Danli Honduras 14°4N 86°35W 88 D2
Danmark = Denmark ■
  Europe 55°45N 10°0E 9 J14
Dannemora U.S.A. 44°43N 73°44W 83 B11
Dannevirke N.Z. 40°12S 176°8E 59 D6
Dannhauser S. Africa 28°0S 30°3E 57 D5
Dansville U.S.A. 42°34N 77°42W 82 D7
Danta India 24°11N 72°46E 42 G5
Dantan India 21°57N 87°20E 43 J12
Dante = Xaafuun
  Somali Rep. 10°25N 51°16E 47 E5
Danube = Dunărea →
  Europe 45°20N 29°40E 17 F15
Danvers U.S.A. 42°34N 70°56W 83 D14
Danville Ill., U.S.A. 40°8N 87°37W 80 E10
Danville Ky., U.S.A. 37°39N 84°46W 81 G11
Danville Pa., U.S.A. 40°58N 76°37W 83 F8
Danville Va., U.S.A. 36°36N 79°23W 81 G14
Danville Vt., U.S.A. 44°25N 72°9W 83 B12
Danzhou China 19°31N 109°33E 38 C7
Danzig = Gdańsk
  Poland 54°22N 18°40E 17 A10
Dapaong Togo 10°55N 0°16E 50 F6
Daqing Shan China 40°40N 111°0E 34 D6
Daqq-e Sorkh, Kavīr
  Iran 33°45N 52°50E 45 C7
Dar Banda Africa 8°0N 23°0E 48 F6
Dar el Beida = Casablanca
  Morocco 33°36N 7°36W 50 B4
Dar es Salaam Tanzania 6°50S 39°12E 54 D4
Dar Mazār Iran 29°14N 57°20E 45 D8
Dar'ā Syria 32°36N 36°7E 46 C5
Dar'ā □ Syria 32°55N 36°10E 46 C5
Dārāb Iran 28°50N 54°30E 45 D7
Daraban Pakistan 31°44N 70°20E 42 D4
Daraina Madag. 13°12S 49°40E 57 A8
Daraj Libya 30°10N 10°28E 51 B8
Dārān Iran 32°59N 50°24E 45 C6
Dārayyā Syria 33°28N 36°15E 46 B5
Darband Pakistan 34°20N 72°50E 42 B5
Darband, Kūh-e Iran 31°34N 57°8E 45 D8
Darbhanga India 26°15N 85°55E 43 F11
D'Arcy Canada 50°33N 122°29W 70 C4
Dardanelle Ark., U.S.A. 35°13N 93°9W 84 D8
Dardanelle Calif.,
  U.S.A. 38°20N 119°50W 78 G7
Dardanelles = Çanakkale Boğazı
  Turkey 40°17N 26°32E 23 D12
Dārestān Iran 29°9N 58°42E 45 D8
Dārfūr Sudan 13°40N 24°0E 51 F10
Dargai Pakistan 34°25N 71°55E 42 B4
Dargaville N.Z. 35°57S 173°52E 59 A4
Darhan Mongolia 49°37N 106°21E 32 B5
Darhan Muminggan Lianheqi
  China 41°40N 110°28E 34 D6
Darıca Turkey 40°45N 29°23E 23 D13
Darién, G. del Colombia 9°0N 77°0W 92 B3
Darién △ Panama 7°36N 77°57W 88 E4
Dariganga = Ovoot
  Mongolia 45°21N 113°45E 34 B7
Darjeeling = Darjiling
  India 27°3N 88°18E 43 F13
Darjiling India 27°3N 88°18E 43 F13
Darkan Australia 33°20S 116°43E 61 F2
Darkhana Pakistan 30°39N 72°11E 42 D5
Darkhazīneh Iran 31°54N 48°39E 45 D6
Darkot Pass Pakistan 36°45N 73°26E 43 A5
Darling → Australia 34°4S 141°54E 63 E3
Darling Downs
  Australia 27°30S 150°30E 63 D5
Darling Ra. Australia 32°30S 116°20E 61 F2
Darlington U.K. 54°32N 1°33W 12 C6
Darlington U.S.A. 34°18N 79°52W 85 D15
Darlington □ U.K. 54°32N 1°33W 12 C6
Darlington, L. S. Africa 33°10S 25°9E 56 E4
Darlot, L. Australia 27°48S 121°35E 61 E3
Darłowo Poland 54°25N 16°25E 16 A9
Darmstadt Germany 49°51N 8°39E 16 D5
Darnah Libya 32°45N 22°45E 51 B10
Darnall S. Africa 29°23S 31°18E 57 D5
Darnley Australia 9°35S 143°46E 62 a
Darnley, C. Antarctica 68°0S 69°0E 5 C6
Darnley B. Canada 69°30N 123°30W 68 D7
Darr → Australia 23°39S 143°50E 62 C3
Darra Pezu Pakistan 32°19N 70°44E 42 C4
Darrequeira Argentina 37°42S 63°10W 94 D3
Darrington U.S.A. 48°15N 121°36W 76 B3
Dart → U.K. 50°24N 3°39W 13 G4
Dart, C. Antarctica 73°6S 126°20W 5 D14
Dartford U.K. 51°26N 0°13E 13 F8
Dartmoor U.K. 50°38N 3°57W 13 G4
Dartmoor △ U.K. 50°37N 3°59W 13 G4
Dartmouth Canada 44°40N 63°30W 73 D7
Dartmouth U.K. 50°21N 3°36W 13 G4
Dartmouth Res.
  Australia 26°4S 145°18E 63 D4

Dartuch, C. = Artrutx, C. de
  Spain 39°55N 3°49E 24 B10
Darvaza Turkmenistan 40°11N 58°24E 28 E6
Darvel, Teluk = Lahad Datu,
  Telok Malaysia 5°0N 118°20E 37 D5
Darwen U.K. 53°42N 2°29W 12 D5
Darwendale Zimbabwe 17°41S 30°33E 57 B5
Darwha India 20°15N 77°45E 40 J10
Darwin Australia 12°25S 130°51E 60 B5
Darwin U.S.A. 36°15N 117°35W 79 J9
Darya Khan Pakistan 31°48N 71°6E 42 D4
Daryācheh-ye Bakhtegān
  Iran 29°40N 53°50E 45 D7
Daryoi Amu = Amudarya →
  Uzbekistan 43°58N 59°34E 28 E6
Dās U.A.E. 25°20N 53°30E 45 E7
Dashen, Ras Ethiopia 13°8N 38°26E 47 E2
Dashetai China 41°0N 109°5E 34 D5
Dashköpri Turkmenistan 36°16N 62°8E 45 B9
Dashoguz Turkmenistan 41°49N 59°58E 28 E6
Dasht → Pakistan 25°10N 61°40E 40 G2
Daska Pakistan 32°20N 74°20E 42 C6
Dasuya India 31°49N 75°38E 42 D6
Datça Turkey 36°46N 27°40E 23 F12
Datia India 25°39N 78°27E 43 G8
Datong China 40°6N 113°18E 34 D7
Dattakhel Pakistan 32°54N 69°46E 42 C3
Datu, Tanjung Indonesia 2°5N 109°39E 36 D3
Datu Piang Phil. 7°2N 124°30E 37 C6
Datuk, Tanjung = Datu, Tanjung
  Indonesia 2°5N 109°39E 36 D3
Daud Khel Pakistan 32°53N 71°34E 42 C4
Daudnagar India 25°2N 84°24E 43 G11
Daugava → Latvia 57°4N 24°3E 9 H21
Daugavpils Latvia 55°53N 26°32E 9 J22
Daulpur India 26°45N 77°59E 42 F7
Dauphin Canada 51°9N 100°5W 71 C8
Dauphin U.S.A. 40°22N 76°56W 82 F8
Dauphin L. Canada 51°20N 99°45W 71 C9
Dauphiné France 45°15N 5°25E 20 D6
Dausa India 26°52N 76°20E 42 F7
Davangere India 14°25N 75°55E 40 M9
Davao Phil. 7°0N 125°40E 37 C7
Davao G. Phil. 6°30N 125°48E 37 C7
Dāvar Panāh = Sarāvān
  Iran 27°25N 62°15E 45 E9
Davenport Calif., U.S.A. 37°1N 122°12W 78 H4
Davenport Iowa, U.S.A. 41°32N 90°35W 80 E8
Davenport Wash., U.S.A. 47°39N 118°9W 76 C4
Davenport Ra. Australia 20°28S 134°0E 62 C1
Davenport Range △
  Australia 20°36S 134°22E 62 C1
Daventry U.K. 52°16N 1°10W 13 E6
David Panama 8°30N 82°30W 88 E3
David City U.S.A. 41°15N 97°8W 80 E5
David Glacier Antarctica 75°20S 162°0E 5 D21
David Gorodok = Davyd Haradok
  Belarus 52°4N 27°8E 17 B14
Davidson Canada 51°16N 105°59W 71 C7
Davidson Mts. U.S.A. 68°41N 142°22W 74 B11
Davis Antarctica 68°34S 77°55E 5 C6
Davis U.S.A. 38°33N 121°44W 78 G5
Davis Dam U.S.A. 35°12N 114°34W 79 K12
Davis Inlet Canada 55°50N 60°59W 73 A7
Davis Mts. U.S.A. 30°50N 103°55W 84 F3
Davis Sea Antarctica 66°0S 92°0E 5 C7
Davis Str. N. Amer. 65°0N 58°0W 69 D19
Davlos Cyprus 35°25N 33°54E 25 D12
Davos Switz. 46°48N 9°49E 20 C8
Davy L. Canada 58°53N 108°18W 71 B7
Davyd Haradok Belarus 52°4N 27°8E 17 B14
Dawei = Tavoy Burma 14°2N 98°12E 38 E2
Dawes Ra. Australia 24°40S 150°40E 62 C5
Dawlish U.K. 50°35N 3°28W 13 G4
Dawna Ra. Burma 16°30N 98°30E 38 D2
Dawros Hd. Ireland 54°50N 8°33W 10 B3
Dawson, I. Chile 53°50S 70°50W 96 G2
Dawson City Canada 64°10N 139°30W 68 E4
Dawson Creek Canada 55°45N 120°15W 70 B4
Dawson Inlet Canada 61°50N 93°25W 71 A10
Dawson Ra. Australia 24°30S 149°48E 62 C4
Dax France 43°44N 1°3W 20 E3
Daxian China 31°15N 107°23E 32 C5
Daxindian China 37°30N 120°50E 35 F11
Daxinggou China 43°25N 129°40E 35 C15
Daxue Shan China 30°30N 101°30E 32 C5
Day Kundī □ Afghan. 34°0N 66°0E 40 C4
Daylesford Australia 37°21S 144°9E 63 F3
Dayr az Zawr Syria 35°20N 40°5E 44 C4
Daysland Canada 52°50N 112°20W 70 C6
Dayton Nev., U.S.A. 39°14N 119°36W 78 F7
Dayton Ohio, U.S.A. 39°45N 84°12W 81 F11
Dayton Pa., U.S.A. 40°53N 79°15W 82 F5
Dayton Tenn., U.S.A. 35°30N 85°1W 85 D12
Dayton Wyo., U.S.A. 44°53N 107°16W 76 D10
Daytona Beach U.S.A. 29°13N 81°1W 85 G14
Dayville U.S.A. 44°28N 119°32W 76 D4
De Aar S. Africa 30°39S 24°0E 56 E3
De Biesbosch △ Neths. 51°45N 4°48E 15 C4
De Funiak Springs
  U.S.A. 30°43N 86°7W 85 F11
De Grey → Australia 20°12S 119°13E 60 D2
De Haan Belgium 51°16N 3°2E 15 C3
De Hoge Veluwe △ Neths. 52°5N 5°46E 15 B5
De Hoop S. Africa 34°30S 20°28E 56 E3
De Kalb Junction U.S.A. 44°30N 75°16W 83 B9
De Kennemerduinen △
  Neths. 52°27N 4°33E 15 B4
De Land U.S.A. 29°2N 81°18W 85 G14
De Leon U.S.A. 32°6N 98°32W 84 E5
De Long Mts. U.S.A. 68°10N 163°30W 74 B7
De Panne Belgium 51°6N 2°34E 15 C2
De Pere U.S.A. 44°27N 88°4W 80 C9
De Queen U.S.A. 34°2N 94°21W 84 D7
De Quincy U.S.A. 30°27N 93°26W 84 F8
De Ruyters U.S.A. 42°45N 75°53W 83 D9

Delgo Sudan 20°6N 30°40E 51 D12
Delhi Canada 42°51N 80°30W 82 D4
Delhi India 28°39N 77°13E 42 E7
Delhi La., U.S.A. 32°28N 91°30W 84 E9
Delhi N.Y., U.S.A. 42°17N 74°55W 83 D10
Delia Canada 51°38N 112°23W 70 C6
Delice Turkey 39°54N 34°2E 19 G5
Delicias Mexico 28°13N 105°28W 86 B3
Deljān Iran 33°59N 50°40E 45 C6
Delisle Canada 65°11N 123°25W 68 C7
Delisle Canada 51°55N 107°8W 71 C7
Deliverance I. Australia 9°31S 141°34E 62 a
Dell City U.S.A. 31°56N 105°12W 84 F2
Dell Rapids U.S.A. 43°50N 96°43W 80 D6
Delmar U.S.A. 42°37N 73°47W 83 D11
Delmenhorst Germany 53°3N 8°37E 16 B5
Delonga, Ostrova
  Russia 76°40N 149°20E 29 B15
Deloraine Australia 41°30S 146°40E 63 G4
Deloraine Canada 49°15N 100°29W 71 D8
Delphi U.S.A. 40°36N 86°41W 80 E10
Delphos U.S.A. 40°51N 84°21E 81 E11
Delportshoop S. Africa 28°22S 24°20E 56 D3
Delray Beach U.S.A. 26°28N 80°4W 85 H14
Delta Colo., U.S.A. 38°44N 108°4W 76 G9
Delta Utah, U.S.A. 39°21N 112°35W 76 G7
Delta Dunărea ○
  Romania 45°15N 29°25E 17 F15
Delta Junction U.S.A. 64°2N 145°44W 68 E2
Deltona U.S.A. 28°54N 81°15W 85 G14
Delungra Australia 29°39S 150°51E 63 D5
Delvada India 20°46N 71°2E 42 J4
Delvinë Albania 39°59N 20°6E 23 E9
Demak Indonesia 6°53S 110°38E 37 G14
Demanda, Sierra de la
  Spain 42°15N 3°0W 21 A4
Demavend = Damāvand,
  Qolleh-ye Iran 35°56N 52°10E 45 C7
Dembia C.A.R. 4°56N 23°53E 54 B1
Dembidolo Ethiopia 8°34N 34°50E 47 F1
Demchok India 32°42N 79°29E 43 C8
Demer → Belgium 50°57N 4°42E 15 D4
Deming N. Mex.,
  U.S.A. 32°16N 107°46W 77 K10
Deming Wash., U.S.A. 48°50N 122°13W 78 B4
Demini → Brazil 0°46S 62°56W 92 D6
Demirci Turkey 39°2N 28°38E 23 E13
Demirköy Turkey 41°49N 27°45E 23 D12
Demopolis U.S.A. 32°31N 87°50W 85 E11
Dempo Indonesia 4°2S 103°15E 36 E2
Den Bosch = 's-Hertogenbosch
  Neths. 51°42N 5°17E 15 C5
Den Burg Neths. 53°3N 4°47E 15 A4
Den Chai Thailand 17°59N 100°4E 38 D3
Den Haag = 's-Gravenhage
  Neths. 52°7N 4°17E 15 B4
Den Helder Neths. 52°57N 4°45E 15 B4
Den Oever Neths. 52°56N 5°2E 15 B5
Denair U.S.A. 37°32N 120°48W 78 H6
Denali = McKinley, Mt.
  U.S.A. 63°4N 151°0W 68 E1
Denau Uzbekistan 38°16N 67°54E 28 F7
Denbigh Canada 45°8N 77°15W 82 A7
Denbigh U.K. 53°12N 3°25W 12 D4
Denbighshire □ U.K. 53°8N 3°22W 12 D4
Dendang Indonesia 3°7S 107°56E 36 E3
Dendermonde Belgium 51°2N 4°5E 15 C4
Dengfeng China 34°25N 113°2E 34 G7
Dengkou China 40°18N 106°55E 34 D4
Denham Australia 25°56S 113°31E 61 E1
Denham, Mt. Jamaica 18°13N 77°32W 88 a
Denham Ra. Australia 21°55S 147°46E 62 C4
Denham Sd. Australia 25°45S 113°15E 61 E1
Denholm Canada 52°39N 108°1W 71 C7
Denia Spain 38°49N 0°8E 21 C6
Denial B. Australia 32°14S 133°32E 63 E1
Deniliquin Australia 35°30S 144°58E 63 F3
Denimoo = Fort Resolution
  Canada 61°10N 113°40W 70 A6
Denison Iowa, U.S.A. 42°1N 95°21W 80 D6
Denison Tex., U.S.A. 33°45N 96°33W 84 E6
Denison Plains Australia 18°35S 128°0E 60 C4
Denizli Turkey 37°42N 29°2E 19 G4
Denman Glacier
  Antarctica 66°45S 99°25E 5 C7
Denmark Australia 34°59S 117°25E 61 F2
Denmark ■ Europe 55°45N 10°0E 9 J14
Denmark Str. Atl. Oc. 66°0N 30°0W 66 C17
Dennery St. Lucia 13°55N 60°54W 89 f
Dennison U.S.A. 40°24N 81°19W 82 F3
Denny U.K. 56°1N 3°55W 11 E5
Denpasar Indonesia 8°39S 115°13E 37 K18
Denpasar ✈ (DPS)
  Indonesia 8°44S 115°10E 37 K18
Denton Mont., U.S.A. 47°19N 109°57W 76 C9
Denton Tex., U.S.A. 33°13N 97°8W 84 E6
D'Entrecasteaux, Pt.
  Australia 34°50S 115°57E 61 F2
D'Entrecasteaux △
  Australia 34°20S 115°33E 61 F2
D'Entrecasteaux Is.
  Papua N. G. 9°0S 151°0E 58 B8
Denver Colo., U.S.A. 39°42N 104°59W 76 G11
Denver Pa., U.S.A. 40°14N 76°8W 83 F8
Denver City U.S.A. 32°58N 102°50W 84 E3
Deoband India 29°42N 77°43E 42 E7
Deogarh India 25°32N 73°54E 42 G5
Deoghar India 24°30N 86°42E 43 G12
Deolali India 19°58N 73°50E 40 K8
Deoli = Devli India 25°50N 75°50E 42 G6
Deora India 26°22N 71°10E 42 F4
Deori India 23°24N 79°1E 43 H8
Deoria India 26°31N 83°48E 43 F10
Deosai Mts. Pakistan 35°40N 75°0E 43 B6
Deosri India 26°46N 90°29E 43 F14
Depalpur India 22°51N 75°33E 42 H6
Deping China 37°25N 116°58E 35 F9

Deposit *U.S.A.* 42°4N 75°25W **83 D9**
Depuch I. *Australia* 20°37S 117°44E **60 D2**
Deputatskiy *Russia* 69°18N 139°54E **29 C14**
Dera Ghazi Khan
  Pakistan 30°5N 70°43E **42 D4**
Dera Ismail Khan
  Pakistan 31°50N 70°50E **42 D4**
Derabugti *Pakistan* 29°2N 69°9E **42 E3**
Derawar Fort *Pakistan* 28°46N 71°20E **42 E4**
Derbent *Russia* 42°5N 48°15E **19 F8**
Derby *Australia* 17°18S 123°38E **60 C3**
Derby *U.K.* 52°56N 1°28W **12 E6**
Derby Conn., *U.S.A.* 41°19N 73°5W **83 E11**
Derby Kans., *U.S.A.* 37°33N 97°16W **80 G5**
Derby N.Y., *U.S.A.* 42°41N 78°58W **82 D6**
Derby City □ *U.K.* 52°56N 1°28W **12 E6**
Derby Line *U.S.A.* 45°0N 72°6W **83 B12**
Derbyshire □ *U.K.* 53°11N 1°38W **12 D6**
Derdepoort *S. Africa* 24°38S 26°24E **56 C4**
Dereham *U.K.* 52°41N 0°57E **13 E8**
Derg → *U.K.* 54°44N 7°26W **10 B4**
Derg, L. *Ireland* 53°0N 8°20W **10 D3**
Deridder *U.S.A.* 30°51N 93°17W **84 F8**
Dermott *U.S.A.* 33°32N 91°26W **84 E9**
Derry = Londonderry
  U.K. 55°0N 7°20W **10 B4**
Derry = Londonderry □
  U.K. 55°0N 7°20W **10 B4**
Derry N.H., *U.S.A.* 42°53N 71°19W **83 D13**
Derry Pa., *U.S.A.* 40°20N 79°18W **82 F5**
Derryveagh Mts. *Ireland* 54°56N 8°11W **10 B3**
Derwent → *Cumb., U.K.* 54°39N 3°33W **12 C4**
Derwent → *Derby, U.K.* 52°57N 1°28W **12 E6**
Derwent → *N. Yorks.,*
  U.K. 53°45N 0°58W **12 D7**
Derwent Water *U.K.* 54°35N 3°9W **12 C4**
Des Moines *Iowa, U.S.A.* 41°35N 93°37W **80 E7**
Des Moines *N. Mex.,*
  U.S.A. 36°46N 103°50W **77 H12**
Des Moines *Wash.,*
  U.S.A. 47°24N 122°19W **78 C4**
Des Moines → *U.S.A.* 40°23N 91°25W **80 E8**
Desaguadero →
  Argentina 34°30S 66°46W **94 C2**
Desaguadero → *Bolivia* 16°35S 69°5W **92 G5**
Desar *Malaysia* 1°31N 104°17E **39 d**
Descanso, Pta. *Mexico* 32°21N 117°3W **79 N9**
Deschaillons-sur-St-Laurent
  Canada 46°32N 72°7W **73 C5**
Deschambault L.
  Canada 54°50N 103°30W **71 C8**
Deschutes → *U.S.A.* 45°38N 120°55W **76 D3**
Dese *Ethiopia* 11°5N 39°40E **47 E2**
Deseado → *Argentina* 47°45S 65°54W **96 F3**
Deseronto *Canada* 44°12N 77°3W **82 B7**
Desert Center *U.S.A.* 33°43N 115°24W **79 M11**
Desert Hot Springs
  U.S.A. 33°58N 116°30W **79 M10**
Deshnok *India* 27°48N 73°21E **42 F5**
Desierto Central de Baja
  California △ *Mexico* 29°40N 114°50W **86 B2**
Desna → *Ukraine* 50°33N 30°32E **17 C16**
Desolación, I. *Chile* 53°0S 74°0W **96 G2**
Despeñaperros, Paso
  Spain 38°24N 3°30W **21 C4**
Dessau *Germany* 51°51N 12°14E **16 C7**
Dessye = Dese *Ethiopia* 11°5N 39°40E **47 E2**
D'Estrees B. *Australia* 35°55S 137°45E **63 F2**
Desuri *India* 25°18N 73°35E **42 G5**
Det Udom *Thailand* 14°54N 105°5E **38 E5**
Dete *Zimbabwe* 18°38S 26°50E **56 B4**
Detmold *Germany* 51°56N 8°52E **16 C5**
Detour, Pt. *U.S.A.* 45°40N 86°40W **80 C10**
Detroit *U.S.A.* 42°19N 83°12W **82 D1**
Detroit Lakes *U.S.A.* 46°49N 95°51W **80 B6**
Deua △ *Australia* 35°32S 149°46E **63 F4**
Deurne *Neths.* 51°27N 5°49E **15 C5**
Deutsche Bucht *Germany* 54°15N 8°0E **16 A5**
Deutschland = Germany ■
  Europe 51°0N 10°0E **16 C6**
Deva *Romania* 45°53N 22°55E **17 F12**
Devakottai *India* 9°55N 78°45E **40 Q11**
Devaprayag *India* 30°13N 78°35E **43 D8**
Deventer *Neths.* 52°15N 6°10E **15 B6**
Deveron → *U.K.* 57°41N 2°32W **11 D6**
Devgadh Bariya *India* 22°40N 73°55E **42 H5**
Devikot *India* 26°42N 71°12E **42 F4**
Devils Den *U.S.A.* 35°46N 119°58W **78 K7**
Devils Hole = Death Valley △
  U.S.A. 36°29N 116°6W **79 J9**
Devils Lake *U.S.A.* 48°7N 98°52W **80 A4**
Devils Paw *Canada* 58°47N 134°0W **70 B2**
Devils Postpile △ *U.S.A.* 37°37N 119°5W **78 H7**
Devils Tower *U.S.A.* 44°35N 104°42W **76 D11**
Devils Tower △
  U.S.A. 44°48N 104°55W **76 D11**
Devine *U.S.A.* 29°8N 98°54W **84 G5**
Devizes *U.K.* 51°22N 1°58W **13 F6**
Devli *India* 25°50N 75°20E **42 G6**
Devon *Canada* 53°24N 113°44W **70 C6**
Devon □ *U.K.* 50°50N 3°40W **13 G4**
Devon I. *Canada* 75°10N 85°0W **69 B15**
Devonport *Australia* 41°10S 146°22E **63 G4**
Devonport *N.Z.* 36°49S 174°49E **59 B6**
Dewas *India* 22°59N 76°3E **42 H7**
Dewetsdorp *S. Africa* 29°33S 26°39E **56 D4**
Dewey *Puerto Rico* 18°18N 65°18W **89 d**
Dexter *Maine, U.S.A.* 45°1N 69°18W **81 C19**
Dexter *Mo., U.S.A.* 36°48N 89°57W **80 G9**
Dexter *N. Mex., U.S.A.* 33°12N 104°22W **77 K11**
Dey-Dey, L. *Australia* 29°12S 131°4E **61 E5**
Deyang *China* 31°3N 104°27E **32 C5**
Deyhūk *Iran* 33°15N 57°30E **45 C8**
Deyyer *Iran* 27°55N 51°55E **45 E6**
Dez → *Iran* 31°39N 48°52E **45 D6**
Dezadeash L. *Canada* 60°28N 136°58W **70 A1**
Dezfūl *Iran* 32°20N 48°30E **45 C6**
Dezhneva, Mys *Russia* 66°5N 169°40W **29 C19**
Dezhou *China* 37°26N 116°18E **34 F9**

Dhadhar → *India* 24°56N 85°24E **43 G11**
Dhahiriya = Aẕ Ẕāhirīyah
  West Bank 31°25N 34°58E **46 D3**
Dhahran = Aẕ Ẕahrān
  Si. Arabia 26°10N 50°7E **45 E6**
Dhak *Pakistan* 32°25N 72°33E **42 C5**
Dhaka *Bangla.* 23°43N 90°26E **43 H14**
Dhaka □ *Bangla.* 24°25N 90°25E **43 G14**
Dhali *Cyprus* 35°1N 33°25E **25 D12**
Dhamār *Yemen* 14°30N 44°20E **47 E3**
Dhampur *India* 29°19N 78°33E **43 E8**
Dhamtari *India* 20°42N 81°35E **41 J12**
Dhanbad *India* 23°50N 86°30E **43 H12**
Dhangarhi *Nepal* 28°55N 80°40E **43 E9**
Dhankuta *Nepal* 26°55N 87°40E **43 F12**
Dhanpuri *India* 23°13N 81°30E **43 H9**
Dhar *India* 22°35N 75°26E **42 H6**
Dharampur *India* 22°13N 75°18E **42 H6**
Dharamsala = Dharmsala
  India 32°16N 76°23E **42 C7**
Dharan *Nepal* 26°49N 87°17E **43 F12**
Dhariwal *India* 31°57N 75°19E **42 D6**
Dharla → *Bangla.* 25°46N 89°42E **43 G13**
Dharmapuri *India* 12°10N 78°10E **40 N11**
Dharmjaygarh *India* 22°28N 83°13E **43 H10**
Dharmsala *India* 32°16N 76°23E **42 C7**
Dharni *India* 21°33N 76°53E **42 J7**
Dharwad *India* 15°30N 75°4E **40 M9**
Dhasan → *India* 25°48N 79°24E **43 G8**
Dhaulagiri *Nepal* 28°39N 83°28E **43 E10**
Dhebar, L. *India* 24°10N 74°0E **42 G6**
Dheftera *Cyprus* 35°5N 33°16E **25 D12**
Dhenkanal *India* 20°45N 85°35E **41 J14**
Dherinia *Cyprus* 35°3N 33°57E **25 D12**
Dhī Qār □ *Iraq* 31°0N 46°15E **44 D5**
Dhiarrizos → *Cyprus* 34°41N 32°34E **25 E11**
Dhībān *Jordan* 31°30N 35°46E **46 D4**
Dhilwan *India* 31°31N 75°21E **42 D6**
Dhimarkhera *India* 23°28N 80°22E **43 H9**
Dhodhekánisos = Dodecanese
  Greece 36°35N 27°0E **23 F12**
Dholka *India* 22°44N 72°29E **42 H5**
Dhoraji *India* 21°45N 70°37E **42 J4**
Dhrangadhra *India* 22°59N 71°31E **42 H4**
Dhrol *India* 22°33N 70°25E **42 H4**
Dhubri *India* 26°2N 89°59E **41 F16**
Dhule *India* 20°58N 74°50E **40 J9**
Di Linh *Vietnam* 11°35N 108°4E **39 G7**
Di Linh, Cao Nguyen
  Vietnam 11°30N 108°0E **39 G7**
Dia *Greece* 35°28N 25°14E **25 D7**
Diablo Range *U.S.A.* 37°20N 121°25W **78 J5**
Diafarabé *Mali* 14°9N 4°57W **50 F5**
Diamante *Argentina* 32°5S 60°40W **94 C3**
Diamante → *Argentina* 34°30S 66°46W **94 C2**
Diamantina *Brazil* 18°17S 43°40W **93 G10**
Diamantina △
  Australia 26°45S 139°10E **63 D2**
Diamantina △ *Australia* 23°33S 141°23E **62 C3**
Diamantina *Brazil* 14°30S 56°30W **93 F7**
Diamond Bar *U.S.A.* 34°1N 117°48W **79 L9**
Diamond Harbour
  India 22°11N 88°14E **43 H13**
Diamond Is. *Australia* 17°25S 151°5E **62 B5**
Diamond Mts. *U.S.A.* 39°40N 115°50W **76 G6**
Diamond Springs
  U.S.A. 38°42N 120°49W **78 G6**
Diaoyu Tai = Senkaku-Shotō
  E. China Sea 25°45N 123°30E **31 M1**
Dībā *U.A.E.* 25°45N 56°16E **45 E8**
Dibai *India* 28°13N 78°15E **42 E8**
Dibaya
  Dem. Rep. of the Congo 6°30S 22°57E **52 F4**
Dibaya-Lubue
  Dem. Rep. of the Congo 4°12S 19°54E **52 E3**
Dibbeen △ *Jordan* 32°20N 35°45E **46 C4**
D'Iberville, Lac *Canada* 55°55N 73°15W **72 A5**
Dibete *Botswana* 23°45S 26°32E **56 C4**
Dibrugarh *India* 27°29N 94°55E **41 F19**
Dickens *U.S.A.* 33°37N 100°50W **84 E4**
Dickinson *U.S.A.* 46°53N 102°47W **80 B2**
Dickson *U.S.A.* 36°5N 87°23W **85 C11**
Dickson City *U.S.A.* 41°28N 75°36W **83 E9**
Didiéni *Mali* 13°53N 8°6W **50 F4**
Didsbury *Canada* 51°35N 114°10W **70 C6**
Didwana *India* 27°23N 74°36E **42 F6**
Diefenbaker, L. *Canada* 51°0N 106°55W **71 C7**
Diego de Almagro *Chile* 26°22S 70°3W **94 B1**
Diego Suarez = Antsiranana
  Madag. 12°25S 49°20E **57 A8**
Diekirch *Lux.* 49°52N 6°10E **15 E6**
Dien Ban *Vietnam* 15°53N 108°16E **38 E7**
Dien Bien *Vietnam* 21°20N 103°0E **38 B4**
Dien Khanh *Vietnam* 12°15N 109°6E **39 F7**
Dieppe *France* 49°54N 1°4E **20 B4**
Dierks *U.S.A.* 34°7N 94°1W **84 D7**
Diest *Belgium* 50°58N 5°4E **15 D5**
Dif *Somali Rep.* 0°59N 40°58E **47 G3**
Differdange *Lux.* 49°31N 5°54E **15 E5**
Dig *India* 27°28N 77°20E **42 F7**
Digba
  Dem. Rep. of the Congo 4°25N 25°48E **54 B2**
Digby *Canada* 44°38N 65°50W **73 D6**
Digges Is. *Canada* 62°40N 77°50W **69 E16**
Diggi *India* 26°22N 75°26E **42 F6**
Dighinala *Bangla.* 23°15N 92°5E **41 H18**
Dighton *U.S.A.* 38°29N 100°28W **80 F3**
Digne-les-Bains *France* 44°5N 6°12E **20 D7**
Digos *Phil.* 6°45N 125°20E **37 C7**
Digul → *Indonesia* 7°7S 138°42E **37 F9**
Dihang = Brahmaputra →
  Asia 23°40N 90°35E **43 H13**
Dijlah, Nahr → *Asia* 31°0N 47°25E **44 D5**
Dijon *France* 47°20N 5°3E **20 C6**
Dikhil *Djibouti* 11°8N 42°20E **47 E3**
Dikkil = Dikhil *Djibouti* 11°8N 42°20E **47 E3**
Diksmuide *Belgium* 51°2N 2°52E **15 C2**
Dikson *Russia* 73°40N 80°5E **28 B9**

Dikti Oros *Greece* 35°8N 25°30E **25 D7**
Dila *Ethiopia* 6°21N 38°22E **47 F2**
Dili *E. Timor* 8°39S 125°34E **37 F7**
Dilley *U.S.A.* 28°40N 99°10W **84 G5**
Dilli = Delhi *India* 28°39N 77°13E **42 E7**
Dillingham *U.S.A.* 59°3N 158°28W **74 D8**
Dillon *Canada* 55°56N 108°35W **71 B7**
Dillon *Mont., U.S.A.* 45°13N 112°38W **76 D7**
Dillon *S.C., U.S.A.* 34°25N 79°22W **85 D15**
Dillon → *Canada* 55°56N 108°56W **71 B7**
Dillsburg *U.S.A.* 40°7N 77°2W **82 F7**
Dilolo
  Dem. Rep. of the Congo 10°28S 22°18E **52 G4**
Dimapur *India* 25°54N 93°45E **32 C4**
Dimas *Mexico* 23°43N 106°47W **86 C3**
Dimashq *Syria* 33°30N 36°18E **46 B5**
Dimashq □ *Syria* 33°30N 36°30E **46 B5**
Dimbaza *S. Africa* 32°50S 27°14E **57 E4**
Dimboola *Australia* 36°28S 142°7E **63 F3**
Dîmbovița = Dâmbovița →
  Romania 44°12N 26°26E **17 F14**
Dimbulah *Australia* 17°8S 145°4E **62 B4**
Dimitrovgrad *Bulgaria* 42°5N 25°35E **23 C11**
Dimitrovgrad *Russia* 54°14N 49°39E **18 D8**
Dimitrovo = Pernik
  Bulgaria 42°35N 23°2E **23 C10**
Dimmitt *U.S.A.* 34°33N 102°19W **84 D3**
Dimona *Israel* 31°2N 35°1E **46 D4**
Dinagat *Phil.* 10°10N 125°40E **37 B7**
Dinajpur *Bangla.* 25°33N 88°43E **41 G16**
Dinan *France* 48°28N 2°2W **20 B2**
Dīnān Āb *Iran* 32°4N 56°49E **45 C8**
Dinant *Belgium* 50°16N 4°55E **15 D4**
Dinapur *India* 25°38N 85°5E **43 G11**
Dīnar, Kūh-e *Iran* 30°42N 51°46E **45 D6**
Dinara Planina *Croatia* 44°0N 16°30E **22 C7**
Dinard *France* 48°38N 2°6W **20 B2**
Dinaric Alps = Dinara Planina
  Croatia 44°0N 16°30E **22 C7**
Dindigul *India* 10°25N 78°0E **40 P11**
Dindori *India* 22°57N 81°5E **43 H9**
Ding Xian = Dingzhou
  China 38°30N 114°59E **34 E8**
Dinga *Pakistan* 25°26N 67°10E **42 G2**
Ding'an *China* 19°42N 110°19E **38 C8**
Dingbian *China* 37°35N 107°32E **34 F4**
Dingle *Ireland* 52°9N 10°17W **10 D1**
Dingle B. *Ireland* 52°3N 10°20W **10 D1**
Dingmans Ferry *U.S.A.* 41°13N 74°55W **83 E10**
Dingo *Australia* 23°38S 149°19E **62 C4**
Dingtao *China* 35°5N 115°35E **34 G8**
Dingwall *U.K.* 57°36N 4°26W **11 D4**
Dingxi *China* 35°30N 104°33E **34 G3**
Dingxiang *China* 38°30N 112°58E **34 E7**
Dingzhou *China* 38°30N 114°59E **34 E8**
Dinh, Mui *Vietnam* 11°22N 109°1E **39 G7**
Dinh Lap *Vietnam* 21°33N 107°6E **38 B6**
Dinin → *Ireland* 52°43N 7°18W **10 D4**
Dinira △ *Venezuela* 9°57N 70°6W **89 E6**
Dinokwe *Botswana* 23°29S 26°37E **56 C4**
Dinorwic *Canada* 49°41N 92°30W **71 D10**
Dinosaur △ *Canada* 50°47N 111°30W **70 C6**
Dinosaur △ *U.S.A.* 40°30N 108°45W **76 F9**
Dinuba *U.S.A.* 36°32N 119°23W **78 J7**
Dionisades *Greece* 35°20N 26°10E **25 D8**
Diourbel *Senegal* 14°39N 16°12W **50 F2**
Dipalpur *Pakistan* 30°40N 73°39E **42 D5**
Dipkarpaz = Rizokarpaso
  Cyprus 35°36N 34°23E **25 D13**
Diplo *Pakistan* 24°35N 69°35E **42 G3**
Dipolog *Phil.* 8°36N 123°20E **37 C6**
Dipperu △ *Australia* 21°56S 148°42E **62 C4**
Dir *Pakistan* 35°8N 71°59E **40 B7**
Dire Dawa *Ethiopia* 9°35N 41°45E **47 F3**
Dirfis Oros *Greece* 38°40N 23°54E **23 E10**
Diriamba *Nic.* 11°51N 86°19W **88 D2**
Dirk Hartog I. *Australia* 25°50S 113°5E **61 E1**
Dirranbandi *Australia* 28°33S 148°17E **63 D4**
Disa *India* 24°18N 72°10E **42 G5**
Disappointment, C.
  U.S.A. 46°18N 124°5W **76 C1**
Disappointment, L.
  Australia 23°20S 122°40E **60 D3**
Disaster B. *Australia* 37°15S 149°58E **63 F4**
Discovery B. *Australia* 38°10S 140°40E **63 F3**
Discovery B. *China* 22°18N 114°1E **33 G11**
Disko = Qeqertarsuaq
  Greenland 69°45N 53°30W **66 C14**
Disney Reef *Tonga* 19°17S 174°7W **59 c**
Diss *U.K.* 52°23N 1°7E **13 E9**
Disteghil Sar *Pakistan* 36°20N 75°12E **43 A6**
District of Columbia □
  U.S.A. 38°55N 77°0W **81 F15**
Distrito Federal □ *Brazil* 15°45S 47°45W **93 G9**
Distrito Federal □
  Mexico 19°15N 99°10W **87 D5**
Diu *India* 20°45N 70°58E **42 J4**
Dīvāndarreh *Iran* 35°55N 47°2E **44 C5**
Divide *U.S.A.* 45°45N 112°45W **76 D7**
Dividing Ra. *Australia* 27°45S 116°0E **61 E2**
Divinópolis *Brazil* 20°10S 44°54W **93 H10**
Divnoye *Russia* 45°55N 43°21E **19 E7**
Divo *Ivory C.* 5°48N 5°15W **50 G4**
Dīwāl Kol *Afghan.* 34°23N 67°52E **42 B2**
Dixie U.S.A. 39°55N 100°19W **78 F6**
Dixon *Calif., U.S.A.* 38°27N 121°49W **78 G5**
Dixon *Ill., U.S.A.* 41°50N 89°29W **80 E9**
Dixon Entrance *U.S.A.* 54°30N 132°0W **68 G5**
Dixville *Canada* 45°4N 71°46W **83 A13**
Diyālā □ *Iraq* 34°0N 45°0E **44 C5**
Diyālā → *Iraq* 33°13N 44°30E **44 C5**
Diyarbakır *Turkey* 37°55N 40°18E **44 B4**
Diyodar *India* 24°8N 71°50E **42 G4**
Djakarta = Jakarta
  Indonesia 6°9S 106°52E **37 G12**
Djamba *Angola* 16°45S 13°58E **56 B1**
Djambala *Congo* 2°32S 14°30E **52 E2**
Djanet *Algeria* 24°35N 9°32E **50 D7**
Djawa = Jawa *Indonesia* 7°0S 110°0E **36 F3**

Djelfa *Algeria* 34°40N 3°15E **50 B6**
Djema *C.A.R.* 6°3N 25°15E **54 A2**
Djerba, Î. de *Tunisia* 33°50N 10°48E **51 B8**
Djerid, Chott *Tunisia* 33°42N 8°30E **50 B7**
Djibouti *Djibouti* 11°30N 43°5E **47 E3**
Djibouti ■ *Africa* 12°0N 43°0E **47 E3**
Djolu *Dem. Rep. of the Congo* 0°35N 22°5E **52 D4**
Djougou *Benin* 9°40N 1°45E **50 G6**
Djoum *Cameroon* 2°41N 12°35E **52 D2**
Djourab, Erg du *Chad* 16°40N 18°50E **51 E9**
Djugu
  Dem. Rep. of the Congo 1°55N 30°35E **54 B3**
Djukbinj △ *Australia* 12°11S 131°2E **60 B5**
Djúpivogur *Iceland* 64°39N 14°17W **8 D6**
Dmitriya Lapteva, Proliv
  Russia 73°0N 140°0E **29 B15**
Dnepr = Dnipro →
  Ukraine 46°30N 32°18E **19 E5**
Dneprodzerzhinsk =
  Dniprodzerzhynsk
  Ukraine 48°32N 34°37E **19 E5**
Dnepropetrovsk =
  Dnipropetrovsk
  Ukraine 48°30N 35°0E **19 E6**
Dnestr = Dnister →
  Europe 46°18N 30°17E **17 E16**
Dnieper = Dnipro →
  Ukraine 46°30N 32°18E **19 E5**
Dniester = Dnister →
  Europe 46°18N 30°17E **17 E16**
Dnipro → *Ukraine* 46°30N 32°18E **19 E5**
Dniprodzerzhynsk
  Ukraine 48°32N 34°37E **19 E5**
Dnipropetrovsk *Ukraine* 48°30N 35°0E **19 E6**
Dnister → *Europe* 46°18N 30°17E **17 E16**
Dno *Russia* 57°50N 29°58E **9 H23**
Dnyapro = Dnipro →
  Ukraine 46°30N 32°18E **19 E5**
Do Gonbadān = Gachsārān
  Iran 30°15N 50°45E **45 D6**
Doaktown *Canada* 46°33N 66°8W **73 C6**
Doan Hung *Vietnam* 21°30N 105°10E **38 B5**
Doany *Madag.* 14°21S 49°30E **57 A8**
Doba *Chad* 8°40N 16°50E **51 G9**
Dobandi *Pakistan* 31°13N 66°50E **42 D2**
Dobbyn *Australia* 19°44S 140°2E **62 B3**
Dobele *Latvia* 56°37N 23°16E **9 H20**
Doberai, Jazirah *Indonesia* 1°25S 133°0E **37 E8**
Doblas *Argentina* 37°5S 64°0W **94 D3**
Dobo *Indonesia* 5°45S 134°15E **37 F8**
Doboj *Bos.-H.* 44°46N 18°4E **23 B8**
Dobrich *Bulgaria* 43°37N 27°49E **23 C12**
Dobruja *Europe* 44°30N 28°15E **17 F15**
Dobrush *Belarus* 52°25N 31°22E **17 B16**
Doc, Mui *Vietnam* 17°58N 106°30E **38 D6**
Docker River = Kaltukatjara
  Australia 24°52S 129°5E **61 D4**
Doctor Arroyo *Mexico* 23°40N 100°11W **86 C4**
Doctor Pedro P. Peña
  Paraguay 22°27S 62°21W **94 A3**
Doda *India* 33°10N 75°34E **43 C6**
Doda, L. *Canada* 49°25N 75°13W **72 C4**
Dodecanese *Greece* 36°35N 27°0E **23 F12**
Dodeanisa = Dodecanese
  Greece 36°35N 27°0E **23 F12**
Dodge City *U.S.A.* 37°45N 100°1W **80 G3**
Dodge L. *Canada* 59°50N 105°36W **71 B7**
Dodgeville *U.S.A.* 42°58N 90°8W **80 D8**
Dodoma *Tanzania* 6°8S 35°45E **54 D4**
Dodoma □ *Tanzania* 6°0S 36°0E **54 D4**
Dodori △ *Kenya* 1°55S 41°7E **54 C5**
Dodsland *Canada* 51°50N 108°45W **71 C7**
Dodson *U.S.A.* 48°24N 108°15W **76 B9**
Doesburg *Neths.* 52°1N 6°9E **15 B6**
Doetinchem *Neths.* 51°59N 6°18E **15 C6**
Dog Creek *Canada* 51°35N 122°14W **70 C4**
Dog L. *Man., Canada* 51°2N 98°31W **71 C9**
Dog L. *Ont., Canada* 48°48N 89°30W **72 C2**
Dogran *Pakistan* 31°48N 73°35E **42 D5**
Doğubayazıt *Turkey* 39°31N 44°5E **44 B5**
Doha = Ad Dawḥah
  Qatar 25°15N 51°35E **45 E6**
Dohazari *Bangla.* 22°10N 92°5E **41 H18**
Dohrighat *India* 26°16N 83°31E **43 F10**
Doi *Indonesia* 2°14N 127°49E **37 D7**
Doi Inthanon △ *Thailand* 18°33N 98°34E **38 C2**
Doi Khuntan △ *Thailand* 18°33N 99°14E **38 C2**
Doi Luang *Thailand* 18°30N 101°0E **38 C3**
Doi Luang △ *Thailand* 19°22N 99°35E **38 C2**
Doi Saket *Thailand* 18°52N 99°9E **38 C2**
Doi Suthep △ *Thailand* 18°49N 98°53E **38 C2**
Dois Irmãos, Sa. *Brazil* 9°0S 42°30W **93 E10**
Dokkum *Neths.* 53°20N 5°59E **15 A5**
Dokri *Pakistan* 27°25N 68°7E **42 F3**
Dolak, Pulau *Indonesia* 8°0S 138°30E **37 F9**
Dolbeau-Mistassini
  Canada 48°53N 72°14W **73 C5**
Dole *France* 47°7N 5°31E **20 C6**
Dolgellau *U.K.* 52°45N 3°53W **12 E4**
Dolgelley = Dolgellau
  U.K. 52°45N 3°53W **12 E4**
Dolinsk *Russia* 47°21N 142°48E **29 E15**
Dollard *Neths.* 53°20N 7°10E **15 A7**
Dolo *Ethiopia* 4°11N 42°3E **47 G3**
Dolomites = Dolomiti
  Italy 46°23N 11°51E **22 A4**
Dolomiti *Italy* 46°23N 11°51E **22 A4**
Dolores *Argentina* 36°20S 57°40W **94 D4**
Dolores *Uruguay* 33°34S 58°15W **94 C4**
Dolores *U.S.A.* 37°28N 108°30W **77 H9**
Dolores → *U.S.A.* 38°49N 108°17W **76 G9**
Dolphin, C. *Falk. Is.* 51°10S 59°0W **96 G5**
Dolphin and Union Str.
  Canada 69°5N 114°45W **68 D7**
Dom Pedrito *Brazil* 31°0S 54°40W **95 C5**
Doma *Zimbabwe* 17°0S 30°40E **55 F3**
Domariaganj → *India* 26°17N 83°44E **43 F10**
Domasi *Malawi* 15°15S 35°22E **55 F4**
Dombarovskiy *Russia* 50°46N 59°32E **28 D6**

Dombås *Norway* 62°4N 9°8E **8 E13**
Dome Argus *Antarctica* 80°50S 76°30E **5 E12**
Dome C. *Antarctica* 75°12S 123°37E **5 D17**
Dome Fuji *Antarctica* 77°20S 39°45E **5 D5**
Domel I. = Letsôk-aw Kyun
  Burma 11°30N 98°25E **39 G2**
Domeyko *Chile* 29°0S 71°0W **94 B1**
Domeyko, Cordillera
  Chile 24°30S 69°0W **94 A2**
Dominador *Chile* 24°21S 69°20W **94 A2**
Dominica ■ *W. Indies* 15°20N 61°20W **89 C7**
Dominica Passage
  W. Indies 15°10N 61°20W **89 C7**
Dominican Rep. ■
  W. Indies 19°0N 70°30W **89 C5**
Domodóssola *Italy* 46°7N 8°17E **20 C8**
Domville, Mt. *Australia* 28°1S 151°15E **63 D5**
Don → *Russia* 47°4N 39°18E **19 E6**
Don → *Aberds., U.K.* 57°11N 2°5W **11 D6**
Don → *S. Yorks., U.K.* 53°41N 0°52W **12 D7**
Don, C. *Australia* 11°18S 131°46E **60 B5**
Don Benito *Spain* 38°53N 5°51W **21 C3**
Don Figuerero Mts.
  Jamaica 18°5S 77°36W **88 a**
Don Sak *Thailand* 9°18N 99°41E **39 H2**
Dona Ana = Nhamaabué
  Mozam. 17°25S 35°5E **55 F4**
Donaghadee *U.K.* 54°39N 5°33W **10 B6**
Donaghmore *Ireland* 52°52N 7°36W **10 D4**
Donald *Australia* 36°23S 143°0E **63 F3**
Donaldsonville *U.S.A.* 30°6N 90°59W **84 F9**
Donalsonville *U.S.A.* 31°3N 84°53W **85 F12**
Donau = Dunărea →
  Europe 45°20N 29°40E **17 F15**
Donauwörth *Germany* 48°43N 10°47E **16 D6**
Doncaster *U.K.* 53°32N 1°6W **12 D6**
Dondo *Angola* 9°45S 14°25E **52 F2**
Dondo *Mozam.* 19°33S 34°46E **55 F3**
Dondo, Teluk *Indonesia* 0°50N 120°30E **37 D6**
Dondra Head *Sri Lanka* 5°55N 80°40E **40 S12**
Donegal *Ireland* 54°39N 8°5W **10 B3**
Donegal □ *Ireland* 54°53N 8°0W **10 B4**
Donegal B. *Ireland* 54°31N 8°49W **10 B3**
Donets → *Russia* 47°33N 40°55E **19 E7**
Donets Basin *Ukraine* 48°0N 38°0E **6 F13**
Donetsk *Ukraine* 48°0N 37°45E **19 E6**
Dong Ba Thin *Vietnam* 12°8N 109°13E **39 F7**
Dong Dang *Vietnam* 21°54N 106°42E **38 B6**
Dong Giam *Vietnam* 19°25N 105°31E **38 C5**
Dong Ha *Vietnam* 16°55N 107°8E **38 D6**
Dong Hene *Laos* 16°40N 105°18E **38 D5**
Dong Hoi *Vietnam* 17°29N 106°36E **38 D6**
Dong Khe *Vietnam* 22°26N 106°27E **38 A6**
Dong Ujimqin Qi *China* 45°32N 116°55E **34 B9**
Dong Van *Vietnam* 23°16N 105°22E **38 A5**
Dong Xoai *Vietnam* 11°32N 106°55E **39 G6**
Dongara *Australia* 29°14S 114°57E **61 E1**
Dongbei *China* 45°0N 125°0E **30 A5**
Dongchuan *China* 26°8N 103°1E **32 D5**
Dongfang *China* 18°50N 108°33E **38 C7**
Dongfeng *China* 42°40N 125°34E **35 C13**
Donggala *Indonesia* 0°30S 119°40E **37 E5**
Donggang *China* 39°52N 124°10E **35 E13**
Dongguang *China* 37°50N 116°30E **34 F9**
Donghae *S. Korea* 37°29N 129°7E **35 F15**
Dongjingcheng *China* 44°5N 129°10E **35 B15**
Dongnae *S. Korea* 35°12N 129°5E **35 G15**
Dongning *China* 44°2N 131°5E **35 B16**
Dongola *Sudan* 19°9N 30°22E **51 E12**
Dongping *China* 35°55N 116°20E **34 G9**
Dongsha Dao *China* 20°50N 116°40E **33 G11**
Dongtai *China* 32°51N 120°21E **35 H11**
Dongting Hu *China* 29°18N 112°45E **33 D6**
Donington, C. *Australia* 34°45S 136°0E **63 E2**
Doniphan *U.S.A.* 36°37N 90°50W **80 G8**
Dønna *Norway* 66°6N 12°30E **8 C15**
Donna *U.S.A.* 26°9N 98°4W **84 H5**
Donnacona *Canada* 46°41N 71°41W **73 C5**
Donnelly's Crossing
  N.Z. 35°42S 173°38E **59 A4**
Donnybrook *Australia* 33°34S 115°48E **61 F2**
Donnybrook *S. Africa* 29°59S 29°48E **57 D4**
Donora *U.S.A.* 40°11N 79°52W **82 F5**
Donostia = Donostia-San
  Sebastián *Spain* 43°17N 1°58W **21 A5**
Donostia-San Sebastián
  Spain 43°17N 1°58W **21 A5**
Donwood *Canada* 44°19N 78°16W **82 B6**
Doomadgee *Australia* 17°56S 138°49E **62 B2**
Doomadgee ◇ *Australia* 17°56S 138°49E **62 B2**
Doon → *U.K.* 55°27N 4°39W **11 F4**
Doon Doon ◇ *Australia* 16°18S 128°14E **60 C4**
Dora, L. *Australia* 22°0S 123°0E **60 D3**
Dora Báltea → *Italy* 45°11N 8°3E **20 D8**
Doran L. *Canada* 61°13N 108°6W **71 A7**
Dorchester *U.K.* 50°42N 2°27W **13 G5**
Dorchester, C. *Canada* 65°27N 77°27W **69 C16**
Dordabis *Namibia* 22°52S 17°38E **56 C2**
Dordogne → *France* 45°2N 0°36W **20 D3**
Dordrecht *Neths.* 51°48N 4°39E **15 C4**
Dordrecht *S. Africa* 31°20S 27°3E **56 E4**
Doré, L. *Canada* 54°46N 107°17W **71 C7**
Dori *Burkina Faso* 14°3N 0°2W **50 F5**
Doring → *S. Africa* 31°54S 18°39E **56 E2**
Doringbos *S. Africa* 31°59S 19°16E **56 E2**
Dorking *U.K.* 51°14N 0°19W **13 F7**
Dornbirn *Austria* 47°25N 9°45E **16 E5**
Dornie *U.K.* 57°17N 5°31W **11 D3**
Dornoch *Canada* 44°18N 80°51W **82 B4**
Dornoch *U.K.* 57°53N 4°2W **11 D4**
Dornoch Firth *U.K.* 57°51N 4°4W **11 D4**
Dornogovĭ □ *Mongolia* 44°0N 110°0E **34 C6**
Doro, Kavo *Greece* 38°0N 24°38E **23 E11**
Dorohoi *Romania* 47°56N 26°23E **17 E14**
Döröö Nuur *Mongolia* 48°0N 93°0E **32 B4**
Dorr *Iran* 33°17N 50°38E **45 C6**
Dorre I. *Australia* 25°13S 113°12E **61 E1**
Dorrigo *Australia* 30°20S 152°44E **63 E5**

Dorris U.S.A. 41°58N 121°55W 76 F3
Dorset Canada 45°14N 78°54W 82 A6
Dorset Ohio, U.S.A. 41°40N 80°40W 82 E4
Dorset Vt., U.S.A. 43°15N 73°5W 83 C11
Dorset □ U.K. 50°45N 2°26W 13 G5
Dortmund Germany 51°30N 7°28E 16 C4
Dörtyol Turkey 36°50N 36°13E 44 B3
Doruma Dem. Rep. of the Congo 4°42N 27°33E 54 B2
Dorüneh Iran 35°10N 57°18E 45 C8
Dos Bahías, C. Argentina 44°58S 65°32W 96 E3
Dos Hermanas Spain 37°16N 5°55W 21 D3
Dos Palos U.S.A. 36°59N 120°37W 78 J6
Dosso Niger 13°0N 3°13E 50 F6
Dothan U.S.A. 31°13N 85°24W 85 F12
Doty U.S.A. 46°38N 123°17W 78 D3
Douai France 50°21N 3°4E 20 A5
Douala Cameroon 4°0N 9°45E 52 D1
Douarnenez France 48°6N 4°21W 20 B1
Double Island Pt. Australia 25°56S 153°11E 63 D5
Double Mountain Fork → U.S.A. 33°16N 100°0W 84 E4
Doubs □ France 46°53N 5°1E 20 C6
Doubtful Sd. N.Z. 45°20S 166°49E 59 F1
Doubtless B. N.Z. 34°55S 173°26E 59 A4
Douglas I. of Man 54°10N 4°28W 12 C3
Douglas S. Africa 29°4S 23°46E 56 D3
Douglas Ariz., U.S.A. 31°21N 109°33W 77 L9
Douglas Ga., U.S.A. 31°31N 82°51W 85 F13
Douglas Wyo., U.S.A. 42°45N 105°24W 76 E11
Douglas Apsley △ Australia 41°45S 148°11E 63 G4
Douglas Chan. Canada 53°40N 129°20W 70 C3
Douglas Pt. Canada 44°19N 81°37W 82 B3
Douglasville U.S.A. 33°45N 84°45W 85 E12
Dounreay U.K. 58°35N 3°44W 11 C5
Dourada, Serra Brazil 13°10S 48°45W 93 F9
Dourados Brazil 22°9S 54°50W 95 A5
Dourados → Brazil 21°58S 54°18W 95 A5
Dourados, Serra dos Brazil 23°30S 53°30W 95 A5
Douro → Europe 41°8N 8°40W 21 B1
Dove → U.K. 52°51N 1°36W 12 E6
Dove Creek U.S.A. 37°46N 108°54W 77 H9
Dover Australia 43°18S 147°2E 63 G4
Dover U.K. 51°7N 1°19E 13 F9
Dover Del., U.S.A. 39°10N 75°32W 81 F16
Dover N.H., U.S.A. 43°12N 70°56W 83 C14
Dover N.J., U.S.A. 40°53N 74°34W 83 F10
Dover Ohio, U.S.A. 40°32N 81°29W 82 F3
Dover, Pt. Australia 32°32S 125°32E 61 F4
Dover, Str. of Europe 51°0N 1°30E 13 G9
Dover-Foxcroft U.S.A. 45°11N 69°13W 81 C19
Dover Plains U.S.A. 41°43N 73°35W 83 E11
Dovey = Dyfi → U.K. 52°32N 4°3W 13 E3
Dovrefjell Norway 62°15N 9°33E 8 E13
Dow Rūd Iran 33°28N 49°4E 45 C6
Dowa Malawi 13°38S 33°58E 55 E3
Dowagiac U.S.A. 41°59N 86°6W 80 E10
Dowerin Australia 31°12S 117°2E 61 F2
Dowgha'i Iran 36°54N 58°32E 45 B8
Dowlatābād Kermān, Iran 28°20N 56°40E 45 D8
Dowlatābād Khorāsān, Iran 35°16N 59°29E 45 C8
Down □ U.K. 54°23N 6°2W 10 B5
Downey Calif., U.S.A. 33°56N 118°9W 79 M8
Downey Idaho, U.S.A. 42°26N 112°7W 76 E7
Downham Market U.K. 52°37N 0°23E 13 E8
Downieville U.S.A. 39°34N 120°50W 78 F6
Downpatrick U.K. 54°20N 5°43W 10 B6
Downpatrick Hd. Ireland 54°20N 9°21W 10 B2
Downsville U.S.A. 42°5N 75°0W 83 D10
Downton, Mt. Canada 52°42N 124°52W 70 C4
Dowsāri Iran 28°25N 57°59E 45 D8
Doyle U.S.A. 40°2N 120°6W 78 E6
Doylestown U.S.A. 40°21N 75°10W 83 F9
Dozois, Rés. Canada 47°30N 77°5W 72 C4
Dra, C. Morocco 28°47N 11°0W 50 C3
Drâa, Hamada du Algeria 28°30N 6°56W 50 C4
Drâa, Oued → Morocco 28°40N 11°10W 50 C3
Drac, Coves del Spain 39°31N 3°19E 24 B10
Drachten Neths. 53°7N 6°5E 15 A6
Drăgășani Romania 44°39N 24°17E 17 F13
Dragichyn Belarus 52°15N 25°8E 17 B13
Dragoman, Prokhod Bulgaria 42°58N 22°53E 23 C10
Dragon's Mouths Venezuela 11°0N 61°50W 93 K15
Draguignan France 43°32N 6°27E 20 E7
Drain U.S.A. 43°40N 123°19W 76 E2
Drake U.S.A. 47°55N 100°23W 80 B3
Drake Passage S. Ocean 58°0S 68°0W 5 B17
Drakensberg S. Africa 31°0S 28°0E 57 D4
Drama Greece 41°9N 24°10E 23 D11
Drammen Norway 59°42N 10°12E 9 G14
Drangajökull Iceland 66°9N 22°15W 8 C2
Dras India 34°25N 75°48E 43 B6
Drastis, Akra Greece 39°48N 19°40E 25 A3
Drau = Drava → Croatia 45°33N 18°55E 23 B8
Drava → Croatia 45°33N 18°55E 23 B8
Drayton Canada 43°46N 80°40W 82 C4
Drayton Valley Canada 53°12N 114°58W 70 C6
Drenthe □ Neths. 52°52N 6°40E 15 B6
Drepano, Akra Greece 35°28N 24°14E 25 D6
Drepanum, C. Cyprus 34°54N 32°19E 25 E11
Dresden Canada 42°35N 82°11W 82 D2
Dresden Germany 51°3N 13°44E 16 C7
Dresden U.S.A. 42°41N 76°57W 82 D8
Dreux France 48°44N 1°23E 20 B4
Driffield U.K. 54°0N 0°26W 12 C7
Driftwood U.S.A. 41°20N 78°8W 82 E6
Driggs U.S.A. 43°44N 111°6W 76 E8
Drin → Albania 41°48N 19°33E 23 C8
Drina → Bos.-H. 44°53N 19°21E 23 B8
Drøbak Norway 59°39N 10°39E 9 G14

Drobeta-Turnu Severin Romania 44°39N 22°41E 17 F12
Drochia Moldova 48°2N 27°48E 17 D14
Drogheda Ireland 53°43N 6°22W 10 C5
Drogichin = Dragichyn Belarus 52°15N 25°8E 17 B13
Drogobych = Drohobych Ukraine 49°20N 23°30E 17 D12
Drohobych Ukraine 49°20N 23°30E 17 D12
Droichead Atha = Drogheda Ireland 53°43N 6°22W 10 C5
Droichead na Bandan = Bandon Ireland 51°44N 8°44W 10 E3
Droichead Nua Ireland 53°11N 6°48W 10 C5
Droitwich U.K. 52°16N 2°8W 13 E5
Drôme → France 44°46N 4°46E 20 D6
Dromedary, C. Australia 36°17S 150°10E 63 F5
Dromore U.K. 54°31N 7°28W 10 B4
Dromore West Ireland 54°15N 8°52W 10 B3
Dronfield U.K. 53°19N 1°27W 12 D6
Dronning Maud Land Antarctica 72°30S 12°0E 5 D3
Dronten Neths. 52°32N 5°43E 15 B5
Druk Yul = Bhutan ■ Asia 27°25N 90°30E 41 F17
Drumbo Canada 43°16N 80°35W 82 C4
Drumcliff Ireland 54°20N 8°29W 10 B3
Drumheller Canada 51°25N 112°40W 70 C6
Drummond U.S.A. 46°40N 113°9W 76 C7
Drummond I. U.S.A. 46°1N 83°39W 81 B12
Drummond Pt. Australia 34°9S 135°16E 63 E2
Drummond Ra. Australia 23°45S 147°10E 62 C4
Drummondville Canada 45°55N 72°25W 72 C5
Drumright U.S.A. 35°59N 96°36W 84 D6
Druskininkai Lithuania 54°3N 23°58E 9 J20
Drut → Belarus 53°8N 30°5E 17 B16
Druzhina Russia 68°14N 145°18E 29 C15
Dry Harbour Mts. Jamaica 18°19N 77°24W 88 a
Dry Tortugas U.S.A. 24°38N 82°55W 85 F13
Dryander △ Australia 20°13S 148°34E 62 b
Dryden Canada 49°47N 92°50W 71 D10
Dryden U.S.A. 42°30N 76°18W 83 D8
Drygalski I. Antarctica 66°0S 92°0E 5 C7
Drygalski Ice Tongue Antarctica 75°24S 163°30E 5 D21
Drysdale → Australia 13°59S 126°51E 60 B4
Drysdale I. Australia 11°41S 136°0E 62 A2
Drysdale River △ Australia 14°56S 127°2E 60 B4
Du Gué → Canada 57°21N 70°45W 72 A5
Du Quoin U.S.A. 38°1N 89°14W 80 G9
Duanesburg U.S.A. 42°45N 74°11W 83 D10
Duaringa Australia 23°42S 149°42E 62 C4
Duarte, Pico Dom. Rep. 19°2N 70°59W 89 C5
Dubai = Dubayy U.A.E. 25°18N 55°20E 45 E7
Dubāsari Moldova 47°15N 29°10E 17 E15
Dubāsari Vdkhr. Moldova 47°30N 29°0E 17 E15
Dubawnt → Canada 64°33N 100°6W 71 A8
Dubawnt L. Canada 63°8N 101°28W 71 A8
Dubayy U.A.E. 25°18N 55°20E 45 E7
Dubbo Australia 32°11S 148°35E 63 E4
Dubele Dem. Rep. of the Congo 2°56N 29°35E 54 B2
Dublin Ireland 53°21N 6°15W 10 C5
Dublin Ga., U.S.A. 32°32N 82°54W 85 E13
Dublin Tex., U.S.A. 32°5N 98°21W 84 E5
Dublin □ Ireland 53°24N 6°20W 10 C5
Dublin ✈ (DUB) Ireland 53°26N 6°15W 10 C5
Dubno Ukraine 50°25N 25°45E 17 C13
Dubois Idaho, U.S.A. 44°10N 112°14W 76 D7
DuBois Pa., U.S.A. 41°7N 78°46W 82 E6
Dubossary = Dubāsari Moldova 47°15N 29°10E 17 E15
Dubossary Vdkhr. = Dubāsari Vdkhr. Moldova 47°30N 29°0E 17 E15
Dubovka Russia 49°5N 44°50E 19 E7
Dubrajpur India 23°48N 87°25E 43 H12
Dubréka Guinea 9°46N 13°31W 50 G3
Dubrovitsa = Dubrovytsya Ukraine 51°31N 26°35E 17 C14
Dubrovnik Croatia 42°39N 18°6E 23 C8
Dubrovytsya Ukraine 51°31N 26°35E 17 C14
Dubuque U.S.A. 42°30N 90°41W 80 D8
Duchesne U.S.A. 40°10N 110°24W 76 F8
Duchess Australia 21°20S 139°50E 62 C2
Ducie I. Pac. Oc. 24°40S 124°48W 65 K15
Duck → U.S.A. 36°2N 87°52W 85 C11
Duck Cr. → Australia 22°37S 116°53E 60 D2
Duck Lake Canada 52°50N 106°16W 71 C7
Duck Mountain △ Canada 51°45N 101°0W 71 C8
Duckwall, Mt. U.S.A. 37°58N 120°7W 78 H6
Dudhi India 24°15N 83°10E 43 G10
Dudinka Russia 69°30N 86°13E 29 C9
Dudley U.K. 52°31N 2°5W 13 E5
Dudwa India 28°30N 80°41E 43 E9
Dudwa △ India 28°30N 80°40E 43 E9
Duero = Douro → Europe 41°8N 8°40W 21 B1
Dufftown U.K. 57°27N 3°8W 11 D5
Dugi Otok Croatia 44°0N 15°3E 16 G8
Duisburg Germany 51°26N 6°45E 16 C4
Duiwelskloof = Modjadjiskloof S. Africa 23°42S 30°10E 57 C5
Dukelský Průsmyk Slovak Rep. 49°25N 21°42E 17 D11
Dukhān Qatar 25°25N 50°50E 45 E6
Duki Pakistan 30°14N 68°25E 40 D6
Duku Nigeria 10°43N 10°43E 51 F8
Dulce → Argentina 30°32S 62°33W 94 C3
Dulce, G. Costa Rica 8°40N 83°20W 88 E3
Dulf Iraq 35°7N 45°51E 44 C5
Duliu China 39°2N 116°55E 34 E9
Dullewala Pakistan 31°50N 71°25E 42 D4
Dullstroom S. Africa 25°27S 30°7E 57 D5
Dulq Maghār Syria 36°22N 38°39E 44 B3

Duluth U.S.A. 46°47N 92°6W 80 B7
Dum Dum India 22°39N 88°26E 43 H13
Dum Duma India 27°40N 95°40E 41 F19
Dūmā Syria 33°34N 36°24E 46 B5
Dumaguete Phil. 9°17N 123°15E 37 C6
Dumai Indonesia 1°35N 101°28E 36 D2
Dumaran Phil. 10°33N 119°50E 37 B5
Dumas Ark., U.S.A. 33°53N 91°29W 84 E9
Dumas Tex., U.S.A. 35°52N 101°58W 84 D4
Dumayr Syria 33°39N 36°42E 46 B5
Dumbarton U.K. 55°57N 4°33W 11 F4
Dumbleyung Australia 33°17S 117°42E 61 F2
Dumfries U.K. 55°4N 3°37W 11 F5
Dumfries & Galloway □ U.K. 55°9N 3°58W 11 F5
Dumka India 24°12N 87°15E 43 G12
Dumoine → Canada 46°13N 77°51W 72 C4
Dumoine, L. Canada 46°55N 77°55W 72 C4
Dumont d'Urville Antarctica 67°0S 110°0E 5 C10
Dumont d'Urville Sea S. Ocean 63°30S 138°0E 5 C9
Dumraon India 25°33N 84°8E 43 G11
Dumyât Egypt 31°24N 31°48E 51 B12
Dún Dealgan = Dundalk Ireland 54°1N 6°24W 10 B5
Dún Garbhán = Dungarvan Ireland 52°5N 7°37W 10 D4
Dún Laoghaire Ireland 53°17N 6°8W 10 C5
Duna = Dunărea → Europe 45°20N 29°40E 17 F15
Dunagiri India 30°31N 79°52E 43 D8
Dunaj = Dunărea → Europe 45°20N 29°40E 17 F15
Dunakeszi Hungary 47°37N 19°8E 17 E10
Dunărea → Europe 45°20N 29°40E 17 F15
Dunaújváros Hungary 46°58N 18°57E 17 E10
Dunav = Dunărea → Europe 45°20N 29°40E 17 F15
Dunay Russia 42°52N 132°22E 30 C6
Dunback N.Z. 45°23S 170°36E 59 F3
Dunbar U.K. 56°0N 2°31W 11 E6
Dunblane U.K. 56°11N 3°58W 11 E5
Duncan Canada 48°45N 123°40W 78 B3
Duncan Ariz., U.S.A. 32°43N 109°6W 77 K9
Duncan Okla., U.S.A. 34°30N 97°57W 84 D6
Duncan, L. Canada 53°29N 77°58W 72 B4
Duncan, L. Canada 62°51N 113°58W 70 A6
Duncan Town Bahamas 22°15N 75°45W 88 B4
Duncannon U.S.A. 40°23N 77°2W 82 F7
Duncansby Head U.K. 58°38N 3°1W 11 C5
Duncansville U.S.A. 40°25N 78°26W 82 F6
Dundalk Canada 44°10N 80°24W 82 B4
Dundalk Ireland 54°1N 6°24W 10 B5
Dundalk U.S.A. 39°15N 76°31W 81 F15
Dundalk Bay Ireland 53°55N 6°15W 10 C5
Dundas = Uummannaq Greenland 77°33N 68°52W 69 B18
Dundas Canada 43°17N 79°59W 82 C5
Dundas, L. Australia 32°35S 121°50E 61 F3
Dundas I. Canada 54°30N 130°50W 70 C2
Dundas Str. Australia 11°15S 131°35E 60 B5
Dundee S. Africa 28°11S 30°15E 57 D5
Dundee U.K. 56°28N 2°59W 11 E6
Dundee U.S.A. 42°32N 76°59W 82 D8
Dundee City □ U.K. 56°30N 2°58W 11 E6
Dundgovi □ Mongolia 45°10N 106°0E 34 B4
Dundrum U.K. 54°16N 5°52W 10 B6
Dundrum B. U.K. 54°13N 5°47W 10 B6
Dunedin N.Z. 45°50S 170°33E 59 F3
Dunedin U.S.A. 28°1N 82°46W 85 G13
Dunfanaghy Ireland 55°11N 7°58W 10 A4
Dunfermline U.K. 56°5N 3°27W 11 E5
Dungannon Canada 43°51N 81°36W 82 C3
Dungannon U.K. 54°31N 6°46W 10 B5
Dungarpur India 23°52N 73°45E 42 H5
Dungarvan Ireland 52°5N 7°37W 10 D4
Dungarvan Harbour Ireland 52°4N 7°35W 10 D4
Dungeness U.K. 50°54N 0°59E 13 G8
Dunglow Ireland 54°57N 8°21W 10 B3
Dungo, L. do Angola 17°15S 19°0E 56 B2
Dungog Australia 32°22S 151°46E 63 E5
Dungu Dem. Rep. of the Congo 3°40N 28°32E 54 B2
Dungun Malaysia 4°45N 103°25E 39 K4
Dunhua China 43°20N 128°14E 35 C15
Dunhuang China 40°8N 94°36E 32 B4
Dunk I. Australia 17°59S 146°29E 62 B4
Dunkeld Australia 33°25S 149°29E 63 E4
Dunkeld U.K. 56°34N 3°35W 11 E5
Dunkerque France 51°2N 2°20E 20 A5
Dunkery Beacon U.K. 51°9N 3°36W 13 F4
Dunkirk = Dunkerque France 51°2N 2°20E 20 A5
Dunkirk U.S.A. 42°29N 79°20W 82 D5
Dúnleary = Dún Laoghaire Ireland 53°17N 6°8W 10 C5
Dunleer Ireland 53°50N 6°24W 10 C5
Dunmanus B. Ireland 51°31N 9°50W 10 E2
Dunmanway Ireland 51°43N 9°6W 10 E2
Dunmara Australia 16°42S 133°25E 62 B1
Dunmore U.S.A. 41°25N 75°38W 83 E9
Dunmore East Ireland 52°9N 6°59W 10 D5
Dunmore Hd. Ireland 52°10N 10°35W 10 D1
Dunmore Town Bahamas 25°30N 76°39W 88 A4
Dunn U.S.A. 35°19N 78°37W 85 D15
Dunnellon U.S.A. 29°3N 82°28W 85 G13
Dunnet Hd. U.K. 58°40N 3°21W 11 C5
Dunning U.S.A. 41°50N 100°6W 80 E3
Dunnville Canada 42°54N 79°36W 82 D5
Dunolly Australia 36°51S 143°44E 63 F3
Dunoon U.K. 55°57N 4°56W 11 F4
Duns U.K. 55°47N 2°20W 11 F6
Dunseith U.S.A. 48°50N 100°3W 80 A3
Dunshaughlin Ireland 53°31N 6°33W 10 C5
Dunsmuir U.S.A. 41°13N 122°16W 76 F2
Dunstable U.K. 51°53N 0°32W 13 F7
Dunstan Mts. N.Z. 44°53S 169°35E 59 F2

Dunster Canada 53°8N 119°50W 70 C5
Dunvegan U.K. 57°27N 6°35W 11 D2
Dunvegan L. Canada 60°8N 107°10W 71 A7
Duolun China 42°12N 116°28E 34 C9
Duong Dong Vietnam 10°13N 103°58E 39 G4
Dupree U.S.A. 45°4N 101°35W 80 C3
Dupuyer U.S.A. 48°13N 112°30W 76 B7
Duque de Caxias Brazil 22°46S 43°18W 95 A7
Durack → Australia 15°33S 127°52E 60 C4
Durack Ra. Australia 16°50S 127°40E 60 C4
Durack River Australia 15°32S 127°39E 60 C4
Durance → France 43°55N 4°45E 20 E6
Durand U.S.A. 44°38N 91°58W 80 C8
Durango Mexico 24°3N 104°39W 86 C4
Durango □ Mexico 24°50N 105°20W 86 C4
Durango U.S.A. 37°16N 107°53W 77 H10
Durant Miss., U.S.A. 33°4N 89°51W 85 E10
Durant Okla., U.S.A. 33°59N 96°25W 84 E6
Durazno Uruguay 33°25S 56°31W 94 C4
Durazzo = Durrës Albania 41°19N 19°28E 23 D8
Durban S. Africa 29°49S 31°1E 57 D5
Durbuy Belgium 50°21N 5°28E 15 D5
Durg = Bhilainagar-Durg India 21°13N 81°26E 41 J12
Durgapur India 23°30N 87°20E 43 H12
Durham Canada 44°10N 80°49W 82 B4
Durham U.K. 54°47N 1°34W 12 C6
Durham Calif., U.S.A. 39°39N 121°48W 78 F5
Durham N.C., U.S.A. 35°59N 78°54W 85 D15
Durham N.H., U.S.A. 43°8N 70°56W 83 C14
Durham □ U.K. 54°42N 1°45W 12 C6
Durlas = Thurles Ireland 52°41N 7°49W 10 D4
Durmā Si. Arabia 24°37N 46°8E 44 E5
Durmitor Montenegro 43°10N 19°0E 23 C8
Durness U.K. 58°34N 4°45W 11 C4
Durrës Albania 41°19N 19°28E 23 D8
Durrow Ireland 52°51N 7°24W 10 D4
Dursey I. Ireland 51°36N 10°12W 10 E1
Dursley U.K. 51°40N 2°21W 13 F5
Dursunbey Turkey 39°35N 28°37E 23 E13
Duru Dem. Rep. of the Congo 4°14N 28°50E 54 B2
Durūz, Jabal ad Jordan 32°35N 36°40E 46 C5
D'Urville, Tanjung Indonesia 1°28S 137°54E 37 E9
D'Urville I. N.Z. 40°50S 173°55E 59 D4
Duryea U.S.A. 41°20N 75°45W 83 E9
Dushak Turkmenistan 37°13N 60°1E 45 B9
Dushanbe Tajikistan 38°33N 68°48E 28 F7
Dushore U.S.A. 41°31N 76°24W 83 E8
Dusky Sd. N.Z. 45°47S 166°30E 59 F1
Dussejour, C. Australia 14°45S 128°13E 60 B4
Düsseldorf Germany 51°14N 6°47E 16 C4
Dutch Harbor U.S.A. 53°53N 166°32W 74 E6
Dutlwe Botswana 23°58S 23°46E 56 C3
Dutton Canada 42°39N 81°30W 82 D3
Dutton → Australia 20°44S 143°10E 62 C3
Dutywa S. Africa 32°8S 28°18E 57 E4
Duwayhin, Khawr U.A.E. 24°20N 51°25E 45 E6
Duyfken Pt. Australia 12°33S 141°38E 62 A3
Duyun China 26°18N 107°29E 32 D5
Dvina, Severnaya → Russia 64°32N 40°30E 18 B7
Dvinsk = Daugavpils Latvia 55°53N 26°32E 9 J22
Dvinskaya Guba Russia 65°0N 39°0E 18 B6
Dwarka India 22°18N 69°8E 42 H3
Dwellingup Australia 32°43S 116°4E 61 F2
Dwight Canada 45°20N 79°1W 82 A5
Dwight U.S.A. 41°5N 88°26W 80 E9
Dyatlovo = Dzyatlava Belarus 53°28N 25°28E 17 B13
Dyce U.K. 57°13N 2°12W 11 D6
Dyer, C. Canada 66°37N 61°16W 69 D19
Dyer Bay Canada 45°10N 81°20W 82 A3
Dyer Plateau Antarctica 70°45S 65°30W 5 D17
Dyersburg U.S.A. 36°3N 89°23W 85 C10
Dyersville U.S.A. 42°29N 91°8W 80 D8
Dyfi → U.K. 52°32N 4°3W 13 E3
Dymer Ukraine 50°47N 30°18E 17 C16
Dysart Australia 22°32S 148°23E 62 C4
Dzaoudzi Mayotte 12°47S 45°16E 53 a
Dzavhan Gol → Mongolia 48°54N 93°23E 32 B4
Dzerzhinsk Russia 56°14N 43°30E 18 C7
Dzhalinda Russia 53°26N 124°0E 29 D13
Dzhambul = Taraz Kazakhstan 42°54N 71°22E 28 E8
Dzhankoy Ukraine 45°40N 34°20E 19 E5
Dzhezkazgan = Zhezqazghan Kazakhstan 47°44N 67°40E 28 E7
Dzhizak = Jizzax Uzbekistan 40°6N 67°50E 28 E7
Dzhugdzur, Khrebet Russia 57°30N 138°0E 29 D14
Dzhungarskiye Vorota = Dzungarian Gate Asia 45°10N 82°0E 32 B3
Działdowo Poland 53°15N 20°15E 17 B11
Dzibilchaltún Mexico 21°10N 89°35W 87 C7
Dzierżoniów Poland 50°45N 16°39E 17 C9
Dzilam de Bravo Mexico 21°24N 88°53W 87 C7
Dzükija △ Lithuania 54°10N 24°30E 9 J21
Dzungaria = Junggar Pendi China 44°30N 86°0E 32 B3
Dzungarian Gate Asia 45°10N 82°0E 32 B3
Dzüünbulag Mongolia 46°58N 106°28E 32 B5
Dzüünharaa Mongolia 48°52N 106°28E 32 B5
Dzüünmod Mongolia 47°45N 106°58E 32 B5
Dzyarzhynsk Belarus 53°40N 27°1E 17 B14
Dzyatlava Belarus 53°28N 25°28E 17 B13

E

E.C. Manning △ Canada 49°5N 120°45W 70 D4
Eabamet L. Canada 51°30N 87°46W 72 B2
Eabametoong Canada 51°30N 88°0W 72 B2
Éadan Doire = Edenderry Ireland 53°21N 7°4W 10 C4
Eads U.S.A. 38°29N 102°47W 76 G12

Eagar U.S.A. 34°6N 109°17W 77 J9
Eagle Alaska, U.S.A. 64°47N 141°12W 68 C5
Eagle Colo., U.S.A. 39°39N 106°50W 76 G10
Eagle → Canada 53°36N 57°26W 73 B8
Eagle Butte U.S.A. 45°0N 101°10W 80 C3
Eagle Grove U.S.A. 42°40N 93°54W 80 D7
Eagle L. Canada 49°42N 93°13W 71 D10
Eagle L. Calif., U.S.A. 40°39N 120°45W 76 F3
Eagle L. Maine, U.S.A. 46°20N 69°22W 81 B19
Eagle Lake Canada 45°8N 78°29W 82 A6
Eagle Lake Maine, U.S.A. 47°3N 68°36W 81 B19
Eagle Lake Tex., U.S.A. 29°35N 96°20W 84 G6
Eagle Mountain U.S.A. 33°49N 115°27W 79 M11
Eagle Nest U.S.A. 36°33N 105°16W 77 H11
Eagle Pass U.S.A. 28°43N 100°30W 84 G4
Eagle Pk. U.S.A. 38°10N 119°25E 78 G7
Eagle Pt. Australia 16°11S 124°23E 60 C3
Eagle River Mich., U.S.A. 47°25N 88°18W 80 B9
Eagle River Wis., U.S.A. 45°55N 89°15W 80 C9
Eaglehawk Australia 36°44S 144°15E 63 F3
Eagles Mere U.S.A. 41°25N 76°33W 83 E8
Ealing □ U.K. 51°31N 0°20W 13 F7
Ear Falls Canada 50°38N 93°13W 71 C10
Earle U.S.A. 35°16N 90°28W 85 D9
Earlimart U.S.A. 35°53N 119°16W 79 K7
Earlville U.S.A. 42°44N 75°32W 83 D9
Earn → U.K. 56°21N 3°18W 11 E5
Earn, L. U.K. 56°23N 4°13W 11 E4
Earnslaw, Mt. N.Z. 44°32S 168°27E 59 F2
Earth U.S.A. 34°14N 102°24W 84 D3
Easley U.S.A. 34°50N 82°36W 85 D13
East Anglia U.K. 52°30N 1°0E 12 E9
East Angus Canada 45°30N 71°40W 73 C5
East Antarctica Antarctica 80°0S 90°0E 5 D7
East Aurora U.S.A. 42°46N 78°37W 82 D6
East Ayrshire □ U.K. 55°26N 4°11W 11 F4
East Bengal Bangla. 24°0N 90°0E 41 G17
East Beskids = Vychodné Beskydy Europe 49°20N 22°0E 17 D11
East Brady U.S.A. 40°59N 79°37W 82 F5
East Branch Clarion River L. U.S.A. 41°35N 78°35W 82 E6
East C. = Dezhneva, Mys Russia 66°5N 169°40W 29 C19
East C. N.Z. 37°42S 178°35E 59 B7
East Caroline Basin Pac. Oc. 4°0N 146°45E 64 G6
East Chicago U.S.A. 41°38N 87°27W 80 E10
East China Sea Asia 30°0N 126°0E 33 C7
East Coulee Canada 51°23N 112°27W 70 C6
East Dereham = Dereham U.K. 52°41N 0°57E 13 E8
East Dunbartonshire □ U.K. 55°57N 4°13W 11 F4
East Falkland Falk. Is. 51°30S 58°30W 96 G5
East Grand Forks U.S.A. 47°56N 97°1W 80 B5
East Greenwich U.S.A. 41°40N 71°27W 83 E13
East Grinstead U.K. 51°7N 0°0 13 F8
East Hartford U.S.A. 41°46N 72°39W 83 E12
East Haydon Australia 18°0S 141°30E 62 B3
East Helena U.S.A. 46°35N 111°56W 76 C8
East Indies Asia 0°0 120°0E 26 J14
East Kilbride U.K. 55°47N 4°11W 11 F4
East Lamma Channel China 22°14N 114°9E 33 G11
East Lansing U.S.A. 42°44N 84°29W 81 D11
East Liverpool U.S.A. 40°37N 80°35W 82 F4
East London S. Africa 33°0S 27°55E 57 E4
East Lothian □ U.K. 55°58N 2°44W 11 F6
East Main = Eastmain Canada 52°10N 78°30W 72 B4
East Mariana Basin Pac. Oc. 12°0N 153°0E 64 F7
East Northport U.S.A. 40°53N 73°20W 83 F11
East Orange U.S.A. 40°46N 74°12W 83 F10
East Pacific Rise Pac. Oc. 15°0S 110°0W 65 J17
East Palestine U.S.A. 40°50N 80°33W 82 F4
East Pine Canada 55°48N 120°12W 70 B4
East Point U.S.A. 33°41N 84°27W 85 E11
East Providence U.S.A. 41°49N 71°23W 83 E13
East Pt. Canada 46°27N 61°58W 73 C7
East Pt. Br. Virgin Is. 18°40N 64°18W 89 e
East Renfrewshire □ U.K. 55°46N 4°21W 11 F4
East Retford = Retford U.K. 53°19N 0°56W 12 D7
East Riding of Yorkshire □ U.K. 53°55N 0°30W 12 D7
East Rochester U.S.A. 43°7N 77°29W 82 C7
East St. Louis U.S.A. 38°37N 90°9W 80 F8
East Schelde = Oosterschelde → Neths. 51°33N 4°0E 15 C4
East Sea = Japan, Sea of Asia 40°0N 135°0E 30 E7
East Siberian Sea Russia 73°0N 160°0E 29 B17
East Stroudsburg U.S.A. 41°1N 75°11W 83 E9
East Sussex □ U.K. 50°56N 0°19E 13 G8
East Tasman Plateau Pac. Oc. 43°30S 152°0E 64 M7
East Tawas U.S.A. 44°17N 83°29W 81 C12
East Timor ■ Asia 8°50S 126°0E 37 F7
East Toorale Australia 30°27S 145°28E 63 E4
East Walker → U.S.A. 38°52N 119°10W 78 G7
East Windsor U.S.A. 40°17N 74°34W 83 F10
Eastbourne N.Z. 41°19S 174°55E 59 D5
Eastbourne U.K. 50°46N 0°18E 13 G8
Eastend Canada 49°32N 108°50W 71 D7
Easter Fracture Zone Pac. Oc. 25°0S 115°0W 65 K16
Easter I. = Pascua, I. de Chile 27°7S 109°23W 65 K17
Eastern □ Kenya 0°0 38°30E 54 C4
Eastern Cape □ S. Africa 32°0S 26°0E 56 E4
Eastern Cr. → Australia 20°40S 141°35E 62 C3
Eastern Desert = Es Sahrâ' Esh Sharqîya Egypt 27°30N 32°30E 51 C12
Eastern Ghats India 14°0N 78°50E 40 N11
Eastern Group = Lau Group Fiji 17°0S 178°30W 59 a

Eastern Group *Australia* 33°30S 124°30E **61 F3**
Eastern Guruma ✧
  Australia 22°0S 117°30E **60 D2**
Eastern Transvaal =
  Mpumalanga □
  S. Africa 26°0S 30°0E **57 D5**
Easterville *Canada* 53°8N 99°49W **71 C9**
Easthampton *U.S.A.* 42°16N 72°40W **83 D12**
Eastlake *U.S.A.* 41°40N 81°26W **82 E3**
Eastland *U.S.A.* 32°24N 98°49W **84 E5**
Eastleigh *U.K.* 50°58N 1°21W **13 G6**
Eastmain *Canada* 52°10N 78°30W **72 B4**
Eastmain → *Canada* 52°27N 78°26W **72 B4**
Eastman *Canada* 45°18N 72°19W **83 A12**
Eastman *U.S.A.* 32°12N 83°11W **85 E13**
Easton *Md., U.S.A.* 38°47N 76°5W **81 F15**
Easton *Pa., U.S.A.* 40°41N 75°13W **83 F9**
Easton *Wash., U.S.A.* 47°14N 121°11W **78 C5**
Eastport *U.S.A.* 44°56N 67°0W **81 C20**
Eastsound *U.S.A.* 48°42N 122°55W **78 B4**
Eaton *U.S.A.* 40°32N 104°42W **76 F11**
Eatonia *Canada* 51°13N 109°25W **71 C7**
Eatonton *U.S.A.* 33°20N 83°23W **85 E13**
Eatontown *U.S.A.* 40°19N 74°4W **83 F10**
Eatonville *U.S.A.* 46°52N 122°16W **78 D4**
Eau Claire *U.S.A.* 44°49N 91°30W **80 C8**
Eau Claire, L. à l' *Canada* 56°10N 74°25W **72 A5**
Eauripik Rise *Pac. Oc.* 2°0N 142°0E **64 G6**
Ebano *Mexico* 22°13N 98°24W **87 C5**
Ebbw Vale *U.K.* 51°46N 3°12W **13 F4**
Ebeltoft *Denmark* 56°12N 10°41E **9 H14**
Ebensburg *U.S.A.* 40°29N 78°44W **82 F6**
Eberswalde-Finow
  Germany 52°50N 13°49E **16 B7**
Ebetsu *Japan* 43°7N 141°34E **30 C10**
Ebey's Landing △
  U.S.A. 48°12N 122°41W **78 B4**
Ebinur Hu *China* 44°55N 82°55E **32 B3**
Ebolowa *Cameroon* 2°55N 11°10E **52 D2**
Ebonda
  Dem. Rep. of the Congo 2°12N 22°21E **52 D4**
Ebre = Ebro → *Spain* 40°43N 0°54E **21 B6**
Ebro → *Spain* 40°43N 0°54E **21 B6**
Ecatepec de Morelos
  Mexico 19°36N 99°3W **87 D5**
Ecbatana = Hamadān
  Iran 34°52N 48°32E **45 C6**
Eceabat *Turkey* 40°11N 26°21E **23 D12**
Ech Chéliff *Algeria* 36°10N 1°20E **50 A6**
Echigo-Sammyaku
  Japan 36°50N 139°50E **31 F9**
Echizen-Misaki *Japan* 35°59N 135°57E **31 G7**
Echo Bay *N.W.T., Canada* 66°5N 117°55W **68 C8**
Echo Bay *Ont., Canada* 46°29N 84°4W **72 C3**
Echoing → *Canada* 55°51N 92°5W **72 B1**
Echternach *Lux.* 49°49N 6°25E **15 E6**
Echuca *Australia* 36°10S 144°45E **63 F3**
Écija *Spain* 37°30N 5°10W **21 D3**
Eclipse I. *Australia* 35°5S 117°58E **61 G2**
Eclipse Is. *Australia* 13°54S 126°19E **60 B4**
Eclipse Sd. *Canada* 72°38N 79°0W **69 C16**
Ecuador ■ *S. Amer.* 2°0S 78°0W **92 D3**
Ed Da'ein *Sudan* 11°26N 26°9E **52 B5**
Ed Damazin *Sudan* 11°46N 34°21E **51 F12**
Ed Dâmer *Sudan* 17°27N 34°0E **51 E12**
Ed Dar el Beida = Casablanca
  Morocco 33°36N 7°36W **50 B4**
Ed Debba *Sudan* 18°0N 30°51E **51 E12**
Ed Déffa *Egypt* 30°40N 26°30E **51 B11**
Ed Dueim *Sudan* 14°0N 32°10E **51 F12**
Edam *Canada* 53°11N 108°46W **71 C7**
Edam *Neths.* 52°31N 5°3E **15 B5**
Eday *U.K.* 59°11N 2°47W **11 B6**
Eddrachillis B. *U.K.* 58°17N 5°14W **11 C3**
Eddystone *U.K.* 50°11N 4°16W **13 G3**
Eddystone Pt. *Australia* 40°59S 148°20E **63 G4**
Ede *Neths.* 52°4N 5°40E **15 B5**
Edehon L. *Canada* 60°25N 97°15W **71 A9**
Eden *Australia* 37°3S 149°55E **63 F4**
Eden *N.C., U.S.A.* 36°29N 79°53W **85 C15**
Eden *N.Y., U.S.A.* 42°39N 78°55W **82 D6**
Eden *Tex., U.S.A.* 31°13N 99°51W **84 F5**
Eden → *U.K.* 54°57N 3°1W **12 C4**
Edenburg *S. Africa* 29°43S 25°58E **56 D4**
Edendale *S. Africa* 29°39S 30°18E **57 D5**
Edenderry *Ireland* 53°21N 7°4W **10 C4**
Edenton *U.S.A.* 36°4N 76°39W **85 C16**
Edenville *S. Africa* 27°37S 27°34E **57 D4**
Eder → *Germany* 51°12N 9°28E **16 C5**
Edessa *Greece* 40°48N 22°5E **23 D10**
Edfu = Idfû *Egypt* 24°55N 32°49E **51 D12**
Edgar *U.S.A.* 40°22N 97°58W **80 E5**
Edgartown *U.S.A.* 41°23N 70°31W **83 E14**
Edge Hill *U.K.* 52°8N 1°26W **13 E6**
Edgefield *U.S.A.* 33°47N 81°56W **85 E14**
Edgeley *U.S.A.* 46°22N 98°43W **80 B4**
Edgemont *U.S.A.* 43°18N 103°50W **80 D2**
Edgeøya *Svalbard* 77°45S 22°30E **4 B9**
Édhessa = Edessa *Greece* 40°48N 22°5E **23 D10**
Edievale *N.Z.* 45°49S 169°22E **59 F2**
Edina *U.S.A.* 40°10N 92°11W **80 E7**
Edinboro *U.S.A.* 41°52N 80°8W **82 E4**
Edinburg *U.S.A.* 26°18N 98°10W **84 H5**
Edinburgh *U.K.* 55°57N 3°13W **11 F5**
Edinburgh ✈ (EDI) *U.K.* 55°54N 3°22W **11 F5**
Edinburgh, City of □
  U.K. 55°57N 3°17W **11 F5**
Edineţ *Moldova* 48°9N 27°18E **17 D14**
Edirne *Turkey* 41°40N 26°34E **23 D12**
Edison *U.S.A.* 48°33N 122°27W **78 B4**
Edithburgh *Australia* 35°5S 137°43E **63 F2**
Edmond *U.S.A.* 35°39N 97°29W **84 D6**
Edmonds *U.S.A.* 47°48N 122°22W **78 C4**
Edmonton *Australia* 17°2S 145°46E **62 B4**
Edmonton *Canada* 53°30N 113°30W **70 C6**
Edmund L. *Canada* 54°45N 93°17W **72 B1**
Edmundston *Canada* 47°23N 68°20W **73 C6**
Edna *U.S.A.* 28°59N 96°39W **84 G6**

Edremit *Turkey* 39°34N 27°0E **23 E12**
Edremit Körfezi *Turkey* 39°30N 26°45E **23 E12**
Edson *Canada* 53°35N 116°28W **70 C5**
Eduardo Castex
  Argentina 35°50S 64°18W **94 D3**
Edward → *Australia* 35°5S 143°30E **63 F3**
Edward, L. *Africa* 0°25S 29°40E **54 C2**
Edward VII Land
  Antarctica 80°0S 150°0W **5 E13**
Edwards *Calif., U.S.A.* 34°50N 117°40W **79 L9**
Edwards *N.Y., U.S.A.* 44°20N 75°15W **83 B9**
Edwards Plateau
  U.S.A. 30°45N 101°20W **84 F4**
Edwardsville *U.S.A.* 41°15N 75°56W **83 E9**
Edzná *Mexico* 19°39N 90°19W **87 D6**
Edzo *Canada* 62°49N 116°4W **70 A5**
Eeklo *Belgium* 51°11N 3°33E **15 C3**
Eesti = Estonia ■ *Europe* 58°30N 25°30E **9 G21**
Effigy Mounds △ *U.S.A.* 43°5N 91°11W **80 D8**
Effingham *U.S.A.* 39°7N 88°33W **80 F9**
Égadi, Ísole *Italy* 37°55N 12°16E **22 F5**
Egan Range *U.S.A.* 39°35N 114°55W **76 G6**
Eganville *Canada* 45°32N 77°5W **82 A7**
Eger *Hungary* 47°53N 20°27E **17 E11**
Eger → *Hungary* 50°9N 12°28E **16 C7**
Egersund *Norway* 58°26N 6°1E **9 G12**
Egg L. *Canada* 55°5N 105°30W **71 B7**
Éghezée *Belgium* 50°35N 4°55E **15 D4**
Egio *Greece* 38°15N 22°5E **23 E10**
Eglinton I. *Canada* 75°48N 118°30W **69 B8**
Egmont *Canada* 49°45N 123°56W **70 D4**
Egmont, C. *N.Z.* 39°16S 173°45E **59 C4**
Egmont, Mt. = Taranaki, Mt.
  N.Z. 39°17S 174°5E **59 C5**
Egmont → *N.Z.* 39°17S 174°4E **59 C5**
Egra *India* 21°54N 87°32E **43 J12**
Eğridir *Turkey* 37°52N 30°51E **19 G5**
Eğridir Gölü *Turkey* 37°53N 30°50E **44 B1**
Egvekinot *Russia* 66°19N 179°50W **29 C19**
Egypt ■ *Africa* 28°0N 31°0E **51 C12**
Ehime □ *Japan* 33°30N 132°40E **31 H6**
Ehrenberg *U.S.A.* 33°36N 114°31W **79 M12**
Eibar *Spain* 43°11N 2°28W **21 A4**
Eidsvold *Australia* 25°25S 151°12E **63 D5**
Eidsvoll *Norway* 60°19N 11°14E **9 F14**
Eielson *U.S.A.* 64°40N 147°4W **74 C10**
Eifel *Germany* 50°15N 6°50E **16 C4**
Eiffel Flats *Zimbabwe* 18°20S 30°0E **55 F3**
Eigg *U.K.* 56°54N 6°10W **11 E2**
Eighty Mile Beach
  Australia 19°30S 120°40E **60 C3**
Eil, L. *U.K.* 56°51N 5°16W **11 E3**
Eildon *L. Australia* 37°10S 146°0E **63 F4**
Eilean Sar = Western Isles □
  U.K. 57°30N 7°10W **11 D1**
Einasleigh *Australia* 18°32S 144°5E **62 B3**
Einasleigh → *Australia* 17°30S 142°17E **62 B3**
Eindhoven *Neths.* 51°26N 5°28E **15 C5**
Eire = Ireland ■ *Europe* 53°50N 7°52W **10 D4**
Eiríksjökull *Iceland* 64°46N 20°24W **8 D3**
Eirunepé *Brazil* 6°35S 69°53W **92 E5**
Eiseb → *Namibia* 20°33S 20°59E **56 C2**
Eisenach *Germany* 50°58N 10°19E **16 C6**
Eisenerz *Austria* 47°32N 14°54E **16 E8**
Eivissa *Spain* 38°54N 1°26E **24 C7**
Ejeda *Madag.* 24°20S 44°31E **57 C7**
Ejutla *Mexico* 16°34N 96°44W **87 D5**
Ekalaka *U.S.A.* 45°53N 104°33W **76 D11**
Ekaterinburg = Yekaterinburg
  Russia 56°50N 60°30E **28 D7**
Ekenäs = Tammisaari
  Finland 60°0N 23°26E **9 G20**
Eketahuna *N.Z.* 40°38S 175°43E **59 D5**
Ekibastuz *Kazakhstan* 51°50N 75°10E **28 D8**
Ekoli *Dem. Rep. of the Congo* 0°23S 24°13E **54 C1**
Eksjö *Sweden* 57°40N 14°58E **9 H16**
Ekuma → *Namibia* 18°40S 16°2E **56 B2**
Ekwan → *Canada* 53°12N 82°15W **72 B3**
Ekwan Pt. *Canada* 53°16N 82°7W **72 B3**
El Aaiún *W. Sahara* 27°9N 13°12W **50 C3**
El Abanico *Chile* 37°20S 71°31W **94 D1**
El 'Agrūd *Egypt* 30°14N 34°24E **46 E3**
El Alamein *Egypt* 30°48N 28°58E **51 B11**
El 'Aqaba, W. → *Egypt* 30°7N 33°54E **46 E2**
El Arīḥā *West Bank* 31°52N 35°27E **46 D4**
El 'Arîsh *Egypt* 31°8N 33°50E **46 D2**
El 'Arîsh, W. → *Egypt* 31°8N 33°47E **46 D2**
El Asnam = Ech Chéliff
  Algeria 36°10N 1°20E **50 A6**
El Bayadh *Algeria* 33°40N 1°1E **50 B6**
El Bluff *Nic.* 11°59N 83°40W **88 D3**
El Cajon *U.S.A.* 32°48N 116°58W **79 N10**
El Calafate *Argentina* 50°19S 72°15W **96 G2**
El Campo *U.S.A.* 29°12N 96°16W **84 G6**
El Capitan *U.S.A.* 37°44N 119°38E **78 H7**
El Carbón *Honduras* 15°25N 85°32W **88 C2**
El Carmen *Colombia* 9°43N 75°8W **92 B3**
El Centro *U.S.A.* 32°48N 115°34W **79 N11**
El Cerro *Bolivia* 17°30S 61°40W **92 G6**
El Compadre *Mexico* 32°20N 116°14W **79 N10**
El Cuy *Argentina* 39°55S 68°25W **96 D3**
El Cuyo *Mexico* 21°31N 87°41W **87 C7**
El Daheir *Egypt* 31°13N 34°10E **46 D3**
El Descanso *Mexico* 32°12N 116°58W **79 N10**
El Desemboque *Mexico* 30°33N 113°1W **86 A2**
El Diviso *Colombia* 1°22N 78°14W **92 C3**
El Djouf *Mauritania* 20°0N 9°0W **50 D4**
El Dorado *Mexico* 24°17N 107°21W **86 C3**
El Dorado *Ark., U.S.A.* 33°12N 92°40W **84 E8**
El Dorado *Kans., U.S.A.* 37°49N 96°52W **80 G5**
El Dorado *Venezuela* 6°55N 61°37W **92 B6**
El Dorado Springs *U.S.A.* 37°52N 94°1W **80 G6**
El Escorial *Spain* 40°35N 4°7W **21 B3**
El Faiyûm *Egypt* 29°19N 30°50E **51 C12**
El Ferrol = Ferrol *Spain* 43°29N 8°15W **21 A1**
El Fuerte *Mexico* 26°25N 108°39W **86 B3**
El Geneina = Al Junaynah
  Sudan 13°27N 22°45E **51 F10**

El Gezira □ *Sudan* 15°0N 33°0E **51 F12**
El Gîza *Egypt* 30°0N 31°12E **51 C12**
El Gogorrón △ *Mexico* 21°49N 100°57W **86 C4**
El Goléa *Algeria* 30°30N 2°50E **50 B6**
El Golfo de Santa Clara
  Mexico 31°42N 114°30W **86 A2**
El Guácharo △ *Venezuela* 10°8N 63°21W **89 D7**
El Guache △ *Venezuela* 9°45N 69°30W **89 E6**
El Iskandarîya *Egypt* 31°13N 29°58E **51 B11**
El Istiwa'iya *Sudan* 5°0N 28°0E **51 G11**
El Jadida *Morocco* 33°11N 8°17W **50 B4**
El Jardal *Honduras* 14°54N 88°50W **88 D2**
El Kef □ *Tunisia* 36°0N 9°0E **51 A7**
El Khârga *Egypt* 25°30N 30°33E **51 C12**
El Khartûm *Sudan* 15°31N 32°35E **51 E12**
El Khartûm Bahrî
  Sudan 15°40N 32°31E **51 E12**
El Kuntilla *Egypt* 30°1N 34°45E **46 E3**
El Leoncito △ *Argentina* 31°58S 69°10W **94 C2**
El Lucero *Mexico* 30°37N 106°31W **86 A3**
El Maestrazgo *Spain* 40°30N 0°25W **21 B5**
El Mahalla el Kubra
  Egypt 31°0N 31°0E **51 B12**
El Malpais △ *U.S.A.* 34°53N 108°0W **77 J10**
El Mansûra *Egypt* 31°0N 31°19E **51 B12**
El Medano *Canary Is.* 28°3N 16°32W **24 F3**
El Ménia = El Goléa
  Algeria 30°30N 2°50E **50 B6**
El Milagro *Argentina* 30°59S 65°59W **94 C2**
El Minyâ *Egypt* 28°7N 30°33E **51 C12**
El Monte *U.S.A.* 34°4N 118°1W **79 L8**
El Obeid *Sudan* 13°8N 30°10E **51 F12**
El Odaiya *Sudan* 12°8N 28°12E **51 F11**
El Oro *Mexico* 19°51N 100°7W **87 D4**
El Oued *Algeria* 33°20N 6°58E **50 B7**
El Palmar △ *Argentina* 32°10S 58°31W **94 C4**
El Palmito, Presa
  Mexico 25°40N 105°30W **86 B3**
El Paso *U.S.A.* 31°45N 106°29W **84 F1**
El Pinacate y Gran Desierto de
  Altar = Gran Desierto del
  Pinacate △ *Mexico* 31°51N 113°32W **86 A2**
El Portal *U.S.A.* 37°41N 119°47W **78 H7**
El Porvenir *Mexico* 31°15N 105°51W **86 A3**
El Prat de Llobregat *Spain* 41°19N 2°5E **21 B7**
El Progreso *Honduras* 15°26N 87°51W **88 C2**
El Pueblito *Mexico* 29°3N 105°4W **86 B3**
El Pueblo *Canary Is.* 28°36N 17°47W **24 F2**
El Puerto de Santa María
  Spain 36°36N 6°13W **21 D2**
El Qâhira *Egypt* 30°2N 31°13E **51 B12**
El Qantara *Egypt* 30°51N 32°20E **46 E1**
El Queseima *Egypt* 30°40N 34°15E **46 E3**
El Real de Santa María
  Panama 8°0N 77°40W **92 B3**
El Reno *U.S.A.* 35°32N 97°57W **84 H6**
El Rey △ *Argentina* 24°40S 64°34W **94 A3**
El Río *U.S.A.* 34°14N 119°10W **79 L7**
El Roque, Pta. *Canary Is.* 28°10N 15°25W **24 F4**
El Rosarito *Mexico* 28°38N 114°4W **86 B2**
El Salto *Mexico* 23°47N 105°22W **86 C3**
El Salvador ■ *Cent. Amer.* 13°50N 89°0W **88 D2**
El Sauce *Nic.* 13°0N 86°40W **88 D2**
El Sueco *Mexico* 29°54N 106°24W **86 B3**
El Suweis *Egypt* 29°58N 32°31E **51 C12**
El Tamarâni, W. → *Egypt* 30°7N 34°43E **46 E3**
El Thamad *Egypt* 29°40N 34°28E **46 F3**
El Tigre *Venezuela* 8°44N 64°15W **92 B6**
El Tîh, Gebel *Egypt* 29°40N 33°50E **46 F2**
El Tofo *Chile* 29°22S 71°18W **94 B1**
El Tránsito *Chile* 28°52S 70°17W **94 B1**
El Tûr *Egypt* 28°14N 33°36E **44 D2**
El Turbio *Argentina* 51°45S 72°5W **96 G2**
El Uqsur *Egypt* 25°41N 32°38E **51 C12**
El Vergel *Mexico* 26°28N 106°22W **86 B3**
El Vigía *Venezuela* 8°38N 71°39W **92 B4**
El Wabeira *Egypt* 29°34N 33°6E **46 F2**
El Wuz *Sudan* 15°5N 30°7E **51 E12**
Elat *Israel* 29°30N 34°56E **46 F3**
Elâzığ *Turkey* 38°37N 39°14E **44 B3**
Elba *Italy* 42°46N 10°17E **22 C4**
Elba *U.S.A.* 31°25N 86°4W **85 F11**
Elbasan *Albania* 41°9N 20°9E **23 D9**
Elbe *U.S.A.* 46°45N 122°10W **78 D4**
Elbe → *Europe* 53°50N 9°0E **16 B5**
Elbert, Mt. *U.S.A.* 39°7N 106°27W **76 G10**
Elberton *U.S.A.* 34°7N 82°52W **85 D13**
Elbeuf *France* 49°17N 1°2E **20 B4**
Elbing = Elbląg *Poland* 54°10N 19°25E **17 A10**
Elbistan *Turkey* 38°13N 37°15E **44 B3**
Elbląg *Poland* 54°10N 19°25E **17 A10**
Elbow *Canada* 51°7N 106°35W **71 C7**
Elbrus *Russia* 43°21N 42°30E **19 F7**
Elburz Mts. = Alborz, Reshteh-ye
  Kühhā-ye *Iran* 36°0N 52°0E **45 B7**
Elche *Spain* 38°15N 0°42W **21 C5**
Elcho I. *Australia* 11°55S 135°45E **62 A2**
Elda *Spain* 38°29N 0°47W **21 C5**
Eldama Ravine *Kenya* 0°3N 35°43E **54 B4**
Elde → *Germany* 53°7N 11°15E **16 B6**
Eldon *Mo., U.S.A.* 38°21N 92°35W **80 F7**
Eldon *Wash., U.S.A.* 47°33N 123°3W **78 C3**
Eldorado *Argentina* 26°28S 54°43W **95 B5**
Eldorado *Mexico* 24°20N 107°22W **86 C3**
Eldorado *Ill., U.S.A.* 37°49N 88°26W **80 G9**
Eldorado *Tex., U.S.A.* 30°52N 100°36W **84 F4**
Eldoret *Kenya* 0°30N 35°17E **54 B4**
Eldred *U.S.A.* 41°58N 78°23W **82 E6**
Elea, C. *Cyprus* 35°19N 34°4E **25 D13**
Eleanora, Pk. *Australia* 32°57S 121°9E **61 F3**
Elefantes → *Africa* 24°10S 32°40E **57 C5**
Elektrostal *Russia* 55°41N 38°32E **18 C6**
Elemi Triangle *Africa* 5°0N 35°20E **54 B4**
Elephant Butte Res.
  U.S.A. 33°9N 107°11W **77 K10**
Elephant I. *Antarctica* 61°0S 55°0W **5 C18**
Eleuthera *Bahamas* 25°0N 76°20W **88 B4**
Elgin *Canada* 44°36N 76°13W **83 B8**

Elgin *U.K.* 57°39N 3°19W **11 D5**
Elgin *Ill., U.S.A.* 42°2N 88°17W **80 D9**
Elgin *N. Dak., U.S.A.* 46°24N 101°51W **80 B3**
Elgin *Oreg., U.S.A.* 45°34N 117°55W **76 D5**
Elgin *Tex., U.S.A.* 30°21N 97°22W **84 F6**
Elgon, Mt. *Africa* 1°10N 34°30E **54 B3**
Eliase *Indonesia* 8°21S 130°48E **37 F8**
Elim *Namibia* 17°48S 15°31E **56 B2**
Elim *S. Africa* 34°35S 19°45E **56 E2**
Elista *Russia* 46°16N 44°14E **19 E7**
Elizabeth *Australia* 34°42S 138°41E **63 E2**
Elizabeth *U.S.A.* 40°39N 74°12W **83 F10**
Elizabeth City *U.S.A.* 36°18N 76°14W **85 C16**
Elizabethton *U.S.A.* 36°21N 82°13W **85 C13**
Elizabethtown *Ky.,*
  U.S.A. 37°42N 85°52W **81 G11**
Elizabethtown *N.Y.,*
  U.S.A. 44°13N 73°36W **83 B11**
Elizabethtown *Pa., U.S.A.* 40°9N 76°36W **83 F8**
Elk *Poland* 53°50N 22°21E **17 B12**
Elk → *Canada* 49°11N 115°14W **70 C5**
Elk → *U.S.A.* 34°46N 87°16W **85 D11**
Elk City *U.S.A.* 35°25N 99°25W **84 D5**
Elk Creek *U.S.A.* 39°36N 122°32W **78 F4**
Elk Grove *U.S.A.* 38°25N 121°22W **78 G5**
Elk Island △ *Canada* 53°35N 112°59W **70 C6**
Elk Lake *Canada* 47°40N 80°25W **72 C3**
Elk Point *Canada* 53°54N 110°55W **71 C6**
Elk River *Idaho, U.S.A.* 46°47N 116°11W **76 C5**
Elk River *Minn., U.S.A.* 45°18N 93°35W **80 C8**
Elkedra → *Australia* 21°8S 136°22E **62 C2**
Elkhart *Ind., U.S.A.* 41°41N 85°58W **81 E11**
Elkhart *Kans., U.S.A.* 37°0N 101°54W **80 G3**
Elkhorn *Canada* 49°59N 101°14W **71 D8**
Elkhorn → *U.S.A.* 41°8N 96°19W **80 E6**
Elkhovo *Bulgaria* 42°10N 26°35E **23 C12**
Elkin *U.S.A.* 36°15N 80°51W **85 C14**
Elkins *U.S.A.* 38°55N 79°51W **81 F14**
Elkland *U.S.A.* 41°59N 77°19W **82 E7**
Elko *Canada* 49°20N 115°10W **70 D5**
Elko *U.S.A.* 40°50N 115°46W **76 F6**
Elkton *U.S.A.* 43°49N 83°11W **82 C1**
Ellas = Greece ■ *Europe* 40°0N 23°0E **23 E9**
Ellef Ringnes I. *Canada* 78°30N 102°2W **69 B11**
Ellen, Mt. *U.S.A.* 44°9N 72°56W **83 B12**
Ellenburg *U.S.A.* 44°54N 73°48W **83 B11**
Ellendale *U.S.A.* 46°0N 98°32W **80 B4**
Ellensburg *U.S.A.* 46°59N 120°34W **78 C5**
Ellenville *U.S.A.* 41°43N 74°24W **83 E10**
Ellerton *Barbados* 13°7N 59°33W **89 g**
Ellery, Mt. *Australia* 37°28S 148°47E **63 F4**
Ellesmere, L. *N.Z.* 43°47S 172°28E **59 G4**
Ellesmere I. *Canada* 79°30N 80°0W **69 B16**
Ellesmere Island = Quttinirpaaq □
  Canada 82°13N 72°13W **69 A17**
Ellesmere Port *U.K.* 53°17N 2°54W **12 D5**
Ellice Is. = Tuvalu ■
  Pac. Oc. 8°0S 178°0E **58 B10**
Ellicottville *U.S.A.* 42°17N 78°40W **82 D6**
Ellington *U.S.A.* 42°13N 79°6W **82 D5**
Elliot *Australia* 17°33S 133°32E **62 B1**
Elliot *S. Africa* 31°22S 27°48E **57 E4**
Elliot Lake *Canada* 46°25N 82°35W **72 C3**
Elliotdale = Xhora
  S. Africa 31°55S 28°38E **57 E4**
Ellis *U.S.A.* 38°56N 99°34W **80 F4**
Elliston *Australia* 33°39S 134°53E **63 E1**
Ellisville *U.S.A.* 31°36N 89°12W **85 F10**
Ellon *U.K.* 57°22N 2°4W **11 D6**
Ellore = Eluru *India* 16°48N 81°8E **41 L12**
Ellsworth *Kans., U.S.A.* 38°44N 98°14W **80 F4**
Ellsworth *Maine, U.S.A.* 44°33N 68°25W **81 C19**
Ellsworth *Mts. Antarctica* 78°30S 85°0W **5 D16**
Ellsworth Land *Antarctica* 76°0S 89°0W **5 D16**
Ellsworth Mts. *Antarctica* 78°30S 85°0W **5 D16**
Ellwood City *U.S.A.* 40°52N 80°17W **82 F4**
Elma *Canada* 49°52N 95°55W **71 D9**
Elma *U.S.A.* 47°0N 123°25W **78 C3**
Elmalı *Turkey* 36°44N 29°56E **19 G4**
Elmhurst *U.S.A.* 41°53N 87°56W **80 E10**
Elmira *Canada* 43°36N 80°33W **82 C4**
Elmira *U.S.A.* 42°6N 76°48W **82 D8**
Elmira Heights *U.S.A.* 42°8N 76°50W **82 D8**
Elmore *Australia* 36°30S 144°37E **63 F3**
Elmshorn *Germany* 53°43N 9°40E **16 B5**
Elmvale *Canada* 44°35N 79°52W **82 B5**
Elora *Canada* 43°41N 80°26W **82 C4**
Elounda *Greece* 35°16N 25°42E **25 D7**
Eloy *U.S.A.* 32°45N 111°33W **77 K8**
Elphin *Canada* 44°55N 76°37W **83 B8**
Elrose *Canada* 51°12N 108°0W **71 C7**
Elsby △ *Australia* 14°55S 133°10E **60 B5**
Elsie *U.S.A.* 45°52N 123°36W **78 E3**
Elsinore = Helsingør
  Denmark 56°2N 12°35E **9 H15**
Eltanin Fracture Zone System
  S. Ocean 54°0S 130°0W **5 B14**
Eltham *N.Z.* 39°26S 174°19E **59 C5**
Eluru *India* 16°48N 81°8E **41 L12**
Elvas *Portugal* 38°50N 7°10W **21 C2**
Elverum *Norway* 60°53N 11°34E **8 F14**
Elvire → *Australia* 17°51S 128°11E **60 C4**
Elvire, Mt. *Australia* 29°22S 119°36E **61 E2**
Elwell, L. = Tiber Res.
  U.S.A. 48°19N 111°6W **76 B8**
Elwood *Ind., U.S.A.* 40°17N 85°50W **81 E11**
Elwood *Nebr., U.S.A.* 40°36N 99°52W **80 E4**
Elx = Elche *Spain* 38°15N 0°42W **21 C5**
Ely *U.K.* 52°24N 0°16E **13 E8**
Ely *Minn., U.S.A.* 47°55N 91°51W **80 B8**
Ely *Nev., U.S.A.* 39°15N 114°54W **76 G6**
Elyria *U.S.A.* 41°22N 82°7W **82 E2**
eMalahleni *S. Africa* 25°51S 29°14E **57 D4**
Emāmrūd *Iran* 36°30N 55°0E **45 B7**
Embarcación *Argentina* 23°10S 64°0W **94 A3**
Embetsu *Japan* 44°44N 141°47E **30 B10**
Embi *Kazakhstan* 48°30N 58°8E **19 E9**
Embi → *Kazakhstan* 46°55N 53°28E **19 E9**
Embonas *Greece* 36°13N 27°51E **25 C9**
Embro *Canada* 43°9N 80°54W **82 C4**

Embrun *France* 44°34N 6°30E **20 D7**
Embu *Kenya* 0°32S 37°38E **54 C4**
Emden *Germany* 53°21N 7°12E **16 B4**
Emerald *Australia* 23°32S 148°10E **62 C4**
Emerald I. *Canada* 76°48N 114°10W **69 B9**
Emerson *Canada* 49°0N 97°10W **71 D9**
Emet *Turkey* 39°20N 39°15E **23 E13**
Emi Koussi *Chad* 19°45N 18°55E **51 E9**
Eminabad *Pakistan* 32°2N 74°8E **42 C6**
Emine, Nos *Bulgaria* 42°40N 27°56E **23 C12**
Emissi, Tarso *Chad* 21°27N 18°36E **51 D9**
Emlenton *U.S.A.* 41°11N 79°43W **82 E5**
Emmaus *S. Africa* 29°2S 25°15E **56 D4**
Emmaus *U.S.A.* 40°32N 75°30W **83 F9**
Emmeloord *Neths.* 52°44N 5°46E **15 B5**
Emmen *Neths.* 52°48N 6°57E **15 B6**
Emmet *Australia* 24°45S 144°30E **62 C3**
Emmetsburg *U.S.A.* 43°7N 94°41W **80 D6**
Emmett *Idaho, U.S.A.* 43°52N 116°30W **76 E5**
Emmett *Mich., U.S.A.* 42°59N 82°46W **82 D2**
Emmonak *U.S.A.* 62°47N 164°31W **74 C7**
Emo *Canada* 48°38N 93°50W **71 D10**
Empalme *Mexico* 27°58N 110°51W **86 B2**
Empangeni *S. Africa* 28°50S 31°52E **57 D5**
Empedrado *Argentina* 28°0S 58°46W **94 B4**
Emperor Seamount Chain
  Pac. Oc. 40°0N 170°0E **64 D9**
Emperor Trough *Pac. Oc.* 43°0N 175°30E **64 C9**
Emporia *Kans., U.S.A.* 38°25N 96°11W **80 F5**
Emporia *Va., U.S.A.* 36°42N 77°32W **81 G15**
Emporium *U.S.A.* 41°31N 78°14W **82 E6**
Empress *Canada* 50°57N 110°0W **71 C7**
Empty Quarter = Rub' al Khālī
  Si. Arabia 19°0N 48°0E **47 D4**
Ems → *Germany* 53°20N 7°12E **16 B4**
Emsdale *Canada* 45°32N 79°19W **82 A5**
Emu *China* 43°40N 128°6E **35 C15**
Emu Park *Australia* 23°13S 150°50E **62 C5**
eMuziwezinto *S. Africa* 30°15S 30°45E **57 E5**
'En 'Avrona *Israel* 29°43N 35°0E **46 F4**
'En Boqeq *Israel* 31°12N 35°21E **46 D4**
'En Gedi *Israel* 31°28N 35°25E **46 D4**
En Nahud *Sudan* 12°45N 28°25E **51 F11**
Ena *Japan* 35°25N 137°25E **31 G8**
Enana *Namibia* 17°30S 16°23E **56 B2**
Enard B. *U.K.* 58°5N 5°20W **11 C3**
Enare = Inarijärvi *Finland* 69°0N 28°0E **8 B23**
Enarotali *Indonesia* 3°55S 136°21E **37 E9**
Encampment *U.S.A.* 41°12N 106°47W **76 F10**
Encantadas, Serra *Brazil* 30°40S 53°0W **95 C5**
Encarnación *Paraguay* 27°15S 55°50W **95 B4**
Encarnación de Díaz
  Mexico 21°31N 102°14W **86 C4**
Encinitas *U.S.A.* 33°3N 117°17W **79 M9**
Encino *U.S.A.* 34°39N 105°28W **77 J11**
Encounter B. *Australia* 35°45S 138°45E **63 F2**
Endako *Canada* 54°6N 125°2W **70 C3**
Endau *Kenya* 1°18S 38°31E **54 C4**
Endau Rompin △
  Malaysia 2°27N 103°45E **39 L4**
Ende *Indonesia* 8°45S 121°40E **37 F6**
Endeavour Str. *Australia* 10°45S 142°0E **62 A3**
Enderbury I. *Kiribati* 3°8S 171°5W **64 H10**
Enderby *Canada* 50°35N 119°10W **70 C5**
Enderby Abyssal Plain
  S. Ocean 60°0S 40°0E **5 C5**
Enderby I. *Australia* 20°35S 116°30E **60 D2**
Enderby Land *Antarctica* 66°0S 53°0E **5 C5**
Enderlin *U.S.A.* 46°38N 97°36W **80 B5**
Enderrocat, C. *Spain* 39°28N 2°43E **24 B9**
Endicott *U.S.A.* 42°6N 76°4W **83 D8**
Endicott Mts. *U.S.A.* 68°0N 152°0W **74 B9**
Endwell *U.S.A.* 42°6N 76°2W **83 D8**
Endyalgout I. *Australia* 11°45S 132°35E **60 B5**
Eneabba *Australia* 29°49S 115°16E **61 E2**
Enewetak Atoll
  Marshall Is. 11°30N 162°15E **64 F8**
Enez *Turkey* 40°45N 26°5E **23 D12**
Enfer, Pte. d' *Martinique* 14°22N 60°54W **88 c**
Enfield *Canada* 44°56N 63°32W **73 D7**
Enfield *Conn., U.S.A.* 41°58N 72°36W **83 E12**
Enfield *N.C., U.S.A.* 36°11N 77°41W **85 C16**
Enfield *N.H., U.S.A.* 43°39N 72°9W **83 C12**
Engadin *Switz.* 46°45N 10°10E **20 C9**
Engaño, C. *Dom. Rep.* 18°30N 68°20W **89 C6**
Engaño, C. *Phil.* 18°35N 122°23E **37 A6**
Engaru *Japan* 44°3N 143°31E **30 B11**
Engcobo = Ngcobo
  S. Africa 31°37S 28°0E **57 E4**
Engels *Russia* 51°28N 46°6E **19 D8**
Engemann L. *Canada* 58°0N 106°55W **71 B7**
Enggano *Indonesia* 5°20S 102°40E **36 F2**
England □ *U.K.* 53°0N 2°0W **13 E5**
England *U.S.A.* 34°33N 91°58W **84 D9**
Englee *Canada* 50°45N 56°5W **73 B8**
Englehart *Canada* 47°49N 79°52W **72 C4**
Englewood *U.S.A.* 39°38N 104°59W **76 G11**
English → *Canada* 49°12N 91°5W **71 C10**
English Bazar = Ingraj Bazar
  India 24°58N 88°10E **43 G13**
English Channel *Europe* 50°0N 2°0W **13 G6**
English Company's Is., The
  Australia 11°50S 136°32E **62 A2**
English River *Canada* 49°14N 91°0W **72 C1**
Enid *U.S.A.* 36°24N 97°53W **84 C6**
Enkhuizen *Neths.* 52°42N 5°17E **15 B5**
Enna *Italy* 37°34N 14°16E **22 F6**
Ennadai L. *Canada* 60°58N 101°20W **71 A8**
Ennedi *Chad* 17°15N 22°0E **51 E10**
Enngonia *Australia* 29°21S 145°50E **63 D4**
Ennis *Ireland* 52°51N 8°59W **10 D3**
Ennis *Mont., U.S.A.* 45°21N 111°44W **76 D8**
Ennis *Tex., U.S.A.* 32°20N 96°38W **84 E6**
Enniscorthy *Ireland* 52°30N 6°34W **10 D5**
Enniskillen *U.K.* 54°21N 7°39W **10 B4**
Ennistimon *Ireland* 52°57N 9°17W **10 D2**
Enns → *Austria* 48°14N 14°32E **16 D8**
Enns *Austria* 48°12N 14°28E **16 D8**
Eno *Finland* 62°47N 30°10E **8 E24**
Enontekiö *Finland* 68°23N 23°37E **8 B20**

Enosburg Falls U.S.A. 44°55N 72°48W 83 B12
Enriquillo, L. Dom. Rep. 18°20N 72°5W 89 C5
Enschede Neths. 52°13N 6°53E 15 B6
Ensenada Argentina 34°55S 57°55W 94 C4
Ensenada Mexico 31°52N 116°37W 86 A1
Ensenada de los Muertos
　Mexico 23°59N 109°51W 86 C2
Ensiola, Pta. de n' Spain 39°7N 2°55E 24 B9
Entebbe Uganda 0°4N 32°28E 54 B3
Enterprise Canada 60°47N 115°45W 70 A5
Enterprise Ala., U.S.A. 31°19N 85°51W 85 F12
Enterprise Oreg., U.S.A. 45°25N 117°17W 76 D5
Entre Ríos Bolivia 21°30S 64°25W 94 A3
Entre Ríos □ Argentina 30°30S 58°30W 94 C4
Entroncamento Portugal 39°28N 8°28W 21 C1
Enugu Nigeria 6°30N 7°30E 50 G7
Enumclaw U.S.A. 47°12N 121°59W 78 C5
Eochail = Youghal
　Ireland 51°56N 7°52W 10 E4
Eólie, Ís. Italy 38°30N 14°57E 22 E6
Epe Neths. 52°21N 5°59E 15 B5
Épernay France 49°3N 3°56E 20 B5
Ephesus Turkey 37°55N 27°22E 23 F12
Ephraim U.S.A. 39°22N 111°35N 76 G8
Ephrata Pa., U.S.A. 40°11N 76°11W 83 F8
Ephrata Wash., U.S.A. 47°19N 119°33W 76 C4
Épinal France 48°10N 6°27E 20 B7
Episkopi Cyprus 34°40N 32°54E 25 E11
Episkopi Greece 35°20N 24°20E 25 D6
Episkopi Bay Cyprus 34°35N 32°50E 25 E11
Epsom U.K. 51°19N 0°16W 13 F7
Epukiro Namibia 21°40S 19°9E 56 C2
Equatoria = El Istiwa'iya
　Sudan 5°0N 28°0E 51 G11
Equatorial Guinea ■ Africa 2°0N 8°0E 52 D1
Er Hai China 25°48N 100°11E 41 G22
Er Rachidia Morocco 31°58N 4°20W 50 B5
Er Rahad Sudan 12°45N 30°32E 51 F12
Er Rif Morocco 35°1N 4°1W 50 A5
Erāwadī Myit = Irrawaddy →
　Burma 15°50N 95°6E 41 M19
Erāwadī Myitwanya = Irrawaddy,
　Mouths of the Burma 15°30N 95°0E 41 M19
Erawan △ Thailand 14°25N 98°58E 38 E2
Erbil = Arbīl Iraq 36°15N 44°5E 44 B5
Erçek Turkey 38°39N 43°36E 44 B4
Erçiyaş Daği Turkey 38°30N 35°28E 44 B2
Érd Hungary 47°22N 18°56E 17 E10
Erdao Jiang → China 42°37N 128°0E 35 C14
Erdek Turkey 40°23N 27°47E 23 D12
Erdene = Ulaan-Uul
　Mongolia 44°13N 111°10E 34 B6
Erdenet Mongolia 49°2N 104°5E 32 B5
Erdenetsogt Mongolia 42°55N 106°5E 34 C4
Erebus, Mt. Antarctica 77°35S 167°0E 5 D11
Erechim Brazil 27°35S 52°15W 95 B5
Ereğli Konya, Turkey 37°31N 34°4E 44 B2
Ereğli Zonguldak, Turkey 41°15N 31°24E 19 F5
Erenhot China 43°48N 112°2E 34 C7
Eresma → Spain 41°26N 4°45W 21 B3
Erfenisdam S. Africa 28°30S 26°50E 56 D4
Erfurt Germany 50°58N 11°2E 16 C6
Ergani Turkey 38°17N 39°49E 44 B3
Ergel Mongolia 43°8N 109°5E 34 C5
Ergeni Vozvyshennost
　Russia 47°0N 44°0E 19 E7
Ergli Latvia 56°54N 25°38E 9 H21
Eriboll, L. U.K. 58°30N 4°42W 11 C4
Érice Italy 38°2N 12°35E 22 E5
Erie U.S.A. 42°8N 80°5W 82 D4
Erie, L. N. Amer. 42°15N 81°0W 82 D4
Erie Canal U.S.A. 43°5N 78°43W 82 C7
Erieau Canada 42°16N 81°57W 82 D3
Erigavo = Ceerigaabo
　Somali Rep. 10°35N 47°20E 47 E4
Erikoussa Greece 39°53N 19°34E 25 A3
Eriksdale Canada 50°52N 98°7W 71 C9
Erimanthos Greece 37°57N 21°50E 23 F9
Erimo-misaki Japan 41°50N 143°15E 30 D11
Erin Canada 43°45N 80°7W 82 C4
Erin Pt. Trin. & Tob. 10°3N 61°39W 93 K15
Erinpura India 25°9N 73°3E 42 G5
Eriskay U.K. 57°4N 7°18W 11 D1
Eritrea ■ Africa 14°0N 38°30E 47 D2
Erlangen Germany 49°36N 11°0E 16 D6
Erldunda Australia 25°14S 133°12E 62 D1
Ermelo Neths. 52°18N 5°35E 15 B5
Ermelo S. Africa 26°31S 29°59E 57 D4
Ermenek Turkey 36°38N 33°0E 44 B2
Ermones Greece 39°37N 19°46E 25 A3
Ermoupoli Greece 37°28N 24°57E 23 F11
Ernakulam India 9°59N 76°22E 40 Q10
Erne → Ireland 54°30N 8°16W 10 B3
Erne, Lower L. U.K. 54°28N 7°47W 10 B4
Erne, Upper L. U.K. 54°14N 7°32W 10 B4
Ernest Giles Ra. Australia 27°0S 123°45E 61 E3
Erode India 11°24N 77°45E 40 P10
Eromanga Australia 26°40S 143°11E 63 D3
Erongo Namibia 21°39S 15°58E 56 C2
Erramala Hills India 15°30N 78°15E 40 M11
Errenteria Spain 43°19N 1°54W 21 A5
Erri-Nundra △ Australia 37°28S 148°56E 63 F4
Errigal Ireland 55°2N 8°6W 10 A3
Erris Hd. Ireland 54°19N 10°0W 10 B1
Erskine U.S.A. 47°40N 96°0W 80 B6
Ertis = Irtysh → Russia 61°4N 68°52E 28 C7
Erwin U.S.A. 36°9N 82°25W 85 C13
Erzgebirge Germany 50°27N 12°55E 16 C7
Erzin Russia 50°15N 95°10E 29 D10
Erzincan Turkey 39°46N 39°30E 44 B3
Erzurum Turkey 39°57N 41°15E 44 B4
Es Caló Spain 38°40N 1°30E 24 C8
Es Canar Spain 39°2N 1°36E 24 B8
Es Mercadal Spain 39°59N 4°5E 24 B11
Es Migjorn Gran Spain 39°57N 4°3E 24 B11
Es Sahrâ' Esh Sharqîya
　Egypt 27°30N 32°30E 51 C12
Es Sinâ' Egypt 29°0N 34°0E 46 F3
Es Vedrà Spain 38°52N 1°12E 24 C7

Esambo
　Dem. Rep. of the Congo 3°48S 23°30E 54 C1
Esan-Misaki Japan 41°40N 141°10E 30 D10
Esashi Hokkaidō, Japan 44°56N 142°35E 30 B11
Esashi Hokkaidō, Japan 41°52N 140°7E 30 D10
Esbjerg Denmark 55°29N 8°29E 9 J13
Esbo = Espoo Finland 60°12N 24°40E 9 F21
Escalante U.S.A. 37°47N 111°36W 77 H8
Escalante → U.S.A. 37°24N 110°57W 77 H8
Escalón Mexico 26°45N 104°20W 86 B4
Escambia → U.S.A. 30°32N 87°11W 85 F11
Escanaba U.S.A. 45°45N 87°4W 80 C10
Esch-sur-Alzette Lux. 49°32N 6°0E 15 E6
Escondido U.S.A. 33°7N 117°5W 79 M9
Escuinapa de Hidalgo
　Mexico 22°50N 105°50W 86 C3
Escuintla Guatemala 14°20N 90°48W 88 D1
Esenguly Turkmenistan 37°37N 53°59E 28 F6
Esfahân Iran 32°39N 51°43E 45 C6
Esfahân □ Iran 32°50N 51°50E 45 C6
Esfarāyen Iran 37°4N 57°30E 45 B8
Esfideh Iran 33°39N 59°46E 45 C8
Esh Sham = Dimashq
　Syria 33°30N 36°18E 46 B5
Esha Ness U.K. 60°29N 1°38W 11 A7
Esher U.K. 51°21N 0°20W 13 F7
Eshkol △ Israel 31°20N 34°30E 46 D3
Eshowe S. Africa 28°50S 31°30E 57 D5
Esigodini Zimbabwe 20°18S 28°56E 57 C4
Esil = Ishim → Russia 57°45N 71°10E 28 D8
Esira Madag. 24°20S 46°42E 57 C8
Esk → Dumf. & Gall., U.K. 54°58N 3°2W 11 G5
Esk → N. Yorks., U.K. 54°30N 0°37W 12 C7
Esk → 26°48N 63°9E 45 E9
Esker Siding Canada 53°53N 66°25W 73 B6
Eskifjörður Iceland 65°3N 13°55W 8 D7
Eskilstuna Sweden 59°22N 16°32E 9 G17
Eskimo Point = Arviat
　Canada 61°6N 93°59W 71 A10
Eskişehir Turkey 39°50N 30°30E 19 G5
Esla → Spain 41°29N 6°3W 21 B2
Eslâmâbâd-e Gharb Iran 34°10N 46°30E 44 C5
Eslâmshahr Iran 35°40N 51°10E 45 C6
Eşme Turkey 38°23N 28°58E 23 E13
Esmeraldas Ecuador 1°0N 79°40W 92 C3
Esna = Isna Egypt 25°17N 32°30E 51 C12
Esnagi L. Canada 48°36N 84°33W 72 C3
Espanola Canada 46°15N 81°46W 72 C3
Espanola U.S.A. 35°59N 106°5W 77 J10
Esparza Costa Rica 9°59N 84°40W 88 E3
Esperance Australia 33°45S 121°55E 61 F3
Esperance B. Australia 33°48S 121°55E 61 F3
Esperance Harbour
　St. Lucia 14°4N 60°55W 89 f
Esperanza Antarctica 65°0S 55°0W 5 C18
Esperanza Argentina 31°29S 61°3W 94 C3
Esperanza Puerto Rico 18°6N 65°28W 89 d
Espichel, C. Portugal 38°22N 9°16W 21 C1
Espigão, Serra do Brazil 26°35S 50°30W 95 B5
Espinazo, Sierra del = Espinhaço,
　Serra do Brazil 17°30S 43°30W 93 G10
Espinhaço, Serra do
　Brazil 17°30S 43°30W 93 G10
Espinho Portugal 41°1N 8°38W 21 B1
Espinilho, Serra do Brazil 28°30S 55°0W 95 B5
Espinosa Brazil 14°57S 42°49W 93 G10
Espírito Santo □ Brazil 20°0S 40°45W 93 H10
Espírito Santo Vanuatu 15°15S 166°50E 58 C9
Espírito Santo, B. del
　Mexico 19°20N 87°35W 87 D7
Espíritu Santo, I.
　Mexico 24°30N 110°22W 86 C2
Espita Mexico 21°1N 88°19W 87 C7
Espoo Finland 60°12N 24°40E 9 F21
Espungabera Mozam. 20°29S 32°45E 57 C5
Esquel Argentina 42°55S 71°20W 96 E2
Esquimalt Canada 48°26N 123°25W 78 B3
Esquina Argentina 30°0S 59°30W 94 C4
Essaouira Morocco 31°32N 9°42W 50 B4
Essebie
　Dem. Rep. of the Congo 2°58N 30°40E 54 B3
Essen Belgium 51°28N 4°28E 15 C4
Essen Germany 51°28N 7°2E 16 C4
Essendon, Mt. Australia 25°0S 120°29E 61 E3
Essequibo → Guyana 6°50N 58°30W 92 B7
Essex Canada 42°10N 82°49W 82 D2
Essex Calif., U.S.A. 34°44N 115°15W 79 L11
Essex N.Y., U.S.A. 44°19N 73°21W 83 B11
Essex □ U.K. 51°54N 0°27E 13 F8
Essex Junction U.S.A. 44°29N 73°7W 83 B11
Esslingen Germany 48°44N 9°18E 16 D5
Estación Camacho
　Mexico 24°25N 102°18W 86 C4
Estación Simón Mexico 24°42N 102°35W 86 C4
Estados, I. de Los
　Argentina 54°40S 64°30W 96 G4
Eştahbânât Iran 29°8N 54°4E 45 D7
Estância Brazil 11°16S 37°26W 93 F11
Estância U.S.A. 34°46N 106°4W 77 J10
Estärm Iran 28°21N 58°21E 45 D8
Estcourt S. Africa 29°0S 29°53E 57 D4
Este △ Dom. Rep. 18°14N 68°42W 89 C6
Estelí Nic. 13°9N 86°22W 88 D2
Estellencs Spain 39°39N 2°29E 24 B9
Esterhazy Canada 50°37N 102°5W 71 C8
Estevan Canada 49°10N 102°59W 71 D8
Estevan Group Canada 53°3N 129°38W 70 C3
Estherville U.S.A. 43°24N 94°50W 80 D6
Eston Canada 51°8N 108°40W 71 C7
Estonia ■ Europe 58°30N 25°30E 9 G21
Estreito Brazil 6°32S 47°25W 93 E9
Estrela, Serra da Portugal 40°10N 7°45W 21 B2
Estremoz Portugal 38°51N 7°39W 21 C2
Estrondo, Serra do Brazil 7°20S 48°0W 93 E9
Esztergom Hungary 47°47N 18°44E 17 E10
Et Tîdra Mauritania 19°45N 16°20W 50 E2
Etah India 27°35N 78°40E 43 F8
Eyre (North), L.
　Australia 28°30S 137°20E 63 D2
Étampes France 48°26N 2°10E 20 B5

Etanga Namibia 17°55S 13°0E 56 B1
Etawah India 26°48N 79°6E 43 F8
Etawney L. Canada 57°50N 96°50W 71 B9
Etchojoa Mexico 26°55N 109°38W 86 B3
eThekwini = Durban
　S. Africa 29°49S 31°1E 57 D5
Ethel U.S.A. 46°32N 122°46W 78 D4
Ethelbert Canada 51°32N 100°25W 71 C8
Ethiopia ■ Africa 8°0N 40°0E 47 F3
Ethiopian Highlands
　Ethiopia 10°0N 37°0E 47 F2
Etive, L. U.K. 56°29N 5°10W 11 E3
Etna Italy 37°50N 14°55E 22 F6
Etoile
　Dem. Rep. of the Congo 11°33S 27°30E 55 E2
Etolin Strait U.S.A. 60°20N 165°15W 74 C6
Etosha △ Namibia 19°0S 16°0E 56 B2
Etosha Pan Namibia 18°40S 16°30E 56 B2
Etowah U.S.A. 35°20N 84°32W 85 D12
Etrek Turkmenistan 37°36N 54°46E 45 B7
Ettelbruck Lux. 49°51N 6°5E 15 E6
Ettrick Water → U.K. 55°31N 2°55W 11 F6
Etuku
　Dem. Rep. of the Congo 3°42S 25°45E 54 C2
Etzná-Tixmucuy = Edzná
　Mexico 19°39N 90°19W 87 D6
Eua Tonga 21°22S 174°56W 59 c
Euboea = Evia Greece 38°30N 24°0E 23 E11
Eucla Australia 31°41S 128°52E 61 F4
Euclid U.S.A. 41°34N 81°32W 82 E3
Eucumbene, L. Australia 36°2S 148°40E 63 F4
Eudora U.S.A. 33°7N 91°16W 84 E9
Eufaula Ala., U.S.A. 31°54N 85°9W 85 F12
Eufaula Okla., U.S.A. 35°17N 95°35W 84 D7
Eufaula L. U.S.A. 35°18N 95°21W 84 D7
Eugene U.S.A. 44°5N 123°4W 76 D2
Eugowra Australia 33°22S 148°24E 63 E4
Eulo Australia 28°10S 145°3E 63 D4
Eungella △ Australia 20°57S 148°40E 62 b
Eunice La., U.S.A. 30°30N 92°25W 84 F8
Eunice N. Mex., U.S.A. 32°26N 103°10W 77 K12
Eupen Belgium 50°37N 6°3E 15 D6
Euphrates = Furât, Nahr al →
　Asia 31°0N 47°25E 44 D5
Eureka Canada 80°0N 85°56W 69 B14
Eureka Calif., U.S.A. 40°47N 124°9W 76 F1
Eureka Kans., U.S.A. 37°49N 96°17W 80 G5
Eureka Mont., U.S.A. 48°53N 115°3W 76 B6
Eureka Nev., U.S.A. 39°31N 115°58W 76 G6
Eureka S. Dak., U.S.A. 45°46N 99°38W 80 C4
Eureka, Mt. Australia 26°35S 121°35E 61 E3
Eureka Sd. Canada 79°0N 85°0W 69 B15
Euroa Australia 36°44S 145°35E 63 F4
Europa, Île Ind. Oc. 22°20S 40°22E 53 J8
Europa, Picos de Spain 43°10N 4°49W 21 A3
Europa, Pt. Gib. 36°3N 5°21W 21 D3
Europe 50°0N 20°0E 6 E10
Europoort Neths. 51°57N 4°10E 15 C4
Eustis U.S.A. 28°51N 81°41W 85 G14
Eutsuk L. Canada 53°20N 126°45W 70 C3
Evale Angola 16°33S 15°44E 56 B2
Evans U.S.A. 40°23N 104°41W 76 F11
Evans, L. Canada 50°50N 77°0W 72 B4
Evans City U.S.A. 40°46N 80°4W 82 F4
Evans Head Australia 29°7S 153°27E 63 D5
Evansburg Canada 53°36N 114°59W 70 C5
Evanston Ill., U.S.A. 42°3N 87°40W 80 D10
Evanston Wyo., U.S.A. 41°16N 110°58W 76 F8
Evansville U.S.A. 37°58N 87°35W 80 G10
Evaz Iran 27°46N 53°59E 45 E7
Eveleth U.S.A. 47°28N 92°32W 80 B7
Evensk Russia 62°12N 159°30E 29 C16
Everard, L. Australia 31°30S 135°0E 63 E2
Everard Ranges Australia 27°5S 132°28E 61 E5
Everest, Mt. Nepal 28°5N 86°58E 43 E12
Everett Pa., U.S.A. 40°1N 78°23W 82 F6
Everett Wash., U.S.A. 47°59N 122°12W 78 C4
Everglades, The U.S.A. 25°50N 81°0W 85 J14
Everglades ∆ U.S.A. 25°30N 81°0W 85 J14
Everglades City U.S.A. 25°52N 81°23W 85 J14
Evergreen Ala., U.S.A. 31°26N 86°57W 85 F11
Evergreen Mont.,
　U.S.A. 48°14N 114°17W 76 B6
Evesham U.K. 52°6N 1°56W 13 E6
Evia Greece 38°30N 24°0E 23 E11
Evje Norway 58°36N 7°51E 9 G12
Évora Portugal 38°33N 7°57W 21 C2
Evowghlī Iran 38°43N 45°13E 44 B5
Évreux France 49°3N 1°8E 20 B4
Évros → Greece 41°40N 26°34E 23 D12
Évry France 48°38N 2°27E 20 B5
Évvoia = Evia Greece 38°30N 24°0E 23 E11
Ewe, L. U.K. 57°49N 5°38W 11 D3
Ewing U.S.A. 42°16N 98°21W 80 D4
Ewo Congo 0°48S 14°45E 52 E2
Exaltación Bolivia 13°10S 65°20W 92 F5
Excelsior Springs U.S.A. 39°20N 94°13W 80 F6
Exe → U.K. 50°41N 3°29W 13 G4
Exeter Canada 43°21N 81°29W 82 C3
Exeter U.K. 50°43N 3°31W 13 G4
Exeter Calif., U.S.A. 36°18N 119°9W 78 J7
Exeter N.H., U.S.A. 42°59N 70°57W 83 D14
Exmoor U.K. 51°12N 3°45W 13 F4
Exmoor ∆ U.K. 51°8N 3°42W 13 F4
Exmouth Australia 21°54S 114°10E 60 D1
Exmouth U.K. 50°37N 3°25W 13 G4
Exmouth G. Australia 22°15S 114°15E 60 D1
Exmouth Plateau Ind. Oc. 19°0S 114°0E 64 J3
Expedition ∆ Australia 25°41S 149°7E 63 D4
Expedition Ra. Australia 24°30S 149°12E 62 C4
Extremadura □ Spain 39°30N 6°5W 21 C2
Exuma Sound Bahamas 24°30N 76°20W 88 B4
Eyasi, L. Tanzania 3°30S 35°0E 54 C4
Eye Pen. U.K. 58°13N 6°10W 11 C2
Eyemouth U.K. 55°52N 2°5W 11 F6
Eyjafjörður Iceland 66°15N 18°30W 8 C4
Eyl Somali Rep. 8°0N 49°50E 47 F4
Eyre (North), L.
　Australia 28°30S 137°20E 63 D2

Eyre (South), L.
　Australia 29°18S 137°25E 63 D2
Eyre, L. Australia 29°30S 137°26E 58 D6
Eyre Mts. N.Z. 45°25S 168°25E 59 F2
Eyre Pen. Australia 33°30S 136°17E 63 E2
Eysturoy Færoe Is. 62°13N 6°54W 8 E9
Eyvän = Jūy Zar Iran 33°50N 46°18E 44 C5
Eyvānkī Iran 35°24N 51°56E 45 C6
Ezine Turkey 39°48N 26°20E 23 E12
Ezouza → Cyprus 34°44N 32°27E 25 E11

F

F.Y.R.O.M. = Macedonia ■
　Europe 41°53N 21°40E 23 D9
Faaa Tahiti 17°34S 149°35W 59 d
Faaone Tahiti 17°40S 149°21W 59 d
Fabala Guinea 9°44N 9°5W 50 G4
Fabens U.S.A. 31°30N 106°10W 84 F1
Fabius U.S.A. 42°50N 75°59W 83 D9
Fabriano Italy 43°20N 12°54E 22 C5
Fachi Niger 18°6N 11°34E 51 E8
Fada Chad 17°13N 21°34E 51 E10
Fada-n-Gourma
　Burkina Faso 12°10N 0°30E 50 F6
Faddeyevskiy, Ostrov
　Russia 76°0N 144°0E 29 B15
Fadghāmī Syria 35°53N 40°52E 44 C4
Faenza Italy 44°17N 11°53E 22 B4
Færoe Is. = Føroyar ☑
　Atl. Oc. 62°0N 7°0W 8 F9
Fāgāras Romania 45°48N 24°58E 17 F13
Fagersta Sweden 60°1N 15°46E 9 F16
Fagnano, L. Argentina 54°30S 68°0W 96 G3
Fahlīān Iran 30°11N 51°28E 45 D6
Fahraj Kermān, Iran 29°0N 59°0E 45 D8
Fahraj Yazd, Iran 31°46N 54°36E 45 D7
Faial Madeira 32°47N 16°53W 24 D3
Faial Azores 38°34N 28°42W 50 a
Fair Haven N.Y., U.S.A. 43°18N 76°34E 43 B7
Fair Haven Vt., U.S.A. 43°36N 73°16W 81 D17
Fair Hd. U.K. 55°14N 6°9W 10 A5
Fair Isle U.K. 59°32N 1°38W 14 B6
Fair Oaks U.S.A. 38°39N 121°16W 78 G5
Fairbanks U.S.A. 64°51N 147°43W 68 E2
Fairbury U.S.A. 40°8N 97°11W 80 E5
Fairfax U.S.A. 44°40N 73°1W 83 B11
Fairfield Ala., U.S.A. 33°29N 86°55W 85 E11
Fairfield Calif., U.S.A. 38°15N 122°3W 78 G4
Fairfield Conn., U.S.A. 41°9N 73°16W 83 E11
Fairfield Idaho, U.S.A. 43°21N 114°44W 76 E6
Fairfield Ill., U.S.A. 38°23N 88°22W 80 F9
Fairfield Iowa, U.S.A. 40°56N 91°57W 80 E8
Fairfield Tex., U.S.A. 31°44N 96°10W 84 F6
Fairford Canada 51°37N 98°38W 71 C9
Fairhope U.S.A. 30°31N 87°54W 85 F11
Fairlie N.Z. 44°5S 170°49E 59 F3
Fairmead U.S.A. 37°5N 120°10W 78 H6
Fairmont Minn., U.S.A. 43°39N 94°28W 80 D6
Fairmont W. Va., U.S.A. 39°29N 80°9W 81 F13
Fairmount Calif., U.S.A. 34°45N 118°26W 79 L8
Fairmount N.Y., U.S.A. 43°3N 76°12W 83 C8
Fairplay U.S.A. 39°15N 106°2W 76 G10
Fairport U.S.A. 43°6N 77°27W 82 C7
Fairport Harbor U.S.A. 41°45N 81°17W 82 E3
Fairview Canada 56°5N 118°25W 70 B5
Fairview Mont., U.S.A. 47°51N 104°3W 76 C11
Fairview Okla., U.S.A. 36°16N 98°29W 84 C5
Fairweather, Mt.
　U.S.A. 58°55N 137°32W 70 B1
Faisalabad Pakistan 31°30N 73°5E 42 D5
Faith U.S.A. 45°2N 102°2W 80 C2
Faizabad India 26°45N 82°10E 43 F10
Fajardo Puerto Rico 18°20N 65°39W 89 d
Fajr, W. → Si. Arabia 29°10N 38°10E 44 D3
Fakenham U.K. 52°51N 0°51E 12 E8
Fakfak Indonesia 2°55S 132°18E 37 E8
Faku China 42°32N 123°21E 35 C12
Falaise France 48°54N 0°12W 20 B3
Falaise, Mui Vietnam 19°6N 105°45E 38 C5
Falam Burma 23°0N 93°45E 41 H18
Falcó, C. des Spain 38°50N 1°23E 24 C7
Falcón, Presa Mexico 26°35N 99°10W 87 B5
Falcon Lake Canada 49°42N 95°15W 71 D9
Falcon Res. U.S.A. 26°34N 99°10W 84 H5
Falconara Maríttima
　Italy 43°37N 13°24E 22 C5
Falcone, C. del Italy 40°58N 8°12E 22 D3
Falconer U.S.A. 42°7N 79°13W 82 D5
Falefa Samoa 13°54S 171°31W 59 b
Falelatai Samoa 13°55S 171°59W 59 b
Falelima Samoa 13°32S 172°41W 59 b
Faleshty = Fălești
　Moldova 47°32N 27°44E 17 E14
Fălești Moldova 47°32N 27°44E 17 E14
Falfurrias U.S.A. 27°14N 98°9W 84 H5
Falher Canada 55°44N 117°15W 70 B5
Faliraki Greece 36°22N 28°12E 25 C10
Falkenberg Sweden 56°54N 12°30E 9 H15
Falkirk U.K. 56°0N 3°47W 11 F5
Falkirk □ U.K. 55°58N 3°49W 11 F5
Falkland U.K. 56°16N 3°12W 11 E5
Falkland Is. ☑ Atl. Oc. 51°30S 59°0W 96 G5
Falkland Sd. Falk. Is. 52°0S 60°0W 96 G5
Fall River U.S.A. 41°43N 71°10W 83 E13
Fallbrook U.S.A. 33°23N 117°15W 79 M9
Fallon U.S.A. 39°28N 118°47W 76 G4
Falls City U.S.A. 40°3N 95°36W 80 E6
Falls Creek U.S.A. 41°9N 78°48W 82 E6
Falmouth Jamaica 18°30N 77°40W 88 a
Falmouth U.K. 50°9N 5°5W 13 G2
Falmouth U.S.A. 41°33N 70°37W 83 E14
Falsa, Pta. Mexico 27°51N 115°3W 86 B1
False B. S. Africa 34°15S 18°40E 56 E2
False C. Honduras 15°12N 83°21W 88 C3
Falso, C. Honduras 15°12N 83°21W 88 C3
Falster Denmark 54°45N 11°55E 9 J14
Falsterbo Sweden 55°23N 12°50E 9 J15

Fălticeni Romania 47°21N 26°20E 17 E14
Falun Sweden 60°37N 15°37E 8 F16
Famagusta Cyprus 35°8N 33°55E 25 D12
Famagusta Bay Cyprus 35°15N 34°0E 25 D13
Famatina, Sierra de
　Argentina 27°30S 68°0W 94 B2
Family L. Canada 51°54N 95°27W 71 C9
Famoso U.S.A. 35°37N 119°12W 79 K7
Fan Xian China 35°55N 115°38E 34 G8
Fanad Hd. Ireland 55°17N 7°38W 10 A4
Fandriana Madag. 20°14S 47°21E 57 C8
Fang Thailand 19°55N 99°13E 38 C2
Fangcheng China 33°18N 112°59E 34 H7
Fangshan China 38°3N 111°25E 34 E6
Fangzi China 36°33N 119°10E 35 F10
Fanjakana Madag. 21°10S 46°53E 57 C8
Fanjiatun China 43°40N 125°15E 35 C13
Fanling China 22°30N 114°8E 33 F11
Fannich, L. U.K. 57°38N 4°59W 11 D4
Fannūj Iran 26°35N 59°38E 45 E8
Fanø Denmark 55°25N 8°25E 9 J13
Fano Italy 43°50N 13°1E 22 C5
Fanshi China 39°12N 113°20E 34 E7
Fao = Al Fāw Iraq 30°0N 48°30E 45 D6
Faqirwali Pakistan 29°27N 73°0E 42 E5
Far East = Dalnevostochnyy □
Far East Asia 40°0N 130°0E 26 E14
Faradje
　Dem. Rep. of the Congo 3°50N 29°45E 54 B2
Farafangana Madag. 22°49S 47°50E 57 C8
Farāh Afghan. 32°20N 62°7E 40 C3
Farāh □ Afghan. 32°25N 62°10E 40 C3
Farahalana Madag. 14°26S 50°10E 57 A9
Faranah Guinea 10°3N 10°45W 50 F3
Farasān, Jazā'ir
　Si. Arabia 16°45N 41°55E 47 D3
Farasan Is. = Farasān, Jazā'ir
　Si. Arabia 16°45N 41°55E 47 D3
Faratsiho Madag. 19°24S 46°57E 57 B8
Fareham U.K. 50°51N 1°11W 13 G6
Farewell, C. N.Z. 40°29S 172°43E 59 D4
Farewell C. = Nunap Isua
　Greenland 59°48N 43°55W 66 D15
Farghona Uzbekistan 40°23N 71°19E 28 E8
Fargo U.S.A. 46°53N 96°48W 80 B5
Fär'iah, W. al →
　West Bank 32°12N 35°27E 46 C4
Faribault U.S.A. 44°18N 93°16W 80 C7
Faridabad India 28°26N 77°19E 42 E6
Faridkot India 30°44N 74°45E 42 D6
Faridpur Bangla. 23°15N 89°55E 43 H13
Faridpur India 28°13N 79°33E 43 E8
Farīmān Iran 35°40N 59°49E 45 C8
Fariones, Pta. Canary Is. 29°13N 13°28E 24 E6
Farleigh Australia 21°4S 149°8E 62 b
Farmerville U.S.A. 32°47N 92°24W 84 E8
Farmingdale U.S.A. 40°12N 74°10W 83 F10
Farmington Canada 55°54N 120°30W 70 B4
Farmington Calif.,
　U.S.A. 37°55N 120°59W 78 H6
Farmington Maine,
　U.S.A. 44°40N 70°9W 81 C18
Farmington Mo., U.S.A. 37°47N 90°25W 80 G8
Farmington N.H., U.S.A. 43°24N 71°4W 83 C13
Farmington N. Mex.,
　U.S.A. 36°44N 108°12W 77 H9
Farmington Utah,
　U.S.A. 40°59N 111°53W 76 F8
Farmington → U.S.A. 41°51N 72°38W 83 E12
Farmville U.S.A. 37°18N 78°24W 81 G14
Farne Is. U.K. 55°38N 1°37W 12 B6
Farnham Canada 45°17N 72°59W 83 A12
Farnham, Mt. Canada 50°29N 116°30W 70 C5
Faro Brazil 2°10S 56°39W 93 D7
Faro Canada 62°11N 133°22W 68 E5
Faro Portugal 37°2N 7°55W 21 D2
Fårö Sweden 57°55N 19°5E 9 H18
Farquhar, C. Australia 23°50S 113°36E 60 D1
Farrars Cr. → Australia 25°35S 140°43E 62 D3
Farrāshband Iran 28°57N 52°5E 45 D7
Farrell U.S.A. 41°13N 80°30W 82 E4
Farrokhī Iran 33°50N 59°31E 45 C8
Farrukhabad India 27°24N 79°34E 43 F8
Fārs □ Iran 29°30N 55°0E 45 D7
Farsala Greece 39°17N 22°23E 23 E10
Fārsī Iran 29°30N 55°40E 45 D7
Farson U.S.A. 42°7N 109°26W 76 E9
Farsund Norway 58°5N 6°55E 9 G12
Fartak, Râs Si. Arabia 28°5N 34°34E 44 D2
Fartak, Ra's Yemen 15°38N 52°15E 47 D5
Fartura, Serra da Brazil 26°21S 52°52W 95 B5
Fārūj Iran 37°14N 58°14E 45 B8
Farvel, Kap = Nunap Isua
　Greenland 59°48N 43°55W 66 D15
Farwell U.S.A. 34°23N 103°2W 84 D3
Faryāb □ Afghan. 36°0N 65°0E 40 B4
Fasā Iran 29°0N 53°39E 45 D7
Fasano Italy 40°50N 17°22E 22 D7
Fastiv Ukraine 50°7N 29°57E 17 C15
Fastnet Rock Ireland 51°22N 9°37W 10 E2
Fastov = Fastiv Ukraine 50°7N 29°57E 17 C15
Fatagar, Tanjung
　Indonesia 2°46S 131°57E 37 E8
Fatehabad Haryana, India 29°31N 75°27E 42 E6
Fatehabad Ut. P., India 27°1N 78°19E 42 F8
Fatehgarh India 27°25N 79°35E 43 F8
Fatehpur Bihar, India 24°38N 85°14E 43 G11
Fatehpur Raj., India 28°0N 74°40E 42 F6
Fatehpur Ut. P., India 25°56N 81°13E 43 G9
Fatehpur Ut. P., India 27°10N 81°13E 43 F9
Fatehpur Sikri India 27°6N 77°40E 42 F6
Fathom Five △ Canada 45°20N 81°40W 82 A3
Fatima Canada 47°24N 61°53W 73 C7
Faulkton U.S.A. 45°2N 99°8W 80 C4
Faure I. Australia 25°52S 113°50E 61 E1
Fauresmith S. Africa 29°44S 25°17E 56 D4

Fauske *Norway* 67°17N 15°25E **8 C16**
Favara *Italy* 37°19N 13°39E **22 F5**
Faváritx, C. de *Spain* 40°0N 4°15E **24 B11**
Favignana *Italy* 37°56N 12°20E **22 F5**
Fawcett, Pt. *Australia* 11°46S 130°2E **60 B5**
Fawn → *Canada* 55°20N 87°35W **72 A2**
Fawnskin *U.S.A.* 34°16N 116°56W **79 L10**
Faxaflói *Iceland* 64°29N 23°0W **8 D2**
Faya-Largeau *Chad* 17°58N 19°6E **51 E9**
Fayd *Si. Arabia* 27°1N 42°52E **44 E4**
Fayette *Ala., U.S.A.* 33°41N 87°50W **85 E11**
Fayette *Mo., U.S.A.* 39°9N 92°41W **80 F7**
Fayette *N.Y., U.S.A.* 42°48N 76°48W **83 D8**
Fayetteville *Ark., U.S.A.* 36°4N 94°10W **84 C7**
Fayetteville *N.C., U.S.A.* 35°3N 78°53W **85 D15**
Fayetteville *N.Y., U.S.A.* 43°1N 76°0W **83 C9**
Fayetteville *Tenn., U.S.A.* 35°9N 86°34W **85 D11**
Faylakah *Kuwait* 29°27N 48°20E **45 D6**
Fazilka *India* 30°27N 74°2E **42 D6**
Fazilpur *Pakistan* 29°18N 70°29E **42 E4**
Feakle *Ireland* 52°56N 8°40W **10 D3**
Feale → *Ireland* 52°27N 9°37W **10 D2**
Fear, C. *U.S.A.* 33°50N 77°58W **85 E16**
Feather → *U.S.A.* 38°47N 121°36W **76 G3**
Feather Falls *U.S.A.* 39°36N 121°16W **78 F5**
Featherston *N.Z.* 41°6S 175°20E **59 D5**
Featherstone *Zimbabwe* 18°42S 30°55E **55 F3**
Fécamp *France* 49°45N 0°22E **20 B4**
Fedala = Mohammedia
  Morocco 33°44N 7°21W **50 B4**
Federación *Argentina* 31°0S 57°55W **94 C4**
Féderal *Argentina* 30°57S 58°48W **96 C5**
Federal Way *U.S.A.* 47°18N 122°19W **78 C4**
Fedeshküh *Iran* 28°49N 53°50E **45 D7**
Fehmarn *Germany* 54°27N 11°7E **16 A6**
Fehmarn Bælt *Europe* 54°35N 11°20E **9 J14**
Fehmarn Belt = Fehmarn Bælt
  Europe 54°35N 11°20E **9 J14**
Fei Xian *China* 35°18N 117°59E **35 G9**
Feijó *Brazil* 8°9S 70°21W **92 E4**
Feilding *N.Z.* 40°13S 175°35E **59 D5**
Feira de Santana *Brazil* 12°15S 38°57W **93 F11**
Feixiang *China* 36°30N 114°45E **34 F8**
Felanitx *Spain* 39°28N 3°9E **24 B10**
Feldkirch *Austria* 47°15N 9°37E **16 E5**
Félicité *Seychelles* 4°19S 55°52E **53 b**
Felipe Carrillo Puerto
  Mexico 19°38N 88°3W **87 D7**
Felixburg *Zimbabwe* 19°29S 30°51E **57 B5**
Felixstowe *U.K.* 51°58N 1°23E **13 F9**
Felton *U.S.A.* 37°3N 122°4W **78 H4**
Femer Bælt = Fehmarn Bælt
  Europe 54°35N 11°20E **9 J14**
Femunden *Norway* 62°10N 11°53E **8 E14**
Fen He → *China* 35°36N 110°42E **34 G6**
Fenelon Falls *Canada* 44°32N 78°45W **82 B6**
Feng Xian *Jiangsu, China* 34°43N 116°35E **34 G9**
Feng Xian *Shaanxi,*
  China 33°54N 106°40E **34 H4**
Fengcheng *China* 40°28N 124°5E **35 D13**
Fengfeng *China* 36°28N 114°8E **34 F8**
Fengning *China* 41°10N 116°33E **34 D9**
Fengqiu *China* 35°2N 114°25E **34 G8**
Fengrun *China* 39°48N 118°8E **35 E10**
Fengtai *China* 39°49N 116°14E **34 E9**
Fengxiang *China* 34°29N 107°25E **34 G4**
Fengyang *China* 32°51N 117°29E **35 H9**
Fengzhen *China* 40°25N 113°2E **34 D7**
Fenoarivo *Fianarantsoa,*
  Madag. 21°43S 46°24E **57 C8**
Fenoarivo *Fianarantsoa,*
  Madag. 20°52S 46°53E **57 C8**
Fenoarivo Afovoany
  Madag. 18°26S 46°34E **57 B8**
Fenoarivo Atsinanana
  Madag. 17°22S 49°25E **57 B8**
Fens, The *U.K.* 52°38N 0°2W **12 E7**
Fenton *U.S.A.* 42°48N 83°42W **81 D12**
Fenxi *China* 36°40N 111°31E **34 F6**
Fenyang *China* 37°18N 111°48E **34 F6**
Feodosiya *Ukraine* 45°2N 35°16E **19 E6**
Ferbane *Ireland* 53°16N 7°50W **10 C4**
Ferdows *Iran* 33°58N 58°2E **45 C8**
Ferfer *Somali Rep.* 5°4N 45°9E **47 F4**
Fergana = Farghona
  Uzbekistan 40°23N 71°19E **28 E8**
Fergus *Canada* 43°43N 80°24W **82 C4**
Fergus Falls *U.S.A.* 46°17N 96°4W **80 B5**
Ferkéssédougou *Ivory C.* 9°35N 5°6W **50 G4**
Ferland *Canada* 50°19N 88°27W **72 B2**
Ferlo, Vallée du *Senegal* 15°15N 14°15W **50 E3**
Fermanagh □ *U.K.* 54°21N 7°40W **10 B4**
Fermo *Italy* 43°9N 13°43E **22 C5**
Fermont *Canada* 52°47N 67°5W **73 B6**
Fermoy *Ireland* 52°9N 8°16W **10 D3**
Fernández *Argentina* 27°55S 63°50W **94 B3**
Fernandina Beach
  U.S.A. 30°40N 81°27W **85 F14**
Fernando de Noronha
  Brazil 4°0S 33°10W **93 D12**
Fernando Póo = Bioko
  Eq. Guin. 3°30N 8°40E **52 D1**
Ferndale *Canada* 44°58N 81°17W **82 B3**
Ferndale *U.S.A.* 48°51N 122°36W **78 B4**
Fernie *Canada* 49°30N 115°5W **70 D5**
Fernlees *Australia* 23°51S 148°7E **62 C4**
Fernley *U.S.A.* 39°36N 119°15W **76 G4**
Fernwood *U.S.A.* 43°16N 73°38W **83 C11**
Ferozepore = Firozpur
  India 30°55N 74°40E **42 D6**
Ferrara *Italy* 44°50N 11°35E **22 B4**
Ferreñafe *Peru* 6°42S 79°50W **92 E3**
Ferrerías *Spain* 39°59N 4°1E **24 B11**
Ferret, C. *France* 44°38N 1°15W **20 D3**
Ferriday *U.S.A.* 31°38N 91°33W **84 F9**
Ferron *U.S.A.* 39°5N 111°8W **76 G8**
Ferrutx, C. de *Spain* 39°47N 3°21E **24 B10**

Ferryland *Canada* 47°2N 52°53W **73 C9**
Fertile *U.S.A.* 47°32N 96°17W **80 B5**
Fès *Morocco* 34°0N 5°0W **50 B5**
Fessenden *U.S.A.* 47°39N 99°38W **80 B4**
Festus *U.S.A.* 38°13N 90°24W **80 F8**
Feteşti *Romania* 44°22N 27°51E **17 F14**
Fethiye *Turkey* 36°36N 29°6E **19 G4**
Fetlar *U.K.* 60°36N 0°52W **11 A8**
Feuilles → *Canada* 58°47N 70°4W **69 F17**
Fezzan *Libya* 27°0N 13°0E **51 C8**
Fiambalá *Argentina* 27°45S 67°37W **94 B2**
Fianarantsoa *Madag.* 21°26S 47°5E **57 C8**
Fianarantsoa □ *Madag.* 19°30S 47°0E **57 B8**
Ficksburg *S. Africa* 28°51S 27°53E **57 D4**
Field → *Australia* 23°48S 138°0E **62 C2**
Field I. *Australia* 12°5S 132°23E **60 B5**
Fier *Albania* 40°43N 19°33E **23 D8**
Fife □ *U.K.* 56°16N 3°1W **11 E5**
Fife ○ *U.K.* 56°15N 3°15W **11 E5**
Fife Ness *U.K.* 56°17N 2°35W **11 E6**
Fifth Cataract *Sudan* 18°22N 33°50E **51 E12**
Figeac *France* 44°37N 2°2E **20 D5**
Figtree *Zimbabwe* 20°22S 28°20E **55 G2**
Figueira da Foz *Portugal* 40°7N 8°54W **21 B1**
Figueres *Spain* 42°18N 2°58E **21 A7**
Figuig *Morocco* 32°5N 1°11W **50 B5**
Fihaonana *Madag.* 18°36S 47°12E **57 B8**
Fiherenana *Madag.* 18°29S 48°24E **57 B8**
Fiherenana → *Madag.* 23°19S 43°37E **57 C7**
Fiji ■ *Pac. Oc.* 17°20S 179°0E **59 a**
Filabusi *Zimbabwe* 20°34S 29°20E **55 G2**
Filadelfia *Paraguay* 22°21S 60°2W **94 A3**
Filchner Ice Shelf *Antarctica* 79°0S 40°0W **5 D1**
Filey *U.K.* 54°12N 0°18E **12 C7**
Filey B. *U.K.* 54°12N 0°15W **12 C7**
Fiffla *Malta* 35°47N 14°24E **25 D1**
Filiatra *Greece* 37°9N 21°35E **23 F9**
Filingué *Niger* 14°21N 3°22E **50 F6**
Filipstad *Sweden* 59°43N 14°9E **9 G16**
Fillmore *Calif., U.S.A.* 34°24N 118°55W **79 L8**
Fillmore *Utah, U.S.A.* 38°58N 112°20W **76 G7**
Fimbul Ice Shelf *S. Ocean* 69°30S 1°0W **5 C2**
Finch *Canada* 45°11N 75°7W **83 A9**
Finch Hatton *Australia* 20°25S 148°39E **62 b**
Findhorn *U.K.* 57°38N 3°38W **11 D5**
Findlay *U.S.A.* 41°2N 83°39W **81 E12**
Fine *U.S.A.* 44°14N 75°8W **83 B9**
Finger L. *Canada* 53°33N 93°30W **72 B1**
Finger Lakes *U.S.A.* 42°40N 76°30W **83 D8**
Fingoè *Mozam.* 14°55S 31°50E **55 E3**
Finisterre, C. = Fisterra, C.
  Spain 42°50N 9°19W **21 A1**
Finke *Australia* 25°34S 134°35E **62 D1**
Finke Gorge △ *Australia* 24°8S 132°49E **60 D5**
Finland ■ *Europe* 63°0N 27°0E **8 E22**
Finland, G. of *Europe* 60°0N 26°0E **9 G22**
Finlay → *Canada* 57°0N 125°10W **70 B3**
Finley *Australia* 35°38S 145°35E **63 F4**
Finley *U.S.A.* 47°31N 97°50W **80 B5**
Finn → *Ireland* 54°51N 7°28W **10 B4**
Finnigan, Mt. *Australia* 15°49S 145°17E **62 B4**
Finniss, C. *Australia* 33°8S 134°51E **63 E1**
Finnmark *Norway* 69°37N 23°57E **8 B20**
Finnsnes *Norway* 69°14N 18°0E **8 B18**
Finspång *Sweden* 58°43N 15°47E **9 G16**
Fiora → *Italy* 42°20N 11°34E **22 C4**
Fiordland △ *N.Z.* 45°46S 167°0E **59 F1**
Fiq *Syria* 32°46N 35°41E **46 C4**
Firat = Furât, Nahr al →
  Asia 31°0N 47°25E **44 D5**
Fire Island △ *U.S.A.* 40°38N 73°8W **83 F11**
Firebag → *Canada* 57°45N 111°21W **71 B6**
Firebaugh *U.S.A.* 36°52N 120°27W **78 J6**
Firedrake L. *Canada* 61°25N 104°30W **71 A8**
Firenze *Italy* 43°46N 11°15E **22 C4**
Firk, Sha'ib → *Iraq* 30°59N 44°34E **44 D5**
Firozabad *India* 27°10N 78°25E **43 F8**
Firozpur *India* 30°55N 74°40E **42 D6**
Firozpur-Jhirka *India* 27°48N 76°57E **42 F7**
Fīrūzābād *Iran* 28°52N 52°35E **45 D7**
Fīrūzkūh *Iran* 35°50N 52°50E **45 C7**
Firvale *Canada* 52°27N 126°13W **70 C3**
Fish → *Namibia* 28°7S 17°10E **56 D2**
Fish → *S. Africa* 31°30S 20°16E **56 E3**
Fish River Canyon
  Namibia 27°40S 17°35E **56 D2**
Fisher B. *Canada* 51°35N 97°13W **71 C9**
Fishers I. *U.S.A.* 41°15N 72°0W **83 E13**
Fishguard *U.K.* 52°0N 4°58W **13 E3**
Fishing L. *Canada* 52°10N 95°24W **71 C9**
Fishkill *U.S.A.* 41°32N 73°54W **83 E11**
Fisterra, C. *Spain* 42°50N 9°19W **21 A1**
Fitchburg *Mass., U.S.A.* 42°35N 71°48W **83 D13**
Fitchburg *Wis., U.S.A.* 42°58N 89°28W **80 D9**
Fitz Roy *Argentina* 47°0S 67°0W **96 F3**
Fitz Roy, Cerro *Argentina* 49°17S 73°5W **96 F2**
Fitzgerald *Canada* 59°51N 111°36W **70 B6**
Fitzgerald *U.S.A.* 31°43N 83°15W **85 F13**
Fitzgerald River △
  Australia 33°53S 119°55E **61 F3**
Fitzmaurice → *Australia* 14°45S 130°5E **60 B5**
Fitzroy → *Queens.,*
  Australia 23°32S 150°52E **62 C5**
Fitzroy → *W. Austral.,*
  Australia 17°31S 123°35E **60 C3**
Fitzroy Crossing
  Australia 18°9S 125°38E **60 C4**
Fitzwilliam I. *Canada* 45°30N 81°45W **82 A3**
Fiume = Rijeka *Croatia* 45°20N 14°21E **16 F8**
Five Points *U.S.A.* 36°26N 120°6W **78 J6**
Fizi *Dem. Rep. of the Congo* 4°17S 28°55E **54 C2**
Flagstaff *U.S.A.* 35°12N 111°39W **77 J8**
Flagstaff L. *U.S.A.* 45°12N 70°18W **83 A14**
Flaherty I. *Canada* 56°15N 79°15W **72 A4**
Flåm *Norway* 60°50N 7°7E **8 F12**
Flambeau → *U.S.A.* 45°18N 91°14W **80 C8**
Flamborough Hd. *U.K.* 54°7N 0°5W **12 C7**
Flaming Gorge ○
  U.S.A. 41°10N 109°25W **76 F9**

Flaming Gorge Res.
  U.S.A. 41°10N 109°25W **76 F9**
Flamingo, Teluk *Indonesia* 5°30S 138°0E **37 F9**
Flanders = Flandre
  Europe 50°50N 2°30E **15 B9**
Flandre *Europe* 50°50N 2°30E **15 B9**
Flandre-Occidentale = West-
  Vlaanderen □ *Belgium* 51°0N 3°0E **15 D2**
Flandre-Orientale = Oost-
  Vlaanderen □ *Belgium* 51°5N 3°50E **15 C3**
Flandreau *U.S.A.* 44°3N 96°36W **80 C5**
Flanigan *U.S.A.* 40°10N 119°53W **78 E7**
Flannan Is. *U.K.* 58°9N 7°52W **11 C1**
Flåsjön *Sweden* 64°5N 15°40E **8 D16**
Flat → *Canada* 61°33N 125°18W **70 A3**
Flat I. *Mauritius* 19°53S 57°35E **53 d**
Flathead L. *U.S.A.* 47°51N 114°8W **76 C6**
Flattery, C. *Australia* 14°58S 145°21E **62 A4**
Flattery, C. *U.S.A.* 48°23N 124°29W **78 B2**
Flatwoods *U.S.A.* 38°31N 82°43W **81 F12**
Fleetwood *U.K.* 53°55N 3°1W **12 D4**
Fleetwood *U.S.A.* 40°27N 75°49W **83 F9**
Flekkefjord *Norway* 58°18N 6°39E **9 G12**
Flemington *U.S.A.* 41°7N 77°28W **82 E7**
Flensburg *Germany* 54°47N 9°27E **16 A5**
Flers *France* 48°47N 0°33W **20 B3**
Flesherton *Canada* 44°16N 80°33W **82 B4**
Flesko, Tanjung
  Indonesia 0°29N 124°30E **37 D6**
Fleurieu Pen. *Australia* 35°40S 138°5E **63 F2**
Flevoland □ *Neths.* 52°30N 5°30E **15 B5**
Flin Flon *Canada* 54°46N 101°53W **71 C8**
Flinders → *Australia* 17°36S 140°36E **62 B3**
Flinders B. *Australia* 34°19S 115°19E **61 F2**
Flinders Group *Australia* 14°11S 144°15E **62 A3**
Flinders I. *S. Austral.,*
  Australia 33°44S 134°41E **63 E1**
Flinders I. *Tas., Australia* 40°0S 148°0E **63 G4**
Flinders Ranges
  Australia 31°30S 138°30E **63 E2**
Flinders Reefs *Australia* 17°37S 148°31E **62 B4**
Flint *U.K.* 53°15N 3°8W **12 D4**
Flint *U.S.A.* 43°1N 83°41W **81 D12**
Flint → *U.S.A.* 30°57N 84°34W **85 F12**
Flint I. *Kiribati* 11°26S 151°48W **65 J12**
Flintshire □ *U.K.* 53°17N 3°17W **12 D4**
Flodden *U.K.* 55°37N 2°8W **12 B5**
Floodwood *U.S.A.* 46°56N 92°55W **80 B7**
Flora *U.S.A.* 38°40N 88°29W **80 F9**
Florala *U.S.A.* 31°0N 86°20W **85 F11**
Florence = Firenze *Italy* 43°46N 11°15E **22 C4**
Florence *Ala., U.S.A.* 34°48N 87°41W **85 D11**
Florence *Ariz., U.S.A.* 33°2N 111°23W **77 K8**
Florence *Colo., U.S.A.* 38°23N 105°8W **76 G11**
Florence *Oreg., U.S.A.* 43°58N 124°7W **76 D1**
Florence *S.C., U.S.A.* 34°12N 79°46W **85 D15**
Florence, L. *Australia* 28°53S 138°9E **63 D2**
Florencia *Colombia* 1°36N 75°36W **92 C3**
Florennes *Belgium* 50°15N 4°35E **15 D4**
Florenville *Belgium* 49°40N 5°19E **15 E5**
Flores *Azores* 39°26N 31°13W **50 a**
Flores *Guatemala* 16°59N 89°50W **88 C2**
Flores *Indonesia* 8°35S 121°0E **37 F6**
Flores I. *Canada* 49°20N 126°10W **70 D3**
Flores Sea *Indonesia* 6°30S 120°0E **37 F6**
Floreşti *Moldova* 47°53N 28°17E **17 E15**
Floresville *U.S.A.* 29°8N 98°10W **84 G5**
Floriano *Brazil* 6°50S 43°0W **93 E10**
Florianópolis *Brazil* 27°30S 48°30W **95 B6**
Florida *Cuba* 21°32N 78°14W **88 B4**
Florida *Uruguay* 34°7S 56°10W **95 C4**
Florida □ *U.S.A.* 28°0N 82°0W **85 G14**
Florida, Straits of *U.S.A.* 25°0N 80°0W **88 B4**
Florida B. *U.S.A.* 25°0N 80°45W **88 B4**
Florida Keys *U.S.A.* 24°40N 81°0W **85 J14**
Florin *U.S.A.* 38°30N 121°24W **78 G5**
Florina *Greece* 40°48N 21°26E **23 D9**
Florissant *U.S.A.* 38°47N 90°19W **80 F8**
Florø *Norway* 61°35N 5°1E **8 F11**
Flower Station *Canada* 45°10N 76°41W **83 A8**
Flowerpot I. *Canada* 45°18N 81°38W **82 A3**
Floydada *U.S.A.* 33°59N 101°20W **84 E4**
Fluk *Indonesia* 1°42S 127°44E **37 E7**
Flushing = Vlissingen
  Neths. 51°26N 3°34E **15 C3**
Fly → *Papua N. G.* 8°25S 143°0E **58 B7**
Flying Fish, C. *Antarctica* 72°6S 102°29W **5 D15**
Foa *Tonga* 19°45S 174°18W **59 c**
Foam Lake *Canada* 51°40N 103°32W **71 C8**
Foça *Turkey* 38°39N 26°46E **23 E12**
Fochabers *U.K.* 57°37N 3°6W **11 D5**
Focşani *Romania* 45°41N 27°15E **17 F14**
Fóggia *Italy* 41°27N 15°34E **22 D6**
Fogo *Canada* 49°43N 54°17W **73 C9**
Fogo *C. Verde Is.* 15°5N 24°20W **50 b**
Fogo I. *Canada* 49°40N 54°5W **73 C9**
Föhr *Germany* 54°43N 8°30E **16 A5**
Foix *France* 42°58N 1°38E **20 E4**
Folda *Nord-Trøndelag,*
  Norway 64°32N 10°30E **8 D14**
Folda *Nordland, Norway* 67°38N 14°50E **8 C16**
Foley *Botswana* 21°34S 27°21E **57 C4**
Foley *U.S.A.* 30°24N 87°41W **85 F11**
Foleyet *Canada* 48°15N 82°25W **72 C3**
Folgefonna *Norway* 60°3N 6°23E **8 F12**
Foligno *Italy* 42°57N 12°42E **22 C5**
Folkestone *U.K.* 51°5N 1°12E **13 F9**
Folkston *U.S.A.* 30°50N 82°0W **85 F13**
Follansbee *U.S.A.* 40°19N 80°35W **82 F4**
Folsom L. *U.S.A.* 38°42N 121°9W **78 G5**
Fomboni *Comoros Is.* 12°18S 43°46E **53 a**
Fond-du-Lac *Canada* 59°19N 107°12W **71 B7**
Fond du Lac *U.S.A.* 43°47N 88°27W **80 D9**
Fond-du-Lac → *Canada* 59°17N 106°0W **71 B7**
Fonda *U.S.A.* 42°57N 74°22W **83 D10**
Fondi *Italy* 41°21N 13°25E **22 D5**
Fongafale *Tuvalu* 8°31S 179°13E **58 B10**
Fonsagrada = A Fonsagrada
  Spain 43°8N 7°4W **21 A2**

Fonseca, G. de
  Cent. Amer. 13°10N 87°40W **88 D2**
Fontainebleau *France* 48°24N 2°40E **20 B5**
Fontana *U.S.A.* 34°6N 117°26W **79 L9**
Fontas → *Canada* 58°14N 121°48W **70 B4**
Fonte Boa *Brazil* 2°33S 66°0W **92 D5**
Fontenay-le-Comte
  France 46°28N 0°48W **20 C3**
Fontenelle Res. *U.S.A.* 42°1N 110°3W **76 E8**
Fontur *Iceland* 66°23N 14°32W **8 C6**
Fonuafo'ou *Tonga* 20°19S 175°25W **59 c**
Fonualei *Tonga* 18°1S 174°19W **59 c**
Foochow = Fuzhou
  China 26°5N 119°16E **33 D6**
Foping *China* 33°41N 108°0E **34 H5**
Foraker, Mt. *U.S.A.* 62°58N 151°24W **74 C9**
Forbes *Australia* 33°22S 148°5E **63 E4**
Forbesganj *India* 26°17N 87°18E **43 F12**
Ford City *Calif., U.S.A.* 35°9N 119°27W **79 K7**
Ford City *Pa., U.S.A.* 40°46N 79°32W **82 F5**
Fords Bridge *Australia* 29°41S 145°29E **63 D4**
Fordyce *U.S.A.* 33°49N 92°25W **84 E8**
Forel, Mt. *Greenland* 66°52N 36°55E **66 C16**
Foremost *Canada* 49°26N 111°34W **70 D6**
Forest *Canada* 43°6N 82°0W **82 C3**
Forest *U.S.A.* 32°22N 89°29W **85 E10**
Forest City *Iowa, U.S.A.* 43°16N 93°39W **80 D7**
Forest City *N.C., U.S.A.* 35°20N 81°52W **85 D14**
Forest City *Pa., U.S.A.* 41°39N 75°28W **83 E9**
Forest Grove *U.S.A.* 45°31N 123°7W **78 E3**
Forestburg *Canada* 52°35N 112°1W **70 C6**
Foresthill *U.S.A.* 39°1N 120°49W **78 F6**
Forestier Pen. *Australia* 43°0S 148°0E **63 G4**
Forestville *Canada* 48°48N 69°2W **73 C6**
Forestville *Calif., U.S.A.* 38°28N 122°54W **78 G4**
Forestville *N.Y., U.S.A.* 42°28N 79°10W **82 D5**
Forfar *U.K.* 56°39N 2°53W **11 E6**
Forillon △ *Canada* 48°46N 64°12W **73 C7**
Forks *U.S.A.* 47°57N 124°23W **78 C2**
Forksville *U.S.A.* 41°29N 76°35W **83 E8**
Forlì *Italy* 44°13N 12°3E **22 B5**
Forman *U.S.A.* 46°7N 97°38W **80 B5**
Formby Pt. *U.K.* 53°33N 3°6W **12 D4**
Formentera *Spain* 38°43N 1°27E **24 C7**
Formentor, C. de *Spain* 39°58N 3°13E **24 B10**
Formentor, Pen. de
  Spain 39°56N 3°11E **24 B10**
Fórmia *Italy* 41°15N 13°37E **22 D5**
Formosa = Taiwan ■
  Asia 23°30N 121°0E **33 D7**
Formosa *Argentina* 26°15S 58°10W **94 B4**
Formosa *Brazil* 15°32S 47°20W **93 G9**
Formosa □ *Argentina* 25°0S 60°0W **94 B4**
Formosa, Serra *Brazil* 12°0S 55°0W **93 F8**
Formosa B. = Ungwana B.
  Kenya 2°45S 40°20E **54 C5**
Fornells *Spain* 40°3N 4°7E **24 A11**
Føroyar ☐ *Atl. Oc.* 62°0N 7°0W **8 F9**
Forres *U.K.* 57°37N 3°37W **11 D5**
Forrest *Australia* 30°51S 128°6E **61 F4**
Forrest, Mt. *Australia* 24°48S 127°45E **61 D4**
Forrest City *U.S.A.* 35°1N 90°47W **85 D9**
Forsayth *Australia* 18°33S 143°34E **62 B3**
Forssa *Finland* 60°49N 23°38E **8 F20**
Forst *Germany* 51°45N 14°37E **16 C8**
Forster *Australia* 32°12S 152°31E **63 E5**
Forsyth *U.S.A.* 46°16N 106°41W **76 C10**
Fort Abbas *Pakistan* 29°12N 72°52E **42 E5**
Fort Albany *Canada* 52°15N 81°35W **72 B3**
Fort Assiniboine
  Canada 54°20N 114°45W **70 C6**
Fort Augustus *U.K.* 57°9N 4°42W **11 D4**
Fort Beaufort *S. Africa* 32°46S 26°40E **56 E4**
Fort Benton *U.S.A.* 47°49N 110°40W **76 C8**
Fort Bragg *U.S.A.* 39°26N 123°48W **76 G2**
Fort Bridger *U.S.A.* 41°19N 110°23W **76 F8**
Fort Chipewyan *Canada* 58°42N 111°8W **71 B6**
Fort Clatsop = Lewis and Clark △
  U.S.A. 46°8N 123°53W **78 D3**
Fort Collins *U.S.A.* 40°35N 105°5W **76 F11**
Fort-Coulonge *Canada* 45°50N 76°45W **72 C4**
Fort Covington *U.S.A.* 44°59N 74°29W **83 B10**
Fort Dauphin = Taolanaro
  Madag. 25°2S 47°0E **57 D8**
Fort Davis *U.S.A.* 30°35N 103°54W **84 F3**
Fort-de-France *Martinique* 14°36N 61°2W **88 c**
Fort Defiance *U.S.A.* 35°45N 109°5W **77 J9**
Fort Dodge *U.S.A.* 42°30N 94°11W **80 D6**
Fort Edward *U.S.A.* 43°16N 73°35W **83 C11**
Fort Erie *Canada* 42°54N 78°56W **82 D6**
Fort Fairfield *U.S.A.* 46°46N 67°50W **81 B20**
Fort Frances *Canada* 48°36N 93°24W **71 D10**
Fort Franklin = Déline
  Canada 65°11N 123°25W **68 D7**
Fort Garland *U.S.A.* 37°26N 105°26W **77 H11**
Fort George = Chisasibi
  Canada 53°50N 79°0W **72 B4**
Fort Good Hope *Canada* 66°14N 128°40W **68 D6**
Fort Hancock *U.S.A.* 31°18N 105°51W **84 F2**
Fort Hope = Eabametoong
  Canada 51°30N 88°0W **72 B2**
Fort Irwin *U.S.A.* 35°16N 116°41W **79 K10**
Fort Kent *U.S.A.* 47°15N 68°36W **81 B19**
Fort Klamath *U.S.A.* 42°42N 122°0W **76 E3**
Fort Laramie *U.S.A.* 42°13N 104°31W **76 E11**
Fort Lauderdale *U.S.A.* 26°7N 80°8W **85 H14**
Fort Liard *Canada* 60°14N 123°30W **70 A4**
Fort Liberté *Haiti* 19°42N 71°51W **89 C5**
Fort Lupton *U.S.A.* 40°5N 104°49W **76 F11**
Fort MacKay *Canada* 57°12N 111°41W **70 B6**
Fort Macleod *Canada* 49°45N 113°30W **70 D6**
Fort McMurray *Canada* 56°44N 111°7W **70 B6**
Fort McPherson
  Canada 67°30N 134°55W **68 D5**

Fort Meade *U.S.A.* 27°45N 81°48W **85 H14**
Fort Morgan *U.S.A.* 40°15N 103°48W **76 F12**
Fort Myers *U.S.A.* 26°39N 81°52W **85 H14**
Fort Nelson *Canada* 58°50N 122°44W **70 B4**
Fort Nelson → *Canada* 59°32N 124°0W **70 B4**
Fort Norman = Tulita
  Canada 64°57N 125°30W **68 E6**
Fort Payne *U.S.A.* 34°26N 85°43W **85 D12**
Fort Peck *U.S.A.* 48°1N 106°27W **76 B10**
Fort Peck Dam *U.S.A.* 48°0N 106°26W **76 C10**
Fort Peck L. *U.S.A.* 48°0N 106°26W **76 C10**
Fort Pierce *U.S.A.* 27°27N 80°20W **85 H14**
Fort Pierre *U.S.A.* 44°21N 100°22W **80 C3**
Fort Portal *Uganda* 0°40N 30°20E **54 B3**
Fort Providence *Canada* 61°3N 117°40W **70 A5**
Fort Qu'Appelle
  Canada 50°45N 103°50W **71 C8**
Fort Resolution *Canada* 61°10N 113°40W **70 A6**
Fort Rixon *Zimbabwe* 20°2S 29°17E **55 G2**
Fort Ross *U.S.A.* 38°32N 123°13W **78 G3**
Fort Rupert = Waskaganish
  Canada 51°30N 78°40W **72 B4**
Fort St. James *Canada* 54°30N 124°10W **70 C4**
Fort St. John *Canada* 56°15N 120°50W **70 B4**
Fort Saskatchewan
  Canada 53°40N 113°15W **70 C6**
Fort Scott *U.S.A.* 37°50N 94°42W **80 G6**
Fort Severn *Canada* 56°0N 87°40W **72 A2**
Fort Shevchenko
  Kazakhstan 44°35N 50°23E **19 F9**
Fort Simpson *Canada* 61°45N 121°15W **70 A4**
Fort Smith *Canada* 60°0N 111°51W **70 B6**
Fort Smith *U.S.A.* 35°23N 94°25W **84 D7**
Fort Stockton *U.S.A.* 30°53N 102°53W **84 F3**
Fort Sumner *U.S.A.* 34°28N 104°15W **77 J11**
Fort Thompson *U.S.A.* 44°3N 99°26W **80 C4**
Fort Union △ *U.S.A.* 35°54N 105°1W **77 J11**
Fort Valley *U.S.A.* 32°33N 83°53W **85 E13**
Fort Vermilion *Canada* 58°24N 116°0W **70 B5**
Fort Walton Beach
  U.S.A. 30°25N 86°36W **85 F11**
Fort Ware *Canada* 57°26N 125°41W **70 B3**
Fort Wayne *U.S.A.* 41°4N 85°9W **81 E11**
Fort William *U.K.* 56°49N 5°7W **11 E3**
Fort Worth *U.S.A.* 32°43N 97°19W **84 E6**
Fort Yates *U.S.A.* 46°5N 100°38W **80 B3**
Fort Yukon *U.S.A.* 66°34N 145°16W **68 D2**
Fortaleza *Brazil* 3°45S 38°35W **93 D11**
Forteau *Canada* 51°28N 56°58W **73 B8**
Fortescue → *Australia* 21°0S 116°4E **60 D2**
Fortescue River Roadhouse
  Australia 21°17S 116°8E **60 D2**
Forth → *U.K.* 56°9N 3°50W **11 E5**
Forth, Firth of *U.K.* 56°5N 2°55W **11 E6**
Fortrose *U.K.* 57°35N 4°9W **11 D4**
Fortuna *Calif., U.S.A.* 40°36N 124°9W **76 F1**
Fortuna *N. Dak., U.S.A.* 48°55N 103°47W **80 A2**
Fortune *Canada* 47°4N 55°50W **73 C8**
Fortune B. *Canada* 47°30N 55°22W **73 C8**
Forūr *Iran* 26°17N 54°32E **45 E7**
Fosen *Norway* 63°50N 10°20E **8 E14**
Foshan *China* 23°6N 113°9E **33 D6**
Fosnavåg *Norway* 62°22N 5°38E **8 E11**
Fossano *Italy* 44°33N 7°43E **20 D7**
Fossil *U.S.A.* 45°0N 120°9W **76 D3**
Fossil Butte △ *U.S.A.* 41°50N 110°27W **76 F8**
Foster *Canada* 45°17N 72°30W **83 A12**
Foster → *Canada* 55°47N 105°49W **71 B7**
Fosters Ra. *Australia* 21°35S 133°48E **62 C1**
Fostoria *U.S.A.* 41°10N 83°25W **81 E12**
Fotadrevo *Madag.* 24°3S 45°1E **57 C8**
Fougères *France* 48°21N 1°14W **20 B3**
Foul Pt. *Sri Lanka* 8°35N 81°18E **40 Q12**
Foula *U.K.* 60°10N 2°5W **11 A6**
Foulness I. *U.K.* 51°36N 0°55E **13 F8**
Foulpointe *Madag.* 17°41S 49°31E **57 B8**
Fouman *Cameroon* 5°45N 10°50E **52 C2**
Foumbouni *Comoros Is.* 11°51S 43°29E **53 a**
Fountain *U.S.A.* 38°41N 104°42W **76 G11**
Fountain Hills *U.S.A.* 33°37N 111°43W **77 K8**
Fountain Springs
  U.S.A. 35°54N 118°51W **79 K8**
Four Mountains, Is. of
  U.S.A. 53°0N 170°0W **74 E5**
Fouriesburg *S. Africa* 28°38S 28°14E **56 D4**
Fourni *Greece* 37°36N 26°32E **23 F12**
Fourth Cataract *Sudan* 18°47N 32°3E **51 E12**
Fouta Djallon *Guinea* 11°20N 12°10W **50 F3**
Foux, Cap-à- *Haiti* 19°43N 73°27W **89 C5**
Foveaux Str. *N.Z.* 46°42S 168°10E **59 G2**
Fowey *U.K.* 50°20N 4°39W **13 G3**
Fowler *Calif., U.S.A.* 36°38N 119°41W **78 J7**
Fowler *Colo., U.S.A.* 38°8N 104°2W **76 G11**
Fowler, Pt. *Australia* 32°2S 132°3E **61 F5**
Fowlers B. *Australia* 31°59S 132°34E **61 F5**
Fowman *Iran* 37°13N 49°19E **45 B6**
Fox → *Canada* 56°3N 93°18W **71 B10**
Fox Creek *Canada* 54°24N 116°48W **70 C5**
Fox Is. *U.S.A.* 53°0N 168°0W **74 E4**
Fox Lake *Canada* 58°28N 114°31W **70 B6**
Fox Valley *Canada* 50°30N 109°25W **71 C7**
Foxboro *Canada* 44°14N 77°26W **82 B7**
Foxboro *U.S.A.* 42°4N 71°15W **83 D13**
Foxdale *Australia* 20°22S 148°35E **62 b**
Foxe Basin *Canada* 66°0N 77°0W **69 D16**
Foxe Chan. *Canada* 65°0N 80°0W **69 E16**
Foxe Pen. *Canada* 65°0N 76°0W **69 E16**
Foxford *Ireland* 53°59N 9°7W **10 C2**
Foxton *N.Z.* 40°29S 175°18E **59 D5**
Foyle, Lough *U.K.* 55°7N 7°4W **10 A4**
Foynes *Ireland* 52°37N 9°7W **10 D2**
Foz do Cunene *Angola* 17°15S 11°48E **56 B1**
Foz do Iguaçu *Brazil* 25°30S 54°30W **95 B5**
Frackville *U.S.A.* 40°47N 76°14W **83 F8**
Fraile Muerto *Uruguay* 32°31S 54°32W **95 C5**
Framingham *U.S.A.* 42°18N 71°24W **83 D13**
Franca *Brazil* 20°33S 47°30W **93 H9**
Francavilla Fontana
  Italy 40°32N 17°35E **23 D7**

France ■ *Europe* 47°0N 3°0E **20 C5**
Frances *Australia* 36°41S 140°55E **63 F3**
Frances → *Canada* 60°16N 129°10W **70 A3**
Frances L. *Canada* 61°23N 129°30W **70 A3**
Franceville *Gabon* 1°40S 13°32E **52 E2**
Franche-Comté □ *France* 46°50N 5°55E **20 C6**
Francis Case, L. *U.S.A.* 43°4N 98°34W **80 D4**
Francisco Beltrão *Brazil* 26°5S 53°4W **95 B5**
Francisco Ignacio Madero
  Coahuila, Mexico 25°48N 103°18W **86 B4**
Francisco Ignacio Madero *Durango,*
  Mexico 24°26N 104°18W **86 C4**
Francisco Ignacio Madero, Presa
  Mexico 28°10N 105°37W **86 B3**
Francistown *Botswana* 21°7S 27°33E **57 C4**
François *Canada* 47°35N 56°45W **73 C8**
François L. *Canada* 54°0N 125°30W **70 C3**
François Peron △
  Australia 25°42S 113°33E **61 E1**
Francs Pk. *U.S.A.* 43°58N 109°20W **76 E9**
Franeker *Neths.* 53°12N 5°33E **15 A5**
Frank Hann △ *Australia* 32°52S 120°19E **61 F3**
Frankford *Canada* 44°12N 77°36W **82 B7**
Frankfort *S. Africa* 27°17S 28°30E **57 D4**
Frankfort *Ind., U.S.A.* 40°17N 86°31W **80 E10**
Frankfort *Kans., U.S.A.* 39°42N 96°25W **80 F5**
Frankfort *Ky., U.S.A.* 38°12N 84°52W **81 F11**
Frankfort *N.Y., U.S.A.* 43°2N 75°4W **83 C9**
Frankfurt *Brandenburg,*
  Germany 52°20N 14°32E **16 B8**
Frankfurt *Hessen, Germany* 50°7N 8°41E **16 C5**
Fränkische Alb *Germany* 49°10N 11°23E **16 D6**
Frankland → *Australia* 35°0S 116°48E **61 G2**
Franklin *Ky., U.S.A.* 36°43N 86°35W **80 G10**
Franklin *La., U.S.A.* 29°48N 91°30W **84 G9**
Franklin *Mass., U.S.A.* 42°5N 71°24W **83 D13**
Franklin *N.H., U.S.A.* 43°27N 71°39W **83 C13**
Franklin *N.Y., U.S.A.* 42°20N 75°9W **83 D9**
Franklin *Nebr., U.S.A.* 40°6N 98°57W **80 E4**
Franklin *Pa., U.S.A.* 41°24N 79°50W **82 E5**
Franklin *Va., U.S.A.* 36°41N 76°56W **81 G15**
Franklin *W. Va., U.S.A.* 38°39N 79°20W **81 F14**
Franklin B. *Canada* 69°45N 126°0W **68 D6**
Franklin D. Roosevelt L.
  U.S.A. 48°18N 118°9W **76 B4**
Franklin-Gordon Wild Rivers △
  Australia 42°19S 145°51E **63 G4**
Franklin I. *Antarctica* 76°10S 168°30E **5 D11**
Franklin I. *Canada* 45°24N 80°20W **82 A4**
Franklin L. *U.S.A.* 40°25N 115°22W **76 F6**
Franklin Mts. *Canada* 65°0N 125°0W **68 D6**
Franklinton *U.S.A.* 30°51N 90°9W **85 F9**
Franklinville *U.S.A.* 42°20N 78°27W **82 D6**
Frankston *Australia* 38°8S 145°8E **63 F4**
Fransfontein *Namibia* 20°12S 15°1E **56 C2**
Frantsa Iosifa, Zemlya
  Russia 82°0N 55°0E **28 A6**
Franz *Canada* 48°25N 84°30W **72 C3**
Franz Josef Land = Frantsa Iosifa,
  Zemlya *Russia* 82°0N 55°0E **28 A6**
Fraser *U.S.A.* 42°32N 82°57W **82 D2**
Fraser → *B.C., Canada* 49°7N 123°11W **78 A3**
Fraser → *Nfld. & L.,*
  Canada 56°39N 62°10W **73 A7**
Fraser, Mt. *Australia* 25°35S 118°20E **61 E2**
Fraser I. *Australia* 25°15S 153°10E **63 D5**
Fraser Lake *Canada* 54°0N 124°50W **70 C4**
Fraserburg *S. Africa* 31°55S 21°30E **56 E3**
Fraserburgh *U.K.* 57°42N 2°1W **11 D6**
Fraserdale *Canada* 49°55N 81°37W **72 C3**
Fray Bentos *Uruguay* 33°10S 58°15W **94 C4**
Fray Jorge △ *Chile* 30°42S 71°40W **94 C1**
Frazier Downs ۞
  Australia 18°48S 121°42E **60 C3**
Fredericia *Denmark* 55°34N 9°45E **9 J13**
Frederick *Md., U.S.A.* 39°25N 77°25W **81 F15**
Frederick *Okla., U.S.A.* 34°23N 99°1W **84 D5**
Frederick *S. Dak., U.S.A.* 45°50N 98°31W **80 C4**
Fredericksburg *Pa.,*
  U.S.A. 40°27N 76°26W **83 F8**
Fredericksburg *Tex.,*
  U.S.A. 30°16N 98°52W **84 F5**
Fredericksburg *Va.,*
  U.S.A. 38°18N 77°28W **81 F15**
Fredericktown *Mo.,*
  U.S.A. 37°34N 90°18W **80 G8**
Fredericktown *Ohio,*
  U.S.A. 40°29N 82°33W **82 F2**
Frederico Westphalen
  Brazil 27°22S 53°24W **95 B5**
Fredericton *Canada* 45°57N 66°40W **73 C6**
Fredericton Junction
  Canada 45°41N 66°40W **73 C6**
Frederikshåb = Paamiut
  Greenland 62°0N 49°43W **4 C5**
Frederikshamn = Hamina
  Finland 60°34N 27°12E **8 F22**
Frederikshavn *Denmark* 57°28N 10°31E **9 H14**
Frederiksted
  U.S. Virgin Is. 17°43N 64°53W **89 C7**
Fredonia *Ariz., U.S.A.* 36°57N 112°32W **77 H7**
Fredonia *Kans., U.S.A.* 37°32N 95°49W **80 G6**
Fredonia *N.Y., U.S.A.* 42°26N 79°20W **82 D5**
Fredrikstad *Norway* 59°13N 10°57E **9 G14**
Free State □ *S. Africa* 28°30S 27°0E **56 D4**
Freehold *U.S.A.* 40°16N 74°17W **83 F10**
Freeland *U.S.A.* 41°1N 75°54W **83 E9**
Freels, C. *Nfld. & L.,*
  Canada 49°15N 53°30W **73 C9**
Freels, C. *Nfld. & L.,*
  Canada 46°37N 53°32W **73 C9**
Freeman *Calif., U.S.A.* 35°35N 117°53W **79 K9**
Freeman *S. Dak., U.S.A.* 43°21N 97°26W **80 D5**
Freeport *Bahamas* 26°30N 78°47W **88 A4**
Freeport *Ill., U.S.A.* 42°17N 89°36W **80 D9**
Freeport *N.Y., U.S.A.* 40°39N 73°35W **83 F11**
Freeport *Ohio, U.S.A.* 40°12N 81°15W **82 F3**
Freeport *Pa., U.S.A.* 40°41N 79°41W **82 F5**

Freeport *Tex., U.S.A.* 28°57N 95°21W **84 G7**
Freetown *S. Leone* 8°30N 13°17W **50 G3**
Freeville *U.S.A.* 42°30N 76°20W **83 D8**
Frégate, L. de la *Canada* 53°15N 74°45W **72 B5**
Fregenal de la Sierra
  Spain 38°10N 6°39W **21 C2**
Fregon *Australia* 26°45S 132°1E **61 E5**
Freibourg = Fribourg
  Switz. 46°49N 7°9E **20 C7**
Freiburg *Germany* 47°59N 7°51E **16 E4**
Freire *Chile* 38°54S 72°38W **96 D2**
Freirina *Chile* 28°30S 71°10W **94 B1**
Freising *Germany* 48°24N 11°45E **16 D6**
Freistadt *Austria* 48°30N 14°30E **16 D8**
Fréjus *France* 43°25N 6°44E **20 E7**
Fremantle *Australia* 32°7S 115°47E **61 F2**
Fremont *Calif., U.S.A.* 37°32N 121°57W **78 H4**
Fremont *Mich., U.S.A.* 43°28N 85°57W **81 D11**
Fremont *Nebr., U.S.A.* 41°26N 96°30W **80 E6**
Fremont *Ohio, U.S.A.* 41°21N 83°7W **81 E12**
Fremont → *U.S.A.* 38°24N 110°42W **76 G8**
Fremont Camp *U.S.A.* 37°53N 121°16W **78 H5**
French Cays = Plana Cays
  Bahamas 22°38N 73°30W **89 B5**
French Creek → *U.S.A.* 41°24N 79°50W **82 E5**
French Frigate Shoals
  U.S.A. 23°45N 166°10W **75 L6**
French Guiana ☒ *S. Amer.* 4°0N 53°0W **93 C8**
French Polynesia ☒
  Pac. Oc. 20°0S 145°0W **65 J13**
Frenchman Cr. →
  N. Amer. 48°31N 107°10W **76 B10**
Frenchman Cr. →
  U.S.A. 40°14N 100°50W **80 E3**
Fresco → *Brazil* 7°15S 51°30W **93 E8**
Freshfield, C. *Antarctica* 68°25S 151°10E **5 C10**
Fresnillo *Mexico* 23°10N 102°53W **86 C4**
Fresno *U.S.A.* 36°44N 119°47W **78 J7**
Fresno Res. *U.S.A.* 48°36N 109°57W **76 B9**
Frew → *Australia* 20°0S 135°38E **62 C2**
Frewsburg *U.S.A.* 42°3N 79°10W **82 D5**
Freycinet △ *Australia* 42°11S 148°19E **63 G4**
Freycinet Pen. *Australia* 42°10S 148°25E **63 G4**
Fria *Guinea* 10°27N 13°38W **50 F3**
Fria, C. *Namibia* 18°0S 12°0E **56 B1**
Friant *U.S.A.* 36°59N 119°43W **78 J7**
Frías *Argentina* 28°40S 65°5W **94 B2**
Fribourg *Switz.* 46°49N 7°9E **20 C7**
Friday Harbor *U.S.A.* 48°32N 123°1W **78 B3**
Friedens *U.S.A.* 40°3N 78°59W **82 F6**
Friedrichshafen *Germany* 47°39N 9°30E **16 E5**
Friendship *U.S.A.* 42°12N 78°8W **82 D6**
Friesland □ *Neths.* 53°5N 5°50E **15 A5**
Frigate *Seychelles* 4°35S 55°56E **53 b**
Frío → *U.S.A.* 28°26N 98°11W **84 G5**
Frio, C. *Brazil* 22°50S 41°50W **90 F6**
Friona *U.S.A.* 34°38N 102°43W **84 D3**
Fritch *U.S.A.* 35°38N 101°36W **84 D4**
Frobisher B. *Canada* 62°30N 66°0W **69 E18**
Frobisher Bay = Iqaluit
  Canada 63°44N 68°31W **69 E18**
Frobisher L. *Canada* 56°20N 108°15W **71 B7**
Frohavet *Norway* 64°0N 9°30E **8 E13**
Frome *U.K.* 51°14N 2°19W **13 F5**
Frome → *U.K.* 50°41N 2°6W **13 G5**
Frome, L. *Australia* 30°45S 139°45E **63 E2**
Front Range *U.S.A.* 40°25N 105°45W **75 G11**
Front Royal *U.S.A.* 38°55N 78°12W **81 F14**
Frontenac △ *Canada* 44°32N 76°30W **83 B8**
Frontera *Canary Is.* 27°47N 17°59W **24 G2**
Frontera *Mexico* 18°32N 92°38W **87 D6**
Fronteras *Mexico* 30°56N 109°31W **86 A3**
Frosinone *Italy* 41°38N 13°19E **22 D5**
Frostburg *U.S.A.* 39°39N 78°56W **81 F14**
Frostisen *Norway* 68°14N 17°10E **8 B17**
Frøya *Norway* 63°43N 8°40E **8 E13**
Frunze = Bishkek
  Kyrgyzstan 42°54N 74°46E **28 E8**
Frutal *Brazil* 20°0S 49°0W **93 H9**
Frýdek-Místek
  Czech Rep. 49°40N 18°20E **17 D10**
Fryeburg *U.S.A.* 44°1N 70°59W **83 B14**
Fu Xian = Wafangdian
  China 39°38N 121°58E **35 E11**
Fu Xian *China* 36°0N 109°20E **34 G5**
Fucheng *China* 37°50N 116°10E **34 F9**
Fuchou = Fuzhou *China* 26°5N 119°16E **33 D6**
Fuchū *Japan* 34°34N 133°14E **31 G6**
Fuencaliente *U.S.A.* 28°28N 17°50W **24 F2**
Fuencaliente, Pta.
  Canary Is. 28°27N 17°51W **24 F2**
Fuengirola *Spain* 36°32N 4°41W **21 D3**
Fuentes de Oñoro *Spain* 40°33N 6°52W **21 B2**
Fuerte → *Mexico* 25°54N 109°22W **86 B3**
Fuerte Olimpo *Paraguay* 21°0S 57°51W **94 A4**
Fuerteventura *Canary Is.* 28°30N 14°0W **24 F6**
Fuerteventura ✈ (FUE)
  Canary Is. 28°24N 13°52W **24 F6**
Fufeng *China* 34°22N 108°0E **34 G5**
Fugou *China* 34°3N 114°25E **34 G8**
Fugu *China* 39°2N 111°3E **34 E6**
Fuhai *China* 47°2N 87°25E **32 B3**
Fuḥaymī *Iraq* 34°16N 42°10E **44 C4**
Fuji *Japan* 35°9N 138°39E **31 G9**
Fuji-Hakone-Izu △
  Japan 35°15N 138°45E **31 G9**
Fuji-San *Japan* 35°22N 138°44E **31 G9**
Fuji-Yoshida *Japan* 35°30N 138°46E **31 G9**
Fujian □ *China* 26°0N 118°0E **33 D6**
Fujinomiya *Japan* 35°10N 138°40E **31 G9**
Fujisawa *Japan* 35°22N 139°29E **31 G9**
Fujiyama, Mt. = Fuji-San
  Japan 35°22N 138°44E **31 G9**
Fukagawa *Japan* 43°43N 142°2E **30 C11**
Fukien = Fujian □ *China* 26°0N 118°0E **33 D6**
Fukuchiyama *Japan* 35°19N 135°9E **31 G7**
Fukue-Shima *Japan* 32°40N 128°45E **31 H4**
Fukui *Japan* 36°5N 136°10E **31 F8**
Fukui □ *Japan* 36°0N 136°12E **31 G8**

Fukuoka *Japan* 33°39N 130°21E **31 H5**
Fukuoka □ *Japan* 33°30N 131°0E **31 H5**
Fukushima *Japan* 37°44N 140°28E **30 F10**
Fukushima □ *Japan* 37°30N 140°15E **30 F10**
Fukuyama *Japan* 34°35N 133°20E **31 G6**
Fulaga *Fiji* 19°8S 178°33W **59 a**
Fulda *U.S.A.* 43°52N 95°36W **80 D6**
Fulda *Germany* 50°32N 9°40E **16 C5**
Fulda → *Germany* 51°25N 9°39E **16 C5**
Fulford Harbour
  Canada 48°47N 123°27W **78 B3**
Fullerton *Calif., U.S.A.* 33°53N 117°56W **79 M9**
Fullerton *Nebr., U.S.A.* 41°22N 97°58W **80 E5**
Fulongquan *China* 44°20N 124°42E **35 B13**
Fulton *Mo., U.S.A.* 38°52N 91°57W **80 F8**
Fulton *N.Y., U.S.A.* 43°19N 76°25W **83 C8**
Funabashi *Japan* 35°45N 140°0E **31 G10**
Funafuti = Fongafale
  Tuvalu 8°31S 179°13E **58 B10**
Funchal *Madeira* 32°38N 16°54W **24 D3**
Funchal ✈ (FNC)
  Madeira 32°42N 16°45W **24 D3**
Fundación *Colombia* 10°31N 74°11W **92 A4**
Fundão *Portugal* 40°8N 7°30W **21 B2**
Fundy, B. of *Canada* 45°0N 66°0W **73 D6**
Fundy △ *Canada* 45°35N 65°10W **73 C6**
Funhalouro *Mozam.* 23°3S 34°25E **57 C5**
Funing *Hebei, China* 39°53N 119°12E **35 E10**
Funing *Jiangsu, China* 33°45N 119°50E **35 H10**
Funiu Shan *China* 33°30N 112°20E **34 H7**
Funtua *Nigeria* 11°30N 7°18E **50 F7**
Fuping *Hebei, China* 38°48N 114°12E **34 E8**
Fuping *Shaanxi, China* 34°42N 109°10E **34 G5**
Furano *Japan* 43°21N 142°23E **30 C11**
Furāt, Nahr al → *Asia* 31°0N 47°25E **44 D5**
Fürg *Iran* 28°18N 55°13E **45 D7**
Furnás *Spain* 39°3N 1°32E **24 B8**
Furnas, Represa de
  Brazil 20°50S 45°30W **95 A6**
Furneaux Group
  Australia 40°10S 147°50E **63 G4**
Furqlus *Syria* 34°36N 37°8E **46 A6**
Fürstenwalde *Germany* 52°22N 14°3E **16 B8**
Fürth *Germany* 49°28N 10°59E **16 D6**
Furukawa *Japan* 38°34N 140°58E **30 E10**
Fury and Hecla Str.
  Canada 69°56N 84°0W **69 D15**
Fusagasugá *Colombia* 4°21N 74°22W **92 C4**
Fushan *Shandong,*
  China 37°30N 121°15E **35 F11**
Fushan *Shanxi, China* 35°58N 111°51E **34 G6**
Fushun *China* 41°50N 123°56E **35 D12**
Fusong *China* 42°20N 127°15E **35 C14**
Futian *China* 22°32N 114°4E **33 F11**
Fuxin *China* 42°5N 121°48E **35 C11**
Fuyang *China* 33°0N 115°48E **34 H8**
Fuyang He → *China* 38°12N 117°0E **34 E9**
Fuyu *Heilongjiang, China* 47°49N 124°27E **33 B7**
Fuyu *Jilin, China* 45°12N 124°43E **35 B13**
Fuyun *China* 47°0N 89°28E **32 B3**
Fuzhou *China* 26°5N 119°16E **33 D6**
Fylde *U.K.* 53°50N 2°58W **12 D5**
Fyn *Denmark* 55°20N 10°30E **9 J14**
Fyne, L. *U.K.* 55°59N 5°23W **11 F3**

G

Gaalkacyo *Somali Rep.* 6°30N 47°30E **47 F4**
Gabba *Australia* 9°45S 142°38E **62 a**
Gabela *Angola* 11°0S 14°24E **52 G2**
Gabès *Tunisia* 33°53N 10°2E **51 B8**
Gabès, G. de *Tunisia* 34°0N 10°30E **51 B8**
Gabon ■ *Africa* 0°10S 10°0E **52 E2**
Gaborone *Botswana* 24°45S 25°57E **56 C4**
Gabriels *U.S.A.* 44°26N 74°12W **83 B10**
Gābrīk *Iran* 25°44N 58°28E **45 E8**
Gabrovo *Bulgaria* 42°52N 25°19E **23 C11**
Gāch Sār *Iran* 36°7N 51°19E **45 B6**
Gachsārān *Iran* 30°15N 50°45E **45 D6**
Gadag *India* 15°30N 75°45E **40 M9**
Gadap *Pakistan* 25°5N 67°28E **42 G2**
Gadarwara *India* 22°50N 78°50E **43 H8**
Gadhada *India* 22°0N 71°35E **42 J4**
Gadra *Pakistan* 25°40N 70°38E **42 G4**
Gadsden *U.S.A.* 34°1N 86°1W **85 D11**
Gadwal *India* 16°10N 77°50E **40 L10**
Gaffney *U.S.A.* 35°5N 81°39W **85 D14**
Gafsa *Tunisia* 34°24N 8°43E **50 B7**
Gagaria *India* 25°43N 70°46E **42 G4**
Gagnoa *Ivory C.* 6°56N 5°16W **50 G4**
Gagnon *Canada* 51°50N 68°5W **73 B6**
Gagnon, L. *Canada* 62°3N 110°27W **71 A6**
Gahini *Rwanda* 1°50S 30°30E **54 C3**
Gahmar *India* 25°27N 83°49E **43 G10**
Gai Xian = Gaizhou
  China 40°22N 122°20E **35 D12**
Gaidouronisi *Greece* 34°53N 25°41E **25 E7**
Gail *U.S.A.* 32°46N 101°27W **84 E4**
Gaillimh = Galway *Ireland* 53°17N 9°3W **10 C2**
Gaines *U.S.A.* 41°46N 77°35W **82 E7**
Gainesville *Fla., U.S.A.* 29°40N 82°20W **85 G13**
Gainesville *Ga., U.S.A.* 34°18N 83°50W **85 D13**
Gainesville *Mo., U.S.A.* 36°36N 92°26W **80 G8**
Gainesville *Tex., U.S.A.* 33°38N 97°8W **84 E6**
Gainsborough *U.K.* 53°24N 0°46W **12 D7**
Gairdner, L. *Australia* 31°30S 136°0E **63 E2**
Gairloch *U.K.* 57°43N 5°41W **11 D3**
Gairloch, L. *U.K.* 57°43N 5°45W **11 D3**
Gaizhou *China* 40°22N 122°20E **35 D12**
Gaj → *Pakistan* 26°26N 67°21E **42 F2**
Gakuch *Pakistan* 36°7N 73°45E **43 A5**
Galán, Cerro *Argentina* 25°55S 66°52W **94 B2**
Galana → *Kenya* 3°9S 40°8E **54 C5**
Galápagos = Colón, Arch. de
  Ecuador 0°0 91°0W **90 D1**
Galapagos Fracture Zone
  Pac. Oc. 2°0N 110°0W **65 G17**

Galapagos Rise *Pac. Oc.* 15°0S 95°0W **65 J18**
Galashiels *U.K.* 55°37N 2°49W **11 F6**
Galateia *Cyprus* 35°25N 34°4E **25 D13**
Galați *Romania* 45°27N 28°2E **17 F15**
Galatina *Italy* 40°10N 18°10E **23 D8**
Galax *U.S.A.* 36°40N 80°56W **81 G13**
Galcaio = Gaalkacyo
  Somali Rep. 6°30N 47°30E **47 F4**
Galdhøpiggen *Norway* 61°38N 8°18E **8 F13**
Galeana *Chihuahua,*
  Mexico 30°7N 107°38W **86 A3**
Galeana *Nuevo León,*
  Mexico 24°50N 100°4W **86 A3**
Galela *Indonesia* 1°50N 127°49E **37 D7**
Galeota Pt. *Trin. & Tob.* 10°8N 60°59W **93 K16**
Galera Pt. *Trin. & Tob.* 10°49N 60°54W **93 K16**
Galesburg *U.S.A.* 40°57N 90°22W **80 E8**
Galestan △ *Iran* 37°30N 56°0E **45 B8**
Galeton *U.S.A.* 41°44N 77°39W **82 E7**
Galich *Russia* 58°22N 42°24E **18 C7**
Galicia □ *Spain* 42°43N 7°45W **21 A2**
Galilee = Hagalil *Israel* 32°53N 35°18E **46 C4**
Galilee, L. *Australia* 22°20S 145°50E **62 C4**
Galilee, Sea of = Yam Kinneret
  Israel 32°45N 35°35E **46 C4**
Galina Pt. *Jamaica* 18°24N 76°58W **88 a**
Galinoporni *Cyprus* 35°31N 34°18E **25 D13**
Galion *U.S.A.* 40°44N 82°47W **82 F2**
Galiuro Mts. *U.S.A.* 32°30N 110°20W **77 K8**
Galiwinku *Australia* 12°5S 135°34E **62 A2**
Gallan Hd. *U.K.* 58°15N 7°2W **11 C1**
Gallatin *U.S.A.* 36°24N 86°27W **85 C11**
Galle *Sri Lanka* 6°5N 80°10E **40 R12**
Gállego → *Spain* 41°39N 0°51W **21 B5**
Gallegos → *Argentina* 51°35S 69°0W **96 G3**
Galley Hd. *Ireland* 51°32N 8°55W **10 E3**
Gallinas, Pta. *Colombia* 12°28N 71°40W **92 A4**
Gallipoli = Gelibolu
  Turkey 40°28N 26°43E **23 D12**
Gallipoli *Italy* 40°3N 17°58E **23 D8**
Gallipolis *U.S.A.* 38°49N 82°12W **81 F12**
Gällivare *Sweden* 67°9N 20°40E **8 C19**
Galloo I. *U.S.A.* 43°55N 76°25W **83 C8**
Galloway *U.K.* 55°1N 4°29W **11 F4**
Galloway, Mull of *U.K.* 54°39N 4°52W **11 G4**
Galloway → *U.K.* 55°3N 4°20W **11 F4**
Gallup *U.S.A.* 35°32N 108°45W **77 J9**
Galoya *Sri Lanka* 8°10N 80°55E **40 Q12**
Galt *U.S.A.* 38°15N 121°18W **78 G5**
Galty Mts. *Ireland* 52°22N 8°10W **10 D3**
Galtymore *Ireland* 52°21N 8°11W **10 D3**
Galugāh *Iran* 36°43N 53°48E **45 B7**
Galva *U.S.A.* 41°10N 90°3W **80 E8**
Galveston *U.S.A.* 29°18N 94°48W **84 G7**
Galveston B. *U.S.A.* 29°36N 94°50W **84 G7**
Gálvez *Argentina* 32°0S 61°14W **94 C3**
Galway *Ireland* 53°17N 9°3W **10 C2**
Galway □ *Ireland* 53°22N 9°1W **10 C2**
Galway B. *Ireland* 53°13N 9°10W **10 C2**
Gam → *Vietnam* 21°55N 105°12E **38 B5**
Gamagōri *Japan* 34°50N 137°14E **31 G8**
Gambat *Pakistan* 27°17N 68°26E **42 F3**
Gambhir → *India* 26°58N 77°27E **42 F6**
Gambia ■ *W. Afr.* 13°25N 16°0W **50 F2**
Gambia → *W. Afr.* 13°28N 16°34W **50 F2**
Gambier, C. *Australia* 11°56S 130°57E **60 B5**
Gambier, Îs.
  French Polynesia 23°8S 134°58W **65 K14**
Gambier Is. *Australia* 35°3S 136°30E **63 F2**
Gambo *Canada* 48°47N 54°13W **73 C9**
Gamboli *Pakistan* 29°53N 68°24E **42 E3**
Gamboma *Congo* 1°55S 15°52E **52 E3**
Gamka → *S. Africa* 33°18S 21°39E **56 E3**
Gamlakarleby = Kokkola
  Finland 63°50N 23°8E **8 E20**
Gammon → *Canada* 51°24N 95°44W **71 C9**
Gammon Ranges △
  Australia 30°38S 139°8E **63 E2**
Gamtoos → *S. Africa* 33°58S 25°1E **56 E4**
Gan Jiang → *China* 29°15N 116°0E **33 D6**
Ganado *U.S.A.* 35°43N 109°33W **77 J9**
Gananoque *Canada* 44°20N 76°10W **83 B8**
Ganāveh *Iran* 29°35N 50°35E **45 D6**
Gäncä *Azerbaijan* 40°45N 46°20E **19 F8**
Gancheng *China* 18°51N 108°37E **38 C7**
Gand = Gent *Belgium* 51°2N 3°42E **15 C3**
Ganda *Angola* 13°3S 14°35E **53 G2**
Gandajika
  Dem. Rep. of the Congo 6°46S 23°58E **52 F4**
Gandak → *India* 25°39N 85°13E **43 G11**
Gandava *Pakistan* 28°32N 67°32E **42 E2**
Gander *Canada* 48°58N 54°35W **73 C9**
Gander L. *Canada* 48°58N 54°35W **73 C9**
Ganderowe Falls
  Zimbabwe 17°20S 29°10E **55 F2**
Gandhi Sagar *India* 24°40N 75°40E **42 G6**
Gandhinagar *India* 23°15N 72°45E **42 H5**
Gandia *Spain* 38°58N 0°9W **21 C5**
Gando, Pta. *Canary Is.* 27°55N 15°22W **24 G4**
Ganedidalem = Gani
  Indonesia 0°48S 128°14E **37 E7**
Ganga → *India* 23°20N 90°30E **43 H14**
Ganga Sagar *India* 21°38N 88°5E **43 J13**
Gangan → *India* 28°38N 78°58E **43 E8**
Ganganagar *India* 29°56N 73°56E **42 E5**
Gangapur *India* 26°32N 76°49E **42 F7**
Gangaw *Burma* 22°5N 94°5E **41 H19**
Gangdisê Shan *China* 31°20N 81°0E **43 D9**
Ganges = Ganga →
  India 23°20N 90°30E **43 H14**
Ganges *Canada* 48°51N 123°31W **70 D4**
Ganges, Mouths of the
  India 21°30N 90°0E **43 J14**
Ganggyeong *S. Korea* 36°10N 127°0E **35 F14**
Ganghwa *S. Korea* 37°45N 126°30E **35 F14**
Gangneung *S. Korea* 37°45N 128°54E **35 F15**
Gangoh *India* 29°46N 77°18E **42 E7**

Gangotri *India* 30°50N 79°10E **43 D8**
Gangotri △ *India* 30°50N 79°10E **43 D8**
Gangseong *S. Korea* 38°24N 128°30E **35 E15**
Gangtok *India* 27°20N 88°37E **41 F16**
Gangu *China* 34°40N 105°15E **34 G3**
Gangyao *China* 44°12N 126°37E **35 B14**
Gani *Indonesia* 0°48S 128°14E **37 E7**
Ganj *India* 27°45N 78°57E **43 F8**
Gannett Peak *U.S.A.* 43°11N 109°39W **76 E9**
Ganquan *China* 36°20N 109°20E **34 F5**
Gansu □ *China* 36°0N 104°0E **34 G3**
Ganta *Liberia* 7°15N 8°59W **50 G4**
Gantheaume, C.
  Australia 36°4S 137°32E **63 F2**
Gantheaume B.
  Australia 27°40S 114°10E **61 E1**
Gantsevichi = Hantsavichy
  Belarus 52°49N 26°30E **17 B14**
Ganyem = Genyem
  Indonesia 2°46S 140°12E **37 E10**
Ganyu *China* 34°50N 119°8E **35 G10**
Ganzhou *China* 25°51N 114°56E **33 D6**
Gao *Mali* 16°15N 0°5W **50 E5**
Gaomi *China* 36°20N 119°42E **35 F10**
Gaoping *China* 35°45N 112°55E **34 G7**
Gaotang *China* 36°50N 116°15E **34 F9**
Gaoua *Burkina Faso* 10°20N 3°8W **50 F5**
Gaoual *Guinea* 11°45N 13°25W **50 F3**
Gaoxiong = Kaohsiung
  Taiwan 22°35N 120°16E **33 D7**
Gaoyang *China* 38°40N 115°45E **34 E8**
Gaoyou Hu *China* 32°45N 119°20E **35 H10**
Gaoyuan *China* 37°8N 117°58E **35 F9**
Gap *France* 44°33N 6°5E **20 D7**
Gapat → *India* 24°30N 82°28E **43 G10**
Gapuwiyak *Australia* 12°25S 135°43E **62 A2**
Gar *China* 32°10N 79°58E **32 C2**
Gara, L. *Ireland* 53°57N 8°26W **10 C3**
Garabogazköl Aylagy
  Turkmenistan 41°0N 53°30E **19 F9**
Garachico *Canary Is.* 28°22N 16°46W **24 F3**
Garachiné *Panama* 8°0N 78°12W **88 E4**
Garafia *Canary Is.* 28°48N 17°57W **24 F2**
Garagum *Turkmenistan* 39°30N 60°0E **45 B8**
Garah *Australia* 29°5S 149°38E **63 D4**
Garajonay *Canary Is.* 28°7N 17°14W **24 F2**
Garamba △
  Dem. Rep. of the Congo 4°10N 29°40E **54 B2**
Garanhuns *Brazil* 8°50S 36°30W **93 E11**
Garautha *India* 25°34N 79°18E **43 G8**
Garawa ۞ *Australia* 16°43S 136°51E **62 B2**
Garba Tula *Kenya* 0°30N 38°32E **54 B4**
Garberville *U.S.A.* 40°6N 123°48W **76 F2**
Garbiyang *India* 30°8N 80°54E **43 D9**
Gard □ *France* 43°51N 4°37E **20 D6**
Garda, L. di *Italy* 45°40N 10°41E **22 B4**
Garde L. *Canada* 62°50N 106°13W **71 A7**
Garden City *Ga., U.S.A.* 32°6N 81°9W **85 E14**
Garden City *Kans.,*
  U.S.A. 37°58N 100°53W **80 G3**
Garden City *Tex.,*
  U.S.A. 31°52N 101°29W **84 F4**
Garden Grove *U.S.A.* 33°47N 117°55W **79 M9**
Gardez *Afghan.* 33°37N 69°9E **42 C3**
Gardiner *Maine, U.S.A.* 44°14N 69°47W **81 C19**
Gardiner *Mont., U.S.A.* 45°2N 110°22W **76 D8**
Gardiners I. *U.S.A.* 41°6N 72°6W **83 E12**
Gardner *U.S.A.* 42°34N 71°59W **83 D13**
Gardner Canal *Canada* 53°27N 128°8W **70 C3**
Gardner Pinnacles
  U.S.A. 25°0N 167°55W **75 L6**
Gardnerville *U.S.A.* 38°56N 119°45W **78 G7**
Gardo = Qardho
  Somali Rep. 9°30N 49°6E **47 F4**
Garey *U.S.A.* 34°53N 120°19W **79 L6**
Garfield *U.S.A.* 47°1N 117°9W **76 C5**
Garforth *U.K.* 53°47N 1°24W **12 D6**
Gargantua, C. *Canada* 47°36N 85°2W **81 B11**
Gargett *Australia* 21°9S 148°46E **62 b**
Garibaldi △ *Canada* 49°50N 122°40W **70 D4**
Gariep, L. *S. Africa* 30°40S 25°40E **56 E4**
Garies *S. Africa* 30°32S 17°59E **56 E2**
Garig Gunak Barlu △
  Australia 11°26S 131°58E **60 B5**
Garigliano → *Italy* 41°13N 13°45E **22 D5**
Garissa *Kenya* 0°25S 39°40E **54 C4**
Garland *Tex., U.S.A.* 32°54N 96°38W **84 E6**
Garland *Utah, U.S.A.* 41°45N 112°10W **76 F7**
Garmāb *Iran* 35°25N 56°45E **45 C8**
Garmisch-Partenkirchen
  Germany 47°30N 11°6E **16 E6**
Garmsār *Iran* 35°20N 52°25E **45 C7**
Garner *U.S.A.* 43°6N 93°36W **80 D7**
Garnett *U.S.A.* 38°17N 95°14W **80 F6**
Garo Hills *India* 25°30N 90°30E **43 G14**
Garoe = Garoowe
  Somali Rep. 8°25N 48°33E **47 F4**
Garonne → *France* 45°2N 0°36W **20 D3**
Garoowe *Somali Rep.* 8°25N 48°33E **47 F4**
Garot *India* 24°19N 75°41E **42 G6**
Garoua *Cameroon* 9°19N 13°21E **51 G8**
Garrauli *India* 25°5N 79°22E **43 G8**
Garrison *Mont., U.S.A.* 46°31N 112°49W **76 C7**
Garrison *N. Dak., U.S.A.* 47°40N 101°25W **80 B3**
Garrison Res. = Sakakawea, L.
  U.S.A. 47°30N 101°25W **80 B3**
Garron Pt. *U.K.* 55°3N 5°59W **11 A6**
Garry → *U.K.* 56°44N 3°47W **11 E5**
Garry, L. *Canada* 65°58N 100°18W **68 D11**
Garrygala *Turkmenistan* 38°31N 56°29E **45 B8**
Garsen *Kenya* 2°20S 40°5E **54 C5**
Garson L. *Canada* 56°19N 110°2W **71 B6**
Garstang *U.K.* 53°55N 2°46W **12 D5**
Garu *India* 23°40N 84°14E **43 H11**
Garub *Namibia* 26°37S 16°0E **56 D2**
Garut *Indonesia* 7°14S 107°53E **37 G12**
Garvie Mts. *N.Z.* 45°30S 168°50E **59 F2**
Garwa = Garoua
  Cameroon 9°19N 13°21E **51 G8**

Garwa *India* 24°11N 83°47E **43** G10
Gary *U.S.A.* 41°36N 87°20W **80** E10
Garzè *China* 31°38N 100°1E **32** C5
Garzón *Colombia* 2°10N 75°40W **92** C3
Gas-San *Japan* 38°32N 140°1E **30** E10
Gasan Kuli = Esenguly
　Turkmenistan 37°37N 53°59E **28** F6
Gascogne *France* 43°45N 0°20E **20** E4
Gascogne, G. de *Europe* 44°0N 2°0W **20** D2
Gascony = Gascogne
　France 43°45N 0°20E **20** E4
Gascoyne → *Australia* 24°52S 113°37E **61** D1
Gascoyne Junction
　Australia 25°2S 115°17E **61** E2
Gashaka *Nigeria* 7°20N 11°29E **51** G8
Gasherbrum *Pakistan* 35°40N 76°40E **43** B7
Gashua *Nigeria* 12°54N 11°0E **51** F8
Gasparillo *Trin. & Tob.* 10°18N 61°26W **93** K15
Gaspé *Canada* 48°52N 64°30W **73** C7
Gaspé, C. de *Canada* 48°48N 64°7W **73** C7
Gaspé Pen. = Gaspésie, Pén. de la
　Canada 48°45N 65°40W **73** C6
Gaspésie, Pén. de la
　Canada 48°45N 65°40W **73** C6
Gaspésie △ *Canada* 48°55N 66°10W **73** C6
Gasteiz = Vitoria-Gasteiz
　Spain 42°50N 2°41W **21** A4
Gastonia *U.S.A.* 35°16N 81°11W **85** D14
Gastre *Argentina* 42°20S 69°15W **96** E3
Gata, C. *Cyprus* 34°34N 33°2E **25** E12
Gata, C. de *Spain* 36°41N 2°13W **21** D4
Gata, Sierra de *Spain* 40°20N 6°45W **21** B2
Gataga → *Canada* 58°35N 126°59W **70** B3
Gatchina *Russia* 59°35N 30°9E **9** G24
Gatehouse of Fleet *U.K.* 54°53N 4°12W **11** G4
Gates *U.S.A.* 43°9N 77°42W **82** C7
Gateshead *U.K.* 54°57N 1°35W **12** C6
Gateshead I. *Canada* 70°36N 100°26W **68** C11
Gatesville *U.S.A.* 31°26N 97°45W **84** F6
Gateway *U.S.A.* 40°38N 73°51W **83** F11
Gaths *Zimbabwe* 20°2S 30°32E **55** G3
Gatineau *Canada* 45°29N 75°39W **83** A9
Gatineau → *Canada* 45°27N 75°42W **72** C4
Gatineau △ *Canada* 45°40N 76°0W **72** C4
Gatton *Australia* 27°32S 152°17E **63** D5
Gatún, L. *Panama* 9°7N 79°56W **88** E4
Gatwick, London ✈ (LGW)
　U.K. 51°10N 0°11W **13** F7
Gatyana *S. Africa* 32°16S 28°31E **57** E4
Gau *Fiji* 18°2S 179°18E **59** a
Gauer L. *Canada* 57°0N 97°50W **71** B9
Gauhati = Guwahati
　India 26°10N 91°45E **41** F17
Gauja → *Latvia* 57°10N 24°16E **9** H21
Gaujas → *Latvia* 57°10N 24°50E **9** H21
Gaula → *Norway* 63°21N 10°14E **8** E14
Gauri Phanta *India* 28°41N 80°36E **43** E9
Gaustatoppen *Norway* 59°48N 8°40E **9** G13
Gauteng □ *S. Africa* 26°0S 28°0E **57** D4
Gāv Koshī *Iran* 28°38N 57°12E **45** D8
Gävakän *Iran* 29°37N 53°10E **45** D7
Gavāter *Iran* 25°10N 61°31E **45** E9
Gävbandī *Iran* 27°12N 53°4E **45** E7
Gavdopoula *Greece* 34°56N 24°0E **25** E6
Gavdos *Greece* 34°50N 24°5E **25** E6
Gaviota *U.S.A.* 34°29N 120°13W **79** L6
Gävkhūnī, Bāţlāq-e *Iran* 32°6N 52°52E **45** C7
Gävle *Sweden* 60°40N 17°9E **8** F17
Gawachab *Namibia* 27°4S 17°55E **56** D2
Gawilgarh Hills *India* 21°15N 76°45E **40** J10
Gawler *Australia* 34°30S 138°42E **63** E2
Gawler Ranges
　Australia 32°30S 135°45E **63** E2
Gaxun Nur *China* 42°22N 100°30E **32** B5
Gay *Russia* 51°27N 58°27E **18** D10
Gaya *India* 24°47N 85°4E **43** G11
Gaya *Niger* 11°52N 3°28E **50** F6
Gaylord *U.S.A.* 45°2N 84°41W **81** C11
Gayndah *Australia* 25°35S 151°32E **63** D5
Gaysin = Haysyn
　Ukraine 48°57N 29°25E **17** D15
Gayvoron = Hayvoron
　Ukraine 48°22N 29°52E **17** D15
Gaza *Gaza Strip* 31°30N 34°28E **46** D3
Gaza □ *Mozam.* 23°10S 32°45E **57** C5
Gaza Strip ■ *Asia* 31°29N 34°25E **46** D3
Gazanjyk = Bereket
　Turkmenistan 39°16N 55°32E **45** B7
Gâzbor *Iran* 28°5N 58°51E **45** D8
Gazi *Dem. Rep. of the Congo* 1°3N 24°30E **54** B1
Gaziantep *Turkey* 37°6N 37°23E **44** B3
Gazimağusa = Famagusta
　Cyprus 35°8N 33°55E **25** D12
Gbadolite
　Dem. Rep. of the Congo 4°17N 21°1E **52** D4
Gbarnga *Liberia* 7°19N 9°13W **50** G4
Gcoverega *Botswana* 19°8S 24°18E **56** B3
Gcuwa *S. Africa* 32°20S 28°11E **57** E4
Gdańsk *Poland* 54°22N 18°40E **17** A10
Gdańska, Zatoka
　Poland 54°30N 19°20E **17** A10
Gdov *Russia* 58°48N 27°55E **9** G22
Gdynia *Poland* 54°35N 18°33E **17** A10
Gebe *Indonesia* 0°5N 129°25E **37** D7
Gebze *Turkey* 40°47N 29°25E **23** D13
Gedaref *Sudan* 14°2N 35°28E **51** F13
Gediz → *Turkey* 38°35N 26°48E **23** E12
Gedser *Denmark* 54°35N 11°55E **9** J14
Gedung, Pulau *Malaysia* 5°17N 100°23E **39** c
Geel *Belgium* 51°10N 4°59E **15** C4
Geelong *Australia* 38°10S 144°22E **63** F3
Geelvink B. = Cenderawasih, Teluk
　Indonesia 3°0S 135°20E **37** E9
Geelvink Chan. *Australia* 28°30S 114°0E **61** E1
Geesthacht *Germany* 53°26N 10°22E **16** B6
Geidam *Nigeria* 12°57N 11°57E **51** F8
Geikie → *Canada* 57°45N 103°52W **71** B8

Geikie Gorge △ *Australia* 18°3S 125°41E **60** C4
Geistown *U.S.A.* 40°18N 78°52W **82** F6
Geita *Tanzania* 2°48S 32°12E **54** C3
Gejiu *China* 23°20N 103°10E **32** D5
Gela *Italy* 37°4N 14°15E **22** F6
Gelang Patah *Malaysia* 1°27N 103°35E **39** d
Gelderland □ *Neths.* 52°5N 6°10E **15** B6
Geldrop *Neths.* 51°25N 5°32E **15** C5
Geleen *Neths.* 50°57N 5°49E **15** D5
Gelib = Jilib *Somali Rep.* 0°29N 42°46E **47** G3
Gelibolu *Turkey* 40°28N 26°43E **23** D12
Gelsenkirchen *Germany* 51°32N 7°6E **16** C4
Gemas *Malaysia* 5°22N 100°1E **39** c
Gelugur *Malaysia* 2°37N 102°36E **39** L4
Gembloux *Belgium* 50°34N 4°43E **15** D4
Gemena
　Dem. Rep. of the Congo 3°13N 19°48E **52** D3
Gemerek *Turkey* 39°15N 36°10E **44** B3
Gemlik *Turkey* 40°26N 29°9E **23** D13
Gemsbok △ *Botswana* 25°5S 21°1E **56** D3
Genadi *Greece* 36°2N 27°56E **25** C9
Genale → *Ethiopia* 6°2N 39°1E **47** F2
General Acha *Argentina* 37°20S 64°38W **94** D3
General Alvear *B. Aires.*
　Argentina 36°0S 60°0W **94** D4
General Alvear *Mendoza,*
　Argentina 35°0S 67°40W **94** D2
General Artigas
　Paraguay 26°52S 56°16W **94** B4
General Belgrano
　Argentina 36°35S 58°47W **94** D4
General Bernardo O'Higgins
　Antarctica 63°0S 58°3W **5** C18
General Cabrera
　Argentina 32°53S 63°52W **94** C3
General Cepeda *Mexico* 25°21N 101°22W **86** B4
General Guido *Argentina* 36°40S 57°50W **94** D4
General Juan Madariaga
　Argentina 37°0S 57°0W **94** D4
General La Madrid
　Argentina 37°17S 61°20W **94** D3
General MacArthur
　Phil. 11°18N 125°28E **37** B7
General Martín Miguel de Güemes
　Argentina 24°50S 65°0W **94** A3
General Pico *Argentina* 35°45S 63°50W **94** D3
General Pinedo
　Argentina 27°15S 61°20W **94** B3
General Pinto *Argentina* 34°45S 61°50W **94** C3
General Roca *Argentina* 39°2S 67°35W **96** D3
General Santos *Phil.* 6°5N 125°14E **37** C7
General Treviño *Mexico* 26°14N 99°29W **87** B5
General Trías *Mexico* 28°21N 106°22W **86** B3
General Viamonte
　Argentina 35°1S 61°3W **94** D3
General Villegas *Argentina* 35°5S 63°0W **94** D3
Genesee *Idaho, U.S.A.* 46°33N 116°56W **76** C5
Genesee *Pa., U.S.A.* 41°59N 77°54W **82** E7
Genesee → *U.S.A.* 43°16N 77°36W **82** C7
Geneseo *Ill., U.S.A.* 41°27N 90°9W **80** E8
Geneseo *N.Y., U.S.A.* 42°48N 77°49W **82** D7
Geneva = Genève *Switz.* 46°12N 6°9E **20** C7
Geneva *Ala., U.S.A.* 31°2N 85°52W **85** F12
Geneva *N.Y., U.S.A.* 42°52N 76°59W **82** D8
Geneva *Nebr., U.S.A.* 40°32N 97°36W **80** E5
Geneva *Ohio, U.S.A.* 41°48N 80°57W **82** E4
Geneva, L. = Léman, L.
　Europe 46°26N 6°30E **20** C7
Genève *Switz.* 46°12N 6°9E **20** C7
Genil → *Spain* 37°42N 5°19W **21** D3
Genk *Belgium* 50°58N 5°32E **15** D5
Gennargentu, Mti. del
　Italy 40°1N 9°19E **22** D3
Genoa = Génova *Italy* 44°25N 8°57E **20** D8
Genoa *Australia* 37°29S 149°35E **63** F4
Genoa *N.Y., U.S.A.* 42°40N 76°32W **83** D8
Genoa *Nebr., U.S.A.* 41°27N 97°44W **80** E5
Genoa *Nev., U.S.A.* 39°2N 119°50W **78** F7
Génova *Italy* 44°25N 8°57E **20** D8
Génova, G. di *Italy* 44°0N 9°0E **22** C3
Genriyetty, Ostrov
　Russia 77°6N 156°30E **29** B16
Gent *Belgium* 51°2N 3°42E **15** C3
Genteng *Bali, Indonesia* 8°22S 114°9E **37** J17
Genteng *Jawa Barat,*
　Indonesia 7°22S 106°24E **37** G12
Genyem *Indonesia* 2°46S 140°12E **37** E10
Geochang *S. Korea* 35°41N 127°55E **35** G14
Geographe B. *Australia* 33°30S 115°15E **61** F2
Geographe Chan.
　Australia 24°30S 113°0E **61** D1
Georga, Zemlya *Russia* 80°30N 49°0E **28** A5
George *S. Africa* 33°58S 22°29E **56** E3
George → *Canada* 58°49N 66°10W **73** A6
George, L. *N.S.W.,*
　Australia 35°10S 149°25E **63** F4
George, L. *S. Austral.,*
　Australia 37°25S 140°0E **63** F3
George, L. *W. Austral.,*
　Australia 22°45S 123°40E **60** D3
George, L. *Uganda* 0°5N 30°10E **54** B3
George, L. *Fla., U.S.A.* 29°17N 81°36W **85** G14
George, L. *N.Y., U.S.A.* 43°37N 73°33W **83** C11
George Gill Ra.
　Australia 24°22S 131°45E **60** D5
George Pt. *Australia* 20°6S 148°36E **62** b
George River = Kangiqsualujjuaq
　Canada 58°30N 65°59W **69** F18
George Sound *N.Z.* 44°52S 167°25E **59** F1
George Town *Australia* 41°6S 146°49E **63** G4
George Town *Bahamas* 23°33N 75°47W **88** B4
George Town *Cayman Is.* 19°20N 81°24W **88** C3
George Town *Malaysia* 5°25N 100°15E **39** c
George V Land *Antarctica* 69°0S 148°0E **5** C10
George VI Sound
　Antarctica 71°0S 68°0W **5** D17
George West *U.S.A.* 28°20N 98°7W **84** G5
Georgetown = Janjanbureh
　Gambia 13°30N 14°47W **50** F3

Georgetown *Australia* 18°17S 143°33E **62** B3
Georgetown *Ont.,*
　Canada 43°40N 79°56W **82** C5
Georgetown *P.E.I.,*
　Canada 46°13N 62°24W **73** C7
Georgetown *Guyana* 6°50N 58°12W **92** B7
Georgetown *Calif.,*
　U.S.A. 38°54N 120°50W **78** G6
Georgetown *Colo.,*
　U.S.A. 39°42N 105°42W **76** G11
Georgetown *Ky., U.S.A.* 38°13N 84°33W **81** F11
Georgetown *N.Y.,*
　U.S.A. 42°46N 75°44W **83** D9
Georgetown *Ohio,*
　U.S.A. 38°52N 83°54W **81** F12
Georgetown *S.C.,*
　U.S.A. 33°23N 79°17W **85** E15
Georgetown *Tex., U.S.A.* 30°38N 97°41W **84** F6
Georgia □ *U.S.A.* 32°50N 83°15W **85** E13
Georgia, Str. of *N. Amer.* 49°25N 124°0W **78** A3
Georgia ■ *Asia* 42°0N 43°0E **19** F7
Georgia Basin *S. Ocean* 55°0S 35°30W **5** B1
Georgian B. *Canada* 45°15N 81°0W **82** A4
Georgian Bay Islands △
　Canada 44°53N 79°52W **82** B5
Georgiyevka *Kazakhstan* 49°19N 84°34E **28** E9
Georgina → *Australia* 23°30S 139°47E **62** C2
Georgina I. *Canada* 44°22N 79°17W **82** B5
Georgioupoli *Greece* 35°20N 24°15E **25** D6
Georgiyevsk *Russia* 44°12N 43°28E **19** F7
Gera *Germany* 50°53N 12°4E **16** C7
Geraardsbergen *Belgium* 50°45N 3°53E **15** D3
Geral, Serra *Brazil* 26°25S 50°0W **95** B6
Geral de Goiás, Serra
　Brazil 12°0S 46°0W **93** F9
Geraldine *U.S.A.* 47°36N 110°16W **76** C8
Geraldton *Australia* 28°48S 114°32E **61** E1
Geraldton *Canada* 49°44N 86°59W **72** C2
Gerdine, Mt. *U.S.A.* 61°35N 152°27W **74** C9
Gereshk *Afghan.* 31°47N 64°35E **40** D4
Gerik *Malaysia* 5°50N 101°15E **39** K3
Gering *U.S.A.* 41°50N 103°40W **80** E2
Gerlach *U.S.A.* 40°39N 119°21W **76** F4
German Bight = Deutsche Bucht
　Germany 54°15N 8°0E **16** A5
Germansen Landing
　Canada 55°43N 124°40W **70** B4
Germantown *U.S.A.* 35°5N 89°49W **85** D10
Germany ■ *Europe* 51°0N 10°0E **16** C6
Germī *Iran* 39°1N 48°3E **45** B6
Germiston *S. Africa* 26°13S 28°10E **57** D4
Gernika-Lumo *Spain* 43°19N 2°40W **21** A4
Gero *Japan* 35°48N 137°14E **31** G8
Gerokgak *Indonesia* 8°11S 114°27E **37** J17
Gerona = Girona *Spain* 41°58N 2°46E **21** B7
Geropotamos → *Greece* 35°3N 24°50E **25** D6
Gerrard *Canada* 50°30N 117°17W **70** C5
Gertak Sanggul *Malaysia* 5°17N 100°12E **39** c
Gertak Sanggul, Tanjung
　Malaysia 5°16N 100°11E **39** c
Gerung *Indonesia* 8°43S 116°7E **37** K19
Geser *Indonesia* 3°50S 130°54E **37** E8
Getafe *Spain* 40°18N 3°43W **21** B4
Gettysburg *Pa., U.S.A.* 39°50N 77°14W **81** F15
Gettysburg *S. Dak., U.S.A.* 45°1N 99°57W **80** C4
Getxo *Spain* 43°21N 2°59W **21** A4
Getz Ice Shelf *Antarctica* 75°0S 130°0W **5** D14
Geyser *U.S.A.* 47°16N 110°30W **76** C8
Geyserville *U.S.A.* 38°42N 122°54W **78** G4
Ghadāf, W. al → *Iraq* 32°56N 43°30E **44** C4
Ghadāmis *Libya* 30°11N 9°29E **51** B8
Ghaggar → *India* 29°30N 74°53E **42** E6
Ghaghara → *India* 25°45N 84°40E **43** G11
Ghaghat → *Bangla.* 25°19N 89°38E **43** G13
Ghagra *India* 23°17N 84°33E **43** H11
Ghagra → *India* 27°29N 81°9E **43** F9
Ghallamane *Mauritania* 23°15N 10°0W **50** D4
Ghana ■ *W. Afr.* 8°0N 1°0W **50** G5
Ghansor *India* 22°39N 80°1E **43** H9
Ghanzi *Botswana* 21°50S 21°34E **56** C3
Gharb Bahr el Ghazâl □
　Sudan 7°30N 27°30E **48** F6
Ghardaïa *Algeria* 32°20N 3°37E **50** B6
Gharm *Tajikistan* 39°0N 70°20E **28** F8
Gharyān *Libya* 32°10N 13°0E **51** B8
Ghat *Libya* 24°59N 10°11E **51** D8
Ghatal *India* 22°40N 87°46E **43** H12
Ghatampur *India* 26°8N 80°13E **43** F9
Ghats, Eastern *India* 14°0N 78°50E **40** N11
Ghats, Western *India* 14°0N 75°0E **40** N9
Ghatsila *India* 22°36N 86°29E **43** H12
Ghaţţī *Si. Arabia* 31°16N 37°31E **44** D3
Ghawdex = Gozo *Malta* 36°3N 14°15E **25** C1
Ghazal, Bahr el → *Chad* 13°0N 15°47E **51** F9
Ghazâl, Bahr el →
　Sudan 9°31N 30°25E **51** G12
Ghaziabad *India* 28°42N 77°26E **42** E7
Ghazipur *India* 25°38N 83°35E **43** G10
Ghaznī *Afghan.* 33°30N 68°28E **42** C3
Ghaznī □ *Afghan.* 32°10N 68°20E **40** C6
Ghent = Gent *Belgium* 51°2N 3°42E **15** C3
Gheorghe Gheorghiu-Dej = Oneşti
　Romania 46°17N 26°47E **17** E14
Ghīnah, Wādī al →
　Si. Arabia 30°27N 38°14E **44** D3
Ghizar → *Pakistan* 36°15N 73°43E **43** A5
Ghotaru *India* 27°20N 70°1E **42** F4
Ghotki *Pakistan* 28°5N 69°21E **42** E3
Ghowr □ *Afghan.* 34°0N 64°20E **40** C4
Ghughri *India* 22°39N 80°41E **43** H9
Ghugus *India* 19°58N 79°12E **40** K11
Ghulam Mohammad Barrage
　Pakistan 25°30N 68°20E **42** G3
Ghūrīān *Afghan.* 34°17N 61°25E **40** B2
Gia Dinh *Vietnam* 10°49N 106°42E **39** G6
Gia Lai = Plei Ku
　Vietnam 13°57N 108°0E **38** F7
Gia Nghia *Vietnam* 11°58N 107°42E **39** G6
Gia Ngoc *Vietnam* 14°50N 108°58E **38** E7

Gia Vuc *Vietnam* 14°42N 108°34E **38** E7
Giamama = Jamaame
　Somali Rep. 0°4N 42°44E **47** G3
Gianitsa *Greece* 40°46N 22°24E **23** D10
Giant Forest *U.S.A.* 36°36N 118°43W **78** J8
Giant Sequoia △
　U.S.A. 36°10N 118°35W **78** K8
Gianyar *Indonesia* 8°32S 115°20E **37** K18
Giarabub = Al Jaghbūb
　Libya 29°42N 24°38E **51** C10
Giarre *Italy* 37°43N 15°11E **22** F6
Gibara *Cuba* 21°9N 76°11W **88** B4
Gibbon *U.S.A.* 40°45N 98°51W **80** E4
Gibeon *Namibia* 25°9S 17°43E **56** D2
Gibraltar ☒ *Europe* 36°7N 5°22W **21** D3
Gibraltar, Str. of *Medit.* 35°55N 5°40W **21** E3
Gibraltar Range △
　Australia 29°31S 152°19E **63** D5
Gibson Desert *Australia* 24°0S 126°0E **60** D4
Gibsons *Canada* 49°24N 123°32W **70** D4
Gibsonville *U.S.A.* 39°46N 120°54W **78** F6
Giddings *U.S.A.* 30°11N 96°56W **84** F6
Giebnegáisi = Kebnekaise
　Sweden 67°53N 18°33E **8** C18
Giessen *Germany* 50°34N 8°41E **16** C5
Gīfan *Iran* 37°54N 57°28E **45** B8
Gift Lake *Canada* 55°53N 115°49W **70** B5
Gifu *Japan* 35°30N 136°45E **31** G8
Gifu □ *Japan* 35°40N 137°0E **31** G8
Giganta, Sa. de la
　Mexico 26°0N 111°39W **86** B2
Gíglio *Italy* 42°20N 10°52E **22** C4
Gijón *Spain* 43°32N 5°42W **21** A3
Gikongoro *Rwanda* 2°28S 29°34E **54** C2
Gil I. *Canada* 53°12N 129°15W **70** C3
Gila → *U.S.A.* 32°43N 114°33W **77** K6
Gila Bend *U.S.A.* 32°57N 112°43W **77** K7
Gila Bend Mts. *U.S.A.* 33°10N 113°0W **77** K7
Gila Cliff Dwellings △
　U.S.A. 33°12N 108°16W **77** K9
Gīlān □ *Iran* 37°0N 50°0E **45** B6
Gilbert → *Australia* 16°35S 141°15E **62** B3
Gilbert Is. *Kiribati* 1°0N 172°0E **58** A10
Gilbert River *Australia* 18°9S 142°52E **62** B3
Gilbert Seamounts
　Pac. Oc. 52°50N 150°10W **4** D18
Gilead *U.S.A.* 44°24N 70°59W **83** B14
Gilf el Kebîr, Hadabat el
　Egypt 23°50N 25°50E **51** D11
Gilford I. *Canada* 50°40N 126°30W **70** C3
Gilgandra *Australia* 31°43S 148°39E **63** E4
Gilgil *Kenya* 0°30S 36°20E **54** C4
Gilgit *India* 35°50N 74°15E **43** B6
Gilgit → *Pakistan* 35°44N 74°37E **43** B6
Gili □ *Mozam.* 16°39S 38°27E **55** F4
Gilimanuk *Indonesia* 8°10S 114°26E **37** J17
Gillam *Canada* 56°20N 94°40W **71** B10
Gillen, L. *Australia* 26°11S 124°38E **61** E3
Gilles, L. *Australia* 32°50S 136°45E **63** E2
Gillette *U.S.A.* 44°18N 105°30W **76** D11
Gilliat *Australia* 20°40S 141°28E **62** C3
Gillingham *U.K.* 51°23N 0°33E **13** F8
Gilmer *U.S.A.* 32°44N 94°57W **84** E7
Gilmore, L. *Australia* 32°29S 121°37E **61** F3
Gilmour *Canada* 44°48N 77°37W **82** B7
Gilroy *U.S.A.* 37°1N 121°34W **78** H5
Gimcheon *S. Korea* 36°11N 128°4E **35** F15
Gimhae *S. Korea* 35°14N 128°53E **35** G15
Gimhwa *S. Korea* 38°17N 127°28E **35** E14
Gimie, Mt. *St. Lucia* 13°54N 61°0W **89** f
Gimje *S. Korea* 35°48N 126°45E **35** G14
Gimli *Canada* 50°40N 97°0W **71** C9
Gin Gin *Australia* 25°0S 151°58E **63** D5
Gingin *Australia* 31°22S 115°54E **61** F2
Gingindlovu *S. Africa* 29°2S 31°30E **57** D5
Ginir *Ethiopia* 7°6N 40°40E **47** F3
Giofyros → *Greece* 35°20N 25°6E **25** D7
Giohar = Jawhar
　Somali Rep. 2°48N 45°30E **47** G4
Giona, Oros *Greece* 38°38N 22°14E **23** E10
Gir □ *India* 21°0N 71°0E **42** J4
Gir Hills *India* 21°0N 71°0E **42** J4
Girab *India* 26°2N 70°38E **42** F4
Girâfi, W. → *Egypt* 29°58N 34°39E **46** F3
Girard *St. Lucia* 13°59N 60°57W **89** f
Girard *Kans., U.S.A.* 37°31N 94°51W **80** G6
Girard *Ohio, U.S.A.* 41°9N 80°42W **82** E4
Girard *Pa., U.S.A.* 42°0N 80°19W **82** E4
Girdle Ness *U.K.* 57°9N 2°3W **11** D6
Giresun *Turkey* 40°55N 38°30E **19** F6
Girga *Egypt* 26°17N 31°55E **51** C12
Giri → *India* 30°28N 77°41E **42** D7
Giridih *India* 24°10N 86°21E **43** G12
Girftu *Kenya* 0°20N 40°29E **47** D5
Giriyondo *S. Africa* 23°15S 31°40E **57** C5
Girne = Kyrenia *Cyprus* 35°20N 33°20E **25** D12
Giron = Kiruna *Sweden* 67°52N 20°15E **8** C19
Girona *Spain* 41°58N 2°46E **21** B7
Gironde → *France* 45°32N 1°7W **20** D3
Girvan *U.K.* 55°14N 4°51W **11** F4
Gisborne *N.Z.* 38°39S 178°5E **59** C7
Gisenyi *Rwanda* 1°41S 29°15E **54** C2
Gislaved *Sweden* 57°19N 13°32E **9** H15
Gitarama *Rwanda* 2°4S 29°45E **54** C2
Gitega *Burundi* 3°26S 29°56E **54** C2
Githio *Greece* 36°46N 22°34E **23** F10
Giuba = Juba →
　Somali Rep. 1°30N 42°35E **47** G3
Giurgiu *Romania* 43°52N 25°57E **17** G13
Giza = El Gîza *Egypt* 30°0N 31°12E **51** C12
Giza Pyramids *Egypt* 29°58N 31°9E **51** C12
Gizab *Afghan.* 33°22N 66°17E **42** C1
Gizhiga *Russia* 62°3N 160°30E **29** C17
Gizhiginskaya Guba
　Russia 61°0N 158°0E **29** C16

Giżycko *Poland* 54°2N 21°48E **17** A11
Gjirokastër *Albania* 40°7N 20°10E **23** D9
Gjoa Haven *Canada* 68°38N 95°53W **68** D12
Gjøvik *Norway* 60°47N 10°43E **8** F14
Glace Bay *Canada* 46°11N 59°58W **73** C8
Glacier △ *Canada* 51°15N 117°30W **70** C5
Glacier Bay △ *U.S.A.* 48°42N 113°48W **76** B7
Glacier Bay *U.S.A.* 58°40N 136°0W **68** F4
Glacier Bay △ *U.S.A.* 58°45N 136°30W **70** B1
Glacier Peak *U.S.A.* 48°7N 121°7W **76** B3
Gladewater *U.S.A.* 32°33N 94°56W **84** E7
Gladstone *Queens.,*
　Australia 23°52S 151°16E **62** C5
Gladstone *S. Austral.,*
　Australia 33°15S 138°22E **63** E2
Gladstone *Canada* 50°13N 98°57W **71** C9
Gladstone *U.S.A.* 45°51N 87°1W **80** C2
Gladwin *U.S.A.* 43°59N 84°29W **81** D11
Glagah *Indonesia* 8°13S 114°18E **37** J17
Glåma = Glomma →
　Norway 59°12N 10°57E **9** G14
Gláma *Iceland* 65°48N 23°0W **8** D2
Glamis *U.S.A.* 32°55N 115°5W **79** N11
Glamorgan, Vale of □
　U.K. 51°28N 3°25W **13** F4
Glasco *Kans., U.S.A.* 39°22N 97°50W **80** F5
Glasco *N.Y., U.S.A.* 42°3N 73°57W **83** D11
Glasgow *U.K.* 55°51N 4°15W **11** F4
Glasgow *Ky., U.S.A.* 37°0N 85°55W **81** G11
Glasgow *Mont., U.S.A.* 48°12N 106°38W **76** B10
Glasgow, City of □ *U.K.* 55°51N 4°12W **11** F4
Glasgow Int. ✈ (GLA)
　U.K. 55°51N 4°21W **11** F4
Glaslyn *Canada* 53°22N 108°21W **71** C7
Glastonbury *U.K.* 51°9N 2°43W **13** F5
Glastonbury *U.S.A.* 41°43N 72°37W **83** E12
Glazov *Russia* 58°9N 52°40E **18** C9
Gleichen *Canada* 50°52N 113°3W **70** C6
Gleiwitz = Gliwice
　Poland 50°22N 18°41E **17** C10
Glen *U.S.A.* 44°7N 71°11W **83** B13
Glen Affric *U.K.* 57°17N 5°1W **11** D3
Glen Canyon *U.S.A.* 37°30N 110°40W **77** H8
Glen Canyon △ *U.S.A.* 37°15N 111°0W **77** H8
Glen Canyon Dam
　U.S.A. 36°57N 111°29W **77** H8
Glen Coe *U.K.* 56°40N 5°0W **11** E3
Glen Cove *U.S.A.* 40°51N 73°38W **83** F11
Glen Garry *U.K.* 57°3N 5°7W **11** D3
Glen Innes *Australia* 29°44S 151°44E **63** D5
Glen Lyon *U.S.A.* 41°10N 76°5W **83** E8
Glen Mor *U.K.* 57°9N 4°37W **11** D4
Glen More *U.K.* 57°8N 3°40W **11** D5
Glen Moriston *U.K.* 57°11N 4°52W **11** D4
Glen Robertson *Canada* 45°22N 74°30W **83** A10
Glen Spean *U.K.* 56°53N 4°40W **11** E4
Glen Ullin *U.S.A.* 46°49N 101°50W **80** B3
Glenarriff △ *Ireland* 55°2N 6°10W **10** A5
Glenbeigh *Ireland* 52°3N 9°58W **10** D2
Glencoe *Canada* 42°45N 81°43W **82** D3
Glencoe *S. Africa* 28°11S 30°11E **57** D5
Glencoe *U.S.A.* 44°46N 94°9W **80** C6
Glencolumbkille *Ireland* 54°43N 8°42W **10** B3
Glendale *Ariz., U.S.A.* 33°32N 112°11W **77** K7
Glendale *Calif., U.S.A.* 34°9N 118°15W **79** L8
Glendale *Zimbabwe* 17°22S 31°5E **55** F3
Glendive *U.S.A.* 47°7N 104°43W **76** B11
Glendo *U.S.A.* 42°30N 105°2W **76** E11
Glenelg → *Australia* 38°4S 140°59E **63** F3
Glenfield *U.S.A.* 43°43N 75°24W **83** C9
Glengad Hd. *Ireland* 55°20N 7°10W **10** A4
Glengarriff *Ireland* 51°45N 9°34W **10** E2
Glenmont *U.S.A.* 40°31N 82°6W **82** F2
Glenmorgan *Australia* 27°14S 149°42E **63** D4
Glenn *U.S.A.* 39°31N 122°1W **78** F4
Glennallen *U.S.A.* 62°7N 145°33W **68** E2
Glennamaddy *Ireland* 53°37N 8°33W **10** C3
Glenns Ferry *U.S.A.* 42°57N 115°18W **76** E6
Glenora *Canada* 44°2N 77°3W **82** B7
Glenorchy *Australia* 42°49S 147°18E **63** G4
Glenore *Australia* 17°50S 141°12E **62** B3
Glenreagh *Australia* 30°2S 153°1E **63** E5
Glenrock *U.S.A.* 42°52N 105°52W **76** E11
Glenrothes *U.K.* 56°12N 3°10W **11** E5
Glens Falls *U.S.A.* 43°19N 73°39W **83** C11
Glenside *U.S.A.* 40°6N 75°9W **83** F9
Glenties *Ireland* 54°49N 8°16W **10** B3
Glenveagh △ *Ireland* 55°3N 8°1W **10** A3
Glenville *U.S.A.* 38°56N 80°50W **81** F13
Glenwood *Canada* 49°0N 54°58W **73** C9
Glenwood *Ark., U.S.A.* 34°20N 93°33W **84** D8
Glenwood *Iowa, U.S.A.* 41°3N 95°45W **80** E6
Glenwood *Minn., U.S.A.* 45°39N 95°23W **80** C6
Glenwood *Wash., U.S.A.* 46°1N 121°17W **78** D5
Glenwood Springs
　U.S.A. 39°33N 107°19W **76** G10
Glettinganes *Iceland* 65°30N 13°37W **8** D7
Glin *Ireland* 52°34N 9°17W **10** D2
Gliwice *Poland* 50°22N 18°41E **17** C10
Globe *U.S.A.* 33°24N 110°47W **77** K8
Głogów *Poland* 51°37N 16°5E **16** C9
Glomma → *Norway* 59°12N 10°57E **9** G14
Glorieuses, Îs. *Ind. Oc.* 11°30S 47°20E **55** a
Glossop *U.K.* 53°27N 1°56W **12** D6
Gloucester *Australia* 32°0S 151°59E **63** E5
Gloucester *U.K.* 51°53N 2°15W **13** F5
Gloucester *U.S.A.* 42°37N 70°40W **83** D14
Gloucester I. *Australia* 20°0S 148°30E **62** b
Gloucester Island △
　Australia 20°2S 148°30E **62** b
Gloucester Point
　U.S.A. 37°15N 76°30W **81** G15
Gloucestershire □ *U.K.* 51°46N 2°15W **13** F5
Gloversville *U.S.A.* 43°3N 74°21W **83** C10
Glovertown *Canada* 48°40N 54°3W **73** C9
Glusk *Belarus* 52°53N 28°41E **17** B15
Gmünd *Austria* 48°45N 15°0E **16** D8
Gmunden *Austria* 47°55N 13°48E **16** E7
Gniezno *Poland* 52°30N 17°35E **17** B9

Gnowangerup Australia 33°58S 117°59E 61 F2
Go Cong Vietnam 10°22N 106°40E 39 G6
Gō-no-ura Japan 33°44N 129°40E 31 H4
Goa India 15°33N 73°59E 40 M8
Goa □ India 15°33N 73°59E 40 M8
Goalen Hd. Australia 36°33S 156°40E 63 F5
Goalpara India 26°10N 90°40E 41 F17
Goaltor India 22°43N 87°10E 43 H12
Goalundo Ghat Bangla. 23°50N 89°47E 43 H13
Goat Fell U.K. 55°38N 5°11W 11 F3
Goba Ethiopia 7°1N 39°59E 47 F2
Goba Mozam. 26°15S 32°13E 57 D5
Gobabis Namibia 22°30S 19°0E 56 C2
Gobi Asia 44°0N 110°0E 34 C6
Gobō Japan 33°53N 135°10E 31 H7
Gochas Namibia 24°59S 18°55E 56 C2
Godalming U.K. 51°11N 0°36W 13 F7
Godavari → India 16°25N 82°18E 41 L13
Godavari Pt. India 17°0N 82°20E 41 L13
Godbout Canada 49°20N 67°38W 73 C6
Godda India 24°50N 87°13E 43 G12
Goderich Canada 43°45N 81°41W 82 C3
Godfrey Ra. Australia 24°0S 117°0E 61 D2
Godhavn = Qeqertarsuaq
  Greenland 69°15N 53°38W 4 C5
Godhra India 22°49N 73°40E 42 H5
Godoy Cruz Argentina 32°56S 68°52W 94 C2
Gods → Canada 56°22N 92°51W 72 A1
Gods L. Canada 54°40N 94°15W 72 A1
Gods River Canada 54°50N 94°5W 71 C10
Godthåb = Nuuk
  Greenland 64°10N 51°35W 67 C14
Goeie Hoop, Kaap die = Good
  Hope, C. of S. Africa 34°24S 18°30E 56 E2
Goéland, L. au Canada 49°50N 76°48W 72 C4
Goélands, L. aux Canada 55°27N 64°17W 73 A7
Goeree Neths. 51°50N 4°0E 15 C3
Goes Neths. 51°30N 3°55E 15 C3
Goffstown U.S.A. 43°1N 71°36W 83 C13
Gogama Canada 47°35N 81°43W 72 C3
Gogebic, L. U.S.A. 46°30N 89°35W 80 B9
Gogra = Ghaghara →
  India 25°45N 84°40E 43 G11
Gogriâl Sudan 8°30N 28°8E 51 G11
Gohana India 29°8N 76°42E 42 E7
Goharganj India 23°1N 77°41E 42 H7
Goi → India 22°4N 74°46E 42 H6
Goiânia Brazil 16°43S 49°20W 93 G9
Goiás Brazil 15°55S 50°10W 93 G8
Goiás □ Brazil 12°10S 48°0W 93 F9
Goio-Erê Brazil 24°12S 53°1W 95 A5
Gojō Japan 34°21N 135°42E 31 G7
Gojra Pakistan 31°10N 72°40E 42 D5
Gökçeada Turkey 40°10N 25°50E 23 D11
Gökova Körfezi Turkey 36°55N 27°50E 23 F12
Göksu → Turkey 36°19N 34°5E 44 B2
Gokteik Burma 22°26N 97°0E 41 H20
Gokurt Pakistan 29°40N 67°26E 42 E2
Gokwe Zimbabwe 18°7S 28°58E 57 B4
Gola India 28°3N 80°32E 43 E9
Golakganj India 26°8N 89°52E 43 F13
Golan Heights = Hagolan
  Syria 33°0N 35°45E 46 C4
Goläshkerd Iran 27°59N 57°16E 45 E8
Golchikha Russia 71°45N 83°30E 4 B12
Golconda U.S.A. 40°58N 117°30W 76 F5
Gold U.S.A. 41°52N 77°50W 82 E7
Gold Beach U.S.A. 42°25N 124°25W 76 E1
Gold Coast W. Afr. 4°0N 1°40W 50 H5
Gold Hill U.S.A. 42°26N 123°3W 76 E2
Gold River Canada 49°46N 126°3W 70 D3
Golden Canada 51°20N 116°59W 70 C5
Golden B. N.Z. 40°40S 172°50E 59 D4
Golden Gate U.S.A. 37°48N 122°29W 77 H2
Golden Gate Highlands △
  S. Africa 28°40S 28°40E 57 D4
Golden Hinde Canada 49°40N 125°44W 70 D3
Golden Lake Canada 45°34N 77°21W 82 A7
Golden Spike △ U.S.A. 41°37N 112°33W 76 F7
Golden Vale Ireland 52°33N 8°17W 10 D3
Goldendale U.S.A. 45°49N 120°50W 76 D3
Goldfield U.S.A. 37°42N 117°14W 77 H5
Goldsand L. Canada 57°2N 101°8W 71 B8
Goldsboro U.S.A. 35°23N 77°59W 85 D16
Goldsmith U.S.A. 31°59N 102°37W 84 F3
Goldthwaite U.S.A. 31°27N 98°34W 84 F5
Goleniów Poland 53°35N 14°50E 16 B8
Golestān □ Iran 37°20N 55°25E 45 B7
Golestānak Iran 30°36N 54°14E 45 D7
Goleta U.S.A. 34°27N 119°50W 79 L7
Golfito Costa Rica 8°41N 83°5W 88 E3
Golfo Aranci Italy 40°59N 9°38E 22 D3
Goliad U.S.A. 28°40N 97°23W 84 G6
Golpāyegān Iran 33°27N 50°18E 45 C6
Golra Pakistan 33°37N 72°56E 42 C5
Golspie U.K. 57°58N 3°59W 11 D5
Goma
  Dem. Rep. of the Congo 1°37S 29°10E 54 C2
Gomal Pass Pakistan 31°56N 69°20E 42 D3
Gomati → India 25°32N 83°11E 43 G10
Gombari
  Dem. Rep. of the Congo 2°45N 29°3E 54 B2
Gombe Nigeria 10°19N 11°2E 51 F8
Gombe → Tanzania 4°38S 31°40E 54 C3
Gombe Stream △
  Tanzania 4°42S 29°37E 54 C2
Gomel = Homyel Belarus 52°28N 31°0E 17 B16
Gomera Canary Is. 28°7N 17°14W 24 F2
Gómez Palacio Mexico 25°34N 103°30W 86 B4
Gomīshān Iran 37°4N 54°6E 45 B7
Gomogomo Indonesia 6°39S 134°43E 37 F8
Gomoh India 23°52N 86°10E 43 H12
Gompa = Ganta Liberia 7°15N 8°59W 50 G4
Gonābād Iran 34°15N 58°45E 45 C8
Gonaïves Haiti 19°20N 72°42W 89 C5
Gonarezhou △ Zimbabwe 22°32S 31°55E 55 G3
Gonâve, G. de la Haiti 19°29N 72°42W 89 C5
Gonâve, Île de la Haiti 18°51N 73°3W 89 C5
Gonbad-e Kāvūs Iran 37°20N 55°25E 45 B7

Gonda India 27°9N 81°58E 43 F9
Gondal India 21°58N 70°52E 42 J4
Gonder Ethiopia 12°39N 37°30E 47 E2
Gondia India 21°23N 80°10E 40 J12
Gondola Mozam. 19°10S 33°37E 55 F3
Gönen Turkey 40°6N 27°39E 23 D12
Gongbei China 22°12N 113°32E 33 G10
Gonghe China 36°18N 100°32E 32 C5
Gongju S. Korea 36°27N 127°7E 35 F14
Gongming China 22°47N 113°53E 33 F10
Gongolgon Australia 30°21S 146°54E 63 E4
Gongzhuling China 43°30N 124°40E 35 C13
Goniri Nigeria 11°30N 12°15E 51 F8
Gonzales Calif., U.S.A. 36°30N 121°26W 78 J5
Gonzales Tex., U.S.A. 29°30N 97°27W 84 G6
González Mexico 22°48N 98°25W 87 C5
Good Hope, C. of S. Africa 34°24S 18°30E 56 E2
Good Hope Lake
  Canada 59°16N 129°18W 70 B3
Gooderham Canada 44°54N 78°21W 82 B6
Goodhouse S. Africa 28°57S 18°13E 56 D2
Gooding U.S.A. 42°56N 114°43W 76 E6
Goodland U.S.A. 39°21N 101°43W 80 F3
Goodlands Mauritius 20°2S 57°39E 53 d
Goodlow Canada 56°20N 120°8W 70 B4
Goodooga Australia 29°3S 147°28E 63 D4
Goodsprings U.S.A. 35°49N 115°27W 79 K11
Goole U.K. 53°42N 0°53W 12 D7
Goolgowi Australia 33°58S 145°41E 63 E4
Goomalling Australia 31°15S 116°49E 61 F2
Goomeri Australia 26°12S 152°6E 63 D5
Goonda Mozam. 19°48S 33°57E 55 F3
Goondiwindi Australia 28°30S 150°21E 63 D5
Goongarrie, L. Australia 30°3S 121°9E 61 F3
Goongarrie △ Australia 30°2S 121°30E 61 F3
Goonyella Australia 21°47S 147°58E 62 C4
Goose → Canada 53°20N 60°35W 73 B7
Goose Creek U.S.A. 32°59N 80°2W 85 E14
Goose L. U.S.A. 41°56N 120°26W 76 F3
Gop India 22°5N 69°50E 42 H3
Gopalganj India 26°28N 84°30E 43 F11
Göppingen Germany 48°42N 9°39E 16 D5
Gorakhpur India 26°47N 83°23E 43 F10
Goražde Bos.-H. 43°38N 18°58E 23 C8
Gorda, Pta. Canary Is. 28°45N 18°0W 24 F2
Gorda, Pta. Nic. 14°20N 83°10W 88 D3
Gordan B. Australia 11°35S 130°10E 60 B5
Gordon U.S.A. 42°48N 102°12W 80 D2
Gordon → Australia 42°27S 145°30E 63 G4
Gordon Bay Canada 45°12N 79°47W 82 A5
Gordon L. Alta., Canada 56°30N 110°25W 71 B6
Gordon L. N.W.T.,
  Canada 63°5N 113°11W 70 A6
Gordonvale Australia 17°5S 145°50E 62 B4
Goré Chad 7°59N 16°31E 51 G9
Gore Ethiopia 8°12N 35°32E 47 F2
Gore N.Z. 46°5S 168°58E 59 G2
Gore Bay Canada 45°57N 82°28W 72 C3
Gorey Ireland 52°41N 6°18W 10 D5
Gorg Iran 29°29N 59°43E 45 D8
Gorgān Iran 36°55N 54°30E 45 B7
Gorgona, I. Colombia 3°0N 78°10W 92 C3
Gorham U.S.A. 44°23N 71°10W 83 B13
Goriganga → India 29°45N 80°23E 43 E9
Gorinchem Neths. 51°50N 4°59E 15 C4
Goris Armenia 39°31N 46°22E 19 G8
Gorizia Italy 45°56N 13°37E 22 B5
Gorkiy = Nizhniy Novgorod
  Russia 56°20N 44°0E 18 C7
Gorkovskoye Vdkhr.
  Russia 57°2N 43°4E 18 C7
Gorleston U.K. 52°35N 1°44E 13 E9
Görlitz Germany 51°9N 14°58E 16 C8
Gorlovka = Horlivka
  Ukraine 48°19N 38°5E 19 E6
Gorman U.S.A. 34°47N 118°51W 79 L8
Gorna Dzhumayo = Blagoevgrad
  Bulgaria 42°2N 23°5E 23 C10
Gorna Oryakhovitsa
  Bulgaria 43°7N 25°40E 23 C11
Gorno-Altay □ Russia 51°0N 86°0E 28 D9
Gorno-Altaysk Russia 51°50N 86°5E 28 D9
Gornozavodsk Russia 46°33N 141°50E 29 E15
Gornyatski Russia 67°32N 64°3E 18 A11
Gornyy Russia 44°57N 133°59E 30 B6
Gorodenka = Horodenka
  Ukraine 48°41N 25°29E 17 D13
Gorodok = Horodok
  Ukraine 49°46N 23°32E 17 D12
Gorokhov = Horokhiv
  Ukraine 50°30N 24°45E 17 C13
Goromonzi Zimbabwe 17°52S 31°22E 55 F3
Gorong, Kepulauan
  Indonesia 3°59S 131°25E 37 E8
Gorongosa △ Mozam. 18°50S 34°29E 57 B5
Gorongose → Mozam. 20°30S 34°40E 57 C5
Gorongoza Mozam. 18°44S 34°2E 55 F3
Gorongoza, Sa. da Mozam. 18°27S 34°2E 55 F3
Gorontalo Indonesia 0°35N 123°5E 37 D6
Gorontalo □ Indonesia 0°50N 122°20E 37 D6
Gort Ireland 53°3N 8°49W 10 C3
Gortis Greece 35°4N 24°58E 25 D6
Goryeong S. Korea 35°44N 128°15E 35 G15
Gorzów Wielkopolski
  Poland 52°43N 15°15E 16 B8
Gosford Australia 33°23S 151°18E 63 E5
Goshen Calif., U.S.A. 36°21N 119°25W 78 J7
Goshen Ind., U.S.A. 41°35N 85°50W 81 E11
Goshen N.Y., U.S.A. 41°24N 74°20W 83 E10
Goshogawara Japan 40°48N 140°27E 30 D10
Goslar Germany 51°54N 10°25E 16 C6
Gospič Croatia 44°35N 15°23E 16 F8
Gosport U.K. 50°48N 1°9W 13 G6
Gosse → Australia 19°32S 134°37E 62 B1
Göta älv → Sweden 57°42N 11°54E 9 H14
Göta kanal Sweden 58°30N 15°58E 9 G16
Götaland Sweden 57°30N 14°30E 9 G16
Göteborg Sweden 57°43N 11°59E 9 H14
Gotha Germany 50°56N 10°42E 16 C6

Gothenburg = Göteborg
  Sweden 57°43N 11°59E 9 H14
Gothenburg U.S.A. 40°56N 100°10W 80 E3
Gotland Sweden 57°30N 18°33E 9 H18
Gotō-Rettō Japan 32°55N 129°5E 31 H4
Gotska Sandön Sweden 58°24N 19°15E 9 G18
Gōtsu Japan 35°0N 132°14E 31 G6
Göttingen Germany 51°31N 9°55E 16 C5
Gottwaldov = Zlín
  Czech Rep. 49°14N 17°40E 17 D9
Goubangzi China 41°20N 121°52E 35 D11
Gouda Neths. 52°1N 4°42E 15 B4
Goudouras, Akra Greece 34°59N 26°6E 25 E8
Gouin, Rés. Canada 48°35N 74°40W 72 C5
Goulburn Australia 34°44S 149°44E 63 E4
Goulburn Is. Australia 11°40S 133°20E 62 A1
Goulimine Morocco 28°56N 10°0W 50 C3
Goundam Mali 16°27N 3°40W 50 E5
Gourits → S. Africa 34°21S 21°52E 56 E3
Gournes Greece 35°19N 25°16E 25 D7
Gourock U.K. 55°57N 4°49W 11 F4
Gouverneur U.S.A. 44°20N 75°28W 83 B9
Gouvia Greece 39°39N 19°50E 25 A3
Gove Peninsula
  Australia 12°17S 136°49E 62 A2
Governador Valadares
  Brazil 18°15S 41°57W 93 G10
Governor's Harbour
  Bahamas 25°10N 76°14W 88 A4
Govindgarh India 24°23N 81°18E 43 G9
Gowan Ra. Australia 25°0S 145°0E 62 C4
Gowanda U.S.A. 42°28N 78°56W 82 D6
Gower U.K. 51°35N 4°10W 13 F3
Gowna, L. Ireland 53°51N 7°34W 10 C4
Goya Argentina 29°10S 59°10W 94 B4
Goyang S. Korea 37°39N 126°50E 33 C7
Goyder Lagoon Australia 27°3S 138°58E 63 D2
Goyllarisquizga Peru 10°31S 76°24W 92 F3
Goz Beïda Chad 12°10N 21°20E 51 F10
Gozo Malta 36°3N 14°15E 25 C1
Graaff-Reinet S. Africa 32°13S 24°32E 56 E3
Gračac Croatia 44°18N 15°57E 16 F8
Gracias a Dios, C.
  Honduras 15°0N 83°10W 88 D3
Graciosa Azores 39°4N 28°0W 50 a
Graciosa, I. Canary Is. 29°15N 13°32W 24 E6
Grado Spain 43°23N 6°4W 21 A2
Grady U.S.A. 34°49N 103°19W 77 J12
Grafham Water U.K. 52°19N 0°18W 13 E7
Grafton Australia 29°38S 152°58E 63 D5
Grafton N. Dak., U.S.A. 48°25N 97°25W 80 A5
Grafton W. Va., U.S.A. 39°21N 80°2W 81 F13
Graham Canada 49°20N 90°30W 72 C1
Graham U.S.A. 33°6N 98°35W 84 E5
Graham, Mt. U.S.A. 32°42N 109°52W 77 K9
Graham Bell, Ostrov = Greem-
  Bell, Ostrov Russia 81°0N 62°0E 28 A7
Graham I. B.C., Canada 53°40N 132°30W 70 C2
Graham I. Nunavut,
  Canada 77°25N 90°30W 69 B13
Graham Land Antarctica 65°0S 64°0W 5 C17
Grahamstown S. Africa 33°19S 26°31E 56 E4
Grahamsville U.S.A. 41°51N 74°33W 83 E10
Grain Coast W. Afr. 4°20N 10°0W 50 H3
Grajagan Indonesia 8°35S 114°13E 37 K17
Grajagan, Teluk
  Indonesia 8°40S 114°18E 37 K17
Grajaú Brazil 5°50S 46°4W 93 E9
Grajaú → Brazil 3°41S 44°48W 93 D10
Grampian U.S.A. 40°58N 78°37W 82 F6
Grampian Highlands = Grampian
  Mts. U.K. 56°50N 4°0W 11 E5
Grampian Mts. U.K. 56°50N 4°0W 11 E5
Grampians, The
  Australia 37°15S 142°20E 63 F3
Gran Canaria Canary Is. 27°55N 15°35W 24 G4
Gran Chaco S. Amer. 25°0S 61°0W 94 B3
Gran Desierto del Pinacate △
  Mexico 31°51N 113°32W 86 A2
Gran Paradiso Italy 45°33N 7°17E 20 D7
Gran Sasso d'Itália Italy 42°27N 13°42E 22 C5
Granada Nic. 11°58N 86°0W 88 D2
Granada Spain 37°10N 3°35W 21 D4
Granada U.S.A. 38°4N 102°19W 76 G12
Granadilla de Abona
  Canary Is. 28°7N 16°33W 24 F3
Granard Ireland 53°47N 7°30W 10 C4
Granbury U.S.A. 32°27N 97°47W 84 E6
Granby Canada 45°25N 72°45W 83 A12
Granby U.S.A. 40°5N 105°56W 76 F11
Grand → Canada 42°51N 79°34W 82 D5
Grand → Mo., U.S.A. 39°23N 93°7W 80 F7
Grand → S. Dak.,
  U.S.A. 45°40N 100°45W 80 C3
Grand Bahama I.
  Bahamas 26°40N 78°30W 88 A4
Grand Baie Mauritius 20°0S 57°35E 53 d
Grand Bank Canada 47°6N 55°48W 73 C8
Grand Bassam Ivory C. 5°10N 3°49W 50 G5
Grand Bend Canada 43°18N 81°45W 82 C3
Grand-Bourg Guadeloupe 15°53N 61°19W 88 b
Grand Canal = Da Yunhe →
  China 39°10N 117°10E 35 E9
Grand Canyon U.S.A. 36°3N 112°9W 77 H7
Grand Canyon △
  U.S.A. 36°15N 112°30W 77 H7
Grand Canyon-Parashant △
  U.S.A. 36°30N 113°45W 77 H7
Grand Cayman
  Cayman Is. 19°20N 81°20W 88 C3
Grand Coulee U.S.A. 47°57N 119°0W 76 C4
Grand Coulee Dam
  U.S.A. 47°57N 118°59W 76 C4
Grand Erg de Bilma Niger 18°30N 14°0E 51 E8
Grand Falls Canada 47°3N 67°44W 73 C6
Grand Falls-Windsor
  Canada 48°56N 55°40W 73 C8
Grand Forks Canada 49°0N 118°30W 70 D5
Grand Forks U.S.A. 47°55N 97°3W 80 B5

Grand Gorge U.S.A. 42°21N 74°29W 83 D10
Grand Haven U.S.A. 43°4N 86°13W 80 D10
Grand I. Mich., U.S.A. 46°31N 86°40W 80 B10
Grand I. N.Y., U.S.A. 43°0N 78°58W 82 D6
Grand Island U.S.A. 40°55N 98°21W 80 E4
Grand Isle La., U.S.A. 29°14N 90°0W 85 G9
Grand Isle Vt., U.S.A. 44°43N 73°18W 83 B11
Grand Junction U.S.A. 39°4N 108°33W 76 G9
Grand L. N.B., Canada 45°57N 66°7W 73 C6
Grand L. Nfld. & L.,
  Canada 49°0N 57°30W 73 C8
Grand L. Nfld. & L.,
  Canada 53°40N 60°30W 73 B7
Grand Lake U.S.A. 40°15N 105°49W 76 F11
Grand Manan I. Canada 44°45N 66°52W 73 D6
Grand Marais Mich.,
  U.S.A. 46°40N 85°59W 81 B11
Grand Marais Minn.,
  U.S.A. 47°45N 90°25W 72 C1
Grand-Mère Canada 46°36N 72°40W 72 C5
Grand Portage U.S.A. 47°58N 89°41W 80 B9
Grand Prairie U.S.A. 32°44N 96°59W 84 E6
Grand Rapids Canada 53°12N 99°19W 71 C9
Grand Rapids Mich.,
  U.S.A. 42°58N 85°40W 81 D11
Grand Rapids Minn.,
  U.S.A. 47°14N 93°31W 80 B7
Grand St-Bernard, Col du
  Europe 45°50N 7°10E 20 D7
Grand Staircase-Escalante △
  U.S.A. 37°25N 111°33W 77 H8
Grand Teton U.S.A. 43°54N 110°50W 76 E8
Grand Teton △ U.S.A. 43°50N 110°50W 76 E8
Grand Union Canal U.K. 52°7N 0°53W 13 E7
Grande → Jujuy,
  Argentina 24°20S 65°2W 94 A2
Grande → Mendoza,
  Argentina 36°52S 69°45W 94 D2
Grande → Bolivia 15°51S 64°39W 92 G6
Grande → Bahia, Brazil 11°30S 44°30W 93 F10
Grande → Minas Gerais,
  Brazil 20°6S 51°4W 93 H8
Grande, B. Argentina 50°30S 68°20W 96 G3
Grande, Rio → N. Amer. 25°58N 97°9W 84 J6
Grande Anse Seychelles 4°18S 55°45E 53 b
Grande Baleine →
  Canada 55°16N 77°47W 72 A4
Grande Cache Canada 53°53N 119°8W 70 C5
Grande Comore
  Comoros 11°35S 43°20E 53 a
Grande-Entrée Canada 47°30N 61°40W 73 C7
Grande Prairie Canada 55°10N 118°50W 70 B5
Grande-Rivière Canada 48°26N 64°30W 73 C7
Grande-Terre Guadeloupe 16°20N 61°25W 88 b
Grande-Vallée Canada 49°14N 65°8W 73 C6
Grande Vigie, Pte. de la
  Guadeloupe 16°32N 61°27W 88 b
Grandfalls U.S.A. 31°20N 102°51W 84 F3
Grands-Jardins △
  Canada 47°41N 70°51W 73 C5
Grandview Canada 51°10N 100°42W 71 C8
Grandview U.S.A. 46°15N 119°54W 76 C4
Graneros Chile 34°5S 70°45W 94 C1
Granger U.S.A. 41°35N 109°58W 76 F9
Grangeville U.S.A. 45°56N 116°7W 76 D5
Granisle Canada 54°53N 126°13W 70 C3
Granite City U.S.A. 38°42N 90°8W 80 F8
Granite Falls U.S.A. 44°49N 95°33W 80 C6
Granite L. Canada 48°8N 57°5W 73 C8
Granite Mt. U.S.A. 33°5N 116°28W 79 M10
Granite Pk. U.S.A. 45°10N 109°48W 76 D9
Graniteville U.S.A. 44°8N 72°29W 83 B12
Granity N.Z. 41°39S 171°51E 59 D3
Granja Brazil 3°7S 40°50W 93 D10
Granollers Spain 41°39N 2°18E 21 B7
Grant U.S.A. 40°50N 101°43W 80 E3
Grant, Mt. U.S.A. 38°34N 118°48W 76 G4
Grant City U.S.A. 40°29N 94°25W 80 E6
Grant I. Australia 11°10S 132°52E 60 B5
Grant Range U.S.A. 38°30N 115°25W 76 G6
Grantham U.K. 52°55N 0°38W 12 E7
Grantown-on-Spey U.K. 57°19N 3°18W 11 D5
Grants U.S.A. 35°9N 107°52W 77 J10
Grants Pass U.S.A. 42°26N 123°19W 76 E2
Grantsville U.S.A. 40°36N 112°28W 76 F7
Granville France 48°50N 1°35W 20 B3
Granville N. Dak.,
  U.S.A. 48°16N 100°47W 80 A3
Granville N.Y., U.S.A. 43°24N 73°16W 83 C11
Granville Ohio, U.S.A. 40°4N 82°31W 82 F2
Granville L. Canada 56°18N 100°30W 71 B8
Graskop S. Africa 24°56S 30°49E 57 C5
Grass → Canada 56°3N 96°33W 71 B9
Grass Range U.S.A. 47°2N 108°48W 76 C9
Grass River △ Canada 54°40N 101°50W 71 C8
Grass Valley Calif.,
  U.S.A. 39°13N 121°4W 78 F6
Grass Valley Oreg.,
  U.S.A. 45°22N 120°47W 76 D3
Grasse France 43°38N 6°56E 20 E7
Grassflat U.S.A. 41°0N 78°6W 82 E6
Grasslands △ Canada 49°11N 107°38W 71 D7
Grassy Australia 40°3S 144°5E 63 G3
Graulhet France 43°45N 1°59E 20 E4
's-Gravenhage Neths. 52°7N 4°17E 15 B4
Gravenhurst Canada 44°52N 79°20W 82 B5
Gravesend Australia 29°35S 150°20E 63 D5
Gravesend U.K. 51°26N 0°22E 13 F8
Gravois, Pointe-à- Haiti 18°15N 73°56W 89 C5
Grayling U.S.A. 44°40N 84°43W 81 C11
Grays U.K. 51°28N 0°21E 13 F8
Grays Harbor U.S.A. 46°59N 124°1W 76 C1
Grays L. U.S.A. 43°4N 111°26W 76 E8
Grays River U.S.A. 46°21N 123°37W 78 D3
Graz Austria 47°4N 15°27E 16 E8
Greasy L. Canada 62°55N 122°12W 70 A4

Great Abaco I. = Abaco I.
  Bahamas 26°25N 77°10W 88 A4
Great Artesian Basin
  Australia 23°0S 144°0E 62 C3
Great Australian Bight
  Australia 33°30S 130°0E 61 F5
Great Bahama Bank
  Bahamas 23°15N 78°0W 88 B4
Great Barrier I. N.Z. 36°11S 175°25E 59 B5
Great Barrier Reef
  Australia 18°0S 146°50E 62 B4
Great Barrier Reef △
  Australia 20°0S 150°0E 62 B4
Great Barrington
  U.S.A. 42°12N 73°22W 83 D11
Great Basalt Wall △
  Australia 19°52S 145°43E 62 B4
Great Basin U.S.A. 40°0N 117°0W 76 G5
Great Basin △ U.S.A. 38°56N 114°15W 76 G6
Great Bear → Canada 65°0N 126°0W 68 C7
Great Bear L. Canada 65°30N 120°0W 68 C8
Great Belt = Store Bælt
  Denmark 55°20N 11°0E 9 J14
Great Bend Kans., U.S.A. 38°22N 98°46W 80 F4
Great Bend Pa., U.S.A. 41°58N 75°45W 83 E9
Great Blasket I. Ireland 52°6N 10°32W 10 D1
Great Britain Europe 54°0N 2°15W 6 E5
Great Camanoe
  Br. Virgin Is. 18°30N 64°35W 89 e
Great Coco I. = Koko Kyunzu
  Burma 14°7N 93°22E 41 M18
Great Codroy Canada 47°51N 59°16W 73 C8
Great Divide, The = Great
  Dividing Ra. Australia 23°0S 146°0E 62 C4
Great Divide Basin
  U.S.A. 42°0N 108°0W 76 E9
Great Dividing Ra.
  Australia 23°0S 146°0E 62 C4
Great Driffield = Driffield
  U.K. 54°0N 0°26W 12 C7
Great Exuma I. Bahamas 23°30N 75°50W 88 B4
Great Falls U.S.A. 47°30N 111°17W 76 C8
Great Fish = Groot-Vis →
  S. Africa 33°28S 27°5E 56 E4
Great Guana Cay
  Bahamas 24°0N 76°20W 88 B4
Great Himalayan △
  India 31°30N 77°30E 42 D7
Great Inagua I. Bahamas 21°0N 73°20W 89 B5
Great Indian Desert = Thar Desert
  India 28°0N 72°0E 42 F5
Great Karoo S. Africa 31°55S 21°0E 56 E3
Great Khingan Mts. = Da
  Hinggan Ling China 48°0N 121°0E 33 B7
Great Lake Australia 41°50S 146°40E 63 G4
Great Lakes N. Amer. 46°0N 84°0W 66 E11
Great Limpopo Transfrontier △
  Africa 23°0S 31°45E 57 C5
Great Malvern U.K. 52°7N 2°18W 13 E5
Great Miami → U.S.A. 39°7N 84°49W 81 F11
Great Ormes Head U.K. 53°20N 3°52W 12 D4
Great Ouse → U.K. 52°48N 0°21E 12 E8
Great Palm I. Australia 18°45S 146°40E 62 B4
Great Pedro Bluff Jamaica 17°51N 77°44W 88 a
Great Pee Dee →
  U.S.A. 33°21N 79°10W 85 E15
Great Plains N. Amer. 47°0N 105°0W 66 E9
Great Ruaha → Tanzania 7°56S 37°52E 54 D4
Great Sacandaga L.
  U.S.A. 43°6N 74°16W 83 C10
Great Saint Bernard Pass = Grand
  St-Bernard, Col du
  Europe 45°50N 7°10E 20 D7
Great Salt Desert = Kavīr, Dasht-e
  Iran 34°30N 55°0E 45 C7
Great Salt Desert = Lūt, Dasht-e
  Iran 31°30N 58°0E 45 D8
Great Salt L. U.S.A. 41°15N 112°40W 76 F7
Great Salt Lake Desert
  U.S.A. 40°50N 113°30W 76 F7
Great Salt Plains L.
  U.S.A. 36°45N 98°8W 84 C5
Great Sand Dunes △
  U.S.A. 37°48N 105°45W 77 H11
Great Sandy △ Australia 26°13S 153°2E 63 D5
Great Sandy Desert
  Australia 21°0S 124°0E 60 D3
Great Sangi = Sangihe, Pulau
  Indonesia 3°35N 125°30E 37 D7
Great Sea Reef Fiji 16°15S 179°0E 59 a
Great Sitkin I. U.S.A. 52°3N 176°6W 74 E4
Great Skellig Ireland 51°47N 10°33W 10 E1
Great Slave L. Canada 61°23N 115°38W 70 A5
Great Smoky Mts. △
  U.S.A. 35°40N 83°40W 85 D13
Great Stour = Stour →
  U.K. 51°18N 1°22E 13 F9
Great Victoria Desert
  Australia 29°30S 126°30E 61 E4
Great Wall Antarctica 62°30S 58°0W 5 C18
Great Wall China 38°30N 109°30E 34 E5
Great Whernside U.K. 54°10N 1°58W 12 C6
Great Yarmouth U.K. 52°37N 1°44E 13 E9
Great Zab = Zāb al Kabīr →
  Iraq 36°1N 43°24E 44 B4
Great Zimbabwe
  Zimbabwe 20°16S 30°54E 55 G3
Greater Antilles W. Indies 17°40N 74°0W 89 C10
Greater London □ U.K. 51°31N 0°6W 13 F7
Greater Manchester □
  U.K. 53°30N 2°15W 12 D5
Greater St. Lucia Wetlands △
  S. Africa 28°6S 32°27E 57 D5
Greater Sudbury = Sudbury
  Canada 46°30N 81°0W 72 C3
Greater Sunda Is. Indonesia 7°0S 112°0E 36 F4
Greco, C. Cyprus 34°57N 34°5E 25 E13
Gredos, Sierra de Spain 40°20N 5°0W 21 B3
Greece U.S.A. 43°13N 77°41W 82 C7

Greece ■ *Europe* 40°0N 23°0E **23 E9**
Greeley *Colo., U.S.A.* 40°25N 104°42W **76 F11**
Greeley *Nebr., U.S.A.* 41°33N 98°32W **80 E4**
Greely Fd. *Canada* 80°30N 85°0W **69 A15**
Greem-Bell, Ostrov *Russia* 81°0N 62°0E **28 A7**
Green ⇨ *Ky., U.S.A.* 37°54N 87°30W **80 G10**
Green ⇨ *Utah, U.S.A.* 38°11N 109°53W **76 G9**
Green B. *U.S.A.* 45°0N 87°30W **80 C10**
Green Bay *U.S.A.* 44°31N 88°0W **80 D9**
Green C. *Australia* 37°13S 150°1E **63 F5**
Green Cove Springs
U.S.A. 29°59N 81°42W **85 G14**
Green Lake *Canada* 54°17N 107°47W **71 C7**
Green Mts. *U.S.A.* 43°45N 72°45W **83 C12**
Green River *Utah,*
U.S.A. 38°59N 110°10W **76 G8**
Green River *Wyo.,*
U.S.A. 41°32N 109°28W **76 F9**
Green Valley *U.S.A.* 31°52N 110°56W **77 L8**
Greenbank *U.S.A.* 48°6N 122°34W **78 B4**
Greenbush *Mich., U.S.A.* 44°35N 83°19W **82 B1**
Greenbush *Minn., U.S.A.* 48°42N 96°11W **80 A5**
Greencastle *U.S.A.* 39°38N 86°52W **80 F10**
Greene *U.S.A.* 42°20N 75°46W **83 D9**
Greeneville *U.S.A.* 36°10N 82°50W **85 C13**
Greenfield *Calif., U.S.A.* 36°19N 121°15W **78 J5**
Greenfield *Calif., U.S.A.* 35°15N 119°0W **79 K8**
Greenfield *Ind., U.S.A.* 39°47N 85°46W **81 F11**
Greenfield *Iowa, U.S.A.* 41°18N 94°28W **80 E6**
Greenfield *Mass.,*
U.S.A. 42°35N 72°36W **83 D12**
Greenfield *Mo., U.S.A.* 37°25N 93°51W **80 G7**
Greenfield Park *Canada* 45°29N 73°28W **83 A11**
Greenland ☒ *N. Amer.* 66°0N 45°0W **67 C15**
Greenland Sea *Arctic* 73°0N 10°0W **4 B7**
Greenock *U.K.* 55°57N 4°46W **11 F4**
Greenore *Ireland* 54°2N 6°8W **10 B5**
Greenore Pt. *Ireland* 52°14N 6°19W **10 D5**
Greenough *Australia* 28°58S 114°43E **61 E1**
Greenough ⇨ *Australia* 28°51S 114°38E **61 E1**
Greenough Pt. *Canada* 44°58N 81°26W **82 B3**
Greenport *U.S.A.* 41°6N 72°22W **83 E12**
Greensboro *Ga., U.S.A.* 33°35N 83°11W **85 E13**
Greensboro *N.C., U.S.A.* 36°4N 79°48W **85 C15**
Greensboro *Vt., U.S.A.* 44°36N 72°18W **83 B12**
Greensburg *Ind., U.S.A.* 39°20N 85°29W **81 F11**
Greensburg *Kans.,*
U.S.A. 37°36N 99°18W **80 G4**
Greensburg *Pa., U.S.A.* 40°18N 79°33W **82 F5**
Greenstone = Geraldton
Canada 49°44N 87°10W **72 C2**
Greenstone Pt. *U.K.* 57°55N 5°37W **11 D3**
Greenvale *Australia* 18°59S 145°7E **62 B4**
Greenville *Liberia* 5°1N 9°6W **50 G4**
Greenville *Ala., U.S.A.* 31°50N 86°38W **85 F11**
Greenville *Calif., U.S.A.* 40°8N 120°57W **78 E6**
Greenville *Maine,*
U.S.A. 45°28N 69°35W **81 C19**
Greenville *Mich., U.S.A.* 43°11N 85°15W **81 D11**
Greenville *Miss., U.S.A.* 33°24N 91°4W **85 E9**
Greenville *Mo., U.S.A.* 37°8N 90°27W **80 G8**
Greenville *N.C., U.S.A.* 35°37N 77°23W **85 H7**
Greenville *N.H., U.S.A.* 42°46N 71°49W **83 D13**
Greenville *N.Y., U.S.A.* 42°25N 74°1W **83 D10**
Greenville *Ohio, U.S.A.* 40°6N 84°38W **81 E11**
Greenville *Pa., U.S.A.* 41°24N 80°23W **82 E4**
Greenville *S.C., U.S.A.* 34°51N 82°24W **85 D13**
Greenville *Tex., U.S.A.* 33°8N 96°7W **84 E6**
Greenwater Lake ○
Canada 52°32N 103°30W **71 C8**
Greenwich *Conn., U.S.A.* 41°2N 73°38W **83 E11**
Greenwich *N.Y., U.S.A.* 43°5N 73°30W **83 C11**
Greenwich *Ohio, U.S.A.* 41°2N 82°31W **82 E2**
Greenwich □ *U.K.* 51°29N 0°1E **13 F8**
Greenwood *Canada* 49°10N 118°40W **70 D5**
Greenwood *Ark., U.S.A.* 35°13N 94°16W **84 D7**
Greenwood *Ind., U.S.A.* 39°37N 86°7W **80 F10**
Greenwood *Miss., U.S.A.* 33°31N 90°11W **85 E9**
Greenwood *S.C., U.S.A.* 34°12N 82°10W **85 D13**
Greenwood, Mt.
Australia 13°48S 130°4E **60 B5**
Gregory *U.S.A.* 43°14N 99°26W **80 D4**
Gregory ⇨ *Australia* 17°53S 139°17E **62 B2**
Gregory, L. *S. Austral.,*
Australia 28°55S 139°0E **63 D2**
Gregory, L. *W. Austral.,*
Australia 20°0S 127°40E **60 D4**
Gregory, L. *W. Austral.,*
Australia 25°38S 119°58E **61 E2**
Gregory △ *Australia* 15°38S 131°15E **60 C5**
Gregory Downs
Australia 18°35S 138°45E **62 B2**
Gregory Ra. *Queens.,*
Australia 19°30S 143°40E **62 B3**
Gregory Ra. *W. Austral.,*
Australia 21°20S 121°12E **60 D3**
Greifswald *Germany* 54°5N 13°23E **16 A7**
Greiz *Germany* 50°39N 12°10E **16 C7**
Gremikha *Russia* 67°59N 39°47E **18 A6**
Grenaa *Denmark* 56°25N 10°53E **9 H14**
Grenada *U.S.A.* 33°47N 89°49W **85 E10**
Grenada ■ *W. Indies* 12°10N 61°40W **89 D7**
Grenadier I. *Canada* 44°3N 76°22W **83 B8**
Grenadines, The
St. Vincent 12°40N 61°20W **89 D7**
Grenen *Denmark* 57°44N 10°40E **9 H14**
Grenfell *Australia* 33°52S 148°8E **63 E4**
Grenfell *Canada* 50°30N 102°56W **71 C8**
Grenoble *France* 45°12N 5°42E **20 D6**
Grenville, C. *Australia* 12°0S 143°13E **62 A3**
Grenville Chan. *Canada* 53°40N 129°46W **70 C3**
Gresham *U.S.A.* 45°30N 122°25W **78 E4**
Gresik *Indonesia* 7°13S 112°38E **37 G15**
Gretna *U.K.* 55°0N 3°3W **11 F5**
Gretna *U.S.A.* 29°54N 90°3W **85 G9**
Grevenmacher *Lux.* 49°41N 6°26E **15 E6**
Grey ⇨ *Canada* 47°34N 57°6W **73 C8**
Grey ⇨ *N.Z.* 42°27S 171°12E **59 E3**
Grey, C. *Australia* 13°0S 136°35E **62 A2**

Grey Is. *Canada* 50°50N 55°35W **69 G20**
Grey Ra. *Australia* 27°0S 143°30E **63 D3**
Greybull *U.S.A.* 44°30N 108°3W **76 D9**
Greymouth *N.Z.* 42°29S 171°13E **59 E3**
Greystones *Ireland* 53°9N 6°5W **10 C5**
Greytown *N.Z.* 41°5S 175°29E **59 D5**
Greytown *S. Africa* 29°1S 30°36E **57 D5**
Gribbell I. *Canada* 53°23N 129°0W **70 C3**
Gridley *U.S.A.* 39°22N 121°42W **78 F5**
Griekwastad *S. Africa* 28°49S 23°15E **56 D3**
Griffin *U.S.A.* 33°15N 84°16W **85 E12**
Griffith *Australia* 34°18S 146°2E **63 E4**
Griffith *Canada* 45°15N 77°10W **82 A7**
Griffith I. *Canada* 44°50N 80°55W **82 B4**
Grimaylov = Hrymayliv
Ukraine 49°20N 26°5E **17 D14**
Grimes *U.S.A.* 39°4N 121°54W **78 F5**
Grimsay *U.K.* 57°29N 7°14W **11 D1**
Grimsby *Canada* 43°12N 79°34W **82 C5**
Grimsby *U.K.* 53°34N 0°5W **12 D7**
Grímsey *Iceland* 66°33N 17°58W **8 C5**
Grimshaw *Canada* 56°10N 117°40W **70 B5**
Grimstad *Norway* 58°20N 8°35E **9 G13**
Grinnell *U.S.A.* 41°45N 92°43W **80 E7**
Grinnell Pen. *Canada* 76°40N 95°0W **69 B13**
Gris-Nez, C. *France* 50°52N 1°35E **20 A4**
Grise Fiord *Canada* 76°25N 82°57W **69 B15**
Groais I. *Canada* 50°55N 55°35W **73 B8**
Groblersdal *S. Africa* 25°15S 29°25E **57 D4**
Grodno = Hrodna
Belarus 53°42N 23°52E **17 B12**
Grodzyanka = Hrodzyanka
Belarus 53°31N 28°42E **17 B15**
Groesbeck *U.S.A.* 31°31N 96°32W **84 F6**
Grójec *Poland* 51°50N 20°58E **17 C11**
Grong *Norway* 64°25N 12°8E **8 D15**
Groningen *Neths.* 53°15N 6°35E **15 A6**
Groningen □ *Neths.* 53°16N 6°40E **15 A6**
Groom *U.S.A.* 35°12N 101°6W **84 D4**
Groot ⇨ *S. Africa* 33°45S 24°36E **56 E3**
Groot-Berg ⇨ *S. Africa* 32°47S 18°8E **56 E2**
Groot-Brakrivier *S. Africa* 34°2S 22°18E **56 E3**
Groot Karasberge
Namibia 27°20S 18°40E **56 D2**
Groot-Kei ⇨ *S. Africa* 32°41S 28°22E **57 E4**
Groot-Vis ⇨ *S. Africa* 33°28S 27°5E **56 E4**
Grootdrink *S. Africa* 28°33S 21°42E **56 D3**
Groote Eylandt *Australia* 14°0S 136°40E **62 A2**
Grootfontein *Namibia* 19°31S 18°6E **56 B2**
Grootlaagte ⇨ *Africa* 20°55S 21°27E **56 C3**
Grootvloer ⇨ *S. Africa* 30°0S 20°40E **56 E3**
Gros C. *Canada* 61°59N 113°32W **70 A6**
Gros Islet *St. Lucia* 14°5N 60°58W **89 f**
Gros Morne △ *Canada* 49°40N 57°50W **73 C8**
Gros Piton *St. Lucia* 13°49N 61°5W **89 f**
Gros Piton Pt. *St. Lucia* 13°49N 61°5W **89 f**
Grossa, Pta. *Spain* 39°6N 1°36E **24 B8**
Grosse Point *U.S.A.* 42°23N 82°54W **82 D2**
Grosser Arber *Germany* 49°6N 13°8E **16 D7**
Grosseto *Italy* 42°46N 11°8E **22 C4**
Grossglockner *Austria* 47°5N 12°40E **16 E7**
Groswater B. *Canada* 54°20N 57°40W **73 B8**
Groton *Conn., U.S.A.* 41°21N 72°5W **83 E12**
Groton *N.Y., U.S.A.* 42°36N 76°22W **83 D8**
Groton *S. Dak., U.S.A.* 45°27N 98°6W **80 C4**
Grouard Mission *Canada* 55°33N 116°9W **70 B5**
Groundhog ⇨ *Canada* 48°45N 82°58W **72 C3**
Grouw *Neths.* 53°5N 5°51E **15 A5**
Grove City *U.S.A.* 41°10N 80°5W **82 E4**
Grove Hill *U.S.A.* 31°42N 87°47W **85 F11**
Groveland *U.S.A.* 37°50N 120°14W **78 H6**
Grover Beach *U.S.A.* 35°7N 120°37W **79 K6**
Groves *U.S.A.* 29°57N 93°54W **84 G8**
Groveton *U.S.A.* 44°36N 71°31W **83 B13**
Groznyy *Russia* 43°20N 45°45E **19 F8**
Grudziądz *Poland* 53°30N 18°47E **17 B10**
Gruinard B. *U.K.* 57°56N 5°35W **11 D3**
Grundy Center *U.S.A.* 42°22N 92°47W **80 D7**
Gruver *U.S.A.* 36°16N 101°24W **84 C4**
Gryazi *Russia* 52°30N 39°58E **18 D6**
Gryazovets *Russia* 58°50N 40°10E **18 C7**
Grytviken *S. Georgia* 54°19S 36°33W **96 G9**
Gua *India* 22°18N 85°20E **43 H11**
Gua Musang *Malaysia* 4°53N 101°58E **39 K3**
Guacanayabo, G. de
Cuba 20°40N 77°20W **88 B4**
Guachipas ⇨ *Argentina* 25°40S 65°30W **94 B2**
Guadalajara *Mexico* 20°40N 103°20W **86 C4**
Guadalajara *Spain* 40°37N 3°12W **21 B4**
Guadalcanal *Solomon Is.* 9°32S 160°12E **58 B9**
Guadales *Argentina* 34°30S 67°55W **94 C2**
Guadalete ⇨ *Spain* 36°35N 6°13W **21 D2**
Guadalquivir ⇨ *Spain* 36°47N 6°22W **21 D2**
Guadalupe = Guadeloupe ☒
W. Indies 16°20N 61°40W **89 b**
Guadalupe *Mexico* 22°45N 102°31W **86 C4**
Guadalupe *U.S.A.* 34°58N 120°34W **79 L6**
Guadalupe ⇨ *U.S.A.* 28°27N 96°47W **84 G6**
Guadalupe, Sierra de
Spain 39°28N 5°30W **21 C3**
Guadalupe Bravos
Mexico 31°20N 106°10W **86 A3**
Guadalupe I. *Pac. Oc.* 29°0N 118°50W **66 G8**
Guadalupe Mts. △
U.S.A. 31°40N 104°30W **84 F2**
Guadalupe Peak *U.S.A.* 31°50N 104°52W **84 F2**
Guadalupe y Calvo
Mexico 26°6N 106°58W **86 B3**
Guadarrama, Sierra de
Spain 41°0N 4°0W **21 B4**
Guadeloupe ☒ *W. Indies* 16°20N 61°40W **88 b**
Guadeloupe △ *Guadeloupe* 16°10N 61°40W **88 b**
Guadeloupe Passage
W. Indies 16°50N 62°15W **89 C7**
Guadiana ⇨ *Portugal* 37°14N 7°22W **21 D2**
Guadix *Spain* 37°18N 3°11W **21 D4**
Guafo, Boca del *Chile* 43°35S 74°0W **96 E2**
Guaico *Trin. & Tob.* 10°35N 61°9W **93 K15**
Guainía ⇨ *Colombia* 2°1N 67°7W **92 C5**

Guaíra *Brazil* 24°5S 54°10W **95 A5**
Guaíra □ *Paraguay* 25°45S 56°30W **94 B4**
Guaire = Gorey *Ireland* 52°41N 6°18W **10 D5**
Guaitecas, Is. *Chile* 44°0S 74°30W **96 E2**
Guajará-Mirim *Brazil* 10°50S 65°20W **92 F5**
Guajira, Pen. de la
Colombia 12°0N 72°0W **92 A4**
Gualán *Guatemala* 15°8N 89°22W **88 C2**
Gualeguay *Argentina* 33°10S 59°14W **94 C4**
Gualeguaychú *Argentina* 33°3S 59°31W **94 C4**
Gualequay ⇨ *Argentina* 33°19S 59°39W **94 C4**
Guam ☒ *Pac. Oc.* 13°27N 144°45E **64 F6**
Guamini *Argentina* 37°1S 62°28W **94 D3**
Guamúchil *Mexico* 25°28N 108°6W **86 B3**
Guana I. *Br. Virgin Is.* 18°30N 64°30W **89 e**
Guanabacoa *Cuba* 23°8N 82°18W **88 B3**
Guanacaste, Cordillera de
Costa Rica 10°40N 85°4W **88 D2**
Guanacaste △
Costa Rica 10°57N 85°30W **88 D2**
Guanaceví *Mexico* 25°56N 105°57W **86 B3**
Guanahani = San Salvador I.
Bahamas 24°0N 74°40W **89 B5**
Guanaja *Honduras* 16°30N 85°55W **88 C2**
Guanajay *Cuba* 22°56N 82°42W **88 B3**
Guanajuato *Mexico* 21°1N 101°15W **86 C4**
Guanajuato □ *Mexico* 21°0N 101°0W **86 C4**
Guandacol *Argentina* 29°30S 68°40W **94 B2**
Guane *Cuba* 22°10N 84°7W **88 B3**
Guangdong □ *China* 23°0N 113°0E **33 D6**
Guangling *China* 39°47N 114°22E **34 E8**
Guangrao *China* 37°5N 118°25E **35 F10**
Guangwu *China* 37°48N 105°57E **34 F3**
Guangxi Zhuangzu Zizhiqu □
China 24°0N 109°0E **33 D5**
Guangzhou *China* 23°6N 113°13E **33 D6**
Guánica *Puerto Rico* 17°58N 66°55W **89 d**
Guanipa ⇨ *Venezuela* 9°56N 62°26W **89 D6**
Guannan *China* 34°8N 119°21E **35 G10**
Guantánamo *Cuba* 20°10N 75°14W **89 B4**
Guantánamo B. *Cuba* 19°59N 75°10W **89 C4**
Guantao *China* 36°42N 115°25E **34 F8**
Guanyun *China* 34°20N 119°18E **35 G10**
Guapay = Grande ⇨
Bolivia 15°51S 64°39W **92 G6**
Guápiles *Costa Rica* 10°10N 83°46W **88 D3**
Guapo B. *Trin. & Tob.* 10°12N 61°41W **93 K15**
Guaporé *Brazil* 28°51S 51°54W **95 B5**
Guaporé ⇨ *Brazil* 11°55S 65°4W **92 F5**
Guaqui *Bolivia* 16°41S 68°54W **92 G5**
Guaramacal △ *Venezuela* 9°13N 70°12W **89 E5**
Guarapari *Brazil* 20°40S 40°30W **95 A7**
Guarapuava *Brazil* 25°20S 51°30W **95 B5**
Guaratinguetá *Brazil* 22°49S 45°9W **95 A6**
Guaratuba *Brazil* 25°53S 48°38W **95 B6**
Guarda *Portugal* 40°32N 7°20W **21 B2**
Guardafui, C. = Asir, Ras
Somali Rep. 11°55N 51°10E **47 E5**
Guárico □ *Venezuela* 8°40N 66°35W **92 B5**
Guarujá *Brazil* 24°2S 46°25W **95 A6**
Guarulhos *Brazil* 23°29S 46°33W **95 A6**
Guasave *Mexico* 25°34N 108°27W **86 B3**
Guasdualito *Venezuela* 7°15N 70°44W **92 B4**
Guatemala *Guatemala* 14°40N 90°22W **88 D1**
Guatemala ■
Cent. Amer. 15°40N 90°30W **88 C1**
Guatemala Basin *Pac. Oc.* 11°0N 95°0W **65 F18**
Guatemala Trench
Pac. Oc. 14°0N 95°0W **66 H10**
Guatopo △ *Venezuela* 10°5N 66°30W **89 D6**
Guatuaro Pt.
Trin. & Tob. 10°19N 60°59W **93 K16**
Guaviare ⇨ *Colombia* 4°3N 67°44W **92 C5**
Guaxupé *Brazil* 21°10S 47°5W **95 A6**
Guayama *Puerto Rico* 17°59N 66°7W **89 d**
Guayaquil *Ecuador* 2°15S 79°52W **92 D3**
Guayaquil *Mexico* 29°59N 115°4W **86 B1**
Guayaquil, G. de *Ecuador* 3°10S 81°0W **92 D2**
Guaymas *Mexico* 27°56N 110°54W **86 B2**
Guba
Dem. Rep. of the Congo 10°38S 26°27E **55 E2**
Gubkin *Russia* 51°17N 37°32E **19 D6**
Gubkinskiy *Russia* 64°27N 76°36E **28 C8**
Gudbrandsdalen *Norway* 61°33N 10°10E **8 F14**
Guddu Barrage *Pakistan* 28°30N 69°50E **42 E3**
Gudur *India* 14°12N 79°55E **40 M11**
Guecho = Getxo *Spain* 43°21N 2°59W **21 A4**
Guékédou *Guinea* 8°40N 10°5W **50 G3**
Guelmine = Goulimine
Morocco 28°56N 10°0W **50 C3**
Guelph *Canada* 43°35N 80°20W **82 C4**
Guéret *France* 46°11N 1°51E **20 C4**
Guerneville *U.S.A.* 38°30N 123°0W **78 G4**
Guernica = Gernika-Lumo
Spain 43°19N 2°40W **21 A4**
Guernsey *U.K.* 49°26N 2°35W **13 H5**
Guernsey *U.S.A.* 42°16N 104°45W **76 E11**
Guerrero □ *Mexico* 17°40N 100°0W **87 D5**
Gügher *Iran* 29°28N 56°27E **45 D8**
Guhakolak, Tanjung
Indonesia 6°50S 105°14E **37 G11**
Guia *Canary Is.* 28°8N 15°38W **24 F4**
Guia de Isora *Canary Is.* 28°12N 16°46W **24 F3**
Guia Lopes da Laguna
Brazil 21°26S 56°7W **95 A4**
Guiana Highlands
S. Amer. 5°10N 60°40W **90 C4**
Guidônia-Montecélio
Italy 42°1N 12°45E **22 C5**
Guijá *Mozam.* 24°27S 33°0E **57 C5**
Guildford *U.K.* 51°14N 0°34W **13 F7**
Guilford *U.S.A.* 41°17N 72°41W **83 E12**
Guilin *China* 25°18N 110°15E **33 D6**
Guillaume-Delisle, L.
Canada 56°15N 76°17W **72 A4**
Guimarães *Brazil* 2°9S 44°42W **93 D10**
Guimaras □ *Phil.* 10°35N 122°37E **37 B6**

Guimarães *Portugal* 41°28N 8°24W **21 B1**
Guimaras □ *Phil.* 10°35N 122°37E **37 B6**
Guinda *U.S.A.* 38°50N 122°12W **78 G4**
Guinea ■ *Africa* 10°20N 11°30W **50 F3**
Guinea, Gulf of *Atl. Oc.* 3°0N 2°30E **49 F4**
Guinea-Bissau ■ *Africa* 12°0N 15°0W **50 F3**
Güines *Cuba* 22°50N 82°0W **88 B3**
Guingamp *France* 48°34N 3°10W **20 B2**
Güiria *Venezuela* 10°32N 62°18W **93 K14**
Guiuan *Phil.* 11°5N 125°55E **37 B7**
Guiyang *China* 26°32N 106°40E **32 D5**
Guizhou □ *China* 27°0N 107°0E **32 D5**
Gujar Khan *Pakistan* 33°16N 73°19E **42 C5**
Gujarat □ *India* 23°20N 71°0E **42 H4**
Gujranwala *Pakistan* 32°10N 74°12E **42 C6**
Gujrat *Pakistan* 32°40N 74°2E **42 C6**
Gulbarga *India* 17°20N 76°50E **40 L10**
Gulbene *Latvia* 57°8N 26°52E **9 H22**
Gulf, The = Persian Gulf
Asia 27°0N 50°0E **45 E6**
Gulf Islands △ *U.S.A.* 30°10N 87°10W **85 F11**
Gulfport *U.S.A.* 30°22N 89°6W **85 F10**
Gulgong *Australia* 32°20S 149°49E **63 E4**
Gulistan *Pakistan* 30°30N 66°35E **42 D2**
Gulja = Yining *China* 43°58N 81°10E **32 B3**
Gull Lake *Canada* 50°10N 108°29W **71 C7**
Gulmarg *India* 34°3N 74°25E **43 B6**
Gülshat *Kazakhstan* 46°38N 74°12E **28 E8**
Gulu *Uganda* 2°48N 32°17E **54 B3**
Gulwe *Tanzania* 6°30S 36°25E **54 D4**
Gumal ⇨ *Pakistan* 31°40N 71°50E **42 D4**
Gumbaz *Pakistan* 30°2N 69°0E **42 D3**
Gumel *Nigeria* 12°39N 9°22E **50 F7**
Gumi *S. Korea* 36°10N 128°12E **35 F15**
Gumla *India* 23°3N 84°33E **43 H11**
Gumlu *Australia* 19°53S 147°41E **62 B4**
Gumma □ *Japan* 36°30N 138°20E **31 F9**
Gumzai *Indonesia* 5°28S 134°42E **37 F8**
Guna *India* 24°40N 77°19E **42 G7**
Gunbalanya *Australia* 12°20S 133°4E **60 B5**
Gundabooka △
Australia 30°30S 145°20E **63 E4**
Gunisao ⇨ *Canada* 53°56N 97°53W **71 C9**
Gunisao L. *Canada* 53°33N 96°15W **71 C9**
Gunjyal *Pakistan* 32°20N 71°55E **42 C4**
Gunnbjørn Fjeld
Greenland 68°55N 29°47W **4 C6**
Gunnedah *Australia* 30°59S 150°15E **63 E5**
Gunnewin *Australia* 25°59S 148°33E **63 D4**
Gunningbar Cr. ⇨
Australia 31°14S 147°6E **63 E4**
Gunnison *Colo.,*
U.S.A. 38°33N 106°56W **76 G10**
Gunnison *Utah, U.S.A.* 39°9N 111°49W **76 G8**
Gunnison ⇨ *U.S.A.* 39°4N 108°35W **76 G9**
Gunsan *S. Korea* 35°59N 126°45E **35 G14**
Guntakal *India* 15°11N 77°27E **40 M10**
Gunter *Canada* 44°52N 77°32W **82 B7**
Guntersville *U.S.A.* 34°21N 86°18W **85 D11**
Guntong *Malaysia* 4°36N 101°3E **39 K3**
Guntur *India* 16°23N 80°30E **41 L12**
Gunungapi *Indonesia* 6°45S 126°30E **37 F7**
Gunungsitoli *Indonesia* 1°15N 97°30E **36 D1**
Gunza *Angola* 10°50S 13°50E **52 G2**
Guo He ⇨ *China* 32°59N 117°10E **35 H9**
Guoyang *China* 33°32N 116°12E **34 H9**
Gupis *Pakistan* 36°15N 73°20E **43 A5**
Gurbantünggüt Shamo
China 45°8N 87°20E **32 B3**
Gurdaspur *India* 32°5N 75°31E **42 C6**
Gurdon *U.S.A.* 33°55N 93°9W **84 E8**
Gurgaon *India* 28°27N 77°1E **42 E7**
Gurgueia ⇨ *Brazil* 6°50S 43°24W **93 E10**
Gurha *India* 25°12N 71°39E **42 G4**
Guri, Embalse de
Venezuela 7°50N 62°52W **92 B6**
Gurkha *Nepal* 28°5N 84°40E **43 E11**
Gurla Mandhata = Naimona'nyi
Feng Nepal 30°26N 81°18E **43 D9**
Gurley *Australia* 29°45S 149°48E **63 D4**
Gurnet Point *U.S.A.* 42°1N 70°34W **83 D14**
Guro *Mozam.* 17°26S 32°30E **55 F3**
Gurué *Mozam.* 15°25S 36°58E **55 F4**
Gurun *Malaysia* 5°49N 100°27E **39 K3**
Gürün *Turkey* 38°43N 37°15E **19 G6**
Gurupá *Brazil* 1°25S 51°35W **93 D8**
Gurupá, I. Grande de
Brazil 1°25S 51°45W **93 D8**
Gurupi *Brazil* 11°43S 49°4W **93 F9**
Gurupi ⇨ *Brazil* 1°13S 46°6W **93 D9**
Guruwe *Zimbabwe* 16°40S 30°42E **57 B5**
Gurvan Sayhan Uul
Mongolia 43°50N 104°0E **34 C9**
Guryev = Atyraü
Kazakhstan 47°5N 52°0E **19 E9**
Gusau *Nigeria* 12°12N 6°40E **50 F7**
Gushan *China* 39°50N 123°35E **35 E12**
Gushgy = Serhetabat
Turkmenistan 35°20N 62°18E **45 C9**
Gusinoozersk *Russia* 51°16N 106°27E **29 D11**
Gustavus *U.S.A.* 58°25N 135°44W **70 B1**
Gustine *U.S.A.* 37°16N 121°0W **78 H6**
Güstrow *Germany* 53°47N 12°10E **16 B7**
Gütersloh *Germany* 51°54N 8°24E **16 C5**
Gutha *Australia* 28°58S 115°55E **61 E2**
Guthalungra *Australia* 19°52S 147°50E **62 B4**
Guthrie *Canada* 44°28N 79°32W **82 B5**
Guthrie *Okla., U.S.A.* 35°53N 97°25W **84 D6**
Guthrie *Tex., U.S.A.* 33°37N 100°19W **84 E4**
Guttenberg *U.S.A.* 42°47N 91°6W **80 D8**
Gutu *Zimbabwe* 19°41S 31°9E **57 B5**
Guwahati *India* 26°10N 91°45E **41 F17**
Guy Fawkes River △
Australia 30°3S 152°20E **63 E5**
Guyana ■ *S. Amer.* 5°0N 59°0W **92 C7**
Guyane française = French
Guiana ☒ *S. Amer.* 4°0N 53°0W **93 C8**

Guyang *China* 41°0N 110°5E **34 D6**
Guyenne *France* 44°30N 0°40E **20 D4**
Guymon *U.S.A.* 36°41N 101°29W **84 C4**
Guyra *Australia* 30°15S 151°40E **63 E5**
Guyuan *Hebei, China* 41°37N 115°40E **34 D8**
Guyuan *Ningxia Huizu,*
China 36°0N 106°20E **34 F4**
Güzelyurt = Morphou
Cyprus 35°12N 32°59E **25 D11**
Guzhen *China* 33°22N 117°18E **35 H9**
Guzmán, L. de *Mexico* 31°20N 107°30W **86 A3**
Gwa *Burma* 17°36N 94°34E **41 L19**
Gwaai *Zimbabwe* 19°15S 27°45E **55 F2**
Gwaai ⇨ *Zimbabwe* 17°59S 26°52E **55 F2**
Gwabegar *Australia* 30°37S 148°59E **63 E4**
Gwādar *Pakistan* 25°10N 62°18E **40 G3**
Gwaii Haanas △
Canada 52°21N 131°26W **70 C2**
Gwalior *India* 26°12N 78°10E **42 F8**
Gwanda *Zimbabwe* 20°55S 29°0E **55 G2**
Gwane
Dem. Rep. of the Congo 4°45N 25°48E **54 B2**
Gwangju *S. Korea* 35°9N 126°54E **35 G14**
Gwanju = Gwangju
S. Korea 35°9N 126°54E **35 G14**
Gweebarra B. *Ireland* 54°51N 8°23W **10 B3**
Gweedore *Ireland* 55°3N 8°13W **10 A3**
Gweru *Zimbabwe* 19°28S 29°45E **55 F2**
Gwinn *U.S.A.* 46°19N 87°27W **80 B10**
Gwydir ⇨ *Australia* 29°27S 149°48E **63 D4**
Gwynedd □ *U.K.* 52°52N 4°10W **12 E3**
Gyandzha = Gäncä
Azerbaijan 40°45N 46°20E **19 F8**
Gyaring Hu *China* 34°50N 97°40E **32 C4**
Gydanskiy Poluostrov
Russia 70°0N 78°0E **28 C8**
Gyeongju *S. Korea* 35°51N 129°14E **35 G15**
Gympie *Australia* 26°11S 152°38E **63 D5**
Gyöngyös *Hungary* 47°48N 19°56E **17 E10**
Györ *Hungary* 47°41N 17°40E **17 E9**
Gypsum Pt. *Canada* 61°53N 114°35W **70 A6**
Gypsumville *Canada* 51°45N 98°40W **71 C9**
Gyula *Hungary* 46°38N 21°17E **17 E11**
Gyumri *Armenia* 40°47N 43°50E **19 F7**
Gyzylarbat = Serdar
Turkmenistan 39°4N 56°23E **45 B8**
Gyzyletrek = Etrek
Turkmenistan 37°36N 54°46E **45 B7**

H

Ha 'Arava ⇨ *Israel* 30°50N 35°20E **46 E4**
Ha Coi *Vietnam* 21°26N 107°46E **38 B6**
Ha Dong *Vietnam* 20°58N 105°46E **38 B5**
Ha Giang *Vietnam* 22°50N 104°59E **38 A5**
Ha Karmel △ *Israel* 32°45N 35°5E **46 C4**
Ha Long, Vinh *Vietnam* 20°56N 107°3E **38 B6**
Ha Tien *Vietnam* 10°23N 104°29E **39 G5**
Ha Tinh *Vietnam* 18°20N 105°54E **38 C5**
Ha Trung *Vietnam* 19°58N 105°50E **38 C5**
Haaksbergen *Neths.* 52°9N 6°45E **15 B6**
Ha'ano *Tonga* 19°41S 174°18W **59 c**
Ha'apai Group *Tonga* 19°47S 174°27W **59 c**
Haapiti *Moorea* 17°34S 149°52W **59 d**
Haapsalu *Estonia* 58°56N 23°30E **9 G20**
Haarlem *Neths.* 52°23N 4°39E **15 B4**
Haast ⇨ *N.Z.* 43°50S 169°2E **59 E2**
Haasts Bluff *Australia* 23°22S 132°0E **60 D5**
Haasts Bluff ◎ *Australia* 23°39S 130°34E **60 D5**
Hab ⇨ *Pakistan* 24°53N 66°41E **42 G3**
Hab Nadi Chauki
Pakistan 25°0N 66°50E **42 G2**
Habahe *China* 48°3N 86°23E **32 B3**
Habaswein *Kenya* 1°2N 39°30E **54 B4**
Habay *Canada* 58°50N 118°44W **70 B5**
Habbānīyah *Iraq* 33°17N 43°29E **44 C4**
Haboro *Japan* 44°22N 141°42E **30 B10**
Habshān *U.A.E.* 23°50N 53°37E **45 F7**
Hachijō-Jima *Japan* 33°5N 139°45E **31 H9**
Hachinohe *Japan* 40°30N 141°29E **30 D10**
Hachiōji *Japan* 35°40N 139°20E **31 G9**
Hackensack *U.S.A.* 40°52N 74°4W **83 F10**
Hackettstown *U.S.A.* 40°51N 74°50W **83 F10**
Hadali *Pakistan* 32°16N 72°11E **42 C5**
Hadarba, Ras *Sudan* 22°4N 36°51E **51 D13**
Hadarom □ *Israel* 31°0N 35°0E **46 E4**
Hadd, Ra's al *Oman* 22°35N 59°50E **47 C6**
Haddington *U.K.* 55°57N 2°47W **11 F6**
Hadejia *Nigeria* 12°30N 10°5E **50 F7**
Hadejia ⇨ *Nigeria* 12°30N 10°0E **50 F7**
Hadera *Israel* 32°27N 34°55E **46 C3**
Hadera, N. ⇨ *Israel* 32°28N 34°52E **46 C3**
Haderslev *Denmark* 55°15N 9°30E **9 J13**
Hadhramaut = Hadramawt
Yemen 15°30N 49°30E **47 D4**
Hadiboh *Yemen* 12°39N 54°2E **47 E5**
Hadley B. *Canada* 72°31N 108°12W **68 C10**
Hadong *S. Korea* 35°5N 127°44E **35 G14**
Hadramawt *Yemen* 15°30N 49°30E **47 D4**
Hadrānīyah *Iraq* 35°38N 43°14E **44 C4**
Hadrian's Wall *U.K.* 55°0N 2°30W **12 B5**
Hae, Ko *Thailand* 7°44N 98°22E **39 a**
Haeju *N. Korea* 38°3N 125°45E **35 E13**
Ha'ena *U.S.A.* 22°14N 159°34W **75 L8**
Haenam *S. Korea* 34°34N 126°35E **35 G14**
Haenertsburg *S. Africa* 24°0S 29°59E **57 C4**
Haerhpin = Harbin
China 45°48N 126°40E **35 B14**
Hafar al Bāṭin *Si. Arabia* 28°32N 45°52E **44 D5**
Hafirat al 'Aydā
Si. Arabia 26°26N 39°12E **44 E3**
Hafit *Oman* 23°59N 55°49E **45 F7**
Hafizabad *Pakistan* 32°5N 73°40E **42 C5**
Haflong *India* 25°10N 93°5E **41 G18**
Haft Gel *Iran* 31°30N 49°32E **45 D6**
Hagalil *Israel* 32°53N 35°18E **46 C4**
Hagemeister I. *U.S.A.* 58°39N 160°54W **74 D7**
Hagen *Germany* 51°21N 7°27E **16 C4**
Hagerman *U.S.A.* 33°7N 104°20W **77 K11**

Hagerman Fossil Beds △
 U.S.A. 42°48N 114°57W **76** E6
Hagerstown U.S.A. 39°39N 77°43W **81** F15
Hagersville Canada 42°58N 80°3W **82** D4
Hagfors Sweden 60°3N 13°45E **9** F15
Hagi Japan 34°30N 131°22E **31** G5
Hagolan Syria 33°0N 35°45E **46** C4
Hagondange France 49°16N 6°11E **20** B7
Hags Hd. Ireland 52°57N 9°28W **10** D2
Hague, C. de la France 49°44N 1°56W **20** B3
Hague, The = 's-Gravenhage
 Neths. 52°7N 4°17E **15** B4
Haguenau France 48°49N 7°47E **20** B7
Hai Duong Vietnam 20°56N 106°19E **38** B6
Haicheng China 40°50N 122°45E **35** D12
Haidar Khel Afghan. 33°58N 68°38E **42** C3
Haidarâbâd = Hyderabad
 India 17°22N 78°29E **40** L11
Haidargarh India 26°37N 81°22E **43** F9
Haifa = Ḥefa Israel 32°46N 35°0E **46** C4
Haikou China 20°1N 110°16E **38** B8
Ḥā'il □ Si. Arabia 26°40N 41°40E **44** E4
Hailar China 49°10N 119°38E **33** B6
Hailey U.S.A. 43°31N 114°19W **76** E6
Haileybury Canada 47°30N 79°38W **72** C4
Hailin China 44°37N 129°30E **35** B15
Hailuoto Finland 65°3N 24°45E **8** D21
Hainan □ China 19°0N 109°30E **38** C7
Hainan Dao China 19°0N 109°30E **38** C7
Hainan Str. = Qiongzhou Haixia
 China 20°10N 110°15E **38** B8
Hainaut □ Belgium 50°30N 4°0E **15** D4
Haines Alaska, U.S.A. 59°14N 135°26W **70** B1
Haines Oreg., U.S.A. 44°55N 117°56W **76** D5
Haines City U.S.A. 28°7N 81°38W **85** G14
Haines Junction
 Canada 60°45N 137°30W **70** A1
Haiphong Vietnam 20°47N 106°41E **38** B6
Haiti ■ W. Indies 19°0N 72°30W **89** C5
Haiya Sudan 18°20N 36°21E **51** E13
Haiyan China 36°53N 100°59E **32** C5
Haiyang China 36°47N 121°9E **35** F11
Haiyuan China 36°35N 105°52E **34** F3
Haizhou China 34°37N 119°7E **35** G10
Haizhou Wan China 34°50N 119°20E **35** G10
Haj 'Ali Qoli, Kavīr Iran 35°55N 54°50E **45** C7
Hajdúböszörmény
 Hungary 47°40N 21°30E **17** E11
Haji Ibrahim Iraq 36°40N 44°30E **44** B5
Hajipur India 25°45N 85°13E **43** G11
Ḥājjīābād Iran 33°37N 60°0E **45** C9
Ḥājjīābād Iran 28°19N 55°55E **45** D7
Ḥājjīābād-e Zarrīn Iran 32°0N 55°0E **45** C7
Hajnówka Poland 52°47N 23°35E **17** B12
Hakansson, Mts.
 Dem. Rep. of the Congo 8°40S 25°45E **55** D2
Hakkâri Turkey 37°34N 43°44E **44** B4
Hakken-Zan Japan 34°10N 135°54E **31** G7
Hakodate Japan 41°45N 140°44E **30** D10
Hakos Namibia 23°13S 16°21E **56** C2
Haku-San Japan 36°9N 136°46E **31** F8
Haku-San △ Japan 36°15N 136°45E **31** F8
Hakui Japan 36°53N 136°47E **31** F8
Hala Pakistan 25°43N 68°20E **40** G6
Ḥalab Syria 36°10N 37°15E **44** B3
Ḥalabjah Iraq 35°10N 45°58E **44** C5
Halaib Sudan 22°12N 36°30E **51** D13
Halaib Triangle Africa 22°30N 35°20E **51** D13
Ḥalāt 'Ammār Si. Arabia 29°10N 36°4E **44** D3
Halbā Lebanon 34°34N 36°6E **46** A5
Halberstadt Germany 51°54N 11°3E **16** C6
Halcombe N.Z. 40°8S 175°30E **59** D5
Halcon Phil. 13°0N 121°30E **37** B6
Halde Fjäll = Haltiatunturi
 Finland 69°17N 21°18E **8** B19
Halden Norway 59°9N 11°23E **9** G14
Haldia Bangla. 22°1N 88°3E **43** H13
Haldwani India 29°31N 79°30E **43** E8
Hale → Australia 24°56S 135°53E **62** C2
Halesowen U.K. 52°27N 2°3W **13** E5
Halesworth U.K. 52°20N 1°31E **13** E9
Haleyville U.S.A. 34°14N 87°37W **85** D11
Half Dome U.S.A. 37°44N 119°32E **78** H7
Halfmoon Bay N.Z. 46°50S 168°5E **59** G2
Halfway → Canada 56°12N 121°32W **70** B4
Halia India 24°50N 82°19E **43** G10
Haliburton Canada 45°3N 78°30W **82** A6
Halifax Australia 18°32S 146°22E **62** B4
Halifax Canada 44°38N 63°35W **73** D7
Halifax U.K. 53°43N 1°52W **12** D6
Halifax U.S.A. 40°25N 76°55W **82** F8
Halifax B. Australia 18°50S 147°0E **62** B4
Halifax I. Namibia 26°38S 15°4E **56** D2
Ḥalīl → Iran 27°40N 58°30E **45** E8
Halkida Greece 38°27N 23°42E **23** E10
Halkirk U.K. 58°30N 3°29W **11** C5
Hall Beach Canada 68°46N 81°12W **69** D15
Hall Pen. Canada 63°30N 66°0W **69** E18
Hall Pt. Australia 15°40S 124°23E **60** C3
Halland Sweden 57°8N 12°47E **9** H15
Hallāniyat, Jazā'ir al
 Oman 17°30N 55°58E **47** D6
Hallasan S. Korea 33°22N 126°32E **35** H14
Halle Belgium 50°44N 4°13E **15** D4
Halle Germany 51°30N 11°56E **16** C6
Hällefors Sweden 59°47N 14°31E **9** G16
Hallett Australia 33°25S 138°55E **63** E2
Hallettsville U.S.A. 29°27N 96°57W **84** G6
Hallim S. Korea 33°24N 126°15E **35** H14
Hallingdalselva →
 Norway 60°23N 9°35E **8** F13
Hallock U.S.A. 48°47N 96°57W **80** A5
Halls Creek Australia 18°16S 127°38E **60** C4
Halls Gap Australia 37°8S 142°34E **63** F3
Halls Lake Canada 45°7N 78°45W **82** A6
Hallsberg Sweden 59°5N 15°7E **9** G16
Hallstead U.S.A. 41°58N 75°45W **83** E9
Halmahera Indonesia 0°40N 128°0E **37** D7
Halmstad Sweden 56°41N 12°52E **9** H15
Hälsingborg = Helsingborg
 Sweden 56°3N 12°42E **9** H15
Hälsingland Sweden 61°40N 16°5E **8** F17
Halstead U.K. 51°57N 0°40E **13** F8
Haltiatunturi Finland 69°17N 21°18E **8** B19
Halton □ U.K. 53°22N 2°45W **12** D5
Haltwhistle U.K. 54°58N 2°26W **12** C5
Ḥālūl Qatar 25°40N 52°40E **45** E7
Halvad India 23°1N 71°11E **42** H4
Ḥalvān Iran 33°57N 56°15E **45** C8
Ham Tan Vietnam 10°40N 107°45E **39** G6
Ham Yen Vietnam 22°4N 105°3E **38** A5
Hamab Namibia 28°7S 19°16E **56** D2
Hamada Japan 34°56N 132°4E **31** G6
Hamadān Iran 34°52N 48°32E **45** C6
Hamadān □ Iran 35°0N 49°0E **45** C6
Ḥamāh Syria 35°5N 36°40E **44** C3
Hamamatsu Japan 34°45N 137°45E **31** G8
Hamar Norway 60°48N 11°7E **8** F14
Hamâta, Gebel Egypt 24°17N 35°0E **44** E2
Hambantota Sri Lanka 6°10N 81°10E **40** R12
Hamber △ Canada 52°20N 118°0W **70** C5
Hamburg Germany 53°33N 9°59E **16** B5
Hamburg Ark., U.S.A. 33°14N 91°48W **84** E9
Hamburg N.Y., U.S.A. 42°43N 78°50W **82** D6
Hamburg Pa., U.S.A. 40°33N 75°59W **83** F9
Ḥamd, W. al →
 Si. Arabia 24°55N 36°20E **44** E3
Hamden U.S.A. 41°23N 72°54W **83** E12
Häme Finland 61°38N 25°10E **8** F21
Hämeenlinna Finland 61°0N 24°28E **8** F21
Hamelin Pool Australia 26°22S 114°20E **61** E1
Hameln Germany 52°6N 9°21E **16** B5
Hamerkaz □ Israel 32°15N 34°55E **46** C3
Hamhũng N. Korea 39°54N 127°30E **35** E14
Hami China 42°55N 93°25E **32** B4
Hamilton Australia 37°45S 142°2E **63** F3
Hamilton Canada 43°15N 79°50W **82** C5
Hamilton N.Z. 37°47S 175°19E **59** B5
Hamilton U.K. 55°46N 4°2W **11** F4
Hamilton Ala., U.S.A. 34°9N 87°59W **85** D11
Hamilton Mont., U.S.A. 46°15N 114°10W **76** C6
Hamilton Ohio, U.S.A. 39°24N 84°34W **81** F11
Hamilton Tex., U.S.A. 31°42N 98°7W **84** F5
Hamilton → Queens.,
 Australia 23°30S 139°47E **62** C2
Hamilton → S. Austral.,
 Australia 26°40S 135°19E **63** D2
Hamilton City U.S.A. 39°45N 122°1W **78** F4
Hamilton I. Australia 20°21S 148°56E **62** b
Hamilton Inlet Canada 54°0N 57°30W **73** B8
Hamilton Mt. U.S.A. 43°25N 74°22W **83** C10
Hamina Finland 60°34N 27°12E **8** F22
Hamirpur H.P., India 31°41N 76°31E **42** D7
Hamirpur Ut. P., India 25°57N 80°9E **43** G8
Hamju N. Korea 39°51N 127°26E **35** E14
Hamlet U.S.A. 34°53N 79°42W **85** D15
Hamley Bridge Australia 34°17S 138°35E **63** E2
Hamlin = Hameln
 Germany 52°6N 9°21E **16** B5
Hamlin N.Y., U.S.A. 43°17N 77°55W **82** C7
Hamlin Tex., U.S.A. 32°53N 100°8W **84** E4
Hamm Germany 51°40N 7°50E **16** C4
Ḥammār, Hawr al Iraq 30°50N 47°10E **44** D5
Hammerfest Norway 70°39N 23°41E **8** A20
Hammond Ind., U.S.A. 41°38N 87°30W **80** E10
Hammond La., U.S.A. 30°30N 90°28W **85** F9
Hammond N.Y., U.S.A. 44°27N 75°42W **83** B9
Hammondsport U.S.A. 42°25N 77°13W **82** D7
Hammonton U.S.A. 39°39N 74°48W **81** F16
Hampden N.Z. 45°18S 170°50E **59** F3
Hampshire □ U.K. 51°7N 1°23W **13** F6
Hampshire Downs U.K. 51°15N 1°10W **13** F6
Hampton N.B., Canada 45°32N 65°51W **73** C6
Hampton Ont., Canada 43°58N 78°45W **82** C6
Hampton Ark., U.S.A. 33°32N 92°28W **84** E8
Hampton Iowa, U.S.A. 42°45N 93°13W **80** D7
Hampton N.H., U.S.A. 42°57N 70°50W **83** D14
Hampton S.C., U.S.A. 32°52N 81°7W **85** E14
Hampton Va., U.S.A. 37°2N 76°21W **81** G15
Hampton Bays U.S.A. 40°53N 72°31E **83** F12
Hampton Tableland
 Australia 32°0S 127°0E **61** F4
Hamyang S. Korea 35°32N 127°42E **35** G14
Han Pijesak Bos.-H. 44°5N 18°57E **23** B8
Hanak Si. Arabia 25°32N 37°0E **44** E3
Hanamaki Japan 39°23N 141°7E **30** E10
Hanang Tanzania 4°30S 35°25E **54** C4
Hanau Germany 50°7N 8°56E **16** C5
Hanbogd = Ihbulag
 Mongolia 43°11N 107°10E **34** C4
Hancheng China 35°31N 110°25E **34** G6
Hancock Mich., U.S.A. 47°8N 88°35W **80** B9
Hancock N.Y., U.S.A. 41°57N 75°17W **83** E9
Hancock Vt., U.S.A. 43°55N 72°50W **83** C12
Handa Japan 34°53N 136°55E **31** G8
Handan China 36°35N 114°28E **34** F8
Handeni Tanzania 5°25S 38°2E **54** D4
Handwara India 34°21N 74°20E **43** B6
Hanegev Israel 30°50N 35°0E **46** E4
Hanford U.S.A. 36°20N 119°39W **78** J7
Hanford Reach △
 U.S.A. 46°40N 119°30W **76** C4
Hang Chat Thailand 18°20N 99°21E **38** C2
Hang Dong Thailand 18°41N 98°55E **38** C2
Hangang → S. Korea 37°50N 126°30E **35** F14
Hangayn Nuruu Mongolia 47°30N 99°0E **32** B4
Hangchou = Hangzhou
 China 30°18N 120°11E **33** C7
Hanggin Houqi China 40°58N 107°4E **34** D4
Hanggin Qi China 39°52N 108°50E **34** E5
Hangu China 39°18N 117°53E **35** E9
Hangzhou China 30°18N 120°11E **33** C7
Hangzhou Wan China 30°15N 120°45E **33** C7
Hanh Mongolia 51°32N 100°35E **32** A5
Hanhongor Mongolia 43°55N 104°28E **34** C3
Hania = Chania Greece 35°30N 24°4E **25** D6
Hanish Si. Arabia 26°35N 48°38E **45** E6
Ḥanīsh Yemen 13°45N 42°46E **47** E3
Hankinson U.S.A. 46°4N 96°54W **80** B5
Hankö Finland 59°50N 22°57E **9** G20
Hanksville U.S.A. 38°22N 110°43W **76** G8
Hanle India 32°42N 79°4E **43** C8
Hanmer Springs N.Z. 42°32S 172°50E **59** E4
Hann → Australia 17°26S 126°17E **60** C4
Hann, Mt. Australia 15°45S 126°0E **60** C4
Hanna Canada 51°40N 111°54W **70** C6
Hanna U.S.A. 41°52N 106°34W **76** F10
Hannah B. Canada 51°40N 80°0W **72** B4
Hannibal Mo., U.S.A. 39°42N 91°22W **80** F8
Hannibal N.Y., U.S.A. 43°19N 76°35W **83** C8
Hanoi Vietnam 21°5N 105°55E **38** B5
Hanover = Hannover
 Germany 52°22N 9°46E **16** B5
Hanover Canada 44°9N 81°2W **82** B3
Hanover S. Africa 31°4S 24°29E **56** E3
Hanover N.H., U.S.A. 43°42N 72°17W **83** C12
Hanover Ohio, U.S.A. 40°4N 82°16W **82** F2
Hanover Pa., U.S.A. 39°48N 76°59W **81** F15
Hanover, I. Chile 51°0S 74°50W **96** G2
Hans Lollik I.
 U.S. Virgin Is. 18°24N 64°53W **89** e
Hansdiha India 24°36N 87°5E **43** G12
Hansi H.P., India 32°27N 77°50E **42** C7
Hansi Haryana, India 29°10N 75°57E **42** E6
Hanson, L. Australia 31°0S 136°15E **63** E2
Hantsavichy Belarus 52°49N 26°30E **17** B14
Hanumangarh India 29°35N 74°19E **42** E6
Hanzhong China 33°10N 107°1E **34** H4
Hanzhuang China 34°33N 117°23E **35** G9
Haora India 22°34N 88°18E **43** H13
Haparanda Sweden 65°52N 24°8E **8** D21
Happy U.S.A. 34°45N 101°52W **84** D4
Happy Camp U.S.A. 41°48N 123°23W **76** F2
Happy Valley-Goose Bay
 Canada 53°15N 60°20W **73** B7
Hapsu N. Korea 41°13N 128°51E **35** D15
Hapur India 28°45N 77°45E **42** E7
Ḥaql Si. Arabia 29°10N 34°58E **46** F3
Har Indonesia 5°16S 133°14E **37** F8
Har-Ayrag Mongolia 45°47N 109°16E **34** B5
Har Hu China 38°20N 97°38E **32** C4
Har Us Nuur Mongolia 48°0N 92°0E **32** B4
Har Yehuda Israel 31°35N 34°57E **46** D3
Ḥaraḍ Si. Arabia 24°22N 49°0E **47** C4
Haramosh Pakistan 35°50N 74°54E **43** B6
Haranomachi Japan 37°38N 140°58E **30** F10
Harare Zimbabwe 17°43S 31°2E **55** F3
Harazé Chad 9°57N 20°48E **51** G10
Harbin China 45°48N 126°40E **35** B14
Harbor Beach U.S.A. 43°51N 82°39W **82** C2
Harborcreek U.S.A. 42°9N 79°57W **82** D5
Harbour Breton Canada 47°29N 55°50W **73** C8
Harbour Deep Canada 50°25N 56°32W **73** B8
Harda India 22°27N 77°5E **42** H7
Hardangerfjorden Norway 60°5N 6°0E **9** F12
Hardangervidda Norway 60°7N 7°20E **8** F12
Hardap □ Namibia 24°29S 17°45E **56** C2
Hardap Dam Namibia 24°32S 17°50E **56** C2
Hardenberg Neths. 52°34N 6°37E **15** B6
Harderwijk Neths. 52°21N 5°38E **15** B5
Hardey → Australia 22°45S 116°8E **60** D2
Hardin U.S.A. 45°44N 107°37W **76** D10
Harding S. Africa 30°35S 29°55E **57** E4
Harding Ra. Australia 16°17S 124°55E **60** C3
Hardisty Canada 52°40N 111°18W **70** C6
Hardoi India 27°26N 80°6E **43** F9
Hardwar = Haridwar
 India 29°58N 78°9E **42** E8
Hardwick U.S.A. 44°30N 72°22W **83** B12
Hardwood Lake Canada 45°12N 77°26W **82** A7
Hardy, Pen. Chile 55°30S 68°20W **96** H3
Hardy, Pte. St. Lucia 14°6N 60°56W **89** f
Hare B. Canada 51°15N 55°45W **73** B8
Hareid Norway 62°22N 6°1E **8** E12
Harer Ethiopia 9°20N 42°8E **47** F3
Hargeisa Somali Rep. 9°30N 44°2E **47** F3
Hari → Indonesia 1°16S 104°5E **36** E2
Haria Canary Is. 29°8N 13°32W **24** E6
Haridwar India 29°58N 78°9E **42** E8
Harim, Jabal al Oman 25°58N 56°14E **45** E8
Haringhata → Bangla. 22°0N 89°58E **41** J16
Harīr, W. al → Syria 32°44N 35°59E **46** C4
Harīrūd → Asia 37°24N 60°38E **45** B9
Härjedalen Sweden 62°22N 13°5E **8** E15
Harlan Iowa, U.S.A. 41°39N 95°19W **80** E6
Harlan Ky., U.S.A. 36°51N 83°19W **81** G12
Harlech U.K. 52°52N 4°6W **12** E3
Harlem U.S.A. 48°32N 108°47W **76** B9
Harlingen Neths. 53°11N 5°25E **15** A5
Harlingen U.S.A. 26°12N 97°42W **84** H6
Harlow U.K. 51°46N 0°8E **13** F8
Harlowton U.S.A. 46°26N 109°50W **76** C9
Harnai Pakistan 30°6N 67°56E **42** D2
Harney Basin U.S.A. 43°0N 119°30W **76** E4
Harney L. U.S.A. 43°14N 119°8W **76** E4
Harney Peak U.S.A. 43°52N 103°32W **80** D3
Harnösand Sweden 62°38N 17°55E **8** E17
Haroldswick U.K. 60°48N 0°50W **11** A8
Harp L. Canada 55°5N 61°50W **73** A7
Harper Liberia 4°25N 7°43W **50** H4
Harper, Mt. U.S.A. 64°14N 143°51W **74** C11
Harrai India 22°37N 79°13E **43** H8
Harrand Pakistan 29°28N 70°3E **42** E4
Harriman U.S.A. 35°56N 84°33W **85** D12
Harrington Harbour
 Canada 50°31N 59°30W **73** B8
Harris U.K. 57°50N 6°55W **11** D2
Harris, L. Australia 31°10S 135°10E **63** E2
Harris, Sd. of U.K. 57°44N 7°6W **11** D1
Harris Pt. Canada 43°6N 82°9W **82** C2
Harrisburg Ill., U.S.A. 37°44N 88°32W **80** G9
Harrisburg Nebr.,
 U.S.A. 41°33N 103°44W **80** E2
Harrisburg Pa., U.S.A. 40°16N 76°53W **82** F8
Harrismith S. Africa 28°15S 29°8E **57** D4
Harrison Ark., U.S.A. 36°14N 93°7W **84** C8
Harrison Maine, U.S.A. 44°7N 70°39W **83** B14
Harrison Nebr., U.S.A. 42°41N 103°53W **80** D2
Harrison, C. Canada 54°55N 57°55W **73** B8
Harrison L. Canada 49°33N 121°50W **70** D4
Harrison Bay U.S.A. 70°40N 151°0W **74** A9
Harrisonburg U.S.A. 38°27N 78°52W **81** F14
Harrisonville U.S.A. 38°39N 94°21W **80** F6
Harriston Canada 43°57N 80°53W **82** C4
Harrisville Mich., U.S.A. 44°39N 83°17W **82** B1
Harrisville N.Y., U.S.A. 44°9N 75°19W **83** B9
Harrisville Pa., U.S.A. 41°8N 80°0W **82** E5
Harrodsburg U.S.A. 37°46N 84°51W **81** G11
Harrogate U.K. 54°0N 1°33W **12** C6
Harrow Canada 42°2N 82°55W **82** D2
Harrow □ U.K. 51°35N 0°21W **13** F7
Harrowsmith Canada 44°24N 76°40W **83** B8
Harry S. Truman Res.
 U.S.A. 38°16N 93°24W **80** F7
Harsīn Iran 34°18N 47°33E **44** C5
Harstad Norway 68°48N 16°30E **8** B17
Harsud India 22°6N 76°44E **42** H7
Hart U.S.A. 43°42N 86°22W **80** D10
Hart, L. Australia 31°10S 136°25E **63** E2
Hartbees → S. Africa 28°45S 20°32E **56** D3
Hartford Conn., U.S.A. 41°46N 72°41W **83** E12
Hartford Ky., U.S.A. 37°27N 86°55W **80** G10
Hartford S. Dak., U.S.A. 43°38N 96°57W **80** D5
Hartford Vt., U.S.A. 43°40N 72°20W **83** C12
Hartford Wis., U.S.A. 43°19N 88°22W **80** D9
Hartford City U.S.A. 40°27N 85°22W **81** E11
Hartland Canada 46°20N 67°32W **73** C6
Hartland Pt. U.K. 51°1N 4°32W **13** F3
Hartlepool U.K. 54°42N 1°13W **12** C6
Hartlepool □ U.K. 54°42N 1°17W **12** C6
Hartley Bay Canada 53°25N 129°15W **70** C3
Hartmannberge Namibia 17°0S 13°0E **56** B1
Hartney Canada 49°30N 100°35W **71** D8
Harts → S. Africa 28°24S 24°17E **56** D3
Harts Range Australia 23°6S 134°55E **62** C1
Hartselle U.S.A. 34°27N 86°56W **85** D11
Hartshorne U.S.A. 34°51N 95°34W **84** D7
Hartstown U.S.A. 41°33N 80°23W **82** E4
Hartsville S.C., U.S.A. 34°23N 80°4W **85** D14
Hartswater S. Africa 27°34S 24°43E **56** D3
Hartwell U.S.A. 34°21N 82°56W **85** D13
Harunabad Pakistan 29°35N 73°8E **42** E5
Harvand Iran 28°25N 55°43E **45** D7
Harvey Australia 33°5S 115°54E **61** F2
Harvey Ill., U.S.A. 41°36N 87°50W **80** E10
Harvey N. Dak., U.S.A. 47°47N 99°56W **80** B4
Harwich U.K. 51°56N 1°17E **13** F9
Haryana □ India 29°0N 76°10E **42** E7
Haryn → Belarus 52°7N 27°17E **17** B14
Harz Germany 51°38N 10°44E **16** C6
Hasa □ Si. Arabia 25°50N 49°0E **45** E6
Hasaheisa Sudan 14°44N 33°20E **51** F12
Ḥasan Kīf Turkey 37°34N 41°23E **44** B4
Hasanābād Iran 32°8N 52°44E **45** C7
Ḥasb, W. → Iraq 31°45N 44°17E **44** D5
Hasdo → India 21°44N 82°44E **43** J10
Hashimoto Japan 34°19N 135°37E **31** G7
Hashtjerd Iran 35°52N 50°40E **45** C6
Hashtpur = Tālesh Iran 37°58N 48°58E **45** B6
Haskell U.S.A. 33°10N 99°44W **84** E5
Haskovo = Khaskovo
 Bulgaria 41°56N 25°30E **23** D11
Haslemere U.K. 51°5N 0°43W **13** F7
Hasselt Belgium 50°56N 5°21E **15** D5
Hassi Messaoud Algeria 31°51N 6°1E **50** B7
Hässleholm Sweden 56°10N 13°46E **9** H15
Hastings N.Z. 39°39S 176°52E **59** C6
Hastings U.K. 50°51N 0°35E **13** G8
Hastings Mich., U.S.A. 42°39N 85°17W **81** D11
Hastings Minn., U.S.A. 44°44N 92°51W **80** C7
Hastings Nebr., U.S.A. 40°35N 98°23W **80** E4
Hastings Ra. Australia 31°15S 152°14E **63** E5
Hat Yai Thailand 7°1N 100°27E **39** J3
Hatanbulag = Ergel
 Mongolia 43°8N 109°5E **34** C5
Hatay Turkey 36°14N 36°10E **44** B3
Hatch U.S.A. 32°40N 107°9W **77** K10
Hatchet L. Canada 58°36N 103°40W **71** B8
Hateruma-Shima Japan 24°3N 123°47E **31** M1
Hatfield Australia 33°54S 143°49E **63** E3
Hatgal Mongolia 50°26N 100°9E **32** A5
Hathras India 27°36N 78°6E **42** F8
Hatia Bangla. 22°30N 91°5E **41** H17
Hato Mayor Dom. Rep. 18°46N 69°15W **89** C6
Hatta India 24°7N 79°36E **43** G8
Hatta U.A.E. 24°45N 56°4E **45** E8
Hattah Australia 34°48S 142°17E **63** E3
Hattah Kulkyne △
 Australia 34°16S 142°33E **63** E3
Hatteras, C. U.S.A. 35°14N 75°32W **85** D17
Hattiesburg U.S.A. 31°20N 89°17W **85** F10
Hatvan Hungary 47°40N 19°45E **17** E10
Hau Duc Vietnam 15°20N 108°13E **38** E7
Haugesund Norway 59°23N 5°13E **9** G11
Haukipudas Finland 65°12N 25°20E **8** D21
Haultain → Canada 55°51N 106°46W **71** B7
Hauraki G. N.Z. 36°35S 175°5E **59** B5
Haut Atlas Morocco 32°30N 5°0W **50** B4
Hautes Fagnes = Hohes Venn
 Belgium 50°30N 6°5E **15** D6
Hauts Plateaux Algeria 35°0N 1°0E **50** B6
Havana = La Habana
 Cuba 23°8N 82°22W **88** B3
Havana U.S.A. 40°18N 90°4W **80** E8
Havant U.K. 50°51N 0°58W **13** G7
Havasor = Kızıl Turkey 38°18N 43°25E **44** B4
Havasu, L. U.S.A. 34°18N 114°28W **79** L12
Havel → Germany 52°50N 12°3E **16** B7
Havelian Pakistan 34°2N 73°10E **42** B5
Havelock Canada 44°26N 77°53W **82** B7
Havelock N.Z. 41°17S 173°48E **59** D4
Havelock U.S.A. 34°53N 76°54W **85** D16
Haverfordwest U.K. 51°48N 4°58W **13** F3
Haverhill U.K. 52°5N 0°28E **13** E8
Haverhill U.S.A. 42°47N 71°5W **83** D13
Haverstraw U.S.A. 41°12N 73°58W **83** E11
Havirga Mongolia 45°41N 113°5E **34** B7
Havířov Czech Rep. 49°46N 18°20E **17** D10
Havlíčkův Brod
 Czech Rep. 49°36N 15°33E **16** D8
Havre U.S.A. 48°33N 109°41W **76** B9
Havre-Aubert Canada 47°12N 61°56W **73** C7
Havre-St.-Pierre Canada 50°18N 63°33W **73** B7
Haw → U.S.A. 35°36N 79°3W **85** D15
Hawai'i U.S.A. 19°30N 155°30W **75** M8
Hawai'i □ U.S.A. 19°30N 156°30W **75** M8
Hawaiian Is. Pac. Oc. 20°30N 156°0W **65** E12
Hawaiian Ridge Pac. Oc. 24°0N 165°0W **65** E11
Hawarden U.S.A. 43°0N 96°29W **80** D5
Hawea, L. N.Z. 44°28S 169°19E **59** F2
Hawera N.Z. 39°35S 174°19E **59** C5
Hawi U.S.A. 20°14N 155°50W **75** L8
Hawick U.K. 55°26N 2°47W **11** F6
Hawk Junction Canada 48°5N 84°38W **72** C3
Hawke B. N.Z. 39°25S 177°20E **59** C6
Hawker Australia 31°59S 138°22E **63** E2
Hawke's Bay Canada 50°36N 57°10W **73** B8
Hawkesbury Canada 45°37N 74°37W **72** C5
Hawkesbury I. Canada 53°37N 129°3W **70** C3
Hawkesbury Pt.
 Australia 11°55S 134°5E **62** A1
Hawkinsville U.S.A. 32°17N 83°28W **85** E13
Hawley Minn., U.S.A. 46°53N 96°19W **80** B5
Hawley Pa., U.S.A. 41°28N 75°11W **83** E9
Ḥawrān, W. → Iraq 33°58N 42°34E **44** C4
Hawsh Mūssá Lebanon 33°45N 35°55E **46** B4
Hawthorne U.S.A. 38°32N 118°38W **76** G4
Hay Australia 34°30S 144°51E **63** E3
Hay → Australia 24°50S 138°0E **62** C2
Hay → Canada 60°50N 116°26W **70** A5
Hay, C. Australia 14°5S 129°29E **60** B4
Hay I. Canada 44°53N 80°58W **82** B4
Hay L. Canada 58°50N 118°50W **70** B5
Hay-on-Wye U.K. 52°5N 3°8W **13** E4
Hay Point Australia 21°18S 149°17E **62** C4
Hay River Canada 60°51N 115°44W **70** A5
Hay Springs U.S.A. 42°41N 102°41W **80** D2
Haya = Tehoru Indonesia 3°23S 129°30E **37** E7
Hayachine-San Japan 39°34N 141°29E **30** E10
Hayastan = Armenia ■
 Asia 40°20N 45°0E **19** F7
Haydān, W. al → Jordan 31°29N 35°34E **46** D4
Hayden U.S.A. 40°30N 107°16W **76** F10
Hayes → Canada 57°3N 92°12W **72** A1
Hayes, Mt. U.S.A. 63°37N 146°43W **74** C10
Hayes Creek Australia 13°43S 131°22E **60** B5
Hayle U.K. 50°11N 5°26W **13** G2
Hayling I. U.K. 50°48N 0°59W **13** G7
Hayman I. Australia 20°4S 148°53E **62** b
Hayrabolu Turkey 41°12N 27°5E **23** D12
Hays Canada 50°6N 111°48W **70** C6
Hays U.S.A. 38°53N 99°20W **80** F4
Haysyn Ukraine 48°57N 29°25E **17** D15
Hayward Calif., U.S.A. 37°40N 122°4W **78** H4
Hayward Wis., U.S.A. 46°1N 91°29W **80** B8
Haywards Heath U.K. 51°0N 0°5W **13** G7
Hazafon □ Israel 32°40N 35°20E **46** C4
Hazar Turkmenistan 39°34N 53°16E **19** G9
Hazārān, Kūh-e Iran 29°35N 57°20E **45** D8
Hazard U.S.A. 37°15N 83°12W **81** G12
Hazaribag India 23°58N 85°26E **43** H11
Hazaribag Road India 24°12N 85°57E **43** G11
Hazelton Canada 55°20N 127°42W **70** B3
Hazelton U.S.A. 46°29N 100°17W **80** B4
Hazen U.S.A. 47°18N 101°38W **80** B3
Hazen, L. Canada 81°47N 71°1W **69** A17
Hazenmore Canada 49°42N 107°35W **71** D7
Hazlehurst Ga., U.S.A. 31°52N 82°36W **85** F13
Hazlehurst Miss., U.S.A. 31°52N 90°24W **85** F9
Hazlet U.S.A. 40°25N 74°12W **83** F10
Hazleton U.S.A. 40°57N 75°59W **83** F9
Hazlett, L. Australia 21°30S 128°48E **60** D4
Hazro Turkey 38°15N 40°47E **44** B4
Head of Bight Australia 31°30S 131°25E **61** F5
Headlands Zimbabwe 18°15S 32°2E **55** F3
Healdsburg U.S.A. 38°37N 122°52W **78** G4
Healdton U.S.A. 34°14N 97°29W **84** H6
Healesville Australia 37°35S 145°30E **63** F4
Healy U.S.A. 63°52N 148°58W **74** C10
Heany Junction Zimbabwe 20°6S 28°54E **57** C4
Heard I. Ind. Oc. 53°6S 72°36E **3** G13
Hearne U.S.A. 30°53N 96°36W **84** F6
Hearst Canada 49°40N 83°41W **72** C3
Heart → U.S.A. 46°46N 100°50W **80** B3
Heart's Content Canada 47°54N 53°27W **73** C9
Heath, Pte. Canada 49°8N 61°40W **73** C7
Heathrow, London ✈ (LHR)
 U.K. 51°28N 0°27W **13** F7
Heavener U.S.A. 34°53N 94°36W **84** D7
Hebbronville U.S.A. 27°18N 98°41W **84** H5
Hebei □ China 39°0N 116°0E **34** E9
Hebel Australia 28°58S 147°42E **63** D4
Heber U.S.A. 34°30N 110°35W **77** J8
Heber Springs U.S.A. 35°30N 92°2W **84** D8
Hebgen L. U.S.A. 44°52N 111°20W **76** D8
Hebi China 35°57N 114°7E **34** G8
Hebrides U.K. 57°30N 7°0W **11** D2
Hebrides, Sea of the U.K. 57°5N 7°0W **11** D2
Hebron = Al Khalīl
 West Bank 31°32N 35°6E **46** D4
Hebron Canada 58°5N 62°30W **69** F19
Hebron N. Dak., U.S.A. 46°54N 102°3W **80** B3
Hebron Nebr., U.S.A. 40°10N 97°35W **80** E5
Hecate Str. Canada 53°10N 130°30W **70** C2
Heceta I. U.S.A. 55°46N 133°40W **70** B2
Hechi China 24°40N 108°2E **32** D5
Hechuan China 30°2N 106°12E **32** C5
Hecla U.S.A. 45°53N 98°9W **80** C4

Hecla I. Canada 51°10N 96°43W 71 C9
Hede Sweden 62°23N 13°30E 8 E15
Hedemora Sweden 60°18N 15°58E 9 F16
Heerde Neths. 52°24N 6°2E 15 B6
Heerenveen Neths. 52°57N 5°55E 15 B5
Heerhugowaard Neths. 52°40N 4°51E 15 B4
Heerlen Neths. 50°55N 5°58E 15 D5
Ḥefa Israel 32°46N 35°0E 46 C4
Ḥefa □ Israel 32°40N 35°0E 46 C4
Hefei China 31°52N 117°18E 33 C6
Hegang China 47°20N 130°19E 33 B8
Hei Ling Chau China 22°15N 114°2E 33 G11
Heichengzhen China 36°24N 106°3E 34 F4
Heidelberg Germany 49°24N 8°42E 16 D5
Heidelberg S. Africa 34°6S 20°59E 56 E3
Heihe China 50°10N 127°30E 33 A7
Heilbron S. Africa 27°16S 27°59E 57 D4
Heilbronn Germany 49°9N 9°13E 16 D5
Heiligenhaus □ Germany 48°0N 126°0E 33 B7
Heilunkiang = Heilongjiang □
China 48°0N 126°0E 33 B7
Heimaey Iceland 63°26N 20°17W 8 E3
Heinola Finland 61°13N 26°2E 8 F22
Heinze Kyun Burma 14°25N 97°45E 38 E1
Heishan China 41°40N 122°5E 35 D12
Heishui China 42°8N 119°30E 35 C10
Hejaz = Ḥijāz Si. Arabia 24°0N 40°0E 44 E3
Hejian China 38°25N 116°5E 34 E9
Hejin China 35°35N 110°42E 34 G6
Hekımhan Turkey 38°50N 37°55E 44 B3
Hekla Iceland 63°56N 19°35W 8 E4
Hekou China 22°30N 103°59E 32 D5
Helan Shan China 38°30N 105°55E 34 E3
Helena Ark., U.S.A. 34°32N 90°36W 85 D9
Helena Mont., U.S.A. 46°36N 112°2W 76 C7
Helendale U.S.A. 34°44N 117°19W 79 L9
Helensburgh U.K. 56°1N 4°43W 11 E4
Helensville N.Z. 36°41S 174°29E 59 B5
Helenvale Australia 15°43S 145°14E 62 B4
Helgeland Norway 66°7N 13°29E 8 C15
Helgoland Germany 54°10N 7°53E 16 A4
Heligoland = Helgoland
Germany 54°10N 7°53E 16 A4
Heligoland B. = Deutsche Bucht
Germany 54°15N 8°0E 16 A5
Hell Hole Gorge △
Australia 25°31S 144°12E 62 D3
Hella Iceland 63°50N 20°24W 8 E3
Hellas = Greece ■ Europe 40°0N 23°0E 23 E9
Hellertown U.S.A. 40°35N 75°21W 83 F9
Hellespont = Çanakkale Boğazı
Turkey 40°17N 26°32E 23 D12
Hellevoetsluis Neths. 51°50N 4°8E 15 C4
Hellín Spain 38°31N 1°40W 21 C5
Hells Canyon △ U.S.A. 45°30N 117°45W 76 D5
Hell's Gate △ Kenya 0°54S 36°19E 54 C4
Helmand □ Afghan. 31°20N 64°0E 40 D4
Helmand → Afghan. 31°12N 61°34E 40 D2
Helmeringhausen
Namibia 25°54S 16°57E 56 D2
Helmond Neths. 51°29N 5°41E 15 C5
Helmsdale U.K. 58°7N 3°39W 11 C5
Helmsdale → U.K. 58°8N 3°43W 11 C5
Helong China 42°40N 129°0E 35 C15
Helper U.S.A. 39°41N 110°51W 76 G8
Helsingborg Sweden 56°3N 12°42E 9 H15
Helsingfors = Helsinki
Finland 60°10N 24°55E 9 F21
Helsingør Denmark 56°2N 12°35E 9 H15
Helsinki Finland 60°10N 24°55E 9 F21
Helston U.K. 50°6N 5°17W 13 G2
Helvellyn U.K. 54°32N 3°1W 12 C4
Helwân Egypt 29°50N 31°20E 51 C12
Hemel Hempstead U.K. 51°44N 0°28W 13 F7
Hemet U.S.A. 33°45N 116°58W 79 M10
Hemingford U.S.A. 42°19N 103°4W 80 D2
Hemis △ India 34°10N 77°15E 42 B7
Hemmingford Canada 45°3N 73°35W 83 A11
Hempstead N.Y., U.S.A. 40°42N 73°37W 83 F11
Hempstead Tex., U.S.A. 30°6N 96°5W 84 F6
Hemse Sweden 57°15N 18°22E 9 H18
Henan □ China 34°0N 114°0E 34 H8
Henares → Spain 40°24N 3°30W 21 B4
Henashi-Misaki Japan 40°37N 139°51E 30 D9
Henderson Argentina 36°18S 61°43W 94 D3
Henderson Ky., U.S.A. 37°50N 87°35W 80 G10
Henderson N.C., U.S.A. 36°20N 78°25W 85 C15
Henderson N.Y., U.S.A. 43°51N 76°11E 83 C8
Henderson Nev., U.S.A. 36°2N 114°58W 79 J12
Henderson Tenn.,
U.S.A. 35°26N 88°38W 85 D10
Henderson Tex., U.S.A. 32°9N 94°48W 84 E7
Henderson I. Pac. Oc. 24°22S 128°19W 65 K15
Hendersonville N.C.,
U.S.A. 35°19N 82°28W 85 D13
Hendersonville Tenn.,
U.S.A. 36°18N 86°37W 85 C11
Hendijân Iran 30°14N 49°43E 45 D6
Hendorābî Iran 26°40N 53°37E 45 E7
Hengcheng China 38°18N 106°28E 34 E4
Hengdaohezi China 44°52N 129°0E 35 B15
Hengduan Shan China 27°30N 99°0E 32 D4
Hengelo Neths. 52°26N 6°48E 15 B6
Henggang China 22°39N 114°12E 33 F11
Hengqin Dao China 22°7N 113°34E 33 G10
Hengshan China 37°58N 109°5E 34 F5
Hengshui China 37°41N 115°40E 34 F8
Hengyang China 26°59N 112°22E 33 D6
Henley-on-Thames U.K. 51°32N 0°54W 13 F7
Henlopen, C. U.S.A. 38°48N 75°6W 81 F8
Hennenman S. Africa 27°59S 27°1E 56 D4
Hennessey U.S.A. 36°6N 97°54W 84 C6
Henri Pittier △
Venezuela 10°26N 67°37W 89 D6
Henrietta N.Y., U.S.A. 43°4N 77°37W 82 C7
Henrietta Tex., U.S.A. 33°49N 98°12W 84 E5
Henrietta, Ostrov = Genriyetty,
Ostrov Russia 77°6N 156°30E 29 B16

Henrietta Maria, C.
Canada 55°9N 82°20W 72 A3
Henry U.S.A. 41°7N 89°22W 80 E9
Henryetta U.S.A. 35°27N 95°59W 84 D7
Henryville Canada 45°8N 73°11W 83 A11
Hensall Canada 43°26N 81°30W 82 C3
Hentiesbaai Namibia 22°8S 14°18E 56 C1
Hentiyn Nuruu
Mongolia 48°30N 108°30E 33 B5
Henty Australia 35°30S 147°3E 63 F4
Henzada Burma 17°38N 95°26E 41 L19
Heppner U.S.A. 45°21N 119°33W 76 D4
Hepworth Canada 44°37N 81°9W 82 B3
Hequ China 39°20N 111°15E 34 E6
Héraðsflói Iceland 65°42N 14°12W 8 D6
Héraðsvötn → Iceland 65°45N 19°25W 8 D4
Heraklion = Iraklio
Greece 35°20N 25°12E 25 D7
Herald Cays Australia 16°58S 149°9E 62 B4
Herãt Afghan. 34°20N 62°7E 40 B3
Herãt □ Afghan. 35°0N 62°0E 40 B3
Herbert Canada 50°30N 107°10W 71 C7
Herbert → Australia 18°31S 146°17E 62 B4
Herberton Australia 17°20S 145°25E 62 B4
Herbertsdale S. Africa 34°1S 21°46E 56 E3
Herceg-Novi Montenegro 42°30N 18°33E 23 C8
Herchmer Canada 57°22N 94°10W 71 B10
Herðubreið Iceland 65°11N 16°21W 8 D5
Hereford U.K. 52°4N 2°43W 13 E5
Hereford U.S.A. 34°49N 102°24W 84 D3
Herefordshire □ U.K. 52°8N 2°40W 13 E5
Herentals Belgium 51°12N 4°51E 15 C4
Herford Germany 52°7N 8°39E 16 B5
Herington U.S.A. 38°40N 96°57W 80 F5
Herkimer U.S.A. 43°2N 74°59W 83 D10
Herlong U.S.A. 40°8N 120°8W 78 E6
Herm U.K. 49°30N 2°28W 13 H5
Hermann U.S.A. 38°42N 91°27W 80 F8
Hermannsburg
Australia 23°57S 132°45E 60 D5
Hermanus S. Africa 34°27S 19°12E 56 E2
Hermidale Australia 31°30S 146°42E 63 E4
Hermiston U.S.A. 45°51N 119°17W 76 D4
Hermon Canada 45°6N 77°37W 82 A7
Hermon U.S.A. 44°28N 75°14W 83 B9
Hermon, Mt. = Shaykh, J. ash
Lebanon 33°25N 35°50E 46 B4
Hermosillo Mexico 29°10N 111°0W 86 B2
Hernád → Hungary 47°56N 21°8E 17 D11
Hernandarias Paraguay 25°20S 54°40W 95 B5
Hernandez U.S.A. 36°24N 120°46W 78 J6
Hernando Argentina 32°28S 63°40W 94 C3
Hernando U.S.A. 34°50N 90°0W 85 D10
Herndon U.S.A. 38°31N 76°51W 82 F8
Herne Germany 51°32N 7°14E 15 C7
Herne Bay U.K. 51°21N 1°8E 13 F9
Herning Denmark 56°8N 8°58E 9 H13
Heroica Caborca = Caborca
Mexico 30°37N 112°6W 86 A2
Heroica Nogales = Nogales
Mexico 31°19N 110°56W 86 A2
Heron Bay Canada 48°40N 86°25W 72 C2
Heron I. Australia 23°27S 151°55E 62 C5
Herradura, Pta. de la
Canary Is. 28°26N 14°8W 24 F5
Herreid U.S.A. 45°50N 100°4W 80 C3
Herrin U.S.A. 37°48N 89°2W 80 G9
Herriot Canada 56°22N 101°16W 71 B8
Herschel I. Canada 69°35N 139°5W 4 C1
Hershey U.S.A. 40°17N 76°39W 83 F8
Herstal Belgium 50°40N 5°38E 15 D5
Hertford U.K. 51°48N 0°4W 13 F7
Hertfordshire □ U.K. 51°51N 0°5W 13 F7
's-Hertogenbosch Neths. 51°42N 5°17E 15 C5
Hertzogville S. Africa 28°9S 25°30E 56 D4
Hervey B. Australia 25°0S 152°52E 62 C5
Herzliyya Israel 32°10N 34°50E 46 C3
Ḥeşãr Fãrs, Iran 29°52N 50°16E 45 D6
Ḥeşãr Markazī, Iran 35°50N 49°12E 45 C6
Heshui China 35°48N 108°0E 34 G5
Heshun China 37°22N 113°32E 34 F7
Hesperia U.S.A. 34°25N 117°18W 79 L9
Hesse = Hessen □
Germany 50°30N 9°0E 16 C5
Hessen □ Germany 50°30N 9°0E 16 C5
Hetauda Nepal 27°25N 85°2E 43 F11
Hetch Hetchy Aqueduct
U.S.A. 37°29N 122°19W 78 H5
Hettinger U.S.A. 46°0N 102°42W 80 B2
Heuksando S. Korea 34°40N 125°30E 35 G13
Heunghae S. Korea 36°12N 129°21E 35 F15
Heuvelton U.S.A. 44°37N 75°25W 83 B9
Hewitt U.S.A. 31°28N 97°12W 84 F6
Hexigten Qi China 43°18N 117°30E 34 C9
Ḥeydarãbãd Iran 30°33N 55°38E 45 D7
Heysham U.K. 54°3N 2°53W 12 C5
Heywood Australia 38°8S 141°37E 63 F3
Heze China 35°14N 115°20E 34 G8
Hi Vista U.S.A. 34°45N 117°46W 79 L9
Hialeah U.S.A. 25°51N 80°16W 85 J14
Hiawatha U.S.A. 39°51N 95°32W 80 F6
Hibbing U.S.A. 47°25N 92°56W 80 B7
Hibernia Reef Australia 12°0S 123°23E 60 B3
Hickman U.S.A. 36°34N 89°11W 80 G9
Hickory U.S.A. 35°44N 81°21W 85 D14
Hicks, Pt. Australia 37°49S 149°17E 63 F4
Hicks L. Canada 61°25N 100°0W 71 A9
Hicksville U.S.A. 40°46N 73°32W 83 F11
Hida-Gawa → Japan 35°26N 137°3E 31 G8
Hida-Sammyaku Japan 36°30N 137°40E 31 F8
Hidaka-Sammyaku
Japan 42°35N 142°45E 30 C11
Hidalgo □ Mexico 20°30N 99°0W 87 C5
Hidalgo, Presa M.
Mexico 26°30N 108°35W 86 B3
Hidalgo del Parral
Mexico 26°56N 105°40W 86 B3
Hierro Canary Is. 27°44N 18°0W 24 G1

Higashiajima-San
Japan 37°40N 140°10E 30 F10
Higashiõsaka Japan 34°39N 135°37E 31 G7
Higgins U.S.A. 36°7N 100°2W 84 C4
Higgins Corner U.S.A. 39°2N 121°5W 78 F5
High Bridge U.S.A. 40°40N 74°54W 83 F10
High Desert U.S.A. 43°40N 120°20W 74 G15
High Island Res. China 22°22N 114°21E 33 G11
High Level Canada 58°31N 117°8W 70 B5
High Point U.S.A. 35°57N 80°0W 85 D15
High Prairie Canada 55°30N 116°30W 70 B5
High River Canada 50°30N 113°50W 70 C6
High Tatra = Tatry
Slovak Rep. 49°20N 20°0E 17 D11
High Veld Africa 27°0S 27°0E 48 J6
High Wycombe U.K. 51°37N 0°45W 13 F7
Highland □ U.K. 57°17N 4°21W 11 D4
Highland Park U.S.A. 42°11N 87°48W 80 D10
Highmore U.S.A. 44°31N 99°27W 80 C4
Highrock L. Canada 55°45N 100°30W 71 B8
Higüey Dom. Rep. 18°37N 68°42W 89 C6
Hiiumaa Estonia 58°50N 22°45E 9 G20
Ḥijãrah, Ṣaḥrã' al Iraq 30°25N 44°30E 44 D5
Ḥijãz Si. Arabia 24°0N 40°0E 44 E3
Hijo = Tagum Phil. 7°33N 125°53E 37 C7
Hikari Japan 33°58N 131°58E 31 H5
Hiko U.S.A. 37°32N 115°14W 78 H11
Hikone Japan 35°15N 136°10E 31 G8
Hikurangi Gisborne, N.Z. 37°55S 178°4E 59 C6
Hikurangi Northland,
N.Z. 35°36S 174°17E 59 A5
Hildesheim Germany 52°9N 9°56E 16 B5
Hill → Australia 30°23S 115°3E 61 F2
Hill City Idaho, U.S.A. 43°18N 115°3W 76 E6
Hill City Kans., U.S.A. 39°22N 99°51W 80 F4
Hill City Minn., U.S.A. 46°59N 93°36W 80 B7
Hill City S. Dak., U.S.A. 43°56N 103°35W 80 D2
Hill Island L. Canada 60°30N 109°50W 71 A7
Hillaby, Mt. Barbados 13°12N 59°35W 89 g
Hillcrest Barbados 13°13N 59°31W 89 g
Hillcrest Center U.S.A. 35°23N 118°57W 79 K8
Hillegom Neths. 52°18N 4°35E 15 B4
Hillsboro Kans., U.S.A. 38°21N 97°12W 80 F5
Hillsboro N. Dak., U.S.A. 47°26N 97°3W 80 B5
Hillsboro Ohio, U.S.A. 39°12N 83°37W 81 F12
Hillsboro Oreg., U.S.A. 45°31N 122°59W 78 E4
Hillsboro Tex., U.S.A. 32°1N 97°8W 84 E6
Hillsborough Grenada 12°28N 61°28W 89 D7
Hillsborough Channel
Australia 20°56S 149°15E 62 b
Hillsdale Mich., U.S.A. 41°56N 84°38W 81 E11
Hillsdale N.Y., U.S.A. 42°11N 73°32W 83 D11
Hillsport Canada 49°27N 85°34W 72 C2
Hillston Australia 33°30S 145°31E 63 E4
Hilo U.S.A. 19°44N 155°5W 75 M8
Hilton U.S.A. 43°17N 77°48W 82 C7
Hilton Head Island
U.S.A. 32°13N 80°45W 85 E14
Hilversum Neths. 52°14N 5°10E 15 B5
Himachal Pradesh □
India 31°30N 77°0E 42 D7
Himalaya Asia 29°0N 84°0E 43 E11
Himalchuli Nepal 28°27N 84°38E 43 E11
Himatnagar India 23°37N 72°57E 42 H5
Himeji Japan 34°50N 134°40E 31 G7
Himi Japan 36°50N 136°55E 31 F8
Ḥimş Syria 34°40N 36°45E 46 A5
Ḥimş □ Syria 34°30N 37°0E 46 A6
Hinche Haiti 19°9N 72°1W 89 C5
Hinchinbrook I.
Australia 18°20S 146°15E 62 B4
Hinchinbrook Island △
Australia 18°14S 146°6E 62 B4
Hinckley U.K. 52°33N 1°22W 13 E6
Hinckley U.S.A. 46°1N 92°56W 80 B7
Hindaun India 26°44N 77°5E 42 F7
Hindmarsh, L. Australia 36°5S 141°55E 63 F3
Hindu Bagh Pakistan 30°56N 67°50E 42 D2
Hindu Kush Asia 36°0N 71°0E 40 B7
Hindupur India 13°49N 77°32E 40 N10
Hines Creek Canada 56°20N 118°40W 70 B5
Hinesville U.S.A. 31°51N 81°36W 85 F14
Hinganghat India 20°30N 78°52E 40 J11
Hingham U.S.A. 48°33N 110°25W 76 B8
Hingir India 21°57N 83°41E 43 J10
Hingoli India 19°41N 77°15E 40 K10
Hinna = Imi Ethiopia 6°28N 42°10E 47 F3
Hinnøya Norway 68°35N 15°50E 8 B16
Hinojosa del Duque Spain 38°30N 5°9W 21 C3
Hinsdale U.S.A. 42°47N 72°29W 83 D12
Hinthada = Henzada
Burma 17°38N 95°26E 41 L19
Hinton Canada 53°26N 117°34W 70 C5
Hinton U.S.A. 37°40N 80°54W 81 G13
Hirado Japan 33°22N 129°33E 31 H4
Hirakud Dam India 21°32N 83°45E 41 J13
Hiran → India 23°6N 79°21E 43 H8
Hirapur India 24°22N 79°13E 43 G8
Hirara Japan 24°48N 125°17E 31 M2
Hiratsuka Japan 35°19N 139°21E 31 G9
Hiroo Japan 42°17N 143°19E 30 C11
Hirosaki Japan 40°34N 140°28E 30 D10
Hiroshima Japan 34°24N 132°30E 31 G6
Hiroshima □ Japan 34°50N 133°0E 31 G6
Hisar India 29°12N 75°45E 42 E6
Hisb, Sha'ib → = Ḥasb, W. →
Iraq 31°45N 44°17E 44 D5
Ḥismã Si. Arabia 28°30N 36°0E 44 D3
Hispaniola W. Indies 19°0N 71°0W 89 C5
Hīt Iraq 33°38N 42°49E 44 C4
Hita Japan 33°20N 130°58E 31 H5
Hitachi Japan 36°36N 140°39E 31 F10
Hitchin U.K. 51°58N 0°16W 13 F7
Hitiaa Tahiti 17°36S 149°18W 59 d
Hitoyoshi Japan 32°13N 130°45E 31 H5
Hitra Norway 63°30N 8°45E 8 E13
Hiva Oa French Polynesia 9°45S 139°0W 65 H14

Hixon Canada 53°25N 122°35W 70 C4
Ḥiyyon, N. → Israel 30°25N 35°10E 46 E4
Hjalmar L. Canada 61°33N 109°25W 71 A7
Hjälmaren Sweden 59°18N 15°40E 9 G16
Hjørring Denmark 57°29N 9°59E 9 H13
Hjort Trench S. Ocean 58°0S 157°30E 5 B10
Hkakabo Razi Burma 28°25N 97°23E 41 E20
Hkamti = Singkaling Hkamti
Burma 26°0N 95°39E 41 G19
Hlobane S. Africa 27°42S 31°0E 57 D5
Hluhluwe S. Africa 28°1S 32°15E 57 D5
Hluhluwe △ S. Africa 28°0S 32°30E 57 D5
Hlyboka Ukraine 48°5N 25°56E 17 D13
Ho Ghana 6°37N 0°27E 50 G6
Ho Chi Minh City = Thanh Pho
Ho Chi Minh Vietnam 10°58N 106°40E 39 G6
Ho Thuong Vietnam 19°32N 105°48E 38 C5
Hoa Binh Vietnam 20°50N 105°20E 38 B5
Hoa Da Vietnam 11°16N 108°40E 39 G7
Hoa Hiep Vietnam 11°34N 105°51E 39 G5
Hoai Nhon Vietnam 14°28N 109°1E 38 E7
Hoang Lien Son Vietnam 22°0N 104°0E 38 A4
Hoanib → Namibia 19°27S 12°46E 56 B2
Hoare B. Canada 65°17N 62°30W 69 D19
Hoarusib → Namibia 19°3S 12°36E 56 B2
Hobart Australia 42°50S 147°21E 63 G4
Hobart U.S.A. 35°1N 99°6W 84 D5
Hobbs U.S.A. 32°42N 103°8W 77 K12
Hobbs Coast Antarctica 74°50S 131°0W 5 D14
Hobe Sound U.S.A. 27°4N 80°8W 85 H14
Hoboken U.S.A. 40°44N 74°3W 83 F10
Hobro Denmark 56°39N 9°46E 9 H13
Hoburgen Sweden 56°55N 18°7E 9 H18
Hobyo Somali Rep. 5°25N 48°30E 47 F4
Hochfeld Namibia 21°28S 17°58E 56 C2
Hodaka-Dake Japan 36°17N 137°39E 31 F8
Hodeida = Al Ḥudaydah
Yemen 14°50N 43°0E 47 E3
Hodgeville Canada 50°7N 106°58W 71 C7
Hodgson Canada 51°13N 97°36W 71 C9
Hódmezővásárhely
Hungary 46°28N 20°22E 17 E11
Hodna, Chott el Algeria 35°26N 4°43E 50 A6
Hodonín Czech Rep. 48°50N 17°10E 17 D9
Hoek van Holland Neths. 52°0N 4°7E 15 C4
Hoengseong S. Korea 37°29N 127°59E 35 F14
Hoeryong N. Korea 42°30N 129°45E 35 C15
Hoeyang N. Korea 38°43N 127°36E 35 E14
Hof Germany 50°19N 11°55E 16 C6
Hofmeyr S. Africa 31°39S 25°50E 56 E4
Höfn Iceland 64°15N 15°13W 8 D6
Hofors Sweden 60°31N 16°15E 9 F17
Hofsjökull Iceland 64°49N 18°48W 8 D4
Hōfu Japan 34°3N 131°34E 31 G5
Hogan Group Australia 39°13S 147°1E 63 F4
Hogarth, Mt. Australia 21°48S 136°58E 62 C2
Hoge Kempen △ Belgium 51°6N 5°35E 15 C5
Hoggar = Ahaggar Algeria 23°0N 6°30E 50 D7
Hogsty Reef Bahamas 21°41N 73°48W 89 B5
Hoh → U.S.A. 47°45N 124°29W 78 C2
Hoh Xil Shan China 35°0N 89°0E 32 C3
Hohenwald U.S.A. 35°33N 87°33W 85 D11
Hoher Rhön = Rhön
Germany 50°24N 9°58E 16 C5
Hohes Venn Belgium 50°30N 6°5E 15 D6
Hohhot China 40°52N 111°40E 34 D6
Hoi An Vietnam 15°30N 108°19E 38 E7
Hoi Xuan Vietnam 20°25N 105°9E 38 B5
Hoisington U.S.A. 38°31N 98°47W 80 F4
Hōjō Japan 33°58N 132°46E 31 H6
Hokianga Harbour
N.Z. 35°31S 173°22E 59 A4
Hokitika N.Z. 42°42S 171°0E 59 E3
Hokkaidō □ Japan 43°30N 143°0E 30 C11
Hola Kenya 1°29S 40°2E 54 B4
Holakas Greece 35°57N 27°53E 25 D9
Holbrook Australia 35°42S 147°18E 63 F4
Holbrook U.S.A. 34°54N 110°10W 77 J8
Holcomb U.S.A. 42°54N 77°25W 82 D7
Holden U.S.A. 39°6N 112°16W 76 G7
Holdenville U.S.A. 35°5N 96°24W 84 D6
Holdrege U.S.A. 40°26N 99°23W 80 E4
Holetown Barbados 13°11N 59°38W 89 g
Holguín Cuba 20°50N 76°20W 88 B4
Hollams Bird I. Namibia 24°40S 14°30E 56 C1
Holland = Netherlands ■
Europe 52°0N 5°30E 15 C5
Holland Mich., U.S.A. 42°47N 86°7W 80 D10
Holland N.Y., U.S.A. 42°38N 78°32W 82 D6
Holland Centre Canada 44°23N 80°47W 82 B4
Holland Patent U.S.A. 43°14N 75°15W 83 C9
Hollandale U.S.A. 33°10N 90°51W 85 E9
Holley U.S.A. 43°14N 78°2W 82 C6
Hollidaysburg U.S.A. 40°26N 78°24W 82 F6
Hollis U.S.A. 34°41N 99°55W 84 D5
Hollister Calif., U.S.A. 36°51N 121°24W 78 J5
Hollister Idaho, U.S.A. 42°21N 114°35W 76 E6
Holly U.S.A. 38°3N 102°7W 76 G12
Holly Hill U.S.A. 29°16N 81°3W 85 G14
Holly Springs U.S.A. 34°46N 89°27W 85 D10
Hollywood U.S.A. 26°0N 80°8W 85 J14
Holman Canada 70°44N 117°44W 68 C8
Hólmavík Iceland 65°42N 21°40W 8 D3
Holmen U.S.A. 43°58N 91°15W 80 D8
Holmes Reefs Australia 16°27S 148°0E 62 B4
Holmsund Sweden 63°41N 20°20E 8 E19
Holroyd → Australia 14°10S 141°36E 62 A3
Holstebro Denmark 56°22N 8°37E 9 H13
Holsworthy U.K. 50°48N 4°22W 13 G3
Holton Canada 54°31N 57°12W 73 B8
Holton U.S.A. 39°28N 95°44W 80 F6
Holtville U.S.A. 32°49N 115°23W 79 N11
Holwerd Neths. 53°22N 5°54E 15 A5
Holy Cross U.S.A. 62°12N 159°46W 74 C8
Holy I. Anglesey, U.K. 53°17N 4°37W 12 D3
Holy I. Northumberland,
U.K. 55°40N 1°47W 12 B6
Holyhead U.K. 53°18N 4°38W 12 D3
Holyoke Colo., U.S.A. 40°35N 102°18W 76 F12
Holyoke Mass., U.S.A. 42°12N 72°37W 83 D12

Holyrood Canada 47°27N 53°8W 73 C9
Homa Bay Kenya 0°36S 34°30E 54 C3
Homalin Burma 24°55N 95°0E 41 G19
Homãnd Iran 32°28N 59°37E 45 C8
Homathko → Canada 51°0N 124°56W 70 C4
Hombori Mali 15°20N 1°38W 50 E5
Home B. Canada 68°40N 67°10W 69 D13
Home Hill Australia 19°43S 147°25E 62 B4
Home Reef Tonga 18°59S 174°47W 59 c
Homedale U.S.A. 43°37N 116°56W 76 E5
Homer Alaska, U.S.A. 59°39N 151°33W 68 F1
Homer La., U.S.A. 32°48N 93°4W 84 E8
Homer N.Y., U.S.A. 42°38N 76°10W 83 D8
Homer City U.S.A. 40°32N 79°10W 82 F5
Homestead Australia 20°20S 145°40E 62 C4
Homestead U.S.A. 25°28N 80°29W 85 J14
Homewood U.S.A. 40°17N 96°50W 78 F6
Homoine Mozam. 23°55S 35°8E 57 C6
Homs = Ḥimş Syria 34°40N 36°45E 46 A5
Homyel Belarus 52°28N 31°0E 17 B16
Hon Chong Vietnam 10°25N 104°30E 39 G5
Hon Hai Vietnam 11°16N 109°0E 39 H7
Hon Me Vietnam 19°23N 105°56E 38 C5
Honan = Henan □ China 34°0N 114°0E 34 H8
Honbetsu Japan 43°7N 143°37E 30 C11
Honcut U.S.A. 39°20N 121°32W 78 F5
Honda, Bahía Cuba 22°54N 83°10W 88 B3
Hondeklipbaai S. Africa 30°19S 17°17E 56 E2
Hondo Japan 32°27N 130°12E 31 H5
Hondo U.S.A. 29°21N 99°9W 84 G5
Hondo, Río → Belize 18°25N 88°21W 87 D7
Honduras ■ Cent. Amer. 14°40N 86°30W 88 D2
Honduras, G. de
Caribbean 16°50N 87°0W 88 C2
Hønefoss Norway 60°10N 10°18E 9 F14
Honesdale U.S.A. 41°34N 75°16W 83 E9
Honey Harbour Canada 44°52N 79°49W 82 B5
Honey L. U.S.A. 40°15N 120°19W 78 E6
Honfleur France 49°25N 0°13E 20 B4
Hong Gai Vietnam 20°57N 107°5E 38 B6
Hong He → China 32°25N 115°35E 34 H8
Hong Kong □ China 22°11N 114°14E 33 G11
Hong Kong Int. ✈ (HKG)
China 22°19N 113°57E 33 G10
Hongcheon S. Korea 37°44N 127°53E 35 F14
Hongjiang China 27°7N 109°59E 33 D5
Hongliu He → China 38°0N 109°50E 34 F5
Hongor Mongolia 45°45N 112°50E 34 B7
Hongsa Laos 19°43N 101°20E 38 C3
Hongseong S. Korea 36°37N 126°38E 35 F14
Hongshui He → China 23°48N 109°30E 33 D5
Hongtong China 36°16N 111°40E 34 F6
Honguedo, Détroit d'
Canada 49°15N 64°0W 73 C7
Hongwon N. Korea 40°0N 127°56E 35 E14
Hongze Hu China 33°15N 118°35E 35 H10
Honiara Solomon Is. 9°27S 159°57E 58 B8
Honiton U.K. 50°47N 3°11W 13 G4
Honjō Japan 39°23N 140°3E 30 E10
Honningsvåg Norway 70°59N 25°59E 8 A21
Honolulu U.S.A. 21°19N 157°52W 75 L8
Honshū Japan 36°0N 138°0E 30 F9
Hood, Pt. Australia 34°23S 119°34E 61 F2
Hood River U.S.A. 45°43N 121°31W 76 D3
Hoodsport U.S.A. 47°24N 123°9W 78 C3
Hoogeveen Neths. 52°44N 6°28E 15 B6
Hoogezand-Sappemeer
Neths. 53°9N 6°45E 15 A6
Hooghly = Hugli →
India 21°56N 88°4E 43 J13
Hooghly-Chinsura = Chunchura
India 22°53N 88°27E 43 H13
Hook Hd. Ireland 52°7N 6°56W 10 D5
Hook I. Australia 20°4S 149°0E 62 b
Hook of Holland = Hoek van
Holland Neths. 52°0N 4°7E 15 C4
Hooker U.S.A. 36°52N 101°13W 84 C4
Hooker Creek = Lajamanu
Australia 18°23S 130°38E 60 C5
Hoonah U.S.A. 58°7N 135°27W 70 B1
Hooper Bay U.S.A. 61°32N 166°6W 74 C6
Hoopeston U.S.A. 40°28N 87°40W 80 E10
Hoopstad S. Africa 27°50S 25°55E 56 D4
Hoorn Neths. 52°38N 5°4E 15 B5
Hoover U.S.A. 33°24N 86°49W 85 E11
Hoover Dam U.S.A. 36°1N 114°44W 79 K12
Hooversville U.S.A. 40°9N 78°55W 82 F6
Hop Bottom U.S.A. 41°42N 75°46W 83 E9
Hope Canada 49°25N 121°25W 70 D4
Hope Ariz., U.S.A. 33°43N 113°42W 79 M13
Hope Ark., U.S.A. 33°40N 93°36W 84 E8
Hope, L. S. Austral.,
Australia 28°24S 139°18E 63 D2
Hope, L. W. Austral.,
Australia 32°35S 120°15E 61 F3
Hope, Pt. U.S.A. 68°21N 166°47W 66 C3
Hope I. Canada 51°9N 80°11W 82 B4
Hope Town Bahamas 26°35N 76°57W 88 A4
Hope Vale ◌ Australia 15°8S 145°15E 62 B4
Hopedale Canada 55°28N 60°13W 73 A7
Hopefield S. Africa 33°3S 18°22E 56 E2
Hopei = Hebei □ China 39°0N 116°0E 34 E9
Hopelchén Mexico 19°46N 89°51W 87 D7
Hopetoun Vic., Australia 35°42S 142°22E 63 F3
Hopetoun W. Austral.,
Australia 33°57S 120°7E 61 F3
Hopetown S. Africa 29°34S 24°3E 56 D3
Hopewell U.S.A. 37°18N 77°17W 81 G15
Hopkins, L. Australia 24°15S 128°35E 60 D4
Hopkinsville U.S.A. 36°52N 87°29W 80 G10
Hopland U.S.A. 38°58N 123°7W 78 G3
Hoquiam U.S.A. 46°59N 123°53W 78 D3
Hordern Hills Australia 20°15S 130°0E 60 D5

Horinger *China* 40°28N 111°48E **34 D6**
Horizontina *Brazil* 27°37S 54°19W **95 B5**
Horlick Mts. *Antarctica* 84°0S 102°0W **5 E15**
Horlivka *Ukraine* 48°19N 38°5E **19 E6**
Hormak *Iran* 29°58N 60°51E **45 D9**
Hormoz *Iran* 27°35N 55°0E **45 E8**
Hormoz, Jaz.-ye *Iran* 27°8N 56°28E **45 E8**
Hormozgān □ *Iran* 27°30N 56°0E **45 E8**
Hormuz, Küh-e *Iran* 27°27N 55°10E **45 E7**
Hormuz, Str. of *The Gulf* 26°30N 56°30E **45 E8**
Horn *Austria* 48°39N 15°40E **16 D8**
Horn → *Canada* 61°30N 118°1W **70 A5**
Horn, Cape = Hornos, C. de
  Chile 55°50S 67°30W **96 H3**
Horn Head *Ireland* 55°14N 8°0W **10 A3**
Horn I. *Australia* 10°37S 142°17E **62 A3**
Horn Plateau *Canada* 62°15N 119°15W **70 A5**
Hornavan *Sweden* 66°15N 17°30E **8 C17**
Hornbeck *U.S.A.* 31°20N 93°24W **84 F8**
Hornbrook *U.S.A.* 41°55N 122°33W **76 F2**
Horncastle *U.K.* 53°13N 0°7W **12 D7**
Hornell *U.S.A.* 42°20N 77°40W **82 D7**
Hornell L. *Canada* 62°20N 119°25W **70 A5**
Hornepayne *Canada* 49°14N 84°48W **72 C3**
Hornings Mills *Canada* 44°9N 80°12W **82 B4**
Hornitos *U.S.A.* 37°30N 120°14W **78 H6**
Hornos, C. de *Chile* 55°50S 67°30W **96 H3**
Hornsby *Australia* 33°42S 151°2E **63 B5**
Hornsea *U.K.* 53°55N 0°11W **12 D7**
Horobetsu = Noboribetsu
  Japan 42°24N 141°6E **30 C10**
Horodenka *Ukraine* 48°41N 25°29E **17 D13**
Horodok Khmelnytskyy,
  Ukraine 49°10N 26°34E **17 D14**
Horodok *Lviv, Ukraine* 49°46N 23°32E **17 D12**
Horokhiv *Ukraine* 50°30N 24°45E **17 C13**
Horqin Youyi Qianqi
  China 46°5N 122°3E **35 A12**
Horqueta *Paraguay* 23°15S 56°55W **94 A4**
Horse Cr. → *U.S.A.* 41°57N 103°58W **76 F12**
Horse I. *Canada* 53°20N 99°6W **71 C9**
Horse Is. *Canada* 50°15N 55°50W **73 B8**
Horsefly L. *Canada* 52°25N 121°0W **70 C4**
Horseheads *U.S.A.* 42°10N 76°49W **82 D8**
Horsens *Denmark* 55°52N 9°51E **9 J13**
Horseshoe Lake *Canada* 45°38N 90°15W **80 C9**
Horsham *Australia* 36°44S 142°13E **63 F3**
Horsham *U.K.* 51°4N 0°20W **13 F7**
Horta *Azores* 38°32N 28°38W **50 a**
Horten *Norway* 59°25N 10°32E **9 G14**
Horton *U.S.A.* 39°40N 95°32W **80 F7**
Horton → *Canada* 69°56N 126°52W **68 D6**
Horwood L. *Canada* 48°5N 82°20W **72 C3**
Hosapete = Hospet
  India 15°15N 76°20E **40 M10**
Ḩoseynābād *Khuzestān,*
  Iran 32°45N 48°20E **45 C6**
Ḩoseynābād *Kordestān,*
  Iran 35°33N 47°8E **44 C5**
Hoshangabad *India* 22°45N 77°45E **42 H7**
Hoshiarpur *India* 31°30N 75°58E **42 D6**
Hospet *India* 15°15N 76°20E **40 M10**
Hoste, I. *Chile* 55°0S 69°0W **96 H3**
Hot *Thailand* 18°8N 98°29E **38 C2**
Hot Creek Range
  U.S.A. 38°40N 116°20W **76 G5**
Hot Springs *Ark., U.S.A.* 34°31N 93°3W **84 D8**
Hot Springs *S. Dak.,*
  U.S.A. 43°26N 103°29W **80 D2**
Hot Springs △ *U.S.A.* 34°31N 93°3W **84 D8**
Hotagen *Sweden* 63°59N 14°12E **8 E16**
Hotan *China* 37°25N 79°55E **32 C2**
Hotan He → *China* 40°22N 80°56E **32 B3**
Hotazel *S. Africa* 27°17S 22°58E **56 D3**
Hotchkiss *U.S.A.* 38°48N 107°43W **76 G10**
Hotham, C. *Australia* 12°2S 131°18E **60 B5**
Hoting *Sweden* 64°8N 16°15E **8 D17**
Hotte, Massif de la *Haiti* 18°30N 73°45W **89 C5**
Hottentotsbaai *Namibia* 26°8S 14°59E **56 D1**
Hou Hai *China* 22°32N 113°56E **33 F10**
Houei Sai *Laos* 20°18N 100°26E **38 B3**
Houffalize *Belgium* 50°8N 5°48E **15 D5**
Houghton *Mich., U.S.A.* 47°7N 88°34W **80 B9**
Houghton *N.Y., U.S.A.* 42°25N 78°10W **82 D6**
Houghton L. *U.S.A.* 44°21N 84°44W **81 C11**
Houghton-le-Spring
  U.K. 54°51N 1°28W **12 C6**
Houhora Heads *N.Z.* 34°49S 173°9E **59 A4**
Houlton *U.S.A.* 46°8N 67°51W **81 B20**
Houma *U.S.A.* 29°36N 90°43W **85 G9**
Housatonic → *U.S.A.* 41°10N 73°7W **83 E11**
Houston *Canada* 54°25N 126°39W **70 C3**
Houston *Mo., U.S.A.* 37°22N 91°58W **80 G9**
Houston *Tex., U.S.A.* 29°45N 95°21W **84 G7**
Hout = Mogwadi →
  S. Africa 23°4S 29°36E **57 C4**
Houtkraal *S. Africa* 30°23S 24°5E **56 E3**
Houtman Abrolhos
  Australia 28°43S 113°48E **61 E1**
Hovd □ *Mongolia* 48°2N 91°37E **32 B4**
Hove *U.K.* 50°50N 0°10W **13 G7**
Hovenweep △ *U.S.A.* 37°20N 109°0W **77 H9**
Hoveyzeh *Iran* 31°27N 48°4E **45 D6**
Hövsgöl Nuur *Mongolia* 51°0N 100°30E **32 A5**
Howar, Wadi → *Sudan* 17°30N 27°8E **51 E11**
Howard *Australia* 25°16S 152°32E **63 D5**
Howard *Pa., U.S.A.* 41°1N 77°40W **82 F7**
Howard *S. Dak., U.S.A.* 44°1N 97°32W **80 C5**
Howe *U.S.A.* 43°48N 113°0W **76 E7**
Howe, C. *Australia* 37°30S 150°0E **63 F5**
Howe, West Cape
  Australia 35°8S 117°36E **61 G2**
Howe I. *Canada* 44°16N 76°17W **83 B8**
Howell *U.S.A.* 42°36N 83°56W **81 D12**
Howick *Canada* 45°11N 73°51W **83 A11**
Howick *S. Africa* 29°28S 30°14E **57 D5**
Howick Group *Australia* 14°20S 145°30E **62 A4**
Howitt, L. *Australia* 27°40S 138°40E **63 D2**

Howland I. *Pac. Oc.* 0°48N 176°38W **64 G10**
Howrah = Haora *India* 22°34N 88°18E **43 H13**
Howth *Ireland* 53°23N 6°6W **10 C5**
Howth Hd. *Ireland* 53°22N 6°4W **10 C5**
Höxter *Germany* 51°46N 9°22E **16 C5**
Hoy *U.K.* 58°50N 3°15W **11 C5**
Høyanger *Norway* 61°13N 6°4E **8 F12**
Hoyerswerda *Germany* 51°26N 14°14E **16 C8**
Hoylake *U.K.* 53°24N 3°10W **12 D4**
Hpa-an = Pa-an *Burma* 16°51N 97°40E **41 L20**
Hpunan Pass *Burma* 27°30N 96°55E **41 F20**
Hradec Králové
  Czech Rep. 50°15N 15°50E **16 C8**
Hrodna *Belarus* 53°42N 23°52E **17 B12**
Hrodzyanka *Belarus* 53°31N 28°42E **17 B15**
Hron → *Slovak Rep.* 47°49N 18°45E **17 E10**
Hrvatska = Croatia ■
  Europe 45°20N 16°0E **16 F9**
Hrymayliv *Ukraine* 49°20N 26°5E **17 D14**
Hsenwi *Burma* 23°22N 97°55E **41 H20**
Hsiamen = Xiamen
  China 24°25N 118°4E **33 D6**
Hsian = Xi'an *China* 34°15N 109°0E **34 G5**
Hsinchu *Taiwan* 24°48N 120°58E **33 D7**
Hsinhailien = Lianyungang
  China 34°40N 119°11E **35 G10**
Hsüchou = Xuzhou
  China 34°18N 117°10E **35 G9**
Hu Xian *China* 34°8N 108°42E **34 G5**
Hua Hin *Thailand* 12°34N 99°58E **38 F2**
Hua Xian *Henan, China* 35°30N 114°30E **34 G8**
Hua Xian *Shaanxi, China* 34°30N 109°48E **34 G5**
Huab → *Namibia* 20°52S 13°25E **56 B2**
Huachinera *Mexico* 30°9N 108°55W **86 A3**
Huacho *Peru* 11°10S 77°35W **92 F3**
Huade *China* 41°55N 113°59E **34 D7**
Huadian *China* 43°0N 126°40E **35 C14**
Huahine, Î.
  French Polynesia 16°46S 150°58W **65 J12**
Huai Hat △ *Thailand* 16°52N 104°17E **38 D5**
Huai He → *China* 33°0N 118°30E **35 C6**
Huai Nam Dang △
  Thailand 19°30N 98°30E **38 C2**
Huai Yot *Thailand* 7°45N 99°37E **39 J2**
Huai'an *Hebei, China* 40°30N 114°20E **34 D8**
Huai'an *Jiangsu, China* 33°30N 119°10E **35 H10**
Huaibei *China* 34°0N 116°48E **34 G9**
Huaide = Gongzhuling
  China 43°30N 124°40E **35 C13**
Huaidezhen *China* 43°48N 124°50E **35 C13**
Huainan *China* 32°38N 116°58E **33 C6**
Huairen *China* 39°48N 113°20E **34 E7**
Huairou *China* 40°20N 116°35E **34 D9**
Huaiyang *China* 33°40N 114°52E **34 H8**
Huaiying *China* 33°30N 119°2E **35 H10**
Huaiyuan *China* 32°55N 117°10E **35 H9**
Huajuapán de León
  Mexico 17°48N 97°46W **87 D5**
Hualapai Peak *U.S.A.* 35°5N 113°54W **77 J7**
Huallaga → *Peru* 5°15S 75°30W **92 E3**
Huambo *Angola* 12°42S 15°54E **53 G3**
Huan Jiang → *China* 34°28N 109°0E **34 G5**
Huan Xian *China* 36°33N 107°7E **34 F4**
Huancabamba *Peru* 5°10S 79°15W **92 E3**
Huancane *Peru* 15°10S 69°44W **92 G5**
Huancavelica *Peru* 12°50S 75°5W **92 F3**
Huancayo *Peru* 12°5S 75°12W **92 F3**
Huanchaca *Bolivia* 20°15S 66°40W **92 H5**
Huang Hai = Yellow Sea
  China 35°0N 123°0E **35 G12**
Huang He → *China* 37°55N 118°50E **35 F10**
Huang Xian *China* 37°38N 120°30E **35 F11**
Huangling *China* 35°34N 109°15E **34 G5**
Huanglong *China* 35°30N 109°59E **34 G5**
Huangshan *China* 29°42N 118°25E **33 D6**
Huangshi *China* 30°10N 115°3E **33 C6**
Huangsongdian *China* 43°45N 127°25E **35 C14**
Huanren *China* 41°23N 125°20E **35 D13**
Huantai *China* 36°58N 117°56E **35 F9**
Huánuco *Peru* 9°55S 76°15W **92 E3**
Huaraz *Peru* 9°30S 77°32W **92 E3**
Huarmey *Peru* 10°5S 78°5W **92 F3**
Huascarán, Nevado *Peru* 9°7S 77°37W **92 E3**
Huasco *Chile* 28°30S 71°15W **94 B1**
Huasco → *Chile* 28°27S 71°13W **94 B1**
Huasna *U.S.A.* 35°6N 120°24W **79 K6**
Huatabampo *Mexico* 26°50N 109°38W **86 B3**
Huauchinango *Mexico* 20°12N 98°3W **87 C5**
Huautla de Jiménez
  Mexico 18°8N 96°51W **87 D5**
Huayin *China* 34°35N 110°5E **34 G6**
Hubballi = Hubli *India* 15°22N 75°15E **40 M9**
Hubbard *Ohio, U.S.A.* 41°9N 80°34W **82 E4**
Hubbard *Tex., U.S.A.* 31°51N 96°48W **84 F6**
Hubbard Glacier
  Canada 60°18N 139°22W **68 E4**
Hubbart Pt. *Canada* 59°21N 94°41W **71 B10**
Hubei □ *China* 31°0N 112°0E **33 C6**
Hubli *India* 15°22N 75°15E **40 M9**
Huch'ang *N. Korea* 41°25N 127°2E **35 D14**
Hucknall *U.K.* 53°3N 1°13W **12 D6**
Huddersfield *U.K.* 53°39N 1°47W **12 D6**
Hudiksvall *Sweden* 61°43N 17°10E **8 F17**
Hudson *Canada* 50°6N 92°9W **72 B1**
Hudson *Mass., U.S.A.* 42°23N 71°34W **83 D13**
Hudson *N.Y., U.S.A.* 42°15N 73°46W **83 D11**
Hudson *Wis., U.S.A.* 44°58N 92°45W **80 C7**
Hudson *Wyo., U.S.A.* 42°54N 108°35W **76 E9**
Hudson → *U.S.A.* 40°42N 74°2W **83 F10**
Hudson, C. *Antarctica* 68°21S 153°45E **5 C20**
Hudson Bay *Nunavut,*
  Canada 60°0N 86°0W **69 F14**
Hudson Bay *Sask.,*
  Canada 52°51N 102°23W **71 C8**
Hudson Falls *U.S.A.* 43°18N 73°35W **83 C11**
Hudson Mts. *Antarctica* 74°32S 99°20W **5 D16**
Hudson Str. *Canada* 62°0N 70°0W **69 E18**
Hudson's Hope *Canada* 56°0N 121°54W **70 B4**
Hue *Vietnam* 16°30N 107°35E **38 D6**

Huehuetenango
  Guatemala 15°20N 91°28W **88 C1**
Huejúcar *Mexico* 22°21N 103°13W **86 C4**
Huelva *Spain* 37°18N 6°57W **21 D2**
Huentelauquén *Chile* 31°38S 71°33W **94 C1**
Huerta, Sa. de la
  Argentina 31°10S 67°30W **94 C2**
Huesca *Spain* 42°8N 0°25W **21 A5**
Huetamo *Mexico* 18°35N 100°53W **86 D4**
Hugh → *Australia* 25°1S 134°1E **62 D1**
Hughenden *Australia* 20°52S 144°10E **62 C3**
Hughesville *U.S.A.* 41°14N 76°44W **83 E8**
Hugli → *India* 21°56N 88°4E **43 J13**
Hugo *Colo., U.S.A.* 39°8N 103°28W **76 G12**
Hugo *Okla., U.S.A.* 34°1N 95°31W **84 D7**
Hugoton *U.S.A.* 37°11N 101°21W **80 G3**
Hui Xian = Huixian
  China 35°27N 113°12E **34 G7**
Hui Xian *China* 33°50N 106°4E **34 H4**
Hui'anbu *China* 37°28N 106°38E **34 F4**
Huichapan *Mexico* 20°23N 99°39W **87 C5**
Huichon *N. Korea* 40°10N 126°16E **35 D14**
Huifa He → *China* 43°0N 127°50E **35 C14**
Huila, Nevado del *Colombia* 3°0N 76°0W **92 C3**
Huimin *China* 37°27N 117°28E **35 F9**
Huinan *China* 42°40N 126°2E **35 C14**
Huinca Renancó
  Argentina 34°51S 64°22W **94 C3**
Huining *China* 35°38N 105°0E **34 G3**
Huinong *China* 39°5N 106°35E **34 E4**
Huiting *China* 34°5N 116°5E **34 G9**
Huixian *China* 35°27N 113°12E **34 G7**
Huixtla *Mexico* 15°9N 92°28W **87 D6**
Huize *China* 26°24N 103°15E **32 D5**
Hukawng Valley
  Burma 26°30N 96°30E **41 F20**
Hukuntsi *Botswana* 23°58S 21°45E **56 C3**
Ḩulayfā' *Si. Arabia* 25°58N 40°45E **44 E4**
Hulin He → *China* 45°0N 122°10E **35 B12**
Hull = Kingston upon Hull
  U.K. 53°45N 0°21W **12 D7**
Hull *Canada* 45°26N 75°43W **83 A9**
Hull → *U.K.* 53°44N 0°20W **12 D7**
Hulst *Neths.* 51°17N 4°2E **15 C4**
Hulun Nur *China* 49°0N 117°30E **33 B6**
Huma, Tanjung *Malaysia* 5°29N 100°16E **39 K3**
Humacao *Puerto Rico* 18°9N 65°50W **89 d**
Humahuaca *Argentina* 23°10S 65°25W **94 A2**
Humaitá *Brazil* 7°35S 63°1W **92 E6**
Humaitá *Paraguay* 27°2S 58°31W **94 B4**
Humansdorp *S. Africa* 34°2S 24°46E **56 E3**
Humbe *Angola* 16°40S 14°55E **56 B1**
Humber → *U.K.* 53°42N 0°27W **12 D7**
Humboldt *Canada* 52°15N 105°9W **71 C7**
Humboldt *Iowa, U.S.A.* 42°44N 94°13W **80 D6**
Humboldt *Tenn., U.S.A.* 35°50N 88°55W **85 D10**
Humboldt → *U.S.A.* 39°59N 118°36W **76 G4**
Humboldt Gletscher =
  Sermersuaq *Greenland* 79°30N 62°0W **69 B19**
Hume *U.S.A.* 36°48N 118°54W **78 J8**
Hume, L. *Australia* 36°0S 147°5E **63 F4**
Humen *China* 22°50N 113°40E **33 F10**
Humenné *Slovak Rep.* 48°55N 21°50E **17 D11**
Humphreys, Mt.
  U.S.A. 37°17N 118°40W **78 H8**
Humphreys Peak
  U.S.A. 35°21N 111°41W **77 J8**
Humptulips *U.S.A.* 47°14N 123°57W **78 C3**
Hun Jiang → *China* 40°50N 125°38E **35 D13**
Húnaflói *Iceland* 65°50N 20°50W **8 D3**
Hunan □ *China* 27°30N 112°0E **33 D6**
Hunchun *China* 42°52N 130°28E **35 C16**
Hundewali *Pakistan* 31°55N 72°38E **42 D5**
Hundred Mile House
  Canada 51°38N 121°18W **70 C4**
Hunedoara *Romania* 45°40N 22°50E **17 F12**
Hung Yen *Vietnam* 20°39N 106°4E **38 B6**
Hunga Ha'apai *Tonga* 20°41S 175°7W **59 c**
Hungary ■ *Europe* 47°20N 19°20E **17 E10**
Hungary, Plain of *Europe* 47°0N 20°0E **6 F10**
Hungerford *Australia* 28°58S 144°24E **63 D3**
Hŭngnam *N. Korea* 39°49N 127°45E **35 E14**
Hunjiang *China* 41°54N 126°26E **35 D14**
Hunsberge *Namibia* 27°45S 17°12E **56 D2**
Hunsrück *Germany* 49°56N 7°27E **16 D4**
Hunstanton *U.K.* 52°56N 0°29E **12 E8**
Hunter *U.S.A.* 42°13N 74°13W **83 D10**
Hunter I. *Australia* 40°30S 144°45E **63 G3**
Hunter I. *Canada* 51°55N 128°0W **70 C3**
Hunter Ra. *Australia* 32°45S 150°15E **63 E5**
Hunters Road *Zimbabwe* 19°9S 29°49E **55 F2**
Hunterville *N.Z.* 39°56S 175°35E **59 C5**
Huntingburg *U.S.A.* 38°18N 86°57W **80 F10**
Huntingdon *Canada* 45°5N 74°10W **83 A10**
Huntingdon *U.K.* 52°20N 0°11W **13 E7**
Huntingdon *U.S.A.* 40°30N 78°1W **82 F6**
Huntington *Ind., U.S.A.* 40°53N 85°30W **81 E11**
Huntington *N.Y.,*
  U.S.A. 40°52N 73°26W **83 F11**
Huntington *Oreg.,*
  U.S.A. 44°21N 117°16W **76 D5**
Huntington *Utah,*
  U.S.A. 39°20N 110°58W **76 G8**
Huntington *W. Va.,*
  U.S.A. 38°25N 82°27W **81 F12**
Huntington Beach
  U.S.A. 33°40N 118°5W **79 M9**
Huntly *N.Z.* 37°34S 175°11E **59 B5**
Huntly *U.K.* 57°27N 2°47W **11 D6**
Huntsville *Canada* 45°20N 79°14W **82 A5**
Huntsville *Ala., U.S.A.* 34°44N 86°35W **85 D11**
Huntsville *Tex., U.S.A.* 30°43N 95°33W **84 F7**
Hunyani → *Zimbabwe* 15°57S 30°39W **55 F3**
Hunyuan *China* 39°42N 113°42E **34 E7**
Hunza → *India* 35°54N 74°20E **43 B6**
Huo Xian = Huozhou
  China 36°36N 111°42E **34 F6**
Huong Khe *Vietnam* 18°13N 105°41E **38 C5**
Huonville *Australia* 43°0S 147°5E **63 G4**

Huozhou *China* 36°36N 111°42E **34 F6**
Hupeh = Hubei □ *China* 31°0N 112°0E **33 C6**
Ḩūr *Iran* 30°50N 57°7E **45 D8**
Hurand *Iran* 38°51N 47°22E **44 B5**
Huraymīla *Si. Arabia* 25°8N 46°8E **44 E5**
Hurd, C. *Canada* 45°13N 81°44W **82 A3**
Hurghada *Egypt* 27°15N 33°50E **51 C12**
Hurley *N. Mex., U.S.A.* 32°42N 108°8W **77 K9**
Hurley *Wis., U.S.A.* 46°27N 90°11W **80 B8**
Huron *Calif., U.S.A.* 36°12N 120°6W **78 J6**
Huron *Ohio, U.S.A.* 41°24N 82°33W **82 E2**
Huron *S. Dak., U.S.A.* 44°22N 98°13W **80 C4**
Huron, L. *U.S.A.* 44°30N 82°40W **82 B2**
Huron East *Canada* 43°37N 81°18W **82 C3**
Hurricane *U.S.A.* 37°11N 113°17W **77 H7**
Hurunui → *N.Z.* 42°54S 173°18E **59 E4**
Húsavík *Iceland* 66°3N 17°21W **8 C5**
Huşi *Romania* 46°41N 28°7E **17 E15**
Hustadvika *Norway* 63°0N 7°0E **8 E12**
Hustontown *U.S.A.* 40°3N 78°2W **82 F6**
Hutchinson *Kans., U.S.A.* 38°5N 97°56W **80 F5**
Hutchinson *Minn.,*
  U.S.A. 44°54N 94°22W **80 C6**
Hutte Sauvage, L. de la
  Canada 56°15N 64°45W **73 A7**
Hutton, Mt. *Australia* 25°51S 148°20E **63 D4**
Huy *Belgium* 50°31N 5°15E **15 D5**
Huzhou *China* 30°51N 120°8E **33 C7**
Hvammstangi *Iceland* 65°24N 20°57W **8 D3**
Hvar *Croatia* 43°11N 16°28E **22 C7**
Hvítá → *Iceland* 64°30N 21°58W **8 D3**
Hwacheon-Cheosuji
  S. Korea 38°5N 127°50E **35 E14**
Hwang Ho = Huang He →
  China 37°55N 118°50E **35 F10**
Hwange *Zimbabwe* 18°18S 26°30E **55 F2**
Hwange △ *Zimbabwe* 19°0S 26°30E **56 B4**
Hyannis *Mass., U.S.A.* 41°39N 70°17W **81 E18**
Hyannis *Nebr., U.S.A.* 42°0N 101°46W **80 E3**
Hyargas Nuur *Mongolia* 49°0N 93°0E **32 B4**
Hydaburg *U.S.A.* 55°15N 132°50W **70 B2**
Hyde Park *U.S.A.* 41°47N 73°56W **83 E11**
Hyden *Australia* 32°24S 118°53E **61 F2**
Hyder *U.S.A.* 55°55N 130°5W **70 B2**
Hyderabad *India* 17°22N 78°29E **40 L11**
Hyderabad *Pakistan* 25°23N 68°24E **42 G3**
Hydra *Greece* 37°20N 23°28E **23 F10**
Hyères *France* 43°8N 6°9E **20 E7**
Hyères, Îs. d' *France* 43°0N 6°20E **20 E7**
Hyesan *N. Korea* 41°20N 128°10E **35 D15**
Hyland → *Canada* 59°52N 128°12W **70 B3**
Hymia *India* 33°40N 78°2E **43 C8**
Hyndman Peak *U.S.A.* 43°45N 114°8W **76 E6**
Hyōgo □ *Japan* 35°15N 134°50E **31 G7**
Hyrum *U.S.A.* 41°38N 111°51W **76 F8**
Hysham *U.S.A.* 46°18N 107°14W **76 C10**
Hythe *U.K.* 51°4N 1°5E **13 F9**
Hyūga *Japan* 32°25N 131°35E **31 H5**
Hyvinge = Hyvinkää
  Finland 60°38N 24°50E **8 F21**
Hyvinkää *Finland* 60°38N 24°50E **8 F21**

I

I-n-Gall *Niger* 16°51N 7°1E **50 E7**
Iaco → *Brazil* 9°3S 68°34W **92 E5**
Iakora *Madag.* 23°6S 46°40E **57 C8**
Ialissos *Greece* 36°24N 28°10E **25 C10**
Ialomiţa → *Romania* 44°42N 27°51E **17 F14**
Iaşi *Romania* 47°10N 27°40E **17 E14**
Ib → *India* 21°34N 83°48E **43 J10**
Iba *Phil.* 15°22N 120°0E **37 A6**
Ibadan *Nigeria* 7°22N 3°58E **50 G6**
Ibagué *Colombia* 4°20N 75°20W **92 C3**
Ibar → *Serbia* 43°43N 20°45E **23 C9**
Ibaraki □ *Japan* 36°10N 140°10E **31 F10**
Ibarra *Ecuador* 0°21N 78°7W **92 C3**
Ibb *Yemen* 14°2N 44°10E **47 E3**
Ibembo
  Dem. Rep. of the Congo 2°35N 23°35E **54 B1**
Ibenga →
  Dem. Rep. of the Congo 2°19N 18°9E **52 D3**
Ibera, L. *Argentina* 28°30S 57°9W **94 B4**
Iberian Peninsula *Europe* 40°0N 5°0W **6 H5**
Iberville *Canada* 45°19N 73°17W **83 A11**
Iberville, Mt. d' *Canada* 58°50N 63°50W **69 F19**
Ibiá *Brazil* 19°30S 46°30W **93 G9**
Ibiapaba, Sa. da *Brazil* 4°0S 41°30W **93 D10**
Ibicuí → *Brazil* 29°25S 56°47W **95 B4**
Ibicuy *Argentina* 33°55S 59°10W **94 C4**
Ibiza = Eivissa *Spain* 38°54N 1°26E **24 C7**
Ibo *Mozam.* 12°22S 40°40E **55 E5**
Ibonma *Indonesia* 3°29S 133°31E **37 E8**
Ibotirama *Brazil* 12°13S 43°12W **93 F10**
Ibrāhīm → *Lebanon* 34°4N 35°38E **46 A4**
'Ibrī *Oman* 23°14N 56°30E **45 F8**
Ibu *Indonesia* 1°35N 127°33E **37 D7**
Ibusuki *Japan* 31°12N 130°40E **31 J5**
Ica *Peru* 14°0S 75°48W **92 F3**
Iça → *Brazil* 2°55S 67°58W **92 D5**
Icacos Pt. *Trin. & Tob.* 10°3N 61°57W **93 K15**
Içana *Brazil* 0°21N 67°19W **92 C5**
Içana → *Brazil* 0°26N 67°19W **92 C5**
Içel = Turkey ... ...
Iceland ■ *Europe* 64°45N 19°0W **8 D4**
Iceland Basin *Atl. Oc.* 61°0N 19°0W **4 C7**
Icelandic Plateau *Arctic* 64°0N 10°0W **4 C7**
Ich'ang = Yichang
  China 30°40N 111°20E **33 C6**
Ichchapuram *India* 19°10N 84°40E **41 K14**
Icheon *S. Korea* 37°17N 127°27E **35 F14**
Ichhawar *India* 23°1N 77°1E **42 H7**
Ichihara *Japan* 35°28N 140°5E **31 G10**
Ichikawa *Japan* 35°44N 139°55E **31 G9**
Ichilo → *Bolivia* 15°57S 64°50W **92 G6**
Ichinohe *Japan* 40°13N 141°17E **30 D10**
Ichinomiya *Japan* 35°18N 136°48E **31 G8**
Ichinoseki *Japan* 38°55N 141°8E **30 E10**
Icod *Canary Is.* 28°22N 16°43W **24 F3**
Icy C. *U.S.A.* 70°20N 161°52W **66 B3**
Ida Grove *U.S.A.* 42°21N 95°28W **80 D6**
Idabel *U.S.A.* 33°54N 94°50W **84 E7**
Idaho □ *U.S.A.* 45°0N 115°0W **76 D6**
Idaho City *U.S.A.* 43°50N 115°50W **76 E6**
Idaho Falls *U.S.A.* 43°30N 112°2W **76 E7**
Idalia △ *Australia* 24°49S 144°36E **62 C3**
Idar-Oberstein *Germany* 49°43N 7°16E **16 D4**
Idensalmi = Iisalmi
  Finland 63°32N 27°10E **8 E22**
Idfû *Egypt* 24°55N 32°49E **51 D12**
Ídhra = Hydra *Greece* 37°20N 23°28E **23 F10**
Idi *Indonesia* 5°2N 97°37E **36 C1**
Idi, Oros = Psiloritis, Oros
  Greece 35°15N 24°45E **25 D6**
Idiofa
  Dem. Rep. of the Congo 4°55S 19°42E **52 E3**
Idlib *Syria* 35°55N 36°36E **44 C3**
Idria *U.S.A.* 36°25N 120°41W **78 J6**
Idutywa = Dutywa
  S. Africa 32°8S 28°18E **57 E4**
Ieper *Belgium* 50°51N 2°53E **15 D2**
Ierapetra *Greece* 35°1N 25°44E **25 E7**
Iesi *Italy* 43°31N 13°14E **22 C5**
Ifakara *Tanzania* 8°8S 36°41E **52 F7**
'Ifāl, W. al → *Si. Arabia* 28°7N 35°3E **44 D2**
Ifanadiana *Madag.* 21°19S 47°39E **57 C8**
Ife *Nigeria* 7°30N 4°31E **50 G6**
Iffley *Australia* 18°53S 141°12E **62 B3**
Iforas, Adrar des *Africa* 19°40N 1°40E **50 E6**
Ifould, L. *Australia* 30°52S 132°6E **61 F5**
Iganga *Uganda* 0°37N 33°28E **54 B3**
Igarapava *Brazil* 20°3S 47°47W **93 H9**
Igarka *Russia* 67°30N 86°33E **28 C9**
Iggesund *Sweden* 61°39N 17°10E **8 F17**
Iglésias *Italy* 39°19N 8°32E **22 E3**
Igloolik = Iglulik
  Canada 69°20N 81°49W **69 D15**
Igluligaarjuk = Chesterfield Inlet
  Canada 63°30N 90°45W **68 E13**
Iglulik *Canada* 69°20N 81°49W **69 D15**
Ignace *Canada* 49°30N 91°40W **72 C1**
İğneada Burnu *Turkey* 41°53N 28°2E **23 D13**
Igoumenitsa *Greece* 39°32N 20°18E **23 E9**
Igrim *Russia* 63°12N 64°30E **28 C7**
Iguaçu → *Brazil* 25°36S 54°36W **95 B5**
Iguaçu, Cat. del *Brazil* 25°41S 54°26W **95 B5**
Iguaçu △ *Brazil* 25°30S 54°0W **95 B5**
Iguaçu Falls = Iguaçu, Cat. del
  Brazil 25°41S 54°26W **95 B5**
Iguala *Mexico* 18°21N 99°32W **87 D5**
Igualada *Spain* 41°37N 1°37E **21 B6**
Iguassu = Iguaçu →
  Brazil 25°36S 54°36W **95 B5**
Iguatu *Brazil* 6°20S 39°18W **93 E11**
Iguazú △ *Argentina* 25°42S 54°22W **95 B5**
Iguidi, Erg *Africa* 27°0N 7°0W **50 C4**
Iharana *Madag.* 13°25S 50°0E **57 A9**
Ihbulag *Mongolia* 43°11N 107°10E **34 C6**
Iheya-Shima *Japan* 27°4N 127°58E **31 L3**
Ihosy *Madag.* 22°24S 46°8E **57 C8**
Ihotry, Farihy *Madag.* 21°56S 43°41E **57 C7**
Ii *Finland* 65°19N 25°22E **8 D21**
Ii-Shima *Japan* 26°43N 127°47E **31 L3**
Iida *Japan* 35°35N 137°50E **31 G8**
Iijoki → *Finland* 65°20N 25°20E **8 D21**
Iisalmi *Finland* 63°32N 27°10E **8 E22**
Iiyama *Japan* 36°51N 138°22E **31 F9**
Iizuka *Japan* 33°38N 130°42E **31 H5**
Ijâfene *Mauritania* 20°40N 8°0W **50 D4**
Ijebu-Ode *Nigeria* 6°47N 3°58E **50 G6**
IJmuiden *Neths.* 52°28N 4°35E **15 B4**
Ijo älv = Iijoki →
  Finland 65°20N 25°20E **8 D21**
IJssel → *Neths.* 52°35N 5°50E **15 B5**
IJsselmeer *Neths.* 52°45N 5°20E **15 B5**
Ijuí *Brazil* 28°23S 53°55W **95 B5**
Ijuí → *Brazil* 27°58S 55°20W **95 B4**
Ikalamavony *Madag.* 21°9S 46°35E **57 C8**
Ikanga *Kenya* 1°42S 38°4E **54 C4**
Ikare *Nigeria* 7°32N 5°40E **50 G7**
Ikaria *Greece* 37°35N 26°10E **23 F12**
Ikeda *Japan* 34°1N 133°48E **31 G6**
Ikela *Dem. Rep. of the Congo* 1°6S 23°6E **52 E4**
Iki *Japan* 33°45N 129°42E **31 H4**
Ikimba L. *Tanzania* 1°30S 31°20E **54 C3**
Ikopa → *Madag.* 16°45S 46°40E **57 B8**
Ikorongo △ *Tanzania* 1°50S 34°53E **54 C3**
Ikparjuk = Arctic Bay
  Canada 73°1N 85°7W **69 C14**
Iksan *S. Korea* 35°59N 127°0E **35 G14**
Ikungu *Tanzania* 1°33S 33°42E **54 C3**
Ikuntji = Haasts Bluff
  Australia 23°22S 132°0E **60 D5**
Ilagan *Phil.* 17°7N 121°53E **37 A6**
Ilaka *Madag.* 19°33S 48°52E **57 B8**
Īlām *Iran* 33°36N 46°36E **44 C5**
Ilam *Nepal* 26°58N 87°58E **43 F12**
Īlām □ *Iran* 33°0N 47°0E **44 C5**
Ilanskiy *Russia* 56°14N 96°3E **29 D10**
Iława *Poland* 53°36N 19°34E **17 B10**
Ile → *Kazakhstan* 45°53N 77°10E **28 E8**
Île-à-la-Crosse *Canada* 55°27N 107°53W **71 B7**
Île-à-la-Crosse, Lac
  Canada 55°40N 107°45W **71 B7**
Île-de-France □ *France* 49°0N 2°20E **20 B5**
Ilebo *Dem. Rep. of the Congo* 4°17S 20°55E **52 E4**
Ilek *Russia* 51°32N 53°21E **28 D6**
Ilek → *Russia* 51°30N 53°22E **18 D9**
Ilesha *Nigeria* 7°37N 4°40E **50 G6**
Ilford *Canada* 56°4N 95°35W **71 B9**
Ilfracombe *Australia* 23°30S 144°30E **62 C3**
Ilfracombe *U.K.* 51°12N 4°8W **13 F3**
Ilha Grande, Represa
  Brazil 23°10S 53°5W **95 A5**
Ilha Grande △ *Brazil* 23°10S 53°20W **95 A5**

Ilhéus *Brazil* 14°49S 39°2W **93** F11
Ili = Ile → *Kazakhstan* 45°53N 77°10E **28** E8
Iliamna L. *U.S.A.* 59°30N 155°0W **74** D8
Ilias, Profitis *Greece* 36°17N 27°56E **25** C9
Iligan *Phil.* 8°12N 124°13E **37** C6
Ilion *U.S.A.* 43°1N 75°2W **83** D9
Ilkeston *U.K.* 52°58N 1°19W **12** E6
Ilkley *U.K.* 53°56N 1°48W **12** D6
Illampu = Ancohuma, Nevado
  Bolivia 16°0S 68°50W **92** G5
Illana B. *Phil.* 7°35N 123°45E **37** C6
Illapel *Chile* 32°0S 71°10W **94** C1
Iller → *Germany* 48°23N 9°58E **16** D6
Illetas *Spain* 39°32N 2°35E **24** B9
Illimani, Nevado *Bolivia* 16°30S 67°50W **92** G5
Illinois □ *U.S.A.* 40°15N 89°30W **80** E9
Illinois → *U.S.A.* 38°58N 90°28W **80** F8
Illizi *Algeria* 26°31N 8°32E **50** C7
Ilma, L. *Australia* 29°13S 127°46E **61** E4
Ilmajoki *Finland* 62°44N 22°34E **8** E20
Ilmen, Ozero *Russia* 58°15N 31°10E **18** C5
Ilo *Peru* 17°40S 71°20W **92** G4
Iloilo *Phil.* 10°45N 122°33E **37** B6
Ilomantsi *Finland* 62°38N 30°57E **8** E24
Ilorin *Nigeria* 8°30N 4°35E **50** G6
Ilwaco *U.S.A.* 46°19N 124°3W **78** D2
Ilwaki *Indonesia* 7°55S 126°30E **37** F7
Imabari *Japan* 34°4N 133°0E **31** G6
Imaloto → *Madag.* 23°27S 45°13E **57** C8
Imandra, Ozero *Russia* 67°30N 33°0E **8** C25
Imanombo *Madag.* 24°26S 45°49E **57** C8
Imari *Japan* 33°15N 129°52E **31** H4
Imatra *Finland* 61°12N 28°48E **8** F23
imeni 26 Bakinskikh Komissarov
  = Neftçala *Azerbaijan* 39°19N 49°12E **45** B6
imeni 26 Bakinskikh Komissarov
  Turkmenistan 39°22N 54°10E **45** B7
imeni Ismail Samani, Pik
  Tajikistan 39°0N 72°2E **28** F8
Imeri, Serra *Brazil* 0°50N 65°25W **92** C5
Imerimandroso *Madag.* 17°26S 48°35E **57** B8
Imlay *U.S.A.* 40°40N 118°9W **76** F4
Imlay City *U.S.A.* 43°2N 83°5W **82** D1
Immingham *U.K.* 53°37N 0°13W **12** D7
Immokalee *U.S.A.* 26°25N 81°25W **85** H14
Imola *Italy* 44°20N 11°42E **22** B4
Imperatriz *Brazil* 5°30S 47°29W **93** E9
Impéria *Italy* 43°53N 8°3E **20** E8
Imperial *Canada* 51°21N 105°28W **71** C7
Imperial *Calif., U.S.A.* 32°51N 115°34W **79** N11
Imperial *Nebr., U.S.A.* 40°31N 101°39W **80** E3
Imperial Beach *U.S.A.* 32°35N 117°6W **79** N9
Imperial Dam *U.S.A.* 32°55N 114°25W **79** N12
Imperial Res. *U.S.A.* 32°53N 114°28W **79** N12
Imperial Valley *U.S.A.* 33°0N 115°30W **79** N11
Imperieuse Reef
  Australia 17°36S 118°50E **60** C2
Impfondo *Congo* 1°40N 18°0E **52** D3
Imphal *India* 24°48N 93°56E **41** G18
İmroz = Gökçeada
  Turkey 40°10N 25°50E **23** D11
Imuris *Mexico* 30°47N 110°52W **86** A2
Imuruan B. *Phil.* 10°40N 119°10E **37** B5
In Guezzam *Algeria* 19°37N 5°52E **50** E7
In Salah *Algeria* 27°10N 2°32E **50** C6
Ina *Japan* 35°50N 137°55E **31** G8
Inagua △ *Bahamas* 21°5N 73°24W **89** B5
Inangahua *N.Z.* 41°52S 171°59E **59** D4
Inanwatan *Indonesia* 2°8S 132°10E **37** E8
Iñapari *Peru* 11°0S 69°40W **92** F5
Inari *Finland* 68°54N 27°1E **8** B22
Inarijärvi *Finland* 69°0N 28°0E **8** B23
Inawashiro-Ko *Japan* 37°29N 140°6E **30** F10
Inca *Spain* 39°43N 2°54E **24** B9
Inca de Oro *Chile* 26°45S 69°54W **94** B2
Incahuasi *Argentina* 27°2S 68°18W **94** B2
Incahuasi *Chile* 29°12S 71°5W **94** B1
İnce Burun *Turkey* 42°7N 34°56E **19** F5
İncesu *Turkey* 38°38N 35°11E **44** B2
Incheon *S. Korea* 37°27N 126°40E **35** F14
İncirliova *Turkey* 37°50N 27°41E **23** F12
Incline Village *U.S.A.* 39°10N 119°58W **76** G4
Incomáti → *Mozam.* 25°46S 32°43E **57** D5
Indalsälven → *Sweden* 62°36N 17°30E **8** E17
Indaw *Burma* 24°15N 96°5E **41** G20
Independence *Calif.,*
  U.S.A. 36°48N 118°12W **78** J8
Independence *Iowa,*
  U.S.A. 42°28N 91°54W **80** D8
Independence *Kans.,*
  U.S.A. 37°14N 95°42W **80** G6
Independence *Ky.,*
  U.S.A. 38°57N 84°33W **81** F11
Independence *Mo., U.S.A.* 39°6N 94°25W **80** F6
Independence Fjord
  Greenland 82°10N 29°0W **4** A6
Independence Mts.
  U.S.A. 41°20N 116°0W **76** F5
Index *U.S.A.* 47°50N 121°33W **78** C5
India ■ *Asia* 20°0N 78°0E **40** K11
Indian → *U.S.A.* 27°59N 80°34W **85** H14
Indian Cabins *Canada* 59°52N 117°40W **70** B5
Indian Harbour *Canada* 54°27N 57°13W **73** B8
Indian Head *Canada* 50°30N 103°41W **71** C8
Indian L. *U.S.A.* 43°46N 74°16W **83** C10
Indian Lake *U.S.A.* 43°47N 74°16W **83** C10
Indian Springs *U.S.A.* 36°35N 115°40W **79** J11
Indiana *U.S.A.* 40°37N 79°9W **82** F5
Indiana □ *U.S.A.* 40°0N 86°0W **81** F11
Indianapolis *U.S.A.* 39°46N 86°9W **80** F10
Indianola *Iowa, U.S.A.* 41°22N 93°34W **80** E7
Indianola *Miss., U.S.A.* 33°27N 90°39W **85** E9
Indiga *Russia* 67°38N 49°9E **18** A8
Indigirka → *Russia* 70°48N 148°54E **29** B15
Indio *U.S.A.* 33°43N 116°13W **79** M10
Indira Gandhi Canal *India* 28°0N 72°0E **42** F5
Indira Sagar *India* 22°15N 76°40E **42** H7

Indo-China *Asia* 15°0N 102°0E **26** G12
Indonesia ■ *Asia* 5°0S 115°0E **36** F5
Indore *India* 22°42N 75°53E **42** H6
Indramayu *Indonesia* 6°20S 108°19E **37** G13
Indravati → *India* 19°20N 80°20E **41** K12
Indre → *France* 47°16N 0°11E **20** C4
Indulkana *Australia* 26°58S 133°5E **63** D1
Indus → *Pakistan* 24°20N 67°47E **42** G2
Indus, Mouths of the
  Pakistan 24°0N 68°0E **42** H3
İnebolu *Turkey* 41°55N 33°40E **19** F5
Infiernillo, Presa del
  Mexico 18°35N 101°50W **86** D4
Ingenio *Canary Is.* 27°55N 15°26W **24** G4
Ingenio Santa Ana
  Argentina 27°25S 65°40W **94** B2
Ingersoll *Canada* 43°4N 80°55W **82** C4
Ingham *Australia* 18°43S 146°10E **62** B4
Ingleborough *U.K.* 54°10N 2°22W **12** C5
Inglewood *Queens.,*
  Australia 28°25S 151°2E **63** D5
Inglewood *Vic., Australia* 36°29S 143°53E **63** F3
Inglewood *N.Z.* 39°9S 174°14E **59** C5
Inglewood *U.S.A.* 33°58N 118°21W **79** M8
Ingólfshöfði *Iceland* 63°48N 16°39W **8** E5
Ingolstadt *Germany* 48°46N 11°26E **16** D6
Ingomar *U.S.A.* 46°35N 107°23W **76** C10
Ingonish *Canada* 46°42N 60°18W **73** C7
Ingraj Bazar *India* 24°58N 88°10E **43** G13
Ingrid Christensen Coast
  Antarctica 69°30S 76°0E **5** C6
Ingulec = Inhulec
  Ukraine 47°42N 33°14E **19** E5
Ingushetia □ *Russia* 43°20N 44°50E **19** F8
Ingwavuma *S. Africa* 27°9S 31°59E **57** D5
Inhaca *Mozam.* 26°1S 32°57E **57** D5
Inhafenga *Mozam.* 20°36S 33°53E **57** C5
Inhambane *Mozam.* 23°54S 35°30E **57** C6
Inhambane □ *Mozam.* 22°30S 34°20E **57** C5
Inhaminga *Mozam.* 18°26S 35°0E **55** F4
Inharrime *Mozam.* 24°30S 35°0E **57** C6
Inharrime → *Mozam.* 24°30S 35°0E **57** C6
Inhulec *Ukraine* 47°42N 33°14E **19** E5
Ining = Yining *China* 43°58N 81°10E **32** B3
Inis = Ennis *Ireland* 52°51N 8°59W **10** D3
Inis Córthaidh = Enniscorthy
  Ireland 52°30N 6°34W **10** D5
Inishbofin *Ireland* 53°37N 10°13W **10** C1
Inisheer *Ireland* 53°3N 9°32W **10** C2
Inishfree B. *Ireland* 55°4N 8°23W **10** A3
Inishkea North *Ireland* 54°9N 10°11W **10** B1
Inishkea South *Ireland* 54°7N 10°12W **10** B1
Inishmaan *Ireland* 53°5N 9°35W **10** C2
Inishmore *Ireland* 53°8N 9°45W **10** C2
Inishmurray I. *Ireland* 54°26N 8°39W **10** B3
Inishowen Pen. *Ireland* 55°14N 7°15W **10** A4
Inishshark *Ireland* 53°37N 10°16W **10** C1
Inishturk *Ireland* 53°42N 10°7W **10** C1
Inishvickillane *Ireland* 52°3N 10°37W **10** D1
Injinoo ◇ *Australia* 10°56S 142°15E **62** A3
Injune *Australia* 25°53S 148°32E **63** D4
Inklin → *N. Amer.* 58°50N 133°10W **70** B2
Inland Kaikoura Ra.
  N.Z. 41°59S 173°41E **59** D4
Inland Sea = Setonaikai
  Japan 34°20N 133°30E **31** G6
Inle L. *Burma* 20°30N 96°58E **41** J20
Inlet *U.S.A.* 43°45N 74°48W **83** C10
Inn → *Austria* 48°35N 13°28E **16** D7
Innamincka *Australia* 27°44S 140°46E **63** D3
Inner Hebrides *U.K.* 57°0N 6°30W **11** E2
Inner Mongolia = Nei Monggol
  Zizhiqu □ *China* 42°0N 112°0E **34** D7
Inner Sound *U.K.* 57°30N 5°55W **11** D3
Innerkip *Canada* 43°13N 80°42W **82** C4
Innetalling I. *Canada* 56°0N 79°0W **72** A4
Innisfail *Australia* 17°33S 146°5E **62** B4
Innisfail *Canada* 52°2N 113°57W **70** C6
In'noshima *Japan* 34°19N 133°10E **31** G6
Innsbruck *Austria* 47°16N 11°23E **16** E6
Inny → *Ireland* 53°30N 7°50W **10** C4
Inongo
  Dem. Rep. of the Congo 1°55S 18°30E **52** E3
Inoucdjouac = Inukjuak
  Canada 58°25N 78°15W **69** F16
Inowrocław *Poland* 52°50N 18°12E **17** B10
Inscription, C. *Australia* 25°29S 112°59E **61** E1
Insein *Burma* 16°50N 96°5E **41** L20
Inta *Russia* 66°5N 60°8E **18** A11
Intendente Alvear
  Argentina 35°12S 63°32W **94** D3
Interlaken *Switz.* 46°41N 7°50E **20** C7
Interlaken *U.S.A.* 42°37N 76°44W **83** D8
International Falls
  U.S.A. 48°36N 93°25W **80** A7
Intiyaco *Argentina* 28°43S 60°5W **94** B3
Inukjuak *Canada* 58°25N 78°15W **69** F16
Inútil, B. *Chile* 53°30S 70°15W **96** G2
Inuvik *Canada* 68°16N 133°40W **68** B6
Inveraray *U.K.* 56°14N 5°5W **11** E3
Inverbervie *U.K.* 56°51N 2°17W **11** E6
Invercargill *N.Z.* 46°24S 168°24E **59** G2
Inverclyde □ *U.K.* 55°55N 4°49W **11** F4
Inverell *Australia* 29°45S 151°8E **63** D5
Invergordon *U.K.* 57°41N 4°10W **11** D4
Inverloch *Australia* 38°38S 145°45E **63** F4
Invermere *Canada* 50°30N 116°2W **70** C5
Inverness *Canada* 46°15N 61°19W **73** C7
Inverness *U.K.* 57°29N 4°13W **11** D4
Inverness *U.S.A.* 28°50N 82°20W **85** G13
Inverurie *U.K.* 57°17N 2°23W **11** D6
Investigator Group
  Australia 34°45S 134°20E **63** E1
Investigator Str.
  Australia 35°30S 137°0E **63** F2
Inya *Russia* 50°28N 86°37E **28** D9
Inyanga *Zimbabwe* 18°12S 32°40E **55** F3
Inyangani *Zimbabwe* 18°5S 32°50E **55** F3

Inyantue *Zimbabwe* 18°33S 26°39E **56** B4
Inyo Mts. *U.S.A.* 36°40N 118°0W **78** J9
Inyokern *U.S.A.* 35°39N 117°49W **79** K9
Inyonga *Tanzania* 6°45S 32°5E **54** D3
Inza *Russia* 53°55N 46°25E **18** D8
Iō-Jima *Japan* 30°48N 130°18E **31** J5
Ioannina *Greece* 39°42N 20°47E **23** E9
Iola *U.S.A.* 37°55N 95°24W **80** G6
Iona *U.K.* 56°20N 6°25W **11** E2
Ione *U.S.A.* 38°21N 120°56W **78** G6
Ionia *U.S.A.* 42°59N 85°4W **81** D11
Ionian Is. = Ionioi Nisoi
  Greece 38°40N 20°0E **23** E9
Ionian Sea *Medit. S.* 37°30N 17°30E **23** E7
Ionioi Nisoi *Greece* 38°40N 20°0E **23** E9
Ios *Greece* 36°41N 25°20E **23** F11
Iowa □ *U.S.A.* 42°18N 93°30W **80** D7
Iowa → *U.S.A.* 41°10N 91°1W **80** E8
Iowa City *U.S.A.* 41°40N 91°32W **80** E8
Iowa Falls *U.S.A.* 42°31N 93°16W **80** D7
Iowa Park *U.S.A.* 33°57N 98°40W **84** E5
Ipala *Tanzania* 4°30S 32°52E **54** C3
Ipameri *Brazil* 17°44S 48°9W **93** G9
Ipatinga *Brazil* 19°32S 42°30W **93** G10
Ipiales *Colombia* 0°50N 77°37W **92** C3
Ipin = Yibin *China* 28°45N 104°32E **32** D5
Ipixuna *Brazil* 7°0S 71°40W **92** E4
Ipoh *Malaysia* 4°35N 101°5E **39** K3
Ippy *C.A.R.* 6°5N 21°7E **52** C4
Ipsala *Turkey* 40°55N 26°23E **23** D12
Ipswich *Australia* 27°35S 152°40E **63** D5
Ipswich *U.K.* 52°4N 1°10E **13** E9
Ipswich *Mass., U.S.A.* 42°41N 70°50W **83** D14
Ipswich *S. Dak., U.S.A.* 45°27N 99°2W **80** C4
Ipu *Brazil* 4°23S 40°44W **93** D10
Iqaluit *Canada* 63°44N 68°31W **69** E18
Iqalukᵗuutiaq = Cambridge Bay
  Canada 69°10N 105°0W **68** D11
Iquique *Chile* 20°19S 70°5W **92** H4
Iquitos *Peru* 3°45S 73°10W **92** D4
Irabu-Jima *Japan* 24°50N 125°10E **31** M2
Iracoubo *Fr. Guiana* 5°30N 53°10W **93** B8
Írafshän *Iran* 26°42N 61°56E **45** E9
Irakli *Greece* 35°20N 25°12E **25** D7
Iraklio *Greece* 35°20N 25°12E **25** D7
Iraklio □ *Greece* 35°10N 25°10E **25** D7
Iráklion = Iraklio *Greece* 35°20N 25°12E **25** D7
Irakliou, Kolpos *Greece* 35°23N 25°8E **25** D7
Irala *Paraguay* 25°55S 54°35W **95** B5
Iran ■ *Asia* 33°0N 53°0E **45** C7
Iran, Pegunungan
  Malaysia 2°20N 114°50E **36** D4
Iran Ra. = Iran, Pegunungan
  Malaysia 2°20N 114°50E **36** D4
Īrānshahr *Iran* 27°15N 60°40E **45** E9
Irapuato *Mexico* 20°41N 101°28W **86** C4
Iraq ■ *Asia* 33°0N 44°0E **44** C5
Irati *Brazil* 25°25S 50°38W **95** B5
Irbid *Jordan* 32°35N 35°48E **46** C4
Irbid □ *Jordan* 32°30N 35°50E **46** C5
Irebu *Dem. Rep. of the Congo* 0°40S 17°46E **52** E3
Ireland ■ *Europe* 53°50N 7°52W **10** C4
Iri = Iksan *S. Korea* 35°59N 127°0E **35** G14
Irian Jaya = Papua □
  Indonesia 4°0S 137°0E **37** E9
Irian Jaya Barat □
  Indonesia 2°5S 132°50E **37** E8
Iringa *Tanzania* 7°48S 35°43E **54** D4
Iringa □ *Tanzania* 7°48S 35°43E **54** D4
Iriomote △ *Japan* 24°29N 123°53E **31** M1
Iriomote-Jima *Japan* 24°19N 123°48E **31** M1
Iriona *Honduras* 15°57N 85°11W **88** C2
Iriri → *Brazil* 3°52S 52°37W **93** D8
Irish Republic ■ *Europe* 53°0N 8°0W **10** C3
Irish Sea *U.K.* 53°38N 4°48W **12** D3
Irkutsk *Russia* 52°18N 104°20E **29** D11
Irma *Canada* 52°55N 111°14W **71** C6
Irō-Zaki *Japan* 34°36N 138°51E **31** G9
Iron Baron *Australia* 32°58S 137°11E **63** E2
Iron Gate = Portile de Fier
  Europe 44°44N 22°30E **17** F12
Iron Knob *Australia* 32°46S 137°8E **63** E2
Iron Mountain *U.S.A.* 45°49N 88°4W **80** C9
Iron Range △ *Australia* 12°34S 143°18E **62** A3
Iron River *U.S.A.* 46°6N 88°39W **80** B9
Irondequoit *U.S.A.* 43°13N 77°35W **82** C7
Ironton *Mo., U.S.A.* 37°36N 90°38W **80** G8
Ironton *Ohio, U.S.A.* 38°32N 82°41W **81** F12
Ironwood *U.S.A.* 46°27N 90°9W **80** B8
Ironwood Forest △
  U.S.A. 32°32N 111°28W **77** K8
Iroquois *Canada* 44°51N 75°19W **83** B9
Iroquois Falls *Canada* 48°46N 80°41W **72** C3
Irpin *Ukraine* 50°30N 30°15E **17** C16
Irrara Cr. → *Australia* 29°35S 145°31E **63** D4
Irrawaddy □ *Burma* 17°0N 95°0E **41** L19
Irrawaddy → *Burma* 15°50N 95°6E **41** M19
Irrawaddy, Mouths of the
  Burma 15°30N 95°0E **41** M19
Irricana *Canada* 51°19N 113°37W **70** C6
Irrunytju *Australia* 26°3S 128°56E **61** E4
Irtysh → *Russia* 61°4N 68°52E **28** C7
Irumu
  Dem. Rep. of the Congo 1°32N 29°53E **54** B2
Irún *Spain* 43°20N 1°52W **21** A5
Irunea = Pamplona-Iruña
  Spain 42°48N 1°38W **21** A5
Irvine *Canada* 49°57N 110°16W **71** D6
Irvine *U.K.* 55°37N 4°41W **11** F4
Irvine *Calif., U.S.A.* 33°41N 117°46W **79** M9
Irvine *Ky., U.S.A.* 37°42N 83°58W **81** G12
Irvinestown *U.K.* 54°28N 7°39W **10** B4
Irving *U.S.A.* 32°48N 96°56W **84** E6
Irvona *U.S.A.* 40°46N 78°33W **82** F6
Irwin → *Australia* 29°15S 114°54E **61** E1
Irymple *Australia* 34°14S 142°8E **63** E3
Isa Khel *Pakistan* 32°41N 71°17E **42** C4
Isaac → *Australia* 22°55S 149°20E **62** C4
Isabel *U.S.A.* 45°24N 101°26W **80** C3
Isabel, I. *Mexico* 21°51N 105°55W **86** C3

Isabela *Phil.* 6°40N 121°59E **37** C6
Isabela *Puerto Rico* 18°30N 67°2W **89** d
Isabella, Cord. *Nic.* 13°30N 85°25W **88** D2
Isabella Ra. *Australia* 21°0S 121°4E **60** D3
Isachsen, C. *Canada* 79°20N 105°28W **69** B10
Ísafjarðardjúp *Iceland* 66°10N 23°0W **8** C2
Ísafjörður *Iceland* 66°5N 23°9W **8** C2
Isagarh *India* 24°48N 77°51E **42** G7
Isahaya *Japan* 32°52N 130°2E **31** H5
Isaka *Tanzania* 3°56S 32°59E **54** C3
Isalo △ *Madag.* 22°23S 45°16E **57** C8
Isan → *India* 26°51N 80°7E **43** F9
Isana → = Içana → *Brazil* 0°26N 67°19W **92** C5
Isangano △ *Zambia* 11°8S 30°35E **55** E3
Isar → *Germany* 48°48N 12°57E **16** D7
Íschia *Italy* 40°44N 13°57E **22** D5
Isdell → *Australia* 16°27S 124°51E **60** C3
Ise *Japan* 34°25N 136°45E **31** G8
Ise-Shima △ *Japan* 34°25N 136°45E **31** G8
Ise-Wan *Japan* 34°43N 136°43E **31** G8
Iseramagazi *Tanzania* 4°37S 32°10E **54** C3
Isère → *France* 44°59N 4°51E **20** D6
Isérnia *Italy* 41°36N 14°14E **22** D6
Isfahan = Eşfahān *Iran* 32°39N 51°43E **45** C6
Ishigaki *Japan* 24°26N 124°10E **31** M2
Ishigaki-Shima *Japan* 24°20N 124°10E **31** M2
Ishikari-Gawa →
  Japan 43°15N 141°23E **30** C10
Ishikari-Sammyaku
  Japan 43°30N 143°0E **30** C11
Ishikari-Wan *Japan* 43°25N 141°1E **30** C10
Ishikawa *Japan* 26°25N 127°49E **31** L3
Ishikawa □ *Japan* 36°30N 136°30E **31** F8
Ishim *Russia* 56°10N 69°30E **28** D7
Ishim → *Russia* 57°45N 71°10E **28** D8
Ishinomaki *Japan* 38°32N 141°20E **30** E10
Ishioka *Japan* 36°11N 140°16E **31** F10
Ishkoman *Pakistan* 36°30N 73°50E **43** A5
Ishpeming *U.S.A.* 46°29N 87°40W **80** B10
Isil Kul *Russia* 54°55N 71°16E **28** D8
Isiolo *Kenya* 0°24N 37°33E **54** B4
Isiro *Dem. Rep. of the Congo* 2°53N 27°40E **54** B2
Isisford *Australia* 24°15S 144°21E **62** C3
İskenderun *Turkey* 36°32N 36°10E **44** B3
İskenderun Körfezi
  Turkey 36°40N 35°50E **19** G6
Iskŭr → *Bulgaria* 43°45N 24°25E **23** C11
İskut → *Canada* 56°45N 131°49W **70** B2
Isla → *U.K.* 56°32N 3°20W **11** E5
Isla Coiba △ *Panama* 7°33N 81°36W **88** E3
Isla de Salamanca △
  Colombia 10°59N 74°40W **89** D5
Isla Gorge △ *Australia* 25°10S 149°57E **62** D4
Isla Isabel △ *Mexico* 21°54N 105°58W **86** C3
Isla Tiburón y San Esteban △
  Mexico 29°0N 112°27W **86** B2
Isla Vista *U.S.A.* 34°25N 119°53W **79** L7
Islam Headworks
  Pakistan 29°49N 72°33E **42** E5
Islamabad *Pakistan* 33°40N 73°10E **42** C5
Islamgarh *Pakistan* 27°51N 70°48E **42** F4
Islamkot *Pakistan* 24°42N 70°13E **42** G4
Islampur *Bihar, India* 25°9N 85°12E **43** G11
Islampur *W. Bengal,*
  India 26°16N 88°12E **43** F13
Island = Iceland ■ *Europe* 64°45N 19°0W **8** D4
Island L. *Canada* 53°47N 94°25W **71** C10
Island Lagoon *Australia* 31°30S 136°40E **63** E2
Island Pond *U.S.A.* 44°49N 71°53W **83** B13
Islands, B. of *Canada* 49°11N 58°15W **73** C8
Islands, B. of *N.Z.* 35°15S 174°6E **59** A5
Islay *U.K.* 55°46N 6°10W **11** F2
Isle → *France* 44°55N 0°15W **20** D3
Isle aux Morts *Canada* 47°35N 59°0W **73** C8
Isle of Wight □ *U.K.* 50°41N 1°17W **13** G6
Isle Royale △ *U.S.A.* 48°0N 88°55W **80** B9
Isleton *U.S.A.* 38°10N 121°37W **78** G5
Ismail = Izmayil
  Ukraine 45°22N 28°46E **17** F15
Ismâ'ilîya *Egypt* 30°37N 32°18E **51** B12
Isna *Egypt* 25°17N 32°30E **51** C12
Isoanala *Madag.* 23°50S 45°44E **57** C8
Isparta *Turkey* 37°47N 30°30E **19** G5
İspica *Italy* 36°47N 14°55E **22** F6
Israel ■ *Asia* 32°0N 34°50E **46** D3
Issoire *France* 45°32N 3°15E **20** D5
Issyk-Kul = Balykchy
  Kyrgyzstan 42°26N 76°12E **32** B2
Issyk-Kul, Ozero = Ysyk-Köl
  Kyrgyzstan 42°25N 77°15E **28** E8
İstanbul *Turkey* 41°0N 28°58E **23** D13
İstanbul Boğazı *Turkey* 41°5N 29°3E **23** D13
Istiea *Greece* 38°57N 23°9E **23** E10
Isto, Mt. *U.S.A.* 69°12N 143°48W **74** B11
Istokpoga, L. *U.S.A.* 27°23N 81°17W **85** H14
Istra *Croatia* 45°10N 14°0E **16** F7
Istres *France* 43°31N 4°59E **20** E6
Istria = Istra *Croatia* 45°10N 14°0E **16** F7
Itá *Paraguay* 25°29S 57°21W **94** B4
Itaberaba *Brazil* 12°32S 40°18W **93** F10
Itabira *Brazil* 19°37S 43°13W **93** G10
Itabirito *Brazil* 20°15S 43°48W **95** A7
Itabuna *Brazil* 14°48S 39°16W **93** F11
Itacaunas → *Brazil* 5°21S 49°8W **93** E9
Itacoatiara *Brazil* 3°8S 58°25W **92** D7
Itaipú, Represa de *Brazil* 25°30S 54°30W **95** B5
Itaituba *Brazil* 4°10S 55°50W **93** D7
Itajaí *Brazil* 27°50S 48°39W **95** B6
Itajubá *Brazil* 22°24S 45°30W **95** A6
Itaka *Tanzania* 8°50S 32°49E **55** D3
Itala △ *S. Africa* 27°30S 31°7E **57** D5
Italy ■ *Europe* 42°0N 13°0E **22** C5
Itamaraju *Brazil* 17°5S 39°32W **93** G11
Itampolo *Madag.* 24°41S 43°57E **57** C7
Itandrano *Madag.* 21°47S 45°17E **57** C8
Itapecuru Mirim *Brazil* 3°24S 44°20W **93** D10
Itaperuna *Brazil* 21°10S 41°54W **95** A7
Itapetininga *Brazil* 23°36S 48°7W **95** A6
Itapeva *Brazil* 23°59S 48°59W **95** A6

Itapicuru → *Bahia,*
  Brazil 11°47S 37°32W **93** F11
Itapicuru → *Maranhão,*
  Brazil 2°52S 44°12W **93** D10
Itapipoca *Brazil* 3°30S 39°35W **93** D11
Itapuá □ *Paraguay* 26°40S 55°40W **95** B4
Itaquí *Brazil* 29°8S 56°30W **94** B4
Itararé *Brazil* 24°6S 49°23W **95** A6
Itarsi *India* 22°36N 77°51E **42** H7
Itati *Argentina* 27°16S 58°15W **94** B4
Itatiaia △ *Brazil* 22°22S 44°38W **95** A7
Itchen → *U.K.* 50°55N 1°22W **13** G6
Itezhi Tezhi, L. *Zambia* 15°30S 25°30E **55** F2
Ithaca = Ithaki *Greece* 38°25N 20°40E **23** E9
Ithaca *U.S.A.* 42°27N 76°30W **83** D8
Ithaki *Greece* 38°25N 20°40E **23** E9
Itiquira → *Brazil* 17°18S 56°44W **93** G7
Itiyuro → *Argentina* 22°40S 63°50W **94** A3
Itō *Japan* 34°58N 139°5E **31** G9
Itoigawa *Japan* 37°2N 137°51E **31** F8
Itonamas → *Bolivia* 12°28S 64°24W **92** F6
Ittoqqortoormiit *Greenland* 70°20N 23°0W **4** B6
Itu *Brazil* 23°17S 47°15W **95** A6
Itu Aba I. *S. China Sea* 10°23N 114°21E **36** B4
Ituiutaba *Brazil* 19°0S 49°25W **93** G9
Itumbiara *Brazil* 18°20S 49°10W **93** G9
Ituna *Canada* 51°10N 103°24W **71** C8
Itunge Port *Tanzania* 9°40S 33°55E **55** D3
Iturbe *Argentina* 23°0S 65°25W **94** A2
Ituri →
  Dem. Rep. of the Congo 1°40N 27°1E **54** B2
Iturup, Ostrov *Russia* 45°0N 148°0E **29** E15
Ituxi → *Brazil* 7°18S 64°51W **92** E6
Itzehoe *Germany* 53°55N 9°31E **16** B5
Ivahona *Madag.* 23°27S 46°10E **57** C8
Ivaí → *Brazil* 23°18S 53°42W **95** A5
Ivalo *Finland* 68°38N 27°35E **8** B22
Ivalojoki → *Finland* 68°40N 27°40E **8** B22
Ivanava *Belarus* 52°7N 25°29E **17** B13
Ivanhoe *Australia* 32°56S 144°20E **63** E3
Ivanhoe *Canada* 48°23N 77°28W **82** B7
Ivanhoe *Calif., U.S.A.* 36°23N 119°13W **78** J7
Ivanhoe *Minn., U.S.A.* 44°28N 96°15W **80** C5
Ivano-Frankivsk
  Ukraine 48°40N 24°40E **17** D13
Ivanovo = Ivanava
  Belarus 52°7N 25°29E **17** B13
Ivanovo *Russia* 57°5N 41°0E **18** C7
Ivato *Madag.* 20°37S 47°10E **57** C8
Ivatsevichy *Belarus* 52°43N 25°21E **17** B13
Ivdel *Russia* 60°42N 60°24E **18** B11
Ivinheima → *Brazil* 23°14S 53°42W **95** A5
Ivinhema *Brazil* 22°10S 53°37W **95** A5
Ivohibe *Madag.* 22°31S 46°57E **57** C8
Ivory Coast *W. Afr.* 4°20N 5°0W **50** H4
Ivory Coast ■ *Africa* 7°30N 5°0W **50** G4
Ivrea *Italy* 45°28N 7°52E **20** D7
Ivujivik *Canada* 62°24N 77°55W **69** E16
Ivvavik △ *Canada* 69°6N 139°30W **68** D4
Ivybridge *U.K.* 50°23N 3°56W **13** G4
Iwaizumi *Japan* 39°50N 141°45E **30** E10
Iwaki *Japan* 37°3N 140°55E **31** F10
Iwakuni *Japan* 34°15N 132°8E **31** G6
Iwamizawa *Japan* 43°12N 141°46E **30** C10
Iwanai *Japan* 42°58N 140°30E **30** C10
Iwata *Japan* 34°42N 137°51E **31** G8
Iwate *Japan* 39°30N 141°30E **30** E10
Iwate-San *Japan* 39°51N 141°0E **30** E10
Iwo *Nigeria* 7°39N 4°9E **50** G6
Iwŏn *N. Korea* 40°19N 128°39E **35** D15
Ixiamas *Bolivia* 13°50S 68°5W **92** F5
Ixopo *S. Africa* 30°11S 30°5E **57** E5
Ixtepec *Mexico* 16°34N 95°6W **87** D5
Ixtlán del Río *Mexico* 21°2N 104°22W **86** C4
Iyo *Japan* 33°45N 132°45E **31** H6
Izabal, L. de *Guatemala* 15°30N 89°10W **88** C2
Izamal *Mexico* 20°56N 89°1W **87** C7
Izena-Shima *Japan* 26°56N 127°56E **31** L3
Izhevsk *Russia* 56°51N 53°14E **18** C9
Izhma → *Russia* 65°19N 52°54E **18** A9
Izmayil *Ukraine* 45°22N 28°46E **17** F15
İzmir *Turkey* 38°25N 27°8E **23** E12
İzmit = Kocaeli *Turkey* 40°45N 29°50E **19** F4
İznik Gölü *Turkey* 40°27N 29°30E **23** D13
Izra *Syria* 32°51N 36°15E **46** C5
Izu-Shotō *Japan* 34°30N 140°0E **31** G10
Izúcar de Matamoros
  Mexico 18°36N 98°28W **87** D5
Izumi-Sano *Japan* 34°23N 135°18E **31** G7
Izumo *Japan* 35°20N 132°46E **31** G6
Izyaslav *Ukraine* 50°5N 26°50E **17** C14

J

J.F.K. Int. ✈ (JFK)
  U.S.A. 40°38N 73°47W **83** F11
J. Strom Thurmond L.
  U.S.A. 33°40N 82°12W **85** E13
Jabalpur *India* 23°9N 79°58E **43** H8
Jabbūl *Syria* 36°4N 37°30E **44** B3
Jabiru *Australia* 12°40S 132°53E **60** B5
Jablah *Syria* 35°20N 36°0E **44** C3
Jablonec nad Nisou
  Czech Rep. 50°43N 15°10E **16** C8
Jaboatão *Brazil* 8°7S 35°1W **93** E11
Jaboticabal *Brazil* 21°15S 48°17W **95** A6
Jaca *Spain* 42°35N 0°33W **21** A5
Jacareí *Brazil* 23°20S 46°0W **95** A6
Jacarèzinho *Brazil* 23°5S 49°58W **95** A6
Jack River △ *Australia* 14°59S 143°12E **62** A3
Jackman *U.S.A.* 45°37N 70°15W **81** C18
Jacksboro *U.S.A.* 33°13N 98°10W **84** E5
Jackson *Barbados* 13°7N 59°36W **89** g
Jackson *Ala., U.S.A.* 31°31N 87°53W **85** F11
Jackson *Calif., U.S.A.* 38°21N 120°46W **78** G6
Jackson *Ky., U.S.A.* 37°33N 83°23W **81** G12
Jackson *Mich., U.S.A.* 42°15N 84°24W **81** D11
Jackson *Minn., U.S.A.* 43°37N 95°1W **80** D6

Jackson *Miss., U.S.A.* 32°18N 90°12W **85** E9
Jackson *Mo., U.S.A.* 37°23N 89°40W **80** G9
Jackson *N.H., U.S.A.* 44°10N 71°11W **83** B13
Jackson *Ohio, U.S.A.* 39°3N 82°39W **81** F12
Jackson *Tenn., U.S.A.* 35°37N 88°49W **85** D10
Jackson *Wyo., U.S.A.* 43°29N 110°46W **76** E8
Jackson B. *N.Z.* 43°58S 168°42E **59** E2
Jackson L. *U.S.A.* 43°52N 110°36W **76** E8
Jacksons *N.Z.* 42°46S 171°32E **59** E3
Jackson's Arm *Canada* 49°52N 56°47W **73** C8
Jacksonville *Ala.,*
  U.S.A. 33°49N 85°46W **85** E12
Jacksonville *Ark., U.S.A.* 34°52N 92°7W **84** D8
Jacksonville *Calif.,*
  U.S.A. 37°52N 120°24W **78** H6
Jacksonville *Fla.,*
  U.S.A. 30°20N 81°39W **85** F14
Jacksonville *Ill., U.S.A.* 39°44N 90°14W **80** F8
Jacksonville *N.C.,*
  U.S.A. 34°45N 77°26W **85** D16
Jacksonville *Tex., U.S.A.* 31°58N 95°17W **84** F7
Jacksonville Beach
  U.S.A. 30°17N 81°24W **85** F14
Jacmel *Haiti* 18°14N 72°32W **89** C5
Jacob Lake *U.S.A.* 36°43N 112°13W **77** H7
Jacobabad *Pakistan* 28°20N 68°29E **42** E3
Jacobina *Brazil* 11°11S 40°30W **93** F10
Jacques-Cartier, Dét. de
  Canada 50°0N 63°30W **73** C7
Jacques-Cartier, Mt.
  Canada 48°57N 66°0W **73** C6
Jacques-Cartier △
  Canada 47°15N 71°33W **73** C5
Jacuí → *Brazil* 30°2S 51°15W **95** C5
Jacumba *U.S.A.* 32°37N 116°11W **79** N10
Jacundá → *Brazil* 1°57S 50°26W **93** D8
Jade City *Canada* 59°15N 129°37W **70** B3
Jaén *Peru* 5°25S 78°40W **92** E3
Jaén *Spain* 37°44N 3°43W **21** D4
Jafarabad *India* 20°52N 71°22E **42** J4
Jaffa = Tel Aviv-Yafo
  Israel 32°4N 34°48E **46** C3
Jaffa, C. *Australia* 36°58S 139°40E **63** F2
Jaffna *Sri Lanka* 9°45N 80°2E **40** Q12
Jaffrey *U.S.A.* 42°49N 72°2W **83** D12
Jagadhri *India* 30°10N 77°20E **42** D7
Jagadishpur *India* 25°30N 84°21E **43** G11
Jagdalpur *India* 19°3N 82°0E **41** K13
Jagersfontein *S. Africa* 29°44S 25°27E **56** D4
Jaghīn → *Iran* 27°17N 57°13E **45** E8
Jagodina *Serbia* 44°5N 21°15E **23** C9
Jagraon *India* 30°50N 75°25E **42** D6
Jagtial *India* 18°50N 79°0E **40** K11
Jaguariaíva *Brazil* 24°10S 49°50W **95** A6
Jaguaribe → *Brazil* 4°25S 37°45W **93** D11
Jagüey Grande *Cuba* 22°35N 81°7W **88** B3
Jahanabad *India* 25°13N 84°59E **43** G11
Jahazpur *India* 25°37N 75°17E **42** G6
Jahrom *Iran* 28°30N 53°31E **45** D7
Jaijon *India* 31°21N 76°9E **42** D7
Jailolo *Indonesia* 1°5N 127°30E **37** D7
Jailolo, Selat *Indonesia* 0°5N 129°5E **37** D7
Jaipur *India* 27°0N 75°50E **42** F6
Jais *India* 26°15N 81°32E **43** F9
Jaisalmer *India* 26°55N 70°54E **42** F4
Jaisinghnagar *India* 23°38N 78°34E **43** H8
Jaitaran *India* 26°12N 73°56E **42** F5
Jaithari *India* 23°14N 78°37E **43** H8
Jājarm *Iran* 36°58N 56°27E **45** B8
Jakam → *India* 23°54N 74°13E **42** H6
Jakarta *Indonesia* 6°9S 106°52E **37** G12
Jakhal *India* 29°48N 75°50E **42** E6
Jakhau *India* 23°13N 68°43E **42** H3
Jakobstad = Pietarsaari
  Finland 63°40N 22°43E **8** E20
Jal *U.S.A.* 32°7N 103°12W **77** K12
Jalājil *Si. Arabia* 25°40N 45°27E **44** E5
Jalālābād *Afghan.* 34°30N 70°29E **42** B4
Jalalabad *India* 27°41N 79°42E **43** F8
Jalalpur Jattan *Pakistan* 32°38N 74°11E **42** C6
Jalama *U.S.A.* 34°29N 120°29W **79** L6
Jalandhar = Jullundur
  India 31°20N 75°40E **42** D6
Jalapa *Guatemala* 14°39N 89°59W **88** D2
Jalapa Enríquez = Xalapa
  Mexico 19°32N 96°55W **87** D5
Jalasjärvi *Finland* 62°29N 22°47E **8** E20
Jalaun *India* 26°8N 79°25E **43** F8
Jaldhaka → *Bangla.* 26°16N 89°16E **43** F13
Jalesar *India* 27°29N 78°19E **42** F8
Jaleswar *Nepal* 26°38N 85°48E **43** F11
Jalgaon *India* 21°0N 75°42E **40** J9
Jalībah *Iraq* 30°35N 46°32E **44** D5
Jalingo *Nigeria* 8°55N 11°25E **51** G8
Jalisco □ *Mexico* 20°20N 103°40W **86** D4
Jalkot *Pakistan* 35°14N 73°24E **43** B5
Jalna *India* 19°48N 75°38E **40** K9
Jalón → *Spain* 41°47N 1°4W **21** B5
Jalor *India* 25°21N 72°37E **42** G5
Jalpa *Mexico* 21°38N 102°58W **86** C4
Jalpaiguri *India* 26°32N 88°46E **41** F16
Jalpan *Mexico* 21°14N 99°29W **87** C5
Jaluit I. *Marshall Is.* 6°0N 169°30E **64** G8
Jalūlā *Iraq* 34°16N 45°10E **44** C5
Jamaame *Somali Rep.* 0°4N 42°44E **47** G3
Jamaica ■ *W. Indies* 18°10N 77°30W **88** a
Jamalpur *Bangla.* 24°52N 89°56E **41** G16
Jamalpur *India* 25°18N 86°28E **43** G12
Jamalpurganj *India* 23°2N 87°59E **43** H13
Jamanxim → *Brazil* 4°43S 56°18W **93** D7
Jambewangi *Indonesia* 8°17S 114°7E **37** J17
Jambi *Indonesia* 1°38S 103°30E **36** E2
Jambi □ *Indonesia* 1°30S 102°30E **36** E2
Jambongan, Pulau
  Malaysia 6°45N 117°20E **36** C5
Jambusar *India* 22°3N 72°51E **42** H5
James → *S. Dak., U.S.A.* 42°52N 97°18W **80** D5
James → *Va., U.S.A.* 36°56N 76°27W **81** G15
James B. *Canada* 54°0N 80°0W **72** B3

James Ranges *Australia* 24°10S 132°30E **60** D5
James Ross I. *Antarctica* 63°58S 57°50W **5** C18
Jamesabad *Pakistan* 25°17N 69°15E **42** G3
Jamestown *Australia* 33°10S 138°32E **63** E2
Jamestown *S. Africa* 31°6S 26°45E **56** E4
Jamestown *N. Dak.,*
  U.S.A. 46°54N 98°42W **80** B4
Jamestown *N.Y., U.S.A.* 42°6N 79°14W **82** D5
Jamestown *Ohio, U.S.A.* 41°29N 80°27W **82** E4
Jamilābād *Iran* 34°24N 48°28E **45** C6
Jamira → *India* 21°35N 88°28E **43** J13
Jamkhandi *India* 16°30N 75°15E **40** L9
Jammu *India* 32°43N 74°54E **42** C6
Jammu & Kashmir □
  India 34°25N 77°0E **43** B7
Jamnagar *India* 22°30N 70°6E **42** H4
Jamni → *India* 25°13N 78°35E **43** G8
Jampur *Pakistan* 29°39N 70°40E **42** E4
Jamrud *Pakistan* 33°59N 71°24E **42** C4
Jämsä *Finland* 61°53N 25°10E **8** F21
Jamshedpur *India* 22°44N 86°12E **43** H12
Jamtara *India* 23°59N 86°49E **43** H12
Jämtland *Sweden* 63°31N 14°0E **8** E16
Jan L. *Canada* 54°56N 102°55W **71** C8
Jan Mayen *Arctic* 71°0N 9°0W **4** B7
Janakpur *India* 26°42N 85°55E **43** F11
Janaúba *Brazil* 15°48S 43°19W **93** G10
Jand *Pakistan* 33°30N 72°6E **42** C5
Jandanku ○ *Australia* 16°20S 135°45E **62** B2
Jandaq *Iran* 34°3N 54°22E **45** C7
Jandía *Canary Is.* 28°6N 14°21W **24** F5
Jandía, Pta. de *Canary Is.* 28°3N 14°31W **24** F5
Jandía △ *Canary Is.* 28°4N 14°19W **24** F5
Jandola *Pakistan* 32°20N 70°9E **42** C4
Jandowae *Australia* 26°45S 151°7E **63** D5
Jangamo *Mozam.* 24°6S 35°21E **57** C6
Janghai *India* 25°33N 82°19E **43** G10
Jangheung *S. Korea* 34°41N 126°52E **35** G14
Janjanbureh *Gambia* 13°30N 14°47W **50** F3
Janjgir *India* 22°1N 82°34E **43** J10
Janjina *Madag.* 20°30S 45°50E **57** C8
Janos *Mexico* 30°54N 108°10W **86** A3
Januária *Brazil* 15°25S 44°25W **93** G10
Janūb Sīnī □ *Egypt* 29°30N 33°50E **46** F2
Janubio *Canary Is.* 28°56N 13°50W **24** F6
Jaora *India* 23°40N 75°10E **42** H6
Japan ■ *Asia* 36°0N 136°0E **31** G8
Japan, Sea of *Asia* 40°0N 135°0E **30** E7
Japan Trench *Pac. Oc.* 32°0N 142°0E **64** D6
Japen = Yapen *Indonesia* 1°50S 136°0E **37** E9
Japla *India* 24°33N 84°1E **43** G11
Japurá → *Brazil* 3°8S 65°46W **92** D5
Jaquarão *Brazil* 32°34S 53°23W **95** C5
Jaqué *Panama* 7°27N 78°8W **88** E4
Jarābulus *Syria* 36°49N 38°1E **44** B3
Jarama → *Spain* 40°24N 3°32W **21** B4
Jaranwala *Pakistan* 31°15N 73°26E **42** D5
Jarash *Jordan* 32°17N 35°54E **46** C4
Jarash □ *Jordan* 32°17N 35°54E **46** C4
Jardim *Brazil* 21°28S 56°2W **94** A4
Jardín América *Argentina* 27°3S 55°14W **95** B4
Jardine River △ *Australia* 11°9S 142°21E **62** A3
Jardines de la Reina, Arch. de los
  Cuba 20°50N 78°50W **88** B4
Jargalang *China* 53°N 122°55E **35** C12
Jari → *Brazil* 1°9S 51°54W **93** D8
Jarīr, W. al → *Si. Arabia* 25°38N 42°30E **44** E4
Jarosław *Poland* 50°2N 22°42E **17** C12
Jarrahdale *Australia* 32°24S 116°5E **61** F2
Jarrahi → *Iran* 30°49N 48°48E **45** D6
Jarres, Plaine des *Laos* 19°27N 103°10E **38** C4
Jartai *China* 39°45N 105°48E **34** E3
Jarud Qi *China* 44°28N 120°50E **35** B11
Järvenpää *Finland* 60°29N 25°5E **8** F21
Jarvis *Canada* 42°53N 80°6W **82** D4
Jarvis I. *Pac. Oc.* 0°15S 160°5W **65** H12
Jarwa *India* 27°38N 82°30E **43** F10
Jasdan *India* 22°2N 71°12E **42** H4
Jashpurnagar *India* 22°54N 84°9E **43** H11
Jasidih *India* 24°31N 86°39E **43** G12
Jāsimīyah *Iraq* 33°45N 44°41E **44** C5
Jasin *Malaysia* 2°20N 102°26E **39** L4
Jāsk *Iran* 25°38N 57°45E **45** E8
Jasło *Poland* 49°45N 21°30E **17** D11
Jaso *India* 24°30N 80°29E **43** G9
Jasper *Alta., Canada* 52°55N 118°5W **70** C5
Jasper *Ont., Canada* 44°52N 75°57W **83** B9
Jasper *Ala., U.S.A.* 33°50N 87°17W **85** E11
Jasper *Fla., U.S.A.* 30°31N 82°57W **85** F13
Jasper *Ind., U.S.A.* 38°24N 86°56W **80** F10
Jasper *Tex., U.S.A.* 30°56N 94°1W **84** F7
Jasper △ *Canada* 52°50N 118°8W **70** C5
Jasrasar *India* 27°43N 73°49E **42** F5
Jászberény *Hungary* 47°30N 19°55E **17** E10
Jataí *Brazil* 17°58S 51°48W **93** G8
Jati *India* 24°20N 68°19E **42** G3
Jatibarang *Indonesia* 6°28S 108°18E **37** G13
Jatiluwih *Indonesia* 8°23S 115°8E **37** J18
Jatinegara *Indonesia* 6°13S 106°52E **37** G12
Játiva = Xàtiva *Spain* 38°59N 0°32W **21** C5
Jaú *Brazil* 22°10S 48°30W **95** A6
Jauja *Peru* 11°45S 75°15W **92** F3
Jaunpur *India* 25°46N 82°44E **43** G10
Java = Jawa *Indonesia* 7°0S 110°0E **36** F3
Java Sea *Indonesia* 4°35S 107°15E **36** E3
Java Trench *Ind. Oc.* 9°0S 105°0E **36** F3
Jawa *Indonesia* 7°0S 110°0E **36** F3
Jawa Barat □ *Indonesia* 7°0S 107°0E **37** G12
Jawa Tengah □ *Indonesia* 7°0S 110°0E **37** G14
Jawa Timur □ *Indonesia* 8°0S 113°0E **37** G15
Jawad *India* 24°36N 74°51E **42** G6
Jawhar *Somali Rep.* 2°48N 45°30E **47** G4
Jawoyn ○ *Australia* 14°16S 132°28E **60** B5
Jay Peak *U.S.A.* 44°55N 72°32E **83** B12
Jayanti *India* 26°45N 89°40E **41** F16
Jayapura *Indonesia* 2°28S 140°38E **37** E10
Jayawijaya, Pegunungan
  Indonesia 5°0S 139°0E **37** F9

Jaynagar *India* 26°43N 86°9E **43** F12
Jaypur = Jeypore *India* 18°50N 82°38E **41** K13
Jayrūd *Syria* 33°49N 36°44E **44** C3
Jayton *U.S.A.* 33°15N 100°34W **84** E4
Jāz Mūriān, Hāmūn-e
  Iran 27°20N 58°55E **45** E8
Jazīreh-ye Shīf *Iran* 29°4N 50°54E **45** D6
Jazminal *Mexico* 24°52N 101°24W **86** C4
Jazzîn *Lebanon* 33°31N 35°35E **46** B4
Jean *U.S.A.* 35°47N 115°20W **79** K11
Jean Marie River
  Canada 61°32N 120°38W **70** A4
Jean-Rabel *Haiti* 19°50N 73°5W **89** C5
Jeanerette *U.S.A.* 29°55N 91°40W **84** G9
Jeanette, Ostrov = Zhannetty,
  Ostrov *Russia* 76°43N 158°0E **29** B16
Jeannette *U.S.A.* 40°20N 79°36W **82** F5
Jebāl Bārez, Kūh-e *Iran* 28°30N 58°20E **45** D8
Jebel, Bahr el → *Sudan* 9°30N 30°25E **51** G12
Jebel Ali = Minā' Jabal 'Alī
  U.A.E. 25°2N 55°8E **45** E7
Jecheon *S. Korea* 37°8N 128°12E **35** F15
Jedburgh *U.K.* 55°29N 2°33W **11** F6
Jedda = Jiddah *Si. Arabia* 21°29N 39°10E **47** C2
Jeddore L. *Canada* 48°3N 55°55W **73** C8
Jefferson *Iowa, U.S.A.* 42°1N 94°23W **80** D6
Jefferson *Ohio, U.S.A.* 41°44N 80°46W **82** E4
Jefferson *Tex., U.S.A.* 32°46N 94°21W **84** E7
Jefferson, Mt. *Nev.,*
  U.S.A. 38°47N 116°56W **76** G5
Jefferson, Mt. *Oreg.,*
  U.S.A. 44°41N 121°48W **76** D3
Jefferson City *Mo.,*
  U.S.A. 38°34N 92°10W **80** F7
Jefferson City *Tenn.,*
  U.S.A. 36°7N 83°30W **85** C13
Jeffersontown *U.S.A.* 38°12N 85°35W **81** F11
Jeffersonville *U.S.A.* 38°17N 85°44W **81** F11
Jeffrey City *U.S.A.* 42°30N 107°49W **76** E10
Jega *Nigeria* 12°15N 4°23E **50** F6
Jeju *S. Korea* 33°31N 126°32E **35** H14
Jeju-do *S. Korea* 33°29N 126°34E **35** H14
Jēkabpils *Latvia* 56°29N 25°57E **9** H21
Jekyll I. *U.S.A.* 31°4N 81°25W **85** F14
Jelenia Góra *Poland* 50°50N 15°45E **16** C8
Jelgava *Latvia* 56°41N 23°49E **9** H20
Jemaja *Indonesia* 3°5N 105°45E **39** L5
Jemaluang *Malaysia* 2°16N 103°52E **39** L4
Jember *Indonesia* 8°11S 113°41E **37** H15
Jena *Germany* 50°54N 11°35E **16** C6
Jena *U.S.A.* 31°41N 92°8W **84** F8
Jenīn *West Bank* 32°28N 35°18E **46** C4
Jenkins *U.S.A.* 37°10N 82°38W **81** G12
Jenner *U.S.A.* 38°27N 123°7W **78** G3
Jennings *U.S.A.* 30°13N 92°40W **84** F8
Jeong-eup *S. Korea* 35°35N 126°50E **35** G14
Jeonju *S. Korea* 35°50N 127°4E **35** G14
Jepara *Indonesia* 7°40S 109°14E **37** G14
Jeparit *Australia* 36°8S 142°1E **63** F3
Jequié *Brazil* 13°51S 40°5W **93** F10
Jequitinhonha *Brazil* 16°30S 41°0W **93** G10
Jequitinhonha →
  Brazil 15°51S 38°53W **93** G11
Jerada *Morocco* 34°17N 2°10W **50** B5
Jeranatul *Malaysia* 3°56N 102°22E **39** L4
Jerejak, Pulau *Malaysia* 5°19N 100°19E **39** c
Jérémie *Haiti* 18°40N 74°10W **89** C5
Jerez, Pta. *Mexico* 22°58N 97°40W **87** C5
Jerez de García Salinas
  Mexico 22°39N 103°0W **86** C4
Jerez de la Frontera *Spain* 36°41N 6°7W **21** D2
Jerez de los Caballeros
  Spain 38°20N 6°45W **21** C2
Jericho = El Arīḥā
  West Bank 31°52N 35°27E **46** D4
Jericho *Australia* 23°38S 146°6E **62** C4
Jerid, Chott el = Djerid, Chott
  Tunisia 33°42N 8°30E **50** B7
Jerilderie *Australia* 35°20S 145°41E **63** F4
Jermyn *U.S.A.* 41°32N 75°33W **83** E9
Jerome *U.S.A.* 42°44N 114°31W **76** E6
Jerramungup *Australia* 33°55S 118°55E **61** F2
Jersey *U.K.* 49°11N 2°7W **13** H5
Jersey City *U.S.A.* 40°42N 74°4W **83** F10
Jersey Shore *U.S.A.* 41°12N 77°15W **82** E7
Jerseyville *U.S.A.* 39°7N 90°20W **80** F8
Jerusalem
  Israel/West Bank 31°47N 35°10E **46** D4
Jervis B. *Australia* 35°8S 150°46E **63** F5
Jervis Inlet *Canada* 50°0N 123°57W **70** C4
Jesi = Iesi *Italy* 43°31N 13°14E **22** C5
Jessore *Bangla.* 23°10N 89°10E **41** H16
Jesup *U.S.A.* 31°36N 81°53W **85** F14
Jesús Carranza *Mexico* 17°26N 95°2W **87** D5
Jesús María *Argentina* 30°59S 64°5W **94** C3
Jetmore *U.S.A.* 38°4N 99°54W **80** F4
Jetpur *India* 21°45N 70°10E **42** J4
Jevnaker *Norway* 60°15N 10°26E **9** F14
Jewett *U.S.A.* 42°20N 81°2W **82** F3
Jewett City *U.S.A.* 41°36N 71°59W **83** E13
Jeypore *India* 18°50N 82°38E **41** K13
Jeybānābād *Iran* 34°58N 48°59E **45** C6
Jha Jha *India* 24°46N 86°22E **43** G12
Jhaarkand = Jharkhand □
  India 24°0N 85°50E **43** H11
Jhabua *India* 22°46N 74°36E **42** H6
Jhajjar *India* 28°37N 76°42E **42** E7
Jhal *Pakistan* 28°17N 67°27E **42** E2
Jhal Jhao *Pakistan* 26°20N 65°35E **40** F4
Jhalawar *India* 24°40N 76°10E **42** G7
Jhalida *India* 23°22N 85°58E **43** H11
Jhalrapatan *India* 24°33N 76°10E **42** G7
Jhang Maghiana
  Pakistan 31°15N 72°22E **42** D5
Jhansi *India* 25°30N 78°36E **43** G8
Jhargram *India* 22°27N 86°59E **43** H12
Jharia *India* 23°45N 86°26E **43** H12
Jharkhand □ *India* 24°0N 85°50E **43** H11

Jharsuguda *India* 21°56N 84°5E **41** J14
Jhelum *Pakistan* 33°0N 73°45E **42** C5
Jhelum → *Pakistan* 31°20N 72°10E **42** D5
Jhilmili *India* 23°24N 82°51E **43** H10
Jhudo *Pakistan* 24°58N 69°18E **42** G3
Jhunjhunu *India* 28°10N 75°30E **42** E6
Ji-Paraná *Brazil* 10°52S 62°57W **92** F6
Ji Xian *Hebei, China* 37°35N 115°30E **34** F8
Ji Xian *Henan, China* 35°22N 114°5E **34** G8
Ji Xian *Shanxi, China* 36°7N 110°40E **34** F6
Ji Xian *Henan, China* 33°59N 113°12E **34** H7
Jia Xian *Shaanxi, China* 38°12N 110°28E **34** E6
Jiamusi *China* 46°40N 130°26E **35** B8
Ji'an *Jiangxi, China* 27°6N 114°59E **35** D6
Ji'an *Jilin, China* 41°5N 126°10E **35** D14
Jianchang *China* 40°55N 120°35E **35** D11
Jianchangying *China* 40°10N 118°50E **35** D10
Jiangcheng *China* 22°36N 101°52E **32** D5
Jiangmen *China* 22°32N 113°0E **33** D6
Jiangsu □ *China* 33°0N 120°0E **35** H11
Jiangxi □ *China* 27°30N 116°0E **33** D6
Jiao Xian = Jiaozhou
  China 36°18N 120°1E **35** F11
Jiaohe *Hebei, China* 38°2N 116°20E **34** E9
Jiaohe *Jilin, China* 43°40N 127°22E **35** C14
Jiaozhou *China* 36°18N 120°1E **35** F11
Jiaozhou Wan *China* 36°5N 120°10E **35** F11
Jiaozuo *China* 35°16N 113°12E **34** G7
Jiawang *China* 34°28N 117°26E **35** G9
Jiaxiang *China* 35°25N 116°20E **34** G9
Jiaxing *China* 30°49N 120°45E **33** C7
Jiayi = Chiai *Taiwan* 23°29N 120°25E **33** D7
Jibuti = Djibouti ■ *Africa* 12°0N 43°0E **47** E3
Jicarón, I. *Panama* 7°10N 81°50W **88** E3
Jiddah *Si. Arabia* 21°29N 39°10E **47** C2
Jido *India* 29°2N 94°58E **41** E19
Jieshou *China* 33°18N 115°22E **34** H8
Jiexiu *China* 37°2N 111°55E **34** F6
Jigalong *Australia* 23°21S 120°47E **60** D3
Jigalong ○ *Australia* 23°21S 120°46E **60** D3
Jigni *India* 25°45N 79°25E **43** G8
Jihlava *Czech Rep.* 49°28N 15°35E **16** D8
Jihlava → *Czech Rep.* 48°55N 16°36E **17** D9
Jijiga *Ethiopia* 9°20N 42°50E **47** F3
Jilib *Somali Rep.* 0°29N 42°46E **47** G3
Jilin *China* 43°44N 126°30E **35** C14
Jilin □ *China* 44°0N 127°0E **35** C14
Jilong = Chilung *Taiwan* 25°3N 121°45E **33** D7
Jim Thorpe *U.S.A.* 40°52N 75°44W **83** F9
Jima *Ethiopia* 7°40N 36°47E **47** F2
Jimbaran, Teluk
  Indonesia 8°46S 115°9E **37** K18
Jiménez *Mexico* 27°8N 104°54W **86** B4
Jimeta *Nigeria* 9°17N 12°28E **52** C2
Jimo *China* 36°23N 120°30E **35** F11
Jin Xian = Jinzhou *Hebei,*
  China 38°2N 115°2E **34** E8
Jin Xian = Jinzhou *Liaoning,*
  China 38°55N 121°42E **35** E11
Jinan *China* 36°38N 117°1E **34** F9
Jincheng *China* 35°29N 112°50E **34** G7
Jincheng *China* 35°29N 112°50E **34** G7
Jind *India* 29°19N 76°22E **42** E7
Jindabyne *Australia* 36°25S 148°35E **63** F4
Jinding *China* 22°22N 113°33E **33** G10
Jindo *S. Korea* 34°28N 126°15E **35** G14
Jindřichův Hradec
  Czech Rep. 49°10N 15°2E **16** D8
Jing He → *China* 34°27N 109°4E **34** G5
Jingbian *China* 37°20N 108°30E **34** F5
Jingchuan *China* 35°20N 107°20E **34** G4
Jingdezhen *China* 29°20N 117°11E **33** D6
Jinggu *China* 23°35N 100°41E **32** D5
Jinghai *China* 38°55N 116°55E **34** E9
Jingle *China* 38°20N 111°55E **34** E6
Jingning *China* 35°30N 105°43E **34** G3
Jingpo Hu *China* 43°55N 128°55E **35** C15
Jingtai *China* 37°10N 104°6E **34** F3
Jingxing *China* 38°2N 114°8E **34** E8
Jingyang *China* 34°30N 108°50E **34** G5
Jingyu *China* 42°25N 126°45E **35** C14
Jingyuan *China* 36°30N 104°40E **34** F3
Jingziguan *China* 33°15N 111°0E **34** H6
Jinhua *China* 29°8N 119°38E **33** D6
Jining *Nei Monggol Zizhiqu,*
  China 41°5N 113°0E **34** D7
Jining *Shandong, China* 35°22N 116°34E **34** G9
Jinja *Uganda* 0°25N 33°12E **54** B3
Jinjang *Malaysia* 3°13N 101°39E **39** L3
Jinji *China* 37°58N 106°8E **34** F4
Jinju *S. Korea* 35°12N 128°2E **35** G15
Jinnah Barrage *Pakistan* 32°58N 71°33E **42** C4
Jinotega *Nic.* 13°6N 85°59W **88** D2
Jinotepe *Nic.* 11°50N 86°10W **88** D2
Jinsha Jiang → *China* 28°50N 104°36E **32** D5
Jinxi *China* 40°52N 120°50E **35** D11
Jinxiang *China* 35°5N 116°22E **34** G9
Jinzhong *China* 37°42N 112°46E **34** F7
Jinzhou *Hebei, China* 38°2N 115°2E **34** E8
Jinzhou *Liaoning, China* 38°55N 121°42E **35** E11
Jiparaná → *Brazil* 8°3S 62°52W **92** E6
Jipijapa *Ecuador* 1°0S 80°40W **92** D2
Jiquilpan *Mexico* 19°57N 102°43W **86** D4
Jirisan *S. Korea* 35°20N 127°44E **35** G14
Jiroft *Iran* 28°45N 57°50E **45** D8
Jishan *China* 35°34N 110°58E **34** G6
Jisr ash Shughūr *Syria* 35°49N 36°18E **44** C3
Jitarning *Australia* 32°48S 117°57E **61** F2
Jitra *Malaysia* 6°16N 100°25E **39** J3
Jiu → *Romania* 43°47N 23°48E **17** F12
Jiudengkou *China* 39°56N 106°40E **34** E4
Jiujiang *China* 29°42N 115°58E **33** D6
Jiulong = Kowloon
  China 22°19N 114°11E **33** G11
Jiuquan *China* 39°50N 98°20E **32** C8
Jiutai *China* 44°10N 125°50E **35** B13
Jiuxincheng *China* 39°17N 115°59E **34** E8

Jiwani *Pakistan* 25°1N 61°44E **40** G2
Jixi *China* 45°20N 130°50E **35** B16
Jiyang *China* 37°0N 117°12E **35** F9
Jiyuan *China* 35°7N 112°57E **34** G7
Jīzān *Si. Arabia* 17°0N 42°20E **47** D3
Jize *China* 36°54N 114°56E **34** F8
Jizl, Wādī al → *Si. Arabia* 25°39N 38°25E **44** E3
Jizō-Zaki *Japan* 35°34N 133°20E **31** G6
Jizzax *Uzbekistan* 40°6N 67°50E **28** E7
Joaçaba *Brazil* 27°5S 51°31W **95** B5
João Pessoa *Brazil* 7°10S 34°52W **93** E12
Joaquín V. González
  Argentina 25°10S 64°0W **94** B3
Jobat *India* 22°25N 74°34E **42** H6
Jodhpur *India* 26°23N 73°8E **42** F5
Jodiya *India* 22°42N 70°18E **42** H4
Joensuu *Finland* 62°37N 29°49E **8** E23
Jōetsu *Japan* 37°12N 138°10E **31** F9
Jofane *Mozam.* 21°15S 34°18E **57** C5
Jogbani *India* 26°25N 87°15E **43** F12
Jõgeva *Estonia* 58°45N 26°24E **9** G22
Jogjakarta = Yogyakarta
  Indonesia 7°49S 110°22E **37** G14
Johannesburg *S. Africa* 26°11S 28°2E **57** D4
Johannesburg *U.S.A.* 35°22N 117°38W **79** K9
Johilla → *India* 23°37N 81°14E **43** H9
John Crow Mts. *Jamaica* 18°5N 76°25W **88** a
John Day *U.S.A.* 44°25N 118°57W **76** D4
John Day → *U.S.A.* 45°44N 120°39W **76** D3
John Day Fossil Beds △
  U.S.A. 44°33N 119°38W **76** D4
John D'or Prairie
  Canada 58°30N 115°8W **70** B5
John H. Kerr Res.
  U.S.A. 36°36N 78°18W **85** C15
John o' Groats *U.K.* 58°38N 3°4W **11** C5
Johnnie *U.S.A.* 36°25N 116°5W **79** J10
John's Ra. *Australia* 21°55S 133°23E **62** C1
Johnson *U.S.A.* 44°38N 72°41W **83** B12
Johnson City *Kans.,*
  U.S.A. 37°34N 101°45W **80** G3
Johnson City *N.Y., U.S.A.* 42°7N 75°58W **83** D9
Johnson City *Tenn.,*
  U.S.A. 36°19N 82°21W **85** C13
Johnson City *Tex., U.S.A.* 30°17N 98°25W **84** F5
Johnsonburg *U.S.A.* 41°29N 78°41W **82** E6
Johnsondale *U.S.A.* 35°58N 118°32W **79** K8
Johnsons Crossing
  Canada 60°29N 133°18W **70** A2
Johnston, L. *Australia* 32°25S 120°30E **61** F3
Johnston Falls = Mambilima Falls
  Zambia 10°31S 28°45E **55** E2
Johnston I. *Pac. Oc.* 17°10N 169°8W **65** F11
Johnstone Str. *Canada* 50°28N 126°0W **70** C3
Johnstown *Ireland* 52°45N 7°33W **10** D4
Johnstown *N.Y., U.S.A.* 43°0N 74°22W **83** C10
Johnstown *Ohio, U.S.A.* 40°9N 82°41W **82** F2
Johnstown *Pa., U.S.A.* 40°20N 78°55W **82** F6
Johor, Selat *Asia* 1°28N 103°47E **39** d
Johor Bahru *Malaysia* 1°28N 103°46E **39** d
Jõhvi *Estonia* 59°22N 27°27E **9** G22
Joinville *Brazil* 26°15S 48°55W **95** B6
Joinville I. *Antarctica* 65°0S 55°30W **5** C18
Jojutla *Mexico* 18°37N 99°11W **87** D5
Jokkmokk *Sweden* 66°35N 19°50E **8** C18
Jökulsá á Bru → *Iceland* 65°40N 14°16W **8** D6
Jökulsá á Fjöllum →
  Iceland 66°10N 16°30W **8** C5
Jolfa *Āzarbājān-e Sharqī,*
  Iran 38°57N 45°38E **44** B5
Jolfa *Eşfahan, Iran* 32°58N 51°37E **45** C6
Joliet *U.S.A.* 41°32N 88°5W **80** E9
Joliette *Canada* 46°3N 73°24W **72** C5
Jolo *Phil.* 6°0N 121°0E **37** C6
Jolon *U.S.A.* 35°58N 121°9W **78** K5
Jombang *Indonesia* 7°33S 112°14E **37** G15
Jonava *Lithuania* 55°8N 24°12E **9** J21
Jones Sound *Canada* 76°0N 85°0W **69** B11
Jonesboro *Ark., U.S.A.* 35°50N 90°42W **85** D9
Jonesboro *La., U.S.A.* 32°15N 92°43W **84** E8
Joniškis *Lithuania* 56°13N 23°35E **9** H20
Jönköping *Sweden* 57°45N 14°8E **9** H16
Jonquière *Canada* 48°27N 71°14W **73** C5
Joplin *U.S.A.* 37°6N 94°31W **80** G6
Jora *India* 26°20N 77°49E **42** F7
Jordan *Mont., U.S.A.* 47°19N 106°55W **76** C10
Jordan *N.Y., U.S.A.* 43°4N 76°29W **83** C8
Jordan ■ *Asia* 31°0N 36°0E **46** E5
Jordan → *Asia* 31°48N 35°32E **46** D4
Jordan Valley *U.S.A.* 42°59N 117°3W **76** E5
Jorhat *India* 26°45N 94°12E **41** F19
Jörn *Sweden* 65°4N 20°1E **8** D19
Jorong *Indonesia* 3°58S 114°56E **36** E4
Jørpeland *Norway* 59°3N 6°1E **9** G12
Jorquera → *Chile* 28°3S 69°58W **94** B2
Jos *Nigeria* 9°53N 8°51E **50** G7
José Batlle y Ordóñez
  Uruguay 33°20S 55°10W **95** C4
Joseph, L. *Canada* 45°10N 79°44W **82** A5
Joseph Bonaparte G.
  Australia 14°35S 128°50E **60** B4
Joseph L. *Canada* 52°45N 65°18W **73** B6
Joshinath *India* 30°34N 79°34E **43** D8
Joshinetsu-Kōgen △
  Japan 36°42N 138°32E **31** F9
Joshua Tree *U.S.A.* 34°8N 116°19W **79** L10
Joshua Tree △ *U.S.A.* 33°55N 116°0W **79** M10
Jost Van Dyke I.
  Br. Virgin Is. 18°29N 64°47W **89** e
Jostedalsbreen *Norway* 61°40N 6°59E **8** F12
Jotunheimen *Norway* 61°35N 8°25E **8** F13
Joubertberge *Namibia* 18°30S 14°0E **56** B1
Jourdanton *U.S.A.* 28°55N 98°33W **84** G5
Jovellanos *Cuba* 22°40N 81°10W **88** B3
Ju Xian *China* 36°35N 118°20E **35** F10
Juan Aldama *Mexico* 24°19N 103°21W **86** C4
Juan Bautista Alberdi
  Argentina 34°26S 61°48W **94** C3
Juan de Fuca, Str of.
  N. Amer. 48°15N 124°0W **78** B3

130 Juán de Nova
INDEX TO WORLD MAPS

Juán de Nova *Ind. Oc.* 17°3S 43°45E 57 B7
Juan Fernández, Arch. de *Pac. Oc.* 33°50S 80°0W 90 G2
Juan José Castelli *Argentina* 25°27S 60°57W 94 B3
Juan L. Lacaze *Uruguay* 34°26S 57°25W 94 C4
Juankoski *Finland* 63°3N 28°19E 8 E23
Juárez *Mexico* 27°37N 100°44W 86 B4
Juárez, Sierra de *Mexico* 32°0N 116°0W 86 A1
Juàzeiro *Brazil* 9°30S 40°30W 93 E10
Juàzeiro do Norte *Brazil* 7°10S 39°18W 93 E11
Jûbâ *Sudan* 4°50N 31°35E 51 H12
Juba → *Somali Rep.* 1°30N 42°35E 47 G3
Jubany *Antarctica* 62°30S 58°0W 5 C18
Jubayl *Lebanon* 34°5N 35°39E 46 A4
Jubbah *Si. Arabia* 28°2N 40°56E 44 D4
Jubbal *India* 31°5N 77°40E 42 D7
Jubbulpore = Jabalpur *India* 23°9N 79°58E 43 H8
Jubilee L. *Australia* 29°0S 126°50E 61 E4
Juby, C. *Morocco* 28°0N 12°59W 50 C3
Júcar = Xúquer → *Spain* 39°5N 0°10W 21 C5
Júcaro *Cuba* 21°37N 78°51W 88 B4
Juchitán de Zaragoza *Mexico* 16°26N 95°1W 87 D5
Judea = Har Yehuda *Israel* 31°35N 34°57E 46 D3
Judith → *U.S.A.* 47°44N 109°39W 76 C9
Judith, Pt. *U.S.A.* 41°22N 71°29W 83 E13
Judith Gap *U.S.A.* 46°41N 109°45W 76 C9
Juigalpa *Nic.* 12°6N 85°26W 88 D2
Juiz de Fora *Brazil* 21°43S 43°19W 95 A7
Jujuy □ *Argentina* 23°20S 65°40W 94 A2
Julesburg *U.S.A.* 40°59N 102°16W 76 F12
Juli *Peru* 16°10S 69°25W 92 G5
Julia Cr. → *Australia* 20°0S 141°11E 62 C3
Julia Creek *Australia* 20°39S 141°44E 62 C3
Juliaca *Peru* 15°25S 70°10W 92 G4
Julian *U.S.A.* 33°4N 116°38W 79 M10
Julian, L. *Canada* 54°25N 77°57W 72 B4
Julianatop *Suriname* 3°40N 56°30W 93 C7
Julianehåb = Qaqortoq *Greenland* 60°43N 46°0W 4 C5
Julimes *Mexico* 28°25N 105°27W 86 B3
Jullundur *India* 31°20N 75°40E 42 D6
Julu *China* 37°15N 115°2E 34 F8
Jumbo *Zimbabwe* 17°30S 30°58E 55 F3
Jumbo Pk. *U.S.A.* 36°12N 114°11W 79 J12
Jumentos Cays *Bahamas* 23°0N 75°40W 88 B4
Jumilla *Spain* 38°28N 1°19W 21 C5
Jumla *Nepal* 29°15N 82°13E 43 E10
Jumna = Yamuna → *India* 25°30N 81°53E 43 G9
Jumunjin *S. Korea* 37°55N 128°54E 35 F15
Junagadh *India* 21°30N 70°30E 42 J4
Junction *Tex., U.S.A.* 30°29N 99°46W 84 F5
Junction *Utah, U.S.A.* 38°14N 112°13W 77 G7
Junction B. *Australia* 11°52S 133°55E 62 A1
Junction City *Kans., U.S.A.* 39°2N 96°50W 80 F5
Junction City *Oreg., U.S.A.* 44°13N 123°12W 76 D2
Junction Pt. *Australia* 11°45S 133°50E 62 A1
Jundah *Australia* 24°46S 143°2E 62 C3
Jundiaí *Brazil* 24°30S 47°0W 95 A6
Juneau *U.S.A.* 58°18N 134°25W 70 B2
Junee *Australia* 34°53S 147°35E 63 E4
Jungfrau *Switz.* 46°32N 7°58E 20 C7
Junggar Pendi *China* 44°30N 86°0E 32 B3
Jungshahi *Pakistan* 24°52N 67°44E 42 G2
Juniata → *U.S.A.* 40°24N 77°1W 82 F7
Junín *Argentina* 34°33S 60°57W 94 C3
Junín de los Andes *Argentina* 39°45S 71°0W 96 D2
Jūniyah *Lebanon* 33°59N 35°38E 46 B4
Juntas *Chile* 28°24S 69°58W 94 B2
Juntura *U.S.A.* 43°45N 118°5W 76 E4
Jur, Nahr el → *Sudan* 8°45N 29°15E 51 G11
Jura = Jura, Mts. du *Europe* 46°40N 6°5E 20 C7
Jura = Schwäbische Alb *Germany* 48°20N 9°30E 16 D5
Jura *U.K.* 56°0N 5°50W 11 F3
Jura, Mts. du *Europe* 46°40N 6°5E 20 C7
Jura, Sd. of *U.K.* 55°57N 5°45W 11 F3
Jurbarkas *Lithuania* 55°4N 22°46E 9 J20
Jurien Bay *Australia* 30°18S 115°2E 61 F2
Jūrmala *Latvia* 56°58N 23°34E 9 H20
Jurong *Singapore* 1°19N 103°42E 39 d
Juruá → *Brazil* 2°37S 65°44W 92 D5
Juruena *Brazil* 13°0S 58°10W 92 F7
Juruena → *Brazil* 7°20S 58°3W 92 E7
Juruti *Brazil* 2°9S 56°4W 93 D7
Justo Daract *Argentina* 33°52S 65°12W 94 C2
Jutaí → *Brazil* 2°43S 66°57W 92 D5
Juticalpa *Honduras* 14°40N 86°12W 88 D2
Jutland = Jylland *Denmark* 56°25N 9°30E 9 H13
Juuka *Finland* 63°13N 29°17E 8 E23
Juventud, I. de la *Cuba* 21°40N 82°40W 88 B3
Jūy Zar *Iran* 33°50N 46°18E 44 C5
Juye *China* 35°22N 116°5E 34 G9
Jwaneng *Botswana* 24°45S 24°50E 53 J4
Jylland *Denmark* 56°25N 9°30E 9 H13
Jyväskylä *Finland* 62°14N 25°50E 8 E21

K

K2 *Pakistan* 35°58N 76°32E 43 B7
Kaakha = Kaka *Turkmenistan* 37°21N 59°36E 45 B8
Kaap Plateau *S. Africa* 28°30S 24°0E 56 D3
Kaapkruis *Namibia* 21°55S 13°57E 56 C1
Kaapstad = Cape Town *S. Africa* 33°55S 18°22E 56 E2
Kabaena *Indonesia* 5°15S 122°0E 37 F6
Kabala *S. Leone* 9°38N 11°37W 50 G3
Kabale *Uganda* 1°15S 30°0E 54 C3
Kabalo *Dem. Rep. of the Congo* 6°0S 27°0E 54 D2
Kabambare *Dem. Rep. of the Congo* 4°41S 27°39E 54 C2
Kabango *Dem. Rep. of the Congo* 8°35S 28°30E 55 D2
Kabanjahe *Indonesia* 3°6N 98°30E 36 D1
Kabara *Fiji* 18°59S 178°56W 59 a
Kabardino-Balkaria □ *Russia* 43°30N 43°30E 19 F7
Kabarega Falls = Murchison Falls *Uganda* 2°15N 31°30E 54 B3
Kabarnet *Kenya* 0°30N 35°45E 54 B4
Kabasalan *Phil.* 7°47N 122°44E 37 C6
Kabat *Indonesia* 8°16S 114°19E 37 J17
Kabin Buri *Thailand* 13°57N 101°43E 38 F3
Kabinakagami L. *Canada* 48°54N 84°25W 72 C3
Kabinda *Dem. Rep. of the Congo* 6°19S 24°20E 52 F4
Kabompo *Zambia* 13°36S 24°14E 55 E1
Kabompo → *Zambia* 14°11S 23°11E 53 G4
Kabondo *Dem. Rep. of the Congo* 8°58S 25°40E 55 D2
Kabongo *Dem. Rep. of the Congo* 7°22S 25°33E 54 D2
Kabrît, G. el *Egypt* 29°42N 33°16E 46 F2
Kabūd Gonbad *Iran* 37°5N 59°45E 45 B8
Kābul *Afghan.* 34°28N 69°11E 42 B3
Kābul □ *Afghan.* 34°30N 69°0E 40 B6
Kābul → *Pakistan* 33°55N 72°14E 42 C5
Kabunga *Dem. Rep. of the Congo* 1°38S 28°3E 54 C2
Kaburuang *Indonesia* 3°50N 126°30E 37 D7
Kabwe *Zambia* 14°30S 28°29E 55 E2
Kachchh, Gulf of *India* 22°50N 69°15E 42 H3
Kachchh, Rann of *India* 24°0N 70°0E 42 H4
Kachchhidhana *India* 21°44N 78°46E 43 J8
Kachebera *Zambia* 13°50S 32°50E 55 E3
Kachikau *Botswana* 18°8S 24°26E 56 B3
Kachin □ *Burma* 26°0N 97°30E 41 G20
Kachira, L. *Uganda* 0°40S 31°7E 54 C3
Kachīry *Kazakhstan* 53°10N 75°50E 28 D8
Kachnara *India* 23°50N 75°6E 42 H6
Kachot *Cambodia* 11°30N 103°3E 39 G4
Kaçkar *Turkey* 40°45N 41°10E 19 F7
Kadam, Mt. *Uganda* 1°45N 34°45E 54 B3
Kadan Kyun *Burma* 12°30N 98°20E 38 F2
Kadanai → *Afghan.* 31°22N 65°45E 42 D1
Kadavu *Fiji* 19°0S 178°15E 59 a
Kadavu Passage *Fiji* 18°45S 178°0E 59 a
Kade *Ghana* 6°7N 0°56W 50 G5
Kadhimain = Al Kāẓimīyah *Iraq* 33°22N 44°18E 44 C5
Kadi *India* 23°18N 72°23E 42 H5
Kadina *Australia* 33°55S 137°43E 63 E2
Kadipur *India* 26°10N 82°23E 43 F10
Kadirli *Turkey* 37°23N 36°5E 44 B3
Kadiyevka = Stakhanov *Ukraine* 48°35N 38°40E 19 E6
Kadoka *U.S.A.* 43°50N 101°31W 80 D3
Kadoma *Zimbabwe* 18°20S 29°52E 55 F2
Kâdugli *Sudan* 11°0N 29°45E 51 F11
Kaduna *Nigeria* 10°30N 7°21E 50 F7
Kaédi *Mauritania* 16°9N 13°28W 50 E3
Kaeng Khoï *Thailand* 14°35N 101°0E 38 E3
Kaeng Krachan △ *Thailand* 12°57N 99°23E 38 F2
Kaeng Tana △ *Thailand* 15°25N 105°32E 38 E5
Kaesŏng *N. Korea* 37°58N 126°35E 35 F14
Kāf *Si. Arabia* 31°25N 37°29E 44 D3
Kafan = Kapan *Armenia* 39°18N 46°27E 44 B5
Kafanchan *Nigeria* 9°40N 8°20E 50 G7
Kafinda *Zambia* 12°32S 30°20E 55 E3
Kafue *Zambia* 15°46S 28°9E 55 F2
Kafue → *Zambia* 15°30S 29°0E 53 H5
Kafue △ *Zambia* 15°12S 25°38E 55 F2
Kafue Flats *Zambia* 15°40S 27°25E 55 F2
Kafulwe *Zambia* 9°0S 29°1E 55 D2
Kaga *Afghan.* 34°14N 70°10E 42 B4
Kaga Bandoro *C.A.R.* 7°0N 19°10E 52 C3
Kagawa □ *Japan* 34°15N 134°0E 31 G7
Kagera □ *Tanzania* 2°0S 31°30E 54 C3
Kagera → *Uganda* 0°57S 31°47E 54 C3
Kağızman *Turkey* 40°5N 43°10E 44 B4
Kagoshima *Japan* 31°35N 130°33E 31 J5
Kagoshima □ *Japan* 31°30N 130°30E 31 J5
Kagul = Cahul *Moldova* 45°50N 28°15E 17 F15
Kahak *Iran* 36°6N 49°46E 45 B6
Kahama *Tanzania* 4°8S 32°30E 54 C3
Kahan *Pakistan* 29°18N 68°54E 42 E3
Kahang *Malaysia* 2°12N 103°32E 39 L4
Kahayan → *Indonesia* 3°40S 114°0E 36 E4
Kahe *Tanzania* 3°30S 37°25E 54 C4
Kahemba *Dem. Rep. of the Congo* 7°18S 18°55E 52 F3
Kahnūj *Iran* 27°55N 57°40E 45 E8
Kahoka *U.S.A.* 40°25N 91°44W 80 E8
Kaho'olawe *U.S.A.* 20°33N 156°37W 75 L8
Kahramanmaraş *Turkey* 37°37N 36°53E 44 B3
Kâhta *Turkey* 37°46N 38°36E 44 B3
Kahului *U.S.A.* 20°54N 156°28W 75 L8
Kahurangi △ *N.Z.* 41°10S 172°32E 59 D4
Kahuta *Pakistan* 33°35N 73°24E 42 C5
Kahuzi-Biega △ *Dem. Rep. of the Congo* 1°50S 27°55E 54 C2
Kai, Kepulauan *Indonesia* 5°55S 132°45E 37 F8
Kai Besar *Indonesia* 5°35S 133°0E 37 F8
Kai Is. = Kai, Kepulauan *Indonesia* 5°55S 132°45E 37 F8
Kai Kecil *Indonesia* 5°45S 132°40E 37 F8
Kaiapoi *N.Z.* 43°24S 172°40E 59 E4
Kaidu He → *China* 41°46N 86°31E 32 B3
Kaieteur Falls *Guyana* 5°1N 59°10W 92 B7
Kaifeng *China* 34°48N 114°21E 34 G8
Kaikohe *N.Z.* 35°25S 173°49E 59 A4
Kaikoura *N.Z.* 42°25S 173°43E 59 E4
Kailash = Kangrinboqe Feng *China* 31°0N 81°25E 43 D9
Kailu *China* 43°38N 121°18E 35 C11
Kailua Kona *U.S.A.* 19°39N 155°59W 75 M8
Kaimana *Indonesia* 3°39S 133°45E 37 E8
Kaimanawa Mts. *N.Z.* 39°15S 175°56E 59 C5
Kaimganj *India* 27°33N 79°24E 43 F8
Kaimur Hills *India* 24°30N 82°0E 43 G10
Kainab → *Namibia* 28°32S 19°34E 56 D2
Kainji Res. *Nigeria* 10°1N 4°40E 50 F6
Kainuu *Finland* 64°30N 29°7E 8 D23
Kaipara Harbour *N.Z.* 36°25S 174°14E 59 B5
Kaipokok B. *Canada* 54°54N 59°47W 73 B8
Kaira *India* 22°45N 72°50E 42 H5
Kairana *India* 29°24N 77°15E 42 E7
Kaironi *Indonesia* 0°47S 133°40E 37 E8
Kairouan *Tunisia* 35°45N 10°5E 51 A8
Kaiserslautern *Germany* 49°26N 7°45E 16 D4
Kaitaia *N.Z.* 35°8S 173°17E 59 A4
Kaitangata *N.Z.* 46°17S 169°51E 59 G2
Kaithal *India* 29°48N 76°26E 42 E7
Kaitu → *Pakistan* 33°10N 70°30E 42 C4
Kaiwi Channel *U.S.A.* 21°15N 157°30W 75 L8
Kaiyuan *Liaoning, China* 42°28N 124°1E 35 C13
Kaiyuan *Yunnan, China* 23°40N 103°12E 32 D5
Kaiyuh Mts. *U.S.A.* 64°30N 158°0W 74 C8
Kajaani *Finland* 64°17N 27°46E 8 D22
Kajabbi *Australia* 20°0S 140°1E 62 C3
Kajana = Kajaani *Finland* 64°17N 27°46E 8 D22
Kajang *Malaysia* 2°59N 101°48E 39 L3
Kajiado *Kenya* 1°53S 36°48E 54 C4
Kajo Kaji *Sudan* 3°58N 31°40E 51 H12
Kaka *Turkmenistan* 37°21N 59°36E 45 B8
Kakabeka Falls *Canada* 48°24N 89°37W 72 C2
Kakadu △ *Australia* 12°0S 132°3E 60 B5
Kakamas *S. Africa* 28°45S 20°33E 56 D3
Kakamega *Kenya* 0°20N 34°46E 54 B3
Kakanui Mts. *N.Z.* 45°10S 170°30E 59 F3
Kakdwip *India* 21°53N 88°11E 43 J13
Kake *Japan* 34°36N 132°19E 31 G6
Kake *U.S.A.* 56°59N 133°57W 70 B2
Kakegawa *Japan* 34°45N 138°1E 31 G9
Kakeroma-Jima *Japan* 28°8N 129°14E 31 K4
Kākhak *Iran* 34°9N 58°38E 45 C8
Kakhovka *Ukraine* 46°45N 33°30E 19 E5
Kakhovske Vdskh. *Ukraine* 47°5N 34°0E 19 E5
Kakinada *India* 16°57N 82°11E 41 L13
Kakisa *Canada* 60°56N 117°25W 70 A5
Kakisa → *Canada* 61°3N 118°10W 70 A5
Kakisa L. *Canada* 60°56N 117°43W 70 A5
Kakogawa *Japan* 34°46N 134°51E 31 G7
Kakuma *Kenya* 3°43N 34°52E 54 B3
Kakwa → *Canada* 54°37N 118°28W 70 C5
Kāl Gūsheh *Iran* 30°59N 58°12E 45 D8
Kal Sefīd *Iran* 34°52N 47°23E 44 C5
Kalaallit Nunaat = Greenland ☒ *N. Amer.* 66°0N 45°0W 67 C15
Kalabagh *Pakistan* 33°0N 71°28E 42 C4
Kalabahi *Indonesia* 8°13S 124°31E 37 F6
Kalach *Russia* 50°22N 41°0E 19 D7
Kaladan → *Burma* 20°20N 93°5E 41 J18
Kaladar *Canada* 44°37N 77°5W 82 B7
Kalahari *Africa* 24°0S 21°30E 56 C3
Kalahari Gemsbok △ *S. Africa* 25°30S 20°30E 56 D3
Kalajoki *Finland* 64°12N 24°10E 8 D21
Kalakamati *Botswana* 20°40S 27°25E 57 C4
Kalakan *Russia* 55°15N 116°45E 29 D12
K'alak'unlun Shank'ou = Karakoram Pass *Asia* 35°33N 77°50E 43 B7
Kalam *Pakistan* 35°34N 72°30E 43 B5
Kalama *Dem. Rep. of the Congo* 2°52S 28°35E 54 C2
Kalama *U.S.A.* 46°1N 122°51W 78 E4
Kalamata *Greece* 37°3N 22°10E 23 F10
Kalamazoo *U.S.A.* 42°17N 85°35W 81 D11
Kalamazoo → *U.S.A.* 42°40N 86°10W 80 D10
Kalambo Falls *Tanzania* 8°37S 31°35E 55 D3
Kalan *Turkey* 39°7N 39°32E 44 B3
Kalannie *Australia* 30°22S 117°5E 61 F2
Kalāntarī *Iran* 32°10N 54°8E 45 C7
Kalao *Indonesia* 7°21S 121°0E 37 F6
Kalaotoa *Indonesia* 7°20S 121°50E 37 F6
Kalasin *Thailand* 16°26N 103°30E 38 D4
Kālat *Iran* 25°29N 59°22E 45 E8
Kalat *Pakistan* 29°8N 66°31E 40 E5
Kalāteh *Iran* 36°33N 55°41E 45 B7
Kalāteh-ye Ganj *Iran* 27°31N 57°55E 45 E8
Kalbā *U.A.E.* 25°5N 56°22E 45 E8
Kalbarri *Australia* 27°40S 114°10E 61 E1
Kalbarri △ *Australia* 27°51S 114°30E 61 E1
Kalburgi = Gulbarga *India* 17°20N 76°50E 40 L10
Kalce *Slovenia* 45°54N 14°13E 16 F8
Kale *Turkey* 37°27N 28°49E 23 F13
Kalegauk Kyun *Burma* 15°33N 97°35E 38 E1
Kalehe *Dem. Rep. of the Congo* 2°6S 28°50E 54 C2
Kalema *Tanzania* 1°12S 31°55E 54 C3
Kalemie *Dem. Rep. of the Congo* 5°55S 29°9E 54 D2
Kalewa *Burma* 23°10N 94°15E 41 H19
Kaleybar *Iran* 38°47N 47°2E 44 B5
Kalgoorlie-Boulder *Australia* 30°40S 121°22E 61 F3
Kali → *India* 27°6N 79°55E 43 F8
Kali Sindh → *India* 25°32N 76°17E 42 G6
Kaliakra, Nos *Bulgaria* 43°21N 28°30E 23 C13
Kalianda *Indonesia* 5°50S 105°45E 36 F3
Kalibo *Phil.* 11°43N 122°22E 37 B6
Kalima *Dem. Rep. of the Congo* 2°33S 26°32E 54 C2
Kalimantan *Indonesia* 0°0 114°0E 36 E4
Kalimantan Barat □ *Indonesia* 0°0 110°30E 36 E4
Kalimantan Selatan □ *Indonesia* 2°30S 115°30E 36 E5
Kalimantan Tengah □ *Indonesia* 2°0S 113°30E 36 E4
Kalimantan Timur □ *Indonesia* 1°30N 116°30E 36 D5
Kálimnos *Greece* 37°0N 27°0E 23 F12
Kalimpong *India* 27°4N 88°35E 43 F13
Kaliningrad *Russia* 54°42N 20°32E 9 J19
Kalinkavichy *Belarus* 52°12N 29°20E 17 B15
Kalinkovichi = Kalinkavichy *Belarus* 52°12N 29°20E 17 B15
Kaliro *Uganda* 0°56N 33°30E 54 B3
Kalispell *U.S.A.* 48°12N 114°19W 76 B6
Kalisz *Poland* 51°45N 18°8E 17 C10
Kaliua *Tanzania* 5°5S 31°48E 54 D3
Kalix = Kalixälven → *Sweden* 65°50N 23°11E 8 D20
Kalix *Sweden* 65°53N 23°12E 8 D20
Kalixälven → *Sweden* 65°50N 23°11E 8 D20
Kalka *India* 30°46N 76°57E 42 D7
Kalkarindji *Australia* 17°30S 130°47E 60 C5
Kalkaska *U.S.A.* 44°44N 85°11W 81 C11
Kalkfeld *Namibia* 20°57S 16°14E 56 C2
Kalkfontein *Botswana* 22°4S 20°57E 56 C3
Kalkrand *Namibia* 24°1S 17°35E 56 C2
Kallavesi *Finland* 62°58N 27°30E 8 E22
Kallsjön *Sweden* 63°38N 13°0E 8 E15
Kalmar *Sweden* 56°40N 16°20E 9 H17
Kalmykia □ *Russia* 46°5N 46°1E 19 E8
Kalna *India* 23°13N 88°25E 43 H13
Kalnai *India* 22°46N 83°30E 43 H10
Kalocsa *Hungary* 46°32N 19°0E 17 E10
Kalokhorio *Cyprus* 34°51N 33°2E 25 E12
Kaloko *Dem. Rep. of the Congo* 6°47S 25°48E 54 D2
Kalol *Gujarat, India* 22°37N 73°31E 42 H5
Kalol *Gujarat, India* 23°15N 72°33E 42 H5
Kalomo *Zambia* 17°0S 26°30E 55 F2
Kalpi *India* 26°8N 79°47E 43 F8
Kaltag *U.S.A.* 64°20N 158°43W 74 C8
Kaltukatjara *Australia* 24°52S 129°5E 61 D4
Kalu *Pakistan* 25°5N 67°39E 42 G2
Kaluga *Russia* 54°35N 36°10E 18 D6
Kalulushi *Zambia* 12°50S 28°3E 55 E2
Kalumburu *Australia* 13°55S 126°35E 60 B4
Kalumburu ✪ *Australia* 14°17S 126°38E 60 B4
Kalush *Ukraine* 49°3N 24°23E 17 D13
Kalutara *Sri Lanka* 6°35N 80°0E 40 R12
Kalya *Russia* 60°15N 59°59E 18 B10
Kalyan *India* 19°15N 73°9E 40 K8
Kama *Dem. Rep. of the Congo* 3°30S 27°5E 54 C2
Kama → *Russia* 55°45N 52°0E 18 C9
Kamachumu *Tanzania* 1°37S 31°37E 54 C3
Kamaishi *Japan* 39°16N 141°53E 30 E10
Kamalia *Pakistan* 30°44N 72°42E 42 D5
Kaman *India* 27°39N 77°16E 42 F6
Kamanjab *Namibia* 19°35S 14°51E 56 B2
Kamapanda *Zambia* 12°5S 24°0E 55 E1
Kamarān *Yemen* 15°21N 42°35E 47 D3
Kamativi *Zimbabwe* 18°20S 27°6E 56 B4
Kambalda West *Australia* 31°10S 121°37E 61 F3
Kambar *Pakistan* 27°37N 68°1E 42 F3
Kambarka *Russia* 56°15N 54°11E 18 C9
Kambolé *Zambia* 8°47S 30°48E 55 D3
Kambos *Cyprus* 35°2N 32°44E 25 D11
Kambove *Dem. Rep. of the Congo* 10°51S 26°33E 55 E2
Kamchatka, Poluostrov *Russia* 57°0N 160°0E 29 D17
Kamchatka Pen. = Kamchatka, Poluostrov *Russia* 57°0N 160°0E 29 D17
Kamchiya → *Bulgaria* 43°4N 27°44E 23 C12
Kame Ruins *Zimbabwe* 20°7S 28°25E 55 G2
Kamen *Russia* 53°50N 81°30E 28 D9
Kamen-Rybolov *Russia* 44°46N 132°2E 30 B6
Kamenjak, Rt *Croatia* 44°47N 13°55E 16 F7
Kamenka *Russia* 65°58N 44°0E 18 A7
Kamenka Bugskaya = Kamyanka-Buzka *Ukraine* 50°8N 24°16E 17 C13
Kamensk Uralskiy *Russia* 56°25N 62°2E 28 D7
Kamenskoye *Russia* 62°45N 165°30E 29 C17
Kameoka *Japan* 35°0N 135°35E 31 G7
Kamet *India* 30°55N 79°35E 43 D8
Kamiah *U.S.A.* 46°14N 116°2W 76 C5
Kamieskroon *S. Africa* 30°9S 17°56E 56 E2
Kamilukuak L. *Canada* 62°22N 101°40W 71 A8
Kamin-Kashyrskyy *Ukraine* 51°39N 24°56E 17 C13
Kamina *Dem. Rep. of the Congo* 8°45S 25°0E 55 D2
Kaminak L. *Canada* 62°10N 95°0W 71 A10
Kaministiquia *Canada* 48°32N 89°35W 72 C1
Kaminoyama *Japan* 38°9N 140°17E 30 E10
Kamiros *Greece* 36°20N 27°56E 25 C9
Kamituga *Dem. Rep. of the Congo* 3°2S 28°10E 54 C2
Kamla → *India* 25°35N 86°36E 43 G12
Kamloops *Canada* 50°40N 120°20W 70 C4
Kamo *Japan* 37°39N 139°3E 30 F9
Kamoke *Pakistan* 32°4N 74°4E 42 C6
Kampala *Uganda* 0°20N 32°30E 54 B3
Kampar *Malaysia* 4°18N 101°9E 39 K3
Kampar → *Indonesia* 0°30N 103°8E 36 D2
Kampen *Neths.* 52°33N 5°53E 15 B5
Kampene *Dem. Rep. of the Congo* 3°36S 26°40E 52 E5
Kamphaeng Phet *Thailand* 16°28N 99°30E 38 D2
Kampolombo, L. *Zambia* 11°37S 29°42E 55 E2
Kampong Chhnang *Cambodia* 12°20N 104°35E 39 F5
Kampong Pengerang *Malaysia* 1°22N 104°7E 39 d
Kampong Punggai *Malaysia* 1°27N 104°18E 39 d
Kampong Saom *Cambodia* 10°38N 103°30E 39 G4
Kampong Saom, Chaak *Cambodia* 10°50N 103°32E 39 G4
Kampong Tanjong Langsat *Malaysia* 1°28N 104°1E 39 d
Kampong Telok Ramunia *Malaysia* 1°22N 104°15E 39 d
Kampot *Cambodia* 10°36N 104°10E 39 G5
Kampuchea = Cambodia ■ *Asia* 12°15N 105°0E 38 F5
Kampung Air Putih *Malaysia* 4°15N 103°10E 39 K4
Kampung Jerangau *Malaysia* 4°50N 103°10E 39 K4
Kampung Raja *Malaysia* 5°45N 102°35E 39 K4
Kampungbaru = Tolitoli *Indonesia* 1°5N 120°50E 37 D6
Kamrau, Teluk *Indonesia* 3°30S 133°36E 37 E8
Kamsack *Canada* 51°34N 101°54W 71 C8
Kamsar *Guinea* 10°40N 14°36W 50 F3
Kamskoye Vdkhr. *Russia* 58°41N 56°7E 18 C10
Kamuchawie L. *Canada* 56°18N 101°59W 71 B8
Kamui-Misaki *Japan* 43°20N 140°21E 30 C10
Kamyanets-Podilskyy *Ukraine* 48°45N 26°40E 17 D14
Kamyanka-Buzka *Ukraine* 50°8N 24°16E 17 C13
Kāmyārān *Iran* 34°47N 46°56E 44 C5
Kamyshin *Russia* 50°10N 45°24E 19 D8
Kanaaupscow → *Canada* 54°2N 76°30W 72 B4
Kanab *U.S.A.* 37°3N 112°32W 77 H7
Kanab Cr. → *U.S.A.* 36°24N 112°38W 77 H7
Kanacea *Lau Group, Fiji* 17°15S 179°6W 59 a
Kanacea *Taveuni, Fiji* 16°59S 179°56E 59 a
Kanaga I. *U.S.A.* 51°45N 177°22W 74 E4
Kanagi *Japan* 40°54N 140°27E 30 D10
Kanairiktok → *Canada* 55°2N 60°18W 73 A7
Kananga *Dem. Rep. of the Congo* 5°55S 22°18E 52 F4
Kanash *Russia* 55°30N 47°32E 18 C8
Kanaskat *U.S.A.* 47°19N 121°54W 78 C5
Kanastraíon, Ákra = Paliouri, Akra *Greece* 39°57N 23°45E 23 E10
Kanawha → *U.S.A.* 38°50N 82°9W 81 F12
Kanazawa *Japan* 36°30N 136°38E 31 F8
Kanchanaburi *Thailand* 14°2N 99°31E 38 E2
Kanchenjunga *Nepal* 27°50N 88°10E 43 F13
Kanchipuram *India* 12°52N 79°45E 40 N11
Kandaghat *India* 30°59N 77°7E 42 D7
Kandahār *Afghan.* 31°32N 65°43E 40 D4
Kandahār □ *Afghan.* 31°0N 65°0E 40 D4
Kandalaksha *Russia* 67°9N 32°30E 8 C25
Kandalakshskiy Zaliv *Russia* 66°0N 35°0E 18 A6
Kandangan *Indonesia* 2°50S 115°20E 36 E5
Kandanghaur *Indonesia* 6°21S 108°6E 37 G13
Kandanos *Greece* 35°19N 23°44E 25 D5
Kandavu = Kadavu *Fiji* 19°0S 178°15E 59 a
Kandavu Passage = Kadavu Passage *Fiji* 18°45S 178°0E 59 a
Kandhkot *Pakistan* 28°16N 69°8E 42 E3
Kandhla *India* 29°18N 77°19E 42 E7
Kandi *Benin* 11°7N 2°55E 50 F6
Kandi *India* 23°58N 88°5E 43 H13
Kandiaro *Pakistan* 27°4N 68°13E 42 F3
Kandla *India* 23°0N 70°10E 42 H4
Kandos *Australia* 32°45S 149°58E 63 E4
Kandreho *Madag.* 17°29S 46°6E 57 B8
Kandy *Sri Lanka* 7°18N 80°43E 40 R12
Kane *U.S.A.* 41°40N 78°49W 82 E6
Kane Basin *Greenland* 79°1N 70°0W 69 B18
Kang *Botswana* 23°41S 22°50E 56 C3
Kang Krung △ *Thailand* 9°30N 98°50E 39 H2
Kangān *Fārs, Iran* 27°50N 52°3E 45 E7
Kangān *Hormozgān, Iran* 25°48N 57°28E 45 E8
Kangar *Malaysia* 6°27N 100°12E 39 J3
Kangaroo I. *Australia* 35°45S 137°0E 63 F2
Kangaroo Mts. *Australia* 23°29S 141°51E 62 C3
Kangasala *Finland* 61°28N 24°4E 8 F21
Kangāvar *Iran* 34°40N 48°0E 45 C6
Kangdong *N. Korea* 39°9N 126°5E 35 E14
Kangean, Kepulauan *Indonesia* 6°55S 115°23E 36 F5
Kangean Is. = Kangean, Kepulauan *Indonesia* 6°55S 115°23E 36 F5
Kanggye *N. Korea* 41°0N 126°35E 35 D14
Kangikajik *Greenland* 70°7N 22°0W 4 B6
Kangiqliniq = Rankin Inlet *Canada* 62°30N 93°0W 68 E13
Kangiqsualujjuaq *Canada* 58°30N 65°59W 69 F18
Kangiqsujuaq *Canada* 61°30N 72°0W 69 E17
Kangiqtugaapik = Clyde River *Canada* 70°30N 68°30W 69 C18
Kangirsuk *Canada* 60°0N 70°0W 69 F18
Kangkar Chemaran *Malaysia* 1°34N 104°12E 39 d
Kangkar Sungai Tiram *Malaysia* 1°35N 103°55E 39 d
Kangkar Teberau *Malaysia* 1°32N 103°51E 39 d
Kangping *China* 42°43N 123°18E 35 C12
Kangra *India* 32°6N 76°16E 42 C7
Kangrinboqe Feng *China* 31°0N 81°25E 43 D9
Kangto *China* 27°50N 92°35E 41 F18
Kanha △ *India* 22°15N 80°40E 43 H9
Kanhar → *India* 24°28N 83°8E 43 G10
Kaniama *Dem. Rep. of the Congo* 7°30S 24°12E 54 D1
Kaniapiskau = Caniapiscau → *Canada* 56°40N 69°30W 73 A6
Kaniapiskau, L. = Caniapiscau, L. *Canada* 54°10N 69°55W 73 B6
Kanin, Poluostrov *Russia* 68°0N 45°0E 18 A8
Kanin Nos, Mys *Russia* 68°39N 43°32E 18 A7
Kanin Pen. = Kanin, Poluostrov *Russia* 68°0N 45°0E 18 A8
Kaniva *Australia* 36°22S 141°18E 63 F3
Kanjut Sar *Pakistan* 36°7N 75°25E 43 A6
Kankaanpää *Finland* 61°44N 22°50E 8 F20
Kankakee *U.S.A.* 41°7N 87°52W 80 E10
Kankakee → *U.S.A.* 41°23N 88°15W 80 E9
Kankan *Guinea* 10°23N 9°15W 50 F4

Kankendy = Xankändi Azerbaijan 39°52N 46°49E 44 B5
Kanker India 20°10N 81°40E 41 J12
Kankroli India 25°4N 73°53E 42 G5
Kannapolis U.S.A. 35°30N 80°37W 85 D14
Kannauj India 27°3N 79°56E 43 F8
Kannod India 22°45N 76°40E 40 H10
Kannur = Cannanore India 11°53N 75°27E 40 P9
Kannyakumari India 8°3N 77°40E 40 Q10
Kano Nigeria 12°2N 8°30E 50 F7
Kan'onji Japan 34°7N 133°39E 31 G6
Kanowit Malaysia 2°14N 112°20E 36 D4
Kanoya Japan 31°25N 130°50E 31 J5
Kanpetlet Burma 21°10N 93°59E 41 J18
Kanpur India 26°28N 80°20E 43 F9
Kansas □ U.S.A. 38°30N 99°0W 80 F4
Kansas → U.S.A. 39°7N 94°37W 80 F6
Kansas City Kans., U.S.A. 39°7N 94°38W 80 F6
Kansas City Mo., U.S.A. 39°6N 94°35W 80 F6
Kansenia Dem. Rep. of the Congo 10°20S 26°0E 55 E2
Kansk Russia 56°20N 95°37E 29 D10
Kansu = Gansu □ China 36°0N 104°0E 34 G3
Kantaphor India 22°35N 76°34E 42 H7
Kantharalak Thailand 14°39N 104°39E 38 E5
Kanthi = Contai India 21°54N 87°46E 43 J12
Kantli → India 28°20N 75°30E 42 E6
Kantō □ Japan 36°15N 139°30E 31 F9
Kantō-Sanchi Japan 35°59N 138°50E 31 G9
Kanturk Ireland 52°11N 8°54W 10 D3
Kanuma Japan 36°34N 139°42E 31 F9
Kanus Namibia 27°50S 18°39E 56 D2
Kanye Botswana 24°55S 25°28E 56 C4
Kanzenze Dem. Rep. of the Congo 10°30S 25°12E 55 E2
Kanzi, Ras Tanzania 7°1S 39°33E 54 D4
Kao Tonga 19°40S 175°1W 59 c
Kao Phara Thailand 8°3N 98°22E 39 a
Kaohsiung Taiwan 22°35N 120°16E 33 D7
Kaokoveld Namibia 19°15S 14°30E 56 B1
Kaolack Senegal 14°5N 16°8W 50 F2
Kaoshan China 44°38N 124°50E 35 B13
Kapa'a U.S.A. 22°5N 159°19W 75 L8
Kapadvanj India 23°5N 73°0E 42 H5
Kapan Armenia 39°18N 46°27E 44 B5
Kapanga Dem. Rep. of the Congo 8°30S 22°40E 52 F4
Kapchagai = Qapshaghay Kazakhstan 43°51N 77°14E 28 E8
Kapedo Kenya 1°10N 36°6E 54 B4
Kapela = Velika Kapela Croatia 45°10N 15°5E 16 F8
Kapema Dem. Rep. of the Congo 10°45S 28°22E 55 E2
Kapenguria Kenya 1°14N 35°7E 54 B4
Kapfenberg Austria 47°26N 15°18E 16 E8
Kapiri Mposhi Zambia 13°59S 28°43E 55 E2
Kāpīsā □ Afghan. 35°0N 69°20E 40 B6
Kapiskau → Canada 52°47N 81°55W 72 B3
Kapit Malaysia 2°0N 112°55E 36 D4
Kapiti I. N.Z. 40°50S 174°56E 59 D5
Kaplan U.S.A. 30°0N 92°17W 84 F8
Kapoe Thailand 9°34N 98°32E 39 H2
Kapoeta Sudan 4°50N 33°35E 51 H12
Kaposvár Hungary 46°25N 17°47E 17 E9
Kapowsin U.S.A. 46°59N 122°13W 78 D4
Kapps Namibia 22°32S 17°18E 56 C2
Kapsabet Kenya 0°12N 35°6E 54 B4
Kapsan N. Korea 41°4N 128°19E 35 D15
Kapsukas = Marijampolė Lithuania 54°33N 23°19E 9 J20
Kaptai L. Bangla. 22°40N 92°20E 41 H18
Kapuas → Indonesia 0°25S 109°20E 36 E3
Kapuas Hulu, Pegunungan Malaysia 1°30N 113°30E 36 D4
Kapuas Hulu Ra. = Kapuas Hulu, Pegunungan Malaysia 1°30N 113°30E 36 D4
Kapulo Dem. Rep. of the Congo 8°18S 29°15E 55 D2
Kapunda Australia 34°20S 138°56E 63 E2
Kapuni N.Z. 39°29S 174°8E 59 C5
Kapurthala India 31°23N 75°25E 42 D6
Kapuskasing Canada 49°25N 82°30W 72 C3
Kapuskasing → Canada 49°49N 82°0W 72 C3
Kaputar, Mt. Australia 30°15S 150°10E 63 E5
Kaputir Kenya 2°5N 35°28E 54 B4
Kara Russia 69°10N 65°0E 28 C7
Kara Bogaz Gol, Zaliv = Garabogazköl Aylagy Turkmenistan 41°0N 53°30E 19 F9
Kara-Kala = Garrygala Turkmenistan 38°31N 56°29E 45 B8
Kara Kalpak Republic = Qoraqalpoghistan □ Uzbekistan 43°0N 58°0E 28 E6
Kara Kum = Garagum Turkmenistan 39°30N 60°0E 45 B8
Kara Sea Russia 75°0N 70°0E 28 B8
Karabiğa Turkey 40°23N 27°17E 23 D12
Karabük Turkey 41°12N 32°37E 19 F5
Karaburun Turkey 38°41N 26°28E 23 E12
Karabutak = Qarabutaq Kazakhstan 49°59N 60°14E 28 E7
Karacabey Turkey 40°12N 28°21E 23 D13
Karacasu Turkey 37°43N 28°35E 23 F13
Karachey-Cherkessia □ Russia 43°40N 41°30E 19 F7
Karachi Pakistan 24°50N 67°0E 42 G2
Karad India 17°15N 74°10E 40 L9
Karaganda = Qaraghandy Kazakhstan 49°50N 73°10E 28 E8
Karagayly = Qaraghayly Kazakhstan 49°26N 76°0E 28 E8
Karaginskiy, Ostrov Russia 58°45N 164°0E 29 D17
Karagiye, Vpadina Kazakhstan 43°27N 51°45E 19 F9
Karagiye Depression = Karagiye, Vpadina Kazakhstan 43°27N 51°45E 19 F9
Karagola Road India 25°29N 87°23E 43 G12
Karaikal India 10°59N 79°50E 40 P11
Karaikkudi India 10°5N 78°45E 40 P11
Karaj Iran 35°48N 51°0E 45 C6
Karajarri ✪ Australia 19°0S 122°30E 60 C3
Karak Malaysia 3°25N 102°2E 39 L4
Karakalpakstan = Qoraqalpoghistan □ Uzbekistan 43°0N 58°0E 28 E6
Karakelong Indonesia 4°35N 126°50E 37 D7
Karakitang Indonesia 3°14N 125°28E 37 D7
Karakol Kyrgyzstan 42°30N 78°20E 32 B2
Karakoram Pass Asia 35°33N 77°50E 43 B7
Karakoram Ra. Pakistan 35°30N 77°0E 43 B7
Karakuwisa Namibia 18°56S 19°40E 56 B2
Karalon Russia 57°5N 115°50E 29 D12
Karama Jordan 31°57N 35°35E 46 D4
Karaman Turkey 37°14N 33°13E 44 B2
Karamay China 45°30N 84°58E 32 B3
Karambu Indonesia 3°53S 116°6E 36 E5
Karamea Bight N.Z. 41°22S 171°40E 59 D3
Karamnasa → India 25°31N 83°52E 43 G10
Karān Si. Arabia 27°43N 49°49E 45 E6
Karand Iran 34°16N 46°15E 44 C5
Karanganyar Indonesia 7°38S 109°37E 37 G13
Karangasem Indonesia 8°27S 115°37E 37 J18
Karanjia India 21°47N 85°58E 43 J11
Karasburg Namibia 28°0S 18°44E 56 D2
Karasino Russia 66°50N 86°50E 28 C9
Karasjok Norway 69°27N 25°30E 8 B21
Karasuk Russia 53°44N 78°2E 28 D8
Karasuyama Japan 36°39N 140°9E 31 F10
Karatau, Khrebet = Qarataū Kazakhstan 43°30N 69°30E 28 E7
Karatax Shan China 35°57N 81°0E 32 C3
Karatsu Japan 33°26N 129°58E 31 H5
Karaul Russia 70°6N 82°15E 28 B9
Karauli India 26°30N 77°4E 42 F7
Karavostasi Cyprus 35°8N 32°50E 25 D11
Karawang Indonesia 6°30S 107°15E 37 G12
Karawanken Europe 46°30N 14°40E 16 E8
Karayazı Turkey 39°41N 42°9E 19 G7
Karazhal = Qarazhal Kazakhstan 48°2N 70°49E 28 E8
Karbalā' Iraq 32°36N 44°3E 44 C5
Karcag Hungary 47°19N 20°57E 17 E11
Karcha → Pakistan 34°45N 76°10E 43 B7
Karchana India 25°17N 81°56E 43 G9
Karditsa Greece 39°23N 21°54E 23 E9
Kärdla Estonia 59°0N 22°45E 9 G20
Kareeberge S. Africa 30°59S 21°50E 56 E3
Kareha → India 25°44N 86°21E 43 G12
Kareima Sudan 18°30N 31°49E 51 E12
Karelia □ Russia 65°30N 32°30E 8 D25
Karelian Republic = Karelia □ Russia 65°30N 32°30E 8 D25
Karera India 25°32N 78°9E 42 G8
Kārevāndar Iran 27°53N 60°44E 45 E9
Kargasok Russia 59°3N 80°53E 28 D9
Kargat Russia 55°10N 80°15E 28 D9
Kargi Kenya 2°31N 37°34E 54 B4
Kargil India 34°32N 76°12E 43 B7
Kargopol Russia 61°30N 38°58E 18 B6
Karhal India 27°1N 78°57E 43 F8
Karīān Iran 26°57N 57°14E 45 E8
Karianga Madag. 22°25S 47°22E 57 C8
Kariba Zimbabwe 16°28S 28°50E 55 F2
Kariba, L. Zimbabwe 16°40S 28°25E 55 F2
Kariba Dam Zimbabwe 16°30S 28°35E 55 F2
Kariba Gorge Zambia 16°30S 28°50E 55 F2
Karibib Namibia 22°0S 15°56E 56 C2
Karijini △ Australia 23°8S 118°15E 60 D2
Karimata, Kepulauan Indonesia 1°25S 109°0E 36 E3
Karimata, Selat Indonesia 2°0S 108°40E 36 E3
Karimata Is. = Karimata, Kepulauan Indonesia 1°25S 109°0E 36 E3
Karimnagar India 18°26N 79°10E 40 K11
Karimun Kecil, Pulau Indonesia 1°8N 103°22E 39 d
Karimunjawa, Kepulauan Indonesia 5°50S 110°30E 36 F4
Karin Somali Rep. 10°50N 45°52E 47 E4
Karīt Iran 33°29N 56°55E 45 C8
Kariya Japan 34°58N 137°1E 31 G8
Kariyangwe Zimbabwe 18°0S 27°38E 57 B4
Karjala Finland 62°0N 30°25E 8 F24
Karkaralinsk = Qarqaraly Kazakhstan 49°26N 75°30E 28 E8
Karkheh → Iran 31°2N 47°29E 44 D5
Karkinitska Zatoka Ukraine 45°56N 33°0E 19 E5
Karkinitskiy Zaliv = Karkinitska Zatoka Ukraine 45°56N 33°0E 19 E5
Karkuk = Kirkūk Iraq 35°30N 44°21E 44 C5
Karlantijpa North ✪ Australia 19°27S 133°33E 60 C5
Karlantijpa South ✪ Australia 20°31S 133°9E 60 D5
Karleby = Kokkola Finland 63°50N 23°8E 8 E20
Karlovac Croatia 45°31N 15°36E 16 F8
Karlovo Bulgaria 42°38N 24°47E 23 C11
Karlovy Vary Czech Rep. 50°13N 12°51E 16 C7
Karlsbad = Karlovy Vary Czech Rep. 50°13N 12°51E 16 C7
Karlsena, Mys Russia 77°0N 67°42E 28 B7
Karlshamn Sweden 56°10N 14°51E 9 H16
Karlskoga Sweden 59°28N 14°33E 9 G16
Karlskrona Sweden 56°10N 15°35E 9 H16
Karlsruhe Germany 49°0N 8°23E 16 D5
Karlstad Sweden 59°23N 13°30E 9 G15
Karlstad U.S.A. 48°35N 96°31W 80 A5
Karmi'el Israel 32°55N 35°18E 46 C4
Karnak Egypt 25°43N 32°39E 51 C12
Karnal India 29°42N 77°2E 42 E7
Karnali → Nepal 28°45N 81°16E 43 E9
Karnaphuli Res. = Kaptai L. Bangla. 22°40N 92°20E 41 H18
Karnaprayag India 30°16N 79°15E 43 D8
Karnataka □ India 13°15N 77°0E 40 N10
Karnes City U.S.A. 28°53N 97°54W 84 G6
Karnische Alpen Europe 46°36N 13°0E 16 E7
Kärnten □ Austria 46°52N 13°30E 16 E8
Karoi Zimbabwe 16°48S 29°45E 55 F2
Karon, Ao Thailand 7°51N 98°17E 39 a
Karonga Malawi 9°57S 33°55E 55 D3
Karoo △ S. Africa 32°18S 22°27E 56 E3
Karoonda Australia 35°1S 139°59E 63 F2
Karor Pakistan 31°15N 70°59E 42 D4
Karora Sudan 17°44N 38°15E 51 E13
Karpasia Cyprus 35°32N 34°15E 25 D13
Karpathos Greece 35°37N 27°10E 23 G12
Karpinsk Russia 59°45N 60°1E 18 C11
Karpogory Russia 64°0N 44°27E 18 B7
Karpuz Burnu = Apostolos Andreas, C. Cyprus 35°42N 34°35E 25 D13
Karratha Australia 20°44S 116°52E 60 D2
Kars Turkey 40°40N 43°5E 19 F7
Karsakpay Kazakhstan 47°55N 66°40E 28 E7
Karshi = Qarshi Uzbekistan 38°53N 65°48E 28 F7
Karsiyang India 26°56N 88°18E 43 F13
Karsog India 31°23N 77°12E 42 D7
Kartala Comoros Is. 11°45S 43°21E 53 a
Kartaly Russia 53°3N 60°40E 28 D7
Kartapur India 31°27N 75°32E 42 D6
Karthaus U.S.A. 41°8N 78°9W 82 E6
Karufa Indonesia 3°50S 133°20E 37 E8
Karuma ⌓ Uganda 2°5N 32°15E 54 B3
Karumba Australia 17°31S 140°50E 62 B3
Karumo Tanzania 2°25S 32°50E 54 C3
Karumwa Tanzania 3°12S 32°38E 54 C3
Kārūn → Iran 30°26N 48°10E 45 D6
Karungu Kenya 0°50S 34°10E 54 C3
Karviná Czech Rep. 49°53N 18°31E 17 D10
Karwan → India 27°26N 78°4E 42 F8
Karwar India 14°55N 74°13E 40 M9
Karwi India 25°12N 80°57E 43 G9
Karymskoye Russia 51°36N 114°21E 29 D12
Kasache Malawi 13°25S 34°20E 55 E3
Kasai → Dem. Rep. of the Congo 3°30S 16°10E 52 E3
Kasai-Oriental □ Dem. Rep. of the Congo 5°0S 24°30E 54 D1
Kasaji Dem. Rep. of the Congo 10°25S 23°27E 55 E1
Kasama Zambia 10°16S 31°9E 55 E3
Kasan N. Korea 41°18N 126°55E 35 D14
Kasandra Kolpos Greece 40°5N 23°30E 23 D10
Kasane Namibia 17°34S 24°50E 56 B3
Kasanga Tanzania 8°30S 31°10E 55 D3
Kasanka △ Zambia 11°34S 30°15E 55 E3
Kasaragod India 12°30N 74°58E 40 N9
Kasba L. Canada 60°20N 102°10W 71 A8
Kāseh Garān Iran 34°5N 46°2E 44 C5
Kasempa Zambia 13°30S 25°44E 55 E2
Kasenga Dem. Rep. of the Congo 10°20S 28°45E 55 E2
Kasese Uganda 0°13N 30°3E 54 B3
Kasewa Zambia 14°28S 28°53E 55 E2
Kasganj India 27°48N 78°42E 43 F8
Kashabowie Canada 48°40N 90°26W 72 C1
Kashaf Iran 35°58N 61°7E 45 C9
Kāshān Iran 34°5N 51°30E 45 C6
Kashechewan Canada 52°18N 81°37W 72 B3
Kashgar = Kashi China 39°30N 76°2E 32 C2
Kashi China 39°30N 76°2E 32 C2
Kashimbo Dem. Rep. of the Congo 11°12S 26°19E 55 E2
Kashipur India 29°15N 79°0E 43 E8
Kashiwazaki Japan 37°22N 138°33E 31 F9
Kashk-e Kohneh Afghan. 34°55N 62°30E 40 B3
Kashkū'īyeh Iran 30°31N 55°40E 45 D7
Kāshmar Iran 35°16N 58°26E 45 C8
Kashmir Asia 34°0N 76°0E 43 C7
Kashmor Pakistan 28°28N 69°32E 42 E3
Kashun Noerh = Gaxun Nur China 42°22N 100°30E 32 B5
Kasiari India 22°8N 87°14E 43 H12
Kasimov Russia 54°55N 41°20E 18 D7
Kasinge Dem. Rep. of the Congo 6°15S 26°58E 54 D2
Kasiruta Indonesia 0°25S 127°12E 37 E7
Kaskaskia → U.S.A. 37°58N 89°57W 80 G9
Kaskattama → Canada 57°3N 90°4W 71 B10
Kaskinen Finland 62°22N 21°15E 8 E19
Kaskö = Kaskinen Finland 62°22N 21°15E 8 E19
Kaslo Canada 49°55N 116°55W 70 D5
Kasmere L. Canada 59°34N 101°10W 71 B8
Kasongo Dem. Rep. of the Congo 4°30S 26°33E 54 C2
Kasongo Lunda Dem. Rep. of the Congo 6°35S 16°49E 52 F3
Kasos Greece 35°20N 26°55E 23 G12
Kassalâ Sudan 15°30N 36°0E 51 E13
Kassel Germany 51°18N 9°26E 16 C5
Kassiopi Greece 39°48N 19°53E 25 A3
Kasson U.S.A. 44°2N 92°45W 80 C7
Kastamonu Turkey 41°25N 33°43E 19 F5
Kasteli Greece 35°29N 23°38E 25 D5
Kastelli Greece 35°12N 25°20E 25 D7
Kasterlee Belgium 51°15N 4°59E 15 C4
Kastoria Greece 40°30N 21°19E 23 D9
Kasulu Tanzania 4°37S 30°5E 54 C3
Kasumi Japan 35°38N 134°38E 31 G7
Kasungu Malawi 13°0S 33°29E 55 E3
Kasungu △ Malawi 12°53S 33°9E 55 E3
Kasur Pakistan 31°5N 74°25E 42 D6
Kata, Ao Thailand 7°48N 98°18E 39 J2
Kata Archanes Greece 35°15N 25°10E 25 D7
Kata Tjuta Australia 25°20S 130°50E 61 E5
Kataba Zambia 16°5S 25°10E 55 F2
Katahdin, Mt. U.S.A. 45°54N 68°56W 81 C19
Kataka = Cuttack India 20°25N 85°57E 41 J14
Katako Kombe Dem. Rep. of the Congo 3°25S 24°20E 54 C1
Katale Tanzania 4°52S 31°7E 54 C3
Katanda Katanga, Dem. Rep. of the Congo 7°52S 24°13E 54 D1
Katanda Nord-Kivu, Dem. Rep. of the Congo 0°55S 29°21E 54 C2
Katanga □ Dem. Rep. of the Congo 8°0S 25°0E 54 D2
Katangi India 21°56N 79°50E 40 J11
Katanning Australia 33°40S 117°33E 61 F2
Katavi △ Tanzania 6°51S 31°3E 54 D3
Katavi Swamp Tanzania 6°50S 31°10E 54 D3
Katerini Greece 40°18N 22°37E 23 D10
Katghora India 22°30N 82°33E 43 H10
Katha Burma 24°10N 96°30E 41 G20
Katherîna, Gebel Egypt 28°30N 33°57E 44 D2
Katherine Australia 14°27S 132°20E 60 B5
Katherine Gorge = Nitmiluk △ Australia 14°6S 132°15E 60 B5
Kathi India 21°47N 74°3E 42 J6
Kathiawar India 22°20N 71°0E 42 H4
Kathikas Cyprus 34°55N 32°25E 25 E11
Kathmandu Nepal 27°45N 85°20E 43 F11
Kathua India 32°23N 75°34E 42 C6
Katihar India 25°34N 87°36E 43 G12
Katima Mulilo Namibia 17°28S 24°13E 56 B3
Katimbira Malawi 12°40S 34°0E 55 E3
Katingan = Mendawai → Indonesia 3°30S 113°0E 36 E4
Katiola Ivory C. 8°10N 5°10W 50 G4
Katiti ✪ Australia 25°1S 131°11E 61 E5
Katmandu = Kathmandu Nepal 27°45N 85°20E 43 F11
Katni = Murwara India 23°46N 80°28E 43 H9
Katni India 23°51N 80°24E 43 H9
Kato Chorio Greece 35°3N 25°47E 25 D7
Kato Korakiana Greece 39°42N 19°45E 25 A3
Káto Pyrgos Cyprus 35°11N 32°41E 25 D11
Katompe Dem. Rep. of the Congo 6°2S 26°23E 54 D2
Katong Singapore 1°18N 103°53E 39 d
Katonga → Uganda 0°34N 31°50E 54 B3
Katoomba Australia 33°41S 150°19E 63 E5
Katowice Poland 50°17N 19°5E 17 C10
Katrine, L. U.K. 56°15N 4°30W 11 E4
Katrineholm Sweden 59°9N 16°12E 9 G17
Katsepe Madag. 15°45S 46°15E 57 B8
Katsina Nigeria 13°0N 7°32E 50 F7
Katsumoto Japan 33°51N 129°42E 31 H4
Katsuura Japan 35°10N 140°20E 31 G10
Katsuyama Japan 36°3N 136°30E 31 F8
Kattavia Greece 35°57N 27°46E 25 D9
Kattegat Denmark 56°40N 11°20E 9 H14
Katumba Dem. Rep. of the Congo 7°40S 25°17E 54 D2
Katwa India 23°30N 88°5E 43 H13
Katwijk Neths. 52°12N 4°24E 15 B4
Kaua'i U.S.A. 22°3N 159°30W 75 L8
Kaudom ⌓ Namibia 18°45S 20°51E 56 B3
Kaufman U.S.A. 32°35N 96°19W 84 E6
Kauhajoki Finland 62°25N 22°10E 8 E20
Kaukauna U.S.A. 44°17N 88°17W 80 C9
Kaukauveld Namibia 20°0S 20°15E 56 C3
Ka'ula I. U.S.A. 21°40N 160°33W 75 L7
Kaunas Lithuania 54°54N 23°54E 9 J20
Kaunia Bangla. 25°46N 89°26E 43 G13
Kautokeino Norway 69°0N 23°4E 8 B20
Kauwapur India 27°31N 82°18E 43 F10
Kavacha Russia 60°16N 169°51E 29 C17
Kavala Greece 40°57N 24°28E 23 D11
Kavalerovo Russia 44°15N 135°4E 30 B7
Kavali India 14°55N 80°1E 40 M12
Kavār Iran 29°11N 52°44E 45 D7
Kavi India 22°12N 72°38E 42 H5
Kavimba Botswana 18°2S 24°38E 56 B3
Kavīr, Dasht-e Iran 34°30N 55°0E 45 C7
Kavīr △ Iran 34°40N 52°0E 45 C7
Kavos Greece 39°23N 20°3E 25 B4
Kaw Fr. Guiana 4°30N 52°15W 93 C8
Kawagama L. Canada 45°18N 78°45W 82 A6
Kawagoe Japan 35°55N 139°29E 31 G9
Kawaguchi Japan 35°52N 139°45E 31 G9
Kawambwa Zambia 9°48S 29°3E 55 D2
Kawanoe Japan 34°1N 133°34E 31 G6
Kawardha India 22°0N 81°17E 43 J9
Kawasaki Japan 35°31N 139°43E 31 G9
Kawasi Indonesia 1°38S 127°28E 37 E7
Kawawachikamach Canada 54°48N 66°50W 73 B6
Kawerau N.Z. 38°7S 176°42E 59 C6
Kawhia N.Z. 38°4S 174°49E 59 C5
Kawhia Harbour N.Z. 38°5S 174°51E 59 C5
Kawio, Kepulauan Indonesia 4°30N 125°30E 37 D7
Kawthaung Burma 10°5N 98°36E 39 H2
Kawthoolei = Kayin □ Burma 18°0N 97°30E 41 L20
Kawthule = Kayin □ Burma 18°0N 97°30E 41 L20
Kaya Burkina Faso 13°4N 1°10W 50 F5
Kayah □ Burma 19°15N 97°15E 41 K20
Kayak I. U.S.A. 59°56N 144°23W 74 D11
Kayan → Indonesia 2°55N 117°35E 36 D5
Kaycee U.S.A. 43°43N 106°38W 76 E10
Kayeli Indonesia 3°20S 127°10E 37 E7
Kayenta U.S.A. 36°44N 110°15W 77 H8
Kayes Mali 14°25N 11°30W 50 F3
Kayin □ Burma 18°0N 97°30E 41 L20
Kayoa Indonesia 0°1N 127°28E 37 D7
Kayomba Zambia 13°11S 24°2E 55 E1
Kayseri Turkey 38°45N 35°30E 44 B2
Kaysville U.S.A. 41°2N 111°56W 76 F8
Kazachye Russia 70°52N 135°58E 29 B14
Kazakhstan ■ Asia 50°0N 70°0E 28 E8
Kazan Russia 55°50N 49°10E 18 C8
Kazan → Canada 64°2N 95°29W 71 A9
Kazan-Rettō Pac. Oc. 25°0N 141°0E 64 E6
Kazanlŭk Bulgaria 42°38N 25°20E 23 C11
Kazatin = Kozyatyn Ukraine 49°45N 28°50E 17 D15
Kāzerūn Iran 29°38N 51°40E 45 D6
Kazi Magomed = Qazımämmäd Azerbaijan 40°3N 49°0E 45 A6
Kazuma Pan △ Zimbabwe 18°20S 25°48E 55 F2
Kazuno Japan 40°10N 140°45E 30 D10
Kazym → Russia 63°54N 65°50E 28 C7
Kea Greece 37°35N 24°22E 23 F11
Keady U.K. 54°15N 6°42W 10 B5
Kearney U.S.A. 40°42N 99°5W 80 E4
Kearney ✪ Australia 20°10S 128°4E 60 D4
Kearny U.S.A. 33°3N 110°55W 77 K8
Kearsarge, Mt. U.S.A. 43°22N 71°50W 83 C13
Keban Turkey 38°50N 38°50E 19 G6
Keban Barajı Turkey 38°41N 38°33E 44 B3
Kebnekaise Sweden 67°53N 18°33E 8 C18
Kebri Dehar Ethiopia 6°45N 44°17E 47 F3
Kebumen Indonesia 7°42S 109°40E 37 G13
Kechika → Canada 59°41N 127°12W 70 B3
Kecskemét Hungary 46°57N 19°42E 17 E10
Kėdainiai Lithuania 55°15N 24°2E 9 J21
Kedarnath India 30°44N 79°4E 43 D8
Kedgwick Canada 47°40N 67°20W 73 C6
Kediri Indonesia 7°51S 112°1E 37 G15
Kedros Oros Greece 35°11N 24°37E 25 D6
Keeler U.S.A. 36°29N 117°52W 78 J9
Keeley L. Canada 54°54N 108°8W 71 C7
Keeling Is. = Cocos Is. Ind. Oc. 12°10S 96°55E 64 J1
Keelung = Chilung Taiwan 25°3N 121°45E 33 D7
Keene Canada 44°15N 78°10W 82 B6
Keene Calif., U.S.A. 35°13N 118°33W 79 K8
Keene N.H., U.S.A. 42°56N 72°17W 83 D12
Keene N.Y., U.S.A. 44°16N 73°46W 83 B11
Keep River △ Australia 15°49S 129°8E 60 C4
Keeper Hill Ireland 52°45N 8°16W 10 D3
Keerweer, C. Australia 14°0S 141°32E 62 A3
Keeseville U.S.A. 44°29N 73°30W 83 B11
Keetmanshoop Namibia 26°35S 18°8E 56 D2
Keewatin Canada 49°46N 94°34W 71 D10
Keewatin → Canada 56°29N 100°46W 71 B8
Kefalonia Greece 38°15N 20°30E 23 E9
Kefamenanu Indonesia 9°28S 124°29E 37 F6
Kefar Sava Israel 32°11N 34°54E 46 C3
Keffi Nigeria 8°55N 7°43E 50 G7
Keflavík Iceland 64°2N 22°35W 8 D2
Keg River Canada 57°54N 117°55W 70 B5
Kegaska Canada 50°9N 61°18W 73 B7
Kehancha Kenya 1°11S 34°37E 54 C3
Keighley U.K. 53°52N 1°54W 12 D6
Keila Estonia 59°18N 24°25E 9 G21
Keimoes S. Africa 28°41S 20°59E 56 D3
Keitele Finland 63°10N 26°20E 8 E22
Keith Australia 36°6S 140°20E 63 F3
Keith U.K. 57°32N 2°57W 11 D6
Keiyasi Fiji 17°53S 177°46E 59 a
Keizer U.S.A. 44°57N 123°1W 76 D2
Kejimkujik △ Canada 44°25N 65°25W 73 D6
Kejserr Franz Joseph Fd. Greenland 73°30N 24°30W 4 B6
Kekri India 26°0N 75°10E 42 G6
Kelan China 38°43N 111°31E 34 E6
Kelang = Klang Malaysia 3°2N 101°26E 39 L3
Kelantan → Malaysia 6°13N 102°14E 39 J4
Kelkit → Turkey 40°45N 36°32E 19 F6
Kellerberrin Australia 31°36S 117°38E 61 F2
Kellett, C. Canada 72°0N 126°0W 4 B1
Kelleys I. U.S.A. 41°36N 82°42W 82 E2
Kellogg U.S.A. 47°32N 116°7W 76 C5
Kells = Ceanannus Mor Ireland 53°44N 6°53W 10 C5
Kélo Chad 9°10N 15°45E 51 G9
Kelokedhara Cyprus 34°48N 32°39E 25 E11
Kelowna Canada 49°50N 119°25W 70 D5
Kelsey Creek Australia 20°26S 148°31E 62 b
Kelseyville U.S.A. 38°59N 122°50W 78 G4
Kelso N.Z. 45°54S 169°15E 59 F2
Kelso U.K. 55°36N 2°26W 11 F6
Kelso U.S.A. 46°9N 122°54W 78 D4
Keluang = Kluang Malaysia 2°3N 103°18E 39 L4
Kelvington Canada 52°10N 103°30W 71 C8
Kem Russia 65°0N 34°38E 18 B5
Kem → Russia 64°57N 34°41E 18 B5
Kema Indonesia 1°22N 125°8E 37 D7
Kemah Turkey 39°32N 39°5E 44 B3
Kemaman Malaysia 4°12N 103°18E 39 K4
Kemano Canada 53°35N 128°0W 70 C3
Kemasik Malaysia 4°25N 103°27E 39 K4
Kemerovo Russia 55°20N 86°5E 28 D9
Kemi Finland 65°44N 24°34E 8 D21
Kemi älv = Kemijoki → Finland 65°47N 24°32E 8 D21
Kemi träsk = Kemijärvi Finland 66°43N 27°22E 8 C22
Kemijärvi Finland 66°43N 27°22E 8 C22
Kemijoki → Finland 65°47N 24°32E 8 D21
Kemmerer U.S.A. 41°48N 110°32W 76 F8
Kemmuna = Comino Malta 36°1N 14°20E 25 C1
Kemp, L. U.S.A. 33°46N 99°9W 84 E5
Kemp Land Antarctica 69°0S 55°0E 5 C5
Kempas Malaysia 1°33N 103°42E 39 d
Kempsey Australia 31°1S 152°50E 63 E5
Kempt, L. Canada 47°25N 74°22W 72 C5
Kempten Germany 47°45N 10°17E 16 E6
Kempton Australia 42°31S 147°12E 63 G4
Kemptville Canada 45°0N 75°38W 83 B9
Ken → India 25°13N 80°27E 43 G9
Kenai U.S.A. 60°33N 151°16W 68 E1
Kenai Mts. U.S.A. 60°0N 150°0W 74 D9
Kenamuke Swamp Sudan 5°55N 33°48E 54 A3
Kendai India 22°45N 82°37E 43 H10
Kendal Indonesia 6°56S 110°14E 37 G14
Kendal U.K. 54°20N 2°44W 12 C5
Kendall Australia 31°35S 152°44E 63 E5
Kendall U.S.A. 25°40N 80°19W 85 J14
Kendall → Australia 14°4S 141°35E 62 A3

Kendallville *U.S.A.* 41°27N 85°16W **81 E11**
Kendari *Indonesia* 3°50S 122°30E **37 E6**
Kendawangan *Indonesia* 2°32S 110°17E **36 E4**
Kendi, Pulau *Malaysia* 5°13N 100°11E **39 c**
Kendrapara *India* 20°35N 86°30E **41 J15**
Kendrew *S. Africa* 32°32S 24°30E **56 E3**
Kene Thao *Laos* 17°44N 101°10E **38 D3**
Kenedy *U.S.A.* 28°49N 97°51W **84 G6**
Kenema *S. Leone* 7°50N 11°14W **50 G3**
Keng Kok *Laos* 16°26N 105°12E **38 D5**
Keng Tawng *Burma* 20°45N 98°18E **41 J21**
Keng Tung *Burma* 21°0N 99°30E **41 J22**
Kengeja *Tanzania* 5°26S 39°45E **54 D4**
Kenhardt *S. Africa* 29°19S 21°12E **56 D3**
Kenitra *Morocco* 34°15N 6°40W **50 B4**
Kenli *China* 37°30N 118°20E **35 F10**
Kenmare *Ireland* 51°53N 9°36W **10 E2**
Kenmare *U.S.A.* 48°41N 102°5W **80 A2**
Kenmare River *Ireland* 51°48N 9°51W **10 E2**
Kennebago Lake *U.S.A.* 45°4N 70°40W **83 A14**
Kennebec *U.S.A.* 43°54N 99°52W **80 D4**
Kennebec → *U.S.A.* 43°45N 69°46W **81 D19**
Kennebunk *U.S.A.* 43°23N 70°33W **83 C14**
Kennedy *Zimbabwe* 18°52S 27°10E **56 B4**
Kennedy Channel
  Arctic 80°50N 66°0W **69 A18**
Kennedy Ra. *Australia* 24°45S 115°10E **61 D2**
Kennedy Range △
  Australia 24°34S 115°2E **61 D2**
Kenner *U.S.A.* 29°59N 90°14W **85 G9**
Kennet → *U.K.* 51°27N 0°57W **13 F7**
Kenneth Ra. *Australia* 23°50S 117°8E **61 D2**
Kennett *U.S.A.* 36°14N 90°3W **80 G8**
Kennewick *U.S.A.* 46°12N 119°7W **76 C4**
Kenniss Lake *Canada* 45°13N 78°36W **82 A6**
Kenogami → *Canada* 51°6N 84°28W **72 B3**
Kenora *Canada* 49°47N 94°29W **71 D10**
Kenosha *U.S.A.* 42°35N 87°49W **80 D10**
Kensington *Canada* 46°28N 63°34W **73 C7**
Kent *Ohio, U.S.A.* 41°9N 81°22W **82 E3**
Kent *Tex., U.S.A.* 31°4N 104°13W **84 F2**
Kent *Wash., U.S.A.* 47°22N 122°14W **78 C4**
Kent □ *U.K.* 51°12N 0°40E **13 F8**
Kent Group *Australia* 39°30S 147°20E **63 F4**
Kent Pen. *Canada* 68°30N 107°0W **68 D10**
Kentaū *Kazakhstan* 43°32N 68°36E **28 E7**
Kentland *U.S.A.* 40°46N 87°27W **80 E10**
Kenton *U.S.A.* 40°39N 83°37W **81 E12**
Kentucky □ *U.S.A.* 37°0N 84°0W **81 G11**
Kentucky → *U.S.A.* 38°41N 85°11W **81 F11**
Kentucky L. *U.S.A.* 37°1N 88°16W **80 G9**
Kentville *Canada* 45°6N 64°29W **73 C7**
Kentwood *U.S.A.* 30°56N 90°31W **85 F9**
Kenya ■ *Africa* 1°0N 38°0E **54 B4**
Kenya, Mt. *Kenya* 0°10S 37°18E **54 C4**
Kenyir, Tasik *Malaysia* 5°3N 102°54E **39 K4**
Keo Neua, Deo *Vietnam* 18°23N 105°10E **38 C5**
Keokuk *U.S.A.* 40°24N 91°24W **80 E8**
Keoladeo △ *India* 27°0N 77°20E **42 F7**
Keonjhargarh *India* 21°28N 85°35E **43 J11**
Kep *Cambodia* 10°29N 104°19E **39 G5**
Kep *Vietnam* 21°24N 106°16E **38 B6**
Kepala Batas *Malaysia* 5°31N 100°26E **39 c**
Kepi *Indonesia* 6°32S 139°19E **37 F9**
Kerala □ *India* 11°0N 76°15E **40 P10**
Kerama-Rettō *Japan* 26°5N 127°15E **31 L3**
Keran *Pakistan* 34°35N 73°59E **43 B5**
Kerang *Australia* 35°40S 143°55E **63 F3**
Keraudren, C. *Australia* 19°58S 119°45E **60 C2**
Kerch *Ukraine* 45°20N 36°20E **19 E6**
Kericho *Kenya* 0°22S 35°15E **54 C4**
Kerinci *Indonesia* 1°40S 101°15E **36 E2**
Kerki = Atamyrat
  Turkmenistan 37°50N 65°12E **28 F7**
Kerkrade *Neths.* 50°53N 6°4E **15 D6**
Kerkyra *Greece* 39°38N 19°50E **25 A3**
Kerkyras, Notio Steno
  Greece 39°34N 20°0E **25 A4**
Kermadec Is. *Pac. Oc.* 30°0S 178°15W **58 E11**
Kermadec Trench
  Pac. Oc. 30°30S 176°0W **64 L10**
Kermān *Iran* 30°15N 57°1E **45 D8**
Kerman *U.S.A.* 36°43N 120°4W **78 J6**
Kermān □ *Iran* 30°0N 57°0E **45 D8**
Kermān, Bīābān-e *Iran* 28°45N 59°45E **45 D8**
Kermānshāh *Iran* 34°23N 47°0E **44 C5**
Kermānshāh □ *Iran* 34°0N 46°30E **44 C5**
Kermit *U.S.A.* 31°52N 103°6W **84 F3**
Kern → *U.S.A.* 35°16N 119°18W **79 K7**
Kernow = Cornwall □
  U.K. 50°26N 4°40W **13 G3**
Kernville *U.S.A.* 35°45N 118°26W **79 K8**
Keroh *Malaysia* 5°43N 101°1E **39 K3**
Kerrera *U.K.* 56°24N 5°33W **11 E3**
Kerrobert *Canada* 51°56N 109°8W **71 C7**
Kerrville *U.S.A.* 30°3N 99°8W **84 F5**
Kerry □ *Ireland* 52°7N 9°35W **10 D2**
Kerry Hd. *Ireland* 52°25N 9°56W **10 D2**
Kerulen → *Asia* 48°48N 117°0E **33 B6**
Kerzaz *Algeria* 29°29N 1°37W **50 C5**
Kesagami → *Canada* 51°50N 79°45W **72 B4**
Kesagami L. *Canada* 50°23N 80°15W **72 B3**
Keşan *Turkey* 40°49N 26°38E **23 D12**
Kesennuma *Japan* 38°54N 141°35E **30 E10**
Keshit *Iran* 29°43N 58°17E **45 D8**
Kestell *S. Africa* 28°17S 28°42E **57 D4**
Kestenga *Russia* 65°50N 31°45E **8 D24**
Keswick *U.K.* 54°36N 3°9W **12 C4**
Ket → *Russia* 58°55N 81°32E **28 D9**
Ketapang *Bali, Indonesia* 8°9S 114°03E **37 J17**
Ketapang *Kalimantan,*
  Indonesia 1°55S 110°0E **36 E4**
Ketchikan *U.S.A.* 55°21N 131°39W **70 B2**
Ketchum *U.S.A.* 43°41N 114°22W **76 E6**
Ketef, Khalig Umm el
  Egypt 23°40N 35°35E **44 F2**
Keti Bandar *Pakistan* 24°8N 67°27E **42 G2**
Ketri *India* 28°1N 75°50E **42 E6**

Kętrzyn *Poland* 54°7N 21°22E **17 A11**
Kettering *U.K.* 52°24N 0°43W **13 E7**
Kettering *U.S.A.* 39°41N 84°10W **81 F11**
Kettle → *Canada* 56°40N 89°34W **71 B11**
Kettle Falls *U.S.A.* 48°37N 118°3W **76 B4**
Kettle Point *Canada* 43°10N 82°1W **82 C2**
Kettle Pt. *Canada* 43°13N 82°1W **82 C2**
Kettleman City *U.S.A.* 36°1N 119°58W **78 J7**
Keuka L. *U.S.A.* 42°30N 77°9W **82 D7**
Keuruu *Finland* 62°16N 24°41E **8 E21**
Kewanee *U.S.A.* 41°14N 89°56W **80 E9**
Kewaunee *U.S.A.* 44°27N 87°31W **80 C10**
Keweenaw B. *U.S.A.* 47°0N 88°15W **80 B9**
Keweenaw Pen. *U.S.A.* 47°15N 88°15W **80 B9**
Keweenaw Pt. *U.S.A.* 47°25N 87°43W **80 B10**
Key, L. *Ireland* 54°0N 8°15W **10 C3**
Key Lake Mine *Canada* 57°5N 105°32W **71 B7**
Key Largo *U.S.A.* 25°5N 80°27W **85 J14**
Key West *U.S.A.* 24°33N 81°48W **88 B3**
Keynsham *U.K.* 51°24N 2°29W **13 F5**
Keyser *U.S.A.* 39°26N 78°59W **81 F14**
Kezhma *Russia* 58°59N 101°9E **29 D11**
Kezi *Zimbabwe* 20°58S 28°32E **57 C4**
Kgalagadi Transfrontier △
  Africa 25°10S 21°0E **56 D3**
Khabarovsk *Russia* 48°30N 135°5E **29 E14**
Khabr *Iran* 28°51N 56°22E **45 D8**
Khābūr → *Syria* 35°17N 40°35E **44 C4**
Khachmas = Xaçmaz
  Azerbaijan 41°31N 48°42E **19 F8**
Khachrod *India* 23°25N 75°20E **42 H6**
Khadro *Pakistan* 26°11N 68°50E **42 F3**
Khadzhilyangar = Dahongliutan
  China 35°45N 79°20E **43 B8**
Khaga *India* 25°47N 81°7E **43 G9**
Khagaria *India* 25°30N 86°32E **43 G12**
Khaipur *Pakistan* 29°34N 72°17E **42 E5**
Khair *India* 27°57N 77°46E **42 F7**
Khairabad *India* 27°33N 80°47E **43 F9**
Khairagarh *India* 21°27N 81°2E **43 J9**
Khairpur *Pakistan* 27°32N 68°49E **42 F3**
Khairpur Nathan Shah
  Pakistan 27°6N 67°44E **42 F2**
Khairwara *India* 23°58N 73°38E **42 H5**
Khaisor → *Pakistan* 31°17N 68°59E **42 D3**
Khajuri Kach *Pakistan* 32°4N 69°51E **42 C3**
Khakassia □ *Russia* 53°0N 90°0E **28 D9**
Khakhea *Botswana* 24°48S 23°22E **56 C3**
Khalafābād *Iran* 30°54N 49°24E **45 D6**
Khalilabad *India* 26°48N 83°5E **43 F10**
Khalīlī *Iran* 27°38N 53°17E **45 E7**
Khalkhāl *Iran* 37°37N 48°32E **45 B6**
Khalkis = Halkida
  Greece 38°27N 23°42E **23 E10**
Khalmer Yu *Russia* 67°58N 65°1E **28 C7**
Khalturin *Russia* 58°40N 48°50E **18 C8**
Khalūf *Oman* 20°30N 58°13E **47 C6**
Kham Keut *Laos* 18°15N 104°43E **38 C5**
Khamaria *India* 23°5N 80°48E **43 H9**
Khambhaliya *India* 22°14N 69°41E **42 H3**
Khambhat *India* 22°23N 72°33E **42 H5**
Khambhat, G. of *India* 20°45N 72°30E **40 J8**
Khamīr *Iran* 26°57N 55°36E **45 E7**
Khamir *Yemen* 16°2N 44°0E **47 D3**
Khamis Mushayt
  Si. Arabia 18°18N 42°44E **47 D3**
Khamsa *Egypt* 30°27N 32°23E **46 E1**
Khān → *Namibia* 22°37S 14°56E **56 C2**
Khān Abū Shāmat *Syria* 33°39N 36°53E **46 B5**
Khān Azād *Iraq* 33°7N 44°22E **44 C5**
Khān Mujiddah *Iraq* 32°21N 43°48E **44 C4**
Khān Shaykhūn *Syria* 35°26N 36°38E **44 C3**
Khan Tengri, Pik *Asia* 42°12N 80°10E **32 B3**
Khān Yūnis *Gaza Strip* 31°21N 34°18E **46 D3**
Khanai *Pakistan* 30°30N 67°8E **42 D2**
Khānaqīn *Iraq* 34°23N 45°25E **44 C5**
Khānbāghī *Iran* 36°10N 55°25E **45 B7**
Khandwa *India* 21°49N 76°22E **40 J10**
Khandyga *Russia* 62°42N 135°35E **29 C14**
Khanewal *Pakistan* 30°20N 71°55E **42 D4**
Khangah Dogran
  Pakistan 31°50N 73°37E **42 D5**
Khanh Duong *Vietnam* 12°44N 108°44E **38 F7**
Khaniá = Chania *Greece* 35°30N 24°4E **25 D6**
Khaniadhana *India* 25°1N 78°8E **42 G8**
Khanka, L. *Asia* 45°0N 132°24E **30 B6**
Khankendy = Xankändi
  Azerbaijan 39°52N 46°49E **44 B5**
Khanna *India* 30°42N 76°16E **42 D7**
Khanozai *Pakistan* 30°37N 67°19E **42 D2**
Khanpur *Pakistan* 28°42N 70°35E **42 E4**
Khanty-Mansiysk *Russia* 61°0N 69°0E **28 C7**
Khao Laem △ *Thailand* 14°56N 98°31E **38 E2**
Khao Laem Res. *Thailand* 14°50N 98°30E **38 E2**
Khao Lak △ *Malaysia* 8°38N 98°18E **39 H2**
Khao Luang △ *Thailand* 8°34N 99°42E **39 H2**
Khao Phlu *Thailand* 9°29N 99°59E **39 b**
Khao Pu-Khao Ya △
  Thailand 7°26N 99°57E **39 J2**
Khao Sam Roi Yot △
  Thailand 12°13N 99°57E **39 F2**
Khao Sok △ *Thailand* 8°55N 98°38E **39 H2**
Khao Yai △ *Thailand* 14°21N 101°29E **38 E3**
Khaoen Si Nakarin △
  Thailand 14°47N 99°0E **38 E2**
Khapalu *Pakistan* 35°10N 76°20E **43 B7**
Khapcheranga *Russia* 49°42N 112°24E **29 E12**
Khaptao △ *Nepal* 29°20N 81°10E **43 E9**
Kharagauli *India* 23°11N 71°46E **42 H4**
Kharagpur *India* 22°20N 87°25E **43 H12**
Kharan Kalat *Pakistan* 28°34N 65°21E **40 E4**
Kharānaq *Iran* 32°20N 54°45E **45 C7**
Kharda *India* 18°40N 75°34E **40 K9**
Khardung La *India* 34°20N 77°43E **43 B7**
Kharg = Khārk, Jazīreh-ye
  Iran 29°15N 50°28E **45 D6**
Khārga, El Wâhât el
  Egypt 25°10N 30°35E **51 C12**
Khargon *India* 21°45N 75°40E **40 J9**

Khari → *India* 25°54N 74°31E **42 G6**
Kharian *Pakistan* 32°49N 73°52E **42 C5**
Khārk, Jazīreh-ye *Iran* 29°15N 50°28E **45 D6**
Kharkiv *Ukraine* 49°58N 36°20E **19 E6**
Kharkov = Kharkiv
  Ukraine 49°58N 36°20E **19 E6**
Kharovsk *Russia* 59°56N 40°13E **18 C7**
Kharsawangarh *India* 22°48N 85°50E **43 H11**
Kharta *Turkey* 40°55N 29°7E **23 D13**
Khartoum = El Khartûm
  Sudan 15°31N 32°35E **51 E12**
Khartum *Canada* 45°15N 77°5W **82 A7**
Khasan *Russia* 42°25N 130°40E **30 C5**
Khashm el Girba *Sudan* 14°59N 35°58E **51 F13**
Khaskovo *Bulgaria* 41°56N 25°30E **23 D11**
Khatanga *Russia* 72°0N 102°20E **29 B11**
Khatanga → *Russia* 72°55N 106°0E **29 B11**
Khatauli *India* 29°17N 77°43E **42 E7**
Khatra *India* 22°59N 86°51E **43 H12**
Khātūnābād *Iran* 30°1N 55°25E **45 D7**
Khatyrka *Russia* 62°3N 175°15E **29 C18**
Khavda *India* 23°51N 69°43E **42 H3**
Khawr Fakkān *U.A.E.* 25°21N 56°22E **45 E8**
Khaybar, Ḥarrat
  Si. Arabia 25°45N 40°0E **44 E4**
Khāzimiyah *Iraq* 34°46N 43°37E **44 C4**
Khe Bo *Vietnam* 19°8N 104°41E **38 C5**
Khe Long *Vietnam* 21°29N 104°46E **38 B5**
Khe Sanh *Vietnam* 16°37N 106°45E **38 D6**
Khed Brahma *India* 24°7N 73°5E **42 G5**
Khekra *India* 28°52N 77°20E **42 E7**
Khemarak Phouminville = Krong
  Kaoh Kong *Cambodia* 11°37N 102°59E **39 G4**
Khemisset *Morocco* 33°50N 6°1W **50 B4**
Khemmarat *Thailand* 16°10N 105°15E **38 D5**
Khenāmān *Iran* 30°27N 56°29E **45 D8**
Khenchela *Algeria* 35°28N 7°11E **50 A7**
Khersān → *Iran* 31°33N 50°22E **45 D6**
Kherson *Ukraine* 46°35N 32°35E **19 E5**
Kheta → *Russia* 71°54N 102°6E **29 B11**
Khewari *Pakistan* 26°36N 68°52E **42 F3**
Khilchipur *India* 24°2N 76°34E **42 G7**
Khilok *Russia* 51°30N 110°45E **29 D12**
Khíos = Hios *Greece* 38°27N 26°9E **23 E12**
Khirsadoh *India* 22°11N 78°47E **43 H8**
Khiuma = Hiiumaa
  Estonia 58°50N 22°45E **9 G20**
Khiva *Uzbekistan* 41°30N 60°18E **28 E7**
Khlong Khlung *Thailand* 16°12N 99°43E **38 D2**
Khmelnik *Ukraine* 49°33N 27°58E **17 D14**
Khmelnytskyy *Ukraine* 49°23N 27°0E **17 D14**
Khmer Rep. = Cambodia ■
  Asia 12°15N 105°0E **38 F5**
Khoai, Hon *Vietnam* 8°26N 104°50E **39 H5**
Khodoriv *Ukraine* 49°24N 24°19E **17 D13**
Khodzent = Khŭjand
  Tajikistan 40°17N 69°37E **28 E7**
Khojak Pass *Afghan.* 30°51N 66°34E **42 D2**
Khok Kloi *Thailand* 8°17N 98°19E **39 a**
Khok Pho *Thailand* 6°43N 101°6E **39 J3**
Khok Samrong *Thailand* 15°3N 100°43E **38 E3**
Kholm *Russia* 57°10N 31°15E **18 C5**
Kholmsk *Russia* 47°40N 142°5E **29 E15**
Khomas Hochland
  Namibia 22°40S 16°0E **56 C2**
Khomeyn *Iran* 33°40N 50°7E **45 C6**
Khomeynī Shahr *Iran* 32°41N 51°41E **45 C6**
Khomodino *Botswana* 22°46S 23°52E **56 C3**
Khon Kaen *Thailand* 16°30N 102°47E **38 D4**
Khong → *Cambodia* 13°32N 105°58E **38 F5**
Khong Sedone *Laos* 15°34N 105°49E **38 E5**
Khonuu *Russia* 66°30N 143°12E **29 C15**
Khoper → *Russia* 49°30N 42°20E **19 D6**
Khorāsān □ *Iran* 34°0N 58°0E **45 C8**
Khorat = Nakhon Ratchasima
  Thailand 14°59N 102°12E **38 E4**
Khorat, Cao Nguyen
  Thailand 15°30N 102°50E **38 E4**
Khorixas *Namibia* 20°16S 14°59E **56 C1**
Khorramābād *Khorāsān,*
  Iran 35°6N 57°57E **45 C8**
Khorramābād *Lorestān,*
  Iran 33°30N 48°25E **45 C6**
Khorrāmshahr *Iran* 30°29N 48°15E **45 D6**
Khorugh *Tajikistan* 37°30N 71°36E **28 F8**
Khosravī *Iran* 30°48N 51°28E **45 D6**
Khosrowābād *Khuzestān,*
  Iran 30°10N 48°25E **45 D6**
Khosrowābād *Kordestān,*
  Iran 35°31N 47°38E **44 C5**
Khost *Pakistan* 30°13N 67°35E **42 D2**
Khosūyeh *Iran* 28°32N 54°26E **45 D7**
Khotyn *Ukraine* 48°31N 26°27E **17 D14**
Khouribga *Morocco* 32°58N 6°57W **50 B4**
Khowst *Afghan.* 33°22N 69°58E **42 C3**
Khowst □ *Afghan.* 33°20N 70°0E **40 C6**
Khoyniki *Belarus* 51°54N 29°55E **17 C15**
Khu Khan *Thailand* 14°42N 104°12E **38 E5**
Khudzhand = Khŭjand
  Tajikistan 40°17N 69°37E **28 E7**
Khuff *Si. Arabia* 24°55N 44°53E **44 E5**
Khūgiānī *Afghan.* 31°34N 66°32E **42 D2**
Khuis *Botswana* 26°40S 21°49E **56 D3**
Khuiyala *India* 27°9N 70°25E **42 F4**
Khujand *Tajikistan* 40°17N 69°37E **28 E7**
Khujner *India* 23°47N 76°36E **42 H7**
Khulna *Bangla.* 22°45N 89°34E **41 H16**
Khulna □ *Bangla.* 22°25N 89°35E **41 H16**
Khumago *Botswana* 20°26S 24°32E **56 C3**
Khunjerab △ *Pakistan* 36°40N 75°30E **43 A6**
Khunjerab Pass = Kinjirap Daban
  Asia 36°40N 75°25E **40 A9**
Khunsorkh *Iran* 27°9N 56°7E **45 E8**
Khunti *India* 23°5N 85°17E **43 H11**
Khūr *Iran* 32°55N 58°18E **45 C8**
Khurai *India* 24°3N 78°23E **42 G8**

Khurayṣ *Si. Arabia* 25°6N 48°2E **45 E6**
Khurja *India* 28°15N 77°58E **42 E7**
Khūrmāl *Iraq* 35°18N 46°2E **44 C5**
Khurr, Wādī al *Iraq* 32°3N 43°52E **44 C4**
Khūsf *Iran* 32°46N 58°53E **45 C8**
Khushab *Pakistan* 32°20N 72°20E **42 C5**
Khust *Ukraine* 48°10N 23°18E **17 D12**
Khuzdar *Pakistan* 27°52N 66°30E **42 F2**
Khūzestān □ *Iran* 31°0N 49°0E **45 D6**
Khvāf *Iran* 34°33N 60°8E **45 C9**
Khvājeh *Iran* 38°9N 46°35E **44 B5**
Khvānsār *Iran* 29°56N 54°8E **45 D7**
Khvor *Iran* 33°45N 55°0E **45 C7**
Khvorgū *Iran* 27°34N 56°27E **45 E8**
Khvoy *Iran* 38°35N 45°0E **44 B5**
Khyber Pass *Afghan.* 34°10N 71°8E **42 B4**
Kia *Fiji* 16°16S 179°8E **59 a**
Kiabukwa
  Dem. Rep. of the Congo 8°40S 24°48E **55 D1**
Kiama *Australia* 34°40S 150°50E **63 E5**
Kiamba *Phil.* 6°2N 124°46E **37 C6**
Kiambi
  Dem. Rep. of the Congo 7°15S 28°0E **54 D2**
Kiambu *Kenya* 1°8S 36°50E **54 C4**
Kiangara *Madag.* 17°58S 47°2E **57 B8**
Kiangsi = Jiangxi □
  China 27°30N 116°0E **33 D6**
Kiangsu = Jiangsu □
  China 33°0N 120°0E **35 H11**
Kibale △ *Uganda* 0°16N 30°18E **54 B3**
Kibanga Port *Uganda* 0°10N 32°58E **54 B3**
Kibara *Tanzania* 2°8S 33°30E **54 C3**
Kibare, Mts.
  Dem. Rep. of the Congo 8°25S 27°10E **54 D2**
Kibira △ *Burundi* 3°6S 30°24E **54 C2**
Kiboga *Uganda* 0°58N 31°45E **54 B3**
Kibombo
  Dem. Rep. of the Congo 3°57S 25°53E **54 C2**
Kibondo *Tanzania* 3°35S 30°45E **54 C3**
Kibre Mengist *Ethiopia* 5°54N 38°59E **47 F2**
Kibris = Cyprus ■ *Asia* 35°0N 33°0E **25 E12**
Kibumbu *Burundi* 3°32S 29°45E **54 C2**
Kibungo *Rwanda* 2°10S 30°32E **54 C3**
Kibuye *Burundi* 3°39S 29°59E **54 C2**
Kibuye *Rwanda* 2°3S 29°21E **54 C2**
Kibwesa *Tanzania* 6°30S 29°58E **54 D2**
Kibwezi *Kenya* 2°27S 37°57E **54 C4**
Kichha *India* 28°53N 79°30E **43 E8**
Kichha → *India* 28°41N 79°18E **43 E8**
Kichmengskiy Gorodok
  Russia 59°59N 45°48E **18 B8**
Kicking Horse Pass
  Canada 51°28N 116°16W **70 C5**
Kidal *Mali* 18°26N 1°22E **50 E6**
Kidderminster *U.K.* 52°24N 2°15W **13 E5**
Kidepo Valley △ *Uganda* 3°52N 33°50E **54 B3**
Kidete *Tanzania* 6°25S 37°17E **54 D4**
Kidnappers, C. *N.Z.* 39°38S 177°5E **59 C6**
Kidsgrove *U.K.* 53°5N 2°14W **12 D5**
Kidston *Australia* 18°52S 144°8E **62 B3**
Kidugallo *Tanzania* 6°49S 38°15E **54 D4**
Kiel *Germany* 54°19N 10°8E **16 A6**
Kiel Canal = Nord-Ostsee-Kanal
  Germany 54°12N 9°32E **16 A5**
Kielce *Poland* 50°52N 20°42E **17 C11**
Kielder Water *U.K.* 55°11N 2°31W **12 B5**
Kieler Bucht *Germany* 54°35N 10°25E **16 A6**
Kien Binh *Vietnam* 9°55N 105°19E **39 H5**
Kien Tan *Vietnam* 10°7N 105°17E **39 G5**
Kienge
  Dem. Rep. of the Congo 10°30S 27°30E **55 E2**
Kiev = Kyyiv *Ukraine* 50°30N 30°28E **17 C16**
Kiffa *Mauritania* 16°37N 11°24W **50 E3**
Kifrī *Iraq* 34°45N 45°0E **44 C5**
Kigali *Rwanda* 1°59S 30°4E **54 C3**
Kigarama *Tanzania* 1°1S 31°50E **54 C3**
Kigezi □ *Tanzania* 0°34S 29°55E **54 C2**
Kigoma □ *Tanzania* 5°0S 30°0E **54 D3**
Kigoma-Ujiji *Tanzania* 4°55S 29°36E **54 C2**
Kigomasha, Ras *Tanzania* 4°58S 38°58E **54 C4**
Kigosi → *Tanzania* 5°0S 31°0E **54 C3**
Kığzı *Turkey* 38°18N 43°25E **44 B4**
Kihnu *Estonia* 58°9N 24°1E **9 G21**
Kii-Sanchi *Japan* 34°20N 136°0E **31 G8**
Kii-Suidō *Japan* 33°40N 134°45E **31 H7**
Kiira Dam *Uganda* 0°25N 33°0E **54 B3**
Kikaiga-Shima *Japan* 28°19N 129°59E **31 K4**
Kikiak = Rigolet *Canada* 54°10N 58°23W **73 B8**
Kikinda *Serbia* 45°50N 20°30E **23 B9**
Kikládhes = Cyclades
  Greece 37°0N 24°30E **23 F11**
Kikwit
  Dem. Rep. of the Congo 5°0S 18°45E **52 F3**
Kilar *India* 33°6N 76°25E **42 C7**
Kilbeggan *Ireland* 53°22N 7°30W **10 C4**
Kilbrannan Sd. *U.K.* 55°37N 5°26E **11 F3**
Kilbuck Mts. *U.S.A.* 60°36N 159°53W **74 C8**
Kilchu *N. Korea* 40°57N 129°25E **35 D15**
Kilcoy *Australia* 26°59S 152°30E **63 D5**
Kilcoy *Ireland* 53°9N 6°55W **10 C5**
Kildare *Ireland* 53°10N 6°50W **10 C5**
Kildare □ *Ireland* 53°10N 6°50W **10 C5**
Kildinstroy *Russia* 68°48N 33°6E **8 B25**
Kilfinnane *Ireland* 52°21N 8°28W **10 D3**
Kilgarvan *Ireland* 51°54N 9°27W **10 D2**
Kilgore *U.S.A.* 32°23N 94°53W **84 E7**
Kilgoris *Kenya* 1°0S 34°53E **54 C3**
Kilifi *Kenya* 3°40S 39°48E **54 C4**
Kilimanjaro *Tanzania* 3°7S 37°20E **54 C4**
Kilimanjaro □ *Tanzania* 4°0S 38°0E **54 C4**
Kilimanjaro △ *Tanzania* 3°5S 37°19E **54 C4**
Kilindini *Kenya* 4°4S 39°40E **54 C4**
Kilis *Turkey* 36°42N 37°6E **44 B3**
Kiliya *Ukraine* 45°28N 29°16E **17 F15**
Kilkee *Ireland* 52°41N 9°39W **10 D2**
Kilkeel *U.K.* 54°4N 6°0W **10 B5**
Kilkenny *Ireland* 52°39N 7°15W **10 D4**
Kilkenny □ *Ireland* 52°35N 7°15W **10 D4**

Kilkieran B. *Ireland* 53°20N 9°41W **10 C2**
Kilkis *Greece* 40°58N 22°57E **23 D10**
Killala *Ireland* 54°13N 9°12W **10 B2**
Killala B. *Ireland* 54°16N 9°8W **10 B2**
Killaloe *Canada* 45°33N 77°25W **82 A7**
Killaloe *Ireland* 52°48N 8°28W **10 D3**
Killarney *Australia* 28°20S 152°18E **63 D5**
Killarney *Canada* 49°10N 99°40W **71 D9**
Killarney *Ireland* 52°4N 9°30W **10 D2**
Killarney △ *Ireland* 52°0N 9°33W **10 D2**
Killary Harbour *Ireland* 53°38N 9°52W **10 C2**
Killdeer *U.S.A.* 47°26N 102°45W **80 B2**
Killeen *U.S.A.* 31°7N 97°44W **84 F6**
Killin *U.K.* 56°28N 4°19W **11 E4**
Killiney *Ireland* 53°15N 6°7W **10 C5**
Killington Pk. *U.S.A.* 43°36N 72°49W **83 C12**
Killini *Greece* 37°54N 22°25E **23 F10**
Killorglin *Ireland* 52°6N 9°47W **10 D2**
Killybegs *Ireland* 54°38N 8°26W **10 B3**
Kilmarnock *U.K.* 55°37N 4°29W **11 F4**
Kilmore *Australia* 37°25S 144°53E **63 F3**
Kilmore Quay *Ireland* 52°10N 6°36W **10 D5**
Kilondo *Tanzania* 9°45S 34°20E **55 D3**
Kilosa *Tanzania* 6°48S 37°0E **54 D4**
Kilrush *Ireland* 52°38N 9°29W **10 D2**
Kilwa Kisiwani *Tanzania* 8°58S 39°32E **55 D4**
Kilwa Kivinje *Tanzania* 8°45S 39°25E **55 D4**
Kilwa Masoko *Tanzania* 8°55S 39°30E **55 D4**
Kilwinning *U.K.* 55°39N 4°43W **11 F4**
Kim *U.S.A.* 37°15N 103°21W **77 H12**
Kimaam *Indonesia* 7°58S 138°53E **37 F9**
Kimamba *Tanzania* 6°45S 37°10E **54 D4**
Kimba *Australia* 33°8S 136°23E **63 E2**
Kimball *Nebr., U.S.A.* 41°14N 103°40W **80 E2**
Kimball *S. Dak., U.S.A.* 43°45N 98°57W **80 D4**
Kimberley *Australia* 16°20S 127°0E **60 C4**
Kimberley *B.C., Canada* 49°40N 115°59W **70 D5**
Kimberley *Ont., Canada* 44°23N 80°32E **82 B4**
Kimberley *S. Africa* 28°43S 24°46E **56 D3**
Kimberly *U.S.A.* 42°32N 114°22W **76 E6**
Kimch'aek *N. Korea* 40°40N 129°10E **35 D15**
Kimchaek *N. Korea* 40°40N 129°10E **35 D15**
Kimhae = Gimhae
  S. Korea 35°14N 128°53E **35 G15**
Kimmirut *Canada* 62°50N 69°50W **69 E18**
Kimpese
  Dem. Rep. of the Congo 5°35S 14°26E **52 F2**
Kimry *Russia* 56°55N 37°15E **18 C6**
Kinabalu, Gunung
  Malaysia 6°3N 116°14E **36 C5**
Kinango *Kenya* 4°8S 39°19E **54 C4**
Kinaskan L. *Canada* 57°38N 130°8E **70 B2**
Kinbasket L. *Canada* 52°0N 118°10W **70 C5**
Kincardine *Canada* 44°10N 81°40W **82 B3**
Kincolith *Canada* 55°0N 129°57W **70 C3**
Kinda *Dem. Rep. of the Congo* 9°18S 25°4E **55 D2**
Kinde *U.S.A.* 43°56N 83°0W **82 C2**
Kinder Scout *U.K.* 53°24N 1°52W **12 D6**
Kindersley *Canada* 51°30N 109°10W **71 C7**
Kindia *Guinea* 10°0N 12°52W **50 F3**
Kindu
  Dem. Rep. of the Congo 2°55S 25°50E **54 C2**
Kineshma *Russia* 57°30N 42°5E **18 C7**
Kinesi *Tanzania* 1°25S 33°50E **54 C3**
King, L. *Australia* 33°10S 119°35E **61 F2**
King, Mt. *Australia* 25°10S 147°30E **62 D4**
King Christian I.
  Canada 77°48N 101°40W **69 B11**
King City *U.S.A.* 36°13N 121°8W **78 J5**
King Cr. → *Australia* 24°35S 139°30E **62 C2**
King Edward →
  Australia 14°14S 126°35E **60 B4**
King Edward Point
  S. Georgia 54°17S 36°30W **96 G9**
King Frederick VI Land = Kong
  Frederik VI Kyst
  Greenland 63°0N 43°0W **4 C5**
King George B. *Falk. Is.* 51°30S 60°30W **96 G4**
King George I. *Antarctica* 60°0S 60°0W **5 C18**
King George Is. *Canada* 57°20N 80°30W **69 F15**
King George Sd. *Australia* 35°5S 118°0E **61 G2**
King I. = Kadan Kyun
  Burma 12°30N 98°20E **38 F2**
King I. *Australia* 39°50S 144°0E **63 F3**
King I. *Canada* 52°10N 127°40W **70 C3**
King Khalid Military City =
  Madinat al Malik Khālid al
  Askarīyah *Si. Arabia* 27°54N 45°31E **44 E5**
King Leopold Ranges
  Australia 17°30S 125°45E **60 C4**
King of Prussia *U.S.A.* 40°5N 75°23W **83 F9**
King Sd. *Australia* 16°50S 123°20E **60 C3**
King Sejong *Antarctica* 62°30S 58°0W **5 C18**
King William I. *Canada* 69°10N 97°25W **68 D12**
King William's Town
  S. Africa 32°51S 27°22E **56 E4**
Kingaok = Bathurst Inlet
  Canada 66°50N 108°1W **68 D10**
Kingaroy *Australia* 26°32S 151°51E **63 D5**
Kingfisher *U.S.A.* 35°52N 97°56W **84 D6**
Kingirbān *Iraq* 34°40N 44°54E **44 C5**
Kingisepp = Kuressaare
  Estonia 58°15N 22°30E **9 G20**
Kingisepp *Russia* 59°25N 28°40E **9 G23**
Kingman *Ariz., U.S.A.* 35°12N 114°4W **79 K12**
Kingman *Kans., U.S.A.* 37°39N 98°7W **80 G4**
Kingoonya *Australia* 30°55S 135°19E **63 E2**
Kingri *Pakistan* 30°27N 69°49E **42 D3**
Kings → *U.S.A.* 36°3N 119°50W **78 J7**
Kings Canyon *Australia* 24°15S 131°34E **60 D5**
Kings Canyon △
  U.S.A. 36°50N 118°40W **78 J8**
King's Lynn *U.K.* 52°45N 0°24E **12 E8**
Kings Park *U.S.A.* 40°53N 73°16W **83 F11**
Kings Peak *U.S.A.* 40°46N 110°23W **76 F8**
Kingsbridge *U.K.* 50°17N 3°47W **13 G4**
Kingsburg *U.S.A.* 36°31N 119°33W **78 J7**
Kingscote *Australia* 35°40S 137°38E **63 F2**
Kingscourt *Ireland* 53°55N 6°48W **10 C5**
Kingsford *U.S.A.* 45°48N 88°4W **80 C9**

Kingsland *U.S.A.* 30°48N 81°41W **85 F14**
Kingsport *U.S.A.* 36°33N 82°33W **85 C13**
Kingston *Canada* 44°14N 76°30W **83 B8**
Kingston *Jamaica* 18°0N 76°50W **88 a**
Kingston *N.Z.* 45°20S 168°43E **59 F2**
Kingston *N.H., U.S.A.* 42°56N 71°3W **83 D13**
Kingston *N.Y., U.S.A.* 41°56N 73°59W **83 E11**
Kingston *Pa., U.S.A.* 41°16N 75°54W **83 E9**
Kingston *R.I., U.S.A.* 41°29N 71°30W **83 E13**
Kingston Pk. *U.S.A.* 35°44N 115°55W **79 K11**
Kingston South East
  Australia 36°51S 139°55E **63 F2**
Kingston upon Hull *U.K.* 53°45N 0°21W **12 D7**
Kingston upon Hull □
  U.K. 53°45N 0°21W **12 D7**
Kingston-upon-Thames □
  U.K. 51°24N 0°17W **13 F7**
Kingstown *St. Vincent* 13°10N 61°10W **89 D7**
Kingstree *U.S.A.* 33°40N 79°50W **85 E15**
Kingsville *Canada* 42°2N 82°45W **82 D2**
Kingsville *U.S.A.* 27°31N 97°52W **84 H6**
Kingussie *U.K.* 57°6N 4°2W **11 D4**
Kingwood *U.S.A.* 30°2N 95°16W **84 F7**
Kınık *Turkey* 39°6N 27°24E **23 E12**
Kinistino *Canada* 52°57N 105°2W **71 C7**
Kinjirap Daban *Asia* 36°40N 75°25E **40 A9**
Kinkala *Congo* 4°18S 14°49E **52 E2**
Kinki □ *Japan* 33°45N 136°0E **31 H8**
Kinleith *N.Z.* 38°20S 175°56E **59 C5**
Kinlochleven *U.K.* 56°43N 5°0W **11 E4**
Kinmount *Canada* 44°48N 78°45W **82 B6**
Kinna *Sweden* 57°32N 12°42E **9 H15**
Kinnairds Hd. *U.K.* 57°43N 2°1W **11 D6**
Kinngait *Canada* 64°14N 76°32W **69 E16**
Kino Nuevo *Mexico* 28°52N 112°3W **86 B2**
Kinoje → *Canada* 52°8N 81°25W **72 B3**
Kinomoto *Japan* 35°30N 136°13E **31 G8**
Kinoni *Uganda* 0°41S 30°28E **54 C3**
Kinoosao *Canada* 57°5N 102°1W **71 B8**
Kinross *U.K.* 56°13N 3°25W **11 E5**
Kinsale *Ireland* 51°42N 8°31W **10 E3**
Kinsale, Old Hd. of
  Ireland 51°37N 8°33W **10 E3**
Kinsha = Chang Jiang →
  China 31°48N 121°10E **33 C7**
Kinshasa
  Dem. Rep. of the Congo 4°20S 15°15E **52 E3**
Kinsley *U.S.A.* 37°55N 99°25W **80 G4**
Kinsman *U.S.A.* 41°26N 80°35W **82 E4**
Kinston *U.S.A.* 35°16N 77°35W **85 D16**
Kintamani *Indonesia* 8°14S 115°19E **37 J18**
Kintore *U.K.* 57°14N 2°20W **11 D6**
Kintore Ra. *Australia* 23°15S 128°47E **60 D4**
Kintyre *U.K.* 55°30N 5°35W **11 F3**
Kintyre, Mull of *U.K.* 55°17N 5°47W **11 F3**
Kinushseo → *Canada* 55°15N 83°45W **72 A3**
Kinuso *Canada* 55°20N 115°25W **70 B5**
Kinvarra *Ireland* 53°8N 8°56W **10 C3**
Kinyangi *Tanzania* 4°25S 34°37E **54 C3**
Kinyeti *Sudan* 3°57N 32°54E **54 B3**
Kinzua *U.S.A.* 41°52N 78°58W **82 E6**
Kiosk *Canada* 46°6N 78°53W **72 C4**
Kiowa *Kans., U.S.A.* 37°1N 98°29W **80 G4**
Kiowa *Okla., U.S.A.* 34°43N 95°54W **84 D7**
Kipahigan L. *Canada* 55°20N 101°55W **71 B8**
Kipanga *Tanzania* 6°15S 35°20E **54 D4**
Kiparissia *Greece* 37°15N 21°40E **23 F9**
Kiparissiakos Kolpos
  Greece 37°25N 21°25E **23 F9**
Kipawa, L. *Canada* 46°50N 79°0W **72 C4**
Kipembawe *Tanzania* 7°38S 33°27E **54 D3**
Kipengere Ra. *Tanzania* 9°12S 34°15E **55 D3**
Kipili *Tanzania* 7°28S 30°32E **54 D3**
Kipini *Kenya* 2°30S 40°32E **54 C5**
Kipling *Canada* 50°6N 102°38W **71 C8**
Kippure *Ireland* 53°11N 6°21W **10 C5**
Kipushi
  Dem. Rep. of the Congo 11°48S 27°12E **55 E2**
Kiranomena *Madag.* 18°17S 46°2E **57 B8**
Kirensk *Russia* 57°50N 107°55E **29 D11**
Kirghiz Range *Asia* 42°40N 73°40E **32 B2**
Kirghizia = Kyrgyzstan ■
  Asia 42°0N 75°0E **28 E8**
Kiribati ■ *Pac. Oc.* 3°0S 180°0E **58 B10**
Kırıkkale *Turkey* 39°51N 33°32E **19 G5**
Kirillov *Russia* 59°49N 38°24E **18 C6**
Kirin = Jilin *China* 43°44N 126°30E **35 C14**
Kirinyaga = Kenya, Mt.
  Kenya 0°10S 37°18E **54 C4**
Kirirom △ *Cambodia* 11°18N 104°5E **39 G5**
Kirishima Yaku △
  Japan 31°24N 130°50E **31 J5**
Kirkby *U.K.* 53°30N 2°54W **12 D5**
Kirkby-in-Ashfield *U.K.* 53°6N 1°14W **12 D6**
Kirkby Lonsdale *U.K.* 54°12N 2°36W **12 C5**
Kirkby Stephen *U.K.* 54°29N 2°21W **12 C5**
Kirkcaldy *U.K.* 56°7N 3°9W **11 E5**
Kirkcudbright *U.K.* 54°50N 4°2W **11 G4**
Kirkenes *Norway* 69°40N 30°5E **8 B24**
Kirkfield *Canada* 44°34N 78°59W **82 B6**
Kirkintilloch *U.K.* 55°56N 4°8W **11 F4**
Kirkjubæjarklaustur
  Iceland 63°47N 18°4W **8 E4**
Kirkkonummi *Finland* 60°8N 24°26E **9 F21**
Kirkland *U.S.A.* 47°40N 122°12W **78 C4**
Kirkland Lake *Canada* 48°9N 80°2W **72 C3**
Kırklareli *Turkey* 41°44N 27°15E **23 D12**
Kirksville *U.S.A.* 40°12N 92°35W **80 E7**
Kirkûk *Iraq* 35°30N 44°21E **44 C5**
Kirkwall *U.K.* 58°59N 2°58W **11 C6**
Kirkwood *S. Africa* 33°22S 25°15E **56 E4**
Kirov *Russia* 58°35N 49°40E **18 C8**
Kirovabad = Gäncä
  Azerbaijan 40°45N 46°20E **19 F8**
Kirovograd = Kirovohrad
  Ukraine 48°35N 32°20E **19 E5**
Kirovohrad *Ukraine* 48°35N 32°20E **19 E5**

Kirovsk *Russia* 67°32N 33°41E **18 A5**
Kirovskiy *Kamchatka,*
  Russia 54°27N 155°42E **29 D16**
Kirovskiy *Primorsk,*
  Russia 45°7N 133°30E **30 B6**
Kirriemuir *U.K.* 56°41N 3°1W **11 E5**
Kirsanov *Russia* 52°35N 42°40E **18 D7**
Kırşehir *Turkey* 39°14N 34°5E **44 B2**
Kirthar → *Pakistan* 25°45N 67°30E **42 F2**
Kirthar Range *Pakistan* 27°0N 67°0E **42 F2**
Kirtland *U.S.A.* 36°44N 108°21W **77 H9**
Kiruna *Sweden* 67°52N 20°15E **8 C19**
Kirundu
  Dem. Rep. of the Congo 0°50S 25°35E **54 C2**
Kiryū *Japan* 36°24N 139°20E **31 F9**
Kisaga *Tanzania* 4°30S 34°23E **54 C3**
Kisanga
  Dem. Rep. of the Congo 2°30S 26°35E **54 D2**
Kisangani
  Dem. Rep. of the Congo 0°35N 25°15E **54 B2**
Kisar *Indonesia* 8°5S 127°10E **37 F7**
Kisarawe *Tanzania* 6°53S 39°0E **54 D4**
Kisarazu *Japan* 35°23N 139°55E **31 G9**
Kiselevsk *Russia* 54°0N 86°39E **28 D9**
Kishanganga →
  Pakistan 34°18N 73°28E **43 B5**
Kishanganj *India* 26°3N 88°14E **43 F13**
Kishangarh *Raj., India* 26°34N 74°52E **42 F6**
Kishangarh *Raj., India* 27°50N 70°30E **42 F4**
Kishinev = Chişinău
  Moldova 47°2N 28°50E **17 E15**
Kishiwada *Japan* 34°28N 135°22E **31 G7**
Kishtwar *India* 33°20N 75°48E **42 C6**
Kisigo → *Tanzania* 6°27S 34°17E **54 D3**
Kisii *Kenya* 0°40S 34°45E **54 C3**
Kisiju *Tanzania* 7°23S 39°19E **54 D4**
Kisizi *Uganda* 1°0S 29°58E **54 C2**
Kiska I. *U.S.A.* 51°59N 177°30E **74 E3**
Kiskőrös *Hungary* 46°37N 19°20E **17 E10**
Kiskunfélegyháza
  Hungary 46°42N 19°53E **17 E10**
Kiskunhalas *Hungary* 46°28N 19°37E **17 E10**
Kislovodsk *Russia* 43°50N 42°45E **19 F7**
Kismaayo *Somali Rep.* 0°22S 42°32E **47 H3**
Kiso-Gawa → *Japan* 35°20N 136°45E **31 G8**
Kiso-Sammyaku *Japan* 35°45N 137°45E **31 G8**
Kisofukushima *Japan* 35°52N 137°43E **31 G8**
Kisoro *Uganda* 1°17S 29°48E **54 C2**
Kissamos = Kasteli
  Greece 35°29N 23°38E **25 D5**
Kissamos, Kolpos *Greece* 35°30N 23°38E **25 D5**
Kissidougou *Guinea* 9°5N 10°5W **50 G3**
Kissimmee *U.S.A.* 28°18N 81°24W **85 G14**
Kissimmee → *U.S.A.* 27°9N 80°52W **85 H14**
Kississing L. *Canada* 55°10N 101°20W **71 B8**
Kissónerga *Cyprus* 34°49N 32°24E **25 E11**
Kisumu *Kenya* 0°3S 34°45E **54 C3**
Kiswani *Tanzania* 4°5S 37°57E **54 C4**
Kiswere *Tanzania* 9°27S 39°30E **55 D4**
Kit Carson *U.S.A.* 38°46N 102°48W **76 G12**
Kita *Mali* 13°5N 9°25W **50 F4**
Kitaibaraki *Japan* 36°50N 140°45E **31 F10**
Kitakami *Japan* 39°20N 141°10E **30 E10**
Kitakami-Gawa →
  Japan 38°25N 141°19E **30 E10**
Kitakami-Sammyaku
  Japan 39°30N 141°30E **30 E10**
Kitakata *Japan* 37°39N 139°52E **30 F9**
Kitakyūshū *Japan* 33°50N 130°50E **31 H5**
Kitale *Kenya* 1°0N 35°0E **54 B4**
Kitami *Japan* 43°48N 143°54E **30 C11**
Kitami-Sammyaku
  Japan 44°22N 142°43E **30 B11**
Kitangiri, L. *Tanzania* 4°5S 34°20E **54 C3**
Kitaya *Tanzania* 10°38S 40°8E **55 E5**
Kitchener *Canada* 43°27N 80°29W **82 C4**
Kitee *Finland* 62°5N 30°8E **8 E24**
Kitega = Gitega *Burundi* 3°26S 29°56E **54 C2**
Kitengo
  Dem. Rep. of the Congo 7°26S 24°8E **54 D1**
Kitgum *Uganda* 3°17N 32°52E **54 B3**
Kíthira = Kythira *Greece* 36°8N 23°0E **23 F10**
Kíthnos *Greece* 37°26N 24°27E **23 F11**
Kiti *Cyprus* 34°50N 33°34E **25 E12**
Kiti, C. *Cyprus* 34°48N 33°36E **25 E12**
Kitimat *Canada* 54°3N 128°38W **70 C3**
Kitinen → *Finland* 67°14N 27°27E **8 C22**
Kitsuki *Japan* 33°25N 131°37E **31 H5**
Kittakittaooloo, L.
  Australia 28°3S 138°14E **63 D2**
Kittanning *U.S.A.* 40°49N 79°31W **82 F5**
Kittatinny Mt. *U.S.A.* 41°19N 74°39W **83 F10**
Kittery *U.S.A.* 43°5N 70°45W **83 C14**
Kittilä *Finland* 67°40N 24°51E **8 C21**
Kitui *Kenya* 1°17S 38°0E **54 C4**
Kitwanga *Canada* 55°6N 128°4W **70 B3**
Kitwe *Zambia* 12°54S 28°13E **55 E2**
Kiunga Marine △ *Kenya* 2°1S 41°14E **54 C5**
Kivarli *India* 24°33N 72°46E **42 G5**
Kivertsi *Ukraine* 50°50N 25°28E **17 C13**
Kividhes *Cyprus* 34°46N 32°51E **25 E11**
Kivu, L.
  Dem. Rep. of the Congo 1°48S 29°0E **54 C2**
Kiwirrkurra *Australia* 22°49S 127°45E **60 D4**
Kiwirrkurra ◎
  Australia 22°49S 127°45E **60 D4**
Kiyev = Kyyiv *Ukraine* 50°30N 30°28E **17 C16**
Kiyevskoye Vdkhr. = Kyyivske
  Vdskh. *Ukraine* 51°0N 30°25E **17 C16**
Kizel *Russia* 59°3N 57°40E **18 C10**
Kiziba-Baluba △ *Congo* 11°50S 28°0E **55 E2**
Kiziguru *Rwanda* 1°46S 30°23E **54 C3**
Kızıl Irmak → *Turkey* 41°44N 35°58E **19 F6**
Kızıl Jilga *China* 35°26N 78°50E **43 B8**
Kızıldağ △ *Turkey* 38°5N 31°20E **44 B1**
Kızılhisar *Turkey* 37°12N 40°40E **44 B4**
Kizimkazi *Tanzania* 6°28S 39°30E **54 D4**
Kizlyar *Russia* 43°51N 46°40E **19 F8**

Kizyl-Arvat = Serdar
  Turkmenistan 39°4N 56°23E **45 B8**
Kjölur *Iceland* 64°50N 19°25W **8 D4**
Kladno *Czech Rep.* 50°10N 14°7E **16 C8**
Klaeng *Thailand* 12°47N 101°39E **38 F3**
Klagenfurt *Austria* 46°38N 14°20E **16 E8**
Klaipėda *Lithuania* 55°43N 21°10E **9 J19**
Klaksvík *Færoe Is.* 62°14N 6°35W **8 E9**
Klamath → *U.S.A.* 41°33N 124°5W **76 F1**
Klamath Falls *U.S.A.* 42°13N 121°46W **76 E3**
Klamath Mts. *U.S.A.* 41°50N 123°20W **76 F2**
Klamono *Indonesia* 1°8S 131°30E **37 E8**
Klang *Malaysia* 3°2N 101°26E **39 L3**
Klappan → *Canada* 58°0N 129°43W **70 B3**
Klarälven → *Sweden* 59°23N 13°32E **9 G15**
Klatovy *Czech Rep.* 49°23N 13°18E **16 D7**
Klawer *S. Africa* 31°44S 18°36E **56 E2**
Klazienaveen *Neths.* 52°44N 7°0E **15 B6**
Kleena Kleene *Canada* 52°0N 124°59W **70 C4**
Klein-Karas *Namibia* 27°33S 18°7E **56 D2**
Klerksdorp *S. Africa* 26°53S 26°38E **56 D4**
Kletsk = Klyetsk *Belarus* 53°5N 26°45E **17 B14**
Kletskiy *Russia* 49°16N 43°11E **19 E7**
Klickitat *U.S.A.* 45°49N 121°9W **76 D3**
Klickitat → *U.S.A.* 45°42N 121°17W **78 E5**
Klidhes *Cyprus* 35°42N 34°36E **25 D13**
Klinaklini → *Canada* 51°21N 125°40W **70 C3**
Klip → *S. Africa* 27°3S 29°3E **57 D4**
Klipdale *S. Africa* 34°19S 19°57E **56 E2**
Klipplaat *S. Africa* 33°1S 24°22E **56 E3**
Kłodzko *Poland* 50°28N 16°38E **17 C9**
Klondike *Canada* 64°0N 139°26W **68 E4**
Klong Wang Chao △
  Thailand 16°20N 99°9E **38 D2**
Klouto *Togo* 6°57N 0°44E **50 G6**
Kluane △ *Canada* 60°45N 139°30W **70 A1**
Kluane L. *Canada* 61°15N 138°40W **68 E4**
Kluang *Malaysia* 2°3N 103°18E **39 L4**
Kluczbork *Poland* 50°58N 18°12E **17 C10**
Klukwan *U.S.A.* 59°24N 135°54W **70 B1**
Klungkung *Indonesia* 8°32S 115°24E **37 K18**
Klyetsk *Belarus* 53°5N 26°45E **17 B14**
Klyuchevskaya, Gora
  Russia 55°50N 160°30E **29 D17**
Klyuchi *Russia* 56°18N 160°51E **29 D17**
Knaresborough *U.K.* 54°1N 1°28W **12 C6**
Knee L. *Man., Canada* 55°3N 94°45W **72 A1**
Knee L. *Sask., Canada* 55°51N 107°0W **71 B7**
Knight Inlet *Canada* 50°45N 125°40W **70 C3**
Knighton *U.K.* 52°21N 3°3W **13 E4**
Knights Ferry *U.S.A.* 37°50N 120°40W **78 H6**
Knights Landing
  U.S.A. 38°48N 121°43W **78 G5**
Knob, C. *Australia* 34°32S 119°16E **61 F2**
Knock *Ireland* 53°48N 8°55W **10 C3**
Knockmealdown Mts.
  Ireland 52°14N 7°56W **10 D4**
Knokke-Heist *Belgium* 51°21N 3°17E **15 C3**
Knóssos *Greece* 35°16N 25°10E **25 D7**
Knowlton *Canada* 45°13N 72°31W **83 A12**
Knox *U.S.A.* 41°18N 86°37W **80 E10**
Knox Coast *Antarctica* 66°30S 108°0E **5 C8**
Knoxville *Iowa, U.S.A.* 41°19N 93°6W **80 E7**
Knoxville *Pa., U.S.A.* 41°57N 77°27W **82 E7**
Knoxville *Tenn., U.S.A.* 35°58N 83°55W **85 D13**
Knud Rasmussen Land
  Greenland 78°0N 60°0W **69 B20**
Knysna *S. Africa* 34°2S 23°2E **56 E3**
Ko Kha *Thailand* 18°11N 99°24E **38 C2**
Ko Tarutao △ *Thailand* 6°31N 99°26E **39 J2**
Ko Yao *Thailand* 8°7N 98°35E **39 a**
Koartac = Quaqtaq
  Canada 60°55N 69°40W **69 E18**
Koba *Indonesia* 6°37S 134°37E **37 F8**
Kobarid *Slovenia* 46°15N 13°30E **16 E7**
Kobayashi *Japan* 31°56N 130°59E **31 J5**
Kōbe *Japan* 34°41N 135°13E **31 G7**
Kōbi-Sho *Japan* 25°56N 123°41E **31 M1**
Kobenhavn *Denmark* 55°40N 12°26E **9 J15**
Koblenz *Germany* 50°21N 7°36E **16 C4**
Kobryn *Belarus* 52°15N 24°22E **17 B13**
Kobuk → *U.S.A.* 66°54N 160°38W **74 B7**
Kocaeli *Turkey* 40°45N 29°50E **19 F4**
Kočani *Macedonia* 41°55N 22°25E **23 D10**
Koch Bihar *India* 26°22N 89°29E **41 F16**
Kochas *India* 25°15N 83°56E **43 G10**
Kochi = Cochin *India* 9°58N 76°20E **40 Q10**
Kōchi *Japan* 33°30N 133°35E **31 H6**
Kōchi □ *Japan* 33°40N 133°30E **31 H6**
Kochiu = Gejiu *China* 23°20N 103°10E **34 D5**
Kodarma *India* 24°28N 85°36E **43 G11**
Kodi *Indonesia* 9°33S 119°0E **60 A2**
Kodiak *U.S.A.* 57°47N 152°24W **74 D9**
Kodiak I. *U.S.A.* 57°30N 152°45W **74 D9**
Kodinar *India* 20°46N 70°46E **42 J4**
Kodinsk *Russia* 58°40N 99°10E **29 D10**
Koedoesberge *S. Africa* 32°40S 20°11E **56 E3**
Koes *Namibia* 26°0S 19°15E **56 D2**
Koffiefontein *S. Africa* 29°30S 25°0E **56 D4**
Kofiau *Indonesia* 1°11S 129°50E **37 E7**
Koforidua *Ghana* 6°3N 0°17W **50 G5**
Kōfu *Japan* 35°40N 138°30E **31 G9**
Koga *Japan* 36°11N 139°43E **31 F9**
Kogaluc → *Canada* 56°12N 61°44W **73 A7**
Køge *Denmark* 55°27N 12°11E **9 J15**
Kogon *Uzbekistan* 39°43N 64°33E **28 F7**
Koh-i-Khurd *Afghan.* 33°30N 65°59E **42 C1**
Koh-i-Maran *Pakistan* 29°18N 66°50E **42 E2**
Koh-i-Khurd *Afghan.* 33°40N 71°29E **42 C4**
Kohkīlūyeh va Būyer Aḥmadī □
  Iran 31°30N 50°30E **45 D6**
Kohima *India* 25°35N 94°10E **41 G19**
Kohkīlūyeh va Būyer Aḥmadī □
  Iran 31°30N 50°30E **45 D6**
Kohler Ra. *Antarctica* 77°0S 110°0W **5 D15**
Kohlu *Pakistan* 29°54N 69°15E **42 E3**
Kohtla-Järve *Estonia* 59°20N 27°20E **9 G22**
Koi Sanjaq *Iraq* 36°5N 44°38E **44 B5**
Koillismaa *Finland* 65°44N 28°36E **8 D23**
Koin *N. Korea* 40°28N 126°18E **35 D14**
Kojŏ *N. Korea* 38°58N 127°58E **35 E14**

Kojonup *Australia* 33°48S 117°10E **61 F2**
Kojūr *Iran* 36°23N 51°43E **45 B6**
Kokand = Qŭqon
  Uzbekistan 40°31N 70°56E **28 E8**
Kokas *Indonesia* 2°42S 132°26E **37 E8**
Kokchetav = Kökshetaū
  Kazakhstan 53°20N 69°25E **28 D7**
Kokemäenjoki →
  Finland 61°32N 21°44E **8 F19**
Kokkola *Finland* 63°50N 23°8E **8 E20**
Koko Kyunzu *Burma* 14°7N 93°22E **41 M18**
Kokomo *U.S.A.* 40°29N 86°8W **80 E10**
Koksan *N. Korea* 38°46N 126°40E **35 E14**
Kökshetaū *Kazakhstan* 53°20N 69°25E **28 D7**
Koksoak → *Canada* 58°30N 68°10W **69 F18**
Kokstad *S. Africa* 30°32S 29°29E **57 E4**
Kokubu *Japan* 31°44N 130°46E **31 J5**
Kola *Indonesia* 5°35S 134°30E **37 F8**
Kola *Russia* 68°45N 33°8E **8 B25**
Kola Pen. = Kolskiy Poluostrov
  Russia 67°30N 38°0E **18 A6**
Kolachi → *Pakistan* 27°8N 67°2E **42 F2**
Kolahoi *India* 34°12N 75°22E **43 B6**
Kolaka *Indonesia* 4°3S 121°46E **37 E6**
Kolar *India* 13°12N 78°15E **40 N11**
Kolar Gold Fields *India* 12°58N 78°16E **40 N11**
Kolaras *India* 25°14N 77°36E **42 G7**
Kolari *Finland* 67°20N 23°48E **8 C20**
Kolayat *India* 27°50N 72°50E **42 F5**
Kolda *Senegal* 12°55N 14°57W **50 F3**
Kolding *Denmark* 55°30N 9°29E **9 J13**
Kolepom = Dolak, Pulau
  Indonesia 8°0S 138°30E **37 F9**
Kolguyev, Ostrov *Russia* 69°20N 48°30E **18 A8**
Kolhapur *India* 16°43N 74°15E **40 L9**
Kolimbia *Greece* 36°15N 28°10E **25 C10**
Kolín *Czech Rep.* 50°2N 15°9E **16 C8**
Kolkas rags *Latvia* 57°46N 22°37E **9 H20**
Kolkata *India* 22°34N 88°21E **43 H13**
Kollam = Quilon *India* 8°50N 76°38E **40 Q10**
Kollum *Neths.* 53°17N 6°10E **15 A6**
Kolmanskop *Namibia* 26°45S 15°14E **56 D2**
Köln *Germany* 50°56N 6°57E **16 C4**
Kolo *Poland* 52°14N 18°40E **17 B10**
Kołobrzeg *Poland* 54°10N 15°35E **16 A8**
Kolokani *Mali* 13°35N 7°45W **50 F4**
Kolomna *Russia* 55°8N 38°45E **18 C6**
Kolomyya *Ukraine* 48°31N 25°2E **17 D13**
Kolonodale *Indonesia* 2°0S 121°19E **37 E6**
Kolosib *India* 24°15N 92°45E **41 G18**
Kolpashevo *Russia* 58°20N 83°5E **28 D9**
Kolpino *Russia* 59°44N 30°39E **18 C5**
Kolskiy Poluostrov
  Russia 67°30N 38°0E **18 A6**
Kolskiy Zaliv *Russia* 69°23N 34°0E **8 B26**
Kolwezi
  Dem. Rep. of the Congo 10°40S 25°25E **55 E2**
Kolyma → *Russia* 69°30N 161°0E **29 C17**
Kolymskoye Nagorye
  Russia 63°0N 157°0E **29 C16**
Kôm Ombo *Egypt* 24°25N 32°52E **51 D12**
Komandorskiye Is. =
  Komandorskiye Ostrova
  Russia 55°0N 167°0E **29 D17**
Komandorskiye Ostrova
  Russia 55°0N 167°0E **29 D17**
Komárno *Slovak Rep.* 47°49N 18°5E **17 E10**
Komatipoort *S. Africa* 25°25S 31°55E **57 D5**
Komatou Yialou *Cyprus* 35°25N 34°8E **25 D13**
Komatsu *Japan* 36°25N 136°30E **31 F8**
Komatsushima *Japan* 34°0N 134°35E **31 H7**
Kome Channel *Uganda* 0°10S 32°53E **54 C3**
Komi *Cyprus* 35°24N 34°0E **25 D13**
Komi □ *Russia* 64°0N 55°0E **18 B10**
Kommunarsk = Alchevsk
  Ukraine 48°30N 38°45E **19 E6**
Kommunizma, Pik = imeni Ismail
  Samani, Pik *Tajikistan* 39°0N 72°2E **28 F8**
Komodo *Indonesia* 8°37S 119°20E **37 F5**
Komoran, Pulau
  Indonesia 8°18S 138°45E **37 F9**
Komoro *Japan* 36°19N 138°26E **31 F9**
Komotini *Greece* 41°9N 25°26E **23 D11**
Kompasberg *S. Africa* 31°45S 24°32E **56 E3**
Kompong Cham
  Cambodia 12°0N 105°30E **39 F5**
Kompong Chhnang = Kampong
  Chhnang *Cambodia* 12°20N 104°35E **39 F5**
Kompong Chikreng
  Cambodia 13°5N 104°18E **38 F5**
Kompong Kleang
  Cambodia 13°6N 104°8E **38 F5**
Kompong Luong
  Cambodia 11°49N 104°48E **39 G5**
Kompong Pranak
  Cambodia 13°35N 104°55E **38 F5**
Kompong Som = Kampong Saom
  Cambodia 10°38N 103°30E **39 G4**
Kompong Som, Chhung =
  Kampong Saom, Chaak
  Cambodia 10°50N 103°32E **39 G4**
Kompong Speu
  Cambodia 11°26N 104°32E **39 G5**
Kompong Sralau
  Cambodia 14°5N 105°46E **38 E5**
Kompong Thom
  Cambodia 12°35N 104°51E **38 F5**
Kompong Trabeck
  Cambodia 13°6N 105°14E **38 F5**
Kompong Trabeck
  Cambodia 11°9N 105°28E **39 G5**
Kompong Trach
  Cambodia 11°25N 105°48E **39 G5**
Kompong Tralach
  Cambodia 11°54N 104°47E **39 G5**
Komrat = Comrat
  Moldova 46°18N 28°40E **17 E15**
Komsberg *S. Africa* 32°40S 20°45E **56 E3**
Komsomolets, Ostrov
  Russia 80°30N 95°0E **29 A10**

Komsomolsk-na-Amur
  Russia 50°30N 137°0E **33 A8**
Kon Tum *Vietnam* 14°24N 108°0E **38 E7**
Kon Tum, Plateau du
  Vietnam 14°30N 108°30E **38 E7**
Konar □ *Afghan.* 34°30N 71°3E **40 B7**
Konāri *Iran* 28°13N 51°36E **45 D6**
Konch *India* 26°0N 79°10E **43 G8**
Konde *Tanzania* 4°57S 39°45E **54 C4**
Kondinin *Australia* 32°34S 118°8E **61 F2**
Kondoa *Tanzania* 4°55S 35°50E **54 C4**
Kondopoga *Russia* 62°12N 34°17E **18 B5**
Kondratyevo *Russia* 57°22N 98°15E **29 D10**
Köneürgench
  Turkmenistan 42°19N 59°10E **28 E6**
Konevo *Russia* 62°8N 39°20E **18 B6**
Kong = Khong →
  Cambodia 13°32N 105°58E **38 F5**
Kong, Koh *Cambodia* 11°20N 103°0E **39 G4**
Kong Christian IX Land
  Greenland 68°0N 36°0W **4 C6**
Kong Christian X Land
  Greenland 74°0N 29°0W **4 B6**
Kong Frederik IX Land
  Greenland 67°0N 52°0W **4 C5**
Kong Frederik VI Kyst
  Greenland 63°0N 43°0W **4 C5**
Kong Frederik VIII Land
  Greenland 78°30N 26°0W **4 B6**
Kong Oscar Fjord
  Greenland 72°20N 24°0W **4 B6**
Konglu *Burma* 27°13N 97°57E **41 F20**
Kongola *Namibia* 17°45S 23°20E **56 B3**
Kongolo *Kasai-Or.,*
  Dem. Rep. of the Congo 5°26S 24°49E **54 D1**
Kongolo *Katanga,*
  Dem. Rep. of the Congo 5°22S 27°0E **54 D2**
Kongsberg *Norway* 59°39N 9°39E **9 G13**
Kongsvinger *Norway* 60°12N 12°2E **9 F15**
Kongur Shan *China* 38°34N 75°18E **32 C2**
Kongwa *Tanzania* 6°11S 36°26E **54 D4**
Koni
  Dem. Rep. of the Congo 10°40S 27°11E **55 E2**
Koni, Mts.
  Dem. Rep. of the Congo 10°36S 27°10E **55 E2**
Konin *Poland* 52°12N 18°15E **17 B10**
Konjic *Bos.-H.* 43°42N 17°58E **23 C7**
Konosha *Russia* 26°49S 117°5E **61 E2**
Kōnosu *Japan* 36°3N 139°31E **31 F9**
Konotop *Ukraine* 51°12N 33°7E **19 D5**
Konqi He → *China* 41°0N 86°0E **32 B3**
Końskie *Poland* 51°15N 20°23E **17 C11**
Konstanz *Germany* 47°40N 9°10E **16 E5**
Kont *Iran* 26°55N 61°50E **45 E9**
Kontagora *Nigeria* 10°23N 5°27E **50 F7**
Kontiolahti *Finland* 62°46N 29°50E **8 E23**
Kontokali *Greece* 39°38N 19°51E **25 A3**
Konya *Turkey* 37°52N 32°35E **44 B2**
Konza *Kenya* 1°45S 37°7E **54 C4**
Koocanusa, L. *Canada* 49°20N 115°15W **76 B6**
Kookynie *Australia* 29°17S 121°22E **61 E3**
Koolyanobbing
  Australia 30°48S 119°36E **61 F2**
Koonibba *Australia* 31°54S 133°25E **63 E1**
Koorawatha *Australia* 34°2S 148°33E **63 E4**
Koorda *Australia* 30°48S 117°35E **61 F2**
Kooskia *U.S.A.* 46°9N 115°59W **76 C6**
Kootenay → *U.S.A.* 49°19N 117°39W **70 D5**
Kootenay △ *Canada* 51°0N 116°0W **70 C5**
Kootenay L. *Canada* 49°45N 116°50W **70 D5**
Kootjieskolk *S. Africa* 31°15S 20°21E **56 E3**
Kopaonik *Serbia* 43°10N 20°50E **23 C9**
Kópavogur *Iceland* 64°6N 21°55W **8 D3**
Koper *Slovenia* 45°31N 13°44E **16 F7**
Kopervik *Norway* 59°17N 5°17E **9 G11**
Kopet Dagh *Asia* 38°0N 58°0E **45 B8**
Kopi *Australia* 33°24S 135°40E **63 E2**
Köping *Sweden* 59°31N 16°3E **9 G17**
Koppeh Dāgh = Kopet Dagh
  Asia 38°0N 58°0E **45 B8**
Koppies *S. Africa* 27°20S 27°30E **57 D4**
Koprivnica *Croatia* 46°12N 16°45E **22 A7**
Köprülü △ *Turkey* 37°20N 31°54E **44 B1**
Kopychyntsi *Ukraine* 49°7N 25°58E **17 D13**
Kora △ *Kenya* 0°14S 38°44E **54 C4**
Korab *Macedonia* 41°44N 20°40E **23 D9**
Koral *India* 21°50N 73°12E **42 J5**
Korba *India* 22°20N 82°40E **43 H10**
Korbu, G. *Malaysia* 4°41N 101°18E **39 K3**
Korçë *Albania* 40°37N 20°50E **23 D9**
Korčula *Croatia* 42°56N 16°57E **22 C7**
Kord Kūy *Iran* 36°48N 54°7E **45 B7**
Kord Sheykh *Iran* 28°31N 52°53E **45 D7**
Kordestān □ *Iran* 36°0N 47°0E **44 C5**
Kordofân *Sudan* 13°0N 29°0E **51 F11**
Korea, North ■ *Asia* 40°0N 127°0E **35 E14**
Korea, South ■ *Asia* 36°0N 128°0E **35 G15**
Korea Bay *Korea* 39°0N 124°0E **35 E13**
Korea Strait *Asia* 34°0N 129°30E **35 H15**
Korets *Ukraine* 50°40N 27°5E **17 C14**
Korhogo *Ivory C.* 9°29N 5°28W **50 G4**
Korinthiakos Kolpos
  Greece 38°16N 22°30E **23 E10**
Korinthos *Greece* 37°56N 22°55E **23 F10**
Korissia, L. *Greece* 39°27N 19°53E **25 B3**
Kōriyama *Japan* 37°24N 140°23E **30 F10**
Korla *China* 41°45N 86°4E **32 B3**
Kormakiti, C. *Cyprus* 35°23N 32°56E **25 D11**
Kornešty = Corneşti
  Moldova 47°21N 28°1E **17 E15**
Koro *Fiji* 17°19S 179°23E **59 a**
Koro *Ivory C.* 8°32N 7°30W **50 G4**
Koro Sea *Fiji* 17°30S 179°45W **59 a**
Korogwe *Tanzania* 5°5S 38°25E **54 D4**
Korolevu *Fiji* 18°12S 177°46E **59 a**
Koronadal *Phil.* 6°12N 125°1E **37 C6**
Koror *Palau* 7°20N 134°28E **64 G5**

Körös → Hungary 46°43N 20°12E 17 E11
Korosten Ukraine 50°54N 28°36E 17 C15
Korostyshev Ukraine 50°19N 29°4E 17 C15
Korovou Fiji 17°47S 178°32E 59 a
Koroyanitu △ Fiji 17°40S 177°35E 59 a
Korraraika, Helodranon' i
Madag. 17°45S 43°57E 57 B7
Korsakov Russia 46°36N 142°42E 29 E15
Korshunovo Russia 58°37N 110°10E 29 D12
Korsør Denmark 55°20N 11°9E 9 J14
Kortrijk Belgium 50°50N 3°17E 15 D3
Korwai India 24°7N 78°5E 42 G8
Koryakskoye Nagorye
Russia 61°0N 171°0E 29 C18
Kos Greece 36°50N 27°15E 23 F12
Kosan N. Korea 38°52N 127°25E 35 E14
Kościan Poland 52°5N 16°40E 17 B9
Kosciusko U.S.A. 33°4N 89°35W 85 E10
Kosciuszko, Mt.
Australia 36°27S 148°16E 63 F4
Kosha Sudan 20°50N 30°30E 51 D12
K'oshih = Kashi China 39°30N 76°2E 32 C2
Koshiki-Rettō Japan 31°45N 129°49E 31 J4
Kosi India 27°48N 77°29E 42 F7
Kosi → India 28°41N 78°57E 43 E8
Košice Slovak Rep. 48°42N 21°15E 17 D11
Koskinou Greece 36°23N 28°13E 25 C10
Koslan Russia 63°34N 49°14E 18 B8
Kosŏng N. Korea 38°40N 128°22E 35 E15
Kosovo □ Europe 42°30N 21°0E 23 C9
Kosovska Mitrovica
Kosovo 42°54N 20°52E 23 C9
Kossou, L. de Ivory C. 6°59N 5°31W 50 G4
Koster S. Africa 25°52S 26°54E 56 D4
Kôstî Sudan 13°8N 32°43E 51 F12
Kostopil Ukraine 50°51N 26°22E 17 C14
Kostroma Russia 57°50N 40°58E 18 C7
Kostrzyn Poland 52°35N 14°39E 16 B8
Koszalin Poland 54°11N 16°8E 16 A9
Kot Addu Pakistan 30°30N 71°0E 42 D4
Kot Kapura India 30°35N 74°50E 42 D6
Kot Moman Pakistan 32°13N 73°0E 42 C5
Kot Sultan Pakistan 30°46N 70°56E 42 D4
Kota India 25°14N 75°49E 42 G6
Kota Barrage India 25°6N 75°51E 42 G6
Kota Belud Malaysia 6°21N 116°26E 36 C5
Kota Bharu Malaysia 6°7N 102°14E 39 J4
Kota Kinabalu Malaysia 6°0N 116°4E 36 C5
Kota Tinggi Malaysia 1°44N 103°53E 39 M4
Kotaagung Indonesia 5°38S 104°29E 36 F2
Kotabaru Indonesia 3°20S 116°20E 36 E5
Kotabumi Indonesia 4°49S 104°54E 36 E2
Kotamobagu Indonesia 0°57N 124°31E 37 D6
Kotapinang Indonesia 1°53N 100°5E 39 M3
Kotcho L. Canada 59°7N 121°12W 70 B4
Kotdwara India 29°45N 78°32E 43 E8
Kotelnich Russia 58°22N 48°24E 18 C8
Kotelnikovo Russia 47°38N 43°8E 19 E7
Kotelnyy, Ostrov
Russia 75°10N 139°0E 29 B14
Kothari → India 25°20N 75°4E 42 G6
Kothi Chhattisgarh, India 23°21N 82°3E 43 H10
Kothi Mad. P., India 24°45N 80°40E 43 G9
Kotiro Pakistan 26°17N 67°13E 42 F2
Kotka Finland 60°28N 26°58E 8 F22
Kotlas Russia 61°17N 46°43E 18 B8
Kotli Pakistan 33°30N 73°55E 42 C5
Kotlik U.S.A. 63°2N 163°33W 74 C7
Kotma India 23°12N 81°58E 43 H9
Kotor Montenegro 42°25N 18°47E 23 C8
Kotovsk Ukraine 47°45N 29°35E 17 E15
Kotputli India 27°43N 76°12E 42 F7
Kotri Pakistan 25°22N 68°22E 42 G3
Kotto → C.A.R. 4°14N 22°2E 52 D4
Kotturu India 14°45N 76°10E 40 M10
Kotu Group Tonga 20°0S 174°45W 59 c
Kotuy → Russia 71°54N 102°6E 29 B11
Kotzebue U.S.A. 66°53N 162°39W 74 B7
Kotzebue Sound U.S.A. 66°20N 163°0W 74 B7
Kouchibouguac △
Canada 46°50N 65°0W 73 C6
Koudougou Burkina Faso 12°10N 2°20W 50 F5
Koufonisi Greece 34°56N 26°8E 25 E8
Kougaberge S. Africa 33°48S 23°50E 56 E3
Kouilou → Congo 4°10S 12°5E 52 E2
Koukdjuak → Canada 66°43N 73°0W 69 D17
Koula Moutou Gabon 1°15S 12°25E 52 E2
Koulen = Kulen
Cambodia 13°50N 104°40E 38 F5
Kouloura Greece 39°42N 19°54E 25 A3
Koumala Australia 21°38S 149°15E 62 C4
Koumra Chad 8°50N 17°35E 51 G9
Kountze U.S.A. 30°22N 94°19W 84 F7
Kouris → Cyprus 34°38N 32°54E 25 E11
Kourou Fr. Guiana 5°9N 52°39W 93 B8
Kouroussa Guinea 10°45N 9°45W 50 F4
Kousseri Cameroon 12°0N 14°55E 51 F8
Koutiala Mali 12°25N 5°23W 50 F4
Kouvola Finland 60°52N 26°43E 8 F22
Kovdor Russia 67°34N 30°24E 8 C24
Kovel Ukraine 51°11N 24°38E 17 C13
Kovrov Russia 56°25N 41°25E 18 C7
Kowanyama Australia 15°29S 141°44E 62 B3
Kowanyama ✪
Australia 15°20S 141°47E 62 B3
Kowloon China 22°19N 114°11E 33 G11
Kowŏn N. Korea 39°26N 127°14E 35 E14
Koyampattur = Coimbatore
India 11°2N 76°59E 40 P10
Köyceğiz Turkey 36°57N 28°40E 23 F13
Koyukuk → U.S.A. 64°55N 157°32W 74 C8
Koza = Okinawa Japan 26°19N 127°46E 31 L3
Kozan Turkey 37°26N 35°50E 44 B2
Kozani Greece 40°19N 21°47E 23 D9
Kozhikode = Calicut
India 11°15N 75°43E 40 P9
Kozhva Russia 65°10N 57°0E 18 A10
Kozyatyn Ukraine 49°45N 28°50E 17 D15
Kozyrevsk Russia 56°3N 159°51E 29 D16
Kpalimé Togo 6°57N 0°44E 50 G6
Kra, Isthmus of = Kra, Kho Khot
Thailand 10°15N 99°30E 39 G2
Kra, Kho Khot Thailand 10°15N 99°30E 39 G2
Kra Buri Thailand 10°22N 98°46E 39 G2
Kraai → S. Africa 30°40S 26°45E 56 E4
Krabi Thailand 8°4N 98°55E 39 H2
Kracheh Cambodia 12°32N 106°10E 38 F6
Kragan Indonesia 6°43S 111°38E 37 G14
Kragerø Norway 58°52N 9°25E 9 G13
Kragujevac Serbia 44°2N 20°56E 23 B9
Krakatau = Rakata, Pulau
Indonesia 6°10S 105°20E 36 F3
Krakatoa = Rakata, Pulau
Indonesia 6°10S 105°20E 36 F3
Krakor Cambodia 12°32N 104°12E 38 F5
Kraków Poland 50°4N 19°57E 17 C10
Kralanh Cambodia 13°35N 103°25E 38 F4
Kraljevo Serbia 43°44N 20°41E 23 C9
Kramatorsk Ukraine 48°50N 37°30E 19 E6
Kramfors Sweden 62°55N 17°48E 8 E17
Kranj Slovenia 46°16N 14°22E 16 E8
Krankskop S. Africa 28°0S 30°47E 57 D5
Krasavino Russia 60°58N 46°29E 18 B8
Kraskino Russia 42°44N 130°48E 30 C5
Kraśnik Poland 50°55N 22°15E 17 C12
Krasnoarmeysk Russia 51°0N 45°42E 28 D5
Krasnodar Russia 45°5N 39°0E 19 E6
Krasnokamensk Russia 50°3N 118°0E 29 D12
Krasnokamsk Russia 58°4N 55°48E 18 C10
Krasnoperekopsk Ukraine 46°0N 33°54E 19 E5
Krasnorechenskiy
Russia 44°41N 135°14E 30 B7
Krasnoselkup Russia 65°20N 82°10E 28 C9
Krasnoturinsk Russia 59°46N 60°12E 18 C11
Krasnoufimsk Russia 56°36N 57°38E 18 C10
Krasnouralsk Russia 58°21N 60°3E 18 C11
Krasnovishersk Russia 60°23N 57°3E 18 B10
Krasnoyarsk Russia 56°8N 93°0E 29 D10
Krasnyy Kut Russia 50°50N 47°0E 19 D8
Krasnyy Luch Ukraine 48°13N 39°0E 19 E6
Krasnyy Yar Russia 46°43N 48°23E 19 E8
Kratie = Kracheh
Cambodia 12°32N 106°10E 38 F6
Krau Indonesia 3°19S 140°5E 37 E10
Kravanh, Chuor Phnum
Cambodia 12°0N 103°32E 39 G4
Krefeld Germany 51°20N 6°33E 16 C4
Kremen Croatia 44°28N 15°53E 16 F8
Kremenchuk Ukraine 49°5N 33°25E 19 E5
Kremenchuksk Vdskh.
Ukraine 49°20N 32°30E 19 E5
Kremenets Ukraine 50°8N 25°43E 17 C13
Kremmling U.S.A. 40°4N 106°24W 76 F10
Krems Austria 48°25N 15°36E 16 D8
Kretinga Lithuania 55°53N 21°15E 9 J19
Kribi Cameroon 2°57N 9°56E 52 D1
Krichev = Krychaw
Belarus 53°40N 31°41E 17 B16
Kril'on, Mys Russia 45°53N 142°5E 30 B11
Krios, Akra Greece 35°13N 23°34E 25 D5
Krishna → India 15°57N 80°59E 41 M12
Krishnanagar India 23°24N 88°33E 43 H13
Kristiansand Norway 58°8N 8°1E 9 G13
Kristianstad Sweden 56°2N 14°9E 9 H16
Kristiansund Norway 63°7N 7°45E 8 E12
Kristiinankaupunki
Finland 62°16N 21°21E 8 E19
Kristinehamn Sweden 59°18N 14°7E 9 G16
Kristinestad =
Kristiinankaupunki
Finland 62°16N 21°21E 8 E19
Kriti Greece 35°15N 25°0E 25 D7
Kritsa Greece 35°10N 25°41E 25 D7
Krivoy Rog = Kryvyy Rih
Ukraine 47°51N 33°20E 19 E5
Krk Croatia 45°8N 14°40E 16 F8
Krokodil = Umgwenya →
Mozam. 25°14S 32°18E 57 D5
Krong Kaoh Kong
Cambodia 11°37N 102°59E 39 G4
Kronprins Frederik Land
Greenland 81°0N 45°0W 4 B5
Kronprins Olav Kyst
Antarctica 69°0S 42°0E 5 C5
Kronprinsesse Märtha Kyst
Antarctica 73°30S 10°0W 5 D2
Kronshtadt Russia 59°57N 29°51E 18 B4
Kroonstad S. Africa 27°43S 27°19E 56 D4
Kropotkin Russia 45°28N 40°28E 19 E7
Krosno Poland 49°42N 21°46E 17 D11
Krotoszyn Poland 51°42N 17°23E 17 C9
Krousonas Greece 35°13N 24°59E 25 D6
Kruger △ S. Africa 24°50S 26°10E 57 C5
Krugersdorp S. Africa 26°5S 27°46E 57 D4
Kruisfontein S. Africa 33°59S 24°43E 56 E3
Krung Thep = Bangkok
Thailand 13°45N 100°35E 38 F3
Krupki Belarus 54°19N 29°8E 17 A15
Kruševac Serbia 43°35N 21°28E 23 C9
Krychaw Belarus 53°40N 31°41E 17 B16
Krymskiy Poluostrov = Krymskyy
Pivostriv Ukraine 45°0N 34°0E 19 F5
Krymskyy Pivostriv
Ukraine 45°0N 34°0E 19 F5
Kryvyy Rih Ukraine 47°51N 33°20E 19 E5
Ksar el Kebir Morocco 35°0N 6°0W 50 B4
Ksar es Souk = Er Rachidia
Morocco 31°58N 4°20W 50 B5
Kuah Malaysia 6°19N 99°51E 39 J2
Kuala Belait Malaysia 4°35N 114°11E 36 D4
Kuala Berang Malaysia 5°5N 103°1E 39 K4
Kuala Dungun = Dungun
Malaysia 4°45N 103°25E 39 K4
Kuala Kangsar Malaysia 4°46N 100°56E 39 K3
Kuala Kelawang Malaysia 2°56N 102°5E 39 L4
Kuala Kerai Malaysia 5°30N 102°12E 39 K4
Kuala Kerian Malaysia 5°10N 100°25E 39 c
Kuala Kubu Bharu
Malaysia 3°34N 101°39E 39 L3
Kuala Lipis Malaysia 4°10N 102°3E 39 K4
Kuala Lumpur Malaysia 3°9N 101°41E 39 L3
Kuala Nerang Malaysia 6°16N 100°37E 39 J3
Kuala Pilah Malaysia 2°45N 102°15E 39 L4
Kuala Rompin Malaysia 2°49N 103°29E 39 L4
Kuala Selangor Malaysia 3°20N 101°15E 39 L3
Kuala Sepetang
Malaysia 4°49N 100°28E 39 K3
Kuala Terengganu
Malaysia 5°20N 103°8E 39 K4
Kualajelai Indonesia 2°58S 110°46E 36 E4
Kualakapuas Indonesia 2°55S 114°20E 36 E4
Kualakurun Indonesia 1°10S 113°50E 36 E4
Kualapembuang
Indonesia 3°14S 112°38E 36 E4
Kualasimpang Indonesia 4°17N 98°3E 36 D1
Kuancheng China 40°37N 118°30E 35 D10
Kuandang Indonesia 0°56N 123°1E 37 D6
Kuandian China 40°45N 124°45E 35 D13
Kuangchou = Guangzhou
China 23°6N 113°13E 33 D6
Kuantan Malaysia 3°49N 103°20E 39 L4
Kuba = Quba Azerbaijan 41°21N 48°32E 19 F8
Kuban → Russia 45°20N 37°30E 19 E6
Kubokawa Japan 33°12N 133°8E 31 H6
Kubu Indonesia 8°16S 115°35E 37 J18
Kubutambahan
Indonesia 8°5S 115°10E 37 J18
Kucar, Tanjung
Indonesia 8°39S 114°34E 37 K18
Kuchaman India 27°13N 74°47E 42 F6
Kuchinda India 21°44N 84°21E 43 J11
Kuching Malaysia 1°33N 110°25E 36 D4
Kuchino-eruba-Jima
Japan 30°28N 130°12E 31 J5
Kuchino-Shima Japan 29°57N 129°55E 31 K4
Kuchinotsu Japan 32°36N 130°11E 31 H5
Kucing = Kuching
Malaysia 1°33N 110°25E 36 D4
Kud → Pakistan 26°5N 66°20E 42 F2
Kuda India 23°10N 71°15E 42 H4
Kudat Malaysia 6°55N 116°55E 36 C5
Kudus Indonesia 6°48S 110°51E 37 G14
Kudymkar Russia 59°1N 54°39E 18 C9
Kueiyang = Guiyang
China 26°32N 106°40E 32 D5
Kufra Oasis = Al Kufrah
Libya 24°17N 23°15E 51 D10
Kufstein Austria 47°35N 12°11E 16 E7
Kugaaruk = Pelly Bay
Canada 68°38N 89°50W 69 D14
Kugluktuk Canada 67°50N 115°5W 68 D8
Kugong I. Canada 56°18N 79°50W 72 A4
Kūh Dasht Iran 33°32N 47°36E 44 C5
Kūh-e-Jebāl Bārez Iran 29°0N 58°0E 45 D8
Kūhak Iran 27°12N 63°10E 45 E9
Kuhan Pakistan 28°19N 67°14E 42 E2
Kūhbonān Iran 31°23N 56°19E 45 D8
Kūhestak Iran 26°47N 57°2E 45 E8
Kuhin Iran 36°22N 49°40E 45 B6
Kūhīrī Iran 26°55N 61°2E 45 E9
Kuhmo Finland 64°7N 29°31E 8 D23
Kūhpāyeh Eşfahan, Iran 32°44N 52°20E 45 C7
Kūhpāyeh Kermān, Iran 30°35N 57°15E 45 D8
Kūhrān, Kūh-e Iran 26°46N 58°12E 45 E8
Kui Buri Thailand 12°3N 99°52E 39 F2
Kuichong China 22°38N 114°25E 33 F11
Kuiseb → Namibia 22°59S 14°31E 56 C1
Kuito Angola 12°22S 16°55E 53 G3
Kuiu I. U.S.A. 57°45N 134°10W 70 B2
Kujang N. Korea 39°57N 126°1E 35 E14
Kuji Japan 40°11N 141°46E 30 D10
Kujū-San Japan 33°5N 131°15E 31 H5
Kukës Albania 42°5N 20°27E 23 C9
Kukup Malaysia 1°20N 103°27E 39 d
Kukup, Pulau Malaysia 1°18N 103°25E 39 d
Kula Turkey 38°32N 28°40E 23 E13
K'ula Shan Bhutan 28°14N 90°36E 32 C4
Kulachi Pakistan 31°56N 70°27E 42 D4
Kulai Malaysia 1°44N 103°35E 39 M4
Kulasekarappattinam
India 8°20N 78°5E 40 Q11
Kuldīga Latvia 56°58N 21°59E 9 H19
Kulen Cambodia 13°50N 104°40E 38 F5
Kulgam India 33°36N 75°2E 43 C6
Kulgera Australia 25°50S 133°18E 62 D1
Kulim Malaysia 5°22N 100°34E 39 K3
Kulin Australia 32°40S 118°2E 61 F2
Kulkayu = Hartley Bay
Canada 53°25N 129°15W 70 C3
Kullu India 31°58N 77°6E 42 D7
Kŭlob Tajikistan 37°55N 69°50E 28 F7
Kulsary = Qulsary
Kazakhstan 46°59N 54°1E 19 E9
Kulti India 23°43N 86°50E 43 H12
Kulunda Russia 52°35N 78°57E 28 D8
Kulungar Afghan. 34°0N 69°2E 42 C3
Kūlvand Iran 31°21N 54°35E 45 D7
Kulwin Australia 35°2S 142°42E 63 F3
Kulyab = Kŭlob
Tajikistan 37°55N 69°50E 28 F7
Kuma → Russia 44°55N 47°0E 19 F8
Kumaganum Nigeria 13°8N 10°38E 51 F8
Kumagaya Japan 36°9N 139°22E 31 F9
Kumai Indonesia 2°44S 111°43E 36 E4
Kumamba, Kepulauan
Indonesia 1°36S 138°45E 37 E9
Kumamoto Japan 32°45N 130°45E 31 H5
Kumamoto □ Japan 32°55N 130°55E 31 H5
Kumanovo Macedonia 42°9N 21°42E 23 C9
Kumara N.Z. 42°37S 171°12E 59 E3
Kumarina Roadhouse
Australia 24°41S 119°32E 61 D2
Kumasi Ghana 6°41N 1°38W 50 G5
Kumba Cameroon 4°36N 9°24E 52 D1
Kumbakonam India 10°58N 79°25E 40 P11
Kumbarilla Australia 27°15S 150°55E 63 D5
Kumbhraj India 24°22N 77°3E 42 G7
Kumbia Australia 26°41S 151°39E 63 D5
Kŭmch'ŏn N. Korea 38°10N 126°29E 35 E14
Kumdok India 33°32N 78°10E 43 C8
Kume-Shima Japan 26°20N 126°47E 31 L3
Kumertau Russia 52°45N 55°57E 18 D10
Kumharsain India 31°19N 77°27E 42 D7
Kumi Uganda 1°30N 33°58E 54 B3
Kumo Nigeria 10°1N 11°12E 51 F8
Kumo älv = Kokemäenjoki →
Finland 61°32N 21°44E 8 F19
Kumon Bum Burma 26°30N 97°15E 41 F20
Kumtag Shamo China 39°40N 92°0E 32 C4
Kunashir, Ostrov Russia 44°0N 146°0E 29 E15
Kunda Estonia 59°30N 26°34E 9 G22
Kunda India 25°43N 81°31E 43 G9
Kundar → Pakistan 31°56N 69°19E 42 D3
Kundelungu △
Dem. Rep. of the Congo 10°30S 27°40E 55 E2
Kundelungu Ouest △
Dem. Rep. of the Congo 9°55S 27°17E 55 D2
Kundian Pakistan 32°27N 71°28E 42 C4
Kundla India 21°21N 71°25E 42 J4
Kung, Ao Thailand 8°5N 98°24E 39 a
Kunga → Bangla. 21°46N 89°30E 43 J13
Kunghit I. Canada 52°6N 131°3W 70 C2
Kungrad = Qŭnghirot
Uzbekistan 43°2N 58°50E 28 E6
Kungsbacka Sweden 57°30N 12°5E 9 H15
Kungur Russia 57°25N 56°57E 18 C10
Kungurri Australia 21°4S 148°45E 62 b
Kunhar → Pakistan 34°20N 73°30E 43 B5
Kuningan Indonesia 6°59S 108°29E 37 G13
Kunlong Burma 23°20N 98°50E 41 H21
Kunlun Shan Asia 36°0N 86°30E 32 C3
Kunming China 25°1N 102°41E 32 D5
Kunmunya ✪ Australia 15°26S 124°42E 60 C3
Kununurra Australia 15°40S 128°50E 60 C4
Kunwari → India 26°26N 79°11E 43 F8
Kunya-Urgench = Köneürgench
Turkmenistan 42°19N 59°10E 28 E6
Kuopio Finland 62°53N 27°35E 8 E22
Kupa → Croatia 45°28N 16°24E 16 F9
Kupang Indonesia 10°19S 123°39E 37 F6
Kupreanof I. U.S.A. 56°50N 133°30W 70 B2
Kupyansk-Uzlovoi
Ukraine 49°40N 37°43E 19 E6
Kuqa China 41°35N 82°30E 32 B3
Kür → Azerbaijan 39°29N 49°15E 19 G8
Kür Dili Azerbaijan 39°3N 49°13E 45 B6
Kura = Kür →
Azerbaijan 39°29N 49°15E 19 G8
Kuranda Australia 16°48S 145°35E 62 B4
Kuranga India 22°4N 69°10E 42 H3
Kurashiki Japan 34°40N 133°50E 31 G6
Kurayn Si. Arabia 27°39N 49°50E 45 E6
Kurayoshi Japan 35°26N 133°50E 31 G6
Kŭrchatov Kazakhstan 50°45N 78°32E 28 D8
Kŭrdzhali Bulgaria 41°38N 25°21E 23 D11
Kure Japan 34°14N 132°32E 31 G6
Kure I. U.S.A. 28°25N 178°25W 75 K4
Kuressaare Estonia 58°15N 22°30E 9 G20
Kurgan Russia 55°26N 65°18E 28 D7
Kuri India 26°37N 70°43E 42 F4
Kuria Maria Is. = Hallāniyat,
Jazā'ir al Oman 17°30N 55°58E 47 D6
Kuridala Australia 21°16S 140°29E 62 C3
Kurigram Bangla. 25°49N 89°39E 41 G16
Kurikka Finland 62°36N 22°24E 8 E20
Kuril Basin Pac. Oc. 47°0N 150°0E 4 E15
Kuril Is. = Kurilskiye Ostrova
Russia 45°0N 150°0E 29 E16
Kuril-Kamchatka Trench
Pac. Oc. 44°0N 153°0E 64 C7
Kurilsk Russia 45°14N 147°53E 29 E15
Kurilskiye Ostrova
Russia 45°0N 150°0E 29 E16
Kurino Japan 31°57N 130°43E 31 J5
Kurinskaya Kosa = Kür Dili
Azerbaijan 39°3N 49°13E 45 B6
Kurlkuta ✪ Australia 24°0S 127°5E 60 D4
Kurnool India 15°45N 78°0E 40 M11
Kuro-Shima Kagoshima,
Japan 30°50N 129°57E 31 J4
Kuro-Shima Okinawa,
Japan 24°14N 124°1E 31 M2
Kurow N.Z. 44°44S 170°29E 59 F3
Kurram → Pakistan 32°36N 71°20E 42 C4
Kurri Kurri Australia 32°50S 151°28E 63 E5
Kurrimine Australia 17°47S 146°6E 62 B4
Kurseong = Karsiyang
India 26°56N 88°18E 43 F13
Kurshskiy Zaliv Russia 55°9N 21°6E 9 J19
Kursk Russia 51°42N 36°11E 18 D6
Kuruçay Turkey 39°39N 38°29E 44 B3
Kurukshetra = Thanesar
India 30°1N 76°52E 42 D7
Kuruktag China 41°0N 89°0E 32 B3
Kuruman S. Africa 27°28S 23°28E 56 D3
Kuruman → S. Africa 26°56S 20°39E 56 D3
Kurume Japan 33°15N 130°30E 31 H5
Kurunegala Sri Lanka 7°30N 80°23E 40 R12
Kurya Russia 61°42N 57°9E 18 B10
Kus Gölü Turkey 40°10N 27°55E 23 D12
Kuşadası Turkey 37°52N 27°15E 23 F12
Kusamba Indonesia 8°34S 115°27E 37 K18
Kusatsu Japan 36°37N 138°36E 31 F9
Kusawa L. Canada 60°20N 136°13W 70 A1
Kushalgarh India 23°10N 74°27E 42 H6
Kushikino Japan 31°44N 130°16E 31 J5
Kushima Japan 31°29N 131°14E 31 J5
Kushimoto Japan 33°28N 135°47E 31 H7
Kushiro Japan 43°0N 144°25E 30 C12
Kushiro-Gawa →
Japan 42°59N 144°23E 30 C12
Kushiro Shitsugen △
Japan 43°9N 144°26E 30 C12
Kūshk Iran 28°46N 56°51E 45 D8
Kushka = Serhetabat
Turkmenistan 35°20N 62°18E 45 C9
Kushol India 33°40N 76°36E 43 C7
Kushtia Bangla. 23°55N 89°5E 41 H16
Kushva Russia 58°18N 59°45E 18 C10
Kuskokwim → U.S.A. 60°5N 162°25W 74 C7
Kuskokwim B. U.S.A. 59°45N 162°25W 74 D7
Kuskokwim Mts.
U.S.A. 62°30N 156°0W 74 C8
Kusmi India 23°17N 83°55E 43 H10
Kusŏng N. Korea 39°59N 125°15E 35 E13
Kussharo-Ko Japan 43°38N 144°21E 30 C12
Kustanay = Qostanay
Kazakhstan 53°10N 63°35E 28 D7
Kut, Ko Thailand 11°40N 102°35E 39 G4
Kuta Indonesia 8°43S 115°11E 37 K18
Kütahya Turkey 39°30N 30°2E 19 G5
Kutaisi Georgia 42°19N 42°40E 19 F7
Kutaraja = Banda Aceh
Indonesia 5°35N 95°20E 36 C1
Kutch, Gulf of = Kachchh, Gulf of
India 22°50N 69°15E 42 H3
Kutch, Rann of = Kachchh, Rann
of India 24°0N 70°0E 42 H4
Kutiyana India 21°36N 70°2E 42 J4
Kutno Poland 52°15N 19°23E 17 B10
Kutse Botswana 21°7S 22°16E 56 C3
Kuttabul Australia 21°1S 148°54E 62 b
Kutu Dem. Rep. of the Congo 2°40S 18°11E 52 E3
Kutum Sudan 14°10N 24°40E 51 F10
Kuujjuaq Canada 58°6N 68°15W 69 F18
Kuujjuarapik Canada 55°20N 77°35W 72 A4
Kuusamo Finland 65°57N 29°8E 8 D23
Kuusankoski Finland 60°55N 26°38E 8 F22
Kuwait = Al Kuwayt
Kuwait 29°30N 48°0E 44 D5
Kuwait ■ Asia 29°30N 47°30E 44 D5
Kuwana Japan 35°5N 136°43E 31 G8
Kuwana → India 26°25N 83°15E 43 F10
Kuybyshev = Samara
Russia 53°8N 50°6E 18 D9
Kuybyshev Russia 55°27N 78°19E 28 D8
Kuybyshevskoye Vdkhr.
Russia 55°2N 49°30E 18 C8
Kuye He → China 38°23N 110°46E 34 E6
Kūyeh Iran 38°45N 47°57E 44 B5
Kuyto, Ozero Russia 65°6N 31°20E 8 D24
Kuyumba Russia 60°58N 96°59E 29 C10
Kuzey Anadolu Dağları
Turkey 41°0N 36°45E 19 F6
Kuznetsk Russia 53°12N 46°40E 18 D8
Kuzomen Russia 66°22N 36°50E 18 A6
Kvænangen Norway 70°5N 21°15E 8 A19
Kvaløya Norway 69°40N 18°30E 8 B18
Kvarner Croatia 44°50N 14°10E 16 F8
Kvarnerič Croatia 44°43N 14°37E 16 F8
Kwabhaca S. Africa 30°51S 29°0E 57 E4
Kwajalein Marshall Is. 9°5N 167°20E 64 G8
Kwakhanai Botswana 21°39S 21°16E 56 C3
Kwakoegron Suriname 5°12N 55°25W 93 B7
Kwale Kenya 4°15S 39°31E 54 C4
KwaMashu S. Africa 29°45S 30°58E 57 D5
Kwando → Africa 18°27S 23°32E 56 B3
Kwangchow = Guangzhou
China 23°6N 113°13E 33 D6
Kwango →
Dem. Rep. of the Congo 3°14S 17°22E 52 E3
Kwangsi-Chuang = Guangxi
Zhuangzu Zizhiqu □
China 24°0N 109°0E 33 D5
Kwangtung = Guangdong □
China 23°0N 113°0E 33 D6
Kwataboahegan →
Canada 51°9N 80°50W 72 B3
Kwatisore Indonesia 3°18S 134°50E 37 E8
KwaZulu Natal □ S. Africa 29°0S 30°0E 57 D5
Kweichow = Guizhou □
China 27°0N 107°0E 32 D5
Kwekwe Zimbabwe 18°58S 29°48E 55 F2
Kwidzyn Poland 53°44N 18°55E 17 B10
Kwilu →
Dem. Rep. of the Congo 3°22S 17°22E 52 E3
Kwinana Australia 32°15S 115°47E 61 F2
Kwoka Indonesia 0°31S 132°27E 37 E8
Kwun Tong China 22°19N 114°13E 33 G11
Kyabra Cr. → Australia 25°36S 142°55E 63 D3
Kyabram Australia 36°19S 145°4E 63 F4
Kyaikto Burma 17°20N 97°3E 38 D1
Kyakhta Russia 50°30N 106°25E 29 D11
Kyambura ⌂ Uganda 0°7S 30°9E 54 C3
Kyancutta Australia 33°8S 135°33E 63 E2
Kyaukpadaung Burma 20°52N 95°8E 41 J19
Kyaukpyu Burma 19°28N 93°30E 41 K18
Kyaukse Burma 21°36N 96°10E 41 J20
Kyburz U.S.A. 38°47N 120°18W 78 G6
Kyelang India 32°35N 77°2E 42 C7
Kyenjojo Uganda 0°40N 30°37E 54 B3
Kyle Canada 50°50N 108°2W 71 C7
Kyle Dam Zimbabwe 20°15S 31°0E 55 G3
Kyle of Lochalsh U.K. 57°17N 5°44W 11 D3
Kymijoki → Finland 60°30N 26°55E 8 F22
Kymmene älv = Kymijoki →
Finland 60°30N 26°55E 8 F22
Kyneton Australia 37°10S 144°29E 63 F3
Kynuna Australia 21°37S 141°55E 62 C3
Kyō-ga-Saki Japan 35°45N 135°15E 31 G7
Kyoga, L. Uganda 1°35N 33°0E 54 B3
Kyogle Australia 28°40S 153°0E 63 D5
Kyŏngju = Gyeongju
S. Korea 35°51N 129°14E 35 G15
Kyongpyaw Burma 17°12N 95°10E 41 L19
Kyŏngsŏng N. Korea 41°35N 129°36E 35 D15
Kyōto Japan 35°0N 135°45E 31 G7
Kyōto □ Japan 35°15N 135°45E 31 G7
Kyparissovouno Cyprus 35°19N 33°10E 25 D12
Kyperounda Cyprus 34°56N 32°58E 25 E11
Kypros = Cyprus ■ Asia 35°0N 33°0E 25 E12
Kyrenia Cyprus 35°20N 33°20E 25 D12
Kyrgyzstan ■ Asia 42°0N 75°0E 28 E8
Kyro älv = Kyrönjoki →
Finland 63°14N 21°45E 8 E19
Kyrönjoki → Finland 63°14N 21°45E 8 E19

Kystatyam Russia 67°20N 123°10E 29 C13
Kythira Greece 36°8N 23°0E 23 F10
Kythréa Cyprus 35°15N 33°29E 25 D12
Kyunhla Burma 23°25N 95°15E 41 H19
Kyūshū Japan 33°0N 131°0E 31 H5
Kyūshū □ Japan 33°0N 131°0E 31 H5
Kyūshū-Palau Ridge
  Pac. Oc. 20°0N 136°0E 64 E5
Kyūshū-Sanchi Japan 32°35N 131°17E 31 H5
Kyustendil Bulgaria 42°16N 22°41E 23 C10
Kyusyur Russia 70°19N 127°30E 29 B13
Kyyiv Ukraine 50°30N 30°28E 17 C16
Kyyivske Vdskh.
  Ukraine 51°0N 30°25E 17 C16
Kyzyl Russia 51°50N 94°30E 32 A4
Kyzyl Kum Uzbekistan 42°30N 65°0E 28 E7
Kyzyl Kyya Kyrgyzstan 40°16N 72°8E 28 E8
Kyzyl Orda = Qyzylorda
  Kazakhstan 44°48N 65°28E 28 E7

L

La Alcarria Spain 40°31N 2°45W 21 B4
La Amistad △ Cent. Amer. 9°28N 83°18W 88 E3
La Asunción Venezuela 11°2N 63°53W 92 A6
La Baie Canada 48°19N 70°53W 73 C5
La Banda Argentina 27°45S 64°10W 94 B3
La Barca Mexico 20°17N 102°34W 86 C4
La Barge U.S.A. 42°16N 110°12W 76 E8
La Barra Nic. 12°54N 83°33W 88 D3
La Belle U.S.A. 26°46N 81°26W 85 H14
La Biche → Canada 59°57N 123°50W 70 B4
La Biche, L. Canada 54°50N 112°3W 70 C6
La Brea Trin. & Tob. 10°15N 61°37W 93 K15
La Calera Chile 32°50S 71°10W 94 C1
La Campana △ Chile 32°58S 71°14W 94 C1
La Canal = Sa Canal
  Spain 38°51N 1°23E 24 C7
La Carlota Argentina 33°30S 63°20W 94 C3
La Ceiba Honduras 15°40N 86°50W 88 C2
La Chaux-de-Fonds Switz. 47°7N 6°50E 20 C7
La Chorrera Panama 8°53N 79°47W 88 E4
La Cocha Argentina 27°50S 65°40W 94 B2
La Concepción Panama 8°31N 82°37W 88 E3
La Concordia Mexico 16°5N 92°38W 87 D6
La Coruña = A Coruña
  Spain 43°20N 8°25W 21 A1
La Crescent U.S.A. 43°50N 91°18W 80 D8
La Crete Canada 58°11N 116°24W 70 B5
La Crosse Kans., U.S.A. 38°32N 99°18W 80 F4
La Crosse Wis., U.S.A. 43°48N 91°15W 80 D8
La Cruz Costa Rica 11°4N 85°39W 88 D2
La Cruz Mexico 23°55N 106°54W 86 C3
La Désirade Guadeloupe 16°18N 61°3W 88 b
La Digue Seychelles 4°20S 55°51E 53 b
La Esperanza Cuba 22°46N 83°44W 88 B3
La Esperanza Honduras 14°15N 88°10W 88 D2
La Estrada = A Estrada
  Spain 42°43N 8°27W 21 A1
La Fayette U.S.A. 34°42N 85°17W 85 D12
La Fé Cuba 22°2N 84°15W 88 B3
La Follette U.S.A. 36°23N 84°7W 85 C12
La Grande U.S.A. 45°20N 118°5W 76 D4
La Grande → Canada 53°50N 79°0W 72 B5
La Grande 3, Rés.
  Canada 53°40N 75°10W 72 B4
La Grande 4, Rés. Canada 54°50N 79°0W 72 B4
La Grange Calif., U.S.A. 37°42N 120°27W 78 H6
La Grange Ga., U.S.A. 33°2N 85°2W 85 E12
La Grange Ky., U.S.A. 38°24N 85°22W 81 F11
La Grange Tex., U.S.A. 29°54N 96°52W 84 G6
La Guaira Venezuela 10°36N 66°56W 92 A5
La Habana Cuba 23°8N 82°22W 88 B3
La Independencia Mexico 16°15N 92°1W 87 D6
La Isabela Dom. Rep. 19°58N 71°2W 89 B5
La Junta U.S.A. 37°59N 103°33W 76 H12
La Laguna Canary Is. 28°28N 16°18W 24 F3
La Libertad = Puerto Libertad
  Mexico 29°55N 112°43W 86 B2
La Libertad Guatemala 16°47N 90°7W 88 C1
La Ligua Chile 32°30S 71°16W 94 C1
La Línea de la Concepción
  Spain 36°15N 5°23W 21 D3
La Loche Canada 56°29N 109°26W 71 B7
La Louvière Belgium 50°27N 4°10E 15 D4
La Lune Trin. & Tob. 10°3N 61°22W 93 K15
La Malbaie Canada 47°40N 70°10W 73 C5
La Malinche △ Mexico 19°15N 98°3W 87 D5
La Mancha Spain 39°10N 2°54W 21 C4
La Martre, L. Canada 63°15N 117°55W 70 A5
La Mesa Mexico 32°30N 116°57W 79 N10
La Mesa U.S.A. 32°46N 117°1W 79 N9
La Mesilla U.S.A. 32°16N 106°48W 77 K10
La Misión Mexico 32°6N 116°53W 86 A1
La Moure U.S.A. 46°21N 98°18W 80 B4
La Negra Chile 23°46S 70°18W 94 A1
La Oliva Canary Is. 28°36N 13°57W 24 F6
La Orotava Canary Is. 28°22N 16°31W 24 F3
La Oroya Peru 11°32S 75°54W 92 F3
La Palma Canary Is. 28°40N 17°50W 24 F2
La Palma Panama 8°15N 78°0W 88 E4
La Palma del Condado
  Spain 37°21N 6°38W 21 D2
La Paloma Chile 30°35S 71°0W 94 C1
La Pampa □ Argentina 36°50S 66°0W 94 D2
La Paragua Venezuela 6°50N 63°20W 92 B6
La Paz Entre Ríos,
  Argentina 30°50S 59°45W 94 C4
La Paz San Luis,
  Argentina 33°30S 67°20W 94 C2
La Paz Bolivia 16°20S 68°10W 92 G5
La Paz Honduras 14°20N 87°47W 88 D2
La Paz Mexico 24°10N 110°18W 86 C2
La Paz Centro Nic. 12°20N 86°41W 88 D2
La Pedrera Colombia 1°18S 69°43W 92 D5
La Pérade Canada 46°35N 72°12W 73 C5
La Perla Mexico 28°18N 104°32W 86 B4

La Perouse Str. Asia 45°40N 142°0E 30 B11
La Pesca Mexico 23°46N 97°47W 87 C5
La Piedad Mexico 20°21N 102°0W 86 C4
La Pine U.S.A. 43°40N 121°30W 76 E3
La Plata Argentina 35°0S 57°55W 94 C4
La Pocatière Canada 47°22N 70°2W 73 C5
La Porte U.S.A. 29°40N 95°1W 84 G7
La Purísima Mexico 26°10N 112°4W 86 B2
La Push U.S.A. 47°55N 124°38W 78 C2
La Quiaca Argentina 22°5S 65°35W 94 A2
La Restinga Canary Is. 27°38N 17°59W 24 G2
La Rioja Argentina 29°20S 67°0W 94 B2
La Rioja □ Argentina 29°30S 67°0W 94 B2
La Rioja □ Spain 42°20N 2°20W 21 A4
La Robla Spain 42°50N 5°41W 21 A3
La Roche-en-Ardenne
  Belgium 50°11N 5°35E 15 D5
La Roche-sur-Yon France 46°40N 1°25W 20 C3
La Rochelle France 46°10N 1°9W 20 C3
La Roda Spain 39°13N 2°15W 21 C4
La Romaine Canada 50°13N 60°40W 73 B7
La Romana Dom. Rep. 18°27N 68°57W 89 C6
La Ronge Canada 55°5N 105°20W 71 B7
La Rumorosa Mexico 32°34N 116°6W 79 N10
La Sabina = Sa Savina
  Spain 38°44N 1°25E 24 C7
La Salle U.S.A. 41°20N 89°6W 80 E9
La Santa Canary Is. 29°5N 13°40W 24 E6
La Sarre Canada 48°45N 79°15W 72 C4
La Scie Canada 49°57N 55°36W 73 C8
La Selva Beach U.S.A. 36°56N 121°51W 78 J5
La Serena Chile 29°55S 71°10W 94 B1
La Seu d'Urgell Spain 42°22N 1°23E 21 A6
La Seyne-sur-Mer France 43°7N 5°52E 20 E6
La Soufrière St. Vincent 13°20N 61°11W 89 D7
La Spézia Italy 44°7N 9°50E 20 D8
La Tagua Colombia 0°3N 74°40W 92 C4
La Tortuga Venezuela 11°0N 65°22W 89 D6
La Trinité Martinique 14°43N 60°58W 88 c
La Tuque Canada 47°30N 72°50W 72 C5
La Unión Chile 40°10S 73°0W 96 E2
La Unión El Salv. 13°20N 87°50W 88 D2
La Unión Mexico 17°58N 101°49W 86 D4
La Urbana Venezuela 7°8N 66°56W 92 B5
La Vache Pt.
  Trin. & Tob. 10°47N 61°28W 93 K15
La Vall d'Uixó Spain 39°49N 0°15W 21 C5
La Vega Dom. Rep. 19°20N 70°30W 89 C5
La Vela de Coro
  Venezuela 11°27N 69°34W 92 A5
La Venta Mexico 18°5N 94°3W 87 D6
La Vergne U.S.A. 36°1N 86°35W 85 C11
La Villa Joiosa = Villajoyosa
  Spain 38°30N 0°12W 21 C5
Laascaanood = Las Anod
  Somali Rep. 8°26N 47°19E 47 F4
Labasa Fiji 16°30S 179°27E 59 a
Labdah = Leptis Magna
  Libya 32°40N 14°12E 51 B8
Labe = Elbe → Europe 53°50N 9°0E 16 B5
Labé Guinea 11°24N 12°16W 50 F3
Laberge, L. Canada 61°11N 135°12W 70 A1
Labinsk Russia 44°40N 40°48E 19 F7
Labis Malaysia 2°22N 103°2E 39 L4
Laborie St. Lucia 13°45N 61°2W 89 f
Laboulaye Argentina 34°10S 63°30W 94 C3
Labrador Canada 53°20N 61°0W 73 B7
Labrador City Canada 52°57N 66°55W 73 B6
Labrador Sea Atl. Oc. 57°0N 54°0W 69 F21
Lábrea Brazil 7°15S 64°51W 92 E6
Labuan Malaysia 5°20N 115°14E 36 C5
Labuan, Pulau Malaysia 5°21N 115°13E 36 C5
Labuha Indonesia 0°30S 127°30E 37 E7
Labuhan Indonesia 6°22S 105°50E 37 G11
Labuhanbajo Indonesia 8°28S 119°54E 37 F6
Labuhanbilik Indonesia 2°31N 100°10E 39 L3
Labuk, Telok Malaysia 6°10N 117°50E 36 C5
Labyrinth, L. Australia 30°40S 135°11E 63 E2
Labytnangi Russia 66°39N 66°21E 18 A12
Lac-Bouchette Canada 48°16N 72°11W 73 C5
Lac Édouard Canada 47°40N 72°16W 72 C5
Lac La Biche Canada 54°45N 111°58W 70 C6
Lac la Martre = Wha Ti
  Canada 63°8N 117°16W 68 E8
Lac La Ronge △ Canada 55°9N 104°41W 71 B7
Lac-Mégantic Canada 45°35N 70°53W 73 C5
Lac Thien Vietnam 12°25N 108°11E 38 F7
Lacanau France 44°58N 1°5W 20 D3
Lacantún → Mexico 16°36N 90°39W 87 D6
Laccadive Is. = Lakshadweep Is.
  India 10°0N 72°30E 3 D13
Lacepede B. Australia 36°40S 139°40E 63 F2
Lacepede Is. Australia 16°55S 122°0E 60 C3
Lacerdónia Mozam. 18°3S 35°35E 55 F4
Lacey U.S.A. 47°7N 122°49W 78 C4
Lachania Greece 35°58N 27°54E 25 D9
Lachhmangarh India 27°50N 75°4E 42 F6
Lachi Pakistan 33°25N 71°20E 42 C4
Lachine Canada 45°26N 73°42W 72 C5
Lachlan → Australia 34°22S 143°55E 63 E3
Lachute Canada 45°39N 74°21W 72 C5
Lackagh Hills Ireland 54°16N 8°10W 10 B3
Lackawanna U.S.A. 42°50N 78°50W 82 D6
Lackawaxen U.S.A. 41°29N 74°59W 83 E10
Lacolle Canada 45°5N 73°22W 83 A11
Lacombe Canada 52°30N 113°44W 70 C6
Laconia U.S.A. 43°32N 71°28W 83 C13
Ladakh Ra. India 34°0N 78°0E 43 C8
Ladismith S. Africa 33°28S 21°15E 56 E3
Lādīz Iran 28°55N 61°15E 45 D9
Ladnun India 27°38N 74°25E 42 F6
Ladoga, L. = Ladozhskoye Ozero
  Russia 61°15N 30°30E 8 F24
Ladozhskoye Ozero
  Russia 61°15N 30°30E 8 F24
Lady Elliott I. Australia 24°7S 152°42E 62 C5
Lady Grey S. Africa 30°43S 27°13E 56 E4
Ladybrand S. Africa 29°9S 27°29E 56 D4

Ladysmith Canada 49°0N 123°49W 78 B3
Ladysmith S. Africa 28°32S 29°46E 57 D4
Ladysmith U.S.A. 45°28N 91°12W 80 C8
Lae Papua N. G. 6°40S 147°2E 58 B7
Laem Hin Khom Thailand 9°25N 99°56E 39 b
Laem Khat Thailand 8°6N 98°26E 39 a
Laem Nga Thailand 8°5N 98°27E 39 a
Laem Ngop Thailand 12°10N 102°26E 39 F4
Laem Phan Wa Thailand 7°47N 98°25E 39 a
Laem Pho Thailand 6°55N 101°19E 39 J3
Laem Phrom Thep Thailand 7°45N 98°19E 39 a
Laem Riang Thailand 8°7N 98°27E 39 a
Laem Sam Rong Thailand 9°35N 100°4E 39 b
Laem Son Thailand 7°59N 98°16E 39 a
Laem Yamu Thailand 7°59N 98°26E 39 a
Laerma Greece 36°9N 27°57E 25 C9
Læsø Denmark 57°15N 11°5E 9 H14
Lafayette Ind., U.S.A. 40°25N 86°54W 80 E10
Lafayette La., U.S.A. 30°14N 92°1W 84 K9
Lafayette Tenn., U.S.A. 36°31N 86°2W 85 C11
Laferte → Canada 61°53N 117°44W 70 A5
Lafia Nigeria 8°30N 8°34E 50 G7
Lafleche Canada 49°45N 106°40W 71 D7
Lagan → U.K. 54°36N 5°55W 10 B6
Lagarfljót → Iceland 65°40N 14°18W 8 D6
Lagdo, L. de Cameroon 8°40N 14°0E 51 G8
Lågen → Oppland, Norway 61°8N 10°25E 8 F14
Lågen → Vestfold, Norway 59°3N 10°3E 9 G14
Lages Brazil 27°48S 50°0W 95 B5
Laghouat Algeria 33°50N 2°59E 50 B6
Lagoa do Peixe △ Brazil 31°12S 50°55W 95 C5
Lagoa Vermelha Brazil 28°13S 51°32W 95 B5
Lagonoy G. Phil. 13°35N 123°50E 37 B6
Lagos Nigeria 6°25N 3°27E 50 G6
Lagos Portugal 37°5N 8°41W 21 D1
Lagos de Moreno
  Mexico 21°21N 101°55W 86 C4
Lagrange = Bidyadanga
  Australia 18°45S 121°43E 60 C3
Lagrange B. Australia 18°38S 121°42E 60 C3
Laguna Brazil 28°30S 48°50W 95 B6
Laguna U.S.A. 35°2N 107°25W 77 J10
Laguna, Sa. de la
  Mexico 23°35N 109°55W 86 C3
Laguna Beach U.S.A. 33°33N 117°47W 79 M9
Laguna de la Restinga △
  Venezuela 10°58N 64°0W 89 D6
Laguna de Lachuá △
  Guatemala 15°55N 90°40W 88 C1
Laguna del Laja △ Chile 37°27S 71°20W 94 D1
Laguna del Tigre △
  Guatemala 17°32N 90°56W 88 C1
Laguna Limpia
  Argentina 26°32S 59°45W 94 B4
Lagunas Chile 21°0S 69°45W 94 A2
Lagunas Peru 5°10S 75°35W 92 E3
Lagunas de Chacahua △
  Mexico 16°0N 97°43W 87 D5
Lagunas de Montebello △
  Mexico 16°4N 91°42W 87 D6
Lahad Datu Malaysia 5°0N 118°20E 37 D5
Lahad Datu, Telok
  Malaysia 4°50N 118°20E 37 D5
Lahan Sai Thailand 14°25N 102°52E 38 E4
Lahanam Laos 16°16N 105°16E 38 D5
Lahar India 26°12N 78°57E 43 F8
Laharpur India 27°43N 80°56E 43 F9
Lahat Indonesia 3°45S 103°30E 36 E2
Lahewa Indonesia 1°22N 97°12E 36 D1
Lāhījān Iran 37°10N 50°6E 45 B6
Lahn → Germany 50°19N 7°37E 16 C4
Laholm Sweden 56°30N 13°2E 9 H15
Lahore Pakistan 31°32N 74°22E 42 D6
Lahri Pakistan 29°11N 68°13E 42 E3
Lāhrūd Iran 38°30N 47°52E 44 B5
Lahti Finland 60°58N 25°40E 8 F21
Lahtis = Lahti Finland 60°58N 25°40E 8 F21
Laï Chad 9°25N 16°18E 51 G9
Lai Chau Vietnam 22°5N 103°3E 38 A4
Laila = Layla Si. Arabia 22°10N 46°40E 47 C4
Laingsburg S. Africa 33°9S 20°52E 56 E3
Lainioälven → Sweden 67°35N 22°40E 8 C20
Lairg U.K. 58°2N 4°24W 11 C4
Laisamis Kenya 1°36N 37°48E 54 B4
Laishui China 39°23N 115°45E 34 E8
Laiwu China 36°15N 117°40E 35 F9
Laixi China 36°50N 120°31E 35 F11
Laiyang China 36°59N 120°45E 35 F11
Laiyuan China 39°20N 114°40E 34 E8
Laizhou China 37°8N 119°57E 35 F10
Laizhou Wan China 37°30N 119°30E 35 F10
Laja → Mexico 20°55N 100°46W 86 C4
Lajamanu Australia 18°23S 130°38E 60 C5
Lak Sao Laos 18°11N 104°59E 38 C5
Lakaband Pakistan 31°2N 69°15E 42 D3
Lake → U.S.A. 44°33N 110°24W 76 D8
Lake Alpine U.S.A. 38°29N 120°0W 78 G7
Lake Andes U.S.A. 43°9N 98°32W 80 D4
Lake Arthur U.S.A. 30°5N 92°41W 84 F8
Lake Bindegolly △
  Australia 28°0S 144°12E 63 D3
Lake Cargelligo
  Australia 33°15S 146°22E 63 E4
Lake Charles U.S.A. 30°14N 93°13W 84 F8
Lake City Colo., U.S.A. 38°2N 107°19W 76 G10
Lake City Fla., U.S.A. 30°11N 82°38W 85 F13
Lake City Mich., U.S.A. 44°20N 85°13W 81 C11
Lake City Minn., U.S.A. 44°27N 92°16W 80 C7
Lake City Pa., U.S.A. 42°1N 80°21W 82 D4
Lake City S.C., U.S.A. 33°52N 79°45W 85 E15
Lake Cowichan Canada 48°49N 124°3W 70 D4
Lake District △ U.K. 54°30N 3°21W 12 C4
Lake Elsinore U.S.A. 33°38N 117°20W 79 M9
Lake Eyre △ Australia 28°40S 137°31E 63 D2
Lake Gairdner △
  Australia 31°41S 135°51E 63 E2
Lake George U.S.A. 43°26N 73°43W 83 C11
Lake Grace Australia 33°7S 118°28E 61 F2
Lake Gregory ☺
  Australia 20°12S 127°27E 60 D4

Lake Harbour = Kimmirut
  Canada 62°50N 69°50W 69 E18
Lake Havasu City
  U.S.A. 34°27N 114°22W 79 L12
Lake Hughes U.S.A. 34°41N 118°26W 79 L8
Lake Isabella U.S.A. 35°38N 118°28W 79 K8
Lake Jackson U.S.A. 29°3N 95°27W 84 G7
Lake King Australia 33°5S 119°45E 61 F2
Lake Lenore Canada 52°24N 104°59W 71 C8
Lake Louise Canada 51°30N 116°10W 70 C5
Lake Mackay ☺
  Australia 22°30S 129°0E 60 D4
Lake Mburo △ Uganda 0°33S 30°56E 54 C3
Lake Mead △
  U.S.A. 36°30N 114°22W 79 K12
Lake Meredith △
  U.S.A. 35°50N 101°50W 84 D4
Lake Mills U.S.A. 43°25N 93°32W 80 D7
Lake Nakuru △ Kenya 0°21S 36°8E 54 C4
Lake Placid U.S.A. 44°17N 73°59W 83 B11
Lake Pleasant U.S.A. 43°28N 74°25W 83 C10
Lake Providence U.S.A. 32°48N 91°10W 84 E9
Lake Roosevelt △
  U.S.A. 48°5N 118°14W 76 B4
Lake St. Peter Canada 45°18N 78°2W 82 A6
Lake Superior △ Canada 47°45N 84°45W 72 C3
Lake Torrens △
  Australia 30°55S 137°40E 63 E2
Lake Village U.S.A. 33°20N 91°17W 84 E9
Lake Wales U.S.A. 27°54N 81°35W 85 H14
Lake Worth U.S.A. 26°37N 80°3W 85 H14
Lakeba Fiji 18°13S 178°47W 59 a
Lakeba Passage Fiji 18°0S 178°45W 59 a
Lakefield Canada 44°25N 78°16W 82 B6
Lakefield △ Australia 15°24S 144°26E 62 B3
Lakehurst U.S.A. 40°1N 74°19W 83 F10
Lakeland Australia 15°49S 144°57E 62 B3
Lakeland U.S.A. 28°3N 81°57W 85 G14
Lakemba = Lakeba Fiji 18°13S 178°47W 59 a
Lakeport Calif., U.S.A. 39°3N 122°55W 78 F4
Lakeport Mich., U.S.A. 43°7N 82°30W 82 C2
Lakes Entrance Australia 37°50S 148°0E 63 F4
Lakeside Calif., U.S.A. 32°52N 116°55W 79 N10
Lakeside Nebr., U.S.A. 42°3N 102°26W 80 D2
Lakeview U.S.A. 42°11N 120°21W 76 E3
Lakeville U.S.A. 44°39N 93°14W 80 C7
Lakewood Colo., U.S.A. 39°42N 105°4W 76 G11
Lakewood N.J., U.S.A. 40°6N 74°13W 83 F10
Lakewood N.Y., U.S.A. 42°6N 79°19W 82 D5
Lakewood Ohio, U.S.A. 41°28N 81°47W 82 E3
Lakewood Wash.,
  U.S.A. 47°11N 122°32W 78 C4
Lakha India 26°9N 70°54E 42 F4
Lakhimpur India 27°57N 80°46E 43 F9
Lakhisarai India 25°11N 86°5E 43 G12
Lakhnadon India 22°36N 79°36E 43 H8
Lakhnau = Lucknow
  India 26°50N 81°0E 43 F9
Lakhonpheng Laos 15°54N 105°34E 38 E5
Lakhpat India 23°48N 68°47E 42 H3
Lakin U.S.A. 37°57N 101°15W 80 G3
Lakitusaki → Canada 54°21N 82°25W 72 B3
Lakki Greece 35°24N 23°57E 25 D5
Lakki Pakistan 32°36N 70°55E 42 C4
Lakonikos Kolpos
  Greece 36°40N 22°40E 23 F10
Lakor Indonesia 8°15S 128°17E 37 F7
Lakota Ivory C. 5°50N 5°30W 50 G4
Lakota U.S.A. 48°2N 98°21W 80 A4
Laksar India 29°46N 78°3E 43 E8
Laksefjorden Norway 70°45N 26°50E 8 A22
Lakselv Norway 70°2N 25°0E 8 A21
Lakshadweep Is. India 10°0N 72°30E 3 D13
Lakshmanpur India 22°58N 83°3E 43 H10
Lakshmikantapur India 22°5N 88°20E 43 H13
Lala Musa Pakistan 32°40N 73°57E 42 C5
Lalaghat India 24°30N 92°40E 41 G18
Lalapanzi Zimbabwe 19°20S 30°15E 55 F3
L'Albufera Spain 39°20N 0°27W 21 C5
Lalganj India 25°52N 85°13E 43 G11
Lalgola India 24°25N 88°15E 43 G13
Lālī Iran 32°21N 49°6E 45 C6
Lalibela Ethiopia 12°3N 39°0E 47 E2
Lalín Spain 42°40N 8°5W 21 A1
Lalitapur Nepal 27°40N 85°20E 43 F11
Lalitpur India 24°42N 78°28E 43 G8
Lalkua India 29°5N 79°31E 43 E8
Lalsot India 26°34N 76°20E 42 F7
Lam Pao Res. Thailand 16°50N 103°15E 38 D4
Lama Kara Togo 9°30N 1°15E 50 G6
Lamae Thailand 9°51N 99°5E 39 H2
Lamar Colo., U.S.A. 38°5N 102°37W 76 G12
Lamar Mo., U.S.A. 37°30N 94°16W 80 G6
Lamas Peru 6°28S 76°31W 92 E3
Lamayuru India 34°25N 76°56E 43 B7
Lambaréné Gabon 0°41S 10°12E 52 E2
Lambasa = Labasa Fiji 16°30S 179°27E 59 a
Lambay I. Ireland 53°29N 6°1W 10 C5
Lambert's Bay S. Africa 32°5S 18°17E 56 E2
Lambeth Canada 42°54N 81°18W 82 D3
Lambomakondro
  Madag. 22°41S 44°44E 57 C7
Lame Deer U.S.A. 45°37N 106°40W 76 D10
Lamego Portugal 41°5N 7°52W 21 B2
Lamèque Canada 47°45N 64°38W 73 C7
Lameroo Australia 35°19S 140°33E 63 F3
Lamesa U.S.A. 32°44N 101°58W 84 E4
Lamia Greece 38°55N 22°26E 23 E10
Lamington △ Australia 28°13S 153°12E 63 D5
Lamma I. China 22°12N 114°7E 33 G11
Lammermuir Hills U.K. 55°50N 2°40W 11 F6
Lamoille → U.S.A. 44°38N 73°13W 83 B11
Lamon B. Phil. 14°30N 122°20E 37 B6
Lamont Canada 53°46N 112°50W 70 C6
Lamont Calif., U.S.A. 35°15N 118°55W 79 K8
Lamont Wyo., U.S.A. 42°13N 107°29W 76 E10

Lampa Peru 15°22S 70°22W 92 G4
Lampang Thailand 18°16N 99°32E 38 C2
Lampasas U.S.A. 31°4N 98°11W 84 F5
Lampazos de Naranjo
  Mexico 27°1N 100°31W 86 B4
Lampedusa Medit. S. 35°36N 12°40E 22 G5
Lampeter U.K. 52°7N 4°4W 13 E3
Lampione Medit. S. 35°33N 12°20E 22 G5
Lampman Canada 49°25N 102°50W 71 D8
Lampung □ Indonesia 5°30S 104°30E 36 F2
Lamta India 22°8N 80°7E 43 H9
Lamu Kenya 2°16S 40°55E 54 C5
Lamy U.S.A. 35°29N 105°53W 77 J11
Lan Xian China 38°15N 111°35E 34 E6
Läna'i U.S.A. 20°50N 156°55W 75 L8
Lanak La China 34°27N 79°32E 43 B8
Lanak'o Shank'ou = Lanak La
  China 34°27N 79°32E 43 B8
Lanark Canada 45°1N 76°22W 83 A8
Lanark U.K. 55°40N 3°47W 11 F5
Lanbi Kyun Burma 10°50N 98°20E 39 G2
Lancang Jiang →
  China 21°40N 101°10E 32 D5
Lancashire □ U.K. 53°50N 2°48W 12 D5
Lancaster Canada 45°10N 74°30W 83 A10
Lancaster U.K. 54°3N 2°48W 12 C5
Lancaster Calif., U.S.A. 34°42N 118°8W 79 L8
Lancaster Ky., U.S.A. 37°37N 84°35W 81 G11
Lancaster N.H., U.S.A. 44°29N 71°34W 83 B13
Lancaster Ohio, U.S.A. 39°43N 82°36W 81 F12
Lancaster Pa., U.S.A. 40°2N 76°19W 83 F8
Lancaster S.C., U.S.A. 34°43N 80°46W 85 D14
Lancaster Wis., U.S.A. 42°51N 90°43W 80 D8
Lancaster Sd. Canada 74°13N 84°0W 69 C15
Lancelin Australia 31°0S 115°18E 61 F2
Lanchow = Lanzhou
  China 36°1N 103°52E 34 F2
Lanciano Italy 42°14N 14°23E 22 C6
Lancun China 36°25N 120°10E 35 F11
Land Between the Lakes △
  U.S.A. 36°25N 88°0W 85 C11
Landeck Austria 47°9N 10°34E 16 E6
Lander U.S.A. 42°50N 108°44W 76 E9
Lander → Australia 22°0S 132°0E 60 D5
Landes France 44°0N 1°0W 20 D3
Landi Kotal Pakistan 34°7N 71°6E 42 B4
Landisburg U.S.A. 40°21N 77°19W 82 F7
Landmannalaugar Iceland 63°59N 19°4W 8 E4
Land's End U.K. 50°4N 5°44W 13 G2
Landsborough Cr. →
  Australia 22°28S 144°35E 62 C3
Landshut Germany 48°34N 12°8E 16 D7
Lanesboro U.S.A. 41°57N 75°34W 83 E9
Lanett U.S.A. 32°52N 85°12W 85 E12
Lang Shan China 41°0N 106°30E 34 D4
Lang Son Vietnam 21°52N 106°42E 38 B6
Lang Suan Thailand 9°57N 99°4E 39 H2
La'nga Co China 30°45N 81°15E 43 D9
Langar Iran 35°23N 60°25E 45 C9
Langara I. Canada 54°14N 133°1W 70 C2
Langarūd Iran 37°11N 50°8E 45 B6
Langdon U.S.A. 48°45N 98°22W 80 A4
Langeberg S. Africa 33°55S 21°0E 56 E3
Langeberge S. Africa 28°15S 22°33E 56 D3
Langeland Denmark 54°56N 10°48E 9 J14
Langenburg Canada 50°51N 101°43W 71 C8
Langholm U.K. 55°9N 3°0W 11 F5
Langjökull Iceland 64°39N 20°12W 8 D3
Langkawi, Pulau
  Malaysia 6°25N 99°45E 39 J2
Langklip S. Africa 28°12S 20°20E 56 D3
Langkon Malaysia 6°30N 116°40E 36 C5
Langley Canada 49°7N 122°39W 78 A4
Langøya Norway 68°45N 14°50E 8 B16
Langreo Spain 43°18N 5°40W 21 A3
Langres France 47°52N 5°20E 20 C6
Langres, Plateau de France 47°45N 5°3E 20 C6
Langsa Indonesia 4°30N 97°57E 36 D1
Langtang △ Nepal 28°10N 85°30E 43 E11
Langtry U.S.A. 29°49N 101°34W 84 G4
Langu Thailand 6°53N 99°47E 39 J2
Languedoc France 43°58N 3°55E 20 E5
Langwang China 22°38N 113°27E 33 F9
Langxiangzhen China 39°43N 116°8E 34 E9
Lanigan Canada 51°51N 105°2W 71 C7
Lankao China 34°48N 114°50E 34 G8
Länkäran Azerbaijan 38°48N 48°52E 45 B6
Lannion France 48°46N 3°29W 20 B2
L'Annonciation Canada 46°25N 74°55W 72 C5
Lansdale U.S.A. 40°14N 75°17W 83 F9
Lansdowne Australia 31°48S 152°30E 63 E5
Lansdowne Canada 44°24N 76°1W 83 B8
Lansdowne India 29°50N 78°41E 43 E8
Lansdowne House = Neskantaga
  Canada 52°14N 87°53W 72 B2
L'Anse U.S.A. 46°45N 88°27W 80 B9
L'Anse au Loup Canada 51°32N 56°50W 73 B8
L'Anse aux Meadows
  Canada 51°36N 55°32W 73 B8
L'Anse à la Raye St. Lucia 13°55N 61°3W 89 f
Lansford U.S.A. 40°50N 75°53W 83 F9
Lansing U.S.A. 42°44N 84°33W 81 D11
Lanta Yai, Ko Thailand 7°35N 99°3E 39 J2
Lantau I. China 22°15N 113°56E 33 G10
Lantian China 34°11N 109°20E 34 G5
Lanus Argentina 34°42S 58°23W 94 C4
Lanusei Italy 39°52N 9°34E 22 E3
Lanzarote Canary Is. 29°0N 13°40W 24 F6
Lanzarote ✈ (ACE)
  Canary Is. 28°57N 13°40W 24 F6
Lanzhou China 36°1N 103°52E 34 F2
Lao Bao Laos 16°35N 106°30E 38 D6
Lao Cai Vietnam 22°30N 103°57E 38 A4
Laoag Phil. 18°7N 120°34E 37 A6
Laoang Phil. 12°32N 125°8E 37 B7
Laoha He → China 43°25N 120°35E 35 C11
Laois □ Ireland 52°57N 7°36W 10 D4
Laon France 49°33N 3°35E 20 B5
Laona U.S.A. 45°34N 88°40W 80 C9

Laos ■ *Asia* 17°45N 105°0E **38** D5
Lapa *Brazil* 25°46S 49°44W **95** B6
Lapeer *U.S.A.* 43°3N 83°19W **81** D12
Lapithos *Cyprus* 35°21N 33°11E **25** D12
Lapland = Lappland
  Europe 68°7N 24°0E **8** B21
LaPorte *Ind., U.S.A.* 41°36N 86°43W **80** E10
Laporte *Pa., U.S.A.* 41°25N 76°30W **83** E8
Lappeenranta *Finland* 61°3N 28°12E **8** F23
Lappland *Europe* 68°7N 24°0E **8** B21
Lappo = Lapua *Finland* 62°58N 23°0E **8** E20
Laprida *Argentina* 37°34S 60°45W **94** D3
Lâpseki *Turkey* 40°20N 26°41E **23** D12
Laptev Sea *Russia* 76°0N 125°0E **29** B13
Lapua *Finland* 62°58N 23°0E **8** E20
L'Áquila *Italy* 42°22N 13°22E **22** C5
Lār *Iran* 27°40N 54°14E **45** E7
Laramie *U.S.A.* 41°19N 105°35W **76** F11
Laramie Mts. *U.S.A.* 42°0N 105°30W **76** F11
Laranjeiras do Sul *Brazil* 25°23S 52°23W **95** B5
Larantuka *Indonesia* 8°21S 122°55E **37** F6
Larat *Indonesia* 7°0S 132°0E **37** F8
Larde *Mozam.* 16°28S 39°43E **55** F4
Larder Lake *Canada* 48°5N 79°40W **72** C4
Lardos *Greece* 36°6N 28°1E **25** C10
Lardos, Akra = Líndos, Ákra
  Greece 36°4N 28°10E **25** C10
Lardos, Ormos *Greece* 36°4N 28°2E **25** C10
Lare *Kenya* 0°20N 37°56E **54** C4
Laredo *U.S.A.* 27°30N 99°30W **84** H5
Laredo Sd. *Canada* 52°30N 128°53W **70** C3
Largo *U.S.A.* 27°54N 82°47W **85** H13
Largs *U.K.* 55°47N 4°52W **11** F4
Lariang *Indonesia* 1°26S 119°17E **37** E5
Larimore *U.S.A.* 47°54N 97°38W **80** B5
Larisa *Greece* 39°36N 22°27E **23** E10
Larkana *Pakistan* 27°32N 68°18E **42** F3
Larnaca *Cyprus* 34°55N 33°38E **25** E12
Larnaca Bay *Cyprus* 34°53N 33°45E **25** E12
Larne *U.K.* 54°51N 5°51W **10** B6
Larned *U.S.A.* 38°11N 99°6W **80** F4
Larose *U.S.A.* 29°34N 90°23W **85** G9
Larrimah *Australia* 15°35S 133°12E **60** C5
Larsen Ice Shelf *Antarctica* 67°0S 62°0W **5** C17
Larvik *Norway* 59°4N 10°2E **9** G14
Las Animas *U.S.A.* 38°4N 103°13W **76** G12
Las Anod *Somali Rep.* 8°26N 47°19E **47** F4
Las Brenãs *Argentina* 27°5S 61°7W **94** B3
Las Cañadas del Teide △
  Canary Is. 28°15N 16°37W **24** F3
Las Cejas *Argentina* 26°53S 64°44W **96** B4
Las Chimeneas *Mexico* 32°8N 116°5W **79** N10
Las Cruces *U.S.A.* 32°19N 106°47W **77** K10
Las Flores *Argentina* 36°10S 59°7W **94** D4
Las Heras *Argentina* 32°51S 68°49W **94** C2
Las Lajas *Argentina* 38°30S 70°25W **96** D2
Las Lomitas *Argentina* 24°43S 60°35W **94** A3
Las Palmas *Argentina* 27°8S 58°45W **94** B4
Las Palmas *Canary Is.* 28°7N 15°26W **24** F4
Las Palmas → *Mexico* 32°31N 116°58W **79** N10
Las Palmas ✈ (LPA)
  Canary Is. 27°55N 15°25W **24** G4
Las Piedras *Uruguay* 34°44S 56°14W **95** C4
Las Pipinas *Argentina* 35°30S 57°19W **94** D4
Las Plumas *Argentina* 43°40S 67°15W **96** E3
Las Rosas *Argentina* 32°30S 61°35W **94** C3
Las Tablas *Panama* 7°49N 80°14W **88** E3
Las Toscas *Argentina* 28°21S 59°18W **94** B4
Las Truchas *Mexico* 17°57N 102°13W **86** D4
Las Tunas *Cuba* 20°58N 76°59W **88** B4
Las Varillas *Argentina* 31°50S 62°50W **94** C3
Las Vegas *N. Mex.,*
  U.S.A. 35°36N 105°13W **77** J11
Las Vegas *Nev., U.S.A.* 36°10N 115°8W **79** J11
Las Vegas McCarran Int. ✈ (LAS)
  U.S.A. 36°5N 115°9W **79** J11
Lascano *Uruguay* 33°35S 54°12W **95** C5
Lash-e Joveyn *Afghan.* 31°45N 61°30E **40** D2
Lashburn *Canada* 53°10N 109°40W **71** C7
Lashio *Burma* 22°56N 97°45E **41** H20
Lashkar *India* 26°10N 78°10E **42** F8
Lasithi *Greece* 35°11N 25°31E **25** D7
Lasithi □ *Greece* 35°5N 25°50E **25** D7
Läsjerd *Iran* 35°24N 53°4E **45** C7
Lassen Pk. *U.S.A.* 40°29N 121°30W **76** F3
Lassen Volcanic △
  U.S.A. 40°30N 121°20W **76** F3
Last Mountain L.
  Canada 51°5N 105°14W **71** C7
Lastchance Cr. →
  U.S.A. 40°2N 121°15W **78** E5
Lastoursville *Gabon* 0°55S 12°38E **52** E2
Lastovo *Croatia* 42°46N 16°55E **22** C7
Lat Yao *Thailand* 15°45N 99°48E **38** E2
Latacunga *Ecuador* 0°50S 78°35W **92** D3
Latakia = Al Lādhiqīyah
  Syria 35°30N 35°45E **44** C2
Latchford *Canada* 47°20N 79°50W **72** C4
Late *Tonga* 18°48S 174°39W **59** c
Latehar *India* 23°45N 84°30E **43** H11
Latham *Australia* 29°44S 116°20E **61** E2
Lathi *India* 27°43N 71°23E **42** F4
Lathrop Wells *U.S.A.* 36°39N 116°24W **79** J10
Latina *Italy* 41°28N 12°52E **22** D5
Latium = Lazio □ *Italy* 42°10N 12°30E **22** C5
Laton *U.S.A.* 36°26N 119°41W **78** J7
Latouche Treville, C.
  Australia 18°27S 121°49E **60** C3
Latrobe *Australia* 41°14S 146°30E **63** G4
Latrobe *U.S.A.* 40°19N 79°23W **82** F5
Latvia ■ *Europe* 56°50N 24°0E **9** H21
Lau Fau Shan *China* 22°28N 113°59E **33** G10
Lau Group *Fiji* 17°0S 178°30W **59** a
Lauchhammer *Germany* 51°29N 13°47E **16** C7
Lauge Koch Kyst
  Greenland 75°45N 57°45W **69** B20
Laughlin *U.S.A.* 35°10N 114°34W **77** J6
Laukaa *Finland* 62°24N 25°56E **8** E21
Launceston *Australia* 41°24S 147°8E **63** G4

Launceston *U.K.* 50°38N 4°22W **13** G3
Laune → *Ireland* 52°7N 9°47W **10** D2
Launglon Bok *Burma* 13°50N 97°54E **38** F1
Laura *Australia* 15°32S 144°32E **62** B3
Laurel *Miss., U.S.A.* 31°41N 89°8W **85** F10
Laurel *Mont., U.S.A.* 45°40N 108°46W **76** D9
Laurel Hill *U.S.A.* 40°14N 79°6W **82** F5
Laurencekirk *U.K.* 56°50N 2°28W **11** E6
Laurens *U.S.A.* 34°30N 82°1W **85** D13
Laurentian Plateau
  Canada 52°0N 70°0W **73** B6
Lauria *Italy* 40°2N 15°50E **22** E6
Laurie L. *Canada* 56°35N 101°57W **71** B8
Laurinburg *U.S.A.* 34°47N 79°28W **85** D15
Laurium *U.S.A.* 47°14N 88°27W **80** B9
Lausanne *Switz.* 46°32N 6°38E **20** C7
Laut *Indonesia* 4°45N 108°0E **36** D3
Laut, Pulau *Indonesia* 3°40S 116°10E **36** E5
Laut Kecil, Kepulauan
  Indonesia 4°45S 115°40E **36** E5
Lautoka *Fiji* 17°37S 177°27E **59** a
Lava Beds △ *U.S.A.* 41°40N 121°30W **76** F3
Lavagh More *Ireland* 54°46N 8°6W **10** B3
Laval *France* 48°4N 0°48W **20** B3
Laval-des-Rapides
  Canada 45°33N 73°42W **72** C5
Lavalle *Argentina* 28°15S 65°15W **94** B2
Lãvän *Iran* 26°48N 53°22E **45** E7
Lavant *Canada* 45°3N 76°42W **83** A8
Lāvar Meydãn *Iran* 30°20N 54°30E **45** D7
Laverton *Australia* 28°44S 122°29E **61** E3
Lavras *Brazil* 21°20S 45°0W **95** A7
Lavrio *Greece* 37°40N 24°4E **23** F11
Lavris *Greece* 35°25N 24°40E **25** D6
Lavumisa *Swaziland* 27°20S 31°55E **57** D5
Lavushi Manda △ *Zambia* 12°46S 31°0E **55** E3
Lawaki *Fiji* 17°40S 178°35E **59** a
Lawas *Malaysia* 4°55N 115°25E **36** D5
Lawele *Indonesia* 5°13S 122°57E **37** F6
Lawn Hill = Boodjamulla △
  Australia 18°15S 138°6E **62** B2
Lawqah *Si. Arabia* 29°49N 42°45E **44** D4
Lawrence *N.Z.* 45°55S 169°41E **59** F2
Lawrence *Ind., U.S.A.* 39°50N 86°2W **80** F10
Lawrence *Kans., U.S.A.* 38°58N 95°14W **80** F6
Lawrence *Mass., U.S.A.* 42°43N 71°10W **83** D13
Lawrenceburg *Ind.,*
  U.S.A. 39°6N 84°52W **81** F11
Lawrenceburg *Tenn.,*
  U.S.A. 35°14N 87°20W **85** D11
Lawrenceville *Ga.,*
  U.S.A. 33°57N 83°59W **85** E13
Lawrenceville *Pa., U.S.A.* 41°59N 77°8W **82** E7
Laws *U.S.A.* 37°24N 118°20W **78** H8
Lawton *U.S.A.* 34°37N 98°25W **84** H5
Lawu *Indonesia* 7°40S 111°13E **37** G14
Laxford, L. *U.K.* 58°24N 5°6W **11** C3
Layla *Si. Arabia* 22°10N 46°40E **47** C4
Laylān *Iraq* 35°18N 44°31E **44** C5
Laysan I. *U.S.A.* 25°50N 171°50W **75** K5
Layton *U.S.A.* 41°4N 111°58W **76** F8
Laytonville *U.S.A.* 39°41N 123°29W **76** G2
Lazarev *Russia* 52°13N 141°30E **29** D15
Lazarev Sea *S. Ocean* 67°30S 30°W **5** C2
Lazarivo *Madag.* 23°54S 44°59E **57** C8
Lázaro Cárdenas
  Mexico 17°55N 102°11W **86** D4
Lazio □ *Italy* 42°10N 12°30E **22** C5
Lazo *Russia* 43°25N 133°55E **30** C6
Le Bic *Canada* 48°20N 68°41W **73** C6
Le Creusot *France* 46°48N 4°24E **20** C6
Le François *Martinique* 14°38N 60°57W **88** c
Le Gosier *Guadeloupe* 16°14N 61°29W **88** b
Le Gris Gris *Mauritius* 20°31S 57°32E **53** d
Le Havre *France* 49°30N 0°5E **20** B4
Le Lamentin *Martinique* 14°35N 61°2W **88** c
Le Mans *France* 48°0N 0°10E **20** C4
Le Marin *Martinique* 14°27N 60°55W **88** c
Le Mars *U.S.A.* 42°47N 96°10W **80** D5
Le Mont-St-Michel
  France 48°40N 1°30W **20** B3
Le Moule *Guadeloupe* 16°20N 61°22W **88** b
Le Moyne, L. *Canada* 56°45N 68°47W **73** A6
Le Port *Réunion* 20°56S 55°18E **53** c
Le Prêcheur *Martinique* 14°50N 61°12W **88** c
Le Puy-en-Velay *France* 45°3N 3°52E **20** D5
Le Raysville *U.S.A.* 41°50N 76°10W **83** E8
Le Robert *Martinique* 14°40N 60°56W **88** c
Le Roy *U.S.A.* 42°58N 77°59W **82** D7
Le St-Esprit *Martinique* 14°34N 60°56W **88** c
Le Sueur *U.S.A.* 44°28N 93°55W **80** C7
Le Tampon *Réunion* 21°16S 55°32E **53** c
Le Thuy *Vietnam* 17°14N 106°49E **38** D6
Le Touquet-Paris-Plage
  France 50°30N 1°36E **20** A4
Le Tréport *France* 50°3N 1°20E **20** A4
Le Verdon-sur-Mer *France* 45°33N 1°4W **20** D3
Lea → *U.K.* 51°31N 0°1E **13** F8
Leach *Cambodia* 12°21N 103°46E **39** F4
Lead *U.S.A.* 44°21N 103°46W **80** C2
Leader *Canada* 50°50N 109°30W **71** C7
Leadville *U.S.A.* 39°15N 106°18W **76** G10
Leaf → *U.S.A.* 30°59N 88°44W **85** F10
Leaf Rapids *Canada* 56°30N 99°59W **71** B9
Leamington *Canada* 42°3N 82°36W **82** D2
Leamington *U.S.A.* 39°32N 112°17W **76** G7
Leamington Spa = Royal
  Leamington Spa *U.K.* 52°18N 1°31W **13** E6
Leandro Norte Alem
  Argentina 27°34S 55°15W **95** B4
Leane, L. *Ireland* 52°2N 9°32W **10** D2
Learmonth *Australia* 22°13S 114°10E **60** D1
Leask *Canada* 53°5N 106°45W **71** C7
Leatherhead *U.K.* 51°18N 0°20W **13** F7
Leavenworth *Kans.,*
  U.S.A. 39°19N 94°55W **80** F6
Leavenworth *Wash.,*
  U.S.A. 47°36N 120°40W **76** C3
Leawood *U.S.A.* 38°58N 94°37W **80** F6

Lebak *Phil.* 6°32N 124°5E **37** C6
Lebam *U.S.A.* 46°34N 123°33W **78** D3
Lebanon *Ind., U.S.A.* 40°3N 86°28W **80** E10
Lebanon *Kans., U.S.A.* 39°49N 98°33W **80** F4
Lebanon *Ky., U.S.A.* 37°34N 85°15W **81** G11
Lebanon *Mo., U.S.A.* 37°41N 92°40W **80** G7
Lebanon *N.H., U.S.A.* 43°39N 72°15W **83** C12
Lebanon *Oreg., U.S.A.* 44°32N 122°55W **76** D2
Lebanon *Pa., U.S.A.* 40°20N 76°26W **83** F8
Lebanon *Tenn., U.S.A.* 36°12N 86°18W **85** C11
Lebanon ■ *Asia* 34°0N 36°0E **46** B5
Lebec *U.S.A.* 34°51N 118°52W **79** L8
Lebel-sur-Quévillon
  Canada 49°3N 76°59W **72** C4
Lebomboberge *S. Africa* 24°30S 32°0E **57** C5
Lębork *Poland* 54°33N 17°46E **17** A9
Lebrija *Spain* 36°53N 6°5W **21** D2
Lebu *Chile* 37°40S 73°47W **94** D1
Lecce *Italy* 40°23N 18°11E **23** D8
Lecco *Italy* 45°51N 9°23E **20** D8
Lech → *Germany* 48°43N 10°56E **16** D6
Lecontes Mills *U.S.A.* 41°5N 78°17W **82** E6
Ledong *China* 18°41N 109°5E **38** C7
Leduc *Canada* 53°15N 113°30W **70** C6
Lee *U.S.A.* 42°19N 73°15W **83** D11
Lee → *Ireland* 51°53N 8°56W **10** E3
Lee Vining *U.S.A.* 37°58N 119°7W **78** H7
Leech L. *U.S.A.* 47°10N 94°24W **80** B6
Leechburg *U.S.A.* 40°37N 79°36W **82** F5
Leeds *U.K.* 53°48N 1°33W **12** D6
Leeds *U.S.A.* 33°33N 86°33W **85** E11
Leek *Neths.* 53°10N 6°24E **15** A6
Leek *U.K.* 53°7N 2°1W **12** D5
Leeman *Australia* 29°57S 114°58E **61** E1
Leeper *U.S.A.* 41°22N 79°18W **82** E5
Leer *Germany* 53°13N 7°26E **16** B4
Leesburg *U.S.A.* 28°49N 81°53W **85** G14
Leeston *N.Z.* 43°45S 172°27E **59** E4
Leesville *U.S.A.* 31°8N 93°16W **84** F8
Leeton *Australia* 34°33S 146°23E **63** E4
Leetonia *U.S.A.* 40°53N 80°45W **82** F4
Leeu Gamka *S. Africa* 32°47S 21°59E **56** E3
Leeuwarden *Neths.* 53°15N 5°48E **15** A5
Leeuwin, C. *Australia* 34°20S 115°9E **61** F2
Leeuwin Naturaliste △
  Australia 34°6S 115°3E **61** F2
Lefka *Cyprus* 35°6N 32°51E **25** D11
Lefkada *Greece* 38°40N 20°43E **23** E9
Lefkimi *Greece* 39°25N 20°3E **25** B4
Lefkímis, Akra *Greece* 39°29N 20°4E **25** B4
Lefkoniko *Cyprus* 35°18N 33°44E **25** D12
Lefroy *Canada* 44°16N 79°34W **82** B5
Lefroy, L. *Australia* 31°21S 121°40E **61** F3
Leganés *Spain* 40°19N 3°45W **21** B4
Legazpi *Phil.* 13°10N 123°45E **37** B6
Legendre I. *Australia* 20°22S 116°55E **60** D2
Leghorn = Livorno *Italy* 43°33N 10°19E **22** C4
Legionowo *Poland* 52°25N 20°50E **17** B11
Legnago *Italy* 45°11N 11°18E **22** B4
Legnica *Poland* 51°12N 16°10E **16** C9
Leh *India* 34°9N 77°35E **43** B7
Lehigh Acres *U.S.A.* 26°36N 81°39W **85** H14
Lehighton *U.S.A.* 40°50N 75°43W **83** F9
Lehututu *Botswana* 23°54S 21°55E **56** C3
Leiah *Pakistan* 30°58N 70°58E **42** D4
Leicester *U.K.* 52°38N 1°8W **13** E6
Leicester City □ *U.K.* 52°38N 1°9W **13** E6
Leicestershire □ *U.K.* 52°41N 1°17W **13** E6
Leichhardt → *Australia* 17°35S 139°48E **62** B2
Leichhardt Ra. *Australia* 20°46S 147°40E **62** C4
Leiden *Neths.* 52°9N 4°30E **15** B4
Leie → *Belgium* 51°2N 3°45E **15** C3
Leimus *Nic.* 14°40N 84°3W **88** D3
Leine → *Germany* 52°43N 9°36E **16** B5
Leinster *Australia* 27°51S 120°36E **61** E3
Leinster □ *Ireland* 53°3N 7°8W **10** C4
Leinster, Mt. *Ireland* 52°37N 6°46W **10** D5
Leipzig *Germany* 51°18N 12°22E **16** C7
Leiria *Portugal* 39°46N 8°53W **21** C1
Leirvik *Norway* 59°47N 5°28E **9** G11
Leisler, Mt. *Australia* 23°23S 129°20E **60** D4
Leith *U.K.* 55°59N 3°11W **11** F5
Leith Hill *U.K.* 51°11N 0°22W **13** F7
Leitir Ceanainn = Letterkenny
  Ireland 54°57N 7°45W **10** B4
Leitrim *Ireland* 54°0N 8°5W **10** B3
Leitrim □ *Ireland* 54°8N 8°0W **10** B4
Leizhou Bandao *China* 21°0N 110°0E **33** D6
Lek → *Neths.* 51°54N 4°35E **15** C4
Leka *Norway* 65°5N 11°35E **8** D14
Leland *Mich., U.S.A.* 45°1N 85°45W **81** C11
Leland *Miss., U.S.A.* 33°24N 90°54W **85** E9
Leleque *Argentina* 42°28S 71°0W **96** E2
Lelystad *Neths.* 52°30N 5°25E **15** B5
Léman, L. *Europe* 46°26N 6°30E **20** C7
Lembar *Indonesia* 8°45S 116°4E **37** K19
Lembuak *Indonesia* 8°36S 116°11E **37** K19
Lemera
  Dem. Rep. of the Congo 3°0S 28°55E **54** C2
Lemhi Ra. *U.S.A.* 44°0N 113°0W **76** D7
Lemmer *Neths.* 52°51N 5°43E **15** B5
Lemmon *U.S.A.* 45°57N 102°10W **80** C2
Lemon Grove *U.S.A.* 32°45N 117°1W **79** N9
Lemoore *U.S.A.* 36°18N 119°46W **78** J7
Lemvig *Denmark* 56°33N 8°20E **9** H13
Lena → *Russia* 72°52N 126°40E **29** B13
Lenadoon Pt. *Ireland* 54°18N 9°3W **10** B2
Lenggong *Malaysia* 5°6N 100°58E **39** K3
Lengua de Vaca, Pta.
  Chile 30°14S 71°38W **94** C1
Lengwe △ *Malawi* 16°14S 34°45E **55** F3
Leninogorsk *Kazakhstan* 50°20N 83°30E **28** D9
Leninsk *Russia* 48°40N 45°15E **19** E8
Leninsk-Kuznetskiy
  Russia 54°44N 86°10E **28** D9
Lenkoran = Länkäran
  Azerbaijan 38°48N 48°52E **45** B6
Lenmalu *Indonesia* 1°45S 130°15E **37** E8

Lennox *U.S.A.* 43°21N 96°53W **80** D5
Lennoxville *Canada* 45°22N 71°51W **83** A13
Lenoir *U.S.A.* 35°55N 81°32W **85** D14
Lenoir City *U.S.A.* 35°48N 84°16W **85** D12
Lenore L. *Canada* 52°30N 104°59W **71** C8
Lenox *U.S.A.* 42°22N 73°17W **83** D11
Lens *France* 50°26N 2°50E **20** A5
Lensk *Russia* 60°48N 114°55E **29** C12
Lentas *Greece* 34°56N 24°56E **25** E6
Lentini *Italy* 37°17N 15°0E **22** F6
Lenwood *U.S.A.* 34°53N 117°7W **79** L9
Lenya *Burma* 11°33N 98°57E **39** G2
Leoben *Austria* 47°22N 15°5E **16** E8
Leodhas = Lewis *U.K.* 58°9N 6°40W **11** C2
Leola *U.S.A.* 45°43N 98°56W **80** C4
Leominster *U.K.* 52°14N 2°43W **13** E5
Leominster *U.S.A.* 42°32N 71°46W **83** D13
León *Mexico* 21°6N 101°41W **86** C4
León *Nic.* 12°20N 86°51W **88** D2
León *Spain* 42°38N 5°34W **21** A3
León *U.S.A.* 40°44N 93°45W **80** E7
Leon → *U.S.A.* 31°14N 97°28W **84** F6
León, Montes de *Spain* 42°30N 6°18W **21** A2
Leonardtown *U.S.A.* 38°17N 76°38W **81** F15
Leonardville *Namibia* 23°29S 18°49E **56** C2
Leone, Amer. Samoa* 14°23S 170°48W **59** b
Leongatha *Australia* 38°30S 145°58E **63** F4
Leonora *Australia* 28°49S 121°19E **61** E3
Leopoldina *Brazil* 21°28S 42°40W **95** A7
Leopoldsburg *Belgium* 51°7N 5°13E **15** C5
Leoti *U.S.A.* 38°29N 101°21W **80** F3
Leova *Moldova* 46°28N 28°15E **17** E15
Leoville *Canada* 53°39N 107°33W **71** C7
Lepel = Lyepyel *Belarus* 54°50N 28°40E **9** J23
Lépo, L. do *Angola* 17°0S 19°0E **56** B2
Leppävirta *Finland* 62°29N 27°46E **8** E22
Leptis Magna *Libya* 32°40N 14°12E **51** B8
Léribe *Lesotho* 28°51S 28°3E **57** D4
Lérida = Lleida *Spain* 41°37N 0°39E **21** B6
Lerwick *U.K.* 60°9N 1°9W **11** A7
Les Cayes *Haiti* 18°15N 73°46W **89** C5
Les Coteaux *Canada* 45°15N 74°13W **83** A10
Les Escoumins *Canada* 48°21N 69°24W **73** C6
Les Sables-d'Olonne
  France 46°30N 1°45W **20** C3
Lesbos *Greece* 39°10N 26°20E **23** E12
Leshan *China* 29°33N 103°41E **32** D5
Leshukonskoye *Russia* 64°54N 45°46E **18** B8
Leshwe →
  Dem. Rep. of the Congo 12°45S 29°30E **55** E2
Leskov I. *Antarctica* 56°0S 28°0W **5** B1
Leskovac *Serbia* 43°0N 21°58E **23** C9
Lesopilnoye *Russia* 46°44N 134°20E **30** A7
Lesotho ■ *Africa* 29°40S 28°0E **57** D4
Lesozavodsk *Russia* 45°30N 133°29E **30** B6
Lesse → *Belgium* 50°15N 4°54E **15** D4
Lesse et Lomme △ *Belgium* 50°8N 5°9E **15** D5
Lesser Antilles *W. Indies* 15°0N 61°0W **89** D7
Lesser Slave L. *Canada* 55°30N 115°25W **70** B5
Lesser Sunda Is. *Indonesia* 8°0S 120°0E **37** F6
Lessines *Belgium* 50°42N 3°50E **15** D3
Lester B. Pearson Int., Toronto ✈
  (YYZ) *Canada* 43°46N 79°35W **82** C5
Lestock *Canada* 51°19N 103°59W **71** C8
Lesuer I. *Australia* 13°50S 127°17E **60** B4
Lesueur △ *Australia* 30°11S 115°10E **61** F2
Lésvos = Lesbos *Greece* 39°10N 26°20E **23** E12
Leszno *Poland* 51°50N 16°30E **17** C9
Letaba *S. Africa* 23°59S 31°50E **57** C5
Letchworth *U.K.* 51°59N 0°13W **13** F7
Lethbridge *Canada* 49°45N 112°45W **70** D6
Lethem *Guyana* 3°20N 59°50W **92** C7
Leti, Kepulauan *Indonesia* 8°10S 128°0E **37** F7
Leti Is. = Leti, Kepulauan
  Indonesia 8°10S 128°0E **37** F7
Letiahau → *Botswana* 21°16S 24°0E **56** C3
Leticia *Colombia* 4°9S 70°0W **92** D5
Leting *China* 39°23N 118°55E **35** E10
Letjiesbos *S. Africa* 32°34S 22°16E **56** E3
Letlhakane *Botswana* 21°27S 25°30E **56** C4
Letlhakeng *Botswana* 24°0S 24°59E **56** C3
Letpadan *Burma* 17°45N 95°45E **41** L19
Letpan *Burma* 19°28N 94°10E **41** K19
Letsôk-aw Kyun *Burma* 11°30N 98°25E **39** G2
Letterkenny *Ireland* 54°57N 7°45W **10** B4
Leucadia *U.S.A.* 33°4N 117°18W **79** M9
Leuchars *U.K.* 56°24N 2°53W **11** E6
Leuser, G. *Indonesia* 3°46N 97°12E **36** D1
Leuven *Belgium* 50°52N 4°42E **15** D4
Leuze-en-Hainaut
  Belgium 50°36N 3°37E **15** D3
Levanger *Norway* 63°45N 11°19E **8** E14
Levelland *U.S.A.* 33°35N 102°23W **84** E3
Leven *U.K.* 56°12N 3°0W **11** E6
Leven, L. *U.K.* 56°12N 3°22W **11** E5
Leven, Toraka *Madag.* 12°30S 47°45E **57** A8
Levin *N.Z.* 40°37S 175°18E **59** D5
Lévis *Canada* 46°48N 71°9W **73** C5
Levis, L. *Canada* 62°37N 117°58W **70** A5
Levittown *N.Y., U.S.A.* 40°44N 73°31W **83** F11
Levittown *Pa., U.S.A.* 40°9N 74°51W **83** F10
Levka Oros *Greece* 35°18N 24°3E **25** D6
Levkás = Lefkada *Greece* 38°40N 20°43E **23** E9
Levkôsia = Nicosia
  Cyprus 35°10N 33°25E **25** D12
Levski grad = Karlovo
  Bulgaria 42°38N 24°47E **23** C11
Levuka *Fiji* 17°34S 179°0E **59** a
Lewes *U.K.* 50°52N 0°1E **13** G8
Lewes *U.S.A.* 38°46N 75°9W **81** F16
Lewis *U.K.* 58°9N 6°40W **11** C2
Lewis → *U.S.A.* 45°51N 122°48W **78** E4
Lewis, Butt of *U.K.* 58°31N 6°16W **11** C2
Lewis and Clark △
  U.S.A. 46°8N 123°53W **78** D3
Lewis Ra. *Australia* 20°3S 128°50E **60** D4
Lewis Range *U.S.A.* 48°5N 113°5W **76** B7

Lewis Run *U.S.A.* 41°52N 78°40W **82** E6
Lewisburg *Pa., U.S.A.* 40°58N 76°54W **82** F8
Lewisburg *Tenn., U.S.A.* 35°27N 86°48W **85** D11
Lewisburg *W. Va.,*
  U.S.A. 37°48N 80°27W **81** G13
Lewisporte *Canada* 49°15N 55°3W **73** C8
Lewiston *Idaho, U.S.A.* 46°25N 117°1W **76** C5
Lewiston *Maine, U.S.A.* 44°6N 70°13W **81** C18
Lewiston *N.Y., U.S.A.* 43°11N 79°3W **82** C5
Lewistown *Mont., U.S.A.* 47°4N 109°26W **76** C9
Lewistown *Pa., U.S.A.* 40°36N 77°34W **82** F7
Lexington *Ill., U.S.A.* 40°39N 88°47W **80** E9
Lexington *Ky., U.S.A.* 38°3N 84°30W **81** F11
Lexington *Mich., U.S.A.* 43°16N 82°32W **82** C2
Lexington *Mo., U.S.A.* 39°11N 93°52W **80** F7
Lexington *N.C., U.S.A.* 35°49N 80°15W **85** D14
Lexington *N.Y., U.S.A.* 42°15N 74°22W **83** D10
Lexington *Nebr., U.S.A.* 40°47N 99°45W **80** E4
Lexington *Ohio, U.S.A.* 40°41N 82°35W **82** F2
Lexington *Tenn., U.S.A.* 35°39N 88°24W **85** D10
Lexington *Va., U.S.A.* 37°47N 79°27W **81** G14
Lexington Park *U.S.A.* 38°16N 76°27W **81** F15
Leyburn *U.K.* 54°19N 1°48W **12** C6
Leyland *U.K.* 53°42N 2°43W **12** D5
Leyte □ *Phil.* 11°0N 125°0E **37** B6
Lezhë *Albania* 41°47N 19°39E **23** D8
Lhasa *China* 29°25N 90°58E **32** D4
Lhazê *China* 29°5N 87°38E **32** D3
L'Hermite, I. *Chile* 55°50S 68°0W **96** H3
Lhokkruet *Indonesia* 4°55N 95°24E **36** D1
Lhokseumawe *Indonesia* 5°10N 97°10E **36** C1
L'Hospitalet de Llobregat
  Spain 41°21N 2°6E **21** B7
Li *Thailand* 17°48N 98°57E **38** D2
Li Xian *Gansu, China* 34°10N 105°5E **34** G3
Li Xian *Hebei, China* 38°30N 115°35E **34** E8
Liancourt Rocks = Tokdo
  Asia 37°15N 131°52E **31** F5
Lianga *Phil.* 8°38N 126°6E **37** C7
Liangcheng *Nei Monggol Zizhiqu,*
  China 40°28N 112°25E **34** D7
Liangcheng *Shandong,*
  China 35°32N 119°37E **35** G10
Liangdang *China* 33°56N 106°18E **34** H4
Liangpran *Indonesia* 1°4N 114°23E **36** D4
Lianshanguan *China* 40°53N 123°43E **35** D12
Lianshui *China* 33°42N 119°20E **35** H10
Lianyungang *China* 34°40N 119°11E **35** G10
Liao He → *China* 41°0N 121°50E **35** D11
Liaocheng *China* 36°28N 115°58E **34** F8
Liaodong Bandao *China* 40°0N 122°30E **35** E12
Liaodong Wan *China* 40°20N 121°10E **35** D11
Liaoning □ *China* 41°40N 122°30E **35** D12
Liaotung, G. of = Liaodong Wan
  China 40°20N 121°10E **35** D11
Liaoyang *China* 41°15N 122°58E **35** D12
Liaoyuan *China* 42°58N 125°2E **35** C13
Liaozhong *China* 41°23N 122°50E **35** D12
Liapades *Greece* 39°42N 19°40E **25** A3
Liard → *Canada* 61°51N 121°18W **70** A4
Liard River *Canada* 59°25N 126°5W **70** B3
Liari *Pakistan* 25°37N 66°30E **42** G2
Libau = Liepāja *Latvia* 56°30N 21°0E **9** H19
Libby *U.S.A.* 48°23N 115°33W **76** B6
Libenge
  Dem. Rep. of the Congo 3°40N 18°55E **52** D3
Liberal *U.S.A.* 37°3N 100°55W **80** G3
Liberec *Czech Rep.* 50°47N 15°7E **16** C8
Liberia *Costa Rica* 10°40N 85°30W **88** D2
Liberia ■ *W. Afr.* 6°30N 9°30W **50** G4
Libertador □ *Chile* 34°15S 70°45W **94** C1
Liberty *Mo., U.S.A.* 39°15N 94°25W **80** F6
Liberty *N.Y., U.S.A.* 41°48N 74°45W **83** E10
Liberty *Pa., U.S.A.* 41°34N 77°6W **82** E7
Liberty *Tex., U.S.A.* 30°3N 94°48W **84** F7
Liberty-Newark Int. ✈ (EWR)
  U.S.A. 40°42N 74°10W **83** F10
Lîbîya, Sahrâ' *Africa* 25°0N 25°0E **51** C10
Libobo, Tanjung
  Indonesia 0°54S 128°28E **37** E7
Libode *S. Africa* 31°33S 29°2E **57** E4
Libong, Ko *Thailand* 7°15N 99°23E **39** J2
Libourne *France* 44°55N 0°14W **20** D3
Libramont *Belgium* 49°55N 5°23E **15** E5
Libreville *Gabon* 0°25N 9°26E **52** D1
Libya ■ *N. Afr.* 27°0N 17°0E **51** C9
Libyan Desert = Lîbîya, Sahrâ'
  Africa 25°0N 25°0E **51** C10
Libyan Plateau = Ed Déffa
  Egypt 30°40N 26°30E **51** B11
Licantén *Chile* 35°55S 72°0W **94** D1
Licata *Italy* 37°6N 13°56E **22** F5
Licheng *China* 36°28N 113°20E **34** F7
Lichfield *U.K.* 52°41N 1°49W **13** E6
Lichinga *Mozam.* 13°13S 35°11E **55** E4
Lichtenburg *S. Africa* 26°8S 26°8E **56** D4
Licking → *U.S.A.* 39°6N 84°30W **81** F11
Licungo → *Mozam.* 16°55S 34°30W —
Lida *Belarus* 53°53N 25°15E **17** B13
Lidköping *Sweden* 58°31N 13°7E **9** G15
Liebig, Mt. *Australia* 23°18S 131°22E **60** D5
Liechtenstein ■ *Europe* 47°8N 9°35E **20** C8
Liège *Belgium* 50°38N 5°35E **15** D5
Liège □ *Belgium* 50°32N 5°35E **15** D5
Liegnitz = Legnica
  Poland 51°12N 16°10E **16** C9
Lieksa *Finland* 63°18N 30°2E **8** E24
Lienart
  Dem. Rep. of the Congo 3°3N 25°31E **54** B2
Lienyünchiangshih =
  Lianyungang *China* 34°40N 119°11E **35** G10
Lienz *Austria* 46°50N 12°46E **16** E7
Liepāja *Latvia* 56°30N 21°0E **9** H19
Lier *Belgium* 51°7N 4°34E **15** C4
Lietuva = Lithuania ■
  Europe 55°30N 24°0E **9** J21
Lièvre → *Canada* 45°31N 75°26W **72** C4
Liffey → *Ireland* 53°21N 6°13W **10** C5
Lifford *Ireland* 54°51N 7°29W **10** B4

Lifudzin *Russia* 44°21N 134°58E **30** B7
Lightning Ridge
  Australia 29°22S 148°0E **63** D4
Ligonha → *Mozam.* 16°54S 39°9E **55** F4
Ligonier *U.S.A.* 40°15N 79°14W **82** F5
Liguria □ *Italy* 44°30N 8°50E **20** D8
Ligurian Sea *Medit. S.* 43°20N 9°0E **22** C3
Lihou Reefs and Cays
  Australia 17°25S 151°40E **62** B5
Lihué Calel △ *Argentina* 38°0S 65°10W **94** D2
Lijiang *China* 26°55N 100°20E **32** D5
Likasi
  Dem. Rep. of the Congo 10°55S 26°48E **55** E2
Likoma I. *Malawi* 12°3S 34°45E **55** E3
Likumburu *Tanzania* 9°43S 35°8E **55** D4
L'Île-Rousse *France* 42°38N 8°57E **20** E8
Lille *France* 50°38N 3°3E **20** A5
Lille Bælt *Denmark* 55°20N 9°45E **9** J13
Lillehammer *Norway* 61°8N 10°30E **8** F14
Lillesand *Norway* 58°15N 8°23E **9** G13
Lillian Pt. *Australia* 27°40S 126°6E **61** E4
Lillooet *Canada* 50°44N 121°57W **70** C4
Lillooet → *Canada* 49°15N 121°57W **70** D4
Lilongwe *Malawi* 14°0S 33°48E **55** E3
Liloy *Phil.* 8°4N 122°39E **37** C6
Lim → *Europe* 43°45N 19°15E **23** C8
Lim Chu Kang *Singapore* 1°26N 103°43E **39** d
Lima *Indonesia* 3°39S 127°58E **37** E7
Lima *Peru* 12°3S 77°2W **92** F3
Lima *Mont., U.S.A.* 44°38N 112°36W **76** D7
Lima *N.Y., U.S.A.* 42°54N 77°36W **82** D7
Lima *Ohio, U.S.A.* 40°44N 84°6W **81** E11
Lima → *Portugal* 41°41N 8°50W **21** B1
Liman *Indonesia* 7°48S 111°45E **37** G14
Limassol *Cyprus* 34°42N 33°1E **25** E12
Limavady *U.K.* 55°3N 6°56W **10** A5
Limay → *Argentina* 39°0S 68°0W **96** D3
Limay Mahuida
  Argentina 37°10S 66°45W **94** D2
Limbang *Brunei* 4°42N 115°6E **36** D5
Limbaži *Latvia* 57°31N 24°42E **9** H21
Limbdi *India* 22°34N 71°51E **42** H4
Limbe *Cameroon* 4°1N 9°10E **52** D1
Limburg *Germany* 50°22N 8°4E **16** C5
Limburg □ *Belgium* 51°2N 5°25E **15** C5
Limburg □ *Neths.* 51°20N 5°55E **15** C5
Limeira *Brazil* 22°35S 47°28W **95** A6
Limerick *Ireland* 52°40N 8°37W **10** D3
Limerick *U.S.A.* 43°41N 70°48W **83** C14
Limerick □ *Ireland* 52°30N 8°50W **10** D3
Limestone *U.S.A.* 42°2N 78°38W **82** D6
Limestone → *Canada* 56°31N 94°7W **71** B10
Limfjorden *Denmark* 56°55N 9°0E **9** H13
Limia = Lima → *Portugal* 41°41N 8°50W **21** B1
Limingen *Norway* 64°48N 13°35E **8** D15
Limmen ⊙ *Australia* 15°15S 135°30E **62** B2
Limmen Bight *Australia* 14°40S 135°35E **62** A2
Limmen Bight →
  Australia 15°7S 135°44E **62** B2
Limnos *Greece* 39°50N 25°5E **23** E11
Limoges *Canada* 45°20N 75°16W **83** A9
Limoges *France* 45°50N 1°15E **20** D4
Limón *Costa Rica* 10°0N 83°2W **88** E3
Limon *U.S.A.* 39°16N 103°41W **76** G12
Limousin □ *France* 45°30N 1°30E **20** D4
Limoux *France* 43°4N 2°12E **20** E5
Limpopo □ *S. Africa* 24°5S 29°0E **57** C4
Limpopo → *Africa* 25°5S 33°30E **57** D5
Limuru *Kenya* 1°2S 36°35E **54** C4
Lin Xian *China* 37°57N 110°58E **34** F6
Linares *Chile* 35°50S 71°40W **94** D1
Linares *Mexico* 24°52N 99°34W **87** C5
Linares *Spain* 38°10N 3°40W **21** C4
Lincang *China* 23°58N 100°1E **32** D5
Lincheng *China* 37°25N 114°30E **34** F8
Lincoln = Beamsville
  Canada 43°12N 79°28W **82** C5
Lincoln *Argentina* 34°55S 61°30W **94** C3
Lincoln *N.Z.* 43°38S 172°30E **59** E4
Lincoln *U.K.* 53°14N 0°32W **12** D7
Lincoln *Calif., U.S.A.* 38°54N 121°17W **78** G5
Lincoln *Ill., U.S.A.* 40°9N 89°22W **80** E9
Lincoln *Kans., U.S.A.* 39°3N 98°9W **80** F4
Lincoln *Maine, U.S.A.* 45°22N 68°30W **81** C19
Lincoln *N.H., U.S.A.* 44°3N 71°40W **83** B13
Lincoln *N. Mex.,
  U.S.A.* 33°30N 105°23W **77** K11
Lincoln *Nebr., U.S.A.* 40°49N 96°41W **80** E6
Lincoln City *U.S.A.* 44°57N 124°1W **76** D1
Lincoln Hav = Lincoln Sea
  Arctic 84°0N 55°0W **69** A21
Lincoln Sea *Arctic* 84°0N 55°0W **69** A21
Lincolnshire □ *U.K.* 53°14N 0°32W **12** D7
Lincolnshire Wolds *U.K.* 53°26N 0°13W **12** D7
Lincolnton *U.S.A.* 35°29N 81°16W **85** D14
Lind *U.S.A.* 46°58N 118°37W **76** C4
Linda *U.S.A.* 39°8N 121°34W **78** F5
Lindeman I. *Australia* 20°27S 149°3E **62** b
Lindeman Islands △
  Australia 20°28S 149°5E **62** b
Linden *Guyana* 6°0N 58°10W **92** B7
Linden *Ala., U.S.A.* 32°18N 87°48W **85** E11
Linden *Calif., U.S.A.* 38°1N 121°5W **78** G5
Linden *Tex., U.S.A.* 33°1N 94°22W **84** E7
Lindenhurst *U.S.A.* 40°41N 73°23W **83** F11
Lindesnes *Norway* 57°58N 7°3E **9** H12
Lindi *Tanzania* 9°58S 39°38E **55** D4
Lindi □ *Tanzania* 9°40S 38°30E **55** D4
Lindi →
  Dem. Rep. of the Congo 0°33N 25°5E **54** B2
Lindley *U.S.A.* 42°1N 77°8W **82** D7
Lindos *Greece* 36°6N 28°10E **25** C10
Lindos, Akra *Greece* 36°4N 28°10E **25** C10
Lindsay *Canada* 44°22N 78°43W **82** B6
Lindsay *Calif., U.S.A.* 36°12N 119°5W **78** J7
Lindsay *Okla., U.S.A.* 34°50N 97°38W **84** D6
Lindsborg *U.S.A.* 38°35N 97°40W **80** F5
Line Islands *Pac. Oc.* 7°0N 160°0W **65** H12
Linesville *U.S.A.* 41°39N 80°26W **82** E4

Linfen *China* 36°3N 111°30E **34** F6
Ling Xian *China* 37°22N 116°30E **34** F9
Lingao *China* 19°56N 109°42E **38** C7
Lingayen *Phil.* 16°1N 120°14E **37** A6
Lingayen G. *Phil.* 16°10N 120°15E **37** A6
Lingbi *China* 33°33N 117°33E **35** H9
Lingchuan *China* 25°45N 113°12E **34** G7
Lingding Yang *China* 22°25N 113°44E **33** G10
Lingen *Germany* 52°31N 7°19E **16** B4
Lingga *Indonesia* 0°12S 104°37E **36** E2
Lingga, Kepulauan
  Indonesia 0°10S 104°30E **36** E2
Lingga Arch. = Lingga,
  Kepulauan *Indonesia* 0°10S 104°30E **36** E2
Lingle *U.S.A.* 42°8N 104°21W **76** E11
Lingqiu *China* 39°28N 114°22E **34** E8
Lingshi *China* 36°48N 111°48E **34** F6
Lingshou *China* 38°20N 114°20E **34** E8
Lingshui *China* 18°27N 110°0E **38** C8
Lingtai *China* 35°0N 107°40E **34** G4
Linguère *Senegal* 15°25N 15°5W **50** E2
Lingwu *China* 38°6N 106°20E **34** E4
Lingyuan *China* 41°10N 119°15E **35** D10
Linhai *China* 28°50N 121°8E **33** D7
Linhares *Brazil* 19°25S 40°4W **93** G10
Linhe *China* 40°48N 107°20E **34** D4
Linjiang *China* 41°50N 127°0E **35** D14
Linkou *China* 45°15N 130°18E **35** B16
Linköping *Sweden* 58°28N 15°36E **9** G16
Linnhe, L. *U.K.* 56°36N 5°25W **11** E3
Linosa *Medit. S.* 35°51N 12°50E **22** G5
Linqi *China* 35°45N 113°52E **34** G7
Linqing *China* 36°50N 115°42E **34** F8
Linqu *China* 36°25N 118°30E **35** F10
Linru *China* 34°11N 112°52E **34** G7
Lins *Brazil* 21°40S 49°44W **95** A6
Linstead *Jamaica* 18°8N 77°2W **88** a
Linta → *Madag.* 25°2S 44°5E **57** D7
Linton *Ind., U.S.A.* 39°2N 87°10W **80** F10
Linton *N. Dak., U.S.A.* 46°16N 100°14W **80** B3
Lintong *China* 34°20N 109°10E **34** G5
Linwood *Canada* 43°35N 80°43W **82** C4
Linxi *China* 43°36N 118°2E **35** C10
Linxia *China* 35°36N 103°10E **32** C5
Linyanti → *Africa* 17°50S 25°5E **56** B4
Linyi *China* 35°5N 118°21E **35** G10
Linz *Austria* 48°18N 14°18E **16** D8
Linzhenzhen *China* 36°30N 109°59E **34** F5
Linzi *China* 36°50N 118°20E **35** F10
Lion, G. du *France* 43°10N 4°0E **20** E6
Lionárisso *Cyprus* 35°28N 34°8E **25** D13
Lions, G. of = Lion, G. du
  France 43°10N 4°0E **20** E6
Lion's Den *Zimbabwe* 17°15S 30°5E **55** F3
Lion's Head *Canada* 44°58N 81°15W **82** B3
Lipa *Phil.* 13°57N 121°10E **37** B6
Lipali *Mozam.* 15°50S 35°50E **55** F4
Lípari *Italy* 38°26N 14°58E **22** E6
Lípari, Is. = Eólie, Ís.
  Italy 38°30N 14°57E **22** E6
Lipcani *Moldova* 48°14N 26°48E **17** D14
Liperi *Finland* 62°31N 29°24E **8** E23
Lipetsk *Russia* 52°37N 39°35E **18** D6
Lipkany = Lipcani
  Moldova 48°14N 26°48E **17** D14
Lipovets *Ukraine* 49°12N 29°1E **17** D15
Lippe → *Germany* 51°39N 6°36E **16** C4
Lipscomb *U.S.A.* 36°14N 100°16W **84** C4
Liptrap, C. *Australia* 38°50S 145°55E **63** F4
Lira *Uganda* 2°17N 32°57E **54** B3
Liria = Lliria *Spain* 39°37N 0°35W **21** C5
Lisala
  Dem. Rep. of the Congo 2°12N 21°38E **52** D4
Lisboa *Portugal* 38°42N 9°8W **21** C1
Lisbon = Lisboa *Portugal* 38°42N 9°8W **21** C1
Lisbon *N. Dak., U.S.A.* 46°27N 97°41W **80** B5
Lisbon *N.H., U.S.A.* 44°13N 71°55W **83** B13
Lisbon *N.Y., U.S.A.* 44°43N 75°19W **83** B9
Lisbon *Ohio, U.S.A.* 40°46N 80°46W **82** F4
Lisbon Falls *U.S.A.* 44°0N 70°4W **81** D18
Lisburn *U.K.* 54°31N 6°3W **10** B5
Lisburne, C. *U.S.A.* 68°53N 166°13W **74** B6
Liscannor B. *Ireland* 52°55N 9°24W **10** D2
Lisdoonvarna *Ireland* 53°2N 9°18W **10** C2
Lishi *China* 37°31N 111°8E **34** F6
Lishu *China* 43°20N 124°18E **35** C13
Lisianski I. *U.S.A.* 26°2N 174°0W **75** K5
Lisichansk = Lysychansk
  Ukraine 48°55N 38°30E **19** E6
Lisieux *France* 49°10N 0°12E **20** B4
Liski *Russia* 51°3N 39°30E **19** D6
Lismore *Australia* 28°44S 153°21E **63** D5
Lismore *Ireland* 52°8N 7°55W **10** D4
Lista *Norway* 58°7N 6°39E **9** G12
Lister, Mt. *Antarctica* 78°0S 162°0E **5** D11
Liston *Australia* 28°39S 152°6E **63** D5
Listowel *Canada* 43°44N 80°58W **82** C4
Listowel *Ireland* 52°27N 9°29W **10** D2
Litani → *Lebanon* 33°20N 35°15E **46** B4
Litchfield *Calif., U.S.A.* 40°24N 120°23W **78** F6
Litchfield *Conn., U.S.A.* 41°45N 73°11W **83** E11
Litchfield *Ill., U.S.A.* 39°11N 89°39W **80** F9
Litchfield *Minn., U.S.A.* 45°8N 94°32W **80** C7
Litchfield △ *Australia* 13°14S 131°1E **60** B5
Lithgow *Australia* 33°25S 150°8E **63** E5
Lithino, Ákra *Greece* 34°55N 24°44E **25** E7
Lithuania ■ *Europe* 55°30N 24°0E **9** J21
Lititz *U.S.A.* 40°9N 76°18W **83** F8
Litoměřice *Czech Rep.* 50°33N 14°10E **16** C8
Little Abaco *Bahamas* 26°50N 77°30W **88** A4
Little Barrier I. *N.Z.* 36°12S 175°8E **59** B5
Little Belt Mts. *U.S.A.* 46°40N 110°45W **76** C8
Little Bighorn Battlefield △
  U.S.A. 45°34N 107°25W **76** D10
Little Blue → *U.S.A.* 39°42N 96°41W **80** F5
Little Buffalo → *Canada* 61°0N 113°46W **70** A6
Little Cayman *Cayman Is.* 19°41N 80°3W **88** C3
Little Churchill →
  Canada 57°30N 95°22W **71** B9

Little Colorado →
  U.S.A. 36°12N 111°48W **77** H8
Little Current *Canada* 45°55N 82°0W **72** C3
Little Current → *Canada* 50°57N 84°36W **72** B3
Little Diomede I.
  U.S.A. 65°45N 168°56W **74** B6
Little Falls *Minn., U.S.A.* 45°59N 94°22W **80** C6
Little Falls *N.Y., U.S.A.* 43°3N 74°51W **83** C10
Little Fork → *U.S.A.* 48°31N 93°35W **80** A7
Little Grand Rapids
  Canada 52°0N 95°29W **71** C9
Little Humboldt →
  U.S.A. 41°1N 117°43W **76** F5
Little Inagua I. *Bahamas* 21°40N 73°50W **89** B5
Little Karoo *S. Africa* 33°45S 21°0E **56** E3
Little Khingan Mts. = Xiao
  Hinggan Ling *China* 49°0N 127°0E **33** B7
Little Lake *U.S.A.* 35°56N 117°55W **79** K9
Little Laut Is. = Laut Kecil,
  Kepulauan *Indonesia* 4°45S 115°40E **36** E5
Little Mecatina = Petit-
  Mécatina → *Canada* 50°40N 59°30W **73** B8
Little Minch *U.K.* 57°35N 6°45W **11** D2
Little Missouri →
  U.S.A. 47°36N 102°25W **80** B2
Little Ouse → *U.K.* 52°22N 1°12E **13** E9
Little Rann *India* 23°25N 71°25E **42** H4
Little Red → *U.S.A.* 35°11N 91°27W **84** D9
Little River *N.Z.* 43°45S 172°49E **59** E4
Little Rock *U.S.A.* 34°45N 92°17W **84** D8
Little Ruaha → *Tanzania* 7°57S 37°53E **54** D4
Little Sable Pt. *U.S.A.* 43°38N 86°33W **80** D10
Little Sioux → *U.S.A.* 41°48N 96°4W **80** E5
Little Smoky →
  Canada 54°44N 117°11W **70** C5
Little Snake → *U.S.A.* 40°27N 108°26W **76** F9
Little Tobago
  Trin. & Tob. 11°18N 60°30W **93** J16
Little Valley *U.S.A.* 42°15N 78°48W **82** D6
Little Wabash → *U.S.A.* 37°55N 88°5W **80** G9
Little White → *U.S.A.* 43°40N 100°40W **80** D3
Little Zab = Zāb aş Şaghīr →
  Iraq 35°17N 43°29E **44** C4
Littlefield *U.S.A.* 33°55N 102°20W **84** E3
Littlehampton *U.K.* 50°49N 0°32W **13** G7
Littleton *U.S.A.* 44°18N 71°46W **83** B13
Liu He → *China* 40°55N 121°35E **35** D11
Liuba *China* 33°38N 106°55E **34** H4
Liugou *China* 40°57N 118°15E **35** D10
Liuhe *China* 42°17N 125°43E **35** C13
Liukang Tenggaja = Sabalana,
  Kepulauan *Indonesia* 6°45S 118°50E **37** F5
Liuli *Tanzania* 11°3S 34°38E **55** E3
Liupanshui *China* 26°38N 104°48E **32** D5
Liuzhou *China* 24°22N 109°22E **33** D5
Liuzhuang *China* 33°12N 120°18E **35** H11
Livadhia *Cyprus* 34°57N 33°38E **25** E12
Livadia *Greece* 38°27N 22°54E **23** E10
Live Oak *Calif., U.S.A.* 39°17N 121°40W **78** F5
Live Oak *Fla., U.S.A.* 30°18N 82°59W **85** F13
Lively *Canada* 46°26N 81°9W **81** B13
Livermore *U.S.A.* 37°41N 121°47W **78** H5
Livermore, Mt. *U.S.A.* 30°38N 104°11W **84** F2
Livermore Falls *U.S.A.* 44°29N 70°11W **81** C18
Liverpool *Australia* 33°54S 150°58E **63** B5
Liverpool *Canada* 44°5N 64°41W **73** D7
Liverpool *U.K.* 53°25N 3°0W **12** D4
Liverpool *U.S.A.* 43°6N 76°13W **83** C8
Liverpool Bay *U.K.* 53°30N 3°20W **12** D4
Liverpool Ra. *Australia* 31°50S 150°30E **63** E5
Livingston *Guatemala* 15°50N 88°50W **88** C2
Livingston *U.K.* 55°54N 3°30W **11** F5
Livingston *Ala., U.S.A.* 32°35N 88°11W **85** E10
Livingston *Calif., U.S.A.* 37°23N 120°43W **78** H6
Livingston *Mont.,
  U.S.A.* 45°40N 110°34W **76** D8
Livingston *S.C., U.S.A.* 33°38N 81°7W **85** E14
Livingston *Tenn.,
  U.S.A.* 36°23N 85°19W **85** C12
Livingston *Tex., U.S.A.* 30°43N 94°56W **84** F7
Livingston, L. *U.S.A.* 30°50N 95°10W **84** F7
Livingston Manor
  U.S.A. 41°54N 74°50W **83** E10
Livingstone *Zambia* 17°46S 25°52E **55** F2
Livingstone Mts. *Tanzania* 9°40S 34°20E **55** D3
Livingstonia *Malawi* 10°38S 34°5E **55** E3
Livny *Russia* 52°30N 37°30E **18** D6
Livonia *Mich., U.S.A.* 42°23N 83°23W **81** D12
Livonia *N.Y., U.S.A.* 42°49N 77°40W **82** D7
Livorno *Italy* 43°33N 10°19E **22** C4
Livramento *Brazil* 30°55S 55°30W **95** C4
Liwale *Tanzania* 9°48S 37°58E **55** D4
Liwonde *Malawi* 15°4S 35°13E **55** F4
Liwonde △ *Malawi* 14°48S 35°20E **55** E4
Lizard I. *Australia* 14°42S 145°30E **62** A4
Lizard Pt. *U.K.* 49°57N 5°13W **13** H2
Ljubljana *Slovenia* 46°4N 14°33E **16** E8
Ljungan → *Sweden* 62°18N 17°23E **8** E17
Ljungby *Sweden* 56°49N 13°55E **9** H15
Ljusdal *Sweden* 61°46N 16°3E **8** F17
Ljusnan → *Sweden* 61°12N 17°8E **8** F17
Ljusne *Sweden* 61°13N 17°7E **8** F17
Llancanelo, Salina
  Argentina 35°40S 69°8W **94** D2
Llandeilo *U.K.* 51°53N 3°59W **13** F4
Llandovery *U.K.* 51°59N 3°48W **13** F4
Llandrindod Wells *U.K.* 52°14N 3°22W **13** E4
Llandudno *U.K.* 53°19N 3°50W **12** D4
Llanelli *U.K.* 51°41N 4°10W **13** F3
Llanes *Spain* 43°25N 4°50W **21** A3
Llangollen *U.K.* 52°58N 3°11W **12** E4
Llanidloes *U.K.* 52°27N 3°31W **13** E4
Llano *U.S.A.* 30°45N 98°41W **84** F5
Llano → *U.S.A.* 30°39N 98°26W **84** F5
Llano Estacado *U.S.A.* 33°30N 103°0W **84** E3
Llanos *S. Amer.* 5°0N 71°35W **92** C4
Llanos de Challe △ *Chile* 28°8S 71°1W **94** B1

Llanquihue, L. *Chile* 41°10S 72°50W **96** E1
Llanwrtyd Wells *U.K.* 52°7N 3°38W **13** E4
Llebeig, C. des *Spain* 39°33N 2°18E **24** B9
Lleida *Spain* 41°37N 0°39E **21** B6
Llentrisca, C. *Spain* 38°52N 1°15E **24** C7
Llera de Canales *Mexico* 23°19N 99°1W **87** C5
Lleyn Peninsula *U.K.* 52°51N 4°36W **12** E3
Llico *Chile* 34°46S 72°5W **94** C1
Lliria *Spain* 39°37N 0°35W **21** C5
Llobregat → *Spain* 41°19N 2°5E **21** B7
Lloret de Mar *Spain* 41°41N 2°53E **21** B7
Lloseta *Spain* 39°43N 2°52E **24** B9
Lloyd B. *Australia* 12°45S 143°27E **62** A3
Lloyd L. *Canada* 57°22N 108°57W **71** B7
Lloydminster *Canada* 53°17N 110°0W **71** C7
Llubí *Spain* 39°42N 3°0E **24** B10
Llucmajor *Spain* 39°29N 2°53E **24** B9
Llullaillaco, Volcán
  S. Amer. 24°43S 68°30W **94** A2
Llullaillaco △ *Chile* 24°50S 68°51W **94** A2
Lo → *Vietnam* 21°18N 105°25E **38** B5
Loa *U.S.A.* 38°24N 111°39W **76** G8
Loa → *Chile* 21°26S 70°41W **94** A1
Loaita I. *S. China Sea* 10°41N 114°25E **36** B4
Loange →
  Dem. Rep. of the Congo 4°17S 20°2E **52** E4
Lobatse *Botswana* 25°12S 25°40E **56** D4
Loberia *Argentina* 38°10S 58°40W **94** D4
Lobito *Angola* 12°18S 13°35E **53** G2
Lobos *Argentina* 35°10S 59°0W **94** D4
Lobos, I. *Mexico* 27°20N 110°36W **86** B2
Lobos, I. de *Canary Is.* 28°45N 13°50W **24** F6
Loc Binh *Vietnam* 21°46N 106°54E **38** B6
Loc Ninh *Vietnam* 11°50N 106°34E **39** G6
Locarno *Switz.* 46°10N 8°47E **20** C8
Loch Baghasdail = Lochboisdale
  U.K. 57°9N 7°20W **11** D1
Loch Garman = Wexford
  Ireland 52°20N 6°28W **10** D5
Loch Lomond and the
  Trossachs △ *U.K.* 56°10N 4°40W **11** E4
Loch Nam Madaidh = Lochmaddy
  U.K. 57°36N 7°10W **11** D1
Lochaber *U.K.* 56°59N 5°1W **11** E3
Locharbriggs *U.K.* 55°7N 3°35W **11** F5
Lochboisdale *U.K.* 57°9N 7°20W **11** D1
Loche, L. La *Canada* 56°30N 109°30W **71** B7
Lochem *Neths.* 52°9N 6°26E **15** B6
Loches *France* 47°7N 1°0E **20** C4
Lochgilphead *U.K.* 56°2N 5°26W **11** E3
Lochinvar △ *Zambia* 15°55N 27°15E **55** F2
Lochinver *U.K.* 58°9N 5°14W **11** C3
Lochmaddy *U.K.* 57°36N 7°10W **11** D1
Lochnagar *Australia* 23°33S 145°38E **62** C4
Lochnagar *U.K.* 56°57N 3°15W **11** E5
Lochy, L. *U.K.* 57°0N 4°53W **11** E4
Lock *Australia* 33°34S 135°46E **63** E2
Lock Haven *U.S.A.* 41°8N 77°28W **82** E7
Lockeford *U.S.A.* 38°10N 121°9W **78** G5
Lockeport *Canada* 43°47N 65°4W **73** D6
Lockerbie *U.K.* 55°7N 3°21W **11** F5
Lockhart *U.S.A.* 29°53N 97°40W **84** G6
Lockhart, L. *Australia* 33°15S 119°3E **61** F2
Lockhart River
  Australia 12°58S 143°30E **62** A3
Lockhart River ⊙
  Australia 12°47S 143°20E **62** A3
Lockney *U.S.A.* 34°7N 101°27W **84** D4
Lockport *U.S.A.* 43°10N 78°42W **82** C6
Lod *Israel* 31°57N 34°54E **46** D3
Lodeinoye Pole *Russia* 60°44N 33°33E **18** B5
Lodge Bay *Canada* 52°14N 55°51W **73** B8
Lodge Grass *U.S.A.* 45°19N 107°22W **76** D10
Lodhran *Pakistan* 29°32N 71°30E **42** E4
Lodi *Italy* 45°19N 9°30E **20** D8
Lodi *Calif., U.S.A.* 38°8N 121°16W **78** G5
Lodi *Ohio, U.S.A.* 41°2N 82°1W **82** E3
Lodja
  Dem. Rep. of the Congo 3°30S 23°23E **54** C1
Lodwar *Kenya* 3°7N 35°36E **54** B4
Łódź *Poland* 51°45N 19°27E **17** C10
Loei *Thailand* 17°29N 101°35E **38** D3
Loengo
  Dem. Rep. of the Congo 4°48S 26°30E **54** C2
Loeriesfontein *S. Africa* 31°0S 19°26E **56** E2
Lofoten *Norway* 68°30N 13°59E **8** B16
Logan *Iowa, U.S.A.* 41°39N 95°47W **80** E6
Logan *Ohio, U.S.A.* 39°32N 82°25W **81** F12
Logan *Utah, U.S.A.* 41°44N 111°50W **76** F8
Logan *W. Va., U.S.A.* 37°51N 81°59W **81** G13
Logan, Mt. *Canada* 60°34N 140°23W **68** E3
Logandale *U.S.A.* 36°36N 114°29W **79** J12
Logansport *Ind., U.S.A.* 40°45N 86°22W **80** E10
Logansport *La., U.S.A.* 31°58N 94°0W **84** F8
Logone → *Chad* 12°6N 15°2E **51** F9
Logroño *Spain* 42°28N 2°27W **21** A4
Lohardaga *India* 23°27N 84°45E **43** H11
Loharia *India* 23°45N 74°14E **42** H6
Loharu *India* 28°27N 75°49E **42** E6
Lohri Wah → *Pakistan* 27°27N 67°37E **42** F2
Loi-kaw *Burma* 19°40N 97°17E **41** K20
Loimaa *Finland* 60°50N 23°5E **8** F20
Loir → *France* 47°33N 0°32W **20** C3
Loire → *France* 47°16N 2°10W **20** C2
Loja *Ecuador* 3°59S 79°16W **92** D3
Loja *Spain* 37°10N 4°10W **21** D3
Loji = Kawasi *Indonesia* 1°38S 127°28E **37** E7
Lokandu
  Dem. Rep. of the Congo 2°30S 25°45E **54** C2
Lokeren *Belgium* 51°6N 3°59E **15** C3
Lokgwabe *Botswana* 24°10S 21°50E **56** C3
Lokichar *Kenya* 2°23N 35°39E **54** B4
Lokichokio *Kenya* 4°19N 34°13E **54** B3
Lokitaung *Kenya* 4°12N 35°48E **54** B4
Lokkan tekojärvi
  Finland 67°55N 27°35E **8** C22
Lokoja *Nigeria* 7°47N 6°45E **50** G7
Lokolo →
  Dem. Rep. of the Congo 1°43S 18°23E **52** E3

Lola, Mt. *U.S.A.* 39°26N 120°22W **78** F6
Lolgorien *Kenya* 1°14S 34°48E **54** C3
Loliondo *Tanzania* 2°2S 35°39E **54** C4
Lolland *Denmark* 54°45N 11°30E **9** J14
Lolo *U.S.A.* 46°45N 114°5W **76** C6
Lom *Bulgaria* 43°48N 23°12E **23** C10
Lom Kao *Thailand* 16°53N 101°14E **38** D3
Lom Sak *Thailand* 16°47N 101°15E **38** D3
Loma *U.S.A.* 47°56N 110°30W **76** C8
Loma Linda *U.S.A.* 34°3N 117°16W **79** L9
Lomaloma *Fiji* 17°17S 178°59W **59** a
Lomami →
  Dem. Rep. of the Congo 0°46N 24°16E **54** B1
Lomas de Zamora
  Argentina 34°45S 58°24W **94** C4
Lombadina *Australia* 16°31S 122°54E **60** C3
Lombárdia □ *Italy* 45°40N 9°30E **20** D8
Lombardy = Lombárdia □
  Italy 45°40N 9°30E **20** D8
Lomblen *Indonesia* 8°30S 123°32E **37** F6
Lombok *Indonesia* 8°45S 116°30E **37** F5
Lombok, Selat *Indonesia* 8°30S 115°50E **37** K18
Lomé *Togo* 6°9N 1°20E **50** G6
Lomela
  Dem. Rep. of the Congo 2°19S 23°15E **52** E4
Lomela →
  Dem. Rep. of the Congo 0°15S 20°40E **52** E4
Lommel *Belgium* 51°14N 5°19E **15** C5
Lomond *Canada* 50°24N 112°36W **70** C6
Lomond, L. *U.K.* 56°8N 4°38W **11** E4
Lomonosov Ridge *Arctic* 88°0N 140°0E **4** A
Lomphat *Cambodia* 13°30N 106°59E **38** F6
Lompobatang *Indonesia* 5°24S 119°56E **37** F5
Lompoc *U.S.A.* 34°38N 120°28W **79** L6
Lomża *Poland* 53°10N 22°2E **17** B12
Lon, Ko *Thailand* 7°47N 98°23E **39** a
Loncoche *Chile* 39°20S 72°50W **96** D2
Londa *India* 15°30N 74°30E **40** M9
Londiani *Kenya* 0°10S 35°33E **54** C4
London *Canada* 42°59N 81°15W **82** D3
London *U.K.* 51°30N 0°3W **13** F7
London *Ky., U.S.A.* 37°8N 84°5W **81** G11
London *Ohio, U.S.A.* 39°53N 83°27W **81** F12
London, Greater □ *U.K.* 51°36N 0°5W **13** F7
London Gatwick ✈ (LGW)
  U.K. 51°10N 0°11W **13** F7
London Heathrow ✈ (LHR)
  U.K. 51°28N 0°27W **13** F7
London Stansted ✈ (STN)
  U.K. 51°54N 0°14E **13** F8
Londonderry *U.K.* 55°0N 7°20W **10** B4
Londonderry □ *U.K.* 55°0N 7°20W **10** B4
Londonderry, C.
  Australia 13°45S 126°55E **60** B4
Londonderry, I. *Chile* 55°0S 71°0W **96** H2
Londres *Argentina* 27°43S 67°7W **96** B3
Londrina *Brazil* 23°18S 51°10W **95** A5
Lone Pine *U.S.A.* 36°36N 118°4W **78** J8
Lonely Mine *Zimbabwe* 19°30S 28°49E **55** F2
Long B. *U.S.A.* 33°35S 78°45W **85** E15
Long Beach *Calif.,
  U.S.A.* 33°46N 118°11W **79** M8
Long Beach *N.Y.,
  U.S.A.* 40°35N 73°39W **83** F11
Long Beach *Wash.,
  U.S.A.* 46°21N 124°3W **78** D2
Long Branch *U.S.A.* 40°18N 74°0W **83** F11
Long Creek *U.S.A.* 44°43N 119°6W **76** D4
Long Eaton *U.K.* 52°53N 1°15E **12** E6
Long I. *Australia* 20°22S 148°51E **62** b
Long I. *Bahamas* 23°20N 75°10W **89** B4
Long I. *Canada* 54°50N 79°20W **72** B4
Long I. *Ireland* 51°30N 9°34W **10** E2
Long I. *U.S.A.* 40°45N 73°30W **83** F11
Long Island Sd. *U.S.A.* 41°10N 73°0W **83** E12
Long L. *Canada* 49°30N 86°50W **72** C2
Long Lake *U.S.A.* 43°58N 74°25W **83** C10
Long Point *Canada* 42°34N 80°25W **82** D4
Long Point B. *Canada* 42°40N 80°10W **82** D4
Long Prairie *U.S.A.* 45°59N 94°52W **80** C6
Long Prairie → *U.S.A.* 46°20N 94°36W **80** B6
Long Pt. *Ont., Canada* 42°35N 80°2W **82** D4
Long Pt. *Ont., Canada* 43°56N 76°53W **83** C8
Long Range Mts.
  Canada 49°30N 57°30W **73** C8
Long Reef *Australia* 14°1S 125°48E **60** B4
Long Sault *Canada* 45°2N 74°53W **83** A10
Long Str. = Longa, Proliv
  Russia 70°0N 175°0E **29** C18
Long Thanh *Vietnam* 10°47N 106°57E **39** G6
Long Xuyen *Vietnam* 10°19N 105°28E **39** G5
Longa, Proliv *Russia* 70°0N 175°0E **29** C18
Longbenton *U.K.* 55°1N 1°31W **12** B6
Longboat Key *U.S.A.* 27°23N 82°39W **85** H13
Longde *China* 35°30N 106°20E **34** G4
Longford *Australia* 41°32S 147°3E **63** G4
Longford *Ireland* 53°43N 7°49W **10** C4
Longford □ *Ireland* 53°42N 7°45W **10** C4
Longhua *Guangdong,
  China* 22°39N 114°0E **33** F11
Longhua *Hebei, China* 41°18N 117°45E **35** D9
Longido *Tanzania* 2°43S 36°42E **54** C4
Longiram *Indonesia* 0°5S 115°45E **36** E5
Longkou *China* 37°40N 120°18E **35** F11
Longlac *Canada* 49°45N 86°25W **72** C2
Longmeadow *U.S.A.* 42°3N 72°34W **83** D12
Longmont *U.S.A.* 40°10N 105°6W **76** F11
Longnawan *Indonesia* 1°51N 114°55E **36** D4
Longreach *Australia* 23°28S 144°14E **62** C3
Longueuil *Canada* 45°31N 73°29W **83** A11
Longview *Tex., U.S.A.* 32°30N 94°44W **84** E7
Longview *Wash., U.S.A.* 46°8N 122°57W **78** D4
Longxi *China* 34°53N 104°40E **34** G3
Longxue Dao *China* 22°41N 113°38E **33** F10
Longyearbyen *Svalbard* 78°13N 15°40E **4** B8
Longkou *U.S.A.* 34°47N 91°54W **84** D9
Lonquimay *Chile* 38°26S 71°14W **96** D2

Lons-le-Saunier *France* 46°40N 5°31E **20** C6
Looe *U.K.* 50°22N 4°28W **13** G3
Lookout, C. *Canada* 55°18N 83°56W **72** A3
Lookout, C. *U.S.A.* 34°35N 76°32W **85** D16
Loolmalasin *Tanzania* 3°0S 35°53E **54** C4
Loon → *Alta., Canada* 57°8N 115°3W **70** B5
Loon → *Man., Canada* 55°53N 101°59W **71** B8
Loon Lake *Canada* 54°2N 109°10W **71** C7
Loongana *Australia* 30°52S 127°5E **61** F4
Loop Hd. *Ireland* 52°34N 9°56W **10** D2
Lop *China* 37°3N 80°11E **32** C3
Lop Buri *Thailand* 14°48N 100°37E **38** E3
Lop Nor = Lop Nur
  China 40°20N 90°10E **32** B4
Lop Nur *China* 40°20N 90°10E **32** B4
Lopatina, Gora *Russia* 50°47N 143°10E **29** D15
Lopatka, Mys *Russia* 50°52N 156°40E **29** D16
Lopez *U.S.A.* 41°27N 76°20W **83** E8
Lopez, C. *Gabon* 0°47S 8°40E **52** E1
Lopphavet *Norway* 70°27N 21°15E **8** A19
Lora → *Afghan.* 31°35N 66°32E **40** D4
Lora, Hāmūn-i- *Pakistan* 29°38N 64°58E **40** E4
Lora Cr. → *Australia* 28°10S 135°22E **63** D2
Lora del Río *Spain* 37°39N 5°33W **21** D3
Lorain *U.S.A.* 41°28N 82°11W **82** E2
Loralai *Pakistan* 30°20N 68°41E **42** D3
Lorca *Spain* 37°41N 1°42W **21** D5
Lord Howe I. *Pac. Oc.* 31°33S 159°6E **58** E8
Lord Howe Rise *Pac. Oc.* 30°0S 162°30E **64** L8
Lordsburg *U.S.A.* 32°21N 108°43W **77** K9
Loreştān □ *Iran* 33°30N 48°40E **45** C6
Loreto *Brazil* 7°5S 45°10W **93** E9
Loreto *Mexico* 26°0N 111°21W **86** B2
Lorient *France* 47°45N 3°23W **20** C2
Lormi *India* 22°17N 81°41E **43** H9
Lorn *U.K.* 56°26N 5°10W **11** E3
Lorn, Firth of *U.K.* 56°20N 5°40W **11** E3
Lorne *Australia* 38°33S 143°59E **63** F3
Lorovouno *Cyprus* 35°8N 32°36E **25** D11
Lorraine □ *France* 48°53N 6°0E **20** B7
Los Alamos *Calif.,*
  U.S.A. 34°44N 120°17W **79** L6
Los Alamos *N. Mex.,*
  U.S.A. 35°53N 106°19W **77** J10
Los Altos *U.S.A.* 37°23N 122°7W **78** H4
Los Andes *Chile* 32°50S 70°40W **94** C1
Los Angeles *Chile* 37°28S 72°23W **94** D1
Los Angeles *U.S.A.* 34°4N 118°15W **79** M8
Los Angeles, Bahia de
  Mexico 28°56N 113°34W **86** B2
Los Angeles Aqueduct
  U.S.A. 35°22N 118°5W **79** K9
Los Angeles Int. ✈ (LAX)
  U.S.A. 33°57N 118°25W **79** M8
Los Banos *U.S.A.* 37°4N 120°51W **78** H6
Los Blancos *Argentina* 23°40S 62°30W **94** A3
Los Cardones △ *Argentina* 25°8S 65°55W **94** B2
Los Chiles *Costa Rica* 11°2N 84°43W **88** D3
Los Cristianos *Canary Is.* 28°3N 16°42W **24** F3
Los Gatos *U.S.A.* 37°14N 121°59W **78** H5
Los Haïtises △ *Dom. Rep.* 19°4N 69°36W **89** C6
Los Hermanos Is.
  Venezuela 11°45N 64°25W **89** D7
Los Islotes *Canary Is.* 29°4N 13°44W **24** E6
Los Llanos de Aridane
  Canary Is. 28°38N 17°54W **24** F2
Los Loros *Chile* 27°50S 70°6W **94** B1
Los Lunas *U.S.A.* 34°48N 106°44W **77** J10
Los Mochis *Mexico* 25°45N 108°57W **86** B3
Los Olivos *U.S.A.* 34°40N 120°7W **79** L6
Los Palacios *Cuba* 22°35N 83°15W **88** B3
Los Queñes *Chile* 35°1S 70°48W **94** D1
Los Reyes de Salgado
  Mexico 19°35N 102°29W **86** D4
Los Roques Is. *Venezuela* 11°50N 66°45W **89** D6
Los Teques *Venezuela* 10°21N 67°2W **92** A5
Los Testigos, Is. *Venezuela* 11°23N 63°6W **92** A6
Los Vilos *Chile* 32°10S 71°30W **94** C1
Lošinj *Croatia* 44°30N 14°30E **16** F8
Loskop Dam *S. Africa* 25°23S 29°20E **57** D4
Lossiemouth *U.K.* 57°42N 3°17W **11** D5
Lostwithiel *U.K.* 50°24N 4°41W **13** G3
Lot → *France* 44°18N 0°20E **20** D4
Lota *Chile* 37°5S 73°10W **94** D1
Loṭfābād *Iran* 37°32N 59°20E **45** B8
Lothair *S. Africa* 26°22S 30°27E **57** D5
Lotta → *Europe* 68°42N 31°6E **8** B24
Loubomo *Congo* 4°9S 12°47E **52** E2
Loudonville *U.S.A.* 40°38N 82°14W **82** F2
Louga *Senegal* 15°45N 16°5W **50** E2
Loughborough *U.K.* 52°47N 1°11W **12** E6
Lougheed I. *Canada* 77°26N 105°6W **69** B10
Loughrea *Ireland* 53°12N 8°33W **10** C3
Louis Trichardt *S. Africa* 23°1S 29°43E **57** C4
Louis XIV, Pte. *Canada* 54°37N 79°45W **72** B4
Louisa *U.S.A.* 38°7N 82°36W **81** F12
Louisbourg *Canada* 45°55N 60°0W **73** C8
Louisburgh *Ireland* 53°46N 9°49W **10** C2
Louise I. *Canada* 52°55N 131°50W **70** C2
Louiseville *Canada* 46°20N 72°56W **72** C5
Louisiade Arch.
  Papua N. G. 11°10S 153°0E **58** C8
Louisiana *U.S.A.* 39°27N 91°3W **80** F8
Louisiana □ *U.S.A.* 30°50N 92°0W **84** F9
Louisville *Ky., U.S.A.* 38°15N 85°46W **81** F11
Louisville *Miss., U.S.A.* 33°7N 89°3W **85** E10
Louisville *Ohio, U.S.A.* 40°50N 81°16W **82** F3
Louisville Ridge
  Pac. Oc. 31°0S 172°30W **64** L10
Loulé *Portugal* 37°9N 8°0W **21** D1
Loup City *U.S.A.* 41°17N 98°58W **80** E4
Loups Marins, Lacs des
  Canada 56°30N 73°45W **72** A5
Lourdes *France* 43°6N 0°3W **20** E3
Lourdes-de-Blanc-Sablon
  Canada 51°24N 57°12W **73** B8
Louroujina *Cyprus* 35°0N 33°28E **25** E12
Louth *Australia* 30°30S 145°8E **63** E4

Louth *Ireland* 53°58N 6°32W **10** C5
Louth *U.K.* 53°22N 0°1W **12** D7
Louth □ *Ireland* 53°56N 6°34W **10** C5
Louvain = Leuven
  Belgium 50°52N 4°42E **15** D4
Louwsburg *S. Africa* 27°37S 31°7E **57** D5
Lovech *Bulgaria* 43°8N 24°42E **23** C11
Loveland *U.S.A.* 40°24N 105°5W **76** F11
Lovell *U.S.A.* 44°50N 108°24W **76** D9
Lovelock *U.S.A.* 40°11N 118°28W **76** F4
Loviisa *Finland* 60°28N 26°12E **8** F22
Loving *U.S.A.* 32°17N 104°6W **77** K11
Lovington *U.S.A.* 32°57N 103°21W **77** K12
Low, L. *Canada* 52°29N 76°17W **72** B4
Low Pt. *Australia* 32°25S 127°25E **61** F4
Low Tatra = Nízké Tatry
  Slovak Rep. 48°55N 19°30E **17** D10
Lowa
  Dem. Rep. of the Congo 1°25S 25°47E **54** C2
Lowa →
  Dem. Rep. of the Congo 1°24S 25°51E **54** C2
Lowell *U.S.A.* 42°38N 71°19W **83** D13
Löwen → *Namibia* 26°51S 18°17E **56** D2
Lower Alkali L. *U.S.A.* 41°16N 120°2W **76** F3
Lower Arrow L. *Canada* 49°40N 118°5W **70** D5
Lower California = Baja California
  Mexico 31°10N 115°12W **86** A1
Lower Hutt *N.Z.* 41°10S 174°55E **59** D5
Lower Lake *U.S.A.* 38°55N 122°37W **78** G4
Lower Manitou L.
  Canada 49°15N 93°0W **71** D10
Lower Post *Canada* 59°58N 128°30W **70** B3
Lower Red L. *U.S.A.* 47°58N 95°0W **80** B6
Lower Saxony = Niedersachsen □
  Germany 52°50N 9°0E **16** B5
Lower Tunguska = Tunguska,
  Nizhnyaya → *Russia* 65°48N 88°4E **29** C9
Lower Zambezi △ *Zambia* 15°25S 29°40E **55** F2
Lowestoft *U.K.* 52°29N 1°45E **13** E9
Lowgar □ *Afghan.* 34°0N 69°0E **40** B6
Lowick → *Canada* 74°33N 97°30W **69** C12
Lowville *U.S.A.* 43°47N 75°29W **83** C9
Loxton *Australia* 34°28S 140°31E **63** E3
Loxton *S. Africa* 31°30S 22°22E **56** E3
Loyalton *U.S.A.* 39°41N 120°14W **78** F6
Loyalty Is. = Loyauté, Îs.
  N. Cal. 20°50S 166°30E **58** D9
Loyang = Luoyang
  China 34°40N 112°26E **34** G7
Loyauté, Îs. *N. Cal.* 20°50S 166°30E **58** D9
Loyev = Loyew *Belarus* 51°56N 30°46E **17** C16
Loyew *Belarus* 51°56N 30°46E **17** C16
Loyoro *Uganda* 3°22N 34°14E **54** B3
Ltalaltuma ◎ *Australia* 23°55S 132°26E **60** D5
Lu Wo *China* 22°33N 114°6E **33** F11
Luachimo *Angola* 7°23S 20°48E **52** F4
Luajan → *India* 24°44N 85°1E **43** G11
Lualaba →
  Dem. Rep. of the Congo 0°26N 25°20E **54** B2
Luambe △ *Zambia* 12°30S 32°15E **55** E3
Luampa *Zambia* 15°4S 24°20E **55** F1
Luan Chau *Vietnam* 21°38N 103°24E **38** B4
Luan He → *China* 39°20N 119°5E **35** E10
Luan Xian *China* 39°40N 118°40E **35** E10
Luancheng *China* 37°53N 114°40E **34** F8
Luanda *Angola* 8°50S 13°15E **52** F2
Luang, Thale *Thailand* 7°30N 100°15E **39** J3
Luang Prabang *Laos* 19°52N 102°10E **38** C4
Luangwa *Zambia* 15°35S 30°16E **55** F3
Luangwa → *Zambia* 14°25S 30°25E **55** E3
Luangwa Valley *Zambia* 13°30S 31°30E **55** E3
Luangue = Loange →
  Dem. Rep. of the Congo 4°17S 20°2E **52** E4
Luanne *China* 40°55N 117°40E **35** D9
Luanping *China* 40°53N 117°23E **35** D9
Luanshya *Zambia* 13°3S 28°28E **55** E2
Luapula □ *Zambia* 11°0S 29°0E **55** E2
Luapula → *Africa* 9°26S 28°33E **55** D2
Luarca *Spain* 43°32N 6°32W **21** A2
Luashi
  Dem. Rep. of the Congo 10°50S 23°36E **55** E1
Luau *Angola* 10°40S 22°10E **52** G4
Lubana, Ozero = Lubānas Ezers
  Latvia 56°45N 27°0E **9** H22
Lubānas Ezers *Latvia* 56°45N 27°0E **9** H22
Lubang Is. *Phil.* 13°50N 120°12E **37** B6
Lubango *Angola* 14°55S 13°30E **53** G2
Lubao
  Dem. Rep. of the Congo 5°17S 25°42E **54** D2
Lubefu
  Dem. Rep. of the Congo 4°47S 24°27E **54** C1
Lubefu →
  Dem. Rep. of the Congo 4°10S 23°0E **54** C1
Lubero = Luofu
  Dem. Rep. of the Congo 0°10S 29°15E **54** C2
Lubicon L. *Canada* 56°23N 115°56W **70** B5
Lubilash →
  Dem. Rep. of the Congo 6°2S 23°45E **52** F4
Lubin *Poland* 51°24N 16°11E **16** C9
Lublin *Poland* 51°12N 22°38E **17** C12
Lubnān = Lebanon ■ *Asia* 34°0N 36°0E **46** B5
Lubnān, Jabal *Lebanon* 33°45N 35°40E **46** B4
Lubny *Ukraine* 50°3N 32°58E **28** D4
Lubongola
  Dem. Rep. of the Congo 2°35S 27°50E **54** C2
Lubudi
  Dem. Rep. of the Congo 9°57S 25°58E **52** F5
Lubudi →
  Dem. Rep. of the Congo 9°0S 25°35E **55** D2
Lubukklinggau *Indonesia* 3°15S 102°55E **36** E2
Lubuksikaping *Indonesia* 0°10N 100°15E **36** D2
Lubumbashi
  Dem. Rep. of the Congo 11°40S 27°28E **55** E2

Lubunda
  Dem. Rep. of the Congo 5°12S 26°41E **54** D2
Lubungu *Zambia* 14°35S 26°24E **55** E2
Lubutu
  Dem. Rep. of the Congo 0°45S 26°30E **54** C2
Luc An Chau *Vietnam* 22°6N 104°43E **38** A5
Lucan *Canada* 43°11N 81°24W **82** C3
Lucania, Mt. *Canada* 61°1N 140°27W **68** E3
Lucas Channel = Main Channel
  Canada 45°21N 81°45W **82** A3
Lucca *Italy* 43°50N 10°29E **22** C4
Luce Bay *U.K.* 54°45N 4°48W **11** G4
Lucea *Jamaica* 18°27N 78°10W **88** a
Lucedale *U.S.A.* 30°56N 88°35W **85** F10
Lucena *Phil.* 13°56N 121°37E **37** B6
Lucena *Spain* 37°27N 4°31W **21** D3
Lučenec *Slovak Rep.* 48°18N 19°42E **17** D10
Lucerne = Luzern *Switz.* 47°3N 8°18E **20** C8
Lucerne *U.S.A.* 39°6N 122°48W **78** F4
Lucerne Valley *U.S.A.* 34°27N 116°57W **79** L10
Lucero *Mexico* 30°49N 106°30W **86** A3
Lucheng *China* 36°20N 113°11E **34** F7
Lucheringo → *Mozam.* 11°43S 36°17E **55** E4
Lucia *U.S.A.* 36°2N 121°33W **78** J5
Lucinda *Australia* 18°32S 146°20E **62** B4
Luckenwalde *Germany* 52°5N 13°10E **16** B7
Luckhoff *S. Africa* 29°44S 24°43E **56** D3
Lucknow *Canada* 43°57N 81°31W **82** C3
Lucknow *India* 26°50N 81°0E **43** F9
Lüda = Dalian *China* 38°50N 121°40E **35** E11
Lüderitz *Namibia* 26°41S 15°8E **56** D2
Lüderitzbaai *Namibia* 26°36S 15°8E **56** D2
Ludhiana *India* 30°57N 75°56E **42** D6
Ludington *U.S.A.* 43°57N 86°27W **80** D10
Ludlow *U.K.* 52°22N 2°42W **13** E5
Ludlow *Calif., U.S.A.* 34°43N 116°10W **79** L10
Ludlow *Pa., U.S.A.* 41°43N 78°56W **82** E6
Ludlow *Vt., U.S.A.* 43°24N 72°42W **83** C12
Ludvika *Sweden* 60°8N 15°14E **9** F16
Ludwigsburg *Germany* 48°53N 9°11E **16** D5
Ludwigshafen *Germany* 49°29N 8°26E **16** D5
Lueki
  Dem. Rep. of the Congo 3°20S 25°48E **54** C2
Luena
  Dem. Rep. of the Congo 9°28S 25°43E **55** D2
Luena *Zambia* 10°40S 30°25E **55** E3
Luena Flats *Zambia* 14°47S 23°17E **53** G4
Luenha = Ruenya →
  Africa 16°24S 33°48E **55** F3
Lüeyang *China* 33°22N 106°10E **34** H4
Lufira →
  Dem. Rep. of the Congo 9°30S 27°0E **55** D2
Lufkin *U.S.A.* 31°21N 94°44W **84** F7
Lufupa
  Dem. Rep. of the Congo 10°37S 24°56E **55** E1
Luga *Russia* 58°40N 29°55E **9** G23
Lugano *Switz.* 46°1N 8°57E **20** C8
Lugansk = Luhansk
  Ukraine 48°38N 39°15E **19** E6
Lugard's Falls *Kenya* 3°6S 38°41E **54** C4
Lugela *Mozam.* 16°25S 36°43E **55** F4
Lugenda → *Mozam.* 11°25S 38°33E **55** E4
Lugh Ganana = Luuq
  Somali Rep. 3°48N 42°34E **47** G3
Lugnaquillia *Ireland* 52°58N 6°28W **10** D5
Lugo *Italy* 44°25N 11°54E **22** B4
Lugo *Spain* 43°2N 7°35W **21** A2
Lugoj *Romania* 45°42N 21°57E **17** F11
Lugovoy = Qulan
  Kazakhstan 42°55N 72°43E **28** E8
Luhansk *Ukraine* 48°38N 39°15E **19** E6
Lui → *Angola* 8°21S 17°33E **52** F3
Luiana *Angola* 17°25S 22°59E **56** B3
Luiana → *Angola* 17°24S 23°3E **53** H4
Luichow Pen. = Leizhou Bandao
  China 21°0N 110°0E **33** D6
Luimneach = Limerick
  Ireland 52°40N 8°37W **10** D3
Luing *U.K.* 56°14N 5°39W **11** E3
Luís Correia *Brazil* 3°0S 41°35W **93** D10
Luitpold Coast *Antarctica* 78°30S 32°0W **5** D1
Luiza *Dem. Rep. of the Congo* 7°40S 22°30E **52** F4
Luizi *Dem. Rep. of the Congo* 6°0S 27°25E **54** D2
Luján *Argentina* 34°45S 59°5W **94** C4
Lukanga Swamp *Zambia* 14°30S 27°40E **55** E2
Lukenie →
  Dem. Rep. of the Congo 3°0S 18°50E **52** E3
Lukolela
  Dem. Rep. of the Congo 5°23S 24°32E **54** D1
Lukosi *Zimbabwe* 18°30S 26°30E **55** F2
Łuków *Poland* 51°55N 22°23E **17** C12
Lukusuzi △ *Zambia* 12°43S 32°36E **55** E3
Luleå *Sweden* 65°35N 22°10E **8** D20
Luleälven → *Sweden* 65°35N 22°10E **8** D20
Lüleburgaz *Turkey* 41°23N 27°22E **23** D12
Lulima
  Dem. Rep. of the Congo 4°12S 25°36E **54** C2
Luling *U.S.A.* 29°41N 97°39W **84** G6
Lulong *China* 39°53N 118°51E **35** E10
Lulonga →
  Dem. Rep. of the Congo 1°0N 18°10E **52** D3
Lulua →
  Dem. Rep. of the Congo 4°30S 20°30E **52** E4
Luma *Amer. Samoa* 14°16S 169°33W **59** b
Lumajang *Indonesia* 8°8S 113°13E **37** H15
Lumbala N'guimbo
  Angola 14°18S 21°18E **53** G4
Lumberton *U.S.A.* 34°37N 79°0W **85** D15
Lumsden *Canada* 50°39N 104°52W **71** C8
Lumsden *N.Z.* 45°44S 168°27E **59** F2
Lumut *Malaysia* 4°13N 100°37E **39** K3
Lumut, Tanjung
  Indonesia 3°50S 105°58E **36** E3
Lund *Sweden* 55°44N 13°12E **9** J15
Lundazi *Zambia* 12°20S 33°7E **55** E3
Lundi → *Zimbabwe* 21°43S 32°34E **55** G3
Lundu *Malaysia* 1°40N 109°50E **36** D3

Lundy *U.K.* 51°10N 4°41W **13** F3
Lune → *U.K.* 54°0N 2°51W **12** C5
Lüneburg *Germany* 53°15N 10°24E **16** B6
Lüneburg Heath = Lüneburger
  Heide *Germany* 53°10N 10°12E **16** B6
Lüneburger Heide
  Germany 53°10N 10°12E **16** B6
Lunenburg *Canada* 44°22N 64°18W **73** D7
Lunéville *France* 48°36N 6°30E **20** B7
Lunga → *Zambia* 14°34S 26°25E **55** E2
Lunga Lunga *Kenya* 4°33S 39°7E **54** C4
Lungleł *India* 22°55N 92°45E **41** H18
Luni *India* 26°0N 73°6E **42** G5
Luni → *India* 24°41N 71°14E **42** G4
Luninets = Luninyets
  Belarus 52°15N 26°50E **17** B14
Luning *U.S.A.* 38°30N 118°11W **76** G4
Luninyets *Belarus* 52°15N 26°50E **17** B14
Lunkaransar *India* 28°29N 73°44E **42** E5
Lunsemfwa → *Zambia* 14°54S 30°12E **55** E3
Lunsemfwa Falls *Zambia* 14°30S 29°6E **55** E2
Luo He → *China* 34°35N 110°20E **34** G6
Luochuan *China* 35°45N 109°26E **34** G5
Luofu
  Dem. Rep. of the Congo 0°10S 29°15E **54** C2
Luohe *China* 33°32N 114°2E **34** H8
Luonan *China* 34°5N 110°10E **34** G6
Luoning *China* 34°35N 111°40E **34** G6
Luoyang *China* 34°40N 112°26E **34** G7
Luozigou *China* 43°42N 130°18E **35** C16
Lupilichi *Mozam.* 11°47S 35°13E **55** E4
Luque *Paraguay* 25°19S 57°25W **94** B4
Luquillo, Sierra de
  Puerto Rico 18°20N 65°47W **89** d
Luray *U.S.A.* 38°40N 78°28W **81** F14
Lurgan *U.K.* 54°28N 6°19W **10** B5
Lúrio *Mozam.* 13°32S 40°30E **55** E5
Lusaka *Zambia* 15°28S 28°16E **55** F2
Lusaka □ *Zambia* 15°30S 29°0E **55** F2
Lusambo
  Dem. Rep. of the Congo 4°58S 23°28E **54** C1
Lusangaye
  Dem. Rep. of the Congo 4°54S 26°0E **54** C2
Luseland *Canada* 52°5N 109°24W **71** C7
Lusenga Plain △ *Zambia* 9°22S 29°14E **55** D2
Lushan *China* 33°45N 112°55E **34** H7
Lushi *China* 34°3N 111°3E **34** G6
Lushnjë *Albania* 40°55N 19°41E **23** D8
Lushoto *Tanzania* 4°47S 38°20E **54** C4
Lushun *China* 38°45N 121°15E **35** E11
Lusk *U.S.A.* 42°46N 104°27W **76** E11
Lüt, Dasht-e *Iran* 31°30N 58°0E **45** D8
Luta = Dalian *China* 38°50N 121°40E **35** E11
Lutherstadt Wittenberg
  Germany 51°53N 12°39E **16** C7
Luton *U.K.* 51°53N 0°24W **13** F7
Luton □ *U.K.* 51°53N 0°24W **13** F7
Łutsel K'e *Canada* 62°24N 110°44W **71** A6
Lutsk *Ukraine* 50°50N 25°15E **17** C13
Lutto = Lotta → *Europe* 68°42N 31°6E **8** B24
Lützow Holmbukta
  Antarctica 69°10S 37°30E **5** C4
Lutzputs *S. Africa* 28°3S 20°40E **56** D3
Luuq *Somali Rep.* 3°48N 42°34E **47** G3
Luverne *Ala., U.S.A.* 31°43N 86°16W **85** F11
Luverne *Minn., U.S.A.* 43°39N 96°13W **80** D5
Luvua
  Dem. Rep. of the Congo 8°48S 25°17E **55** D2
Luvua →
  Dem. Rep. of the Congo 6°50S 27°30E **54** D2
Luvuvhu → *S. Africa* 22°25S 31°18E **57** C5
Luwegu → *Tanzania* 8°31S 37°23E **55** D4
Luwero *Uganda* 0°50N 32°28E **54** B3
Luwuk *Indonesia* 0°56S 122°47E **37** E6
Luxembourg *Lux.* 49°37N 6°9E **15** E6
Luxembourg □ *Belgium* 49°58N 5°30E **15** E5
Luxembourg ■ *Europe* 49°45N 6°0E **15** E5
Luxembourg ✈ (LUX)
  Lux. 49°37N 6°10E **15** E6
Luxi *China* 24°27N 98°36E **32** D4
Luxor = El Uqsur *Egypt* 25°41N 32°38E **51** C12
Luyi *China* 33°50N 115°35E **34** H8
Luza *Russia* 60°39N 47°10E **18** B8
Luzern *Switz.* 47°3N 8°18E **20** C8
Luziânia *Brazil* 16°20S 48°0W **93** G9
Luzon *Phil.* 16°0N 121°0E **37** A6
Lviv *Ukraine* 49°50N 24°0E **17** D13
Lvov = Lviv *Ukraine* 49°50N 24°0E **17** D13
Lyakhavichy *Belarus* 53°2N 26°32E **17** B14
Lyakhovskiye, Ostrova
  Russia 73°40N 141°0E **29** B15
Lyal I. *Canada* 44°57N 81°24E **82** B3
Lybster *U.K.* 58°18N 3°15W **11** C5
Lycksele *Sweden* 64°38N 18°40E **8** D18
Lydda = Lod *Israel* 31°57N 34°54E **46** D3
Lyddan I. *Antarctica* 74°0S 21°0W **5** D2
Lydenburg *S. Africa* 25°10S 30°29E **57** D5
Lydia *Turkey* 38°48N 28°19E **23** E13
Lyell *N.Z.* 41°48S 172°4E **59** D4
Lyell I. *Canada* 52°40N 131°35W **70** C2
Lyepyel *Belarus* 54°50N 28°40E **9** J23
Lykens *U.S.A.* 40°34N 76°42W **83** F8
Lyman *U.S.A.* 41°20N 110°18W **76** F8
Lyme B. *U.K.* 50°42N 2°53W **13** G4
Lyme Regis *U.K.* 50°43N 2°57W **13** G5
Lymington *U.K.* 50°45N 1°32W **13** G6
Łyna → *Poland* 54°37N 21°14E **17** A11
Lynchburg *U.S.A.* 37°25N 79°9W **81** G14
Lynd → *Australia* 16°28S 143°18E **62** B3
Lynd Ra. *Australia* 25°30S 149°20E **63** D4
Lynden *Canada* 43°14N 80°9W **82** C4
Lynden *U.S.A.* 48°57N 122°27W **78** B4
Lyndhurst *Australia* 30°15S 138°18E **63** E2
Lyndon → *Australia* 23°29S 114°6E **61** D1
Lyndonville *N.Y., U.S.A.* 43°20N 78°23W **82** C6
Lyndonville *Vt., U.S.A.* 44°31N 72°1W **83** B12
Lyngen *Norway* 69°45N 20°30E **8** B19
Lynher Reef *Australia* 15°27S 121°55E **60** C3

Lynn *U.S.A.* 42°28N 70°57W **83** D14
Lynn Canal *U.S.A.* 58°50N 135°15W **74** D12
Lynn Haven *U.S.A.* 30°15N 85°39W **85** F12
Lynn Lake *Canada* 56°51N 101°3W **71** B8
Lynnwood *U.S.A.* 47°49N 122°18W **78** C4
Lynton *U.K.* 51°13N 3°50W **13** F4
Lyntupy *Belarus* 55°4N 26°23E **9** J22
Lynx L. *Canada* 62°25N 106°15W **71** A7
Lyon *France* 45°46N 4°50E **20** D6
Lyonnais *France* 45°45N 4°15E **20** D6
Lyons = Lyon *France* 45°46N 4°50E **20** D6
Lyons *Ga., U.S.A.* 32°12N 82°19W **85** E13
Lyons *Kans., U.S.A.* 38°21N 98°12W **80** F4
Lyons *N.Y., U.S.A.* 43°5N 77°0W **82** C7
Lyons → *Australia* 25°2S 115°9E **61** E2
Lyons Falls *U.S.A.* 43°37N 75°22W **83** C9
Lys = Leie → *Belgium* 51°2N 3°45E **15** C3
Lysi *Cyprus* 35°6N 33°41E **25** D12
Lysva *Russia* 58°7N 57°49E **18** C10
Lysychansk *Ukraine* 48°55N 38°30E **19** E6
Lytham St. Anne's *U.K.* 53°45N 3°0W **12** D4
Lyttelton *N.Z.* 43°35S 172°44E **59** E4
Lytton *Canada* 50°13N 121°31W **70** C4
Lyubertsy *Russia* 55°40N 37°51E **18** C6
Lyuboml *Ukraine* 51°11N 24°4E **17** C13

M

Ma → *Vietnam* 19°47N 105°56E **38** C5
Ma'adaba *Jordan* 30°43N 35°47E **46** E4
Maamba *Zambia* 17°17S 26°28E **56** B4
Ma'ān *Jordan* 30°12N 35°44E **46** E4
Ma'ān □ *Jordan* 30°0N 36°0E **46** F5
Maanselkä *Finland* 63°52N 28°32E **8** E23
Ma'anshan *China* 31°44N 118°29E **33** C6
Maarianhamina = Mariehamn
  Finland 60°5N 19°55E **9** F18
Ma'arrat an Nu'mān
  Syria 35°43N 36°43E **44** C3
Maas → *Neths.* 51°45N 4°32E **15** C4
Maaseik *Belgium* 51°6N 5°45E **15** C5
Maasin *Phil.* 10°8N 124°50E **37** B6
Maastricht *Neths.* 50°50N 5°40E **15** D5
Maave *Mozam.* 21°4S 34°47E **57** C5
Mababe Depression
  Botswana 18°50S 24°15E **56** B3
Mabalane *Mozam.* 23°37S 32°31E **57** C5
Mabel L. *Canada* 50°35N 118°43W **70** C5
Mabenge
  Dem. Rep. of the Congo 4°15N 24°12E **54** B1
Maberly *Canada* 44°50N 76°32W **83** B8
Mablethorpe *U.K.* 53°20N 0°15E **12** D8
Maboma
  Dem. Rep. of the Congo 2°30N 28°10E **54** B2
Mabuasehube △
  Botswana 25°5S 21°10E **56** D3
Mabuiag *Australia* 9°57S 142°11E **62** a
Mac Bac *Vietnam* 9°46N 106°7E **39** H6
Macachín *Argentina* 37°10S 63°43W **94** D3
Macaé *Brazil* 22°20S 41°43W **95** A7
McAlester *U.S.A.* 34°56N 95°46W **84** D7
McAllen *U.S.A.* 26°12N 98°14W **84** H5
MacAlpine L. *Canada* 66°32N 102°45W **68** D11
Macamic *Canada* 48°45N 79°0W **72** C4
Macao = Macau *China* 22°12N 113°33E **33** G10
Macapá *Brazil* 0°5N 51°4W **93** C8
Macarao △ *Venezuela* 10°22N 67°7W **89** D6
McArthur → *Australia* 15°54S 136°40E **62** B2
McArthur, Port *Australia* 16°4S 136°23E **62** B2
Macau *Brazil* 5°15S 36°40W **93** E11
Macau *China* 22°12N 113°33E **33** G10
McBride *Canada* 53°20N 120°19W **70** C4
McCall *U.S.A.* 44°55N 116°6W **76** D5
McCamey *U.S.A.* 31°8N 102°14W **84** F3
McCammon *U.S.A.* 42°39N 112°12W **76** E7
McCarran Int., Las Vegas ✈ (LAS)
  U.S.A. 36°5N 115°9W **79** J11
McCauley I. *Canada* 53°40N 130°15W **70** C2
McCleary *U.S.A.* 47°3N 123°16W **78** C3
Macclenny *U.S.A.* 30°17N 82°7W **85** F13
Macclesfield *U.K.* 53°15N 2°8W **12** D5
M'Clintock Chan.
  Canada 72°0N 102°0W **68** C11
McClintock Ra.
  Australia 18°44S 127°38E **60** C4
McCloud *U.S.A.* 41°15N 122°8W **76** F2
McCluer I. *Australia* 11°5S 133°0E **60** B5
McClure *U.S.A.* 40°42N 77°19W **82** F7
McClure, L. *U.S.A.* 37°35N 120°16W **78** H6
M'Clure Str. *Canada* 75°0N 119°0W **69** C8
McClusky *U.S.A.* 47°29N 100°27W **80** B3
McComb *U.S.A.* 31°15N 90°27W **85** F9
McCook *U.S.A.* 40°12N 100°38W **80** E3
McCreary *Canada* 50°47N 99°29W **71** C9
McCullough Mt.
  U.S.A. 35°35N 115°13W **79** K11
McCusker → *Canada* 55°32N 108°39W **71** B7
McDermitt *U.S.A.* 41°59N 117°43W **76** F5
McDonald *U.S.A.* 40°22N 80°14W **82** F4
Macdonald, L. *Australia* 23°30S 129°0E **60** D4
McDonald Is. *Ind. Oc.* 53°0S 73°0E **3** G13
MacDonnell Ranges
  Australia 23°40S 133°0E **60** D5
MacDowell L. *Canada* 52°15N 92°45W **72** B1
Macduff *U.K.* 57°40N 2°31W **11** D6
Macedonia *U.S.A.* 41°19N 81°31W **82** E3
Macedonia □ *Greece* 40°39N 22°0E **23** D10
Macedonia ■ *Europe* 41°53N 21°40E **23** D9
Maceió *Brazil* 9°40S 35°41W **93** E11
Macerata *Italy* 43°18N 13°27E **22** C5
McFarland *U.S.A.* 35°41N 119°14W **79** K7
McFarlane → *Canada* 59°12N 107°58W **71** B7
Macfarlane, L. *Australia* 32°0S 136°40E **63** E2
McGehee *U.S.A.* 33°38N 91°24W **84** E9
McGill *U.S.A.* 39°23N 114°47W **76** G6
Macgillycuddy's Reeks
  Ireland 51°58N 9°45W **10** E2
McGraw *U.S.A.* 42°36N 76°8W **83** D8

McGregor U.S.A. 43°1N 91°11W **80** D8
McGregor Ra. Australia 27°0S 142°45E **63** D3
McGuire, Mt. Australia 20°18S 148°23E **62** b
Mach Pakistan 29°50N 67°20E **42** E2
Māch Kowr Iran 25°48N 61°28E **45** E9
Machado = Jiparaná → Brazil 8°3S 62°52W **92** E6
Machagai Argentina 26°56S 60°2W **94** B3
Machakos Kenya 1°30S 37°15E **54** C4
Machala Ecuador 3°20S 79°57W **92** D3
Machanga Mozam. 20°59S 35°0E **57** C6
Machattie, L. Australia 24°50S 139°48E **62** C2
Machava Mozam. 25°54S 32°28E **57** D5
Machece Mozam. 19°15S 35°32E **55** F4
Macheke Zimbabwe 18°5S 31°51E **57** B5
Machhu → India 23°6N 70°46E **42** H4
Machiara △ Pakistan 34°40N 73°30E **42** B5
Machias Maine, U.S.A. 44°43N 67°28W **81** C20
Machias N.Y., U.S.A. 42°25N 78°29W **82** D6
Machichi → Canada 57°3N 92°6W **71** B10
Machico Madeira 32°43N 16°44W **24** D3
Machilipatnam India 16°12N 81°8E **41** L12
Machiques Venezuela 10°4N 72°34W **92** A4
Machu Picchu Peru 13°8S 72°30W **92** F4
Machynlleth U.K. 52°35N 3°50W **13** E4
Macia Mozam. 25°2S 33°8E **57** D5
McIlwraith Ra. Australia 13°50S 143°20E **62** A3
McInnes L. Canada 52°13N 93°45W **71** C10
McIntosh U.S.A. 45°55N 101°21W **80** C3
McIntosh L. Canada 55°45N 105°0W **71** B8
Macintosh Ra. Australia 27°39S 125°32E **61** E4
Macintyre → Australia 28°37S 150°47E **63** D5
Mackay Australia 21°8S 149°11E **62** K7
Mackay U.S.A. 43°55N 113°37W **76** E7
MacKay → Canada 57°10N 111°38W **70** B6
Mackay, L. Australia 22°30S 129°0E **60** D4
McKay Ra. Australia 23°0S 122°30E **60** D3
McKeesport U.S.A. 40°20N 79°51W **82** F5
McKellar Canada 45°30N 79°55W **82** A5
McKenna U.S.A. 46°56N 122°33W **78** D4
Mackenzie Canada 55°20N 123°5W **70** B4
McKenzie U.S.A. 36°8N 88°31W **85** C10
Mackenzie → Australia 23°38S 149°46E **62** C4
Mackenzie → Canada 69°10N 134°20W **68** D5
McKenzie → U.S.A. 44°7N 123°6W **76** D2
Mackenzie Bay Canada 69°0N 137°30W **66** C6
Mackenzie City = Linden Guyana 6°0N 58°10W **92** B7
Mackenzie King I. Canada 77°45N 111°0W **69** B9
Mackenzie Mts. Canada 64°0N 130°0W **68** E6
Mackinac, Straits of U.S.A. 45°50N 84°40W **75** F23
Mackinaw City U.S.A. 45°47N 84°44W **81** C11
McKinlay Australia 21°16S 141°18E **62** C3
McKinlay → Australia 20°50S 141°28E **62** C3
McKinley, Mt. U.S.A. 63°4N 151°0W **68** E1
McKinley Sea Arctic 82°0N 0°0 **4** A7
McKinney U.S.A. 33°12N 96°37W **84** E6
Mackinnon Road Kenya 3°40S 39°1E **54** C4
McKittrick U.S.A. 35°18N 119°37W **79** K7
Macklin Canada 52°20N 109°56W **71** C7
Macksville Australia 30°40S 152°56E **63** E5
McLaughlin U.S.A. 45°49N 100°49W **80** C3
Maclean Australia 29°26S 153°16E **63** D5
McLean U.S.A. 35°14N 100°36W **84** D4
McLeansboro U.S.A. 38°6N 88°32W **80** F9
Maclear S. Africa 31°2S 28°23E **57** E4
Maclear, C. Malawi 13°58S 34°49E **55** E3
Macleay → Australia 30°56S 153°0E **63** E5
McLennan Canada 55°42N 116°50W **70** B5
McLeod → Canada 54°9N 115°44W **70** C5
MacLeod, L. Australia 24°9S 113°47E **61** D1
MacLeod B. Canada 62°53N 110°0W **71** A7
MacLeod Lake Canada 54°58N 123°0W **70** C4
McLoughlin, Mt. U.S.A. 42°27N 122°19W **76** E2
McMechen U.S.A. 39°57N 80°44W **82** G4
McMinnville Oreg., U.S.A. 45°13N 123°12W **76** D2
McMinnville Tenn., U.S.A. 35°41N 85°46W **85** D12
McMurdo Antarctica 77°0S 140°0E **5** D11
McMurdo Sd. Antarctica 77°0S 170°0E **5** D11
McMurray = Fort McMurray Canada 56°44N 111°7W **70** B6
McMurray U.S.A. 48°19N 122°14W **78** B4
Maçobere Mozam. 21°13S 32°47E **55** G3
Macodoene Mozam. 23°32S 35°5E **57** C6
Macomb U.S.A. 40°27N 90°40W **80** E8
Mâcon France 46°19N 4°50E **20** C6
Macon Ga., U.S.A. 32°51N 83°38W **85** E13
Macon Miss., U.S.A. 33°7N 88°34W **85** E10
Macon Mo., U.S.A. 39°44N 92°28W **80** F7
Macossa Mozam. 17°55S 33°56E **55** F3
Macoun L. Canada 56°32N 103°40W **71** B8
Macovane Mozam. 21°30S 35°2E **57** C6
McPherson U.S.A. 38°22N 97°40W **80** F5
McPherson Pk. U.S.A. 34°53N 119°53W **79** L7
McPherson Ra. Australia 28°15S 153°15E **63** D5
Macquarie → Australia 30°7S 147°24E **63** E4
Macquarie Harbour Australia 42°15S 145°23E **63** G4
Macquarie Is. Pac. Oc. 54°36S 158°55E **64** N7
Macquarie Ridge S. Ocean 57°0S 159°0E **5** B10
MacRobertson Land Antarctica 71°0S 64°0E **5** D6
Macroom Ireland 51°54N 8°57W **10** E3
MacTier Canada 45°8N 79°47W **82** A5
Macubela Mozam. 16°53S 37°49E **55** F4
Macuira △ Colombia 12°9N 71°21W **89** D5
Macuiza Mozam. 18°7S 34°29E **55** F3
Macumba → Australia 27°52S 137°12E **63** D2
Macuro Venezuela 10°42N 61°55W **93** K15
Macusani Peru 14°4S 70°29W **92** F4
Macuse Mozam. 17°45S 37°10E **55** F4
Macuspana Mexico 17°46N 92°36W **87** D6
Macusse Angola 17°48S 20°23E **56** B3
Ma'dabā □ Jordan 31°43N 35°47E **46** D4
Madadeni S. Africa 27°43S 30°3E **57** D5
Madagascar ■ Africa 20°0S 47°0E **57** C8
Madā'in Sālih Si. Arabia 26°46N 37°57E **44** E3
Madama Niger 22°0N 13°40E **51** D8
Madame, I. Canada 45°30N 60°58W **73** C7
Madang Papua N. G. 5°12S 145°49E **58** B7
Madaripur Bangla. 23°19N 90°15E **41** H17
Madauk Burma 17°56N 96°52E **41** L20
Madawaska Canada 45°30N 78°0W **82** A7
Madawaska → Canada 45°27N 76°21W **82** A7
Madaya Burma 22°12N 96°10E **41** H20
Maddalena Italy 41°16N 9°23E **22** D3
Madeira Atl. Oc. 32°50N 17°0W **24** D3
Madeira → Brazil 3°22S 58°45W **92** D7
Madeleine, Îs. de la Canada 47°30N 61°40W **73** C7
Madera Mexico 29°12N 108°7W **86** B3
Madera Calif., U.S.A. 36°57N 120°3W **78** J6
Madera Pa., U.S.A. 40°49N 78°26W **82** F6
Madha India 18°0N 75°30E **40** L9
Madhavpur India 21°15N 69°58E **42** J3
Madhepura India 26°11N 86°23E **43** F12
Madhubani India 26°21N 86°7E **43** F12
Madhupur India 24°16N 86°39E **43** G12
Madhya Pradesh □ India 22°50N 78°0E **42** J8
Madidi → Bolivia 12°32S 66°52W **92** F5
Madikeri India 12°30N 75°45E **40** N9
Madikwe ⌓ S. Africa 27°38S 32°15E **57** D5
Madill U.S.A. 34°6N 96°46W **84** D6
Madimba Dem. Rep. of the Congo 4°58S 15°5E **52** E3
Ma'din Syria 35°45N 39°36E **44** C3
Madinat al Malik Khālid al Askarīyah Si. Arabia 27°54N 45°31E **44** E5
Madingou Congo 4°10S 13°33E **52** E2
Madirovalo Madag. 16°26S 46°32E **57** B8
Madison Calif., U.S.A. 38°41N 121°59W **78** G5
Madison Fla., U.S.A. 30°28N 83°25W **85** F13
Madison Ind., U.S.A. 38°44N 85°23W **81** F11
Madison Nebr., U.S.A. 41°50N 97°27W **80** E5
Madison Ohio, U.S.A. 41°46N 81°3W **82** E3
Madison S. Dak., U.S.A. 44°0N 97°7W **80** C5
Madison Wis., U.S.A. 43°4N 89°24W **80** D9
Madison → U.S.A. 45°56N 111°31W **76** D8
Madison Heights U.S.A. 37°25N 79°8W **81** G14
Madisonville Ky., U.S.A. 37°20N 87°30W **80** G10
Madisonville Tex., U.S.A. 30°57N 95°55W **84** F7
Madista Botswana 21°15S 25°6E **56** C4
Madiun Indonesia 7°38S 111°32E **37** G14
Mado Gashi Kenya 0°44N 39°10E **54** B4
Madoc Canada 44°30N 77°28W **82** B7
Madona Latvia 56°53N 26°5E **9** H22
Madrakah, Ra's al Oman 19°0N 57°50E **47** D6
Madras = Chennai India 13°8N 80°19E **40** N12
Madras = Tamil Nadu □ India 11°0N 77°0E **40** P10
Madras U.S.A. 44°38N 121°8W **76** D3
Madre, L. U.S.A. 25°15N 97°30W **84** J6
Madre, Sierra Phil. 17°0N 122°0E **37** A6
Madre de Dios → Bolivia 10°59S 66°8W **92** F5
Madre de Dios, I. Chile 50°20S 75°10W **96** G1
Madre del Sur, Sierra Mexico 17°30N 100°0W **87** D5
Madre Occidental, Sierra Mexico 27°0N 107°0W **86** B3
Madre Oriental, Sierra Mexico 25°0N 100°0W **86** C5
Madri India 24°16N 73°32E **42** G5
Madrid Spain 40°24N 3°42W **21** B4
Madrid U.S.A. 44°45N 75°8W **83** B9
Madula Dem. Rep. of the Congo 0°27N 25°22E **54** B2
Madura Australia 31°55S 127°0E **61** F4
Madura Indonesia 7°30S 114°0E **37** G15
Madura, Selat Indonesia 7°30S 113°20E **37** G15
Madurai India 9°55N 78°10E **40** Q11
Madurantakam India 12°30N 79°50E **40** N11
Mae Chan Thailand 20°9N 99°52E **38** B2
Mae Hong Son Thailand 19°16N 97°56E **38** C2
Mae Khlong → Thailand 13°24N 100°0E **38** F3
Mae Phrik Thailand 17°27N 99°7E **38** D2
Mae Ping △ Thailand 17°37N 98°51E **38** D2
Mae Ramat Thailand 16°58N 98°31E **38** D2
Mae Rim Thailand 18°54N 98°57E **38** C2
Mae Sai Thailand 20°20N 99°55E **38** B2
Mae Sot Thailand 16°43N 98°34E **38** D2
Mae Suai Thailand 19°39N 99°33E **38** C2
Mae Tha Thailand 18°28N 99°8E **38** C2
Mae Wong △ Thailand 15°54N 99°12E **38** E2
Mae Yom △ Thailand 18°43N 100°15E **38** C3
Maebashi Japan 36°24N 139°4E **31** F9
Maelpaeg L. Canada 48°20N 56°30W **73** C8
Maesteg U.K. 51°36N 3°40W **13** F4
Maestra, Sierra Cuba 20°15N 77°0W **88** B4
Maevatanana Madag. 16°56S 46°49E **57** B8
Mafeking = Mafikeng S. Africa 25°50S 25°38E **56** D4
Mafeking Canada 52°40N 101°10W **71** C8
Mafeteng Lesotho 29°51S 27°15E **56** D4
Maffra Australia 37°53S 146°58E **63** F4
Mafia I. Tanzania 7°45S 39°50E **54** D4
Mafikeng S. Africa 25°50S 25°38E **56** D4
Mafra Brazil 26°10S 49°55W **95** B6
Mafra Portugal 38°55N 9°20W **21** C1
Mafungabusi Plateau Zimbabwe 18°30S 29°8E **55** F2
Magadan Russia 59°38N 150°50E **29** D16
Magadi Kenya 1°54S 36°19E **54** C4
Magadi, L. Kenya 1°54S 36°19E **54** C4
Magaliesburg S. Africa 26°0S 27°32E **57** D4
Magallanes, Estrecho de Chile 52°30S 75°0W **96** G2
Magangué Colombia 9°14N 74°45W **92** B4
Magdagachi Russia 53°27N 125°48E **29** D13
Magdalen Is. = Madeleine, Îs. de la Canada 47°30N 61°40W **73** C7
Magdalena Argentina 35°5S 57°30W **94** D4
Magdalena Bolivia 13°13S 63°57W **92** F6
Magdalena U.S.A. 34°7N 107°15W **77** J10
Magdalena → Colombia 11°6N 74°51W **92** A4
Magdalena → Mexico 30°40N 112°25W **86** A2
Magdalena, B. Mexico 24°35N 112°0W **86** C2
Magdalena, I. Mexico 24°40N 112°15W **86** C2
Magdalena, Llano de Mexico 25°0N 111°25W **86** C2
Magdalena de Kino Mexico 30°38N 110°57W **86** A2
Magdeburg Germany 52°7N 11°38E **16** B6
Magdelaine Cays Australia 16°33S 150°18E **62** B5
Magee U.S.A. 31°52N 89°44W **85** F10
Magelang Indonesia 7°29S 110°13E **37** G14
Magellan's Str. = Magallanes, Estrecho de Chile 52°30S 75°0W **96** G2
Magenta, L. Australia 33°30S 119°2E **61** F2
Magerøya Norway 71°3N 25°40E **8** A21
Maggiore, Lago Italy 45°57N 8°39E **20** D8
Maggotty Jamaica 18°9N 77°46W **88** a
Maghâgha Egypt 28°38N 30°50E **51** C12
Magherafelt U.K. 54°45N 6°37W **10** B5
Maghreb N. Afr. 32°0N 4°0W **50** B5
Magistralnyy Russia 56°16N 107°36E **29** D11
Magnetic Pole (North) Canada 82°42N 114°24W **4** A2
Magnetic Pole (South) Antarctica 64°8S 138°8E **5** C9
Magnitogorsk Russia 53°27N 59°4E **18** D10
Magnolia Ark., U.S.A. 33°16N 93°14W **84** E8
Magnolia Miss., U.S.A. 31°9N 90°28W **85** F9
Mago Fiji 17°26S 179°8W **59** a
Magog Canada 45°18N 72°9W **83** A12
Magoro Uganda 1°45N 34°12E **54** B3
Magoša = Famagusta Cyprus 35°8N 33°55E **25** D12
Magoulades Greece 39°45N 19°42E **25** A3
Magoye Zambia 16°1S 27°30E **55** F2
Magpie, L. Canada 51°0N 64°41W **73** B7
Magrath Canada 49°25N 112°50W **70** D6
Magu Tanzania 2°30S 33°30E **54** C3
Maguarinho, C. Brazil 0°15S 48°30W **93** D9
Magude Mozam. 25°2S 32°40E **57** D5
Mağusa = Famagusta Cyprus 35°8N 33°55E **25** D12
Maguse L. Canada 61°37N 95°10W **71** A9
Maguse Pt. Canada 61°20N 93°50W **71** A10
Magvana India 23°13N 69°22E **42** H3
Magwe Burma 20°10N 95°0E **41** J19
Magyarorszag = Hungary ■ Europe 47°20N 19°20E **17** E10
Maha Sarakham Thailand 16°12N 103°16E **38** D4
Mahābād Iran 36°50N 45°45E **44** B5
Mahabharat Lekh Nepal 28°30N 82°0E **43** E10
Mahabo Madag. 20°23S 44°40E **57** C7
Mahadeo Hills India 22°20N 78°30E **43** H8
Mahaffey U.S.A. 40°53N 78°44W **82** F6
Mahagi Dem. Rep. of the Congo 2°20N 31°0E **54** B3
Mahajamba → Madag. 15°33S 47°8E **57** B8
Mahajamba, Helodranon' i Madag. 15°24S 47°5E **57** B8
Mahajan India 28°48N 73°56E **42** E5
Mahajanga Madag. 15°40S 46°25E **57** B8
Mahajanga □ Madag. 17°0S 47°0E **57** B8
Mahajilo → Madag. 19°42S 45°22E **57** B8
Mahakam → Indonesia 0°35S 117°17E **36** E5
Mahalapye Botswana 23°1S 26°51E **56** C4
Mahale Mts. Tanzania 6°20S 30°0E **54** D3
Mahale Mts. △ Tanzania 6°10S 29°50E **54** D2
Maḥallāt Iran 33°55N 50°30E **45** C6
Māhān Iran 30°5N 57°18E **45** D8
Mahan → India 23°30N 82°50E **43** H10
Mahanadi → India 20°20N 86°25E **41** J15
Mahananda → India 25°12N 87°52E **43** G12
Mahanoro Madag. 19°54S 48°48E **57** B8
Mahanoy City U.S.A. 40°49N 76°9W **83** F8
Maharashtra □ India 20°30N 75°30E **40** J9
Mahasham, W. → Egypt 30°15N 34°10E **46** E3
Mahasoa Madag. 22°12S 46°6E **57** C8
Mahasolo Madag. 19°7S 46°22E **57** B8
Mahattat ash Shīdīyah Jordan 29°55N 35°55E **46** F4
Mahattat 'Unayzah Jordan 30°30N 35°47E **46** E4
Mahavavy → Madag. 15°57S 45°54E **57** B8
Mahaxay Laos 17°22N 105°12E **38** D5
Mahbubnagar India 16°45N 77°59E **40** L10
Mahda U.A.E. 25°20N 56°15E **45** E8
Maḥḍah Oman 24°24N 55°59E **45** E7
Mahdia Tunisia 35°28N 11°0E **51** A8
Mahe India 33°10N 78°32E **43** C8
Mahé Seychelles 5°0S 55°30E **53** b
Mahé ✈ (SEZ) Seychelles 4°40S 55°31E **53** b
Mahébourg Mauritius 20°24S 57°42E **53** d
Mahendragarh India 28°17N 76°14E **42** E7
Mahendranagar Nepal 28°55N 80°20E **43** E9
Mahenge Tanzania 8°45S 36°41E **55** D4
Maheno N.Z. 45°10S 170°50E **59** F3
Mahesana India 23°39N 72°26E **42** H5
Maheshwar India 22°11N 75°35E **42** H6
Mahgawan India 26°29N 78°37E **43** F8
Mahi → India 22°15N 72°55E **42** H5
Mahia Pen. N.Z. 39°9S 177°55E **59** C6
Mahilyow Belarus 53°55N 30°18E **17** B16
Mahina Tahiti 17°30S 149°27W **59** d
Mahinerangi, L. N.Z. 45°50S 169°56E **59** F2
Mahmud Kot Pakistan 30°16N 71°0E **42** D4
Mahnomen U.S.A. 47°19N 95°58W **80** B6
Mahoba India 25°15N 79°55E **43** G8
Mahón = Maó Spain 39°53N 4°16E **24** B11
Mahone Bay Canada 44°27N 64°23W **73** D7
Mahopac U.S.A. 41°22N 73°45W **83** E11
Mahuva India 21°5N 71°48E **42** J4
Mai-Ndombe, L. Dem. Rep. of the Congo 2°0S 18°20E **52** E3
Mai Thon, Ko Thailand 7°40N 98°28E **39** a
Maicuru → Brazil 2°14S 54°17W **93** D8
Maidan Khula Afghan. 33°36N 69°50E **42** C3
Maidenhead U.K. 51°31N 0°42W **13** F7
Maidstone Canada 53°5N 109°20W **71** C7
Maidstone U.K. 51°16N 0°32E **13** F8
Maiduguri Nigeria 12°0N 13°20E **51** F8
Maigh Nuad = Maynooth Ireland 53°23N 6°34W **10** C5
Maihar India 24°16N 80°45E **43** G9
Maikala Ra. India 22°0N 81°0E **41** J12
Maiko △ Dem. Rep. of the Congo 0°30S 27°50E **54** C2
Mailani India 28°17N 80°21E **43** E9
Mailsi Pakistan 29°48N 72°15E **42** E5
Main → Germany 50°0N 8°18E **16** C5
Main → U.K. 54°48N 6°18W **10** B5
Main Channel Canada 45°21N 81°45W **82** A3
Main Range △ Australia 28°11S 152°27E **63** D5
Main Ridge Trin. & Tob. 11°16N 60°40W **93** J16
Maine France 48°20N 0°15W **20** C3
Maine □ U.S.A. 45°20N 69°0W **81** C19
Maine → Ireland 52°9N 9°45W **10** D2
Maine, G. of U.S.A. 43°0N 68°30W **81** D19
Maingkwan Burma 26°15N 96°37E **41** F20
Mainistir an Corann = Midleton Ireland 51°55N 8°10W **10** E3
Mainit, L. Phil. 9°31N 125°30E **37** C7
Mainland Orkney, U.K. 58°59N 3°8W **11** C5
Mainland Shet., U.K. 60°15N 1°22W **11** A7
Mainpuri India 27°18N 79°4E **43** F8
Maintirano Madag. 18°3S 44°1E **57** B7
Mainz Germany 50°1N 8°14E **16** C5
Maio C. Verde Is. 15°10N 23°10W **50** b
Maipú Argentina 36°52S 57°50W **94** D4
Maiquetía Venezuela 10°36N 66°57W **92** A5
Mairabari India 26°30N 92°22E **41** F18
Maisi Cuba 20°17N 74°9W **89** B5
Maisí, Pta. de Cuba 20°10N 74°10W **89** B5
Maitland N.S.W., Australia 32°33S 151°36E **63** E5
Maitland S. Austral., Australia 34°23S 137°40E **63** E2
Maitland → Canada 43°45N 81°43W **82** C3
Maitri Antarctica 70°0S 3°0W **5** D3
Maíz, Is. del Nic. 12°15N 83°4W **88** D3
Maizuru Japan 35°25N 135°22E **31** G7
Majalengka Indonesia 6°50S 108°13E **37** G13
Majanji Uganda 0°16N 34°0E **54** B3
Majene Indonesia 3°38S 118°57E **37** E5
Majete ⌓ Malawi 15°54S 34°34E **55** F3
Majorca = Mallorca Spain 39°30N 3°0E **24** B10
Majuro Marshall Is. 7°9N 171°12E **64** G9
Maka Senegal 13°40N 14°10W **50** F3
Makaha Zimbabwe 17°20S 32°39E **57** B5
Makalamabedi Botswana 20°19S 23°51E **56** C3
Makale Indonesia 3°6S 119°51E **37** E5
Makalu-Barun △ Nepal 27°45N 87°10E **43** F12
Makamba Burundi 4°8S 29°49E **54** C2
Makarikari = Makgadikgadi Salt Pans Botswana 20°40S 25°45E **56** C4
Makarov Basin Arctic 87°0N 150°0W **4** A
Makarovo Russia 57°40N 107°45E **29** D11
Makasar = Ujung Pandang Indonesia 5°10S 119°20E **37** F5
Makasar, Selat Indonesia 1°0S 118°20E **37** E5
Makasar, Str. of = Makasar, Selat Indonesia 1°0S 118°20E **37** E5
Makat = Maqat Kazakhstan 47°39N 53°19E **19** E9
Makedonija = Macedonia ■ Europe 41°53N 21°40E **23** D9
Makeni S. Leone 8°55N 12°5W **50** G3
Makeyevka = Makiyivka Ukraine 48°0N 38°0E **19** E6
Makgadikgadi △ Botswana 20°27S 24°47E **56** C3
Makgadikgadi Salt Pans Botswana 20°40S 25°45E **56** C4
Makhachkala Russia 43°0N 47°30E **19** F8
Makhado = Louis Trichardt S. Africa 23°1S 29°43E **57** C4
Makham, Ao Thailand 7°51N 98°25E **39** a
Makhfar al Buşayyah Iraq 30°0N 46°10E **44** D5
Makhmūr Iraq 35°46N 43°35E **44** C4
Makian Indonesia 0°20N 127°20E **37** D7
Makindu Kenya 2°18S 37°50E **54** C4
Makīnsk Kazakhstan 52°37N 70°26E **28** D8
Makira = San Cristóbal Solomon Is. 10°30S 161°0E **58** C9
Makiyivka Ukraine 48°0N 38°0E **19** E6
Makkah Si. Arabia 21°30N 39°54E **47** C2
Makkovik Canada 55°10N 59°10W **73** A8
Makó Hungary 46°14N 20°33E **17** E11
Makogai Fiji 17°28S 179°0E **59** a
Makokou Gabon 0°40N 12°50E **52** D2
Makongo Dem. Rep. of the Congo 3°25N 26°17E **54** B2
Makoro Dem. Rep. of the Congo 3°10N 29°59E **54** B2
Makrai India 22°2N 77°0E **42** H7
Makran Coast Range Pakistan 25°40N 64°0E **40** G4
Makrana India 27°2N 74°46E **42** F6
Makrigialos Greece 35°2N 25°59E **25** D7
Mākū Iran 39°15N 44°31E **44** B5
Makunda Botswana 22°30S 20°7E **56** C3
Makurazaki Japan 31°15N 130°20E **31** J5
Makurdi Nigeria 7°43N 8°35E **50** G7
Makushin Volcano U.S.A. 53°53N 166°55W **74** E6
Makūyeh Iran 28°7N 53°9E **45** D7
Makwassie S. Africa 27°17S 26°0E **56** D4
Makwiro Zimbabwe 17°58S 30°25E **57** B5
Mal B. Ireland 52°50N 9°30W **10** D2
Mala = Mallow Ireland 52°8N 8°39W **10** D3
Mala ✿ Australia 21°39S 130°45E **60** D5
Mala, Pta. Panama 7°28N 80°2W **88** E3
Malabar Coast India 11°0N 75°0E **40** P9
Malacca, Straits of Indonesia 3°0N 101°0E **39** L3
Malad City U.S.A. 42°12N 112°15W **76** E7
Maladzyechna Belarus 54°20N 26°50E **17** A14
Málaga Spain 36°43N 4°23W **21** D3
Malagarasi Tanzania 5°5S 30°50E **54** D3
Malagarasi → Tanzania 5°12S 29°47E **54** D2
Malagasy Rep. = Madagascar ■ Africa 20°0S 47°0E **57** C8
Malahide Ireland 53°26N 6°9W **10** C5
Malaimbandy Madag. 20°20S 45°36E **57** C8
Malaita Solomon Is. 9°0S 161°0E **58** B9
Malakâl Sudan 9°33N 31°40E **51** G12
Malakand Pakistan 34°40N 71°55E **42** B4
Malakula Vanuatu 16°15S 167°30E **58** C9
Malakwal Pakistan 32°34N 73°13E **42** C5
Malamala Indonesia 3°21S 120°55E **37** E6
Malanda Australia 17°22S 145°35E **62** B4
Malang Indonesia 7°59S 112°45E **37** G15
Malanga Mozam. 13°28S 36°7E **55** E4
Malangen Norway 69°24N 18°37E **8** B18
Malanje Angola 9°36S 16°17E **52** F3
Mälaren Sweden 59°30N 17°10E **9** G17
Malargüe Argentina 35°32S 69°30W **94** D2
Malartic Canada 48°9N 78°9W **72** C4
Malaryta Belarus 51°50N 24°3E **17** C13
Malaspina Glacier U.S.A. 59°50N 140°30W **74** D11
Malatya Turkey 38°25N 38°20E **44** B3
Malawi ■ Africa 11°55S 34°0E **55** E3
Malawi, L. Africa 12°30S 34°30E **55** E3
Malay Pen. Asia 7°25N 100°0E **39** J3
Malaya Vishera Russia 58°55N 32°25E **18** C5
Malaybalay Phil. 8°5N 125°7E **37** C7
Malāyer Iran 34°19N 48°51E **45** C6
Malaysia ■ Asia 5°0N 110°0E **39** K4
Malazgirt Turkey 39°10N 42°33E **44** B4
Malbon Australia 21°5S 140°17E **62** C3
Malbooma Australia 30°41S 134°11E **63** E1
Malbork Poland 54°3N 19°1E **17** B10
Malcolm Australia 28°51S 121°25E **61** E3
Malcolm, Pt. Australia 33°48S 123°45E **61** F3
Maldah India 25°2N 88°9E **43** G13
Maldegem Belgium 51°14N 3°26E **15** C3
Malden Mass., U.S.A. 42°26N 71°3W **83** D13
Malden Mo., U.S.A. 36°34N 89°57W **80** G9
Malden I. Kiribati 4°3S 155°1W **65** H12
Maldives ■ Ind. Oc. 5°0N 73°0E **26** H9
Maldon U.K. 51°44N 0°42E **13** F8
Maldonado Uruguay 34°59S 55°0W **95** C5
Maldonado, Pta. Mexico 16°20N 98°33W **87** D5
Malé Karpaty Slovak Rep. 48°30N 17°20E **17** D9
Maleas, Akra Greece 36°28N 23°7E **23** F10
Malebo, Pool Africa 4°17S 15°20E **52** E3
Malegaon India 20°30N 74°38E **40** J9
Malei Mozam. 17°12S 36°58E **55** F4
Malek Kandī Iran 37°9N 46°6E **44** B5
Malela Dem. Rep. of the Congo 4°22S 26°8E **54** C2
Malema Mozam. 14°57S 37°20E **55** E4
Maleme Greece 35°31N 23°49E **25** D5
Malerkotla India 30°32N 75°58E **42** D6
Males Greece 35°6N 25°35E **25** D7
Malgomaj Sweden 64°40N 16°30E **8** D17
Malha Sudan 15°8N 25°10E **51** E11
Malhargarh India 24°17N 74°59E **42** G6
Malheur → U.S.A. 44°4N 116°59W **76** D5
Malheur L. U.S.A. 43°20N 118°48W **76** E4
Mali ■ Africa 17°0N 3°0W **50** E5
Mali → Burma 25°42N 97°30E **41** G20
Mali Kyun Burma 13°0N 98°20E **38** F2
Malia Greece 35°17N 25°32E **25** D7
Malia, Kolpos Greece 35°19N 25°27E **25** D7
Malibu U.S.A. 34°2N 118°41W **79** L8
Maliku Indonesia 0°39S 123°16E **37** E6
Malili Indonesia 2°42S 121°6E **37** E6
Malimba, Mts. Dem. Rep. of the Congo 7°30S 29°30E **54** D2
Malin Hd. Ireland 55°23N 7°23W **10** A4
Malin Pen. Ireland 55°20N 7°17W **10** A4
Malindi Kenya 3°12S 40°5E **54** C5
Malindi Marine ⌓ Kenya 3°15S 40°7E **54** C5
Malines = Mechelen Belgium 51°2N 4°29E **15** C4
Malino Indonesia 1°0N 121°0E **37** D6
Malinyi Tanzania 8°56S 36°0E **55** D4
Malita Phil. 6°19N 125°39E **37** C7
Maliwun Burma 10°17N 98°40E **39** G2
Maliya India 23°5N 70°46E **42** H4
Malka Mari △ Kenya 4°11N 40°46E **54** B5
Malkara Turkey 40°53N 26°53E **23** D12
Mallacoota Inlet Australia 37°34S 149°40E **63** F4
Mallaig U.K. 57°0N 5°50W **11** D3
Mallawan India 27°4N 80°12E **43** F9
Mallawi Egypt 27°44N 30°44E **51** C12
Mallicolo = Malakula Vanuatu 16°15S 167°30E **58** C9
Mallorca Spain 39°30N 3°0E **24** B10
Mallorytown Canada 44°29N 75°53W **83** B9
Mallow Ireland 52°8N 8°39W **10** D3
Malmberget Sweden 67°11N 20°40E **8** C19
Malmédy Belgium 50°25N 6°2E **15** D6
Malmesbury S. Africa 33°28S 18°41E **56** E2
Malmivaara = Malmberget Sweden 67°11N 20°40E **8** C19
Malmö Sweden 55°36N 12°59E **9** J15
Malolo Fiji 17°45S 177°11E **59** a
Malolos Phil. 14°50N 120°49E **37** B6
Malolotja ⌓ Swaziland 26°4S 31°6E **57** D5
Malombe L. Malawi 14°40S 35°15E **55** E4
Malone U.S.A. 44°51N 74°18W **83** B10
Måløy Norway 61°57N 5°6E **8** F11

Malpaso *Canary Is.* 27°43N 18°3W **24** G1
Malpaso, Presa =
Netzahualcóyotl, Presa
Mexico 17°8N 93°35W **87** D6
Malpelo, I. de *Colombia* 4°3N 81°35W **92** C2
Malpur *India* 23°21N 73°27E **42** H5
Malpura *India* 26°17N 75°23E **42** F6
Malta *Idaho, U.S.A.* 42°18N 113°22W **76** E7
Malta *Mont., U.S.A.* 48°21N 107°52W **76** B10
Malta ■ *Europe* 35°55N 14°26E **25** D2
Maltahöhe *Namibia* 24°55S 17°0E **56** C2
Malton *Canada* 43°42N 79°38W **82** C5
Malton *U.K.* 54°8N 0°49W **12** C7
Maluku *Indonesia* 1°0S 127°0E **37** E7
Maluku □ *Indonesia* 3°0S 128°0E **37** E7
Maluku Sea = Molucca Sea
Indonesia 0°0 125°0E **37** E6
Malvan *India* 16°2N 73°30E **40** L8
Malvern *U.S.A.* 34°22N 92°49W **84** D8
Malvern Hills *U.K.* 52°0N 2°19W **13** E5
Malvinas, Is. = Falkland Is. ☑
Atl. Oc. 51°30S 59°0W **96** G5
Malya *Tanzania* 3°5S 33°38E **54** C3
Malyn *Ukraine* 50°46N 29°3E **17** C15
Malyy Lyakhovskiy, Ostrov
Russia 74°7N 140°36E **29** B15
Malyy Taymyr, Ostrov
Russia 78°6N 107°15E **29** B11
Mama *Russia* 58°18N 112°54E **29** D12
Mamanguape *Brazil* 6°50S 35°4W **93** E11
Mamanuca Group *Fiji* 17°35S 177°5E **59** a
Mamarr Mitlā *Egypt* 30°2N 32°54E **46** E1
Mamasa *Indonesia* 2°55S 119°20E **37** E5
Mambasa
Dem. Rep. of the Congo 1°22N 29°3E **54** B2
Mamberamo → *Indonesia* 2°0S 137°50E **37** E9
Mambilima Falls *Zambia* 10°31S 28°45E **55** E2
Mambirima
Dem. Rep. of the Congo 11°25S 27°33E **55** E2
Mambo *Tanzania* 4°52S 38°22E **54** C4
Mambrui *Kenya* 3°5S 40°5E **54** C5
Mamburao *Phil.* 13°13N 120°39E **37** B6
Mameigwess L. *Canada* 52°35N 87°50W **72** B2
Mammoth *U.S.A.* 32°43N 110°39W **77** K8
Mammoth Cave △
U.S.A. 37°8N 86°13W **80** G10
Mamoré → *Bolivia* 10°23S 65°53W **92** F5
Mamou *Guinea* 10°15N 12°0W **50** F3
Mamoudzou *Mayotte* 12°48S 45°14E **53** a
Mampikony *Madag.* 16°6S 47°38E **57** B8
Mamuju *Indonesia* 2°41S 118°50E **37** E5
Mamuno *Botswana* 22°16S 20°1E **56** C3
Man *Ivory C.* 7°30N 7°40W **50** G4
Man, I. of *U.K.* 54°15N 4°30W **12** C3
Man-Bazar *India* 23°4N 86°39E **43** H12
Man Na *Burma* 23°27N 97°19E **41** H20
Mänä *U.S.A.* 22°2N 159°47W **75** L8
Mana → *Fr. Guiana* 5°45N 53°55W **93** B8
Mana Pools △ *Zimbabwe* 15°56S 29°25E **55** F2
Manaar, G. of = Mannar, G. of
Asia 8°30N 79°0E **40** Q11
Manacapuru *Brazil* 3°16S 60°37W **92** D6
Manacor *Spain* 39°34N 3°13E **24** B10
Manado *Indonesia* 1°29N 124°51E **37** D6
Managua *Nic.* 12°6N 86°20W **88** D2
Managua, L. de *Nic.* 12°20N 86°30W **88** D2
Manakara *Madag.* 22°8S 48°1E **57** C8
Manali *India* 32°16N 77°10E **42** C7
Manama = Al Manāmah
Bahrain 26°10N 50°30E **45** E6
Manambao → *Madag.* 17°35S 44°0E **57** B7
Manambato *Madag.* 13°43S 49°7E **57** A8
Manambolo → *Madag.* 19°18S 44°22E **57** B7
Manambolosy *Madag.* 16°2S 49°40E **57** B8
Mananara *Madag.* 16°10S 49°46E **57** B8
Mananara → *Madag.* 23°21S 47°42E **57** C8
Mananara △ *Madag.* 16°14S 49°45E **57** B8
Mananjary *Madag.* 21°13S 48°20E **57** C8
Manantenina *Madag.* 24°17S 47°19E **57** C8
Manaos = Manaus *Brazil* 3°0S 60°0W **92** D7
Manapire → *Venezuela* 7°42N 66°7W **92** B5
Manapouri *N.Z.* 45°34S 167°39E **59** F1
Manapouri, L. *N.Z.* 45°32S 167°32E **59** F1
Manār, Jabal *Yemen* 14°2N 44°17E **47** E3
Manaravolo *Madag.* 23°59S 45°39E **57** C8
Manas *China* 44°17N 85°56E **32** B3
Manas → *India* 26°12N 90°40E **41** F17
Manas He → *China* 45°38N 85°12E **32** B3
Manaslu *Nepal* 28°33N 84°33E **43** E11
Manasquan *U.S.A.* 40°8N 74°3W **83** F10
Manassa *U.S.A.* 37°11N 105°56W **77** H11
Manatí *Puerto Rico* 18°26N 66°29W **89** d
Manaung *Burma* 18°45N 93°40E **41** K18
Manaus *Brazil* 3°0S 60°0W **92** D7
Manawan L. *Canada* 55°24N 103°14W **71** B8
Manbij *Syria* 36°31N 37°57E **44** B3
Manchegorsk *Russia* 67°54N 32°58E **28** C4
Manchester *U.K.* 53°29N 2°12W **12** D5
Manchester *Calif., U.S.A.* 38°58N 123°41W **78** G3
Manchester *Conn., U.S.A.* 41°47N 72°31W **83** E12
Manchester *Ga., U.S.A.* 32°51N 84°37W **85** E12
Manchester *Iowa, U.S.A.* 42°29N 91°27W **80** D8
Manchester *Ky., U.S.A.* 37°9N 83°46W **81** G12
Manchester *N.H., U.S.A.* 42°59N 71°28W **83** D13
Manchester *N.Y., U.S.A.* 42°56N 77°16W **82** D7
Manchester *Pa., U.S.A.* 40°4N 76°43W **83** F8
Manchester *Tenn., U.S.A.* 35°29N 86°5W **85** D11
Manchester *Vt., U.S.A.* 43°10N 73°5W **83** C11
Manchester Int. ✈ (MAN)
U.K. 53°21N 2°17W **12** D5
Manchester L. *Canada* 61°28N 107°29W **71** A7
Manchhar L. *Pakistan* 26°25N 67°39E **42** F2
Manchuria = Dongbei
China 45°0N 125°0E **30** A5
Manchurian Plain *China* 47°0N 124°0E **26** D14

Mand → *India* 21°42N 83°15E **43** J10
Mand → *Iran* 28°20N 52°30E **45** D7
Manda *Ludewe, Tanzania* 10°30S 34°40E **55** E3
Manda *Mbeya, Tanzania* 7°58S 32°29E **54** D3
Manda *Mbeya, Tanzania* 8°30S 32°49E **55** D3
Mandabé *Madag.* 21°0S 44°55E **57** C7
Mandaguari *Brazil* 23°32S 51°42W **95** A5
Mandah = Töhöm
Mongolia 44°27N 108°2E **34** B5
Mandal *Norway* 58°2N 7°25E **9** G12
Mandala, Puncak
Indonesia 4°44S 140°20E **37** E10
Mandalay *Burma* 22°0N 96°4E **41** J20
Mandale = Mandalay
Burma 22°0N 96°4E **41** J20
Mandalgarh *India* 25°12N 75°6E **42** G6
Mandalgovi *Mongolia* 45°45N 106°10E **34** B4
Mandali *Iraq* 33°43N 45°28E **44** C5
Mandan *U.S.A.* 46°50N 100°54W **80** B3
Mandar, Teluk *Indonesia* 3°35S 119°15E **37** E5
Mandaue *Phil.* 10°20N 123°56E **37** B6
Mandera *Kenya* 3°55N 41°53E **54** B5
Mandeville *Jamaica* 18°2N 77°31W **88** a
Mandi *India* 31°39N 76°58E **42** D7
Mandi Burewala *Pakistan* 30°9N 72°41E **42** D5
Mandi Dabwali *India* 29°58N 74°42E **42** E6
Mandimba *Mozam.* 14°20S 35°40E **55** E4
Mandioli *Indonesia* 0°40S 127°20E **37** E7
Mandla *India* 22°39N 80°30E **43** H9
Mandorah *Australia* 12°32S 130°42E **60** B5
Mandoto *Madag.* 19°34S 46°17E **57** B8
Mandra *Pakistan* 33°23N 73°12E **42** C5
Mandrare → *Madag.* 25°10S 46°30E **57** D8
Mandritsara *Madag.* 15°50S 48°49E **57** B8
Mandronarivo *Madag.* 21°7S 45°38E **57** C8
Mandsaur *India* 24°3N 75°8E **42** G6
Mandurah *Australia* 32°36S 115°48E **61** F2
Mandvi *India* 22°51N 69°22E **42** H3
Mandya *India* 12°30N 77°0E **40** N10
Mandzai *Pakistan* 30°55N 67°6E **42** D2
Maneh *Iran* 37°39N 57°7E **45** B8
Manera *Madag.* 22°55S 44°20E **57** C7
Maneroo Cr. →
Australia 23°21S 143°53E **62** C3
Manfalût *Egypt* 27°20N 30°52E **51** C12
Manfredónia *Italy* 41°38N 15°55E **22** D6
Mangabeiras, Chapada das
Brazil 10°0S 46°30W **93** F9
Mangaia *Cook Is.* 21°55S 157°55W **65** K12
Mangalia *Romania* 43°50N 28°35E **17** G15
Mangalore *India* 12°55N 74°47E **40** N9
Mangaluru = Mangalore
India 12°55N 74°47E **40** N9
Mangan *India* 27°31N 88°32E **43** F13
Mangawan *India* 24°41N 81°33E **43** G9
Mangaweka *N.Z.* 39°48S 175°47E **59** C5
Manggar *Indonesia* 2°50S 108°10E **36** E3
Manggawitu *Indonesia* 4°8S 133°32E **37** E8
Mangghystaū Tübegi
Kazakhstan 44°30N 52°30E **28** E6
Manggis *Indonesia* 8°29S 115°31E **37** J18
Mangindrano *Madag.* 14°17S 48°58E **57** A8
Mangkalihat, Tanjung
Indonesia 1°2N 118°59E **37** D5
Mangkururrpa ◎
Australia 20°35S 129°43E **60** D4
Mangla *Pakistan* 33°7N 73°39E **42** C5
Mangla Dam *Pakistan* 33°9N 73°44E **43** C5
Manglaur *India* 29°44N 77°49E **42** E7
Mangnai *China* 37°52N 91°43E **32** C4
Mangnai Zhen *China* 38°24N 90°14E **32** C4
Mango *Togo* 10°20N 0°30E **50** F6
Mango *Tonga* 20°17S 174°29W **59** c
Mangoche *Malawi* 14°25S 35°16E **55** E4
Mangoky → *Madag.* 21°29S 43°41E **57** C7
Mangole *Indonesia* 1°50S 125°55E **37** E6
Mangombe
Dem. Rep. of the Congo 1°20S 26°48E **54** C2
Mangonui *N.Z.* 35°1S 173°32E **59** A4
Mangoro → *Madag.* 20°0S 48°45E **57** B8
Mangrol *Mad. P., India* 21°7N 70°7E **42** J4
Mangrol *Raj., India* 25°20N 76°31E **42** G6
Mangueira, L. da *Brazil* 33°0S 52°50W **95** C5
Mangum *U.S.A.* 34°53N 99°30W **84** D5
Mangyshlak, Poluostrov =
Mangghystaū Tübegi
Kazakhstan 44°30N 52°30E **28** E6
Manhattan *U.S.A.* 39°11N 96°35W **80** F5
Manhiça *Mozam.* 25°23S 32°49E **57** D5
Mania → *Madag.* 19°42S 45°22E **57** B8
Manica *Mozam.* 18°58S 32°59E **57** B5
Manica □ *Mozam.* 19°10S 33°45E **57** B5
Manicaland □ *Zimbabwe* 19°0S 32°30E **55** F3
Manicoré *Brazil* 5°48S 61°16W **92** E6
Manicouagan →
Canada 49°30N 68°30W **73** C6
Manicouagan, Rés.
Canada 51°5N 68°40W **73** B6
Maniema □
Dem. Rep. of the Congo 3°0S 26°0E **54** C2
Manifah *Si. Arabia* 27°44N 49°0E **45** E6
Manifold, C. *Australia* 22°41S 150°50E **62** C5
Manigotagan *Canada* 51°6N 96°18W **71** C9
Manigotagan → *Canada* 51°7N 96°20W **71** C9
Manihari *India* 25°21N 87°38E **43** G12
Manihiki *Cook Is.* 10°24S 161°1W **65** J11
Manihiki Plateau
Pac. Oc. 11°0S 164°0W **65** J11
Manika, Plateau de la
Dem. Rep. of the Congo 10°0S 25°5E **55** E2
Manikpur *India* 25°4N 81°7E **43** G9
Manila *Phil.* 14°35N 120°58E **37** B6
Manila *U.S.A.* 40°59N 109°43W **76** F9
Manila B. *Phil.* 14°40N 120°35E **37** B6
Manilla *Australia* 30°45S 150°43E **63** E5
Maningrida *Australia* 12°3S 134°13E **62** A1
Manipur □ *India* 25°0N 94°0E **41** G19
Manipur → *Burma* 23°45N 94°20E **41** H19

Manisa *Turkey* 38°38N 27°30E **23** E12
Manistee *U.S.A.* 44°15N 86°19W **80** C10
Manistee → *U.S.A.* 44°15N 86°21W **80** C10
Manistique *U.S.A.* 45°57N 86°15W **80** C10
Manitoba □ *Canada* 53°30N 97°0W **71** B9
Manitoba, L. *Canada* 51°0N 98°45W **71** C9
Manitou *Canada* 49°15N 98°32W **71** D9
Manitou, L. *Canada* 50°55N 65°17W **73** B6
Manitou Is. *Canada* 45°8N 86°0W **81** C11
Manitou L. *Canada* 52°43N 109°43W **71** C7
Manitou Springs
U.S.A. 38°52N 104°55W **76** G11
Manitoulin I. *Canada* 45°40N 82°30W **72** C3
Manitouwadge *Canada* 49°8N 85°48W **72** C2
Manitowoc *U.S.A.* 44°5N 87°40W **80** C10
Manizales *Colombia* 5°5N 75°32W **92** B3
Manja *Madag.* 21°26S 44°20E **57** C7
Manjacaze *Mozam.* 24°45S 34°0E **57** C5
Manjakandriana *Madag.* 18°55S 47°47E **57** B8
Manjhand *Pakistan* 25°50N 68°10E **42** G3
Manjimup *Australia* 34°15S 116°6E **61** F2
Manjra → *India* 18°49N 77°52E **40** K10
Mankato *Kans., U.S.A.* 39°47N 98°13W **80** F4
Mankato *Minn., U.S.A.* 44°10N 94°0W **80** C6
Mankayane *Swaziland* 26°40S 31°4E **57** D5
Mankera *Pakistan* 31°23N 71°26E **42** D4
Mankono *Ivory C.* 8°1N 6°10W **50** G4
Manlay = Üydzin
Mongolia 44°9N 107°0E **34** B4
Manmad *India* 20°18N 74°28E **40** J9
Mann Ranges *Australia* 26°6S 130°5E **61** E5
Manna *Indonesia* 4°25S 102°55E **36** E2
Mannahill *Australia* 32°25S 140°0E **63** E3
Mannar *Sri Lanka* 9°1N 79°54E **40** Q11
Mannar, G. of *Asia* 8°30N 79°0E **40** Q11
Mannar I. *Sri Lanka* 9°5N 79°45E **40** Q11
Mannheim *Germany* 49°29N 8°29E **16** D5
Manning *Canada* 56°53N 117°39W **70** B5
Manning *Oreg., U.S.A.* 45°45N 123°13W **78** E3
Manning *S.C., U.S.A.* 33°42N 80°13W **85** E14
Mannum *Australia* 34°50S 139°20E **63** E2
Manoharpur *India* 22°23N 85°12E **43** H11
Manokwari *Indonesia* 0°54S 134°0E **37** E8
Manombo *Madag.* 22°57S 43°28E **57** C7
Manono
Dem. Rep. of the Congo 7°15S 27°25E **54** D2
Manono *Samoa* 13°50S 172°5W **59** b
Manorhamilton *Ireland* 54°18N 8°9W **10** B3
Manosque *France* 43°49N 5°47E **20** E6
Manotick *Canada* 45°13N 75°41W **83** A9
Manouane → *Canada* 49°30N 71°10W **73** C5
Manouane, L. *Canada* 50°45N 70°45W **73** B5
Manp'o *N. Korea* 41°6N 126°24E **35** D14
Manpojin = Manp'o
N. Korea 41°6N 126°24E **35** D14
Manpur *Chhattisgarh,
India* 23°17N 83°35E **43** H10
Manpur *Mad. P., India* 22°26N 75°37E **42** H6
Manresa *Spain* 41°48N 1°50E **21** B6
Mansa *Gujarat, India* 23°27N 72°45E **42** H5
Mansa *Punjab, India* 30°0N 75°27E **42** E6
Mansa *Zambia* 11°13S 28°55E **55** E2
Mansehra *Pakistan* 34°20N 73°15E **42** B5
Mansel I. *Canada* 62°0N 80°0W **69** E15
Mansfield *Australia* 37°4S 146°6E **63** F4
Mansfield *U.K.* 53°9N 1°11W **12** D6
Mansfield *La., U.S.A.* 32°2N 93°43W **84** E8
Mansfield *Mass., U.S.A.* 42°2N 71°13W **83** D13
Mansfield *Ohio, U.S.A.* 40°45N 82°31W **82** F2
Mansfield *Pa., U.S.A.* 41°48N 77°5W **82** E7
Mansfield *Tex., U.S.A.* 32°33N 97°8W **84** E6
Mansfield, Mt. *U.S.A.* 44°33N 72°49W **83** B12
Manson Creek *Canada* 55°37N 124°32W **70** B4
Manta *Ecuador* 1°0S 80°40W **92** D2
Mantadia △ *Madag.* 18°54S 48°21E **57** B8
Mantalingajan, Mt.
Phil. 8°55N 117°45E **36** C5
Mantare *Tanzania* 2°42S 33°13E **54** C3
Manteca *U.S.A.* 37°48N 121°13W **78** H5
Manteo *U.S.A.* 35°55N 75°40W **85** D17
Mantes-la-Jolie *France* 48°58N 1°41E **20** B4
Manthani *India* 18°40N 79°35E **40** K11
Manti *U.S.A.* 39°16N 111°38W **76** G8
Mantiqueira, Serra da
Brazil 22°0S 44°0W **95** A7
Manton *U.S.A.* 44°25N 85°24W **81** C11
Mántova *Italy* 45°9N 10°48E **22** B4
Mänttä *Finland* 62°3N 24°40E **8** E21
Mantua = Mántova *Italy* 45°9N 10°48E **22** B4
Manú *Peru* 12°10S 70°51W **92** F4
Manú → *Peru* 12°16S 70°55W **92** F4
Manu'a Is. *Amer. Samoa* 14°13S 169°35W **59** b
Manuel Alves → *Brazil* 11°19S 48°28W **93** F9
Manui *Indonesia* 3°35S 123°5E **37** E6
Manukau *N.Z.* 37°0S 174°52E **59** B5
Manuripi → *Bolivia* 11°6S 67°36W **92** F5
Many *U.S.A.* 31°34N 93°29W **84** F8
Manyallaluk ◎
Australia 14°16S 132°49E **60** B5
Manyani *Kenya* 3°5S 38°30E **54** C4
Manyara, L. *Tanzania* 3°40S 35°50E **54** C4
Manyara △ *Tanzania* 3°35S 35°50E **54** C4
Manych-Gudilo, Ozero
Russia 46°24N 42°38E **19** E7
Manyonga → *Tanzania* 4°10S 34°15E **54** C3
Manyoni *Tanzania* 5°45S 34°55E **54** D3
Manzai *Pakistan* 32°12N 70°15E **42** C4
Manzanar △ *U.S.A.* 36°44N 118°9W **78** J7
Manzanares *Spain* 39°2N 3°22W **21** C4
Manzanillo *Cuba* 20°20N 77°31W **88** B4
Manzanillo *Mexico* 19°3N 104°20W **86** D4
Manzanillo, Pta. *Panama* 9°30N 79°40W **88** E4
Manzano Mts. *U.S.A.* 34°40N 106°20W **77** J10
Manzarīyeh *Iran* 34°53N 50°50E **45** C6
Manzhouli *China* 49°35N 117°25E **33** B6
Manzini *Swaziland* 26°30S 31°25E **57** D5
Manzur Vadisi △ *Turkey* 39°10N 39°30E **44** B3
Mao *Chad* 14°4N 15°19E **51** F9
Maó *Spain* 39°53N 4°16E **24** B11

Maoke, Pegunungan
Indonesia 3°40S 137°30E **37** E9
Maolin *China* 43°58N 123°30E **35** C12
Maoming *China* 21°50N 110°54E **33** D6
Maoxing *China* 45°28N 124°40E **35** B13
Mapam Yumco *China* 30°45N 81°28E **43** D9
Mapastepec *Mexico* 15°26N 92°54W **87** D6
Maphrao, Ko *Thailand* 7°56N 98°26E **39** a
Mapia, Kepulauan
Indonesia 0°50N 134°20E **37** D8
Mapimí *Mexico* 25°49N 103°51W **86** B4
Mapimí, Bolsón de
Mexico 27°0N 104°15W **86** B4
Mapinga *Tanzania* 6°40S 39°12E **54** D4
Mapinhane *Mozam.* 22°20S 35°0E **57** C6
Maple Creek *Canada* 49°55N 109°29W **71** D7
Maple Valley *U.S.A.* 47°25N 122°3W **78** C4
Mapleton *U.S.A.* 44°2N 123°52W **76** D2
Mapoon ◎ *Australia* 11°44S 142°8E **62** A3
Mapuera → *Brazil* 1°5S 57°2W **92** D7
Mapulanguene *Mozam.* 24°29S 32°6E **57** C5
Mapungubwe △
S. Africa 22°12S 29°22E **55** G2
Maputo *Mozam.* 25°58S 32°32E **57** D5
Maputo □ *Mozam.* 26°0S 32°25E **57** D5
Maputo, B. de *Mozam.* 25°50S 32°45E **57** D5
Maputo △ *Mozam.* 26°23S 32°48E **57** D5
Maqat *Kazakhstan* 47°39N 53°19E **19** E9
Maqên *China* 34°24N 100°6E **32** C5
Maqiaohe *China* 44°40N 130°30E **35** B16
Maqnā *Si. Arabia* 28°25N 34°50E **44** D2
Maquan He = Brahmaputra →
Asia 23°40N 90°35E **43** H13
Maquela do Zombo *Angola* 6°0S 15°15E **52** F3
Maquinchao *Argentina* 41°15S 68°50W **96** E3
Maquoketa *U.S.A.* 42°4N 90°40W **80** D8
Mar *Canada* 44°49N 81°12W **82** B3
Mar, Serra do *Brazil* 25°30S 49°0W **95** B6
Mar Chiquita, L.
Argentina 30°40S 62°50W **94** C3
Mar del Plata *Argentina* 38°0S 57°30W **94** D4
Mar Menor *Spain* 37°40N 0°45W **21** D5
Mara *Tanzania* 1°30S 34°32E **54** C3
Mara □ *Tanzania* 1°45S 34°20E **54** C3
Maraã *Brazil* 1°52S 65°25W **92** D5
Maraã *Tahiti* 17°46S 149°34W **59** d
Marabá *Brazil* 5°20S 49°5W **93** E9
Maraboon, L. *Australia* 23°41S 148°0E **62** C4
Maracá, I. de *Brazil* 2°10N 50°30W **93** C8
Maracaibo *Venezuela* 10°40N 71°37W **92** A4
Maracaibo, L. de
Venezuela 9°40N 71°30W **92** B4
Maracaju *Brazil* 21°38S 55°9W **95** A4
Maracas Bay Village
Trin. & Tob. 10°46N 61°28W **93** K15
Maracay *Venezuela* 10°15N 67°28W **92** A5
Marādah *Libya* 29°15N 19°15E **51** C9
Maradi *Niger* 13°29N 7°20E **50** F7
Marāgheh *Iran* 37°30N 46°12E **44** B5
Marāh *Si. Arabia* 25°0N 45°35E **44** E5
Marajó, I. de *Brazil* 1°0S 49°30W **93** D9
Marākand *Iran* 38°51N 45°16E **44** B5
Marakele △ *S. Africa* 32°14S 25°27E **57** E4
Maralal *Kenya* 1°0N 36°38E **54** B4
Maralinga *Australia* 30°13S 131°32E **61** F5
Maralinga Tjarutja ◎
Australia 29°30S 131°0E **61** E5
Marambio *Antarctica* 64°0S 56°0W **5** C18
Maran *Malaysia* 3°35N 102°45E **39** L4
Marana *U.S.A.* 32°27N 111°13W **77** K8
Maranboy *Australia* 14°40S 132°39E **60** B5
Marand *Iran* 38°30N 45°45E **44** B5
Marang *Malaysia* 5°12N 103°13E **39** K4
Maranguape *Brazil* 3°55S 38°50W **93** D11
Maranhão = São Luís
Brazil 2°39S 44°15W **93** D10
Maranhão □ *Brazil* 5°0S 46°0W **93** E9
Maranoa → *Australia* 27°50S 148°37E **63** D4
Marañón → *Peru* 4°30S 73°35W **92** D4
Marão *Mozam.* 24°18S 34°2E **57** C5
Maraş = Kahramanmaraş
Turkey 37°37N 36°53E **44** B3
Marathasa *Cyprus* 34°59N 32°51E **25** E11
Marathon *Australia* 20°51S 143°32E **62** C3
Marathon *Canada* 48°44N 86°23W **72** C2
Marathon *N.Y., U.S.A.* 42°27N 76°2W **83** D8
Marathon *Tex., U.S.A.* 30°12N 103°15W **84** F3
Marathóvouno *Cyprus* 35°13N 33°37E **25** D12
Maratua *Indonesia* 2°10N 118°35E **37** D5
Maraval *Trin. & Tob.* 10°42N 61°31W **93** K15
Maravatío *Mexico* 19°54N 100°27W **86** D4
Marāwih *U.A.E.* 24°18N 53°18E **45** E7
Marbella *Spain* 36°30N 4°57W **21** D3
Marble Bar *Australia* 21°9S 119°44E **60** D2
Marble Falls *U.S.A.* 30°35N 98°16W **84** F5
Marblehead *Mass.,
U.S.A.* 42°29N 70°51W **83** D14
Marblehead *Ohio, U.S.A.* 41°32N 82°44W **82** E2
Marburg *Germany* 50°47N 8°46E **16** C5
Marca, Pta. do *Angola* 16°31S 11°43E **53** H2
March *U.K.* 52°33N 0°5E **13** E8
Marche *France* 46°5N 1°20E **20** C4
Marche-en-Famenne
Belgium 50°14N 5°19E **15** D5
Marchena *Spain* 37°18N 5°23W **21** D3
Marco Island *U.S.A.* 25°58N 81°44W **85** J14
Marcos Juárez *Argentina* 32°42S 62°5W **94** C3
Marcus Baker, Mt.
U.S.A. 61°26N 147°45W **74** C10
Marcus I. = Minami-Tori-Shima
Pac. Oc. 24°20N 153°58E **64** E7
Marcy, Mt. *U.S.A.* 44°7N 73°56W **83** B11
Mardan *Pakistan* 34°20N 72°0E **42** B5
Mardie *Australia* 21°12S 115°59E **60** D2
Mardin *Turkey* 37°20N 40°43E **44** B4
Maree, L. *U.K.* 57°40N 5°26W **11** D3
Mareeba *Australia* 16°59S 145°28E **62** B4
Mareetsane *S. Africa* 26°9S 25°25E **56** D4

Marek = Stanke Dimitrov
Bulgaria 42°17N 23°9E **23** C10
Marengo *U.S.A.* 41°48N 92°4W **80** E7
Marerano *Madag.* 21°23S 44°52E **57** C7
Marfa *U.S.A.* 30°19N 104°1W **84** F2
Marfa Pt. *Malta* 35°59N 14°19E **25** d1
Margaret → *Australia* 18°9S 125°41E **60** C4
Margaret Bay *Canada* 51°20N 127°35W **70** C3
Margaret L. *Canada* 58°56N 115°25W **70** B5
Margaret River *Australia* 33°57S 115°4E **61** F2
Margarita, I. de *Venezuela* 11°0N 64°0W **92** A6
Margaritovo *Russia* 43°25N 134°45E **30** C7
Margate *S. Africa* 30°50S 30°20E **57** E5
Margate *U.K.* 51°23N 1°23E **13** F9
Margherita Pk. *Uganda* 0°22N 29°51E **54** B3
Marghilon *Uzbekistan* 40°27N 71°42E **28** E8
Mārgow, Dasht-e
Afghan. 30°40N 62°30E **40** D3
Marguerite *Canada* 52°30N 122°25W **70** C4
Mari El □ *Russia* 56°30N 48°0E **18** C8
Mari Indus *Pakistan* 32°57N 71°34E **42** C4
Mari Republic = Mari El □
Russia 56°30N 48°0E **18** C8
María de la Salut *Spain* 39°40N 3°5E **24** B10
María Elena *Chile* 22°18S 69°40W **94** A2
María Grande *Argentina* 31°45S 59°55W **94** C4
Maria I. *N. Terr.,
Australia* 14°52S 135°45E **62** A2
Maria I. *Tas., Australia* 42°35S 148°0E **63** G4
Maria van Diemen, C.
N.Z. 34°29S 172°40E **59** A4
Mariakani *Kenya* 3°50S 39°27E **54** C4
Mariala △ *Australia* 25°57S 145°8E **63** D4
Marian *Australia* 21°9S 148°57E **62** b
Marian L. *Canada* 63°0N 116°15W **70** A5
Mariana Trench *Pac. Oc.* 13°0N 145°0E **64** F6
Marianna *Ark., U.S.A.* 34°46N 90°46W **85** D9
Marianna *Fla., U.S.A.* 30°46N 85°14W **85** F12
Marías → *U.S.A.* 47°56N 110°30W **76** C8
Marías, Islas *Mexico* 21°25N 106°28W **86** C3
Mariato, Punta *Panama* 7°12N 80°52W **88** E3
Maribor *Slovenia* 46°36N 15°40E **16** E8
Marico → *Africa* 23°35S 26°57E **56** C4
Maricopa *Ariz., U.S.A.* 33°4N 112°3W **77** K7
Maricopa *Calif., U.S.A.* 35°4N 119°24W **79** K7
Marié → *Brazil* 0°27S 66°26W **92** D5
Marie Byrd Land
Antarctica 79°30S 125°0W **5** D14
Marie-Galante
Guadeloupe 15°56N 61°16W **88** b
Mariecourt = Kangiqsujuaq
Canada 61°30N 72°0W **69** E17
Mariehamn *Finland* 60°5N 19°55W **9** F18
Mariembourg *Belgium* 50°6N 4°31E **15** D4
Mariental *Namibia* 24°36S 18°0E **56** C2
Marienville *U.S.A.* 41°28N 79°8W **82** E5
Marietta *Ga., U.S.A.* 33°57N 84°33W **85** E12
Marietta *Ohio, U.S.A.* 39°25N 81°27W **81** F13
Marieville *Canada* 45°26N 73°10W **83** A11
Mariinsk *Russia* 56°10N 87°20E **28** D9
Marijampolė *Lithuania* 54°33N 23°19E **9** J20
Marília *Brazil* 22°13S 50°0W **95** A6
Marín *Spain* 42°23N 8°42W **21** A1
Marinduque *Phil.* 13°25N 122°0E **37** B6
Marine City *U.S.A.* 42°43N 82°30W **82** D2
Marinette *U.S.A.* 45°6N 87°38W **80** C10
Maringá *Brazil* 23°26S 52°2W **95** A5
Marion *Ala., U.S.A.* 32°38N 87°19W **85** E11
Marion *Ill., U.S.A.* 37°44N 88°56W **80** G9
Marion *Ind., U.S.A.* 40°32N 85°40W **81** E11
Marion *Iowa, U.S.A.* 42°2N 91°36W **80** D9
Marion *Kans., U.S.A.* 38°21N 97°1W **80** F5
Marion *N.C., U.S.A.* 35°41N 82°1W **85** D13
Marion *Ohio, U.S.A.* 40°35N 83°8W **81** E12
Marion *Va., U.S.A.* 36°50N 81°31W **81** G13
Marion, L. *U.S.A.* 33°28N 80°10W **85** E14
Mariposa *U.S.A.* 37°29N 119°58W **78** H7
Mariscal Estigarribia
Paraguay 22°3S 60°40W **94** A3
Maritime Alps = Maritimes, Alpes
Europe 44°10N 7°10E **20** D7
Maritimes, Alpes *Europe* 44°10N 7°10E **20** D7
Maritsa = Evros →
Greece 41°40N 26°34E **23** D12
Maritsa *Greece* 36°22N 28°8E **25** C10
Mariupol *Ukraine* 47°5N 37°31E **19** E6
Mariusa △ *Venezuela* 9°24N 61°27W **89** D7
Marīvān *Iran* 35°30N 46°25E **44** C5
Marj 'Uyūn *Lebanon* 33°21N 35°34E **46** B4
Markam *China* 29°42N 98°38E **41** E21
Markazi □ *Iran* 35°0N 49°30E **45** C6
Markdale *Canada* 44°19N 80°39W **82** B4
Marked Tree *U.S.A.* 35°32N 90°25W **85** D9
Market Drayton *U.K.* 52°54N 2°29W **12** E5
Market Harborough
U.K. 52°29N 0°55W **13** E7
Market Rasen *U.K.* 53°24N 0°20W **12** D7
Markham *Canada* 43°52N 79°16W **82** C5
Markham, Mt. *Antarctica* 83°0S 164°0E **5** E11
Markleeville *U.S.A.* 38°42N 119°47W **78** G7
Markovo *Russia* 64°40N 170°24E **29** C18
Marks *Russia* 51°45N 46°50E **18** D8
Marksville *U.S.A.* 31°8N 92°4W **84** F8
Marla *Australia* 27°19S 133°33E **63** D1
Marlbank *Canada* 44°26N 77°6W **82** B7
Marlboro *U.S.A.* 41°36N 73°59W **83** E11
Marlborough *Australia* 22°46S 149°52E **62** C4
Marlborough *U.S.A.* 42°21N 71°33W **83** D13
Marlborough Downs
U.K. 51°27N 1°53W **13** F6
Marlin *U.S.A.* 31°18N 96°54W **84** F6
Marlow *U.S.A.* 34°39N 97°58W **84** D6
Marmagao *India* 15°25N 73°56E **40** M8

Marmara *Turkey* 40°35N 27°34E **23** D12
Marmara, Sea of = Marmara
  Denizi *Turkey*
Marmara Denizi *Turkey* 40°45N 28°15E **23** D13
Marmaris *Turkey* 36°50N 28°14E **23** F13
Marmion, Mt. *Australia* 29°16S 119°50E **61** E2
Marmion L. *Canada* 48°55N 91°20W **72** C1
Marmolada, Mte. *Italy* 46°26N 11°51E **22** A4
Marmora *Canada* 44°28N 77°41W **82** B7
Marmugao = Marmagao
  India 15°25N 73°56E **40** M8
Marne → *France* 48°47N 2°29E **20** B5
Maro Reef *U.S.A.* 25°25N 170°35W **75** K5
Maroala *Madag.* 15°23S 47°59E **57** B8
Maroantsetra *Madag.* 15°26S 49°44E **57** B8
Maroelaboom *Namibia* 19°15S 18°53E **56** B2
Marofandilia *Madag.* 20°7S 44°34E **57** C7
Marojejy △ *Madag.* 14°26S 49°21E **57** A8
Marolambo *Madag.* 20°2S 48°7E **57** C8
Maromandia *Madag.* 14°13S 48°5E **57** A8
Maromokotro *Madag.* 14°0S 49°0E **57** A8
Marondera *Madag.* 18°5S 31°42E **55** F3
Maroni → *Fr. Guiana* 5°30N 54°0W **93** B8
Maroochydore *Australia* 26°29S 153°5E **63** D5
Maroona *Australia* 37°27S 142°54E **63** F3
Marosakoa *Madag.* 15°26S 46°38E **57** B8
Maroseranana *Madag.* 18°32S 48°51E **57** B8
Marotandrano *Madag.* 16°10S 48°50E **57** B8
Marotaolano *Madag.* 12°47S 49°15E **57** A8
Maroua *Cameroon* 10°40N 14°20E **51** F8
Marovato *Madag.* 15°48S 48°5E **57** B8
Marovoay *Madag.* 16°6S 46°39E **57** B8
Marquard *S. Africa* 28°40S 27°28E **56** D4
Marquesas Fracture Zone
  Pac. Oc. 9°0S 125°0W **65** H15
Marquesas Is. = Marquises, Îs.
  French Polynesia 9°30S 140°0W **65** H14
Marquette *U.S.A.* 46°33N 87°24W **80** B10
Marquis *St. Lucia* 14°2N 60°54W **89** f
Marquises, Îs.
  French Polynesia 9°30S 140°0W **65** H14
Marra, Djebel *Sudan* 13°10N 24°22E **51** F10
Marracuene *Mozam.* 25°45S 32°35E **57** D5
Marrakech *Morocco* 31°9N 8°0W **50** B4
Marrawah *Australia* 40°55S 144°42E **63** G3
Marree *Australia* 29°39S 138°1E **63** D2
Marrero *U.S.A.* 29°53N 90°6W **85** G9
Marrimane *Mozam.* 22°58S 33°34E **57** C5
Marromeu *Mozam.* 18°15S 36°25E **57** B6
Marromeu △ *Mozam.* 19°0S 36°0E **57** B6
Marrowie Cr. →
  Australia 33°23S 145°40E **63** E4
Marrubane *Mozam.* 18°0S 37°0E **55** F4
Marrupa *Mozam.* 13°8S 37°30E **55** E4
Mars Hill *U.S.A.* 46°31N 67°52W **81** B20
Marsá 'Alam *Egypt* 25°5N 34°54E **47** E1
Marsá Matrûh *Egypt* 31°19N 27°9E **51** B11
Marsabit *Kenya* 2°18N 38°0E **54** B4
Marsabit △ *Kenya* 2°23N 37°56E **54** B4
Marsala *Italy* 37°48N 12°26E **22** F5
Marsalforn *Malta* 36°4N 14°16E **25** C1
Marsden *Australia* 33°47S 147°32E **63** E4
Marseille *France* 43°18N 5°23E **20** E6
Marseilles = Marseille
  France 43°18N 5°23E **20** E6
Marsh I. *U.S.A.* 29°34N 91°53W **84** G9
Marshall *Ark., U.S.A.* 35°55N 92°38W **84** D8
Marshall *Mich., U.S.A.* 42°16N 84°58W **81** D11
Marshall *Minn., U.S.A.* 44°27N 95°47W **80** C6
Marshall *Mo., U.S.A.* 39°7N 93°12W **80** F7
Marshall *Tex., U.S.A.* 32°33N 94°23W **84** E7
Marshall → *Australia* 22°59S 136°59E **62** C2
Marshall Is. ■ *Pac. Oc.* 9°0N 171°0E **58** A10
Marshalltown *U.S.A.* 42°3N 92°55W **80** D7
Marshbrook *Zimbabwe* 18°33S 31°9E **57** B5
Marshfield *Mo., U.S.A.* 37°15N 92°54W **80** G7
Marshfield *Vt., U.S.A.* 44°20N 72°20W **83** B12
Marshfield *Wis., U.S.A.* 44°40N 90°10W **80** C8
Marshûn *Iran* 36°19N 49°23E **45** B6
Märsta *Sweden* 59°37N 17°52E **9** G17
Mart *U.S.A.* 31°33N 96°50W **84** F6
Martaban *Burma* 16°30N 97°35E **41** L20
Martaban, G. of *Burma* 16°5N 96°30E **41** L20
Martapura *Kalimantan,*
  Indonesia 3°22S 114°47E **36** E4
Martapura *Sumatera,*
  Indonesia 4°19S 104°22E **36** E2
Marte R. Gómez, Presa
  Mexico 26°10N 99°0W **87** B5
Martelange *Belgium* 49°49N 5°43E **15** E5
Martha's Vineyard
  U.S.A. 41°25N 70°38W **83** E14
Martigny *Switz.* 46°6N 7°3E **20** C7
Martigues *France* 43°24N 5°4E **20** E6
Martin *Slovak Rep.* 49°6N 18°58E **17** D10
Martin *S. Dak., U.S.A.* 43°11N 101°44W **80** D3
Martin *Tenn., U.S.A.* 36°21N 88°51W **85** C10
Martin L. *U.S.A.* 32°41N 85°55W **85** E12
Martina Franca *Italy* 40°42N 17°20E **22** D7
Martinborough *N.Z.* 41°14S 175°29E **59** D5
Martinez *Calif., U.S.A.* 38°1N 122°8W **78** G4
Martinez *Ga., U.S.A.* 33°31N 82°5W **85** E13
Martinique ☑ *W. Indies* 14°40N 61°0W **88** c
Martinique Passage
  W. Indies 15°15N 61°0W **89** C7
Martinópolis *Brazil* 22°11S 51°12W **95** A5
Martins Ferry *U.S.A.* 40°6N 80°44W **82** F4
Martinsburg *Pa., U.S.A.* 40°19N 78°20W **82** F6
Martinsburg *W. Va.,*
  U.S.A. 39°27N 77°58W **81** F15
Martinsville *Ind.,*
  U.S.A. 39°26N 86°25W **80** F10
Martinsville *Va., U.S.A.* 36°41N 79°52W **81** G14
Marton *N.Z.* 40°4S 175°23E **59** D5
Martos *Spain* 37°44N 3°58W **21** D4
Martu ✪ *Australia* 22°30S 122°30E **60** D3
Marudi *Malaysia* 4°11N 114°19E **36** D4
Maruf *Afghan.* 31°30N 67°6E **40** D5

Marugame *Japan* 34°15N 133°40E **31** G6
Marunga *Angola* 17°28S 20°2E **56** B3
Marungu, Mts.
  Dem. Rep. of the Congo 7°30S 30°0E **54** D3
Maruwa ♦ *Australia* 22°30S 127°30E **60** D4
Marv Dasht *Iran* 29°50N 52°40E **45** D7
Marvast *Iran* 30°30N 54°15E **45** D7
Marvel Loch *Australia* 31°28S 119°29E **61** F2
Marwar *India* 25°43N 73°45E **42** G5
Mary *Turkmenistan* 37°40N 61°50E **45** B9
Maryborough = Port Laoise
  Ireland 53°2N 7°18W **10** C4
Maryborough *Queens.,*
  Australia 25°31S 152°37E **63** D5
Maryborough *Vic.,*
  Australia 37°3S 143°44E **63** F3
Maryfield *Canada* 49°50N 101°35W **71** D8
Maryland ☐ *U.S.A.* 39°0N 76°30W **81** F15
Maryland Junction
  Zimbabwe 17°45S 30°31E **55** F3
Maryport *U.K.* 54°44N 3°28W **12** C4
Mary's Harbour *Canada* 52°18N 55°51W **73** B8
Marystown *Canada* 47°10N 55°10W **73** C8
Marysville *Calif., U.S.A.* 39°9N 121°35W **78** F5
Marysville *Kans., U.S.A.* 39°51N 96°39W **80** F5
Marysville *Mich., U.S.A.* 42°54N 82°29W **82** D2
Marysville *Ohio, U.S.A.* 40°14N 83°22W **81** E12
Marysville *Wash., U.S.A.* 48°3N 122°11W **78** B4
Maryville *Mo., U.S.A.* 40°21N 94°52W **80** E6
Maryville *Tenn., U.S.A.* 35°46N 83°58W **85** D13
Marzûq *Libya* 25°53N 13°57E **51** C8
Marzûq, Idehân *Libya* 24°50N 13°51E **51** D8
Masada *Israel* 31°15N 35°20E **46** D4
Masahunga *Tanzania* 2°6S 33°18E **54** C3
Masai *Kenya* 1°29N 103°55E **39** d
Masai Mara △ *Kenya* 1°25S 35°5E **54** C4
Masai Steppe *Tanzania* 4°30S 36°30E **54** C4
Masaka *Uganda* 0°21S 31°45E **54** C3
Masalembo, Kepulauan
  Indonesia 5°35S 114°30E **36** F4
Masalima, Kepulauan
  Indonesia 5°4S 117°5E **36** F5
Masamba *Indonesia* 2°30S 120°15E **37** E6
Masan *S. Korea* 35°11N 128°32E **35** G15
Masandam, Ra's *Oman* 26°30N 56°30E **45** E8
Masasi *Tanzania* 10°45S 38°52E **54** E4
Masaya *Nic.* 12°0N 86°7W **88** D2
Masbate *Phil.* 12°21N 123°36E **37** B6
Mascara *Algeria* 35°26N 0°6E **50** A6
Mascota *Mexico* 20°32N 104°49W **86** C4
Masela *Indonesia* 8°9S 129°51E **37** F7
Maseru *Lesotho* 29°18S 27°30E **56** D4
Mashaba *Zimbabwe* 20°2S 30°29E **55** G3
Mashābih *Si. Arabia* 25°35N 36°30E **44** E3
Mashatu △ *Botswana* 22°45S 29°5E **57** C4
Masherbrum *Pakistan* 35°38N 76°18E **43** B7
Mashhad *Iran* 36°20N 59°35E **45** B8
Mashīz *Iran* 29°56N 56°37E **45** D8
Mäshkel, Hämün-i-
  Pakistan 28°20N 62°56E **45** D9
Mashki Chāh *Pakistan* 29°5N 62°30E **40** E3
Mashonaland *Zimbabwe* 16°30S 31°0E **53** H6
Mashonaland Central ☐
  Zimbabwe 17°30S 31°0E **57** B5
Mashonaland East ☐
  Zimbabwe 18°0S 32°0E **57** B5
Mashonaland West ☐
  Zimbabwe 17°30S 29°30E **57** B4
Mashrakh *India* 26°7N 84°48E **43** F11
Masi Manimba
  Dem. Rep. of the Congo 4°40S 17°54E **52** E3
Masig *Australia* 9°45S 143°24E **62** a
Masindi *Uganda* 1°40N 31°43E **54** B3
Masindi Port *Uganda* 1°43N 32°2E **54** B3
Masinga Res. *Kenya* 0°58S 37°38E **54** C4
Masiri *Iran* 30°55N 49°46E **45** D6
Masisi
  Dem. Rep. of the Congo 1°23S 28°49E **54** C2
Masjed Soleyman *Iran* 31°55N 49°18E **45** D6
Mask, L. *Ireland* 53°36N 9°22W **10** C2
Maskin *Oman* 23°44N 56°52E **45** F8
Masoala, Tanjon' i
  Madag. 15°59S 50°13E **57** B9
Masoala △ *Madag.* 15°30S 50°12E **57** B9
Masoarivo *Madag.* 19°3S 44°19E **57** B7
Masohi = Amahai
  Indonesia 3°20S 128°55E **37** E7
Masomeloka *Madag.* 20°17S 48°37E **57** C8
Mason *Nev., U.S.A.* 38°56N 119°8W **78** G4
Mason *Tex., U.S.A.* 30°45N 99°14W **84** F5
Mason City *U.S.A.* 43°9N 93°12W **80** D7
Maspalomas *Canary Is.* 27°46N 15°35W **24** G4
Maspalomas, Pta.
  Canary Is. 27°43N 15°36W **24** G4
Masqat *Oman* 23°37N 58°36E **47** C6
Massa *Italy* 44°1N 10°9E **20** D9
Massachusetts ☐ *U.S.A.* 42°30N 72°0W **83** D13
Massachusetts B.
  U.S.A. 42°25N 70°50W **83** D14
Massakory *Chad* 13°0N 15°49E **51** F9
Massamba *Mozam.* 15°58S 33°31E **57** F3
Massanella *Spain* 39°48N 2°51E **24** B9
Massangena *Mozam.* 21°34S 33°0E **57** C5
Massango *Angola* 8°2S 16°21E **52** F3
Massawa = Mitsiwa
  Eritrea 15°35N 39°25E **47** D2
Massena *U.S.A.* 44°56N 74°54W **83** B10
Massenya *Chad* 11°21N 16°9E **51** F9
Masset *Canada* 54°2N 132°10W **70** C2
Massiah Street *Barbados* 13°9N 59°29E **89** g
Massif Central *France* 44°55N 3°0E **20** D5
Massillon *U.S.A.* 40°48N 81°32W **82** F3
Massinga *Mozam.* 23°15S 35°22E **57** C6
Massingir *Mozam.* 23°51S 32°4E **57** C5
Masson-Angers *Canada* 45°32N 75°25W **83** A9
Masson I. *Antarctica* 66°10S 93°20E **5** C7
Mastanli = Momchilgrad
  Bulgaria 41°33N 25°23E **23** D11

Masterton *N.Z.* 40°56S 175°39E **59** D5
Mastic *U.S.A.* 40°47N 72°54W **83** F12
Mastuj *Pakistan* 36°20N 72°36E **43** A5
Mastung *Pakistan* 29°50N 66°56E **40** E5
Masty *Belarus* 53°27N 24°38E **17** B13
Masuda *Japan* 34°40N 131°51E **31** G5
Masuku = Franceville
  Gabon 1°40S 13°32E **52** E2
Masurian Lakes = Mazurski,
  Pojezierze *Poland* 53°50N 21°0E **17** B11
Masvingo *Zimbabwe* 20°8S 30°49E **55** G3
Masvingo ☐ *Zimbabwe* 21°0S 31°30E **55** G3
Maswa △ *Tanzania* 2°58S 34°19E **54** C3
Maşyāf *Syria* 35°4N 36°20E **44** C3
Mata-au = Clutha →
  N.Z. 46°20S 169°49E **59** G2
Matabeleland *Zimbabwe* 18°0S 27°0E **53** H5
Matabeleland North ☐
  Zimbabwe 19°0S 28°0E **55** F2
Matabeleland South ☐
  Zimbabwe 21°0S 29°0E **55** G2
Matachewan *Canada* 47°56N 80°39W **72** C3
Matadi
  Dem. Rep. of the Congo 5°52S 13°31E **52** F2
Matagalpa *Nic.* 13°0N 85°58W **88** D2
Matagami *Canada* 49°45N 77°34W **72** C4
Matagami, L. *Canada* 49°50N 77°40W **72** C4
Matagorda B. *U.S.A.* 28°40N 96°12W **84** G6
Matagorda I. *U.S.A.* 28°15N 96°30W **84** G6
Mataiea *Tahiti* 17°46S 149°25W **59** d
Matak *Indonesia* 3°18N 106°16E **36** D3
Matala *Greece* 34°59N 24°45E **25** E6
Matam *Senegal* 15°34N 13°17W **50** E3
Matamoros *Campeche,*
  Mexico 18°50N 90°50W **87** D6
Matamoros *Coahuila,*
  Mexico 25°32N 103°15W **86** B4
Matamoros *Tamaulipas,*
  Mexico 25°53N 97°30W **87** B5
Ma'ṭan as Sarra *Libya* 21°45N 22°0E **51** D10
Matandu → *Tanzania* 8°45S 34°19E **55** D3
Matane *Canada* 48°50N 67°33W **73** C6
Matanomadh *India* 23°33N 68°57E **42** H3
Matanzas *Cuba* 23°0N 81°40W **88** B3
Matapa *Botswana* 23°11S 24°39E **56** C3
Matapan, C. = Tenaro, Akra
  Greece 36°22N 22°27E **23** F10
Matapédia *Canada* 48°0N 66°59W **73** C6
Matapo △ *Zimbabwe* 20°30S 29°40E **55** G2
Matara *Sri Lanka* 5°58N 80°30E **40** S12
Mataram *Indonesia* 8°35S 116°7E **37** K18
Matarani *Peru* 17°0S 72°10W **92** G4
Mataranka *Australia* 14°55S 133°4E **60** B5
Matarma, Râs *Egypt* 30°27N 32°44E **46** E1
Mataró *Spain* 41°32N 2°29E **21** B7
Matatiele *S. Africa* 30°20S 28°49E **57** E4
Mataura *N.Z.* 46°11S 168°51E **59** G2
Matavai, B. de *Tahiti* 17°30S 149°23W **59** d
Matehuala *Mexico* 23°39N 100°39W **86** C4
Mateke Hills *Zimbabwe* 21°48S 31°0E **55** G3
Matelot *Trin. & Tob.* 10°50N 61°7W **93** K15
Matera *Italy* 40°40N 16°36E **22** D7
Matetsi *Zimbabwe* 18°12S 26°0E **55** F2
Matheniko △ *Uganda* 2°49N 34°27E **54** B3
Mathis *U.S.A.* 28°6N 97°50W **84** G6
Mathraki *Greece* 39°48N 19°31E **25** A3
Mathura *India* 27°30N 77°40E **42** F7
Mati *Phil.* 6°55N 126°15E **37** C7
Matiali *India* 26°56N 88°49E **43** F13
Matías Romero *Mexico* 16°53N 95°2W **87** D5
Matibane *Mozam.* 14°49S 40°45E **55** E5
Matiri Ra. *N.Z.* 41°38S 172°20E **59** D4
Matjiesfontein *S. Africa* 33°14S 20°35E **56** E3
Matla → *India* 21°40N 88°40E **43** J13
Matlamanyane
  Botswana 19°33S 25°57E **56** B4
Matli *Pakistan* 25°2N 68°39E **42** G3
Matlock *U.K.* 53°9N 1°33W **12** D6
Mato Grosso ☐ *Brazil* 14°0S 55°0W **93** F8
Mato Grosso, Planalto do
  Brazil 15°0S 55°0W **93** G8
Mato Grosso do Sul ☐
  Brazil 18°0S 55°0W **93** G8
Matobo = Matapo △
  Zimbabwe 20°30S 29°40E **55** G2
Matochkin Shar, Proliv
  Russia 73°23N 55°12E **28** B6
Matopo Hills *Zimbabwe* 20°36S 28°20E **55** G2
Matopos *Zimbabwe* 20°20S 28°29E **55** G2
Matosinhos *Portugal* 41°11N 8°42W **21** B1
Matroosberg *S. Africa* 33°23S 19°40E **56** E2
Matsue *Japan* 35°25N 133°10E **31** G6
Matsum, Ko *Thailand* 9°22N 99°59E **39** b
Matsumae *Japan* 41°26N 140°7E **30** D10
Matsumoto *Japan* 36°15N 138°0E **31** F9
Matsusaka *Japan* 34°34N 136°32E **31** G8
Matsuura *Japan* 33°20N 129°49E **31** H4
Matsuyama *Japan* 33°45N 132°45E **31** H6
Mattagami → *Canada* 50°43N 81°29W **72** B3
Mattancheri *India* 9°50N 76°15E **40** Q10
Mattawa *Canada* 46°20N 78°45W **72** C4
Matterhorn *Switz.* 45°58N 7°39E **20** D7
Matthew Town
  Bahamas 20°57N 73°40W **89** B5
Matthews Ridge *Guyana* 7°37N 60°10W **92** B6
Mattice *Canada* 49°40N 83°20W **72** C3
Mattituck *U.S.A.* 40°59N 72°32W **83** F12
Mattō *Japan* 36°31N 136°34E **31** F8
Mattoon *U.S.A.* 39°29N 88°23W **80** F9
Matuba *Mozam.* 24°28S 32°49E **57** C5
Matucana *Peru* 11°55S 76°25W **92** F3
Matuku *Fiji* 19°10S 179°44E **59** a
Matún = Khowst
  Afghan. 33°22N 69°58E **42** C3
Matura B. *Trin. & Tob.* 10°39N 61°1W **93** K15
Maturín *Venezuela* 9°45N 63°11W **92** B6
Matusadona △ *Zimbabwe* 16°58S 28°42E **55** F2
Mau *Mad. P., India* 26°17N 78°41E **43** F8

Mau *Ut. P., India* 25°56N 83°33E **43** G10
Mau *Ut. P., India* 25°17N 81°23E **43** G9
Mau Escarpment *Kenya* 0°40S 36°0E **54** C4
Mau Ranipur *India* 25°16N 79°8E **43** G8
Maua *Kenya* 0°14N 37°56E **54** C4
Maua *Mozam.* 13°53S 37°10E **55** E4
Maubeuge *France* 50°17N 3°57E **20** A6
Maubin *Burma* 16°44N 95°39E **41** L19
Maud, Pt. *Australia* 23°6S 113°45E **60** D1
Maude *Australia* 34°29S 144°18E **63** E3
Maud Rise *S. Ocean* 66°0S 3°0E **5** C3
Maudin Sun *Burma* 16°0N 94°30E **41** M19
Maués *Brazil* 3°20S 57°45W **92** D7
Mauganj *India* 24°50N 81°55E **43** G9
Maughold Hd. *I. of Man* 54°18N 4°18W **12** C3
Maui *U.S.A.* 20°48N 156°20W **75** L8
Maulamyaing = Moulmein
  Burma 16°30N 97°40E **41** L20
Maule ☐ *Chile* 36°5S 72°30W **94** D1
Maumee *U.S.A.* 41°34N 83°39W **81** E12
Maumee → *U.S.A.* 41°42N 83°28W **81** E12
Maumere *Indonesia* 8°38S 122°13E **37** F6
Maun *Botswana* 20°0S 23°26E **56** C3
Mauna Kea *U.S.A.* 19°50N 155°28W **75** M8
Mauna Loa *U.S.A.* 19°30N 155°35W **75** M8
Maunath Bhanjan = Mau
  India 25°56N 83°33E **43** G10
Maungmagan Kyunzu
  Burma 14°0N 97°48E **38** E1
Maungu *Kenya* 3°33S 38°45E **54** C4
Maupin *U.S.A.* 45°11N 121°5W **76** D3
Maurepas, L. *U.S.A.* 30°15N 90°30W **85** F9
Maurice, L. *Australia* 29°30S 131°0E **61** E5
Mauricie △ *Canada* 46°45N 73°0W **72** C5
Mauritania ■ *Africa* 20°50N 10°0W **50** E3
Mauritius ■ *Ind. Oc.* 20°0S 57°0E **53** d
Mauston *U.S.A.* 43°48N 90°5W **80** D8
Mavli *India* 24°45N 73°55E **42** G5
Mavuradonha Mts.
  Zimbabwe 16°30S 31°30E **55** F3
Mawa
  Dem. Rep. of the Congo 2°45N 26°40E **54** B2
Mawai *India* 22°30N 81°4E **43** H9
Mawana *India* 29°6N 77°58E **42** E7
Mawand *Pakistan* 29°33N 68°38E **42** E3
Mawjib, W. al → *Jordan* 31°28N 35°36E **46** D4
Mawk Mai *Burma* 20°14N 97°37E **41** J20
Mawlaik *Burma* 23°40N 94°26E **41** H19
Mawlamyine = Moulmein
  Burma 16°30N 97°40E **41** L20
Mawqaq *Si. Arabia* 27°25N 41°8E **44** E4
Mawson Base *Antarctica* 67°30S 62°53E **5** C6
Mawson Coast *Antarctica* 68°30S 63°0E **5** C6
Max *U.S.A.* 47°49N 101°18W **80** B3
Maxcanú *Mexico* 20°35N 90°0W **87** C6
Maxesibeni *S. Africa* 30°49S 29°23E **57** E4
Maxhamish L. *Canada* 59°50N 123°17W **70** B4
Maxixe *Mozam.* 23°54S 35°17E **57** C6
Maxville *Canada* 45°17N 74°51W **83** A10
Maxwell *U.S.A.* 39°17N 122°11W **78** F4
Maxwelton *Australia* 20°43S 142°41E **62** C3
May, C. *U.S.A.* 38°56N 74°58W **81** F16
May Pen *Jamaica* 17°58N 77°15W **88** a
Maya → *Russia* 60°28N 134°28E **29** D14
Maya Mts. *Belize* 16°30N 89°0W **87** D7
Mayaguana *Bahamas* 22°30N 72°44W **89** B5
Mayagüez *Puerto Rico* 18°12N 67°9W **89** d
Mayāmey *Iran* 36°24N 55°42E **45** B7
Mayanup *Australia* 33°57S 116°27E **61** F2
Mayapán *Mexico* 20°29N 89°11W **87** C7
Mayarí *Cuba* 20°40N 75°41W **89** B4
Mayaro B. *Trin. & Tob.* 10°14N 60°59W **93** K16
Maybell *U.S.A.* 40°31N 108°5W **76** F9
Maybole *U.K.* 55°21N 4°42W **11** F4
Maydān *Iraq* 34°55N 45°37E **44** C5
Maydena *Australia* 42°45S 146°30E **63** G4
Mayen *Germany* 50°18N 7°13E **16** C4
Mayenne *France* 48°20N 0°38W **20** B3
Mayenne → *France* 47°30N 0°32W **20** C3
Mayer *U.S.A.* 34°24N 112°14W **77** J7
Mayerthorpe *Canada* 53°57N 115°8W **70** C5
Mayfield *Ky., U.S.A.* 36°44N 88°38W **85** C10
Mayfield *N.Y., U.S.A.* 43°6N 74°16W **83** C10
Mayhill *U.S.A.* 32°53N 105°29W **77** K11
Maykop *Russia* 44°35N 40°10E **19** F7
Maymyo *Burma* 22°2N 96°28E **38** A1
Maynard *Mass., U.S.A.* 42°26N 71°27W **83** D13
Maynard *Wash., U.S.A.* 47°59N 122°55W **78** C4
Maynard Hills *Australia* 28°28S 119°49E **61** E2
Mayne → *Australia* 23°40S 141°55E **62** C3
Maynooth *Canada* 45°13N 77°56W **82** A7
Maynooth *Ireland* 53°23N 6°34W **10** C5
Mayo *Canada* 63°38N 135°57W **68** E4
Mayo ☐ *Ireland* 53°53N 9°3W **10** C2
Mayon Volcano *Phil.* 13°15N 123°41E **37** B6
Mayor I. *N.Z.* 37°16S 176°17E **59** B6
Mayotte ☑ *Ind. Oc.* 12°50S 45°10E **53** a
Maysān ☐ *Iraq* 31°55N 47°15E **44** D5
Maysville *U.S.A.* 38°39N 83°46W **81** F12
Mayu *Indonesia* 1°30N 126°30E **37** D7
Mayville *N. Dak., U.S.A.* 47°30N 97°20W **80** B5
Mayville *N.Y., U.S.A.* 42°15N 79°30W **82** D5
Mazabuka *Zambia* 15°52S 27°44E **55** F2
Mazagán = El Jadida
  Morocco 33°11N 8°17W **50** B4
Mazagão *Brazil* 0°7S 51°16W **93** D8
Mazán *Peru* 3°30S 73°0W **92** D4
Mazapil *Mexico* 24°39N 101°34W **86** C4
Mazar *China* 36°32N 77°1E **32** C2
Mazara del Vallo *Italy* 37°39N 12°35E **22** F5
Mazarrón *Spain* 37°38N 1°19W **21** D5
Mazaruni → *Guyana* 6°25N 58°35W **92** B7
Mazatán *Mexico* 29°0N 110°8W **86** B2
Mazatenango *Guatemala* 14°35N 91°30W **88** D1
Mazatlán *Mexico* 23°13N 106°25W **86** C3
Mažeikiai *Lithuania* 56°20N 22°20E **9** H20
Māzhān *Iran* 32°30N 59°0E **45** C8
Mazīnān *Iran* 36°19N 56°56E **45** B8
Mazoe *Mozam.* 16°42S 33°7E **55** F3
Mazoe → *Mozam.* 16°20S 33°30E **55** F3
Mazowe *Zimbabwe* 17°28S 30°58E **55** F3

Mazurski, Pojezierze
  Poland 53°50N 21°0E **17** B11
Mazyr *Belarus* 51°59N 29°15E **17** B15
Mba *Fiji* 17°33S 177°41E **59** a
Mbabane *Swaziland* 26°18S 31°6E **57** D5
Mbaïki *C.A.R.* 3°53N 18°1E **52** D3
Mbala *Zambia* 8°46S 31°24E **55** D3
Mbalabala *Zimbabwe* 20°27S 29°3E **57** C4
Mbale *Uganda* 1°8N 34°12E **54** B3
Mbalmayo *Cameroon* 3°33N 11°33E **52** D2
Mbamba Bay *Tanzania* 11°13S 34°49E **55** E3
Mbandaka
  Dem. Rep. of the Congo 0°1N 18°18E **52** D3
Mbanza Congo *Angola* 6°18S 14°16E **52** F2
Mbanza Ngungu
  Dem. Rep. of the Congo 5°12S 14°53E **52** F2
Mbarangandu *Tanzania* 10°11S 36°48E **55** D4
Mbarara *Uganda* 0°35S 30°40E **54** C3
Mbenga = Beqa *Fiji* 18°23S 178°8E **59** a
Mbengu ♦ *Tanzania* 9°25S 39°50E **55** D4
Mberengwa *Zimbabwe* 20°29S 29°57E **55** G2
Mberengwa, Mt.
  Zimbabwe 20°37S 29°55E **55** G2
Mbesuma *Zambia* 10°0S 32°2E **55** E3
Mbeya *Tanzania* 8°54S 33°29E **55** D3
Mbeya ☐ *Tanzania* 8°15S 33°30E **55** D3
Mbhashe → *S. Africa* 32°15S 28°54E **57** E4
Mbinga *Tanzania* 10°50S 35°0E **55** E4
Mbini = Río Muni ☐
  Eq. Guin. 1°30N 10°0E **52** D2
Mbizi *Zimbabwe* 21°23S 31°1E **55** G3
Mbouda *Cameroon* 5°38N 10°15E **50** G8
M'boukou, L. de
  Cameroon 6°23N 12°50E **52** C2
Mbour *Senegal* 14°22N 16°54W **50** F2
Mbuji-Mayi
  Dem. Rep. of the Congo 6°9S 23°40E **54** D1
Mbulu *Tanzania* 3°45S 35°30E **54** C4
Mburucuyá *Argentina* 28°1S 58°14W **94** B4
Mburucuyá △ *Argentina* 28°1S 58°12W **94** B4
Mchinja *Tanzania* 9°44S 39°45E **55** D4
Mchinji *Malawi* 13°47S 32°58E **55** E3
Mdantsane *S. Africa* 32°56S 27°46E **57** E4
Mead, L. *U.S.A.* 36°0N 114°44W **79** J12
Meade *U.S.A.* 37°17N 100°20W **80** G3
Meade River = Atqasuk
  U.S.A. 70°28N 157°24W **74** A8
Meadow Lake *Canada* 54°10N 108°26W **71** C7
Meadow Lake △ *Canada* 54°27N 109°0W **71** C7
Meadow Valley Wash →
  U.S.A. 36°40N 114°34W **79** J12
Meadville *U.S.A.* 41°39N 80°9W **82** E4
Meaford *Canada* 44°36N 80°35W **82** B4
Mealy Mts. *Canada* 53°10N 58°0W **73** B8
Meander River *Canada* 59°2N 117°42W **70** B5
Meares, C. *U.S.A.* 45°37N 124°0W **76** D1
Mearim → *Brazil* 3°4S 44°35W **93** D10
Meath ☐ *Ireland* 53°40N 6°57W **10** C5
Meath Park *Canada* 53°27N 105°22W **71** C7
Meaux *France* 48°58N 2°50E **20** B5
Mebechi-Gawa →
  Japan 40°31N 141°31E **30** D10
Mebulu, Tanjung
  Indonesia 8°50S 115°5E **37** K18
Mecanhelas *Mozam.* 15°12S 35°54E **55** F4
Mecca = Makkah
  Si. Arabia 21°30N 39°54E **47** C2
Mecca *U.S.A.* 33°34N 116°5W **79** M10
Mechanicsburg *U.S.A.* 40°13N 77°1W **82** F7
Mechanicville *U.S.A.* 42°54N 73°41W **83** D11
Mechelen *Belgium* 51°2N 4°29E **15** C4
Mecheria *Algeria* 33°35N 0°18W **50** B5
Mecklenburg *Germany* 53°33N 11°40E **16** B7
Mecklenburger Bucht
  Germany 54°20N 11°40E **16** A6
Meconta *Mozam.* 14°59S 39°50E **55** E4
Mecubúri *Mozam.* 14°39S 38°54E **55** E4
Mecubúri → *Mozam.* 14°10S 40°30E **55** E5
Mecúfi *Mozam.* 13°20S 40°32E **55** E5
Medan *Indonesia* 3°40N 98°38E **36** D1
Médanos de Coro △
  Venezuela 11°35N 69°44W **89** D6
Medanosa, Pta. *Argentina* 48°8S 66°0W **96** F3
Médéa *Algeria* 36°12N 2°50E **50** A6
Medellín *Colombia* 6°15N 75°35W **92** B3
Medelpad *Sweden* 62°33N 16°30E **8** E17
Medemblik *Neths.* 52°46N 5°8E **15** B5
Medford *Mass., U.S.A.* 42°25N 71°7W **83** D13
Medford *Oreg., U.S.A.* 42°19N 122°52W **76** E2
Medford *Wis., U.S.A.* 45°9N 90°20W **80** C8
Medgidia *Romania* 44°15N 28°19E **17** F15
Media Agua *Argentina* 31°58S 68°25W **94** C2
Media Luna *Argentina* 34°45S 66°44W **94** C2
Medianeira *Brazil* 25°17S 54°5W **95** B5
Mediaş *Romania* 46°9N 24°22E **17** E13
Medicine Bow *U.S.A.* 41°54N 106°12W **76** F10
Medicine Bow Mts.
  U.S.A. 40°40N 106°0W **76** F10
Medicine Bow Pk.
  U.S.A. 41°21N 106°19W **76** F10
Medicine Hat *Canada* 50°0N 110°45W **71** D6
Medicine Lake *U.S.A.* 48°30N 104°30W **76** B11
Medicine Lodge *U.S.A.* 37°17N 98°35W **80** G4
Medina = Al Madīnah
  Si. Arabia 24°35N 39°52E **44** E3
Medina *N. Dak., U.S.A.* 46°54N 99°18W **80** B4
Medina *N.Y., U.S.A.* 43°13N 78°23W **82** C6
Medina *Ohio, U.S.A.* 41°8N 81°52W **82** E3
Medina → *U.S.A.* 29°16N 98°29W **84** G5
Medina del Campo *Spain* 41°18N 4°55W **21** B3
Medina L. *U.S.A.* 29°32N 98°56W **84** G5
Medina Sidonia *Spain* 36°28N 5°57W **21** D3
Medinipur *India* 22°25N 87°21E **43** H12
Mediterranean Sea *Europe* 35°0N 15°0E **6** H7
Médoc *France* 45°10N 0°50W **20** D3
Medveditsa → *Russia* 49°35N 42°41E **19** E7
Medvezhi, Ostrava
  Russia 71°0N 161°0E **29** B17
Medvezhyegorsk *Russia* 63°0N 34°25E **18** B5

Medway □ *U.K.* 51°25N 0°32E **13** F8
Medway ➤ *U.K.* 51°27N 0°46E **13** F8
Meekatharra *Australia* 26°32S 118°29E **61** E2
Meeker *U.S.A.* 40°2N 107°55W **76** F10
Meerut *India* 29°1N 77°42E **42** E7
Meeteetse *U.S.A.* 44°9N 108°52W **76** D9
Mega *Ethiopia* 3°57N 38°19E **47** G2
Megara *Greece* 37°58N 23°22E **23** F10
Megasini *India* 21°38N 86°21E **43** J12
Meghalaya □ *India* 25°50N 91°0E **41** G17
Meghna ➤ *Bangla.* 22°50N 90°50E **41** H17
Megion *Russia* 61°3N 76°6E **28** C8
Mégiscane, L. *Canada* 48°35N 75°55W **72** C4
Meharry, Mt. *Australia* 22°59S 118°35E **60** D2
Mehlville *U.S.A.* 38°31N 90°19W **80** F8
Mehndawal *India* 26°58N 83°5E **43** F10
Mehr Jān *Iran* 33°50N 55°6E **45** C7
Mehrābād *Iran* 36°53N 47°55E **44** B5
Mehrān *Iran* 33°7N 46°10E **44** C5
Mehrān ➤ *Iran* 26°45N 55°26E **45** E7
Mehrgarh *Pakistan* 29°30N 67°30E **42** E2
Mehriz *Iran* 31°35N 54°28E **45** D7
Mei Xian *China* 34°18N 107°55E **34** G4
Meighen I. *Canada* 80°0N 99°30W **69** B12
Meihekou *China* 42°32N 125°40E **35** C13
Meiktila *Burma* 20°53N 95°54E **41** J19
Meissen *Germany* 51°9N 13°29E **16** C7
Meizhou *China* 24°16N 116°6E **33** D6
Meja *India* 25°9N 82°7E **43** G10
Mejillones *Chile* 23°10S 70°30W **94** A1
Mekele *Ethiopia* 13°33N 39°30E **47** E2
Mekerghene, Sebkra
   Algeria 26°21N 1°30E **50** C6
Mekhtar *Pakistan* 30°30N 69°15E **40** D6
Meknès *Morocco* 33°57N 5°33W **50** B4
Mekong ➤ *Asia* 9°30N 106°15E **39** H6
Mekongga *Indonesia* 3°39S 121°15E **37** E6
Mekvari = Kür ➤
   Azerbaijan 39°29N 49°15E **19** G8
Melagiri Hills *India* 12°20N 77°30E **40** N10
Melaka *Malaysia* 2°15N 102°15E **39** L4
Melalap *Malaysia* 5°10N 116°5E **36** C5
Melambes *Greece* 35°8N 24°40E **25** D6
Melanesia *Pac. Oc.* 4°0S 155°0E **64** H7
Melanesian Basin *Pac. Oc.* 0°5N 160°35E **64** G8
Melaya *Indonesia* 8°17S 114°30E **37** J17
Melbourne *Australia* 37°48S 144°58E **63** F4
Melbourne *U.S.A.* 28°5N 80°37W **85** G14
Melchor Múzquiz
   Mexico 27°53N 101°31W **86** B4
Melchor Ocampo
   Mexico 24°51N 101°39W **86** C4
Mélèzes ➤ *Canada* 57°40N 69°29W **72** A5
Melfort *Canada* 52°50N 104°37W **71** C8
Melfort *Zimbabwe* 18°0S 31°25E **55** F3
Melhus *Norway* 63°17N 10°18E **8** E14
Melilla *N. Afr.* 35°21N 2°57W **21** E4
Melipilla *Chile* 33°42S 71°15W **94** C1
Melissa *Canada* 45°24N 79°14W **82** A5
Melissa, Akra *Greece* 35°6N 24°33E **25** D6
Melita *Canada* 49°15N 101°0W **71** D8
Melitopol *Ukraine* 46°50N 35°22E **19** E6
Melk *Austria* 48°13N 15°20E **16** D8
Mellansel *Sweden* 63°26N 18°19E **8** E18
Mellen *U.S.A.* 46°20N 90°40W **80** B8
Mellerud *Sweden* 58°41N 12°28E **9** G15
Mellette *U.S.A.* 45°9N 98°30W **80** C4
Mellieha *Malta* 35°57N 14°22E **25** D1
Melo *Uruguay* 32°20S 54°10W **95** C5
Melolo *Indonesia* 9°53S 120°40E **37** F6
Melouprey *Cambodia* 13°48N 105°16E **38** F5
Melrhir, Chott *Algeria* 34°13N 6°30E **50** B7
Melrose *Australia* 32°42S 146°57E **63** E4
Melrose *U.K.* 55°36N 2°43W **11** F6
Melrose *Minn., U.S.A.* 45°40N 94°49W **80** C7
Melrose *N. Mex.,*
   U.S.A. 34°26N 103°38W **77** J12
Melstone *U.S.A.* 46°36N 107°52W **76** C10
Melton Mowbray *U.K.* 52°47N 0°54W **12** E7
Melun *France* 48°32N 2°39E **20** B5
Melville *Canada* 50°55N 102°50W **71** C8
Melville, C. *Australia* 14°11S 144°30E **62** A3
Melville, L. *Canada* 53°30N 60°0W **73** B8
Melville B. *Australia* 12°0S 136°45E **62** A2
Melville B. *Greenland* 75°30N 63°0W **69** B19
Melville I. *Australia* 11°30S 131°0E **60** B5
Melville I. *Canada* 75°30N 112°0W **69** B9
Melville Pen. *Canada* 68°0N 84°0W **69** D15
Melvin, Lough *Ireland* 54°26N 8°10W **10** B3
Memba *Mozam.* 14°11S 40°30E **55** E5
Memboro *Indonesia* 9°30S 119°30E **60** A2
Memel = Klaipėda
   Lithuania 55°43N 21°10E **9** J19
Memel *S. Africa* 27°38S 29°36E **57** D4
Memmingen *Germany* 47°58N 10°10E **16** E6
Mempawah *Indonesia* 0°30N 109°5E **36** D3
Memphis *Mich., U.S.A.* 42°54N 82°46W **82** D2
Memphis *Tenn., U.S.A.* 35°8N 90°2W **85** D9
Memphis *Tex., U.S.A.* 34°44N 100°33W **84** D4
Memphrémagog, L.
   N. Amer. 45°8N 72°17W **83** B12
Mena *U.S.A.* 34°35N 94°15W **84** D7
Menai Strait *U.K.* 53°11N 4°13W **12** D3
Ménaka *Mali* 15°59N 2°18E **50** E6
Menan = Chao Phraya ➤
   Thailand 13°40N 100°31E **38** F3
Menard *U.S.A.* 30°55N 99°47W **84** F5
Menard Fracture Zone
   Pac. Oc. 43°0S 97°0W **65** M18
Mendaña Fracture Zone
   Pac. Oc. 16°0S 91°0W **65** J18
Mendawai ➤ *Indonesia* 3°30S 113°0E **36** E4
Mende *France* 44°31N 3°30E **20** D5
Mendeleyev Ridge *Arctic* 80°0N 178°0W **4** B17
Mendhar *India* 33°35N 74°10E **43** C6
Mendip Hills *U.K.* 51°17N 2°40W **13** F5
Mendocino *U.S.A.* 39°19N 123°48W **76** G2
Mendocino, C. *U.S.A.* 40°26N 124°25W **76** F1

Mendocino Fracture Zone
   Pac. Oc. 40°0N 142°0W **65** D13
Mendota *Calif., U.S.A.* 36°45N 120°23W **78** J6
Mendota *Ill., U.S.A.* 41°33N 89°7W **80** E9
Mendoyo *Indonesia* 8°23S 114°42E **37** J17
Mendoza *Argentina* 32°50S 68°52W **94** C2
Mendoza □ *Argentina* 33°0S 69°0W **94** C2
Mene Grande *Venezuela* 9°49N 70°56W **92** B4
Menemen *Turkey* 38°34N 27°3E **23** E12
Menen *Belgium* 50°47N 3°7E **15** D3
Menggala *Indonesia* 4°30S 105°15E **36** E3
Mengjin *China* 34°55N 112°45E **34** G7
Mengyin *China* 35°40N 117°58E **35** G9
Mengzi *China* 23°20N 103°22E **32** D5
Menihek *Canada* 54°28N 56°36W **73** B6
Menihek L. *Canada* 54°0N 67°0W **73** B6
Menin = Menen *Belgium* 50°47N 3°7E **15** D3
Menindee *Australia* 32°20S 142°25E **63** E3
Menindee L. *Australia* 32°20S 142°25E **63** E3
Meningie *Australia* 35°50S 139°18E **63** F2
Menjangan, Pulau
   Indonesia 8°7S 114°31E **37** J17
Menlo Park *U.S.A.* 37°27N 122°12W **78** H4
Menngen ☼ *Australia* 15°21S 131°16E **60** C5
Menominee *U.S.A.* 45°6N 87°37W **80** C10
Menominee ➤ *U.S.A.* 45°6N 87°35W **80** C10
Menomonie *U.S.A.* 44°53N 91°55W **80** C8
Menongue *Angola* 14°48S 17°52E **53** G3
Menorca *Spain* 40°0N 4°0E **24** B11
Mentakab *Malaysia* 3°29N 102°21E **39** L4
Mentawai, Kepulauan
   Indonesia 2°0S 99°0E **36** E1
Menton *France* 43°50N 7°29E **20** E7
Mentor *U.S.A.* 41°40N 81°21W **82** E3
Menzelinsk *Russia* 55°47N 53°11E **18** C9
Menzies *Australia* 29°40S 121°2E **61** E3
Meob B. *Namibia* 24°25S 14°34E **56** C1
Me'ona *Israel* 33°1N 35°15E **46** A4
Meoqui *Mexico* 28°17N 105°29W **86** B3
Mepaco *Mozam.* 15°57S 30°48E **55** F3
Meppel *Neths.* 52°42N 6°12E **15** B6
Merak *Indonesia* 6°10N 106°26E **37** F12
Meramangye, L.
   Australia 28°25S 132°13E **61** E5
Meran = Merano *Italy* 46°40N 11°9E **22** A4
Merano *Italy* 46°40N 11°9E **22** A4
Merauke *Indonesia* 8°29S 140°24E **37** F10
Merbein *Australia* 34°10S 142°2E **63** E3
Merbuk, Gunung
   Indonesia 8°13S 114°39E **37** J17
Merca = Marka
   Somali Rep. 1°48N 44°50E **47** G3
Merced *U.S.A.* 37°18N 120°29W **78** H6
Merced ➤ *U.S.A.* 37°21N 120°59W **78** H6
Merced Pk. *U.S.A.* 37°36N 119°24W **78** H7
Mercedes *B. Aires,*
   Argentina 34°40S 59°30W **94** C4
Mercedes *Corrientes,*
   Argentina 29°10S 58°5W **94** B4
Mercedes *San Luis,*
   Argentina 33°40S 65°21W **94** C2
Mercedes *Uruguay* 33°12S 58°0W **94** C4
Merceditas *Chile* 28°20S 70°35W **94** B1
Mercer *N.Z.* 37°16S 175°5E **59** B5
Mercer *U.S.A.* 41°14N 80°15W **82** E4
Mercer Island *U.S.A.* 47°34N 122°13W **78** C4
Mercury *U.S.A.* 36°40N 115°59W **79** J11
Mercy, C. *Canada* 65°0N 63°30W **69** E19
Mere *U.K.* 51°6N 2°16W **13** F5
Meredith, C. *Falk. Is.* 52°15S 60°40W **96** G4
Meredith, L. *U.S.A.* 35°43N 101°33W **84** D4
Mergui *Burma* 12°26N 98°34E **38** F2
Mergui Arch. = Myeik Kyunzu
   Burma 11°30N 97°30E **39** G1
Mérida *Mexico* 20°58N 89°37W **87** C7
Mérida *Spain* 38°55N 6°25W **21** C2
Mérida *Venezuela* 8°24N 71°8W **92** B4
Mérida, Cord. de *Venezuela* 9°0N 71°0W **92** B4
Meriden *U.K.* 52°26N 1°38W **13** E6
Meriden *U.S.A.* 41°32N 72°48W **83** E12
Meridian *Calif., U.S.A.* 39°9N 121°55W **78** F5
Meridian *Idaho, U.S.A.* 43°37N 116°24W **76** E5
Meridian *Miss., U.S.A.* 32°22N 88°42W **85** E10
Merinda *Australia* 20°2S 148°11E **62** C4
Merir *Pac. Oc.* 4°10N 132°30E **37** D8
Meriruma *Brazil* 1°15N 54°50W **93** C8
Merkel *U.S.A.* 32°28N 100°1W **84** E4
Mermaid Reef *Australia* 17°6S 119°36E **60** C2
Merredin *Australia* 31°28S 118°18E **61** F2
Merrick *U.K.* 55°8N 4°28W **11** F4
Merrickville *Canada* 44°55N 75°50W **83** B9
Merrill *Oreg., U.S.A.* 42°1N 121°36W **76** E3
Merrill *Wis., U.S.A.* 45°11N 89°41W **80** C9
Merrimack ➤ *U.S.A.* 42°49N 70°49W **83** D14
Merriman *U.S.A.* 42°55N 101°42W **80** D3
Merritt *Canada* 50°10N 120°45W **70** C4
Merritt Island *U.S.A.* 28°21N 80°42W **85** G14
Merriwa *Australia* 32°6S 150°22E **63** E5
Merry I. *Canada* 55°29N 77°31W **72** A4
Merryville *U.S.A.* 30°45N 93°33W **84** F8
Mersch *Lux.* 49°44N 6°7E **15** E6
Mersea I. *U.K.* 51°47N 0°58E **13** F8
Merseburg *Germany* 51°22N 11°59E **16** C6
Mersey ➤ *U.K.* 53°25N 3°1W **12** D4
Merseyside □ *U.K.* 53°31N 3°2W **12** D4
Mersin = İçel *Turkey* 36°51N 34°36E **44** B2
Mersing *Malaysia* 2°25N 103°50E **39** L4
Merta *India* 26°39N 74°4E **42** F6
Merta Road *India* 26°43N 73°55E **42** F5
Merthyr Tydfil *U.K.* 51°45N 3°22W **13** F4
Merthyr Tydfil □ *U.K.* 51°46N 3°21W **13** F4
Merti *Kenya* 1°4N 38°40E **54** B4
Mértola *Portugal* 37°40N 7°40W **21** D2
Mertzon *U.S.A.* 31°16N 100°49W **84** F4
Meru *Kenya* 0°3N 37°40E **54** B4
Meru *Tanzania* 3°15S 36°46E **54** C4
Meru △ *Kenya* 0°5N 38°10E **54** B4
Mesa *U.S.A.* 33°25N 111°50W **77** K8
Mesa Verde △ *U.S.A.* 37°11N 108°29W **77** H9

Mesanagros *Greece* 36°1N 27°49E **25** C9
Mesaoría *Cyprus* 35°12N 33°14E **25** D12
Mesgouez, L. *Canada* 51°20N 75°0W **72** B5
Meshed = Mashhad *Iran* 36°20N 59°35E **45** B8
Meshgīn Shahr *Iran* 38°30N 47°45E **44** B5
Meshoppen *U.S.A.* 41°36N 76°3W **83** E8
Mesilinka ➤ *Canada* 56°6N 124°30W **70** B4
Mesologi *Greece* 38°21N 21°28E **23** E9
Mesongi *Greece* 39°29N 19°56E **25** B3
Mesopotamia = Al Jazirah
   Iraq 33°30N 44°0E **44** C5
Mesopotamia *U.S.A.* 41°27N 80°57W **82** E4
Mesquite *U.S.A.* 36°48N 114°4W **77** H6
Messaad *Algeria* 34°8N 3°30E **50** B6
Messalo ➤ *Mozam.* 12°25S 39°15E **55** E4
Messara, Kolpos *Greece* 35°6N 24°47E **25** D6
Messina = Musina
   S. Africa 22°20S 30°5E **57** C5
Messina *Italy* 38°11N 15°34E **22** E6
Messina, Str. di *Italy* 38°15N 15°35E **22** E6
Messini *Greece* 37°4N 22°1E **23** F10
Messiniakos Kolpos
   Greece 36°45N 22°5E **23** F10
Mesta = Nestos ➤
   Europe 40°54N 24°49E **23** D11
Meta ➤ *S. Amer.* 6°12N 67°28W **92** B5
Meta Incognita Pen.
   Canada 62°45N 68°30W **69** E18
Metabetchouan *Canada* 48°26N 71°52W **73** C5
Metairie *U.S.A.* 29°59N 90°9W **85** G9
Metaline Falls *U.S.A.* 48°52N 117°22W **76** B5
Metán *Argentina* 25°30S 65°0W **94** B3
Metangula *Mozam.* 12°40S 34°50E **55** E3
Metcalfe *Canada* 45°14N 75°28W **83** A9
Metema *Ethiopia* 12°58N 36°12E **47** E2
Metengobalame *Mozam.* 14°49S 34°30E **55** E3
Methven *N.Z.* 43°38S 171°40E **59** E3
Metil *Mozam.* 16°24S 39°0E **55** F4
Metlakatla *U.S.A.* 55°8N 131°35W **68** F5
Metropolis *U.S.A.* 37°9N 88°44W **80** G9
Metropolitana □ *Chile* 33°30S 70°50W **94** C1
Metu *Ethiopia* 8°18N 35°35E **47** F2
Metz *France* 49°8N 6°10E **20** B7
Meulaboh *Indonesia* 4°11N 96°3E **36** D1
Meureudu *Indonesia* 5°19N 96°10E **36** C1
Meuse ➤ *Europe* 50°45N 5°41E **15** D5
Mexia *U.S.A.* 31°41N 96°29W **84** F6
Mexicali *Mexico* 32°40N 115°30W **79** N11
Mexican Plateau *Mexico* 25°0N 104°0W **66** G9
Mexican Water *U.S.A.* 36°57N 109°32W **77** H9
México *Mexico* 19°24N 99°9W **87** D5
Mexico *Maine, U.S.A.* 44°34N 70°33W **83** B14
Mexico *Mo., U.S.A.* 39°10N 91°53W **80** F8
Mexico *N.Y., U.S.A.* 43°28N 76°14W **83** C8
México □ *Mexico* 19°20N 99°30W **87** D5
Mexico ■ *Cent. Amer.* 25°0N 105°0W **86** C4
México, Ciudad de
   Mexico 19°24N 99°9W **87** D5
Mexico, G. of *Cent. Amer.* 25°0N 90°0W **87** C7
Mexico B. *U.S.A.* 43°35N 76°20W **83** C8
Meydān-e Naftūn *Iran* 31°56N 49°18E **45** D6
Meydani, Ra's-e *Iran* 25°24N 59°6E **45** E8
Meyers Chuck *U.S.A.* 55°45N 132°15W **70** B2
Meymaneh *Afghan.* 35°53N 64°38E **40** B4
Mezen *Russia* 65°50N 44°20E **18** A7
Mezen ➤ *Russia* 65°44N 44°22E **18** A7
Mézenc, Mt. *France* 44°54N 4°11E **20** D6
Mezhdurechensk *Russia* 53°41N 88°3E **28** D9
Mezhdurechenskiy
   Russia 59°36N 65°56E **28** D7
Mezőkövesd *Hungary* 47°49N 20°35E **17** E11
Mezőtúr *Hungary* 47°1N 20°41E **17** E11
Mezquital *Mexico* 23°29N 104°23W **86** C4
Mfolozi ➤ *S. Africa* 28°25S 32°26E **57** D5
Mgeta *Tanzania* 8°22S 36°6E **55** D4
Mhlaba Hills *Zimbabwe* 18°30S 30°30E **55** F3
Mhow *India* 22°33N 75°50E **42** H6
Miahuatlán *Mexico* 16°20N 96°36W **87** D5
Miami *Fla., U.S.A.* 25°46N 80°11W **85** J14
Miami *Okla., U.S.A.* 36°53N 94°53W **84** C7
Miami *Tex., U.S.A.* 35°42N 100°38W **84** D4
Miami Beach *U.S.A.* 25°47N 80°7W **85** J14
Mian Xian *China* 33°10N 106°32E **34** H4
Mianchi *China* 34°48N 111°48E **34** G6
Miandarreh *Iran* 35°37N 53°39E **45** C7
Miandowāb *Iran* 37°0N 46°5E **44** B5
Miandrivazo *Madag.* 19°31S 45°29E **57** B8
Mīāneh *Iran* 37°30N 47°40E **44** B5
Mianwali *Pakistan* 32°38N 71°28E **42** C4
Mianyang *China* 31°22N 104°47E **32** C5
Miarinarivo *Antananarivo,*
   Madag. 18°57S 46°55E **57** B8
Miarinarivo *Toamasina,*
   Madag. 16°38S 48°15E **57** B8
Miarirarivaratra *Madag.* 20°13S 47°31E **57** C8
Miass *Russia* 54°59N 60°6E **18** D11
Mica *S. Africa* 24°9S 30°33E **57** B5
Michalovce *Slovak Rep.* 48°47N 21°58E **17** D11
Michigan □ *U.S.A.* 44°0N 85°0W **81** C11
Michigan, L. *U.S.A.* 44°0N 87°0W **80** D10
Michigan City *U.S.A.* 41°43N 86°54W **80** E10
Michipicoten I. *Canada* 47°40N 85°40W **72** C2
Michoacán □ *Mexico* 19°0N 102°0W **86** D4
Michurin *Bulgaria* 42°9N 27°51E **23** C12
Michurinsk *Russia* 52°58N 40°27E **18** D7
Micoud *St. Lucia* 13°49N 60°54W **89** f
Micronesia *Pac. Oc.* 11°0N 160°0E **64** G7
Micronesia, Federated States of ■
   Pac. Oc. 9°0N 150°0E **58** A8
Mid-Pacific Seamounts
   Pac. Oc. 18°0N 177°0W **64** F10
Midai *Indonesia* 3°0N 107°47E **36** D3
Midale *Canada* 49°25N 103°20W **71** D8
Middelburg *Neths.* 51°30N 3°36E **15** C3
Middelburg *Eastern Cape,*
   S. Africa 31°30S 25°0E **56** E4
Middelburg *Mpumalanga,*
   S. Africa 25°49S 29°28E **57** D4

Middelpos *S. Africa* 31°55S 20°13E **56** E3
Middelwit *S. Africa* 24°51S 27°3E **56** C4
Middle Alkali L. *U.S.A.* 41°27N 120°5W **76** F3
Middle America Trench =
   Guatemala Trench
   Pac. Oc. 14°0N 95°0W **66** H10
Middle Bass I. *U.S.A.* 41°41N 82°48W **82** E2
Middle East *Asia* 35°0N 40°0E **26** C5
Middle Fork Feather ➤
   U.S.A. 38°33N 121°30W **78** F5
Middle I. *Australia* 34°6S 123°11E **61** F3
Middle Loup ➤ *U.S.A.* 41°17N 98°24W **80** E4
Middleboro *U.S.A.* 41°54N 70°55W **83** E14
Middleburg *Fla., U.S.A.* 30°4N 81°52W **85** G13
Middleburg *Pa., U.S.A.* 40°47N 77°3W **82** F7
Middleburgh *U.S.A.* 42°36N 74°20W **83** D10
Middlebury *U.S.A.* 44°1N 73°10W **83** B11
Middlefield *U.S.A.* 41°27N 81°4W **82** E3
Middlemount *Australia* 22°50S 148°40E **62** C4
Middleport *N.Y., U.S.A.* 43°13N 78°29W **82** C6
Middleport *Ohio, U.S.A.* 39°0N 82°3W **81** F12
Middlesboro *U.S.A.* 36°36N 83°43W **81** G12
Middlesbrough *U.K.* 54°35N 1°13W **12** C6
Middlesbrough □ *U.K.* 54°28N 1°13W **12** C6
Middlesex *Belize* 17°2N 88°31W **88** C2
Middlesex *N.J., U.S.A.* 40°36N 74°30W **83** F10
Middlesex *N.Y., U.S.A.* 42°42N 77°16W **82** D7
Middleton *Australia* 22°22S 141°32E **62** C3
Middleton *Canada* 44°57N 65°4W **73** D6
Middleton Cr. ➤
   Australia 22°35S 141°51E **62** C3
Middleton I. *U.S.A.* 59°26N 146°20W **74** D10
Middletown *N. Ireland* 54°17N 6°51W **10** B5
Middletown *Calif.,*
   U.S.A. 38°45N 122°37W **78** G4
Middletown *Conn.,*
   U.S.A. 41°34N 72°39W **83** E12
Middletown *N.Y.,*
   U.S.A. 41°27N 74°25W **83** E10
Middletown *Ohio,*
   U.S.A. 39°31N 84°24W **81** F11
Middletown *Pa., U.S.A.* 40°12N 76°44W **83** F8
Midge Point *Australia* 20°39S 148°43E **62** b
Midhurst *Canada* 44°26N 79°43W **82** B5
Midhurst *U.K.* 50°59N 0°44W **13** G7
Midi, Canal du ➤ *France* 43°45N 1°21E **20** E4
Midland *Australia* 31°54S 116°1E **61** F2
Midland *Canada* 44°45N 79°50W **82** B5
Midland *Calif., U.S.A.* 33°52N 114°48W **79** M12
Midland *Mich., U.S.A.* 43°37N 84°14W **81** D11
Midland *Pa., U.S.A.* 40°39N 80°27W **82** F4
Midland *Tex., U.S.A.* 32°0N 102°3W **84** F3
Midlands □ *Zimbabwe* 19°40S 29°0E **55** F2
Midleton *Ireland* 51°55N 8°10W **10** E3
Midlothian *U.S.A.* 32°30N 97°0W **84** E6
Midlothian □ *U.K.* 55°51N 3°5W **11** F5
Midnapore = Medinipur
   India 22°25N 87°21E **43** H12
Midongy, Tangorombohitr' i
   Madag. 23°30S 47°0E **57** C8
Midongy Atsimo *Madag.* 23°35S 47°1E **57** C8
Midway Is. *Pac. Oc.* 28°13N 177°22W **75** K4
Midway Wells *U.S.A.* 32°41N 115°7W **79** N11
Midwest *U.S.A.* 42°0N 90°0W **75** G22
Midwest *Wyo., U.S.A.* 43°25N 106°16W **76** E10
Midwest City *U.S.A.* 35°27N 97°24W **84** D6
Midyat *Turkey* 37°25N 41°23E **44** B4
Midzör *Bulgaria* 43°24N 22°42E **23** C10
Mie □ *Japan* 34°30N 136°10E **31** G8
Międzychód *Poland* 52°35N 15°53E **16** B8
Międzyrzec Podlaski
   Poland 51°58N 22°45E **17** C12
Mielec *Poland* 50°15N 21°25E **17** C11
Mienga *Angola* 17°12S 19°48E **56** B2
Miercurea-Ciuc
   Romania 46°21N 25°48E **17** E13
Mieres *Spain* 43°18N 5°48W **21** A3
Mifflintown *U.S.A.* 40°34N 77°24W **82** F7
Mifraz Hefa *Israel* 32°52N 35°0E **46** C4
Migori *Kenya* 1°4S 34°28E **54** C3
Miguel Alemán, Presa
   Mexico 18°15N 96°32W **87** D5
Mihara *Japan* 34°24N 133°5E **31** G6
Mikese *Tanzania* 6°48S 37°55E **54** D4
Mikhaylovgrad = Montana
   Bulgaria 43°27N 23°16E **23** C10
Mikhaylovka *Russia* 50°3N 43°5E **19** D7
Mikines *Greece* 37°43N 22°46E **23** F10
Mikkeli *Finland* 61°43N 27°15E **8** F22
Mikkwa ➤ *Canada* 58°25N 114°46W **70** B6
Mikonos = Mykonos
   Greece 37°30N 25°25E **23** F11
Mikumi *Tanzania* 7°26S 37°0E **54** D4
Mikumi △ *Tanzania* 7°35S 37°15E **54** D4
Mikun *Russia* 62°20N 50°0E **18** B9
Milaca *U.S.A.* 45°45N 93°39W **80** C7
Milagro *Ecuador* 2°11S 79°36W **92** D3
Milan = Milano *Italy* 45°28N 9°10E **20** D8
Milan *Mo., U.S.A.* 40°12N 93°7W **80** E7
Milan *Tenn., U.S.A.* 35°55N 88°46W **85** D10
Milange *Mozam.* 16°3S 35°45E **55** F4
Milano *Italy* 45°28N 9°10E **20** D8
Milanoa *Madag.* 13°35S 49°47E **57** A8
Milâs *Turkey* 37°20N 27°50E **23** F12
Milatos *Greece* 35°18N 25°34E **25** D7
Milazzo *Italy* 38°13N 15°15E **22** E6
Milbank *U.S.A.* 45°13N 96°38W **80** C5
Milbanke Sd. *Canada* 52°19N 128°33W **70** C3
Milden *Canada* 51°29N 107°32W **71** C7
Mildenhall *U.K.* 52°21N 0°32E **13** E8
Mildmay *Canada* 44°3N 81°7W **82** B3
Mildura *Australia* 34°13S 142°9E **63** E3
Miles *Australia* 26°40S 150°9E **63** D5
Miles City *U.S.A.* 46°25N 105°51W **76** C11
Milestone *Canada* 49°59N 104°31W **71** D8
Miletus *Turkey* 37°30N 27°18E **23** F12
Milford *Calif., U.S.A.* 40°10N 120°22W **78** E6
Milford *Del., U.S.A.* 38°55N 75°26W **81** F16
Milford *Mass., U.S.A.* 42°8N 71°31W **83** D13

Milford *N.H., U.S.A.* 42°50N 71°39W **83** D13
Milford *N.Y., U.S.A.* 42°35N 74°56W **83** D10
Milford *Pa., U.S.A.* 41°19N 74°48W **83** E10
Milford *Utah, U.S.A.* 38°24N 113°1W **76** G7
Milford Haven *U.K.* 51°42N 5°7W **13** F2
Milford Sd. *N.Z.* 44°34S 167°47E **59** F1
Milford Sound *N.Z.* 44°41S 167°55E **59** F1
Milh, Baḥr al = Razāzah,
   Buḩayrat ar *Iraq* 32°40N 43°35E **44** C4
Milikapiti *Australia* 11°26S 130°40E **60** B5
Miling *Australia* 30°30S 116°17E **61** F2
Milk River *Canada* 49°10N 112°5W **70** D6
Mill ➤ *U.S.A.* 42°57N 83°23W **82** E7
Mill I. *Antarctica* 66°0S 101°30E **5** C8
Mill I. *Canada* 63°58N 77°47W **69** E16
Mill Valley *U.S.A.* 37°54N 122°32W **78** H4
Millau *France* 44°8N 3°4E **20** D5
Millbridge *Canada* 44°41N 77°36W **82** B7
Millbrook *Canada* 44°10N 78°29W **82** B6
Millbrook *Ala., U.S.A.* 32°29N 86°22W **85** E11
Millbrook *N.Y., U.S.A.* 41°47N 73°42W **83** E11
Mille Lacs, L. des *Canada* 48°45N 90°35W **72** C1
Mille Lacs L. *U.S.A.* 46°15N 93°39W **80** B7
Milledgeville *U.S.A.* 33°5N 83°14W **85** E13
Millen *U.S.A.* 32°48N 81°57W **85** E14
Millennium I. = Caroline I.
   Kiribati 9°58S 150°13W **65** H12
Miller *U.S.A.* 44°31N 98°59W **80** C4
Miller Lake *Canada* 45°6N 81°26W **82** A3
Millersburg *Ohio, U.S.A.* 40°33N 81°55W **82** F3
Millersburg *Pa., U.S.A.* 40°32N 76°58W **82** F8
Millerton *U.S.A.* 41°57N 73°31W **83** E11
Millerton L. *U.S.A.* 37°1N 119°41W **78** J7
Millet *St. Lucia* 13°55N 60°59W **89** f
Millheim *U.S.A.* 40°54N 77°29W **82** F7
Millicent *Australia* 37°34S 140°21E **63** F3
Millington *U.S.A.* 35°20N 89°53W **85** D10
Millinocket *U.S.A.* 45°39N 68°43W **81** C19
Millmerran *Australia* 27°53S 151°16E **63** D5
Millom *U.K.* 54°13N 3°16W **12** C4
Mills L. *Canada* 61°30N 118°20W **70** A5
Millsboro *U.S.A.* 40°0N 80°0W **82** G5
Millstream Chichester △
   Australia 21°35S 117°6E **60** D2
Millstreet *Ireland* 52°4N 9°4W **10** D2
Milltown Malbay *Ireland* 52°52N 9°24W **10** D2
Millville *U.S.A.* 39°24N 75°2W **81** F16
Millville *Pa., U.S.A.* 41°7N 76°32W **83** E8
Millwood L. *U.S.A.* 33°42N 93°58W **84** E8
Milne ➤ *Australia* 21°10S 137°33E **62** C2
Milo *U.S.A.* 45°15N 68°59W **81** C19
Milon, Akra *Greece* 36°15N 28°11E **25** C10
Milos *Greece* 36°44N 24°25E **23** F11
Milparinka *Australia* 29°46S 141°57E **63** D3
Milpitas *U.S.A.* 37°26N 121°55W **78** H5
Milton *N.S., Canada* 44°4N 64°45W **73** D7
Milton *Ont., Canada* 43°31N 79°53W **82** C5
Milton *N.Z.* 46°7S 169°59E **59** G2
Milton *Calif., U.S.A.* 38°3N 120°51W **78** G6
Milton *Fla., U.S.A.* 30°38N 87°3W **85** F11
Milton *Pa., U.S.A.* 41°1N 76°51W **82** F8
Milton *Vt., U.S.A.* 44°38N 73°7W **83** B11
Milton-Freewater
   U.S.A. 45°56N 118°23W **76** D4
Milton Keynes *U.K.* 52°1N 0°44W **13** E7
Milton Keynes □ *U.K.* 52°1N 0°44W **13** E7
Milverton *Canada* 43°34N 80°55W **82** C4
Milwaukee *U.S.A.* 43°2N 87°54W **80** D10
Milwaukee Deep *Atl. Oc.* 19°50N 68°0W **89** C6
Milwaukie *U.S.A.* 45°26N 122°38W **78** E4
Mimili *Australia* 27°0S 132°42E **61** E5
Min Jiang ➤ *Fujian,*
   China 26°0N 119°35E **33** D6
Min Jiang ➤ *Sichuan,*
   China 28°45N 104°40E **32** D5
Min Xian *China* 34°25N 104°5E **34** G3
Minā' Jabal 'Alī *U.A.E.* 25°2N 55°8E **45** E7
Mina Pirquitas
   Argentina 22°40S 66°30W **94** A2
Mīnā Su'ud *Si. Arabia* 28°45N 48°28E **45** D6
Mīnā'al Aḩmadī *Kuwait* 29°5N 48°10E **45** D6
Minago ➤ *Canada* 54°33N 98°59W **71** C9
Minaki *Canada* 49°59N 94°40W **71** D10
Minamata *Japan* 32°10N 130°30E **31** H5
Minami-Arapusa △
   Japan 35°30N 138°9E **31** G9
Minami-Tori-Shima
   Pac. Oc. 24°20N 153°58E **64** E7
Minas *Uruguay* 34°20S 55°10W **95** C4
Minas, Sierra de las
   Guatemala 15°9N 89°31W **88** C2
Minas Basin *Canada* 45°20N 64°12W **73** C7
Minas Gerais □ *Brazil* 18°50S 46°0W **93** G9
Minatitlán *Mexico* 17°59N 94°31W **87** D6
Minbu *Burma* 20°10N 94°52E **41** J19
Minchinabad *Pakistan* 30°10N 73°34E **42** D5
Mindanao *Phil.* 8°0N 125°0E **37** C7
Mindanao Sea = Bohol Sea
   Phil. 9°0N 124°0E **37** C6
Mindanao Trench
   Pac. Oc. 12°0N 126°6E **37** B7
Mindelo *C. Verde Is.* 16°24N 25°0W **50** b
Minden *Canada* 44°55N 78°43W **82** B6
Minden *Germany* 52°17N 8°55E **16** B5
Minden *La., U.S.A.* 32°37N 93°17W **84** E8
Minden *Nev., U.S.A.* 38°57N 119°46W **78** G7
Mindibungu = Billiluna
   Australia 19°37S 127°41E **60** C4
Mindiptana *Indonesia* 5°55S 140°22E **37** F10
Mindoro *Phil.* 13°0N 121°0E **37** B6
Mindoro Str. *Phil.* 12°30N 120°30E **37** B6
Mine *Japan* 34°12S 131°7E **31** G5
Minehead *U.K.* 51°12N 3°29W **13** F4
Mineola *N.Y., U.S.A.* 40°44N 73°38W **83** F11
Mineola *Tex., U.S.A.* 32°40N 95°29W **84** E7
Mineral King *U.S.A.* 36°27N 118°36W **78** J8
Mineral Wells *U.S.A.* 32°48N 98°7W **84** E5
Miners Bay *Canada* 44°49N 78°46W **82** B6
Minersville *U.S.A.* 40°41N 76°16W **83** F8

Minerva *N.Y., U.S.A.* 43°47N 73°59W **83** C11
Minerva *Ohio, U.S.A.* 40°44N 81°6W **82** F3
Minetto *U.S.A.* 43°24N 76°28W **83** C8
Minfeng *China* 37°4N 82°46E **32** C3
Mingāçevir Su Anbarı
  Azerbaijan 40°57N 46°50E **19** F8
Mingan *Canada* 50°20N 64°0W **73** B7
Mingechaurskoye Vdkhr. =
  Mingāçevir Su Anbarı
  Azerbaijan 40°57N 46°50E **19** F8
Mingela *Australia* 19°52S 146°38E **62** B4
Mingenew *Australia* 29°12S 115°21E **61** E2
Mingera Cr. →
  Australia 20°38S 137°45E **62** C2
Mingin *Burma* 22°50N 94°30E **41** H19
Mingo Junction *U.S.A.* 40°19N 80°37W **82** F4
Mingora *Pakistan* 34°48N 72°22E **43** B5
Mingteke Daban = Mintaka Pass
  Pakistan 37°0N 74°58E **43** A6
Mingyuegue *China* 43°2N 128°50E **35** C15
Minho = Miño → *Spain* 41°52N 8°40W **21** A2
Minho *Portugal* 41°25N 8°20N **21** B1
Minidoka *U.S.A.* 42°45N 113°29W **76** E7
Minigwal, L. *Australia* 29°31S 123°14E **61** E3
Minilya → *Australia* 23°45S 114°0E **61** D1
Minilya Roadhouse
  Australia 23°55S 114°0E **61** D1
Minipi L. *Canada* 52°25N 60°45W **73** B7
Minjilang *Australia* 11°8S 132°33E **60** B5
Mink L. *Canada* 61°54N 117°40W **70** A5
Minna *Nigeria* 9°37N 6°30E **50** G7
Minneapolis *Kans., U.S.A.* 39°8N 97°42W **80** F5
Minneapolis *Minn., U.S.A.* 44°57N 93°16W **80** C7
Minnedosa *Canada* 50°14N 99°50W **71** C9
Minnesota □ *U.S.A.* 46°0N 94°15W **80** B6
Minnesota → *U.S.A.* 44°54N 93°9W **80** C7
Minnewaukan *U.S.A.* 48°4N 99°15W **80** A4
Minnipa *Australia* 32°51S 135°9E **63** E2
Minnitaki L. *Canada* 49°57N 92°10W **72** C1
Mino *Japan* 35°32N 136°55E **31** G8
Miño → *Spain* 41°52N 8°40W **21** A2
Minorca = Menorca *Spain* 40°0N 4°0E **24** B11
Minot *U.S.A.* 48°14N 101°18W **80** A3
Minqin *China* 38°38N 103°20E **34** E2
Minsk *Belarus* 53°52N 27°30E **17** B14
Mińsk Mazowiecki
  Poland 52°10N 21°33E **17** B11
Mintabie *Australia* 27°15S 133°7E **63** D1
Mintaka Pass *Pakistan* 37°0N 74°58E **43** A6
Minto *Canada* 46°5N 66°5W **73** C6
Minto, L. *Canada* 57°13N 75°0W **72** A5
Minton *Canada* 49°10N 104°35W **71** D8
Minturn *U.S.A.* 39°35N 106°26W **76** G10
Minudasht *Iran* 37°17N 56°7E **45** B8
Minusinsk *Russia* 53°43N 91°20E **29** D10
Minutang *India* 28°15N 96°30E **41** E20
Minvoul *Gabon* 2°9N 12°8E **52** D2
Minzhong *China* 22°37N 113°30E **33** F10
Miquelon *Canada* 49°25N 76°27W **72** C4
Miquelon *St-P. & M.* 47°8N 56°22W **73** C8
Mīr Kūh *Iran* 26°22N 58°55E **45** E8
Mīr Shahdād *Iran* 26°15N 58°29E **45** E8
Mira *Italy* 45°26N 12°8E **22** B5
Mira por vos Cay
  Bahamas 22°9N 74°30W **89** B5
Mirabello, Kolpos *Greece* 35°10N 25°50E **25** D7
Mirador-Río Azul △
  Guatemala 17°45N 89°50W **88** C2
Miraj *India* 16°50N 74°45E **40** L9
Miram Shah *Pakistan* 33°0N 70°2E **42** C4
Miramar *Argentina* 38°15S 57°50W **94** D4
Miramar *Mozam.* 23°50S 35°35E **57** C6
Miramichi *Canada* 47°2N 65°28W **73** C6
Miramichi B. *Canada* 47°15N 65°0W **73** C7
Miranda *Brazil* 20°10S 56°15W **93** H7
Miranda → *Brazil* 19°25S 57°20W **92** G7
Miranda de Ebro *Spain* 42°41N 2°57W **21** A4
Miranda do Douro
  Portugal 41°30N 6°16W **21** B2
Mirandópolis *Brazil* 21°9S 51°6W **95** A5
Mirango *Malawi* 13°32S 34°58E **55** E3
Mirani *Australia* 21°8S 148°53E **62** b
Mirassol *Brazil* 20°46S 49°28W **95** A6
Mirbāţ *Oman* 17°0N 54°45E **47** D5
Mires *Greece* 35°4N 24°56E **25** D6
Miri *Malaysia* 4°23N 113°59E **36** D4
Miriam Vale *Australia* 24°20S 151°33E **62** C5
Mirim, L. S. Amer. 32°45S 52°50W **95** C5
Miriuwung Gajerrong ⊕
  Australia 15°0S 128°45E **60** C4
Mīrjāveh *Iran* 29°1N 61°30E **45** D9
Mirnyy *Antarctica* 66°50S 92°30E **5** C14
Mirnyy *Russia* 62°33N 113°53E **29** C12
Mirokhan *Pakistan* 27°46N 68°6E **42** F3
Mirond L. *Canada* 55°6N 102°47W **71** B8
Mirpur *Pakistan* 33°32N 73°56E **43** C5
Mirpur Batoro *Pakistan* 24°44N 68°16E **42** G3
Mirpur Bibiwari *Pakistan* 28°33N 67°44E **42** E2
Mirpur Khas *Pakistan* 25°30N 69°0E **42** G3
Mirpur Sakro *Pakistan* 24°33N 67°41E **42** G2
Mirs Bay = Tai Pang Wan
  China 22°33N 114°24E **33** F11
Mirtağ *Turkey* 38°23N 41°56E **44** B4
Mirtoo Sea *Greece* 37°0N 23°20E **23** F10
Miryang *S. Korea* 35°31N 128°44E **35** G15
Mirzapur *India* 25°10N 82°34E **43** G10
Mirzapur-cum-Vindhyachal =
  Mirzapur *India* 25°10N 82°34E **43** G10
Misantla *Mexico* 19°56N 96°50W **87** D5
Misawa *Japan* 40°41N 141°24E **30** D10
Miscou I. *Canada* 47°57N 64°31W **73** C7
Mish'āb, Ra's al
  Si. Arabia 28°15N 48°43E **45** D6
Mishamo *Tanzania* 5°41S 30°41E **54** D3
Mishan *China* 45°37N 131°48E **30** B5
Mishawaka *U.S.A.* 41°40N 86°11W **80** E10
Mishima *Japan* 35°10N 138°52E **31** G9
Misión *Mexico* 32°6N 116°53W **79** N10

Misiones □ *Argentina* 27°0S 55°0W **95** B5
Misiones □ *Paraguay* 27°0S 56°0W **94** B4
Miskah *Si. Arabia* 24°49N 42°56E **44** E4
Miskitos, Cayos *Nic.* 14°26N 82°50W **88** D3
Miskolc *Hungary* 48°7N 20°50E **17** D11
Misoke
  Dem. Rep. of the Congo 0°42S 28°2E **54** C2
Misool *Indonesia* 1°52S 130°10E **37** E8
Mişr = Egypt ■ *Africa* 28°0N 31°0E **51** C12
Mişrātah *Libya* 32°24N 15°3E **51** B9
Missanabie *Canada* 48°20N 84°6W **72** C3
Missinaibi → *Canada* 50°43N 81°29W **72** B3
Missinaibi L. *Canada* 48°23N 83°40W **72** C3
Mission *Canada* 49°10N 122°15W **70** D4
Mission *S. Dak., U.S.A.* 43°18N 100°39W **80** D3
Mission *Tex., U.S.A.* 26°13N 98°20W **84** H5
Mission Beach *Australia* 17°53S 146°6E **62** B4
Mission Viejo *U.S.A.* 33°36N 117°40W **79** M9
Missisa L. *Canada* 52°20N 85°7W **72** B2
Missisicabi → *Canada* 51°14N 79°31W **72** B4
Mississagi → *Canada* 46°15N 83°9W **72** C3
Mississauga *Canada* 43°32N 79°35W **82** C5
Mississippi □ *U.S.A.* 33°0N 90°0W **85** E10
Mississippi → *U.S.A.* 29°9N 89°15W **85** G10
Mississippi L. *Canada* 45°5N 76°10W **83** A8
Mississippi River Delta
  U.S.A. 29°10N 89°15W **85** G10
Mississippi Sd. *U.S.A.* 30°20N 89°0W **85** F10
Missoula *U.S.A.* 46°52N 114°1W **76** C6
Missouri □ *U.S.A.* 38°25N 92°30W **80** F7
Missouri → *U.S.A.* 38°49N 90°7W **80** F8
Missouri City *U.S.A.* 29°37N 95°32W **84** G7
Missouri Valley *U.S.A.* 41°34N 95°53W **80** E6
Mist *U.S.A.* 45°59N 123°15W **78** E3
Mistassibi → *Canada* 48°53N 72°13W **73** B5
Mistassini *Canada* 48°53N 72°12W **73** C5
Mistassini → *Canada* 48°42N 72°20W **73** C5
Mistassini, L. *Canada* 51°0N 73°30W **72** B5
Mistastin L. *Canada* 55°57N 63°20W **73** A7
Mistinibi, L. *Canada* 55°56N 64°17W **73** A7
Mistissini *Canada* 48°53N 72°12W **73** C5
Misty L. *Canada* 58°53N 101°40W **71** B8
Misurata = Mişrātah
  Libya 32°24N 15°3E **51** B9
Mitande *Mozam.* 14°6S 35°58E **55** E4
Mitchell *Australia* 26°29S 147°58E **63** D4
Mitchell *Canada* 43°28N 81°12W **82** C3
Mitchell *Nebr., U.S.A.* 41°57N 103°49W **80** E2
Mitchell *Oreg., U.S.A.* 44°34N 120°9W **76** D3
Mitchell *S. Dak., U.S.A.* 43°43N 98°2W **80** D4
Mitchell → *Australia* 15°12S 141°35E **62** B3
Mitchell, Mt. *U.S.A.* 35°46N 82°16W **85** D13
Mitchell-Alice Rivers △
  Australia 15°28S 142°5E **62** B3
Mitchell Ra. *Australia* 12°49S 135°36E **62** A2
Mitchelstown *Ireland* 52°15N 8°16W **10** D3
Mitha Tiwana *Pakistan* 32°13N 72°6E **42** C5
Mithi *Pakistan* 24°44N 69°48E **42** G3
Mithrao *Pakistan* 27°28N 69°40E **42** F3
Mitilini *Greece* 39°6N 26°35E **23** E12
Mitla Pass = Mamarr Mitlā
  Egypt 30°2N 32°54E **46** E1
Mito *Japan* 36°20N 140°30E **31** F10
Mitrovica = Kosovska Mitrovica
  Kosovo 42°54N 20°52E **23** C9
Mitsamiouli *Comoros Is.* 11°20S 43°16E **53** a
Mitsinjo *Madag.* 16°1S 45°52E **57** B8
Mitsiwa *Eritrea* 15°35N 39°25E **47** D2
Mitsukaidō *Japan* 36°1N 139°59E **31** F9
Mittagong *Australia* 34°28S 150°29E **63** E5
Mittimatalik = Pond Inlet
  Canada 72°40N 77°0W **69** C16
Mitú *Colombia* 1°15N 70°13W **92** C4
Mitumba *Tanzania* 7°8S 31°2E **54** D3
Mitumba, Mts.
  Dem. Rep. of the Congo 7°0S 27°30E **54** D2
Mitwaba
  Dem. Rep. of the Congo 8°2S 27°17E **55** D2
Mityana *Uganda* 0°23N 32°2E **54** B3
Mixteco → *Mexico* 18°11N 98°30W **87** D5
Miyagi □ *Japan* 38°15N 140°45E **30** E10
Miyah, W. el → *Syria* 34°44N 39°57E **44** C3
Miyake-Jima *Japan* 34°5N 139°30E **31** G9
Miyako *Japan* 39°40N 141°59E **30** E10
Miyako-Jima *Japan* 24°45N 125°20E **31** M2
Miyako-Rettō *Japan* 24°24N 125°0E **31** M2
Miyakonojō *Japan* 31°40N 131°5E **31** J5
Miyani *India* 21°50N 69°26E **42** J3
Miyanoura-Dake *Japan* 30°20N 130°31E **31** J5
Miyazaki *Japan* 31°56N 131°30E **31** J5
Miyazaki □ *Japan* 32°30N 131°30E **31** H5
Miyazu *Japan* 35°35N 135°10E **31** G7
Miyet, Bahr el = Dead Sea
  Asia 31°30N 35°30E **46** D4
Miyoshi *Japan* 34°48N 132°51E **31** G6
Miyun *China* 40°28N 116°50E **34** D9
Miyun Shuiku *China* 40°30N 117°0E **35** D9
Mizdah *Libya* 31°30N 13°0E **51** B8
Mizen Hd. *Cork, Ireland* 51°27N 9°50W **10** E2
Mizen Hd. *Wicklow, Ireland* 52°51N 6°4W **10** D5
Mizhi *China* 37°47N 110°12E **34** F6
Mizoram □ *India* 23°30N 92°40E **41** H18
Mizpe Ramon *Israel* 30°34N 34°49E **46** E3
Mizuho *Antarctica* 70°30S 41°0E **5** D5
Mizusawa *Japan* 39°8N 141°8E **30** E10
Mjölby *Sweden* 58°20N 15°10E **9** G16
Mjøsa *Norway* 60°40N 11°0E **8** F14
Mkata *Tanzania* 5°45S 38°20E **54** D4
Mkhaya △ *Tanzania* 26°34S 31°45E **57** D5
Mkhuze △ *S. Africa* 27°27S 29°30E **57** D4
Mkokotoni *Tanzania* 5°55S 39°15E **54** D4
Mkomazi *Tanzania* 4°40S 38°7E **54** C4
Mkomazi → *S. Africa* 30°12S 30°50E **57** E5
Mkomazi △ *Tanzania* 4°4S 30°2E **54** C3
Mkulwe *Tanzania* 8°37S 32°27E **54** D3
Mkumbi, Ras *Tanzania* 7°38S 39°55E **54** D4
Mkushi *Zambia* 14°25S 29°15E **55** E2
Mkushi River *Zambia* 13°32S 29°45E **55** E2
Mkuze *S. Africa* 27°10S 32°0E **57** D5

Mladá Boleslav
  Czech Rep. 50°27N 14°53E **16** C8
Mlala Hills *Tanzania* 6°50S 31°40E **54** D3
Mlange = Mulanje, Mt.
  Malawi 16°2S 35°33E **55** F4
Mława *Poland* 53°9N 20°25E **17** B11
Mlawula → *Swaziland* 26°12S 32°2E **57** D5
Mljet *Croatia* 42°43N 17°30E **22** C7
Mmabatho *S. Africa* 25°49S 25°30E **56** D4
Mmathubudukwane *S. Africa* 24°10S 28°55E **57** C4
Mo i Rana *Norway* 66°20N 14°7E **8** C16
Moa *Australia* 10°11S 142°16E **62** a
Moa *Cuba* 20°40N 74°56W **89** B4
Moa *Indonesia* 8°0S 128°0E **37** F7
Moa → *S. Leone* 6°59N 11°36W **50** G3
Moab *U.S.A.* 38°35N 109°33W **76** G9
Moala *Fiji* 18°36S 179°53E **59** a
Moama *Australia* 36°7S 144°46E **63** F3
Moamba *Mozam.* 25°36S 32°15E **57** D5
Moapa *U.S.A.* 36°40N 114°37W **79** J12
Moate *Ireland* 53°24N 7°44W **10** C4
Moba *Dem. Rep. of the Congo* 7°0S 29°48E **54** D2
Mobārakābād *Iran* 28°24N 53°20E **45** D7
Mobaye *C.A.R.* 4°25N 21°5E **52** D4
Moberly *U.S.A.* 39°25N 92°26W **80** F7
Moberly Lake *Canada* 55°50N 121°44W **70** B4
Mobile *U.S.A.* 30°41N 88°3W **85** F10
Mobile B. *U.S.A.* 30°30N 88°0W **85** F11
Mobridge *U.S.A.* 45°32N 100°26W **80** C3
Moc Chau *Vietnam* 20°50N 104°38E **38** B5
Moc Hoa *Vietnam* 10°46N 105°56E **39** G5
Mocabe Kasari
  Dem. Rep. of the Congo 9°58S 26°12E **55** D2
Moçambique = Mozambique ■
  Africa 19°0S 35°0E **55** F4
Moçâmbique *Mozam.* 15°3S 40°42E **55** F5
Mocanaqua *U.S.A.* 41°9N 76°8W **83** E8
Moce *Fiji* 18°40S 178°29W **59** a
Mochima △ *Venezuela* 10°30N 64°5W **89** D7
Mochos *Greece* 35°16N 25°27E **25** D7
Mochudi *Botswana* 24°27S 26°7E **56** C4
Mocimboa da Praia
  Mozam. 11°25S 40°20E **55** E5
Moclips *U.S.A.* 47°14N 124°13W **78** C2
Mocoa *Colombia* 1°7N 76°35W **92** C3
Mococa *Brazil* 21°28S 47°0W **95** A6
Mocorito *Mexico* 25°29N 107°55W **86** B3
Moctezuma *Mexico* 29°48N 109°42W **86** B3
Moctezuma → *Mexico* 21°59N 98°34W **87** C5
Mocuba *Mozam.* 16°54S 36°57E **55** F4
Modane *France* 45°12N 6°40E **20** D7
Modasa *India* 23°30N 73°21E **42** H5
Modder → *S. Africa* 29°2S 24°37E **56** D3
Modderrivier *S. Africa* 29°2S 24°38E **56** D3
Módena *Italy* 44°40N 10°55E **22** B4
Modena *U.S.A.* 37°48N 113°56W **77** H7
Modesto *U.S.A.* 37°39N 121°0W **78** H6
Módica *Italy* 36°52N 14°46E **22** F6
Modimolle *S. Africa* 24°42S 28°22E **57** C4
Modjadjiskloof *S. Africa* 23°42S 30°10E **57** C5
Moe *Australia* 38°12S 146°19E **63** F4
Moebase *Mozam.* 17°3S 38°41E **55** F4
Moengo *Suriname* 5°45N 54°20W **93** B8
Moffat *U.K.* 55°21N 3°27W **11** F5
Moga *India* 30°48N 75°8E **42** D6
Mogadishu = Muqdisho
  Somali Rep. 2°2N 45°25E **47** G4
Mogador = Essaouira
  Morocco 31°32N 9°42W **50** B4
Mogalakwena →
  S. Africa 22°38S 28°40E **57** C4
Mogami-Gawa →
  Japan 38°45N 140°0E **30** E10
Mogán *Canary Is.* 27°53N 15°43W **24** G4
Mogaung *Burma* 25°20N 97°0E **41** G20
Mogi das Cruzes *Brazil* 23°31S 46°11W **95** A6
Mogi-Guaçu → *Brazil* 20°53S 48°10W **95** A6
Mogi-Mirim *Brazil* 22°29S 47°0W **93** H9
Mogilev = Mahilyow
  Belarus 53°55N 30°18E **17** B16
Mogilev-Podolskiy = Mohyliv-
  Podilskyy *Ukraine* 48°26N 27°48E **17** D14
Mogincual *Mozam.* 15°35S 40°25E **55** F5
Mogocha *Russia* 53°40N 119°50E **29** D12
Mogok *Burma* 23°0N 96°40E **41** H20
Mogollon Rim *U.S.A.* 34°10N 110°50W **77** J8
Mogumber *Australia* 31°2S 116°3E **61** F2
Mogwadi → *S. Africa* 23°4S 29°36E **57** C4
Mohács *Hungary* 45°58N 18°41E **17** F10
Mohales Hoek *Lesotho* 30°7S 27°26E **56** E4
Mohall *U.S.A.* 48°46N 101°31W **80** A3
Mohammadābād *Iran* 37°52N 59°5E **45** B8
Mohammedia *Morocco* 33°44N 7°21W **50** B4
Mohana → *India* 24°43N 85°0E **43** G11
Mohanlalganj *India* 26°41N 80°58E **43** F9
Mohave, L. *U.S.A.* 35°12N 114°34W **79** K12
Mohawk → *U.S.A.* 42°47N 73°41W **83** D11
Mohéli *Comoros Is.* 12°20S 43°40E **53** a
Mohenjodaro *Pakistan* 27°19N 68°7E **42** F3
Moher, Cliffs of *Ireland* 52°58N 9°27W **10** D2
Mohicanville Res. *U.S.A.* 40°45N 82°9W **82** F2
Mohns Ridge *Arctic* 72°30N 5°0W **4** B7
Mohoro *Tanzania* 8°6S 39°8E **54** D4
Mohsenābād *Iran* 36°40N 59°35E **45** B8
Mohyliv-Podilskyy
  Ukraine 48°26N 27°48E **17** D14
Moidart, L. *U.K.* 56°47N 5°52W **11** E3
Moira → *Canada* 44°21N 77°24W **82** B7
Moisaküla *Estonia* 58°3N 25°12E **9** G21
Moisie *Canada* 50°12N 66°1W **73** B6
Moisie → *Canada* 50°14N 66°5W **73** B6
Mojave *U.S.A.* 35°3N 118°10W **79** K8
Mojave → *U.S.A.* 35°7N 115°32W **79** K11
Mojave Desert *U.S.A.* 35°0N 116°30W **79** L10
Mojo *Bolivia* 21°48S 65°33W **94** A2
Mojokerto *Indonesia* 7°28S 112°26E **37** G15
Mokai *N.Z.* 38°32S 175°56E **59** C5
Mokameh *India* 25°24N 85°55E **43** G11

Mokau *N.Z.* 38°42S 174°39E **59** C5
Mokelumne → *U.S.A.* 38°13N 121°28W **78** G5
Mokelumne Hill
  U.S.A. 38°18N 120°43W **78** G6
Mokhotlong *Lesotho* 29°22S 29°2E **57** D4
Mokoan, L. *Australia* 36°27S 146°5E **63** C4
Mokokchung *India* 26°15N 94°30E **41** F19
Mokolo → *S. Africa* 23°14S 27°43E **57** C4
Mokopane *S. Africa* 24°10S 28°55E **57** C4
Mokpo *S. Korea* 34°50N 126°25E **35** G14
Mokra Gora *Europe* 42°50N 20°30E **23** C9
Mol *Belgium* 51°11N 5°5E **15** C5
Molchanovo *Russia* 57°40N 83°50E **28** D9
Mold *U.K.* 53°9N 3°8W **12** D4
Moldavia = Moldova ■
  Europe 47°0N 28°0E **17** E15
Moldavia *Romania* 46°30N 27°0E **17** E14
Molde *Norway* 62°45N 7°9E **8** E12
Moldova ■ *Europe* 47°0N 28°0E **17** E15
Moldoveanu, Vf.
  Romania 45°36N 24°45E **17** F13
Mole → *U.K.* 51°24N 0°21W **13** F7
Molepolole *Botswana* 24°28S 25°28E **56** C4
Molfetta *Italy* 41°12N 16°36E **22** D7
Moline *U.S.A.* 41°30N 90°31W **80** E8
Molinos *Argentina* 25°28S 66°15W **94** B2
Moliro
  Dem. Rep. of the Congo 8°12S 30°30E **54** D3
Mollendo *Peru* 17°0S 72°0W **92** G4
Mollerin, L. *Australia* 30°30S 117°35E **61** F2
Molo *Kenya* 0°15S 35°44E **54** C4
Molodechno = Maladzyechna
  Belarus 54°20N 26°50E **17** A14
Molodezhnaya *Antarctica* 67°40S 45°51E **5** C9
Moloka'i *U.S.A.* 21°8N 157°0W **75** L8
Molokai Fracture Zone
  Pac. Oc. 28°0N 125°0W **65** E15
Molong *Australia* 33°5S 148°54E **63** E4
Molopo → *Africa* 28°30S 20°12E **56** D3
Molson L. *Canada* 54°22N 96°40W **71** C9
Molteno *S. Africa* 31°22S 26°22E **56** E4
Molu *Indonesia* 6°45S 131°40E **37** F8
Molucca Sea *Indonesia* 0°0 125°0E **37** E6
Moluccas = Maluku
  Indonesia 1°0S 127°0E **37** E7
Moma
  Dem. Rep. of the Congo 1°35S 23°52E **54** C1
Moma *Mozam.* 16°47S 39°4E **55** F4
Mombasa *Kenya* 4°3S 39°40E **54** C4
Mombetsu *Japan* 44°21N 143°22E **30** B11
Momchilgrad *Bulgaria* 41°33N 25°23E **23** D11
Momi *Dem. Rep. of the Congo* 1°42S 27°0E **54** C2
Mompós *Colombia* 9°14N 74°26W **92** B4
Møn *Denmark* 54°57N 12°20E **9** J15
Mon □ *Burma* 16°0N 97°30E **41** L20
Mona, Canal de la = Mona
  Passage *W. Indies* 18°30N 67°45W **89** C6
Mona, Isla *Puerto Rico* 18°5N 67°54W **89** C6
Mona, Pta. *Costa Rica* 9°37N 82°36W **88** E3
Mona Passage *W. Indies* 18°30N 67°45W **89** C6
Monaca *U.S.A.* 40°41N 80°17W **82** F4
Monaco ■ *Europe* 43°46N 7°23E **20** E7
Monadhliath Mts. *U.K.* 57°10N 4°4W **11** D4
Monadnock, Mt. *U.S.A.* 42°52N 72°7W **83** D12
Monaghan *Ireland* 54°15N 6°57W **10** B5
Monaghan □ *Ireland* 54°11N 6°56W **10** B5
Monahans *U.S.A.* 31°36N 102°54W **84** F3
Monapo *Mozam.* 14°56S 40°19E **55** E5
Monar, L. *U.K.* 57°26N 5°8W **11** D3
Monarch Mt. *Canada* 51°55N 125°57W **70** C3
Monashee Mts. *Canada* 51°0N 118°43W **70** C5
Monasterevin *Ireland* 53°8N 7°4W **10** C4
Monastir = Bitola
  Macedonia 41°1N 21°20E **23** D9
Monastir *Tunisia* 35°50N 10°49E **51** A8
Moncayo, Sierra del
  Spain 41°48N 1°50W **21** B5
Monchegorsk *Russia* 67°54N 32°58E **8** C25
Mönchengladbach
  Germany 51°11N 6°27E **16** C4
Monchique *Portugal* 37°19N 8°38W **21** D1
Moncks Corner *U.S.A.* 33°12N 80°1W **85** E14
Monclova *Mexico* 26°54N 101°25W **86** B4
Moncton *Canada* 46°7N 64°51W **73** C7
Mondego → *Portugal* 40°9N 8°52W **21** B1
Mondeodo *Indonesia* 3°34S 122°9E **37** E6
Mondovì *Italy* 44°23N 7°49E **20** D7
Mondrain I. *Australia* 34°9S 122°14E **61** F3
Moneague *Jamaica* 18°16N 77°7W **88** a
Moneron, Ostrov
  Russia 46°15N 141°16E **30** A10
Monessen *U.S.A.* 40°9N 79°54W **82** F5
Monett *U.S.A.* 36°55N 93°55W **80** G7
Moneymore *U.K.* 54°41N 6°40W **10** B5
Monforte de Lemos *Spain* 42°31N 7°33W **21** A2
Mong Cai *Vietnam* 21°27N 107°54E **38** B6
Mong Hsu *Burma* 21°54N 98°30E **41** J21
Mong Kung *Burma* 21°35N 97°35E **41** J21
Mong Nai *Burma* 20°32N 97°46E **41** J20
Mong Pawk *Burma* 22°4N 99°16E **41** H21
Mong Ton *Burma* 20°17N 98°45E **41** J21
Mong Wa *Burma* 21°26N 100°27E **41** J22
Mong Yai *Burma* 22°21N 98°3E **41** H21
Mongalla *S. Sudan* 5°8N 31°42E **51** G12
Mongers, L. *Australia* 29°25S 117°5E **61** E2
Monghyr = Munger
  India 25°23N 86°30E **43** G12
Mongibello = Etna *Italy* 37°50N 14°55E **22** F6
Mongo *Chad* 12°14N 18°43E **51** F9
Mongolia ■ *Asia* 47°0N 103°0E **32** B5
Mongolia, Plateau of
  Asia 45°0N 105°0E **26** D12
Mongu *Zambia* 15°16S 23°12E **53** H4
Môngua *Angola* 16°43S 15°20E **56** B2
Monifieth *U.K.* 56°30N 2°48W **11** E6
Monkey Bay *Malawi* 14°7S 35°1E **55** E4
Monkey Mia *Australia* 25°48S 113°43E **61** E1
Monkey River *Belize* 16°22N 88°29W **87** D7
Monkland *Canada* 45°11N 74°52W **83** A10

Monkoto
  Dem. Rep. of the Congo 1°38S 20°35E **52** E4
Monkton *Canada* 43°35N 81°5W **82** C3
Monmouth *U.K.* 51°48N 2°42W **13** F5
Monmouth *Ill., U.S.A.* 40°55N 90°39W **80** E8
Monmouth *Oreg.,*
  U.S.A. 44°51N 123°14W **76** D2
Monmouthshire □ *U.K.* 51°48N 2°54W **13** F5
Mono *Pac. Nic.* 12°0N 83°30W **88** D3
Mono L. *U.S.A.* 38°1N 119°1W **78** H7
Monolith *U.S.A.* 35°7N 118°22W **79** K8
Monolithos *Greece* 36°7N 27°45E **25** C9
Monongahela *U.S.A.* 40°12N 79°56W **82** F5
Monópoli *Italy* 40°57N 17°18E **22** D7
Monos I. *Trin. & Tob.* 10°42N 61°44W **93** K15
Monroe *Ga., U.S.A.* 33°47N 83°43W **85** E13
Monroe *La., U.S.A.* 32°30N 92°7W **84** E8
Monroe *Mich., U.S.A.* 41°55N 83°24W **81** E12
Monroe *N.C., U.S.A.* 34°59N 80°33W **85** D14
Monroe *N.Y., U.S.A.* 41°20N 74°11W **83** E10
Monroe *Utah, U.S.A.* 38°38N 112°7W **76** G7
Monroe *Wash., U.S.A.* 47°51N 121°58W **78** C5
Monroe *Wis., U.S.A.* 42°36N 89°38W **80** D9
Monroe City *U.S.A.* 39°39N 91°44W **80** F8
Monroeton *U.S.A.* 41°43N 76°29W **83** E8
Monroeville *Ala.,*
  U.S.A. 31°31N 87°20W **85** F11
Monroeville *Pa., U.S.A.* 40°26N 79°45W **82** F5
Monrovia *Liberia* 6°18N 10°47W **50** G3
Mons *Belgium* 50°27N 3°58E **15** D3
Monse *Indonesia* 4°7S 123°15E **37** E6
Mont-de-Marsan *France* 43°54N 0°31W **20** E3
Mont-Joli *Canada* 48°37N 68°10W **73** C6
Mont-Laurier *Canada* 46°35N 75°30W **72** C4
Mont-Louis *Canada* 49°15N 65°44W **73** C6
Mont-St-Michel, Le
  France 48°40N 1°30W **20** B3
Mont-Tremblant △
  Canada 46°30N 74°30W **72** C5
Montagne d'Ambre △
  Madag. 12°37S 49°8E **57** A8
Montagu *S. Africa* 33°45S 20°8E **56** E3
Montagu I. *Antarctica* 58°25S 26°20W **5** B1
Montague *Canada* 46°10N 62°39W **73** C7
Montague, I. *Mexico* 31°45N 114°48W **86** A2
Montague I. *U.S.A.* 60°0N 147°30W **74** D10
Montague Ra. *Australia* 27°15S 119°30E **61** E2
Montague Sd. *Australia* 14°28S 125°20E **60** B4
Montalbán *Spain* 40°50N 0°45W **21** B5
Montalvo *U.S.A.* 34°15N 119°12W **79** L7
Montana *Bulgaria* 43°27N 23°16E **23** C10
Montaña *Peru* 6°0S 73°0W **92** E4
Montana □ *U.S.A.* 47°0N 110°0W **76** C9
Montaña Clara, I.
  Canary Is. 29°17N 13°33W **24** E6
Montargis *France* 47°59N 2°43E **20** C5
Montauban *France* 44°2N 1°21E **20** D4
Montauk *U.S.A.* 41°3N 71°57W **83** E13
Montauk Pt. *U.S.A.* 41°4N 71°51W **83** E13
Montbéliard *France* 47°31N 6°48E **20** C7
Montceau-les-Mines
  France 46°40N 4°23E **20** C6
Montclair *U.S.A.* 40°49N 74°12W **83** F10
Monte Albán *Mexico* 17°2N 96°46W **87** D5
Monte Alegre *Brazil* 2°0S 54°0W **93** D8
Monte Azul *Brazil* 15°9S 42°53W **93** G10
Monte-Carlo *Monaco* 43°44N 7°25E **20** E7
Monte Caseros
  Argentina 30°10S 57°50W **94** C4
Monte Comán *Argentina* 34°40S 67°53W **94** C2
Monte Cristi *Dom. Rep.* 19°52N 71°39W **89** C5
Monte Lindo →
  Paraguay 23°56S 57°12W **94** A4
Monte Patria *Chile* 30°42S 70°58W **94** C1
Monte Quemado
  Argentina 25°53S 62°41W **94** B3
Monte Rio *U.S.A.* 38°28N 123°0W **78** G4
Monte Santu, C. di *Italy* 40°5N 9°44E **22** D3
Monte Vista *U.S.A.* 37°35N 106°9W **77** H10
Monteagudo *Argentina* 27°14S 54°8W **95** B5
Montebello *U.S.A.* 34°1N 118°6W **79** M8
Montebello Is. *Australia* 20°30S 115°45E **60** D2
Montecarlo *Argentina* 26°34S 54°47W **95** B5
Montecito *U.S.A.* 34°26N 119°40W **79** L7
Montecristo *Italy* 42°20N 10°19E **22** C4
Montego Bay *Jamaica* 18°28N 77°55W **88** a
Montélimar *France* 44°33N 4°45E **20** D6
Montello *U.S.A.* 41°16N 114°12W **76** F6
Montemorelos *Mexico* 25°12N 99°49W **87** B5
Montenegro *Brazil* 29°39S 51°29W **95** B5
Montenegro ■ *Europe* 42°40N 19°20E **23** C8
Montepuez *Mozam.* 13°8S 38°59E **55** E4
Montepuez → *Mozam.* 12°32S 40°27E **55** E5
Monterey *U.S.A.* 36°37N 121°55W **78** J5
Monterey B. *U.S.A.* 36°45N 122°0W **78** J5
Montería *Colombia* 8°46N 75°53W **92** B3
Monteros *Argentina* 27°11S 65°30W **94** B2
Monterrey *Mexico* 25°40N 100°19W **86** B4
Montes Azules △ *Mexico* 16°21N 91°3W **87** D6
Montes Claros *Brazil* 16°30S 43°50W **93** G10
Montesano *U.S.A.* 46°59N 123°36W **78** D3
Montesilvano *Italy* 42°29N 14°8E **22** C6
Montevideo *Uruguay* 34°50S 56°11W **95** C4
Montevideo *U.S.A.* 44°57N 95°43W **80** C6
Montezuma *U.S.A.* 41°35N 92°32W **80** E7
Montezuma Castle △
  U.S.A. 34°39N 111°45W **77** J8
Montgomery *U.K.* 52°34N 3°8W **13** E4
Montgomery *Ala.,*
  U.S.A. 32°23N 86°19W **85** E11
Montgomery *Pa., U.S.A.* 41°10N 76°53W **82** E8
Montgomery *W. Va.,*
  U.S.A. 38°11N 81°19W **81** F13
Montgomery City
  U.S.A. 38°59N 91°30W **80** F8
Monticello *Ark., U.S.A.* 33°38N 91°47W **84** E9
Monticello *Fla., U.S.A.* 30°33N 83°52W **85** F13
Monticello *Ind., U.S.A.* 40°45N 86°46W **80** E10
Monticello *Iowa, U.S.A.* 42°15N 91°12W **80** D8

Monticello *Ky., U.S.A.* 36°50N 84°51W **81** G11
Monticello *Minn., U.S.A.* 45°18N 93°48W **80** C7
Monticello *Miss., U.S.A.* 31°33N 90°7W **85** F9
Monticello *N.Y., U.S.A.* 41°39N 74°42W **83** E10
Monticello *Utah, U.S.A.* 37°52N 109°21W **77** H9
Montijo *Portugal* 38°41N 8°54W **21** C1
Montilla *Spain* 37°36N 4°40W **21** D3
Montluçon *France* 46°22N 2°36E **20** C5
Montmagny *Canada* 46°58N 70°34W **73** C5
Montmartre *Canada* 50°14N 103°27W **71** C8
Monto *Australia* 24°52S 151°6E **62** C5
Montongbuwoh *Indonesia* 8°33S 116°4E **37** K19
Montoro *Spain* 38°1N 4°27W **21** C3
Montour Falls *U.S.A.* 42°21N 76°51W **82** D8
Montoursville *U.S.A.* 41°15N 76°55W **82** E8
Montpelier *Idaho, U.S.A.* 42°19N 111°18W **76** E8
Montpelier *Vt., U.S.A.* 44°16N 72°35W **83** B12
Montpellier *France* 43°37N 3°52E **20** E5
Montréal *Canada* 45°30N 73°33W **83** A11
Montreal *→ Canada* 47°14N 84°39W **72** C3
Montreal L. *Canada* 54°20N 105°45W **71** C7
Montreal Lake *Canada* 54°3N 105°46W **71** C7
Montreux *Switz.* 46°26N 6°55E **20** C7
Montrose *U.K.* 56°44N 2°27N **11** E6
Montrose *Colo., U.S.A.* 38°29N 107°53W **76** G10
Montrose *Pa., U.S.A.* 41°50N 75°53W **83** E9
Monts, Pte. des *Canada* 49°20N 67°12W **73** C6
Montserrat ☑ *W. Indies* 16°40N 62°10W **89** C7
Montuiri *Spain* 39°34N 2°59E **24** B9
Monywa *Burma* 22°7N 95°11E **41** H19
Monza *Italy* 45°35N 9°16E **20** D8
Monze *Zambia* 16°17S 27°29E **55** F2
Monze, C. *Pakistan* 24°47N 66°37E **42** G2
Monzón *Spain* 41°52N 0°10E **21** B6
Mooers *U.S.A.* 44°58N 73°35W **83** B11
Mooi *→ S. Africa* 28°45S 30°34E **57** D5
Mooi River *S. Africa* 29°13S 29°50E **57** D4
Moomba *Australia* 28°6S 140°12E **63** A3
Moonah *→ Australia* 22°3S 138°33E **62** C2
Moonda, L. *Australia* 25°52S 140°25E **62** D3
Moonie *Australia* 27°46S 150°20E **63** D5
Moonie *→ Australia* 29°19S 148°43E **63** D4
Moonta *Australia* 34°6S 137°32E **63** E2
Moora *Australia* 30°37S 115°58E **61** F2
Moorcroft *U.S.A.* 44°16N 104°57W **76** D11
Moore *→ Australia* 31°22S 115°30E **61** F2
Moore, L. *Australia* 29°50S 117°35E **61** E2
Moore Falls *Canada* 44°48N 78°48W **82** B6
Moore Park *Australia* 24°43S 152°17E **62** C5
Moore River △ *Australia* 31°7S 115°39E **61** F2
Moorea *French Polynesia* 17°30S 149°50W **59** d
Moorefield *U.S.A.* 39°4N 78°58W **81** F14
Moorfoot Hills *U.K.* 55°44N 3°8W **11** F5
Moorhead *U.S.A.* 46°53N 96°45W **80** B5
Moorpark *U.S.A.* 34°17N 118°53W **79** L8
Moorreesburg *S. Africa* 33°6S 18°38E **56** E2
Moorrinya △ *Australia* 21°42S 144°58E **62** C3
Moose *→ Canada* 51°20N 80°25W **72** B3
Moose *→ U.S.A.* 43°38N 75°24W **83** C9
Moose Creek *Canada* 45°15N 74°58W **83** A10
Moose Factory *Canada* 51°16N 80°32W **72** B3
Moose Jaw *Canada* 50°24N 105°30W **71** C7
Moose Jaw *→ Canada* 50°34N 105°18W **71** C7
Moose Lake *Canada* 53°46N 100°8W **71** C8
Moose Lake *U.S.A.* 46°27N 92°46W **80** B7
Moose Mountain ○ *Canada* 49°48N 102°25W **71** D8
Moosehead L. *U.S.A.* 45°38N 69°40W **81** C19
Mooselookmeguntic L. *U.S.A.* 44°55N 70°49W **83** B14
Moosomin *Canada* 50°9N 101°40W **71** C8
Moosonee *Canada* 51°17N 80°39W **72** B3
Moosup *U.S.A.* 41°43N 71°53W **83** E13
Mopane *S. Africa* 22°37S 29°52E **57** C4
Mopeia Velha *Mozam.* 17°30S 35°40E **55** F4
Mopipi *Botswana* 21°6S 24°55E **56** C3
Mopoi *C.A.R.* 5°6N 26°54E **54** A2
Mopti *Mali* 14°30N 4°0W **50** F5
Moqor *Afghan.* 32°50N 67°42E **42** C2
Moquegua *Peru* 17°15S 70°46W **92** G4
Mora *Sweden* 61°2N 14°38E **8** F16
Mora *Minn., U.S.A.* 45°53N 93°18W **80** C7
Mora *N. Mex., U.S.A.* 35°58N 105°20W **77** J11
Moradabad *India* 28°50N 78°50E **43** E8
Morafenobe *Madag.* 17°50S 44°53E **57** B7
Moramanga *Madag.* 18°56S 48°12E **57** B8
Moran *Kans., U.S.A.* 37°55N 95°10W **80** G6
Moran *Wyo., U.S.A.* 43°50N 110°31W **76** E8
Moranbah *Australia* 22°1S 148°6E **62** C4
Morang = Biratnagar *Nepal* 26°27N 87°17E **43** F12
Morant Bay *Jamaica* 17°53N 76°25W **88** a
Morant Cays *Jamaica* 17°22N 76°0W **88** C4
Morant Pt. *Jamaica* 17°55N 76°12W **88** a
Morar *India* 26°14N 78°14E **42** F8
Morar, L. *U.K.* 56°57N 5°40W **11** E3
Moratuwa *Sri Lanka* 6°45N 79°55E **40** R11
Morava *→ Serbia* 44°36N 21°4E **23** B9
Morava *→ Slovak Rep.* 48°10N 16°59E **17** D9
Moravia *U.S.A.* 42°43N 76°25W **83** D8
Moravian Hts. = Českomoravská Vrchovina *Czech Rep.* 49°30N 15°40E **16** D8
Morawa *Australia* 29°13S 116°0E **61** E2
Morawhanna *Guyana* 8°30N 59°40W **92** B7
Moray □ *U.K.* 57°31N 3°18W **11** D5
Moray Firth *U.K.* 57°40N 3°52W **11** D5
Morbi *India* 22°50N 70°42E **42** H4
Morden *Canada* 49°15N 98°10W **71** D9
Mordovian Republic = Mordvinia □ *Russia* 54°20N 44°30E **18** D7
Mordvinia □ *Russia* 54°20N 44°30E **18** D7
Moreau *→ U.S.A.* 45°18N 100°43W **80** C3
Morebeng *S. Africa* 23°30S 29°55E **57** C4
Morecambe *U.K.* 54°5N 2°52W **12** C5

Morecambe B. *U.K.* 54°7N 3°0W **12** C5
Moree *Australia* 29°28S 149°54E **63** D4
Morehead *U.S.A.* 38°11N 83°26W **81** F12
Morehead City *U.S.A.* 34°43N 76°43W **85** D16
Morel *→ India* 26°13N 76°36E **42** F7
Morelia *Mexico* 19°42N 101°7W **86** D4
Morella *Australia* 23°0S 143°52E **62** C3
Morella *Spain* 40°35N 0°5W **21** B5
Morelos *Mexico* 26°42N 107°40W **86** B3
Morelos □ *Mexico* 18°45N 99°0W **87** D5
Morena *India* 26°30N 78°4E **42** F8
Morena, Sierra *Spain* 38°20N 4°0W **21** C3
Moreno Valley *U.S.A.* 33°56N 117°14W **79** M10
Moresby I. *Canada* 52°30N 131°40W **70** C2
Moreton I. *Australia* 27°10S 153°25E **63** D5
Moreton Island △ *Australia* 27°2S 153°24E **63** D5
Morgan *U.S.A.* 41°2N 111°41W **76** F8
Morgan City *U.S.A.* 29°42N 91°12W **84** G9
Morgan Hill *U.S.A.* 37°8N 121°39W **78** H5
Morganfield *U.S.A.* 37°41N 87°55W **80** G10
Morganton *U.S.A.* 35°45N 81°41W **85** D14
Morgantown *U.S.A.* 39°38N 79°57W **81** F14
Morgenzon *S. Africa* 26°45S 29°36E **57** D4
Morghak *Iran* 29°7N 57°54E **45** D8
Morhar *→ India* 25°29N 85°11E **43** G11
Mori *Japan* 42°6N 140°35E **30** C10
Moriarty *U.S.A.* 34°59N 106°3W **77** J10
Morice L. *Canada* 53°50N 127°40W **70** C3
Morinville *Canada* 53°49N 113°41W **70** C6
Morioka *Japan* 39°45N 141°8E **30** E10
Moris *Mexico* 28°10N 108°32W **86** B3
Morlaix *France* 48°36N 3°52W **20** B2
Mornington *Australia* 38°15S 145°5E **63** F4
Mornington, I. *Chile* 49°50S 75°30W **96** F1
Mornington I. *Australia* 16°30S 139°30E **62** B2
Moro *Pakistan* 26°40N 68°0E **42** F2
Moro *→ Pakistan* 29°42N 67°22E **42** E2
Moro G. *Phil.* 6°30N 123°0E **37** C6
Morocco ■ *N. Afr.* 32°0N 5°50W **50** B4
Morogoro *Tanzania* 6°50S 37°40E **54** D4
Morogoro □ *Tanzania* 8°0S 37°0E **54** D4
Moroleón *Mexico* 20°8N 101°12W **86** C4
Morombe *Madag.* 21°45S 43°22E **57** C7
Morón *Argentina* 34°39S 58°37W **94** C4
Morón *Cuba* 22°8N 78°39W **88** B4
Mörön *Mongolia* 49°38N 100°9E **32** B4
Morón de la Frontera *Spain* 37°6N 5°28W **21** D3
Morona *→ Peru* 4°40S 77°10W **92** D3
Morondava *Madag.* 20°17S 44°17E **57** C7
Morongo Valley *U.S.A.* 34°3N 116°37W **79** L10
Moroni *Comoros Is.* 11°40S 43°16E **53** a
Moroni *U.S.A.* 39°32N 111°35W **76** G8
Morotai *Indonesia* 2°10N 128°30E **37** D7
Moroto *Uganda* 2°28N 34°42E **54** B3
Moroto, Mt. *Uganda* 2°30N 34°43E **54** B3
Morpeth *Canada* 42°23N 81°50W **82** D3
Morpeth *U.K.* 55°10N 1°41W **12** B6
Morphou *Cyprus* 35°12N 32°59E **25** D11
Morphou Bay *Cyprus* 35°15N 32°50E **25** D11
Morrilton *U.S.A.* 35°9N 92°44W **84** D8
Morrinhos *Brazil* 17°45S 49°10W **93** G9
Morrinsville *N.Z.* 37°40S 175°32E **59** B5
Morris *Canada* 49°25N 97°22W **71** D9
Morris *Ill., U.S.A.* 41°22N 88°26W **80** E9
Morris *Minn., U.S.A.* 45°35N 95°55W **80** C6
Morris *N.Y., U.S.A.* 42°33N 75°15W **83** D9
Morris *Pa., U.S.A.* 41°35N 77°17W **82** E7
Morris, Mt. *Australia* 26°9S 131°4E **61** E5
Morris Jesup, Kap *Greenland* 83°40N 34°0W **66** A16
Morrisburg *Canada* 44°55N 75°7W **83** B9
Morristown *Ariz., U.S.A.* 33°51N 112°37W **77** K7
Morristown *N.J., U.S.A.* 40°48N 74°29W **83** F10
Morristown *N.Y., U.S.A.* 44°35N 75°39W **83** B9
Morristown *Tenn., U.S.A.* 36°13N 83°18W **85** C13
Morrisville *N.Y., U.S.A.* 42°53N 75°35W **83** D9
Morrisville *Pa., U.S.A.* 40°13N 74°47W **83** F10
Morrisville *Vt., U.S.A.* 44°34N 72°36W **83** B12
Morro, Pta. *Chile* 27°6S 71°0W **94** B1
Morro Bay *U.S.A.* 35°22N 120°51W **78** K6
Morro del Jable *Canary Is.* 28°3N 14°23W **24** F5
Morro Jable, Pta. de *Canary Is.* 28°2N 14°20W **24** F5
Morrocoy △ *Venezuela* 10°48N 68°13W **89** D6
Morrosquillo, G. de *Colombia* 9°35N 75°40W **88** E4
Morrumbene *Mozam.* 23°31S 35°16E **57** C6
Morshansk *Russia* 53°28N 41°50E **18** D7
Morteros *Argentina* 30°50S 62°0W **94** C3
Mortlach *Canada* 50°27N 106°4W **71** C7
Mortlake *Australia* 38°5S 142°50E **63** F3
Morton *Tex., U.S.A.* 33°44N 102°46W **84** E3
Morton *Wash., U.S.A.* 46°34N 122°17W **78** D4
Moruga *Trin. & Tob.* 10°4N 61°16W **93** K15
Morundah *Australia* 34°57S 146°19E **63** E4
Moruya *Australia* 35°58S 150°3E **63** F4
Morvan *France* 47°5N 4°3E **20** C6
Morven *Australia* 26°22S 147°5E **63** D4
Morvern *U.K.* 56°38N 5°44W **11** E3
Morwell *Australia* 38°10S 146°22E **63** F4
Morzhovets, Ostrov *Russia* 66°44N 42°35E **18** A7
Mosakahiken = Moose Lake *Canada* 53°46N 100°8W **71** C8
Moscos Is. *Burma* 14°0N 97°30E **38** F1
Moscow = Moskva *Russia* 55°45N 37°37E **18** C6
Moscow *Idaho, U.S.A.* 46°44N 117°0W **76** C5
Moscow *Pa., U.S.A.* 41°20N 75°31W **83** E9
Mosel *→ Europe* 50°22N 7°36E **20** A7
Moselle = Mosel *→ Europe* 50°22N 7°36E **20** A7
Moses Lake *U.S.A.* 47°8N 119°17W **76** C4
Mosgiel *N.Z.* 45°53S 170°21E **59** F3

Moshaweng *→ S. Africa* 26°35S 22°50E **56** D3
Moshchnyy, Ostrov *Russia* 60°1N 27°50E **9** F22
Moshi *Tanzania* 3°22S 37°18E **54** C4
Moshupa *Botswana* 24°46S 25°29E **56** C4
Mosjøen *Norway* 65°51N 13°12E **8** D15
Moskenesøya *Norway* 67°58N 13°0E **8** C15
Moskenstraumen *Norway* 67°47N 12°45E **8** C15
Moskva *Russia* 55°45N 37°37E **18** C6
Mosomane *Botswana* 24°2S 26°19E **56** C4
Mosonmagyaróvár *Hungary* 47°52N 17°18E **17** E9
Mosquera *Colombia* 2°35N 78°24W **92** C3
Mosquero *U.S.A.* 35°47N 103°58W **77** J12
Mosquitia *Honduras* 15°20N 84°10W **88** C3
Mosquito Coast = Mosquitia *Honduras* 15°20N 84°10W **88** C3
Mosquito Creek L. *U.S.A.* 41°18N 80°46W **82** E4
Mosquito L. *Canada* 62°35N 103°20W **71** A8
Mosquitos, G. de los *Panama* 9°15N 81°10W **88** E3
Moss *Norway* 59°27N 10°40E **9** G14
Moss Vale *Australia* 34°32S 150°25E **63** E5
Mossbank *Canada* 49°56N 105°56W **71** D7
Mossburn *N.Z.* 45°41S 168°15E **59** F2
Mosselbaai *S. Africa* 34°11S 22°8E **56** E3
Mossendjo *Congo* 2°55S 12°42E **52** E2
Mossgiel *Australia* 33°15S 144°5E **63** E3
Mossman *Australia* 16°21S 145°15E **62** B4
Mossoró *Brazil* 5°10S 37°15W **93** E11
Mossuril *Mozam.* 14°58S 40°42E **55** E5
Most *Czech Rep.* 50°31N 13°38E **16** C7
Mosta *Malta* 35°55N 14°26E **25** D1
Mostaganem *Algeria* 35°54N 0°5E **50** A6
Mostar *Bos.-H.* 43°22N 17°50E **23** C7
Mostardas *Brazil* 31°2S 50°51W **95** C5
Mostiska = Mostyska *Ukraine* 49°48N 23°4E **17** D12
Mosty = Masty *Belarus* 53°27N 24°38E **17** B13
Mostyska *Ukraine* 49°48N 23°4E **17** D12
Mosul = Al Mawşil *Iraq* 36°15N 43°5E **44** B4
Motagua *→ Guatemala* 15°44N 88°14W **88** C2
Motala *Sweden* 58°32N 15°1E **9** G16
Motaze *Mozam.* 24°48S 32°52E **57** C5
Moth *India* 25°43N 78°57E **43** G8
Motherwell *U.K.* 55°47N 3°58W **11** F5
Motihari *India* 26°30N 84°55E **43** F11
Motozintla de Mendoza *Mexico* 15°22N 92°14W **87** D6
Motril *Spain* 36°31N 3°37W **21** D4
Mott *U.S.A.* 46°23N 102°20W **80** B2
Motueka *N.Z.* 41°7S 173°1E **59** D4
Motueka *→ N.Z.* 41°5S 173°1E **59** D4
Motul *Mexico* 21°6N 89°17W **87** C7
Mouchalagane *→ Canada* 50°56N 68°41W **73** B6
Moudros *Greece* 39°50N 25°18E **23** E11
Mouhoun = Black Volta *→ Africa* 8°41N 1°33W **50** G5
Mouila *Gabon* 1°50S 11°0E **52** E2
Moulamein *Australia* 35°3S 144°1E **63** F3
Moule à Chique, C. *St. Lucia* 13°43N 60°57W **89** f
Mouliana *Greece* 35°10N 25°59E **25** D7
Moulins *France* 46°35N 3°19E **20** C5
Moulmein *Burma* 16°30N 97°40E **41** L20
Moulouya, O. *→ Morocco* 35°5N 2°25W **50** B5
Moultrie *U.S.A.* 31°11N 83°47W **85** F13
Moultrie, L. *U.S.A.* 33°20N 80°5W **85** E14
Mound City *Mo., U.S.A.* 40°7N 95°14W **80** E6
Mound City *S. Dak., U.S.A.* 45°44N 100°4W **80** C3
Moundou *Chad* 8°40N 16°10E **51** G9
Moundsville *U.S.A.* 39°55N 80°44W **82** G4
Moung *Cambodia* 12°46N 103°27E **38** F4
Mount Airy *U.S.A.* 36°31N 80°37W **85** C14
Mount Albert *Canada* 44°8N 79°19W **82** B5
Mount Aspiring △ *N.Z.* 44°19S 168°47E **59** F2
Mount Barker *S. Austral., Australia* 35°5S 138°52E **63** F2
Mount Barker *W. Austral., Australia* 34°38S 117°40E **61** F2
Mount Barnett Roadhouse *Australia* 16°39S 125°57E **60** C4
Mount Bellew Bridge *Ireland* 53°28N 8°31W **10** C3
Mount Brydges *Canada* 42°54N 81°29W **82** D3
Mount Burr *Australia* 37°34S 140°26E **63** F3
Mount Carmel = Ha Karmel △ *Israel* 32°45N 35°5E **46** C4
Mount Carmel *Ill., U.S.A.* 38°25N 87°46W **80** F10
Mount Carmel *Pa., U.S.A.* 40°47N 76°26W **83** F8
Mount Clemens *U.S.A.* 42°35N 82°53W **82** D2
Mount Coolon *Australia* 21°25S 147°25E **62** C4
Mount Darwin *Zimbabwe* 16°47S 31°38E **55** F3
Mount Desert I. *U.S.A.* 44°21N 68°20W **81** C19
Mount Dora *U.S.A.* 28°48N 81°38W **85** G14
Mount Ebenezer *Australia* 25°6S 132°34E **61** E5
Mount Edziza △ *Canada* 57°30N 130°45W **70** B2
Mount Elgon △ *E. Afr.* 1°4N 34°42E **54** B3
Mount Field △ *Australia* 42°39S 146°35E **63** G4
Mount Fletcher *S. Africa* 30°40S 28°30E **57** E4
Mount Forest *Canada* 43°59N 80°43W **82** C4
Mount Frankland △ *Australia* 34°47S 116°37E **61** F2
Mount Frederick ○ *Australia* 19°39S 129°18E **60** C4
Mount Gambier *Australia* 37°50S 140°46E **63** F3
Mount Garnet *Australia* 17°37S 145°6E **62** B4
Mount Holly *U.S.A.* 39°59N 74°47W **83** G10

Mount Holly Springs *U.S.A.* 40°7N 77°12W **82** F7
Mount Hope *N.S.W., Australia* 32°51S 145°51E **63** E4
Mount Hope *S. Austral., Australia* 34°7S 135°23E **63** E2
Mount Isa *Australia* 20°42S 139°26E **62** C2
Mount James ○ *Australia* 24°51S 116°54E **61** D2
Mount Jewett *U.S.A.* 41°44N 78°39W **82** E6
Mount Kaputar △ *Australia* 30°16S 150°10E **63** E5
Mount Kenya △ *Kenya* 0°7S 37°21E **54** C4
Mount Kisco *U.S.A.* 41°12N 73°44W **83** E11
Mount Laguna *U.S.A.* 32°52N 116°25W **79** N10
Mount Larcom *Australia* 23°48S 150°59E **62** C5
Mount Lofty Ranges *Australia* 34°35S 139°5E **63** E2
Mount Magnet *Australia* 28°2S 117°47E **61** E2
Mount Maunganui *N.Z.* 37°40S 176°14E **59** B6
Mount Molloy *Australia* 16°42S 145°20E **62** B4
Mount Morgan *Australia* 23°40S 150°25E **62** C5
Mount Morris *U.S.A.* 42°44N 77°52W **82** D7
Mount Pearl *Canada* 47°31N 52°47W **73** C9
Mount Penn *U.S.A.* 40°20N 75°54W **83** F9
Mount Perry *Australia* 25°13S 151°42E **63** D5
Mount Pleasant *Iowa, U.S.A.* 40°58N 91°33W **80** E8
Mount Pleasant *Mich., U.S.A.* 43°36N 84°46W **81** D11
Mount Pleasant *Pa., U.S.A.* 40°9N 79°33W **82** F5
Mount Pleasant *S.C., U.S.A.* 32°47N 79°52W **85** E15
Mount Pleasant *Tenn., U.S.A.* 35°32N 87°12W **85** D11
Mount Pleasant *Tex., U.S.A.* 33°9N 94°58W **84** E7
Mount Pleasant *Utah, U.S.A.* 39°33N 111°27W **76** G8
Mount Pocono *U.S.A.* 41°7N 75°22W **83** E9
Mount Rainier △ *U.S.A.* 46°55N 121°50W **78** D5
Mount Revelstoke △ *Canada* 51°5N 118°30W **70** C5
Mount Robson ○ *Canada* 53°0N 119°0W **70** C5
Mount St. Helens ○ *U.S.A.* 46°14N 122°11W **78** D4
Mount Selinda *Zimbabwe* 20°24S 32°43E **57** C5
Mount Shasta *U.S.A.* 41°19N 122°19W **76** F2
Mount Signal *U.S.A.* 32°39N 115°37W **79** N11
Mount Sterling *Ill., U.S.A.* 39°59N 90°45W **80** F8
Mount Sterling *Ky., U.S.A.* 38°4N 83°56W **81** F12
Mount Surprise *Australia* 18°10S 144°17E **62** B3
Mount Union *U.S.A.* 40°23N 77°53W **82** F7
Mount Upton *U.S.A.* 42°26N 75°23W **83** D9
Mount Vernon *Ill., U.S.A.* 38°19N 88°55W **80** F9
Mount Vernon *Ind., U.S.A.* 37°56N 87°54W **80** G10
Mount Vernon *N.Y., U.S.A.* 40°54N 73°49W **83** F11
Mount Vernon *Ohio, U.S.A.* 40°23N 82°29W **82** F2
Mount Vernon *Wash., U.S.A.* 48°25N 122°20W **78** B4
Mount William △ *Australia* 40°56S 148°14E **63** G4
Mountain Ash *U.K.* 51°40N 3°23W **13** F4
Mountain Center *U.S.A.* 33°42N 116°44W **79** M10
Mountain City *Nev., U.S.A.* 41°50N 115°58W **76** F6
Mountain City *Tenn., U.S.A.* 36°29N 81°48W **85** C14
Mountain Dale *U.S.A.* 41°41N 74°32W **83** E10
Mountain Grove *U.S.A.* 37°8N 92°16W **80** G7
Mountain Home *Ark., U.S.A.* 36°20N 92°23W **84** C8
Mountain Home *Idaho, U.S.A.* 43°8N 115°41W **76** E6
Mountain Iron *U.S.A.* 47°32N 92°37W **80** B7
Mountain Pass *U.S.A.* 35°29N 115°35W **79** K11
Mountain View *Ark., U.S.A.* 35°52N 92°7W **84** D8
Mountain View *Calif., U.S.A.* 37°23N 122°5W **78** H4
Mountain Zebra △ *S. Africa* 32°14S 25°27E **56** E4
Mountainair *U.S.A.* 34°31N 106°15W **77** J10
Mountlake Terrace *U.S.A.* 47°47N 122°18W **78** C4
Mountmellick *Ireland* 53°7N 7°20W **10** C4
Mountrath *Ireland* 53°0N 7°28W **10** D4
Moura *Australia* 24°35S 149°58E **62** C4
Moura *Brazil* 1°32S 61°38W **92** D6
Moura *Portugal* 38°7N 7°30W **21** C2
Mourdi, Dépression du *Chad* 18°10N 23°0E **51** E10
Mourilyan *Australia* 17°35S 146°3E **62** B4
Mourne *→ U.K.* 54°52N 7°26W **10** B4
Mourne Mts. *U.K.* 54°10N 6°0W **10** B5
Mournies *Greece* 35°29N 24°1E **25** D6
Mouscron *Belgium* 50°45N 3°12E **15** D3
Moussoro *Chad* 13°41N 16°35E **51** F9
Moutong *Indonesia* 0°28N 121°13E **37** D6
Movas *Mexico* 28°10N 109°25W **86** B3
Moville *Ireland* 55°11N 7°3W **10** A4
Mowandjum *Australia* 17°22S 123°40E **60** C3
Moy *→ Ireland* 54°8N 9°8W **10** B2
Moya *Comoros Is.* 12°18S 44°18E **53** a
Moyale *Ethiopia* 3°34N 39°5E **54** B4
Moyale *Kenya* 3°30N 39°4E **54** B4

Moyen Atlas *Morocco* 33°0N 5°0W **50** B4
Moyo *Indonesia* 8°10S 117°40E **36** F5
Moyobamba *Peru* 6°0S 77°0W **92** E3
Moyowosi *→ Tanzania* 3°50S 31°0E **54** C3
Moyyero *→ Russia* 68°44N 103°42E **29** C11
Moyynqum *Kazakhstan* 44°12N 71°0E **32** D2
Moyynty *Kazakhstan* 47°10N 73°18E **28** E8
Mozambique = Moçambique *Mozam.* 15°3S 40°42E **55** F5
Mozambique ■ *Africa* 19°0S 35°0E **55** F4
Mozambique Chan. *Africa* 17°30S 42°30E **57** B7
Mozdok *Russia* 43°45N 44°48E **19** F7
Mozdūrān *Iran* 36°9N 60°35E **45** B9
Mozhnābād *Iran* 34°7N 60°6E **45** C9
Mozyr = Mazyr *Belarus* 51°59N 29°15E **17** B15
Mpanda *Tanzania* 6°23S 31°1E **54** D3
Mphoeng *Zimbabwe* 21°10S 27°51E **55** G2
Mpika *Zambia* 11°51S 31°25E **55** E3
Mpulungu *Zambia* 8°51S 31°5E **55** D3
Mpumalanga *S. Africa* 29°50S 30°33E **57** D5
Mpumalanga □ *S. Africa* 26°0S 30°0E **57** D5
Mpwapwa *Tanzania* 6°23S 36°30E **54** D4
Mqanduli *S. Africa* 31°49S 28°45E **57** E4
Msaken *Tunisia* 35°49N 10°33E **51** A8
Msambansovu *Zimbabwe* 15°50S 30°3E **55** F3
M'sila *Algeria* 35°30N 4°29E **50** A6
Msoro *Zambia* 13°35S 31°50E **55** E3
Mstislavl = Mstsislaw *Belarus* 54°0N 31°50E **17** A16
Mstsislaw *Belarus* 54°0N 31°50E **17** A16
Mtama *Tanzania* 10°17S 39°21E **55** E4
Mtamvuna = Mthamvuna *→ S. Africa* 31°6S 30°12E **57** E5
Mthamvuna *→ S. Africa* 31°6S 30°12E **57** E5
Mthatha *S. Africa* 31°36S 28°49E **57** E4
Mtilikwe *→ Zimbabwe* 21°9S 31°30E **55** G3
Mtito Andei *Kenya* 2°41S 38°10E **54** C4
Mtubatuba *S. Africa* 28°30S 32°8E **57** D5
Mtwalume *S. Africa* 30°30S 30°38E **57** E5
Mtwara-Mikindani *Tanzania* 10°20S 40°20E **55** E5
Mu Gia, Deo *Vietnam* 17°40N 105°47E **38** D5
Mu Ko Chang △ *Thailand* 11°59N 102°22E **39** G4
Mu Us Shamo *China* 39°0N 109°0E **34** E5
Muang Chiang Rai = Chiang Rai *Thailand* 19°52N 99°50E **38** C2
Muang Khong *Laos* 14°7N 105°51E **38** E5
Muang Lamphun *Thailand* 18°40N 99°2E **38** C2
Muang Mai *Thailand* 8°5N 98°21E **39** a
Muang Pak Beng *Laos* 19°54N 101°8E **38** C3
Muar *Malaysia* 2°3N 102°34E **39** L4
Muarabungo *Indonesia* 1°28S 102°52E **36** E2
Muaraenim *Indonesia* 3°40S 103°50E **36** E2
Muarajuloi *Indonesia* 0°12S 114°3E **36** E4
Muarakaman *Indonesia* 0°2S 116°45E **36** E5
Muaratebo *Indonesia* 1°30S 102°26E **36** E2
Muaratembesi *Indonesia* 1°42S 103°8E **36** E2
Muaratewe *Indonesia* 0°58S 114°52E **36** E4
Mubarakpur *India* 26°6N 83°18E **43** F10
Mubarraz = Al Mubarraz *Si. Arabia* 25°30N 49°40E **45** E6
Mubende *Uganda* 0°33N 31°22E **54** B3
Mubi *Nigeria* 10°18N 13°16E **51** F8
Mucajaí *→ Brazil* 2°25N 60°52W **92** C6
Muchachos, Roque de los *Canary Is.* 28°44N 17°52W **24** F2
Muchinga Mts. *Zambia* 11°30S 31°30E **55** E3
Muck *U.K.* 56°50N 6°15W **11** E2
Muckadilla *Australia* 26°35S 148°23E **63** D4
Muckaty ○ *Australia* 18°37S 133°52E **62** B1
Muckle Flugga *U.K.* 60°51N 0°54W **11** A8
Mucuri *Brazil* 18°0S 39°36W **93** G11
Mucusso *Angola* 18°1S 21°25E **56** B3
Muda *Canary Is.* 28°34N 13°57W **24** F6
Mudanjiang *China* 44°38N 129°30E **35** B15
Mudanya *Turkey* 40°25N 28°50E **23** D13
Muddy Cr. *→ U.S.A.* 38°24N 110°42W **76** G8
Mudgee *Australia* 32°32S 149°31E **63** E4
Mudjatik *→ Canada* 56°1N 107°36W **71** B7
Muecate *Mozam.* 14°55S 39°40E **55** E4
Mueda *Mozam.* 11°36S 39°28E **55** E4
Mueller Ranges *Australia* 18°18S 126°46E **60** C4
Muende *Mozam.* 14°28S 33°0E **55** E3
Muerto, Mar *Mexico* 16°10N 94°10W **87** D6
Mufulira *Zambia* 12°32S 28°15E **55** E2
Mufumbiro Range *Africa* 1°25S 29°30E **54** C2
Mughal Sarai *India* 25°18N 83°7E **43** G10
Mughayrā' *Si. Arabia* 29°17N 37°41E **44** D3
Mugi *Japan* 33°40N 134°25E **31** H7
Mugila, Mts. *Dem. Rep. of the Congo* 7°0S 28°50E **54** D2
Muğla *Turkey* 37°15N 28°22E **23** F13
Mugu *Nepal* 29°45N 82°30E **43** E10
Muhala *Congo* 7°0S 28°50E **54** D2
Muhammad, Râs *Egypt* 27°44N 34°16E **44** E2
Muhammad Qol *Sudan* 20°53N 37°9E **51** D13
Muhammadabad *India* 26°4N 83°25E **43** F10
Muhesi *→ Tanzania* 7°0S 35°20E **54** D4
Mühlhausen *Germany* 51°12N 10°27E **16** C6
Mühlig Hofmann fjell *Antarctica* 72°30S 5°0E **5** D3
Muhos *Finland* 64°47N 25°59E **8** D21
Muhu *Estonia* 58°36N 23°11E **9** G20
Muhutwe *Tanzania* 1°35S 31°45E **54** C3
Mui Wo *China* 22°16N 113°59E **33** G10
Muine Bheag *Ireland* 52°42N 6°58W **10** D5
Muineachán = Monaghan *Ireland* 54°15N 6°57W **10** B5
Muir, L. *Australia* 34°30S 116°40E **61** F2
Muir of Ord *U.K.* 57°32N 4°28W **11** D4
Mujeres, I. *Mexico* 21°13N 86°43W **88** B2
Mujnak = Muynak *Uzbekistan* 43°44N 59°10E **28** E6
Muka, Tanjung *Malaysia* 5°28N 100°11E **39** c
Mukacheve *Ukraine* 48°27N 22°45E **17** D12

Mukachevo = Mukacheve
  Ukraine 48°27N 22°45E **17** D12
Mukah *Malaysia* 2°55N 112°5E **36** D4
Mukandwara *India* 24°49N 75°59E **42** G6
Mukawwa, Geziret
  Egypt 23°55N 35°53E **44** F2
Mukdahan *Thailand* 16°32N 104°43E **38** D5
Mukden = Shenyang
  China 41°48N 123°27E **35** D12
Mukerian *India* 31°57N 75°37E **42** D6
Mukinbudin *Australia* 30°55S 118°5E **61** F2
Mukishi
  Dem. Rep. of the Congo 8°30S 24°44E **55** D1
Mukomuko *Indonesia* 2°30S 101°10E **36** E2
Mukomwenze
  Dem. Rep. of the Congo 6°49S 27°15E **54** D2
Mukono *Uganda* 0°21N 32°45E **54** B3
Muktsar *India* 30°30N 74°30E **42** D6
Mukur = Moqor *Afghan.* 32°50N 67°42E **42** C2
Mukutawa → *Canada* 53°10N 97°24W **71** C9
Mukwela *Zambia* 17°0S 26°40E **55** F2
Mula *Spain* 38°3N 1°33W **21** C5
Mula → *Pakistan* 27°57N 67°36E **42** F2
Mulange
  Dem. Rep. of the Congo 3°40S 27°10E **54** C2
Mulanje, Mt. *Malawi* 16°2S 35°33E **55** F4
Mulchatna → *U.S.A.* 59°40N 157°7W **74** D8
Mulchén *Chile* 37°45S 72°20W **94** D1
Mulde → *Germany* 51°53N 12°15E **16** C7
Mule Creek Junction
  U.S.A. 43°23N 104°13W **76** E11
Muleba *Tanzania* 1°50S 31°37E **54** C3
Mulegé *Mexico* 26°53N 111°59W **86** B2
Muleshoe *U.S.A.* 34°13N 102°43W **84** D3
Mulgrave *Canada* 45°38N 61°31W **73** C7
Mulgrave I. = Badu
  Australia 10°7S 142°11E **62** a
Mulhacén *Spain* 37°4N 3°20W **21** D4
Mulhouse *France* 47°40N 7°20E **20** C7
Mulifanua *Samoa* 13°50S 171°59W **59** b
Muling *China* 44°35N 130°10E **35** B16
Mull *U.K.* 56°25N 5°56W **11** E3
Mull, Sound of *U.K.* 56°30N 5°50W **11** E3
Mullach Íde = Malahide
  Ireland 53°26N 6°9W **10** C5
Mullaittivu *Sri Lanka* 9°15N 80°49E **40** Q12
Mullen *U.S.A.* 42°3N 101°1W **80** D3
Mullengudgery
  Australia 31°43S 147°23E **63** B4
Mullens *U.S.A.* 37°35N 81°23W **81** G13
Muller, Pegunungan
  Indonesia 0°30N 113°30E **36** D4
Mullet Pen. *Ireland* 54°13N 10°2W **10** B1
Mullewa *Australia* 28°29S 115°30E **61** E2
Mulligan → *Australia* 25°0S 139°0E **62** D2
Mullingar *Ireland* 53°31N 7°21W **10** C4
Mullins *U.S.A.* 34°12N 79°15W **85** D15
Mullumbimby *Australia* 28°30S 153°30E **63** D5
Mulobezi *Zambia* 16°45S 25°7E **55** F2
Mulonga Plain *Zambia* 16°20S 22°40E **53** H4
Mulroy B. *Ireland* 55°15N 7°46W **10** A4
Multan *Pakistan* 30°15N 71°36E **42** D4
Mulumbe, Mts.
  Dem. Rep. of the Congo 8°40S 27°30E **55** D2
Mulungushi Dam
  Zambia 14°48S 28°48E **55** E2
Mulvane *U.S.A.* 37°29N 97°15W **80** G6
Mulwala, L. *Australia* 35°59S 146°1E **63** C4
Mumbai *India* 18°56N 72°50E **40** K8
Mumbwa *Zambia* 15°0S 27°0E **55** F2
Mumias *Kenya* 0°20N 34°29E **54** C4
Mun → *Thailand* 15°19N 105°30E **38** E5
Muna *Indonesia* 5°0S 122°30E **37** F6
Munabao *India* 25°45N 70°17E **42** G4
Munamagi *Estonia* 57°43N 27°4E **9** H22
Muncan *Indonesia* 8°34S 115°11E **37** K18
Muncar *Indonesia* 8°26S 114°20E **37** J17
München *Germany* 48°8N 11°34E **16** D6
München-Gladbach =
  Mönchengladbach
  Germany 51°11N 6°27E **16** C4
Muncho Lake *Canada* 59°0N 125°50W **70** B3
Munch'ŏn *N. Korea* 39°14N 127°19E **35** E14
Muncie *U.S.A.* 40°12N 85°23W **81** E11
Muncoonie L. West
  Australia 25°12S 138°40E **62** D2
Mundabbera *Australia* 25°36S 151°18E **63** D5
Munday *U.S.A.* 33°27N 99°38W **84** E5
Münden *Germany* 51°25N 9°38E **16** C5
Mundiwindi *Australia* 23°47S 120°9E **60** D3
Mundo Novo *Brazil* 11°50S 40°29W **93** F10
Mundra *India* 22°54N 69°48E **42** H3
Mundrabilla *Australia* 31°52S 127°51E **61** F4
Mungallala *Australia* 26°28S 147°34E **63** D4
Mungallala Cr. →
  Australia 28°53S 147°5E **63** D4
Mungana *Australia* 17°8S 144°27E **62** B3
Mungaoli *India* 24°24N 78°7E **42** G8
Mungari *Mozam.* 17°12S 33°30E **55** F3
Mungbere
  Dem. Rep. of the Congo 2°36N 28°28E **54** B2
Munger *India* 22°4N 81°43E **43** G12
Mungeranie *Australia* 28°1S 138°39E **63** D2
Mungilli → *Australia* 25°14S 124°17E **61** E3
Mungkan Kandju △
  Australia 13°35S 142°52E **62** A3
Mungkarta ◎ *Australia* 20°22S 134°2E **62** C1
Munich = München
  Germany 48°8N 11°34E **16** D6
Munising *U.S.A.* 46°25N 86°40W **80** B10
Munku-Sardyk *Russia* 51°45N 100°20E **29** D11
Munnsville *U.S.A.* 42°58N 75°35W **83** D9
Muñoz Gamero, Pen.
  Chile 52°30S 73°5W **96** G2
Munroe L. *Canada* 59°13N 98°35W **71** B9
Munsan *S. Korea* 37°51N 126°48E **35** F14
Münster *Germany* 51°58N 7°37E **16** C4
Munster □ *Ireland* 52°18N 8°44W **10** D3

Muntadgin *Australia* 31°45S 118°33E **61** F2
Muntok *Indonesia* 2°5S 105°10E **36** E3
Muong Beng *Laos* 20°23N 101°46E **38** B3
Muong Boum *Vietnam* 22°24N 102°49E **38** A4
Muong Et *Laos* 20°49N 104°1E **38** B5
Muong Hai *Laos* 21°3N 101°49E **38** B3
Muong Hiem *Laos* 20°5N 103°22E **38** B4
Muong Houn *Laos* 20°8N 101°23E **38** B3
Muong Hung *Vietnam* 20°56N 103°53E **38** B4
Muong Kau *Laos* 15°6N 105°47E **38** E5
Muong Khao *Laos* 19°38N 103°32E **38** C4
Muong Khoua *Laos* 21°5N 102°31E **38** B4
Muong Liep *Laos* 18°29N 101°40E **38** C3
Muong May *Laos* 14°49N 106°56E **38** E6
Muong Ngeun *Laos* 20°36N 101°3E **38** B3
Muong Ngoi *Laos* 20°43N 102°41E **38** B4
Muong Nhie *Vietnam* 22°12N 102°28E **38** A4
Muong Nong *Laos* 16°22N 106°30E **38** D6
Muong Ou Tay *Laos* 22°7N 101°48E **38** A3
Muong Oua *Laos* 18°18N 101°20E **38** C3
Muong Peun *Laos* 20°13N 103°52E **38** B4
Muong Phalane *Laos* 16°39N 105°34E **38** D5
Muong Phieng *Laos* 19°6N 101°32E **38** C3
Muong Phine *Laos* 16°32N 106°2E **38** D6
Muong Sai *Laos* 20°42N 101°59E **38** B3
Muong Saiapoun *Laos* 18°24N 101°31E **38** C3
Muong Sen *Vietnam* 19°24N 104°8E **38** C5
Muong Sing *Laos* 21°11N 101°9E **38** B3
Muong Son *Laos* 20°27N 103°19E **38** B4
Muong Soui *Laos* 19°33N 102°52E **38** C4
Muong Va *Laos* 21°53N 102°19E **38** B4
Muong Xia *Vietnam* 20°19N 104°50E **38** B5
Muonio *Finland* 67°57N 23°40E **8** C20
Muonio älv = Muonionjoki →
  Finland 67°11N 23°34E **8** C20
Muonioälven = Muonionjoki →
  Finland 67°11N 23°34E **8** C20
Muonionjoki → *Finland* 67°11N 23°34E **8** C20
Mupa → *Mozam.* 18°58S 35°54E **55** F4
Muping *China* 37°22N 121°36E **35** F11
Muqdisho *Somali Rep.* 2°2N 45°25E **47** G4
Mur → *Austria* 46°18N 16°52E **17** E9
Murakami *Japan* 38°14N 139°29E **30** E9
Muralag = Prince of Wales I.
  Australia 10°40S 142°10E **62** A3
Murallón, Cerro *Chile* 49°48S 73°30W **96** F2
Muranda *Rwanda* 1°52S 29°20E **54** C2
Murang'a *Kenya* 0°45S 37°9E **54** C4
Murashi *Russia* 59°30N 49°0E **18** C8
Murat → *Turkey* 38°46N 40°0E **19** G7
Muratlı *Turkey* 41°10N 27°29E **23** D12
Murayama *Japan* 38°30N 140°25E **30** E10
Murchison → *Australia* 27°45S 114°0E **61** E1
Murchison, Mt.
  Antarctica 73°25S 166°20E **5** D11
Murchison Falls *Uganda* 2°15N 31°30E **54** B3
Murchison Falls △
  Uganda 2°17N 31°48E **54** B3
Murchison Ra. *Australia* 20°0S 134°10E **62** C1
Murchison Rapids
  Malawi 15°55S 34°35E **55** F3
Murchison Roadhouse
  Australia 27°39S 114°14E **61** E1
Murcia *Spain* 38°5N 1°10W **21** D5
Murcia □ *Spain* 37°50N 1°30W **21** D5
Murdo *U.S.A.* 43°53N 100°43W **80** D3
Murdoch Pt. *Australia* 14°37S 144°55E **62** A3
Mureş → *Romania* 46°15N 20°13E **17** E11
Mureşul = Mureş →
  Romania 46°15N 20°13E **17** E11
Murewa *Zimbabwe* 17°39S 31°47E **57** B5
Murfreesboro *N.C.,*
  U.S.A. 36°27N 77°6W **85** C16
Murfreesboro *Tenn.,*
  U.S.A. 35°51N 86°24W **85** D11
Murgap = Murghob
  Tajikistan 38°10N 74°2E **28** F8
Murgap → *Turkmenistan* 38°18N 61°12E **45** B9
Murgenella *Australia* 11°34S 132°56E **60** B5
Murgha Kibzai *Pakistan* 30°44N 69°25E **42** D3
Murghob *Tajikistan* 38°10N 74°2E **28** F8
Murgon *Australia* 26°15S 151°54E **63** D5
Muri *India* 23°22N 85°52E **43** H11
Muria *Indonesia* 6°36S 110°53E **37** G14
Muriaé *Brazil* 21°8S 42°23W **95** A7
Muriel Mine *Zimbabwe* 17°14S 30°40E **55** F3
Müritz *Germany* 53°25N 12°42E **16** B7
Murliganj *India* 25°54N 86°59E **43** G12
Murmansk *Russia* 68°57N 33°10E **8** B25
Murmashi *Russia* 68°47N 32°42E **8** B25
Muro *Spain* 39°44N 3°3E **24** B10
Murom *Russia* 55°35N 42°3E **18** C7
Muroran *Japan* 42°25N 141°0E **30** C10
Muroto *Japan* 33°18N 134°9E **31** H7
Muroto-Misaki *Japan* 33°15N 134°10E **31** H7
Murphy *U.S.A.* 43°13N 116°33W **76** E5
Murphys *U.S.A.* 38°8N 120°28W **78** G6
Murray *Australia* 9°56S 144°2E **62** a
Murray *Ky., U.S.A.* 36°37N 88°19W **80** G9
Murray *Utah, U.S.A.* 40°40N 111°53W **76** F8
Murray → *Australia* 35°20S 139°22E **63** F2
Murray, L. *U.S.A.* 34°3N 81°13W **85** D14
Murray Bridge *Australia* 35°6S 139°14E **63** F2
Murray Fracture Zone
  Pac. Oc. 35°0N 130°0W **65** D14
Murray Harbour *Canada* 46°0N 62°28W **73** C7
Murray River △
  Australia 34°23S 140°32E **63** E3
Murraysburg *S. Africa* 31°58S 23°47E **56** E3
Murree *Pakistan* 33°56N 73°28E **42** C5
Murrieta *U.S.A.* 33°33N 117°13W **79** M9
Murrumbidgee →
  Australia 34°43S 143°12E **63** E3
Murrumburrah
  Australia 34°32S 148°22E **63** E4
Murrurundi *Australia* 31°42S 150°51E **63** E5
Murshidabad *India* 24°11N 88°19E **43** G13
Murtle L. *Canada* 52°8N 119°38W **70** C5
Murtoa *Australia* 36°35S 142°28E **63** F3

Murungu *Tanzania* 4°12S 31°10E **54** C3
Mururoa
  French Polynesia 21°52S 138°55W **65** K14
Murwara *India* 23°46N 80°28E **43** H9
Murwillumbah
  Australia 28°18S 153°27E **63** D5
Mürzzuschlag *Austria* 47°36N 15°41E **16** E8
Muş *Turkey* 38°45N 41°30E **44** B4
Mûsa, Gebel *Egypt* 28°33N 33°59E **44** D2
Musa Khel *Pakistan* 30°59N 69°52E **42** D3
Mûsa Qal'eh *Afghan.* 32°20N 64°50E **40** C4
Musafirkhana *India* 26°22N 81°48E **43** F9
Musala *Bulgaria* 42°13N 23°37E **23** C10
Musala *Indonesia* 1°41N 98°28E **36** D1
Musan *N. Korea* 42°12N 129°12E **35** C15
Musangu
  Dem. Rep. of the Congo 10°28S 23°55E **55** E1
Musasa *Tanzania* 3°25S 31°30E **54** C3
Musay'īd *Qatar* 25°0N 51°33E **45** E6
Muscat = Masqaṭ *Oman* 23°37N 58°36E **47** C6
Muscatine *U.S.A.* 41°25N 91°3W **80** E8
Muscle Shoals *U.S.A.* 34°45N 87°40W **85** D11
Musengezi = Unsengedsi →
  Zimbabwe 15°43S 31°14E **55** F3
Musgrave Harbour
  Canada 49°27N 53°58W **73** C9
Musgrave Ranges
  Australia 26°0S 132°0E **61** E5
Mushie
  Dem. Rep. of the Congo 2°56S 16°55E **52** E3
Musi → *Indonesia* 2°20S 104°56E **36** E2
Musina *S. Africa* 22°20S 30°5E **57** C5
Muskeg → *Canada* 60°20N 123°20W **70** A4
Muskegon *U.S.A.* 43°14N 86°16W **80** D10
Muskegon → *U.S.A.* 43°14N 86°21W **80** D10
Muskegon Heights
  U.S.A. 43°12N 86°16W **80** D10
Muskogee *U.S.A.* 35°45N 95°22W **84** D7
Muskoka, L. *Canada* 45°0N 79°25W **82** B5
Muskoka Falls *Canada* 44°59N 79°17W **82** B5
Muslīmiyah *Syria* 36°19N 37°12E **44** B3
Musofu *Zambia* 13°30S 29°0E **55** E2
Musoma *Tanzania* 1°30S 33°48E **54** C3
Musquaro, L. *Canada* 50°38N 61°5W **73** B7
Musquodoboit Harbour
  Canada 44°50N 63°9W **73** D7
Musselburgh *U.K.* 55°57N 3°2W **11** F5
Musselshell → *U.S.A.* 47°21N 107°57W **76** C10
Mussende *Angola* 10°32S 16°5E **52** G3
Mussoorie *India* 30°27N 78°6E **42** D8
Mussuco *Angola* 17°2S 19°3E **56** B2
Mustafakemalpaşa
  Turkey 40°2N 28°24E **23** D13
Mustang *Nepal* 29°10N 83°55E **43** E10
Musters, L. *Argentina* 45°20S 69°25W **96** F3
Musudan *N. Korea* 40°50N 129°43E **35** D15
Muswellbrook *Australia* 32°16S 150°56E **63** E5
Mût *Egypt* 25°28N 28°58E **51** C11
Mut *Turkey* 36°40N 33°28E **44** B2
Mutanda *Mozam.* 21°0S 33°34E **57** C5
Mutanda *Zambia* 12°24S 26°13E **55** E2
Mutare *Zimbabwe* 18°58S 32°38E **55** F3
Mutawintji △ *Australia* 31°10S 142°30E **63** E3
Mutha *Kenya* 1°48S 38°26E **54** C4
Muting *Indonesia* 7°23S 140°20E **37** F10
Mutki = Mirtağ *Turkey* 38°23N 41°56E **44** B4
Mutoko *Zimbabwe* 17°24S 32°13E **57** B5
Mutomo *Kenya* 1°51S 38°12E **54** C4
Mutoray *Russia* 60°56N 101°0E **29** C11
Mutsamudu *Comoros Is.* 12°10S 44°25E **53** a
Mutshatsha
  Dem. Rep. of the Congo 10°35S 24°20E **55** E1
Mutsu *Japan* 41°5N 140°55E **30** D10
Mutsu-Wan *Japan* 41°5N 140°55E **30** D10
Muttaburra *Australia* 22°38S 144°29E **62** C3
Mutton I. *Ireland* 52°49N 9°32W **10** D2
Mutuáli *Mozam.* 14°55S 37°0E **55** E4
Mutumba *Burundi* 3°25S 29°21E **54** C2
Muweilih *Egypt* 30°42N 34°19E **46** E3
Muy Muy *Nic.* 12°39N 85°36W **88** D2
Muyinga *Burundi* 3°14S 30°33E **54** C3
Muynak *Uzbekistan* 43°44N 59°10E **28** E6
Muyunkum, Peski = Moyynqum
  Kazakhstan 44°12N 71°0E **32** B2
Muz Tag *China* 36°25N 87°25E **32** C3
Muzaffarabad *Pakistan* 34°25N 73°30E **43** B5
Muzaffargarh *Pakistan* 30°5N 71°14E **42** D4
Muzaffarnagar *India* 29°26N 77°40E **42** E7
Muzaffarpur *India* 26°7N 85°23E **43** F11
Muzafirpur *Pakistan* 28°58N 69°9E **42** E3
Muzhi *Russia* 65°25N 64°40E **18** A11
Muztagh-Ata *China* 38°17N 75°7E **32** C2
Mvuma *Zimbabwe* 19°16S 30°30E **55** F3
Mvurwi *Zimbabwe* 17°0S 30°57E **55** F3
Mwadui *Tanzania* 3°26S 33°32E **54** C3
Mwali = Mohéli
  Comoros Is. 12°20S 43°40E **53** a
Mwambo *Tanzania* 10°30S 40°22E **55** E5
Mwandi *Zambia* 17°30S 24°51E **55** F1
Mwanza
  Dem. Rep. of the Congo 7°55S 26°43E **54** D2
Mwanza *Tanzania* 2°30S 32°58E **54** C3
Mwanza *Zambia* 16°58S 24°28E **55** F1
Mwanza □ *Tanzania* 2°0S 33°0E **54** C3
Mwaya *Tanzania* 9°32S 33°55E **55** D3
Mweelrea *Ireland* 53°39N 9°49W **10** C2
Mweka
  Dem. Rep. of the Congo 4°50S 21°34E **52** E4
Mwene-Ditu
  Dem. Rep. of the Congo 6°35S 22°27E **52** F4
Mwenezi *Zimbabwe* 21°15S 30°48E **55** G3
Mwenezi → *Mozam.* 22°40S 31°50E **55** G3
Mwenga
  Dem. Rep. of the Congo 3°1S 28°28E **54** C2
Mweru, L. *Zambia* 9°0S 28°40E **55** D2
Mweru Wantipa △
  Zambia 8°39S 29°25E **55** D2

Mweza Range *Zimbabwe* 21°0S 30°0E **55** G3
Mwilambwe
  Dem. Rep. of the Congo 8°7S 25°5E **54** D2
Mwimbi *Tanzania* 8°38S 31°39E **55** D3
Mwingi *Kenya* 0°56S 38°4E **54** C4
Mwinilunga *Zambia* 11°43S 24°25E **55** E1
My Tho *Vietnam* 10°29N 106°23E **39** G6
Myajlar *India* 26°15N 70°20E **42** F4
Myanaung *Burma* 18°18N 95°22E **41** K19
Myanmar = Burma ■
  Asia 21°0N 96°30E **41** J20
Myaungmya *Burma* 16°30N 94°40E **41** L19
Mycenæ = Mikines
  Greece 37°43N 22°46E **23** F10
Myeik Kyunzu *Burma* 11°30N 97°30E **39** G1
Myerstown *U.S.A.* 40°22N 76°19W **83** F8
Myingyan *Burma* 21°30N 95°20E **41** J19
Myitkyina *Burma* 25°24N 97°26E **41** G20
Mykines *Færoe Is.* 62°7N 7°35W **8** E9
Mykolayiv *Ukraine* 46°58N 32°0E **19** E5
Mykonos *Greece* 37°30N 25°25E **23** F11
Mymensingh *Bangla.* 24°45N 90°24E **41** G17
Mynydd Du *U.K.* 51°52N 3°50W **13** F4
Mýrdalsjökull *Iceland* 63°40N 19°6W **8** E4
Myrtle Beach *U.S.A.* 33°42N 78°53W **85** D15
Myrtle Creek *U.S.A.* 43°1N 123°17W **76** E2
Myrtle Point *U.S.A.* 43°4N 124°8W **76** E1
Myrtou *Cyprus* 35°18N 33°4E **25** D12
Mysia *Turkey* 39°50N 27°0E **23** E12
Mysore = Karnataka □
  India 13°15N 77°0E **40** N10
Mysore *India* 12°17N 76°41E **40** N10
Mystic *U.S.A.* 41°21N 71°58W **83** E13
Mysuru = Mysore *India* 12°17N 76°41E **40** N10
Myszków *Poland* 50°45N 19°22E **17** C10
Mytishchi *Russia* 55°50N 37°50E **18** C6
Mývatn *Iceland* 65°36N 17°0W **8** D5
Mzimba *Malawi* 11°55S 33°39E **55** E3
Mzimkulu → *S. Africa* 30°44S 30°28E **57** E5
Mzimvubu → *S. Africa* 31°38S 29°33E **57** E4
Mzuzu *Malawi* 11°30S 33°55E **55** E3

N

Na Clocha Liatha = Greystones
  Ireland 53°9N 6°5W **10** C5
Na Hearadh = Harris
  U.K. 57°50N 6°55W **11** D2
Na Noi *Thailand* 18°19N 100°43E **38** C3
Na Phao *Laos* 17°35N 105°44E **38** D5
Na Sam *Vietnam* 22°3N 106°37E **38** A6
Na San *Vietnam* 21°12N 104°2E **38** B5
Na Thon *Thailand* 9°32N 99°56E **39** b
Naab → *Germany* 49°1N 12°2E **16** D6
Naantali *Finland* 60°29N 22°2E **9** F20
Naas *Ireland* 53°12N 6°40W **10** C5
Nababeep *S. Africa* 29°36S 17°46E **56** D2
Nabadwip = Navadwip
  India 23°34N 88°20E **43** H13
Nabawa *Australia* 28°30S 114°48E **61** E1
Nabberu, L. *Australia* 25°50S 120°30E **61** E3
Naberezhnyye Chelny
  Russia 55°42N 52°19E **18** C9
Nabeul *Tunisia* 36°30N 10°44E **51** A8
Nabha *India* 30°26N 76°14E **42** D7
Nabīd *Iran* 29°40N 57°38E **45** D8
Nabire *Indonesia* 3°15S 135°26E **37** E9
Nabisar *Pakistan* 25°8N 69°40E **42** G3
Nabisipi → *Canada* 50°14N 62°13W **73** B7
Nabiswera *Uganda* 1°27N 32°15E **54** B3
Nâblus = Nâbulus
  West Bank 32°14N 35°15E **46** C4
Naboomspruit *S. Africa* 24°32S 28°40E **57** C4
Nabouwalu *Fiji* 17°0S 178°45E **59** a
Nâbulus *West Bank* 32°14N 35°15E **46** C4
Nacala *Mozam.* 14°32S 40°34E **55** E5
Nacaome *Honduras* 13°31N 87°30W **88** D2
Nacaroa *Mozam.* 14°22S 39°56E **55** E4
Naches *U.S.A.* 46°44N 120°42W **78** D6
Naches → *U.S.A.* 46°38N 120°31W **78** D6
Nachicapau, L. *Canada* 56°40N 68°5W **73** A6
Nachingwea *Tanzania* 10°23S 38°49E **55** E4
Nachna *India* 27°34N 71°41E **42** F4
Nacimiento, L. *U.S.A.* 35°46N 120°53W **78** K6
Naco *Mexico* 31°19N 109°56W **86** A3
Nacogdoches *U.S.A.* 31°36N 94°39W **84** F7
Nácori Chico *Mexico* 29°40N 108°57W **86** B3
Nacozari de García
  Mexico 30°25N 109°38W **86** A3
Nada *Fiji* 16°54S 177°27E **59** a
Nâdendal = Naantali
  Finland 60°29N 22°2E **9** F20
Nadi *Fiji* 17°42S 177°20E **59** a
Nadiad *India* 22°41N 72°56E **42** H5
Nador *Morocco* 35°14N 2°58W **50** B5
Nadur *Malta* 36°2N 14°18E **25** C1
Nadūshan *Iran* 32°2N 53°35E **45** C7
Nadvirna *Ukraine* 48°37N 24°30E **17** D13
Nadvoitsy *Russia* 63°52N 34°14E **18** B5
Nadvornaya = Nadvirna
  Ukraine 48°37N 24°30E **17** D13
Nadym *Russia* 65°35N 72°42E **28** C8
Nadym → *Russia* 66°12N 72°0E **28** C8
Nærbø *Norway* 58°40N 5°39E **9** G11
Næstved *Denmark* 55°13N 11°44E **9** J14
Nafarroa = Navarra □ *Spain* 42°40N 1°40W **21** A5
Nafpaktos *Greece* 38°24N 21°50E **23** E9
Nafplio *Greece* 37°33N 22°50E **23** F10
Naft-e Safīd *Iran* 31°40N 49°17E **45** D6
Naftshahr *Iran* 34°0N 45°30E **44** C5
Nafud Desert = An Nafūd
  Si. Arabia 28°15N 41°0E **44** D4
Naga *Phil.* 13°38N 123°15E **37** B6
Nagagami → *Canada* 49°40N 84°40W **72** C3
Nagai *Japan* 38°6N 140°2E **30** E10
Nagaland □ *India* 26°0N 94°30E **41** G19
Nagano *Japan* 36°40N 138°10E **31** F9
Nagano □ *Japan* 36°15N 138°0E **31** F9

Nagaoka *Japan* 37°27N 138°51E **31** F9
Nagaon = Nowgong
  India 26°20N 92°50E **41** F18
Nagappattinam *India* 10°46N 79°51E **40** P11
Nagar → *Bangla.* 24°27N 89°12E **43** G13
Nagar Parkar *Pakistan* 24°28N 70°46E **42** G4
Nagasaki *Japan* 32°47N 129°50E **31** H4
Nagasaki □ *Japan* 32°50N 129°40E **31** H4
Nagato *Japan* 34°19N 131°5E **31** G5
Nagaur *India* 27°15N 73°45E **42** F5
Nagda *India* 23°27N 75°25E **42** H6
Nagercoil *India* 8°12N 77°26E **40** Q10
Nagina *India* 29°30N 78°30E **43** E8
Nagīneh *Iran* 34°20N 57°15E **45** C8
Nagir *Pakistan* 36°12N 74°42E **43** A6
Nagles Mts. *Ireland* 52°8N 8°30W **10** D3
Nagod *India* 24°34N 80°36E **43** G9
Nagoorin *Australia* 24°17S 151°15E **62** C5
Nagorno-Karabakh □
  Azerbaijan 39°55N 46°45E **44** B5
Nagornyy *Russia* 55°58N 124°57E **29** D13
Nagoya *Japan* 35°10N 136°50E **31** G8
Nagpur *India* 21°8N 79°10E **40** J11
Nagua *Dom. Rep.* 19°23N 69°50W **89** C6
Naguabo *Puerto Rico* 18°13N 65°44W **89** d
Nagurunguru ◎
  Australia 16°45S 129°45E **60** C4
Nagykanizsa *Hungary* 46°28N 17°0E **17** E9
Nagykőrös *Hungary* 47°5N 19°48E **17** E10
Naha *Japan* 26°13N 127°42E **31** L3
Nahan *India* 30°33N 77°18E **42** D7
Nahanni △ *Canada* 61°36N 125°41W **70** A4
Nahanni Butte *Canada* 61°2N 123°31W **70** A4
Nahargarh *Mad. P., India* 24°10N 75°14E **42** G6
Nahargarh *Raj., India* 24°55N 76°50E **42** G7
Nahariyya *Israel* 33°1N 35°5E **44** C2
Nahāvand *Iran* 34°10N 48°22E **45** C6
Nahuel Huapí, L.
  Argentina 41°0S 71°32W **96** E2
Nahuelbuta △ *Chile* 37°44S 72°57W **94** D1
Nai Yong *Thailand* 8°14N 98°22E **39** a
Naicá *Mexico* 27°53N 105°31W **86** B3
Naicam *Canada* 52°30N 104°30W **71** C8
Naikoon △ *Canada* 53°55N 131°55W **70** C2
Naimisharanya *India* 27°21N 80°30E **43** F9
Naimona'nyi Feng *Nepal* 30°26N 81°18E **43** D9
Nain *Canada* 56°34N 61°40W **73** A7
Nā'īn *Iran* 32°54N 53°0E **45** C7
Naini Tal *India* 29°30N 79°30E **43** E8
Nainpur *India* 22°30N 80°10E **43** H9
Nainwa *India* 25°46N 75°51E **42** G6
Nairai *Fiji* 17°49S 179°15E **59** a
Nairn *U.K.* 57°35N 3°53W **11** D5
Nairobi *Kenya* 1°17S 36°48E **54** C4
Nairobi △ *Kenya* 1°22S 36°50E **54** C4
Naissaar *Estonia* 59°34N 24°29E **9** G21
Naitaba *Fiji* 17°0S 179°16W **59** a
Naivasha *Kenya* 0°40S 36°30E **54** C4
Naivasha, L. *Kenya* 0°48S 36°20E **54** C4
Najaf = An Najaf *Iraq* 32°3N 44°15E **44** C5
Najafābād *Iran* 32°40N 51°15E **45** C6
Najd *Si. Arabia* 26°30N 42°0E **47** B3
Najibabad *India* 29°40N 78°20E **42** E8
Najin *N. Korea* 42°12N 130°15E **35** C16
Najmah *Si. Arabia* 26°42N 50°6E **45** E6
Najrān *Si. Arabia* 17°34N 44°18E **47** D3
Naju *S. Korea* 35°3N 126°43E **35** G14
Nakadōri-Shima *Japan* 32°57N 129°4E **31** H4
Nakalagba
  Dem. Rep. of the Congo 2°50N 27°58E **54** B2
Nakaminato *Japan* 36°21N 140°36E **31** F10
Nakamura *Japan* 32°59N 132°56E **31** H6
Nakano *Japan* 36°45N 138°22E **31** F9
Nakano-Shima *Japan* 29°51N 129°52E **31** K4
Nakashibetsu *Japan* 43°33N 144°59E **30** C12
Nakfa *Eritrea* 16°40N 38°32E **47** D2
Nakha Yai, Ko *Thailand* 8°3N 98°28E **39** a
Nakhichevan = Naxçıvan
  Azerbaijan 39°12N 45°15E **44** B5
Nakhichevan Rep. = Naxçıvan □
  Azerbaijan 39°45N 45°26E **44** B5
Nakhl *Egypt* 29°55N 33°43E **46** F2
Nakhl-e Taqī *Iran* 27°28N 52°36E **45** E7
Nakhodka *Russia* 42°53N 132°54E **30** C6
Nakhon Nayok
  Thailand 14°12N 101°13E **38** E3
Nakhon Pathom
  Thailand 13°49N 100°3E **38** F3
Nakhon Phanom
  Thailand 17°23N 104°43E **38** D5
Nakhon Ratchasima
  Thailand 14°59N 102°12E **38** E4
Nakhon Sawan
  Thailand 15°35N 100°10E **38** E3
Nakhon Si Thammarat
  Thailand 8°29N 100°0E **39** H3
Nakhon Thai *Thailand* 17°5N 100°44E **38** D3
Nakhtarana *India* 23°20N 69°15E **42** H3
Nakina *Canada* 50°10N 86°40W **72** B2
Nakodar *India* 31°8N 75°31E **42** D6
Naktong → *S. Korea* 35°7N 128°57E **35** G15
Nakuru *Kenya* 0°15S 36°4E **54** C4
Nakuru, L. *Kenya* 0°23S 36°5E **54** C4
Nakusp *Canada* 50°20N 117°45W **70** D5
Nal *Pakistan* 27°40N 66°12E **42** F2
Nal → *Pakistan* 25°20N 65°30E **42** G1
Nalázi *Mozam.* 24°3S 33°20E **57** C5
Nalchik *Russia* 43°30N 43°33E **19** F7
Nalgonda *India* 17°6N 79°15E **40** L11
Nalhati *India* 24°17N 87°52E **43** G12
Naliya *India* 23°16N 68°50E **42** H3
Nallamalai Hills *India* 15°30N 78°50E **40** M11
Nalubaale Dam *Uganda* 0°30N 33°5E **54** B3
Nam Can *Vietnam* 8°46N 104°59E **39** H5
Nam-ch'on *N. Korea* 38°15N 126°26E **35** E14
Nam Co *China* 30°30N 90°45E **32** C4
Nam Du, Hon *Vietnam* 9°41N 104°21E **39** H5
Nam Nao △ *Thailand* 16°44N 101°32E **38** D3

Nam Ngum Res. *Laos* 18°35N 102°34E 38 C4
Nam-Phan *Vietnam* 10°30N 106°0E 39 G6
Nam Phong *Thailand* 16°42N 102°52E 38 D4
Nam Tha *Laos* 20°58N 101°30E 38 B3
Nam Tok *Thailand* 14°21N 99°4E 38 E2
Namacunde *Angola* 17°18S 15°50E 56 B2
Namacurra *Mozam.* 17°30S 36°50E 57 B6
Namak, Daryācheh-ye
 Iran 34°30N 52°0E 45 C7
Namak, Kavir-e *Iran* 34°30N 57°30E 45 C8
Namakzār, Daryācheh-ye
 Iran 34°0N 60°30E 45 C9
Namaland *Namibia* 26°0S 17°0E 56 C2
Namanga *Kenya* 2°33S 36°47E 54 C4
Namangan *Uzbekistan* 41°0N 71°40E 28 E8
Namapa *Mozam.* 13°43S 39°50E 55 E4
Namaqualand *S. Africa* 30°0S 17°25E 56 D2
Namasagali *Uganda* 1°2N 33°0E 54 B3
Namber *Indonesia* 1°2S 134°49E 37 E8
Nambour *Australia* 26°32S 152°58E 63 D5
Nambouwalu = Nabouwalu
 Fiji 17°0S 178°45E 59 a
Nambucca Heads
 Australia 30°37S 153°0E 63 E5
Nambung △ *Australia* 30°30S 115°5E 61 F2
Namcha Barwa *China* 29°40N 95°10E 32 D4
Namche Bazar *Nepal* 27°51N 86°47E 43 F12
Namchonjŏm = Nam-ch'on
 N. Korea 38°15N 126°26E 35 E14
Namecunda *Mozam.* 14°54S 37°37E 55 E4
Namenalala *Fiji* 17°8S 179°9E 59 a
Nameponda *Mozam.* 15°50S 39°50E 55 F4
Nametil *Mozam.* 15°40S 39°21E 55 F4
Namew L. *Canada* 54°14N 101°56W 71 C8
Namgia *India* 31°48N 78°40E 43 D8
Namialo *Mozam.* 14°55S 39°59E 55 E4
Namib Desert *Namibia* 22°30S 15°0E 56 C2
Namib-Naukluft △
 Namibia 24°40S 15°16E 56 C2
Namibe *Angola* 15°7S 12°11E 53 H2
Namibe □ *Angola* 16°35S 12°30E 56 B1
Namibia ■ *Africa* 22°0S 18°9E 56 C2
Namibwoestyn = Namib Desert
 Namibia 22°30S 15°0E 56 C2
Namlea *Indonesia* 3°18S 127°5E 37 E7
Namoi → *Australia* 30°12S 149°30E 63 E4
Nampa *U.S.A.* 43°34N 116°34W 76 E5
Namp'o *N. Korea* 38°52N 125°10E 35 E13
Nampō-Shotō *Japan* 32°0N 140°0E 31 J10
Nampula *Mozam.* 15°6S 39°15E 55 F4
Namrole *Indonesia* 3°46S 126°46E 37 E7
Namse Shankou *China* 30°0N 82°25E 43 E10
Namsen → *Norway* 64°28N 11°37E 8 D14
Namsos *Norway* 64°29N 11°30E 8 D14
Namtok Chat Trakan △
 Thailand 17°17N 100°40E 38 D3
Namtok Mae Surin △
 Thailand 18°55N 98°2E 38 C2
Namtsy *Russia* 62°43N 129°37E 29 C13
Namtu *Burma* 23°5N 97°28E 41 H20
Namtumbo *Tanzania* 10°30S 36°4E 55 E4
Namu *Canada* 51°52N 127°50W 70 C3
Namuka-i-Lau *Fiji* 18°53S 178°37W 59 a
Namur *Belgium* 50°27N 4°52E 15 D4
Namur □ *Belgium* 50°17N 5°0E 15 D4
Namuruputh *Kenya* 4°34N 35°57E 54 B4
Namutoni *Namibia* 18°49S 16°55E 56 B2
Namwala *Zambia* 15°44S 26°30E 55 F2
Namwon *S. Korea* 35°23N 127°23E 35 G14
Namyang *N. Korea* 42°57N 129°52E 35 C15
Nan *Thailand* 18°48N 100°46E 38 C3
Nan → *Thailand* 15°42N 100°9E 38 E3
Nan-ch'ang = Nanchang
 China 28°42N 115°55E 33 D6
Nanaimo *Canada* 49°10N 124°0W 70 D4
Nānākuli *U.S.A.* 21°24N 158°9W 75 L8
Nanam *N. Korea* 41°44N 129°40E 35 D15
Nanango *Australia* 26°40S 152°0E 63 D5
Nanao *Japan* 37°0N 137°0E 31 F8
Nanchang *China* 28°42N 115°55E 33 D6
Nanching = Nanjing
 China 32°2N 118°47E 33 C6
Nanchong *China* 30°43N 106°2E 32 C5
Nancy *France* 48°42N 6°12E 20 B7
Nanda Devi *India* 30°23N 79°59E 43 D8
Nanda Devi △ *India* 30°30N 79°50E 43 D8
Nanda Kot *India* 30°17N 80°5E 43 D9
Nandan *Japan* 34°10N 134°42E 31 G7
Nanded *India* 19°10N 77°20E 40 K10
Nandewar Ra. *Australia* 30°15S 150°35E 63 E5
Nandi = Nadi *Fiji* 17°42S 177°20E 59 a
Nandi *Zimbabwe* 20°58S 31°44E 55 G3
Nandigram *India* 22°1N 87°58E 43 H12
Nandurbar *India* 21°20N 74°15E 40 J9
Nandyal *India* 15°30N 78°30E 40 M11
Nang Rong *Thailand* 14°38N 102°48E 38 E4
Nanga-Eboko *Cameroon* 4°41N 12°22E 52 D2
Nanga Parbat *Pakistan* 35°10N 74°35E 43 B6
Nangade *Mozam.* 11°5S 39°36E 55 E4
Nangapinoh *Indonesia* 0°20S 111°44E 36 E4
Nangarhār □ *Afghan.* 34°20N 70°0E 40 B7
Nangatayap *Indonesia* 1°32S 110°34E 36 E4
Nangeya Mts. *Uganda* 3°30N 33°30E 54 B3
Nangong *China* 37°23N 115°22E 34 F8
Nanhuang *China* 36°58N 121°48E 35 F11
Nanisivik *Canada* 73°2N 84°33W 69 C15
Nanjeko *Zambia* 15°31S 23°30E 55 F1
Nanjing *China* 32°2N 118°47E 33 C6
Nanjirinji *Tanzania* 9°41S 39°5E 55 D4
Nankana Sahib *Pakistan* 31°27N 73°38E 42 D5
Nanking = Nanjing
 China 32°2N 118°47E 33 C6
Nankoku *Japan* 33°39N 133°44E 31 H6
Nanlang *China* 22°30N 113°32E 33 G10
Nanning *China* 22°48N 108°20E 32 D5
Nannup *Australia* 33°59S 115°48E 61 F2
Nanpara *India* 27°52N 81°33E 43 F9
Nanpi *China* 38°2N 116°45E 34 E9
Nanping *China* 26°38N 118°10E 33 D6

Nanripe *Mozam.* 13°52S 38°52E 55 E4
Nansei-Shotō = Ryūkyū-rettō
 Japan 26°0N 126°0E 31 M3
Nansen Basin *Arctic* 84°0N 50°0E 4 A10
Nansen Sd. *Canada* 81°0N 91°0W 69 A13
Nansha *China* 22°45N 113°34E 33 F10
Nanshan I. *S. China Sea* 15°45N 115°49E 36 B5
Nansio *Tanzania* 2°3S 33°4E 54 C3
Nantawarrinna ☼
 Australia 30°49S 138°58E 63 B2
Nantes *France* 47°12N 1°33W 20 C3
Nanticoke *U.S.A.* 41°12N 76°0W 83 E8
Nanton *Canada* 50°21N 113°46W 70 C6
Nantong *China* 32°1N 120°52E 33 C7
Nantou *China* 22°32N 113°55E 33 F10
Nantucket *U.S.A.* 41°17N 70°6W 81 E18
Nantucket I. *U.S.A.* 41°16N 70°5W 81 E18
Nantulo *Mozam.* 12°33S 38°45E 55 E4
Nantwich *U.K.* 53°4N 2°31W 12 D5
Nanty Glo *U.S.A.* 40°28N 78°50W 82 F6
Nanuku Passage *Fiji* 16°45S 179°15W 59 a
Nanuque *Brazil* 17°50S 40°21W 93 G10
Nanusa, Kepulauan
 Indonesia 4°45N 127°1E 37 D7
Nanutarra Roadhouse
 Australia 22°32S 115°30E 60 D2
Nanyang *China* 33°11N 112°30E 34 H7
Nanyuki *Kenya* 0°2N 37°4E 54 B4
Nao, C. de la *Spain* 38°44N 0°14E 21 C6
Naococane, L. *Canada* 52°50N 70°45W 73 B5
Napa *U.S.A.* 38°18N 122°17W 78 G4
Napa → *U.S.A.* 38°10N 122°19W 78 G4
Napanee *Canada* 44°15N 77°0W 82 B8
Napanoch *U.S.A.* 41°44N 74°22W 83 E10
Nape *Laos* 18°18N 105°6E 38 C5
Nape Pass = Keo Neua, Deo
 Vietnam 18°23N 105°10E 38 C5
Napier *N.Z.* 39°30S 176°56E 59 C6
Napier Broome B.
 Australia 14°2S 126°37E 60 B4
Napier Pen. *Australia* 12°4S 135°43E 62 A2
Napierville *Canada* 45°11N 73°25W 83 A11
Naples = Nápoli *Italy* 40°50N 14°15E 22 D6
Naples *U.S.A.* 26°8N 81°48W 85 H14
Napo → *Peru* 3°20S 72°40W 92 D4
Napoleon *N. Dak., U.S.A.* 46°30N 99°46W 80 B4
Napoleon *Ohio, U.S.A.* 41°23N 84°8W 81 E11
Nápoli *Italy* 40°50N 14°15E 22 D6
Napopo
 Dem. Rep. of the Congo 4°15N 28°0E 54 B2
Naqadeh *Iran* 36°57N 45°23E 44 B5
Naqb, Ra's an *Jordan* 29°48N 35°44E 46 F4
Naqqāsh *Iran* 35°40N 49°6E 45 C6
Nara *Japan* 34°40N 135°49E 31 G7
Nara *Mali* 15°10N 7°20W 50 E4
Nara □ *Japan* 34°30N 136°0E 31 G8
Nara Canal *Pakistan* 24°30N 69°20E 42 G3
Nara Visa *U.S.A.* 35°37N 103°6W 77 J12
Naracoorte *Australia* 36°58S 140°45E 63 F3
Naradhan *Australia* 33°34S 146°17E 63 E4
Naraini *India* 25°11N 80°29E 43 G9
Naranjos *Mexico* 21°21N 97°41W 87 C5
Narasapur *India* 16°26N 81°40E 41 L12
Narathiwat *Thailand* 6°30N 101°48E 39 J3
Narayangadh = Bharatpur
 Nepal 27°34N 84°10E 43 F11
Narayanganj *Bangla.* 23°40N 90°33E 41 H17
Narayanpet *India* 16°45N 77°30E 40 L10
Narberth *U.K.* 51°47N 4°44W 13 F3
Narbonne *France* 43°11N 3°0E 20 E5
Nardīn *Iran* 37°3N 55°59E 45 B7
Nardò *Italy* 40°11N 18°2E 23 D8
Narembeen *Australia* 32°7S 118°24E 61 F2
Narendranagar *India* 30°10N 78°18E 42 D8
Nares Str. *Arctic* 80°0N 70°0W 69 B18
Naretha *Australia* 31°0S 124°45E 61 F3
Narew → *Poland* 52°26N 20°41E 17 B11
Nari → *Pakistan* 28°0N 67°40E 42 F2
Narin *Afghan.* 36°5N 69°0E 40 A6
Narindra, Helodranon' i
 Madag. 14°55S 47°30E 57 A8
Narita *Japan* 35°47N 140°19E 31 G10
Nariva Swamp
 Trin. & Tob. 10°26N 61°4W 93 K15
Narmada → *India* 21°38N 72°36E 42 J5
Narnaul *India* 28°5N 76°11E 42 E7
Narooma *Australia* 36°14S 150°4E 63 F5
Narowal *Pakistan* 32°6N 74°52E 42 C6
Narrabri *Australia* 30°19S 149°46E 63 E4
Narran → *Australia* 28°37S 148°12E 63 D4
Narrandera *Australia* 34°42S 146°31E 63 E4
Narrogin *Australia* 32°58S 117°14E 61 F2
Narromine *Australia* 32°12S 148°12E 63 E4
Narrow Hills △ *Canada* 54°0N 104°37W 71 C8
Narsimhapur *India* 22°54S 79°14E 43 H8
Narsinghgarh *India* 23°45N 76°40E 42 H7
Naruto *Japan* 34°11N 134°37E 31 G7
Narva *Estonia* 59°23N 28°12E 18 C4
Narva → *Russia* 59°27N 28°2E 9 G23
Narva Bay = Narva Laht
 Estonia 59°35N 27°35E 9 G22
Narva Laht *Estonia* 59°35N 27°35E 9 G22
Narvik *Norway* 68°28N 17°26E 8 B17
Narwana *India* 29°39N 76°6E 42 E7
Narwinbi ☼ *Australia* 16°7S 136°17E 62 B2
Naryan-Mar *Russia* 67°42N 53°12E 18 A9
Naryn *Kyrgyzstan* 41°26N 75°58E 28 E8
Naryn Qum *Kazakhstan* 47°30N 49°23E 8 E16
Nasa *Norway* 66°29N 15°23E 8 C16
Nasau *Fiji* 17°19S 179°27E 59 a
Nasca = Nazca *Peru* 14°50S 74°57W 92 F4
Naseby *N.Z.* 45°1S 170°10E 59 F3
Naselle *U.S.A.* 46°22N 123°49W 78 D3
Naser, Buheirat en
 Egypt 23°0N 32°30E 51 D12
Nashik = Nasik *India* 19°58N 73°50E 40 K8

Nashua *Mont., U.S.A.* 48°8N 106°22W 76 B10
Nashua *N.H., U.S.A.* 42°45N 71°28W 83 D13
Nashville *Ark., U.S.A.* 33°57N 93°51W 84 E8
Nashville *Ga., U.S.A.* 31°12N 83°15W 85 F13
Nashville *Tenn., U.S.A.* 36°10N 86°47W 85 C11
Nasik *India* 19°58N 73°50E 40 K8
Nasirabad *India* 26°15N 74°45E 42 F6
Nasirabad *Pakistan* 28°23N 68°24E 42 E3
Nasiri = Ahvāz *Iran* 31°20N 48°40E 45 D6
Nasiriyah = An Nāşirīyah
 Iraq 31°0N 46°15E 44 D5
Naskaupi → *Canada* 53°47N 60°51W 73 B7
Naşrābād *Iran* 34°8N 51°26E 45 C6
Naşrīān-e Pā'īn *Iran* 32°52N 46°52E 44 C5
Nass → *Canada* 55°0N 129°40W 70 C3
Nassau *Bahamas* 25°5N 77°20W 88 A4
Nassau *U.S.A.* 42°31N 73°37W 83 D11
Nassau, B. *Chile* 55°20S 68°0W 96 H3
Nasser, L. = Naser, Buheirat en
 Egypt 23°0N 32°30E 51 D12
Nässjö *Sweden* 57°39N 14°42E 9 H16
Nastapoka → *Canada* 56°55N 76°33W 72 A4
Nastapoka, Is. *Canada* 56°55N 76°50W 72 A4
Nata *Botswana* 20°12S 26°12E 56 C4
Nata → *Botswana* 20°14S 26°10E 56 C4
Natal *Brazil* 5°47S 35°13W 93 E11
Natal *Indonesia* 0°35N 99°7E 36 D1
Natal Drakensberg △
 S. Africa 29°27S 29°30E 57 D4
Naţanz *Iran* 33°30N 51°55E 45 C6
Natashquan *Canada* 50°14N 61°46W 73 B7
Natashquan → *Canada* 50°7N 61°50W 73 B7
Natchez *U.S.A.* 31°34N 91°24W 84 F9
Natchitoches *U.S.A.* 31°46N 93°5W 84 F8
Natewa B. *Fiji* 16°35S 179°40E 59 a
Nathalia *Australia* 36°1S 145°13E 63 F4
Nathdwara *India* 24°55N 73°50E 42 G5
Nati, Pta. *Spain* 40°3N 3°50E 24 A10
Natimuk *Australia* 36°42S 142°0E 63 F3
Nation → *Canada* 55°30N 123°32W 70 B4
National City *U.S.A.* 32°40N 117°5W 79 N9
Natitingou *Benin* 10°20N 1°26E 50 F6
Natividad, I. *Mexico* 27°52N 115°11W 86 B1
Natkyizin *Burma* 14°57N 97°59E 38 E1
Natron, L. *Tanzania* 2°20S 36°0E 54 C4
Natrona Heights *U.S.A.* 40°37N 79°44W 82 F5
Natukanaoka Pan
 Namibia 18°40S 15°45E 56 B2
Natuna Besar, Kepulauan
 Indonesia 4°0N 108°15E 36 D3
Natuna Is. = Natuna Besar,
 Kepulauan *Indonesia* 4°0N 108°15E 36 D3
Natuna Selatan, Kepulauan
 Indonesia 2°45N 109°0E 36 D3
Natural Bridge *U.S.A.* 44°5N 75°30W 83 B9
Natural Bridges △
 U.S.A. 37°36N 110°0W 77 H9
Naturaliste, C. *Tas.,*
 Australia 40°50S 148°15E 63 G4
Naturaliste, C. *W. Austral.,*
 Australia 33°32S 115°0E 61 F2
Naturaliste Plateau
 Ind. Oc. 34°0S 112°0E 64 L3
Nau Qala *Afghan.* 34°5N 68°5E 42 B3
Naugatuck *U.S.A.* 41°30N 73°3W 83 E11
Naujaat = Repulse Bay
 Canada 66°30N 86°30W 69 D14
Naumburg *Germany* 51°9N 11°47E 16 C6
Nauru ■ *Pac. Oc.* 1°0S 166°0E 58 B9
Naushahra = Nowshera
 Pakistan 34°0N 72°0E 40 C8
Naushahro *Pakistan* 26°50N 68°7E 42 F3
Naushon I. *U.S.A.* 41°29N 70°45W 83 E14
Nausori *Fiji* 18°2S 178°32E 59 a
Nauta *Peru* 4°31S 73°35W 92 D4
Nautanwa *India* 27°20N 83°25E 43 F10
Naute □ *Namibia* 26°55S 17°57E 56 D2
Nautla *Mexico* 20°13N 96°47W 87 C5
Nava *Mexico* 28°25N 100°45W 86 B4
Navadwip *India* 23°34N 88°20E 43 H13
Navahrudak *Belarus* 53°40N 25°50E 17 B13
Navajo Res. *U.S.A.* 36°48N 107°36W 77 H10
Navalmoral de la Mata
 Spain 39°52N 5°33W 21 C3
Navan = An Uaimh
 Ireland 53°39N 6°41W 10 C5
Navarin, Mys *Russia* 62°15N 179°5E 29 C18
Navarino, I. *Chile* 55°0S 67°40W 96 H3
Navarra □ *Spain* 42°40N 1°40W 21 A5
Navarre *U.S.A.* 40°43N 81°31W 82 F3
Navarro *U.S.A.* 39°11N 123°45W 78 F3
Navasota *U.S.A.* 30°23N 96°5W 84 F6
Navassa I. *W. Indies* 18°30N 75°0W 89 C5
Naver → *U.K.* 58°32N 4°14W 11 C4
Navibandar *India* 21°26N 69°48E 42 J3
Navidad *Chile* 33°57S 71°50W 94 C1
Naviraí *Brazil* 23°8S 54°13W 95 A5
Naviti *Fiji* 17°7S 177°15E 59 a
Navlakhi *India* 22°58N 70°28E 42 H4
Năvodari *Romania* 44°19N 28°36E 17 F15
Navoiy *Uzbekistan* 40°9N 65°22E 28 E7
Navojoa *Mexico* 27°6N 109°26W 86 B3
Navolato *Mexico* 24°47N 107°42W 86 C3
Navsari *India* 20°57N 72°59E 40 J8
Nawa Kot *Pakistan* 28°21N 71°24E 42 E4
Nawab Khan *Pakistan* 30°17N 69°12E 42 D3
Nawabganj *Ut. P., India* 26°56N 81°14E 43 F9
Nawabganj *Ut. P., India* 28°32N 79°40E 43 E8
Nawabshah *Pakistan* 26°15N 68°25E 42 F3
Nawada *India* 24°50N 85°33E 43 G11
Nawakot *Nepal* 27°55N 85°10E 43 F11
Nawalgarh *India* 27°50N 75°15E 42 F6
Nawanshahr *India* 32°33N 74°48E 43 C6
Nawar, Dasht-i- *Afghan.* 33°52N 68°0E 42 C3
Nawoiy = Navoiy
 Uzbekistan 40°9N 65°22E 28 E7
Naxçıvan *Azerbaijan* 39°12N 45°15E 44 B5
Naxçıvan □ *Azerbaijan* 39°25N 45°26E 44 B5

Naxos *Greece* 37°8N 25°25E 23 F11
Nay, Mui = Varela, Mui
 Vietnam 12°54N 109°26E 38 F7
Nāy Band *Būshehr, Iran* 27°20N 52°40E 45 E7
Nāy Band *Khorāsān, Iran* 32°20N 57°34E 45 C8
Nayakhan *Russia* 61°56N 159°0E 29 C16
Nayarit □ *Mexico* 22°0N 105°0W 86 C4
Nayau *Fiji* 18°6S 178°10E 59 a
Nayoro *Japan* 44°21N 142°28E 30 B11
Naypyidaw *Burma* 19°44N 96°12E 38 C1
Nayyāl, W. → *Si. Arabia* 28°35N 39°4E 44 D3
Nazaré *Brazil* 13°2S 39°0W 93 F11
Nazareth = Nazerat
 Israel 32°43N 35°17E 46 C4
Nazareth *U.S.A.* 40°44N 75°19W 83 F9
Nazarovo *Russia* 57°2N 90°40E 29 D10
Nazas *Mexico* 25°14N 104°8W 86 B4
Nazas → *Mexico* 25°12N 104°12W 86 B4
Nazca *Peru* 14°50S 74°57W 92 F4
Nazca Ridge *Pac. Oc.* 20°0S 80°0W 65 K19
Naze *Japan* 28°22N 129°27E 31 K4
Naze, The *U.K.* 51°53N 1°18E 13 F9
Nazerat *Israel* 32°43N 35°17E 46 C4
Nāzik *Iran* 39°1N 45°4E 44 B5
Nazilli *Turkey* 37°55N 28°15E 23 F13
Nazko *Canada* 53°1N 123°37W 70 C4
Nazko → *Canada* 53°7N 123°34W 70 C4
Nazret *Ethiopia* 8°32N 39°22E 47 F2
Nchanga *Zambia* 12°30S 27°49E 55 E2
Ncheu *Malawi* 14°50S 34°47E 55 E3
Ndala *Tanzania* 4°45S 33°15E 54 C3
Ndalatando *Angola* 9°12S 14°48E 52 F2
Ndareda *Tanzania* 4°12S 35°30E 54 C4
Ndélé *C.A.R.* 8°25N 20°36E 52 C4
Ndjamena *Chad* 12°10N 14°59E 51 F8
Ndola *Zambia* 13°0S 28°34E 55 E2
Ndomo △ *S. Africa* 26°52S 32°15E 57 D5
Ndoto Mts. *Kenya* 2°0N 37°0E 54 B4
Nduguti *Tanzania* 4°18S 34°41E 54 C3
Neagh, Lough *U.K.* 54°37N 6°25W 10 B5
Neah Bay *U.S.A.* 48°22N 124°37W 78 B2
Neale, L. *Australia* 24°15S 130°0E 60 D5
Neales → *Australia* 28°8S 136°47E 63 D2
Neapoli *Greece* 35°15N 25°37E 25 D7
Near Is. *U.S.A.* 52°30N 174°0E 74 E2
Neath *U.K.* 51°39N 3°48W 13 F4
Neath Port Talbot □
 U.K. 51°42N 3°45W 13 F4
Nebbi *Uganda* 2°28N 31°6E 54 B3
Nebine Cr. → *Australia* 29°27S 146°56E 63 D4
Nebitdag = Balkanabat
 Turkmenistan 39°30N 54°22E 45 B7
Nebo *Australia* 21°42S 148°42E 62 C4
Nebraska □ *U.S.A.* 41°30N 99°30W 80 E4
Nebraska City *U.S.A.* 40°41N 95°52W 80 E6
Nébrodi, Monti *Italy* 37°54N 14°35E 22 F6
Necedah *U.S.A.* 44°2N 90°4W 80 C8
Nechako → *Canada* 53°55N 122°42W 70 C4
Neches → *U.S.A.* 29°58N 93°51W 84 G8
Neckar → *Germany* 49°27N 8°29E 16 D5
Necker I. *U.S.A.* 23°35N 164°42W 75 L7
Necochea *Argentina* 38°30S 58°50W 94 D4
Nederland = Netherlands ■
 Europe 52°0N 5°30E 15 C5
Needles *Canada* 49°53N 118°7W 70 D5
Needles *U.S.A.* 34°51N 114°37W 79 L12
Needles, The *U.K.* 50°39N 1°35W 13 G6
Neembucú □ *Paraguay* 27°0S 58°0W 94 B4
Neemuch = Nimach
 India 24°30N 74°56E 42 G6
Neenah *U.S.A.* 44°11N 88°28W 80 C9
Neepawa *Canada* 50°15N 99°30W 71 C9
Neftçala *Azerbaijan* 39°19N 49°12E 45 B6
Neftegorsk *Russia* 53°1N 142°58E 29 D15
Neftekumsk *Russia* 44°46N 44°50E 19 F7
Nefteyugansk *Russia* 61°5N 72°42E 28 C8
Nefyn *U.K.* 52°56N 4°31W 12 E3
Negapatam = Nagappattinam
 India 10°46N 79°51E 40 P11
Negara *Indonesia* 8°22S 114°37E 37 J17
Negaunee *U.S.A.* 46°30N 87°36W 80 B10
Negele *Ethiopia* 5°20N 39°36E 47 F2
Negev Desert = Hanegev
 Israel 30°50N 35°0E 46 E4
Negombo *Sri Lanka* 7°12N 79°50E 40 R11
Negotin *Serbia* 44°16N 22°37E 23 B10
Negra, Pta. *Mauritania* 22°54N 16°18W 50 D2
Negra, Pta. *Peru* 6°6S 81°10W 92 E2
Negrais, C. = Maudin Sun
 Burma 16°0N 94°30E 41 M19
Negril *Jamaica* 18°22N 78°20W 88 a
Negro → *Argentina* 41°2S 62°47W 96 E4
Negro → *Brazil* 3°0S 60°0W 92 D7
Negro → *Uruguay* 33°24S 58°22W 94 C4
Negros *Phil.* 9°30N 122°40E 37 C6
Neguac *Canada* 47°15N 65°5W 73 C6
Nehalem → *U.S.A.* 45°40N 123°56W 78 E3
Nehāvand *Iran* 35°56N 49°31E 45 C6
Nehbandān *Iran* 31°35N 60°5E 45 D9
Nei Monggol Zizhiqu □
 China 42°0N 112°0E 34 D7
Neiafu *Tonga* 18°39S 173°59W 59 c
Neiges, Piton des *Réunion* 21°5S 55°29E 53 c
Neijiang *China* 29°35N 104°55E 32 D5
Neilingding Dao *China* 22°25N 113°48E 33 G10
Neillsville *U.S.A.* 44°34N 90°36W 80 C8
Neilton *U.S.A.* 47°25N 123°53W 78 C2
Neiqiu *China* 37°15N 114°30E 34 F8
Neiva *Colombia* 2°56N 75°18W 92 C3
Neixiang *China* 33°10N 111°52E 34 H6
Nejanilini L. *Canada* 59°33N 97°48W 71 B9
Nejd = Najd *Si. Arabia* 26°30N 42°0E 44 E4
Nekā *Iran* 36°39N 53°19E 45 B7
Nekemte *Ethiopia* 9°4N 36°30E 47 F2
Nekso *Denmark* 55°4N 15°8E 9 J16
Nelia *Australia* 20°39S 142°12E 62 C3
Neligh *U.S.A.* 42°8N 98°2W 80 D4
Nelkan *Russia* 57°40N 136°4E 29 D14
Nellore *India* 14°27N 79°59E 40 M11

Nelson *Canada* 49°30N 117°20W 70 D5
Nelson *N.Z.* 41°18S 173°16E 59 D4
Nelson *U.K.* 53°50N 2°13W 12 D5
Nelson *Ariz., U.S.A.* 35°31N 113°19W 77 J7
Nelson *Nev., U.S.A.* 35°42N 114°49W 79 K12
Nelson → *Canada* 54°33N 98°2W 71 C9
Nelson, C. *Australia* 38°26S 141°32E 63 F3
Nelson, Estrecho *Chile* 51°30S 75°0W 96 G2
Nelson Forks *Canada* 59°30N 124°0W 70 B4
Nelson House *Canada* 55°47N 98°51W 71 B9
Nelson L. *Canada* 55°48N 100°7W 71 B8
Nelson Lakes △ *N.Z.* 41°55S 172°44E 59 D4
Nelspoort *S. Africa* 32°7S 23°0E 56 E3
Nelspruit *S. Africa* 25°29S 30°59E 57 D5
Néma *Mauritania* 16°40N 7°15W 50 E4
Neman = Nemunas →
 Lithuania 55°25N 21°10E 9 J19
Nembrala *Indonesia* 10°53S 122°50E 60 D3
Nemeiben L. *Canada* 55°20N 105°20W 71 B7
Nemiscau *Canada* 51°18N 76°54W 72 B4
Nemiscau, L. *Canada* 51°25N 76°40W 72 B4
Nemunas → *Lithuania* 55°25N 21°10E 9 J19
Nemuro *Japan* 43°20N 145°35E 30 C12
Nemuro-Kaikyō *Japan* 43°30N 145°30E 30 C12
Nen Jiang → *China* 45°28N 124°30E 35 B13
Nenagh *Ireland* 52°52N 8°11W 10 D3
Nenana *U.S.A.* 64°34N 149°5W 74 C10
Nenasi *Malaysia* 3°9N 103°23E 39 L4
Nene → *U.K.* 52°49N 0°11E 13 E8
Nenjiang *China* 49°10N 125°10E 33 B7
Neno *Malawi* 15°25S 34°40E 55 F3
Neodesha *U.S.A.* 37°25N 95°41W 80 G6
Neora Valley △ *India* 27°0N 88°45E 43 F13
Neosho *U.S.A.* 36°52N 94°22W 80 G6
Neosho → *U.S.A.* 36°48N 95°18W 84 C7
Nepal ■ *Asia* 28°0N 84°30E 43 F11
Nepalganj *Nepal* 28°5N 81°40E 43 E9
Nepalganj Road *India* 28°1N 81°41E 43 E9
Nephi *U.S.A.* 39°43N 111°50W 76 G8
Nephin *Ireland* 54°1N 9°22W 10 B2
Nephin Beg Range *Ireland* 54°0N 9°40W 10 C2
Neptune *U.S.A.* 40°13N 74°2W 83 F10
Neqáb *Iran* 36°42N 57°25E 45 B8
Nerang *Australia* 27°58S 153°20E 63 D5
Nerastro, Sarīr *Libya* 24°20N 20°37E 51 D10
Nerchinsk *Russia* 52°0N 116°39E 29 D12
Néret, L. *Canada* 54°45N 70°44W 73 B5
Neretva → *Croatia* 43°1N 17°27E 23 C7
Neringa *Lithuania* 55°20N 21°5E 9 J19
Neris → *Lithuania* 55°8N 24°16E 9 J21
Neryungri *Russia* 57°38N 124°28E 29 D13
Nescopeck *U.S.A.* 41°3N 76°12W 83 E8
Neskantaga *Canada* 52°14N 87°53W 72 B2
Ness, L. *U.K.* 57°15N 4°32W 11 D4
Ness City *U.S.A.* 38°27N 99°54W 80 F4
Nesterov *Ukraine* 50°4N 23°58E 17 C12
Nestos → *Europe* 40°54N 24°49E 23 D11
Nesvizh = Nyasvizh
 Belarus 53°14N 26°38E 17 B14
Netanya *Israel* 32°20N 34°51E 46 C3
Netarhat *India* 23°29N 84°16E 43 H11
Nete → *Belgium* 51°7N 4°14E 15 C4
Netherdale *Australia* 21°10S 148°33E 62 b
Netherlands ■ *Europe* 52°0N 5°30E 15 C5
Netherlands Antilles ☑
 W. Indies 12°15N 69°0W 92 A5
Netrang *India* 21°39N 73°21E 42 J5
Nettilling L. *Canada* 66°30N 71°0W 69 D17
Netzahualcóyotl, Presa
 Mexico 17°8N 93°35W 87 D6
Neubrandenburg
 Germany 53°33N 13°15E 16 B7
Neuchâtel *Switz.* 47°0N 6°55E 20 C7
Neuchâtel, Lac de *Switz.* 46°53N 6°50E 20 C7
Neufchâteau *Belgium* 49°50N 5°25E 15 E5
Neumünster *Germany* 54°4N 9°58E 16 A5
Neunkirchen *Germany* 49°20N 7°9E 16 D4
Neuquén *Argentina* 38°55S 68°0W 96 D3
Neuquén □ *Argentina* 38°0S 69°50W 94 D2
Neuruppin *Germany* 52°55N 12°48E 16 B7
Neuse → *U.S.A.* 35°6N 76°29W 85 D16
Neusiedler See *Austria* 47°50N 16°47E 17 E9
Neustrelitz *Germany* 53°21N 13°4E 16 B7
Neva → *Russia* 59°56N 30°20E 18 C5
Nevada *Iowa, U.S.A.* 42°1N 93°27W 80 D7
Nevada *Mo., U.S.A.* 37°51N 94°22W 80 G6
Nevada □ *U.S.A.* 39°0N 117°0W 76 G5
Nevada City *U.S.A.* 39°16N 121°1W 78 F6
Nevado, Cerro *Argentina* 35°30S 68°32W 94 D2
Nevado de Colima = Volcán de
 Colima △ *Mexico* 19°30N 103°40W 86 D4
Nevado de Tres Cruces △
 Chile 27°13S 69°5W 94 B2
Nevel *Russia* 56°0N 29°55E 18 C4
Nevelsk *Russia* 46°40N 141°51E 29 E15
Nevers *France* 47°0N 3°9E 20 C5
Nevertire *Australia* 31°50S 147°44E 63 E4
Neville *Canada* 49°58N 107°39W 71 D7
Nevinnomyssk *Russia* 44°40N 42°0E 19 F7
Nevis *St. Kitts & Nevis* 17°0N 62°30W 89 C7
Nevşehir *Turkey* 38°33N 34°40E 44 B2
Nevyansk *Russia* 57°30N 60°13E 18 C11
New Aiyansh *Canada* 55°12N 129°4W 70 B3
New Albany *Ind.,*
 U.S.A. 38°18N 85°49W 81 F11
New Albany *Miss.,*
 U.S.A. 34°29N 89°0W 85 D10
New Albany *Pa., U.S.A.* 41°36N 76°27W 83 E8
New Amsterdam *Guyana* 6°15N 57°36W 92 B7
New Baltimore *U.S.A.* 42°41N 82°44W 82 D2
New Bedford *U.S.A.* 41°38N 70°56W 83 E14
New Berlin *N.Y., U.S.A.* 42°37N 75°20W 83 D9
New Berlin *Pa., U.S.A.* 40°50N 76°57W 82 F8
New Bern *U.S.A.* 35°7N 77°3W 85 D16
New Bethlehem *U.S.A.* 41°0N 79°20W 82 F5
New Bight *Bahamas* 24°19N 75°24W 89 B4
New Bloomfield *U.S.A.* 40°25N 77°11W 82 F7

New Boston U.S.A. 33°28N 94°25W 84 E7
New Braunfels U.S.A. 29°42N 98°8W 84 G5
New Brighton N.Z. 43°29S 172°43E 59 E4
New Brighton U.S.A. 40°42N 80°19W 82 F4
New Britain Papua N. G. 5°50S 150°20E 58 B8
New Britain U.S.A. 41°40N 72°47W 83 E12
New Brunswick U.S.A. 40°30N 74°27W 83 F10
New Brunswick □ Canada 46°50N 66°30W 73 C6
New Caledonia ☒ Pac. Oc. 21°0S 165°0E 58 D9
New Caledonia Trough Pac. Oc. 30°0S 165°0E 64 L8
New Castile = Castilla-La Mancha □ Spain 39°30N 3°30W 21 C4
New Castle Ind., U.S.A. 39°55N 85°22W 81 F11
New Castle Pa., U.S.A. 41°0N 80°21W 82 F4
New City U.S.A. 41°9N 73°59W 83 E11
New Concord U.S.A. 39°59N 81°54W 82 G3
New Cumberland U.S.A. 40°30N 80°36W 82 F4
New Cuyama U.S.A. 34°57N 119°38W 79 L7
New Delhi India 28°36N 77°11E 42 E7
New Denver Canada 50°0N 117°25W 70 D5
New Don Pedro Res. U.S.A. 37°43N 120°24W 78 H6
New England U.S.A. 43°0N 71°0W 75 G25
New England N. Dak., U.S.A. 46°32N 102°52W 80 B2
New England Ra. Australia 30°20S 151°45E 63 E5
New Forest △ U.K. 50°53N 1°34W 13 G6
New Galloway U.K. 55°5N 4°9W 11 F4
New Glasgow Canada 45°35N 62°36W 73 C7
New Guinea Oceania 4°0S 136°0E 58 B6
New Hamburg Canada 43°23N 80°42W 82 C4
New Hampshire □ U.S.A. 44°0N 71°30W 83 C13
New Hampton U.S.A. 43°3N 92°19W 80 D7
New Hanover S. Africa 29°22S 30°31E 57 D5
New Hartford U.S.A. 43°4N 75°18W 83 C9
New Haven Conn., U.S.A. 41°18N 72°55W 83 E12
New Haven Mich., U.S.A. 42°44N 82°48W 82 D2
New Haven N.Y., U.S.A. 43°28N 76°18W 83 C8
New Hazelton Canada 55°20N 127°30W 70 B3
New Hebrides = Vanuatu ■ Pac. Oc. 15°0S 168°0E 58 C9
New Holland U.S.A. 40°6N 76°5W 83 F8
New Iberia U.S.A. 30°1N 91°49W 84 F9
New Ireland Papua N. G. 3°20S 151°50E 58 B8
New Jersey □ U.S.A. 40°0N 74°30W 81 F16
New Kensington U.S.A. 40°34N 79°46W 82 F5
New Lexington U.S.A. 39°43N 82°13W 81 F12
New Liskeard Canada 47°31N 79°41W 72 C4
New London Conn., U.S.A. 41°22N 72°6W 83 E12
New London Ohio, U.S.A. 41°5N 82°24W 82 E2
New London Wis., U.S.A. 44°23N 88°45W 80 C9
New Madrid U.S.A. 36°36N 89°32W 80 G9
New Martinsville U.S.A. 39°39N 80°52W 81 F13
New Meadows U.S.A. 44°58N 116°18W 76 D5
New Melones L. U.S.A. 37°57N 120°31W 78 H6
New Mexico □ U.S.A. 34°30N 106°0W 77 J11
New Milford Conn., U.S.A. 41°35N 73°25W 83 E11
New Milford Pa., U.S.A. 41°52N 75°44W 83 E9
New Moore I. Ind. Oc. 21°37N 89°10E 43 J13
New Norcia Australia 30°57S 116°13E 61 F2
New Norfolk Australia 42°46S 147°2E 63 G4
New Orleans U.S.A. 29°57N 90°4W 85 G9
New Philadelphia U.S.A. 40°30N 81°27W 82 F3
New Plymouth N.Z. 39°4S 174°5E 59 C5
New Plymouth U.S.A. 43°58N 116°49W 76 E5
New Port Richey U.S.A. 28°16N 82°43W 85 G13
New Providence Bahamas 25°25N 78°35W 88 A4
New Quay U.K. 52°13N 4°21W 13 E3
New Radnor U.K. 52°15N 3°9W 13 E4
New Richmond Canada 48°15N 65°45W 73 C6
New Richmond U.S.A. 45°7N 92°32W 80 C7
New River Gorge ⌓ U.S.A. 37°53N 81°5W 81 G13
New Roads U.S.A. 30°42N 91°26W 84 F9
New Rochelle U.S.A. 40°55N 73°46W 83 F11
New Rockford U.S.A. 47°41N 99°8W 80 B4
New Romney U.K. 50°59N 0°57E 13 G8
New Ross Ireland 52°23N 6°57W 10 D5
New Salem U.S.A. 46°51N 101°25W 80 B3
New Scone = Scone U.K. 56°25N 3°24W 11 E5
New Siberian I. = Novaya Sibir, Ostrov Russia 75°10N 150°0E 29 B16
New Siberian Is. = Novosibirskiye Ostrova Russia 75°0N 142°0E 29 B15
New Smyrna Beach U.S.A. 29°1N 80°56W 85 G14
New South Wales □ Australia 33°0S 146°0E 63 E4
New Tecumseth = Alliston Canada 44°9N 79°52W 82 B5
New Town U.S.A. 47°59N 102°30W 80 B2
New Tredegar U.K. 51°44N 3°16W 13 F4
New Ulm U.S.A. 44°19N 94°28W 80 C6
New Waterford Canada 46°13N 60°4W 73 C7
New Westminster Canada 49°13N 122°55W 78 A4
New York U.S.A. 40°43N 74°0W 83 F11
New York □ U.S.A. 43°0N 75°0W 83 D9
New York J.F. Kennedy Int. ✈ (JFK) U.S.A. 40°38N 73°47W 83 F11
New Zealand ■ Oceania 40°0S 176°0E 59 D6
Newaj → India 24°24N 76°49E 42 G7
Newala Tanzania 10°58S 39°18E 55 E4
Newark Del., U.S.A. 39°41N 75°46W 81 F16
Newark N.J., U.S.A. 40°44N 74°10W 83 F10
Newark N.Y., U.S.A. 43°3N 77°6W 82 C7
Newark Ohio, U.S.A. 40°3N 82°24W 82 F2
Newark Liberty Int. ✈ (EWR) U.S.A. 40°42N 74°10W 83 F10
Newark-on-Trent U.K. 53°5N 0°48W 12 D7
Newark Valley U.S.A. 42°14N 76°11W 83 D8
Newberg U.S.A. 45°18N 122°58W 76 D2
Newberry Mich., U.S.A. 46°21N 85°30W 81 B11
Newberry S.C., U.S.A. 34°17N 81°37W 85 D14
Newberry Springs U.S.A. 34°50N 116°41W 79 L10
Newboro L. Canada 44°38N 76°20W 83 B8
Newbridge = Droichead Nua Ireland 53°11N 6°48W 10 C5
Newburgh Canada 44°19N 76°52W 82 B8
Newburgh U.S.A. 41°30N 74°1W 83 E10
Newbury U.K. 51°24N 1°20W 13 F6
Newbury N.H., U.S.A. 43°19N 72°3W 83 B12
Newbury Vt., U.S.A. 44°5N 72°4W 83 B12
Newburyport U.S.A. 42°49N 70°53W 83 D14
Newcastle Australia 33°0S 151°46E 63 E5
Newcastle N.B., Canada 47°1N 65°38W 73 C6
Newcastle Ont., Canada 43°55N 78°35W 72 D4
Newcastle S. Africa 27°45S 29°58E 57 D4
Newcastle U.K. 54°13N 5°54W 10 B6
Newcastle Calif., U.S.A. 38°53N 121°8W 78 G5
Newcastle Wyo., U.S.A. 43°50N 104°11W 76 E11
Newcastle Emlyn U.K. 52°2N 4°28W 13 E3
Newcastle Ra. Australia 15°45S 130°15E 60 C5
Newcastle-under-Lyme U.K. 53°1N 2°14W 12 D5
Newcastle-upon-Tyne U.K. 54°58N 1°36W 12 C6
Newcastle Waters Australia 17°30S 133°28E 62 B1
Newcastle West Ireland 52°27N 9°3W 10 D2
Newcomb U.S.A. 43°58N 74°10W 83 C10
Newcomerstown U.S.A. 40°16N 81°36W 82 F3
Newdegate Australia 33°6S 119°0E 61 F2
Newell Australia 16°20S 145°16E 62 B4
Newell U.S.A. 44°43N 103°25W 80 C2
Newenham, C. U.S.A. 58°39N 162°11W 74 D7
Newfane U.S.A. 43°17N 78°43W 82 C6
Newfield U.S.A. 42°18N 76°33W 83 D8
Newfound L. U.S.A. 43°40N 71°47W 83 C13
Newfoundland Canada 49°0N 55°0W 73 C8
Newfoundland U.S.A. 41°18N 75°19W 83 E9
Newfoundland & Labrador □ Canada 53°0N 58°0W 73 B8
Newhaven U.K. 50°47N 0°3E 13 G8
Newkirk U.S.A. 36°53N 97°3W 84 C6
Newlyn U.K. 50°6N 5°34W 13 G2
Newman Australia 23°18S 119°45E 60 D2
Newman U.S.A. 37°19N 121°1W 78 H5
Newmarket Canada 44°3N 79°28W 82 B5
Newmarket Ireland 52°13N 9°0W 10 D2
Newmarket U.K. 52°15N 0°25E 13 E8
Newmarket U.S.A. 43°5N 70°56W 83 C14
Newnan U.S.A. 33°23N 84°48W 85 E12
Newport Ireland 53°53N 9°33W 10 C2
Newport I. of W., U.K. 50°42N 1°17W 13 G6
Newport Newport, U.K. 51°35N 3°0W 13 F5
Newport Ark., U.S.A. 35°37N 91°16W 84 D9
Newport Ky., U.S.A. 39°5N 84°29W 81 F11
Newport N.H., U.S.A. 43°22N 72°10W 83 C12
Newport N.Y., U.S.A. 43°11N 75°1W 83 C9
Newport Oreg., U.S.A. 44°39N 124°3W 76 D1
Newport Pa., U.S.A. 40°29N 77°8W 82 F7
Newport R.I., U.S.A. 41°29N 71°19W 83 E13
Newport Tenn., U.S.A. 35°58N 83°11W 85 D13
Newport Vt., U.S.A. 44°56N 72°13W 83 B12
Newport Wash., U.S.A. 48°11N 117°3W 76 B5
Newport □ U.K. 51°33N 3°1W 13 F4
Newport Beach U.S.A. 33°37N 117°56W 79 M9
Newport News U.S.A. 36°58N 76°25W 81 G15
Newport Pagnell U.K. 52°5N 0°43W 13 E7
Newquay U.K. 50°25N 5°6W 13 G2
Newry U.K. 54°11N 6°21W 10 B5
Newry Islands △ Australia 20°51S 148°56E 62 b
Newton Ill., U.S.A. 38°59N 88°10W 80 F9
Newton Iowa, U.S.A. 41°42N 93°3W 80 E7
Newton Kans., U.S.A. 38°3N 97°21W 80 F5
Newton Mass., U.S.A. 42°21N 71°12W 83 D13
Newton Miss., U.S.A. 32°19N 89°10W 85 E10
Newton N.C., U.S.A. 35°40N 81°13W 85 D14
Newton N.J., U.S.A. 41°3N 74°45W 83 E10
Newton Tex., U.S.A. 30°51N 93°46W 84 F8
Newton Abbot U.K. 50°32N 3°37W 13 G4
Newton Aycliffe U.K. 54°37N 1°34W 12 C6
Newton Falls N.Y., U.S.A. 44°12N 74°59W 83 B10
Newton Falls Ohio, U.S.A. 41°11N 80°59W 82 E4
Newton Stewart U.K. 54°57N 4°30W 11 G4
Newtonmore U.K. 57°4N 4°8W 11 D4
Newtown U.K. 52°31N 3°19W 13 E4
Newtownabbey U.K. 54°40N 5°56W 10 B6
Newtownards U.K. 54°36N 5°42W 10 B6
Newtownbarry = Bunclody Ireland 52°39N 6°40W 10 D5
Newtownstewart U.K. 54°43N 7°23W 10 B4
Newville U.S.A. 40°10N 77°24W 82 F7
Neya Russia 58°21N 43°49E 18 C7
Neyrīz Iran 29°15N 54°19E 45 D7
Neyshābūr Iran 36°10N 58°50E 45 B8
Nezhin = Nizhyn Ukraine 51°5N 31°55E 19 D5
Nezperce U.S.A. 46°14N 116°14W 76 C5
Ngaanyatjarra ☼ Australia 22°40S 127°0E 60 D4
Ngabang Indonesia 0°23N 109°55E 36 D3
Ngabordamlu, Tanjung Indonesia 6°56S 134°11E 37 F8
N'Gage Angola 7°46S 15°15E 52 F3
Ngaliwurru Nungali ☼ Australia 15°42S 130°4E 60 C5
Ngalurrtju ☼ Australia 22°44S 132°5E 60 D5
Ngami Depression Botswana 20°30S 22°46E 56 C3
Ngamo Zimbabwe 19°3S 27°32E 55 F2
Nganglong Kangri China 33°0N 81°0E 43 C9
Ngao Thailand 18°46N 99°59E 38 C2
Ngaoundéré Cameroon 7°15N 13°35E 52 C2
Ngapara N.Z. 44°57S 170°46E 59 F3
Ngara Tanzania 2°29S 30°40E 54 C3
Ngarluma ☼ Australia 21°30S 118°30E 60 D2
Ngawi Indonesia 7°24S 111°26E 37 G14
Ngcobo S. Africa 31°37S 28°0E 57 E4
Ngeru Uganda 0°27N 33°10E 54 B3
Nghia Lo Vietnam 21°33N 104°28E 38 B5
Ngoma Malawi 13°8S 33°45E 55 E3
Ngomahura Zimbabwe 20°26S 30°43E 55 G3
Ngomba Tanzania 8°20S 32°53E 55 D3
Ngomeni, Ras Kenya 2°59S 40°14E 54 C5
Ngong Kenya 1°22S 36°39E 54 C4
Ngoring Hu China 34°55N 97°5E 32 C4
Ngorongoro Tanzania 3°11S 35°32E 54 C4
Ngorongoro ⌓ Tanzania 2°40S 35°30E 54 C4
Ngozi Burundi 2°54S 29°50E 54 C2
Ngudu Tanzania 2°58S 33°25E 54 C3
Nguigmi Niger 14°20N 13°20E 51 F8
Nguiu Australia 11°46S 130°38E 60 B5
Ngukurr Australia 14°44S 134°44E 62 A1
Ngundu Zimbabwe 18°11S 31°15E 55 F3
Ngunga Tanzania 3°37S 33°37E 54 C3
Nguru Nigeria 12°56N 10°29E 51 F8
Nguru Mts. Tanzania 6°0S 37°30E 54 D4
Ngusi Malawi 14°0S 34°50E 55 E3
Nguyen Binh Vietnam 22°39N 105°56E 38 A5
Nha Trang Vietnam 12°16N 109°10E 39 F7
Nhacoongo Mozam. 24°18S 35°14E 57 C6
Nhamaabué Mozam. 17°25S 35°5E 55 F4
Nhamundá → Brazil 2°12S 56°41W 93 D7
Nhangulaze, L. Mozam. 24°0S 34°30E 57 C5
Nharnuwangga, Wajarri and Ngarlawangga ☼ Australia 24°50S 118°0E 61 D2
Nhill Australia 36°18S 141°40E 63 F3
Nho Quan Vietnam 20°18N 105°45E 38 B5
Nhulunbuy Australia 12°10S 137°20E 62 A2
Nia-nia Dem. Rep. of the Congo 1°30N 27°40E 54 B2
Niafounké Mali 16°0N 4°5W 50 E5
Niagara Falls Canada 43°7N 79°5W 82 C5
Niagara Falls U.S.A. 43°5N 79°4W 82 C6
Niagara-on-the-Lake Canada 43°15N 79°4W 82 C5
Niah Malaysia 3°58N 113°46E 36 D4
Niamey Niger 13°27N 2°6E 50 F6
Niangara Dem. Rep. of the Congo 3°42N 27°50E 54 B2
Niantic U.S.A. 41°20N 72°11W 83 E12
Nias Indonesia 1°0N 97°30E 36 D1
Niassa □ Mozam. 13°30S 36°0E 55 E4
Niassa ⌓ Mozam. 12°4S 36°57E 55 E4
Nibāk Si. Arabia 24°25N 50°50E 45 E7
Nicaragua ■ Cent. Amer. 11°40N 85°30W 88 D2
Nicaragua, L. de Nic. 12°0N 85°30W 88 D2
Nicastro Italy 38°59N 16°19E 22 E7
Nice France 43°42N 7°14E 20 E7
Niceville U.S.A. 30°31N 86°30W 85 F11
Nichicun, L. Canada 53°5N 71°0W 73 B5
Nichinan Japan 31°38N 131°23E 31 J5
Nicholás, Canal W. Indies 23°30N 80°5W 88 B3
Nicholasville U.S.A. 37°53N 84°34W 81 G11
Nichols U.S.A. 42°1N 76°22W 83 D8
Nicholson Australia 18°2S 128°54E 60 C4
Nicholson U.S.A. 41°37N 75°47W 83 E9
Nicholson → Australia 17°31S 139°36E 62 B2
Nicholson L. Canada 62°40N 102°40W 71 A8
Nicholson Ra. Australia 27°15S 116°45E 61 E2
Nicholville U.S.A. 44°41N 74°39W 83 B10
Nicobar Is. Ind. Oc. 8°0N 93°30E 27 H11
Nicola Canada 50°12N 120°40W 70 C4
Nicolls Town Bahamas 25°8N 78°0W 88 A4
Nicosia Cyprus 35°10N 33°25E 25 D12
Nicoya Costa Rica 10°9N 85°27W 88 D2
Nicoya, G. de Costa Rica 10°0N 85°0W 88 E3
Nicoya, Pen. de Costa Rica 9°45N 85°40W 88 E2
Nidd → U.K. 53°59N 1°23W 12 D6
Niedersachsen □ Germany 52°50N 9°0E 16 B5
Niekerkshoop S. Africa 29°19S 22°51E 56 D3
Niemba Dem. Rep. of the Congo 5°58S 28°24E 54 D2
Niemen = Nemunas → Lithuania 55°25N 21°10E 9 J19
Nienburg Germany 52°39N 9°13E 16 B5
Nieu Bethesda S. Africa 31°51S 24°34E 56 E3
Nieuw Amsterdam Suriname 5°53N 55°5W 93 B7
Nieuw Nickerie Suriname 6°0N 56°59W 93 B7
Nieuwoudtville S. Africa 31°23S 19°7E 56 E2
Nieuwpoort Belgium 51°8N 2°45E 15 C2
Nieves, Pico de las Canary Is. 27°57N 15°35W 24 G4
Niğde Turkey 37°58N 34°40E 44 B2
Nigel S. Africa 26°27S 28°25E 57 D4
Niger ■ W. Afr. 17°30N 10°0E 50 E7
Niger → W. Afr. 5°33N 6°33E 50 G7
Nigeria ■ W. Afr. 8°30N 8°0E 50 G7
Nighasin India 28°14N 80°52E 43 E9
Nightcaps N.Z. 45°57S 168°2E 59 F2
Nihoa U.S.A. 23°6N 161°58W 75 L7
Nihon = Japan ■ Asia 36°0N 136°0E 31 G8
Nii-Jima Japan 34°20N 139°15E 31 G9
Niigata Japan 37°58N 139°0E 30 F9
Niigata □ Japan 37°15N 138°45E 31 F9
Niihama Japan 33°55N 133°16E 31 H6
Ni'ihau U.S.A. 21°54N 160°9W 75 L7
Niimi Japan 34°59N 133°28E 31 G6
Niitsu Japan 37°48N 139°7E 30 F9
Nijil Jordan 30°32N 35°33E 46 E4
Nijkerk Neths. 52°13N 5°30E 15 B5
Nijmegen Neths. 51°50N 5°52E 15 C5
Nijverdal Neths. 52°22N 6°28E 15 B6
Nīk Pey Iran 36°50N 48°10E 45 B6
Nikel Russia 69°24N 30°13E 8 B24
Nikiniki Indonesia 9°49S 124°30E 60 A3
Nikkō Japan 36°45N 139°35E 31 F9
Nikkō △ Japan 36°56N 139°37E 31 F9
Nikolayev = Mykolayiv Ukraine 46°58N 32°0E 19 E5
Nikolayevsk Russia 50°0N 45°35E 19 E8
Nikolayevsk-na-Amur Russia 53°8N 140°44E 29 D15
Nikolskoye Russia 55°12N 166°0E 29 D17
Nikopol Ukraine 47°35N 34°25E 19 E5
Nīkshahr Iran 26°15N 60°10E 45 E9
Nikšić Montenegro 42°50N 18°57E 23 C8
Nîl, Nahr en → Africa 30°10N 31°6E 51 B12
Nîl el Abyad → Sudan 15°38N 32°31E 51 E12
Nîl el Azraq → Sudan 15°38N 32°31E 51 E12
Nila Indonesia 6°44S 129°31E 37 F7
Niland U.S.A. 33°14N 115°31W 79 M11
Nile = Nîl, Nahr en → Africa 30°10N 31°6E 51 B12
Niles Mich., U.S.A. 41°50N 86°15W 80 E10
Niles Ohio, U.S.A. 41°11N 80°46W 82 E4
Nim Ka Thana India 27°44N 75°48E 42 F6
Nimach India 24°30N 74°56E 42 G6
Nimbahera India 24°37N 74°45E 42 G6
Nîmes France 43°50N 4°23E 20 E6
Nimfaíon, Ákra = Pines, Ákra Greece 40°5N 24°20E 23 D11
Nimmitabel Australia 36°29S 149°15E 63 F4
Nīnawá Iraq 36°25N 43°10E 44 B4
Nīnawá □ Iraq 36°15N 43°0E 44 B4
Nindigully Australia 28°21S 148°50E 63 D4
Ninepin Group China 22°16N 114°21E 33 G11
Nineveh = Nīnawá Iraq 36°25N 43°10E 44 B4
Ning Xian China 35°30N 107°58E 34 G4
Ningaloo Marine ⌓ Australia 22°23S 113°32E 60 D1
Ning'an China 44°22N 129°20E 35 B15
Ningbo China 29°51N 121°28E 33 D7
Ningcheng China 41°32N 119°53E 35 D10
Ningjin China 37°35N 114°57E 34 F8
Ningjing Shan China 30°0N 98°20E 41 E21
Ningling China 34°25N 115°22E 34 G8
Ningpo = Ningbo China 29°51N 121°28E 33 D7
Ningqiang China 32°47N 106°15E 34 H4
Ningshan China 33°21N 108°21E 34 H5
Ningsia Hui A.R. = Ningxia Huizu Zizhiqu □ China 38°0N 106°0E 34 F4
Ningwu China 39°0N 112°18E 34 E7
Ningxia Huizu Zizhiqu □ China 38°0N 106°0E 34 F4
Ningyang China 35°47N 116°45E 34 G9
Ninh Binh Vietnam 20°15N 105°55E 38 B5
Ninh Giang Vietnam 20°44N 106°24E 38 B6
Ninh Hoa Vietnam 12°30N 109°7E 38 F7
Ninh Ma Vietnam 12°48N 109°21E 38 F7
Ninove Belgium 50°51N 4°2E 15 D4
Nioaque Brazil 21°5S 55°50W 95 A4
Niobrara U.S.A. 42°45N 98°2W 80 D4
Niobrara → U.S.A. 42°46N 98°3W 80 D4
Nioro du Sahel Mali 15°15N 9°30W 50 E4
Niort France 46°19N 0°29W 20 C3
Nipawin Canada 53°20N 104°0W 71 C8
Nipigon Canada 49°0N 88°17W 72 C2
Nipigon, L. Canada 49°50N 88°30W 72 C2
Nipishish L. Canada 54°12N 60°45W 73 B7
Nipissing, L. Canada 46°20N 80°0W 72 C4
Nipomo U.S.A. 35°3N 120°29W 79 K6
Nippon = Japan ■ Asia 36°0N 136°0E 31 G8
Nipton U.S.A. 35°28N 115°16W 79 K11
Niquelândia Brazil 14°33S 48°23W 93 F9
Nīr Iran 38°2N 47°59E 44 B5
Nirasaki Japan 35°42N 138°27E 31 G9
Nirmal India 19°3N 78°20E 40 K11
Nirmali India 26°20N 86°35E 43 F12
Niš Serbia 43°19N 21°58E 23 C9
Nişāb Si. Arabia 29°11N 44°43E 44 D5
Nişāb Yemen 14°25N 46°29E 47 E4
Nishinomiya Japan 34°45N 135°20E 31 G7
Nishino'omote Japan 30°43N 130°59E 31 J5
Nishiwaki Japan 34°59N 134°58E 31 G7
Niskibi → Canada 56°29N 88°9W 72 A2
Nisqually → U.S.A. 47°7N 122°42W 78 C4
Nissaki Greece 39°43N 19°52E 25 A3
Nissum Bredning Denmark 56°40N 8°20E 9 H13
Nistru = Dnister → Europe 46°18N 30°17E 17 E16
Nisutlin → Canada 60°14N 132°34W 70 A2
Nitchequon Canada 53°10N 70°58W 73 B5
Niterói Brazil 22°53S 43°7W 95 A7
Nith → Canada 43°12N 80°23W 82 C4
Nith → U.K. 55°14N 3°33W 11 F5
Nitmiluk △ Australia 14°6S 132°15E 60 B5
Nitra Slovak Rep. 48°19N 18°4E 17 D10
Nitra → Slovak Rep. 47°46N 18°10E 17 E10
Niue Pac. Oc. 19°2S 169°54W 65 J11
Niut Indonesia 0°55N 110°6E 36 D4
Niuzhuang China 40°58N 122°28E 35 D12
Nivala Finland 63°56N 24°57E 8 E21
Nivelles Belgium 50°35N 4°20E 15 D4
Nivernais France 47°15N 3°30E 20 C5
Niverville Canada 49°36N 97°3W 71 D9
Niwas India 23°3N 80°26E 43 H9
Nixa U.S.A. 37°3N 93°18W 80 G7
Nixon U.S.A. 29°16N 97°46W 84 G6
Nizamabad India 18°45N 78°7E 40 K11
Nizamghat India 28°20N 95°45E 41 E19
Nizhne Kolymsk Russia 68°34N 160°55E 29 C17
Nizhnekamsk Russia 55°38N 51°49E 18 C9
Nizhneudinsk Russia 54°54N 99°3E 29 D10
Nizhnevartovsk Russia 60°56N 76°38E 28 C8
Nizhniy Bestyakh Russia 61°57N 129°54E 29 C13
Nizhniy Novgorod Russia 56°20N 44°0E 18 C7
Nizhniy Tagil Russia 57°55N 59°57E 18 C10
Nizhyn Ukraine 51°5N 31°55E 19 D5
Nizip Turkey 37°5N 37°50E 44 B3
Nízké Tatry Slovak Rep. 48°55N 19°30E 17 D10
Nizwá Oman 22°56N 57°32E 47 C6
Njakwa Malawi 11°1S 33°56E 55 E3
Njanji Zambia 14°25S 31°46E 55 E3
Njazidja = Grande Comore Comoros Is. 11°35S 43°20E 53 a
Njinjo Tanzania 8°48S 38°54E 55 D4
Njombe Tanzania 9°20S 34°50E 55 D3
Njombe → Tanzania 6°56S 35°6E 54 D4
Nkana Zambia 12°50S 28°8E 55 E2
Nkandla S. Africa 28°37S 31°5E 57 D5
Nkawkaw Ghana 6°36N 0°49W 50 G5
Nkayi Zimbabwe 19°41S 29°20E 55 F2
Nkhotakota Malawi 12°56S 34°15E 55 E3
Nkhotakota ⌓ Malawi 12°50S 34°0E 55 E3
Nkondwe Tanzania 5°51S 30°51E 54 D3
Nkongsamba Cameroon 4°55N 9°55E 52 D1
Nkurenkuru Namibia 17°42S 18°32E 56 B2
Nmai → Burma 25°30N 97°25E 41 G20
Noakhali Bangla. 22°48N 91°10E 41 H17
Nobel Canada 45°25N 80°6W 82 A4
Nobeoka Japan 32°36N 131°41E 31 H5
Noblesville U.S.A. 40°3N 86°1W 80 E10
Noboribetsu Japan 42°24N 141°6E 30 C10
Noccundra Australia 27°50S 142°36E 63 D3
Nocera Inferiore Italy 40°44N 14°38E 22 D6
Nocona U.S.A. 33°47N 97°44W 84 E6
Noda Japan 35°56N 139°52E 31 G9
Nogales Mexico 31°19N 110°56W 86 A2
Nogales U.S.A. 31°21N 110°56W 77 L8
Nōgata Japan 33°48N 130°44E 31 H5
Noggerup Australia 33°32S 116°5E 61 F2
Noginsk Russia 64°30N 90°50E 29 C10
Nogliki Russia 51°50N 143°10E 29 D15
Nogoa → Australia 23°40S 147°55E 62 C4
Nogoyá Argentina 32°24S 59°48W 94 C4
Nohar India 29°11N 74°49E 42 E6
Nohta India 23°40N 79°34E 43 H8
Noires, Mts. France 48°11N 3°40W 20 B2
Noirmoutier, Î. de France 46°58N 2°10W 20 C2
Nojane Botswana 23°15S 20°14E 56 C3
Nojima-Zaki Japan 34°54N 139°53E 31 G9
Nok Kundi Pakistan 28°50N 62°45E 40 E3
Nok Ta Phao, Ko Thailand 9°23N 99°40E 39 b
Nokaneng Botswana 19°40S 22°17E 56 B3
Nokia Finland 61°30N 23°30E 8 F20
Nokomis Canada 51°35N 105°0W 71 C8
Nokomis L. Canada 57°0N 103°0W 71 B8
Nola C.A.R. 3°35N 16°4E 52 D3
Noma Omuramba → Namibia 18°52S 20°53E 56 B3
Nombre de Dios Panama 9°34N 79°28W 88 E4
Nome U.S.A. 64°30N 165°25W 74 C6
Nomo-Zaki Japan 32°35N 129°44E 31 H4
Nomuka Tonga 20°17S 174°48W 59 c
Nomuka Group Tonga 20°20S 174°48W 59 c
Nonacho L. Canada 61°42N 109°40W 71 A7
Nonda Australia 20°40S 142°28E 62 C3
Nong Chang Thailand 15°23N 99°51E 38 E2
Nong Het Laos 19°29N 103°59E 38 C4
Nong Khai Thailand 17°50N 102°46E 38 D4
Nong'an China 44°25N 125°5E 35 B13
Nongoma S. Africa 27°58S 31°35E 57 D5
Nongsa Indonesia 1°11N 104°8E 39 d
Nonoava Mexico 27°28N 106°44W 86 B3
Nonsan S. Korea 36°12N 127°5E 35 F14
Nonthaburi Thailand 13°50N 100°29E 38 F3
Noonamah Australia 12°40S 131°4E 60 B5
Noondie, L. Australia 28°30S 119°30E 61 E2
Noonkanbah ☼ Australia 18°30S 124°50E 60 C3
Noord Brabant □ Neths. 51°40N 5°0E 15 C5
Noord Holland □ Neths. 52°30N 4°45E 15 B4
Noordbeveland Neths. 51°35N 3°50E 15 C3
Noordoostpolder Neths. 52°45N 5°45E 15 B5
Noordwijk Neths. 52°14N 4°26E 15 B4
Noosa Heads Australia 26°25S 153°6E 63 D5
Nootka I. Canada 49°32N 126°42W 70 D3
Nopiming ⌓ Canada 50°30N 95°37W 71 C9
Noralee Canada 53°59N 126°26W 70 C3
Noranda = Rouyn-Noranda Canada 48°20N 79°0W 72 C4
Norco U.S.A. 33°56N 117°33W 79 M9
Nord-Kivu □ Dem. Rep. of the Congo 1°0S 29°0E 54 C2
Nord-Ostsee-Kanal Germany 54°12N 9°32E 16 A5
Nordaustlandet Svalbard 79°14N 23°0E 4 B9
Nordegg Canada 52°29N 116°5W 70 C5
Norderney Germany 53°42N 7°9E 16 B4
Norderstedt Germany 53°42N 10°1E 16 B5
Nordfjord Norway 61°55N 5°30E 8 F11
Nordfriesische Inseln Germany 54°40N 8°20E 16 A5
Nordhausen Germany 51°30N 10°47E 16 C6
Norðoyar Færoe Is. 62°17N 6°35W 8 E9
Nordkapp Norway 71°10N 25°50E 8 A21
Nordkapp Svalbard 80°31N 20°0E 4 A9
Nordkinnhalvøya Norway 70°55N 27°40E 8 A22
Nordrhein-Westfalen □ Germany 51°45N 7°30E 16 C4
Nordvik Russia 74°2N 111°32E 29 B12
Nore → Ireland 52°25N 6°58W 10 D4
Noreland Canada 44°43N 78°48W 82 B6
Norfolk = Simcoe Canada 42°50N 80°23W 82 D4
Norfolk N.Y., U.S.A. 44°48N 74°59W 83 B10
Norfolk Nebr., U.S.A. 42°2N 97°25W 80 D5
Norfolk Va., U.S.A. 36°50N 76°17W 81 G15
Norfolk □ U.K. 52°39N 0°54E 13 E8
Norfolk Broads △ U.K. 52°45N 1°30E 13 E9
Norfolk I. Pac. Oc. 28°58S 168°3E 58 D9
Norfolk Ridge Pac. Oc. 29°0S 168°0E 64 K8
Norfork L. U.S.A. 36°15N 92°14W 84 C8
Norge = Norway ■ Europe 63°0N 11°0E 8 E14
Norilsk Russia 69°20N 88°6E 29 C9

Norma, Mt. *Australia* 20°55S 140°42E **62 C3**
Normal *U.S.A.* 40°31N 88°59W **80 E9**
Norman *U.S.A.* 35°13N 97°26W **84 D6**
Norman → *Australia* 19°18S 141°51E **62 B3**
Norman Wells *Canada* 65°17N 126°51W **68 D6**
Normanby → *Australia* 14°23S 144°10E **62 A3**
Normandie *France* 48°45N 0°10E **20 B4**
Normandin *Canada* 48°49N 72°31W **72 C5**
Normandy = Normandie
　France 48°45N 0°10E **20 B4**
Normanhurst, Mt.
　Australia 25°4S 122°30E **61 E3**
Normanton *Australia* 17°40S 141°10E **62 B3**
Normétal *Canada* 49°0N 79°22W **72 C4**
Norquay *Canada* 51°53N 102°5W **71 C8**
Norquinco *Argentina* 41°51S 70°55W **96 E2**
Norrbottens län □
　Sweden 66°50N 20°0E **8 C19**
Norris Point *Canada* 49°31N 57°53W **73 C8**
Norristown *U.S.A.* 40°7N 75°21W **83 F9**
Norrköping *Sweden* 58°37N 16°11E **9 G17**
Norrland *Sweden* 62°15N 15°45E **8 E16**
Norrtälje *Sweden* 59°46N 18°42E **9 G18**
Norseman *Australia* 32°8S 121°43E **61 F3**
Norsk *Russia* 52°30N 130°5E **29 D14**
Norte, Pta. del *Canary Is.* 27°51N 17°57W **24 G2**
Norte, Serra do *Brazil* 11°20S 59°0W **92 F7**
North, C. *Canada* 47°2N 60°20W **73 C7**
North Adams *U.S.A.* 42°42N 73°7W **83 D11**
North America 40°0N 100°0W **66 F10**
North Arm *Canada* 62°0N 114°30W **70 A5**
North Augusta *U.S.A.* 33°30N 81°59W **85 E14**
North Australian Basin
　Ind. Oc. 14°30S 116°30E **60 B2**
North Ayrshire □ *U.K.* 55°45N 4°44W **11 F4**
North Bass I. *U.S.A.* 41°40N 82°56W **82 E2**
North Battleford
　Canada 52°50N 108°17W **71 C7**
North Bay *Canada* 46°20N 79°30W **72 C4**
North Belcher Is. *Canada* 56°50N 79°50W **72 A4**
North Bend *Oreg.,*
　U.S.A. 43°24N 124°14W **76 E1**
North Bend *Pa., U.S.A.* 41°20N 77°42W **82 E7**
North Bend *Wash.,*
　U.S.A. 47°30N 121°47W **78 C5**
North Bennington
　U.S.A. 42°56N 73°15W **83 D11**
North Berwick *U.K.* 56°4N 2°42W **11 E6**
North Berwick *U.S.A.* 43°18N 70°44W **83 C14**
North Bruce *Canada* 44°22N 81°26W **82 B3**
North C. *Canada* 47°5N 64°0W **73 C7**
North C. *N.Z.* 34°23S 173°4E **59 A4**
North Canadian →
　U.S.A. 35°22N 95°37W **84 D7**
North Canton *U.S.A.* 40°53N 81°24W **82 F3**
North Cape = Nordkapp
　Norway 71°10N 25°50E **8 A21**
North Caribou L.
　Canada 52°50N 90°40W **72 B1**
North Carolina □
　U.S.A. 35°30N 80°0W **85 D15**
North Cascades △
　U.S.A. 48°45N 121°10W **76 B3**
North Channel *Canada* 46°0N 83°0W **72 C3**
North Channel *U.K.* 55°13N 5°52W **11 F3**
North Charleston
　U.S.A. 32°53N 79°58W **85 E15**
North Chicago *U.S.A.* 42°19N 87°51W **80 D10**
North Collins *U.S.A.* 42°35N 78°56W **82 D6**
North Creek *U.S.A.* 43°42N 73°59W **83 C11**
North Dakota □
　U.S.A. 47°30N 100°15W **80 B3**
North Downs *U.K.* 51°19N 0°21E **13 F8**
North East *U.S.A.* 42°13N 79°50W **82 D5**
North East Frontier Agency =
　Arunachal Pradesh □
　India 28°0N 95°0E **41 F19**
North East Lincolnshire □
　U.K. 53°34N 0°2W **12 D7**
North Eastern □ *Kenya* 1°30N 40°0E **54 B5**
North Esk → *U.K.* 56°46N 2°24W **11 E6**
North European Plain
　Europe 55°0N 25°0E **6 E10**
North Foreland *U.K.* 51°22N 1°28E **13 F9**
North Fork *U.S.A.* 37°14N 119°21W **78 H7**
North Fork American →
　U.S.A. 38°57N 120°59W **78 G5**
North Fork Feather →
　U.S.A. 38°33N 121°30W **78 F5**
North Fork Grand →
　U.S.A. 45°47N 102°16W **80 C2**
North Fork Red →
　U.S.A. 34°24N 99°14W **84 D5**
North Frisian Is. = Nordfriesische
　Inseln *Germany* 54°40N 8°20E **16 A5**
North Gower *Canada* 45°8N 75°43W **83 A9**
North Hd. *Australia* 30°14S 114°59E **61 F1**
North Henik L. *Canada* 61°45N 97°40W **71 A9**
North Highlands
　U.S.A. 38°40N 121°23W **78 G5**
North Horr *Kenya* 3°20N 37°8E **54 B4**
North I. *Kenya* 4°5N 36°5E **54 B4**
North I. *N.Z.* 38°0S 175°0E **59 C5**
North I. *Seychelles* 3°35S 5°3b
North Kingsville *U.S.A.* 41°54N 80°42W **82 E4**
North Kitui □ *Kenya* 0°15S 38°29E **54 C4**
North Knife → *Canada* 58°53N 94°45W **71 B10**
North Koel → *India* 24°45N 83°50E **43 G10**
North Korea ■ *Asia* 40°0N 127°0E **35 E14**
North Lakhimpur *India* 27°14N 94°7E **41 F19**
North Lanarkshire □
　U.K. 55°52N 3°56W **11 F5**
North Las Vegas *U.S.A.* 36°11N 115°7W **79 J11**
North Lincolnshire □
　U.K. 53°36N 0°30W **12 D7**
North Little Rock
　U.S.A. 34°45N 92°16W **84 D8**
North Loup → *U.S.A.* 41°17N 98°24W **80 E4**
North Luangwa △ *Zambia* 11°49S 32°9E **55 E3**

North Magnetic Pole
　Canada 82°42N 114°24W **4 A2**
North Mankato *U.S.A.* 44°10N 94°2W **80 C6**
North Minch *U.K.* 58°5N 5°55W **11 C3**
North Moose L. *Canada* 54°4N 100°12W **71 C8**
North Myrtle Beach
　U.S.A. 33°48N 78°42W **85 E15**
North Nahanni →
　Canada 62°15N 123°20W **70 A4**
North Olmsted *U.S.A.* 41°25N 81°56W **82 E3**
North Ossetia □ *Russia* 43°30N 44°30E **19 F7**
North Pagai, I. = Pagai Utara,
　Pulau *Indonesia* 2°35S 100°0E **36 E2**
North Palisade *U.S.A.* 37°6N 118°31W **78 H8**
North Platte *U.S.A.* 41°8N 100°46W **80 E3**
North Platte → *U.S.A.* 41°7N 100°42W **80 E3**
North Pole *Arctic* 90°0N 0°0 **4 A**
North Portal *Canada* 49°0N 102°33W **71 D8**
North Powder *U.S.A.* 45°2N 117°55W **76 D5**
North Pt. *Barbados* 13°20N 59°37W **89 g**
North Pt. *Trin. & Tob.* 11°21N 60°31W **93 J16**
North Pt. *U.S.A.* 45°2N 83°16W **82 A1**
North Rhine Westphalia =
　Nordrhein-Westfalen □
　Germany 51°45N 7°30E **16 C4**
North River *Canada* 53°49N 57°6W **73 B8**
North Ronaldsay *U.K.* 59°22N 2°26W **11 B6**
North Saskatchewan →
　Canada 53°15N 105°5W **71 C7**
North Sea *Europe* 56°0N 4°0E **6 D6**
North Seal → *Canada* 58°50N 98°7W **71 B9**
North Slope ☆ *U.S.A.* 69°15N 152°0W **74 B9**
North Somerset □ *U.K.* 51°24N 2°45W **13 F5**
North Sydney *Canada* 46°12N 60°15W **73 C7**
North Syracuse *U.S.A.* 43°8N 76°7W **83 C8**
North Taranaki Bight
　N.Z. 38°50S 174°15E **59 C5**
North Thompson →
　Canada 50°40N 120°20W **70 C4**
North Tonawanda
　U.S.A. 43°2N 78°53W **82 C6**
North Troy *U.S.A.* 45°0N 72°24W **83 B12**
North Twin I. *Canada* 53°20N 80°0W **72 B4**
North Tyne → *U.K.* 55°0N 2°8W **12 C5**
North Uist *U.K.* 57°40N 7°15W **11 D1**
North Vancouver
　Canada 49°19N 123°4W **78 A3**
North Vernon *U.S.A.* 39°0N 85°38W **81 F11**
North Wabasca L.
　Canada 56°0N 113°55W **70 B6**
North Walsham *U.K.* 52°50N 1°22E **12 E9**
North West = Severo-Zapadnyy □
　Russia 65°0N 40°0E **28 C4**
North-West □ *S. Africa* 27°0S 25°0E **56 D4**
North West C. *Australia* 21°45S 114°9E **60 D1**
North West Frontier □
　Pakistan 34°0N 72°0E **42 C4**
North West Highlands
　U.K. 57°33N 4°58W **11 D4**
North West River
　Canada 53°30N 60°10W **73 B7**
North Western □ *Zambia* 13°30S 25°30E **55 E2**
North Wildwood *U.S.A.* 39°0N 74°48W **81 F16**
North York Moors *U.K.* 54°23N 0°53W **12 C7**
North York Moors △
　U.K. 54°27N 0°51W **12 C7**
North Yorkshire □ *U.K.* 54°15N 1°25W **12 C6**
Northallerton *U.K.* 54°20N 1°26W **12 C6**
Northam *Australia* 31°35S 116°42E **61 F2**
Northam *S. Africa* 24°56S 27°18E **56 C4**
Northampton *Australia* 28°27S 114°33E **61 E1**
Northampton *U.K.* 52°15N 0°53W **13 E7**
Northampton *Mass.,*
　U.S.A. 42°19N 72°38W **83 D12**
Northampton *Pa.,*
　U.S.A. 40°41N 75°30W **83 F9**
Northamptonshire □
　U.K. 52°16N 0°55W **13 E7**
Northbridge *U.S.A.* 42°9N 71°39W **83 D13**
Northbrook *Canada* 44°44N 77°9W **82 B7**
Northcliffe *Australia* 34°39S 116°7E **61 F2**
Northeast Pacific Basin
　Pac. Oc. 32°0N 145°0W **65 D13**
Northeast Providence Chan.
　W. Indies 26°0N 76°0W **88 A4**
Northern = Limpopo □
　S. Africa 24°5S 29°0E **57 C4**
Northern □ *Malawi* 11°0S 34°0E **55 E3**
Northern □ *Zambia* 10°30S 31°0E **55 E3**
Northern Areas □
　Pakistan 36°30N 73°0E **43 A5**
Northern Cape □ *S. Africa* 30°0S 20°0E **56 D3**
Northern Circars *India* 17°30N 82°30E **41 L13**
Northern Indian L.
　Canada 57°20N 97°20W **71 B9**
Northern Ireland □ *U.K.* 54°45N 7°0W **10 B5**
Northern Lau Group
　Fiji 17°30S 178°59W **59 a**
Northern Light L.
　Canada 48°15N 90°39W **72 C1**
Northern Marianas ☑
　Pac. Oc. 17°0N 145°0E **64 F6**
Northern Province □
　S. Africa 24°0S 29°0E **57 C4**
Northern Range
　Trin. & Tob. 10°46N 61°15W **93 K15**
Northern Sporades
　Greece 39°15N 23°30E **23 E10**
Northern Territory □
　Australia 20°0S 133°0E **60 D5**
Northfield *Minn., U.S.A.* 44°27N 93°9W **80 C7**
Northfield *Vt., U.S.A.* 44°9N 72°40W **83 B12**
Northland □ *N.Z.* 35°30S 173°30E **59 A4**
Northome *U.S.A.* 47°52N 94°17W **80 B6**
Northport *Ala., U.S.A.* 33°14N 87°35W **85 E11**
Northport *Wash.,*
　U.S.A. 48°55N 117°48W **76 B5**
Northumberland □ *U.K.* 55°12N 2°0W **12 B6**

Northumberland, C.
　Australia 38°5S 140°40E **63 F3**
Northumberland Is.
　Australia 21°30S 149°50E **62 C4**
Northumberland Str.
　Canada 46°20N 64°0W **73 C7**
Northville *Canada* 43°10N 81°56W **82 C3**
Northville *U.S.A.* 43°13N 74°11W **83 C10**
Northwest Pacific Basin
　Pac. Oc. 32°0N 165°0E **64 D8**
Northwest Providence Channel
　W. Indies 26°0N 78°0W **88 A4**
Northwest Territories □
　Canada 63°0N 118°0W **68 C8**
Northwich *U.K.* 53°15N 2°31W **12 D5**
Northwood *Iowa, U.S.A.* 43°27N 93°13W **80 D7**
Northwood *N. Dak.,*
　U.S.A. 47°44N 97°34W **80 B5**
Norton *U.S.A.* 39°50N 99°53W **80 F4**
Norton *Zimbabwe* 17°52S 30°40E **55 F3**
Norton Sd. *U.S.A.* 63°50N 164°0W **74 C7**
Norwalk *Calif., U.S.A.* 33°54N 118°4W **79 M8**
Norwalk *Conn., U.S.A.* 41°7N 73°22W **83 E11**
Norwalk *Iowa, U.S.A.* 41°29N 93°41W **80 E7**
Norwalk *Ohio, U.S.A.* 41°15N 82°37W **82 E2**
Norway *Maine, U.S.A.* 44°13N 70°32W **81 C18**
Norway *Mich., U.S.A.* 45°47N 87°55W **80 C10**
Norway ■ *Europe* 63°0N 11°0E **8 E14**
Norway House *Canada* 53°59N 97°50W **71 C9**
Norwegian B. *Canada* 77°30N 90°0W **69 B14**
Norwegian Basin *Atl. Oc.* 68°0N 2°0W **4 C7**
Norwegian Sea *Atl. Oc.* 66°0N 1°0E **6 B6**
Norwich *Canada* 42°59N 80°36W **82 D4**
Norwich *U.K.* 52°38N 1°18E **13 E9**
Norwich *Conn., U.S.A.* 41°31N 72°5W **83 E12**
Norwich *N.Y., U.S.A.* 42°32N 75°32W **83 D9**
Norwood *Canada* 44°23N 77°59W **82 B7**
Norwood *U.S.A.* 44°45N 75°0W **83 B9**
Nosappu-Misaki *Japan* 45°26N 141°39E **30 C12**
Noshiro *Japan* 40°12N 140°0E **30 D10**
Noṣratābād *Iran* 29°55N 60°0E **45 D8**
Noss Hd. *U.K.* 58°28N 3°3W **11 C5**
Nossob → *S. Africa* 26°55S 20°45E **56 D3**
Nosy Barren *Madag.* 18°25S 43°40E **53 H8**
Nosy Bé *Madag.* 13°25S 48°15E **53 G9**
Nosy Boraha *Madag.* 16°50S 49°55E **57 B8**
Nosy Lava *Madag.* 14°33S 47°36E **57 A8**
Nosy Varika *Madag.* 20°35S 48°32E **57 C8**
Noteć → *Poland* 52°44N 15°26E **16 B8**
Notikewin → *Canada* 57°2N 117°38W **70 B5**
Notodden *Norway* 59°35N 9°17E **9 G13**
Notre Dame B. *Canada* 49°45N 55°30W **73 C8**
Notre-Dame-de-Koartac =
　Quaqtaq *Canada* 60°55N 69°40W **69 E18**
Notre-Dame-des-Bois
　Canada 45°24N 71°4W **83 A13**
Notre-Dame-d'Ivugivic = Ivujivik
　Canada 62°24N 77°55W **69 E16**
Notre-Dame-du-Nord
　Canada 47°36N 79°30W **72 C4**
Nottawasaga B. *Canada* 44°35N 80°15W **82 B4**
Nottaway → *Canada* 51°22N 78°55W **72 B4**
Nottingham *U.K.* 52°58N 1°10W **12 E6**
Nottingham, City of □
　U.K. 52°58N 1°10W **12 E6**
Nottingham I. *Canada* 63°20N 77°55W **69 E16**
Nottinghamshire □ *U.K.* 53°10N 1°3W **12 D6**
Nottoway → *U.S.A.* 36°33N 76°55W **81 G15**
Notwane → *Botswana* 23°35S 26°58E **56 C4**
Nouâdhibou *Mauritania* 20°54N 17°0W **50 D2**
Nouâdhibou, Râs
　Mauritania 20°50N 17°0W **50 D2**
Nouakchott *Mauritania* 18°9N 15°58W **50 E2**
Nouméa *N. Cal.* 22°17S 166°30E **58 D9**
Noupoort *S. Africa* 31°10S 24°57E **56 E3**
Nouveau Comptoir = Wemindji
　Canada 53°0N 78°49W **72 B4**
Nouvelle Amsterdam, Î.
　Ind. Oc. 38°30S 77°30E **3 F13**
Nouvelle-Calédonie = New
　Caledonia ☑ *Pac. Oc.* 21°0S 165°0E **58 D9**
Nova Esperança *Brazil* 23°8S 52°24W **95 A5**
Nova Friburgo *Brazil* 22°16S 42°30W **95 A7**
Nova Iguaçu *Brazil* 22°45S 43°28W **95 A7**
Nova Iorque *Brazil* 7°0S 44°5W **93 E10**
Nova Lamego
　Guinea-Biss. 12°19N 14°11W **50 F3**
Nova Lusitânia *Mozam.* 19°50S 34°34E **55 F3**
Nova Mambone *Mozam.* 21°0S 35°3E **57 C6**
Nova Scotia □ *Canada* 45°10N 63°0W **73 C7**
Nova Sofala *Mozam.* 20°7S 34°42E **57 C5**
Nova Venécia *Brazil* 18°45S 40°24W **93 G10**
Nova Zagora *Bulgaria* 42°32N 26°1E **23 C11**
Novar *Canada* 45°27N 79°15W **82 A5**
Novara *Italy* 45°28N 8°38E **20 D8**
Novato *U.S.A.* 38°6N 122°35W **78 G4**
Novaya Ladoga *Russia* 60°7N 32°16E **18 B5**
Novaya Lyalya *Russia* 59°4N 60°45E **18 C11**
Novaya Sibir, Ostrov
　Russia 75°10N 150°0E **29 B16**
Novaya Zemlya *Russia* 75°0N 56°0E **28 B6**
Nové Zámky *Slovak Rep.* 48°2N 18°8E **17 D10**
Novgorod *Russia* 58°30N 31°25E **18 C5**
Novgorod-Severskiy = Novhorod-
　Siverskyy *Ukraine* 52°2N 33°10E **18 D5**
Novhorod-Siverskyy
　Ukraine 52°2N 33°10E **18 D5**
Novi Lígure *Italy* 44°46N 8°47E **20 D8**
Novi Pazar *Serbia* 43°12N 20°28E **23 C9**
Novi Sad *Serbia* 45°18N 19°52E **23 B8**
Novo Hamburgo *Brazil* 29°37S 51°7W **95 B5**
Novo Mesto *Slovenia* 45°47N 15°12E **20 B6**
Novoaltaysk *Russia* 53°30N 84°0E **28 D9**
Novocherkassk *Russia* 47°27N 40°15E **19 E7**
Novodvinsk *Russia* 64°25N 40°42E **18 B7**
Novogrudok = Navahrudak
　Belarus 53°40N 25°50E **17 B13**
Novohrad-Volynskyy
　Ukraine 50°34N 27°35E **17 C14**

Novokachalinsk *Russia* 45°5N 132°0E **30 B5**
Novokuybyshevsk *Russia* 53°7N 49°58E **18 D8**
Novokuznetsk *Russia* 53°45N 87°10E **28 D9**
Novolazarevskaya
　Antarctica 71°0S 12°0E **5 D3**
Novomoskovsk *Russia* 54°5N 38°15E **18 D6**
Novorossiysk *Russia* 44°43N 37°46E **19 F6**
Novorybnoye *Russia* 72°50N 105°50E **29 B11**
Novoselytsya *Ukraine* 48°14N 26°15E **17 D14**
Novoshakhtinsk *Russia* 47°46N 39°58E **19 E6**
Novosibirsk *Russia* 55°0N 83°5E **28 D9**
Novosibirskiye Ostrova
　Russia 75°0N 142°0E **29 B15**
Novotroitsk *Russia* 51°10N 58°15E **18 D10**
Novouzensk *Russia* 50°32N 48°17E **19 D8**
Novovolynsk *Ukraine* 50°45N 24°4E **17 C13**
Novska *Croatia* 45°19N 17°0E **22 B7**
Novvy Bor *Russia* 66°43N 52°19E **18 A9**
Novyy Port *Russia* 67°40N 72°30E **28 C8**
Novyy Urengoy *Russia* 65°48N 76°52E **28 C8**
Nowa Sól *Poland* 51°48N 15°44E **16 C8**
Nowata *U.S.A.* 36°42N 95°38W **84 C7**
Nowbarān *Iran* 35°8N 49°42E **45 C6**
Nowghāb *Iran* 33°53N 59°4E **45 C8**
Nowgong *Assam, India* 26°20N 92°50E **41 F18**
Nowgong *Mad. P., India* 25°4N 79°27E **43 G8**
Nowra *Australia* 34°53S 150°35E **63 E5**
Nowshera *Pakistan* 34°0N 72°0E **40 C8**
Nowy Sącz *Poland* 49°40N 20°41E **17 D11**
Nowy Targ *Poland* 49°29N 20°2E **17 D11**
Nowy Tomyśl *Poland* 52°19N 16°10E **16 B9**
Noxen *U.S.A.* 41°25N 76°4W **83 E8**
Noyabr'sk *Russia* 64°34N 76°21E **28 C8**
Noyon *France* 49°34N 2°59E **20 B5**
Noyon *Mongolia* 43°2N 102°4E **34 C2**
Nqutu *S. Africa* 28°13S 30°32E **57 D5**
Nsanje *Malawi* 16°55S 35°12E **55 F4**
Nsawam *Ghana* 5°50N 0°24W **50 G5**
Nseluka *Zambia* 9°58S 31°16E **55 D3**
Nsomba *Zambia* 10°45S 29°51E **55 E2**
Ntaria ☉ *Australia* 24°0S 132°41E **60 D5**
Ntungamo *Uganda* 0°56S 30°17E **54 C3**
Nu Jiang → *China* 29°58N 97°25E **32 D4**
Nu Shan *China* 26°0N 99°20E **41 G21**
Nuba Mts. = Nubah, Jibalan
　Sudan 12°0N 31°0E **51 F12**
Nubah, Jibalan *Sudan* 12°0N 31°0E **51 F12**
Nubia *Africa* 21°0N 32°0E **48 D7**
Nubian Desert = Nûbîya, Es Sahrâ
　en *Sudan* 21°30N 33°30E **51 D12**
Nûbîya, Es Sahrâ en
　Sudan 21°30N 33°30E **51 D12**
Nuboai *Indonesia* 2°10S 136°30E **37 E9**
Nubra → *India* 34°35N 77°35E **43 B7**
Nueces → *U.S.A.* 27°51N 97°30W **84 H6**
Nueltin L. *Canada* 60°30N 99°30W **71 A9**
Nuestra Señora del Rosario de
　Caá-Catí *Argentina* 27°45S 57°36W **94 B4**
Nueva Ciudad Guerrero
　Mexico 26°34N 99°12W **87 B5**
Nueva Gerona *Cuba* 21°53N 82°49W **88 B3**
Nueva Palmira *Uruguay* 33°52S 58°20W **94 C4**
Nueva Rosita *Mexico* 27°57N 101°13W **86 B4**
Nueva San Salvador
　El Salv. 13°40N 89°18W **88 D2**
Nuéve de Julio *Argentina* 35°30S 61°0W **94 D3**
Nuevitas *Cuba* 21°30N 77°20W **88 B4**
Nuevo, G. *Argentina* 43°0S 64°30W **96 E4**
Nuevo Casas Grandes
　Mexico 30°25N 107°55W **86 A3**
Nuevo Laredo *Mexico* 27°30N 99°31W **87 B5**
Nuevo León □ *Mexico* 25°20N 100°0W **86 C5**
Nuevo Rocafuerte
　Ecuador 0°55S 75°27W **92 D3**
Nugget Pt. *N.Z.* 46°27S 169°50E **59 G2**
Nuhaka *N.Z.* 39°3S 177°45E **59 C6**
Nukey Bluff *Australia* 32°26S 135°29E **63 E2**
Nukhayb *Iraq* 32°4N 42°3E **44 C4**
Nuku Hiva
　French Polynesia 8°54S 140°6W **65 H13**
Nuku'alofa *Tonga* 21°10S 175°12W **59 c**
Nukus *Uzbekistan* 42°27N 59°41E **28 E6**
Nulato *U.S.A.* 64°43N 158°6W **74 C8**
Nullagine *Australia* 21°53S 120°7E **60 D3**
Nullagine → *Australia* 21°20S 120°20E **60 D3**
Nullarbor *Australia* 31°28S 130°55E **61 F5**
Nullarbor △ *Australia* 32°39S 130°0E **61 F5**
Nullarbor Plain *Australia* 31°10S 129°0E **61 F4**
Numalla, L. *Australia* 28°43S 144°20E **63 D3**
Numan *Nigeria* 9°29N 12°3E **51 G8**
Numata *Japan* 36°45N 139°4E **31 F9**
Numazu *Japan* 35°7N 138°51E **31 G9**
Numbulwar *Australia* 14°15S 135°45E **62 A2**
Numfoor *Indonesia* 1°0S 134°50E **37 E8**
Numurkah *Australia* 36°5S 145°26E **63 F4**
Nunaksaluk I. *Canada* 55°49N 60°20W **73 A7**
Nunap Isua *Greenland* 59°48N 43°55W **66 D15**
Nunavik *Greenland* 71°50N 54°25W **69 C21**
Nunavut □ *Canada* 66°0N 85°0W **69 D15**
Nunda *U.S.A.* 42°35N 77°56W **82 D7**
Nuneaton *U.K.* 52°32N 1°27W **13 E6**
Nungarin *Australia* 31°12S 118°6E **61 F2**
Nungo *Mozam.* 13°23S 37°43E **55 E4**
Nungwe *Tanzania* 2°48S 32°2E **54 C3**
Nunivak I. *U.S.A.* 60°10N 166°30W **74 C6**
Nunkun *India* 33°57N 76°2E **43 C7**
Núoro *Italy* 40°20N 9°20E **22 D3**
Nūr *Iran* 36°33N 52°1E **45 B7**
Nūrābād *Hormozgān, Iran* 27°47N 57°12E **45 E8**
Nūrābād *Lorestān, Iran* 34°5N 47°58E **44 C5**
Nuremberg = Nürnberg
　Germany 49°27N 11°3E **16 D6**
Nuri *Mexico* 28°5N 109°22W **86 B3**
Nuriootpa *Australia* 34°27S 139°0E **63 E2**
Nuristān □ *Afghan.* 35°20N 71°0E **40 B7**
Nurmes *Finland* 63°33N 29°10E **8 E23**
Nürnberg *Germany* 49°27N 11°3E **16 D6**

Nurpur *Pakistan* 31°53N 71°54E **42 D4**
Nurran, L. = Terewah, L.
　Australia 29°52S 147°35E **63 D4**
Nurrari Lakes *Australia* 29°1S 130°5E **61 E5**
Nusa Barung *Indonesia* 8°30S 113°30E **37 H15**
Nusa Dua *Indonesia* 8°48S 115°14E **37 K18**
Nusa Kambangan
　Indonesia 7°40S 108°10E **37 G13**
Nusa Tenggara Barat □
　Indonesia 8°50S 117°30E **36 F5**
Nusa Tenggara Timur □
　Indonesia 9°30S 122°0E **37 F6**
Nusaybin *Turkey* 37°3N 41°10E **19 G7**
Nushki *Pakistan* 29°35N 66°0E **42 E2**
Nuuk *Greenland* 64°10N 51°35W **67 C14**
Nuupere, Pte. *Moorea* 17°36S 149°47W **59 d**
Nuwakot *Nepal* 28°10N 83°55E **43 E10**
Nuwaybi', W. an □
　Si. Arabia 29°18N 34°57E **46 F3**
Nuweiba' *Egypt* 28°59N 34°39E **46 F3**
Nuwerus *S. Africa* 31°8S 18°24E **56 E2**
Nuweveldberge *S. Africa* 32°10S 21°45E **56 E3**
Nuyts, Pt. *Australia* 35°4S 116°38E **61 G2**
Nuyts Arch. *Australia* 32°35S 133°20E **63 E1**
Nxai Pan △ *Botswana* 19°50S 24°46E **56 B3**
Nxaunxau *Botswana* 18°57S 21°4E **56 B3**
Nyabing *Australia* 33°33S 118°9E **61 F2**
Nyagan *Russia* 62°30N 65°38E **28 C7**
Nyahanga *Tanzania* 2°20S 33°37E **54 C3**
Nyahua *Tanzania* 5°25S 33°23E **54 D3**
Nyahururu *Kenya* 0°2N 36°27E **54 B4**
Nyainqêntanglha Shan
　China 30°0N 90°0E **32 D3**
Nyakanazi *Tanzania* 3°2S 31°10E **54 C3**
Nyâlâ *Sudan* 12°2N 24°58E **51 F10**
Nyamandhlovu
　Zimbabwe 19°55S 28°16E **55 F2**
Nyambiti *Tanzania* 2°48S 33°27E **54 C3**
Nyamira *Kenya* 0°36S 34°52E **54 C3**
Nyamwaga *Tanzania* 1°27S 34°33E **54 C3**
Nyandekwa *Tanzania* 3°57S 32°32E **54 C3**
Nyandoma *Russia* 61°40N 40°12E **18 B7**
Nyanga △ *Zimbabwe* 18°17S 32°46E **55 F3**
Nyanguge *Tanzania* 2°30S 33°12E **54 C3**
Nyanza *Rwanda* 2°20S 29°42E **54 C2**
Nyanza □ *Kenya* 0°10S 34°15E **54 C3**
Nyanza-Lac *Burundi* 4°21S 29°36E **54 C2**
Nyasa, L. = Malawi, L.
　Africa 12°30S 34°30E **55 E3**
Nyasvizh *Belarus* 53°14N 26°38E **17 B14**
Nyazepetrovsk *Russia* 56°3N 59°36E **18 C10**
Nyazura *Zimbabwe* 18°40S 32°16E **55 F3**
Nyazwidzi → *Zimbabwe* 20°0S 31°17E **55 G3**
Nybro *Sweden* 56°44N 15°55E **9 H16**
Nyda *Russia* 66°40N 72°58E **28 C8**
Nyeboe Land *Greenland* 82°0N 57°0W **69 A20**
Nyeri *Kenya* 0°23S 36°56E **54 C4**
Nyika △ *Malawi* 10°30S 33°53E **55 E3**
Nyimba *Zambia* 14°33S 30°50E **55 E3**
Nyíregyháza *Hungary* 47°58N 21°47E **17 E11**
Nyiru, Mt. *Kenya* 2°8N 36°50E **54 B4**
Nykarleby = Uusikaarlepyy
　Finland 63°32N 22°31E **8 E20**
Nykøbing *Nordjylland,*
　Denmark 56°48N 8°51E **9 H13**
Nykøbing *Sjælland,*
　Denmark 54°56N 11°52E **9 J14**
Nykøbing *Sjælland,*
　Denmark 55°55N 11°40E **9 J14**
Nyköping *Sweden* 58°45N 17°1E **9 G17**
Nylstroom = Modimolle
　S. Africa 24°42S 28°22E **57 C4**
Nymagee *Australia* 32°7S 146°20E **63 E4**
Nymboida △ *Australia* 29°38S 152°26E **63 D5**
Nynäshamn *Sweden* 58°54N 17°57E **9 G17**
Nyngan *Australia* 31°30S 147°8E **63 E4**
Nyoma Rap *India* 33°10N 78°40E **43 C8**
Nyoman = Nemunas →
　Lithuania 55°25N 21°10E **9 J19**
Nysa *Poland* 50°30N 17°22E **17 C9**
Nysa → *Europe* 52°4N 14°46E **16 B8**
Nyslott = Savonlinna
　Finland 61°52N 28°53E **8 F23**
Nyssa *U.S.A.* 43°53N 117°0W **76 E5**
Nystad = Uusikaupunki
　Finland 60°47N 21°25E **8 F19**
Nyunzu
　Dem. Rep. of the Congo 5°57S 27°58E **54 D2**
Nyurba *Russia* 63°17N 118°28E **29 C12**
Nzega *Tanzania* 4°10S 33°12E **54 C3**
Nzérékoré *Guinea* 7°49N 8°48W **50 G4**
Nzeto *Angola* 7°10S 12°52E **52 F2**
Nzilo, Chutes de
　Dem. Rep. of the Congo 10°18S 25°27E **55 E2**
Nzubuka *Tanzania* 4°45S 32°50E **54 C3**
Nzwani = Anjouan
　Comoros Is. 12°15S 44°20E **53 a**

O

O Le Pupū Pu'e △
　Samoa 13°59S 171°43W **59 b**
Ō-Shima *Hokkaidō,*
　Japan 41°30N 139°22E **30 D9**
Ō-Shima *Shizuoka, Japan* 34°44N 139°24E **31 G9**
Oa, Mull of *U.K.* 55°35N 6°20W **11 F2**
Oacoma *U.S.A.* 43°48N 99°24W **80 D4**
Oahe, L. *U.S.A.* 44°27N 100°24W **80 C3**
Oahe Dam *U.S.A.* 44°27N 100°24W **80 C4**
O'ahu *U.S.A.* 21°28N 157°58W **75 L8**
Oak Harbor *U.S.A.* 48°18N 122°39W **78 B4**
Oak Hill *U.S.A.* 37°59N 81°9W **81 G13**
Oak Island *U.S.A.* 33°55N 78°10W **85 E15**
Oak Ridge *U.S.A.* 36°1N 84°16W **85 C12**
Oak View *U.S.A.* 34°24N 119°18W **79 L7**
Oakan-Dake *Japan* 43°27N 144°10E **30 C12**

Oakdale *Calif., U.S.A.* 37°46N 120°51W **78** H6
Oakdale *La., U.S.A.* 30°49N 92°40W **84** F8
Oakes *U.S.A.* 46°8N 98°6W **80** B4
Oakesdale *U.S.A.* 47°8N 117°15W **76** C5
Oakey *Australia* 27°25S 151°43E **63** D5
Oakfield *U.S.A.* 43°4N 78°16W **82** C6
Oakham *U.K.* 52°40N 0°43W **13** E7
Oakhurst *U.S.A.* 37°19N 119°40W **78** H7
Oakland *Calif., U.S.A.* 37°48N 122°16W **78** H4
Oakland *Pa., U.S.A.* 41°57N 75°36W **83** E9
Oakley *Idaho, U.S.A.* 42°15N 113°53W **76** E7
Oakley *Kans., U.S.A.* 39°8N 100°51W **80** F4
Oakover → *Australia* 21°0S 120°40E **60** D3
Oakridge *U.S.A.* 43°45N 122°28W **76** E2
Oakville *Canada* 43°27N 79°41W **82** C5
Oakville *U.S.A.* 46°51N 123°14W **78** D3
Oamaru *N.Z.* 45°5S 170°59E **59** F3
Oasis *Calif., U.S.A.* 37°29N 117°55W **78** H9
Oasis *Calif., U.S.A.* 33°28N 116°6W **79** M10
Oates Land *Antarctica* 69°0S 160°0E **5** C11
Oatman *U.S.A.* 35°1N 114°19W **79** K12
Oaxaca *Mexico* 17°3N 96°43W **87** D5
Oaxaca □ *Mexico* 17°0N 96°30W **87** D5
Ob → *Russia* 66°45N 69°30E **28** C7
Oba *Canada* 49°4N 84°7W **72** C3
Obama *Japan* 35°30N 135°45E **31** G7
Oban *U.K.* 56°25N 5°29W **11** E3
Obbia = Hobyo
  Somali Rep. 5°25N 48°30E **47** F4
Oberá *Argentina* 27°21S 55°2W **95** B4
Oberhausen *Germany* 51°28N 6°51E **16** C4
Oberlin *Kans., U.S.A.* 39°49N 100°32W **80** F3
Oberlin *La., U.S.A.* 30°37N 92°46W **84** F8
Oberlin *Ohio, U.S.A.* 41°18N 82°13W **82** E2
Oberon *Australia* 33°45S 149°52E **63** E4
Obi, Kepulauan *Indonesia* 1°23S 127°45E **37** E7
Obihiro *Japan* 42°56N 143°12E **30** C11
Obilatu *Indonesia* 1°25S 127°20E **37** E7
Obluchye *Russia* 49°1N 131°4E **29** E14
Obo *C.A.R.* 5°20N 26°32E **54** A2
Oboyan *Russia* 51°15N 36°21E **28** D4
Obozerskaya = Obozerskiy
  Russia 63°34N 40°21E **18** B7
Obozerskiy *Russia* 63°34N 40°21E **18** B7
Observatory Inlet
  Canada 55°10N 129°54W **70** B3
Obshchi Syrt *Russia* 52°0N 53°0E **6** E16
Obskaya Guba *Russia* 69°0N 73°0E **28** C8
Obuasi *Ghana* 6°17N 1°40W **50** G5
Ocala *U.S.A.* 29°11N 82°8W **85** G13
Ocampo *Chihuahua,*
  Mexico 28°11N 108°23W **86** B3
Ocampo *Tamaulipas,*
  Mexico 22°50N 99°20W **87** C5
Ocaña *Spain* 39°55N 3°30W **21** C4
Occidental, Cordillera
  Colombia 5°0N 76°0W **92** C3
Occidental, Grand Erg
  Algeria 30°20N 1°0E **50** B6
Ocean City *Md., U.S.A.* 38°20N 75°5W **81** F16
Ocean City *N.J., U.S.A.* 39°17N 74°35W **81** F16
Ocean City *Wash.,*
  U.S.A. 47°4N 124°10W **78** C2
Ocean Falls *Canada* 52°18N 127°48W **70** C3
Ocean I. = Banaba
  Kiribati 0°45S 169°50E **64** H8
Ocean Park *U.S.A.* 46°30N 124°3W **78** D2
Oceano *U.S.A.* 35°6N 120°37W **79** K6
Oceanport *U.S.A.* 40°19N 74°3W **83** F10
Oceanside *U.S.A.* 33°12N 117°23W **79** M9
Ochil Hills *U.K.* 56°14N 3°40W **11** E5
Ocho Rios *Jamaica* 18°24N 77°6W **88** a
Ocilla *U.S.A.* 31°36N 83°15W **85** F13
Ocmulgee → *U.S.A.* 31°58N 82°33W **85** F13
Ocniţa *Moldova* 48°25N 27°30E **17** D14
Oconee → *U.S.A.* 31°58N 82°33W **85** F13
Oconomowoc *U.S.A.* 43°7N 88°30W **80** D9
Oconto *U.S.A.* 44°53N 87°52W **80** C10
Oconto Falls *U.S.A.* 44°52N 88°9W **80** C9
Ocosingo *Mexico* 16°53N 92°6W **87** D6
Ocotal *Nic.* 13°41N 86°31W **88** D2
Ocotlán *Jalisco, Mexico* 20°21N 102°46W **86** C4
Ocotlán *Oaxaca, Mexico* 16°48N 96°40W **87** D5
Ōda *Japan* 35°11N 132°30E **31** G6
Ódáðahraun *Iceland* 65°5N 17°0W **8** D5
Ōdaejin *N. Korea* 41°34N 129°40E **30** D4
Odate *Japan* 40°16N 140°34E **30** D10
Odawara *Japan* 35°20N 139°6E **31** G9
Odda *Norway* 60°3N 6°35E **9** F12
Odei → *Canada* 56°6N 96°54W **71** B9
Ödemiş *Turkey* 38°15N 28°0E **23** E13
Odendaalsrus *S. Africa* 27°48S 26°45E **56** D4
Odense *Denmark* 55°22N 10°23E **9** J14
Oder → *Europe* 53°33N 14°38E **16** B8
Odesa *Ukraine* 46°30N 30°45E **19** E5
Odessa = Odesa *Ukraine* 46°30N 30°45E **19** E5
Odessa *Canada* 44°17N 76°43W **83** B8
Odessa *Tex., U.S.A.* 31°52N 102°23W **84** F3
Odessa *Wash., U.S.A.* 47°20N 118°41W **76** C4
Odiakwe *Botswana* 20°12S 25°17E **56** C4
Odienné *Ivory C.* 9°30N 7°34W **50** G4
Odintsovo *Russia* 55°40N 37°16E **18** C6
O'Donnell *U.S.A.* 32°58N 101°50W **84** E4
O'Donnell Pt. *Canada* 45°5N 80°5W **82** A4
Odorheiu Secuiesc
  Romania 46°21N 25°21E **17** E13
Odra = Oder → *Europe* 53°33N 14°38E **16** B8
Odzi *Zimbabwe* 19°0S 32°20E **57** B5
Odzi → *Zimbabwe* 19°45S 32°23E **57** B5
Oeiras *Brazil* 7°0S 42°8W **93** E10
Oelrichs *U.S.A.* 43°11N 103°14W **80** D2
Oelwein *U.S.A.* 42°41N 91°55W **80** D8
Oeno I. *Pac. Oc.* 24°0S 131°0W **65** K14
Oenpelli = Gunbalanya
  Australia 12°20S 133°4E **60** B5
Ofanto → *Italy* 41°22N 16°13E **22** D7
Offa *Nigeria* 8°13N 4°42E **50** G6
Offaly □ *Ireland* 53°15N 7°30W **10** C4

Offenbach *Germany* 50°6N 8°44E **16** C5
Offenburg *Germany* 48°28N 7°56E **16** D4
Officer Cr. → *Australia* 27°46S 132°30E **61** E5
Ofolanga *Tonga* 19°38S 174°27W **59** c
Ofotfjorden *Norway* 68°27N 17°0E **8** B17
Ofu *Amer. Samoa* 14°11S 169°41W **59** b
Ōfunato *Japan* 39°4N 141°43E **30** E10
Oga *Japan* 39°55N 139°50E **30** E9
Oga-Hantō *Japan* 39°58N 139°47E **30** E9
Ogaden *Ethiopia* 7°30N 45°30E **47** F3
Ōgaki *Japan* 35°21N 136°37E **31** G8
Ogallala *U.S.A.* 41°8N 101°43W **80** E3
Ogasawara Gunto
  Pac. Oc. 27°0N 142°0E **27** F16
Ogbomosho *Nigeria* 8°1N 4°11E **50** G6
Ogden *U.S.A.* 41°13N 111°58W **76** F8
Ogdensburg *U.S.A.* 44°42N 75°30W **83** B9
Ogea Driki *Fiji* 19°12S 178°27W **59** a
Ogea Levu *Fiji* 19°8S 178°24W **59** a
Ogeechee → *U.S.A.* 31°50N 81°3W **85** F14
Ogilby *U.S.A.* 32°49N 114°50W **79** N12
Ōglio → *Italy* 45°2N 10°39E **22** B4
Ogmore *Australia* 22°37S 149°35E **62** C4
Ogoki *Canada* 51°38N 85°58W **72** B2
Ogoki → *Canada* 51°38N 85°57W **72** B2
Ogoki L. *Canada* 50°50N 87°10W **72** B2
Ogoki Res. *Canada* 50°45N 88°15W **72** B2
Ogooué → *Gabon* 1°0S 9°0E **52** E1
Ogowe = Ogooué → *Gabon* 1°0S 9°0E **52** E1
Ogre *Latvia* 56°49N 24°36E **9** H21
Ogurchinskiy, Ostrov
  Turkmenistan 38°55N 53°2E **45** B7
Ohai *N.Z.* 45°55S 168°0E **59** F2
Ohakune *N.Z.* 39°24S 175°24E **59** C5
Ohata *Japan* 41°24N 141°10E **30** D10
Ohau, L. *N.Z.* 44°15S 169°53E **59** F2
Ohio □ *U.S.A.* 40°15N 82°45W **82** E2
Ohio → *U.S.A.* 36°59N 89°8W **80** G9
Ohře → *Czech Rep.* 50°30N 14°10E **16** C8
Ohrid *Macedonia* 41°8N 20°52E **23** D9
Ohridsko Jezero
  Macedonia 41°8N 20°52E **23** D9
Ohrigstad *S. Africa* 24°39S 30°36E **57** C5
Oiapoque *Brazil* 3°50N 51°50W **93** C8
Oikou *China* 38°35N 117°42E **35** E9
Oil City *U.S.A.* 41°26N 79°42W **82** E5
Oil Springs *Canada* 42°47N 82°7W **82** D2
Oildale *U.S.A.* 35°25N 119°1W **79** K7
Oise → *France* 49°0N 2°4E **20** B5
Oistins *Barbados* 13°4N 59°33W **89** g
Oistins B. *Barbados* 13°4N 59°33W **89** g
Ōita *Japan* 33°14N 131°36E **31** H5
Ōita □ *Japan* 33°15N 131°30E **31** H5
Oiticica *Brazil* 5°3S 41°5W **93** E10
Ojai *U.S.A.* 34°27N 119°15W **79** L7
Ojinaga *Mexico* 29°34N 104°25W **86** B4
Ojiya *Japan* 37°18N 138°48E **31** F9
Ojo Caliente *Mexico* 21°53N 102°15W **86** C4
Ojo de Liebre, L.
  Mexico 27°45N 114°15W **86** B2
Ojos del Salado, Cerro
  Argentina 27°0S 68°40W **94** B2
Oka → *Russia* 56°20N 43°59E **18** C7
Okaba *Indonesia* 8°6S 139°42E **37** F9
Okahandja *Namibia* 22°0S 16°59E **56** C2
Okanagan L. *Canada* 50°0N 119°30W **70** D5
Okandja *Gabon* 0°35S 13°45E **52** E2
Okanogan *U.S.A.* 48°22N 119°35W **76** B4
Okanogan → *U.S.A.* 48°6N 119°44W **76** B4
Okanogan Range
  N. Amer. 49°0N 119°55W **70** D5
Okapi △
  Dem. Rep. of the Congo 2°30N 27°20E **54** B2
Okaputa *Namibia* 20°5S 17°0E **56** C2
Okara *Pakistan* 30°50N 73°31E **42** D5
Okaukuejo *Namibia* 19°10S 16°0E **56** B2
Okavango Delta
  Botswana 18°45S 22°45E **56** B3
Okavango Swamp = Okavango
  Delta *Botswana* 18°45S 22°45E **56** B3
Okaya *Japan* 36°5N 138°10E **31** F9
Okayama *Japan* 34°40N 133°54E **31** G6
Okayama □ *Japan* 35°0N 133°50E **31** G6
Okazaki *Japan* 34°57N 137°10E **31** G8
Okeechobee *U.S.A.* 27°15N 80°50W **85** H14
Okeechobee, L. *U.S.A.* 27°0N 80°50W **85** H14
Okefenokee → *U.S.A.* 30°40N 82°18W **85** F13
Okefenokee Swamp
  U.S.A. 30°40N 82°20W **85** F13
Okehampton *U.K.* 50°44N 4°0W **13** G4
Okha *India* 22°27N 69°4E **42** H3
Okha *Russia* 53°40N 143°0E **29** D15
Okhotsk *Russia* 59°20N 143°10E **29** D15
Okhotsk, Sea of *Asia* 55°0N 145°0E **29** D15
Okhotskiy Perevoz
  Russia 61°52N 135°35E **29** C14
Okhtyrka *Ukraine* 50°25N 35°0E **19** D5
Oki-Shotō *Japan* 36°5N 133°15E **31** F6
Okiep *S. Africa* 29°39S 17°53E **56** D2
Okinawa *Japan* 26°19N 127°46E **31** L4
Okinawa □ *Japan* 26°40N 128°0E **31** L4
Okinawa-Guntō *Japan* 26°40N 128°0E **31** L4
Okinawa-Jima *Japan* 26°32N 128°0E **31** L4
Okino-erabu-Shima
  Japan 27°21N 128°33E **31** L4
Oklahoma □ *U.S.A.* 35°20N 97°30W **84** D6
Oklahoma City *U.S.A.* 35°30N 97°30W **84** D6
Okmulgee *U.S.A.* 35°37N 95°58W **84** D7
Oknitsa = Ocniţa
  Moldova 48°25N 27°30E **17** D14
Okolo *Uganda* 2°37N 31°8E **54** B3
Okolona *U.S.A.* 34°0N 88°45W **85** E10
Okombahe *Namibia* 21°23S 15°22E **56** C2
Okotoks *Canada* 50°43N 113°58W **70** C6
Oksovskiy *Russia* 62°33N 39°57E **18** B6
Oktyabrsk = Qandyaghash
  Kazakhstan 49°28N 57°25E **19** E10

Oktyabrskiy = Aktsyabrski
  Belarus 52°38N 28°53E **17** B15
Oktyabrskiy *Bashkortostan,*
  Russia 54°28N 53°28E **18** D9
Oktyabrskiy *Kamchatka,*
  Russia 52°39N 156°14E **29** D16
Oktyabrskoy Revolyutsii, Ostrov
  Russia 79°30N 97°0E **29** B10
Okuru *N.Z.* 43°55S 168°55E **59** E2
Okushiri-Tō *Japan* 42°15N 139°30E **30** C9
Okwa → *Botswana* 22°30S 23°0E **56** C3
Ola *Russia* 59°35N 151°17E **29** D16
Ola *U.S.A.* 35°2N 93°13W **84** D8
Ólafsfjörður *Iceland* 66°4N 18°39W **8** C4
Ólafsvík *Iceland* 64°53N 23°43E **8** D2
Olancha *U.S.A.* 36°17N 118°1W **79** J8
Olancha Pk. *U.S.A.* 36°16N 118°7W **79** J8
Olanchito *Honduras* 15°30N 86°30W **88** C2
Öland *Sweden* 56°45N 16°38E **9** H17
Olary *Australia* 32°18S 140°19E **63** E3
Olascoaga *Argentina* 35°15S 60°39W **94** D3
Olathe *U.S.A.* 38°53N 94°49W **80** F6
Olavarría *Argentina* 36°55S 60°20W **94** D3
Oława *Poland* 50°57N 17°20E **17** C9
Ólbia *Italy* 40°55N 9°31E **22** D3
Olcott *U.S.A.* 43°20N 78°42W **82** C6
Old Bahama Chan. = Bahama,
  Canal Viejo de
  W. Indies 22°10N 77°30W **88** B4
Old Baldy Pk. = San Antonio, Mt.
  U.S.A. 34°17N 117°38W **79** L9
Old Bridge *U.S.A.* 40°25N 74°22W **83** F10
Old Castile = Castilla y Leon □
  Spain 42°0N 5°0W **21** B3
Old Crow *Canada* 67°30N 139°55W **68** D4
Old Dale *U.S.A.* 34°8N 115°47W **79** L11
Old Forge *N.Y., U.S.A.* 43°43N 74°58W **83** C10
Old Forge *Pa., U.S.A.* 41°22N 75°45W **83** E9
Old Mapoon ◇ *Australia* 11°5S 142°22E **62** A3
Old Perlican *Canada* 48°5N 53°1W **73** C9
Old Shinyanga *Tanzania* 3°33S 33°27E **54** C3
Old Speck Mt. *U.S.A.* 44°34N 70°57W **83** B14
Old Town *U.S.A.* 44°56N 68°39W **81** C19
Old Washington *U.S.A.* 40°2N 81°27W **82** F3
Old Wives L. *Canada* 50°5N 106°0W **71** C7
Oldbury *U.K.* 51°38N 2°33W **13** F5
Oldcastle *Ireland* 53°46N 7°10W **10** C4
Oldeani *Tanzania* 3°22S 35°35E **54** C4
Oldenburg *Germany* 53°9N 8°13E **16** B5
Oldenzaal *Neths.* 52°19N 6°53E **15** B6
Oldham *U.K.* 53°33N 2°7W **12** D5
Oldman → *Canada* 49°57N 111°42W **70** D6
Oldmeldrum *U.K.* 57°20N 2°19W **11** D6
Olds *Canada* 51°50N 114°10W **70** C6
Olduvai Gorge *Tanzania* 2°57S 35°23E **54** C4
Oldziyt *Mongolia* 44°40N 109°1E **34** B5
Olean *U.S.A.* 42°5N 78°26W **82** D6
Olekma → *Russia* 60°22N 120°42E **29** C13
Olekminsk *Russia* 60°25N 120°30E **29** C13
Oleksandriya *Ukraine* 50°37N 26°19E **17** C14
Olema *U.S.A.* 38°3N 122°47W **78** G4
Olenegorsk *Russia* 68°9N 33°18E **8** B25
Olenek *Russia* 68°28N 112°18E **29** C12
Olenek → *Russia* 73°0N 120°10E **29** B13
Oléron, Î. d' *France* 45°55N 1°15W **20** D3
Oleśnica *Poland* 51°13N 17°22E **17** C9
Olevsk *Ukraine* 51°12N 27°39E **17** C14
Olga, L. *Canada* 49°47N 77°15W **72** C4
Olgas, The = Kata Tjuta
  Australia 25°20S 130°50E **61** E5
Ölgiy *Mongolia* 48°56N 89°57E **32** B3
Olhão *Portugal* 37°3N 7°48W **21** D2
Olifants = Elefantes →
  Africa 24°10S 32°40E **57** C5
Olifants → *Namibia* 25°30S 19°30E **56** C2
Olifantshoek *S. Africa* 27°57S 22°42E **56** D3
Ólimbos, Óros = Olymbos Oros
  Greece 40°6N 22°23E **23** D10
Olímpia *Brazil* 20°44S 48°54W **95** A6
Olinda *Brazil* 8°1S 34°51W **93** E12
Oliva *Argentina* 32°0S 63°38W **94** C3
Olivares, Cerro los
  Argentina 30°18S 69°55W **94** C2
Olive Branch *U.S.A.* 34°57N 89°49W **85** D10
Olivehurst *U.S.A.* 39°6N 121°34W **78** F5
Olivenza *Spain* 38°41N 7°9W **21** C2
Oliver *Canada* 49°13N 119°37W **70** D5
Oliver L. *Canada* 56°56N 103°22W **71** B8
Ollagüe *Chile* 21°15S 68°10W **94** A2
Olmaliq *Uzbekistan* 40°50N 69°35E **28** E7
Olney *Ill., U.S.A.* 38°44N 88°5W **80** F9
Olney *Tex., U.S.A.* 33°22N 98°45W **84** E5
Oloitokitok *Kenya* 2°56S 37°30E **54** C4
Olomane → *Canada* 50°14N 60°37W **73** B7
Olomouc *Czech Rep.* 49°38N 17°12E **17** D9
Olonets *Russia* 61°0N 32°54E **18** B5
Olongapo *Phil.* 14°50N 120°18E **37** B6
Olosega *Amer. Samoa* 14°10S 169°37W **59** b
Olosenga = Swains I.
  Amer. Samoa 11°11S 171°4W **65** J11
Olot *Spain* 42°11N 2°30E **21** A7
Olovyannaya *Russia* 50°58N 115°35E **29** D12
Oloy → *Russia* 66°29N 159°29E **29** C16
Olsztyn *Poland* 53°48N 20°29E **17** B11
Olt → *Romania* 43°43N 24°51E **17** G13
Olteniţa *Romania* 44°7N 26°42E **17** F14
Olton *U.S.A.* 34°11N 102°8W **84** D3
Olymbos *Cyprus* 35°21N 33°45E **25** D12
Olymbos Oros *Greece* 40°6N 22°23E **23** D10
Olympia *Greece* 37°39N 21°39E **23** F9
Olympia *U.S.A.* 47°3N 122°53W **78** D4
Olympic Dam *Australia* 30°30S 136°55E **63** E2
Olympic Mts. *U.S.A.* 47°55N 123°45W **78** C3
Olympus *Cyprus* 34°56N 32°52E **25** E11
Olympus, Mt. = Olymbos Oros
  Greece 40°6N 22°23E **23** D10
Olympus, Mt. = Uludağ
  Turkey 40°4N 29°13E **23** D13

Olympus, Mt. *U.S.A.* 47°48N 123°43W **78** C3
Olyphant *U.S.A.* 41°27N 75°36W **83** E9
Olyutorskiy, Mys
  Russia 59°55N 170°27E **29** D18
Om → *Russia* 54°59N 73°22E **28** D8
Om Koi *Thailand* 17°48N 98°22E **38** D2
Ōma *Japan* 41°45N 141°5E **30** D10
Ōmachi *Japan* 36°30N 137°50E **31** F8
Omae-Zaki *Japan* 34°36N 138°14E **31** G9
Ōmagari *Japan* 39°27N 140°29E **30** E10
Omagh *U.K.* 54°36N 7°19W **10** B4
Omagh □ *U.K.* 54°35N 7°15W **10** B4
Omaha *U.S.A.* 41°17N 95°58W **80** E6
Omak *U.S.A.* 48°25N 119°31W **76** B4
Omalos *Greece* 35°19N 23°55E **25** D5
Oman ■ *Asia* 23°0N 58°0E **47** C6
Oman, G. of *Asia* 24°30N 58°30E **45** E8
Omaruru *Namibia* 21°26S 16°0E **56** C2
Omaruru → *Namibia* 22°7S 14°15E **56** C1
Omate *Peru* 16°45S 71°0W **92** G4
Ombai, Selat *Indonesia* 8°30S 124°50E **37** F6
Omboué *Gabon* 1°35S 9°15E **52** E1
Ombrone → *Italy* 42°42N 11°5E **22** C4
Omdurmân *Sudan* 15°40N 32°28E **51** E12
Omemee *Canada* 44°18N 78°33W **82** B6
Omeonga
  Dem. Rep. of the Congo 3°40S 24°22E **54** C1
Ometepe, I. de *Nic.* 11°32N 85°35W **88** D2
Ometepec *Mexico* 16°41N 98°25W **87** D5
Ominato *Japan* 41°17N 141°10E **30** D10
Omineca → *Canada* 56°3N 124°16W **70** B4
Omineca Mts. *Canada* 56°30N 125°30W **70** B3
Omitara *Namibia* 22°16S 18°2E **56** C2
Ōmiya = Saitama *Japan* 35°54N 139°38E **31** G9
Ommen *Neths.* 52°31N 6°26E **15** B6
Ömnögovĭ □ *Mongolia* 43°15N 104°0E **34** C5
Omo → *Ethiopia* 6°25N 36°10E **47** F2
Omodhos *Cyprus* 34°51N 32°48E **25** E11
Omolon → *Russia* 68°42N 158°36E **29** C16
Omono-Gawa → *Japan* 39°46N 140°3E **30** E10
Ompha *Canada* 45°0N 76°50W **83** B8
Omsk *Russia* 55°0N 73°12E **28** D8
Omsukchan *Russia* 62°32N 155°48E **29** C16
Ōmu *Japan* 44°34N 142°58E **30** B11
Omul, Vf. *Romania* 45°27N 25°29E **17** F13
Ōmura *Japan* 32°56N 129°57E **31** H4
Omuramba Omatako →
  Namibia 17°45S 20°25E **56** B2
Omuramba Ovambo →
  Namibia 18°45S 16°59E **56** B2
Ōmuta *Japan* 33°5N 130°26E **31** H5
Onaga *U.S.A.* 39°29N 96°10W **80** F5
Onalaska *U.S.A.* 43°53N 91°14W **80** D8
Onancock *U.S.A.* 37°43N 75°45W **81** G16
Onang *Indonesia* 3°2S 118°49E **37** E5
Onangue, L. *Gabon* 0°57S 10°4E **52** E2
Onaping L. *Canada* 47°3N 81°30W **72** C3
Onavas *Mexico* 28°31N 109°35W **86** B3
Onawa *U.S.A.* 42°2N 96°6W **80** D5
Oncócua *Angola* 16°30S 13°25E **56** B1
Onda *Spain* 39°55N 0°17W **21** C5
Ondangwa *Namibia* 17°57S 16°4E **56** B2
Ondjiva *Angola* 16°48S 15°50E **56** B2
Öndörhaan *Mongolia* 47°19N 110°39E **34** B6
Öndörshil *Mongolia* 45°13N 108°5E **34** B5
Öndverðarnes *Iceland* 64°52N 24°0W **8** D2
One Arm Point *Australia* 16°26S 123°3E **60** C3
One Arm Point ◇
  Australia 16°31S 122°53E **60** C3
One Tree *Australia* 34°11S 144°43E **63** E3
Oneata *Fiji* 18°26S 178°25W **59** a
Onega *Russia* 64°0N 38°10E **18** B6
Onega → *Russia* 63°58N 38°2E **18** B6
Onega, G. of = Onezhskaya Guba
  Russia 64°24N 36°38E **18** B6
Onega, L. = Onezhskoye Ozero
  Russia 61°44N 35°22E **18** B6
Oneida *U.S.A.* 43°6N 75°39W **83** C9
Oneida L. *U.S.A.* 43°12N 75°54W **83** C9
O'Neill *U.S.A.* 42°27N 98°39W **80** D4
Onekotan, Ostrov
  Russia 49°25N 154°45E **29** E16
Onema
  Dem. Rep. of the Congo 4°35S 24°30E **54** C1
Oneonta *U.S.A.* 42°27N 75°4W **83** D9
Oneşti *Romania* 46°17N 26°47E **17** E14
Onezhskaya Guba
  Russia 64°24N 36°38E **18** B6
Onezhskoye Ozero
  Russia 61°44N 35°22E **18** B6
Ongarue *N.Z.* 38°42S 175°19E **59** C5
Ongerup *Australia* 33°58S 118°28E **61** F2
Ongjin *N. Korea* 37°56N 125°21E **35** F13
Ongkharak *Thailand* 14°8N 101°1E **38** E3
Ongniud Qi *China* 43°0N 118°38E **35** C10
Ongoka
  Dem. Rep. of the Congo 1°20S 26°0E **54** C2
Ongole *India* 15°33N 80°2E **40** M12
Ongon = Havirga
  Mongolia 45°41N 113°5E **34** B7
Onida *U.S.A.* 44°42N 100°4W **80** C3
Onilahy → *Madag.* 23°34S 43°45E **57** C7
Onitsha *Nigeria* 6°6N 6°42E **50** G7
Ono *Fiji* 18°55S 178°29E **59** a
Onoda *Japan* 33°59N 131°11E **31** G5
Onslow *Australia* 21°40S 115°12E **60** D2
Onslow B. *U.S.A.* 34°20N 77°15W **85** D16
Ontake-San *Japan* 35°53N 137°29E **31** G8
Ontario *Calif., U.S.A.* 34°4N 117°39W **79** L9
Ontario *Oreg., U.S.A.* 44°2N 116°58W **76** D5
Ontario □ *Canada* 48°0N 83°0W **72** B2
Ontario, L. *N. Amer.* 43°20N 78°0W **82** C7
Ontonagon *U.S.A.* 46°52N 89°19W **80** B9
Onyx *U.S.A.* 35°41N 118°14W **79** K8
Oodnadatta *Australia* 27°33S 135°30E **63** D2
Ooldea *Australia* 30°27S 131°50E **61** F5

Oombulgurri *Australia* 15°15S 127°45E **60** C4
Oombulgurri ◇
  Australia 15°10S 127°50E **60** C4
Oorindi *Australia* 20°40S 141°1E **62** C3
Oost-Vlaanderen □
  Belgium 51°5N 3°50E **15** C3
Oostende *Belgium* 51°15N 2°54E **15** C2
Oosterhout *Neths.* 51°39N 4°47E **15** C4
Oosterschelde → *Neths.* 51°33N 4°0E **15** C4
Oosterwolde *Neths.* 53°0N 6°17E **15** B6
Ootacamund = Udagamandalam
  India 11°30N 76°44E **40** P10
Ootsa L. *Canada* 53°50N 126°2W **70** C3
Ooty = Udagamandalam
  India 11°30N 76°44E **40** P10
Op Luang △ *Thailand* 18°12N 98°32E **38** C2
Opala
  Dem. Rep. of the Congo 0°40S 24°20E **54** C1
Opanake *Sri Lanka* 6°35N 80°40E **40** R12
Opasatika *Canada* 49°30N 82°50W **72** C3
Opasquia △ *Canada* 53°33N 93°5W **72** B1
Opava *Czech Rep.* 49°57N 17°58E **17** D9
Opelika *U.S.A.* 32°39N 85°23W **85** E12
Opelousas *U.S.A.* 30°32N 92°5W **84** F8
Opémisca, L. *Canada* 49°56N 74°52W **72** C5
Opheim *U.S.A.* 48°51N 106°24W **76** B10
Ophthalmia Ra.
  Australia 23°15S 119°30E **60** D2
Opinaca → *Canada* 52°15N 78°2W **72** B4
Opinaca, Rés. *Canada* 52°39N 76°20W **72** B4
Opinnagau → *Canada* 54°12N 82°25W **72** B3
Opiscotéo, L. *Canada* 53°10N 68°10W **73** B6
Opobo *Nigeria* 4°35N 7°34E **50** H7
Opole *Poland* 50°42N 17°58E **17** C9
Oponono L. *Namibia* 18°8S 15°45E **56** B2
Oporto = Porto *Portugal* 41°8N 8°40W **21** B1
Opotiki *N.Z.* 38°1S 177°19E **59** C6
Opp *U.S.A.* 31°17N 86°16W **85** F11
Oppdal *Norway* 62°35N 9°41E **8** E13
Opportunity *U.S.A.* 47°39N 117°15W **76** C5
Opua *N.Z.* 35°19S 174°9E **59** A5
Opunake *N.Z.* 39°26S 173°52E **59** C4
Opuwo *Namibia* 18°3S 13°45E **56** B1
Ora *Cyprus* 34°51N 33°12E **25** E12
Oracle *U.S.A.* 32°37N 110°46W **77** K8
Oradea *Romania* 47°2N 21°58E **17** E11
Öræfajökull *Iceland* 64°2N 16°39W **8** D5
Orai *India* 25°58N 79°30E **43** G8
Oral = Zhayyq →
  Kazakhstan 47°0N 51°48E **19** E9
Oral *Kazakhstan* 51°20N 51°20E **19** D9
Oran *Algeria* 35°45N 0°39W **50** A5
Orange *Australia* 33°15S 149°7E **63** E4
Orange *France* 44°8N 4°47E **20** D6
Orange *Calif., U.S.A.* 33°47N 117°51W **79** M9
Orange *Mass., U.S.A.* 42°35N 72°19W **83** D12
Orange *Tex., U.S.A.* 30°6N 93°44W **84** F8
Orange *Va., U.S.A.* 38°15N 78°7W **81** F14
Orange → *S. Africa* 28°41S 16°28E **56** D2
Orange, C. *Brazil* 4°20N 51°30W **93** C8
Orange Cove *U.S.A.* 36°38N 119°19W **78** J7
Orange Free State = Free State □
  S. Africa 28°30S 27°0E **56** D4
Orange Grove *U.S.A.* 27°58N 97°56W **84** H6
Orange Walk *Belize* 18°6N 88°33W **87** D7
Orangeburg *U.S.A.* 33°30N 80°52W **85** E14
Orangeville *Canada* 43°55N 80°5W **82** C4
Orango *Guinea-Biss.* 11°5N 16°0W **50** F2
Oranienburg *Germany* 52°45N 13°14E **16** B7
Oranje = Orange →
  S. Africa 28°41S 16°28E **56** D2
Oranjemund *Namibia* 28°38S 16°29E **56** D2
Oranjerivier *S. Africa* 29°40S 24°12E **56** D3
Oranjestad *Aruba* 12°32N 70°2W **89** D5
Orapa *Botswana* 21°15S 25°30E **53** J5
Oras *Phil.* 12°9N 125°28E **37** B7
Orbetello *Italy* 42°27N 11°13E **22** C4
Orbisonia *U.S.A.* 40°15N 77°54W **82** F7
Orbost *Australia* 37°40S 148°29E **63** F4
Orcadas *Antarctica* 60°44S 44°37W **5** C18
Orcas I. *U.S.A.* 48°42N 122°56W **78** B4
Orchard City *U.S.A.* 38°50N 107°58W **76** G10
Orchard Homes *U.S.A.* 46°55N 114°4W **76** C6
Orchila, I. *Venezuela* 11°48N 66°10W **89** D6
Orchilla, Pta. *Canary Is.* 27°42N 18°10W **24** G1
Orcutt *U.S.A.* 34°52N 120°27W **79** L6
Ord *U.S.A.* 41°36N 98°56W **80** E4
Ord → *Australia* 15°33S 128°15E **60** C4
Ord, Mt. *Australia* 17°20S 125°34E **60** C4
Ord Mts. *U.S.A.* 34°39N 116°45W **79** L10
Orderville *U.S.A.* 37°17N 112°38W **77** H7
Ordos = Mu Us Shamo
  China 39°0N 109°0E **34** E5
Ordu *Turkey* 40°55N 37°53E **19** F6
Ordway *U.S.A.* 38°13N 103°46W **76** G12
Ore *Dem. Rep. of the Congo* 3°17N 29°30E **54** B2
Ore Mts. = Erzgebirge
  Germany 50°27N 12°55E **16** C7
Örebro *Sweden* 59°20N 15°18E **9** G16
Oregon *U.S.A.* 42°1N 89°20W **80** E9
Oregon □ *U.S.A.* 44°0N 121°0W **76** E3
Oregon City *U.S.A.* 45°21N 122°36W **78** E4
Oregon Dunes
  U.S.A. 43°40N 124°10W **76** E1
Orekhovo-Zuyevo
  Russia 55°50N 38°55E **18** C6
Orel *Russia* 52°57N 36°3E **18** D6
Orem *U.S.A.* 40°19N 111°42W **76** F8
Ören *Turkey* 37°3N 27°57E **23** F12
Orenburg *Russia* 51°45N 55°6E **18** D10
Orense = Ourense *Spain* 42°19N 7°55W **21** A2
Orepuki *N.Z.* 46°19S 167°46E **59** G1
Orestes Pereyra *Mexico* 26°30N 105°39W **86** B3
Orestiada *Greece* 41°30N 26°33E **23** D12
Orfanos Kolpos *Greece* 40°33N 24°0E **23** D11
Orford Ness *U.K.* 52°5N 1°35E **13** E9
Organ Pipe Cactus △
  U.S.A. 32°0N 112°52W **77** K7

150 Organos, Pta. de los INDEX TO WORLD MAPS

Organos, Pta. de los *Canary Is.* 28°12N 17°17W 24 F2
Orgaz *Spain* 39°39N 3°53W 21 C4
Orgeyev = Orhei *Moldova* 47°24N 28°50E 17 E15
Orhaneli *Turkey* 39°54N 28°59E 23 E13
Orhangazi *Turkey* 40°29N 29°18E 23 D13
Orhei *Moldova* 47°24N 28°50E 17 E15
Orhon Gol → *Mongolia* 50°21N 106°0E 32 A5
Oriental, Cordillera *Colombia* 6°0N 73°0W 92 B4
Oriental, Grand Erg *Algeria* 30°0N 6°30E 50 B7
Orientale □ *Dem. Rep. of the Congo* 2°20N 26°0E 54 B2
Oriente *Argentina* 38°44S 60°37W 94 D3
Orihuela *Spain* 38°7N 0°55W 21 C5
Orillia *Canada* 44°40N 79°24W 82 B5
Orinoco → *Venezuela* 9°15N 61°30W 92 B6
Orion *Canada* 49°27N 110°49W 71 D6
Oriskany *U.S.A.* 43°10N 75°20W 83 C9
Orissa □ *India* 20°0N 84°0E 41 K14
Orissaare *Estonia* 58°34N 23°5E 9 G20
Oristano *Italy* 39°54N 8°36E 22 E3
Oristano, G. di *Italy* 39°50N 8°29E 22 E3
Orizaba *Mexico* 18°51N 97°6W 87 D5
Orizaba, Pico de *Mexico* 18°58N 97°15W 87 D5
Orkanger *Norway* 63°18N 9°52E 8 E13
Orkla → *Norway* 63°18N 9°51E 8 E13
Orkney *S. Africa* 26°58S 26°40E 56 D4
Orkney □ *U.K.* 59°2N 3°13W 11 B5
Orkney Is. *U.K.* 59°0N 3°0W 11 B6
Orland *U.S.A.* 39°45N 122°12W 78 F4
Orlando *U.S.A.* 28°32N 81°22W 85 G14
Orléanais *France* 48°0N 2°0E 20 C5
Orléans *France* 47°54N 1°52E 20 C4
Orleans *U.S.A.* 44°49N 72°12W 83 B12
Orléans, Î. d' *Canada* 46°54N 70°58W 73 C5
Ormara *Pakistan* 25°16N 64°33E 40 G4
Ormoc *Phil.* 11°0N 124°37E 37 B6
Ormond *N.Z.* 38°33S 177°56E 59 C6
Ormond Beach *U.S.A.* 29°17N 81°3W 85 G14
Ormskirk *U.K.* 53°35N 2°54W 12 D5
Ormstown *Canada* 45°8N 74°0W 83 A11
Örnsköldsvik *Sweden* 63°17N 18°40E 8 E18
Oro *N. Korea* 40°1N 127°27E 35 D14
Oro → *Mexico* 25°35N 105°2W 86 B3
Oro Grande *U.S.A.* 34°36N 117°20W 79 L9
Oro Valley *U.S.A.* 32°26N 110°58W 77 K8
Orocué *Colombia* 4°48N 71°20W 92 C4
Orofino *U.S.A.* 46°29N 116°15W 76 C5
Orohena, Mt. *Tahiti* 17°37S 149°28W 59 d
Orol Dengizi = Aral Sea *Asia* 44°30N 60°0E 28 E7
Oromocto *Canada* 45°54N 66°29W 73 C6
Orono *Canada* 43°59N 78°37W 82 C6
Orono *U.S.A.* 44°53N 68°40W 81 C19
Oronsay *U.K.* 56°1N 6°15W 11 E2
Oroqen Zizhiqi *China* 50°34N 123°43E 33 A7
Oroquieta *Phil.* 8°32N 123°44E 37 C6
Orosei *Italy* 40°23N 9°42E 22 D3
Orosháza *Hungary* 46°32N 20°42E 17 E11
Orotukan *Russia* 62°16N 151°42E 29 C16
Oroville *Calif., U.S.A.* 39°31N 121°33W 78 F5
Oroville *Wash., U.S.A.* 48°56N 119°26W 76 B4
Oroville, L. *U.S.A.* 39°33N 121°29W 78 F5
Orroroo *Australia* 32°43S 138°38E 63 E2
Orrville *U.S.A.* 40°50N 81°46W 82 F3
Orsha *Belarus* 54°30N 30°25E 18 D5
Orsk *Russia* 51°12N 58°34E 28 D6
Orşova *Romania* 44°41N 22°25E 17 F12
Ortaca *Turkey* 36°49N 28°45E 23 F13
Ortegal, C. *Spain* 43°43N 7°52W 21 A2
Orthez *France* 43°29N 0°48W 20 E3
Ortigueira *Spain* 43°40N 7°50W 21 A2
Orting *U.S.A.* 47°6N 122°12W 78 C4
Ortles *Italy* 46°31N 10°33E 20 C9
Ortón → *Bolivia* 10°50S 67°0W 92 F5
Ortonville *U.S.A.* 45°19N 96°27W 80 C5
Orūmīyeh *Iran* 37°40N 45°0E 44 B5
Orūmīyeh, Daryācheh-ye *Iran* 37°50N 45°30E 44 B5
Oruro *Bolivia* 18°0S 67°9W 92 G5
Orust *Sweden* 58°10N 11°40E 9 G14
Oruzgān □ *Afghan.* 33°0N 66°0E 40 C5
Orvieto *Italy* 42°43N 12°7E 22 C5
Orwell *N.Y., U.S.A.* 43°35N 75°50W 83 C9
Orwell *Ohio, U.S.A.* 41°32N 80°52W 82 E4
Orwell → *U.K.* 51°59N 1°18E 13 F9
Orwigsburg *U.S.A.* 40°38N 76°6W 83 F8
Oryakhovo *Bulgaria* 43°40N 23°57E 23 C10
Oryol = Orel *Russia* 52°57N 36°3E 18 D6
Osa *Russia* 57°17N 55°26E 18 C10
Osa, Pen. de *Costa Rica* 8°0N 84°0W 88 E3
Osage *U.S.A.* 43°17N 92°49W 80 D7
Osage → *U.S.A.* 38°36N 91°57W 80 F8
Osage City *U.S.A.* 38°38N 95°50W 80 F6
Ōsaka *Japan* 34°42N 135°30E 31 G7
Osan *S. Korea* 37°11N 127°4E 35 F14
Osawatomie *U.S.A.* 38°31N 94°57W 80 F6
Osborne *U.S.A.* 39°26N 98°42W 80 F4
Osceola *Ark., U.S.A.* 35°42N 89°58W 85 D10
Osceola *Iowa, U.S.A.* 41°2N 93°46W 80 E7
Oscoda *U.S.A.* 44°26N 83°20W 82 B1
Ösel = Saaremaa *Estonia* 58°30N 22°30E 9 G20
Osgoode *Canada* 45°8N 75°36W 83 A9
Osh *Kyrgyzstan* 40°37N 72°49E 32 B2
Oshakati *Namibia* 17°45S 15°40E 53 H3
Oshawa *Canada* 43°50N 78°50W 82 C6
Oshigambo *Namibia* 17°45S 16°5E 56 B2
Oshkosh *Nebr., U.S.A.* 41°24N 102°21W 80 E2
Oshkosh *Wis., U.S.A.* 44°1N 88°33W 80 C9
Oshmyany = Ashmyany *Belarus* 54°26N 25°52E 17 A13
Oshnovīyeh *Iran* 37°2N 45°6E 44 B5
Oshogbo *Nigeria* 7°48N 4°37E 50 G6
Oshtorīnān *Iran* 34°1N 48°38E 45 C6
Oshwe *Dem. Rep. of the Congo* 3°25S 19°28E 52 E3
Osijek *Croatia* 45°34N 18°41E 23 B8
Osipovichi = Asipovichy *Belarus* 53°19N 28°33E 17 B15
Osiyan *India* 26°43N 72°55E 42 F5
Osizweni *S. Africa* 27°49S 30°7E 57 D5
Oskaloosa *U.S.A.* 41°18N 92°39W 80 E7
Oskarshamn *Sweden* 57°15N 16°27E 9 H17
Oskélanéo *Canada* 48°5N 75°15W 72 C4
Öskemen *Kazakhstan* 50°0N 82°36E 28 E9
Oslo *Norway* 59°54N 10°43E 9 G14
Oslofjorden *Norway* 59°20N 10°35E 9 G14
Osmanabad *India* 18°5N 76°10E 40 K10
Osmaniye *Turkey* 37°5N 36°10E 44 B3
Osnabrück *Germany* 52°17N 8°3E 16 B5
Osório *Brazil* 29°53S 50°17W 95 B5
Osorno *Chile* 40°25S 73°0W 96 E2
Osorno, Vol. *Chile* 41°0S 72°30W 96 D2
Osoyoos *Canada* 49°0N 119°30W 70 D5
Osøyro *Norway* 60°9N 5°30E 8 F11
Ospika → *Canada* 56°20N 124°0W 70 B4
Osprey Reef *Australia* 13°52S 146°36E 62 A4
Oss *Neths.* 51°46N 5°32E 15 C5
Ossa, Mt. *Australia* 41°52S 146°3E 63 G4
Ossa, Oros *Greece* 39°47N 22°42E 23 E10
Ossabaw I. *U.S.A.* 31°50N 81°5W 85 F14
Ossining *U.S.A.* 41°10N 73°55W 83 E11
Ossipee *U.S.A.* 43°41N 71°7W 83 C13
Ossokmanuan L. *Canada* 53°25N 65°0W 73 B7
Ossora *Russia* 59°20N 163°13E 29 D17
Ostend = Oostende *Belgium* 51°15N 2°54E 15 C2
Oster *Ukraine* 50°57N 30°53E 17 C16
Österbotten = Pohjanmaa *Finland* 62°58N 22°50E 8 E20
Osterburg *U.S.A.* 40°16N 78°31W 82 F6
Österdalälven *Sweden* 61°30N 13°45E 8 F15
Østerdalen *Norway* 61°40N 10°50E 8 F14
Östermyra = Seinäjoki *Finland* 62°40N 22°51E 8 E20
Österreich = Austria ■ *Europe* 47°0N 14°0E 16 E8
Östersund *Sweden* 63°10N 14°38E 8 E16
Ostfriesische Inseln *Germany* 53°42N 7°0E 16 B4
Ostrava *Czech Rep.* 49°51N 18°18E 17 D10
Ostróda *Poland* 53°42N 19°58E 17 B10
Ostroh *Ukraine* 50°20N 26°30E 17 C14
Ostrołęka *Poland* 53°4N 21°32E 17 B11
Ostrów Mazowiecka *Poland* 52°50N 21°51E 17 B11
Ostrów Wielkopolski *Poland* 51°36N 17°44E 17 C9
Ostrowiec-Świętokrzyski *Poland* 50°55N 21°22E 17 C11
Ostuni *Italy* 40°44N 17°35E 23 D7
Ōsumi-Kaikyō *Japan* 30°55N 131°0E 31 J5
Ōsumi-Shotō *Japan* 30°30N 130°0E 31 J5
Osuna *Spain* 37°14N 5°8W 21 D3
Oswegatchie → *U.S.A.* 44°42N 75°30W 83 B9
Oswego *U.S.A.* 43°27N 76°31W 83 C8
Oswego → *U.S.A.* 43°27N 76°30W 83 C8
Oswestry *U.K.* 52°52N 3°3W 12 E4
Oświęcim *Poland* 50°2N 19°11E 17 C10
Otago □ *N.Z.* 45°15S 170°0E 59 F2
Otago Harbour *N.Z.* 45°47S 170°42E 59 F3
Otaheite B. *Trin. & Tob.* 10°15N 61°30W 93 K15
Ōtake *Japan* 34°12N 132°13E 31 G6
Otaki *N.Z.* 40°45S 175°10E 59 D5
Otaru *Japan* 43°10N 141°0E 30 C10
Otaru-Wan = Ishikari-Wan *Japan* 43°25N 141°1E 30 C10
Otavalo *Ecuador* 0°13N 78°20W 92 C3
Otavi *Namibia* 19°40S 17°24E 56 B2
Otchinjau *Angola* 16°30S 13°56E 56 B1
Otego *U.S.A.* 42°23N 75°10W 83 D9
Otelnuk, L. *Canada* 56°9N 68°12W 73 A6
Othello *U.S.A.* 46°50N 119°10W 76 C4
Otish, Mts. *Canada* 52°22N 70°30W 73 B5
Otjiwarongo *Namibia* 20°30S 16°33E 56 C2
Oto Tolu Group *Tonga* 20°21S 174°32W 59 c
Otoineppu *Japan* 44°44N 142°16E 30 B11
Otorohanga *N.Z.* 38°12S 175°14E 59 C5
Otoskwin → *Canada* 52°13N 88°6W 72 B2
Otra → *Norway* 58°9N 8°1E 9 G13
Otranto *Italy* 40°9N 18°28E 23 D8
Otranto, C. d' *Italy* 40°7N 18°30E 23 D8
Otranto, Str. of *Italy* 40°15N 18°40E 23 D8
Otse *S. Africa* 25°2S 25°45E 56 D4
Otsego L. *U.S.A.* 42°45N 74°53W 83 D10
Ōtsu *Japan* 35°0N 135°50E 31 G7
Ōtsuki *Japan* 35°36N 138°57E 31 G9
Ottawa = Outaouais → *Canada* 45°27N 74°8W 72 C5
Ottawa *Canada* 45°26N 75°42W 83 A9
Ottawa *Ill., U.S.A.* 41°21N 88°51W 80 E9
Ottawa *Kans., U.S.A.* 38°37N 95°16W 80 F6
Ottawa Is. *Canada* 59°35N 80°10W 69 F15
Otter Cr. → *U.S.A.* 44°13N 73°17W 83 B11
Otter Lake *Canada* 45°17N 79°56W 82 A5
Otterville *Canada* 42°55N 80°36W 82 D4
Ottery St. Mary *U.K.* 50°44N 3°17W 13 G4
Otto Beit Bridge *Zimbabwe* 15°59S 28°56E 55 F2
Ottosdal *S. Africa* 26°46S 25°59E 56 D4
Ottumwa *U.S.A.* 41°1N 92°25W 80 E7
Oturkpo *Nigeria* 7°16N 8°8E 50 G7
Otway, B. *Chile* 53°30S 74°0W 96 G2
Otway, C. *Australia* 38°52S 143°30E 63 F3
Otwock *Poland* 52°5N 21°20E 17 B11
Ou → *Laos* 20°4N 102°13E 38 B4
Ou Neua *Laos* 22°18N 101°48E 38 A3
Ou-Sammyaku *Japan* 39°20N 140°35E 30 E10
Ouachita → *U.S.A.* 31°38N 91°49W 84 F9
Ouachita, L. *U.S.A.* 34°34N 93°12W 84 D8
Ouachita Mts. *U.S.A.* 34°30N 94°30W 84 D7
Ouagadougou *Burkina Faso* 12°25N 1°30W 50 F5
Ouahigouya *Burkina Faso* 13°31N 2°25W 50 F5
Ouahran = Oran *Algeria* 35°45N 0°39W 50 A5
Ouallene *Algeria* 24°41N 1°11E 50 D6
Ouarâne *Mauritania* 21°0N 10°30W 50 D3
Ouargla *Algeria* 31°59N 5°16E 50 B7
Ouarra → *C.A.R.* 5°5N 24°26E 52 C4
Ouarzazate *Morocco* 30°55N 6°50W 50 B4
Oubangi → *Dem. Rep. of the Congo* 0°30S 17°50E 52 E3
Ouddorp *Neths.* 51°50N 3°57E 15 C3
Oude Rijn → *Neths.* 52°12N 4°24E 15 B4
Oudenaarde *Belgium* 50°50N 3°37E 15 D3
Oudtshoorn *S. Africa* 33°35S 22°14E 56 E3
Ouessant, Î. d' *France* 48°28N 5°6W 20 B1
Ouesso *Congo* 1°37N 16°5E 52 D3
Ouest, Pte. de l' *Canada* 49°52N 64°40W 73 C7
Ouezzane *Morocco* 34°51N 5°35W 50 B4
Oughter, L. *Ireland* 54°1N 7°28W 10 B4
Oughterard *Ireland* 53°26N 9°18W 10 C2
Ouidah *Benin* 6°25N 2°0E 50 G6
Oujda *Morocco* 34°41N 1°55W 50 B5
Oulainen *Finland* 64°17N 24°47E 8 D21
Oulu *Finland* 65°1N 25°29E 8 D21
Oulujärvi *Finland* 64°25N 27°15E 8 D22
Oulujoki → *Finland* 65°1N 25°30E 8 D21
Oum Chalouba *Chad* 15°48N 20°46E 51 E10
Oum Hadjer *Chad* 13°18N 19°41E 51 F9
Ounasjoki → *Finland* 66°31N 25°40E 8 C21
Ounguati *Namibia* 22°0S 15°46E 56 C2
Ounianga Kébir *Chad* 19°4N 20°29E 51 E10
Our → *Lux.* 49°55N 6°5E 15 E6
Ouray *U.S.A.* 38°1N 107°40W 77 G10
Ourense *Spain* 42°19N 7°55W 21 A2
Ouricuri *Brazil* 7°53S 40°5W 93 E10
Ourinhos *Brazil* 23°0S 49°54W 95 A6
Ouro Fino *Brazil* 22°16S 46°25W 95 A6
Ouro Prêto *Brazil* 20°20S 43°30W 95 A7
Ourthe → *Belgium* 50°29N 5°35E 15 D5
Ouse → *E. Sussex, U.K.* 50°47N 0°4E 13 G8
Ouse → *N. Yorks., U.K.* 53°44N 0°55W 12 D7
Outaouais → *Canada* 45°27N 74°8W 72 C5
Outardes → *Canada* 49°24N 69°30W 73 C6
Outer Hebrides *U.K.* 57°30N 7°40W 11 D1
Outjo *Namibia* 20°5S 16°7E 56 C2
Outlook *Canada* 51°30N 107°0W 71 C7
Outokumpu *Finland* 62°43N 29°1E 8 E23
Ouyen *Australia* 35°1S 142°22E 63 F3
Ovalau *Fiji* 17°40S 178°48E 59 a
Ovalle *Chile* 30°33S 71°18W 94 C1
Ovamboland *Namibia* 18°30S 16°0E 56 B2
Overflakkee *Neths.* 51°44N 4°10E 15 C4
Overijssel □ *Neths.* 52°25N 6°35E 15 B6
Overland Park *U.S.A.* 38°58N 94°40W 80 F6
Overlander Roadhouse *Australia* 26°19S 114°28E 61 E1
Overton *U.S.A.* 36°33N 114°27W 79 J12
Övertorneå *Sweden* 66°23N 23°38E 8 C20
Ovid *U.S.A.* 42°41N 76°49W 83 D8
Oviedo *Spain* 43°25N 5°50W 21 A3
Ovīšrags *Latvia* 57°33N 21°44E 9 H19
Ovoot *Mongolia* 45°21N 113°45E 34 B7
Övör Hangay □ *Mongolia* 45°0N 102°30E 34 B2
Øvre Årdal *Norway* 61°19N 7°48E 8 F12
Ovruch *Ukraine* 51°25N 28°45E 17 C15
Owaka *N.Z.* 46°27S 169°40E 59 G2
Owambo = Ovamboland *Namibia* 18°30S 16°0E 56 B2
Owasco L. *U.S.A.* 42°50N 76°31W 83 D8
Owase *Japan* 34°7N 136°12E 31 G8
Owatonna *U.S.A.* 44°5N 93°14W 80 C7
Owbeh *Afghan.* 34°28N 63°10E 40 B3
Owego *U.S.A.* 42°6N 76°16W 83 D8
Owen Falls Dam = Nalubaale Dam *Uganda* 0°30N 33°5E 54 B3
Owen Sound *Canada* 44°35N 80°55W 82 B4
Owen Stanley Ra. *Papua N. G.* 8°30S 147°0E 58 B7
Oweniny → *Ireland* 54°8N 9°34W 10 B2
Owens → *U.S.A.* 36°32N 117°59W 78 J9
Owens L. *U.S.A.* 36°26N 117°57W 79 J9
Owensboro *U.S.A.* 37°46N 87°7W 80 G10
Owl → *Canada* 57°51N 92°44W 71 B10
Owo *Nigeria* 7°10N 5°39E 50 G7
Owosso *U.S.A.* 43°0N 84°10W 81 D11
Owyhee *U.S.A.* 41°57N 116°6W 76 F5
Owyhee → *U.S.A.* 43°49N 117°2W 76 E5
Owyhee, L. *U.S.A.* 43°38N 117°14W 76 E5
Ox Mts. = Slieve Gamph *Ireland* 54°6N 9°0W 10 B3
Öxarfjörður *Iceland* 66°15N 16°45W 8 C5
Oxbow *Canada* 49°14N 102°10W 71 D8
Oxelösund *Sweden* 58°43N 17°5E 9 G17
Oxford *N.Z.* 43°18S 172°11E 59 E4
Oxford *U.K.* 51°46N 1°15W 13 F6
Oxford *Mass., U.S.A.* 42°7N 71°52W 83 D13
Oxford *Miss., U.S.A.* 34°22N 89°31W 85 D10
Oxford *N.C., U.S.A.* 36°19N 78°35W 85 C15
Oxford *N.Y., U.S.A.* 42°27N 75°36W 83 D9
Oxford *Ohio, U.S.A.* 39°31N 84°45W 81 F11
Oxford L. *Canada* 54°51N 95°37W 71 C9
Oxfordshire □ *U.K.* 51°48N 1°16W 13 F6
Oxnard *U.S.A.* 34°12N 119°11W 79 L7
Oxus = Amudarya → *Uzbekistan* 43°58N 59°34E 28 E6
Oya *Malaysia* 2°55N 111°55E 36 D4
Oyama *Japan* 36°18N 139°48E 31 F9
Oyem *Gabon* 1°34N 11°31E 52 D2
Oyen *Canada* 51°22N 110°28W 71 C6
Oykel → *U.K.* 57°56N 4°26W 11 D4
Oymyakon *Russia* 63°25N 142°44E 29 C15
Oyo *Nigeria* 7°46N 3°56E 50 G6
Oyster Bay *U.S.A.* 40°52N 73°32W 83 F11
Ōyübari *Japan* 43°1N 142°5E 30 C11
Ozamiz *Phil.* 8°15N 123°50E 37 C6
Ozark *Ala., U.S.A.* 31°28N 85°39W 85 F12
Ozark *Ark., U.S.A.* 35°29N 93°50W 84 D8
Ozark *Mo., U.S.A.* 37°1N 93°12W 80 G7
Ozark Plateau *U.S.A.* 37°20N 91°40W 80 G8
Ozarks, L. of the *U.S.A.* 38°12N 92°38W 80 F7
Ózd *Hungary* 48°14N 20°15E 17 D11
Ozernovskiy *Russia* 51°30N 156°31E 29 D16
Ozette, L. *U.S.A.* 48°6N 124°38W 78 B2
Ozieri *Italy* 40°35N 9°0E 22 D3
Ozona *U.S.A.* 30°43N 101°12W 84 F4
Ozuluama *Mexico* 21°40N 97°51W 87 C5

P

Pa-an *Burma* 16°51N 97°40E 41 L20
Pa Mong Dam *Thailand* 18°0N 102°22E 38 D4
Pa Sak → *Thailand* 15°30N 101°0E 38 E3
Paamiut *Greenland* 62°0N 49°43W 4 C5
Paarl *S. Africa* 33°45S 18°56E 56 E2
Pab Hills *Pakistan* 26°30N 66°45E 42 F2
Pabbay *U.K.* 57°46N 7°14W 11 D1
Pabianice *Poland* 51°40N 19°20E 17 C10
Pabna *Bangla.* 24°1N 89°18E 41 G16
Pabo *Uganda* 3°1N 32°10E 54 B3
Pacaja → *Brazil* 1°56S 50°50W 93 D8
Pacaraima, Sa. *S. Amer.* 4°0N 62°30W 92 C6
Pacasmayo *Peru* 7°20S 79°35W 92 E3
Pachitea → *Peru* 8°46S 74°33W 92 E4
Pachmarhi *India* 22°28N 78°26E 43 H8
Pachnes *Greece* 35°16N 24°4E 25 D6
Pachpadra *India* 25°58N 72°10E 42 G5
Pachuca *Mexico* 20°7N 98°44W 87 C5
Pacific Antarctic Ridge *Pac. Oc.* 43°0S 115°0W 5 B13
Pacific Grove *U.S.A.* 36°38N 121°56W 78 J5
Pacific Ocean 10°0N 140°0W 65 G14
Pacific Rim △ *Canada* 48°40N 124°45W 78 B2
Pacifica *U.S.A.* 37°37N 122°27W 78 H4
Pacitan *Indonesia* 8°12S 111°7E 37 H14
Packwood *U.S.A.* 46°36N 121°40W 78 D5
Padaido, Kepulauan *Indonesia* 1°15S 136°30E 37 E9
Padang *Riau, Indonesia* 1°30N 102°30E 39 M4
Padang *Sumatera Barat, Indonesia* 1°0S 100°20E 36 E2
Padang Endau *Malaysia* 2°40N 103°38E 39 L4
Padangpanjang *Indonesia* 0°40S 100°20E 36 E2
Padangsidempuan *Indonesia* 1°30N 99°15E 36 D1
Paddle Prairie *Canada* 57°57N 117°29W 70 B5
Paderborn *Germany* 51°42N 8°45E 16 C5
Padma *India* 24°12N 85°22E 43 G11
Pádova *Italy* 45°25N 11°53E 22 B4
Padra *India* 22°15N 73°7E 42 H5
Padrauna *India* 26°54N 83°59E 43 F10
Padre I. *U.S.A.* 27°10N 97°25W 84 H6
Padre Island ⌂ *U.S.A.* 27°0N 97°25W 84 H6
Padstow *U.K.* 50°33N 4°58W 13 G3
Padua = Pádova *Italy* 45°25N 11°53E 22 B4
Paducah *Ky., U.S.A.* 37°5N 88°37W 80 G9
Paducah *Tex., U.S.A.* 34°1N 100°18W 84 D4
Paea *Tahiti* 17°41S 149°35W 59 d
Paeroa *N.Z.* 37°23S 175°41E 59 B5
Pafúri *Mozam.* 22°28S 31°17E 57 C5
Pag *Croatia* 44°25N 15°3E 16 F8
Pagadian *Phil.* 7°55N 123°30E 37 C6
Pagai Selatan, Pulau *Indonesia* 3°0S 100°15E 36 E2
Pagai Utara, Pulau *Indonesia* 2°35S 100°0E 36 E2
Pagalu = Annobón *Atl. Oc.* 1°25S 5°36E 49 G4
Pagara *India* 24°22N 80°1E 43 G9
Pagastikos Kolpos *Greece* 39°15N 23°0E 23 E10
Pagatan *Indonesia* 3°33S 115°59E 36 E5
Page *U.S.A.* 36°57N 111°27W 77 H8
Paget, Mt. *S. Georgia* 54°26S 36°31W 96 G9
Pago Pago *Amer. Samoa* 14°16S 170°43W 59 b
Pagosa Springs *U.S.A.* 37°16N 107°1W 77 H10
Pagwa River *Canada* 50°2N 85°14W 72 B2
Pāhala *U.S.A.* 19°12N 155°29W 75 M8
Pahang → *Malaysia* 3°30N 103°9E 39 L4
Pahiatua *N.Z.* 40°27S 175°50E 59 D5
Pahokee *U.S.A.* 26°50N 80°40W 85 H14
Pahrump *U.S.A.* 36°12N 115°59W 79 J11
Pahute Mesa *U.S.A.* 37°20N 116°45W 78 H10
Pai *Thailand* 19°19N 98°27E 38 C2
Paicines *U.S.A.* 36°44N 121°17W 78 J5
Paide *Estonia* 58°53N 25°33E 9 G21
Paignton *U.K.* 50°26N 3°35W 13 G4
Päijänne *Finland* 61°30N 25°30E 8 F21
Pailani *India* 25°45N 80°26E 43 G9
Pailin *Cambodia* 12°46N 102°36E 38 F4
Painan *Indonesia* 1°21S 100°34E 36 E2
Painesville *U.S.A.* 41°43N 81°15W 82 E3
Paint Hills = Wemindji *Canada* 53°0N 78°49W 72 B4
Paint L. *Canada* 55°28N 97°57W 71 B9
Painted Desert *U.S.A.* 36°0N 111°0W 77 H8
Paintsville *U.S.A.* 37°49N 82°48W 81 G12
País Vasco □ *Spain* 42°50N 2°45W 21 A4
Paisley *Canada* 44°18N 81°16W 82 B3
Paisley *U.K.* 55°50N 4°25W 11 F4
Paisley *U.S.A.* 42°42N 120°32W 76 E3
Paita *Peru* 5°11S 81°9W 92 E2
Pajares, Puerto de *Spain* 42°58N 5°46W 21 A3
Pak Lay *Laos* 18°15N 101°27E 38 C3
Pak Phanang *Thailand* 8°21N 100°12E 39 H3
Pak Sane *Laos* 18°22N 103°39E 38 C4
Pak Song *Laos* 15°11N 106°14E 38 E6
Pak Suong *Laos* 19°58N 102°15E 38 C4
Pak Tam Chung *China* 22°24N 114°19E 33 G11
Pakaur *India* 24°38N 87°51E 43 G12
Pakch'ŏn *N. Korea* 39°44N 125°35E 35 E13
Pakenham *Canada* 45°18N 76°18W 83 A8
Pakhuis *S. Africa* 32°9S 19°5E 56 E2
Pakistan ■ *Asia* 30°0N 70°0E 42 E4
Pakkading *Laos* 18°19N 103°59E 38 C4
Pakokku *Burma* 21°20N 95°0E 41 J19
Pakowki L. *Canada* 49°20N 111°0W 71 D6
Pakpattan *Pakistan* 30°25N 73°27E 42 D5
Paktīā □ *Afghan.* 33°30N 69°15E 40 C6
Paktīkā □ *Afghan.* 32°30N 69°0E 40 C6
Pakwach *Uganda* 2°28N 31°27E 54 B3
Pakxe *Laos* 15°5N 105°52E 38 E5
Pal Lahara *India* 21°27N 85°11E 43 J11
Pala *Chad* 9°25N 15°5E 51 G9
Pala *Dem. Rep. of the Congo* 6°45S 29°30E 54 D2
Pala *U.S.A.* 33°22N 117°5W 79 M9
Palabek *Uganda* 3°22N 32°33E 54 B3
Palacios *U.S.A.* 28°42N 96°13W 84 G6
Palagruža *Croatia* 42°24N 16°15E 22 C7
Palakkad = Palghat *India* 10°46N 76°42E 40 P10
Palam *India* 19°0N 77°0E 40 K10
Palampur *India* 32°10N 76°30E 42 C7
Palana *Australia* 39°45S 147°55E 63 F4
Palana *Russia* 59°10N 159°59E 29 D16
Palanan *Phil.* 17°8N 122°29E 37 A6
Palanan Pt. *Phil.* 17°17N 122°30E 37 A6
Palandri *Pakistan* 33°42N 73°40E 43 C5
Palanga *Lithuania* 55°58N 21°3E 9 J19
Palangkaraya *Indonesia* 2°16S 113°56E 36 E4
Palani Hills *India* 10°14N 77°33E 40 P10
Palanpur *India* 24°10N 72°25E 42 G5
Palapye *Botswana* 22°30S 27°7E 56 C4
Palas *Pakistan* 35°4N 73°14E 43 B5
Palasponga *India* 21°47N 85°34E 43 J11
Palatka *Russia* 60°6N 150°54E 29 C16
Palatka *U.S.A.* 29°39N 81°38W 85 G14
Palau ■ *Palau* 7°30N 134°30E 58 A6
Palauk *Burma* 13°10N 98°40E 38 F2
Palawan *Phil.* 9°30N 118°30E 36 C5
Palayankottai *India* 8°45N 77°45E 40 Q10
Paldiski *Estonia* 59°23N 24°9E 9 G21
Palekastro *Greece* 35°12N 26°15E 25 D8
Paleleh *Indonesia* 1°10N 121°50E 37 D6
Palembang *Indonesia* 3°0S 104°50E 36 E2
Palencia *Spain* 42°1N 4°34W 21 A3
Palenque *Mexico* 17°29N 92°1W 87 D6
Paleochora *Greece* 35°16N 23°39E 25 D5
Paleokastritsa *Greece* 39°40N 19°41E 25 A3
Paleometokho *Cyprus* 35°7N 33°11E 25 D12
Palermo *Italy* 38°7N 13°22E 22 E5
Palermo *U.S.A.* 39°26N 121°33W 76 G3
Palestina *Chile* 23°50S 69°47W 96 A3
Palestine *Asia* 32°0N 35°0E 46 D4
Palestine *U.S.A.* 31°46N 95°38W 84 F7
Paletwa *Burma* 21°10N 92°50E 41 J18
Palghat *India* 10°46N 76°42E 40 P10
Palgrave, Mt. *Australia* 23°22S 115°58E 60 D2
Pali *India* 25°50N 73°20E 42 G5
Palikir *Micronesia* 6°55N 158°9E 64 G7
Palioúri, Akra *Greece* 39°57N 23°45E 23 E10
Palisades Res. *U.S.A.* 43°20N 111°12W 76 E8
Paliseul *Belgium* 49°54N 5°8E 15 E5
Palitana *India* 21°32N 71°49E 42 J4
Palizada *Mexico* 18°15N 92°5W 87 D6
Palk Bay *Asia* 9°30N 79°15E 40 Q11
Palk Strait *Asia* 10°0N 79°45E 40 Q11
Palkānah *Iraq* 35°49N 44°26E 44 C5
Palkot *India* 22°53N 84°39E 43 H11
Pallanza = Verbánia *Italy* 45°56N 8°33E 20 D8
Pallarenda *Australia* 19°12S 146°46E 62 B4
Pallinup → *Australia* 34°27S 118°50E 61 F2
Pallisa *Uganda* 1°12N 33°43E 54 B3
Pallu *India* 28°59N 74°14E 42 E6
Palm Bay *U.S.A.* 28°2N 80°35W 85 G14
Palm Beach *U.S.A.* 26°43N 80°2W 85 H14
Palm Coast *U.S.A.* 29°35N 81°12W 85 G14
Palm Desert *U.S.A.* 33°43N 116°22W 79 M10
Palm-Grove △ *Australia* 24°57S 149°21E 62 C4
Palm Is. *Australia* 18°40S 146°35E 62 B4
Palm Springs *U.S.A.* 33°50N 116°33W 79 M10
Palma *Mozam.* 10°46S 40°29E 55 E5
Palma, B. de *Spain* 39°30N 2°39E 24 B9
Palma de Mallorca *Spain* 39°35N 2°39E 24 B9
Palma Nova = Palmanova *Spain* 39°32N 2°34E 24 B9
Palma Soriano *Cuba* 20°15N 76°0W 88 B4
Palmanova *Spain* 39°32N 2°34E 24 B9
Palmares *Brazil* 8°41S 35°28W 93 E11
Palmas *Brazil* 26°29S 52°0W 95 B5
Palmas, C. *Liberia* 4°27N 7°46W 50 H4
Pálmas, G. di *Italy* 39°0N 8°30E 22 E3
Palmdale *U.S.A.* 34°35N 118°7W 79 L8
Palmeira das Missões *Brazil* 27°55S 53°17W 95 B5
Palmeira dos Índios *Brazil* 9°25S 36°37W 93 E11
Palmer *Antarctica* 64°35S 65°0W 5 C17
Palmer *U.S.A.* 61°36N 149°7W 68 E2
Palmer → *Australia* 16°0S 142°26E 62 B3
Palmer Arch. *Antarctica* 64°15S 65°0W 5 C17
Palmer Lake *U.S.A.* 39°7N 104°55W 76 G11
Palmer Land *Antarctica* 73°0S 63°0W 5 D18
Palmerston *Australia* 12°31S 130°59E 60 B5
Palmerston *Canada* 43°50N 80°51W 82 C4
Palmerston *N.Z.* 45°29S 170°43E 59 F3
Palmerston North *N.Z.* 40°21S 175°39E 59 D5
Palmerton *U.S.A.* 40°48N 75°37W 83 F9
Palmetto *U.S.A.* 27°31N 82°34W 85 H13
Palmi *Italy* 38°21N 15°51E 22 E6
Palmira *Argentina* 32°59S 68°34W 94 C2
Palmira *Colombia* 3°32N 76°16W 92 C3
Palmyra = Tudmur *Syria* 34°36N 38°15E 44 C3
Palmyra *Mo., U.S.A.* 39°48N 91°32W 80 F8
Palmyra *N.J., U.S.A.* 40°0N 75°1W 83 F9
Palmyra *N.Y., U.S.A.* 43°5N 77°18W 82 C7
Palmyra *Pa., U.S.A.* 40°18N 76°36W 83 F8
Palmyra Is. *Pac. Oc.* 5°52N 162°5W 65 G11
Palo Alto *U.S.A.* 37°27N 122°10W 78 H4
Palo Seco *Trin. & Tob.* 10°4N 61°36W 93 K15
Palo Verde *U.S.A.* 33°26N 114°44W 79 M12
Palo Verde △ *Costa Rica* 10°21N 85°21W 88 D2
Palomar Mt. *U.S.A.* 33°22N 116°50W 79 M10
Palopo *Indonesia* 3°0S 120°16E 37 E6
Palos, C. de *Spain* 37°38N 0°40W 21 D5

Palos Verdes, Pt.
  U.S.A. 33°46N 118°25W 79 M8
Palos Verdes Estates
  U.S.A. 33°48N 118°23W 79 M8
Palu Indonesia 1°0S 119°52E 37 E5
Palu Turkey 38°45N 40°0E 44 B3
Paluma Ra. Australia 19°9S 146°22E 62 B4
Palwal India 28°8N 77°19E 42 E7
Pamanukan Indonesia 6°16S 107°49E 37 G12
Pamekasan Indonesia 7°10S 113°28E 37 G15
Pamenang Indonesia 8°24S 116°6E 37 J19
Pamiers France 43°7N 1°39E 20 E4
Pamir Tajikistan 37°40N 73°0E 28 F8
Pamlico → U.S.A. 35°20N 76°28W 85 D16
Pamlico Sd. U.S.A. 35°20N 76°0W 85 D17
Pampa U.S.A. 35°32N 100°58W 84 D4
Pampa de las Salinas
  Argentina 32°1S 66°58W 94 C2
Pampanua Indonesia 4°16S 120°8E 37 E6
Pampas Argentina 35°0S 63°0W 94 D3
Pampas Peru 12°20S 74°50W 92 F4
Pamplona Colombia 7°23N 72°39W 92 B4
Pamplona-Iruña Spain 42°48N 1°38W 21 A5
Pampoenpoort S. Africa 31°3S 22°40E 56 E3
Pan de Azúcar Chile 24°55S 68°10W 94 A2
Pan de Azúcar △ Chile 26°0S 70°40W 94 B1
Pana U.S.A. 39°23N 89°5W 80 F9
Panaca U.S.A. 37°47N 114°23W 77 H6
Panaitan Indonesia 6°36S 105°12E 37 G11
Panaji India 15°25N 73°50E 40 M8
Panama ■ Cent. Amer. 8°48N 79°55W 88 E4
Panamá Panama 9°0N 79°25W 88 E4
Panamá, G. de Panama 8°4N 79°20W 88 E4
Panama, Isthmus of
  Cent. Amer. 9°0N 79°0W 66 J12
Panama Basin Pac. Oc. 5°0N 83°30W 65 G19
Panama Canal Panama 9°10N 79°37W 88 E4
Panama City U.S.A. 30°10N 85°40W 85 F12
Panamint Range
  U.S.A. 36°20N 117°20W 79 J9
Panamint Springs
  U.S.A. 36°20N 117°28W 79 J9
Panão Peru 9°55S 75°55W 92 E3
Panare Thailand 6°51N 101°30E 39 J3
Panay Phil. 11°10N 122°30E 37 B6
Panay, G. Phil. 11°0N 122°30E 37 B6
Panayarvi △ Russia 66°16N 30°10E 8 C24
Pančevo Serbia 44°52N 20°41E 23 B9
Panda Mozam. 24°2S 34°45E 57 C5
Pandan Malaysia 1°32N 103°46E 39 d
Pandan Phil. 11°45N 122°10E 37 B6
Pandan, Selat Singapore 1°15N 103°44E 39 d
Pandan Tampoi = Tampoi
  Malaysia 1°30N 103°39E 39 d
Pandegelang Indonesia 6°25S 106°5E 37 G12
Pandhana India 21°42N 76°13E 42 J7
Pandharpur India 17°41N 75°20E 40 L9
Pando Uruguay 34°44S 56°0W 95 C4
Pando, L. = Hope, L.
  Australia 28°24S 139°18E 63 D2
Pandokratoras Greece 39°45N 19°50E 25 A3
Pandora Costa Rica 9°43N 83°3W 88 E3
Panevėžys Lithuania 55°42N 24°25E 9 J21
Pang-Long Burma 23°11N 98°45E 41 H21
Pang Sida △ Thailand 14°5N 102°17E 38 E4
Pang-Yang Burma 22°7N 98°48E 41 H21
Panga
  Dem. Rep. of the Congo 1°52N 26°18E 54 B2
Pangalanes, Canal des =
  Ampangalana, Lakandranon'
  Madag. 22°48S 47°50E 57 C8
Pangani Tanzania 5°25S 38°58E 54 D4
Pangani → Tanzania 5°26S 38°58E 54 D4
Pangfou = Bengbu
  China 32°58N 117°20E 35 H9
Pangil
  Dem. Rep. of the Congo 3°10S 26°35E 54 C2
Pangkah, Tanjung
  Indonesia 6°51S 112°33E 37 G15
Pangkajene Indonesia 4°46S 119°34E 37 E5
Pangkalanbrandan
  Indonesia 4°1N 98°20E 36 D1
Pangkalanbuun
  Indonesia 2°41S 111°37E 36 E4
Pangkalpinang Indonesia 2°0S 106°0E 36 E3
Pangkor, P. Malaysia 4°13N 100°34E 39 K3
Pangnirtung = Pangnirtung
  Canada 66°8N 65°43W 69 D18
Pangnirtung Canada 66°8N 65°43W 69 D18
Pangody Russia 65°52N 74°27E 28 C8
Pangong Tso = Bangong Co
  China 33°45N 78°43E 43 C8
Panguitch U.S.A. 37°50N 112°26W 77 H7
Panguturan Group Phil. 6°18N 120°34E 37 C6
Panhandle U.S.A. 35°21N 101°23W 84 D4
Pani Mines India 22°29N 73°50E 42 H5
Pania-Mutombo
  Dem. Rep. of the Congo 5°11S 23°51E 54 D1
Panikota I. India 20°46N 71°21E 42 J4
Panipat India 29°25N 77°2E 42 E7
Panjal Range = Pir Panjal Range
  India 32°30N 76°50E 42 C7
Panjang, Hon Vietnam 9°20N 103°28E 39 H4
Panjgur Pakistan 27°0N 64°5E 40 F4
Panjim = Panaji India 15°25N 73°50E 40 M8
Panjin China 41°3N 122°2E 35 D12
Panjnad → Pakistan 28°57N 70°30E 42 E4
Panjnad Barrage
  Pakistan 29°22N 71°15E 42 E4
Panjwai Afghan. 31°26N 65°27E 42 D1
Panna India 24°40N 80°15E 43 G9
Panna △ India 24°40N 80°0E 43 G8
Panna Hills India 24°40N 81°15E 43 G9
Pannawonica Australia 21°39S 116°19E 60 D2
Pannga, Tanjung
  Indonesia 8°54S 116°2E 37 K19
Pano Akil Pakistan 27°51N 69°7E 42 F3
Pano Lefkara Cyprus 34°53N 33°20E 25 E12

Pano Panayia Cyprus 34°55N 32°38E 25 E11
Panorama Brazil 21°21S 51°51W 95 A5
Panormos Greece 35°25N 24°41E 25 D6
Pansemal India 21°39N 74°42E 42 J6
Panshan = Panjin China 41°3N 122°2E 35 D12
Panshi China 42°58N 126°5E 35 C14
Pantanal Brazil 17°30S 57°40W 92 H7
Pantanos de Centla △
  Mexico 18°25N 92°25W 87 D6
Pantar Indonesia 8°28S 124°10E 37 F6
Pante Macassar E. Timor 9°30S 123°58E 37 F6
Pantelleria Italy 36°50N 11°57E 22 F4
Pánuco Mexico 22°3N 98°10W 87 C5
Panzhihua China 26°33N 101°44E 32 D5
Paola Malta 35°52N 14°30E 25 D2
Paola U.S.A. 38°35N 94°53W 80 F6
Paonia U.S.A. 38°52N 107°36W 76 G10
Paopao Moorea 17°30S 149°49W 59 d
Paoting = Baoding
  China 38°50N 115°28E 34 E8
Paot'ou = Baotou China 40°32N 110°2E 34 D6
Paoua C.A.R. 7°9N 16°20E 52 G3
Pápa Hungary 47°22N 17°30E 17 E9
Papa Stour U.K. 60°20N 1°42W 11 A7
Papagayo → Mexico 16°46N 99°43W 87 D5
Papagayo, G. de
  Costa Rica 10°30N 85°50W 88 D2
Papakura N.Z. 37°4S 174°59E 59 B5
Papantla Mexico 20°27N 97°19W 87 C5
Papar Malaysia 5°45N 116°0E 36 C5
Papara Tahiti 17°43S 149°31W 59 d
Paparoa △ N.Z. 42°7S 171°26E 59 E3
Papeete Tahiti 17°32S 149°34W 59 d
Papenoo Tahiti 17°30S 149°25W 59 d
Papenoo → Tahiti 17°30S 149°25W 59 d
Papetoai Moorea 17°29S 149°52W 59 d
Paphos Cyprus 34°46N 32°25E 25 E11
Papoose Chile 25°0S 70°30W 94 B1
Papoutsa Cyprus 34°54N 33°4E 25 E12
Papua □ Indonesia 4°0S 137°0E 37 E9
Papua, G. of Papua N. G. 9°0S 144°50E 58 B7
Papua New Guinea ■
  Oceania 8°0S 145°0E 58 B7
Papudo Chile 32°29S 71°27W 94 C1
Papun Burma 18°2N 97°30E 41 K20
Papunya Australia 23°15S 131°54E 60 D5
Pará = Belém Brazil 1°20S 48°30W 93 D9
Pará □ Brazil 3°20S 52°0W 93 D8
Paraburdoo Australia 23°14S 117°32E 60 D2
Paracatu Brazil 17°10S 46°50W 93 G9
Paracel Is. S. China Sea 15°50N 112°0E 36 A4
Parachilna Australia 31°10S 138°21E 63 E2
Parachinar Pakistan 33°55N 70°5E 42 C4
Paradip India 20°15N 86°35E 41 J15
Paradise Calif., U.S.A. 39°46N 121°37W 78 F5
Paradise Nev., U.S.A. 36°5N 115°8W 79 J11
Paradise → Canada 53°27N 57°19W 73 B8
Paradise Hill Canada 53°32N 109°28W 71 C7
Paradise River Canada 53°27N 57°17W 73 B8
Paradise Valley U.S.A. 41°30N 117°32W 76 F5
Paradisi Greece 36°18N 28°7E 25 C10
Parado Indonesia 8°42S 118°30E 37 F5
Paragould U.S.A. 36°3N 90°29W 85 C9
Paragua → Venezuela 6°55N 62°55W 92 B6
Paraguaçu → Brazil 12°45S 38°54W 93 F11
Paraguaçu Paulista
  Brazil 22°22S 50°35W 95 A5
Paraguaná, Pen. de
  Venezuela 12°0N 70°0W 92 A5
Paraguarí Paraguay 25°36S 57°0W 94 B4
Paraguarí □ Paraguay 26°0S 57°10W 94 B4
Paraguay ■ S. Amer. 23°0S 57°0W 94 A4
Paraguay → Paraguay 27°18S 58°38W 94 B4
Paraíba = João Pessoa
  Brazil 7°10S 34°52W 93 E12
Paraíba □ Brazil 7°0S 36°0W 93 E11
Paraíba do Sul → Brazil 21°37S 41°3W 95 A7
Parainen Finland 60°18N 22°18E 9 F20
Paraíso Mexico 18°24N 93°14W 87 D6
Parak Iran 27°38N 52°25E 45 E7
Parakou Benin 9°25N 2°40E 50 G6
Paralimni Cyprus 35°2N 33°58E 25 D12
Paramaribo Suriname 5°50N 55°10W 93 B7
Páramos del Batallón y La
  Negra △ Venezuela 8°2N 71°55W 89 E5
Paramushir, Ostrov
  Russia 50°24N 156°0E 29 D16
Paran → Israel 30°20N 35°10E 46 E4
Paraná Argentina 31°45S 60°30W 94 C3
Paraná Brazil 12°30S 47°48W 93 F9
Paraná □ Brazil 24°30S 51°0W 95 A5
Paraná → Argentina 33°43S 59°15W 94 C4
Paranaguá Brazil 25°30S 48°30W 95 B6
Paranaíba Brazil 19°40S 51°11W 93 G8
Paranaíba → Brazil 20°6S 51°4W 93 H8
Paranapanema → Brazil 22°40S 53°9W 95 A5
Paranapiacaba, Serra do
  Brazil 24°31S 48°35W 95 A6
Paranavaí Brazil 23°4S 52°56W 95 A5
Parang Maguindanao,
  Phil. 7°23N 124°16E 37 C6
Parang Sulu, Phil. 5°55N 120°54E 37 C6
Parângul Mare, Vf.
  Romania 45°20N 23°37E 17 F12
Paraparaumu N.Z. 40°57S 175°3E 59 D5
Parbati → Mad. P., India 25°50N 76°30E 42 G7
Parbati → Raj., India 26°54N 77°53E 42 F7
Parbhani India 19°8N 76°52E 40 K10
Parchim Germany 53°26N 11°52E 16 B6
Pardes Hanna-Karkur
  Israel 32°28N 34°57E 46 C3
Pardo → Bahia, Brazil 15°40S 39°0W 93 G11
Pardo → Mato Grosso,
  Brazil 21°46S 52°9W 95 A5
Pardoo Roadhouse
  Australia 20°6S 119°3E 60 D2
Pardubice Czech Rep. 50°3N 15°45E 16 C8
Pare Indonesia 7°43S 112°12E 37 G15

Pare Mts. Tanzania 4°0S 37°45E 54 C4
Parecis, Serra dos Brazil 13°0S 60°0W 92 F7
Paren Russia 62°30N 163°15E 29 C17
Parent Canada 47°55N 74°35W 72 C5
Parent, L. Canada 48°31N 77°1W 72 C4
Parepare Indonesia 4°0S 119°40E 37 E5
Parga Greece 39°15N 20°29E 23 E9
Pargas = Parainen
  Finland 60°18N 22°18E 9 F20
Pargo, Pta. do Madeira 32°49N 17°17W 24 D2
Parham Canada 44°39N 76°43W 83 B8
Paria → Venezuela 10°20N 62°0W 93 K14
Paria, G. de Venezuela 10°20N 62°0W 93 K14
Pariaguán Venezuela 8°51N 64°34W 92 B6
Paricutín, Cerro
  Mexico 19°28N 102°15W 86 D4
Parigi Indonesia 0°50S 120°5E 37 E6
Parika Guyana 6°50N 58°20W 92 B7
Parikkala Finland 61°33N 29°31E 8 F23
Parima, Serra Brazil 2°30N 64°0W 92 C6
Parinari Peru 4°35S 74°25W 92 D4
Pariñas, Pta. Peru 4°30S 82°0W 90 D2
Parintins Brazil 2°40S 56°50W 93 D7
Paripat Kyun Burma 14°52N 93°41E 41 M18
Paris Canada 43°12N 80°25E 82 C4
Paris France 48°53N 2°20E 20 B5
Paris Idaho, U.S.A. 42°14N 111°24W 76 E8
Paris Ky., U.S.A. 38°13N 84°15W 81 F11
Paris Tenn., U.S.A. 36°18N 88°19W 85 C10
Paris Tex., U.S.A. 33°40N 95°33W 84 E7
Parish U.S.A. 43°25N 76°8W 83 C8
Parishville U.S.A. 44°38N 74°49W 83 B10
Pariti Indonesia 10°1S 123°45E 60 B3
Park U.S.A. 48°45N 122°18W 78 B4
Park City U.S.A. 37°48N 97°20W 80 G5
Park Falls U.S.A. 45°56N 90°27W 80 C8
Park Head Canada 44°36N 81°9W 82 B3
Park Hills U.S.A. 37°53N 90°28W 80 G9
Park Range U.S.A. 40°41N 106°41W 76 F10
Park Rapids U.S.A. 46°55N 95°4W 80 B6
Park River U.S.A. 48°24N 97°45W 80 A5
Park Rynie S. Africa 30°25S 30°45E 57 E5
Parkā Bandar Iran 25°55N 59°35E 45 E8
Parkano Finland 62°1N 23°0E 8 E20
Parker Ariz., U.S.A. 34°9N 114°17W 79 L12
Parker Pa., U.S.A. 41°5N 79°41W 82 E5
Parker Dam U.S.A. 34°18N 114°8W 79 L12
Parkersburg U.S.A. 39°16N 81°34W 81 F13
Parkes Australia 33°9S 148°11E 63 E4
Parkfield U.S.A. 35°54N 120°26W 78 K6
Parkhill Canada 43°15N 81°38W 82 C3
Parkland U.S.A. 47°9N 122°26W 78 C4
Parkston U.S.A. 43°24N 97°59W 80 D5
Parksville Canada 49°20N 124°21W 70 D4
Parkway U.S.A. 38°32N 121°26W 78 G5
Parla Spain 40°14N 3°46W 21 B4
Parma Italy 44°48N 10°20E 20 D9
Parma Idaho, U.S.A. 43°47N 116°57W 76 E5
Parma Ohio, U.S.A. 41°24N 81°43W 82 E3
Parnaguá Brazil 10°10S 44°38W 93 F10
Parnaíba Brazil 2°54S 41°47W 93 D10
Parnaíba → Brazil 3°0S 41°50W 93 D10
Parnassós Greece 38°35N 22°30E 23 E10
Pärnu Estonia 58°28N 24°33E 9 G21
Paro Dzong Bhutan 27°23N 89°53E 43 F13
Paroo → Australia 31°28S 143°32E 63 E3
Paros Greece 37°5S 25°12E 23 F11
Parowan U.S.A. 37°51N 112°50W 77 H7
Parral Chile 36°10S 71°52W 94 D1
Parramatta Australia 33°48S 151°1E 63 B5
Parras Mexico 25°25N 102°11W 86 B4
Parrett → U.K. 51°12N 3°1W 13 F4
Parris I. U.S.A. 32°20N 80°41W 85 E14
Parrsboro Canada 45°30N 64°25W 73 C7
Parry Channel Canada 74°45N 94°0W 69 C13
Parry I. Canada 45°18N 80°10W 82 A4
Parry Is. Canada 77°0N 110°0W 69 B10
Parry Sound Canada 45°20N 80°0W 82 A5
Parsaloi Kenya 1°16N 36°51E 54 B4
Parsnip → Canada 55°10N 123°2W 70 B4
Parsons U.S.A. 37°20N 95°16W 80 G6
Parsons Ra. Australia 13°30S 135°15E 62 A2
Partinico Italy 38°3N 13°7E 22 E5
Partizansk Russia 43°8N 133°9E 30 C6
Partridge I. Canada 55°59N 87°37W 72 A2
Partry Mts. Ireland 53°40N 9°28W 10 C2
Paru → Brazil 1°33S 52°38W 93 D8
Parvān □ Afghan. 35°0N 69°0E 40 B6
Parvatipuram India 18°50N 83°25E 41 K13
Parvatsar India 26°52N 74°49E 42 F6
Parys S. Africa 26°54S 27°27E 56 D4
Pas, Pta. des Spain 38°46N 1°26E 24 C7
Pas, The Canada 53°45N 101°15W 71 C8
Pasadena Canada 49°1N 57°36W 73 C8
Pasadena Calif., U.S.A. 34°9N 118°8W 79 L8
Pasadena Tex., U.S.A. 29°43N 95°13W 84 G7
Pasaje → Argentina 25°39S 63°56W 94 B3
Pasar Indonesia 8°27S 114°54E 37 J17
Pascagoula U.S.A. 30°21N 88°33W 85 F10
Pascagoula → U.S.A. 30°23N 88°37W 85 F10
Pașcani Romania 47°14N 26°45E 17 E14
Pasco U.S.A. 46°14N 119°6W 76 C4
Pasco I. Australia 20°57S 115°20E 60 D2
Pasco, I. de Chile 27°7S 109°23W 65 K17
Pasfield L. Canada 58°24N 105°20W 71 B7
Pasir Mas Malaysia 6°2N 102°8E 39 J4
Pasir Panjang Singapore 1°18N 103°46E 39 d
Pasir Putih Malaysia 5°50N 102°24E 39 K4
Pasirian Indonesia 8°13S 113°8E 37 H15
Pasirkuning Indonesia 0°30S 104°33E 36 E2
Paskūh Iran 27°34N 61°39E 45 E9
Pasley, C. Australia 33°52S 123°35E 61 F3
Pašman Croatia 43°58N 15°20E 16 G8
Pasni Pakistan 25°15N 63°27E 40 G3
Paso Bravo △ Paraguay 22°32S 57°5W 94 A4
Paso Cantinela
  Mexico 32°33N 115°47W 79 N11
Paso de Indios Argentina 43°55S 69°0W 96 E3

Paso de los Libres
  Argentina 29°44S 57°10W 94 B4
Paso de los Toros
  Uruguay 32°45S 56°30W 94 C4
Paso Robles U.S.A. 35°38N 120°41W 78 K6
Paspébiac Canada 48°3N 65°17W 73 C6
Pasrur Pakistan 32°16N 74°43E 42 C6
Passage East Ireland 52°14N 7°0W 10 D5
Passage West Ireland 51°52N 8°21W 10 E3
Passaic U.S.A. 40°51N 74°7W 83 F10
Passau Germany 48°34N 13°28E 16 D7
Passero, C. Italy 36°41N 15°10E 22 F6
Passo Fundo Brazil 28°10S 52°20W 95 B5
Passos Brazil 20°45S 46°37W 93 H9
Pastavy Belarus 55°4N 26°50E 9 J22
Pastaza → Peru 4°50S 76°52W 92 D3
Pasto Colombia 1°13N 77°17W 92 C3
Pasuruan Indonesia 7°40S 112°44E 37 G15
Patagonia U.S.A. 31°33N 110°45W 77 L8
Patagonia Argentina 45°0S 69°0W 96 F3
Patambar Iran 29°45N 60°17E 45 D9
Patan = Lalitapur Nepal 27°40N 85°20E 43 F11
Patan = Somnath India 20°53N 70°22E 42 J4
Patan India 23°54N 72°14E 42 H5
Patani Indonesia 0°20N 128°50E 37 D7
Pataudi India 28°18N 76°48E 42 E7
Patchewollock Australia 35°22S 142°12E 63 F3
Patchogue U.S.A. 40°46N 73°1W 83 F11
Pate Kenya 2°10S 41°0E 54 C5
Patea N.Z. 39°45S 174°30E 59 C5
Patensie S. Africa 33°46S 24°49E 56 E3
Paternò Italy 37°34N 14°54E 22 F6
Pateros U.S.A. 48°3N 119°54W 76 B4
Paterson U.S.A. 40°54N 74°9W 83 F10
Paterson Ra. Australia 21°45S 122°10E 60 D3
Pathankot India 32°18N 75°45E 42 C6
Pathein = Bassein
  Burma 16°45N 94°30E 41 L19
Pathfinder Res. U.S.A. 42°28N 106°51W 76 E10
Pathiu Thailand 10°42N 99°19E 39 G2
Pathum Thani Thailand 14°1N 100°32E 38 E3
Pati Indonesia 6°45S 111°1E 37 G14
Patía → Colombia 2°13N 78°40W 92 C3
Patiala Punjab, India 30°23N 76°26E 42 D7
Patiala Ut. P., India 27°43N 79°1E 43 F8
Patkai Bum India 27°0N 95°30E 41 F19
Patmos Greece 37°21N 26°36E 23 F12
Patna India 25°35N 85°12E 43 G11
Pato Branco Brazil 26°13S 52°40W 95 B5
Patong, Ao Thailand 7°54N 98°17E 39 a
Patonga Uganda 2°45N 33°15E 54 B3
Patos Brazil 6°55S 37°16W 93 E11
Patos, L. dos Brazil 31°20S 51°0W 95 C5
Patos, Río de los →
  Argentina 31°18S 69°25W 94 C2
Patos de Minas Brazil 18°35S 46°32W 93 G9
Patquía Argentina 30°2S 66°55W 94 C2
Patra Greece 38°14N 21°47E 23 E9
Patraikós Kolpos Greece 38°17N 21°30E 23 E9
Patras = Patra Greece 38°14N 21°47E 23 E9
Patriot Hills Antarctica 82°20S 81°25W 5 E16
Patrocínio Brazil 18°57S 47°0W 93 G9
Pattani Thailand 6°48N 101°15E 39 J3
Pattaya Thailand 12°52N 100°55E 38 F3
Patten U.S.A. 46°0N 68°38W 81 B19
Patterson Calif., U.S.A. 37°28N 121°8W 78 H5
Patterson La., U.S.A. 29°42N 91°18W 85 G9
Patterson, Mt. U.S.A. 38°29N 119°20W 78 G7
Patti Punjab, India 31°17N 74°54E 42 D6
Patti Ut. P., India 25°55N 82°12E 43 G10
Patton U.S.A. 40°38N 78°39W 82 F6
Patuakhali Bangla. 22°20N 90°25E 41 H17
Patuanak Canada 55°55N 107°43W 71 B7
Patuca → Honduras 15°50N 84°18W 88 C3
Patuca, Punta Honduras 15°49N 84°14W 88 C3
Patuca □ Honduras 14°30N 85°30W 88 D3
Patvinsuo △ Finland 63°7N 30°45E 8 E24
Pátzcuaro Mexico 19°31N 101°38W 86 D4
Pau France 43°19N 0°25W 20 E3
Paudash Canada 44°59N 77°58W 82 B7
Pauk Burma 21°27N 94°30E 41 J19
Paul I. Canada 56°30N 61°20W 73 A7
Paul Smiths U.S.A. 44°26N 74°15W 83 B10
Paulatuk Canada 69°25N 124°0W 68 D7
Paulding Bay S. Ocean 66°0S 118°0E 5 C8
Paulistana Brazil 8°9S 41°9W 93 E10
Paulo Afonso Brazil 9°21S 38°15W 93 E11
Paulpietersburg S. Africa 27°23S 30°50E 57 D5
Pauls Valley U.S.A. 34°44N 97°13W 84 H6
Pauma Valley U.S.A. 33°16N 116°58W 79 M10
Pauri India 30°9N 78°47E 43 D8
Päveh Iran 35°3N 46°22E 44 C5
Pavia Italy 45°7N 9°8E 20 D8
Pavilion U.S.A. 42°52N 78°1W 82 D6
Pavlistan = Pavlohrad
  Ukraine 48°30N 35°52E 19 E6
Pavlodar Kazakhstan 52°33N 77°0E 28 D8
Pavlograd = Pavlohrad
  Ukraine 48°30N 35°52E 19 E6
Pavlohrad Ukraine 48°30N 35°52E 19 E6
Pavlovo Russia 55°58N 43°5E 18 C7
Pavlovsk Russia 50°26N 40°5E 19 E7
Pavlovskaya Russia 46°17N 39°47E 19 E6
Pawai, Pulau Singapore 1°11N 103°44E 39 d
Pawayan India 28°4N 80°6E 43 E9
Pawhuska U.S.A. 36°40N 96°20W 84 C6
Pawling U.S.A. 41°34N 73°36W 83 E11
Pawnee U.S.A. 36°20N 96°48W 84 C6
Pawnee City U.S.A. 40°7N 96°9W 80 E5
Pawtucket U.S.A. 41°53N 71°23W 83 E13
Paxi Greece 39°14N 20°12E 23 E9
Paximadia Greece 35°0N 24°35E 25 E6
Paxton U.S.A. 40°27N 88°6W 80 E9
Payakumbuh Indonesia 0°20S 100°35E 36 E2
Payette U.S.A. 44°5N 116°56W 76 D5
Payne Bay = Kangirsuk
  Canada 60°0N 70°0W 69 F17
Payne L. Canada 59°30N 74°30W 69 F17
Paynes Find Australia 29°15S 117°42E 61 E2

Paynesville U.S.A. 45°23N 94°43W 80 C6
Paysandú Uruguay 32°19S 58°8W 94 C4
Payson Ariz., U.S.A. 34°14N 111°20W 77 J8
Payson Utah, U.S.A. 40°3N 111°44W 76 F8
Paz → Guatemala 13°44N 90°10W 88 D1
Paz, B. de la Mexico 24°9N 110°25W 86 C2
Pāzanān Iran 30°35N 49°59E 45 D6
Pazardzhik Bulgaria 42°12N 24°20E 23 C11
Pe Ell U.S.A. 46°34N 123°18W 78 D3
Peabody U.S.A. 42°31N 70°56W 83 D14
Peace → Canada 59°0N 111°25W 70 B6
Peace Point Canada 59°7N 112°27W 70 B6
Peace River Canada 56°15N 117°18W 70 B5
Peach Springs U.S.A. 35°32N 113°25W 77 J7
Peachland Canada 49°47N 119°45W 70 D5
Peachtree City U.S.A. 33°25N 84°35W 85 E12
Peak, The = Kinder Scout
  U.K. 53°24N 1°52W 12 D6
Peak Charles △
  Australia 32°42S 121°10E 61 F3
Peak District △ U.K. 53°24N 1°46W 12 D6
Peak Hill Australia 32°47S 148°11E 63 E4
Peak Ra. Australia 22°50S 148°20E 62 C4
Peake Cr. → Australia 28°2S 136°7E 63 D2
Peale, Mt. U.S.A. 38°26N 109°14W 76 G9
Pearblossom U.S.A. 34°30N 117°55W 79 L9
Pearl → U.S.A. 30°11N 89°32W 85 F10
Pearl and Hermes Reef
  U.S.A. 27°55N 175°45W 75 K4
Pearl River U.S.A. 41°4N 74°2W 83 E10
Pearsall U.S.A. 28°54N 99°6W 84 G5
Pearson Int. Toronto ✈ (YYZ)
  Canada 43°46N 79°35W 82 C5
Peary Land Greenland 82°40N 33°0W 4 A6
Pease → U.S.A. 34°12N 99°2W 84 D5
Peawanuck Canada 55°15N 85°12W 72 A2
Pebane Mozam. 17°10S 38°8E 55 F4
Pebas Peru 3°10S 71°46W 92 D4
Pebble Beach U.S.A. 36°34N 121°57W 78 J5
Peć Kosovo 42°40N 20°17E 23 C9
Pechenga Russia 69°29N 31°4E 8 B24
Pechenizhyn Ukraine 48°30N 24°48E 17 D13
Pechiguera, Pta.
  Canary Is. 28°51N 13°53W 24 F6
Pechora Russia 65°10N 57°11E 18 A10
Pechora → Russia 68°13N 54°15E 18 A9
Pechorskaya Guba Russia 68°40N 54°0E 18 A9
Pechory Russia 57°48N 27°40E 9 H22
Pecos N. Mex., U.S.A. 35°35N 105°41W 77 J11
Pecos Tex., U.S.A. 31°26N 103°30W 84 F3
Pecos → U.S.A. 29°42N 101°22W 84 G4
Pécs Hungary 46°5N 18°15E 17 E10
Pedasi Panama 7°32N 80°2W 88 E3
Peddie S. Africa 33°14S 27°7E 57 E4
Pedernales Dom. Rep. 18°2N 71°44W 89 C5
Pedieos → Cyprus 35°10N 33°54E 25 D12
Pedirka Desert Australia 26°47S 134°11E 63 A1
Pedra Azul Brazil 16°2S 41°17W 93 G10
Pedra Lume C. Verde Is. 16°40N 22°52W 50 b
Pedreiras Brazil 4°32S 44°40W 93 D10
Pedro Afonso Brazil 9°0S 48°10W 93 E9
Pedro Cays Jamaica 17°5N 77°48W 88 C4
Pedro de Valdivia Chile 22°55S 69°38W 94 A2
Pedro Juan Caballero
  Paraguay 22°30S 55°40W 95 A4
Pee Dee = Great Pee Dee →
  U.S.A. 33°21N 79°10W 85 E15
Peebinga Australia 34°52S 140°57E 63 E3
Peebles U.K. 55°40N 3°11W 11 F5
Peekskill U.S.A. 41°17N 73°55W 83 E11
Peel I. of Man 54°13N 4°40W 12 C3
Peel → Australia 30°50S 150°29E 63 E5
Peel → Canada 67°0N 135°0W 68 D5
Peel Sd. Canada 73°0N 96°0W 68 C12
Peera Peera Poolanna L.
  Australia 26°30S 138°0E 63 D2
Peerless Lake Canada 56°37N 114°40W 70 B6
Peers Canada 53°40N 116°0W 70 C5
Pegasus Bay N.Z. 43°20S 173°10E 59 E4
Pegu Burma 17°20N 96°29E 41 L20
Pegu Yoma Burma 19°0N 96°0E 41 K20
Pehuajó Argentina 35°45S 62°0W 94 D3
Pei Xian = Pizhou
  China 34°44N 116°55E 34 G9
Peine Chile 23°45S 68°8W 94 A2
Peine Germany 52°19N 10°14E 16 B6
Peip'ing = Beijing China 39°53N 116°21E 34 E9
Peipus, L. = Chudskoye, Ozero
  Russia 58°13N 27°30E 9 G22
Peixe Brazil 12°0S 48°40W 93 F9
Peixe → Brazil 21°31S 51°58W 93 H8
Pekalongan Indonesia 6°53S 109°40E 37 G13
Pekan Malaysia 3°30N 103°25E 39 L4
Pekan Nenas Malaysia 1°31N 103°31E 39 d
Pekanbaru Indonesia 0°30N 101°15E 36 D2
Pekin U.S.A. 40°35N 89°40W 80 E9
Peking = Beijing China 39°53N 116°21E 34 E9
Pekutatan Indonesia 8°25S 114°49E 37 J17
Pelabuhan Klang
  Malaysia 3°0N 101°23E 39 L3
Pelabuhan Ratu, Teluk
  Indonesia 7°5S 106°30E 37 G12
Pelabuhanratu Indonesia 7°0S 106°32E 37 G12
Pelagie, Is. Italy 35°39N 12°33E 22 G5
Pelaihari Indonesia 3°55S 114°45E 36 E4
Peleaga, Vf. Romania 45°22N 22°55E 17 F12
Pelée, Mt. Martinique 14°48N 61°10W 88 c
Pelee, Pt. Canada 41°54N 82°31W 72 D3
Pelee I. Canada 41°47N 82°40W 82 E2
Pelekech Kenya 3°52N 35°8E 54 B4
Peleng Indonesia 1°20S 123°30E 37 E6
Pelentong Malaysia 1°32N 103°49E 39 d
Pelican U.S.A. 57°58N 136°14W 70 B1
Pelican L. Canada 52°28N 100°20W 71 C8
Pelican Narrows
  Canada 55°10N 102°56W 71 B8
Peljesac Croatia 42°55N 17°25E 22 C7
Pelkosenniemi Finland 67°6N 27°28E 8 C22

Pella *S. Africa* 29°1S 19°6E **56** D2
Pella *U.S.A.* 41°25N 92°55W **80** E7
Pello *Finland* 66°47N 23°59E **8** C20
Pelly → *Canada* 62°47N 137°19W **70** A1
Pelly Bay *Canada* 68°38N 89°50W **69** D14
Peloponnese → *Greece* 37°10N 22°0E **23** F10
Pelorus Sd. *N.Z.* 40°59S 173°59E **59** D4
Pelotas *Brazil* 31°42S 52°23W **95** C5
Pelotas → *Brazil* 27°28S 51°55W **95** B5
Pelvoux, Massif du
  France 44°52N 6°20E **20** D7
Pemalang *Indonesia* 6°53S 109°23E **37** G13
Pemanggil, Pulau
  Malaysia 2°37N 104°21E **39** L5
Pematangsiantar *Indonesia* 2°57N 99°5E **36** D1
Pemba *Mozam.* 12°58S 40°30E **55** E5
Pemba *Zambia* 16°30S 27°28E **55** F2
Pemba Channel *Tanzania* 5°0S 39°37E **54** D4
Pemba I. *Tanzania* 5°0S 39°45E **54** D4
Pemberton *Australia* 34°30S 116°0E **61** F2
Pemberton *Canada* 50°25N 122°50W **70** C4
Pembina → *U.S.A.* 54°45N 114°17W **70** D6
Pembina → *U.S.A.* 54°45N 114°17W **70** D6
Pembroke *Canada* 45°50N 77°7W **72** C4
Pembroke *U.K.* 51°41N 4°55W **13** F3
Pembrokeshire □ *U.K.* 51°52N 4°56W **13** F3
Pembrokeshire Coast △
  U.K. 51°50N 5°2W **13** F2
Pen-y-Ghent *U.K.* 54°10N 2°14W **12** C5
Penal *Trin. & Tob.* 10°9N 61°29W **93** K15
Penang = Pinang
  Malaysia 5°25N 100°15E **39** c
Penápolis *Brazil* 21°30S 50°0W **95** A6
Peñarroya-Pueblonuevo
  Spain 38°19N 5°16W **21** C3
Penarth *U.K.* 51°26N 3°11W **13** F4
Peñas, C. de *Spain* 43°42N 5°52W **21** A3
Peñas, G. de *Chile* 47°0S 75°0W **96** F2
Peñas del Chache
  Canary Is. 29°6N 13°33W **24** E6
Pench △ *India* 21°45N 79°20E **43** J8
Penchʼi = Benxi *China* 41°20N 123°48E **35** D12
Pend Oreille → *U.S.A.* 49°4N 117°37W **76** B5
Pend Oreille, L. *U.S.A.* 48°10N 116°21W **76** B5
Pendembu *S. Leone* 9°7N 11°14W **50** G3
Pendleton *U.S.A.* 45°40N 118°47W **76** D4
Pendra *India* 22°46N 81°57E **43** H9
Penedo *Brazil* 10°15S 36°36W **93** F11
Penelokan *Indonesia* 8°17S 115°22E **37** J18
Penetanguishene
  Canada 44°50N 79°55W **82** B5
Penfield *U.S.A.* 41°13N 78°35W **82** E6
Peng Chau *China* 22°17N 114°2E **33** G11
Pengalengan *Indonesia* 7°9S 107°30E **37** G12
Penge *Kasai-Or.,*
  Dem. Rep. of the Congo 5°30S 24°33E **54** D1
Penge *Sud-Kivu,*
  Dem. Rep. of the Congo 4°27S 28°25E **54** C2
Penglai *China* 37°48N 120°42E **35** F11
Penguin *Australia* 41°8S 146°6E **63** G4
Penhalonga *Zimbabwe* 18°52S 32°40E **55** F3
Peniche *Portugal* 39°19N 9°22W **21** C1
Penicuik *U.K.* 55°50N 3°13W **11** F5
Penida, Nusa *Indonesia* 8°45S 115°30E **37** K18
Peninsular Malaysia □
  Malaysia 4°0N 102°0E **39** L4
Penitente, Serra do *Brazil* 8°45S 46°20W **93** E9
Penkridge *U.K.* 52°44N 2°6W **12** E5
Penn Hills *U.S.A.* 40°28N 79°52W **82** F5
Penn Yan *U.S.A.* 42°40N 77°3W **82** D7
Pennant *Canada* 50°32N 108°14W **71** C7
Penner → *India* 14°35N 80°10E **40** M12
Pennines *U.K.* 54°45N 2°27W **12** C5
Pennington *U.S.A.* 39°15N 121°47W **78** F5
Pennsburg *U.S.A.* 40°23N 75°29W **83** F9
Pennsylvania □ *U.S.A.* 40°45N 77°30W **81** E15
Penny *Canada* 53°51N 121°20W **70** C4
Penobscot → *U.S.A.* 44°30N 68°48W **81** C19
Penobscot B. *U.S.A.* 44°35N 68°50W **81** C19
Penola *Australia* 37°25S 140°48E **63** F3
Penong *Australia* 31°56S 133°1E **61** F5
Penonomé *Panama* 8°31N 80°21W **88** E3
Penrhyn *Cook Is.* 9°0S 158°0W **65** H12
Penrith *Australia* 33°43S 150°38E **63** E5
Penrith *U.K.* 54°40N 2°45W **12** C5
Penryn *U.K.* 50°9N 5°7W **13** G2
Pensacola *U.S.A.* 30°25N 87°13W **85** F11
Pensacola Mts. *Antarctica* 84°0S 40°0W **5** E1
Pense *Canada* 50°25N 104°59W **71** C8
Penshurst *Australia* 37°49S 142°20E **63** F3
Penticton *Canada* 49°30N 119°38W **70** D5
Pentland *Australia* 20°32S 145°25E **62** C4
Pentland Firth *U.K.* 58°43N 3°10W **11** C5
Pentland Hills *U.K.* 55°48N 3°25W **11** F5
Pentland Hills △ *U.K.* 55°50N 3°20W **11** F5
Penza *Russia* 53°15N 45°5E **18** D8
Penzance *U.K.* 50°7N 5°33W **13** G2
Penzhino *Russia* 63°30N 167°55E **29** C17
Penzhinskaya Guba
  Russia 61°30N 163°0E **29** C17
Peoria *Ariz., U.S.A.* 33°43N 112°14W **77** K7
Peoria *Ill., U.S.A.* 40°42N 89°36W **80** E9
Pepacton Res. *U.S.A.* 42°5N 74°58W **83** D10
Pepani → *S. Africa* 25°49S 22°47E **56** D3
Pera Hd. *Australia* 12°55S 141°37E **62** A3
Perabumulih *Indonesia* 3°27S 104°15E **36** E2
Perak → *Malaysia* 4°0N 100°50E **39** K3
Perama *Kerkyra, Greece* 39°34N 19°54E **25** A3
Perama *Kriti, Greece* 35°20N 24°40E **25** D6
Perancak *Indonesia* 8°24S 114°37E **37** J17
Peräpohjola *Finland* 66°16N 26°10E **8** C22
Percé *Canada* 48°31N 64°13W **73** C7
Perche, Collines du
  France 48°30N 0°40E **20** B4
Percival Lakes *Australia* 21°25S 125°0E **60** D4
Percy Is. *Australia* 21°39S 150°16E **62** C5
Perdido, Mte. *Spain* 42°40N 0°5E **21** A6
Perdu, Mt. = Perdido, Mte.
  Spain 42°40N 0°5E **21** A6
Pereira *Colombia* 4°49N 75°43W **92** C3
Perenjori *Australia* 29°26S 116°16E **61** E2
Pereyaslav-Khmelnytskyy
  Ukraine 50°3N 31°28E **19** D5
Pérez, I. *Mexico* 22°24N 89°42W **87** C7
Pergamino *Argentina* 33°52S 60°30W **94** C3
Pergau → *Malaysia* 5°23N 102°2E **39** K3
Perham *U.S.A.* 46°36N 95°34W **80** B6
Perhentian, Kepulauan
  Malaysia 5°54N 102°42E **39** K4
Péribonka → *Canada* 48°45N 72°5W **73** C5
Péribonka, L. *Canada* 50°1N 71°10W **73** B5
Perico *Argentina* 24°20S 65°5W **94** A2
Pericos *Mexico* 25°3N 107°42W **86** B3
Périgueux *France* 45°10N 0°42E **20** D4
Perijá, Sierra de *Colombia* 9°30N 73°3W **92** B4
Perijá △ *Venezuela* 9°30N 72°55W **89** E5
Peristerona → *Cyprus* 35°8N 33°5E **25** D12
Perkasie *U.S.A.* 40°22N 75°18W **83** F9
Perlas, Arch. de las
  Panama 8°41N 79°7W **88** E4
Perlas, Punta de *Nic.* 12°30N 83°30W **88** D3
Perm *Russia* 58°0N 56°10E **18** C10
Pernambuco = Recife
  Brazil 8°0S 35°0W **93** E12
Pernambuco □ *Brazil* 8°0S 37°0W **93** E11
Pernatty Lagoon
  Australia 31°30S 137°12E **63** E2
Pernik *Bulgaria* 42°35N 23°2E **23** C10
Peron Is. *Australia* 13°9S 130°4E **60** B5
Peron Pen. *Australia* 26°0S 113°10E **61** E1
Perow *Canada* 54°35N 126°10W **70** C3
Perpignan *France* 42°42N 2°53E **20** E5
Perris *U.S.A.* 33°47N 117°14W **79** M9
Perry *Fla., U.S.A.* 30°7N 83°35W **85** F13
Perry *Ga., U.S.A.* 32°28N 83°44W **85** E13
Perry *Iowa, U.S.A.* 41°51N 94°6W **80** E6
Perry *N.Y., U.S.A.* 42°42N 78°0W **82** D7
Perry *Okla., U.S.A.* 36°17N 97°14W **84** C6
Perryton *U.S.A.* 36°24N 100°48W **84** C4
Perryville *U.S.A.* 37°43N 89°52W **80** G9
Persepolis *Iran* 29°55N 52°50E **45** D7
Pershotravensk *Ukraine* 50°13N 27°40E **17** C14
Persia = Iran ■ *Asia* 33°0N 53°0E **45** C7
Persian Gulf *Asia* 27°0N 50°0E **45** E6
Perth *Australia* 31°57S 115°52E **61** F2
Perth *Canada* 44°55N 76°15W **83** B8
Perth *U.K.* 56°24N 3°26W **11** E5
Perth & Kinross □ *U.K.* 56°45N 3°55W **11** E5
Perth Amboy *U.S.A.* 40°30N 74°15W **83** F10
Perth-Andover *Canada* 46°44N 67°42W **73** C6
Perth Basin *Ind. Oc.* 30°0S 108°0E **64** L2
Peru *Ind., U.S.A.* 40°45N 86°4W **80** E10
Peru *N.Y., U.S.A.* 44°35N 73°32W **83** B11
Peru ■ *S. Amer.* 4°0S 75°0W **92** D4
Peru Basin *Pac. Oc.* 20°0S 95°0W **65** J18
Peru-Chile Trench
  Pac. Oc. 20°0S 72°0W **92** G3
Perúgia *Italy* 43°7N 12°23E **22** C5
Pervomaysk *Ukraine* 48°10N 30°46E **19** E5
Pervouralsk *Russia* 56°59N 59°59E **18** C10
Pésaro *Italy* 43°54N 12°55E **22** C5
Pescara *Italy* 42°28N 14°13E **22** C6
Peshawar *Pakistan* 34°2N 71°37E **42** B4
Peshkopi *Albania* 41°41N 20°25E **23** D9
Peshtigo *U.S.A.* 45°3N 87°45W **80** C10
Pesqueira *Brazil* 8°20S 36°42W **93** E11
Petah Tiqwa *Israel* 32°6N 34°53E **46** C3
Petaling Jaya *Malaysia* 3°4N 101°42E **39** L3
Petaloudes *Greece* 36°18N 28°5E **25** C10
Petaluma *U.S.A.* 38°14N 122°39W **78** G4
Pétange *Lux.* 49°33N 5°55E **15** E5
Petaro *Pakistan* 25°31N 68°18E **42** G3
Petatlán *Mexico* 17°31N 101°16W **86** D4
Petauke *Zambia* 14°14S 31°20E **55** E3
Petawawa *Canada* 45°54N 77°17W **72** C4
Petén Itzá, L. *Guatemala* 16°58N 89°50W **88** C2
Peter I. *Br. Virgin Is.* 18°22N 64°35W **89** e
Peter I. Øy *Antarctica* 69°0S 91°0W **5** C16
Peter Pond L. *Canada* 55°55N 108°44W **71** B7
Peterbell *Canada* 48°36N 83°21W **72** C3
Peterborough *Australia* 32°58S 138°51E **63** E2
Peterborough *Canada* 44°20N 78°20W **82** B6
Peterborough *U.K.* 52°35N 0°15W **13** E7
Peterborough *U.S.A.* 42°53N 71°57W **83** D13
Peterborough □ *U.K.* 52°35N 0°15W **13** E7
Peterculter *U.K.* 57°6N 2°16W **11** D6
Peterhead *U.K.* 57°31N 1°48W **11** D7
Peterlee *U.K.* 54°47N 1°20W **12** C6
Petermann ۞ *Australia* 24°58S 130°0E **61** E4
Petermann Gletscher
  Greenland 80°30N 60°0W **69** A20
Petermann Ranges
  Australia 26°0S 130°30E **61** E5
Petersburg *Alaska,*
  U.S.A. 56°48N 132°58W **68** F5
Petersburg *Pa., U.S.A.* 40°34N 78°3W **82** F6
Petersburg *Va., U.S.A.* 37°14N 77°24W **81** G15
Petersburg *W. Va., U.S.A.* 39°1N 79°5W **81** F14
Petersfield *U.K.* 51°1N 0°56W **13** F7
Petit-Canal *Guadeloupe* 16°25N 61°31W **88** b
Petit Goâve *Haiti* 18°27N 72°51W **89** C5
Petit Lac Manicouagan
  Canada 51°25N 67°40W **73** B6
Petit-Mécatina →
  Canada 50°40N 59°30W **73** B8
Petit-Mécatina, Î. du
  Canada 50°30N 59°25W **73** B8
Petit Piton *St. Lucia* 13°51N 61°5W **89** f
Petit-Saguenay *Canada* 48°15N 70°4W **73** C5
Petitcodiac *Canada* 45°57N 65°11W **73** C6
Petite Terre, Îles de la
  Guadeloupe 16°13N 61°9W **88** b
Petitot → *Canada* 60°14N 123°29W **70** A4
Petitsikapau L. *Canada* 54°37N 66°25W **73** B6
Petlad *India* 22°30N 72°45E **42** H5
Peto *Mexico* 20°8N 88°55W **87** C7
Petone *N.Z.* 41°13S 174°53E **59** D5
Petorca *Chile* 32°15S 70°56W **94** C1
Petoskey *U.S.A.* 45°22N 84°57W **81** C11
Petra *Jordan* 30°20N 35°22E **46** E4
Petra *Spain* 39°37N 3°6E **24** B10
Petra, Ostrova *Russia* 76°15N 118°30E **29** B12
Petra Velikogo, Zaliv
  Russia 42°40N 132°0E **30** C6
Petre, Pt. *Canada* 43°50N 77°9W **82** C7
Petrich *Bulgaria* 41°24N 23°13E **23** D10
Petrified Forest △ *U.S.A.* 35°0N 109°30W **77** J9
Petrolândia *Brazil* 9°5S 38°20W **93** E11
Petrolia *Canada* 42°54N 82°9W **82** D2
Petrolina *Brazil* 9°24S 40°30W **93** E10
Petropavl *Kazakhstan* 54°53N 69°13E **28** D7
Petropavlovsk = Petropavl
  Kazakhstan 54°53N 69°13E **28** D7
Petropavlovsk-Kamchatskiy
  Russia 53°3N 158°43E **29** D16
Petrópolis *Brazil* 22°33S 43°9W **95** A7
Petroșani *Romania* 45°28N 23°20E **17** F12
Petrovaradin *Serbia* 45°16N 19°55E **23** B8
Petrovsk *Russia* 52°22N 45°19E **18** D8
Petrovsk-Zabaykalskiy
  Russia 51°20N 108°55E **29** D11
Petrozavodsk *Russia* 61°41N 34°20E **18** B5
Petrus Steyn *S. Africa* 27°38S 28°8E **57** D4
Petrusburg *S. Africa* 29°4S 25°26E **56** D4
Peumo *Chile* 34°21S 71°12W **94** C1
Peureulak *Indonesia* 4°48N 97°45E **36** D1
Pevek *Russia* 69°41N 171°19E **29** C18
Pforzheim *Germany* 48°52N 8°41E **16** D5
Pha Taem △ *Thailand* 15°32N 105°30E **38** E5
Phaestos *Greece* 35°2N 24°50E **25** D6
Phagwara *India* 31°10N 75°40E **42** D6
Phala *Botswana* 23°45S 26°50E **56** C4
Phalera = Phulera *India* 26°52N 75°16E **42** F6
Phalodi *India* 27°12N 72°24E **42** F5
Phaluai, Ko *Thailand* 9°32N 99°41E **39** b
Phan *Thailand* 19°28N 99°43E **38** C2
Phan Rang *Vietnam* 11°34N 109°0E **39** G7
Phan Ri = Hoa Da
  Vietnam 11°16N 108°40E **39** G7
Phan Si Pan *Vietnam* 22°18N 103°46E **38** A4
Phan Thiet *Vietnam* 11°1N 108°9E **39** G7
Phanat Nikhom
  Thailand 13°27N 101°11E **38** F3
Phangan, Ko *Thailand* 9°45N 100°0E **39** b
Phangnga *Thailand* 8°28N 98°30E **39** H2
Phangnga, Ao *Thailand* 8°16N 98°33E **39** a
Phanom Sarakham
  Thailand 13°45N 101°21E **38** F3
Phaphund *India* 26°36N 79°28E **43** F8
Pharenda *India* 27°5N 83°17E **43** F10
Pharr *U.S.A.* 26°12N 98°11W **84** H5
Phatthalung *Thailand* 7°39N 100°6E **39** J3
Phayao *Thailand* 19°11N 99°55E **38** C2
Phelps *U.S.A.* 42°58N 77°3W **82** D7
Phelps L. *Canada* 59°15N 103°15W **71** B8
Phenix City *U.S.A.* 32°28N 85°0W **85** E12
Phet Buri *Thailand* 13°1N 99°55E **38** F2
Phetchabun *Thailand* 16°25N 101°8E **38** D3
Phetchabun, Thiu Khao
  Thailand 16°0N 101°20E **38** E3
Phetchaburi = Phet Buri
  Thailand 13°1N 99°55E **38** F2
Phi Phi, Ko *Thailand* 7°45N 98°46E **39** J2
Phiafay *Laos* 14°48N 106°0E **38** E6
Phibun Mangsahan
  Thailand 15°14N 105°14E **38** E5
Phichai *Thailand* 17°22N 100°10E **38** D3
Phichit *Thailand* 16°26N 100°22E **38** D3
Philadelphia *Miss.,*
  U.S.A. 32°46N 89°7W **85** E10
Philadelphia *N.Y., U.S.A.* 44°9N 75°43W **83** B9
Philadelphia *Pa., U.S.A.* 39°57N 75°9W **83** G9
Philip *U.S.A.* 44°2N 101°40W **80** C3
Philip Smith Mts. *U.S.A.* 68°0N 148°0W **74** B10
Philippeville *Belgium* 50°12N 4°33E **15** D4
Philippi *U.S.A.* 39°9N 80°3W **81** F13
Philippi L. *Australia* 24°20S 138°55E **62** C2
Philippine Basin *Pac. Oc.* 17°0N 132°0E **64** F5
Philippine Sea *Pac. Oc.* 18°0N 125°0E **64** F4
Philippine Trench = Mindanao
  Trench *Pac. Oc.* 12°0N 126°6E **37** B7
Philippines ■ *Asia* 12°0N 123°0E **37** B6
Philippolis *S. Africa* 30°15S 25°16E **56** E4
Philippopolis = Plovdiv
  Bulgaria 42°8N 24°44E **23** C11
Philipsburg *Canada* 45°2N 73°5W **83** A11
Philipsburg *Mont.,*
  U.S.A. 46°20N 113°18W **76** C7
Philipsburg *Pa., U.S.A.* 40°54N 78°13W **82** F6
Philipstown = Daingean
  Ireland 53°18N 7°17W **10** C4
Philipstown *S. Africa* 30°28S 24°30E **56** E3
Phillip I. *Australia* 38°30S 145°12E **63** F4
Phillips *U.S.A.* 45°42N 90°24W **80** C8
Phillipsburg *Kans.,*
  U.S.A. 39°45N 99°19W **80** F4
Phillipsburg *N.J., U.S.A.* 40°42N 75°12W **83** F9
Philmont *U.S.A.* 42°15N 73°39W **83** D11
Philomath *U.S.A.* 44°32N 123°22W **76** D2
Phimai *Thailand* 15°13N 102°30E **38** E4
Phitsanulok *Thailand* 16°50N 100°12E **38** D3
Phnom Kulen △
  Cambodia 13°38N 104°15E **38** F5
Phnom Penh *Cambodia* 11°33N 104°55E **39** G5
Phnum Penh = Phnom Penh
  Cambodia 11°33N 104°55E **39** G5
Phoenicia *U.S.A.* 42°5N 74°14W **83** D10
Phoenix *Mauritius* 20°17S 57°30E **53** d
Phoenix *Ariz., U.S.A.* 33°26N 112°4W **77** K7
Phoenix *N.Y., U.S.A.* 43°14N 76°18W **83** C8
Phoenix Is. *Kiribati* 3°30S 172°0W **64** H10
Phoenixville *U.S.A.* 40°8N 75°31W **83** F9
Phon *Thailand* 15°49N 102°36E **38** E4
Phon Tiou *Laos* 17°53N 104°37E **38** D5
Phong → *Thailand* 16°23N 102°56E **38** D4
Phong Saly *Laos* 21°42N 102°9E **38** B4
Phong Tho *Vietnam* 22°32N 103°21E **38** A4
Phonhong *Laos* 18°30N 102°25E **38** C4
Phonum *Thailand* 8°49N 98°48E **39** H2
Phra Nakhon Si Ayutthaya
  Thailand 14°25N 100°30E **38** E3
Phra Pradaeng *Thailand* 13°39N 100°33E **38** F3
Phra Thong, Ko *Thailand* 9°5N 98°17E **39** H2
Phrae *Thailand* 18°7N 100°9E **38** C3
Phrom Phiram *Thailand* 17°2N 100°12E **38** D3
Phu Bia *Laos* 19°10N 103°0E **38** C4
Phu Chong-Na Yoi △
  Thailand 14°25N 105°30E **38** E5
Phu Dien *Vietnam* 18°58N 105°31E **38** C5
Phu Hin Rang Kla △
  Thailand 17°0N 100°59E **38** D3
Phu Kradung △ *Thailand* 17°2N 101°44E **38** D3
Phu Loi *Laos* 20°14N 103°14E **38** B4
Phu Luang △ *Thailand* 17°15N 101°29E **38** D3
Phu Ly *Vietnam* 20°35N 105°50E **38** B5
Phu Phan △ *Thailand* 17°20N 103°56E **38** D4
Phu Quoc, Dao *Vietnam* 10°20N 104°0E **39** G4
Phu Tho *Vietnam* 21°24N 105°13E **38** B5
Phu Wiang △ *Thailand* 16°39N 102°23E **38** D4
Phuc Yen *Vietnam* 21°16N 105°45E **38** B5
Phuket *Thailand* 7°53N 98°24E **39** a
Phuket, Ko *Thailand* 8°0N 98°22E **39** a
Phul *India* 30°19N 75°14E **42** D6
Phulad *India* 25°38N 73°49E **42** G5
Phulchari *Bangla.* 25°11N 89°37E **43** G13
Phulera *India* 26°52N 75°16E **42** F6
Phulpur *India* 25°31N 82°49E **43** G10
Phun Phin *Thailand* 9°7N 99°12E **39** b
Phuntsholing *Bhutan* 26°51N 89°23E **43** F13
Pia ۞ *Australia* 27°5S 116°23E **61** E2
Piacenza *Italy* 45°1N 9°40E **20** D8
Piai, Tanjung *Malaysia* 1°17N 103°30E **39** d
Pian Cr. → *Australia* 30°2S 148°12E **63** E4
Pian-Upe *Uganda* 1°44N 34°20E **54** B3
Pianosa *Italy* 42°35N 10°5E **22** C4
Piapot *Canada* 49°59N 109°8W **71** D7
Piatra Neamț *Romania* 46°56N 26°21E **17** E14
Piauí □ *Brazil* 7°0S 43°0W **93** E10
Piauí → *Brazil* 6°38S 42°42W **93** E10
Piave → *Italy* 45°32N 12°44E **22** B5
Pibor Post *Sudan* 6°47N 33°3E **51** G12
Picardie □ *France* 49°50N 3°0E **20** B5
Picardy = Picardie □
  France 49°50N 3°0E **20** B5
Picayune *U.S.A.* 30°32N 89°41W **85** F10
Pichhor *India* 25°58N 78°20E **43** F8
Pichilemu *Chile* 34°22S 72°0W **94** C1
Pichor *India* 25°11N 78°11E **42** G8
Pickerel L. *Canada* 48°40N 91°25W **72** C1
Pickering *U.K.* 54°15N 0°46W **12** C7
Pickering, Vale of *U.K.* 54°14N 0°45W **12** C7
Pickle Lake *Canada* 51°30N 90°12W **72** B1
Pickwick L. *U.S.A.* 35°4N 88°15W **85** D10
Pico *Azores* 38°28N 28°20W **50** a
Pico Bonito △ *Honduras* 15°34N 86°48W **88** C2
Pico Truncado *Argentina* 46°40S 68°0W **96** F3
Picos *Brazil* 7°5S 41°28W **93** E10
Picton *Canada* 44°1N 77°9W **82** B7
Picton *N.Z.* 41°18S 174°3E **59** D5
Pictou *Canada* 45°41N 62°42W **73** C7
Picture Butte *Canada* 49°55N 112°45W **70** D6
Pictured Rocks △
  U.S.A. 46°30N 86°30W **80** B10
Picún Leufú *Argentina* 39°30S 69°5W **96** D3
Pidurutalagala *Sri Lanka* 7°10N 80°50E **40** R12
Piedmont = Piemonte □
  Italy 45°0N 8°0E **20** D7
Piedmont *Ala., U.S.A.* 33°55N 85°37W **85** E12
Piedmont *S.C., U.S.A.* 34°42N 82°28W **85** F11
Piedras Negras *Mexico* 28°42N 100°31W **86** B4
Pieksämäki *Finland* 62°18N 27°10E **8** E22
Pielinen *Finland* 63°15N 29°40E **8** E23
Piemonte □ *Italy* 45°0N 8°0E **20** D7
Pienaarsrivier *S. Africa* 25°15S 28°18E **57** D4
Piercefield *U.S.A.* 44°13N 74°35W **83** B10
Pierceland *Canada* 54°20N 109°46W **71** C7
Pierpont *U.S.A.* 41°45N 80°34W **82** E4
Pierre *U.S.A.* 44°22N 100°21W **80** C4
Pierrefonds *Canada* 45°29N 73°51W **83** A11
Pierreville *Trin. & Tob.* 10°16N 61°0W **93** K16
Piet Retief *S. Africa* 27°1S 30°50E **57** D5
Pietarsaari *Finland* 63°40N 22°43E **8** E20
Pietermaritzburg
  S. Africa 29°35S 30°25E **57** D5
Pietersburg = Polokwane
  S. Africa 23°54S 29°25E **57** C4
Pietrosul, Vf. *Maramureş,*
  Romania 47°35N 24°43E **17** E13
Pietrosul, Vf. *Suceava,*
  Romania 47°12N 25°18E **17** E13
Pigeon L. *Canada* 44°27N 78°30E **82** B6
Piggott *U.S.A.* 36°23N 90°11W **85** C9
Pigüe *Argentina* 37°36S 62°25W **94** D3
Pihani *India* 27°36N 80°15E **43** F9
Pihlajavesi *Finland* 61°45N 28°45E **8** F23
Pijijiapan *Mexico* 15°42N 93°14W **87** D6
Pikangikum *Canada* 51°49N 94°0W **71** C10
Pikes Peak *U.S.A.* 38°50N 105°3W **76** G11
Piketberg *S. Africa* 32°55S 18°40E **56** E2
Pikeville *U.S.A.* 37°29N 82°31W **81** G12
Pikou *China* 39°18N 122°22E **35** E12
Pikwitonei *Canada* 55°35N 97°9W **71** B9
Piła *Poland* 53°10N 16°48E **17** B9
Pilanesberg *S. Africa* 25°15S 27°4E **56** D4
Pilani *India* 28°22N 75°33E **42** E6
Pilar *Paraguay* 26°50S 58°20W **94** B4
Pilaya → *Bolivia* 20°55S 64°4W **94** A3
Pilbara *Australia* 21°15S 118°16E **60** D2
Pilcomaya → *Paraguay* 25°21S 57°42W **94** B4
Pilgrim's Rest *S. Africa* 24°55S 30°44E **57** C5
Pilibhit *India* 28°40N 79°50E **43** E8
Pilica → *Poland* 51°52N 21°17E **17** C11
Pilipinas = Philippines ■
  Asia 12°0N 123°0E **37** B6
Pilkhawa *India* 28°43N 77°42E **42** E7
Pilliga *Australia* 30°21S 148°54E **63** E4
Pilos *Greece* 36°55N 21°42E **23** F9
Pilot Mound *Canada* 49°15N 98°54W **71** D9
Pilot Point *U.S.A.* 33°24N 96°58W **84** E6
Pilot Rock *U.S.A.* 45°29N 118°50W **76** D4
Pima *U.S.A.* 32°54N 109°50W **77** K9
Pimba *Australia* 31°18S 136°46E **63** E2
Pimenta Bueno *Brazil* 11°35S 61°10W **92** F6
Pimentel *Peru* 6°45S 79°55W **92** E2
Pin Valley △ *India* 31°50N 77°50E **42** D7
Pinang *Malaysia* 5°25N 100°15E **39** c
Pinar, C. des *Spain* 39°53N 3°12E **24** B10
Pinar del Río *Cuba* 22°26N 83°40W **88** B3
Pınarhisar *Turkey* 41°37N 27°30E **23** D12
Pinatubo, Mt. *Phil.* 15°8N 120°21E **37** A6
Pinawa *Canada* 50°9N 95°50W **71** C9
Pincher Creek *Canada* 49°30N 113°57W **70** D6
Pinchi L. *Canada* 54°38N 124°30W **70** C4
Pinckneyville *U.S.A.* 38°5N 89°23W **80** F9
Pińczów *Poland* 50°32N 20°32E **17** C11
Pindar *Australia* 28°30S 115°47E **61** E2
Pindera Downs ۞
  Australia 29°24S 142°37E **63** A3
Pindi Gheb *Pakistan* 33°14N 72°21E **42** C5
Pindos Oros *Greece* 40°0N 21°0E **23** E9
Pindus Mts. = Pindos Oros
  Greece 40°0N 21°0E **23** E9
Pine → *B.C., Canada* 56°8N 120°43W **70** B4
Pine → *Sask., Canada* 58°50N 105°38W **71** B7
Pine Bluff *U.S.A.* 34°13N 92°1W **84** D8
Pine Bluffs *U.S.A.* 41°11N 104°4W **76** F11
Pine City *U.S.A.* 45°50N 92°59W **80** C7
Pine Cr. → *U.S.A.* 41°10N 77°16W **82** E7
Pine Creek *Australia* 13°50S 131°50E **60** B5
Pine Falls *Canada* 50°34N 96°11W **71** C9
Pine Flat L. *U.S.A.* 36°50N 119°20W **78** J7
Pine Grove *U.S.A.* 40°33N 76°23W **83** F8
Pine Hill *Australia* 23°38S 146°57E **62** C4
Pine Pass *Canada* 55°25N 122°42W **70** B4
Pine Point *Canada* 60°50N 114°28W **70** A6
Pine Ridge *U.S.A.* 43°2N 102°33W **80** D2
Pine River *Canada* 51°45N 100°30W **71** C8
Pine River *U.S.A.* 46°43N 94°24W **80** B6
Pine Valley *U.S.A.* 32°50N 116°32W **79** N10
Pinecrest *U.S.A.* 38°12N 120°1W **78** G6
Pinedale *Calif., U.S.A.* 36°50N 119°48W **78** J7
Pinedale *Wyo., U.S.A.* 42°52N 109°52W **76** E9
Pinega → *Russia* 64°30N 44°19E **18** B8
Pinehouse L. *Canada* 55°32N 106°35W **71** B7
Pineimuta → *Canada* 52°8N 88°33W **72** B1
Pinerolo *Italy* 44°53N 7°21E **20** D7
Pines, Akra *Greece* 40°5N 24°20E **23** D11
Pinetop-Lakeside *U.S.A.* 34°9N 109°58W **77** J9
Pinetown *S. Africa* 29°48S 30°54E **57** D5
Pineville *U.S.A.* 31°19N 92°26W **84** F8
Ping → *Thailand* 15°42N 100°9E **38** E3
Pingaring *Australia* 32°40S 118°32E **61** F2
Pingding *China* 37°47N 113°38E **34** F7
Pingdingshan *China* 33°43N 113°27E **34** H7
Pingdong *Taiwan* 22°39N 120°30E **33** D7
Pingdu *China* 36°42N 119°59E **35** F10
Pingelly *Australia* 32°32S 117°5E **61** F2
Pingliang *China* 35°35N 106°31E **34** G4
Pingliu *China* 39°31N 112°30E **34** E7
Pingluo *China* 38°52N 106°30E **34** E4
Pingquan *China* 41°1N 118°37E **35** D10
Pingrup *Australia* 33°32S 118°29E **61** F2
P'ingtung *Taiwan* 22°38N 120°30E **33** D7
Pingwu *China* 32°25N 104°30E **34** H3
Pingxiang *China* 22°6N 106°46E **32** D5
Pingyao *China* 37°12N 112°10E **34** F7
Pingyi *China* 35°30N 117°35E **35** G9
Pingyin *China* 36°20N 116°25E **34** F9
Pingyuan *China* 37°10N 116°22E **34** F9
Pinheiro *Brazil* 2°31S 45°5W **93** D9
Pinheiro Machado
  Brazil 31°34S 53°23W **95** C5
Pinhel *Portugal* 40°50N 7°1W **21** B2
Pini *Indonesia* 0°10N 98°40E **36** D1
Pinios → *Greece* 39°55N 22°41E **23** E10
Pinjarra *Australia* 32°37S 115°52E **61** F2
Pink Mountain *Canada* 57°3N 122°52W **70** B4
Pinnacles △ *U.S.A.* 36°25N 121°12W **78** J5
Pinnaroo *Australia* 35°17S 140°53E **63** F3
Pinon Hills *U.S.A.* 34°26N 117°39W **79** L9
Pinos *Mexico* 22°18N 101°34W **86** C4
Pinos, Mt. *U.S.A.* 34°49N 119°8W **79** L7
Pinos Pt. *U.S.A.* 36°38N 121°57W **77** H3
Pinrang *Indonesia* 3°46S 119°41E **37** E5
Pins, Pte. aux *Canada* 42°15N 81°51W **82** D3
Pinsk *Belarus* 52°10N 26°1E **17** B14
Pintados *Chile* 20°35S 69°40W **92** H5
Pinyug *Russia* 60°5N 48°0E **18** B8
Pioche *U.S.A.* 37°56N 114°27W **77** H6
Piombino *Italy* 42°55N 10°32E **22** C4
Pioner, Ostrov *Russia* 79°50N 92°0E **29** B10
Piopiotaki = Milford Sd.
  N.Z. 44°41S 167°47E **59** F1
Piorini, L. *Brazil* 3°15S 62°35W **92** D6
Piotrków Trybunalski
  Poland 51°23N 19°43E **17** C10
Pîp *Iran* 26°45N 60°10E **45** E9
Pipar *India* 26°25N 73°31E **42** F5
Pipar Road *India* 26°27N 73°27E **42** F5
Piparia *Mad. P., India* 22°45N 78°23E **42** H8
Piparia *Mad. P., India* 21°49N 77°37E **42** J7
Pipestone *U.S.A.* 44°0N 96°19W **80** D5
Pipestone → *Canada* 52°53N 89°23W **72** B2
Pipestone Cr. →
  Canada 49°38N 100°15W **71** D8
Piplan *Pakistan* 32°17N 71°21E **42** C4
Piploda *India* 23°37N 74°56E **42** H6
Pipmuacan, Rés. *Canada* 49°45N 70°30W **73** C5

Pippingarra *Australia* 20°27S 118°42E **60** D2
Piqua *U.S.A.* 40°9N 84°15W **81** E11
Piquiri → *Brazil* 24°3S 54°14W **95** A5
Pir Panjal Range *India* 32°30N 76°50E **42** C7
Piracicaba *Brazil* 22°45S 47°40W **95** A6
Piracuruca *Brazil* 3°50S 41°50W **93** D10
Pirae *Tahiti* 17°31S 149°32W **59** d
Piræus = Pireas *Greece* 37°57N 23°42E **23** F10
Piraiévs = Pireas *Greece* 37°57N 23°42E **23** F10
Pirajuí *Brazil* 21°59S 49°29W **95** A6
Piram I. *India* 21°36N 72°21E **42** J5
Pirané *Argentina* 25°42S 59°6W **94** B4
Pīrānshahr *Iran* 36°41N 45°8E **44** B5
Pirapora *Brazil* 17°20S 44°56W **93** G10
Pirawa *India* 24°10N 76°2E **42** G7
Pireas *Greece* 37°57N 23°42E **23** F10
Pirgos *Greece* 37°40N 21°27E **23** F9
Piribebuy *Paraguay* 25°26S 57°2W **94** B4
Pirimapun *Indonesia* 6°20S 138°24E **37** F9
Pirin Planina *Bulgaria* 41°40N 23°30E **23** D10
Pirineos = Pyrénées
  Europe 42°45N 0°18E **20** E4
Piripiri *Brazil* 4°15S 41°46W **93** D10
Pirlangimpi *Australia* 11°24S 130°26E **60** B5
Pirmasens *Germany* 49°12N 7°36E **16** D4
Pirot *Serbia* 43°9N 22°33E **23** C10
Piru *Indonesia* 3°4S 128°12E **37** E7
Piru *U.S.A.* 34°25N 118°48W **79** L8
Pisa *Italy* 43°43N 10°23E **22** C4
Pisagua *Chile* 19°40S 70°15W **92** G4
Pisco *Peru* 13°50S 76°12W **92** F3
Písek *Czech Rep.* 49°19N 14°10E **16** D8
Pishan *China* 37°30N 78°33E **32** C2
Pīshīn *Iran* 26°6N 61°47E **45** E9
Pishin *Pakistan* 30°35N 67°0E **42** D2
Pishin Lora → *Pakistan* 29°9N 64°5E **42** E1
Pising *Indonesia* 5°8S 121°53E **37** F6
Pismo Beach *U.S.A.* 35°9N 120°38W **79** K6
Pissis, Cerro *Argentina* 27°45S 68°48W **94** B2
Pissouri *Cyprus* 34°40N 32°42E **25** E11
Pistóia *Italy* 43°55N 10°54E **22** C4
Pistol B. *Canada* 62°25N 92°37W **71** A10
Pisuerga → *Spain* 41°33N 4°52W **21** B3
Pit → *U.S.A.* 40°47N 122°6W **76** F2
Pitarpunga L. *Australia* 34°24S 143°30E **63** E3
Pitcairn I. *Pac. Oc.* 25°5S 130°5W **65** K14
Pitch L. *Trin. & Tob.* 10°12N 61°39W **93** K15
Piteå *Sweden* 65°20N 21°25E **8** D19
Piteälven → *Sweden* 65°20N 21°25E **8** D19
Pitești *Romania* 44°52N 24°54E **17** F13
Pithapuram *India* 17°10N 82°15E **41** L13
Pithara *Australia* 30°20S 116°35E **61** F2
Pithoragarh *India* 29°35N 80°23E **43** E9
Pithoro *Pakistan* 25°31N 69°23E **42** G3
Pitlochry *U.K.* 56°42N 3°44W **11** E5
Pitsilia *Cyprus* 34°55N 33°0E **25** E12
Pitt I. *Canada* 53°30N 129°50W **70** C3
Pittsburg *Calif., U.S.A.* 38°2N 121°53W **78** G5
Pittsburg *Kans., U.S.A.* 37°25N 94°42W **80** G6
Pittsburg *Tex., U.S.A.* 33°0N 94°59W **84** E7
Pittsburgh *U.S.A.* 40°26N 79°58W **82** F5
Pittsfield *Ill., U.S.A.* 39°36N 90°49W **80** F8
Pittsfield *Maine, U.S.A.* 44°47N 69°23W **81** C19
Pittsfield *Mass., U.S.A.* 42°27N 73°15W **83** D11
Pittsfield *N.H., U.S.A.* 43°18N 71°20W **83** C13
Pittston *U.S.A.* 41°19N 75°47W **83** E9
Pittsworth *Australia* 27°41S 151°37E **63** D5
Pituri → *Australia* 22°35S 138°30E **62** C2
Pixley *U.S.A.* 35°58N 119°18W **78** K7
Pizhou *China* 34°44N 116°55E **34** G9
Placentia *Canada* 47°0N 54°0W **73** C9
Placentia B. *Canada* 47°0N 54°40W **73** C9
Placerville *U.S.A.* 38°44N 120°48W **78** G6
Placetas *Cuba* 22°15N 79°44W **88** B4
Plainfield *N.J., U.S.A.* 40°37N 74°25W **83** F10
Plainfield *Ohio, U.S.A.* 40°13N 81°43W **82** F3
Plainfield *Vt., U.S.A.* 44°17N 72°26W **83** B12
Plains *Mont., U.S.A.* 47°28N 114°53W **76** C6
Plains *Tex., U.S.A.* 33°11N 102°50W **84** J3
Plainview *Nebr., U.S.A.* 42°21N 97°47W **80** D6
Plainview *Tex., U.S.A.* 34°11N 101°43W **84** D4
Plainwell *U.S.A.* 42°27N 85°38W **81** D11
Plaistow *U.S.A.* 42°50N 71°6W **83** D13
Plaka, Ákra *Greece* 35°11N 26°19E **25** D8
Plana Cays *Bahamas* 22°38N 73°30W **89** B5
Planada *U.S.A.* 37°16N 120°19W **78** H6
Plano *U.S.A.* 33°1N 96°42W **84** E6
Plant City *U.S.A.* 28°1N 82°7W **85** M4
Plaquemine *U.S.A.* 30°17N 91°14W **84** F9
Plasencia *Spain* 40°3N 6°8W **21** B2
Plaster City *U.S.A.* 32°47N 115°51W **79** N11
Plaster Rock *Canada* 46°53N 67°22W **73** C6
Plastun *Russia* 44°45N 136°19E **30** B8
Plata, Río de la →
  S. Amer. 34°45S 57°30W **94** C4
Plátani → *Italy* 37°23N 13°16E **22** F5
Plátanos *Greece* 35°28N 23°33E **25** D5
Platte *U.S.A.* 43°23N 98°51W **80** D5
Platte → *Mo., U.S.A.* 39°16N 94°50W **80** F6
Platte → *Nebr., U.S.A.* 41°4N 95°53W **80** E6
Platteville *U.S.A.* 42°44N 90°29W **80** D8
Plattsburgh *U.S.A.* 44°42N 73°28W **83** B11
Plattsmouth *U.S.A.* 41°1N 95°53W **80** E6
Plauen *Germany* 50°30N 12°8E **16** C7
Plavinas *Latvia* 56°35N 25°46E **9** H21
Playa Blanca *Canary Is.* 28°55N 13°37W **24** F6
Playa Blanca Sur
  Canary Is. 28°51N 13°50W **24** F6
Playa de las Americas
  Canary Is. 28°5N 16°43W **24** F3
Playa de Mogán
  Canary Is. 27°48N 15°47W **24** G4
Playa del Carmen *Mexico* 20°37N 87°4W **87** C7
Playa del Inglés
  Canary Is. 27°45N 15°33W **24** G4
Playa Esmeralda
  Canary Is. 28°8N 14°16W **24** F5

Playgreen L. *Canada* 54°0N 98°15W **71** C9
Pleasant Bay *Canada* 46°51N 60°48W **73** C7
Pleasant Hill *U.S.A.* 37°57N 122°4W **78** H4
Pleasant Mount *U.S.A.* 41°44N 75°26W **83** E9
Pleasanton *Calif.,*
  U.S.A. 37°39N 121°52W **78** H5
Pleasanton *Tex., U.S.A.* 28°58N 98°29W **84** G5
Pleasantville *N.J.,*
  U.S.A. 39°24N 74°32W **81** F16
Pleasantville *Pa., U.S.A.* 41°35N 79°34W **82** E5
Plei Ku *Vietnam* 13°57N 108°0E **38** F7
Plenty → *Australia* 23°25S 136°31E **62** C2
Plenty, B. of *N.Z.* 37°45S 177°0E **59** B6
Plentywood *U.S.A.* 48°47N 104°34W **76** B11
Plesetsk *Russia* 62°43N 40°20E **18** B7
Plessisville *Canada* 46°14N 71°47W **73** C5
Plétipi, L. *Canada* 51°44N 70°6W **73** B5
Pleven *Bulgaria* 43°26N 24°37E **23** C11
Plevlja *Montenegro* 43°21N 19°21E **23** C8
Plevna *Canada* 44°58N 76°59W **82** B8
Płock *Poland* 52°32N 19°40E **17** B10
Plöckenstein *Germany* 48°46N 13°51E **16** D7
Ploiești *Romania* 44°57N 26°5E **17** F14
Plonge, Lac la *Canada* 55°8N 107°20W **71** B7
Plovdiv *Bulgaria* 42°8N 24°44E **23** C11
Plover Cove Res. *China* 22°28N 114°15E **33** G11
Plum *U.S.A.* 40°29N 79°47W **82** F5
Plum I. *U.S.A.* 41°11N 72°12W **83** E12
Plumas *U.S.A.* 39°45N 120°4W **78** F6
Plummer *U.S.A.* 47°20N 116°53W **76** C5
Plumridge Lakes
  Australia 29°26S 125°16E **61** E4
Plumtree *Zimbabwe* 20°27S 27°55E **55** G2
Plungė *Lithuania* 55°53N 21°59E **9** J19
Plymouth *Trin. & Tob.* 11°14N 60°48W **93** J16
Plymouth *U.K.* 50°22N 4°10W **13** G3
Plymouth *Calif., U.S.A.* 38°29N 120°51W **78** G6
Plymouth *Ind., U.S.A.* 41°21N 86°19W **80** E10
Plymouth *Mass., U.S.A.* 41°57N 70°40W **83** E14
Plymouth *N.H., U.S.A.* 43°46N 71°41W **83** C13
Plymouth *N.C., U.S.A.* 35°52N 76°43W **85** D16
Plymouth *Pa., U.S.A.* 41°14N 75°57W **83** E9
Plymouth *Wis., U.S.A.* 43°45N 87°59W **80** D10
Plympton-Wyoming = Wyoming
  Canada 42°57N 82°7W **82** D2
Plynlimon = Pumlumon Fawr
  U.K. 52°28N 3°46W **13** E4
Plyusa *Russia* 58°28N 29°27E **9** G23
Plzeň *Czech Rep.* 49°45N 13°22E **16** D7
Pmere Nyente ◎
  Australia 24°15S 136°10E **62** C2
Po → *Italy* 44°57N 12°4E **22** B5
Po Hai = Bo Hai *China* 39°0N 119°0E **35** E10
Po Toi *China* 22°10N 114°16E **33** G11
Pobeda *Russia* 65°12N 146°12E **29** C15
Pobedy, Pik *Kyrgyzstan* 42°0N 79°58E **32** B2
Pocahontas *Ark., U.S.A.* 36°16N 90°58W **85** C9
Pocahontas *Iowa, U.S.A.* 42°44N 94°40W **80** D6
Pocatello *U.S.A.* 42°52N 112°27W **76** E7
Pocomoke City *U.S.A.* 38°5N 75°34W **81** F16
Poços de Caldas *Brazil* 21°50S 46°33W **95** A6
Podgorica *Montenegro* 42°30N 19°19E **23** C8
Podilska Vysochyna
  Ukraine 49°0N 28°0E **17** D14
Podolsk *Russia* 55°25N 37°30E **18** C6
Podporozhye *Russia* 60°55N 34°2E **18** B5
Pofadder *S. Africa* 29°10S 19°22E **56** D2
Pogranichnyy *Russia* 44°25N 131°24E **30** B5
Poh *Indonesia* 0°46S 122°51E **37** E6
Pohang *S. Korea* 36°1N 129°23E **35** F15
Pohjanmaa *Finland* 62°58N 22°50E **8** E20
Pohnpei *Micronesia* 6°55N 158°10E **64** G7
Pohri *India* 25°32N 77°22E **42** G6
Poinsett, C. *Antarctica* 65°42S 113°18E **5** C8
Point Arena *U.S.A.* 38°55N 123°41W **78** G3
Point Baker *U.S.A.* 56°21N 133°37W **70** B2
Point Fortin
  Trin. & Tob. 10°10N 61°42W **93** K15
Point Hope *U.S.A.* 68°21N 166°47W **74** B6
Point L. *Canada* 65°15N 113°4W **68** D9
Point Lisas *Trin. & Tob.* 10°24N 61°29W **93** K15
Point Pedro *Sri Lanka* 9°50N 80°15E **40** Q12
Point Pelee △ *Canada* 41°57N 82°31W **82** E2
Point Pleasant *N.J.,*
  U.S.A. 40°5N 74°4W **83** F10
Point Pleasant *W. Va.,*
  U.S.A. 38°51N 82°8W **81** F12
Point Reyes △ *U.S.A.* 38°10N 122°55W **78** G2
Pointe-à-Pitre *Guadeloupe* 16°10N 61°32W **88** b
Pointe-au-Pic = La Malbaie
  Canada 47°40N 70°10W **73** C5
Pointe-Claire *Canada* 45°26N 73°50W **83** A11
Pointe-Gatineau *Canada* 45°27N 75°41W **83** A9
Pointe-Noire *Congo* 4°48S 11°53E **52** E2
Pointe-Noire *Guadeloupe* 16°14N 61°47W **88** b
Poipet *Cambodia* 13°39N 102°33E **38** F4
Poisonbush Ra.
  Australia 22°30S 121°30E **60** D3
Poissonnier Pt.
  Australia 19°57S 119°10E **60** C2
Poitiers *France* 46°35N 0°20E **20** C4
Poitou *France* 46°40N 0°10W **20** C3
Pojoaque *U.S.A.* 35°54N 106°1W **77** J10
Pokaran *India* 26°55N 71°55E **42** F4
Pokataroo *Australia* 29°30S 148°36E **63** D4
Pokhara *Nepal* 28°14N 83°58E **43** E10
Poko *Dem. Rep. of the Congo* 3°7N 26°52E **54** B2
Pokrovsk *Russia* 61°29N 129°0E **29** C13
Pola = Pula *Croatia* 44°54N 13°57E **16** F7
Polacca *U.S.A.* 35°50N 110°23W **77** J8
Polan *Iran* 25°30N 61°10E **45** E9
Poland *U.S.A.* 43°13N 75°3W **83** C9
Poland ■ *Europe* 52°0N 20°0E **17** C10
Polar Bear △ *Canada* 55°0N 83°45W **72** A2
Polatsk *Belarus* 55°30N 28°50E **9** J23
Polcura *Chile* 37°17S 71°43W **94** D1
Polesye = Pripet Marshes
  Europe 52°10N 28°10E **17** B15
Polevskoy *Russia* 56°26N 60°11E **18** C11

Police *Poland* 53°33N 14°33E **16** B8
Police, Pte. *Seychelles* 4°51S 55°32E **53** b
Poligiros *Greece* 40°23N 23°25E **23** D10
Polillo Is. *Phil.* 14°56N 122°0E **37** B6
Polis *Cyprus* 35°2N 32°26E **25** D11
Polk *U.S.A.* 41°22N 79°56W **82** E5
Pollachi *India* 10°35N 77°0E **40** P10
Pollença *Spain* 39°54N 3°1E **24** B10
Pollença, B. de *Spain* 39°53N 3°8E **24** B10
Polnovat *Russia* 63°50N 65°54E **28** C7
Polokwane *S. Africa* 23°54S 29°25E **57** C4
Polokwane → *S. Africa* 22°25S 30°5E **57** C5
Polonne *Ukraine* 50°6N 27°30E **17** C14
Polonnoye = Polonne
  Ukraine 50°6N 27°30E **17** C14
Polson *U.S.A.* 47°41N 114°9W **76** C6
Poltava *Ukraine* 49°35N 34°35E **19** E5
Põltsamaa *Estonia* 58°39N 25°58E **9** G21
Polunochnoye *Russia* 60°52N 60°25E **28** C7
Põlva *Estonia* 58°3N 27°3E **9** G22
Polyarny *Russia* 69°8N 33°20E **8** B25
Polyarnyye Zori *Russia* 67°22N 32°30E **8** C25
Polynesia *Pac. Oc.* 10°0S 162°0W **65** F11
Polynésie française = French
  Polynesia ☑ *Pac. Oc.* 20°0S 145°0W **65** J13
Pombal *Portugal* 39°55N 8°40W **21** C1
Pombia *Greece* 35°0N 24°51E **25** E6
Pomene *Mozam.* 22°53S 35°33E **57** C6
Pomeroy *Ohio, U.S.A.* 39°2N 82°2W **81** F12
Pomeroy *Wash., U.S.A.* 46°28N 117°36W **76** C5
Pomézia *Italy* 41°40N 12°30E **22** D5
Pomona *Australia* 26°22S 152°52E **63** D5
Pomona *U.S.A.* 34°4N 117°45W **79** L9
Pomorskie, Pojezierze
  Poland 53°40N 16°37E **17** B9
Pomos *Cyprus* 35°9N 32°33E **25** D11
Pomos, C. *Cyprus* 35°10N 32°33E **25** D11
Pompano Beach *U.S.A.* 26°14N 80°7W **85** H14
Pompeys Pillar *U.S.A.* 45°59N 107°57W **76** D10
Pompeys Pillar △
  U.S.A. 46°0N 108°0W **76** D10
Pompton Lakes *U.S.A.* 41°0N 74°17W **83** F10
Ponape = Pohnpei
  Micronesia 6°55N 158°10E **64** G7
Ponask L. *Canada* 54°0N 92°41W **72** B1
Ponca *U.S.A.* 42°34N 96°43W **80** D5
Ponca City *U.S.A.* 36°42N 97°5W **84** C6
Ponce *Puerto Rico* 18°1N 66°37W **89** d
Ponchatoula *U.S.A.* 30°26N 90°26W **85** F9
Poncheville, L. *Canada* 50°10N 76°55W **72** B4
Pond *U.S.A.* 35°43N 119°20W **79** K7
Pond Inlet *Canada* 72°40N 77°0W **69** C16
Pondicherry = Puducherry
  India 11°59N 79°50E **40** P11
Ponds, I. of *Canada* 53°27N 55°52W **73** B8
Ponferrada *Spain* 42°32N 6°35W **21** A2
Ponnani *India* 10°45N 75°59E **40** P9
Ponoka *Canada* 52°42N 113°40W **70** C6
Ponoy *Russia* 67°0N 41°13E **18** A7
Ponoy → *Russia* 66°59N 41°17E **18** A7
Ponta Delgada *Azores* 37°44N 25°40W **50** a
Ponta do Sol *Madeira* 32°42N 17°7W **24** D2
Ponta Grossa *Brazil* 25°7S 50°10W **95** B5
Ponta Porã *Brazil* 22°20S 55°35W **95** A4
Pontarlier *France* 46°54N 6°20E **20** C7
Pontchartrain, L. *U.S.A.* 30°5N 90°5W **85** F9
Ponte do Pungué
  Mozam. 19°30S 34°33E **55** F3
Ponte Nova *Brazil* 20°25S 42°54W **95** A7
Ponteix *Canada* 49°46N 107°29W **71** D7
Pontevedra *Spain* 42°26N 8°40W **21** A1
Pontiac *Ill., U.S.A.* 40°53N 88°38W **80** E9
Pontiac *Mich., U.S.A.* 42°38N 83°18W **81** D12
Pontian Kechil *Malaysia* 1°29N 103°23E **39** d
Pontianak *Indonesia* 0°3S 109°15E **36** E3
Pontine Is. = Ponziane, Ísole
  Italy 40°55N 12°57E **22** D5
Pontine Mts. = Kuzey Anadolu
  Dağları *Turkey* 41°0N 36°45E **19** F6
Pontivy *France* 48°5N 2°58W **20** B2
Pontoise *France* 49°3N 2°5E **20** B5
Ponton → *Canada* 58°27N 116°11W **70** B5
Pontypool *Canada* 44°6N 78°38W **82** B6
Pontypool *U.K.* 51°42N 3°2W **13** F4
Ponziane, Ísole *Italy* 40°55N 12°57E **22** D5
Poochera *Australia* 32°43S 134°51E **63** E1
Poole *U.K.* 50°43N 1°59W **13** G6
Poole □ *U.K.* 50°43N 1°59W **13** G6
Poona = Pune *India* 18°29N 73°57E **40** K8
Pooncarie *Australia* 33°22S 142°31E **63** E3
Poopelloe L. *Australia* 31°40S 144°0E **63** E3
Poopó, L. de *Bolivia* 18°30S 67°35W **92** G5
Popayán *Colombia* 2°27N 76°36W **92** C3
Poperinge *Belgium* 50°51N 2°42E **15** D2
Popilta L. *Australia* 33°10S 141°42E **63** E3
Popio L. *Australia* 33°10S 141°52E **63** E3
Poplar *U.S.A.* 48°7N 105°12W **76** B11
Poplar → *Canada* 53°0N 97°19W **71** C9
Poplar Bluff *U.S.A.* 36°46N 90°24W **80** G8
Poplarville *U.S.A.* 30°51N 89°32W **85** F10
Popocatépetl, Volcán
  Mexico 19°2N 98°38W **87** D5
Popokabaka
  Dem. Rep. of the Congo 5°41S 16°40E **52** F3
Poprad *Slovak Rep.* 49°3N 20°18E **17** D11
Porali → *Pakistan* 25°58N 66°26E **42** G2
Porbandar *India* 21°44N 69°43E **42** J3
Porcher I. *Canada* 53°50N 130°30W **70** C2
Porcupine *U.S.A.* 59°11N 104°46W **71** B8
Porcupine → *Canada* 66°34N 145°19W **68** D2
Porcupine Gorge △
  Australia 20°22S 144°26E **62** C3
Pordenone *Italy* 45°57N 12°39E **22** B5
Pori *Finland* 61°29N 21°48E **8** F19
Porkhov *Russia* 57°45N 29°38E **9** H23
Porlamar *Venezuela* 10°57N 63°51W **92** A6
Pormpuraaw *Australia* 14°59S 141°26E **62** A3

Pormpuraaw ◎
  Australia 14°55S 141°47E **62** A3
Poronaysk *Russia* 49°13N 143°0E **29** E15
Poroshiri-Dake *Japan* 42°41N 142°52E **30** C11
Poroto Mts. *Tanzania* 9°0S 33°30E **55** D3
Porpoise B. *Antarctica* 66°0S 127°0E **5** C9
Porreres *Spain* 39°31N 3°2E **24** B10
Porsangerfjorden
  Norway 70°40N 25°40E **8** A21
Porsgrunn *Norway* 59°10N 9°40E **9** G13
Port Alberni *Canada* 49°14N 124°50W **70** D4
Port Alfred *S. Africa* 33°36S 26°55E **56** E4
Port Alice *Canada* 50°20N 127°25W **70** C3
Port Allegany *U.S.A.* 41°48N 78°17W **82** E6
Port Allen *U.S.A.* 30°27N 91°12W **84** F9
Port Alma *Australia* 23°38S 150°53E **62** C5
Port Alma *Canada* 42°10N 82°14W **82** D2
Port Angeles *U.S.A.* 48°7N 123°27W **78** B3
Port Antonio *Jamaica* 18°10N 76°26W **88** a
Port Aransas *U.S.A.* 27°50N 97°4W **84** M6
Port Arthur *Australia* 43°7S 147°50E **63** G4
Port Arthur *U.S.A.* 29°54N 93°56W **84** G8
Port au Choix *Canada* 50°43N 57°22W **73** B8
Port au Port B. *Canada* 48°40N 58°50W **73** C8
Port-au-Prince *Haiti* 18°40N 72°20W **89** C5
Port Augusta *Australia* 32°30S 137°50E **63** E2
Port Austin *U.S.A.* 44°3N 83°1W **82** B2
Port Bell *Uganda* 0°18N 32°35E **54** B3
Port Bergé Vaovao
  Madag. 15°33S 47°40E **57** B8
Port Blandford *Canada* 48°20N 54°10W **73** C9
Port Bradshaw
  Australia 12°30S 137°20E **62** A2
Port Broughton
  Australia 33°37S 137°56E **63** E2
Port Bruce *Canada* 42°39N 81°0W **82** D4
Port Burwell *Canada* 42°40N 80°48W **82** D4
Port Canning *India* 22°23N 88°40E **43** H13
Port Carling *Canada* 45°7N 79°35W **82** A5
Port-Cartier *Canada* 50°2N 66°50W **73** B6
Port Chalmers *N.Z.* 45°49S 170°30E **59** F3
Port Charlotte *U.S.A.* 26°59N 82°6W **85** H13
Port Chester *U.S.A.* 41°0N 73°40W **83** F11
Port Clements *Canada* 53°40N 132°10W **70** C2
Port Clinton *U.S.A.* 41°31N 82°56W **81** E12
Port Colborne *Canada* 42°50N 79°10W **82** D5
Port Coquitlam *Canada* 49°15N 122°45W **78** A4
Port Credit *Canada* 43°33N 79°35W **82** C5
Port Curtis *Australia* 23°57S 151°20E **62** C5
Port d'Alcúdia *Spain* 39°50N 3°7E **24** B10
Port Dalhousie *Canada* 43°13N 79°16W **82** C5
Port d'Andratx *Spain* 39°32N 2°23E **24** B9
Port Darwin *Australia* 12°24S 130°45E **60** B5
Port Darwin *Falk. Is.* 51°50S 59°0W **96** G5
Port Davey *Australia* 43°16S 145°55E **63** G4
Port-de-Paix *Haiti* 19°50N 72°50W **89** C5
Port de Pollença *Spain* 39°54N 3°4E **24** B10
Port de Sóller *Spain* 39°48N 2°42E **24** B9
Port Dickson *Malaysia* 2°30N 101°49E **39** L3
Port Douglas *Australia* 16°30S 145°30E **62** B4
Port Dover *Canada* 42°47N 80°12W **82** D4
Port Edward *Canada* 54°12N 130°10W **70** C2
Port Elgin *Canada* 44°25N 81°25W **82** B3
Port Elizabeth *S. Africa* 33°58S 25°40E **56** E4
Port Ellen *U.K.* 55°38N 6°11W **11** F2
Port Erin *I. of Man* 54°5N 4°45W **12** C3
Port Essington *Australia* 11°15S 132°10E **60** B5
Port Ewen *U.S.A.* 41°54N 73°59W **83** E11
Port Fairy *Australia* 38°22S 142°12E **63** F3
Port Gamble *U.S.A.* 47°51N 122°34W **78** C4
Port Germein *Australia* 33°1S 138°1E **63** E2
Port Gibson *U.S.A.* 31°58N 90°59W **84** F9
Port Glasgow *U.K.* 55°56N 4°41W **11** F4
Port Harcourt *Nigeria* 4°40N 7°10E **50** H7
Port Hardy *Canada* 50°41N 127°30W **70** C3
Port Harrison = Inukjuak
  Canada 58°25N 78°15W **69** F16
Port Hawkesbury
  Canada 45°36N 61°22W **73** C7
Port Hedland *Australia* 20°25S 118°35E **60** D2
Port Henry *U.S.A.* 44°3N 73°28W **83** B11
Port Hood *Canada* 46°0N 61°32W **73** C7
Port Hope *Canada* 43°56N 78°20W **82** C6
Port Hope *U.S.A.* 43°57N 82°43W **82** C2
Port Hope Simpson
  Canada 52°33N 56°18W **73** B8
Port Hueneme *U.S.A.* 34°7N 119°12W **79** L7
Port Huron *U.S.A.* 42°58N 82°26W **82** D2
Port Jefferson *U.S.A.* 40°57N 73°3W **83** F11
Port Jervis *U.S.A.* 41°22N 74°41W **83** E10
Port Kelang = Pelabuhan Klang
  Malaysia 3°0N 101°23E **39** L3
Port Kenny *Australia* 33°10S 134°41E **63** E1
Port Laoise *Ireland* 53°2N 7°18W **10** C4
Port Lavaca *U.S.A.* 28°37N 96°38W **84** G6
Port Leyden *U.S.A.* 43°35N 75°21W **83** C9
Port Lincoln *Australia* 34°42S 135°52E **63** E2
Port Loko *S. Leone* 8°48N 12°46W **50** G3
Port-Louis *Guadeloupe* 16°28N 61°32W **88** b
Port Louis *Mauritius* 20°10S 57°30E **53** d
Port MacDonnell
  Australia 38°5S 140°48E **63** F3
Port McNeill *Canada* 50°35N 127°6W **70** C3
Port Macquarie
  Australia 31°25S 152°25E **63** E5
Port Maria *Jamaica* 18°22N 76°54W **88** a
Port Matilda *U.S.A.* 40°48N 78°3W **82** F6
Port McNicoll *Canada* 44°44N 79°48W **82** B5
Port Mellon *Canada* 49°32N 123°31W **70** D4
Port-Menier *Canada* 49°51N 64°15W **73** C7
Port Moody *Canada* 49°17N 122°51W **78** A4
Port Morant *Jamaica* 17°54N 76°19W **88** a
Port Moresby *Papua N. G.* 9°24S 147°8E **58** B7
Port Musgrave
  Australia 11°55S 141°50E **62** A3

Port Neches *U.S.A.* 30°0N 93°59W **84** G8
Port Nolloth *S. Africa* 29°17S 16°52E **56** D2
Port Nouveau-Québec =
  Kangiqsualujjuaq
  Canada 58°30N 65°59W **69** F18
Port of Climax *Canada* 49°10N 108°20W **71** D7
Port of Coronach
  Canada 49°7N 105°31W **71** D7
Port of Spain
  Trin. & Tob. 10°40N 61°31W **93** K15
Port Orange *U.S.A.* 29°9N 80°59W **85** G14
Port Orchard *U.S.A.* 47°32N 122°38W **78** C4
Port Orford *U.S.A.* 42°45N 124°30W **76** E1
Port Pegasus *N.Z.* 47°12S 167°41E **59** G1
Port Perry *Canada* 44°6N 78°56W **82** B6
Port Phillip B. *Australia* 38°10S 144°50E **63** F3
Port Pirie *Australia* 33°10S 138°1E **63** E2
Port Renfrew *Canada* 48°30N 124°20W **78** B2
Port Roper *Australia* 14°45S 135°25E **62** A2
Port Rowan *Canada* 42°40N 80°30W **82** D4
Port Safaga = Bûr Safâga
  Egypt 26°43N 33°57E **44** E2
Port Said = Bûr Sa'îd
  Egypt 31°16N 32°18E **51** B12
Port St. Joe *U.S.A.* 29°49N 85°18W **85** G12
Port St. Johns = Umzimvubu
  S. Africa 31°38S 29°33E **57** E4
Port St. Lucie *U.S.A.* 27°18N 80°21W **85** H14
Port Sanilac *U.S.A.* 43°26N 82°33W **82** C2
Port Severn *Canada* 44°48N 79°43W **82** B5
Port Shepstone *S. Africa* 30°44S 30°28E **57** E5
Port Simpson *Canada* 54°30N 130°20W **70** C2
Port Stanley = Stanley
  Falk. Is. 51°40S 59°51W **96** G5
Port Stanley *Canada* 42°40N 81°10W **82** D3
Port Sudan = Bûr Sûdân
  Sudan 19°32N 37°9E **51** E13
Port Sulphur *U.S.A.* 29°29N 89°42W **85** G10
Port Talbot *U.K.* 51°35N 3°47W **13** F4
Port Townsend *U.S.A.* 48°7N 122°45W **78** B4
Port-Vendres *France* 42°32N 3°8E **20** E5
Port Vila *Vanuatu* 17°45S 168°18E **58** C9
Port Vladimir *Russia* 69°25N 33°6E **8** B25
Port Wakefield *Australia* 34°12S 138°10E **63** E2
Port Washington
  U.S.A. 43°23N 87°53W **80** D10
Porta Orientalis *Romania* 45°6N 22°18E **17** F12
Portacloy *Ireland* 54°20N 9°46W **10** B2
Portadown *U.K.* 54°25N 6°27W **10** B5
Portage *Pa., U.S.A.* 40°23N 78°41W **82** F6
Portage *Wis., U.S.A.* 43°33N 89°28W **80** D9
Portage la Prairie
  Canada 49°58N 98°18W **71** D9
Portageville *U.S.A.* 36°26N 89°42W **80** G9
Portalegre *Portugal* 39°19N 7°25W **21** C2
Portales *U.S.A.* 34°11N 103°20W **77** J12
Portarlington *Ireland* 53°9N 7°14W **10** C4
Portbou *Spain* 42°25N 3°9E **21** A7
Porter L. *N.W.T., Canada* 61°41N 108°5W **71** A7
Porter L. *Sask., Canada* 56°20N 107°20W **71** B7
Porterville *S. Africa* 33°0S 19°0E **56** E2
Porterville *U.S.A.* 36°4N 119°1W **78** J8
Porthcawl *U.K.* 51°29N 3°42W **13** F4
Porthill *U.S.A.* 48°59N 116°30W **76** B5
Porthmadog *U.K.* 52°55N 4°8W **12** E3
Portile de Fier *Europe* 44°42N 22°30E **17** F12
Portimão *Portugal* 37°8N 8°32W **21** D1
Portishead *U.K.* 51°29N 2°46W **13** F5
Portknockie *U.K.* 57°42N 2°51W **11** D6
Portland *N.S.W.,*
  Australia 33°20S 150°0E **63** E5
Portland *Vic., Australia* 38°20S 141°35E **63** F3
Portland *Conn., U.S.A.* 41°34N 72°38W **83** E12
Portland *Maine, U.S.A.* 43°39N 70°16W **81** D18
Portland *Mich., U.S.A.* 42°52N 84°54W **81** D11
Portland *Oreg., U.S.A.* 45°32N 122°37W **78** E4
Portland *Tex., U.S.A.* 27°53N 97°20W **84** H6
Portland, I. of *U.K.* 50°33N 2°26E **13** G5
Portland B. *Australia* 38°15S 141°45E **63** F3
Portland Bight *Jamaica* 17°52N 77°5W **88** a
Portland Bill *U.K.* 50°31N 2°28W **13** G5
Portland Canal *U.S.A.* 55°56N 130°0W **70** B2
Portland Int. ✈ (PDX)
  U.S.A. 45°35N 122°36W **78** E4
Portland Pt. *Jamaica* 17°42N 77°11W **88** a
Portmadoc = Porthmadog
  U.K. 52°55N 4°8W **12** E3
Portmore *Jamaica* 17°53N 76°53W **88** a
Porto *France* 42°16N 8°42E **20** E8
Porto *Portugal* 41°8N 8°40W **21** B1
Pôrto Alegre *Brazil* 30°5S 51°10W **95** C5
Porto Colom *Spain* 39°26N 3°15E **24** B10
Porto Cristo *Spain* 39°33N 3°20E **24** B10
Porto de Moz *Brazil* 1°41S 52°13W **93** D8
Pôrto Empédocle *Italy* 37°17N 13°32E **22** F5
Porto Esperança *Brazil* 19°37S 57°29W **92** G7
Porto Franco *Brazil* 6°20S 47°24W **93** E9
Porto Inglês = C. Verde Is. 14°15N 23°10W **50** b
Porto Mendes *Brazil* 24°30S 54°15W **95** A5
Porto Moniz *Madeira* 32°52N 17°11W **24** D2
Porto Murtinho *Brazil* 21°45S 57°55W **92** H7
Porto Nacional *Brazil* 10°40S 48°30W **93** F9
Porto-Novo *Benin* 6°23N 2°42E **50** G6
Porto Primavera, Represa
  Brazil 22°10S 52°45W **95** A5
Porto Santo, I. de
  Madeira 33°45N 16°25W **50** B2
Pôrto São José *Brazil* 22°43S 53°10W **95** A5
Porto Seguro *Brazil* 16°26S 39°5W **93** G11
Porto Tórres *Italy* 40°50N 8°24E **22** D3
Porto União *Brazil* 26°10S 51°10W **95** B5
Porto-Vecchio *France* 41°35N 9°16E **20** F8
Pôrto Velho *Brazil* 8°46S 63°54W **92** E6
Porto Walter *Brazil* 8°15S 72°40W **92** E4
Portobelo *Panama* 9°35N 79°42W **88** E4
Portoferráio *Italy* 42°48N 10°20E **22** C4

Portola *U.S.A.* 39°49N 120°28W **78** F6
Portopetro *Spain* 39°22N 3°13E **24** B10
Portoscuso *Italy* 39°12N 8°24E **22** E3
Portoviejo *Ecuador* 1°7S 80°28W **92** D2
Portpatrick *U.K.* 54°51N 5°7W **11** G3
Portree *U.K.* 57°25N 6°12W **11** D2
Portrush *U.K.* 55°12N 6°40W **10** A5
Portsmouth *Dominica* 15°34N 61°27W **89** C7
Portsmouth *U.K.* 50°48N 1°6W **13** G6
Portsmouth *N.H., U.S.A.* 43°5N 70°45W **83** C14
Portsmouth *Ohio, U.S.A.* 38°44N 82°57W **81** F12
Portsmouth *R.I., U.S.A.* 41°36N 71°15W **83** E13
Portsmouth *Va., U.S.A.* 36°58N 76°23W **81** G15
Portsmouth □ *U.K.* 50°48N 1°6W **13** G6
Portsoy *U.K.* 57°41N 2°41W **11** D6
Portstewart *U.K.* 55°11N 6°43W **10** A5
Porttipahdan tekojärvi *Finland* 68°5N 26°40E **8** B22
Portugal ■ *Europe* 40°0N 8°0W **21** C1
Portumna *Ireland* 53°6N 8°14W **10** C3
Portville *U.S.A.* 42°3N 78°20W **82** D6
Poruma *Australia* 10°2S 143°4E **62** a
Porvenir *Chile* 53°10S 70°16W **96** G2
Posadas *Argentina* 27°30S 55°50W **95** B4
Posht-e Badam *Iran* 33°2N 55°23E **45** C7
Poso *Indonesia* 1°20S 120°55E **37** E6
Posse *Brazil* 14°4S 46°18W **93** F9
Possession I. *Antarctica* 72°4S 172°0E **5** D11
Possum Kingdom L. *U.S.A.* 32°52N 98°26W **84** E5
Post *U.S.A.* 33°12N 101°23W **84** E4
Post Falls *U.S.A.* 47°43N 116°57W **76** C5
Postavy = Pastavy *Belarus* 55°4N 26°50E **9** J22
Poste-de-la-Baleine = Kuujjuarapik *Canada* 55°20N 77°35W **72** A4
Postmasburg *S. Africa* 28°18S 23°5E **56** D3
Postojna *Slovenia* 45°46N 14°12E **16** F8
Poston *U.S.A.* 34°0N 114°24W **79** M12
Postville *Canada* 54°54N 59°47W **73** B8
Posyet *Russia* 42°39N 130°48E **30** C5
Potchefstroom *S. Africa* 26°41S 27°7E **56** D4
Poteau *U.S.A.* 35°3N 94°37W **84** D7
Poteet *U.S.A.* 29°2N 98°35W **84** G5
Potenza *Italy* 40°38N 15°48E **22** D6
Poteriteri, L. *N.Z.* 46°5S 167°10E **59** G1
Potgietersrus = Mokopane *S. Africa* 24°10S 28°55E **57** C4
Poti *Georgia* 42°10N 41°38E **19** F7
Potiskum *Nigeria* 11°39N 11°2E **51** F8
Potomac → *U.S.A.* 38°0N 76°23W **81** F14
Potosí *Bolivia* 19°38S 65°50W **92** G5
Potosi Mt. *U.S.A.* 35°57N 115°29W **79** K11
Pototan *Phil.* 10°54N 122°38E **37** B6
Potrerillos *Chile* 26°30S 69°30W **94** B2
Potsdam *Germany* 52°23N 13°3E **16** B7
Potsdam *U.S.A.* 44°40N 74°59W **83** B10
Pottersville *U.S.A.* 43°43N 73°50W **83** C11
Pottstown *U.S.A.* 40°15N 75°39W **83** F9
Pottsville *U.S.A.* 40°41N 76°12W **83** F8
Pottuvil *Sri Lanka* 6°55N 81°50E **40** R12
Pouce Coupé *Canada* 55°40N 120°10W **70** B4
Poughkeepsie *U.S.A.* 41°42N 73°56W **83** E11
Poulaphouca Res. *Ireland* 53°8N 6°30W **10** C5
Poulsbo *U.S.A.* 47°44N 122°38W **78** C4
Poultney *U.S.A.* 43°31N 73°14W **83** C11
Poulton-le-Fylde *U.K.* 53°51N 2°58W **12** D5
Pouso Alegre *Brazil* 22°14S 45°57W **95** A6
Pouthisat *Cambodia* 12°34N 103°50E **38** F4
Považská Bystrica *Slovak Rep.* 49°8N 18°27E **17** D10
Povenets *Russia* 62°50N 34°50E **18** B5
Poverty B. *N.Z.* 38°43S 178°2E **59** C7
Póvoa de Varzim *Portugal* 41°25N 8°46W **21** B1
Povorotnyy, Mys *Russia* 42°40N 133°2E **30** C6
Povungnituk = Puvirnituq *Canada* 60°2N 77°10W **69** E16
Powassan *Canada* 46°5N 79°25W **72** C4
Poway *U.S.A.* 32°58N 117°2W **79** N9
Powder → *U.S.A.* 46°45N 105°26W **76** C11
Powder River *U.S.A.* 43°2N 106°59W **76** E10
Powell *U.S.A.* 44°45N 108°46W **76** D9
Powell, L. *U.S.A.* 36°57N 111°29W **77** H8
Powell River *Canada* 49°50N 124°35W **70** D4
Powers *U.S.A.* 45°41N 87°32W **80** C10
Pownal *U.S.A.* 42°45N 73°14W **83** D11
Powys □ *U.K.* 52°20N 3°20W **13** E4
Poyang Hu *China* 29°5N 116°20E **33** D6
Poyarkovo *Russia* 49°36N 128°41E **29** E13
Poza Rica *Mexico* 20°33N 97°27W **87** C5
Požarevac *Serbia* 44°35N 21°18E **23** B9
Poznań *Poland* 52°25N 16°55E **17** B9
Pozo *U.S.A.* 35°20N 120°24W **79** K6
Pozo Almonte *Chile* 20°10S 69°50W **92** H5
Pozo Colorado *Paraguay* 23°30S 58°45W **94** A4
Pozoblanco *Spain* 38°23N 4°51W **21** C3
Pozzuoli *Italy* 40°49N 14°7E **22** D6
Prachin Buri *Thailand* 14°0N 101°25E **38** F3
Prachuap Khiri Khan *Thailand* 11°49N 99°48E **39** G2
Prado *Brazil* 17°20S 39°13W **93** G11
Prague = Praha *Czech Rep.* 50°4N 14°25E **16** C8
Praha *Czech Rep.* 50°4N 14°25E **16** C8
Praia *C. Verde Is.* 15°2N 23°34W **50** b
Prainha *Brazil* 1°45S 53°30W **93** D8
Prainha Nova *Brazil* 7°10S 60°30W **92** E6
Prairie *Australia* 20°50S 144°35E **62** C3
Prairie City *U.S.A.* 44°28N 118°43W **76** D4
Prairie Dog Town Fork Red → *U.S.A.* 34°34N 99°58W **84** D5
Prairies, L. of the *Canada* 51°16N 101°32W **71** C8
Pran Buri *Thailand* 12°23N 99°55E **38** F2
Prapat *Indonesia* 2°41N 98°58E **36** D1
Praslin *Seychelles* 4°18S 55°45E **53** b

Prasonisi, Akra *Greece* 35°42N 27°46E **25** D9
Prata *Brazil* 19°25S 48°54W **93** G9
Pratabpur *India* 23°28N 83°15E **43** H10
Pratapgarh *Raj., India* 24°2N 74°40E **42** G6
Pratapgarh *Ut. P., India* 25°56N 81°59E **43** G9
Prato *Italy* 43°53N 11°6E **22** C4
Pratt *U.S.A.* 37°39N 98°44W **80** G4
Prattville *U.S.A.* 32°28N 86°29W **85** E11
Pravia *Spain* 43°30N 6°12W **21** A2
Praya *Indonesia* 8°39S 116°17E **36** F5
Prayag = Allahabad *India* 25°25N 81°58E **43** G9
Preble *U.S.A.* 42°44N 76°8W **83** D8
Precipice △ *Australia* 25°18S 150°5E **63** D5
Precordillera *Argentina* 30°0S 69°1W **94** C2
Preeceville *Canada* 51°57N 102°40W **71** C8
Preiļi *Latvia* 56°18N 26°43E **9** H22
Premont *U.S.A.* 27°22N 98°7W **84** H5
Prentice *U.S.A.* 45°33N 90°17W **80** C8
Preobrazheniye *Russia* 42°54N 133°54E **30** C6
Preparis I. = Pariparit Kyun *Burma* 14°52N 93°41E **41** M18
Preparis North Channel *Ind. Oc.* 15°27N 94°5E **41** M18
Preparis South Channel *Ind. Oc.* 14°33N 93°30E **41** M18
Přerov *Czech Rep.* 49°28N 17°27E **17** D9
Prescott *Canada* 44°45N 75°30W **83** B9
Prescott *Ariz., U.S.A.* 34°33N 112°28W **77** J7
Prescott *Ark., U.S.A.* 33°48N 93°23W **84** E8
Prescott Valley *U.S.A.* 34°40N 112°18W **77** J7
Preservation Inlet *N.Z.* 46°8S 166°35E **59** G1
Presho *U.S.A.* 43°54N 100°3W **80** D3
Presidencia de la Plaza *Argentina* 27°0S 59°50W **94** B4
Presidencia Roque Saenz Peña *Argentina* 26°45S 60°30W **94** B3
Presidente Epitácio *Brazil* 21°56S 52°6W **93** H8
Presidente Hayes □ *Paraguay* 24°0S 59°0W **94** A4
Presidente Prudente *Brazil* 22°5S 51°25W **95** A5
Presidio *Mexico* 29°29N 104°23W **86** B4
Presidio *U.S.A.* 29°34N 104°22W **84** G2
Prešov *Slovak Rep.* 49°0N 21°15E **17** D11
Prespa, L. = Prespansko Jezero *Macedonia* 40°55N 21°0E **23** D9
Prespansko Jezero *Macedonia* 40°55N 21°0E **23** D9
Presque I. *U.S.A.* 42°10N 80°6W **82** D4
Presque Isle *U.S.A.* 46°41N 68°1W **81** B19
Prestatyn *U.K.* 53°20N 3°24W **12** D4
Presteigne *U.K.* 52°17N 3°0W **13** E5
Preston *Canada* 43°23N 80°21W **82** C4
Preston *U.K.* 53°46N 2°42W **12** D5
Preston *Idaho, U.S.A.* 42°6N 111°53W **76** E8
Preston *Minn., U.S.A.* 43°40N 92°5W **80** D7
Preston, C. *Australia* 20°51S 116°12E **60** D2
Prestonsburg *U.S.A.* 37°40N 82°47W **81** G12
Prestwick *U.K.* 55°29N 4°37W **11** F4
Pretoria *S. Africa* 25°44S 28°12E **57** D4
Preveza *Greece* 38°57N 20°45E **23** E9
Prey Veng *Cambodia* 11°35N 105°29E **39** G5
Pribilof Is. *U.S.A.* 57°0N 170°0W **74** D6
Příbram *Czech Rep.* 49°41N 14°2E **16** D8
Price *U.S.A.* 39°36N 110°49W **76** G8
Price I. *Canada* 52°23N 128°41W **70** C3
Prichard *U.S.A.* 30°44N 88°5W **85** F10
Priekule *Latvia* 56°26N 21°35E **9** H19
Prienai *Lithuania* 54°38N 23°57E **9** J20
Prieska *S. Africa* 29°40S 22°42E **56** D3
Priest L. *U.S.A.* 48°35N 116°52W **76** B5
Priest River *U.S.A.* 48°11N 116°55W **76** B5
Priest Valley *U.S.A.* 36°10N 120°39W **78** J6
Prievidza *Slovak Rep.* 48°46N 18°36E **17** D10
Prikaspiyskaya Nizmennost = Caspian Depression *Eurasia* 47°0N 48°0E **19** E8
Prilep *Macedonia* 41°21N 21°32E **23** D9
Priluki = Pryluky *Ukraine* 50°30N 32°24E **19** D5
Prime Seal I. *Australia* 40°3S 147°43E **63** G4
Primo Tapia *Mexico* 32°16N 116°54W **79** N10
Primorskiy Kray □ *Russia* 45°0N 135°0E **30** B7
Primrose L. *Canada* 54°55N 109°45W **71** C7
Prince Albert *Canada* 53°15N 105°50W **71** C7
Prince Albert *S. Africa* 33°12S 22°2E **56** E3
Prince Albert △ *Canada* 54°0N 106°25W **71** C7
Prince Albert Mts. *Antarctica* 76°0S 161°30E **5** D11
Prince Albert Pen. *Canada* 72°30N 116°0W **68** C8
Prince Albert Sd. *Canada* 70°25N 115°0W **68** C9
Prince Alfred, C. *Canada* 74°20N 124°40W **4** B1
Prince Charles I. *Canada* 67°47N 76°12W **69** D16
Prince Charles Mts. *Antarctica* 72°0S 67°0E **5** D6
Prince Edward Fracture Zone *Ind. Oc.* 46°0S 35°0E **5** A4
Prince Edward I. □ *Canada* 46°20N 63°20W **73** C7
Prince Edward Is. *Ind. Oc.* 46°35S 38°0E **3** G11
Prince George *Canada* 53°55N 122°50W **70** C4
Prince of Wales, C. *U.S.A.* 65°36N 168°5W **74** B6
Prince of Wales I. *Australia* 10°40S 142°10E **62** A3
Prince of Wales I. *Canada* 73°0N 99°0W **68** C12
Prince of Wales I. *U.S.A.* 55°47N 132°50W **70** B2
Prince of Wales Icefield *Canada* 78°15N 79°0W **69** B16
Prince of Wales Str. *Canada* 73°0N 117°0W **68** C8
Prince Patrick I. *Canada* 77°0N 120°0W **69** B8

Prince Regent Inlet *Canada* 73°0N 90°0W **69** C14
Prince Rupert *Canada* 54°20N 130°20W **70** C2
Prince William Sd. *U.S.A.* 60°40N 147°0W **68** E2
Princes Town *Trin. & Tob.* 10°16N 61°23W **93** K15
Princess Charlotte B. *Australia* 14°25S 144°0E **62** A3
Princess Elizabeth Trough *S. Ocean* 64°10S 83°0E **5** C7
Princess May Ranges *Australia* 15°30S 125°30E **60** C4
Princess Royal I. *Canada* 53°0N 128°40W **70** C3
Princeton *Canada* 49°27N 120°30W **70** D4
Princeton *Calif., U.S.A.* 39°24N 122°1W **78** F4
Princeton *Ill., U.S.A.* 41°23N 89°28W **80** E9
Princeton *Ind., U.S.A.* 38°21N 87°34W **80** F10
Princeton *Ky., U.S.A.* 37°7N 87°53W **80** G10
Princeton *Mo., U.S.A.* 40°24N 93°35W **80** E7
Princeton *N.J., U.S.A.* 40°21N 74°39W **83** F10
Princeton *W. Va., U.S.A.* 37°22N 81°6W **81** G13
Príncipe *São Tomé & Príncipe* 1°37N 7°25E **48** F4
Príncipe da Beira *Brazil* 12°20S 64°30W **92** F6
Prineville *U.S.A.* 44°18N 120°51W **76** D3
Prins Harald Kyst *Antarctica* 70°0S 35°1E **5** D4
Prinsesse Astrid Kyst *Antarctica* 70°45S 12°30E **5** D3
Prinsesse Ragnhild Kyst *Antarctica* 70°15S 27°30E **5** D4
Prinzapolca *Nic.* 13°20N 83°35W **88** D3
Priozersk *Russia* 61°2N 30°7E **8** F24
Pripet = Prypyat → *Europe* 51°20N 30°15E **17** C16
Pripet Marshes *Europe* 52°10N 28°10E **17** B15
Pripyat Marshes = Pripet Marshes *Europe* 52°10N 28°10E **17** B15
Pripyats = Prypyat → *Europe* 51°20N 30°15E **17** C16
Priština *Kosovo* 42°40N 21°13E **23** C9
Privas *France* 44°45N 4°37E **20** D6
Privolzhskaya Vozvyshennost *Russia* 51°0N 46°0E **19** D8
Privolzhskiy □ *Russia* 56°0N 50°0E **28** D6
Prizren *Kosovo* 42°13N 20°45E **23** C9
Probolinggo *Indonesia* 7°46S 113°13E **37** G15
Proctor *U.S.A.* 43°40N 73°2W **83** C11
Proddatur *India* 14°45N 78°30E **40** M11
Prodhromos *Cyprus* 34°57N 32°50E **25** E11
Profília *Greece* 36°5N 27°51E **25** C9
Profondeville *Belgium* 50°23N 4°52E **15** D4
Progreso *Coahuila, Mexico* 27°28N 100°59W **86** B4
Progreso *Yucatán, Mexico* 21°20N 89°40W **87** C7
Progress *Antarctica* 66°22S 76°22E **5** C12
Progress *Russia* 49°45N 129°37E **29** E13
Prokopyevsk *Russia* 54°0N 86°45E **28** D9
Prokuplje *Serbia* 43°16N 21°36E **23** C9
Prome *Burma* 18°49N 95°13E **41** K19
Prophet → *Canada* 58°48N 122°40W **70** B4
Prophet River *Canada* 58°6N 122°43W **70** B4
Propriá *Brazil* 10°13S 36°51W **93** F11
Propriano *France* 41°41N 8°52E **20** F8
Proserpine *Australia* 20°21S 148°36E **62** b
Prosna → *Poland* 52°6N 17°44E **17** B9
Prospect *U.S.A.* 43°18N 75°9W **83** C9
Prosser *U.S.A.* 46°12N 119°46W **76** C4
Prostějov *Czech Rep.* 49°30N 17°9E **17** D9
Proston *Australia* 26°8S 151°32E **63** D5
Provence *France* 43°40N 5°46E **20** E6
Providence *Ky., U.S.A.* 37°24N 87°46W **80** G10
Providence *R.I., U.S.A.* 41°49N 71°24W **83** E13
Providence Bay *Canada* 45°41N 82°15W **72** C3
Providence Mts. *U.S.A.* 35°10N 115°15W **79** K11
Providencia, I. de *Colombia* 13°25N 81°26W **88** D3
Provideniya *Russia* 64°23N 173°18W **29** C19
Provincetown *U.S.A.* 42°3N 70°11W **81** D18
Provins *France* 48°33N 3°15E **20** B5
Provo *U.S.A.* 40°14N 111°39W **76** F8
Provost *Canada* 52°25N 110°20W **71** C6
Prudhoe Bay *U.S.A.* 70°18N 148°22W **74** A10
Prudhoe I. *Australia* 21°19S 149°41E **62** C4
Prud'homme *Canada* 52°20N 105°54W **71** C7
Pruszków *Poland* 52°9N 20°49E **17** B11
Prut → *Romania* 45°28N 28°10E **17** F15
Pruzhany *Belarus* 52°33N 24°28E **17** B13
Prydz B. *Antarctica* 69°0S 74°0E **5** C6
Pryluky *Ukraine* 50°30N 32°24E **19** D5
Pryor *U.S.A.* 36°19N 95°19W **84** C7
Prypyat → *Europe* 51°20N 30°15E **17** C16
Przemyśl *Poland* 49°50N 22°45E **17** D12
Przhevalsk = Karakol *Kyrgyzstan* 42°30N 78°20E **32** B2
Psara *Greece* 38°37N 25°38E **23** E11
Psiloritis, Oros *Greece* 35°15N 24°45E **25** D6
Psira *Greece* 35°12N 25°52E **25** D7
Pskov *Russia* 57°50N 28°25E **9** H23
Ptich → *Belarus* 52°9N 28°52E **17** B15
Ptichia = Vidos *Greece* 39°38N 19°55E **25** A3
Ptsich → *Belarus* 52°9N 28°52E **17** B15
Pu Xian *China* 36°24N 111°6E **34** F6
Pua *Thailand* 19°11N 100°55E **38** C3
Puán *Argentina* 37°30S 62°45W **94** D3
Pu'apu'a *Samoa* 13°34S 172°9W **59** b
Pucallpa *Peru* 8°25S 74°30W **92** E4
Puch'on = Bucheon *S. Korea* 37°28N 126°45E **35** F14
Pucheng *China* 35°40N 115°12W **79** K11
Pudasjärvi *Finland* 65°23N 26°53E **8** D22
Pudozh *Russia* 61°48N 36°32E **18** B6
Puducherry *India* 11°59N 79°50E **40** P11
Pudukkottai *India* 10°28N 78°47E **40** P11
Puebla *Mexico* 19°3N 98°12W **87** D5
Puebla □ *Mexico* 18°50N 98°0W **87** D5
Pueblo *U.S.A.* 38°16N 104°37W **76** G11

Puelches *Argentina* 38°5S 65°51W **94** D2
Puelén *Argentina* 37°32S 67°38W **94** D2
Puente Alto *Chile* 33°32S 70°35W **94** C1
Puente-Genil *Spain* 37°22N 4°47W **21** D3
Puerca, Pta. *Puerto Rico* 18°13N 65°36W **89** d
Puerco → *U.S.A.* 34°22N 107°50W **77** J10
Puerto Aisén *Chile* 45°27S 73°0W **96** F2
Puerto Ángel *Mexico* 15°40N 96°29W **87** D5
Puerto Arista *Mexico* 15°56N 93°48W **87** D6
Puerto Armuelles *Panama* 8°20N 82°51W **88** E3
Puerto Ayacucho *Venezuela* 5°40N 67°35W **92** B5
Puerto Barrios *Guatemala* 15°40N 88°32W **88** C2
Puerto Bermejo *Argentina* 26°55S 58°34W **94** B4
Puerto Bermúdez *Peru* 10°20S 74°58W **92** F4
Puerto Bolívar *Ecuador* 3°19S 79°55W **92** D3
Puerto Cabello *Venezuela* 10°28N 68°1W **92** A5
Puerto Cabezas *Nic.* 14°0N 83°30W **88** D3
Puerto Cabo Gracias á Dios *Nic.* 15°0N 83°10W **88** D3
Puerto Carreño *Colombia* 6°12N 67°22W **92** B5
Puerto Castilla *Honduras* 16°0N 86°0W **88** C2
Puerto Chicama *Peru* 7°45S 79°20W **92** E3
Puerto Coig *Argentina* 50°54S 69°15W **96** G3
Puerto Cortés *Honduras* 15°51N 88°0W **88** C2
Puerto Cumarebo *Venezuela* 11°29N 69°30W **92** A5
Puerto de Alcudia = Port d'Alcúdia *Spain* 39°50N 3°7E **24** B10
Puerto de Cabrera *Spain* 39°8N 2°56E **24** B9
Puerto de Gran Tarajal *Canary Is.* 28°13N 14°1W **24** F5
Puerto de la Cruz *Canary Is.* 28°24N 16°32W **24** F3
Puerto de los Angeles △ *Mexico* 23°39N 105°45W **86** C3
Puerto de Pozo Negro *Canary Is.* 28°19N 13°55W **24** F6
Puerto de Sóller = Port de Sóller *Spain* 39°48N 2°42E **24** B9
Puerto del Carmen *Canary Is.* 28°55N 13°38W **24** F6
Puerto del Rosario *Canary Is.* 28°30N 13°52W **24** F6
Puerto Deseado *Argentina* 47°55S 66°0W **96** F3
Puerto Escondido *Mexico* 15°50N 97°0W **87** D5
Puerto Heath *Bolivia* 12°34S 68°39W **92** F5
Puerto Inírida *Colombia* 3°53N 67°52W **92** C5
Puerto Juárez *Mexico* 21°11N 86°49W **87** C7
Puerto La Cruz *Venezuela* 10°13N 64°38W **92** A6
Puerto Leguízamo *Colombia* 0°12S 74°46W **92** D4
Puerto Lempira *Honduras* 15°16N 83°36W **88** C3
Puerto Libertad *Mexico* 29°55N 112°43W **86** B2
Puerto Limón *Colombia* 3°23N 73°30W **92** C4
Puerto Lobos *Argentina* 42°0S 65°3W **96** E3
Puerto Madryn *Argentina* 42°48S 65°4W **96** E3
Puerto Maldonado *Peru* 12°30S 69°10W **92** F5
Puerto Manatí *Cuba* 21°22N 76°50W **88** B4
Puerto Montt *Chile* 41°28S 73°0W **96** E2
Puerto Morazán *Nic.* 12°51N 87°11W **88** D2
Puerto Morelos *Mexico* 20°50N 86°52W **87** C7
Puerto Natales *Chile* 51°45S 72°15W **96** G2
Puerto Oscuro *Chile* 31°24S 71°35W **94** C1
Puerto Padre *Cuba* 21°13N 76°35W **88** B4
Puerto Páez *Venezuela* 6°13N 67°28W **92** B5
Puerto Peñasco *Mexico* 31°20N 113°33W **86** A2
Puerto Pinasco *Paraguay* 22°36S 57°50W **94** A4
Puerto Plata *Dom. Rep.* 19°48N 70°45W **89** C5
Puerto Pollensa = Port de Pollença *Spain* 39°54N 3°4E **24** B10
Puerto Princesa *Phil.* 9°46N 118°45E **37** C5
Puerto Quepos *Costa Rica* 9°29N 84°6W **88** E3
Puerto Rico *Canary Is.* 27°47N 15°42W **24** G4
Puerto Rico ☑ *W. Indies* 18°15N 66°45W **89** d
Puerto Rico Trench *Atl. Oc.* 19°50N 66°0W **89** C6
Puerto San Julián *Argentina* 49°18S 67°43W **96** F3
Puerto Santa Cruz *Argentina* 50°0S 68°32W **96** G3
Puerto Sastre *Paraguay* 22°2S 57°55W **94** A4
Puerto Suárez *Bolivia* 18°58S 57°52W **92** G7
Puerto Vallarta *Mexico* 20°37N 105°15W **86** C3
Puerto Varas *Chile* 41°19S 72°59W **96** E2
Puerto Wilches *Colombia* 7°21N 73°54W **92** B4
Puertollano *Spain* 38°43N 4°7W **21** C3
Pueu *Tahiti* 17°44S 149°13W **59** d
Pueyrredón, L. *Argentina* 47°20S 72°0W **96** F2
Puffin I. *Ireland* 51°50N 10°24W **10** E1
Pugachev *Russia* 52°0N 48°49E **18** D8
Pugal *India* 28°30N 72°48E **42** E5
Puge *Tanzania* 4°45S 33°11E **54** C3
Puget Sound *U.S.A.* 47°50N 122°30W **76** C2
Pugödong *N. Korea* 42°5N 130°0E **35** C16
Pugu *Tanzania* 6°55S 39°4E **54** D4
Pūgūnzī *Iran* 25°49N 59°10E **45** E8
Puig Major *Spain* 39°48N 2°47E **24** B9
Puigcerdà *Spain* 42°24N 1°50E **21** A6
Puigpunyent *Spain* 39°38N 2°32E **24** B9
Pujon-ho *N. Korea* 40°35N 127°35E **35** D14
Pukaki, L. *N.Z.* 44°4S 170°1E **59** F3
Pukapuka *Cook Is.* 10°53S 165°49W **65** J11
Pukaskwa △ *Canada* 48°20N 86°0W **72** C2
Pukatawagan *Canada* 55°45N 101°20W **71** B8
Pukchin *N. Korea* 40°12N 125°45E **35** D13
Pukch'ŏng *N. Korea* 40°14N 128°10E **35** D15
Pukekohe *N.Z.* 37°12S 174°55E **59** B5
Pukhrayan *India* 26°14N 79°51E **43** F8
Puksoozero *Russia* 61°42N 40°32E **18** B7
Pula *Croatia* 44°54N 13°57E **16** F7
Pulacayo *Bolivia* 20°25S 66°41W **92** H5
Pulai *Malaysia* 1°20N 103°31E **39** d

Pulaski *N.Y., U.S.A.* 43°34N 76°8W **83** C8
Pulaski *Tenn., U.S.A.* 35°12N 87°2W **85** D11
Pulaski *Va., U.S.A.* 37°3N 80°47W **81** G13
Pulau → *Indonesia* 5°50S 138°15E **37** F9
Pulawy *Poland* 51°23N 21°59E **17** C11
Pulga *U.S.A.* 39°48N 121°29W **78** F5
Pulicat L. *India* 13°40N 80°15E **40** N12
Pullman *U.S.A.* 46°44N 117°10W **76** C5
Pulog, Mt. *Phil.* 16°40N 120°50E **37** A6
Pultusk *Poland* 52°43N 21°6E **17** B11
Pumlumon Fawr *U.K.* 52°28N 3°46W **13** E4
Puná, I. *Ecuador* 2°55S 80°5W **92** D2
Punakaiki *N.Z.* 42°7S 171°15E **59** E3
Punakha Dzong *Bhutan* 27°42N 89°52E **41** F16
Punasar *India* 27°6N 73°6E **42** F5
Punata *Bolivia* 17°32S 65°50W **92** G5
Punch *India* 33°48N 74°4E **43** C6
Punch → *Pakistan* 33°12N 73°40E **42** C5
Punda Maria *S. Africa* 22°40S 31°5E **57** C5
Pune *India* 18°29N 73°57E **40** K8
P'ungsan *N. Korea* 40°50N 128°9E **35** D15
Pungue, Ponte de *Mozam.* 19°0S 34°0E **55** F3
Punjab □ *India* 31°0N 76°0E **42** D7
Punjab □ *Pakistan* 32°0N 72°30E **42** E6
Puno *Peru* 15°55S 70°3W **92** G4
Punpun → *India* 25°31N 85°18E **43** G11
Punta, Cerro de *Puerto Rico* 18°10N 66°37W **89** d
Punta Alta *Argentina* 38°53S 62°4W **96** D4
Punta Arenas *Chile* 53°10S 71°0W **96** G2
Punta del Díaz *Chile* 28°0S 70°45W **94** B1
Punta del Hidalgo *Canary Is.* 28°33N 16°19W **24** F3
Punta Gorda *Belize* 16°10N 88°45W **87** D7
Punta Gorda *U.S.A.* 26°56N 82°3W **85** H13
Punta Prieta *Mexico* 28°58N 114°17W **86** B2
Punta Prima *Spain* 28°24N 16°32W **24** F3
Puntarenas *Costa Rica* 10°0N 84°50W **88** E3
Puntland *Somali Rep.* 8°0N 49°0E **47** F4
Punto Fijo *Venezuela* 11°50N 70°13W **92** A4
Punxsutawney *U.S.A.* 40°57N 78°59W **82** F6
Pupuan *Indonesia* 8°19S 115°0E **37** J18
Puquio *Peru* 14°45S 74°10W **92** F4
Pur → *Russia* 67°31N 77°55E **28** C8
Puracé, Vol. *Colombia* 2°21N 76°23W **92** C3
Puralia = Puruliya *India* 23°17N 86°24E **43** H12
Puranpur *India* 28°31N 80°9E **43** E9
Purbeck, Isle of *U.K.* 50°39N 1°59W **13** G5
Purcell *U.S.A.* 35°1N 97°22W **84** D6
Purcell Mts. *Canada* 49°55N 116°15W **70** D5
Purdy *Canada* 45°19N 77°44W **82** A7
Puri *India* 19°50N 85°58E **41** K14
Purmerend *Neths.* 52°32N 4°58E **15** B4
Purnia *India* 25°45N 87°31E **43** G12
Purnululu △ *Australia* 17°20S 128°20E **60** C4
Pursat = Pouthisat *Cambodia* 12°34N 103°50E **38** F4
Purukcahu *Indonesia* 0°35S 114°35E **36** E4
Puruliya *India* 23°17N 86°24E **43** H12
Purus → *Brazil* 3°42S 61°28W **92** D6
Puruvesi *Finland* 61°50N 29°30E **8** F23
Purvis *U.S.A.* 31°9N 89°25W **85** F10
Purwa *India* 26°28N 80°47E **43** F9
Purwo, Tanjung *Indonesia* 8°44S 114°21E **37** K18
Purwodadi *Indonesia* 7°7S 110°55E **37** G14
Purwokerto *Indonesia* 7°25S 109°14E **37** G13
Puryŏng *N. Korea* 42°5N 129°43E **35** C15
Pusa *India* 25°59N 85°41E **43** G11
Pusan = Busan *S. Korea* 35°5N 129°0E **35** G15
Pushkin *Russia* 59°45N 30°25E **9** G24
Pushkino *Russia* 51°16N 47°0E **18** D8
Put-in-Bay *U.S.A.* 41°39N 82°49W **82** E2
Putahow L. *Canada* 59°54N 100°40W **71** B8
Putao *Burma* 27°28N 97°30E **41** F20
Putaruru *N.Z.* 38°2S 175°50E **59** C5
Putignano *Italy* 40°51N 17°7E **22** D7
Puting, Tanjung *Indonesia* 3°31S 111°46E **36** E4
Putnam *U.S.A.* 41°55N 71°55W **83** E13
Putorana, Gory *Russia* 69°0N 95°0E **29** C10
Putrajaya *Malaysia* 2°55N 101°40E **39** L3
Puttalam *Sri Lanka* 8°1N 79°55E **40** Q11
Puttgarden *Germany* 54°30N 11°10E **16** A6
Putumayo → *S. Amer.* 3°7S 67°58W **92** D5
Putussibau *Indonesia* 0°50N 112°56E **36** D4
Puvirnituq *Canada* 60°2N 77°10W **69** E16
Puy-de-Dôme *France* 45°46N 2°57E **20** D5
Puyallup *U.S.A.* 47°12N 122°18W **78** C4
Puyang *China* 35°40N 115°1E **34** G8
Pūzeh Rīg *Iran* 27°20N 58°40E **45** E8
Pwani □ *Tanzania* 7°0S 39°0E **54** D4
Pweto *Dem. Rep. of the Congo* 8°25S 28°51E **55** D2
Pwllheli *U.K.* 52°53N 4°25W **12** E3
Pyaozero, Ozero *Russia* 66°5N 30°58E **8** C24
Pyapon *Burma* 16°20N 95°40E **41** L19
Pyasina → *Russia* 73°30N 87°0E **28** B9
Pyatigorsk *Russia* 44°2N 43°6E **19** F7
Pyè = Prome *Burma* 18°49N 95°13E **41** K19
Pyinmana *Burma* 19°45N 96°12E **41** K20
Pyŏktong *N. Korea* 40°50N 125°50E **35** D13
Pyŏnggang *N. Korea* 38°24N 127°17E **35** E14
Pyŏngtaek *S. Korea* 37°1N 127°4E **35** F14
Pyŏngyang *N. Korea* 39°0N 125°30E **35** E13
Pyote *U.S.A.* 31°32N 103°8W **84** F3
Pyramid L. *U.S.A.* 40°1N 119°35W **76** F4
Pyramid Pk. *U.S.A.* 36°25N 116°37W **79** J10
Pyramids *Egypt* 29°58N 31°9E **51** C12
Pyrénées *Europe* 42°45N 0°18E **20** E4
Pyu *Burma* 18°30N 96°28E **41** K20

Q

Qaanaaq *Greenland* 77°30N 69°10W **69** B18
Qachasnek *S. Africa* 30°6S 28°42E **57** E4
Qa'el Jafr *Jordan* 30°20N 36°25E **46** E5
Qa'emābād *Iran* 31°44N 60°2E **45** D9
Qā'emshahr *Iran* 36°30N 52°53E **45** B7
Qagan Nur *China* 43°30N 114°55E **34** C8
Qahar Youyi Zhongqi
China 41°12N 112°40E **34** D7
Qahremānshahr = Kermānshāh
Iran 34°23N 47°0E **44** C5
Qaidam Pendi *China* 37°0N 95°0E **32** C4
Qajarīyeh *Iran* 31°1N 48°22E **45** D6
Qala, Ras il *Malta* 36°2N 14°20E **25** C1
Qala-i-Jadid = Spīn Būldak
Afghan. 31°1N 66°25E **42** D2
Qala Point = Qala, Ras il
Malta 36°2N 14°20E **25** C1
Qala Viala *Pakistan* 30°49N 67°17E **42** D2
Qala Yangi *Afghan.* 34°20N 66°30E **42** B2
Qal'at al Akhḑar *Si. Arabia* 28°4N 37°9E **44** E3
Qal'at Dīzah *Iraq* 36°11N 45°7E **44** B5
Qal'at Şāliḩ *Iraq* 31°31N 47°16E **44** D5
Qal'at Sukkar *Iraq* 31°51N 46°5E **44** D5
Qamani'tuaq = Baker Lake
Canada 64°20N 96°3W **68** E12
Qamdo *China* 31°15N 97°6E **32** C4
Qamea *Fiji* 16°45S 179°45W **59** a
Qamruddin Karez
Pakistan 31°45N 68°20E **42** D3
Qandahār = Kandahār
Afghan. 31°32N 65°43E **40** D4
Qandahār = Kandahār □
Afghan. 31°0N 65°0E **40** D4
Qandyaghash
Kazakhstan 49°28N 57°25E **19** E10
Qapān *Iran* 37°40N 55°47E **45** B7
Qapshaghay *Kazakhstan* 43°51N 77°14E **28** E8
Qaqortoq *Greenland* 60°43N 46°0W **4** C5
Qara Qash → *China* 35°0N 78°30E **43** B8
Qarabutaq *Kazakhstan* 49°59N 60°14E **28** E7
Qaraghandy *Kazakhstan* 49°50N 73°10E **28** E8
Qaraghayly *Kazakhstan* 49°26N 76°0E **28** E8
Qārah *Si. Arabia* 29°55N 40°3E **44** D4
Qarataū *Ongtüstik Qazaqstan,*
Kazakhstan 43°30N 69°30E **28** E7
Qarataū *Zhambyl,*
Kazakhstan 43°10N 70°28E **28** E8
Qarazhal *Kazakhstan* 48°2N 70°49E **28** E8
Qardho *Somali Rep.* 9°30N 49°6E **47** F4
Qareh → *Iran* 39°25N 47°22E **44** B5
Qareh Tekān *Iran* 36°38N 49°29E **45** B6
Qarnein *U.A.E.* 24°56N 52°52E **45** E7
Qarqan He → *China* 39°30N 88°30E **32** C3
Qarqaraly *Kazakhstan* 49°26N 75°30E **28** E8
Qarshi *Uzbekistan* 38°53N 65°48E **28** F7
Qartabā *Lebanon* 34°4N 35°50E **46** A4
Qārūh *Kuwait* 28°49N 48°46E **45** D6
Qaryat al Gharab *Iraq* 31°27N 44°48E **44** D5
Qaryat al 'Ulyā *Si. Arabia* 27°33N 47°42E **44** E5
Qasr 'Amra *Jordan* 31°48N 36°35E **44** D3
Qaşr-e Qand *Iran* 26°15N 60°45E **45** E9
Qaşr-e Shīrīn *Iran* 34°31N 45°35E **44** C5
Qasr Farâfra *Egypt* 27°0N 28°1E **51** C11
Qasuittuq = Resolute
Canada 74°42N 94°54W **69** C13
Qatanā *Syria* 33°26N 36°4E **46** B5
Qatar ■ *Asia* 25°30N 51°15E **45** E6
Qatlīsh *Iran* 37°50N 57°19E **45** B8
Qattâra, Munkhafed el
Egypt 29°30N 27°30E **51** C11
Qattâra Depression = Qattâra,
Munkhafed el *Egypt* 29°30N 27°30E **51** C11
Qawām al Ḩamzah = Al Ḩamzah
Iraq 31°43N 44°58E **44** D5
Qāyen *Iran* 33°40N 59°10E **45** C8
Qazaqstan = Kazakhstan ■
Asia 50°0N 70°0E **28** E8
Qazımämmäd *Azerbaijan* 40°3N 49°0E **45** A6
Qazvīn *Iran* 36°15N 50°0E **45** B6
Qazvīn □ *Iran* 36°20N 50°0E **45** B6
Qena *Egypt* 26°10N 32°43E **51** C12
Qeqertarsuaq *Greenland* 69°15N 53°38W **4** C5
Qeqertarsuaq
Greenland 69°45N 53°30W **66** C14
Qeshlāq *Iran* 34°55N 46°28E **44** C5
Qeshm *Iran* 26°55N 56°10E **45** E8
Qeys *Iran* 26°32N 53°58E **45** E7
Qezel Owzen → *Iran* 36°45N 49°22E **45** B6
Qezi'ot *Israel* 30°52N 34°26E **46** E3
Qi Xian *China* 34°40N 114°48E **34** G8
Qian Gorlos *China* 45°5N 124°42E **35** B13
Qian Hai *China* 22°32N 113°54E **33** F10
Qian Xian *China* 34°31N 108°15E **34** G5
Qianshan *China* 22°15N 113°31E **33** G10
Qianyang *China* 34°40N 107°8E **34** G4
Qi'ao *China* 22°25N 113°39E **33** G10
Qi'ao Dao *China* 22°25N 113°38E **33** G10
Qiemo *China* 38°8N 85°32E **32** C3
Qijiaojing *China* 43°28N 91°36E **32** B4
Qikiqtarjuaq *Canada* 67°33N 63°0W **69** D19
Qila Saifullāh *Pakistan* 30°45N 68°17E **42** D3
Qilian Shan *China* 38°30N 96°0E **32** C4
Qin He → *China* 35°1N 113°22E **34** G7
Qin Ling = Qinling Shandi
China 33°50N 108°10E **34** H5
Qin'an *China* 34°48N 105°40E **34** G3
Qing Xian *China* 38°35N 116°45E **34** E9
Qingcheng *China* 37°15N 117°40E **35** F9
Qingdao *China* 36°5N 120°20E **35** F11
Qingfeng *China* 35°52N 115°8E **34** G8
Qinghai □ *China* 36°0N 98°0E **32** C4
Qinghai Hu *China* 36°40N 100°10E **32** C5
Qinghecheng *China* 41°28N 124°15E **35** D13
Qinghemen *China* 41°48N 121°25E **35** D11
Qingjian *China* 37°8N 110°8E **34** F6
Qingjiang = Huaiyin
China 33°30N 119°2E **35** H10
Qingshui *China* 34°48N 106°8E **34** G4
Qingshuihe *China* 39°55N 111°35E **34** E6
Qingtongxia Shuiku
China 37°50N 105°58E **34** F3
Qingxu *China* 37°34N 112°22E **34** F7
Qingyang *China* 36°2N 107°55E **34** F4
Qingyuan *China* 42°10N 124°55E **35** C13
Qingyun *China* 37°45N 117°20E **35** F9
Qinhuangdao *China* 39°56N 119°30E **35** E10
Qinling Shandi *China* 33°50N 108°10E **34** H5
Qinshui *China* 35°40N 112°8E **34** G7
Qinyang = Jiyuan *China* 35°7N 112°57E **34** G7
Qinyuan *China* 36°29N 112°20E **34** F7
Qinzhou *China* 21°58N 108°38E **32** D5
Qionghai *China* 19°15N 110°26E **38** C8
Qiongzhou Haixia
China 20°10N 110°15E **38** B8
Qiqihar *China* 47°26N 124°0E **33** B7
Qira *China* 37°0N 80°48E **32** C3
Qiraïya, W. → *Egypt* 30°27N 34°0E **46** E3
Qiryat Ata *Israel* 32°47N 35°6E **46** C4
Qiryat Gat *Israel* 31°32N 34°46E **46** D3
Qiryat Mal'akhi *Israel* 31°44N 34°44E **46** D3
Qiryat Shemona *Israel* 33°13N 35°35E **46** B4
Qiryat Yam *Israel* 32°51N 35°4E **46** C4
Qishan *China* 34°25N 107°38E **34** G4
Qitai *China* 44°2N 89°35E **32** B3
Qitaihe *China* 45°48N 130°51E **30** B5
Qixia *China* 37°17N 120°52E **35** F11
Qızılağac Körfäzi
Azerbaijan 39°9N 49°0E **45** B6
Qojūr *Iran* 36°12N 47°55E **44** B5
Qom *Iran* 34°40N 51°0E **45** C6
Qom □ *Iran* 34°40N 51°0E **45** C6
Qomolangma Feng = Everest, Mt.
Nepal 28°5N 86°58E **43** E12
Qomsheh *Iran* 32°0N 51°55E **45** D6
Qoqek = Tacheng *China* 46°40N 82°58E **32** B3
Qoqon = Qŭqon
Uzbekistan 40°31N 70°56E **28** E8
Qoraqalpoghistan □
Uzbekistan 43°0N 58°0E **28** E6
Qorveh *Iran* 35°10N 47°48E **44** C5
Qosshaghyl *Kazakhstan* 46°40N 54°0E **19** E9
Qostanay *Kazakhstan* 53°10N 63°35E **28** D7
Quabbin Res. *U.S.A.* 42°20N 72°20W **83** D12
Quairading *Australia* 32°0S 117°21E **61** F2
Quakertown *U.S.A.* 40°26N 75°21W **83** F9
Qualicum Beach
Canada 49°22N 124°26W **70** D4
Quambatook *Australia* 35°49S 143°34E **63** F3
Quambone *Australia* 30°57S 147°53E **63** E4
Quamby *Australia* 20°22S 140°17E **62** C3
Quan Long = Ca Mau
Vietnam 9°7N 105°8E **39** H5
Quanah *U.S.A.* 34°18N 99°44W **84** D5
Quang Ngai *Vietnam* 15°13N 108°58E **38** E7
Quang Tri *Vietnam* 16°45N 107°13E **38** D6
Quang Yen *Vietnam* 20°56N 106°52E **38** B6
Quantock Hills *U.K.* 51°8N 3°10W **13** F4
Quanzhou *China* 24°55N 118°34E **33** D6
Qu'Appelle → *Canada* 50°33N 103°53W **71** C8
Quaqtaq *Canada* 60°55N 69°40W **69** E18
Quaraí *Brazil* 30°15S 56°20W **94** C4
Quartu Sant'Élena *Italy* 39°15N 9°10E **22** E3
Quartzsite *U.S.A.* 33°40N 114°13W **79** M12
Quatre Bornes *Mauritius* 20°15S 57°28E **53** d
Quatsino Sd. *Canada* 50°25N 127°58W **70** C3
Quba *Azerbaijan* 41°21N 48°32E **19** F8
Qūchān *Iran* 37°10N 58°27E **45** B8
Queanbeyan *Australia* 35°17S 149°14E **63** F4
Québec *Canada* 46°52N 71°13W **73** C5
Québec □ *Canada* 48°0N 74°0W **73** C6
Quebrada del Condorito △
Argentina 31°49S 64°40W **94** C3
Queen Alexandra Ra.
Antarctica 85°0S 170°0E **5** E11
Queen Charlotte City
Canada 53°15N 132°2W **70** C2
Queen Charlotte Is.
Canada 53°20N 132°10W **70** C2
Queen Charlotte Sd.
Canada 51°0N 128°0W **70** C3
Queen Charlotte Strait
Canada 50°45N 127°10W **70** C3
Queen Elizabeth △ *Uganda* 0°0 30°0E **54** C3
Queen Elizabeth ⌓ *U.K.* 56°7N 4°30W **11** E4
Queen Elizabeth Is.
Canada 76°0N 95°0W **69** B13
Queen Mary Land
Antarctica 70°0S 95°0E **5** D7
Queen Maud G.
Canada 68°15N 102°30W **68** D11
Queen Maud Land = Dronning
Maud Land *Antarctica* 72°30S 12°0E **5** D3
Queen Maud Mts.
Antarctica 86°0S 160°0W **5** E13
Queens Channel
Australia 15°0S 129°30E **60** C4
Queenscliff *Australia* 38°16S 144°39E **63** F3
Queensland □ *Australia* 22°0S 142°0E **62** C3
Queenstown *Australia* 42°4S 145°35E **63** G4
Queenstown *N.Z.* 45°1S 168°40E **59** F2
Queenstown *Singapore* 1°18N 103°48E **39** d
Queenstown *S. Africa* 31°52S 26°52E **56** E4
Queets *U.S.A.* 47°32N 124°19W **78** C2
Queguay Grande →
Uruguay 32°9S 58°9W **94** C4
Queimadas *Brazil* 11°0S 39°38W **93** F11
Quelimane *Mozam.* 17°53S 36°58E **55** F4
Quellón *Chile* 43°7S 73°37W **96** E2
Quelpart = Jeju-do
S. Korea 33°29N 126°34E **35** H14
Quemado *N. Mex.,*
U.S.A. 34°20N 108°30W **77** J9
Quemado *Tex., U.S.A.* 28°56N 100°37W **84** G4
Quemú-Quemú
Argentina 36°3S 63°36W **94** D3
Quequén *Argentina* 38°30S 58°30W **94** D4
Querétaro *Mexico* 20°36N 100°23W **86** C4
Querétaro □ *Mexico* 21°0N 99°55W **86** C5
Queshan *China* 32°55N 114°2E **34** H8
Quesnel *Canada* 53°0N 122°30W **70** C4
Quesnel → *Canada* 52°58N 122°29W **70** C4
Quesnel L. *Canada* 52°30N 121°20W **70** C4
Questa *U.S.A.* 36°42N 105°36W **77** H11
Quetico ⌓ *Canada* 48°30N 91°45W **72** C1
Quetta *Pakistan* 30°15N 66°55E **42** D2
Quezaltenango
Guatemala 14°50N 91°30W **88** D1
Quezon City *Phil.* 14°37N 121°2E **37** B6
Qufār *Si. Arabia* 27°26N 41°37E **44** E4
Qui Nhon *Vietnam* 13°40N 109°13E **38** F7
Quibala *Angola* 10°46S 14°59E **52** G2
Quibaxe *Angola* 8°24S 14°27E **52** F2
Quibdó *Colombia* 5°42N 76°40W **92** B3
Quiberon *France* 47°29N 3°9W **20** C2
Quiet L. *Canada* 61°5N 133°5W **70** A2
Quiindy *Paraguay* 25°58S 57°14W **94** B4
Quilá *Mexico* 24°23N 107°13W **86** C3
Quilán, C. *Chile* 43°15S 74°30W **96** E2
Quilcene *U.S.A.* 47°49N 122°53W **78** C4
Quilimarí *Chile* 32°5S 71°30W **94** C1
Quilino *Argentina* 30°14S 64°29W **94** C3
Quillabamba *Peru* 12°50S 72°50W **92** F4
Quillagua *Chile* 21°40S 69°40W **94** A2
Quillota *Chile* 32°54S 71°16W **94** C1
Quilmes *Argentina* 34°43S 58°15W **94** C4
Quilon *India* 8°50N 76°38E **40** Q10
Quilpie *Australia* 26°35S 144°11E **63** D3
Quilpué *Chile* 33°5S 71°33W **94** C1
Quilua *Mozam.* 16°17S 39°54E **55** F4
Quimilí *Argentina* 27°40S 62°30W **94** B3
Quimper *France* 48°0N 4°9W **20** B1
Quimperlé *France* 47°53N 3°33W **20** C2
Quinault → *U.S.A.* 47°21N 124°18W **78** C2
Quincy *Calif., U.S.A.* 39°56N 120°57W **78** F6
Quincy *Fla., U.S.A.* 30°35N 84°34W **85** F12
Quincy *Ill., U.S.A.* 39°56N 91°23W **80** F8
Quincy *Mass., U.S.A.* 42°14N 71°0W **83** D14
Quincy *Wash., U.S.A.* 47°14N 119°51W **76** C4
Quines *Argentina* 32°13S 65°48W **94** C2
Quinga *Mozam.* 15°49S 40°15E **55** F5
Quintana Roo □ *Mexico* 19°40N 88°30W **87** D7
Quintanar de la Orden
Spain 39°36N 3°5W **21** C4
Quintero *Chile* 32°45S 71°30W **94** C1
Quirihue *Chile* 36°15S 72°35W **94** D1
Quirimbas △ *Mozam.* 12°30S 40°15E **55** E5
Quirindi *Australia* 31°28S 150°40E **63** E5
Quirinópolis *Brazil* 18°32S 50°30W **93** G8
Quissanga *Mozam.* 12°24S 40°28E **55** E5
Quissico *Mozam.* 24°42S 34°44E **57** C5
Quitilipi *Argentina* 26°50S 60°13W **94** B3
Quitman *U.S.A.* 30°47N 83°34W **85** F13
Quito *Ecuador* 0°15S 78°35W **92** D3
Quixadá *Brazil* 4°55S 39°0W **93** D11
Quixaxe *Mozam.* 15°17S 40°4E **55** F5
Qulan *Kazakhstan* 42°55N 72°43E **28** E8
Qul'ân, Jazâ'ir *Egypt* 24°22N 35°31E **44** E2
Qulsary *Kazakhstan* 46°59N 54°1E **19** E9
Qumbu *S. Africa* 31°10S 28°48E **57** E4
Quneitra *Syria* 33°7N 35°48E **46** B4
Qŭnghirot *Uzbekistan* 43°2N 58°50E **28** E6
Quoin I. *Australia* 14°54S 129°32E **60** B4
Quoin Pt. *S. Africa* 34°46S 19°37E **56** E2
Quorn *Australia* 32°25S 138°5E **63** E2
Qŭqon *Uzbekistan* 40°31N 70°56E **28** E8
Qurimbas *Mozam.* 12°20S 40°10E **55** E5
Qurnat as Sawdā'
Lebanon 34°18N 36°6E **46** A5
Quşaybā' *Si. Arabia* 26°53N 43°35E **44** E4
Qusaybah *Iraq* 34°24N 40°59E **44** C4
Quseir *Egypt* 26°7N 34°16E **44** E2
Qūshchī *Iran* 37°59N 45°3E **44** B5
Quthing *Lesotho* 30°25S 27°36E **57** E4
Qūţīābād *Iran* 35°47N 48°30E **45** C6
Quttinirpaaq △ *Canada* 82°13N 72°13W **69** A17
Quwo *China* 35°38N 111°25E **34** G6
Quyang *China* 38°35N 114°40E **34** E8
Quynh Nhai *Vietnam* 21°49N 103°33E **38** B4
Quyon *Canada* 45°31N 76°14W **83** A8
Quzhou *China* 28°57N 118°54E **33** D6
Quzi *China* 36°20N 107°20E **34** F4
Qyzylorda *Kazakhstan* 44°48N 65°28E **28** E7

R

Ra, Ko *Thailand* 9°13N 98°16E **39** H2
Raahe *Finland* 64°40N 24°28E **8** D21
Raalte *Neths.* 52°23N 6°16E **15** B6
Raasay *U.K.* 57°25N 6°4W **11** D2
Raasay, Sd. of *U.K.* 57°30N 6°8W **11** D2
Raba *Indonesia* 8°36S 118°55E **37** F5
Rába → *Hungary* 47°38N 17°38E **17** E9
Rabai *Kenya* 3°50S 39°31E **54** C4
Rabat = Victoria *Malta* 36°3N 14°14E **25** C1
Rabat *Malta* 35°53N 14°24E **25** D1
Rabat *Morocco* 34°2N 6°48W **50** B4
Rabaul *Papua N. G.* 4°24S 152°18E **58** B8
Rabbit Flat *Australia* 20°11S 130°1E **60** D5
Rabbit Lake Mine *Canada* 58°4N 104°5W **71** B8
Rabi *Fiji* 16°30S 179°59W **59** a
Rābigh *Si. Arabia* 22°50N 39°5E **47** C2
Râbniţa *Moldova* 47°45N 29°0E **17** E15
Rābor *Iran* 29°17N 56°55E **45** D8
Rabwah = Chenab Nagar
Pakistan 31°45N 72°55E **42** D5
Race, C. *Canada* 46°40N 53°5W **73** C9
Rach Gia *Vietnam* 10°5N 105°5E **39** G5
Rachid *Mauritania* 18°45N 11°35W **50** E3
Racibórz *Poland* 50°7N 18°18E **17** C10
Racine *U.S.A.* 42°44N 87°47W **80** D10
Rackerby *U.S.A.* 39°26N 121°22W **78** F5
Radama, Nosy *Madag.* 14°0S 47°47E **57** A8
Radama, Saikanosy
Madag. 14°16S 47°53E **57** A8
Rădăuţi *Romania* 47°50N 25°59E **17** E13
Radcliff *U.S.A.* 37°51N 85°57W **81** G11
Radekhiv *Ukraine* 50°25N 24°32E **17** C13
Radekhov = Radekhiv
Ukraine 50°25N 24°32E **17** C13
Radford *U.S.A.* 37°8N 80°34W **81** G13
Radhanpur *India* 23°50N 71°38E **42** H4
Radhwa, Jabal *Si. Arabia* 24°34N 38°18E **44** E3
Radisson *Qué., Canada* 53°47N 77°37W **72** B4
Radisson *Sask., Canada* 52°30N 107°20W **71** C7
Radium Hot Springs
Canada 50°35N 116°2W **70** C5
Radnor Forest *U.K.* 52°17N 3°10W **13** E4
Radom *Poland* 51°23N 21°12E **17** C11
Radomsko *Poland* 51°5N 19°28E **17** C10
Radomyshl *Ukraine* 50°30N 29°12E **17** C15
Radstock, C. *Australia* 33°12S 134°20E **63** E1
Raduzhnyy *Russia* 62°5N 77°28E **28** C8
Radviliškis *Lithuania* 55°49N 23°33E **9** J20
Radville *Canada* 49°30N 104°15W **71** D8
Rae *Canada* 62°50N 116°3W **70** A5
Rae Bareli *India* 26°18N 81°20E **43** F9
Rae Isthmus *Canada* 66°40N 87°30W **69** D14
Raeren *Belgium* 50°41N 6°7E **15** D6
Raeside, L. *Australia* 29°20S 122°0E **61** E3
Raetihi *N.Z.* 39°25S 175°17E **59** C5
Rafaela *Argentina* 31°10S 61°30W **94** C3
Rafah *Gaza Strip* 31°18N 34°14E **46** D3
Rafai *C.A.R.* 4°59N 23°58E **54** B1
Rafḩā *Si. Arabia* 29°35N 43°35E **44** D4
Rafsanjān *Iran* 30°30N 56°5E **45** D8
Raft Pt. *Australia* 16°4S 124°26E **60** C3
Râgâ *Sudan* 8°28N 25°41E **51** G11
Ragachow *Belarus* 53°8N 30°5E **17** B16
Ragama *Sri Lanka* 7°0N 79°50E **40** R11
Ragged, Mt. *Australia* 33°27S 123°25E **61** F3
Ragged Pt. *Barbados* 13°10N 59°26W **89** g
Raghunathpalli *India* 22°14N 84°48E **43** H11
Raghunathpur *India* 23°33N 86°40E **43** H12
Raglan *N.Z.* 37°55S 174°55E **59** B5
Ragusa *Italy* 36°55N 14°44E **22** F6
Raha *Indonesia* 4°55S 123°0E **37** E6
Rahaeng = Tak *Thailand* 16°52N 99°8E **38** D2
Rahatgarh *India* 23°47N 78°22E **43** H8
Rahimyar Khan *Pakistan* 28°30N 70°25E **42** E4
Rāhjerd *Iran* 34°22N 50°22E **45** C6
Rahole ⌓ *Kenya* 0°5N 38°57E **54** B4
Rahon *India* 31°3N 76°7E **42** D7
Raiatéa, Î.
French Polynesia 16°50S 151°25W **65** J12
Raichur *India* 16°10N 77°20E **40** L10
Raiganj *India* 25°37N 88°10E **43** G13
Raigarh *India* 21°56N 83°25E **41** J13
Raijua *Indonesia* 10°37S 121°36E **37** F6
Raikot *India* 30°41N 75°42E **42** D6
Railton *Australia* 41°25S 146°28E **63** G4
Rainbow Bridge ⌓
U.S.A. 37°5N 110°58W **77** H8
Rainbow Lake *Canada* 58°30N 119°23W **70** B5
Rainier *U.S.A.* 46°53N 122°41W **78** D4
Rainier, Mt. *U.S.A.* 46°52N 121°46W **78** D5
Rainy L. *Canada* 48°42N 93°10W **71** D10
Rainy River *Canada* 48°43N 94°29W **71** D10
Raippaluoto *Finland* 63°13N 21°14E **8** E19
Raipur *India* 21°17N 81°45E **41** J12
Raisen *India* 23°20N 77°48E **42** H8
Raisio *Finland* 60°28N 22°11E **9** F20
Raj Nandgaon *India* 21°5N 81°5E **41** J12
Raj Nilgiri *India* 21°28N 86°46E **43** J12
Raja, Ujung *Indonesia* 3°40N 96°25E **36** D1
Raja Ampat, Kepulauan
Indonesia 0°30S 130°0E **37** E8
Rajahmundry *India* 17°1N 81°48E **41** L12
Rajaji △ *India* 30°10N 78°20E **42** D8
Rajang → *Malaysia* 2°30N 112°0E **36** D4
Rajanpur *Pakistan* 29°6N 70°19E **42** E4
Rajapalaiyam *India* 9°25N 77°35E **40** Q10
Rajasthan □ *India* 26°45N 73°30E **42** F5
Rajasthan Canal = Indira Gandhi
Canal *India* 28°0N 72°0E **42** F5
Rajauri *India* 33°25N 74°21E **43** C6
Rajgarh *Mad. P., India* 24°2N 76°45E **42** G7
Rajgarh *Raj., India* 27°14N 76°38E **42** F7
Rajgarh *Raj., India* 28°40N 75°25E **42** E6
Rajgir *India* 25°2N 85°25E **43** G11
Rajkot *India* 22°15N 70°56E **42** H4
Rajmahal Hills *India* 24°30N 87°30E **43** G12
Rajpipla *India* 21°50N 73°30E **40** J8
Rajpur *India* 22°18N 74°21E **42** H6
Rajpura *India* 30°25N 76°32E **42** D7
Rajsamand = Kankroli
India 25°4N 73°53E **42** G5
Rajshahi *Bangla.* 24°22N 88°39E **41** G16
Rajshahi □ *Bangla.* 25°0N 89°0E **43** G13
Rajula *India* 21°3N 71°26E **42** J4
Rakaia *N.Z.* 43°45S 172°1E **59** E4
Rakaia → *N.Z.* 43°36S 172°15E **59** E4
Rakan, Ra's *Qatar* 26°10N 51°20E **45** E6
Rakaposhi *Pakistan* 36°10N 74°25E **43** A6
Rakata, Pulau *Indonesia* 6°10S 105°20E **36** F3
Rakhiv *Ukraine* 48°3N 24°12E **17** D13
Rakhni *Pakistan* 30°4N 69°56E **42** D3
Rakhni → *Pakistan* 29°31N 69°36E **42** E3
Rakiraki *Fiji* 17°22S 178°11E **59** a
Rakitnoye *Russia* 45°36N 134°17E **30** B7
Rakiura = Stewart I.
N.Z. 46°58S 167°54E **59** G1
Rakiura △ *N.Z.* 47°0S 167°50E **59** G1
Rakops *Botswana* 21°1S 24°28E **56** C3
Rakvere *Estonia* 59°20N 26°25E **9** G22
Raleigh *U.S.A.* 35°47N 78°39W **85** D15
Ralik Chain *Pac. Oc.* 8°0N 168°0E **64** G8
Ralls *U.S.A.* 33°41N 101°24W **84** E4
Ralston *U.S.A.* 41°30N 76°57W **82** E8
Ram → *Canada* 62°1N 123°41W **70** A4
Rām Allāh *West Bank* 31°55N 35°10E **46** D4
Rama *Nic.* 12°9N 84°15W **88** D3
Ramakona *India* 21°43N 78°50E **43** J8
Rāmallāh = Rām Allāh
West Bank 31°55N 35°10E **46** D4
Raman *Thailand* 6°29N 101°18E **39** J3
Ramanathapuram *India* 9°25N 78°55E **40** Q11
Ramanetaka, B. de
Madag. 14°13S 47°52E **57** A8
Ramanujganj *India* 23°48N 83°42E **43** H10
Ramat Gan *Israel* 32°4N 34°48E **46** C3
Ramatlhabama *S. Africa* 25°37S 25°33E **56** D4
Ramban *India* 33°14N 75°12E **43** C6
Rambi = Rabi *Fiji* 16°30S 179°59W **59** a
Rambipuji *Indonesia* 8°12S 113°37E **37** H15
Rame Hd. *Australia* 37°47S 149°30E **63** F4
Ramechhap *Nepal* 27°25N 86°10E **43** F12
Ramganga → *India* 27°5N 79°58E **43** F8
Ramgarh *Jharkhand,*
India 23°40N 85°35E **43** H11
Ramgarh *Raj., India* 27°16N 75°14E **42** F6
Ramgarh *Raj., India* 27°30N 70°36E **42** F4
Rāmhormoz *Iran* 31°15N 49°35E **45** D6
Ramīān *Iran* 37°3N 55°16E **45** B7
Ramingining *Australia* 12°19S 135°3E **62** A2
Ramla *Israel* 31°55N 34°52E **46** D3
Ramm = Rum *Jordan* 29°39N 35°26E **46** F4
Ramm, Jabal *Jordan* 29°35N 35°24E **46** F4
Ramnad = Ramanathapuram
India 9°25N 78°55E **40** Q11
Ramnagar *Jammu & Kashmir,*
India 32°47N 75°18E **43** C6
Ramnagar *Uttarakhand,*
India 29°24N 79°7E **43** E8
Râmnicu Sărat *Romania* 45°26N 27°3E **17** F14
Râmnicu Vâlcea
Romania 45°9N 24°21E **17** F13
Ramona *U.S.A.* 33°2N 116°52W **79** M10
Ramore *Canada* 48°30N 80°25W **72** C3
Ramotswa *Botswana* 24°50S 25°52E **56** C4
Rampur *H.P., India* 31°26N 77°43E **42** D7
Rampur *Mad. P., India* 23°25N 73°53E **42** H5
Rampur *Ut. P., India* 28°50N 79°5E **43** E8
Rampur Hat *India* 24°10N 87°50E **43** G12
Rampura *India* 24°30N 75°27E **42** G6
Ramrama Tola *India* 21°52N 79°55E **43** J8
Ramree I. *Burma* 19°0N 93°40E **41** K19
Rāmsar *Iran* 36°53N 50°41E **45** B6
Ramsey *I. of Man* 54°20N 4°22W **12** C3
Ramsey *U.S.A.* 41°4N 74°9W **83** E10
Ramsey L. *Canada* 47°13N 82°15W **72** C3
Ramsgate *U.K.* 51°20N 1°25E **13** F9
Ramtek *India* 21°20N 79°15E **40** J11
Ramu *Kenya* 3°55N 41°10E **54** B5
Rana Pratap Sagar Dam
India 24°58N 75°38E **42** G6
Ranaghat *India* 23°15N 88°35E **43** H13
Ranahu *Pakistan* 25°55N 69°45E **42** G3
Ranau *Malaysia* 6°2N 116°40E **36** C5
Rancagua *Chile* 34°10S 70°50W **94** C1
Rancheria → *Canada* 60°13N 129°7W **70** A3
Ranchester *U.S.A.* 44°54N 107°10W **76** D10
Ranchi *India* 23°19N 85°27E **43** H11
Rancho Cordova
U.S.A. 38°36N 121°18W **78** G5
Rancho Cucamonga
U.S.A. 34°10N 117°30W **79** L9
Randalstown *U.K.* 54°45N 6°19W **10** B5
Randers *Denmark* 56°29N 10°1E **9** H14
Randfontein *S. Africa* 26°8S 27°45E **57** D4
Randle *U.S.A.* 46°32N 121°57W **78** D5
Randolph *Mass., U.S.A.* 42°10N 71°2W **83** D13
Randolph *N.Y., U.S.A.* 42°10N 78°59W **82** D6
Randolph *Utah, U.S.A.* 41°40N 111°11W **76** F8
Randolph *Vt., U.S.A.* 43°55N 72°40W **83** C12
Randsburg *U.S.A.* 35°22N 117°39W **79** K9
Råneälven → *Sweden* 65°50N 22°20E **8** D20
Rangae *Thailand* 6°19N 101°44E **39** J3
Rangaunu B. *N.Z.* 34°51S 173°15E **59** A4
Range, The *Zimbabwe* 19°2S 31°2E **55** F3
Rangeley *U.S.A.* 44°58N 70°39W **83** B14
Rangeley L. *U.S.A.* 44°55N 70°43W **83** B14
Rangely *U.S.A.* 40°5N 108°48W **76** F9
Ranger *U.S.A.* 32°28N 98°41W **84** E5
Rangia *India* 26°28N 91°38E **41** F17
Rangiora *N.Z.* 43°19S 172°36E **59** E4
Rangitaiki → *N.Z.* 37°54S 176°49E **59** B6
Rangitata → *N.Z.* 43°45S 171°15E **59** E3
Rangitoto ke te tonga = D'Urville
I. *N.Z.* 40°50S 173°55E **59** D4
Rangkasbitung
Indonesia 6°21S 106°15E **37** G12
Rangon → *Burma* 16°28N 96°40E **41** L20
Rangoon *Burma* 16°45N 96°20E **41** L20
Rangpur *Bangla.* 25°42N 89°22E **41** G16
Rangsang *Indonesia* 1°20N 103°30E **39** M4
Rangsit *Thailand* 13°59N 100°37E **38** F3
Ranibennur *India* 14°35N 75°30E **40** M9
Raniganj *Ut. P., India* 27°3N 82°13E **43** F9
Raniganj *W. Bengal, India* 23°40N 87°5E **41** H15
Ranikhet *India* 29°39N 79°25E **43** E8
Raniwara *India* 24°50N 72°10E **42** G5
Rāniyah *Iraq* 36°15N 44°53E **44** B5
Ranka *India* 23°59N 83°47E **43** H10
Ranken → *Australia* 20°31S 137°36E **62** C2
Rankin *U.S.A.* 31°13N 101°56W **84** F4
Rankin Inlet *Canada* 62°30N 93°0W **68** E13
Rankins Springs
Australia 33°49S 146°14E **63** E4
Rannoch, L. *U.K.* 56°41N 4°20W **11** E4
Rannoch Moor *U.K.* 56°38N 4°48W **11** E4
Ranobe, Helodranon' i
Madag. 23°3S 43°33E **57** C7
Ranohira *Madag.* 22°29S 45°24E **57** C8
Ranomafana *Toamasina,*
Madag. 18°57S 48°50E **57** B8
Ranomafana *Toliara,*
Madag. 24°34S 47°0E **57** C8
Ranomafana △ *Madag.* 21°16S 47°25E **57** C8
Ranomena *Madag.* 23°25S 47°17E **57** C8

Ranong *Thailand* 9°56N 98°40E **39** H2
Ranotsara Nord *Madag.* 22°48S 46°36E **57** C8
Rānsa *Iran* 33°39N 48°18E **45** C6
Ransiki *Indonesia* 1°30S 134°10E **37** E8
Rantabe *Madag.* 15°42S 49°39E **57** B8
Rantauprapat *Indonesia* 2°15N 99°50E **36** D1
Rantemario *Indonesia* 3°15S 119°57E **37** E5
Ranthambore △ *India* 26°10N 76°30E **42** F7
Rantoul *U.S.A.* 40°19N 88°9W **80** E9
Raohe *China* 46°47N 134°0E **30** A7
Raoyang *China* 38°15N 115°45E **34** E8
Rap, Ko *Thailand* 9°19N 99°58E **39** b
Rapa *French Polynesia* 27°35S 144°20W **65** K13
Rapa Nui = Pascua, I. de
   Chile 27°7S 109°23W **65** K17
Rapallo *Italy* 44°21N 9°14E **20** D8
Rapar *India* 23°34N 70°38E **42** H4
Rāpch *Iran* 25°40N 59°15E **45** E8
Rapel, Lago *Chile* 34°20S 71°14W **94** C1
Raper, C. *Canada* 69°44N 67°6W **69** D18
Rapid City *U.S.A.* 44°5N 103°14W **80** C2
Rapid River *U.S.A.* 45°55N 86°58W **80** C10
Rapla *Estonia* 59°1N 24°52E **9** G21
Rapti → *India* 26°18N 83°41E **43** F10
Raquette → *U.S.A.* 45°0N 74°42W **83** B10
Raquette Lake *U.S.A.* 43°49N 74°40W **83** C10
Rara △ *Nepal* 29°30N 82°10E **43** E10
Rarotonga *Cook Is.* 21°30S 160°0W **65** K12
Ra's al 'Ayn *Syria* 36°45N 40°12E **44** B4
Ra's al Khaymah *U.A.E.* 25°50N 55°59E **45** E7
Ra's aţ Ţīb *Tunisia* 37°1N 11°2E **22** F4
Rasa, Pta. *Argentina* 36°20S 56°41W **94** D4
Rasca, Pta. de la
   Canary Is. 27°59N 16°41W **24** G3
Raseiniai *Lithuania* 55°25N 23°5E **9** J20
Rashmi *India* 25°4N 74°22E **42** G6
Rasht *Iran* 37°20N 49°40E **45** B6
Rasi Salai *Thailand* 15°20N 104°9E **38** E5
Rason L. *Australia* 28°45S 124°25E **61** E3
Rasul *Pakistan* 32°42N 73°34E **42** C5
Rasra *India* 25°50N 83°50E **43** G10
Rat → *Canada* 49°35N 97°10W **71** D9
Rat Buri *Thailand* 13°30N 99°54E **38** F2
Rat Islands *U.S.A.* 52°0N 178°0E **74** E3
Rat L. *Canada* 56°10N 99°40W **71** B9
Ratak Chain *Pac. Oc.* 1°0N 170°0E **64** G8
Ratangarh *India* 28°5N 74°35E **42** E6
Raţāwī *Iraq* 30°38N 47°13E **44** D5
Rath *India* 25°36N 79°37E **43** G8
Rath Luirc *Ireland* 52°21N 8°40W **10** D3
Rathangan *Ireland* 53°13N 7°1W **10** C4
Rathdrum *Ireland* 52°56N 6°14W **10** D5
Rathenow *Germany* 52°37N 12°19E **16** B7
Rathkeale *Ireland* 52°32N 8°56W **10** D3
Rathlin I. *U.K.* 55°18N 6°14W **10** A5
Rathmelton *Ireland* 55°2N 7°38W **10** A4
Ratibor = Racibórz
   Poland 50°7N 18°18E **17** C10
Ratlam *India* 23°20N 75°0E **42** H6
Ratmanova Ostrov
   Russia 65°46N 169°6W **74** B6
Ratnagiri *India* 16°57N 73°18E **40** L8
Ratodero *Pakistan* 27°48N 68°18E **42** F3
Raton *U.S.A.* 36°54N 104°24W **77** H11
Rattaphum *Thailand* 7°8N 100°16E **39** J3
Rattray Hd. *U.K.* 57°38N 1°50W **11** D7
Ratz, Mt. *Canada* 57°23N 132°12W **70** B2
Raub *Malaysia* 3°47N 101°52E **39** L3
Rauch *Argentina* 36°45S 59°5W **94** D4
Raudales *Mexico* 17°27N 93°39W **87** D6
Raufarhöfn *Iceland* 66°27N 15°57W **8** C6
Raufoss *Norway* 60°44N 10°37E **8** F14
Raukumara Ra. *N.Z.* 38°5S 177°55E **59** C6
Rauma *Finland* 61°10N 21°30E **8** F19
Raumo = Rauma
   Finland 61°10N 21°30E **8** F19
Raung, Gunung *Indonesia* 8°8S 114°3E **37** J17
Raurkela *India* 22°14N 84°50E **43** H11
Rausu-Dake *Japan* 44°4N 145°7E **30** B12
Rava-Ruska *Ukraine* 50°15N 23°42E **17** C12
Rava Russkaya = Rava-Ruska
   Ukraine 50°15N 23°42E **17** C12
Ravalli *U.S.A.* 47°17N 114°11W **76** C6
Ravānsar *Iran* 34°43N 46°40E **44** C5
Rāvar *Iran* 31°20N 56°51E **45** D8
Ravena *U.S.A.* 42°28N 73°49W **83** D11
Ravenna *Italy* 44°25N 12°12E **22** B5
Ravenna *Nebr., U.S.A.* 41°1N 98°55W **80** E4
Ravenna *Ohio, U.S.A.* 41°9N 81°15W **82** E3
Ravensburg *Germany* 47°46N 9°36E **16** E5
Ravenshoe *Australia* 17°37S 145°29E **62** B4
Ravensthorpe *Australia* 33°35S 120°2E **61** F3
Ravenswood *Australia* 20°6S 146°54E **62** C4
Ravenswood *U.S.A.* 38°57N 81°46W **81** F13
Ravi → *Pakistan* 30°35N 71°49E **42** D4
Rawalpindi *Pakistan* 33°38N 73°8E **42** C5
Rawang *Malaysia* 3°20N 101°35E **39** L3
Rawene *N.Z.* 35°25S 173°32E **59** A4
Rawlinna *Australia* 30°58S 125°28E **61** F4
Rawlins *U.S.A.* 41°47N 107°14W **76** F10
Rawlinson Ra. *Australia* 24°40S 128°30E **61** D4
Rawson *Argentina* 43°15S 65°5W **96** E3
Raxaul *India* 26°59N 84°51E **43** F11
Ray *U.S.A.* 48°21N 103°10W **80** A2
Ray, C. *Canada* 47°33N 59°15W **73** C8
Ray Mts. *U.S.A.* 66°0N 152°0W **74** B9
Raya Ring, Ko *Thailand* 8°18N 98°29E **39** a
Rayadurg *India* 14°40N 76°50E **40** M10
Rayagada *India* 19°15N 83°20E **41** K13
Rāyen *Iran* 29°34N 57°26E **45** D8
Rayleigh *U.K.* 51°36N 0°37E **13** F8
Raymond *Canada* 49°30N 112°35W **70** D6
Raymond *Calif., U.S.A.* 37°13N 119°54W **78** H7
Raymond *N.H., U.S.A.* 43°2N 71°11W **83** C13
Raymond *Wash.,*
   U.S.A. 46°41N 123°44W **78** D3
Raymondville *U.S.A.* 26°29N 97°47W **84** H6
Raymore *Canada* 51°25N 104°31W **71** C8

Rayón *Mexico* 29°43N 110°35W **86** B2
Rayong *Thailand* 12°40N 101°20E **38** F3
Raystown L. *U.S.A.* 40°25N 78°5W/ **82** F6
Rayville *U.S.A.* 32°29N 91°46W **84** E9
Raz, Pte. du *France* 48°2N 4°47W **20** C1
Razan *Iran* 35°23N 49°2E **45** C6
Razāzah, Buḩayrat ar
   Iraq 32°40N 43°35E **44** C4
Razāzah, L. = Razāzah, Buḩayrat
   ar *Iraq* 32°40N 43°35E **44** C4
Razdel'naya = Rozdilna
   Ukraine 46°50N 30°2E **17** E16
Razdolnoye *Russia* 43°30N 131°52E **30** C5
Razeh *Iran* 32°47N 48°9E **45** C6
Razgrad *Bulgaria* 43°33N 26°34E **23** C12
Razim, Lacul *Romania* 44°50N 29°0E **17** F15
Razmak *Pakistan* 32°45N 69°50E **42** C3
Re, Cu Lao *Vietnam* 15°22N 109°8E **38** E7
Ré, Î. de *France* 46°12N 1°30W **20** C3
Reading *U.K.* 51°27N 0°58W **13** F7
Reading *U.S.A.* 40°20N 75°56W **83** F9
Reading □ *U.K.* 51°27N 0°58W **13** F7
Realicó *Argentina* 35°0S 64°15W **94** D3
Ream *Cambodia* 10°34N 103°39E **39** G4
Ream △ *Cambodia* 10°30N 103°45E **39** G4
Reay Forest *U.K.* 58°22N 4°55W **11** C4
Rebecca, L. *Australia* 30°0S 122°15E **61** F3
Rebi *Indonesia* 6°23S 134°7E **37** F8
Rebiana *Libya* 24°12N 22°10E **51** D10
Rebiana, Sahrâ' *Libya* 24°30N 21°0E **51** D10
Reboly *Russia* 63°49N 30°47E **8** E24
Recherche, Arch. of the
   Australia 34°15S 122°50E **61** F3
Rechna Doab *Pakistan* 31°35N 73°30E **42** D5
Rechytsa *Belarus* 52°21N 30°24E **17** B16
Recife *Brazil* 8°0S 35°0W **93** E12
Recife *Seychelles* 4°36S 55°42E **53** b
Recklinghausen *Germany* 51°37N 7°12E **15** C7
Reconquista *Argentina* 29°10S 59°45W **94** B4
Recreo *Argentina* 29°25S 65°10W **94** B2
Red → *U.S.A.* 31°1N 91°45W **84** F9
Red Bank *U.S.A.* 40°21N 74°5W **83** F10
Red Bay *Canada* 51°44N 56°25W **73** B8
Red Bluff *U.S.A.* 40°11N 122°15W **76** F2
Red Bluff Res. *U.S.A.* 31°54N 103°55W **77** L12
Red Cliffs *Australia* 34°19S 142°11E **63** E3
Red Cloud *U.S.A.* 40°5N 98°32W **80** E4
Red Creek *U.S.A.* 43°14N 76°45W **83** C8
Red Deer *Canada* 52°20N 113°50W **70** C6
Red Deer → *Alta.,*
   Canada 50°58N 110°0W **71** C7
Red Deer → *Man.,*
   Canada 52°53N 101°1W **71** C8
Red Deer L. *Canada* 52°55N 101°20W **71** C8
Red Hook *U.S.A.* 41°55N 73°53W **83** E11
Red Indian L. *Canada* 48°35N 57°0W **73** C8
Red L. *Canada* 51°3N 93°49W **71** C10
Red Lake *Canada* 51°3N 93°49W **71** C10
Red Lake Falls *U.S.A.* 47°53N 96°16W **80** B5
Red Lake Road *Canada* 49°59N 93°25W **71** C10
Red Lodge *U.S.A.* 45°11N 109°15W **76** D9
Red Mountain *U.S.A.* 35°37N 117°38W **79** K9
Red Oak *U.S.A.* 41°1N 95°14W **80** E6
Red River of the North →
   N. Amer. 49°0N 97°15W **80** A5
Red Rock *Canada* 48°55N 88°15W **72** C2
Red Rock, L. *U.S.A.* 41°22N 92°59W **80** E7
Red Rocks Pt. *Australia* 32°13S 127°32E **61** F4
Red Sea *Asia* 25°0N 36°0E **47** C2
Red Slate Mt. *U.S.A.* 37°31N 118°52W **78** H8
Red Sucker L. *Canada* 54°9N 93°40W **72** B1
Red Tower Pass = Turnu Roşu, P.
   Romania 45°33N 24°17E **17** F13
Red Wing *U.S.A.* 44°34N 92°31W **80** C7
Redang *Malaysia* 5°49N 103°2E **39** K4
Redange *Lux.* 49°46N 5°52E **15** E5
Redcar *U.K.* 54°37N 1°4W **12** C6
Redcar & Cleveland □
   U.K. 54°29N 1°0W **12** C7
Redcliff *Canada* 50°10N 110°50W **76** A8
Redcliffe *Australia* 27°12S 153°6E **63** D5
Redcliffe, Mt. *Australia* 28°30S 121°30E **61** E3
Redding *U.S.A.* 40°35N 122°24W **76** F2
Redditch *U.K.* 52°18N 1°55W **13** E6
Redford *U.S.A.* 44°38N 73°48W **83** B11
Redhead *Trin. & Tob.* 10°44N 60°58W **93** K16
Redlands *U.S.A.* 34°4N 117°11W **79** M9
Redmond *Oreg., U.S.A.* 44°17N 121°11W **76** D3
Redmond *Wash., U.S.A.* 47°40N 122°7W **78** C4
Redon *France* 47°40N 2°6W **20** C2
Redonda *Antigua & B.* 16°58N 62°19W **89** C7
Redondela *Spain* 42°15N 8°38W **21** A1
Redondo Beach *U.S.A.* 33°50N 118°23W **79** M8
Redoubt Volcano
   U.S.A. 60°29N 152°45W **74** C9
Redruth *U.K.* 50°14N 5°14W **13** G2
Redvers *Canada* 49°35N 101°40W **71** D8
Redwater *Canada* 53°55N 113°6W **70** C6
Redwood *U.S.A.* 44°18N 75°48W **83** B9
Redwood △ *U.S.A.* 41°40N 124°5W **76** F1
Redwood City *U.S.A.* 37°29N 122°13W **78** H4
Redwood Falls *U.S.A.* 44°32N 95°7W **80** C6
Ree, L. *Ireland* 53°35N 8°0W **10** C3
Reed City *U.S.A.* 43°53N 85°31W **81** D11
Reed L. *Canada* 54°38N 100°30W **71** C8
Reedley *U.S.A.* 36°36N 119°27W **78** J7
Reedsburg *U.S.A.* 43°32N 90°0W **80** D8
Reedsport *U.S.A.* 43°42N 124°6W **76** E1
Reedsville *U.S.A.* 40°39N 77°35W **82** F7
Reefton *N.Z.* 42°6S 171°51E **59** E3
Reese → *U.S.A.* 40°48N 117°4W **76** F5
Refugio *U.S.A.* 28°18N 97°17W **84** G6
Regana, C. de *Spain* 39°16N 2°43E **24** B9
Regensburg *Germany* 49°1N 12°6E **16** D7
Reggâne = Zaouiet Reggâne
   Algeria 26°32N 0°3E **50** C6

Réggio di Calábria *Italy* 38°6N 15°39E **22** E6
Réggio nell'Emília *Italy* 44°43N 10°36E **22** B4
Reghin *Romania* 46°46N 24°42E **17** E13
Regina *Canada* 50°27N 104°35W **71** C8
Regina Beach *Canada* 50°47N 105°0W **71** C8
Registro *Brazil* 24°29S 47°49W **95** A6
Rehar → *India* 23°55N 82°40E **43** H10
Rehli *India* 23°38N 79°5E **43** H8
Rehoboth *Namibia* 23°15S 17°4E **56** C2
Rehovot *Israel* 31°54N 34°48E **46** D3
Reichenbach *Germany* 50°37N 12°17E **16** C7
Reid *Australia* 30°49S 128°26E **61** F4
Reidsville *U.S.A.* 36°21N 79°40W **85** C15
Reigate *U.K.* 51°14N 0°12W **13** F7
Reims *France* 49°15N 4°1E **20** B6
Reina Adelaida, Arch.
   Chile 52°20S 74°0W **96** G2
Reina Sofia, Tenerife ✈ (TFS)
   Canary Is. 28°3N 16°33W **24** F3
Reindeer → *Canada* 55°36N 103°11W **71** B8
Reindeer I. *Canada* 52°30N 98°0W **71** C9
Reindeer L. *Canada* 57°15N 102°15W **71** B8
Reinga, C. *N.Z.* 34°25S 172°43E **59** A4
Reinosa *Spain* 43°2N 4°15W **21** A3
Reitz *S. Africa* 27°48S 28°29E **57** D4
Reivilo *S. Africa* 27°36S 24°8E **56** D3
Remanso *Brazil* 9°41S 42°4W **93** E10
Remarkable, Mt.
   Australia 32°48S 138°10E **63** E2
Rembang *Indonesia* 6°42S 111°21E **37** G14
Remedios *Panama* 8°15N 81°50W **88** E3
Remeshk *Iran* 26°55N 58°50E **45** E8
Remich *Lux.* 49°32N 6°22E **15** E6
Ren Xian *China* 37°8N 114°40E **34** F8
Rendang *Indonesia* 8°26S 115°25E **37** J18
Rendsburg *Germany* 54°17N 9°39E **16** A5
Renfrew *Canada* 45°30N 76°40W **83** A8
Renfrewshire □ *U.K.* 55°49N 4°38W **11** F4
Rengat *Indonesia* 0°30S 102°45E **36** E2
Rengo *Chile* 34°24S 70°50W **94** C1
Reni = Taranagar *India* 28°43N 74°50E **42** E6
Reni *Ukraine* 45°28N 28°15E **17** F15
Renmark *Australia* 34°11S 140°43E **63** E3
Rennell Sd. *Canada* 53°23N 132°35W **70** C2
Renner Springs
   Australia 18°20S 133°47E **62** B1
Rennes *France* 48°7N 1°41W **20** B3
Rennick Glacier
   Antarctica 70°30S 161°45E **5** D21
Rennie L. *Canada* 61°32N 105°35W **71** A7
Reno *U.S.A.* 39°31N 119°48W **78** F7
Reno → *Italy* 44°38N 12°16E **22** B5
Renovo *U.S.A.* 41°20N 77°45W **82** E7
Renqiu *China* 38°43N 116°5E **34** E9
Rensselaer *Ind., U.S.A.* 40°57N 87°9W **80** E10
Rensselaer *N.Y., U.S.A.* 42°38N 73°45W **83** D11
Renton *U.S.A.* 47°28N 122°12W **78** C4
Renukoot *India* 24°12N 83°2E **43** G10
Reotipur *India* 25°33N 83°45E **43** G10
Republic *Mo., U.S.A.* 37°7N 93°29W **80** G7
Republic *Wash., U.S.A.* 48°39N 118°44W **76** B4
Republican → *U.S.A.* 39°4N 96°48W **80** F5
Repulse B. *Australia* 20°35S 148°46E **62** b
Repulse Bay *Canada* 66°30N 86°30W **69** D14
Requena *Peru* 5°5S 73°52W **92** E4
Requena *Spain* 39°30N 1°4W **21** C5
Reserve *U.S.A.* 33°43N 108°45W **77** K9
Resht = Rasht *Iran* 37°20N 49°40E **45** B6
Resistencia *Argentina* 27°30S 59°0W **94** B4
Reşiţa *Romania* 45°18N 21°53E **17** F11
Reso = Raisio *Finland* 60°28N 22°11E **9** F20
Resolute *Canada* 74°42N 94°54W **69** C13
Resolution I. *Canada* 61°30N 65°0W **69** E19
Resolution I. *N.Z.* 45°40S 166°40E **59** F1
Ressano Garcia *Mozam.* 25°25S 32°0E **57** D5
Reston *Canada* 49°33N 101°6W **71** D8
Retalhuleu *Guatemala* 14°33N 91°46W **88** D1
Retenue, L. de
   Dem. Rep. of the Congo 11°0S 27°0E **55** E2
Retford *U.K.* 53°19N 0°56W **12** D7
Rethimno *Greece* 35°18N 24°30E **25** D6
Rethimno □ *Greece* 35°23N 24°28E **25** D6
Reti *Pakistan* 28°5N 69°48E **42** E3
Réunion ☑ *Ind. Oc.* 21°0S 56°0E **53** c
Reus *Spain* 41°10N 1°5E **21** B6
Reutlingen *Germany* 48°29N 9°12E **16** D5
Reval = Tallinn *Estonia* 59°22N 24°48E **9** G21
Revda *Russia* 56°48N 59°57E **18** C10
Revelganj *India* 25°50N 84°40E **43** G11
Revelstoke *Canada* 51°0N 118°10W **70** C5
Reventazón *Peru* 6°10S 80°58W **92** E2
Revilla Gigedo, Is. de
   Pac. Oc. 18°40N 112°0W **86** D2
Revúe → *Mozam.* 19°50S 34°0E **55** F3
Rewa *India* 24°33N 81°25E **43** G9
Rewari *India* 28°15N 76°40E **42** E7
Rexburg *U.S.A.* 43°49N 111°47W **76** E8
Rexdale *Canada* 43°43N 79°34W **82** c
Rey *Iran* 35°35N 51°25E **45** C6
Rey, I. del *Panama* 8°20N 78°30W **88** E4
Rey, L. del *Mexico* 27°1N 103°26W **86** B4
Rey Malabo *Eq. Guin.* 3°45N 8°50E **52** D1
Reyðarfjörður *Iceland* 65°2N 14°13W **8** D6
Reyes, Pt. *U.S.A.* 38°0N 123°0W **78** H3
Reykjahlið *Iceland* 65°40N 16°55W **8** D5
Reykjanes *Iceland* 63°48N 22°40W **8** E2
Reykjavík *Iceland* 64°10N 21°57W **8** D3
Reynolds Ra. *Australia* 22°30S 133°0E **60** D5
Reynoldsville *U.S.A.* 41°6N 78°53W **82** E6
Reynosa *Mexico* 26°7N 98°18W **87** B5
Rēzekne *Latvia* 56°30N 27°17E **9** H22
Rezvān *Iran* 27°34N 56°6E **45** E8
Rhayader *U.K.* 52°18N 3°29W **13** E4
Rhein → *U.K.* 51°52N 6°2E **15** C6
Rhein-Main-Donau-Kanal
   Germany 49°1N 11°27E **16** D6
Rheine *Germany* 52°17N 7°26E **16** B4
Rheinland-Pfalz □ *Germany* 50°0N 7°0E **16** C4

Rhin = Rhein → *Europe* 51°52N 6°2E **15** C6
Rhine = Rhein → *Europe* 51°52N 6°2E **15** C6
Rhinebeck *U.S.A.* 41°56N 73°55W **83** E11
Rhineland-Palatinate =
   Rheinland-Pfalz □
   Germany 50°0N 7°0E **16** C4
Rhinelander *U.S.A.* 45°38N 89°25W **80** C9
Rhinns Pt. *U.K.* 55°40N 6°29W **11** F2
Rhino Camp *Uganda* 3°0N 31°22E **54** B3
Rhir, Cap *Morocco* 30°38N 9°54W **50** B4
Rhode Island □ *U.S.A.* 41°40N 71°30W **83** E13
Rhodes *Greece* 36°15N 28°10E **25** C10
Rhodope Mts. = Rhodopi Planina
   Bulgaria 41°40N 24°20E **23** D11
Rhodopi Planina
   Bulgaria 41°40N 24°20E **23** D11
Rhön *Germany* 50°24N 9°58E **16** C5
Rhondda *U.K.* 51°39N 3°31W **13** F4
Rhondda Cynon Taff □
   U.K. 51°42N 3°27W **13** F4
Rhône → *France* 43°28N 4°42E **20** E6
Rhum *U.K.* 57°0N 6°20W **11** E2
Rhyl *U.K.* 53°20N 3°29W **12** D4
Riachão *Brazil* 7°20S 46°37W **93** E9
Riasi *India* 33°10N 74°50E **43** C6
Riau □ *Indonesia* 0°0 102°35E **36** E2
Riau, Kepulauan
   Indonesia 0°30N 104°20E **36** D2
Riau Arch. = Riau, Kepulauan
   Indonesia 0°30N 104°20E **36** D2
Ribadeo *Spain* 43°35N 7°5W **21** A2
Ribas do Rio Pardo
   Brazil 20°27S 53°46W **93** H8
Ribaué *Mozam.* 14°57S 38°17E **55** E4
Ribble → *U.K.* 53°52N 2°25W **12** D5
Ribe *Denmark* 55°19N 8°44E **9** J13
Ribeira Brava *Madeira* 32°41N 17°4W **24** D2
Ribeira Grande *C. Verde Is.* 17°0N 25°4W **50** b
Ribeirão Prêto *Brazil* 21°10S 47°50W **95** A6
Riberalta *Bolivia* 11°0S 66°0W **92** F5
Riccarton *N.Z.* 43°32S 172°37E **59** E4
Rice *U.S.A.* 34°5N 114°51W **79** L12
Rice L. *Canada* 44°12N 78°10W **82** B6
Rice Lake *U.S.A.* 45°30N 91°44W **80** C8
Rich, C. *Canada* 44°43N 80°38W **82** B4
Richards Bay *S. Africa* 28°48S 32°6E **57** D5
Richardson → *Canada* 58°25N 111°14W **71** B6
Richardson Lakes
   U.S.A. 44°46N 70°58W **81** C18
Richardson Springs
   U.S.A. 39°51N 121°46W **78** F5
Riche, C. *Australia* 34°36S 118°47E **61** F2
Richey *U.S.A.* 47°39N 105°4W **76** C11
Richfield *U.S.A.* 38°46N 112°5W **76** G7
Richfield Springs
   U.S.A. 42°51N 74°59W **83** D10
Richford *U.S.A.* 45°0N 72°40W **83** B12
Richibucto *Canada* 46°42N 64°54W **73** C7
Richland *Ga., U.S.A.* 32°5N 84°40W **85** E12
Richland *Wash., U.S.A.* 46°17N 119°18W **76** C4
Richland Center *U.S.A.* 43°21N 90°23W **80** D8
Richlands *U.S.A.* 37°6N 81°48W **81** G13
Richmond *Australia* 20°43S 143°8E **62** C3
Richmond *N.Z.* 41°20S 173°12E **59** D4
Richmond *U.K.* 54°25N 1°43W **12** C6
Richmond *Calif., U.S.A.* 37°56N 122°21W **78** H4
Richmond *Ind., U.S.A.* 39°50N 84°53W **81** F11
Richmond *Ky., U.S.A.* 37°45N 84°18W **81** G11
Richmond *Mich., U.S.A.* 42°49N 82°45W **82** D2
Richmond *Mo., U.S.A.* 39°17N 93°58W **80** F7
Richmond *Tex., U.S.A.* 29°35N 95°46W **84** G7
Richmond *Utah, U.S.A.* 41°56N 111°48W **76** F8
Richmond *Va., U.S.A.* 37°33N 77°27W **81** G15
Richmond *Vt., U.S.A.* 44°24N 72°59W **83** B12
Richmond Hill *Canada* 43°52N 79°27W **82** C5
Richmond Ra. *Australia* 29°0S 152°45E **63** D5
Richmondville *U.S.A.* 42°38N 74°33W **83** D10
Richtersveld △ *S. Africa* 28°15S 17°10E **56** D2
Richville *U.S.A.* 44°25N 75°23W **83** B9
Richwood *U.S.A.* 38°14N 80°32W **81** F13
Ridder = Leninogorsk
   Kazakhstan 50°20N 83°30E **28** D9
Riddlesburg *U.S.A.* 40°9N 78°15W **82** F6
Ridgecrest *U.S.A.* 35°38N 117°40W **79** K9
Ridgefield *Conn., U.S.A.* 41°17N 73°30W **83** E11
Ridgefield *Wash.,*
   U.S.A. 45°49N 122°45W **78** E4
Ridgeland *Miss., U.S.A.* 32°26N 90°8W **85** E9
Ridgeland *S.C., U.S.A.* 32°29N 80°59W **85** E14
Ridgetown *Canada* 42°26N 81°52W **82** D3
Ridgewood *U.S.A.* 40°59N 74°7W **83** F10
Ridgway *U.S.A.* 41°25N 78°44W **82** E6
Riding Mountain △
   Canada 50°50N 100°0W **71** C9
Ridley, Mt. *Australia* 33°12S 122°7E **61** F3
Riebeek-Oos *S. Africa* 33°10S 26°10E **56** E4
Ried *Austria* 48°14N 13°30E **16** D7
Riesa *Germany* 51°17N 13°17E **16** C7
Riet → *S. Africa* 29°0S 23°54E **56** D3
Rietbron *S. Africa* 32°54S 23°10E **56** E3
Rietfontein *Namibia* 21°58S 20°58E **56** C3
Rieti *Italy* 42°24N 12°51E **22** C5
Rif = Er Rif *Morocco* 35°1N 4°1W **50** A5
Riffe L. *U.S.A.* 46°32N 122°26W **78** D4
Rifle *U.S.A.* 39°32N 107°47W **76** G10
Rift Valley *Africa* 7°0N 30°0E **48** G7
Rift Valley □ *Kenya* 0°20N 36°0E **54** B4
Riga *Latvia* 56°53N 24°8E **9** H21
Riga, G. of *Latvia* 57°40N 23°45E **9** H20
Rīgān *Iran* 28°37N 58°58E **45** D8
Rīgas Jūras Līcis = Riga, G. of
   Latvia 57°40N 23°45E **9** H20
Rigaud *Canada* 45°29N 74°18W **83** A10
Rigby *U.S.A.* 43°40N 111°55W **76** E8
Rīgestān *Afghan.* 30°15N 65°0E **40** D4
Riggins *U.S.A.* 45°25N 116°19W **76** D5
Rigolet *Canada* 54°10N 58°23W **73** B8
Rihand Dam *India* 24°9N 83°2E **43** G10
Riihimäki *Finland* 60°45N 24°48E **8** F21

Riiser-Larsen-halvøya
   Antarctica 68°0S 35°0E **5** C4
Riiser-Larsen Ice Shelf
   S. Ocean 74°0S 19°0W **5** D2
Riiser-Larsen Sea *S. Ocean* 67°30S 22°0E **5** C4
Rijeka *Croatia* 45°20N 14°21E **16** F8
Rijssen *Neths.* 52°19N 6°31E **15** B6
Rikuchū-Kaigan △
   Japan 39°20N 142°0E **30** E10
Rikuzentakada *Japan* 39°0N 141°40E **30** E10
Riley *U.S.A.* 43°32N 119°28W **76** E4
Rima → *Nigeria* 13°4N 5°10E **50** F7
Rimah, Wadi ar →
   Si. Arabia 26°5N 41°30E **44** E4
Rimau, Pulau *Malaysia* 5°15N 100°16E **39** c
Rimbey *Canada* 52°35N 114°15W **70** C6
Rimersburg *U.S.A.* 41°3N 79°30W **82** E5
Rímini *Italy* 44°3N 12°33E **22** B5
Rimouski *Canada* 48°27N 68°30W **73** C6
Rimrock *U.S.A.* 46°40N 121°7W **78** D5
Rinca *Indonesia* 8°45S 119°35E **37** F5
Rincón de Romos
   Mexico 22°14N 102°18W **86** C4
Rinconada *Argentina* 22°26S 66°10W **94** A2
Rind → *India* 25°53N 80°33E **43** G9
Ringas *India* 27°21N 75°34E **42** F6
Ringgold Is. *Fiji* 16°15S 179°25W **59** a
Ringkøbing *Denmark* 56°5N 8°15E **9** H13
Ringvassøya *Norway* 69°56N 19°15E **8** B18
Ringwood *U.S.A.* 41°7N 74°15W **83** E10
Rinjani *Indonesia* 8°24S 116°28E **36** F5
Rio Branco *Brazil* 9°58S 67°49W **92** E5
Río Branco *Uruguay* 32°40S 53°40W **95** C5
Río Bravo *Mexico* 25°59N 98°6W **87** B5
Río Bravo △ *N. Amer.* 29°2N 102°45W **86** B4
Rio Bravo del Norte →
   Mexico 25°57N 97°9W **87** B5
Rio Brilhante *Brazil* 21°48S 54°33W **95** A5
Rio Claro *Brazil* 22°19S 47°35W **95** A6
Rio Claro *Trin. & Tob.* 10°20N 61°25W **93** K15
Río Colorado *Argentina* 39°0S 64°0W **96** D4
Río Cuarto *Argentina* 33°10S 64°25W **94** C3
Rio das Pedras *Mozam.* 23°8S 35°28E **57** C5
Rio de Janeiro *Brazil* 23°0S 43°12W **95** A7
Rio de Janeiro □ *Brazil* 22°50S 43°0W **95** A7
Rio do Sul *Brazil* 27°13S 49°37W **95** B6
Río Dulce △ *Guatemala* 15°43N 88°50W **88** C2
Río Gallegos *Argentina* 51°35S 69°15W **96** G3
Río Grande *Argentina* 53°50S 67°45W **96** G3
Rio Grande *Brazil* 32°0S 52°20W **95** C5
Río Grande *Mexico* 23°50N 103°2W **86** C4
Río Grande *Puerto Rico* 18°23N 65°50W **89** d
Río Grande → *N. Amer.* 25°58N 97°9W **84** H5
Rio Grande City *U.S.A.* 26°23N 98°49W **84** H5
Rio Grande de Santiago →
   Mexico 21°36N 105°26W **86** C3
Rio Grande do Norte □
   Brazil 5°40S 36°0W **93** E11
Rio Grande do Sul □
   Brazil 30°0S 53°0W **95** C5
Rio Hato *Panama* 8°22N 80°10W **88** E3
Río Lagartos *Mexico* 21°36N 88°10W **87** C7
Rio Largo *Brazil* 9°28S 35°50W **93** E12
Río Mulatos *Bolivia* 19°40S 66°50W **92** G5
Río Muni □ *Eq. Guin.* 1°30N 10°0E **52** D2
Rio Negro *Brazil* 26°0S 49°55W **95** B6
Rio Pardo *Brazil* 30°0S 52°30W **95** C5
Río Pilcomayo △
   Argentina 25°5S 58°5W **94** B4
Río Platano △ *Honduras* 15°45N 85°0W **88** C3
Rio Rancho *U.S.A.* 35°14N 106°41W **77** J10
Río Segundo *Argentina* 31°40S 63°59W **94** C3
Río Tercero *Argentina* 32°15S 64°8W **94** C3
Rio Verde *Brazil* 17°50S 51°0W **93** G8
Río Verde *Mexico* 21°56N 99°59W **87** C5
Rio Vista *U.S.A.* 38°10N 121°42W **78** G5
Riobamba *Ecuador* 1°50S 78°45W **92** D3
Ríohacha *Colombia* 11°33N 72°55W **92** A4
Riosucio *Colombia* 7°27N 77°7W **92** B3
Riou L. *Canada* 59°7N 106°25W **71** B7
Ripley *Canada* 44°4N 81°35W **82** B3
Ripley *Calif., U.S.A.* 33°32N 114°39W **79** M12
Ripley *N.Y., U.S.A.* 42°16N 79°43W **82** D5
Ripley *Tenn., U.S.A.* 35°45N 89°32W **85** D10
Ripley *W. Va., U.S.A.* 38°49N 81°43W **81** F13
Ripon *U.K.* 54°9N 1°31W **12** C6
Ripon *Calif., U.S.A.* 37°44N 121°7W **78** H5
Ripon *Wis., U.S.A.* 43°51N 88°50W **80** D9
Rishā', W. ar → *Si. Arabia* 25°33N 44°5E **44** E5
Rishiri-Rebun-Sarobetsu △
   Japan 45°26N 141°30E **30** B10
Rishiri-Tō *Japan* 45°11N 141°15E **30** B10
Rishon le Ziyyon *Israel* 31°58N 34°48E **46** D3
Rison *U.S.A.* 33°58N 92°11W **84** E8
Risør *Norway* 58°43N 9°13E **9** G13
Rita Blanca Cr. →
   U.S.A. 35°40N 102°29W **84** D3
Ritter, Mt. *U.S.A.* 37°41N 119°12W **78** H7
Rittman *U.S.A.* 40°58N 81°47W **82** F3
Ritzville *U.S.A.* 47°8N 118°23W **76** C4
Riva del Garda *Italy* 45°53N 10°50E **22** B4
Rivadavia *B. Aires,*
   Argentina 35°29S 62°59W **94** D3
Rivadavia *Mendoza,*
   Argentina 33°13S 68°30W **94** C2
Rivadavia *Salta, Argentina* 24°5S 62°54W **94** A3
Rivadavia *Chile* 29°57S 70°35W **94** B1
Rivas *Nic.* 11°30N 85°50W **88** D2
Rivash *Iran* 35°28N 58°26E **45** C8
River Cess *Liberia* 5°30N 9°32W **50** G4
River Jordan *Canada* 48°26N 124°3W **78** B2
Rivera *Argentina* 37°12S 63°14W **94** D3
Rivera *Uruguay* 31°0S 55°50W **95** C4
Riverbank *U.S.A.* 37°44N 120°56W **78** H6
Riverdale *U.S.A.* 36°26N 119°52W **78** J7
Riverhead *U.S.A.* 40°55N 72°40W **83** F12
Riverhurst *Canada* 50°55N 106°50W **71** C7
Rivers *Canada* 50°2N 100°14W **71** C8
Rivers Inlet *Canada* 51°42N 127°15W **70** C3

Riversdale *Canada* 44°5N 81°20W **82 B3**
Riversdale *S. Africa* 34°7S 21°15E **56 E3**
Riverside *U.S.A.* 33°59N 117°22W **79 M9**
Riverton *Australia* 34°10S 138°46E **63 E2**
Riverton *Canada* 51°1N 97°0W **71 C9**
Riverton *N.Z.* 46°21S 168°0E **59 G2**
Riverton *U.S.A.* 43°2N 108°23W **76 E9**
Riviera *U.S.A.* 35°4N 114°35W **79 K12**
Riviera di Levante *Italy* 44°15N 9°30E **20 D8**
Riviera di Ponente *Italy* 44°10N 8°20E **20 D8**
Rivière-au-Renard
  Canada 48°59N 64°23W **73 C7**
Rivière-du-Loup *Canada* 47°50N 69°30W **73 C6**
Rivière-Pentecôte *Canada* 49°57N 67°1W **73 C6**
Rivière-Pilote *Martinique* 14°26N 60°53W **88 c**
Rivière St-Paul *Canada* 51°28N 57°45W **73 B8**
Rivière-Salée *Martinique* 14°31N 61°0W **88 c**
Rivne *Ukraine* 50°40N 26°10E **17 C14**
Rívoli *Italy* 45°3N 7°31E **20 D7**
Rivoli B. *Australia* 37°32S 140°3E **63 F3**
Riyadh = Ar Riyāḍ
  Si. Arabia 24°41N 46°42E **44 E5**
Riyadh al Khabrā'
  Si. Arabia 26°2N 43°33E **44 E4**
Rize *Turkey* 41°0N 40°30E **19 F7**
Rizhao *China* 35°25N 119°30E **35 G10**
Rizokarpaso *Cyprus* 35°36N 34°23E **25 D13**
Rizzuto, C. *Italy* 38°53N 17°5E **22 E7**
Rjukan *Norway* 59°54N 8°33E **9 G13**
Road Town *Br. Virgin Is.* 18°27N 64°37W **89 e**
Roan Plateau *U.S.A.* 39°20N 109°20W **76 G9**
Roanne *France* 46°3N 4°4E **20 C6**
Roanoke *Ala., U.S.A.* 33°9N 85°22W **85 E12**
Roanoke *Va., U.S.A.* 37°16N 79°56W **81 G14**
Roanoke → *U.S.A.* 35°57N 76°42W **85 D16**
Roanoke I. *U.S.A.* 35°53N 75°39W **85 D17**
Roanoke Rapids *U.S.A.* 36°28N 77°40W **85 C16**
Roatán *Honduras* 16°18N 86°35W **88 C2**
Robāt Sang *Iran* 35°35N 59°10E **45 C8**
Robāṭkarīm *Iran* 35°25N 50°59E **45 C6**
Robbins I. *Australia* 40°42S 145°0E **63 G4**
Robe → *Australia* 21°42S 116°15E **60 D2**
Robe *Australia* 33°17S 123°51E ...
Robert Bourassa, Rés.
  Canada 53°40N 76°55W **72 B4**
Robert Lee *U.S.A.* 31°54N 100°29W **84 F4**
Robertsdale *U.S.A.* 40°11N 78°6W **82 F6**
Robertsganj *India* 24°44N 83°4E **43 G10**
Robertson *S. Africa* 33°46S 19°50E **56 E2**
Robertson I. *Antarctica* 65°15S 59°30W **5 C18**
Robertson Ra. *Australia* 23°15S 121°0E **60 D3**
Robertstown *Australia* 33°58S 139°5E **63 E2**
Roberval *Canada* 48°32N 72°15W **73 C5**
Robeson Chan. *N. Amer.* 82°0N 61°30W **69 A19**
Robesonia *U.S.A.* 40°21N 76°8W **83 F8**
Robinson *U.S.A.* 39°0N 87°44W **80 F10**
Robinson → *Australia* 16°3S 137°16E **62 B2**
Robinson Crusoe I.
  Pac. Oc. 33°38S 78°52W **90 F2**
Robinson Ra. *Australia* 25°40S 119°0E **61 E2**
Robinvale *Australia* 34°40S 142°45E **63 E3**
Roblin *Canada* 51°14N 101°21W **71 C8**
Roboré *Bolivia* 18°10S 59°45W **92 G7**
Robson, Mt. *Canada* 53°10N 119°10W **70 C5**
Robstown *U.S.A.* 27°47N 97°40W **84 H6**
Roca, C. da *Portugal* 38°40N 9°31W **21 C1**
Roca Partida, I. *Mexico* 19°1N 112°2W **86 D2**
Rocas, I. *Brazil* 4°0S 34°1W **93 D12**
Rocha *Uruguay* 34°30S 54°25W **95 C5**
Rochdale *U.K.* 53°38N 2°9W **12 D5**
Rochefort *Belgium* 50°9N 5°12E **15 D5**
Rochefort *France* 45°56N 0°57W **20 D3**
Rochelle *U.S.A.* 41°56N 89°4W **80 E9**
Rocher River *Canada* 61°23N 112°44W **70 A6**
Rochester *U.K.* 51°23N 0°31E **13 F8**
Rochester *Ind., U.S.A.* 41°4N 86°13W **80 E10**
Rochester *Minn., U.S.A.* 44°1N 92°28W **80 C7**
Rochester *N.H., U.S.A.* 43°18N 70°59W **83 C14**
Rochester *N.Y., U.S.A.* 43°10N 77°37W **82 C7**
Rock → *Canada* 60°7N 127°7W **70 A3**
Rock, The *Australia* 35°15S 147°2E **63 F4**
Rock Creek *U.S.A.* 41°40N 80°52W **82 E4**
Rock Falls *U.S.A.* 41°47N 89°41W **80 E9**
Rock Hill *U.S.A.* 34°56N 81°1W **85 D14**
Rock Island *U.S.A.* 41°30N 90°34W **80 E8**
Rock Port *U.S.A.* 40°25N 95°31W **80 E6**
Rock Rapids *U.S.A.* 43°26N 96°10W **80 D5**
Rock Sound *Bahamas* 24°54N 76°12W **88 B4**
Rock Springs *Mont.,*
  U.S.A. 46°49N 106°15W **76 C10**
Rock Springs *Wyo.,*
  U.S.A. 41°35N 109°14W **76 F9**
Rock Valley *U.S.A.* 43°12N 96°18W **80 D5**
Rockall *Atl. Oc.* 57°37N 13°42W **6 D3**
Rockdale *Tex., U.S.A.* 30°39N 97°0W **84 F6**
Rockdale *Wash., U.S.A.* 47°22N 121°28W **78 C5**
Rockeby = Mungkan Kandju ○
  Australia 13°35S 142°52E **62 A3**
Rockefeller Plateau
  Antarctica 76°0S 130°0W **5 E14**
Rockford *U.S.A.* 42°16N 89°6W **80 D9**
Rockglen *Canada* 49°11N 105°57W **71 D7**
Rockhampton *Australia* 23°22S 150°32E **62 C5**
Rockingham *Australia* 32°15S 115°38E **61 F2**
Rockingham *N.C.,*
  U.S.A. 34°57N 79°46W **85 D15**
Rockingham *Vt.,*
  U.S.A. 43°11N 72°29W **83 C12**
Rockingham B. *Australia* 18°5S 146°10E **62 B4**
Rocklake *U.S.A.* 48°47N 99°15W **80 A4**
Rockland *Canada* 45°33N 75°17W **83 A9**
Rockland *Idaho, U.S.A.* 42°34N 112°53W **76 E7**
Rockland *Maine, U.S.A.* 44°6N 69°7W **81 C19**
Rockland *Mich., U.S.A.* 46°44N 89°11W **80 B9**
Rocklin *U.S.A.* 38°48N 121°14W **78 G5**
Rockly B. *Trin. & Tob.* 11°9N 60°46W **93 J16**
Rockmart *U.S.A.* 34°0N 85°3W **85 D12**
Rockport *Mass., U.S.A.* 42°39N 70°37W **83 D14**
Rockport *Tex., U.S.A.* 28°2N 97°3W **84 G6**
Rocksprings *U.S.A.* 30°1N 100°13W **84 F4**

Rockville *Conn., U.S.A.* 41°52N 72°28W **83 E12**
Rockville *Md., U.S.A.* 39°5N 77°9W **81 F15**
Rockwall *U.S.A.* 32°56N 96°28W **84 E6**
Rockwell City *U.S.A.* 42°24N 94°38W **80 D6**
Rockwood *Canada* 43°37N 80°8W **82 C4**
Rockwood *Maine,*
  U.S.A. 45°41N 69°45W **81 C19**
Rockwood *Tenn.,*
  U.S.A. 35°52N 84°41W **85 D12**
Rocky Ford *U.S.A.* 38°3N 103°43W **76 G12**
Rocky Gully *Australia* 34°30S 116°57E **61 F2**
Rocky Harbour *Canada* 49°36N 57°55W **73 C8**
Rocky Island L. *Canada* 46°55N 83°0W **72 C3**
Rocky Lane *Canada* 58°31N 116°22W **70 B5**
Rocky Mount *U.S.A.* 35°57N 77°48W **85 D16**
Rocky Mountain △
  U.S.A. 40°25N 105°45W **76 F11**
Rocky Mountain House
  Canada 52°22N 114°55W **70 C6**
Rocky Mts. *N. Amer.* 49°0N 115°0W **76 B6**
Rod *Pakistan* 28°10N 63°5E **40 E3**
Roda *Greece* 39°48N 19°46E **25 A3**
Rødbyhavn *Denmark* 54°39N 11°22E **9 J14**
Roddickton *Canada* 50°51N 56°8W **73 B8**
Rodez *France* 44°21N 2°33E **20 D5**
Ródhos = Rhodes
  Greece 36°15N 28°10E **25 C10**
Rodia *Greece* 35°22N 25°1E **25 D7**
Rodna ○ *Australia* 23°45S 132°4E **60 D5**
Rodney *Canada* 42°34N 81°41W **82 D3**
Rodney, C. *N.Z.* 36°17S 174°50E **59 B5**
Ródopos *Greece* 35°34N 23°45E **25 D5**
Rodrigues *Ind. Oc.* 19°45S 63°20E **3 E13**
Roe → *U.K.* 55°6N 6°59W **10 A5**
Roebling *U.S.A.* 40°7N 74°47W **83 F10**
Roebourne *Australia* 20°44S 117°9E **60 D2**
Roebuck B. *Australia* 18°5S 122°20E **60 C3**
Roebuck Roadhouse
  Australia 17°59S 122°36E **60 C3**
Roermond *Neths.* 51°12N 6°0E **15 C6**
Roes Welcome Sd.
  Canada 65°0N 87°0W **69 E14**
Roeselare *Belgium* 50°57N 3°7E **15 D3**
Rogachev = Ragachow
  Belarus 53°8N 30°5E **17 B16**
Rogagua, L. *Bolivia* 13°43S 66°50W **92 F5**
Rogatyn *Ukraine* 49°24N 24°36E **17 D13**
Rogers *U.S.A.* 36°20N 94°7W **84 C7**
Rogers City *U.S.A.* 45°25N 83°49W **81 C12**
Rogersville *Canada* 46°44N 65°26W **73 C6**
Roggan → *Canada* 54°24N 79°25W **72 B4**
Roggan L. *Canada* 54°8N 77°50W **72 B4**
Roggeveen Basin
  Pac. Oc. 31°30S 95°30W **65 L18**
Roggeveldberge *S. Africa* 32°10S 20°10E **56 E3**
Rogoaguado, L. *Bolivia* 12°45S 65°30W **92 F5**
Rogojampi *Indonesia* 8°19S 114°17E **37 J17**
Rogue → *U.S.A.* 42°26N 124°26W **76 E1**
Rohnert Park *U.S.A.* 38°16N 122°40W **78 G4**
Rohri *Pakistan* 27°45N 68°51E **42 F3**
Rohri Canal *Pakistan* 26°15N 68°27E **42 F3**
Rohtak *India* 28°55N 76°43E **42 E7**
Roi Et *Thailand* 16°4N 103°40E **38 D4**
Roja *Latvia* 57°29N 22°43E **9 H20**
Rojas *Argentina* 34°10S 60°45W **94 C3**
Rojo, C. *Mexico* 21°33N 97°20W **87 C5**
Rokan → *Indonesia* 2°0N 100°50E **36 D2**
Rokiškis *Lithuania* 55°55N 25°35E **9 J21**
Rolândia *Brazil* 23°18S 51°23W **95 A5**
Rolla *Mo., U.S.A.* 37°57N 91°46W **80 G8**
Rolla *N. Dak., U.S.A.* 48°52N 99°37W **80 A4**
Rolleston *Australia* 24°28S 148°35E **62 C4**
Rollingstone *Australia* 19°2S 146°24E **62 B4**
Roma *Australia* 26°32S 148°49E **63 D4**
Roma *Italy* 41°54N 12°28E **22 D5**
Roma *Sweden* 57°32N 18°26E **9 H18**
Roma-Los Saenz *U.S.A.* 26°24N 99°1W **84 H5**
Romain, C. *U.S.A.* 33°0N 79°22W **85 E15**
Romaine → *Canada* 50°18N 63°47W **73 B7**
Roman *Romania* 46°57N 26°55E **17 E14**
Romang *Indonesia* 7°30S 127°20E **37 F7**
Români *Egypt* 30°59N 32°38E **46 E1**
Romania ■ *Europe* 46°0N 25°0E **17 F12**
Romano, Cayo *Cuba* 22°0N 77°30W **88 B4**
Romans-sur-Isère *France* 45°3N 5°3E **20 D6**
Romanzof C. *U.S.A.* 61°49N 166°6W **74 C6**
Romblon *Phil.* 12°33N 122°17E **37 B6**
Rome = Roma *Italy* 41°54N 12°28E **22 D5**
Rome *Ga., U.S.A.* 34°15N 85°10W **85 D12**
Rome *N.Y., U.S.A.* 43°13N 75°27W **83 C9**
Rome *Pa., U.S.A.* 41°51N 76°21W **83 E8**
Romney *U.S.A.* 39°21N 78°45W **81 F14**
Romney Marsh *U.K.* 51°2N 0°54E **13 F8**
Rømø *Denmark* 55°10N 8°30E **9 J13**
Romorantin-Lanthenay
  France 47°21N 1°45E **20 C4**
Romsdalen *Norway* 62°25N 7°52E **8 E12**
Romsey *U.K.* 51°0N 1°29W **13 G6**
Ron *Vietnam* 17°53N 106°27E **38 D6**
Rona *U.K.* 57°34N 5°59W **11 D3**
Ronan *U.S.A.* 47°32N 114°6W **76 C6**
Roncador, Cayos
  Colombia 13°32N 80°4W **88 D3**
Roncador, Serra do
  Brazil 12°30S 52°30W **93 F8**
Ronda *Spain* 36°46N 5°12W **21 D3**
Rondane *Norway* 61°57N 9°50E **8 F13**
Rondônia □ *Brazil* 11°0S 63°0W **92 F6**
Rondonópolis *Brazil* 16°28S 54°38W **93 G8**
Rondu *Pakistan* 35°32N 75°10E **43 B6**
Rong, Koh *Cambodia* 10°45N 103°15E **39 G4**
Ronge, L. la *Canada* 55°6N 105°17W **71 B7**
Rønne *Denmark* 55°6N 14°43E **9 J16**
Ronne Ice Shelf
  Antarctica 77°30S 60°0W **5 D18**
Ronsard, C. *Australia* 24°46S 113°10E **61 D1**
Ronse *Belgium* 50°45N 3°35E **15 D3**
Roodepoort *S. Africa* 26°11S 27°54E **57 D4**

Roof Butte *U.S.A.* 36°28N 109°5W **77 H9**
Rooiboklaagte →
  Namibia 20°50S 21°0E **56 C3**
Rooiu, Mt. *Tahiti* 17°49S 149°12W **59 d**
Roorkee *India* 29°52N 77°59E **42 E7**
Roosendaal *Neths.* 51°32N 4°29E **15 C4**
Roosevelt *U.S.A.* 40°18N 109°59W **76 F9**
Roosevelt → *Brazil* 7°35S 60°20W **92 E6**
Roosevelt *Canada* 58°26N 125°20W **70 B3**
Roosevelt I. *Antarctica* 79°30S 162°0W **5 D12**
Roper → *Australia* 14°43S 135°27E **62 A2**
Roper Bar *Australia* 14°44S 134°44E **62 A1**
Roper River = St. Vidgeon's ○
  Australia 14°47S 134°53E **62 A1**
Roque Pérez *Argentina* 35°25S 59°24W **94 D4**
Roquetas de Mar *Spain* 36°46N 2°36W **21 D4**
Roraima □ *Brazil* 2°0N 61°30W **92 C6**
Roraima, Mt. *Venezuela* 5°10N 60°40W **92 B6**
Røros *Norway* 62°35N 11°23E **8 E14**
Ros Comáin = Roscommon
  Ireland 53°38N 8°11W **10 C3**
Rosa *Zambia* 9°33S 31°15E **55 D3**
Rosa, Monte *Europe* 45°57N 7°53E **20 D7**
Rosalia *U.S.A.* 47°14N 117°22W **76 C5**
Rosamond *U.S.A.* 34°52N 118°10W **79 L8**
Rosário *Argentina* 33°0S 60°40W **94 C3**
Rosário *Brazil* 3°0S 44°15W **93 D10**
Rosario *Baja Calif.,*
  Mexico 30°0N 115°50W **86 B1**
Rosario *Sinaloa, Mexico* 22°58N 105°53W **86 C3**
Rosario *Paraguay* 24°30S 57°35W **94 A4**
Rosario de la Frontera
  Argentina 25°50S 65°0W **94 B3**
Rosario de Lerma
  Argentina 24°59S 65°35W **94 A2**
Rosario del Tala
  Argentina 32°20S 59°10W **94 C4**
Rosário do Sul *Brazil* 30°15S 54°55W **95 C5**
Rosarito *Mexico* 32°20N 117°2W **79 N9**
Roscoe *U.S.A.* 41°56N 74°55W **83 E10**
Roscommon *Ireland* 53°38N 8°11W **10 C3**
Roscommon □ *Ireland* 53°49N 8°23W **10 C3**
Roscrea *Ireland* 52°57N 7°49W **10 D4**
Rose → *Australia* 14°16S 135°45E **62 A2**
Rose, L. *Bahamas* 21°0N 73°30W **89 B5**
Rose Belle *Mauritius* 20°24S 57°36E **53 d**
Rose Blanche *Canada* 47°38N 58°45W **73 C8**
Rose Hill *Mauritius* 20°14S 57°27E **53 d**
Rose Pt. *Canada* 54°11N 131°39W **70 C2**
Rose Valley *Canada* 52°19N 103°49W **71 C8**
Roseau *Dominica* 15°17N 61°24W **89 C7**
Roseau *U.S.A.* 48°51N 95°46W **80 A6**
Rosebery *Australia* 41°46S 145°33E **63 G4**
Rosebud *S. Dak., U.S.A.* 43°14N 100°51W **80 D3**
Rosebud *Tex., U.S.A.* 31°4N 96°59W **84 F6**
Roseburg *U.S.A.* 43°13N 123°20W **76 E2**
Rosedale *U.S.A.* 33°51N 91°2W **85 E9**
Rosehearty *U.K.* 57°42N 2°7W **11 D6**
Roseires Res. *Sudan* 11°51N 34°23E **51 F12**
Roseland *U.S.A.* 38°25N 122°43W **78 G4**
Rosemary *Canada* 50°46N 112°5W **70 C6**
Rosenberg *U.S.A.* 29°34N 95°49W **84 G7**
Rosenheim *Germany* 47°51N 12°7E **16 E7**
Roses, G. de *Spain* 42°10N 3°15E **21 A7**
Rosetown *Canada* 51°35N 107°59W **71 C7**
Roseville *Calif., U.S.A.* 38°45N 121°17W **78 G5**
Roseville *Mich., U.S.A.* 42°30N 82°56W **82 D2**
Roseville *Pa., U.S.A.* 41°51N 76°57W **83 E8**
Rosewood *Australia* 27°38S 152°36E **63 D5**
Roshkhvār *Iran* 34°58N 59°37E **45 C8**
Rosignano Maríttimo
  Italy 43°24N 10°28E **22 C4**
Rosignol *Guyana* 6°15N 57°30W **92 B7**
Roșiori de Vede *Romania* 44°9N 25°0E **17 F13**
Roskilde *Denmark* 55°38N 12°3E **9 J15**
Roslavl *Russia* 53°57N 32°55E **18 D5**
Rosmead *S. Africa* 31°29S 25°8E **56 E4**
Rosolini *Italy* 36°36N 16°39E **22 F6**
Rossburn *Canada* 50°40N 100°49W **71 C8**
Rosseau *Canada* 45°16N 79°39W **82 A5**
Rosseau, L. *Canada* 45°10N 79°35W **82 A5**
Rosses, The *Ireland* 55°2N 8°20W **10 A3**
Rossignol, L. *Canada* 52°43N 73°40W **72 B5**
Rossignol L. *Canada* 44°12N 65°10W **73 D6**
Rossiya = Russia ■
  Eurasia 62°0N 105°0E **29 C11**
Rossland *Canada* 49°6N 117°50W **70 D5**
Rosslare *Ireland* 52°17N 6°24W **10 D5**
Rosslare Harbour *Ireland* 52°15N 6°20W **10 D5**
Rossmore *Canada* 44°8N 77°23W **82 B7**
Rosso *Mauritania* 16°40N 15°45W **50 E2**
Rossosh *Russia* 50°15N 39°28E **19 D6**
Røssvatnet *Norway* 65°45N 14°5E **8 D16**
Røst *Norway* 67°32N 12°0E **8 C15**
Rosthern *Canada* 52°40N 106°20W **71 C7**
Rostock *Germany* 54°5N 12°8E **16 A7**
Rostov *Don, Russia* 47°15N 39°45E **19 E6**
Rostov *Yaroslavl, Russia* 57°14N 39°25E **18 C6**
Roswell *Ga., U.S.A.* 34°2N 84°22W **85 D12**
Roswell *N. Mex.,*
  U.S.A. 33°24N 104°32W **77 K11**
Rotan *U.S.A.* 32°51N 100°28W **84 E4**
Rother → *U.K.* 50°59N 0°45E **13 G8**
Rothera *Antarctica* 67°34S 68°8W **5 C17**

Rotherham *U.K.* 53°26N 1°20W **12 D6**
Rothes *U.K.* 57°32N 3°13W **11 D5**
Rothesay *Canada* 45°23N 66°0W **73 C6**
Rothesay *U.K.* 55°50N 5°3W **11 F3**
Roti *Indonesia* 10°50S 123°0E **37 F6**
Roto *Australia* 33°0S 145°30E **63 E4**
Rotondo, Mte. *France* 42°14N 9°8E **20 E8**
Rotoroa, L. *N.Z.* 41°55S 172°39E **59 D4**
Rotorua *N.Z.* 38°9S 176°16E **59 C6**
Rotorua, L. *N.Z.* 38°5S 176°18E **59 C6**
Rotterdam *Neths.* 51°55N 4°30E **15 C4**
Rotterdam *U.S.A.* 42°48N 74°1W **83 D10**
Rottnest I. *Australia* 32°0S 115°27E **61 F2**
Rottumeroog *Neths.* 53°33N 6°34E **15 A6**
Rottweil *Germany* 48°9N 8°37E **16 D5**
Rotuma *Fiji* 12°25S 177°5E **58 C10**
Roubaix *France* 50°40N 3°10E **20 A5**
Rouen *France* 49°27N 1°4E **20 B4**
Rouleau *Canada* 50°10N 104°56W **71 C8**
Roulpmaulpma ○
  Australia 23°52S 133°0E **60 D5**
Round I. *Mauritius* 19°51S 57°45E **53 d**
Round Mountain
  U.S.A. 38°43N 117°4W **76 G5**
Round Mt. *Australia* 30°26S 152°16E **63 E5**
Round Rock *U.S.A.* 30°31N 97°41W **84 F6**
Roundup *U.S.A.* 46°27N 108°33W **76 C9**
Rousay *U.K.* 59°10N 3°2W **11 B5**
Rouses Point *U.S.A.* 44°59N 73°22W **83 B11**
Rouseville *U.S.A.* 41°28N 79°42W **82 E5**
Rousse = Ruse *Bulgaria* 43°48N 25°59E **23 C12**
Roussillon *France* 42°30N 2°35E **20 E5**
Rouxville *S. Africa* 30°25S 26°50E **56 E4**
Rouyn-Noranda *Canada* 48°20N 79°0W **72 C4**
Rovaniemi *Finland* 66°29N 25°41E **8 C21**
Rovereto *Italy* 45°53N 11°3E **22 B4**
Rovigo *Italy* 45°4N 11°47E **22 B4**
Rovinj *Croatia* 45°5N 13°40E **16 F7**
Rovno = Rivne *Ukraine* 50°40N 26°10E **17 C14**
Rovuma = Ruvuma →
  Tanzania 10°29S 40°28E **55 E5**
Row'ān *Iran* 35°8N 48°51E **45 C6**
Rowena *Australia* 29°48S 148°55E **63 D4**
Rowley I. *Canada* 69°6N 77°52W **69 D16**
Rowley Shoals *Australia* 17°30S 119°0E **60 C2**
Roxas *Phil.* 11°36N 122°49E **37 B6**
Roxboro *U.S.A.* 36°24N 78°59W **85 C15**
Roxborough
  Trin. & Tob. 11°15N 60°35W **93 J16**
Roxburgh *N.Z.* 45°33S 169°19E **59 F2**
Roxbury *N.Y., U.S.A.* 42°17N 74°33W **83 D10**
Roxbury *Pa., U.S.A.* 40°6N 77°39W **82 F7**
Roxby Downs *Australia* 30°43S 136°46E **63 E2**
Roy *Mont., U.S.A.* 47°20N 108°58W **76 C9**
Roy *N. Mex., U.S.A.* 35°57N 104°12W **77 J11**
Roy *Utah, U.S.A.* 41°10N 112°2W **76 F7**
Royal Bardia △ *Nepal* 28°20N 81°20E **43 E9**
Royal Canal *Ireland* 53°30N 7°13W **10 C4**
Royal Chitawan △
  Nepal 26°30N 84°30E **43 F11**
Royal Geographical Society Is.
  Canada 68°50N 100°15W **68 D11**
Royal Leamington Spa
  U.K. 52°18N 1°31W **13 E6**
Royal Natal △ *S. Africa* 28°43S 28°51E **57 D4**
Royal Tunbridge Wells
  U.K. 51°7N 0°16E **13 F8**
Royale, Isle *U.S.A.* 48°0N 88°54W **80 B9**
Royan *France* 45°37N 1°2W **20 D3**
Royston *U.K.* 52°3N 0°0 **13 E7**
Rozdilna *Ukraine* 46°50N 30°2E **17 E16**
Rozhyshche *Ukraine* 50°54N 25°15E **17 C13**
Rtishchevo *Russia* 52°18N 43°46E **18 D7**
Ruacaná *Namibia* 17°27S 14°21E **56 B1**
Ruahá △ *Tanzania* 7°41S 34°30E **54 D3**
Ruahine Ra. *N.Z.* 39°55S 176°2E **59 C6**
Ruapehu *N.Z.* 39°17S 175°35E **59 C6**
Ruapuke I. *N.Z.* 46°46S 168°31E **59 G2**
Ruāq, W. → *Egypt* 30°0N 33°49E **46 F2**
Rub' al Khālī *Si. Arabia* 19°0N 48°0E **47 D4**
Rubeho Mts. *Tanzania* 6°50S 36°25E **54 D4**
Rubh a' Mhail *U.K.* 55°56N 6°8W **11 F2**
Rubha Hunish *U.K.* 57°42N 6°20W **11 D2**
Rubha Robhanais = Lewis, Butt of
  U.K. 58°31N 6°16W **11 C2**
Rubicon → *U.S.A.* 38°53N 121°4W **78 G5**
Rubio *Venezuela* 7°43N 72°22W **92 B4**
Rubondo △ *Tanzania* 2°18S 31°58E **54 C3**
Rubtsovsk *Russia* 51°30N 81°10E **28 D9**
Ruby L. *U.S.A.* 40°10N 115°28W **76 F6**
Ruby Mts. *U.S.A.* 40°30N 115°20W **76 F6**
Rubyvale *Australia* 23°25S 147°42E **62 C4**
Rūd Sar *Iran* 37°8N 50°18E **45 B6**
Rudall *Australia* 33°43S 136°17E **63 E2**
Rudall → *Australia* 22°34S 122°13E **60 D3**
Rudall River △
  Australia 22°38S 122°30E **60 D3**
Rudbar *Iran* 36°48N 49°23E **45 B6**
Rudewa *Tanzania* 10°7S 34°40E **55 E3**
Rudnyy *Kazakhstan* 52°57N 63°7E **28 D7**
Rudolfa, Ostrov *Russia* 81°45N 58°30E **28 A6**
Rudyard *U.S.A.* 46°14N 84°36W **81 B11**
Ruenya → *Africa* 16°24S 33°48E **55 F3**
Ruffling Pt. *Br. Virgin Is.* 18°44N 64°27W **89 e**
Rufiji → *Tanzania* 7°50S 39°15E **54 D4**
Rufino *Argentina* 34°20S 62°50W **94 C3**
Rufunsa *Zambia* 15°4S 29°34E **55 F2**
Rugby *U.K.* 52°23N 1°16W **13 E6**
Rugby *U.S.A.* 48°22N 100°0W **80 A4**
Rügen *Germany* 54°22N 13°24E **16 A7**
Ruhengeri *Rwanda* 1°30S 29°36E **54 C2**
Ruhnu *Estonia* 57°48N 23°15E **9 H20**
Ruhr → *Germany* 51°27N 6°43E **16 C4**
Ruhuhu → *Tanzania* 10°31S 34°34E **55 E3**
Ruidoso *U.S.A.* 33°20N 105°41W **77 K11**
Ruivo, Pico *Madeira* 32°45N 16°56W **24 D3**
Rujm Tal'at al Jamā'ah
  Jordan 30°24N 35°30E **46 E4**
Ruk *Pakistan* 27°50N 68°42E **42 F3**

Rukhla *Pakistan* 32°27N 71°57E **42 C4**
Ruki →
  Dem. Rep. of the Congo 0°5N 18°17E **52 E3**
Rukwa □ *Tanzania* 7°0S 31°30E **54 D3**
Rukwa, L. *Tanzania* 8°0S 32°20E **54 D3**
Rulenge *Burundi* 2°43S 30°37E **54 C3**
Rulhieres, C. *Australia* 13°56S 127°22E **60 B4**
Rum = Rhum *U.K.* 57°0N 6°20W **11 E2**
Rum *Jordan* 29°39S 35°26E **46 F4**
Rum Cay *Bahamas* 23°40N 74°58W **89 B5**
Rum Jungle *Australia* 13°0S 130°59E **60 B5**
Ruma △ *Kenya* 0°39S 34°18E **54 C3**
Rumāḥ *Si. Arabia* 25°29N 47°10E **44 E5**
Rumania = Romania ■
  Europe 46°0N 25°0E **17 F12**
Rumaylah *Iraq* 30°47N 47°37E **44 D5**
Rumbêk *Sudan* 6°54N 29°37E **51 G11**
Rumford *U.S.A.* 44°33N 70°33W **83 B14**
Rumia *Poland* 54°37N 18°25E **17 A10**
Rumoi *Japan* 43°56N 141°39E **30 C10**
Rumonge *Burundi* 3°59S 29°26E **54 C2**
Rumphi *Malawi* 11°1S 33°52E **55 E3**
Rumson *U.S.A.* 40°23N 74°0W **83 F11**
Runan *China* 33°0N 114°30E **34 H8**
Runanga *N.Z.* 42°25S 171°15E **59 E3**
Runaway, C. *N.Z.* 37°32S 177°59E **59 B6**
Runaway Bay *Jamaica* 18°27N 77°20W **88 a**
Runcorn *U.K.* 53°21N 2°44W **12 D5**
Rundu *Namibia* 17°52S 19°43E **56 B2**
Rungwa *Tanzania* 6°55S 33°32E **54 D3**
Rungwa → *Tanzania* 7°36S 31°50E **54 D3**
Rungwa △ *Tanzania* 6°53S 34°2E **54 D3**
Rungwe *Tanzania* 9°11S 33°32E **55 D3**
Rungwe, Mt. *Tanzania* 9°8S 33°40E **52 F6**
Runton Ra. *Australia* 23°31S 123°6E **60 D3**
Ruo Shui → *China* 41°0N 100°16E **32 B5**
Ruokolahti *Finland* 61°17N 28°50E **8 F23**
Ruoqiang *China* 38°55N 88°10E **32 C3**
Rupa *India* 27°15N 92°21E **41 F18**
Rupar *India* 31°2N 76°38E **42 D7**
Rupat *Indonesia* 1°45N 101°40E **36 D2**
Rupen → *India* 23°28N 71°31E **42 H4**
Rupert *U.S.A.* 42°37N 113°41W **76 E7**
Rupert → *Canada* 51°29N 78°45W **72 B4**
Rupert B. *Canada* 51°35N 79°0W **72 B4**
Rupert House = Waskaganish
  Canada 51°30N 78°40W **72 B4**
Rupsa *India* 21°37N 87°1E **43 J12**
Rurrenabaque *Bolivia* 14°30S 67°32W **92 F5**
Rusambo *Zimbabwe* 16°30S 32°4E **55 F3**
Rusape *Zimbabwe* 18°35S 32°8E **55 F3**
Ruschuk = Ruse
  Bulgaria 43°48N 25°59E **23 C12**
Ruse *Bulgaria* 43°48N 25°59E **23 C12**
Rush *Ireland* 53°31N 6°6W **10 C5**
Rushan *China* 36°56N 121°30E **35 F11**
Rushden *U.K.* 52°18N 0°35W **13 E7**
Rushmore, Mt. *U.S.A.* 43°53N 103°28W **76 D3**
Rushville *Ill., U.S.A.* 40°7N 90°34W **80 E8**
Rushville *Ind., U.S.A.* 39°37N 85°27W **81 F11**
Rushville *Nebr., U.S.A.* 42°43N 102°28W **80 D2**
Russas *Brazil* 4°55S 37°50W **93 D11**
Russell *Canada* 50°50N 101°20W **71 C8**
Russell *Kans., U.S.A.* 38°54N 98°52W **80 F4**
Russell *N.Y., U.S.A.* 44°27N 75°9W **83 B9**
Russell *Pa., U.S.A.* 41°56N 79°8W **82 E5**
Russell Cave ○ *U.S.A.* 34°59N 85°49W **85 D12**
Russell L. *Man., Canada* 56°15N 101°30W **71 B8**
Russell L. *N.W.T.,*
  Canada 63°5N 115°44W **70 A5**
Russellkonda *India* 19°57N 84°42E **41 K14**
Russellville *Ala., U.S.A.* 34°30N 87°44W **85 D11**
Russellville *Ark., U.S.A.* 35°17N 93°8W **84 D8**
Russellville *Ky., U.S.A.* 36°51N 86°53W **80 G10**
Russia ■ *Eurasia* 62°0N 105°0E **29 C11**
Russian → *U.S.A.* 38°27N 123°8W **78 G3**
Rustam Shahr *Pakistan* 26°58N 66°6E **42 F2**
Rustavi *Georgia* 41°30N 45°0E **19 F8**
Rustenburg *S. Africa* 25°41S 27°14E **56 D4**
Ruston *U.S.A.* 32°32N 92°38W **84 E8**
Rutana *Burundi* 3°55S 30°0E **54 C3**
Ruteng *Indonesia* 8°35S 120°30E **37 F6**
Rutenga *Zimbabwe* 21°15S 30°44E **55 G3**
Ruth *U.S.A.* 43°42N 82°45W **82 C2**
Rutherford *U.S.A.* 38°26N 122°24W **78 G4**
Rutland *U.S.A.* 43°37N 72°58W **83 C12**
Rutland □ *U.K.* 52°38N 0°40W **13 E7**
Rutland Water *U.K.* 52°39N 0°38W **13 E7**
Rutledge → *Canada* 61°4N 112°0W **71 A6**
Rutledge L. *Canada* 61°33N 110°47W **71 A6**
Rutog *China* 33°27N 79°42E **32 C2**
Rutshuru
  Dem. Rep. of the Congo 1°13S 29°25E **54 C2**
Ruvu *Tanzania* 6°49S 38°43E **54 D4**
Ruvu → *Tanzania* 6°23S 38°52E **54 D4**
Ruvuba △ *Burundi* 3°3S 29°33E **54 C2**
Ruvuma □ *Tanzania* 10°20S 36°0E **55 E4**
Ruvuma → *Tanzania* 10°29S 40°28E **55 E5**
Ruwais *U.A.E.* 24°5N 52°50E **45 E7**
Ruwenzori *Africa* 0°30N 29°55E **54 B2**
Ruwenzori △ *Uganda* 0°20N 30°0E **54 B2**
Ruya → *Zimbabwe* 16°27S 32°5E **55 F3**
Ruyigi *Burundi* 3°29S 30°15E **54 C3**
Ružomberok *Slovak Rep.* 49°3N 19°17E **17 D10**
Rwanda ■ *Africa* 2°0S 30°0E **54 C3**
Ryan, L. *U.K.* 55°0N 5°2W **11 G3**
Ryazan *Russia* 54°40N 39°40E **18 D6**
Ryazhsk *Russia* 53°45N 40°3E **18 D7**
Rybachiy Poluostrov
  Russia 69°43N 32°0E **8 B25**
Rybache = Balykchy
  Kyrgyzstan 42°26N 76°12E **32 B2**
Rybinsk *Russia* 58°5N 38°50E **18 C6**
Rybinskoye Vdkhr.
  Russia 58°30N 38°25E **18 C6**
Rybnitsa = Râbniţa
  Moldova 47°45N 29°0E **17 E15**
Rycroft *Canada* 55°45N 118°40W **70 B5**

Ryde U.K. 50°43N 1°9W 13 G6
Ryderwood U.S.A. 46°23N 123°3W 78 D3
Rye U.K. 50°57N 0°45E 13 G8
Rye → U.K. 54°11N 0°44W 12 C7
Rye Bay U.K. 50°52N 0°49E 13 G8
Rye Patch Res. U.S.A. 40°28N 118°19W 76 F4
Ryegate U.S.A. 46°18N 109°15W 76 C9
Ryley Canada 53°17N 112°26W 70 C6
Rylstone Australia 32°46S 149°58E 63 E4
Ryn Peski = Naryn Qum
  Kazakhstan 47°30N 49°0E 28 E5
Ryōtsu Japan 38°5N 138°26E 30 E9
Rypin Poland 53°3N 19°25E 17 B10
Ryūgasaki Japan 35°54N 140°11E 31 G10
Ryukyu Is. = Ryūkyū-rettō
  Japan 26°0N 126°0E 31 M3
Ryūkyū-rettō Japan 26°0N 126°0E 31 M3
Rzeszów Poland 50°5N 21°58E 17 C11
Rzhev Russia 56°20N 34°20E 18 C5

S

Sa Thailand 18°34N 100°45E 38 C3
Sa Cabaneta Spain 39°37N 2°45E 24 B9
Sa Canal Spain 38°51N 1°23E 24 C7
Sa Conillera Spain 38°59N 1°13E 24 C7
Sa Dec Vietnam 10°20N 105°46E 39 G5
Sa Dragonera Spain 39°35N 2°19E 24 B9
Sa Kaeo Thailand 13°49N 102°4E 38 F4
Sa Mesquida Spain 39°55N 4°16E 24 B11
Sa Pa Vietnam 22°20N 103°47E 38 A4
Sa Savina Spain 38°44N 1°25E 24 C7
Sa'ādatābād Fārs, Iran 30°10N 53°5E 45 D7
Sa'ādatābād Hormozgān,
  Iran 28°3N 55°53E 45 D7
Sa'ādatābād Kermān,
  Iran 29°40N 55°51E 45 D7
Saale → Germany 51°56N 11°54E 16 C6
Saalfeld Germany 50°38N 11°21E 16 C6
Saanich Canada 48°29N 123°26W 78 B3
Saar → Europe 49°41N 6°32E 15 E6
Saarbrücken Germany 49°14N 6°59E 16 D4
Saaremaa Estonia 58°30N 22°30E 9 G20
Saarijärvi Finland 62°43N 25°16E 8 E21
Saariselkä Finland 68°16N 28°15E 8 B23
Sab 'Ābar Syria 33°46N 37°41E 44 C3
Saba W. Indies 17°38N 63°14W 89 C7
Šabac Serbia 44°48N 19°42E 23 B8
Sabadell Spain 41°28N 2°7E 21 B7
Sabah □ Malaysia 6°0N 117°0E 36 C5
Sabak Malaysia 3°46N 100°58E 39 L3
Sabalān, Kūhhā-ye Iran 38°15N 47°45E 44 B5
Sabalana, Kepulauan
  Indonesia 6°45S 118°50E 37 F5
Sábana de la Mar
  Dom. Rep. 19°7N 69°24W 89 C6
Sábanalarga Colombia 10°38N 74°55W 92 A4
Sabang Indonesia 5°50N 95°15E 36 C1
Sabarmati → India 22°18N 72°22E 42 H5
Sabattis U.S.A. 44°6N 74°40W 83 B10
Saberania Indonesia 2°5S 138°18E 37 E9
Sabhā Libya 27°9N 14°29E 51 C8
Sabi → India 28°29N 76°44E 42 E7
Sabie S. Africa 25°10S 30°48E 57 D5
Sabinal Mexico 30°57N 107°30W 86 A3
Sabinal U.S.A. 29°19N 99°28W 84 G5
Sabinas Mexico 27°51N 101°7W 86 B4
Sabinas → Mexico 27°37N 100°42W 86 B4
Sabinas Hidalgo
  Mexico 26°30N 100°10W 86 B4
Sabine → U.S.A. 29°59N 93°47W 84 G8
Sabine L. U.S.A. 29°53N 93°51W 84 G8
Sabine Pass U.S.A. 29°44N 93°54W 84 H8
Sablayan Phil. 12°50N 120°50E 37 B6
Sable Canada 55°30N 68°21W 73 A6
Sable, C. Canada 43°29N 65°38W 73 D6
Sable, C. U.S.A. 25°9N 81°8W 88 A3
Sable I. Canada 44°0N 60°0W 73 D8
Sabrina Coast Antarctica 68°0S 120°0E 5 C9
Sabulubbek Indonesia 1°36S 98°40E 36 E1
Sabzevār Iran 36°15N 57°40E 45 B8
Sabzvārān = Jiroft Iran 28°45N 57°50E 45 D8
Sac City U.S.A. 42°25N 95°0W 80 D6
Săcele Romania 45°37N 25°41E 17 F13
Sacheon S. Korea 35°0N 128°6E 35 G15
Sachigo → Canada 55°6N 88°58W 72 A2
Sachigo, L. Canada 53°50N 92°12W 72 B1
Sachimbo Angola 9°14S 20°16E 52 F4
Sachsen □ Germany 50°55N 13°10E 16 C7
Sachsen-Anhalt □
  Germany 52°0N 12°0E 16 C7
Sackets Harbor U.S.A. 43°57N 76°7W 83 C8
Sackville Canada 45°54N 64°22W 73 C7
Saco Maine, U.S.A. 43°30N 70°27W 83 C14
Saco Mont., U.S.A. 48°28N 107°21W 76 B10
Sacramento U.S.A. 38°35N 121°29W 78 G5
Sacramento → U.S.A. 38°3N 121°56W 78 G5
Sacramento Mts.
  U.S.A. 32°30N 105°30W 77 K11
Sacramento Valley
  U.S.A. 39°30N 122°0W 78 G5
Sada-Misaki Japan 33°20N 132°1E 31 H6
Sadabad India 27°27N 78°3E 42 F8
Sadani Tanzania 5°58S 38°35E 54 D4
Sadani △ Tanzania 6°3S 38°47E 54 D4
Sadao Thailand 6°38N 100°26E 39 J3
Sadd el Aali Egypt 23°54N 32°54E 51 D12
Saddle Mt. U.S.A. 45°58N 123°41W 78 E3
Sadimi
  Dem. Rep. of the Congo 9°25S 23°32E 55 D1
Sado Japan 38°0N 138°25E 30 F9
Sadra India 23°21N 72°43E 42 H5
Sadri India 25°11N 73°26E 42 G5
Sæby Denmark 57°21N 10°30E 9 H14
Saegertown U.S.A. 41°43N 80°9W 82 E4
Şafājah Si. Arabia 26°25N 39°0E 44 E3
Safata B. Samoa 14°0S 171°50W 59 b

Safford U.S.A. 32°50N 109°43W 77 K9
Saffron Walden U.K. 52°1N 0°16E 13 E8
Safi Morocco 32°18N 9°20W 50 B4
Şafiābād Iran 36°45N 57°58E 45 B8
Safid Dasht Iran 33°27N 48°11E 45 C6
Safid Kūh Afghan. 34°45N 63°0E 40 B3
Safid Rūd → Iran 37°23N 50°11E 45 B6
Şāfītā Syria 34°48N 36°7E 44 C3
Safipur India 26°44N 80°21E 43 F9
Safune Samoa 13°25S 172°21W 59 b
Şafwān Iraq 30°7N 47°43E 44 D5
Sag Harbor U.S.A. 41°0N 72°18W 83 F12
Saga Japan 33°15N 130°16E 31 H5
Saga □ Japan 33°15N 130°20E 31 H5
Sagae Japan 38°22N 140°17E 30 E10
Sagaing Burma 21°52N 95°59E 41 J19
Sagamore U.S.A. 40°46N 79°14W 82 F5
Saganaga L. Canada 48°14N 90°52W 80 A8
Sagar Karnataka, India 14°14N 75°6E 40 M9
Sagar Mad. P., India 23°50N 78°44E 43 H8
Sagara, L. Tanzania 5°20S 31°0E 54 D3
Sagarmatha = Everest, Mt.
  Nepal 28°5N 86°58E 43 E12
Sagarmatha △ Nepal 27°55N 86°45E 43 F12
Saginaw U.S.A. 43°26N 83°56W 81 D12
Saginaw B. U.S.A. 43°50N 83°40W 81 D12
Saglouc = Salluit
  Canada 62°14N 75°38W 69 E16
Sagone France 42°7N 8°42E 20 E8
Sagua la Grande Cuba 22°50N 80°10W 88 B3
Saguache U.S.A. 38°5N 106°8W 76 G10
Saguaro △ U.S.A. 32°12N 110°38W 77 K8
Saguenay → Canada 48°22N 71°0W 73 C5
Sagunt Spain 39°42N 0°18W 21 C5
Sagunto = Sagunt Spain 39°42N 0°18W 21 C5
Sagwara India 23°41N 74°1E 42 H6
Sahagún Spain 42°18N 5°2W 21 A3
Saḥam al Jawlān Syria 32°45N 35°55E 46 C4
Sahamandrevo Madag. 23°15S 45°35E 57 C8
Sahand, Kūh-e Iran 37°44N 46°27E 44 B5
Sahara Africa 23°0N 5°0E 50 D6
Saharan Atlas = Saharien, Atlas
  Algeria 33°30N 1°0E 50 B6
Saharanpur India 29°58N 77°33E 42 E7
Saharien, Atlas Algeria 33°30N 1°0E 50 B6
Saharsa India 25°53N 86°36E 43 G12
Sahasinaka Madag. 21°49S 47°49E 57 C8
Sahaswan India 28°5N 78°45E 43 E8
Saheira, W. el → Egypt 30°5N 33°25E 46 E2
Sahel Africa 16°0N 5°0E 50 E5
Sahibganj India 25°12N 87°40E 43 G12
Sāhilīyah Iraq 33°43N 42°42E 44 C4
Sahiwal Pakistan 30°45N 73°8E 42 D5
Şahneh Iran 34°29N 47°41E 44 C5
Sahrawi = Western Sahara ■
  Africa 25°0N 13°0W 50 D3
Sahuaripa Mexico 29°3N 109°14W 86 B3
Sahuarita U.S.A. 31°57N 110°58W 77 L8
Sahuayo de Díaz Mexico 20°4N 102°43W 86 C4
Sai → India 25°39N 82°47E 43 G10
Sai Buri Thailand 6°43N 101°45E 39 J3
Sai Kung China 22°23N 114°16E 33 G11
Sai Twong △ Thailand 15°56N 101°10E 38 E3
Sai Yok △ Thailand 14°25N 98°40E 38 E2
Saibai I. Australia 9°25S 142°40E 62 a
Sa'id Bundās Sudan 8°24N 24°48E 51 G10
Sa'īdābād = Sīrjān Iran 29°30N 55°45E 45 D7
Sa'īdābād Iran 36°8N 54°11E 45 B7
Sa'īdīyeh Iran 36°20N 48°55E 45 B6
Saidpur Bangla. 25°48N 89°0E 41 G16
Saidpur India 25°33N 83°11E 43 G10
Saidu Sharif Pakistan 34°43N 72°24E 43 B5
Saigō Japan 36°12N 133°20E 31 F6
Saigon = Thanh Pho Ho Chi Minh
  Vietnam 10°58N 106°40E 39 G6
Saijō Japan 33°55N 133°11E 31 H6
Saikai △ Japan 33°12N 129°36E 31 H4
Saikanosy Masoala
  Madag. 15°45S 50°10E 57 B9
Saikhoa Ghat India 27°50N 95°40E 41 F19
Saiki Japan 32°58N 131°51E 31 H5
Şā'īl Si. Arabia 27°28N 41°45E 44 E4
Sailana India 23°28N 74°55E 42 H6
Sailolof Indonesia 1°15S 130°46E 37 E8
Saimaa Finland 61°15N 28°15E 8 F23
Saimen = Saimaa
  Finland 61°15N 28°15E 8 F23
Şa'in Dezh Iran 36°40N 46°25E 44 B5
St. Abb's Head U.K. 55°55N 2°8W 11 F6
St. Alban's Canada 47°51N 55°50W 73 C8
St. Albans U.K. 51°45N 0°19W 13 F7
St. Albans Vt., U.S.A. 44°49N 73°5W 83 B11
St. Albans W. Va.,
  U.S.A. 38°23N 81°50W 81 F13
St. Alban's Head U.K. 50°34N 2°4W 13 G5
St. Albert Canada 53°37N 113°32W 70 C6
St-André Réunion 20°57S 55°39E 53 c
St. Andrew's Canada 47°45N 59°15W 73 C8
St. Andrews U.K. 56°20N 2°47W 11 E6
St-Anicet Canada 45°8N 74°22W 83 A10
St. Annes Canada 49°40N 96°39W 71 D9
St. Ann's B. Canada 46°22N 60°25W 73 C7
St. Ann's Bay Jamaica 18°26N 77°12W 88 a
St. Anthony Canada 51°22N 55°35W 73 B8
St. Anthony U.S.A. 43°58N 111°41W 76 E8
St-Antoine Canada 46°22N 64°45W 73 C7
St. Arnaud Australia 36°40S 143°16E 63 F3
St-Augustin Canada 51°13N 58°38W 73 B8
St-Augustin → Canada 51°16N 58°40W 73 B8
St. Augustine U.S.A. 29°54N 81°19W 85 G14
St. Austell U.K. 50°20N 4°47W 13 G3
St. Barbe Canada 51°12N 56°46W 73 B8
St-Barthélemy W. Indies 17°50N 62°50W 89 C7
St. Bees Hd. U.K. 54°31N 3°38W 12 C4
St. Bees I. Australia 20°56S 149°26E 62 b
St-Benoît Réunion 21°2S 55°43E 53 c
St. Bride's Canada 46°56N 54°10W 73 C9
St. Brides B. U.K. 51°49N 5°9W 13 F2
St-Brieuc France 48°30N 2°46W 20 B2

St. Catharines Canada 43°10N 79°15W 82 C5
St. Catherine I. U.S.A. 31°40N 81°10W 85 F14
St. Catherine's Pt. U.K. 50°34N 1°18W 13 G6
St-Chamond France 45°28N 4°31E 20 D6
St. Charles Ill., U.S.A. 41°54N 88°19W 80 E9
St. Charles Md., U.S.A. 38°36N 76°56W 81 F15
St. Charles Mo., U.S.A. 38°47N 90°29W 80 F8
St. Charles Va., U.S.A. 36°48N 83°4W 81 G12
St. Christopher-Nevis = St. Kitts &
  Nevis ■ W. Indies 17°20N 62°40W 89 C7
St. Clair Mich., U.S.A. 42°50N 82°30W 82 D2
St. Clair Pa., U.S.A. 40°43N 76°12W 83 F8
St. Clair → U.S.A. 42°38N 82°31W 82 D2
St. Clair, L. N. Amer. 42°27N 82°39W 82 D2
St. Clairsville U.S.A. 40°5N 80°54W 82 F4
St. Claude Canada 49°40N 98°20W 71 D9
St. Clears U.K. 51°49N 4°31E 13 F3
St. Cloud Fla., U.S.A. 28°15N 81°17W 85 G14
St. Cloud Minn., U.S.A. 45°34N 94°10W 80 C6
St. Cricq, C. Australia 25°17S 113°6E 61 E1
St. Croix U.S. Virgin Is. 17°45N 64°45W 89 C7
St. Croix → U.S.A. 44°45N 92°48W 80 C7
St. Croix Falls U.S.A. 45°24N 92°38W 80 C7
St. David's Canada 48°12N 58°52W 73 C8
St. David's U.K. 51°53N 5°16W 13 F2
St. David's Head U.K. 51°54N 5°19W 13 F2
St-Denis France 48°56N 2°20E 20 B5
St-Denis Réunion 20°52S 55°27E 53 c
St-Denis ✈ (RUN) Réunion 20°53S 55°32E 53 c
St-Dizier France 48°38N 4°56E 20 B6
St. Elias, Mt. U.S.A. 60°18N 140°56W 68 E3
St. Elias Mts. N. Amer. 60°33N 139°28W 70 A1
St-Étienne France 45°27N 4°22E 20 D6
St. Eugène Canada 45°30N 74°28W 83 A10
St. Eustatius W. Indies 17°20N 63°0W 89 C7
St-Félicien Canada 48°40N 72°25W 72 C5
St-Flour France 45°2N 3°6E 20 D5
St. Francis Canada 39°47N 101°48W 80 F3
St. Francis → U.S.A. 34°38N 90°36W 85 D9
St. Francis, C. S. Africa 34°14S 24°49E 56 E3
St. Francisville U.S.A. 30°47N 91°23W 84 F9
St-François, L. Canada 45°10N 74°22W 83 A10
St-Gabriel Canada 46°17N 73°24W 72 C5
St. Gallen = Sankt Gallen
  Switz. 47°26N 9°22E 20 C8
St-Gaudens France 43°6N 0°44E 20 E4
St. George Australia 28°1S 148°30E 63 D4
St. George N.B., Canada 45°11N 66°50W 73 C6
St. George Ont., Canada 43°15N 80°15W 82 C4
St. George S.C., U.S.A. 33°11N 80°35W 85 E14
St. George Utah, U.S.A. 37°6N 113°35W 77 H7
St. George, C. Canada 48°30N 59°16W 73 C8
St. George, C. U.S.A. 29°40N 85°5W 85 G12
St. George I. U.S.A. 56°35N 169°35W 74 D6
St. George Ra. Australia 18°40S 125°0E 60 C4
St. George's Canada 48°26N 58°31W 73 C8
St-Georges Canada 46°8N 70°40W 73 C5
St. George's Grenada 12°5N 61°43W 89 D7
St. George's B. Canada 48°24N 58°53W 73 C8
St. Georges Basin N.S.W.,
  Australia 35°7S 150°36E 63 F5
St. Georges Basin W. Austral.,
  Australia 15°23S 125°2E 60 C4
St. George's Channel
  Europe 52°0N 6°0W 10 E6
St. Georges Hd.
  Australia 35°12S 150°42E 63 F5
St. Gotthard P. = San Gottardo, P.
  del Switz. 46°33N 8°33E 20 C8
St. Helena Atl. Oc. 15°58S 5°42W 48 H3
St. Helena U.S.A. 38°30N 122°28W 76 G2
St. Helena, Mt. U.S.A. 38°40N 122°36W 78 G4
St. Helena B. S. Africa 32°40S 18°10E 56 E2
St. Helens Australia 41°20S 148°15E 63 G4
St. Helens U.K. 53°27N 2°44W 12 D5
St. Helens U.S.A. 45°52N 122°48W 78 E4
St. Helens, Mt. U.S.A. 46°12N 122°12W 78 D4
St. Helier U.K. 49°10N 2°7W 13 H5
St-Hubert Belgium 50°2N 5°23E 15 D5
St-Hubert Canada 45°29N 73°25W 83 A11
St-Hyacinthe Canada 45°40N 72°58W 72 C5
St. Ignace U.S.A. 45°52N 84°44W 81 C11
St. Ignace I. Canada 48°45N 88°0W 72 C2
St. Ignatius U.S.A. 47°19N 114°6W 76 C6
St. Ives Cambs., U.K. 52°20N 0°4W 13 E7
St. Ives Corn., U.K. 50°12N 5°30W 13 G2
St. James U.S.A. 43°59N 94°38W 80 D6
St-Jean → Canada 50°17N 64°20W 73 B7
St-Jean, L. Canada 48°40N 72°0W 73 C5
St-Jean-Port-Joli Canada 47°15N 70°13W 73 C5
St-Jean-sur-Richelieu
  Canada 45°20N 73°20W 83 A11
St-Jérôme Canada 45°47N 74°0W 72 C5
St. John Canada 45°20N 66°8W 73 C6
St. John U.S.A. 38°0N 98°46W 80 F4
St. John → N. Amer. 45°12N 66°5W 81 C20
St. John, C. Canada 50°0N 55°32W 73 C8
St. John I. U.S. Virgin Is. 18°20N 64°42W 89 e
St. John's Antigua & B. 17°6N 61°51W 89 C7
St. John's Canada 47°35N 52°40W 73 C9
St. Johns Ariz., U.S.A. 34°30N 109°22W 77 J9
St. Johns Mich., U.S.A. 43°0N 84°33W 81 D11
St. John's Pt. Ireland 54°34N 8°27W 10 B3
St. Johns → U.S.A. 30°24N 81°24W 85 F14
St. Johnsbury U.S.A. 44°25N 72°1W 83 B12
St. Johnsville U.S.A. 43°0N 74°43W 83 C10
St. Joseph Canada 43°24N 81°42W 82 C3
St-Joseph Martinique 14°39N 61°4W 88 c
St-Joseph Réunion 21°22S 55°37E 53 c
St. Joseph La., U.S.A. 31°55N 91°14W 84 F9
St. Joseph Mo., U.S.A. 39°46N 94°50W 80 F6
St. Joseph → U.S.A. 42°7N 86°29W 80 D10
St. Joseph, I. Canada 46°12N 83°58W 72 C3
St. Joseph, L. Canada 51°10N 90°35W 72 B1
St-Jovite Canada 46°8N 74°38W 72 C5
St. Kilda U.K. 57°49N 8°34W 14 C2
St. Kitts & Nevis ■
  W. Indies 17°20N 62°40W 89 C7

St. Laurent Canada 50°25N 97°58W 71 C9
St. Lawrence Australia 22°16S 149°31E 62 C4
St. Lawrence Canada 46°54N 55°23W 73 C8
St. Lawrence → Canada 49°30N 66°0W 73 C6
St. Lawrence, Gulf of
  Canada 48°25N 62°0W 73 C7
St. Lawrence I. U.S.A. 63°30N 170°30W 74 C5
St. Lawrence Islands △
  Canada 44°27N 75°52W 83 B9
St. Léonard Canada 47°12N 67°58W 73 C6
St-Leu Réunion 21°9S 55°18E 53 c
St-Lô France 49°7N 1°5W 20 B3
St-Louis Guadeloupe 15°56N 61°19W 88 b
St-Louis Réunion 21°16S 55°25E 53 c
St. Louis Senegal 16°8N 16°27W 50 E2
St. Louis U.S.A. 38°37N 90°11W 80 F8
St. Louis → U.S.A. 46°44N 92°9W 80 B7
St. Lucia ■ W. Indies 14°0N 60°57W 89 f
St. Lucia, L. S. Africa 28°5S 32°30E 57 D5
St. Lucia Channel
  W. Indies 14°15N 61°0W 89 D7
St. Maarten ☑ W. Indies 18°0N 63°5W 89 C7
St. Magnus B. U.K. 60°25N 1°35W 11 A7
St-Malo France 48°39N 2°1W 20 B2
St-Marc Haiti 19°10N 72°41W 89 C5
St. Maries U.S.A. 47°19N 116°35W 76 C5
St-Martin ☑ W. Indies 18°0N 63°0W 89 C7
St-Martin, C. Martinique 14°52N 61°14W 88 c
St. Martin, L. Canada 51°40N 98°30W 71 C9
St. Martins Barbados 13°5N 59°28W 89 g
St. Mary Pk. Australia 31°32S 138°34E 63 E2
St. Marys Australia 41°35S 148°11E 63 G4
St. Marys Canada 43°20N 81°10W 82 C3
St. Mary's Corn., U.K. 49°55N 6°18W 13 H1
St. Mary's Orkney, U.K. 58°54N 2°54W 11 C6
St. Marys Ga., U.S.A. 30°44N 81°33W 85 F14
St. Marys Pa., U.S.A. 41°26N 78°34W 82 E6
St. Mary's, C. Canada 46°50N 53°50W 73 C9
St. Mary's B. Canada 46°50N 53°50W 73 C9
St-Mathieu, Pte. France 48°20N 4°45W 20 B1
St. Matthew I. U.S.A. 60°24N 172°42W 74 C5
St-Maurice → Canada 46°21N 72°31W 72 C5
St. Mawes U.K. 50°10N 5°2W 13 G2
St-Nazaire France 47°17N 2°12W 20 C2
St. Neots U.K. 52°14N 0°15W 13 E7
St-Niklaas Belgium 51°10N 4°8E 15 C4
St-Omer France 50°45N 2°15E 20 A5
St-Pamphile Canada 46°58N 69°48W 73 C6
St-Pascal Canada 47°32N 69°48W 73 C6
St. Paul Canada 54°0N 111°17W 70 C6
St-Paul Réunion 20°59S 55°17E 53 c
St. Paul Minn., U.S.A. 44°56N 93°5W 80 C7
St. Paul Nebr., U.S.A. 41°13N 98°27W 80 E4
St-Paul → Canada 51°27N 57°42W 73 B8
St. Paul, I. Ind. Oc. 38°55S 77°34E 3 F13
St. Paul I. Canada 47°12N 60°9W 73 C7
St. Peter U.S.A. 44°20N 93°57W 80 C7
St. Peter Port U.K. 49°26N 2°33W 13 H5
St. Peters N.S., Canada 45°40N 60°53W 73 C7
St. Peters P.E.I., Canada 46°25N 62°35W 73 C7
St. Petersburg = Sankt-Peterburg
  Russia 59°55N 30°20E 9 G24
St. Petersburg U.S.A. 27°46N 82°40W 85 H13
St-Phillippe Réunion 21°21S 55°44E 53 c
St-Pie Canada 45°30N 72°54W 83 A12
St-Pierre Martinique 14°45N 61°10W 88 c
St-Pierre Réunion 21°19S 55°28E 53 c
St-Pierre St-P. & M. 46°46N 56°12W 73 C8
St-Pierre, L. Canada 46°12N 72°52W 72 C5
St-Pierre-et-Miquelon ☑
  N. Amer. 46°55N 56°10W 73 C8
St-Quentin Canada 47°30N 67°23W 73 C6
St-Quentin France 49°50N 3°16E 20 B5
St. Regis U.S.A. 47°18N 115°6W 76 C6
St. Regis Falls U.S.A. 44°40N 74°32W 83 B10
St-Sébastien, Tanjon' i
  Madag. 12°26S 48°44E 57 A8
St-Siméon Canada 47°51N 69°54W 73 C6
St. Simons I. U.S.A. 31°12N 81°15W 85 F14
St. Simons Island U.S.A. 31°9N 81°22W 85 F14
St. Stephen Canada 45°16N 67°17W 73 C6
St. Thomas Canada 42°45N 81°10W 82 D3
St. Thomas I.
  U.S. Virgin Is. 18°20N 64°55W 89 e
St-Tite Canada 46°45N 72°34W 72 C5
St-Tropez France 43°17N 6°38E 20 E7
St-Troud = St. Truiden
  Belgium 50°48N 5°10E 15 D5
St. Truiden Belgium 50°48N 5°10E 15 D5
St. Vidgeon's ◇
  Australia 14°47S 134°53E 62 A1
St. Vincent = São Vicente
  C. Verde Is. 17°0N 25°0W 50 b
St. Vincent, G. Australia 35°0S 138°0E 63 F2
St. Vincent & the Grenadines ■
  W. Indies 13°0N 61°10W 89 D7
St. Vincent Passage
  W. Indies 13°30N 61°0W 89 D7
St-Vith Belgium 50°17N 6°9E 15 D6
St. Walburg Canada 53°39N 109°12W 71 C7
Ste-Agathe-des-Monts
  Canada 46°3N 74°17W 72 C5
Ste-Anne Guadeloupe 16°13N 61°24W 88 b
Ste-Anne Seychelles 4°36S 55°31E 53 b
Ste-Anne Réunion 21°5S 55°37E 53 c
Ste-Anne-des-Monts
  Canada 49°8N 66°30W 73 C6
Ste. Genevieve U.S.A. 37°59N 90°2W 80 G9
Ste-Marguerite →
  Canada 50°9N 66°36W 73 B6
Ste-Marie Canada 46°26N 71°0W 73 C5
Ste-Marie Martinique 14°48N 61°1W 88 c
Ste-Marie, Ile = Nosy Boraha
  Madag. 16°50S 49°55E 57 B8

Ste-Rose Guadeloupe 16°20N 61°45W 88 b
Ste-Rose Réunion 21°8S 55°45E 53 c
Ste. Rose du Lac Canada 51°4N 99°30W 71 C9
Saintes France 45°45N 0°37W 20 D3
Saintes, Îs. des Guadeloupe 15°50N 61°35W 88 b
Saintfield U.K. 54°28N 5°49W 10 B6
Saintonge France 45°40N 0°50W 20 D3
Saipan N. Marianas 15°12N 145°45E 64 F6
Sairang India 23°50N 92°45E 41 H18
Sairecábur, Cerro
  Bolivia 22°43S 67°54W 94 A2
Saitama Japan 35°54N 139°38E 31 G9
Saitama □ Japan 36°25N 139°30E 31 F9
Saiyid Pakistan 33°7N 73°2E 42 C5
Sajama Bolivia 18°7S 69°0W 92 G5
Sajószentpéter Hungary 48°12N 20°44E 17 D11
Sajum India 33°20N 79°0E 43 C8
Sak → S. Africa 30°52S 20°25E 56 E3
Saka Kenya 0°9S 39°20E 54 B4
Sakai Japan 34°34N 135°27E 31 G7
Sakaide Japan 34°19N 133°50E 31 G6
Sakaiminato Japan 35°38N 133°11E 31 G6
Sakākah Si. Arabia 30°0N 40°8E 44 D4
Sakakawea, L. U.S.A. 47°30N 101°25W 80 B3
Sakami → Canada 53°40N 76°40W 72 B4
Sakami, L. Canada 53°15N 77°0W 72 B4
Sakania
  Dem. Rep. of the Congo 12°43S 28°30E 55 E2
Sakaraha Madag. 22°55S 44°32E 57 C7
Sakartvelo = Georgia ■
  Asia 42°0N 43°0E 19 F7
Sakarya Turkey 40°48N 30°25E 19 F5
Sakashima-Guntō Japan 24°46N 124°0E 31 M2
Sakata Japan 38°55N 139°50E 30 E9
Sakchu N. Korea 40°23N 125°2E 35 D13
Sakeny → Madag. 20°0S 45°25E 57 C8
Sakha □ Russia 66°0N 130°0E 29 C14
Sakhalin Russia 51°0N 143°0E 29 D15
Sakhalinskiy Zaliv
  Russia 54°0N 141°0E 29 D15
Šakiai Lithuania 54°59N 23°2E 9 J20
Sakon Nakhon Thailand 17°10N 104°9E 38 D5
Sakrand Pakistan 26°10N 68°15E 42 F3
Sakri India 26°13N 86°5E 43 F12
Sakrivier S. Africa 30°54S 20°28E 56 E3
Sakti India 22°2N 82°58E 43 H10
Sakuma Japan 35°3N 137°49E 31 G8
Sakurai Japan 34°30N 135°51E 31 G7
Sal C. Verde Is. 16°45N 22°55W 50 b
Sal Rei C. Verde Is. 16°11N 22°53W 50 b
Sala Sweden 59°58N 16°35E 9 G17
Sala Consilina Italy 40°23N 15°36E 22 D6
Sala-y-Gómez Pac. Oc. 26°28S 105°28W 65 K17
Sala y Gómez Ridge
  Pac. Oc. 25°0S 98°0W 65 K18
Salaberry-de-Valleyfield
  Canada 45°15N 74°8W 83 A10
Salada, L. Mexico 32°20N 115°40W 77 N10
Saladas Argentina 28°15S 58°40W 94 B4
Saladillo Argentina 35°40S 59°55W 94 D4
Salado → B. Aires,
  Argentina 35°44S 57°22W 94 D4
Salado → La Pampa,
  Argentina 37°30S 67°0W 96 D3
Salado → Santa Fe,
  Argentina 31°40S 60°41W 94 C3
Salado → Mexico 26°52N 99°19W 84 H5
Salaga Ghana 8°31N 0°31W 50 G5
Sālah Syria 32°40N 36°45E 46 C5
Şalāḩ ad Dīn □ Iraq 35°35N 43°35E 44 C4
Salakos Greece 36°17N 27°57E 25 C9
Salālah Oman 16°56N 53°59E 47 D5
Salamanca Chile 31°46S 70°59W 94 C1
Salamanca Spain 40°58N 5°39W 21 B3
Salamanca U.S.A. 42°10N 78°43W 82 D6
Salāmatābād Iran 35°39N 47°50E 44 C5
Salamina Greece 37°56N 23°30E 25 F10
Salamís Cyprus 35°11N 33°54E 25 D12
Salar de Atacama Chile 23°30S 68°25W 94 A2
Salar de Uyuni Bolivia 20°30S 67°45W 92 H5
Salatiga Indonesia 7°19S 110°30E 37 G14
Salavat Russia 53°21N 55°55E 18 D10
Salaverry Peru 8°15S 79°0W 92 E3
Salawati Indonesia 1°7S 130°52E 37 E8
Salaya India 22°19N 69°35E 42 H3
Salayar Indonesia 6°7S 120°30E 37 F6
S'Albufera Spain 39°47N 3°7E 24 B10
Salcombe U.K. 50°14N 3°47W 13 G4
Saldanha S. Africa 33°0S 17°58E 56 E2
Saldanha B. S. Africa 33°6S 18°0E 56 E2
Saldus Latvia 56°38N 22°30E 9 H20
Sale Australia 38°6S 147°6E 63 F4
Salé Morocco 34°3N 6°48W 50 B4
Sale U.K. 53°26N 2°19W 12 D5
Salekhard Russia 66°30N 66°35E 28 C7
Salelologa Samoa 13°41S 172°11W 59 b
Salem India 11°40N 78°11E 40 P11
Salem Ill., U.S.A. 38°38N 88°57W 80 F9
Salem Ind., U.S.A. 38°36N 86°6W 80 F10
Salem Mass., U.S.A. 42°31N 70°53W 83 D14
Salem Mo., U.S.A. 37°39N 91°32W 80 G8
Salem N.H., U.S.A. 42°45N 71°12W 83 D13
Salem N.J., U.S.A. 39°34N 75°28W 81 F16
Salem Ohio, U.S.A. 40°54N 80°52W 82 F4
Salem Oreg., U.S.A. 44°56N 123°2W 76 D2
Salem S. Dak., U.S.A. 43°44N 97°23W 80 D5
Salem Va., U.S.A. 37°18N 80°3W 81 G13
Salerno Italy 40°41N 14°47E 22 D6
Salford U.K. 53°30N 2°18W 12 D5
Salgótarján Hungary 48°5N 19°47E 17 D10
Salgueiro Brazil 8°4S 39°6W 93 E11
Salibabu Indonesia 3°51N 126°40E 37 D7
Salibea = Salybia
  Trin. & Tob. 10°43N 61°2W 93 K15
Salida U.S.A. 38°32N 106°0W 75 H18
Salihli Turkey 38°28N 28°8E 23 E13
Salihorsk Belarus 52°51N 27°27E 17 B14
Salima Malawi 13°47S 34°28E 53 G6

Salina *Italy* 38°34N 14°50E **22 E6**
Salina *Kans., U.S.A.* 38°50N 97°33W **80 F5**
Salina *Utah, U.S.A.* 38°58N 111°51W **76 G8**
Salina Cruz *Mexico* 16°10N 95°12W **87 D5**
Salinas *Brazil* 16°10S 42°10W **93 G10**
Salinas *Ecuador* 2°10S 80°58W **92 D2**
Salinas *U.S.A.* 36°40N 121°39W **78 J5**
Salinas → *Guatemala* 16°28N 90°31W **87 D6**
Salinas → *U.S.A.* 36°45N 121°48W **78 J5**
Salinas, B. de *Nic.* 11°4N 85°45W **88 D2**
Salinas, Pampa de las
Argentina 31°58S 66°42W **94 C2**
Salinas Ambargasta
Argentina 29°0S 65°0W **94 B3**
Salinas de Hidalgo
Mexico 22°38N 101°43W **86 C4**
Salinas Grandes *Argentina* 30°0S 65°0W **94 C3**
Salinas Pueblo Missions △
U.S.A. 34°6N 106°4W **77 J10**
Salinas Valley *U.S.A.* 36°15N 121°10W **78 J5**
Saline → *Ark., U.S.A.* 33°10N 92°8W **84 E8**
Saline → *Kans., U.S.A.* 38°52N 97°30W **80 F5**
Salines, C. de ses *Spain* 39°16N 3°4E **24 B10**
Salinópolis *Brazil* 0°40S 47°20W **93 D9**
Salisbury *Australia* 34°46S 138°38E **63 E2**
Salisbury *U.K.* 51°4N 1°47W **13 F6**
Salisbury *Md., U.S.A.* 38°22N 75°36W **81 F16**
Salisbury *N.C., U.S.A.* 35°40N 80°29W **85 D14**
Salisbury I. *Canada* 63°30N 77°0W **69 E16**
Salisbury Plain *U.K.* 51°14N 1°55W **13 F6**
Salkhad *Syria* 32°29N 36°43E **46 C5**
Salla *Finland* 66°50N 28°49E **8 C23**
Salliq = Coral Harbour
Canada 64°8N 83°10W **69 E15**
Sallisaw *U.S.A.* 35°28N 94°47W **84 D7**
Salluit *Canada* 62°14N 75°38W **69 E16**
Salmās *Iran* 38°11N 44°47E **44 B5**
Salmo *Canada* 49°10N 117°20W **70 D5**
Salmon *U.S.A.* 45°11N 113°54W **76 D7**
Salmon → *Canada* 54°3N 122°40W **70 C4**
Salmon → *U.S.A.* 45°51N 116°47W **76 D5**
Salmon Arm *Canada* 50°40N 119°15W **70 C5**
Salmon Gums *Australia* 32°59S 121°38E **61 F3**
Salmon Pt. *Canada* 43°52N 77°15W **82 C7**
Salmon River Mts.
U.S.A. 44°50N 115°30W **76 D6**
Salmon River Res.
U.S.A. 43°32N 75°55W **83 C9**
Salo *Finland* 60°22N 23°10E **9 F20**
Salome *U.S.A.* 33°47N 113°37W **79 M13**
Salon *India* 26°2N 81°27E **43 F9**
Salon-de-Provence *France* 43°39N 5°6E **20 E6**
Salonica = Thessaloniki
Greece 40°38N 22°58E **23 D10**
Salonta *Romania* 46°49N 21°42E **17 E11**
Salpausselkä *Finland* 61°3N 26°15E **8 F22**
Salsacate *Argentina* 31°20S 65°5W **94 C2**
Salsk *Russia* 46°28N 41°30E **19 E7**
Salso → *Italy* 37°6N 13°57E **22 F5**
Salt → *Canada* 60°0N 112°25W **70 B6**
Salt → *U.S.A.* 33°23N 112°19W **77 K7**
Salt Fork Red → *U.S.A.* 34°27N 99°21W **84 D5**
Salt L. *Australia* 30°6S 142°8E **63 E3**
Salt Lake City *U.S.A.* 40°45N 111°53W **76 F8**
Salt Range *Pakistan* 32°30N 72°25E **42 C5**
Salta *Argentina* 24°57S 65°25W **94 A2**
Salta □ *Argentina* 24°48S 65°30W **94 A2**
Saltash *U.K.* 50°24N 4°14W **13 G3**
Saltburn by the Sea *U.K.* 54°35N 0°58W **12 C7**
Saltcoats *U.K.* 55°38N 4°47W **11 F4**
Saltee Is. *Ireland* 52°7N 6°37W **10 D5**
Saltfjellet *Norway* 66°40N 15°15E **8 C16**
Saltfjorden *Norway* 67°15N 14°10E **8 C16**
Saltillo *Mexico* 25°25N 101°0W **86 B4**
Salto *Argentina* 34°20S 60°15W **94 C3**
Salto *Uruguay* 31°27S 57°50W **94 C4**
Salto → *Italy* 42°26E 12°25E **22 C5**
Salto del Guaíra *Paraguay* 24°3S 54°17W **95 A5**
Salton City *U.S.A.* 33°18N 115°57W **79 M11**
Salton Sea *U.S.A.* 33°15N 115°45W **79 M11**
Saltsburg *U.S.A.* 40°29N 79°27W **82 F5**
Saluda → *U.S.A.* 34°1N 81°4W **85 D14**
Salûm *Egypt* 31°31N 25°7E **51 B11**
Salur *India* 18°27N 83°18E **41 K13**
Salvador *Brazil* 13°0S 38°30W **93 F11**
Salvador *Canada* 52°10N 109°32W **71 C7**
Salvador, El ■
Cent. Amer. 13°50N 89°0W **88 D2**
Salvador, L. *U.S.A.* 29°43N 90°15W **85 G9**
Salween → *Burma* 16°31N 97°37E **41 L20**
Salyan *Azerbaijan* 39°33N 48°59E **46 B6**
Salybia *Trin. & Tob.* 10°43N 61°2W **93 K15**
Salzach → *Austria* 48°12N 12°56E **16 D7**
Salzburg *Austria* 47°48N 13°2E **16 E7**
Salzgitter *Germany* 52°9N 10°19E **16 B6**
Salzwedel *Germany* 52°52N 11°10E **16 B6**
Sam *India* 26°50N 70°31E **42 F4**
Sam Neua *Laos* 20°29N 104°5E **38 B5**
Sam Ngao *Thailand* 17°18N 99°0E **38 D2**
Sam Rayburn Res. *U.S.A.* 31°4N 94°5W **84 F7**
Sam Son *Vietnam* 19°44N 105°54E **38 C5**
Sam Teu *Laos* 19°59N 104°38E **38 C5**
Sama de Langreo = Langreo
Spain 43°18N 5°40W **21 A3**
Samagaltay *Russia* 50°36N 95°3E **29 D10**
Samales Group *Phil.* 6°0N 122°0E **37 C6**
Samana *India* 30°10N 76°13E **42 D7**
Samana Cay *Bahamas* 23°3N 73°45W **89 B5**
Samanga *Tanzania* 8°20S 39°13E **55 D4**
Samangān □ *Afghan.* 36°15N 68°3E **40 B5**
Samangwa
Dem. Rep. of the Congo 4°23S 24°10E **54 C1**
Samani *Japan* 42°7N 142°56E **30 C11**
Samar *Phil.* 12°0N 125°0E **37 B7**
Samara *Russia* 53°8N 50°6E **18 D9**
Samaria = Shōmrōn
West Bank 32°15N 35°13E **46 C4**
Samaria △ *Greece* 35°17N 23°58E **25 D5**
Samarinda *Indonesia* 0°30S 117°9E **36 E5**

Samarkand = Samarqand
Uzbekistan 39°40N 66°55E **28 F7**
Samarqand *Uzbekistan* 39°40N 66°55E **28 F7**
Sāmarrā' *Iraq* 34°12N 43°52E **44 C4**
Samastipur *India* 25°50N 85°50E **43 G11**
Samba
Dem. Rep. of the Congo 4°38S 26°22E **54 C2**
Samba *India* 32°32N 75°10E **43 C6**
Sambalpur *India* 21°28N 84°4E **41 J14**
Sambar, Tanjung
Indonesia 2°59S 110°19E **36 E4**
Sambas *Indonesia* 1°20N 109°20E **36 D3**
Sambava *Madag.* 14°16S 50°10E **57 A9**
Sambawizi *Zimbabwe* 18°24S 26°13E **55 F2**
Sambhajinagar = Aurangabad
India 19°50N 75°23E **40 K9**
Sambhal *India* 28°35N 78°37E **43 E8**
Sambhar *India* 26°52N 75°6E **42 F6**
Sambhar L. *India* 26°55N 75°12E **42 F6**
Sambiase *Italy* 38°58N 16°17E **22 E7**
Sambir *Ukraine* 49°30N 23°10E **17 D12**
Sambor *Cambodia* 12°46N 106°0E **38 F6**
Samborombón, B.
Argentina 36°5S 57°20W **94 D4**
Samburu △ *Kenya* 0°37N 37°51E **54 B4**
Samcheok *S. Korea* 37°30N 129°10E **35 F15**
Same *Tanzania* 4°2S 37°38E **54 C4**
Samfya *Zambia* 11°22S 29°31E **55 E2**
Samo Alto *Chile* 30°22S 71°0W **94 C1**
Samoa ■ *Pac. Oc.* 14°0S 172°0W **59 b**
Samokov *Bulgaria* 42°18N 23°35E **23 C10**
Samos *Greece* 37°45N 26°50E **23 F12**
Samothráki = Mathráki
Greece 39°48N 19°31E **25 A3**
Samothráki *Greece* 40°28N 25°28E **23 D11**
Sampacho *Argentina* 33°20S 64°50W **94 C3**
Sampalan *Indonesia* 8°41S 115°34E **37 K18**
Sampang *Indonesia* 7°11S 113°13E **37 G15**
Sampit *Indonesia* 2°34S 113°0E **36 E4**
Sampit, Teluk *Indonesia* 3°5S 113°3E **36 E4**
Samrong *Cambodia* 14°15N 103°30E **38 E4**
Samrong *Thailand* 15°10N 100°40E **38 E3**
Samsø *Denmark* 55°50N 10°35E **9 J14**
Samsun *Turkey* 41°15N 36°22E **19 F6**
Samui, Ko *Thailand* 9°30N 100°0E **39 b**
Samusole
Dem. Rep. of the Congo 10°2S 24°0E **55 E1**
Samut Prakan *Thailand* 13°40N 100°36E **38 F3**
Samut Songkhram
Thailand 13°24N 100°1E **38 F3**
Samwari *Pakistan* 28°30N 66°46E **42 E2**
San *Mali* 13°15N 4°57W **50 F5**
San → *Cambodia* 13°32N 105°57E **38 F5**
San → *Poland* 50°45N 21°51E **17 C11**
San Agustin, C. *Phil.* 6°20N 126°13E **37 C7**
San Agustín de Valle Fértil
Argentina 30°35S 67°30W **94 C2**
San Ambrosio *Pac. Oc.* 26°28S 79°53W **90 F3**
San Andreas *U.S.A.* 38°12N 120°41W **78 G6**
San Andrés, I. de
Caribbean 12°42N 81°46W **88 D3**
San Andres Mts.
U.S.A. 33°0N 106°30W **77 K10**
San Andrés Tuxtla
Mexico 18°27N 95°13W **87 D5**
San Angelo *U.S.A.* 31°28N 100°26W **84 F4**
San Anselmo *U.S.A.* 37°59N 122°34W **78 H4**
San Antonio *Belize* 16°15N 89°2W **87 D7**
San Antonio *Chile* 33°40S 71°40W **94 C1**
San Antonio *N. Mex.,*
U.S.A. 33°55N 106°52W **77 K10**
San Antonio *Tex.,*
U.S.A. 29°25N 98°29W **84 G5**
San Antonio → *U.S.A.* 28°30N 96°54W **84 G6**
San Antonio, C.
Argentina 36°15S 56°40W **94 D4**
San Antonio, C. de *Cuba* 21°50N 84°57W **88 B3**
San Antonio, Mt.
U.S.A. 34°17N 117°38W **79 L9**
San Antonio de los Baños
Cuba 22°54N 82°31W **88 B3**
San Antonio de los Cobres
Argentina 24°10S 66°17W **94 A2**
San Antonio Oeste
Argentina 40°40S 65°0W **96 E4**
San Ardo *U.S.A.* 36°1N 120°54W **78 J6**
San Augustin *Canary Is.* 27°47N 15°32W **24 G4**
San Augustine *U.S.A.* 31°32N 94°7W **84 F7**
San Bartolomé
Canary Is. 28°59N 13°37W **24 F6**
San Bartolomé de Tirajana
Canary Is. 27°54N 15°34W **24 G4**
San Benedetto del Tronto
Italy 42°57N 13°53E **22 C5**
San Benedicto, I.
Mexico 19°18N 110°49W **86 D2**
San Benito *U.S.A.* 26°8N 97°38W **84 H6**
San Benito → *U.S.A.* 36°53N 121°34W **78 J5**
San Benito Mt. *U.S.A.* 36°22N 120°37W **78 J6**
San Bernardino *U.S.A.* 34°7N 117°19W **79 L9**
San Bernardino Mts.
U.S.A. 34°10N 116°45W **79 L10**
San Bernardino Str. *Phil.* 13°0N 125°0E **37 B7**
San Bernardo *Chile* 33°40S 70°50W **94 C1**
San Bernardo, I. de
Colombia 9°45N 75°50W **92 B3**
San Blas *Mexico* 26°5N 108°46W **86 B3**
San Blas, Arch. de
Panama 9°50N 78°31W **88 E4**
San Blas, C. *U.S.A.* 29°40N 85°21W **85 G12**
San Borja *Bolivia* 14°50S 66°52W **92 F5**
San Carlos = Sant Carles
Spain 39°3N 1°34E **24 B8**
San Carlos *Argentina* 33°50S 69°0W **94 C2**

San Carlos *Chile* 36°10S 72°0W **94 D1**
San Carlos *Baja Calif. S.,*
Mexico 24°47N 112°7W **86 C2**
San Carlos *Coahuila,*
Mexico 29°1N 100°51W **86 B4**
San Carlos *Nic.* 11°12N 84°50W **88 D3**
San Carlos *Phil.* 10°29N 123°25E **37 B6**
San Carlos *Uruguay* 34°46S 54°58W **95 C5**
San Carlos *U.S.A.* 33°21N 110°27W **77 K8**
San Carlos *Venezuela* 9°40N 68°36W **92 B5**
San Carlos de Bariloche
Argentina 41°10S 71°25W **96 E2**
San Carlos de Bolívar
Argentina 36°15S 61°6W **94 D3**
San Carlos del Zulia
Venezuela 9°1N 71°55W **92 B4**
San Carlos L. *U.S.A.* 33°11N 110°32W **77 K8**
San Clemente *Chile* 35°30S 71°29W **94 D1**
San Clemente *U.S.A.* 33°26N 117°37W **79 M9**
San Clemente I. *U.S.A.* 32°53N 118°29W **79 N8**
San Cristóbal = Es Migjorn Gran
Spain 39°57N 4°3E **24 B11**
San Cristóbal *Argentina* 30°20S 61°10W **94 C3**
San Cristóbal *Dom. Rep.* 18°25N 70°6W **89 C5**
San Cristóbal *Solomon Is.* 10°30S 161°0E **58 C9**
San Cristóbal *Venezuela* 7°46N 72°14W **92 B4**
San Cristóbal de las Casas
Mexico 16°45N 92°38W **87 D6**
San Diego *Calif., U.S.A.* 32°42N 117°9W **79 N9**
San Diego *Tex., U.S.A.* 27°46N 98°14W **84 H5**
San Diego, C. *Argentina* 54°40S 65°10W **96 G3**
San Diego de la Unión
Mexico 21°28N 100°52W **86 C4**
San Diego Int. ✈ (SAN)
U.S.A. 32°44N 117°11W **79 N9**
San Dimitri, Ras *Malta* 36°4N 14°11E **25 C1**
San Dimitri Point = San Dimitri,
Ras *Malta* 36°4N 14°11E **25 C1**
San Estanislao *Paraguay* 24°39S 56°26W **94 A4**
San Felipe *Chile* 32°43S 70°42W **94 C1**
San Felipe *Mexico* 31°1N 114°52W **86 A2**
San Felipe *Venezuela* 10°20N 68°44W **92 A5**
San Felipe → *U.S.A.* 33°10N 115°49W **79 M11**
San Félix *Chile* 28°56S 70°28W **94 B1**
San Félix *Pac. Oc.* 26°23S 80°0W **90 F2**
San Fernando = Sant Ferran
Spain 38°42N 1°28E **24 C7**
San Fernando *Chile* 34°30S 71°0W **94 C1**
San Fernando *Mexico* 24°51N 98°10W **87 C5**
San Fernando *La Union,*
Phil. 16°40N 120°23E **37 A6**
San Fernando *Pampanga,*
Phil. 15°5N 120°37E **37 A6**
San Fernando *Spain* 36°28N 6°17W **21 D2**
San Fernando
Trin. & Tob. 10°16N 61°28W **93 K15**
San Fernando de Apure
Venezuela 7°54N 67°15W **92 B5**
San Fernando de Atabapo
Venezuela 4°3N 67°42W **92 C5**
San Francisco *Argentina* 31°30S 62°5W **94 C3**
San Francisco *U.S.A.* 37°46N 122°23W **78 H4**
San Francisco →
U.S.A. 32°59N 109°22W **77 K9**
San Francisco, C. de
Colombia 6°18N 77°29W **90 C3**
San Francisco, Paso de
S. Amer. 27°0S 68°0W **94 B2**
San Francisco de Macorís
Dom. Rep. 19°19N 70°15W **89 C5**
San Francisco del Monte de Oro
Argentina 32°36S 66°8W **94 C2**
San Francisco del Oro
Mexico 26°52N 105°51W **86 B3**
San Francisco Int. ✈ (SFO)
U.S.A. 37°37N 122°22W **78 H4**
San Francisco Javier = Sant
Francesc de Formentera
Spain 38°42N 1°26E **24 C7**
San Gabriel *Chile* 33°47S 70°15W **94 C1**
San Gabriel Chilac
Mexico 18°19N 97°21W **87 D5**
San Gabriel Mts.
U.S.A. 34°17N 117°38W **79 L9**
San Gavino Monreale
Italy 39°33N 8°47E **22 E3**
San German *Puerto Rico* 18°4N 67°4W **89 d**
San Gorgonio Mt.
U.S.A. 34°6N 116°50W **79 L10**
San Gottardo, P. del
Switz. 46°33N 8°33E **20 C8**
San Gregorio *Uruguay* 32°37S 55°40W **95 C4**
San Gregorio *U.S.A.* 37°20N 122°23W **78 H4**
San Guillermo △
Argentina 27°50S 69°45W **94 B2**
San Ignacio *Belize* 17°10N 89°5W **87 D7**
San Ignacio *Bolivia* 16°20S 60°55W **92 G6**
San Ignacio *Mexico* 27°27N 112°51W **86 B2**
San Ignacio *Paraguay* 26°52S 57°3W **94 B4**
San Ignacio, L. *Mexico* 26°54N 113°13W **86 B2**
San Ildefonso, C. *Phil.* 16°0N 122°1E **37 A6**
San Isidro *Argentina* 34°29S 58°31W **94 C4**
San Jacinto *U.S.A.* 33°47N 116°57W **79 M10**
San Jaime = Sant Jaume
Spain 39°54N 4°4E **24 B11**
San Javier *Misiones,*
Argentina 27°55S 55°5W **95 B4**
San Javier *Santa Fe,*
Argentina 30°40S 59°55W **94 C4**
San Javier *Bolivia* 16°18S 62°30W **92 G6**
San Javier *Chile* 35°40S 71°45W **94 D1**
San Jerónimo Taviche
Mexico 16°44N 96°35W **87 D5**
San Joaquin *U.S.A.* 36°36N 120°11W **78 J6**
San Joaquin → *U.S.A.* 38°4N 121°51W **78 G5**
San Joaquin Valley
U.S.A. 37°20N 121°0W **78 J6**
San Jon *U.S.A.* 35°6N 103°20W **77 J12**

San Jordi = Sant Jordi
Spain 39°33N 2°46E **24 B9**
San Jorge *Argentina* 31°54S 61°50W **94 C3**
San Jorge, B. *Mexico* 31°20N 113°20W **86 A2**
San Jorge, G. *Argentina* 46°0S 66°0W **96 F3**
San José = San Josep
Spain 38°55N 1°18E **24 C7**
San José *Argentina* 32°12S 58°15W **94 C4**
San José *Costa Rica* 9°55N 84°2W **88 E3**
San José *Guatemala* 14°0N 90°50W **88 D1**
San Jose *Mind. Occ., Phil.* 12°27N 121°4E **37 B6**
San Jose *Nueva Ecija,*
Phil. 15°45N 120°55E **37 A6**
San Jose *U.S.A.* 37°20N 121°53W **78 H5**
San Jose → *U.S.A.* 34°25N 106°45W **77 J10**
San Jose de Buenavista
Phil. 10°45N 121°56E **37 B6**
San José de Chiquitos
Bolivia 17°53S 60°50W **92 G6**
San José de Feliciano
Argentina 30°26S 58°46W **94 C4**
San José de Jáchal
Argentina 30°15S 68°46W **94 C2**
San José de Mayo
Uruguay 34°27S 56°40W **94 C4**
San José del Cabo
Mexico 23°3N 109°41W **86 C3**
San José del Guaviare
Colombia 2°35N 72°38W **92 C4**
San Josep *Spain* 38°55N 1°18E **24 C7**
San Juan *Argentina* 31°30S 68°30W **94 C2**
San Juan *Puerto Rico* 18°28N 66°7W **89 d**
San Juan □ *Argentina* 31°9S 69°0W **94 C2**
San Juan → *Argentina* 32°20S 67°25W **94 C2**
San Juan → *Nic.* 10°56N 83°42W **88 D3**
San Juan → *U.S.A.* 37°16N 110°26W **77 H8**
San Juan Bautista = Sant Joan de
Labritja *Spain* 39°5N 1°31E **24 B8**
San Juan Bautista
Paraguay 26°37S 57°6W **94 B4**
San Juan Bautista
U.S.A. 36°51N 121°32W **78 J5**
San Juan Capistrano
U.S.A. 33°30N 117°40W **79 M9**
San Juan Cr. → *U.S.A.* 35°40N 120°22W **78 J5**
San Juan de Guadelupe
Mexico 24°38N 102°44W **86 C4**
San Juan de la Costa
Mexico 24°20N 110°41W **86 C2**
San Juan de los Lagos
Mexico 21°15N 102°18W **86 C4**
San Juan de los Morros
Venezuela 9°55N 67°21W **92 B5**
San Juan del Norte *Nic.* 10°58N 83°40W **88 D3**
San Juan del Norte, B. de
Nic. 11°0N 83°40W **88 D3**
San Juan del Río *Mexico* 20°23N 100°0W **87 C5**
San Juan del Sur *Nic.* 11°20N 85°51W **88 D2**
San Juan I. *U.S.A.* 48°32N 123°5W **78 B3**
San Juan Island △
U.S.A. 48°35N 123°8W **78 B4**
San Juan Mts. *U.S.A.* 37°30N 107°0W **77 H10**
San Justo *Argentina* 30°47S 60°30W **94 C3**
San Kamphaeng *Thailand* 18°45N 99°8E **38 C2**
San Lázaro, C. *Mexico* 24°50N 112°18W **86 C2**
San Leandro *U.S.A.* 37°42N 122°9W **78 H4**
San Lorenzo = Sant Llorenç des
Cardassar *Spain* 39°37N 3°17E **24 B10**
San Lorenzo *Argentina* 32°45S 60°45W **94 C3**
San Lorenzo *Ecuador* 1°15N 78°50W **92 C3**
San Lorenzo *Paraguay* 25°20S 57°32W **94 B4**
San Lorenzo → *Mexico* 24°15N 107°24W **86 C3**
San Lorenzo, I. *Mexico* 28°38N 112°51W **86 B2**
San Lorenzo, Mte.
Argentina 47°40S 72°20W **96 F2**
San Lucas = Cabo San Lucas
Mexico 22°53N 109°54W **86 C3**
San Lucas *Bolivia* 20°5S 65°7W **92 H5**
San Lucas *Mexico* 27°10N 112°14W **86 B2**
San Lucas *U.S.A.* 36°8N 121°1W **78 J5**
San Lucas, C. *Mexico* 22°52N 109°53W **86 C3**
San Luis *Argentina* 33°20S 66°20W **94 C2**
San Luis *Cuba* 22°17N 83°46W **88 B3**
San Luis *Guatemala* 16°14N 89°27W **88 C2**
San Luis *Ariz., U.S.A.* 32°29N 114°47W **77 K6**
San Luis *Colo., U.S.A.* 37°12N 105°25W **77 H11**
San Luis □ *Argentina* 34°0S 66°0W **94 C2**
San Luis, I. *Mexico* 29°58N 114°26W **86 B2**
San Luis, Sierra de
Argentina 32°30S 66°10W **94 C2**
San Luis de la Paz
Mexico 21°18N 100°31W **86 C4**
San Luis Obispo *U.S.A.* 35°17N 120°40W **79 K6**
San Luis Potosí *Mexico* 22°9N 100°59W **86 C4**
San Luis Potosí □ *Mexico* 23°0N 101°0W **86 C4**
San Luis Res. *U.S.A.* 37°4N 121°5W **78 H5**
San Luis Río Colorado
Mexico 32°29N 114°58W **86 A2**
San Manuel *U.S.A.* 32°36N 110°38W **77 K8**
San Marcos *Guatemala* 14°59N 91°52W **88 D1**
San Marcos *Calif.,*
U.S.A. 33°9N 117°10W **79 M9**
San Marcos *Tex., U.S.A.* 29°53N 97°56W **84 G6**
San Marino *San Marino* 43°55N 12°30E **16 G7**
San Marino ■ *Europe* 43°56N 12°25E **22 C5**
San Martín *Antarctica* 68°11S 67°0W **5 C17**
San Martín → *Bolivia* 13°8S 63°43W **92 F6**
San Martín, L. *Argentina* 48°50S 72°50W **96 F2**
San Martin de los Andes
Argentina 40°10S 71°20W **96 E2**
San Mateo = Sant Mateu
Spain 39°3N 1°23E **24 B7**
San Mateo *U.S.A.* 37°34N 122°19W **78 H4**
San Matías *Bolivia* 16°25S 58°20W **92 G7**
San Matías, G. *Argentina* 41°30S 64°0W **96 E4**

San Miguel = Sant Miquel
Spain 39°3N 1°26E **24 B7**
San Miguel *El Salv.* 13°30N 88°12W **88 D2**
San Miguel *Panama* 8°27N 78°55W **88 E4**
San Miguel *U.S.A.* 35°45N 120°42W **78 K6**
San Miguel → *Bolivia* 13°52S 63°56W **92 F6**
San Miguel de Tucumán
Argentina 26°50S 65°20W **94 B2**
San Miguel del Monte
Argentina 35°23S 58°50W **94 D4**
San Miguel I. *U.S.A.* 34°2N 120°23W **79 L6**
San Nicolás *Canary Is.* 27°58N 15°47W **24 G4**
San Nicolás de los Arroyos
Argentina 33°25S 60°10W **94 C3**
San Nicolás I. *U.S.A.* 33°15N 119°30W **79 M7**
San Onofre *U.S.A.* 33°22N 117°34W **79 M9**
San Pablo *Bolivia* 21°43S 66°38W **94 A2**
San Pablo *U.S.A.* 37°58N 122°21W **78 H4**
San Pedro *B. Aires,*
Argentina 33°40S 59°40W **94 C4**
San Pedro *Misiones,*
Argentina 26°30S 54°10W **95 B5**
San Pedro *Chile* 33°54S 71°28W **94 C1**
San Pedro *Ivory C.* 4°50N 6°33W **50 H4**
San Pedro *Mexico* 23°55N 110°17W **86 C3**
San Pedro □ *Paraguay* 24°0S 57°0W **94 A4**
San Pedro → *Chihuahua,*
Mexico 28°20N 106°10W **86 B3**
San Pedro → *Nayarit,*
Mexico 21°45N 105°30W **86 C3**
San Pedro → *U.S.A.* 32°59N 110°47W **77 K8**
San Pedro, Pta. *Chile* 25°30S 70°38W **94 B1**
San Pedro Channel
U.S.A. 33°30N 118°25W **79 M8**
San Pedro de Atacama
Chile 22°55S 68°15W **94 A2**
San Pedro de Jujuy
Argentina 24°12S 64°55W **94 A3**
San Pedro de las Colonias
Mexico 25°45N 102°59W **86 B4**
San Pedro de Macorís
Dom. Rep. 18°30N 69°18W **89 C6**
San Pedro del Norte *Nic.* 13°4N 84°33W **88 D3**
San Pedro del Paraná
Paraguay 26°43S 56°13W **94 B4**
San Pedro Mártir, Sierra
Mexico 31°0N 115°30W **86 A1**
San Pedro Mártir △
Mexico 31°0N 115°21W **86 A1**
San Pedro Ocampo = Melchor
Ocampo *Mexico* 24°51N 101°39W **86 C4**
San Pedro Pochutla
Mexico 15°44N 96°28W **87 D5**
San Pedro Sula *Honduras* 15°30N 88°0W **88 C2**
San Pietro *Italy* 39°8N 8°17E **22 E3**
San Rafael *Argentina* 34°40S 68°21W **94 C2**
San Rafael *Calif., U.S.A.* 37°58N 122°32W **78 H4**
San Rafael *N. Mex.,*
U.S.A. 35°7N 107°53W **77 J10**
San Rafael Mt. *U.S.A.* 34°41N 119°52W **79 L7**
San Rafael Mts. *U.S.A.* 34°40N 119°50W **79 L7**
San Ramón de la Nueva Orán
Argentina 23°10S 64°20W **94 A3**
San Remo *Italy* 43°49N 7°46E **20 E7**
San Roque *Argentina* 28°25S 58°45W **94 B4**
San Roque *Spain* 36°17N 5°21W **21 D3**
San Rosendo *Chile* 37°16S 72°43W **94 D1**
San Saba *U.S.A.* 31°12N 98°43W **84 F5**
San Salvador *El Salv.* 13°40N 89°10W **88 D2**
San Salvador de Jujuy
Argentina 24°10S 64°48W **94 A3**
San Salvador I. *Bahamas* 24°0N 74°40W **89 B5**
San Sebastián = Donostia-San
Sebastián *Spain* 43°17N 1°58W **21 A5**
San Sebastián *Argentina* 53°10S 68°30W **96 G3**
San Sebastián *Puerto Rico* 18°20N 66°59W **89 d**
San Sebastián de la Gomera
Canary Is. 28°5N 17°7W **24 F2**
San Serra = Son Serra
Spain 39°43N 3°13E **24 B10**
San Severo *Italy* 41°41N 15°23E **22 C6**
San Simeon *U.S.A.* 35°39N 121°11W **78 K5**
San Simon *U.S.A.* 32°16N 109°14W **77 K9**
San Telmo = Sant Elm
Spain 39°35N 2°21E **24 B9**
San Telmo *Mexico* 30°58N 116°6W **86 A1**
San Tiburcio *Mexico* 24°8N 101°32W **86 C4**
San Valentin, Mte. *Chile* 46°30S 73°30W **96 F2**
San Vicente de Cañete
Peru 13°8S 76°30W **92 F3**
San Vicente de la Barquera
Spain 43°23N 4°29W **21 A3**
San Vito *Costa Rica* 8°50N 82°58W **88 E3**
Sana' *Yemen* 15°27N 44°12E **47 D3**
Sana → *Bos.-H.* 45°3N 16°23E **16 F9**
Sanae IV *Antarctica* 70°20S 9°0W **5 D2**
Sanaga → *Cameroon* 3°35N 9°38E **52 D1**
Sanak I. *U.S.A.* 54°25N 162°40W **74 E7**
Sanaloa, Presa *Mexico* 24°50N 107°20W **86 C3**
Sanana *Indonesia* 2°4S 125°58E **37 E7**
Sanand *India* 22°59N 72°25E **42 H5**
Sanandaj *Iran* 35°18N 47°1E **44 C5**
Sanandita *Bolivia* 21°40S 63°45W **94 A3**
Sanawad *India* 22°11N 76°5E **42 H7**
Sancellas = Sencelles
Spain 39°39N 2°54E **24 B9**
Sanchahe *China* 44°50N 126°2E **35 B14**
Sánchez *Dom. Rep.* 19°15N 69°36W **89 C6**
Sanchor *India* 24°45N 71°55E **42 G4**
Sancti Spíritus *Cuba* 21°52N 79°33W **88 B4**
Sancy, Puy de *France* 45°32N 2°50E **20 D5**
Sand → Polokwane →
S. Africa 22°25S 30°5E **57 C5**
Sand Hills *U.S.A.* 42°10N 101°30W **80 D3**
Sand Lakes △ *Canada* 57°51N 98°32W **71 B9**
Sand Springs *U.S.A.* 36°9N 96°7W **84 C6**
Sanda *Japan* 34°53N 135°14E **31 G7**

Sandakan *Malaysia* 5°53N 118°4E **36 C5**
Sandan = Sambor
  Cambodia 12°46N 106°0E **38 F6**
Sandanski *Bulgaria* 41°35N 23°16E **23 D10**
Sanday *U.K.* 59°16N 2°31W **11 B6**
Sandefjord *Norway* 59°10N 10°15E **9 G14**
Sanders *U.S.A.* 35°13N 109°20W **77 J9**
Sanderson *U.S.A.* 30°9N 102°24W **84 F3**
Sandersville *U.S.A.* 32°59N 82°48W **85 E13**
Sandfire Roadhouse
  Australia 19°45S 121°15E **60 C3**
Sandfly L. *Canada* 55°43N 106°6W **71 B7**
Sandfontein *Namibia* 23°48S 19°1E **56 C2**
Sandheads, The *India* 21°10N 88°20E **43 J13**
Sandía *Peru* 14°10S 69°30W **92 F5**
Sandila *India* 27°5N 80°31E **43 F9**
Sandnes *Norway* 58°50N 5°45E **9 G11**
Sandnessjøen *Norway* 66°2N 12°38E **8 C15**
Sandoa
  Dem. Rep. of the Congo 9°41S 23°0E **52 F4**
Sandomierz *Poland* 50°40N 21°43E **17 C11**
Sandover → *Australia* 21°43S 136°32E **62 C2**
Sandoway = Thandwe
  Burma 18°20N 94°30E **41 K19**
Sandoy *Færoe Is.* 61°52N 6°46W **8 F9**
Sandpoint *U.S.A.* 48°17N 116°33W **76 B5**
Sandray *U.K.* 56°53N 7°31W **11 E1**
Sandringham *U.K.* 52°51N 0°31E **12 E8**
Sandstone *Australia* 27°59S 119°16E **61 E2**
Sandusky *Mich., U.S.A.* 43°25N 82°50W **82 C2**
Sandusky *Ohio, U.S.A.* 41°27N 82°42W **82 E2**
Sandveld *Namibia* 21°25S 20°0E **56 C3**
Sandviken *Sweden* 60°38N 16°46E **8 F17**
Sandwich, C. *Australia* 18°14S 146°18E **62 B4**
Sandwich B. *Canada* 53°40N 57°15W **73 B8**
Sandwich B. *Namibia* 23°25S 14°20E **56 C1**
Sandy *Oreg., U.S.A.* 45°24N 122°16W **78 E4**
Sandy *Pa., U.S.A.* 41°6N 78°46W **82 E6**
Sandy *Utah, U.S.A.* 40°32N 111°50W **76 F8**
Sandy Bay *Canada* 55°31N 102°19W **71 B8**
Sandy Bight *Australia* 33°50S 123°20E **61 F3**
Sandy C. *Queens.,*
  Australia 24°42S 153°15E **62 C5**
Sandy C. *Tas., Australia* 41°25S 144°45E **63 G3**
Sandy Cay *Bahamas* 23°13N 75°18W **89 B4**
Sandy Cr. → *Australia* 31°54S 145°18E **63 B4**
Sandy Cr. → *U.S.A.* 41°51N 109°47W **76 F9**
Sandy Creek *U.S.A.* 43°38N 76°5W **83 C8**
Sandy L. *Canada* 53°2N 93°0W **72 B1**
Sandy Lake *Canada* 53°0N 93°15W **72 B1**
Sandy Valley *U.S.A.* 35°49N 115°38W **79 K11**
Sanford *Fla., U.S.A.* 28°48N 81°16W **85 G14**
Sanford *Maine, U.S.A.* 43°27N 70°47W **83 C14**
Sanford *N.C., U.S.A.* 35°29N 79°10W **85 D15**
Sanford → *Australia* 27°22S 115°53E **61 E2**
Sanford, Mt. *U.S.A.* 62°13N 144°8W **68 E3**
Sang-i-Masha *Afghan.* 33°8N 67°27E **42 C2**
Sanga *Mozam.* 12°22S 35°21E **55 E4**
Sanga → *Congo* 1°5S 17°0E **52 E3**
Sangamner *India* 19°37N 74°15E **40 K9**
Sangān *Iran* 34°23N 60°15E **45 C9**
Sangar *Afghan.* 32°56N 65°30E **42 C1**
Sangar *Russia* 64°2N 127°31E **29 C13**
Sangar Sarai *Afghan.* 34°27N 70°35E **42 B4**
Sangarh → *Pakistan* 30°43N 70°44E **42 D4**
Sangay *Ecuador* 2°0S 78°20W **92 D3**
Sange
  Dem. Rep. of the Congo 6°58S 28°21E **54 D2**
Sangeang *Indonesia* 8°12S 119°6E **37 F5**
Sanger *U.S.A.* 36°42N 119°33W **78 J7**
Sangerhausen *Germany* 51°28N 11°18E **16 C6**
Sanggan He → *China* 38°12N 117°15E **34 E9**
Sanggau *Indonesia* 0°5N 110°30E **36 D4**
Sangihe, Kepulauan
  Indonesia 3°0N 125°30E **37 D7**
Sangihe, Pulau *Indonesia* 3°35N 125°30E **37 D7**
Sangju *S. Korea* 36°25N 128°10E **35 F15**
Sangkapura *Indonesia* 5°52S 112°40E **36 F4**
Sangkhla Buri *Thailand* 14°57N 98°28E **38 E2**
Sangkulirang *Indonesia* 0°59N 117°58E **36 D5**
Sangla *Pakistan* 31°43N 73°23E **42 D5**
Sangli *India* 16°55N 74°33E **40 L9**
Sangmélima *Cameroon* 2°57N 12°1E **52 D2**
Sango *Zimbabwe* 18°44S 31°44E **55 F3**
Sangod *India* 24°55N 76°17E **42 G7**
Sangre de Cristo Mts.
  U.S.A. 37°30N 105°20W **77 H11**
Sangre Grande
  Trin. & Tob. 10°35N 61°8W **93 K15**
Sangrur *India* 30°14N 75°50E **42 D6**
Sangudo *Canada* 53°50N 114°54W **70 C6**
Sangue → *Brazil* 11°1S 58°39W **92 F7**
Sanibel *U.S.A.* 26°27N 82°1W **85 H13**
Sanikluaq *Canada* 56°32N 79°14W **72 A4**
Sanin-Kaigan △ *Japan* 35°39N 134°37E **31 G7**
Sanirajak = Hall Beach
  Canada 68°46N 81°12W **69 D15**
Sanjawi *Pakistan* 30°17N 68°21E **42 D3**
Sanje *Uganda* 0°49S 31°30E **54 C3**
Sanjo *Japan* 37°37N 138°57E **30 F9**
Sankh → *India* 22°15N 84°48E **43 H11**
Sankt Gallen *Switz.* 47°26N 9°22E **20 C8**
Sankt Michel = Mikkeli
  Finland 61°43N 27°15E **8 F22**
Sankt Moritz *Switz.* 46°30N 9°51E **20 C8**
Sankt-Peterburg *Russia* 59°55N 30°20E **9 G24**
Sankt Pölten *Austria* 48°12N 15°38E **16 D8**
Sankuru →
  Dem. Rep. of the Congo 4°17S 20°25E **52 E4**
Sanliurfa *Turkey* 37°12N 38°50E **44 B3**
Sanlúcar de Barrameda
  Spain 36°46N 6°21W **21 D2**
Sanmenxia *China* 34°47N 111°12E **34 G6**
Sanming *China* 26°15N 117°40E **33 D6**
Sannicandro Gargánico
  Italy 41°50N 15°34E **22 D6**
Sânnicolau Mare
  Romania 46°5N 20°39E **17 E11**

Sannieshof *S. Africa* 26°30S 25°47E **56 D4**
Sannīn, J. *Lebanon* 33°57N 35°52E **46 B4**
Sanniquellie *Liberia* 7°19N 8°38W **50 G4**
Sanok *Poland* 49°35N 22°10E **17 D12**
Sanquhar *U.K.* 55°22N 3°54W **11 F5**
Sans Souci *Trin. & Tob.* 10°50N 61°0W **93 K16**
Sant Antoni de Portmany
  Spain 38°59N 1°19E **24 C7**
Sant Carles *Spain* 39°3N 1°34E **24 B8**
Sant Elm *Spain* 39°35N 2°21E **24 B9**
Sant Feliu de Guíxols *Spain* 41°45N 3°1E **21 B7**
Sant Ferran *Spain* 38°42N 1°28E **24 C7**
Sant Francesc de Formentera
  Spain 38°42N 1°26E **24 C7**
Sant Jaume *Spain* 39°54N 4°4E **24 B11**
Sant Joan *Spain* 39°36N 3°4E **24 B10**
Sant Joan de Labritja *Spain* 39°5N 1°31E **24 B8**
Sant Jordi *Ibiza, Spain* 38°53N 1°24E **24 C7**
Sant Jordi *Mallorca, Spain* 39°33N 2°46E **24 B9**
Sant Jordi, G. de *Spain* 40°53N 1°2E **21 B6**
Sant Llorenç des Cardassar
  Spain 39°37N 3°17E **24 B10**
Sant Mateu *Spain* 39°3N 1°23E **24 B7**
Sant Miquel *Spain* 39°3N 1°26E **24 B7**
Sant Salvador *Spain* 39°27N 3°11E **24 B10**
Santa Agnés *Spain* 39°3N 1°21E **24 B7**
Santa Ana *Bolivia* 13°50S 65°40W **92 F5**
Santa Ana *El Salv.* 14°0N 89°31W **88 D2**
Santa Ana *Mexico* 30°33N 111°7W **86 A2**
Santa Ana *U.S.A.* 33°46N 117°52W **79 M9**
Sant' Antíoco *Italy* 39°4N 8°27E **22 E3**
Santa Bárbara *Chile* 37°40S 72°1W **94 D1**
Santa Bárbara *Honduras* 14°53N 88°14W **88 D2**
Santa Bárbara *Mexico* 26°48N 105°49W **86 B3**
Santa Barbara *U.S.A.* 34°25N 119°42W **79 L7**
Santa Barbara Channel
  U.S.A. 34°15N 120°0W **79 L7**
Santa Barbara I. *U.S.A.* 33°29N 119°2W **79 M7**
Santa Catalina, Gulf of
  U.S.A. 33°10N 117°50W **79 N9**
Santa Catalina, I.
  Mexico 25°40N 110°47W **86 B2**
Santa Catalina I.
  U.S.A. 33°23N 118°25W **79 M8**
Santa Catarina □ *Brazil* 27°25S 48°30W **95 B6**
Santa Catarina, I. de
  Brazil 27°30S 48°40W **95 B6**
Santa Cecília *Brazil* 26°56S 50°18W **95 B5**
Santa Clara *Cuba* 22°20N 80°0W **88 B4**
Santa Clara *Calif.,*
  U.S.A. 37°21N 121°57W **78 H5**
Santa Clara *N.Y.,*
  U.S.A. 44°38N 74°27W **83 B10**
Santa Clara *Utah, U.S.A.* 37°8N 113°39W **77 H7**
Santa Clara de Olimar
  Uruguay 32°50S 54°54W **95 C5**
Santa Clara Valley
  U.S.A. 36°50N 121°30W **78 J5**
Santa Clarita *U.S.A.* 34°24N 118°33W **79 L8**
Santa Clotilde *Peru* 2°33S 73°45W **92 D4**
Santa Coloma de Gramenet
  Spain 41°27N 2°13E **21 B7**
Santa Cruz *Bolivia* 17°43S 63°10W **92 G6**
Santa Cruz *Chile* 34°38S 71°27W **94 C1**
Santa Cruz *Costa Rica* 10°15N 85°35W **88 D2**
Santa Cruz *Madeira* 32°42N 16°46W **24 D3**
Santa Cruz *Phil.* 14°20N 121°24E **37 B6**
Santa Cruz → *Argentina* 50°10S 68°20W **96 G3**
Santa Cruz de la Palma
  Canary Is. 28°41N 17°46W **24 F2**
Santa Cruz de la Palma ✈ (SPC)
  Canary Is. 28°40N 17°45W **24 F2**
Santa Cruz de Tenerife
  Canary Is. 28°28N 16°15W **24 F3**
Santa Cruz del Norte
  Cuba 23°9N 81°55W **88 B3**
Santa Cruz del Sur *Cuba* 20°44N 78°0W **88 B4**
Santa Cruz do Rio Pardo
  Brazil 22°54S 49°37W **95 A6**
Santa Cruz do Sul *Brazil* 29°42S 52°25W **95 B5**
Santa Cruz I. *U.S.A.* 34°1N 119°43W **79 M7**
Santa Cruz Is. *Solomon Is.* 10°30S 166°0E **58 C9**
Santa Cruz Mts. *Jamaica* 17°58N 77°43W **88 a**
Santa Domingo, Cay
  Bahamas 21°25N 75°15W **88 B4**
Santa Elena *Argentina* 30°58S 59°47W **94 C4**
Santa Elena, C.
  Costa Rica 10°54N 85°56W **88 D2**
Santa Eulària des Riu
  Spain 38°59N 1°32E **24 C8**
Santa Fé *Argentina* 31°35S 60°41W **94 C3**
Santa Fe *U.S.A.* 35°41N 105°57W **77 J11**
Santa Fé □ *Argentina* 31°50S 60°55W **94 C3**
Santa Fé do Sul *Brazil* 20°13S 50°56W **93 H8**
Santa Filomena *Brazil* 9°6S 45°50W **93 E9**
Santa Gertrudis *Spain* 39°0N 1°26E **24 C7**
Santa Inês *Brazil* 13°17S 39°48W **93 F11**
Santa Inés, I. *Chile* 54°0S 73°0W **96 G2**
Santa Isabel *Argentina* 36°10S 66°54W **94 D2**
Santa Isabel do Morro
  Brazil 11°34S 50°40W **93 F8**
Santa Lucía *Corrientes,*
  Argentina 28°58S 59°5W **94 B4**
Santa Lucía *San Juan,*
  Argentina 31°30S 68°30W **94 C2**
Santa Lucía *Uruguay* 34°27S 56°24W **94 C4**
Santa Lucia Range
  U.S.A. 36°0N 121°20W **78 K5**
Santa Luzia *C. Verde Is.* 16°50N 24°35W **50 b**
Santa Margalida *Spain* 39°42N 3°6E **24 B10**
Santa Margarita
  Argentina 38°28S 61°35W **94 D3**
Santa Margarita
  U.S.A. 35°23N 120°37W **78 K6**
Santa Margarita →
  U.S.A. 33°13N 117°23W **79 M9**
Santa Margarita, I.
  Mexico 24°27N 111°50W **86 C2**

Santa María *Argentina* 26°40S 66°0W **94 B2**
Santa Maria *Azores* 36°58N 25°6W **50 a**
Santa Maria *Brazil* 29°40S 53°48W **95 B5**
Santa Maria *C. Verde Is.* 16°31N 22°53W **50 b**
Santa María *U.S.A.* 34°57N 120°26W **79 L6**
Santa María → *Mexico* 31°0N 107°14W **86 A3**
Santa Maria, B. de
  Mexico 25°4N 108°6W **86 B3**
Santa Maria da Vitória
  Brazil 13°24S 44°12W **93 F10**
Santa María del Camí
  Spain 39°38N 2°47E **24 B9**
Santa Maria di Léuca, C.
  Italy 39°47N 18°22E **23 E8**
Santa Marta *Colombia* 11°15N 74°13W **92 A4**
Santa Marta, Sierra Nevada de
  Colombia 10°55N 73°50W **92 A4**
Santa Marta Grande, C.
  Brazil 28°43S 48°50W **95 B6**
Santa Maura = Lefkada
  Greece 38°40N 20°43E **23 E9**
Santa Monica *U.S.A.* 34°1N 118°29W **79 M8**
Santa Monica Mts. △
  U.S.A. 34°4N 118°44W **79 L8**
Santa Paula *U.S.A.* 34°21N 119°4W **79 L7**
Santa Ponça *Spain* 39°30N 2°28E **24 B9**
Santa Rosa *La Pampa,*
  Argentina 36°40S 64°17W **94 D3**
Santa Rosa *San Luis,*
  Argentina 32°21S 65°10W **94 C2**
Santa Rosa *Brazil* 27°52S 54°29W **95 B5**
Santa Rosa *Calif.,*
  U.S.A. 38°26N 122°43W **78 G4**
Santa Rosa *N. Mex.,*
  U.S.A. 34°57N 104°41W **77 J11**
Santa Rosa and San Jacinto
  Mts. △ *U.S.A.* 33°28N 116°20W **79 M10**
Santa Rosa de Copán
  Honduras 14°47N 88°46W **88 D2**
Santa Rosa de Río Primero
  Argentina 31°8S 63°20W **94 C3**
Santa Rosa del Sara
  Bolivia 17°7S 63°35W **92 G6**
Santa Rosa I. *Calif.,*
  U.S.A. 33°58N 120°6W **79 M6**
Santa Rosa I. *Fla.,*
  U.S.A. 30°20N 86°50W **85 F11**
Santa Rosa Range
  U.S.A. 41°45N 117°40W **76 F5**
Santa Rosalía *Mexico* 27°19N 112°17W **86 B2**
Santa Sylvina *Argentina* 27°50S 61°10W **94 B3**
Santa Tecla = Nueva San
  Salvador *El Salv.* 13°40N 89°18W **88 D2**
Santa Teresa *Argentina* 33°25S 60°47W **94 C3**
Santa Teresa *Australia* 24°8S 134°22E **62 C1**
Santa Teresa *Mexico* 25°17N 97°51W **87 B5**
Santa Teresa △ *Uruguay* 33°57S 53°31W **95 C5**
Santa Teresita *Argentina* 36°32S 56°41W **94 D4**
Santa Vitória do Palmar
  Brazil 33°32S 53°25W **95 C5**
Santa Ynez → *U.S.A.* 34°41N 120°36W **79 L6**
Santa Ynez Mts. *U.S.A.* 34°30N 120°0W **79 L6**
Santa Ysabel *U.S.A.* 33°7N 116°40W **79 M10**
Santai *China* 31°5N 104°58E **32 C5**
Santana *Madeira* 32°48N 16°52W **24 D3**
Santana, Coxilha de
  Brazil 30°50S 55°35W **95 C4**
Santana do Livramento
  Brazil 30°55S 55°30W **95 C4**
Santander *Spain* 43°27N 3°51W **21 A4**
Santander Jiménez
  Mexico 24°13N 98°28W **87 C5**
Santanilla, Is. *Honduras* 17°22N 83°57W **88 C3**
Santanyí *Spain* 39°20N 3°5E **24 B10**
Santaquin *U.S.A.* 39°59N 111°47W **76 G8**
Santarém *Brazil* 2°25S 54°42W **93 D8**
Santarém *Portugal* 39°12N 8°42W **21 C1**
Santaren Channel
  W. Indies 24°0N 79°30W **88 B4**
Santee *U.S.A.* 32°50N 116°58W **79 N10**
Santee → *U.S.A.* 33°7N 79°17W **85 E15**
Santiago = Río Grande de
  Santiago → *Mexico* 21°36N 105°26W **86 C3**
Santiago = São Tiago
  C. Verde Is. 15°0N 23°40W **50 b**
Santiago *Brazil* 29°11S 54°52W **95 B5**
Santiago *Canary Is.* 28°2N 17°12W **24 F2**
Santiago *Chile* 33°26S 70°40W **94 C1**
Santiago *Panama* 8°0N 81°0W **88 E3**
Santiago → *Peru* 4°27S 77°38W **92 D3**
Santiago de Compostela
  Spain 42°52N 8°37W **21 A1**
Santiago de Cuba *Cuba* 20°0N 75°49W **88 C4**
Santiago de los Caballeros
  Dom. Rep. 19°30N 70°40W **89 C5**
Santiago del Estero
  Argentina 27°50S 64°15W **94 B3**
Santiago del Estero □
  Argentina 27°40S 63°15W **94 B3**
Santiago del Teide
  Canary Is. 28°17N 16°48W **24 F3**
Santiago Ixcuintla
  Mexico 21°49N 105°13W **86 C3**
Santiago Jamiltepec
  Mexico 16°17N 97°49W **87 D5**
Santiago Papasquiaro
  Mexico 25°3N 105°25W **86 C3**
Santiago Pinotepa Nacional
  Mexico 16°19N 98°1W **87 D5**
Santiaguillo, L. de
  Mexico 24°48N 104°48W **86 C4**
Santo Amaro *Brazil* 12°30S 38°43W **93 F11**
Santo Anastácio *Brazil* 21°58S 51°39W **95 A5**
Santo André *Brazil* 23°39S 46°29W **95 A6**
Santo Ângelo *Brazil* 28°15S 54°15W **95 B5**
Santo Antão *C. Verde Is.* 16°52N 25°10W **50 b**
Santo Antônio do Içá
  Brazil 3°5S 67°57W **92 D5**

Santo Antônio do Leverger
  Brazil 15°52S 56°5W **93 G7**
Santo Domingo
  Dom. Rep. 18°30N 69°59W **89 C6**
Santo Domingo *Baja Calif.,*
  Mexico 30°43N 116°2W **86 A1**
Santo Domingo *Baja Calif. S.,*
  Mexico 25°29N 111°55W **86 B2**
Santo Domingo *Nic.* 12°14N 84°59W **88 D3**
Santo Domingo de los Colorados
  Ecuador 0°15S 79°9W **92 D3**
Santo Domingo Pueblo
  U.S.A. 35°31N 106°22W **77 J10**
Santo Tomás *Mexico* 31°33N 116°24W **86 A1**
Santo Tomás *Peru* 14°26S 72°8W **92 F4**
Santo Tomé *Argentina* 28°40S 56°5W **94 B4**
Santo Tomé de Guayana = Ciudad
  Guayana *Venezuela* 8°0N 62°30W **92 B6**
Santoña *Spain* 43°29N 3°27W **21 A4**
Santorini *Greece* 36°23N 25°27E **23 F11**
Santos *Brazil* 24°0S 46°20W **95 A6**
Santos Dumont *Brazil* 22°55S 43°10W **95 A7**
Santuario de Aves Laguna
  Colorada △ *Bolivia* 22°10S 67°45W **94 A2**
Sanur *Indonesia* 8°41S 115°15E **37 K18**
Sanwer *India* 22°59N 75°50E **42 H6**
Sanxia Shuiku *China* 30°10N 108°0E **33 C5**
Sanxiang *China* 22°21N 113°25E **33 G9**
Sanya *China* 18°14N 109°29E **38 C7**
Sanyuan *China* 34°35N 108°58E **34 G5**
São Bernardo do Campo
  Brazil 23°45S 46°34W **95 A6**
São Borja *Brazil* 28°39S 56°0W **95 B4**
São Carlos *Brazil* 22°0S 47°50W **95 A6**
São Cristóvão *Brazil* 11°1S 37°15W **93 F11**
São Domingos *Brazil* 13°25S 46°19W **93 F9**
São Filipe *C. Verde Is.* 15°2N 24°30W **50 b**
São Francisco *Brazil* 16°0S 44°50W **93 G10**
São Francisco →
  Brazil 10°30S 36°24W **93 F11**
São Francisco do Sul
  Brazil 26°15S 48°36W **95 B6**
São Gabriel *Brazil* 30°20S 54°20W **95 C5**
São Gonçalo *Brazil* 22°48S 43°5W **95 A7**
Sao Hill *Tanzania* 8°20S 35°12E **55 D4**
São João da Boa Vista
  Brazil 22°0S 46°52W **95 A6**
São João da Madeira
  Portugal 40°54N 8°30W **21 B1**
São João del Rei *Brazil* 21°8S 44°15W **95 A7**
São João do Araguaia
  Brazil 5°23S 48°46W **93 E9**
São João do Piauí *Brazil* 8°21S 42°15W **93 E10**
São Joaquim *Brazil* 28°18S 49°56W **95 B6**
São Joaquim △ *Brazil* 28°12S 49°37W **95 B6**
São Jorge *Azores* 38°38N 28°3W **50 a**
São Jorge, Pta. de
  Madeira 32°50N 16°53W **24 D3**
São José *Brazil* 27°38S 48°39W **95 B6**
São José do Norte *Brazil* 32°1S 52°3W **95 C5**
São José do Rio Preto
  Brazil 20°50S 49°20W **95 A6**
São José dos Campos
  Brazil 23°7S 45°52W **95 A6**
São Leopoldo *Brazil* 29°50S 51°10W **95 B5**
São Lourenço *Brazil* 22°7S 45°3W **95 A6**
São Lourenço → *Brazil* 17°53S 57°27W **93 G7**
São Lourenço, Pta. de
  Madeira 32°44N 16°39W **24 D3**
São Lourenço do Sul
  Brazil 31°22S 51°58W **95 C5**
São Luís *Brazil* 2°39S 44°15W **93 D10**
São Luís Gonzaga *Brazil* 28°25S 55°0W **95 B5**
São Marcos → *Brazil* 18°15S 47°37W **93 G9**
São Marcos, B. de *Brazil* 2°0S 44°0W **93 D10**
São Mateus *Brazil* 18°44S 39°50W **93 G11**
São Mateus do Sul
  Brazil 25°52S 50°23W **95 B5**
São Miguel *Azores* 37°47N 25°30W **50 a**
São Miguel do Oeste
  Brazil 26°45S 53°34W **95 B5**
São Nicolau *C. Verde Is.* 16°20N 24°20W **50 b**
São Paulo *Brazil* 23°32S 46°38W **95 A6**
São Paulo □ *Brazil* 22°0S 49°0W **95 A6**
São Paulo de Olivença
  Brazil 3°27S 68°48W **92 D5**
São Roque *Madeira* 32°46N 16°48W **24 D3**
São Roque, C. de *Brazil* 5°30S 35°16W **93 E11**
São Sebastião, I. de
  Brazil 23°50S 45°18W **95 A6**
São Sebastião do Paraíso
  Brazil 20°54S 46°59W **95 A6**
São Tiago *C. Verde Is.* 15°0N 23°40W **50 b**
São Tomé
  São Tomé & Príncipe 0°10N 6°39E **48 F4**
São Tomé *C. Verde Is.* 22°0S 40°59W **95 A7**
São Tomé & Príncipe ■
  Africa 0°12N 6°39E **49 F4**
São Vicente *Brazil* 23°57S 46°23W **95 A6**
São Vicente *C. Verde Is.* 17°0N 25°0W **50 b**
São Vicente, C. de *Portugal* 37°0N 9°0W **21 D1**
Saona, I. *Dom. Rep.* 18°10N 68°40W **89 C6**
Saône → *France* 45°44N 4°50E **20 D6**
Saonek *Indonesia* 0°22S 130°55E **37 E8**
Sapam, Ao *Thailand* 8°0N 98°26E **39 a**
Saparua *Indonesia* 3°33S 128°40E **37 E7**
Sapele *Nigeria* 5°50N 5°40E **50 G7**
Sapelo I. *U.S.A.* 31°25N 81°12W **85 F14**
Sapi △ *Zimbabwe* 15°48S 29°42E **55 F2**
Saposoa *Peru* 6°55S 76°45W **92 E3**
Sapphire *Australia* 23°28S 147°43E **62 C4**
Sappho *U.S.A.* 48°4N 124°16W **78 B2**
Sapporo *Japan* 43°0N 141°21E **30 C10**
Sapulpa *U.S.A.* 35°59N 96°5W **84 D6**
Saqqez *Iran* 36°15N 46°20E **44 B5**
Sar Dasht *Āzarbāyjān-e Gharbī,*
  Iran 36°9N 45°28E **44 B5**
Sar Dasht *Khuzestān, Iran* 32°32N 48°52E **45 C6**

Sar-e Pol □ *Afghan.* 36°20N 65°50E **40 B4**
Sar Gachīneh = Yāsūj
  Iran 30°31N 51°31E **45 D6**
Sar Planina *Macedonia* 42°0N 21°0E **23 C9**
Sara Buri = Saraburi
  Thailand 14°30N 100°55E **38 E3**
Sarāb *Iran* 37°55N 47°40E **44 B5**
Sarābādī *Iraq* 33°1N 44°48E **44 C5**
Saraburi *Thailand* 14°30N 100°55E **38 E3**
Saradiya *India* 21°34N 70°2E **42 J4**
Saragossa = Zaragoza
  Spain 41°39N 0°53W **21 B5**
Saraguro *Ecuador* 3°35S 79°16W **92 D3**
Sarahs *Turkmenistan* 36°32N 61°13E **45 B9**
Sarai Naurang *Pakistan* 32°50N 70°47E **42 C4**
Saraikela *India* 22°42N 85°56E **43 H11**
Sarajevo *Bos.-H.* 43°52N 18°26E **23 C8**
Saran, Gunung *Indonesia* 0°30S 111°25E **36 E4**
Saranac Lake *U.S.A.* 44°20N 74°10W **83 B10**
Saranac Lakes *U.S.A.* 44°20N 74°28W **83 B10**
Saranda *Tanzania* 5°45S 34°59E **54 D3**
Sarandí del Yí *Uruguay* 33°18S 55°38W **95 C4**
Sarandí Grande
  Uruguay 33°44S 56°20W **94 C4**
Sarangani B. *Phil.* 6°0N 125°13E **37 C7**
Sarangani Is. *Phil.* 5°25N 125°25E **37 C7**
Sarangarh *India* 21°30N 83°5E **41 J13**
Saransk *Russia* 54°10N 45°10E **18 D8**
Sarapul *Russia* 56°28N 53°48E **18 C9**
Sarasota *U.S.A.* 27°20N 82°32W **85 H13**
Saratoga *Calif., U.S.A.* 37°16N 122°2W **78 H4**
Saratoga *Wyo., U.S.A.* 41°27N 106°49W **76 F10**
Saratoga △ *U.S.A.* 43°0N 73°38W **83 D11**
Saratoga L. *U.S.A.* 43°1N 73°44W **83 C11**
Saratoga Springs *U.S.A.* 43°5N 73°47W **83 C11**
Saratok *Malaysia* 1°55N 111°17E **36 D4**
Saratov *Russia* 51°30N 46°2E **19 D8**
Sarāvān *Iran* 27°25N 62°15E **45 E9**
Saravane *Laos* 15°43N 106°25E **38 E6**
Sarawak □ *Malaysia* 2°0N 113°0E **36 D4**
Saray *Turkey* 41°26N 27°55E **23 D12**
Sarayköy *Turkey* 37°55N 28°54E **23 F13**
Sarbāz *Iran* 26°38N 61°19E **45 E9**
Sarbīsheh *Iran* 32°30N 59°40E **45 C8**
Sarda → *India* 27°21N 81°23E **43 F9**
Sardegna □ *Italy* 40°0N 9°0E **22 D3**
Sardhana *India* 29°9N 77°39E **42 E7**
Sardina, Pta. *Canary Is.* 28°9N 15°44W **24 F4**
Sardinia = Sardegna □
  Italy 40°0N 9°0E **22 D3**
Sardis *Turkey* 38°28N 27°58E **23 E12**
Sārdūīyeh = Dar Mazār
  Iran 29°14N 57°20E **45 D8**
Saren *Indonesia* 8°26S 115°34E **37 J18**
S'Arenal *Spain* 39°30N 2°45E **24 B9**
Sarera, G. of *Indonesia* 2°0S 135°0E **58 B6**
Sargasso Sea *Atl. Oc.* 27°0N 72°0W **66 G13**
Sargodha *Pakistan* 32°10N 72°40E **42 C5**
Sarh *Chad* 9°5N 18°23E **51 G9**
Sārī *Iran* 36°30N 53°4E **45 B7**
Saria *India* 21°38N 83°22E **43 J10**
Sariab *Pakistan* 30°6N 66°59E **42 D2**
Sarigöl *Turkey* 38°14N 28°41E **23 E13**
Sarikei *Malaysia* 2°8N 111°30E **36 D4**
Sarila *India* 25°46N 79°41E **43 G8**
Sarina *Australia* 21°22S 149°13E **62 C4**
Sarita *U.S.A.* 27°13N 97°47W **84 H6**
Sariwŏn *N. Korea* 38°31N 125°46E **35 E13**
Sarju → *India* 27°21N 81°23E **43 F9**
Sark *U.K.* 49°25N 2°22W **13 H5**
Sarköy *Turkey* 40°36N 27°6E **23 D12**
Sarkari Tala *India* 27°39N 70°52E **42 F4**
Sarlat-la-Canéda *France* 44°54N 1°13E **20 D4**
Sarmi *Indonesia* 1°49S 138°44E **37 E9**
Sarmiento *Argentina* 45°35S 69°5W **96 F3**
Särna *Sweden* 61°41N 13°8E **8 F15**
Sarnia *Canada* 42°58N 82°23W **82 D2**
Sarolangun *Indonesia* 2°19S 102°42E **36 E2**
Saronikos Kolpos
  Greece 37°45N 23°45E **23 F10**
Saros Körfezi *Turkey* 40°30N 26°15E **23 D12**
Sarpsborg *Norway* 59°16N 11°7E **9 G14**
Sarqan *Kazakhstan* 45°24N 79°55E **32 B2**
Sarre = Saar → *Europe* 49°41N 6°32E **15 E6**
Sarreguemines *France* 49°5N 7°4E **20 B7**
Sarthe → *France* 47°33N 0°31W **20 C3**
Saruna → *Pakistan* 26°31N 67°7E **42 F2**
Sarvar *India* 26°4N 75°0E **42 F6**
Sarvestān *Iran* 29°20N 53°10E **45 D7**
Sary-Tash *Kyrgyzstan* 39°44N 73°15E **28 F8**
Saryshaghan *Kazakhstan* 46°12N 73°38E **28 E8**
Sasan Gir *India* 21°10N 70°36E **42 J4**
Sasaram *India* 24°57N 84°5E **43 G11**
Sasebo *Japan* 33°10N 129°43E **31 H4**
Saser Kangri *India* 34°50N 77°50E **43 B7**
Saskatchewan □
  Canada 54°40N 106°0W **71 C7**
Saskatchewan →
  Canada 53°37N 100°40W **71 C8**
Saskatoon *Canada* 52°10N 106°38W **71 C7**
Saskylakh *Russia* 71°55N 114°1E **29 B12**
Saslaya △ *Nic.* 13°45N 85°4W **88 D2**
Sasolburg *S. Africa* 26°46S 27°49E **57 D4**
Sasovo *Russia* 54°25N 41°55E **18 D7**
Sassandra *Ivory C.* 4°55N 6°8W **50 H4**
Sassandra → *Ivory C.* 4°58N 6°5W **50 H4**
Sássari *Italy* 40°43N 8°34E **22 D3**
Sassnitz *Germany* 54°29N 13°39E **16 A7**
Sassuolo *Italy* 44°33N 10°47E **22 B4**
Sasyk, Ozero *Ukraine* 45°45N 29°20E **17 F15**
Sata-Misaki *Japan* 31°0N 130°40E **31 J5**
Satadougou *Mali* 12°25N 11°25W **50 F2**
Satakunda = Satakunta
  Finland 61°45N 23°0E **8 F20**
Satakunta *Finland* 61°45N 23°0E **8 F20**

Satara *India* 17°44N 73°58E **40 L8**
Satara *S. Africa* 24°29S 31°47E **57 C5**
Satbarwa *India* 23°55N 84°16E **43 H11**
Satevó *Mexico* 27°57N 106°7W **86 B3**
Satilla ➤ *U.S.A.* 30°59N 81°29W **85 F14**
Satka *Russia* 55°3N 59°1E **18 C10**
Satmala Hills *Andhra Pradesh, India* 19°45N 78°45E **40 K11**
Satmala Hills *Maharashtra, India* 20°15N 74°40E **40 J9**
Satna *India* 24°35N 80°50E **43 G9**
Sátoraljaújhely *Hungary* 48°25N 21°41E **17 D11**
Satpura △ *India* 22°40N 78°15E **42 H8**
Satpura Ra. *India* 21°25N 76°10E **40 J10**
Satsuna-Shotō *Japan* 30°0N 130°0E **31 K5**
Sattahip *Thailand* 12°41N 100°54E **38 F3**
Satu Mare *Romania* 47°46N 22°55E **17 E12**
Satui *Indonesia* 3°50S 115°27E **36 E5**
Satun *Thailand* 6°43N 100°2E **39 J3**
Satupa'itea *Samoa* 13°45S 172°18W **59 b**
Saturnina ➤ *Brazil* 12°15S 58°10W **92 F7**
Sauce *Argentina* 30°5S 58°46W **94 C4**
Sauceda *Mexico* 25°46N 101°19W **86 B4**
Saucillo *Mexico* 28°1N 105°17W **86 B3**
Sauda *Norway* 59°40N 6°20E **9 G12**
Sauðarkrókur *Iceland* 65°45N 19°40W **8 D4**
Saudi Arabia ■ *Asia* 26°0N 44°0E **44 B3**
Sauerland *Germany* 51°12N 7°59E **16 C4**
Saugeen ➤ *Canada* 44°30N 81°22W **82 B3**
Saugerties *U.S.A.* 42°5N 73°57W **83 D11**
Saugus *U.S.A.* 34°25N 118°32W **79 L8**
Sauk Centre *U.S.A.* 45°44N 94°57W **80 C6**
Sauk Rapids *U.S.A.* 45°35N 94°10W **80 C6**
Sault Ste. Marie *Canada* 46°30N 84°20W **72 C3**
Sault Ste. Marie *U.S.A.* 46°30N 84°21W **81 B11**
Saumlaki *Indonesia* 7°55S 131°20E **37 F8**
Saumur *France* 47°15N 0°5W **20 C3**
Saunders, C. *N.Z.* 45°53S 170°45E **59 F3**
Saunders I. *Antarctica* 57°48S 26°28W **5 B1**
Saunders Pt. *Australia* 27°52S 125°38E **61 E4**
Saurimo *Angola* 9°40S 20°12E **52 F4**
Sausalito *U.S.A.* 37°51N 122°29W **78 H4**
Savá *Honduras* 15°32N 86°15W **88 C2**
Sava ➤ *Serbia* 44°50N 20°26E **23 B9**
Savage *U.S.A.* 47°27N 104°21W **76 C11**
Savage I. = Niue *Pac. Oc.* 19°2S 169°54W **65 J11**
Savage River *Australia* 41°31S 145°14E **63 G4**
Savai'i *Samoa* 13°28S 172°24W **59 b**
Savalou *Benin* 7°57N 1°58E **50 G6**
Savane *Mozam.* 19°37S 35°8E **55 F4**
Savanna *U.S.A.* 42°5N 90°8W **80 D8**
Savanna-la-Mar *Jamaica* 18°10N 78°10W **88 a**
Savannah *Ga., U.S.A.* 32°5N 81°6W **85 E14**
Savannah *Mo., U.S.A.* 39°56N 94°50W **80 F6**
Savannah *Tenn., U.S.A.* 35°14N 88°15W **85 D10**
Savannah ➤ *U.S.A.* 32°2N 80°53W **85 E14**
Savannakhet *Laos* 16°30N 104°49E **38 D5**
Savant L. *Canada* 50°16N 90°44W **72 B1**
Savant Lake *Canada* 50°14N 90°40W **72 B1**
Savarkundla = Kundla *India* 21°21N 71°25E **42 J4**
Save ➤ *Mozam.* 21°16S 34°0E **57 C5**
Sāveh *Iran* 35°2N 50°20E **45 C6**
Savelugu *Ghana* 9°38N 0°54W **50 G5**
Savo *Finland* 62°45N 27°30E **8 E22**
Savoie □ *France* 45°26N 6°25E **20 D7**
Savolax = Savo *Finland* 62°45N 27°30E **8 E22**
Savona *Italy* 44°17N 8°30E **20 D8**
Savona *U.S.A.* 42°17N 77°13W **82 D7**
Savonlinna *Finland* 61°52N 28°53E **8 F23**
Savoy = Savoie □ *France* 45°26N 6°25E **20 D7**
Savur *Turkey* 37°34N 40°53E **44 B4**
Savusavu *Fiji* 16°34S 179°15E **59 a**
Savusavu B. *Fiji* 16°45S 179°15E **59 a**
Sawahlunto *Indonesia* 0°40S 100°52E **36 E2**
Sawai *Indonesia* 3°0S 129°5E **37 E7**
Sawai Madhopur *India* 26°0N 76°25E **42 G7**
Sawaleke *Fiji* 17°59S 179°18E **59 a**
Sawang Daen Din *Thailand* 17°28N 103°28E **38 D4**
Sawankhalok *Thailand* 17°19N 99°50E **38 D2**
Sawara *Japan* 35°55N 140°30E **31 G10**
Sawatch Range *U.S.A.* 39°0N 106°30W **76 G10**
Sawel Mt. *U.K.* 54°50N 7°2W **10 B4**
Sawi *Thailand* 10°14N 99°5E **39 G2**
Sawmills *Zimbabwe* 19°30S 28°2E **55 F2**
Sawtooth △ *U.S.A.* 44°0N 114°50W **76 D6**
Sawtooth Range *U.S.A.* 44°3N 114°58W **76 D6**
Sawu *Indonesia* 10°35S 121°50E **37 F6**
Sawu Sea *Indonesia* 9°30S 121°50E **37 F6**
Saxby ➤ *Australia* 18°25S 140°53E **62 B3**
Saxmundham *U.K.* 52°13N 1°30E **13 E9**
Saxony = Sachsen □ *Germany* 50°55N 13°10E **16 C7**
Saxony, Lower = Niedersachsen □ *Germany* 52°50N 9°0E **16 B5**
Saxton *U.S.A.* 40°13N 78°15W **82 F6**
Sayabec *Canada* 48°35N 67°41W **73 C6**
Sayaboury *Laos* 19°15N 101°45E **38 C3**
Sayán *Peru* 11°8S 77°12W **92 F3**
Sayan, Vostochnyy *Russia* 54°0N 96°0E **29 D10**
Sayan, Zapadnyy *Russia* 52°30N 94°0E **32 A4**
Sayanogorsk *Russia* 53°5N 91°23E **29 D10**
Saydā *Lebanon* 33°35N 35°25E **46 B4**
Sayhandulaan = Oldziyt *Mongolia* 44°40N 109°1E **34 B5**
Sayḩūt *Yemen* 15°12N 51°10E **47 D5**
Saylac *Somali Rep.* 11°21N 43°30E **47 E3**
Saynshand = Buyant-Uhaa *Mongolia* 44°55N 110°11E **33 B6**
Sayre *Okla., U.S.A.* 35°18N 99°38W **84 D5**
Sayre *Pa., U.S.A.* 41°59N 76°32W **83 E8**
Sayreville *U.S.A.* 40°28N 74°22W **83 F10**
Sayula *Mexico* 19°52N 103°36W **86 D4**
Sayward *Canada* 50°21N 125°55W **70 C3**

Sazanit *Albania* 40°30N 19°20E **23 D8**
Sázava ➤ *Czech Rep.* 49°53N 14°24E **16 D8**
Sazin *Pakistan* 35°35N 73°30E **43 B5**
Scafell Pike *U.K.* 54°27N 3°14W **12 C4**
Scalloway *U.K.* 60°9N 1°17W **11 A7**
Scalpay *U.K.* 57°18N 6°0W **11 D3**
Scandia *Canada* 50°20N 112°2W **70 C6**
Scandicci *Italy* 43°45N 11°11E **22 C4**
Scandinavia *Europe* 64°0N 12°0E **8 E15**
Scapa Flow *U.K.* 58°53N 3°3W **11 C5**
Scappoose *U.S.A.* 45°45N 122°53W **78 E4**
Scarba *U.K.* 56°11N 5°43W **11 E3**
Scarborough *Trin. & Tob.* 11°11N 60°42W **93 J16**
Scarborough *U.K.* 54°17N 0°24W **12 C7**
Scariff I. *Ireland* 51°44N 10°15W **10 E1**
Scarp *U.K.* 58°1N 7°8W **11 C1**
Scebeli = Shabeelle ➤ *Somali Rep.* 2°0N 44°0E **47 G3**
Schaffhausen *Switz.* 47°42N 8°39E **20 C8**
Schagen *Neths.* 52°49N 4°48E **15 B4**
Schaghticoke *U.S.A.* 52°54N 73°35W **83 D11**
Schefferville *Canada* 54°48N 66°50W **73 B6**
Schelde ➤ *Belgium* 51°15N 4°16E **15 C4**
Schell Creek Ra. *U.S.A.* 39°25N 114°40W **76 G6**
Schellsburg *U.S.A.* 40°3N 78°39W **82 F6**
Schenectady *U.S.A.* 42°49N 73°57W **83 D11**
Schenevus *U.S.A.* 42°33N 74°50W **83 D10**
Schiedam *Neths.* 51°55N 4°25E **15 C4**
Schiermonnikoog *Neths.* 53°30N 6°15E **15 A6**
Schio *Italy* 45°43N 11°21E **22 B4**
Schiphol, Amsterdam ✈ (AMS) *Neths.* 52°18N 4°45E **15 B4**
Schleswig *Germany* 54°31N 9°34E **16 A5**
Schleswig-Holstein □ *Germany* 54°30N 9°30E **16 A5**
Schœlcher *Martinique* 14°36N 61°7W **88 c**
Schoharie *U.S.A.* 42°40N 74°19W **83 D10**
Schoharie Cr. ➤ *U.S.A.* 42°57N 74°18W **83 D10**
Scholls *U.S.A.* 45°24N 122°56W **78 E4**
Schouten I. *Australia* 42°20S 148°20E **63 G4**
Schouten Is. = Supiori *Indonesia* 1°0S 136°0E **37 E9**
Schouwen *Neths.* 51°43N 3°45E **15 C3**
Schreiber *Canada* 48°45N 87°20W **72 C2**
Schroffenstein *Namibia* 27°11S 18°42E **56 D2**
Schroon Lake *U.S.A.* 43°50N 73°46W **83 C11**
Schuler *Canada* 50°20N 110°6W **71 C6**
Schumacher *Canada* 48°30N 81°16W **72 C3**
Schurz *U.S.A.* 38°57N 118°49W **76 G4**
Schuyler *U.S.A.* 41°27N 97°4W **80 E5**
Schuylerville *U.S.A.* 43°6N 73°35W **83 C11**
Schuylkill ➤ *U.S.A.* 39°53N 75°12W **83 G9**
Schuylkill Haven *U.S.A.* 40°37N 76°11W **83 F8**
Schwäbische Alb *Germany* 48°20N 9°30E **16 D5**
Schwaner, Pegunungan *Indonesia* 1°0S 112°30E **36 E4**
Schwarzrand *Namibia* 25°37S 16°50E **56 D2**
Schwarzwald *Germany* 48°30N 8°20E **16 D5**
Schwatka Mts. *U.S.A.* 67°20N 156°30W **74 B8**
Schwedt *Germany* 53°3N 14°16E **16 B8**
Schweinfurt *Germany* 50°3N 10°14E **16 C6**
Schweiz = Switzerland ■ *Europe* 46°30N 8°0E **20 C8**
Schweizer-Reneke *S. Africa* 27°11S 25°18E **56 D4**
Schwenningen = Villingen-Schwenningen *Germany* 48°3N 8°26E **16 D5**
Schwerin *Germany* 53°36N 11°22E **16 B6**
Schwyz *Switz.* 47°2N 8°39E **20 C8**
Sciacca *Italy* 37°31N 13°3E **22 F5**
Scilla *Italy* 38°15N 15°43E **22 E6**
Scilly, Isles of *U.K.* 49°56N 6°22W **13 H1**
Scioto ➤ *U.S.A.* 38°44N 83°1W **81 F12**
Scituate *U.S.A.* 42°12N 70°44W **83 D14**
Scobey *U.S.A.* 48°47N 105°25W **76 B11**
Scone *Australia* 32°5S 150°52E **63 E5**
Scone *U.K.* 56°25N 3°24W **11 E5**
Scoresbysund = Ittoqqortoormiit *Greenland* 70°20N 23°0W **4 B6**
Scotia *Calif., U.S.A.* 40°29N 124°6W **76 F1**
Scotia *N.Y., U.S.A.* 42°50N 73°58W **83 D11**
Scotia Sea *Antarctica* 56°5S 56°0W **5 B18**
Scotland *Canada* 43°1N 80°22W **82 C4**
Scotland *U.S.A.* 43°9N 97°43W **80 D5**
Scotland □ *U.K.* 57°0N 4°0W **11 E5**
Scott *Antarctica* 77°0S 165°0E **5 D11**
Scott, C. *Australia* 13°30S 129°49E **60 B4**
Scott City *U.S.A.* 38°29N 100°54W **80 F3**
Scott Glacier *Antarctica* 66°15S 100°5E **5 C8**
Scott I. *Antarctica* 67°0S 179°0E **5 C11**
Scott Is. *Canada* 50°48N 128°40W **70 C3**
Scott L. *Canada* 59°55N 106°18W **71 B7**
Scott Reef *Australia* 14°0S 121°50E **60 B3**
Scottburgh *S. Africa* 30°15S 30°47E **57 E5**
Scottdale *U.S.A.* 40°6N 79°35W **82 F5**
Scottish Borders □ *U.K.* 55°35N 2°50W **11 F6**
Scotts Valley *U.S.A.* 37°3N 122°1W **78 H4**
Scottsbluff *U.S.A.* 41°52N 103°40W **80 E2**
Scottsboro *U.S.A.* 34°40N 86°2W **85 D11**
Scottsburg *U.S.A.* 38°41N 85°47W **81 F11**
Scottsdale *Australia* 41°9S 147°31E **63 G4**
Scottsdale *U.S.A.* 33°40N 111°53W **77 K7**
Scottsville *Ky., U.S.A.* 36°45N 86°11W **80 G10**
Scottsville *N.Y., U.S.A.* 43°2N 77°47W **82 D7**
Scottville *U.S.A.* 43°58N 86°17W **80 D10**
Scranton *U.S.A.* 41°25N 75°40W **83 E9**
Scugog, L. *Canada* 44°10N 78°55W **82 B6**
Scunthorpe *U.K.* 53°36N 0°39W **12 D7**
Scutari = Shkodër *Albania* 42°4N 19°32E **23 C8**
Sea Is. *U.S.A.* 31°30N 81°7W **85 F14**
Seabrook, L. *Australia* 30°55S 119°40E **61 F2**
Seaford *Australia* 38°10S 145°11E **63 F4**
Seaford *U.S.A.* 38°39N 75°37W **81 F16**
Seaforth *Australia* 20°55S 148°57E **62 b**
Seaforth *Canada* 43°35N 81°25W **82 C3**
Seaforth, L. *U.K.* 57°52N 6°36W **11 D2**

Seagraves *U.S.A.* 32°57N 102°34W **84 E3**
Seaham *U.K.* 54°50N 1°20W **12 C6**
Seal ➤ *Canada* 59°4N 94°48W **71 B10**
Seal L. *Canada* 54°20N 61°30W **73 B7**
Sealy *U.S.A.* 29°47N 96°9W **84 G6**
Searchlight *U.S.A.* 35°28N 114°55W **79 K12**
Searcy *U.S.A.* 35°15N 91°44W **84 D9**
Searles L. *U.S.A.* 35°44N 117°21W **79 K9**
Seascale *U.K.* 54°24N 3°29W **12 C4**
Seaside *Calif., U.S.A.* 36°37N 121°50W **78 J5**
Seaside *Oreg., U.S.A.* 46°0N 123°56W **78 E3**
Seaspray *Australia* 38°25S 147°15E **63 F4**
Seattle *U.S.A.* 47°36N 122°19W **78 C4**
Seattle-Tacoma Int. ✈ (SEA) *U.S.A.* 47°27N 122°18W **78 C4**
Seba *Indonesia* 10°29S 121°50E **60 B3**
Sebago L. *U.S.A.* 43°52N 70°34W **83 C14**
Sebago Lake *U.S.A.* 43°51N 70°34W **83 C14**
Sebastián Vizcaíno, B. *Mexico* 28°0N 114°30W **86 B2**
Sebastopol = Sevastopol *Ukraine* 44°35N 33°30E **19 F5**
Sebastopol *U.S.A.* 38°24N 122°49W **78 G4**
Sebewaing *U.S.A.* 43°44N 83°27W **81 D12**
Sebha = Sabhā *Libya* 27°9N 14°29E **51 C8**
Şebinkarahisar *Turkey* 40°22N 38°28E **19 F6**
Sebring *Fla., U.S.A.* 27°30N 81°27W **85 H14**
Sebring *Ohio, U.S.A.* 40°55N 81°2W **82 F3**
Sebta = Ceuta *N. Afr.* 35°52N 5°18W **21 E3**
Sebuku *Indonesia* 3°30S 116°25E **36 E5**
Sebuku, Teluk *Malaysia* 4°0N 118°10E **36 D5**
Sechelt *Canada* 49°25N 123°42W **70 D4**
Sechura, Desierto de *Peru* 6°0S 80°30W **92 E2**
Secretary I. *N.Z.* 45°15S 166°56E **59 F1**
Secunderabad *India* 17°28N 78°30E **40 L11**
Security *U.S.A.* 38°45N 104°45W **76 G11**
Sedalia *U.S.A.* 38°42N 93°14W **80 F8**
Sedan *France* 49°43N 4°57E **20 B6**
Sedan *U.S.A.* 37°8N 96°11W **80 G5**
Seddon *N.Z.* 41°40S 174°7E **59 D5**
Seddonville *N.Z.* 41°33S 172°1E **59 D4**
Sedé Boqér *Israel* 30°52N 34°47E **46 E3**
Sedeh *Fārs, Iran* 30°45N 52°11E **45 D7**
Sedeh *Khorāsān, Iran* 33°20N 59°14E **45 C8**
Séderot *Israel* 31°32N 34°37E **46 D3**
Sédhiou *Senegal* 12°44N 15°30W **50 F2**
Sedley *Canada* 50°10N 104°0W **71 C8**
Sedona *U.S.A.* 34°52N 111°46W **77 J8**
Sedova, Pik *Russia* 73°29N 54°58E **28 B6**
Sedro-Woolley *U.S.A.* 48°30N 122°14W **78 B4**
Seeheim *Namibia* 26°50S 17°45E **56 D2**
Seeis *Namibia* 22°29S 17°39E **56 C2**
Seekoei ➤ *S. Africa* 30°18S 25°1E **56 E4**
Seeley's Bay *Canada* 44°29N 76°14W **83 B8**
Seferihisar *Turkey* 38°10N 26°50E **23 E12**
Sefophe *Botswana* 22°11S 27°58E **55 G2**
Seg-ozero *Russia* 63°20N 33°46E **18 B5**
Segamat *Malaysia* 2°30N 102°50E **39 L4**
Segesta *Italy* 37°56N 12°50E **22 F5**
Seget *Indonesia* 1°24S 130°58E **37 E8**
Segezha *Russia* 63°44N 34°19E **18 B5**
Ségou *Mali* 13°30N 6°16W **50 F4**
Segovia = Coco ➤ *Cent. Amer.* 15°0N 83°8W **88 D3**
Segovia *Spain* 40°57N 4°10W **21 B3**
Segre ➤ *Spain* 41°40N 0°43E **21 B6**
Seguam I. *U.S.A.* 52°19N 172°30W **74 E5**
Séguéla *Ivory C.* 7°55N 6°40W **50 G4**
Seguin *U.S.A.* 29°34N 97°58W **84 G6**
Segundo ➤ *Argentina* 30°53S 62°44W **94 C3**
Segura ➤ *Spain* 38°3N 0°44W **21 C5**
Seh Konj, Kūh-e *Iran* 30°6N 57°30E **45 D8**
Seh Qal'eh *Iran* 33°40N 58°24E **45 C8**
Sehitwa *Botswana* 20°30S 22°30E **56 C3**
Sehlabathebe △ *Lesotho* 29°53S 29°7E **57 D4**
Sehore *India* 23°10N 77°5E **42 H7**
Sehwan *Pakistan* 26°28N 67°53E **42 F2**
Seikan Tunnel *Japan* 41°28N 140°10E **30 D10**
Seil *U.K.* 56°18N 5°38W **11 E3**
Seiland *Norway* 70°25N 23°15E **8 A20**
Seiling *U.S.A.* 36°9N 98°56W **84 C5**
Seinäjoki *Finland* 62°40N 22°51E **8 E20**
Seine ➤ *France* 49°26N 0°26E **20 B4**
Seistan = Sīstān *Asia* 30°50N 61°0E **45 D9**
Seistan, Daryācheh-ye = Sīstān, Daryācheh-ye *Iran* 31°0N 61°0E **45 D9**
Sekayu *Indonesia* 2°51S 103°51E **36 E2**
Seke *Tanzania* 3°20S 33°31E **54 C3**
Sekenke *Tanzania* 4°18S 34°11E **54 C3**
Sekondi-Takoradi *Ghana* 4°58N 1°45W **50 H5**
Sekudai *Malaysia* 1°32N 103°39E **39 d**
Sekuma *Botswana* 24°36S 23°50E **56 C3**
Selah *U.S.A.* 46°39N 120°32W **76 C3**
Selama *Malaysia* 5°12N 100°42E **39 K3**
Selaru *Indonesia* 8°9S 131°0E **37 F8**
Selatan, Selat *Malaysia* 5°15N 100°20E **39 c**
Selawik L. *U.S.A.* 66°30N 160°45W **74 B7**
Selby *U.K.* 53°47N 1°5W **12 D6**
Selby *U.S.A.* 45°31N 100°2W **80 C3**
Selçuk *Turkey* 37°56N 27°22E **23 F12**
Selden *U.S.A.* 39°33N 100°34W **80 F3**
Sele ➤ *Italy* 40°29N 14°56E **22 D6**
Selebi-Phikwe *Botswana* 21°58S 27°48E **57 C4**
Selemdzha ➤ *Russia* 51°42N 128°53E **29 D13**
Selenga = Selenge Mörön ➤ *Asia* 52°16N 106°16E **32 A5**
Selenge Mörön ➤ *Asia* 52°16N 106°16E **32 A5**
Seletan, Tanjung *Indonesia* 4°10S 114°40E **36 E4**
Seletytengiz *Mauritania* 15°20N 11°0W **50 F2**
Seligman *U.S.A.* 35°20N 112°53W **77 J7**
Selinda Spillway ➤ *Botswana* 18°35S 23°10E **56 B3**
Selinsgrove *U.S.A.* 40°48N 76°52W **82 F8**
Selkirk *Canada* 50°10N 96°55W **71 C9**
Selkirk *U.K.* 55°33N 2°50W **11 F6**
Selkirk I. = Horse I. *Canada* 53°20N 99°6W **71 C9**
Selkirk Mts. *Canada* 51°15N 117°40W **68 G8**
Sellafield *U.K.* 54°25N 3°29W **12 C4**
Sellia *Greece* 35°12N 24°23E **25 D6**
Sells *U.S.A.* 31°55N 111°53W **77 L8**
Selma *Ala., U.S.A.* 32°25N 87°1W **85 E11**
Selma *Calif., U.S.A.* 36°34N 119°37W **78 J7**
Selma *N.C., U.S.A.* 35°32N 78°17W **85 D15**
Selmer *U.S.A.* 35°10N 88°36W **85 D10**
Selous *Tanzania* 8°37S 37°42E **55 D4**
Selowandoma Falls *Zimbabwe* 21°15S 31°50E **55 G3**
Selpele *Indonesia* 0°1S 130°5E **37 E8**
Selsey Bill *U.K.* 50°43N 0°47W **13 G7**
Seltso *Russia* 53°22N 34°4E **18 D5**
Selu *Indonesia* 7°32S 130°55E **37 F8**
Selva *Argentina* 29°50S 62°0W **94 B3**
Selva *Spain* 39°46N 2°54E **24 B9**
Selva Lancandona = Montes Azules △ *Mexico* 16°21N 91°3W **87 D6**
Selvagens, Ilhas *Madeira* 30°5N 15°55W **50 B2**
Selvas *Brazil* 6°30S 67°0W **92 E5**
Selwyn L. *Canada* 60°0N 104°30W **71 B8**
Selwyn Mts. *Canada* 63°0N 130°0W **68 E5**
Selwyn Ra. *Australia* 21°10S 140°0E **62 C3**
Seman ➤ *Albania* 40°47N 19°30E **23 D8**
Semarang *Indonesia* 7°0S 110°26E **37 G14**
Sembabule *Uganda* 0°4S 31°25E **54 C3**
Sembawang *Singapore* 1°27N 103°50E **39 d**
Sembung *Indonesia* 8°28S 115°11E **37 J18**
Semenanjung Blambangan *Indonesia* 8°42S 114°29E **37 K17**
Semeru *Indonesia* 8°4S 112°55E **37 H15**
Semey *Kazakhstan* 50°30N 80°10E **28 D9**
Seminoe Res. *U.S.A.* 42°9N 106°55W **76 E10**
Seminole *Okla., U.S.A.* 35°14N 96°41W **84 D6**
Seminole *Tex., U.S.A.* 32°43N 102°39W **84 E3**
Seminole Draw ➤ *U.S.A.* 32°27N 102°20W **84 E3**
Semipalatinsk = Semey *Kazakhstan* 50°30N 80°10E **28 D9**
Semirara Is. *Phil.* 12°0N 121°20E **37 B6**
Semisopochnoi I. *U.S.A.* 51°55N 179°36E **74 E3**
Semitau *Indonesia* 0°29N 111°57E **36 D4**
Semliki ➤ *Uganda* 0°49N 30°4E **54 B3**
Semmering ✠ *Austria* 47°41N 15°45E **16 E8**
Semnān *Iran* 35°40N 53°23E **45 C7**
Semnān □ *Iran* 36°0N 54°0E **45 C7**
Semporna *Malaysia* 4°30N 118°33E **37 D5**
Semuda *Indonesia* 2°51S 112°58E **36 E4**
Sen ➤ *Cambodia* 12°32N 104°28E **38 F5**
Senā *Iran* 28°27N 51°36E **45 D6**
Sena *Mozam.* 17°25S 35°0E **55 F4**
Sena Madureira *Brazil* 9°5S 68°45W **92 E5**
Senador Pompeu *Brazil* 5°40S 39°20W **93 E11**
Senang, Pulau *Singapore* 1°11N 103°52E **39 d**
Senanga *Zambia* 16°7S 23°16E **53 H4**
Senatobia *U.S.A.* 34°37N 89°58W **85 D10**
Sencelles *Spain* 39°39N 2°54E **24 B9**
Sendai *Kagoshima, Japan* 31°50N 130°20E **31 J5**
Sendai *Miyagi, Japan* 38°15N 140°53E **30 E10**
Sendai-Wan *Japan* 38°15N 141°0E **30 E10**
Sendhwa *India* 21°41N 75°6E **42 J6**
Seneca *U.S.A.* 34°41N 82°57W **85 D13**
Seneca Falls *U.S.A.* 42°55N 76°48W **83 D8**
Seneca L. *U.S.A.* 42°40N 76°54W **82 D8**
Senecaville L. *U.S.A.* 39°55N 81°25W **82 G3**
Senegal ■ *W. Afr.* 14°30N 14°30W **50 F3**
Sénégal ➤ *W. Afr.* 15°48N 16°32W **50 E2**
Senegambia *Africa* 12°45N 12°0W **48 E2**
Senekal *S. Africa* 28°20S 27°36E **57 D4**
Senga Hill *Zambia* 9°19S 31°11E **55 D3**
Senge Khambab = Indus ➤ *Pakistan* 24°20N 67°47E **42 G2**
Sengerema *Tanzania* 2°42S 32°35E **54 C3**
Sengua ➤ *Zimbabwe* 17°7S 28°5E **55 F2**
Senhor-do-Bonfim *Brazil* 10°30S 40°10W **93 F10**
Senigállia *Italy* 43°43N 13°13E **22 C5**
Senj *Croatia* 45°0N 14°58E **16 F8**
Senja *Norway* 69°25N 17°30E **8 B17**
Senkaku-Shotō *E. China Sea* 25°45N 123°30E **31 M1**
Senkuang *Indonesia* 1°11N 104°2E **39 d**
Senlis *France* 49°13N 2°35E **20 B5**
Senmonorom *Cambodia* 12°27N 107°12E **38 F6**
Senneterre *Canada* 48°25N 77°15W **72 C4**
Seno *Laos* 16°35N 104°50E **38 D5**
Senqu = Orange ➤ *S. Africa* 28°41S 16°28E **56 D2**
Sens *France* 48°11N 3°15E **20 B5**
Senta *Serbia* 45°55N 20°3E **23 B9**
Sentani *Indonesia* 2°36S 140°37E **37 E10**
Sentery = Lubao *Dem. Rep. of the Congo* 5°17S 25°42E **54 D2**
Sentinel *U.S.A.* 32°52N 113°13W **77 K7**
Sentosa *Singapore* 1°16N 103°50E **39 d**
Seo de Urgel = La Seu d'Urgell *Spain* 42°22N 1°23E **21 A6**
Seogwipo *S. Korea* 33°13N 126°34E **35 H14**
Seohara *India* 29°15N 78°33E **43 E8**
Seonath ➤ *India* 21°44N 82°28E **43 J10**
Seondha *India* 26°9N 78°48E **43 F8**
Seongnam *S. Korea* 37°26N 127°8E **35 F14**
Seoni *India* 22°5N 79°30E **43 H8**
Seoni Malwa *India* 22°27N 77°28E **43 H8**
Seonsan *S. Korea* 36°14N 128°17E **35 F15**
Seosan *S. Korea* 36°47N 126°27E **35 F14**
Seoul = Sŏul *S. Korea* 37°31N 126°58E **35 F14**
Sepīdān *Iran* 30°20N 52°5E **45 D7**
Sep'o *N. Korea* 38°57N 127°25E **35 E14**
Sepone *Laos* 16°45N 106°13E **38 D6**
Sept-Îles *Canada* 50°13N 66°22W **73 B6**
Sequim *U.S.A.* 48°5N 123°6W **78 B3**
Sequoia △ *U.S.A.* 36°30N 118°30W **78 J8**
Seraing *Belgium* 50°35N 5°32E **15 D5**

Serakhis ➤ *Cyprus* 35°13N 32°55E **25 D11**
Seram *Indonesia* 3°10S 129°0E **37 E7**
Seram Sea *Indonesia* 2°30S 128°30E **37 E7**
Serampore = Shrirampur *India* 22°44N 88°21E **43 H13**
Serangantsara *Madag.* 18°30S 49°5E **57 B8**
Serang *Indonesia* 6°8S 106°10E **37 G12**
Serangoon *Singapore* 1°23N 103°54E **39 d**
Serasan *Indonesia* 2°29N 109°4E **36 D3**
Serbia ■ *Europe* 43°20N 20°0E **23 B9**
Serdar *Turkmenistan* 39°4N 56°23E **45 B8**
Serdobsk *Russia* 52°28N 44°10E **18 D7**
Seremban *Malaysia* 2°43N 101°53E **39 L3**
Serengeti △ *Tanzania* 2°11S 35°0E **54 C4**
Serengeti Plain *Tanzania* 2°40S 35°0E **54 C4**
Serenje *Zambia* 13°14S 30°15E **55 E3**
Sereth = Siret ➤ *Romania* 45°24N 28°1E **17 F14**
Sergeya Kirova, Ostrova *Russia* 77°30N 90°0E **29 B10**
Sergino *Russia* 62°25N 65°12E **28 C7**
Sergipe □ *Brazil* 10°30S 37°30W **93 F11**
Sergiyev Posad *Russia* 56°20N 38°10E **18 C6**
Serhetabat *Turkmenistan* 35°20N 62°18E **45 C9**
Seria *Brunei* 4°37N 114°23E **36 D4**
Serian *Malaysia* 1°10N 110°31E **36 D4**
Seribu, Kepulauan *Indonesia* 5°36S 106°33E **36 F3**
Sericho *Kenya* 1°5N 39°5E **54 B4**
Serifos *Greece* 37°9N 24°30E **23 F11**
Sérigny ➤ *Canada* 56°47N 66°0W **73 A6**
Seringapatam Reef *Australia* 13°38S 122°5E **60 B3**
Seririt *Indonesia* 8°12S 114°56E **37 J17**
Serkout *Algeria* 23°56N 6°47E **50 D7**
Sermata *Indonesia* 8°15S 128°50E **37 F7**
Sermersuaq *Greenland* 79°30N 62°0W **69 B19**
Serov *Russia* 59°29N 60°35E **18 C11**
Serowe *Botswana* 22°25S 26°43E **56 C4**
Serpentine Lakes *Australia* 28°30S 129°10E **61 E4**
Serpent's Mouth = Sierpe, Bocas de la *Venezuela* 10°0N 61°30W **93 L15**
Serpukhov *Russia* 54°55N 37°28E **18 D6**
Serra do Navio *Brazil* 0°59N 52°3W **93 C8**
Serranía San Luís △ *Paraguay* 22°35S 57°22W **94 A4**
Serranía San Rafael △ *Paraguay* 26°30S 56°0W **95 B4**
Serres *Greece* 41°5N 23°31E **23 D10**
Serrezuela *Argentina* 30°40S 65°20W **94 C2**
Serrinha *Brazil* 11°39S 39°0W **93 F11**
Sertanópolis *Brazil* 23°4S 51°2W **95 A5**
Serua *Indonesia* 6°18S 130°1E **37 F8**
Serui *Indonesia* 1°53S 136°10E **37 E9**
Serule *Botswana* 21°57S 27°20E **56 C4**
Ses Salines *Spain* 39°21N 3°3E **24 B10**
Sese Is. *Uganda* 0°20S 32°20E **54 C3**
Sesepe *Indonesia* 1°30S 127°59E **37 E7**
Sesfontein *Namibia* 19°7S 13°39E **56 B1**
Sesheke *Zambia* 17°29S 24°13E **56 B3**
S'Espalmador *Spain* 38°47N 1°26E **24 C7**
S'Espardell *Spain* 38°48N 1°29E **24 C7**
S'Estanyol *Spain* 39°22N 2°54E **24 B9**
Setana *Japan* 42°26N 139°51E **30 C9**
Sète *France* 43°25N 3°42E **20 E5**
Sete Lagoas *Brazil* 19°27S 44°16W **93 G10**
Sétif *Algeria* 36°9N 5°26E **50 A7**
Seto *Japan* 35°14N 137°6E **31 G8**
Setonaikai *Japan* 34°20N 133°30E **31 G6**
Setonaikai △ *Japan* 34°15N 133°15E **31 G6**
Settat *Morocco* 33°0N 7°40W **50 B4**
Setting L. *Canada* 55°0N 98°38W **71 C9**
Settle *U.K.* 54°5N 2°16W **12 C5**
Settlement, The *Br. Virgin Is.* 18°43N 64°22W **89 e**
Settlers *S. Africa* 25°2S 28°30E **57 C4**
Setúbal *Portugal* 38°30N 8°58W **21 C1**
Setúbal, B. de *Portugal* 38°40N 8°56W **21 C1**
Seul, Lac *Canada* 50°20N 92°30W **72 B1**
Sevan, Ozero = Sevana Lich *Armenia* 40°30N 45°20E **44 A5**
Sevana Lich *Armenia* 40°30N 45°20E **44 A5**
Sevastopol *Ukraine* 44°35N 33°30E **19 F5**
Seven Sisters *Canada* 54°56N 128°10W **70 C3**
Severn ➤ *Canada* 56°2N 87°36W **72 A2**
Severn ➤ *U.K.* 51°35N 2°40W **13 F5**
Severnaya Zemlya *Russia* 79°0N 100°0E **29 B11**
Severnyye Uvaly *Russia* 60°0N 50°0E **18 C8**
Severo-Kurilsk *Russia* 50°40N 156°8E **29 D16**
Severo-Yeniseyskiy *Russia* 60°22N 93°1E **29 C10**
Severo-Zapadnyy □ *Russia* 65°0N 40°0E **28 C4**
Severobaykalsk *Russia* 55°39N 109°19E **29 D11**
Severodvinsk *Russia* 64°27N 39°58E **18 B6**
Severomorsk *Russia* 69°5N 33°27E **8 B25**
Severouralsk *Russia* 60°9N 59°57E **18 B10**
Seversk *Russia* 56°36N 84°49E **28 D9**
Sevier ➤ *U.S.A.* 39°4N 113°6W **76 G7**
Sevier Desert *U.S.A.* 39°40N 112°45W **76 G7**
Sevier L. *U.S.A.* 38°54N 113°9W **76 G7**
Sevilla *Spain* 37°23N 5°58W **21 D2**
Seville = Sevilla *Spain* 37°23N 5°58W **21 D2**
Sevlievo *Bulgaria* 43°2N 25°6E **23 C11**
Sewani *India* 28°58N 75°39E **42 E6**
Seward *Alaska, U.S.A.* 60°7N 149°27W **68 E2**
Seward *Nebr., U.S.A.* 40°55N 97°6W **80 E5**
Seward *Pa., U.S.A.* 40°25N 79°1W **82 F5**
Seward Peninsula *U.S.A.* 65°30N 166°0W **74 B6**
Sewell *Chile* 34°10S 70°23W **94 C1**
Sewer *Indonesia* 5°53S 134°40E **37 F8**
Sewickley *U.S.A.* 40°32N 80°12W **82 F4**
Sexsmith *Canada* 55°21N 118°47W **70 B5**
Seychelles ■ *Ind. Oc.* 5°0S 56°0E **53 b**
Seyðisfjörður *Iceland* 65°16N 13°57W **8 D7**
Seydişehir *Turkey* 37°25N 31°51E **19 G5**

Seydvān *Iran* 38°34N 45°2E **44** B5
Seyhan → *Turkey* 36°43N 34°53E **44** B2
Seym → *Ukraine* 51°27N 32°34E **19** D5
Seymour *Australia* 37°2S 145°10E **63** F4
Seymour *Conn., U.S.A.* 41°24N 73°4W **83** E11
Seymour *Ind., U.S.A.* 38°58N 85°53W **81** F11
Seymour *Tex., U.S.A.* 33°35N 99°16W **84** E5
Sfântu Gheorghe
　Romania 45°52N 25°48E **17** F13
Sfax *Tunisia* 34°49N 10°48E **51** B8
Sha Tau Kok *China* 22°33N 114°12E **33** G11
Sha Tin *China* 22°23N 114°12E **33** G11
Shaanxi □ *China* 35°0N 109°0E **34** G5
Shaba = Katanga □
　Dem. Rep. of the Congo 8°0S 25°0E **54** D2
Shaba △ *Kenya* 0°38N 37°48E **54** B4
Shabeelle → *Somali Rep.* 2°0N 44°0E **47** G3
Shabogamo L. *Canada* 53°15N 66°30W **73** B6
Shabunda
　Dem. Rep. of the Congo 2°40S 27°16E **54** C2
Shache *China* 38°20N 77°10E **32** C2
Shackleton Fracture Zone
　S. Ocean 60°0S 60°0W **5** B18
Shackleton Ice Shelf
　Antarctica 66°0S 100°0E **5** C8
Shackleton Inlet
　Antarctica 83°0S 160°0E **5** E11
Shādegān *Iran* 30°40N 48°38E **45** D6
Shadi *India* 33°24N 77°14E **43** C7
Shadrinsk *Russia* 56°5N 63°32E **28** D7
Shadyside *U.S.A.* 39°58N 80°45W **82** G4
Shafter *U.S.A.* 35°30N 119°16W **79** K7
Shaftesbury *U.K.* 51°0N 2°11W **13** F5
Shaftsbury *U.S.A.* 43°0N 73°11W **83** D11
Shagram *Pakistan* 36°24N 72°20E **43** A5
Shah Alam *Malaysia* 3°5N 101°32E **39** L3
Shah Alizai *Pakistan* 29°25N 66°33E **42** E2
Shah Bunder *Pakistan* 24°13N 67°56E **42** G2
Shahabad *Punjab, India* 30°10N 76°55E **42** D7
Shahabad *Raj., India* 25°15N 77°11E **42** G7
Shahabad *Ut. P., India* 27°36N 79°56E **43** F8
Shahadpur *Pakistan* 25°55N 68°35E **42** G3
Shahbā *Syria* 32°52N 36°38E **46** C5
Shahdād *Iran* 30°30N 57°40E **45** D8
Shahdād, Namakzār-e
　Iran 30°20N 58°20E **45** D8
Shahdadkot *Pakistan* 27°50N 67°55E **42** F2
Shahdol *India* 23°19N 81°26E **43** H9
Shahe *China* 37°0N 114°32E **34** F8
Shahganj *India* 26°3N 82°44E **43** F10
Shahgarh *India* 27°15N 69°50E **42** F3
Shahjahanpur *India* 27°54N 79°57E **43** F8
Shahpur = Salmās *Iran* 38°11N 44°47E **44** B5
Shahpur *India* 22°12N 77°58E **42** H7
Shahpur *Baluchistan,*
　Pakistan 28°46N 68°27E **42** E3
Shahpur *Punjab, Pakistan* 32°17N 72°26E **42** C5
Shahpur Chakar *Pakistan* 26°9N 68°39E **42** F3
Shahpura *Mad. P., India* 23°10N 80°45E **43** H9
Shahpura *Raj., India* 25°38N 74°56E **42** G6
Shahr-e Bābak *Iran* 30°7N 55°9E **45** D7
Shahr-e Kord *Iran* 32°15N 50°55E **45** C6
Shāhrakht *Iran* 33°38N 60°16E **45** C9
Shahreza = Qomsheh
　Iran 32°0N 51°55E **45** D6
Shahrig *Pakistan* 30°15N 67°40E **42** D2
Shāhrud = Emāmrūd
　Iran 36°30N 55°0E **45** B7
Shahukou *China* 40°20N 112°18E **34** D7
Shaikhabad *Afghan.* 34°2N 68°45E **42** B3
Shajapur *India* 23°27N 76°21E **42** H7
Shajing *China* 22°44N 113°48E **33** F10
Shakargarh *Pakistan* 32°17N 75°10E **42** C6
Shakawe *Botswana* 18°28S 21°49E **56** B3
Shaker Heights *U.S.A.* 41°28N 81°32W **82** E3
Shakhtersk *Russia* 49°10N 142°8E **29** E15
Shakhty *Russia* 47°40N 40°16E **19** E7
Shakhunya *Russia* 57°40N 46°46E **18** C8
Shaki *Nigeria* 8°41N 3°21E **50** G6
Shaksam Valley *Asia* 36°0N 76°20E **43** A7
Shallow Lake *Canada* 44°36N 81°5W **82** B3
Shalqar *Kazakhstan* 47°48N 59°39E **28** E6
Shām *Iran* 26°39N 57°21E **45** E8
Shām, Bādiyat ash *Asia* 32°0N 40°0E **44** C3
Shamāl Sīnî □ *Egypt* 30°30N 33°30E **46** E2
Shamattawa *Canada* 55°51N 92°5W **72** A1
Shamattawa → *Canada* 55°1N 85°23W **72** A2
Shamil *Iran* 27°30N 56°55E **45** E8
Shāmkūh *Iran* 35°47N 57°50E **45** C8
Shamli *India* 29°32N 77°18E **42** E7
Shammar, Jabal *Si. Arabia* 27°40N 41°0E **44** E4
Shamo = Gobi *Asia* 44°0N 110°0E **34** C6
Shamo, L. *Ethiopia* 5°45N 37°30E **47** F2
Shamokin *U.S.A.* 40°47N 76°34W **83** F8
Shamrock *Canada* 45°23N 76°50W **83** A8
Shamrock *U.S.A.* 35°13N 100°15W **84** D4
Shamva *Zimbabwe* 17°20S 31°32E **55** F3
Shan □ *Burma* 21°30N 98°30E **41** J21
Shan Xian *China* 34°50N 116°5E **34** G9
Shanchengzhen *China* 42°20N 125°20E **35** C13
Shāndak *Iran* 28°28N 60°27E **45** D9
Shandon *U.S.A.* 35°39N 120°23W **78** K6
Shandong □ *China* 36°0N 118°0E **35** G10
Shandong Bandao *China* 37°0N 121°0E **35** F11
Shandur Pass *Pakistan* 36°4N 72°31E **43** A5
Shang Xian = Shangzhou
　China 33°50N 109°58E **34** H5
Shangalowe
　Dem. Rep. of the Congo 10°50S 26°30E **55** E2
Shangani *Zimbabwe* 19°41S 29°20E **57** B4
Shangani → *Zimbabwe* 18°41S 27°10E **55** F2
Shangbancheng *China* 40°18N 118°1E **35** D10
Shangdu *China* 41°30N 113°30E **34** D7
Shanghai *China* 31°15N 121°26E **33** C7
Shanghe *China* 37°20N 117°10E **35** F9
Shangnan *China* 33°32N 110°50E **34** H6
Shangqiu *China* 34°26N 115°36E **34** G8

Shangrao *China* 28°25N 117°59E **33** D6
Shangri-La = Zhongdian
　China 27°48N 99°42E **32** D4
Shangshui *China* 33°42N 114°35E **33** C6
Shangzhi *China* 45°22N 127°56E **35** B14
Shangzhou *China* 33°50N 109°58E **34** H5
Shanhetun *China* 44°33N 127°15E **35** B14
Shanklin *U.K.* 50°38N 1°11W **13** G6
Shannon *N.Z.* 40°33S 175°25E **59** D5
Shannon → *Ireland* 52°35N 9°30W **10** D2
Shannon ✈ (SNN)
　Ireland 52°42N 8°57W **10** D3
Shannon, Mouth of the
　Ireland 52°30N 9°55W **10** D2
Shannon △ *Australia* 34°35S 116°25E **61** F2
Shannonbridge *Ireland* 53°17N 8°3W **10** C3
Shansi = Shanxi □ *China* 37°0N 112°0E **34** F7
Shantar, Ostrov Bolshoy
　Russia 55°9N 137°40E **29** D14
Shantipur *India* 23°17N 88°25E **43** H13
Shantou *China* 23°18N 116°40E **33** D6
Shantung = Shandong □
　China 36°0N 118°0E **35** G10
Shanxi □ *China* 37°0N 112°0E **34** F7
Shanyang *China* 33°31N 109°55E **34** H5
Shanyin *China* 39°25N 112°56E **34** E7
Shaoguan *China* 24°48N 113°35E **33** D6
Shaoxing *China* 30°0N 120°35E **33** D7
Shaoyang *China* 27°14N 111°25E **33** D6
Shap *U.K.* 54°32N 2°40W **12** C5
Shapinsay *U.K.* 59°3N 2°51W **11** B6
Shaqra' *Si. Arabia* 25°15N 45°16E **44** E5
Shaqrā' *Yemen* 13°22N 45°44E **47** E4
Sharafkhāneh *Iran* 38°11N 45°29E **44** B5
Sharbot Lake *Canada* 44°46N 76°41W **83** B8
Shari *Japan* 43°55N 144°40E **30** C12
Sharjah = Ash Shāriqah
　U.A.E. 25°23N 55°26E **45** E7
Shark B. *Australia* 25°30S 113°32E **61** E1
Shark Bay △ *Australia* 25°30S 113°30E **61** E1
Sharm el Sheikh *Egypt* 27°53N 34°18E **51** C12
Sharon *Canada* 44°6N 79°26W **82** B5
Sharon *Mass., U.S.A.* 42°7N 71°11W **83** D13
Sharon *Pa., U.S.A.* 41°14N 80°31W **82** E4
Sharon Springs *Kans.,*
　U.S.A. 38°54N 101°45W **80** F3
Sharon Springs *N.Y.,*
　U.S.A. 42°48N 74°37W **83** D10
Sharp Pt. *Australia* 10°58S 142°43E **62** A3
Sharpe L. *Canada* 54°24N 93°40W **72** B1
Sharpsville *U.S.A.* 41°15N 80°29W **82** E4
Sharqi, Al Jabal ash
　Lebanon 33°40N 36°10E **46** B5
Sharya *Russia* 58°22N 45°20E **18** C8
Shashemene *Ethiopia* 7°13N 38°33E **47** F2
Shashi *Botswana* 21°15S 27°27E **57** C4
Shashi *China* 30°25N 112°14E **33** C6
Shashi → *Africa* 21°14S 29°20E **55** G2
Shasta, Mt. *U.S.A.* 41°25N 122°12W **76** F2
Shasta L. *U.S.A.* 40°43N 122°25W **76** F2
Shatsky Rise *Pac. Oc.* 34°0N 158°0E **64** D7
Shatt al Arab *Asia* 29°57N 48°34E **45** D6
Shaunavon *Canada* 49°35N 108°25W **71** D7
Shaver L. *U.S.A.* 37°9N 119°18W **78** H7
Shaw → *Australia* 20°21S 119°17E **60** D2
Shaw I. *Australia* 20°30S 149°2E **62** b
Shawanaga *Canada* 45°31N 80°17W **82** A4
Shawangunk Mts.
　U.S.A. 41°35N 74°30W **83** E10
Shawano *U.S.A.* 44°47N 88°36W **80** C9
Shawinigan *Canada* 46°35N 72°50W **72** C5
Shawmari, J. ash *Jordan* 30°35N 36°35E **46** E5
Shawnee *U.S.A.* 35°20N 96°55W **84** D6
Shay Gap *Australia* 20°30S 120°10E **60** D3
Shaybārā *Si. Arabia* 25°26N 36°47E **44** E3
Shaykh, J. ash *Lebanon* 33°25N 35°50E **46** B4
Shaykh Miskīn *Syria* 32°49N 36°9E **46** C5
Shaykh Sa'd *Iraq* 32°34N 46°17E **44** C5
Shāzand *Iran* 33°56N 49°24E **45** C6
She Xian *China* 36°30N 113°40E **34** F7
Shebele = Shabeelle →
　Somali Rep. 2°0N 44°0E **47** G3
Sheboygan *U.S.A.* 43°46N 87°45W **80** D10
Shediac *Canada* 46°14N 64°32W **73** C7
Sheelin, L. *Ireland* 53°48N 7°20W **10** C4
Sheenjek → *U.S.A.* 66°45N 144°33W **74** B11
Sheep Haven *Ireland* 55°11N 7°52W **10** A4
Sheep Range *U.S.A.* 36°35N 115°15W **79** J11
Sheerness *U.K.* 51°26N 0°47E **13** F8
Sheet Harbour *Canada* 44°56N 62°31W **73** D7
Sheffield *U.K.* 53°23N 1°28W **12** D6
Sheffield *Ala., U.S.A.* 34°46N 87°41W **85** D11
Sheffield *Mass., U.S.A.* 42°5N 73°21W **83** D11
Sheffield *Pa., U.S.A.* 41°42N 79°3W **82** E5
Sheikhpura *India* 25°9N 85°53E **43** G11
Shekhupura *Pakistan* 31°42N 73°58E **42** D5
Shekou *China* 22°30N 113°55E **33** G10
Shelburne *N.S., Canada* 43°47N 65°20W **73** D6
Shelburne *Ont., Canada* 44°4N 80°15W **82** B4
Shelburne *U.S.A.* 44°23N 73°14W **83** B11
Shelburne B. *Australia* 11°50S 142°50E **62** A3
Shelburne Falls *U.S.A.* 42°36N 72°45W **83** D12
Shelby *Mich., U.S.A.* 43°37N 86°22W **80** D10
Shelby *Miss., U.S.A.* 33°57N 90°46W **85** E9
Shelby *Mont., U.S.A.* 48°30N 111°51W **76** B8
Shelby *N.C., U.S.A.* 35°17N 81°32W **85** D14
Shelby *Ohio, U.S.A.* 40°53N 82°40W **82** F2
Shelbyville *Ill., U.S.A.* 39°24N 88°48W **80** F9
Shelbyville *Ind., U.S.A.* 39°31N 85°47W **81** F11
Shelbyville *Ky., U.S.A.* 38°13N 85°14W **81** F11
Shelbyville *Tenn.,*
　U.S.A. 35°29N 86°28W **85** D11
Sheldrake *Canada* 50°20N 64°51W **73** B7
Shelikhova, Zaliv
　Russia 59°30N 157°0E **29** D16
Shelikof Strait *U.S.A.* 57°30N 155°0W **74** D9
Shell Lakes *Australia* 29°20S 127°30E **61** E4

Shellbrook *Canada* 53°13N 106°24W **71** C7
Shellharbour *Australia* 34°31S 150°51E **63** E5
Shelter I. *U.S.A.* 41°4N 72°20W **83** E12
Shelton *Conn., U.S.A.* 41°19N 73°5W **83** E11
Shelton *Wash., U.S.A.* 47°13N 123°6W **78** C3
Shen Xian *China* 36°15N 115°40E **34** F8
Shenandoah *Iowa,*
　U.S.A. 40°46N 95°22W **80** E6
Shenandoah *Pa., U.S.A.* 40°49N 76°12W **83** F8
Shenandoah *Va.,*
　U.S.A. 38°29N 78°37W **81** F14
Shenandoah → *U.S.A.* 39°19N 77°44W **81** F15
Shenandoah △ *U.S.A.* 38°35N 78°22W **81** F14
Shenchi *China* 39°8N 112°10E **34** E7
Shendam *Nigeria* 8°49N 9°30E **50** G7
Shendî *Sudan* 16°46N 33°22E **51** E12
Shengfang *China* 39°3N 116°42E **34** E9
Shenjingzi *China* 44°40N 124°30E **35** B13
Shenmu *China* 38°50N 110°29E **34** E6
Shenqiu *China* 33°25N 115°5E **34** H8
Shensi = Shaanxi □
　China 35°0N 109°0E **34** G5
Shenyang *China* 41°48N 123°27E **35** D12
Shenzhen *China* 22°32N 114°5E **33** F10
Shenzhen ✈ (SZX)
　China 22°41N 113°49E **33** F10
Shenzhen Shuiku *China* 22°34N 114°8E **33** F11
Shenzhen Wan *China* 22°27N 113°55E **33** G10
Sheo *India* 26°11N 71°15E **42** F4
Sheopur Kalan *India* 25°40N 76°40E **42** G7
Shepetivka *Ukraine* 50°10N 27°10E **17** C14
Shepparton *Australia* 36°23S 145°26E **63** F4
Sheppey, I. of *U.K.* 51°25N 0°48E **13** F8
Shepton Mallet *U.K.* 51°11N 2°33W **13** F5
Sheqi *China* 33°12N 112°57E **34** H7
Sher Qila *Pakistan* 36°7N 74°2E **43** A6
Sher *Pakistan* 36°7N 74°2E **43** A6
Sherborne *U.K.* 50°57N 2°31W **13** G5
Sherbro I. *S. Leone* 7°30N 12°40W **50** G3
Sherbrooke *N.S., Canada* 45°8N 61°59W **73** C7
Sherbrooke *Qué.,*
　Canada 45°28N 71°57W **83** A13
Sherburne *U.S.A.* 42°41N 75°30W **83** D9
Shergarh *India* 26°20N 72°18E **42** F5
Sherghati *India* 24°34N 84°47E **43** G11
Sheridan *Ark., U.S.A.* 34°19N 92°24W **84** D8
Sheridan *Wyo., U.S.A.* 44°48N 106°58W **76** D10
Sheringham *U.K.* 52°56N 1°13E **12** E9
Sherkin I. *Ireland* 51°28N 9°26W **10** E2
Sherkot *India* 29°22N 78°35E **43** E8
Sherlovaya Gora
　Russia 50°34N 116°15E **29** D12
Sherman *N.Y., U.S.A.* 42°9N 79°35W **82** D5
Sherman *Tex., U.S.A.* 33°38N 96°36W **84** E6
Sherpur *India* 25°34N 83°47E **43** G10
Sherridon *Canada* 55°8N 101°5W **71** B8
Sherwood Forest *U.K.* 53°6N 1°7W **12** D6
Sherwood Park *Canada* 53°31N 113°19W **70** C6
Sheslay → *Canada* 58°48N 132°5W **70** B2
Shethanei L. *Canada* 58°48N 97°50W **71** B9
Shetland □ *U.K.* 60°30N 1°30W **11** A7
Shetland Is. *U.K.* 60°30N 1°30W **11** A7
Shetrunji → *India* 21°19N 72°7E **42** J5
Sheung Shui *China* 22°31N 114°7E **33** F11
Shey-Phoksundo △
　Nepal 29°30N 82°45E **43** E10
Sheyenne → *U.S.A.* 47°2N 96°50W **80** B5
Shiashkotan, Ostrov
　Russia 48°49N 154°6E **29** E16
Shibām *Yemen* 15°59N 48°36E **47** D4
Shibata *Japan* 37°57N 139°20E **30** F9
Shibecha *Japan* 43°17N 144°36E **30** C12
Shibetsu *Japan* 44°10N 142°23E **30** B11
Shibogama L. *Canada* 53°35N 88°15W **72** B2
Shibushi *Japan* 31°25N 131°8E **31** J5
Shickshinny *U.S.A.* 41°9N 76°9W **83** E8
Shickshock Mts. = Chic-Chocs,
　Mts. *Canada* 48°55N 66°0W **73** C6
Shidao *China* 36°50N 122°25E **35** F12
Shido *Japan* 34°19N 134°10E **31** G7
Shiel, L. *U.K.* 56°48N 5°34W **11** E3
Shield, C. *Australia* 13°20S 136°20E **62** A2
Shiĕli *Kazakhstan* 44°20N 66°15E **28** E7
Shiga □ *Japan* 35°20N 136°0E **31** G8
Shiguaigou *China* 40°52N 110°15E **34** D6
Shihchiachuangi = Shijiazhuang
　China 38°2N 114°28E **34** E8
Shihezi *China* 44°15N 86°2E **32** B3
Shijiazhuang *China* 38°2N 114°28E **34** E8
Shikarpur *India* 28°17N 78°7E **42** E8
Shikarpur *Pakistan* 27°57N 68°39E **42** F3
Shikohabad *India* 27°6N 78°36E **43** F8
Shikoku □ *Japan* 33°30N 133°30E **31** H6
Shikoku-Sanchi *Japan* 33°30N 133°30E **31** H6
Shikotan, Ostrov *Asia* 43°47N 146°44E **29** E15
Shikotsu-Ko *Japan* 42°45N 141°25E **30** C10
Shikotsu-Tōya △ *Japan* 44°4N 145°8E **30** C10
Shiliu = Changjiang
　China 19°20N 108°55E **38** C7
Shilka *Russia* 52°0N 115°55E **29** D12
Shilka → *Russia* 53°20N 121°26E **29** D13
Shillelagh *Ireland* 52°45N 6°32W **10** D5
Shillington *U.S.A.* 40°18N 75°58W **83** F9
Shillong *India* 25°35N 91°53E **41** G17
Shilo *West Bank* 32°4N 35°18E **46** C4
Shilou *China* 37°0N 110°48E **34** F6
Shimabara *Japan* 32°48N 130°20E **31** H5
Shimada *Japan* 34°49N 138°10E **31** G9
Shimane □ *Japan* 35°0N 132°30E **31** G6
Shimanovsk *Russia* 52°15N 127°30E **29** D13
Shimba Hills △ *Kenya* 4°14S 39°25E **54** C4
Shimizu *Japan* 35°0N 138°30E **31** G9
Shimla *India* 31°2N 77°9E **42** D7
Shimodate *Japan* 36°20N 139°55E **31** F9
Shimoga *India* 13°57N 75°32E **40** N9
Shimoni *Kenya* 4°38S 39°20E **54** C4
Shimonoseki *Japan* 33°58N 130°55E **31** H5

Shimpuru Rapids
　Namibia 17°45S 19°55E **56** B2
Shin, L. *U.K.* 58°5N 4°30W **11** C4
Shinano-Gawa →
　Japan 36°50N 138°30E **31** F9
Shinās *Oman* 24°46N 56°28E **45** E8
Shindand *Afghan.* 33°12N 62°8E **40** D3
Shinglehouse *U.S.A.* 41°58N 78°12W **82** E6
Shingū *Japan* 33°40N 135°55E **31** H7
Shingwidzi *S. Africa* 23°5S 31°25E **57** C5
Shinjō *Japan* 38°46N 140°18E **30** E10
Shinkolobwe
　Dem. Rep. of the Congo 11°10S 26°40E **52** G5
Shinshār *Syria* 34°36N 36°43E **46** A5
Shinyanga *Tanzania* 3°45S 33°27E **54** C3
Shinyanga □ *Tanzania* 3°50S 34°0E **54** C3
Shio-no-Misaki *Japan* 33°25N 135°45E **31** H7
Shiogama *Japan* 38°19N 141°1E **30** E10
Shiojiri *Japan* 36°6N 137°58E **31** F8
Shipchenski Prokhod
　Bulgaria 42°45N 25°15E **23** C11
Shiping *China* 23°45N 102°23E **32** D5
Shippagan *Canada* 47°45N 64°45W **73** C7
Shippensburg *U.S.A.* 40°3N 77°31W **82** F7
Shippenville *U.S.A.* 41°15N 79°28W **82** E5
Shiprock *U.S.A.* 36°47N 108°41W **77** H9
Shiqma, N. → *Israel* 31°37N 34°30E **46** D3
Shiquan *China* 33°5N 108°15E **34** H5
Shiquan He = Indus →
　Pakistan 24°20N 67°47E **42** G2
Shīr Kūh *Iran* 31°39N 54°3E **45** D7
Shiragami-Misaki
　Japan 41°24N 140°12E **30** D10
Shirakawa *Fukushima,*
　Japan 37°7N 140°13E **31** F10
Shirakawa *Gifu, Japan* 36°17N 136°56E **31** F8
Shirane-San *Gumma,*
　Japan 36°48N 139°22E **31** F9
Shirane-San *Yamanashi,*
　Japan 35°42N 138°9E **31** G9
Shiraoi *Japan* 42°33N 141°21E **30** C10
Shīrāz *Iran* 29°42N 52°30E **45** D7
Shire → *Africa* 17°42S 35°19E **55** F4
Shiretoko-Misaki
　Japan 44°21N 145°20E **30** B12
Shirinab → *Pakistan* 30°15N 66°28E **42** D2
Shiriya-Zaki *Japan* 41°25N 141°30E **30** D10
Shiroishi *Japan* 38°0N 140°37E **30** F10
Shirshov Ridge *Pac. Oc.* 58°0N 170°0E **64** B8
Shīrvān *Iran* 37°30N 57°50E **45** B8
Shirwa, L. = Chilwa, L.
　Malawi 15°15S 35°40E **55** F4
Shishaldin Volcano
　U.S.A. 54°45N 163°58W **74** E7
Shivamogga = Shimoga
　India 13°57N 75°32E **40** N9
Shivpuri *India* 25°26N 77°42E **42** G7
Shixian *China* 43°5N 129°50E **35** C15
Shiyan *China* 32°35N 110°50E **34** G6
Shiyan Shuiku *China* 22°42N 113°54E **33** F10
Shizuishan *China* 39°15N 106°50E **34** E4
Shizuoka *Japan* 34°57N 138°24E **31** G9
Shizuoka □ *Japan* 35°15N 138°40E **31** G9
Shklov = Shklow
　Belarus 54°16N 30°15E **17** A16
Shklow *Belarus* 54°16N 30°15E **17** A16
Shkodër *Albania* 42°4N 19°32E **23** C8
Shkumbini → *Albania* 41°2N 19°31E **23** D8
Shmidta, Ostrov *Russia* 81°0N 91°0E **29** A10
Shō-Gawa → *Japan* 36°47N 137°4E **31** F8
Shoal L. *Canada* 49°33N 95°1W **71** D9
Shoal Lake *Canada* 50°30N 100°35W **71** C8
Shōdo-Shima *Japan* 34°30N 134°15E **31** G7
Sholapur = Solapur
　India 17°43N 75°56E **40** L9
Shōmrōn *West Bank* 32°15N 35°13E **46** C4
Shoreham *U.S.A.* 43°53N 73°18W **83** C11
Shoreham by Sea *U.K.* 50°50N 0°16W **13** G7
Shori → *Pakistan* 28°29N 69°44E **42** E3
Shorkot *Pakistan* 30°50N 72°0E **42** D4
Shorkot Road *Pakistan* 30°47N 72°15E **42** D5
Shoshone *Calif.,*
　U.S.A. 35°58N 116°16W **79** K10
Shoshone *Idaho, U.S.A.* 42°56N 114°25W **76** E6
Shoshone L. *U.S.A.* 44°22N 110°43W **76** D8
Shoshone Mts. *U.S.A.* 39°20N 117°25W **76** G5
Shoshong *Botswana* 22°56S 26°31E **56** C4
Shoshoni *U.S.A.* 43°14N 108°7W **76** E9
Shouguang *China* 37°52N 118°45E **35** F10
Shouyang *China* 37°54N 113°8E **34** F7
Show Low *U.S.A.* 34°15N 110°2W **77** J8
Shpola *Ukraine* 49°1N 31°30E **19** E5
Shreveport *U.S.A.* 32°31N 93°45W **84** E8
Shrewsbury *U.K.* 52°43N 2°45W **13** E5
Shri Mohangarh *India* 27°17N 71°18E **42** F4
Shrirampur *India* 22°44N 88°21E **43** H13
Shropshire □ *U.K.* 52°36N 2°45W **13** E5
Shū *Kazakhstan* 43°36N 73°42E **28** E8
Shu → *Kazakhstan* 45°0N 67°44E **28** E7
Shuangcheng *China* 45°20N 126°15E **35** B14
Shuanggou *China* 34°2N 117°30E **35** G9
Shuangliao *China* 43°29N 123°30E **35** C12
Shuangshanzi *China* 40°20N 119°8E **35** D10
Shuangyang *China* 43°28N 125°40E **35** C13
Shuangyashan *China* 46°28N 131°5E **33** B8
Shuguri Falls *Tanzania* 8°33S 37°22E **54** D4
Shuiye *China* 36°7N 114°8E **34** F8
Shujalpur *India* 23°18N 76°46E **42** H7
Shukpa Kunzang *India* 34°22N 78°22E **43** B8
Shulan *China* 44°28N 127°0E **35** B14
Shule *China* 39°25N 76°3E **32** C2
Shule He → *China* 40°20N 92°50E **32** B4
Shumagin Is. *U.S.A.* 55°7N 160°30W **74** D7
Shumen *Bulgaria* 43°18N 26°55E **23** C12
Shumikha *Russia* 55°10N 63°15E **28** D7
Shungnak *U.S.A.* 66°52N 157°9W **74** B8
Shuo Xian = Shuozhou
　China 39°20N 112°33E **34** E7
Shuozhou *China* 39°20N 112°33E **34** E7

Shūr → *Fārs, Iran* 28°30N 55°0E **45** D7
Shūr → *Kermān, Iran* 30°52N 57°37E **45** D8
Shūr → *Yazd, Iran* 31°45N 55°15E **45** C6
Shūr Āb *Iran* 34°23N 51°11E **45** C6
Shūr Gaz *Iran* 29°10N 59°20E **45** D8
Shūrāb *Iran* 33°43N 56°29E **45** C8
Shūrjestān *Iran* 31°24N 52°25E **45** D7
Shūsf *Iran* 31°50N 60°5E **45** D9
Shūshtar *Iran* 32°0N 48°50E **45** D6
Shuswap L. *Canada* 50°55N 119°3W **70** C5
Shute Harbour △
　Australia 20°17S 148°47E **62** b
Shuyang *China* 34°10N 118°42E **35** G10
Shūzū *Iran* 29°52N 54°30E **45** D7
Shwebo *Burma* 22°30N 95°45E **41** H19
Shwegu *Burma* 24°15N 96°26E **41** G20
Shweli → *Burma* 23°45N 96°45E **41** H20
Shymkent *Kazakhstan* 42°18N 69°36E **28** E7
Shyok *India* 34°13N 78°12E **43** B8
Shyok → *Pakistan* 35°13N 75°53E **43** B6
Si Kiang = Xi Jiang →
　China 22°5N 113°20E **33** D6
Si Lanna △ *Thailand* 19°17N 99°12E **38** C2
Si Nakarin Res. *Thailand* 14°35N 99°0E **38** E2
Si-ngan = Xi'an *China* 34°15N 109°0E **34** G5
Si Prachan *Thailand* 14°37N 100°9E **38** E3
Si Racha *Thailand* 13°10N 100°48E **38** F3
Si Xian *China* 33°30N 117°50E **35** H9
Siachen Glacier *Asia* 35°20N 77°30E **43** B7
Siahaf → *Pakistan* 29°3N 68°57E **42** E3
Siahan Range *Pakistan* 27°30N 64°40E **40** F4
Siaksriindrapura
　Indonesia 0°51N 102°0E **36** D2
Sialkot *Pakistan* 32°32N 74°30E **42** C6
Siam = Thailand ■ *Asia* 16°0N 102°0E **38** E4
Sian = Xi'an *China* 34°15N 109°0E **34** G5
Sian Ka'an △ *Mexico* 19°35N 87°40W **87** D7
Siantan *Indonesia* 3°10N 106°15E **36** D3
Siāreh *Iran* 28°5N 60°14E **45** D9
Siargao I. *Phil.* 9°52N 126°3E **37** C7
Siari *Pakistan* 34°55N 76°40E **43** B7
Siasi *Phil.* 5°34N 120°50E **37** C6
Siau *Indonesia* 2°50N 125°25E **37** D7
Šiauliai *Lithuania* 55°56N 23°15E **9** J20
Sibā', Gebel el *Egypt* 25°45N 34°10E **44** E2
Sibang *Indonesia* 8°34S 115°13E **37** K18
Sibay *Russia* 52°42N 58°39E **18** D10
Sibayi, L. *S. Africa* 27°20S 32°45E **57** D5
Šibenik *Croatia* 43°48N 15°54E **22** C6
Siberia = Sibirskiy □
　Russia 58°0N 90°0E **29** D11
Siberia *Russia* 60°0N 100°0E **4** D13
Siberut *Indonesia* 1°30S 99°0E **36** E1
Sibi *Pakistan* 29°30N 67°54E **42** E2
Sibil = Oksibil *Indonesia* 4°59S 140°35E **37** E10
Sibiloi △ *Kenya* 4°0N 36°20E **54** B4
Sibirskiy □ *Russia* 58°0N 90°0E **29** D10
Sibirtsevo *Russia* 44°12N 132°26E **30** B5
Sibiti *Congo* 3°38S 13°19E **52** E2
Sibiu *Romania* 45°45N 24°9E **17** F13
Sibley *U.S.A.* 43°24N 95°45W **80** D6
Siborongborong *Indonesia* 2°13N 98°59E **39** L2
Sibsagar *India* 27°0N 94°36E **41** F19
Sibu *Malaysia* 2°18N 111°49E **36** D4
Sibuco *Phil.* 7°20N 122°10E **37** C6
Sibuguey B. *Phil.* 7°50N 122°45E **37** C6
Sibut *C.A.R.* 5°46N 19°10E **52** C3
Sibutu *Phil.* 4°45N 119°30E **37** D5
Sibutu Passage *E. Indies* 4°50N 120°0E **37** D6
Sibuyan I. *Phil.* 12°25N 122°40E **37** B6
Sibuyan Sea *Phil.* 12°30N 122°20E **37** B6
Sicamous *Canada* 50°49N 119°0W **70** C5
Siccus → *Australia* 31°55S 139°17E **63** E2
Sichon *Thailand* 9°0N 99°54E **39** H2
Sichuan □ *China* 30°30N 103°0E **32** C5
Sicilia *Italy* 37°30N 14°30E **22** F6
Sicily = Sicilia *Italy* 37°30N 14°30E **22** F6
Sicily, Str. of *Medit. S.* 37°35N 11°56E **22** F4
Sico → *Honduras* 15°58N 84°58W **88** C3
Sicuani *Peru* 14°21S 71°10W **92** F4
Sidári *Greece* 39°47N 19°41E **25** A3
Siddhapur *India* 23°56N 72°25E **42** H5
Siddipet *India* 18°5N 78°51E **40** K11
Sideros, Akra *Greece* 35°19N 26°19E **25** D8
Sidhauli *India* 27°17N 80°50E **43** F9
Sidhi *India* 24°25N 81°53E **43** G9
Sidi-bel-Abbès *Algeria* 35°13N 0°39W **50** A5
Sidi Ifni *Morocco* 29°29N 10°12W **50** C3
Sidikalang *Indonesia* 2°45N 98°19E **39** L2
Sidlaw Hills *U.K.* 56°32N 3°2W **11** E5
Sidley, Mt. *Antarctica* 77°2S 126°2W **5** D14
Sidmouth *U.K.* 50°40N 3°15W **13** G4
Sidmouth, C. *Australia* 13°25S 143°36E **62** A3
Sidney *Canada* 48°39N 123°24W **78** B3
Sidney *Mont., U.S.A.* 47°43N 104°9W **76** C11
Sidney *N.Y., U.S.A.* 42°19N 75°24W **83** D9
Sidney *Nebr., U.S.A.* 41°8N 102°59W **80** E2
Sidney *Ohio, U.S.A.* 40°17N 84°9W **81** E11
Sidney Lanier, L. *U.S.A.* 34°10N 84°4W **85** D12
Sidoarjo *Indonesia* 7°27S 112°43E **37** G15
Sidon = Saydā *Lebanon* 33°35N 35°25E **46** B4
Sidra, G. of = Surt, Khalīj
　Libya 31°40N 18°30E **51** B9
Siedlce *Poland* 52°10N 22°20E **17** B12
Sieg → *Germany* 50°46N 7°6E **16** C4
Siegen *Germany* 50°51N 8°0E **16** C5
Siem Pang *Cambodia* 14°7N 106°23E **38** E6
Siem Reap = Siemreab
　Cambodia 13°20N 103°52E **38** F4
Siemreab *Cambodia* 13°20N 103°52E **38** F4
Siena *Italy* 43°19N 11°21E **22** C4
Sieradz *Poland* 51°37N 18°41E **17** C10
Sierpe, Bocas de la
　Venezuela 10°0N 61°30W **93** L15
Sierra Blanca *U.S.A.* 31°11N 105°22W **84** F2
Sierra Blanca Peak
　U.S.A. 33°23N 105°49W **77** K11

Sierra City *U.S.A.* 39°34N 120°38W **78** F6
Sierra Colorada
  Argentina 40°35S 67°50W **96** E3
Sierra de Agalta △
  Honduras 15°1N 85°48W **88** C2
Sierra de Bahoruco △
  Dom. Rep. 18°10N 71°25W **89** C5
Sierra de La Culata △
  Venezuela 8°45N 71°10W **89** E5
Sierra de Lancandón △
  Guatemala 16°59N 90°23W **88** C1
Sierra de las Quijadas △
  Argentina 32°29S 67°5W **94** C2
Sierra de San Luis △
  Venezuela 11°20N 69°43W **89** D6
Sierra de San Pedro Mártir △
  Mexico 31°10N 115°30W **86** A1
Sierra Gorda *Chile* 22°50S 69°15W **94** A2
Sierra Leone ■ *W. Afr.* 9°0N 12°0W **50** G3
Sierra Madre *Mexico* 16°0N 93°0W **87** D6
Sierra Madre Occidental
  Mexico 27°0N 107°0W **86** B3
Sierra Madre Oriental
  Mexico 25°0N 100°0W **86** C5
Sierra Mojada *Mexico* 27°18N 103°41W **86** B4
Sierra Nevada *Spain* 37°3N 3°15W **21** D4
Sierra Nevada *U.S.A.* 39°0N 120°30W **78** H8
Sierra Nevada △
  Venezuela 8°35N 70°45W **89** E5
Sierra Nevada de Santa Marta △
  Colombia 10°56N 73°36W **89** D5
Sierra Vista *U.S.A.* 31°33N 110°18W **77** L8
Sierraville *U.S.A.* 39°36N 120°22W **78** F6
Sifnos *Greece* 37°0N 24°45E **23** F11
Sifton *Canada* 51°21N 100°8W **71** C8
Sifton Pass *Canada* 57°52N 126°15W **70** B3
Sig *Algeria* 35°32N 0°12W **50** A5
Sigatoka *Fiji* 18°8S 177°32E **59** a
Sighetu-Marmaţiei
  Romania 47°57N 23°52E **17** E12
Sighişoara *Romania* 46°12N 24°50E **17** E13
Sigli *Indonesia* 5°25N 96°0E **36** C1
Siglufjörður *Iceland* 66°12N 18°55W **8** C4
Signal de Botrang *Belgium* 50°29N 6°4E **15** D6
Signal Pk. *U.S.A.* 33°20N 114°2W **79** M12
Signy I. *Antarctica* 60°43S 45°36W **5** C18
Sígsig *Ecuador* 3°0S 78°50W **92** D3
Sigüenza *Spain* 41°3N 2°40W **21** B4
Siguiri *Guinea* 11°31N 9°10W **50** F4
Sigulda *Latvia* 57°10N 24°55E **9** H21
Sihora *India* 23°29N 80°6E **43** H9
Siikajoki → *Finland* 64°50N 24°43E **8** D21
Siilinjärvi *Finland* 63°4N 27°39E **8** E22
Sijarira Ra. = Chizarira
  Zimbabwe 17°36S 27°45E **55** F2
Sika *India* 22°26N 69°47E **42** H3
Sikanni Chief →
  Canada 57°47N 122°15W **70** B4
Sikao *Thailand* 7°34N 99°21E **39** J2
Sikar *India* 27°33N 75°10E **42** F6
Sikasso *Mali* 11°18N 5°35W **50** F4
Sikeston *U.S.A.* 36°53N 89°35W **80** G9
Sikhote Alin, Khrebet
  Russia 45°0N 136°0E **30** B8
Sikhote Alin Ra. = Sikhote Alin,
  Khrebet *Russia* 45°0N 136°0E **30** B8
Sikinos *Greece* 36°40N 25°8E **23** F11
Sikkim □ *India* 27°50N 88°30E **41** F16
Sil → *Spain* 42°27N 7°43W **21** A2
Silacayoapan *Mexico* 17°30N 98°9W **87** D5
Silawad *India* 21°54N 74°54E **42** J6
Silchar *India* 24°49N 92°48E **41** G18
Siler City *U.S.A.* 35°44N 79°28W **85** D15
Silesia = Śląsk *Poland* 51°0N 16°30E **16** C9
Silgarhi Doti *Nepal* 29°15N 81°0E **43** E9
Silghat *India* 26°35N 93°0E **41** F18
Silhouette *Seychelles* 4°29S 55°12E **53** b
Silifke *Turkey* 36°22N 33°58E **44** B2
Siliguri = Shiliguri *India* 26°45N 88°25E **41** F16
Siling Co *China* 31°50N 89°20E **32** C3
Silistra *Bulgaria* 44°6N 27°19E **23** B12
Silivri *Turkey* 41°4N 28°14E **23** D13
Siljan *Sweden* 60°55N 14°45E **8** F16
Silkeborg *Denmark* 56°10N 9°32E **9** H13
Silkwood *Australia* 17°45S 146°2E **62** B4
Sillajhuay, Cordillera
  Chile 19°46S 68°40W **92** G5
Sillamäe *Estonia* 59°24N 27°45E **9** G22
Silloth *U.K.* 54°52N 3°23W **12** C4
Siloam Springs *U.S.A.* 36°11N 94°32W **84** C7
Silopi *Turkey* 37°15N 42°27E **44** B4
Silsbee *U.S.A.* 30°21N 94°11W **84** F7
Šilutė *Lithuania* 55°21N 21°33E **9** J19
Silvan *Turkey* 38°7N 41°2E **44** B4
Silvani *India* 23°18N 78°25E **43** H8
Silver City *U.S.A.* 32°46N 108°17W **77** K9
Silver Cr. → *U.S.A.* 43°16N 119°13W **76** E4
Silver Creek *U.S.A.* 42°33N 79°10W **82** D5
Silver L. *U.S.A.* 38°39N 120°6W **78** G6
Silver Lake *Calif.,*
  U.S.A. 35°21N 116°7W **79** K10
Silver Lake *Oreg., U.S.A.* 43°8N 121°3W **76** E3
Silvermine Mts. *Ireland* 52°47N 8°15W **10** D3
Silverton *Tex., U.S.A.* 34°28N 101°19W **84** D4
Silvies → *U.S.A.* 43°34N 119°2W **76** E4
Simaltala *India* 24°43N 86°33E **43** G12
Simanggang = Sri Aman
  Malaysia 1°15N 111°32E **36** D4
Simard, L. *Canada* 47°40N 78°40W **72** C4
Simav *Turkey* 39°4N 28°58E **23** E13
Simba *Tanzania* 2°10S 37°36E **54** C4
Simbirsk = Ulyanovsk
  Russia 54°20N 48°25E **18** D8
Simbo *Tanzania* 4°51S 29°41E **54** C2
Simcoe *Canada* 42°50N 80°20W **82** D4
Simcoe, L. *Canada* 44°25N 79°20W **82** B5
Simdega *India* 22°37N 84°31E **43** H11
Simeria *Romania* 45°51N 23°1E **17** F12

Simeulue *Indonesia* 2°45N 95°45E **36** D1
Simferopol *Ukraine* 44°55N 34°3E **19** F5
Simi *Greece* 36°35N 27°50E **23** F12
Simi Valley *U.S.A.* 34°16N 118°47W **79** L8
Simikot *Nepal* 30°0N 81°50E **43** E9
Simla = Shimla *India* 31°2N 77°9E **42** D7
Simlipal △ *India* 21°45N 86°30E **43** J12
Simmie *Canada* 49°56N 108°6W **71** D7
Simmler *U.S.A.* 35°21N 119°59W **79** K7
Simo älv = Simojoki →
  Finland 65°35N 25°1E **8** D21
Simojoki → *Finland* 65°35N 25°1E **8** D21
Simojovel *Mexico* 17°12N 92°38W **87** D6
Simonette → *Canada* 55°9N 118°15W **70** B5
Simonstown *S. Africa* 34°14S 18°26E **56** E2
Simpang Empat *Malaysia* 5°27N 100°29E **39** c
Simplonpass *Switz.* 46°15N 8°3E **20** C8
Simpson Desert *Australia* 25°0S 137°0E **62** D2
Simpson Desert △
  Australia 24°59S 138°21E **62** C2
Simpson Pen. *Canada* 68°34N 88°45W **69** D14
Simrishamn *Sweden* 55°33N 14°22E **9** J16
Simsbury *U.S.A.* 41°53N 72°48W **83** E12
Simushir, Ostrov
  Russia 46°50N 152°30E **29** E16
Sin Cowe I. *S. China Sea* 9°53N 114°19E **36** C4
Sina Dhaqo *Somali Rep.* 5°50N 47°0E **47** F4
Sinabang *Indonesia* 2°30N 96°24E **36** D1
Sinai = Es Sînâ' *Egypt* 29°0N 34°0E **46** F3
Sinai, Mt. = Mûsa, Gebel
  Egypt 28°33N 33°59E **44** D2
Sinaloa □ *Mexico* 25°0N 107°30W **86** C3
Sinaloa de Leyva
  Mexico 25°50N 108°14W **86** B3
Sinarades *Greece* 39°34N 19°51E **25** A3
Sincelejo *Colombia* 9°18N 75°24W **92** B3
Sinch'ang *N. Korea* 40°7N 128°28E **35** D15
Sinch'ŏn *N. Korea* 38°17N 125°21E **35** E13
Sinclair *U.S.A.* 41°47N 107°7W **76** F10
Sinclair Mills *Canada* 54°5N 121°40W **70** C4
Sinclair's B. *U.K.* 58°31N 3°5W **11** C5
Sinclairville *U.S.A.* 42°16N 79°16W **82** D5
Sincorá, Serra do *Brazil* 13°30S 41°0W **93** F10
Sind = Sindh □ *Pakistan* 26°0N 69°0E **42** G3
Sind → *Jammu & Kashmir,*
  India 34°18N 74°45E **43** B6
Sind → *Mad. P., India* 26°26N 79°13E **43** F8
Sind Sagar Doab *Pakistan* 32°0N 71°30E **42** C4
Sindangan *Phil.* 8°10N 123°5E **37** C6
Sindangbarang *Indonesia* 7°27S 107°1E **37** G12
Sinde *Zambia* 17°28S 25°51E **55** F2
Sindh □ = Indus →
  Pakistan 24°20N 67°47E **42** G2
Sindh □ *Pakistan* 26°0N 69°0E **42** G3
Sindri *India* 23°45N 86°42E **43** H12
Sines *Portugal* 37°56N 8°51W **21** D1
Sines, C. de *Portugal* 37°58N 8°53W **21** D1
Sineu *Spain* 39°38N 3°1E **24** B10
Sing Buri *Thailand* 14°53N 100°25E **38** E3
Singa *Sudan* 13°10N 33°57E **51** F12
Singalila △ *India* 27°10N 88°5E **43** F13
Singapore ■ *Asia* 1°17N 103°51E **39** d
Singapore, Straits of *Asia* 1°15N 104°0E **39** d
Singapore Changi ✈ (SIN)
  Singapore 1°23N 103°59E **39** M4
Singaraja *Indonesia* 8°7S 115°6E **37** J18
Singatoka = Sigatoka *Fiji* 18°8S 177°32E **59** a
Singida *Tanzania* 4°49S 34°48E **54** C3
Singida □ *Tanzania* 6°0S 34°30E **54** D3
Singkaling Hkamti
  Burma 26°0N 95°39E **41** G19
Singkang *Indonesia* 4°8S 120°1E **37** E6
Singkawang *Indonesia* 1°0N 108°57E **36** D3
Singkep *Indonesia* 0°30S 104°25E **36** E2
Singkil *Indonesia* 2°17N 97°49E **39** L1
Singleton *Australia* 32°33S 151°0E **63** E5
Singleton, Mt. *N. Terr.,*
  Australia 22°0S 130°46E **60** D5
Singleton, Mt. *W. Austral.,*
  Australia 29°27S 117°15E **61** E2
Singoli *India* 25°0N 75°22E **42** G6
Singora = Songkhla
  Thailand 7°13N 100°37E **39** J3
Sinhüng *N. Korea* 40°11N 127°34E **35** D14
Siniscóla *Italy* 40°34N 9°41E **22** D3
Sinjai *Indonesia* 5°7S 120°20E **37** F6
Sinjär *Iraq* 36°19N 41°52E **44** B4
Sinkat *Sudan* 18°55N 36°49E **51** E13
Sinkiang = Xinjiang Uygur
  Zizhiqu □ *China* 42°0N 86°0E **32** B3
Sinmak *N. Korea* 38°25N 126°14E **35** E14
Sinmi-do *N. Korea* 39°33N 124°53E **35** E13
Sinnamary *Fr. Guiana* 5°25N 53°0W **93** B8
Sinni → *Italy* 40°8N 16°41E **22** D7
Sinop *Turkey* 42°1N 35°11E **19** F6
Sinor *India* 21°55N 73°20E **42** J5
Sinp'o *N. Korea* 40°0N 128°13E **35** E15
Sinsk *Russia* 61°8N 126°48E **29** C13
Sintang *Indonesia* 0°5N 111°35E **36** D4
Sinton *U.S.A.* 28°2N 97°31W **84** G6
Sintra *Portugal* 38°47N 9°25W **21** C1
Sinŭiju *N. Korea* 40°5N 124°24E **35** D13
Siófok *Hungary* 46°54N 18°3E **17** E10
Sion *Switz.* 46°14N 7°20E **20** C7
Sion Mills *U.K.* 54°48N 7°29W **10** B4
Sionainn = Shannon →
  Ireland 52°35N 9°30W **10** D2
Sioux Center *U.S.A.* 43°5N 96°11W **80** D5
Sioux City *U.S.A.* 42°30N 96°24W **80** D5
Sioux Falls *U.S.A.* 43°33N 96°44W **80** D5
Sioux Lookout *Canada* 50°10N 91°50W **72** B1
Sioux Narrows *Canada* 49°25N 94°10W **71** D10
Sipadan *Malaysia* 4°6N 118°38E **37** D5
Siparia *Trin. & Tob.* 10°8N 61°31W **93** K15
Siping *China* 43°8N 124°21E **35** C13
Sipiwesk L. *Canada* 55°5N 97°35W **71** B9
Siple *Antarctica* 75°0S 74°0W **5** D7
Sipra → *India* 23°55N 75°28E **42** H6

Sipura *Indonesia* 2°18S 99°40E **36** E1
Siquia → *Nic.* 12°10N 84°20W **88** D3
Siquijor *Phil.* 9°12N 123°35E **37** C6
Siquirres *Costa Rica* 10°6N 83°30W **88** D3
Şīr Abu Nu'ayr *U.A.E.* 25°20N 54°20E **45** E7
Şīr Banī Yās *U.A.E.* 24°19N 52°37E **45** E7
Sir Edward Pellew Group
  Australia 15°40S 137°10E **62** B2
Sir Graham Moore Is.
  Australia 13°53S 126°34E **60** B4
Sir James MacBrien, Mt.
  Canada 62°7N 127°41W **68** E6
Sira → *Norway* 58°23N 6°34E **9** G12
Siracusa *Italy* 37°4N 15°17E **22** F6
Sirajganj *Bangla.* 24°25N 89°47E **43** G13
Sirathu *India* 25°39N 81°19E **43** G9
Sīrdān *Iran* 36°39N 49°12E **45** B6
Siren *U.S.A.* 45°47N 92°24W **80** C7
Sirer *Spain* 38°56N 1°22E **24** C7
Siret → *Romania* 45°24N 28°1E **17** F14
Sirghāyā *Syria* 33°51N 36°8E **46** B5
Sirina *Thailand* 8°6N 98°17E **39** a
Sirmaur *India* 24°51N 81°23E **43** G9
Sirmilik △ *Canada* 72°50N 80°35W **69** C15
Sirohi *India* 24°52N 72°53E **42** G5
Sironj *India* 24°5N 77°39E **42** G7
Síros = Ermoupoli
  Greece 37°28N 24°57E **23** F11
Sirr, Nafud as *Si. Arabia* 25°33N 44°35E **44** E5
Sirretta Pk. *U.S.A.* 35°56N 118°19W **79** K8
Sīrrī *Iran* 25°55N 54°32E **45** E7
Sirsa *India* 29°33N 75°4E **42** E6
Sirsa → *India* 26°51N 79°4E **43** F8
Sisak *Croatia* 45°30N 16°21E **16** F9
Sisaket *Thailand* 15°8N 104°23E **38** E5
Sishen *S. Africa* 27°47S 22°59E **56** D3
Sishui *Henan, China* 34°48N 113°15E **34** G7
Sishui *Shandong, China* 35°42N 117°18E **35** G9
Sisipuk L. *Canada* 55°45N 101°50W **71** B8
Sisophon *Cambodia* 13°38N 102°59E **38** F4
Sisseton *U.S.A.* 45°40N 97°3W **80** C5
Sīstān *Asia* 30°50N 61°0E **45** D9
Sīstān, Daryācheh-ye *Iran* 31°0N 61°0E **45** D9
Sīstān va Balūchestān □
  Iran 27°0N 62°0E **45** E9
Sisters *U.S.A.* 44°18N 121°33W **76** D3
Sisters, The *Seychelles* 4°16S 55°52E **53** b
Siswa Bazar *India* 27°9N 83°46E **43** F10
Sitamarhi *India* 26°37N 85°30E **43** F11
Sitampiky *Madag.* 16°41S 46°6E **57** B8
Sitapur *India* 27°38N 80°45E **43** F9
Siteki *Swaziland* 26°32S 31°58E **57** D5
Sitges *Spain* 41°17N 1°47E **21** B6
Sitia *Greece* 35°13N 26°6E **25** D8
Sitito-Ozima Ridge
  Pac. Oc. 23°0N 143°0E **64** E6
Sitka *U.S.A.* 57°3N 135°20W **70** B1
Sitoti *Botswana* 23°15S 23°40E **56** C3
Sittang Myit → *Burma* 17°20N 96°45E **41** L20
Sittard *Neths.* 51°0N 5°52E **15** C5
Sittingbourne *U.K.* 51°20N 0°45E **13** F8
Sittoung = Sittang Myit →
  Burma 17°20N 96°45E **41** L20
Sittwe *Burma* 20°18N 92°45E **41** J18
Situbondo *Indonesia* 7°42S 114°0E **37** G16
Si'umu *Samoa* 14°1S 171°48W **59** b
Siuna *Nic.* 13°37N 84°45W **88** D3
Siuri *India* 23°50N 87°34E **43** H12
Sīvand *Iran* 30°5N 52°55E **45** D7
Sivas *Turkey* 39°43N 36°58E **44** B3
Siverek *Turkey* 37°50N 39°19E **44** B3
Sivomaskinskiy *Russia* 66°40N 62°35E **18** A11
Sivrihisar *Turkey* 39°30N 31°35E **19** G5
Sîwa *Egypt* 29°11N 25°31E **51** C11
Sîwa, El Wâhât es *Egypt* 29°10N 25°30E **48** D6
Siwa Oasis = Sîwa, El Wâhât es
  Egypt 29°10N 25°30E **48** D6
Siwalik Range *Nepal* 28°0N 83°0E **43** F10
Siwan *India* 26°13N 84°21E **43** F11
Siwana *India* 25°38N 72°25E **42** G5
Six Cross Roads *Barbados* 13°7N 59°28E **89** g
Sixmilebridge *Ireland* 52°44N 8°46W **10** D3
Sixth Cataract *Sudan* 16°20N 32°42E **51** E12
Siyah Kuh, Kavīr-e *Iran* 32°55N 53°55E **45** C7
Siziwang Qi *China* 41°25N 111°40E **34** D6
Sjælland *Denmark* 55°30N 11°30E **9** J14
Sjumen = Shumen
  Bulgaria 43°18N 26°55E **23** C12
Skadarsko Jezero *Europe* 42°10N 19°20E **23** C8
Skaftafell *Iceland* 64°1N 17°0W **8** D5
Skaftafell △ *Iceland* 64°9N 16°50W **8** D5
Skaftafellsjökull *Iceland* 65°54N 19°35W **8** D4
Skagastølstindane
  Norway 61°28N 7°52E **8** F12
Skagaströnd *Iceland* 65°50N 20°19W **8** D3
Skagen *Denmark* 57°43N 10°35E **9** H14
Skagerrak *Denmark* 57°30N 9°0E **9** H13
Skagit → *U.S.A.* 48°23N 122°22W **78** B4
Skagway *U.S.A.* 59°28N 135°19W **68** F4
Skala-Podilska *Ukraine* 48°50N 26°15E **17** D14
Skala-Podolskaya = Skala-
  Podilska *Ukraine* 48°50N 26°15E **17** D14
Skalat *Ukraine* 49°23N 25°55E **17** D13
Skåne *Sweden* 55°59N 13°30E **9** J15
Skaneateles *U.S.A.* 42°57N 76°26W **83** D8
Skaneateles L. *U.S.A.* 42°51N 76°22W **83** D8
Skardu *Pakistan* 35°20N 75°44E **43** B6
Skarżysko-Kamienna
  Poland 51°7N 20°52E **17** C11
Skeena → *Canada* 54°9N 130°5W **70** C2
Skeena Mts. *Canada* 56°40N 128°30W **70** B3
Skegness *U.K.* 53°9N 0°20E **12** D8
Skeldon = Corriverton
  Guyana 5°55N 57°20W **92** B7
Skeleton Coast *Namibia* 20°0S 13°0E **54** J2
Skeleton Coast △ *Namibia* 20°0S 13°0E **56** C1
Skellefteå *Sweden* 64°45N 20°50E **8** D19
Skellefteälven →
  Sweden 64°45N 21°10E **8** D19
Skelleftehamn *Sweden* 64°40N 21°9E **8** D19

Skerries, The *U.K.* 53°25N 4°36W **12** D3
Ski *Norway* 59°43N 10°52E **9** G14
Skiathos *Greece* 39°12N 23°30E **23** E10
Skibbereen *Ireland* 51°33N 9°16W **10** E2
Skiddaw *U.K.* 54°39N 3°9W **12** C4
Skidegate *Canada* 53°15N 132°1W **70** C2
Skien *Norway* 59°12N 9°35E **9** G13
Skierniewice *Poland* 51°58N 20°10E **17** C11
Skihist, Mt. *Canada* 50°12N 121°54W **70** C4
Skikda *Algeria* 36°50N 6°58E **50** A7
Skilloura *Cyprus* 35°14N 33°10E **25** D12
Skipton *U.K.* 53°58N 2°3W **12** D5
Skirmish Pt. *Australia* 11°59S 134°17E **62** A1
Skiros *Greece* 38°55N 24°34E **23** E11
Skive *Denmark* 56°33N 9°2E **9** H13
Skjálfandafljót → *Iceland* 65°59N 17°25W **8** D5
Skjálfandi *Iceland* 66°5N 17°30W **8** C5
Skole *Ukraine* 49°3N 23°30E **17** D12
Skopelos *Greece* 39°9N 23°47E **23** E10
Skopi *Greece* 35°11N 26°2E **25** D8
Skopje *Macedonia* 42°1N 21°26E **23** C9
Skövde *Sweden* 58°24N 13°50E **9** G15
Skovorodino *Russia* 54°0N 124°0E **29** D13
Skowhegan *U.S.A.* 44°46N 69°43W **81** C19
Skull *Ireland* 51°32N 9°34W **10** E2
Skunk → *U.S.A.* 40°42N 91°7W **80** E8
Skuodas *Lithuania* 56°16N 21°33E **9** H19
Skvyra *Ukraine* 49°44N 29°40E **17** D15
Skye *U.K.* 57°15N 6°10W **11** D2
Skykomish *U.S.A.* 47°42N 121°22W **76** C3
Skyros = Skiros *Greece* 38°55N 24°34E **23** E11
Slade Point *Australia* 21°4S 149°13E **62** b
Slade Pt. *Australia* 21°5S 149°13E **62** b
Slættaratindur *Faeroe Is.* 62°18N 7°1W **8** E9
Slagelse *Denmark* 55°23N 11°19E **9** J14
Slamet *Indonesia* 7°16S 109°8E **37** G13
Slane *Ireland* 53°42N 6°33W **10** C5
Slaney → *Ireland* 52°26N 6°33W **10** D5
Slangberge *S. Africa* 31°32S 20°48E **56** E3
Slate Is. *Canada* 48°40N 87°0W **72** C2
Slatina *Romania* 44°28N 24°22E **17** F13
Slatington *U.S.A.* 40°45N 75°37W **83** F9
Slaton *U.S.A.* 33°26N 101°39W **84** E4
Slave → *Canada* 61°18N 113°39W **70** A6
Slave Coast *W. Afr.* 6°0N 2°30E **50** G6
Slave Lake *Canada* 55°17N 114°43W **70** B6
Slave Pt. *Canada* 61°11N 115°56W **70** A5
Slavgorod *Russia* 53°1N 78°37E **28** D8
Slavonski Brod *Croatia* 45°11N 18°1E **23** B8
Slavuta *Ukraine* 50°15N 27°2E **17** C14
Slavyanka *Russia* 42°53N 131°21E **30** C5
Slavyansk = Slovyansk
  Ukraine 48°55N 37°36E **19** E6
Slawharad *Belarus* 53°27N 31°0E **17** B16
Sleaford *U.K.* 53°0N 0°24W **12** D7
Sleaford B. *Australia* 34°55S 135°45E **63** E2
Sleat, Sd. of *U.K.* 57°5N 5°47W **11** D3
Sleeper Is. *Canada* 58°30N 81°0W **69** F15
Sleeping Bear Dunes △
  U.S.A. 44°50N 86°5W **80** C10
Sleepy Eye *U.S.A.* 44°18N 94°43W **80** C6
Slemon L. *Canada* 63°13N 116°4W **70** A5
Slide Mt. *U.S.A.* 42°0N 74°25W **83** E10
Slidell *U.S.A.* 30°17N 89°47W **85** F10
Sliema *Malta* 35°55N 14°30E **25** D2
Slieve Aughty *Ireland* 53°4N 8°30W **10** C3
Slieve Bloom *Ireland* 53°4N 7°40W **10** C4
Slieve Donard *Ireland* 54°11N 5°55W **10** B6
Slieve Gamph *Ireland* 54°6N 9°0W **10** B3
Slieve Gullion *Ireland* 54°7N 6°26W **10** B5
Slieve League *Ireland* 54°40N 8°42W **10** B3
Slieve Mish *Ireland* 52°12N 9°50W **10** D2
Slievenamon *Ireland* 52°25N 7°34W **10** D4
Sligeach = Sligo *Ireland* 54°16N 8°28W **10** B3
Sligo *Ireland* 54°16N 8°28W **10** B3
Sligo *U.S.A.* 41°6N 79°29W **82** E5
Sligo □ *Ireland* 54°8N 8°42W **10** B3
Sligo B. *Ireland* 54°18N 8°40W **10** B3
Slite *Sweden* 57°42N 18°48E **9** H18
Sliven *Bulgaria* 42°42N 26°19E **23** C12
Sloan *U.S.A.* 35°57N 115°13W **79** K11
Sloansville *U.S.A.* 42°45N 74°22W **83** D10
Slobodskoy *Russia* 58°40N 50°6E **18** C9
Slobozia *Romania* 44°34N 27°23E **17** F14
Slocan *Canada* 49°48N 117°28W **70** D5
Slonim *Belarus* 53°4N 25°19E **17** B13
Slough *U.K.* 51°30N 0°36W **13** F7
Slough □ *U.K.* 51°30N 0°36W **13** F7
Sloughhouse *U.S.A.* 38°26N 121°12W **78** G5
Slovak Rep. ■ *Europe* 48°30N 20°0E **17** D10
Slovakia = Slovak Rep. ■
  Europe 48°30N 20°0E **17** D10
Slovakian Ore Mts. = Slovenské
  Rudohorie *Slovak Rep.* 48°45N 20°0E **17** D10
Slovenia ■ *Europe* 45°58N 14°30E **16** F8
Slovenija = Slovenia ■
  Europe 45°58N 14°30E **16** F8
Slovenská = Slovak Rep. ■
  Europe 48°30N 20°0E **17** D10
Slovenské Rudohorie
  Slovak Rep. 48°45N 20°0E **17** D10
Slovyansk *Ukraine* 48°55N 37°36E **19** E6
Sluch → *Ukraine* 51°37N 26°38E **17** C14
Sluis *Neths.* 51°18N 3°23E **15** C3
Słupsk *Poland* 54°30N 17°3E **17** A9
Slurry *S. Africa* 25°49S 25°42E **56** D4
Slutsk *Belarus* 53°2N 27°31E **17** B14
Slyne Hd. *Ireland* 53°25N 10°10W **10** C1
Slyudyanka *Russia* 51°40N 103°40E **29** D11
Småland *Sweden* 57°15N 15°25E **9** H16
Smalltree L. *Canada* 61°0N 105°0W **71** A8
Smallwood Res. *Canada* 54°0N 64°0W **73** B7
Smarhon *Belarus* 54°20N 26°24E **17** A14
Smartt Syndicate Dam
  S. Africa 30°45S 23°10E **56** E3
Smartville *U.S.A.* 39°13N 121°18W **78** F5
Smeaton *Canada* 53°30N 104°49W **71** C8

Smederevo *Serbia* 44°40N 20°57E **23** B9
Smerwick Harbour
  Ireland 52°12N 10°23W **10** D1
Smethport *U.S.A.* 41°49N 78°27W **82** E6
Smidovich *Russia* 48°36N 133°49E **29** E14
Smith *Canada* 55°10N 114°0W **70** B6
Smith Center *U.S.A.* 39°47N 98°47W **80** F4
Smith I. *Canada* 60°45N 78°25W **69** E16
Smith Islands △ *Australia* 20°40S 149°9E **62** b
Smith River △ *U.S.A.* 41°55N 124°0W **76** F2
Smithburne → *Australia* 17°3S 140°57E **62** B3
Smithers *Canada* 54°45N 127°10W **70** C3
Smithfield *S. Africa* 30°9S 26°30E **57** E4
Smithfield *N.C., U.S.A.* 35°31N 78°21W **85** D15
Smithfield *Utah, U.S.A.* 41°50N 111°50W **76** F8
Smiths Falls *Canada* 44°55N 76°0W **83** B9
Smithton *Australia* 40°53S 145°6E **63** G4
Smithville *Canada* 43°6N 79°33W **82** C5
Smithville *U.S.A.* 30°1N 97°10W **84** F6
Smoke Creek Desert
  U.S.A. 40°30N 119°40W **76** F4
Smoky → *Canada* 56°10N 117°21W **70** B5
Smoky Bay *Australia* 32°22S 134°13E **63** E1
Smoky Hill → *U.S.A.* 39°4N 96°48W **80** F5
Smoky Hills *U.S.A.* 39°15N 99°30W **80** F4
Smoky Lake *Canada* 54°10N 112°30W **70** C6
Smøla *Norway* 63°23N 8°3E **8** E13
Smolensk *Russia* 54°45N 32°5E **18** D5
Smolikas, Oros *Greece* 40°9N 20°58E **23** D9
Smolyan *Bulgaria* 41°36N 24°38E **23** D11
Smooth Rock Falls
  Canada 49°17N 81°37W **72** C3
Smoothstone L. *Canada* 54°40N 106°50W **71** C7
Smorgon = Smarhon
  Belarus 54°20N 26°24E **17** A14
Smyrna = İzmir *Turkey* 38°25N 27°8E **23** E12
Smyrna *U.S.A.* 39°18N 75°36W **81** F16
Snæfell *Iceland* 64°48N 15°34W **8** D6
Snaefell *I. of Man* 54°16N 4°27W **12** C3
Snæfellsjökull *Iceland* 64°49N 23°46W **8** D2
Snake → *U.S.A.* 46°12N 119°2W **76** C4
Snake I. *Australia* 38°47S 146°33E **63** F4
Snake Range *U.S.A.* 39°0N 114°20W **76** G6
Snake River Plain
  U.S.A. 42°50N 114°0W **76** E7
Snåsavatnet *Norway* 64°12N 12°0E **8** D15
Sneek *Neths.* 53°2N 5°40E **15** A5
Sneem *Ireland* 51°50N 9°54W **10** E2
Sneeuberge *S. Africa* 31°46S 24°20E **56** E3
Snelling *U.S.A.* 37°31N 120°26W **78** H6
Snežka *Europe* 50°41N 15°50E **16** C8
Snizort, L. *U.K.* 57°33N 6°28W **11** D2
Snøhetta *Norway* 62°19N 9°16E **8** E13
Snohomish *U.S.A.* 47°55N 122°6W **78** C4
Snoul *Cambodia* 12°4N 106°26E **39** F6
Snover *U.S.A.* 43°27N 82°58W **82** C2
Snow Hill *U.S.A.* 38°11N 75°24W **81** F16
Snow Lake *Canada* 54°52N 100°3W **71** C8
Snow Mt. *Calif., U.S.A.* 39°23N 122°45W **78** F4
Snow Mt. *Maine, U.S.A.* 45°18N 70°48W **83** A14
Snow Shoe *U.S.A.* 41°2N 77°57W **82** E7
Snowbird L. *Canada* 60°45N 103°0W **71** A8
Snowdon *U.K.* 53°4N 4°5W **12** D3
Snowdonia △ *U.K.* 53°7N 3°59W **12** D4
Snowdrift = Łutsel K'e
  Canada 62°24N 110°44W **71** A6
Snowdrift → *Canada* 62°24N 110°44W **71** A6
Snowflake *U.S.A.* 34°30N 110°5W **77** J8
Snowtown *Australia* 33°46S 138°14E **63** E2
Snowville *U.S.A.* 41°58N 112°43W **76** F7
Snowy → *Australia* 37°46S 148°30E **63** F4
Snowy Mt. *U.S.A.* 43°42N 74°23W **83** C10
Snowy Mts. *Australia* 36°30S 148°20E **63** F4
Snug Corner *Bahamas* 22°33N 73°52W **89** B5
Snug Harbour *Canada* 45°22N 80°17W **82** A4
Snyatyn *Ukraine* 48°27N 25°38E **17** D13
Snyder *Okla., U.S.A.* 34°40N 98°57W **84** D5
Snyder *Tex., U.S.A.* 32°44N 100°55W **84** E4
Soahanina *Madag.* 18°42S 44°13E **57** B7
Soalala *Madag.* 16°6S 45°20E **57** B8
Soamanonga *Madag.* 23°52S 44°47E **57** C7
Soan → *Pakistan* 33°1N 71°44E **42** C4
Soanierana-Ivongo
  Madag. 16°55S 49°35E **57** B8
Soanindrariny *Madag.* 19°54S 47°14E **57** B8
Soavina *Madag.* 19°9S 46°45E **57** B8
Soavinandriana *Madag.* 19°9S 46°45E **57** B8
Sobat, Nahr → *Sudan* 9°22N 31°33E **51** G12
Sobhapur *India* 22°47N 78°17E **42** H8
Sobradinho, Represa de
  Brazil 9°30S 42°0W **93** E10
Sobral *Brazil* 3°50S 40°20W **93** D10
Soc Giang *Vietnam* 22°54N 106°1E **38** A6
Soc Trang *Vietnam* 9°37N 105°50E **39** H5
Socastee *U.S.A.* 33°41N 78°59W **85** E15
Soch'e = Shache *China* 38°20N 77°10E **32** C2
Sochi *Russia* 43°35N 39°40E **19** F6
Société, Îs. de la
  French Polynesia 17°0S 151°0W **65** J12
Society Is. = Société, Îs. de la
  French Polynesia 17°0S 151°0W **65** J12
Socompa, Portezuelo de
  Chile 24°27S 68°18W **94** A2
Socorro *N. Mex., U.S.A.* 34°4N 106°54W **77** J10
Socorro *Tex., U.S.A.* 31°39N 106°18W **84** F1
Socorro, I. *Mexico* 18°45N 110°58W **86** D2
Socotra *Yemen* 12°30N 54°0E **47** E5
Soda L. *U.S.A.* 35°10N 116°4W **77** J5
Soda Plains *India* 35°30N 79°0E **43** B8
Soda Springs *U.S.A.* 42°39N 111°36W **76** E8
Sodankylä *Finland* 67°29N 26°40E **8** C22
Soddy-Daisy *U.S.A.* 35°17N 85°10W **85** D12
Söderhamn *Sweden* 61°18N 17°10E **8** F17
Söderköping *Sweden* 58°31N 16°20E **9** G17
Södermanland *Sweden* 58°56N 16°55E **9** G17

Södertälje *Sweden* 59°12N 17°39E **9** G17
Sodiri *Sudan* 14°27N 29°0E **51** F11
Sodus *U.S.A.* 43°14N 77°4W **82** C7
Sodwana Bay △ *S. Africa* 27°35S 32°43E **57** D5
Soe *Indonesia* 9°52S 124°17E **60** A3
Soekmekaar = Morebeng
  S. Africa 23°30S 29°55E **57** C4
Soest *Neths.* 52°9N 5°19E **15** B5
Sofala □ *Mozam.* 19°30S 34°30E **57** B5
Sofia = Sofiya *Bulgaria* 42°45N 23°20E **23** C10
Sofia → *Madag.* 15°27S 47°23E **57** B8
Sofiya *Bulgaria* 42°45N 23°20E **23** C10
Sofu-Gan *Japan* 29°49N 140°21E **31** K10
Sogamoso *Colombia* 5°43N 72°56W **92** B4
Sogār *Iran* 25°53N 58°6E **45** E8
Sogndalsfjøra *Norway* 61°14N 7°5E **8** F12
Søgne *Norway* 58°5N 7°48E **9** G12
Sognefjorden *Norway* 61°10N 5°50E **8** F11
Soh *Iran* 33°26N 51°27E **45** C6
Sohâg *Egypt* 26°33N 31°43E **51** C12
Sohagpur *India* 22°42N 78°12E **42** H8
Soignies *Belgium* 50°35N 4°5E **15** D4
Soissons *France* 49°25N 3°19E **20** B5
Sōja *Japan* 34°40N 133°45E **31** G6
Sojat *India* 25°55N 73°45E **42** G5
Sokal *Ukraine* 50°31N 24°15E **17** C13
Sokcho *S. Korea* 38°12N 128°36E **35** E15
Söke *Turkey* 37°48N 27°28E **23** F12
Sokelo
  Dem. Rep. of the Congo 9°55S 24°36E **55** D1
Sokhumi *Georgia* 43°0N 41°0E **19** F7
Soko Is. *China* 22°10N 113°54E **33** G10
Sokodé *Togo* 9°0N 1°11E **50** G6
Sokol *Russia* 59°30N 40°5E **18** C7
Sokółka *Poland* 53°25N 23°30E **17** B12
Sokołów Podlaski
  Poland 52°25N 22°15E **17** B12
Sokoto *Nigeria* 13°2N 5°16E **50** F7
Sol Iletsk *Russia* 51°10N 55°0E **18** D10
Solai *Kenya* 0°2N 36°12E **54** B4
Solan *India* 30°55N 77°7E **42** D7
Solana Beach *U.S.A.* 32°58N 117°16W **79** N9
Solander I. *N.Z.* 46°34S 166°54E **59** G1
Solano *Phil.* 16°31N 121°15E **37** A6
Solapur *India* 17°43N 75°56E **40** L9
Soldotna *U.S.A.* 60°29N 151°3W **68** E1
Soléa *Cyprus* 35°5N 33°4E **25** D12
Soledad *Colombia* 10°55N 74°46W **92** A4
Soledad *U.S.A.* 36°26N 121°20W **78** J5
Soledad *Venezuela* 8°10N 63°34W **92** B6
Solent, The *U.K.* 50°45N 1°25W **13** G6
Solfonntaggen *Norway* 60°2N 6°57E **9** F12
Solhan *Turkey* 38°57N 41°3E **44** B4
Soligalich *Russia* 59°5N 42°10E **18** C7
Soligorsk = Salihorsk
  Belarus 52°51N 27°27E **17** B14
Solihull *U.K.* 52°26N 1°47W **13** E6
Solikamsk *Russia* 59°38N 56°50E **18** C10
Solila *Madag.* 21°25S 46°37E **57** C8
Solimões = Amazonas →
  S. Amer. 0°5S 50°0W **93** D8
Solingen *Germany* 51°10N 7°5E **16** C4
Sollefteå *Sweden* 63°12N 17°20E **8** E17
Sóller *Spain* 39°46N 2°43E **24** B9
Solo → *Indonesia* 6°47S 112°22E **37** G15
Sologne *France* 47°40N 1°45E **20** C4
Solok *Indonesia* 0°45S 100°40E **36** E2
Sololá *Guatemala* 14°49N 91°10W **88** D1
Sololo *Kenya* 3°33N 38°39E **54** B4
Solomon, N. Fork →
  U.S.A. 39°29N 98°26W **80** F4
Solomon, S. Fork →
  U.S.A. 39°25N 99°12W **80** F4
Solomon Is. ■ *Pac. Oc.* 6°0S 155°0E **58** B8
Solomon Rise *Pac. Oc.* 1°0N 157°0E **64** G7
Solon *China* 46°32N 121°10E **33** B7
Solon Springs *U.S.A.* 46°22N 91°49W **80** B8
Solor *Indonesia* 8°27S 123°0E **37** F6
Solothurn *Switz.* 47°13N 7°32E **20** C7
Šolta *Croatia* 43°24N 16°15E **22** C7
Solṭānābād *Khorāsān,*
  Iran 34°13N 59°58E **45** C8
Solṭānābād *Khorāsān, Iran* 36°29N 58°5E **45** B8
Solunska Glava
  Macedonia 41°44N 21°31E **23** D9
Solvang *U.S.A.* 34°36N 120°8W **79** L6
Solvay *U.S.A.* 43°3N 76°13W **83** D8
Sölvesborg *Sweden* 56°5N 14°35E **9** H16
Solvychegodsk *Russia* 61°21N 46°56E **18** B8
Solway Firth *U.K.* 54°49N 3°35W **12** C4
Solwezi *Zambia* 12°11S 26°21E **55** E2
Sōma *Japan* 37°40N 140°50E **30** F10
Soma *Turkey* 39°10N 27°35E **23** E12
Somabhula *Zimbabwe* 19°42S 29°40E **57** B4
Somali Pen. *Africa* 7°0N 46°0E **48** F8
Somali Rep. ■ *Africa* 7°0N 47°0E **47** F4
Somalia = Somali Rep. ■
  Africa 7°0N 47°0E **47** F4
Somaliland □ *Somali Rep.* 9°0N 46°0E **47** F4
Sombor *Serbia* 45°46N 19°9E **23** B8
Sombra *Canada* 42°43N 82°29W **82** D2
Sombrerete *Mexico* 23°38N 103°39W **86** C4
Sombrero *Anguilla* 18°37N 63°30W **89** C7
Somdari *India* 25°47N 72°38E **42** G5
Somers *U.S.A.* 48°5N 114°13W **76** B6
Somerset *Ky., U.S.A.* 37°5N 84°36W **81** G11
Somerset *Mass., U.S.A.* 41°47N 71°8W **83** E13
Somerset *Pa., U.S.A.* 40°1N 79°5W **82** F5
Somerset □ *U.K.* 51°9N 3°0W **13** F5
Somerset East *S. Africa* 32°42S 25°35E **56** E4
Somerset I. *Canada* 73°30N 93°0W **68** A12
Somerset West *S. Africa* 34°8S 18°50E **56** E2
Somersworth *U.S.A.* 43°16N 70°52W **83** C14
Somerton *U.S.A.* 32°36N 114°43W **77** K6
Somerville *U.S.A.* 40°35N 74°38W **83** F10
Someş → *Romania* 47°49N 22°43E **17** E12
Somme → *France* 50°11N 1°38E **20** A4
Somnath *India* 20°53N 70°22E **42** J4

Somosierra, Puerto de
  Spain 41°4N 3°35W **21** B4
Somosomo *Fiji* 16°47S 179°58W **59** a
Somosomo Str. *Fiji* 16°0S 180°0E **59** a
Somoto *Nic.* 13°28N 86°37W **88** D2
Somport, Tunnel de
  Spain 42°48N 0°31W **20** E3
Son → *India* 25°42N 84°52E **43** G11
Son Ha *Vietnam* 15°3N 108°34E **38** E7
Son Hoa *Vietnam* 13°2N 108°58E **38** F7
Son La *Vietnam* 21°20N 103°50E **38** B4
Son Morrell *Spain* 39°44N 3°20E **24** B10
Son Rapinya *Spain* 39°35N 2°37E **24** B9
Son Sardina *Spain* 39°37N 2°40E **24** B9
Son Serra *Spain* 39°43N 3°13E **24** B10
Son Tay *Vietnam* 21°8N 105°30E **38** B5
Soná *Panama* 8°0N 81°20W **88** E3
Sonamarg *India* 34°18N 75°21E **43** B6
Sonamukhi *India* 23°18N 87°27E **43** H12
Sonar → *India* 24°24N 79°56E **43** G8
Sŏnch'ŏn *N. Korea* 39°48N 124°55E **35** E13
Sondags → *S. Africa* 33°44S 25°51E **56** E4
Sondar *India* 33°28N 75°56E **43** C6
Sóndrio *Italy* 46°10N 9°52E **20** C8
Sone *Mozam.* 17°23S 34°55E **55** F3
Sonepur *India* 20°55N 83°50E **41** J13
Song *Thailand* 18°28N 100°11E **38** C3
Song Cau *Vietnam* 13°27N 109°18E **38** F7
Song Hong → *Vietnam* 22°0N 104°0E **32** D5
Song Xian *China* 34°12N 112°8E **34** G7
Songan *Indonesia* 8°13S 115°24E **37** J18
Songea *Tanzania* 10°40S 35°40E **54** G6
Songgang *China* 22°46N 113°50E **33** F10
Songhua Hu *China* 43°35N 126°50E **35** C14
Songhua Jiang →
  China 47°45N 132°30E **33** B8
Songimvelo △ *S. Africa* 25°50S 31°2E **57** D5
Sŏngjin = Kimch'aek
  N. Korea 40°40N 129°10E **35** D15
Songkhla *Thailand* 7°13N 100°37E **39** J3
Songnim *N. Korea* 38°45N 125°39E **35** E13
Songo *Mozam.* 15°34S 32°38E **55** F3
Songo *Sudan* 9°47N 24°21E **51** G10
Songpan *China* 32°40N 103°30E **32** C5
Songwe
  Dem. Rep. of the Congo 3°20S 26°16E **54** C2
Songwe → *Africa* 9°44S 33°58E **55** D3
Sonhat *India* 23°29N 82°31E **43** H10
Sonid Youqi *China* 42°45N 112°48E **34** C7
Sonipat *India* 29°0N 77°5E **42** E7
Sonkach *India* 22°59N 76°21E **42** H7
Sonmiani *Pakistan* 25°25N 66°40E **42** G2
Sonmiani B. *Pakistan* 25°15N 66°30E **42** G2
Sono → *Brazil* 9°58S 48°11W **93** E9
Sonoma *U.S.A.* 38°18N 122°28W **78** G4
Sonora *Calif., U.S.A.* 37°59N 120°23W **78** H6
Sonora *Tex., U.S.A.* 30°34N 100°39W **84** F4
Sonora □ *Mexico* 29°20N 110°40W **86** B2
Sonora → *Mexico* 29°5N 110°55W **86** B2
Sonoran Desert
  U.S.A. 33°40N 113°30W **79** L12
Sonoyta *Mexico* 31°51N 112°50W **86** A2
Sonsonate *El Salv.* 13°43N 89°44W **88** D2
Soochow = Suzhou
  China 31°19N 120°38E **33** C7
Sooke *Canada* 48°13N 123°43W **78** B3
Soomaaliya = Somali Rep. ■
  Africa 7°0N 47°0E **47** F4
Sop Hao *Laos* 20°33N 104°27E **38** B5
Sop Prap *Thailand* 17°53N 99°20E **38** D2
Sopi *Indonesia* 2°34N 128°28E **37** D7
Sopot *Poland* 54°27N 18°31E **17** A10
Sopron *Hungary* 47°45N 16°32E **17** E9
Sopur *India* 34°18N 74°27E **43** B6
Sør-Rondane *Antarctica* 72°0S 25°0E **5** D4
Sorah *Pakistan* 27°13N 68°56E **42** F3
Saraon *India* 25°37N 81°51E **43** G9
Sord = Swords *Ireland* 53°28N 6°13W **10** C5
Sorel-Tracy *Canada* 46°0N 73°10W **72** C5
Sórgono *Italy* 40°1N 9°6E **22** D3
Soria *Spain* 41°43N 2°32W **21** B4
Soriano *Uruguay* 33°24S 58°19W **94** C4
Sorkh, Kuh-e *Iran* 35°40N 58°30E **45** C8
Soroca *Moldova* 48°8N 28°12E **17** D15
Sorocaba *Brazil* 23°31S 47°27W **95** A6
Sorochinsk *Russia* 52°26N 53°10E **18** D9
Soroki = Soroca *Moldova* 48°8N 28°12E **17** D15
Sorong *Indonesia* 0°55S 131°15E **37** E8
Soroni *Greece* 36°21N 28°1E **25** C10
Soroti *Uganda* 1°43N 33°35E **54** B3
Sørøya *Norway* 70°40N 22°30E **8** A20
Sørøysundet *Norway* 70°25N 23°0E **8** A20
Sorrell *Australia* 42°47S 147°34E **63** G4
Sorrento *Italy* 40°37N 14°22E **22** D6
Sorsele *Sweden* 65°31N 17°30E **8** D17
Sorsogon *Phil.* 13°0N 124°0E **37** B6
Sortavala *Russia* 61°42N 30°41E **8** F24
Sortland *Norway* 68°42N 15°25E **8** B16
Soscumica, L. *Canada* 50°15N 77°27W **72** B4
Sosnogorsk *Russia* 63°37N 53°51E **18** B9
Sosnowiec *Poland* 50°20N 19°10E **17** C10
Sossus Vlei *Namibia* 24°40S 15°23E **56** C2
Sot → *India* 27°27N 79°37E **43** F8
Sotavento *C. Verde Is.* 15°0N 25°0W **50** b
Sotik *Kenya* 0°41S 35°7E **54** C4
Sotkamo *Finland* 64°8N 28°23E **8** D23
Soto la Marina *Mexico* 23°46N 98°13W **87** C5
Soto la Marina →
  Mexico 23°45N 97°45W **87** C5
Sotuta *Mexico* 20°36N 89°1W **87** C7
Souanké *Congo* 2°10N 14°3E **52** D2
Souda *Greece* 35°29N 24°4E **25** D6
Soudas, Ormos *Greece* 35°25N 24°10E **25** D6
Souderton *U.S.A.* 40°19N 75°19W **83** F9
Soufrière *Guadeloupe* 16°5N 61°40W **88** b
Soufrière *St. Lucia* 13°51N 61°3W **89** f
Soufrière Bay *Dominica* 15°13N 61°22W **89** f

Soukhouma *Laos* 14°38N 105°48E **38** E5
Sŏul = Seoul *S. Korea* 37°31N 126°58E **35** F14
Sound, The *U.K.* 50°20N 4°10W **13** G3
Sources, Mt. aux *Lesotho* 28°45S 28°50E **57** D4
Soure *Brazil* 0°35S 48°30W **93** D9
Souris *Man., Canada* 49°40N 100°20W **71** D8
Souris *P.E.I., Canada* 46°21N 62°15W **73** C7
Souris → *N. Amer.* 49°40N 99°34W **80** A4
Sousa *Brazil* 6°45S 38°10W **93** E11
Sousse *Tunisia* 35°50N 10°38E **51** A8
Sout → *S. Africa* 31°35S 18°24E **56** E2
South Africa ■ *Africa* 32°0S 23°0E **56** E3
South America 10°0S 60°0W **90** E5
South Aulatsivik I.
  Canada 56°45N 61°30W **73** A7
South Australia □
  Australia 32°0S 139°0E **63** E2
South Australian Basin
  Ind. Oc. 38°0S 126°0E **64** L4
South Ayrshire □ *U.K.* 55°18N 4°41W **11** F4
South Baldy Pk. *U.S.A.* 34°6N 107°11W **77** J10
South Bass I. *U.S.A.* 41°39N 82°49W **82** E2
South Bend *Ind., U.S.A.* 41°41N 86°15W **80** E10
South Bend *Wash.,*
  U.S.A. 46°40N 123°48W **78** D3
South Boston *U.S.A.* 36°42N 78°54W **81** G14
South Branch *Canada* 47°55N 59°2W **73** C8
South Brook *Canada* 49°26N 56°5W **73** C8
South Bruny I. *Australia* 43°20S 147°15E **63** G4
South Carolina □ *U.S.A.* 34°0N 81°0W **85** E14
South Charleston
  U.S.A. 38°22N 81°44W **81** F13
South China Sea *Asia* 10°0N 113°0E **36** C4
South Cumberland Is. △
  Australia 20°42S 149°11E **62** b
South Dakota □ *U.S.A.* 44°15N 100°0W **80** C4
South Dayton *U.S.A.* 42°21N 79°3W **82** D5
South Deerfield *U.S.A.* 42°29N 72°37W **83** D12
South Downs *U.K.* 50°52N 0°25W **13** G7
South East C. *Australia* 43°40S 146°50E **63** G4
South East Is. *Australia* 34°17S 123°30E **61** F3
South Esk → *U.K.* 56°43N 2°31W **11** E6
South Fiji Basin *Pac. Oc.* 26°0S 175°0E **64** K9
South Foreland *U.K.* 51°8N 1°24E **13** F9
South Fork American →
  U.S.A. 38°57N 120°59W **78** G5
South Fork Feather →
  U.S.A. 39°17N 121°36W **78** F5
South Fork Grand →
  U.S.A. 45°43N 102°17W **80** C2
South Fork Milk →
  U.S.A. 48°4N 106°19W **76** B10
South Fork Republican →
  U.S.A. 40°3N 101°31W **80** E3
South Georgia *Antarctica* 54°30S 37°0W **96** G9
South Gloucestershire □
  U.K. 51°32N 2°28W **13** F5
South Hadley *U.S.A.* 42°16N 72°35W **83** D12
South Haven *U.S.A.* 42°24N 86°16W **80** D10
South Henik L. *Canada* 61°30N 97°20W **71** A9
South Horr *Kenya* 2°12N 36°56E **54** B4
South I. *Kenya* 2°36N 36°35E **54** B4
South I. *N.Z.* 44°0S 170°0E **59** F3
South Indian Lake
  Canada 56°47N 98°56W **71** B9
South Invercargill *N.Z.* 46°26S 168°23E **59** G2
South Island △ *U.S.A.* 2°39N 36°35E **54** B4
South Kitui △ *Kenya* 1°48S 38°46E **54** C4
South Knife → *Canada* 58°55N 94°37W **71** B10
South Koel → *India* 22°32N 85°14E **43** H11
South Korea ■ *Asia* 36°0N 128°0E **35** G15
South Lake Tahoe
  U.S.A. 38°57N 119°59W **78** G6
South Lanarkshire □
  U.K. 55°37N 3°53W **11** F5
South Loup → *U.S.A.* 41°4N 98°39W **80** E4
South Luangwa △ *Zambia* 13°0S 31°20E **55** E3
South Magnetic Pole
  Antarctica 64°8S 138°8E **5** C9
South Milwaukee
  U.S.A. 42°55N 87°52W **80** D10
South Molton *U.K.* 51°1N 3°51W **13** F4
South Moose L. *Canada* 53°49N 100°1W **71** C8
South Nahanni →
  Canada 61°3N 123°21W **70** A4
South Nation → *Canada* 45°34N 75°6W **83** A9
South Natuna Is. = Natuna
  Selatan, Kepulauan
  Indonesia 2°45N 109°0E **36** D3
South Negril Pt. *Jamaica* 18°16N 78°22W **88** a
South Orkney Is.
  Antarctica 63°0S 45°0W **5** C18
South Ossetia □ *Georgia* 42°21N 44°2E **19** F7
South Otselic *U.S.A.* 42°38N 75°46W **83** D9
South Pagai, I. = Pagai Selatan,
  Pulau *Indonesia* 3°0S 100°15E **36** E2
South Paris *U.S.A.* 44°14N 70°31W **83** B14
South Pittsburg *U.S.A.* 35°1N 85°42W **85** D12
South Platte → *U.S.A.* 41°7N 100°42W **80** E3
South Pole *Antarctica* 90°0S 0°0 **5** E
South Porcupine *Canada* 48°30N 81°12W **72** C3
South Portland *U.S.A.* 43°38N 70°15W **81** D18
South Pt. *Barbados* 13°2N 59°32W **89** g
South River *Canada* 45°52N 79°23W **72** C4
South River *U.S.A.* 40°27N 74°23W **83** F10
South Ronaldsay *U.K.* 58°48N 2°58W **11** C6
South Rukuru → *Malawi* 10°44S 34°14E **55** E3
South Sandwich Is.
  Antarctica 57°0S 27°0W **5** B1
South Sandwich Trench
  Atl. Oc. 56°0S 24°0W **5** B1
South Saskatchewan →
  Canada 53°15N 105°5W **71** C7
South Seal → *Canada* 58°48N 98°8W **71** B9
South Shetland Is.
  Antarctica 62°0S 59°0W **5** C18
South Shields *U.K.* 55°0N 1°25W **12** C6
South Sioux City *U.S.A.* 42°28N 96°24W **80** D5

South Sister *U.S.A.* 44°4N 121°51W **76** D3
South Talpatti = New Moore I.
  Ind. Oc. 21°37N 89°10E **43** J13
South Taranaki Bight
  N.Z. 39°40S 174°5E **59** C5
South Tasman Rise
  S. Ocean 48°0S 146°0E **5** A10
South Thompson →
  Canada 50°40N 120°20W **70** C4
South Twin I. *Canada* 53°7N 79°52W **72** B4
South Tyne → *U.K.* 54°59N 2°8W **12** C5
South Uist *U.K.* 57°20N 7°15W **11** D1
South Valley *U.S.A.* 35°1N 106°41W **77** J10
South Wellesley Is.
  Australia 16°58S 139°17E **62** B2
South West C. *Australia* 43°34S 146°3E **63** G4
South West C. *N.Z.* 47°17S 167°28E **59** G1
South Williamsport
  U.S.A. 41°13N 77°0W **82** E8
South Yorkshire □ *U.K.* 53°27N 1°36W **12** D6
Southampton *Canada* 44°30N 81°25W **82** B3
Southampton *U.K.* 50°54N 1°23W **13** G6
Southampton □ *U.K.* 50°54N 1°23W **13** G6
Southampton I. *Canada* 64°30N 84°0W **69** E15
Southaven *U.S.A.* 34°59N 90°0W **85** D9
Southbank *Canada* 54°2N 125°46W **70** C3
Southbridge *N.Z.* 43°48S 172°16E **59** E4
Southbridge *U.S.A.* 42°5N 72°2W **83** D12
Southend *Canada* 56°19N 103°22W **71** B8
Southend-on-Sea *U.K.* 51°32N 0°44E **13** F8
Southend-on-Sea □ *U.K.* 51°32N 0°44E **13** F8
Southern □
  Russia 44°0N 40°0E **28** E5
Southern □ *Malawi* 15°0S 35°0E **55** F4
Southern □ *Zambia* 16°20S 26°20E **55** F2
Southern Alps *N.Z.* 43°41S 170°11E **59** E3
Southern Cross
  Australia 31°12S 119°15E **61** F2
Southern Indian L.
  Canada 57°10N 98°30W **71** B9
Southern Lau Group
  Fiji 18°40S 178°40W **59** a
Southern Ocean *Antarctica* 62°0S 60°0E **5** C6
Southern Pines *U.S.A.* 35°11N 79°24W **85** D15
Southern Uplands *U.K.* 55°28N 3°52W **11** F5
Southington *U.S.A.* 41°36N 72°53W **83** E12
Southland □ *N.Z.* 45°30S 168°0E **59** F1
Southold *U.S.A.* 41°4N 72°26W **83** E12
Southport *Australia* 27°58S 153°25E **63** D5
Southport *U.K.* 53°39N 3°0W **12** D4
Southport *U.S.A.* 42°3N 76°49W **82** D8
Southwest △ *Australia* 43°8S 146°5E **63** G4
Southwest Pacific Basin
  Pac. Oc. 40°0S 140°0W **5** A12
Southwold *U.K.* 52°20N 1°41E **13** E9
Southwood △ *Australia* 27°48S 150°8E **63** D5
Soutpansberg *S. Africa* 23°0S 29°30E **57** C4
Sovetsk *Kaliningrad, Russia* 55°6N 21°50E **9** J19
Sovetsk *Kirov, Russia* 57°38N 48°53E **18** C8
Sovetskaya Gavan
  Russia 48°58N 140°18E **29** E15
Soweto *S. Africa* 26°14S 27°52E **57** D4
Sowma'eh Sarā *Iran* 37°17N 49°18E **45** B6
Sōya-Kaikyō = La Perouse Str.
  Asia 45°40N 142°0E **30** B11
Sōya-Misaki *Japan* 45°30N 141°55E **30** B10
Soyo *Angola* 6°13S 12°20E **52** F2
Sozh → *Belarus* 51°57N 30°48E **17** B16
Spa *Belgium* 50°29N 5°53E **15** D5
Spain ■ *Europe* 39°0N 4°0W **21** B4
Spalding *Australia* 33°30S 138°37E **63** E2
Spalding *U.K.* 52°48N 0°9W **12** E7
Spanaway *U.S.A.* 47°6N 122°26W **78** C4
Spangler *U.S.A.* 40°39N 78°48W **82** F6
Spanish *Canada* 46°12N 82°20W **72** C3
Spanish Fork *U.S.A.* 40°7N 111°39W **76** F8
Spanish Town
  Br. Virgin Is. 17°43N 64°26W **89** e
Spanish Town *Jamaica* 18°0N 76°57W **88** a
Sparks *U.S.A.* 39°32N 119°45W **78** F7
Sparta = Sparti *Greece* 37°5N 22°25E **23** F10
Sparta *Mich., U.S.A.* 43°10N 85°42W **81** D11
Sparta *N.J., U.S.A.* 41°2N 74°38W **83** E10
Sparta *Wis., U.S.A.* 43°56N 90°49W **80** D8
Spartanburg *U.S.A.* 34°56N 81°57W **85** D14
Sparti *Greece* 37°5N 22°25E **23** F10
Spartivento, C. *Calabria,*
  Italy 37°55N 16°4E **22** F7
Spartivento, C. *Sard., Italy* 38°53N 8°50E **22** E3
Sparwood *Canada* 49°44N 114°53W **70** D6
Spassk Dalniy *Russia* 44°40N 132°48E **30** B6
Spatha, Akra *Greece* 35°42N 23°43E **25** D5
Spatsizi → *Canada* 57°42N 128°7W **70** B3
Spatsizi Plateau Wilderness △
  Canada 57°40N 128°0W **70** B3
Spean → *U.K.* 56°55N 4°59W **11** E4
Spearfish *U.S.A.* 44°30N 103°52W **80** C2
Spearman *U.S.A.* 36°12N 101°12W **84** C4
Speculator *U.S.A.* 43°30N 74°22W **83** C10
Speightstown *Barbados* 13°15N 59°39W **89** g
Speke Gulf *Tanzania* 2°20S 32°50E **54** C3
Spence Bay = Taloyoak
  Canada 69°32N 93°32W **68** D13
Spencer *Idaho, U.S.A.* 44°22N 112°11W **76** D7
Spencer *Iowa, U.S.A.* 43°9N 95°9W **80** D6
Spencer *N.Y., U.S.A.* 42°13N 76°30W **83** D8
Spencer *Nebr., U.S.A.* 42°53N 98°42W **80** D4
Spencer, C. *Australia* 35°20S 136°53E **63** F2
Spencer B. *Namibia* 25°30S 14°47E **56** D1
Spencer G. *Australia* 34°0S 137°20E **63** E2
Spencerville *Canada* 44°51N 75°33W **83** B9
Spences Bridge *Canada* 50°25N 121°20W **70** C4
Spennymoor *U.K.* 54°42N 1°36W **12** C6
Spenser Mts. *N.Z.* 42°15S 172°45E **59** E4
Sperrin Mts. *U.K.* 54°50N 7°0W **10** B5
Spey → *U.K.* 57°40N 3°6W **11** D5
Speyer *Germany* 49°29N 8°25E **16** D5
Spezand *Pakistan* 29°59N 67°0E **42** E2

Spiddle *Ireland* 53°15N 9°18W **10** C2
Spili *Greece* 35°13N 24°31E **25** D6
Spīn Būldak *Afghan.* 31°1N 66°25E **42** D2
Spinalonga *Greece* 35°18N 25°44E **25** D7
Spinifex ○ *Australia* 28°30S 128°30E **61** E4
Spirit Lake *U.S.A.* 46°15N 122°9W **78** D4
Spirit River *Canada* 55°45N 118°50W **70** B5
Spiritwood *Canada* 53°24N 107°33W **71** C7
Spithead *U.K.* 50°45N 1°10W **13** G6
Spitzbergen = Svalbard
  Arctic 78°0N 17°0E **4** B8
Spjelkavik *Norway* 62°28N 6°22E **8** E12
Split *Croatia* 43°31N 16°26E **22** C7
Split L. *Canada* 56°8N 96°15W **71** B9
Split Lake *Canada* 56°8N 96°15W **71** B9
Spofford *U.S.A.* 29°10N 100°25W **84** G4
Spokane *U.S.A.* 47°40N 117°24W **76** C5
Spoleto *Italy* 42°44N 12°44E **22** C5
Spooner *U.S.A.* 45°50N 91°53W **80** C8
Sporyy Navolok, Mys
  Russia 75°50N 68°40E **28** B7
Sprague *U.S.A.* 47°18N 117°59W **76** C5
Spratly I. *S. China Sea* 8°38N 111°55E **36** C4
Spratly Is. *S. China Sea* 8°20N 112°0E **36** C4
Spray *U.S.A.* 44°50N 119°48W **76** D4
Sprengisandur *Iceland* 64°52N 18°7W **8** D4
Spring City *U.S.A.* 40°11N 75°33W **83** F9
Spring Creek *U.S.A.* 40°44N 115°35W **76** F6
Spring Garden *U.S.A.* 39°52N 120°47W **78** F6
Spring Hall *Barbados* 13°18N 59°36W **89** g
Spring Hill *U.S.A.* 28°27N 82°41W **85** G13
Spring Mts. *U.S.A.* 36°0N 115°45W **79** J11
Spring Valley *Calif.,*
  U.S.A. 32°44N 116°59W **79** N10
Spring Valley *Nev.,*
  U.S.A. 36°6N 115°14W **79** J11
Springbok *S. Africa* 29°42S 17°54E **56** D2
Springboro *U.S.A.* 41°48N 80°22W **82** E4
Springdale *Canada* 49°30N 56°6W **73** C8
Springdale *U.S.A.* 36°11N 94°8W **84** C7
Springer *U.S.A.* 36°22N 104°36W **77** H11
Springerville *U.S.A.* 34°8N 109°17W **77** J9
Springfield *Canada* 42°50N 80°56W **82** D4
Springfield *N.Z.* 43°19S 171°56E **59** E3
Springfield *Colo.,*
  U.S.A. 37°24N 102°37W **77** H12
Springfield *Ill., U.S.A.* 39°48N 89°39W **80** F9
Springfield *Mass., U.S.A.* 42°6N 72°35W **83** D12
Springfield *Mo., U.S.A.* 37°13N 93°17W **80** G7
Springfield *Ohio, U.S.A.* 39°55N 83°49W **81** F12
Springfield *Oreg., U.S.A.* 44°3N 123°1W **76** D2
Springfield *Tenn.,*
  U.S.A. 36°31N 86°53W **85** C11
Springfield *Vt., U.S.A.* 43°18N 72°29W **83** C12
Springfontein *S. Africa* 30°15S 25°40E **56** E4
Springhill *Canada* 45°40N 64°4W **73** C7
Springhill *U.S.A.* 33°0N 93°28W **84** E8
Springhouse *Canada* 51°56N 122°7W **70** C4
Springs *S. Africa* 26°13S 28°25E **57** D4
Springvale *U.S.A.* 43°28N 70°48W **83** C14
Springville *Calif., U.S.A.* 36°8N 118°49W **78** J8
Springville *N.Y., U.S.A.* 42°31N 78°40W **82** D6
Springville *Utah, U.S.A.* 40°10N 111°37W **76** F8
Springwater *U.S.A.* 42°38N 77°35W **82** D7
Spruce-Creek *U.S.A.* 40°36N 78°9W **82** F6
Spruce Knob-Seneca Rocks △
  U.S.A. 38°50N 79°30W **81** F14
Spruce Mt. *U.S.A.* 44°12N 72°19W **83** B12
Sprucedale *Canada* 45°29N 79°28W **82** A5
Spur *U.S.A.* 33°28N 100°52W **84** J4
Spurn Hd. *U.K.* 53°35N 0°8E **12** D8
Spuzzum *Canada* 49°37N 121°23W **70** D4
Squam L. *U.S.A.* 43°45N 71°32W **83** C13
Squamish *Canada* 49°45N 123°10W **70** D4
Square Islands *Canada* 52°47N 55°47W **73** B8
Squires, Mt. *Australia* 26°14S 127°28E **61** E4
Srbija = Serbia ■ *Europe* 43°20N 20°0E **23** B9
Sre Ambel *Cambodia* 11°8N 103°46E **39** G4
Sre Khtum *Cambodia* 12°10N 106°52E **39** F6
Sre Umbell = Sre Ambel
  Cambodia 11°8N 103°46E **39** G4
Srebrenica *Bos.-H.* 44°6N 19°18E **23** B8
Sredinny Ra. = Sredinnyy Khrebet
  Russia 57°0N 160°0E **29** D17
Sredinnyy Khrebet
  Russia 57°0N 160°0E **29** D17
Srednekolymsk *Russia* 67°27N 153°40E **29** C16
Śrem *Poland* 52°6N 17°2E **17** B9
Sremska Mitrovica
  Serbia 44°59N 19°38E **23** B8
Srepok → *Cambodia* 13°33N 106°16E **38** F6
Sretensk *Russia* 52°10N 117°40E **29** D12
Sri Aman *Malaysia* 1°15N 111°32E **36** D4
Sri Lanka ■ *Asia* 7°30N 80°50E **40** R12
Srikakulam *India* 18°14N 83°58E **41** K13
Srinagar *India* 34°5N 74°50E **43** B6
Srono *Indonesia* 8°24S 114°16E **37** J17
Ssese Is. = Sese Is. *Uganda* 0°20S 32°20E **54** C3
Staaten → *Australia* 16°24S 141°17E **62** B3
Staaten River △
  Australia 16°15S 142°40E **62** B3
Stadskanaal *Neths.* 53°4N 6°55E **15** A6
Staffa *U.K.* 56°27N 6°21W **11** E2
Stafford *U.K.* 52°49N 2°7W **12** E5
Stafford *U.S.A.* 37°58N 98°36W **80** G4
Stafford Springs *U.S.A.* 41°57N 72°18W **83** E12
Staffordshire □ *U.K.* 52°53N 2°10W **12** E5
Staines *U.K.* 51°26N 0°29W **13** F7
Stakhanov *Ukraine* 48°35N 38°40E **19** E6
Stalida *Greece* 35°17N 25°25E **25** D7
Stalowa Wola *Poland* 50°34N 22°3E **17** C12
Stalybridge *U.K.* 53°28N 2°3W **12** D5
Stamford *Australia* 21°15S 143°46E **62** C3
Stamford *U.K.* 52°39N 0°29W **12** E7
Stamford *Conn., U.S.A.* 41°3N 73°32W **83** E11
Stamford *N.Y., U.S.A.* 42°25N 74°38W **83** D10

Stamford Tex., U.S.A. 32°57N 99°48W 84 E5
Stampriet Namibia 24°20S 18°28E 56 C2
Stamps U.S.A. 33°22N 93°30W 84 E8
Standerton S. Africa 26°55S 29°7E 57 D4
Standish U.S.A. 43°59N 83°57W 81 D12
Stanford S. Africa 34°26S 19°29E 56 E2
Stanford U.S.A. 47°9N 110°13W 76 C8
Stanger S. Africa 29°27S 31°14E 57 D5
Stängselåsen = Salpausselkä Finland 61°3N 26°15E 8 F22
Stanislaus → U.S.A. 37°40N 121°14W 78 H5
Stanke Dimitrov Bulgaria 42°17N 23°9E 23 C10
Stanley Australia 40°46S 145°19E 63 G4
Stanley China 22°13N 114°12E 33 G11
Stanley Falk. Is. 51°40S 59°51W 96 G5
Stanley U.K. 54°53N 1°41W 12 C6
Stanley Idaho, U.S.A. 44°13N 114°56W 76 D6
Stanley N. Dak., U.S.A. 48°19N 102°23W 80 A2
Stanley N.Y., U.S.A. 42°48N 77°6W 82 D7
Stanley Mission Canada 55°25N 104°33W 71 B8
Stannards U.S.A. 42°5N 77°55W 82 D7
Stanovoy Khrebet Russia 55°0N 130°0E 29 D14
Stanovoy Ra. = Stanovoy Khrebet Russia 55°0N 130°0E 29 D14
Stansmore Ra. Australia 21°23S 128°33E 60 D4
Stansted, London ✕ (STN) U.K. 51°54N 0°14E 13 F8
Stanthorpe Australia 28°36S 151°59E 63 D5
Stanton U.S.A. 32°8N 101°48W 84 E4
Stanwood U.S.A. 48°15N 122°23W 78 B4
Staples Canada 42°10N 82°35W 82 D2
Staples U.S.A. 46°21N 94°48W 80 B6
Stapleton U.S.A. 41°29N 100°31W 80 E3
Star City Canada 52°50N 104°20W 71 C8
Star Lake U.S.A. 44°10N 75°2W 83 B9
Stara Planina Bulgaria 43°15N 23°0E 23 C10
Stara Zagora Bulgaria 42°26N 25°39E 23 C11
Starachowice Poland 51°3N 21°2E 17 C11
Staraya Russa Russia 57°58N 31°23E 18 C5
Starbuck I. Kiribati 5°37S 155°55W 65 H12
Starcke △ Australia 14°56S 145°2E 62 A4
Stargard Szczeciński Poland 53°20N 15°0E 16 B8
Staritsa Russia 56°33N 34°55E 18 C5
Starke U.S.A. 29°57N 82°7W 85 G13
Starkville U.S.A. 33°28N 88°49W 85 E10
Starogard Gdański Poland 53°59N 18°30E 17 B10
Starokonstantinov = Starokonstyantyniv Ukraine 49°48N 27°10E 17 D14
Starokonstyantyniv Ukraine 49°48N 27°10E 17 D14
Start Pt. U.K. 50°13N 3°39W 13 G4
Staryy Chartoriysk Ukraine 51°15N 25°54E 17 C13
Staryy Oskol Russia 51°19N 37°55E 19 D6
State College U.S.A. 40°48N 77°52W 82 F7
Stateline U.S.A. 38°57N 119°56W 78 G7
Staten, I. = Estados, I. de Los Argentina 54°40S 64°30W 96 G4
Staten I. U.S.A. 40°35N 74°9W 83 F10
Statesboro U.S.A. 32°27N 81°47W 85 E14
Statesville U.S.A. 35°47N 80°53W 85 D14
Statia = St. Eustatius W. Indies 17°20N 63°0W 89 C7
Stauffer U.S.A. 34°45N 119°3W 79 L7
Staunton Ill., U.S.A. 39°1N 89°47W 80 F9
Staunton Va., U.S.A. 38°9N 79°4W 81 F14
Stavanger Norway 58°57N 5°40E 9 G11
Staveley N.Z. 43°40S 171°32E 59 E3
Stavelot Belgium 50°23N 5°55E 15 D5
Stavern Norway 59°0N 10°1E 9 G14
Stavoren Neths. 52°53N 5°22E 15 B5
Stavropol Russia 45°5N 42°0E 19 E7
Stavros Cyprus 35°1N 32°38E 25 D11
Stavros Greece 35°12N 24°45E 25 D6
Stavros, Akra Greece 35°26N 24°58E 25 D6
Stawell Australia 37°5S 142°47E 63 F3
Stawell → Australia 20°20S 142°55E 62 C3
Stayner Canada 44°25N 80°5W 82 B4
Stayton U.S.A. 44°48N 122°48W 76 D2
Steamboat Springs U.S.A. 40°29N 106°50W 76 F10
Steele U.S.A. 46°51N 99°55W 80 B4
Steelton U.S.A. 40°14N 76°50W 82 F8
Steen River Canada 59°40N 117°12W 70 B5
Steens Mt. U.S.A. 42°35N 118°40W 76 E4
Steenwijk Neths. 52°47N 6°7E 15 B6
Steep Pt. Australia 26°8S 113°8E 61 E1
Steep Rock Canada 51°30N 98°48W 71 C9
Stefanie L. = Chew Bahir Ethiopia 4°40N 36°50E 47 G2
Stefansson Bay Antarctica 67°20S 59°8E 5 C5
Stefansson I. Canada 73°20N 105°45W 69 C10
Steiermark □ Austria 47°26N 15°0E 16 E8
Steilacoom U.S.A. 47°10N 122°36W 78 C4
Steilrandberge Namibia 17°45S 13°20E 56 B1
Steinbach Canada 49°32N 96°40W 71 D9
Steinhausen Namibia 21°49S 18°20E 56 C2
Steinkjer Norway 64°1N 11°31E 8 D14
Steinkopf S. Africa 29°18S 17°43E 56 D2
Stellarton Canada 45°32N 62°30W 73 C7
Stellenbosch S. Africa 33°58S 18°50E 56 E2
Stendal Germany 52°36N 11°53E 16 B6
Steornabhaigh = Stornoway U.K. 58°13N 6°23W 11 C2
Stepanakert = Xankändi Azerbaijan 39°52N 46°49E 44 B5
Stephens Creek Australia 31°50S 141°30E 63 E3
Stephens I. Canada 54°10N 130°45W 70 C2
Stephens L. Canada 56°32N 95°0W 71 B9
Stephenville Canada 48°31N 58°35W 73 C8
Stephenville U.S.A. 32°13N 98°12W 84 E5
Steppe Asia 50°0N 50°0E 26 C7
Sterkstroom S. Africa 31°32S 26°32E 56 E4
Sterling Colo., U.S.A. 40°37N 103°13W 76 F12
Sterling Ill., U.S.A. 41°48N 89°42W 80 E9
Sterling Kans., U.S.A. 38°13N 98°12W 80 F4
Sterling City U.S.A. 31°51N 101°0W 84 F4
Sterling Heights U.S.A. 42°35N 83°2W 81 D12
Sterling Run U.S.A. 41°25N 78°12W 82 E6
Sterlitamak Russia 53°40N 56°0E 18 D10
Sternes Greece 35°30N 24°9E 25 D6
Stettin = Szczecin Poland 53°27N 14°27E 16 B8
Stettiner Haff Germany 53°47N 14°15E 16 B8
Stettler Canada 52°19N 112°40W 70 C6
Steubenville U.S.A. 40°22N 80°37W 82 F4
Stevenage U.K. 51°55N 0°13W 13 F7
Stevens Point U.S.A. 44°31N 89°34W 80 C9
Stevenson U.S.A. 45°42N 121°53W 78 E5
Stevenson → Australia 27°6S 135°33E 63 D2
Stevenson L. Canada 53°55N 96°0W 71 C9
Stevensville U.S.A. 46°30N 114°5W 76 C6
Stewart Canada 55°56N 129°57W 70 B3
Stewart U.S.A. 39°5N 119°46W 78 F7
Stewart → Canada 63°19N 139°26W 68 E4
Stewart, C. Australia 11°57S 134°56E 62 A1
Stewart, I. Chile 54°50S 71°15W 96 G2
Stewart I. N.Z. 46°58S 167°54E 59 G1
Stewarts Point U.S.A. 38°39N 123°24W 78 G3
Stewartville U.S.A. 43°51N 92°29W 80 D7
Stewiacke Canada 45°9N 63°22W 73 C7
Steynsburg S. Africa 31°15S 25°49E 56 E4
Steyr Austria 48°3N 14°25E 16 D8
Steytlerville S. Africa 33°17S 24°19E 56 E3
Stigler U.S.A. 35°15N 95°8W 84 D7
Stikine → Canada 56°40N 132°30W 70 B2
Stilfontein S. Africa 26°51S 26°50E 56 D4
Stillwater N.Z. 42°27S 171°20E 59 E3
Stillwater N.Y., U.S.A. 42°55N 73°41W 83 D11
Stillwater Okla., U.S.A. 36°7N 97°4W 84 C6
Stillwater Range U.S.A. 39°50N 118°5W 76 G4
Stillwater Res. U.S.A. 43°54N 75°3W 83 C9
Stilwell U.S.A. 35°49N 94°38W 84 D7
Stînga Nistrului □ Moldova 47°20N 29°15E 17 E15
Štip Macedonia 41°42N 22°10E 23 D10
Stirling Canada 44°18N 77°33W 82 B7
Stirling U.K. 56°8N 3°57W 11 E5
Stirling □ U.K. 56°12N 4°18W 11 E4
Stirling Ra. Australia 34°23S 118°0E 61 F2
Stirling Range △ Australia 34°26S 118°20E 61 F2
Stittsville Canada 45°15N 75°55W 83 A9
Stjernøya Norway 70°20N 22°40E 8 A20
Stjørdalshalsen Norway 63°29N 10°51E 8 E14
Stockerau Austria 48°24N 16°12E 16 D9
Stockholm Sweden 59°19N 18°4E 9 G18
Stockport U.K. 53°25N 2°9W 12 D5
Stocksbridge U.K. 53°29N 1°35W 12 D6
Stockton Calif., U.S.A. 37°58N 121°17W 78 H5
Stockton Kans., U.S.A. 39°26N 99°16W 80 F4
Stockton Mo., U.S.A. 37°42N 93°48W 80 G7
Stockton-on-Tees U.K. 54°35N 1°19W 12 C6
Stockton-on-Tees □ U.K. 54°35N 1°19W 12 C6
Stockton Plateau U.S.A. 30°30N 102°30W 84 F3
Stoeng Treng Cambodia 13°31N 105°58E 38 F5
Stoer, Pt. of U.K. 58°16N 5°23W 11 C3
Stoke-on-Trent U.K. 53°1N 2°11W 12 D5
Stoke-on-Trent □ U.K. 53°1N 2°11W 12 D5
Stokes △ Australia 33°45S 121°11E 61 F3
Stokes Bay Canada 45°0N 81°28W 82 B3
Stokes Pt. Australia 40°10S 143°56E 63 G3
Stokes Ra. Australia 15°50S 130°50E 60 C5
Stokksnes Iceland 64°14N 14°58W 8 D6
Stokmarknes Norway 68°34N 14°54E 8 B16
Stolac Bos.-H. 43°5N 17°59E 23 C7
Stolbovoy, Ostrov Russia 74°44N 135°14E 29 B14
Stolbtsy = Stowbtsy Belarus 53°30N 26°43E 17 B14
Stolin Belarus 51°53N 26°50E 17 C14
Stomio Greece 35°21N 23°32E 25 D5
Stone U.K. 52°55N 2°9W 12 E5
Stoneboro U.S.A. 41°20N 80°7W 82 E4
Stonehaven U.K. 56°59N 2°12W 11 E6
Stonehenge Australia 24°22S 143°17E 62 C3
Stonehenge U.K. 51°9N 1°45W 13 F6
Stonewall Canada 50°10N 97°19W 71 C9
Stony I. U.S.A. 43°53N 76°19W 83 C8
Stony L. Man., Canada 58°51N 98°40W 71 B9
Stony L. Ont., Canada 44°30N 78°5W 82 B6
Stony Point U.S.A. 41°14N 73°59W 83 E11
Stony Pt. U.S.A. 43°50N 76°18W 83 C8
Stony Rapids Canada 59°16N 105°50W 71 B7
Stony Tunguska = Tunguska, Podkamennaya → Russia 61°50N 90°13E 29 C10
Stonyford U.S.A. 39°23N 122°33W 78 F4
Stora Lulevatten Sweden 67°10N 19°30E 8 C18
Storavan Sweden 65°45N 18°10E 8 D18
Stord Norway 59°52N 5°23E 9 G11
Store Bælt Denmark 55°20N 11°0E 9 J14
Storkerson Pen. Canada 72°30N 106°30W 68 C10
Storm B. Australia 43°10S 147°30E 63 G4
Storm Lake U.S.A. 42°39N 95°13W 80 D6
Stormberge S. Africa 31°16S 26°17E 56 E4
Stormsrivier S. Africa 33°59S 23°52E 56 E3
Stornoway U.K. 58°13N 6°23W 11 C2
Storozhinets = Storozhynets Ukraine 48°14N 25°45E 17 D13
Storozhynets Ukraine 48°14N 25°45E 17 D13
Storrs U.S.A. 41°49N 72°15W 83 E12
Storsjön Sweden 63°9N 14°30E 8 E16
Storuman Sweden 65°5N 17°10E 8 D17
Storuman, L. Sweden 65°13N 16°50E 8 D17
Stouffville Canada 43°58N 79°15W 82 C5
Stoughton Canada 49°40N 103°0W 71 D8
Stour → Dorset, U.K. 50°43N 1°47W 13 G6
Stour → Kent, U.K. 51°18N 1°22E 13 F9
Stour → Suffolk, U.K. 51°57N 1°4E 13 F9
Stourbridge U.K. 52°28N 2°8W 13 E5
Stout L. Canada 52°0N 94°40W 71 C10
Stove Pipe Wells Village U.S.A. 36°35N 117°11W 79 J9
Stow U.S.A. 41°10N 81°27W 82 E3
Stowbtsy Belarus 53°30N 26°43E 17 B14
Stowmarket U.K. 52°12N 1°0E 13 E9
Strabane U.K. 54°50N 7°27W 10 B4
Strahan Australia 42°9S 145°20E 63 G4
Stralsund Germany 54°18N 13°4E 16 A7
Strand S. Africa 34°9S 18°48E 56 E2
Stranda Møre og Romsdal, Norway 62°19N 6°58E 8 E12
Stranda Nord-Trøndelag, Norway 63°33N 10°14E 8 E14
Strangford L. U.K. 54°30N 5°37W 10 B6
Stranorlar Ireland 54°48N 7°46W 10 B4
Stranraer U.K. 54°54N 5°1W 11 G3
Strasbourg Canada 51°4N 104°55W 71 C8
Strasbourg France 48°35N 7°42E 20 B7
Stratford Canada 43°23N 81°0W 82 C4
Stratford N.Z. 39°20S 174°19E 59 C5
Stratford Calif., U.S.A. 36°11N 119°49W 78 J7
Stratford Conn., U.S.A. 41°12N 73°8W 83 E11
Stratford Tex., U.S.A. 36°20N 102°4W 84 C3
Stratford-upon-Avon U.K. 52°12N 1°42W 13 E6
Strath Spey U.K. 57°9N 3°49W 11 D5
Strathalbyn Australia 35°13S 138°53E 63 F2
Strathaven U.K. 55°40N 4°5W 11 F4
Strathcona ⌂ Canada 49°38N 125°40W 70 D3
Strathmore Canada 51°5N 113°18W 70 C6
Strathmore U.K. 56°37N 3°7W 11 E5
Strathmore U.S.A. 36°9N 119°4W 78 J7
Strathnaver Canada 53°20N 122°33W 70 C4
Strathpeffer U.K. 57°35N 4°32W 11 D4
Strathroy Canada 42°58N 81°38W 82 D3
Strathy Pt. U.K. 58°36N 4°1W 11 C4
Strattanville U.S.A. 41°12N 79°19W 82 E5
Stratton U.S.A. 45°8N 70°26W 83 A14
Stratton Mt. U.S.A. 43°4N 72°55W 83 C12
Straubing Germany 48°52N 12°34E 16 D7
Straumnes Iceland 66°26N 23°8W 8 C2
Strawberry → U.S.A. 40°10N 110°24W 76 F8
Streaky B. Australia 32°48S 134°13E 63 E1
Streaky Bay Australia 32°51S 134°18E 63 E1
Streator U.S.A. 41°8N 88°50W 80 E9
Streetsboro U.S.A. 41°14N 81°21W 82 E3
Streetsville Canada 43°35N 79°42W 82 C5
Streng → Cambodia 13°12N 103°37E 38 F4
Streymoy Færoe Is. 62°8N 7°5W 8 E9
Strezhevoy Russia 60°42N 77°34E 28 C8
Strimonas → Greece 40°46N 23°51E 23 D10
Strokestown Ireland 53°46N 8°7W 10 C3
Stroma U.K. 58°41N 3°7W 11 C5
Strómboli Italy 38°47N 15°13E 22 E6
Stromeferry U.K. 57°21N 5°33W 11 D3
Stromness U.K. 58°58N 3°17W 11 C5
Stromsburg U.S.A. 41°7N 97°36W 80 E5
Strömstad Sweden 58°56N 11°10E 9 G14
Strömsund Sweden 63°51N 15°33E 8 E16
Strongsville U.S.A. 41°19N 81°50W 82 E3
Stronsay U.K. 59°7N 2°35W 11 B6
Stroud U.K. 51°45N 2°13W 13 F5
Stroud Road Australia 32°18S 151°57E 63 E5
Stroudsburg U.S.A. 40°59N 75°12W 83 F9
Stroumbi Cyprus 34°53N 32°29E 25 E11
Struer Denmark 56°30N 8°35E 9 H13
Strugi Krasnyye Russia 58°21N 29°1E 9 G23
Strumica Macedonia 41°28N 22°41E 23 D10
Struthers U.S.A. 41°4N 80°39W 82 E4
Stryker U.S.A. 48°41N 114°46W 76 B6
Stryy Ukraine 49°16N 23°48E 17 D12
Strzelecki Cr. → Australia 29°37S 139°59E 63 D2
Strzelecki Desert Australia 29°30S 140°0E 63 D3
Stuart Fla., U.S.A. 27°12N 80°15W 85 H14
Stuart Nebr., U.S.A. 42°36N 99°8W 80 D4
Stuart → Canada 54°0N 123°35W 70 C4
Stuart Bluff Ra. Australia 22°50S 131°52E 60 D5
Stuart I. U.S.A. 63°35N 162°30W 74 C7
Stuart L. Canada 54°30N 124°30W 70 C4
Stuart Ra. Australia 29°10S 134°56E 63 D1
Stull L. Canada 54°24N 92°34W 72 B1
Stung Treng = Stoeng Treng Cambodia 13°31N 105°58E 38 F5
Stupart → Canada 56°0N 93°25W 72 A1
Sturge I. Antarctica 67°26S 164°47E 5 C11
Sturgeon B. Canada 52°0N 97°50W 71 C9
Sturgeon Bay U.S.A. 44°50N 87°23W 80 C10
Sturgeon Falls Canada 46°25N 79°57W 72 C4
Sturgeon L. Alta., Canada 55°6N 117°32W 70 B5
Sturgeon L. Ont., Canada 50°0N 90°45W 72 C1
Sturgeon L. Ont., Canada 44°28N 78°43W 82 B6
Sturgis Canada 51°56N 102°36W 71 C8
Sturgis Mich., U.S.A. 41°48N 85°25W 81 E11
Sturgis S. Dak., U.S.A. 44°25N 103°31W 80 C2
Sturt △ Australia 27°17S 141°37E 63 D3
Sturt Cr. → Australia 19°8S 127°50E 60 C4
Sturt Stony Desert Australia 28°30S 141°0E 63 D3
Stutterheim S. Africa 32°33S 27°28E 56 E4
Stuttgart Germany 48°48N 9°11E 16 D5
Stuttgart U.S.A. 34°30N 91°33W 84 D9
Stuyvesant U.S.A. 42°23N 73°45W 83 D11
Stykkishólmur Iceland 65°2N 22°40W 8 D2
Styria = Steiermark □ Austria 47°26N 15°0E 16 E8
Su Xian = Suzhou China 33°41N 116°59E 34 H9
Suakin Sudan 19°8N 37°20E 51 E13
Suan N. Korea 38°42N 126°22E 35 E14
Suar India 29°2N 79°3E 43 E8
Şubā Si. Arabia 27°10N 35°40E 44 E2
Subang Indonesia 6°34S 107°45E 37 G12
Subansiri → India 26°48N 93°50E 41 F18
Subarnarekha → India 22°34N 87°24E 43 H12
Subayhah Si. Arabia 30°2N 38°50E 44 D3
Subi Indonesia 2°58N 108°50E 36 D3
Subotica Serbia 46°6N 19°39E 23 A8
Suceava Romania 47°38N 26°16E 17 E14
Suchan = Partizansk Russia 43°8N 133°9E 30 C6
Suchil Mexico 23°39N 103°54W 86 C4
Suchou = Suzhou China 31°19N 120°38E 33 C7
Süchow = Xuzhou China 34°18N 117°10E 35 G9
Suck → Ireland 53°17N 8°3W 10 C3
Sucre Bolivia 19°0S 65°15W 92 G5
Sucuriú → Brazil 20°47S 51°38W 93 H8
Sud, Pte. du Canada 49°3N 62°14W 73 C7
Sud-Kivu □ Dem. Rep. of the Congo 3°0S 28°30E 54 C2
Sud-Ouest, Pte. Canada 49°23N 63°36W 73 C7
Sud Ouest, Pte. Mauritius 20°28S 57°18E 53 d
Sudan U.S.A. 34°4N 102°31W 84 D3
Sudan ■ Africa 15°0N 30°0E 51 E11
Sudbury Canada 46°30N 81°0W 72 C3
Sudbury U.K. 52°2N 0°45E 13 E8
Sûdd Sudan 8°20N 30°0E 51 G12
Sudeten Mts. = Sudety Europe 50°20N 16°45E 17 C9
Sudety Europe 50°20N 16°45E 17 C9
Suðuroy Færoe Is. 61°32N 6°50W 8 F9
Sudi Tanzania 10°11S 39°57E 55 E4
Sudirman, Pegunungan Indonesia 4°30S 137°0E 37 E9
Sudong, Pulau Singapore 1°13N 103°44E 39 d
Sueca Spain 39°12N 0°21W 21 C5
Suemez I. U.S.A. 55°15N 133°20W 70 B2
Suez = El Suweis Egypt 29°58N 32°31E 51 C12
Suez, G. of = Suweis, Khalîg el Egypt 28°40N 33°0E 51 C12
Suez Canal = Suweis, Qanâ es Egypt 31°0N 32°20E 51 B12
Suffield Canada 50°12N 111°10W 70 C6
Suffolk U.S.A. 36°44N 76°35W 81 G15
Suffolk □ U.K. 52°16N 1°0E 13 E9
Sugar Grove U.S.A. 41°59N 79°20W 82 E5
Sugarcreek U.S.A. 41°25N 79°52W 82 E5
Sugarive → India 26°16N 86°24E 43 F12
Sugluk = Salluit Canada 62°14N 75°38W 69 E16
Şuḩār Oman 24°20N 56°40E 45 E8
Sühbaatar Mongolia 50°17N 106°10E 32 A5
Sühbaatar □ Mongolia 45°30N 114°0E 34 B8
Suhl Germany 50°36N 10°43E 16 C6
Sui Pakistan 28°37N 69°19E 42 E3
Sui Xian China 34°25N 115°2E 34 G8
Suide China 37°30N 110°12E 34 F6
Suifenhe China 44°25N 131°10E 35 B16
Suihua China 46°32N 126°55E 33 B7
Suining Jiangsu, China 33°56N 117°58E 35 H9
Suining Sichuan, China 30°26N 105°35E 32 C5
Suiping China 33°10N 113°59E 34 H7
Suir → Ireland 52°16N 7°9W 10 D4
Suisse = Switzerland ■ Europe 46°30N 8°0E 20 C8
Suisun City U.S.A. 38°15N 122°2W 78 G4
Suiyang China 44°30N 130°56E 35 B16
Suizhong China 40°21N 120°20E 35 D11
Sujangarh India 27°42N 74°31E 42 F6
Sukabumi Indonesia 6°56S 106°50E 37 G12
Sukadana Indonesia 1°10S 110°0E 36 E4
Sukagawa Japan 37°17N 140°23E 31 F10
Sukaraja Indonesia 2°28S 110°25E 36 E4
Sukawati Indonesia 8°35S 115°17E 37 K18
Sukch'ŏn N. Korea 39°22N 125°35E 35 E13
Sukhona → Russia 61°15N 46°39E 18 C6
Sukhothai Thailand 17°1N 99°49E 38 D2
Sukhumi = Sokhumi Georgia 43°0N 41°0E 19 F7
Sukkur Pakistan 27°42N 68°54E 42 F3
Sukkur Barrage Pakistan 27°40N 68°50E 42 F3
Sukri → India 25°4N 71°43E 42 G4
Sukumo Japan 32°56N 132°44E 31 H6
Sukunka → Canada 55°45N 121°15W 70 B4
Sula, Kepulauan Indonesia 1°45S 125°0E 37 E7
Sulaco → Honduras 15°2N 87°44W 88 C2
Sulaiman Range Pakistan 30°30N 69°50E 42 D3
Sūlār Iran 31°53N 51°54E 45 D6
Sulawesi Indonesia 2°0S 120°0E 37 E6
Sulawesi Barat □ Indonesia 3°0S 119°0E 37 E5
Sulawesi Sea = Celebes Sea Indonesia 3°0N 123°0E 37 D6
Sulawesi Selatan □ Indonesia 2°30S 120°0E 37 E6
Sulawesi Tengah □ Indonesia 1°30S 121°0E 37 E6
Sulawesi Tenggara □ Indonesia 3°50S 122°0E 37 E6
Sulawesi Utara □ Indonesia 1°0N 124°0E 37 D6
Sulima S. Leone 6°58N 11°32W 50 G3
Sulina Romania 45°10N 29°40E 17 F15
Sulitjelma Norway 67°9N 16°3E 8 C17
Sullana Peru 4°52S 80°39W 92 D2
Sullivan Ill., U.S.A. 39°36N 88°37W 80 F9
Sullivan Ind., U.S.A. 39°6N 87°24W 80 F10
Sullivan Mo., U.S.A. 38°13N 91°10W 80 F8
Sullivan Bay Canada 50°55N 126°50W 70 C3
Sullivan I. = Lanbi Kyun Burma 10°50N 98°20E 39 G2
Sullom Voe U.K. 60°27N 1°20W 11 A7
Sulphur La., U.S.A. 30°14N 93°23W 84 F8
Sulphur Okla., U.S.A. 34°31N 96°58W 84 D6
Sulphur Pt. Canada 60°56N 114°48W 70 A6
Sulphur Springs U.S.A. 33°8N 95°36W 84 E7
Sultan Canada 47°36N 82°47W 72 C3
Sultan U.S.A. 47°52N 121°49W 78 C5
Sultan Hamud Kenya 2°1S 37°22E 54 C4
Sultanābād = Arāk Iran 34°0N 49°40E 45 C6
Sultanpur Mad. P., India 23°9N 77°56E 42 H8
Sultanpur Punjab, India 31°13N 75°11E 42 D6
Sultanpur Ut. P., India 26°18N 82°4E 43 F10
Sulu Arch. Phil. 6°0N 121°0E 37 C6
Sulu Sea E. Indies 8°0N 120°0E 37 C6
Sulūq Libya 31°44N 20°14E 51 B10
Sulzberger Ice Shelf Antarctica 78°0S 150°0W 5 E13
Sumalata Indonesia 1°0N 122°31E 37 D6
Sumampa Argentina 29°25S 63°29W 94 B3
Sumatera Indonesia 0°40N 100°20E 36 D2
Sumatera Barat □ Indonesia 1°0S 101°0E 36 E2
Sumatera Utara □ Indonesia 2°30N 98°0E 36 D1
Sumatra = Sumatera Indonesia 0°40N 100°20E 36 D2
Sumba Indonesia 9°45S 119°35E 37 F5
Sumba, Selat Indonesia 9°0S 118°40E 37 F5
Sumbawa Indonesia 8°26S 117°30E 36 F5
Sumbawa Besar Indonesia 8°30S 117°26E 36 F5
Sumbawanga □ Tanzania 8°0S 31°30E 52 F6
Sumbe Angola 11°10S 13°48E 52 G2
Sumbu △ Zambia 8°43S 30°22E 55 D3
Sumburgh Hd. U.K. 59°52N 1°17W 11 B7
Sumdeo India 31°26N 78°44E 43 D8
Sumdo China 35°6N 78°41E 43 B8
Sumedang Indonesia 6°52S 107°55E 37 G12
Šumen = Shumen Bulgaria 43°18N 26°55E 23 C12
Sumenep Indonesia 7°1S 113°52E 37 G15
Sumgait = Sumqayıt Azerbaijan 40°34N 49°38E 19 F8
Summer L. U.S.A. 42°50N 120°45W 76 E3
Summerland Canada 49°32N 119°41W 70 D5
Summerside Canada 46°24N 63°47W 73 C7
Summersville U.S.A. 38°17N 80°51W 81 F13
Summerville Ga., U.S.A. 34°29N 85°21W 85 D12
Summerville S.C., U.S.A. 33°1N 80°11W 85 E14
Summit Lake Canada 54°20N 122°40W 70 C4
Summit Peak U.S.A. 37°21N 106°42W 77 H10
Sumner Iowa, U.S.A. 42°51N 92°6W 80 D7
Sumner Wash., U.S.A. 47°12N 122°14W 78 C4
Sumoto Japan 34°21N 134°54E 31 G7
Šumperk Czech Rep. 49°59N 16°59E 17 D9
Sumqayıt Azerbaijan 40°34N 49°38E 19 F8
Sumter U.S.A. 33°55N 80°21W 85 E14
Sumy Ukraine 50°57N 34°50E 19 D5
Sun City S. Africa 25°17S 27°3E 56 D4
Sun City Ariz., U.S.A. 33°35N 112°16W 77 K7
Sun City Calif., U.S.A. 33°42N 117°11W 79 M9
Sun City Center U.S.A. 27°43N 82°21W 85 H13
Sun Lakes U.S.A. 33°10N 111°52W 77 K8
Sun Valley U.S.A. 43°42N 114°21W 76 E6
Sunagawa Japan 43°29N 141°55E 30 C10
Sunan N. Korea 39°15N 125°40E 35 E13
Sunart, L. U.K. 56°42N 5°43W 11 E3
Sunburst U.S.A. 48°53N 111°55W 76 B8
Sunbury Australia 37°35S 144°44E 63 F3
Sunbury U.S.A. 40°52N 76°48W 83 F8
Sunchales Argentina 30°58S 61°35W 94 C3
Suncheon S. Korea 34°52N 127°31E 35 G14
Suncho Corral Argentina 27°55S 63°27W 94 B3
Sunch'on N. Korea 39°25N 125°56E 35 E13
Suncook U.S.A. 43°8N 71°27W 83 C13
Sunda, Selat Indonesia 6°20S 105°30E 36 F3
Sunda Is. Indonesia 5°0S 105°0E 64 H2
Sunda Str. = Sunda, Selat Indonesia 6°20S 105°30E 36 F3
Sunda Trench = Java Trench Ind. Oc. 9°0S 105°0E 36 F3
Sundance Canada 56°32N 94°4W 71 B10
Sundance U.S.A. 44°24N 104°23W 76 D11
Sundar Nagar India 31°32N 76°53E 42 D7
Sundarbans Asia 22°0N 89°0E 41 J16
Sundarbans △ India 22°0N 88°45E 43 J13
Sundargarh India 22°4N 84°5E 41 H14
Sundays = Sondags → S. Africa 33°44S 25°51E 56 E4
Sunderland Canada 44°16N 79°4W 82 B5
Sunderland U.K. 54°55N 1°23W 12 C6
Sundown △ Australia 28°49S 151°38E 63 D5
Sundre Canada 51°49N 114°38W 70 C6
Sundsvall Sweden 62°23N 17°17E 8 E17
Sung Hei Vietnam 10°20N 106°2E 39 G6
Sungai Acheh Malaysia 5°8N 100°30E 39 c
Sungai Kolok Thailand 6°2N 101°58E 39 J3
Sungai Lembing Malaysia 3°55N 103°3E 39 L4
Sungai Petani Malaysia 5°37N 100°30E 39 K3
Sungaigerong Indonesia 2°59S 104°52E 36 E2
Sungailiat Indonesia 1°51S 106°8E 36 E3
Sungaipenuh Indonesia 2°1S 101°20E 36 E2
Sungari = Songhua Jiang → China 47°45N 132°30E 33 B8
Sunghua Chiang = Songhua Jiang → China 47°45N 132°30E 33 B8
Sunland Park U.S.A. 31°50N 106°40W 77 L10
Sunndalsøra Norway 62°40N 8°33E 8 E13
Sunnyside U.S.A. 46°20N 120°0W 76 C4
Sunnyvale U.S.A. 37°23N 122°2W 78 H4
Sunrise Manor U.S.A. 36°12N 115°4W 79 J11
Suntar Russia 62°15N 117°30E 29 C12
Suomenselkä Finland 62°52N 24°0E 8 E21
Suomi = Finland ■ Europe 63°0N 27°0E 8 E22
Suomussalmi Finland 64°54N 29°10E 8 D23
Suoyarvi Russia 62°3N 32°20E 18 B5
Supai U.S.A. 36°15N 112°41W 77 H7
Supaul India 26°10N 86°40E 43 F12
Superior Ariz., U.S.A. 33°18N 111°6W 77 K8
Superior Mont., U.S.A. 47°12N 114°53W 76 C6
Superior Nebr., U.S.A. 40°1N 98°4W 80 E4
Superior Wis., U.S.A. 46°44N 92°6W 80 B7
Superior, L. N. Amer. 47°0N 87°0W 72 C2
Suphan Buri Thailand 14°14N 100°10E 38 E3
Suphan Dağı Turkey 38°54N 42°48E 44 B4
Supiori Indonesia 1°0S 136°0E 37 E9
Supung Shuiku China 40°35N 124°50E 35 D13
Sūq ash Shuyūkh Iraq 30°53N 46°28E 44 D5
Sūq Suwayq Si. Arabia 24°23N 38°27E 44 E3

Suqian China 33°54N 118°8E 35 H10
Suquṭra = Socotra Yemen 12°30N 54°0E 47 E5
Sūr Lebanon 33°19N 35°16E 46 B4
Şūr Oman 22°34N 59°32E 47 C6
Sur, Pt. U.S.A. 36°18N 121°54W 78 J5
Sura → Russia 56°6N 46°0E 18 C8
Surab Pakistan 28°25N 66°15E 42 E2
Surabaja = Surabaya Indonesia 7°17S 112°45E 37 G15
Surabaya Indonesia 7°17S 112°45E 37 G15
Surakarta Indonesia 7°35S 110°48E 37 G14
Surat Australia 27°10S 149°6E 63 D4
Surat India 21°12N 72°55E 40 J8
Surat Thani Thailand 9°6N 99°20E 39 H2
Suratgarh India 29°18N 73°55E 42 E5
Şuraymilā Si. Arabia 25°7N 46°7E 44 E5
Surf U.S.A. 34°41N 120°36W 79 L6
Surfers Paradise Australia 28°0S 153°25E 63 D5
Surgut Russia 61°14N 73°20E 28 C8
Suriapet India 17°10N 79°40E 40 L11
Surigao Phil. 9°47N 125°29E 37 C7
Surin Thailand 14°50N 103°34E 38 E4
Surin Nua, Ko Thailand 9°30N 97°55E 39 H1
Surinam = Suriname ■ S. Amer. 4°0N 56°0W 93 C7
Suriname ■ S. Amer. 4°0N 56°0W 93 C7
Suriname → Suriname 5°50N 55°15W 93 B7
Sürmaq Iran 31°3N 52°48E 45 D7
Surrey Canada 49°7N 122°45W 78 A4
Surrey □ U.K. 51°15N 0°31W 13 F7
Sursand India 26°39N 85°43E 43 F11
Sursar → India 26°14N 87°3E 43 F12
Surt Libya 31°11N 16°39E 51 B9
Surt, Khalīj Libya 31°40N 18°30E 51 B9
Surtanahu Pakistan 26°22N 70°0E 42 F4
Surtsey Iceland 63°20N 20°30W 8 E3
Suruga-Wan Japan 34°45N 138°30E 31 G9
Süsah Libya 32°52N 21°59E 51 B10
Susaki Japan 33°22N 133°17E 31 H6
Süsangerd Iran 31°35N 48°6E 45 D6
Susanville U.S.A. 40°25N 120°39W 76 F3
Susner India 23°57N 76°5E 42 H7
Susquehanna U.S.A. 41°57N 75°36W 83 E9
Susquehanna → U.S.A. 39°33N 76°5W 83 G8
Susques Argentina 23°35S 66°25W 94 A2
Sussex Canada 45°45N 65°37W 73 C6
Sussex U.S.A. 41°13N 74°37W 83 E10
Sussex, E. □ U.K. 51°0N 0°0E 13 G8
Sussex, W. □ U.K. 51°0N 0°30W 13 G7
Sustut → Canada 56°20N 127°30W 70 B3
Susuman Russia 62°47N 148°10E 29 C15
Susunu Indonesia 3°7S 133°39E 37 E8
Susurluk Turkey 39°54N 28°8E 23 E13
Sutay Uul Asia 46°35N 93°38E 32 B4
Sutherland S. Africa 32°24S 20°40E 56 E3
Sutherland U.K. 58°12N 4°50W 11 C4
Sutherland U.S.A. 41°10N 101°8W 80 E3
Sutherland Falls N.Z. 44°48S 167°46E 59 F1
Sutherlin U.S.A. 43°23N 123°19W 76 E2
Suthri India 23°3N 68°55E 42 H3
Sutlej → Pakistan 29°23N 71°3E 42 E4
Sutter U.S.A. 39°10N 121°45W 78 F5
Sutter Buttes U.S.A. 39°12N 121°49W 78 F5
Sutter Creek U.S.A. 38°24N 120°48W 78 G6
Sutton Canada 45°6N 72°37W 83 A12
Sutton Nebr., U.S.A. 40°36N 97°52W 80 E5
Sutton W. Va., U.S.A. 38°40N 80°43W 81 F13
Sutton → Canada 55°15N 83°45W 72 A3
Sutton Coldfield U.K. 52°35N 1°49W 13 E6
Sutton in Ashfield U.K. 53°8N 1°16W 12 D6
Sutton L. Canada 54°15N 84°42W 72 B3
Suttor → Australia 21°36S 147°2E 62 C4
Suttsu Japan 42°48N 140°14E 30 C10
Sutwik I. U.S.A. 56°34N 157°12W 74 D8
Suva Fiji 18°6S 178°30E 59 a
Suva Planina Serbia 43°10N 22°5E 23 C10
Suvorov Is. = Suwarrow Is. Cook Is. 13°15S 163°5W 65 J11
Suwałki Poland 54°8N 22°59E 17 A12
Suwana Indonesia 8°44S 115°36E 37 K18
Suwannaphum Thailand 15°33N 103°47E 38 E4
Suwannee → U.S.A. 29°17N 83°10W 85 G13
Suwanose-Jima Japan 29°38N 129°43E 31 K4
Suwarrow Is. Cook Is. 13°15S 163°5W 65 J11
Suweis, Khalig el Egypt 28°40N 33°0E 51 C12
Suweis, Qanâ es Egypt 31°0N 32°20E 51 B12
Suwon S. Korea 37°17N 127°1E 35 F14
Suzdal Russia 56°29N 40°26E 18 C5
Suzhou Anhui, China 33°41N 116°59E 34 H9
Suzhou Jiangsu, China 31°19N 120°38E 33 C7
Suzu Japan 37°25N 137°17E 31 F8
Suzu-Misaki Japan 37°31N 137°21E 31 F8
Suzuka Japan 34°55N 136°36E 31 G8
Svalbard Arctic 78°0N 17°0E 4 B8
Svalbard Radio = Longyearbyen Svalbard 78°13N 15°40E 4 B8
Svappavaara Sweden 67°40N 21°3E 8 C19
Svartisen Norway 66°40N 13°59E 8 C15
Svay Chek Cambodia 13°48N 102°58E 38 F4
Svay Rieng Cambodia 11°9N 105°45E 39 G5
Svealand □ Sweden 60°20N 15°0E 9 G16
Sveg Sweden 62°2N 14°21E 8 E16
Svendborg Denmark 55°4N 10°35E 9 J14
Sverdrup Chan. Canada 79°56N 96°25W 69 B12
Sverdrup Is. Canada 79°0N 97°0W 66 B10
Sverige = Sweden ■ Europe 57°0N 15°0E 9 H16
Svetlaya Russia 46°33N 138°18E 30 A7
Svetlogorsk = Svyetlahorsk Belarus 52°38N 29°46E 17 B15
Svir → Russia 60°30N 32°48E 18 B5
Svishtov Bulgaria 43°36N 25°23E 23 C11
Svislach Belarus 53°3N 24°2E 17 B13
Svizzera = Switzerland ■ Europe 46°30N 8°0E 20 C8
Svobodnyy Russia 51°20N 128°0E 29 D13

Svolvær Norway 68°15N 14°34E 8 B16
Svyetlahorsk Belarus 52°38N 29°46E 17 B15
Swabian Alps = Schwäbische Alb Germany 48°20N 9°30E 16 D5
Swaffham U.K. 52°39N 0°42E 13 E8
Swains I. Amer. Samoa 11°11S 171°4W 65 J11
Swainsboro U.S.A. 32°36N 82°20W 85 E13
Swakop → Namibia 22°38S 14°36E 56 C2
Swakopmund Namibia 22°37S 14°30E 56 C1
Swale → U.K. 54°5N 1°20W 12 C6
Swan → Australia 32°3S 115°45E 61 F2
Swan → Canada 52°30N 100°45W 71 C8
Swan Hill Australia 35°20S 143°33E 63 F3
Swan Hills Canada 54°43N 115°24W 70 C5
Swan Is. = Santanilla, Is. Honduras 17°22N 83°57W 88 C3
Swan L. Man., Canada 52°30N 100°40W 71 C8
Swan L. Ont., Canada 54°16N 91°11W 72 B1
Swan Ra. U.S.A. 48°0N 113°45W 76 C7
Swan River Canada 52°10N 101°16W 71 C8
Swanage U.K. 50°36N 1°58W 13 G6
Swansea Australia 42°8S 148°4E 63 G4
Swansea Canada 43°38N 79°28W 82 C5
Swansea U.K. 51°37N 3°57W 13 F4
Swansea □ U.K. 51°38N 4°3W 13 F3
Swartberge S. Africa 33°20S 22°0E 56 E3
Swartmodder S. Africa 28°1S 20°32E 56 D3
Swartnossob → Namibia 23°8S 18°42E 56 C2
Swartruggens S. Africa 25°39S 26°42E 56 D4
Swastika Canada 48°7N 80°6W 72 C3
Swat → Pakistan 34°40N 72°5E 43 B5
Swatow = Shantou China 23°18N 116°40E 33 D6
Swaziland ■ Africa 26°30S 31°30E 57 D5
Sweden ■ Europe 57°0N 15°0E 9 H16
Sweet Grass U.S.A. 48°59N 111°58W 76 B8
Sweet Home U.S.A. 44°24N 122°44W 76 D2
Sweetwater Nev., U.S.A. 38°27N 119°9W 78 G7
Sweetwater Tenn., U.S.A. 35°36N 84°28W 85 D12
Sweetwater Tex., U.S.A. 32°28N 100°25W 84 E4
Sweetwater → U.S.A. 42°31N 107°2W 76 E10
Swellendam S. Africa 34°1S 20°26E 56 E3
Świdnica Poland 50°50N 16°30E 17 C9
Świdnik Poland 51°13N 22°39E 17 C12
Świebodzin Poland 52°15N 15°31E 16 B8
Świecie Poland 53°25N 18°30E 17 B10
Swift Current Canada 50°20N 107°45W 71 C7
Swift Current → Canada 50°38N 107°44W 71 C7
Swilly, L. Ireland 55°12N 7°33W 10 A4
Swindon U.K. 51°34N 1°46W 13 F6
Swindon □ U.K. 51°34N 1°46W 13 F6
Swinemünde = Świnoujście Poland 53°54N 14°16E 16 B8
Swinford Ireland 53°57N 8°58W 10 C3
Świnoujście Poland 53°54N 14°16E 16 B8
Switzerland ■ Europe 46°30N 8°0E 20 C8
Swords Ireland 53°28N 6°13W 10 C5
Swoyerville U.S.A. 41°18N 75°53W 83 E9
Sydenham → Canada 42°33N 82°25W 82 D2
Sydney Australia 33°52S 151°12E 63 E5
Sydney Canada 46°7N 60°7W 73 C7
Sydney L. Canada 50°41N 94°25W 71 C10
Sydney Mines Canada 46°18N 60°15W 73 C7
Sydprøven = Alluitsup Paa Greenland 60°30N 45°35W 4 C5
Sydra, G. of = Surt, Khalīj Libya 31°40N 18°30E 51 B9
Sykesville U.S.A. 41°3N 78°50W 82 E6
Syktyvkar Russia 61°45N 50°40E 18 B9
Sylacauga U.S.A. 33°10N 86°15W 85 E11
Sylarna Sweden 63°2N 12°13E 8 E15
Sylhet Bangla. 24°54N 91°52E 41 G17
Sylhet □ Bangla. 24°50N 91°50E 41 G17
Sylt Germany 54°54N 8°22E 16 A5
Sylvan Beach U.S.A. 43°12N 75°44W 83 C9
Sylvan Lake Canada 52°20N 114°3W 70 C6
Sylvania Ga., U.S.A. 32°45N 81°38W 85 E14
Sylvania Ohio, U.S.A. 41°43N 83°42W 81 E12
Sylvester U.S.A. 31°32N 83°50W 85 F13
Sym Russia 60°20N 88°18E 28 C9
Synnot Ra. Australia 16°30S 125°20E 60 C4
Syowa Antarctica 68°50S 12°0E 5 C5
Syracuse Kans., U.S.A. 37°59N 101°45W 80 G3
Syracuse N.Y., U.S.A. 43°3N 76°9W 83 C8
Syracuse Nebr., U.S.A. 40°39N 96°11W 80 E5
Syrdarya → Kazakhstan 46°3N 61°0E 28 E7
Syria ■ Asia 35°0N 38°0E 44 C3
Syrian Desert = Shām, Bādiyat ash Asia 32°0N 40°0E 44 C3
Syros = Ermoupoli Greece 37°28N 24°57E 23 F11
Syzran Russia 53°12N 48°30E 18 D8
Szczecin Poland 53°27N 14°27E 16 B8
Szczecinek Poland 53°43N 16°41E 17 B9
Szczeciński, Zalew = Stettiner Haff Germany 53°47N 14°15E 16 B8
Szczytno Poland 53°33N 21°0E 17 B11
Szechwan = Sichuan □ China 30°30N 103°0E 32 C5
Szeged Hungary 46°16N 20°10E 17 E11
Székesfehérvár Hungary 47°15N 18°25E 17 E10
Szekszárd Hungary 46°22N 18°42E 17 E10
Szentes Hungary 46°39N 20°21E 17 E11
Szolnok Hungary 47°10N 20°15E 17 E11
Szombathely Hungary 47°14N 16°38E 17 E9

T

Ta Khli Thailand 15°15N 100°21E 38 E3
Ta Khli Khok Thailand 15°18N 100°20E 38 E3
Ta Lai Vietnam 11°24N 107°23E 39 G6
Tabacal Argentina 23°15S 64°15W 94 A3
Tabaco Phil. 13°22N 123°44E 37 B6
Ţābah Si. Arabia 26°55N 42°38E 44 E4
Tabanan Indonesia 8°32S 115°8E 37 K18

Ţabas Khorāsān, Iran 32°48N 60°12E 45 C9
Ţabas Yazd, Iran 33°35N 56°55E 45 C8
Tabasará, Serranía de Panama 8°35N 81°40W 88 E3
Tabasco □ Mexico 18°0N 92°40W 87 D6
Tabāsīn Iran 31°12N 57°54E 45 D8
Tabatinga, Serra da Brazil 10°30S 44°0W 93 F10
Taber Canada 49°47N 112°8W 70 D6
Tablas Phil. 12°25N 122°2E 37 B6
Table, Pte. de la Réunion 21°14S 55°48E 53 c
Table B. Canada 53°40N 56°25W 73 B8
Table B. S. Africa 33°35S 18°25E 56 E2
Table Mountain △ S. Africa 34°20S 18°28E 56 E2
Table Mt. S. Africa 33°58S 18°26E 56 E2
Table Rock L. U.S.A. 36°36N 93°19W 80 G7
Tabletop, Mt. Australia 23°24S 147°11E 62 C4
Tábor Czech Rep. 49°25N 14°39E 16 D8
Tabora Tanzania 5°2S 32°50E 54 D3
Tabora □ Tanzania 5°0S 33°0E 54 D3
Tabou Ivory C. 4°30N 7°20W 50 H4
Tabrīz Iran 38°7N 46°20E 44 B5
Tabuaeran Kiribati 3°51N 159°22W 65 G12
Tabūk Si. Arabia 28°23N 36°36E 44 D3
Tabūk □ Si. Arabia 28°0N 37°10E 44 E3
Tacámbaro de Codallos Mexico 19°14N 101°28W 86 D4
Tacheng China 46°40N 82°58E 32 B3
Tach'ing Shan = Daqing Shan China 40°40N 111°0E 34 D6
Tacloban Phil. 11°15N 124°58E 37 B6
Tacna Peru 18°0S 70°20W 92 G4
Tacoma U.S.A. 47°14N 122°26W 78 C4
Tacuarembó Uruguay 31°45S 56°0W 95 C4
Tademaït, Plateau du Algeria 28°30N 2°30E 50 C6
Tadjoura Djibouti 11°50N 42°55E 47 E3
Tadmor N.Z. 41°27S 172°45E 59 D4
Tadoule L. Canada 58°36N 98°20W 71 B9
Tadoussac Canada 48°11N 69°42W 73 C6
Tadzhikistan = Tajikistan ■ Asia 38°30N 70°0E 28 F8
Taegu = Daegu S. Korea 35°50N 128°37E 35 G15
Taegwan N. Korea 40°13N 125°12E 35 D13
Taejŏn = Daejeon S. Korea 36°20N 127°28E 35 F14
Taen, Ko Thailand 9°22N 99°57E 39 b
Tafalla Spain 42°30N 1°41W 21 A5
Tafelbaai = Table B. S. Africa 33°35S 18°25E 56 E2
Tafermaar Indonesia 6°47S 134°10E 37 F8
Tafi Viejo Argentina 26°43S 65°17W 94 B2
Tafīhān Iran 29°25N 52°39E 45 D7
Tafresh Iran 34°45N 49°57E 45 C6
Taft Iran 31°45N 54°14E 45 D7
Taft Phil. 11°57N 125°30E 37 B7
Taft U.S.A. 35°8N 119°28W 79 K7
Taftān, Kūh-e Iran 28°40N 61°0E 45 D9
Taga Samoa 13°46S 172°28W 59 b
Taga Dzong Bhutan 27°5N 89°55E 41 F16
Taganrog Russia 47°12N 38°50E 19 E6
Tagbilaran Phil. 9°39N 123°51E 37 C6
Tagish Canada 60°19N 134°16W 70 A2
Tagish L. Canada 60°10N 134°20W 70 A2
Tagliamento → Italy 45°38N 13°6E 22 B5
Tagomago Spain 39°2N 1°39E 24 B8
Taguatinga Brazil 12°27S 46°22W 93 F10
Tagum Phil. 7°33N 125°53E 37 C7
Tagus = Tejo → Europe 38°40N 9°24W 21 C1
Tahakopa N.Z. 46°30S 169°23E 59 G2
Tahan, Gunung Malaysia 4°34N 102°17E 39 K4
Tahat Algeria 23°18N 5°33E 50 D7
Tāherī Iran 27°43N 52°20E 45 E7
Tahiti French Polynesia 17°37S 149°27W 59 d
Tahiti, I. Tahiti 17°37S 149°27W 59 d
Tahlequah U.S.A. 35°55N 94°58W 84 D7
Tahoe, L. U.S.A. 39°6N 120°2W 78 G6
Tahoe City U.S.A. 39°10N 120°9W 78 F6
Tahoka U.S.A. 33°10N 101°48W 84 E4
Taholah U.S.A. 47°21N 124°17W 78 C2
Tahoua Niger 14°57N 5°16E 50 F7
Tahrūd Iran 29°26N 57°49E 45 D8
Tahsis Canada 49°55N 126°40W 70 D3
Tahta Egypt 26°44N 31°32E 51 C12
Tahulandang Indonesia 2°27N 125°23E 37 D7
Tahuna Indonesia 3°38N 125°30E 37 D7
Tai Au Mun China 22°18N 114°17E 33 G11
Tai Mo Shan China 22°25N 114°7E 33 G11
Tai O China 22°15N 113°52E 33 G10
Tai Pang Wan China 22°33N 114°24E 33 F11
Tai Po China 22°27N 114°10E 33 G11
Tai Rom Yen △ Thailand 8°45N 99°30E 39 H2
Tai Shan China 36°25N 117°20E 35 F9
Tai Yue Shan = Lantau I. China 22°15N 113°56E 33 G10
Tai'an China 36°12N 117°8E 35 F9
Taiarapu, Presqu'île de Tahiti 17°47S 149°14W 59 d
Taibei = T'aipei Taiwan 25°4N 121°29E 33 D7
Taibique Canary Is. 27°42N 17°58W 24 G2
Taibus Qi China 41°54N 115°22E 34 D8
T'aichung Taiwan 24°9N 120°37E 33 D7
Taieri → N.Z. 46°3S 170°12E 59 G3
Taigu China 37°28N 112°30E 34 F7
Taihang Shan China 36°0N 113°30E 34 G7
Taihape N.Z. 39°41S 175°48E 59 C5
Taihe China 33°20N 115°42E 34 H8
Tailem Bend Australia 35°12S 139°29E 63 F2
Taimyr Peninsula = Taymyr, Poluostrov Russia 75°0N 100°0E 29 B11
Tain U.K. 57°49N 4°4W 11 D4
T'ainan Taiwan 23°0N 120°10E 33 D7
Taipa China 22°10N 113°35E 33 G10
T'aipei Taiwan 25°4N 121°29E 33 D7

Taiping Malaysia 4°51N 100°44E 39 K3
Taipingzhen China 33°35N 111°42E 34 H6
Tairbeart = Tarbert U.K. 57°54N 6°49W 11 D2
Taita Hills Kenya 3°25S 38°15E 54 C4
Taitao, Pen. de Chile 46°30S 75°0W 96 F2
T'aitung Taiwan 22°43N 121°4E 33 D7
Taivalkoski Finland 65°33N 28°12E 8 D23
Taiwan ■ Asia 23°30N 121°0E 33 D7
Taiyiba Israel 32°36N 35°27E 46 C4
Taiyuan China 37°52N 112°33E 34 F7
Taizhong = T'aichung Taiwan 24°9N 120°37E 33 D7
Ta'izz Yemen 13°35N 44°2E 47 E3
Tājābād Iran 30°2N 54°24E 45 D7
Tajikistan ■ Asia 38°30N 70°0E 28 F8
Tajima Japan 37°12N 139°46E 31 F9
Tajo = Tejo → Europe 38°40N 9°24W 21 C1
Tajrīsh Iran 35°48N 51°25E 45 C6
Tak Thailand 16°52N 99°8E 38 D2
Takāb Iran 36°24N 47°7E 44 B5
Takachiho Japan 32°42N 131°18E 31 H5
Takachu Botswana 22°37S 21°58E 56 C3
Takada Japan 37°7N 138°15E 31 F9
Takahagi Japan 36°43N 140°45E 31 F10
Takaka N.Z. 40°51S 172°50E 59 D4
Takamaka Seychelles 4°50S 55°30E 53 b
Takamatsu Japan 34°20N 134°5E 31 G7
Takaoka Japan 36°47N 137°0E 31 F8
Takapuna N.Z. 36°47S 174°47E 59 B5
Takasaki Japan 36°20N 139°0E 31 F9
Takatsuki Japan 34°51N 135°37E 31 G7
Takaungu Kenya 3°38S 39°52E 54 C4
Takayama Japan 36°18N 137°11E 31 F8
Take-Shima Japan 30°49N 130°26E 31 J5
Takefu Japan 35°50N 136°10E 31 G8
Takengon Indonesia 4°45N 96°50E 36 D1
Takeo Japan 33°12N 130°1E 31 H5
Takeshima = Tokdo Asia 37°15N 131°52E 31 F5
Tākestān Iran 36°0N 49°40E 45 C6
Taketa Japan 32°58N 131°24E 31 H5
Takev Cambodia 10°59N 104°47E 39 G5
Takh India 33°6N 77°32E 43 C7
Takhmau Cambodia 11°29N 104°57E 39 G5
Takht-Sulaiman Pakistan 31°40N 69°58E 42 D3
Takikawa Japan 43°33N 141°54E 30 C10
Takla L. Canada 55°15N 125°45W 70 B3
Takla Landing Canada 55°30N 125°50W 70 B3
Takla Makan China 38°0N 83°0E 32 C3
Taklamakan Shamo = Takla Makan China 38°0N 83°0E 32 C3
Taksimo Russia 56°20N 114°52E 29 D12
Taku → Canada 58°30N 133°50W 70 B2
Takua Pa Thailand 8°52N 98°21E 39 H2
Takua Thung Thailand 8°24N 98°27E 39 a
Tal Halāl Iran 31°45N 54°14E 45 D7
Tala Uruguay 34°21S 55°46W 95 C4
Talagang Pakistan 32°55N 72°25E 42 C5
Talagante Chile 33°40S 70°50W 94 C1
Talamanca, Cordillera de Cent. Amer. 9°20N 83°20W 88 E3
Talara Peru 4°38S 81°18W 92 D2
Talas Kyrgyzstan 42°30N 72°13E 28 E8
Talâta Egypt 30°36N 32°20E 46 E1
Talaud, Kepulauan Indonesia 4°30N 126°50E 37 D7
Talaud Is. = Talaud, Kepulauan Indonesia 4°30N 126°50E 37 D7
Talavera de la Reina Spain 39°55N 4°46W 21 C3
Talayan Phil. 6°52N 124°24E 37 C6
Talbandh India 22°3N 86°20E 43 H12
Talbot, C. Australia 13°48S 126°43E 60 B4
Talbragar → Australia 32°12S 148°37E 63 E4
Talca Chile 35°28S 71°40W 94 D1
Talcahuano Chile 36°40S 73°10W 94 D1
Talcher India 21°0N 85°18E 41 J14
Taldy Kurgan = Taldyqorghan Kazakhstan 45°10N 78°45E 28 E8
Taldyqorghan Kazakhstan 45°10N 78°45E 28 E8
Tālesh Iran 37°58N 48°58E 45 B6
Tālesh, Kühhā-ye Iran 37°42N 48°55E 45 B6
Tali Post Sudan 5°55N 30°44E 51 G12
Taliabu Indonesia 1°50S 125°0E 37 E6
Talibon Phil. 10°9N 124°20E 37 B6
Talihina U.S.A. 34°45N 95°3W 84 D7
Taliwang Indonesia 8°50S 116°55E 36 F5
Tall 'Afar Iraq 36°22N 42°27E 44 B4
Tall Kalakh Syria 34°41N 36°15E 46 A5
Talladega U.S.A. 33°26N 86°6W 85 E11
Tallahassee U.S.A. 30°27N 84°17W 85 F12
Tallangatta Australia 36°15S 147°19E 63 F4
Tallering Pk. Australia 28°6S 115°37E 61 E2
Talli Pakistan 29°32N 68°8E 42 E3
Tallinn Estonia 59°22N 24°48E 9 G21
Tallmadge U.S.A. 41°6N 81°27W 82 E3
Tallulah U.S.A. 32°25N 91°11W 84 E9
Talnakh Russia 69°29N 88°22E 29 C9
Taloyoak Canada 69°32N 93°32W 68 D13
Talpa de Allende Mexico 20°23N 104°51W 86 C4
Talparo Trin. & Tob. 10°30N 61°17W 93 K15
Talsi Latvia 57°10N 22°30E 9 H20
Taltal Chile 25°23S 70°33W 94 B1
Taltson → Canada 61°24N 112°46W 70 A6
Talwood Australia 28°29S 149°29E 63 D4
Talyawalka Cr. → Australia 32°28S 142°22E 63 E3
Tam Ky Vietnam 15°34N 108°12E 38 E7
Tam Quan Vietnam 14°35N 109°3E 38 E7
Tama U.S.A. 41°58N 92°35W 80 E7
Tama Abu, Banjaran Malaysia 3°10N 115°5E 36 D5
Tamale Ghana 9°22N 0°50W 50 G5
Taman Negara △ Malaysia 4°38N 102°26E 39 K4

Tamano Japan 34°29N 133°59E 31 G6
Tamanrasset Algeria 22°50N 5°30E 50 D7
Tamaqua U.S.A. 40°48N 75°58W 83 F9
Tamar → U.K. 50°27N 4°15W 13 G3
Tamar Mauritius 20°19S 57°22E 53 d
Tamarin Mauritius 20°19S 57°20E 53 d
Tamarinda Spain 39°55N 3°49E 24 B10
Tamashima Japan 34°32N 133°40E 31 G6
Tamatave = Toamasina Madag. 18°10S 49°25E 57 B8
Tamaulipas □ Mexico 24°0N 98°45W 87 C5
Tamaulipas, Sierra de Mexico 23°30N 98°20W 87 C5
Tamazula Mexico 24°57N 106°57W 86 C3
Tamazunchale Mexico 21°16N 98°47W 87 C5
Tambach Kenya 0°36N 35°31E 54 B4
Tambacounda Senegal 13°45N 13°40W 50 F3
Tambelan, Kepulauan Indonesia 1°0N 107°30E 36 D3
Tambellup Australia 34°4S 117°37E 61 F2
Tambo Australia 24°54S 146°14E 62 C4
Tambo de Mora Peru 13°30S 76°8W 92 F3
Tambohorano Madag. 17°30S 43°58E 57 B7
Tambora Indonesia 8°12S 118°5E 36 F5
Tamboura C.A.R. 5°10N 25°12E 54 A2
Tambov Russia 52°45N 41°28E 18 D7
Tambuku Indonesia 7°8S 113°40E 37 G15
Tâmega → Portugal 41°5N 8°21W 21 B1
Tamenglong India 25°0N 93°35E 41 G18
Tamiahua, L. de Mexico 21°35N 97°35W 87 C5
Tamil Nadu □ India 11°0N 77°0E 40 P10
Tamluk India 22°18N 87°58E 43 H12
Tammerfors = Tampere Finland 61°30N 23°50E 8 F20
Tammisaari Finland 60°0N 23°26E 9 G20
Tampa U.S.A. 27°56N 82°27W 85 H13
Tampa, Tanjung Indonesia 8°55S 116°12E 37 K18
Tampa B. U.S.A. 27°50N 82°30W 85 H13
Tampere Finland 61°30N 23°50E 8 F20
Tampico Mexico 22°13N 97°51W 87 C5
Tampin Malaysia 2°28N 102°13E 39 L4
Tampoi Malaysia 1°30N 103°39E 39 d
Tamu Burma 24°13N 94°12E 41 G19
Tamworth Australia 31°7S 150°58E 63 E5
Tamworth Canada 44°29N 77°0W 82 B8
Tamworth U.K. 52°39N 1°41W 13 E6
Tan An Vietnam 10°32N 106°25E 39 G6
Tan Chau Vietnam 10°48N 105°12E 39 G5
Tan-Tan Morocco 28°29N 11°1W 50 C3
Tana → Kenya 2°32S 40°31E 54 C5
Tana → Norway 70°30N 28°14E 8 A23
Tana, L. Ethiopia 13°5N 37°30E 47 E2
Tana River Primate △ Kenya 1°55S 40°7E 54 C5
Tanabe Japan 33°44N 135°22E 31 H7
Tanafjorden Norway 70°45N 28°25E 8 A23
Tanaga I. U.S.A. 51°48N 177°53W 74 E4
Tanahbala Indonesia 0°30S 98°30E 36 E1
Tanahgrogot Indonesia 1°55S 116°15E 36 E5
Tanahjampea Indonesia 7°10S 120°35E 37 F6
Tanahmasa Indonesia 0°12S 98°39E 36 E1
Tanahmerah Indonesia 6°5S 140°16E 37 F10
Tanakpur India 29°5N 80°7E 43 E9
Tanakura Japan 37°10N 140°20E 31 F10
Tanami Desert Australia 18°50S 132°0E 60 C5
Tanana U.S.A. 65°10N 152°4W 74 B9
Tanana → U.S.A. 65°10N 151°58W 68 D1
Tananarive = Antananarivo Madag. 18°55S 47°31E 57 B8
Tánaro → Italy 44°55N 8°40E 20 D8
Tancheng China 34°25N 118°20E 35 G10
Tanch'ŏn N. Korea 40°27N 128°54E 35 D15
Tanda Ut. P., India 26°33N 82°35E 43 F10
Tanda Ut. P., India 28°57N 78°56E 43 E8
Tandag Phil. 9°4N 126°9E 37 C7
Tandaia Tanzania 9°25S 34°15E 55 D3
Tandil Argentina 37°15S 59°6W 94 D4
Tandil, Sa. del Argentina 37°30S 59°0W 94 D4
Tandlianwala Pakistan 31°3N 73°9E 42 D5
Tando Adam Pakistan 25°45N 68°40E 42 G3
Tando Allahyar Pakistan 25°28N 68°43E 42 G3
Tando Bago Pakistan 24°47N 68°58E 42 G3
Tando Mohommed Khan Pakistan 25°8N 68°32E 42 G3
Tandou L. Australia 32°40S 142°5E 63 E3
Tandoureh △ Iran 37°50N 59°0E 45 B8
Tandragee U.K. 54°21N 6°24W 10 B5
Tane-ga-Shima Japan 30°30N 131°0E 31 J5
Taneatua N.Z. 38°4S 177°1E 59 C6
Tanen Tong Dan = Dawna Ra. Burma 16°30N 98°30E 38 D2
Tanezrouft Algeria 23°9N 0°11E 50 D6
Tang, Koh Cambodia 10°16N 103°7E 39 G4
Tang, Ra's-e Iran 25°21N 59°52E 45 E8
Tang Krasang Cambodia 12°34N 105°3E 38 F5
Tanga Tanzania 5°5S 39°2E 54 D4
Tanga □ Tanzania 5°20S 38°0E 54 D4
Tanganyika, L. Africa 6°40S 30°0E 54 D3
Tanger Morocco 35°50N 5°49W 50 A4
Tangerang Indonesia 6°11S 106°37E 37 G12
Tanggu China 39°2N 117°40E 35 E9
Tanggula Shan China 32°40N 92°10E 32 C4
Tanggula Shankou China 32°42N 92°27E 32 C4
Tanghla Range = Tanggula Shan China 32°40N 92°10E 32 C4
Tangier = Tanger Morocco 35°50N 5°49W 50 A4
Tangjia Indonesia 22°22N 113°35E 33 G10
Tangjia Wan China 22°21N 113°36E 33 G10
Tangorin Australia 21°47S 144°12E 62 C3
Tangorombohitr'i Makay Madag. 21°0S 45°15E 57 C8
Tangra Yumco China 31°0N 86°38E 32 C3
Tangshan China 39°38N 118°10E 35 E10
Tangtou China 35°28N 118°30E 35 G10

INDEX TO WORLD MAPS

Tessaoua **167**

Tanimbar, Kepulauan *Indonesia* 7°30S 131°30E **37** F8
Tanimbar Is. = Tanimbar, Kepulauan *Indonesia* 7°30S 131°30E **37** F8
Taninthari = Tenasserim *Burma* 12°6N 99°3E **39** F2
Tanjay *Phil.* 9°30N 123°5E **37** C6
Tanjong Malim *Malaysia* 3°42N 101°31E **39** L3
Tanjong Pelepas *Malaysia* 1°21N 103°33E **39** d
Tanjore = Thanjavur *India* 10°48N 79°12E **40** P11
Tanjung *Bali, Indonesia* 8°21S 116°9E **37** J19
Tanjung *Kalimantan, Indonesia* 2°10S 115°25E **36** E5
Tanjung Tokong *Malaysia* 5°28N 100°18E **39** c
Tanjungbalai *Indonesia* 2°55N 99°44E **36** D1
Tanjungbatu *Indonesia* 2°23N 118°3E **36** D5
Tanjungkarang Telukbetung = Bandar Lampung *Indonesia* 5°20S 105°10E **36** F3
Tanjungpandan *Indonesia* 2°43S 107°38E **36** E3
Tanjungpinang *Indonesia* 1°5N 104°30E **36** D2
Tanjungredeb *Indonesia* 2°9N 117°29E **36** D5
Tanjungselor *Indonesia* 2°55N 117°25E **36** D5
Tank *Pakistan* 32°14N 70°25E **42** C4
Tankhala *India* 21°58N 73°47E **42** J5
Tankwa-Karoo △ *S. Africa* 32°14S 19°50E **56** E2
Tannersville *U.S.A.* 41°3N 75°18W **83** E9
Tannu Ola *Asia* 51°0N 94°0E **29** D10
Tannum Sands *Australia* 23°57S 151°22E **62** C5
Tanout *Niger* 14°50N 8°55E **50** F7
Tanta *Egypt* 30°45N 30°57E **51** B12
Tantoyuca *Mexico* 21°21N 98°14W **87** C5
Tantung = Dandong *China* 40°10N 124°20E **35** D13
Tanunda *Australia* 34°30S 139°0E **63** E2
Tanzania ■ *Africa* 6°0S 34°0E **54** D3
Tanzhou *China* 22°16N 113°28E **33** G9
Tanzilla → *Canada* 58°8N 130°43W **70** B2
Tao, Ko *Thailand* 10°5N 99°52E **39** G2
Tao'an = Taonan *China* 45°22N 122°40E **35** B12
Tao'er He → *China* 45°45N 124°5E **35** B13
Taolanaro *Madag.* 25°2S 47°0E **57** D8
Taole *China* 38°48N 106°40E **34** E4
Taonan *China* 45°22N 122°40E **35** B12
Taos *U.S.A.* 36°24N 105°35W **77** H11
Taoudenni *Mali* 22°40N 3°55W **50** D5
Tapa *Estonia* 59°15N 25°50E **9** G21
Tapa Shan = Daba Shan *China* 32°0N 109°0E **33** C5
Tapachula *Mexico* 14°54N 92°17W **87** E6
Tapah *Malaysia* 4°12N 101°15E **39** K3
Tapajós → *Brazil* 2°24S 54°41W **93** D8
Tapaktuan *Indonesia* 3°15N 97°10E **36** D1
Tapanahoni → *Suriname* 4°20N 54°25W **93** C8
Tapanui *N.Z.* 45°56S 169°18E **59** F2
Tapauá → *Brazil* 5°40S 64°21W **92** E6
Tapes *Brazil* 30°40S 51°23W **95** C5
Tapeta *Liberia* 6°29N 8°52W **50** G4
Taphan Hin *Thailand* 16°13N 100°26E **38** D3
Tapirapecó, Serra *Venezuela* 1°10N 65°0W **92** C6
Tapo-Capara △ *Venezuela* 7°55N 71°15W **89** E5
Tapti → *India* 21°8N 72°41E **40** J8
Tapuae-o-Uenuku *N.Z.* 42°0S 173°39E **59** E4
Tapul Group *Phil.* 5°35N 120°50E **37** C6
Tapurucuará *Brazil* 0°24S 65°2W **92** D5
Ţaqţaq *Iraq* 35°53N 44°35E **44** C5
Taquara *Brazil* 29°36S 50°46W **95** B5
Taquari → *Brazil* 19°15S 57°17W **92** G7
Tara *Australia* 27°17S 150°31E **63** D5
Tara *Canada* 44°28N 81°9W **82** B3
Tara *Russia* 56°55N 74°24E **28** D8
Tara *Zambia* 16°58S 26°45E **55** F2
Tara → *Montenegro* 43°21N 18°51E **23** C8
Tarābulus *Lebanon* 34°31N 35°50E **46** A4
Tarābulus *Libya* 32°49N 13°7E **51** B8
Tarābulus *N. Afr.* 31°0N 13°0E **51** B8
Taradehi *India* 23°18N 79°21E **43** H8
Tarajalejo *Canary Is.* 28°12N 14°7W **24** F5
Tarakan *Indonesia* 3°20N 117°35E **36** D5
Tarakit, Mt. *Kenya* 2°2N 35°10E **54** B4
Tarama-Jima *Japan* 24°39N 124°42E **31** M2
Taran, Mys *Russia* 54°56N 19°59E **9** J18
Taranagar *India* 28°43N 74°50E **42** E6
Taranaki ☐ *N.Z.* 39°25S 174°30E **59** C5
Taranaki, Mt. *N.Z.* 39°17S 174°5E **59** C5
Tarancón *Spain* 40°1N 3°1W **21** B4
Tarangire △ *Tanzania* 4°21S 36°7E **54** C4
Taransay *U.K.* 57°54N 7°0W **11** D1
Táranto *Italy* 40°28N 17°14E **22** D7
Táranto, G. di *Italy* 40°8N 17°20E **22** D7
Tarapacá *Colombia* 2°56S 69°46W **92** D5
Tarapacá ☐ *Chile* 20°45S 69°30W **94** A2
Tarapoto *Peru* 6°30S 76°20W **92** E3
Tararua Ra. *N.Z.* 40°45S 175°25E **59** D5
Tarashcha *Ukraine* 49°30N 30°31E **17** D16
Tarauacá *Brazil* 8°6S 70°48W **92** E4
Tarauacá → *Brazil* 6°42S 69°48W **92** E5
Taravao *Tahiti* 17°43S 149°18W **59** d
Taravao, Isthme de *Tahiti* 17°43S 149°19W **59** d
Tarawa *Kiribati* 1°30N 173°0E **64** G9
Tarawera *N.Z.* 39°2S 176°36E **59** C6
Tarawera, L. *N.Z.* 38°13S 176°27E **59** C6
Taraz *Kazakhstan* 42°54N 71°22E **28** E8
Tarazona *Spain* 41°55N 1°43W **21** B5
Tarbagatay, Khrebet *Kazakhstan* 48°0N 83°0E **28** E9
Tarbat Ness *U.K.* 57°52N 3°47W **11** D5
Tarbela Dam *Pakistan* 34°8N 72°52E **42** B5
Tarbert *Ireland* 52°34N 9°22W **10** D2
Tarbert *Argyll & Bute, U.K.* 55°52N 5°25W **11** F3
Tarbert *W. Isles, U.K.* 57°54N 6°49W **11** D2
Tarbes *France* 43°15N 0°3E **20** E4
Tarboro *U.S.A.* 35°54N 77°32W **85** D16
Tarcoola *Australia* 30°44S 134°36E **63** E1
Tarcoon *Australia* 30°15S 146°43E **63** E4
Taree *Australia* 31°50S 152°30E **63** E5
Tarfaya *Morocco* 27°55N 12°55W **50** C3
Târgovişte *Romania* 44°55N 25°27E **17** F13
Târgu Jiu *Romania* 45°5N 23°19E **17** F12
Târgu Mureş *Romania* 46°31N 24°38E **17** E13
Ţarif *U.A.E.* 24°3N 53°46E **45** E7
Tarifa *Spain* 36°1N 5°36W **21** D3
Tarija *Bolivia* 21°30S 64°40W **94** A3
Tarija ☐ *Bolivia* 21°30S 63°30W **94** A3
Tariku → *Indonesia* 2°55S 138°26E **37** E9
Tarim Basin = Tarim Pendi *China* 40°0N 84°0E **32** B3
Tarim He → *China* 39°30N 88°30E **32** C3
Tarim Pendi *China* 40°0N 84°0E **32** B3
Taritatu → *Indonesia* 2°54S 138°27E **37** E9
Tarka → *S. Africa* 32°10S 26°0E **56** E4
Tarka La *Bhutan* 27°12N 89°44E **43** F13
Tarkastad *S. Africa* 32°0S 26°16E **56** E4
Tarkhankut, Mys *Ukraine* 45°25N 32°30E **19** E5
Tarko Sale *Russia* 64°55N 77°50E **28** C8
Tarkwa *Ghana* 5°20N 2°0W **50** G5
Tarlac *Phil.* 15°29N 120°35E **37** A6
Tarma *Peru* 11°25S 75°45W **92** F3
Tarn → *France* 44°5N 1°6E **20** E4
Târnăveni *Romania* 46°19N 24°13E **17** E13
Tarnobrzeg *Poland* 50°35N 21°41E **17** C11
Tarnów *Poland* 50°3N 21°0E **17** C11
Tarnowskie Góry *Poland* 50°27N 18°54E **17** C10
Ţārom *Iran* 28°11N 55°46E **45** D7
Taroom *Australia* 25°36S 149°48E **63** D4
Taroudannt *Morocco* 30°30N 8°52W **50** B4
Tarpon Springs *U.S.A.* 28°9N 82°45W **85** G13
Tarrafal *C. Verde Is.* 15°18N 23°39W **50** b
Tarragona *Spain* 41°5N 1°17E **21** B6
Tarraleah *Australia* 42°17S 146°26E **63** G4
Tarrasa = Terrassa *Spain* 41°34N 2°1E **21** B7
Tarrytown *U.S.A.* 41°4N 73°52W **83** E11
Tarshiha = Me'ona *Israel* 33°1N 35°15E **46** B4
Tarsus *Turkey* 36°58N 34°55E **44** B2
Tartagal *Argentina* 22°30S 63°50W **94** A3
Tartu *Estonia* 58°20N 26°44E **9** G22
Ţarţūs *Syria* 34°55N 35°55E **44** C2
Tarumizu *Japan* 31°29N 130°42E **31** J5
Tarutao = Ko Tarutao △ *Thailand* 6°31N 99°26E **39** J2
Tarutao, Ko *Thailand* 6°33N 99°40E **39** J2
Tarutung *Indonesia* 2°0N 98°54E **36** D1
Taseko → *Canada* 52°8N 123°45W **70** C4
Tash-Kömür *Kyrgyzstan* 41°40N 72°10E **28** E8
Tash-Kumyr = Tash-Kömür *Kyrgyzstan* 41°40N 72°10E **28** E8
Tashauz = Dashoguz *Turkmenistan* 41°49N 59°58E **28** E6
Tashi Chho Dzong = Thimphu *Bhutan* 27°31N 89°45E **41** F16
Ţashk, Daryācheh-ye *Iran* 29°45N 53°35E **45** D7
Tashkent = Toshkent *Uzbekistan* 41°20N 69°10E **28** E7
Tashtagol *Russia* 52°47N 87°53E **28** D9
Tasiilaq *Greenland* 65°40N 37°20W **4** C6
Tasik Kenyir *Malaysia* 5°5N 102°45E **39** K4
Tasikmalaya *Indonesia* 7°18S 108°12E **37** G13
Tåsjön *Sweden* 64°15N 15°40E **8** D16
Taskan *Russia* 62°59N 150°20E **29** C16
Tasman B. *N.Z.* 40°59S 173°25E **59** D4
Tasman Basin *Pac. Oc.* 46°0S 158°0E **64** M7
Tasman Mts. *N.Z.* 41°3S 172°25E **59** D4
Tasman Pen. *Australia* 43°10S 148°0E **63** G4
Tasman Sea *Pac. Oc.* 36°0S 160°0E **58** E9
Tasmania ☐ *Australia* 42°0S 146°30E **63** G4
Tasmanian Wilderness World Heritage Area △ *Australia* 43°0S 146°0E **63** G4
Tassili n'Ajjer *Algeria* 25°47N 8°1E **50** C7
Tassili-Oua-n-Ahaggar *Algeria* 20°41N 5°30E **50** D7
Tat Ton △ *Thailand* 15°57N 102°2E **38** E4
Tata *Morocco* 29°46N 7°56W **50** C4
Tatabánya *Hungary* 47°32N 18°25E **17** E10
Tatahouine *Tunisia* 32°56N 10°27E **51** B8
Tataouine *Tunisia* 32°57N 10°29E **51** B8
Tatar Republic = Tatarstan ☐ *Russia* 55°30N 51°30E **18** C9
Tatarbunary *Ukraine* 45°50N 29°39E **17** F15
Tatarsk *Russia* 55°14N 76°0E **28** D8
Tatarskiy Proliv *Russia* 50°0N 141°0E **29** E15
Tatarstan ☐ *Russia* 55°30N 51°30E **18** C9
Tatatua, Pte. *Tahiti* 17°44S 149°8W **59** d
Tateyama *Japan* 35°0N 139°50E **31** G9
Tathlina L. *Canada* 60°33N 117°39W **70** A5
Tathra *Australia* 36°44S 149°59E **63** F4
Tatinnai L. *Canada* 60°55N 97°40W **71** A9
Tatla Lake *Canada* 52°0N 124°20W **70** C4
Tatnam, C. *Canada* 57°16N 91°0W **71** B10
Tatra = Tatry *Slovak Rep.* 49°20N 20°0E **17** D11
Tatry *Slovak Rep.* 49°20N 20°0E **17** D11
Tatshenshini → *Canada* 59°28N 137°45W **70** B1
Tatsuno *Japan* 34°52N 134°33E **31** G7
Tatta *Pakistan* 24°42N 67°55E **42** G2
Tatuí *Brazil* 23°25S 47°53W **95** A6
Tatum *U.S.A.* 33°16N 103°19W **77** K12
Tat'ung = Datong *China* 40°6N 113°18E **34** D7
Tatvan *Turkey* 38°31N 42°15E **44** B4
Ta'ū *Amer. Samoa* 14°15S 169°30W **59** b
Taubaté *Brazil* 23°0S 45°36W **95** A6
Tauern *Austria* 47°15N 12°40E **16** E7
Taumarunui *N.Z.* 38°53S 175°15E **59** C5
Taumaturgo *Brazil* 8°54S 72°51W **92** E4
Taung *S. Africa* 27°33S 24°47E **56** D3
Taungdwingyi *Burma* 20°1N 95°40E **41** J19
Taunggyi *Burma* 20°50N 97°0E **41** J20
Taungup *Burma* 18°51N 94°14E **41** K19
Taunsa *Pakistan* 30°42N 70°39E **42** D4
Taunsa Barrage *Pakistan* 30°42N 70°50E **42** D4
Taunton *U.K.* 51°1N 3°5W **13** F4
Taunton *U.S.A.* 41°54N 71°6W **83** E13
Taunus *Germany* 50°13N 8°34E **16** C5
Taupo *N.Z.* 38°41S 176°7E **59** C6
Taupo, L. *N.Z.* 38°46S 175°55E **59** C5
Tauragė *Lithuania* 55°14N 22°16E **9** J20
Tauranga *N.Z.* 37°42S 176°11E **59** B6
Tauranga Harb. *N.Z.* 37°30S 176°5E **59** B6
Taureau, Rés. *Canada* 46°46N 73°50W **72** C5
Taurianova *Italy* 38°21N 16°1E **22** E7
Taurus Mts. = Toros Dağları *Turkey* 37°0N 32°30E **44** B2
Tautira *Tahiti* 17°44S 149°9W **59** d
Tauyskaya Guba *Russia* 59°20N 150°20E **29** D16
Tavan Bogd Uul *Mongolia* 49°10N 87°49E **32** B3
Tavastehus = Hämeenlinna *Finland* 61°0N 24°28E **8** F21
Tavda *Russia* 58°7N 65°8E **28** D7
Tavda → *Russia* 57°47N 67°18E **28** D7
Taverner B. *Canada* 67°12N 72°25W **69** D17
Taveta *Kenya* 3°23S 37°37E **54** C4
Taveuni *Fiji* 16°51S 179°58W **59** a
Tavira *Portugal* 37°8N 7°40W **21** D2
Tavistock *Canada* 43°19N 80°50W **82** C4
Tavistock *U.K.* 50°33N 4°9W **13** G3
Tavoy *Burma* 14°2N 98°12E **38** E2
Tavrichanka *Russia* 43°18N 131°59E **30** C5
Tavua *Fiji* 17°37S 177°5E **59** a
Tavuki *Fiji* 19°7S 178°8E **59** a
Taw → *U.K.* 51°4N 4°4W **13** F3
Tawa → *India* 22°48N 77°48E **42** H8
Tawas City *U.S.A.* 44°16N 83°31W **81** C12
Tawau *Malaysia* 4°20N 117°55E **36** D5
Tawi-Tawi *Phil.* 5°10N 120°15E **37** C6
Taxco *Mexico* 18°33N 99°36W **87** D5
Taxila *Pakistan* 33°42N 72°52E **42** C5
Taxkorgan Tajik Zizhixian *China* 37°49N 75°14E **32** C2
Tay → *U.K.* 56°37N 3°38W **11** E5
Tay, Firth of *U.K.* 56°25N 3°8W **11** E5
Tay, L. *Australia* 32°55S 120°48E **61** F3
Tay, L. *U.K.* 56°32N 4°8W **11** E4
Tay ⌓ *U.K.* 56°43N 3°59W **11** E5
Tay Ninh *Vietnam* 11°20N 106°5E **39** G6
Tayabamba *Peru* 8°15S 77°16W **92** E3
Taygetos Oros *Greece* 37°0N 22°23E **23** F10
Taylakova *Russia* 59°13N 74°0E **28** D8
Taylor *Canada* 56°13N 120°40W **70** B4
Taylor *Nebr., U.S.A.* 41°46N 99°23W **80** E4
Taylor *Pa., U.S.A.* 41°23N 75°43W **83** E9
Taylor *Tex., U.S.A.* 30°34N 97°25W **84** F6
Taylor, Mt. *U.S.A.* 35°14N 107°37W **77** J10
Taylorville *U.S.A.* 39°33N 89°18W **80** F9
Taymā *Si. Arabia* 27°35N 38°45E **44** E3
Taymyr, Oz. *Russia* 74°20N 102°0E **29** B11
Taymyr, Poluostrov *Russia* 75°0N 100°0E **29** B11
Taypaq *Kazakhstan* 49°0N 51°47E **19** E9
Tayport *U.K.* 56°27N 2°52W **11** E6
Tayrona △ *Colombia* 11°20N 74°2W **89** D5
Tayshet *Russia* 55°58N 98°1E **29** D10
Taytay *Phil.* 10°45N 119°30E **37** B5
Tāyyebād *Iran* 34°45N 60°45E **45** C9
Tāyyebād ☐ *Iran* 34°44N 60°44E **45** C9
Taz → *Russia* 67°32N 78°40E **28** C8
Taza *Morocco* 34°16N 4°6W **50** B5
Tāza Khurmātū *Iraq* 35°18N 44°20E **44** C5
Tazawa-Ko *Japan* 39°43N 140°40E **30** E10
Tazerbo *Libya* 25°45N 21°0E **51** C10
Tazin → *Canada* 59°48N 109°55W **71** B7
Tazin L. *Canada* 59°44N 108°42W **71** B7
Tazovskiy *Russia* 67°30N 78°44E **28** C8
Tbilisi *Georgia* 41°43N 44°50E **19** F7
Tchad = Chad ■ *Africa* 15°0N 17°15E **51** F8
Tchad, L. *Chad* 13°30N 14°30E **51** F8
Tch'eng-tou = Chengdu *China* 30°38N 104°2E **32** C5
Tchentlo L. *Canada* 55°15N 125°0W **70** B4
Tchibanga *Gabon* 2°45S 11°0E **52** E2
Tch'ong-k'ing = Chongqing *China* 29°35N 106°25E **32** D5
Tczew *Poland* 54°8N 18°50E **17** A10
Te Anau, L. *N.Z.* 45°15S 167°45E **59** F1
Te Aroha *N.Z.* 37°32S 175°44E **59** B5
Te Awamutu *N.Z.* 38°1S 175°20E **59** C5
Te Ika a Maui = North I. *N.Z.* 38°0S 175°0E **59** C5
Te Kuiti *N.Z.* 38°20S 175°11E **59** C5
Te Puke *N.Z.* 37°46S 176°22E **59** B6
Te Waewae B. *N.Z.* 46°13S 167°33E **59** G1
Te Wai Pounamu = South I. *N.Z.* 44°0S 170°0E **59** F3
Teague *U.S.A.* 31°38N 96°17W **84** F6
Teahupoo *Tahiti* 17°50S 149°16W **59** d
Teapa *Mexico* 17°33N 92°57W **87** D6
Tebakang *Malaysia* 1°6N 110°30E **36** D4
Teberu *Malaysia* 1°30N 103°42E **39** d
Tébessa *Algeria* 35°22N 8°8E **50** A7
Tebicuary → *Paraguay* 26°36S 58°16W **94** B4
Tebingtinggi *Riau, Indonesia* 1°0N 102°45E **36** E2
Tebingtinggi *Sumatera Utara, Indonesia* 3°20N 99°9E **36** D1
Tecate *Mexico* 32°34N 116°38W **79** N10
Tecka *Argentina* 43°29S 70°48W **96** E2
Tecomán *Mexico* 18°55N 103°53W **86** D4
Tecopa *U.S.A.* 35°51N 116°13W **79** K10
Tecoripa *Mexico* 28°37N 109°57W **86** B3
Tecuala *Mexico* 22°23N 105°27W **86** C3
Tecuci *Romania* 45°51N 27°27E **17** F14
Tecumseh *Canada* 42°19N 82°54W **82** D2
Tecumseh *Mich., U.S.A.* 42°0N 83°57W **81** D12
Tecumseh *Okla., U.S.A.* 35°15N 96°56W **84** D6
Tedzhen = Tejen *Turkmenistan* 37°23N 60°31E **28** F7
Tees → *U.K.* 54°37N 1°10W **12** C6
Tees B. *U.K.* 54°40N 1°9W **12** C6
Teeswater *Canada* 43°59N 81°17W **82** C3
Tefé *Brazil* 3°25S 64°50W **92** D6
Tegal *Indonesia* 6°52S 109°8E **37** G13
Tegallalang *Indonesia* 8°27S 115°17E **37** J18
Tegalsari *Indonesia* 8°25S 114°8E **37** J17
Tegid, L. = Bala, L. *U.K.* 52°53N 3°37W **12** E4
Tegucigalpa *Honduras* 14°5N 87°14W **88** D2
Tehachapi *U.S.A.* 35°8N 118°27W **79** K8
Tehachapi Mts. *U.S.A.* 35°0N 118°30W **79** L8
Teheran = Tehrān *Iran* 35°41N 51°25E **45** C6
Tehoru *Indonesia* 3°23S 129°30E **37** E7
Tehrān *Iran* 35°41N 51°25E **45** C6
Tehrān ☐ *Iran* 35°30N 51°30E **45** C6
Tehri *India* 30°23N 78°29E **43** D8
Tehuacán *Mexico* 18°27N 97°23W **87** D5
Tehuantepec *Mexico* 16°21N 95°13W **87** D5
Tehuantepec, G. de *Mexico* 15°50N 95°12W **87** D5
Tehuantepec, Istmo de *Mexico* 17°15N 94°30W **87** D6
Teide, Pico de *Canary Is.* 28°15N 16°38W **24** F3
Teifi → *U.K.* 52°5N 4°41W **13** E3
Teign → *U.K.* 50°32N 3°32W **13** G4
Teignmouth *U.K.* 50°33N 3°31W **13** G4
Tejakula *Indonesia* 8°8S 115°20E **37** J18
Tejam *India* 29°57N 80°11E **43** E9
Tejen *Turkmenistan* 37°23N 60°31E **28** F7
Tejen → *Turkmenistan* 37°24N 60°38E **45** B9
Tejo → *Europe* 38°40N 9°24W **21** C1
Tejon Pass *U.S.A.* 34°49N 118°53W **79** L8
Tekamah *U.S.A.* 41°47N 96°13W **80** E5
Tekapo, L. *N.Z.* 43°53S 170°33E **59** E3
Tekax *Mexico* 20°12N 89°17W **87** C7
Tekeli *Kazakhstan* 44°50N 79°0E **28** E8
Tekirdağ *Turkey* 40°58N 27°30E **23** D12
Tekkali *India* 18°37N 84°15E **41** K14
Tekoa *U.S.A.* 47°14N 117°4W **76** C5
Tekong Besar, Pulau *Singapore* 1°25N 104°3E **39** d
Tel Aviv ✈ (TLV) *Israel* 32°5N 34°49E **46** C3
Tel Aviv-Yafo *Israel* 32°4N 34°48E **46** C3
Tel Lakhish *Israel* 31°34N 34°51E **46** D3
Tel Megiddo *Israel* 32°35N 35°11E **46** C4
Tela *Honduras* 15°40N 87°28W **88** C2
Telanaipura = Jambi *Indonesia* 1°38S 103°30E **36** E2
Telavi *Georgia* 42°0N 45°30E **19** F8
Telde *Canary Is.* 27°59N 15°25W **24** G4
Telegraph Creek *Canada* 58°0N 131°10W **70** B2
Telekhany = Tsyelyakhany *Belarus* 52°30N 25°46E **17** B13
Telemark *Norway* 59°15N 7°40E **9** G12
Telén *Argentina* 36°15S 65°31W **94** D2
Teleng *Iran* 25°47N 61°3E **45** E9
Teles Pires → *Brazil* 7°21S 58°3W **92** E7
Telescope Pk. *U.S.A.* 36°10N 117°5W **79** J9
Telford *U.K.* 52°40N 2°27W **13** E5
Telford and Wrekin ☐ *U.K.* 52°45N 2°27W **12** E5
Telkwa *Canada* 54°41N 127°5W **70** C3
Tell City *U.S.A.* 37°57N 86°46W **80** G10
Teller *U.S.A.* 65°16N 166°22W **74** B6
Tellicherry *India* 11°45N 75°30E **40** P9
Telluride *U.S.A.* 37°56N 107°49W **77** H10
Teloloapán *Mexico* 18°21N 99°51W **87** D5
Telpos Iz *Russia* 63°16N 59°13E **18** B10
Telsen *Argentina* 42°30S 66°50W **96** E3
Telšiai *Lithuania* 55°59N 22°14E **9** J20
Teluk Anson = Teluk Intan *Malaysia* 4°3N 101°0E **39** K3
Teluk Bahang *Malaysia* 5°28N 100°13E **39** c
Teluk Betung = Bandar Lampung *Indonesia* 5°20S 105°10E **36** F3
Teluk Intan *Malaysia* 4°3N 101°0E **39** K3
Teluk Kumbar *Malaysia* 5°18N 100°14E **39** c
Telukbutun *Indonesia* 4°13N 108°12E **36** D3
Telukdalem *Indonesia* 0°33N 97°50E **36** D1
Tema *Ghana* 5°41N 0°0 **50** G5
Temagami, L. *Canada* 47°0N 80°10W **72** C3
Temax *Mexico* 21°9N 88°56W **87** C7
Temba *S. Africa* 25°20S 28°17E **57** D4
Tembagapura *Indonesia* 4°20S 137°0E **37** E9
Tembe *Dem. Rep. of the Congo* 0°16S 28°14E **54** C2
Tembe ⌓ *S. Africa* 26°51S 32°24E **57** D5
Temblor Range *U.S.A.* 35°20N 119°50W **79** K7
Teme → *U.K.* 52°11N 2°13W **13** E5
Temecula *U.S.A.* 33°30N 117°9W **79** M9
Temengor, Tasik *Malaysia* 5°24N 101°18E **39** K3
Temerloh *Malaysia* 3°27N 102°25E **39** L4
Teminabuan *Indonesia* 1°26S 132°1E **37** E8
Temir *Kazakhstan* 49°1N 57°14E **19** E10
Temirtau *Kazakhstan* 50°5N 72°56E **32** A2
Temirtau *Russia* 53°10N 87°30E **28** D9
Témiscamie → *Canada* 50°59N 73°5W **73** B5
Témiscaming *Canada* 46°44N 79°5W **72** C4
Témiscamingue, L. *Canada* 47°10N 79°25W **72** C4
Temosachic *Mexico* 28°57N 107°51W **86** B3
Tempe *U.S.A.* 33°24N 111°54W **77** K8
Tempiute *U.S.A.* 37°39N 115°38W **78** H11
Temple *U.S.A.* 31°6N 97°21W **84** F6
Temple B. *Australia* 12°15S 143°3E **62** A3
Templemore *Ireland* 52°47N 7°51W **10** D4
Templeton *U.S.A.* 35°33N 120°42W **78** K6
Templeton → *Australia* 21°0S 138°40E **62** C2
Tempoal de Sánchez *Mexico* 21°31N 98°23W **87** C5
Temuco *Chile* 38°45S 72°40W **96** D2
Temuka *N.Z.* 44°14S 171°17E **59** F3
Tenabo *Mexico* 20°3N 90°14W **87** C6
Tenaha *U.S.A.* 31°57N 94°15W **84** F7
Tenakee Springs *U.S.A.* 57°47N 135°13W **70** B1
Tenali *India* 16°15N 80°35E **41** L12
Tenancingo de Degollado *Mexico* 18°58N 99°36W **87** D5
Tenango del Valle *Mexico* 19°7N 99°33W **87** D5
Tenaro, Akra *Greece* 36°22N 22°27E **23** F10
Tenasserim *Burma* 12°6N 99°3E **39** F2
Tenasserim ☐ *Burma* 14°0N 98°30E **38** F2
Tenby *U.K.* 51°40N 4°42W **13** F3
Tenda, Colle di *France* 44°7N 7°36E **20** D7
Tendaho *Ethiopia* 11°48N 40°54E **47** E3
Tendukhera *India* 23°24N 79°33E **43** H8
Teneguía, Volcanes de *Canary Is.* 28°28N 17°51W **24** F2
Ténéré, Erg du *Niger* 17°35N 10°55E **51** E8
Tenerife *Canary Is.* 28°15N 16°35W **24** F3
Tenerife, Pico *Canary Is.* 27°43N 18°1W **24** G1
Tenerife Norte ✈ (TFN) *Canary Is.* 28°28N 16°17W **24** F3
Tenerife Sur ✈ (TFS) *Canary Is.* 28°3N 16°33W **24** F3
Teng Xian *China* 35°5N 117°10E **35** G9
Tengah, Kepulauan *Indonesia* 7°5S 118°15E **36** F5
Tengchong *China* 25°0N 98°28E **32** D4
Tengchowfu = Penglai *China* 37°48N 120°42E **35** F11
Tenggarong *Indonesia* 0°24S 116°58E **36** E5
Tengger Shamo *China* 38°0N 104°0E **32** C5
Tenggol, Pulau *Malaysia* 4°48N 103°41E **39** K4
Tengiz Köli *Kazakhstan* 50°30N 69°0E **32** A1
Teniente Enciso △ *Paraguay* 21°5S 61°8W **94** A3
Teniente Rodolfo Marsh *Antarctica* 62°30S 58°0W **5** C18
Tenino *U.S.A.* 46°51N 122°51W **78** D4
Tenkasi *India* 8°55N 77°20E **40** Q10
Tenke *Katanga, Dem. Rep. of the Congo* 11°22S 26°40E **55** E2
Tenke *Katanga, Dem. Rep. of the Congo* 10°32S 26°7E **55** E2
Tennant Creek *Australia* 19°30S 134°15E **62** B1
Tennessee ☐ *U.S.A.* 36°0N 86°30W **85** D11
Tennessee → *U.S.A.* 37°4N 88°34W **85** C10
Teno, Pta. de *Canary Is.* 28°21N 16°55W **24** F3
Tenom *Malaysia* 5°4N 115°57E **36** C5
Tenosique *Mexico* 17°29N 91°26W **87** D6
Tenryū-Gawa → *Japan* 35°39N 137°48E **31** G8
Tenterden *U.K.* 51°4N 0°42E **13** F8
Tenterfield *Australia* 29°0S 152°0E **63** D5
Teófilo Otoni *Brazil* 17°50S 41°30W **93** G10
Tepa *Indonesia* 7°52S 129°31E **37** F7
Tepalcatepec → *Mexico* 18°35N 101°59W **86** D4
Tepehuanes *Mexico* 25°21N 105°44W **86** B3
Tepetongo *Mexico* 22°28N 103°9W **86** C4
Tepic *Mexico* 21°30N 104°54W **86** C4
Teplice *Czech Rep.* 50°40N 13°48E **16** C7
Tepoca, C. *Mexico* 30°20N 112°25W **86** A2
Tequila *Mexico* 20°54N 103°47W **86** C4
Ter → *Spain* 42°2N 3°12E **21** A7
Ter Apel *Neths.* 52°53N 7°5E **15** B7
Téra *Niger* 14°0N 0°45E **50** F6
Teraina *Kiribati* 4°43N 160°25W **65** G12
Téramo *Italy* 42°39N 13°42E **22** C5
Terang *Australia* 38°15S 142°55E **63** F3
Terang, Teluk *Indonesia* 8°44S 116°0E **37** K19
Terceira *Azores* 38°43N 27°13W **50** a
Tercero → *Argentina* 32°58S 61°47W **94** C3
Terebovlya *Ukraine* 49°18N 25°44E **17** D13
Terek → *Russia* 44°0N 47°30E **19** F8
Terepaima △ *Venezuela* 9°58N 69°17W **89** E6
Teresina *Brazil* 5°9S 42°45W **93** E10
Terewah, L. *Australia* 29°52S 147°35E **63** D4
Teridgerie Cr. → *Australia* 30°25S 148°50E **63** E4
Termas de Río Hondo *Argentina* 27°29S 64°52W **94** B3
Termez = Termiz *Uzbekistan* 37°15N 67°15E **28** F7
Términi Imerese *Italy* 37°59N 13°42E **22** F5
Términos, L. de *Mexico* 18°37N 91°33W **87** D6
Termiz *Uzbekistan* 37°15N 67°15E **28** F7
Térmoli *Italy* 42°0N 15°0E **22** C6
Ternate *Indonesia* 0°45N 127°25E **37** D7
Terneuzen *Neths.* 51°20N 3°50E **15** C3
Terney *Russia* 45°3N 136°37E **30** B8
Terni *Italy* 42°34N 12°37E **22** C5
Ternopil *Ukraine* 49°30N 25°40E **17** D13
Ternopol = Ternopil *Ukraine* 49°30N 25°40E **17** D13
Terowie *Australia* 33°8S 138°55E **63** E2
Terra Bella *U.S.A.* 35°58N 119°3W **79** K7
Terra Nova △ *Canada* 48°33N 53°55W **73** C9
Terrace *Canada* 54°30N 128°35W **70** C3
Terrace Bay *Canada* 48°47N 87°5W **72** C2
Terracina *Italy* 41°17N 13°15E **22** D5
Terralba *Italy* 39°43N 8°39E **22** E3
Terrassa *Spain* 41°34N 2°1E **21** B7
Terre Haute *U.S.A.* 39°28N 87°25W **80** F10
Terrebonne B. *U.S.A.* 29°5N 90°35W **85** G9
Terrell *U.S.A.* 32°44N 96°17W **84** E6
Terrenceville *Canada* 47°40N 54°44W **73** C9
Terry *U.S.A.* 46°47N 105°19W **76** C11
Terryville *U.S.A.* 41°41N 73°3W **83** E11
Terschelling *Neths.* 53°25N 5°20E **15** A5
Teruel *Spain* 40°22N 1°8W **21** B5
Tervola *Finland* 66°6N 24°49E **8** C21
Teryaweynya L. *Australia* 32°18S 143°22E **63** E3
Teshio *Japan* 44°53N 141°44E **30** B10
Teshio-Gawa → *Japan* 44°53N 141°45E **30** B10
Tesiyn Gol → *Mongolia* 50°40N 93°20E **32** A4
Teslin *Canada* 60°10N 132°43W **70** A2
Teslin → *Canada* 61°34N 134°35W **70** A2
Teslin L. *Canada* 60°15N 132°57W **70** A2
Tessalit *Mali* 20°12N 1°0E **50** D6
Tessaoua *Niger* 13°47N 7°56E **50** F7

Test → U.K. 50°56N 1°29W 13 G6
Testigos, Is. Los Venezuela 11°23N 63°7W 89 D7
Tetachuck L. Canada 53°18N 125°55W 70 C3
Tetas, Pta. Chile 23°31S 70°38W 94 A1
Tete Mozam. 16°13S 33°33E 55 F3
Tete □ Mozam. 15°15S 32°40E 55 F3
Teterev → Ukraine 51°1N 30°5E 17 C16
Teteven Bulgaria 42°58N 24°17E 23 C11
Tethul → Canada 60°35N 112°12W 70 A6
Tetiyev Ukraine 49°22N 29°38E 17 D15
Tetlit Zheh = Fort McPherson
  Canada 67°30N 134°55W 68 D5
Teton → U.S.A. 47°56N 110°31W 76 C8
Tétouan Morocco 35°35N 5°21W 50 A4
Tetovo Macedonia 42°1N 20°59E 23 C9
Tetufera, Mt. Tahiti 17°40S 149°26W 59 d
Teuco → Argentina 25°35S 60°11W 94 B3
Teulon Canada 50°23N 97°16W 71 C9
Teun Indonesia 6°59S 129°8E 37 F7
Teuri-Tō Japan 44°26N 141°19E 30 B10
Teutoburger Wald
  Germany 52°5N 8°22E 16 B5
Tevere → Italy 41°44N 12°14E 22 D5
Teverya Israel 32°47N 35°32E 46 C4
Teviot → U.K. 55°29N 2°38W 11 F6
Tewantin Australia 26°27S 153°3E 63 D5
Tewkesbury U.K. 51°59N 2°9W 13 F5
Texada I. Canada 49°40N 124°25W 70 D4
Texarkana Ark., U.S.A. 33°26N 94°2W 84 E7
Texarkana Tex., U.S.A. 33°26N 94°3W 84 E7
Texas Australia 28°49S 151°9E 63 D5
Texas □ U.S.A. 31°40N 98°30W 84 F5
Texas City U.S.A. 29°24N 94°54W 84 G7
Texel Neths. 53°5N 4°50E 15 A4
Texline U.S.A. 36°23N 103°2W 84 C3
Texoma, L. U.S.A. 33°50N 96°34W 84 E6
Teyateyaneng Lesotho 29°7S 27°34E 53 K5
Tezin Afghan. 34°24N 69°30E 42 B3
Teziutlán Mexico 19°49N 97°21W 87 D5
Tezpur India 26°40N 92°45E 41 F18
Tezzeron L. Canada 54°43N 124°30W 70 C4
Tha-anne → Canada 60°31N 94°37W 71 A10
Tha Deua Laos 17°57N 102°53E 38 D4
Tha Deua Laos 19°26N 101°50E 38 D3
Tha Li Thailand 17°37N 101°25E 38 D3
Tha Pla Thailand 17°48N 100°32E 38 D3
Tha Rua Thailand 14°34N 100°44E 38 E3
Tha Sala Thailand 8°40N 99°56E 39 H2
Tha Song Yang Thailand 17°34N 97°55E 38 D1
Thaba Putsoa Lesotho 29°45S 28°0E 57 D4
Thabana Ntlenyana
  Lesotho 29°30S 29°16E 57 D4
Thabazimbi S. Africa 24°40S 27°21E 57 C4
Thādiq Si. Arabia 25°18N 45°52E 44 E5
Thai Binh Vietnam 20°35N 106°1E 38 B6
Thai Muang Thailand 8°24N 98°16E 39 H2
Thai Nguyen Vietnam 21°35N 105°55E 38 B5
Thailand ■ Asia 16°0N 102°0E 38 E4
Thailand, G. of Asia 11°30N 101°0E 39 G3
Thakhek Laos 17°25N 104°45E 38 D5
Thal Pakistan 33°28N 70°33E 42 C4
Thal Desert Pakistan 31°10N 71°30E 42 D4
Thala La = Hkakabo Razi
  Burma 28°25N 97°23E 41 E20
Thalabarivat Cambodia 13°33N 105°57E 38 F5
Thalassery = Tellicherry
  India 11°45N 75°30E 40 P9
Thallon Australia 28°39S 148°49E 63 D4
Thalu, Ko Thailand 9°26N 99°54E 39 b
Thames N.Z. 37°7S 175°34E 59 B5
Thames → Canada 42°20N 82°25W 82 D2
Thames → U.K. 51°29N 0°34E 13 F8
Thames → U.S.A. 41°18N 72°5W 83 E12
Thames Estuary U.K. 51°29N 0°52E 13 F8
Thamesford Canada 43°4N 81°0W 82 C4
Thamesville Canada 42°33N 81°59W 82 D3
Than India 22°34N 71°11E 42 H4
Than Uyen Vietnam 22°0N 103°54E 38 B4
Thana Gazi India 27°25N 76°19E 42 F7
Thandla India 23°0N 74°34E 42 H6
Thandwe Burma 18°20N 94°30E 41 K19
Thane India 19°12N 72°59E 40 K8
Thanesar India 30°1N 76°52E 42 D7
Thanet, I. of U.K. 51°21N 1°20E 13 F9
Thangool Australia 24°38S 150°42E 62 C5
Thanh Hoa Vietnam 19°48N 105°46E 38 C5
Thanh Hung Vietnam 9°55N 105°43E 39 H5
Thanh Pho Ho Chi Minh
  Vietnam 10°58N 106°40E 39 G6
Thanh Thuy Vietnam 22°55N 104°51E 38 A5
Thanjavur India 10°48N 79°12E 40 P11
Thanlwin = Salween →
  Burma 16°31N 97°37E 41 L20
Thano Bula Khan
  Pakistan 25°22N 67°50E 42 G2
Thaolintoa L. Canada 61°30N 96°25W 71 A9
Thap Lan △ Thailand 14°15N 102°16E 38 E4
Thap Sakae Thailand 11°30N 99°37E 39 G2
Thap Than Thailand 15°27N 99°54E 38 E2
Thar Desert India 28°0N 72°0E 42 F5
Tharad India 24°30N 71°44E 42 G4
Thargomindah
  Australia 27°58S 143°46E 63 D3
Tharp Fracture Zone
  S. Ocean 54°0S 135°0W 5 B14
Tharrawaddy Burma 17°38N 95°48E 41 L19
Tharthār, Buḥayrat ath
  Iraq 34°0N 43°15E 44 C4
Tharthar, L. = Tharthār,
  Buḥayrat ath Iraq 34°0N 43°15E 44 C4
Tharthār, W. ath → Iraq 34°32N 43°15E 44 C4
Thasos Greece 40°40N 24°40E 23 D11
That Khe Vietnam 22°16N 106°28E 38 A6
Thatcher Ariz., U.S.A. 32°51N 109°46W 77 K9
Thatcher Colo., U.S.A. 37°33N 104°7W 77 H11
Thaton Burma 16°55N 97°22E 41 L20
Thaungdut Burma 24°30N 94°40E 41 G19
Thayer U.S.A. 36°31N 91°33W 80 G8
Thayetmyo Burma 19°20N 95°10E 41 K19

Thazi Burma 21°0N 96°5E 41 J20
Thbeng Meanchey
  Cambodia 13°49N 104°58E 38 F5
The Broads U.K. 52°45N 1°30E 12 E9
The Everglades U.S.A. 25°50N 81°0W 85 J14
The Gulf = Persian Gulf
  Asia 27°0N 50°0E 45 E6
The Hague = 's-Gravenhage
  Neths. 52°7N 4°17E 15 B4
The Pas Canada 53°45N 101°15W 71 C8
The Wash U.K. 52°58N 0°20E 12 E8
The Weald U.K. 51°4N 0°20E 13 F8
Thebes = Thiva Greece 38°19N 23°19E 23 E10
Thebes Egypt 25°40N 32°35E 51 C12
Thedford U.S.A. 41°59N 100°35W 80 E3
Theebine Australia 25°57S 152°34E 63 D5
Thekulthili L. Canada 61°3N 110°0W 71 A7
Thelon → Canada 64°16N 96°4W 71 A8
Theodore Australia 24°55S 150°3E 62 C5
Theodore Canada 51°26N 102°55W 71 C8
Theodore U.S.A. 30°33N 88°10W 85 F10
Theodore Roosevelt △
  U.S.A. 47°0N 103°25W 80 B2
Theodore Roosevelt L.
  U.S.A. 33°40N 111°10W 77 K8
Thepha Thailand 6°52N 100°58E 39 J3
Theresa U.S.A. 44°13N 75°48W 83 B9
Thermopolis U.S.A. 43°39N 108°13W 76 E9
Thessalon Canada 46°20N 83°30W 72 C3
Thessalonica, Gulf of =
  Thessaloniki Kolpos
  Greece 40°15N 22°45E 23 D10
Thessaloniki Greece 40°38N 22°58E 23 D10
Thessaloniki Kolpos
  Greece 40°15N 22°45E 23 D10
Thetford U.K. 52°25N 0°45E 13 E8
Thetford Mines Canada 46°8N 71°18W 73 C5
Theun → Laos 18°19N 104°0E 38 C5
Theunissen S. Africa 28°26S 26°43E 56 D4
Thevenard Australia 32°9S 133°38E 63 E1
Thibodaux U.S.A. 29°48N 90°49W 85 G9
Thicket Portage Canada 55°19N 97°42W 71 B9
Thief River Falls U.S.A. 48°7N 96°10W 80 A5
Thiel Mts. Antarctica 85°15S 91°0W 5 E16
Thiers France 45°52N 3°33E 20 D5
Thiès Senegal 14°50N 16°51W 50 F2
Thika Kenya 1°1S 37°5E 54 C4
Thimphu Bhutan 27°31N 89°45E 41 F16
Thina → S. Africa 31°18S 29°13E 57 E4
Þingvallavatn Iceland 64°11N 21°9W 8 D3
Thionville France 49°20N 6°10E 20 B7
Thira = Santorini
  Greece 36°23N 25°27E 23 F11
Third Cataract Sudan 19°42N 30°20E 51 E12
Thirsk U.K. 54°14N 1°19W 12 C6
Thiruvananthapuram =
  Trivandrum India 8°41N 77°0E 40 Q10
Thisted Denmark 56°58N 8°40E 9 H13
Thistle I. Australia 35°0S 136°8E 63 F2
Thithia = Cicia Fiji 17°45S 179°18W 59 a
Thiva Greece 38°19N 23°19E 23 E10
Þjórsá → Iceland 63°47N 20°48W 8 E3
Thlewiaza → Canada 60°29N 94°40W 71 A10
Thmar Puok Cambodia 13°57N 103°4E 38 F4
Tho Vinh Vietnam 19°16N 105°42E 38 C5
Thoa → Canada 60°31N 109°47W 71 A7
Thoen Thailand 17°43N 99°12E 38 D2
Thoeng Thailand 19°41N 100°12E 38 C3
Thohoyandou S. Africa 22°58S 30°29E 53 J6
Tholdi Pakistan 35°5N 76°6E 43 B7
Thomas, L. Australia 26°4S 137°58E 63 D2
Thomas Hubbard, C.
  Canada 82°0N 94°25W 69 A13
Thomaston U.S.A. 32°53N 84°20W 85 E12
Thomasville Ala.,
  U.S.A. 31°55N 87°44W 85 F11
Thomasville Ga., U.S.A. 30°50N 83°59W 85 F13
Thomasville N.C., U.S.A. 35°53N 80°5W 85 D14
Thompson Canada 55°45N 97°52W 71 B9
Thompson U.S.A. 41°52N 75°31W 83 E9
Thompson → Canada 50°15N 121°24W 70 C4
Thompson → U.S.A. 39°46N 93°37W 80 F7
Thompson Falls U.S.A. 47°36N 115°21W 76 C6
Thompson Pk. U.S.A. 41°0N 123°2W 76 F2
Thompson Springs
  U.S.A. 38°58N 109°43W 76 G9
Thompsontown U.S.A. 40°33N 77°14W 82 F7
Thomson U.S.A. 33°28N 82°30W 85 E13
Thomson → Australia 25°11S 142°53E 62 C3
Thong Yang Thailand 9°28N 99°56E 39 b
Thoothukudi = Tuticorin
  India 8°50N 78°12E 40 Q11
Þórisvatn Iceland 64°20N 18°55W 8 D4
Thornaby on Tees U.K. 54°33N 1°18W 12 C6
Thornbury Canada 44°34N 80°26W 82 B4
Thorne U.K. 53°37N 0°57W 12 D7
Thornton Canada 44°16N 79°42W 82 B5
Thornton U.S.A. 39°52N 104°58W 76 G11
Thorold Canada 43°7N 79°12W 82 C5
Thouin, C. Australia 20°20S 118°10E 60 D2
Thousand Islands U.S.A. 44°20N 76°0W 83 B9
Thousand Oaks U.S.A. 34°10N 118°50W 79 L8
Thrace Turkey 41°0N 27°0E 23 D12
Three Forks U.S.A. 45°54N 111°33W 76 D8
Three Gorges Res. = Sanxia
  Shuiku China 30°40N 111°10E 33 C5
Three Hills Canada 51°43N 113°15W 70 C6
Three Hummock I.
  Australia 40°25S 144°55E 63 G3
Three Pagodas Pass Asia 15°20N 98°30E 38 E2
Three Points, C. Ghana 4°42N 2°6W 50 H5
Three Rivers Calif.,
  U.S.A. 36°26N 118°54W 78 J8
Three Rivers Tex.,
  U.S.A. 28°28N 98°11W 84 G5
Three Springs Australia 29°32S 115°45E 61 E2

Thrissur = Trichur
  India 10°30N 76°18E 40 P10
Throssell, L. Australia 27°33S 124°10E 61 E3
Throssell Ra. Australia 22°3S 121°43E 60 D3
Thrushton △ Australia 27°47S 147°40E 63 D4
Thua → Kenya 1°31S 39°30E 54 C4
Thuan Hoa Vietnam 8°58N 105°30E 39 H5
Thubun Lakes Canada 61°30N 112°0W 71 A6
Thuin Belgium 50°20N 4°17E 15 D4
Thule = Qaanaaq
  Greenland 77°30N 69°10W 69 B18
Thule Air Base = Uummannaq
  Greenland 77°33N 68°52W 69 B18
Thun Switz. 46°45N 7°38E 20 C7
Thunder B. U.S.A. 45°0N 83°20W 82 B1
Thunder Bay Canada 48°20N 89°15W 72 C2
Thung Salaeng Luang △
  Thailand 16°43N 100°50E 38 D3
Thung Song Thailand 8°10N 99°40E 39 H2
Thunkar Bhutan 27°55N 91°0E 41 F17
Thuong Tra Vietnam 16°2N 107°42E 38 D6
Thüringer Wald Germany 50°35N 11°0E 16 C6
Thuringowa □
  Australia 19°18S 146°43E 62 B4
Thurles Ireland 52°41N 7°49W 10 D4
Thurrock □ U.K. 51°31N 0°23E 13 F8
Thursday I. Australia 10°30S 142°3E 62 A3
Thurso Canada 45°36N 75°15W 72 C4
Thurso U.K. 58°36N 3°32W 11 C5
Thurso → U.K. 58°36N 3°32W 11 C5
Thurston I. Antarctica 72°0S 100°0W 5 D16
Thutade L. Canada 57°0N 126°55W 70 B3
Thyolo Malawi 16°7S 35°5E 55 F4
Ti-Tree Australia 22°5S 133°22E 62 C1
Tian Shan Asia 40°30N 76°0E 32 B3
Tianjin China 39°7N 117°12E 35 E9
Tianshifu China 41°17N 124°22E 35 D13
Tianshui China 34°32N 105°40E 34 G3
Tianyar Indonesia 8°12S 115°30E 37 J18
Tianzhen China 40°24N 114°5E 34 D8
Tianzhuangtai China 40°43N 122°5E 35 D12
Tiarei Tahiti 17°33S 149°20W 59 d
Tiaret Algeria 35°20N 1°21E 50 A6
Tibagi Brazil 24°30S 50°24W 95 A5
Tibagi → Brazil 22°47S 51°1W 95 A5
Tībastī, Sarīr Libya 22°50N 18°30E 51 D9
Tibati Cameroon 6°22N 12°30E 52 C2
Tiber = Tevere → Italy 41°44N 12°14E 22 D5
Tiber Res. U.S.A. 48°19N 111°6W 76 B8
Tiberias = Teverya Israel 32°47N 35°32E 46 C4
Tiberias, L. = Yam Kinneret
  Israel 32°45N 35°35E 46 C4
Tibesti Chad 21°0N 17°30E 51 D9
Tibet = Xizang Zizhiqu □
  China 32°0N 88°0E 32 C3
Tibet, Plateau of Asia 32°0N 86°0E 26 E10
Tibooburra Australia 29°26S 142°1E 63 D3
Tiburón, I. Mexico 29°0N 112°25W 86 B2
Ticino → Italy 45°9N 9°14E 20 D8
Ticonderoga U.S.A. 43°51N 73°26W 83 C11
Ticul Mexico 20°24N 89°32W 87 C7
Tidaholm Sweden 58°12N 13°58E 9 G15
Tiddim Burma 23°28N 93°45E 41 H18
Tidioute U.S.A. 41°41N 79°24W 82 E5
Tidjikja Mauritania 18°29N 11°35W 50 E3
Tidore Indonesia 0°40N 127°25E 37 D7
Tiefa China 42°28N 123°26E 35 C12
Tiegang Shuiku China 22°37N 113°53E 33 F10
Tiel Neths. 51°53N 5°26E 15 C5
Tieling China 42°20N 123°55E 35 C12
Tielt Belgium 51°0N 3°20E 15 C3
Tien Shan = Tian Shan
  Asia 40°30N 76°0E 32 B3
Tien-tsin = Tianjin
  China 39°7N 117°12E 35 E9
Tien Yen Vietnam 21°20N 107°24E 38 B6
T'ienching = Tianjin
  China 39°7N 117°12E 35 E9
Tientsin = Tianjin China 39°7N 117°12E 35 E9
Tierra Amarilla Chile 27°28S 70°18W 94 B1
Tierra Amarilla
  U.S.A. 36°42N 106°33W 77 H10
Tierra Colorada Mexico 17°11N 99°32W 87 D5
Tierra de Campos Spain 42°10N 4°50W 21 A3
Tierra del Fuego, I. Grande de
  Argentina 54°0S 69°0W 96 G3
Tiétar → Spain 39°50N 6°1W 21 C3
Tieté → Brazil 20°40S 51°35W 95 A5
Tiffin U.S.A. 41°7N 83°11W 81 E12
Tifrah Israel 31°19N 34°42E 46 D3
Tifu Indonesia 3°39S 126°24E 37 E7
Tighina Moldova 46°50N 29°30E 17 E15
Tigil Russia 57°49N 158°40E 29 D16
Tignish Canada 46°58N 64°2W 73 C7
Tigre → Peru 4°30S 74°10W 92 D4
Tigre → Venezuela 9°20N 62°30W 92 B6
Tigris = Dijlah, Nahr →
  Asia 31°0N 47°25E 44 D5
Tigyaing Burma 23°45N 96°10E 41 H20
Tīhāmah Asia 16°15N 43°23E 47 D3
Tijara India 27°56N 76°31E 42 F7
Tijuana Mexico 32°32N 117°1W 79 N9
Tikal △ Guatemala 17°13N 89°24W 88 C2
Tikamgarh India 24°44N 78°50E 43 G8
Tikchik Lakes U.S.A. 60°0N 159°0W 74 D8
Tikhoretsk Russia 45°56N 40°5E 19 E7
Tikhvin Russia 59°35N 33°30E 18 C5
Tikirarjuaq = Whale Cove
  Canada 62°10N 92°34W 71 A10
Tikrīt Iraq 34°35N 43°37E 44 C4
Tiksi Russia 71°40N 128°45E 29 B13
Tilamuta Indonesia 0°32N 122°23E 37 D6
Tilburg Neths. 51°31N 5°6E 15 C5
Tilbury Canada 42°17N 82°23W 82 D2
Tilbury U.K. 51°27N 0°22E 13 F8

Tilcara Argentina 23°36S 65°23W 94 A2
Tilden U.S.A. 42°3N 97°50W 80 D5
Tilhar India 28°0N 79°45E 43 F8
Tilichiki Russia 60°27N 166°5E 29 C17
Tilissos Greece 35°20N 25°1E 25 D7
Till → U.K. 55°41N 2°13W 12 B5
Tillamook U.S.A. 45°27N 123°51W 76 D2
Tillsonburg Canada 42°53N 80°44W 82 D4
Tillyeria Cyprus 35°6N 32°40E 25 D11
Tilos Greece 36°27N 27°27E 23 F12
Tilpa Australia 30°57S 144°24E 63 E3
Tilt → U.K. 56°46N 3°51N 11 C5
Tilton U.S.A. 43°27N 71°36W 83 C13
Tiltonsville U.S.A. 40°10N 80°41W 82 F4
Timanfaya △ Canary Is. 29°0N 13°46W 24 E6
Timanskiy Kryazh Russia 65°58N 50°5E 18 A9
Timaru N.Z. 44°23S 171°14E 59 F3
Timau Kenya 0°4N 37°15E 54 B4
Timbaki Greece 35°4N 24°45E 25 D6
Timber Creek Australia 15°40S 130°29E 60 C5
Timber Lake U.S.A. 45°26N 101°5W 80 C3
Timber Mt. U.S.A. 37°6N 116°28W 78 H10
Timbué, Ponta Mozam. 18°47S 36°22E 55 F4
Timbuktu = Tombouctou
  Mali 16°50N 3°0W 50 E5
Timi Cyprus 34°44N 32°31E 25 E11
Timimoun Algeria 29°14N 0°16E 50 C6
Timiris, Râs Mauritania 19°21N 16°30W 50 E2
Timiskaming, L. =
  Témiscamingue, L.
  Canada 47°10N 79°25W 72 C4
Timișoara Romania 45°43N 21°15E 17 F11
Timmins Canada 48°28N 81°25W 72 C3
Timok → Serbia 44°10N 22°40E 23 B10
Timoleague Ireland 51°39N 8°46W 10 E3
Timor Asia 9°0S 125°0E 37 F7
Timor Leste = East Timor ■
  Asia 8°50S 126°0E 37 F7
Timor Sea Ind. Oc. 12°0S 127°0E 60 B4
Tin Can Bay Australia 25°56S 153°0E 63 D5
Tin Mt. U.S.A. 36°50N 117°10W 78 J9
Tina → Thina → S. Africa 31°18S 29°13E 57 E4
Tina, Khalîg el Egypt 31°10N 32°40E 46 D1
Tinaca Pt. Phil. 5°30N 125°25E 37 C7
Tinajo Canary Is. 29°4N 13°42W 24 E6
Tindal Australia 14°31S 132°22E 60 B5
Tindouf Algeria 27°42N 8°10W 50 C4
Tinfunque △ Paraguay 23°55S 60°17W 94 A3
Tinggi, Pulau Malaysia 2°18N 104°7E 39 L4
Tingo María Peru 9°10S 75°54W 92 E3
Tingrela Ivory C. 10°27N 6°25W 50 F4
Tinh Bien Vietnam 10°36N 104°57E 39 G5
Tinian N. Marianas 15°0N 145°38E 64 F6
Tinnevelly = Tirunelveli
  India 8°45N 77°45E 40 Q10
Tinogasta Argentina 28°5S 67°32W 94 B2
Tinos Greece 37°33N 25°8E 23 F11
Tinpahar India 24°59N 87°44E 43 G12
Tintina Argentina 27°2S 62°45W 94 B3
Tintinara Australia 35°48S 140°2E 63 F3
Tioga N. Dak., U.S.A. 48°24N 102°56W 80 A2
Tioga Pa., U.S.A. 41°55N 77°8W 82 E7
Tioman, Pulau Malaysia 2°50N 104°10E 39 L5
Tionesta U.S.A. 41°30N 79°28W 82 E5
Tipperary Ireland 52°28N 8°10W 10 D3
Tipperary □ Ireland 52°37N 7°55W 10 D4
Tipton Calif., U.S.A. 36°4N 119°19W 78 J7
Tipton Iowa, U.S.A. 41°46N 91°8W 80 E8
Tipton Mt. U.S.A. 35°32N 114°12W 79 K12
Tiptonville U.S.A. 36°23N 89°29W 85 C10
Tīrān Iran 32°45N 51°8E 45 C6
Tiranë Albania 41°18N 19°49E 23 D8
Tirari Desert Australia 28°22S 138°7E 63 D2
Tiraspol Moldova 46°55N 29°35E 17 E15
Tire Turkey 38°5N 27°45E 23 E12
Tirebolu Turkey 40°58N 38°45E 19 F6
Tiree U.K. 56°31N 6°55W 11 E2
Tiree, Passage of U.K. 56°30N 6°30W 11 E2
Tîrgoviște = Târgoviște
  Romania 44°55N 25°27E 17 F13
Tîrgu Jiu = Târgu Jiu
  Romania 45°5N 23°19E 17 F12
Tîrgu Mureş = Târgu Mureş
  Romania 46°31N 24°38E 17 E13
Tirich Mir Pakistan 36°15N 71°55E 40 A7
Tiritiri o te Moana = Southern
  Alps N.Z. 43°41S 170°11E 59 E3
Tírnavos Greece 39°45N 22°18E 23 E10
Tirodi India 21°40N 79°44E 40 J11
Tirol □ Austria 47°3N 10°43E 16 E6
Tirso → Italy 39°53N 8°32E 22 E3
Tiruchchirappalli India 10°45N 78°45E 40 P11
Tirunelveli India 8°45N 77°45E 40 Q10
Tirupati India 13°39N 79°25E 40 N11
Tiruppur India 11°5N 77°22E 40 P10
Tiruvannamalai India 12°15N 79°5E 40 N11
Tisa India 32°50N 76°9E 42 C7
Tisa → Serbia 45°15N 20°17E 23 B9
Tisdale Canada 52°50N 104°0W 71 C8
Tishomingo U.S.A. 34°14N 96°41W 84 D6
Tisza = Tisa → Serbia 45°15N 20°17E 23 B9
Tit-Ary Russia 71°55N 127°2E 29 B13
Tithwal Pakistan 34°21N 73°50E 43 B5
Titicaca, L. S. Amer. 15°30S 69°30W 92 G5
Titiwa Nigeria 12°14N 12°53E 51 F8
Titule
  Dem. Rep. of the Congo 3°15N 25°31E 54 B2
Titusville Fla., U.S.A. 28°37N 80°49W 85 G14
Titusville Pa., U.S.A. 41°38N 79°41W 82 E5
Tivaouane Senegal 14°56N 16°45W 50 F2
Tiverton Canada 44°16N 81°32W 82 B3
Tiverton U.K. 50°54N 3°29W 13 G4
Tívoli Italy 41°58N 12°45E 22 D5
Tiwi □ Australia 11°33S 130°42E 60 B5
Tizi-Ouzou Algeria 36°42N 4°3E 50 A6
Tizimín Mexico 21°9N 88°9W 87 C7
Tiznit Morocco 29°48N 9°45W 50 C4

Tjeggelvas Sweden 66°37N 17°45E 8 C17
Tjieggelvas = Tjeggelvas
  Sweden 66°37N 17°45E 8 C17
Tjirebon = Cirebon
  Indonesia 6°45S 108°32E 37 G13
Tjirrkarli ⊙ Australia 26°0S 125°28E 61 E4
Tjluring Indonesia 8°25S 114°13E 37 J17
Tjörn Sweden 58°0N 11°35E 9 H14
Tjukayirla Roadhouse
  Australia 27°9S 124°34E 61 E3
Tjurabalan ⊙ Australia 19°50S 128°0E 60 C4
Tlacotalpan Mexico 18°37N 95°40W 87 D5
Tlahualilo de Zaragoza
  Mexico 26°7N 103°27W 86 B4
Tlaquepaque Mexico 20°39N 103°19W 86 C4
Tlaxcala Mexico 19°19N 98°14W 87 D5
Tlaxcala □ Mexico 19°30N 98°10W 87 D5
Tlaxiaco Mexico 17°25N 97°35W 87 D5
Tlemcen Algeria 34°52N 1°21W 50 B5
To Bong Vietnam 12°45N 109°16E 38 F7
Toa Payoh Singapore 1°20N 103°51E 39 d
Toad → Canada 59°25N 124°57W 70 B4
Toad River Canada 58°51N 125°14W 70 B3
Toamasina Madag. 18°10S 49°25E 57 B8
Toamasina □ Madag. 18°0S 49°0E 57 B8
Toay Argentina 36°43S 64°38W 94 D3
Toba Japan 34°30N 136°51E 31 G8
Toba, Danau Indonesia 2°30N 97°30E 36 D1
Toba Kakar Pakistan 31°30N 69°0E 42 D3
Toba Tek Singh Pakistan 30°55N 72°25E 42 D5
Tobago Trin. & Tob. 11°10N 60°30W 93 J16
Tobelo Indonesia 1°45N 127°56E 37 D7
Tobermory Canada 45°12N 81°40W 82 A3
Tobermory U.K. 56°38N 6°5W 11 E2
Tobi Pac. Oc. 2°40N 131°10E 37 D8
Tobi-Shima Japan 41°12N 139°34E 30 D9
Tobin, L. Australia 21°45S 125°49E 60 D4
Tobin, L. Canada 53°35N 103°30W 71 C8
Tobin, Mt. U.S.A. 40°24N 117°32W 76 F5
Toboali Indonesia 3°0S 106°25E 36 E3
Tobol → Russia 58°10N 68°12E 28 D7
Toboli Indonesia 0°38S 120°5E 37 E6
Tobolsk Russia 58°15N 68°10E 28 D7
Tobruk = Tubruq Libya 32°7N 23°55E 51 B10
Tobyhanna U.S.A. 41°11N 75°25W 83 E9
Tobyl = Tobol → Russia 58°10N 68°12E 28 D7
Tocantinópolis Brazil 6°20S 47°25W 93 E9
Tocantins □ Brazil 10°0S 48°0W 93 F9
Tocantins → Brazil 1°45S 49°10W 93 D9
Toccoa U.S.A. 34°35N 83°19W 85 D13
Tochi → Pakistan 32°49N 70°41E 42 C4
Tochigi Japan 36°25N 139°45E 31 F9
Tochigi □ Japan 36°45N 139°45E 31 F9
Toco Trin. & Tob. 10°49N 60°57W 93 K16
Toconao Chile 23°11S 68°1W 94 A2
Tocopilla Chile 22°5S 70°10W 94 A1
Tocumwal Australia 35°51S 145°31E 63 F4
Tocuyo → Venezuela 11°3N 68°23W 89 D6
Todd → Australia 24°52S 135°48E 62 C2
Todeli Indonesia 1°40S 124°29E 37 E6
Todenyang Kenya 4°35N 35°56E 54 B4
Todgarh India 25°42N 73°58E 42 G5
Todos os Santos, B. de
  Brazil 12°48S 38°38W 93 F11
Todos Santos Mexico 23°26N 110°13W 86 C2
Toe Hd. U.K. 57°50N 7°8W 11 D1
Tofield Canada 53°25N 112°40W 70 C6
Tofino Canada 49°11N 125°55W 70 D3
Tofua Tonga 19°45S 175°5W 59 c
Tōgane Japan 35°33N 140°22E 31 G10
Togian, Kepulauan
  Indonesia 0°20S 121°50E 37 E6
Togliatti Russia 53°32N 49°24E 18 D8
Togo ■ W. Afr. 8°30N 1°35E 50 G6
Togtoh China 40°15N 111°10E 34 D6
Tohiea, Mt. Moorea 17°33S 149°49W 59 d
Tōhoku □ Japan 39°50N 141°45E 30 E10
Tōhōm Mongolia 44°27N 108°2E 34 B5
Toinya Sudan 6°17N 29°46E 51 G11
Toiyabe Range U.S.A. 39°30N 117°0W 76 G5
Tojikiston = Tajikistan ■
  Asia 38°30N 70°0E 28 F8
Tojo Indonesia 1°20S 121°15E 37 E6
Tōjō Japan 34°53N 133°16E 31 G6
Tok U.S.A. 63°20N 142°59W 68 E3
Tokachi-Dake Japan 43°17N 142°5E 30 C11
Tokachi-Gawa →
  Japan 42°44N 143°42E 30 C11
Tokala Indonesia 1°30S 121°40E 37 E6
Tōkamachi Japan 37°8N 138°43E 31 F9
Tokanui N.Z. 46°34S 168°56E 59 G2
Tokara-Rettō Japan 29°37N 129°43E 31 K4
Tokarahi N.Z. 44°56S 170°39E 59 F3
Tokashiki-Shima Japan 26°11N 127°21E 31 L3
Tokat Turkey 40°22N 36°35E 19 F6
Tokch'ŏn N. Korea 39°45N 126°18E 35 E14
Tokdo Asia 37°15N 131°52E 31 F5
Tokeland U.S.A. 46°42N 123°59W 78 D3
Tokelau Is. ☒ Pac. Oc. 9°0S 171°45W 64 H10
Tokmak Kyrgyzstan 42°49N 75°15E 28 E8
Toko Ra. Australia 23°5S 138°20E 62 C2
Tokoro-Gawa → Japan 44°7N 144°5E 30 B12
Toku Tonga 18°10S 174°11W 59 c
Tokuno-Shima Japan 27°56N 128°55E 31 L4
Tokushima Japan 34°4N 134°34E 31 G7
Tokushima □ Japan 33°55N 134°0E 31 H7
Tokuyama Japan 34°3N 131°50E 31 G5
Tōkyō Japan 35°43N 139°45E 31 G9
Tolbukhin = Dobrich
  Bulgaria 43°37N 27°49E 23 C12
Toledo Brazil 24°44S 53°45W 95 A5
Toledo Spain 39°50N 4°2W 21 C3
Toledo Ohio, U.S.A. 41°39N 83°33W 81 E12
Toledo Oreg., U.S.A. 44°37N 123°56W 76 D2
Toledo Wash., U.S.A. 46°26N 122°51W 78 D4
Toledo, Montes de Spain 39°33N 4°20W 21 C3
Toledo Bend Res. U.S.A. 31°11N 93°34W 84 F8
Tolga Australia 17°15S 145°29E 62 B4
Toliara Madag. 23°21S 43°40E 57 C7

Toliara □ Madag. 21°0S 45°0E 57 C8
Tolima Colombia 4°40N 75°19W 92 C3
Tolitoli Indonesia 1°5N 120°50E 37 D6
Tollhouse U.S.A. 37°1N 119°24W 78 H7
Tolo, Teluk Indonesia 2°20S 122°10E 37 E6
Tolo Harbour China 22°27N 114°12E 33 G11
Toluca Mexico 19°17N 99°40W 87 D5
Tolyatti = Togliatti
  Russia 53°32N 49°24E 18 D8
Tom Burke S. Africa 23°5S 28°0E 57 C4
Tom Price Australia 22°40S 117°48E 60 D2
Tomah U.S.A. 43°59N 90°30W 80 D8
Tomahawk U.S.A. 45°28N 89°44W 80 C9
Tomakomai Japan 42°38N 141°36E 30 C10
Tomales U.S.A. 38°15N 122°53W 78 G4
Tomales B. U.S.A. 38°15N 123°58W 78 G3
Tomanivi Fiji 17°37S 178°1E 59 a
Tomar Portugal 39°36N 8°25W 21 C1
Tomaszów Mazowiecki
  Poland 51°30N 20°2E 17 C10
Tomatlán Mexico 19°56N 105°15W 86 D3
Tombador, Serra do Brazil 12°0S 58°0W 92 F7
Tombigbee → U.S.A. 31°8N 87°57W 85 F11
Tombouctou Mali 16°50N 3°0W 50 E5
Tombstone U.S.A. 31°43N 110°4W 77 L8
Tombua Angola 15°55S 11°55E 56 B1
Tomé Chile 36°36S 72°57W 94 D1
Tomelloso Spain 39°10N 3°2W 21 C4
Tomini Indonesia 0°30S 120°30E 37 D6
Tomini, Teluk Indonesia 0°10S 121°0E 37 E6
Tomintoul U.K. 57°15N 3°23W 11 D5
Tomkinson Ranges
  Australia 26°11S 129°5E 61 E4
Tommot Russia 59°4N 126°20E 29 D13
Tomnop Ta Suos
  Cambodia 11°20N 104°15E 39 G5
Tomo → Colombia 5°20N 67°48W 92 B5
Toms Place U.S.A. 37°34N 118°41W 78 H8
Toms River U.S.A. 39°58N 74°12W 83 G10
Tomsk Russia 56°30N 85°5E 28 D9
Tonalá Chiapas, Mexico 16°4N 93°45W 87 D6
Tonalá Jalisco, Mexico 20°37N 103°14W 86 C4
Tonantins Brazil 2°45S 67°45W 92 D5
Tonasket U.S.A. 48°42N 119°26W 76 B4
Tonawanda U.S.A. 43°1N 78°53W 82 D6
Tonb Iran 26°15N 55°15E 45 E7
Tonbridge U.K. 51°11N 0°17E 13 F8
Tondano Indonesia 1°35N 124°54E 37 D6
Tondoro Namibia 17°45S 18°50E 56 B2
Tone → Australia 34°25S 116°25E 61 F2
Tone-Gawa → Japan 35°44N 140°51E 31 F9
Tonekābon Iran 36°45N 51°12E 45 B6
Tong Xian China 39°55N 116°35E 34 E9
Tong-Yeong S. Korea 34°50N 128°20E 35 G15
Tonga ■ Pac. Oc. 19°50S 174°30W 59 c
Tonga Trench Pac. Oc. 18°0S 173°0W 64 J10
Tongaat S. Africa 29°33S 31°9E 57 D5
Tongareva = Penrhyn
  Cook Is. 9°0S 158°0W 65 H12
Tongariro △ N.Z. 39°8S 175°33E 59 C5
Tongatapu Tonga 21°10S 175°10W 59 c
Tongatapu Group Tonga 21°0S 175°0W 59 c
Tongchuan China 35°6N 109°3E 34 G5
Tongeren Belgium 50°47N 5°28E 15 D5
Tonggu Jiao China 22°22N 113°37E 33 G10
Tongguan China 34°40N 110°25E 34 G6
Tonghua China 41°42N 125°58E 35 D13
Tongjosŏn Man
  N. Korea 39°30N 128°0E 35 E15
Tongking, G. of = Tonkin, G. of
  Asia 20°0N 108°0E 38 C7
Tongliao China 43°38N 122°18E 35 C12
Tongling China 30°55N 117°48E 33 C6
Tongobory Madag. 23°32S 44°20E 57 C7
Tongoy Chile 30°16S 71°31W 94 C1
Tongres = Tongeren
  Belgium 50°47N 5°28E 15 D5
Tongsa Dzong Bhutan 27°31N 90°31E 41 F17
Tongshi China 18°30N 109°20E 38 C7
Tongue U.K. 58°29N 4°25W 11 C4
Tongue → U.S.A. 46°25N 105°52W 76 C11
Tongwei China 35°0N 105°5E 34 G3
Tongxin China 36°59N 105°58E 34 F3
Tongyang N. Korea 39°9N 126°53E 35 E14
Tongyu China 44°45N 123°4E 35 B12
Tonj Sudan 7°20N 28°44E 51 G11
Tonk India 26°6N 75°54E 42 F6
Tonkawa U.S.A. 36°41N 97°18W 84 C6
Tonkin = Bac Phan
  Vietnam 22°0N 105°0E 38 B5
Tonkin, G. of Asia 20°0N 108°0E 38 C7
Tonle Sap Cambodia 13°0N 104°0E 38 F5
Tono Japan 39°19N 141°32E 30 E10
Tonopah U.S.A. 38°4N 117°14W 77 G5
Tonosí Panama 7°20N 80°20W 88 E3
Tons → Haryana, India 30°30N 77°39E 42 D7
Tons → Ut. P., India 26°1N 83°33E 43 F10
Tønsberg Norway 59°19N 10°25E 9 G14
Tonto △ U.S.A. 33°39N 111°7W 77 K8
Tonumea Tonga 20°30S 174°30W 59 c
Toobanna Australia 18°42S 146°9E 62 B4
Toodyay Australia 31°34S 116°28E 61 F2
Tooele U.S.A. 40°32N 112°18W 76 F7
Toompine Australia 27°15S 144°19E 63 D3
Toora Australia 38°39S 146°23E 63 F4
Toora-Khem Russia 52°28N 96°17E 29 D10
Toowoomba Australia 27°32S 151°56E 63 D5
Top Springs Australia 16°37S 131°51E 60 C5
Topaz U.S.A. 38°41N 119°30W 78 G7
Topeka U.S.A. 39°3N 95°40W 80 F6
Topley Canada 54°49N 126°18W 70 C3
Topocalma, Pta. Chile 34°10S 72°2W 94 C1
Topock U.S.A. 34°46N 114°29W 79 L12
Topol'čany Slovak Rep. 48°35N 18°12E 17 D10
Topolobampo Mexico 25°36N 109°3W 86 B3
Topozero, Ozero Russia 65°35N 32°0E 8 D25
Toppenish U.S.A. 46°23N 120°19W 76 C3
Toraka Vestale Madag. 16°20S 43°58E 57 B7

Torata Peru 17°23S 70°1W 92 G4
Torbalı Turkey 38°10N 27°21E 23 E12
Torbat-e Heydārīyeh
  Iran 35°15N 59°12E 45 C8
Torbat-e Jām Iran 35°16N 60°35E 45 C9
Torbay Canada 47°40N 52°42W 73 C9
Torbay □ U.K. 50°26N 3°31W 13 G4
Tordesillas Spain 41°30N 5°0W 21 B3
Torfaen □ U.K. 51°43N 3°3W 13 F4
Torgau Germany 51°34N 13°0E 16 C7
Torhout Belgium 51°5N 3°7E 15 C3
Tori-Shima Japan 30°29N 140°19E 31 J10
Torilla Pen. Australia 22°29S 150°5E 62 C5
Torino Italy 45°3N 7°40E 20 D7
Torit Sudan 4°27N 32°31E 51 H12
Torkamān Iran 37°35N 47°23E 44 B5
Tormes → Spain 41°18N 6°29W 21 B2
Tornado Mt. Canada 49°55N 114°40W 70 D6
Torneå = Tornio Finland 65°50N 24°12E 8 D21
Torneälven → Europe 65°50N 24°12E 8 D21
Torneträsk Sweden 68°24N 19°15E 8 B18
Torngat Mts. Canada 59°0N 63°40W 69 F19
Tornio Finland 65°50N 24°12E 8 D21
Tornionjoki = Torneälven →
  Europe 65°50N 24°12E 8 D21
Tornquist Argentina 38°8S 62°15W 94 D3
Toro Spain 39°59N 4°8E 24 B11
Toro, Cerro del Chile 29°10S 69°50W 94 B2
Toro △ Uganda 1°5N 30°22E 54 C3
Toro Pk. U.S.A. 33°34N 116°24W 79 M10
Toronto Canada 43°39N 79°20W 82 C5
Toronto U.S.A. 40°28N 80°36W 82 F4
Toronto Lester B. Pearson Int. ✈
  (YYZ) Canada 43°46N 79°35W 82 C5
Toropets Russia 56°30N 31°40E 18 C5
Tororo Uganda 0°45N 34°12E 54 B3
Toros Dağları Turkey 37°0N 32°30E 44 B2
Torpa India 22°57N 85°6E 43 H11
Torquay U.K. 50°27N 3°32W 13 G4
Torrance U.S.A. 33°50N 118°20W 79 M8
Torre de Moncorvo
  Portugal 41°12N 7°8W 21 B2
Torre del Greco Italy 40°47N 14°22E 22 D6
Torrejón de Ardoz Spain 40°27N 3°29W 21 B4
Torrelavega Spain 43°20N 4°5W 21 A3
Torremolinos Spain 36°38N 4°30W 21 D3
Torrens, L. Australia 31°0S 137°50E 63 E2
Torrens Cr. → Australia 22°23S 145°9E 62 C4
Torrens Creek Australia 20°48S 145°3E 62 C4
Torrent Spain 39°27N 0°28W 21 C5
Torreón Mexico 25°33N 103°26W 86 B4
Torres Brazil 29°21S 49°44W 95 B5
Torres Mexico 28°46N 110°47W 86 B2
Torres Strait Australia 9°50S 142°20E 62 a
Torres Vedras Portugal 39°5N 9°15W 21 C1
Torrevieja Spain 37°59N 0°42W 21 D5
Torrey U.S.A. 38°18N 111°25W 76 G8
Torridge → U.K. 51°0N 4°13W 13 G3
Torridon, L. U.K. 57°35N 5°50W 11 D3
Torrington Conn., U.S.A. 41°48N 73°7W 83 E11
Torrington Wyo.,
  U.S.A. 42°4N 104°11W 76 E11
Tórshavn Færoe Is. 62°5N 6°56W 8 E9
Tortola Br. Virgin Is. 18°19N 64°45W 89 e
Tortosa Spain 40°49N 0°31E 21 B6
Tortosa, C. Spain 40°41N 0°52E 21 B6
Tortue, Î. de la Haiti 20°5N 72°57W 89 B5
Tortuguero △ Costa Rica 10°31N 83°29W 88 D3
Torūd Iran 35°25N 55°5E 45 C7
Toruń Poland 53°2N 18°39E 17 B10
Tory Hill Canada 44°58N 78°16W 82 B6
Tory I. Ireland 55°16N 8°14W 10 A3
Tosa Japan 33°24N 133°23E 31 H6
Tosa-Shimizu Japan 32°52N 132°58E 31 H6
Tosa-Wan Japan 33°15N 133°30E 31 H6
Toscana □ Italy 43°25N 11°0E 22 C4
Toshka, Buheirat en
  Egypt 22°50N 31°0E 51 D12
Toshka Lakes = Toshka, Buheirat
  en Egypt 22°50N 31°0E 51 D12
Toshkent Uzbekistan 41°20N 69°10E 28 E7
Tostado Argentina 29°15S 61°50W 94 B3
Tostón, Pta. de Canary Is. 28°42N 14°2W 24 F5
Tosu Japan 33°22N 130°31E 31 H5
Toteng Botswana 20°22S 22°58E 56 C3
Totma Russia 60°0N 42°40E 18 C7
Totnes U.K. 50°26N 3°42W 13 G4
Totness Suriname 5°53N 56°19W 93 B7
Totonicapán Guatemala 14°58N 91°12W 88 D1
Totoya, I. Fiji 18°57S 179°50W 59 a
Totten Glacier Antarctica 66°45S 116°10E 5 C8
Tottenham Australia 32°14S 147°21E 63 E4
Tottenham Canada 44°1N 79°49W 82 B5
Tottori Japan 35°30N 134°15E 31 G7
Tottori □ Japan 35°30N 134°12E 31 G7
Toubkal, Djebel Morocco 31°0N 8°0W 50 B4
Tougan Burkina Faso 13°11N 2°58W 50 F5
Touggourt Algeria 33°6N 6°4E 50 B7
Toul France 48°40N 5°53E 20 B6
Toulon France 43°10N 5°55E 20 E6
Toulouse France 43°37N 1°27E 20 E4
Toummo Niger 22°45N 14°8E 51 D8
Toungoo Burma 19°0N 96°30E 41 K20
Touraine France 47°20N 0°30E 20 C4
Tourcoing France 50°42N 3°10E 20 A5
Touriñán, C. Spain 43°3N 9°18E 21 A1
Tournai Belgium 50°35N 3°25E 15 D3
Tournon-sur-Rhône
  France 45°4N 4°50E 20 D6
Tours France 47°22N 0°40E 20 C4
Toussoro, Mt. C.A.R. 9°7N 23°14E 52 C4
Touws → S. Africa 33°45S 21°11E 56 E3
Touwsrivier S. Africa 33°20S 20°2E 56 E3
Towada Japan 40°37N 141°13E 30 D10
Towada-Hachimantai △
  Japan 40°28N 140°55E 30 D10
Towada-Ko Japan 40°28N 140°55E 30 D10
Towanda U.S.A. 41°46N 76°27W 83 E8
Tower U.S.A. 47°48N 92°17W 80 B7

Towerhill Cr. →
  Australia 22°28S 144°35E 62 C3
Towner U.S.A. 48°21N 100°25W 80 A3
Townsend U.S.A. 46°19N 111°31W 76 C8
Townshend I. Australia 22°10S 150°31E 62 C5
Towot Sudan 6°12N 34°25E 54 A3
Towraghondī Afghan. 35°13N 62°16E 40 B3
Towson U.S.A. 39°24N 76°36W 81 F15
Towuti, Danau Indonesia 2°45S 121°32E 37 E6
Toya-Ko Japan 42°35N 140°51E 30 C10
Toyama Japan 36°40N 137°15E 31 F8
Toyama □ Japan 36°45N 137°30E 31 F8
Toyama-Wan Japan 37°0N 137°30E 31 F8
Toyapakeh Indonesia 8°41S 115°29E 37 K18
Toyohashi Japan 34°45N 137°25E 31 G8
Toyokawa Japan 34°48N 137°27E 31 G8
Toyonaka Japan 34°46N 135°28E 31 G7
Toyooka Japan 35°35N 134°48E 31 G7
Toyota Japan 35°3N 137°7E 31 G8
Tozeur Tunisia 33°56N 8°8E 50 B7
Trá Lí = Tralee Ireland 52°16N 9°42W 10 D2
Trá Mhór = Tramore
  Ireland 52°10N 7°10W 10 D4
Tra On Vietnam 9°58N 105°55E 39 H5
Trabzon Turkey 41°0N 39°45E 19 F6
Tracadie Canada 47°30N 64°55W 73 C7
Tracy Canada 46°1N 73°9W 72 C5
Tracy Calif., U.S.A. 37°44N 121°26W 78 H5
Tracy Minn., U.S.A. 44°14N 95°37W 80 C6
Trafalgar, C. Spain 36°10N 6°2W 21 D2
Trail Canada 49°5N 117°40W 70 D5
Trainor L. Canada 60°24N 120°17W 70 A4
Trakai △ Lithuania 54°30N 25°10E 9 J21
Trákhonas Cyprus 35°12N 33°21E 25 D12
Tralee Ireland 52°16N 9°42W 10 D2
Tralee B. Ireland 52°17N 9°55W 10 D2
Tramore Ireland 52°10N 7°10W 10 D4
Tramore B. Ireland 52°9N 7°10W 10 D4
Tramuntana, Serra de
  Spain 39°48N 2°54E 24 B9
Tran Ninh, Cao Nguyen
  Laos 19°30N 103°10E 38 C4
Tranås Sweden 58°3N 14°59E 9 G16
Trancas Argentina 26°11S 65°20W 94 B2
Trang Thailand 7°33N 99°38E 39 J2
Trangahy Madag. 19°7S 44°31E 57 B7
Trangan Indonesia 6°40S 134°20E 37 F8
Trangie Australia 32°4S 148°0E 63 E4
Trani Italy 41°17N 16°25E 22 D7
Tranoroa Madag. 24°42S 45°4E 57 C8
Tranqueras Uruguay 31°13S 55°45W 95 C4
Transantarctic Mts.
  Antarctica 85°0S 170°0W 5 E12
Transilvania Romania 46°30N 24°0E 17 E12
Transilvanian Alps = Carpații
  Meridionali Romania 45°30N 25°0E 17 F13
Transnistria = Stînga Nistrului □
  Moldova 47°20N 29°15E 17 E15
Transylvania = Transilvania
  Romania 46°30N 24°0E 17 E12
Trápani Italy 38°1N 12°29E 22 E5
Trapper Pk. U.S.A. 45°54N 114°18W 76 D6
Traralgon Australia 38°12S 146°34E 63 F4
Trasimeno, L. Italy 43°8N 12°6E 22 C5
Trat Thailand 12°14N 102°33E 39 F4
Tratani → Pakistan 29°19N 68°20E 42 E3
Traun Austria 48°14N 14°15E 16 D8
Travellers L. Australia 33°20S 142°0E 63 E3
Travemünde Germany 53°57N 10°52E 16 B6
Travers, Mt. N.Z. 42°1S 172°45E 59 E4
Traverse City U.S.A. 44°46N 85°38W 81 C11
Travis, L. U.S.A. 30°24N 97°55W 84 F5
Travnik Bos.-H. 44°17N 17°39E 23 B7
Trawbreaga B. Ireland 55°20N 7°25W 10 A4
Trébbia → Italy 45°4N 9°41E 20 D8
Trebíč Czech Rep. 49°14N 15°55E 16 D8
Trebinje Bos.-H. 42°44N 18°22E 23 C8
Trebonne Australia 18°37S 146°5E 62 B4
Tregaron U.K. 52°14N 3°56W 13 E4
Tregrosse Is. Australia 17°41S 150°43E 62 B5
Treherne Canada 49°38N 98°42W 71 D9
Treinta y Tres Uruguay 33°16S 54°17W 95 C5
Trelawney Zimbabwe 17°30S 30°30E 57 B5
Trelew Argentina 43°10S 65°20W 96 E3
Trelleborg Sweden 55°20N 13°10E 9 J15
Tremadog Bay U.K. 52°51N 4°18W 12 E3
Tremonton U.S.A. 41°43N 112°10W 76 F7
Tremp Spain 42°10N 0°52E 21 A6
Trenche → Canada 47°46N 72°53W 72 C5
Trenčín Slovak Rep. 48°52N 18°4E 17 D10
Trenggalek Indonesia 8°3S 111°43E 37 H14
Trenque Lauquen
  Argentina 36°5S 62°45W 94 D3
Trent → Canada 44°6N 77°34W 82 B7
Trent → U.K. 53°41N 0°42W 12 D7
Trento Italy 46°4N 11°8E 22 A4
Trenton Canada 44°10N 77°34W 82 B7
Trenton Mo., U.S.A. 40°5N 93°37W 80 E7
Trenton N.J., U.S.A. 40°14N 74°46W 83 F10
Trenton Nebr., U.S.A. 40°11N 101°1W 80 E3
Trepassey Canada 46°43N 53°25W 73 C9
Tres Arroyos Argentina 38°26S 60°20W 94 D3
Três Corações Brazil 21°44S 45°15W 95 A6
Três Lagoas Brazil 20°50S 51°43W 93 H8
Tres Lomas Argentina 36°27S 62°51W 94 D3
Tres Montes, C. Chile 46°50S 75°30W 96 F1
Tres Pinos U.S.A. 36°48N 121°19W 78 J5
Três Pontas Brazil 21°23S 45°29W 95 A6
Tres Puentes Chile 27°50S 70°15W 94 B1
Tres Puntas, C. Argentina 47°0S 66°0W 96 F3
Três Rios Brazil 22°6S 43°15W 95 A7
Tres Valles Mexico 18°15N 96°8W 87 D5
Tresco U.K. 49°57N 6°20W 13 H1
Treviso Italy 45°40N 12°15E 22 B5
Triabunna Australia 42°30S 147°55E 63 G4
Trianda Greece 36°25N 28°10E 25 C10
Triangle Zimbabwe 21°2S 31°28E 57 C5
Tribal Areas □ Pakistan 33°0N 70°0E 42 C4

Tribulation, C. Australia 16°5S 145°29E 62 B4
Tribune U.S.A. 38°28N 101°45W 80 F3
Trichinopoly = Tiruchchirappalli
  India 10°45N 78°45E 40 P11
Trichur India 10°30N 76°18E 40 P10
Trichy = Tiruchchirappalli
  India 10°45N 78°45E 40 P11
Trida Australia 33°1S 145°1E 63 E4
Trier Germany 49°45N 6°38E 16 D4
Trieste Italy 45°40N 13°46E 22 B5
Triglav Slovenia 46°21N 13°50E 16 E7
Trikala Greece 39°34N 21°47E 23 E9
Trikomo Cyprus 35°17N 33°52E 25 D12
Trikora, Puncak
  Indonesia 4°15S 138°45E 37 E9
Trim Ireland 53°33N 6°48W 10 C5
Trimmu Dam Pakistan 31°10N 72°8E 42 D5
Trincomalee Sri Lanka 8°38N 81°15E 40 Q12
Trindade Brazil 16°40S 49°30W 93 G9
Trindade, I. Atl. Oc. 20°20S 29°50W 2 F8
Trinidad Bolivia 14°46S 64°50W 92 F6
Trinidad Cuba 21°48N 80°0W 88 B4
Trinidad Trin. & Tob. 10°30N 61°15W 93 K15
Trinidad Uruguay 33°30S 56°50W 94 C4
Trinidad U.S.A. 37°10N 104°31W 77 H11
Trinidad → Mexico 17°49N 95°9W 87 D5
Trinidad & Tobago ■
  W. Indies 10°30N 61°20W 89 D7
Trinity Canada 48°59N 53°55W 73 C9
Trinity U.S.A. 30°57N 95°22W 84 F7
Trinity → Calif., U.S.A. 41°11N 123°42W 76 F2
Trinity → Tex., U.S.A. 29°45N 94°43W 84 G7
Trinity B. Canada 48°20N 53°10W 73 C9
Trinity Hills Trin. & Tob. 10°7N 61°7W 93 K15
Trinity Is. U.S.A. 56°33N 154°25W 74 D9
Trinity Range U.S.A. 40°10N 118°40W 76 F4
Trinkitat Sudan 18°45N 37°51E 51 E13
Trinway U.S.A. 40°9N 82°1W 82 F2
Triolet Mauritius 20°4S 57°32E 53 d
Tripoli = Tarābulus
  Lebanon 34°31N 35°50E 46 A4
Tripoli = Tarābulus Libya 32°49N 13°7E 51 B8
Tripoli Greece 37°31N 22°25E 23 F10
Tripolitania = Tarābulus
  N. Afr. 31°0N 13°0E 51 B8
Tripura □ India 24°0N 92°0E 41 H18
Triplyos Cyprus 35°2N 32°42E 25 D11
Tristan da Cunha Atl. Oc. 37°6S 12°20W 49 K2
Trisul India 30°19N 79°47E 43 D8
Trivandrum India 8°41N 77°0E 40 Q10
Trnava Slovak Rep. 48°23N 17°35E 17 D9
Trochu Canada 51°50N 113°13W 70 C6
Trodely I. Canada 52°15N 79°26W 72 B4
Troglav Croatia 43°56N 16°36E 22 C7
Troilus, L. Canada 50°50N 74°35W 72 B5
Trois-Pistoles Canada 48°5N 69°10W 73 C6
Trois-Rivières Canada 46°25N 72°34W 72 C5
Trois-Rivières Guadeloupe 15°57N 61°40W 88 b
Troitsk Russia 54°10N 61°35E 28 D7
Troitsko Pechorsk
  Russia 62°40N 56°10E 18 B10
Trölladyngja Iceland 64°54N 17°16W 8 D5
Trollhättan Sweden 58°17N 12°20E 9 G15
Trollheimen Norway 62°46N 9°1E 8 E13
Trombetas → Brazil 1°55S 55°35W 93 D7
Tromsø Norway 69°40N 18°56E 8 B18
Tron Thailand 17°28N 100°7E 38 D3
Trona U.S.A. 35°46N 117°23W 79 K9
Tronador, Mte.
  Argentina 41°10S 71°50W 96 E2
Trøndelag Norway 64°17N 11°50E 8 D14
Trondheim Norway 63°36N 10°25E 8 E14
Trondheimsfjorden
  Norway 63°35N 10°30E 8 E14
Troodos Cyprus 34°55N 32°52E 25 E11
Troon U.K. 55°33N 4°39W 11 F4
Tropic U.S.A. 37°37N 112°5W 77 H7
Trostan U.K. 55°3N 6°10W 10 A5
Trou Gras Pt. St. Lucia 13°51N 60°53W 89 f
Trout → Canada 61°19N 119°51W 70 A5
Trout L. N.W.T., Canada 60°40N 121°14W 70 A4
Trout L. Ont., Canada 51°20N 93°15W 71 C10
Trout Lake Canada 56°30N 114°32W 70 B6
Trout Lake U.S.A. 46°0N 121°32W 78 E5
Trout River Canada 49°29N 58°8W 73 C8
Trout Run U.S.A. 41°23N 77°3W 82 E7
Trouville-sur-Mer France 49°21N 0°5E 20 B4
Trowbridge U.K. 51°18N 2°12W 13 F5
Troy Turkey 39°57N 26°12E 23 E12
Troy Ala., U.S.A. 31°48N 85°58W 85 F12
Troy Kans., U.S.A. 39°47N 95°5W 80 F6
Troy Mo., U.S.A. 38°59N 90°59W 80 F8
Troy Mont., U.S.A. 48°28N 115°53W 76 B6
Troy N.Y., U.S.A. 42°44N 73°41W 83 D11
Troy Ohio, U.S.A. 40°2N 84°12W 81 E11
Troy Pa., U.S.A. 41°47N 76°47W 83 E8
Troyes France 48°19N 4°3E 20 B6
Truchas Pk. U.S.A. 35°58N 105°39W 77 J11
Trucial States = United Arab
  Emirates ■ Asia 23°50N 54°0E 45 F7
Truckee U.S.A. 39°20N 120°11W 78 F6
Trudovoye Russia 43°17N 132°5E 30 C6
Trujillo Honduras 16°0N 86°0W 88 C2
Trujillo Peru 8°6S 79°0W 92 E3
Trujillo Spain 39°28N 5°55W 21 C3
Trujillo U.S.A. 35°32N 104°42W 77 J11
Trujillo Venezuela 9°22N 70°38W 92 B4
Truk Micronesia 7°25N 151°46E 64 G7
Trumann U.S.A. 35°41N 90°31W 85 D9
Trumanburg U.S.A. 42°33N 76°40W 83 D8
Trumbull, Mt. U.S.A. 36°25N 113°19W 77 H7
Trundle Australia 32°53S 147°35E 63 E4
Trung-Phan = Annam
  Vietnam 16°0N 108°0E 38 E7
Truro Canada 45°21N 63°14W 73 C7
Truro U.K. 50°16N 5°4W 13 G2
Truskavets Ukraine 49°17N 23°30E 17 D12
Trutch Canada 57°44N 122°57W 70 B4

Truth or Consequences
  U.S.A. 33°8N 107°15W 77 K10
Trutnov Czech Rep. 50°37N 15°54E 16 C8
Tryonville U.S.A. 41°42N 79°48W 82 E5
Tsandi Namibia 17°42S 14°50E 56 B1
Tsaratanana Madag. 16°47S 47°39E 57 B8
Tsaratanana, Mt. de =
  Maromokotro Madag. 14°0S 49°0E 57 A8
Tsaratanana △ Madag. 13°5S 48°52E 57 A8
Tsau Botswana 20°8S 22°22E 56 C3
Tsavo Kenya 2°59S 38°28E 54 C4
Tsavo East △ Kenya 2°44S 38°47E 54 C4
Tsavo West △ Kenya 3°19S 37°57E 54 C4
Tsentralnyy □ Russia 52°0N 40°0E 28 D4
Tses Namibia 25°58S 18°8E 56 D2
Tsetserleg Mongolia 47°36N 101°32E 32 B5
Tsévié Togo 6°25N 1°20E 50 G6
Tshabong Botswana 26°2S 22°29E 56 D3
Tshane Botswana 24°5S 21°54E 56 C3
Tshela
  Dem. Rep. of the Congo 4°57S 13°4E 52 E2
Tshesebe Botswana 21°51S 27°32E 57 C4
Tshibeke
  Dem. Rep. of the Congo 2°40S 28°35E 54 C2
Tshibinda
  Dem. Rep. of the Congo 2°23S 28°43E 54 C2
Tshikapa
  Dem. Rep. of the Congo 6°28S 20°48E 52 F4
Tshilenge
  Dem. Rep. of the Congo 6°17S 23°48E 54 D1
Tshinsenda
  Dem. Rep. of the Congo 12°20S 28°0E 55 E2
Tshofa
  Dem. Rep. of the Congo 5°13S 25°16E 54 D2
Tshwane = Pretoria
  S. Africa 25°44S 28°12E 57 D4
Tshwane Botswana 22°24S 22°1E 56 C3
Tsigara Botswana 20°22S 25°54E 56 C4
Tsihombe Madag. 25°10S 45°41E 57 D8
Tsiigehtchic Canada 67°15N 134°0W 68 D5
Ts'il-os △ Canada 51°13N 123°59W 70 C4
Tsimlyansk Res. = Tsimlyanskoye
  Vdkhr. Russia 48°0N 43°0E 19 E7
Tsimlyanskoye Vdkhr.
  Russia 48°0N 43°0E 19 E7
Tsinan = Jinan China 36°38N 117°1E 34 F9
Tsineng S. Africa 27°5S 23°5E 56 D3
Tsing Yi China 22°21N 114°6E 33 G11
Tsinghai = Qinghai □
  China 36°0N 98°0E 32 C4
Tsingtao = Qingdao
  China 36°5N 120°20E 35 F11
Tsingy de Bemaraha △
  Madag. 18°35S 45°25E 57 B8
Tsingy de Namoroka △
  Madag. 16°29S 45°25E 57 B8
Tsinjoarivo Madag. 19°37S 47°40E 57 B8
Tsinjomitondraka Madag. 15°40S 47°8E 57 B8
Tsirigo = Kythira Greece 36°8N 23°0E 23 F10
Tsiroanomandidy Madag. 18°46S 46°2E 57 B8
Tsitsikamma △ S. Africa 34°3S 23°40E 56 E3
Tsivory Madag. 24°4S 46°5E 57 C8
Tskhinvali Georgia 42°14N 44°1E 19 F7
Tsna → Russia 54°55N 41°58E 18 D7
Tso Moriri, L. India 32°50N 78°20E 43 C8
Tsobis Namibia 19°27S 17°30E 56 B2
Tsodilo Hill Botswana 18°49S 21°43E 56 B3
Tsogttsetsiy = Baruunsuu
  Mongolia 43°43N 105°35E 34 C3
Tsolo S. Africa 31°18S 28°37E 57 E4
Tsomo S. Africa 32°0S 27°42E 57 E4
Tsu Japan 34°45N 136°25E 31 G8
Tsu L. Canada 60°40N 111°52W 70 A6
Tsuchiura Japan 36°5N 140°15E 31 F10
Tsuen Wan China 22°22N 114°6E 33 G11
Tsugaru-Kaikyō Japan 41°35N 141°0E 30 D10
Tsumeb Namibia 19°9S 17°44E 56 B2
Tsumis Namibia 23°39S 17°29E 56 C2
Tsuruga Japan 35°45N 136°2E 31 G8
Tsurugi-San Japan 33°51N 134°6E 31 H7
Tsuruoka Japan 38°44N 139°50E 30 E9
Tsushima Gifu, Japan 35°10N 136°43E 31 G8
Tsushima Nagasaki,
  Japan 34°20N 129°20E 31 G4
Tsuyama Japan 35°3N 134°0E 31 G7
Tsyelyakhany Belarus 52°30N 25°46E 17 B13
Tuaim = Tuam Ireland 53°31N 8°51W 10 C3
Tual Indonesia 5°38S 132°44E 37 F8
Tualatin U.S.A. 45°23N 122°45W 78 E4
Tuam Ireland 53°31N 8°51W 10 C3
Tuamotu, Îs.
  French Polynesia 17°0S 144°0W 65 J13
Tuamotu Arch. = Tuamotu, Îs.
  French Polynesia 17°0S 144°0W 65 J13
Tuamotu Ridge Pac. Oc. 20°0S 138°0W 65 K14
Tuan Giao Vietnam 21°35N 103°25E 38 B4
Tuao Phil. 17°55N 121°22E 37 A6
Tuapse Russia 44°5N 39°10E 19 F6
Tuas Singapore 1°19N 103°39E 39 d
Tuatapere N.Z. 46°8S 167°41E 59 G1
Tuba City U.S.A. 36°8N 111°14W 77 H8
Tubani Indonesia 6°54S 112°3E 37 G15
Tubani Namibia 24°46S 24°18E 56 C3
Tubarão Brazil 28°30S 49°0W 95 B6
Tûbâs West Bank 32°20N 35°22E 46 C4
Tubas → Namibia 22°54S 14°35E 56 C1
Tübingen Germany 48°31N 9°4E 16 D5
Tubou Fiji 18°13S 178°48W 59 a
Tubruq Libya 32°7N 23°55E 51 B10
Tubuaï, Îs.
  French Polynesia 25°0S 150°0W 65 K13
Tuc Trung Vietnam 11°1N 107°12E 39 G6
Tucacas Venezuela 10°48N 68°19W 92 A5
Tuchitua Canada 60°55N 129°13W 70 A3
Tuchodi → Canada 58°17N 123°42W 70 B4
Tuckanarra Australia 27°7S 118°5E 61 E2
Tucson U.S.A. 32°13N 110°58W 77 K8
Tucumán □ Argentina 26°48S 66°2W 94 B2

Tucumcari U.S.A. 35°10N 103°44W 77 J12
Tucupita Venezuela 9°2N 62°3W 92 B6
Tucuruí Brazil 3°42S 49°44W 93 D9
Tucuruí, Represa de Brazil 4°0S 49°30W 93 D9
Tudela Spain 42°4N 1°39W 21 A5
Tudmur Syria 34°36N 38°15E 44 C3
Tudor, L. Canada 55°50N 65°25W 73 A6
Tuen Mun China 22°24N 113°59E 33 G10
Tugela → S. Africa 29°14S 31°30E 57 D5
Tuguegarao Phil. 17°35N 121°42E 37 A6
Tugur Russia 53°44N 136°45E 29 D14
Tui Spain 42°3N 8°39W 21 A1
Tuineje Canary Is. 28°19N 14°3W 24 F5
Tukangbesi, Kepulauan Indonesia 6°0S 124°0E 37 F6
Tukarak I. Canada 56°15N 78°45W 72 A4
Tukayyid Iraq 29°47N 45°36E 44 D5
Tuktoyaktuk Canada 69°27N 133°2W 68 D5
Tuktut Nogait △ Canada 69°15N 122°0W 68 D7
Tukums Latvia 56°58N 23°10E 9 H20
Tukuyu Tanzania 9°17S 33°35E 55 D3
Tula Hidalgo, Mexico 20°3N 99°21W 87 C5
Tula Tamaulipas, Mexico 23°0N 99°43W 87 C5
Tula Russia 54°13N 37°38E 18 D6
Tulach Mhór = Tullamore Ireland 53°16N 7°31W 10 C4
Tulancingo Mexico 20°5N 98°22W 87 C5
Tulare U.S.A. 36°13N 119°21W 78 J7
Tulare Lake Bed U.S.A. 36°0N 119°48W 78 K7
Tularosa U.S.A. 33°5N 106°1W 77 K10
Tulbagh S. Africa 33°16S 19°6E 56 E2
Tulcán Ecuador 0°48N 77°43W 92 C3
Tulcea Romania 45°13N 28°46E 17 F15
Tulchyn Ukraine 48°41N 28°49E 17 D15
Tūleh Iran 34°35N 52°33E 45 C7
Tulemalu L. Canada 62°58N 99°25W 71 A9
Tuli Zimbabwe 21°58S 29°13E 55 G2
Tulia U.S.A. 34°32N 101°46W 84 D4
Tulita Canada 64°57N 125°30W 68 E6
Ţūlkarm West Bank 32°19N 35°2E 46 C4
Tulla Ireland 52°53N 8°46W 10 D3
Tullahoma U.S.A. 35°22N 86°13W 85 D11
Tullamore Australia 32°39S 147°36E 63 E4
Tullamore Ireland 53°16N 7°31W 10 C4
Tulle France 45°16N 1°46E 20 D4
Tullow Ireland 52°49N 6°45W 10 D5
Tully Australia 17°56S 145°55E 62 B4
Tully U.S.A. 42°48N 76°7W 83 D8
Tulsa U.S.A. 36°10N 95°55W 84 C7
Tulsequah Canada 58°39N 133°35W 70 B2
Tuluá Colombia 4°6N 76°11W 92 C3
Tulun Russia 54°32N 100°35E 29 D11
Tulungagung Indonesia 8°5S 111°54E 37 H14
Tuma → Nic. 13°6N 84°35W 88 D3
Tumacacori ⌂ U.S.A. 31°35N 111°6W 77 L8
Tumaco Colombia 1°50N 78°45W 92 C3
Tumakuru = Tumkur India 13°18N 77°6E 40 N10
Tumatumari Guyana 5°20N 58°55W 92 B7
Tumba Sweden 59°12N 17°48E 9 G17
Tumba, L. Dem. Rep. of the Congo 0°50S 18°0E 52 E3
Tumbarumba Australia 35°44S 148°0E 63 F4
Tumbaya Argentina 23°50S 65°26W 94 A2
Tumbes Peru 3°37S 80°27W 92 D2
Tumbler Ridge Canada 55°8N 121°0W 70 B4
Tumbwe Dem. Rep. of the Congo 11°25S 27°15E 55 E2
Tumby Bay Australia 34°21S 136°8E 63 E2
Tumd Youqi China 40°30N 110°30E 34 D6
Tumen China 43°0N 129°50E 30 C4
Tumen Jiang → China 42°20N 130°35E 35 C16
Tumeremo Venezuela 7°18N 61°30W 92 B6
Tumkur India 13°18N 77°6E 40 N10
Tump Pakistan 26°7N 62°16E 40 F3
Tumpat Malaysia 6°11N 102°10E 39 J4
Tumu Ghana 10°56N 1°56W 50 F5
Tumucumaque, Serra Brazil 2°0N 55°0W 93 C8
Tumut Australia 35°16S 148°13E 63 F4
Tumwater U.S.A. 47°1N 122°54W 78 C4
Tuna India 22°59N 70°5E 42 H4
Tunapuna Trin. & Tob. 10°38N 61°24W 93 K15
Tunas de Zaza Cuba 21°39N 79°34W 88 B4
Tunbridge Wells = Royal Tunbridge Wells U.K. 51°7N 0°16E 13 F8
Tuncurry Australia 32°17S 152°29E 63 E5
Tundla India 27°12N 78°17E 42 F8
Tunduru Tanzania 11°8S 37°25E 55 E4
Tundzha → Bulgaria 41°40N 26°35E 23 C11
Tung Chung China 22°17N 113°57E 33 G10
Tung Lung Chau China 22°15N 114°17E 33 G11
Tungabhadra → India 15°57N 78°15E 40 M11
Tungla Nic. 13°24N 84°21W 88 D3
Tungsten Canada 61°57N 128°16W 70 A3
Tunguska, Nizhnyaya → Russia 65°48N 88°4E 29 C9
Tunguska, Podkamennaya → Russia 61°50N 90°13E 29 C10
Tunica U.S.A. 34°41N 90°23W 85 D9
Tunis Tunisia 36°50N 10°11E 50 A7
Tunisia ■ Africa 33°30N 9°10E 51 A7
Tunja Colombia 5°33N 73°25W 92 B4
Tunkhannock U.S.A. 41°32N 75°57W 83 E9
Tunliu China 36°13N 112°52E 34 F7
Tunnel Creek △ Australia 17°41S 125°18E 60 C4
Tunnsjøen Norway 64°45N 13°25E 8 D15
Tunungayualok I. Canada 56°0N 61°0W 73 A7
Tunuyán Argentina 33°35S 69°0W 94 C2
Tunuyán → Argentina 33°33S 67°30W 94 C2
Tuolumne U.S.A. 37°58N 120°15W 78 H6
Tuolumne → U.S.A. 37°36N 121°13W 78 H5
Tūp Āghāj Iran 36°3N 47°50E 44 B5
Tupã Brazil 21°57S 50°28W 95 A5
Tupelo U.S.A. 34°16N 88°43W 85 D10
Tupinambarana, I. Brazil 3°0S 58°0W 92 D7
Tupiza Bolivia 21°30S 65°40W 94 A2
Tupman U.S.A. 35°18N 119°21W 79 K7
Tupper Canada 55°32N 120°1W 70 B4
Tupper L. U.S.A. 44°10N 74°32W 83 B10
Tupper Lake U.S.A. 44°14N 74°28W 83 B10
Tupungato, Cerro S. Amer. 33°15S 69°50W 94 C2
Tuquan China 45°18N 121°38E 35 B11
Túquerres Colombia 1°5N 77°37W 92 C3
Tura Russia 64°20N 100°17E 29 C11
Turabah Si. Arabia 28°20N 43°15E 44 D4
Tūrān Iran 35°39N 56°42E 45 C8
Turan Russia 51°55N 94°0E 29 D10
Ţurayf Si. Arabia 31°41N 38°39E 44 D3
Turda Romania 46°34N 23°47E 17 E12
Turek Poland 52°3N 18°30E 17 B10
Turén Venezuela 9°17N 69°6W 92 B5
Turfan = Turpan China 43°58N 89°10E 32 B3
Turfan Basin = Turpan Pendi China 42°40N 89°25E 32 B3
Turfan Depression = Turpan Pendi China 42°40N 89°25E 32 B3
Turgeon → Canada 50°0N 78°56W 72 C4
Tŭrgovishte Bulgaria 43°17N 26°38E 23 C12
Turgutlu Turkey 38°30N 27°43E 23 E12
Turgwe → Zimbabwe 21°31S 32°15E 57 C5
Turia → Spain 39°27N 0°19W 21 C5
Turiaçu Brazil 1°40S 45°19W 93 D9
Turiaçu → Brazil 1°36S 45°19W 93 D9
Turin = Torino Italy 45°3N 7°40E 20 D7
Turkana, L. Africa 3°30N 36°5E 54 B4
Turkestan = Türkistan Kazakhstan 43°17N 68°16E 28 E7
Turkey ■ Eurasia 39°0N 36°0E 19 G6
Turkey Creek = Warmun Australia 17°2S 128°12E 60 C4
Türkistan Kazakhstan 43°17N 68°16E 28 E7
Türkmenabat Turkmenistan 39°6N 63°34E 45 B9
Türkmenbashi Turkmenistan 40°5N 53°5E 45 A7
Turkmenistan ■ Asia 39°0N 59°0E 28 F6
Turks & Caicos Is. ☒ W. Indies 21°20N 71°20W 89 B5
Turks Island Passage W. Indies 21°30N 71°30W 89 B5
Turku Finland 60°30N 22°19E 9 F20
Turkwel → Kenya 3°6N 36°6E 54 B4
Turlock U.S.A. 37°30N 120°51W 78 H6
Turnagain Australia 9°34S 142°17E 62 a
Turnagain → Canada 59°12N 127°35W 70 B3
Turnagain, C. N.Z. 40°28S 176°38E 59 D6
Turneffe Is. Belize 17°20N 87°50W 87 D7
Turner U.S.A. 48°51N 108°24W 76 B9
Turner Pt. Australia 11°47S 133°32E 62 A1
Turner Valley Canada 50°40N 114°17W 70 C6
Turners Falls U.S.A. 42°36N 72°33W 83 D12
Turnhout Belgium 51°19N 4°57E 15 C4
Turnor L. Canada 56°35N 108°35W 71 B7
Tŭrnovo = Veliko Tŭrnovo Bulgaria 43°5N 25°41E 23 C11
Turnu Măgurele Romania 43°46N 24°56E 17 G13
Turnu Roşu, P. Romania 45°33N 24°17E 17 F13
Turpan China 43°58N 89°10E 32 B3
Turpan Pendi China 42°40N 89°25E 32 B3
Turriff U.K. 57°32N 2°27W 11 D6
Tursāq Iraq 33°27N 45°47E 44 C5
Turtle Head I. Australia 10°56S 142°37E 62 A3
Turtle L. Canada 53°36N 108°38W 71 C7
Turtle Lake U.S.A. 47°31N 100°53W 80 B3
Turtleford Canada 53°23N 108°57W 71 C7
Turuépano △ Venezuela 10°34N 62°43W 89 D7
Turukhansk Russia 65°21N 88°5E 29 C9
Tuscaloosa U.S.A. 33°12N 87°34W 85 E11
Tuscany = Toscana ☐ Italy 43°25N 11°0E 22 C4
Tuscarawas → U.S.A. 40°24N 81°25W 82 F3
Tuscarora Mt. U.S.A. 40°55N 77°55W 82 F7
Tuscola Ill., U.S.A. 39°48N 88°17W 80 F9
Tuscola Tex., U.S.A. 32°12N 99°48W 84 E5
Tuscumbia U.S.A. 34°44N 87°42W 85 D11
Tuskegee U.S.A. 32°25N 85°42W 85 E12
Tuticorin India 8°50N 78°12E 40 Q11
Tutóia Brazil 2°45S 42°20W 93 D10
Tutong Brunei 4°47N 114°40E 36 D4
Tutrakan Bulgaria 44°2N 26°40E 23 B12
Tuttle Creek L. U.S.A. 39°15N 96°36W 80 F5
Tuttlingen Germany 47°58N 8°48E 16 E5
Tutuala E. Timor 8°25S 127°15E 37 F7
Tutuila Amer. Samoa 14°19S 170°50W 59 b
Tutume Botswana 20°30S 27°5E 53 J5
Tuul Gol → Mongolia 48°30N 104°25E 32 B5
Tuva ☐ Russia 51°30N 95°0E 29 D10
Tuvalu ■ Pac. Oc. 8°0S 178°0E 58 B10
Tuvuca Fiji 17°40S 178°48W 59 a
Tuxpan Mexico 20°57N 97°24W 87 C5
Tuxtla Gutiérrez Mexico 16°45N 93°7W 87 D6
Tuy = Tui Spain 42°3N 8°39W 21 A1
Tuy An Vietnam 13°17N 109°16E 38 F7
Tuy Duc Vietnam 12°15N 107°27E 39 F6
Tuy Hoa Vietnam 13°5N 109°10E 38 F7
Tuy Phong Vietnam 11°14N 108°43E 39 G7
Tuya L. Canada 59°7N 130°35W 70 B2
Tuyen Hoa Vietnam 17°50N 106°10E 38 D6
Tuyen Quang Vietnam 21°50N 105°10E 38 B5
Tūysarkān Iran 34°33N 48°27E 45 C6
Tuz Gölü Turkey 38°42N 33°18E 19 G5
Ţūz Khurmātū Iraq 34°56N 44°38E 44 C5
Tuzigoot △ U.S.A. 34°46N 112°2W 77 J7
Tuzla Bos.-H. 44°34N 18°41E 23 B8
Tver Russia 56°55N 35°55E 18 C6
Twain U.S.A. 40°1N 121°3W 78 E5
Twain Harte U.S.A. 38°2N 120°14W 78 G6
Tweed Canada 44°29N 77°19W 82 B7
Tweed → U.K. 55°45N 2°0W 11 F6
Tweed Heads Australia 28°10S 153°31E 63 D5
Tweedsmuir ⌂ Canada 53°0N 126°20W 70 C3
Twentynine Palms U.S.A. 34°8N 116°3W 79 L10
Twillingate Canada 49°42N 54°45W 73 C9
Twin Bridges U.S.A. 45°33N 112°20W 76 D7
Twin Falls Canada 53°30N 64°32W 73 B7
Twin Falls U.S.A. 42°34N 114°28W 76 E6
Twin Valley U.S.A. 47°16N 96°16W 80 B5
Twinsburg U.S.A. 41°19N 81°26W 82 E3
Twitchell Res. U.S.A. 34°59N 120°19W 79 L6
Two Harbors U.S.A. 47°2N 91°40W 80 B8
Two Hills Canada 53°43N 111°52W 70 C6
Two Rivers U.S.A. 44°9N 87°34W 80 C10
Two Rocks Australia 31°30S 115°35E 61 F2
Twofold B. Australia 37°8S 149°59E 63 F4
Tyachiv Ukraine 48°1N 23°35E 17 D12
Tychy Poland 50°9N 18°59E 17 C10
Tyler Minn., U.S.A. 44°17N 96°8W 80 C5
Tyler Tex., U.S.A. 32°21N 95°18W 84 E7
Tynda Russia 55°10N 124°43E 29 D13
Tyndall U.S.A. 43°0N 97°50W 80 D5
Tyne → U.K. 54°59N 1°32W 12 C6
Tyne & Wear ☐ U.K. 55°6N 1°17W 12 B6
Tynemouth U.K. 55°1N 1°26W 12 B6
Tyre = Sūr Lebanon 33°19N 35°16E 46 B4
Tyrifjorden Norway 60°2N 10°8E 9 F14
Tyrol = Tirol ☐ Austria 47°3N 10°43E 16 E6
Tyrone U.S.A. 40°40N 78°14W 82 F6
Tyrone ☐ U.K. 54°38N 7°11W 10 B4
Tyrrell → Australia 35°26S 142°51E 63 F3
Tyrrell, L. Australia 35°20S 142°50E 63 F3
Tyrrell L. Canada 63°7N 105°27W 71 A7
Tyrrhenian Sea Medit. S. 40°0N 12°30E 22 E5
Tysfjorden Norway 68°7N 16°25E 8 B17
Tyulgan Russia 52°22N 56°12E 18 D10
Tyumen Russia 57°11N 65°29E 28 D7
Tywi → U.K. 51°48N 4°21W 13 F3
Tywyn U.K. 52°35N 4°5W 13 E3
Tzaneen S. Africa 23°47S 30°9E 57 C5
Tzermiado Greece 35°12N 25°29E 25 D7
Tzukong = Zigong China 29°15N 104°48E 32 D5

U

U.S.A. = United States of America ■ N. Amer. 37°0N 96°0W 75 H20
U.S. Virgin Is. ☒ W. Indies 18°20N 65°0W 89 e
Uanle Uen = Wanleweyne Somali Rep. 2°37N 44°54E 47 G3
Uatumã → Brazil 2°26S 57°37W 92 D7
Uaupés Brazil 0°8S 67°5W 92 D5
Uaupés → Brazil 0°2N 67°16W 92 C5
Uaxactún Guatemala 17°25N 89°29W 88 C2
Ubá Brazil 21°8S 43°0W 95 A7
Ubaitaba Brazil 14°18S 39°20W 93 F11
Ubangi = Oubangi → Dem. Rep. of the Congo 0°30S 17°50E 52 E3
Ubauro Pakistan 28°15N 69°45E 42 E3
Ubayyiḑ, W. al → Iraq 32°34N 43°48E 44 C4
Ube Japan 33°56N 131°15E 31 H5
Úbeda Spain 38°3N 3°23W 21 C4
Uberaba Brazil 19°50S 47°55W 93 G9
Uberlândia Brazil 19°0S 48°20W 93 G9
Ubin, Pulau Singapore 1°24N 103°57E 39 d
Ubly U.S.A. 43°42N 82°55W 82 C2
Ubolratna Res. Thailand 16°45N 102°30E 38 D4
Ubombo S. Africa 27°31S 32°4E 57 D5
Ubon Ratchathani Thailand 15°15N 104°50E 38 E5
Ubondo Dem. Rep. of the Congo 0°55S 25°42E 54 C2
Ubort → Belarus 52°6N 28°30E 17 B15
Ubud Indonesia 8°30S 115°16E 37 J18
Ubundu Dem. Rep. of the Congo 0°22S 25°30E 54 C2
Ucayali → Peru 4°30S 73°30W 92 D4
Uchab Namibia 19°47S 17°42E 56 B2
Uchiura-Wan Japan 42°25N 140°40E 30 C10
Uchquduq Uzbekistan 41°50N 62°50E 28 E7
Uchur → Russia 58°48N 130°35E 29 D14
Ucluelet Canada 48°57N 125°32W 70 D3
Uda → Russia 54°42N 135°14E 29 D14
Udachnyy Russia 66°25N 112°24E 29 C12
Udagamandalam India 11°30N 76°44E 40 P10
Udainagar India 22°33N 76°13E 42 H7
Udaipur India 24°36N 73°44E 42 G5
Udaipur Garhi Nepal 27°0N 86°35E 43 F12
Udala India 21°35N 86°34E 43 J12
Uddevalla Sweden 58°21N 11°55E 9 G14
Uddjaure Sweden 65°56N 17°49E 8 D17
Uden Neths. 51°40N 5°37E 15 C5
Udgir India 18°25N 77°5E 40 K10
Udhampur India 33°0N 75°5E 43 C6
Údine Italy 46°3N 13°14E 22 A5
Udintsev Fracture Zone S. Ocean 57°0S 145°0W 5 B13
Udmurtia ☐ Russia 57°30N 52°30E 18 C9
Udon Thani Thailand 17°29N 102°46E 38 D4
Udong Cambodia 11°48N 104°45E 39 G5
Udskaya Guba Russia 54°50N 135°45E 29 D14
Udu Pt. Fiji 16°9S 179°57W 59 a
Udupi India 13°25N 74°42E 40 N9
Udzungwa △ Tanzania 7°52S 36°35E 54 D4
Udzungwa Range Tanzania 9°30S 35°10E 55 D4
Ueda Japan 36°24N 138°16E 31 F9
Uedineniya, Os. Russia 78°0N 85°0E 4 B12
Uele → Dem. Rep. of the Congo 3°45N 24°45E 52 D4
Uelen Russia 66°10N 170°0W 29 C19
Uelzen Germany 52°57N 10°32E 16 B6
Ufa Russia 54°45N 55°55E 18 D10
Ufa → Russia 54°40N 56°0E 18 D10
Ugab → Namibia 20°55S 13°30E 56 C1
Ugalla → Tanzania 5°8S 30°42E 54 D3
Ugalla River ⌂ Tanzania 5°50S 31°54E 54 D3
Uganda ■ Africa 2°0N 32°0E 54 B3
Ugie S. Africa 31°10S 28°13E 57 E4
Uglegorsk Russia 49°5N 142°2E 29 E15
Ugljan Croatia 44°12N 15°10E 16 F8
Ugolnye Kopi Russia 64°44N 177°42E 29 C18
Uhlenhorst Namibia 23°45S 17°55E 56 C2
Uhrichsville U.S.A. 40°24N 81°21W 82 F3
Uibhist a Deas = South Uist U.K. 57°20N 7°15W 11 D1
Uibhist a Tuath = North Uist U.K. 57°40N 7°15W 11 D1
Uig U.K. 57°35N 6°21W 11 D2
Uíge Angola 7°30S 14°40E 52 F2
Uiha Tonga 19°54S 174°25W 59 c
Uijeongbu S. Korea 37°44N 127°2E 35 F14
Ŭiju N. Korea 40°15N 124°35E 35 D13
Uinta Mts. U.S.A. 40°45N 110°30W 76 F8
Uis Namibia 21°8S 14°49E 56 C1
Uiseong S. Korea 36°21N 128°45E 35 F15
Uitenhage S. Africa 33°40S 25°28E 56 E4
Uithuizen Neths. 53°24N 6°41E 15 A6
Ujh → India 32°10N 75°18E 42 C6
Ujhani India 28°0N 79°6E 43 F8
Uji-guntō Japan 31°15N 129°25E 31 J4
Ujjain India 23°9N 75°43E 42 H6
Ujung Pandang Indonesia 5°10S 119°20E 37 F5
Uka Russia 57°50N 162°0E 29 D17
Ukara I. Tanzania 1°50S 33°0E 54 C3
Uke-Shima Japan 28°2N 129°14E 31 K4
Ukerewe I. Tanzania 2°0S 33°0E 54 C3
Ukhrul India 25°10N 94°25E 41 G19
Ukhta Russia 63°34N 53°41E 18 B9
Ukiah U.S.A. 39°9N 123°13W 78 F3
Ukmergė Lithuania 55°15N 24°45E 9 J21
Ukraine ■ Europe 49°0N 32°0E 19 E5
Ukwi Botswana 23°29S 20°30E 56 C3
Ulaan-Uul Mongolia 44°13N 111°10E 34 B6
Ulaanbaatar Mongolia 47°55N 106°53E 32 B5
Ulaangom Mongolia 50°5N 92°10E 32 A4
Ulaanjirem Mongolia 45°5N 105°30E 34 B3
Ulak I. U.S.A. 51°22N 178°57W 74 E4
Ulamba Dem. Rep. of the Congo 9°3S 23°38E 55 D1
Ulan Bator = Ulaanbaatar Mongolia 47°55N 106°53E 32 B5
Ulan Ude Russia 51°45N 107°40E 29 D11
Ulanhad = Chifeng China 42°18N 118°58E 35 C10
Ulaya Morogoro, Tanzania 7°3S 36°55E 54 D4
Ulaya Tabora, Tanzania 4°25S 33°30E 54 C3
Ulcinj Montenegro 41°58N 19°10E 23 D8
Ulco S. Africa 28°21S 24°15E 56 D3
Ule älv = Oulujoki → Finland 65°1N 25°30E 8 D21
Ule träsk = Oulujärvi Finland 64°25N 27°15E 8 D22
Uleåborg = Oulu Finland 65°1N 25°29E 8 D21
Ulefoss Norway 59°17N 9°16E 9 G13
Ulhasnagar India 19°15N 73°10E 40 K8
Uliastay Mongolia 47°56N 97°28E 32 B4
Uljin S. Korea 36°59N 129°24E 35 F15
Ulladulla Australia 35°21S 150°29E 63 F5
Ullapool U.K. 57°54N 5°9W 11 D3
Ulleungdo S. Korea 37°30N 130°30E 31 F5
Ullswater Canada 45°12N 79°29W 82 A5
Ullswater U.K. 54°34N 2°52W 12 C5
Ulm Germany 48°23N 9°58E 16 D5
Ulmarra Australia 29°37S 153°4E 63 D5
Ulonguè Mozam. 14°37S 34°19E 55 E3
Ulricehamn Sweden 57°46N 13°26E 9 H15
Ulsan S. Korea 35°20N 129°15E 35 G15
Ulsta U.K. 60°30N 1°9W 11 A7
Ulster ☐ U.K. 54°35N 6°30W 10 B5
Ulubat Gölü Turkey 40°9N 28°35E 23 D13
Uludağ Turkey 40°4N 29°13E 23 D13
Uluguru Mts. Tanzania 7°15S 37°40E 54 D4
Ulungur He → China 47°1N 87°24E 32 B3
Ulungur Hu China 47°20N 87°10E 32 B3
Uluru Australia 25°23S 131°5E 61 E5
Uluru-Kata Tjuta △ Australia 25°19S 131°1E 61 E5
Ulutau Kazakhstan 48°39N 67°1E 28 E7
Uluwatu Indonesia 8°50S 115°5E 37 K18
Ulva U.K. 56°29N 6°13W 11 E2
Ulverston U.K. 54°13N 3°5W 12 C4
Ulverstone Australia 41°11S 146°11E 63 G4
Ulya Russia 59°10N 142°0E 29 D15
Ulyanovsk Russia 54°20N 48°25E 18 D8
Ulyasutay = Uliastay Mongolia 47°56N 97°28E 32 B4
Ulysses Kans., U.S.A. 37°35N 101°22W 80 G3
Ulysses Pa., U.S.A. 41°54N 77°46W 82 E7
Ulysses, Mt. Canada 57°20N 124°5W 70 B4
Umala Bolivia 17°25S 68°5W 92 G5
'Umān = Oman ■ Asia 23°0N 58°0E 47 C6
Uman Ukraine 48°40N 30°12E 17 D16
Umaria India 23°35N 80°50E 43 H9
Umarkot Pakistan 25°15N 69°40E 42 G3
Umarpada India 21°27N 73°30E 42 J5
Umatilla U.S.A. 45°55N 119°21W 76 D4
Umba Russia 66°42N 34°11E 18 A5
Umbagog L. U.S.A. 44°46N 71°3W 83 B13
Umbakumba Australia 13°47S 136°50E 62 A2
Umbrella Mts. N.Z. 45°35S 169°5E 59 F2
Umeå Sweden 63°45N 20°20E 8 E19
Umeälven → Sweden 63°45N 20°20E 8 E19
Umera Indonesia 0°12S 129°37E 37 E7
Umfuli → Zimbabwe 17°30S 29°23E 55 F2
Umfurudzi ⌂ Zimbabwe 17°6S 31°40E 55 F3
Umgusa Zimbabwe 19°29S 27°52E 55 F2
Umgwenya → Mozam. 25°14S 32°18E 57 D5
Umiujaq Canada 56°33N 76°33W 72 A4
Umkomaas S. Africa 30°13S 30°48E 57 E5
Umlazi S. Africa 29°59S 30°54E 53 L6
Umm ad Daraj, J. Jordan 32°18N 35°48E 46 C4
Umm al Qaywayn U.A.E. 25°30N 55°35E 45 E7
Umm al Qittayn Jordan 32°18N 36°40E 46 C5
Umm Bāb Qatar 25°12N 50°48E 45 E6
Umm Durman = Omdurmân Sudan 15°40N 32°28E 51 E12
Umm el Fahm Israel 32°31N 35°9E 46 C4
Umm Keddada Sudan 13°33N 26°35E 51 F11
Umm Lajj Si. Arabia 25°0N 37°23E 44 E3
Umm Qasr Iraq 30°1N 47°58E 44 D5
Umm Ruwaba Sudan 12°50N 31°20E 51 F12
Umnak I. U.S.A. 53°15N 168°20W 74 E6
Umniati → Zimbabwe 16°49S 28°45E 55 F2
Umpqua → U.S.A. 43°40N 124°12W 76 E1
Umreth India 22°41N 73°4E 42 H5
Umtata = Mthatha S. Africa 31°36S 28°49E 57 E4
Umuarama Brazil 23°45S 53°20W 95 A5
Umvukwe Ra. Zimbabwe 16°45S 30°45E 55 F3
Umzimvubu S. Africa 31°38S 29°33E 57 E4
Umzingwane → Zimbabwe 22°12S 29°56E 55 G2
Umzinto = eMuziwezinto S. Africa 30°15S 30°45E 57 E5
Una India 20°46N 71°8E 42 J4
Una → Bos.-H. 45°0N 16°20E 16 F9
Unadilla U.S.A. 42°20N 75°19W 83 D9
Unalakleet U.S.A. 63°52N 160°47W 74 C7
Unalaska U.S.A. 53°53N 166°32W 74 E6
Unalaska I. U.S.A. 53°35N 166°50W 74 E6
'Unayzah Si. Arabia 26°6N 43°58E 44 E4
'Unayzah, J. Asia 32°12N 39°18E 44 C3
Uncía Bolivia 18°25S 66°40W 92 G5
Uncompahgre Peak U.S.A. 38°4N 107°28W 76 G10
Uncompahgre Plateau U.S.A. 38°20N 108°15W 76 G9
Undara Volcanic △ Australia 18°14S 144°41E 62 B3
Underbool Australia 35°10S 141°51E 63 F3
Underwood Canada 44°18N 81°29W 82 B3
Ungarie Australia 33°38S 146°56E 63 E4
Ungarra Australia 34°12S 136°2E 63 E2
Ungava, Pén. d' Canada 60°0N 74°0W 69 F17
Ungava B. Canada 59°30N 67°30W 69 F18
Ungeny = Ungheni Moldova 47°11N 27°51E 17 E14
Unggi N. Korea 42°16N 130°28E 35 C16
Ungheni Moldova 47°11N 27°51E 17 E14
Ungwana B. Kenya 2°45S 40°20E 54 C5
União da Vitória Brazil 26°13S 51°5W 95 B5
Unimak I. U.S.A. 54°45N 164°0W 74 E7
Unimak Pass. U.S.A. 54°15N 164°30W 74 E7
Union Miss., U.S.A. 32°34N 89°7W 85 E10
Union Mo., U.S.A. 38°27N 91°0W 80 F8
Union S.C., U.S.A. 34°43N 81°37W 85 D14
Union City Calif., U.S.A. 37°36N 122°1W 78 H4
Union City N.J., U.S.A. 40°45N 74°2W 83 F10
Union City Pa., U.S.A. 41°54N 79°51W 82 E5
Union City Tenn., U.S.A. 36°26N 89°3W 85 C10
Union Dale U.S.A. 41°43N 75°29W 83 E9
Union Gap U.S.A. 46°33N 120°28W 76 C3
Union Springs Ala., U.S.A. 32°9N 85°43W 85 E12
Union Springs N.Y., U.S.A. 42°50N 76°41W 83 D8
Uniondale S. Africa 33°39S 23°7E 56 E3
Uniontown U.S.A. 39°54N 79°44W 81 F14
Unionville U.S.A. 40°29N 93°1W 80 E7
United Arab Emirates ■ Asia 23°50N 54°0E 45 F7
United Kingdom ■ Europe 53°0N 2°0W 14 E6
United States of America ■ N. Amer. 37°0N 96°0W 75 H20
Unity Canada 52°30N 109°5W 71 C7
University Park U.S.A. 32°17N 106°45W 77 K10
University Place U.S.A. 47°14N 122°33W 78 C4
Unjha India 23°46N 72°24E 42 H5
Unnao India 26°35N 80°30E 43 F9
Unsengedsi → Zimbabwe 15°43S 31°14E 55 F3
Unst U.K. 60°44N 0°53W 11 A8
Unuk → Canada 56°5N 131°3W 70 B2
Unzen-Amakusa △ Japan 32°15N 130°10E 31 H5
Uozu Japan 36°48N 137°24E 31 F8
Upata Venezuela 8°1N 62°24W 92 B6
Upemba, L. Dem. Rep. of the Congo 8°30S 26°20E 55 D2
Upemba △ Dem. Rep. of the Congo 9°0S 26°35E 55 D2
Upernavik Greenland 72°49N 56°20W 4 B5
Upington S. Africa 28°25S 21°15E 56 D3
Upleta India 21°46N 70°16E 42 J4
'Upolu Samoa 13°58S 172°0W 59 b
Upper Alkali L. U.S.A. 41°47N 120°8W 76 F3
Upper Arrow L. Canada 50°30N 117°50W 70 C5
Upper Daly ✪ Australia 14°26S 131°3E 60 B5
Upper Darby U.S.A. 39°55N 75°16W 81 F16
Upper Foster L. Canada 56°47N 105°20W 71 B7
Upper Hutt N.Z. 41°8S 175°5E 59 D5
Upper Klamath L. U.S.A. 42°25N 121°55W 76 E3
Upper Lake U.S.A. 39°10N 122°54W 78 F4
Upper Liard Canada 60°3N 128°54W 70 A3
Upper Manzanilla Trin. & Tob. 10°31N 61°4W 93 K15
Upper Missouri Breaks ⌂ U.S.A. 47°50N 109°55W 76 C9
Upper Musquodoboit Canada 45°10N 62°58W 73 C7
Upper Red L. U.S.A. 48°8N 94°45W 80 A6
Upper Sandusky U.S.A. 40°50N 83°17W 81 E12
Upper Volta = Burkina Faso ■ Africa 12°0N 1°0W 50 F5
Uppland Sweden 59°59N 17°48E 9 G17
Uppsala Sweden 59°53N 17°38E 9 G17
Upshi India 33°48N 77°52E 43 C7
Upton U.S.A. 44°6N 104°38W 76 D11
Uqsuqtuuq = Gjoa Haven Canada 68°38N 95°53W 68 D12
Ur Iraq 30°55N 46°25E 44 D5

Urad Qianqi *China* 40°40N 108°30E **34** D5
Urakawa *Japan* 42°9N 142°47E **30** C11
Ural = Uralskiy ⇨ *Russia* 64°0N 70°0E **28** C7
Ural = Zhayyq ⇨
  Kazakhstan 47°0N 51°48E **19** E9
Ural *Australia* 33°21S 146°12E **63** E4
Ural Mts. = Uralskie Gory
  Eurasia 60°0N 59°0E **18** C10
Uralla *Australia* 30°37S 151°29E **63** E5
Uralsk = Oral *Kazakhstan* 51°20N 51°20E **19** D9
Uralskiy ⇨ *Russia* 64°0N 70°0E **28** C7
Uralskie Gory *Eurasia* 60°0N 59°0E **18** C10
Urambo *Tanzania* 5°4S 32°0E **54** D3
Urandangi *Australia* 21°32S 138°14E **62** C2
Uranium City *Canada* 59°34N 108°37W **71** B7
Urapuntja = Utopia
  Australia 22°14S 134°33E **62** C1
Uraricoera ⇨ *Brazil* 3°2N 60°30W **92** C6
Urasoe *Japan* 26°15N 127°43E **31** L3
Urawa = Saitama *Japan* 35°54N 139°38E **31** G9
Uray *Russia* 60°5N 65°15E **28** C7
'Uray'irah *Si. Arabia* 25°57N 48°53E **45** E6
Urbana *Ill., U.S.A.* 40°7N 88°12W **80** E3
Urbana *Ohio, U.S.A.* 40°7N 83°45W **81** E12
Urbandale *U.S.A.* 41°38N 93°43W **80** E7
Urbino *Italy* 43°43N 12°38E **22** C5
Urbión, Picos de *Spain* 42°1N 2°52W **21** A4
Urcos *Peru* 13°40S 71°38W **92** F4
Urdinarrain *Argentina* 32°37S 58°52W **94** C4
Ure ⇨ *U.K.* 54°5N 1°20W **12** C6
Urengoy *Russia* 65°58N 78°22E **28** C8
Ures *Mexico* 29°26N 110°24W **86** B2
Urewera △ *N.Z.* 38°29S 177°7E **59** C6
Urfa = Şanlıurfa *Turkey* 37°12N 38°50E **44** B3
Urganch *Uzbekistan* 41°40N 60°41E **28** E7
Urgench = Urganch
  Uzbekistan 41°40N 60°41E **28** E7
Ürgüp *Turkey* 38°38N 34°56E **44** B2
Uri *India* 34°8N 74°2E **43** B6
Uribia *Colombia* 11°43N 72°16W **92** A4
Uriondo *Bolivia* 21°41S 64°41W **94** A3
Urique *Mexico* 27°13N 107°55W **86** B3
Urique ⇨ *Mexico* 26°29N 107°58W **86** B3
Urk *Neths.* 52°39N 5°36E **15** B5
Urla *Turkey* 38°20N 26°47E **23** E12
Urmia = Orūmīyeh *Iran* 37°40N 45°0E **44** B5
Uroševac *Kosovo* 42°23N 21°10E **23** C9
Uroyan, Montañas de
  Puerto Rico 18°12N 67°0W **89** d
Urrampinyi Iltjiltarri ☺
  Australia 24°20S 132°10E **60** D5
Uruaçu *Brazil* 14°30S 49°10W **93** F9
Uruapan *Mexico* 19°24N 102°3W **86** D4
Urubamba ⇨ *Peru* 10°43S 73°48W **92** F4
Urucará *Brazil* 2°32S 57°45W **92** D7
Uruçuí *Brazil* 7°20S 44°28W **93** E10
Uruguai ⇨ *Brazil* 26°0S 53°30W **95** B5
Uruguaiana *Brazil* 29°50S 57°0W **94** B4
Uruguay ■ *S. Amer.* 32°30S 56°30W **94** C4
Uruguay ⇨ *S. Amer.* 34°12S 58°18W **94** C4
Urumchi = Ürümqi
  China 43°45N 87°45E **32** B3
Ürümqi *China* 43°45N 87°45E **32** B3
Uruna ☺ *Australia* 24°3S 133°1E **60** D5
Urup, Ostrov *Russia* 46°0N 151°0E **29** E16
Ürzhar *Kazakhstan* 47°5N 81°38E **28** E9
Usa ⇨ *Russia* 66°16N 59°49E **18** A10
Uşak *Turkey* 38°43N 29°28E **19** G4
Usakos *Namibia* 21°54S 15°31E **56** C2
Usedom *Germany* 53°55N 14°2E **16** B8
Useless Loop *Australia* 26°8S 113°23E **61** E1
Ushakova, Ostrov *Russia* 82°0N 80°0E **29** A8
Ushant = Ouessant, Î. d'
  France 48°28N 5°6W **20** B1
Ushashi *Tanzania* 1°59S 33°57E **54** C3
'Ushayrah *Si. Arabia* 25°35N 45°47E **44** E5
Ushibuka *Japan* 32°11N 130°1E **31** H5
Üshtöbe *Kazakhstan* 45°16N 78°0E **28** E8
Ushuaia *Argentina* 54°50S 68°23W **96** G3
Ushumun *Russia* 52°47N 126°32E **29** D13
Usinsk *Russia* 65°57N 57°27E **18** A10
Usk *Canada* 54°38N 128°26W **70** C3
Usk ⇨ *U.K.* 51°33N 2°58W **13** F5
Uska *India* 27°12N 83°7E **43** F10
Usman *Russia* 52°5N 39°48E **18** D6
Usoke *Tanzania* 5°8S 32°24E **54** D3
Usolye-Sibirskoye
  Russia 52°48N 103°40E **29** D11
Uspallata, P. de
  Argentina 32°37S 69°22W **94** C2
Ussuriysk *Russia* 43°48N 131°59E **30** C5
Ussurka *Russia* 45°12N 133°31E **30** B6
Ust-Chaun *Russia* 68°47N 170°30E **29** C18
Ust-Ilimsk *Russia* 58°3N 102°39E **29** D11
Ust-Ishim *Russia* 57°45N 71°10E **28** D8
Ust-Kamchatsk *Russia* 56°10N 162°28E **29** D17
Ust-Kamenogorsk = Öskemen
  Kazakhstan 50°0N 82°36E **28** E9
Ust-Khayryuzovo
  Russia 57°15N 156°45E **29** D16
Ust-Kut *Russia* 56°50N 105°42E **29** D11
Ust-Kuyga *Russia* 70°1N 135°43E **29** B14
Ust-Maya *Russia* 60°30N 134°28E **29** C14
Ust-Mil *Russia* 59°40N 133°11E **29** D14
Ust-Nera *Russia* 64°35N 143°15E **29** C15
Ust-Nyukzha *Russia* 56°34N 121°37E **29** D13
Ust-Olenek *Russia* 73°0N 120°5E **29** B12
Ust-Omchug *Russia* 61°9N 149°38E **29** C15
Ust-Port *Russia* 69°40N 84°26E **28** C9
Ust-Tsilma *Russia* 65°28N 52°11E **18** A9
Ust-Urt = Ustyurt Plateau
  Asia 44°0N 55°0E **28** E6
Ust-Usa *Russia* 66°2N 56°57E **18** A10
Ust-Vorkuta *Russia* 67°24N 64°0E **18** A11
Ústí nad Labem *Czech Rep.* 50°41N 14°3E **16** C8
Ústica *Italy* 38°42N 13°11E **22** E5
Ustinov = Izhevsk
  Russia 56°51N 53°14E **18** C9
Ustyurt Plateau *Asia* 44°0N 55°0E **28** E6

Usu *China* 44°27N 84°40E **32** B3
Usuki *Japan* 33°8N 131°49E **31** H5
Usulután *El Salv.* 13°25N 88°28W **88** D2
Usumacinta ⇨ *Mexico* 18°24N 92°38W **87** D6
Usumbura = Bujumbura
  Burundi 3°16S 29°18E **54** C2
Usure *Tanzania* 4°40S 34°22E **54** C3
Usutuo ⇨ *Mozam.* 26°48S 32°7E **57** D5
Uta *Indonesia* 4°33S 136°0E **37** E9
Utah □ *U.S.A.* 39°20N 111°30W **76** G8
Utah L. *U.S.A.* 40°12N 111°48W **76** F8
Utara, Selat *Malaysia* 5°28N 100°20E **39** c
Utarni *India* 26°5N 71°58E **42** F4
Utatlan *Guatemala* 15°2N 91°11W **88** C1
Ute Creek ⇨ *U.S.A.* 35°21N 103°50W **77** J12
Utena *Lithuania* 55°27N 25°40E **9** J21
Utete *Tanzania* 8°0S 38°45E **54** D4
Uthai Thani *Thailand* 15°22N 100°3E **38** E3
Uthal *Pakistan* 25°44N 66°40E **42** G2
Utiariti *Brazil* 13°0S 58°10W **92** F7
Utica *N.Y., U.S.A.* 43°6N 75°14W **83** C9
Utica *Ohio, U.S.A.* 40°14N 82°27W **82** F2
Utikuma L. *Canada* 55°50N 115°30W **70** B5
Utila *Honduras* 16°6N 86°56W **88** C2
Utopia *Australia* 22°14S 134°33E **62** C1
Utraula *India* 27°19N 82°25E **43** F10
Utrecht *Neths.* 52°5N 5°8E **15** B5
Utrecht *S. Africa* 27°38S 30°20E **57** D5
Utrecht □ *Neths.* 52°6N 5°7E **15** B5
Utrera *Spain* 37°12N 5°48W **21** D3
Utsjoki ⇨ *Finland* 69°51N 26°59E **8** B22
Utsunomiya *Japan* 36°30N 139°50E **31** F9
Uttar Pradesh □ *India* 27°0N 80°0E **43** F9
Uttaradit *Thailand* 17°36N 100°5E **38** D3
Uttarakhand □ *India* 30°0N 79°30E **43** D8
Utterson *Canada* 45°12N 79°19W **82** A5
Uttoxeter *U.K.* 52°54N 1°52W **12** E6
Utuado *Puerto Rico* 18°16N 66°42W **89** d
Uummannaq *Avannaarsua,*
  Greenland 77°33N 68°52W **69** B18
Uummannaq *Kitaa,*
  Greenland 70°58N 52°17W **4** B5
Uummannarsuaq = Nunap Isua
  Greenland 59°48N 43°55W **66** D15
Uusikaarlepyy *Finland* 63°32N 22°31E **8** E20
Uusikaupunki *Finland* 60°47N 21°25E **8** F19
Uva *Russia* 56°59N 52°13E **18** C9
Uvalde *U.S.A.* 29°13N 99°47W **84** G5
Uvat *Russia* 59°5N 68°50E **28** D7
Uvinza *Tanzania* 5°5S 30°24E **54** D3
Uvira *Dem. Rep. of the Congo* 3°22S 29°3E **54** C2
Uvs Nuur *Mongolia* 50°20N 92°30E **32** A4
'Uwairidh, Ḥarrat al
  Si. Arabia 26°50N 38°0E **44** E3
Uwajima *Japan* 33°10N 132°35E **31** H6
Uwanda △ *Tanzania* 7°46S 32°0E **54** D3
Uweinat, Jebel *Sudan* 21°54N 24°58E **51** D10
Uxbridge *Canada* 44°6N 79°7W **82** B5
Uxin Qi *China* 38°50N 109°5E **34** E5
Uxmal *Mexico* 20°22N 89°46W **87** C7
Üydzin *Mongolia* 44°9N 107°0E **34** B4
Uyo *Nigeria* 5°1N 7°53E **50** G7
Uyûn Mûsa *Egypt* 29°53N 32°40E **46** F1
Uyuni *Bolivia* 20°28S 66°47W **92** H5
Uzbekistan ■ *Asia* 41°30N 65°0E **28** E7
Uzboy ⇨ *Turkmenistan* 39°30N 55°0E **45** B7
Uzen, Bolshoi = Uzen, Mal ⇨
  Kazakhstan 49°4N 49°44E **19** E8
Uzen, Mal ⇨ *Kazakhstan* 49°4N 49°44E **19** E8
Uzerche *France* 45°25N 1°34E **20** D4
Uzh ⇨ *Ukraine* 51°15N 30°12E **17** C16
Uzhgorod = Uzhhorod
  Ukraine 48°36N 22°18E **17** D12
Uzhhorod *Ukraine* 48°36N 22°18E **17** D12
Užice *Serbia* 43°55N 19°50E **23** C8
Uzunköprü *Turkey* 41°16N 26°43E **23** D12

V

Vaal ⇨ *S. Africa* 29°4S 23°38E **56** D3
Vaal Dam *S. Africa* 27°0S 28°14E **57** D4
Vaalbos △ *S. Africa* 28°22S 24°20E **56** D3
Vaalwater *S. Africa* 24°15S 28°8E **57** C4
Vaasa *Finland* 63°6N 21°38E **8** E19
Vác *Hungary* 47°49N 19°10E **17** E10
Vacaria *Brazil* 28°31S 50°52W **95** B5
Vacata *Fiji* 17°15S 179°31W **59** a
Vacaville *U.S.A.* 38°21N 121°59W **78** G5
Vach = Vakh ⇨ *Russia* 60°45N 76°45E **28** C8
Vache, Î. à *Haiti* 18°2N 73°35W **89** C5
Vacoas *Mauritius* 20°18S 57°29E **53** d
Vadakara = Badagara
  India 11°35N 75°40E **40** P9
Vadnagar *India* 23°47N 72°40E **42** H5
Vadodara *India* 22°20N 73°10E **42** H5
Vadsø *Norway* 70°3N 29°50E **8** A23
Vaduz *Liech.* 47°8N 9°31E **20** C8
Værøy *Norway* 67°40N 12°40E **8** C15
Vágar *Færoe Is.* 62°5N 7°15W **8** E9
Vagia, Akra *Greece* 36°15N 28°11E **25** C10
Vágsfjorden *Norway* 68°50N 16°50E **8** B17
Váh ⇨ *Slovak Rep.* 47°43N 18°7E **17** D9
Vahsel B. *Antarctica* 75°0S 35°0W **5** D1
Váhtjer = Gällivare
  Sweden 67°9N 20°40E **8** C19
Vaï *Greece* 35°15N 26°18E **25** D8
Vaihiria, L. *Tahiti* 17°40S 149°25W **59** d
Vail *U.S.A.* 39°40N 106°20W **75** H18
Vairao *Tahiti* 17°47S 149°17W **59** d
Vaisali ⇨ *India* 26°28N 78°53E **43** F8
Vaitogi *Amer. Samoa* 14°24S 170°44W **59** b
Vakh ⇨ *Russia* 60°45N 76°45E **28** C8
Val-d'Or *Canada* 48°7N 77°47W **72** C4
Val Marie *Canada* 49°15N 107°45W **71** D7
Valaam *Russia* 61°22N 30°57E **9** B24
Valahia *Romania* 44°35N 25°0E **17** F13
Valandovo *Macedonia* 41°19N 22°34E **23** D10
Valatie *U.S.A.* 42°24N 73°40W **83** D11

Valcheta *Argentina* 40°40S 66°8W **96** E3
Valdai Hills = Valdayskaya
  Vozvyshennost *Russia* 57°0N 33°30E **18** C5
Valdayskaya Vozvyshennost
  Russia 57°0N 33°30E **18** C5
Valdepeñas *Spain* 38°43N 3°25W **21** C4
Valdés, Pen. *Argentina* 42°30S 63°45W **96** E4
Valdez *U.S.A.* 61°7N 146°16W **68** E2
Valdivia *Chile* 39°50S 73°14W **96** D2
Valdivia Abyssal Plain
  S. Ocean 62°30S 70°0E **5** C6
Valdosta *U.S.A.* 30°50N 83°17W **85** F13
Valdres *Norway* 61°5N 9°5E **8** F13
Vale *U.S.A.* 43°59N 117°15W **76** E5
Vale of Glamorgan □
  U.K. 51°28N 3°25W **13** F4
Valemount *Canada* 52°50N 119°15W **70** C5
Valença *Brazil* 13°20S 39°5W **93** F11
Valença do Piauí *Brazil* 6°20S 41°45W **93** E10
Valence *France* 44°57N 4°54E **20** D6
Valencia *Spain* 39°27N 0°23W **21** C5
Valencia *Trin. & Tob.* 10°39N 61°11W **93** K15
Valencia *U.S.A.* 34°48N 106°43W **77** J10
Valencia *Venezuela* 10°11N 68°0W **92** A5
Valencia □ *Spain* 39°20N 0°40W **21** C5
Valencia, G. de *Spain* 39°30N 0°20E **21** C6
Valencia de Alcántara
  Spain 39°25N 7°14W **21** C2
Valencia I. *Ireland* 51°54N 10°22W **10** E1
Valenciennes *France* 50°20N 3°34E **20** A5
Valentim, Sa. do *Brazil* 6°0S 43°30W **93** E10
Valentin *Russia* 43°8N 134°17E **30** C7
Valentine *Nebr., U.S.A.* 42°52N 100°33W **80** D3
Valentine *Tex., U.S.A.* 30°35N 104°30W **84** F2
Valera *Venezuela* 9°19N 70°37W **92** B4
Valga *Estonia* 57°47N 26°2E **9** H22
Valier *U.S.A.* 48°18N 112°16W **76** B7
Valjevo *Serbia* 44°18N 19°53E **23** B8
Valka *Latvia* 57°46N 26°3E **9** H22
Valkeakoski *Finland* 61°16N 24°2E **8** F21
Valkenswaard *Neths.* 51°21N 5°29E **15** C5
Vall de Uxó = La Vall d'Uixó
  Spain 39°49N 0°15W **21** C5
Valladolid *Mexico* 20°41N 88°12W **87** C7
Valladolid *Spain* 41°38N 4°43W **21** B3
Valldemossa *Spain* 39°43N 2°37E **24** B9
Valle de la Pascua
  Venezuela 9°13N 66°0W **92** B5
Valle de las Palmas
  Mexico 32°20N 116°43W **79** N10
Valle de Santiago
  Mexico 20°23N 101°12W **86** C4
Valle de Zaragoza
  Mexico 27°25N 105°50W **86** B3
Valle Fértil, Sierra del
  Argentina 30°20S 68°0W **94** C2
Valle Gran Rey *Canary Is.* 28°5N 17°20W **24** F2
Valle Hermoso *Mexico* 25°35N 97°40W **87** B5
Valle Nacional *Mexico* 17°47N 96°18W **87** D5
Valledupar *Colombia* 10°29N 73°15W **92** A4
Vallehermoso *Canary Is.* 28°10N 17°15W **24** F2
Vallejo *U.S.A.* 38°7N 122°14W **78** G4
Vallenar *Chile* 28°30S 70°50W **94** B1
Valletta *Malta* 35°54N 14°31E **25** D2
Valley Center *U.S.A.* 33°13N 117°2W **79** M9
Valley City *U.S.A.* 46°55N 98°0W **80** B5
Valley Falls *Oreg.,*
  U.S.A. 42°29N 120°17W **76** E3
Valley Falls *R.I., U.S.A.* 41°54N 71°24W **83** E13
Valley of Flowers △
  India 30°50N 79°40E **43** D8
Valley Springs *U.S.A.* 38°12N 120°50W **78** G6
Valley View *U.S.A.* 40°39N 76°33W **83** F8
Valley Wells *U.S.A.* 35°27N 115°46W **79** K11
Valleyview *Canada* 55°5N 117°17W **70** B5
Vallimanca, Arroyo
  Argentina 35°40S 59°10W **94** D4
Valls *Spain* 41°18N 1°15E **21** B6
Valmiera *Latvia* 57°37N 25°29E **9** H21
Valognes *France* 49°30N 1°28W **20** B3
Valona = Vlorë *Albania* 40°32N 19°28E **23** D8
Valozhyn *Belarus* 54°3N 26°30E **17** A14
Valparaíso *Mexico* 22°46N 103°34W **86** C4
Valparaiso *U.S.A.* 41°28N 87°4W **80** E10
Valparaíso □ *Chile* 33°2S 71°40W **94** C1
Valsad *India* 20°40N 72°58E **40** J8
Valverde *Canary Is.* 27°48N 17°55W **24** G2
Valverde del Camino
  Spain 37°35N 6°47W **21** D2
Vamizi, I. *Mozam.* 11°2S 40°40E **55** E5
Vammala *Finland* 61°20N 22°54E **8** F20
Vamos *Greece* 35°24N 24°13E **25** D6
Van *Turkey* 38°30N 43°20E **44** B4
Van, L. = Van Gölü
  Turkey 38°30N 43°0E **44** B4
Van Alstyne *U.S.A.* 33°25N 96°35W **84** E6
Van Blommestein Meer
  Suriname 4°45N 55°5W **93** C7
Van Buren *Canada* 47°10N 67°58W **73** C6
Van Buren *Ark., U.S.A.* 35°26N 94°21W **84** D7
Van Buren *Maine,*
  U.S.A. 47°10N 67°58W **81** B20
Van Buren *Mo., U.S.A.* 37°0N 91°1W **80** G8
Van Canh *Vietnam* 13°37N 109°0E **38** F7
Van Diemen, C. *N. Terr.,*
  Australia 11°9S 130°24E **60** B5
Van Diemen, C. *Queens.,*
  Australia 16°30S 139°46E **62** B2
Van Diemen G. *Australia* 11°45S 132°0E **60** B5
Van Gölü *Turkey* 38°30N 43°0E **44** B4
Van Horn *U.S.A.* 31°3N 104°50W **84** F2
Van Ninh *Vietnam* 12°42N 109°14E **38** F7
Van Rees, Pegunungan
  Indonesia 2°35S 138°15E **37** E9
Van Wert *U.S.A.* 40°52N 84°35W **81** E11
Van Yen *Vietnam* 21°4N 104°42E **38** B5

Van Zylsrus *S. Africa* 26°52S 22°4E **56** D3
Vanadzor *Armenia* 40°48N 44°30E **19** F7
Vanavara *Russia* 60°22N 102°16E **29** C11
Vancouver *Canada* 49°15N 123°7W **78** A3
Vancouver *U.S.A.* 45°38N 122°40W **78** E4
Vancouver, C. *Australia* 35°2S 118°11E **61** G2
Vancouver I. *Canada* 49°50N 126°0W **78** B2
Vancouver Int. ✈ (YVR)
  Canada 49°10N 123°10W **78** A3
Vanda = Vantaa *Finland* 60°18N 24°56E **9** F21
Vandalia *Ill., U.S.A.* 38°58N 89°6W **80** F9
Vandalia *Mo., U.S.A.* 39°19N 91°29W **80** F8
Vandenberg Village
  U.S.A. 34°43N 120°28W **79** L6
Vandergrift *U.S.A.* 40°36N 79°34W **82** F5
Vanderhoof *Canada* 54°0N 124°0W **70** C4
Vanderkloof Dam
  S. Africa 30°4S 24°40E **56** E3
Vanderlin I. *Australia* 15°44S 137°2E **62** B2
Vänern *Sweden* 58°47N 13°30E **9** G15
Vänersborg *Sweden* 58°26N 12°19E **9** G15
Vang Vieng *Laos* 18°58N 102°32E **38** C4
Vanga *Kenya* 4°35S 39°12E **54** C4
Vangaindrano *Madag.* 23°21S 47°36E **57** C8
Vanguard *Canada* 49°55N 107°20W **71** D7
Vanino *Russia* 48°50N 140°5E **29** E15
Vankleek Hill *Canada* 45°32N 74°40W **83** A10
Vännäs *Sweden* 63°58N 19°48E **8** E18
Vannes *France* 47°40N 2°47W **20** C2
Vannøya *Norway* 70°6N 19°50E **8** A18
Vanrhynsdorp *S. Africa* 31°36S 18°44E **56** E2
Vansbro *Sweden* 60°32N 14°15E **9** F16
Vansittart B. *Australia* 14°3S 126°17E **60** B4
Vansittart I. *Canada* 65°50N 84°0W **69** D15
Vantaa *Finland* 60°18N 24°56E **9** F21
Vanua Balavu *Fiji* 17°12S 178°55W **59** a
Vanua Levu *Fiji* 16°33S 179°15E **59** a
Vanua Vatu *Fiji* 18°22S 179°15W **59** a
Vanuatu ■ *Pac. Oc.* 15°0S 168°0E **58** C9
Vanwyksvlei *S. Africa* 30°18S 21°49E **56** E3
Vapnyarka *Ukraine* 48°32N 28°45E **17** D15
Var ⇨ *France* 43°39N 7°12E **20** E7
Varāmīn *Iran* 35°20N 51°39E **45** C6
Varāmīn □ *Iran* 35°18N 51°35E **45** B6
Varanasi *India* 25°22N 83°0E **43** G10
Varangerfjorden *Norway* 70°3N 29°25E **8** A23
Varangerhalvøya
  Norway 70°25N 29°30E **8** A23
Varaždin *Croatia* 46°20N 16°20E **16** E9
Varberg *Sweden* 57°6N 12°20E **9** H15
Vardak □ *Afghan.* 34°0N 68°0E **40** B6
Vardar = Axios ⇨
  Greece 40°57N 22°35E **23** D10
Varde *Denmark* 55°38N 8°29E **9** J13
Vardø *Norway* 70°23N 31°5E **8** A24
Varella, Mui *Vietnam* 12°54N 109°26E **38** F7
Varéna *Lithuania* 54°12N 24°30E **9** J21
Varese *Italy* 45°48N 8°50E **20** D8
Varginha *Brazil* 21°33S 45°25W **95** A6
Varillas *Chile* 24°0S 70°10W **94** A1
Varkaus *Finland* 62°19N 27°50E **8** E22
Varna *Bulgaria* 43°13N 27°56E **23** C12
Värnamo *Sweden* 57°10N 14°3E **9** H16
Vars *Canada* 45°21N 75°21W **83** A9
Varysburg *U.S.A.* 42°46N 78°19W **82** D6
Varzaneh *Iran* 32°25N 52°40E **45** C7
Vasa = Vaasa *Finland* 63°6N 21°38E **8** E19
Vasa Barris ⇨ *Brazil* 11°10S 37°10W **93** F11
Vascongadas = País Vasco □
  Spain 42°50N 2°45W **21** A4
Vasht = Khāsh *Iran* 28°15N 61°15E **45** D9
Vasilevichi *Belarus* 52°15N 29°50E **17** B15
Vasilkov = Vasylkiv
  Ukraine 50°7N 30°15E **17** C16
Vaslui *Romania* 46°38N 27°42E **17** E14
Vassar *Canada* 49°10N 95°55W **71** D9
Vassar *U.S.A.* 43°22N 83°35W **81** D12
Västerås *Sweden* 59°37N 16°38E **9** G17
Västerbotten *Sweden* 64°36N 20°4E **8** D19
Västerdalälven ⇨ *Sweden* 60°30N 14°7E **8** F16
Västervik *Sweden* 57°43N 16°33E **9** H17
Västmanland *Sweden* 59°45N 16°20E **9** G17
Vasto *Italy* 42°8N 14°40E **22** C6
Vasylkiv *Ukraine* 50°7N 30°15E **17** C16
Vatersay *U.K.* 56°55N 7°32W **11** E1
Vati *Greece* 35°57N 27°53E **25** D9
Vatican City ■ *Europe* 41°54N 12°27E **22** D5
Vatili *Cyprus* 35°6N 33°40E **25** D12
Vatiu = Atiu *Cook Is.* 20°0S 158°10W **65** J12
Vatnajökull *Iceland* 64°30N 16°48W **8** D5
Vatoa *Fiji* 19°50S 178°13W **59** a
Vatólakos *Greece* 35°27N 23°53E **25** D6
Vatoloha *Madag.* 17°52S 47°48E **57** B8
Vatomandry *Madag.* 19°20S 48°59E **57** B8
Vatra-Dornei *Romania* 47°22N 25°22E **17** E13
Vatrak ⇨ *India* 23°9N 73°2E **42** H5
Vättern *Sweden* 58°25N 14°30E **9** G16
Vatu Vara *Fiji* 17°26S 179°31W **59** a
Vatulele *Fiji* 18°33S 177°37E **59** a
Vaudreuil-Dorion
  Canada 45°23N 74°3W **83** A10
Vaughn *Mont., U.S.A.* 47°33N 111°33W **76** C8
Vaughn *N. Mex.,*
  U.S.A. 34°36N 105°13W **77** J11
Vaujours L. *Canada* 55°27N 74°15W **72** A5
Vaupés = Uaupés ⇨
  Brazil 0°2N 67°16W **92** C5
Vaupés □ *Colombia* 1°0N 71°0W **92** C4
Vauxhall *Canada* 50°5N 112°9W **70** C6
Vav *India* 24°22N 71°31E **42** G4
Vavatenina *Madag.* 17°28S 49°12E **57** B8
Vava'u *Tonga* 18°36S 174°0W **59** c
Vava'u Group *Tonga* 18°40S 174°0W **59** c
Vawkavysk *Belarus* 53°9N 24°30E **17** B13
Vaygach, Ostrov *Russia* 70°0N 60°0E **28** C6
Veaikevárri = Svappavaara
  Sweden 67°40N 21°3E **8** C19
Vechte ⇨ *Neths.* 52°34N 6°6E **15** B6
Vedea ⇨ *Romania* 43°42N 25°41E **17** G13

Vedia *Argentina* 34°30S 61°31W **94** C3
Veendam *Neths.* 53°5N 6°52E **15** A6
Veenendaal *Neths.* 52°2N 5°34E **15** B5
Vefsna ⇨ *Norway* 65°48N 13°10E **8** D15
Vega *Norway* 65°40N 11°55E **8** D14
Vega *U.S.A.* 35°15N 102°26W **84** D3
Vega Baja *Puerto Rico* 18°27N 66°23W **89** d
Vegreville *Canada* 53°30N 112°5W **70** C6
Vejer de la Frontera
  Spain 36°15N 5°59W **21** D3
Vejle *Denmark* 55°43N 9°30E **9** J13
Velas, C. *Costa Rica* 10°21N 85°52W **88** D2
Velasco, Sierra de
  Argentina 29°20S 67°10W **94** B2
Velddrif *S. Africa* 32°42S 18°11E **56** E2
Velebit Planina *Croatia* 44°50N 15°20E **16** F8
Veles *Macedonia* 41°46N 21°47E **23** D9
Vélez-Málaga *Spain* 36°48N 4°5W **21** D3
Vélez Rubio *Spain* 37°41N 2°5W **21** D4
Velhas ⇨ *Brazil* 17°13S 44°49W **93** G10
Velika Kapela *Croatia* 45°10N 15°5E **16** F8
Velikaya ⇨ *Russia* 57°48N 28°10E **18** C4
Velikaya Kema *Russia* 45°30N 137°12E **30** B8
Veliki Ustyug *Russia* 60°47N 46°20E **18** B8
Velikiye Luki *Russia* 56°25N 30°32E **18** C5
Veliko Tŭrnovo *Bulgaria* 43°5N 25°41E **23** C11
Velikonda Range *India* 14°45N 79°10E **40** M11
Velletri *Italy* 41°41N 12°47E **22** D5
Vellore *India* 12°57N 79°10E **40** N11
Velsk *Russia* 61°10N 42°5E **18** B7
Veluwezoom △ *Neths.* 52°5N 6°0E **15** B6
Velva *U.S.A.* 48°4N 100°56W **80** A3
Venado *Mexico* 22°56N 101°6W **86** C4
Venado Tuerto *Argentina* 33°50S 62°0W **94** C3
Vendée □ *France* 46°50N 1°35W **20** C2
Vendôme *France* 47°47N 1°3E **20** C4
Venézia *Italy* 45°27N 12°21E **22** B5
Venézia, G. di *Italy* 45°15N 13°0E **22** B5
Venezuela ■ *S. Amer.* 8°0N 66°0W **92** B5
Venezuela, G. de
  Venezuela 11°30N 71°0W **92** A4
Vengurla *India* 15°53N 73°45E **40** M8
Venice = Venézia *Italy* 45°27N 12°21E **22** B5
Venice *U.S.A.* 27°6N 82°27W **85** H13
Venkatapuram *India* 18°20N 80°30E **41** K12
Venlo *Neths.* 51°22N 6°11E **15** C6
Vennachar Junction
  Canada 45°5N 77°14W **82** A7
Vennesla *Norway* 58°15N 7°59E **9** G12
Venray *Neths.* 51°31N 6°0E **15** C6
Ventana, Punta de la
  Mexico 24°4N 109°48W **86** C3
Ventana, Sa. de la
  Argentina 38°0S 62°30W **94** D3
Ventersburg *S. Africa* 28°7S 27°9E **56** D4
Venterstad *S. Africa* 30°47S 25°48E **56** E4
Ventnor *U.K.* 50°36N 1°12W **13** G6
Ventoténe *Italy* 40°47N 13°25E **22** D5
Ventoux, Mt. *France* 44°10N 5°17E **20** D6
Ventspils *Latvia* 57°25N 21°32E **9** H19
Ventuari ⇨ *Venezuela* 3°58N 67°2W **92** C5
Ventucopa *U.S.A.* 34°50N 119°29W **79** L7
Ventura *U.S.A.* 34°17N 119°18W **79** L7
Vénus, Pte. *Tahiti* 17°29S 149°29W **59** d
Venus B. *Australia* 38°40S 145°42E **63** F4
Venustiano Carranza
  Mexico 16°15N 115°53W **86** A1
Vera *Argentina* 29°30S 60°20W **94** B3
Vera *Spain* 37°15N 1°51W **21** D5
Veracruz *Mexico* 19°11N 96°8W **87** D5
Veracruz □ *Mexico* 19°0N 96°15W **87** D5
Veraval *India* 20°53N 70°27E **42** J4
Verbánia *Italy* 45°56N 8°33E **20** D8
Vercelli *Italy* 45°19N 8°25E **20** D8
Verdalsøra *Norway* 63°48N 11°30E **8** E14
Verde ⇨ *Argentina* 41°56N 65°5W **96** E3
Verde ⇨ *Goiás, Brazil* 18°1S 50°14W **93** G8
Verde ⇨ *Mato Grosso do Sul,*
  Brazil 21°25S 52°20W **93** H8
Verde ⇨ *Chihuahua,*
  Mexico 26°29N 107°58W **86** B3
Verde ⇨ *Oaxaca, Mexico* 15°59N 97°50W **87** D5
Verde ⇨ *Veracruz,*
  Mexico 21°10N 102°50W **86** C4
Verde ⇨ *Paraguay* 23°9S 57°37W **94** A4
Verde ⇨ *U.S.A.* 33°33N 111°40W **74** J17
Verde, Cay *Bahamas* 23°0N 75°5W **88** B4
Verden *Germany* 52°55N 9°14E **16** B5
Verdi *U.S.A.* 39°31N 119°59W **78** F7
Verdun *France* 49°9N 5°24E **20** B6
Vereeniging *S. Africa* 26°38S 27°57E **57** D4
Verga, C. *Guinea* 10°30N 14°10W **50** F3
Vergemont Cr. ⇨
  Australia 24°16S 143°16E **62** C3
Vergennes *U.S.A.* 44°10N 73°15W **83** B11
Veria *Greece* 40°34N 22°12E **23** D10
Verín *Spain* 41°57N 7°27W **21** B2
Verkhnetulomskoye Vdkhr.
  Russia 68°36N 31°12E **8** B24
Verkhnevilyuysk
  Russia 63°27N 120°18E **29** C13
Verkhniy Baskunchak
  Russia 48°14N 46°44E **19** E8
Verkhoyansk *Russia* 67°35N 133°25E **29** C14
Verkhoyansk Ra. =
  Verkhoyanskiy Khrebet
  Russia 66°0N 129°0E **29** C13
Verkhoyanskiy Khrebet
  Russia 66°0N 129°0E **29** C13
Vermilion *Canada* 53°20N 110°50W **71** C6
Vermilion *U.S.A.* 41°25N 82°22W **82** E2
Vermilion ⇨ *Canada* 53°22N 110°51W **71** C6
Vermilion B. *U.S.A.* 29°42N 92°0W **84** G9
Vermilion Bay *Canada* 49°51N 93°34W **71** D10
Vermilion L. *U.S.A.* 47°53N 92°26W **80** B7
Vermillion ⇨ *Canada* 47°38N 72°56W **72** C5
Vermont □ *U.S.A.* 44°0N 73°0W **83** C12

Vernadsky *Antarctica* 65°0S 64°0W **5** C17
Vernal *U.S.A.* 40°27N 109°32W **76** F9
Vernalis *U.S.A.* 37°36N 121°17W **78** H5
Verner *Canada* 46°25N 80°8W **72** C3
Verneukpan *S. Africa* 30°0S 21°0E **56** E3
Vernon *Canada* 50°20N 119°15W **70** C5
Vernon *U.S.A.* 34°9N 99°17W **84** D5
Vernonia *U.S.A.* 45°52N 123°11W **78** D2
Vero Beach *U.S.A.* 27°38N 80°24W **85** H14
Véroia = Veria *Greece* 40°34N 22°12E **23** D10
Verona *Canada* 44°29N 76°42W **83** B8
Verona *Italy* 45°27N 10°59E **22** B4
Versailles *France* 48°48N 2°7E **20** B5
Vert, C. *Senegal* 14°45N 17°30W **50** F2
Verulam *S. Africa* 29°38S 31°2E **57** D5
Verviers *Belgium* 50°37N 5°52E **15** D5
Veselovskoye Vdkhr.
Russia 46°58N 41°25E **19** E7
Vesoul *France* 47°40N 6°11E **20** C7
Vesterålen *Norway* 68°45N 15°0E **8** B16
Vestfjorden *Norway* 67°55N 14°0E **8** C16
Vestmannaeyjar *Iceland* 63°27N 20°15W **8** E3
Vestspitsbergen *Svalbard* 78°40N 17°0E **4** B8
Vestvågøya *Norway* 68°18N 13°50E **8** B15
Vesuvio *Italy* 40°49N 14°26E **22** D6
Vesuvius, Mt. = Vesuvio
Italy 40°49N 14°26E **22** D6
Veszprém *Hungary* 47°8N 17°57E **17** E9
Vetlanda *Sweden* 57°24N 15°3E **9** H16
Vetlugu ➤ *Russia* 56°36N 46°4E **18** C8
Vettore, Mte. *Italy* 42°49N 13°16E **22** C5
Veurne *Belgium* 51°5N 2°40E **15** C2
Veys *Iran* 31°30N 49°0E **45** D6
Vezhen *Bulgaria* 42°50N 24°20E **23** C11
Vi Thanh *Vietnam* 9°42N 105°26E **39** H5
Viacha *Bolivia* 16°39S 68°18W **92** G5
Viamão *Brazil* 30°5S 51°0W **95** C5
Viana *Brazil* 3°13S 44°55W **93** D10
Viana do Alentejo
Portugal 38°17N 7°59W **21** C2
Viana do Castelo *Portugal* 41°42N 8°50W **21** B1
Vianden *Lux.* 49°56N 6°12E **15** E6
Viangchan = Vientiane
Laos 17°58N 102°36E **38** D4
Vianópolis *Brazil* 16°40S 48°35W **93** G9
Vianos *Greece* 35°2N 25°21E **25** D7
Viaréggio *Italy* 43°52N 10°14E **22** C4
Vibo Valéntia *Italy* 38°40N 16°6E **22** E7
Viborg *Denmark* 56°27N 9°23E **9** H13
Vic *Spain* 41°58N 2°19E **21** B7
Vicenza *Italy* 45°33N 11°33E **22** B4
Vich = Vic *Spain* 41°58N 2°19E **21** B7
Vichada ➤ *Colombia* 4°55N 67°50W **92** C5
Vichy *France* 46°9N 3°26E **20** C5
Vicksburg *Ariz.,*
U.S.A. 33°45N 113°45W **79** M13
Vicksburg *Miss., U.S.A.* 32°21N 90°53W **85** J9
Victor *India* 21°0N 71°30E **42** J4
Victor Harbor *Australia* 35°30S 138°37E **63** F2
Victoria *Argentina* 32°40S 60°10W **94** C3
Victoria *Canada* 48°30N 123°25W **78** B3
Victoria *Chile* 38°13S 72°20W **96** D2
Victoria *China* 22°17N 114°9E **33** G1
Victoria *Malta* 36°3N 14°14E **25** C1
Victoria *Seychelles* 4°38S 55°28E **53** b
Victoria *Kans., U.S.A.* 38°52N 99°9W **80** F4
Victoria *Tex., U.S.A.* 28°48N 97°0W **84** G6
Victoria □ *Australia* 37°0S 144°0E **63** F3
Victoria ➤ *Australia* 15°10S 129°40E **60** C4
Victoria, Grand L.
Canada 47°31N 77°30W **72** C4
Victoria, L. *Africa* 1°0S 33°0E **54** C3
Victoria, L. *Australia* 33°57S 141°15E **63** E3
Victoria, Mt. *Burma* 21°14N 93°55E **41** J18
Victoria Beach *Canada* 50°40N 96°35W **71** C9
Victoria de Durango = Durango
Mexico 24°3N 104°39W **86** C4
Victoria de las Tunas = Las Tunas
Cuba 20°58N 76°59W **88** B4
Victoria Falls *Zimbabwe* 17°58S 25°52E **55** F2
Victoria Harbour
Canada 44°45N 79°45W **82** B5
Victoria I. *Canada* 71°0N 111°0W **68** D9
Victoria L. *Canada* 48°20N 57°27W **73** C8
Victoria Ld. *Antarctica* 75°0S 160°0E **5** D11
Victoria Nile ➤ *Uganda* 2°14N 31°26E **54** B3
Victoria Pk. *Belize* 16°48N 88°37W **87** D7
Victoria River *Australia* 15°12S 131°0E **60** C5
Victoria Str. *Canada* 69°31N 100°30W **68** D11
Victoria West *S. Africa* 31°25S 23°4E **56** E3
Victoriaville *Canada* 46°4N 71°56W **73** C5
Victorica *Argentina* 36°20S 65°30W **94** D2
Victorville *U.S.A.* 34°32N 117°18W **79** L9
Vicuña *Chile* 30°0S 70°50W **94** C1
Vicuña Mackenna
Argentina 33°53S 64°25W **94** C3
Vidal *U.S.A.* 34°7N 114°31W **79** L12
Vidalia *U.S.A.* 32°13N 82°25W **85** E13
Vidin *Bulgaria* 43°59N 22°50E **23** C10
Vidisha *India* 23°28N 77°53E **42** H7
Vidos *Greece* 39°38N 19°55E **25** A3
Vidzy *Belarus* 55°23N 26°37E **9** J22
Viedma *Argentina* 40°50S 63°0W **96** E4
Viedma, L. *Argentina* 49°30S 72°30W **96** F2
Vielsalm *Belgium* 50°17N 5°54E **15** D5
Vieng Pou Kha *Laos* 20°41N 101°4E **38** B3
Vienna = Wien *Austria* 48°12N 16°22E **16** D9
Vienna *Canada* 42°41N 80°48W **82** D4
Vienna *Ill., U.S.A.* 37°25N 88°54W **80** G9
Vienna *Mo., U.S.A.* 38°11N 91°57W **80** F8
Vienne *France* 45°31N 4°53E **20** D6
Vienne ➤ *France* 47°13N 0°5E **20** C4
Vientiane *Laos* 17°58N 102°36E **38** D4
Vientos, Paso de los
Caribbean 20°0N 74°0W **89** C5
Vieques *Puerto Rico* 18°8N 65°25W **89** d
Vierge Pt. *St. Lucia* 13°49N 60°53W **89** f
Vierzon *France* 47°13N 2°5E **20** C5
Viet Tri *Vietnam* 21°18N 105°25E **38** B5

Vietnam ■ *Asia* 19°0N 106°0E **38** C6
Vieux Fort *St. Lucia* 13°46N 60°58W **89** f
Vigan *Phil.* 17°35N 120°28E **37** A6
Vigévano *Italy* 45°19N 8°51E **20** D8
Vigia *Brazil* 0°50S 48°5W **93** D9
Vigía Chico *Mexico* 19°46N 87°35W **87** D7
Víglas, Ákra *Greece* 35°54N 27°51E **25** D9
Vigo *Spain* 42°12N 8°41W **21** A1
Vihowa *Pakistan* 31°8N 70°30E **42** D4
Vihowa ➤ *Pakistan* 31°8N 70°41E **42** D4
Vijayawada *India* 16°31N 80°39E **41** L12
Vijosë ➤ *Albania* 40°37N 19°24E **23** D8
Vík *Iceland* 63°25N 19°1W **8** E4
Vikeke = Viqueque
E. Timor 8°52S 126°23E **37** F7
Viking *Canada* 53°7N 111°50W **70** C6
Vikna *Norway* 64°55N 10°58E **8** D14
Vila da Maganja *Mozam.* 17°18S 37°30E **55** F4
Vila da Ribeira Brava
C. Verde Is. 16°32N 24°25W **50** b
Vila do Bispo *Portugal* 37°5N 8°53W **21** D1
Vila Franca de Xira
Portugal 38°57N 8°59W **21** C1
Vila Gamito *Mozam.* 14°12S 33°0E **55** E3
Vila Gomes da Costa
Mozam. 24°20S 33°37E **57** C5
Vila Machado *Mozam.* 19°15S 34°14E **55** F3
Vila Mouzinho *Mozam.* 14°48S 34°25E **55** E3
Vila Nova de Gaia *Portugal* 41°8N 8°37W **21** B1
Vila Real *Portugal* 41°17N 7°48W **21** B2
Vila-Real *Spain* 39°55N 0°3W **21** C5
Vila Real de Santo António
Portugal 37°10N 7°28W **21** D2
Vila Vasco da Gama
Mozam. 14°54S 32°14E **55** E3
Vila Velha *Brazil* 20°20S 40°17W **95** A7
Vilagarcía de Arousa
Spain 42°34N 8°46W **21** A1
Vilaine ➤ *France* 47°30N 2°27W **20** C2
Vilanandro, Tanjona
Madag. 16°11S 44°27E **57** B7
Vilanculos *Mozam.* 22°1S 35°17E **57** C6
Vilanova i la Geltrú *Spain* 41°13N 1°40E **21** B6
Vileyka *Belarus* 54°30N 26°53E **17** A14
Vilhelmina *Sweden* 64°35N 16°39E **8** D17
Vilhena *Brazil* 12°40S 60°5W **92** F6
Viliya = Neris ➤
Lithuania 55°8N 24°16E **9** J21
Viljandi *Estonia* 58°28N 25°30E **9** G21
Vilkitskogo, Proliv
Russia 78°0N 103°0E **29** B11
Vilkovo = Vylkove
Ukraine 45°28N 29°32E **17** F15
Villa Abecia *Bolivia* 21°0S 68°18W **94** A2
Villa Ana *Argentina* 28°28S 59°40W **94** B4
Villa Ángela *Argentina* 27°34S 60°45W **94** B3
Villa Bella *Bolivia* 10°25S 65°22W **92** F5
Villa Cañás *Argentina* 34°0S 61°35W **94** C3
Villa Constitución
Argentina 33°15S 60°20W **94** C3
Villa de Arriaga *Mexico* 21°56N 101°20W **86** C4
Villa de María *Argentina* 29°55S 63°43W **94** B3
Villa de Méndez *Mexico* 25°7N 98°34W **87** B5
Villa Dolores *Argentina* 31°58S 65°15W **94** C2
Villa Frontera *Mexico* 26°56N 101°27W **86** B4
Villa Gesell *Argentina* 37°15S 56°55W **94** D4
Villa Guillermina
Argentina 28°15S 59°29W **94** B4
Villa Hayes *Paraguay* 25°5S 57°20W **94** B4
Villa Hidalgo *Mexico* 24°15N 99°26W **87** C5
Villa Iris *Argentina* 38°12S 63°12W **94** D3
Villa María *Argentina* 32°20S 63°10W **94** C3
Villa Mazán *Argentina* 28°40S 66°30W **94** B2
Villa Montes *Bolivia* 21°10S 63°30W **94** A3
Villa Ocampo *Argentina* 28°30S 59°20W **94** B4
Villa Ocampo *Mexico* 26°27N 105°31W **86** B3
Villa Ojo de Agua
Argentina 29°30S 63°44W **94** B3
Villa San Martín
Argentina 28°15S 64°9W **94** B3
Villa Unión *Mexico* 23°12N 106°14W **86** C3
Villacarlos *Spain* 39°53N 4°17E **24** B11
Villacarrillo *Spain* 38°7N 3°3W **21** C4
Villach *Austria* 46°37N 13°51E **16** E7
Villafranca de Bonany
Spain 39°34N 3°5E **24** B10
Villagrán *Mexico* 24°29N 99°29W **87** C5
Villaguay *Argentina* 32°0S 59°0W **94** C4
Villahermosa *Mexico* 17°59N 92°55W **87** D6
Villajoyosa *Spain* 38°30N 0°12W **21** C5
Villalba *Spain* 43°26N 7°40W **21** A2
Villanueva *U.S.A.* 35°16N 105°22W **77** J11
Villanueva de la Serena
Spain 38°59N 5°50W **21** C3
Villanueva y Geltrú = Vilanova i
la Geltrú *Spain* 41°13N 1°40E **21** B6
Villarreal = Vila-Real
Spain 39°55N 0°3W **21** C5
Villarrica *Chile* 39°15S 72°15W **96** D2
Villarrica *Paraguay* 25°40S 56°30W **94** B4
Villarrobledo *Spain* 39°18N 2°36W **21** C4
Villavicencio *Argentina* 32°28S 69°0W **94** C2
Villavicencio *Colombia* 4°9N 73°37W **92** C4
Villaviciosa *Spain* 43°32N 5°27W **21** A3
Villazón *Bolivia* 22°0S 65°35W **94** A2
Ville-Marie *Canada* 47°20N 79°30W **72** C4
Ville Platte *U.S.A.* 30°41N 92°17W **84** F8
Villena *Spain* 38°39N 0°52W **21** C5
Villeneuve-d'Ascq *France* 50°38N 3°9E **20** A5
Villeneuve-sur-Lot *France* 44°24N 0°42E **20** D4
Villiers *S. Africa* 27°2S 28°36E **57** D4
Villingen-Schwenningen
Germany 48°3N 8°26E **16** D5
Villmanstrand = Lappeenranta
Finland 61°3N 28°12E **8** F23
Vilnius *Lithuania* 54°38N 25°19E **9** J21
Vilvoorde *Belgium* 50°56N 4°26E **15** D4

Vilyuchinsk *Russia* 52°55N 158°24E **29** D16
Vilyuy ➤ *Russia* 64°24N 126°26E **29** C13
Vilyuysk *Russia* 63°40N 121°35E **29** C13
Viña del Mar *Chile* 33°0S 71°30W **94** C1
Vinarós *Spain* 40°30N 0°27E **21** B6
Vincennes *U.S.A.* 38°41N 87°32W **80** F10
Vincennes Bay *S. Ocean* 66°0S 109°0E **5** C8
Vincent *U.S.A.* 34°33N 118°11W **79** L8
Vinchina *Argentina* 28°45S 68°15W **94** B2
Vindelälven ➤ *Sweden* 63°55N 19°50E **8** E18
Vindeln *Sweden* 64°12N 19°43E **8** D18
Vindhya Ra. *India* 22°50N 77°0E **42** H7
Vineland *U.S.A.* 39°29N 75°2W **81** F16
Vinh *Vietnam* 18°45N 105°38E **38** C5
Vinh Linh *Vietnam* 17°4N 107°2E **38** D6
Vinh Long *Vietnam* 10°16N 105°57E **39** G5
Vinh Yen *Vietnam* 21°21N 105°35E **38** B5
Vinita *U.S.A.* 36°39N 95°9W **84** C7
Vinkovci *Croatia* 45°19N 18°48E **23** B8
Vinnitsa = Vinnytsya
Ukraine 49°15N 28°30E **17** D15
Vinnytsya *Ukraine* 49°15N 28°30E **17** D15
Vinson Massif *Antarctica* 78°35S 85°25W **5** D16
Vinton *Calif., U.S.A.* 39°48N 120°10W **78** F6
Vinton *Iowa, U.S.A.* 42°10N 92°1W **80** D7
Vinton *La., U.S.A.* 30°11N 93°35W **84** F8
Violet Valley ☉
Australia 17°10S 127°55E **60** C4
Viqueque *E. Timor* 8°52S 126°23E **37** F7
Virac *Phil.* 13°30N 124°20E **37** B6
Virachey *Cambodia* 13°59N 106°49E **38** F6
Virachey △ *Cambodia* 14°14N 106°55E **38** E6
Virago Sd. *Canada* 54°0N 132°30W **70** C2
Viramgam *India* 23°5N 72°0E **42** H5
Viranşehir *Turkey* 37°13N 39°45E **44** B3
Virawah *Pakistan* 24°31N 70°46E **42** G4
Virden *Canada* 49°50N 100°56W **71** D8
Vire *France* 48°50N 0°53W **20** B3
Vírgenes, C. *Argentina* 52°19S 68°21W **96** G3
Virgin ➤ *U.S.A.* 36°28N 114°21W **77** H6
Virgin Gorda *Br. Virgin Is.* 18°30N 64°26W **89** e
Virgin Is. (British) ☑
W. Indies 18°30N 64°30W **89** e
Virgin Is. (U.S.) ☑
W. Indies 18°20N 65°0W **89** e
Virgin Islands △
U.S. Virgin Is. 18°21N 64°43W **89** C7
Virginia *S. Africa* 28°8S 26°55E **56** D4
Virginia *U.S.A.* 47°31N 92°32W **80** B7
Virginia □ *U.S.A.* 37°30N 78°45W **81** G14
Virginia Beach *U.S.A.* 36°49N 76°9W **81** F16
Virginia City *Mont.,*
U.S.A. 45°18N 111°56W **76** D8
Virginia City *Nev.,*
U.S.A. 39°19N 119°39W **78** F7
Virginia Falls *Canada* 61°38N 125°42W **70** A3
Virginiatown *Canada* 48°9N 79°36W **72** C4
Viroqua *U.S.A.* 43°34N 90°53W **80** D8
Virovitica *Croatia* 45°51N 17°21E **22** B7
Virpur *India* 21°51N 70°42E **42** J4
Virton *Belgium* 49°35N 5°32E **15** E5
Virudunagar *India* 9°30N 77°58E **40** Q10
Virunga △
Dem. Rep. of the Congo 0°5N 29°38E **54** B2
Vis *Croatia* 43°4N 16°10E **22** C7
Visalia *U.S.A.* 36°20N 119°18W **78** J7
Visayan Sea *Phil.* 11°30N 123°30E **37** B6
Visby *Sweden* 57°37N 18°18E **9** H18
Viscount Melville Sd.
Canada 74°10N 108°0W **69** C10
Visé *Belgium* 50°44N 5°41E **15** D5
Vise, Ostrov *Russia* 79°33N 76°50E **28** B8
Višegrad *Bos.-H.* 43°47N 19°17E **23** C8
Viseu *Brazil* 1°10S 46°5W **93** D9
Viseu *Portugal* 40°40N 7°55W **21** B2
Vishakhapatnam *India* 17°45N 83°20E **41** L13
Visnagar *India* 23°45N 72°32E **42** H5
Viso, Mte. *Italy* 44°38N 7°5E **20** D7
Visokoi I. *Antarctica* 56°43S 27°15W **5** M9
Vista *U.S.A.* 33°12N 117°14W **79** M9
Vistula = Wisła ➤
Poland 54°22N 18°55E **17** A10
Vitebsk = Vitsyebsk
Belarus 55°10N 30°15E **18** C5
Viterbo *Italy* 42°25N 12°6E **22** C5
Viti Levu *Fiji* 17°30S 177°30E **59** a
Vitigudino *Spain* 41°1N 6°26W **21** B2
Vitim *Russia* 59°28N 112°35E **29** D12
Vitim ➤ *Russia* 59°26N 112°34E **29** D12
Vitória *Brazil* 20°20S 40°22W **93** H10
Vitória da Conquista
Brazil 14°51S 40°51W **93** F10
Vitória de Santo Antão
Brazil 8°10S 35°20W **93** E11
Vitoria-Gasteiz *Spain* 42°50N 2°41W **21** A4
Vitsyebsk *Belarus* 55°10N 30°15E **18** C5
Vittória *Italy* 36°57N 14°32E **22** F6
Vittório Véneto *Italy* 45°59N 12°18E **22** B5
Viveiro *Spain* 43°39N 7°38W **21** A2
Vivian *U.S.A.* 32°53N 93°59W **84** E8
Viwa *Fiji* 17°10S 177°58E **59** a

Vogelkop = Doberai, Jazirah
Indonesia 1°25S 133°0E **37** E8
Vogelsberg *Germany* 50°31N 9°12E **16** C5
Voghera *Italy* 44°59N 9°1E **20** D8
Vohibinany *Madag.* 18°49S 49°4E **57** B8
Vohilava *Madag.* 21°4S 48°0E **57** C8
Vohimarina = Iharana
Madag. 13°25S 50°0E **57** A9
Vohimena, Tanjon' i
Madag. 25°36S 45°8E **57** D8
Vohipeno *Madag.* 22°22S 47°51E **57** C8
Voi *Kenya* 3°25S 38°32E **54** C4
Voiron *France* 45°22N 5°35E **20** D6
Voisey B. *Canada* 56°15N 61°50W **73** A7
Vojmsjön *Sweden* 65°0N 16°24E **8** D17
Vojvodina □ *Serbia* 45°20N 20°0E **23** B9
Volborg *U.S.A.* 45°51N 105°41W **76** D11
Volcán de Colima △
Mexico 19°30N 103°40W **86** D4
Volcano Is. = Kazan-Rettō
Pac. Oc. 25°0N 141°0E **64** E6
Volcans △ *Rwanda* 1°30S 29°26E **54** C2
Volda *Norway* 62°9N 6°5E **8** E12
Volga = Privolzhskiy □
Russia 56°0N 50°0E **28** D6
Volga ➤ *Russia* 46°0N 48°30E **19** E8
Volga Hts. = Privolzhskaya
Vozvyshennost *Russia* 51°0N 46°0E **19** D8
Volgodonsk *Russia* 47°33N 42°5E **19** E7
Volgograd *Russia* 48°40N 44°25E **19** E7
Volgogradskoye Vdkhr.
Russia 50°0N 45°20E **19** D8
Volkhov ➤ *Russia* 60°8N 32°20E **18** B5
Volkovysk = Vawkavysk
Belarus 53°9N 24°30E **17** B13
Volksrust *S. Africa* 27°24S 29°53E **57** D4
Volochanka *Russia* 71°0N 94°28E **29** B10
Volodymyr-Volynskyy
Ukraine 50°50N 24°18E **17** C13
Vologda *Russia* 59°10N 39°45E **18** C6
Volos *Greece* 39°24N 22°59E **23** E10
Volosovo *Russia* 59°27N 29°32E **9** G23
Volovets *Ukraine* 48°43N 23°11E **17** D12
Volozhin = Valozhyn
Belarus 54°3N 26°30E **17** A14
Volsk *Russia* 52°5N 47°22E **18** D8
Volta ➤ *Ghana* 5°46N 0°41E **48** F4
Volta, L. *Ghana* 7°30N 0°0 **50** G6
Volta Redonda *Brazil* 22°31S 44°5W **95** A7
Voltaire, C. *Australia* 14°16S 125°35E **60** B4
Volterra *Italy* 43°24N 10°51E **22** C4
Volturno ➤ *Italy* 41°1N 13°55E **22** D5
Volzhskiy *Russia* 48°56N 44°46E **19** E7
Vomo *Fiji* 17°30S 177°15E **59** a
Vondrozo *Madag.* 22°49S 47°20E **57** C8
Vopnafjörður *Iceland* 65°45N 14°50W **8** D6
Vorkuta *Russia* 67°48N 64°20E **18** A11
Vormsi *Estonia* 59°1N 23°13E **9** G20
Voronezh *Russia* 51°40N 39°10E **19** D6
Võrts Järv *Estonia* 58°16N 26°3E **9** G22
Võru *Estonia* 57°48N 26°54E **9** H22
Vosges *France* 48°20N 7°10E **20** B7
Voss *Norway* 60°38N 6°26E **8** F12
Vostok *Antarctica* 78°30S 106°50E **5** D8
Vostok I. *Kiribati* 10°5S 152°23W **65** J12
Votkinsk *Russia* 57°0N 53°55E **18** C9
Votkinskoye Vdkhr.
Russia 57°22N 55°12E **18** C10
Votsuri-Shima *Japan* 25°45N 123°29E **31** M1
Vouga ➤ *Portugal* 40°41N 8°40W **21** B1
Vouxa, Ákra *Greece* 35°37N 23°32E **25** D5
Voyageurs △ *U.S.A.* 48°32N 93°0W **80** A7
Voynitsa *Russia* 65°10N 30°20E **8** D24
Voyvozh *Russia* 62°56N 54°56E **18** B10
Vozhe, Ozero *Russia* 60°45N 39°0E **18** B6
Voznesensk *Ukraine* 47°35N 31°21E **19** E5
Voznesenye *Russia* 61°0N 35°28E **18** B6
Vrangel *Russia* 42°43N 133°5E **30** C6
Vrangelya, Ostrov
Russia 71°0N 180°0E **29** B18
Vranje *Serbia* 42°34N 21°54E **23** C9
Vratsa *Bulgaria* 43°15N 23°30E **23** C10
Vrbas ➤ *Bos.-H.* 45°8N 17°29E **22** B7
Vrede *S. Africa* 27°24S 29°6E **57** D4
Vredefort *S. Africa* 27°0S 27°22E **56** D4
Vredenburg *S. Africa* 32°56S 18°0E **56** E2
Vredendal *S. Africa* 31°41S 18°35E **56** E2
Vrindavan *India* 27°37N 77°40E **42** F7
Vrsses *Greece* 35°23N 24°13E **25** D6
Vršac *Serbia* 45°8N 21°30E **23** B9
Vryburg *S. Africa* 26°55S 24°45E **56** D3
Vryheid *S. Africa* 27°45S 30°47E **57** D5
Vu Liet *Vietnam* 18°43N 105°23E **38** C5
Vukovar *Croatia* 45°21N 18°59E **23** B8
Vuktyl *Russia* 63°52N 57°20E **28** C6
Vulcan *Canada* 50°25N 113°15W **70** C6
Vulcan *Romania* 45°23N 23°17E **17** F12
Vulcanești *Moldova* 45°41N 28°18E **17** F15
Vulcano *Italy* 38°24N 14°58E **22** E6
Vulkanesthy = Vulcanești
Moldova 45°41N 28°18E **17** F15
Vunduzi ➤ *Mozam.* 18°56S 34°1E **55** F3
Vung Tau *Vietnam* 10°21N 107°4E **39** G6
Vunisea *Fiji* 19°3S 178°10E **59** a
Vwaza △ *Malawi* 10°58S 33°25E **55** E3
Vyartsilya *Russia* 62°8N 30°45E **8** E24
Vyatka = Kirov *Russia* 58°35N 49°40E **18** C8
Vyatka ➤ *Russia* 55°37N 51°28E **18** C9
Vyatskiye Polyany *Russia* 56°14N 51°5E **18** C9
Vyazemskiy *Russia* 47°32N 134°45E **29** E14
Vyazma *Russia* 55°10N 34°15E **18** C5
Vyborg *Russia* 60°43N 28°47E **8** F23
Vychegda ➤ *Russia* 61°18N 46°36E **18** B8
Vychodné Beskydy
Europe 49°20N 22°0E **17** D11
Vyg-ozero *Russia* 63°47N 34°29E **18** B5
Vylkove *Ukraine* 45°28N 29°32E **17** F15
Vynohradiv *Ukraine* 48°9N 23°2E **17** D12
Vyrnwy, L. *U.K.* 52°48N 3°31W **12** E4
Vyshniy Volochek
Russia 57°30N 34°30E **18** C5
Vyshzha = imeni 26 Bakinskikh
Komissarov
Turkmenistan 39°22N 54°10E **45** B7
Vyškov *Czech Rep.* 49°17N 17°0E **17** D9
Vytegra *Russia* 61°0N 36°27E **18** B6

W

W.A.C. Bennett Dam
Canada 56°2N 122°6W **70** B4
Wa *Ghana* 10°7N 2°25W **50** F5
Waal ➤ *Neths.* 51°37N 5°0E **15** C5
Waalwijk *Neths.* 51°42N 5°4E **15** C5
Waanyi-Garawa ☉
Australia 18°2S 137°33E **62** B2
Wabakimi △ *Canada* 50°43N 89°29W **72** B2
Wabana *Canada* 47°40N 53°0W **73** C9
Wabasca-Desmarais
Canada 55°57N 113°56W **70** B6
Wabash *U.S.A.* 40°48N 85°49W **81** E11
Wabash ➤ *U.S.A.* 37°48N 88°2W **80** G9
Wabigoon L. *Canada* 49°44N 92°44W **71** D10
Wabowden *Canada* 54°55N 98°38W **71** C9
Wabuk Pt. *Canada* 55°20N 85°5W **72** A2
Wabush *Canada* 52°55N 66°52W **73** B6
Waco *U.S.A.* 31°33N 97°9W **84** F6
Waconichi, L. *Canada* 50°8N 74°0W **72** B5
Wad Hamid *Sudan* 16°30N 32°45E **51** E12
Wad Thana *Pakistan* 27°22N 66°23E **42** F2
Wad Medanî *Sudan* 14°28N 33°30E **51** F12
Wadai *Africa* 12°0N 19°0E **48** E5
Wadayama *Japan* 35°19N 134°52E **31** G7
Waddeneilanden *Neths.* 53°25N 5°10E **15** A5
Waddenzee *Neths.* 53°6N 5°10E **15** A5
Waddington *U.S.A.* 44°52N 75°12W **83** B9
Waddington, Mt.
Canada 51°23N 125°15W **70** C3
Waddy Pt. *Australia* 24°58S 153°21E **63** C5
Wadebridge *U.K.* 50°31N 4°51E **13** G3
Wadena *Canada* 51°57N 103°47W **71** C8
Wadena *U.S.A.* 46°26N 95°8W **80** B6
Wadeye *Australia* 14°28S 129°52E **60** B4
Wadhams *Canada* 51°30N 127°30W **70** C3
Wādī as Sīr *Jordan* 31°56N 35°49E **46** D4
Wadi Halfa *Sudan* 21°53N 31°19E **51** D12
Wadi Rum △ *Jordan* 29°30S 35°20E **46** F4
Wadsworth *Nev.,*
U.S.A. 39°38N 119°17W **76** G4
Wadsworth *Ohio, U.S.A.* 41°2N 81°44W **82** E3
Waegwan *S. Korea* 35°59N 128°23E **35** G15
Wafangdian *China* 39°38N 121°58E **35** E11
Wafrah *Kuwait* 28°33N 47°56E **44** D5
Wagait ☉ *Australia* 13°1S 130°5E **60** B5
Wageningen *Neths.* 51°58N 5°40E **15** C5
Wager B. *Canada* 65°26N 88°40W **69** D14
Wagga Wagga *Australia* 35°7S 147°24E **63** F4
Waghete *Indonesia* 4°10S 136°50E **37** E9
Wagin *Australia* 33°17S 117°25E **61** F2
Wagner *U.S.A.* 43°5N 98°18W **80** D4
Wagon Mound *U.S.A.* 36°1N 104°42W **77** H11
Wagoner *U.S.A.* 35°58N 95°22W **84** D7
Wah *Pakistan* 33°45N 72°40E **42** C5
Wahai *Indonesia* 2°48S 129°35E **37** E7
Wâhid *Egypt* 30°48N 32°21E **46** E1
Wahnai *Afghan.* 32°40N 65°50E **42** C1
Wahoo *U.S.A.* 41°13N 96°37W **80** E5
Wahpeton *U.S.A.* 46°16N 96°36W **80** B5
Waialua *N.Z.* 21°34N 158°8W **75** L8
Waiau ➤ *N.Z.* 42°47S 173°22E **59** E4
Waibeem *Indonesia* 0°30S 132°59E **37** E8
Waigeo *Indonesia* 0°20S 130°40E **37** E8
Waihi *N.Z.* 37°23S 175°52E **59** B5
Waihou ➤ *N.Z.* 37°15S 175°40E **59** B5
Waika
Dem. Rep. of the Congo 2°22S 25°42E **54** C2
Waikabubak *Indonesia* 9°45S 119°25E **37** F5
Waikaremoana, L. *N.Z.* 38°49S 177°9E **59** C6
Waikari *N.Z.* 42°58S 172°41E **59** E4
Waikato ➤ *N.Z.* 37°23S 174°43E **59** B5
Waikelo *Indonesia* 9°24S 119°19E **60** A2
Waikokopu *N.Z.* 39°3S 177°52E **59** C6
Waikouaiti *N.Z.* 45°36S 170°41E **59** F3
Wailingding Dao *China* 22°6N 114°2E **33** G11
Waimakariri ➤ *N.Z.* 43°24S 172°42E **59** E4
Waimate *N.Z.* 44°45S 171°3E **59** F3
Wainganga ➤ *India* 18°50N 79°55E **40** K11
Waingapu *Indonesia* 9°35S 120°11E **37** F6
Waini ➤ *Guyana* 8°20N 59°50W **92** B7
Wainwright *Canada* 52°50N 110°50W **71** C6
Waiouru *N.Z.* 39°28S 175°41E **59** C5
Waipara *N.Z.* 43°3S 172°46E **59** E4
Waipawa *N.Z.* 39°56S 176°38E **59** C6
Waipiro *N.Z.* 38°2S 178°22E **59** C7
Waipoua Forest *N.Z.* 35°39S 173°33E **59** A4
Waipu *N.Z.* 35°59S 174°29E **59** A5
Waipukurau *N.Z.* 40°1S 176°33E **59** D6
Wairakei *N.Z.* 38°37S 176°6E **59** C6
Wairarapa, L. *N.Z.* 41°14S 175°15E **59** D5
Wairoa *N.Z.* 39°3S 177°25E **59** C6
Waitaki ➤ *N.Z.* 44°56S 171°7E **59** F3
Waitangi *N.Z.* 35°16S 174°5E **59** A5
Waitara *N.Z.* 38°59S 174°15E **59** C5
Waitomo Caves *N.Z.* 38°16S 175°7E **59** C5
Waitsburg *U.S.A.* 46°16N 118°9W **76** C4
Waiuku *N.Z.* 37°15S 174°45E **59** B5
Wajima *Japan* 37°30N 137°0E **31** F8
Wajir *Kenya* 1°42N 40°5E **54** B5
Wakasa *Japan* 35°20N 134°24E **31** G7
Wakasa-Wan *Japan* 35°40N 135°30E **31** G7
Wakatipu, L. *N.Z.* 45°5S 168°33E **59** F2
Wakaw *Canada* 52°39N 105°44W **71** C7

Wakaya *Fiji* 17°37S 179°0E **59 a**
Wakayama *Japan* 34°15N 135°15E **31 G7**
Wakayama □ *Japan* 33°50N 135°30E **31 H7**
Wake Forest *U.S.A.* 35°59N 78°30W **85 D15**
Wake I. *Pac. Oc.* 19°18N 166°36E **64 F8**
WaKeeney *U.S.A.* 39°1N 99°53W **80 F4**
Wakefield *Jamaica* 18°26N 77°42W **88 a**
Wakefield *N.Z.* 41°24S 173°5E **59 D4**
Wakefield *U.K.* 53°41N 1°29W **12 D6**
Wakefield *Mass., U.S.A.* 42°30N 71°5W **83 D13**
Wakefield *Mich., U.S.A.* 46°29N 89°56W **80 B9**
Wakkanai *Japan* 45°28N 141°35E **30 B10**
Wakkerstroom *S. Africa* 27°24S 30°10E **57 D5**
Wakool *Australia* 35°28S 144°23E **63 F3**
Wakool → *Australia* 35°5S 143°33E **63 F3**
Wakre *Indonesia* 0°19S 131°5E **37 E8**
Wakuach, L. *Canada* 55°34N 67°32W **73 A6**
Walagunya ◊ *Australia* 23°10S 120°50E **60 D3**
Walamba *Zambia* 13°30S 28°42E **55 E2**
Wałbrzych *Poland* 50°45N 16°18E **16 C9**
Walbury Hill *U.K.* 51°21N 1°28W **13 F6**
Walcha *Australia* 30°55S 151°31E **63 E5**
Walcheren *Neths.* 51°30N 3°35E **15 C3**
Walcott *U.S.A.* 41°46N 106°51W **76 F10**
Walcz *Poland* 53°17N 16°27E **16 B9**
Waldburg Ra. *Australia* 24°40S 117°35E **61 D2**
Walden *Colo., U.S.A.* 40°44N 106°17W **76 F10**
Walden *N.Y., U.S.A.* 41°34N 74°11W **83 E10**
Waldport *U.S.A.* 44°26N 124°4W **76 D1**
Waldron *U.S.A.* 34°54N 94°5W **84 D7**
Walebing *Australia* 30°41S 116°13E **61 F2**
Wales □ *U.K.* 52°19N 4°43W **13 E3**
Wales I. *Canada* 68°1N 86°40W **69 D14**
Walgett *Australia* 30°0S 148°5E **63 E4**
Walgreen Coast
  Antarctica 75°15S 105°0W **5 D15**
Walker *U.S.A.* 47°6N 94°35W **80 B6**
Walker, L. *Canada* 50°20N 67°11W **73 B6**
Walker L. *Canada* 54°42N 95°57W **71 C9**
Walker L. *U.S.A.* 38°42N 118°43W **76 G4**
Walkerston *Australia* 21°11S 149°8E **62 b**
Walkerton *Canada* 44°10N 81°10W **82 B3**
Wall *U.S.A.* 44°0N 102°8W **80 C2**
Walla Walla *U.S.A.* 46°4N 118°20W **76 C4**
Wallace *Idaho, U.S.A.* 47°28N 115°56W **76 C6**
Wallace *N.C., U.S.A.* 34°44N 77°59W **85 D16**
Wallaceburg *Canada* 42°34N 82°23W **82 D2**
Wallachia = Valahia
  Romania 44°35N 25°0E **17 F13**
Wallal *Australia* 26°32S 146°7E **63 D4**
Wallam Cr. →
  Australia 28°40S 147°20E **63 D4**
Wallambin, L. *Australia* 30°57S 117°35E **61 F2**
Wallangarra *Australia* 28°56S 151°58E **63 D5**
Wallaroo *Australia* 33°56S 137°39E **63 E2**
Wallenpaupack, L.
  U.S.A. 41°25N 75°15W **83 E9**
Wallingford *Conn.,*
  U.S.A. 41°27N 72°50W **83 E12**
Wallingford *Vt., U.S.A.* 43°28N 72°58W **83 C12**
Wallis & Futuna, Is.
  Pac. Oc. 13°18S 176°10W **58 C11**
Wallowa *U.S.A.* 45°34N 117°32W **76 D5**
Wallowa Mts. *U.S.A.* 45°20N 117°30W **76 D5**
Walls *U.K.* 60°14N 1°33W **11 A7**
Walls of Jerusalem △
  Australia 41°56S 146°15E **63 G4**
Wallula *U.S.A.* 46°5N 118°54W **76 C4**
Wallumbilla *Australia* 26°33S 149°9E **63 D4**
Walmsley L. *Canada* 63°25N 108°36W **71 A7**
Walney, I. of *U.K.* 54°6N 3°15W **12 C4**
Walnut Canyon △
  U.S.A. 35°15N 111°20W **77 J8**
Walnut Creek *U.S.A.* 37°54N 122°4W **78 H4**
Walnut Ridge *U.S.A.* 36°4N 90°57W **85 C9**
Walpole *Australia* 34°58S 116°44E **61 F2**
Walpole *U.S.A.* 42°9N 71°15W **83 D13**
Walpole-Nornalup △
  Australia 35°0S 116°45E **61 G2**
Walsall *U.K.* 52°35N 1°58W **13 E6**
Walsenburg *U.S.A.* 37°38N 104°47W **77 H11**
Walsh *U.S.A.* 37°23N 102°17W **77 H12**
Walsh → *Australia* 16°31S 143°42E **62 B3**
Walsingham *Canada* 42°40N 80°31W **82 D4**
Walter F. George Res.
  U.S.A. 31°38N 85°4W **85 F12**
Walterboro *U.S.A.* 32°55N 80°40W **85 E14**
Walters *U.S.A.* 34°22N 98°19W **84 D5**
Waltham *U.S.A.* 42°23N 71°14W **83 D13**
Waltman *U.S.A.* 43°4N 107°12W **76 E10**
Walton *U.S.A.* 42°10N 75°8W **83 D9**
Walton-on-the-Naze *U.K.* 51°51N 1°17E **13 F9**
Walvis Bay *Namibia* 23°0S 14°28E **56 C1**
Walvisbaai = Walvis Bay
  Namibia 23°0S 14°28E **56 C1**
Wamba
  Dem. Rep. of the Congo 2°10N 27°57E **54 B2**
Wamba *Kenya* 0°58N 37°19E **54 B4**
Wambardi ◊ *Australia* 16°2S 130°55E **60 C5**
Wamego *U.S.A.* 39°12N 96°18W **80 F5**
Wamena *Indonesia* 4°4S 138°57E **37 E9**
Wampana Karlantijpa ◊
  Australia 17°45S 132°10E **60 C5**
Wampaya ◊ *Australia* 17°20S 135°0E **62 B2**
Wampsville *U.S.A.* 43°4N 75°42W **83 C9**
Wamsutter *U.S.A.* 41°40N 107°58W **76 F10**
Wamulan *Indonesia* 3°27S 126°7E **37 E7**
Wan Xian *China* 38°47N 115°7E **34 E8**
Wana *Pakistan* 32°20N 69°32E **42 C3**
Wanaaring *Australia* 29°38S 144°9E **63 D3**
Wanaka *N.Z.* 44°42S 169°9E **59 F2**
Wanaka, L. *N.Z.* 44°33S 169°7E **59 F2**
Wanapitei L. *Canada* 46°45N 80°40W **72 C3**
Wandel Sea = McKinley Sea
  Arctic 82°0N 0°0 **4 A7**
Wanderer *Zimbabwe* 19°36S 30°1E **55 F3**
Wandhari *Pakistan* 27°42N 66°48E **42 F2**
Wandoan *Australia* 26°5S 149°55E **63 D4**
Wanfu *China* 40°8N 122°38E **35 D12**

Wang → *Thailand* 17°8N 99°2E **38 D2**
Wang Noi *Thailand* 14°13N 100°44E **38 E3**
Wang Saphung
  Thailand 17°18N 101°46E **38 D3**
Wang Thong *Thailand* 16°50N 100°26E **38 D3**
Wanga
  Dem. Rep. of the Congo 2°58N 29°12E **54 B2**
Wangal *Indonesia* 6°8S 134°9E **37 F8**
Wanganella *Australia* 35°6S 144°49E **63 F3**
Wanganui *N.Z.* 39°56S 175°3E **59 C5**
Wangaratta *Australia* 36°21S 146°19E **63 F4**
Wangary *Australia* 34°35S 135°29E **63 E2**
Wangdu *China* 38°40N 115°7E **34 E8**
Wangerooge *Germany* 53°47N 7°54E **16 B4**
Wangiwangi *Indonesia* 5°22S 123°37E **37 F6**
Wangqing *China* 43°12N 129°42E **35 C15**
Wanimiyn → *Australia* 15°55S 130°49E **60 C5**
Wanjina Wunggurr Wilinggin ◊
  Australia 16°0S 127°0E **60 C4**
Wankaner *India* 22°35N 71°0E **42 H4**
Wanless *Canada* 54°11N 101°21W **71 C8**
Wanlaweyne *Somali Rep.* 2°37N 44°54E **47 G3**
Wanneroo *Australia* 31°42S 115°46E **61 F2**
Wanning *China* 18°48N 110°22E **38 C8**
Wannoo Billabong Roadhouse
  Australia 27°25S 115°49E **61 E2**
Wanon Niwat *Thailand* 17°38N 103°46E **38 D4**
Wanqinsha *China* 22°43N 113°33E **33 F10**
Wanquan *China* 40°50N 114°40E **34 D8**
Wanrong *China* 35°25N 110°50E **34 G6**
Wanshan Qundao
  China 21°57N 113°45E **33 G10**
Wantage *U.K.* 51°35N 1°25W **13 F6**
Wanxian *China* 30°42N 108°20E **32 C5**
Wanzai *China* 22°12N 113°31E **33 G10**
Wapakoneta *U.S.A.* 40°34N 84°12W **81 E11**
Wapato *U.S.A.* 46°27N 120°25W **76 C3**
Wapawekka L. *Canada* 54°55N 104°40W **71 C8**
Wapikopa L. *Canada* 52°56N 87°53W **72 B2**
Wapiti → *Canada* 55°5N 118°18W **70 B5**
Wappingers Falls
  U.S.A. 41°36N 73°55W **83 E11**
Wapsipinicon → *U.S.A.* 41°44N 90°19W **80 E8**
Wapusk △ *Canada* 57°46N 93°22W **71 B10**
Warakurna *Australia* 24°59S 128°17E **61 D4**
Warangal *India* 17°58N 79°35E **40 L11**
Waraseoni *India* 21°45N 80°2E **43 J9**
Waratah *Australia* 41°30S 145°30E **63 G4**
Waratah B. *Australia* 38°54S 146°5E **63 F4**
Warburton *Vic.,*
  Australia 37°47S 145°42E **63 F4**
Warburton *W. Austral.,*
  Australia 26°8S 126°35E **61 E4**
Warburton ◊ *Australia* 26°7S 126°34E **61 E4**
Warburton → *Australia* 28°4S 137°28E **63 D2**
Warburton Groove
  Australia 28°18S 137°8E **63 A2**
Warburton Ra.
  Australia 25°55S 126°28E **61 E4**
Ward *N.Z.* 41°49S 174°11E **59 D5**
Ward → *Australia* 26°28S 146°6E **63 D4**
Ward Mt. *U.S.A.* 37°12N 118°54W **78 H8**
Warden *S. Africa* 27°50S 29°0E **57 D4**
Wardha *India* 20°45N 78°39E **40 J11**
Wardha → *India* 19°57N 79°11E **40 K11**
Wardsville *Canada* 42°39N 81°45W **82 D3**
Ware *U.K.* 51°49N 0°1W **13 F8**
Ware *U.S.A.* 42°16N 72°14W **83 D12**
Waregem *Belgium* 50°53N 3°27E **15 D3**
Wareham *U.S.A.* 41°46N 70°43W **83 E14**
Waremme *Belgium* 50°43N 5°15E **15 D5**
Warialda *Australia* 29°29S 150°33E **63 D5**
Wariap *Indonesia* 1°30S 134°5E **37 E8**
Warin Chamrap
  Thailand 15°12N 104°53E **38 E5**
Warkopi *Indonesia* 1°12S 134°9E **37 E8**
Warm Springs *U.S.A.* 38°10N 116°20W **77 G5**
Warman *Canada* 52°19N 106°30W **71 C7**
Warmbad = Bela Bela
  S. Africa 24°51S 28°19E **57 C4**
Warmbad *Namibia* 28°25S 18°42E **56 D2**
Warminster *U.K.* 51°12N 2°10W **13 F5**
Warminster *U.S.A.* 40°12N 75°6W **83 F9**
Warmun *Australia* 17°2S 128°12E **60 C4**
Warner Mts. *U.S.A.* 41°40N 120°15W **76 F3**
Warner Robins *U.S.A.* 32°37N 83°36W **85 E13**
Waroona *Australia* 32°50S 115°58E **61 F2**
Warrabri ◊ *Australia* 21°1S 134°19E **62 C1**
Warracknabeal *Australia* 36°9S 142°26E **63 F3**
Warragul *Australia* 38°10S 145°58E **63 F4**
Warrego → *Australia* 30°24S 145°21E **63 E4**
Warrego Ra. *Australia* 24°58S 146°0E **62 C4**
Warren *Australia* 31°42S 147°51E **63 E4**
Warren *Ark., U.S.A.* 33°37N 92°4W **84 E8**
Warren *Mich., U.S.A.* 42°28N 83°1W **81 D12**
Warren *Minn., U.S.A.* 48°12N 96°46W **80 A5**
Warren *Ohio, U.S.A.* 41°14N 80°49W **82 E4**
Warren *Pa., U.S.A.* 41°51N 79°9W **82 E5**
Warrenpoint *U.K.* 54°6N 6°15W **10 B5**
Warrensburg *Mo.,*
  U.S.A. 38°46N 93°44W **80 F7**
Warrensburg *N.Y.,*
  U.S.A. 43°29N 73°46W **83 C11**
Warrenton *S. Africa* 28°9S 24°47E **56 D3**
Warrenton *U.S.A.* 46°10N 123°56W **78 D3**
Warri *Nigeria* 5°30N 5°41E **50 G7**
Warrington *U.K.* 53°24N 2°35W **12 D5**
Warrington *U.S.A.* 30°23N 87°17W **85 F11**
Warrnambool *Australia* 38°25S 142°30E **63 F3**
Warroad *U.S.A.* 48°54N 95°19W **80 A6**
Warruwi *Australia* 11°36S 133°20E **62 A1**
Warsa *Indonesia* 0°47S 135°55E **37 E9**
Warsak Dam *Pakistan* 34°11N 71°19E **42 B4**
Warsaw = Warszawa
  Poland 52°14N 21°0E **17 B11**
Warsaw *Ind., U.S.A.* 41°14N 85°51W **81 E11**
Warsaw *N.Y., U.S.A.* 42°45N 78°8W **82 D6**
Warsaw *Ohio, U.S.A.* 40°20N 82°0W **82 F3**

Warszawa *Poland* 52°14N 21°0E **17 B11**
Warta → *Poland* 52°35N 14°39E **16 B8**
Warthe = Warta →
  Poland 52°35N 14°39E **16 B8**
Waru *Indonesia* 3°30S 130°36E **37 E8**
Warumungu ◊
  Australia 19°15S 134°44E **62 B1**
Warwick *Australia* 28°10S 152°1E **63 D5**
Warwick *U.K.* 52°18N 1°35W **13 E6**
Warwick *N.Y., U.S.A.* 41°16N 74°22W **83 E10**
Warwick *R.I., U.S.A.* 41°42N 71°28W **83 E13**
Warwickshire □ *U.K.* 52°14N 1°38W **13 E6**
Wasaga Beach *Canada* 44°31N 80°1W **82 B4**
Wasagaming *Canada* 50°39N 99°58W **71 C9**
Wasatch Ra. *U.S.A.* 40°0N 111°30W **76 F8**
Wasbank *S. Africa* 28°15S 30°9E **57 D5**
Wasco *Calif., U.S.A.* 35°36N 119°20W **79 K7**
Wasco *Oreg., U.S.A.* 45°36N 120°42W **76 D3**
Waseca *U.S.A.* 44°5N 93°30W **80 C7**
Wasekamio L. *Canada* 56°45N 108°45W **71 B7**
Wash, The *U.K.* 52°58N 0°20E **12 E8**
Washago *Canada* 44°45N 79°20W **82 B5**
Washburn *N. Dak.,*
  U.S.A. 47°17N 101°2W **80 B3**
Washburn *Wis., U.S.A.* 46°40N 90°54W **80 B8**
Washim *India* 20°3N 77°0E **40 J10**
Washington *U.K.* 54°55N 1°30W **12 C6**
Washington *D.C., U.S.A.* 38°53N 77°2W **81 F15**
Washington *Ga.,*
  U.S.A. 33°44N 82°44W **85 E13**
Washington *Ind.,*
  U.S.A. 38°40N 87°10W **80 F10**
Washington *Iowa,*
  U.S.A. 41°18N 91°42W **80 E8**
Washington *Mo., U.S.A.* 38°33N 91°1W **80 F8**
Washington *N.C.,*
  U.S.A. 35°33N 77°3W **85 D16**
Washington *N.J.,*
  U.S.A. 40°46N 74°59W **83 F10**
Washington *Pa., U.S.A.* 40°10N 80°15W **82 F4**
Washington *Utah,*
  U.S.A. 37°8N 113°31W **77 H7**
Washington □ *U.S.A.* 47°30N 120°30W **76 C3**
Washington, Mt.
  U.S.A. 44°16N 71°18W **83 B13**
Washington Court House
  U.S.A. 39°32N 83°26W **81 F12**
Washington I. *U.S.A.* 45°23N 86°54W **80 C10**
Washougal *U.S.A.* 45°35N 122°21W **78 E4**
Washpool △ *Australia* 29°22S 152°20E **63 D5**
Wasian *Indonesia* 1°47S 133°19E **37 E8**
Wasilla *U.S.A.* 61°35N 149°26W **68 E2**
Wasini Marine △ *Kenya* 4°33S 39°14E **54 C4**
Wasior *Indonesia* 2°43S 134°30E **37 E8**
Wāsiṭ □ *Iraq* 32°50N 45°50E **44 C5**
Waskaganish *Canada* 51°30N 78°40W **72 B4**
Waskaiowaka L.
  Canada 56°33N 96°23W **71 B9**
Waskesiu Lake *Canada* 53°55N 106°5W **71 C7**
Wasserkuppe *Germany* 50°29N 9°55E **16 C5**
Waswanipi *Canada* 49°40N 76°29W **72 C4**
Waswanipi, L. *Canada* 49°35N 76°40W **72 C4**
Watampone *Indonesia* 4°29S 120°25E **37 E6**
Watamu *Kenya* 3°23S 40°0E **54 C5**
Watarrka △ *Australia* 24°20S 131°30E **60 D5**
Water Park Pt.
  Australia 22°56S 150°47E **62 C5**
Water Valley *U.S.A.* 34°10N 89°38W **85 D10**
Waterberg Plateau △
  Namibia 20°25S 17°18E **56 C2**
Waterberge *S. Africa* 24°10S 28°0E **57 C4**
Waterbury *Conn., U.S.A.* 41°33N 73°3W **83 E11**
Waterbury *Vt., U.S.A.* 44°20N 72°46W **83 B12**
Waterbury L. *Canada* 58°10N 104°22W **71 B8**
Waterdown *Canada* 43°20N 79°53W **82 C5**
Waterford *Canada* 42°56N 80°17W **82 D4**
Waterford *Ireland* 52°15N 7°8W **10 D4**
Waterford *Calif., U.S.A.* 37°38N 120°46W **78 H6**
Waterford *Pa., U.S.A.* 41°57N 79°59W **82 E5**
Waterford □ *Ireland* 52°10N 7°40W **10 D4**
Waterford Harbour
  Ireland 52°8N 6°58W **10 D5**
Waterhen L. *Canada* 52°10N 99°40W **71 C9**
Waterloo *Belgium* 50°43N 4°25E **15 D4**
Waterloo *Ont., Canada* 43°30N 80°32W **82 C4**
Waterloo *Qué., Canada* 45°22N 72°32W **83 A12**
Waterloo *Ill., U.S.A.* 38°20N 90°9W **80 F8**
Waterloo *Iowa, U.S.A.* 42°30N 92°21W **80 D7**
Waterloo *N.Y., U.S.A.* 42°54N 76°52W **82 D7**
Watersmeet *U.S.A.* 46°16N 89°11W **80 B9**
Waterton Lakes △
  Canada 48°45N 115°0W **70 D6**
Watertown *Conn.,*
  U.S.A. 41°36N 73°7W **83 E11**
Watertown *N.Y., U.S.A.* 43°59N 75°55W **83 C9**
Watertown *S. Dak.,*
  U.S.A. 44°54N 97°7W **80 C5**
Watertown *Wis., U.S.A.* 43°12N 88°43W **80 D9**
Waterval-Boven *S. Africa* 25°40S 30°18E **57 D5**
Waterville *Canada* 45°16N 71°54W **83 A13**
Waterville *Maine,*
  U.S.A. 44°33N 69°38W **81 C19**
Waterville *N.Y., U.S.A.* 42°56N 75°23W **83 D9**
Waterville *Wash., U.S.A.* 47°39N 120°4W **76 C3**
Watervliet *U.S.A.* 42°44N 73°42W **83 D11**
Wates *Indonesia* 7°51S 110°10E **37 G14**
Watford *Canada* 42°57N 81°53W **82 D3**
Watford *U.K.* 51°40N 0°24W **13 F7**
Watford City *U.S.A.* 47°48N 103°17W **80 B2**
Wathaman → *Canada* 57°16N 102°59W **71 B8**
Wathaman L. *Canada* 56°58N 103°44W **71 B8**
Watheroo *Australia* 30°15S 116°0E **61 F2**
Watheroo △ *Australia* 30°19S 115°48E **61 F2**
Wating *China* 35°40N 106°38E **34 G4**
Watkins Glen *U.S.A.* 42°23N 76°52W **82 D8**
Watling I. = San Salvador I.
  Bahamas 24°0N 74°40W **89 B5**
Watonga *U.S.A.* 35°51N 98°25W **84 D5**

Watrous *Canada* 51°40N 105°25W **71 C7**
Watrous *U.S.A.* 35°48N 104°59W **77 J11**
Watsa
  Dem. Rep. of the Congo 3°4N 29°30E **54 B2**
Watseka *U.S.A.* 40°47N 87°44W **80 E10**
Watson *Canada* 52°10N 104°30W **71 C8**
Watson Lake *Canada* 60°6N 128°49W **70 A3**
Watsontown *U.S.A.* 41°5N 76°52W **82 E8**
Watsonville *U.S.A.* 36°55N 121°45W **78 J5**
Wattiwarriganna Cr. →
  Australia 28°57S 136°10E **63 D2**
Watubela, Kepulauan
  Indonesia 4°28S 131°35E **37 E8**
Watubela Is. = Watubela,
  Kepulauan *Indonesia* 4°28S 131°35E **37 E8**
Wau = Wâw *Sudan* 7°45N 28°1E **51 G11**
Waubamik *Canada* 45°27N 80°1W **82 A4**
Waubay *U.S.A.* 45°20N 97°18W **80 C5**
Wauchope *N.S.W.,*
  Australia 31°28S 152°45E **63 E5**
Wauchope *N. Terr.,*
  Australia 20°36S 134°15E **62 C1**
Wauchula *U.S.A.* 27°33N 81°49W **85 H14**
Waukarlycarly, L.
  Australia 21°18S 121°56E **60 D3**
Waukegan *U.S.A.* 42°22N 87°50W **80 D10**
Waukesha *U.S.A.* 43°1N 88°14W **80 D9**
Waukon *U.S.A.* 43°16N 91°29W **80 D8**
Waupaca *U.S.A.* 44°21N 89°5W **80 C9**
Waupun *U.S.A.* 43°38N 88°44W **80 D9**
Waurika *U.S.A.* 34°10N 98°0W **84 D6**
Wausau *U.S.A.* 44°58N 89°38W **80 C9**
Wautoma *U.S.A.* 44°4N 89°18W **80 C9**
Wauwatosa *U.S.A.* 43°2N 88°0W **80 D9**
Wave Hill = Kalkarindji
  Australia 17°30S 130°47E **60 C5**
Wave Rock △ *Australia* 32°26S 118°53E **61 F2**
Waveney → *U.K.* 52°35N 1°39E **13 E9**
Waverley *N.Z.* 39°46S 174°37E **59 C5**
Waverly *Iowa, U.S.A.* 42°44N 92°29W **80 D7**
Waverly *N.Y., U.S.A.* 42°1N 76°32W **83 E8**
Wavre *Belgium* 50°43N 4°38E **15 D4**
Wâw *Sudan* 7°45N 28°1E **51 G11**
Wāw al Kabīr *Libya* 25°20N 16°43E **51 C9**
Wawa *Canada* 47°59N 84°47W **72 C3**
Wawanesa *Canada* 49°36N 99°40W **71 D9**
Wawona *U.S.A.* 37°32N 119°39W **78 H7**
Waxahachie *U.S.A.* 32°24N 96°51W **84 E6**
Way, L. *Australia* 26°45S 120°16E **61 E3**
Waya *Fiji* 17°19S 177°10E **59 a**
Waycross *U.S.A.* 31°13N 82°21W **85 F13**
Wayland *U.S.A.* 42°34N 77°35W **82 D7**
Wayne *Nebr., U.S.A.* 42°14N 97°1W **80 D5**
Wayne *W. Va., U.S.A.* 38°13N 82°27W **81 F12**
Waynesboro *Ga., U.S.A.* 33°6N 82°1W **85 E13**
Waynesboro *Miss.,*
  U.S.A. 31°40N 88°39W **85 F10**
Waynesboro *Pa.,*
  U.S.A. 39°45N 77°35W **81 F15**
Waynesboro *Va., U.S.A.* 38°4N 78°53W **81 F14**
Waynesburg *U.S.A.* 39°54N 80°11W **81 F13**
Waynesville *U.S.A.* 35°28N 82°58W **85 D13**
Waynoka *U.S.A.* 36°35N 98°53W **84 C5**
Wazirabad *Pakistan* 32°30N 74°8E **42 C6**
Wazirstan *Pakistan* 33°0N 70°0E **42 C4**
We *Indonesia* 5°51N 95°18E **36 C1**
Weald, The *U.K.* 51°4N 0°20E **13 F8**
Wear → *U.K.* 54°55N 1°23W **12 C6**
Weatherford *Okla.,*
  U.S.A. 35°32N 98°43W **84 D5**
Weatherford *Tex., U.S.A.* 32°46N 97°48W **84 E6**
Weaverville *U.S.A.* 40°44N 122°56W **76 F2**
Webb City *U.S.A.* 37°9N 94°28W **80 G6**
Webequie *Canada* 52°59N 87°21W **72 B2**
Webster *Mass., U.S.A.* 42°3N 71°53W **83 D13**
Webster *N.Y., U.S.A.* 43°13N 77°26W **82 C7**
Webster *S. Dak., U.S.A.* 45°20N 97°31W **80 C5**
Webster City *U.S.A.* 42°28N 93°49W **80 D7**
Webster Springs *U.S.A.* 38°29N 80°25W **81 F13**
Webuye *Kenya* 0°37N 34°46E **54 B3**
Weda *Indonesia* 0°21N 127°50E **37 D7**
Weda, Teluk *Indonesia* 0°20N 128°0E **37 D7**
Weddell Abyssal Plain
  S. Ocean 65°0S 20°0W **5 C2**
Weddell I. *Falk. Is.* 51°50S 61°0W **96 G4**
Weddell Sea *Antarctica* 72°30S 40°0W **5 D1**
Wedderburn *Australia* 36°26S 143°33E **63 F3**
Wedgeport *Canada* 43°44N 65°59W **73 D6**
Wedza *Zimbabwe* 18°40S 31°33E **55 F3**
Wee Waa *Australia* 30°11S 149°26E **63 E4**
Weed *U.S.A.* 41°25N 122°23W **76 F2**
Weed Heights *U.S.A.* 38°59N 119°13W **78 G7**
Weedsport *U.S.A.* 43°2N 76°33W **83 C8**
Weedville *U.S.A.* 41°17N 78°30W **82 E6**
Weenen *S. Africa* 28°48S 30°7E **57 D5**
Weert *Neths.* 51°15N 5°43E **15 C5**
Wei He → *Hebei, China* 36°10N 115°45E **34 F8**
Wei He → *Shaanxi,*
  China 34°38N 110°15E **34 G6**
Weichang *China* 41°58N 117°49E **35 D9**
Weichuan *China* 34°20N 113°59E **34 G7**
Weiden *Germany* 49°41N 12°10E **16 D7**
Weifang *China* 36°44N 119°7E **35 F10**
Weihai *China* 37°30N 122°6E **35 F12**
Weimar *Germany* 50°58N 11°19E **16 C6**
Weinan *China* 34°31N 109°29E **34 G5**
Weipa *Australia* 12°40S 141°50E **62 A3**
Weir → *Australia* 28°20S 149°50E **63 D4**
Weir → *Canada* 56°54N 93°21W **71 B10**
Weir River *Canada* 56°49N 94°6W **71 B10**
Weirton *U.S.A.* 40°24N 80°35W **82 F4**
Weiser *U.S.A.* 44°15N 116°58W **76 D5**
Weishan *China* 34°47N 117°5E **35 G9**
Weiyuan *China* 35°7N 104°10E **34 G3**
Wejherowo *Poland* 54°35N 18°12E **17 A10**
Wekusko L. *Canada* 54°40N 99°50W **71 C9**
Welch *U.S.A.* 37°26N 81°35W **81 G13**

Welford △ *Australia* 25°5S 143°16E **62 D3**
Welkom *S. Africa* 28°0S 26°46E **56 D4**
Welland *Canada* 43°0N 79°15W **82 D5**
Welland → *U.K.* 52°51N 0°5W **13 E7**
Wellesley Is. *Australia* 16°42S 139°30E **62 B2**
Wellesley Islands ◊
  Australia 16°32S 139°23E **62 B2**
Wellingborough *U.K.* 52°19N 0°41W **13 E7**
Wellington *Australia* 32°35S 148°59E **63 E4**
Wellington *Canada* 43°57N 77°20W **82 C7**
Wellington *N.Z.* 41°19S 174°46E **59 D5**
Wellington *S. Africa* 33°38S 19°1E **56 E2**
Wellington *Somst., U.K.* 50°58N 3°13W **13 G4**
Wellington *Telford & Wrekin,*
  U.K. 52°42N 2°30W **13 E5**
Wellington *Colo.,*
  U.S.A. 40°42N 105°0W **76 F11**
Wellington *Kans., U.S.A.* 37°16N 97°24W **80 G5**
Wellington *Nev., U.S.A.* 38°45N 119°23W **78 G7**
Wellington *Ohio, U.S.A.* 41°10N 82°13W **82 E2**
Wellington *Tex., U.S.A.* 34°51N 100°13W **84 D4**
Wellington, I. *Chile* 49°30S 75°0W **96 F2**
Wellington, L. *Australia* 38°6S 147°20E **63 F4**
Wellington Chan. *Canada* 75°0N 93°0W **69 C13**
Wells *U.K.* 51°13N 2°39W **13 F5**
Wells *Maine, U.S.A.* 43°20N 70°35W **83 C14**
Wells *N.Y., U.S.A.* 43°24N 74°17W **83 C10**
Wells *Nev., U.S.A.* 41°7N 114°58W **76 F6**
Wells, L. *Australia* 26°44S 123°15E **61 E3**
Wells, Mt. *Australia* 17°25S 127°8E **60 C4**
Wells Gray △ *Canada* 52°30N 120°15W **70 C4**
Wells River *U.S.A.* 44°9N 72°4W **83 B12**
Wells-next-the-Sea *U.K.* 52°57N 0°51E **12 E8**
Wellsboro *U.S.A.* 41°45N 77°18W **82 E7**
Wellsburg *U.S.A.* 40°16N 80°37W **82 F4**
Wellsville *N.Y., U.S.A.* 42°7N 77°57W **82 D7**
Wellsville *Ohio, U.S.A.* 40°36N 80°39W **82 F4**
Wellsville *Utah, U.S.A.* 41°38N 111°56W **76 F8**
Wellton *U.S.A.* 32°40N 114°8W **77 K6**
Wels *Austria* 48°9N 14°1E **16 D8**
Welshpool *U.K.* 52°39N 3°8W **13 E4**
Welwyn Garden City
  U.K. 51°48N 0°12W **13 F7**
Wem *U.K.* 52°52N 2°44W **12 E5**
Wembere → *Tanzania* 4°10S 34°15E **54 C3**
Wemindji *Canada* 53°0N 78°49W **72 B4**
Wemyss *Canada* 44°52N 76°23W **83 B8**
Wen Xian *China* 34°55N 113°5E **34 G7**
Wenatchee *U.S.A.* 47°25N 120°19W **76 C3**
Wenchang *China* 19°38N 110°42E **38 C8**
Wenchi *Ghana* 7°46N 2°8W **50 G5**
Wenchow = Wenzhou
  China 28°0N 120°38E **33 D7**
Wenden *U.S.A.* 33°49N 113°33W **79 M13**
Wendeng *China* 37°15N 122°5E **35 F12**
Wendesi *Indonesia* 2°30S 134°17E **37 E8**
Wendover *U.S.A.* 40°44N 114°2W **76 F6**
Wenlock → *Australia* 12°2S 141°55E **62 A3**
Wenshan *China* 23°20N 104°18E **32 D5**
Wenshang *China* 35°45N 116°30E **34 G9**
Wenshui *China* 37°26N 112°1E **34 F7**
Wensleydale *U.K.* 54°17N 2°0W **12 C6**
Wensu *China* 41°15N 80°10E **32 B3**
Wensum → *U.K.* 52°40N 1°15E **12 E8**
Wentworth *Australia* 34°2S 141°54E **63 E3**
Wentzel L. *Canada* 59°2N 114°28W **70 B6**
Wenut *Indonesia* 3°11S 133°19E **37 E8**
Wenxi *China* 35°20N 111°10E **34 G6**
Wenxian *China* 32°43N 104°36E **34 H3**
Wenzhou *China* 28°0N 120°38E **33 D7**
Weott *U.S.A.* 40°20N 123°55W **76 F2**
Wepener *S. Africa* 29°42S 27°3E **56 D4**
Werda *Botswana* 25°24S 23°15E **56 D3**
Weri *Indonesia* 3°10S 132°38E **37 E8**
Werra → *Germany* 51°24N 9°39E **16 C5**
Werrimull *Australia* 34°25S 141°38E **63 E3**
Werris Creek *Australia* 31°18S 150°38E **63 E5**
Weser → *Germany* 53°36N 8°28E **16 B5**
Wesiri *Indonesia* 7°30S 126°30E **37 F7**
Weslaco *U.S.A.* 26°10N 97°58W **84 H6**
Weslemkoon L. *Canada* 45°2N 77°25W **82 A7**
Wesleyville *Canada* 49°9N 53°33W **73 C9**
Wesleyville *U.S.A.* 42°9N 80°1W **82 D4**
Wessel, C. *Australia* 10°59S 136°46E **62 A2**
Wessel Is. *Australia* 11°10S 136°45E **62 A2**
Wessington Springs
  U.S.A. 44°5N 98°34W **80 C4**
West *U.S.A.* 31°48N 97°6W **84 F6**
West → *U.S.A.* 42°52N 72°33W **83 D12**
West Allis *U.S.A.* 43°1N 88°0W **80 D9**
West Antarctica
  Antarctica 80°0S 90°0W **5 D15**
West Baines →
  Australia 15°38S 129°59E **60 C4**
West Bank ■ *Asia* 32°6N 35°13E **46 C4**
West Bend *U.S.A.* 43°25N 88°11W **80 D9**
West Bengal □ *India* 23°0N 88°0E **43 H13**
West Berkshire □ *U.K.* 51°25N 1°17W **13 F6**
West Beskids = Západné Beskydy
  Europe 49°30N 19°0E **17 D10**
West Branch *U.S.A.* 44°17N 84°14W **81 C11**
West Branch Susquehanna
  U.S.A. 40°53N 76°48W **83 F8**
West Bromwich *U.K.* 52°32N 1°59W **13 E6**
West Burra *U.K.* 60°5N 1°21W **11 A7**
West Canada Cr. →
  U.S.A. 43°1N 74°58W **83 C10**
West Caroline Basin
  Pac. Oc. 4°0N 138°0E **64 G5**
West Chazy *U.S.A.* 44°49N 73°28W **83 B11**
West Chester *U.S.A.* 39°58N 75°36W **83 G9**
West Coast △ *Namibia* 21°53S 14°14E **56 C1**
West Coast △ *S. Africa* 33°13S 18°0E **56 E2**
West Columbia *U.S.A.* 29°9N 95°39W **84 G7**
West Covina *U.S.A.* 34°4N 117°54W **79 L9**
West Des Moines *U.S.A.* 41°35N 93°43W **80 E7**
West Dunbartonshire □
  U.K. 55°59N 4°30W **11 F4**
West End *Bahamas* 26°41N 78°58W **88 A4**

West Falkland *Falk. Is.* 51°40S 60°0W **96** G4
West Fargo *U.S.A.* 46°52N 96°54W **80** B5
West Fiji Basin *Pac. Oc.* 17°0S 173°0E **64** J9
West Fjord = Vestfjorden
  Norway 67°55N 14°0E **8** C16
West Fork Trinity →
  U.S.A. 32°48N 96°54W **84** E6
West Frankfort *U.S.A.* 37°54N 88°55W **80** G9
West Grand L. *U.S.A.* 45°14N 67°51W **81** C20
West Hartford *U.S.A.* 41°45N 72°44W **83** E12
West Haven *U.S.A.* 41°17N 72°57W **83** E12
West Hazleton *U.S.A.* 40°58N 76°0W **83** F9
West Helena *U.S.A.* 34°33N 90°38W **85** D9
West Hurley *U.S.A.* 41°59N 74°7W **83** E10
West Ice Shelf *Antarctica* 67°0S 85°0E **5** C7
West Indies *Cent. Amer.* 15°0N 65°0W **89** D7
West Jordan *U.S.A.* 40°36N 111°56W **76** F8
West Lamma Channel
  China 22°14N 114°4E **33** G11
West Linn *U.S.A.* 45°21N 122°36W **78** E4
West Lorne *Canada* 42°36N 81°36W **82** D3
West Lothian □ *U.K.* 55°54N 3°36W **11** F5
West Lunga → *Zambia* 13°6S 24°39E **55** E1
West MacDonnell △
  Australia 23°38S 132°59E **60** D5
West Mariana Basin
  Pac. Oc. 15°0N 137°0E **64** F5
West Memphis *U.S.A.* 35°8N 90°10W **85** D9
West Midlands □ *U.K.* 52°26N 2°0W **13** E6
West Mifflin *U.S.A.* 40°21N 79°52W **82** F5
West Milford *U.S.A.* 41°8N 74°22W **83** E10
West Milton *U.S.A.* 41°1N 76°50W **82** E8
West Monroe *U.S.A.* 32°31N 92°9W **84** E8
West Newton *U.S.A.* 40°14N 79°46W **82** F5
West Nicholson *Zimbabwe* 21°2S 29°20E **55** G2
West Odessa *U.S.A.* 31°50N 102°30W **84** F3
West Palm Beach
  U.S.A. 26°43N 80°3W **85** H14
West Plains *U.S.A.* 36°44N 91°51W **80** G8
West Point *Miss.,*
  U.S.A. 33°36N 88°39W **85** E10
West Point *N.Y., U.S.A.* 41°24N 73°58W **83** E11
West Point *Nebr., U.S.A.* 41°51N 96°43W **80** E6
West Point *Va., U.S.A.* 37°32N 76°48W **81** G15
West Point L. *U.S.A.* 33°8N 85°0W **85** E12
West Pt. = Ouest, Pte. de l'
  Canada 49°52N 64°40W **73** C7
West Pt. *Australia* 35°1S 135°56E **63** F2
West Road → *Canada* 53°18N 122°53W **70** C4
West Rutland *U.S.A.* 43°36N 73°3W **83** C11
West Schelde = Westerschelde →
  Neths. 51°25N 3°25E **15** C3
West Seneca *U.S.A.* 42°51N 78°48W **82** D6
West Siberian Plain *Russia* 62°0N 75°0E **26** B9
West Sussex □ *U.K.* 50°55N 0°30W **13** G7
West-Terschelling *Neths.* 53°22N 5°13E **15** A5
West Valley City *U.S.A.* 40°42N 111°58W **76** F8
West Virginia □ *U.S.A.* 38°45N 80°30W **81** F13
West-Vlaanderen □
  Belgium 51°0N 3°0E **15** D2
West Walker → *U.S.A.* 38°54N 119°9W **78** G7
West Wyalong *Australia* 33°56S 147°10E **63** E4
West Yellowstone
  U.S.A. 44°40N 111°6W **76** D8
West Yorkshire □ *U.K.* 53°45N 1°40W **12** D6
Westall, Pt. *Australia* 32°55S 134°4E **63** E1
Westbrook *U.S.A.* 43°41N 70°22W **81** D18
Westbury *Australia* 41°30S 146°51E **63** G4
Westby *U.S.A.* 48°52N 104°3W **76** B11
Westend *U.S.A.* 35°42N 117°24W **79** K9
Westerland *Germany* 54°54N 8°17E **16** A5
Westerly *U.S.A.* 41°22N 71°50W **83** E13
Western □ *Kenya* 0°30N 34°30E **54** B3
Western □ *Zambia* 15°0S 24°4E **55** F1
Western Australia □
  Australia 25°0S 118°0E **61** E2
Western Cape □ *S. Africa* 34°0S 20°0E **56** E3
Western Dvina = Daugava →
  Latvia 57°4N 24°3E **9** H21
Western Ghats *India* 14°0N 75°0E **40** N9
Western Isles □ *U.K.* 57°30N 7°10W **11** D1
Western Sahara ■ *Africa* 25°0N 13°0W **50** D3
Western Samoa = Samoa ■
  Pac. Oc. 14°0S 172°0W **59** b
Western Sierra Madre = Madre
  Occidental, Sierra
  Mexico 27°0N 107°0W **86** B3
Westernport *U.S.A.* 39°29N 79°3W **81** F14
Westerschelde → *Neths.* 51°25N 3°25E **15** C3
Westerwald *Germany* 50°38N 7°56E **16** C4
Westfield *Mass., U.S.A.* 42°7N 72°45W **83** D12
Westfield *N.Y., U.S.A.* 42°20N 79°35W **82** D5
Westfield *Pa., U.S.A.* 41°55N 77°32W **82** E7
Westhill *U.K.* 57°9N 2°19W **11** D6
Westhope *U.S.A.* 48°55N 101°1W **80** A3
Westland □ *N.Z.* 43°16S 170°16E **59** E2
Westland Bight *N.Z.* 42°55S 170°5E **59** E3
Westlock *Canada* 54°9N 113°55W **70** C6
Westmar *Australia* 27°55S 149°44E **63** D4
Westmeath □ *Ireland* 53°33N 7°34W **10** C4
Westminster *Calif.,*
  U.S.A. 33°45N 118°0W **79** M8
Westminster *Colo.,*
  U.S.A. 39°50N 105°2W **76** G11
Westminster *Md.,*
  U.S.A. 39°34N 76°59W **81** F15
Westmont *U.S.A.* 40°19N 78°58W **82** F6
Westmoreland *Barbados* 13°13N 59°37W **89** g
Westmorland *U.S.A.* 33°2N 115°37W **79** M11
Weston *Oreg., U.S.A.* 45°49N 118°26W **76** D4
Weston *W. Va., U.S.A.* 39°2N 80°28W **81** F13
Weston I. *Canada* 52°33N 79°36W **72** B4
Weston-super-Mare *U.K.* 51°21N 2°58W **13** F5
Westover *U.S.A.* 40°45N 78°40W **82** F6
Westport *Canada* 44°40N 76°25W **83** B8
Westport *Ireland* 53°48N 9°31W **10** C2
Westport *N.Z.* 41°46S 171°37E **59** D3
Westport *N.Y., U.S.A.* 44°11N 73°26W **83** B11
Westport *Oreg., U.S.A.* 46°8N 123°23W **78** D3

Westport *Wash., U.S.A.* 46°53N 124°6W **78** D2
Westray *Canada* 53°36N 101°24W **71** C8
Westray *U.K.* 59°18N 3°0W **11** B5
Westree *Canada* 47°26N 81°34W **72** C3
Westville *U.S.A.* 39°8N 120°42W **78** F6
Westwood *U.S.A.* 40°18N 121°0W **76** F3
Wetar *Indonesia* 7°48S 126°30E **37** F7
Wetaskiwin *Canada* 52°55N 113°24W **70** C6
Wete *Tanzania* 5°4S 39°43E **54** D4
Wetherby *U.K.* 53°56N 1°23W **12** D6
Wethersfield *U.S.A.* 41°42N 72°40W **83** E12
Wetteren *Belgium* 51°0N 3°53E **15** D3
Wetzlar *Germany* 50°32N 8°31E **16** C5
Wewoka *U.S.A.* 35°9N 96°30W **84** D6
Wexford *Ireland* 52°20N 6°28W **10** D5
Wexford □ *Ireland* 52°20N 6°25W **10** D5
Wexford Harbour *Ireland* 52°20N 6°25W **10** D5
Weyburn *Canada* 49°40N 103°50W **71** D8
Weymouth *Canada* 44°30N 66°1W **73** D6
Weymouth *U.K.* 50°37N 2°28W **13** G5
Weymouth *U.S.A.* 42°13N 70°58W **83** D14
Weymouth, C. *Australia* 12°37S 143°27E **62** A3
Wha Ti *Canada* 63°8N 117°16W **68** E8
Whakaari *N.Z.* 37°30S 177°13E **59** B6
Whakatane *N.Z.* 37°57S 177°1E **59** B6
Whale = Baleine →
  Canada 58°15N 67°40W **73** A6
Whale Cove *Canada* 62°10N 92°34W **71** A10
Whales, B. of *Antarctica* 78°0S 160°0W **5** D12
Whalsay *U.K.* 60°22N 0°59W **11** A8
Whangamata *N.Z.* 37°12S 175°53E **59** B5
Whangamomona *N.Z.* 39°8S 174°44E **59** C5
Whanganui → *N.Z.* 39°17S 174°53E **59** C5
Whangarei *N.Z.* 35°43S 174°21E **59** A5
Whangarei Harb. *N.Z.* 35°45S 174°28E **59** A5
Wharekauri = Chatham Is.
  Pac. Oc. 44°0S 176°40W **64** M10
Wharfe → *U.K.* 53°51N 1°9W **12** D5
Wharfedale *U.K.* 54°6N 2°1W **12** C5
Wharton *N.J., U.S.A.* 40°54N 74°35W **83** F10
Wharton *Pa., U.S.A.* 41°31N 78°1W **82** E6
Wharton *Tex., U.S.A.* 29°19N 96°6W **84** G6
Wharton Basin *Ind. Oc.* 22°0S 92°0E **64** K1
Wheatland *Calif., U.S.A.* 39°1N 121°25W **78** F5
Wheatland *Wyo.,*
  U.S.A. 42°3N 104°58W **76** E11
Wheatley *Canada* 42°6N 82°27W **82** D2
Wheaton *Md., U.S.A.* 39°3N 77°3W **81** F15
Wheaton *Minn., U.S.A.* 45°48N 96°30W **80** C5
Wheelbarrow Pk.
  U.S.A. 37°26N 116°5W **78** H10
Wheeler *Oreg., U.S.A.* 45°41N 123°53W **76** D2
Wheeler *Tex., U.S.A.* 35°27N 100°16W **84** D4
Wheeler → *Canada* 57°26N 67°13W **73** A6
Wheeler L. *U.S.A.* 34°48N 87°23W **85** D11
Wheeler Pk. *N. Mex.,*
  U.S.A. 36°34N 105°25W **77** H11
Wheeler Pk. *Nev.,*
  U.S.A. 38°57N 114°15W **76** G6
Wheeler Ridge *U.S.A.* 35°0N 118°57W **79** L8
Wheelersburg *U.S.A.* 38°44N 82°51W **81** F12
Wheeling *U.S.A.* 40°4N 80°43W **82** F4
Whernside *U.K.* 54°14N 2°24W **12** C5
Whiddy I. *Ireland* 51°41N 9°31W **10** E2
Whim Creek *Australia* 20°50S 117°49E **60** D2
Whiskey Jack L.
  Canada 58°23N 101°55W **71** B8
Whiskeytown-Shasta-Trinity △
  U.S.A. 40°45N 122°15W **76** F2
Whistleduck Cr. →
  Australia 20°15S 135°18E **62** C2
Whistler *Canada* 50°7N 122°58W **70** C4
Whitby *Canada* 43°52N 78°56W **82** C6
Whitby *U.K.* 54°29N 0°37W **12** C7
White → *Ark., U.S.A.* 33°57N 91°5W **84** E9
White → *Ind., U.S.A.* 38°25N 87°45W **80** F10
White → *S. Dak., U.S.A.* 43°42N 99°27W **80** D4
White → *Utah, U.S.A.* 33°14N 100°56W **84** E4
White → *Vt., U.S.A.* 43°37N 72°20W **83** C12
White → *Wash., U.S.A.* 47°12N 122°15W **78** C4
White, L. *Australia* 21°9S 128°56E **60** D4
White B. *Canada* 50°0N 56°35W **73** C8
White Bird *U.S.A.* 45°46N 116°18W **76** D5
White Butte *U.S.A.* 46°23N 103°18W **80** B2
White City *U.S.A.* 38°47N 122°51W **76** E2
White Cliffs *Australia* 30°50S 143°10E **63** E3
White Hall *U.S.A.* 39°26N 90°24W **80** F8
White Haven *U.S.A.* 41°4N 75°47W **83** E9
White Horse, Vale of
  U.K. 51°37N 1°30W **13** F6
White I. = Whakaari
  N.Z. 37°30S 177°13E **59** B6
White L. *Canada* 45°18N 76°31W **83** A8
White L. *U.S.A.* 29°44N 92°30W **84** G8
White Lake *Canada* 45°21N 76°29W **83** A8
White Mountain Peak
  U.S.A. 37°38N 118°15W **77** H4
White Mts. *Calif.,*
  U.S.A. 37°30N 118°15W **78** H8
White Mts. *N.H.,*
  U.S.A. 44°15N 71°15W **83** B13
White Mts. △ *Australia* 20°43S 145°12E **62** C4
White Nile = Nil el Abyad →
  Sudan 15°38N 32°31E **51** E12
White Otter L. *Canada* 49°5N 91°55W **72** C1
White Pass *U.S.A.* 46°38N 121°24W **78** D5
White Plains *U.S.A.* 41°2N 73°46W **83** E11
White River *Canada* 48°35N 85°20W **72** C2
White River *U.S.A.* 43°34N 100°45W **80** D3
White Rock *Canada* 49°2N 122°48W **78** A4
White Rock *U.S.A.* 35°50N 106°12W **77** J10
White Russia = Belarus ■
  Europe 53°30N 27°0E **17** B14
White Sands △ *U.S.A.* 32°46N 106°20W **77** K10
White Sea = Beloye More
  Russia 66°30N 38°0E **8** C25
White Sulphur Springs *Mont.,*
  U.S.A. 46°33N 110°54W **76** C8

White Sulphur Springs *W. Va.,*
  U.S.A. 37°48N 80°18W **81** G13
White Swan *U.S.A.* 46°23N 120°44W **78** D6
Whitecliffs *N.Z.* 43°26S 171°55E **59** E3
Whitecourt *Canada* 54°10N 115°45W **70** C5
Whiteface Mt. *U.S.A.* 44°22N 73°54W **83** B11
Whitefield *U.S.A.* 44°23N 71°37W **83** B13
Whitefish *U.S.A.* 48°25N 114°20W **76** B6
Whitefish B. *U.S.A.* 46°40N 84°55W **72** C3
Whitefish L. *Canada* 62°41N 106°48W **71** A7
Whitefish Pt. *U.S.A.* 46°45N 84°59W **81** B11
Whitegull, L. = Goélands, L. aux
  Canada 55°27N 64°17W **73** A7
Whitehall *Mich., U.S.A.* 43°24N 86°21W **80** D10
Whitehall *Mont., U.S.A.* 45°52N 112°6W **76** D7
Whitehall *N.Y., U.S.A.* 43°33N 73°24W **83** C11
Whitehall *Wis., U.S.A.* 44°22N 91°19W **80** C9
Whitehaven *U.K.* 54°33N 3°35W **12** C4
Whitehorse *Canada* 60°43N 135°3W **70** A1
Whitemark *Australia* 40°7S 148°3E **63** G4
Whiteriver *U.S.A.* 33°50N 109°58W **77** K9
Whitesand → *Canada* 55°0N 74°0W **73** A5
Whitesands *S. Africa* 34°23S 20°50E **56** E3
Whitesboro *N.Y., U.S.A.* 43°7N 75°18W **83** C9
Whitesboro *Tex., U.S.A.* 33°39N 96°54W **84** E6
Whiteshell △ *Canada* 50°0N 95°40W **71** D9
Whiteville *U.S.A.* 34°20N 78°42W **85** D15
Whitewater *U.S.A.* 42°50N 88°44W **80** D9
Whitewater Baldy
  U.S.A. 33°20N 108°39W **77** K9
Whitewater L. *Canada* 50°50N 89°10W **72** B2
Whitewood *Australia* 21°28S 143°30E **62** C3
Whitewood *Canada* 50°20N 102°20W **71** C8
Whithorn *U.K.* 54°44N 4°26W **11** G4
Whitianga *N.Z.* 36°47S 175°41E **59** B5
Whitman *U.S.A.* 42°5N 70°56W **83** D14
Whitney *Canada* 45°31N 78°14W **82** A6
Whitney, Mt. *U.S.A.* 36°35N 118°18W **78** J8
Whitney Point *U.S.A.* 42°20N 75°58W **83** D9
Whitstable *U.K.* 51°21N 1°3E **13** F9
Whitsunday I. *Australia* 20°15S 149°4E **62** b
Whitsunday Islands △
  Australia 20°15S 149°0E **62** b
Whittier *Alaska, U.S.A.* 60°47N 148°41W **74** C10
Whittier *Calif., U.S.A.* 33°58N 118°2W **79** M8
Whittlesea *Australia* 37°27S 145°9E **63** F4
Wholdaia L. *Canada* 60°43N 104°20W **71** A8
Whyalla *Australia* 33°2S 137°30E **63** E2
Wiang Kosai △ *Thailand* 17°54N 99°29E **38** C2
Wiang Sa *Thailand* 18°34N 100°45E **38** C3
Wiarton *Canada* 44°40N 81°10W **82** B3
Wiay *U.K.* 57°24N 7°13W **11** D1
Wibaux *U.S.A.* 46°59N 104°11W **76** C11
Wichian Buri *Thailand* 15°39N 101°7E **38** E3
Wichita *U.S.A.* 37°42N 97°20W **80** G6
Wichita Falls *U.S.A.* 33°54N 98°30W **84** E5
Wick *U.K.* 58°26N 3°5W **11** C5
Wickenburg *U.S.A.* 33°58N 112°44W **77** K7
Wickepin *Australia* 32°50S 117°30E **61** F2
Wickham *Australia* 20°42S 117°11E **60** D2
Wickham, C. *Australia* 39°35S 143°57E **63** F3
Wickliffe *U.S.A.* 41°36N 81°28W **82** E3
Wicklow *Ireland* 52°59N 6°3W **10** D5
Wicklow □ *Ireland* 52°57N 6°25W **10** D5
Wicklow Hd. *Ireland* 52°58N 6°0W **10** D6
Wicklow Mts. *Ireland* 52°58N 6°26W **10** C5
Wicklow Mts. △ *Ireland* 53°6N 6°21W **10** C5
Widgeegoara Cr. →
  Australia 28°51S 146°34E **63** D4
Widgiemooltha
  Australia 31°30S 121°34E **61** F3
Widnes *U.K.* 53°23N 2°45W **12** D5
Wieluń *Poland* 51°15N 18°34E **17** C10
Wien *Austria* 48°12N 16°22E **16** D9
Wiener Neustadt *Austria* 47°49N 16°16E **16** E9
Wiesbaden *Germany* 50°4N 8°14E **16** C5
Wigan *U.K.* 53°33N 2°38W **12** D5
Wiggins *Colo., U.S.A.* 40°14N 104°4W **76** F11
Wiggins *Miss., U.S.A.* 30°51N 89°8W **85** F10
Wight, I. of *U.K.* 50°41N 1°17W **13** G6
Wigston *U.K.* 52°35N 1°6W **13** E6
Wigton *U.K.* 54°53N 4°27W **11** G4
Wigtown *U.K.* 54°53N 4°27W **11** G4
Wigtown B. *U.K.* 54°46N 4°15W **11** G4
Wik and Wikway People ◎
  Australia 13°55S 142°28E **62** A3
Wilber *U.S.A.* 40°29N 96°58W **80** E5
Wilberforce *Canada* 45°2N 78°13W **82** A6
Wilberforce, C. *Australia* 11°54S 136°35E **62** A2
Wilburton *U.S.A.* 34°55N 95°19W **84** D7
Wilcannia *Australia* 31°30S 143°26E **63** E3
Wilcox *U.S.A.* 41°35N 78°41W **82** E6
Wildrose *U.S.A.* 36°14N 117°11W **79** J9
Wildspitze *Austria* 46°53N 10°53E **16** E6
Wilge → *S. Africa* 27°3S 28°20E **57** D4
Wilhelm II Coast *Antarctica* 68°0S 90°0E **5** C7
Wilhelmshaven *Germany* 53°31N 8°7E **16** B5
Wilhelmstal *Namibia* 21°58S 16°21E **56** C2
Wilkes Land *Antarctica* 69°0S 120°0E **5** D9
Wilkie *Canada* 52°27N 108°42W **71** C7
Wilkinsburg *U.S.A.* 40°26N 79°52W **82** F5
Wilkinson Lakes
  Australia 29°40S 132°39E **61** E5
Willandra Creek →
  Australia 33°22S 145°52E **63** E4
Willapa B. *U.S.A.* 46°40N 124°0W **76** C1
Willapa Hills *U.S.A.* 46°35N 123°25W **78** D3
Willard *U.S.A.* 41°3N 82°44W **82** E2
Willare Bridge Roadhouse
  Australia 17°43S 123°38E **60** C3
Willcox *U.S.A.* 32°15N 109°50W **77** K9
Willemstad *Neth. Ant.* 12°5N 68°55W **89** D6
William → *Canada* 59°8N 109°19W **71** B7
William 'Bill' Dannelly Res.
  U.S.A. 32°6N 87°24W **85** E11
William Creek *Australia* 28°58S 136°22E **63** D2
Williams *Australia* 33°2S 116°52E **61** F2
Williams *Ariz., U.S.A.* 35°15N 112°11W **77** J7

Williams *Calif., U.S.A.* 39°9N 122°9W **78** F4
Williams Harbour
  Canada 52°33N 55°47W **73** B8
Williams Lake *Canada* 52°10N 122°10W **70** C4
Williamsburg *Ky.,*
  U.S.A. 36°44N 84°10W **81** G11
Williamsburg *Pa.,*
  U.S.A. 40°28N 78°12W **82** F6
Williamsburg *Va.,*
  U.S.A. 37°16N 76°43W **81** G15
Williamson *N.Y., U.S.A.* 43°14N 77°11W **82** C7
Williamson *W. Va.,*
  U.S.A. 37°41N 82°17W **81** G12
Williamsport *U.S.A.* 41°15N 77°1W **82** E7
Williamston *U.S.A.* 35°51N 77°4W **85** D16
Williamstown *Australia* 37°51S 144°52E **63** F3
Williamstown *Ky.,*
  U.S.A. 38°38N 84°34W **81** F11
Williamstown *Mass.,*
  U.S.A. 42°43N 73°12W **83** D11
Williamstown *N.Y.,*
  U.S.A. 43°26N 75°53W **83** C9
Willimantic *U.S.A.* 41°43N 72°13W **83** E12
Willingboro *U.S.A.* 40°3N 74°54W **81** E16
Williston *S. Africa* 31°20S 20°53E **56** E3
Williston *Fla., U.S.A.* 29°23N 82°27W **85** G13
Williston *N. Dak., U.S.A.* 48°9N 103°37W **80** A2
Williston L. *Canada* 56°0N 124°0W **70** B4
Willits *U.S.A.* 39°25N 123°21W **76** G2
Willmar *U.S.A.* 45°7N 95°3W **80** C6
Willmore Wilderness △
  Canada 53°45N 119°30W **70** C5
Willoughby *U.S.A.* 41°39N 81°24W **82** E3
Willow Bunch *Canada* 49°20N 105°35W **71** D7
Willow L. *Canada* 62°10N 119°8W **70** A5
Willow Wall, The *China* 42°10N 122°0E **35** C12
Willowick *U.S.A.* 41°38N 81°28W **82** E3
Willowlake → *Canada* 62°42N 123°8W **70** A4
Willowmore *S. Africa* 33°15S 23°30E **56** E3
Willows *U.S.A.* 39°31N 122°12W **78** F4
Willowvale = Gatyana
  S. Africa 32°16S 28°31E **57** E4
Wills, L. *Australia* 21°25S 128°51E **60** D4
Wills Cr. → *Australia* 22°43S 140°2E **62** C3
Willsboro *U.S.A.* 44°21N 73°24W **83** B11
Willunga *Australia* 35°15S 138°30E **63** F2
Wilmette *U.S.A.* 42°4N 87°42W **80** D10
Wilmington *Australia* 32°39S 138°7E **63** E2
Wilmington *Del.,*
  U.S.A. 39°45N 75°33W **81** F16
Wilmington *N.C.,*
  U.S.A. 34°14N 77°55W **85** D16
Wilmington *Ohio,*
  U.S.A. 39°27N 83°50W **81** F12
Wilmington *Vt., U.S.A.* 42°52N 72°52W **83** D12
Wilmslow *U.K.* 53°19N 2°13W **12** D5
Wilpena Cr. →
  Australia 31°25S 139°29E **63** E2
Wilsall *U.S.A.* 45°59N 110°38W **76** D8
Wilson *N.C., U.S.A.* 35°44N 77°55W **85** D16
Wilson *N.Y., U.S.A.* 43°19N 78°50W **82** C6
Wilson *Pa., U.S.A.* 40°41N 75°15W **83** F9
Wilson → *Australia* 16°48S 128°16E **60** C4
Wilson Bluff *Australia* 31°41S 129°0E **61** F4
Wilson Inlet *Australia* 35°0S 117°22E **61** G2
Wilsons Promontory
  Australia 38°59S 146°23E **63** F4
Wilton *U.S.A.* 47°10N 100°47W **80** B4
Wilton → *Australia* 14°45S 134°33E **62** A1
Wiltshire □ *U.K.* 51°18N 1°53W **13** F6
Wiltz *Lux.* 49°57N 5°55E **15** E5
Wiluna *Australia* 26°36S 120°14E **61** E3
Wimborne Minster *U.K.* 50°48N 1°59W **13** G6
Wimmera → *Australia* 36°8S 141°56E **63** F3
Winam G. *Kenya* 0°20S 34°15E **54** C3
Winburg *S. Africa* 28°30S 27°2E **56** D4
Winchendon *U.S.A.* 42°41N 72°3W **83** D12
Winchester *U.K.* 51°4N 1°18W **13** F6
Winchester *Conn.,*
  U.S.A. 41°53N 73°9W **83** E11
Winchester *Idaho,*
  U.S.A. 46°14N 116°38W **76** C5
Winchester *Ind., U.S.A.* 40°10N 84°59W **81** E11
Winchester *Ky., U.S.A.* 37°59N 84°11W **81** G11
Winchester *N.H.,*
  U.S.A. 42°46N 72°23W **83** D12
Winchester *Nev., U.S.A.* 36°7N 115°7W **79** J11
Winchester *Tenn.,*
  U.S.A. 35°11N 86°7W **85** D11
Winchester *Va., U.S.A.* 39°11N 78°10W **81** F14
Wind → *U.S.A.* 43°12N 108°12W **76** E9
Wind Cave △ *U.S.A.* 43°32N 103°17W **80** D2
Wind River Range
  U.S.A. 43°0N 109°30W **76** E9
Windamere, L. *Australia* 32°48S 149°51E **63** B4
Windau = Ventspils
  Latvia 57°25N 21°32E **9** H19
Windber *U.S.A.* 40°14N 78°50W **82** F6
Winder *U.S.A.* 34°0N 83°45W **85** D13
Windermere *U.S.A.* 54°23N 2°55W **12** C5
Windhoek *Namibia* 22°35S 17°4E **56** C2
Windidda ◎ *Australia* 26°23S 122°12E **61** E3
Windjana Gorge △
  Australia 17°51S 125°0E **60** C3
Windom *U.S.A.* 43°52N 95°7W **80** D6
Windorah *Australia* 25°24S 142°36E **62** D3
Window Rock *U.S.A.* 35°41N 109°3W **77** J9
Windrush → *U.K.* 51°43N 1°24W **13** F6
Windsor *Australia* 33°37S 150°50E **63** E5
Windsor *N.S., Canada* 44°59N 64°5W **73** D7
Windsor *Ont., Canada* 42°18N 83°0W **82** D2
Windsor *U.K.* 51°29N 0°36W **13** F7
Windsor *Calif., U.S.A.* 38°33N 122°49W **76** G2
Windsor *Colo., U.S.A.* 40°29N 104°54W **76** F11
Windsor *Conn., U.S.A.* 41°50N 72°39W **83** E12
Windsor *Mo., U.S.A.* 38°32N 93°31W **80** F7
Windsor *N.Y., U.S.A.* 42°5N 75°37W **83** D9
Windsor *Vt., U.S.A.* 43°29N 72°24W **83** C12

Windsor & Maidenhead □
  U.K. 51°29N 0°40W **13** F7
Windsorton *S. Africa* 28°16S 24°44E **56** D3
Windward Is. *W. Indies* 13°0N 61°0W **89** D7
Windward Passage = Vientos,
  Paso de los *Caribbean* 20°0N 74°0W **89** C5
Winefred L. *Canada* 55°30N 110°30W **71** B6
Winfield *U.S.A.* 37°15N 96°59W **80** G5
Wingate Mts. *Australia* 14°25S 130°40E **60** B5
Wingellina = Irrunytju
  Australia 26°3S 128°56E **61** E4
Wingham *Australia* 31°48S 152°22E **63** E5
Wingham *Canada* 43°55N 81°20W **82** C3
Winisk → *Canada* 55°17N 85°5W **72** A2
Winisk L. *Canada* 52°55N 87°22W **72** B2
Wink *U.S.A.* 31°45N 103°9W **84** F3
Winkler *Canada* 49°10N 97°56W **71** D9
Winlock *U.S.A.* 46°30N 122°56W **78** D4
Winneba *Ghana* 5°25N 0°36W **50** G5
Winnebago, L. *U.S.A.* 44°0N 88°26W **80** D9
Winnecke Cr. →
  Australia 18°35S 131°34E **60** C5
Winnemucca *U.S.A.* 40°58N 117°44W **76** F5
Winnemucca L. *U.S.A.* 40°7N 119°21W **76** F4
Winner *U.S.A.* 43°22N 99°52W **80** D4
Winnett *U.S.A.* 47°0N 108°21W **76** C9
Winnfield *U.S.A.* 31°56N 92°38W **84** F8
Winnibigoshish, L.
  U.S.A. 47°27N 94°13W **80** B6
Winnipeg *Canada* 49°54N 97°9W **71** D9
Winnipeg → *Canada* 50°38N 96°19W **71** C9
Winnipeg, L. *Canada* 52°0N 97°0W **71** C9
Winnipeg Beach *Canada* 50°30N 96°58W **71** C9
Winnipegosis *Canada* 51°39N 99°55W **71** C9
Winnipegosis L. *Canada* 52°30N 100°0W **71** C9
Winnipesaukee, L.
  U.S.A. 43°38N 71°21W **83** C13
Winnisquam L. *U.S.A.* 43°33N 71°31W **83** C13
Winnsboro *La., U.S.A.* 32°10N 91°43W **84** E9
Winnsboro *S.C., U.S.A.* 34°23N 81°5W **85** D14
Winnsboro *Tex., U.S.A.* 32°58N 95°17W **84** E7
Winokapau, L. *Canada* 53°15N 62°50W **73** B7
Winona *Minn., U.S.A.* 44°3N 91°39W **80** C8
Winona *Miss., U.S.A.* 33°29N 89°44W **85** E10
Winooski *U.S.A.* 44°29N 73°11W **83** B11
Winooski → *U.S.A.* 44°32N 73°17W **83** B11
Winschoten *Neths.* 53°9N 7°3E **15** A7
Winsford *U.K.* 53°12N 2°31W **12** D5
Winslow = Bainbridge Island
  U.S.A. 47°38N 122°32W **78** C4
Winslow *U.S.A.* 35°2N 110°42W **77** J8
Winsted *U.S.A.* 41°55N 73°4W **83** E11
Winston-Salem *U.S.A.* 36°6N 80°15W **85** C14
Winter Garden *U.S.A.* 28°34N 81°35W **85** G14
Winter Haven *U.S.A.* 28°1N 81°44W **85** G14
Winter Park *U.S.A.* 28°36N 81°20W **85** G14
Winterhaven *U.S.A.* 32°44N 114°38W **79** N12
Winters *U.S.A.* 38°32N 121°58W **78** G5
Winterset *U.S.A.* 41°20N 94°1W **80** E6
Wintersville *U.S.A.* 40°23N 80°42W **82** F4
Winterswijk *Neths.* 51°58N 6°43E **15** C6
Winterthur *Switz.* 47°30N 8°44E **20** C8
Winthrop *U.S.A.* 48°28N 120°10W **76** B3
Winton *Australia* 22°24S 143°3E **62** C3
Winton *N.Z.* 46°8S 168°20E **59** G2
Wirlyajarrayi ◎
  Australia 21°45S 132°35E **60** D5
Wirralla *Australia* 32°24S 134°31E **63** E1
Wisbech *U.K.* 52°41N 0°9E **13** E8
Wisconsin □ *U.S.A.* 44°45N 89°30W **80** C9
Wisconsin → *U.S.A.* 43°0N 91°15W **80** D8
Wisconsin Rapids
  U.S.A. 44°23N 89°49W **80** C9
Wisdom *U.S.A.* 45°37N 113°27W **76** D7
Wiseman *U.S.A.* 67°25N 150°6W **74** B9
Wishaw *U.K.* 55°46N 3°54W **11** F5
Wishek *U.S.A.* 46°16N 99°33W **80** B4
Wisła → *Poland* 54°22N 18°55E **17** A10
Wismar *Germany* 53°54N 11°29E **16** B6
Wisner *U.S.A.* 41°59N 96°55W **80** E5
Witbank = eMalahleni
  S. Africa 25°51S 29°14E **57** D4
Witdraai *S. Africa* 26°58S 20°48E **56** D3
Witham → *U.K.* 51°48N 0°40E **13** F8
Witham *U.K.* 52°59N 0°2E **12** E7
Withernsea *U.K.* 53°44N 0°1E **12** D8
Witjira △ *Australia* 26°22S 135°37E **63** D2
Witless Bay *Canada* 47°17N 52°50W **73** C9
Witney *U.K.* 51°48N 1°28W **13** F6
Witnossob → *Namibia* 23°55S 18°45E **56** D3
Witrivier *S. Africa* 25°20S 31°0E **57** D5
Wittenberge *Germany* 53°0N 11°45E **16** B6
Wittenoom *Australia* 22°15S 118°20E **60** D2
Witu *Kenya* 2°23S 40°26E **54** C5
Witvlei *Namibia* 22°23S 18°32E **56** C2
Wiwon *N. Korea* 40°54N 126°3E **35** D14
Wkra → *Poland* 52°27N 20°44E **17** B11
Wlingi *Indonesia* 8°5S 112°25E **37** H15
Włocławek *Poland* 52°40N 19°3E **17** B10
Włodawa *Poland* 51°33N 23°31E **17** C12
Woburn *U.S.A.* 42°29N 71°9W **83** D13
Wodian *China* 32°50N 112°35E **34** H7
Wodonga *Australia* 36°5S 146°50E **63** F4
Wokam *Indonesia* 5°45S 134°28E **37** F8
Woking *U.K.* 51°19N 0°34W **13** F7
Wokingham *U.K.* 51°24N 0°49W **13** F7
Wokingham □ *U.K.* 51°25N 0°51W **13** F7
Wolf → *Canada* 60°17N 132°33W **70** A2
Wolf Creek *U.S.A.* 47°0N 112°4W **76** C7
Wolf L. *Canada* 60°24N 131°40W **70** A2
Wolfe Creek Crater △
  Australia 19°10S 127°47E **60** C4
Wolfe I. *Canada* 44°7N 76°20W **83** B8
Wolfeboro *U.S.A.* 43°35N 71°13W **83** C13
Wolfsberg *Austria* 46°50N 14°52E **16** E8
Wolfsburg *Germany* 52°25N 10°48E **16** B6
Wolin *Poland* 53°50N 14°37E **16** B8
Wollaston, Is. *Chile* 55°40S 67°30W **96** H3

Wollaston L. *Canada* 58°7N 103°10W **71** B8
Wollaston Lake *Canada* 58°3N 103°33W **71** B8
Wollaston Pen. *Canada* 69°30N 115°0W **68** D9
Wollongong *Australia* 34°25S 150°54E **63** E5
Wolmaransstad *S. Africa* 27°12S 25°59E **56** D4
Wolseley *S. Africa* 33°26S 19°7E **56** E2
Wolsey *U.S.A.* 44°25N 98°28W **80** C4
Wolstenholme, C.
Canada 62°35N 77°30W **66** C12
Wolvega *Neths.* 52°52N 6°0E **15** B6
Wolverhampton *U.K.* 52°35N 2°7W **13** E5
Wondai *Australia* 26°20S 151°49E **63** D5
Wongalarroo L. *Australia* 31°32S 144°0E **63** E3
Wongan Hills *Australia* 30°51S 116°37E **61** F2
Wonju *S. Korea* 37°22N 127°58E **35** F14
Wonosari *Indonesia* 7°58S 110°36E **37** G14
Wonosobo *Indonesia* 7°22S 109°54E **37** G13
Wonowon *Canada* 56°44N 121°48W **70** B4
Wŏnsan *N. Korea* 39°11N 127°27E **35** E14
Wonthaggi *Australia* 38°37S 145°37E **63** F4
Wood Buffalo △ *Canada* 59°0N 113°41W **70** B6
Wood Is. *Australia* 16°24S 123°19E **60** C3
Wood L. *Canada* 55°17N 103°17W **71** B8
Woodah, I. *Australia* 13°27S 136°10E **62** A2
Woodbourne *U.S.A.* 41°46N 74°36W **83** E10
Woodbridge *Canada* 43°47N 79°36W **82** C5
Woodbridge *U.K.* 52°6N 1°20E **13** E9
Woodburn *Australia* 29°6S 153°23E **63** A5
Woodburn *U.S.A.* 45°9N 122°51W **76** D2
Woodenbong *Australia* 28°24S 152°39E **63** D5
Woodend *Australia* 37°20S 144°33E **63** F3
Woodford *Australia* 26°58S 152°47E **63** D5
Woodfords *U.S.A.* 38°47N 119°50W **78** G7
Woodlake *U.S.A.* 36°25N 119°6W **78** J7
Woodland *Calif., U.S.A.* 38°41N 121°46W **78** G5
Woodland *Maine, U.S.A.* 45°9N 67°25W **81** C20
Woodland *Pa., U.S.A.* 41°0N 78°21W **82** F6
Woodland *Wash.,*
U.S.A. 45°54N 122°45W **78** E4
Woodland Caribou △
Canada 51°0N 94°45W **71** C10
Woodlands *Singapore* 1°26N 103°46E **39** d
Woodlands, The *U.S.A.* 30°9N 95°29W **84** F7
Woodonga *Australia* 36°10S 146°50E **63** F4
Woodridge *Canada* 49°20N 96°9W **71** D9
Woodroffe, Mt.
Australia 26°20S 131°45E **61** E5
Woods, L. *Australia* 17°50S 133°30E **62** B1
Woods, L. of the
N. Amer. 49°15N 94°45W **71** D10
Woods Bay *Canada* 45°8N 79°59W **82** A5
Woodstock *Australia* 19°35S 146°50E **62** B4
Woodstock *N.B., Canada* 46°11N 67°37W **73** C6
Woodstock *Ont., Canada* 43°10N 80°45W **82** C4
Woodstock *U.K.* 51°51N 1°20W **13** F6
Woodstock *Ill., U.S.A.* 42°19N 88°27W **80** D9
Woodstock *N.Y., U.S.A.* 42°2N 74°7W **83** D10
Woodstock *Vt., U.S.A.* 43°37N 72°31W **83** C12
Woodsville *U.S.A.* 44°9N 72°2W **83** B13
Woodview *Canada* 44°35N 78°8W **82** B6
Woodville *N.Z.* 40°20S 175°53E **59** D5
Woodville *Miss., U.S.A.* 31°6N 91°18W **84** F9
Woodville *Tex., U.S.A.* 30°47N 94°25W **84** F7
Woodward *U.S.A.* 36°26N 99°24W **84** C5
Woody *U.S.A.* 35°42N 118°50W **79** K8
Woody ➔ *Canada* 52°31N 100°51W **71** C8
Woolacombe *U.K.* 51°10N 4°13W **13** F3
Woolamai, C. *Australia* 38°30S 145°23E **63** F4
Wooler *U.K.* 55°33N 2°1W **12** B5
Woolgoolga *Australia* 30°6S 153°11E **63** E5
Woomera *Australia* 31°5S 136°50E **63** E2
Woonsocket *R.I., U.S.A.* 42°0N 71°31W **83** E13
Woonsocket *S. Dak.,*
U.S.A. 44°3N 98°17W **80** C4
Wooramel ➔ *Australia* 25°47S 114°10E **61** E1
Wooramel Roadhouse
Australia 25°45S 114°17E **61** E1
Wooroonooran △
Australia 16°26S 146°°E **62** B4
Wooster *U.S.A.* 40°48N 81°56W **82** F3
Worcester *S. Africa* 33°39S 19°27E **56** E2
Worcester *U.K.* 52°11N 2°12W **13** E5
Worcester *Mass.,*
U.S.A. 42°16N 71°48W **83** D13
Worcester *N.Y., U.S.A.* 42°36N 74°45W **83** D10
Worcestershire □ *U.K.* 52°13N 2°10W **13** E5
Workington *U.K.* 54°39N 3°33W **12** C4
Worksop *U.K.* 53°18N 1°7W **12** D6
Workum *Neths.* 52°59N 5°26E **15** B5
Worland *U.S.A.* 44°1N 107°57W **76** D10
Worms *Germany* 49°37N 8°21E **16** D5
Worsley *Canada* 56°31N 119°8W **70** B5
Wortham *U.S.A.* 31°47N 96°28W **84** F6
Worthing *Barbados* 13°5N 59°35W **89** g
Worthing *U.K.* 50°49N 0°21W **13** G7
Worthington *Minn.,*
U.S.A. 43°37N 95°36W **80** D6
Worthington *Pa., U.S.A.* 40°50N 79°38W **82** F5
Wosi *Indonesia* 0°15S 128°0E **37** E7
Wote *Kenya* 1°47S 37°38E **54** C4
Wotjalum ✪ *Australia* 16°30S 123°45E **60** C3
Wotjobaluk ✪ *Australia* 37°0S 142°0E **63** C3
Wou-han = Wuhan *China*
Wousi = Wuxi *China* 31°33N 120°18E **33** C7
Wowoni *Indonesia* 4°5S 123°5E **37** E6
Wrangel I. = Vrangelya, Ostrov
Russia 71°0N 180°0E **29** B18
Wrangell *U.S.A.* 56°28N 132°23W **70** B2
Wrangell Mts. *U.S.A.* 61°30N 142°0W **68** E3
Wrath, C. *U.K.* 58°38N 5°1W **11** C3
Wray *U.S.A.* 40°5N 102°13W **76** F12
Wrekin, The *U.K.* 52°41N 2°32W **13** E5
Wrexham *U.K.* 53°3N 3°0W **12** D4
Wrexham □ *U.K.* 53°1N 2°58W **12** D5
Wright *Fla., U.S.A.* 30°27N 86°38W **85** F11
Wright *Wyo., U.S.A.* 43°45N 105°28W **76** E11
Wright Pt. *Canada* 43°48N 81°44W **82** C3

Wrightson, Mt. *U.S.A.* 31°42N 110°51W **77** L8
Wrightwood *U.S.A.* 34°22N 117°38W **79** L9
Wrigley *Canada* 63°16N 123°37W **68** E7
Wrocław *Poland* 51°5N 17°5E **17** C9
Września *Poland* 52°21N 17°36E **17** B9
Wu Jiang ➔ *China* 29°40N 107°20E **32** D5
Wu Kau Tang *China* 22°30N 114°14E **33** F11
Wu'an *China* 36°40N 114°15E **34** F8
Wubin *Australia* 30°6S 116°37E **61** F2
Wubu *China* 37°28N 110°42E **34** F6
Wuchang *China* 44°55N 127°5E **35** B14
Wucheng *China* 37°12N 116°20E **34** F9
Wuchuan *China* 41°5N 111°28E **34** D6
Wudi *China* 37°40N 117°35E **35** F9
Wuding He ➔ *China* 37°2N 110°23E **34** F6
Wudinna *Australia* 33°0S 135°22E **63** E2
Wudu *China* 33°22N 104°54E **34** H3
Wuguishan *China* 22°25N 113°25E **33** G9
Wugullar = Beswick
Australia 14°34S 132°53E **60** B5
Wuhai *China* 39°47N 106°52E **32** C5
Wuhan *China* 30°31N 114°18E **33** C6
Wuhe *China* 33°10N 117°50E **35** H9
Wuhsi = Wuxi *China* 31°33N 120°18E **33** C7
Wuhu *China* 31°22N 118°21E **33** C6
Wukari *Nigeria* 7°51N 9°42E **50** G7
Wulajie *China* 44°6N 126°33E **35** B14
Wulanbulang *China* 41°5N 110°55E **34** D6
Wular L. *India* 34°20N 74°30E **43** B6
Wulian *China* 35°40N 119°12E **35** G10
Wuliaru *Indonesia* 7°27S 131°0E **37** F8
Wulumuchi = Ürümqi
China 43°45N 87°45E **32** B3
Wundanyi *Kenya* 3°24S 38°22E **54** C4
Wunnummin L. *Canada* 52°55N 89°10W **72** B2
Wuntho *Burma* 23°55N 95°45E **41** H19
Wupatki △ *U.S.A.* 35°35N 111°20W **77** J8
Wuppertal *Germany* 51°16N 7°12E **16** C4
Wuppertal *S. Africa* 32°13S 19°12E **56** E2
Wuqing *China* 39°23N 117°4E **35** E9
Wurralibi ✪ *Australia* 15°43S 137°1E **62** B2
Wurtsboro *U.S.A.* 41°35N 74°29W **83** E10
Würzburg *Germany* 49°46N 9°55E **16** D5
Wushan *China* 34°43N 104°53E **34** G3
Wushi *China* 41°9N 79°13E **32** B2
Wutai *China* 38°40N 113°12E **34** E7
Wuting = Huimin
China 37°27N 117°28E **35** F9
Wutonghaolai *China* 42°50N 120°5E **35** C11
Wutongqiao *China* 29°22N 103°50E **32** D5
Wuwei *China* 37°57N 102°34E **32** C5
Wuxi *China* 31°33N 120°18E **33** C7
Wuxiang *China* 36°49N 112°50E **34** F7
Wuyang *China* 33°25N 113°35E **34** H7
Wuyi *China* 37°46N 115°56E **34** F8
Wuyi Shan *China* 27°0N 117°0E **33** D6
Wuyuan *China* 41°2N 108°20E **34** D5
Wuzhai *China* 38°54N 111°48E **34** E6
Wuzhi Shan *China* 18°45N 109°45E **38** C7
Wuzhong *China* 38°2N 106°12E **34** E4
Wuzhou *China* 23°30N 111°18E **33** D6
Wyaaba Cr. ➔
Australia 16°27S 141°35E **62** B3
Wyalkatchem *Australia* 31°8S 117°22E **61** F2
Wyalusing *U.S.A.* 41°40N 76°16W **83** E8
Wyandotte *U.S.A.* 42°12N 83°9W **81** D12
Wyandra *Australia* 27°12S 145°56E **63** D4
Wyangala, L. *Australia* 33°54S 149°0E **63** E4
Wyara, L. *Australia* 28°42S 144°14E **63** D3
Wycheproof *Australia* 36°5S 143°17E **63** F3
Wycliffe Well *Australia* 20°48S 134°14E **62** C1
Wye ➔ *U.K.* 51°38N 2°40W **13** F5
Wyemandoo *Australia* 28°28S 118°29E **61** E2
Wymondham *U.K.* 52°35N 1°7E **13** E9
Wymore *U.S.A.* 40°7N 96°40W **80** E5
Wyndham *Australia* 15°33S 128°3E **60** C4
Wyndham *N.Z.* 46°20S 168°51E **59** G2
Wynne *U.S.A.* 35°14N 90°47W **85** D9
Wynyard *Australia* 41°5S 145°44E **63** G4
Wynyard *Canada* 51°45N 104°10W **71** C8
Wyola L. *Australia* 29°8S 130°17E **61** E5
Wyoming *Canada* 42°57N 82°7W **82** D2
Wyoming □ *U.S.A.* 43°0N 107°30W **76** E10
Wyomissing *U.S.A.* 40°20N 75°59W **83** F9
Wyong *Australia* 33°14S 151°24E **63** E5
Wytheville *U.S.A.* 36°57N 81°5W **81** G13

X

Xaafuun *Somali Rep.* 10°25N 51°16E **47** E5
Xaafuun, Ras *Somali Rep.* 10°27N 51°24E **47** E5
Xaçmaz *Azerbaijan* 41°31N 48°42E **19** F8
Xai-Xai *Mozam.* 25°6S 33°31E **57** D5
Xainza *China* 30°58N 88°35E **32** C3
Xalapa *Mexico* 19°32N 96°55W **87** D5
Xangongo *Angola* 16°45S 15°5E **56** B2
Xankändi *Azerbaijan* 39°52N 46°49E **44** B5
Xanthi *Greece* 41°10N 24°58E **23** D11
Xanxerê *Brazil* 26°53S 52°23W **95** B5
Xapuri *Brazil* 10°35S 68°35W **92** F5
Xar Moron He ➔
China 43°25N 120°35E **35** C11
Xátiva *Spain* 38°59N 0°32W **21** C5
Xau, L. *Botswana* 21°15S 24°44E **56** C3
Xavantina *Brazil* 21°15S 52°48W **95** A5
Xenia *U.S.A.* 39°41N 83°56W **81** F12
Xeropotamos ➔
Cyprus 34°42N 32°33E **25** E11
Xhora *S. Africa* 31°55S 28°38E **57** E4
Xhumo *Botswana* 21°7S 24°35E **56** C3
Xi Jiang ➔ *China* 22°5N 113°20E **33** D6
Xi Xian *China* 36°41N 110°58E **34** F6
Xia Xian *China* 35°8N 111°12E **34** G6
Xiachengzi *China* 44°40N 130°18E **35** B16
Xiaguan *China* 25°32N 100°16E **32** D5
Xiajin *China* 36°56N 116°0E **34** F9
Xiamen *China* 24°25N 118°4E **33** D6

Xi'an *China* 34°15N 109°0E **34** G5
Xian Xian *China* 38°12N 116°6E **34** E9
Xiang Jiang ➔ *China* 28°55N 112°50E **33** D6
Xiangcheng *Henan,*
China 33°29N 114°52E **34** H8
Xiangcheng *Henan,*
China 33°50N 113°27E **34** H7
Xiangfan *China* 32°2N 112°8E **33** C6
Xianggang = Hong Kong □
China 22°11N 114°14E **33** G11
Xianghuang Qi *China* 42°2N 113°50E **34** C7
Xiangning *China* 35°58N 110°50E **34** G6
Xiangquan *China* 36°30N 113°1E **34** F7
Xiangquan He = Sutlej ➔
Pakistan 29°23N 71°3E **42** E4
Xiangshui *China* 34°12N 119°33E **35** G10
Xiangtan *China* 27°51N 112°54E **33** D6
Xianyang *China* 34°20N 108°40E **34** G5
Xiao Hinggan Ling *China* 49°0N 127°0E **33** B7
Xiao Xian *China* 34°15N 116°55E **34** G9
Xiaoyi *China* 37°8N 111°48E **34** F6
Xiawa *China* 42°35N 120°38E **35** C11
Xiayi *China* 34°15N 116°10E **34** G9
Xichang *China* 27°51N 102°19E **32** D5
Xichuan *China* 33°0N 111°30E **34** H6
Xieng Khouang *Laos* 19°17N 103°25E **38** C4
Xifei He ➔ *China* 32°45N 116°40E **34** H9
Xifeng *Gansu, China* 35°40N 107°40E **34** G4
Xifeng *Liaoning, China* 42°42N 124°45E **35** C13
Xifengzhen = Xifeng
China 35°40N 107°40E **34** G4
Xigazê *China* 29°5N 88°45E **32** D3
Xihe *China* 34°2N 105°20E **34** G3
Xihua *China* 33°45N 114°30E **34** H8
Xili Shuiku *China* 22°36N 113°57E **33** F10
Xiliao He ➔ *China* 43°32N 123°35E **35** C12
Xilinhot *China* 43°52N 116°2E **34** C9
Ximana *Mozam.* 19°24S 33°58E **55** F3
Xin Xian = Xinzhou
China 38°22N 112°46E **34** E7
Xinavane *Mozam.* 25°2S 32°47E **57** D5
Xinbin *China* 41°40N 125°2E **35** D13
Xincun *China* 38°15N 117°45E **35** E9
Xing Xian *China* 38°27N 111°7E **34** E6
Xing'an *China* 25°38N 110°40E **33** D6
Xingcheng *China* 40°40N 120°45E **35** D11
Xinghe *China* 40°55N 113°55E **34** D7
Xinghua *China* 32°58N 119°48E **35** H10
Xinglong *China* 40°25N 117°30E **35** D9
Xingping *China* 34°20N 108°28E **34** G5
Xingtai *China* 37°3N 114°32E **34** F8
Xingu ➔ *Brazil* 1°30S 51°53W **93** D8
Xingyang *China* 34°45N 112°52E **34** G7
Xingyi *China* 25°3N 104°59E **32** D5
Xinhe *China* 37°30N 115°15E **34** F8
Xining *China* 36°34N 101°40E **32** C5
Xinjiang *China* 35°34N 111°11E **34** G6
Xinjiang Uygur Zizhiqu □
China 42°0N 86°0E **32** C3
Xinjin = Pulandian
China 39°25N 121°58E **35** E11
Xinken *China* 22°39N 113°55E **33** F10
Xinle *China* 38°25N 114°40E **34** E8
Xinlitun *China* 42°0N 122°8E **35** D12
Xinmin *China* 41°59N 122°50E **35** D12
Xinwan *China* 22°47N 113°40E **33** F10
Xinxiang *China* 35°18N 113°50E **34** G7
Xinzhan *China* 43°50N 127°18E **35** C14
Xinzheng *China* 34°20N 113°45E **34** G7
Xinzhou *Hainan, China* 19°43N 109°17E **38** C7
Xinzhou *Shanxi, China* 38°22N 112°46E **34** E7
Xiongyuecheng *China* 40°12N 122°5E **35** D12
Xiping *Henan, China* 33°22N 114°5E **34** H8
Xiping *Henan, China* 33°25N 111°8E **34** H6
Xique-Xique *Brazil* 10°50S 42°40W **93** F10
Xisha Qundao = Paracel Is.
S. China Sea 15°50N 112°0E **36** A4
Xiuyan *China* 40°18N 123°11E **35** D12
Xixabangma Feng
China 28°20N 85°40E **43** E11
Xixia *China* 33°25N 111°29E **34** H6
Xixiang *China* 33°0N 107°44E **34** H4
Xixón = Gijón *Spain* 43°32N 5°42W **21** A3
Xiyang *China* 37°38N 113°38E **34** F7
Xizang Zizhiqu □ *China* 32°0N 88°0E **32** C3
Xlendi *Malta* 36°1N 14°12E **25** C1
Xochob *Mexico* 19°21N 89°48W **87** D7
Xuan Loc *Vietnam* 10°56N 107°14E **39** G6
Xuanhua *China* 40°40N 115°2E **34** D8
Xuchang *China* 34°2N 113°48E **34** G7
Xun Xian *China* 35°42N 114°33E **34** G8
Xunyang *China* 32°48N 109°22E **34** H5
Xunyi *China* 35°8N 108°20E **34** G5
Xúquer ➔ *Spain* 39°5N 0°10W **21** C5
Xushui *China* 39°2N 115°40E **34** E8
Xuyen Moc *Vietnam* 10°34N 107°25E **39** G6
Xuzhou *China* 34°18N 117°10E **35** G9
Xylophagou *Cyprus* 34°54N 33°51E **25** E12

Y

Ya Xian = Sanya *China* 18°14N 109°29E **38** C7
Yaamba *Australia* 23°8S 150°22E **62** C5
Yaapeet *Australia* 35°45S 142°3E **63** F3
Yablonovyy Khrebet
Russia 53°0N 114°0E **29** D12
Yablonovyy Ra. = Yablonovyy
Khrebet *Russia* 53°0N 114°0E **29** D12
Yabrai Shan *China* 39°40N 103°0E **34** E2
Yabrūd *Syria* 33°58N 36°39E **46** B5
Yabucoa *Puerto Rico* 18°3N 65°53W **89** d
Yacheng *China* 18°22N 109°6E **38** C7
Yacuiba *Bolivia* 22°0S 63°43W **94** A3
Yacuma ➔ *Bolivia* 13°38S 65°23W **92** F5
Yadgir *India* 16°45N 77°5E **40** L10

Yadkin ➔ *U.S.A.* 35°23N 80°4W **85** D14
Yadua *Fiji* 16°49S 178°18E **59** a
Yaeyama-Rettō *Japan* 24°30N 123°40E **31** M1
Yagasa Cluster *Fiji* 18°57S 178°28W **59** a
Yagodnoye *Russia* 62°33N 149°40E **29** C15
Yahila
Dem. Rep. of the Congo 0°13N 24°28E **54** B1
Yahk *Canada* 49°6N 116°10W **70** D5
Yahuma
Dem. Rep. of the Congo 1°0N 23°10E **52** D4
Yaita *Japan* 36°48N 139°56E **31** F9
Yaiza *Canary Is.* 28°57N 13°46W **24** F6
Yakima *U.S.A.* 46°36N 120°31W **76** C3
Yakima ➔ *U.S.A.* 46°15N 119°14W **76** C4
Yakishiri-Jima *Japan* 44°26N 141°25E **30** B10
Yakobi I. *U.S.A.* 58°0N 136°30W **70** B1
Yakovlevka *Russia* 44°26N 133°28E **30** B6
Yaku-Shima *Japan* 30°20N 130°30E **31** J5
Yakumo *Japan* 42°15N 140°16E **30** C10
Yakutat *U.S.A.* 59°33N 139°44W **68** F4
Yakutat B. *U.S.A.* 59°45N 140°45W **74** D11
Yakutia = Sakha □
Russia 66°0N 130°0E **29** C14
Yakutsk *Russia* 62°5N 129°50E **29** C13
Yala *Thailand* 6°33N 101°18E **39** J3
Yalata *Australia* 31°59S 132°26E **61** F5
Yalata ✪ *Australia* 31°55S 132°7E **61** F5
Yalboroo *Australia* 20°50S 148°40E **62** b
Yale *U.S.A.* 43°8N 82°48W **82** C2
Yalgorup △ *Australia* 32°39S 115°38E **61** F2
Yalinga *C.A.R.* 6°33N 23°10E **52** C4
Yalkabul, Pta. *Mexico* 21°32N 88°37W **87** C7
Yalleroi *Australia* 24°3S 145°42E **62** C4
Yalobusha ➔ *U.S.A.* 33°33N 90°10W **85** E9
Yalong Jiang ➔ *China* 26°40N 101°55E **32** D5
Yalova *Turkey* 40°41N 29°15E **23** D13
Yalu Jiang ➔ *China* 39°55N 124°19E **35** E13
Yam *Australia* 9°54S 142°46E **62** a
Yam Ha Melaḥ = Dead Sea
Asia 31°30N 35°30E **46** D4
Yam Kinneret *Israel* 32°45N 35°35E **46** C4
Yam Kinnneret *Israel* 32°45N 35°35E **46** C4
Yamada *Japan* 33°33N 130°49E **31** H5
Yamagata *Japan* 38°15N 140°15E **30** E10
Yamagata □ *Japan* 38°30N 140°0E **30** E10
Yamaguchi *Japan* 34°10N 131°32E **31** G5
Yamaguchi □ *Japan* 34°20N 131°40E **31** G5
Yamal, Poluostrov *Russia* 71°0N 70°0E **28** B8
Yamal Pen. = Yamal, Poluostrov
Russia 71°0N 70°0E **28** B8
Yamanashi □ *Japan* 35°40N 138°40E **31** G9
Yamantau, Gora *Russia* 54°15N 58°6E **18** D10
Yamato Ridge
Sea of Japan 39°20N 135°0E **30** E7
Yamba *Australia* 29°26S 153°23E **63** D5
Yambarran Ra.
Australia 15°10S 130°25E **60** C5
Yâmbiô *Sudan* 4°35N 28°16E **51** H11
Yambol *Bulgaria* 42°30N 26°30E **23** C12
Yamburg *Russia* 68°21N 77°8E **28** C8
Yamdena *Indonesia* 7°45S 131°20E **37** F8
Yame *Japan* 33°13N 130°35E **31** H5
Yamethin *Burma* 20°29N 96°18E **41** J20
Yamma Yamma, L.
Australia 26°16S 141°20E **63** D3
Yamoussoukro *Ivory C.* 6°49N 5°17W **50** G4
Yampa ➔ *U.S.A.* 40°32N 108°59W **76** F9
Yampi Sd. *Australia* 16°8S 123°38E **60** C3
Yampil *Moldova* 48°15N 28°15E **17** D15
Yampol = Yampil
Moldova 48°15N 28°15E **17** D15
Yamuna ➔ *India* 25°30N 81°53E **43** G9
Yamunanagar *India* 30°7N 77°17E **42** D7
Yamzho Yumco *China* 28°48N 90°35E **32** D4
Yana ➔ *Russia* 71°30N 136°0E **29** B14
Yanagawa *Japan* 33°10N 130°24E **31** H5
Yanai *Japan* 33°58N 132°7E **31** H6
Yan'an *China* 36°35N 109°26E **34** F5
Yanaul *Russia* 56°25N 55°0E **18** C10
Yanbu 'al Baḥr *Si. Arabia* 24°0N 38°5E **44** F3
Yanchang *China* 36°43N 110°1E **34** F6
Yancheng *Henan, China* 33°35N 114°0E **34** H8
Yancheng *Jiangsu, China* 33°23N 120°8E **35** H11
Yanchep *Australia* 31°33S 115°37E **61** F2
Yanchi *China* 37°48N 107°20E **34** F4
Yanchuan *China* 36°51N 110°10E **34** F6
Yanco Cr. ➔ *Australia* 35°14S 145°35E **63** F4
Yandeyarra ✪ *Australia* 21°17S 118°24E **60** D2
Yandicoogina *Australia* 22°49S 119°10E **60** D2
Yandoon *Burma* 17°0N 95°40E **41** L19
Yang Xian *China* 33°15N 107°30E **34** H4
Yang-yang *S. Korea* 38°4N 128°38E **35** E15
Yangambi
Dem. Rep. of the Congo 0°47N 24°24E **54** B1
Yangcheng *China* 35°28N 112°22E **34** G7
Yangch'ü = Taiyuan
China 37°52N 112°33E **34** F7
Yanggao *China* 40°21N 113°55E **34** D7
Yanggu *China* 36°8N 115°43E **34** F8
Yangliuqing *China* 39°2N 117°5E **35** E9
Yangon = Rangoon
Burma 16°45N 96°20E **41** L20
Yangpingguan *China* 32°58N 106°5E **34** H4
Yangquan *China* 37°58N 113°31E **34** F7
Yangtse = Chang Jiang ➔
China 31°48N 121°10E **33** C7
Yangtze Kiang = Chang Jiang ➔
China 31°48N 121°10E **33** C7
Yangyuan *China* 40°1N 114°10E **34** D8
Yangzhou *China* 32°21N 119°26E **33** C6
Yanji *China* 42°59N 129°30E **35** C15
Yankton *U.S.A.* 42°53N 97°23W **80** D5
Yankunytjatjara-Antakirinja ✪
Australia 27°20S 134°30E **63** A1
Yanonge
Dem. Rep. of the Congo 0°35N 24°38E **54** B1
Yanqi *China* 42°5N 86°35E **32** B3
Yanqing *China* 40°30N 115°58E **34** D8

Yanshan *China* 38°4N 117°22E **35** E9
Yanshou *China* 45°28N 128°22E **35** B15
Yantabulla *Australia* 29°21S 145°0E **63** D4
Yantai *China* 37°34N 121°22E **35** F11
Yantian *China* 22°35N 114°16E **33** F11
Yanuca *Fiji* 18°24S 178°0E **59** a
Yanzhou *China* 35°35N 116°49E **34** G9
Yao Noi, Ko *Thailand* 8°7N 98°37E **39** a
Yao Xian *China* 34°55N 108°59E **34** G5
Yao Yai, Ko *Thailand* 8°0N 98°35E **39** a
Yaoundé *Cameroon* 3°50N 11°35E **52** D2
Yaowan *China* 34°15N 118°3E **35** G10
Yap *Pac. Oc.* 9°30N 138°10E **64** G5
Yapen *Indonesia* 1°50S 136°0E **37** E9
Yapen, Selat *Indonesia* 1°20S 136°10E **37** E9
Yapero *Indonesia* 4°59S 137°11E **37** E9
Yappar ➔ *Australia* 18°22S 141°16E **62** B3
Yapuparra ✪ *Australia* 27°15S 126°20E **61** E4
Yaqaga *Fiji* 16°35S 178°36E **59** a
Yaqui ➔ *Mexico* 27°37N 110°39W **86** B2
Yar-Sale *Russia* 66°50N 70°50E **28** C8
Yaraka *Australia* 24°53S 144°3E **62** C3
Yaransk *Russia* 57°22N 47°49E **18** C8
Yare ➔ *U.K.* 52°35N 1°38E **13** E9
Yaremcha *Ukraine* 48°27N 24°33E **17** D13
Yarensk *Russia* 62°11N 49°15E **18** B8
Yarí ➔ *Colombia* 0°20S 72°20W **92** D4
Yarkand = Shache
China 38°20N 77°10E **32** C2
Yarkant He ➔ *China* 40°26N 80°59E **32** B3
Yarker *Canada* 44°23N 76°46W **83** B8
Yarkhun ➔ *Pakistan* 36°17N 72°30E **43** A5
Yarlung Ziangbo Jiang =
Brahmaputra ➔
Asia 23°40N 90°35E **43** H13
Yarmouth *Canada* 43°50N 66°7W **73** D6
Yarmūk ➔ *Syria* 32°42N 35°40E **46** C4
Yaroslavl *Russia* 57°35N 39°55E **18** C6
Yarqa, W. ➔ *Egypt* 30°0N 33°49E **46** F2
Yarra Yarra Lakes
Australia 29°40S 115°45E **61** E2
Yarram *Australia* 38°29S 146°39E **63** F4
Yarraman *Australia* 26°50S 152°0E **63** D5
Yarras *Australia* 31°25S 152°20E **63** E5
Yarrie *Australia* 20°40S 120°12E **60** D3
Yartsevo *Russia* 60°20N 90°0E **29** C10
Yarumal *Colombia* 6°58N 75°24W **92** B3
Yasawa *Fiji* 16°47S 177°31E **59** a
Yasawa Group *Fiji* 17°0S 177°23E **59** a
Yaselda *Belarus* 52°7N 26°28E **17** B14
Yasin *Pakistan* 36°24N 73°23E **43** A5
Yasinski, L. *Canada* 53°16N 77°35W **72** B4
Yasinya *Ukraine* 48°16N 24°21E **17** D13
Yasothon *Thailand* 15°50N 104°10E **38** E5
Yass *Australia* 34°49S 148°54E **63** E4
Yāsūj *Iran* 30°31N 51°31E **45** D6
Yatağan *Turkey* 37°20N 28°10E **23** F13
Yates Center *U.S.A.* 37°53N 95°44W **80** G7
Yathkyed L. *Canada* 62°40N 98°0W **71** A9
Yatsushiro *Japan* 32°30N 130°40E **31** H5
Yatta Plateau *Kenya* 2°0S 38°0E **54** C4
Yauco *Puerto Rico* 18°2N 66°51W **89** d
Yavari ➔ *Peru* 4°21S 70°2W **92** D4
Yávaros *Mexico* 26°42N 109°31W **86** B3
Yavatmal *India* 20°20N 78°15E **40** J11
Yavne *Israel* 31°52N 34°45E **46** D3
Yavoriv *Ukraine* 49°55N 23°20E **17** D12
Yavorov = Yavoriv
Ukraine 49°55N 23°20E **17** D12
Yawatahama *Japan* 33°27N 132°24E **31** H6
Yawri B. *S. Leone* 8°22N 13°0W **50** G3
Yaxian = Sanya *China* 18°14N 109°29E **38** C7
Yazd *Iran* 31°55N 54°27E **45** D7
Yazd □ *Iran* 32°0N 55°0E **45** D7
Yazd-e Khvāst *Iran* 31°31N 52°7E **45** D7
Yazman *Pakistan* 29°8N 71°45E **42** E4
Yazoo ➔ *U.S.A.* 32°22N 90°54W **85** E9
Yazoo City *U.S.A.* 32°51N 90°25W **85** E9
Ybycuí △ *Paraguay* 26°5S 56°46W **94** B4
Ybytyruzú △ *Paraguay* 25°56S 56°11W **95** B4
Ye *Burma* 15°15N 97°15E **38** E1
Ye Xian *China* 33°35N 113°25E **34** H7
Yebyu *Burma* 14°15N 98°13E **38** E2
Yecheng *China* 37°54N 77°26E **32** C2
Yecheon *S. Korea* 36°39N 128°27E **35** F15
Yecla *Spain* 38°35N 1°5W **21** C5
Yécora *Mexico* 28°20N 108°58W **86** B3
Yedintsy = Edineț
Moldova 48°9N 27°18E **17** D14
Yegros *Paraguay* 26°20S 56°25W **94** B4
Yehbuah *Indonesia* 8°23S 114°45E **37** J17
Yehuda, Midbar *Israel* 31°35N 35°15E **46** D4
Yei *Sudan* 4°9N 30°40E **51** H12
Yekaterinburg *Russia* 56°50N 60°30E **28** D7
Yelarbon *Australia* 28°33S 150°38E **63** D5
Yelets *Russia* 52°40N 38°30E **18** D6
Yelizavetgrad = Kirovohrad
Ukraine 48°35N 32°20E **19** E5
Yelizovo *Russia* 53°11N 158°23E **29** D16
Yell *U.K.* 60°35N 1°5W **11** A7
Yell Sd. *U.K.* 60°33N 1°15W **11** A7
Yellow = Huang He ➔
China 37°55N 118°50E **35** F10
Yellow Sea *China* 35°0N 123°0E **35** G12
Yellowhead Pass
Canada 52°53N 118°25W **70** C5
Yellowknife *Canada* 62°27N 114°29W **70** A6
Yellowknife ➔ *Canada* 62°31N 114°19W **70** A6
Yellowstone □
U.S.A. 47°59N 103°59W **76** C12
Yellowstone △ *U.S.A.* 44°40N 110°30W **76** D8
Yellowstone ➔ *U.S.A.* 47°59N 103°59W **76** B12
Yelsk *Belarus* 51°50N 29°10E **17** C15
Yemen ■ *Asia* 15°0N 44°0E **47** E3
Yen Bai *Vietnam* 21°42N 104°52E **38** B5
Yenangyaung *Burma* 20°30N 95°0E **41** J19
Yenbo = Yanbu 'al Baḥr
Si. Arabia 24°0N 38°5E **44** F3
Yenda *Australia* 34°13S 146°14E **63** E4

Yeni Erenköy = Yialousa
  Cyprus 35°32N 34°10E 25 D13
Yenice Turkey 39°55N 27°17E 23 E12
Yenisey → Russia 71°50N 82°40E 28 B9
Yeniseysk Russia 58°27N 92°13E 29 D10
Yeniseyskiy Zaliv Russia 72°20N 81°0E 28 B9
Yenyuka Russia 57°57N 121°15E 29 D13
Yeo → U.K. 51°2N 2°49W 13 G5
Yeo, L. Australia 28°0S 124°30E 61 E3
Yeo I. Canada 45°24N 81°48W 82 A3
Yeoju S. Korea 37°20N 127°35E 35 F14
Yeola India 20°2N 74°30E 40 J9
Yeong-wol S. Korea 37°11N 128°28E 35 F15
Yeongcheon S. Korea 35°58N 128°56E 35 G15
Yeongdeok S. Korea 36°24N 129°22E 35 F15
Yeongdeungpo
  S. Korea 37°31N 126°54E 35 F14
Yeongdong S. Korea 36°10N 127°46E 35 F14
Yeongju S. Korea 36°50N 128°40E 35 F15
Yeosu S. Korea 34°47N 127°45E 35 G14
Yeotmal = Yavatmal
  India 20°20N 78°15E 40 J11
Yeovil U.K. 50°57N 2°38W 13 G5
Yeppoon Australia 23°5S 150°47E 62 C5
Yerbent Turkmenistan 39°30N 58°50E 28 F6
Yerbogachen Russia 61°16N 108°0E 29 C11
Yerevan Armenia 40°10N 44°31E 44 A5
Yerington U.S.A. 38°59N 119°10W 76 G4
Yermo U.S.A. 34°54N 116°50W 79 L10
Yermak Kazakhstan 52°2N 76°55E 28 D8
Yerólakkos Cyprus 35°11N 33°15E 25 D12
Yeropol Russia 65°15N 168°40E 29 C17
Yeroskipos Cyprus 34°46N 32°28E 25 E11
Yershov Russia 51°23N 48°27E 19 D8
Yerushalayim = Jerusalem
  Israel/West Bank 31°47N 35°10E 46 D4
Yes Tor U.K. 50°41N 4°0W 13 G4
Yesan S. Korea 36°41N 126°51E 35 F14
Yeso U.S.A. 34°26N 104°37W 77 J11
Yessey Russia 68°29N 102°10E 29 C11
Yetman Australia 28°56S 150°48E 63 D5
Yeu, Î. d' France 46°42N 2°20W 20 C2
Yevpatoriya Ukraine 45°15N 33°20E 19 E5
Yeysk Russia 46°40N 38°12E 19 E6
Yezd = Yazd Iran 31°55N 54°27E 45 D7
Ygatimi Paraguay 24°5S 55°40W 95 A4
Yhati Paraguay 25°45S 56°35W 94 B4
Yhú Paraguay 25°0S 56°0W 95 B4
Yí → Uruguay 33°7S 57°8W 94 C4
Yi 'Allaq, G. Egypt 30°21N 33°31E 46 E2
Yi He → China 34°10N 118°8E 35 G10
Yi Xian Hebei, China 39°20N 115°30E 34 E8
Yi Xian Liaoning, China 41°30N 121°22E 35 D11
Yialiás → Cyprus 35°9N 33°44E 25 D12
Yialousa Cyprus 35°32N 34°10E 25 D13
Yibin China 28°45N 104°32E 32 D5
Yichang China 30°40N 111°20E 33 C6
Yicheng China 35°42N 111°40E 34 G6
Yichuan China 36°2N 110°10E 34 F6
Yichun China 47°44N 128°52E 33 B7
Yidu China 36°43N 118°28E 35 F10
Yijun China 35°28N 109°8E 34 G5
Yıldız Dağları Turkey 41°48N 27°36E 23 D12
Yilehuli Shan China 51°20N 124°20E 33 A7
Yimianpo China 45°7N 128°2E 35 B15
Yinchuan China 38°30N 106°15E 34 E4
Yindarlgooda, L.
  Australia 30°40S 121°52E 61 F3
Yindjibarndi ⊙ Australia 22°0S 118°35E 60 D2
Ying He → China 32°30N 116°30E 34 H9
Ying Xian China 39°32N 113°10E 34 E7
Yingkou China 40°37N 122°18E 35 D12
Yingualyalya ⊙
  Australia 18°49S 129°12E 60 C4
Yining China 43°58N 81°10E 32 B3
Yiningarra ⊙ Australia 20°53S 129°27E 60 D4
Yinmabin Burma 22°10N 94°55E 41 H19
Yirga Alem Ethiopia 6°48N 38°22E 47 F2
Yirrkala Australia 12°14S 136°56E 62 A2
Yishan China 24°28N 108°38E 32 D5
Yishui China 35°47N 118°30E 35 G10
Yishun Singapore 1°26N 103°51E 39 d
Yitong China 43°13N 125°20E 35 C13
Yixing China 31°21N 119°48E 33 C6
Yiyang Henan, China 34°27N 112°10E 34 G7
Yiyang Hunan, China 28°35N 112°18E 33 D6
Yli-Kitka Finland 66°8N 28°30E 8 C23
Ylitornio Finland 66°19N 23°39E 8 C20
Ylivieska Finland 64°4N 24°28E 8 D21
Yoakum U.S.A. 29°17N 97°9W 84 G6
Yog Pt. Phil. 14°6N 124°12E 37 B6
Yogyakarta Indonesia 7°49S 110°22E 37 G14
Yogyakarta □ Indonesia 7°48S 110°22E 37 G14
Yoho △ Canada 51°25N 116°30W 70 C5
Yojoa, L. de Honduras 14°53N 88°0W 88 D2
Yok Don △ Vietnam 12°50N 107°40E 38 F6
Yokadouma Cameroon 3°26N 14°55E 52 D2
Yokkaichi Japan 34°55N 136°38E 31 G8
Yoko Cameroon 5°32N 12°20E 52 C2
Yokohama Japan 35°27N 139°28E 31 G9
Yokosuka Japan 35°20N 139°40E 31 G9
Yokote Japan 39°20N 140°30E 30 E10
Yola Nigeria 9°10N 12°29E 51 G8
Yolaina, Cordillera de
  Nic. 11°30N 84°0W 88 D3
Yolöten Turkmenistan 37°18N 62°21E 45 B9
Yom → Thailand 15°35N 100°1E 38 E3
Yonago Japan 35°25N 133°19E 31 G6
Yonaguni-Jima Japan 24°27N 123°0E 31 M1
Yonezawa Japan 37°57N 140°4E 30 F10
Yong Peng Malaysia 2°0N 103°3E 39 M4
Yong Sata Thailand 7°8N 99°41E 39 J2
Yongam'po N. Korea 39°56N 124°23E 35 E13
Yongcheng China 33°55N 116°20E 34 H9
Yongdeng China 36°38N 103°25E 34 F2
Yonghe China 36°46N 110°38E 34 F6
Yŏnghŭng N. Korea 39°31N 127°18E 35 E14
Yongji China 34°52N 110°28E 34 G6

Yongnian China 36°47N 114°29E 34 F8
Yongning China 38°15N 106°14E 34 E4
Yongqing China 39°25N 116°28E 34 E9
Yonibana S. Leone 8°30N 12°19W 50 G3
Yonkers U.S.A. 40°56N 73°52W 83 F11
Yonne □ France 48°23N 3°58E 20 B5
York Australia 31°52S 116°47E 61 F2
York U.K. 53°58N 1°6W 12 D6
York Ala., U.S.A. 32°29N 88°18W 85 E10
York Nebr., U.S.A. 40°52N 97°36W 80 E5
York Pa., U.S.A. 39°58N 76°44W 81 F15
York, C. Australia 10°42S 142°31E 62 A3
York, City of □ U.K. 53°58N 1°6W 12 D6
York, Kap Greenland 75°55N 66°25W 69 B18
York, Vale of U.K. 54°15N 1°25W 12 C6
York Sd. Australia 15°0S 125°5E 60 C4
Yorke Pen. Australia 34°50S 137°40E 63 E2
Yorkshire Dales △ U.K. 54°12N 2°10W 12 C5
Yorkshire Wolds U.K. 54°8N 0°31W 12 C7
Yorkton Canada 51°11N 102°28W 71 C8
Yorkville U.S.A. 38°52N 123°13W 78 G3
Yoro Honduras 15°9N 87°7W 88 C2
Yoron-Jima Japan 27°2N 128°26E 31 L4
Yos Sudarso, Pulau = Dolak,
  Pulau Indonesia 8°0S 138°30E 37 F9
Yosemite △ U.S.A. 37°45N 119°40W 78 H7
Yosemite Village
  U.S.A. 37°45N 119°35W 78 H7
Yoshino-Kumano △
  Japan 34°12N 135°55E 31 H8
Yoshkar Ola Russia 56°38N 47°55E 18 C8
Yotvata Israel 29°55N 35°2E 46 F4
Youbou Canada 48°53N 124°13W 78 B2
Youghal Ireland 51°56N 7°52W 10 E4
Youghal B. Ireland 51°55N 7°49W 10 E4
Young Australia 34°19S 148°18E 63 E4
Young Canada 51°47N 105°45W 71 C7
Young Uruguay 32°44S 57°36W 94 C4
Young I. Antarctica 66°25S 162°24E 5 C11
Younghusband, L.
  Australia 30°50S 136°5E 63 E2
Younghusband Pen.
  Australia 36°0S 139°25E 63 F2
Youngstown Canada 51°35N 111°10W 71 C6
Youngstown N.Y., U.S.A. 43°15N 79°3W 82 C5
Youngstown Ohio, U.S.A. 41°6N 80°39W 82 E4
Youngsville U.S.A. 41°51N 79°19W 82 E5
Youngwood U.S.A. 40°14N 79°34W 82 F5
Youyu China 40°10N 112°20E 34 D7
Yozgat Turkey 39°51N 34°47E 19 G5
Ypacaraí △ Paraguay 25°18S 57°19W 94 B4
Ypané → Paraguay 23°29S 57°19W 94 A4
Ypres = Ieper Belgium 50°51N 2°53E 15 D2
Yreka U.S.A. 41°44N 122°38W 76 F2
Ystad Sweden 55°26N 13°50E 9 J15
Ysyk-Köl = Balykchy
  Kyrgyzstan 42°26N 76°12E 32 B2
Ysyk-Köl Kyrgyzstan 42°25N 77°15E 28 E8
Ythan → U.K. 57°19N 1°59W 11 D7
Ytyk-Kyuyel Russia 62°30N 133°45E 29 C14
Yu Jiang → China 23°22N 110°3E 33 D6
Yu Xian = Yuzhou
  China 34°10N 113°28E 34 G7
Yu Xian Hebei, China 39°50N 114°35E 34 E8
Yu Xian Shanxi, China 38°5N 113°20E 34 E7
Yuan Jiang → China 28°55N 111°50E 33 D6
Yuanqu China 35°18N 111°40E 34 G6
Yuanyang China 35°3N 113°58E 34 G7
Yuba → U.S.A. 39°8N 121°36W 78 F5
Yuba City U.S.A. 39°8N 121°37W 78 F5
Yūbari Japan 43°4N 141°59E 30 C10
Yūbetsu Japan 44°13N 143°50E 30 B11
Yucatán □ Mexico 20°50N 89°0W 87 C7
Yucatán, Canal de
  Caribbean 22°0N 86°30W 88 B2
Yucatán, Península de
  Mexico 19°30N 89°0W 66 H11
Yucatan Basin Cent. Amer. 19°0N 86°0W 87 D7
Yucatan Channel = Yucatán,
  Canal de Caribbean 22°0N 86°30W 88 B2
Yucca U.S.A. 34°52N 114°9W 79 L12
Yucca Valley U.S.A. 34°8N 116°27W 79 L10
Yucheng China 36°55N 116°32E 34 F9
Yuci = Jinzhong China 37°42N 112°46E 34 F7
Yuen Long China 22°26N 114°2E 33 G11
Yuendumu Australia 22°16S 131°49E 60 D5
Yuendumu ⊙ Australia 22°21S 131°40E 60 D5
Yugorenok Russia 59°47N 137°40E 29 D14
Yukon U.S.A. 35°31N 97°45W 84 D6
Yukon → U.S.A. 62°32N 163°54W 74 C7
Yukon Flats U.S.A. 66°40N 145°45W 74 B10
Yukon Territory □
  Canada 63°0N 135°0W 68 E5
Yukta Russia 63°26N 105°42E 29 C11
Yukuhashi Japan 33°44N 130°59E 31 H5
Yulara Australia 25°10S 130°55E 61 E5
Yule → Australia 20°41S 118°17E 60 D2
Yuleba Australia 26°37S 149°42E 63 D4
Yulin Hainan, China 18°10N 109°31E 38 C7
Yulin Shaanxi, China 38°20N 109°30E 34 E5
Yuma Ariz., U.S.A. 32°43N 114°37W 79 N12
Yuma Colo., U.S.A. 40°8N 102°43W 76 F12
Yuma, B. de Dom. Rep. 18°20N 68°35W 89 C6
Yumbe Uganda 3°28N 31°15E 54 B3
Yumbi
  Dem. Rep. of the Congo 1°12S 26°15E 54 C2
Yumen China 39°50N 97°30E 32 C8
Yuna Australia 28°20S 115°0E 61 E2
Yuncheng Henan, China 35°36N 115°57E 34 G8
Yuncheng Shanxi, China 35°2N 111°0E 34 G6
Yungas Bolivia 17°0S 66°0W 92 G5
Yungay Chile 37°10S 72°5W 94 D1
Yunkanjini ⊙ Australia 22°33S 131°6E 60 D5
Yunnan □ China 25°0N 102°0E 32 D5
Yunta Australia 32°34S 139°36E 63 E2
Yunxi China 33°0N 110°22E 34 H6
Yupanqui Basin Pac. Oc. 19°0S 101°0W 65 J17
Yuraygir △ Australia 29°45S 153°15E 63 D5
Yurga Russia 55°42N 84°51E 28 D9

Yurimaguas Peru 5°55S 76°7W 92 E3
Yurubí △ Venezuela 10°26N 68°42W 89 D6
Yuscarán Honduras 13°58N 86°45W 88 D2
Yushe China 37°4N 112°58E 34 F7
Yushu Jilin, China 44°43N 126°38E 35 B14
Yushu Qinghai, China 33°5N 96°55E 32 C4
Yutai China 35°0N 116°45E 34 G9
Yutian Hebei, China 39°53N 117°45E 35 E9
Yutian Sinkiang-Uigur,
  China 36°52N 81°42E 32 C3
Yuxarı Qarabağ =
  Nagorno-Karabakh □
  Azerbaijan 39°55N 46°45E 44 B5
Yuxi China 24°30N 102°35E 32 D5
Yuzawa Japan 39°10N 140°30E 30 E10
Yuzhno-Kurilsk Russia 44°1N 145°51E 29 E15
Yuzhno-Sakhalinsk
  Russia 46°58N 142°45E 29 E15
Yuzhnyy □ Russia 44°0N 40°0E 28 E5
Yuzhou China 34°10N 113°28E 34 G7
Yvetot France 49°37N 0°44E 20 B4

Z

Zaanstad Neths. 52°27N 4°50E 15 B4
Zāb al Kabīr → Iraq 36°1N 43°24E 44 B4
Zāb aş Şaghīr → Iraq 35°17N 43°29E 44 C4
Zabaykalsk Russia 49°40N 117°25E 29 E12
Zabol Iran 31°0N 61°32E 45 D9
Zābol □ Afghan. 32°0N 67°0E 40 D5
Zābolī Iran 27°10N 61°35E 45 E9
Zabrze Poland 50°18N 18°50E 17 C10
Zacapa Guatemala 14°59N 89°31W 88 D2
Zacapu Mexico 19°50N 101°43W 86 D4
Zacatecas Mexico 22°47N 102°35W 86 C4
Zacatecas □ Mexico 23°0N 103°0W 86 C4
Zacatecoluca El Salv. 13°29N 88°51W 88 D2
Zachary U.S.A. 30°39N 91°9W 84 F9
Zacoalco de Torres
  Mexico 20°14N 103°35W 86 C4
Zacualtipán Mexico 20°39N 98°36W 87 C5
Zadar Croatia 44°8N 15°14E 16 F8
Zadetkyi Kyun Burma 10°0N 98°25E 39 G2
Zafarqand Iran 33°11N 52°29E 45 C7
Zafra Spain 38°26N 6°30W 21 C2
Żagań Poland 51°39N 15°22E 16 C8
Zagaoua Chad 15°30N 22°24E 51 E10
Zagazig Egypt 30°40N 31°30E 51 B12
Zāgheh Iran 33°30N 48°42E 45 C6
Zagreb Croatia 45°50N 15°58E 16 F9
Zāgros, Kūhhā-ye Iran 33°45N 48°5E 45 C6
Zagros Mts. = Zāgros, Kūhhā-ye
  Iran 33°45N 48°5E 45 C6
Zahamena △ Madag. 17°37S 48°49E 57 B8
Zāhedān Fārs, Iran 28°46N 53°52E 45 D7
Zāhedān Sīstān va Balūchestān,
  Iran 29°30N 60°50E 45 D9
Zahlah Lebanon 33°52N 35°50E 46 B4
Zaïre = Congo → Africa 6°4S 12°24E 52 F2
Zaječar Serbia 43°53N 22°18E 23 C10
Zaka Zimbabwe 20°20S 31°29E 57 C5
Zakamensk Russia 50°23N 103°17E 29 D11
Zakhodnaya Dzvina =
  Daugava → Latvia 57°4N 24°3E 9 H21
Zākhū Iraq 37°10N 42°50E 44 B4
Zakinthos = Zakynthos
  Greece 37°47N 20°54E 23 F9
Zakopane Poland 49°18N 19°57E 17 D10
Zakros Greece 35°6N 26°10E 25 D8
Zakynthos Greece 37°47N 20°54E 23 F9
Zalaegerszeg Hungary 46°53N 16°47E 17 E9
Zalari Russia 53°33N 102°30E 29 D11
Zalău Romania 47°12N 23°3E 17 E12
Zaleshchiki = Zalishchyky
  Ukraine 48°45N 25°45E 17 D13
Zalew Wiślany Poland 54°20N 19°50E 17 A10
Zalishchyky Ukraine 48°45N 25°45E 17 D13
Zama L. Canada 58°45N 119°5W 70 B5
Zambeke
  Dem. Rep. of the Congo 2°8N 25°17E 54 B2
Zambeze → Africa 18°35S 36°20E 55 F4
Zambezi = Zambeze →
  Africa 18°35S 36°20E 55 F4
Zambezi Zambia 13°30S 23°15E 53 G4
Zambezi △ Zimbabwe 17°54S 25°41E 55 F2
Zambezia □ Mozam. 16°15S 37°30E 55 F4
Zambia ■ Africa 15°0S 28°0E 55 F2
Zamboanga Phil. 6°59N 122°3E 37 C6
Zamora Mexico 19°59N 102°16W 86 D4
Zamora Spain 41°30N 5°45W 21 B3
Zamość Poland 50°43N 23°15E 17 C12
Zandā China 31°32N 79°50E 32 C2
Zandvoort Neths. 52°22N 4°32E 15 B4
Zanesville U.S.A. 39°56N 82°1W 82 G2
Zangābād Iran 38°26N 46°44E 44 B5
Zangue → Mozam. 17°50S 35°21E 55 F4
Zanjān Iran 36°40N 48°35E 45 B6
Zanjān □ Iran 37°20N 49°30E 45 B6
Zanjān → Iran 37°8N 47°47E 45 B6
Zante = Zakynthos
  Greece 37°47N 20°54E 23 F9
Zanthus Australia 31°2S 123°34E 61 F3
Zanzibar Tanzania 6°12S 39°12E 54 D4
Zaouiet El-Kala = Bordj Omar
  Driss Algeria 28°10N 6°40E 50 C7
Zaouiet Reggâne Algeria 26°32N 0°3E 50 C6
Zap Suyu = Zāb al Kabīr →
  Iraq 36°1N 43°24E 44 B4
Zapadnaya Dvina = Daugava →
  Latvia 57°4N 24°3E 9 H21
Zapadné Beskydy Europe 49°30N 19°0E 17 D10
Zapala Argentina 39°0S 70°5W 96 D2
Zapaleri, Cerro Bolivia 22°49S 67°11W 94 A2
Zapata U.S.A. 26°55N 99°16W 84 H5
Zapolyarnyy Russia 69°26N 30°51E 8 B24
Zapopán Mexico 20°43N 103°24W 86 C4

Zaporizhzhya Ukraine 47°50N 35°10E 19 E6
Zaporozhye = Zaporizhzhya
  Ukraine 47°50N 35°10E 19 E6
Zara Turkey 39°58N 37°43E 44 B3
Zaragoza Coahuila,
  Mexico 28°29N 100°55W 86 B4
Zaragoza Nuevo León,
  Mexico 23°58N 99°46W 87 C5
Zaragoza Spain 41°39N 0°53W 21 B5
Zarand Kermān, Iran 30°46N 56°34E 45 D8
Zarand Markazī, Iran 35°18N 50°25E 45 C6
Zaranj Afghan. 30°55N 61°55E 40 D2
Zarasai Lithuania 55°40N 26°20E 9 J22
Zárate Argentina 34°7S 59°0W 94 C4
Zard, Kūh-e Iran 32°22N 50°4E 45 C6
Zāreh Iran 35°7N 49°9E 45 C6
Zaria Nigeria 11°0N 7°40E 50 F7
Zarneh Iran 33°55N 46°10E 44 C5
Zaros Greece 35°8N 24°54E 25 D6
Zarqā', Nahr az →
  Jordan 32°10N 35°37E 46 C4
Zarrīn Iran 32°46N 54°37E 45 C7
Zaruma Ecuador 3°40S 79°38W 92 D3
Zary Poland 51°37N 15°10E 16 C8
Zarzis Tunisia 33°31N 11°2E 51 B8
Zaskar → India 34°13N 77°20E 43 B7
Zaskar Mts. India 33°15N 77°30E 43 C7
Zastron S. Africa 30°18S 27°7E 56 E4
Zavāreh Iran 33°29N 52°28E 45 C7
Zave Zimbabwe 17°6S 30°1E 57 B5
Zavitinsk Russia 50°10N 129°20E 29 D13
Zavodovski, I. Antarctica 56°0S 27°45W 5 B1
Zawiercie Poland 50°30N 19°24E 17 C10
Zāwiyat al Baydā = Al Baydā
  Libya 32°50N 21°44E 51 B10
Zāyā Iraq 33°33N 44°13E 44 C5
Zāyandeh → Iran 32°35N 52°0E 45 C7
Zaysan Kazakhstan 47°28N 84°52E 32 B3
Zaysan Köli Kazakhstan 48°0N 83°0E 28 E9
Zayū China 28°48N 97°27E 41 E20
Zazafotsy Madag. 21°11S 46°21E 57 C8
Zbarazh Ukraine 49°43N 25°44E 17 D13
Zdolbuniv Ukraine 50°30N 26°15E 17 C14
Zduńska Wola Poland 51°37N 18°59E 17 C10
Zeballos Canada 49°59N 126°50W 70 D3
Zebediela S. Africa 24°20S 29°17E 57 C4
Zeebrugge Belgium 51°19N 3°12E 15 C3
Zeehan Australia 41°52S 145°25E 63 G4
Zeeland □ Neths. 51°30N 3°50E 15 C3
Zeerust S. Africa 25°31S 26°4E 56 D4
Zefat Israel 32°58N 35°29E 46 C4
Zehak Iran 30°53N 61°42E 45 D9
Zeil, Mt. Australia 23°30S 132°23E 60 D5
Zeila = Saylac
  Somali Rep. 11°21N 43°30E 47 E3
Zeist Neths. 52°5N 5°15E 15 B5
Zeitz Germany 51°2N 12°7E 16 C7
Zelenogorsk Russia 60°12N 29°43E 8 F23
Zelenograd Russia 56°1N 37°12E 18 C6
Zelienople U.S.A. 40°48N 80°8W 82 F4
Zémio C.A.R. 5°2N 25°5E 54 A2
Zempoala Mexico 19°27N 96°23W 87 D5
Zemun Serbia 44°51N 20°25E 23 B9
Zenica Bos.-H. 44°10N 17°57E 23 B7
Žepče Bos.-H. 44°28N 18°2E 23 B8
Zevenaar Neths. 51°56N 6°5E 15 C6
Zeya Russia 53°48N 127°14E 29 D13
Zeya → Russia 51°42N 128°53E 29 D13
Zêzere → Portugal 39°28N 8°20W 21 C1
Zghartā Lebanon 34°21N 35°53E 46 A4
Zgorzelec Poland 51°10N 15°0E 16 C8
Zhabinka Belarus 52°13N 24°2E 17 B13
Zhambyl = Taraz
  Kazakhstan 42°54N 71°22E 28 E8
Zhangaözen Kazakhstan 43°18N 52°48E 19 F9
Zhangaqazaly Kazakhstan 45°48N 62°6E 28 E7
Zhangbei China 41°10N 114°45E 34 D8
Zhangguangcai Ling
  China 45°0N 129°0E 35 B15
Zhangjiabian China 22°33N 113°28E 33 F9
Zhangjiakou China 40°48N 114°55E 34 D8
Zhangwu China 42°43N 123°52E 35 C12
Zhangye China 38°50N 100°23E 32 C5
Zhangzhou China 24°30N 117°35E 33 D6
Zhanhua China 37°40N 118°8E 35 F10
Zhanjiang China 21°15N 110°20E 33 D6
Zhannetty, Ostrov
  Russia 76°43N 158°0E 29 B16
Zhanyi China 25°38N 103°48E 32 D5
Zhanyu China 44°30N 122°30E 35 B12
Zhao Xian China 37°43N 114°45E 34 F8
Zhaocheng China 36°22N 111°38E 34 F6
Zhaotong China 27°20N 103°44E 32 D5
Zhaoyuan Heilongjiang,
  China 45°27N 125°0E 35 B13
Zhaoyuan Shandong,
  China 37°20N 120°23E 35 F11
Zhari Namco China 31°6N 85°36E 32 C3
Zharkent Kazakhstan 44°10N 80°0E 28 E8
Zhashkiv Ukraine 49°15N 30°5E 17 D16
Zhashui China 33°40N 109°8E 34 H5
Zhayylma Kazakhstan 51°37N 61°33E 28 D7
Zhayyq → Kazakhstan 47°0N 51°48E 19 E9
Zhdanov = Mariupol
  Ukraine 47°5N 37°31E 19 E6
Zhecheng China 34°7N 115°20E 34 G8
Zhejiang □ China 29°0N 120°0E 33 D7
Zheleznodorozhnyy
  Russia 62°35N 50°55E 18 B9
Zheleznogorsk-Ilimskiy
  Russia 56°34N 104°8E 29 D11
Zhen'an China 33°20N 109°9E 34 H5
Zhengding China 38°8N 114°32E 34 E8
Zhengzhou China 34°45N 113°34E 34 G7
Zhenlai China 45°50N 123°5E 35 B12
Zhenping China 33°10N 112°16E 34 H7
Zhenyuan China 35°35N 107°30E 34 G4
Zhetiqara Kazakhstan 52°11N 61°12E 28 D7
Zhezqazghan Kazakhstan 47°44N 67°40E 28 E7

Zhidan China 36°48N 108°48E 34 F5
Zhigansk Russia 66°48N 123°27E 29 C13
Zhilinda Russia 70°0N 114°20E 29 C12
Zhitomir = Zhytomyr
  Ukraine 50°20N 28°40E 17 C15
Zhlobin Belarus 52°55N 30°0E 17 B16
Zhmerynka Ukraine 49°2N 28°2E 17 D15
Zhob Pakistan 31°20N 69°31E 42 D3
Zhob → Pakistan 32°4N 69°50E 42 C3
Zhodzina Belarus 54°5N 28°17E 17 A15
Zhokhova, Ostrov
  Russia 76°4N 152°40E 29 B16
Zhongdian China 27°48N 99°42E 32 D4
Zhongning China 37°29N 105°40E 34 F3
Zhongshan Antarctica 69°0S 39°50E 5 C6
Zhongshan China 22°26N 113°20E 33 G6
Zhongshankou China 41°14N 104°10E 34 D6
Zhongtiao Shan China 35°0N 111°10E 34 G6
Zhongwei China 37°30N 105°12E 34 F3
Zhongyang China 37°20N 111°11E 34 F6
Zhosaly Kazakhstan 45°29N 64°4E 28 E7
Zhoucun China 36°47N 117°48E 35 F9
Zhouzhi China 34°10N 108°12E 34 G5
Zhuanghe China 39°40N 123°0E 35 E12
Zhucheng China 36°0N 119°27E 35 G10
Zhugqu China 33°40N 104°30E 34 H3
Zhuhai China 22°17N 113°34E 33 G10
Zhujiang Kou China 22°20N 113°45E 33 G10
Zhumadian China 32°59N 114°2E 34 H8
Zhuo Xian = Zhuozhou
  China 39°28N 115°58E 34 E8
Zhuolu China 40°20N 115°12E 34 D8
Zhuozhou China 39°28N 115°58E 34 E8
Zhuozi China 41°0N 112°25E 34 D7
Zhuzhou China 27°49N 113°12E 33 D6
Zhytomyr Ukraine 50°20N 28°40E 17 C15
Ziarat Pakistan 30°25N 67°49E 42 D2
Zibo China 36°47N 118°3E 35 F10
Zichang China 37°18N 109°40E 34 F5
Zidi = Wandhari
  Pakistan 27°42N 66°48E 42 F2
Zielona Góra Poland 51°57N 15°31E 16 C8
Zierikzee Neths. 51°40N 3°55E 15 C3
Zigong China 29°15N 104°48E 32 D5
Ziguey Chad 14°43N 15°50E 51 F8
Ziguinchor Senegal 12°35N 16°20W 50 F2
Zihuatanejo Mexico 17°39N 101°33W 86 D4
Žilina Slovak Rep. 49°12N 18°42E 17 D10
Zillah Libya 28°30N 17°33E 51 C9
Zima Russia 54°0N 102°5E 29 D11
Zimapán Mexico 20°45N 99°21W 87 C5
Zimba Zambia 17°20S 26°11E 55 F2
Zimbabwe Zimbabwe 20°16S 30°54E 55 G3
Zimbabwe ■ Africa 19°0S 30°0E 55 F3
Zimnicea Romania 43°40N 25°22E 17 G13
Zinave △ Mozam. 21°35S 33°40E 57 C5
Zinder Niger 13°48N 9°0E 50 F7
Zinga Tanzania 9°16S 38°49E 54 D4
Zion △ U.S.A. 37°15N 113°5W 77 H7
Ziros Greece 35°5N 26°8E 25 D8
Zirreh, Gowd-e Afghan. 29°45N 62°0E 40 E3
Zitácuaro Mexico 19°24N 100°22W 86 D4
Zitundo Mozam. 26°48S 32°47E 57 D5
Ziwa Maghariba = Kagera □
  Tanzania 2°0S 31°30E 54 C3
Ziway, L. Ethiopia 8°0N 38°50E 47 F2
Ziyang China 32°32N 108°31E 34 H5
Zlatograd Bulgaria 41°22N 25°7E 23 D11
Zlatoust Russia 55°10N 59°40E 18 C10
Zlín Czech Rep. 49°14N 17°40E 17 D9
Zmeinogorsk Kazakhstan 51°10N 82°13E 28 D9
Znojmo Czech Rep. 48°50N 16°2E 16 D9
Zobeyrī Iran 34°10N 46°40E 44 C5
Zobia Dem. Rep. of the Congo 3°0N 25°59E 54 B2
Zoetermeer Neths. 52°3N 4°30E 15 B4
Zohreh → Iran 30°16N 51°15E 45 D6
Zolochiv Ukraine 49°45N 24°51E 17 D13
Zomba Malawi 15°22S 35°19E 55 F4
Zongo
  Dem. Rep. of the Congo 4°20N 18°35E 52 D3
Zonguldak Turkey 41°28N 31°50E 19 F5
Zonqor Pt. Malta 35°52N 14°34E 25 C2
Zorritos Peru 3°43S 80°40W 92 D2
Zou Xiang China 35°30N 116°58E 34 G9
Zouar Chad 20°30N 16°32E 51 D9
Zouérate = Zouîrât
  Mauritania 22°44N 12°21W 50 D3
Zouîrât Mauritania 22°44N 12°21W 50 D3
Zoutkamp Neths. 53°20N 6°18E 15 A6
Zrenjanin Serbia 45°22N 20°23E 23 B9
Zufār Oman 17°40N 54°0E 47 D5
Zug Switz. 47°10N 8°31E 20 C8
Zugspitze Germany 47°25N 10°59E 16 E6
Zuid-Holland □ Neths. 52°0N 4°35E 15 C4
Zuidbeveland Neths. 51°30N 3°50E 15 C3
Zuidhorn Neths. 53°15N 6°23E 15 A6
Zula Eritrea 15°17N 39°40E 47 D2
Zumbo Mozam. 15°35S 30°26E 55 F3
Zumpango Mexico 19°48N 99°6W 87 D5
Zunhua China 40°18N 117°58E 35 D9
Zuni Pueblo U.S.A. 35°4N 108°51W 77 J9
Zunyi China 27°42N 106°53E 32 D5
Zurbātīyah Iraq 33°9N 46°3E 44 C5
Zürich Switz. 47°22N 8°32E 20 C8
Zutphen Neths. 52°9N 6°12E 15 B6
Zuurberg △ S. Africa 33°12S 25°32E 56 E4
Zuwārah Libya 32°58N 12°1E 51 B8
Zūzan Iran 34°22N 59°53E 45 C8
Zvishavane Zimbabwe 20°17S 30°2E 55 G3
Zvolen Slovak Rep. 48°33N 19°10E 17 D10
Zwettl Austria 48°35N 15°9E 16 D8
Zwickau Germany 50°44N 12°30E 16 C7
Zwolle Neths. 52°31N 6°6E 15 B6
Zwolle U.S.A. 31°38N 93°39W 84 F8
Żyrardów Poland 52°3N 20°28E 17 B11
Zyryan Kazakhstan 49°43N 84°20E 28 E9
Zyryanka Russia 65°45N 150°51E 29 C16
Zyryanovsk = Zyryan
  Kazakhstan 49°43N 84°20E 28 E9
Żywiec Poland 49°42N 19°10E 17 D10